GATE

Mechanical Engineering

Second Edition

D.P. Sharma
Associate Professor
Department of Mechanical Engineering
Rajasthan Technical University, Kota
Rajasthan

PHI Learning Private Limited
Delhi-110092
2020

₹ 795.00

GATE—Mechanical Engineering, Second Edition
D.P. Sharma

ISBN-978-93-89347-36-4 (Print Book)
ISBN-978-93-89347-33-3 (e-Book)

Second Printing (Second Edition) ... ... November, 2019

Published by Asoke K. Ghosh, PHI Learning Private Limited, Rimjhim House, 111, Patparganj Industrial Estate, Delhi-110092 and Printed by Rajkamal Electric Press, Plot No. 2, Phase IV, HSIDC, Kundli-131028, Sonepat, Haryana.

Contents

Preface

The book, GATE Mechanical Engineering is an outcome of classroom tested notes by the author, refined over the years while teaching and guiding students. In GATE only score matters. The students must have their own strategy, both for preparation and writing the examination and have to practice many difficult questions to score high. They study most part of the course during their graduation, but still everything has to be revised and requires practice. From a practice point of view, this book is very useful. In this book, the type, level and length of problems have been kept relevant and as close to the recent GATE trends as possible.

In order to have an overview of the examination pattern, the book provides solved previous years' questions with step-by-step solutions so that students can practice those questions straightway. It is advised to the students that they should solve questions without looking into the solutions given in the book. It is good to struggle with the difficult questions which develop problem solving skills. A large number of diagrams given in the book provide ease in understanding the concepts, which make the reading more fruitful. The book is designed in such a manner that even average students can score high percentile if they practice more and more based on the fundamental concepts.

I wish the readers all the best!

D.P. Sharma

Preface

Acknowledgements

I am very grateful to my uncle Shri J.C. Sharma for his inspiration and encouragement to complete the book in the best possible way. I am very thankful to my wife Krishna for helping me in preparation of the book, without her, I could not think to complete this book. I am also thankful to my family members, whose encouragement and blessings have helped me in bringing out this text.

I thank Hon'ble Vice-Chancellor, Rajasthan Technical University, Kota, Head of Department (Mechanical); faculty members; and students who encouraged me and gave suggestions and helpful comments during the preparation of the manuscript.

I would like to acknowledge editorial and production staff of PHI Learning for their excellent help in producing this book on time.

I welcome all constructive suggestions for further improving the quality of this book.

D.P. Sharma

SYLLABUS

GATE Mechanical Engineering

Section 1: Engineering Mathematics

Linear Algebra: Matrix algebra, systems of linear equations, eigenvalues and eigenvectors.

Calculus: Functions of single variable, limit, continuity and differentiability, mean value theorems, indeterminate forms; evaluation of definite and improper integrals; double and triple integrals; partial derivatives, total derivative, Taylor series (in one and two variables), maxima and minima, Fourier series; gradient, divergence and curl, vector identities, directional derivatives, line, surface and volume integrals, applications of Gauss, Stokes and Green's theorems.

Differential equations: First order equations (linear and nonlinear); higher order linear differential equations with constant coefficients; Euler-Cauchy equation; initial and boundary value problems; Laplace transforms; solutions of heat, wave and Laplace's equations.

Complex variables: Analytic functions; Cauchy-Riemann equations; Cauchy's integral theorem and integral formula; Taylor and Laurent series.

Probability and Statistics: Definitions of probability, sampling theorems, conditional probability; mean, median, mode and standard deviation; random variables, binomial, Poisson and normal distributions.

Numerical Methods: Numerical solutions of linear and non-linear algebraic equations; integration by trapezoidal and Simpson's rules; single and multi-step methods for differential equations.

Section 2: Applied Mechanics and Design

Engineering Mechanics: Free-body diagrams and equilibrium; trusses and frames; virtual work; kinematics and dynamics of particles and of rigid bodies in plane motion; impulse and momentum (linear and angular) and energy formulations, collisions.

Mechanics of Materials: Stress and strain, elastic constants, Poisson's ratio; Mohr's circle for plane stress and plane strain; thin cylinders; shear force and bending moment diagrams; bending and shear stresses; deflection of beams; torsion of circular shafts; Euler's theory of columns; energy methods; thermal stresses; strain gauges and rosettes; testing of materials with universal testing machine; testing of hardness and impact strength.

Theory of Machines: Displacement, velocity and acceleration analysis of plane mechanisms; dynamic analysis of linkages; cams; gears and gear trains; flywheels and governors; balancing of reciprocating and rotating masses; gyroscope.

Vibrations: Free and forced vibration of single degree of freedom systems, effect of damping; vibration isolation; resonance; critical speeds of shafts.

Machine Design: Design for static and dynamic loading; failure theories; fatigue strength and the S-N diagram; principles of the design of machine elements such as bolted, riveted and welded joints; shafts, gears, rolling and sliding contact bearings, brakes and clutches, springs.

Section 3: Fluid Mechanics and Thermal Sciences

Fluid Mechanics: Fluid properties; fluid statics, manometry, buoyancy, forces on submerged bodies, stability of floating bodies; control-volume analysis of mass, momentum and energy; fluid acceleration; differential equations of continuity and momentum; Bernoulli's equation; dimensional analysis; viscous flow of incompressible fluids, boundary layer, elementary turbulent flow, flow through pipes, head losses in pipes, bends and fittings.

Heat-transfer: Modes of heat transfer; one dimensional heat conduction, resistance concept and electrical analogy, heat transfer through fins; unsteady heat conduction, lumped parameter system, Heisler's charts; thermal boundary layer, dimensionless parameters in free and forced convective heat transfer, heat transfer correlations for flow over flat plates and through pipes, effect of turbulence; heat exchanger performance, LMTD and NTU methods; radiative heat transfer, Stefan-Boltzmann law, Wien's displacement law, black and grey surfaces, view factors, radiation network analysis.

Thermodynamics: Thermodynamic systems and processes; properties of pure substances, behaviour of ideal and real gases; zeroth and first laws of thermodynamics, calculation of work and heat in various processes; second law of thermodynamics; thermodynamic property charts and tables, availability and irreversibility; thermodynamic relations.

Applications: Power Engineering: Air and gas compressors; vapour and gas power cycles, concepts of regeneration and reheat. I.C. Engines: Air-standard Otto, Diesel and dual cycles. Refrigeration and air-conditioning: Vapour and gas refrigeration and heat pump cycles; properties of moist air, psychrometric chart, basic psychrometric processes. Turbomachinery: Impulse and reaction principles, velocity diagrams, Pelton-Wheel, Francis and Kaplan turbines.

Section 4: Materials, Manufacturing and Industrial Engineering

Engineering Materials: Structure and properties of engineering materials, phase diagrams, heat treatment, stress-strain diagrams for engineering materials.

Casting, Forming and Joining Processes: Different types of castings, design of patterns, moulds and cores; solidification and cooling; riser and gating design. Plastic deformation and yield criteria; fundamentals of hot and cold working processes; load estimation for bulk (forging, rolling, extrusion, drawing) and sheet (shearing, deep drawing, bending) metal forming processes; principles of powder metallurgy. Principles of welding, brazing, soldering and adhesive bonding.

Machining and Machine Tool Operations: Mechanics of machining; basic machine tools; single and multi-point cutting tools, tool geometry and materials, tool life and wear; economics of machining; principles of non-traditional machining processes; principles of work holding, design of jigs and fixtures.

Metrology and Inspection: Limits, fits and tolerances; linear and angular measurements; comparators; gauge design; interferometry; form and finish measurement; alignment and testing methods; tolerance analysis in manufacturing and assembly.

Computer Integrated Manufacturing: Basic concepts of CAD/CAM and their integration tools.

Production Planning and Control: Forecasting models, aggregate production planning, scheduling, materials requirement planning.

Inventory Control: Deterministic models; safety stock inventory control systems.

Operations Research: Linear programming, simplex method, transportation, assignment, network flow models, simple queuing models, PERT and CPM.

General Aptitude

Verbal Ability: English grammar, sentence completion, verbal analogies, word groups, instructions, critical reasoning and verbal deduction.

Numerical Ability: Numerical computation, numerical estimation, numerical reasoning and data interpretation.

1 Linear Algebra

GATE Mechanical Engg.

GATE Syllabus

Linear Algebra: Matrix algebra, Systems of linear equations, Eigenvalues and Eigenvectors.

Chapter Outline

1.1 KEY CONCEPTS AND FORMULAS

Matrix

Matrix is a rectangular array of numbers arranged in rows and columns. It is written as follows:

$$\begin{bmatrix} a_{11} & a_{12} & \cdots & a_{1n} \\ a_{21} & a_{22} & \cdots & a_{2n} \\ \cdots & \cdots & \cdots & \cdots \\ a_{m1} & a_{m2} & \cdots & a_{mn} \end{bmatrix}$$

The array is called a m by n matrix.

Types of Matrices

Row matrix, Column matrix, Square matrix, Null matrix or Zero matrix, Diagonal matrix, Unit or Identity matrix, Orthogonal matrix, Symmetric matrix, Skew-Symmetric matrix, Triangular matrix, Sub-matrix, Non-singular matrix, Involutory matrix, Nilpotent matrix, Idempotent matrix, Hermitian, Skew-Hermitian, Unitary matrices

Trace of a Square Matrix

The sum of the main diagonal elements of a square matrix A is called the *trace of A*.

$$\text{trace } A = a_{11} + a_{22} + a_{33} + \ldots + a_{nn}$$

Properties of Transposes (T)

If A and B are matrices (with orders such that the given matrix operations are defined) and c is a scalar, then the following properties are true.

- $(A^T)^T = A$
- $(A+B)^T = A^T + B^T$
- $(cA)^T = c(A)^T$
- $(AB)^T = B^T A^T$

Determinant

If a matrix is square, the elements of the matrix may be combined to compute a real-valued number called a *determinant*. It can be denoted by the symbol Δ, or by $|A|$, or by $\det(A)$.

Minors and Cofactors of a Matrix

If A is a square matrix, then the minor M_{ij} of the element a_{ij} is the determinant of the matrix obtained by deleting the ith row and jth column of A. The cofactor C_{ij} is given by

$$C_{ij} = (-1)^{i+j} M_{ij}$$

Determinant of a Matrix

If A is a square matrix (of order 2 or greater), then the determinant of A is the sum of the entries in the first row of A multiplied by their cofactors. That is,

$$|A| = \sum_{j=1}^{n} a_{1j}C_{1j} = a_{11}C_{11} + a_{12}C_{12} + \cdots + a_{1n}C_{1n}$$

Expansion by Cofactors

Let A be a square matrix of order n. Then the determinant of A is given by

$$|A| = \sum_{j=1}^{n} a_{ij}C_{ij}$$

$= a_{i1}C_{i1} + a_{i2}C_{i2} + \cdots + a_{in}C_{in}$ (ith row expansion)

$= a_{1j}C_{1j} + a_{2j}C_{2j} + \cdots + a_{nj}C_{nj}$ (jth column expansion)

Determinant of a Triangular Matrix

If A is a triangular matrix of order n, then its determinant is the product of the entries on the main diagonal. That is,

$$|A| = a_{11} \times a_{22} \times a_{33} \times \cdots \times a_{nn}$$

Conditions That Yield a Zero Determinant

If A is a square matrix and any of the following conditions is true, then $|A| = 0$.

- An entire row (or an entire column) consists of zeros.
- Two rows (or two column) are equal.
- On row (or column) is a multiple of another row (or column).

Applications of Determinants

Area of a Triangle in the *xy*-plane

The area of the triangle whose vertices are (x_1, y_1), (x_2, y_2) and (x_3, y_3) is given by

$$\text{Area} = \pm\frac{1}{2}\begin{vmatrix} x_1 & y_1 & 1 \\ x_2 & y_2 & 1 \\ x_3 & y_3 & 1 \end{vmatrix}$$ where the sign ($\pm$) is chosen to give a positive area.

Equation of Line in the *xy*-plane

The equation of line passing through the distinct points (x_1, y_1), and (x_2, y_2) is given by

$$\begin{vmatrix} x & y & 1 \\ x_1 & y_1 & 1 \\ x_2 & y_2 & 1 \end{vmatrix} = 0$$

Equation of Plane

The equation of the plane passing through the distinct point (x_1, y_1, z_1), (x_2, y_2, z_2) and (x_3, y_3, z_3) is given by

$$\begin{vmatrix} x & y & z & 1 \\ x_1 & y_1 & z_1 & 1 \\ x_2 & y_2 & z_2 & 1 \\ x_3 & y_3 & z_3 & 1 \end{vmatrix} = 0$$

Volume of a Tetrahedron

The volume of the tetrahedron whose vertices are (x_1, y_1, z_1), (x_2, y_2, z_2), (x_3, y_3, z_3) and (x_4, y_4, z_4) is given by

$$\text{Volume} = \pm\frac{1}{6}\begin{vmatrix} x_1 & y_1 & z_1 & 1 \\ x_2 & y_2 & z_2 & 1 \\ x_3 & y_3 & z_3 & 1 \\ x_4 & y_4 & z_4 & 1 \end{vmatrix}$$

where the sign ($\pm$) is chosen to give a positive volume.

Rank of Matrix

The rank of a matrix can be described as the order of the largest non-zero determinant that can be formed from the elements of the given matrix.

A matrix A is said to have rank r if it contains at least one square sub-matrix of r rows with a non-zero determinant, while all square sub-matrices of (R + 1) rows, or more, have zero determinants.

Rank of Matrix by Elementary Row (or Column) Transformations of a Matrix

Rank of matrix can be easily calculated by applying elementary row (column) transformations given as follow:

- Interchange any two rows or columns.
- Multiplication of the elements of row (or column) by a non-zero number k.
- The addition to the elements of ith row (column) and the corresponding elements of any other row say jth row (or column) multiplied by a non-zero number k.

Note: The rank of a matrix does not alter by applying elementary row transformations (or column transformation).

Echelon Form of a Matrix

A matrix A is said to be in Echelon form, if

- All the non zero rows, if any, proceed the zero rows.

- The number of zero proceeding the first nonzero element in a row is less than that the number of such zeros in the succeeding (or next) row.
- The first nonzero element in every row is unity

e.g., the matrix $\begin{bmatrix} 1 & 2 & 4 & 0 & 3 \\ 0 & 1 & 3 & 5 & 7 \\ 0 & 0 & 1 & 2 & 0 \\ 0 & 0 & 0 & 0 & 0 \end{bmatrix}$ is in echelon form.

Note: When a matrix is converted in Echelon form, then the number of nonzero rows of the matrix is the rank of the matrix.

If all the elements of a matrix A are zero, then A is said to be of rank zero. (Null matrix have zero rank)

Singular and Non-singular Matrices

If A is a square matrix of order n and if the rank of $A = n$, then $|A| \neq 0$ and A is said to be *non singular*.

If, however, $|A| = 0$, then A is said to be *singular*.

Inverse of a Matrix

An $n \times n$ matrix A is invertible (or non singular) if there exists an $n \times n$ matrix B such that

$$AB = BA = I_n$$

where I_n is the identity matrix of order n. The matrix B is called the (multiplicative) inverse of A. A matrix that does not have an inverse is called *non-invertible* (or singular).

Important Observations Regarding the Inverse

- For a matrix A to have an inverse, it must be square.
- The inverse of A will also be square and of the same dimension as A.
- Not every square matrix has an inverse.

Method to Find the Inverse of a Matrix by Gauss-Jordan Elimination Method

Let A be a square matrix of order n.

- Write the $n \times 2n$ matrix that consists of the given matrix A on the left and the $n \times n$ identity matrix I on the right to obtain $[A : I]$. Note that we separate the matrices A and I by a dotted line. We call this process adjoining the matrices A and I.
- If possible, row reduce A to I using elementary row operations on the entire matrix $[A : I]$. The result will be the matrix $[I : A^{-1}]$. If this is not possible, then A is not invertible.
- Check your work by multiplying to see that $AA^{-1} = I = A^{-1}A$.

Adjoint of a Matrix

The cofactor C_{ij} of a matrix A is defined to be $(-1)^{i+j}$ times the determinant of the matrix obtained by deleting the ith row and jth column of A. If A is a square matrix, then the matrix of cofactors of A has the form:

$$\begin{bmatrix} C_{11} & C_{12} & \cdots & C_{1n} \\ C_{21} & C_{22} & \cdots & C_{2n} \\ \cdot & \cdot & & \cdot \\ \cdot & \cdot & \cdots & \cdot \\ \cdot & \cdot & & \cdot \\ C_{n1} & C_{n2} & \cdots & C_{nn} \end{bmatrix}$$

The transpose of this matrix is called the adjoint of A and is denoted by adj(A). That is,

$$\text{adj}(A) = \begin{bmatrix} C_{11} & C_{21} & \cdots & C_{n1} \\ C_{12} & C_{22} & \cdots & C_{n2} \\ \cdot & \cdot & & \cdot \\ \cdot & \cdot & \cdots & \cdot \\ \cdot & \cdot & & \cdot \\ C_{1n} & C_{2n} & \cdots & C_{nn} \end{bmatrix}$$

Inverse of a Matrix by Adjoint

If A is an $n \times n$ invertible, then

$$A^{-1} = \frac{1}{|A|}\text{adj}(A)$$

Properties of Inverse and Adjoint of Matrices

For two non-singular matrices A and B of order n, k is a positive integer, and c is a scalar, then the following are true:

- $(AB)^{-1} = B^{-1}A^{-1}$ • $(A^{-1})^{-1} = A$
- $(A+B)^{-1} \neq A^{-1}+B^{-1}$ (in general)
- $(A^T)^{-1} = (A^{-1})^T$
- $(A^{-1})^n = A^{-n}$ for any positive integer n.
- $(cA)^{-1} = \frac{1}{c}A^{-1}, c \neq 0$
- $(A^k)^{-1} = \underbrace{A^{-1}A^{-1} \cdots A^{-1}}_{k \text{ factors}}$
- $A^pA^q = A^{p+q}$; • $(A^p)^q = A^{pq}$
- adj AB = (adj B)(adj A)
- adj (adj$A$) = $(\det A)^{n-2}A$ if $\det A \neq 0$

Representation of System of Equations

An $(m \times n)$ system of equations having the form:

$$\left.\begin{array}{l} a_{11}x_1 + a_{12}x_2 + \ \ldots \ + a_{1n}x_n = b_1 \\ a_{21}x_1 + a_{22}x_2 + \ \ldots \ + a_{2n}x_n = b_2 \\ \ldots\ldots\ldots\ldots\ldots\ldots\ldots\ldots\ldots \\ a_{m1}x_1 + a_{m2}x_2 + \ \ldots \ + a_{mn}x_n = b_m \end{array}\right\}$$

Can be represented by the matrix form $AX = B$,

$$\text{where } A = \begin{bmatrix} a_{11} & a_{12} & \cdots & a_{1n} \\ a_{21} & a_{22} & \cdots & a_{2n} \\ \cdot & \cdot & & \cdot \\ \cdot & \cdot & \cdots & \cdot \\ \cdot & \cdot & & \cdot \\ a_{m1} & a_{m2} & \cdots & a_{mn} \end{bmatrix}, X = \begin{bmatrix} x_1 \\ x_2 \\ \cdot \\ \cdot \\ \cdot \\ x_n \end{bmatrix}, \text{ and } B = \begin{bmatrix} b_1 \\ b_2 \\ \cdot \\ \cdot \\ \cdot \\ b_m \end{bmatrix}$$

- If $B \neq 0$, that is, at least one of the elements $b_1, b_2, \ldots, b_m$ is not zero, then the system of equations is called *non-homogeneous.*
- If $B = 0$, then the system of equation is called *homogeneous.*

Solution of System of Linear Equations

Matrix Method

System of equation in matrix form is given by $AX = B$.

When A is a non-singular matrix, then A^{-1} exists and hence $A^{-1}A = I$.

$$A^{-1}AX = A^{-1}B \Rightarrow X = A^{-1}B = \frac{\text{adj}\,A}{|A|}B$$

E-Row Transformations Method (Gauss-Elimination Method)

To solve the equation $AX = B$, we perform elementary row operations on both A and B so that the matrix A be reduced to triangular form.

Cramer's Rule

If a system of n linear equations in n variable has a coefficient matrix with a non-zero determinant $|A|$, then the solution to the system ($AX = B$) is given by

$$x_i = \frac{|A_i|}{|A|}, \ i = 1, 2, 3, \ldots, n$$

where $|A_i|$ is the determinant of the matrix A_i obtained by replacing the ith column of A by the right hand side column B.

- When $|A| \neq 0$, the system of equations is consistent and the unique solution is obtained.
- When $|A| = 0$, and one or more of $|A_i|, i = 1, 2, 3, \ldots, n$ are not zero, then the system of equation has no solution, that is the system is inconsistent.
- When $|A| = 0$, and all $|A_i| = 0, i = 1, 2, 3, \ldots, n$ then the system of equations is consistent and has infinite number of solutions.

Rouche's Theorem

The system of equations $AX = B$ is consistent, if and only if the coefficient matrix A and the augmented matrix $[A{:}B]$ are of the same rank.

Thus, to discuss the consistency of the equation $AX = B$ (m equations in n unknowns), the following procedure is adopted:

We first find rank A and rank $[A{:}B]$.

- If $\text{rank}(A) \neq \text{rank}[A{:}B]$, the equations are *inconsistent.* (no solution)
- If $\text{rank}(A) = \text{rank}[A{:}B] = n$ (number of unknowns), the equations are consistent and have a *unique solution.*
- In particular, if A is a non-singular (square) matrix, the system $AX = B$ has a unique solution.
- If $\text{rank}(A) = \text{rank}[A{:}B] < n$ (number of unknowns), the equations are consistent and have an *infinite number* of solutions.

Definitions

- A set of values of $x_1, x_2, x_3, \ldots, x_n$ which satisfy all the given m equations simultaneously is called a *solution of the system.*
- When the system of equations has a solution, it is said to be *consistent.* Otherwise, the system is said to be *inconsistent.*
- When a system has only one solution, it is called the *unique solution.*
- A consistent system may have either only one or infinitely many solutions.
- The necessary and sufficient condition for the consistency of a system of linear non-homogeneous equations is provided by a theorem, called *Rouches's theorem.*

System of Homogeneous Linear Equation

Consider the system of homogeneous linear equation $AX = O$ (m equations in n unknowns)

- This system is always consistent, as rank $(A) = \text{rank}(A{:}O)$. If the coefficient matrix A is *non-singular*, the system has a *unique solution*, namely, $x_1 = x_2 = x_3 = \ldots = x_n = 0$. This unique solution is called the *trivial solution.*
- If the coefficient matrix A is *singular,* i.e., If $|A| = 0$, the system has an infinite number of non-zero or non-trivial solution.

Eigenvalue and Eigenvector

Let A be an $n \times n$ matrix. The scalar λ is called an eigenvalue of A if there is a non-zero vector $\boldsymbol{x}$ such that $A\boldsymbol{x} = \lambda \boldsymbol{x}$, The vector $\boldsymbol{x}$ is called an eigenvector of A corresponding to λ.

Finding the Eigenvalues and Eigenvectors

Let A be an $n \times n$ matrix.

Form the characteristic equation $|A - \lambda I| = 0$. It will be a polynomial equation of degree n in the variable λ.

Find the real roots of the characteristic equation. These are the eigenvalues of A.

For each eigenvalue λ_i, find the eigenvectors corresponding to λ_i by solving the homogeneous system $(A - \lambda_i I)x = 0$. This requires row-reducing an $n \times n$ matrix. The resulting reduced row-echelon form must have at least one row of zeros.

Properties of Eigenvalues

- Matrix A and A^T have same eigenvalues.
- Sum of eigenvalues = trace of matrix.
- Product of eigenvalues of matrix A = Determinant of matrix A.
- If $\lambda_1, \lambda_2, \lambda_3, \ldots, \lambda_n$ are the eigenvalues of a matrix A, then

  1. $k\lambda_1, k\lambda_2, k\lambda_3, \ldots, k\lambda_n$ are the eigenvalues of the matrix kA, where k is a non-zero scalar.
  2. $\lambda_1^p, \lambda_2^p, \lambda_3^p, \ldots, \lambda_n^p$ are the eigenvalues of the matrix A^p, where k is a positive integer.
  3. $\frac{1}{\lambda_1}, \frac{1}{\lambda_2}, \frac{1}{\lambda_3}, \ldots, \frac{1}{\lambda_n}$ are the eigenvalues of the inverse matrix A^{-1}, provided $\lambda_r \neq 0$.

- For a real matrix A, if $\alpha + i\beta$ is an eigenvalue, then its conjugate $\alpha - i\beta$ is also eigenvalue (since the characteristic equation has real coefficients). When the matrix A is complex, this properties does not hold.

1.2 SOLVED EXAMPLES

Previous Years GATE Questions

Example 1.1

The lowest eigenvalue of the 2×2 matrix $\begin{bmatrix} 4 & 2 \\ 1 & 3 \end{bmatrix}$ is__.

GATE 2015

Solution

Given: Matrix $A = \begin{bmatrix} 4 & 2 \\ 1 & 3 \end{bmatrix}$

The characteristic equation of this matrix is given by

$$|A - \lambda I| = 0$$

or $$\begin{vmatrix} 4-\lambda & 2 \\ 1 & 3-\lambda \end{vmatrix} = 0$$

or $$(4-\lambda)(3-\lambda) - 2 = 0$$

or $$(\lambda - 5)(\lambda - 2) = 0$$

or $$\lambda_1 = 5, \lambda_2 = 2$$

Lowest eigenvalue of matrix is 2.

Example 1.2

If any two column of a determinant $P = \begin{bmatrix} 4 & 7 & 8 \\ 3 & 1 & 5 \\ 9 & 6 & 2 \end{bmatrix}$ are interchanged, which one of the following statements regarding the value of the determinant is CORRECT?

(A) Absolute value remains unchanged but sign will change

(B) Both absolute value and sign will change

(C) Absolute value will change but sign will not change

(D) Both absolute value and sign will remain unchanged

GATE 2015

Solution

If two column of a determinants are interchanged, then the absolute value of determinant remains unchanged but sign will change.

Example 1.3

Given that the determinant of the matrix $\begin{bmatrix} 1 & 3 & 0 \\ 2 & 6 & 4 \\ -1 & 0 & 2 \end{bmatrix}$ is -12, the determinant of the matrix $\begin{bmatrix} 2 & 6 & 0 \\ 4 & 12 & 8 \\ -2 & 0 & 4 \end{bmatrix}$ is

(A) – 96 (B) – 24 (C) 24 (D) 96

GATE 2014

Solution

Given: $$\begin{vmatrix} 1 & 3 & 0 \\ 2 & 6 & 4 \\ -1 & 0 & 2 \end{vmatrix} = -12$$

$$\begin{vmatrix} 2 & 6 & 0 \\ 4 & 12 & 8 \\ -2 & 0 & 4 \end{vmatrix} = 2^3 \begin{vmatrix} 1 & 3 & 0 \\ 2 & 6 & 4 \\ -1 & 0 & 2 \end{vmatrix}$$

$$= 2^3 \times (-12)$$

$$\begin{vmatrix} 2 & 6 & 0 \\ 4 & 12 & 8 \\ -2 & 0 & 4 \end{vmatrix} = -96$$

Example 1.4

The matrix from of the linear system $\frac{dx}{dt} = 3x - 5y$ and $\frac{dy}{dt} = 4x + 8y$ is

(A) $\frac{d}{dt}\begin{bmatrix} x \\ y \end{bmatrix} = \begin{bmatrix} 3 & -5 \\ 4 & 8 \end{bmatrix}\begin{bmatrix} x \\ y \end{bmatrix}$ (B) $\frac{d}{dt}\begin{bmatrix} x \\ y \end{bmatrix} = \begin{bmatrix} 3 & 8 \\ 4 & -5 \end{bmatrix}\begin{bmatrix} x \\ y \end{bmatrix}$

(C) $\frac{d}{dt}\begin{bmatrix} x \\ y \end{bmatrix} = \begin{bmatrix} 4 & -5 \\ 3 & 8 \end{bmatrix}\begin{bmatrix} x \\ y \end{bmatrix}$ (D) $\frac{d}{dt}\begin{bmatrix} x \\ y \end{bmatrix} = \begin{bmatrix} 4 & 8 \\ 3 & -5 \end{bmatrix}\begin{bmatrix} x \\ y \end{bmatrix}$

GATE 2014

Solution

Given: Linear system

$$\frac{dx}{dt} = 3x - 5y$$

$$\frac{dy}{dt} = 4x + 8y$$

System of equation in matrix form $(Ax = B)$ is

$$\begin{bmatrix} 3 & -5 \\ 4 & 8 \end{bmatrix}\begin{bmatrix} x \\ y \end{bmatrix} = \begin{bmatrix} dx/dt \\ dy/dt \end{bmatrix}$$

or $$\begin{bmatrix} 3 & -5 \\ 4 & 8 \end{bmatrix}\begin{bmatrix} x \\ y \end{bmatrix} = \frac{d}{dt}\begin{bmatrix} x \\ y \end{bmatrix}$$

$$\frac{d}{dt}\begin{bmatrix} x \\ y \end{bmatrix} = \begin{bmatrix} 3 & -5 \\ 4 & 8 \end{bmatrix}\begin{bmatrix} x \\ y \end{bmatrix}$$

Example 1.5

The eigenvalues of a symmetric matrix are all

(A) Complex with non-zero positive imaginary part

(B) Complex with non-zero negative imaginary part

(C) Real (D) Pure imaginary

GATE 2013

Solution

The eigenvalues of symmetric matrix $[A^T = A]$ are real.

Example 1.6

The system of algebraic given below has

$$x + 2y + z = 4$$
$$2x + y + 2z = 5$$
$$x - y + z = 1$$

(A) A unique solution of $x = 1$, $y = 1$ and $z = 1$

(B) Only the two solutions of $(x = 1, y = 1, z = 1)$ and $(x = 2, y = 1, z = 0)$

(C) Infinite number of solutions

(D) No feasible solution

GATE 2012

Solution

The given system of equations in matrix form $(AX = B)$ is

$$\begin{bmatrix} 1 & 2 & 1 \\ 2 & 1 & 2 \\ 1 & -1 & 1 \end{bmatrix}\begin{bmatrix} x \\ y \\ z \end{bmatrix} = \begin{bmatrix} 4 \\ 5 \\ 1 \end{bmatrix}$$

Augmented matrix $[A{:}B] = \begin{bmatrix} 1 & 2 & 1 & 4 \\ 2 & 1 & 2 & 5 \\ 1 & -1 & 1 & 1 \end{bmatrix}$

$$[A{:}B] \sim \begin{bmatrix} 1 & 2 & 1 & 4 \\ 0 & -3 & 0 & -3 \\ 0 & -3 & 0 & -3 \end{bmatrix} \begin{matrix} \\ \leftarrow R_2 - 2R_1 \\ \leftarrow R_3 - R_1 \end{matrix}$$

$$[A{:}B] \sim \begin{bmatrix} 1 & 2 & 1 & 4 \\ 0 & -3 & 0 & -3 \\ 0 & 0 & 0 & 0 \end{bmatrix} \begin{matrix} \\ \\ \leftarrow R_3 - R_2 \end{matrix}$$

$\text{rank}(A) = \text{rank}(A{:}B) = 2 < 3$

Hence,

System has infinite number of solutions

Example 1.7

Consider the following system of equations:

$$2x_1 + x_2 + x_3 = 0$$
$$x_2 - x_3 = 0$$
$$x_1 + x_2 = 0$$

The system has

(A) A unique solution (B) Infinite number of solutions

(C) No solution (D) Five solution

GATE 2011

Solution

The given system of equations in matrix form $(AX = B)$ is

$$\begin{bmatrix} 2 & 1 & 1 \\ 0 & 1 & -1 \\ 1 & 1 & 0 \end{bmatrix}\begin{bmatrix} x_1 \\ x_2 \\ x_3 \end{bmatrix} = \begin{bmatrix} 0 \\ 0 \\ 0 \end{bmatrix}$$

$$\text{Augmented matrix } [A:B] = \begin{bmatrix} 2 & 1 & 1 & 0 \\ 0 & 1 & -1 & 0 \\ 1 & 1 & 0 & 0 \end{bmatrix}$$

$$[A:B] \sim \begin{bmatrix} 2 & 1 & 1 & 0 \\ 0 & 1 & -1 & 0 \\ 0 & \frac{1}{2} & -\frac{1}{2} & 0 \end{bmatrix} \leftarrow R_3 - \frac{1}{2}R_1$$

$$[A:B] \sim \begin{bmatrix} 2 & 1 & 1 & 0 \\ 0 & 1 & -1 & 0 \\ 0 & 0 & 0 & 0 \end{bmatrix} \leftarrow R_3 - \frac{1}{2}R_2$$

$\text{rank}(A) = \text{rank}(A{:}B) = 2 < 3$

Hence,

System has infinite number of solutions

Example 1.8

One of the eigenvectors of the matrix $A = \begin{bmatrix} 2 & 2 \\ 1 & 3 \end{bmatrix}$ is

(A) $\begin{bmatrix} 2 \\ -1 \end{bmatrix}$ (B) $\begin{bmatrix} 2 \\ 1 \end{bmatrix}$ (C) $\begin{bmatrix} 4 \\ 1 \end{bmatrix}$ (D) $\begin{bmatrix} 1 \\ -1 \end{bmatrix}$

GATE 2010

Solution

Given: Matrix $A = \begin{bmatrix} 2 & 2 \\ 1 & 3 \end{bmatrix}$

The characteristic equation of this matrix is

$$|A - \lambda I| = 0$$

$$\begin{bmatrix} 2-\lambda & 2 \\ 1 & 3-\lambda \end{bmatrix} = 0 \quad \text{or} \quad \lambda^2 - 5\lambda + 4 = 0$$

or $\quad (\lambda - 1)(\lambda - 4) = 0$

Eigen values are $\lambda = 1, 4$

The eigenvalue problem is $\quad [A - \lambda I]X = 0$

$$\begin{bmatrix} 2-\lambda & 2 \\ 1 & 3-\lambda \end{bmatrix}\begin{bmatrix} x_1 \\ x_2 \end{bmatrix} = \begin{bmatrix} 0 \\ 0 \end{bmatrix}$$

Putting $\lambda = 1$; $\quad \begin{bmatrix} 1 & 2 \\ 1 & 2 \end{bmatrix}\begin{bmatrix} x_1 \\ x_2 \end{bmatrix} = \begin{bmatrix} 0 \\ 0 \end{bmatrix}$

From which $\quad x_1 + 2x_2 = 0$

$\quad x_1 + 2x_2 = 0$

Solution of above equations is $x_2 = k$, $x_1 = -2k$

$$X_1 = \begin{bmatrix} x_1 \\ x_2 \end{bmatrix} = \begin{bmatrix} -2k \\ k \end{bmatrix} = -k\begin{bmatrix} 2 \\ -1 \end{bmatrix}$$

$\begin{bmatrix} 2 \\ -1 \end{bmatrix}$ is one of the eigenvector

Example 1.9

For a matrix $[M] = \begin{bmatrix} 3/5 & 4/5 \\ x & 3/5 \end{bmatrix}$, the transpose of the matrix is equal to the inverse of the matrix, $[M]^T = [M]^{-1}$. The value of x is given by

(A) $-\frac{4}{5}$ (B) $-\frac{3}{5}$ (C) $\frac{3}{5}$ (D) $\frac{4}{5}$

GATE 2009

Solution

Given: Matrix $[M] = \begin{bmatrix} 3/5 & 4/5 \\ x & 3/5 \end{bmatrix}$ and $[M]^T = [M]^{-1}$

Now, $\quad [M]^T = [M]^{-1}$

Matrix property; $[M]^T[M] = [M]^{-1}[M] = I$

$$\begin{bmatrix} 3/5 & x \\ 4/5 & 3/5 \end{bmatrix}\begin{bmatrix} 3/5 & 4/5 \\ x & 3/5 \end{bmatrix} = \begin{bmatrix} 1 & 0 \\ 0 & 1 \end{bmatrix}$$

or

$$\begin{bmatrix} \left(\frac{3}{5}\right)^2 + x^2 & \left(\frac{3}{5}\right)\left(\frac{4}{5}\right) + \left(\frac{3}{5}\right)x \\ \left(\frac{3}{5}\right)\left(\frac{4}{5}\right) + \left(\frac{3}{5}\right)x & \left(\frac{4}{5}\right)^2 + \left(\frac{3}{5}\right)^2 \end{bmatrix} = \begin{bmatrix} 1 & 0 \\ 0 & 1 \end{bmatrix}$$

From which $\quad \frac{3}{5} \times \frac{4}{5} + \frac{3}{5}x = 0$

$$x = -\frac{4}{5}$$

Example 1.10

The matrix $\begin{bmatrix} 1 & 2 & 4 \\ 3 & 0 & 6 \\ 1 & 1 & p \end{bmatrix}$ has one eigenvalue equal to 3. The sum of the other two eigenvalues is

(A) p (B) $p-1$ (C) $p-2$ (D) $p-3$

GATE 2008

Solution

Sum of eigenvalues of matrix = trace of matrix

= Sum of diagonal elements

Let λ_2 and λ_3 be the other two eigenvalues

$$3+\lambda_2+\lambda_3=1+0+p$$

$$\lambda_2+\lambda_3=p-2$$

Example 1.11

For what value of a, if any, will the following system of equations in x, y and z have a solution?

$$2x+3y=4$$
$$x+y+z=4$$
$$x+2y-z=a$$

(A) Any real number (B) 0

(C) 1 (D) There is no such value

GATE 2008

Solution

The given system of equations in matrix form ($AX=B$) is

$$\begin{bmatrix}2 & 3 & 0\\1 & 1 & 1\\1 & 2 & -1\end{bmatrix}\begin{bmatrix}x\\y\\z\end{bmatrix}=\begin{bmatrix}4\\4\\a\end{bmatrix}$$

$$\text{Augmented matrix }[A{:}B]=\begin{bmatrix}2 & 3 & 0 & 4\\1 & 1 & 1 & 4\\1 & 2 & -1 & a\end{bmatrix}$$

$$[A{:}B]\sim\begin{bmatrix}2 & 3 & 0 & 4\\0 & -1/2 & 1 & 2\\0 & 1/2 & -1 & a-2\end{bmatrix}\begin{matrix}\\ \leftarrow R_2-\frac{1}{2}R_1\\ \leftarrow R_3-\frac{1}{2}R_1\end{matrix}$$

$$[A{:}B]\sim\begin{bmatrix}2 & 3 & 0 & 4\\0 & -1/2 & 1 & 2\\0 & 0 & 0 & a\end{bmatrix}\begin{matrix}\\ \\ \leftarrow R_3+R_2\end{matrix}$$

If $a\neq 0$, $\text{rank}(A)=2$ and $\text{rank}(A{:}B)=3$. Hence, the system will have no solution.

If $a=0$, $\text{rank}(A)=\text{rank}(A{:}B)=2<3$, then the system will be consistent and will have infinite number of solution.

Example 1.12

The eigenvectors of the matrix $\begin{bmatrix}1 & 2\\0 & 2\end{bmatrix}$ are written in the form $\begin{bmatrix}1\\a\end{bmatrix}$ and $\begin{bmatrix}1\\b\end{bmatrix}$. What is $a+b$?

(A) 0 (B) 1/2 (C) 1 (D) 2

GATE 2007

Solution

Given: Matrix $A=\begin{bmatrix}1 & 2\\0 & 2\end{bmatrix}$

The characteristic equation of this matrix A is given by

$$|A-\lambda I|=0$$

$$\begin{vmatrix}1-\lambda & 2\\0 & 2-\lambda\end{vmatrix}=0 \quad \text{or} \quad (1-\lambda)(2-\lambda)=0$$

Roots are: $\lambda=1,2$

Now, $[A-\lambda I]X=0$

$$\begin{bmatrix}1-\lambda & 2\\0 & 2-\lambda\end{bmatrix}X=\begin{bmatrix}0\\0\end{bmatrix}$$

Putting $\lambda=1$ and $X=\begin{bmatrix}1\\a\end{bmatrix}$

$$\begin{bmatrix}1-1 & 2\\0 & 2-1\end{bmatrix}\begin{bmatrix}1\\a\end{bmatrix}=\begin{bmatrix}0\\0\end{bmatrix}$$

From which

$$a=0 \qquad \text{(i)}$$

Putting $\lambda=2$ and $X=\begin{bmatrix}1\\b\end{bmatrix}$

$$\begin{bmatrix}1-2 & 2\\0 & 2-2\end{bmatrix}\begin{bmatrix}1\\b\end{bmatrix}=\begin{bmatrix}0\\0\end{bmatrix}$$

or $$\begin{bmatrix}-1 & 2\\0 & 0\end{bmatrix}\begin{bmatrix}1\\b\end{bmatrix}=\begin{bmatrix}0\\0\end{bmatrix} -1+2b=0$$

$$b=\frac{1}{2} \qquad \text{(ii)}$$

Equations (i) and (ii) give

$$a+b=0+\frac{1}{2}$$

$$a+b=\frac{1}{2}$$

Example 1.13

If a square matrix A is real and symmetric, then the eigenvalues

(A) are always real

(B) are always real and positive

(C) are always real and non-negative

(D) occur in complex conjugate pairs

GATE 2007

Solution

The eigenvalues of symmetric matrix is always real.

Example 1.14

Multiplication of matrices E and F is G. Matrices E and G are

$E=\begin{bmatrix}\cos\theta & -\sin\theta & 0\\ \sin\theta & \cos\theta & 0\\ 0 & 0 & 1\end{bmatrix}$ and $G=\begin{bmatrix}1 & 0 & 0\\ 0 & 1 & 0\\ 0 & 0 & 1\end{bmatrix}$. What is the matrix F?

(A) $\begin{bmatrix}\cos\theta & -\sin\theta & 0\\ \sin\theta & \cos\theta & 0\\ 0 & 0 & 1\end{bmatrix}$ (B) $\begin{bmatrix}\sin\theta & \cos\theta & 0\\ -\cos\theta & \sin\theta & 0\\ 0 & 0 & 1\end{bmatrix}$

(C) $\begin{bmatrix}\cos\theta & \sin\theta & 0\\ -\sin\theta & \cos\theta & 0\\ 0 & 0 & 1\end{bmatrix}$ (D) $\begin{bmatrix}\sin\theta & -\cos\theta & 0\\ \cos\theta & \sin\theta & 0\\ 0 & 0 & 1\end{bmatrix}$

GATE 2006

Solution

Given that multiplication of matrices E and F is G and $E\times F=G$.

where $G=\begin{bmatrix}1 & 0 & 0\\ 0 & 1 & 0\\ 0 & 0 & 1\end{bmatrix}$ is unit matrix

$E\times F=G=I\Rightarrow E\times E^{-1}=I$

Hence matrix F is the inverse of matrix E.

$$E=\begin{bmatrix}\cos\theta & -\sin\theta & 0\\ \sin\theta & \cos\theta & 0\\ 0 & 0 & 1\end{bmatrix}$$

$$E^{-1}=\frac{\text{adj }E}{|E|}=\frac{1}{1}\begin{bmatrix}\cos\theta & -\sin\theta & 0\\ \sin\theta & \cos\theta & 0\\ 0 & 0 & 1\end{bmatrix}^T$$

$$E^{-1}=\begin{bmatrix}\cos\theta & \sin\theta & 0\\ -\sin\theta & \cos\theta & 0\\ 0 & 0 & 1\end{bmatrix}$$

$$F=E^{-1}=\begin{bmatrix}\cos\theta & \sin\theta & 0\\ -\sin\theta & \cos\theta & 0\\ 0 & 0 & 1\end{bmatrix}$$

Example 1.15

Match List-I with List-II and select the correct answer using the codes given below the lists.

List-I	List-II
P. Singular matrix	1. Determinant is not defined
Q. Non-square matrix	2. Determinant is always one
R. Real symmetric	3. Determinant is zero
S. Orthogonal matrix	4. Eigenvalues are always real
	5. Eigenvalues are not defined

(A) P-3, Q-1, R-4, S-2 (B) P-2, Q-3, R-4, S-1

(C) P-3, Q-2, R-5, S-4 (D) P-3, Q-4, R-2, S-1

GATE 2006

Solution

Correct match

P. Singular matrix $\rightarrow$ 3. Determinant is zero

Q. Non-square matrix $\rightarrow$ 1. Determinant is not defined

R. Real symmetric $\rightarrow$ 4. Eigenvalues are always real

S. Orthogonal matrix $\rightarrow$ 2. Determinant is always one

Example 1.16

Eigenvalues of a matrix $S=\begin{bmatrix}3 & 2\\ 2 & 3\end{bmatrix}$ are 5 and 1. What are the eigenvalues of the matrix $S^2=SS$?

(A) 1 and 25 (B) 6 and 4

(C) 5 and 1 (D) 2 an 10

GATE 2006

Solution

If $\lambda_1,\lambda_2,\lambda_3,\ldots,\lambda_n$ are the eigenvalues of matrix A, then the eigenvalues of matrix A^m will be $\lambda_1^m,\lambda_2^m,\lambda_3^m,\ldots,\lambda_n^m$.

Matrix S has eigenvalues 1 and 5.

Thus, matrix S^2 has eigenvalues 1^2 and 5^2.

Eigenvalues of the matrix S^2 are 1 and 25.

Example 1.17

Which one of the following is an eigenvector of the matrix $\begin{bmatrix}5 & 0 & 0 & 0\\ 0 & 5 & 0 & 0\\ 0 & 0 & 2 & 1\\ 0 & 0 & 3 & 1\end{bmatrix}$?

(A) $\begin{bmatrix}1\\ -2\\ 0\\ 0\end{bmatrix}$ (B) $\begin{bmatrix}0\\ 0\\ 1\\ 0\end{bmatrix}$ (C) $\begin{bmatrix}1\\ 0\\ 0\\ -2\end{bmatrix}$ (D) $\begin{bmatrix}0\\ 0\\ 1\\ 0\end{bmatrix}$

GATE 2005

Solution

The characteristic equation of this matrix is $|A-\lambda I|=0$

$$|A-\lambda I|=\begin{bmatrix}5-\lambda & 0 & 0 & 0\\ 0 & 5-\lambda & 0 & 0\\ 0 & 0 & 2-\lambda & 1\\ 0 & 0 & 3 & 1-\lambda\end{bmatrix}=0$$

or $|A-\lambda I| = (5-\lambda)(5-\lambda)[(2-\lambda)(1-\lambda)-3] = 0$

or $(5-\lambda)(5-\lambda)(\lambda^2-3\lambda-1) = 0$

Roots are: $\lambda = 5, 5, \frac{3\pm\sqrt{13}}{2}$

Substituting $\lambda = 5$ in $[A-\lambda I]X = 0$

$$\begin{bmatrix} 5-5 & 0 & 0 & 0 \\ 0 & 5-5 & 0 & 0 \\ 0 & 0 & 2-5 & 1 \\ 0 & 0 & 3 & 1-5 \end{bmatrix}\begin{bmatrix} x_1 \\ x_2 \\ x_3 \\ x_4 \end{bmatrix} = \begin{bmatrix} 0 \\ 0 \\ 0 \\ 0 \end{bmatrix}$$

or
$$\begin{bmatrix} 0 & 0 & 0 & 0 \\ 0 & 0 & 0 & 0 \\ 0 & 0 & -3 & 1 \\ 0 & 0 & 3 & -4 \end{bmatrix}\begin{bmatrix} x_1 \\ x_2 \\ x_3 \\ x_4 \end{bmatrix} = \begin{bmatrix} 0 \\ 0 \\ 0 \\ 0 \end{bmatrix}$$

From which

$$5x_3 = 0$$
$$-3x_3 + x_4 = 0$$
$$3x_3 - 4x_4 = 0$$

Solving equation, we get $x_3 = 0$, $x_4 = 0$, x_1 and x_2 may be any real number.

The eigenvector corresponding to $\lambda = 5$, may be written as

$$X = \begin{bmatrix} x_1 \\ x_2 \\ x_3 \\ x_4 \end{bmatrix} = \begin{bmatrix} k_1 \\ k_2 \\ 0 \\ 0 \end{bmatrix}$$

Since choice (A) is only matrix in this form with both x_3 and $x_4 = 0$, so it is the correct answer.

Example 1.18

A is a 3×4 real matrix and $Ax = b$ is an inconsistant system of equations. The highest possible rank of A is

(A) 1 (B) 2 (C) 3 (D) 4

GATE 2005

Solution

Rank of matrix A; $\text{rank}(A_{m\times n}) \le \min(m,n)$

Highest possible rank of A = Least value of 3 and 4.

Highest possible rank of A = 3

However, if the rank of A = 3 then rank of $[A:B]$ also would be 3, which means the system would become consistent. But it is given that the system is inconsistent. so the maximum rank of A could be 2.

The highest possible rank of A is 2.

Example 1.19

The sum of the eigenvalues of the given matrix

$$\begin{bmatrix} 1 & 1 & 3 \\ 1 & 5 & 1 \\ 3 & 1 & 1 \end{bmatrix}$$

(A) 5 (B) 7 (C) 9 (D)18

GATE 2004

Solution

Given: Matrix $A = \begin{bmatrix} 1 & 1 & 3 \\ 1 & 5 & 1 \\ 3 & 1 & 1 \end{bmatrix}$

Sum of eigenvalues of matrix

= Sum of diagonal elements of given matrix

Sum of eigenvalues $= 1+5+1$

Sum of eigenvalues $= 7$

Example 1.20

For which value of x will the matrix given below become singular ?

$$\begin{bmatrix} 8 & x & 0 \\ 4 & 0 & 2 \\ 12 & 6 & 0 \end{bmatrix}$$

(A) 4 (B) 6 (C) 8 (D)12

GATE 2004

Solution

Determinant of singular matrix is zero.

$$\begin{vmatrix} 8 & x & 0 \\ 4 & 0 & 2 \\ 12 & 6 & 0 \end{vmatrix} = 0$$

or $8\times(0-12) - x\times(0-24) + 0\times(24-0) = 0$

$$x = 4$$

Example 1.21

For the matrix $\begin{bmatrix} 4 & 1 \\ 1 & 4 \end{bmatrix}$, the eigenvalues are

(A) 3 and −3 (B) −3 and −5 (C) 3 and 5 (D) 5 and 0

GATE 2003

Solution

Given: Matrix $A = \begin{bmatrix} 4 & 1 \\ 1 & 4 \end{bmatrix}$

The characteristic equation of this matrix is given by

$$|A-\lambda I|=0 \qquad \text{or} \qquad \begin{vmatrix} 4-\lambda & 1 \\ 1 & 4-\lambda \end{vmatrix}=0$$

or $\quad (4-\lambda)(4-\lambda)-1=0$

or $\quad \lambda^2-8\lambda+15=0$

or $\quad (\lambda-5)(\lambda-3)=0$

Roots are: $\lambda_1=5, \lambda_2=3$

Hence,

The eigenvalues of matrix A are 5 and 3.

Example 1.22

Consider the system of simultaneous equations

$$x+2y+z=6$$
$$2x+y+2z=6$$
$$x+y+z=5$$

This system has

(A) Unique solution (B) Infinite number of solutions

(C) No solution (D) Exactly two solutions

GATE 2003

Solution

The given system of equations in matrix form $(AX=B)$ is

$$\begin{bmatrix} 1 & 2 & 1 \\ 2 & 1 & 2 \\ 1 & 1 & 1 \end{bmatrix}\begin{bmatrix} x \\ y \\ z \end{bmatrix}=\begin{bmatrix} 6 \\ 6 \\ 5 \end{bmatrix}$$

Augmented matrix $[A:B]=\begin{bmatrix} 1 & 2 & 1 & 6 \\ 2 & 1 & 2 & 6 \\ 1 & 1 & 1 & 5 \end{bmatrix}$

$$[A:B]\sim\begin{bmatrix} 1 & 2 & 1 & 6 \\ 0 & -3 & 0 & -6 \\ 0 & -1 & 0 & -1 \end{bmatrix}\begin{matrix} \\ \leftarrow R_2-2R_1 \\ \leftarrow R_3-R_1 \end{matrix}$$

$$[A:B]\sim\begin{bmatrix} 1 & 2 & 1 & 6 \\ 0 & -3 & 0 & -6 \\ 0 & 0 & 0 & 0 \end{bmatrix}\begin{matrix} \\ \\ \leftarrow R_3-\frac{1}{3}R_2 \end{matrix}$$

Rank of matrix A; $\quad \text{rank}(A)=2$

Rank of matrix $[A:B]$; $\text{rank}[A:B]=3$

Since, $\quad \text{rank}[A]\neq\text{rank}[A:B]$

Hence,

System has no solution.

Example 1.23

Consider the system of equations given below:

$$x+y=2$$
$$2x+2y=5$$

This system has

(A) One solution (B) No solution

(C) Infinite solution (D) Four solutions

GATE 2001

Solution

The given system of equations in matrix form

$(AX=B)$ is $\begin{bmatrix} 1 & 1 \\ 2 & 2 \end{bmatrix}\begin{bmatrix} x \\ y \end{bmatrix}=\begin{bmatrix} 2 \\ 5 \end{bmatrix}$

Augmented matrix $[A:B]=\begin{bmatrix} 1 & 1 & 2 \\ 2 & 2 & 5 \end{bmatrix}$

$$[A:B]\sim\begin{bmatrix} 1 & 1 & 2 \\ 0 & 0 & 1 \end{bmatrix}\begin{matrix} \\ \leftarrow R_2-2R_1 \end{matrix}$$

$\text{rank}(A)=1$, $\text{rank}(A:B)=2$

$\text{rank}(A)<\text{rank}(A:B)$

The system of equation is inconsistent (no solution)

System has no solution.

Example 1.24

The three characteristic roots of the following matrix A,

$$A=\begin{bmatrix} 1 & 2 & 3 \\ 0 & 2 & 3 \\ 0 & 0 & 2 \end{bmatrix} \text{ are}$$

(A) 1, 2, 3 (B) 1, 2, 2 (C) 1, 0, 0 (D) 0, 2, 3

GATE 2000

Solution

Let λ_1, λ_2 and λ_3 be the characteristic roots of matrix A.

The characteristic equation of matrix A is $|A-\lambda I|=0$

$$\begin{vmatrix} 1-\lambda & 2 & 3 \\ 0 & 2-\lambda & 3 \\ 0 & 0 & 2-\lambda \end{vmatrix}=0$$

or $\quad (1-\lambda)(2-\lambda)(2-\lambda)=0$

$$\lambda_1=1, \lambda_2=2, \lambda_3=2$$

Three characteristic roots are 1, 2, 2.

Example 1.25

Rank of the matrix given $\begin{bmatrix} 3 & 2 & -9 \\ -6 & -4 & 18 \\ 12 & 8 & -36 \end{bmatrix}$ is

(A) 1 (B) 2 (C) 3 (D) $\sqrt{2}$

GATE 1999

Solution

$$A = \begin{bmatrix} 3 & 2 & -9 \\ -6 & -4 & 18 \\ 12 & 8 & -36 \end{bmatrix}$$

$$A \sim \begin{bmatrix} 3 & 2 & -9 \\ 0 & 0 & 0 \\ 0 & 0 & 0 \end{bmatrix} \begin{matrix} \\ \leftarrow R_2 + 2R_1 \\ \leftarrow R_3 - 4R_1 \end{matrix}$$

From which

rank $(A) = 1$

Example 1.26

The eigenvalues of the matrix $\begin{bmatrix} 5 & 3 \\ 3 & -3 \end{bmatrix}$ are

(A) 6, –4 (B) 5,6 (C) –3,–4 (D) –4, 6

GATE 1999

Solution

Given: Matrix $A = \begin{bmatrix} 5 & 3 \\ 3 & -3 \end{bmatrix}$

The characteristic equation of this matrix is given by

$$|A - \lambda I| = 0 \quad \Rightarrow \quad \begin{vmatrix} 5-\lambda & 5 \\ 3 & -3-\lambda \end{vmatrix} = 0$$

or $(5-\lambda)(-3-\lambda) - 9 = 0$

or $(\lambda - 6)(\lambda + 4) = 0$

$$\lambda_1 = 6, \lambda_2 = -4$$

Eigenvalues of matrix are 6 and –4.

Example 1.27

The solution to the system of equations

$$\begin{bmatrix} 2 & 5 \\ -4 & 3 \end{bmatrix}\begin{bmatrix} x \\ y \end{bmatrix} = \begin{bmatrix} 2 \\ -30 \end{bmatrix}$$

is

(A) 6, 2 (B) –6, 2 (C) –6, – 2 (D) 6, – 2

GATE 2016

Solution

Given system of equations

$$\begin{bmatrix} 2 & 5 \\ -4 & 3 \end{bmatrix}\begin{bmatrix} x \\ y \end{bmatrix} = \begin{bmatrix} 2 \\ -30 \end{bmatrix}$$

$$\begin{bmatrix} 2 & 5 \\ 0 & 13 \end{bmatrix}\begin{bmatrix} x \\ y \end{bmatrix} = \begin{bmatrix} 2 \\ -26 \end{bmatrix} \leftarrow R_2 + 2R_1$$

or $2x + 5y = 2$ (i)

$13y = -26$ (ii)

Equations (i) and (ii) give

$$x = 6, \ y = -2$$

(6, – 2)

Example 1.28

The condition for which the eigenvalues of the matrix

$$A = \begin{bmatrix} 2 & 1 \\ 1 & k \end{bmatrix}$$

are positive, is

(A) $k > \frac{1}{2}$ (B) $k > -2$ (C) $k > 0$ (D) $k > -\frac{1}{2}$

GATE 2016

Solution

Let λ_1 and λ_2 be the eigenvalues (positive) of given matrix A.

The sum of the eigenvalues of a matrix is equal to the sum of the elements of principal diagonal that is always greater than zero.

Trace of matrix A = Sum of eigenvalues > 0

$$2 + k = \lambda_1 + \lambda_2 > 0$$

$k > -2$

Example 1.29

A real square matrix A is called skew-symmetric if

(A) $A^T = A$ (B) $A^T = A^{-1}$

(C) $A^T = -A$ (D) $A^T = A + A^{-1}$

GATE 2016

Solution

Matrix A is called skew-symmetric if

$A^T = -A$

Example 1.30

The product of eigenvalues of the matrix P is

$$P = \begin{bmatrix} 2 & 0 & 1 \\ 4 & -3 & 3 \\ 0 & 2 & -1 \end{bmatrix}$$

(A) – 6 (B) 2 (C) 6 (D) – 2

GATE 2017

Solution

We know that the product of eigenvalues of matrix P = determinant of matrix P

Product of eigenvalues of matrix P

$$= \begin{vmatrix} 2 & 0 & 1 \\ 4 & -3 & 3 \\ 0 & 2 & -1 \end{vmatrix}$$

$= 2(-3 \times -1 - 2 \times 3) - 0(4 \times -1 - 0 \times 3) + 1(4 \times 2 - 0 \times -3)$

$= 2$

Product of eigenvalues of $P = 2$

Example 1.31

The determinant of a 2×2 matrix is 50. If one eigenvalue of the matrix is 10, the other eigenvalue is______.

GATE 2017

Solution

Let λ = other eigenvalue

We know that

Product of eigenvalues = Determinant of matrix

$$10 \times \lambda = 50$$

Other eigenvalue $\lambda = 5$

Example 1.32

Consider the matrix $\mathbf{A} = \begin{bmatrix} 50 & 70 \\ 70 & 80 \end{bmatrix}$ whose eigenvectors corresponding to eigenvalues λ_1 and λ_2 are $\mathbf{x}_1 = \begin{bmatrix} 70 \\ \lambda_1 - 50 \end{bmatrix}$ and $\mathbf{x}_2 = \begin{bmatrix} \lambda_2 - 80 \\ 70 \end{bmatrix}$, respectively. The value of $\mathbf{x}_1^T \mathbf{x}_2$ is ______.

GATE 2017

Solution

Sum of eigenvalue $= \lambda_1 + \lambda_2 =$ trace of A $= 50 + 80$

$$\lambda_1 + \lambda_2 = 130$$

$$\mathbf{x}_1^T \mathbf{x}_2 = [70 \quad \lambda_1 - 50] \begin{bmatrix} \lambda_2 - 80 \\ 70 \end{bmatrix}$$

$$= 70(\lambda_1 + \lambda_2 - 130) = 70(130 - 130)$$

$$\mathbf{x}_1^T \mathbf{x}_2 = 0$$

Example 1.33

The rank of the matrix $\begin{bmatrix} -4 & 1 & -1 \\ -1 & -1 & -1 \\ 7 & -3 & 1 \end{bmatrix}$ is

(A) 1 (B) 2 (C) 3 (D) 4

GATE 2018

Solution

Matrix $A = \begin{bmatrix} -4 & 1 & -1 \\ -1 & -1 & -1 \\ 7 & -3 & 1 \end{bmatrix}$

$$A = \begin{bmatrix} -1 & -1 & -1 \\ -4 & 1 & -1 \\ 7 & -3 & 1 \end{bmatrix} R_2 \leftrightarrow R_1$$

$$A = \begin{bmatrix} -1 & -1 & -1 \\ 0 & 5 & 3 \\ 0 & -10 & -6 \end{bmatrix} \begin{matrix} \\ R_2 - 4R_1 \\ R_3 + 7R_1 \end{matrix}$$

$$A = \begin{bmatrix} -1 & -1 & -1 \\ 0 & 5 & 3 \\ 0 & 0 & 0 \end{bmatrix} \begin{matrix} \\ \\ R_3 + 2R_2 \end{matrix}$$

Number of non-zero rows = 2

Rank = 2

Example 1.34

If $A = \begin{bmatrix} 1 & 2 & 3 \\ 0 & 4 & 5 \\ 0 & 0 & 1 \end{bmatrix}$ then $\det(A^{-1})$ is________.

GATE 2018

Solution

$$\det A = 1 \times 4 \times 1 = 4$$

$$\det(A^{-1}) = \frac{1}{4}$$

$$\det(A^{-1}) = 0.25$$

Example 1.35

Consider the matrix

$$P = \begin{bmatrix} 1 & 1 & 0 \\ 0 & 1 & 1 \\ 0 & 0 & 1 \end{bmatrix}$$

The number of distinct eigenvalues of P is

(A) 0 (B) 1 (C) 2 (D) 3

GATE 2019

Solution

We know that the eigenvalues of upper triangular matrix are its diagonal elements.

Eigenvalues of matrix $P = \begin{bmatrix} 1 & 1 & 0 \\ 0 & 1 & 1 \\ 0 & 0 & 1 \end{bmatrix}$ are 1, 1 and 1.

Number of distinct eigenvalues of $P = 1$

Example 1.36

The set of equations

$$x + y + z = 1$$
$$ax - ay + 3z = 5$$
$$5x - 3y + az = 6$$

has infinite solutions, if $a =$

(A) −3 (B) 3 (C) 4 (D) − 4

GATE 2019

Solution

The given system of equations in matrix form $(AX = B)$ is

$$\begin{bmatrix} 1 & 1 & 1 \\ a & -a & 3 \\ 5 & -3 & a \end{bmatrix}\begin{bmatrix} x \\ y \\ z \end{bmatrix} = \begin{bmatrix} 1 \\ 5 \\ 6 \end{bmatrix}$$

Augmented matrix $[A:B] = \begin{bmatrix} 1 & 1 & 1 & 1 \\ a & -a & 3 & 5 \\ 5 & -3 & a & 6 \end{bmatrix}$

$$[A:B] = \begin{bmatrix} 1 & 1 & 1 & 1 \\ 0 & -2a & 3-a & 5-a \\ 0 & -8 & a-5 & 1 \end{bmatrix} \begin{matrix} \\ \leftarrow R_2 - aR_1 \\ \leftarrow R_3 - 5R_1 \end{matrix}$$

$$[A:B] = \begin{bmatrix} 1 & 1 & 1 & 1 \\ 0 & -2a & 3-a & 5-a \\ 0 & 0 & a^2 - a - 12 & 5a - 20 \end{bmatrix} \begin{matrix} \\ \\ \leftarrow aR_3 - 4R_2 \end{matrix}$$

To have infinite number of solution

$$a^2 - a - 12 = 0 \text{ and } 5a - 20 = 0$$

or $(a-4)(a+3) = 0$ and $(a-4) = 0$

or $a = 4, a = -3$ and $a = 4$

From which

a must be equal to 4 only

Example 1.37

In matrix equation $[A]\{X\} = \{R\}$,

$$[A] = \begin{bmatrix} 4 & 8 & 4 \\ 8 & 16 & -4 \\ 4 & -4 & 15 \end{bmatrix}, \{X\} = \begin{bmatrix} 2 \\ 1 \\ 4 \end{bmatrix} \text{ and } \{R\} = \begin{bmatrix} 32 \\ 16 \\ 64 \end{bmatrix}$$

One of the eigenvalues of matrix $[A]$ is

(A) 4 (B) 8 (C) 15 (D) 16

GATE 2019

Solution

Given: $[A]\{X\} = \{R\} \Rightarrow \begin{bmatrix} 4 & 8 & 4 \\ 8 & 16 & -4 \\ 4 & -4 & 15 \end{bmatrix}\begin{bmatrix} 2 \\ 1 \\ 4 \end{bmatrix} = \begin{bmatrix} 32 \\ 16 \\ 64 \end{bmatrix}$

or $\begin{bmatrix} 4 & 8 & 4 \\ 8 & 16 & -4 \\ 4 & -4 & 15 \end{bmatrix}\begin{bmatrix} 2 \\ 1 \\ 4 \end{bmatrix} = 16\begin{bmatrix} 2 \\ 1 \\ 4 \end{bmatrix}$

The above equation is of the form $AX = \lambda X$; where λ is an eigenvalue.

Thus,

One of the eigenvalues of matrix must be 16

1.3 PRACTICE PAPER

Time: 3 Hours **Max. Marks:100**

Q.1 to Q.30 carry one mark each.

Q.1 to Q.20 Multiple Choice Questions

Q.1 If A and B are any two square matrices of order 2×2, then $(A + B)^2$ is equal to

(A) $A^2 + 2AB + B^2$ (B) $A^2 + 2BA + B^2$

(C) $A^2 + AB - BA + B^2$ (D) $A^2 + AB + BA + B^2$

Q.2 If A is an orthogonal matrix, then A^{-1} equals

(A) A (B) A^T (C) A^2 (D) None of these

Q.3 Let A be a square matrix of order n and Δ denotes $\det(A)$, then $\det(2A)$ is equal to

(A) $2^n\Delta$ (B) $2n\Delta$ (C) 2Δ (D) $\dfrac{\Delta}{2^n}$

Q.4 The eigenvalues of the matrix $\begin{bmatrix} 1 & 4 \\ 3 & 2 \end{bmatrix}$ are

(A) 1, 4 (B) 3, 2 (C) 5, −2 (D) 3, 4

Q.5 If a square matrix A satisfies the equation

$I + A + A^2 + \ldots + A^k = 0$, then A^{-1} is equal to

(A) A^{k-1} (B) A^k (C) A^{k+1} (D) A^{k+2}

Q.6 If $A=\begin{bmatrix}2 & 3 & 0\\1 & -1 & 1\\2 & 0 & 1\end{bmatrix}$ and $B=\begin{bmatrix}1 & -1 & 2\\0 & 1 & -1\\1 & 2 & 1\end{bmatrix}$, then $\det(AB)$ is equal to

(A) 0 (B) 1 (C) 2 (D) 3

Q.7 The characteristic roots of matrix $\begin{bmatrix}1 & 1 & 1\\1 & 1 & 1\\1 & 1 & 1\end{bmatrix}$ are

(A) 0,1, 2 (B) 0, 2, 3 (C) 0, 1, 3 (D) 0, 0, 3

Q.8 If A be a non-zero square matrix of order n, then

(A) the matrix $A+A^T$ is anti-symmetric, but the matrix $A-A^T$ is symmetric

(B) the matrix $A+A^T$ is symmetric, but the matrix $A-A^T$ is anti-symmetric

(C) Both $A+A^T$ and $A-A^T$ are symmetric

(D) Both $A+A^T$ and $A-A^T$ are anti-symmetric

Q.9 If A is an orthogonal matrix, then

(A) $|A|=0$ (B) $|A|=\pm 1$

(C) $|A|=\pm 2$ (D) None of these

Q.10 Let A be a non-singular matrix. Then $|\text{adj}A|$ is equal to

(A) $|A|^n$ (B) $|A|^{n-1}$ (C) $|A|^{n-2}$ (D) None of these

Q.11 If $A=\begin{bmatrix}\cos x & \sin x\\-\sin x & \cos x\end{bmatrix}$ and $A\,\text{adj}A=k\begin{bmatrix}1 & 0\\0 & 1\end{bmatrix}$, then the value of k is

(A) $\sin x\cos x$ (B) 1 (C) 2 (D) 3

Q.12 The matrix $\begin{bmatrix}1 & 2 & 4\\3 & 0 & 6\\1 & 1 & p\end{bmatrix}$ has one eigenvalue equal to 3. The sum of the other two eigenvalues is

(A) p (B) $p-1$ (C) $p-2$ (D) $p-3$

Q.13 Let A, B and C be the square matrices, then which of the following is true

(A) $A(BC)=(AB)C$ (B) $(AB)^T=A^TB^T$

(C) $(A+B)C=CA+CB$ (D) $(A+B)^2=A^2+2AB+B^2$

Q.14 Let $A=\begin{bmatrix}1 & 2 & 0\\2 & 3 & 2\\3 & 1 & 2\end{bmatrix}$ and $B=\dfrac{A-A^T}{2}$, then matrix B is

(A) Symmetric (B) Skew-symmetric

(C) Diagonal (D) Unit matrix

Q.15 Let A and B be two square matrices of the same order and the rank of B^TA^T is n, then rank of AB is

(A) n (B) $n-1$ (C) $n+1$ (D) None of these

Q.16 The trace and determinant of 2×2 matrix are known to be -2 and -35 respectively. Its eigenvalues are

(A) -30 and -5 (B) -37 and -1

(C) -7 and 5 (D) 17.5 and -2

Q.17 If A and B are square matrices of the same order, then which of the following statements cannot be true

(A) $(A+B)^{-1}=B^{-1}+A^{-1}$

(B) $(AB)^{-1}=B^{-1}A^{-1}$

(C) $AB=0\Rightarrow |A|=0$ *or* $|B|=0$

(D) $\text{adj}(AB)=(\text{adj}B)(\text{adj}A)$

Q.18 If the characteristic equation of a matrix A is $\lambda^3-\lambda+1=0$, then A^3 is equal to

(A) A (B) $A-I$ (C) A^2 (D) A^2+A-I

Q.19 If $A=\begin{bmatrix}1 & 1\\1 & 1\end{bmatrix}$ and $n\varepsilon N$, then A^n is equal to

(A) 2^nA (B) $2^{n-1}A$ (C) nA (D) None of these

Q.20 If A and B are symmetric matrices of the same order then matrix $(AB-BA)$ is

(A) Symmetric matrix (B) Skew-symmetric matrix

(C) Null matrix (D) Unit matrix

Q.21 to Q.30 Numerical Answer Questions

Q.21 If A is a non-zero column matrix of order 4×1 and B is a non-zero row matrix of order 1×3, then rank of matrix AB equals___.

Q.22 If $A=\begin{bmatrix}1 & -1 & 2\\0 & 1 & -1\\1 & 2 & 1\end{bmatrix}$ then $\det(A^{-1})$ is equal to___.

Q.23 If A is a skew-symmetric matrix, then trace of A is___.

Q.24 The sum of the eigenvalues of the matrix $\begin{bmatrix}1 & 1 & 3\\1 & 5 & 1\\3 & 1 & 1\end{bmatrix}$ is___.

Q.25 The rank of the matrix $\begin{bmatrix} 3 & 2 & -9 \\ -6 & -4 & 18 \\ 12 & 8 & -36 \end{bmatrix}$ is___.

Q.26 The eigenvalues of the matrix A given below are 15, 3 and 0.

$$A = \begin{bmatrix} 8 & -6 & 2 \\ -6 & n & -4 \\ 2 & -4 & 3 \end{bmatrix}$$

Determinant of the matrix A is______.

Q.27 The rank of a null matrix is_______.

Q.28 Rank of matrix $\begin{bmatrix} 1 & 0 & 0 & 0 \\ 1 & 2 & 0 & 0 \\ 2 & 2 & 3 & 0 \\ 7 & 5 & 3 & 4 \end{bmatrix}$ is_______.

Q.29 A is a 3×4 real matrix and $Ax = B$ is an inconsistent system of equations. The highest possible rank of A is___.

Q.30 The eigenvalues of a square matrix A are 1, 2 and 3. The trace of the matrix $(2A)$_____.

Q.31 to Q.65 carry two marks each.

Q.31 to Q.50 Multiple Choice Questions

Q.31 The equation of plane passing through the points (0,1,0), (−1,3,2) and (−2,0,1) is

(A) $4x - 3y + 5z + 3 = 0$ (B) $4x - y + 5z + 2 = 0$

(C) $-3x + 2y + 4z = 0$ (D) None of these

Q.32 The values of λ and μ for which the system of equations

$$\begin{cases} x + y + z = 6 \\ x + 2y + 3z = 10 \\ x + 2y + \lambda z = \mu \end{cases}$$

has no solutions, are

(A) $\lambda = 3, \mu = 10$ (B) $\lambda = 3$, μ has any value

(C) $\lambda = 3, \mu \neq 10$ (D) None of these

Q.33 For any two 2×2 symmetric matrices A and B consider the following statements:

1. $(A + B)$ is a symmetric matrix
2. (AB) is a symmetric matrix
3. $AB = (BA)^T$
4. $A^T B = AB^T$

Of these statements

(A) 2 , 3 and 4 are correct (B) 1, 3 and 4 are correct

(C) 1 and 2 are correct (D) 1, 2 , 3 and 4 are correct

Q.34 If $P + Q = \begin{bmatrix} 1 & -1 \\ 3 & 0 \end{bmatrix}$ and $P - Q = \begin{bmatrix} 3 & 1 \\ 1 & 4 \end{bmatrix}$ then PQ is

(A) $\begin{bmatrix} 4 & 1 \\ 4 & 4 \end{bmatrix}$ (B) $\begin{bmatrix} 1 & 1 \\ 3 & 4 \end{bmatrix}$

(C) $\begin{bmatrix} -2 & -2 \\ 0 & -6 \end{bmatrix}$ (D) $\begin{bmatrix} 3 & -1 \\ 1 & 0 \end{bmatrix}$

Q.35 If $R = \begin{bmatrix} 1 & 0 & -1 \\ 2 & 1 & -1 \\ 2 & 3 & 2 \end{bmatrix}$, the top row of R^{-1} is

(A) $[5 \quad 6 \quad 4]$ (B) $[5 \quad -3 \quad 1]$

(C) $[2 \quad 0 \quad -1]$ (D) $\begin{bmatrix} 2 & -1 & \frac{1}{2} \end{bmatrix}$

Q.36 If $A = \begin{bmatrix} 1 & 0 \\ 1/2 & 1 \end{bmatrix}$, then A^{50} is

(A) $\begin{bmatrix} 1 & 0 \\ 0 & 50 \end{bmatrix}$ (B) $\begin{bmatrix} 1 & 0 \\ 50 & 1 \end{bmatrix}$

(C) $\begin{bmatrix} 1 & 25 \\ 50 & 1 \end{bmatrix}$ (D) $\begin{bmatrix} 1 & 0 \\ 25 & 1 \end{bmatrix}$

Q.37 If $X = \begin{bmatrix} 3 & -4 \\ 1 & -1 \end{bmatrix}$, then X^n is

(A) $\begin{bmatrix} 3n & -4n \\ n & -n \end{bmatrix}$ (B) $\begin{bmatrix} 2+n & 5-n \\ n & -n \end{bmatrix}$

(C) $\begin{bmatrix} 3^n & (-4)^n \\ 1^n & (-1)^n \end{bmatrix}$ (D) $\begin{bmatrix} 2n+1 & -4n \\ n & -2n+1 \end{bmatrix}$

Q.38 The three characteristic roots of the following matrix

$A = \begin{bmatrix} 1 & 2 & 3 \\ 0 & 2 & 3 \\ 0 & 0 & 2 \end{bmatrix}$ are

(A) 1, 2, 3 (B) 1, 2, 2 (C) 1, 0, 0 (D) 0, 2, 3

Q.39 If for $AX = B$, $B = \begin{bmatrix} 9 \\ 52 \\ 0 \end{bmatrix}$ and

$A^{-1} = \begin{bmatrix} 3 & -1/2 & -1/2 \\ -4 & 3/4 & 5/4 \\ 2 & -1/4 & -3/4 \end{bmatrix}$ then X is equal to

(A) $\begin{bmatrix}1\\3\\5\end{bmatrix}$ (B) $\begin{bmatrix}-1/2\\-1/2\\2\end{bmatrix}$ (C) $\begin{bmatrix}-4\\2\\3\end{bmatrix}$ (D) $\begin{bmatrix}3\\3/4\\-3/4\end{bmatrix}$

Q.40 The following set of equations has

$$3x+2y+z=4$$
$$x-y+z=2$$
$$-2x+2z=5$$

(A) No solution (B) A unique solution

(C) Multiple solutions (D) An inconsistency

Q.41 Let $A=\begin{bmatrix}2&1&3\\1&2&0\\2&1&-1\end{bmatrix}$ then $\det(A^{-1})$ is equal to

(A) $-\frac{1}{12}$ (B) $-\frac{1}{15}$ (C) $-\frac{1}{18}$ (D) $-\frac{1}{24}$

Q.42 The characteristic equation of matrix

$$A=\begin{bmatrix}2&2&1\\1&3&1\\1&2&2\end{bmatrix} \text{ is}$$

(A) $\lambda^3-7\lambda^2+11\lambda-5=0$ (B) $\lambda^3+7\lambda^2+11\lambda-5=0$

(C) $\lambda^3+7\lambda^2-11\lambda-5=0$ (D) $\lambda^3+7\lambda^2+11\lambda+5=0$

Q.43 The eigenvalues of a square matrix A are 1 and 3. Then A^3 is equal to

(A) $12A-13I$ (B) $13A-12I$

(C) $12(A-I)$ (D) $13(A-I)$

Q.44 Matrix A is a square matrix of order 4 and I is a unit matrix, then it is true that

(A) $\det(2A)=16\det(A)$ (B) $\det(-A)=-\det(A)$

(C) $\det(2A)=2\det(A)$ (D) $\det(A+I)=\det(A)+I$

Q.45 If $A=\begin{bmatrix}1&a\\0&1\end{bmatrix}$, then $\lim_{n\to\infty}\frac{1}{n}A^n$

(A) $\begin{bmatrix}0&a\\0&0\end{bmatrix}$ (B) $\begin{bmatrix}0&0\\0&0\end{bmatrix}$

(C) $\begin{bmatrix}0&1\\0&0\end{bmatrix}$ (D) Does not exist

Q.46 If $A=\begin{bmatrix}3&8\\2&1\end{bmatrix}$, then A^{-1} is

(A) $\frac{1}{13}\begin{bmatrix}3&2\\8&1\end{bmatrix}$ (B) $-\frac{1}{13}\begin{bmatrix}1&-8\\-2&3\end{bmatrix}$

(C) $-\frac{1}{13}\begin{bmatrix}3&2\\8&1\end{bmatrix}$ (D) $\frac{1}{13}\begin{bmatrix}1&-8\\-2&8\end{bmatrix}$

Q.47 Consider the following statements relating to matrix operation:

1. If A is a $m\times n$ matrix, then B has to be a $n\times m$ matrix for AB and BA to be defined.
2. If $(A+B)$ and AB are defined, then A and B must be square matrices of the same order.
3. If AB and BA are both defined, then $AB=0$ implies $BA=0$, where 0 is the null matrix.

Of these statements

(A) 1 and 2 are correct (B) 1 and 3 are correct

(C) 2 and 3 are correct (D) 1, 2 and 3 are correct

Q.48 Consider the following statements relating to any two matrices A and B such that AB is defined:

1. $(AB)^{-1}=B^{-1}A^{-1}$
2. $(AB)^T=B^TA^T$
3. rank $(AB)\le\min[\text{rank}(A),\text{rank}(B)]$

Of these statements

(A) 1, 2 and 3 are correct (B) 1and 2 are correct

(C) 1and 3 are correct (D) 2 and 3 are correct

Q.49 If $A=\begin{bmatrix}-1&2\\3&-5\end{bmatrix}$, then its inverse is

(A) $\begin{bmatrix}-5&-2\\-3&-1\end{bmatrix}$ (B) $\begin{bmatrix}5&2\\3&1\end{bmatrix}$

(C) $\begin{bmatrix}-5&2\\3&-1\end{bmatrix}$ (D) $\begin{bmatrix}5&3\\2&1\end{bmatrix}$

Q.50 If $A=\begin{bmatrix}3&2\\1&4\end{bmatrix}$, then $A\,\text{adj}(A)$ equals

(A) $\begin{bmatrix}10&0\\0&10\end{bmatrix}$ (B) $\begin{bmatrix}0&10\\10&0\end{bmatrix}$

(C) $\begin{bmatrix}10&1\\1&10\end{bmatrix}$ (D) None of these

Q.51 to Q.65 Numerical Answer Questions

Q.51 Consider the following matrix $A=\begin{bmatrix}2&3\\x&y\end{bmatrix}$. If the eigenvalues of A are 4 and 8, then the value of x is______.

Q.52 Let $A=\begin{bmatrix}2 & -0.1\\0 & 3\end{bmatrix}$ and $A^{-1}=\begin{bmatrix}1/2 & a\\0 & b\end{bmatrix}$, then $(a+b)$ is equal to______.

Q.53 If $A=\begin{bmatrix}1 & 3\\3 & 4\end{bmatrix}$ and $A^2-kA-5I_2=0$, then the value of k is______.

Q.54 If $A=\begin{bmatrix}-8 & 5\\2 & 4\end{bmatrix}$ then $|A^2+4A+42I|$ is equal to___.

Q.55 If $A+B=\begin{bmatrix}0 & 0\\2 & 1\end{bmatrix}$ and $A-B=\begin{bmatrix}0 & 2\\0 & 1\end{bmatrix}$, then $\det(A)$ is equal to______.

Q.56 The system of equations

$$\left.\begin{array}{l}2x+y=5\\x-3y=-1\\3x+4y=k\end{array}\right\}\text{ is consistent, when } k \text{ is\_\_\_\_\_.}$$

Q.57 If $A=\begin{bmatrix}0 & 1 & 0 & 0\\0 & 2 & 0 & 1\\0 & 3 & 2 & 0\\1 & 4 & 1 & 0\end{bmatrix}$, then $\det(A^{-1})$ is equal to___.

Q.58 If $A=\begin{bmatrix}1 & 1 & 1\\1 & 2 & -3\\2 & -1 & 3\end{bmatrix}$ and $B=\text{adj}(A)$, then the value of B_{23}(the element in B belonging to second row and third column) is______.

Q.59 If $A=\begin{bmatrix}-5 & -3\\2 & 0\end{bmatrix}$, then $|A^3|$ is equal to_______.

Q.60 The sum of the eigenvalues of the inverse of $A=\begin{bmatrix}2 & 0 & 0\\1 & 3 & 0\\3 & 1 & 1\end{bmatrix}$ is ______.

Q.61 The minimum and the maximum eigenvalues of the matrix $\begin{bmatrix}1 & 1 & 3\\1 & 5 & 1\\3 & 1 & 1\end{bmatrix}$ are –2 and 6, respectively. What is the other eigenvalue?_________.

Q.62 If $A=\begin{bmatrix}2x & 0\\x & x\end{bmatrix}$ and $A^{-1}=\begin{bmatrix}1 & 0\\-1 & 2\end{bmatrix}$, then the value of x is_____.

Q.63 If A and B are matrices of order 4×4 such that $A=5B$ and $|A|=\alpha\cdot|B|$, then α is _________.

Q.64 If $\det(A)=0.5$, where $A=\begin{bmatrix}a & b & c\\d & e & f\\g & b & c\end{bmatrix}$ then $\det(2A)^{-1}$ is equal to _____.

Q.65 Let A be a 3×3 matrix with eigenvalues $1, -1, 0$. Then the determinant of $I+A^{100}$ is _____.

1.4 SOLUTION TO PRACTICE PAPER

Q.1 Ans:(D)

A and B are two square matrices

$$(A+B)^2=(A+B)(A+B)$$

or $(A+B)^2=(A+B)A+(A+B)B$

or $(A+B)^2=A^2+BA+AB+B^2$

$$(A+B)^2=A^2+AB+BA+B^2$$

Q.2 Ans:(B)

If $AA^T=I$, then matrix A is orthogonal.

or $A^{-1}AA^T=A^{-1}I \Rightarrow IA^T=A^{-1}I$

$$A^{-1}=A^T$$

Q.3 Ans:(A)

If matrix A is of order n, and k is constant, then

$$\det(kA)=k^n\det(A)$$

Substituting $n=2$ and $k=2$, we have

or $\det(2A)=2^2\det(A)$

$$\det(2A)=2^2\Delta$$

Q.4 Ans:(C)

Given: Matrix $A=\begin{bmatrix}1 & 4\\3 & 2\end{bmatrix}$

The characteristic equation of this matrix is given by

$$|A-\lambda I|=0 \quad\Rightarrow\quad \begin{vmatrix}1-\lambda & 4\\3 & 2-\lambda\end{vmatrix}=0$$

or $(1-\lambda)(2-\lambda)-12=0$

or $(\lambda-5)(\lambda+2)=0$

$$\lambda_1=5, \lambda_2=-2$$

Therefore,

The eigenvalues of A are $5, -2$.

Q.5 Ans:(B)

Given: $I+A+A^2+\ldots+A^k=0$ (i)

Multiplying by $\mathbf{A}^{-1}$, we get

$A^{-1} + I + A + A^2 + \ldots + A^{k-1} = 0$ (ii)

From equations (i) and (ii), we obtain

$$A^{-1} - A^k = 0$$

$$A^{-1} = A^k$$

Q.6 Ans:(C)

Given: Matrices $A = \begin{bmatrix} 2 & 3 & 0 \\ 1 & -1 & 1 \\ 2 & 0 & 1 \end{bmatrix}$ and $B = \begin{bmatrix} 1 & -1 & 2 \\ 0 & 1 & -1 \\ 1 & 2 & 1 \end{bmatrix}$

Determinant of matrix *A*;

$$|A| = 2 \times (-1-0) - 3 \times (1-2) + 0 \times (0+2) = 1$$

Determinant of matrix *B*;

$$|B| = 1 \times (1+2) - 0 \times (-1-4) + 1 \times (1-2) = 2$$

Determinant of matrix AB: $|AB| = |A| \times |B|$

$$\det(AB) = 1 \times 2$$

$$\det(AB) = 2$$

Q.7 Ans:(D)

Given: Matrix $A = \begin{bmatrix} 1 & 1 & 1 \\ 1 & 1 & 1 \\ 1 & 1 & 1 \end{bmatrix}$

Eigenvalues of *A* are the roots of the characteristic polynomial given below

$$|A - \lambda I| = 0 \Rightarrow \begin{bmatrix} 1-\lambda & 1 & 1 \\ 1 & 1-\lambda & 1 \\ 1 & 1 & 1-\lambda \end{bmatrix} = 0$$

From which

$$\lambda^2(\lambda - 3) = 0$$

Eigenvalues are

$$0, 0, 3$$

Q.8 Ans:(B)

If *A* be a non-zero square matrix of order n, then

$$A = \frac{1}{2}(A + A^T) + \frac{1}{2}(A - A^T)$$

where

$\frac{1}{2}(A + A^T)$ is symmetric matrix

$\frac{1}{2}(A - A^T)$ is anti-symmetric matrix

Q.9 Ans:(B)

If $A A^T = I$, then matrix *A* is orthogonal.

$$|A A^T| = 1$$

or $|A||A^T| = 1$, since $|A| = |A^T|$

or $|A|^2 = 1$

$$|A| = \pm 1$$

Q.10 Ans:(B)

Let n be the order of matrix *A*

$$A^{-1} = \frac{\text{adj}(A)}{|A|}$$

or $\text{adj}(A) = |A| A^{-1}$

or $|\text{adj}(A)| = |A|^n |A^{-1}| = \frac{|A|^n}{|A|}$

$$|\text{adj}(A)| = |A|^{n-1}$$

Q.11 Ans:(B)

$$A^{-1} = \frac{\text{adj } A}{|A|} \text{ or } I = AA^{-1} = \frac{A \text{ adj } A}{|A|}$$

or $A \text{ adj } A = |A| I = |A| \begin{bmatrix} 1 & 0 \\ 0 & 1 \end{bmatrix}$

where $k = |A| = \begin{vmatrix} \cos x & \sin x \\ -\sin x & \cos x \end{vmatrix} = \cos^2 x + \sin^2 x$

$$k = 1$$

Q.12 Ans:(C)

Given: Matrix $A = \begin{bmatrix} 1 & 2 & 4 \\ 3 & 0 & 6 \\ 1 & 1 & p \end{bmatrix}$

Let λ_1 and λ_2 be the other two eigenvalues.

Sum of the eigenvalues = trace of matrix

$$3 + \lambda_1 + \lambda_2 = 1 + 0 + p$$

Sum of the other two eigenvalues $\lambda_1 + \lambda_2 = p - 2$

Q.13 Ans:(A)

$$A(BC) = (AB)C$$

Q.14 Ans:(B)

For any square matrix *A*,

Matrix $B = \frac{A - A^T}{2}$ is skew-symmetric matrix.

Q.15 Ans:(A)

Properties of transpose matrices; $(AB)^T = B^T A^T$

Thus,

rank of matrix $(B^T A^T)$ = rank of $(AB) = n$

Q.16 Ans:(C)

Let λ_1 and λ_2 be the eigenvalues of matrix.

$$\text{trace}(A) = -2 = \lambda_1 + \lambda_2 \quad \text{(i)}$$

and $\det(A) = -35 = \lambda_1\lambda_2$ (ii)

Solving equations (i) and (ii), we obtain λ_1 and $\lambda_2 = 5, -7$

Eigenvalues are -7 and 5

Q.17 Ans:(C)

$(A+B)^{-1} = B^{-1} + A^{-1}$ is true

$(AB)^{-1} = B^{-1}A^{-1}$ is true

$AB = O \Rightarrow |A| = 0$ or $|B| = 0$ is not true

$\text{adj}(AB) = (\text{adj}B)(\text{adj}A)$ is true

Q.18 Ans:(B)

The characteristic equation of a matrix A is

$$\lambda^3 - \lambda + 1 = 0$$

By Cayley-Hamilton theorem

$$A^3 - A + I = 0$$

$$A^3 = A - I$$

Q.19 Ans:(B)

The characteristic equation of A is $|A - \lambda I| = 0$

or $\begin{bmatrix} 1-\lambda & 1 \\ 1 & 1-\lambda \end{bmatrix} = 0$

or $\lambda^2 - 2\lambda = 0$

By Cayley-Hemilton theorem $A^2 - 2A = 0$

or $A^2 = 2A$

$$A^3 = A^2A = 2AA = 2A^2 = 2^2A$$

$$A^4 = A^3A = 2^2AA = 2^2A^2 = 2^2 2A = 2^3A$$

Similarly, $A^5 = 2^4A$

$$A^n = 2^{n-1}A$$

Q.20 Ans:(C)

If matrices A and B are symmetric matrix of the same order, then $AB = BA$. Thus

$AB - BA = 0$ Null matrix

Q.21 Ans:[1]

Order of matrix A is 4×1;

Rank of matrix $r(A) = \min(4, 1) = 1$

Order of matrix B is 1×3;

Rank of matrix $r(B) = \min(1, 3) = 1$

Rank of matrix $r(AB) = \min\{r(A), r(B)\} = 1$

$$r(AB) = 1$$

Q.22 Ans:[0.5]

Given: Matrix $A = \begin{bmatrix} 1 & -1 & 2 \\ 0 & 1 & -1 \\ 1 & 2 & 1 \end{bmatrix}$

Determinant of matrix A

$$\det(A) = 1 \times (1+2) + 1 \times (1-2) = 2$$

$$\det(A^{-1}) = \frac{1}{\det(A)} = \frac{1}{2}$$

$$\det(A^{-1}) = 0.5$$

Q.23 Ans:[0]

Diagonal elements of skew-symmetric matrix are zero.

Trace (A) = Sum of diagonal elements

trace $(A) = 0$.

Q.24 Ans:[7]

Diagonal elements of the matrix $\begin{bmatrix} 1 & 1 & 3 \\ 1 & 5 & 1 \\ 3 & 1 & 1 \end{bmatrix}$ are 1,5,1.

Sum of eigenvalues = Sum of diagonal elements.

Sum of eigenvalues $= 1 + 5 + 1 = 7$

Q.25 Ans:[1]

Matrix $A = \begin{bmatrix} 3 & 2 & -9 \\ -6 & -4 & 18 \\ 12 & 8 & -36 \end{bmatrix}$

or $A = \begin{bmatrix} 3 & 2 & -9 \\ 0 & 0 & 0 \\ 0 & 0 & 0 \end{bmatrix} \begin{matrix} \\ \leftarrow R_2 + 2R_1 \\ \leftarrow R_3 - 4R_1 \end{matrix}$, $|A| = 0$

and determinant of all 2×2 minors are zero.

Therefore,

The rank of given matrix is 1.

Q.26 Ans:[0]

Determinant of matrix = product of eigenvalues

Determinant of matrix $= 15 \times 3 \times 0 = 0$

Determinant of matrix $= 0$

Q.27 Ans:[0]

The rank of a null matrix is 0

Q.28 Ans:[4]

Determinant of matrix A;

$$|A| = \begin{vmatrix} 1 & 0 & 0 & 0 \\ 1 & 2 & 0 & 0 \\ 2 & 2 & 3 & 0 \\ 7 & 5 & 3 & 4 \end{vmatrix} = 1\times 2\times 3\times 4 = 24 \neq 0$$

Therefore,

Rank of given matrix is 4

Q.29 Ans:[2]

Highest rank of matrix $A =$ least value of 3 and 4 $= 3$

If the rank of $A = 3$ then rank of $[A \ |B]$ also would be 3, which means the system would become consistent. But it is given that system is inconsistent. Thus,

Maximum rank of A is 2

Q.30 Ans:[12]

If $\lambda_1, \lambda_2, \ldots, \lambda_n$ are the eigenvalues of A, then $k\lambda_1, k\lambda_2, \ldots, k\lambda_n$ are the eigenvalues of kA.

Eigenvalues of matrix $2A$ are 2, 4, 6

trace of matrix $2A =$ sum of eigenvalues

$$\text{trace}(2A) = 2+4+6$$

$$\text{trace}(2A) = 12$$

Q.31 Ans:(A)

The equation of plane passing through the points $(0,1,0)$, $(-1,3,2)$ and $(-2,0,1)$ is given by

$$\begin{vmatrix} x & y & z & 1 \\ 0 & 1 & 0 & 1 \\ -1 & 3 & 2 & 1 \\ -2 & 0 & 1 & 1 \end{vmatrix} = 0$$

From which

$$4x - 3y + 5z + 3 = 0$$

Q.32 Ans:(C)

The given system of equations in matrix form $(AX = B)$ is

$$\begin{bmatrix} 1 & 1 & 1 \\ 1 & 2 & 3 \\ 1 & 2 & \lambda \end{bmatrix}\begin{bmatrix} x \\ y \\ z \end{bmatrix} = \begin{bmatrix} 6 \\ 10 \\ \mu \end{bmatrix}$$

Augmented matrix $[A{:}B] = \begin{bmatrix} 1 & 1 & 1 & 6 \\ 1 & 2 & 3 & 10 \\ 1 & 2 & \lambda & \mu \end{bmatrix}$

$$[A{:}B] \sim \begin{bmatrix} 1 & 1 & 1 & 6 \\ 0 & 1 & 2 & 4 \\ 0 & 1 & \lambda-1 & \mu-6 \end{bmatrix} \begin{matrix} \\ \leftarrow R_2 - R_1 \\ \leftarrow R_3 - R_1 \end{matrix}$$

$$[A{:}B] \sim \begin{bmatrix} 1 & 1 & 1 & 6 \\ 0 & 1 & 2 & 4 \\ 0 & 0 & \lambda-3 & \mu-10 \end{bmatrix} \begin{matrix} \\ \\ \leftarrow R_3 - R_2 \end{matrix}$$

There is no solution $\text{rank}[A{:}B] \neq \text{rank}A$

Now let $\text{rank}[A{:}B] = 3$, $\text{rank}[A] = 2$

so that $\lambda - 3 = 0$, $\mu - 10 \neq 0$

Thus

$$\lambda = 3 \text{ and } \mu \neq 10$$

Q.33 Ans:(D)

For any two 2×2 symmetric matrices A and B.

$(A+B)$ is a symmetric matrix . . . correct

(AB) is a symmetric matrix . . . correct

$AB = (BA)^T$ . . . correct

$A^T B = AB^T$ . . . correct

Q.34 Ans:(C)

Given: Matrices $P+Q = \begin{bmatrix} 1 & -1 \\ 3 & 0 \end{bmatrix}$ and $P-Q = \begin{bmatrix} 3 & 1 \\ 1 & 4 \end{bmatrix}$

From which

$$P = \frac{(P+Q)+(P-Q)}{2} = \begin{bmatrix} 2 & 0 \\ 2 & 2 \end{bmatrix}$$

and $$Q = \frac{(P+Q)-(P-Q)}{2} = \begin{bmatrix} -1 & -1 \\ 1 & -2 \end{bmatrix}$$

Now, $$PQ = \begin{bmatrix} 2 & 0 \\ 2 & 2 \end{bmatrix}\begin{bmatrix} -1 & -1 \\ 1 & -2 \end{bmatrix}$$

$$PQ = \begin{bmatrix} -2 & -2 \\ 0 & -6 \end{bmatrix}$$

Q.35 Ans:(B)

Determinant of matrix R;

$$|R| = \begin{vmatrix} 1 & 0 & -1 \\ 2 & 1 & -1 \\ 2 & 3 & 2 \end{vmatrix}$$

$$= 1\times(2+3) - 0\times(4+2) - 1\times(6-2) = 1$$

and $$\text{adj}\,R = \begin{bmatrix} 5 & -6 & 4 \\ -3 & 4 & -3 \\ 1 & -1 & 1 \end{bmatrix}^T = \begin{bmatrix} 5 & -3 & 1 \\ -6 & 4 & -1 \\ 4 & -3 & 1 \end{bmatrix}$$

$$R^{-1} = \frac{\text{adj}\,R}{|R|} = \frac{1}{1}\begin{bmatrix} 5 & -3 & 1 \\ -6 & 4 & -1 \\ 4 & -3 & 1 \end{bmatrix}$$

Top row of R^{-1} is $[5 \ \ -3 \ \ 1]$

Q.36 Ans:(D)

Given: Matrix $A = \begin{bmatrix} 1 & 0 \\ 1/2 & 1 \end{bmatrix}$

The characteristic equation of A is $|A - \lambda I| = 0$

$$\Rightarrow \quad \begin{vmatrix} 1-\lambda & 0 \\ 1/2 & 1-\lambda \end{vmatrix} = 0 \quad \text{or} \quad \lambda^2 - 2\lambda + 1 = 0$$

By Cayley-Hamilton theorem $A^2 - 2A + I = 0$

or $\quad A^2 = 2A - I$

and $\quad A^3 = A^2 A = (2A - I)A$

$= 2A^2 - A = 2(2A - I) - A = 3A - 2I$

Similarly $\quad A^n = nA - (n-1)I$

Substituting $n = 50$,

$$A^{50} = 50A - 49I = 50\begin{bmatrix} 1 & 0 \\ 1/2 & 1 \end{bmatrix} - 49\begin{bmatrix} 1 & 0 \\ 0 & 1 \end{bmatrix}$$

$$A^{50} = \begin{bmatrix} 1 & 0 \\ 25 & 1 \end{bmatrix}$$

Q.37 Ans:(D)

Given: Matrix $X = \begin{bmatrix} 3 & -4 \\ 1 & -1 \end{bmatrix}$

The characteristic equation of X is $|X - \lambda I| = 0$

or $\quad \begin{vmatrix} 3-\lambda & -4 \\ 1 & -1-\lambda \end{vmatrix} = 0$

or $\quad (\lambda + 1)(\lambda - 3) + 4 = 0 \Rightarrow \quad \lambda^2 - 2\lambda + 1 = 0$

By Cayley-Hamilton theorem $X^2 - 2X + I = 0$

or $\quad X^2 = 2X - I$

and $\quad X^3 = X^2 X = (2X - I)X$

$= 2X^2 - X = 2(2X - I) - X = 3X - 2I$

Similarly $\quad X^4 = 4X - 3I$

$\ldots X^n = nX - (n-1)I$

$$X^n = n\begin{bmatrix} 3 & -4 \\ 1 & -1 \end{bmatrix} - (n-1)\begin{bmatrix} 1 & 0 \\ 0 & 1 \end{bmatrix}$$

$$X^n = \begin{bmatrix} 2n+1 & -4n \\ n & -2n+1 \end{bmatrix}$$

Q.38 Ans:(B)

The characteristic equation is

$$|A - \lambda I| = \begin{bmatrix} 1-\lambda & 2 & 3 \\ 0 & 2-\lambda & 3 \\ 0 & 0 & 2-\lambda \end{bmatrix} = 0$$

or $\quad (1-\lambda)(2-\lambda)(2-\lambda) = 0$

$\lambda = 1, 2, 2$

Characteristic roots are 1, 2, 2

Q.39 Ans:(A)

$$AX = B \quad \Rightarrow \quad A^{-1}AX = A^{-1}B$$

or $\quad X = A^{-1}B$

or $\quad X = \begin{bmatrix} 3 & -1/2 & -1/2 \\ -4 & 3/4 & 5/4 \\ 2 & -1/4 & -3/4 \end{bmatrix}\begin{bmatrix} 9 \\ 52 \\ 0 \end{bmatrix} = \begin{bmatrix} 1 \\ 3 \\ 5 \end{bmatrix}$

$$X = \begin{bmatrix} 1 \\ 3 \\ 5 \end{bmatrix}$$

Q.40 Ans:(B)

Given set of equation can be written as $Ax = B$

or $\quad \begin{bmatrix} 3 & 2 & 1 \\ 1 & -1 & 1 \\ -2 & 0 & 2 \end{bmatrix}\begin{bmatrix} x \\ y \\ z \end{bmatrix} = \begin{bmatrix} 4 \\ 2 \\ 5 \end{bmatrix}$

and $|A| = 3 \times (-2 - 0) - 2 \times (2 + 2) + 1 \times (0 - 2) = 16$

Since $|A| \neq 0$, thus there exist a unique solution

Q.41 Ans:(A)

Given: Matrix $\quad A = \begin{bmatrix} 2 & 1 & 3 \\ 1 & 2 & 0 \\ 2 & 1 & -1 \end{bmatrix}$

$$\det(A) = \begin{vmatrix} 2 & 1 & 3 \\ 1 & 2 & 0 \\ 2 & 1 & -1 \end{vmatrix}$$

$$= 2 \times (-2 - 0) - 1 \times (-1 - 0) + 3 \times (1 - 4) = -12$$

$$\det(A^{-1}) = \frac{1}{\det(A)} = -\frac{1}{12}$$

$$\det(A^{-1}) = -\frac{1}{12}$$

Q.42 Ans:(A)

The characteristic equation of matrix A is $|A - \lambda I| = 0$

or $\begin{vmatrix} 2-\lambda & 2 & 1 \\ 1 & 3-\lambda & 1 \\ 1 & 2 & 2-\lambda \end{vmatrix} = 0$

From which

$$\lambda^3 - 7\lambda^2 + 11\lambda - 5 = 0$$

Q.43 Ans:(B)

Eigenvalues of square matrix are 1 and 3.

The characteristic equation of A is $(\lambda - 1)(\lambda - 3) = 0$

$$\lambda^2 - 4\lambda + 3 = 0$$

By Cayley-Hamilton theorem

$$A^2 - 4A + 3I = 0$$

or $A^2 = 4A - 3I$

Multiplying by A, we obtain

$$A^3 = 4A^2 - 3A$$

or $A^3 = 4(4A - 3I) - 3A$

$$A^3 = 13A - 12I$$

Q.44 Ans:(A)

We know $\det(kA) = k^n \det(A)$

$$\det(2A) = 2^4 \det(A)$$

$$\det(2A) = 16\det(A)$$

Q.45 Ans:(A)

The characteristic equation of A is $|A - \lambda I| = 0$

or $\begin{vmatrix} 1-\lambda & a \\ 0 & 1-\lambda \end{vmatrix} = 0$

or $\lambda^2 - 2\lambda + 1 = 0$

By Cayley-Hamilton theorem,

$$A^2 - 2A + I = 0 \quad \text{or} \quad A^2 = 2A - I$$

and $A^3 = A^2 A = (2A - I)A$

$$= 2A^2 - A = 2(2A - I) - A = 3A - 2I$$

Similarly

$$A^n = nA - (n-1)I = n\begin{bmatrix} 1 & a \\ 0 & 1 \end{bmatrix} - (n-1)\begin{bmatrix} 1 & 0 \\ 0 & 1 \end{bmatrix}$$

$$A^n = \begin{bmatrix} 1 & na \\ 0 & 1 \end{bmatrix}$$

$$\lim_{n\to\infty} \frac{1}{n} A^n = \lim_{n\to\infty} \begin{bmatrix} 1/n & a \\ 0 & 1/n \end{bmatrix} = \begin{bmatrix} 0 & a \\ 0 & 0 \end{bmatrix}$$

$$\lim_{n\to\infty} \frac{1}{n} A^n = \begin{bmatrix} 0 & a \\ 0 & 0 \end{bmatrix}$$

Q.46 Ans:(B)

Given: Matrix $A = \begin{bmatrix} 3 & 8 \\ 2 & 1 \end{bmatrix}$

$$|A| = -13$$

$$\text{adj}(A) = \begin{bmatrix} 1 & -2 \\ -8 & 3 \end{bmatrix}^T = \begin{bmatrix} 1 & -8 \\ -2 & 3 \end{bmatrix}$$

$$A^{-1} = \frac{\text{adj}(A)}{|A|} = -\frac{1}{13}\begin{bmatrix} 1 & -8 \\ -2 & 3 \end{bmatrix}$$

Q.47 Ans:(A)

1. If A is a $m \times n$ matrix, then B has to be a $n \times m$ matrix for AB and BA to be defined.

2. If $(A+B)$ and AB are defined, then A and B must be square matrices of the same order.

Q.48 Ans:(A)

1. $(AB)^{-1} = B^{-1}A^{-1}$ correct

2. $(AB)^T = B^T A^T$ correct

3. $\text{rank}(AB) \le \min[\text{rank}(A), \text{rank}(B)]$ correct

Q.49 Ans:(B)

Given: Matrix $A = \begin{bmatrix} -1 & 2 \\ 3 & -5 \end{bmatrix}$

$$|A| = 5 - 6 = -1$$

$$\text{adj}(A) = \begin{bmatrix} -5 & -3 \\ -2 & -1 \end{bmatrix}^T = \begin{bmatrix} -5 & -2 \\ -3 & -1 \end{bmatrix}$$

$$A^{-1} = \frac{\text{adj}(A)}{|A|} = \frac{1}{-1}\begin{bmatrix} -5 & -2 \\ -3 & -1 \end{bmatrix}$$

$$A^{-1} = \begin{bmatrix} 5 & 2 \\ 3 & 1 \end{bmatrix}$$

Q.50 Ans:(A)

$$A^{-1} = \frac{\text{adj}(A)}{|A|} \quad \text{or} \quad I = \frac{A\,\text{adj}(A)}{|A|}$$

or $A\,\text{adj}(A) = |A|I = 10\begin{bmatrix} 1 & 0 \\ 0 & 1 \end{bmatrix}$

$$A\,\text{adj}(A) = \begin{bmatrix} 10 & 0 \\ 0 & 10 \end{bmatrix}$$

Q.51 Ans:[– 4]

Given: Matrix $A = \begin{bmatrix} 2 & 3 \\ x & y \end{bmatrix}$

Trace of matrix A = Sum of eigenvalues

$$2 + y = 4 + 8$$
$$y = 10$$

Determinant of A = Product of eigenvalues

$$2y - 3x = 4 \times 8$$
$$2 \times 10 - 3x = 32$$
$$x = -4$$

Q.52 Ans:[0.35]

Given: Matrices $A = \begin{bmatrix} 2 & -0.1 \\ 0 & 3 \end{bmatrix}$ and $A^{-1} = \begin{bmatrix} 1/2 & a \\ 0 & b \end{bmatrix}$

we have $AA^{-1} = I$

$$\begin{bmatrix} 2 & -0.1 \\ 0 & 3 \end{bmatrix}\begin{bmatrix} 0.5 & a \\ 0 & b \end{bmatrix} = \begin{bmatrix} 1 & 0 \\ 0 & 1 \end{bmatrix}$$

$$\begin{bmatrix} 1 & 2a - 0.1b \\ 0 & 3b \end{bmatrix} = \begin{bmatrix} 1 & 0 \\ 0 & 1 \end{bmatrix}$$

From which

$$3b = 1 \Rightarrow b = \frac{1}{3}$$
$$2a - 0.1b = 0$$
$$\Rightarrow \quad 2a - 0.1 \times \frac{1}{3} = 0 \quad \text{or} \quad a = \frac{0.1}{6}$$
$$a + b = \frac{1}{3} + \frac{0.1}{6} = \frac{2.1}{6}$$
$$a + b = 0.35$$

Q.53 Ans:[5]

The characteristic equation of A is $|A - \lambda I| = 0$

or $$\begin{vmatrix} 1-\lambda & 3 \\ 3 & 4-\lambda \end{vmatrix} = 0$$

or $$\lambda^2 - 5\lambda - 5 = 0$$

By Cayley-Hamilton theorem,

$$A^2 - 5A - 5I_2 = 0$$

Compare with given equation $A^2 - kA - 5I_2 = 0$

From which

$$k = 5$$

Q.54 Ans:[84]

The characteristic equation of A is $|A - \lambda I| = 0$

$$\begin{vmatrix} -8-\lambda & 5 \\ 2 & 4-\lambda \end{vmatrix} = 0$$

or $$\lambda^2 + 4\lambda - 42 = 0$$

By Cayley-Hamilton theorem,

$$A^2 + 4A - 42I = 0$$

or $$A^2 + 4A + 42I = 84I$$

$$|A^2 + 4A + 42I| = 84$$

Q.55 Ans:[–1]

Given: Matrices $A + B = \begin{bmatrix} 0 & 0 \\ 2 & 1 \end{bmatrix}$ and $A - B = \begin{bmatrix} 0 & 2 \\ 0 & 1 \end{bmatrix}$

$$A = \frac{(A+B) + (A-B)}{2} = \begin{bmatrix} 0 & 1 \\ 1 & 1 \end{bmatrix}$$

$$\det(A) = \begin{vmatrix} 0 & 1 \\ 1 & 1 \end{vmatrix} = 0 - 1$$

$$\det(A) = -1$$

Q.56 Ans:[10]

A system of equations is said to be consistent if they have one or more solution.

$$2x + y = 5 \qquad \text{(i)}$$
$$x - 3y = -1 \qquad \text{(ii)}$$
$$3x + 4y = k \qquad \text{(iii)}$$

Solving for x, y from equations (i) and (ii), we obtain

$$x = 2, \; y = 1$$

Substituting $x = 2$ and $y = 1$ in equation (iii);

$$3 \times 2 + 4 \times 1 = k$$
$$k = 10$$

Q.57 Ans:[0.5]

Given: Matrix $A = \begin{bmatrix} 0 & 1 & 0 & 0 \\ 0 & 2 & 0 & 1 \\ 0 & 3 & 2 & 0 \\ 1 & 4 & 1 & 0 \end{bmatrix}$

$$|A| = -1\begin{vmatrix} 0 & 0 & 1 \\ 0 & 2 & 0 \\ 1 & 1 & 0 \end{vmatrix} = 2$$

$$\det(A^{-1}) = \frac{1}{\det(A)} = \frac{1}{2}$$

$$\det(A^{-1}) = 0.5$$

Q.58 Ans:[4]

Given: Matrix $A = \begin{bmatrix} 1 & 1 & 1 \\ 1 & 2 & -3 \\ 2 & -1 & 3 \end{bmatrix}$

$$B = \text{adj}(A) = \begin{bmatrix} 3 & -9 & -5 \\ -4 & 1 & 3 \\ -5 & 4 & 1 \end{bmatrix}^T = \begin{bmatrix} 3 & -4 & -5 \\ -9 & 1 & (4) \\ -5 & 3 & 1 \end{bmatrix}$$

$$B = \begin{bmatrix} 3 & -4 & -5 \\ -9 & 1 & (4) \\ -5 & 3 & 1 \end{bmatrix}$$

$$B_{23} = 4$$

Q.59 Ans:[-924]

The characteristic equation of A is $|A - \lambda I| = 0$

or $\begin{bmatrix} -5-\lambda & -3 \\ 2 & -\lambda \end{bmatrix} = 0$

or $\lambda^2 + 5\lambda + 6 = 0$

By Caley-Hamilton theorem

$$A^2 + 5A + 6I = 0$$

or $A^2 = -5A - 6I$

$$A^3 = A^2 A = (-5A - 6I)A$$

$$= -5A^2 - 6A = -5(-5A - 6I) - 6A$$

$$= 19A + 30I$$

or $A^3 = 19A + 30I = 19\begin{bmatrix} -5 & -3 \\ 2 & 0 \end{bmatrix} + 30\begin{bmatrix} 1 & 0 \\ 0 & 1 \end{bmatrix}$

or $A^3 = \begin{bmatrix} -65 & -57 \\ 18 & 30 \end{bmatrix}$

$$|A^3| = -924$$

Q.60 Ans:[1.83]

Let $\lambda_1, \lambda_2, \lambda_3$ be the eigenvalues of matrix A.

The characteristic equation of A is $|A - \lambda I| = 0$

$$\begin{bmatrix} 2-\lambda & 0 & 0 \\ 1 & 3-\lambda & 0 \\ 3 & 1 & 1-\lambda \end{bmatrix} = 0$$

or $(2-\lambda)(3-\lambda)(1-\lambda) = 0$

or $\lambda_1 = 2,\ \lambda_2 = 3$ and $\lambda_3 = 1$

Eigenvalues of the inverse of $A = \begin{bmatrix} 2 & 0 & 0 \\ 1 & 3 & 0 \\ 3 & 1 & 1 \end{bmatrix}$ are

$$\frac{1}{2}, \frac{1}{3} \text{ and } \frac{1}{1}$$

Sum of eigenvalues of inverse of $A = \frac{1}{2} + \frac{1}{3} + \frac{1}{1} = \frac{11}{6}$

Sum of eigenvalues of inverse of $A = 1.83$

Q.61 Ans:[3]

Let λ be the other eigenvalue.

Trace of matrix A = Sum of eigenvalues

$$1 + 5 + 1 = -2 + \lambda + 6$$

$$\lambda = 3$$

Q.62 Ans:[0.5]

Given: Matrices $A = \begin{bmatrix} 2x & 0 \\ x & x \end{bmatrix}$ and $A^{-1} = \begin{bmatrix} 1 & 0 \\ -1 & 2 \end{bmatrix}$

Now $AA^{-1} = I$ or $\begin{bmatrix} 2x & 0 \\ x & x \end{bmatrix}\begin{bmatrix} 1 & 0 \\ -1 & 2 \end{bmatrix} = \begin{bmatrix} 1 & 0 \\ 0 & 1 \end{bmatrix}$

or $\begin{bmatrix} 2x & 0 \\ 0 & 2x \end{bmatrix} = \begin{bmatrix} 1 & 0 \\ 0 & 1 \end{bmatrix}$

From which $2x = 1$

$$x = 0.5$$

Q.63 Ans:[625]

Order of matrices A and B are 4, and $A = 5B$

$$\det(A) = \alpha \det(B)$$

or $\det(5B) = \alpha \det(B)$

or $5^4 \det(B) = \alpha \det(B)$

or $\alpha = 5^4$

$$\alpha = 625$$

Q.64 Ans:[0.25]

Order of given matrix is 3

$$\det(2A)^{-1} = \frac{1}{\det(2A)} = \frac{1}{2^3 \det(A)}$$

$$\det(2A)^{-1} = \frac{1}{2^3 \times 0.5} = \frac{1}{4}$$

$$\det(2A)^{-1} = 0.25$$

Q.65 Ans:[4]

Eigenvalues of matrix A are $1, -1, 0$, then

Eigenvalues of matrix A^{100} are $1^{100}, (-1)^{100}, 0^{100}$

or Eigenvalues of matrix A^{100} are $1, 1, 0$

and Eigenvalues of matrix $(I + A^{100})$ are

$$1+1,\ 1+1,\ 1+0$$

Therefore,

Determinant of matrix $I + A^{100}$

$$= (1+1)(1+1)(1+0)$$

Determinant of matrix $I + A^{100} = 4$

2 Calculus

GATE Syllabus

Calculus: Functions of single variable, Limit, Continuity and differentiability, Mean value theorems, Indeterminate forms, Evaluation of definite and improper integrals, Double and triple integrals, Partial derivatives, Total derivative, Taylor series (in one and two variables), Maxima and minima, Fourier series; gradient, Divergence and Curl, Vector identities, Directional derivatives, Line, Surface and Volume integrals, Applications of Gauss, Stokes and Green's theorems.

Chapter Outline

2.1 KEY CONCEPTS AND FORMULAS

Limit, Continuity and Differentiability

Function

A function is a mathematical rule that assigns to each input value gives one and only one output value.

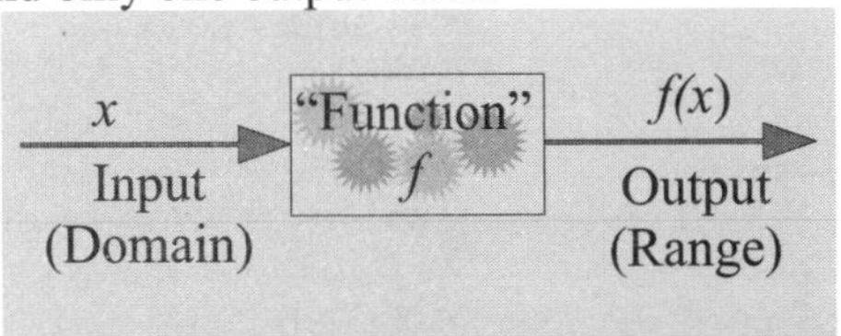

A flow diagram for a function f.

Limit

If $f(x)$ gets closer to a number L as x gets closer and closer to c from either side, then L is the limit of $f(x)$ as x approaches c.

$$\lim_{x\to c} f(x) = L$$

$$\Rightarrow \lim_{x\to c^+} f(x) = L \text{ and } \lim_{x\to c^-} f(x) = L$$

Continuity

A function f is continuous at $x = c$, if

(a) $f(c)$ is exists (b) $\lim_{x\to c} f(x)$ exists (c) $\lim_{x\to c} f(x) = f(c)$

If $f(x)$ is not continuous at $x = c$, it is said to have a *discontinuity* there.

Differentiability

A function $f(x)$ is differentiable at $x = c$ if

$$\lim_{h\to 0^+} \frac{f(c+h)-f(c)}{h} = \lim_{h\to 0^-} \frac{f(c-h)-f(c)}{-h}$$

Derivative (Differential Coefficient)

The derivative of the function f with respect to the variable

x is the function f' whose value at x is

$f'(x) = \lim_{h \to 0} \frac{f(x+h) - f(x)}{h}$ provided the limit exists.

Differentiation Rules

- $\frac{d}{dx}(x^n) = nx^{n-1}$
- $\frac{d}{dx}(c) = 0$
- $\frac{d}{dx}(cf) = c\frac{d}{dx}(f)$
- $\frac{d}{dx}(f+g) = \frac{df}{dx} + \frac{dg}{dx}$
- $\frac{d}{dx}(fg) = f\frac{dg}{dx} + g\frac{df}{dx}$
- $\frac{d}{dx}\left(\frac{f}{g}\right) = \frac{g\frac{df}{dx} - f\frac{dg}{dx}}{g^2}$
- $\frac{d}{dx} f_1\{f_2(x)\} = \frac{d}{dt} f_1(t) \times \frac{dt}{dx}$, where, $t = f_2(x)$

Geometric Interpretation of the Derivative

The derivative $f'(x)$ expresses the slope of the tangent to the curve $y = f(x)$ as a function of the x-coordinate of the point of tangency.

Derivative of Some Standard Function

- $\frac{d}{dx} x^n = nx^{n-1}$
- $\frac{d}{dx} \sin x = \cos x$
- $\frac{d}{dx} \cos x = -\sin x$
- $\frac{d}{dx} e^n = e^x$
- $\frac{d}{dx} \log x = \frac{1}{x}$
- $\frac{d}{dx} c = 0$
- $\frac{d}{dx} \log_a {}^x = \frac{1}{x \log a}$
- $\frac{d}{dx} \tan x = \sec^2 x$
- $\frac{d}{dx} \cot n = \text{cosec}^2 n$
- $\frac{d}{dx} \sec x = \sec x \tan x$
- $\frac{d}{dx} \text{cosec}\, x = -\text{cosec}\, x \cot x$
- $\frac{d}{dx} \sin^{-1} x = \frac{1}{\sqrt{1-x^2}}$
- $\frac{d}{dx} \cos^{-1} x = -\frac{1}{\sqrt{1-x^2}}$
- $\frac{d}{dx} \tan^{-1} x = \frac{1}{1+x^2}$
- $\frac{d}{dx} \cot^{-1} x = -\frac{1}{1+x^2}$
- $\frac{d}{dx} \sec^{-1} x = \frac{1}{x\sqrt{x^2-1}}$
- $\frac{d}{dx} \text{cosec}^{-1} = -\frac{1}{x\sqrt{x^2-1}}$

Chain Rule (Differentiation of function)

Suppose y is a differentiable function of u and u is a differentiable function of x. Then y can be regarded as a function of x and

$$\frac{dy}{dx} = \frac{dy}{du} \times \frac{du}{dx}$$

That is, the derivative of y with respect to x is the derivative of y with respect to u times the derivative of u with respect to x.

The chain rule in functional notation:

If $g(u)$ and $h(x)$ are differentiable function, then

$$\frac{d}{dx} g[h(x)] = g'[h(x)]h'(x)$$

The chain rule for powers:

$$\frac{d}{dx}[h(x)]^n = n[h(x)]^{n-1}\frac{d}{dx}h(x)$$

Logarithmic Differentiation

Let $y = u^v$, where u and v are both function of x taking logarithms, we have $\log y = v \log u$. Differentiating w.r.t. x, we have

Let $y = [f_1(x)]^{f_2(x)}$ then $\log y = f_2(x) \log f_1(x)$

$$\frac{1}{y}\frac{dy}{dx} = \frac{f_2(x)}{f_1(x)} f_1'(x) + \log f_1(x) f_2'(x)$$

or $$\frac{dy}{dx} = y\left(\frac{f_2(x)}{f_1(x)} f_1'(x) + \log f_1(x) f_2'(x)\right)$$

Differentiation of the Product of any Number of Functions

Let $y = f_1(x), f_2(x), f_3(x) \ldots f_n(x)$ then

$\log y = \log f_1(x) + \log f_2(x) + \log f_3(x) \ldots \log f_n(x)$

$$\therefore \quad \frac{1}{y}\frac{dy}{dx} = \frac{f_1'(x)}{f_1(x)} + \frac{f_2'(x)}{f_2(x)} + \ldots . \frac{f_n'(x)}{f_n(x)}$$

$$\frac{dy}{dx} = [f_1(x) f_2(x) \ldots f_n(x)]\left[\frac{f_1'(x)}{f_1(x)} + \frac{f_2'(x)}{f_2(x)} + \ldots \frac{f_n'(x)}{f_n(x)}\right]$$

Differentiation of Implicit Function

If the relation between y and x is represented by an equation from which y cannot be easily expressed in terms of x, then y is called an *implicit function* of x.

To find $\frac{dy}{dx}$ of implicit function:

Differentiate both sides of the equation with respect to x.

Solve the differentiated equation algebraically for $\frac{dy}{dx}$.

Parametric Equations

Let $x = f_1(t)$ and $y = f_2(t)$, then $\frac{dy}{dx} = \frac{dy}{dt} \cdot \frac{dt}{dx} = \frac{dy/dt}{dx/dt}$

Differentiation of Infinite Series

Let $y=[f(x)]^{[f(x)]^{\cdot^{\cdot^{\infty}}}}$ then $y=[f(x)]^{y}$

or $\log y = y \log f(x)$

Differentiating $\frac{1}{y}\cdot\frac{dy}{dx}=\frac{yf'(x)}{f(x)}+\log f(x)\frac{dy}{dx}$

$$\frac{dy}{dx}=\frac{\frac{yf'(x)}{f(x)}}{\left[\frac{1}{y}-\log f(x)\right]}=\frac{y^2 f'(x)}{f(x)[1-y\log f(x)]}$$

Differentiation with Respect to a Given Function of x

Let $y=f(x)$, $z=g(x)$, $\frac{dy}{dz}=\frac{dy}{dx}\cdot\frac{dx}{dz}=\frac{f'(x)}{g'(x)}$

Leibnitz's Theorem

Let u and v be any function of x, then

$$\frac{d^n}{dx}(uv)=$$

$$\left(\frac{d^n u}{dx}\right)v+{}^nc_1\left(\frac{d^{n-1}u}{dx}\right)\left(\frac{dv}{dx}\right)+{}^nc_r\left(\frac{d^{n-r}u}{dx}\right)\left(\frac{d^r v}{dx}\right)+{}^nc_n u\cdot\left(\frac{d^n v}{dx}\right)$$

Expansion of Functions

Maclaurin's Theorem

$$f(x)=f(0)+xf'(0)+\frac{x^2}{2!}f''(0)+\ldots\frac{x^n}{n!}f^n(0)$$

Taylor's Theorem

$$f(a+h)=f(a)+hf'(a)+\frac{h^2}{2!}f''(a)+\ldots\frac{h^n}{n!}f^n(a)$$

$$f(b)=f(a)+(b-a)f'(a)+\frac{(b-a)^2}{2!}f''(a)+\ldots$$

$$f(x)=f(a)+(x-a)f'(a)+\frac{(x-a)^2}{2!}f''(a)+\ldots\frac{(x-a)^n}{n!}f^n(a)+\ldots$$

Rolle's Theorem

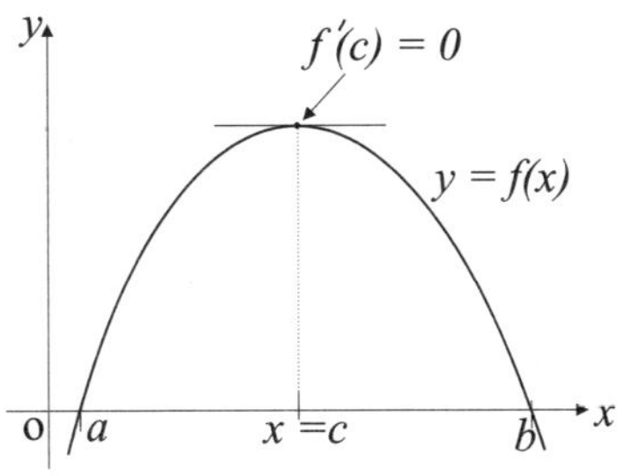

Suppose that $y=f(x)$ is continuous at every point of the closed interval $[a,b]$ and differentiable at every point of its interior (a,b).

If $f(a)=f(b)=0$, then there is at least one number c in (a,b) at which

$$f'(c)=0$$

If $f(x)$ is discontinuous at any point between a and b, or if $f'(x)$ does not exist at some point, the theorem may not be true.

The Mean Value Theorem

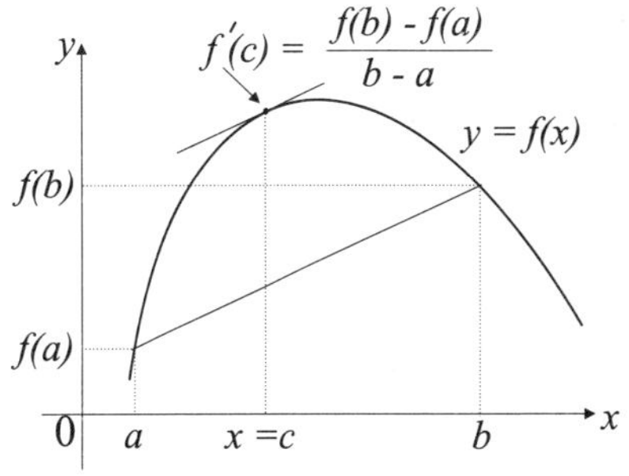

Suppose $y=f(x)$ is continuous on a closed interval $[a,b]$ and differentiable on the interval's interior (a,b). Then there is at least one point c in (a,b) at which

$$f'(c)=\frac{f(b)-f(a)}{b-a}$$

Maxima and Minima

I. Condition for maximum or minimum of $f(x)$ at $x=a$
$f'(a)=0$

II. $f''(a)=-ve$ value $\leftarrow$ maximum

$f''(a)=+ve$ value $\leftarrow$ minimum

Partial Derivatives

Suppose $z=f(x,y)$. The partial derivative of f with respect to x is denoted by $\frac{\partial z}{\partial x}$ or $f_x(x,y)$.

Partial derivative of f with respect to y is denoted by $\frac{\partial z}{\partial y}$ or $f_y(x,y)$.

Partial derivative of f_x with respect to x is

$$f_{xx}=(f_x)_x \text{ or } \frac{\partial^2 z}{\partial x^2}=\frac{\partial}{\partial x}\left(\frac{\partial z}{\partial x}\right).$$

Partial derivative of f_x with respect to y is

$$f_{xy}=(f_x)_y \text{ or } \frac{\partial^2 z}{\partial y\partial x}=\frac{\partial}{\partial y}\left(\frac{\partial z}{\partial x}\right).$$

Partial derivative of f_y with respect to x is

$$f_{yx} = (f_y)_x \quad \text{or} \quad \frac{\partial^2 z}{\partial x \partial y} = \frac{\partial}{\partial x}\left(\frac{\partial z}{\partial y}\right).$$

Partial derivative of f_y with respect to y is

$$f_{yy} = (f_y)_y \quad \text{or} \quad \frac{\partial^2 z}{\partial y^2} = \frac{\partial}{\partial y}\left(\frac{\partial z}{\partial y}\right).$$

Total Differential Coefficient

If $u = f(x, y)$, where $x = \phi(t)$, and $y = \psi(t)$ then

$$\frac{du}{dt} = \frac{\partial u}{\partial x}\cdot\frac{dx}{dt} + \frac{\partial u}{\partial y}\cdot\frac{dy}{dt}$$

Approximation Formula

Suppose z is a function of x and y. If Δx denotes a small change in x and Δy denotes a small change in y, the corresponding change in z is

$$\Delta z \approx \frac{\partial z}{\partial x}\Delta x + \frac{\partial z}{\partial y}\Delta y$$

Chain Rule for Partial Derivatives

Suppose $z = f(x, y)$ each of which is a function of t. Then z can be regarded as a function of t and

$$\frac{dz}{dt} = \frac{\partial z}{\partial x}\frac{dx}{dt} + \frac{\partial z}{\partial y}\frac{dy}{dt}$$

Homogeneous Functions

An expression in which every term is of the same degree is called a *homogeneous function*. Thus,

$$a_0 x^n + a_1 x^{n-1} y + a_2 x^{n-2} y^2 + \ldots a_{n-1} x \cdot y^{n-1} + a_n y^n$$

is a homogeneous function of x and y of degree n.

This can also be written as:

$$x^n\left\{a_0 + a_1\left(\frac{y}{x}\right) + a_2\left(\frac{y}{x}\right)^2 + \ldots a_{n-1}\left(\frac{y}{x}\right)^{n-1} + a_{n1}\left(\frac{y}{x}\right)^n\right\}$$

Euler's Theorem

If $f(x, y)$ is a homogeneous function of x and y of degree n, then $x\frac{\partial f}{\partial x} + y\frac{\partial f}{\partial y} = nf$.

If $f(x_1, x_2, x_3, \ldots, x_n)$ is a homogeneous function of $x_1, x_2, \ldots, x_n$ of degree n, then

$$x_1\frac{\partial f}{\partial x_1} + x_2\frac{\partial f}{\partial x_2} + \ldots + x_3\frac{\partial f}{\partial x_3} = nf.$$

Taylor's Theorem for Function of Two Variables

$$f(x+h, y+k) = f(x, y) + \left(h\frac{\partial f}{\partial x} + k\frac{\partial f}{\partial y}\right) + \frac{1}{2!}\left[h^2\frac{\partial^2 f}{\partial x^2} + 2hk\frac{\partial^2 f}{\partial x \partial y} + k^2\frac{\partial^2 f}{\partial y^2}\right] + \ldots$$

Change of Variables

If $u = f(x, y)$, where $x = \phi(t_1, t_2)$, and $y = \psi(t_1, t_2)$ then

$$\frac{\partial u}{\partial t_1} = \frac{\partial u}{\partial x}\cdot\frac{\partial x}{\partial t_1} + \frac{\partial u}{\partial y}\cdot\frac{\partial y}{\partial t_1} \text{ and } \frac{\partial u}{\partial t_2} = \frac{\partial u}{\partial x}\cdot\frac{\partial x}{\partial t_2} + \frac{\partial u}{\partial y}\cdot\frac{\partial y}{\partial t_2}$$

Maxima and Minima (Two independent variables)

I. Necessary condition that $f(x, y)$ should have a maximum or minimum at $x = a,\ y = b$ is that

$$\left(\frac{\partial f}{\partial x}\right)_{\substack{x=a\\y=b}} = 0, \left(\frac{\partial f}{\partial y}\right)_{\substack{x=a\\y=b}} = 0$$

II. $\left[\left(\frac{\partial^2 f}{\partial x^2}\right)\left(\frac{\partial^2 f}{\partial y^2}\right) - \left(\frac{\partial^2 f}{\partial x \partial y}\right)\right]_{\substack{x=a\\y=b}} > 0$ and

$$\left(\frac{\partial^2 f}{\partial x^2}\right)_{\substack{x=a\\y=b}} = -ve \text{ value (Maximum)}$$

$\left[\left(\frac{\partial^2 f}{\partial x^2}\right)\left(\frac{\partial^2 f}{\partial y^2}\right) - \left(\frac{\partial^2 f}{\partial x \partial y}\right)\right]_{\substack{x=a\\y=b}} > 0$ and

$$\left(\frac{\partial^2 f}{\partial x^2}\right)_{\substack{x=a\\y=b}} = +ve \text{ value (Minimum)}$$

Jacobian's

If u and v are function of two independent variables x and y, the determinant $\begin{vmatrix} \frac{\partial u}{\partial x} & \frac{\partial u}{\partial y} \\ \frac{\partial v}{\partial x} & \frac{\partial v}{\partial y} \end{vmatrix}$ is called the *Jacobian* (J) of u, v with respect to x, y and is written as $\frac{\partial(u, v)}{\partial(x, y)}$ or sometimes as $J(u, v)$.

Similarly, if u, v, w are functions of three independent variables x, y, z, the Jacobian of u, v, w with respect to x, y, z is

$$\frac{\partial(u, v, w)}{\partial(x, y, z)} = \begin{vmatrix} \frac{\partial u}{\partial x} & \frac{\partial u}{\partial y} & \frac{\partial u}{\partial z} \\ \frac{\partial v}{\partial x} & \frac{\partial v}{\partial y} & \frac{\partial v}{\partial z} \\ \frac{\partial w}{\partial x} & \frac{\partial w}{\partial y} & \frac{\partial w}{\partial z} \end{vmatrix}$$

$$\frac{\partial x}{\partial u} = \left(\frac{\partial v}{\partial y}\right) / J; \qquad \frac{\partial x}{\partial v} = -\left(\frac{\partial u}{\partial y}\right) / J$$

$$\frac{\partial y}{\partial u} = -\left(\frac{\partial v}{\partial x}\right) / J; \qquad \frac{\partial y}{\partial v} = \left(\frac{\partial u}{\partial x}\right) / J$$

Anti-derivative

A function $F(x)$ for which $F'(x) = f(x)$

for every x in the domain of F is said to be an anti-derivative (or indefinite integral) of f.

Important Integrals

- $\int x^n dx = \frac{x^{n+1}}{n+1} + C, n \neq -1$
- $\int \frac{dx}{\sqrt{1-x^2}} = \sin^{-1} x + C$
- $\int \sin x \, dx = -\cos x + C$
- $\int \frac{dx}{1+x^2} = \tan^{-1} x + C$
- $\int \cos x \, dx = \sin x + C$
- $\int e^x \, dx = e^x + C$
- $\int \sec^2 x \, dx = \tan x + C$
- $\int a^x \, dx = \frac{a^x}{\log a} + C$
- $\int \text{cosec}^2 x \, dx = -\cot x + C$
- $\int \frac{dx}{x} = \log|x| + C$
- $\int \sec x \tan x \, dx = \sec x + C$
- $\int \frac{dx}{x\sqrt{x^2-1}} = \sec^{-1} x + C$

Constant Multiple Rule for Integrals

$$\int cf(x)dx = c\int f(x)dx$$

Integral Form of the Chain Rule

$$\int g(u)\frac{du}{dx}dx = \int g(x)\,du$$

Integration by Parts

$$\int f(x)g(x)\,dx = f(x)G(x) - \int f'(x)G(x)\,dx,$$

where G is an anti-derivative of g

Definite Integrals

$\int_a^b f(x)\,dx$ is called the definite integral of $f(x)$ from a to b or between the limits a and b.

General Properties of the Definite Integral

Let $\int f(x)\,dx = F(x)$, so that $\int_a^b f(x)\,dx = F(b) - F(a)$

(I) $\int_a^b f(x)\,dx = \int_a^b f(t)\,dt$

(II) $\int_a^b f(x)\,dx = -\int_b^a f(x)\,dx$

(III) $\int_a^b f(x)\,dx = \int_a^c f(x)\,dx + \int_c^b f(x)\,dx$

(IV) $\int_0^a f(x)\,dx = \int_0^a f(a-x)\,dx$

(V) $\int_{-a}^a f(x)\,dx = 0$; if $f(x)$ is odd function

$= 2\int_0^a f(x)\,dx$; if $f(x)$ is even function

(VI) $\int_a^{2a} f(x)\,dx = 2\int_0^a f(x)\,dx$, if $f(2a-x) = f(x)$

$= 0$ if $f(2a-x) = -f(x)$

Rules for Definite Integrals

- $\int_a^a f(x)\,dx = 0$
- $\int_a^b f(x)\,dx + \int_b^c f(x)\,dx = \int_a^c f(x)\,dx$
- $\int_a^b f(x)\,dx = \int_{a-c}^{b-c} f(x+c)\,dx$

Fundamental Theorem of Calculus

If f is continuous on $[a, b]$, then $F(x) = \int_a^x f(t)\,dt$ has a derivative at every point of $[a, b]$ and

$$\frac{dF}{dx} = \frac{d}{dx}\int_a^x f(t)\,dt = f(x) \quad , \ a \le x \le b.$$

Leibniz Rule

If f is continuous on $[a, b]$, and $u(x)$ and $v(x)$ are differentiable function of x whose values lie in $[a, b]$, then

$$\frac{d}{dx}\int_{u(x)}^{v(x)} f(t)\,dt = f(v(x))\frac{dv}{dx} - f(u(x))\frac{du}{dx}$$

Area and Volume

Area under a Curve

Suppose $f(x)$ is continuous and $f(x) \ge 0$ on the integral $a \le x \le b$. Then the region R under the curve $y = f(x)$ and between $x = a$ and $x = b$ has area

$$\text{Area of } R = \int_a^b f(x)dx$$

Area between Two Curves

If $f(x)$ and $g(x)$ are continuous on the interval $a \le x \le b$ with $f(x) \ge g(x)$, and if R is the region bounded by the graph of f and g and the vertical lines $x = a$ and $x = b$, then

$$\text{Area of } R = \int_a^b [f(x) - g(x)]\, dx$$

Volume

Suppose $f(x)$ is continuous and non-negative on $a \le x \le b$ and let R be the region under the curve $y = f(x)$ between $x = a$ and $x = b$. Then the solid S formed by revolving R about the x-axis has volume

$$\text{Volume of } S = \pi \int_a^b [f(x)]^2 dx$$

Fundamental Theorem of Calculus

Suppose f is continuos on the interval $a \le x \le b$, which is divided into n equal subinterval of length Δx by $x_1, x_2, \ldots, x_n$, where x_j is the left-hand endpoint of the jth subinterval. Then,

$$\lim_{n\to\infty} \sum_{j=1}^{n} f(x_j)\Delta x = \int_a^b f(x)dx = F(b) - F(a)$$

where F is any anti-derivative of f.

The integral as the limit of sum

$$\int_a^b f(x)dx = \lim_{n\to\infty} h[f(a) + f(a+h) + f(a+2h) + \ldots + f\{a+(n-1)h\}]$$

where $b - a = nh$.

Summation of series:

$$\lim_{n\to\infty} \sum_{r=0}^{r=n-1} \{f(a+rh)\}\, h = \int_a^b f(x)\, dx, \quad \text{where } nh = b - a$$

Or more conveniently, by the formula, derived from the above by putting $a = 0$ and $b = 1$,

$$\lim_{n\to\infty} \sum_{r=0}^{r=n-1} \left\{ f\left(\frac{r}{n}\right)\right\} \frac{1}{n} = \int_0^1 f(x)\, dx$$

Fourier Series

Fourier series is an infinite series representation of periodic function in terms of the trigonometric sine and cosine functions.

If $f(x)$ be a function of x known in the interval $0 \le x \le 2\pi$, we can write

$$f(x) = a_0 + a_1 \cos x + a_2 \cos 2x + \ldots + a_n \cos nx + \ldots$$
$$+ b_1 \sin x + b_2 \sin 2x + \ldots + b_n \sin nx + \ldots$$

or $$f(x) = a_0 + \sum_{n=1}^{n=\infty} (a_n \cos nx + b_n \sin nx)$$

where $a_0 = \frac{1}{2\pi}\int_0^{2\pi} f(x)dx$, $a_n = \frac{1}{\pi}\int_0^{2\pi} f(x)\cos nx\, dx$

and $b_n = \frac{1}{\pi}\int_0^{2\pi} f(x)\sin nx\, dx$

If $f(x)$ is given in the interval $-\pi \le x \le \pi$, we can write

$$f(x) = a_0 + \sum_{n=1}^{n=\infty} (a_n \cos nx + b_n \sin nx)$$

where $a_0 = \frac{1}{2\pi}\int_{-\pi}^{\pi} f(x)dx$, $\quad a_n = \frac{1}{\pi}\int_{-\pi}^{\pi} f(x)\cos nx\, dx$

and $b_n = \frac{1}{\pi}\int_{-\pi}^{\pi} f(x)\sin nx\, dx$

Scalar and Vector

A *scalar* is quantity that is determined by its magnitude, its number of units measured on a suitable scale. For example, temperature, voltage, length, etc. are scalars.

A *vector* is a quantity that is determined by both its magnitude and its direction; thus, it is an arrow or directed line segment. For example, force, velocity, displacement, acceleration, etc. are vectors.

Representation of vector is:

$\mathbf{a} = [a_1, a_2, a_3] = a_1\mathbf{i} + a_2\mathbf{j} + a_3\mathbf{k}$ and the magnitude (or length) of a vector a is $|\mathbf{a}| = \sqrt{a_1^2 + a_2^2 + a_3^2}$

Dot Product or Scalar Product

The scalar product or dot product $\mathbf{A}\cdot\mathbf{B}$ (read "A dot B") of two vectors **A** and **B** is the product of their lengths times the cosine of their angle $\mathbf{A}\cdot\mathbf{B} = |\mathbf{A}||\mathbf{B}|\cos\theta$,

The angle between two non-zero vectors **A** and **B** is

$$\theta = \cos^{-1}\left(\frac{\mathbf{A}\cdot\mathbf{B}}{|\mathbf{A}||\mathbf{B}|}\right)$$

Cross Product or Vector Product

The vector product of two vector **A** and **B** is denoted by $\mathbf{A}\times\mathbf{B}$ (read "A cross B") and defined as

$$\mathbf{A}\times\mathbf{B} = |\mathbf{A}||\mathbf{B}|\sin\theta\, n$$

Where n unit vector perpendicular to **A** and **B**, θ is the angle between **A** and **B**.

Product of Three Vectors

The scalar triple product of three vectors **A**, **B** and **C** is denoted by denoted by [**A B C**] and is defined by

$$[\mathbf{A}\ \mathbf{B}\ \mathbf{C}] = (\mathbf{A}\times\mathbf{B})\cdot\mathbf{C}$$

The vector triple product of three vectors **A**, **B** and **C** is

$$(\mathbf{A}\times\mathbf{B})\times\mathbf{C} = (\mathbf{A}\cdot\mathbf{C})\mathbf{B} - (\mathbf{B}\cdot\mathbf{C})\mathbf{A}$$

The absolute value of the scalar triple product is the volume of the parallelepiped (Parallelogram sided box) with **A**, **B**, **C** as edge vectors.

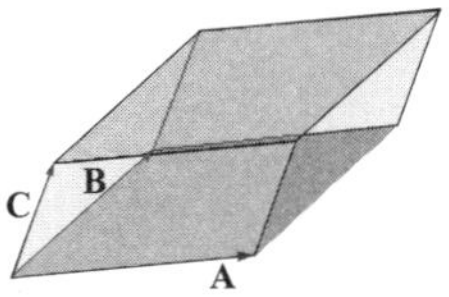

Let $\mathbf{A} = a_1\mathbf{i} + a_2\mathbf{j} + a_3\mathbf{k}$, $\mathbf{B} = b_1\mathbf{i} + b_2\mathbf{j} + b_3\mathbf{k}$, and $\mathbf{C} = c_1\mathbf{i} + c_2\mathbf{j} + c_3\mathbf{k}$, then

$$(\mathbf{A}\ \ \mathbf{B}\ \ \mathbf{C}) = (\mathbf{A}\times\mathbf{B})\cdot\mathbf{C} = \begin{vmatrix} a_1 & b_1 & c_1 \\ a_2 & b_2 & c_2 \\ a_3 & b_3 & c_3 \end{vmatrix}$$

Scalar and Vector Fields

A variable quantity whose value at any point in a region of space depends upon the position of the point, is called a *point function*. There are two types of point functions.

Scalar Point Function: Let R be a region of space at each point of which a scalar $f = f(x, y, z)$ given, then f is called a *scalar function* and R is called a *scalar field.*

Vector Point Function: Let R be a region of space at each point of which a vector $\mathbf{V} = \mathbf{V}(x, y, z)$ is given, then $\mathbf{V}$ is called a *vector point function* and R is called a *vector field.*

Limit of a Vector Function

Let $\mathbf{r}(t) = f(t)\mathbf{i} + g(t)\mathbf{j} + h(t)\mathbf{k}$ be a vector valued function of t. The limit of $\mathbf{r}(t)$ as t approaches the number t_0 is the vector $\mathbf{L}$ if and only if the limit of $|\mathbf{r}(t) - \mathbf{L}|$ as t approaches t_0 is zero. In symbols

$$\mathbf{L} = \lim_{t\to t_0} \mathbf{r}(t) \Leftrightarrow \lim_{t\to t_0} |\mathbf{r}(t) - \mathbf{L}| = 0.$$

Continuity of vector valued function:

A vector function $\mathbf{r}(t)$ is continuous at a point $t = t_0$ in its domain if $\lim_{t\to t_0} \mathbf{r}(t) = \mathbf{r}(t_0)$. The function is continuous if it is continuous at every point in its domain.

Derivatives of Vector Function

The vector function $\mathbf{r}(t) = f(t)\mathbf{i} + g(t)\mathbf{j} + h(t)\mathbf{k}$ is differentiable at $t = t_0$ if f, g and h are differentiable at t_0. Also $\mathbf{r}$ is said to be differentiable if it is differentiable at every point of its domain. At any point t at which $\mathbf{r}$ is differentiable, its derivative is the vector

$$\frac{d\mathbf{r}}{dt} = \lim_{\Delta t\to 0} \frac{\mathbf{r}(t+\Delta t) - \mathbf{r}(t)}{\Delta t} = \frac{df}{dt}\mathbf{i} + \frac{dg}{dt}\mathbf{j} + \frac{dh}{dt}\mathbf{k}$$

The curve traced by $\mathbf{r}$ is smooth if $\frac{d\mathbf{r}}{dt}$ is continuous and never 0 i.e., if f, g, and h have continuous first derivative that are not simultaneously 0.

Integration of Vector Functions

Let the $\mathbf{f}(t)$ and $\mathbf{F}(t)$ be two vector functions such that $\frac{d}{dt}\mathbf{F}(t) = \mathbf{f}(t)$, then $\mathbf{F}(t)$ is called the indefinite integral of $\mathbf{f}(t)$ with respect to t and symbolically we write $\int \mathbf{f}(t)\,dt = \mathbf{F}(t)$.

If c is any arbitrary constant vector independent of t, then $\frac{d}{dt}\{\mathbf{F}(t) + c\} = \mathbf{f}(t) \Rightarrow \int \mathbf{f}(t)\,dt = \mathbf{F}(t) + c$

Differentiation Rules for Vector Functions

If $\mathbf{u}$, $\mathbf{v}$, and $\mathbf{w}$ are differentiable vector functions of a scalar t and ϕ is a differentiable scalar function of the same variable t then

- $\frac{d}{dt}(c\mathbf{u}) = c\frac{d\mathbf{u}}{dt}$ (any number c)
- $\frac{d}{dt}(\mathbf{u}+\mathbf{v}) = \frac{d\mathbf{u}}{dt} + \frac{d\mathbf{v}}{dt}$
- $\frac{d}{dt}(\mathbf{u}\cdot\mathbf{v}) = \frac{d\mathbf{u}}{dt}\cdot\mathbf{v} + \mathbf{u}\cdot\frac{d\mathbf{v}}{dt}$
- $\frac{d}{dt}(\mathbf{u}\times\mathbf{v}) = \frac{d\mathbf{u}}{dt}\times\mathbf{v} + \mathbf{u}\times\frac{d\mathbf{v}}{dt}$
- $\frac{d}{dt}(\phi\,\mathbf{u}) = \phi\frac{d\mathbf{u}}{dt} + \mathbf{u}\frac{d\phi}{dt}$
- $\frac{d}{dt}[\mathbf{u}\ \mathbf{v}\ \mathbf{w}] = \left[\frac{d\mathbf{u}}{dt}\ \mathbf{v}\ \mathbf{w}\right] + \left[\mathbf{u}\ \frac{d\mathbf{v}}{dt}\ \mathbf{w}\right] + \left[\mathbf{u}\ \mathbf{v}\ \frac{d\mathbf{w}}{dt}\right]$
- $\frac{d}{dt}\{\mathbf{u}\times(\mathbf{v}\times\mathbf{w})\}$

$$= \frac{d\mathbf{u}}{dt}\times(\mathbf{v}\times\mathbf{w}) + \mathbf{u}\times\left(\frac{d\mathbf{v}}{dt}\times\mathbf{w}\right) + \mathbf{u}\times\left(\mathbf{v}\times\frac{d\mathbf{w}}{dt}\right)$$

If $\mathbf{u}$ has a constant length, then $\mathbf{u}\cdot\frac{d\mathbf{u}}{dt} = 0$. If $\mathbf{u}$ has a constant direction, then $\mathbf{u}\times\frac{d\mathbf{u}}{dt} = 0$.

Some Important Rules For Integration

- $\int\left(\frac{d\mathbf{u}}{dt}\cdot\mathbf{v} + \mathbf{u}\cdot\frac{d\mathbf{v}}{dt}\right)dt = \mathbf{u}\cdot\mathbf{v} + c$
- $\int\left(2\mathbf{u}\cdot\frac{d\mathbf{u}}{dt}\right)dt = \mathbf{u}^2 + c$
- $\int\left(2\frac{d\mathbf{u}}{dt}\cdot\frac{d^2\mathbf{u}}{dt^2}\right)dt = \left(\frac{d\mathbf{u}}{dt}\right)^2 + c$
- $\int\left(\mathbf{u}\times\frac{d^2\mathbf{u}}{dt^2}\right)dt = \mathbf{u}\times\frac{d\mathbf{u}}{dt} + c$

- $\int\left(\mathbf{a}\times\frac{d\mathbf{u}}{dt}\right)dt=\mathbf{a}\times\mathbf{u}+c$, where $\mathbf{a}$ is a constant.

Length of Curve

The length of a smooth curve $\mathbf{r}(t)=f(t)\,\mathbf{i}+g(t)\,\mathbf{j}+h(t)\,\mathbf{k},\ a\le t\le b$ that is traced exactly once as t increases from $t=a$ to $t=b$ is

$$L=\int_a^b\sqrt{\left(\frac{df}{dt}\right)^2+\left(\frac{dg}{dt}\right)^2+\left(\frac{dh}{dt}\right)^2}\,dt$$

In short form, $L=\int_a^b|\mathbf{v}|\,dt$, where $\mathbf{v}=\frac{d\mathbf{r}}{dt}$.

Unit Tangent Vector

The unit tangent vector of a differentiable curve $\mathbf{r}(t)$ is

$$\mathbf{T}=\frac{d\mathbf{r}}{ds}=\frac{d\mathbf{r}}{dt}\Big/\frac{ds}{dt}=\frac{\mathbf{v}}{|\mathbf{v}|},\quad\text{where }\mathbf{v}=\frac{d\mathbf{r}}{dt}.$$

Gradient

Let $f(x, y, z)$ be defined and differentiable at each point (x, y, z) in a certain region of space (i.e., defines a differentiable scalar field). Then the gradient of f, written as ∇f or grad f, is defined as:

$$\nabla f=\left(\mathbf{i}\frac{\partial}{\partial x}+\mathbf{j}\frac{\partial}{\partial y}+\mathbf{k}\frac{\partial}{\partial z}\right)f=\frac{\partial f}{\partial x}\mathbf{i}+\frac{\partial f}{\partial y}\mathbf{j}+\frac{\partial f}{\partial z}\mathbf{k}$$

Geometrical Significance of Gradient

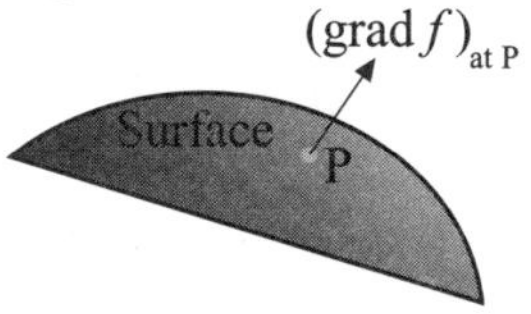

∇f represents a vector normal to the surface $f(x, y, z)=0$ and has a magnitude equal to the rate of change of f along this normal.

∇f is the maximum rate of change of f and the magnitude of this maximum is $|\nabla f|$.

Directional Derivative

The directional derivative of a surface field f at a point P (x, y, z) in the direction of a unit vector $\mathbf{b}$ is given by

$$\frac{df}{ds}=\mathbf{b}\cdot\nabla f$$

Tangent Plane and Normal

The equation of the tangent plane to the surface $f(x, y, z)=0$ at the point (X, Y, Z) is

$$(x-X)\frac{\partial f}{\partial x}+(y-Y)\frac{\partial f}{\partial y}+(z-Z)\frac{\partial f}{\partial z}=0$$

or $\quad(\mathbf{r}-\mathbf{R})\cdot\nabla f=0$

where $\mathbf{R}=X\,\mathbf{i}+Y\,\mathbf{j}+Z\,\mathbf{k},\ \mathbf{r}=x\,\mathbf{i}+y\,\mathbf{j}+z\,\mathbf{k}$.

The equation of the normal to the surface $f(x, y, z)$ at the point (x, y, z) is

$$\frac{x-X}{\frac{\partial f}{\partial x}}=\frac{y-Y}{\frac{\partial f}{\partial y}}=\frac{z-Z}{\frac{\partial f}{\partial z}}$$

Tangent Line

The equation of the tangent line at a point on the curve of intersection of the surfaces $f_1(x, y, z)=0$ and $f_2(x, y, z)=0$ is

$$[(x-X)\mathbf{i}+(y-Y)\mathbf{j}+(z-Z)\mathbf{k}]\times[\text{grad } f_1\times\text{grad } f_2]=0$$

or $\quad(\mathbf{r}-\mathbf{R})\times(\text{grad } f_1\times\text{grad } f_2)=0$

where $\quad\mathbf{R}=X\,\mathbf{i}+Y\,\mathbf{j}+Z\,\mathbf{k},\ \mathbf{r}=x\,\mathbf{i}+y\,\mathbf{j}+z\,\mathbf{k}$

Divergence

Let $\mathbf{V}$ be any differentiable vector point function. Then the divergence of $\mathbf{V}$ written as $\nabla\cdot\mathbf{V}$ or *div* $\mathbf{V}$ is defined by

$$\text{div }\mathbf{V}=\nabla\cdot\mathbf{V}=\left(\mathbf{i}\frac{\partial}{\partial x}+\mathbf{j}\frac{\partial}{\partial y}+\mathbf{k}\frac{\partial}{\partial z}\right)\cdot\mathbf{V}$$

$$=\mathbf{i}\cdot\frac{\partial\mathbf{V}}{\partial x}+\mathbf{j}\cdot\frac{\partial\mathbf{V}}{\partial y}+\mathbf{k}\cdot\frac{\partial\mathbf{V}}{\partial z}=\sum\mathbf{i}\cdot\frac{\partial\mathbf{V}}{\partial x}$$

If $\mathbf{V}=\mathbf{V}_1\mathbf{i}+\mathbf{V}_2\mathbf{j}+\mathbf{V}_3\mathbf{k}$ then $\text{div}\,\mathbf{V}=\frac{\partial\mathbf{V}_1}{\partial x}+\frac{\partial\mathbf{V}_2}{\partial y}+\frac{\partial\mathbf{V}_3}{\partial z}$.

The divergence of a vector point function is a scalar point function.

Solenoidal Vector: A vector $\mathbf{V}$ is said to be solenoidal if div $\mathbf{V}=0$.

Curl

Let $\mathbf{V}$ be any given differentiable vector point function. Then the curl $\mathbf{V}$ or rotation of $\mathbf{V}$, written as $\nabla\times\mathbf{V}$, curl $\mathbf{V}$ or rot $\mathbf{V}$ is defined as

$$\text{curl }\mathbf{V}=\nabla\times\mathbf{V}=\left(\mathbf{i}\frac{\partial}{\partial x}+\mathbf{j}\frac{\partial}{\partial y}+\mathbf{k}\frac{\partial}{\partial z}\right)\times\mathbf{V}$$

$$=\mathbf{i}\times\frac{\partial\mathbf{V}}{\partial x}+\mathbf{j}\times\frac{\partial\mathbf{V}}{\partial y}+\mathbf{k}\times\frac{\partial\mathbf{V}}{\partial z}=\sum\mathbf{i}\times\frac{\partial\mathbf{V}}{\partial x}$$

If $\mathbf{V}=\mathbf{V}_1\mathbf{i}+\mathbf{V}_2\mathbf{j}+\mathbf{V}_3\mathbf{k}$ then

$$\text{curl }\mathbf{V}=\nabla\times\mathbf{V}=\begin{bmatrix}\mathbf{i} & \mathbf{j} & \mathbf{k}\\ \frac{\partial}{\partial x} & \frac{\partial}{\partial y} & \frac{\partial}{\partial z}\\ \mathbf{V}_1 & \mathbf{V}_2 & \mathbf{V}_3\end{bmatrix}$$

Irrotational Vector: A vector $\mathbf{V}$ is said to be irrotational if curl $\mathbf{V}=0$.

Line Integrals

Any integral which is to be evaluated along a curve is called a *line integral.*

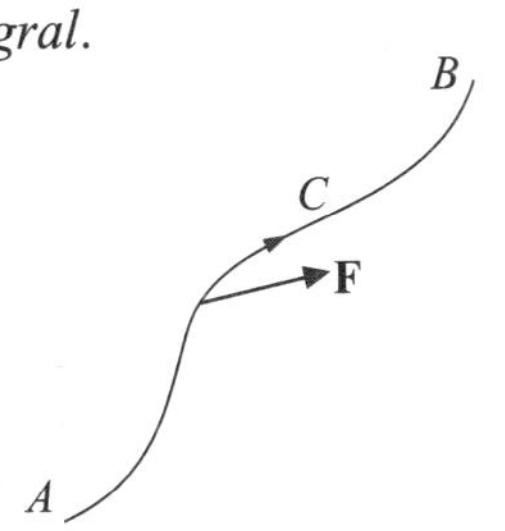

A line integral of a vector function $\mathbf{F}(r)$ over a curve C is defined by:

$$\int_c \mathbf{F}(r)\cdot dr$$

Line integral in component form:

$$\int_c \mathbf{F}(r)\cdot dr = \int_c (F_1dx+F_2dy+F_3dz)$$

Line integral in parametric form:

$$\int_c \mathbf{F}(r)\cdot dr = \int_c \mathbf{F}(r)\frac{dr}{dt}\cdot dr$$

$$=\int_{t_1}^{t_2}\left(F_1\frac{dx}{dt}+F_2\frac{dy}{dt}+F_3\frac{dz}{dt}\right)dt$$

Work done by a (variable) force $\mathbf{F}$ from A to B alone the path C is $W=\int_A^B \mathbf{F}(r)\cdot dr$

Circulation

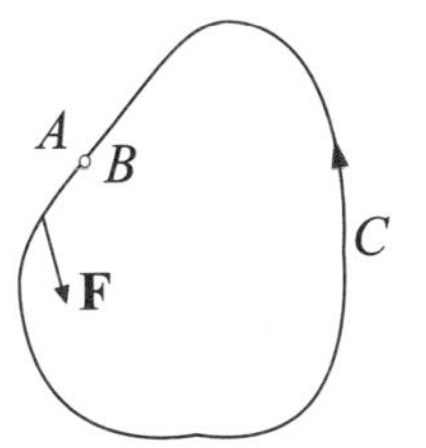

If C is a closed curve (i.e., a curve which does not intersect itself anywhere), then the tangent line integral of $\mathbf{F}$ around C is called the circulation of $\mathbf{F}$ about C.

$$\oint_c \mathbf{F}\cdot dr$$

If $\int_A^B \mathbf{F}\cdot dr$ is independent of the path C joining A and B, then $\mathbf{F}$ is called a *conservative field.*

If $\mathbf{F}$ is conservative field then $\mathbf{F}$ is the gradient of some function ϕ.

$\Rightarrow \mathbf{F} = \text{grad}\ \phi.$ or $\text{curl}\ \mathbf{F} = \text{curl grad}\ \phi = 0$

The ϕ is called the *scalar potential.*

If $\oint_C \mathbf{F}\cdot dr = 0$, then the field $\mathbf{F}$ is conservative on C.

Surface and Volume Integrals

Surface Integrals

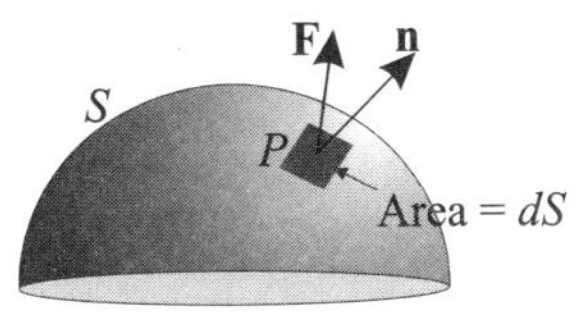

Any integral which is to be evaluated over a surface is called a *surface integral.* It is written as:

$\iint_s \mathbf{F}\cdot\mathbf{n}\,dS$, where $\mathbf{n}$ is the normal unit vector at point P of surface S.

$\iint_s \mathbf{F}\cdot\mathbf{n}\,dS$ is also called flux of $\mathbf{F}$ over S.

We can write

$$\iint_S \mathbf{F}\cdot\mathbf{n}\,dS = \iint (F_1\cos\alpha+F_2\cos\beta+F_3\cos\gamma)\,dS$$

$$=\int F_1dy\,dz+\int F_2dz\,dx+\int F_3dxdy$$

Volume Integral

Any integral which is to be evaluated over a volume is called a *volume integral.*

If $\mathbf{V}$ is a volume bounded by a surface S, then the triple integrals $\iiint_V \phi\,dV$ and $\iiint_V \mathbf{F}\cdot dV$ are called volume integrals.

Green's Theorem

Let R be a closed bounded region in the x-y plane whose boundary C consists of finitely many lines. Let $\mathbf{M}$ and $\mathbf{N}$ be continuous function of x and y having continuous partial derivatives $\frac{\partial \mathbf{M}}{\partial y}$ and $\frac{\partial \mathbf{N}}{\partial x}$ in R. Then

$$\oint_C (\mathbf{M}\,dx+\mathbf{N}\,dx) = \iint_R\left(\frac{\partial \mathbf{N}}{\partial x}-\frac{\partial \mathbf{M}}{dy}\right)dx\,dy$$

where C is traversed in the counter-clockwise direction.

Divergence Theorem of Gauss

If V is the volume bounded by a closed surface S and $\mathbf{F}$ is a vector point function which is continuous and has continuous first partial derivatives in V. Then

$$\iiint_V \nabla\cdot\mathbf{F}\,dV = \iint_S \mathbf{F}\cdot\mathbf{n}\,dS$$

Where $\mathbf{n}$ is the outwards drawn unit normal vector to S.

The surface integral of the normal component of a vector $\mathbf{F}$ taken over a closed surface is equal to the integral of the divergence of **F** taken over the volume enclosed by the surface.

Let $\mathbf{F} = F_1\,\mathbf{i} + F_2\mathbf{j} + F_3\,\mathbf{k}$, then $\nabla \cdot \mathbf{F} = \frac{\partial F_1}{\partial x} + \frac{\partial F_2}{\partial y} + \frac{\partial F_3}{\partial z}$

Divergence theorem of Gauss can be written as:

$$\iint_S (F_1\,\mathbf{i} + F_2\mathbf{j} + F_3\,\mathbf{k}) \cdot \mathbf{n}\, dS$$

$$= \iiint_V \left(\frac{\partial F_1}{\partial x} + \frac{\partial F_2}{\partial y} + \frac{\partial F_3}{\partial z} \right) dx\, dy\, dz$$

Stoke's Theorem

If S be an open surface bounded by a closed curve C and **F** be any vector point function having continuous first order partial derivatives, then

$$\oint_C \mathbf{F} \cdot dr = \iint_S \text{curl } \mathbf{F} \cdot \mathbf{n}\ dS = \iint_S (\nabla \times \mathbf{F}) \cdot \mathbf{n}\, dS$$

Where C is traversed in the positive direction. The direction of C is positive if an observer, walking on the boundary of S in this direction with his head pointing in the direction of outwards drawn normal **n** to S, has the surface on the left.

The line integral of the tangential component of vector **F** taken around a simple closed curve C is equal to surface integral of the normal component of the curl of **F** taken over any surface S having C as its boundary.

Let $\mathbf{F} = F_1\mathbf{i} + F_2\mathbf{j} + F_3\mathbf{k}$ and unit normal vector of surface S $\mathbf{n} = \cos\alpha\ \mathbf{i} + \cos\beta\ \mathbf{j} + \cos\gamma\ \mathbf{k}$, then

$$\oint_C \mathbf{F} \cdot dr = \oint_C F_1 dx + F_2 dy + F_3 dz$$

$$= \iint_S \left[\left(\frac{\partial F_3}{\partial y} - \frac{\partial F_2}{\partial z} \right) \cos\alpha + \left(\frac{\partial F_1}{\partial z} - \frac{\partial F_3}{\partial x} \right) \cos\beta + \left(\frac{\partial F_2}{\partial x} - \frac{\partial F_1}{\partial y} \right) \cos\gamma \right] dS$$

2.2 SOLVED EXAMPLES

Previous Years GATE Questions

Example 2.1

At $x = 0$, the function $f(x) = |x|$ has

(A) A minimum

(B) A maximum

(C) A point of inflexion

(D) Neither a maximum nor minimum

GATE 2015

Solution

Figure shows the graph of function $f(x) = |x|$

From the graph function $f(x)$ is minimum at $x = 0$.

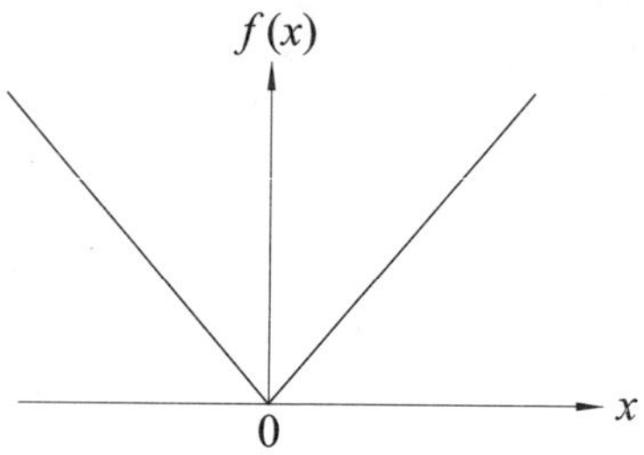

Graph function $f(x) = |x|$

Example 2.2

The value of $\lim_{x \to 0} \frac{1 - \cos(x^2)}{2x^4}$ is

(A) 0 (B) $\frac{1}{2}$ (C) $\frac{1}{4}$ (D) Undefined

GATE 2015

Solution

$$\lim_{x \to 0} \frac{1 - \cos(x^2)}{2x^4}$$

or $$\lim_{x \to 0} \frac{1 - \left[1 - \frac{(x^2)^2}{2!} + \frac{(x^2)^4}{4!} - \frac{(x^2)^6}{6!} + \ldots\right]}{2x^4}$$

$$\lim_{x \to 0} \frac{1 - \cos(x^2)}{2x^4}$$

$$= \lim_{x \to 0} \frac{1}{4} - \frac{x^4}{2 \times 4!} + \frac{x^8}{2 \times 6!} + \ldots$$

$$= \frac{1}{4} - 0 + 0 + 0\ldots$$

$$\lim_{x \to 0} \frac{1 - \cos(x^2)}{2x^4} = \frac{1}{4}$$

Example 2.3

Consider a spatial curve in three-dimensional space given in parametric form by $x(t) = \cos t$, $y(t) = \sin t$, $z(t) = \frac{2}{\pi} t$, $0 \le t \le \frac{\pi}{2}$. The length of the curve is _______.

GATE 2015

Solution

Equation of curve $x(t) = \cos t$, $y(t) = \sin t$, $z = \frac{2}{\pi} t$

Length of curve from $t = 0$ to $t = \frac{\pi}{2}$ is

$$L = \int_0^{\pi/2} \sqrt{\left(\frac{dx}{dt}\right)^2 + \left(\frac{dy}{dt}\right)^2 + \left(\frac{dz}{dt}\right)^2}\, dt$$

or $$L = \int_0^{\pi/2} \sqrt{\left(\frac{d}{dt}\cos t\right)^2 + \left(\frac{d}{dt}\sin t\right)^2 + \left(\frac{d}{dt}\frac{2}{\pi}t\right)^2}\, dt$$

or $$L = \int_0^{\pi/2} \sqrt{\cos^2 t + \sin^2 t + \frac{4}{\pi^2}}\, dt$$

or $$L = \sqrt{\frac{\pi^2+4}{\pi^2}} \int_0^{\pi/2} dt = \sqrt{\frac{\pi^2+4}{2\pi}}$$

$$L = 1.48 \text{ units}$$

Example 2.4

Curl of vector $\mathbf{V}(x, y, z) = 2x^2\mathbf{i} + 3z^2\mathbf{j} + y^3\mathbf{k}$ at $x = y = z = 1$ is

(A) $-3i$ (B) $3i$ (C) $3i - 4j$ (D) $3i - 6k$

GATE 2015

Solution

Given: Vector $\mathbf{V}(x, y, z) = 2x^2\mathbf{i} + 3z^2\mathbf{j} + y^3\mathbf{k}$

$$\text{Curl}\,\mathbf{V} = \begin{vmatrix} \mathbf{i} & \mathbf{j} & \mathbf{k} \\ \frac{\partial}{\partial x} & \frac{\partial}{\partial y} & \frac{\partial}{\partial z} \\ 2x^2 & 3z^2 & y^3 \end{vmatrix}$$

or $$\text{Curl}\,\mathbf{V} = (3y^2 - 6z)\,\mathbf{i} - 0\mathbf{j} + 0\mathbf{k}$$

Curl $\mathbf{V}$ at $x = y = z = 1$

$$\text{Curl}\,\mathbf{V} = -3i$$

Example 2.5

The surface integral $\iint_S \frac{1}{\pi}(9xi - 3yj)\cdot\mathbf{n}\,dS$ over the sphere given by $x^2 + y^2 + z^2 = 9$ is________.

GATE 2015

Solution

Let $$\iint_S \frac{1}{\pi}(9x\,i - 3y\,j)\cdot\mathbf{n}\,dS = \iint_S \mathbf{F}\cdot\mathbf{n}\,dS,$$

where $$\mathbf{F} = \frac{1}{\pi}(9x\,i - 3y\,j)\cdot\mathbf{n}\,dS$$

$$\text{div}\,\mathbf{F} = \nabla\mathbf{F} = \frac{\partial}{\partial x}\left(\frac{9x}{\pi}\right) + \frac{\partial}{\partial y}\left(-\frac{3y}{\pi}\right) = \frac{9}{\pi} - \frac{3}{\pi}$$

or $$\text{div}\,\mathbf{F} = \frac{6}{\pi}$$

Using divergence theorem $\iint_S \mathbf{F}\cdot\mathbf{n}\,dS = \iiint_V \text{div}\,\mathbf{F}\cdot dV$

$$\iint_S \frac{1}{\pi}(9xi - 3yj)\cdot\mathbf{n}\,dS = \iiint_V \frac{6}{\pi}\,dV$$

or $$\iint_S \frac{1}{\pi}(9xi - 3yj)\cdot\mathbf{n}\,dS = \frac{6}{\pi}\times\frac{4}{3}\pi\times 3^3$$

$$\iint_S \frac{1}{\pi}(9xi - 3yj)\cdot\mathbf{n}\,dS = 216$$

Example 2.6

The value of $\lim_{x\to 0}\left(\frac{-\sin x}{2\sin x + x\cos x}\right)$ is________.

GATE 2015

Solution

$$\lim_{x\to 0}\left(\frac{-\sin x}{2\sin x + x\cos x}\right) \qquad \left[\text{This is of form } \frac{0}{0}\right]$$

Applying L-hospital's therorem

$$\lim_{x\to 0}\left(\frac{-\sin x}{2\sin x + x\cos x}\right) = \lim_{x\to 0}\left(\frac{-\cos x}{2\cos x + \cos x - x\sin x}\right)$$

$$= \frac{-1}{2+1-0}$$

$$\lim_{x\to 0}\left(\frac{-\sin x}{2\sin x + x\cos x}\right) = -\frac{1}{3}$$

Example 2.7

The value of $\int_C [(3x - 8y^2)dx + (4y - 6xy)dy]$, where C is region bounded by $x = 0$, $y = 0$ and $x + y = 1$ is________.

GATE 2105

Solution

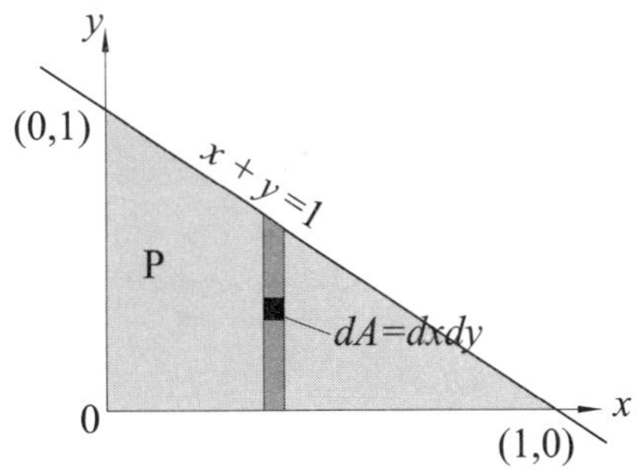

Let $$\int_C [(3x - 8y^2)dx + (4y - 6xy)dy] = \int_C Mdx + Ndy$$

where $M = (3x - 8y^2)$ and $N = (4y - 6xy)$

Applying Green theorem

$$\int_C Mdx + Ndy = \iint_S \left(\frac{\partial N}{\partial x} - \frac{\partial M}{\partial y}\right)dx\,dy$$

$$\int_C [(3x-8y^2)dx + (4y-6xy)dy]$$

$$= \int_0^1 \int_0^{1-x} \left(\frac{\partial}{\partial x}(4y-6xy) - \frac{\partial}{\partial y}(3x-8y^2) \right) dx\, dy$$

$$= \int_0^1 \int_0^{1-x} 10y\, dx\, dy = 10\int_0^1 \left[\frac{y^2}{2}\right]_0^{1-x} dx$$

$$= 5\int_0^1 (1-x)^2 dx$$

$$\int_C [(3x-8y^2)dx + (4y-6xy)dy] = \frac{5}{3}$$

Example 2.8

$\lim_{x \to 0} \frac{x - \sin x}{1 - \cos x}$ is

(A) 0 (B) 1 (C) 3 (D) Not defined

GATE 2014

Solution

$$\lim_{x \to 0} \frac{x-\sin x}{1-\cos x} \qquad \left[\text{This is of form } \frac{0}{0}\right]$$

Applying L-hospital's therorem

$$\lim_{x \to 0} \frac{x-\sin x}{1-\cos x} = \lim_{x \to 0} \frac{1-\cos x}{\sin x} \qquad \left[\text{This is of form } \frac{0}{0}\right]$$

or $$\lim_{x \to 0} \frac{x-\sin x}{1-\cos x} = \lim_{x \to 0} \frac{\sin x}{\cos x} = 0$$

$$\lim_{x \to 0}\left(\frac{x-\sin x}{1-\cos x}\right) = 0$$

Example 2.9

The integral $\oint_C (ydx - xdy)$ is evaluated along the circle $x^2 + y^2 = \frac{1}{4}$ traversed in counter clockwise direction. The integral is equal to

(A) 0 (B) $-\frac{\pi}{4}$ (C) $-\frac{\pi}{2}$ (D) $\frac{\pi}{4}$

GATE 2014

Solution

By Green theorem in plane region bounded by a single closed curve $x^2 + y^2 = \frac{1}{4}$, we have

$$\iint_S \left(\frac{\partial N}{\partial x} - \frac{\partial M}{\partial y} \right) dx\, dy = \oint_C Mdx + Ndy$$

Here $M = y, N = -x$

$$\oint_C (ydx - xdy) = \iint_S \left(\frac{\partial}{\partial x}(-x) - \frac{\partial}{\partial y}(y) \right) dx\, dy$$

or $$\oint_C (ydx - xdy) = \iint_S -2dx\, dy = -2A$$

Substituting $A = \pi \times r^2 = \pi \times \left(\frac{1}{2}\right)^2$ in above equation, we get

or $$\oint_C (ydx - xdy) = -2 \times \pi \times \left(\frac{1}{2}\right)^2$$

$$\oint_C (ydx - xdy) = -\frac{\pi}{2}$$

Example 2.10

The following surface integral is to be evaluated over a sphere for the given steady velocity vector field $\mathbf{F} = x\mathbf{i} + y\mathbf{j} + z\mathbf{k}$ defined with respect to a Cartesian coordinate system having, **i, j,** and **k** as unit base vectors

$$\iint_S \frac{1}{4}(\mathbf{F}.\mathbf{n})\, dA$$

where S is the sphere, $x^2 + y^2 + z^2 = 1$ and **n** is the outward unit normal vector to the sphere. The value of the surface integral is

(A) π (B) 2π (C) $\frac{3}{4}\pi$ (D) 4π

GATE 2013

Solution

By Divergence theorem, we have

$$\iint_S \mathbf{F}\cdot\mathbf{n}\, dA = \iiint_V \text{div}\, \mathbf{F}\, dV$$

or $$\iint_S \frac{1}{4}(\mathbf{F}\cdot\mathbf{n})\, dA = \iiint_V \frac{1}{4}\text{div}\, \mathbf{F}\, dV$$

Vector field $\mathbf{F} = x\mathbf{i} + y\mathbf{j} + z\mathbf{k}$

and $$\text{div}\, \mathbf{F} = \frac{\partial}{\partial x}(x) + \frac{\partial}{\partial x}(y) + \frac{\partial}{\partial x}(z) = 3$$

$$\iint_S \frac{1}{4}(\mathbf{F}\cdot\mathbf{n})\, dA = \iiint_V \frac{1}{4} \times 3\, dV = \frac{3}{4}V$$

or $$\iint_S \frac{1}{4}(\mathbf{F}\cdot\mathbf{n})\, dA = \frac{3}{4} \times \frac{4}{3}\pi \times 1^3$$

$$\iint_S \frac{1}{4}(\mathbf{F}\cdot\mathbf{n})\, dA = \pi$$

Example 2.11

Consider the function $f(x)=|x|$ in the interval $-1 \le x \le 1$. At the point $x=0$, $f(x)$ is

(A) Continuous and differentiable

(B) Non-continuous and differentiable

(C) Continuous and non-differentiable

(D) Neither continuous nor differentiable

GATE 2012

Solution

Limit of $f(x)=|x|$ at $x=0$; $\lim_{x\to 0+}|x| = \lim_{x\to 0-}|x| = 0$

Therefore, the function $f(x)=|x|$ is continuous at $x=0$.

At $x=0$;

$$\lim_{h\to 0+}\frac{f(x+h)-f(x)}{h} = \lim_{h\to 0+}\frac{x+h-x}{h} = +1$$

$$\lim_{h\to 0-}\frac{f(x-h)-f(x)}{h} = \lim_{h\to 0+}\frac{x-h-x}{h} = -1$$

From which

$$\lim_{h\to 0+}\frac{f(x+h)-f(x)}{h} \ne \lim_{h\to 0-}\frac{f(x-h)-f(x)}{h}$$

Therefore, the function $f(x)=|x|$ is non-differentiable at $x=0$.

Function $f(x)=|x|$ is continuous and non-differentiable at $x=0$.

Example 2.12

$\lim_{x\to 0}\left(\frac{1-\cos x}{x^2}\right)$ is

(A) $\frac{1}{4}$ (B) 1 (C) $\frac{1}{2}$ (D) 2

GATE 2012

Solution

$$\lim_{x\to 0}\left(\frac{1-\cos x}{x^2}\right) \qquad \left[\text{This is of form } \frac{0}{0}\right]$$

Applying L-hospital's therorem

$$\lim_{x\to 0}\left(\frac{1-\cos x}{x^2}\right) = \lim_{x\to 0}\frac{\sin x}{2x} = \lim_{x\to 0}\frac{\cos x}{2} = \frac{1}{2}$$

$$\lim_{x\to 0}\left(\frac{1-\cos x}{x^2}\right) = \frac{1}{2}$$

Example 2.13

The area enclosed between the straight line $y=x$ and the parabola $y=x^2$ in the $x-y$ plane is

(A) $\frac{1}{6}$ (B) $\frac{1}{3}$ (C) $\frac{1}{4}$ (D) $\frac{1}{2}$

GATE 2012

Solution

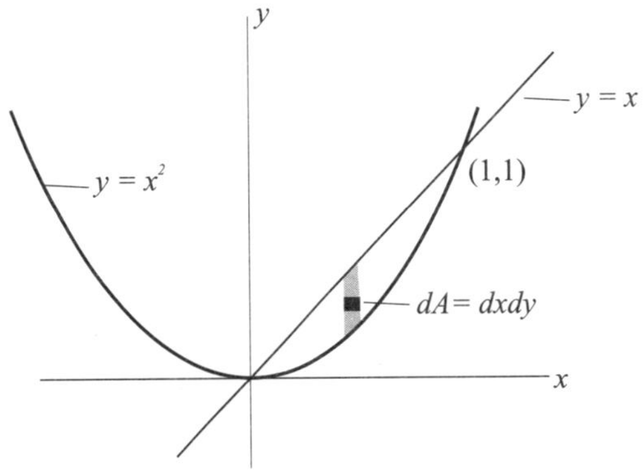

Coordinate of intersection point of the straight line $y=x$ and the parabola $y=x^2$ are (0,0) and (1,1).

The area enclosed between curves is given by

$$A = \int_0^1 \int_{y=x^2}^{y=x} dxdy$$

$$A = \int_0^1 (x-x^2)dx = \frac{1}{2} - \frac{1}{3}$$

$$A = \frac{1}{6}$$

Example 2.14

For the spherical surface $x^2+y^2+z^2=1$, the unit outward normal vector at the point $\left(\frac{1}{\sqrt{2}}, \frac{1}{\sqrt{2}}, 0\right)$ is given by

(A) $\frac{1}{\sqrt{2}}\mathbf{i} + \frac{1}{\sqrt{2}}\mathbf{j}$ (B) $\mathbf{k}$

(C) $\frac{1}{\sqrt{2}}\mathbf{i} - \frac{1}{\sqrt{2}}\mathbf{j}$ (D) $\frac{1}{\sqrt{3}}\mathbf{i} + \frac{1}{\sqrt{3}}\mathbf{j} + \frac{1}{\sqrt{3}}\mathbf{k}$

GATE 2012

Solution

Equation of spherical surface is $f = x^2+y^2+z^2-1$

∇f is the vector normal to the surface f.

$$\nabla f = \mathbf{i}\frac{\partial}{\partial x}(x^2+y^2+z^2-1) + \mathbf{j}\frac{\partial}{\partial y}(x^2+y^2+z^2-1) + \mathbf{k}\frac{\partial}{\partial z}(x^2+y^2+z^2-1)$$

or $\nabla f = 2x\,\mathbf{i} + 2y\,\mathbf{j} + 2z\,\mathbf{k}$

$$(\nabla f)_{\left(\frac{1}{\sqrt{2}},\frac{1}{\sqrt{2}},0\right)} = \sqrt{2}\,\mathbf{i} + \sqrt{2}\,\mathbf{j}$$

Unit vector normal to surface f;

$$\mathbf{n} = \frac{\sqrt{2}\,\mathbf{i} + \sqrt{2}\,\mathbf{j}}{\sqrt{(\sqrt{2})^2 + (\sqrt{2})^2}}$$

$$\mathbf{n} = \frac{1}{\sqrt{2}}\mathbf{i} + \frac{1}{\sqrt{2}}\mathbf{j}$$

Example 2.15

At $x = 0$, the function $f(x) = x^3 + 1$ has

(A) A maximum value (B) A singularity

(C) A minimum value (D) A point of infexion

GATE 2012

Solution

$$f(x) = x^3 + 1$$

$$\frac{d}{dx}f(x) = \frac{d}{dx}(x^3 + 1) = 3x^2$$

$$\frac{d^2}{dx^2}f(x) = \frac{d^2}{dx^2}(x^3 + 1) = 6x$$

At $x = 0$; $f'(0) = 0$ and $f''(0) = 0$

Therefore,

Function $f(x) = x^3 + 1$ has infexion at $x = 0$

Example 2.16

If $f(x)$ is an even function and a is a positive real number, then $\int_{-a}^{a} f(x)\,dx$ equal

(A) 0 (B) $2a$ (C) a (D) $2\int_0^a f(x)\,dx$

GATE 2011

Solution

From the properties of the definite integral, if $f(x)$ is an even function then

$$\int_{-a}^{a} f(x)\,dx = 2\int_0^a f(x)\,dx$$

Example 2.17

What is $\lim_{\theta \to 0} \frac{\sin\theta}{\theta}$ equal to?

(A) θ (B) 0 (C) $\sin\theta$ (D) 1

GATE 2011

Solution

$$\lim_{\theta \to 0} \frac{\sin\theta}{\theta} \qquad \left[\text{This is of form } \frac{0}{0}\right]$$

Applying L-hospital's theorem

$$\lim_{\theta \to 0} \frac{\sin\theta}{\theta} = \lim_{\theta \to 0} \frac{\cos\theta}{1} = 1$$

$$\lim_{\theta \to 0} \frac{\sin\theta}{\theta} = 1$$

Example 2.18

A series expansion for the function $\sin\theta$ is

(A) $1 - \frac{\theta^2}{2!} + \frac{\theta^4}{4!} - \ldots$ (B) $1 + \theta + \frac{\theta^2}{2!} + \frac{\theta^3}{3!} + \ldots$

(C) $\theta - \frac{\theta^3}{3!} + \frac{\theta^5}{5!} - \ldots$ (D) $\theta + \frac{\theta^3}{3!} + \frac{\theta^5}{5!} + \ldots$

GATE 2011

Solution

Maclaurin's theorem is given by

$$f(x) = f(0) + xf'(0) + \frac{x^2}{2!}f''(0) + \frac{x^3}{3!}f'''(0) + \frac{x^4}{4!}f^{iv}(0) + \ldots$$

Putting $f(x) = \sin\theta$, we have

$$\sin\theta = \sin 0 + \theta\cos 0 + \frac{\theta^2}{2!}(-\sin 0) + \frac{\theta^3}{3!}(-\cos 0) + \frac{\theta^4}{4!}(\sin 0) + \ldots$$

$$\sin\theta = \theta - \frac{\theta^3}{3!} + \frac{\theta^5}{5!} + \ldots$$

Example 2.19

The parabolic arc $y = \sqrt{x}, 1 \le x \le 2$ is revolved around the x-axis. The volume of the solid of revolution is

(A) $\frac{\pi}{4}$ (B) $\frac{\pi}{2}$ (C) $\frac{3\pi}{4}$ (D) $\frac{3\pi}{2}$

GATE 2010

Solution

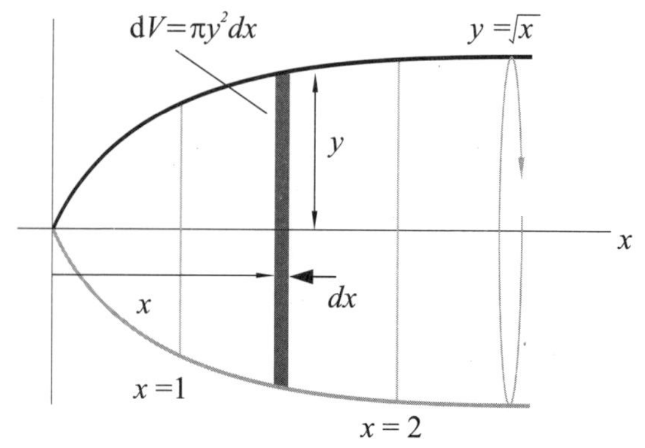

The volume of a solid generated by revolution about the

x-axis from $x = 1$ to $x = 2$ is

$$V = \int_1^2 \pi y^2 dx$$

or $$V = \int_1^2 \pi(\sqrt{x})^2 dx$$

or $$V = \pi \left[\frac{x^2}{2}\right]_1^2$$

$$V = \frac{3}{2}\pi$$

Example 2.20

The value of the integral $\int_{-\infty}^{\infty} \frac{dx}{1+x^2}$ is

(A) $-\pi$ (B) $-\frac{\pi}{2}$ (C) $\frac{\pi}{2}$ (D) π

GATE 2010

Solution

$$\int_{-\infty}^{\infty} \frac{dx}{1+x^2} = [\tan^{-1} x]_{-\infty}^{\infty}$$

or $$\int_{-\infty}^{\infty} \frac{dx}{1+x^2} = \tan^{-1}(\infty) - \tan^{-1}(-\infty)$$

or $$\int_{-\infty}^{\infty} \frac{dx}{1+x^2} = \frac{\pi}{2} - \left(-\frac{\pi}{2}\right)$$

$$\int_{-\infty}^{\infty} \frac{dx}{1+x^2} = \pi$$

Example 2.21

Vorticity vector of a flow field is given as $\mathbf{V} = 2xy\ \mathbf{i} - x^2 z\ \mathbf{j}$. The vorticity vector at $(1,1,1)$ is

(A) $4\mathbf{i} - \mathbf{j}$ (B) $4\mathbf{i} - \mathbf{k}$ (C) $\mathbf{i} - 4\mathbf{j}$ (D) $\mathbf{i} - 4\mathbf{k}$

GATE 2010

Solution

Vorticity vector = Curl (velocity vector)

Vorticity vector ; $$\text{Curl } \mathbf{V} = \begin{vmatrix} i & j & k \\ \frac{\partial}{\partial x} & \frac{\partial}{\partial y} & \frac{\partial}{\partial z} \\ 2xy & -x^2 z & 0 \end{vmatrix}$$

Vorticity vector ; $\text{Curl } \mathbf{V} = x^2\mathbf{i} - 2(xz + x)\mathbf{k}$

Vorticity vector at $(1,1,1)$,

$$\text{Curl } \mathbf{V} = \mathbf{i} - 4\mathbf{k}$$

Example 2.22

The area enclosed between the curves $y^2 = 4x$ and $x^2 = 4y$ is

(A) $\frac{16}{3}$ (B) 8 (C) $\frac{32}{3}$ (D) 16

GATE 2009

Solution

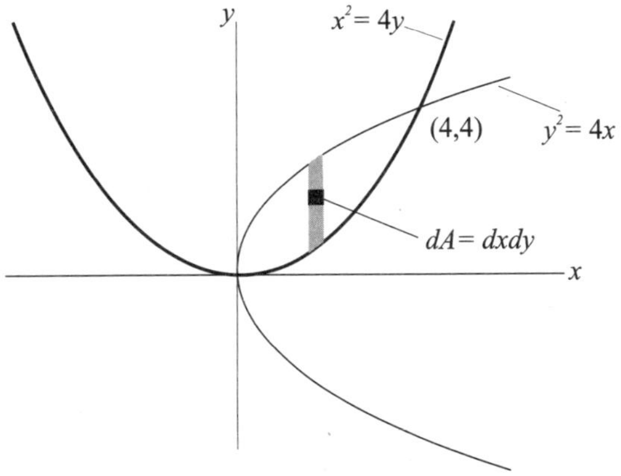

Coordinates of intersection points is obtained by solving $y^2 = 4x$ and $x^2 = 4y$

$$\left(\frac{x^2}{4}\right)^2 = 4x \Rightarrow x(x^3 - 4^3) = 0$$

$$x = 0, 4$$

Thus, Coordinate are (0,0) and (4,4)

Area enclosed between the curves $y^2 = 4x$ and $x^2 = 4y$ is

$$A = \int_0^4 \int_{\frac{x^2}{4}}^{\sqrt{4x}} dxdy$$

or $$A = \int_0^4 \left(\sqrt{4x} - \frac{x^2}{4}\right) dx$$

$$A = \frac{16}{3}$$

Example 2.23

The divergence of the vector field $3xz\, i + 2xy\, j - yz^2 k$ at a point $(1,1,1)$ is equal to

(A) 7 (B) 4 (C) 3 (D) 0

GATE 2009

Solution

Vector field $\mathbf{F} = 3xz\,\mathbf{i} + 2xy\,\mathbf{j} - yz^2\mathbf{k}$

$$\text{Div}\,\mathbf{F} = \left(i\frac{\partial}{\partial x} + j\frac{\partial}{\partial y} + k\frac{\partial}{\partial z}\right)\cdot(3xz\,i + 2xy\,j - yz^2k)$$

or $$\text{Div}\,\mathbf{F} = \frac{\partial}{\partial x}(3xz) + \frac{\partial}{\partial y}(2xy) + \frac{\partial}{\partial z}(-yz^2)$$

$$\text{Div}\,\mathbf{F} = 3z + 2x - 2yz$$

Divergence at (1,1,1), $\text{Div}\,\mathbf{F} = 3 + 2 - 2 = 3$

$$\text{Div}\,\mathbf{F} = 3$$

Example 2.24

A path AB in the form of one quarter of a circle of unit radius is shown in the figure. Integration of $(x+y)^2$ on path AB traversed in a counter-clockwise sense is

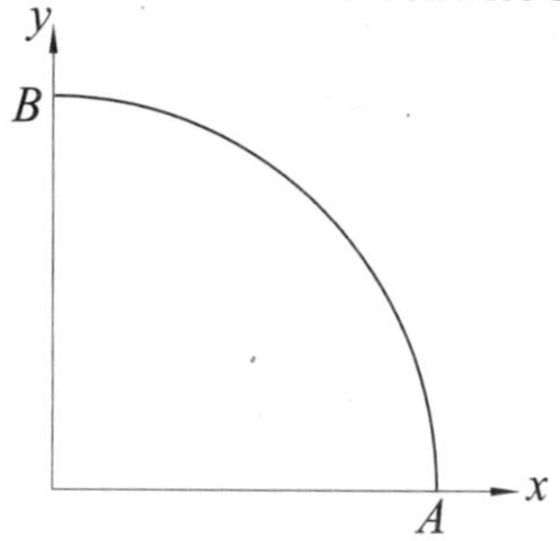

(A) $\frac{\pi}{2} - 1$ (B) $\frac{\pi}{2} + 1$ (C) $\frac{\pi}{2}$ (D) 1

GATE 2009

Solution

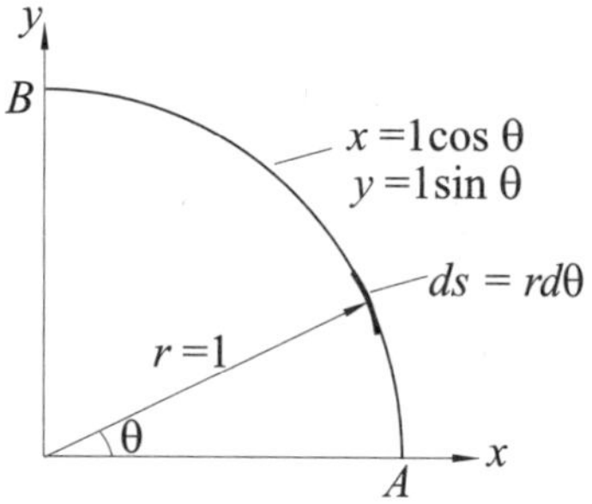

Parametric equation of circle of unit radius is

$x = \cos\theta,\ y = \sin\theta.$

Path AB varies from $\theta = 0$ to $\theta = \frac{\pi}{2}$

$$\int_{\text{Path } AB}(x+y)^2\,ds = \int_0^{\frac{\pi}{2}}(\cos\theta + \sin\theta)^2 1.\,d\theta$$

or $$\int_{\text{Path } AB}(x+y)^2\,ds = \theta + \left.\frac{-\cos 2\theta}{2}\right]_0^{\frac{\pi}{2}}$$

$$\int_{\text{Path } AB}(x+y)^2\,ds = \frac{\pi}{2} + 1$$

Example 2.25

In the Taylor series expansion of e^x about $x = 2$, the coefficient of $(x-2)^4$ is

(A) $\frac{1}{4!}$ (B) $\frac{2^4}{4!}$ (C) $\frac{e^2}{4!}$ (D) $\frac{e^4}{4!}$

GATE 2008

Solution

Taylor's Theorem is given by

$$f(x) = f(a) + (x-a)f'(a) + \frac{(x-a)^2}{2!}f''(a) + \ldots\frac{(x-a)^n}{n!}f^n(a) + \ldots$$

Putting $f(x) = e^x$ and $a = 2$

$$e^x = f(2) + (x-2)f'(2) + \frac{(x-2)^2}{2!}f''(2) + \ldots\frac{(x-2)^4}{4!}f^4(2) + \ldots\frac{(x-2)^n}{n!}f^n(2) + \ldots$$

Coefficient of $(x-2)^4$ is $\frac{1}{4!}f^{iv}(2) = \frac{1}{4!}e^2$

$$\text{Coefficient of } (x-2)^4 \text{ is } \frac{1}{4!}e^2$$

Example 2.26

The value of $\lim_{x\to 8}\frac{x^{\frac{1}{3}} - 2}{x - 8}$ is

(A) $\frac{1}{16}$ (B) $\frac{1}{12}$ (C) $\frac{1}{8}$ (D) $\frac{1}{4}$

GATE 2008

Solution

$$\lim_{x\to 8}\frac{x^{\frac{1}{3}} - 2}{x - 8} \qquad \left[\text{This is of form } \frac{0}{0}\right]$$

Applying L-hospital's theorem

$$\lim_{x\to 8}\frac{x^{\frac{1}{3}} - 2}{x - 8} = \lim_{x\to 8}\frac{1}{3}\frac{x^{-\frac{2}{3}}}{1} = \lim_{x\to 8}\frac{1}{3}\frac{8^{-\frac{2}{3}}}{1} = \frac{1}{12}$$

$$\lim_{x\to 8}\frac{x^{\frac{1}{3}} - 2}{x - 8} = \frac{1}{12}$$

Example 2.27

The divergence of the vector field
$(x-y)\mathbf{i} + (y-z)\mathbf{j} + (x+y+z)\mathbf{k}$ is

(A) 0 (B) 1 (C) 2 (D) 3

GATE 2008

Solution

Vector field $\mathbf{F} = (x-y)\mathbf{i} + (y-z)\mathbf{j} + (x+y+z)\mathbf{k}$

$$\text{Div}\,\mathbf{F} = \left(\mathbf{i}\frac{\partial}{\partial x} + \mathbf{j}\frac{\partial}{\partial y} + \mathbf{k}\frac{\partial}{\partial z}\right)\cdot[(x-y)\mathbf{i} + (y-z)\mathbf{j} + (x+y+z)\mathbf{k}]$$

or $\text{Div}\,\mathbf{F} = \frac{\partial}{\partial x}(x-y) + \frac{\partial}{\partial y}(y-z) + \frac{\partial}{\partial z}(x+y+z)$

or $\text{Div}\,\mathbf{F} = 1+1+1$

$$\text{Div}\,\mathbf{F} = 3$$

Example 2.28

Consider the shaded triangular region P shown in the figure. What is $\iint_P xy\,dx\,dy$?

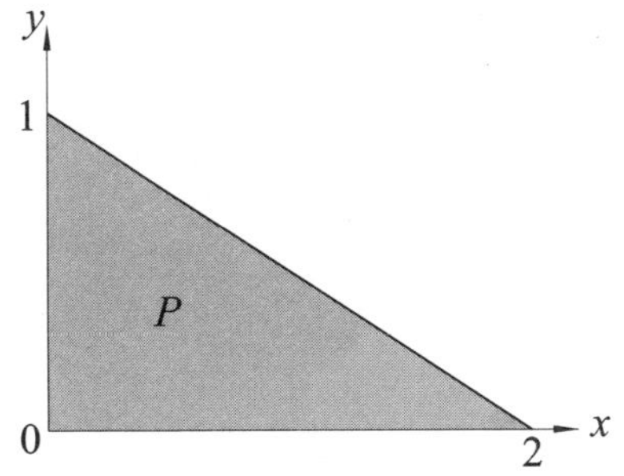

(A) $\frac{1}{6}$ (B) $\frac{2}{9}$ (C) $\frac{1}{16}$ (D) 1

GATE 2008

Solution

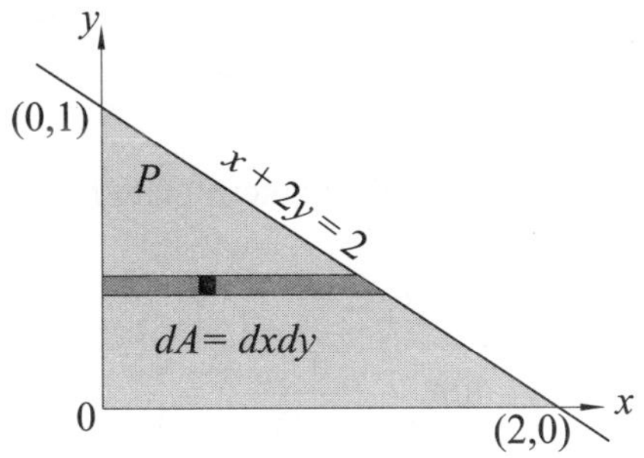

Equation of straight line $\frac{x}{2} + \frac{y}{1} = 1$

$$\iint_P xydxdy = \int_0^1 \int_0^{2-2y} (xydx)dy$$

or $$\iint_P xydxdy = \int_0^1 \left[\frac{yx^2}{2}\right]_0^{2-2y} dy$$

or $$\iint_P xydxdy = \int_0^1 \frac{y(2-2y)^2}{2}dy = \frac{1}{6}$$

$$\iint_P xydxdy = \frac{1}{6}$$

Example 2.29

The directional derivative of the scalar function $f(x, y, z) = x^2 + 2y^2 + z$ at the point $P = (1,1,2)$ in the direction of the vector $\mathbf{a} = 3i - 4j$ is

(A) –4 (B) –2 (C) –1 (D)1

GATE 2008

Solution

Scalar function $f(x, y, z) = x^2 + 2y^2 + z$

$$\nabla \mathbf{f} = \left(i\frac{\partial}{\partial x} + j\frac{\partial}{\partial y} + k\frac{\partial}{\partial z}\right)\cdot(x^2 + 2y^2 + z)$$

or $$\nabla \mathbf{f} = 2x\,i + 4y\,j + k$$

$$(\nabla \mathbf{f})_{(1,1,2)} = 2i + 4j + k$$

Directional derivative at $P = (1,1,2)$ in the direction $\mathbf{a} = 3i - 4j$ is

$$(\nabla \mathbf{f})\cdot \mathbf{a} = 2i + 4j + k)\cdot\frac{(3i-4j)}{\sqrt{3^2+4^2}}$$

$$(\nabla \mathbf{f})\cdot \mathbf{a} = -2$$

Example 2.30

Let $f = y^x$. What is $\frac{\partial^2 f}{\partial x \partial y}$ at $x = 2$, $y = 1$?

(A) 0 (B) ln 2 (C) 1 (D) $\frac{1}{\ln 2}$

GATE 2008

Solution

Given that $f = y^x$

$$\frac{\partial f}{\partial y} = xy^{x-1}$$

$$\frac{\partial^2 f}{\partial x \partial y} = \frac{\partial}{\partial x}\left(\frac{\partial f}{\partial y}\right) = \frac{\partial}{\partial x}xy^{x-1}$$

or $$\frac{\partial^2 f}{\partial x \partial y} = y^{x-1} + xy^{x-1}\ln y$$

$$\left(\frac{\partial^2 f}{\partial x \partial y}\right)_{(2,1)} = 1^{2-1} + 2\times 1^{2-1}\times \ln 1$$

$$\left(\frac{\partial^2 f}{\partial x \partial y}\right)_{(2,1)} = 1$$

Example 2.31

Consider the function $f(x) = 2x^3 - 3x^2$ in the domain $[-1,2]$. The global minimum of $f(x)$ is__________.

GATE 2016

Solution

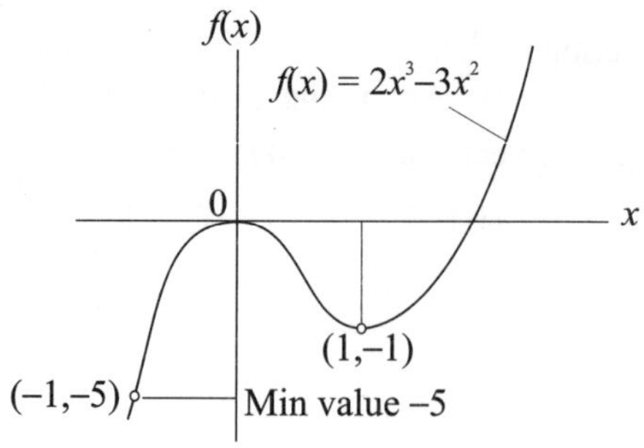

Graph of $f(x) = 2x^3 - 3x^2$

Figure shows the graph of $f(x) = 2x^3 - 3x^2$ in the domain $[-1, 2]$.

Now $f'(x) = 6x^2 - 6x = 0$

$$6x(x-1) = 0$$

$$x = 0, x = 1$$

The value of $f(x)$ at $x = 0$, 1, −1, and 2, we have $f(0) = 0$, $f(1) = -1$, $f(-1) = -5$, $f(2) = 4$

Therefore, minimum value of $f(x)$ in the domain $[-1, 2]$ is −5.

Example 2.32

The values of x for which the function

$$f(x) = \frac{x^2 - 3x - 4}{x^2 + 3x - 4}$$

is NOT continuous are

(A) 4 and −1 (B) 4 and 1

(C) − 4 and 1 (D) − 4 and −1

GATE 2016

Solution

Function $f(x) = \dfrac{x^2 - 3x - 4}{x^2 + 3x - 4}$

or $f(x) = \dfrac{x^2 - 3x - 4}{(x+4)(x-1)}$

The function $f(x)$ is not continuous at $x = -4$ and $x = 1$.

− 4 and 1

Example 2.33

A scalar potential ϕ has the following gradient:

$$\nabla\phi = yz\,i + xz\,j + xy\,k.$$

Consider the integral $\int_C \nabla\phi \cdot dr$ on the curve $r = xi + yj + zk$. The curve C is parameterised as follows:

$$\begin{cases} x = t \\ y = t^2 \text{ and } 1 \le t \le 3 \\ z = 3t^2 \end{cases}$$

The value of the integral is ________.

GATE 2016

Solution

Substituting $x = t$, $y = t^2$, $z = 3t^2$ in

$\nabla\phi = yz\,i + xz\,j + xy\,k$ and $r = xi + yj + zk$, we have

$\nabla\phi = 3t^4\,i + 3t^3\,j + t^3\,k$ and $r = t\,i + t^2 j + 3t^2\,k$

$dr = (i + 2t\,j + 6t\,k)\,dt$

Now $\int_C \nabla\phi \cdot dr = (3t^4\,i + 3t^3\,j + t^3\,k)\cdot(i + 2t\,j + 6t\,k)\,dt$

or $\int_C \nabla\phi \cdot dr = \int_1^3 15t^4\,dt = 3[t^5]_1^3$

$$\int_C \nabla\phi \cdot dr = 726$$

Example 2.34

$\lim_{x\to 0} \dfrac{\log_e(1+4x)}{e^{3x} - 1}$ is equal to

(A) 0 (B) $\frac{1}{12}$ (C) $\frac{4}{3}$ (D) 1

GATE 2016

Solution

$\lim_{x\to 0} \dfrac{\log_e(1+4x)}{e^{3x} - 1} \leftarrow \dfrac{0}{0}$ indeterminate form

Applying L' Hospital's rule

$$\lim_{x\to 0} \frac{\log_e(1+4x)}{e^{3x} - 1} = \lim_{x\to 0} \frac{4}{(1+4x)3e^{3x}} = \frac{4}{3}$$

$$\lim_{x\to 0} \frac{\log_e(1+4x)}{e^{3x} - 1} = \frac{4}{3}$$

Example 2.35

The value of the line integral $\int_C \mathbf{F} \cdot \mathbf{r}'\, ds$, where C is a circle of radius $\dfrac{4}{\sqrt{\pi}}$ units is ________.

Here, $\mathbf{F}(x, y) = y\,i + 2x\,j$ and $\mathbf{r}'$ is the unit tangent vector on the curve C at an arc length s from a reference point on the curve. $\mathbf{i}$ and $\mathbf{j}$ are the basis vectors in the x-y Cartesian reference. In evaluating the line integral, the curve has to be traversed in the counterclockwise direction.

GATE 2016

Solution

Equation of circle of radius $\frac{4}{\sqrt{\pi}}$ units in parametric form

is $x=\frac{4}{\sqrt{\pi}}\cos\theta$, $y=\frac{4}{\sqrt{\pi}}\sin\theta$

Unit tangent vector $\mathbf{r}'=\frac{d\mathbf{r}}{ds}$

Now $$\int_C \mathbf{F}\cdot\mathbf{r}'\,ds=\int_C \mathbf{F}\cdot\frac{d\mathbf{r}}{ds}\,ds=\int_C \mathbf{F}\cdot d\mathbf{r}$$

$$=\int_C (y\mathbf{i}+2x\,\mathbf{j})\cdot(dx\,\mathbf{i}+dy\,\mathbf{j})$$

or

$$\int_C \mathbf{F}\cdot\mathbf{r}'\,ds=\int_0^{2\pi}\left(\frac{4}{\sqrt{\pi}}\sin\theta\,\mathbf{i}+2\frac{4}{\sqrt{\pi}}\cos\theta\,\mathbf{j}\right)\cdot\left(-\frac{4}{\sqrt{\pi}}\sin\theta\,\mathbf{i}+\frac{4}{\sqrt{\pi}}\cos\theta\,\mathbf{j}\right)d\theta$$

or $$\int_C \mathbf{F}\cdot\mathbf{r}'\,ds=\left(\frac{4}{\sqrt{\pi}}\right)^2\int_0^{2\pi}(3\cos^2\theta-1)\,d\theta=16$$

$$\int_C \mathbf{F}\cdot\mathbf{r}'\,ds=16$$

Example 2.36

$\lim_{x\to\infty}\sqrt{x^2+x-1}-x$ is

(A) 0 (B) ∞ (C) $\frac{1}{2}$ (D) $-\infty$

GATE 2016

Solution

Given: $\lim_{x\to\infty}\sqrt{x^2+x-1}-x$

Let $y=\frac{1}{x}$

$$\lim_{x\to\infty}\sqrt{x^2+x-1}-x=\lim_{y\to 0}\sqrt{\frac{1}{y^2}+\frac{1}{y}-1}-\frac{1}{y}$$

$$=\lim_{y\to 0}\frac{\sqrt{1+y-y^2}-1}{y} \qquad \frac{0}{0}\text{ indeterminate form}$$

Applying L-Hospital rule

$$\lim_{x\to\infty}\sqrt{x^2+x-1}-x=\lim_{y\to 0}\frac{1-2y}{2\sqrt{1+y-y^2}}=+\frac{1}{2}$$

$$\lim_{x\to\infty}\sqrt{x^2+x-1}-x=\frac{1}{2}$$

Example 2.37

The value of $\lim_{x\to 0}\frac{x^3-\sin x}{x}$ is

(A) 0 (B) 3 (C) 1 (D) -1

GATE 2017

Solution

$$\lim_{x\to 0}\frac{x^3-\sin x}{x}=\lim_{x\to 0}\left(\frac{x^3}{x}-\frac{\sin x}{x}\right)=\lim_{x\to 0}x^2-\lim_{x\to 0}\left(\frac{\sin x}{x}\right)$$

$$\lim_{x\to 0}\frac{x^3-\sin x}{x}=0-1=-1$$

$$\lim_{x\to 0}\frac{x^3-\sin x}{x}=-1$$

Example 2.38

A parametric curve defined by $x=\cos\left(\frac{\pi u}{2}\right)$, $y=\sin\left(\frac{\pi u}{2}\right)$ in the range $0\le u\le 1$ is rotated about the x–axis by 360 degrees. Area of the surface generated is

(A) $\frac{\pi}{2}$ (B) π (C) 2π (D) 4π

GATE 2017

Solution

The following graph of $x=\cos\left(\frac{\pi u}{2}\right)$, $y=\sin\left(\frac{\pi u}{2}\right)$ in the range $0\le u\le 1$ is sketched.

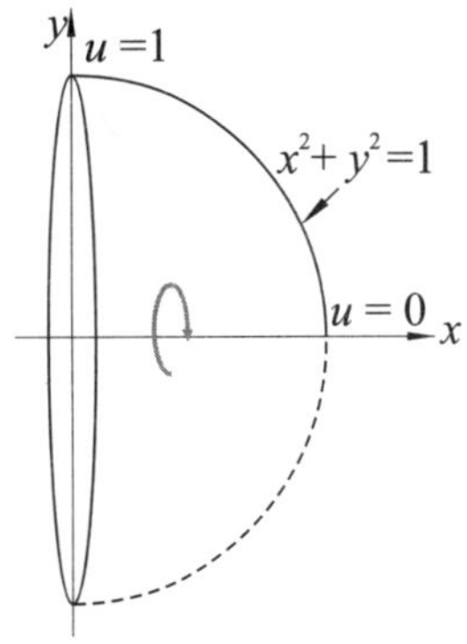

The surface area of solid generated by revolving about x-axis $=\frac{1}{2}$(Surface area of sphere) $=\frac{1}{2}\times 4\pi\times 1^2$

Surface area $=2\pi$

Example 2.39

For the vector $\mathbf{V}=2yz\,\mathbf{i}+3xz\,\mathbf{j}+4xy\,\mathbf{k}$, the value of $\nabla\cdot(\nabla\times\mathbf{V})$ is______.

GATE 2017

Solution

$$\nabla \times \mathbf{V} = \begin{vmatrix} \mathbf{i} & \mathbf{j} & \mathbf{k} \\ \frac{\partial}{\partial x} & \frac{\partial}{\partial y} & \frac{\partial}{\partial z} \\ 2yz & 3xz & 4xy \end{vmatrix} = x\,\mathbf{i} - 2y\,\mathbf{j} + z\,\mathbf{k}$$

$$\nabla \cdot (\nabla \times \mathbf{V}) = \left(\mathbf{i}\frac{\partial}{\partial x} + \mathbf{j}\frac{\partial}{\partial y} + \mathbf{k}\frac{\partial}{\partial z}\right) \cdot (x\,\mathbf{i} - 2y\,\mathbf{j} + z\,\mathbf{k})$$

or $\quad \nabla \cdot (\nabla \times \mathbf{V}) = 1 - 2 + 1 = 0$

$$\nabla \cdot (\nabla \times \mathbf{V}) = 0$$

Example 2.40

The divergence of the vector $-y\,\mathbf{i} + x\,\mathbf{j}$ is________.

GATE 2017

Solution

Let $\mathbf{u} = -y\,\mathbf{i} + x\,\mathbf{j}$

Divergence of $\mathbf{u} = \nabla \cdot \mathbf{u} = \left(\mathbf{i}\frac{\partial}{\partial x} + \mathbf{j}\frac{\partial}{\partial y}\right) \cdot (-y\,\mathbf{i} + x\,\mathbf{j})$

$$\nabla \cdot \mathbf{u} = 0$$

Example 2.41

The surface integral $\iint_S \mathbf{F} \cdot \mathbf{n}\, dS$ over the surface S of the sphere $x^2 + y^2 + z^2 = 9$,

where $\mathbf{F} = (x + y)\,\mathbf{i} + (x + z)\,\mathbf{j} + (y + z)\,\mathbf{k}$ and $\mathbf{n}$ is the unit outward surface normal, yields ______.

GATE 2017

Solution

Given: $\mathbf{F} = (x + y)\,\mathbf{i} + (x + z)\,\mathbf{j} + (y + z)\,\mathbf{k}$

Using divergence theorem $\iint_S \mathbf{F.n}\, dS = \iiint_V (div\mathbf{F})dV$

Where V is volume of given surface of sphere $x^2 + y^2 + z^2 = 3^2$

$$div\,\mathbf{F} = \frac{\partial}{\partial x}(x + y) + \frac{\partial}{\partial y}(x + z) + \frac{\partial}{\partial z}(y + z) = 2$$

$$\iint_S \mathbf{F.n}\, dS = \iiint_V 2dV = 2V = 2 \times \frac{4}{3} \times \pi \times 3^3$$

$$\iint_S \mathbf{F.n}\, dS = 72\pi$$

$$\iint_S \mathbf{F.n}\, dS = 226.19$$

Example 2.42

According to the Mean Value Theorem, for a continuous function $f(x)$ in the interval $[a, b]$, there exists a value ξ in this interval such that

$$\int_a^b f(x)dx =$$

(A) $f(\xi)(b - a)$ (B) $f(b)(\xi - a)$ (C) $f(a)(b - \xi)$ (D) 0

GATE 2018

Solution

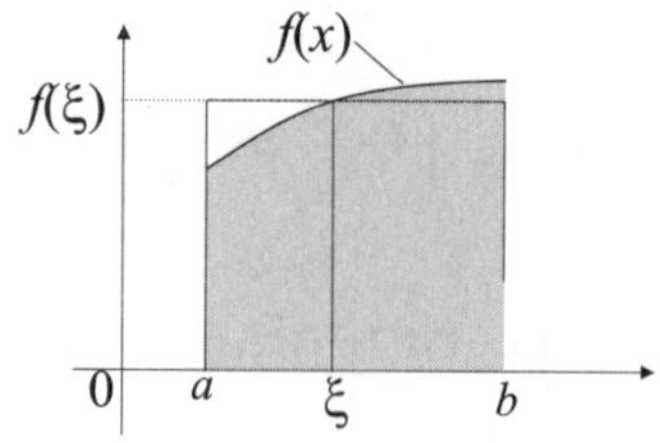

$$\int_a^b f(x)dx = \text{Area under the curve } f(x)$$

$$\int_a^b f(x)dx = f(\xi)(b - a)$$

Example 2.43

The value of the integral

$$\oiint_S \mathbf{r} \cdot \mathbf{n}\; dS$$

over the closed surface S bounding a volume V, where $\mathbf{r} = x\,\mathbf{i} + y\,\mathbf{j} + z\,\mathbf{k}$ is the position vector and $\mathbf{n}$ is the normal to the surface S, is

(A) V (B) $2V$ (C) $3V$ (D) $4V$

GATE 2018

Solution

Divergence theorem $\quad \oiint_S \mathbf{r} \cdot \mathbf{n}\, dS = \iiint_V div\,\mathbf{r}\, dV$

$$\oiint_S \mathbf{r} \cdot \mathbf{n}\, dS = \iiint_V 3\, dV$$

$$\oiint_S \mathbf{r} \cdot \mathbf{n}\, dS = 3V$$

Example 2.44

The Fourier cosine series for an even function $f(x)$ is given by

$$f(x) = a_o + \sum_{n=1}^{\infty} a_n \cos(nx)$$

The value of the coefficient a_2 for the function $f(x) = \cos^2(x)$ in $[0, \pi]$ is

(A) – 0.5 (B) 0.0 (C) 0.5 (D) 1.0

GATE 2018

Solution

Function $f(x)=\cos^2(x)$

or $f(x)=\dfrac{1+\cos 2x}{2}=\dfrac{1}{2}+\dfrac{1}{2}\cos 2x$

or $f(x)=\dfrac{1}{2}+0\times\cos x+\dfrac{1}{2}\times\cos 2x$

Compare with $f(x)=a_o+\sum_{n=1}^{\infty}a_n\cos(nx)$, we have

$$a_o=1,\ a_1=0,\ a_2=\frac{1}{2}$$

$$a_2=0.5$$

Example 2.45

The divergence of the vector field $\mathbf{u}=e^x(\cos y\,\mathbf{i}+\sin y\,\mathbf{j})$ is

(A) 0 (B) $e^x\cos y+e^x\sin y$

(C) $2e^x\cos y$ (D) $2e^x\sin y$

GATE 2018

Solution

Given vector field $\mathbf{u}=e^x(\cos y\,\mathbf{i}+\sin y\,\mathbf{j})$

Divergence of the vector field $\mathbf{u}$ is

$$\nabla.\mathbf{u}=\frac{\partial}{\partial x}(e^x\cos y)+\frac{\partial}{\partial y}(e^x\sin y)$$

$$\nabla.\mathbf{u}=e^x\cos y+e^x\cos y$$

$$\nabla.\mathbf{u}=2e^x\cos y$$

Example 2.46

For a position vector $\mathbf{r}=x\,\mathbf{i}+y\,\mathbf{j}+z\,\mathbf{k}$ the norm of the vector can be defined as $|\mathbf{r}|=\sqrt{x^2+y^2+z^2}$. Given a function $\phi=\ln|\mathbf{r}|$, its gradient $\nabla\phi$ is

(A) $\mathbf{r}$ (B) $\dfrac{\mathbf{r}}{|\mathbf{r}|}$ (C) $\dfrac{\mathbf{r}}{\mathbf{r}\cdot\mathbf{r}}$ (D) $\dfrac{\mathbf{r}}{|\mathbf{r}|^3}$

GATE 2018

Solution

Given: Function $\phi=\ln|\mathbf{r}|$

$$\nabla\phi=\mathbf{i}\frac{\partial}{\partial x}\ln(\sqrt{x^2+y^2+z^2}+\mathbf{j}\frac{\partial}{\partial y}\ln(\sqrt{x^2+y^2+z^2}$$

$$+\mathbf{k}\frac{\partial}{\partial z}\ln(\sqrt{x^2+y^2+z^2}$$

$$\nabla\phi=\frac{x\mathbf{i}+y\mathbf{i}+z\mathbf{k}}{(\sqrt{x^2+y^2+z^2})^2}=\frac{\mathbf{r}}{\mathbf{r}\cdot\mathbf{r}}$$

$$\nabla\phi=\frac{\mathbf{r}}{\mathbf{r}\cdot\mathbf{r}}$$

Example 2.47

A parabola $x=y^2$ with $0\le x\le 1$ is shown in the figure. The volume of the solid of rotation obtained by rotating the shaded area by 360° around the x – axis is

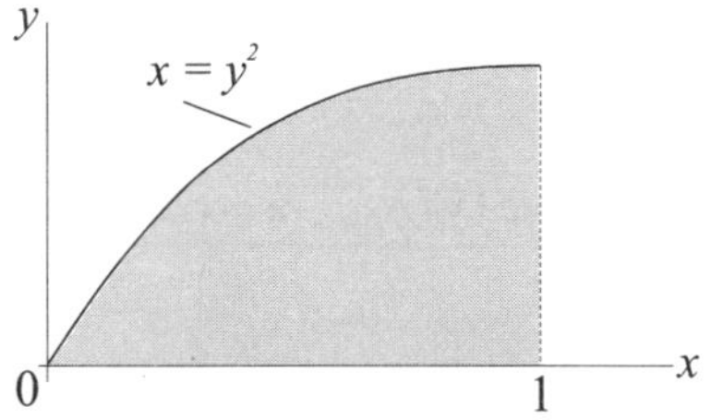

(A) $\dfrac{\pi}{4}$ (B) $\dfrac{\pi}{2}$ (C) π (D) 2π

GATE 2019

Solution

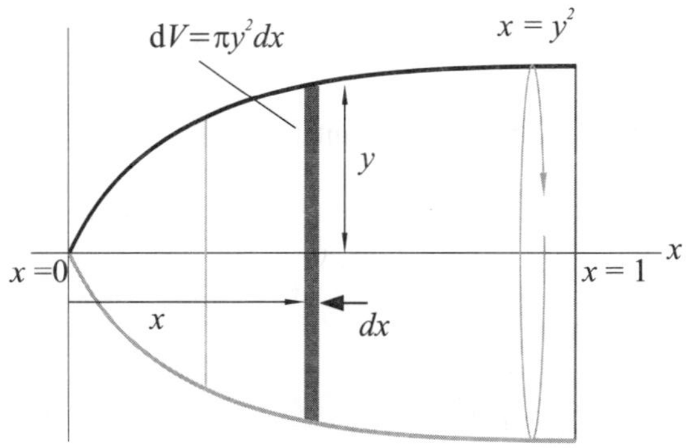

The volume of a solid generated by revolution about x –axis from $x=0$ to $x=1$ is

$$V=\int_0^1\pi y^2\,dx$$

$$V=\int_0^1\pi x\,dx=\pi\left[\frac{x^2}{2}\right]_0^1$$

$$V=\frac{\pi}{2}$$

Example 2.48

The directional derivative of the function $f(x,y)=x^2+y^2$ along a line directed from $(0,0)$ to $(1,1)$, evaluated at the point $x=1,\ y=1$ is

(A) $\sqrt{2}$ (B) 2 (C) $2\sqrt{2}$ (D) $4\sqrt{2}$

GATE 2019

Solution

Gradient of given function $f(x,y)=x^2+y^2$ is

$$grad\ f = \nabla f = i\frac{\partial}{\partial x}(x^2 + y^2) + j\frac{\partial}{\partial y}(x^2 + y^2)$$

$$grad\ f = \nabla f = 2x\,i + 2y\,j$$

$$(\nabla f)_{(1,1)} = 2i + 2j$$

Line directed from (0,0) to (1,1) is $\mathbf{a} = (1-0)i + (1-0)j$

Unit vector of **a**; $\hat{\mathbf{a}} = \frac{i+j}{\sqrt{2}}$

Directional derivative $(\nabla f)_{(1,1)} \cdot \hat{\mathbf{a}} = (2i + 2j)\cdot\left(\frac{i+j}{\sqrt{2}}\right)$

$$(\nabla f)_{(1,1)} \cdot \hat{\mathbf{a}} = 2\sqrt{2}$$

2.3 PRACTICE PAPER

Time: 3 hours **Max. Marks:100**

Q.1 to Q.30 carry one mark each

Q.1 to Q.20 Multiple Choice Questions

Q.1 Given the following limits:

1. $\lim_{x\to 0} \frac{\sin x}{x} = 1$

2. $\lim_{x\to\infty}\left(1+\frac{1}{x}\right)^x = 1$

3. $\lim_{x\to 0} \frac{\log(x+1)}{x} = 1$

which of these are correct?

(A) 1, 2 and 3 (B) 1 and 2 (C) 1 and 3 (D) 2 and 3

Q.2 If $f(x) = \begin{cases} 0\ ; & \text{when } -\pi \le x \le 0 \\ x^2\ ; & \text{when } 0 \le x \le \pi \end{cases}$ and

$f(x) = a_0 + \sum_{n=1}^{n=\infty}(a_n \cos nx + b_n \sin nx)$ is its Fourier series expansion then a_0 is equal to

(A) π^2 (B) $\frac{\pi^2}{2}$ (C) $\frac{\pi^2}{6}$ (D) $\frac{\pi^2}{9}$

Q.3 $\lim_{n\to\infty}\left[\frac{1}{n+1} + \frac{1}{n+2} + \frac{1}{n+3} + \ldots + \frac{1}{2n}\right]$ is equal to

(A) $\log_e 2$ (B) 2 (C) e^2 (D) 0

Q.4 If $a < b$; then $\int_a^b (|x-a| + |x-b|)\,dx$ is equal to

(A) $\frac{(b-a)^2}{2}$ (B) $\frac{b^2-a^2}{2}$

(C) $\frac{a^3-b^3}{2}$ (D) $(b-a)^2$

Q.5 The value of the double integral $\int_0^1\int_x^{1/x}\frac{x}{1+y^2}\,dx\,dy$ is

(A) 0 (B) $\pi/4$

(C) $\tan^{-1}(2)$ (D) None of these

Q.6 p is a polynomial such that $p'(0) = p''(0) = 1$ while $p'''(0) = 2$, if p is of the third degree, then $p'(x)$ is

(A) $2x^2 + x + 1$ (B) $x^2 + x + 2$

(C) $x^2 + x + 1$ (D) $x^2 + 2x + 1$

Q.7 If $f = \sin^{-1}\left(\frac{x^2+y^2}{x+y}\right)$, then $x\frac{\partial f}{\partial x} + y\frac{\partial f}{\partial y}$ is

(A) f (B) $2f$ (C) $\tan f$ (D) $\sin f$

Q.8 If the function $f(x) = \begin{cases} 2x+1; & x \le 1 \\ \alpha x^2 + \beta x; & x > 1 \end{cases}$ is differentiable for every x, then the values of α and β are given by

(A) $\alpha = 0, \beta = 2$ (B) $\alpha = 3, \beta = 0$

(C) $\alpha = 4, \beta = -1$ (D) $\alpha = -1, \beta = 4$

Q.9 $\lim_{n\to\infty}\left\{\left(1+\frac{1}{n}\right)^n + \left(1+\frac{1}{n}\right)^{-n}\right\}$

(A) Exists and is equal to 0 (B) Does not exists

(C) Exists and is equal to $e + \frac{1}{e}$ (D) Exists and is equal to e

Q.10 Consider the function $f(x) = x(1-x)$. The function:

(A) Attains minima at $x = \frac{1}{2}$ and $\frac{3}{4}$

(B) Is discontinuous in the given interval

(C) Is negative at a few points in the given interval

(D) Has a maximum at $x = \frac{1}{2}$

Q.11 $\int_0^{2a} f(x)\,dx = 2\int_0^a f(x)\,dx$ is

(A) Always true

(B) True only when $f(a) = f(a+x)$

(C) True only when $f(x) = f(2a - x)$

(D) True only when $f(2a - x) = -f(x)$

Q.12 If the vector

$\mathbf{F} = (x + 2y + az)\,\mathbf{i} - (2x + 3y + z)\,\mathbf{j} + (4x - y + 2z)\,\mathbf{k}$ is irrotational, then

(A) $a = 4$ (B) $a = -2$ (C) $a = -1$ (D) $a = 2$

Q.13 The value of $\int_0^{\pi/2} \frac{\sqrt{\cos x}}{\sqrt{\sin x} + \sqrt{\cos x}}\, dx$ is

(A) $\frac{\pi}{2}$ (B) $\frac{\pi}{4}$ (C) $\frac{\pi}{8}$ (D) $\frac{\pi}{6}$

Q.14 If C is closed curve $x = a\cos\theta$, $y = b\sin\theta$, then $\frac{1}{2}\oint_C (x\,dy - y\,dx)$ is

(A) ab (B) 0 (C) πab (D) 1

Q.15 If the closed curve of the region bounded by $y = x$ and $y = x^2$ then $\oint_C (xy + y^2)\,dx + x^2 dy$ is

(A) $-\frac{1}{20}$ (B) $-\frac{3}{20}$ (C) 4 (D) 2

Q.16 If S is the surface of cube bounded by the planes $x = 0, x = a, y = 0, y = a, z = 0, z = a$, then $\iint_S (x\,\mathbf{i} + y\mathbf{j} + z\,\mathbf{k})\cdot\mathbf{n}\,dS$ is

(A) a^3 (B) $8a^3$ (C) $3a^3$ (D) 0

Q.17 If $u = x^2 - y^2 + 4z$ then $\nabla^2 u$ is

(A) 0 (B) 2 (C) 4 (D) 8

Q.18 If S is any closed surface enclosing a volume V and $\mathbf{F} = x\,\mathbf{i} + 2y\,j + 3z\,\mathbf{k}$, then $\iint_s \mathbf{F}\cdot\mathbf{n}\,dS$ is

(A) V (B) $2V$ (C) $6V$ (D) 0

Q.19 If $\mathbf{r} = 5t^2\mathbf{i} + t\,\mathbf{j} - t^3\mathbf{k}$, then $\int_{t=1}^{t=2} \left(\mathbf{r} \times \frac{d^2\mathbf{r}}{dt^2}\right) dt$ is

(A) $2\mathbf{i}$ (B) $-14\mathbf{i} + 75\mathbf{j} - 15\mathbf{k}$

(C) $5\mathbf{i} + \mathbf{j} - 3\mathbf{k}$ (D) 0

Q.20 If $\mathbf{a}$ is a constant vector and $\mathbf{r}$ is a position vector, then grad$(\mathbf{r}\cdot\mathbf{a})$ is

(A) 0 (B) $\mathbf{r}$ (C) $\mathbf{a}$ (D) 1

Q.21 to Q.30 Numerical Answer Questions

Q.21 $\int_0^1 \frac{|x|}{x}\,dx$ is equal to__________.

Q.22 If $\int_1^x f(t) = x\cos\pi x$, then $f(4)$ is__________.

Q.23 If $\lim_{x\to 0}(1+x)^{\frac{1}{x}} = e$, then $\lim_{n\to\infty}\left(\frac{n}{n+1}\right)^{2n}$ is ________.

Q.24 The derivative of $\tan^{-1}\left(\frac{2x}{1-x^2}\right)$ with respect to $\cos^{-1}\left(\frac{1-x^2}{1+x^2}\right)$ is________.

Q.25 A cube is expanding in such a way that its edge is changing at a rate of 5 cm/s. If its edge is 4 cm long, then the rate of change(in cm^3/s) of its volume is_____.

Q.26 If $\mathbf{a} = 2\mathbf{i} + 3\,\mathbf{j} - m\mathbf{k}$ and $|\nabla\mathbf{a}\cdot\mathbf{r}| = \sqrt{14}$ then m is_______.

Q.27 If curve C is circle $x^2 + y^2 = 1$, then $\oint_c (\cos x\sin y - xy)dx + \sin x\cos y\,dy$ is ________.

Q.28 If $\mathbf{V} = (x + 3y)\,i + (y - 2z)\,j + (x + az)\,k$ is solenoidal, then the value of a is ________.

Q.29 If $\mathbf{r} = \begin{cases} 2\mathbf{i} - \mathbf{j} + 2\mathbf{k};\ \text{when } t = 2 \\ 4\mathbf{i} - 2\mathbf{j} + 3\mathbf{k};\ \text{when } t = 3 \end{cases}$, then $\int_2^3 \left(\mathbf{r}\cdot\frac{d\mathbf{r}}{dt}\right)dt$ is_______.

Q.30 If $\mathbf{r}$ is a position vector, then curl $\mathbf{r}$ is equal to_____.

Q.31 to Q.65 carry two marks each.

Q.31 to Q.50 Multiple Choice Questions

Q.31 If $V = f(y - z,\ z - x,\ x - y)$, then $\frac{\partial V}{\partial x} + \frac{\partial V}{\partial y} + \frac{\partial V}{\partial z}$ is equal to

(A) V (B) $2V$ (C) $3V$ (D) 0

Q.32 Consider the following statements:

If $f(x) = \begin{cases} x & ;\ 0 < x < 1 \\ 3 - x & ;\ 1 \le x \le 2 \end{cases}$, then

1. $\lim_{x\to 1-0} f(x) = 1$
2. $\lim_{x\to 1+0} f(x) = 2$
3. $\lim_{x\to 1} f(x) = 2$,

Of these statements

(A) 1 and 3 are correct (B) 1, 2 and 3 are correct

(C) 1 and 2 are correct (D) 2 alone is correct

Q.33 A hemispherical bowl of radius r is filled with water up to depth equal to half of the radius. The volume of water in the bowl is

(A) $\frac{2}{3}\pi r^3$ (B) $\frac{5}{24}\pi r^3$ (C) $\frac{5}{12}\pi r^3$ (D) $\frac{1}{3}\pi r^3$

Q.34 Changing the order of the integration in the double integral

$I = \int_0^8 \int_{\frac{x}{4}}^{2} f(x, y)\, dy\, dx$ leads to $I = \int_r^s \int_p^q f(x, y)\, dx\, dy$,

the value of q and s are, respectively

(A) $4y, 2$ (B) $16y^2, 8$ (C) $x, 2$ (D) $x, 8$

Q.35 The figure bounded by the graphs of $y^2 = 4x$, $y = 0$ and $x = 1$, is rotated round the line $x = 1$. The volume of the resulting solid is

(A) $\frac{16\pi}{15}$ (B) $\frac{15\pi}{16}$ (C) $\frac{16\pi}{5}$ (D) $\frac{5\pi}{16}$

Q.36 The Fourier series expansion of the function $f(x) = x\,;[-\pi, \pi]$ is

(A) $x = 2\left(\sin x - \frac{1}{2}\sin 2x + \frac{1}{3}\sin 3x - \frac{1}{4}\sin 4x + \ldots\right)$

(B) $x = 2\left(\cos x - \frac{1}{2}\cos 2x + \frac{1}{3}\cos 3x - \frac{1}{4}\cos 4x + \ldots\right)$

(C) $x = \sin x - \sin 2x + \sin 3x - \sin 4x + \ldots$

(D) $x = 2\left(\cos x - \cos 2x + \cos 3x - \frac{1}{2}\cos 4x + \ldots\right)$

Q.37 If $y = (\sin x)^{\sin x^{\cdot^{\cdot^{\infty}}}}$ then $\frac{dy}{dx}$ is

(A) $\frac{y^2 \cot x}{1 - y\log \sin x}$ (B) $\frac{y^2 \cot x}{1 + y\log \sin x}$

(C) $\frac{y^2 \cot x}{1 + y\log \sin x}$ (D) None of these

Q.38 The perimeter of the cardioid $r = 2(1 + \cos\theta)$ is

(A) 12 (B) 8 (C) 16 (D) 24

Q.39 If $u = \sin^{-1}\left(\frac{x^{\frac{1}{3}} + y^{\frac{1}{3}}}{x + y}\right)^{\frac{1}{2}}$, then $x\frac{\partial u}{\partial x} + y\frac{\partial u}{\partial y}$ is

(A) $-\frac{1}{3}\tan u$ (B) $-\frac{1}{12}\tan u$

(C) $\frac{12}{\tan u}$ (D) $\frac{-12}{\tan u}$

Q.40 If $f(x) = \begin{cases} ax + b; & x \le \frac{\pi}{4} \\ \cos x; & x > \frac{\pi}{4} \end{cases}$ then $f(x)$ is differentiable at $x = \frac{\pi}{4}$ if

(A) $a = -\frac{1}{\sqrt{2}}, b = \frac{1 + \frac{\pi}{4}}{\sqrt{2}}$ (B) $a = \frac{1}{\sqrt{2}}, b = \frac{1 + \frac{\pi}{4}}{\sqrt{2}}$

(C) $a = b = \frac{1}{\sqrt{2}}$ (D) $a = b = -\frac{1}{\sqrt{2}}$

Q.41 If $z = e^x \sin y$, $x = \log_e t$ and $y = t^2$, then $\frac{dz}{dt}$ is given by the expression

(A) $\frac{e^x}{t}(\sin y - 2t^2 \cos y)$ (B) $\frac{e^x}{t}(\sin y + 2t^2 \cos y)$

(C) $\frac{e^x}{t}(\cos y + 2t^2 \sin y)$ (D) $\frac{e^x}{t}(\cos y - 2t^2 \sin y)$

Q.42 The area included between the parabolas $y^2 = 8(x + 2)$ and $y^2 = 8(2 - x)$ is equal to

(A) $\frac{64}{3}$ (B) $\frac{32}{3}$ (C) $\frac{16}{3}$ (D) 0

Q.43 If $\mathbf{F} = xy\,\mathbf{i} + yz\,\mathbf{j} + zx\,\mathbf{k}$ and curve C is $\mathbf{r} = t\,\mathbf{i} + t^2\mathbf{j} + t^3\mathbf{k}$, then $\int_{t=-1}^{t=1} \mathbf{F}\cdot d\mathbf{r}$. is

(A) $\frac{1}{7}$ (B) $\frac{2}{7}$ (C) $\frac{10}{7}$ (D) 0

Q.44 The area of the cardioid $r = 1 + \cos\theta$ is equal to

(A) 4π (B) 8π (C) $\frac{3\pi}{2}$ (D) 2π

Q.45 If **a** is a constant vector, then div $(\mathbf{r} \times \mathbf{a})$ is

(A) 0 (B) **a** (C) **r** (D) 3**a**

Q.46 If **a** is a constant vector, then grad $(\mathbf{r} \cdot \mathbf{a})$ is

(A) 0 (B) **r** (C) **a** (D) 2**a**

Q.47 If **a** and **b** are constant vector then grad $[\mathbf{r}\ \ \mathbf{a}\ \ \mathbf{b}]$ is

(A) $\mathbf{a} \times \mathbf{b}$ (B) 0 (C) 1 (D) **a**

Q.48 The length of the curve $y = \log \sec x$ from $x = 0$ to $x = \frac{\pi}{3}$ is equal to

(A) $\log(3 + \sqrt{2})$ (B) $\log(2 + \sqrt{3})$

(C) $\log(x + \sqrt{3})$ (D) $\log 2\cos x$

Q.49 The directional derivative of $f = x^2 - 2y^2 + 4z^2$ at the point (1, 1, –1) in the direction of $2\mathbf{i} + \mathbf{j} - \mathbf{k}$ is

(A) $\frac{8}{\sqrt{3}}$ (B) $\frac{8}{\sqrt{6}}$ (C) 4 (D) 0

Q.50 The length of one turn of the helix $\mathbf{r} = \cos t\,\mathbf{i} + \sin t\,\mathbf{j} + t\,\mathbf{k}$ is

(A) 2π (B) $2\sqrt{2}\,\pi$ (C) $2\sqrt{3}\,\pi$ (D) π

Q.51 to Q.65 Numerical Answer Questions

Q.51 If the function $f(x) = \frac{(5+x)(2+x)}{1+x}$; $x > 0$, then the minimum value of $f(x)$ is________

Q.52 $\lim_{x\to 0} \frac{e^x - \left(1 + x + \frac{x^2}{2}\right)}{x^3}$ is equal to _________.

Q.53 The difference of maximum and minimum values of $\sqrt{3}\,\sin x + \cos x$ is _________.

Q.54 The area of the region in the first quadrant bounded by the y-axis and the curves $y = \sin x$ and $y = \cos x$ is__.

Q.55 The length of the cycloid $x = (t + \sin t)$, $y = (1 - \cos t)$ between $(0,0)$ and $(\pi, 2)$ is____.

Q.56 The area of the loop of the curve $5y^2 = x^2(5 - x)$ is____.

Q.57 The area of the surface of the solid generated by the revolving of the line segment $y = 2x$ from $x = 0$ to $x = 2$ about the x-axis is equal to______.

Q.58 If $f'(x) = \frac{x^2}{2} + kx + 1$ and $f(0) = 0,\ f(3) = 15$ then the value of k is equal to________.

Q.59 If $\lim_{x\to 0} \frac{x(1 - \cos x) - ax^2 \sin x}{x^5}$ exists and is finite, then the value of 'a' must be _______.

Q.60 The area of the region in first quadrant enclosed between the curve $y = x^3$ and the line $y = x$ is_______.

Q.61 The sides of a right angled triangle are 12 cm and 13 cm respectively. The first side decreases at the rate of 1 cm/s and the second increases at the rate of 1.5 cm/s. The rate of change of the area (in cm^2 / s) after 4 s is________.

Q.62 The greatest rate of increase of $u = xyz^2$ at the point (1, 0, 3) is ________.

Q.63 The distance between the origin and the point nearest to it on the surface $z^2 = 1 + xy$ is _______.

Q.64 If S is the surface of the sphere $x^2 + y^2 + z^2 = 4$ then $\iint_S (x+z)\,dy\,dz + (y+z)\,dz\,dx + (x+y)\,dx\,dy$ is __.

Q.65 If $\mathbf{A} + \mathbf{B} + \mathbf{C} = 0$ and $|\mathbf{A}| = 3, |\mathbf{B}| = 5, |\mathbf{C}| = 7$, then the angle (in degree) between $\mathbf{A}$ and $\mathbf{B}$ is________.

2.4 SOLUTION TO PRACTICE PAPER

Q.1 Ans:(C)

1. $\lim_{x\to 0} \frac{\sin x}{x} = \lim_{x\to 0} \frac{\cos x}{1} = 1$ (correct)

2. $\lim_{x\to\infty} \left(1 + \frac{1}{x}\right)^x = e$ (wrong)

3. $\lim_{x\to 0} \frac{\log(x+1)}{x} = \lim_{x\to 0} \frac{1}{x+1} = 1$ (correct)

Q.2 Ans:(C)

The Fourier series of function $f(x)$ in the interval $-\pi \le x \le \pi$ is

$$f(x) = a_0 + \sum_{n=1}^{n=\infty} (a_n \cos nx + b_n \sin nx)$$

where $a_0 = \frac{1}{2\pi} \int_{-\pi}^{\pi} f(x)dx$

$$a_0 = \frac{1}{2\pi} \int_{-\pi}^{\pi} f(x)dx = \frac{1}{2\pi}\left[\int_{-\pi}^{0} 0\,dx + \int_{0}^{\pi} x^2 dx\right]$$

$$a_0 = \frac{\pi^2}{6}$$

Q.3 Ans:(A)

$$\lim_{n\to\infty}\left[\frac{1}{n+1} + \frac{1}{n+2} + \frac{1}{n+3} + \ldots + \frac{1}{2n}\right]$$

$$= \lim_{n\to\infty} \sum_{r=1}^{n} \frac{1}{n+r} = \lim_{n\to\infty} \sum_{r=1}^{n} \frac{\frac{1}{n}}{1 + \frac{r}{n}}$$

Now to write the limit as a definite integral

$= \lim_{n\to\infty} \sum_{r=1}^{n}$ by $\int$ and lower limit $\lim_{n\to\infty}\left[\frac{r}{n}\right]_{r=1} = 0$, upper limit $\lim_{n\to\infty}\left[\frac{r}{n}\right]_{r=n} = 1$

The given series

$$\int_0^1 \frac{dx}{1+x} = [\log(1+x)]_0^1 = \log 2$$

Q.4 Ans:(D)

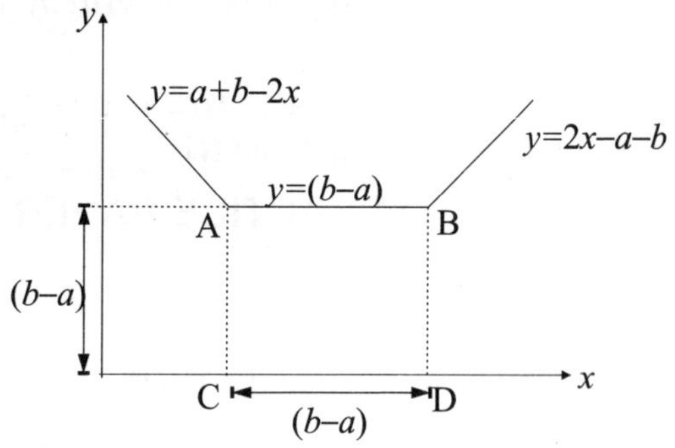

Graph of $|x-a|+|x-b|$

Figure shows the graph of function $|x-a|+|x-b|$

$\int_a^b (|x-a|+|x-b|)\,dx$ represents the area under the curve from $x = a$ to $x = b$. That is

$$\int_a^b (|x-a|+|x-b|)\,dx = (b-a)^2$$

Q.5 Ans:(B)

$$\int_0^1\int_x^{1/x} \frac{x}{1+y^2}\,dx\,dy = \int_0^1\left(\int_x^{1/x} \frac{1}{1+y^2}\,dy\right)x dx$$

$$= \int_0^1 [\tan^{-1} y]_x^{1/x}\, x\,dx,$$

$$= \int_0^1 \tan^{-1}\infty\, x\,dx = \frac{\pi}{2}\int_0^1 x\,dx$$

$$= \frac{\pi}{2}\left[\frac{x^2}{2}\right]_x^1 = \frac{\pi}{4}$$

$$\int_0^1\int_x^{1/x} \frac{x}{1+y^2}\,dx\,dy = \frac{\pi}{4}$$

Q.6 Ans:(C)

Let $p(x) = A + Bx + Cx^2 + Dx^3$

$p'(x) = B + 2Cx + 3Dx^2 \Rightarrow p'(0) = B = 1$

$p''(x) = 2C + 6Dx;\ \ p''(0) = 2C = 1 \Rightarrow C = \frac{1}{2}$

$p'''(x) = 6D = 2;\ \ \ p''(0) = 6D = 2 \Rightarrow D = \frac{1}{3}$

$p'(x) = B + 2\times\frac{1}{2}x + 3\times\frac{1}{3}x^2$

$$p'(x) = 1 + x + x^2$$

Q.7 Ans:(C)

We have $\quad f = \sin^{-1}\left(\frac{x^2+y^2}{x+y}\right)$

or $\quad \sin f = x\left(\frac{1+\left(\frac{y}{x}\right)^2}{1+\frac{y}{x}}\right)$

or $\quad u = \sin f = x\phi\left(\frac{y}{x}\right) = x\left(\frac{1+\left(\frac{y}{x}\right)^2}{1+\frac{y}{x}}\right)$

Applying Euler's theorem $x\frac{\partial u}{\partial x} + y\frac{\partial u}{\partial y} = nu$

or $\quad x\frac{\partial}{\partial x}(\sin f) + y\frac{\partial}{\partial y}(\sin f) = 1\times\sin f$

$$x\frac{\partial f}{\partial x} + y\frac{\partial f}{\partial y} = \tan f$$

Q.8 Ans:(D)

Function $f(x)$ is differentiable at $x = 1$ if

$$f(1-0) = f(1+0)$$

and $\quad f'(1-0) = f'(1+0)$

From which

$$\alpha + \beta = 3 \quad \text{and } 2\alpha + \beta = 2$$

Solving the equations, we get

$$\alpha = -1,\ \beta = 4$$

Q.9 Ans:(C)

$$\lim_{n\to\infty}\left\{\left(1+\frac{1}{n}\right)^n + \left(1+\frac{1}{n}\right)^{-n}\right\}$$

We know that $\lim_{n\to\infty}\left(1+\frac{1}{n}\right)^n = e$

$$\lim_{n\to\infty}\left\{\left(1+\frac{1}{n}\right)^n + \left(1+\frac{1}{n}\right)^{-n}\right\}$$

$$= \lim_{n\to\infty}\left(1+\frac{1}{n}\right)^n + \lim_{n\to\infty}\left\{\left(1+\frac{1}{n}\right)^n\right\}^{-1}$$

$$\lim_{n\to\infty}\left\{\left(1+\frac{1}{n}\right)^n + \left(1+\frac{1}{n}\right)^{-n}\right\} = e + \frac{1}{e}$$

Q.10 Ans:(D)

The following graph of function $f(x)=x(1-x)$ is sketched.

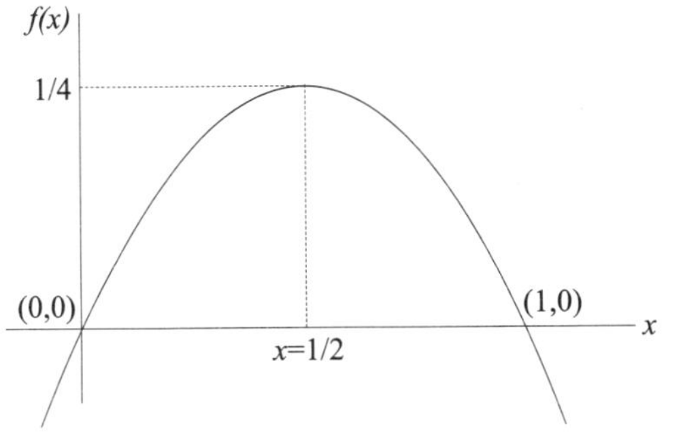

Graph of $f(x)=x(1-x)$

From the graph, we can easily see that it has a maximum at $x=\frac{1}{2}$, and it is continuous function.

Q.11 Ans:(C)

$$\int_0^{2a} f(x)\,dx=\int_0^{a} f(x)\,dx+\int_a^{2a} f(x)\,dx$$

or $$\int_0^{2a} f(x)\,dx=\int_0^{a} f(x)\,dx+\int_0^{a} f(2a-y)\,dy,$$

where $x=2a-y$

or $$\int_0^{2a} f(x)\,dx=\int_0^{a} f(x)\,dx+\int_0^{a} f(2a-x)\,dx$$

$$=2\int_0^{a} f(x)\,dx \quad \text{or} \quad 0$$

or $$\int_0^{2a} f(x)\,dx=0; \quad \text{if } f(2a-x)=-f(x)$$

$$\int_0^{2a} f(x)\,dx=2\int_0^{a} f(x)\,dx; \quad \text{if } f(2a-x)=f(x)$$

Q.12 Ans:(A)

The vector **F** is said to be irrotational, if curl $\mathbf{F}=0$

$$\text{curl}\,\mathbf{F}=\begin{vmatrix} \mathbf{i} & \mathbf{j} & \mathbf{k} \\ \frac{\partial}{\partial x} & \frac{\partial}{\partial y} & \frac{\partial}{\partial z} \\ x+2y+az & -2x-3y-z & 4x-y+2z \end{vmatrix}=0$$

or $$\mathbf{i}\times 0-\mathbf{j}(4-a)+\mathbf{k}\times 0=0$$

From which

$$a=4$$

Q.13 Ans:(B)

Let $$I=\int_0^{\pi/2}\frac{\sqrt{\cos x}}{\sqrt{\sin x}+\sqrt{\cos x}}\,dx \qquad \text{(i)}$$

Applying the property of definite integral,

$$I=\int_0^{\pi/2}\frac{\sqrt{\cos\left(\frac{\pi}{2}-x\right)}}{\sqrt{\sin\left(\frac{\pi}{2}-x\right)}+\sqrt{\cos\left(\frac{\pi}{2}-x\right)}}\,dx$$

or $$I=\int_0^{\pi/2}\frac{\sqrt{\sin x}}{\sqrt{\sin x}+\sqrt{\cos x}}\,dx \qquad \text{(ii)}$$

Adding equation (i) and (ii), we obtain

$$2I=\int_0^{\pi/2}\frac{\sqrt{\sin x}+\sqrt{\cos x}}{\sqrt{\sin x}+\sqrt{\cos x}}\,dx=\int_0^{\pi/2}dx$$

or $$2I=\frac{\pi}{2} \Rightarrow I=\frac{\pi}{4}$$

$$\int_0^{\pi/2}\frac{\sqrt{\cos x}}{\sqrt{\sin x}+\sqrt{\cos x}}\,dx=\frac{\pi}{4}$$

Q.14 Ans:(C)

By Green theorem in plane region bounded by a simple closed curve C, then

$$\iint\left(\frac{\partial N}{\partial x}-\frac{\partial M}{\partial y}\right)dxdy=\oint_C Mdx+Ndy$$

Putting $M=-y$ and $N=x$, we have

$$\oint_C xdy-ydx=\iint\left(\frac{\partial x}{\partial x}-\frac{\partial(-y)}{\partial y}\right)dxdy$$

or $$\oint_C xdy-ydx=2\iint_R dxdy=2A$$

where A is the area bounded by curve C

or $$A=\frac{1}{2}\oint_C xdy-ydx$$

Area of ellipse

$$A=\frac{1}{2}\oint_C xdy-ydx$$

$$=\frac{1}{2}\int_{\theta=0}^{\theta=2\pi}\left[a\cos\theta\frac{\partial(a\sin\theta)}{\partial\theta}-a\sin\theta\frac{\partial(a\cos\theta)}{\partial\theta}\right]d\theta$$

$$=\frac{1}{2}ab\int_{\theta=0}^{\theta=2\pi}d\theta=\pi ab$$

$$\frac{1}{2}\oint_C xdy-ydx=\pi ab$$

Q.15 Ans:(A)

Applying Green's theorem in plane, we have

$$\iint_R \left(\frac{\partial N}{\partial x} - \frac{\partial M}{\partial y}\right) dxdy = \oint_C Mdx + Ndy$$

$$\oint_C (xy + y^2)\, dx + x^2 dy$$

$$= \iint_R \left(\frac{\partial}{\partial x}(x^2) - \frac{\partial}{\partial y}(xy + y^2)\right) dxdy$$

$$= \iint_R (x - 2y) dxdy = \int_0^1 \int_{x^2}^{x} (x - 2y) dydx$$

$$= \int_0^1 [xy - y^2]_{y=x^2}^{y=x}\, dx = \int_0^1 [x^4 - x^3] dx$$

$$\oint_C (xy + y^2)\, dx + x^2 dy = -\frac{1}{20}$$

Q.16 Ans:(C)

By divergence theorem, we have

$$\iint_S \mathbf{F} \cdot \mathbf{n}\, dS = \iiint_V \text{div } \mathbf{F}\, dV$$

Substituting $\mathbf{F} = x\ \mathbf{i} + y\,\mathbf{j} + z\,\mathbf{k}$, we have

$$\iint_S (x\,\mathbf{i} + y\,\mathbf{j} + z\,\mathbf{k}) \cdot \mathbf{n}\, dS = \iiint_V \text{div}(x\,\mathbf{i} + y\,\mathbf{j} + z\,\mathbf{k})\, dV$$

or $\iint_S (x\,\mathbf{i} + y\,\mathbf{j} + z\,\mathbf{k}) \cdot \mathbf{n}\, dS = 3V$,

where V is the volume of cube.

$$\iint_S (x\,\mathbf{i} + y\,\mathbf{j} + z\,\mathbf{k}) \cdot \mathbf{n}\, dS = 3a^3$$

Q.17 Ans:(A)

We know that

$$\nabla^2 u = \nabla \cdot \nabla u = \left(\mathbf{i}\frac{\partial}{\partial x} + \mathbf{j}\frac{\partial}{\partial y} + \mathbf{k}\frac{\partial}{\partial z}\right) \cdot \left(\mathbf{i}\frac{\partial u}{\partial x} + \mathbf{j}\frac{\partial u}{\partial y} + \mathbf{k}\frac{\partial u}{\partial z}\right)$$

or $\nabla^2 u = \dfrac{\partial^2 u}{\partial x^2} + \dfrac{\partial^2 u}{\partial y^2} + \dfrac{\partial^2 u}{\partial z^2}$

Substituting $u = x^2 - y^2 + 4z$, we have

$$\nabla^2 u = \frac{\partial^2}{\partial x^2}(x^2 - y^2 + 4z) + \frac{\partial^2}{\partial y^2}(x^2 - y^2 + 4z) + \frac{\partial^2}{\partial z^2}(x^2 - y^2 + 4z)$$

or $\nabla^2 u = 2 - 2 + 0$

$$\nabla^2 u = 0$$

Q.18 Ans:(C)

By divergence theorem, we have

$$\iint_S \mathbf{F} \cdot \mathbf{n}\, dS = \iiint_V \text{div } \mathbf{F}\, dV$$

Substituting $\mathbf{F} = x\ \mathbf{i} + 2y\,\mathbf{j} + 3z\,\mathbf{k}$, we have

$$\iint_S \mathbf{F} \cdot \mathbf{n}\, dS = \iiint_V \text{div}(x\,\mathbf{i} + 2y\,\mathbf{j} + 3z\,\mathbf{k})\, dV$$

or $\iint_S \mathbf{F} \cdot \mathbf{n}\, dS = \iiint_V (1 + 2 + 3) dV = 6\iiint_V dV$

$$\iint_S \mathbf{F} \cdot \mathbf{n}\, dS = 6\text{V}$$

Q.19 Ans:(B)

We have $\dfrac{d}{dt}\left(\mathbf{r} \times \dfrac{d\mathbf{r}}{dt}\right) = \mathbf{r} \times \dfrac{d^2\mathbf{r}}{dt^2}$

$$\int_{t=1}^{t=2} \left(\mathbf{r} \times \frac{d^2\mathbf{r}}{dt^2}\right) dt = \left[\mathbf{r} \times \frac{d\mathbf{r}}{dt}\right]_{t=1}^{t=2}$$

$$\int_{t=1}^{t=2} \left(\mathbf{r} \times \frac{d^2\mathbf{r}}{dt^2}\right) dt = [(5t^2\mathbf{i} + t\,\mathbf{j} - t^3\mathbf{k}) \times (10t\,\mathbf{i} + \mathbf{j} - 3t^2\mathbf{k})]_{t=1}^{t=2}$$

or $\displaystyle\int_{t=1}^{t=2} \left(\mathbf{r} \times \frac{d^2\mathbf{r}}{dt^2}\right) dt = \begin{vmatrix} \mathbf{i} & \mathbf{j} & \mathbf{k} \\ 5t^2 & t & -t^3 \\ 10t & 1 & -3t^2 \end{vmatrix}_{t=1}^{t=2}$

$$\int_{t=1}^{t=2} \left(\mathbf{r} \times \frac{d^2\mathbf{r}}{dt^2}\right) dt = -14\mathbf{i} + 75\mathbf{j} - 15\mathbf{k}$$

Q.20 Ans:(C)

Let $\mathbf{a} = a_1\ \mathbf{i} + a_2\mathbf{j} + a_3\mathbf{k}$ and $\mathbf{r} = x\,\mathbf{i} + y\,\mathbf{j} + z\,\mathbf{k}$

Now $\mathbf{r} \cdot \mathbf{a} = (x\,\mathbf{i} + y\,\mathbf{j} + z\,\mathbf{k}) \cdot (a_1\ \mathbf{i} + a_2\mathbf{j} + a_3\mathbf{k})$

or $\mathbf{r} \cdot \mathbf{a} = a_1 x + a_2 y + a_3 z$

$$\text{grad}(\mathbf{r}.\,\mathbf{a}) = i\frac{\partial}{\partial x}(a_1 x + a_2 y + a_3 z) + j\frac{\partial}{\partial y}(a_1 x + a_2 y + a_3 z) + k\frac{\partial}{\partial z}(a_1 x + a_2 y + a_3 z)$$

or $\text{grad}(\mathbf{r}.\,\mathbf{a}) = a_1\ \mathbf{i} + a_2\mathbf{j} + a_3\mathbf{k}$

$$\text{grad}(\mathbf{r}.\,\mathbf{a}) = \mathbf{a}$$

Q.21 Ans:[1]

For $x > 0$, $|x| = x$

$$\int_0^1 \frac{|x|}{x} dx = \int_0^1 \frac{x}{x} dx = \int_0^1 1\, dx = 1$$

$$\int_0^1 \frac{|x|}{x} dx = 1$$

Q.22 Ans:[1]

We have $\int_0^x f(t) = x \cos \pi x$

Applying Leibniz rule,

differentiate with respect to x, we obtain

$$\frac{d}{dx}\int_0^x f(t) = \frac{d}{dx} x \cos \pi x = \cos \pi x - \pi x \sin \pi x$$

or $f(x) = \cos \pi x - \pi x \sin \pi x$

or $f(4) = \cos 4\pi - 4\pi \sin 4\pi$

$$f(4) = 1$$

Q.23 Ans:[0.135]

$$\lim_{n\to\infty}\left(\frac{n}{n+1}\right)^{2n} = \lim_{n\to\infty}\left(\frac{1}{1+\frac{1}{n}}\right)^{2n}$$

$$= \lim_{n\to\infty}\left(\frac{1}{1+\frac{1}{n}}\right)^{2n} = \lim_{x\to 0}\left(\frac{1}{1+x}\right)^{\frac{2}{x}}$$

$$= \lim_{x\to 0}\left(\frac{1}{(1+x)^{\frac{1}{x}}}\right)^{2} = \left(\frac{1}{e}\right)^2$$

or $$\lim_{n\to\infty}\left(\frac{n}{n+1}\right)^{2n} = \frac{1}{e^2}$$

$$\lim_{n\to\infty}\left(\frac{n}{n+1}\right)^{2n} = 0.135$$

Q.24 Ans:[1]

Let $y = \tan^{-1}\left(\frac{2x}{1-x^2}\right)$, $z = \cos^{-1}\left(\frac{1-x^2}{1+x^2}\right)$ and $x = \tan\theta$

$$y = \tan^{-1}\left(\frac{2\tan\theta}{1-\tan^2\theta}\right) = \tan^{-1}(\tan 2\theta) = 2\theta$$

$$z = \cos^{-1}\left(\frac{1-\cos^2\theta}{1+\cos^2\theta}\right) = \cos^{-1}(\cos 2\theta) = 2\theta$$

$$\frac{dy}{dz} = \frac{dy/d\theta}{dz/d\theta} = \frac{2}{2}$$

$$\frac{dy}{dz} = 1$$

Q.25 Ans:[240]

Let x be the side of the cube.

Volume of cube $V = x^3$; differentiate with respect to time t, we obtain

$$\frac{dV}{dt} = 3x^2 \frac{dx}{dt}$$

Rate of change of its volume $\frac{dV}{dt} = 3 \times 4^2 \times 5$

$$\frac{dV}{dt} = 240\,\text{cm}^3/\text{s}$$

Q.26 Ans:[1]

Let $\mathbf{r} = x\,\mathbf{i} + y\,\mathbf{j} + z\,\mathbf{k}$

$$\mathbf{a}\cdot\mathbf{r} = (2\mathbf{i} + 3\mathbf{j} - m\,\mathbf{k})\cdot(x\,\mathbf{i} + y\,\mathbf{j} + z\,\mathbf{k})$$

or $\mathbf{a}\cdot\mathbf{r} = 2x + 3y - mz$

$\therefore$ $\nabla\mathbf{a}\cdot\mathbf{r} = 2\mathbf{i} + 3\mathbf{j} - m\,\mathbf{k}$

or $|\nabla\mathbf{a}\cdot\mathbf{r}| = \sqrt{4+9+m^2} = \sqrt{14}$

$$m = 1$$

Q.27 Ans:[0]

By Green theorem in plane region bounded by a simple closed curve C, we have

$$\iint\left(\frac{\partial N}{\partial x} - \frac{\partial M}{\partial y}\right)dxdy = \oint_C M dx + N dy$$

Here $M = \cos x \sin y - xy$, $N = \sin x \cos y$

$$\oint_C (\cos x \sin y - xy)\,dx + \sin x \cos y\,dy = \iint_R x dx dy$$

$$= \int_{-1}^{1}\int_{-\sqrt{1-x^2}}^{\sqrt{1-x^2}} x dx dy$$

$$= \int_{-1}^{1} x \times 2\sqrt{1-x^2}\,dx$$

$$\oint_C (\cos x \sin y - xy)\,dx + \sin x \cos y\,dy = 0$$

Q.28 Ans:[–2]

A vector $\mathbf{V}$ is said to be solenoidal if div $\mathbf{V} = 0$

$$\text{div}\,\mathbf{V} = \nabla\cdot\text{V} = \frac{\partial}{\partial x}(x+3y) + \frac{\partial}{\partial y}(y-2z) + \frac{\partial}{\partial z}(x+az)$$

$$\text{div}\,\mathbf{V} = 1 + 1 + a = 0$$

$$a = -2$$

Q.29 Ans:[10]

We have $\frac{d}{dt}(\mathbf{r}^2) = 2\mathbf{r}\cdot\frac{d\mathbf{r}}{dt}$

or $\int\left(\mathbf{r}\cdot\frac{d\mathbf{r}}{dt}\right)dt = \frac{1}{2}\mathbf{r}^2 + c$

or $\int_{t=2}^{t=3}\left(\mathbf{r}\cdot\frac{d\mathbf{r}}{dt}\right)dt = \frac{1}{2}[\mathbf{r}^2]_{t=2}^{t=3} = \frac{1}{2}[\mathbf{r}^2]_{t=3} - \frac{1}{2}[\mathbf{r}^2]_{t=2}$

$$= \frac{1}{2}[\{4^2 + (-2)^2 + (3)^2\} - \{(2)^2 + (-1)^2 + (2)^2\}]$$

$$\int_{t=2}^{t=3}\left(\mathbf{r}\cdot\frac{d\mathbf{r}}{dt}\right)dt = 10$$

Q.30 Ans:[0]

Position vector $\mathbf{r} = x\,\mathbf{i} + y\,\mathbf{j} + z\,\mathbf{k}$

$$\text{curl } \mathbf{r} = \nabla\times\boldsymbol{r} = \begin{bmatrix} i & j & k \\ \frac{\partial}{\partial x} & \frac{\partial}{\partial y} & \frac{\partial}{\partial z} \\ x & y & z \end{bmatrix} = \mathbf{i}\times 0 - \mathbf{j}\times 0 + \mathbf{k}\times 0$$

$$\text{curl } \mathbf{r} = 0$$

Q.31 Ans:(D)

Given: $V = f(y-z,\ z-x,\ x-y)$, let $p = y-z$, $q = z-x$ and $r = x-y$.

$$\frac{\partial V}{\partial x} = \frac{\partial V}{\partial p}\frac{\partial p}{\partial x} + \frac{\partial V}{\partial q}\frac{\partial q}{\partial x} + \frac{\partial V}{\partial r}\frac{\partial r}{\partial x}$$

$$= \frac{\partial V}{\partial p}\times 0 + \frac{\partial V}{\partial q}\times -1 + \frac{\partial V}{\partial r}\times 1$$

or $\frac{\partial V}{\partial x} = -\frac{\partial V}{\partial q} + \frac{\partial V}{\partial r}$

Similarly $\frac{\partial V}{\partial y} = \frac{\partial V}{\partial p} - \frac{\partial V}{\partial r}$

and $\frac{\partial V}{\partial z} = -\frac{\partial V}{\partial p} + \frac{\partial V}{\partial q}$

From which,

$$\frac{\partial V}{\partial x} + \frac{\partial V}{\partial y} + \frac{\partial V}{\partial z} = -\frac{\partial V}{\partial q} + \frac{\partial V}{\partial r} + \frac{\partial V}{\partial p} - \frac{\partial V}{\partial r} - \frac{\partial V}{\partial p} + \frac{\partial V}{\partial q} = 0$$

$$\frac{\partial V}{\partial x} + \frac{\partial V}{\partial y} + \frac{\partial V}{\partial z} = 0$$

Q.32 Ans:(B)

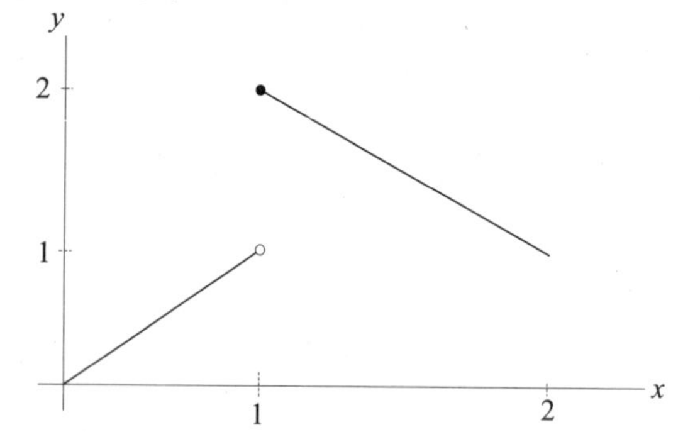

Graph of function $f(x)$

Graph of function $f(x) = \begin{cases} x & ;\ 0<x<1 \\ 3-x & ;\ 1\le x\le 2 \end{cases}$, is drawn above. From which

1. $f(1-0) = 1$ (correct)
2. $f(1+0) = 3-1 = 2$ (correct)
3. $f(1) = 3-1 = 2$ (correct)

Q.33 Ans:(B)

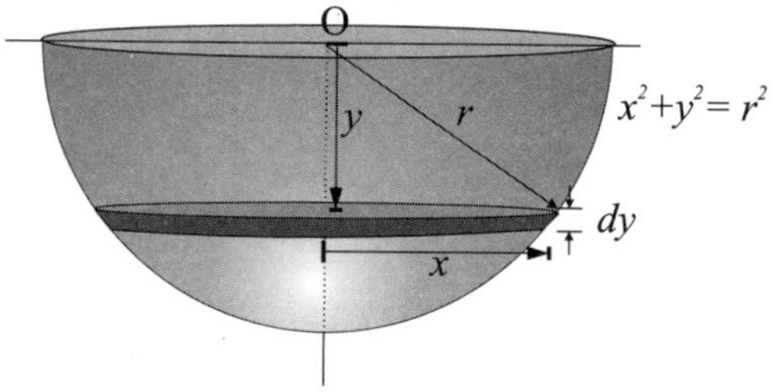

Volume of water in bowl $V = \int_{r/2}^{r}\pi x^2 dy$

$$V = \int_{r/2}^{r}\pi(r^2 - y^2)\,dy = \pi\left[r^2 y - \frac{y^3}{3}\right]_{r/2}^{r}$$

$$V = \frac{5}{24}\pi r^3$$

Q.34 Ans:(A)

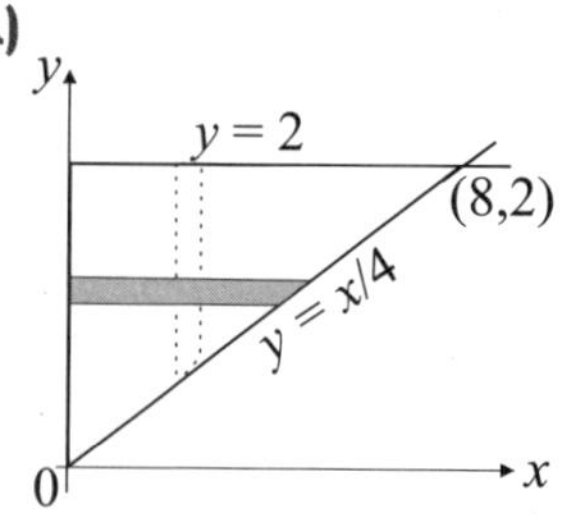

The given limits show that the region of integration is bounded by the lines $y = \frac{x}{4}$, $y = 2$, $x = 0$ and $x = 8$

$$I = \int_0^8 \int_{\frac{x}{4}}^{2} f(x, y)\, dy\, dx = \int_r^s \int_p^q f(x, y)\, dx\, dy \qquad \text{(i)}$$

by changing order $\quad I = \int_0^2 \int_0^{4y} f(x, y)\, dx\, dy \qquad$ (ii)

Compare Equation (i) with Equation (ii), we find

$$q = 4y, s = 2$$

Q.35 Ans:(A)

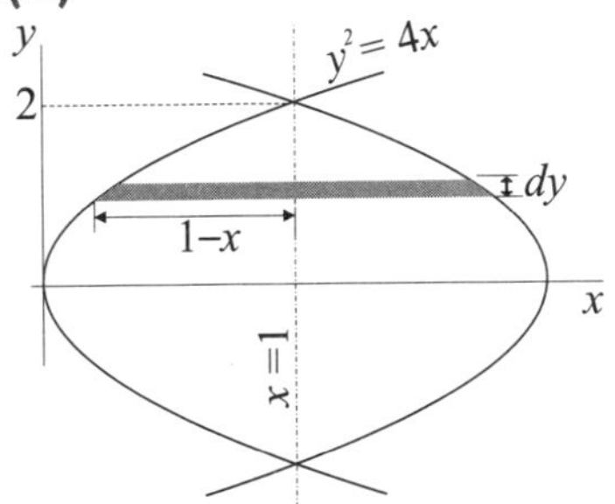

Consider an element of thickness dy and radius $(1-x)$.

The volume of element is

$$dV = \pi(1-x)^2 dy$$

Volume from $y=0$ to $y=2$; $\quad V = \int_{y=0}^{y=2} \pi(1-x)^2 dy$

or $\quad V = \int_{y=0}^{y=2} \pi\left(1-\frac{y^2}{4}\right)^2 dy = \pi\int_0^2 \left(1-\frac{y^2}{2}+\frac{y^4}{16}\right)dy$

From which

$$V = \frac{16}{15}\pi$$

Q.36 Ans:(A)

The function is odd in the given interval. Therefore

$$a_0 = a_n = 0$$

and $\quad b_n = \frac{2}{\pi}\int_0^{\pi} x\sin nx dx = \frac{2}{\pi}\left[x\left(\frac{-\cos nx}{n}\right)-\left(\frac{-\sin nx}{n^2}\right)\right]_0^{\pi}$

or $\quad b_n = \frac{-2\cos n\pi}{n} = -2\frac{(-1)^n}{n}$

Hence

$$x = 2\left(\sin x - \frac{1}{2}\sin 2x + \frac{1}{3}\sin 3x - \frac{1}{4}\sin 4x + \ldots\right)$$

Q.37 Ans:(A)

We have $\quad y = (\sin x)^{\sin x^{\cdot^{\cdot^{\cdot^{\infty}}}}}$ or $\quad y = (\sin x)^y$

Taking log $\quad \ln y = y\ln(\sin x)$

Differentiating $\quad \frac{1}{y}\frac{dy}{dx} = y\cot x + \ln(\sin x)\frac{dy}{dx}$

From which

$$\frac{dy}{dx} = \frac{y^2\cot x}{1 - y\ln\sin x}$$

Q.38 Ans:(C)

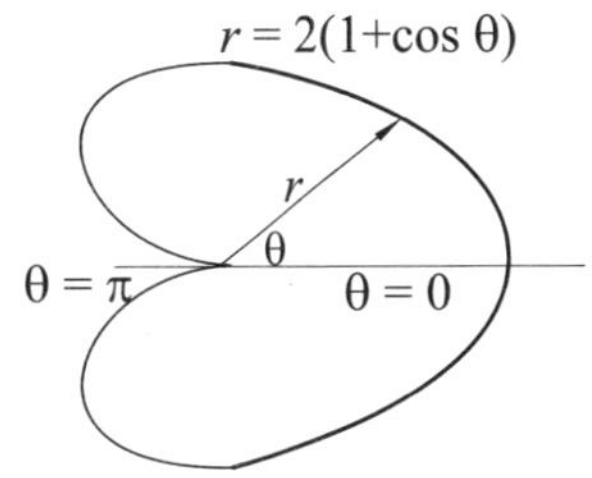

Perimeter of the cardioid $S = 2\int_0^{\pi}\sqrt{r^2+\left(\frac{dr}{d\theta}\right)^2}\,d\theta$

$$S = 2\int_0^{\pi}\sqrt{\{2(1+\cos\theta)\}^2+\left(\frac{d}{d\theta}2(1+\cos\theta)\right)^2}\,d\theta$$

$$S = 8\int_0^{\pi}\cos\frac{\theta}{2}\,d\theta = 16\left[\sin\frac{\theta}{2}\right]_0^{\pi}$$

$$S = 16$$

Q.39 Ans:(A)

We have $\quad u = \sin^{-1}\left(\frac{x^{\frac{1}{3}}+y^{\frac{1}{3}}}{x+y}\right)^{\frac{1}{2}}$

or $\quad \sin u = \left(\frac{x^{\frac{1}{3}}+y^{\frac{1}{3}}}{x+y}\right)^{\frac{1}{2}} = x^{-\frac{1}{3}}\left(\frac{1+\left(\frac{y}{x}\right)^{\frac{1}{3}}}{1+\left(\frac{y}{x}\right)}\right)^{\frac{1}{2}}$

or $\quad \sin u = x^{-\frac{1}{3}} f\left(\frac{y}{x}\right)$

Applying Euler's theorem,

$$x\frac{\partial}{\partial x}(\sin u) + y\frac{\partial}{\partial y}(\sin u) = -\frac{1}{3}\sin u$$

or $\quad \cos u\, x\frac{\partial u}{\partial x} + \cos u\, y\frac{\partial u}{\partial y} = -\frac{1}{3}\sin u$

$$x\frac{\partial u}{\partial x} + y\frac{\partial u}{\partial y} = -\frac{1}{3}\tan u$$

Q.40 Ans:(A)

The function $f(x)$ is differentiable at $x=\frac{\pi}{4}$, if

$$f\left(\frac{\pi}{4}-0\right)=f\left(\frac{\pi}{4}+0\right) \text{and } f'\left(\frac{\pi}{4}-0\right)=f'\left(\frac{\pi}{4}+0\right)$$

From which

$$a=-\frac{1}{\sqrt{2}} \quad \text{and } \frac{a\pi}{4}+b=\frac{1}{\sqrt{2}} \Rightarrow b=\frac{1+\frac{\pi}{4}}{\sqrt{2}}$$

$$b=\frac{1+\frac{\pi}{4}}{\sqrt{2}},\ a=-\frac{1}{\sqrt{2}}$$

Q.41 Ans:(B)

We have $\quad \frac{dz}{dt}=\frac{\partial z}{\partial x}\frac{dx}{dt}+\frac{\partial z}{\partial y}\frac{dy}{dt}$

Substituting $\frac{\partial z}{\partial x}=e^x \sin y$, $\frac{\partial z}{\partial y}=e^x \cos y$, $\frac{dx}{dt}=\frac{1}{t}$ and $\frac{dy}{dt}=2t$

or $\quad \frac{dz}{dt}=e^x \sin y \times \frac{1}{t}+e^x \cos y \times 2t$

$$\frac{dz}{dt}=\frac{e^x}{t}(\sin y+2t^2 \cos y)$$

Q.42 Ans:(A)

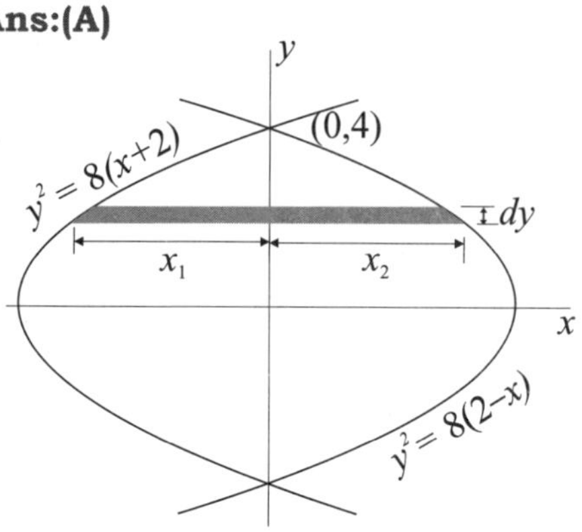

Parabolas $y^2=8(x+2)$ and $y^2=8(2-x)$ are intersect at (0,4) and (0,–4).

Required area $A=2\int_0^4 (x_1+x_2)dy$

or $\quad A=2\int_0^4\left[-\left(-2+\frac{y^2}{8}\right)+\left(2-\frac{y^2}{8}\right)\right]dy$

or $\quad A=4\int_0^4\left(2-\frac{y^2}{8}\right)dy$

or $\quad A=4\left[2y-\frac{y^3}{24}\right]_0^4$

$$A=\frac{64}{3}$$

Q.43 Ans:(C)

If curve C $\quad \mathbf{r}=t\,\mathbf{i}+t^2\mathbf{j}+t^3\mathbf{k}=x\mathbf{i}+y\mathbf{j}+z\mathbf{k}$

Therefore, $x=t,\ y=t^2$ and $z=t^3$ and

$\frac{d\mathbf{r}}{dt}=\mathbf{i}+2t\,\mathbf{j}+3t^2\,\mathbf{k}$

$\mathbf{F}=xy\mathbf{i}+yz\,\mathbf{j}+zx\,\mathbf{k}=t^3\mathbf{i}+t^5\mathbf{j}+t^4\mathbf{k}$

Hence, $\int_C \mathbf{F}\cdot d\mathbf{r}=\int_{t=-1}^{t=1}\left(\mathbf{F}\cdot\frac{d\mathbf{r}}{dt}\right)dt$

$$\int_C \mathbf{F}\cdot d\mathbf{r}=\int_{t=-1}^{t=1}\{(t^3\mathbf{i}+t^5\mathbf{j}+t^4\mathbf{k})\cdot(\mathbf{i}+2t\,\mathbf{j}+3t^2\,\mathbf{k})\}dt$$

$$=\int_{t=-1}^{t=1}(t^3+5t^6)dt$$

$$\int_C \mathbf{F}\cdot d\mathbf{r}=\frac{10}{7}$$

Q.44 Ans:(C)

Area of curve $r=f(\theta)$ from θ_1 to θ_2 is given by

$$A=\int_{\theta_1}^{\theta_2}\frac{1}{2}r^2 d\theta$$

Area of cardioid $A=2\int_0^{\pi}\frac{1}{2}(1+\cos\theta)^2 d\theta$

or $\quad A=4\int_{\theta_1}^{\theta_2}\cos^4\frac{\theta}{2}d\theta$

or $\quad A=8\frac{\Gamma\left(\frac{4+1}{2}\right)\Gamma\left(\frac{0+1}{2}\right)}{2\Gamma\left(\frac{4+0+2}{2}\right)}$

$$A=\frac{3}{2}\pi$$

Q.45 Ans:(A)

Let $\mathbf{a}=a_1\,\mathbf{i}+a_2\mathbf{j}+a_3\mathbf{k}$ and $\mathbf{r}=x\,\mathbf{i}+y\,\mathbf{j}+z\,\mathbf{k}$

Now $\quad \mathbf{r}\times\mathbf{a}=\begin{vmatrix} i & j & k \\ x & y & z \\ a_1 & a_2 & a_3 \end{vmatrix}$

$$=\mathbf{i}(a_3y-a_2z)-\mathbf{j}(a_3x-a_1z)+\mathbf{k}(a_2x-a_1y)$$

$\therefore\quad \text{div}(\mathbf{r}\times\mathbf{a}) = \mathbf{i}\times 0 - \mathbf{j}\times 0 + \mathbf{k}\times 0 = 0$

$$\text{div}(\mathbf{r}\times\mathbf{a}) = 0$$

Q.46 Ans:(C)

Let $\mathbf{a} = a_1\,\mathbf{i} + a_2\mathbf{j} + a_3\mathbf{k}$ and $\mathbf{r} = x\,\mathbf{i} + y\,\mathbf{j} + z\,\mathbf{k}$

$$\mathbf{r}\cdot\mathbf{a} = (x\,\mathbf{i} + y\,\mathbf{j} + z\,\mathbf{k})\cdot(a_1\,\mathbf{i} + a_2\mathbf{j} + a_3\mathbf{k})$$

or $\mathbf{r}\cdot\mathbf{a} = a_1x + a_2y + a_3z$

or $\text{grad}(\mathbf{r}\cdot\mathbf{a}) = \mathbf{i}\dfrac{\partial}{\partial x}(a_1x) + \mathbf{j}\dfrac{\partial}{\partial x}(a_2y) + \mathbf{k}\dfrac{\partial}{\partial x}(a_3z)$

or $\quad \text{grad}(\mathbf{r}\cdot\mathbf{a}) = a_1\mathbf{i} + a_2\mathbf{j} + a_3\mathbf{k} = \mathbf{a}$

$$\text{grad}(\mathbf{r}\cdot\mathbf{a}) = \mathbf{a}$$

Q.47 Ans:(A)

Let $\mathbf{a} = a_1\,\mathbf{i} + a_2\mathbf{j} + a_3\mathbf{k}$, $\mathbf{b} = b_1\,\mathbf{i} + b_2\mathbf{j} + b_3\mathbf{k}$ and $\mathbf{r} = x\,\mathbf{i} + y\,\mathbf{j} + z\,\mathbf{k}$

$$\mathbf{a}\times\mathbf{b} = \begin{vmatrix} i & j & k \\ a_1 & a_2 & a_3 \\ b_1 & b_2 & b_3 \end{vmatrix}$$

$$= \mathbf{i}\,(a_2b_3 - a_3b_2) - \mathbf{j}(a_1b_3 - a_3b_1) + \mathbf{k}(a_1b_2 - a_2b_1)$$

$[\mathbf{r}\ \mathbf{a}\ \mathbf{b}] = \mathbf{r}\cdot(\mathbf{a}\times\mathbf{b})$

$= (x\mathbf{i} + y\mathbf{j} + z\mathbf{k})\cdot\{\mathbf{i}\,(a_2b_3 - a_3b_2) - \mathbf{j}(a_1b_3 - a_3b_1) + \mathbf{k}\,(a_1b_2 - a_2b_1)\}$

or $\quad [\mathbf{r}\ \mathbf{a}\ \mathbf{b}] = x(a_2b_3 - a_3b_2) - y(a_1b_3 - a_3b_1) + z(a_1b_2 - a_2b_1)$

$\therefore\quad \text{grad}[\mathbf{r}\ \mathbf{a}\ \mathbf{b}] = \mathbf{i}\,(a_2b_3 - a_3b_2) - \mathbf{j}(a_1b_3 - a_3b_1) + \mathbf{k}\,(a_1b_2 - a_2b_1)$

$$\text{grad}[\mathbf{r}\ \mathbf{a}\ \mathbf{b}] = \mathbf{a}\times\mathbf{b}$$

Q.48 Ans:(B)

Length of curve $y = f(x)$ between $x = a$ and $x = b$ is given by:

$$S = \int_a^b \sqrt{1 + \left(\frac{dy}{dx}\right)^2}\,dx$$

$$S = \int_0^{\pi/3} \sqrt{1 + \left(\frac{d}{dx}\log\sec x\right)^2}\,dx = \int_0^{\pi/3}\sqrt{1 + \tan^2 x}\,dx$$

or $\quad S = \displaystyle\int_0^{\pi/3}\sec x\,dx = \int_0^{\pi/3}\frac{\cos x}{1 - \sin^2 x}\,dx$

or
$$S = \frac{1}{2}\int_0^{\pi/3}\left(\frac{\cos x}{1 - \sin x} + \frac{\cos x}{1 + \sin x}\right)dx$$
$$= \frac{1}{2}\left[\log\frac{1 + \sin x}{1 - \sin x}\right]_0^{\pi/3}$$

or $\quad S = \dfrac{1}{2}\log\dfrac{2 + \sqrt{3}}{2 - \sqrt{3}} = \log(2 + \sqrt{3})$

$$S = \log(2 + \sqrt{3})$$

Q.49 Ans:(B)

We have $f = x^2 - 2y^2 + 4z^2$

$\therefore\quad \text{grad}\,f = 2x\,\mathbf{i} - 4y\,\mathbf{j} + 8z\,\mathbf{k}$

$\quad\quad \text{grad}\,f = 2\,\mathbf{i} - 4\,\mathbf{j} - 8\,\mathbf{k}$ at the point (1, 1, –1)

If $\mathbf{a}$ be the unit vector in the direction of the vector $2\,\mathbf{i} + \mathbf{j} - \mathbf{k}$, then

$$\mathbf{a} = \frac{2\,\mathbf{i} + \mathbf{j} - \mathbf{k}}{\sqrt{4 + 1 + 1}} = \frac{2\,\mathbf{i} + \mathbf{j} - \mathbf{k}}{\sqrt{6}}$$

Therefore, the required directional derivative is

$$\text{grad}\,\mathbf{f}\cdot\mathbf{a} = (2\,\mathbf{i} - 4\,\mathbf{j} - 8\,\mathbf{k})\cdot\left(\frac{2\,\mathbf{i} + \mathbf{j} - \mathbf{k}}{\sqrt{6}}\right)$$

$$\text{grad}\,\mathbf{f}\cdot\mathbf{a} = \left(\frac{4 - 4 + 8}{\sqrt{6}}\right)$$

$$\text{grad}\,\mathbf{f}\cdot\mathbf{a} = \frac{8}{\sqrt{6}}$$

Q.50 Ans:(B)

Length of one turn (from $t = 0$ to $t = 2\pi$) of the helix

$$L = \int_{t=0}^{t=2\pi}\left|\frac{d\mathbf{r}}{dt}\right|dt$$

Substituting equation of helix $\mathbf{r} = \cos t\,\mathbf{i} + \sin t\,\mathbf{j} + t\,\mathbf{k}$, we have

$$L = \int_{t=0}^{t=2\pi}\left|\frac{d}{dt}(\cos t\,\mathbf{i} + \sin t\,\mathbf{j} + t\,\mathbf{k})\right|dt$$

or $\quad L = \displaystyle\int_{t=0}^{t=2\pi}\left|\sqrt{\cos^2 t + \sin^2 t + 1^2}\right|dt$

or $\quad L = \sqrt{2}\displaystyle\int_{t=0}^{t=2\pi}dt$

$$L = 2\sqrt{2}\pi$$

Q.51 Ans:[9]

We have $\quad f(x) = \dfrac{(5 + x)(2 + x)}{1 + x}$; let $1 + x = y$

$$f(y) = \frac{(y + 4)(y + 1)}{y} = y + 5 + \frac{4}{y}$$

or $\quad f(y) = \left(\sqrt{y} - \dfrac{2}{\sqrt{y}}\right)^2 + 9$

Function $f(y)$ is minimum when $\left(\sqrt{y} - \dfrac{2}{\sqrt{y}}\right)^2$ is minimum; that is zero.

Therefore,

$$[f(x)]_{min} = 9$$

Q.52 Ans:[0.166]

$$\lim_{x\to 0}\frac{e^x - \left(1+x+\frac{x^2}{2}\right)}{x^3}$$

$$= \lim_{x\to 0}\frac{1+x+\frac{x^2}{2!}+\frac{x^3}{3!}+\ldots\left(1+x+\frac{x^2}{2}\right)}{x^3}$$

or $$\lim_{x\to 0}\frac{e^x - \left(1+x+\frac{x^2}{2}\right)}{x^3} = \lim_{x\to 0}\frac{\frac{x^3}{3!}+\frac{x^4}{4!}+\ldots}{x^3}$$

$$= \lim_{x\to 0}\frac{1}{3!}+\frac{x}{4!}+\ldots = \frac{1}{3!}+\frac{0}{4!}+\frac{0}{5!}+\ldots.$$

or $$\lim_{x\to 0}\frac{e^x - \left(1+x+\frac{x^2}{2}\right)}{x^3} = \frac{1}{6}$$

$$\lim_{x\to 0}\frac{e^x - \left(1+x+\frac{x^2}{2}\right)}{x^3} = 0.166$$

Q.53 Ans:[4]

Let $y = \sqrt{3}\sin x + \cos x$

or $$y = \sqrt{(\sqrt{3})^2+1^2}\left[\frac{\sqrt{3}}{\sqrt{(\sqrt{3})^2+1^2}}\sin x + \frac{1}{\sqrt{(\sqrt{3})^2+1^2}}\cos x\right]$$

or $y = 2\sin(x+\phi) \Rightarrow y_{max} = 2,\ y_{min} = -2$

$$y_{max} - y_{min} = 4$$

Q.54 Ans:[0.414]

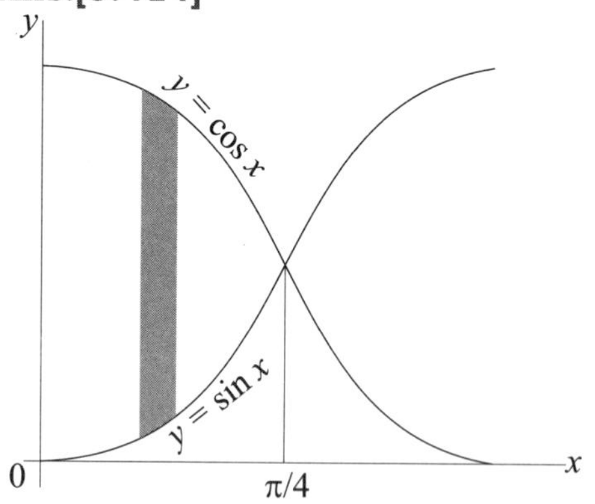

The area of the region in the first quadrant bounded by the y-axis and the curves $y = \sin x$ and $y = \cos x$ is

$$A = \int_0^{\pi/4}(\cos x - \sin x)dx$$

or $$A = [\sin x + \cos x]_0^{\pi/4}$$

or $$A = \left(\sin\frac{\pi}{4}+\cos\frac{\pi}{4}\right) - [\sin 0 + \cos 0]$$

or $$A = \sqrt{2} - 1$$

$$A = 0.414$$

Q.55 Ans:[4]

Length of cycloid $$S = \int_{t_1}^{t_2}\sqrt{\left(\frac{dx}{dt}\right)^2 + \left(\frac{dy}{dt}\right)^2}\,dt$$

Substituting $x = 1+\cos t$ and $y = \sin t$, we have

$$S = \int_0^{\pi}\sqrt{(1+\cos t)^2 + (\sin t)^2}\,dt$$

or $$S = \sqrt{2}\int_0^{\pi}\sqrt{1+\cos t}\,dt$$

or $$S = 2\int_0^{\pi}\cos\frac{t}{2}\,dt$$

$$S = 4$$

Q.56 Ans:[13.3]

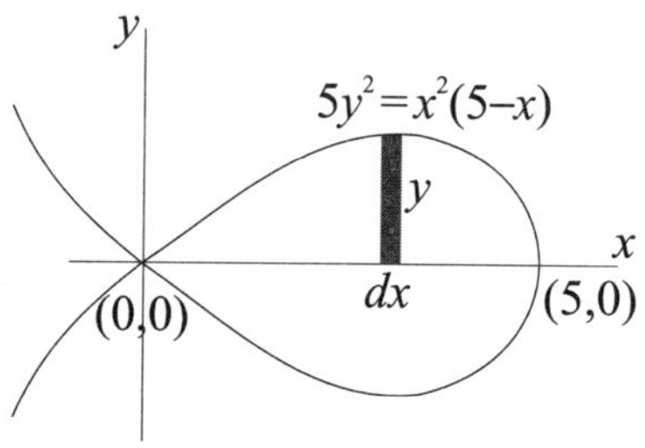

Area of loop $A = 2\int_0^5 y\,dx$

or $$A = 2\int_0^5 \frac{x}{\sqrt{5}}\sqrt{5-x}\,dx$$

Substituting $x = 5\sin^2\theta$ and $dx = 10\sin\theta\cos\theta d\theta$ in above equation, we have

$$A = 2\int_0^{\frac{\pi}{2}}\frac{5\sin^2\theta}{\sqrt{5}}\sqrt{5-5\sin^2\theta}\times 10\sin\theta\cos\theta d\theta$$

or $$A = 100\int_0^{\frac{\pi}{2}}\sin^3\theta\cos^2\theta\,d\theta$$

From which

$$A = \frac{80}{3}\sqrt{\pi} = 13.3$$

Q.57 Ans:[33.5]

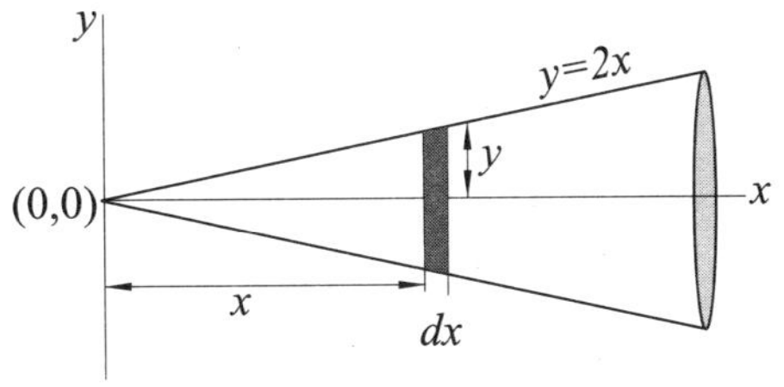

Consider an element of thickness dx and radius y.

The volume of element $dV = \pi y^2 dx$

or $dV = \pi(2x)^2 dx$

Volume from $x = 0$ to $x = 2$, $V = \int_0^2 \pi(2x)^2 dx$

or $V = 4\pi\int_0^2 x^2 dx = \frac{32\pi}{3}$

$V = 33.5$

Q.58 Ans:[1.66]

We have $f'(x) = \frac{x^2}{2} + kx + 1$

or $\frac{d}{dx} f(x) = \frac{x^2}{2} + kx + 1$

or $f(x) = \frac{x^3}{6} + \frac{k}{2}x^2 + x + c$

or $f(0) = \frac{0^3}{6} + \frac{k}{2}0^2 + 0 + c = 0 \Rightarrow c = 0$

or $f(3) = \frac{3^3}{6} + \frac{k}{2}3^2 + 3 + 0 = 15 \Rightarrow k = \frac{5}{3}$

$k = 1.66$

Q.59 Ans:[0.5]

$$\lim_{x\to 0} \frac{x(1-\cos x) - ax^2 \sin x}{x^5}$$

$$= \lim_{x\to 0} \frac{x\left[1-\left(1-\frac{x^2}{2!}+\frac{x^4}{4!}-\frac{x^6}{6!}+\ldots\right)\right] - ax^2\left(x-\frac{x^3}{3!}+\frac{x^5}{5!}+\ldots\right)}{x^5}$$

$$\lim_{x\to 0} \frac{x(1-\cos x) - ax^2 \sin x}{x^5}$$

$$= \lim_{x\to 0} \frac{1}{x^2}\left(\frac{1}{2!}-a\right) - \left(\frac{1}{4!}-\frac{a}{3!}\right) + x^2\left(\frac{1}{6!}-\frac{a}{5!}\right) + \ldots$$

is exist, if $\left(\frac{1}{2!}-a\right) = 0$

$a = 0.5$

Q.60 Ans:[0.25]

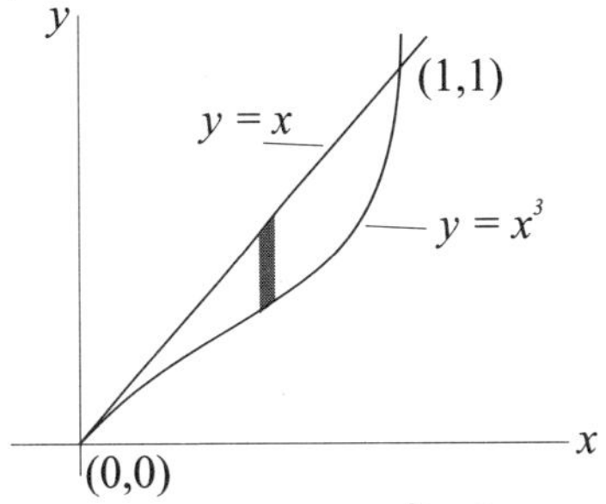

Area between curve $y = x$ and $y = x^3$ in first quadrant is

$$A = \int_0^1 (x - x^3)dx$$

or $A = \left[\frac{x^2}{2} - \frac{x^4}{4}\right]_0^0 = \frac{1}{4}$

$A = 0.25$

Q.61 Ans:[–3.5]

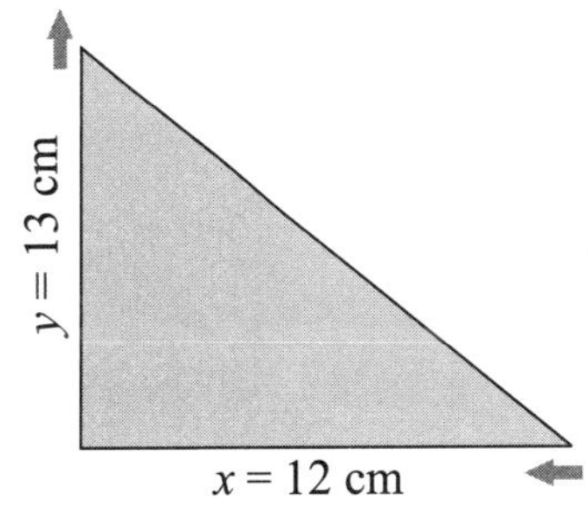

Let $x = 12$ cm and $y = 13$ cm

After 4 s

$x = 12 - 1 \times 4 = 8$ cm and $y = 13 + 1.5 \times 4 = 19$ cm

Area of triangle $A = \frac{1}{2}xy$

$$\frac{dA}{dt} = \frac{1}{2}\left(x\frac{dy}{dt} + y\frac{dx}{dt}\right)$$

Substituting $x = 8$ cm, $y = 19$ cm, $\frac{dx}{dt} = -1$ cm/s and $\frac{dy}{dt} = 1.5$ cm/s, we obtain

$$\frac{dA}{dt} = \frac{1}{2}(8 \times 1.5 + 19 \times -1)$$

$\frac{dA}{dt} = -3.5\ \text{cm}^2/\text{s}$

Q.62 Ans:[9]

We have $u = xyz^2$

$\therefore \ \nabla u = yz^2\mathbf{i} + xz^2\mathbf{j} + 2xyz\,\mathbf{k}$

or $\nabla u = 9\mathbf{j}$ at the point (1, 0, 3)

The greatest rate of increase of u at the point (1,0,3) is

$$|\nabla u| = 9$$

Q.63 Ans:[1]

Let the point $P(x, y, z)$ on the surface $z^2 = 1 + xy$

The distance of P from origin is

$$S = \sqrt{(x-0)^2 + (y-0)^2 (z-0)^2} = \sqrt{x^2 + y^2 + z^2}$$

$$S = \sqrt{x^2 + y^2 + 1 + xy} = \sqrt{u}$$

The distance S is shortest: $\frac{\partial u}{\partial x} = 0 = 2x + y$ and

$$\frac{\partial u}{\partial y} = 0 = 2y + x$$

Solving, we get $x = 0$ $y = 0$ is only the solution

Now, $r = \frac{\partial^2 u}{\partial x^2} = 2,\ s = \frac{\partial^2 u}{\partial x \partial y} = 1,\ t = \frac{\partial^2 u}{\partial y^2} = 2,$

since $rt - s^2 = 4 - 1 = 3 > 0$ and $r > 2$

So, it is a minimum at $(0,0)$, $z = 1 + xy = 1 + 0 = 1$

The coordinate of nearest point on surface from origin is (0, 0, 1)

$$S_{\min} = \sqrt{0^2 + 0^2 + 1^2}$$

$$S_{\min} = 1$$

Q.64 Ans:[100.5]

By divergence theorem, the given surface integral is equal to the volume integral

$$\iint_s (x+z)\,dy\,dz + (y+z)\,dz\,dx + (x+y)\,dx\,dy$$

$$= \iiint_V \left(\frac{\partial}{\partial x}(x+z) + \frac{\partial}{\partial y}(y+z) + \frac{\partial}{\partial z}(x+y) \right) dxdydz$$

$$= 3\iiint_V dxdydz = 3V$$

$$= 3 \times \frac{4}{3}\pi \times 2^3 = 32\pi$$

where V is the volume of sphere of radius 2.

100.5

Q.65 Ans:[60]

Given $\mathbf{A} + \mathbf{B} + \mathbf{C} = 0$ and $|\mathbf{A}| = 3, |\mathbf{B}| = 5, |\mathbf{C}| = 7$

or $\mathbf{A} + \mathbf{B} = -\mathbf{C}$

or $|\mathbf{A} + \mathbf{B}| = |-\mathbf{C}| \ \Rightarrow \ \mathbf{A}^2 + 2\mathbf{A}\cdot\mathbf{B} + \mathbf{B}^2 = \mathbf{C}^2$

or $9 + 2\mathbf{A}\cdot\mathbf{B} + 25 = 49$

or $\mathbf{A}\cdot\mathbf{B} = \frac{15}{2}$

or $|\mathbf{A}|\cdot|\mathbf{B}|\cos\theta = \frac{15}{2} \Rightarrow 3 \times 5\cos\theta = \frac{15}{2}$

or $\cos\theta = \frac{1}{2} \quad \Rightarrow \theta = 60°$

The angle (in degree) between **A** and **B** is $\theta = 60°$

3 Differential Equations and Laplace Transform

GATE Mechanical Engg.

GATE Syllabus

Differential equations: First order equations (linear and nonlinear); Higher order linear differential equations with constant coefficients; Euler-Cauchy equation; Initial and boundary value problems; Laplace transforms; Solutions of heat, wave and Laplace's equations.

Chapter Outline

3.1 KEY CONCEPTS AND FORMULAS

Differential Equations

An equation involving differentials or differential coefficient is called a *differential equation*.

Degree and Order of Differential Equation

The *degree* of a differential equation is the degree of the highest differential coefficient which occur in it, after the differential equation has been cleared of radicals and fractions.

The *order* of a differential equation is the order of the highest differential coefficient appearing in the equation.

Differential Equation of First Order and First Degree

A differential equation of the form

$$M + N\frac{dy}{dx} = 0 \qquad \text{or} \qquad Mdx + Ndy = 0$$

where M and N are functions x and y or are constants.

- **Case 1**: Variables separable

If an equation is of the form $f_1(x)dx = f_2(y)dy$, then its solution, by integration, is $\int f_1(x)dx = \int f_2(y)dy + c$, where c is an arbitrary constant.

- **Case 2**: Homogeneous equations

Differential equation of the form $\frac{dy}{dx} = \frac{f_1(x, y)}{f_2(x, y)}$, where $f_1(x, y)$ and $f_2(x, y)$ are homogeneous function of x and y of same degree.

Such equation can be solved by putting $y = vx$ and $\frac{dy}{dx} = v + x\frac{dv}{dx}$

- **Case 3**: An equation reducible to homogeneous form

Differential equation of the form $\frac{dy}{dx}=\frac{ax+by+c}{Ax+By+C}$ where $\frac{a}{b}\neq\frac{A}{B}$

Substituting $x=X+h$, $y=Y+k$ and $\frac{dy}{dx}=\frac{dY}{dX}$, choose h and k such that $ah+bk+c=0$ and $Ah+Bk+C=0$.

- **Case 4**: Linear differential equation

A differential equation of the form $\frac{dy}{dx}+Py=Q$, where P and Q are constants or function of x alone(and not of y) is called a *linear differential equation* of the first order in y.

Solution is $y\times \text{IF}=\int Q\times \text{IF}\,dx+c$, where integrating factor, $\text{IF}=e^{\int Pdx}$

- **Case 5**: Equation reducible to the linear form

A differential equation of the form $\frac{dy}{dx}+Py=Qy^n$, where P and Q are constants or function of x alone and n is a constant other than zero or unity is called the *Benoulli's equation* or *extended form of linear equation.*

This type of equation can be reduced to the linear form on dividing y^n and putting $\frac{1}{y^{n-1}}$ equal to v.

$$\frac{dv}{dx}+P(1-n)v=Q(1-n)$$

- **Case 6**: Exact differential equation

A differential equation of the form $Mdx+Ndy=0$; where M and N are functions of x and y or constants is said to be exact if the expression on the left hand side can be obtained directly by differenting some function of x and y. If $f(x, y)$ be such a function, we must have $d[f(x, y)]=Mdx+Ndy$.

or $\frac{\partial f}{\partial x}dx+\frac{\partial f}{\partial y}dy=Mdx+Ndy$

Necessary condition is $\frac{\partial M}{\partial y}=\frac{\partial N}{\partial x}$.

Integrating Factor

A differential equation of the type $Mdx+Ndy=0$ which is not exact can sometimes be made exact by multiplying the equation by some function of x and y, which is called an *integrating factor.*

- **Method I**: Integrating factor found by inspection

(a) $d\left(\frac{y}{x}\right)=\frac{xdy-ydx}{x^2}$

(b) $d\left(\frac{x}{y}\right)=\frac{ydx-xdy}{y^2}$

(c) $d(xy)=xdy+ydx$

- **Method II**: In the differential equation $Mdx+Ndy=0$, if $M=yf_1(xy)$ and $N=xf_2(xy)$, then $\frac{1}{Mx-Ny}$ is an integrating factor provided $Mx-Ny\neq 0$.
- **Method III**: In the differential equation $Mdx+Ndy=0$, if $\frac{1}{N}\left(\frac{\partial M}{\partial y}-\frac{\partial N}{\partial x}\right)$ is function of x alone, say $f(x)$, then the integrating factor is $e^{\int f(x)dx}$.
- **Method IV**: In the differential equation $Mdx+Ndy=0$, if $\frac{1}{M}\left(\frac{\partial N}{\partial x}-\frac{\partial M}{\partial y}\right)$ is function of y alone, say $f(y)$, then the integrating factor is $e^{\int f(y)dy}$.
- **Method V**: If the equation $Mdx+Ndy=0$ is homogeneous then $\frac{1}{Mx+Ny}$ is an integration factor, provided $Mx+Ny\neq 0$.
- **Method VI**: If the equation be of the form $x^a y^b(my\,dx+nx\,dy)+x^c y^d(py\,dx+qx\,dy)=0$, where a, b, m, n, c, p and q are constants, then the integrating factor is $x^h y^k$, where h, k can be obtained by applying the condition that after multiplication by $x^h y^k$ the equation is exact.

Linear Differential Equation with Constant Coefficients

General form of equation

$$\frac{d^n y}{dx^n}+P_1\frac{d^{n-1}y}{dx^{n-1}}+P_2\frac{d^{n-2}y}{dx^{n-2}}+...+P_n y=Q$$

where Q and $P_1, P_2, P_3, ...P_n$ are all constants or function of x.

or $F(D)y=Q$

Complete solution of equation of differential equation

$y=$ Complementay function (CF) + Particular integral (PI)

Auxiliary equation

$m^n+P_1m^{n-1}+P_2m^{n-2}+...+P_n=0$, if the roots of auxiliary equation are $m_1, m_2, m_3, ...m_n$ then

$$\text{CF}=C_1e^{m_1x}+C_2e^{m_2x}+C_3e^{m_3x}+...C_ne^{m_nx}$$

- Auxiliary equation having two equal roots

$$\text{CF}=(C_1x+C_2)e^{m_1x}+C_3e^{m_3x}+C_4e^{m_4x}+...C_ne^{m_nx}$$

- Auxiliary equation having imaginary roots

$$CF = C_1 e^{(\alpha+i\beta)x} + C_2 e^{(\alpha-i\beta)x}$$

or $$CF = e^{\alpha x}(A\cos\beta x + B\sin\beta x)$$

Particular integral $PI = \frac{1}{F(D)}Q$

- $PI = \frac{1}{F(D)}e^{ax} = \frac{1}{F(a)}e^{ax}$, if $F(a) \neq 0$
- $PI = \frac{1}{F(D^2)}\sin ax = \frac{1}{F(-a^2)}\sin ax$, if $F(-a^2) \neq 0$
- $PI = \frac{1}{F(D^2)}\cos ax = \frac{1}{F(-a^2)}\cos ax$, if $F(-a^2) \neq 0$
- $PI = \frac{1}{D^2+a^2}\sin ax = -\frac{x}{2a}\cos ax$
- $PI = \frac{1}{D^2+a^2}\cos ax = \frac{x}{2a}\sin ax$
- $PI = \frac{1}{F(D)}x^m = [F(D)]^{-1}x^m$
- $PI = \frac{1}{F(D)}e^{ax}V = e^{ax}\frac{1}{F(D+a)}V$
- $PI = \frac{1}{F(D)}e^{ax} = \frac{1}{\phi(a)}e^{ax}x,$

where $F(D) = (D-a)\phi(D)$, if $F(a) = 0$

- $PI = \frac{1}{F(D)}x.V = x.\frac{1}{F(D)}V - \frac{F'(D)}{\{F'(D)\}^2}V$

Equation of the First Order but not of the First Degree

A differential equations which involve $p\left(=\frac{dy}{dx}\right)$ in degree higher than first can be solved for p and is of the form $\{p-f_1(x,y)\}\{p-f_2(x,y)\}...\{p-f_n(x,y)\}=0$, then each factor equated to zero gives a differential equation of the first degree and of first order which can be easily solved.

Equation Solvable for *x*

This type of equation can put in the form $y = f(x,p)$, then differentiating with respect to x, we get $p = F\left(x, p, \frac{dp}{dx}\right)$ which is an equation involving two variables x and p and its solution may be obtained as $\phi(x,p,c)=0$.

Equation Solvable for *y*

This type of equation can be put in the form $x = f(y,p)$, then differentiating with respect to y, we get $\frac{1}{p} = F\left(y, p, \frac{dp}{dy}\right)$, which is an equation involving two variables y and p and its solution may be obtained as $\phi(y,p,c)=0$.

Cauchy's-Euler's Equations

$$a_0x^n\frac{d^ny}{dx^n} + a_1x^{n-1}\frac{d^{n-1}y}{dx^{n-1}} + a_2x^{n-2}\frac{d^{n-2}y}{dx^{n-2}} + ... + a_{n-1}x\frac{dy}{dx} + a_ny = F(x),$$

where $a_0, a_1, a_2, ... a_n$ are all constants and $F(x)$ is a function of x.

By substitution $x = e^t$, Cauchy's-Euler's equation can be transformed into linear differential equation with constant coefficient with t as the independent variable.

Heat, Wave and Laplace's Equations

Heat Equation

$$\frac{\partial u}{\partial t} = c^2\left(\frac{\partial^2 u}{\partial x^2} + \frac{\partial^2 u}{\partial y^2} + \frac{\partial^2 u}{\partial z^2}\right);$$ 3-dimensional heat equation

$$\frac{\partial u}{\partial t} = c^2\left(\frac{\partial^2 u}{\partial x^2} + \frac{\partial^2 u}{\partial y^2}\right);$$ 2 – dimensional heat equation

$$\frac{\partial u}{\partial t} = c^2\frac{\partial^2 u}{\partial x^2};$$ 1 –dimensional heat equation

Wave Equation

$$\frac{\partial^2 u}{\partial t^2} = c^2\left(\frac{\partial^2 u}{\partial x^2} + \frac{\partial^2 u}{\partial y^2} + \frac{\partial^2 u}{\partial z^2}\right);$$ 3-dimensional wave equation

$$\frac{\partial^2 u}{\partial t^2} = c^2\left(\frac{\partial^2 u}{\partial x^2} + \frac{\partial^2 u}{\partial y^2}\right);$$ 2 –dimensional wave equation

$$\frac{\partial^2 u}{\partial t^2} = c^2\frac{\partial^2 u}{\partial x^2};$$ 1 –dimensional wave equation

Laplace's Equation

$$\frac{\partial^2 u}{\partial x^2} + \frac{\partial^2 u}{\partial y^2} + \frac{\partial^2 u}{\partial z^2} = 0;$$ 3-dimensional Laplace equation (3-dimensional steady state heat equation)

Method of Separation of Variables

Separation of variable is a technique to solve partial differential equation (P.D.E). For a P.D.E in the function u of two independent variable x and y, assume that the required solution is separable, i.e.,

$$u(x,y) = X(x)Y(y)$$

where $X(x)$ is a function x alone and $Y(y)$ is a function y alone. Then substitution of u and its derivatives reduces the the P.D.E to the form

$$f(X, X', X'', ...) = \phi(Y, Y', Y'', ...)$$

which is separable in X and Y.

Laplace Transform

Let $F(t)$ be a function of t specified for $t>0$. Then the Laplace transform of $F(t)$, denoted by $L\{F(t)\}$, is defined by $L\{F(t)\} = f(s) = \int_0^\infty e^{-st} F(t)\,dt$; provided that the integral exists.

Laplace Transforms of Some Elementary Functions

$F(t)$	$L\{F(t)\}$	
• 1	$\frac{1}{s}$	$s>0$
• t^n	$\frac{n!}{s^{n+1}}$	$s>0$
• e^{at}	$\frac{1}{s-a}$	$s>a$
• $\sin at$	$\frac{a}{s^2+a^2}$	$s>0$
• $\cos at$	$\frac{s}{s^2+a^2}$	$s>0$
• $\sinh at$	$\frac{a}{s^2-a^2}$	$s>\lvert a\rvert$
• $\cosh at$	$\frac{s}{s^2-a^2}$	$s>\lvert a\rvert$

- Linearity property

  If c_1 and c_2 are any constants, then

  $$L\{c_1F_1(t)+c_2F_2(t)\} = c_1L\{F_1(t)\}+c_2L\{F_2(t)\} = c_1f_1(s)+c_2f_2(s)$$

- First translation or shifting property

  If $L\{F(t)\}=f(s)$, then $L\{e^{at}F(t)\}=f(s-a)$

- Second translation or shifting property

  If $L\{F(t)\}=f(s)$ and $G(t)=\begin{cases} F(t-a) & t>a \\ 0 & t<a \end{cases}$, then

  $$L\{G(t)\}=e^{-as}f(s)$$

- Change of scale property

  If $L\{F(t)\}=f(s)$, then $L\{F(at)\}=\frac{1}{a}f\left(\frac{s}{a}\right)$

- Laplace transform of derivatives

  If $L\{F(t)\}=f(s)$, then $L\{F'(t)\}=sf(s)-F(0)$

  $$L\{F^{(n)}(t)\}=s^n f(s)-s^{n-1}F(0)-s^{n-2}F'(0)-\ldots-sF^{n-2}(0)-F^{n-1}(0).$$

If $F(t), F'(t),\ldots F^{(n-1)}(t)$ are continuous for $0\le t\le N$ and of exponential order for $t>N$ while $F^{(n)}(t)$ is sectionally continuous for $0\le t\le N$.

Case 1: if $n=1 \Rightarrow L\{F'(t)\}=sf(s)-F(0)$,

Case 2: if $n=2 \Rightarrow L\{F''(t)\}=s^2f(s)-sF(0)-F'(0)$

- Laplace transform of integrals

  If $L\{F(t)\}=f(s)$, then $L\left\{\int_0^t F(u)\,du\right\}=\frac{f(s)}{s}$

- Multiplication by t^n

  If $L\,F(t)=f(s)$, then

  $$L\{t^nF(t)\}=(-1)^n\frac{d^n}{ds^n}f(s)=(-1)^n f^{(n)}(s)$$

- Division by t

  If $L\{F(t)\}=f(s)$, then $L\left\{\frac{F(t)}{t}\right\}=\int_s^\infty f(u)\,du$

  provided $\lim_{t\to 0}\frac{F(t)}{t}$ exists.

- Periodic Functions

  Let $F(t)$ have period $T>0$ so that $F(t+T)=F(T)$,

  then $L\{F(t)\}=\frac{\int_0^T e^{-st}F(t)\,dt}{1-e^{-sT}}$.

Inverse Laplace Transform

If the Laplace transform of a function $F(t)$ is $f(s)$, i.e., if $L\{F(t)\}=f(s)$, then $F(t)$ is called an *inverse Laplace transform* of $f(s)$ and we write symbolically $F(t)=L^{-1}\{f(s)\}$ where L^{-1} is called the *inverse Laplace transformation operator*.

- Linearity property

  If c_1 and c_2 are any constants, then

  $$L^{-1}\{c_1f_1(s)+c_2f_2(s)\}$$
  $$=c_1L^{-1}\{f_1(s)\}+c_2L^{-1}\{f_2(s)\}=c_1F_1(t)+c_2F_2(t)$$

- First translation or shifting property

  If $L^{-1}\{f(s)\}=F(t)$, then $L^{-1}\{f(s-a)\}=e^{at}F(t)$

- Second translation or shifting property

  If $L^{-1}\{f(s)\}=F(t)$, then

  $$L^{-1}\{e^{-as}f(s)\}=\begin{cases} F(t-a) & t>a \\ 0 & t<a \end{cases}$$

- Change of scale property

  If $L^{-1}\{f(s)\}=F(t)$, then $L^{-1}\{f(ks)\}=\frac{1}{k}F\left(\frac{t}{k}\right)$

- Inverse Laplace transform of derivatives

  If $L^{-1}\{f(s)\}=F(t)$, then

  $$L^{-1}\{f^n(s)\}=L^{-1}\left\{\frac{d^n}{ds^n}f(s)\right\}=(-1)^n t^n F(t)$$

- Inverse Laplace transform of integrals

  If $L^{-1}\{f(s)\}=F(t)$, then $L^{-1}\left\{\int_s^\infty f(u)\,du\right\}=\dfrac{F(t)}{t}$

- Multiplication by s^n

  If $L^{-1}\{f(s)\}=F(t)$ and $F(0)=0$, then

  $L^{-1}\{s\,f(s)\}=F'(t)$

- Division by s

  If $L^{-1}\{f(s)\}=F(t)$, then $L^{-1}\left\{\dfrac{f(s)}{s}\right\}=\int_0^t F(u)\,du$

3.2 SOLVED EXAMPLES

Previous Years GATE Questions

Example 3.1

Find the solution of $\dfrac{d^2y}{dx^2}=y$, which passes through the origin and the point $\left(\ln 2, \dfrac{3}{4}\right)$.

(A) $y=\dfrac{1}{2}e^x-e^{-x}$ (B) $y=\dfrac{1}{2}(e^x+e^{-x})$

(C) $y=\dfrac{1}{2}(e^x-e^{-x})$ (D) $y=\dfrac{1}{2}e^x+e^{-x}$

GATE 2015

Solution

The given differential equation can be written as $\dfrac{d^2y}{dx^2}-y=0$.

Writing D for $\dfrac{d}{dx}$, the equation is $(D^2-1)y=0$.

Auxiliary equation is $m^2-1=0$, giving $m=+1,-1$

The solution is $y=c_1e^x+c_2e^{-x}$.

Putting given boundary conditions (a) $x=0,\ y=0$ and (b) $x=\ln 2,\ y=\dfrac{3}{4}$

$$0=c_1+c_2 \qquad \text{(i)}$$

and $$\frac{3}{4}=c_1e^{\ln 2}+c_2e^{-\ln 2}$$

$$\frac{3}{4}=2c_1+\frac{c_2}{2} \qquad \text{(ii)}$$

Solving Equations (i) and (ii), we have $c_1=\dfrac{1}{2},\ c_2=-\dfrac{1}{2}$

Thus, the solution equation is

$$y=y=c_1e^x+c_2e^{-x}=\frac{1}{2}e^x-\frac{1}{2}e^{-x}$$

$$y=\frac{1}{2}(e^x-e^{-x})$$

Example 3.2

The Laplace transform of e^{i5t} where $i=\sqrt{-1}$, is

(A) $\dfrac{s-5i}{s^2-25}$ (B) $\dfrac{s+5i}{s^2+25}$

(C) $\dfrac{s+5i}{s^2-25}$ (D) $\dfrac{s-5i}{s^2+25}$

GATE 2015

Solution

$$L(e^{i5t})=\int_0^\infty e^{-st}\times e^{i5t}dt=\int_0^\infty e^{-(s-5i)t}dt$$

or $$L(e^{i5t})=\frac{1}{s-5i}$$

or $$L(e^{i5t})=\frac{1}{s-5i}\times\frac{s+5i}{s+5i}=\frac{s+5i}{s^2-25i^2}$$

$$L(e^{i5t})=\frac{s+5i}{s^2+25}$$

Example 3.3

Consider the following differential equation $\dfrac{dy}{dt}=-5y$, initial condition: $y=2$ at $t=0$. The value of y at $t=3$ is

(A) $-5e^{-10}$ (B) $2e^{-10}$ (C) $2e^{-15}$ (D) $-15e^2$

GATE 2015

Solution

Given differential equation $\dfrac{dy}{dt}=-5y$

or $$\frac{dy}{y}=-5\,dt$$

Integrating $\displaystyle\int\frac{dy}{y}=-5\int dt+c$

or $\ln y=-5t+c$

Putting initial value $t=0$, $y=2$, we have $\ln 2=c$

Thus, the solution is $\ln y=-5t+\ln 2$

or $$\ln\frac{y}{2}=-5t$$

or $$y=2e^{-5t}$$

The value of y at $t=3$ is $y=2e^{-5\times 3}$

$$y=2e^{-15}$$

Example 3.4

Laplace transform of the function $f(t)$ is given by $f(s) = L\{f(t)\} = \int_0^\infty f(t)e^{-st}dt$. Laplace transform of the function shown below is given by

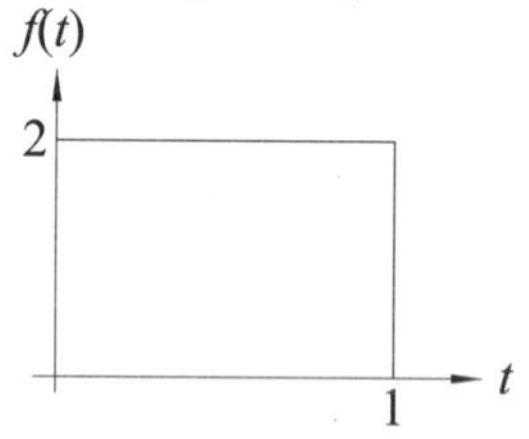

(A) $\frac{1-e^{-2s}}{s}$ (B) $\frac{1-e^{-s}}{2s}$

(C) $\frac{2-2e^{-s}}{s}$ (D) $\frac{1-2e^{-s}}{s}$

GATE 2015

Solution

The function of given graph is

$$f(t) = \begin{cases} 2, & 0 < t < 1 \\ 0, & t > 1 \end{cases}$$

Laplace transform of the function $f(t)$ is

$$L\{f(t)\} = \int_0^\infty f(t)e^{-st}dt = \int_0^1 2\,e^{-st}dt + \int_1^\infty 0\,e^{-st}dt$$

or $L\{f(t)\} = \int_0^1 2\,e^{-st}dt = \frac{2}{-s}[e^{-st}]_0^1 = \frac{2}{-s}[e^{-s} - 1]_0^1$

$$L\{f(t)\} = \frac{2-2e^{-s}}{s}$$

Example 3.5

If $y = f(x)$ is the solution of $\frac{d^2y}{dx^2} = 0$, with the boundary conditions $y = 5$ at $x = 0$, and $\frac{dy}{dx} = 2$ at $x = 10$, $f(15) =$___.

GATE 2014

Solution

Integration given differential equation $\frac{d^2y}{dx^2} = 0$, we obtain

$$\frac{dy}{dx} = c_1 \text{ and } y = c_1x + c_2$$

Putting given boundary conditions (a) $x = 0$, $y = 5$ and (b) $x = 10$, $\frac{dy}{dx} = 2$

We obtain $c_1 = 2$ and $c_2 = 5$

The complete solution is $y = 2x + 5$

The value of y at $x = 15$ is $y = 2 \times 15 + 5 = 35$

$$y(15) = 35$$

Example 3.6

The function $f(t)$ satisfies the differential equation $\frac{d^2f}{dt^2} + f = 0$, and the auxiliary conditions, $f(0) = 0$, $\frac{df}{dt}(0) = 4$. The Laplace transform of $f(t)$ is given by

(A) $\frac{2}{s+1}$ (B) $\frac{4}{s+1}$ (C) $\frac{4}{s^2+1}$ (D) $\frac{2}{s^4+1}$

GATE 2013

Solution

Given differential equation $\frac{d^2f(t)}{dt^2} + f(t) = 0$

Laplace transform of $f''(t) + f(t) = 0$ is

$$L(f'' + f) = L(0)$$

$$s^2L\{f(t)\} - sf(0) - f'(0) + L\{f(t)\} = L\{0\}$$

Putting $f(0) = 0$, $\frac{df}{dt}(0) = 4$;

$$s^2L\{f(t)\} - s \times 0 - 4 + L\{f(t)\} = 0$$

or $L\{f(t)\}(s^2 + 1) = 4$

$$L\{f(t)\} = \frac{4}{(s^2+1)}$$

Example 3.7

The solution of the differential equation $\frac{d^2u}{dx^2} - k\frac{du}{dx} = 0$; where k is a constant subjected to the boundary conditions $u(0) = 0$ and $u(L) = U$ is

(A) $u = U\frac{x}{L}$ (B) $u = U\left(\frac{1-e^{kx}}{1-e^{kL}}\right)$

(C) $u = U\left(\frac{1-e^{-kx}}{1-e^{-kL}}\right)$ (D) $u = U\left(\frac{1+e^{-kx}}{1+e^{kL}}\right)$

GATE 2013

Solution

Let $p = \frac{du}{dx}$, the differential equation reduces to

$$\frac{dp}{dx} - k\,p = 0 \Rightarrow \frac{dp}{p} = k\,dx$$

Integrating $\int \frac{dp}{p} = \int k\,dx + c_1$

or $\ln p = kx + c_1$

or $p = c e^{kx} \Rightarrow \frac{du}{dx} = c e^{kx}$

Integrating, we have

$$\int du = \int c e^{kx} dx + B \Rightarrow u = \frac{c}{k} e^{kx} + B$$

or $u = A e^{kx} + B$

Putting the boundary conditions (a) $x = 0$, $u = 0$ and (b) $x = L, u = U$

$$A + B = 0 \quad \text{(i)}$$

$$A e^{kL} + B = U \quad \text{(ii)}$$

Solving equations, we obtain

$$A = \frac{U}{e^{kL} - 1} \text{ and } B = \frac{-U}{e^{kL} - 1}$$

The solution is $u = e^{kx} \frac{U}{e^{kL} - 1} - \frac{U}{e^{kL} - 1}$

$$u = U\left(\frac{e^{kx} - 1}{e^{kL} - 1}\right)$$

Example 3.8

The inverse Laplace transform of the function $F(s) = \frac{1}{s(s+1)}$ is given by

(A) $f(t) = \sin t$ (B) $f(t) = e^{-t}$

(C) $f(t) = e^{-t} \sin t$ (D) $f(t) = 1 - e^{-t}$

GATE 2012, 2009

Solution

Given function $F(s) = \frac{1}{s(s+1)}$

or $F(s) = \frac{1}{s} - \frac{1}{s+1}$

Inverse Laplace transform of the function $F(s)$ is

$$f(t) = L^{-1}\left(\frac{1}{s}\right) - L^{-1}\left(\frac{1}{s+1}\right)$$

$$f(t) = 1 - e^{-t}$$

Example 3.9

Consider the differential equation $x^2 \frac{d^2y}{dx^2} + x\frac{dy}{dx} - 4y = 0$ with the boundary conditions of $y(0) = 0$ and $y(1) = 1$. The complete solution of the differential equation is

(A) x^2 (B) $e^x \sin\left(\frac{\pi x}{2}\right)$

(C) $\sin\left(\frac{\pi x}{2}\right)$ (D) $e^{-x} \sin\left(\frac{\pi x}{2}\right)$

GATE 2012

Solution

Given differential equation $x^2 \frac{d^2y}{dx^2} + x\frac{dy}{dx} - 4y = 0$

Let $x = e^t$, substituting $x^2 \frac{d^2y}{dx^2} = \frac{d}{dt}\left(\frac{d}{dt} - 1\right)y$ and $x\frac{dy}{dx} = \frac{dy}{dt}$, the differential equation reduces to

$$\frac{d}{dt}\left(\frac{d}{dt} - 1\right)y + \frac{dy}{dt} - 4y = 0$$

or $\frac{d^2y}{dt^2} - 4y = 0$

Auxiliary equation $m^2 - 4 = 0$; giving roots $m = 2, -2$

The solution is $y = c_1 e^{2t} + c_2 e^{-2t}$

or $y = c_1 (e^t)^2 + c_2 (e^t)^{-2} = c_1 x^2 + \frac{c_2}{x^2}$

Put boundary conditions $y(0) = 0$ and $y(1) = 1$

$$0 = c_1 \times 0^2 + \frac{c_2}{0^2} \Rightarrow c_2 = 0$$

$$1 = c_1 \times 1^2 + \frac{0}{1^2} \Rightarrow c_1 = 1$$

Thus, the solution is

$$y = x^2$$

Example 3.10

Consider the differential equation $\frac{dy}{dx} = (1 + y^2)x$. The general solution with constant c is

(A) $y = \tan\frac{x^2}{2} + \tan c$ (B) $y = \tan^2\left(\frac{x}{2}\right) + c$

(C) $y = \tan^2\left(\frac{x}{2} + c\right)$ (D) $y = \tan\left(\frac{x^2}{2} + c\right)$

GATE 2011

Solution

The given differential equation can be written as

$$\frac{dy}{1+y^2} = xdx.$$

Integrating $\int \frac{dy}{1+y^2} = \int xdx + c$

or $\tan^{-1} y = \frac{x^2}{2} + c$

$$y = \tan\left(\frac{x^2}{2} + c\right)$$

Example 3.11

The Laplace transform of the function $f(t)$ is $\frac{1}{s^2(s+1)}$. The function $f(t)$ is

(A) $t-1+e^{-t}$ (B) $t+1+e^{-t}$

(C) $-1+e^{-t}$ (D) $2t+e^{t}$

GATE 2010

Solution

Let $f(s) = \frac{1}{s^2(s+1)} = \frac{A}{s} + \frac{B}{s^2} + \frac{C}{s+1}$

$$\frac{1}{s^2(s+1)} = \frac{A\times s(s+1)}{s} + \frac{B(s+1)}{s^2} + \frac{Cs^2}{s+1}$$

$$= \frac{(A+C)s^2 + (A+B)s + B}{s^2(s+1)}$$

Coefficient of s^2, $A+C=0$

Coefficient of s, $A+B=0$

and $B=1$

Solving, we get $A=-1, C=1$

$$\frac{1}{s^2(s+1)} = \frac{-1}{s} + \frac{1}{s^2} + \frac{1}{s+1}$$

$$f(t) = L^{-1}\left[\frac{1}{s^2(s+1)}\right]$$

$$= L^{-1}\left(-\frac{1}{s}\right) + L^{-1}\left(\frac{1}{s^2}\right) + L^{-1}\left(\frac{1}{s+1}\right)$$

$$L^{-1}\left[\frac{1}{s^2(s+1)}\right] = -1+t+e^{-t}$$

$$f(t) = -1+t+e^{-t}$$

Example 3.12

The solution of $x\frac{dy}{dx} + y = x^4$ with the condition $y(1) = \frac{6}{5}$ is

(A) $y = \frac{x^4}{5} + \frac{1}{x}$ (B) $y = \frac{4x^4}{5} + \frac{4}{5x}$

(C) $y = \frac{x^4}{5} + 1$ (D) $y = \frac{x^5}{5} + 1$

GATE 2009

Solution

Given differential equation $x\frac{dy}{dx} + y = x^4$

$\frac{dy}{dx} + \left(\frac{1}{x}\right)y = x^3$ [Which is first order linear differential equation $\frac{dy}{dx} + P(x)\,y = Q(x)$]

Integrating factor $\text{IF} = e^{\int \frac{1}{x}dx} = e^{\ln x} = x$

The solution is $y(\text{IF}) = \int Q\,(\text{IF})\,dx + c$

$$yx = \int x^3 \times x\,dx + c$$

or $yx = \frac{x^5}{5} + c$

Putting $x=1$, $y = \frac{6}{5}$, we have $\frac{6}{5}\times 1 = \frac{1^5}{5} + c \Rightarrow c=1$

Thus, the solution is

$$y = \frac{x^4}{5} + \frac{1}{x}$$

Example 3.13

Given that $\ddot{x} + 3x = 0$, and $x(0)=1$, $\dot{x}(0)=0$. What is $x(1)$?

(A) –0.99 (B) –0.16 (C) 0.16 (D) 0.99

GATE 2008

Solution

Given differential equation $\ddot{x} + 3x = 0$

The auxiliary equation is $m^2 + 3 = 0$

Roots are $m = \sqrt{3}\,i, -\sqrt{3}\,i$

The solution is $x = c_1 \cos\sqrt{3}\,t + c_2 \sin\sqrt{3}\,t$

Putting boundary conditions $x(0)=1$ and $\dot{x}(0)=0$

$$c_1\cos\sqrt{3}\times 0 + c_2 \sin\sqrt{3}\times 0 = 1 \Rightarrow c_1 = 1$$

$$\sqrt{3}\times 1\times \sin\sqrt{3}\times 0 + \sqrt{3}\,c_2\cos\sqrt{3}\times 0 = 0 \Rightarrow c_2 = 0$$

Thus, the solution is

$$x = \cos\sqrt{3}\,t$$

Value of x at $t=1$ is

$$x(1) = \cos\sqrt{3}\times 1 = 0.99$$

$$x(1) = 0.99$$

Example 3.14

It is given that $y''+2y'+y=0$, $y(0)=0$, $y(1)=0$. What is $y(0.5)$?

(A) 0 (B) 0.37 (C) 0.62 (D) 1.13

GATE 2008

Solution

The given differential equation can be written as

$$(D^2+2D+1)y=0$$

Now auxiliary equation is $m^2+2m+1=0$

Roots are $m=-1,-1$

The solution is $y=(c_1+c_2x)e^{-x}$

Putting boundary values $y(0)=0$ and $y(1)=0$

$$0=(c_1+c_2\times 0)e^{-0} \Rightarrow c_1=0$$

$$0=(c_1+c_2\times 1)e^{-1} \Rightarrow c_2=0$$

The value of y at $x=0.5$ is

$$y=(0+0\times 0.5)e^{-0.5}$$

$$y(0.5)=0$$

Example 3.15

The solution of $\frac{dy}{dx}=y^2$ with initial value $y(0)=1$ is bounded in the interval

(A) $-\infty \le x \le \infty$ (B) $-\infty \le x \le 1$

(C) $x<1, x>1$ (D) $-2 \le x \le 2$

GATE 2007

Solution

Given differential equation $\frac{dy}{dx}=y^2$

or $\frac{dy}{y^2}=dx$

Integrating $\int \frac{dy}{y^2}=\int dx$

or $-\frac{1}{y}=x+c$

or $y=-\frac{1}{x+c}$

Putting initial value $y(0)=1$

$$1=-\frac{1}{0+c} \Rightarrow c=-1$$

$$y=-\frac{1}{x-1}$$

At $x=1$; $y=\infty$

Thus, y is bounded in $x>1$ and $x<1$

$$1<x<1$$

Example 3.16

The solution of the differential equation

$$\frac{dy}{dx}+2xy=e^{-x^2} \text{ with } y(0)=1 \text{ is}$$

(A) $(1-x)e^{+x^2}$ (B) $(1+x)e^{-x^2}$

(C) $(1-x)e^{-x^2}$ (D) None of these

GATE 2006

Solution

The given differential equation

$\frac{dy}{dx}+(2x)y=e^{-x^2}$ which is a linear differential equation

Integrating factor, $\text{IF}=e^{\int 2x dx}=e^{x^2}$

The solution is $y(\text{IF})=\int Q(\text{IF})dx+c$

$$y(e^{x^2})=\int e^{-x^2}(e^{x^2})dx+c$$

$$y(e^{x^2})=x+c$$

Putting initial value $y(0)=1$

$$1\times(e^{0^2})=0+c \Rightarrow c=1$$

Thus, the complete solution is

$$y=e^{-x^2}(x+1)$$

Example 3.17

For $\frac{d^2y}{dx^2}+4\frac{dy}{dx}+3y=3e^{2x}$, the particular integral is

(A) $\frac{1}{15}e^{2x}$ (B) $\frac{1}{5}e^{2x}$

(C) $3e^{2x}$ (D) $c_1e^{-x}+c_2e^{-3x}$

GATE 2006

Solution

Writing D for $\frac{d}{dx}$, the equation is

$$(D^2+4D+3)y=3e^{2x}$$

Particular integral $\text{PI}=\frac{3e^{2x}}{D^2+4D+3}$

Now since $\frac{1}{f(D)}e^{ax}=\frac{1}{f(a)}e^{ax}$ $[f(a)\neq 0]$

$$\text{PI} = \frac{3e^{2x}}{2^2+4\times 2+3} = \frac{3e^{2x}}{15}$$

$$\text{PI} = \frac{e^{2x}}{5}$$

Example 3.18

If $x^2\frac{dy}{dx}+2xy=\frac{2\ln x}{x}$ and $y(1)=0$, then what is $y(e)$?

(A) e (B) 1 (C) $\frac{1}{e}$ (D) $\frac{1}{e^2}$

GATE 2005

Solution

The given differential equation can be written as

$$\frac{dy}{dx}+\frac{2}{x}y=\frac{2\ln x}{x^3}$$ [This is first order linear differential equation]

Integrating factor, $\text{IF} = e^{\int \frac{2}{x}dx} = e^{2\ln x} = x^2$

The solution is $y(\text{IF}) = \int Q(\text{IF})dx + c$

$$y(x^2) = \int \frac{2\ln x}{x^3}(x^2)dx + c$$

or $y(x^2) = (\ln x)^2 + c$

Putting initial value $y(1)=0$, we have

$$0\times(1^2) = (\ln 1)^2 + c \Rightarrow c=0$$

Thus, the solution is $y=\left(\frac{\ln x}{x}\right)^2$

Value of y at $x=e$

$$y=\left(\frac{\ln e}{e}\right)^2=\frac{1}{e^2}$$

$$y(e)=\frac{1}{e^2}$$

Example 3.19

Linked Answer Questions

The complete solution of the ordinary differential equation

$$\frac{d^2y}{dx^2}+p\frac{dy}{dx}+qy=0 \text{ is } y=c_1e^{-x}+c_2e^{-3x}$$

Q19(a) Then, p and q are

(A) $p=3, q=3$ (B) $p=3, q=4$

(C) $p=4, q=3$ (D) $p=4, q=4$

Q19(b) Which of the following is a solution of the differential equation

$$\frac{d^2y}{dx^2}+p\frac{dy}{dx}+(q+1)y=0$$

(A) e^{-3x} (B) xe^{-x} (C) xe^{-2x} (D) x^2e^{-2x}

GATE 2005

Solution

(a) Given equation $\frac{d^2y}{dx^2}+p\frac{dy}{dx}+qy=0$

Its solution is $y=c_1e^{-x}+c_2e^{-3x}$

Roots are $-1, -3$

So roots of auxiliary equation $m^2+pm+q=0$ are $-1, -3$

Sum of roots $-p=-1-3=-4$

$$p=4$$

Product of roots $q=-1\times -3=3$

$$q=4$$

$$p=4, q=4$$

(b) Given equation $\frac{d^2y}{dx^2}+p\frac{dy}{dx}+(q+1)y=0$

Substituting $p=4$, $q=4$; $\frac{d^2y}{dx^2}+4\frac{dy}{dx}+(3+1)y=0$

$(D^2+4D+4)y=0$

Auxiliary equation $(m+2)^2=0$; giving $m=-2,-2$

Thus, solution is $y=(c_1+c_2x)e^{-2x}$

If $c_1=0$, $c_2=1$ then the solution

$$y=xe^{-2x}$$

Example 3.20

A delayed unit step function is defined as

$$u(t-a)=\begin{cases}0, & \text{for } t<a\\ 1, & \text{for } t\ge a\end{cases}.$$

Its Laplace transform is

(A) ae^{-as} (B) $\frac{e^{-as}}{a}$ (C) $\frac{e^{as}}{s}$ (D) $\frac{e^{as}}{a}$

GATE 2004

Solution

$$L[u(t-a)]=\int_0^\infty e^{-st}\,u(t-a)dt$$

or $$u(t-a)=\int_0^a e^{-st}\times 0dt+\int_a^\infty e^{-st}\times 1dt$$

or $u(t-a) = 0 + \int_a^{\infty} e^{-st}\, dt$

or $u(t-a) = \left[\frac{e^{-st}}{-s}\right]_a^{\infty} = \frac{e^{-as}}{s}$

$$u(t-a) = \frac{e^{-as}}{s}$$

Example 3.21

The solution of the differential equation $\frac{dy}{dx} + y^2 = 0$ is

(A) $y = \frac{1}{x+c}$ (B) $y = -\frac{x^3}{3} + c$

(C) ce^x (D) Unsolvable as equation is no-linear

GATE 2003

Solution

Given differential equation $-\frac{dy}{y^2} = dx$

Integrating $-\int \frac{dy}{y^2} = \int dx + c$

or $\frac{1}{y} = x + c$

The solution is

$$y = \frac{1}{x+c}$$

Example 3.22

If $f(t)$ is a function defined for all $t \geq 0$, its Laplace transform $F(s)$ is defined as

(A) $\int_0^{\infty} e^{st} f(t)\, dt$ (B) $\int_0^{\infty} e^{-st} f(t)\, dt$

(C) $\int_0^{\infty} e^{ist} f(t)\, dt$ (D) $\int_0^{\infty} e^{-ist} f(t)\, dt$

GATE 2016

Solution

By the definition of Laplace transform of $f(t)$ for all $t \geq 0$ is

$$L\{f(t)\} = \int_0^{\infty} e^{-st} f(t)\, dt$$

Example 3.23

If $y = f(x)$ satisfies the boundary value problem $y'' + 9y = 0$, $y(0) = 0$, $y\left(\frac{\pi}{2}\right) = \sqrt{2}$ then $y\left(\frac{\pi}{4}\right)$ is___.

GATE 2016

Solution

The given differential equation can be written as $(D^2 + 9)y = 0$.

Now auxiliary equation $m^2 + 9 = 0$

Roots are $m = 3i, -3i$

The solution is $y = c_1 \cos 3x + c_2 \sin 3x$

Substituting boundary values $y(0) = 0$ and $y\left(\frac{\pi}{2}\right) = \sqrt{2}$, we get

$$c_1 = 0 \quad \text{and} \quad c_1 \cos\frac{3\pi}{2} + c_2 \sin\frac{3\pi}{2} = \sqrt{2}$$

$$c_2 = -\sqrt{2}$$

Solution is $y = -\sqrt{2}\sin 3x$

$$y\left(\frac{\pi}{4}\right) = -\sqrt{2}\sin\frac{3\pi}{4} = -1$$

$$y\left(\frac{\pi}{4}\right) = -1$$

Example 3.24

Laplace transform of $\cos(\omega t)$ is

(A) $\frac{s}{s^2+\omega^2}$ (B) $\frac{\omega}{s^2+\omega^2}$

(C) $\frac{s}{s^2-\omega^2}$ (D) $\frac{\omega}{s^2-\omega^2}$

GATE 2016

Solution

$$L(\cos\omega t) = \frac{\omega}{s^2+\omega^2}$$

Example 3.25

Consider the following partial differential equation for $u(x, y)$ with the constant $c > 1$:

$$\frac{\partial u}{\partial y} + c\frac{\partial u}{\partial x} = 0$$

Solution of this equation is

(A) $u(x, y) = f(x + cy)$ (B) $u(x, y) = f(x - cy)$

(C) $u(x, y) = f(cx + y)$ (D) $u(x, y) = f(cx - y)$

GATE 2017

Solution

Option (A);

$$\frac{\partial}{\partial y} f(x+cy) + c\frac{\partial}{\partial x} f(x+cy) = 2cf'(x+cy)$$

Incorrect (A)

Option (B);

$$\frac{\partial}{\partial y} f(x-cy) + c\frac{\partial}{\partial x} f(x-cy) = 0 \qquad \text{correct (B)}$$

Option (C);

$$\frac{\partial}{\partial y} f(cx+y) + c\frac{\partial}{\partial x} f(cx+y) = (1+c^2)f'(cx+y)$$

Incorrect (C)

Option (D);

$$\frac{\partial}{\partial y} f(cx-y) + c\frac{\partial}{\partial x} f(cx-y) = -(1+c^2)f'(cx-y)$$

Incorrect (D)

Example 3.26

The differential equation $\frac{d^2y}{dx^2} + 16y = 0$ for $y(x)$ with the two boundary conditions $\left.\frac{dy}{dx}\right|_{x=0} = 1$ and $\left.\frac{dy}{dx}\right|_{x=\frac{\pi}{2}} = -1$ has

(A) no solution (B) exactly two solutions

(C) exactly one solution (D) infinitely many solutions

GATE 2017

Solution

Given differential equation $\frac{d^2y}{dx^2} + 16y = 0$ and boundary conditions (i) $\left.\frac{dy}{dx}\right|_{x=0} = 1$ and (ii) $\left.\frac{dy}{dx}\right|_{x=\frac{\pi}{2}} = -1$

Auxiliary equation is $m^2 + 16 = 0$, giving $m = 4i, -4i$.

The solution is $y = -c_1 \cos 4x + c_2 \sin 4x$

$$\frac{dy}{dx} = -4c_1 \sin 4x + 4c_2 \cos 4x$$

$$\left.\frac{dy}{dx}\right]_{x=0} = -4c_1 \times 0 + 4c_2 \times 1 = 1 \quad \Rightarrow \quad c_2 = \frac{1}{4}$$

$$\left.\frac{dy}{dx}\right]_{x=\frac{\pi}{2}} = -4c_1 \times 0 + 4c_2 \times -1 = -1 \Rightarrow \quad c_2 = -\frac{1}{4}$$

$c_2 = \frac{1}{4}$ and $-\frac{1}{4}$; two values not possible

Hence there is no solution.

Example 3.27

The Laplace transform of $t\,e^t$ is

(A) $\frac{s}{(s+1)^2}$ (B) $\frac{1}{(s-1)^2}$ (C) $\frac{1}{(s+1)^2}$ (D) $\frac{s}{s-1}$

GATE 2017

Solution

Using formula $L(t^n e^{at}) = \frac{n!}{(s-a)^{n+1}}$

$$L(t\,e^t) = \frac{1!}{(s-1)^{1+1}}$$

$$L(t\,e^t) = \frac{1}{(s-1)^2}$$

Example 3.28

Consider the differential equation $3y''(x) + 27y(x) = 0$ with initial conditions $y(0) = 0$ and $y'(0) = 2000$. The value of y at $x = 1$ is____.

GATE 2017

Solution

Given: Differential equation $3y''(x) + 27y(x) = 0$ and initial conditions (i) $y(0) = 0$ and (ii) $y'(0) = 2000$.

Auxillary equation $3m^2 + 27 = 0 \Rightarrow m = +3i, -3i$

The solution is $y = c_1 \cos 3x + c_2 \sin 3x$

Initial conditions (i) $y(0) = 0;\ 0 = c_1 + c_2 \times 0 \quad \Rightarrow \quad c_1 = 0$

(ii) $y'(0) = 2000;\quad 2000 = 0 + 3c_2 \times 1 \quad \Rightarrow \quad c_2 = \frac{2000}{3}$

$$y = \frac{2000}{3} \sin 3x$$

$$y_{x=1} = \frac{2000}{3} \sin(3 \times 1)$$

$$y_{x=1} = 94.08$$

Example 3.29

An explicit forward Euler method is used to numerically integrate the differential equation

$$\frac{dy}{dx} = y$$

using a time step of 0.1. With the initial condition $y(0) = 1$, the value of $y(1)$ computed by this method is ______.

GATE 2018

Solution

Given: Differential equation $\frac{dy}{dx} = y$, initial value

$y(0)=1$ and $h=0.1$

$$y_n = y_{n-1} + \left(\frac{dy}{dx}\right)_{x_{n-1}} h \quad \Rightarrow \quad y_n = y_{n-1} + y_{x_{n-1}} h$$

$$y_1 = y_0 + y_0 \times h; \qquad x_0 = 0,\ y_0 = 1$$

$$y_1 = 1 + 1\times 0.1 = 1.1; \qquad x_1 = 0.1,\ y_1 = 1.1$$

$$y_2 = 1.1 + 1.1\times 0.1 = 1.21; \qquad x_2 = 0.2,\ y_2 = 1.21$$

$$y_3 = 1.21 + 1.21\times 0.1 = 1.331; \quad x_3 = 0.3,\ y_3 = 1.331$$

$$y_{10} = 2.5937; \qquad x_{10} = 1.0,\ y_{10} = 2.5937$$

$$y(1) = 2.5937$$

Example 3.30

$F(s)$ is the Laplace transform of the function

$$f(t) = 2t^2 e^{-t}$$

$F(1)$ is ________ .

GATE 2018

Solution

We know that $\qquad L(e^{-t}) = \dfrac{1}{s+1}$

Laplace transform property $\quad L(t^n F(t)) = (-1)^n \dfrac{d^n}{ds^n} f(s)$

$$L(2t^2e^{-t}) = 2(-1)^2 \frac{d^2}{ds^2}\left(\frac{1}{s+1}\right)$$

$$L(2t^2e^{-t}) = \frac{4}{(s+1)^3} = F(s)$$

$$F(1) = \frac{4}{(1+1)^3} = 0.5$$

$$F(1) = 0.5$$

Example 3.31

Consider a function u which depends on position x and time t. The partial differential equation

$$\frac{\partial u}{\partial t} = \frac{\partial^2 u}{\partial x^2}$$

is known as the

(A) Wave equation (B) Heat equation

(C) Laplace's equation (D) Elasticity equation

GATE 2018

Solution

$\dfrac{\partial u}{\partial t} = \dfrac{\partial^2 u}{\partial x^2}$ is one dimensional unsteady without heat generation heat equation.

Heat equation

Example 3.32

If y is the solution of the differential equation $y^3 \dfrac{dy}{dx} + x^3 = 0,\ y(0) = 1$, the value of $y(-1)$ is

(A) – 2 (B) – 1 (C) 0 (D)1

GATE 2018

Solution

Given: Differential equation $y^3 \dfrac{dy}{dx} + x^3 = 0$ and $y(0) = 1$

$$y^3 \frac{dy}{dx} + x^3 = 0 \quad \Rightarrow \quad y^3 dy + x^3 dx = 0$$

$$x^4 + y^4 = c$$

Putting $x = 0,\ y = 1;\quad 0^4 + 1^4 = c \Rightarrow \quad c = 1$

Solution of equation $\qquad y = (1 - x^4)^{\frac{1}{4}}$

Putting $x = -1;\quad y = \{1 - (-1)^4\}^{\frac{1}{4}} = 0$

$$y(-1) = 0$$

Example 3.33

Given the ordinary differential equation

$$\frac{d^2y}{dx^2} + \frac{dy}{dx} - 6y = 0$$

with $y(0) = 0$ and $\dfrac{dy}{dx}(0) = 1$, the value of $y(1)$ is _____ .

GATE 2018

Solution

Given differential equation can be written as

$$(D^2 + D - 6)y = 0$$

Auxiliary equation $\quad m^2 + m - 6 = 0 \Rightarrow (m+3)(m-2) = 0$

Roots are $m = -3, 2$

The solution is $\quad y = c_1 e^{-3x} + c_2 e^{2x}$

Putting $x = 0,\ y = 0; \qquad c_1 + c_2 = 0 \qquad$ (i)

$$\frac{dy}{dx} = -3c_1 e^{-3x} + 2c_2 e^{2x}$$

Putting $x = 0,\ \dfrac{dy}{dx} = 1; \qquad -3c_1 + 2c_2 = 1 \qquad$ (ii)

Equations (i) and (ii) give $\qquad c_1 = -\dfrac{1}{5},\ c_2 = -\dfrac{1}{5} \qquad y(0) = 1$

$$y=-\frac{1}{5}e^{-3x}+\frac{1}{5}e^{2x}$$

$$y(1)=-\frac{1}{5}e^{-3}+\frac{1}{5}e^{2}=1.467$$

$$y(1)=1.467$$

Example 3.34

For the equation $\frac{dy}{dx}+7x^2y=0$, if $y(0)=\frac{3}{7}$, then the value of $y(1)$ is

(A) $\frac{7}{3}e^{-7/3}$ (B) $\frac{7}{3}e^{-3/7}$ (C) $\frac{3}{7}e^{-7/3}$ (D) $\frac{3}{7}e^{-3/7}$

GATE 2019

Solution

Given differential equation $\frac{dy}{dx}+7x^2y=0$, which is a linear differential equation.

Integrating factor, $IF=e^{\int 7x^2dx}=e^{\frac{7}{3}x^3}$

The solution is $y(IF)=\int Q\,(IF)dx+c$

$$ye^{\frac{7}{3}x^3}=\int 0\times e^{\frac{7}{3}x^3}dx+c$$

or $$y=ce^{-\frac{7}{3}x^3}$$

Putting initial value $y(0)=\frac{3}{7}$; $\quad c=\frac{3}{7}$

Thus, the complete solution is $y=\frac{3}{7}e^{-\frac{7}{3}x^3}$

Value of y at $x=1$; $\quad y_{(x=1)}=\frac{3}{7}e^{-\frac{7}{3}\times 1^3}=\frac{3}{7}e^{-\frac{7}{3}}$

$$y(1)=\frac{3}{7}e^{-\frac{7}{3}}$$

Example 3.35

The differential equation $\frac{dy}{dx}+4y=5$ is valid in the domain $0\le x\le 1$ with $y(0)=2.25$. The solution of the differential equation is

(A) $y=e^{-4x}+5$ (B) $y=e^{-4x}+1.25$

(C) $y=e^{4x}+5$ (D) $y=e^{4x}+1.25$

GATE 2019

Solution

Given differential equation $\frac{dy}{dx}+4y=5$, which is a linear differential equation.

Integrating factor, $IF=e^{\int 4dx}=e^{4x}$

The solution is $y(IF)=\int Q\,(IF)dx+c$

$$ye^{4x}=\int 5\times e^{4x}dx+c$$

or $$ye^{4x}=\frac{5}{4}e^{4x}+c$$

Putting initial value $y(0)=2.25$; $\quad c=1$

Thus, the complete solution is $ye^{4x}=1.25e^{4x}+1$

$$y=e^{-4x}+1.25$$

Example 3.36

The differential equation is given as

$$x^2\frac{d^2y}{dx^2}-2x\frac{dy}{dx}+2y=4$$

The solution of the differential equation in terms of arbitrary constant C_1 and C_2 is

(A) $y=C_1x^2+C_2x+2$ (B) $y=\frac{C_1}{x^2}+C_2x+2$

(C) $y=C_1x^2+C_2x+4$ (D) $y=\frac{C_1}{x^2}+C_2x+4$

GATE 2019

Solution

Differential equation $x^2\frac{d^2y}{dx^2}-2x\frac{dy}{dx}+2y=4$

or $\quad (x^2D^2-2xD+2)y=4 \quad \left[\text{where } D=\frac{d}{dx}\right]$

Putting $x=e^z$ or $z=\ln x$ and $D_1=\frac{d}{dz}$, the given equation reduces to

$$[D_1(D_1-1)-2D_1+2]y=4$$

or $$(D_1^2-3D_1+2)y=4$$

The auxiliary equation is $m^2-3m+2=0$

or $\quad (m-2)(m-1)=0 \quad \Rightarrow m=2,\, m=1$

Complementary function, $\text{CF}=c_1e^{2z}+c_2e^{z}$

Particular Integral, $\text{PI}=\frac{4}{D_1^2-3D_1+2}e^{0z}=\frac{4}{0-0+2}=2$

The general solution $y=\text{CF}+\text{PI}$

$$y=c_1e^{2z}+c_2e^{z}+2 \quad \text{Substituting } z=\ln x$$

$$y=c_1e^{2\times\ln x}+c_2e^{\ln x}+2$$

$$y=c_1x^2+c_2x+2$$

3.3 PRACTICE PAPER

Time: 3 hours **Max. Marks:100**

Q.1 to Q.30 carry one mark each

Q.1 The following differential equation has

$$\left(\frac{d^2y}{dx^2}\right)^2 = \left[1+\left(\frac{dy}{dx}\right)^2\right]^3$$

(A) Degree $=2$, order $=2$ (B) Degree $=3$, order $=2$

(C) Degree $=2$, order $=3$ (D) Degree $=6$, order $=2$

Q.2 Solution of $(xy^2+x)\,dx+(yx^2+y)\,dy=0$ is

(A) $(1+x^2)(1+y^2)=c$ (B) $1+x^2=c(1+y^2)$

(C) $\tan^{-1}x+\tan^{-1}y=c$ (D) None of these

Q.3 Equation of motion of simple pendulum $l\frac{d^2\theta}{dt^2}+g\theta=0$ given that $\theta=\theta_0$ and $\frac{d\theta}{dt}=0$ when $t=0$. Relation between angular displacement (θ) and time t is

(A) $\theta=\theta_0\cos\sqrt{\frac{g}{l}}\,t$ (B) $\theta=\theta_0\sin\sqrt{\frac{g}{l}}\,t$

(C) $\theta=\theta_0 e^{-\sqrt{\frac{g}{l}}t}$ (D) None of these

Q.4 The differential equation of the family of curves $y=Ae^{3x}+Be^{5x}$, where A and B are constants, is

(A) $\frac{d^2y}{dx^2}-8\frac{dy}{dx}-15y=0$ (B) $\frac{d^2y}{dx^2}-8\frac{dy}{dx}+15y=0$

(C) $\frac{d^2y}{dx^2}+8\frac{dy}{dx}-15y=0$ (D) None of these

Q.5 Solution of $\frac{dy}{dx}=\cos(x+y)$ is

(A) $\tan\frac{x+y}{2}=x+c$ (B) $\sin\frac{x+y}{2}=x+c$

(C) No solution (D) None of these

Q.6 Solution of $\log\left(\frac{dy}{dx}\right)=ax+by$ is

(A) $be^{ax}=ay+c$ (B) $be^{ax}+ae^{-by}+cab=0$

(C) No solution (D) None of these

Q.7 Partial differential equation $\frac{\partial^2u}{\partial x^2}=\frac{1}{c^2}\frac{\partial^2u}{\partial t^2}$ represents

(A) One-dimensional wave equation

(B) Two-dimensional wave equation

(C) One-dimensional heat equation

(D) None of these

Q.8 The differential equation $9yy'+4x=0$ represents

(A) Circle (B) Ellipse

(C) Straight line (D) Hyperbola

Q.9 Solution of $v\frac{dv}{dx}=g,\ v(0)=u$ is

(A) $v^2=2gx$ (B) $v^2=u^2+2gx$

(C) $x=ut+gt^2$ (D) None of these

Q.10 The differential equation $y\,dx-2x\,dy=0$, represents a

(A) Family of straight lines (B) Family of parabolas

(C) Family of circles (D) Family of catenaries

Q.11 If the solution of $\frac{d^2y}{dx^2}+\lambda y=0$ is given by $y=A\cos 3x+B\sin 3x$, then value of λ is

(A) 3 (B) −3 (C) 9 (D) −9

Q.12 Integrating factor (IF) of differential equation $x\frac{dy}{dx}-3y=x^2$ is

(A) e^{-x} (B) $\frac{1}{x^3}$ (C) e^{-3x} (D) None of these

Q.13 The solution of $\frac{dy}{dx}=xy+x+y+1$ is

(A) $y=ce^{x+\frac{x^2}{2}}-1$ (B) $y=ce^{x^2}+2$

(C) $\log(y+1)=cx$ (D) None of these

Q.14 Laplace tranform of $(4te^{-t})$ is equal to

(A) $\frac{4}{(s+1)^2}$ (B) $\frac{4}{s^2}$ (C) $\frac{4}{(s-1)^2}$ (D) None of these

Q.15 $\int_0^\infty t^n e^{-st}\,dt$ is equal to

(A) $\frac{n!}{s^{n+1}}$ (B) $\frac{n!}{s^n}$ (C) $\frac{(n-1)!}{s^n}$ (D) None of these

Q.16 Laplace transform of $(e^{-3t}\sin 2t)$ is equal to

(A) $\frac{2}{s^2+6s+13}$ (B) $\frac{2}{s^2+4}$

(C) $\frac{3}{s^2+4}$ (D) None of these

Q.17 The inverse Laplace transform of the function $F(s)=\frac{1}{s(s+1)}$ is given by

(A) $f(t)=1-e^{-t}$ (B) $f(t)=e^{-t}$

(C) $f(t)=e^{-t}\sin t$ (D) $f(t)=e^{-t}\sin t$

Q.18 The inverse Laplace transform of the function $f(s)=\left(\frac{9s-8}{s^2-2s}\right)$ is equal to

(A) $\sin(2t+3)$ (B) te^{2t}

(C) $4t+5e^{2t}$ (D) None of these

Q.19 Laplace transform of (e^{-at+b}) is equal to

(A) $\frac{e^b}{s+a}$ (B) $\frac{1}{s+a}$ (C) $\frac{e^a}{s+b}$ (D) $\frac{as-b}{s+a}$

Q.20 Laplace transform of (cosh at) is equal to

(A) $\frac{a}{s^2+a^2}$ (B) $\frac{s}{s^2+a^2}$

(C) $\frac{a}{s^2-a^2}$ (D) $\frac{s}{s^2-a^2}$

Q.21 The degree of differential equation

$$\left(\frac{d^2y}{dx^2}\right)^{\frac{2}{3}}+\left(\frac{d^3y}{dx^3}\right)^{\frac{3}{2}}=0, \text{ is}$$

(A) 3 (B) 5 (C) 4 (D) 9

Q.22 The solution of the equation $(x+y-2)dy=(x+y)dx$, is

(A) $y+x=\ln(y-x+1)+c$ (B) $y-x=\ln(x+y-1)+c$

(C) $y-2x=\ln(x+y-1)+c$ (D) $y+2x=\ln(x+y+1)+c$

Q.23 The solution of differential equation

$$(x+1)\frac{dy}{dx}+1=e^{-y}, \text{ is}$$

(A) $(x+1)e^y=x+c$ (B) $(x+1)(1+e^y)=c$

(C) $\frac{x+1}{1+e^y}=c$ (D) $\frac{x+1}{1-e^y}=c$

Q.24 The family of straight lines passing through the origin is represented by the differential equation

(A) $ydx+xdy=0$ (B) $xdx+ydy=0$

(C) $xdy-ydx=0$ (D) $ydy-xdx=0$

Q.25 The general solution of the differential equation $\frac{d^2y}{dx^2}+4y=\sin^2 x$ is given by

(A) $y=c_1e^{2x}+c_2e^{-2x}+2\sin x\cos x$

(B) $y=c_1\cos 2x+c_2\sin 2x+\frac{1}{8}-\frac{x}{8}\sin 2x$

(C) $y=(c_1+c_2\cos 2x)e^{-2x}-\frac{x}{8}\cos 2x$

(D) $y=c_1\cos(2x+c_2)+\frac{1}{8}$

Q.26 The particular integral of the differential equation $(D^2+4)y=x$ is

(A) xe^{-2x} (B) $x\cos 2x$ (C) $x\sin 2x$ (D) $\frac{x}{4}$

Q.27 A solution curve of the equation $xy'=2y$, passing through (1, 2), also passes through coordinate

(A) (2, 1) (B) (0, 0) (C) (4, 24) (D) (24, 4)

Q.28 If in a culture of yeast, y_0 is the amount of yeast present initially, and the rate of growth $\frac{dy}{dx}$ is proportional to the amount y at time t and if y doubles in one day, the amount expected after 3 days equals

(A) $3y_0$ (B) $8y_0$ (C) $9y_0$ (D) $27y_0$

Q.29 The particular integral of $(D^2+a^2)y=\sin ax$ $\left(D\equiv\frac{d}{dx}\right)$ is

(A) $-\frac{x}{2a}\cos ax$ (B) $\frac{x}{2a}\cos ax$

(C) $-\frac{ax}{2}\cos ax$ (D) $\frac{ax}{2}\cos ax$

Q.30 $e^{-x}(c_1\cos\sqrt{3}x+c_2\sin\sqrt{3}x)+c_3e^{2x}$ is the general solution of

(A) $\frac{d^3y}{dx^3}+4y=0$ (B) $\frac{d^3y}{dx^3}+8y=0$

(C) $\frac{d^3y}{dx^3}-8y=0$ (D) $\frac{d^3y}{dx^3}-2\frac{d^2y}{dx^2}+\frac{dy}{dx}-2y=0$

Q.31 to Q.65 carry two marks each

Q.31 The equation of the curve that passes through the point (1, 2) and has at every point $\frac{dy}{dx}=-\frac{2xy}{1+x^2}$ is

(A) $y(x^2+1)=4$ (B) $y=4\log(1+x^2)$

(C) $y=4x^2$ (D) None of these

Q.32 Solution of $\frac{dy}{dx}=\frac{y}{x}+\sin\frac{y}{x}$ is

(A) $y=c\cos\frac{y}{x}$ (B) $y=2x\log cx$

(C) $\tan\left(\frac{y}{2x}\right) = cx$ (D) None of these

Q.33 The solution of differential equation $\frac{dy}{dx} = \frac{1}{x+y+1}$ is

(A) $y = \log(x+y+2)+c$ (B) $y = \log(x+y+1)+c$

(C) $y + \log(x+y) = c$ (D) $y + \log(x+y+1) = c$

Q.34 The solution of the equation $\frac{d^2y}{dx^2} + \frac{dy}{dx} - 2y = 0,$ with $y(0)=0,\ y'(0)=3$, is

(A) $e^x + e^{-2x}$ (B) $e^x - e^{-2x}$

(C) $e^x - e^{2x}$ (D) $e^x + e^{2x}$

Q.35 The differential equation $y\frac{dy}{dx} + x = A$, where A is a constant, represents a set of:

(A) Circles centred at y-axis (B) Circles centred at x-axis

(C) Parabolas (D) Ellipses

Q.36 Laplace transform of $(t\,e^{-2t}\sin t)$ is equal to

(A) $\frac{2s+4}{(s^2+4s+5)^2}$ (B) $\frac{2s+4}{(s^2+5)^2}$

(C) $\frac{2s+4}{(s^2+4s)^2}$ (D) None of these

Q.37 A particle moves from a point P with an acceleration k times its distance from P with starting velocity $\sqrt{k}$. The velocity of the particle at a distance 2 units from P is

(A) $\sqrt{5k}$ units (B) $\sqrt{3k}$ units

(C) $\sqrt{7k}$ units (D) $\sqrt{5}\ k$ units

Q.38 The general solution of the differential equation $\frac{d^2y}{dx^2} + 2\frac{dy}{dx} + y = e^{-x}\cos x,$ is

(A) $(c_1 + c_2x + \sin x)e^{-x}$ (B) $(c_1 + c_2x - \sin x)e^{-x}$

(C) $(c_1 + c_2x + \cos x)e^{-x}$ (D) $(c_1 + c_2x - \cos x)e^{-x}$

Q.39 The solution of differential equation $(x+y)^2\frac{dy}{dx} = a^2$ is

(A) $y + x = a\tan\left(\frac{y-c}{a}\right)$ (B) $y - x = a\tan(y-c)$

(C) $y - x = \tan\left(\frac{y-c}{a}\right)$ (D) $a(y-x) = \tan\left(\frac{y-c}{a}\right)$

Q.40 Solution of heat conduction equation (in polar coordinates) $\frac{d^2T}{dr^2} + \frac{1}{r}\frac{dT}{dr} = 0$ is

(A) $T = c_1 r + c_2$ (B) $T = c_1 \log r + c_2$

(C) $T = c_1 e^r + c_2$ (D) None of these

Q.41 The decay rate of radium at any time t is proportional to its mass at that time. The mass is M_0 at time $t = 0$. The time when the mass will be halved is

(A) $\frac{\log 3}{3k}$ (B) $\frac{\log 2}{2k}$ (C) $\frac{\log 2}{k}$ (D) None of these

(where, k is constant)

Q.42 A spherical rain drop evaporates at a rate proportional to its surface area. If its radius is originally 3 mm and after one hour it is reduced to 2 mm. The expression for the radius of the rain drop at any time t is

(A) $r = 3 - t$ (B) $r = 3 + t$ (C) $r = 2 - t$ (D) $r = 2 + t$

Q.43 The differential equation of the family of all circle passing through the origin and having the centres on the x-axis is

(A) $2xy\frac{dy}{dx} + (x^2 + y^2) = 0$ (B) $2xy\frac{dy}{dx} + (x^2 - y^2) = 0$

(C) $2xy\frac{dy}{dx} - (x^2 - y^2) = 0$ (D) None of these

Q.44 The rate at which bacteria multiply is proportional to the instantaneous number present. If the original number doubles in 2 hours, then it will triple in:

(A) $2\frac{\log 3}{\log 2}$ (B) $2\frac{\log 2}{\log 3}$

(C) $\frac{\log 3}{\log 2}$ (D) $\frac{\log 2}{\log 3}$

Q.45 Particular integral of differential equation $\frac{d^2y}{d^2x} + 4\frac{dy}{dx} + 3y = 3e^{2x}$ is

(A) $\frac{1}{15}e^{2x}$ (B) $\frac{1}{5}e^{2x}$

(C) $3e^{2x}$ (D) $c_1e^{-x} + c_2e^{-3x}$

Q.46 Laplace transform of $(t\sin 2t)$ is equal to

(A) $\frac{2}{s^2+4}$ (B) $\frac{2}{s^2+4s+4}$

(C) $\frac{4s}{(s^2+4)^2}$ (D) None of these

Q.47 Laplace transform of $(\sin^2 t)$ is

(A) $\frac{2}{s(s^2+4)}$ (B) $\frac{1}{s^2+4}$

(C) $\frac{1}{s(s^2+2)}$ (D) None of these

Q.48 Inverse Laplace transform of $\left(\frac{1}{s^2+4s}\right)$ is

(A) $1-e^{-4t}$ (B) $\frac{1}{4}(1-e^{-4t})$

(C) te^{-4t} (D) None of these

Q.49 By means of a suitable transform of the independent variable t, the differential equation

$x\frac{d^2y}{dx^2}+2\frac{dy}{dx}=6x+\frac{1}{x}$, reduces to the form

(A) $\frac{d^2y}{dt^2}+2\frac{dy}{dt}=6e^{2t}+1$ (B) $\frac{d^2y}{dt^2}=6e^{2t}+\ln t$

(C) $\frac{d^2y}{dt^2}+\frac{dy}{dt}=6e^{2t}+1$ (D) $\frac{d^2y}{dt^2}=6e^{t}+1$

Q.50 Solution of the following initial value problems $y''+a\,y'-2a^2y=0,\ \ y(0)=6,\ y'(0)=0$, is

(A) $y=2e^{-2at}+4e^{at}$ (B) $y=4e^{-2at}+2e^{at}$

(C) $y=2e^{-2at}$ (D) $y=4e^{at}$

Q.51 The general solution of the differential equation

$\frac{d^2y}{dx^2}+9y=\sin^3 x$, is

(A) $y=A\cos(3x+B)+\frac{1}{24}\sin x-\sin 3x$

(B) $y=Ae^{3x}+Be^{-3x}+\frac{1}{32}\sin x+\frac{1}{2}\cos 3x$

(C) $y=A+Bxe^{3x}+2\sin x-\frac{5}{13}\sin 3x$

(D) $y=A\sin(3x+B)+\frac{3}{32}\sin x+\frac{x}{24}\cos 3x$

Q.52 The maximum value of the solution $y(t)$ of the differential equation $y(t)+\ddot{y}(t)=0$ with initial conditions $\dot{y}(0)=1$ and $y(0)=1$, for $t\geq 0$ is

(A) $\sqrt{2}$ (B) $\sqrt{3}$ (C) $\sqrt{8}$ (D) $\sqrt{5}$

Q.53 A solution of the following differential equation is given by $\frac{d^2y}{dx^2}-5\frac{dy}{dx}+6y=0$

(A) $y=Ae^{-2x}+Be^{-3x}$ (B) $y=Ae^{-2x}$

(C) $y=Ae^{5x}+Be^{6x}$ (D) $y=Ae^{2x}+Be^{3x}$

Q.54 The solution of the differential equation $\frac{d^2y}{dx^2}+y=0$ satisfying the conditions $y(0)=1,\ y(\pi/2)=2$, is

(A) $\cos x+2\sin x$ (B) $\cos x+\sin x$

(C) $2\cos x+\sin x$ (D) $2(\cos x+\sin x)$

Q.55 If $x=A\cos(mt-\alpha)$ then the differential equation satisfying the relation is

(A) $\frac{dx}{dt}=1-x^2$ (B) $\frac{d^2x}{dt^2}=-\alpha^2x$

(C) $\frac{d^2x}{dt^2}=-m^2x$ (D) $\frac{dx}{dt}=-m^2x$

Q.56 The solution of the differential equation

$y''+(3i-1)y'-3i\,y=0$, is

(A) $y=c_1e^{x}+c_2e^{3ix}$ (B) $y=c_1e^{-x}+c_2e^{3ix}$

(C) $y=c_1e^{x}+c_2e^{-3ix}$ (D) $y=c_1e^{-x}+c_2e^{-3ix}$

Q.57 The general solution of the differential equation

$\frac{dy}{dx}=\frac{y}{x}+\tan\frac{y}{x}$, is

(A) $\sin\frac{y}{x}=c$ (B) $\cos\frac{y}{x}=cx$

(C) $\sin\frac{y}{x}=cx$ (D) $\cos\frac{y}{x}=c$

Q.58 The Laplace transform of the function $(\sin^2 2t)$ is

(A) $\frac{1}{2s}-\frac{s}{2(s^2+16)}$ (B) $\frac{s}{s^2+16}$

(C) $\frac{s}{2}-\frac{s}{(s^2+16)}$ (D) $\frac{s}{s^2+4}$

Q.59 With initial condition $x(1)=0.5$, the solution of the differential equation $t\frac{dx}{dt}+x=t$, is

(A) $x=t-\frac{1}{2}$ (B) $x=t^2-\frac{1}{2}$

(C) $x=\frac{t^2}{2}$ (D) $x=\frac{t}{2}$

Q.60 The solution of the first order differential equation $x'(t)=-3x(t),\ x(0)=x_0$ is

(A) $x(t)=x_0e^{-3t}$ (B) $x(t)=x_0e^{-3}$

(C) $x(t)=x_0e^{-\frac{1}{3}}$ (D) $x(t)=x_0e^{-t}$

Q.61 Solution of $\frac{dy}{dx}=-\frac{x}{y}$ at $x=1$ and $y=\sqrt{3}$ is

(A) $x - y^2 = -2$ (B) $x + y^2 = 4$

(C) $x^2 - y^2 = 4$ (D) $x^2 + y^2 = 4$

Q.62 A body originally at 60°C cools down to 40°C in 15 minutes when kept in air at a temperature of 25°C. What will be the temperature of the body at the end of 30 minutes?

(A) 31.5°C (B) 28.5°C (C) 34.5°C (D) None of these

Q.63 The solution for the differential equation $\frac{dy}{dx} = x^2 y$ with the condition that $y = 1$ at $x = 0$ is

(A) $y = e^{\frac{1}{2x}}$ (B) $\ln(y) = \frac{x^3}{3} + 4$

(C) $\ln(y) = \frac{x^2}{2}$ (D) $y = e^{\frac{x^3}{3}}$

Q.64 A spherical naphthalene ball exposed to the atmosphere loses volume at a rate proportional to its instantaneous surface area due to evaporation. If the initial diameter of the ball is 2 cm and the diameter reduces to 1 cm after 3 months, the ball completely evaporates in (months).

(A) 4 (B) 5 (C) 6 (D) 7

Q.65 The number N of bacteria in a culture grew at a rate proportional to N. The value of N was initially 100 and increased to 332 in one hour, what would be the value of N after $1\frac{1}{2}$ hours

(A) 408 (B) 506 (C) 558 (D) 605

3.4 SOLUTION OF PRACTICE PAPER

Q.1 Ans:(A)

Order is highest derivative term, so order = 2

Degree is power of highest derivative term, so degree = 2

$$\text{Degree} = 2, \text{ order} = 2$$

Q.2 Ans:(A)

Given differential equation

$(x y^2 + x)\,dx + (yx^2 + y)\,dy = 0$

or $x(y^2+1)\,dx + y(x^2+1)\,dy = 0$

or $\left(\frac{x}{x^2+1}\right)dx + \left(\frac{y}{y^2+1}\right)dy = 0$

This is variable separable form.

Integrating, we have

$$\int\left(\frac{x}{x^2+1}\right)dx + \int\left(\frac{y}{y^2+1}\right)dy = c_1$$

or $\ln(x^2+1) + \ln(y^2+1) = c$

or $\ln(x^2+1)(y^2+1) = c$

The solution is

$$(x^2+1)(y^2+1) = c$$

Q.3 Ans:(A)

The given equation can be written as

$$\frac{d^2\theta}{dt^2} + \frac{g}{l}\theta = 0 \quad \text{or} \quad \left(D^2 + \frac{g}{l}\right)\theta = 0$$

Now auxiliary equation is $m^2 + \frac{g}{l} = 0$

Roots are $m = +\sqrt{\frac{g}{l}}\,i, -\sqrt{\frac{g}{l}}\,i$

Thus, the solution is $\theta = c_1 \cos\sqrt{\frac{g}{l}}\,t + c_2 \sin\sqrt{\frac{g}{l}}\,t$

Putting boundary values (a) $\theta = \theta_0$ at $t = 0$, (b) $\frac{d\theta}{dt} = 0$ at $t = 0$.

$$\theta_0 = c_1 \cos\sqrt{\frac{g}{l}} \times 0 + c_2 \sin\sqrt{\frac{g}{l}} \times 0 \quad \Rightarrow \quad c_1 = \theta_0$$

$$0 = -\theta_0\, c_1\sqrt{\frac{g}{l}} \sin\sqrt{\frac{g}{l}} \times 0 + c_2\sqrt{\frac{g}{l}} \cos\sqrt{\frac{g}{l}} \times 0 \quad \Rightarrow \quad c_2 = 0$$

Thus, required solution is

$$\theta = \theta_0 \cos\sqrt{\frac{g}{l}}\,t$$

Q.4 Ans:(B)

The solution of differential equation $\frac{d^2y}{dx^2} - (m_1 + m_2)\frac{dy}{dx} + m_1 m_2 y = 0$ is $y = A\,e^{m_1 x} + B\,e^{m_2 x}$.

$m_1 = 3$ and $m_2 = 5$ of given equation of curve $y = A\,e^{3x} + B\,e^{5x}$.

Thus, the differential equation of curve is

$$\frac{d^2y}{dx^2} - (3+5)\frac{dy}{dx} + 3 \times 5y = 0$$

$$\frac{d^2y}{dx^2} - 8\frac{dy}{dx} + 15y = 0$$

Q.5 Ans:(A)

Given differential equation $\frac{dy}{dx} = \cos(x+y)$

Let $v = x + y \quad \Rightarrow \quad \frac{dv}{dx} = 1 + \frac{dy}{dx}$

$\frac{dy}{dx} = \cos(x+y) \quad \Rightarrow \quad \frac{dv}{dx} - 1 = \cos v$

or $\frac{dv}{1+\cos v} = dx$

Integrating $\int \frac{dv}{1+\cos v} = \int dx + c$

or $\int \frac{1}{2}\sec^2\frac{v}{2}\,dv = x + c$

or $\tan\left(\frac{v}{2}\right) = x + c$

$$\tan\left(\frac{x+y}{2}\right) = x + c$$

Q.6 Ans:(B)

Given equation $\log\left(\frac{dy}{dx}\right) = ax + by$

or $\frac{dy}{dx} = e^{ax+by}$

or $\frac{dy}{dx} = e^{ax}e^{by}$

or $\int e^{-by}dy = \int e^{ax}dx + c$

Integrating $\int e^{-by}dy = \int e^{ax}dx + c$

or $\frac{e^{-by}}{-b} = \frac{e^{ax}}{a} + c$

$$ae^{-by} + be^{ax} + abc = 0$$

Q.7 Ans:(A)

Three-dimensional wave equation is given by

$$\frac{\partial^2 u}{\partial x^2} + \frac{\partial^2 u}{\partial y^2} + \frac{\partial^2 u}{\partial z^2} = \frac{1}{c^2}\frac{\partial^2 u}{\partial t^2}$$

$\frac{\partial^2 u}{\partial x^2} = \frac{1}{c^2}\frac{\partial^2 u}{\partial t^2}$ One-dimensional wave equation

Q.8 Ans:(B)

The given differential equation can be written as

$$9y\frac{dy}{dx} + 4x = 0$$

or $9y\,dy + 4x\,dx = 0$

Integrating $\int 9y\,dy + \int 4x\,dx = c_1$

or $\frac{9y^2}{2} + \frac{4x^2}{2} = c_1$

$\frac{x^2}{3^2} + \frac{y^2}{2^2} =$ constant. This is the equation of ellipse.

Q.9 Ans:(B)

Given differential equation $v\frac{dv}{dx} = g$

or $vdv = gdx$

Integrating $\int vdv = \int gdx + c$

or $\frac{v^2}{2} = gx + c$

Putting initial value; $x = 0$, $v = u$

$$\frac{u^2}{2} = g \times 0 + c \quad \Rightarrow \quad c = \frac{u^2}{2}$$

or $\frac{v^2}{2} = gx + \frac{u^2}{2}$

$$v^2 = u^2 + 2gx$$

Q.10 Ans:(B)

Given differential equation: $y\,dx - 2x\,dy = 0$

or $\frac{dx}{x} - 2\frac{dy}{y} = 0$

Integrating, we have $\int\frac{dx}{x} - 2\int\frac{dy}{y} = c_1$

or $\ln x - 2\ln y = c_1$

or $\ln\left(\frac{x}{y^2}\right) = c_1 \Rightarrow \left(\frac{x}{y^2}\right) = e^{c_1} = c$

The solution is

$x = cy^2$. This is the equation of parabola.

Q.11 Ans:(C)

Writing D for $\frac{d}{dx}$, the equation is

$$(D^2 + \lambda)y = 0$$

Now, auxiliary equation is $m^2 + \lambda = 0$;

giving $m = +\sqrt{\lambda}\,i,\ -\sqrt{\lambda}\,i$

Thus, the solution is

$$y = c_1\cos\sqrt{\lambda}\,x + c_2\sin\sqrt{\lambda}\,x \qquad \text{(i)}$$

Given solution is $y = A\cos 3x + B\sin 3x$ (ii)

From equation (i) and (ii), we get

$$\sqrt{\lambda} = 3$$

$$\lambda = 9$$

Q.12 Ans:(B)

Differential equation $x\dfrac{dy}{dx} - 3y = x^2$

$$\frac{dy}{dx} - \left(\frac{3}{x}\right)y = x$$

This is the linear differential equation

Integrating factor (IF), $e^{\int Pdx} = e^{-\int \frac{3}{x}dx} = e^{-3\log x} = \dfrac{1}{x^3}$

$$\text{IF} = \frac{1}{x^3}$$

Q.13 Ans:(A)

Given differential equation $\dfrac{dy}{dx} = xy + x + y + 1$

or $\dfrac{dy}{dx} = x(y+1) + (y+1)$

or $\dfrac{dy}{dx} = (x+1)(y+1)$

Integrating $\displaystyle\int \frac{dy}{(y+1)} = \int (x+1)dx + c_1$

or $\ln(y+1) = \dfrac{x^2}{2} + x + c_1$

or $y + 1 = ce^{\left(\frac{x^2}{2}+x\right)}$

$$y = ce^{x+\frac{x^2}{2}} - 1$$

Q.14 Ans:(A)

Using formula $L(t^n e^{at}) = \dfrac{n!}{(s-a)^{n+1}}$, we obtain

$$L(4te^{-t}) = 4 \times \frac{1!}{(s+1)^{1+1}}$$

$$L(4te^{-t}) = \frac{4}{(s+1)^2}$$

Q.15 Ans:(A)

By the definition of Laplace transform

$$L(t^n) = \int_0^\infty t^n e^{-st}\, dt = \frac{n!}{s^{n+1}}$$

$$L(t^n) = \frac{n!}{s^{n+1}}$$

Q.16 Ans:(A)

We know that $L(\sin at) = \dfrac{a}{s^2 + a^2}$

By first shifting theorem, replace s by $s-a$ in $F(s)$, the Laplace transform of $(e^{-3t}\sin 2t)$ is

$$L(e^{-3t}\sin 2t) = \frac{2}{(s+3)^2 + (2)^2}$$

$$L(e^{-3t}\sin 2t) = \frac{2}{s^2 + 6s + 13}$$

Q.17 Ans:(A)

$$F(s) = \frac{1}{s(s+1)} = \frac{1}{s} - \frac{1}{s+1}$$

$$L^{-1}\{F(s)\} = L^{-1}\left\{\frac{1}{s(s+1)}\right\} = L^{-1}\left(\frac{1}{s}\right) - L^{-1}\left(\frac{1}{s+1}\right)$$

$$L^{-1}\left\{\frac{1}{s(s+1)}\right\} = 1 - e^{-t}$$

Q.18 Ans:(C)

$$f(s) = \left(\frac{9s-8}{s^2-2s}\right) = \frac{9s-8}{s(s-2)}$$

Let $\dfrac{9s-8}{s(s-2)} = \dfrac{A}{s} + \dfrac{B}{s-2}$

Solving $A = 4,\ B = 5$

$$\frac{9s-8}{s(s-2)} = \frac{4}{s} + \frac{5}{s-2}$$

$$L^{-1}\left[\frac{9s-8}{s(s-2)}\right] = L^{-1}\left(\frac{4}{s}\right) + L^{-1}\left(\frac{5}{s-2}\right)$$

$$L^{-1}\left[\frac{9s-8}{s(s-2)}\right] = 4t + 5e^{2t}$$

Q.19 Ans:(A)

$$L(e^{-at+b}) = L(e^{-at} \times e^b)$$

or $L(e^{-at+b}) = e^b L(e^{-at})$

$$L(e^{-at+b}) = \frac{e^b}{s+a}$$

Q.20 Ans:(D)

$$\cosh at = \frac{e^{at} + e^{-at}}{2}$$

$$L(\cosh at) = L\left(\frac{e^{at}}{2}\right) + L\left(\frac{e^{-at}}{2}\right)$$

or $L(\cosh at) = \frac{1}{2}\left(\frac{1}{s-a}\right) + \frac{1}{2}\left(\frac{1}{s+a}\right)$

or $L(\cosh at) = \frac{s}{(s-a)(s+a)}$

$$L(\cosh at) = \frac{s}{s^2 - a^2}$$

Q.21 Ans:(D)

Given differential equation $\left(\frac{d^2y}{dx^2}\right)^{\frac{2}{3}} + \left(\frac{d^3y}{dx^3}\right)^{\frac{3}{2}} = 0$

Removing radical power $\left(\frac{d^2y}{dx^2}\right)^{\frac{2}{3}\times 6} = (-1)^{\times 6}\left(\frac{d^3y}{dx^3}\right)^{\frac{3}{2}\times 6}$

or $\left(\frac{d^3y}{dx^3}\right)^9 - \left(\frac{d^2y}{dx^2}\right)^4 = 0$

Degree is power of the highest derivative term, so degree $=9$

$$\text{Degree} = 9$$

Q.22 Ans:(B)

The equation can be written as $\frac{dy}{dx} = \frac{x+y}{x+y-2}$

Let $x + y = v \quad \Rightarrow \frac{dy}{dx} = \frac{dv}{dx} - 1$

$\frac{dv}{dx} - 1 = \frac{v}{v-2}$ or $\frac{dv}{dx} = \frac{2v-2}{v-2}$

Integrating $\int \frac{v-2}{v-1} dv = 2\int dx + c$

or $\int\left(1 - \frac{1}{v-1}\right) dv = 2\int dx + c$

or $v - \ln(v-1) = 2x + c$

or $x + y - \ln(x+y-1) = 2x + c$

$$y - x = \ln(x+y-1) + c$$

Q.23 Ans:(A)

Given differential equation: $(x+1)\frac{dy}{dx} + 1 = e^{-y}$

or $\frac{dy}{e^{-y} - 1} = \frac{dx}{x+1}$

Integrating, $\int \frac{e^y}{1-e^y} dy = \int \frac{dx}{x+1} + c_1$

or $-\ln(1-e^y) = \ln(x+1) + c_1$

or $\ln(x+1)(1-e^y) = -c_1$

or $(x+1)(1-e^y) = c_2$

$$(x+1)e^y = x + c$$

Q.24 Ans:(C)

The family of straight lines passing through the origin is given by

$$y = mx \qquad \text{(i)}$$

Differentiating with respect to x

$$\frac{dy}{dx} = m \qquad \text{(ii)}$$

Eliminating m from Equations (i) and (ii),we get

$$\frac{dy}{dx} = \frac{y}{x} \quad \Rightarrow x\,dy = y\,dx$$

$$y\,dx - x\,dy = 0$$

Q.25 Ans:(B)

The given differential equation can be written as

$$(D^2 + 4)y = \sin^2 x$$

Auxiliary equation $m^2 + 4 = 0$

Roots are $m = 2i, -2i$

Complementary function, $\text{CF} = c_1 \cos 2x + c_2 \sin 2x$

Particular integral, $\text{PI} = \frac{1}{D^2+4}\sin^2 x$

$$\text{PI} = \frac{1}{D^2+4}\left(\frac{1-\cos 2x}{2}\right) = \frac{1}{D^2+4}\left(\frac{1}{2} - \frac{\cos 2x}{2}\right)$$

or $\text{PI} = \frac{1}{D^2+4} \times \frac{1}{2} - \frac{1}{D^2+4} \times \frac{\cos 2x}{2}$

or $\text{PI} = \frac{1}{2} \times \frac{1}{4} - \frac{1}{2}\frac{x \sin 2x}{2 \times 2}$

or $\text{PI} = \frac{1}{8} - \frac{x}{8}\sin 2x$

The general solution $y = \text{CF} + \text{PI}$

$$y = c_1 \cos 2x + c_2 \sin 2x + \frac{1}{8} - \frac{x}{8}\sin 2x$$

Q.26 Ans:(D)

Given differential equation: $(D^2 + 4)y = x$

Particular integral, $\text{PI} = \frac{1}{D^2+4}x$

or $\text{PI} = \frac{1}{4}\left(1 + \frac{D^2}{4}\right)^{-1} x$

$$=\frac{1}{4}\left(1-\frac{D^2}{4}+\frac{1}{2!}\left(\frac{D^2}{4}\right)^2-\frac{1}{3!}\left(\frac{D^2}{4}\right)^3+\ldots\right)x$$

or $\quad \text{PI}=\frac{1}{4}(x-0+0-0+\ldots)$

$$\text{PI}=\frac{x}{4}$$

Q.27 Ans:(B)

Given differential equation of curve $xy'=2y$

or $\quad x\frac{dy}{dx}=2y$

Integrating $\int\frac{dy}{y}=2\int\frac{dx}{x}+c$

or $\quad \ln y=2\ln x+c$

or $\quad y=kx^2$

The equation passing through (1, 2);

$$2=k1^2 \Rightarrow k=2$$

Therefore, the equation of curve $\quad y=2x^2$

Curve $(y=2x^2)$ passes through (0, 0)

Q.28 Ans:(B)

Rate of growth $\quad \frac{dy}{dt}\propto y$

$$\frac{dy}{dt}=ky \quad \text{or} \quad \frac{dy}{y}=kdt$$

Integrating $\int_{y_0}^{y}\frac{dy}{y}=k\int_0^t dt$

or $\quad \ln\frac{y}{y_0}=kt$

or $\quad y=y_0e^{kt}$

y is double in one day; $\quad 2y_0=y_0e^{k\times1} \Rightarrow e^k=2$

Amount after 3 days $\quad y=y_0e^{k\times3}=y_0(e^k)^3$

or $\quad y=y_0(2)^3$

$$y=8y_0$$

Q.29 Ans:(A)

Given differential equation $(D^2+a^2)y=\sin ax$

$$\text{PI}=\frac{1}{D^2+a^2}\sin ax \qquad [F(-a^2)=0]$$

$$\text{PI}=-\frac{x\cos ax}{2a}$$

Q.30 Ans:(C)

Given solution of a differential equation is

$$e^{-x}(c_1\cos\sqrt{3}x+c_2\sin\sqrt{3}x)+c_3e^{2x}$$

From solution given, the roots of auxiliary equation are

$$-1+\sqrt{3}\,i,\ -1-\sqrt{3}\,i \text{ and } 2$$

Thus, the auxiliary equation

$$[m-(-1+\sqrt{3}\,i)][m-(-1-\sqrt{3}\,i)][m-2]=0$$

or $\quad (m-2)(m^2+2m+4)=0$

or $\quad m^3-8=0$

Thus, the differential equation is $\quad (D^3-8)y=0$

$$\frac{d^3y}{dx^3}-8y=0$$

Q.31 Ans:(A)

Differential equation of curve $\frac{dy}{dx}=-\frac{2xy}{1+x^2}$

or $\quad \frac{dy}{y}=-\frac{2x}{1+x^2}dx$

Integrating, $\int\frac{dy}{y}=-\int\frac{2x}{1+x^2}dx+c_1$

or $\quad \ln y=-\ln(1+x^2)+c_1$

or $\quad \ln y(1+x^2)=c_1$

or $\quad y(1+x^2)=c$

Curve passes through (1, 2); $2(1+1^2)=c$

$$c=4$$

Thus, the required equation of curve

$$y(1+x^2)=4$$

Q.32 Ans:(C)

Given differential equation $\frac{dy}{dx}=\frac{y}{x}+\sin\frac{y}{x}$

Putting $v=\frac{y}{x}$, the equation reduces to

$$x\frac{dv}{dx}+v=v+\sin v$$

Integrating, $\int\frac{dv}{\sin v}=\int\frac{dx}{x}+c_1$

or $\ln\left(\tan\dfrac{v}{2}\right) = \ln(x) + c_1$

or $\tan\dfrac{v}{2} = cx \Rightarrow \tan\dfrac{y}{2x} = cx$

$$\tan\frac{y}{2x} = cx$$

Q.33 Ans:(A)

Given differential equation $\dfrac{dy}{dx} = \dfrac{1}{x+y+1}$

Put $x + y + 1 = v$ and $\dfrac{dy}{dx} = \dfrac{dv}{dx} - 1$

or $\dfrac{dv}{dx} - 1 = \dfrac{1}{v}$

Integrating $\int \dfrac{v}{v+1}dv = \int dx + c_1$

or $\int\left(1 - \dfrac{1}{v+1}\right)dv = \int dx + c_1$

or $v - \log(v+1) = x + c_1$

or $x + y + 1 - \log(x + y + 1 + 1) = x + c_1$

Thus, required solution is

$$y = \log(x + y + 2) + c$$

Q.34 Ans:(B)

Given differential equation $\dfrac{d^2y}{dx^2} + \dfrac{dy}{dx} - 2y = 0$

Writing D for $\dfrac{d}{dx}$, the equation reduces to

$$(D^2 + D - 2)y = 0$$

Auxiliary equation is $m^2 + m - 2 = 0$

or $(m+2)(m-1) = 0$; giving $m = -2, 1$

The solution is $y = c_1e^x + c_2e^{-2x}$

Putting $y(0) = 0,\ y'(0) = 3$

$c_1 + c_2 = 0$ (i)

$c_1 - 2c_2 = 3$ (ii)

From equations (i) and (ii), $c_2 = -1, c_1 = 1$

Thus, required solution is

$$y = e^x - e^{-2x}$$

Q.35 Ans:(B)

Given differential equation $y\dfrac{dy}{dx} + x = A$

or $ydy = (A - x)dx$

Integrating, $\int ydy = \int (A - x)dx + c_1$

or $\dfrac{y^2}{2} = Ax - \dfrac{x^2}{2}c_1$

or $x^2 + y^2 - 2Ax = 2c_1$

or $x^2 - 2Ax + y^2 = c$

This is the equation of circle of center at x-axis.

Circle of center at x-axis

Q.36 Ans:(A)

We have $L(\sin t) = \dfrac{1}{s^2+1}$

$$L(e^{-2t}\sin t) = \frac{1}{(s+2)^2+1} = \frac{1}{(s^2+4s+5)}$$

Using first shift theorem

$$L(t \times e^{-2t}\sin t) = -\frac{d}{ds}\left[\frac{1}{(s^2+4s+5}\right]$$

$$L(t \cdot e^{-2t}\sin t) = \frac{2s+4}{(s^2+4s+5)^2}$$

Q.37 Ans:(A)

Acceleration of particle $\dfrac{dv}{dt} = kx$

or $\dfrac{dv}{dt} = \dfrac{dx}{dt}\dfrac{dv}{dx} = v\dfrac{dv}{dx} = kx$

or $vdv = kxdx$

Integrating, $\int vdv = \int kxdx + c$

or $\dfrac{v^2}{2} = k\dfrac{x^2}{2} + c$

Starting velocity $= \sqrt{k}$; $\dfrac{(\sqrt{k})^2}{2} = k\dfrac{0^2}{2} + c$

$$c = \frac{k}{2}$$

The solution is $\dfrac{v^2}{2} = k\dfrac{x^2}{2} + \dfrac{k}{2}$

or $v = \sqrt{k(x^2+1)}$

The velocity of the particle at a distance 2 units form P is

$$v = \sqrt{k(2^2+1)} = \sqrt{k \times 5}$$

$$v = \sqrt{5k}$$

Q.38 Ans:(D)

Given differential equation $\dfrac{d^2y}{dx^2}+2\dfrac{dy}{dx}+y=e^{-x}\cos x$

The equation can be written as $(D^2+2D+1)y=e^{-x}\cos x$

Here auxiliary equation $m^2+2m+1=0$, giving $m=-1,-1$

Complementary function, $\text{CF}=(c_1+c_2x)e^{-x}$

Now particular integral, $\text{PI}=\dfrac{1}{D^2+2D+1}e^{-x}\cos x$

$$\text{PI}=e^{-x}\frac{1}{(D-1)^2+2(D-1)+1}\cos x$$

or $$\text{PI}=e^{-x}\frac{1}{D^2}\cos x=e^{-x}\int\int\cos x\,dx$$

or $$\text{PI}=-e^{-x}\cos x$$

The general solution is $y=\text{CF}+\text{PI}$

$$y=(c_1+c_2x)e^{-x}-e^{-x}\cos x$$

$$y=(c_1+c_2x-\cos x)e^{-x}$$

Q.39 Ans:(A)

Given differential equation $(x+y)^2\dfrac{dy}{dx}=a^2$

Let $x+y=v \quad\Rightarrow\quad \dfrac{dy}{dx}=\dfrac{dv}{dx}-1$

$$v^2\left(\frac{dv}{dx}-1\right)=a^2 \text{ or } \frac{dv}{dx}=\frac{a^2+v^2}{v^2}$$

or $$\frac{dv}{dx}=\frac{a^2+v^2}{v^2}$$

Integrating $\displaystyle\int\frac{v^2}{a^2+v^2}dv=\int dx+c$

$$v-\frac{a^2}{a}\tan^{-1}\frac{v}{a}=x+c$$

$$x+y-a\tan^{-1}\frac{x+y}{a}=x+c$$

Thus, required solution

$$y+x=a\tan\left(\frac{y-c}{a}\right)$$

Q.40 Ans:(B)

Given differential equation can be written as

$$r\frac{d^2T}{dr^2}+\frac{dT}{dr}=0$$

or $$\frac{d}{dr}\left(r\frac{dT}{dr}\right)=0$$

or $$r\frac{dT}{dr}=c_1 \quad\Rightarrow\quad dT=c_1\frac{dr}{r}$$

or $$\int dT=c_1\int\frac{dr}{r}+c_2$$

$$T=c_1\log r+c_2$$

Q41 Ans:(C)

Decay rate $\propto$ mass

$$-\frac{dm}{dt}\propto m \quad\Rightarrow\quad -\frac{dm}{dt}=k\,m$$

or $$-\frac{dm}{m}=k\,dt$$

Integrating, the above equation, we get

$$\int_{M_0}^{M_0/2}\frac{dm}{m}=-k\int_0^T dt$$

or $$\log\left(\frac{M_0/2}{M_0}\right)=-kT$$

$$T=\frac{\log 2}{k}$$

Q.42 Ans:(A)

Evaporation rate $\propto$ surface area

$$-\frac{dV}{dt}\propto A \quad\Rightarrow\quad -\frac{dV}{dt}=\lambda\ A$$

Substituting $V=\dfrac{4}{3}\pi r^3,\ A=4\pi r^2$, we have

$$-\frac{d}{dt}\left(\frac{4}{3}\pi r^3\right)=\lambda\ 4\pi r^2$$

or $$\frac{4}{3}\pi\times 3r^2\frac{dr}{dt}=-\lambda\times 4\pi r^2$$

or $$\frac{dr}{dt}=-\lambda$$

Integrating $\displaystyle\int dr=-\int\lambda\,dt$

$$r=-\lambda t+c$$

Boundary values at $t=0, r=3$ mm, and $t=1$ hr, $r=2$ mm.

From which $c=3,\ \lambda=1$

$$r=3-t$$

Q.43 Ans:(B)

Equation of circle $(x-a)^2+y^2=a^2$

$$x^2-2ax+y^2=0 \qquad \text{(i)}$$

$$2x - 2a + 2y\frac{dy}{dx} = 0 \qquad \text{(Multiplying by } x)$$

$$2xy\frac{dy}{dx} + 2x^2 - 2ax = 0 \qquad \text{(ii)}$$

From Equation (i) and (ii), $2xy\frac{dy}{dx} + 2x^2 - x^2 - y^2 = 0$

$$2xy\frac{dy}{dx} + (x^2 - y^2) = 0$$

Q.44 Ans:(A)

$$\frac{dn}{dt} \propto n \Rightarrow \frac{dn}{dt} = \lambda n \quad \Rightarrow \frac{dn}{n} = \lambda dt$$

Integrating $\int_n^{2n} \frac{dn}{n} = \int_0^2 \lambda dt$

From which $\lambda = \frac{\log 2}{2}$

$$\int_n^{3n} \frac{dn}{n} = \frac{\log 2}{2}\int_0^T dt$$

or $\log 3 = \frac{\log 2}{2} \times T$

$$T = 2\frac{\log 3}{\log 2}$$

Q.45 Ans:(B)

Differential equation $\frac{d^2y}{dx^2} + 4\frac{dy}{dx} + 3y = 3e^{2x}$

or $(D^2 + 4D + 3)y = 3e^{2x}$

Particular integral, $\text{PI} = \frac{3e^{2x}}{D^2 + 4D + 3}$

$$\text{PI} = \frac{3e^{2x}}{2^2 + 4 \times 2 + 3} = \frac{3e^{2x}}{15}$$

$$\text{PI} = \frac{e^{2x}}{5}$$

Q.46 Ans:(C)

$$L(\sin 2t) = \frac{2}{s^2 + 2^2}$$

Applying Laplace theorem, we get

$$L\{t^n f(t)\} = (-1)^n \frac{d^n}{ds^n} F(s)$$

$$L(t \sin 2t) = -\frac{d}{ds}\left(\frac{2}{s^2 + 2^2}\right) = \frac{4s}{(s^2 + 2^2)^2}$$

$$L(t \sin 2t) = \frac{4s}{(s^2 + 2^2)^2}$$

Q.47 Ans:(A)

Given: $f(t) = \sin^2 t$

We have $f(0) = 0$, $f'(t) = 2\sin t \cos t = \sin 2t$

[Theorem $L(f') = sL(f) - f(0)$]

or $L(\sin 2t) = \frac{2}{s^2 + 4} = sLf(t)$

or $\frac{2}{s^2 + 4} = sL(\sin^2 t)$

$$L(\sin^2 t) = \frac{2}{s(s^2 + 4)}$$

Q.48 Ans:(B)

$$L^{-1}\frac{1}{(s^2 + 4s)} = L^{-1}\frac{1}{s(s+4)}$$

$$= \frac{1}{4}\left[L^{-1}\left(\frac{1}{s}\right) - L^{-1}\left(\frac{1}{(s+4)}\right)\right]$$

$$L^{-1}\frac{1}{(s^2 + 4s)} = \frac{1}{4}(1 - e^{-4t})$$

Q.49 Ans:(C)

Given differential equation

$$x\frac{d^2y}{dx^2} + 2\frac{dy}{dx} = 6x + \frac{1}{x}$$

Multiplying by x, the equation reduces

$$x^2\frac{d^2y}{dx^2} + 2x\frac{dy}{dx} = 6x^2 + 1$$

Let $x = e^t$

Substituting $x^2\frac{d^2y}{dx^2} = \frac{d^2y}{dt^2} - \frac{dy}{dt}$, $x\frac{dy}{dx} = \frac{dy}{dt}$ and $x^2 = e^{2t}$,

we have

$$\frac{d^2y}{dt^2} - \frac{dy}{dt} + 2\frac{dy}{dt} = 6e^{2t} + 1$$

$$\frac{d^2y}{dt^2} + \frac{dy}{dt} = 6e^{2t} + 1$$

Q.50 Ans:(A)

The given differential equation can be written as

$$(D^2 + aD - 2a^2)y = 0$$

Auxiliary equation $m^2 + am - 2a^2 = 0$

or $(m + 2a)(m - a) = 0$

Roots are $m = a, -2a$

The solution is $y = c_1 e^{at} + c_2 e^{-2at}$

Putting boundary conditions $y(0)=6,\ y'(0)=0$

$$c_1 + c_2 = 6 \quad \text{(i)}$$

$$ac_1 - 2ac_2 = 0 \quad \text{(ii)}$$

Solving Equations (i) and (ii); $c_1 = 4,\ c_2 = 2$

Thus, required solution is

$$y = 4e^{at} + 2e^{-2at}$$

Q.51 Ans:(D)

The given differential equation can be written as

$$(D^2+9)y = \sin^3 x$$

Auxiliary equation $m^3 + 9 = 0$, giving $m = 3i, -3i$

Complementary function,

$$\text{CF} = c_1 \cos 3x + c_2 \sin 3x = A \sin(3x+B)$$

Particular integral, $\text{PI} = \dfrac{1}{D^2+9}\sin^3 x$

or $\text{PI} = \dfrac{1}{D^2+9}\left(\dfrac{3}{4}\sin x - \dfrac{1}{4}\sin 3x\right)$

or $\text{PI} = \dfrac{3}{4}\dfrac{1}{D^2+9}\sin x - \dfrac{1}{4}\dfrac{1}{D^2+9}\sin 3x$

or $\text{PI} = \dfrac{3}{4}\times\dfrac{\sin x}{-1^2+9} - \dfrac{1}{4}\times\dfrac{x\cos 3x}{2\times 3}$

or $\text{PI} = \dfrac{3}{32}\sin x + \dfrac{x}{24}\cos 3x$

Thus, required solution is $y = \text{CF} + \text{PI}$

$$y = A\sin(3x+B) + \frac{3}{32}\sin x + \frac{x}{24}\cos 3x$$

Q.52 Ans:(A)

Given differential equation $y(t) + \ddot{y}(t) = 0$

Writing D for $\dfrac{d}{dx}$, the equation reduces to $(1+D^2)y=0$

Auxiliary equation $1 + m^2 = 0$

Root are $m = -i, i$

Solution is $y = A\cos t + B\sin t$

Putting initial conditions $\dot{y}(0) = 1$ and $y(0) = 1$

$$1 = A\cos 0 + B\sin 0 \ \Rightarrow\ A = 1$$

$$1 = -A\sin 0 + B\cos 0 \Rightarrow\ B = 1$$

Thus, the complete solution is $y = \cos t + \sin t$

$$y = \sqrt{2}\sin\left(t + \frac{\pi}{4}\right)$$

Maximum value of y is

$$y_{\max} = \sqrt{2}$$

Q.53 Ans:(D)

Given differential equation $\dfrac{d^2y}{dx^2} - 5\dfrac{dy}{dx} + 6y = 0$

Writing D for $\dfrac{d}{dx}$, the equation reduces to

$(D^2 - 5D + 6)y = 0$

Auxiliary equation $m^2 - 5m + 6 = 0$, giving $m = 2, 3$

Thus, the solution is

$$y = A\,e^{2x} + B\,e^{3x}$$

Q.54 Ans:(A)

The given differential equation can be written as

$$(D^2+1)y = 0$$

Auxiliary equation $m^2 + 1 = 0$

Root are $m = i, -i$

The solution is $y = c_1\cos x + c_2 \sin x$

Putting given conditions $y(0) = 1,\ y(\pi/2) = 2$

$$c_1 + c_2 \times 0 = 1 \quad \Rightarrow \quad c_1 = 1$$

$$c_1 \times 0 + c_2 = 2 \quad \Rightarrow \quad c_2 = 2$$

Thus, the solution is

$$y = \cos x + 2\sin x$$

Q.55 Ans:(C)

$$x = A\cos(mt - \alpha) \quad \text{(i)}$$

Differentiating two time with respect to t

$$\frac{dx}{dt} = -mA\sin(mt-\alpha)$$

$$\frac{d^2x}{dt^2} = -m^2 A\cos(mt-\alpha) \quad \text{(ii)}$$

From Equation (i) and (ii), we get

$$\frac{d^2x}{dt^2} = -m^2 x$$

Q.56 Ans:(C)

The given differential equation can be written as

$$(D^2 + (3i-1)D - 3i)y = 0$$

Auxiliary equation $m^2 + (3i-1)m - 3i = 0$

$$m^2 + 3im - m - 3i = 0$$

or $(m-1)(m+3i) = 0$

Roots are $m = 1, -3i$

Thus, the solution is

$$y = c_1 e^{x} + c_2 e^{-3ix}$$

Q.57 Ans:(C)

Given differential equation $\dfrac{dy}{dx} = \dfrac{y}{x} + \tan\dfrac{y}{x}$

Putting $y = vx \Rightarrow x\dfrac{dv}{dx} + v = v + \tan v$

or $\quad x\dfrac{dv}{dx} = \tan v$

Integrating $\displaystyle\int \frac{dv}{\tan v} = \int \frac{dx}{x} + c_1$

or $\quad \ln(\sin v) = \ln(x) + c_1$

or $\quad \sin v = cx$

$$\sin\left(\frac{y}{x}\right) = cx$$

Q.58 Ans:(C)

$$L(\sin^2 2t) = L\left\{\frac{1-\cos 4t}{2}\right\}$$

or $\quad L(\sin^2 2t) = L\left(\dfrac{1}{2}\right) - L\left(\dfrac{1}{2}\cos 4t\right)$

$$L(\sin^2 2t) = \frac{s}{2} - \frac{s}{s^2+4^2}$$

Q.59 Ans:(D)

The given differential equation can be written as $\dfrac{dx}{dt} + \left(\dfrac{1}{t}\right)x = 1$ [which is a linear differential equation]

Integrating factor, $\quad \text{IF} = e^{\int \frac{1}{t}dt} = e^{\ln t} = t$

The solution is $\quad x(\text{IF}) = \int Q(\text{IF})dt + c$

or $\quad xt = \int 1 \times t\, dt + c$

or $\quad xt = \dfrac{t^2}{2} + c$

or $\quad x = \dfrac{t}{2} + \dfrac{c}{t}$

Putting initial condition $x(1) = 0.5$

$$0.5 = \frac{1}{2} + \frac{c}{1} \Rightarrow c = 0$$

Thus, the required solution is

$$x = \frac{t}{2}$$

Q.60 Ans:(A)

Given differential equation $\quad x'(t) = -3x(t)$

$$\frac{dx}{dt} = -3x \quad \text{or} \quad \frac{dx}{x} = -3dt$$

Integrating $\displaystyle\int \frac{dx}{x} = -\int 3dt + c_1$

or $\quad \ln x = -3t + c_1$

or $\quad x = ce^{-3t}$

Putting initial condition $\quad x(0) = x_0$

$$x_0 = ce^{-3\times 0} \Rightarrow c = x_0$$

Thus, the solution is

$$x = x_0 e^{-3t}$$

Q.61 Ans:(D)

Given differential equation $\quad \dfrac{dy}{dx} = -\dfrac{x}{y}$

or $\quad y\,dy + x\,dx = 0$

Integrating, we have $\int y\,dy + \int x\,dx = c_1$

or $\quad x^2 + y^2 = 2c_1$

or $\quad x^2 + y^2 = c$

Putting initial value $x = 1,\ y = \sqrt{3}$

$$1^2 + (\sqrt{3})^2 = c \Rightarrow c = 4$$

The complete solution is

$$x^2 + y^2 = 4$$

Q.62 Ans:(A)

Newton's law of cooling $\quad \dfrac{d\theta}{dt} = -k(\theta - \theta_0)$

or $\quad \dfrac{d\theta}{\theta - \theta_0} = -k\,dt$

Integrating $\displaystyle\int \frac{d\theta}{\theta - \theta_0} = -\int k\,dt + c_1$

or $\quad \ln(\theta - \theta_0) = -kt + c_1$

or $\quad \theta - \theta_0 = ce^{-kt}$

Putting given temperature $\theta_0 = 25°\text{C}$, and $t = 0, \theta = 60°\text{C}$

$$60 - 25 = ce^{-k\times 0} \Rightarrow c = 35$$

$$\theta = 25 + 35e^{-kt}$$

Temperature of body becomes 40°C after 15 minutes

$$40 = 25 + 35e^{-k\times 15}$$

$$e^{-15k} = \frac{3}{7}$$

Now temperature at $t = 30$ minutes, $\theta = 25 + 35\,e^{-k\times 30}$

$$\theta = 25 + 35(e^{-15k})^2 = 25 + 35 \times \left(\frac{3}{7}\right)^2$$

$$\theta = 31.5°\text{C}$$

Q.63 Ans:(D)

Given differential equation $\dfrac{dy}{dx} = x^2 y$

or $\dfrac{dy}{y} = x^2 dx$

After integrating, we get $\ln y = \dfrac{x^3}{3} + c$

or $y = c_1 e^{\frac{x^3}{3}}$

Now at $x = 0$, $y = 1$; $1 = c_1 e^0 \Rightarrow c_1 = 1$

$$y = e^{\frac{x^3}{3}}$$

Q.64 Ans:(C)

$\dfrac{dV}{dt} \propto -A$ or $\dfrac{dV}{dt} = -k\,A$

Substituting $V = \dfrac{4}{3}\pi r^3$ and $A = 4\pi r^3$

$$\frac{d}{dt}\left(\frac{4}{3}\pi r^3\right) = -k\,(4\pi r^3)$$

$$\frac{dr}{dt} = -k \quad \Rightarrow \quad r = -kt + c$$

Given conditions (a) $t = 0$, $d = 2$ cm (b) $t = 3$ months, $d = 1$cm

$$1 = -k \times 0 + c \quad \Rightarrow \quad c = 1$$

$$0.5 = -k \times 3 + c \;\Rightarrow\; k = \frac{0.5}{3}$$

Substituting $k = \dfrac{0.5}{3}$, $c = 1$, we have

$$r = -\frac{0.5}{3}t + 1$$

Let T be time for completely evaporation $(r = 0)$ of ball

$$0 = -\frac{0.5}{3}T + 1$$

or $T = \dfrac{3}{0.5}$

$$T = 6 \text{ months}$$

Q.65 Ans:(D)

Growth rate of culture $\dfrac{dN}{dt} \propto N$

$$\frac{dN}{dt} = kN$$

or $\dfrac{dN}{N} = kdt$

Integrating $\displaystyle\int_{100}^{N} \frac{dN}{N} = \int_0^t kdt$

or $N = 100\,e^{kt}$

$N = 332$ in time $t = 1$ hr $\quad 332 = 100\,e^{k\times 1}$

$e^k = 3.32$

N after $1\frac{1}{2}$ hr, $\quad N = 100\,e^{k\times 1.5} = 100\,(e^k)^{1.5}$

$N = 100\,e^{k\times 1.5} = 100 \times 3.32^{1.5} = 605$

$$N = 605$$

4 Complex Variables Numerical Methods Probability and Statistics

GATE Mechanical Engg.

GATE Syllabus

Complex variables: Analytic functions; Cauchy-Riemann equations; Cauchy's integral theorem and integral formula; Taylor and Laurent series. Probability and Statistics: Definitions of probability, sampling theorems, conditional probability; Mean, median, mode and standard deviation; Random variables, Binomial, Poisson and Normal distributions. Numerical Methods: Numerical solutions of linear and non-linear algebraic equations; Integration by Trapezoidal and Simpson's rules; Single and multi-step methods for differential equations.

Chapter Outline

4.1 KEY CONCEPTS AND FORMULAS

Basic Concepts of Complex Analysis

Complex Numbers

A complex number z is an ordered pair (x, y) of real numbers x and y.

$z \equiv (x, y) = x + i\,y$; Re $z = x$ (Real part), Im $z = y$ (Imaginary part) and $i = \sqrt{-1}$ (Imaginary part)

Addition and Subtraction of Complex Numbers

Let $z_1 = x_1 + iy_1$ and $z_2 = x_2 + iy_2$, then

$$z_1 + z_2 = (x_1 + x_2) + i(y_1 + y_2)$$

and $$z_1 - z_2 = (x_1 - x_2) + i(y_1 - y_2)$$

Multiplication of Complex Numbers

$$z_1\, z_2 = (x_1\, x_2) - y_1\, y_2 + i(x_1 y_2 + x_2 y_1)$$

Division of Complex Numbers

$$z = \frac{z_1}{z_2} = x + iy,$$

where $x = \dfrac{x_1 x_2 + y_1 y_2}{x_2^{\,2} + y_2^{\,2}}, \quad y = \dfrac{x_2 y_1 + x_1 y_2}{x_2^{\,2} + y_2^{\,2}}, \quad z_2 \neq 0$

Practical rule $z = \dfrac{z_1}{z_2} = \dfrac{x_1 + iy_1}{x_2 + iy_2}$

$$z = \left(\frac{x_1 + iy_1}{x_2 - iy_2}\right) \times \left(\frac{x_2 - iy_2}{x_2 + iy_2}\right) = x + iy$$

Complex Conjugate Number

The conjugate of the number $z = x + iy$ is $\bar{z} = x - iy$

$$\text{Re } z = x = \frac{1}{2}(z + \bar{z}) \text{ and } \text{Im } z = x = \frac{1}{2i}(z - \bar{z})$$

Polar Form of Complex Numbers

Let (x, y) be the coordinate in cartesian coordinate system and (r, θ) be the coordinate in polar coordinates, then $x = r\cos\theta, \quad y = r\sin\theta$

$\therefore \quad z = x + iy = r(\cos\theta + i\sin\theta)$

Here

$r = |z| = \sqrt{x^2 + y^2} = \sqrt{z\bar{z}}$ (absolute value/modulus of z),

$\theta = \arg z = \tan^{-1}\dfrac{y}{x}$ (Argument of z)

De Moivre's Formula

$$(\cos\theta + i\sin\theta)^n = \cos n\theta + i\sin n\theta$$

Analyticity

A function $f(z)$ is said to be analytic at a point z_0 if f is differentiable not only at z_0 but at every point of some neitherhood of z_0.

Cauchy Riemann (C-R) Equations

If $f(z) = u(x, y) + iv(x, y)$ is differentiable at z then at this point the first order partial derivatives of u and v exist and satisfy the Cauchy Riemann equations.

$$\frac{\partial u}{\partial x} = \frac{\partial v}{\partial y} \text{ and } \frac{\partial u}{\partial y} = -\frac{\partial v}{\partial x} \quad \text{Cartesian coordinate}$$

$$\frac{\partial u}{\partial r} = \frac{1}{r}\frac{\partial v}{\partial \theta} \text{ and } \frac{\partial v}{\partial r} = -\frac{1}{r}\frac{\partial u}{\partial \theta} \quad \text{Polar coordinate}$$

Cauchy's Integral Theorem

If $f(z)$ is analytic in a simply connected domain D. Let C be any simple closed curve in D enclosing any point z_o in D. Then

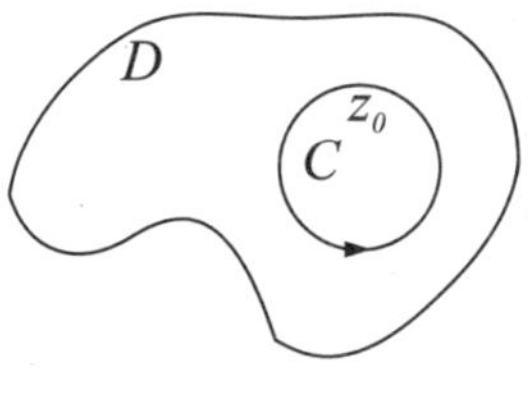

$$\oint_C \frac{f(z)}{z - z_0} dz = 2\pi i f(z_0)$$

where C is traversed in counter clockwise direction.

$$f^n(z_0) = \frac{n!}{2\pi i}\oint_C \frac{f(z)}{(z - z_0)^{n+1}} dz \qquad n = 1, 2, \ldots$$

Taylor's Series (Theorem)

A function $f(z)$ which is analytic at all points within a circle C with centre at z_0 and of radius R can be represented uniquely as a convergent power series in C known as the *Taylor's series* given by

$$f(z) = \sum_{n=0}^{\infty} a_n (z - z_0)^n \quad \text{where} \quad a_n = \frac{f^n(z_0)}{n!}$$

Laurent Series

Let $f(z)$ be analytic on two concentric circle C_1 and C_2 with centre z_0 and radii R_1 and R_2 and in the annulus region $R_1 < |z - z_0| < R_2$. Then $f(z)$ is uniquely represented by a convergent Laurent series given by

$$f(z) = \sum_{z=0}^{\infty} a_n (z - z_0)^n + \sum_{z=1}^{\infty} \frac{b_n}{(z - z_0)^n}$$

Probability

Experiment: An experiment is the process of observing a phenomenon that has variation in its outcomes.

Sample space : The sample space associated with an experiment is the collection of all possible distinct outcomes of the experiment. It is denoted by S.

Element: Each outcome of an experiment is called an element (simple event, or elementary event) of the sample space.

Event: An event is the collection of elementary outcomes possessing a designated feature.

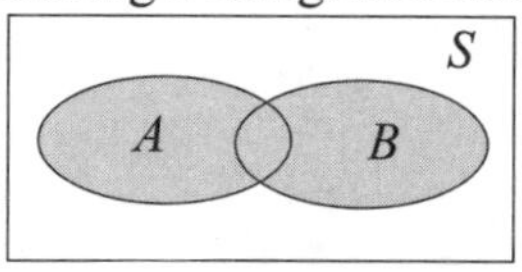

$A \cup B$

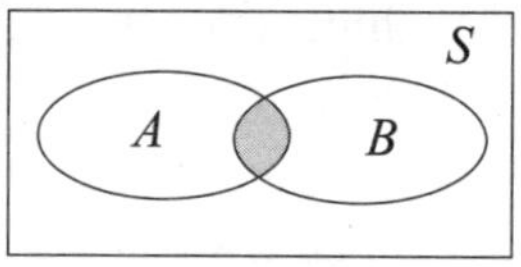

$A \cap B$

Probability: It is a number measure of uncertainty with value from 0 to 1. A value close to 0 indicates an event is extremely unlikely and a value close to 1 indicates an event is very likely, with the intermediate value interpreted accordingly.

An experiment has n mutually exclusive, equally likely and exhaustive cases, out of which m are favourable to the happening of the event A, then the probability of the happening of A is denoted by $P(A)$ and is defined as:

$$P(A) = \frac{m}{n} = \frac{\text{Number cases favourable to } A}{\text{Total (exhaustive) number of cases}}$$

Axioms of Probability

Axiom 1: $0 \le P(A) \le 1$ for each event A in S.

Axiom 2: $P(S) = 1$.

Axiom 3: For mutually exclusive event A and B $(A \cap B = \phi)$;

$$P(A \cup B) = P(A) + P(B).$$

Basic Theorem for Probability

Complementation rule

$$P(\bar{A}) = 1 - P(A)$$

Addition rule for mutually exclusive events

$$P(A_1 \cup A_2 \cup A_3 \cup ... A_m)$$
$$= P(A_1) + P(A_2) + P(A_3) + ... + P(A_m)$$

Addition rule for arbitrary events

$$P(A \cup B) = P(A) + P(B) - P(A \cap B)$$

Conditional Probability

(i) The conditional probability of an event B given an event A, denoted as $P\left(\frac{B}{A}\right)$, is

$$P\left(\frac{B}{A}\right) = \frac{P(A \cap B)}{P(A)}$$

(ii) The conditional probability of an event A given an event B is

$$P\left(\frac{A}{B}\right) = \frac{P(A \cap B)}{P(B)}$$

Multiplication rule

$$P(A \cap B) = P(A) P\left(\frac{B}{A}\right)$$

$$P(A \cap B) = P(A) P(B) \quad \text{(Independent events)}$$

Arithmetic Mean (AM)

(i) $\text{A.M.} = \frac{\Sigma x}{n}$

(ii) $\text{A.M.} = A + \frac{\Sigma d}{n}$ (For an individual series)

where $d = x - A$, where A is the assumed mean.

(iii) $\text{A.M.} = \frac{\Sigma f x}{\Sigma f}$ (For a frequency distribution)

(iv) $\text{A.M.} = A + \frac{\Sigma f d}{\Sigma f}$, (Short cut method)

where $d = x - A$, where A is the assumed mean.

(v) $\text{A.M.} = A + \left(\frac{\Sigma f u}{\Sigma f}\right) h$ (Step deviation method)

where A is the assumed mean and $u = \frac{x - A}{h}$.

Weighted Arithmetic Mean

If $w_1, w_2, w_3, ..., w_n$ are the weights assigned to the values $x_1, x_2, x_3, ..., x_n$ respectively, then the weighted average is

$$\text{Weighted arithmetic mean} = \frac{w_1 x_1 + w_2 x_2 + ... + w_n x_n}{w_1 + w_2 + ... + w_n}$$

Median

Median is defined as the middle most or the central value of the variable in a set of observations, when the observations are arranged either in ascending or in descending order of their magnitudes. It divides the arranged series in two equal parts. Median is a position average, whereas, the arithmetic mean is the calculated average. When a series consists of an number of terms, median is the arithmetic mean of the two central items. It is generally denoted by M.

When the series is continuous. In this case, the data is given in the form of a frequency table with class-interval, etc., and following formula is used to calculate the median.

$$M = L + \frac{\frac{n}{2} - C}{f} \times i$$

where

L = lower limit of the class in which the median lies

n = total number of frequencies, $n = \Sigma f$

f = frequency of the class in which the median lies

C = cumulative frequency of the class preceding the median class

i = width of class-interval of the class in which the median lies

Mode

Mode is defined as that value in a series which occurs most frequently. In a frequency distribution, mode is that variable which has the maximum frequency.

$$\text{Mode} = l + \frac{l_m - l_1}{2f_m - f_1 - f_2} \times i$$

Where

l = lower limit of the modal class

i = width of the modal class

f_1 = frequency of the class preceding modal class

f_m = frequency of the modal class

f_2 = frequency of the class succeeding modal class.

The above formula fails to give the mode. In this case, the modal value lies in a class other than the one containing maximum frequency. In such cases, we take help of the following formula:

Mode $= l + \frac{f_2}{f_1 + f_2} \times i$, where l, f_1, f_2, i have usual meaning.

Geometric Mean (*G*)

$$G = (x_1, x_2, x_3, ..., x_n)^{\frac{1}{n}}.$$

Geometric Mean for Frequency Distribution

Geometric Mean of n values $x_1, x_2, x_3, ..., x_n$ of a variate x occurring with frequency $f_1, f_2, f_3, ..., f_n$ respectively is given by $G = [x^{f_1}.x_2^{f_2}.x_3^{f_3}...x_n^{f_n}]^{\frac{1}{n}}$

or $$G = \text{anti-log}\left\{\frac{\sum_{i=1}^{n} f_i \log x_i}{n}\right\}$$

Harmonic Mean

The harmonic mean of n items $x_1, x_2, x_3, ..., x_n$ is

$$\text{Harmonic mean} = \frac{n}{\frac{1}{x_1}+\frac{1}{x_2}+\frac{1}{x_3}+...+\frac{1}{x_n}}$$

$$\text{Harmonic mean} = \frac{f_1+f_2+f_3+...+f_n}{\frac{f_1}{x_1}+\frac{f_2}{x_2}+\frac{f_3}{x_3}+...+\frac{f_n}{x_n}}$$

Measures of Dispersion

The degree to which numerical data tend to spread about an average value is called the *dispersion of the data.* Measures of dispersion are (i) Range (ii) Mean deviation (ii) Standard deviation.

Range

$$\text{Range} = L - S \text{ and coefficient of range} = \frac{L-S}{L+S}$$

where $L =$ largest value; $S =$ smallest value.

Standard Deviation (σ)

The positive square root of the average of squared deviations of all observations taken from their mean is called *standard deviation.*

The square of the standard deviation is called variance (σ^2).

$$\sigma = \sqrt{\frac{(x-\bar{x})^2}{n}} = \sqrt{\frac{\Sigma d^2}{n}}$$

where $d = x - \bar{x}$ (For ungrouped data)

$$\sigma = \sqrt{\frac{\Sigma d^2}{n} - \left(\frac{\Sigma d}{n}\right)^2}, \text{ where } d = x - A, A = \text{assumed mean}$$

$$\sigma = \sqrt{\frac{\Sigma f(x-\bar{x})^2}{n}}; \qquad \text{(For grouped data)}$$

Binomial Distribution

Probability of r successes is $P(r) = {}^nC_r\, q^{n-r} p^r$,

where $p =$ probability of success and $q =$ probability of failure $= 1 - p$

Mean of Binomial distribution $= np$

Variance of Binomial distribution $= npq$

Poisson Distribution

Probability of r successes is $P(r) = \frac{e^{-m} m^r}{r!}$

Mean of Poisson distribution $\mu = m$

Variance $\sigma^2 = m$

Standard deviation $= \sqrt{\text{Variance}} = \sqrt{m}$

Conditions under which Poisson distribution can be derived from Binomial distribution

(i) Probability of the occurrence (P) of the event is very small.

(ii) Number of trials n is very-very large.

(iii) np is a finite quantity (say $np = m$, m is called the parameter of the Poisson distribution)

Normal Distribution

The normal distribution is also known as *Gaussion distribution* or a *normal curve.* It is a continuous distribution. Normal distribution is also a limiting form of the Binomial distribution under the following conditions:

(i) Number of trials(n) is infinitely large.

(ii) Neither p nor q is very small, i.e., p and q are fairly near equal.

The probability function of the normal distribution with mean μ and standard deviation σ is given by

$$P(x) = \frac{1}{\sigma\sqrt{2\pi}} e^{-\frac{(x-\mu)^2}{2\sigma^2}}, \quad -\infty \le x \le \infty$$

Standard Normal Distribution

A random variable z which has a normal distribution with mean $\mu = 0$ and standard deviation $\sigma = 1$ is said to have a standard normal distribution. Its density function is given by

$$f(z) = \frac{1}{\sqrt{2\pi}} e^{-\frac{z^2}{2}}, \quad -\infty < z < \infty$$

Numerical Solution of Linear Algebraic Equations

An $(m \times n)$ system of equations having the form

$$\left.\begin{aligned} a_{11}x_1 + a_{12}x_2 + \ldots + a_{1n}x_n &= b_1 \\ a_{21}x_1 + a_{22}x_2 + \ldots + a_{2n}x_n &= b_2 \\ \ldots\ldots\ldots\ldots\ldots\ldots\ldots\ldots\ldots \\ a_{m1}x_1 + a_{m2}x_2 + \ldots + a_{mn}x_n &= b_m \end{aligned}\right\}$$

Can be represented by the matrix form $AX = B$,

$$\text{Where } A = \begin{bmatrix} a_{11} & a_{12} & \cdots & a_{1n} \\ a_{21} & a_{22} & \cdots & a_{2n} \\ \cdot & \cdot & & \cdot \\ \cdot & \cdot & \cdots & \cdot \\ \cdot & \cdot & & \cdot \\ a_{m1} & a_{m2} & \cdots & a_{mn} \end{bmatrix}, X = \begin{bmatrix} x_1 \\ x_2 \\ \cdot \\ \cdot \\ \cdot \\ x_n \end{bmatrix} \text{ and } B = \begin{bmatrix} b_1 \\ b_2 \\ \cdot \\ \cdot \\ \cdot \\ b_m \end{bmatrix}$$

(i) If $B \neq 0$, that is, at least one of the elements $b_1, b_2, \ldots, b_m$ is not zero, then the system of equations is called *non-homogeneous.*

(b) If $B = 0$, then the system of equation is called *homogeneous.*

Matrix Inversion Method

System of equation in matrix form is given by $AX = B$

When A is a non-singular matrix, then A^{-1} exists and hence $A\,A^{-1} = I$

$$A^{-1}A\,X = A^{-1}B$$

$$X = A^{-1}B = \frac{\text{adj}A}{|A|}B$$

Cramer's Rule

If a system of n linear equations in n variables has a coefficient matrix with a non-zero determinant $|A|$, then the solution to the system ($AX = B$) is given by

$$x_i = \frac{|A_i|}{|A|}, \quad i = 1, 2, 3, \ldots, n$$

Where $|A_i|$ is the determinant of the matrix A_i obtained by replacing the ith column of A by the right hand side column vector B.

(i) When $|A| \neq 0$, the system of equations is consistent and the unique solution is obtained.

(ii) When $|A| = 0$, and one or more of $|A_i|$, $i = 1, 2, 3, \ldots, n$ are not zero, then the system of equation has no solution, that is the system is inconsistent.

(iii) When $|A| = 0$, and all $|A_i| = 0$, $i = 1, 2, 3, \ldots, n$ then the system of equations is consistent and has infinite number of solutions.

Gauss Elimination Method (E Row Transformations Method)

To solve the equation $AX = B$, we perform elementary row operations on both A and B so that the matrix A be reduced to triangular form.

Gauss-Seidal Iterative Method

This method is applicable only when each equation of the system contains one coefficient much larger than the other in the equation and the larger coefficients in different equations correspond to the different variables. Such a system is known as *diagonal system.* It can be arranged in such a way that the largest coefficients lie on the diagonal.

Consider a system of 3 non-homogenous linear equations in 3 variables.

$$\left.\begin{aligned} a_{11}x_1 + a_{12}x_2 + a_{13}x_3 &= b_1 \\ a_2x_1 + a_{22}x_2 + a_{23}x_3 &= b_2 \\ a_{31}x_1 + a_{32}x_2 + a_{33}x_3 &= b_3 \end{aligned}\right\} \quad (4.1)$$

Assuming that x_1, x_2, x_3 respectively have largest coefficients in the 1st, 2nd, 3rd equations of (4.1), i.e., a_{11}, a_{22}, a_{33} are largest (4.1). We can write the system (4.1) as

$$\left.\begin{aligned} x_1 &= \frac{1}{a_{11}}[b_1 - a_{12}x_2 - a_{13}x_3] \\ x_2 &= \frac{1}{a_{22}}[b_2 - a_{21}x_1 - a_{23}x_3] \\ x_3 &= \frac{1}{a_{33}}[b_3 - a_{31}x_1 - a_{32}x_2] \end{aligned}\right\} \quad (4.2)$$

For the first iteration, starting from $x_2 = 0, x_3 = 0$, we have

$$\left.\begin{aligned} x_1^{(1)} &= \frac{1}{a_{11}}b_1 \\ x_2^{(1)} &= \frac{1}{a_{22}}[b_2 - a_{21}x_1^{(1)} - 0] \\ x_3^{(1)} &= \frac{1}{a_{33}}[b_3 - a_{31}x_1^{(1)} - a_{32}x_2^{(1)}] \end{aligned}\right\} \quad (4.3)$$

For the second iteration, we have

$$\left.\begin{aligned} x_1^{(2)} &= \frac{1}{a_{11}}[b_1 - a_{12}x_2^{(1)} - a_{13}x_3^{(1)}] \\ x_2^{(2)} &= \frac{1}{a_{22}}[b_2 - a_{21}x_1^{(2)} - a_{23}x_3^{(1)}] \\ x_3^{(2)} &= \frac{1}{a_{33}}[b_3 - a_{31}x_1^{(2)} - a_{32}x_2^{(2)}] \end{aligned}\right\} \quad (4.4)$$

Similar, for the third iteration, we have

$$\left.\begin{aligned} x_1^{(3)} &= \frac{1}{a_{11}}[b_1 - a_{12}x_2^{(2)} - a_{13}x_3^{(2)}] \\ x_2^{(3)} &= \frac{1}{a_{22}}[b_2 - a_{21}x_1^{(3)} - a_{33}x_3^{(2)}] \\ x_3^{(3)} &= \frac{1}{a_{33}}[b_3 - a_{31}x_1^{(3)} - a_{32}x_2^{(3)}] \end{aligned}\right\} \quad (4.5)$$

And so on, so forth, until we get the roots within the desired agree of accuracy.

Bisection Method

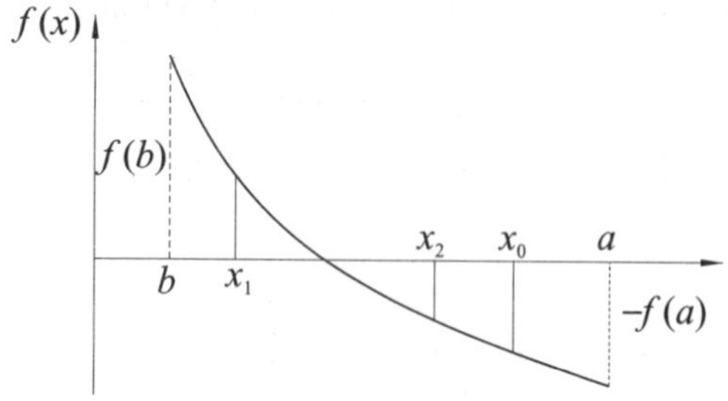

This method is based on the intermediate value theorem which states that if a function $f(x)$ is continuous between a and b, $f(a)$ and $f(b)$ are of opposite signs than there exists at least one root between a and b.

Working rule

(i) Find $f(a)$ and $f(b)$

(ii) Let $f(a)$ be negative and $f(b)$ be positive, then take $\alpha = \frac{a+b}{2}$

(iii) If $f(\alpha) = 0$, then α is a required root. If $f(\alpha) > 0$ then roots lie between a and α.

If $f(\alpha) < 0$ then roots lies between α and b.

(iv) Repeat the process until we get the root correct up to desired level of accuracy.

Regula-Falsi Method

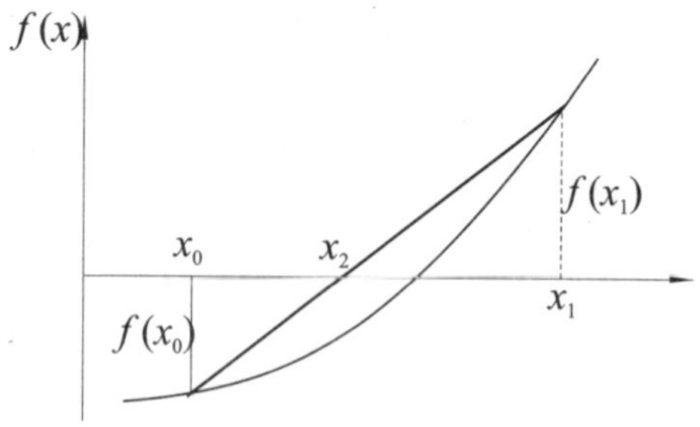

If the root $f(x) = 0$ belongs to the interval (x_0, x_1), $f(x_0)$ and $f(x_1)$ are of opposite sign [say $f(x_0) < 0$, $f(x_1) > 0$, then

$$\frac{f(x_1)}{x_1 - x_2} = \frac{f(x_0)}{x_2 - x_0}$$

or $$x_2 = \frac{x_0 f(x_1) - x_1 f(x_0)}{f(x_1) - f(x_0)}$$

$$x_{n+1} = \frac{x_{n-1} f(x_n) - x_n f(x_{n-1})}{f(x_n) - f(x_{n-1})}$$

Newton Raphson Method

Let x_0 be an approximate root of $f(x) = 0$ and let $x_1 = x_0 + h$ be the correct root so that $f(x_1) = 0$.

Expanding $f(x_0 + h) = 0$ by Taylor's series, we obtain

$$f(x_0 + h) = f(x_0) + h f'(x_0) + \frac{h^2}{2!} f'(x_0) + \ldots$$

Neglecting second and high order derivatives

$$f(x_0) + h f'(x_0) = 0$$

which gives $h = -\frac{f(x_0)}{f'(x_0)}$

A better approximation than x_0 is therefore given by x_1

$$x_1 = x_0 - \frac{f(x_0)}{f'(x_0)}$$

Successive approximation are $x_2, x_3, x_4, \ldots, x_{n+1}$, where

$$x_{n+1} = x_n - \frac{f(x_n)}{f'(x_n)} \quad \text{Newton Raphson formula}$$

Integration by Trapezoidal Rule and Simpson's Rule

Trapezoidal rule

Let $y = f(x)$ be a function defined on $[a, b]$ which is subdivided into n equal sub-intervals each of width h so that $b - a = nh$, then

$$\int_{x_0}^{x_0+nh} f(x)dx = \frac{h}{2}[y_0 + 2(y_1 + y_2 + \ldots + y_{n-1}) + y_n]$$

where n is any positive integer and y_n is the value of $f(x)$ for $x = a + nh$.

Simpson's $\frac{1}{3}$ Rule

Let $y = f(x)$ be a function defined on $[a, b]$ which is divided into n (even number) equal parts of width h so that $b - a = nh$ and y_n is the value of $f(x)$, then for $x = a + nh$, then

$$\int_{x_0}^{x_0+nh} f(x)\,dx$$

$$= \frac{h}{3}[y_0 + 4(y_1 + y_3 + \ldots + y_{n-1}) + 2(y_2 + y_4 + \ldots + y_{n-2}) + y_n]$$

Picard's Iterative Method

Differential equation $\frac{dy}{dx} = f(x, y)$ and initial value $y(x_0) = y_0$

On integration $\int_{y_0}^{y=y^{(1)}} dy = \int_{x_0}^{x} f(x, y_0)\, dx$

First approximation $y^{(1)} = y_0 + \int_{x_0}^{x} f(x, y_0)\, dx$

Second approximation $y^{(2)} = y_0 + \int_{x_0}^{x} f(x, y^{(1)})\, dx$

nth iterative value (approximate value)

$$y^{(n)} = y_0 + \int_{x_0}^{x} f(x, y^{(n-1)})\, dx$$

Euler's Method

Differential equation $\frac{dy}{dx} = f(x, y)$ and initial value $y(x_0) = y_0$

$$y - y_0 = \left(\frac{dy}{dx}\right)_{P_0}(x - x_0)\text{; when } x - x_0 = h\text{, then}$$

$$y_1^{(1)} = y_0^{(0)} + h\left(\frac{dy}{dx}\right)_{P_0}$$

Similarly, $y_2^{(2)} = y_1^{(1)} + h\left(\frac{dy}{dx}\right)_{P_1}$

$$y_n^{(n)} = y_{n-1}^{(n-)} + h\left(\frac{dy}{dx}\right)_{P_{n-1}}$$

Modified Euler's Method

Differential equation $\frac{dy}{dx} = f(x, y)$ and initial value $y(x_0) = y_0$

$$y_1^{(1)} = y_0^{(0)} + \frac{h}{2}\left[\left(\frac{dy}{dx}\right)_{P_0} + \left(\frac{dy}{dx}\right)_{P^{(1)}}\right]$$

Similarly, $y_2^{(2)} = y_1^{(1)} + \frac{h}{2}\left[\left(\frac{dy}{dx}\right)_{P_1^{(1)}} + \left(\frac{dy}{dx}\right)_{P_2^{(2)}}\right]$

$$y_n^{(n)} = y_{n-1}^{(n-1)} + \frac{h}{2}\left[\left(\frac{dy}{dx}\right)_{P_{n-1}^{(n-1)}} + \left(\frac{dy}{dx}\right)_{P_n^{(n)}}\right]$$

4.2 SOLVED EXAMPLES

Previous Years GATE Questions

Example 4.1

The values of function $f(x)$ at 5 discrete points are given below:

x	0	0.1	0.2	0.3	0.4
$f(x)$	0	10	40	90	160

Using trapezoidal rule with step size of 0.1, the value of $\int_0^{0.4} f(x)dx$ is___.

GATE 2015

Solution

i	0	1	2	3	4
x	0	0.1	0.2	0.3	0.4
$f(x)$	0	10	40	90	160

By trapezoidal rule,

$$\int_0^{0.4} f(x)dx = \frac{h}{2}[f(x_0) + 2\{f(x_1) + f(x_2) + f(x_3)\} + f(x_4)]$$

Substituting the value of $f(x_0)$, $f(x_1)$, $f(x_2)$, $f(x_3)$ and $f(x_4)$ from given table, we have

$$\int_0^{0.4} f(x)\, dx = \frac{0.1}{2}[0 + 2\{10 + 40 + 90\} + 160]$$

$$\int_0^{0.4} f(x)dx = 22$$

Example 4.2

If $P(X) = \frac{1}{4}$, $P(Y) = \frac{1}{3}$, and $P(X \cap Y) = \frac{1}{12}$, the value of $P(Y / X)$ is

(A) $\frac{1}{4}$ (B) $\frac{4}{25}$ (C) $\frac{1}{3}$ (D) $\frac{29}{50}$

GATE 2015

Solution

Given: $P(X) = \frac{1}{4}$, $P(Y) = \frac{1}{3}$, and $P(X \cap Y) = \frac{1}{12}$

$$P(Y / X)=\frac{P(X \cap Y)}{P(X)}$$

or $$P(Y / X)=\frac{1/12}{1/4}$$

$$P(Y / X)=\frac{1}{3}$$

Example 4.3

Using a unit step size, the value of integral $\int_1^2 x \ln x \, dx$ by trapezoidal rule is___.

GATE 2015

Solution

Function $f(x)=x \ln x$,

Unit step size $h=1$

i	0	1
x	1	2
$f(x)=x \ln x$	0	1.3862

By trapezoidal rule,

$$\int_1^2 x \ln x \, dx=\frac{h}{2}[f(x_0)+f(x_1)]$$

Substituting the value of $f(x_0)$ and $f(x_1)$ from given table, we have

$$\int_1^2 x \ln x \, dx=\frac{1}{2}[0+1.3862]$$

$$\int_1^2 x \ln x \, dx=0.6931$$

Example 4.4

Newton-Raphson method is used to find the roots of the equation, $x^3+2x^2+3x-1=0$. If the initial guess is $x_0=1$, then the value of x after 2nd iteration is______.

GATE 2015

Solution

Given: $f(x)=x^3+2x^2+3x-1$

$$f'(x)=3x^2+4x+3$$

By Newton-Raphson method, $x_{n+1}=x_n-\frac{f(x_n)}{f'(x_n)}$

$$x_{n+1}=x_n-\frac{x_n^3+2x_n^2+3x_n^3-1}{3x_n^2+4x_n+3}$$

or $$x_{n+1}=\frac{2x_n^3+2x_n^2+1}{3x_n^2+4x_n+3}$$

Putting $n=0$ and initial guess $x_0=1$;

$$x_1=\frac{2x_0^3+2x_0^2+1}{3x_0^2+4x_0+3}=\frac{2\times1^3+2\times1^2+1}{3\times1^2+4\times1+3}$$

$$x_1=0.5$$

Now, $$x_2=\frac{2x_1^3+2x_1^2+1}{3x_1^2+4x_1+3}=\frac{2\times0.5^3+2\times0.5^2+1}{3\times0.5^2+4\times0.5+3}$$

$$x_2=0.3043$$

Example 4.5

Simpson's $\frac{1}{3}$ rule is used to integrate the function $f(x)=\frac{3}{5}x^2+\frac{9}{5}$ between $x=0$ and $x=1$ using the least number of equal sub-intervals. The value of the integral is____.

GATE 2015

Solution

i	0	1	2	3	4	5
x	0	0.2	0.4	0.6	0.8	1
$f(x)=\frac{3}{5}x^2+\frac{9}{5}$	1.8	1.824	1.896	2.016	2.184	2.4

By Simpson's $\frac{1}{3}$ rule,

$$\int_0^1\left(\frac{3}{5}x^2+\frac{9}{5}\right)dx$$

$$=\frac{h}{3}[f(x_0)+4\{f(x_1)+f(x_3)\}+2\{f(x_2)+f(x_4)\}+f(x_5)]$$

$$=\frac{0.2}{3}[1.8+4\{1.824+2.016\}+2\{1.896+2.184\}+2.4]$$

$$\int_0^1\left(\frac{3}{5}x^2+\frac{9}{5}\right)dx=1.848$$

Example 4.6

Given two complex numbers $z_1=5+(5\sqrt{3})i$ and $z_2=\frac{2}{\sqrt{3}}+2i$, the argument of $\frac{z_1}{z_2}$ in degrees is

(A) 0 (B) 30 (C) 60 (D) 90

GATE 2015

Solution

Given: $z_1 = 5 + (5\sqrt{3})i$ and $z_2 = \frac{2}{\sqrt{3}} + 2i$

$$z_1 = 5 + (5\sqrt{3})i = \sqrt{5^2 + (5\sqrt{3})^2}\, e^{\frac{\pi}{3}i}$$

or $$z_1 = 10\, e^{\frac{\pi}{3}i}$$

$$z_2 = \frac{2}{\sqrt{3}} + 2i = \sqrt{\left(\frac{2}{\sqrt{3}}\right)^2 + (2)^2}\, e^{\frac{\pi}{3}i}$$

or $$z_2 = \frac{4}{\sqrt{3}} e^{\frac{\pi}{3}i}$$

Now, $$\frac{z_1}{z_2} = \frac{10\, e^{\frac{\pi}{3}i}}{\frac{4}{\sqrt{3}} e^{\frac{\pi}{3}i}} = 2.5\, e^{0i}$$

Argument of $\frac{z_1}{z_2} = 0$

Example 4.7

In the following table, x is a discrete random variable and $p(x)$ is the probability density. The standard deviation of x is

x	1	2	3
$p(x)$	0.3	0.6	0.1

(A) 0.18 (B) 0.36 (C) 0.54 (D) 0.6

GATE 2014

Solution

x_i	1	2	3
$p(x_i)$	0.3	0.6	0.1

Mean μ = Expectation = $E(x) = \sum x_i p(x_i)$

$$\mu = 1 \times 0.3 + 2 \times 0.6 + 3 \times 0.1$$

$$\mu = 1.8$$

Variance $\sigma^2 = \sum x_i^2 f(x_i) - \mu^2$

$$\sigma^2 = 1^2 \times 0.3 + 2^2 \times 0.6 + 3^2 \times 0.1 - 1.8^2$$

or $$\sigma^2 = 0.36$$

Standard deviation $\sigma = 0.6$

Example 4.8

Using the trapezoidal rule, and dividing the interval of integration into three equal sub-interval, the definite integral $\int_{-1}^{+1} |x|\, dx$ is

GATE 2014

Solution

i	0	1	2
x	−1	0	1
$f(x) = \lvert x \rvert$	1	0	1

By trapezoidal rule,

$$\int_{-1}^{1} |x|\, dx = \frac{h}{2}[f(x_0) + 2\{f(x_1) + f(x_2)]$$

Substituting the value of $f(x_0), f(x_1)$, and $f(x_2)$ from given table, we have

$$\int_{-1}^{1} |x|\, dx = \frac{1}{2}[1 + 2 \times 0 + 1]$$

$$\int_{-1}^{1} |x|\, dx = 1$$

Example 4.9

The product of two complex numbers $1 + i$ and $2 - 5i$, is

(A) $7 - 3i$ (B) $-3 - 4i$ (C) $3 - 4i$ (D) $7 + 3i$

GATE 2011

Solution

Product of two complex numbers $1 + i$ and $2 - 5i$ is

$$z = (1 + i)(2 - 5i)$$

or $$z = 2 + 2i - 5i - 5i^2 = 2 + 2i - 5i + 5$$

$$z = 7 - 3i$$

Example 4.10

An analytic function of a complex variable $z = x + iy$ is expressed as $f(z) = u(x, y) + i\, v(x, y)$, where $i = \sqrt{-1}$. If $u = xy$, the expression for v should be

(A) $\frac{(x+y)^2}{2} + k$ (B) $\frac{x^2 - y^2}{2} + k$

(C) $\frac{y^2 - x^2}{2} + k$ (D) $\frac{(x-y)^2}{2} + k$

GATE 2009

Solution

Given $u = xy$ and function $f(z) = u(x, y) + i\,v(x, y)$ is analytic.

Function $f(z)$ must satisfy the Cauchy-Reimann equation.

$$\frac{\partial u}{\partial x} = \frac{\partial v}{\partial y} \Rightarrow \frac{\partial v}{\partial y} = y \text{ or } \partial v = y\partial y$$

Integrating we have $v = \dfrac{y^2}{2} + f(x)$ (i)

and $\dfrac{\partial u}{\partial y} = -\dfrac{\partial v}{\partial x} \Rightarrow \dfrac{\partial v}{\partial x} = -x$ (ii)

From equations (i) and (ii), we get

$$\frac{\partial}{\partial x}\left(\frac{y^2}{2} + f(x)\right) = -x \quad \text{or} \quad \frac{\partial}{\partial x} f(x) = -x$$

or $f(x) = -\dfrac{x^2}{2} + k$

Substituting $f(x) = -\dfrac{x^2}{2} + k$ in Equation (i), we get

$$v = \frac{y^2}{2} - \frac{x^2}{2} + k$$

$$v = \frac{y^2 - x^2}{2} + k$$

Example 4.11

The modulus of the complex number $\left(\dfrac{3+4i}{1-2i}\right)$ is

(A) 5 (B) $\sqrt{5}$ (C) $\dfrac{1}{\sqrt{5}}$ (D) $\dfrac{1}{5}$

GATE 2010

Solution

Let $z = \dfrac{3+4i}{1-2i}$

or $z = \dfrac{3+4i}{1-2i} \times \dfrac{1+2i}{1+2i} = \dfrac{3+4i+6i+8i^2}{1-4i^2}$

or $z = \dfrac{3+4i+6i-8}{1+4} = -1+2i$

Modulus of z, $|z| = \sqrt{(-1)^2 + (2)^2} = \sqrt{5}$

$$\text{Modulus of } \left(\frac{3+4i}{1-2i}\right) \text{ is } |z| = \sqrt{5}$$

Example 4.12

The integral $\oint f(z)dz$ evaluated around the unit circle on the complex plane for $f(z) = \dfrac{\cos z}{z}$ is

(A) $2\pi i$ (B) $4\pi i$ (C) $-2\pi i$ (D) 0

GATE 2008

Solution

$f(z) = \dfrac{\cos z}{z}$ has single pole at $z = 0$ and it is inside unit circle on complex plane.

Cauchy's integral theorem, $\oint_C \dfrac{f(z)}{z-a} dz = 2\pi i\, f(a)$

Now, $\oint_C \dfrac{\cos z}{z} dz = \oint_C \dfrac{\cos z}{z-0} dz = 2\pi i \cos 0$

$$\oint_C \frac{\cos z}{z} dz = 2\pi i$$

Example 4.13

A single die is thrown twice. What is the probability that the sum is neither 8 nor 9?

(A) $\dfrac{1}{9}$ (B) $\dfrac{5}{36}$ (C) $\dfrac{1}{4}$ (D) $\dfrac{3}{4}$

GATE 2005

Solution

Sample space $= 6 \times 6 = 36$

Number of ways in which sum is either 8 or 9

(2,6), (3,5), (4,4), (5,3), (6,2), (3,6), (4,5), (5,4), (6,3) $= 9$ ways

Therefore, probability of getting sum 8 or 9 $= \dfrac{9}{36} = \dfrac{1}{4}$

So probability of not getting sum 8 nor 9, $P = 1 - \dfrac{1}{4} = \dfrac{3}{4}$

$$P = \frac{3}{4}$$

Example 4.14

A lot has 10% defective items. Ten items are chosen randomly from this lot. The probability that exactly 2 of the chosen items are defective is

(A) 0.0036 (B) 0.1937 (C) 0.2234 (D) 0.3874

GATE 2005

Solution

Applying Binomial distribution theorem, we get

$$P(x) = {}^nC_x p^x q^{n-x}$$

Probability of defective item $p = 0.1$

Probability of non-defective item $q = 1 - p = 0.9$

Probability that exactly 2 of the chosen items defective is

$$P_{(x=2)} = {}^{10}C_2\,(0.1)^2(0.9)^{10-2}$$

$$P = 0.1937$$

Example 4.15

A coin is tossed 4 times. What is the probability of getting heads exactly 3 times?

(A) $\frac{1}{4}$ (B) $\frac{3}{8}$ (C) $\frac{1}{2}$ (D) $\frac{3}{4}$

GATE 2008

Solution

Using Binomial distribution theorem $P(x) = {}^nC_x p^x q^{n-x}$, we get

Probability of getting head, $p(\text{head}) = \frac{1}{2}$

Probability of not getting head, $q = 1 - \frac{1}{2} = \frac{1}{2}$

Probability of getting head exactly 3 times is

$$P_{(x=3)} = {}^{40}C_3\,(0.5)^3(0.5)^1 = 0.25$$

$$P = \frac{1}{4}$$

Example 4.16

If three coins are tossed simultaneously, the probability of getting at least one head is

(A) $\frac{1}{8}$ (B) $\frac{3}{8}$ (C) $\frac{1}{2}$ (D) $\frac{7}{8}$

GATE 2009

Solution

Applying Binomial distribution theorem

$$P = P(\text{head}) = \frac{1}{2}$$

$$n = 3$$

$$x \geq 1 \text{ (at least one head)}$$

Probability of getting at least one head is

$$P_{(x\geq 1)} = 1 - P_{(x=0)}$$

or $$P_{(x\geq 1)} = 1 - {}^3C_0\left(\frac{1}{2}\right)^0\left(1-\frac{1}{2}\right)^{3-0}$$

or $$P_{(x\geq 1)} = 1 - \left(\frac{1}{2}\right)^3 = \frac{7}{8}$$

Probability of getting at least one head $P = \frac{7}{8}$

Example 4.17

A box contains 5 black and 5 red balls. Two balls are randomly picked one after another from the box, without replacement. The probability for both balls being red is

(A) $\frac{1}{90}$ (B) $\frac{1}{2}$ (C) $\frac{19}{90}$ (D) $\frac{2}{9}$

GATE 2003

Solution

Each event is independent

Probability of drawing two red balls

$$P = P_{(\text{first ball is red})} \times P_{(\text{second ball is red given that first ball is red})}$$

$$P = \frac{5}{10} \times \frac{4}{9}$$

$$P = \frac{2}{9}$$

Example 4.18

From a pack of regular playing cards, two cards are drawn at random. What is the probability that both cards will be kings, if first card is NOT replaced

(A) $\frac{1}{26}$ (B) $\frac{1}{52}$ (C) $\frac{1}{169}$ (D) $\frac{1}{221}$

GATE 2004

Solution

Number of cards $= 52$

Number of kings $= 4$

Probability that both cards are kings

$$P = \frac{{}^4C_2 \times {}^{48}C_0}{{}^{52}C_0}$$

$$P = \frac{1}{221}$$

Example 4.19

A box contains 20 defective items and 80 non-defective items. If two items are selected at random without replacement, what will be the probability that both items are defective?

(A) $\frac{1}{5}$ (B) $\frac{1}{25}$ (C) $\frac{20}{99}$ (D) $\frac{19}{495}$

GATE 2006

Solution

Number of defective items $= 20$

Number of non-defective items $= 80$

Probability that both items are defective

$$P = \frac{{}^{20}C_2 \times {}^{80}C_0}{{}^{100}C_2}$$

$$P = \frac{19}{495}$$

Example 4.20

A box contains 4 red balls and 6 black balls. Three balls are selected randomly from the box one after another, without replacement. The probability that the selected set contains one red ball and two black balls is

(A) $\frac{1}{20}$ (B) $\frac{1}{12}$ (C) $\frac{3}{10}$ (D) $\frac{1}{2}$

GATE 200

Solution

Box contains 4 red balls and 6 black balls

Probability that 1 ball is red and 2 balls are black.

$$P = \frac{{}^{4}C_1 \times {}^{6}C_2}{{}^{10}C_3} = \frac{60}{120}$$

$$P = \frac{1}{2}$$

Example 4.21

Consider the continuous random variable with probability density function

$$f(x) = \begin{cases} 1+x & \text{for } -1 \le x \le 0 \\ 1-x & \text{for } \;\; 0 \le x \le 1 \end{cases}$$

The standard deviation of the random variable is

(A) $\frac{1}{\sqrt{3}}$ (B) $\frac{1}{\sqrt{6}}$ (C) $\frac{1}{3}$ (D) $\frac{1}{6}$

GATE 2006

Solution

Mean

$$\mu = E(x) = \int_{-\infty}^{\infty} xf(x)dx = \int_{-1}^{0} x(1+x)dx + \int_{0}^{1} x(1-x)dx$$

$$\mu = E(x) = 0$$

Variance $\sigma^2 = E(x^2) - [E(x)]^2 = \int_{-\infty}^{\infty} x^2 f(x)dx - 0^2$

$$\sigma^2 = \int_{-1}^{0} x^2(1+x)\,dx + \int_{0}^{1} x^2(1-x)\,dx$$

or $\sigma^2 = \frac{1}{6}$

Standard deviation, $\sigma = \sqrt{\text{Variance}} = \frac{1}{\sqrt{6}}$

Standard deviation, $\sigma = \frac{1}{\sqrt{6}}$

Example 4.22

An unbiased coin is tossed five times. The outcome of each toss is either a head or a tail. The probability of getting at least one head is

(A) $\frac{1}{32}$ (B) $\frac{13}{32}$ (C) $\frac{16}{32}$ (D) $\frac{31}{32}$

GATE 2011

Solution

Applying Binomial distribution theorem

$$P = P(\text{head}) = \frac{1}{2}$$

$$n = 5$$

$$x \ge 1 \text{ (at least one head)}$$

Probability of getting at least one head is

$$P_{(x\ge 1)} = 1 - P_{(x=0)}$$

or $P_{(x\ge 1)} = 1 - {}^{5}C_0 \left(\frac{1}{2}\right)^0 \left(1-\frac{1}{2}\right)^{5-0}$

or $P_{(x\ge 1)} = 1 - \frac{1}{32} = \frac{31}{32}$

Probability of getting at least one head $P = \frac{31}{32}$

Example 4.23

Let X be a normal random variable with mean 1 and variance 4. The probability $P\{X<0\}$ is

(A) 0.5

(B) Greater than zero and less than 0.5

(C) Greater than 0.5 and less than 1.0

(D) 1.0

GATE 2013

Solution

Given: Mean $\mu = 1$, Variance $\sigma^2 = 4 \Rightarrow \sigma = 2$

Standard normal variate, $z = \frac{x-\mu}{\sigma}$

Standard normal variate of $x < 0$ is $z = \frac{0-1}{2} = -0.5$

Probability at $z = -0.5$ is less than 0.5 and greater than 0

Example 4.24

With a 1 unit change in *b*, what is the change in *x* in the solution of the system of equations $x + y = 2$, $1.01x + 0.99y = b$?

(A) Zero (B) 2 units (C) 50 units (D) 100 units

GATE 2005

Solution

Given system of equations

$$x + y = 2 \quad \text{(i)}$$

$$1.01x + 0.99y = b \quad \text{(ii)}$$

Eliminating *y* from Equations (ii) and (i), we have

$$(1.01 - 0.99)x = b - 2 \times 0.99$$

$$x = 50b - 99$$

From which

$$\Delta x = 50\Delta b$$

Putting given $\Delta b = 1$

$$\Delta x = 50$$

1 unit change in *b*, change in *x* would be 50 units

Example 4.25

Starting from $x_0 = 1$, one step of Newton-Raphson method in solving the equation $x^3 + 3x - 7 = 0$ gives the next value (x_1) as

(A) $x_1 = 0.5$ (B) $x_1 = 1.406$ (C) $x_1 = 1.5$ (D) $x_1 = 2$

GATE 2005

Solution

Given: $f(x) = x^3 + 3x - 7 = 0$

$$f'(x) = 3x^2 + 3$$

The Newton-Raphson iterative formula is

$$x_{n+1} = x_n - \frac{f(x_n)}{f'(x_n)}$$

$$x_{n+1} = x_n - \frac{x_n^3 + 3x_n - 7}{3x_n^2 + 3} = \frac{2x_n^3 + 7}{3x_n^2 + 3}$$

or $$x_1 = \frac{2x_0^3 + 7}{3x_0^2 + 3}$$

Putting $x_0 = 1$; $$x_1 = \frac{2 \times 1^3 + 7}{3 \times 1^2 + 3}$$

$$x_1 = 1.5$$

Example 4.26

A calculator has accuracy up to 8 digits after decimal place. The value of $\int_0^{2\pi} \sin x \, dx$, when evaluated using this calculator by trapezoidal method with 8 equal intervals, to 5 significant digits is

(A) 0.00000 (B) 1.0000 (C) 0.00500 (D) 0.00025

GATE 2007

Solution

Step size $h = \frac{2\pi - 0}{8} = \frac{\pi}{4}$

i	0	1	2	3	4	5	6	7	8
x	0	$\frac{\pi}{4}$	$\frac{\pi}{2}$	$\frac{3\pi}{4}$	π	$\frac{5\pi}{4}$	$\frac{6\pi}{4}$	$\frac{7\pi}{4}$	2π
$\sin x$	0	0.70710	1	0.70710	0	–0.70710	–1	–0.70710	0

By trapezoidal rule,

$$\int_0^{2\pi} f(x)dx = \frac{h}{2}[y_0 + 2(y_1 + y_2 + y_3 + y_4 + y_5 + y_6 + y_7) + y_8]$$

$$\int_0^{2\pi} \sin x \, dx$$

$$= \frac{\pi/4}{2}[0 + 2(0.70710 + 1 + 0.70710 + 0 - 0.70710 - 1 - 0.70710) + 0]$$

$$\int_0^{2\pi} \sin x \, dx = 0.00000$$

Example 4.27

Torque exerted on a flywheel over a cycle is listed in the table. Flywheel energy (in J per unit cycle) using Simpson's rule is

Angle (degree)	0	60	120	180	240	300	360
Torque, (Nm)	0	1066	–323	0	323	–355	0

(A) 542 (B) 993 (C) 1444 (D) 1986

GATE 2010

Solution

i	0	1	2	3	4	5	6
Angle θ	0	60	120	180	240	300	360
Torque T (Nm)	0	1066	–323	0	323	–355	0

Flywheel energy $E = \int_0^{2\pi} T \, d\theta$, where T is torque exerted.

Flywheel energy by Simpson's Rule is

$$E = \int_0^{2\pi} T\, d\theta = \frac{h}{3}[T_0 + 4(T_1 + T_3 + T_5) + 2(T_2 + T_4) + T_6]$$

$$E = \frac{\pi/3}{3}[0 + 4(1066 + 0 - 355) + 2(-323 + 323) + 0]$$

$$E = 993$$

Example 4.28

The integral $\int_1^3 \frac{1}{x} dx$, when evaluated by using Simpson's 1/3 rule on two equal sub-intervals each of length 1, equals

(A) 1.000 (B) 1.098 (C) 1.111 (D) 1.120

GATE 2011

Solution

$$\text{Step size } h = \frac{3-1}{2} = 1$$

i	0	1	2
x	1	2	3
$y = \frac{1}{x}$	1	$\frac{1}{2}$	$\frac{1}{3}$

By Simpson's $\frac{1}{3}$ rule,

$$\int_1^3 \frac{1}{x} dx = \frac{h}{3}[f(0) + 4f(1) + f(2)]$$

or

$$\int_1^3 \frac{1}{x} dx = \frac{1}{3}\left[1 + 4 \times \frac{1}{2} + \frac{1}{3}\right]$$

$$\int_1^3 \frac{1}{x} dx = 1.111$$

Example 4.29

$f(z) = u(x, y) + i\,v(x, y)$ is an analytic function of complex variable $z = x + iy$ where $i = \sqrt{-1}$. If $u(x, y) = 2xy$, then $v(x, y)$ may be expressed as

(A) $-x^2 + y^2$ + constant (B) $x^2 - y^2$ + constant

(C) $x^2 + y^2$ + constant (D) $-(x^2 + y^2)$ + constant

GATE 2016

Solution

Given: $u(x, y) = 2xy$ and function $f(z) = u(x, y) + i\,v(x, y)$ is analytic.

Function $f(z)$ must satisfy the Cauchy-Reimann equation.

$$\frac{\partial u}{\partial x} = \frac{\partial v}{\partial y} \Rightarrow \frac{\partial v}{\partial y} = 2y \text{ or } \partial v = 2y\partial y$$

By integration we have $v = y^2 + f(x)$ (i)

and $\frac{\partial u}{\partial y} = -\frac{\partial v}{\partial x} \Rightarrow \frac{\partial v}{\partial x} = -2x$ (ii)

From Equations (i) and (ii), we get

$$\frac{\partial}{\partial x}(y^2 + f(x)) = -2x \quad \text{or} \quad \frac{\partial}{\partial x} f(x) = -2x$$

or $f(x) = -x^2 + k$

Substituting $f(x) = -x^2 + k$ in Equation (i), we get

$$v = y^2 - x^2 + k$$

$$v = y^2 - x^2 + \text{constant}$$

Example 4.30

Consider a Poisson distribution for the tossing of a biased coin. The mean for this distribution is μ. The standard deviation for this distribution is given by

(A) $\sqrt{\mu}$ (B) μ^2 (C) μ (D) $\frac{1}{\mu}$

GATE 2016

Solution

Mean of Poission distribution $= \mu$

$$\text{Standard deviation } \sigma = \sqrt{\mu}$$

Example 4.31

Solve the equation $x = 10\cos(x)$ using the Newton-Raphson method. The initial guess is $x = \frac{\pi}{4}$. The value of the predicted root after the first iteration, up to second decimal, is ________

GATE 2016

Solution

Given: $f(x) = x - 10\cos x$

$f'(x) = 1 + 10\sin x$

By Newton-Raphson method, $x_{n+1} = x_n - \frac{f(x_n)}{f'(x_n)}$

$$x_{n+1} = x_n - \frac{x_n - 10\cos x_n}{1 + 10\sin x_n} = \frac{10x_n \sin x_n + 10\cos x_n}{1 + 10\sin x_n}$$

Putting $n = 0$ and initial guess $x_0 = \frac{\pi}{4}$;

$$x_1 = \frac{10x_0 \sin x_0 + 10\cos x_0}{1+10\sin x_0} = \frac{10\times\frac{\pi}{4}\sin\frac{\pi}{4}+10\cos\frac{\pi}{4}}{1+10\sin\frac{\pi}{4}}$$

or $$x_1 = \frac{10}{10+\sqrt{2}}\left(\frac{\pi}{4}+1\right)$$

$$x_1 = 1.5641$$

Example 4.32

Gauss-Seidel method is used to solve the following equations (as per the given order):

$$x_1 + 2x_2 + 3x_3 = 5$$
$$2x_1 + 3x_2 + x_3 = 1$$
$$3x_1 + 2x_2 + x_3 = 3$$

Assuming initial guess as $x_1 = x_2 = x_3 = 0$, the value of x_3 after the first iteration is _____.

GATE 2016

Solution

The system of equations

$$x_1 + 2x_2 + 3x_3 = 5 \quad \text{(i)}$$
$$2x_1 + 3x_2 + x_3 = 1 \quad \text{(ii)}$$
$$3x_1 + 2x_2 + x_3 = 3 \quad \text{(iii)}$$

Substituting $x_2 = 0$ and $x_3 = 0$ in Equation (i), we have

$$x_1^{(1)} + 2\times 0 + 3\times 0 = 5 \quad \text{or} \quad x_1^{(1)} = 5$$

Substituting $x_1^{(1)} = 5$ and $x_3 = 0$ in Equation (ii), we have

$$2\times 5 + 3x_2^{(1)} + 0 = 1 \quad \text{or} \quad x_2^{(1)} = -3$$

Substituting $x_1^{(1)} = 5$ and $x_2^{(1)} = -3$ in Equation (iii), we have

$$3\times 5 + 2\times -3 + x_3^{(1)} = 3$$

or $$x_3^{(1)} = -6$$

$$x_3^{(1)} = -6$$

Example 4.33

A function f of the complex variable $z = x + i\,y$ is given as $f(x, y) = u(x, y) + i\,v(x, y)$ where $u(x, y) = 2kxy$ and $v(x, y) = x^2 - y^2$. The value of k, for which the function is analytic, is _____.

GATE 2016

Solution

Given: $u(x, y) = 2kxy$ and function $f(z) = u(x, y) + i\,v(x, y)$ is analytic.

Function $f(z)$ must satisfy the Cauchy-Reimann equation.

$$\frac{\partial u}{\partial x} = \frac{\partial v}{\partial y} \Rightarrow \frac{\partial v}{\partial y} = 2ky \quad \text{or} \quad \partial v = 2ky\partial y$$

By integration we have $v = ky^2 + f(x)$ (i)

and $$\frac{\partial u}{\partial y} = -\frac{\partial v}{\partial x} \Rightarrow \frac{\partial v}{\partial x} = -2kx \quad \text{(ii)}$$

From Equations (i) and (ii), we get

$$\frac{\partial}{\partial x}(ky^2 + f(x)) = -2kx \quad \text{or} \quad \frac{\partial}{\partial x}f(x) = -2kx$$

or $$f(x) = -kx^2 + c$$

Substituting $f(x) = -kx^2 + c$ in Equation (i), we get

$$v = ky^2 - kx^2 + c$$

Compare with given equation $v(x, y) = x^2 - y^2$, we obtain

$$k = 1 \text{ and } c = 0$$

$$k = 1$$

Example 4.34

Numerical integration using trapezoidal rule gives the best result for a single variable function, which is

(A) Linear (B) Parabolic

(C) Logarithmic (D) Hyperbolic

GATE 2016

Solution

Numerical integration using trapezoidal rule gives the best result for a single variable function, which is linear.

Example 4.35

The value of $\oint_\Gamma \frac{3z-5}{(z-1)(z-2)}dz$ along a closed path Γ is equal to $4\pi i$ where $z = x + i\,y$ and $i = \sqrt{-1}$. The correct path Γ is

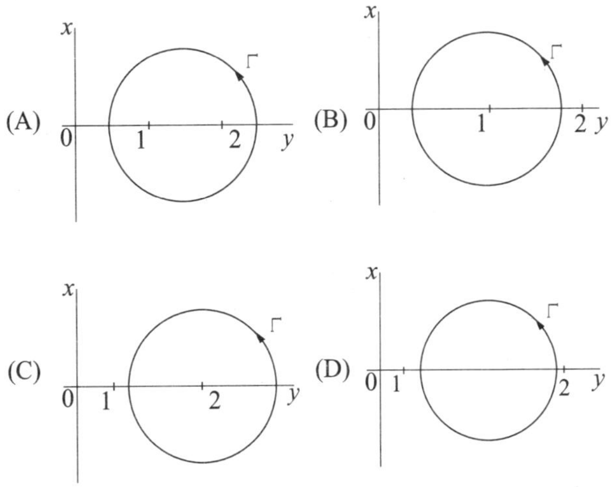

GATE 2016

Solution

Given $\oint_\Gamma \frac{3z-5}{(z-1)(z-2)}dz = 4\pi i$

$$\oint_\Gamma \frac{3z-5}{(z-1)(z-2)}dz = \oint_\Gamma \frac{\left(\frac{3z-5}{z-2}\right)}{(z-1)}dz = 4\pi i$$

Applying Cauchy's integral theorem, using

$f(z) = \left(\frac{3z-5}{z-2}\right)$ and $a = 1$, we have

$$\oint_\Gamma \frac{\left(\frac{3z-5}{z-2}\right)}{(z-1)}dz = 2\pi i f(a) = 2\pi i\left(\frac{3\times 1-5}{1-2}\right) = 4\pi i$$

The pole at 1 is inside and pole at 2 is outside the circle. Therefore, option B is correct.

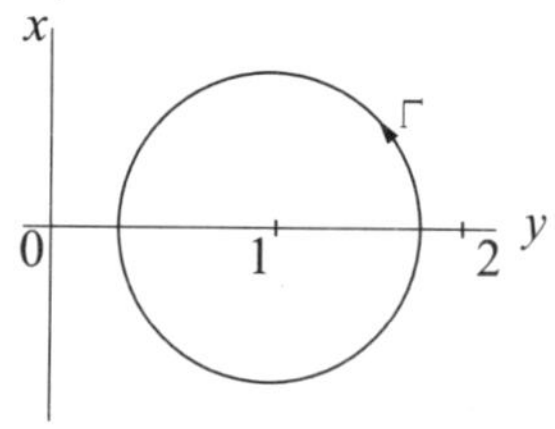

Example 4.36

The probability that a screw manufactured by a company is defective is 0.1. The company sells screws in packets containing 5 screws and gives a guarantee of replacement if one or more screws in the packet are found to be defective. The probability that a packet would have to be replaced is____.

GATE 2016

Solution

The probability that a screw is defective is constant, $p = 0.1$. We use the Binomial distribution for this situation.

$$P(r) = {}^nC_r p^r (1-p)^{n-r}$$

Probability that one or more screws in the packet defective $P(r \geq 1) = 1 - P(r < 1)$

$$P(r \geq 1) = 1 - P(r = 0) = 1 - {}^5C_0 (0.1)^0 (0.9)^{5-0}$$

The probability that a packet would have to be replaced is

$$P(r \geq 1) = 0.40951$$

Example 4.37

The error in numerically computing the integral $\int_0^\pi (\sin x + \cos x)dx$ using the trapezoidal rule with three intervals of equal length between 0 and π is ______.

GATE 2016

Solution

Step size $h = \frac{\pi - 0}{3} = \frac{\pi}{3}$

x	0	$\frac{\pi}{3}$	$\frac{2\pi}{3}$	π
$\sin x + \cos x$	1	1.3660	0.3660	−1

By trapezoidal rule,

$$\int_0^\pi (\sin x + \cos x)dx = \frac{h}{2}[y_0 + 2(y_1 + y_2) + y_3]$$

$$\int_0^\pi (\sin x + \cos x)dx = \frac{\pi/3}{2}[1 + 2(1.3660 + 0.3660) - 1]$$

$$\int_0^\pi (\sin x + \cos x)dx = 1.8137$$

Exact value of $\int_0^\pi (\sin x + \cos x)dx = [-\cos x + \sin x]_0^\pi = 2$

$$\text{Error} = 2 - 1.8137$$

$$\text{Error} = 0.187$$

Example 4.38

The area (in percentage) under standard normal distribution curve of random variable z within limits from −3 to +3 is____.

GATE 2016

Solution

The area under standard normal distribution curve of random variable z within limits from −3 to +3 is 99.74%.

Example 4.39

The root of the function $f(x) = x^3 + x - 1$ obtained after first iteration on application of Newton-Raphson scheme using an initial guess of $x_0 = 1$ is

(A) 0.682 (B) 0.686 (C) 0.750 (D) 1.000

GATE 2016

Solution

Given: Equation $f(x) = x^3 + x - 1 \quad \Rightarrow \quad f'(x) = 3x^2 + 1$

By Newton's-Raphson method,

$$x_{n+1} = x_n - \frac{f(x_n)}{f'(x_n)} = x_n - \frac{x_n^3 + x_n - 1}{3x_n^2 + 1} = \frac{2x_n^3 + 1}{3x_n^2 + 1}$$

Substituting initial guess of $x_0 = 1$;

$$x_1 = \frac{2x_0^3+1}{3x_0^2+1} = \frac{2\times1^3+1}{3\times1^3+1} = \frac{3}{4}$$

$$x_1 = 0.75$$

Example 4.40

Three cards were drawn from a pack of 52 cards. The probability that they are a king, a queen, and a jack is

(A) $\frac{16}{5525}$ (B) $\frac{64}{2197}$ (C) $\frac{3}{13}$ (D) $\frac{8}{16575}$

GATE 2016

Solution

Number of cards = 52

3 cards is drawn in $^{52}C_3$. There are 4 kings, 4 queens and 4 jacks in pack of 52 cards.

The probability that they are a king, a queen, and a jack is

$$= \frac{^4C_1 \times {}^4C_1 \times {}^4C_1}{^{52}C_3} = \frac{16}{5525}$$

$$\frac{16}{5525}$$

Example 4.41

A six-face fair dice is rolled a large number of times. The mean value of the outcomes is_______.

GATE 2017

Solution

The probabilities corresponding to the outcomes are

Face	1	2	3	4	5	6
$P(x)$	$\frac{1}{6}$	$\frac{1}{6}$	$\frac{1}{6}$	$\frac{1}{6}$	$\frac{1}{6}$	$\frac{1}{6}$

Mean $E(x) = \sum x P(x)$

$$= 1\times\frac{1}{6} + 2\times\frac{1}{6} + 3\times\frac{1}{6} + 4\times\frac{1}{6} + 5\times\frac{1}{6} + 6\times\frac{1}{6}$$

$$\text{Mean} = 3.5$$

Example 4.42

P(0, 3), Q(0.5, 4), and R (1, 5) are three points on the curve defined by $f(x)$. Numerical integration is carried out using both Trapezoidal rule and Simpson's rule within limits $x = 0$ and $x = 1$ for the curve. The difference between the two results will be.

(A) 0 (B) 0.25 (C) 0.5 (D) 1

GATE 2017

Solution

	P	Q	R
x	0	0.5	1
$f(x)$	3	4	5

Trapezoidal rule $\int_0^1 f(x)dx = \frac{h}{2}[f(x_0) + 2f(x_1) + f(x_2)]$

$$\int_0^1 f(x)dx = \frac{0.5}{2}(3 + 2\times4 + 5) = 4$$

Simpson's rule $\int_0^1 f(x)dx = \frac{h}{3}[f(x_0) + 4f(x_1) + f(x_2)]$

$$\int_0^1 f(x)dx = \frac{0.5}{3}(3 + 4\times4 + 5) = 4$$

$$\text{Difference} = 4 - 4 = 0$$

Example 4.43

Two coins are tossed simultaneously. The probability (upto two decimal points accuracy) of getting at least one head is___.

GATE 2017

Solution

Total numbers of outcomes = 4 (HH,HT,TH,TT)

Favourable outcomes(at least one head) = 3 (HH,HT,TH)

Probability of getting at least one head = $\frac{3}{4}$

Probability of getting at least one head = 0.75

Example 4.44

A sample of 15 data is a follows: 17, 18, 17, 17, 13, 18, 5, 5, 6, 7, 8, 9, 20, 17, 3. The mode of the data is

(A) 4 (B) 13 (C) 17 (D) 20

GATE 2017

Solution

Data which occurs most is 17

Mode =17

Example 4.45

If $f(z) = (x^2 + ay^2) + i\,bxy$ is a complex analytic function of $z = x + i\,y$, where $i = \sqrt{-1}$, then

(A) $a = -1, b = -1$ (B) $a = -1, b = 2$

(C) $a = 1, b = 2$ (D) $a = 2, b = 2$

GATE 2017

Solution

Let $f(z) = u + iv$, where $u = x^2 + ay^2 v = bxy$. The function $f(z)$ is analytic function, applying Cauchy Riemann (C-R) equation

$$\frac{\partial u}{\partial y} = -\frac{\partial v}{\partial x} \Rightarrow 2x = bx$$

$$b = 2$$

and $$\frac{\partial u}{\partial x} = \frac{\partial v}{\partial y} \Rightarrow 2ay = -by$$

$$a = -\frac{b}{2} = -1$$

$$a = -1,\ b = 2$$

Example 4.46

Four red balls, four green balls and four blue balls are put in a box. Three balls are pulled out of the box at random one after another without replacement. The probability that all the three balls are red is

(A) $\frac{1}{72}$ (B) $\frac{1}{55}$ (C) $\frac{1}{36}$ (D) $\frac{1}{27}$

GATE 2018

Solution

Box contains 4 red balls, 4 green balls and 4 blue balls.

Probability that all the three balls are red, is

$$P = \frac{^4C_1}{^{12}C_1} \times \frac{^3C_1}{^{11}C_1} \times \frac{^2C_1}{^{10}C_1}$$

$$P = \frac{4}{12} \times \frac{3}{11} \times \frac{2}{10} = \frac{1}{55}$$

$$\text{Probability } P = \frac{1}{55}$$

Example 4.47

$F(z)$ is a function of the complex variable $z = x + iy$ given by

$$F(z) = iz + k\,Re(z) + i\,Im(z)$$

For what value of k will $F(z)$ satisfy the Cauchy- Riemann equations?

(A) 0 (B) 1 (C) – 1 (D) y

GATE 2018

Solution

Given function $F(z) = iz + k\,Re(z) + i\,Im(z)$

$$u + iv = i(x + iy) + kx + iy$$

or $$u + iv = kx - y + i(x + y)$$

where $u = kx - y$ and $v = x + y$

Function $F(z)$ satisfy the Cauchy-Riemann equation

$$\frac{\partial u}{\partial x} = \frac{\partial v}{\partial y} \Rightarrow k = 1$$

$$k = 1$$

Example 4.48

A six-faced fair dice is rolled five times. The probability (in %) of obtaining "ONE" at least four times is

(A) 33.3 (B) 3.33 (C) 0.33 (D) 0.0033

GATE 2018

Solution

A dice is rolled 5 times, $n = 5$

Probability of getting 1, $p = \frac{1}{6}$

$$q = 1 - \frac{1}{6} = \frac{5}{6}$$

Probability of getting 1 at least 4 times is

$$P(r \geq 4) = P(r = 4) + P(r = 5)$$

$$P(r \geq 4) = {^5C_4} p^4 q^{5-4} + {^5C_5} p^5 q^0$$

$$P(r \geq 4) = 5 \times \left(\frac{1}{6}\right)^4 \left(\frac{5}{6}\right)^1 + 1 \times \left(\frac{1}{6}\right)^5 \left(\frac{5}{6}\right)^0 = 0.0033$$

$$\%\ \text{Probability} = 0.33$$

Example 4.49

Let X_1, X_2 be two independent normal random variables with means μ_1, μ_2 and standard deviations σ_1, σ_2, respectively. Consider $Y = X_1 - X_2$; $\mu_1 = \mu_2 = 1$, $\sigma_1 = 1, \sigma_2 = 2$. Then,

(A) Y is normally distributed with mean 0 and variance 1

(B) Y is normally distributed with mean 0 and variance 5

(C) Y has mean 0 and variance 5, but is NOT normally distributed

(D) Y has mean 0 and variance 1, but is NOT normally distributed

GATE 2018

Solution

Given that $\mu_1 = 1, \mu_2 = 1, \sigma_1 = 1, \sigma_2 = 2$ and $Y = X_1 - X_2$.

X_1 and X_2 are two independent random variable.

$$Y = X_1 - X_2$$

$$\mu(Y) = \mu(X_1) - \mu(X_2) = 1 - 1 = 0$$

$$\text{Var}(Y) = \text{Var}(X_1 - X_2)$$

$$\text{Var}(Y) = \text{Var}(X_1) + \text{Var}(X_2) - \text{Cov}(X_1 X_2)$$

Since X_1 and X_2 are two independent random variables.

$$\text{Var}(Y) = \text{Var}(X_1) + \text{Var}(X_2)$$

$$\text{Var}(Y) = \sigma_1^2 + \sigma_2^2 = 1 + 4$$

$$\text{Var}(Y) = 5$$

Example 4.50

Let z be a complex variable. For a counter-clockwise integration around a unit circle C, centred at origin,

$$\int_C \frac{1}{5z-4} dz = A\pi i,$$

the value of A is

(A) 2/5 (B) 1/2 (C) 2 (D) 4/5

GATE 2018

Solution

Applying Cauchy's integral theorem

$$\int_C \frac{f(z)}{z - z_o} dz = 2\pi i f(z_o)$$

$$\int_C \frac{1}{5z-4} dz = \int_C \frac{\frac{1}{5}}{z - \frac{4}{5}} dz$$

$$\int_C \frac{\frac{1}{5}}{z - \frac{4}{5}} dz = 2\pi i \times \frac{1}{5} = A\pi i$$

$$A = \frac{2}{5}$$

Example 4.51

Let X_1 and X_2 be two independent exponentially distributed random variables with means 0.5 and 0.25, respectively. Then $Y = \min(X_1, X_2)$ is

(A) exponentially distributed with mean 1/6

(B) exponentially distributed with mean 2

(C) normally distributed with mean 3/4

(D) normally distributed with mean 1/6

GATE 2018

Solution

$$\text{Mean}(X_1) = 0.5 \Rightarrow \frac{1}{\lambda_1} = 0.5$$

$$\lambda_1 = 2$$

$$\text{Mean}(X_2) = 0.25 \quad \Rightarrow \frac{1}{\lambda_2} = 0.25 \qquad \lambda_2 = 4$$

$$\text{Mean}(Y) = \frac{1}{\lambda_1 + \lambda_2} = \frac{1}{2+4} = \frac{1}{6}$$

Exponentially distributed with mean $= \frac{1}{6}$

Example 4.52

The lengths of a large stock of titanium rods follow a normal distribution with a mean (μ) of 440 mm and a standard deviation (σ) of 1 mm. What is the percentage of rods whose lengths lie between 438 mm and 441 mm?

(A) 81.85% (B) 68.4% (C) 99.75% (D) 86.64%

GATE 2019

Solution

Given: Mean $\mu = 440$ mm, Standard deviation $\sigma = 1$ mm

Random variable $z = \frac{x-\mu}{\sigma} = \frac{x-440}{1}$

For $x = 438$ mm; $z_1 = \frac{438-440}{1} = -2$

For $x = 441$ mm; $z_2 = \frac{441-440}{1} = 1$

Percentage of rods whose length lie between 438 mm and 441 mm is

= Area of normal distribution curve from $z_1 = -2$ to $z_2 = 1$

$$p(438 < x < 441) = p(-2 < x < 0) + p(0 < z < 1)$$

$$p(438 < x < 441) = \left(\frac{95.44}{2} + \frac{68.26}{2}\right)\%$$

$$p(438 < x < 441) = 81.85\%$$

Example 4.53

Evaluation of $\int_2^4 x^3 dx$ using a 2-equal-segment trapezoidal rule gives a value of ________.

GATE 2019

Solution

Let $f(x) = x^3$, $a = 2$, $b = 4$ and $n = 2$

$$h = \frac{b-a}{n} = \frac{4-2}{2} = 1$$

i	0	1	2
x	2	3	4
$f(x)$	8	27	64

Using Trapezoidal rule

$$\int_a^b f(x)dx = \frac{h}{2}[(y_0 + y_n) + 2(y_1 + y_2 + \ldots + y_{n-1})]$$

$$\int_2^4 x^3 dx = \frac{1}{2}[(8+64) + 2(27)] = 63$$

$$\int_2^4 x^3 dx = 63$$

Example 4.54

A harmonic function is analytic if it satisfies the Laplace equation. If $u(x, y) = 2x^2 - 2y^2 + 4xy$ is a harmonic function, then its conjugate harmonic function $v(x, y)$ is

(A) $4xy - 2x^2 + 2y^2 + \text{constant}$

(B) $2y^2 - 4xy + \text{constant}$

(C) $2x^2 - 2y^2 + xy + \text{constant}$

(D) $-4xy + 2y^2 - 2x^2 + \text{constant}$

GATE 2019

Solution

Given: $u(x, y) = 2x^2 - 2y^2 + 4xy$

$$\frac{\partial u}{\partial x} = 4x + 4y, \frac{\partial u}{\partial y} = 4x - 4y$$

By Cauchy - Reimann equations $\frac{\partial u}{\partial x} = \frac{\partial v}{\partial y}$ and $\frac{\partial u}{\partial y} = -\frac{\partial v}{\partial x}$

$$\frac{\partial v}{\partial y} = 4x + 4y \Rightarrow \quad v = 4xy + 2y^2 + \phi(x) + c$$

$$-\frac{\partial v}{\partial x} = 4x - 4y \Rightarrow -\frac{\partial}{\partial x}(4xy + 2y^2 + \phi(x) + c) = 4x - 4y$$

or $\frac{\partial}{\partial x}\phi(x) = -4x \quad \Rightarrow \quad \phi(x) = -\int 4x dx = -2x^2$

$$v = 4xy + 2y^2 - 2x^2 + c$$

$$v = 4xy - 2x^2 + 2y^2 + c$$

Example 4.55

An analytic function $f(z)$ of complex variable $z = x + iy$ may be written as $f(z) = u(x, y) + iv(x, y)$. Then, $u(x, y)$ and $v(x, y)$ must satisfy

(A) $\frac{\partial u}{\partial x} = \frac{\partial v}{\partial y}$ and $\frac{\partial u}{\partial y} = \frac{\partial v}{\partial x}$

(B) $\frac{\partial u}{\partial x} = \frac{\partial v}{\partial y}$ and $\frac{\partial u}{\partial y} = -\frac{\partial v}{\partial x}$

(C) $\frac{\partial u}{\partial x} = -\frac{\partial v}{\partial y}$ and $\frac{\partial u}{\partial y} = \frac{\partial v}{\partial x}$

(D) $\frac{\partial u}{\partial x} = -\frac{\partial v}{\partial y}$ and $\frac{\partial u}{\partial y} = -\frac{\partial v}{\partial x}$

GATE 2019

Solution

An analytic function $f(z)$ must satisfy the Cauchy - Reimann equation:

$$\frac{\partial u}{\partial x} = \frac{\partial v}{\partial y} \text{ and } \frac{\partial u}{\partial y} = -\frac{\partial v}{\partial x}$$

Example 4.56

If x is the mean of data 3, x, 2 and 4, then the mode is______.

GATE 2019

Solution

$$\text{Mean } x = \frac{3 + x + 2 + 4}{4}$$

$$x = 3$$

Data are 3, 3, 2, 4

Data which occurs most is 3

Mode = 3

Example 4.57

The derivative of $f(x) = \cos(x)$ can be estimated using the approximation $f'(x) = \frac{f(x+h) - f(x-h)}{2h}$. The percentage error is calculated as $\left(\frac{\text{Exact value} - \text{Approximate value}}{\text{Exact value}}\right) \times 100$. The percentage error in the derivative of $f(x)$ at $x = \pi/6$ radian, choosing $h = 0.1$ radian, is

(A) $< 0.1\%$

(B) $> 0.1\%$ and $< 1\%$

(C) $> 1\%$ and $< 5\%$

(D) $> 5\%$

GATE 2019

Solution

Given function $f(x) = \cos(x)$

$f'(x) = -\sin(x)$

Approximate value

$$= \frac{f(x+h) - f(x-h)}{2h} = \frac{\cos(x+h) - \cos(x-h)}{2h}$$

$$= -\frac{2\sin x \sin(h)}{2h} = -\sin x\left(\frac{\sin h}{h}\right)$$

$$\%\text{ Error} = \left(\frac{\text{Exact value} - \text{Approximate value}}{\text{Exact value}}\right) \times 100$$

$$\%\text{ Error} = \left(1 - \frac{\sin h}{h}\right) \times 100 = \left(1 - \frac{\sin(0.1\pi/180)}{0.1}\right) \times 100$$

$$\%\text{ Error} = 0.166\%$$

Example 4.58

The probability that a part manufactured by a company will be defective is 0.05. If 15 such parts are selected randomly and inspected, then the probability that at least two parts will be defective is _____. (round off to two decimal places)

GATE 2019

Solution

Given: Probability of defective part $p=0.05$

$q=1-p=0.95$

Number of trials(parts) $n=15$

Probability that at least two parts will be defective

$$p(r\geq 2)=1-[p(r=0)+p(r=1)]$$

$$p(r\geq 2)=1-({}^{n}C_{r=0}p^{0}q^{n}+{}^{n}C_{r=1}p^{1}q^{n-1})$$

$$p(r\geq 2)=1-[{}^{15}C_{0}(0.05)^{0}(0.95)^{15}+{}^{15}C_{0}(0.05)^{1}(0.95)^{15-1}]$$

$$p(r\geq 2)=0.17$$

4.3 PRACTICE PAPER

Time: 3 hours **Max. Marks: 100**

Q.1 to Q.30 carry one mark each

Q.1 to Q.20 Multiple Choice Questions

Q.1 If $x=\sqrt{-1}$, then the value of x^x is

(A) $e^{-\frac{\pi}{2}}$ (B) $e^{\frac{\pi}{2}}$ (C) x (D) 1

Q.2 Square roots of $-i$ (where $i=\sqrt{-1}$) are

(A) $i, -i$

(B) $\cos\left(-\frac{\pi}{4}\right)+i\sin\left(-\frac{\pi}{4}\right), \cos\left(\frac{3\pi}{4}\right)+i\sin\left(\frac{3\pi}{4}\right)$

(C) $\cos\left(\frac{\pi}{4}\right)+i\sin\left(\frac{3\pi}{4}\right), \cos\left(\frac{3\pi}{4}\right)+i\sin\left(\frac{\pi}{4}\right)$

(D) $\cos\left(\frac{3\pi}{4}\right)+i\sin\left(-\frac{3\pi}{4}\right), \cos\left(-\frac{3\pi}{4}\right)+i\sin\left(\frac{3\pi}{4}\right)$

Q.3 There are two containers, with one containing 4 red and 3 green balls and the other containing 3 blue and 4 green balls. One ball is drawn at random from each container. The probability that one of the balls is red and the other is blue will be

(A) $\frac{1}{7}$ (B) $\frac{9}{49}$ (C) $\frac{12}{49}$ (D) $\frac{3}{7}$

Q.4 Match List-I with List-II and select the correct answer using the codes given below the lists:

List-I	List-II
(a) Newton-Raphson method	(1) Solving nonlinear equations
(b) Runge-Kutta method equations	(2) Solving simultaneous linear equations
(c) Simpson's Rule equations	(3) Solving ordinary differential equation
(d) Gauss elimination	(4) Numerical integration
	(5) Interpolation
	(6) Calculation of Eigenvalues

(A) a-6 b-1 c-5 d-3 (B) a-1 b-6 c-4 d-3

(C) a-1 b-3 c-4 d-2 (D) a-5 b-3 c-4 d-1

Q.5 Let $P(E)$ denotes the probability of the event E. Given $P(A)=1$, $P(B)=1/2$, the value of $P(A/B)$ and $P(B/A)$ respectively are

(A) $\frac{1}{4}, \frac{1}{2}$ (B) $\frac{1}{2}, \frac{1}{4}$ (C) $\frac{1}{2}, 1$ (D) $1, \frac{1}{2}$

Q.6 A box contains 10 screws, 3 of which are defective. Two screws are drawn at random with replacement. The probability that none of the two screws is defective will be

(A) 100 % (B) 50 % (C) 49 % (D) None of these

Q.7 A fair coin is tossed independently four times. The probability of the event "the number of times heads show up is more than the number of times tails show up" is

(A) $\frac{1}{16}$ (B) $\frac{1}{8}$ (C) $\frac{1}{4}$ (D) $\frac{5}{16}$

Q.8 If a fair coin is tossed four times. What is the probability that two heads and two tails will result

(A) $\frac{3}{8}$ (B) $\frac{1}{2}$ (C) $\frac{5}{8}$ (D) $\frac{3}{4}$

Q.9 If probability density function of a random variable X is

$$f(x)=\begin{cases}x^2, & \text{for } -1\leq x\leq 1\\ 0, & \text{for any other value of } x\end{cases}$$

then, the percentage probability $P\left(-\frac{1}{3}\leq x\leq\frac{1}{3}\right)$ is

(A) 0.0247 (B) 0.247 (C) 0.472 (D) 0.647

Q.10 A continuous random variable X has a probability density function $f(x)=e^{-x}; 0<x<\infty$. Then $P(X>1)$ is

(A) 0.368 (B) 0.5 (C) 0.632 (D) 1.0

Q.11 Given that one root of the equation $x^3 - 10x^2 + 31x - 30 = 0$ is 5, the other roots are

(A) 2 and 3 (B) 2 and 4

(C) 3 and 4 (D) −2 and −3

Q.12 The square root of a number N is to be obtained by applying the Newton-Raphson iterations to the equation $x^2 - N = 0$. If i denotes the iteration index, the correct iterative scheme will be

(A) $x_{i+1} = \frac{1}{2}\left(x_i + \frac{N}{x_i}\right)$ (B) $x_{i+1} = \frac{1}{2}\left(x_i^2 + \frac{N}{x_i^2}\right)$

(C) $x_{i+1} = \frac{1}{2}\left(x_i + \frac{N^2}{x_i}\right)$ (D) $x_{i+1} = \frac{1}{2}\left(x_i - \frac{N}{x_i}\right)$

Q.13 If $f(z) = c_0 + c_1 z^{-1}$, then $\oint_{\text{unit circle}} \frac{1 + f(z)}{z} dz$ is given by

(A) $2\pi c_1$ (B) $2\pi(1 + c_0)$

(C) $2\pi i c_i$ (D) $2\pi i(1 + c_0)$

Q.14 When the Newton-Raphson method is applied to solve the equation $f(x) = x^3 + 2x - 1 = 0$, the solution at the end of the first iteration with the initial guess value at $x_0 = 1.2$ is

(A) −0.82 (B) 0.49 (C) 0.705 (D) 1.69

Q.15 Let $x^2 - 117 = 0$. The iterative steps for the solution using Newton-Raphson method is given by

(A) $x_{k+1} = \frac{1}{2}\left(x_k + \frac{117}{x_k}\right)$ (B) $x_{k+1} = x_k - \frac{117}{x_k}$

(C) $x_{k+1} = x_k - \frac{x_k}{117}$ (D) $x_{k+1} = x_k - \frac{1}{2}\left(x_k + \frac{117}{x_k}\right)$

Q.16 The complex numbers $z = x + iy$ which satisfy the equation $|z + 1| = 1$, lie on

(A) y-axis

(B) x-axis

(C) circle with center $(-1, 0)$ and radius 1

(D) None of these

Q.17 In a box there are 2 red, 3 black and 4 white balls. Out of these, three balls are drawn together. The probability of these being of same colour is

(A) $\frac{1}{84}$ (B) $\frac{1}{21}$ (C) $\frac{5}{84}$ (D) None of these

Q.18 If the probability function of the normal distribution is $P(x) = \frac{1}{\sqrt{2\pi}} e^{-\frac{x^2}{2}}$, then its mean and standard deviation are, respectively

(A) 0 and 0 (B) 0 and 1 (C) 1 and 1 (D) None of these

Q.19 The probability that a person hits a target is 0.003. What is the probability of hitting the target with 2 or more bullet if the number of shot is 2000?

(A) $1 - e^{-6}$ (B) $1 - e^{6}$ (C) $1 - 7e^{6}$ (D) $1 - 7e^{-6}$

Q.20 The roots of equation $x^3 - 3x + 1 = 0$ lies between

(A) 1 and 2 (B) 0 and 1 (C) 1 and −1 (D) 0 and −1

Q.21 to Q.30 Numerical Answer Questions

Q.21 A fair dice is rolled twice. The probability that an odd number will follow an even number is___.

Q.22 A faire coin is tossed 6 times. What is the probability that ONLY the first two tosses will yield heads?___.

Q.23 A box contains 4 white balls and 3 red balls. In succession, two balls are randomly selected and removed from the box. Give that the first removed ball is white, the probability that the second removed ball is red is________.

Q.24 If X is uniformly distributed over (0,10), the probability that $3 < X < 8$ is____________.

Q.25 An examination consists of two papers, Paper 1 and Paper 2. The probability of failing in Paper 1 is 0.3 and that in Paper 2 is 0.2. Given that a student has failed in Paper 2, the probability of failing in Paper 1 is 0.6. The probability of a student failing in both the papers is______.

Q.26 Starting with $x_0 = 1$, the next approximation x_1 to $2^{\frac{1}{3}}$ obtained by Newton-Rapshon method is_____.

Q.27 For a Binomial distribution, mean is 6 and variance is 2. The number of Bernoulli trials is__________.

Q.28 Area between $\mu - 3\sigma$ and $\mu + 3\sigma$ in normal distribution curve is (approximate)_______%.

Q.29 Three coins are tossed, the probability of getting at least two head is_______.

Q.30 If x is a continuous random variable with probability density function given by

$$f(x) = \begin{cases} kx^2, & 0 \le x < 2 \\ 2k, & 2 \le x \le 4 \end{cases}$$, then the value of k is___.

Q.31 to Q.65 carry two marks each

Q.31 to Q.50 Multiple Choice Questions

Q.31 For an analytic function, $f(x+iy) = u(x, y) + i\,v(x, y)$, u is given by $u = 3x^2 - 3y^2$. The expression for v, considering k to be constant is

(A) $3y^2 - 3x^2 + k$ (B) $6x - 6y + k$

(C) $6y - 6x + k$ (D) $6xy + k$

Q.32 Using Cauchy's integral theorem, the value of the integral (integration being taken in counter clockwise direction) $\oint \frac{z^3 - 6}{3z - i}\,dz$ is

(A) $\frac{2\pi}{81} - 4\pi i$ (B) $\frac{\pi}{8} - 6\pi i$

(C) $\frac{4\pi}{81} - 6\pi i$ (D) 1

Q.33 The value of the integral $\oint_C \frac{\cos(2\pi z)}{(2z-1)(z-3)}\,dz$ (where C is a closed curve given by $|z| = 1$) is

(A) $-\pi i$ (B) $\frac{\pi}{5} i$ (C) $\frac{2\pi}{5} i$ (D) πi

Q.34 The integral $\oint \frac{z^2 - 4}{z^2 + 4}\,dz$ evaluated anti-clockwise around the circle $|z - i| = 2$, where $i = \sqrt{-1}$, is

(A) -4π (B) 0 (C) $2 + \pi$ (D) $2 + 2i$

Q.35 The value of $\oint_C \frac{dz}{(1+z^2)}$ where C is the counter $\left|z - \frac{i}{2}\right| = 1$, is

(A) $2\pi i$ (B) π (C) $\tan^{-1} z$ (D) $\pi i \tan^{-1} z$

Q.36 The value of the contour integral $\oint_{|z-i|=2} \frac{1}{z^2+4}\,dz$ in positive sense is

(A) $\frac{\pi}{2} i$ (B) $-\frac{\pi}{2}$ (C) $-\frac{\pi}{2} i$ (D) $\frac{\pi}{2}$

Q.37 The residue of the function $f(z) = \frac{1}{(z+2)^2(z-2)^2}$ at $z = 2$, is

(A) $-\frac{1}{32}$ (B) $-\frac{1}{16}$ (C) $\frac{1}{16}$ (D) $\frac{1}{32}$

Q.38 A loaded dice has following probability distribution of occurrences:

Dice value	1	2	3	4	5	6
Probability	$\frac{1}{4}$	$\frac{1}{8}$	$\frac{1}{8}$	$\frac{1}{8}$	$\frac{1}{8}$	$\frac{1}{4}$

If three identical dice as the above are thrown, the probability of occurrence of values 1, 5 and 6 on the three dice is

(A) Same as that of occurrence of 3, 4, 5

(B) Same as that of occurrence of 1, 2, 5

(C) $\frac{1}{128}$ (D) $\frac{5}{8}$

Q.39 The annual precipitation data of a city is normally distributed with mean and standard deviation as 1000 mm and 200 mm, respectively. The probability (%) that the annual precipitation will be more than 1200 mm is

(A) $< 50\%$ (B) 50% (C) 75 % (D) 100 %

Q.40 The following equation needs to be numerically solved using the Newton-Rapshon method.

$$x^3 + 4x - 9 = 0$$

The iterative equation for this purpose is (k indicates the iteration level)

(A) $x_{k+1} = \frac{2x_k^3 + 9}{3x_k^2 + 4}$ (B) $x_{k+1} = \frac{3x_k^3 + 4}{2x_k^2 + 9}$

(C) $x_{k+1} = x_k - 3x_k^2 + 4$ (D) $x_{k+1} = \frac{4x_k^2 + 3}{9x_k^2 + 2}$

Q.41 Equation $e^x - 1 = 0$ is required to be solved using Newton's method with an initial guess $x_0 = -1$. Then, after one step of Newton's method, estimate x_1 of the solution will be given by

(A) 0.71828 (B) 0.36784

(C) 0.20587 (D) 0.00000

Q.42 The Newton-Raphson iteration $x_{n+1} = \frac{1}{2}\left(x_n + \frac{R}{x_n}\right)$ can be used to compute the

(A) Square of R (B) Reciprocal of R

(C) Square root of R (D) Logarithm of R

Q.43 Consider the series $x_{n+1} = \frac{x_n}{2} + \frac{9}{8x_n}$, $x_0 = 0.5$ obtained from the Newton-Raphson method. The series converges to

(A) 1.5 (B) $\sqrt{2}$ (C) 1.6 (D) 1.4

Q.44 The estimate of $\int_{0.5}^{1.5} \frac{dx}{x}$ obtained using Simpson's rule with three-point function evaluation exceeds the exact value by

(A) 0.235 (B) 0.068 (C) 0.024 (D) 0.012

Q.45 What is the magnitude as the error (correct to two decimal places) in the estimation of following integral using Simpson 1/3 rule. Take the step length as 1.

$$\int_0^4 (x^4 + 10)dx$$

(A) 0.53 (B) 0.34 (C) 0.22 (D) 0.12

Q.46 The differential equation $\frac{dy}{dx} = 0.25y^2$ is to be solved using the backward (implicit) Euler's method with the boundary condition $y = 1$ at $x = 0$ and with a step size of 1. What would be the value of y at $x = 1$?

(A) 1.33 (B) 1.67 (C) 2.00 (D) 2.33

Q.47 While numerically solving the differential equation $\frac{dy}{dx} + 2xy^2 = 0$, $y(0) = 1$ using Euler's predictor corrector (improved Euler-Cauchy) with a step size of 0.2, the value of y after the first step is

(A) 1.00 (B) 1.03 (C) 0.97 (D) 0.96

Q.48 Function $f(z) = (x^2 - 2xy + py^2) + i(qx^2 - y^2 + 2xy)$. If $f(z)$ is a analytic, then the value of p and q are

(A) 1,1 (B) –1,1 (C) 1,–1 (D) None of these

Q.49 Using Cauchy's integral theorem, the value of the integral (integration being taken in counter clockwise direction) $\oint_C \frac{z^3 - 6}{3z - i} dz$ is

(A) $\frac{2\pi}{81} - 4\pi i$ (B) $\frac{\pi}{8} - 6\pi i$ (C) $\frac{2\pi}{81} - 6\pi i$ (D) 1

Q.50 Suppose p is the number of cars per minute passing through a certain road junction between 5 PM, and p has Poission's distribution with mean 3. What is the probability of observing fewer than 3 cars during any given minutes in this interval?

(A) $\frac{8}{2e^3}$ (B) $\frac{9}{2e^3}$ (C) $\frac{17}{2e^3}$ (D) $\frac{26}{2e^3}$

Q.51 to Q.65 Numerical Answer Questions

Q.51 A probability density function is of the form $P(x) = k\,e^{-|x|};\ x \in (-\infty, \infty)$. The value of k is____.

Q.52 Find the value of λ such that $f(x)$ is valid probability density function

$$f(x) = \begin{cases} \lambda(x-1)(2-x); & \text{for } 1 \le x \le 2 \\ 0 & ; \text{ otherwise} \end{cases}$$

λ =______.

Q.53 The value of the integral $I = \frac{1}{\sqrt{2\pi}} \int_0^\infty \exp\left(-\frac{x^2}{8}\right) dx$ is_____.

Q.54 The following table gives values of a function $f(x)$ obtained for values of x at intervals of 0.25.

x	0	0.25	0.5	0.75	1.0
$f(x)$	1	0.9412	0.8	0.64	0.50

The value of the integral of the function between the limits 0 to 1 using Simpson's rule is_______.

Q.55 Consider a differential equation $\frac{dy}{dx} - y = x$ with the initial condition $y(0) = 0$. Using Euler's first order method with a step size of 0.1, the value of $y(0.3)$ is__________.

Q.56 By Simpson's rule, the value of $\int_{-3}^{3} x^4 dx$ by taking 6 sub-intervals is_________.

Q.57 Given system of equations

$27x + 6y - z = 85, 6x + 15y + 2z = 72$ and $x + y + 54z = 110$

The first approximation value of x by Gauss-seidel iteration method is ___.

Q.58 A river is 80 m wide. Its depth d m and corresponding distance x m from one bank is given below in the table

x (in m)	0	10	20	30	40	50	60	70	80
d (in m)	0	4	7	9	12	15	14	8	3

The approximate area (in m^2) of cross-section of river by trapezoidal rule is______.

Q.59 The probability of an event A occurring is 0.5 and of occurring is 0.3. If A and B are mutually exclusive events, then the probability of neither A nor B occurring is______.

Q.60 If the initial approximate root (x_0) of equation $x^3 - 10 = 0$ is 2.5, then second approximate root (x_2) is__.

Q.61 Find the fourth approximation of the root of the equation $x^3 + x - 11 = 0$, between 2 and 3, using bisection method______.

Q.62 Sum of deviation of a set of values $x_1, x_2, x_3 \ldots x_n$ measured from 50 is -10 and the sum of deviation of values from 46 is 70. The mean of values $x_1, x_2, x_3 \ldots x_n$ is____.

Q.63 A fair coin is tossed till a head appears for the first time. The probability that the number of required tosses is odd, is___.

Q.64 An examination paper contains 150 multiple-choice questions of one mark each, with each question having four choices. Each incorrect answer fetches −0.25 mark. Suppose 1000 students choose all their answers randomly with uniform probability. The sum total of the expected marks obtained by all these students is________.

Q.65 In an experiment, positive and negative value are equally likely to occur. The probability of obtaining at most one negative value in five trials is_______.

4.4 SOLUTION TO PRACTICE PAPER

Q.1 Ans:(A)

Given: $x = \sqrt{-1}$

$$x = \sqrt{-1} = \cos\frac{\pi}{2} + i\sin\frac{\pi}{2}$$

or $x = \cos\frac{\pi}{2} + i\sin\frac{\pi}{2} = e^{\frac{\pi}{2}i}$

Now $x^x = \left\{e^{\frac{\pi}{2}i}\right\}^i = e^{\frac{\pi}{2}i^2} = e^{-\frac{\pi}{2}}$

$$x^x = e^{-\frac{\pi}{2}}$$

Q.2 Ans:(B)

We know that

$$-i = \cos\left(-\frac{\pi}{2}\right) + i\sin\left(-\frac{\pi}{2}\right)$$

$$= \cos\left(\frac{3\pi}{2}\right) + i\sin\left(\frac{3\pi}{2}\right)$$

Square root of $-i$

$$\sqrt{-i} = \left[\cos\left(-\frac{\pi}{2}\right) + i\sin\left(-\frac{\pi}{2}\right)\right]^{\frac{1}{2}}$$

$$= \left[\cos\left(\frac{3\pi}{2}\right) + i\sin\left(\frac{3\pi}{2}\right)\right]^{\frac{1}{2}}$$

$$\sqrt{-i} = \cos\left(-\frac{\pi}{4}\right) + i\sin\left(-\frac{\pi}{4}\right)$$

$$= \cos\left(\frac{3\pi}{4}\right) + i\sin\left(\frac{3\pi}{4}\right)$$

$$\sqrt{-i} = \cos\left(-\frac{\pi}{4}\right) + i\sin\left(-\frac{\pi}{4}\right)$$

$$\sqrt{-i} = \cos\left(\frac{3\pi}{4}\right) + i\sin\left(\frac{3\pi}{4}\right)$$

Q.3 Ans:(C)

Number of balls in each container = 7

1 ball is drawn in $^7C_1$ ways = 7

Probability of getting one ball is red and another is blue

$= P(\text{first ball is red and second ball is blue}) = \frac{4}{7} \times \frac{3}{7}$

$$P(\text{first ball is red and second ball is blue}) = \frac{12}{49}$$

Q.4 Ans:(C)

Correct Match:

List-I	List-II
(a) Newton-Raphson method	(1) Solving nonlinear equations
(b) Runge-Kutta method equations	(3) Solving ordinary differential equation
(c) Simpson's Rule equations	(4) Numerical integration
(d) Gauss elimination	(2) Solving simultaneous linear equations

Q.5 Ans:(D)

Given: $P(A) = 1$ and $P(B) = \frac{1}{2}$

Both the events are independent

$$P(A \cap B) = P(A)P(B) = 1 \times \frac{1}{2} = \frac{1}{2}$$

$$P(A/B) = \frac{P(A \cap B)}{P(B)} = \frac{1/2}{1/2} = 1$$

$$P(B/A) = \frac{P(A \cap B)}{P(A)} = \frac{1/2}{1} = \frac{1}{2}$$

$$P(A/B) = 1, P(B/A) = \frac{1}{2}$$

Q.6 Ans:(C)

Probability of defective screw $p = \frac{3}{10}$

$n = 2$ and $x = 0$ (no defective)

Applying Binomial distribution theorem,

$$P(x) = {}^nC_x\, p^x q^{n-x}$$

Probability of none of two screw is defective

$$P_{(x=0)} = {}^2C_0 \left(\frac{3}{10}\right)^0 \left(1 - \frac{3}{10}\right)^{2-0}$$

$$P_{(x=0)} = \left(\frac{7}{10}\right)^2 = 0.49$$

$$P = 49\,\%$$

Q.7 Ans:(D)

Number of toss = 4

Probability (Number of heads > Number of tails)

$$= P(\text{4 heads and 0 tail or 3 heads and 1 tail})$$

$$= {}^4C_4 \left(\frac{1}{2}\right)^4 \left(1 - \frac{1}{2}\right)^0 + {}^4C_3 \left(\frac{1}{2}\right)^3 \left(1 - \frac{1}{2}\right)^1$$

$$= \frac{1}{16} + \frac{4}{16} = \frac{5}{16}$$

Probability (Number of heads > Number of tails) $= \dfrac{5}{16}$

Q.8 Ans:(A)

Probability of getting head, $p = \dfrac{1}{2}$

Applying Binomial distribution theorem,

$$P(x) = {}^nC_x\, p^x q^{n-x}$$

$$P_{(x=2)} = {}^4C_2 \left(\frac{1}{2}\right)^2 \left(1 - \frac{1}{2}\right)^{4-2}$$

or $$P_{(x=2)} = \frac{4!}{2!\,2!}\left(\frac{1}{2}\right)^2 \left(\frac{1}{2}\right)^2$$

$$P_{(x=2)} = \frac{3}{8}$$

Q.9 Ans:(A)

Given: $$f(x) = \begin{cases} x^2, & \text{for } -1 \le x \le 1 \\ 0, & \text{for any other value of } x \end{cases}$$

Probability $$P\left(-\frac{1}{3} \le x \le \frac{1}{3}\right) = \int_{-\frac{1}{3}}^{\frac{1}{3}} f(x)dx = \int_{-\frac{1}{3}}^{\frac{1}{3}} x^2 dx$$

or $$P\left(-\frac{1}{3} \le x \le \frac{1}{3}\right) = \left[\frac{x^3}{3}\right]_{-\frac{1}{3}}^{\frac{1}{3}} = \frac{2}{81}$$

$$P\left(-\frac{1}{3} \le x \le \frac{1}{3}\right) = \frac{2}{81}$$

Q.10 Ans:(A)

Given: $f(x) = e^{-x};\ 0 < x < \infty$

$$P(X > 1) = \int_1^{\infty} f(x)\,dx = \int_1^{\infty} e^{-x} dx$$

or $$P(X > 1) = [-e^{-x}]_1^{\infty} = e^{-1}$$

$$P(X > 1) = 0.368$$

Q.11 Ans:(A)

Given: One root of the equation $x^3 - 10x^2 + 31x - 30 = 0$ is 5.

Therefore, the equation $x^3 - 10x^2 + 31x - 30 = 0$ is divisible by $(x - 5)$.

$$\frac{x^3 - 10x^2 + 31x - 30}{x - 5} = x^2 - 5x + 6$$

and $$x^2 - 5x + 6 = (x - 2)(x - 3) = 0$$

Thus, the roots of equation $x^3 - 10x^2 + 31x - 30 = 0$ are 5, 2 and 3.

Other two roots are 2 and 3.

Q.12 Ans:(A)

The Newton-Raphson iterative formula is

$$x_{i+1} = x_i - \frac{f(x_i)}{f'(x_i)}$$

or $$x_{i+1} = x_i - \frac{(x_i^2 - N)}{2x_i}$$

or $$x_{i+1} = \frac{2x_i^2 - x_i^2 + N}{2x_i} = \frac{x_i^2 + N}{2x_i}$$

$$x_{i+1} = \frac{1}{2}\left(x_i + \frac{N}{x_i}\right)$$

Q.13 Ans:(D)

It has one pole at origin, which is inside the unit circle.

So, $$\oint_{\text{unit circle}} \frac{1 + f(z)}{z} dz = 2\pi i\, F(a) = 2\pi i[(1 + f(z)]_{z=0}$$

$$\oint_{\text{unit circle}} \frac{1 + f(z)}{z} dz = 2\pi i\,(1 + c_0)$$

Q.14 Ans:(C)

The Newton-Raphson iterative formula is

$$x_{n+1} = x_n - \frac{f(x_n)}{f'(x_n)}$$

$$x_{n+1} = x_n - \frac{x_n^2 + 2x_n - 1}{2x_n + 2}$$

or $$x_{n+1} = \frac{2x_n^3 + 1}{3x_n^3 + 2}$$

Putting initial guess value $x_0 = 1.2$

$$x_1 = \frac{2 \times 1.2^3 + 1}{3 \times 1.2^2 + 2}$$

$$x_1 = 0.705$$

Q.15 Ans:(A)

The Newton-Raphson iterative formula is

$$x_{k+1} = x_k - \frac{f(x_k)}{f'(x_k)}$$

$$x_{k+1} = x_k - \frac{(x_k^2 - 117)}{2x_k}$$

or $$x_{k+1} = \frac{x_k^2 + 117}{2x_k}$$

$$x_{k+1} = \frac{1}{2}\left(x_k + \frac{117}{x_k}\right)$$

Q.16 Ans:(C)

Given: $|z+1| = 1 \quad \Rightarrow \quad |x + iy + 1| = 1$

or $(x+1)^2 + y^2 = 1^2$

This is the equation of circle of center $(-1, 0)$ and radius 1.

Q.17 Ans:(C)

Total number of balls in box $= 2 + 3 + 4 = 9$

3 balls are drawn in ${}^9C_3$ ways $= \frac{9!}{6! \times 3!} = \frac{9 \times 8 \times 7}{3 \times 2} = 84$

Favorable way of getting 3 black (same colour) balls

$$= {}^3C_3 = 1$$

Favorable way of getting 3 white (same colour) balls

$$= {}^4C_3 = 4$$

Probability of getting same colour ball

$$= \frac{{}^3C_3 + {}^4C_3}{{}^9C_3} = \frac{1+4}{84} = \frac{5}{84}$$

$$P = \frac{5}{84}$$

Q.18 Ans:(B)

Compare $P(x) = \frac{1}{\sqrt{2\pi}} e^{-\frac{x^2}{2}}$ with standard form of normal distribution

$$P(x) = \frac{1}{\sigma\sqrt{2\pi}} e^{-\frac{1}{2}\left(\frac{x-\mu}{\sigma}\right)^2}$$

From which $\mu = 0$ and $\sigma = 1$

Mean $\mu = 0$, standard deviation $\sigma = 1$

Q.19 Ans:(D)

$P(x > 2) = 1 - P(x < 2) = 1 - [P(x=0) + P(x=1)]$

Applying Poisson distribution, $\quad P_{(x=k)} = \frac{\lambda^k}{k!} e^{-\lambda}$

$$\lambda = \mu = np = 2000 \times 0.003 = 6$$

$$P(x > 2) = 1 - \left[\frac{6^0}{0!} e^{-6} + \frac{6^1}{1!} e^{-6}\right]$$

$$= 1 - (e^{-6} + 6e^{-6})$$

$$P(x > 2) = 1 - 7e^{-6}$$

Q.20 Ans:(B)

Given: $f(x) = x^3 - 3x + 1$

Substituting $x = 0$, $f(0) = 0^3 - 3 \times 0 + 1 = 1$ (Positive value)

Substituting $x = 1$, $f(1) = 1^3 - 3 \times 1 + 1 = -2$ (Negative value)

Roots lie between 0 and 1.

Q.21 Ans:[0.25]

$P_{\text{odd}} = \frac{3}{6}$ and $P_{\text{even}} = \frac{3}{6}$

Since both events are independent of each other.

$$P_{(\text{odd/even})} = \frac{3}{6} \times \frac{3}{6}$$

$$P_{(\text{odd/even})} = \frac{1}{4}$$

Q.22 Ans:[0.01562]

P(ONLY the first two tosses are heads)

$= P$ (H, H, T, T, T, T)

Since each toss is independent

Thus, required probability

$$P = P(\text{H}) \times P(\text{H}) \times P(\text{T}) \times P(\text{T}) \times P(\text{T}) \times P(\text{T})$$

or $$P = [P(\text{H})]^2 \times [P(\text{T})]^4$$

or $$P=\left(\frac{1}{2}\right)^2\times\left(\frac{1}{2}\right)^4=\left(\frac{1}{2}\right)^6$$

$$P=0.01562$$

Q.23 Ans:[0.5]

P(2nd ball is red / 1st ball is white)

$$=\frac{P(\text{2nd ball is red and 1st ball is white})}{P(\text{1st ball is white})}$$

P(2nd ball is red /1st ball is white)

$$=\frac{P(\text{1st ball is white and 2nd ball is red})}{P(\text{1st ball is white})}$$

$$P(\text{2nd ball is red /1st ball is white})=\frac{\frac{4}{7}\times\frac{3}{6}}{\frac{4}{7}}=\frac{3}{6}$$

$$P(\text{2nd ball is red/1st ball is white})=\frac{1}{2}$$

Q.24 Ans:[0.5]

Probability function $f(x)=\frac{1}{10-1}=\frac{1}{10}$

$$P(3<x<8)=\int_3^8 f(x)dx=\int_3^8\frac{1}{10}dx$$

$$P(3<x<8)=\frac{8-3}{10}=\frac{5}{10}$$

$$P(3<x<8)=\frac{1}{2}$$

Q.25 Ans:[0.12]

A denotes the event of failing in Paper 1

B denotes the event of failing in Paper 2

Given: $P(A)=0.3, P(B)=0.2$ and $P(A/B)=0.6$

Probability of failing in both papers

$$P(A\cap B)=P(B)\times P(A/B)$$

or $$P(A\cap B)=0.2\times 0.6=0.12$$

Probability of failing in both papers $=0.12$

Q.26 Ans:[1.33]

Given: $x=2^{\frac{1}{3}}\Rightarrow x^3-2=0$

Let $f(x)=x^3-2\Rightarrow f'(x)=3x^2$

Newton's-Raphson formula

$$x_1=x_0-\frac{f(x_0)}{f'(x_0)}$$

$$\Rightarrow\quad x_1=x_0-\frac{x_0^3-2}{3x_0^2}=\frac{2x_0^3+2}{3x_0^2}$$

Substituting $x_0=1$, $x_1=\frac{2\times1^3+2}{3\times1^2}$

$$x_1=\frac{4}{3}=1.33$$

Q.27 Ans:[9]

Mean $np=6$ (i)

Variance $npq=2$ (ii)

From Equation (i) and (ii), we have $q=\frac{2}{6}=\frac{1}{3}$

$p+q=1$ or $p=1-q=1-\frac{1}{3}=\frac{2}{3}$

From Equation (i) $n\times\frac{2}{3}=6$

Number of trial $n=9$

Q.28 Ans:[99.73]

Area between $\mu-3\sigma$ and $\mu+3\sigma$ in normal distribution curve is 99.73%

Q.29 Ans:[0.5]

S={HHT, THH, HTH, HHT, TTT, TTH, THT, HTT} $\leftarrow$8 (total number of cases)

If A is the required the event, then

A={HHT, THH, HTH, HHT} $\leftarrow$4 (number of cases favourable to A)

Hence, the required probability is given by

$$P(A)=\frac{\text{Number of cases favourable to }A}{\text{Total number of cases}}$$

$$P(A)=\frac{4}{8}=0.5$$

Q.30 Ans:[0.15]

Property of probability function $\int_0^4 f(x)\,dx=1$

$$\int_0^2 f(x)dx+\int_2^4 f(x)dx=1$$

$$\int_0^2 kx^2dx+\int_2^4 2kdx=1 \quad\text{or}\quad \frac{k}{3}[x^3]_0^2+2k[x]_2^4=1$$

or $$\frac{8k}{3}+4k=1$$

$$k=\frac{3}{20}=0.15$$

Q.31 Ans:(D)

Given: $u = 3x^2 - 3y^2$ and $f(x+iy) = u(x,y) + i\,v(x,y)$ is analytic

Since $f(z)$ is an analytic. Cauchy-Riemann equations are satisfied.

$$\frac{\partial u}{\partial x} = \frac{\partial v}{\partial y} \quad \Rightarrow \quad \frac{\partial v}{\partial y} = 6x,$$

Integrating, we get $\int \partial v = \int 6x\partial y + f(x)$

$$v = 6xy + f(x)$$

and $$\frac{\partial u}{\partial y} = -\frac{\partial v}{\partial x} \quad \Rightarrow \quad -6y = \frac{\partial}{\partial x}(6xy + f(x))$$

or $$\frac{\partial}{\partial x} f(x) = 0$$

$$f(x) = k$$

From which

$$v = 6xy + k$$

Q.32 Ans:(A)

Cauchy's integral theorem, $\oint_C \frac{f(z)}{z-a}\,dz = 2\pi i\,f(a)$

Now $$\oint_C \frac{z^3-6}{3z-i}\,dz = \frac{1}{3}\oint_C \frac{z^3-6}{z-\frac{i}{3}}\,dz$$

Applying Cauchy's integral theorem,

$$\frac{1}{3}\oint_C \frac{z^3-6}{z-\frac{i}{3}}\,dz = \frac{1}{3}2\pi i\left[\left(\frac{i}{3}\right)^3 - 6\right]$$

or $$\frac{1}{3}\oint_C \frac{z^3-6}{z-\frac{i}{3}}\,dz = \frac{1}{3}2\pi i\left[\left(\frac{i}{3}\right)^3 - 6\right]$$

$$\oint_C \frac{z^3-6}{3z-i}\,dz = \frac{1}{3}\oint_C \frac{z^3-6}{z-\frac{i}{3}}\,dz = \frac{2\pi}{81} - 4\pi i$$

Q.33 Ans:(C)

$$I = \oint_C \frac{\cos(2\pi z)}{(2z-1)(z-3)}\,dz$$

or $$I = \frac{1}{2}\oint_C \frac{\left(\frac{\cos(2\pi z)}{z-3}\right)}{\left(z-\frac{1}{2}\right)}\,dz$$

Since $z = \frac{1}{2}$ is a point within $|z| = 1$ (clockwise curve C), we can use Cauchy's integral theorem

$$\frac{1}{2}\oint_C \frac{\left(\frac{\cos(2\pi z)}{z-3}\right)}{\left(z-\frac{1}{2}\right)}\,dz = \frac{1}{2}2\pi i\,f(a)$$

$$\frac{1}{2}\oint_C \frac{\left(\frac{\cos(2\pi z)}{z-3}\right)}{\left(z-\frac{1}{2}\right)}\,dz = \frac{1}{2}2\pi i\frac{\cos\left(2\pi\times\frac{1}{2}\right)}{\frac{1}{2}-3}$$

$$\oint_C \frac{\cos(2\pi z)}{(2z-1)(z-3)}\,dz = \frac{1}{2}\oint_C \frac{\left(\frac{\cos(2\pi z)}{z-3}\right)}{\left(z-\frac{1}{2}\right)}\,dz = \frac{2\pi}{5}i$$

Q.34 Ans:(A)

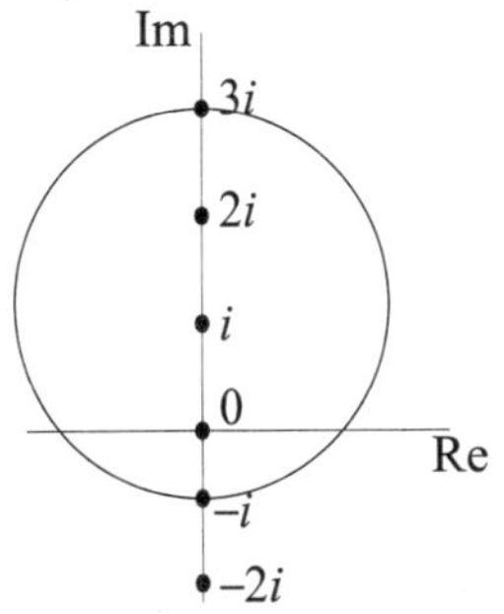

$$\oint \frac{z^2-4}{z^2+4}\,dz = \oint \frac{z^2-4}{(z+2i)(z-2i)}\,dz$$

Poles are at $2i$ and $-2i$

Pole $2i$ inside and pole $-2i$ is outside the circle $|z-i| = 2$

$$\oint \frac{z^2-4}{z^2+4}\,dz = \oint \frac{\frac{z^2-4}{z+2i}}{(z-2i)}\,dz = 2\pi i\left(\frac{(2i)^2-4}{2i+2i}\right)$$

$$\oint \frac{z^2-4}{z^2+4}\,dz = -4\pi$$

Q.35 Ans:(B)

$$\oint \frac{dz}{(1+z^2)} = \oint \frac{dz}{(z-i)(z+i)}$$

Poles at i is inside and $-i$ is outside the circle $\left|z - \frac{i}{2}\right| = 1.$

$$\oint \frac{dz}{(1+z^2)} = \oint \frac{\frac{1}{z+i}}{(z-i)}\,dz = 2\pi i\,f(a) = 2\pi i\left(\frac{1}{i+i}\right)$$

$$\oint \frac{dz}{(1+z^2)} = \pi$$

Q.36 Ans:(D)

$$\oint_{|z-i|=2} \frac{1}{z^2+4} dz = \oint_{|z-i|=2} \frac{1}{(z+2i)(z-2i)} dz$$

Poles $2i$ inside and $-2i$ outside the circle $|z-i|=2$

$$\oint_{|z-i|=2} \frac{1}{z^2+4} dz = \oint_{|z-i|=2} \frac{\frac{1}{z+2i}}{(z-2i)} dz = 2\pi i f(a)$$

$$\oint_{|z-i|=2} \frac{1}{z^2+4} dz = \oint_{|z-i|=2} \frac{\frac{1}{z+2i}}{(z-2i)} dz = 2\pi i \left(\frac{1}{2i+2i}\right)$$

$$\oint_{|z-i|=2} \frac{1}{z^2+4} dz = \frac{\pi}{2}$$

Q.37 Ans:(A)

Since $\lim_{z\to 2}[(z-2)^2 f(z)]$ is finite and non-zero, $f(z)$ has a pole of order two at $z=2$.

The residue at $z=a$ is given for a pole of order n as

$$\text{Res } f(a) = \frac{1}{(n-1)!}\left\{\frac{d^{n-1}}{dz^{n-1}}(z-a)^n f(z)\right\}_{z=2}$$

Here $n=2$ (pole of order 2) and $a=2$

$$\text{Res } f(2) = \frac{1}{(2-1)!}\left\{\frac{d}{dz}(z-2)^2 \frac{1}{(z+2)^2(z-2)^2}\right\}_{z=2}$$

or $$\text{Res } f(2) = \left\{\frac{d}{dz}\frac{1}{(z+2)^2}\right\}_{z=2}$$

or $$\text{Res } f(2) = \left\{-\frac{2}{(z+2)^3}\right\}_{z=2}$$

$$\text{Res } f(2) = -\frac{1}{32}$$

Q.38 Ans:(C)

Dice value	1	2	3	4	5	6
Probability	$\frac{1}{4}$	$\frac{1}{8}$	$\frac{1}{8}$	$\frac{1}{8}$	$\frac{1}{8}$	$\frac{1}{4}$

Since each events is independent,

$$P(1,5,6) = \frac{1}{4}\times\frac{1}{8}\times\frac{1}{4} = \frac{1}{128}$$

$$P(3,4,5) = \frac{1}{8}\times\frac{1}{8}\times\frac{1}{8} = \frac{1}{512}$$

$$P(1,2,5) = \frac{1}{4}\times\frac{1}{8}\times\frac{1}{8} = \frac{1}{256}$$

Probability of occurrence of values 1, 5 and 6 is

$$P(1,5 \text{ and } 6) = \frac{1}{4}\times\frac{1}{8}\times\frac{1}{4} = \frac{1}{128}$$

Q.39 Ans:(A)

Given: Mean, $\mu = 1000$ mm

Standard deviation, $\sigma = 200$ mm

Standard normal variate, $z = \frac{x-\mu}{\sigma}$

Standard normal variate for $x > 1200$ is

$$z = \frac{1200-1000}{200} = 1$$

From normal distribution table (0.3413 at $z = 1.00$)

The probability that the annual precipitation will be more than 1200 mm is $(0.5000 - 0.3413) = 0.1587$ or 15.87 %.

Less than 50 %

Q.40 Ans:(A)

Given: $f(x) = x^3 + 4x - 9$

$$f'(x) = 3x^2 + 4$$

By Newton-Raphson method,

$$x_{k+1} = x_{k+1} - \frac{f(x_k)}{f'(x_k)}$$

or $$x_{k+1} = x_{k+1} - \frac{x_k^3 + 4x_k - 9}{3x_k^2 + 4}$$

$$x_{k+1} = \frac{2x_k^3 + 9}{3x_k^2 + 4}$$

Q.41 Ans:(A)

Given: $f(x) = e^x - 1$

$$f'(x) = e^x$$

The Newton-Raphson iterative equation is

$$x_{i+1} = x_{i+1} - \frac{f(x_i)}{f'(x_i)}$$

$$x_{i+1} = x_i - \frac{(e^{x_i} - 1)}{e^{x_i}}$$

$$x_{i+1} = \frac{e^{x_i}(x_i - 1) + 1}{e^{x_i}}$$

Now put $i = 0$; $x_1 = \frac{e^{x_0}(x_0 - 1) + 1}{e^{x_0}}$

Putting initial guess $x_0 = -1$;

$$x_1 = \frac{e^{-1}(-1-1)+1}{e^{-1}} = 0.71828$$

$$x_1 = 0.71828$$

Q.42 Ans:(C)

Given: $x_{n+1} = \frac{1}{2}\left(x_n + \frac{R}{x_n}\right)$

At convergence $x_{n+1} = x_n = \alpha$

$$\alpha = \frac{1}{2}\left(\alpha + \frac{R}{\alpha}\right)$$

or $$2\alpha = \alpha + \frac{R}{\alpha}$$

$$\alpha = \sqrt{R}$$

Q.43 Ans:(A)

Given: $x_{n+1} = \frac{x_n}{2} + \frac{9}{8x_n}$ and $x_0 = 0.5$

Series converges as $n \to \infty$

$$x_{n+1} = x_n = \alpha$$

$$\alpha = \frac{\alpha}{2} + \frac{9}{8\alpha}$$

or $$\alpha = \frac{4\alpha^2 + 9}{8\alpha}$$

or $$\alpha^2 = \frac{9}{4} = \left(\frac{3}{2}\right)^2$$

$$\alpha = 1.5$$

Q.44 Ans:(D)

Exact value of $\int_{0.5}^{1.5} \frac{dx}{x} = [\ln x]_{0.5}^{1.5} = 1.0986$

i	0	1	2
x	0.5	1.0	1.5
$y = \frac{1}{x}$	$\frac{1}{0.5}$	1	$\frac{1}{1.5}$

Approximate value by Simpson's rule with 3 points is

$$I = \frac{h}{3}[f(0) + 4f(1) + f(2)]$$

or $$I = \frac{0.5}{3}\left(\frac{1}{0.5} + 4\times\frac{1}{1.0} + \frac{1}{1.5}\right)$$

$$I = 1.1111$$

Approximate value – Exact value = 1.1111 – 1.0986

Approximate value – Exact value = 0.012

Q.45 Ans:(A)

Exact value of integral

$$I = \int_0^4 (x^4 + 10)dx = \left[\frac{x^5}{5} + 10x\right]_0^4 = \frac{4^5}{5} + 10\times 4$$

$I = 244.8$

i	0	1	2	3	4
x	0	1	2	3	4
$f(x) = x^4 + 10$	10	11	26	91	266

Using Simpson's rule, we have

$$\int_0^4 (x^4 + 10)\,dx = \frac{h}{3}[f(0) + 4\{f(1) + f(3)\} + 2f(2) + f(4)]$$

or $$\int_0^4 (x^4 + 10)\,dx = \frac{1}{3}[10 + 4\{11 + 91\} + 2\times 26 + 266]$$

or $$\int_0^4 (x^4 + 10)\,dx = 245.33$$

Thus,

The magnitude of error= 245.33 – 244.8 = 0.53

Q.46 Ans:(C)

Given: $\frac{dy}{dx} = 0.25y^2$, $y = 1$ at $x = 0$ and $h = 1$

By backward(implicit) Euler's method,

$$y_{k+1} = y_k + h\,f(x_{k+1}, y_{k+1})$$

$$y_{k+1} = y_k + h\times 0.25\,y_{k+1}^2$$

$$0.25h\,y_{k+1}^2 - y_{k+1} + y_k = 0$$

Putting $k = 0$; $\quad 0.25h\,y_1^2 - y_1 + y_0 = 0$

Putting $y_0 = 1$ and $h = 1$, we have

$$0.25\,y_1^2 - y_1 + 1 = 0$$

$$y_1 = \frac{1 \pm \sqrt{1 - 4\times 0.25}}{2\times 0.25} = 2$$

$$y_1 = 2$$

Q.47 Ans:(D)

Given: $\frac{dy}{dx} + 2xy^2 = 0$; $y(0) = 1$ and $h = 0.2$

$$y_1^* = y_0 + h(-2x_0 y_0^2)$$

$$y_1^* = 1 + 0.2(-2 \times 0 \times 1^2)$$

$$y_1^* = 1$$

$$y_1 = y_0 + \frac{h}{2}(-2x_0 y_0^2 - 2x_1 y^{*2}_1)$$

$$y_1 = 1 + \frac{02}{2}(-2 \times 0 \times 1^2 - 2 \times 0.2 \times 1^2)$$

$$y_1 = 0.96$$

Q.48 Ans:(B)

$f(z) = (x^2 - 2xy + py^2) + i(qx^2 - y^2 + 2xy) = u + iv$

From which $u = x^2 - 2xy + py^2$, $v = qx^2 - y^2 + 2xy)$

$$\frac{\partial u}{\partial x} = 2x - 2y \quad \text{and} \quad \frac{\partial v}{\partial x} = 2qx + 2y$$

$$\frac{\partial u}{\partial y} = -2x + 2py \quad \text{and} \quad \frac{\partial v}{\partial y} = -2y + 2x$$

Since $f(z)$ is a analytic, Cauchy-Riemann equations are satisfied.

$$\frac{\partial u}{\partial x} = \frac{\partial v}{\partial y} \quad \text{and} \quad \frac{\partial u}{\partial y} = -\frac{\partial v}{\partial x} \quad \Rightarrow \quad -2x + 2py = -2qx - 2y$$

From which

$$p = -1, q = 1$$

Q.49 Ans:(A)

Cauchy's integral theorem, $\oint_C \frac{f(z)}{z-a} dz = 2\pi i f(a)$

Now $\oint_C \frac{z^3 - 6}{3z - i} dz = \frac{1}{3} \oint_C \frac{z^3 - 6}{z - \frac{i}{3}} dz$

Applying Cauchy's integral theorem, using $f(z) = z^3 - 6$ and $a = \frac{i}{3}$, we have

$$\frac{1}{3} \oint_C \frac{z^3 - 6}{z - \frac{i}{3}} dz = \frac{1}{3}\left[2\pi i f\left(\frac{i}{3}\right)\right] = \frac{2\pi}{3} i\left[\left(\frac{i}{3}\right)^3 - 6\right]$$

$$= \frac{2\pi}{3}\left[\frac{i^4}{27} - 6i\right]$$

$$\oint_C \frac{z^3 - 6}{3z - i} dz == \frac{2\pi}{81} - 4\pi i$$

Q.50 Ans:(C)

Applying Poisson distribution formula $P(x) = \frac{e^{-\lambda}\lambda^x}{x!}$

Mean, $\lambda = 3$

Probability of observing fewer than 3 cars

$$P = p(x=0) + p(x=1) + p(x=2)$$

$$= \frac{e^{-3}3^0}{0!} + \frac{e^{-3}3^1}{1!} + \frac{e^{-3}3^2}{2!}$$

$$P = \frac{17}{2e^3}$$

Q.51 Ans:[0.5]

Probability density function $p(x) = ke^{-|x|}; x \in (-\infty, \infty)$

$$\int_{-\infty}^{\infty} p(x) dx = 1 \quad \Rightarrow \quad \int_{-\infty}^{\infty} ke^{-|x|} dx = 1$$

or $\int_{-\infty}^{0} ke^{x} dx + \int_{0}^{\infty} ke^{-x} dx = 1$

or $k + k = 1$

$$k = 0.5$$

Q.52 Ans:[6]

Probability density function

$$f(x) = \begin{cases} \lambda(x-1)(2-x) & \text{for } 1 \le x \le 2 \\ 0 & \text{otherwise} \end{cases}$$

$$\int_{-\infty}^{\infty} f(x) dx = 1$$

or $\int_{-\infty}^{\infty} f(x) dx = \int_{-\infty}^{1} f(x) dx + \int_{1}^{2} f(x) dx + \int_{2}^{\infty} f(x) dx = 1$

or $\int_{-\infty}^{1} 0\, dx + \int_{1}^{2} \lambda(x-1)(2-x) dx + \int_{2}^{\infty} 0 dx = 1$

or $\int_{1}^{2} \lambda(-x^2 + 3x - 2) dx = 1$

$$\lambda = 6$$

Q.53 Ans:[1]

$$I = \frac{1}{\sqrt{2\pi}} \int_0^{\infty} \exp\left(-\frac{x^2}{8}\right) dx \qquad \text{(i)}$$

Normal distribution probability density function is given by

$$f(x) = \frac{1}{\sigma\sqrt{2\pi}} e^{-\frac{(x-\mu)^2}{2\sigma^2}}; -\infty < x < \infty$$

$$\int_{-\infty}^{\infty} \frac{1}{\sigma\sqrt{2\pi}} e^{-\frac{(x-\mu)^2}{2\sigma^2}} dx = 1$$

or $2\int_{0}^{\infty} \frac{1}{\sigma\sqrt{2\pi}} e^{-\frac{(x-\mu)^2}{2\sigma^2}} dx = 1$

Putting $\mu = 0$ and $\sigma = 2$

$$2 \times \frac{1}{2\sqrt{2\pi}} \int_0^\infty e^{-\frac{x^2}{8}} dx = 1 \qquad \text{(ii)}$$

Comparing Equation (i) and (ii), we have

$$\frac{1}{\sqrt{2\pi}} \int_0^\infty \exp\left(-\frac{x^2}{8}\right) dx = 1$$

Q.54 Ans:[0.7854]

i	0	1	2	3	4
x	0	0.25	0.5	0.75	1.0
$f(x)$	1	0.9412	0.8	0.64	0.50

Using Simpson's rule,we have

$$I = \frac{h}{3}[f(0) + 4\{f(1) + f(3)\} + 2f(2) + f(4)]$$

or $$I = \frac{0.25}{3}[1 + 4\{0.9412 + 0.64\} + 2 \times 0.8 + 0.50]$$

$$I = 0.7854$$

Q.55 Ans:[0.031]

Given: $\frac{dy}{dx} = x + y$; $y(0) = 0$ and step size $h = 0.1$

Euler's first order formula $y_{i+1} = y_i + hf(x_i, y_i)$

$$y_1 = y_0 + h(x_0 + y_0),\ x_1 = x_0 + h$$

$$y_1 = 0 + 0.1(0 + 0) = 0$$

$$x_1 = x_0 + h = 0 + 0.1 = 0.1$$

$$y_2 = y_1 + h(x_1 + y_1), x_2 = x_1 + h$$

$$y_2 = 0 + 0.1(0.1 + 0) = 0.01$$

$$x_2 = x_1 + h = 0.1 + 0.1 = 0.2$$

$$y_3 = y_2 + h(x_2 + y_2), x_3 = x_2 + h$$

$$y_3 = 0.01 + 0.1\ (0.2 + 0.01) = 0.031,$$

$$x_3 = x_2 + h = 0.2 + 0.1 = 0.3$$

$$y_3 = 0.031, \text{ at } x_3 = 0.3$$

Q.56 Ans:[98]

For six sub-interval $h = \frac{3-(-3)}{6} = 1$

x	−3	−2	−1	0	1	2	3
$y = x^4$	81	16	1	0	1	16	81

Using Simpson's $\frac{1}{3}$ rule, we have

$$\int_{-3}^{3} x^4 dx = \frac{h}{3}[(y_0 + y_6) + 4(y_1 + y_3 + y_5) + 2(y_2 + y_4)]$$

or $$\int_{-3}^{3} x^4 dx = \frac{1}{3}[(81 + 81) + 4(16 + 0 + 16) + 2(1 + 1)]$$

or $$\int_{-3}^{3} x^4 dx = \frac{1}{3}[162 + 128 + 4]$$

$$\int_{-3}^{3} x^4 dx = 98$$

Q.57 Ans:[3.15]

We solve each equation of the system for the unknown with the largest coefficient in terms of the remaining unknowns,

$$x = \frac{1}{27}(85 - 6y + z)$$

$$y = \frac{1}{15}(72 - 6x - 2z)$$

$$z = \frac{1}{54}(110 - x - y)$$

Starting with $y = 0,\ z = 0$, we have

$$x^{(1)} = \frac{1}{27}(85 + 0) = 3.15 \text{ (First approximation)}$$

Q.58 Ans:[705]

x	0	10	20	30	40	50	60	70	80
d	0	4	7	9	12	15	14	8	3

Here $h = 10$

Using trapezoidal rule, we have

$$\text{Area} = \frac{h}{2}[f(0) + 2\{f(1) + f(2) + f(3) + \ldots\} + f(8)]$$

$$\text{Area} = \frac{10}{2}[0 + 3 + 2(4 + 7 + 9 + 12 + 15 + 14 + 8)]$$

$$\text{Area} = 705 \text{ m}^2$$

Q.59 Ans:[0.2]

Given: $P(A) = 0.5$, $P(B) = 0.3$ and event A and B are mutually exclusive.

$$P(\text{neither } A \text{ nor } B) = 1 - (0.5 + 0.3)$$

$$P(\text{neither } A \text{ nor } B) = 0.2$$

Q.60 Ans:[2.155]

Given: Equation $f(x) = x^3 - 10 \quad \Rightarrow \quad f'(x) = 3x^2$

By Newton Raphson method, we have

$$x_{n+1} = x_n - \frac{f(x_n)}{f'(x_n)} = x_n - \frac{x_n^3 - 10}{3x_n^2} = \frac{2x_n^3 + 10}{3x_n^2}$$

First approximate root, $x_1 = \frac{2x_0^3 + 10}{3x_0^2} = \frac{2 \times (2.5)^3 + 10}{3 \times (2.5)^2}$

or $\quad x_1 = 2.2$

Second approximate root, $x_2 = \frac{2x_1^3 + 10}{3x_1^2}$

or $\quad x_2 = \frac{2 \times (2.2)^3 + 10}{3 \times (2.2)^2} = 2.155$

$$x_2 = 2.15537$$

Q.61 Ans:[2.062]

Let $f(x) = x^3 + x - 11$,

$f(2) = 8 + 2 - 11 = -1\,(-\text{ve})$

$f(3) = 27 + 3 - 11 = 19\,(+\text{ve})$

Therefore, one root lies between 2 and 3.

First approximation to the root $= \frac{2+3}{2} = 2.5$

Now $\quad f(2.5) = 2.5^3 + 2.5 - 11 = 7.125 < 0$

Therefore, root lies between 2 and 2.5.

Second approximation to the root $= \frac{2+2.5}{2} = 2.25$

Now $f(2.25) = 2.25^3 + 2.25 - 11 = 2.6406 < 0.$

Therefore, root lies between 2 and 2.25.

Third approximation to the root $= \frac{2+2.25}{2} = 2.125$

Now $f(2.125) = 2.125^3 + 2.125 - 11 = 0.7207 < 0.$

Therefore, root lies between 2 and 2.125.

Fourth approximation to the root is $\frac{2+2.125}{2} = 2.0625$

Q.62 Ans:[49.5]

Given: Deviation $\sum_{i=1}^{i=n}(x_i - 50) = -10$

or $\quad \left(\sum_{i=1}^{i=n} x_i\right) - 50n = -10 \qquad$ (i)

and $\quad$ deviation $\sum_{i=1}^{i=n}(x_i - 46) = 70$

or $\quad \left(\sum_{i=1}^{i=n} x_i\right) - 46n = 70 \qquad$ (ii)

Subtracting Equation (ii) from Equation (i), we get

$4n = 80$

$n = 20$

Putting $n = 20$ in Equation (i), we get

$\left(\sum_{i=1}^{i=20} x_i\right) - 50 \times 20 = -10$

or $\quad \left(\sum_{i=1}^{i=20} x_i\right) = 990$

Thus, $\quad$ the mean is $\mu = \frac{\left(\sum_{i=1}^{i=20} x_i\right)}{n} = \frac{990}{20}$

Mean $\mu = 49.5$

Q.63 Ans:[0.6666]

P(no. of tosses is odd) = P(no. of tosses is 1, 3, 5, 7,...)

P(no. of tosses is 1) = P(head in first toss) $= \frac{1}{2}$

P(no. of tosses is 3)

= P(tail in first and second toss, head in third toss)

$= \frac{1}{2} \times \frac{1}{2} \times \frac{1}{2} = \left(\frac{1}{2}\right)^3$

P(no.of tosses is 5)

= P(tail in first, second, thired, and fourth toss, head in fifth toss) $= \left(\frac{1}{2}\right)^5$

Similarly

P(no. of tosses is odd) $= \frac{1}{2} + \left(\frac{1}{2}\right)^3 + \left(\frac{1}{2}\right)^5 + \left(\frac{1}{2}\right)^7 + \ldots$

$$= \frac{\frac{1}{2}}{1 - \left(\frac{1}{2}\right)^2}$$

P(no. of tosses is odd) $= \frac{2}{3}$

Q.64 Ans:[9375]

Let the marks obtained per question be a random variable X.

Its probability distribution table is

X	1	−0.25
$P(X)$	$\frac{1}{4}$	$\frac{3}{4}$

Expected marks per questions $= E(X)$

$$= \sum x P(X)$$

$$= 1 \times \frac{1}{4} + (0.25) \times \frac{3}{4}$$

$$= \frac{1}{16} \text{ marks}$$

Total marks per students expected for 150 questions

$$= \frac{1}{16} \times 150 = \frac{75}{8}$$

Total expected marks of 1000 students

$$= \frac{75}{8} \times 1000 = 9375 \text{ marks}$$

Q.65 Ans:[0.1875]

Given: $p = \frac{1}{2}$, $q = \frac{1}{2}$ and number of trials $n = 5$

Let x be number of negative value in 5 trials

P(at most one negative value) $= p(x=0) + p(x=1)$

$$P = {}^5C_0 \left(\frac{1}{2}\right)^0 \left(\frac{1}{2}\right)^5 + {}^5C_1 \left(\frac{1}{2}\right)^1 \left(\frac{1}{2}\right)^4$$

$$P = \frac{6}{32}$$

5 Engineering Mechanics

GATE Syllabus

Free-body diagrams and equilibrium; Trusses and frames; Virtual work; Kinematics and dynamics of particles and of rigid bodies in plane motion; Impulse and momentum (linear and angular); Energy formulations, Collisions.

Chapter Outline

5.1 KEY CONCEPTS AND FORMULAS

Statics of Particles and Rigid Bodies

System of Forces

Concurrent forces: Two or more forces that act at the same point are called concurrent forces.

Coplanar forces: Two or more forces whose directed arrows lie in the same plane are called coplanar forces.

Parallelogram Law of Forces

If two forces acting at a point, be represented, in magnitude and direction by the sides of a parallelogram drawn from the point, their resultant is represented both in magnitude and direction, by the diagonal of the parallelogram drawn through that point.

Resultant, $R = \sqrt{P^2 + Q^2 + 2PQ\cos\theta}$

Direction of resultant $\alpha = \tan^{-1}\left(\dfrac{Q\sin\theta}{P + Q\cos\theta}\right)$

Resolution of Force

In resolution, a single force F acting on a particle may be replaced by two or more forces which together, have the same effect on the particle. These forces are called components of the original force F, and the process of substituting them is called resolving the force F into component.

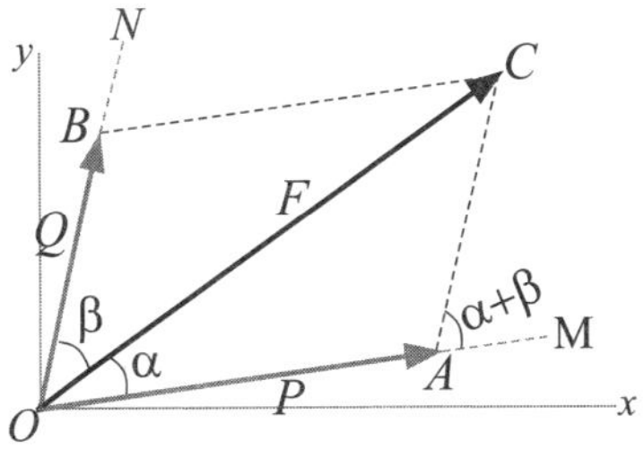

Component $\quad P = F\dfrac{\sin\beta}{\sin(\alpha+\beta)}$

Component $\quad Q = F\dfrac{\sin\alpha}{\sin(\alpha+\beta)}$

Rectangular components of a force in space

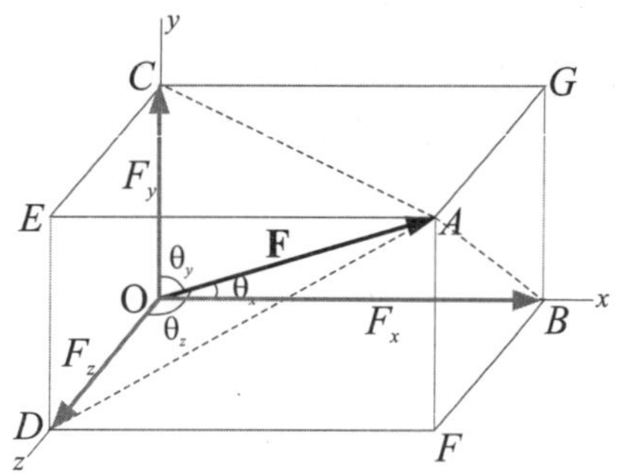

$\mathbf{F} = F_x\mathbf{i} + F_y\mathbf{j} + F_z\mathbf{k}$, $\mathrm{F} = \sqrt{F_x^2 + F_y^2 + F_z^2}$

Component of **F** along *x*-direction $F_x = F\cos\theta_x$

Component of **F** along *y*-direction $F_y = F\cos\theta_y$

Component of **F** along *z*-direction $F_z = F\cos\theta_z$

$\theta_x = \cos^{-1}\left(\frac{F_x}{F}\right)$, $\theta_y = \cos^{-1}\left(\frac{F_y}{F}\right)$ and $\theta_z = \cos^{-1}\left(\frac{F_z}{F}\right)$

$\cos^2\theta_x + \cos^2\theta_y + \cos^2\theta_z = 1$

Moment of Force

The moment of a force is measure of its tendency to cause a body to rotate about a specific point or axis. This is different from the tendency for a body to move, or translate, in the direction of force.

$$M_0 = Fd = Fr\sin\theta$$

In vector form $\mathbf{M_0} = \mathbf{r} \times \mathbf{F}$

Couples

The moment produced by two equal, opposite, and non-collinear forces is called a *couple*. It does not produce any translation, but produces only rotation. The resultant force of a couple is zero, ($M = Fd$).

Free Body Diagram

A free-body diagram is a sketch of the body that shows the body(by it self, free of the other parts of the system) and all the forces applied to it, that is, all forces acting on the body.

Static Equilibrium

A body is said to be in static equilibrium when the resultant force on it must be zero and the body must have no tendency to rotate. This second condition of equilibrium requires that the net moment about any point be zero.

Conditions for equilibrium: First condition: $\sum \mathbf{F} = 0$ and Second condition: $\sum \mathbf{M} = 0$

Lami's Theorem

If a body is in equilibrium under the action of only three coplanar and concurrent forces, Lami's theorem can be used.

Lami's theorem states: If a body is in equilibrium under the action of three forces, each force is proportional to the sine of angle between the other forces.

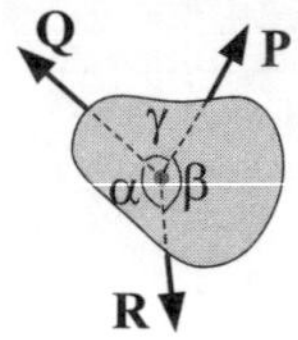

Mathematically,

$$\frac{P}{\sin\alpha} = \frac{Q}{\sin\beta} = \frac{R}{\sin\gamma}$$

Friction

When a body slides over another body, a force is exerted at the surface of contact by a stationary body on the moving body. This resisting force is called the *force of friction* and acts in a direction opposite to the direction of motion.

Static and Kinetic Friction

The force of static friction between any two surfaces in contact is opposite the applied force and can have values given by $F_s \le \mu_s R$ where μ_s is called the *coefficient of static friction.*

When the block is on the verge of slipping, force of static friction is $F_s \le \mu_s R$

The force of kinetic friction acting on an object is opposite to the direction of motion of the object is given by $F_k = \mu_k R$ where μ_k is a constant called the *coefficient of kinetic friction.*

Laws of Solid Friction (Laws of Coulomb Friction)

The force of friction acts in the opposite direction in which surface is having tendency to move.

The force of friction is equal to the force applied to the surface, so long as the surface is at rest.

When the surface is on the point of motion, the force of friction is maximum and this maximum frictional force is called the *limiting friction force.*

The limiting frictional force bears a constant ratio to the normal reaction between two surfaces.

The limiting frictional force does not depend upon the shape and areas of the surfaces in contact.

The ratio between limiting friction and normal reaction is slightly less when the two surfaces are in motion.

The force of friction is independent of the velocity of sliding.

Angle of Friction

It is the angle ϕ which reaction R subtends with the normal to the plane, when the body just starts sliding over the horizontal plane. This angle is also known as *limiting angle* of reaction or friction.

$$\text{Limiting angle of friction } \phi = \tan^{-1}\mu$$

Angle of Repose

The maximum angle θ of the inclined plane, at which a block resting on it is about to slide down is called the *angle of repose*, and it is equal to the angle of friction between the block and the inclined plane.

Belt Friction

Tension ratio of belt $\frac{T_1}{T_2} = e^{\mu\theta}$. This relation is valid only when the belt is on the point of slipping on the drum.

Rolling Friction

$$F = \frac{a}{h}W = \mu_r W$$

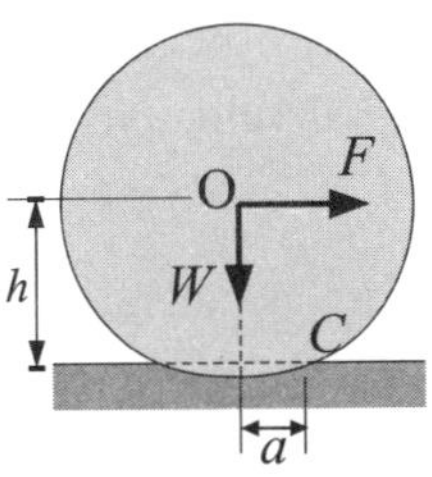

Where, ratio $\mu_r = \frac{a}{h}$ is called the *coefficient of rolling resistance*.

The body, rolls without sliding if $\mu > \frac{a}{h}$. The body will slide, if $\mu < \frac{a}{h}$.

Trusses and Frames

Truss: A truss is an articulated structure composed of straight members arranged and connected in such a way that they transmit primarily axial forces. If all the members lie in one plane it is called a *plane truss*. A three-dimensional truss is called a *space truss*.

Frames: These are structures composed of jointed members any one of which has more than two forces acting on it. Frames are structures which are designed to support applied loads and are usually fixed in position.

Equations of Equilibrium

A structure or one of its member is in equilibrium when it maintains a balance of force and moment. In general this requires that the force and moment equations of equilibrium be satisfied along *x*, *y* and *z*-axis, namely,

$$\sum F_x = 0, \sum F_y = 0, \sum F_z = 0,$$
$$\sum M_x = 0, \sum M_y = 0 \text{ and } \sum M_z = 0$$

Whenever these equations are applied, it is first necessary to draw a free-body diagram of the truss or its members. If a member is selected, it must be isolated from its supports and surroundings and its outlined shapes drawn. All the forces and couple moments must be shown that act on the member.

Classification of Truss

(a) **Efficient or perfect truss**: A truss is said to be perfect when the number of members in the truss are just sufficient to prevent distortion of its shape when loaded with external load. A perfect truss has to satisfy the following equation $m = 2j - 3$, where m = number of members.

(b) **Imperfect truss**: An imperfect truss is that which does not satisfy the equation $m = 2j - 3$. In other words, a truss in which the number of member is more or less than $2j - 3$. The imperfect truss may be further classified into the following two types: (i) Deficient truss, and (ii) Redundant truss.

Deficient truss: A deficient truss is an imperfect truss, in which the number of members are less than $2j - 3$.

Redundant truss: A Redundant truss is an imperfect truss, in which the number of members are more than $2j - 3$.

Basic Assumptions of Truss Analysis

A plane truss can be defined as a structure composed of number of bars, all lying in one plane and hinged together at their ends in such a manner as to form a rigid configuration.

(i) Members are connected at their ends by smooth frictionless pins.

(ii) Loads and reactions are applied to the truss at joints only.

(iii) The centroidal axis of each member is straight and coincides with the line connecting the joint centres at the end of the member.

(iv) All members function as two-force members, i.e., they are subjected to either tension or compression.

Methods of Truss Analysis: (i) Method of joints (ii) Method of sections and (iii) Graphical methods.

Method of Joints

If a truss is in equilibrium, then each of its joints must also be in equilibrium. Hence, the method of joints consists of satisfying the equilibrium conditions $\sum F_x = 0$ and $\sum F_y = 0$ for the forces exerted on the pin at each joint of the truss.

Method of Sections

The method of joints is most effective when the forces in all the members of a truss are to be determined. If, however, the force in only one member or the forces in a very few members are to be found then method of sections is more efficient. The method of section consists of satisfying the equilibrium conditions $\sum F_x = 0$, $\sum F_y = 0$ and $\sum M_z = 0$ for portion of truss.

Virtual Work

When a system or a body is in equilibrium under the action of number of forces, there is no displacement and accordingly no work is done. However, if the system is imagined to undergo any arbitrary but small displacement, some work can be imagined to have been done.

The imaginary small displacement given to the system is

called *virtual displacement*. The product of the net resultant force and the virtual displacement in the direction of force is called *virtual work*.

Principle of Virtual Work

If a body is in equilibrium the total virtual work of the external forces acting on the body is zero for any virtual displacement of the body.

Active Forces

Active forces are external forces capable of doing virtual work during possible virtual displacement.

Stability of Equilibrium

Stable equilibrium: Stable equilibrium occurs if the potential energy V is a minimum.

Unstable equilibrium: Unstable equilibrium occurs if the potential energy V is a maximum.

Neutral equilibrium: Neutral equilibrium exists if a system remains in any position in which it is placed.

Kinematics of Particles and Rigid Bodies

Rectilinear Motion: Velocity and Acceleration

Average velocity, $v_{avg} = \dfrac{\Delta s}{\Delta t}$

Instantaneous velocity, $v = \dfrac{ds}{dt}$

Acceleration, $a = \dfrac{dv}{dt}$

$$a = \frac{d^2 s}{dt^2} \quad \text{or} \quad a = \frac{dv}{ds}\frac{ds}{dt} = v\frac{dv}{ds}$$

Equations of Motion: Rectilinear

Velocity as a function of time, $v = u + at$

Position as a function of time, $s = ut + \dfrac{1}{2}at^2$

Velocity as a function of position, $v^2 = u^2 + 2as$

Curvilinear Motion: Velocity and Acceleration

Instantaneous velocity, $v = \dfrac{dr}{dt}$

Instantaneous acceleration, $a = \dfrac{dv}{dt}$

Angular Velocity and Angular Acceleration

Angular velocity, $\omega = \dot{\theta} = \dfrac{d\theta}{dt}$

Angular acceleration, $\alpha = \dfrac{d^2\theta}{dt^2}, \quad \alpha = \omega\dfrac{d\omega}{d\theta}$

Equations of Motion: Circular

Angular velocity as a function of time

$$\omega = \omega_0 + \alpha t$$

Angular displacement as a function of time

$$\theta = \omega_0 t + \frac{1}{2}\alpha t^2$$

Angular velocity as a function of angular displacement

$$\omega^2 = \omega_0^2 + 2\alpha\theta$$

Radial and Transverse Velocities and Accelerations

Radial velocity, $v_r = \dfrac{dr}{dt}$

Radial acceleration, $a_r = \dfrac{d^2 r}{dt^2} - r\left(\dfrac{d\theta}{dt}\right)^2$

Transverse velocity, $v_\theta = r\dfrac{d\theta}{dt}$

Transverse acceleration, $a_\theta = \dfrac{1}{r}\dfrac{d}{dt}\left(r^2\dfrac{d\theta}{dt}\right)$

Resultant velocity, $v = \sqrt{\left(\dfrac{dr}{dt}\right)^2 + \left(r\dfrac{d\theta}{dt}\right)^2}$

Resultant acceleration, $a = \sqrt{a_r^2 + a_\theta^2}$

Projectiles

A path followed by a particle when it is projected into the space making certain angle with the horizontal is known as projectile.

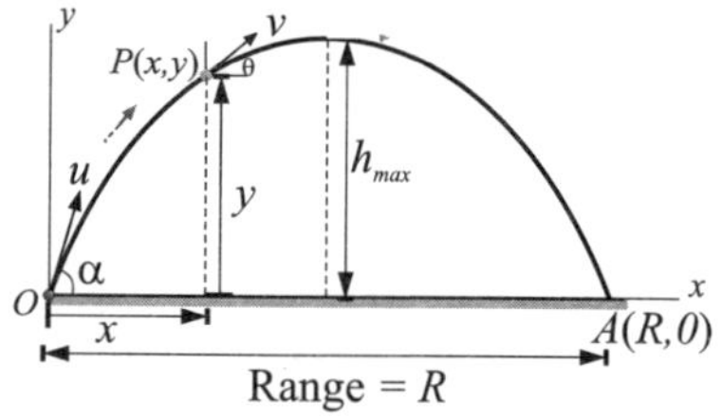

Equation of trajectory, $y = x\tan\alpha - \dfrac{1}{2}\dfrac{gx^2}{u^2\cos^2\alpha}$

Maximum height, $h_{max} = \dfrac{u^2\sin^2\alpha}{2g}$

Time of flight, $T = \dfrac{2u\sin\alpha}{g}$

Range, $R = \dfrac{u^2\sin 2\alpha}{g}$

Maximum value of range

$$R_{max} = \frac{u^2}{g} \qquad \left[\sin 2\alpha = 1 \Rightarrow \alpha = \frac{\pi}{4}\right]$$

Velocity and direction of motion

$$v = \sqrt{u^2 - 2ugt\sin\alpha + g^2t^2}, \; \theta = \tan^{-1}\left(\frac{u\sin\alpha - gt}{u\cos\alpha}\right)$$

$$v = \sqrt{u^2 - 2gy}, \; \theta = \tan^{-1}\left(\frac{\sqrt{u^2\sin^2\alpha - 2gy}}{u\cos\alpha}\right)$$

Dynamics of Particles and Rigid Bodies

Newton's Second Law

$\sum F = ma$ for a particle

$\sum F = \sum ma_G$ for a system of particles (or rigid body)

Equation of Motion: Rectangular Coordinate

$$\sum F_x = ma_x; \quad \sum F_y = ma_y; \quad \sum F_z = ma_z$$

Equation of Motion: Radial and Transverse Components

Radial force, $\sum F_r = m\left[\frac{d^2r}{dt^2} - r\left(\frac{d\theta}{dt}\right)^2\right]$

Transverse force, $\sum F_\theta = m\left[r\frac{d^2\theta}{dt^2} + 2\frac{dr}{dt}\frac{d\theta}{dt}\right]$

Equation of Motion in Plane for a Rigid Body

$$\sum F = ma_G \quad \text{and} \quad \sum \tau = I_G\,\alpha$$

Impulse and Momentum

Linear Momentum

It is defined as the product of the mass and the velocity of the particle ($p = mv$).

Principle of momentum for a particle: The force that acts on a particle is equal to the time rate of change of the momentum of the particle.

$$F = \frac{dp}{dt} \quad \text{or} \quad F = \frac{d(mv)}{dt} = m\frac{dv}{dt} + v\frac{dm}{dt}$$

Impulse

It is defined as the product of force and time. Impulse (**I**) is a vector quantity.

$$\mathbf{I} = F\,\Delta t \quad \text{or} \quad \mathbf{I} = \int_{t_1}^{t_2} F\,dt$$

Principle of linear impulse and momentum of a particle

Impulse = change in linear momentum

Initial momentum + Impulse = Final momentum

$$m(v_x)_1 + \int_{t_1}^{t_2} \mathbf{F}_x dt = m(v_x)_2$$

$$m(v_y)_1 + \int_{t_1}^{t_2} \mathbf{F}_y dt = m(v_y)_2$$

$$m(v_z)_1 + \int_{t_1}^{t_2} \mathbf{F}_z dt = m(v_z)_2$$

Conservation of Linear Momentum

If the resultant force on a particle is zero during an interval of time, linear momentum of particle remains constant ($mv_1 = mv_2$).

Angular Momentum

The angular momentum of a particle about point O is defined as the moment of the linear momentum vector $m\mathbf{v}$ about the point O ($H_o = r \times m\mathbf{v}$).

Angular Impulse

The product of moment and time is defined as angular impulse. $I = M_o\Delta t$

Principle of angular momentum and impulse

Angular impulse = Change in angular momentum

Impact

A collision between two bodies which occurs in a very small interval of time, and during which the two bodies exert on each other relatively large forces, is called an impact. In general, there are two type of impact (i) central impact, (ii) oblique impact.

Central impact occurs when the direction of motion of the mass centres of the two colliding particles is along a line passing through the mass centres of the particles.

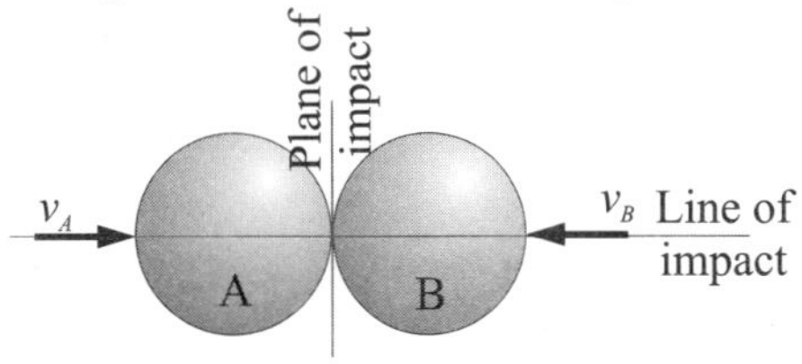

Central impact

Oblique impact occurs when the motion of one or both of the particles is at an angle with the line of impact.

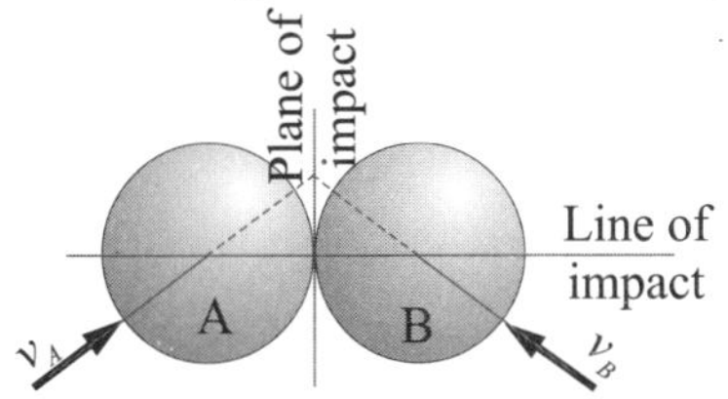

Oblique impact

Coefficient of Restitution

It is the ratio the restitution impulse to the deformation impulse.

Mathematically, $e = \dfrac{\int R\,dt}{\int P\,dt}$ or $e = \dfrac{v_B - v_A}{u_A - u_B}$

Perfectly plastic impact $e = 0$ and perfectly elastic impact $e = 1$

System of Variable Mass

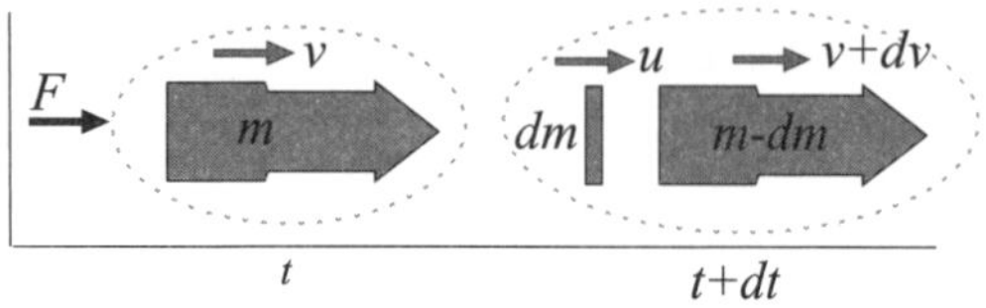

$$F = m\frac{dv}{dt} - v_{\text{rel}}\frac{dm}{dt} \qquad \text{losing mass}$$

$$F = m\frac{dv}{dt} + v_{\text{rel}}\frac{dm}{dt} \qquad \text{gaining mass}$$

Thrust (reaction) $T = v_{\text{rel}}\dfrac{dm}{dt}$

Work and Energy

Work

Work of a force $U_{P-Q} = \int_P^Q (F_x dx + F_y dy + F_z dz)$

Work of the weight, $U_{1-2} = -W\,\Delta y$

Work of a spring force, $U_{1-2} = \frac{1}{2}k(x_2^2 - x_1^2)$

Work of a Couple, $U = \int_{\theta_1}^{\theta_2} M\,d\theta$

Work of a constant force in rectilinear motion

$$U_{1-2} = F\cos\theta\,(x_2 - x_1)$$

Power

Power is the time rate at which work is performed,

$$P = \frac{dU}{dt}. \quad P = \mathbf{F}\cdot\mathbf{v} \quad \text{and} \quad P = \tau\cdot\omega$$

Energy

Energy is defined as the capacity to do work.

Translation kinetic energy, $T = \frac{1}{2}mv_G^2$

Rotation kinetic energy about fixed axis, $T = \frac{1}{2}I_0\,\omega^2$

Total kinetic energy, $T = \frac{1}{2}m v_G^2 + \frac{1}{2}I_G\omega^2$

Principle of Work and Energy

The work done by a system of forces acting on a body during a displacement is equal to the change in kinetic energy of the body during the same displacement.

$$U_{1-2} = \frac{1}{2}mv_2^{\,2} - \frac{1}{2}mv_1^{\,2}$$

Conservative and Non-conservative Forces

Conservative force: A force is said to be conservative if the work done by the force on a system that moves between two configurations is independent of the path the system takes.

Non-conservative force: A force is said to be non-conservative if the work done by a force on a system depends on the path the system follows.

Conservation of Energy

When a rigid body, or a system of rigid bodies, moves under the action of conservative forces, the sum of the kinetic energy and the potential energy of the system remains constant.

$$T + V = \text{constant} \qquad \text{or} \qquad \Delta T + \Delta V = 0$$

5.2 SOLVED EXAMPLES

Previous Years GATE Questions

Example 5.1

A small ball of mass 1 kg moving with a velocity of 12 m/s undergoes a direct central impact with a stationary ball of mass 2 kg. The impact is perfectly elastic. The speed (in m/s) of 2 kg mass ball after the impact will be_________

GATE 2015

Solution

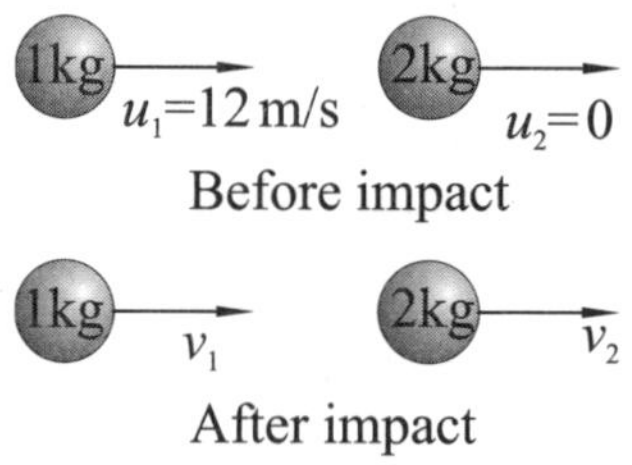

Linear momentum is conserved

$$m_1u_1 + m_2u_2 = m_1v_1 + m_2v_2$$

$$1\times 12 + 2\times 0 = 1\times v_1 + 2\times v_2$$

or $\quad v_1 + 2v_2 = 12 \qquad$ (i)

Coefficent of restitution, $e = 1 = \dfrac{v_2 - v_1}{u_1 - u_2}$

$$v_2 - v_1 = 12 - 0 \qquad \text{(ii)}$$

From Equations (i) and (ii) we obtain $v_2 = 8$

$$\text{Velocity of 2 kg ball after impact } v_2 = 8 \text{ m/s}$$

Example 5.2

The initial velocity of an object is 40 m/s. The acceleration a of the object is given by the following expression:

$$a = -0.1\,v$$

where v is the instantaneous velocity of the object. The velocity of the object after 3 s will be____.

GATE 2015

Solution

Acceleration of the object $\quad a = -0.1\,v$

$$\frac{dv}{dt} = -0.1\,v \qquad \text{or} \qquad \frac{dv}{v} = -0.1\,dt$$

or $$\int_{v=40}^{v} \frac{dv}{v} = \int_{t=0}^{t=3} -0.1\,dt \Rightarrow \ln\left(\frac{v}{40}\right) = -0.1 \times 3$$

or $$v = 40e^{-0.3}$$

$$v = 29.63 \text{ m/s}$$

Example 5.3

In a certain slider crank mechanism, lengths of crank and connecting rod are equal. If the crank rotates with a uniform angular speed of 14 rad/s and the crank length is 300 mm, the maximum acceleration of the slider (in m/s^2) is____.

GATE 2015

Solution

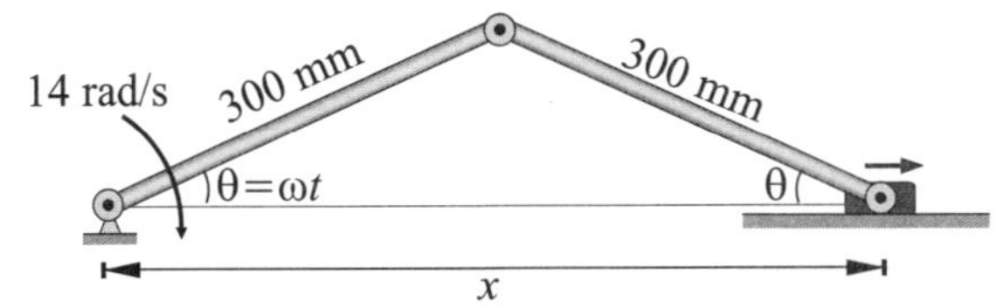

Position of slider from crank pin, $\quad x = 2 \times 300 \cos \omega t$

Acceleration of slider, $\quad a = \dfrac{d^2x}{dt^2} = -600\,\omega^2 \cos \omega t$

Maximum acceleration of slider $\quad a_{max} = -\dfrac{600}{1000} \times 14^2$

$$a_{max} = 117.6 \text{ m/s}^2$$

Example 5.4

A weight of 500 N is supported by two metallic ropes as shown in the figure. The values of tensions T_1 and T_2 are respectively.

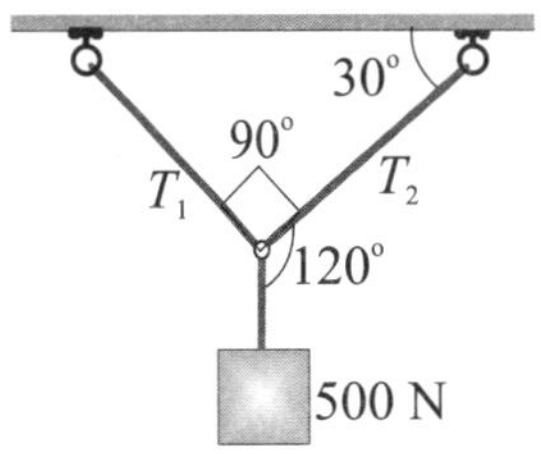

(A) 433 N and 250 N (B) 250 N and 433 N

(C) 253.5 N and 250 N (D) 250 N and 353.5 N

GATE 2015

Solution

Applying Lami's theorem,

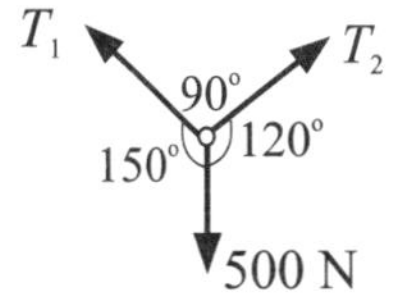

$$\frac{T_1}{\sin 120} = \frac{T_2}{\sin 150} = \frac{500}{\sin 90}$$

From which

$$T_1 = 500 \times \frac{\sin 120}{\sin 90} \quad \text{and} \quad T_2 = 500 \frac{\sin 150}{\sin 90}$$

$$T_1 = 433 \text{ N and } T_2 = 250 \text{ N}$$

Example 5.5

Figure shows a wheel rotating about O. Two points A and B located along the radius of wheel have speeds of 80 m/s and 140 m/s respectively. The distance between the points A and B is 300 mm. The diameter of the wheel (in mm) is___.

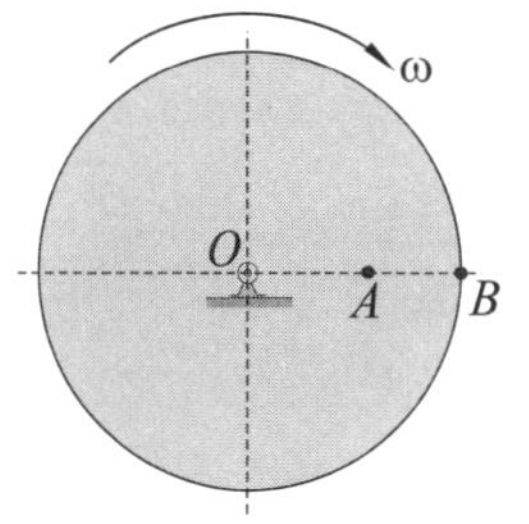

GATE 2015

Solution

Let d be diameter of wheel.

Velocity of point B, $\quad v_B = \omega \times OB = 140$

$$\omega \times \frac{d}{2} = 140 \qquad \text{(i)}$$

Velocity of point A, $\quad v_A = \omega \times OA = 80$

$$\omega \times \left(\frac{d}{2} - 0.3\right) = 80 \qquad \text{(ii)}$$

From Equations (i) and (ii), we have

$$\frac{\frac{d}{2} - 0.3}{\frac{d}{2}} = \frac{80}{140}$$

$$d = 1.4\,\text{m}$$

$$d = 1400\,\text{mm}$$

Example 5.6

A bullet spin as the spot is fired from a gun. For this purpose, two helical slots as shown in the figure are cut in the barrel. Projections A and B on the bullet engage in each of the slots. Helical slots are such that one turn of helix is completed over a distance of 0.5 m. If velocity of bullet when it exits the barrel is 20 m/s, its spinning speed in rad/s is____.

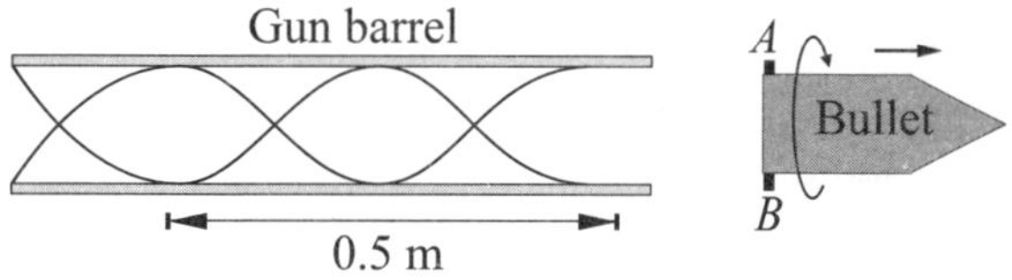

GATE 2015

Solution

Distance moved in one turn of bullet is $L = 0.5\,\text{m}$

Time taken in one turn $\quad t = \frac{0.5}{20}\,\text{s}$

Angular velocity, $\omega = \frac{2\pi}{t}$

$$\omega = \frac{2\pi}{\left(\frac{0.5}{20}\right)} = \frac{40\pi}{0.5}$$

or $\quad \omega = \frac{40\pi}{0.5}$

$$\omega = 251.3\,\text{rad/s}$$

Example 5.7

The value of moment of inertia of the section shown in the figure about the axis XX is

(A) $8.5050 \times 10^6\ \text{mm}^4$ (B) $6.8850 \times 10^6\ \text{mm}^4$

(C) $7.7625 \times 10^6\ \text{mm}^4$ (D) $8.5725 \times 10^6\ \text{mm}^4$

GATE 2015

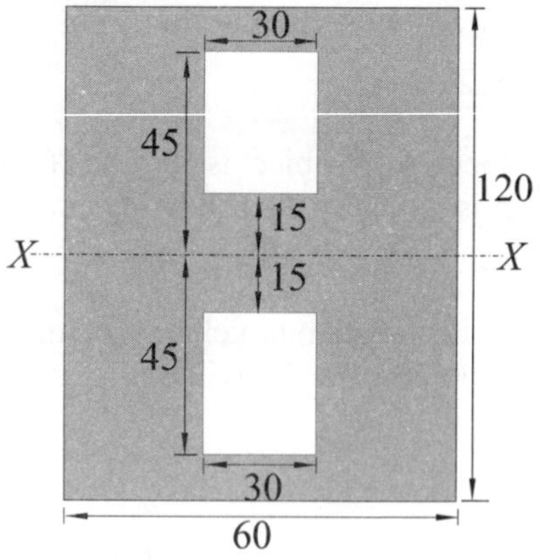

All dimensions are in 'mm'

Solution

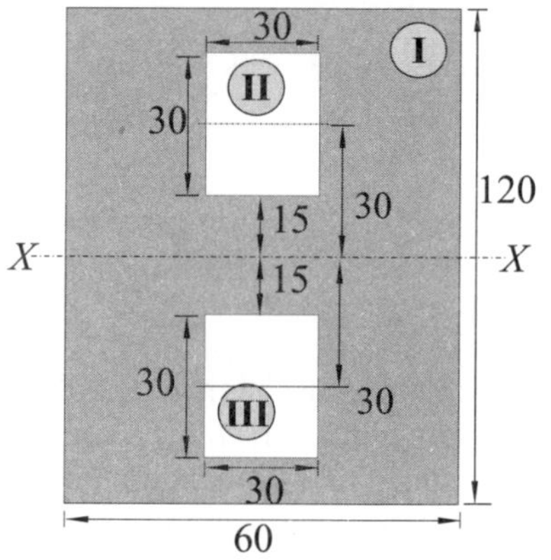

Moment of inertia (MOI) of the section about XX axis

= MOI of section I about XX − MOI of removed section II and III about XX axis.

$$= \frac{60 \times 120^3}{12} - 2\left(\frac{30 \times 30^3}{12} + 30 \times 30 \times 30^2\right)$$

MOI of section about $X\,X$ axis $= 6.8850 \times 10^6\,\text{mm}^4$

Example 5.8

A swimmer can swim 10 km in 2 h when swimming along the flow of a river. While swimming against the flow, she takes 5 h for the same distance. Her speed in still water (in km/h) is ________.

GATE 2015

Solution

Let u be the velocity of flow and v be the velocity of swimmer.

Resultant of velocity of swimmer along flow is

$$u + v = \frac{10}{2} = 5\,\text{km/h} \qquad \text{(i)}$$

Resultant of velocity of swimmer against flow is

$$v-u=\frac{10}{5}=2 \text{ km/h} \qquad \text{(ii)}$$

From Equations (i) and (ii), we have

$$v=3.5 \text{ km/h and } u=1.5 \text{ km/h}$$

Speed of swimmer in still water $v=3.5$ km/h

Example 5.9

A wheel of radius r rolls without slipping on a horizontal surface shown below. If the velocity of point P is 10 m/s in the horizontal direction, the magnitude of the velocity of point Q (in m/s) is_____.

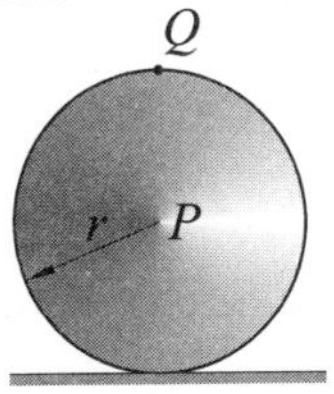

GATE 2015

Solution

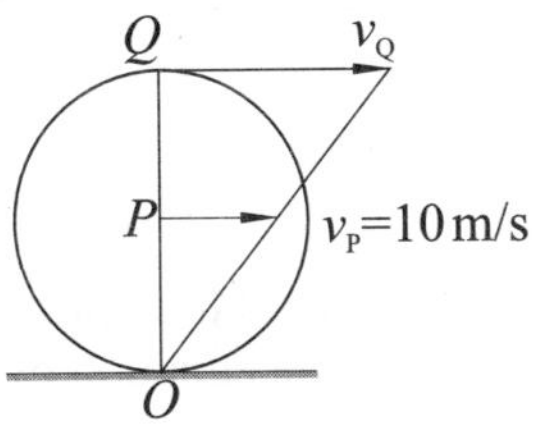

Let O be the instantaneous centre.

From the geometry of figure, $\frac{v_P}{OP}=\frac{v_Q}{OQ}$

or $$v_Q=v_P\frac{OQ}{OP}$$

or $$v_Q=10\times\frac{2r}{r}$$

$$v_Q=20 \text{ m/s}$$

Example 5.10

Two identical trusses supported a load of 100 N as shown in the figure. The length of each truss is 0.1 m; cross-sectional area is 200 mm^2, Young's modulus $E=200$ GPa. The force in the truss AC (in N) is____.

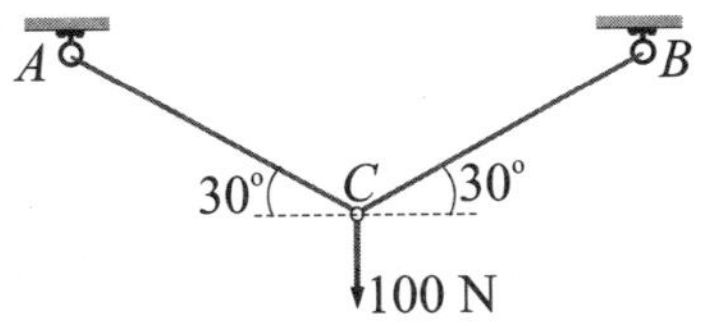

GATE 2015

Solution

Applying Lami's theorem

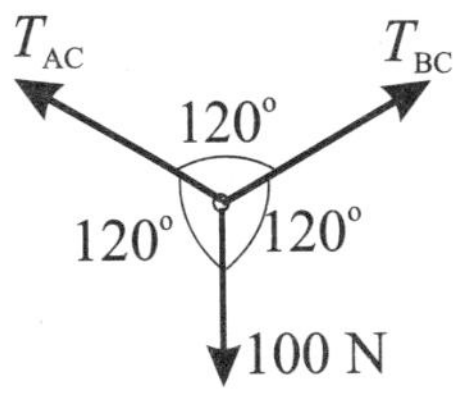

$$\frac{100}{\sin 120}=\frac{T_{AC}}{\sin 120}=\frac{T_{BC}}{\sin 120}$$

or $$T_{AC}=T_{BC}=100\times\frac{\sin 120}{\sin 120}$$

From which

$$T_{AC}=T_{BC}=100 \text{ N}$$

Example 5.11

Consider an ant crawling along the curve $(x-2)^2+y^2=4$, where x and y are in metres, the ant starts at the point (4, 0) and moves counter-clockwise with a speed of 1.57 m/s. The time taken by the ant to reach the point (2, 2) is (in seconds) ______.

GATE 2015

Solution

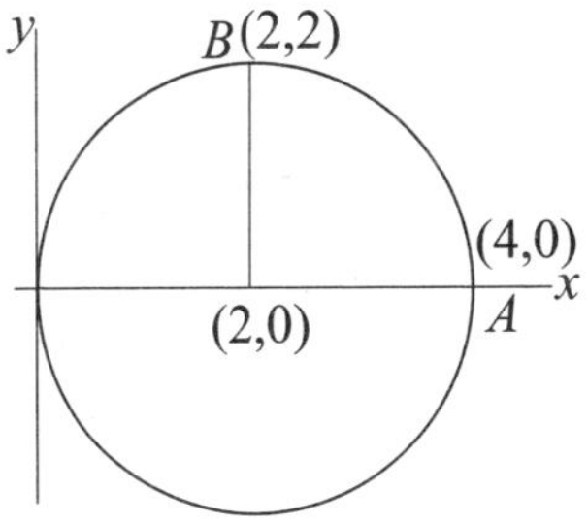

Length of path AB

$$\text{arc } AB=\frac{2\pi r}{4}=\frac{2\pi\times 2}{4}=\pi$$

Time taken by the ant to reach the point $B(2,2)$ is

$$t=\frac{\text{arc } AB}{\text{speed of ant}}=\frac{\pi}{1.57}$$

$$t=2 \text{ s}$$

Example 5.12

For the truss shown in figure, the magnitude of the force in member PR and the support reaction at R are respectively

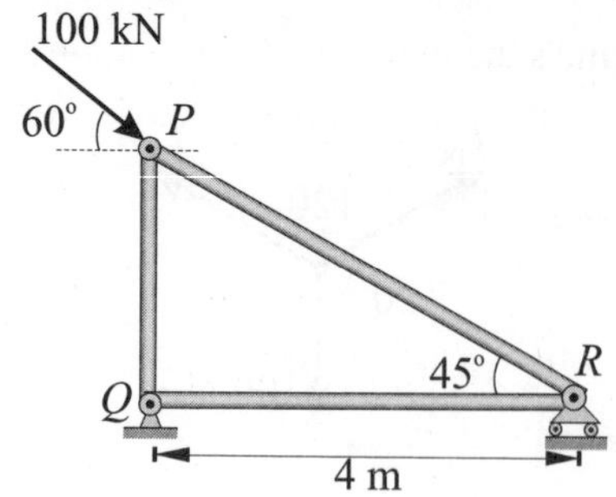

(A) 122.47 kN and 50 kN (B) 70.71kN and 100 kN

(C) 70.71 kN and 50 kN (D) 81.65 kN and 100 kN

GATE 2015

Solution

Consider the joint P

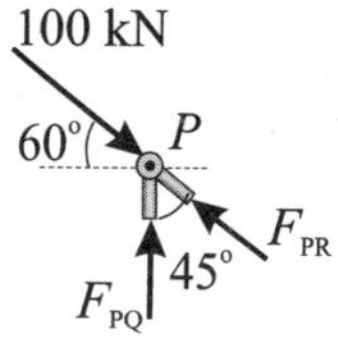

$$\sum F_x = 0$$

or $100\cos 60 - F_{PR}\sin 45 = 0$

$$F_{PR} = 100\frac{\cos 60}{\sin 45}$$

$$F_{PR} = 122.47\,\text{kN}$$

Taking moment about Q; $100\cos 60 \times PQ - R_R \times QR = 0$

or $R_R = 100\cos 60 \times \dfrac{PQ}{QR}$

or $R_R = 100\cos 60 \times \tan 45$

$$R_R = 50\,\text{kN}$$

Example 5.13

A ball of mass 0.1 kg, initially at rest, is dropped from height of 1 m. Ball hits the ground and bounces off the ground. Upon impact with the ground, the velocity reduces by 20%. The height (in m) to which the ball will rise is ___.

GATE 2015

Solution

Velocity of ball just before impact

$$v = \sqrt{2g \times 1} = \sqrt{2g}$$

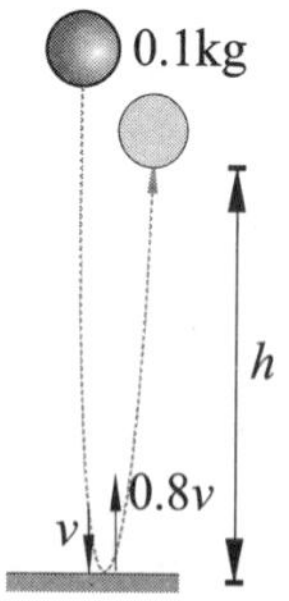

Velocity of ball just after impact $= 0.8v$

Let h be the maximum height of ball rise.

$$v^2 = u^2 + 2(-g)h$$

$$0^2 = (0.8v)^2 - 2gh$$

or $h = \dfrac{(0.8v)^2}{2g}$

$$= \frac{(0.8\sqrt{2g})^2}{2g}$$

$$h = 0.64\,\text{m}$$

Example 5.14

A single device shown in given figure, derive the relationship between forces P and all terms of the angle θ.

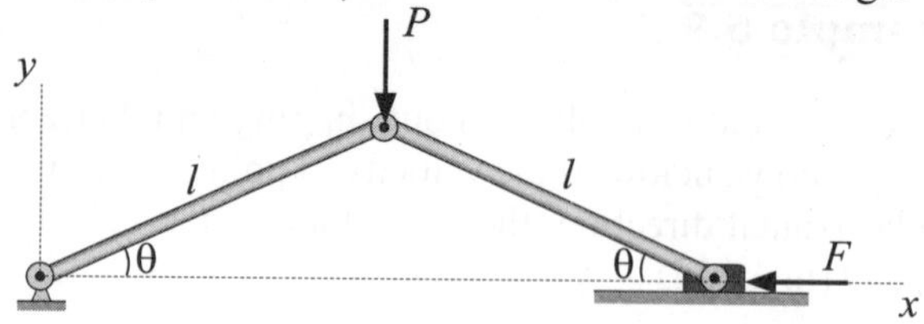

GATE 2000

Solution

Figure shows the active force diagram of the device.

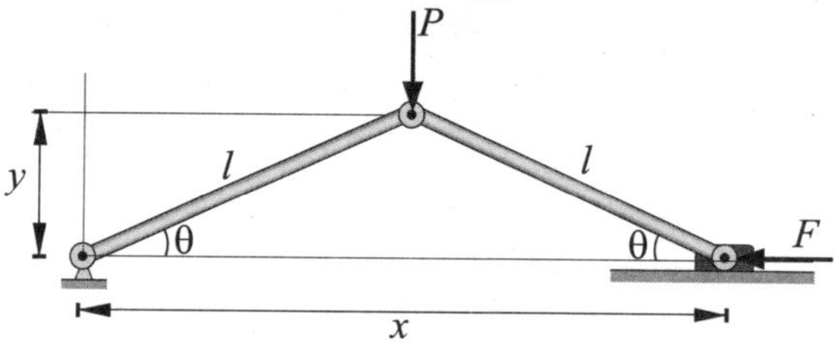

Give the system a small virtual displacement such that θ changes into $\theta + \delta\theta$, then the equation of virtual work is

$$\delta u = 0 \Rightarrow -F\delta x - P\delta y = 0$$

From geometry of figure,

$$x = 2l\cos\theta \Rightarrow \delta x = -2l\sin\theta\delta\theta$$

$$y = l\sin\theta \Rightarrow \delta y = l\cos\theta\delta\theta$$

From which $-F \times -2l\sin\theta\delta\theta - P \times l\cos\theta\delta\theta = 0$

$$P = 2F\tan\theta$$

Example 5.15

Common Data for Questions (a) and (b)

Two steel truss members, AC and BC, each having cross-sectional area of 100 mm^2, are subjected to a horizontal force F as shown in figure. All the joints are hinged.

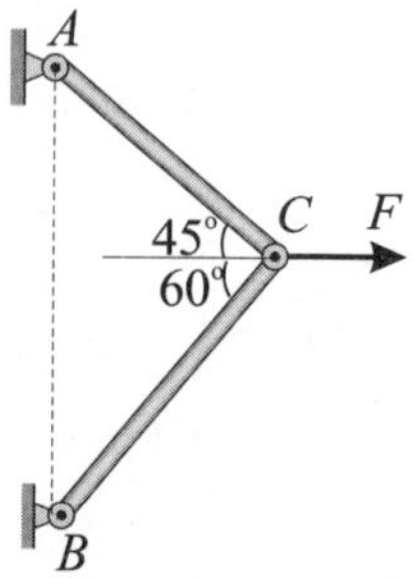

(a) If $F = 1$ kN, the magnitude of the vertical reaction force developed at the point B in kN is

(A) 0.63 (B) 1.26 (C) 0.32 (D) 1.46

(b) The maximum force F in kN that can be applied at C such that the axial stress in any of the truss member DOES NOT exceed 100 MPa is

(A) 8.17 (B) 14.14 (C) 11.15 (D) 22.30

GATE 2012

Solution

(a) Consider the joint C.

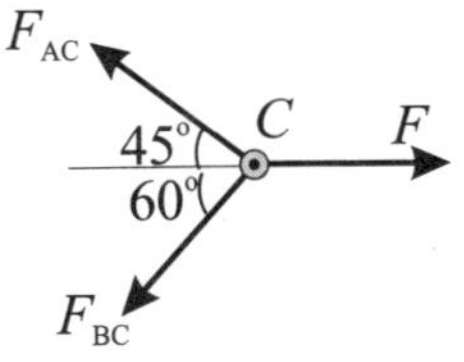

Summing forces along x and y direction

$$\sum F_x = 0; \quad F - F_{AC}\cos 45 - F_{BC}\cos 60 = 0$$

$$F - \frac{F_{AC}}{\sqrt{2}} - \frac{F_{BC}}{2} = 0 \qquad \text{(i)}$$

$$\sum F_y = 0 \Rightarrow \quad F_{AC}\sin 45 - F_{BC}\sin 60 = 0$$

$$\frac{F_{AC}}{\sqrt{2}} = \frac{\sqrt{3}}{2} F_{BC}$$

or $$F_{AC} = \frac{\sqrt{3}}{\sqrt{2}} F_{BC} \qquad \text{(ii)}$$

From Equations (i) and (ii), we obtain

$$F_{BC} = \frac{2F}{\sqrt{3}+1}, \; F_{AC} = \frac{\sqrt{6}F}{\sqrt{3}+1}$$

Now, consider joint B

Vertical component of force $(F_V)_B = F_{BC}\cos 30$

or $$(F_V)_B = \frac{2F}{\sqrt{3}+1}\cos 30 = \frac{\sqrt{3}F}{\sqrt{3}+1}$$

or $$(F_V)_B = \frac{\sqrt{3}\times 1}{\sqrt{3}+1}$$

$$(F_V)_B = 0.633\text{kN}$$

(b) Maximum tensile force is in member AC, that is,

$$F_{AC} = \frac{\sqrt{6}}{\sqrt{3}+1} F$$

Stress in member AC, $\sigma_{AC} = \dfrac{F_{AC}}{A}$

or $$\sigma_{AC} = \frac{\sqrt{6}}{(\sqrt{3}+1)}\frac{F}{A} = 100\times 10^6 \text{ N/m}^2$$

or $$F = \frac{(\sqrt{3}+1)\times \dfrac{100}{(1000)^2}\times 100\times 10^6}{\sqrt{6}} \text{ N}$$

$$F = 11.15\text{N}$$

Example 5.16

A block R of mass 100 kg is placed on a blocks of mass 150 kg shown in the figure. Block R is tied to the wall by a massless and inextensible string PQ. If the coefficient of static friction for all surfaces is 0.4, the minimum force F (kN) needed to move the block S is

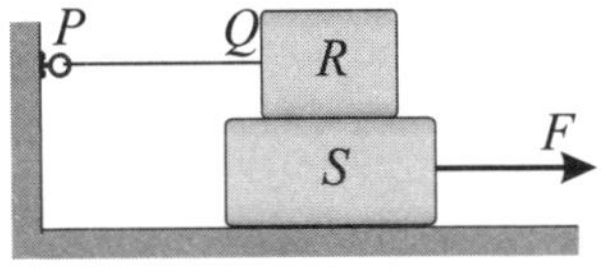

(A) 0.69 (B) 0.88 (C) 0.98 (D) 1.37

GATE 2014

Solution

Figure shows the free-body diagrams of block R and S when block S is just about to slip.

Consider block R

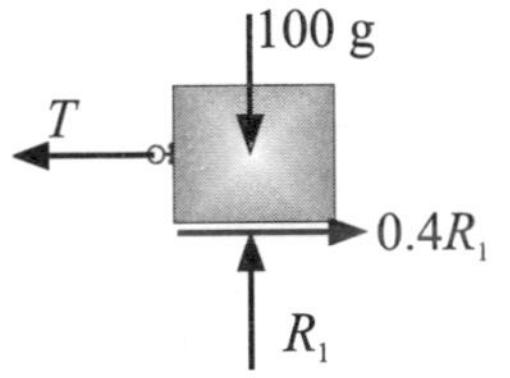

FBD of block R

Equilibrium equation, $\sum F_V = 0$

$$R_1 - 100g = 0$$

$$R_1 = 100g$$

Consider block S

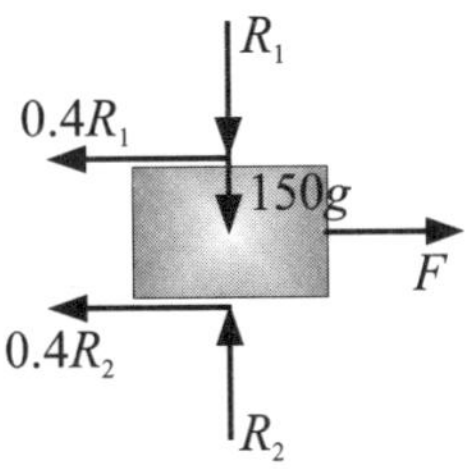

FBD of block S

Equilibrium equations

$$\sum F_V = 0 \Rightarrow \quad R_2 - R_1 - 150g = 0$$

$$R_2 = 100g + 150g$$

or $\quad R_2 = 250g$

$$\sum F_H = 0 \Rightarrow F - 0.4R_1 - 0.4R_2 = 0$$

$$F = 0.4(R_1 + R_2)$$

Substituting $R_1 = 100g$ and $R_2 = 250g$, we have

$$F = 0.4(100g + 250g)$$

or $\quad F = 1373.4\,\text{N}$

$$F = 13734\,\text{kN}$$

Example 5.17

A block weighing 200 N is in contact with a level plane whose coefficients of static and kinetic friction are 0.4 and 0.2 respectively. The block is acted upon by a horizontal force (in N) $P = 10\,t$, where t denotes the time in seconds. The velocity (in m/s) of the block attained after 10 s is ___.

GATE 2014

Solution

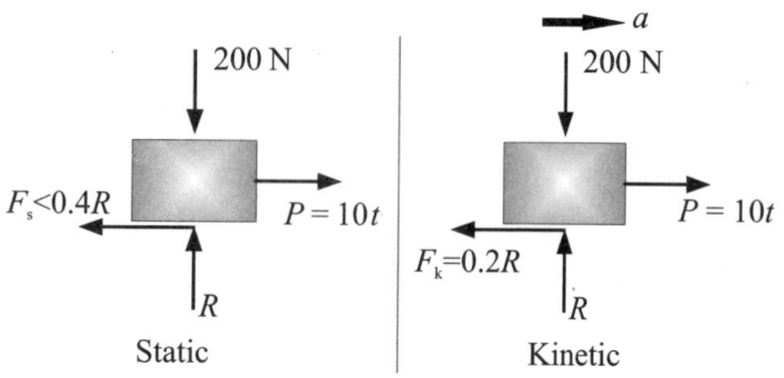

Let t_0 be the time of start motion.

$$10t_0 = 0.4R \quad \text{or} \quad 10t_0 = 0.4 \times 200$$

$$t_0 = 8\,\text{s}$$

Applying equation of motion ($t > 8\,\text{s}$) $\; P - F_k = ma$

or $\quad 10t - 0.2 \times 200 = \dfrac{200}{9.81}a$

or $\quad 10t - 40 = 20.38\dfrac{dv}{dt}$

or $\quad \displaystyle\int_8^{10} (10t - 40)dt = 20.38\int_0^v dv$

From which

$$v = 4.9\,\text{m/s}$$

Example 5.18

A block weighing 981 N is resting on a horizontal surface. The coefficient of friction between the block and the horizontal surface is $\mu = 0.2$. A vertical cable attached to the block provides partial support as shown. A man can pull horizontally with a force of 100 N. What will be the tension, T (in N) in the cable if the man is just able to move the block to the right?

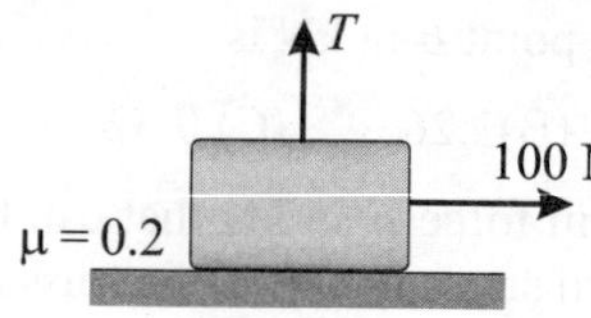

(A) 176.2 (B) 196.0 (C) 481.0 (D) 981.0

GATE 2009

Solution

Figure shows the free body diagram of block when it is just about to slide.

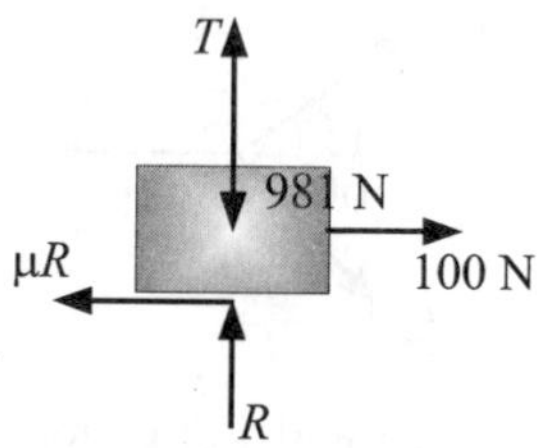

The equilibrium equation are

$$\sum F_V = 0 \Rightarrow \quad T + R - 981 = 0$$

$$R = 981 - T \qquad \text{(i)}$$

$$\sum F_H = 0 \Rightarrow 100 - \mu R = 0$$

$$100 = 0.2R \qquad \text{(ii)}$$

Solving for T from Equations (i) and (ii), we have

$$100 = 0.2(981 - T)$$

$$T = 481.0\,\text{N}$$

Example 5.19

The figure shows a pair of pin-jointed gripper tongs holding an object weighting 2000 N. The coefficient of friction (μ) at the gripper surface is 0.1, XX is the line of action of the input force and YY is the line of application of gripping force. If the pin-joint is assumed to be frictionless, then magnitude of force F required to hold the weight is

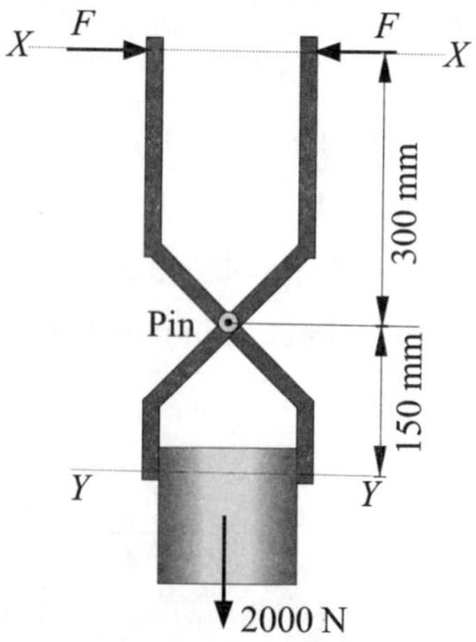

(A) 1000 N (B) 2000 N (C) 2500 N (D) 5000 N

GATE 2004

Solution

Free body diagram for the one lever of tong and object are shown in the figure.

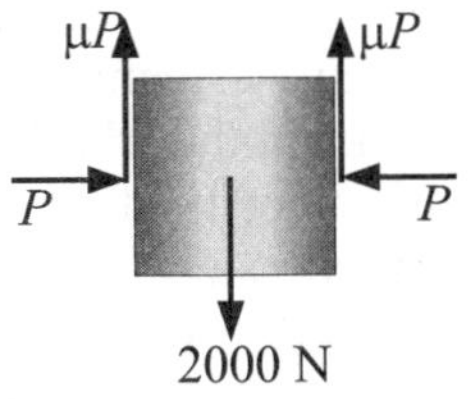

FBD of Object

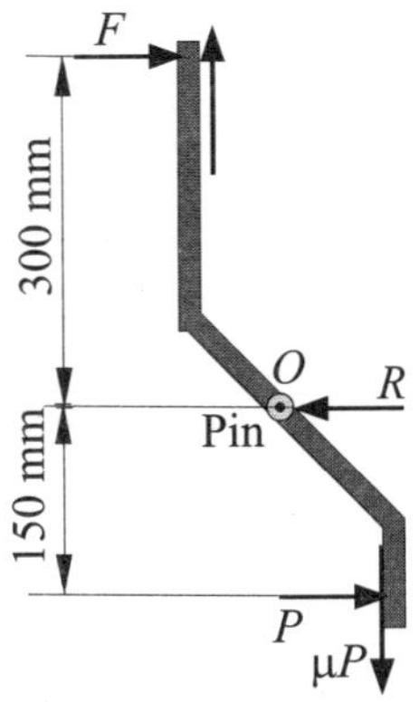

FBD of Lever

The equation $\sum M_o = 0$, applied to the free body diagram of lever, gives

$$F \times 300 - P \times 150 = 0$$

or $\quad P = 2F$

Summing forces along vertical of block yields

$$2\mu P - 2000 = 0$$

or $\quad 2\mu \times 2F = 2000$

or $\quad F = \dfrac{2000}{4\mu} = \dfrac{2000}{4 \times 0.1}$

$$F = 5000\text{ N}$$

Example 5.20

A force of 400 N is applied to the brake drum of 0.5 m diameter in a band-brake system as shown in the figure, where the wrapping angle is 180°. If the coefficient of friction between the drum and the band is 0.25, the braking torque applied, in Nm is

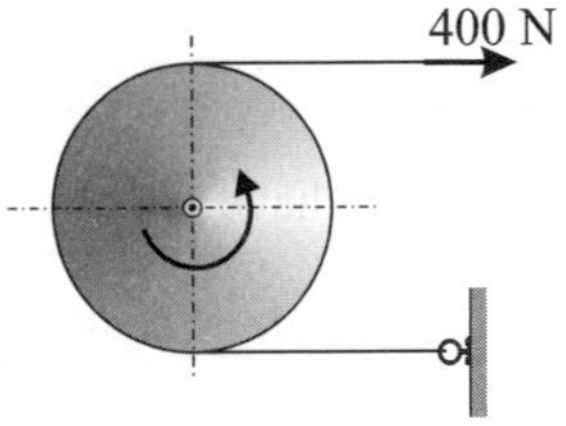

(A) 100.6 (B) 22.1 (C) 54.4 (D) 15.7

GATE 2012

Solution

Let T_1 and T_2 be the tensions of tight and slack side of band.

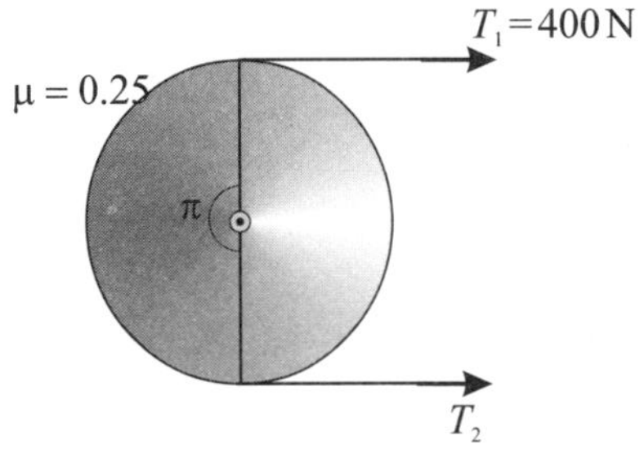

Tensions ratio $\quad \dfrac{T_1}{T_2} = e^{\mu\theta} \quad$ or $\quad \dfrac{400}{T_2} = e^{0.25\times\pi}$

From which $\quad T_2 = 182.37\text{ N}$

Braking torque $\quad \tau = (T_1 - T_2)r$

$$\tau = (400 - 182.37) \times \frac{0.5}{2}$$

$$\tau = 54.4\text{ Nm}$$

Example 5.21

A flat belt open drive transmits 1.5 kW of power. The coefficient of friction between the belt and the drive pulley is 0.25 and the lap angle is 159°. The drive pulley is rotating in the clockwise direction with the linear belt velocity of 3.75 m/s. Determine the x and y components of the reaction force on the drive pulley shaft.

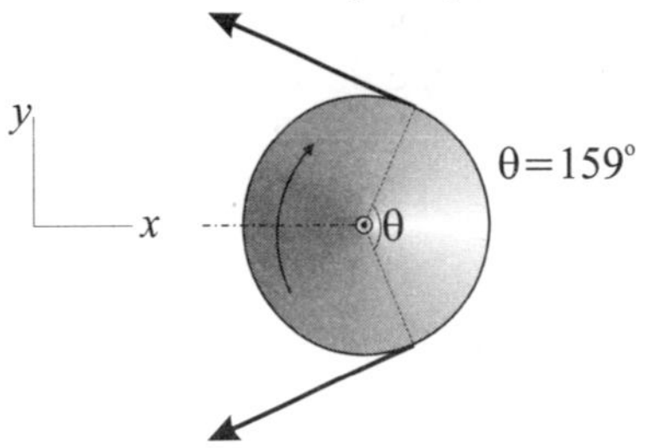

GATE 1999

Solution

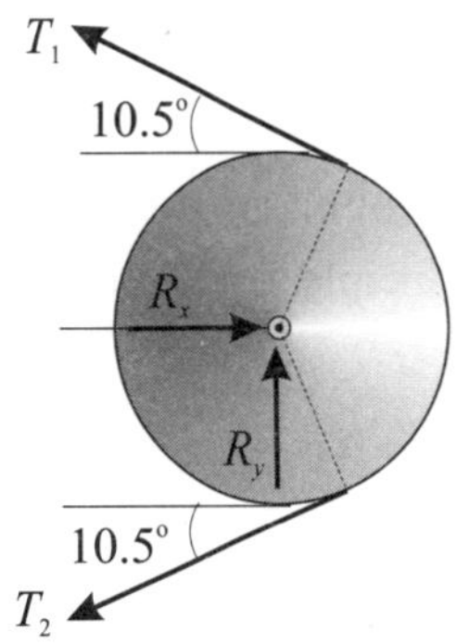

Let T_1 and T_2 be the tensions of belt on tight and slack side.

Tension ratio $\frac{T_1}{T_2} = e^{\mu\theta}$

or $\frac{T_1}{T_2} = e^{0.25\times\frac{\pi}{180}\times 159}$

or $\frac{T_1}{T_2} = 2$

Power transmitted $P = (T_1 - T_2)v$

$$1.5\times 10^3 = (2T_2 - T_2)\times 3.75$$

From which $T_2 = 400$ N and $T_1 = 2\times T_2 = 800$ N

Summing forces along x and y directions

$$R_x - T_1\cos 10.5 - T_2\cos 10.5 = 0$$

or $R_x = 800\cos 10.5 + 400\cos 10.5$

$$R_x = 1179.9\text{ N} \rightarrow$$

$$R_y + T_1\sin 10.5 - T_2\sin 10.5 = 0$$

or $R_y = -800\sin 10.5 + 400\sin 10.5 = 0$

$$R_y = 351.8\text{ N} \downarrow$$

Example 5.22

A bullet of mas m travels at a very high velocity v (as shown in the figure) and gets embedded inside the block of mass M initially at rest on a rough horizontal floor. The block with the bullet is seen to move a distance S along the floor. Assuming μ to be the coefficient of kinetic friction between the block and the floor and g the acceleration due to gravity, what is the velocity v of the bullet?

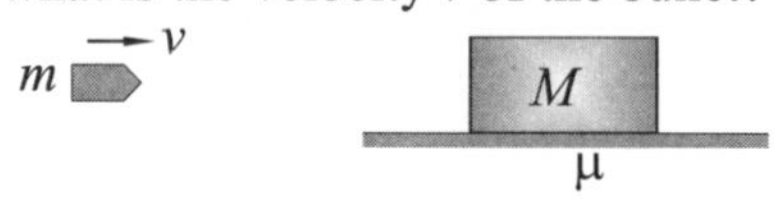

(A) $\frac{M+m}{m}\sqrt{2\mu g S}$ (B) $\frac{M-m}{m}\sqrt{2\mu g S}$

(C) $\frac{\mu(M+m)}{m}\sqrt{2g S}$ (D) $\frac{M}{m}\sqrt{2\mu g S}$

GATE 2013

Solution

Let V be the velocity of block just after impact.

Applying the principle of conservation of linear momentum

$$mv = (M+m)V \quad \text{or} \quad V = \frac{m}{(M+m)}v$$

Friction force acting on sliding block is

$$F_f = \mu(M+m)g$$

Now, applying the work-energy principle

Kinetic energy of block and bullet = Work against friction force

$$\frac{1}{2}(M+m)V^2 = F_f \times S$$

or $\frac{1}{2}(M+m)\left\{\frac{m}{(M+m)}v\right\}^2 = \mu(M+m)g\times S$

$$v = \frac{M+m}{m}\sqrt{2\mu g S}$$

Example 5.23

A 1 kg mass of clay, moving with a velocity of 10 m/s, strikes a stationary wheel and sticks to it. The solid wheel has a mass of 20 kg and a radius of 1 m. Assuming that the wheel and the ground are both rigid and the wheel is set into pure rolling motion, the angular velocity of the wheel immediately after the impact is approximately

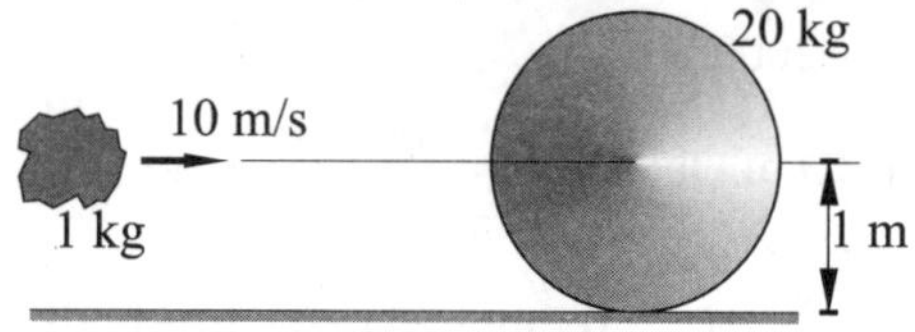

(A) Zero (B) $\frac{1}{3}$ rad/s (C) $\sqrt{\frac{10}{3}}$ rad/s (D) $\frac{10}{3}$ rad/s

GATE 2005

Solution

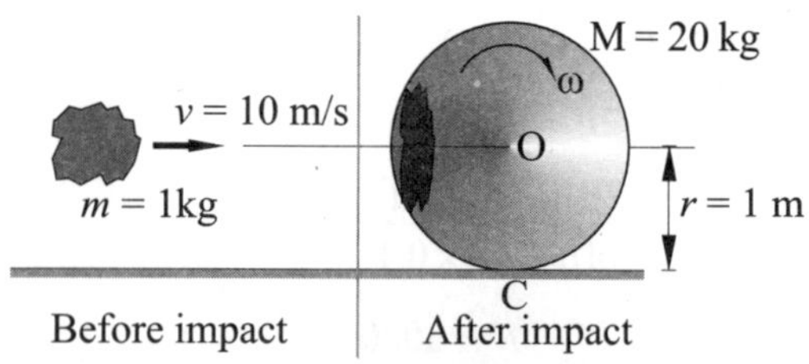

Let ω be the angular velocity of wheel after the impact.

Applying the principle of conservation of angular momentum about C.

$$mv\times r = I_C\omega$$

or $mv\times r = \frac{3}{2}(M+m)r^2\omega$

or $\omega = \frac{2mv}{3(M+m)r}$

Substituting given data, we have

$$\omega = \frac{2\times 1\times 10}{3(20+1)\times 1}$$

or $\omega = \frac{20}{62}$ rad/s $\approx \frac{1}{3}$ rad/s

$$\omega = \frac{1}{3}\text{ rad/s}$$

Example 5.24

The 2 kg mass C moving horizontally to the right, with a velocity of 5 m/s, strikes the 8 kg mass B at the lower end of the rigid massless rod AB. The rod is suspended from a frictionless hinge at A and is initially at rest. If the coefficient of restitution between mass C and B is one, determine the angular velocity of the rod AB immediately after impact.________.

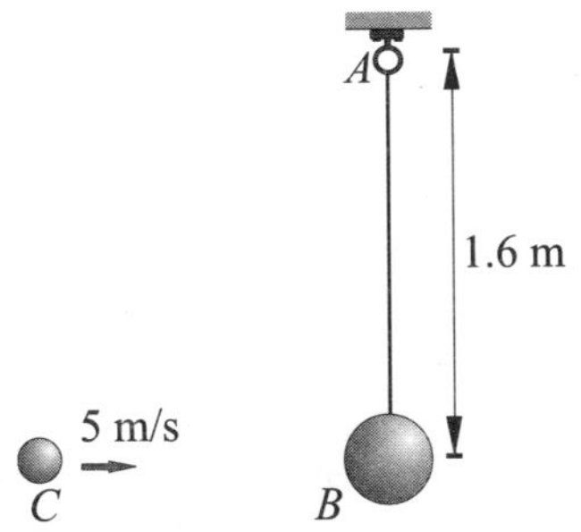

GATE 2001

Solution

Let v_B be the velocity of mass B after impact.

Applying the conservation of linear momentum.

$$m_c u_c + m_B u_B = m_c v_c + m_B v_B$$

$$2\times 5 + 8\times 0 = 2v_c + 8v_B$$

$$v_c + 4v_B = 5 \qquad \text{(i)}$$

Coefficient of restitution, $e = \dfrac{v_c - v_B}{u_B - u_C}$

$$e = 1 = \frac{v_c - v_B}{0-5}$$

$$v_B - v_c = 5 \qquad \text{(ii)}$$

From Equations (i) and (ii), we obtain

$$v_B = 2 \text{ m/s}$$

Angular velocity of rod AB, $\omega = \dfrac{v_B}{AB} = \dfrac{2}{1.6}$

$$\omega = 1.25 \text{ rad/s}$$

Example 5.25

A straight rod of length $L(t)$, hinged at one end and freely extensible at the other end, rotates through an angle $\theta(t)$ about the hinge. At time t, $L(t) = 1\,\text{m}$, $\dot{L}(t) = 1\,\text{m/s}$, $\theta(t) = \dfrac{\pi}{4}$ rad and $\dot{\theta}(t) = 1$ rad/s. The magnitude of the velocity at the other end of the rod is

(A) 1m/s (B) $\sqrt{2}$ m/s (C) $\sqrt{3}$ m/s (D) 2 m/s

GATE 2008

Solution

Radial velocity is given by $v_r = \dfrac{dr}{dt}$

Transverse velocity is given by $v_\theta = r\dfrac{d\theta}{dt}$

Therefore, resultant velocity, $v = \sqrt{v_r^2 + v_\theta^2}$

or $$v = \sqrt{\left(\frac{dr}{dt}\right)^2 + \left(r\frac{d\theta}{dt}\right)^2}$$

Substituting given data $L(t) = r = 1\,m$, $\dot{L}(t) = \dfrac{dr}{dt} = 1$ m/s, $\theta(t) = \dfrac{\pi}{4}$ and $\dot{\theta}(t) = \dfrac{\pi}{4}$ rad/s, we obtain

$$v = \sqrt{1^2 + (1\times 1)^2}$$

$$v = \sqrt{2} \text{ m/s}$$

Example 5.26

A block of mass M is released from point P on a rough inclined plane with inclination angle θ, shown in the figure below. The coefficient of friction is μ. If $\mu < \tan\theta$, then the time taken by the block to reach another point Q on the inclined plane, where $PQ = S$, is

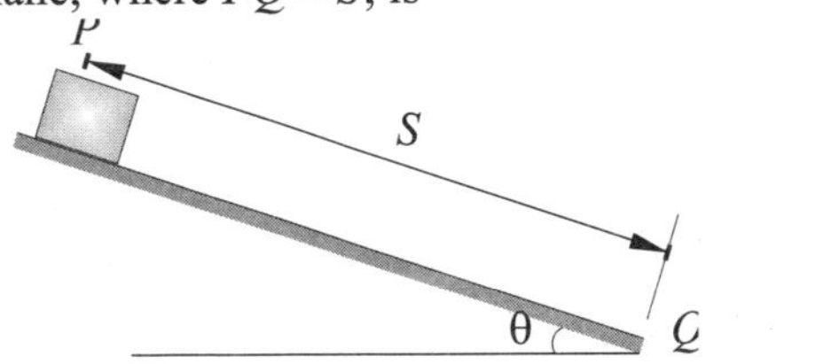

(A) $\sqrt{\dfrac{2S}{g\cos\theta(\tan\theta - \mu)}}$ (B) $\sqrt{\dfrac{2S}{g\cos\theta(\tan\theta + \mu)}}$

(C) $\sqrt{\dfrac{2S}{g\sin\theta(\tan\theta - \mu)}}$ (D) $\sqrt{\dfrac{2S}{g\sin\theta(\tan\theta + \mu)}}$

GATE 2007

Solution

Let a be the acceleration of block. Free-body diagram of block is shown in figure. Applying equation of motion along plane; $mg\sin\theta - \mu R = ma$

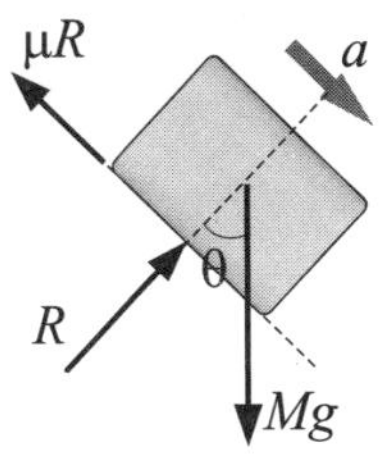

Substituting $R = mg\cos\theta$

$$mg\sin\theta - \mu mg\cos\theta = ma$$

or $$a = g(\sin\theta - \mu\cos\theta)$$

Equation of motion, $S = ut + \dfrac{1}{2}at^2$

or $$S = 0\times t + \frac{1}{2}g(\sin\theta - \mu\cos\theta)t^2$$

or $$t^2 = \frac{2S}{g(\sin\theta - \mu\cos\theta)}$$

$$t = \sqrt{\frac{2S}{g\cos\theta(\tan\theta - \mu)}}$$

Example 5.27

Data for Q (a) and Q(b) are given below.

A reel of mass 'm' and radius of gyration 'k' is rolling down smoothly from rest with one end of the thread wound on it held in the ceiling as depicted in the figure. Consider the thickness of the thread and its mass negligible in caparison with the radius 'r' of the hub and the reel mass 'm'. Symbol 'g' represents the acceleration due to gravity.

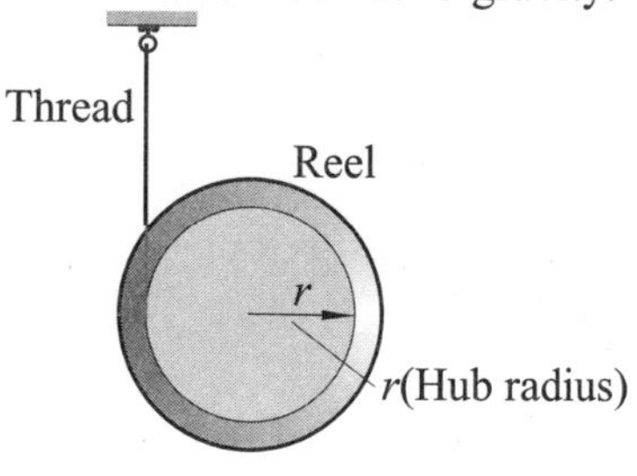

Q(a) The linear acceleration of the reel is

(A) $\frac{gr^2}{r^2+k^2}$ (B) $\frac{gk^2}{r^2+k^2}$

(C) $\frac{grk}{r^2+k^2}$ (D) $\frac{mgr^2}{r^2+k^2}$

Q(b) The tension in the thread is

(A) $\frac{mgr^2}{r^2+k^2}$ (B) $\frac{mgk^2}{r^2+k^2}$

(C) $\frac{mgrk}{r^2+k^2}$ (D) $\frac{mg}{r^2+k^2}$

GATE 2003

Solution

(a) Let T and a be the tension of thread and acceleration of reel, respectively. Figure shows the free body diagram of reel.

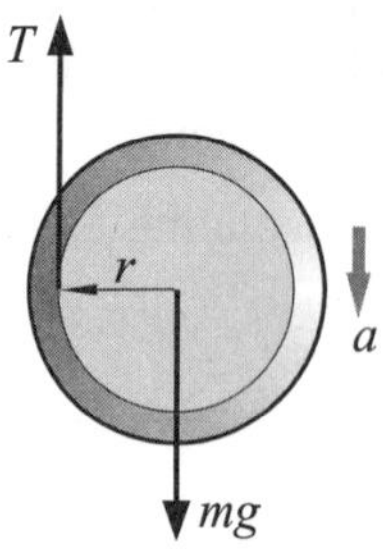

Applying equations of motion

$$\sum F_V = ma$$

$$mg - T = ma \quad \text{(i)}$$

$$\sum \tau = I\alpha$$

$$T \times r = I\alpha = I\frac{a}{r}$$

or $$T = I\frac{a}{r^2} \quad \text{(ii)}$$

Eliminating T and a from Equations (i) and (ii), we obtain

$$mg - I\frac{a}{r^2} = ma \quad \text{or} \quad a = \frac{mg}{m + \frac{I}{r^2}} = \frac{mg}{m + \frac{mk^2}{r^2}}$$

Linear acceleration, $$a = \frac{gr^2}{(r^2+k^2)}$$

(b) From Equation (ii) $T = I\frac{a}{r^2}$

Substituting $a = \frac{gr^2}{(r^2+k^2)}$, we have

$$T = \frac{I}{r^2} \times \frac{gr^2}{(r^2+k^2)} = \frac{mk^2}{r^2} \times \frac{gr^2}{(r^2+k^2)}$$

$$T = \frac{mgk^2}{(r^2+k^2)}$$

Example 5.28

A circular disk of radius R rolls without slipping at velocity v. The magnitude of the velocity at point P (see figure) is

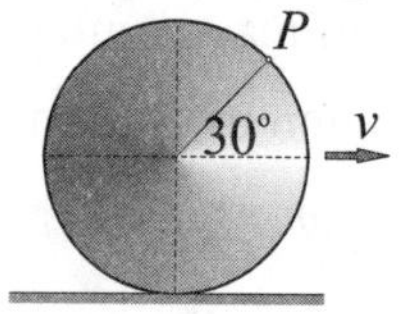

(A) $\sqrt{3}\,v$ (B) $\frac{\sqrt{3}}{2}v$ (C) $\frac{v}{2}$ (D) $\frac{2}{\sqrt{3}}v$

GATE 2008

Solution

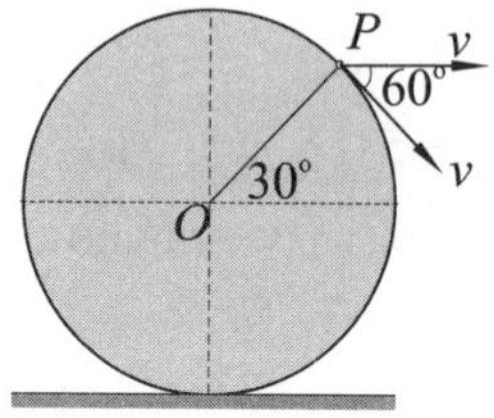

Because of disk rolls without slipping, the velocity of its centre is v in horizontal direction and velocity of point P with respect to center is v perpendicular to OP.

Thus, the components of resultant velocity of point P are shown in the figure.

Hence, the resultant velocity is

$$v_R = \sqrt{v^2 + v^2 + 2v \times v\cos 60}$$

$$v_R = \sqrt{3}\,v$$

Example 5.29

A stone with mass of 0.1 kg is catapulted as shown in the figure. The total force F_x (in N) exerted by the rubber band as a function of distance x (in m) is given by $F_x = 300x^2$. If the stone is displaced by 0.1 m from the un-stretched position ($x = 0$) of the rubber band, the energy stored in the rubber band is

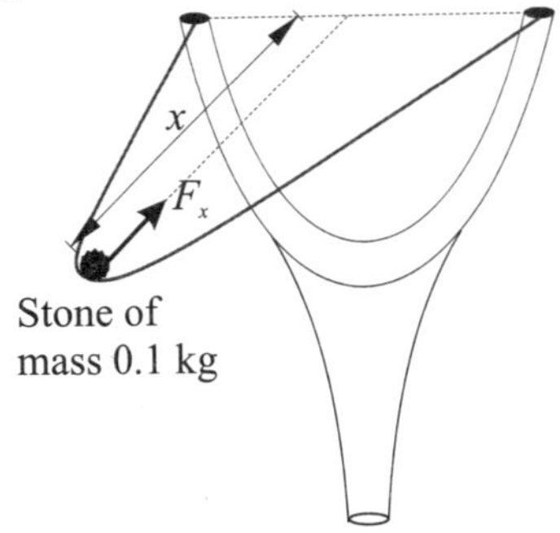

(A) 0.01J (B) 1 J (C) 0.1 J (D) 10 J

GATE 2011

Solution

Energy stored in the rubber band is

$$u = \int F_x dx$$

or $$u = \int_0^{0.1} 300x^2 dx$$

or $$u = \left[300 \times \frac{x^3}{3}\right]_0^{0.1}$$

$$u = 0.1 \text{ J}$$

Example 5.30

A rigid ball of weight 100 N is suspended with the help of a string. The ball is pulled by a horizontal force F such that the string makes an angle of 30^0 with the vertical. The magnitude of force F (in N) is_____.

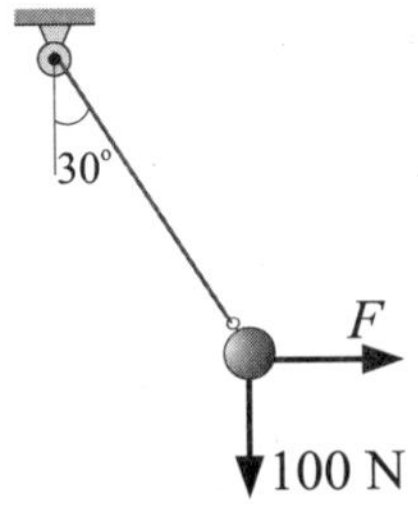

GATE 2016

Solution

Free body diagram of ball is shown in figure.

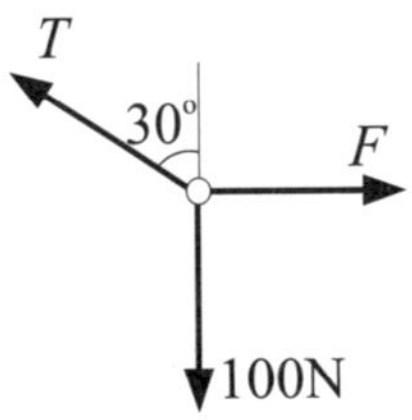

Applying Lami's theorem,

$$\frac{T}{\sin 90} = \frac{F}{\sin(180-30)} = \frac{100}{\sin(90+30)}$$

or $$F = 100\frac{\sin(180-30)}{\sin(90+30)}$$

$$F = 57.73 \text{ N}$$

Example 5.31

A point mass M is released from rest and slides down a spherical bowl (of radius R) from a height H as shown in the figure below. The surface of the bowl is smooth (no friction). The velocity of the mass at the bottom of the bowl is

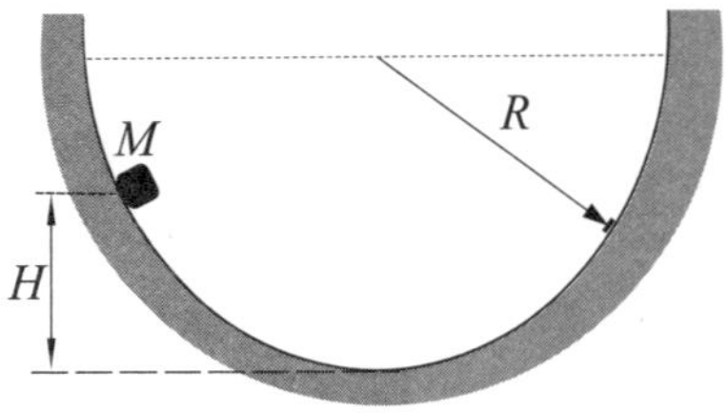

(A) $\sqrt{gH}$ (B) $\sqrt{2gR}$ (C) $\sqrt{2gH}$ (D) 0

GATE 2016

Solution

Let v be the velocity of mass at bottom of bowl.

Applying the principle of conservation energy, we have

$$MgH = Mg \times 0 + \frac{1}{2}Mv^2$$

$$v = \sqrt{2gH}$$

Example 5.32

A block of mass m rests on an inclined plane and is attached by a string to the wall as shown in the figure. The coefficient of static friction between the plane and the block is 0.25. The string can withstand a maximum force of 20 N. The maximum value of the mass (m) for which the string will not break and the block will be in static equilibrium is __________ kg.

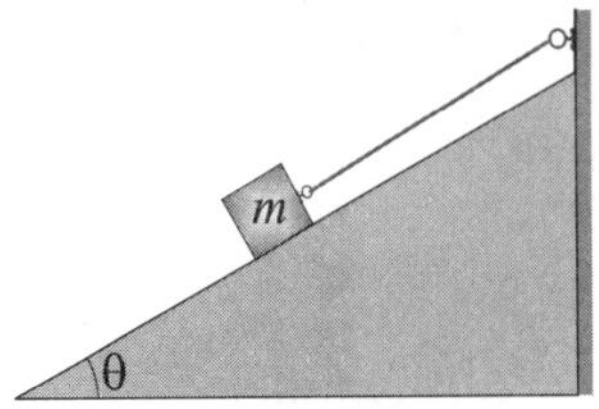

Take $\cos\theta = 0.8$, $\sin\theta = 0.6$, and acceleration due to gravity $g = 10 \text{ m/s}^2$.

GATE 2016

Solution

Figure shows the free-body diagram of mass when the string is just about to break.

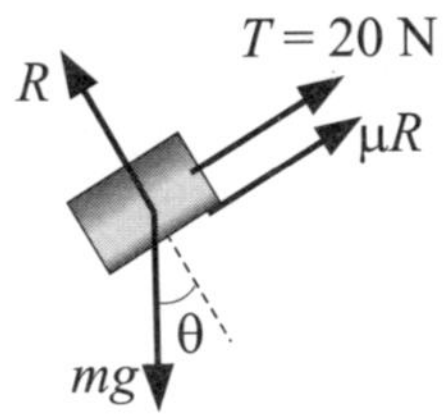

Resolving the forces along the plane and perpendicular direction.

$$R - mg\cos\theta = 0 \text{ or } R = mg\cos\theta$$

$$T + \mu R - mg\sin\theta = 0$$

or $$20 + 0.25 \times mg\cos\theta - mg\sin\theta = 0$$

or $$m = \frac{20}{g(\sin\theta - 0.25\cos\theta)}$$

or $$m = \frac{20}{10 \times (0.6 - 0.25 \times 0.8)} = 5$$

$$m = 5\text{ kg}$$

Example 5.33

A two-member truss PQR is supporting a load W. The axial forces in members PQ and QR are respectively

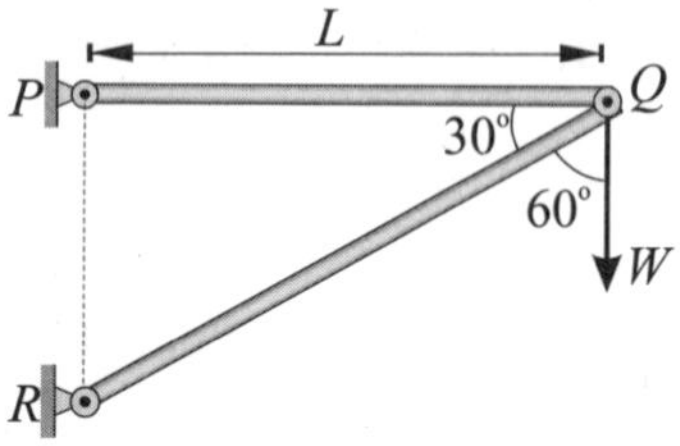

(A) $2W$ tensile and $\sqrt{3}W$ compressive

(B) $\sqrt{3}W$ tensile and $2W$ compressive

(C) $\sqrt{3}W$ compressive and $2W$ tensile

(D) $2W$ compressive and $\sqrt{3}W$ tensile

GATE 2016

Solution

Free body diagram of joint Q is shown in figure.

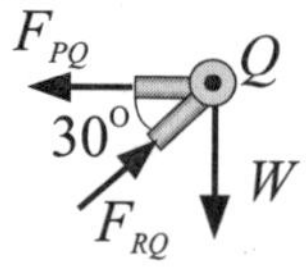

$$\sum F_y = 0 \Rightarrow F_{RQ}\sin 30 - W = 0$$

or $$F_{RQ} = \frac{W}{\sin 30}$$

$$F_{RQ} = 2W \text{ (compressive)}$$

$$\sum F_x = 0 \Rightarrow F_{RQ}\cos 30 - F_{PQ} = 0$$

or $$2W \times \frac{\sqrt{3}}{2} = F_{PQ}$$

$$F_{PQ} = \sqrt{3}W \text{ (tensile)}$$

$$F_{PQ} = \sqrt{3}W \text{ (tensile) and } F_{RQ} = 2W \text{ (compressive)}$$

Example 5.34

A point mass having mass M is moving with a velocity V at an angle θ to the wall as shown in the figure. The mass undergoes a perfectly elastic collision with the smooth wall and rebounds. The total change (final minus initial) in the momentum of the mass is

(A) $-2MV\cos\theta\,\mathbf{j}$

(B) $2MV\sin\theta\,\mathbf{j}$

(C) $2MV\cos\theta\,\mathbf{j}$

(D) $-2MV\sin\theta\,\mathbf{j}$

GATE 2016

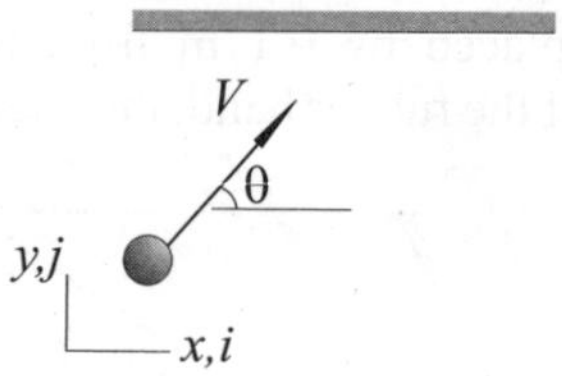

Solution

Since the wall is smooth, change in linear momentum in x-direction is zero.

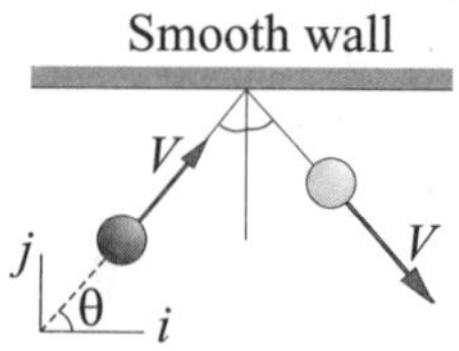

Change in linear momentum in y- direction

$= -MV\cos(90-\theta) - MV\cos(90-\theta) = -2MV\sin\theta$

Change in linear momentum $= 0\,\mathbf{i} - 2MV\sin\theta\,\mathbf{j}$

Change in linear momentum $= -2MV\sin\theta\,\mathbf{j}$

Example 5.35

A mass of 2000 kg is currently being lowered at a velocity of 2 m/s from the drum as shown in the figure. The mass moment of inertia of the drum is 150 $\text{kg}\cdot\text{m}^2$. On applying the brake, the mass is brought to rest in a distance of 0.5 m. The energy absorbed by the brake (in kJ) is____.

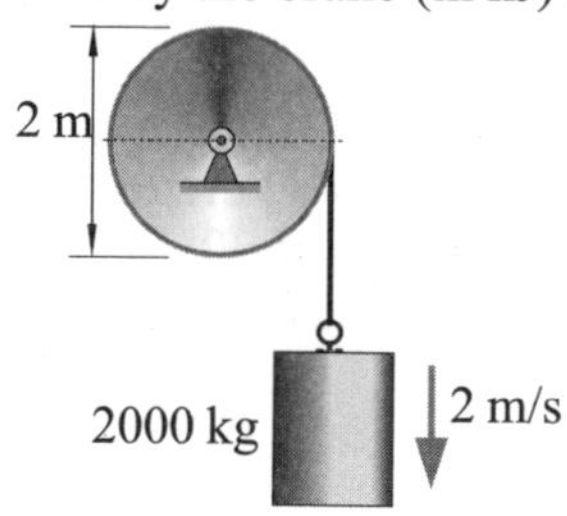

GATE 2016

Solution

Energy absorbed by brake

= Kinetic energy of drum and mass + Potential energy of mass

Energy absorbed by brake $= \left(\frac{1}{2}I\omega^2 + \frac{1}{2}mv^2\right) + mgh$

Energy absorbed by brake

$$= \left(\frac{1}{2} \times 150 \times \left(\frac{2}{1}\right)^2 + \frac{1}{2} \times 2000 \times 2^2\right) + 2000 \times 9.81 \times 0.5$$

Energy absorbed by brake = 14110 J

Energy absorbed by brake = 14.110 kJ

Example 5.36

A force F is acting on a bent bar which is clamped at one end as shown in the figure.

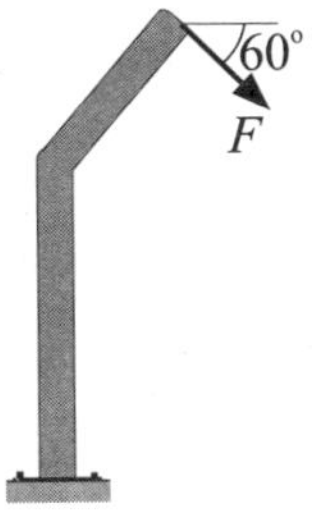

The CORRECT free body diagram is

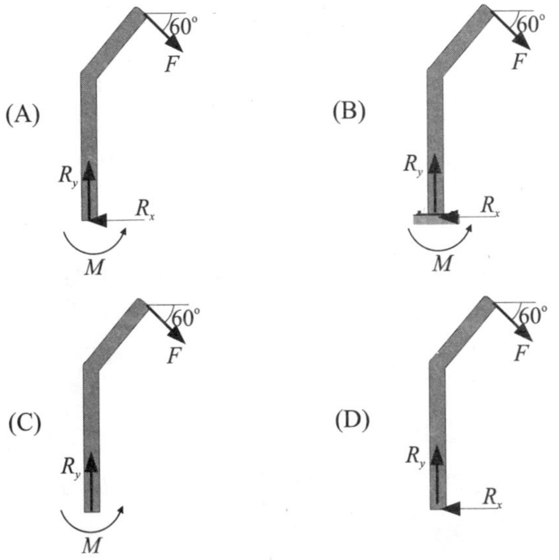

GATE 2016

Solution

Option (A) is the correct Free body diagram of bent bar.

Example 5.37

An inextensible massless string goes over a frictionless pulley. Two weights of 100 N and 200 N are attached to the two ends of the string. The weights are released from rest, and start moving due to gravity. The tension in the string (in N) is ______.

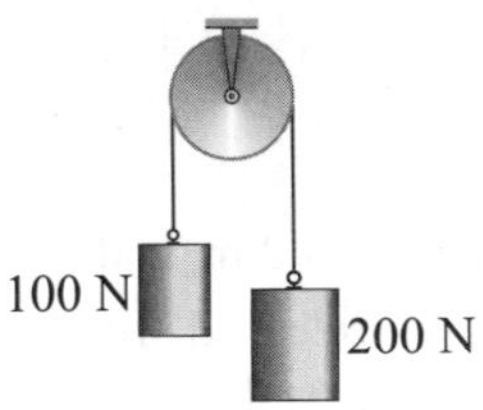

GATE 2016

Solution

Let T and a be the tension of string and acceleration of weights respectively.

Applying the equation of motion for weights.

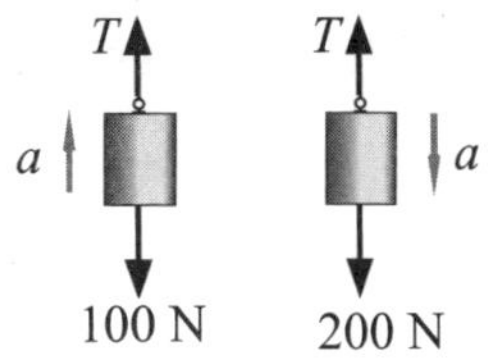

$$200 - T = \frac{200}{g} a$$

or $$T - 100 = \frac{100}{g} a$$

From which we get

$$T = \frac{400}{3}$$

$$T = 133.33\text{ N}$$

Example 5.38

A circular disc of radius 100 mm and mass 1 kg, initially at rest at position A, rolls without slipping down a curved path as shown in figure. The speed v of the disk when it reaches position B is_____ m/s.

Acceleration due to gravity $g = 10\ \text{m/s}^2$.

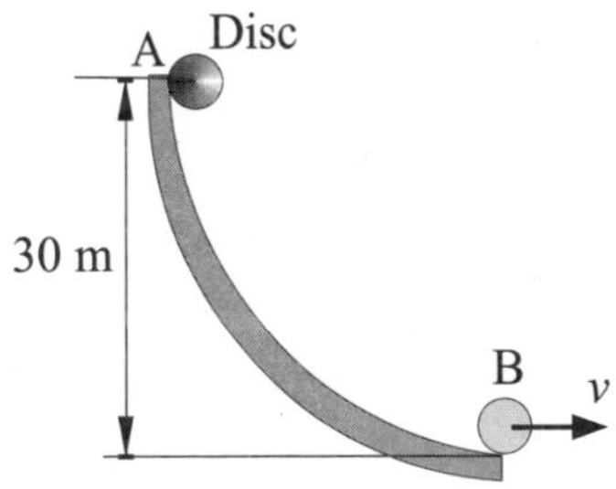

GATE 2016

Solution

Applying the principle of conservation of energy.

$$mgh = \frac{1}{2} I\omega^2 + \frac{1}{2} mv^2$$

or $$mgh = \frac{1}{2} \times \frac{1}{2} m r^2 \left(\frac{v}{r}\right)^2 + \frac{1}{2} mv^2$$

or $$mgh = \frac{3}{4} mv^2$$

$$v = \sqrt{\frac{4}{3} gh} = \sqrt{\frac{4}{3} \times 10 \times 30}$$

$$v = 20\text{ m/s}$$

Example 5.39

A particle of unit mass is moving on a plane. Its trajectory, in polar coordinates, is given by $r(t) = t^2, \theta(t) = t$, where t is time. The kinetic energy of the particle at time $t = 2$ is

(A) 4 (B) 12 (C) 16 (D) 24

GATE 2017

Solution

Given: Coordinates of moving particle, $r = t^2, \theta = t$

Radial velocity $v_r = \frac{dr}{dt} = 2t$

Transverse velocity $v_\theta = r\frac{d\theta}{dt} = t^2 \times 1 = t^2$

Resultant velocity $V = \sqrt{v_r^2 + v_\theta^2} = \sqrt{(2t)^2 + (t^2)^2}$

$$V_{t=2} = \sqrt{(2\times 2)^2 + (2^2)^2} = 4\sqrt{2}$$

Kinetic energy $\text{KE} = \frac{1}{2}mV^2 = \frac{1}{2}\times 1\times (4\sqrt{2})^2$

$$\text{Kinetic energy KE} = 16$$

Example 5.40

The following figure shows the velocity time plot for a particle travelling along a straight line. The distance covered by the particle from $t = 0$ to $t = 5$ s is_______m.

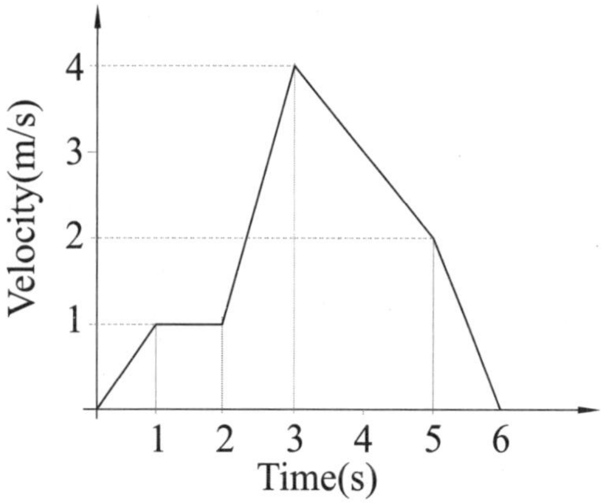

GATE 2017

Solution

Distance covered from $t = 0$ to $t = 5\,s$ $\quad S = \int_0^5 V dt$

$$S = \frac{1}{2}\times 1\times 1 + 1(2-1) + 1\times 1 + \frac{1}{2}\times 1\times (4-1) + \frac{1}{2}\times 2\times 2 + 2\times 2 = 10$$

$$S = 10\text{ m}$$

Example 5.41

Two disks A and B with identical mass (m) and radius (R) are initially at rest. They roll down from the top of identical inclined planes without slipping. Disk A has all of its mass concentrated at the rim, while Disk B has its mass uniformly distributed. At the bottom of the plane, the ratio of velocity of the center of disk A to the velocity of the center of disk B is.

(A) $\sqrt{\frac{3}{4}}$ (B) $\sqrt{\frac{3}{2}}$ (C) 1 (D) $\sqrt{2}$

GATE 2017

Solution

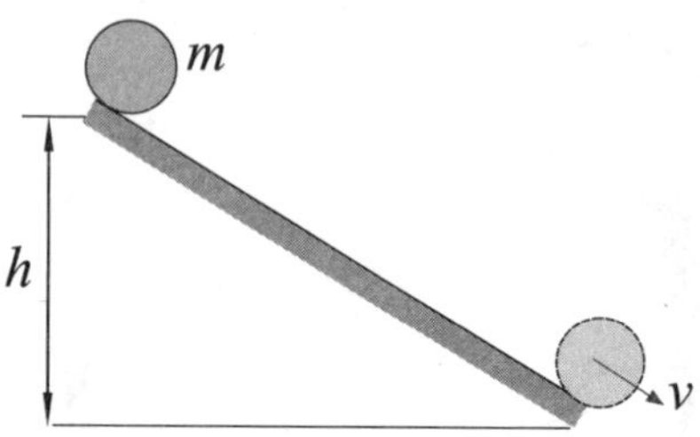

Applying the principle of conservation of energy

$$mgh = \frac{1}{2}mv^2 + \frac{1}{2}I\omega^2$$

For disk A

$$mgh = \frac{1}{2}mv_A^2 + \frac{1}{2}mr^2\left(\frac{v_A}{r}\right)^2; \qquad [I_A = mr^2]$$

$$v_A = \sqrt{gh} \qquad \text{(i)}$$

For disk B

$$mgh = \frac{1}{2}mv_B^2 + \frac{1}{2}\times\frac{1}{2}mr^2\left(\frac{v_B}{r}\right)^2; \quad \left[I_B = \frac{1}{2}mr^2\right]$$

$$v_B = \sqrt{\frac{4}{3}gh} \qquad \text{(ii)}$$

From equations (i) and (ii), we obtain

$$\frac{v_A}{v_B} = \sqrt{\frac{3}{4}}$$

Example 5.42

The rod PQ of length $L = \sqrt{2}$ m, and uniformly distributed mass of $M = 10$ kg, is released from rest at the position shown in the figure. The ends slide along the frictionless faces OP and OQ. Assume acceleration due to gravity, $g = 10$ m/s^2. The mass moment of inertia of the rod about its centre of mass and an axis perpendicular to the plane of the figure is ($ML^2/12$). At this instant, the magnitude of angular acceleration (in radian/s^2) of the rod is______.

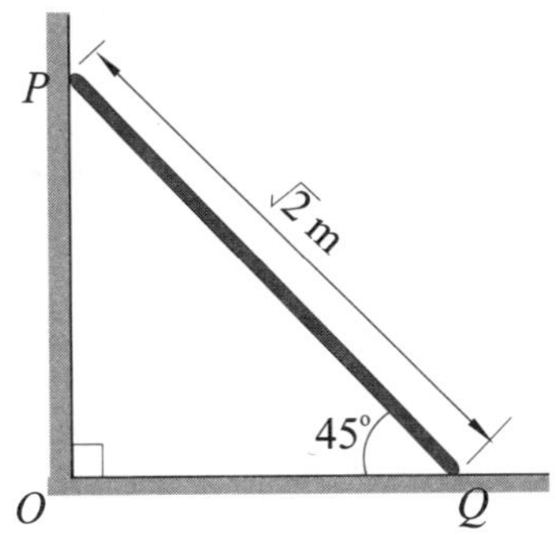

GATE 2017

Solution

Moment of inertia of rod about I

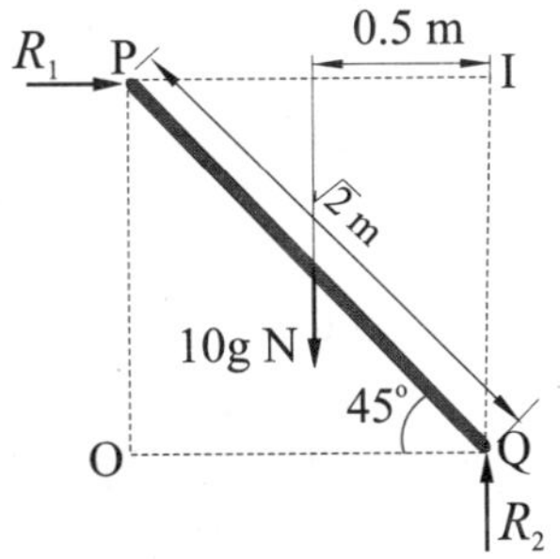

$$I_I = I_G + M(IG)^2 = \frac{10 \times \sqrt{2}^2}{12} + 10 \times \left(\frac{1}{\sqrt{2}}\right)^2 = \frac{20}{3} \text{ kgm}^2$$

Moment about I, $M = I\alpha$

$$10g \times 0.5 = \frac{20}{3}\alpha$$

$$g \times 0.5 = \frac{2}{3}\alpha$$

Angular acceleration α = 7.5 rad/s

Example 5.43

A bar of uniform cross section and weighing 100 N is held horizontally using two massless and inextensible strings $S1$ and $S2$ as shown in the figure.

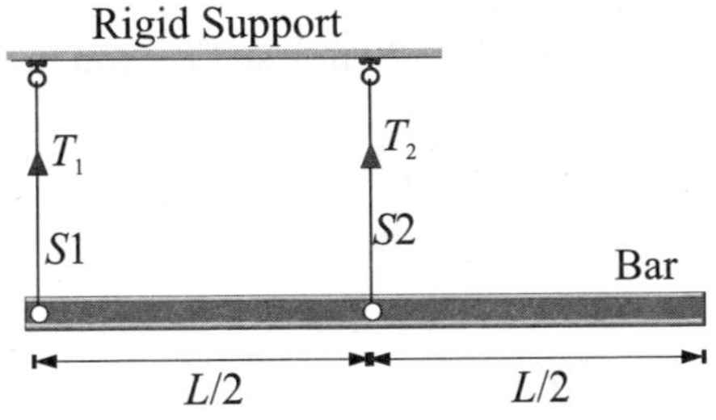

The tensions in the strings are

(A) $T_1 = 100$ N and $T_2 = 0$ N (B) $T_1 = 0$ N and $T_2 = 100$ N

(C) $T_1 = 75$ N and $T_2 = 25$ N (D) $T_1 = 25$ N and $T_2 = 75$ N

GATE 2018

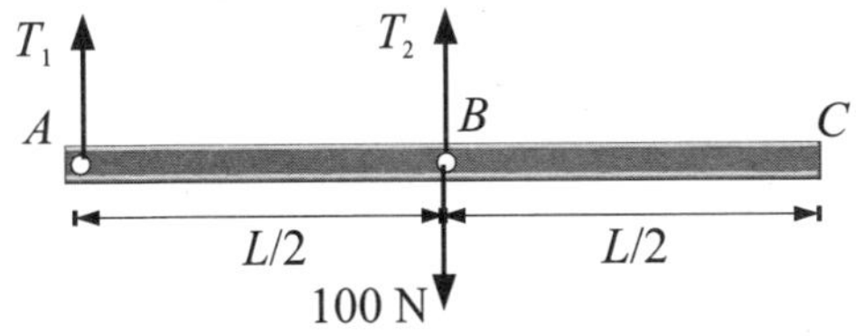

Solution

Figure shows the free body diagram of bar.

Applying equilibrium equations.

$$\sum M_A = 0 \Rightarrow T_2 \times \frac{L}{2} - 100 \times \frac{L}{2} = 0$$

$$T_2 = 100 \text{ N}$$

$$\sum F_y = 0 \Rightarrow T_1 + T_2 = 100 \text{ N}$$

$$T_1 = 0 \text{ N}$$

$$T_1 = 0 \text{ N}, T_2 = 100 \text{ N}$$

Example 5.44

A point mass is shot vertically up from ground level with a velocity of 4 m /s at time, $t = 0$. It loses 20% of its impact velocity after each collision with the ground. Assuming that the acceleration due to gravity is 10 m/s^2 and that air resistance is negligible, the mass stops bouncing and comes to complete rest on the ground after a total time (in seconds) of

(A) 1 (B) 2 (C) 4 (D) ∞

GATE 2018

Solution

Equation of motion for first throw, $v = u + gt$

$$0 = 4 - 10t$$

$$t = \frac{4}{10} \text{ s}$$

Velocity of mass after first collision, $u_1 = 0.8 \times 4$ m/s

$$0 = 0.8 \times 4 - 10t_1 \quad \text{or} \quad t_1 = \frac{0.8 \times 4}{10} \text{ s}$$

Velocity of mass after second collision,

$$u_2 = 0.8 \times 0.8 \times 4 = 0.8^2 \times 4 \text{ m/s}$$

$$0 = 0.8^2 \times 4 - 10t_2 \quad \text{or} \quad t_2 = \frac{0.8^2 \times 4}{10} \text{ s}$$

Velocity of mass after third collision,

$$u_3 = 0.8 \times 0.8 \times 0.8 \times 4 = 0.8^3 \times 4 \text{ m/s}$$

$$0 = 0.8^3 \times 4 - 10t_3$$

$$t_3 = \frac{0.8^3 \times 4}{10}\ \text{s}$$

....

$$t_n = \frac{0.8^n \times 4}{10}$$

So, $t, t_1, t_2, t_3, \_\_\_$ are forming GP series.

Total time $T = 2(t + t_1 + t_2 + t_3 + \_\_\_)$

$$T = 2\left(\frac{4}{10} + \frac{0.8 \times 4}{10} + \frac{0.8^2 \times 4}{10} + \frac{0.8^3 \times 4}{10} + \text{---}\right)$$

$$T = 2 \times \frac{\frac{4}{10}}{1 - 0.8}$$

$$T = 4\ \text{s}$$

Example 5.45

The schematic of an external drum rotating clockwise engaging with a short shoe is shown in the figure. The shoe is mounted at point Y on a rigid lever XYZ hinged at point X. A force $F = 100$ is applied at the free end of the lever as shown. Given that the coefficient of friction between the shoe and the drum is 0.3, the braking torque (in Nm) applied on the drum is _______ . (All dimensions are in mm)

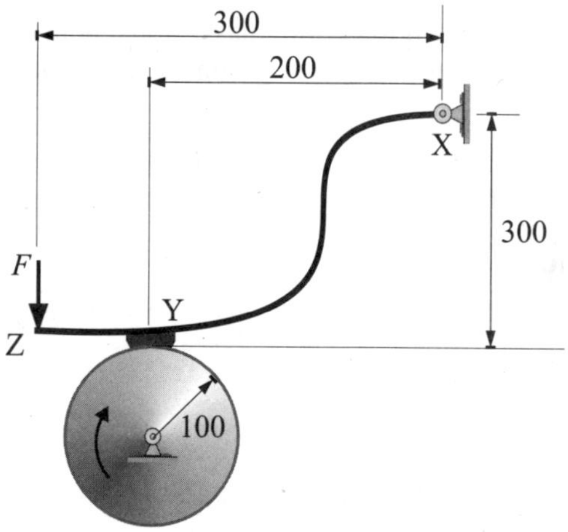

GATE 2018

Solution

Free body diagram of lever is shown in figure.

Taking moment about X.

$$\sum M_X = 0 \Rightarrow R \times 200 - F \times 300 - \mu R \times 300 = 0$$

$$R \times 200 - 100 \times 300 - 0.3 \times R \times 300 = 0$$

$$R = 272.7\ \text{N}$$

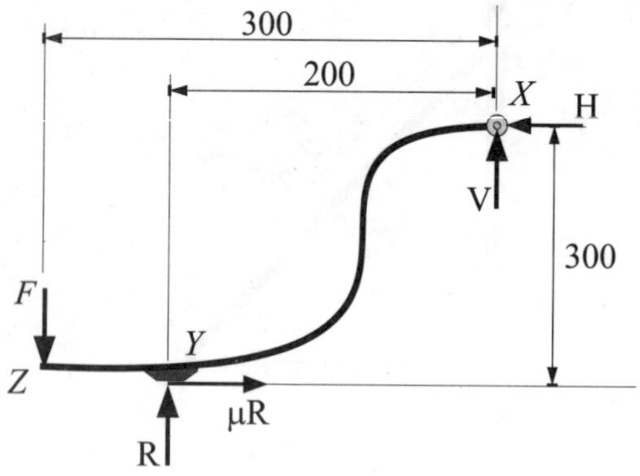

Free body Diagram

Breaking torque, $M = \mu R \times r = 0.3 \times 272.7 \times \frac{100}{1000}$

$$M = 8.18\ \text{Nm}$$

Example 5.46

Block P of mass 2 kg slides down the surface and has a speed 20 m/s at the lowest point, Q, where the local radius of curvature is 2 m as shown in the figure. Assuming g = 10 m/s^2, the normal force (in N) at Q is _______ .

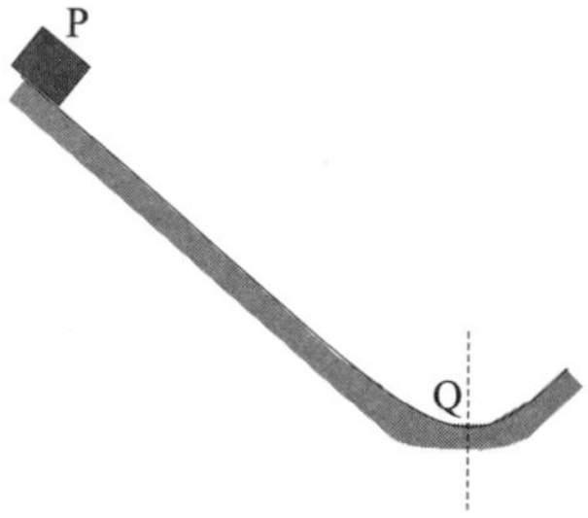

GATE 2018

Solution

Figure shows the free-body diagram of block at lowest point Q.

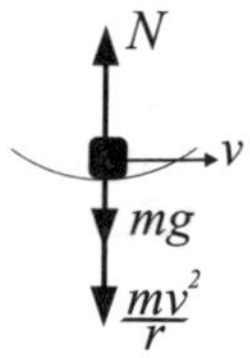

$$\sum F_y = 0 \quad \Rightarrow N - mg - \frac{mv^2}{r} = 0$$

or $$N = mg + \frac{mv^2}{r}$$

Substituting $m = 2$ kg, $v = 20$ m/s and $r = 2$ m, we have

$$N = 2 \times 10 + \frac{2 \times 20^2}{2}$$

$$N = 420\ \text{N}$$

Example 5.47

A ball is dropped from rest from a height of 1 m in a frictionless tube as shown in the figure. If the tube profile is approximated by two straight lines (ignoring the curved portion), the total distance travelled (in m) by the ball is________.

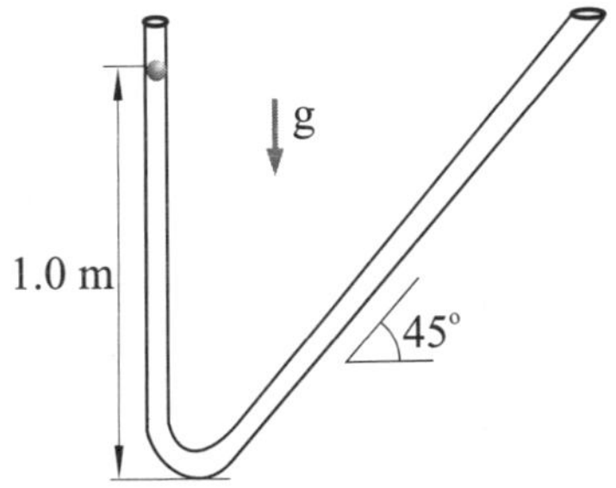

GATE 2018

Solution

Total distance travelled

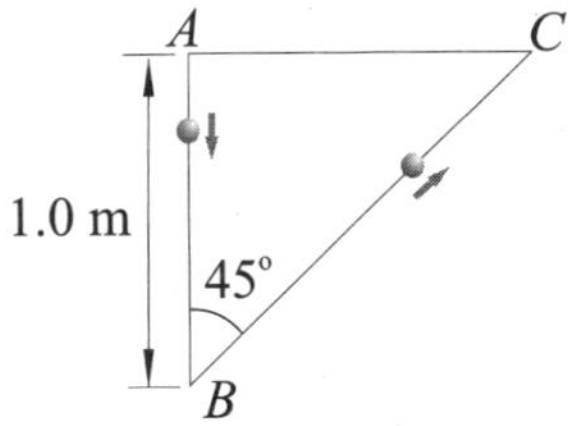

$$S = AB + BC$$

$$S = 1 + \frac{1}{\sin 45} = 1 + \sqrt{2}$$

$$S = 2.41\,\text{m}$$

Example 5.48

In a rigid body in plane motion, the point R is accelerating with respect to point P at $10\angle 180^\circ$ m/s^2. If the instantaneous acceleration of point Q is zero, the acceleration (in m/s^2) of point R is

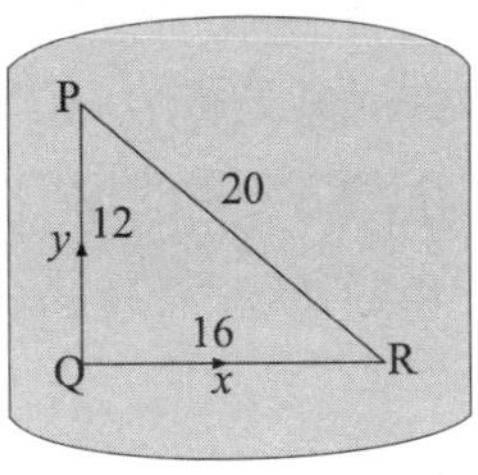

(A) $8\angle 233^\circ$ (B) $10\angle 225^\circ$ (C) $10\angle 217^\circ$ (D) $8\angle 217^\circ$

GATE 2018

Solution

As acceleration of point Q is zero. So this region the body is hinged at point Q.

Figure shows the direction of acceleration.

Let ω be the angular velocity of body.

Radial acceleration of point R $\quad a_R = \omega^2 \times QR = 16\omega^2$

Radial acceleration of point P $\quad a_P = \omega^2 \times PQ = 12\omega^2$

Acceleration of point R with respect to point P

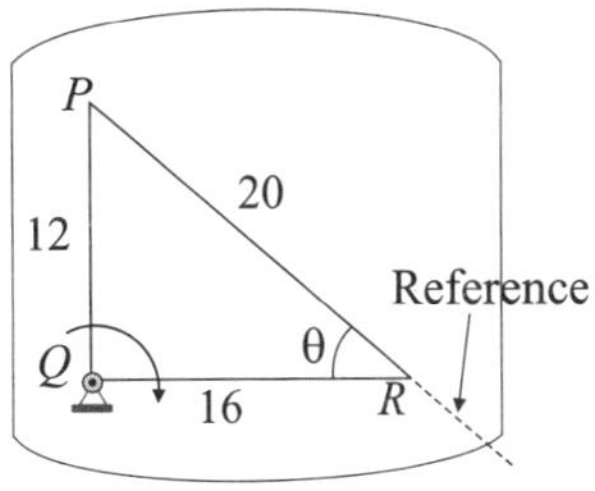

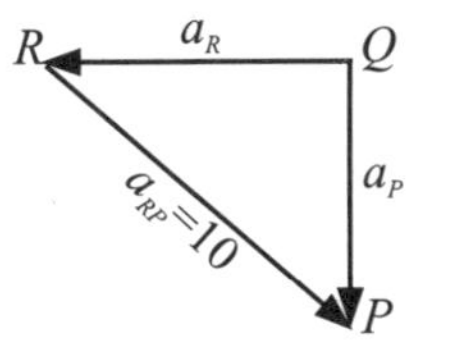

Acceleration diagram

$$\sqrt{(16\omega^2)^2 + (12\omega^2)^2} = 10$$

$$\omega^2 = 0.5$$

Acceleration of point R $\quad a_R = 16\omega^2 = 16 \times 0.5 = 8\ \text{m/s}^2$

In $\Delta\, PQR$, $\quad \theta = \tan^{-1}\left(\frac{PQ}{RQ}\right) = \tan^{-1}\left(\frac{12}{16}\right) = 36.869^\circ$

Direction of a_R from the reference $(180 + 36.869) = 217^\circ$

Acceleration of point R is $8\angle 217^\circ$

Example 5.49

A force of 100 N is applied to the centre of a circular disc, of mass 10 kg and radius 1 m, resting on a floor as shown in the figure. If the disc rolls without slipping on the floor, the linear acceleration (in m/s^2) of the centre of the disc is________.

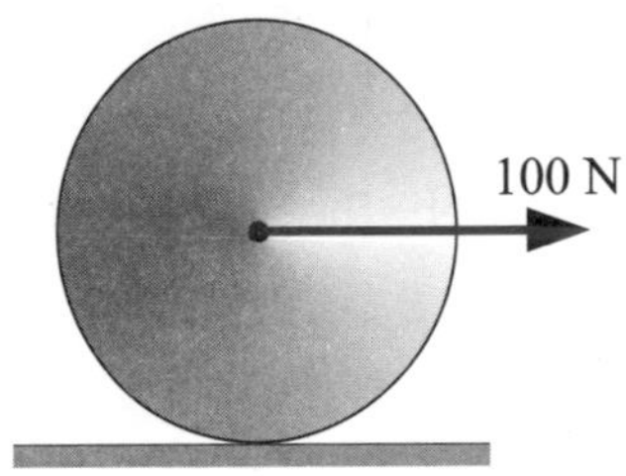

GATE 2018

Solution

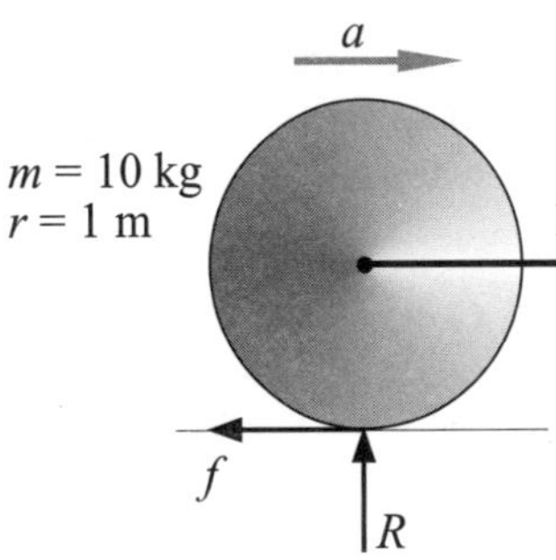

Applying equation of motion

$$\sum F = ma \quad \Rightarrow \quad 100 - f = 10a \qquad \text{(i)}$$

$$\sum \tau = I\alpha \quad \Rightarrow \quad f\,r = I\alpha$$

$$f = \frac{I}{r^2}a = \frac{\frac{mr^2}{2}}{r^2}a = \frac{m}{2}a = \frac{10a}{2}$$

or $\quad f = 5a \quad$ (ii)

Equations (i) and (ii) give $a = \frac{100}{15} = 6.66$

$$a = 6.66 \text{ m/s}^2$$

Example 5.50

A block of mass 10 kg rests on a horizontal floor. The acceleration due to gravity is 9.81 m/s^2. The coefficient of static friction between the floor and the block is 0.2. A horizontal force of 10 N is applied on the block as shown in the figure. The magnitude of force of friction (in N) on the block is ______

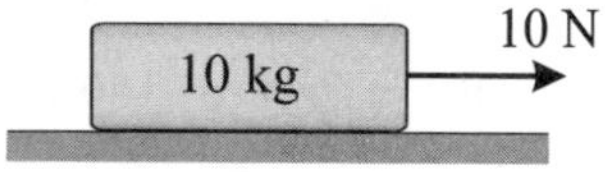

GATE 2019

Solution

Figure shows the free-body diagram of body.

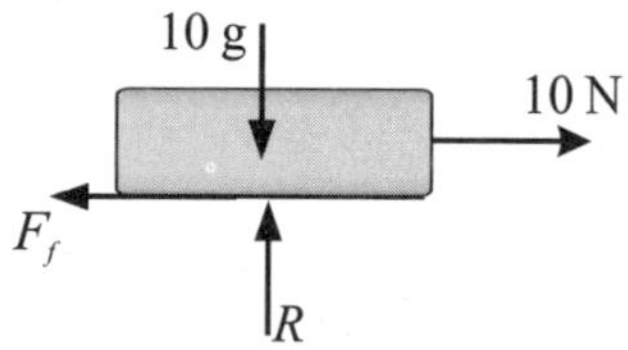

Friction force $F_f = 10\text{ N}$ [because $10\text{ N} < \mu R (= 19.62\text{ N})$]

$$F_f = 10\text{ N}$$

Example 5.51

A car having weight W is moving in the direction as shown in the figure. The center of gravity (CG) of the car is located at height h from the ground, midway between the front and rear wheels. The distance between the front and rear wheels is l. The acceleration of the car is a, and acceleration due to gravity is g. The reactions on the front wheels (R_f) and rear wheels (R_r) are given by

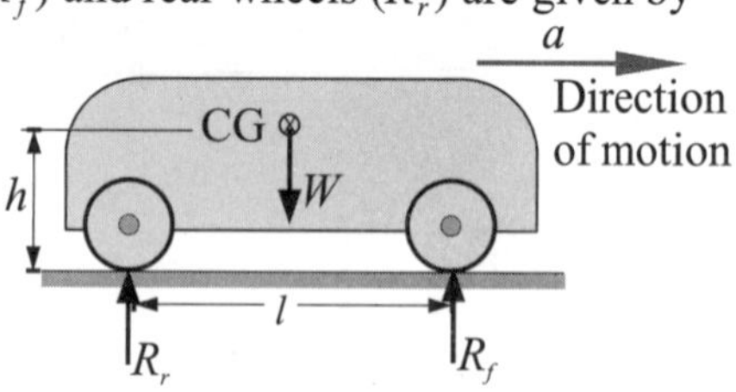

(A) $R_f = R_r = \frac{W}{2} - \frac{W}{g}\left(\frac{h}{l}\right)a$

(B) $R_f = \frac{W}{2} + \frac{W}{g}\left(\frac{h}{l}\right)a$; $R_r = \frac{W}{2} - \frac{W}{g}\left(\frac{h}{l}\right)a$

(C) $R_f = \frac{W}{2} - \frac{W}{g}\left(\frac{h}{l}\right)a$; $R_r = \frac{W}{2} + \frac{W}{g}\left(\frac{h}{l}\right)a$

(D) $R_f = R_r = \frac{W}{2} + \frac{W}{g}\left(\frac{h}{l}\right)a$

GATE 2019

Solution

Free body diagram of car is shown in figure.

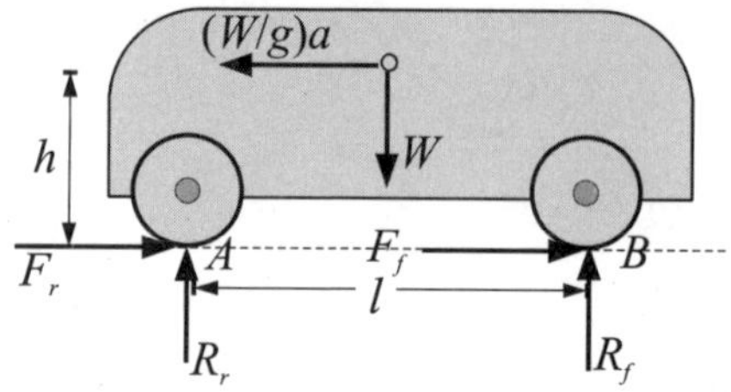

Applying equilibrium equations

$$\sum M_A = 0 \quad \Rightarrow W \times \frac{l}{2} - \left(\frac{W}{g}a\right) \times h - R_f \times l = 0$$

$$R_f = \frac{W}{2} - \frac{W}{g}\left(\frac{h}{l}\right)a$$

$$\sum F_v = 0 \Rightarrow R_f + R_r = W$$

or $\quad R_r = W - \left\{\frac{W}{2} - \frac{W}{g}\left(\frac{h}{l}\right)a\right\}$

or $\quad R_r = \frac{W}{2} + \frac{W}{g}\left(\frac{h}{l}\right)a$

$$R_f = \frac{W}{2} - \frac{W}{g}\left(\frac{h}{l}\right)a \; ; \; R_r = \frac{W}{2} + \frac{W}{g}\left(\frac{h}{l}\right)a$$

Example 5.52

A truss is composed of member AB, BC, CD, AD and BD, as shown in the figure. A vertical load of 10 kN is applied at point D. The magnitude of force (in kN) in the member BC is __________.

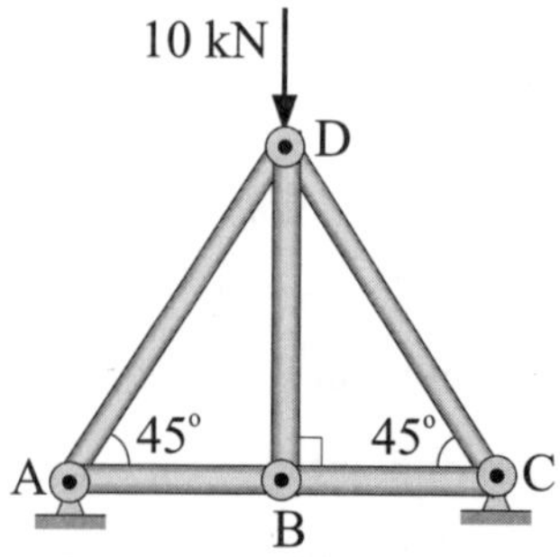

GATE 2019

Solution

Reactions at supports $R_A = R_C = \frac{10}{2} = 5\text{ N}$

Consider joint C

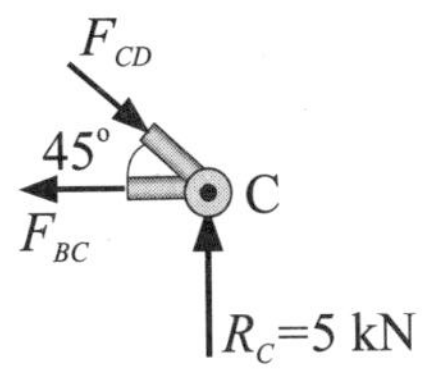

$$\sum F_y = 0 \Rightarrow F_{CD}\sin 45 = 5$$

$$F_{CD} = 5\sqrt{2}\text{ kN}$$

$$\sum F_x = 0 \Rightarrow F_{CD}\cos 45 - F_{BC} = 0$$

$$F_{BC} = 5\sqrt{2} \times \frac{1}{\sqrt{2}} = 5\text{ kN}$$

$$F_{BC} = 5\text{ kN}$$

Example 5.53

The figure shows an idealized plane truss. If a horizontal force of of 300 N is applied at point A, then the magnitude of the force produced in member CD is ______ N.

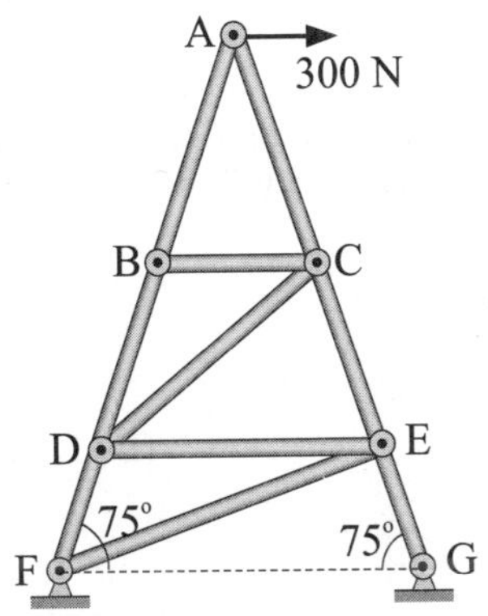

GATE 2019

Solution

Look for joint geometries that have three and four members for which two are collinear. We have

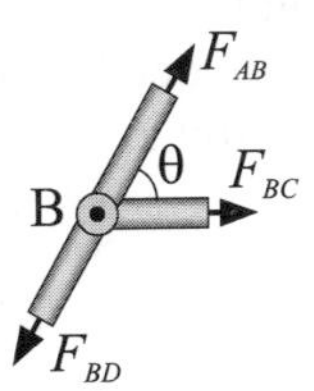

Joint B

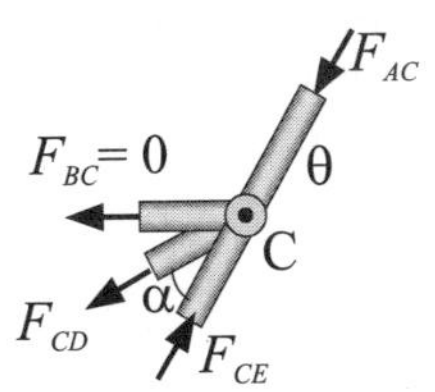

Joint C

Joint B

$$F_{BC}\sin\theta = 0$$

$$F_{BC} = 0$$

Joint C

$$F_{CD}\sin\alpha = 0$$

$$F_{CD} = 0$$

Example 5.54

A ball of mass 3 kg moving with a velocity of 4 m/s undergoes a perfectly-elastic direct-central impact with a stationary ball of mass *m*. After the impact is over, the kinetic energy of the 3 kg ball is 6 J. The possible value(s) of *m* is/are

(A) 1 kg only (B) 6 kg only

(C)1 kg, 6 kg (D) 1kg, 9 kg

GATE 2019

Solution

Given: $m_1 = 3$ kg, $u_1 = 4$ m/s, $m_2 = m$ kg, $u_2 = 0$ m/s and Coefficient of restitution, $e = 1$

Let v_2 be the velocity of mass *m* after impact.

Applying the conservation of linear momentum.

$$m_1u_1 + m_2u_2 = m_1v_1 + m_2v_2$$

$$3 \times 4 + m \times 0 = 3v_1 + mv_2$$

$$3v_1 + mv_2 = 12 \quad \text{(i)}$$

Coefficient of restitution, $e = \frac{v_2 - v_1}{u_1 - u_2} \Rightarrow \frac{v_2 - v_1}{4 - 0} = 1$

$$v_2 - v_1 = 4 \quad \text{(ii)}$$

From Equations (i) and (ii), we obtain

$$m = \frac{12 - 3v_1}{4 + v_1}\text{ kg}$$

Given kinetic energy of the 3 kg ball is 6 J; $\frac{1}{2} \times 3 \times v_1^2 = 6$

$$v_1 = \pm 2\text{ m/s}$$

$$m = \frac{12 - 3 \times (\pm 2)}{4 + (\pm 2)} = 1\text{ and }9$$

$$m = 1\text{ kg and }9\text{ kg}$$

5.3 PRACTICE PAPER

Time: 3 hours **Max. Marks: 100**

Q.1 to Q.30 carry one mark each

Q.1 to Q.20 Multiple Choice Questions

Q.1 A spring scale indicates a tension *T* in the right hand cable of the pulley system shown in figure. Neglecting the mass of the pulley and ignoring friction between the cable and pulley, the weight *W* is

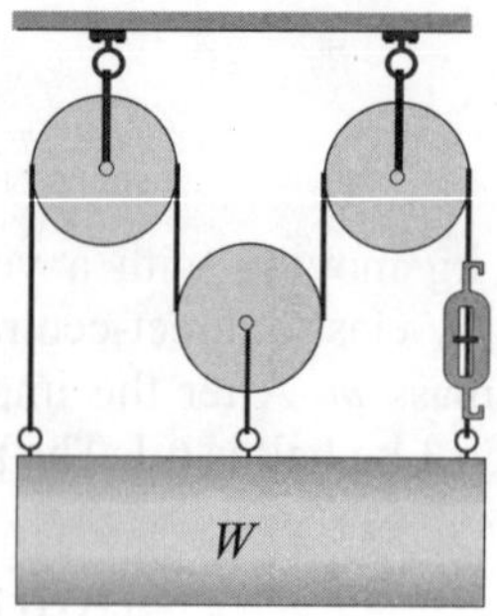

(A) $2T$ (B) $3T$ (C) $4T$ (D) $T(1+e^{4\pi})g$

Q.2 Block A of mass M rest on a table as shown in figure. The coefficient of friction between block and the table is μ. The maximum weight of block B which would keep the system in equilibrium is

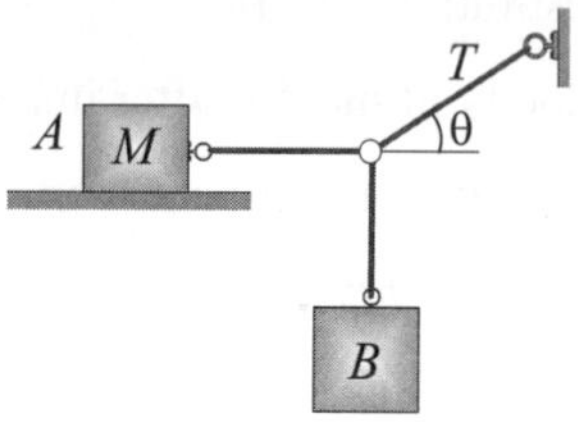

(A) $\mu Mg \tan\theta$ (B) Mg (C) μMg (D) $\mu Mg \cos\theta$

Q.3 A block of mass m is released at rest from a point P of a rough circular path of radius r as shown in the figure. There is a spring of stiffness k at the other end of the path (acceleration due to gravity = g). The maximum spring deflection is

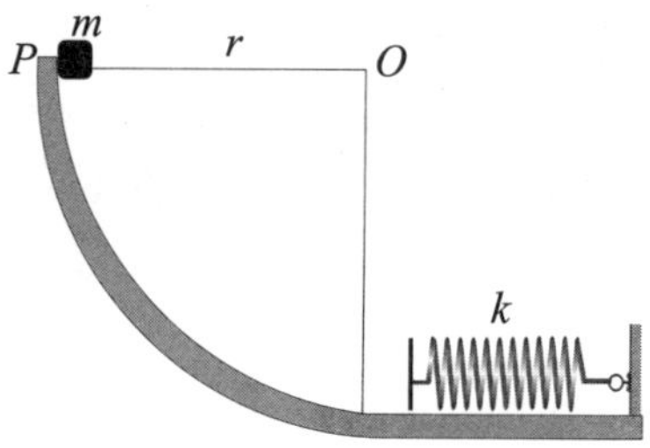

(A) Independent of r (B) More than $\sqrt{\frac{2mgr}{k}}$

(C) Equal to $\sqrt{\frac{2mgr}{k}}$ (D) Less than $\sqrt{\frac{2mgr}{k}}$

Q.4 The relation between forces P and Q for equilibrium of four bar linkage shown in the position is

(A) $P = Q$ (B) $P = Q\tan\theta$

(C) $P = Q\cot\theta$ (D) $Q = P\cos\theta$

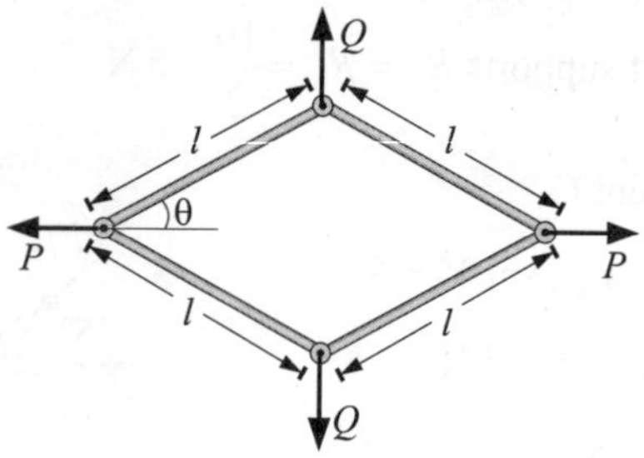

Q.5 A ball of mass m strikes the ground at angle α (as shown in figure) and is deflected at angle β as shown in figure. The coefficient of restitution is

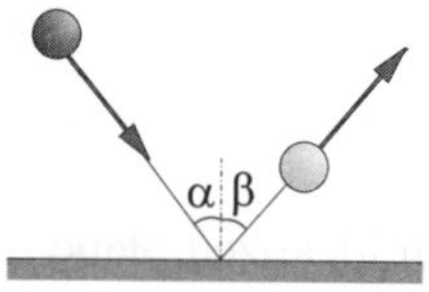

(A) $\frac{\tan\alpha}{\tan\beta}$ (B) $\frac{\cos\alpha}{\cos\beta}$ (C) $\frac{\sin\alpha}{\sin\beta}$ (D) $\frac{\tan\beta}{\tan\alpha}$

Q.6 An aeroplane is flying horizontally at a velocity u. It drops a packet from a height h. The time taken by the packet to reach the ground will be

(A) $\frac{u}{g}$ (B) $\frac{u}{g} + \sqrt{\frac{2h}{g}}$

(C) $\sqrt{\frac{2h}{g}}$ (D) None of these

Q.7 A particle projected from the lowest point with velocity u moves along the inside of the arc of smooth vertical circle of radius r. It will oscillate about the lowest point, if:

(A) $u^2 > 2gr$ (B)) $u^2 < 2gr$

(C) $u^2 > 5gr$ (D) $u^2 = 5gr$

Q.8 A square thin sheet of side l and uniform mass per unit area σ is used to form a hollow cylinder. The moment of inertia of this cylinder about the central axis is

(A) $\frac{2\sigma l^4}{\pi^2}$ (B) $\frac{\sigma l^4}{4\pi^2}$ (C) σl^4 (D) $\frac{2\sigma l^4}{3\sqrt{2}\,\pi^2}$

Q.9 A man is pulling a bucket of water up to the roof of the building of 6 m height. The total weight of the rope is 20 N and the weight of the bucket with water is 100 N. The work done (in N.m) by the man is

(A) 660 (B) 720 (C) 600 (D) 675

Q.10 Figure shows the system of linkage under the static equilibrium. Which one of the following option is true?

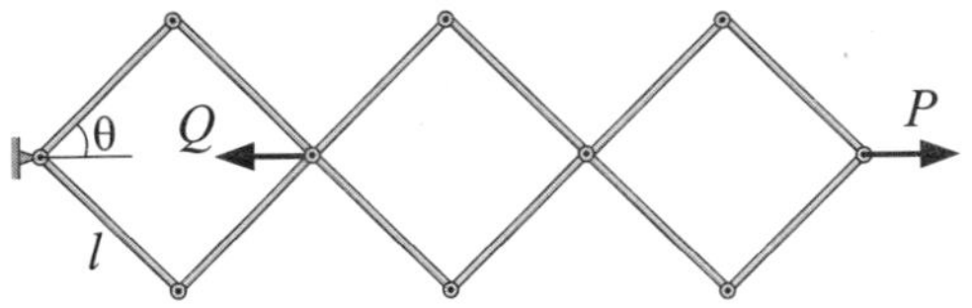

(A) $P = Q$ (B) $P = 3Q$ (C) $3P = Q$ (D) $P = 2Q$

Q.11 A thin string of negligible mass with one end fixed to the roof is wound around a circular disc of radius 2 m and mass 10 kg as shown below. The disc rolls vertically down under the action of its own weight. Considering acceleration due to gravity as 10 m/s^2, the tension in the string is

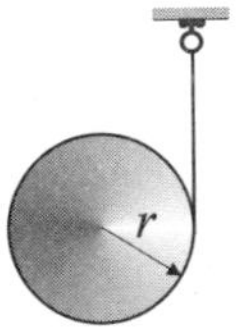

(A) 0 N (B) 25.0 N (C) 33.3 N (D) 50 N

Q.12 When a ball of weight W rests on a spring of constant k, it produces a static deflection of 3 cm. If the ball is now dropped from a height of $h = 30$ cm as shown in the figure, the spring will get compressed by

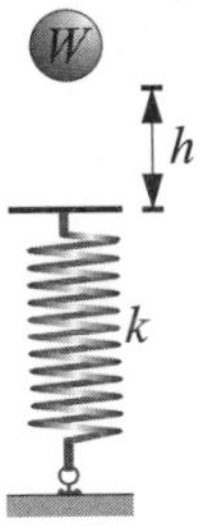

(A) 2.45 cm (B) 13.4 cm (C) 16.7 cm (D) 14.7 cm

Q.13 A mass of 2 kg is hung by a string of length 1.5 m as shown in figure. The mass revolves in a horizontal circular path at 50 revolutions per minute.

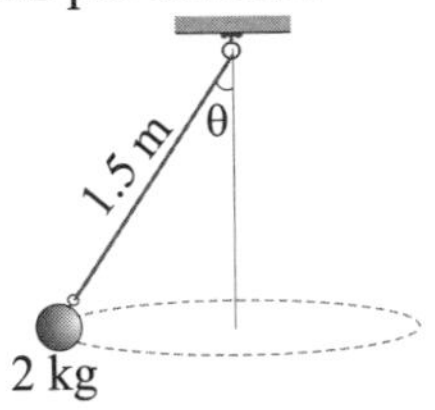

The tension in the string (in N) is

(A) $\frac{25\pi}{3}$ (B) $\frac{25\pi^2}{3}$ (C) $\frac{50\pi}{3}$ (D) $\frac{50\pi^2}{3}$

Q.14 A 2 kg mass, initially at rest, is acted upon by a time-varying force whose profile is as shown in graph. The distance (in m) travelled by the mass in 2 s is

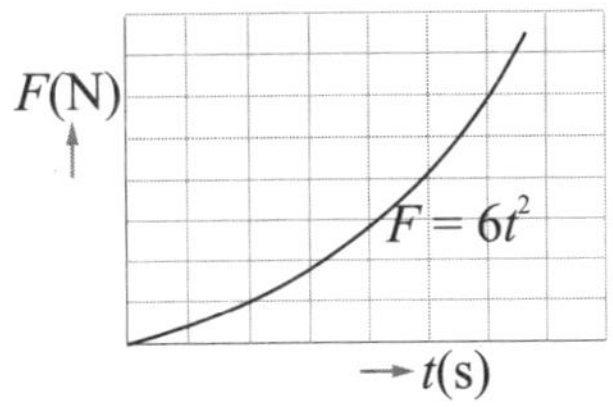

(A) 24 (B) 12 (C) 8 (D) 4

Q.15 A cubical block of side a is moving with velocity v on a horizontal smooth plane as shown in figure. It hits a ridge at point O. The angular velocity of the block just after it hits O is

(A) $\frac{3v}{4a}$ (B) $\frac{3v}{2a}$ (C) $\frac{2v}{3a}$ (D) $\frac{v}{a}$

Q.16 A thin circular ring of mass M and radius R is rotating about its axis with a constant angular velocity ω. Two objects each of mass m are attached gently to the opposite ends of a diameter of the ring. The wheel now rotates with an angular velocity

(A) $\omega \frac{M}{(m+M)}$ (B) $\omega \frac{(M-2m)}{(M+2m)}$

(C) $\omega \frac{M}{(M+2m)}$ (D) $\omega \frac{(M+2m)}{M}$

Q.17 A wheel of centroidal radius of gyration k is rolling on a horizontal surface with constant velocity. It comes across an obstruction of height h. Because of its rolling speed, just overcomes the obstruction. To determine v, one should use the principle (s) of conservation of

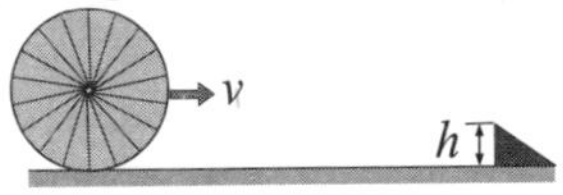

(A) Energy (B) Linear momentum

(C) Energy and linear momentum

(D) Energy and angular momentum

Q.18 A bullet of mass 0.1 kg is fired with a velocity of u from a gun of mass 10 kg. The ratio of kinetic energy of bullet to gun is

(A) 1 (B) 10 (C) 100 (D) 1000

Q.19 Starting from rest, a body slides down a 45° inclined plane in twice the time it takes to slide down the same distance in the absence of friction. The coefficient of friction between the body and the inclined plane is

(A) 0.33 (B) 0.25 (C) 0.75 (D) 0.80

Q.20 Thin wire of length L and uniform linear mass density ρ is bent into a circular loop with center O as shown in figure. The moment of inertia of the loop about the x-axis is

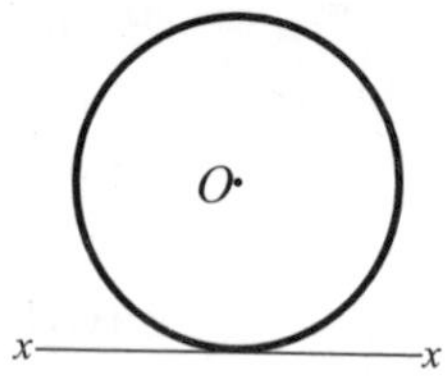

(A) $\frac{\rho L^3}{8\pi^3}$ (B) $\frac{\rho L^3}{16\pi^3}$ (C) $\frac{5\rho L^3}{16\pi^2}$ (D) $\frac{3\rho L^3}{8\pi^2}$

Q.21 to Q.30 Numerical Answer Questions

Q.21 A thin uniform rectangular plate of length 2 m and width 1 m is suspended from a corner as shown in figure. The equilibrium angle θ will be

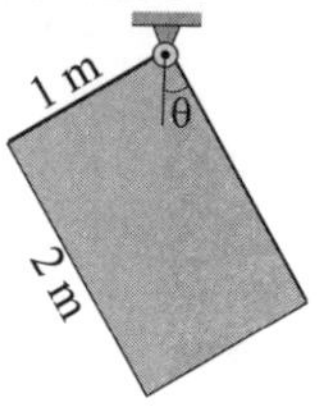

Q.22 A particle rests at the origin. It moves along x-axis with an acceleration $x - x^2$, where x is the distance (in m) of the particle at time t. The particle next comes to rest after it has covered a distance (in m) is_________.

Q.23 A bullet is fired from a gun. The force on the bullet is given by $F = 600 - 2\times10^5 t$, where F is in N and t in s. The force on the bullet becomes zero as soon as it leaves the barrel. The average impulse (in N.s) imparted to the bullet is______.

Q.24 The potential energy of a mechanical system is given by $V = 8x^3 + 6x^2 - 7x$, where x is in meters. The system is under static equilibrium at x =______m.

Q.25 The force in the member PR of the truss shown is______.

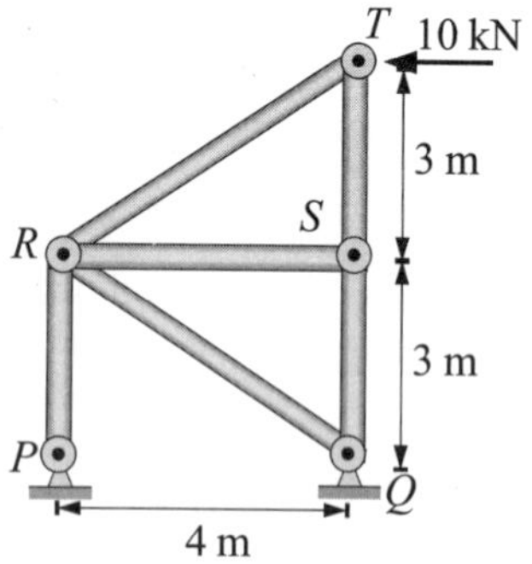

Q.26 A car is moving along a circular horizontal track of radius 10 m with a constant speed of 10 m/s. A plumb bob is suspended from the roof of the car by a light rigid rod of length 1.0 m. The angle (in degree) made by the rod with the track is ($g = 10\ \text{m/s}^2$)______.

Q.27 A homogeneous wire $ABCD$ is bent as shown and supported by a pin at C. The length l (in m) for which the portion BCD of the wire remain horizontal, is______.

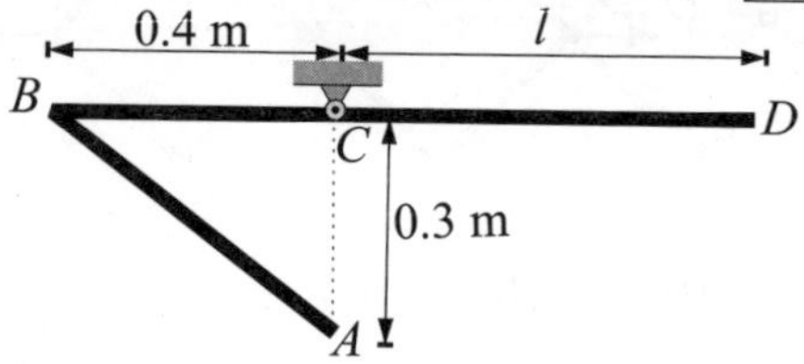

Q.28 A rod of length 1 m is sliding in a corner as shown in figure. At an instant when the rod makes an angle of 60° with the horizontal plane, the velocity of point A on the rod is 1 m/s. The angular velocity (in rad/s) of the rod at this instant is______.

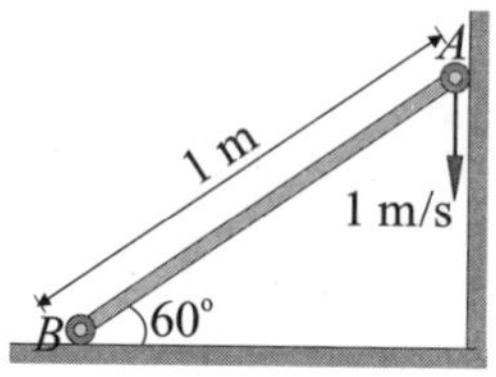

Q.29 A uniform stiff rod of length 300 mm and having a weight of 300 N is pivoted at one end and connected to a spring at the other end (See figure). For keeping the rod vertical in a stable position the minimum value of spring constant k (in N/m) needed is______.

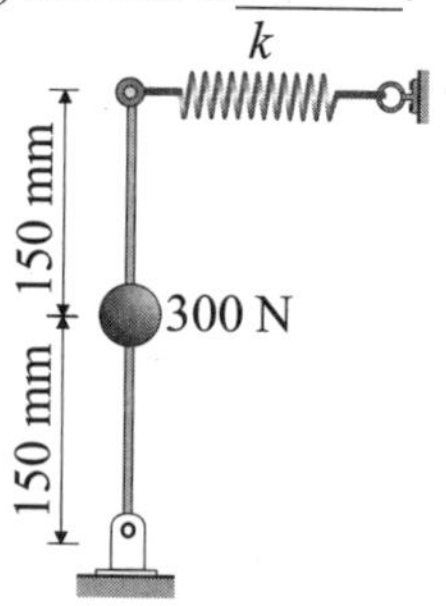

Q.30 A man weighing 600 N stands on a horizontal beam of negligible weight at C and holds a string passing over two smooth pulleys and attached to point B on the beam as shown in the figure. The tension(in N) in the string is__.

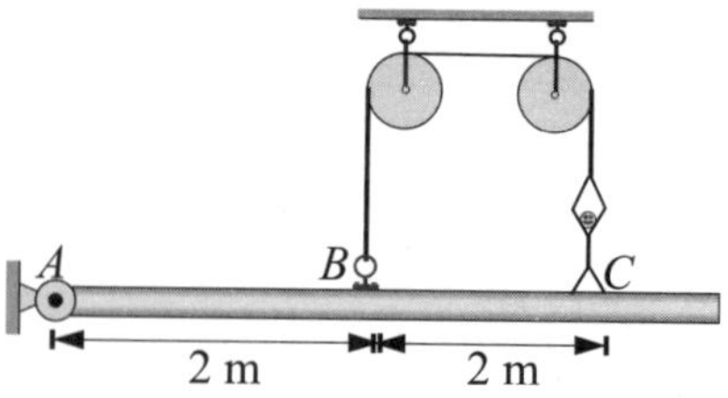

Q.31 to Q.65 carry two marks each

Q.31 to Q.50 Multiple Choice Questions

Q.31 Two equal spheres of weight W are suspended by

strings as shown in figure. They are also interconnected by a horizontal weightless rod. For a given applied force P, applied horizontally, the inclination "θ" of the strings with the vertical is

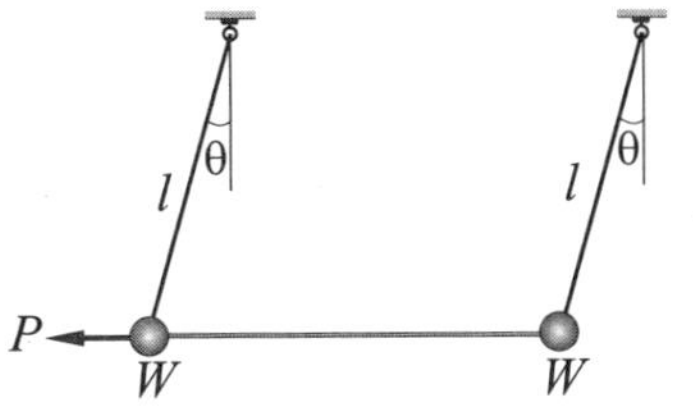

(A) $\tan^{-1}\left(\frac{P}{2W}\right)$ (B) $\tan^{-1}\left(\frac{P}{W}\right)$

(C) $\sin^{-1}\left(\frac{P}{2W}\right)$ (D) None of these

Q.32 A thin circular ring of mass per unit length ρ and radius r is rotating at an angular speed ω shown in figure. The tension in the ring is

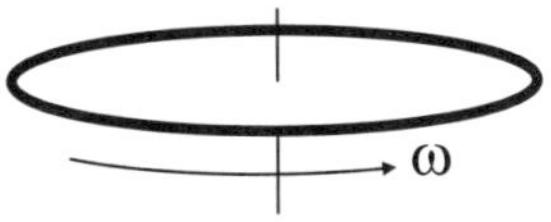

(A) $\rho\omega^2 r^2$ (B) $\frac{1}{2}\rho\omega^2 r^2$

(C) $2\pi\rho\omega^2 r^3$ (D) None of these

Q.33 The simple pendulum shown in figure is released from rest at A with the string horizontal and swings downward under the influence of gravity. The tension in the string at angle θ is

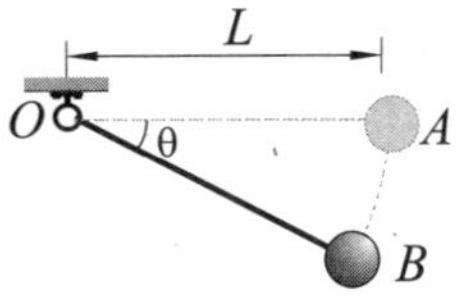

(A) $mg\cos\theta$ (B) $2mg\sin\theta$ (C) $3mg\sin\theta$ (D) 0

Q.34 A uniform pole of weight W and length l leans on a smooth wall as shown. Coefficient of friction = μ for the contact between the floor and the pole. Find the maximum distance d that it can be placed without slipping.

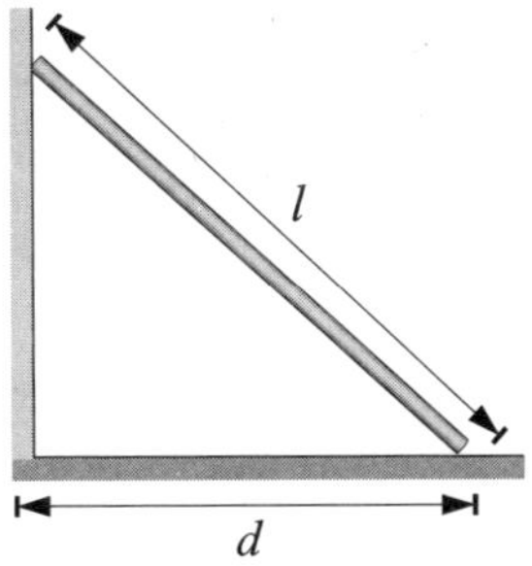

(A) $\frac{2\mu l}{\sqrt{1+4\mu^2}}$ (B) $\frac{2\mu l}{\sqrt{1+2\mu^2}}$

(C) $\frac{2\mu l}{3}$ (D) μl

Q.35 The force in the member AC of the loaded frame shown in figure, is

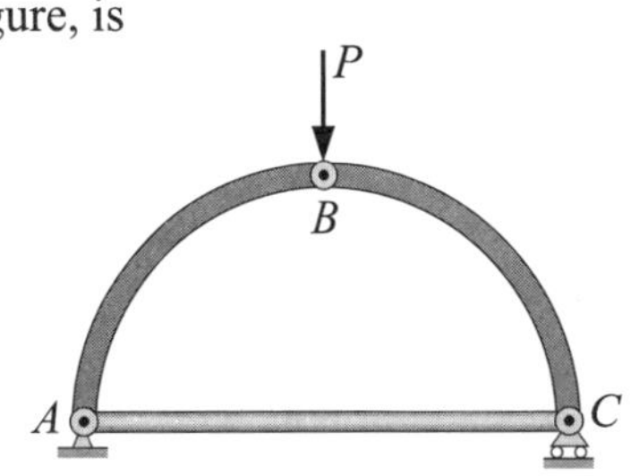

(A) P (compression) (B) $2P$ (tension)

(C) $\frac{P}{2}$ (tension) (D) $1.5P$ (tension)

Q.36 A rocket is fired vertically with a constant velocity v from the station. Its flight is tracked by radar from point O. The angular velocity ω of radar is

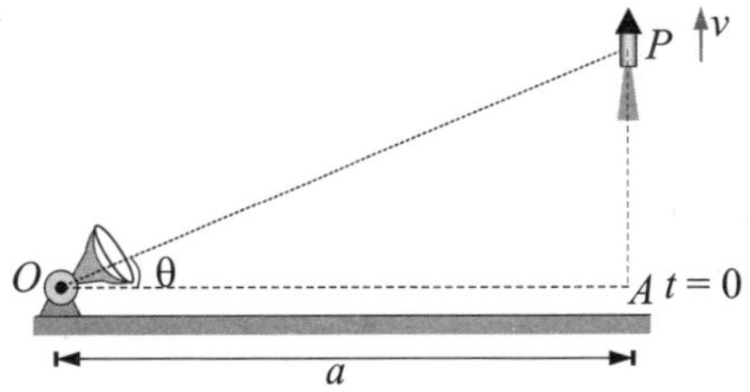

(A) $\omega = \text{constant}$ (B) $\omega = \frac{av}{a^2 + v^2t^2}$

(C) $\omega = \frac{v}{a}$ (D) $\omega = \frac{v}{\sqrt{a^2 + v^2t^2}}$

Q.37 A solid sphere of mass m and radius r rolls down a plane inclined at θ with the horizontal. The acceleration of the sphere will be

(A) $\frac{2}{3}g\sin\theta$ (B) $\frac{5}{7}g\sin\theta$

(C) $\frac{3}{7}g\sin\theta$ (D) None of these

Q.38 A particle of mass m moves in a straight line under an attractive force $m\mu x$ towards a fixed point O on the line, x being the distance of the particle from O. If $x = a$ and $v = 0$, then the velocity of the particle at a distance x is given by:

(A) $\mu(a - x)$ (B) $\mu(x - a)$

(C) $\sqrt{\mu(a^2 - x^2)}$ (D) $-\mu\sqrt{(a^2 - x^2)}$

Q.39 Two identical springs are arranged in series and subjected to a force F as shown in figure. The strain energy stored in one spring is

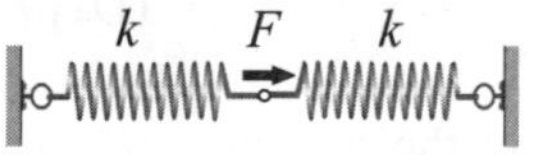

(A) $\frac{F^2}{2k}$ (B) $\frac{F^2}{4k}$ (C) $\frac{F^2}{8k}$ (D) $\frac{F^2}{16k}$

Q.40 Five weightless rods of equal length are joined together so as to form a rhombus $ABCD$ with one diagonal. If weight W be attached to C and system be suspended from A. The compressed force in BD is

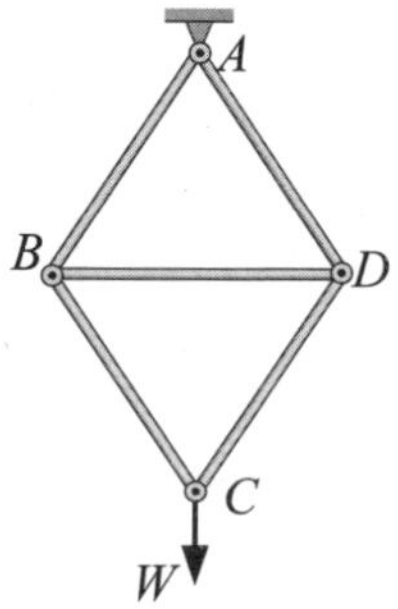

(A) $\sqrt{3}\,W$ (B) $\frac{W}{\sqrt{3}}$ (C) W (D) $\sqrt{2}\,W$

Q.41 A uniform chain of length l and mass m is lying on smooth table and one third of its length is hanging vertically down over the edge of the table. The work required to pull the hanging part on the table is

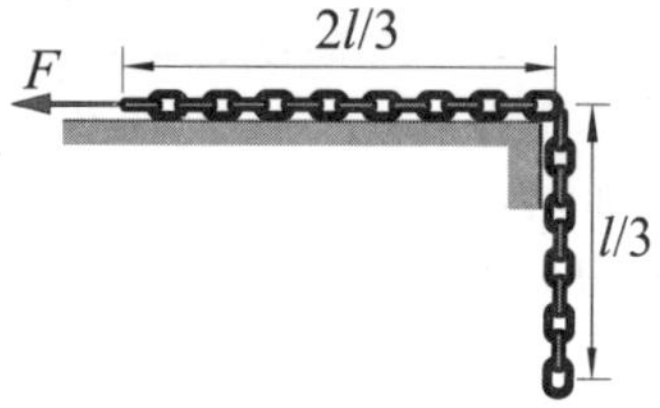

(A) mgl (B) $\frac{mgl}{18}$ (C) $\frac{mgl}{9}$ (D) $\frac{mgl}{\sqrt{2}}$

Q.42 $ABCD$ is a channel in the vertical plane, $BCDE$ being a circular loop with radius r. If a block is released from point A, the minimum height h such that the block completes the loop is

(A) $3r$ (B) $4r$

(C) $\frac{5}{2}r$ (D) $\frac{7}{2}r$

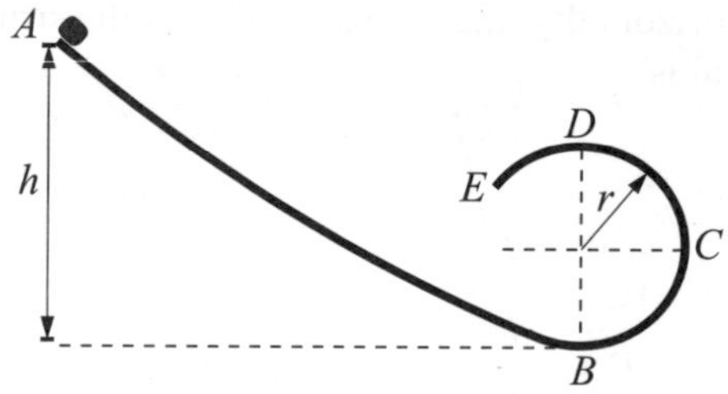

Q.43 The collar A moves down with a constant velocity v_A as shown in figure. The velocity of block B is

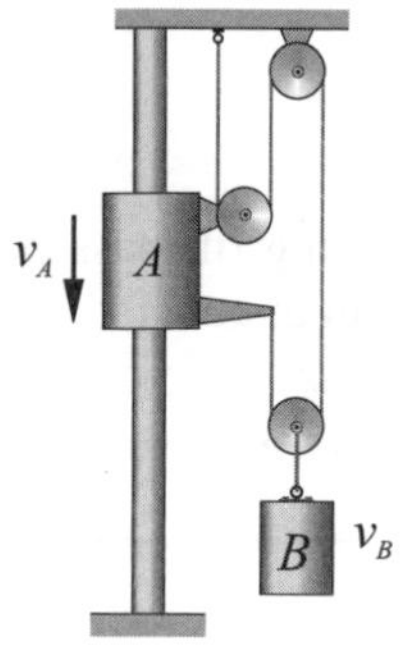

(A) $v_B = \frac{v_A}{2}\uparrow$ (B) $v_B = v_A \uparrow$

(C) $v_B = \frac{v_A}{4}\uparrow$ (D) $v_B = \frac{v_A}{4}\downarrow$

Q.44 A uniform sphere of mass m and radius r is placed in a corner with an initial counter clockwise angular velocity ω as shown in figure. Kinetic coefficient of friction between sphere and both surfaces is μ. The number of rotation before sphere comes to rest is

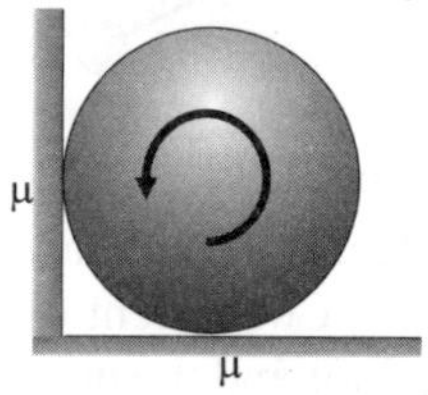

(A) $n = \frac{\omega^2 r(1+\mu^2)}{10\mu g\pi(1+\mu)}$ (B) $n = \frac{\omega^2 r(1+\mu^2)}{8\mu g\pi(1+\mu)}$

(C) $n = \frac{\omega^2 r(1+\mu^2)}{8\mu g\pi}$ (D) None of these

Q.45 A shot of mass 0.2 kg fired at the bob of a pendulum of mass 1.0 kg hits it with a velocity of 20 m/s and remains stuck to it after impact. After impact the bob will swing from its initial position to an approximate height h of

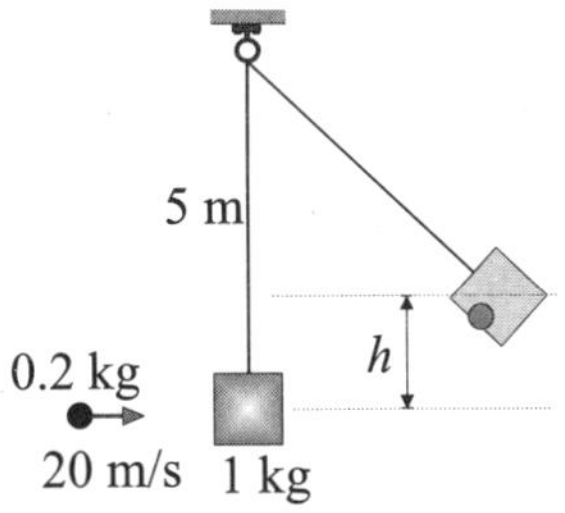

(A) 10 m (B) 4.08 m (C) 3.39 m (D) 0.56m

Q.46 The elevation of the load is controlled by the adjusting screw which connects joint A and C(see figure). The tensile force in adjusting screw AC is

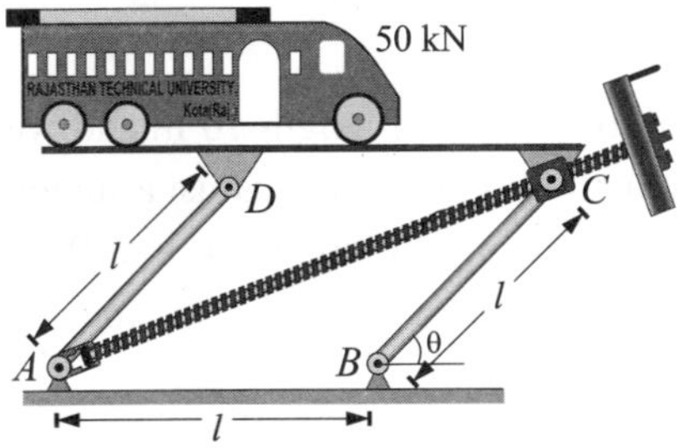

(A) $\dfrac{100\cos\theta}{\sin\frac{\theta}{2}}$ kN (B) $50\cos\theta$ kN

(C) $\dfrac{50\cos\theta}{\sin\frac{\theta}{2}}$ kN (D) None of these

Q47 The system shown in figure is released from rest. Neglecting the rotational inertia of body A, the velocity of body B as a function of the distance fall h is

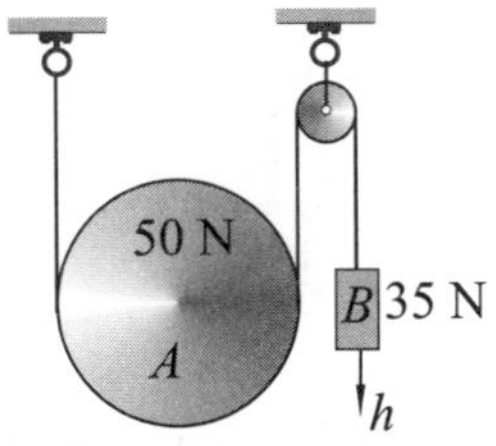

(A) $\sqrt{0.42gh}$ (B) $\sqrt{gh}$

(C) $\sqrt{1.22gh}$ (D) None of these

Q48 A rigid rod of length L and weight W rests on a small roller at B and leans against a vertical wall at A as shown. Assume the surface of the wall is smooth. Find the length of the rod that is in equilibrium for the given configuration in terms of a and θ.

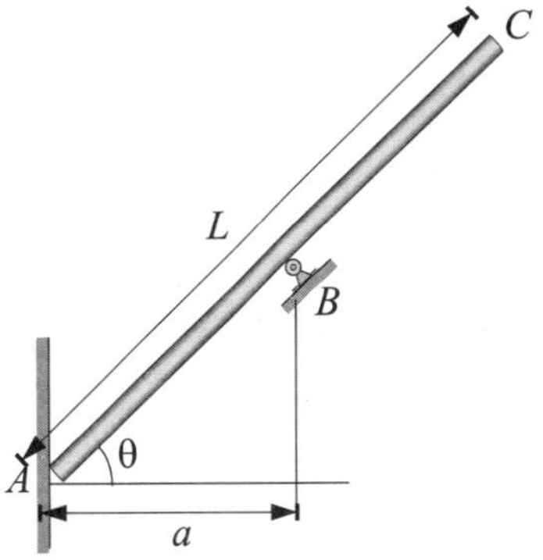

(A) $L = \dfrac{4a}{\cos\theta}$ (B) $L = \dfrac{2a}{\cos^3\theta}$

(C) $L = \dfrac{a}{\cos^2\theta}$ (D) $L = \dfrac{a}{2\cos\theta}$

Q.49 The rigid links PQ and PR of length L each are connected to three sliders P, Q and R, by pin joints as shown in figure. The sliders, Q and R, slide in the y-direction while the slider P, slide in the x-direction. When the slider P, is at the position $x = 40$ mm, its velocity is 30 mm/s along the positive x-direction. At that instant, the velocity of slider, Q will be

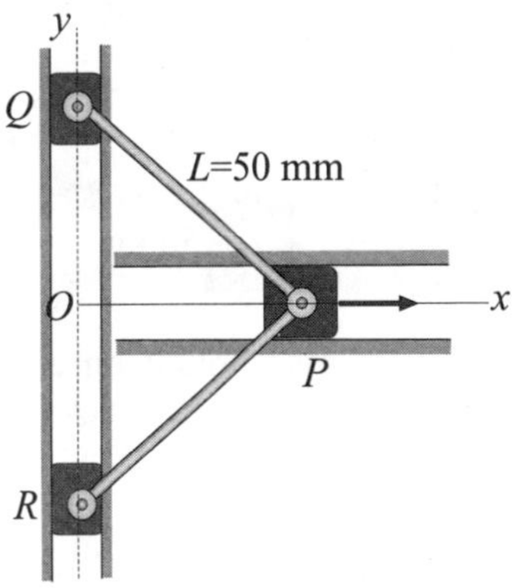

(A) 40 mm/s along the positive y-direction

(B) 40 mm/s along the negative y-direction

(C) 22.5 mm/s along the positive y-direction

(D) 22.5 mm/s along the negative y-direction

Q.50 A member ABC of weight 2 kN/m hinged at A is held such that AB is in the horizontal position by cable attached at C, whose other end is fixed to the wall (see figure). The tension(in kN) in the cable under the weight of member is

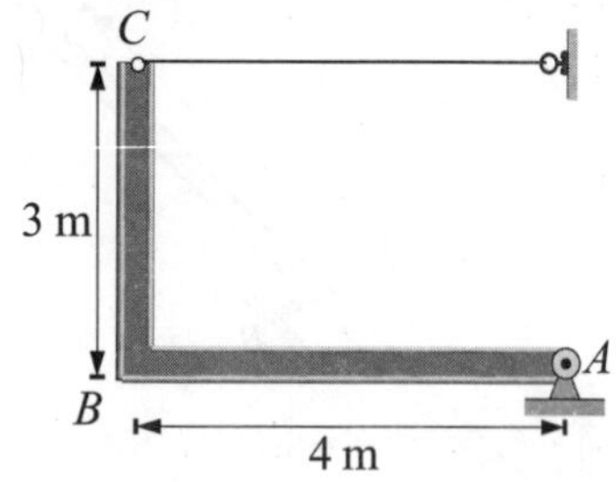

(A) 14.1 kN (B) 15.6 kN 40 kN (D) 13.3 kN

Q.51 to Q.65 Numerical Answer Questions

Q.51 A particle is projected from a point on the x-axis in vertical x-y plane. If the trajectory above the x-axis is given by $x^2 + 4y - 8 = 0$, then the velocity (in m/s) of projection is______.

Q.52 A cable is used to support blocks A and B as shown in figure. Block A is supported by a small wheel that is free to roll on the cable. The displacement y (in m) of block A for equilibrium is______.

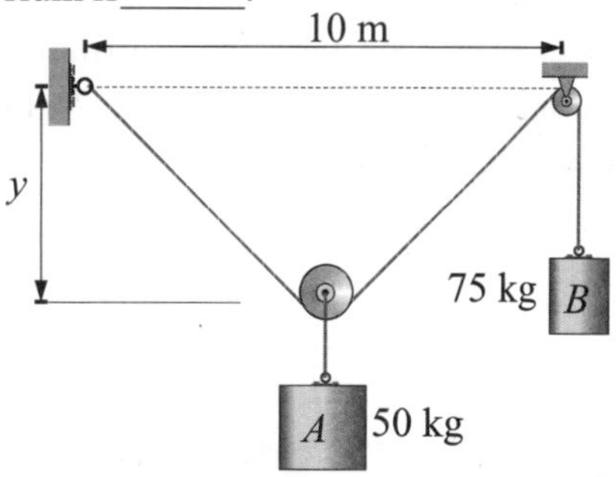

Q.53 A force $F = 2\,\text{N}$ is applied on a block of mass $M = 0.5\,\text{kg}$ as shown in figure. The block is constrained to move along the horizontal direction in a guideway. Neglect any friction between the block and the guideway. The distance (in m) travelled by the block in 2 s starting from rest is______.

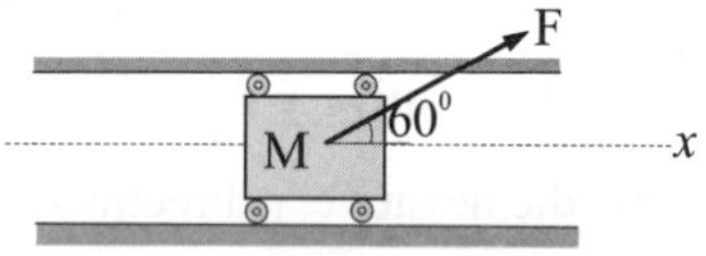

Q.54 The blocks P and Q are connected by a string, which passes over a pulley as shown in the figure. The block P is sliding on an inclined surface. Ignoring the masses of the string and the pulley, the tension in the string is (neglect all friction)______.

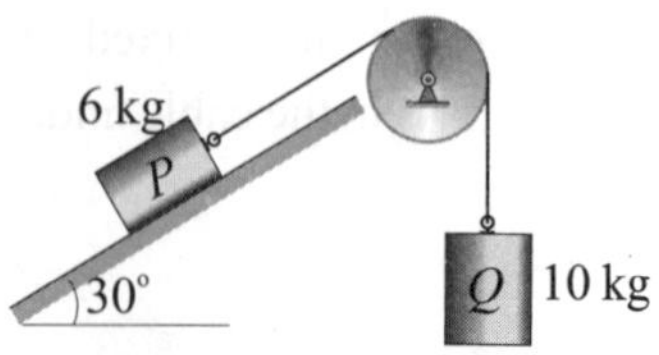

Q.55 A rectangular box of mass 80 kg rests on a rough horizontal surface as shown in figure. The static coefficient of friction between the contacting surfaces is 0.25. The maximum value of 'h' at which a horizontal force P can be applied so that the box can slide without toppling is______.

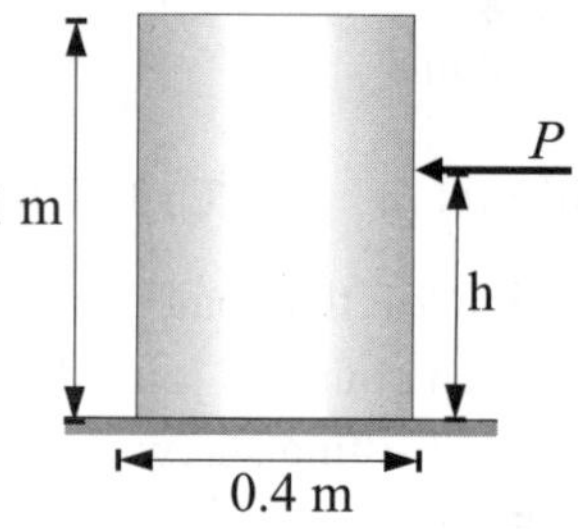

Q.56 A uniform ladder of length 10 m and weight 100 N rests on a smooth floor at A and against a smooth wall at B as shown in figure. A horizontal rope PQ prevents the ladder from sliding. The tension of the rope is______.

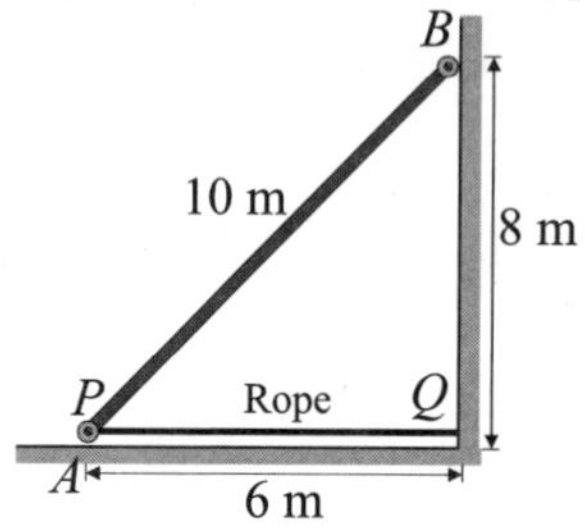

Q.57 A weight W is supported by two cables as shown in figure. The tension T_2 in the cable making angle θ will be the minimum when the value of θ is______.

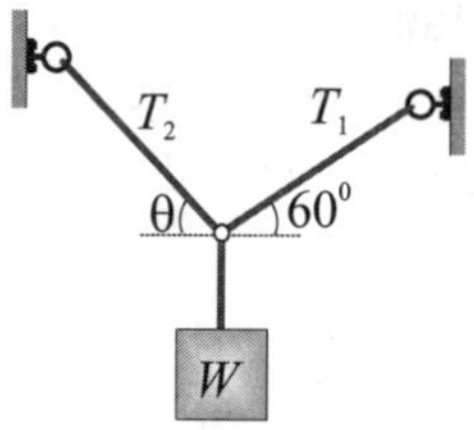

Q.58 A ladder 5 m long rests on a rough horizontal plane and smooth vertical wall. The ladder is about to slip on the rough plane when its lower end is at a distance 4 m from the wall. The coefficient of friction is______.

Q.59 A block has a mass of 20 kg is attached with two springs and is released from rest when $h = 0$. The springs are unstreched when $h = 0$. The velocity of block at $h = 3$ m is______.

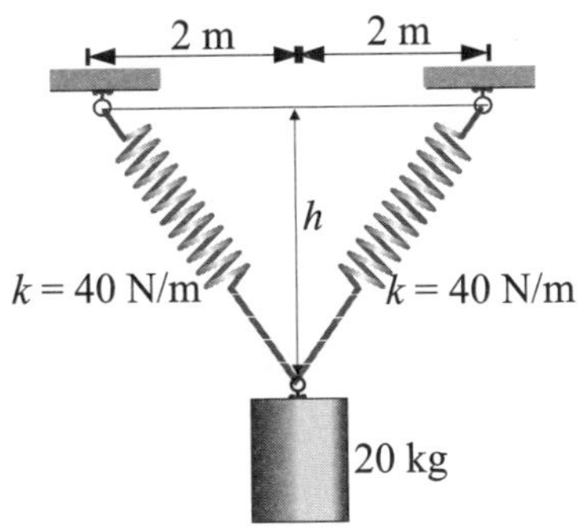

Q.60 The force F (in N) needed to get 300 N block moving to the right with coefficient of static friction of all surfaces being 0.2 is______.

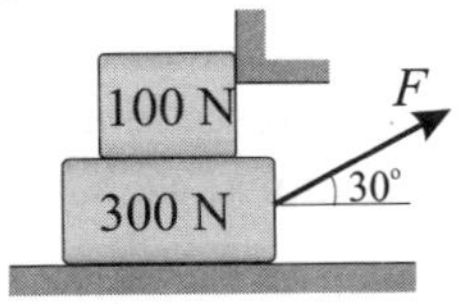

Q.61 A projectile is fired with a velocity $3\sqrt{2}$ m/s from a point at height $H = 0.8$ m at an angle 45° with respect to the horizontal direction as shown in figure. The horizontal distance S (in metres) travelled by the projectile when it hits the ground, is

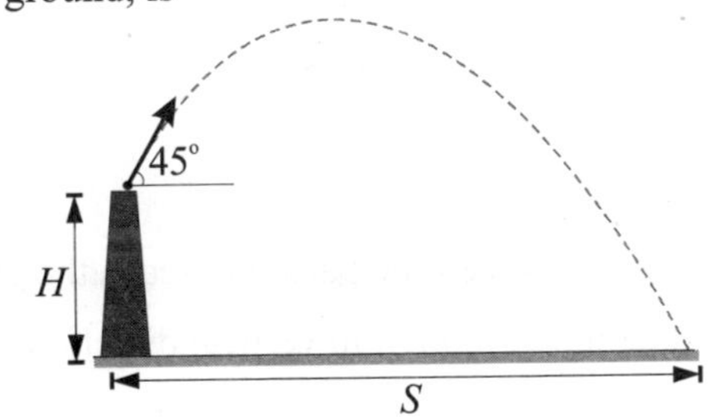

Q.62 Rod AB, whose end B is hinged, touches a semi-circular cylinder at point A as shown in figure. There is no friction between the cylindrical surface and the rod. If the cylinder moves with a constant velocity of 10 m/s in the horizontal direction as shown, then the angular velocity ω of the rod AB at that instant is______.

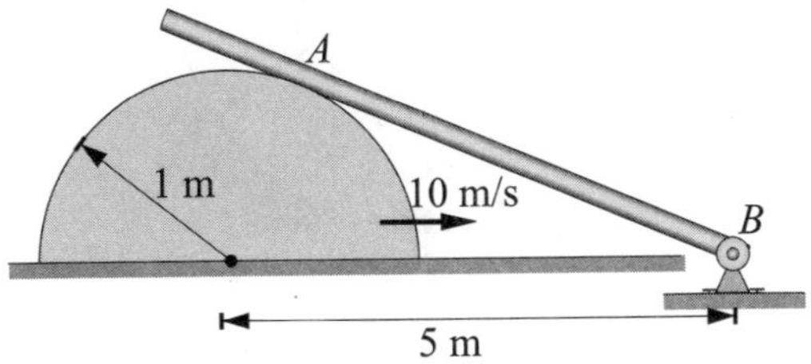

Q.63 A disc of mass $M = 14$ kg and radius 1 m is attached to a spring which has a stiffness $k = 75$ N/m and an un-stretched length of 4 m. If the disc is released from rest in the position shown in the figure and the disc rolls without slipping, angular velocity (in rad/s) of disc at the center C is______.

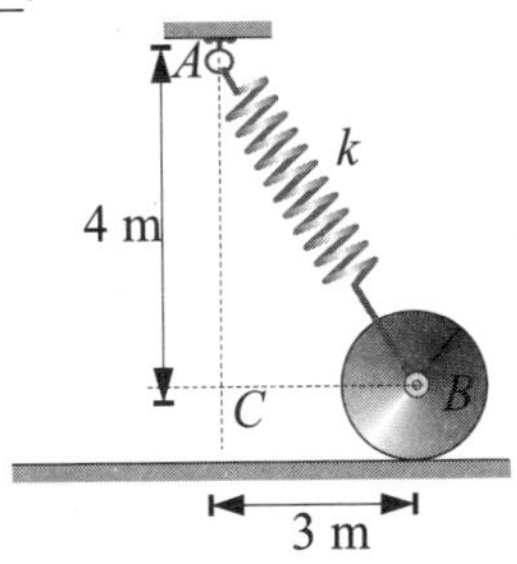

Q.64 In the figure below, a cylinder of radius 0.2 m and mass 10 kg is rolling down freely on an inclined plane without slipping. The inclined plane is rough and is at an angle of 30° with the horizontal. The friction force between the cylinder and the inclined plane is______.

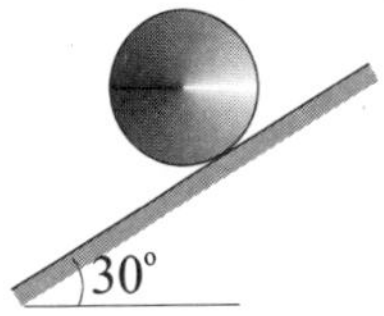

Q.65 A particle of mass m is rest at A, when it is slightly displaced and allowed to slide down the cylindrical surface of radius r as shown in figure. Neglecting the friction, the value of θ (in degree) when the particle leaves the surface is______.

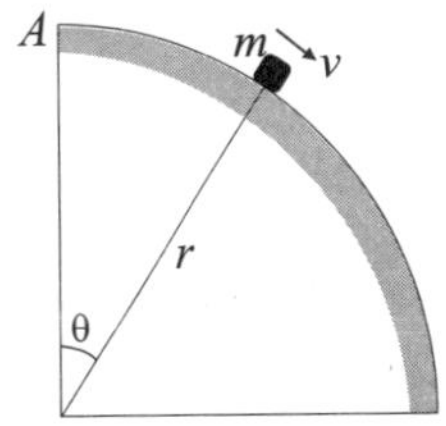

5.4 SOLUTION TO PRACTICE PAPER

Q.1 Ans:(C)

Figure shows the free body diagram. Let T be the tension of cable.

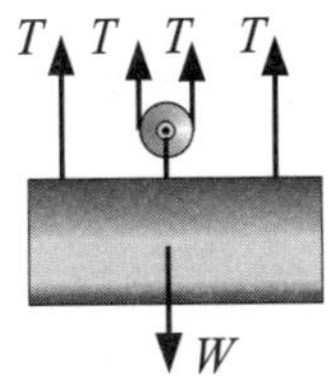

Applying equilibrium equation $\sum F_y = 0$

$$T + T + T + T - W = 0$$

$$W = 4T$$

Q.2 Ans:(A)

Figure shows the free-body diagrams.

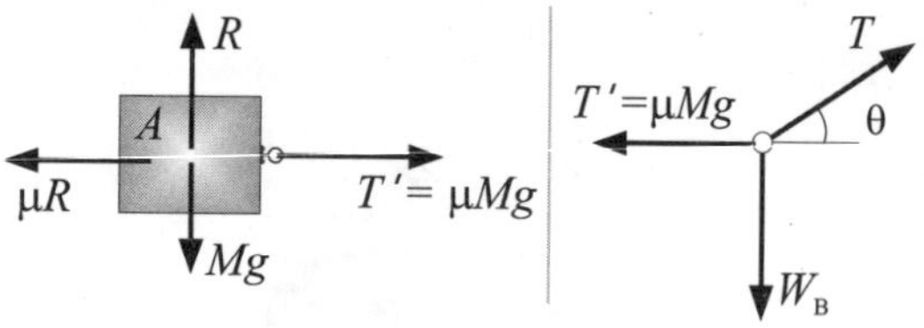

Applying equilibrium equations;

$\sum F_y = 0 \Rightarrow \quad T\sin\theta = W_B \qquad$ (i)

$\sum F_y = 0 \Rightarrow \quad T\cos\theta = \mu Mg \qquad$ (ii)

Eliminating T from Equations (i) and (ii), we obtain

$$\tan\theta = \frac{W_B}{\mu Mg}$$

$$W_B = \mu Mg\tan\theta$$

Q.3 Ans:(D)

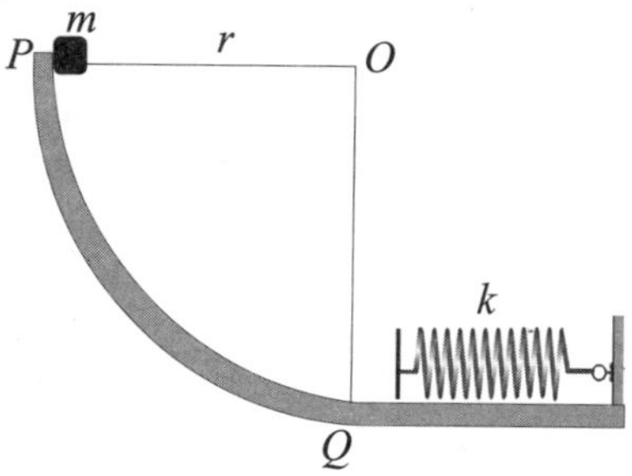

Applying work-energy equation between P and Q.

$$mgr = \frac{1}{2}kx^2 + \text{Work against friction } (W)$$

Maximum spring deflection $x = \sqrt{\dfrac{2(mgr - W)}{k}}$

or $\quad x = \sqrt{\dfrac{2mgr}{k} - \dfrac{2W}{k}}$

or $\quad x < \sqrt{\dfrac{2mgr}{k}}$

Maximum spring deflection less than $\sqrt{\dfrac{2mgr}{k}}$

Q.4 Ans:(C)

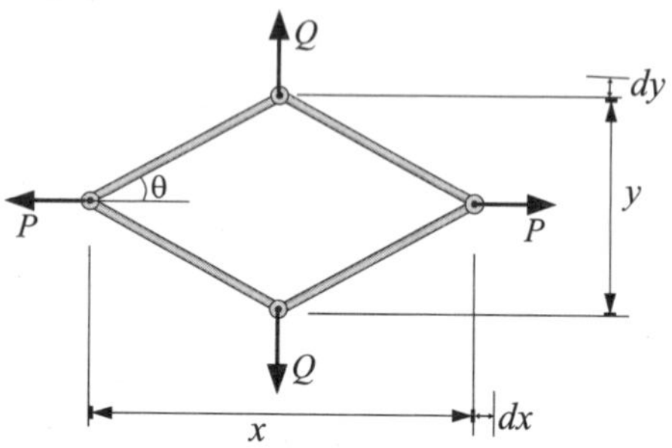

Applying the principle of virtual work.

Virtual work $\quad du = Pdx + Qdy = 0$

$$Pd(2l\cos\theta) + Qd(2l\sin\theta) = 0$$

or $\quad -2Pl\sin\theta d\theta + 2Ql\cos\theta d\theta = 0$

From which

$$P = Q\cot\theta$$

Q.5 Ans:(A)

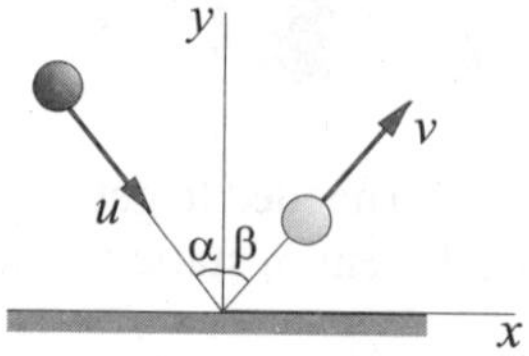

Let e be the coefficient of restitution. Using equations for collision in x and y-directions, we have

$v\sin\beta = u\sin\alpha \qquad$ (i)

$v\cos\beta = eu\cos\alpha \qquad$ (ii)

From Equations (i) and (ii), we obtain

$$\frac{\cos\beta}{\sin\beta} = e\frac{\cos\alpha}{\sin\alpha}$$

$$e = \frac{\tan\alpha}{\tan\beta}$$

Q.6 Ans:(C)

Let t be the time taken by the packet to reach the ground.

Applying equation of motion in vertical direction

$$h = 0 \times t + \frac{1}{2}gt^2$$

$$t = \sqrt{\frac{2h}{g}}$$

Q.7 Ans:(B)

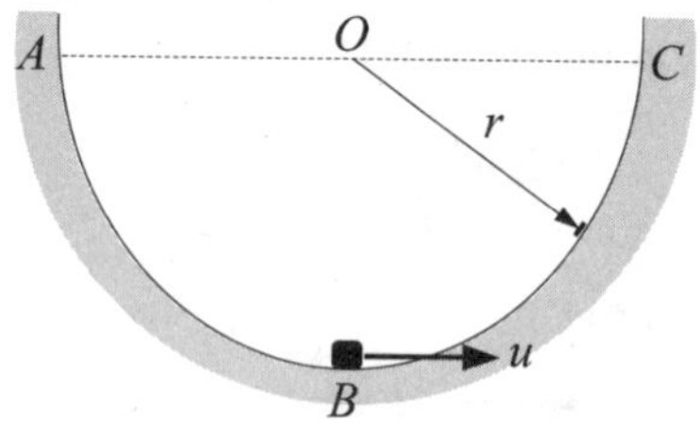

Condition for particle oscillate in vertical circle is: its circular amplitude < arc BC

Applying the principle of conservation of energy between B and C.

$$\frac{1}{2}mu^2 + mg0 < \frac{1}{2}m \times 0^2 + mgr$$

$$u^2 < 2gr$$

Q.8 Ans:(B)

Mass of cylinder $m = \sigma\,(l \times l)$, radius of cylinder $r = \dfrac{l}{2\pi}$.

Moment of inertia of cylinder, $I = mr^2$

$$I = \sigma\,(l \times l) \times \left(\frac{l}{2\pi}\right)^2$$

$$I = \frac{\sigma l^4}{4\pi^2}$$

Q.9 Ans:(A)

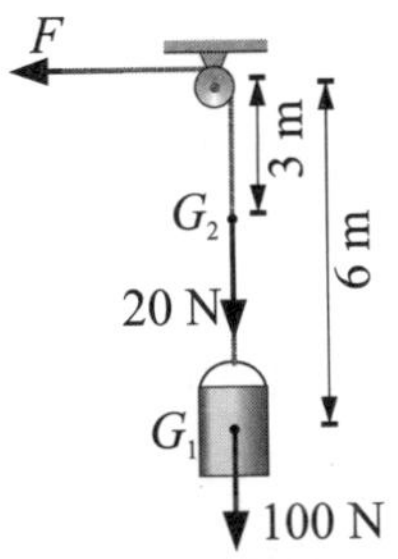

G_1 and G_2 are the center of gravity of bucket and rope respectively.

Work done by the man $W = 100 \times 6 + 20 \times 3$

$$W = 660 \text{ J}$$

Q.10 Ans:(C)

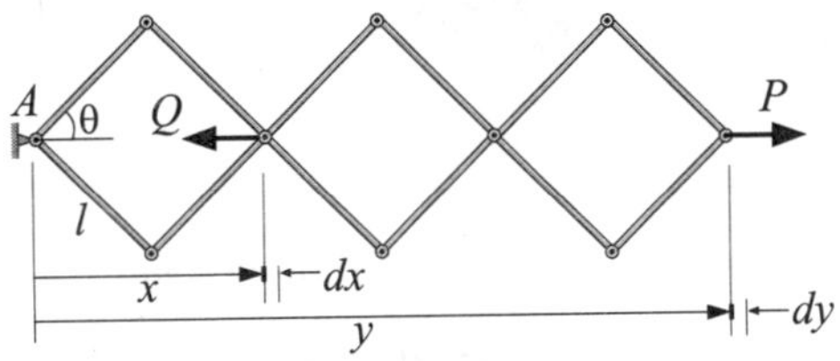

Applying the principle of virtual work.

Virtual work $du = Pdy - Qdx = 0$

$$Pd(6l\cos\theta) + Qd(2l\cos\theta) = 0$$

From which

$$Q = 3P$$

Q.11 Ans:(C)

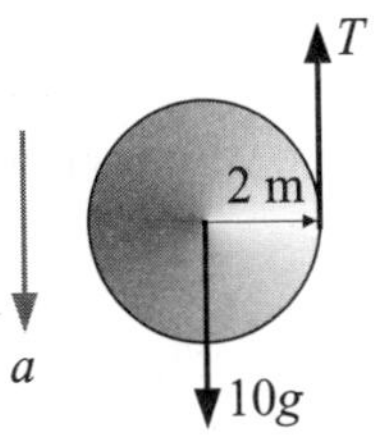

Applying Newton's second law, we write

$$\sum F_y = ma \Rightarrow \quad 10g - T = 10a \qquad \text{(i)}$$

$$\tau = I\alpha \quad \Rightarrow \quad T \times 2 = \frac{1}{2} \times 10 \times 2^2 \times \frac{a}{2}$$

or $\quad T = 5a \qquad$ (ii)

Eliminating a from equations (i) and (ii), we obtain

$$10g - T = 10 \times \frac{T}{5} \quad \Rightarrow \quad T = \frac{10}{3}g = \frac{10 \times 10}{3}$$

$$T = 33.3 \text{ N}$$

Q.12 Ans:(C)

Let x be compression of spring.

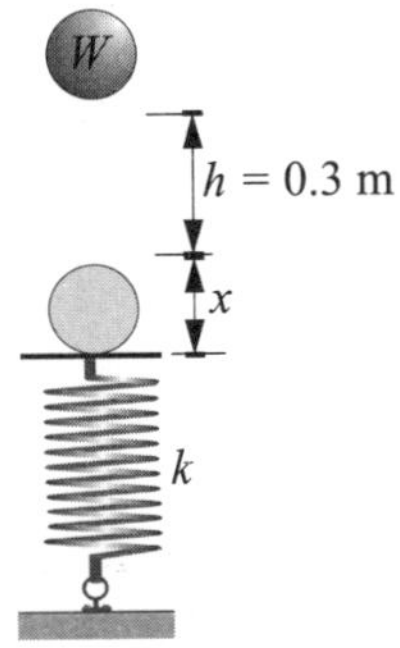

Applying the principle of conservation of energy.

$$W(h + x) = \frac{1}{2}kx^2 \quad \Rightarrow \quad \frac{W}{k}(h + x) = \frac{1}{2}x^2$$

Substituting $\dfrac{W}{k} = 0.03$

$$0.03(h + x) = \frac{1}{2}x^2 \quad \Rightarrow \quad x^2 - 0.06x - 0.018 = 0$$

Solving for x, we obtain

$$x = 16.74 \text{ cm}$$

Q.13 Ans:(B)

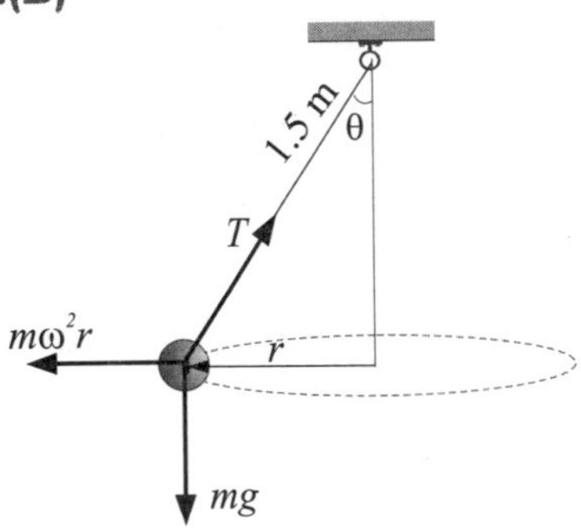

Resolving the forces along horizontal direction

$$T\sin\theta = m\omega^2 r$$

or $\quad T\sin\theta = m\omega^2 \times 1.5\sin\theta$

or $$T = 2\left(\frac{2\pi\times 50}{60}\right)^2 \times 1.5$$

$$T = \frac{25\pi^2}{3}\,\text{N}$$

Q.14 Ans:(D)

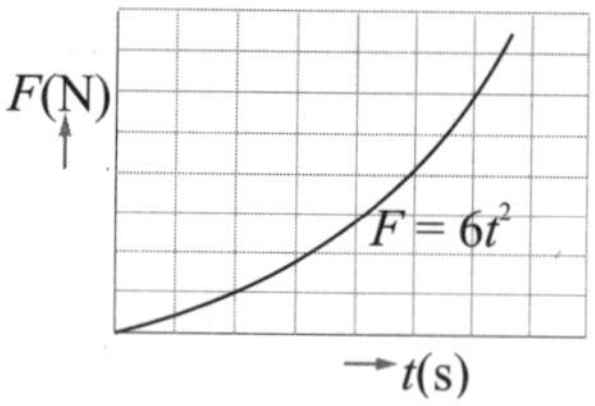

$$F = ma \Rightarrow 6t^2 = 2\frac{dv}{dt}$$

or $$dv = 3t^2 dt$$

Integration above equation, $$\int_0^v dv = \int_0^t 3t^2 dt$$

or $$v = t^3 \Rightarrow \frac{dx}{dt} = t^3$$

After integration, $$\int_0^s dx = \int_0^2 t^3 dt$$

$$S = 4\,\text{m}$$

Q.15 Ans:(A)

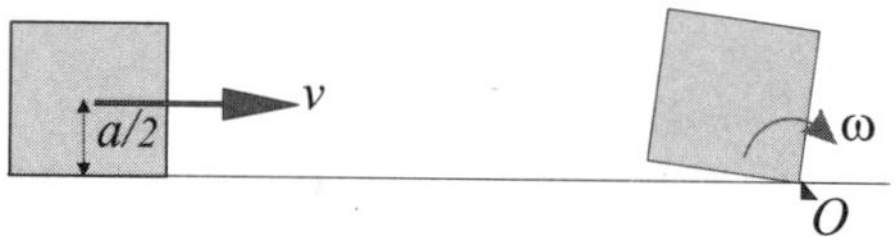

Applying principle of conservation of angular momentum about O.

$$Mv \times \frac{a}{2} = I_o\omega$$

or $$Mv \times \frac{a}{2} = \frac{2}{3}Ma^2\omega$$

$$\omega = \frac{3v}{4a}$$

Q.16 Ans:(C)

Applying the principle of conservation of angular momentum.

$$I_1\omega_1 = I_2\omega_2$$

or $$MR^2\omega = (MR^2 + 2mR^2)\omega_2$$

From which, we obtain

$$\omega_2 = \frac{M}{(M+2m)}\omega$$

Q.17 Ans:(D)

To determine v, following principles are used

(i) Conservation of angular momentum

(ii) Conservation of energy.

Q.18 Ans:(C)

Let u and V be the velocity of bullet and recoil velocity of gun respectively.

Given: mass of bullet $m = 0.1\,\text{kg}$ and mass of gun $M = 10$ kg.

Applying the principle of conservation of linear momentum

$$mu + MV = 0 \quad \Rightarrow 0.1u + 10(-V) = 0$$

or $$\frac{u}{V} = \frac{10}{0.1} = 100$$

Ratio of kinetic energy of bullet to gun

$$= \frac{\frac{1}{2}mu^2}{\frac{1}{2}MV^2} = \frac{m}{M}\left(\frac{u}{V}\right)^2 = \frac{0.1}{10}\times 100^2$$

Ratio of kinetic energy of bullet to gun = 100

Q.19 Ans:(C)

Let μ be the coefficient of friction between body and plane.

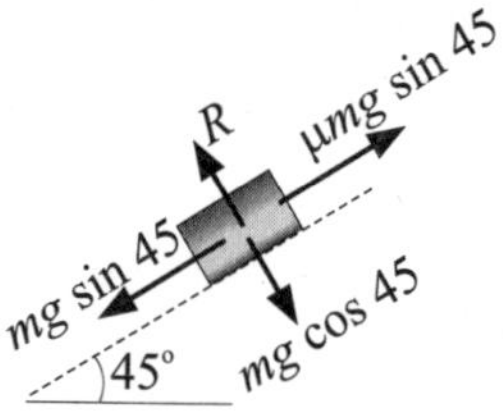

Applying Newton's second law along plane

$$\sum F = ma \Rightarrow mg\sin 45 - \mu mg\cos 45 = ma$$

Acceleration of body $a = \frac{g}{\sqrt{2}}(1-\mu)$

Let S be the distance of plane

$$S = ut + \frac{1}{2}at^2 \quad \Rightarrow S = 0\times t + \frac{1}{2}at^2$$

$$t = \sqrt{\frac{2S}{a}} = \sqrt{\frac{2S}{\frac{g}{\sqrt{2}}(1-\mu)}} = \sqrt{\frac{2\sqrt{2}S}{g(1-\mu)}}$$

Time taken to slide down with friction, $t_1 = \sqrt{\frac{2\sqrt{2}S}{g(1-\mu)}}$

Time taken to slide down without friction, $t_2 = \sqrt{\frac{2\sqrt{2}S}{g}}$

Given that $t_1 = 2t_2 \Rightarrow \sqrt{\frac{2\sqrt{2}S}{g(1-\mu)}} = 2\sqrt{\frac{2\sqrt{2}S}{g}}$

From which $\mu = \frac{3}{4}$

$$\mu = 0.75$$

Q.20 Ans:(D)

Mass of ring $= \rho L$, Radius of ring $r = \frac{L}{2\pi}$

Moment of inertia about x-x, $I_{xx} = \frac{3}{2} m r^2$

or $I_{xx} = \frac{3}{2}\rho L \times \left(\frac{L}{2\pi}\right)^2 = \frac{3\rho L^3}{8\pi^2}$

$$I_{xx} = \frac{3\rho L^3}{8\pi^2}$$

Q.21 Ans:[26.5]

Two force system is under equilibrium if line of action of weight mg passing through hinge O as shown in figure.

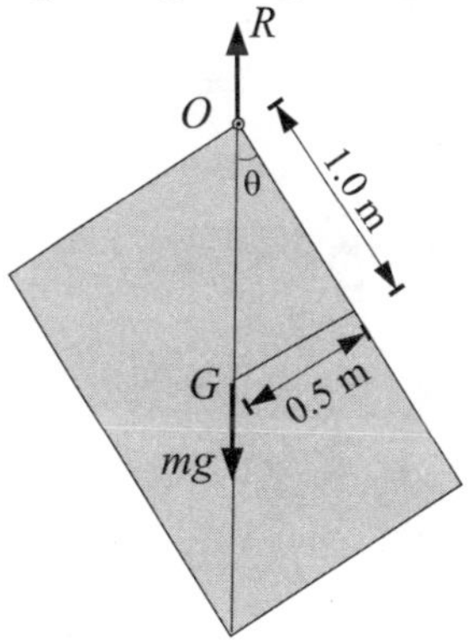

In triangle OGA, $\tan\theta = \frac{0.5}{1} \Rightarrow \theta = \tan^{-1} 0.5$

$$\theta = 26.5°$$

Q.22 Ans:[1.5]

Given; $a = x - x^2$ and initial value $v = 0$ at $x = 0$

$a = v\frac{dv}{dx} = x - x^2 \Rightarrow \frac{v^2}{2} = \frac{x^2}{2} - \frac{x^3}{3} + C_1 \Rightarrow C_1 = 0$

From which

$$v = \sqrt{x^2 - \frac{2}{3}x^3} = 0 \Rightarrow x = \frac{3}{2}, 0$$

$$x = \frac{3}{2} = 1.5\text{ m}$$

Q.23 Ans:[0.9]

Figure shown the graph between F and t.

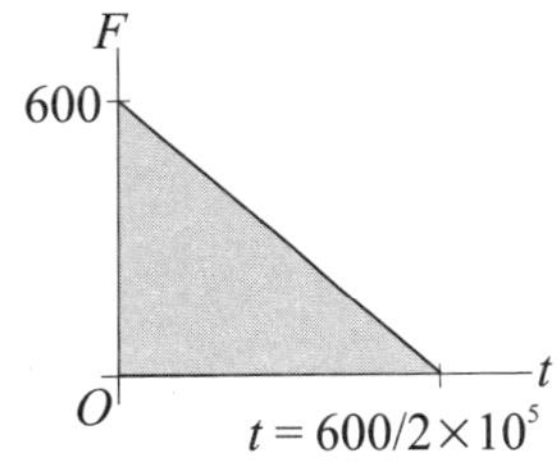

Average impulse, $I = \int F dt$

$$I = \frac{1}{2} \times 600 \times \frac{600}{2 \times 10^5}$$

$$I = 0.9\text{ Ns}$$

Q.24 Ans:[0.345]

Potential energy of system $V = 8x^3 + 6x^2 - 7x$

System is under static equilibrium,

if $\frac{dV}{dx} = 0$ and $\frac{d^2V}{dx^2} = +\text{ve}$

$$\frac{d}{dx}(8x^3 + 6x^2 - 7x) = 0$$

or $24x^2 + 12x - 7 = 0$

Solving for x, we obtain

$$x = 0.345\text{ m}$$

Q.25 Ans:[15]

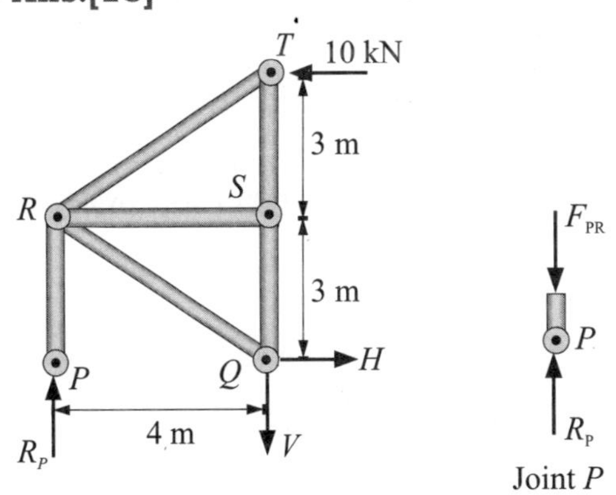

Figure shown the free body diagram of entire truss. Taking moment about Q.

$$R_P \times 4 - 10 \times 6 = 0$$

$$R_P = 15\text{ kN}$$

Now consider joint P:

$\sum F_y = 0 \Rightarrow R_P - F_{PR} = 0$

$$F_{PR} = 15\text{ kN (compression)}$$

Q.26 Ans:[45]

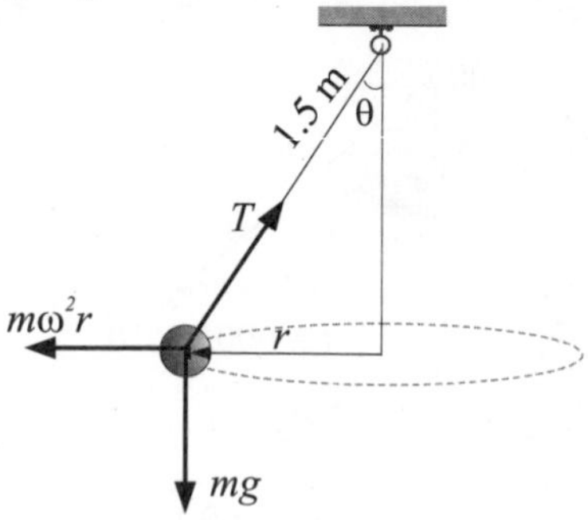

Figure shows the free-body diagram of plumb bob.

Applying equilibrium equations

$$T\cos\theta = mg \qquad \text{and} \qquad T\sin\theta = \frac{mv^2}{r}$$

From which, we obtain $\tan\theta = \dfrac{v^2}{rg}$

or $$\theta = \tan^{-1}\frac{v^2}{rg} = \tan^{-1}\frac{10^2}{10\times 10}$$

$$\theta = 45°$$

Q.27 Ans:[0.6]

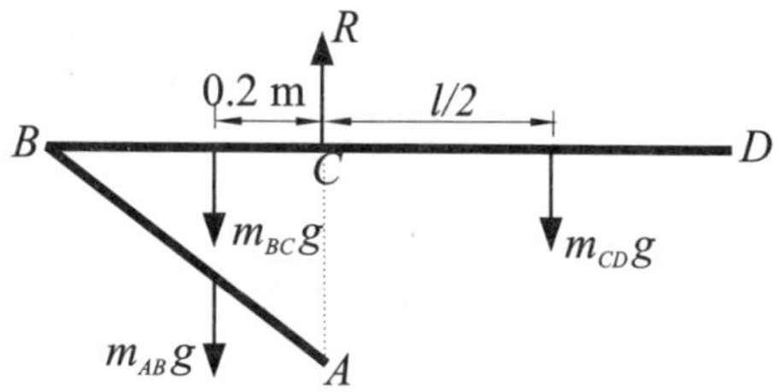

Let λ be the linear density(kg/m) of wire. Masses of wire segments BC, CD and AB are

$m_{BC} = 0.4\lambda$, $m_{CD} = l\times\lambda$ and $m_{AB} = AB\times\lambda = 0.5\lambda$

Taking moment of weights of about C, we have

$$M_C = m_{CD}g\times\frac{l}{2} - m_{BC}g\times 0.2 - m_{AB}g\times 0.2$$

Portion BCD of wire remain horizontal if $M_C = 0$.

$$m_{CD}g\times\frac{l}{2} - m_{BC}g\times 0.2 - m_{AB}g\times 0.2 = 0$$

or $$m_{CD}\times\frac{l}{2} - m_{BC}\times 0.2 - m_{AB}\times 0.2 = 0$$

or $$l\lambda\times\frac{l}{2} - 0.4\lambda\times 0.2 - 0.5\lambda\times 0.2 = 0$$

From which

$$l = 0.6\text{ m}$$

Q.28 Ans:[2]

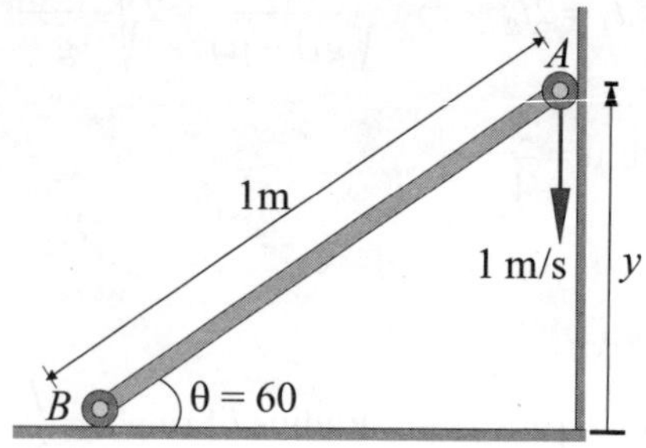

In triangle ABC, $\quad \sin\theta = \dfrac{y}{1}$

Differentiate with respect to time t;

$$\cos\theta\frac{d\theta}{dt} = \frac{dy}{dt}$$

Angular velocity of rod $\dfrac{d\theta}{dt} = \dfrac{1}{\cos\theta}\dfrac{dy}{dt}$

or $$\left(\frac{d\theta}{dt}\right)_{\theta=60^0} = \frac{1}{\cos 60}\times 1 = 2$$

$$\omega_{\theta=60^0} = 2\text{ rad/s}$$

Q.29 Ans:[500]

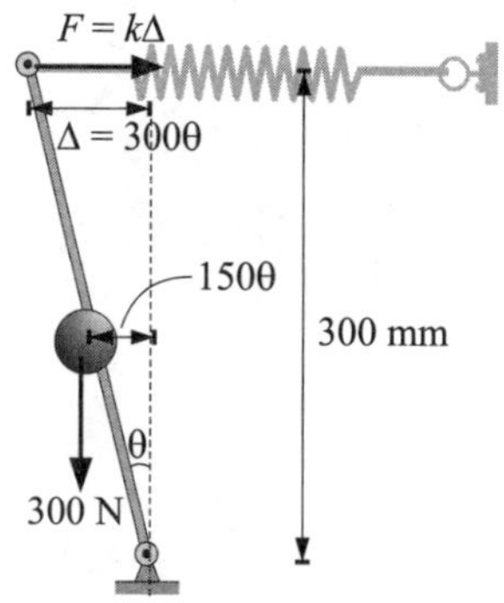

The system is displaced at small angle θ.

The system is stable equilibrium if

$$F\times\frac{300}{1000} \geq 300\times\frac{150}{1000}\theta$$

or $$\left(k\frac{300}{1000}\theta\right)\times\frac{300}{1000} \geq 300\times\frac{150}{1000}\theta$$

$$k_{min} = 500\text{ N/m}$$

Q.30 Ans:[400]

Let T be the tension of string. Figure shows the free body diagram of beam.

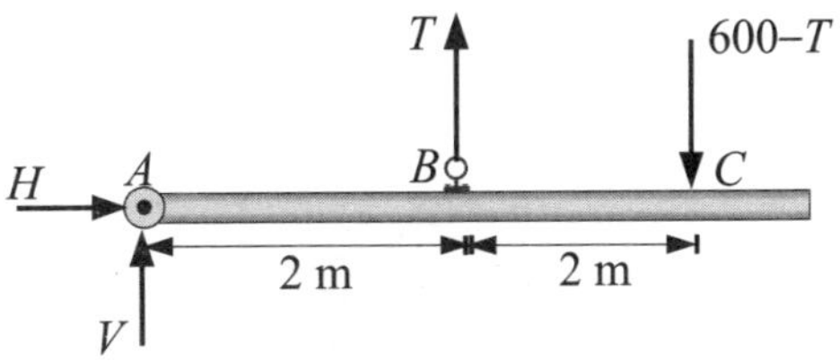

Taking moment about A; $(600-T)\times 4 - T\times 2 = 0$

or $\quad 2400 - 4T - 2T = 0$

$$T = 400\text{ N}$$

Q.31 Ans:(A)

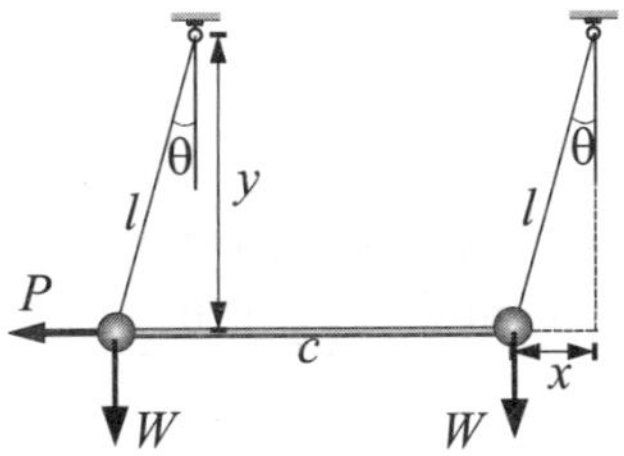

Applying the principle of virtual work (Refer figure)

$$P\,d(c+x) + W\,dy + W\,dy = 0$$

or $\quad P\,dx + 2W\,dy = 0$

or $\quad P\,d(l\sin\theta) + 2W\,d(l\cos\theta) = 0$

or $\quad P\,l\cos\theta d\theta + 2W\times -l\sin\theta d\theta = 0$

or $\quad P = 2W\tan\theta \Rightarrow \tan\theta = \dfrac{P}{2W}$

$$\theta = \tan^{-1}\left(\frac{P}{2W}\right)$$

Q.32 Ans:(A)

Figure shows the free-body diagram of an element of ring. Resolving the forces along radial direction

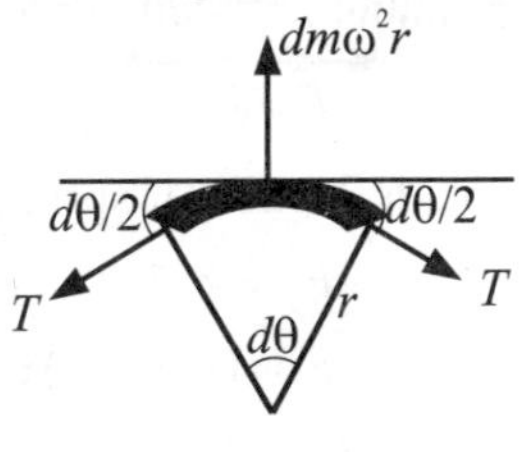

$$\sum F_r = 0 \;\Rightarrow dm\omega^2 r - T\sin\frac{d\theta}{2} - T\sin\frac{d\theta}{2} = 0$$

or $\quad dm\omega^2 r - Td\theta = 0$

or $\quad \rho r d\theta\omega^2 r - Td\theta = 0$

$$T = \rho\omega^2 r^2$$

Q.33 Ans:(C)

Let v be the velocity at B,

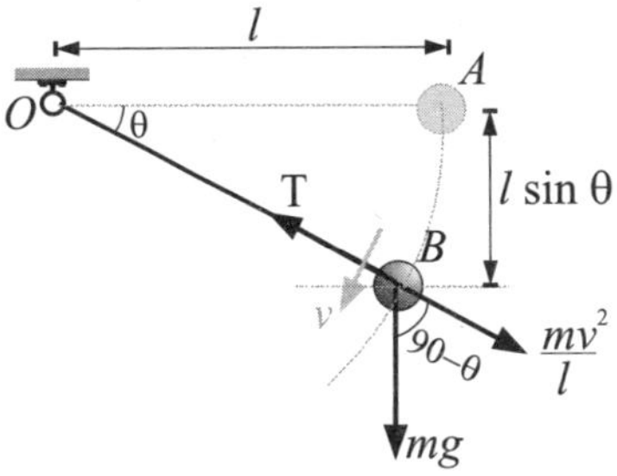

Tension of rope $T = mg\cos(90-\theta) + \dfrac{mv^2}{l}$

$$T = mg\sin\theta + \frac{mv^2}{l} \qquad \text{(i)}$$

Applying the principle of conservation of energy between A and B, we have

$$mgl\sin\theta = \frac{1}{2}mv^2$$

or $\quad mv^2 = 2mgl\sin\theta \qquad$ (ii)

From Equations (i) and (ii), we obtain

$$T = mg\sin\theta + \frac{2mgl\sin\theta}{l}$$

From which

$$T = 3mg\sin\theta$$

Q.34 Ans:(A)

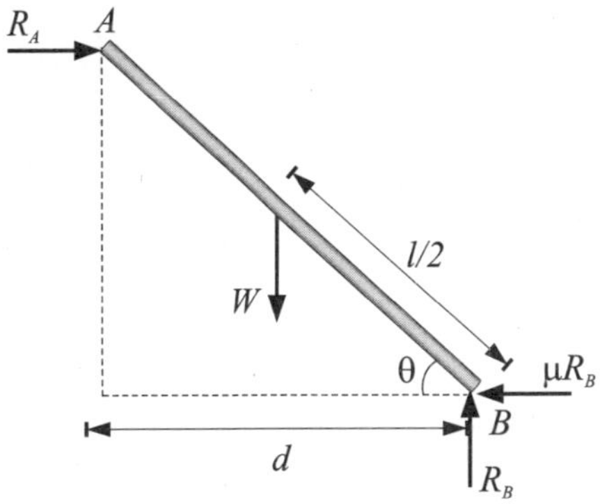

Figure shows the free-body diagram of pole.

Applying equilibrium equations

$$\sum F_H = 0 \quad \Rightarrow \quad R_A = \mu R_B \qquad \text{(i)}$$

$$\sum F_V = 0 \quad \Rightarrow \quad R_B = W \qquad \text{(ii)}$$

Taking moment about B

$$R_A \times l\sin\theta - W\times\frac{1}{2}\cos\theta = 0 \qquad \text{(iii)}$$

From Equations (i), (ii) and (iii), we obtain

$$\mu W\times l\sqrt{1-\cos^2\theta} - W\times\frac{l}{2}\cos\theta = 0$$

or $$2\mu \times l\sqrt{1-\left(\frac{d}{l}\right)^2} = \frac{d}{l}$$

From which

$$d = \frac{2\mu l}{\sqrt{1+4\mu^2}}$$

Q.35 Ans:(C)

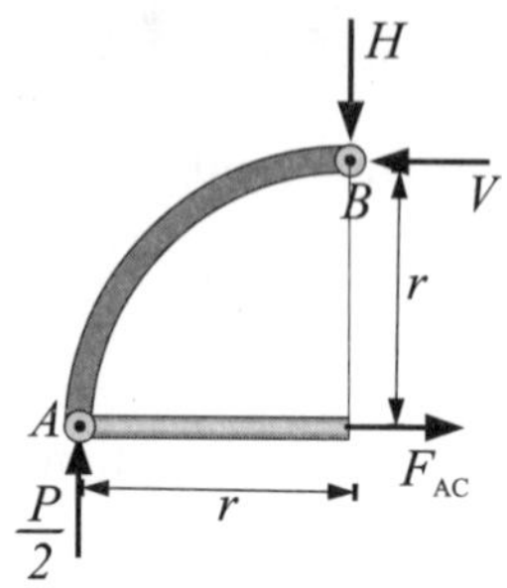

Reaction of supports $R_A = R_C = \frac{P}{2}$

Figure shows the free-body diagram of left half portion. Taking moment about B.

$$\frac{P}{2} \times r - F_{AC} \times r = 0$$

$$F_{AC} = \frac{P}{2} \text{ (tension)}$$

Q.36 Ans:(B)

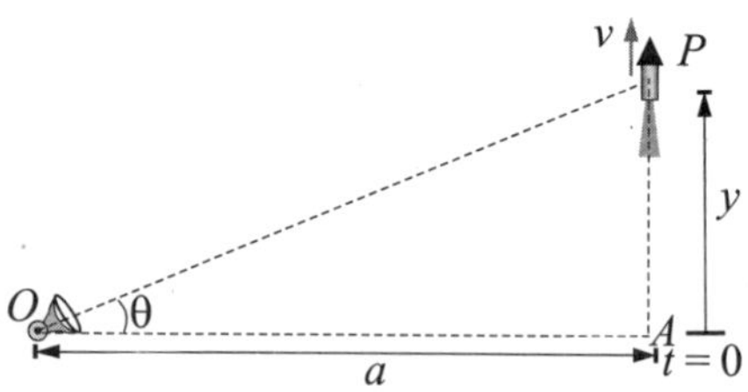

In triangle ΔOPA

$$\tan\theta = \frac{y}{a}$$

Differentiate with respect to t, we obtain

$$\sec^2\theta \frac{d\theta}{dt} = \frac{1}{a}\frac{dy}{dt}$$

or $$\frac{d\theta}{dt} = \frac{1}{a} \times \frac{1}{1+\tan^2\theta} v = \frac{1}{a} \times \frac{1}{1+\left(\frac{y}{a}\right)^2} v$$

or $$\frac{d\theta}{dt} = \frac{a}{a^2+y^2} v,$$ Substituting $y = vt$, we obtain

$$\omega = \frac{a}{a^2+v^2t^2} v$$

Q.37 Ans:(B)

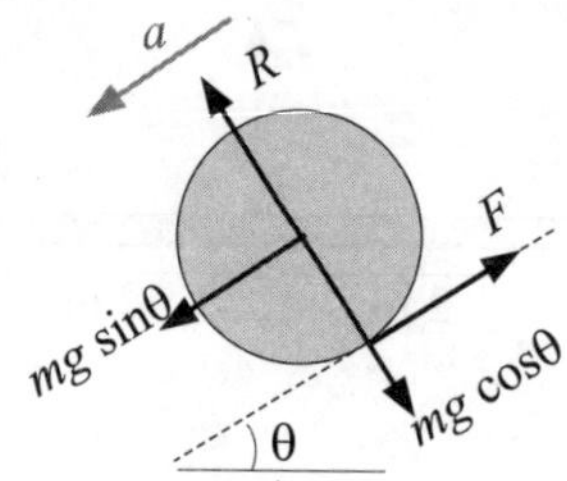

Applying Newton's second law, we write

$$\sum F = ma \Rightarrow mg\sin\theta - F = ma \quad \text{(i)}$$

$$\tau = I\alpha \Rightarrow F \times r = I\frac{a}{r}$$

or $$F = \frac{I}{r^2} a \quad \text{(ii)}$$

Eliminating a from Equations (i) and (ii), we obtain

$$a = \frac{g\sin\theta}{1+\frac{I}{mr^2}} = \frac{g\sin\theta}{1+\frac{\frac{2}{5}mr^2}{mr^2}}$$

$$\text{Acceleration, } a = \frac{5}{7} g\sin\theta$$

Q.38 Ans:(C)

Equation of motion of particle is given by $F = -m\mu x$

or $$mv\frac{dv}{dx} = -m\mu x$$

Integration $$\int_0^v v\,dv = -\int_a^x \mu x\,dx \Rightarrow \frac{v^2}{2} = \frac{\mu}{2}(a^2 - x^2)$$

$$v = \sqrt{\mu(a^2 - x^2)}$$

Q.39 Ans:(C)

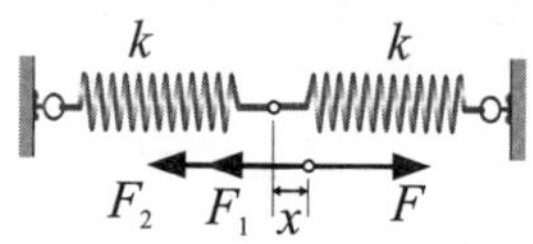

Let x be the common deflection of spring

$$F_1 = k_1 x, \qquad F_2 = k_2 x$$

$$F = F_1 + F_2 \qquad F = (k_1 + k_2)x$$

$$x = \frac{F}{(k_1+k_2)} = \frac{F}{2k} \quad \text{and } F_1 = F_2 = \frac{F}{2}$$

Strain energy stored in one spring

$$U_1 = \frac{1}{2}kx^2 = \frac{1}{2}k\left(\frac{F}{2k}\right)^2$$

$$U_1 = \frac{F^2}{8k}$$

Q.40 Ans:(B)

Applying principle of virtual work

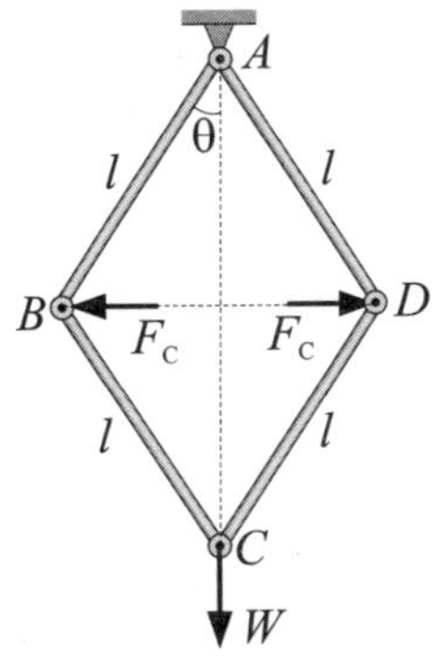

$$du = Wd(AC) + F_c d(BD) = 0$$

or $\quad Wd(2l\cos\theta) + F_c d(2l\sin\theta) = 0$

or $\quad -W2l\sin\theta d\theta + F_c 2l\cos\theta d\theta = 0$

or $\quad F_c = W\tan\theta$

or $\quad F_c = W\tan 30 \qquad [\text{at } \theta = 30]$

$$F_C = \frac{W}{\sqrt{3}}$$

Q.41 Ans:(B)

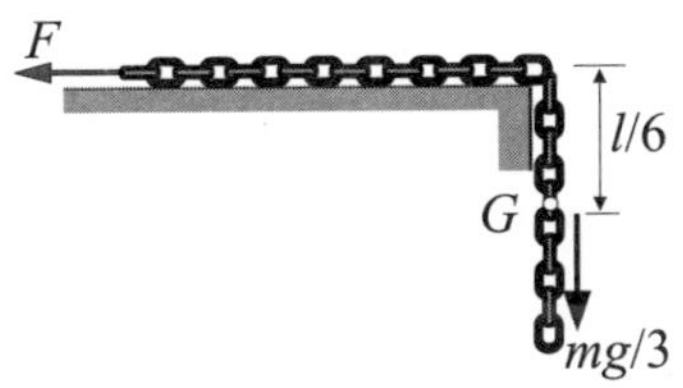

Location of center of gravity of chain is $\frac{l}{6}$ below surface.

The work required to pull chain is

$$W = \frac{mg}{3} \times \frac{l}{6}$$

$$W = \frac{mgl}{18}$$

Q.42 Ans:(C)

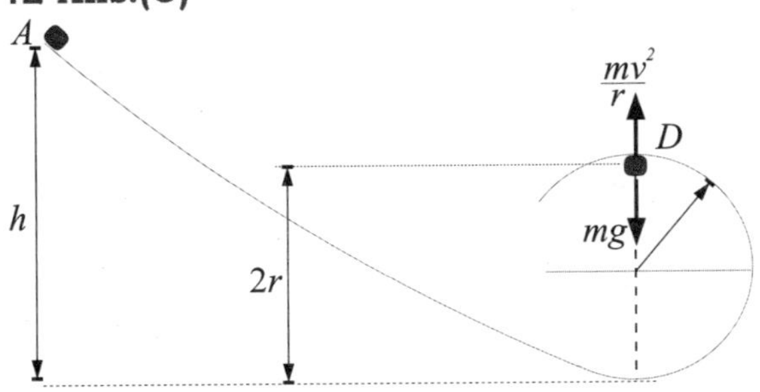

At point D; $\frac{mv^2}{r} = mg$

$$v^2 = rg \qquad \text{(i)}$$

Applying principle of conservation of energy between A and D,

$$mg(h - 2r) = \frac{1}{2}mv^2 \qquad \text{(ii)}$$

From Equations (i) and (ii), we obtain

$$mg(h - 2r) = \frac{1}{2}m \times rg$$

$$h = \frac{5}{2}r$$

Q.43 Ans:(A)

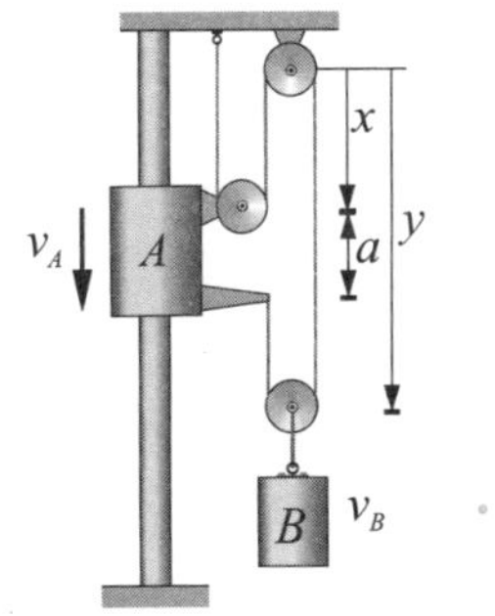

Length of rope $l = 3x + a + 2(y - x - a) = \text{constant}$

or $\quad l = x + 2y - a = \text{constant}$

Differentiate with respect to t, we get

$$\frac{dx}{dt} + 2\frac{dy}{dt} = 0$$

or $\quad v_A + 2v_B = 0 \quad \Rightarrow \quad v_B = -\frac{v_A}{2}$

$$v_B = \frac{v_A}{2}\uparrow$$

Q.44 Ans:(A)

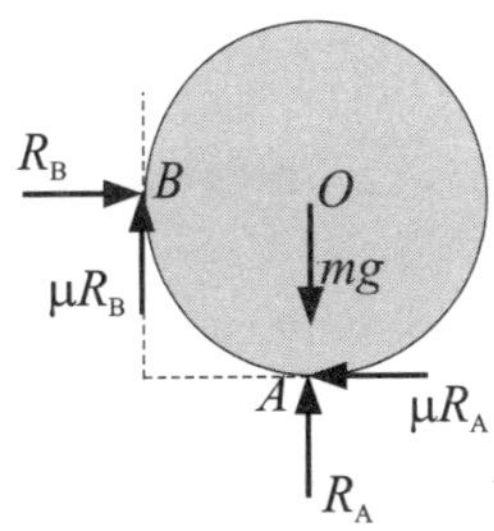

Figure shows the free-body diagram of rotating sphere. Using equilibrium equations, we have

$$\sum F_V = 0 \;\Rightarrow\; R_A + \mu R_B = mg \qquad \text{(i)}$$

$$\sum F_H = 0 \;\Rightarrow\; R_B - \mu R_A = 0 \qquad \text{(ii)}$$

From which

$$R_A = \frac{mg}{1+\mu^2} \text{ and } R_B = \frac{\mu\, mg}{1+\mu^2}$$

Applying work-energy equation, we write

Kinetic energy = Work-done against friction

$$\frac{1}{2}I\omega^2 = \mu R_A 2\pi rn + \mu R_B 2\pi rn$$

or $$\frac{1}{2}\times\frac{2}{5}mr^2\times\omega^2 = \mu 2\pi rn\left(\frac{mg}{1+\mu^2}+\frac{\mu\, mg}{1+\mu^2}\right)$$

From which

$$n = \frac{\omega^2 r(1+\mu^2)}{10\mu g\pi(1+\mu)}$$

Q.45 Ans:(D)

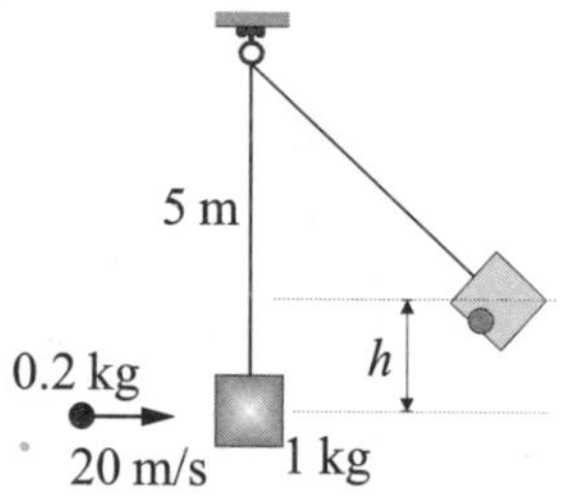

Let V be the velocity of bob just after impact.

Applying the law of conservation of linear momentum.

$$mu = (m+M)V \quad\Rightarrow\quad V = \frac{m}{m+M}u$$

$$V = \frac{02}{02+1}\times 20 = \frac{10}{3}\text{ m/s}$$

Now applying the principle of conservation of energy

$$\frac{1}{2}(m+M)V^2 = (m+M)gh$$

or $$h = \frac{V^2}{2g} = \frac{\left(\frac{10}{3}\right)^2}{2\times 9.81}$$

$$h = 0.566\text{ m}$$

Q.46 Ans:(C)

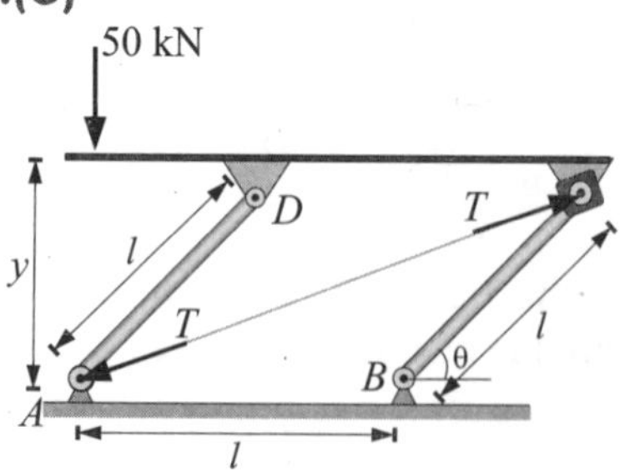

Principle of virtual work $du = 0$

$$-50\,dy - Td(AC) = 0$$

or $$-50\,d(l\sin\theta) - Td(2l\cos\frac{\theta}{2}) = 0$$

or $$-50\,l\cos\theta d\theta + Tl\sin\frac{\theta}{2}d\theta = 0$$

$$T = \frac{50\cos\theta}{\sin\frac{\theta}{2}}\text{ kN}$$

Q.47 Ans:(A)

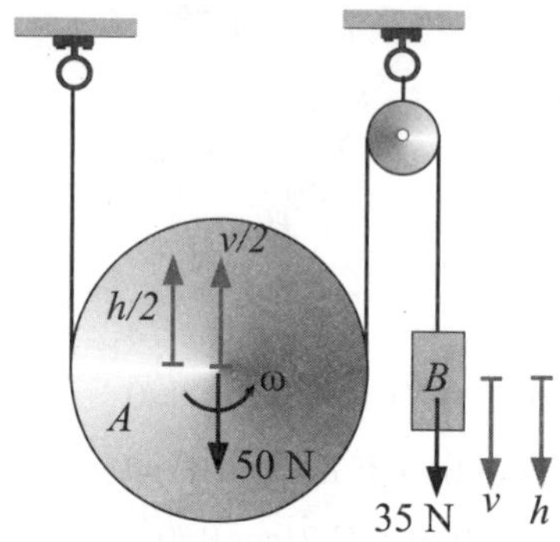

Applying principle of conservation of energy

Change of potential energy = Kinetic energy

$$35h - 50\times\frac{h}{2} = \frac{1}{2}\times\frac{35}{g}v^2 + \frac{1}{2}\times\frac{50}{g}\left(\frac{v}{2}\right)^2$$

or $$10h = \left(\frac{35}{2g}+\frac{50}{8g}\right)v^2$$

or $$v^2 = \frac{10h\times 8g}{190}$$

$$v = \sqrt{0.42gh}$$

Q.48 Ans:(B)

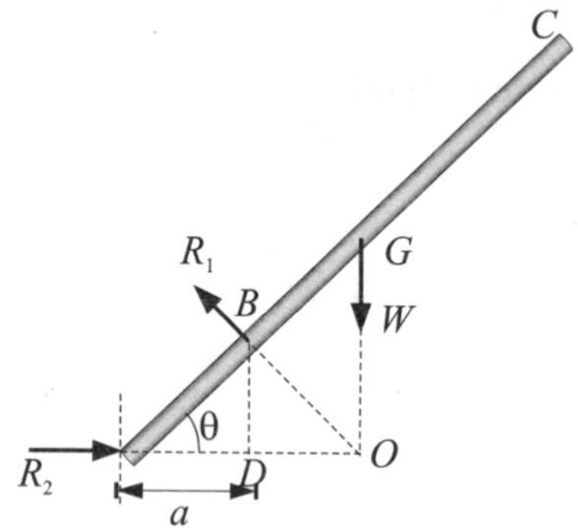

Free-body diagram of rigid rod is shown in figure.

In $\Delta\, AOG$; $OA = \frac{L}{2}\cos\theta$

In $\Delta\, AOB$; $AB = \left(\frac{L}{2}\cos\theta\right)\cos\theta$

In $\Delta\, ABD$; $AD = AB\cos\theta$

or $$a = \left(\frac{L}{2}\cos\theta\right)\cos\theta\cos\theta$$

$$L = \frac{2a}{\cos^3\theta}$$

Q.49 Ans:(B)

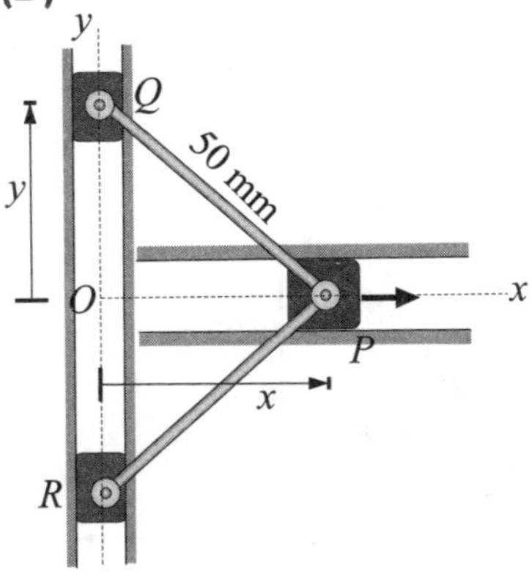

Let $OP = x$ and $OQ = y$

In ΔOPQ ; $x^2 + y^2 = 50^2$

Differentiate with respect to t, we get

$$2x\frac{dx}{dt} + 2y\frac{dy}{dt} = 0 \Rightarrow \frac{dy}{dt} = -\left(\frac{x}{y}\right) \times \frac{dx}{dt}$$

or $$\frac{dy}{dt} = -\frac{x}{\sqrt{50^2 - x^2}} \times \frac{dx}{dt} = -\frac{40}{\sqrt{50^2 - 40^2}} \times 30$$

$$\frac{dy}{dt} = -40 \text{ mm/s}$$

40 mm/s along the negative y-direction

Q.50 Ans:(D)

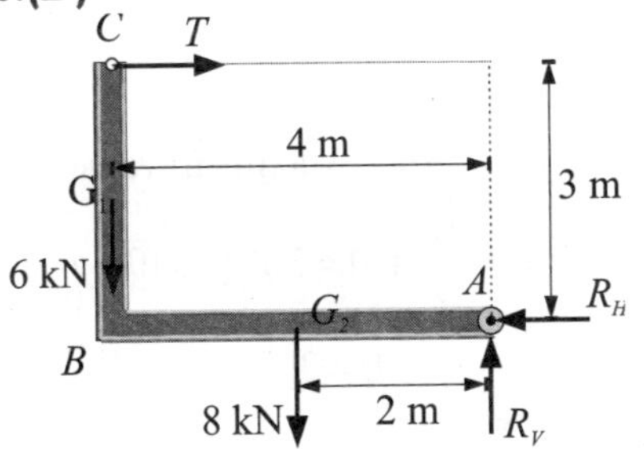

Figure shows the free-body diagram

Taking moment about A, we have

$$T \times 3 - 6 \times 4 - 8 \times 2 = 0$$

or $$T = \frac{24 + 16}{3} = \frac{40}{3}$$

$$T = 13.3 \text{ kN}$$

Q.51 Ans:[7.67]

Figure shows the path of particle on x - $y$plane

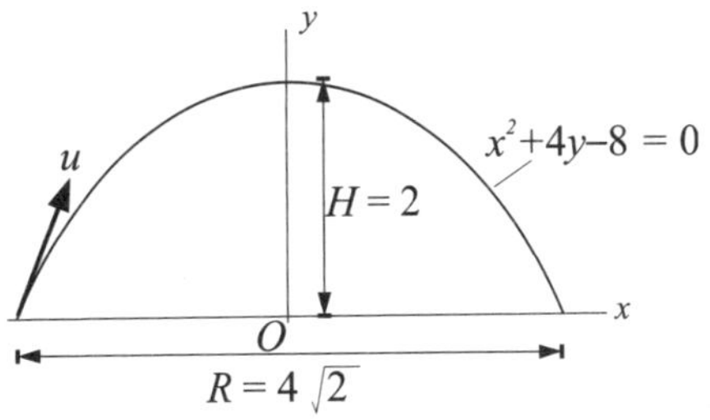

Range, $$R = 4\sqrt{2} = \frac{u^2 \sin 2\alpha}{g} \quad \text{(i)}$$

Maximum height, $$H_{\max} = 2 = \frac{u^2 \sin^2\alpha}{2g} \quad \text{(ii)}$$

Eliminating u^2 from Equations (i) and (ii), we obtain

$$\tan\alpha = \sqrt{2} \Rightarrow \sin\alpha = \frac{\sqrt{2}}{\sqrt{3}}$$

From Equation (ii), we obtain $$2 = \frac{u^2}{2g}\left(\frac{\sqrt{2}}{\sqrt{3}}\right)^2$$

$$u^2 = 6g$$

$$u = \sqrt{6g} = 7.67 \text{ m/s}$$

Q.52 Ans:[1.76]

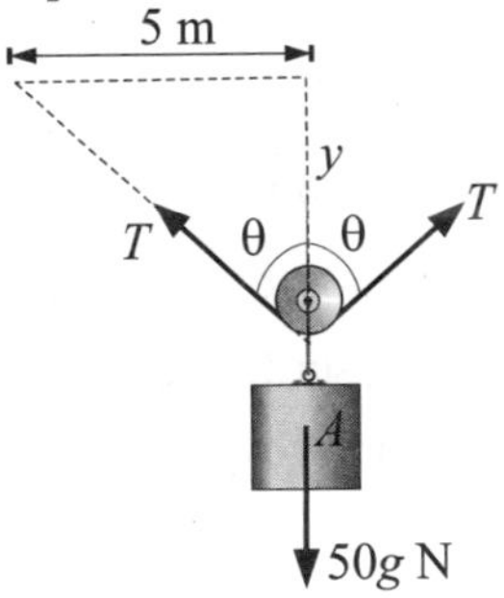

Tension in cable, $T = 75g$ N

$$\sum F_y = 0 \Rightarrow 75g\cos\theta \times 2 = 50g$$

or $$\cos\theta = \frac{1}{3}$$

From the geometry of figure, $$\cos\theta = \frac{y}{\sqrt{5^2 + y^2}}$$

$$\cos\theta = \frac{y}{\sqrt{5^2 + y^2}} = \frac{1}{3}$$

From which

$$y = 1.76 \text{ m}$$

Q.53 Ans:[4]

Applying Newton second law along guide way.

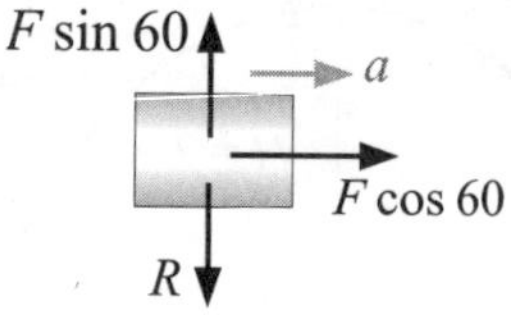

$F\cos 60 = ma$ or $2\cos 60 = 0.5\,a$

$a = 2\text{ m/s}^2$

Equation of uniform acceleration motion, $S = ut + \frac{1}{2}at^2$

$S = \frac{1}{2}\times 2\times 2^2$

$S = 4\text{ m}$

Q.54 Ans:[29.43]

Let a and T be the acceleration of masses and tension of cable respectively.

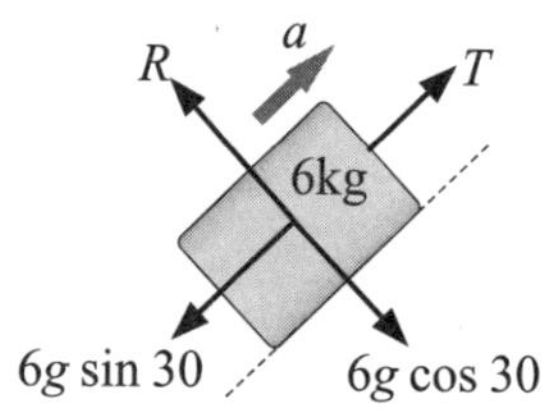

Free body diagram of block P

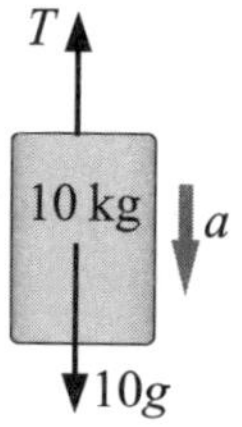

Free body diagram of block Q

Applying Newton's second law

for block Q; $\quad 10g - T = 10a \quad$ (i)

for block P; $\quad T - 6g\sin 30 = 6a \quad$ (ii)

From Equations (i) and (ii), we obtain

$T = 3g$

$T = 29.43\text{ N}$

Q.55 Ans:[0.8]

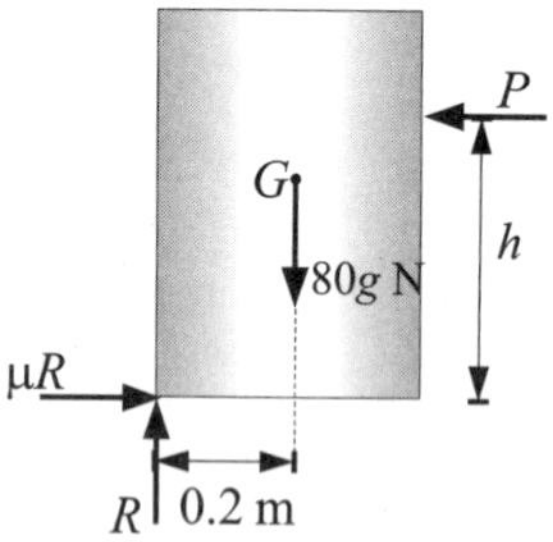

Figure shows the free-body diagram of box.

When box is about to slide; $\quad P = \mu R = 0.25\times 80g$

or $\quad P = 196.2\text{ N}$

When box is about to topple; $P\times h = 80g\times 0.2$

or $\quad h = \frac{80g\times 02}{196.2} = 0.8$

$h = 0.8\text{ m}$

Q.56 Ans:[37.5]

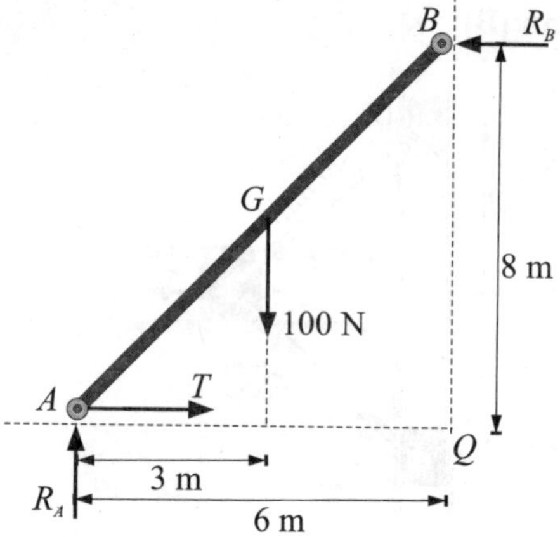

Let T be the tension of rope. Applying equilibrium equation.

$\sum F_y = 0 \quad \Rightarrow \quad R_A - 100 = 0$

or $\quad R_A = 100\text{ N}$

$\sum M_B = 0 \quad \Rightarrow \quad R_A\times 6 - T\times 8 - 100\times 3 = 0$

or $\quad 100\times 6 - T\times 8 - 100\times 3 = 0$

$T = 37.5\text{ N}$

Q.57 Ans:[30]

Using Lami's theorem, we have

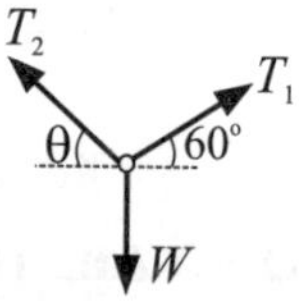

$$T_2 = W\frac{\sin(90+60)}{\sin(180-\theta-60)} = W\frac{\cos 60}{\sin(\theta+60)}$$

$$(T_2)_{\text{Min}} = W\frac{\cos 60}{\sin(\theta+60)} \leftarrow \text{Maximum value} = 1$$

$$(T_2)_{\text{Min}} = W\cos 60 = \frac{W}{2} \text{ at } \theta = 30° \;[\sin(\theta+60) = 1 = \sin 90]$$

$\theta = 30°$

Q.58 Ans:[0.66]

Figure shows the free body diagram of ladder.

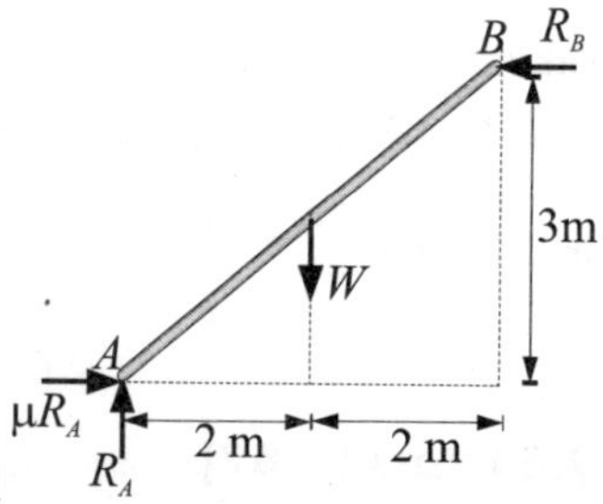

Applying equilibrium equations;

$\sum F_H = 0$

$\Rightarrow \quad \mu R_A - R_B = 0$

$\sum F_V = 0$

$\Rightarrow \quad R_A - W = 0$

From which $R_A = W$ and $R_B = \mu W$

$$\sum M_A = 0 \Rightarrow W \times 2 - R_B \times 3 = 0$$

or $$W \times 2 - \mu W \times 3 = 0$$

$$\mu = \frac{2}{3} = 0.66$$

Q.59 Ans:[6.96]

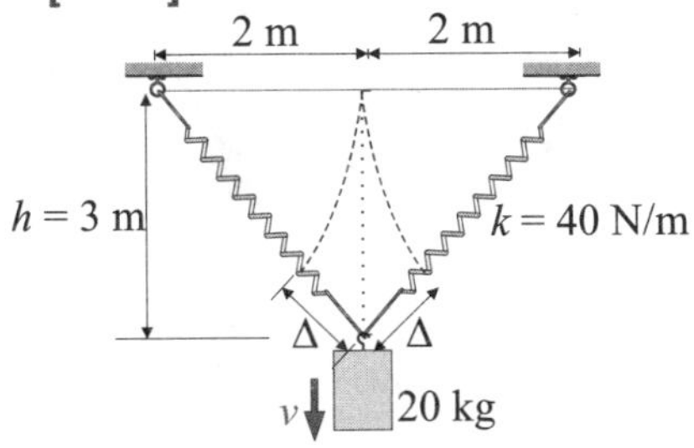

Applying principle of conservation of energy, we have

$$mgh = \left(\frac{1}{2}k\Delta^2\right) \times 2 + \frac{1}{2}mv^2$$

or $$20 \times 9.81 \times 3 = \frac{1}{2} \times 40 \times [\sqrt{2^2 + 3^2} - 2]^2 \times 2 + \frac{1}{2} \times 20 \times v^2$$

or $$588.6 = 103.11 + 10 \times v^2$$

$$v = 6.96 \text{ m/s}$$

Q.60 Ans:[103.51]

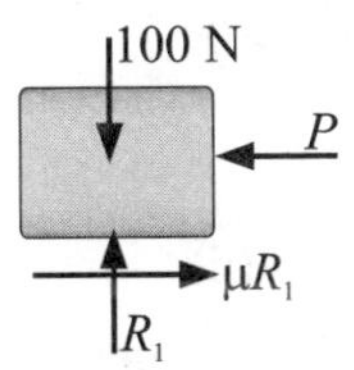

Free body diagram of 100 N body

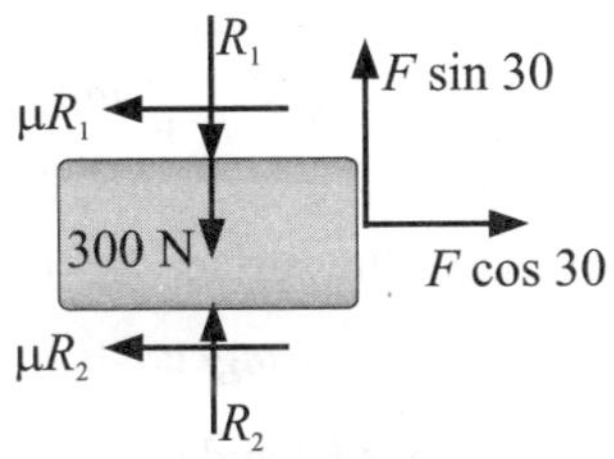

Free body diagram of 300 N body

Free-body diagram of blocks are shown in figure.

Consider 100 N block

$$\sum F_y = 0 \Rightarrow R_1 = 100$$

Friction force $= \mu R_1 = 0.2 \times 100 = 20$ N

Now consider 300 N block

$$\sum F_y = 0 \Rightarrow R_2 - 100 - 300 + F \sin 30 = 0$$

$$R_2 = 400 - \frac{F}{2}$$

$$\sum F_x = 0 \Rightarrow F \cos 30 - \mu R_2 - \mu R_1 = 0$$

or $$\frac{\sqrt{3}}{2}F - 0.2\left(400 - \frac{F}{2}\right) - 20 = 0$$

or $$F = \frac{100 \times 2}{\sqrt{3} + 0.2}$$

$$F = 103.51 \text{ N}$$

Q.61 Ans:[2.43]

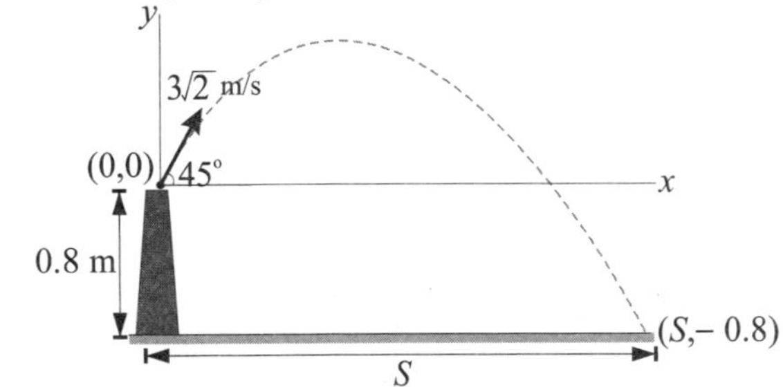

Applying equation of path of projectile

$$y = x \tan\theta - \frac{gx^2}{2u^2 \cos^2\theta}$$

$$-0.8 = S \tan 45 - \frac{9.81 \times S^2}{2(3\sqrt{2})^2 \cos^2 45}$$

or $$S^2 - 1.834S - 1.467 = 0$$

Solving for S, we obtain

$$S = 2.43 \text{ m}$$

Q.62 Ans:[0.408]

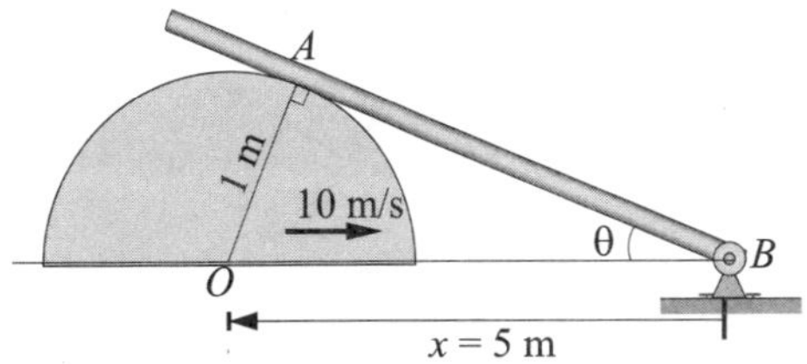

Geometry of figure; $\sin\theta = \frac{OA}{OB} = \frac{1}{x}$

Differentiating with respect to time t, we obtain

$$\cos\theta \frac{d\theta}{dt} = -\frac{1}{x^2}\frac{dx}{dt}$$

Angular velocity, $$\frac{d\theta}{dt} = \frac{-\frac{1}{x^2}\frac{dx}{dt}}{\cos\theta} = \frac{-\frac{1}{x^2}\frac{dx}{dt}}{\sqrt{25 - x^2} / 5}$$

$$= \frac{-\frac{1}{5^2}(-10)}{\sqrt{24}/5} = \frac{5}{\sqrt{24}}$$

$$\omega = 0.408 \text{ rad/s}$$

Q.63 Ans:[1.889]

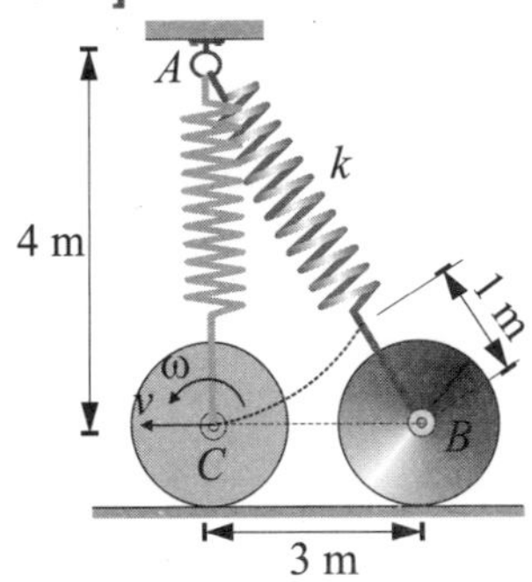

Applying the principle of conservation of energy between B and C, we write

$$\frac{1}{2}k\Delta^2 = \frac{1}{2}I\omega^2 + \frac{1}{2}mv^2$$

Substituting $I = \frac{1}{2}mr^2$ and $\omega = \frac{v}{r}$, we have

$$\frac{1}{2}k\Delta^2 = \frac{1}{2}\times\frac{1}{2}mr^2\frac{v^2}{r^2} + \frac{1}{2}mv^2 = \frac{3}{4}mv^2$$

or $$\frac{1}{2}\times 75\times(\sqrt{4^2+3^2}-4) = \frac{3}{4}\times 14v^2$$

Velocity $v = 1.889$ m/s and angular velocity $\omega = \frac{v}{r} = \frac{1.889}{1}$

$$\omega = 1.889 \text{ rad/s}$$

Q.64 Ans:[16.35]

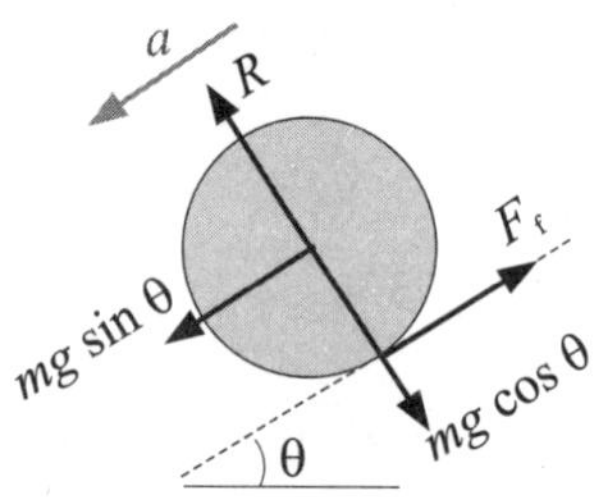

Applying Newton's second law, we write

$$\sum F = ma \Rightarrow mg\sin\theta - F_f = ma \quad \text{(i)}$$

$$\tau = I\alpha \Rightarrow F_f \times r = I\frac{a}{r}$$

or $$a = \frac{F_f \times r^2}{I}$$

Substituting $I = \frac{1}{2}mr^2$, we have

$$a = \frac{2F_f}{m} \quad \text{(ii)}$$

Eliminating a from Equations (i) and (ii), we obtain

$$F_f = \frac{1}{3}mg\sin\theta = \frac{1}{3}\times 10\times 9.81\sin 30$$

$$F_f = 1635 \text{ N}$$

Q.65 Ans:[48.18]

Let v be the velocity of particle at C. Applying the principle of conservation of energy between A and C, we write

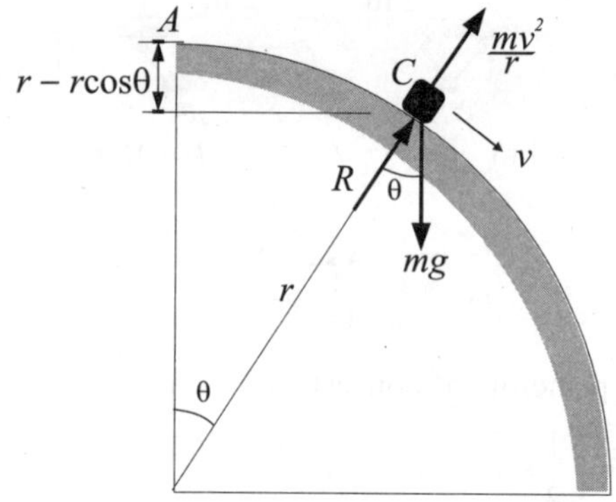

$$mg(r - r\cos\theta) = \frac{1}{2}mv^2$$

or $$mv^2 = 2mgr(1-\cos\theta) \quad \text{(i)}$$

Resolving the forces along perpendicular to the contact surface.

$$\sum F_r = 0 \quad \Rightarrow \quad R + \frac{mv^2}{r} - mg\cos\theta = 0$$

Particle leave the surface $R = 0$;

$$mv^2 = mgr\cos\theta \quad \text{(ii)}$$

From Equations (i) and (ii), we obtain

$$mgr\cos\theta = 2\,mgr\,(1-\cos\theta)$$

or $$\cos\theta = \frac{2}{3}$$

$$\theta = 48.18°$$

6 Strength of Materials

GATE Mechanical Engg.

GATE Syllabus

Stress and strain, Elastic constants, Poisson's ratio; Mohr's circle for plane stress and plane strain; Thin cylinders; Shear force and bending moment diagrams; Bending and shear stresses; Deflection of beams; Torsion of circular shafts; Euler's theory of columns; Energy methods; Thermal stresses; Strain gauges and rosettes; Testing of materials with universal testing machine; Testing of hardness and impact strength.

Chapter Outline

6.1 KEY CONCEPTS AND FORMULAS

Stresses and Strains

Stress: Stress is the intensity of internal force. A body must be able to withstand the intensity of internal force; if not, the body may rapture or deform excessively. Stress (force intensity) is a force divided by the area over which the force is distributed.

When some external forces are applied to a body, then the body offers resistance to these forces. This internal resisting force per unit area is called *stress*.

Types of stress

(i) Tensile or compressive stress

$$\sigma = \lim_{\Delta A \to 0} \frac{\Delta F}{\Delta A} = \frac{dF}{dA}$$

(ii) Shear stress

$$\tau_x = \lim_{\Delta A \to 0} \frac{\Delta F_x}{\Delta A} = \frac{dF_x}{dA}$$

(iii) Normal stress

$$\sigma_n = \lim_{\Delta A \to 0} \frac{\Delta F_n}{\Delta A} = \frac{dF_n}{dA}$$

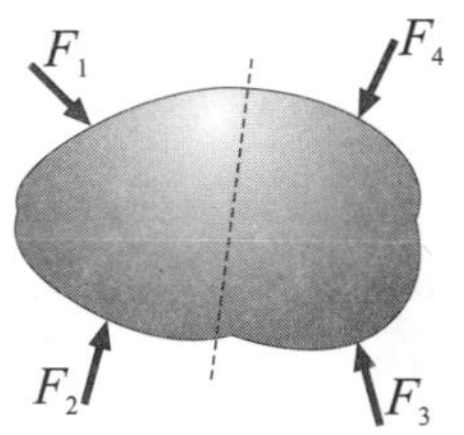

Body

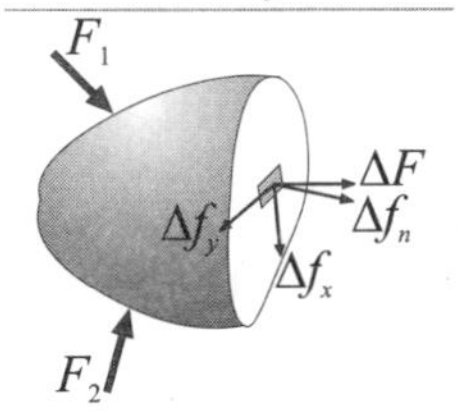

Free body diagram

Strain: Strain (deformation per unit length) is the quantity used to measure the intensity of a deformation.

Types of strain

(i) Normal strain ε, (ii) Shear strain ϕ and (iii) Volumetric strain ε_V

Hook's law

This law states that within elastic limits, strain is proportional to stress.

Stress $\propto$ Strain

$\sigma = E\varepsilon,\ \tau = G\phi,\ p = K\varepsilon_v$

Relation between Elastic Constants

$$E = 2G(1+\nu),\ E = 3K(1-2\nu) \text{ and } E = \frac{9KG}{G+3K}$$

Thermal Stress

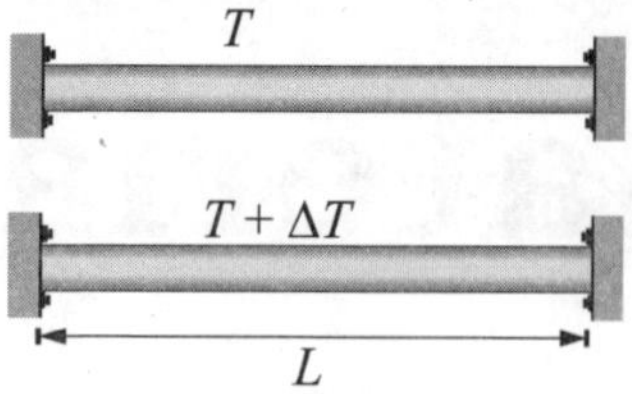

When a temperature change takes place while member is restrained, stresses (thermal stresses) are induced in the member.

Stress, $\sigma = E \times \text{strain}$

Thermal strain, $\varepsilon = \frac{dL}{L} = \alpha \Delta T$

$$\sigma = E\alpha\,\Delta T$$

Stress-Strain Diagram

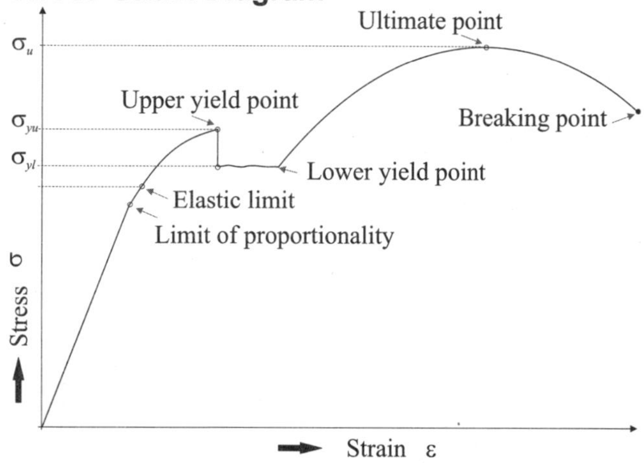

Stress-strain diagram of ductile material

Elastic Limit

The elastic limit is the maximum stress for which the material acts elastically. For stresses above the elastic limit, some strains (deformation) remain when the load is removed.

Ultimate Strength

The maximum stress developed in a material before rupture is called the ultimate strength.

Ductility

It is defined as the capacity for plastic deformation in tension or shear.

Poisson's Ratio

The ratio of the lateral or perpendicular strain to the longitudinal of axial strain is called *Poisson's ratio.*

Poisson's ratio, $\nu = -\frac{\varepsilon_{\text{lateral}}}{\varepsilon_{\text{longitudinal}}}$

Complex and Principal Stresses

Biaxial Stresses Combined with Shear Stresses

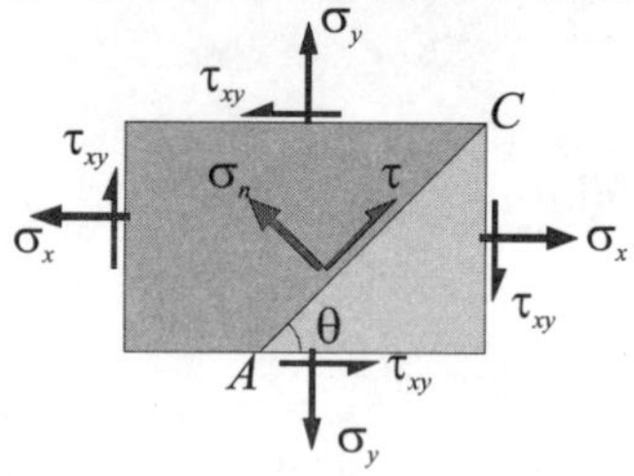

$$\sigma_n = \frac{1}{2}(\sigma_y + \sigma_x) + \frac{1}{2}(\sigma_y - \sigma_x)\cos 2\theta + \tau_{xy}\sin 2\theta$$

$$\tau = \frac{1}{2}(\sigma_y - \sigma_x)\sin 2\theta + \tau_{xy}\cos 2\theta$$

σ_n is maximum or minimum (and $\tau = 0$) at

$$\theta = \frac{1}{2}\tan^{-1}\frac{2\tau_{xy}}{\sigma_y - \sigma_x}$$

Principal Stresses

Two values of σ_n, one of which is maximum and the other minimum, which are the two principal stresses σ_1 and σ_2 respectively.

Principal stresses

$$\sigma_{1,2} = \frac{1}{2}(\sigma_y + \sigma_x) \pm \frac{1}{2}\sqrt{(\sigma_y - \sigma_x)^2 + 4\tau_{xy}^2}$$

$$\tau_{\max} = \pm\frac{1}{2}\sqrt{(\sigma_y - \sigma_x)^2 + 4\tau_{xy}^2}$$

$$\tau_{\max} = \frac{1}{2}(\sigma_1 - \sigma_2)$$

Mohr's Circle

Eliminating $\sin 2\theta$ and $\cos 2\theta$ from

$$\sigma_n = \frac{1}{2}(\sigma_y + \sigma_x) + \frac{1}{2}(\sigma_y - \sigma_x)\cos 2\theta + \tau_{xy}\sin 2\theta$$

and $\tau = \frac{1}{2}(\sigma_y - \sigma_x)\sin 2\theta + \tau_{xy}\cos 2\theta$, we get

$$\left[\sigma_n - \frac{\sigma_y + \sigma_x}{2}\right]^2 + \tau^2 = \left(\sqrt{\left(\frac{\sigma_y - \sigma_x}{2}\right)^2 + \tau_{xy}^2}\right)^2$$

This is the equation of circle (Mohr's circle) of center

$\left(\frac{\sigma_y + \sigma_x}{2}, 0\right)$ and radius $\sqrt{\left(\frac{\sigma_y - \sigma_x}{2}\right)^2 + \tau_{xy}^2}$

Thin Pressure Vessels

Stresses in a Thin Cylindrical Vessel

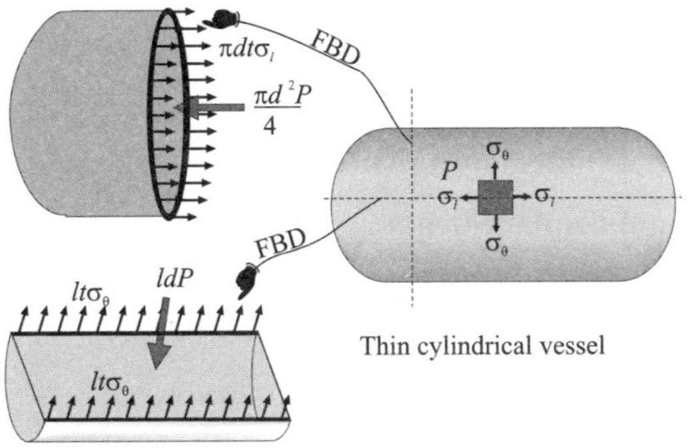

Thin cylindrical vessel

Hoop stress $\sigma_\theta = \dfrac{Pd}{2t}$

Longitudinal stress $\sigma_l = \dfrac{Pd}{4t}$

Maximum shear stress $\tau_{max} = \dfrac{Pd}{8t}$

Hoop strain $\varepsilon_\theta = \dfrac{1}{E}(\sigma_\theta - \nu\sigma_l) = \dfrac{Pd}{4tE}(2-\nu)$

Longitudinal strain $\varepsilon_l = \dfrac{1}{E}(\sigma_l - \nu\sigma_\theta) = \dfrac{Pd}{4tE}(1-2\nu)$

Volume of cylinder $V = \dfrac{\pi}{4}d^2 l$

Volumetric strain $\varepsilon_V = 2\varepsilon_\theta + \varepsilon_l = \dfrac{Pd}{2tE}(2.5-2\nu)$

Stresses in a Thin Spherical Vessel

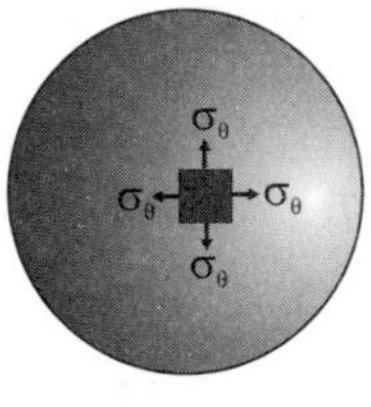

Spherical Shell

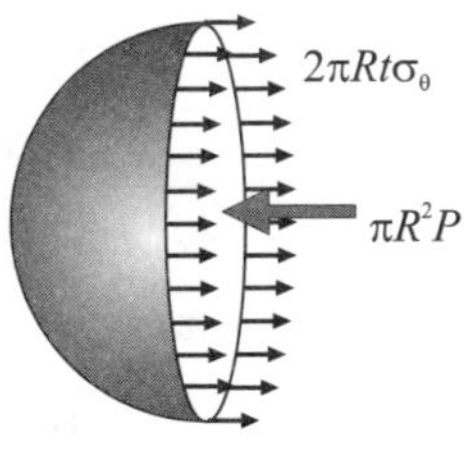

Free body diagram

Hoop stress $\sigma_\theta = \dfrac{Pd}{4t}$

Hoop strain $\varepsilon_\theta = \dfrac{1}{E}(\sigma_\theta - \nu\sigma_\theta) = \dfrac{Pd}{4tE}(1-\nu)$

Volumetric strain $\varepsilon_V = \dfrac{3Pd}{4tE}(1-\nu)$

Change in volume $dV = V\dfrac{3Pd}{4tE}(1-\nu)$

Shear Forces and Bending Moments

Shear Force

The shear force S at any cross-section of a horizontal beam is the algebraic sum of the vertical projection of all forces (including reactions) to the left of the given cross-section. (where, in the sum, the projection of a force is positive if its direction is upward and negative if its direction is downward.

Bending Moment

The bending moment M at any cross-section of a horizontal beam is the sum of the moments about the given cross-section of all the forces (including support reactions) to the left of the cross-section. (where, in the sum, a clockwise moment is positive and a anti-clockwise moment is negative).

Shear Force and Bending Moment Diagram

The graphical representation of Shear force in which y-axis represents shear force and x-axis represents the position of the section is called *shear force diagram* (SFD).

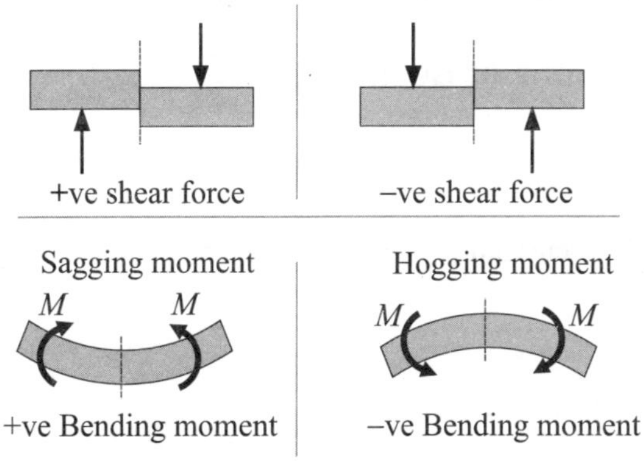

The graph in which y-axis represents bending moment and x-axis represents the position of the section is called *bending moment diagram* (BMD).

The points (other than ends) in a beam at which bending moment is zero, called *points of contraflexure* or *point of inflexion*.

Relationship between Shear Force and Bending Moment

Intensity of loading $\omega = -\dfrac{dS}{dx}$, Shear force $S = \dfrac{dM}{dx}$

Intensity of loading $\omega = -\dfrac{dS}{dx} = -\dfrac{d^2M}{dx^2}$

Sign Convention of Shear Force and Bending Moment

Shear force is assumed to be positive if it produces a clockwise moment and negative if it produces an anticlockwise moment.

or

The shear force is positive if the net resultant external force to the left of a section is upward.

Positive bending moment produces compression on the top fibre of the beam and negative bending moment produces tension on the top fibre of the beam.

Stresses in Beams

Bending formula, $\frac{M}{I} = \frac{\sigma}{y} = \frac{E}{R}$

Section modulus, $z = \frac{I}{y}$

Flitched Beams

A flitched beam is made of two or more different materials and rigidly connected together.

Horizontal Shear Stress in Beam

$\tau = \frac{dM}{dx} \cdot \frac{1}{Ib} \int_y^{h/2} bydy$ or $\tau = \frac{SA\bar{y}}{Ib}$ where S is the shear force at the section.

Deflections of Beams

$$\text{Radius of curvature } R = \frac{\left\{1 + \left(\frac{dy}{dx}\right)^2\right\}^{\frac{3}{2}}}{\frac{d^2y}{dx^2}}$$

If curvature is very small then $\frac{1}{R} \approx \frac{d^2y}{dx^2}$

or $\frac{1}{R} = -\frac{d\theta}{ds} = -\frac{M}{EI} = \frac{d^2y}{dx^2}$ or $EI\frac{d^2y}{dx^2} = -M$

Slope of the beam, $\frac{dy}{dx} = -\int \frac{M}{EI} dx$

Deflection, $y = -\iint \frac{M}{EI} dx.dx$

Macaulay's method, moment area method and conjugate beam method are generally used to determine the slop and deflection at a point of beam.

Fixed Beams

A fixed or built-in beam has both of its ends rigidly fixed so that the slop at the ends remains zero.

Torsion

Torsion of circular shaft

Torsion formula $\frac{T}{J} = \frac{\tau}{r} = \frac{G\theta}{l}$

Shear stress $\tau = \left(\frac{G\theta}{l}\right)r$

$T_{hollow} = \frac{\pi}{16}\frac{(D^4 - d^4)}{D}\tau$ and $T_{solid} = \frac{\pi}{16}D^3\tau$ (for same outer radius and stress)

Power transmitted by a shaft $P = T\omega$

Torsional displacements

$$\theta = \int \frac{T\,dx}{GJ} \quad \text{or} \quad \theta = \sum_{i=1}^{n} \frac{T_i L_i}{G_i J_i}$$

Combined Stresses

Axial, Bending and Torsional Stresses

If a body is subjected to axial, bending and torsional stresses then direct stress $\sigma_d = \frac{P}{A}$, bending stress $\sigma_b = \frac{M}{I}y$ and torsional stress (shear) $\tau = \frac{T}{J}r$.

The principal stresses under the combined action of these stresses

$$\sigma_{1,2} = \frac{\sigma_d + \sigma_b}{2} \pm \frac{1}{2}\sqrt{(\sigma_d - \sigma_b)^2 + 4\tau^2}$$

Maximum shear stress $\tau_{max} = \frac{1}{2}\sqrt{(\sigma_d - \sigma_b)^2 + 4\tau^2}$

For a circular shaft of diameter *d*

Direct stress $\sigma_d = \frac{4P}{\pi d^2}$, bending stress $\sigma_b = \frac{32M}{\pi d^3}$ and torsional stress (shear) $\tau = \frac{16T}{\pi d^3}$

$$\sigma_{1,2} = \frac{\frac{4P}{\pi d^2} + \frac{32M}{\pi d^3}}{2} \pm \frac{1}{2}\sqrt{\left(\frac{4P}{\pi d^2} - \frac{32M}{\pi d^3}\right)^2 + 4\left(\frac{16T}{\pi d^3}\right)^2}$$

$$\tau_{max} = \frac{1}{2}\sqrt{\left(\frac{4P}{\pi d^2} - \frac{32M}{\pi d^3}\right)^2 + 4\left(\frac{16T}{\pi d^3}\right)^2}$$

If $P = 0$;

$$\sigma_{1,2} = \frac{16}{\pi d^3}(M \pm \sqrt{M^2 + T^2})$$

$$= \frac{32}{\pi d^3}\left[\frac{1}{2}(M \pm \sqrt{M^2 + T^2})\right]$$

$$= \frac{32}{\pi d^3}M_{eq}$$

$$\tau_{max} = \frac{16}{\pi d^3}(\sqrt{M^2 + T^2})$$

$$= \frac{16}{\pi d^3}T_{eq}$$

Equivalent bending moment $M_{eq} = \frac{1}{2}(M \pm \sqrt{M^2 + T^2})$

Equivalent torque $T_{eq} = \sqrt{M^2 + T^2}$

Eccentric Loading for Short Column without Buckling

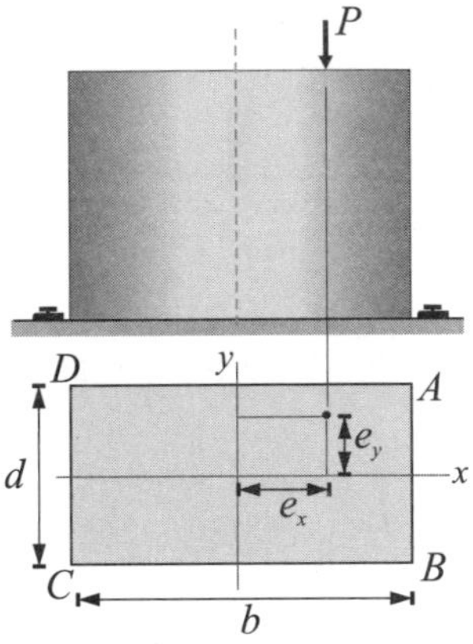

Resultant stress $\sigma_r = \sigma_d \pm \sigma_b$

where, direct stress $\sigma_d = \frac{P}{A}$ (compressive stress)

Bending stress $\sigma_b = \frac{M}{I} y$

or $\sigma_b = \pm \frac{Pe_x}{I_{yy}} x \pm \frac{Pe_y}{I_{xx}} y$

Resultant stress $\sigma_r = \left[\frac{P}{A} \pm \frac{Pe_x}{I_{yy}} x \pm \frac{Pe_y}{I_{xx}} y\right]$

Stress at A $(\sigma_r)_A = \frac{P}{A}\left[1 + \frac{6e_x}{b} + \frac{6e_y}{d}\right]$

Stress at B $(\sigma_r)_B = \frac{P}{A}\left[1 + \frac{6e_x}{b} - \frac{6e_y}{d}\right]$

Stress at C $(\sigma_r)_C = \frac{P}{A}\left[1 - \frac{6e_x}{b} - \frac{6e_y}{d}\right]$

Stress at D $(\sigma_r)_D = \frac{P}{A}\left[1 - \frac{6e_x}{b} + \frac{6e_y}{d}\right]$

For no tensile stress $(\sigma_r)_C = 0 \Rightarrow 0 = \frac{P}{A}\left[1 - \frac{6e_x}{b} - \frac{6e_y}{d}\right]$

or $\frac{e_x}{b} + \frac{e_y}{d} = \frac{1}{6}$ ← This equation represents a straight line.

Columns

Slenderness ratio: The ratio of the length of the column to the least radius of gyration is called the *slenderness ratio.*

Buckling factor: It is the ratio of equivalent length of column to the minimum radius of gyration.

Buckling load: The minimum axial load at which the column tends to have lateral displacement or buckle is called the *buckling* or *crippling* or *critical load.*

Safe load: The safe load for the column is the load under which the column will not buckle.

Equivalent length: Equivalent length for a column is the length which gives the same buckling load as given by a both ends hinged column.

Short column: A column for which the slenderness ratio is less than 32 is called a *short column.*

Medium column: A column for which the slenderness ratio lies between 32 and 120 is called a *medium column.*

Long column: A column for which the slenderness ratio is more than 120 is called a *long column.*

Euler's Theory of Buckling of Columns

Assumptions:

1. The column is initially straight and the applied load is truly axial.
2. The material of the column is homogeneous, linear and isotropic.
3. The length of the column is very large as compared to the cross-sectional dimensions of the column.
4. The cross-section of the column is uniform throughout.
5. The shortening of the column due to axial compression is negligible.
6. The self weight of the column is neglected.
7. The ends of column are frictionless.

Column with Pinned Ends

Critical load (Euler load) $P_{cr} = \frac{\pi^2 EI}{l^2}$; where $I = A k^2$, $A =$ area of cross-section of the column, $k =$ least radius of gyration. $P_{cr} = \frac{\pi^2 EA}{\left(\frac{l}{k}\right)^2}$, where $\frac{l}{k} =$ slenderness ratio.

Column Fixed at the Base and Free at the Top

Critical load (Euler load) $P_{cr} = \frac{\pi^2 EI}{4l^2}$ or $P_{cr} = \frac{\pi^2 EI}{(2l)^2}$

Equivalent (Effective) length $l_{eq} = 2l$

Column with Both Ends Fixed against Rotation

Critical load (Euler load) $P_{cr} = \dfrac{4\pi^2 EI}{l^2}$ or $P_{cr} = \dfrac{\pi^2 EI}{\left(\dfrac{l}{2}\right)^2}$

Equivalent (Effective) length $l_{eq} = \dfrac{l}{2}$

Column Fixed at the Base and Pinned at the Top

Critical load (Euler load) $P_{cr} = \dfrac{2\pi^2 EI}{l^2}$ or $P_{cr} = \dfrac{\pi^2 EI}{\left(\dfrac{l}{2}\right)^2}$

Equivalent (Effective) length $l_{eq} = \dfrac{l}{2}$

Rankine Formula

$\dfrac{1}{P} = \dfrac{1}{P_{com}} + \dfrac{1}{P_{cr}}$ where $P_{com} = \sigma_c A$ (compressive load)

$P_{cr} = \dfrac{\pi^2 EI}{l^2}$ (critical load)

$P = \dfrac{\sigma_c A}{1 + a\left(\dfrac{l_{eq}}{k}\right)^2}$ where $a = \dfrac{\sigma_c}{\pi^2 E}$ is a constant for a material

Secant Formula for Long Column

$$\sigma_{max} = \frac{P}{A}\left[1 + \frac{e\,y_c}{k^2}.\sec\sqrt{\frac{P}{EI}}.\frac{l_{eq}}{2}\right]$$

Energy Methods

Strain energy: The work done is straining the material, within the elastic limits, is known as *strain energy*.

Proof resilience: The maximum strain energy that can be stored in a material without permanent deformation is called *proof resilience*.

Modulus of resilience: The maximum strain energy stored in the body per unit volume is known as *modulus of resilience*.

Proof load: The maximum load which can be applied to a member without its being permanently deformed is called *proof load*.

Strain Energy for Axial Loading

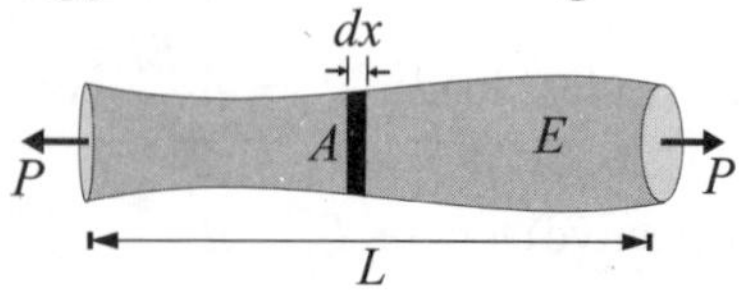

$$U = \int_V \frac{\sigma^2}{2E} dV \quad \text{where } \sigma = \frac{P}{A} \text{ and } dV = A\,dx$$

or $$U = \int_0^L \frac{P^2}{2EA} dx$$

Strain Energy for Torsion Loading

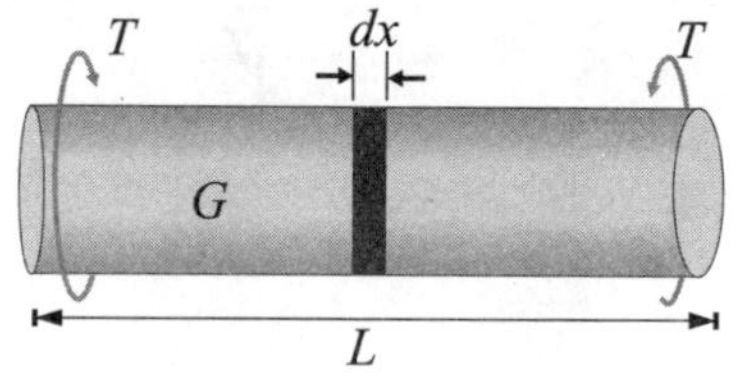

$$U = \int_V \frac{\tau^2}{2G} dV \quad \text{where } \tau = \frac{T}{J} r \text{ and } dV = dA\,dx$$

or $$U = \int_0^L \frac{T^2}{2GJ} dx$$

Strain Energy for Bending Loads

The strain energy in the beam resulting from the bending moment M is

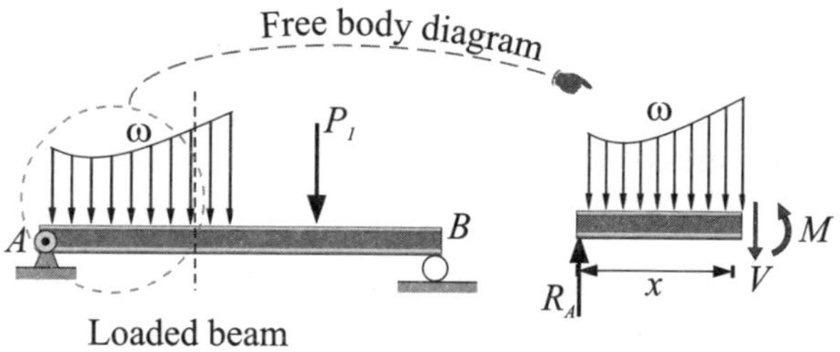

$$U = \int_V \frac{\sigma^2}{2E} dV = \int_V \frac{\left(\dfrac{M}{I} y\right)^2}{2E} dV$$

where $\sigma = \dfrac{M}{I} y$ and $dV = dA\,dx$

$$U = \int_0^L \frac{M^2}{2EI} dx$$

Castigliano's Theorem

The partial derivatives of the strain energy of a structure with respect to any load is equal to the displacement corresponding to that load.

$$\delta_i = \frac{\partial U}{\partial P_i}$$

Strain Gauges

Strain gauges are constructed from a single wire that is wound back and forth. The gauge is attached to the surface of an object with wires in the direction where the strain is to be measured. The electrical resistance in the wire change when they are elongated.

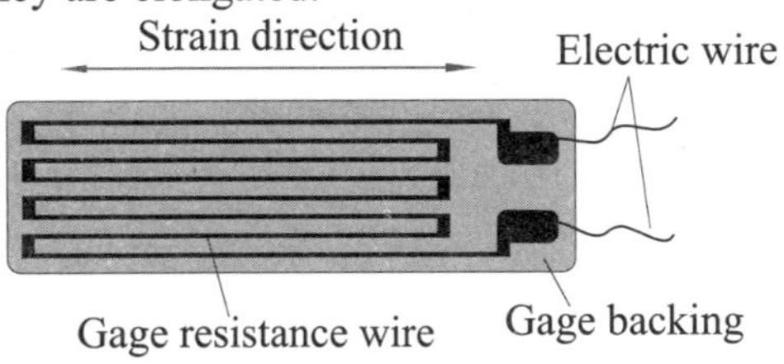

Strain Rosettes

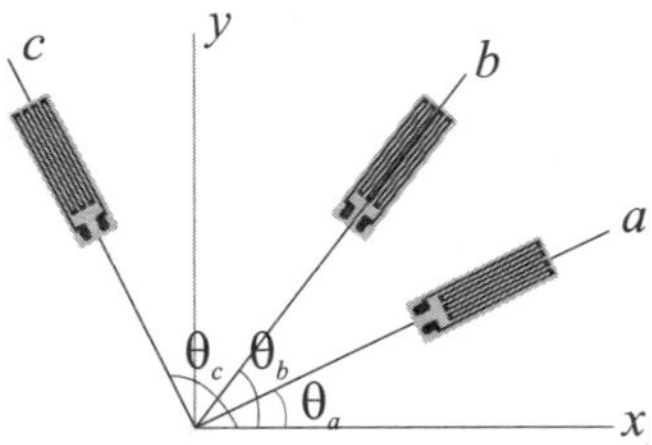

Any three strain gauges used together at one location on a stressed object is called a *strain rosette*.

Three gauges are attached to the object in any three different angles. Three gauges give three equations, these are

$$\varepsilon_a = \frac{\varepsilon_x + \varepsilon_y}{2} + \frac{\varepsilon_x - \varepsilon_y}{2}\cos 2\theta_a + \frac{\gamma_{xy}}{2}\sin 2\theta_a$$

$$\varepsilon_b = \frac{\varepsilon_x + \varepsilon_y}{2} + \frac{\varepsilon_x - \varepsilon_y}{2}\cos 2\theta_b + \frac{\gamma_{xy}}{2}\sin 2\theta_b$$

$$\varepsilon_c = \frac{\varepsilon_x + \varepsilon_y}{2} + \frac{\varepsilon_x - \varepsilon_y}{2}\cos 2\theta_c + \frac{\gamma_{xy}}{2}\sin 2\theta_c$$

Strain Rosette-45°

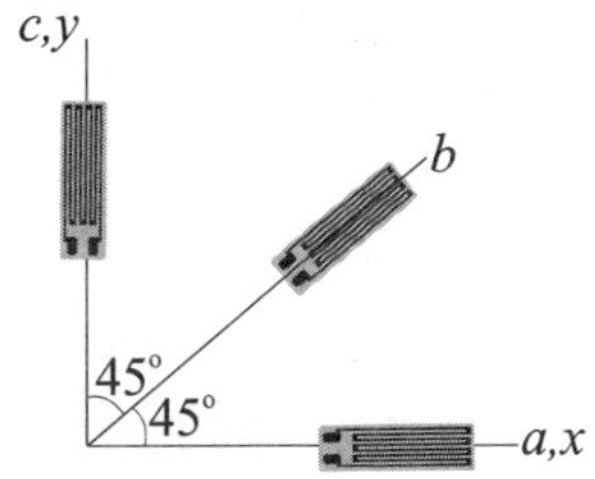

$$\varepsilon_a = \frac{\varepsilon_x + \varepsilon_y}{2} + \frac{\varepsilon_x - \varepsilon_y}{2}, \qquad \varepsilon_b = \frac{\varepsilon_x + \varepsilon_y}{2} + \frac{\gamma_{xy}}{2}$$

$$\varepsilon_c = \frac{\varepsilon_x + \varepsilon_y}{2} - \frac{\varepsilon_x - \varepsilon_y}{2}$$

Solving for ε_x, ε_y and γ_{xy} gives

$$\varepsilon_x = \varepsilon_a, \varepsilon_y = \varepsilon_b, \gamma_{xy} = 2\varepsilon_b - (\varepsilon_a + \varepsilon_c)$$

Strain Rosette-60°

$$\varepsilon_x = \varepsilon_a$$

$$\varepsilon_y = \frac{2\varepsilon_b + 2\varepsilon_c - \varepsilon_a}{3}$$

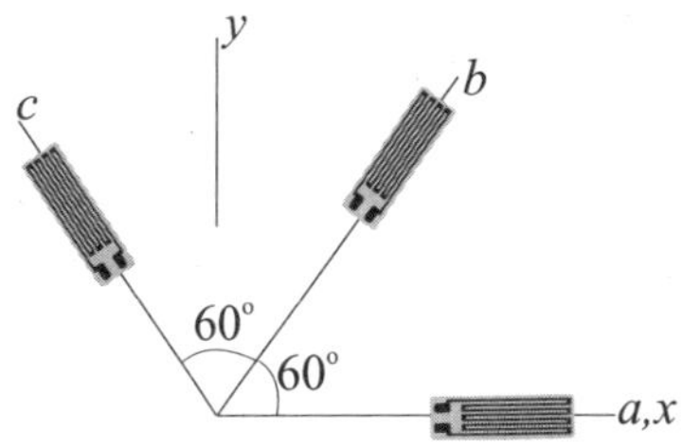

$$\gamma_{xy} = \frac{2\varepsilon_b - 2\varepsilon_c}{\sqrt{3}}$$

Hardness

Hardness is the property of a material that enables it to resist plastic deformation, usually by penetration.

Hardness test methods are as follows:

Rockwell Hardness Test

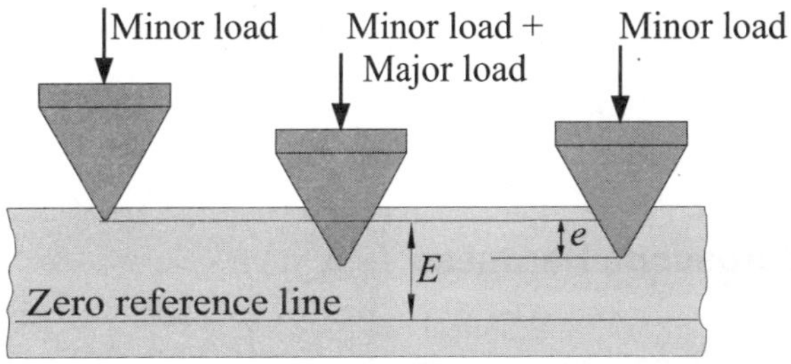

This method consists of indenting the test material with a diamond cone or hardened steel ball indenter.

Rockwell hardness number, $HR = E - e$

$$HR = 130 - \frac{\text{Depth of penetration (in mm)}}{0.002}$$

where E = constant depending on form of indenter (100 units for diamond indenter, 130 units for steel ball indenter and e = permanent increase in depth of penetration due to major load.

Brinell Hardness Test

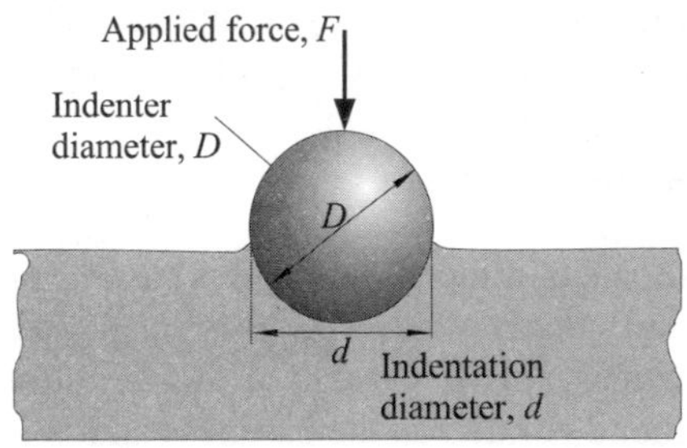

This method consists of indenting the test material with a 10 mm diameter hardened steel or carbinde ball subjected to a load 3000 kg (for softer material 1500 kg or 500 kg)

Brinell hardness number, $BHN = \dfrac{F}{\frac{\pi}{2}D(D - \sqrt{D^2 - d^2})}$

Vickers Hardness Test

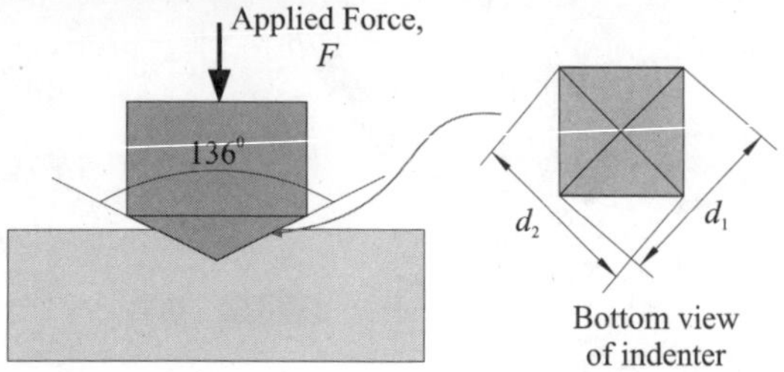

This method consists of indenting the test material with a diamond indenter, in the form of a right pyramid with a square base and an angle of 136° between opposite faces subjected to a load of 1 to 100 kgf. The full load is normally applied for 10 to 15 s.

$$\text{Vickers hardness,} \quad HV = \frac{2F \sin \dfrac{136^\circ}{2}}{\left(\dfrac{d_1 + d_1}{2}\right)^2}$$

or $HV = 1.854 \dfrac{F}{d^2}$ (approximate), where $d = \left(\dfrac{d_1 + d_1}{2}\right)$

Scleroscope Hardness Test

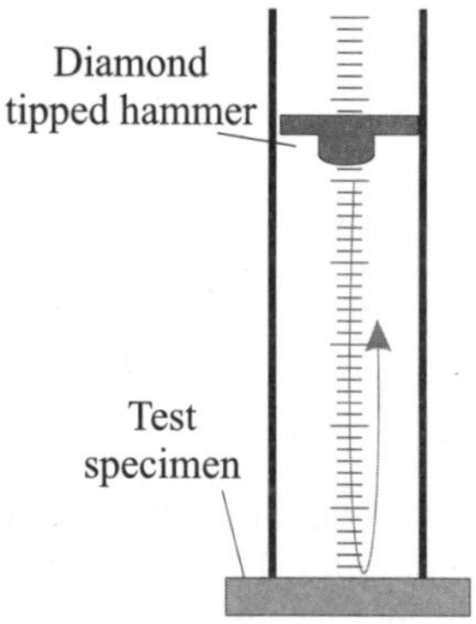

The scleroscope test consists of dropping a diamond tipped hammer, which falls inside a glass tube under the force of its own weight from a fixed height, onto the test specimen. The height of the rebound travel of the hammer is measured on a graduated scale.

Moh's Hardness Scale

The Moh's scale of mineral hardness is based on the ability of one natural sample of mineral to scratch another mineral visibly. It consists of 10 minerals arranged in order form 1 to 10. Diamond is rated as the hardness and is indexed as 10, talc as the softest with index number 1. Each mineral in the scale will scratch all those below it as follow:

Hardness	Mineral
10	Diamond
9	Corundum
8	Topaz
7	Quartz
6	Orthoclase
5	Apatite
4	Fluorite
3	Calcite
2	Gypsum
1	Talc

Knoop Hardness Test

In this test, a predetermined test force is applied with a pyramid-shaped diamond indenter for a specified dwell time period. The indenter used on a Knoop test is pyramid-shaped but more elongated than the indenter used on a Vickers test. After this dwell period, the force is removed. Unlike the Vickers test where the indentation length on the vertical and horizontal axes are measured and averaged, the Knoop method only uses the long axis.

$KHN = \dfrac{P}{0.07028\, d^2}$, where P = applied load in N, d = long diagonal of impression in mm.

Universal Testing Machines (UTM)

A universal testing machine also known as a materials testing machine and can be used to test the tensile and compressive properties of materials.

Impact Strength

An impact test measures how much energy is absorbed when an object fractures or breaks under a high speed collision.

Toughness: It is the amount of energy a material can absorb before fracturing or breaking.

Impact Testing Methods

The notched test specimen is broken by the impact of a heavy pendulum or hammer, falling at a predetermined velocity through a fixed distance. The test measures the energy absorbed by the fractured specimen.

Charpy Impact Test

The Charpy impact test is a dynamic test in which a test piece U-notched or V-notched in the middle and supported at each end, is broken by a single blow of a freely swinging pendulum. The energy absorbed is measured. This absorbed energy is a measure of the impact strength of material.

Izod Impact Test

The Izod impact test is a dynamic test in which a test piece V-notched test piece, gripped vertically, is broken by a single blow of a freely swinging pendulum. The blow is struck on the same face as the notch and at the fixed height above it. The energy absorbed is measured.

6.2 SOLVED EXAMPLES

Previous Years GATE Questions

Example 6.1

A rod is subjected to a uniaxial load within linear elastic limit. When the change in the stress is 200 MPa, the change in the strain is 0.001. If the Poisson's ratio of the rod is 0.3 the modulus of rigidity (in GPa) is_____.

GATE 2015

Solution

Modulus of elasticity $E = \frac{\sigma}{\varepsilon} = \frac{200}{0.001}$ MPa

or $E = 200\,\text{GPa}$

Relation between E, G and ν is given by

$$E = 2G(1+\nu)$$

or $G = \frac{E}{2(1+\nu)} = \frac{200}{2(1+0.3)}$

$$G = 76.92\,\text{GPa}$$

Example 6.2

A cantilever OP is connected to another beam PQ with a pin joint as shown in figure. A load of 10 kN is applied at the mid-point of PQ. The magnitude of bending movement (in kNm) at fixed end O is

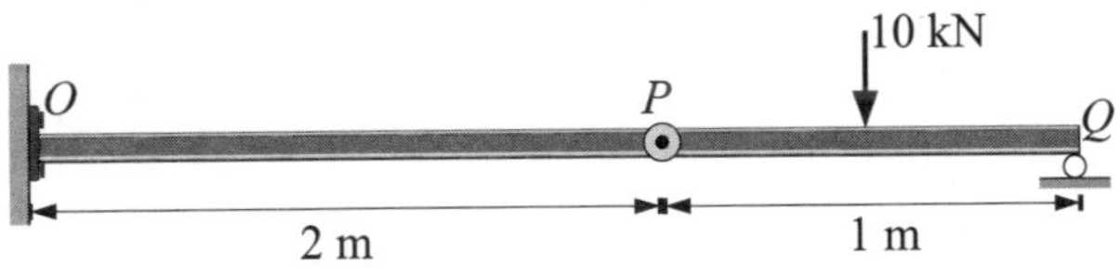

(A) 2.5 (B) 5 (C) 10 (D) 25

GATE 2015

Solution

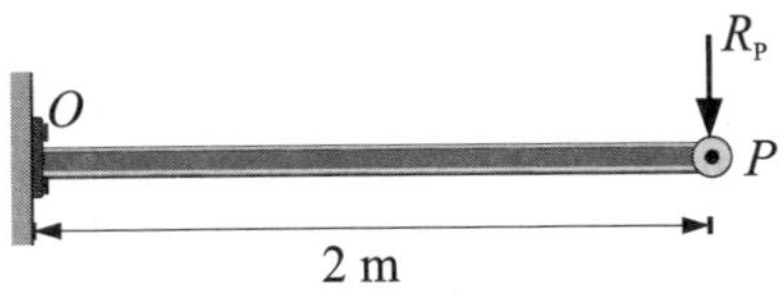

(a) Cantilever beam OP

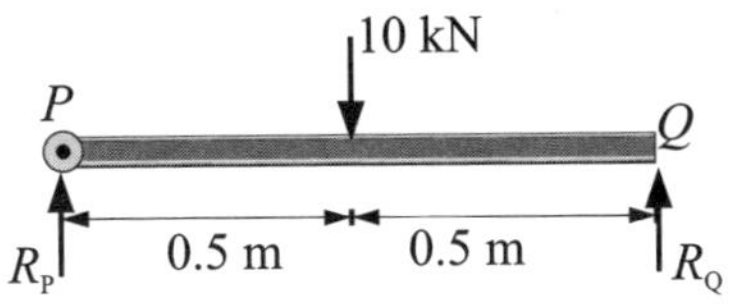

(b) Simply supported beam PQ

Let R_P be the reaction at the pin joint P and consider the beam PQ.

Reaction at the pin joint P; $R_P = R_Q = \frac{10}{2} = 5\,\text{kN}$

Now, consider the cantilever beam OP.

Bending moment at fixed end O is $M_O = R_P \times OP$

$$M_O = 5 \times 2$$

$$M_O = 10\ \text{kNm}$$

Example 6.3

A cantilever beam with square cross-section of 6 mm side is subjected to a load of 2 kN normal to the top surface as shown in figure. The Young's modulus of elasticity of the material of the beam is 210 GPa. The magnitude of slope (in radian) at Q (20 mm from the fixed end) is____.

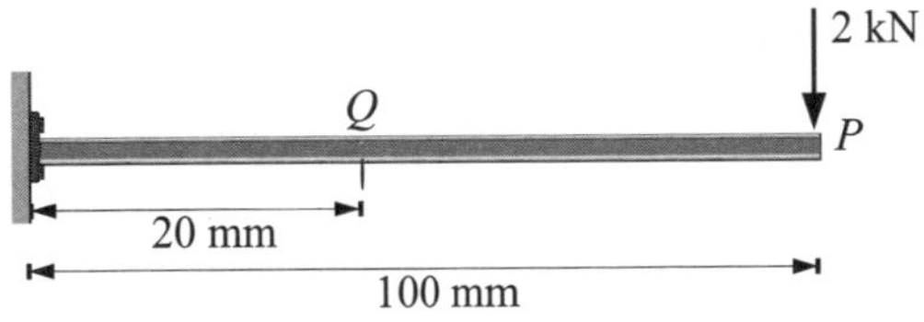

GATE 2015

Solution

Consider the section x-x at distance x from free end P.

Bending moment x-x ; $M_{xx} = 2000x$

Bending equation $EI\frac{d^2y}{dx^2} = -M_{xx}$

$$EI\frac{d^2y}{dx^2} = -2000x$$

Integrating $EI\frac{dy}{dx} = -1000x^2 + c$

Applying boundary condition $\frac{dy}{dx} = 0$ at $x = 0.1$ m, we obtain $c = 1000 \times 0.1^2 = 10$

$$EI\frac{dy}{dx} = -1000x^2 + 10$$

Slop at Q ($x = 80$ mm); $\left(\frac{dy}{dx}\right)_Q = \frac{-1000 \times 0.08^2 + 10}{EI}$

$$\left(\frac{dy}{dx}\right)_Q = \frac{3.6}{E\frac{d^4}{12}} = \frac{3.6 \times 12}{Ed^4} = \frac{3.6 \times 12}{210 \times 10^9\left(\frac{6}{1000}\right)^4}$$

Slope at Q $\left(\frac{dy}{dx}\right)_Q = 0.158$

Example 6.4

In a plane stress condition, the components of stress at a

point are $\sigma_x = 20$ MPa, $\sigma_y = 80$ MPa and $\tau_{xy} = 40$ MPa. The maximum shear stress (in MPa) at the point is

(A) 20 (B) 25 (C) 50 (D) 100

GATE 2015

Solution

Given: $\sigma_x = 20$ MPa, $\sigma_y = 80$ MPa and $\tau_{xy} = 40$ MPa

Maximum shear stress $\tau_{max} = \sqrt{\left(\frac{\sigma_y - \sigma_x}{2}\right)^2 + \tau_{xy}^2}$

$$\tau_{max} = \sqrt{\left(\frac{80-20}{2}\right)^2 + 40^2}$$

$$\tau_{max} = 50\text{ MPa}$$

Example 6.5

A cylindrical tank with closed ends is filled with compressed air at a pressure of 500 kPa, the inner radius of the tank is 2 m, and it has wall thickness of 10 mm. The magnitude of maximum in-plane shear stress (in MPa) is_____.

GATE 2015

Solution

Given: $P = 500$ kPa, $d = 4$ m and $t = \frac{10}{1000}$ m

Maximum in plane shear stress $\tau_{max} = \frac{\sigma_\theta - \sigma_l}{2}$

or $$\tau_{max} = \frac{\frac{pd}{2t} - \frac{pd}{4t}}{2} = \frac{pd}{8t}$$

$$\tau_{max} = \frac{500 \times 10^3 \times 4}{8 \times \frac{10}{1000}}$$

$$= 25 \times 10^6 \text{ Pa}$$

$$\tau_{max} = 25\text{ MPa}$$

Example 6.6

For the overhanging beam shown in figure, the magnitude of maximum bending moment (in kNm) is________.

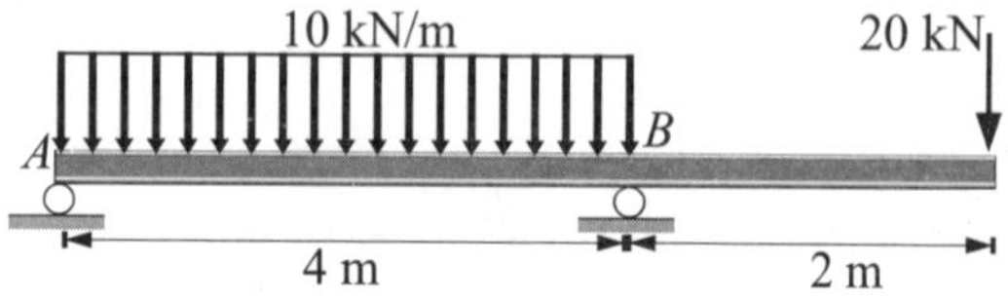

GATE 2015

Solution

Free body diagram of beam is shown in the figure.

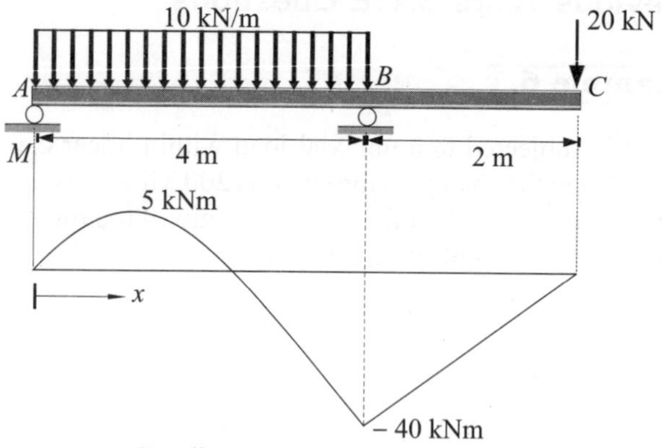

Bending moment diagram

Applying equilibrium equations, we have

$$R_A + R_B = 60\text{ kN} \quad \text{(i)}$$

$$R_B \times 4 - 10 \times 4 \times 2 - 20 \times 6 = 0 \quad \text{(ii)}$$

From equations (i) and (ii), we have

$$R_A = 10\text{ kN and } R_B = 50\text{ kN}$$

Consider portion *AB* ($0 \le x \le 4$)

Bending moment $M = 10x - 5x^2$

Maximum bending moment in portion AB at $x = 1$; $M = 5$ kNm

Consider portion *BC* ($4 \le x \le 6$)

Bending moment $M = 10x - 40(x-2) + 50(x-4)$

$M = 20x - 120$

Maximum bending moment in portion BC at $x = 4$

$M = -40$ kNm

$$M_{max} = 40\text{ kNm (magnitude) at } x = 4\text{ m}$$

Example 6.7

Consider a stepped shaft subjected to a twisting moment applied at B as shown in the figure. Assume shear modulus $G = 77$ GPa. The angle of twist at C (in degrees) is____.

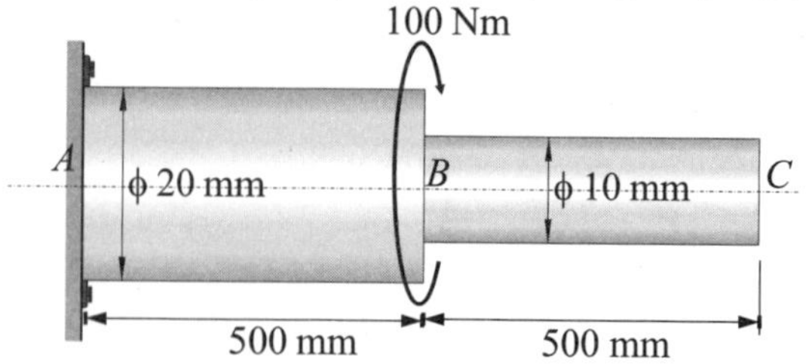

GATE 2015

Solution

Angle of twist $\theta = \frac{Tl}{GJ}$

or $$\theta = \frac{100 \times \frac{500}{1000}}{77 \times 10^9 \times \frac{\pi\left(\frac{20}{1000}\right)^4}{32}} \text{ radians}$$

or $$\theta = 0.0413 \text{ radians}$$

or $$\theta = 0.0413 \times \frac{180}{\pi} \text{ degrees}$$

$$\theta = 2.36 \text{ degrees}$$

Example 6.8

Consider a steel (Young's modulus $E = 200\text{GPa}$) column hinged on both sides. Its height is 1.0 m and cross-section is $10\,\text{mm} \times 20\,\text{mm}$. The lowest Euler critical buckling load (in N) is _______.

GATE 2015

Solution

Euler critical buckling load for column hinged on both ends

$$P_{cr} = \frac{\pi^2 EI}{l^2}$$

or $$P_{cr} = \frac{\pi^2 E\left(\frac{bd^3}{12}\right)}{l^2}$$

or $$P_{cr} = \frac{\pi^2 \times 200 \times 10^9\left(\frac{0.002 \times 0.001^3}{12}\right)}{1^2}$$

$$P_{cr} = 3289\,\text{N}$$

Example 6.9

A cantilever beam with flexural rigidity of $200\,\text{Nm}^2$ is loaded as shown in the figure. The deflection (in mm) at the tip of the beam is _______.

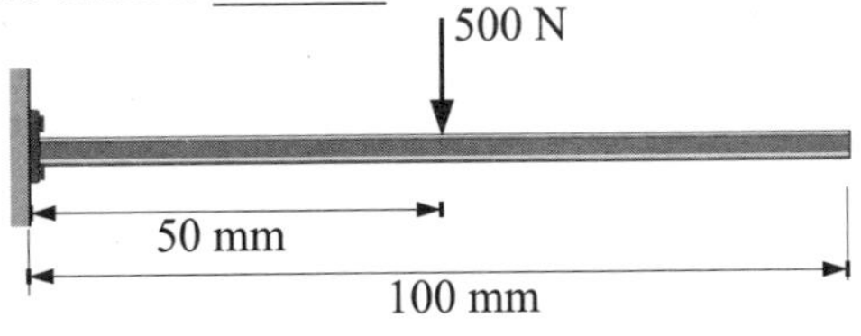

GATE 2015

Solution

Deflection at free end $\Delta = \Delta_1 + \Delta_2$ where $\Delta_1 = \frac{P L_1^3}{3EI}$

and $$\Delta_2 = \theta \times L_2 = \frac{P L_1^3}{2EI} \times L_2$$

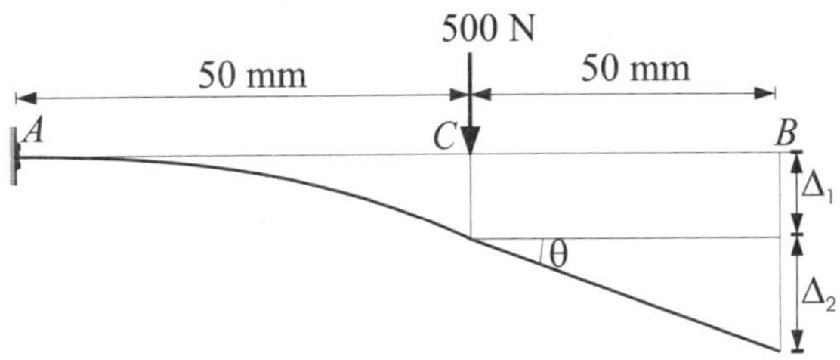

$$\Delta = \frac{P L_1^3}{3EI} + \frac{P L_1^2}{2EI} L_2$$

or $$\Delta = \frac{P}{EI}\left(\frac{L_1^3}{3} + \frac{L_1^2 L_2}{2}\right)$$

or $$\Delta = \frac{500}{200}\left(\frac{0.05^3}{3} + \frac{0.05^3}{2}\right)$$

or $$\Delta = 2.6 \times 10^{-4}\,\text{m}$$

$$\Delta = 0.26 \text{ mm}$$

Example 6.10

The figure below shows a steel rod of 25 mm^2 cross-sectional area. It is loaded at four points, *K*, *L*, *M*, and *N*. Assume $E_{steel} = 200\text{GPa}$. The total change in length of the rod due to loading is

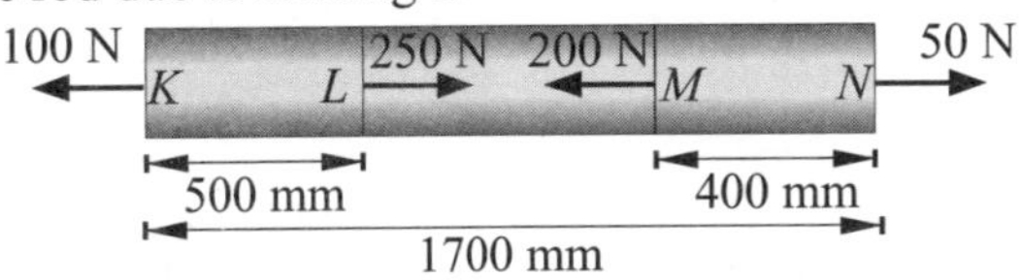

(A) $1.0\mu\text{m}$ (B) $-10.0\mu\text{m}$ (C) $16.0\mu\text{m}$ (D) $-20.0\mu\text{m}$

GATE 2004

Solution

The forces transmitted by cross-sections in intervals *KL*, *LM* and *MN* of the rod shown in figure are obtained by using the free-body diagram shown in figure.

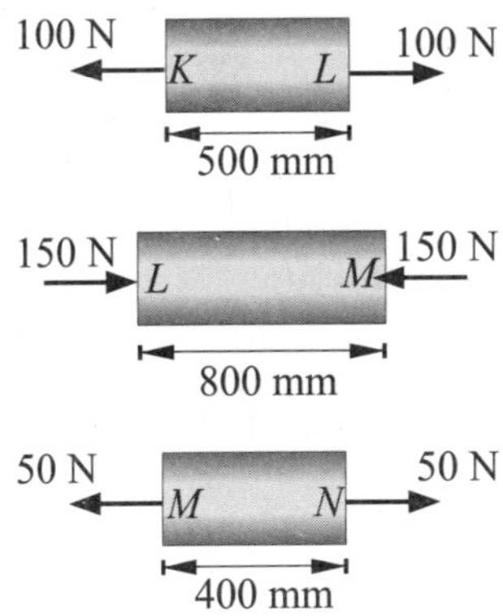

FBD of *KL*, *LM* and *MN*

Applying deformation equation $\Delta = \frac{FL}{AE}$

For segment *KL*, $$\Delta_{KL} = \frac{100\times\frac{500}{1000}}{\frac{25}{(1000)^2}\times 200\times 10^9}$$

$$\Delta_{KL} = 1.0\times 10^{-5}\text{ m}$$

For segment *LM*, $$\Delta_{LM} = -\frac{150\times\frac{800}{1000}}{\frac{25}{(1000)^2}\times 200\times 10^9}$$

$$\Delta_{LM} = -2.4\times 10^{-5}\text{ m}$$

For segment *MN*, $$\Delta_{MN} = \frac{50\times\frac{400}{1000}}{\frac{25}{(1000)^2}\times 200\times 10^9}$$

$$\Delta_{MN} = 0.4\times 10^{-5}\text{ m}$$

Thus, total change in length

$$\Delta = 1.0\times 10^{-5} - 2.4\times 10^{-5} + 0.4\times 10^{-5}\text{ m}$$

$$\Delta = -10\mu\text{m}$$

Example 6.11

A $200\times 100\times 50\text{ mm}^3$ steel block is subjected to a hydrostatic pressure of 15 MPa.

The Young's modulus and poisson's ratio of the material are 200 GPa and 0.3 respectively. The change in the volume of the block in mm^3 is

(A) 85 (B) 90 (C) 100 (D) 110

GATE 2007

Solution

Bulk modulus, $$K = \frac{\text{Normal stress}}{\text{Volumetric strain}} = \frac{p}{\frac{\Delta V}{V}}$$

or $$\Delta V = \frac{pV}{K}$$

Relation between bulk modulus, *K* and Young's modulus, *E* is given by $E = 3K(1-2v)$

Hence,

$$\Delta V = \frac{pV}{\frac{E}{3(1-2v)}} = \frac{3pV(1-2v)}{E}$$

Substituting given data, gives

$$\Delta V = \frac{3\times 15\times 10^6\times 200\times 100\times 50\times 10^{-9}(1-2\times 0.3)}{200\times 10^9}$$

or $$\Delta V = 9\times 10^{-8}\text{ m}^3$$

Change in volume $\Delta V = 90\text{ mm}^3$

Example 6.12

In a simply-supported beam loaded as shown below, the maximum bending moment in Nm is

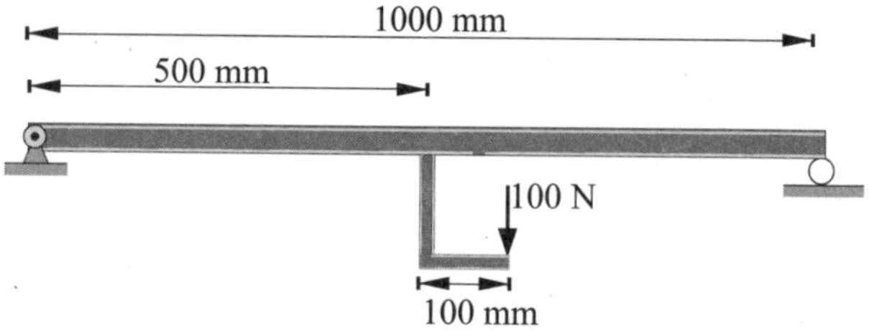

(A) 25 (B) 30 (C) 35 (D) 60

GATE 2007

Solution

By transferring a load 100 N by a force 100 N and a moment 10 Nm. We draw free body diagram of beam as shown in figure and applying equation of equilibrium, we have

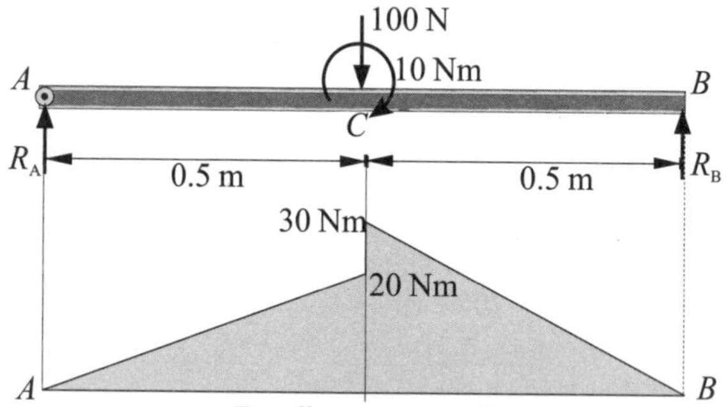

Bending moment diagram

$\sum F_y = 0,\quad R_A + R_B = 100\text{ N}$

$\sum M_A = 0,\quad R_B\times 1 - 100\times 0.5 - 10 = 0$

From which $R_A = 40$ N and $R_B = 60$ N

Consider segment *AC* ($0 < x < 0.5$) of beam

Bending moment $M_x = R_A x$; $0 < x < 0.5$

$M_x = 40x$

Consider segment *CB* ($0.5 < x < 1$) of beam

Bending moment $M_x = R_A x + 10 - 100(x - 0.5)$; $(0.5 < x < 1)$

$$M_x = 60 - 60x$$

Bending moment at $x = (0.5-0)$; $M_x = 40\times 0.5 = 20\text{ Nm}$

$x = (0.5+0)$; $M_x = 60 - 60\times 0.5 = 30\text{ Nm}$

Maximum bending moment $M_{max} = 30\text{ Nm}$

Example 6.13

A uniformly loaded propped cantilever beam and its free body diagram are shown below. The reactions are:

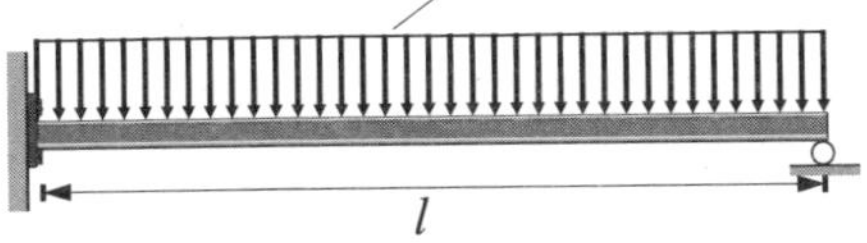

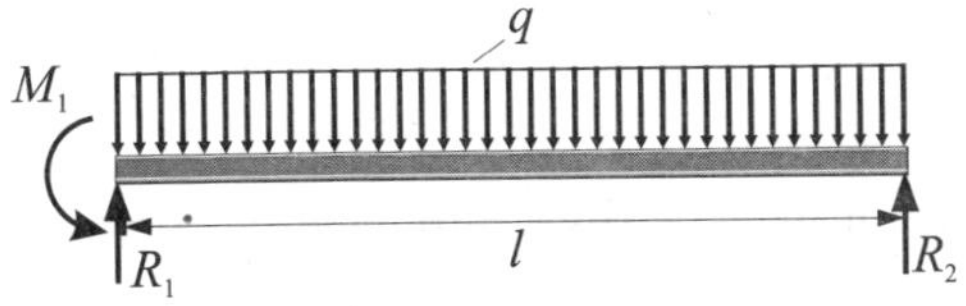

(A) $R_1 = \frac{5ql}{8}, R_2 = \frac{3ql}{8}, M_1 = \frac{ql^2}{8}$

(B) $R_1 = \frac{3ql}{8}, R_2 = \frac{5ql}{8}, M_1 = \frac{ql^2}{8}$

(C) $R_1 = \frac{5ql}{8}, R_2 = \frac{3ql}{8}, M_1 = 0$

(D) $R_1 = \frac{3ql}{8}, R_2 = \frac{5ql}{8}, M_1 = 0$

GATE 2007

Solution

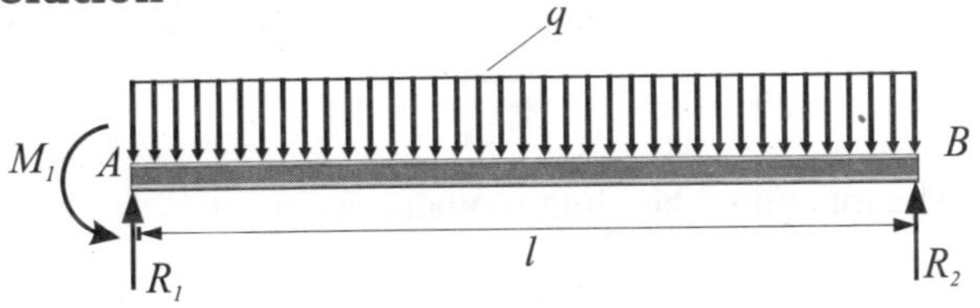

Applying equilibrium equations

$$\sum F_V = 0 \quad \Rightarrow \quad R_1 + R_2 = ql \qquad \text{(i)}$$

$$\sum M_A = 0 \quad \Rightarrow \quad R_2 \times l + M_1 - ql\frac{l}{2} = 0 \qquad \text{(ii)}$$

Deflection at free end $= 0 \Rightarrow \frac{ql^4}{8EI} - \frac{R_2 l^3}{3EI} = 0$

$$R_2 = \frac{3ql}{8} \qquad \text{(iii)}$$

Solving equation (i), (ii) and (iii), we obtain

$$R_1 = \frac{5ql}{8}, R_2 = \frac{3ql}{8}, M_1 = \frac{ql^2}{8}$$

Example 6.14

A simply supported beam of length L is subjected to a varying distributed load $\sin\left(\frac{3\pi x}{L}\right)$ N/m, where the distance x is measured from the left support. The magnitude of the vertical reaction force in Newton at the left support is

(A) Zero (B) $\frac{L}{3\pi}$ (C) $\frac{L}{\pi}$ (D) $\frac{2L}{\pi}$

GATE 2013

Solution

Figure shows free body diagram of varying load beam. Applying the equilibrium equation.

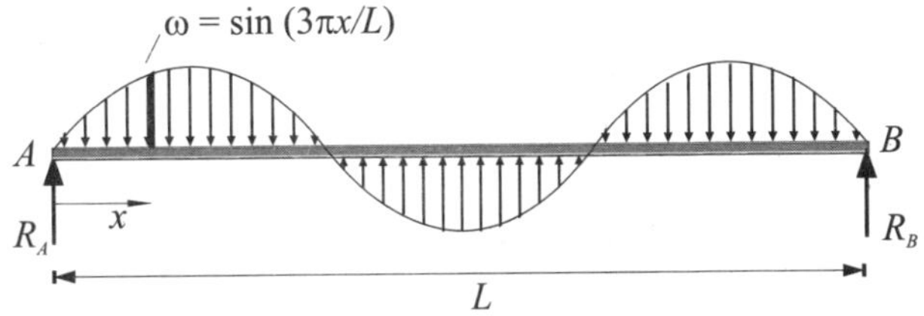

$$\sum M_A = 0 \quad \Rightarrow \quad R_B \times L = \int_0^L \omega dx \times x$$

$$R_B = \frac{1}{L}\int_0^L x \sin\left(\frac{3\pi x}{L}\right) dx$$

Solving integration, we obtain

$$R_B = \frac{L}{3\pi}$$

Due to symmetric loading; $R_B = R_A = \frac{L}{3\pi}$

$$R_A = \frac{L}{3\pi}$$

Example 6.15

Consider the signboard mounting shown in figure given below. The wind load acting perpendicular to the plane of the figure is $F = 100$ N. We wish to limit the deflection, due to bending, at point A of the hollow cylindrical pole of outer diameter 150 mm to 5 mm. Find the wall thickness for the pole. Assume 2.0×10^{11} N/m^2.

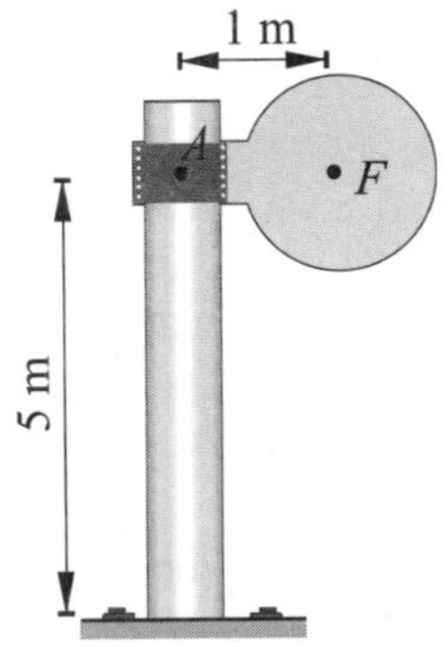

GATE 1999

Solution

Let t be the wall thickness of pole.

Inner diameter of hollow cylinder $d = (150 - 2t)$ mm

Deflection at A due to point load F is

$$\delta = \frac{Fl^3}{3EI}$$

Substituting given data, gives

$$\frac{5}{1000} = \frac{100 \times 5^3}{3 \times 2.0 \times 10^{11} \times I}$$

$$I = 416.66 \times 10^{-8}\ \text{m}^4$$

or $$\frac{\pi}{64}[150^4 - (150-2t)^4] = 416.66 \times 10^4\ \text{mm}^4$$

From which

$$t = 3.36\ \text{mm}$$

Example 6.16

A triangular shaped cantilever beam of uniform thickness is shown in the figure. The Young's modulus of the materials of the beam is E. A concentrated load P is applied at the free end of the beam.

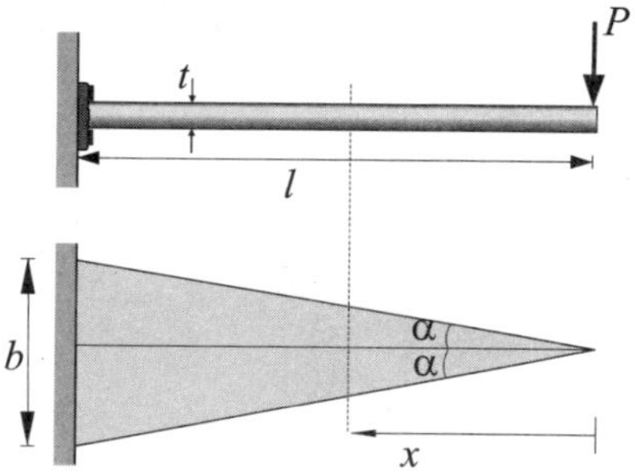

(a) The area moment of inertia about the neural axis of a cross-section at a distance x measure from the free end is

(A) $\frac{bxt^3}{6l}$ (B) $\frac{bxt^3}{24l}$ (C) $\frac{bxt^3}{12l}$ (D) $\frac{xt^3}{12}$

(b) The maximum deflection of the beam is

(A) $\frac{24Pl^3}{Ebt^3}$ (B) $\frac{8Pl^3}{Ebt^3}$ (C) $\frac{12Pl^3}{Ebt^3}$ (D) $\frac{6Pl^3}{Ebt^3}$

GATE 2011

Solution

(a) Let b_x be the width of beam at x-x.

$$\frac{b_x}{x} = \frac{b}{l} \Rightarrow b_x = \frac{b}{l}x$$

Area moment of inertia about the neutral axis is

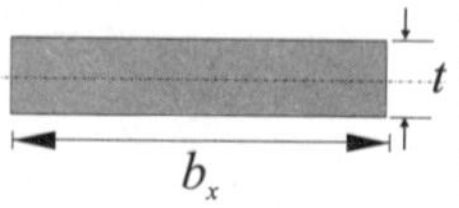

$$I_x = \frac{b_x t^3}{12} = \frac{\left(\frac{b}{l}x\right)t^3}{12}$$

$$I_x = \frac{bxt^3}{12l}$$

(b) Bending moment at x-x, $M_x = Px$

Strain energy due to bending is

$$U = \int_0^l \frac{M_x^2 dx}{2EI_x}$$

or $$U = \int_0^l \frac{(Px)^2 dx}{2E \times \left(\frac{bxt^3}{12l}\right)}$$

or $$U = 3\frac{P^2l^3}{Ebt^3}$$

Deflection of free end (by Castigliano's theorem)

$$\Delta = \frac{\partial U}{\partial P} = \frac{\partial}{\partial P}\left(3\frac{P^2l^3}{Ebt^3}\right)$$

$$\Delta = \frac{6Pl^3}{Ebt^3}$$

Example 6.17

A massless beam has a loading pattern as shown in figure. The beam is of rectangular cross-section with a width of 30 mm and height of 100 mm.

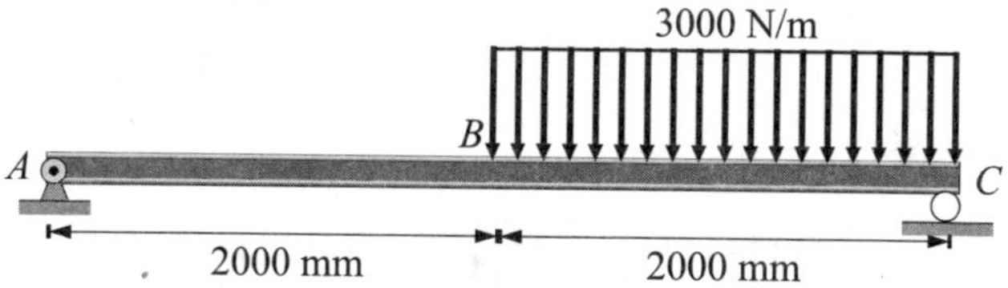

(a) The maximum bending moment occurs at

(A) Location B

(B) 2675 mm to the right of A

(C) 2500 mm to the right of A

(D) 3225 mm to the right of A

(b) The maximum magnitude of bending stress (in MPa) is given by

(A) 60.0 (B) 67.5 (C) 200.0 (D) 225.0

GATE 2010

Solution

(a) The free body diagram of the beam is shown in figure. The reaction at support A and C are determined by using the equilibrium equation

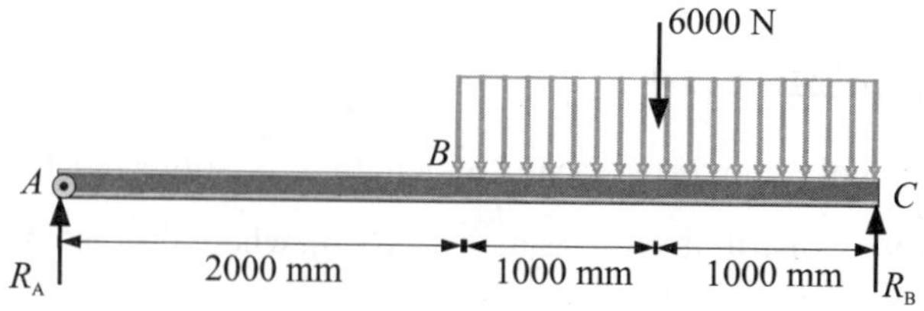

$$\sum M_A = 0 \Rightarrow R_B \times 4 - 3000 \times 2 \times 3 = 0$$

$$R_C = 4500\,\text{N}$$

$$\sum F_V = 0 \quad \Rightarrow \quad R_A + R_C = 6000$$

or $$R_A + 4500 = 6000$$

$$R_A = 1500\,\text{N}$$

Consider segment *AB* ($0 < x < 2000$)

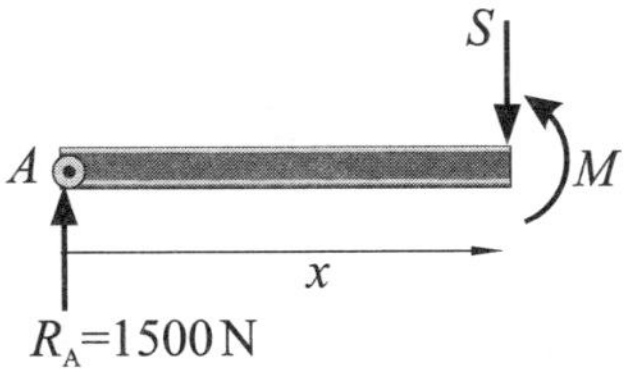

Figure shows the free body diagram of segment of length x ($0 < x < 2000$)

Applying equilibrium equations, we have

$$\sum F_y = 0 \Rightarrow 1500 - S = 0$$

Shear force $S = 1500$ N (i)

$$\sum M = 0 \Rightarrow 1500x - M = 0$$

Bending moment $M = 1500\,x$ (ii)

Consider segment *BC* ($2000 < x < 4000$)

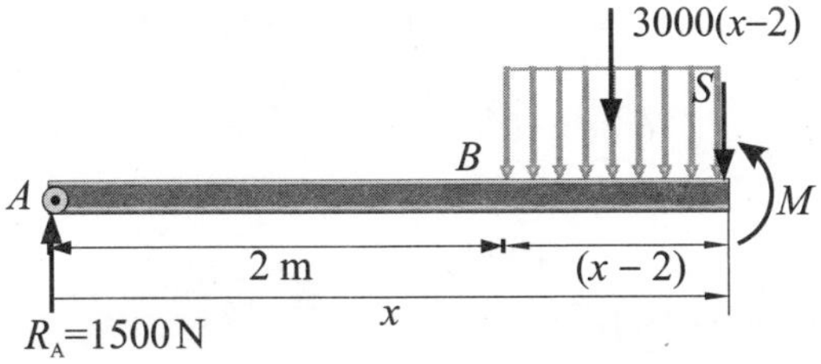

Figure shows the free body diagram of segment of length x ($2000 < x < 4000$)

Applying equilibrium equations, we have

$$\sum F_y = 0 \Rightarrow 1500 - 3000(x-2) - S = 0$$

Shear force $S = (7500 - 3000x)$ N (iii)

$$\sum M = 0 \Rightarrow 1500x - \frac{3000(x-2)^2}{2} - M = 0$$

Bending moment

$$M = 1500x - \frac{3000(x-2)^2}{2} \qquad \text{(iv)}$$

Maximum bending occurs where shear force is zero. [Refer Equation (iii)]

$$S = (7500 - 3000x) = 0$$

or $$x = 2.5\,\text{m} \qquad \Rightarrow \quad x = 2500\,\text{mm}$$

The maximum bending moment occurs at 2500 mm to the right of A

(b) Maximum bending moment

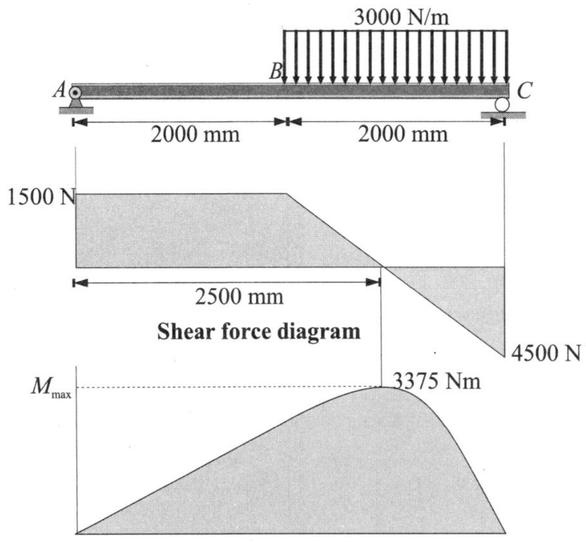

Shear force diagram

Bending moment diagram

$$M_{\max} = \left[1500x - \frac{3000(x-2)^2}{2}\right]_{x=2.5}$$

$$M_{\max} = \left[1500 \times 2.5 - \frac{3000(2.5-2)^2}{2}\right]$$

$$M_{\max} = 3375\,\text{Nm}$$

Maximum bending stress is

$$\sigma_{\max} = \frac{M_{\max}}{I} y_{\max} = \frac{M_{\max}}{\frac{bd^3}{12}} \times \frac{d}{2}$$

or $$\sigma_{\max} = \frac{6M_{\max}}{bd^2}$$

or $$\sigma_{max} = \frac{6 \times 3375}{\frac{30}{1000} \times \left(\frac{100}{1000}\right)^2}\,\text{N/m}^2$$

$$\sigma_{max} = 67.5\,\text{MPa}$$

Example 6.18

For the component loaded with a force F as shown in the figure, the axial stress at the corner point P is

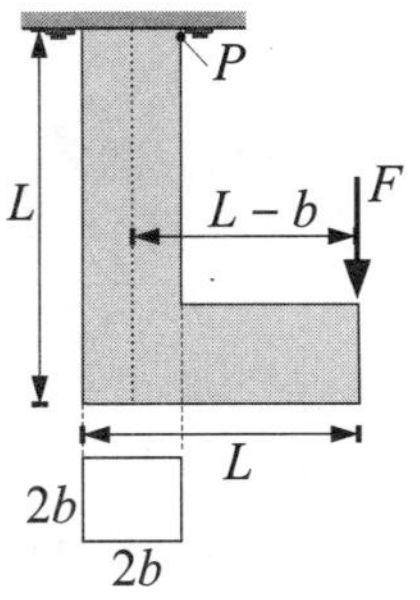

(A) $\dfrac{F(3L-b)}{4b^3}$ (B) $\dfrac{F(3L+b)}{4b^3}$

(C) $\dfrac{F(3L+4b)}{4b^3}$ (D) $\dfrac{F(3L-2b)}{4b^3}$

GATE 2008

Solution

Axial stress at P = Bending stress (σ_b) + Direct stress (σ_d)

Direct stress $\sigma_d = \dfrac{F}{A} = \dfrac{F}{2b \times 2b}$

$$\sigma_d = \frac{F}{4b^2} \quad \text{(Tensile stress)}$$

Bending stress $\sigma_b = \dfrac{M}{I} y$ (Tensile stress)

Substituting $M = F(L-b)$, $I = \dfrac{2b(2b)^3}{12} = \dfrac{4}{3}b^4$ and $y = \dfrac{2b}{2}$, we have

$$\sigma_b = \frac{F(L-b)}{\frac{4}{3}b^4} \times b$$

or $$\sigma_b = \frac{3F(L-b)}{4b^3}$$

Thus,

Axial stress at P is $$\sigma = \frac{3F(L-b)}{4b^3} + \frac{F}{4b^2}$$

$$\sigma = \frac{F(3L-2b)}{4b^3}$$

Example 6.19

A cylindrical container of radius $R = 1$ m, wall thickness 1 mm is filled with water up to a depth of 2 m and suspended along its upper rim. The density of water is 1000 kg/m^3 and acceleration due to gravity is 10 m/s^2. The self-weight of the cylinder is negligible. The formula for hoop stress in a thin-walled cylinder can be used at all points along the height of the cylindrical container.

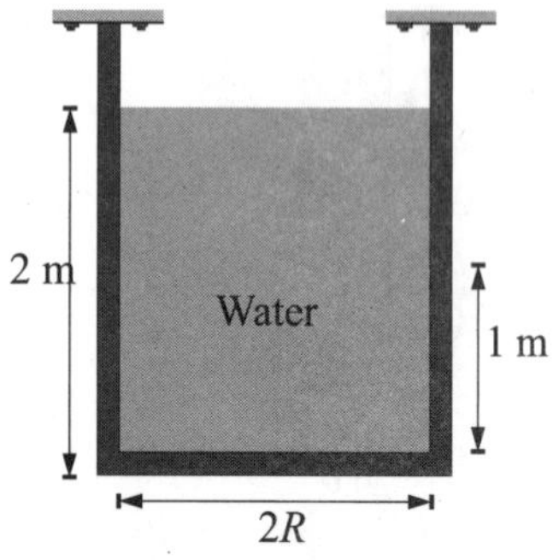

(a) The axial and circumferential stress (σ_a, σ_c) experienced by the cylinder wall at mid-depth (1m as shown) are

(A) (10,10) MPa (B) (5,10) MPa

(C) (10,5) MPa (D) (5,5) MPa

(b) If the Young's modulus and poisson's ratio of the container material are 100GPa and 0.3, respectively, the axial strain in the cylinder wall at mid-depth is

(A) 2×10^{-5} (B) 6×10^{-5}

(C) 7×10^{-5} (D) 1.2×10^{-4}

GATE 2008

Solution

(a) Pressure at depth 1 m from free surface of water is

$$P = \rho g h = 1000 \times 10 \times 1$$
$$P = 1 \times 10^4 \text{ N/m}^2$$

Weight of water, $W = rgAH = 1000 \times 10 \times \dfrac{\pi}{4}(2)^2 \times 2$

$$W = 6.28 \times 10^4 \text{N}$$

Therefore, axial stress (longitudinal stress) $\sigma_a = \dfrac{W}{\pi d t}$

$$\sigma_a = \frac{6.28 \times 10^4}{\pi \times 2 \times \frac{1}{1000}}$$

or $$\sigma_a = 1 \times 10^7 \text{N/m}^2$$

$$\sigma_a = 10 \text{ MPa}$$

Circumferential stress (hoop stress) is given by

$$\sigma_c = \frac{Pd}{2t}$$

$$\sigma_c = \frac{1 \times 10^4 \times 2 \times 1}{2 \times \frac{1}{1000}}$$

$$\sigma_c = 10 \text{ MPa}$$

(*b*) Axial strain of cylinder at mid depth is

$$\varepsilon_a = \frac{\sigma_a}{E} - \nu \frac{\sigma_c}{E}$$

or $$\varepsilon_a = \frac{10 \times 10^6}{100 \times 10^9} - 0.3 \frac{10 \times 10^6}{100 \times 10^9}$$

$$\varepsilon_a = 7 \times 10^{-5}$$

Example 6.20

A torque T is applied at the free end of a stepped rod of circular cross-sections as shown in the figure. The shear modulus of the material of the rod is G. The expression of d to produce an angular twist θ at the free end is

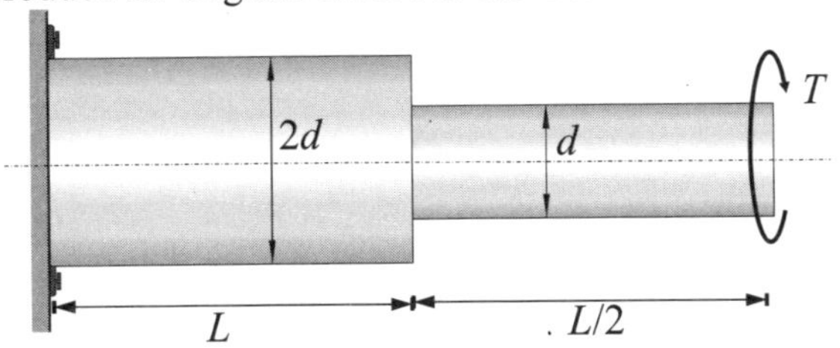

(A) $\left(\dfrac{32TL}{\pi\theta G}\right)^{\frac{1}{4}}$ (B) $\left(\dfrac{16TL}{\pi\theta G}\right)^{\frac{1}{4}}$

(C) $\left(\dfrac{18TL}{\pi\theta G}\right)^{\frac{1}{4}}$ (D) $\left(\dfrac{2TL}{\pi\theta G}\right)^{\frac{1}{4}}$

GATE 2011

Solution

Angle of twist, $\theta = \theta_1 + \theta_2$

Angle of twist for part I, $\theta_1 = \dfrac{T_1 l_1}{G_1 J_1} = \dfrac{T \times \dfrac{L}{2}}{G \times \dfrac{\pi d^4}{32}}$

$$\theta_1 = \frac{16TL}{\pi G d^4}$$

Angle of twist for part II, $\theta_2 = \dfrac{T_2 l_2}{G_2 J_2} = \dfrac{T \times L}{G \times \dfrac{\pi (2d)^4}{32}}$

$$\theta_2 = \frac{2TL}{\pi G d^4}$$

From which

$$\theta = \theta_1 + \theta_2 = \frac{16TL}{\pi G d^4} + \frac{2TL}{\pi G d^4}$$

or $\theta = \dfrac{18TL}{\pi G d^4}$

$$d = \left(\frac{18TL}{\pi G \theta}\right)^{\frac{1}{4}}$$

Example 6.21

A solid shaft of diameter, d and length, L is fixed at both the ends. A torque, T_0 is applied at a distance $L/4$ from the left end as shown in the figure given below.

The maximum shear stress in the shaft is

(A) $\dfrac{16T_0}{\pi d^3}$ (B) $\dfrac{12T_0}{\pi d^3}$ (C) $\dfrac{8T_0}{\pi d^3}$ (D) $\dfrac{4T_0}{\pi d^3}$

GATE 2009

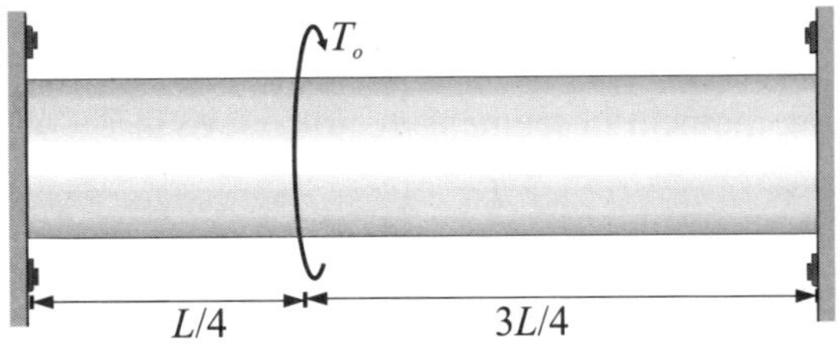

Solution

Let T_A and T_B be the torque reactions at fixed ends. Equilibrium equations are

$$T_A + T_B = T_0 \quad \text{(i)}$$

Angle of twist, $\theta = \dfrac{T_A \times \dfrac{L}{4}}{GJ} = \dfrac{T_B \times \dfrac{3L}{4}}{GJ}$

$$3T_B = T_A \quad \text{(ii)}$$

From Equations (i) and (ii), we obtain

$$T_A = \frac{T_0}{4} \text{ and } T_B = \frac{3T_0}{4} \quad \leftarrow T_{max}$$

Maximum shear stress $\tau_{max} = \dfrac{T_{max}}{J} \times r$

$$\tau_{max} = \frac{\dfrac{3T_0}{4}}{\dfrac{\pi d^4}{32}} \times \frac{d}{2}$$

$$\tau_{max} = \frac{12T_0}{\pi d^3}$$

Example 6.22

The strain energy stored in the beam with flexural rigidity EI and loaded as shown in the figure is

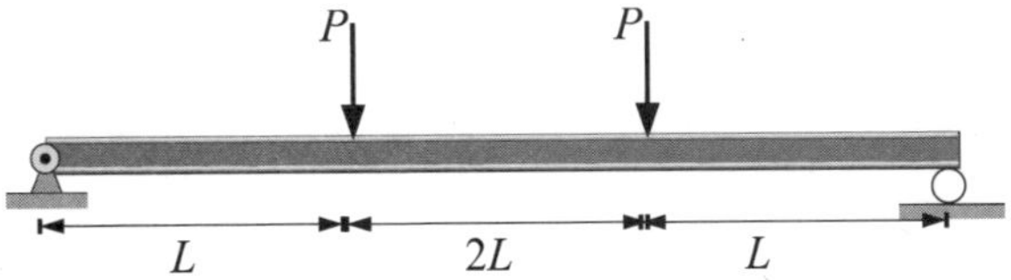

(A) $\dfrac{P^2 L^3}{3EI}$ (B) $\dfrac{2P^2 L^3}{3EI}$

(C) $\dfrac{4P^2 L^3}{3EI}$ (D) $\dfrac{8P^2 L^3}{3EI}$

GATE 2008

Solution

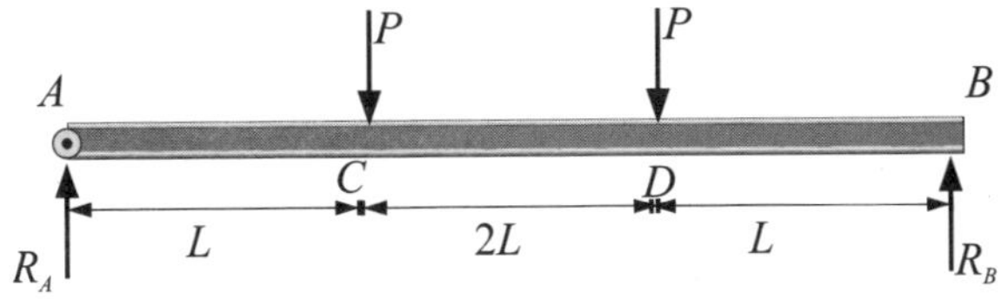

Reactions at supports

$$R_A = R_B = P$$

Bending moment in segment AC ($0 < x < L$) is

$$M = Px; \qquad 0 < x < L$$

Bending moment in segment CD ($L < x < 3L$) is

$$M = Px - P(x - L) = PL; \qquad L < x < 3L$$

Bending moment in segment DB ($3L < x < 4L$) is

$$M = Px - P(x - L) - P(x - 2L)$$

$$M = P(2L - x); \; 3L < x < 4L$$

Strain energy stored in beam is

$$U = \int_0^L \frac{M^2 dx}{2EI} + \int_L^{3L} \frac{M^2 dx}{2EI} + \int_{3L}^{4L} \frac{M^2 dx}{2EI}$$

or $$U = \int_0^L \frac{(Px)^2 dx}{2EI} + \int_L^{3L} \frac{(PL)^2 dx}{2EI} + \int_{3L}^{4L} \frac{[P(2L - x]^2 dx}{2EI}$$

or $$U = \frac{P^2L^3}{6EI} + \frac{2P^2L^3}{2EI} + \frac{P^2L^3}{6EI}$$

$$U = \frac{4}{3}\frac{P^2L^3}{EI}$$

Example 6.23

The rod PQ of length L and with flexural rigidity EI is hinged at both ends. For what minimum force F is it expected to buckle?

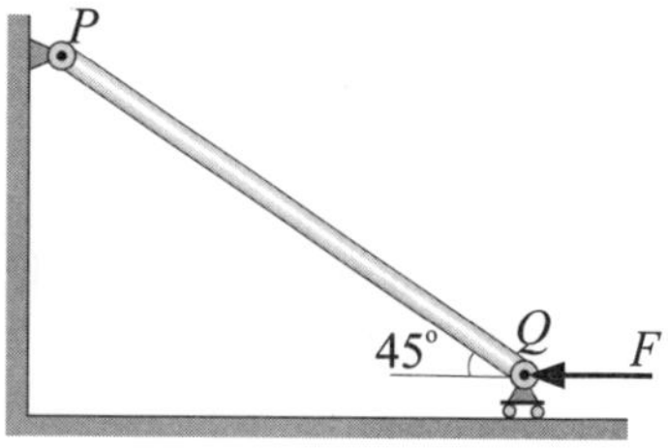

(A) $\frac{\pi^2 EI}{L^2}$ (B) $\frac{\sqrt{2}\pi^2 EI}{L^2}$ (C) $\frac{\pi^2 EI}{\sqrt{2}L^2}$ (D) $\frac{\pi^2 EI}{2L^2}$

GATE 2008

Solution

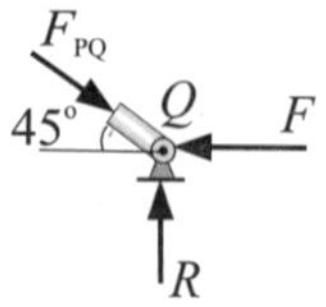

Consider the joint Q.

Free body diagram of joint Q is shown in figure.

Summing forces along x-direction.

$$F_{PQ}\cos 45 - F = 0$$

or $$F_{PQ} = \sqrt{2}F$$

Critical load (Euler load) for the column with pinned ends is

$$P_{cr} = \frac{\pi^2 EI}{L^2} = \sqrt{2}F$$

$$F = \frac{\pi^2 EI}{\sqrt{2}L^2}$$

Example 6.24

A solid steel cube constructed on all six faces is heated so that the temperature rises uniformly by ΔT. If the thermal coefficient of the material is α. Young's modulus is E and the poissons's ratio is ν, the thermal stress developed in the cube due to heating is

(A) $-\frac{\alpha(\Delta T)E}{(1-2\nu)}$ (B) $-\frac{3\alpha(\Delta T)E}{(1-2\nu)}$

(C) $-\frac{2\alpha(\Delta T)E}{(1-2\nu)}$ (D) $-\frac{\alpha(\Delta T)E}{3(1-2\nu)}$

GATE 2012

Solution

Thermal strain of each side of cube

$$\frac{\Delta l}{l} = \alpha\Delta T \qquad \text{(i)}$$

Let σ be the stress developed in the cube.

Strain $$\frac{\Delta l}{l} = \frac{\sigma}{E} - \nu\frac{\sigma}{E} - \nu\frac{\sigma}{E}$$

$$\frac{\Delta l}{l} = \frac{\sigma}{E}(1 - 2\nu) \qquad \text{(ii)}$$

From Equations (i) and (ii), we obtain

$$\alpha\Delta T = \frac{\sigma}{E}(1 - 2\nu)$$

or $$\sigma = \frac{E\alpha\Delta T}{(1 - 2\nu)} \qquad \text{compression}$$

$$\sigma = -\frac{E\alpha\Delta T}{(1 - 2\nu)}$$

Example 6.25

In the figure, the load P = 1 N, length L = 1 m, Young's modulus E = 70 GPa, and the cross-section of the links is a square with dimension 10 mm × 10 mm. All joints are pin joints. The stress (in Pa) in the link AB is ___________.

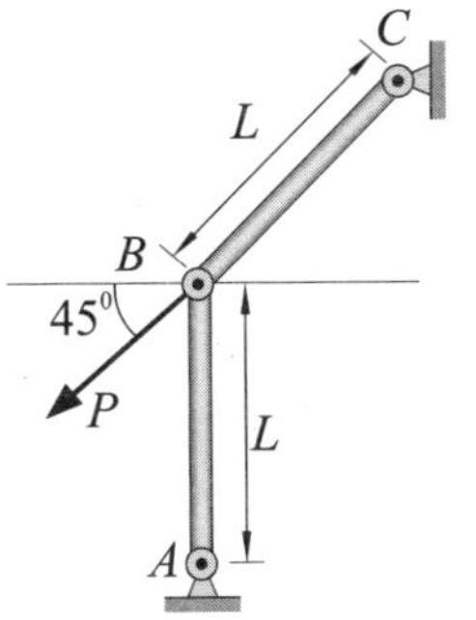

(Indicate compressive stress by a negative sign and tensile stress by a positive sign.)

GATE 2016

Solution

Consider the joint B.

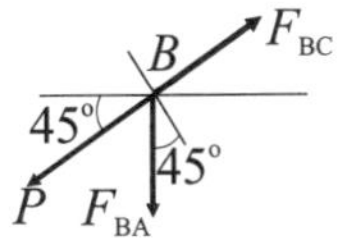

$$F_{BA}\cos 45 = 0 \quad \Rightarrow \quad F_{BA} = 0$$

$$F_{BC} - F_{BA}\sin 45 - P = 0$$

$$F_{BC} = P$$

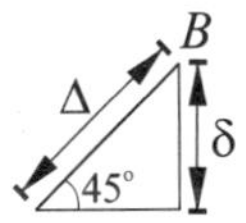

Extension of link BC; $\Delta = \dfrac{F_{BC}L}{AE} = \dfrac{PL}{AE}$

Contraction of link AB; $\delta = \Delta\sin 45 = \dfrac{1}{\sqrt{2}}\dfrac{PL}{AE}$

Stress in link AB; $\sigma_{AB} = \dfrac{E\delta}{L} = \dfrac{E}{L}\times\dfrac{1}{\sqrt{2}}\dfrac{PL}{AE} = \dfrac{P}{\sqrt{2}A}$

$$\sigma_{AB} = \frac{1}{\sqrt{2}\times\dfrac{10}{1000}\times\dfrac{10}{1000}} \text{ (Compressive)}$$

$$\sigma_{AB} = -7071.06 \text{ N/m}^2$$

Example 6.26

The cross-sections of two hollow bars made of the same material are concentric circles as shown in the figure. It is given that $r_3 > r_1$ and $r_4 > r_2$, and that the areas of the cross-sections are the same. J_1 and J_2 are the torsional rigidities of the bars on the left and right, respectively. The ratio $\dfrac{J_2}{J_1}$ is

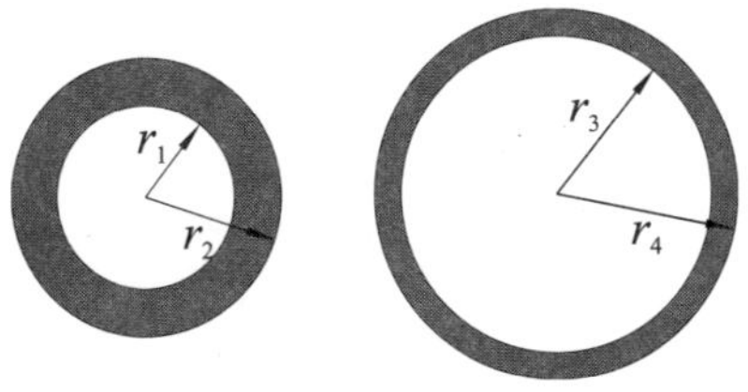

(A) >1 (B) < 0.5

(C) $=1$ (D) Between 0.5 and 1

GATE 2016

Solution

Cross-sectional area $A_1 = A_2$

$$\pi(r_2^2 - r_1^2) = \pi(r_4^2 - r_3^2)$$

or

$$(r_2^2 - r_1^2) = (r_4^2 - r_3^2)$$

Torsional rigidity ratio

$$= \frac{J_2}{J_1} = \left(\frac{GI_P}{l}\right)_2 \Big/ \left(\frac{GI_P}{l}\right)_1 = \frac{I_{P2}}{I_{P1}}$$

$$\frac{J_2}{J_1} = \frac{\frac{\pi}{2}(r_4^4 - r_3^4)}{\frac{\pi}{2}(r_2^4 - r_1^4)} = \frac{(r_4^2 - r_3^2)\times(r_4^2 + r_3^2)}{(r_2^2 - r_1^2)\times(r_2^2 + r_1^2)} = \frac{(r_4^2 + r_3^2)}{(r_2^2 + r_1^2)}$$

But $r_3 > r_1$ and $r_4 > r_2$; $\dfrac{(r_4^2 + r_3^2)}{(r_2^2 + r_1^2)} > 1$

Thus,

$$\frac{J_2}{J_1} > 1$$

Example 6.27

A cantilever beam having square cross-section of side a is subjected to an end load. If a is increased by 19%, the tip deflection decreases approximately by

(A) 19% (B) 29% (C) 41% (D) 50%

GATE 2016

Solution

The deflection of end of cantilever beam $\delta = \dfrac{PL^3}{3EI}$

$$\delta = \frac{PL^3}{3E\left(\dfrac{a\times a^3}{12}\right)} = \frac{4PL^3}{Ea^4}$$

Side a is increased by 19%. The deflection is

$$\delta' = \frac{4PL^3}{E(1.19a)^4} = 0.5\frac{4PL^3}{Ea^4}$$

$$\delta' = (1 - 0.5)\delta$$

Deflection decreases by 50%

Example 6.28

A horizontal bar with a constant cross-section is subjected to loading as shown in the figure. The Young's moduli for the sections AB and BC are $3E$ and E, respectively. For the deflection at C to be zero, the ratio P/F is ________.

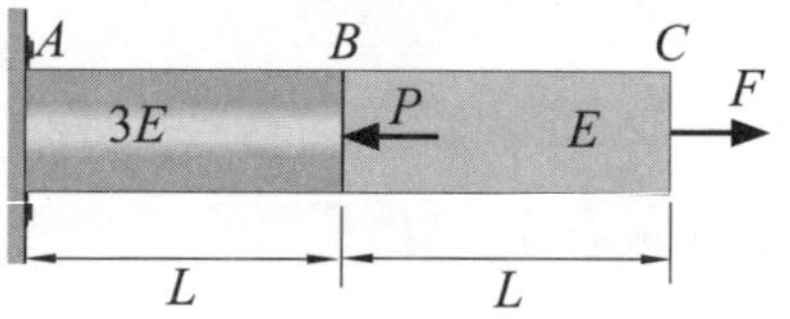

GATE 2016

Solution

The free-body diagram of bar AB and BC are shown in figure.

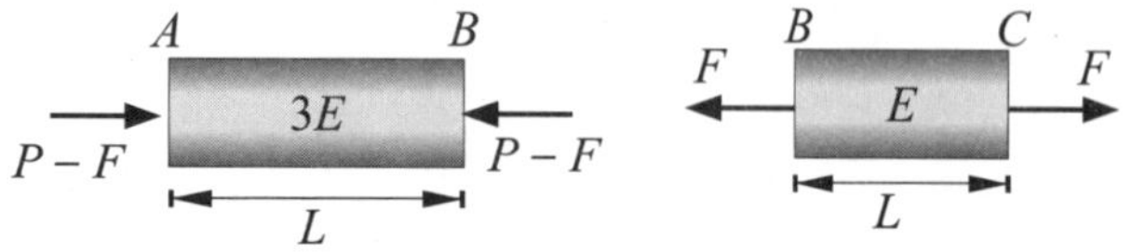

Compression Tension

Net deflection C = Deflection of BC (extension) – Deflection of AB (compression)

Net deflection at C, $\dfrac{FL}{AE} - \dfrac{(P-F)L}{A \times 3E} = 0$

$$\frac{P}{F} = 4$$

Example 6.29

The figure shows cross-section of a beam subjected to bending. The area moment of inertia (in mm^4) of this cross-section about its base is _____.

GATE 2016

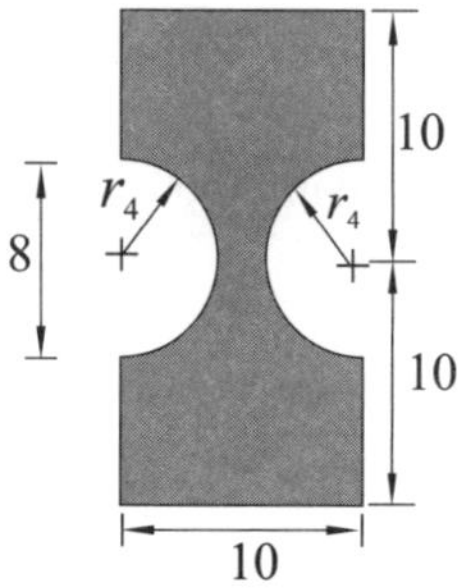

All dimensions are in mm

Solution

Moment of inertia about centroidal axis

$$I_G = \frac{bd^3}{12} - \frac{\pi r^4}{4}$$

Area of cross-section, $A = bd - \pi r^2$

Applying parallel axis theorem,

Moment of area about its base parallel to centroidal axis,

$$I_o = I_G + Ah^2$$

$$I_o = \left(\frac{bd^3}{12} - \frac{\pi r^4}{4}\right) + (bd - \pi r^2)\left(\frac{d}{2}\right)^2$$

Substituting $b = 10$ mm, $d = 20$ mm and $r = 4$ mm

$$I_o = \left(\frac{10 \times 20^3}{12} - \frac{\pi \times 4^4}{4}\right) + (10 \times 20 - \pi \times 4^2)\left(\frac{20}{2}\right)^2$$

$$I_o = 21439.06 \text{ mm}^4$$

Example 6.30

A simply-supported beam of length $3L$ is subjected to the loading shown in the figure.

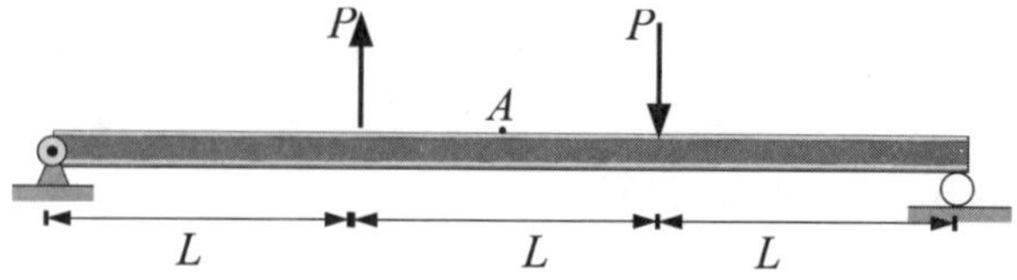

It is given that $P = 1$ N, $L = 1$ m and Young's modulus E = 200 GPa. The cross-section is a square with dimension 10 mm × 10 mm. The bending stress (in Pa) at the point A located at the top surface of the beam at a distance of 1.5 L from the left end is _________.

(Indicate compressive stress by a negative sign and tensile stress by a positive sign.)

GATE 2016

Solution

Let R_c and R_D be the reactions at supports C and D.

$$\sum M = 0 \quad \Rightarrow R_C \times 3L - P \times 2L + P \times L = 0$$

$$R_C = \frac{P}{3}$$

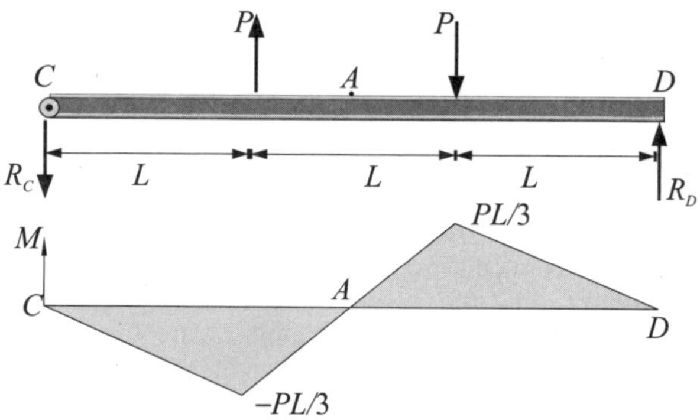

Bending moment diagram

Bending moment diagram is shown in figure.

Bending moment at A; $M_A = \dfrac{P}{3} \times \dfrac{3L}{2} - \dfrac{PL}{2}$

$$M_A = 0$$

Bending stress at A; $\sigma_A = \dfrac{M_A y}{I} = \dfrac{0 \times y}{I}$

$$\sigma_A = 0$$

Example 6.31

A shaft with a circular cross-section is subjected to pure twisting moment. The ratio of the maximum shear stress to the largest principal stress is

(A) 2.0 (B) 1.0 (C) 0.5 (D) 0

GATE 2016

Solution

Let T be the twisting moment.

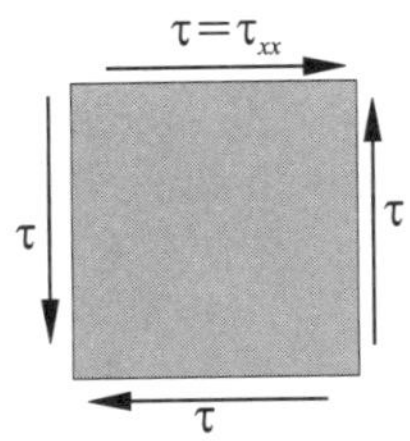

Maximum shear stress,

$$\tau = \frac{T}{J} r_{\max} = \frac{16T}{\pi d^3}$$

Principle stresses

$$\sigma_{1,2} = \frac{\sigma_x + \sigma_y}{2} \pm \sqrt{\left(\frac{\sigma_y - \sigma_x}{2}\right)^2 + \tau_{xy}^2}$$

Substituting $\sigma_x = \sigma_y = 0$ and $\tau_{xy} = \tau$, we have

Largest principle stress $\sigma_{\max} = \tau$

$$\frac{\tau}{\sigma_{\max}} = 1$$

Example 6.32

A thin cylindrical pressure vessel with closed-ends is subjected to internal pressure. The ratio of circumferential (hoop) stress to the longitudinal stress is

(A) 0.25 (B) 0.50 (C) 1.0 (D) 2.0

GATE 2016

Solution

Let P, d and t be the pressure, diameter and thickness of thin cylinder respectively.

Hoop stress $\sigma_\theta = \dfrac{Pd}{2t}$

Longitudinal stress $\sigma_l = \dfrac{Pd}{4t}$

Therefore $\dfrac{\sigma_\theta}{\sigma_l} = \dfrac{Pd}{2t} \Big/ \dfrac{Pd}{4t} = 2$

$$\frac{\sigma_\theta}{\sigma_l} = 2$$

Example 6.33

A machine element XY, fixed at end X, is subjected to an axial load P, transverse load F, and a twisting moment T at its free end Y. The most critical point from the strength point of view is a

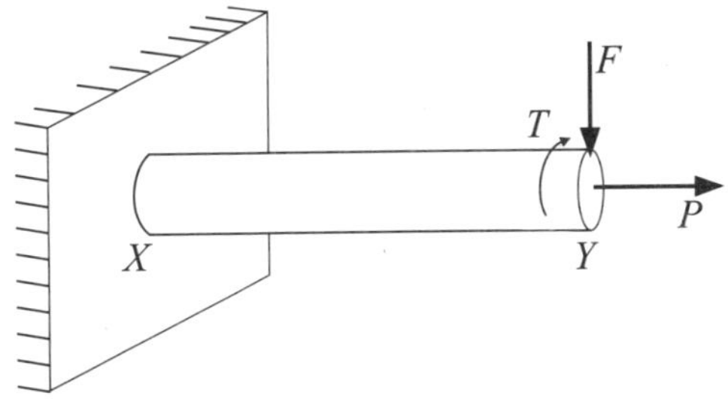

(A) Point on the circumference at location Y

(B) Point at the center at location Y

(C) Point on the circumference at location X

(D) Point at the center at location X

GATE 2016

Solution

There are three types of stresses in the machine element.

1. Direct stress $\sigma_d = \dfrac{P}{A}$; Uniform and constant from Y to X.

2. Bending stress $\sigma_b = \dfrac{M}{I} y_{\max}$; Maximum on circumference and increases from Y to X.

3. Torsion stress $\tau = \dfrac{T}{J} r_{\max}$; Maximum on circumference and constant from Y to X.

From which, we get

The most critical point from the strength point of view is a point on the circumference at location X.

Example 6.34

A rigid horizontal rod of length $2L$ is fixed to a circular cylinder of radius R as shown in the figure. Vertical forces of magnitude P are applied at the two ends as shown in the figure. The shear modulus for the cylinder is G and the Young's modulus is E.

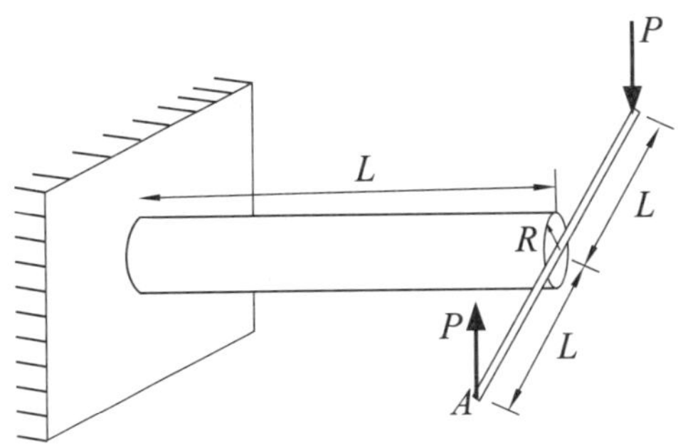

The vertical deflection at point A is

(A) $\dfrac{PL^3}{\pi R^4 G}$ (B) $\dfrac{PL^3}{\pi R^4 E}$ (C) $\dfrac{2PL^3}{\pi R^4 E}$ (D) $\dfrac{4PL^3}{\pi R^4 G}$

GATE 2016

Solution

Resultant force at end of cylinder $= P - P = 0$

Therefore, deflection due to bending $= 0$

Twisting moment on circular cylinder

$$T = PL + PL = 2PL$$

$$\text{Angle of twist } \theta = \frac{TL}{GJ} = \frac{2PL \times L}{G \times \frac{\pi R^4}{2}}$$

$$\theta = \frac{4PL^2}{\pi R^4 G}$$

Deflection at point A due to twisting moment;

$$\delta_A = L\theta = L \times \frac{4PL^2}{\pi R^4 G}$$

$$\delta_A = \frac{4PL^3}{\pi R^4 G}$$

Example 6.35

A simply supported beam of length $2L$ is subjected to a moment M at the mid-point $x = 0$ as shown in the figure. The deflection in the domain $0 \le x \le L$ is given by

$$\delta = \frac{-Mx}{12EIL}(L - x)(x + c)$$

where E is the Young's modulus, I is the area moment of inertia and c is a constant (to be determined).

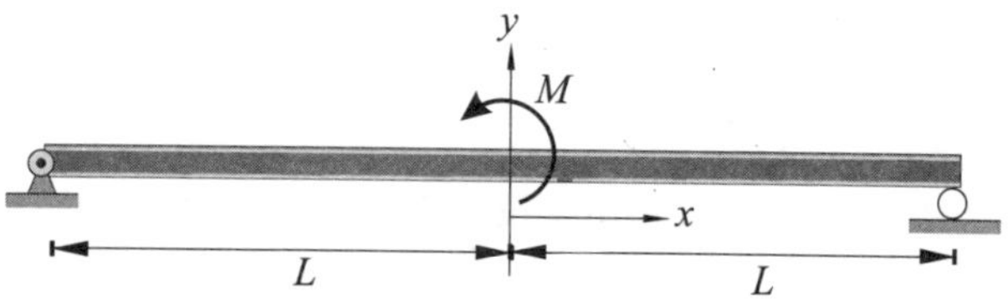

The slope at the center $x = 0$ is

(A) $\frac{ML}{2EI}$ (B) $\frac{ML}{3EI}$ (C) $\frac{ML}{6EI}$ (D) $\frac{ML}{12EI}$

GATE 2016

Solution

The deflection in the domain $0 \le x \le L$ is

$$\delta = \frac{-Mx}{12EIL}(L - x)(x + c)$$

Boundary value; $x = L, \delta = 0$ and $x = -L, \delta = 0$

$$0 = \frac{-M \times -L}{12EIL}(L + L)(-L + c)$$

$$c = L$$

$$\delta = \frac{Mx(x^2 - L^2)}{12EIL}$$

$$\text{Slope of beam } \theta = \frac{d\delta}{dx} = \frac{M(3x^2 - L^2)}{12EIL}$$

$$\text{Slope of beam at center } x = 0;\ \theta_{x=0} = \frac{ML}{12EI}$$

Example 6.36

A circular metallic rod of length 250 mm is placed between two rigid immovable walls as shown in the figure. The rod is in perfect contact with the wall on the left side and there is a gap of 0.2 mm between the rod and the wall on the right side. If the temperature of the rod is increased by 200°C, the axial stress developed in the rod is _______ MPa.

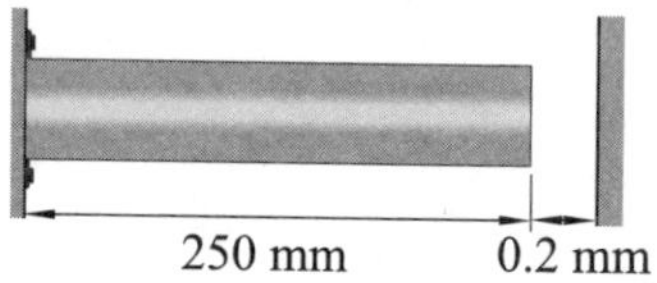

Young's modulus of the material of the rod is 200 GPa and the coefficient of thermal expansion is 10^{-5} per °C.

GATE 2016

Solution

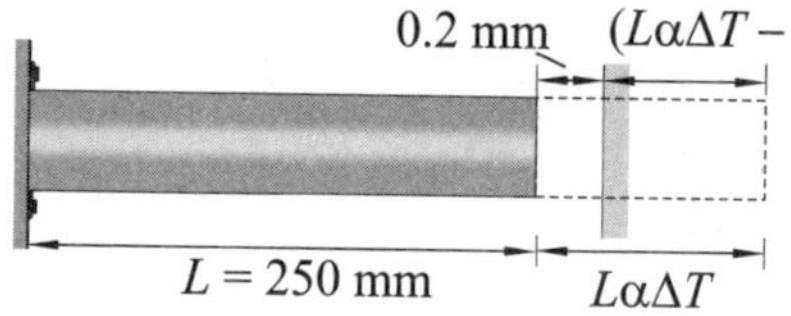

$$\text{Strain of rod} \quad \varepsilon = \frac{L\alpha\,\Delta T - 0.2}{L}$$

$$\text{Stress} \quad \sigma = E\varepsilon = E\left(\frac{L\alpha\,\Delta T - 0.2}{L}\right) = E\left(\alpha\,\Delta T - \frac{0.2}{L}\right)$$

$$\sigma = 200 \times 10^9\left(10^{-5} \times 200 - \frac{0.2}{250}\right)$$

$$\sigma = 240\,\text{MPa}$$

Example 6.37

The cross-sections of two solid bars made of the same material are shown in the figure. The square cross-section has flexural (bending) rigidity I_1, while the circular cross-section has flexural rigidity I_2. Both sections have the same cross-sectional area. The ratio I_1/I_2 is

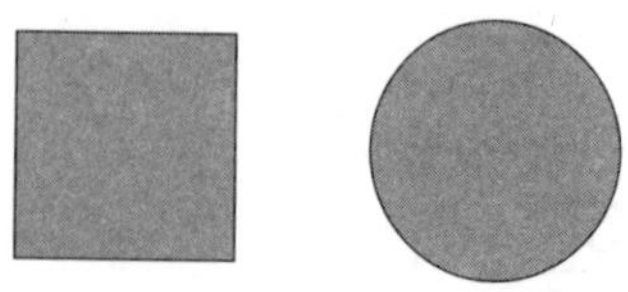

(A) $\frac{1}{\pi}$ (B) $\frac{2}{\pi}$ (C) $\frac{\pi}{3}$ (D) $\frac{\pi}{6}$

GATE 2016

Solution

Let a be side of square section and r be the radius of circular section.

Area of cross-section $a^2 = \pi r^2$

Flexural rigidity ratio $= \frac{(EI)_{\text{square}}}{(EI)_{\text{circle}}} = \frac{a^4/12}{\pi r^4/4} = \frac{a^4}{3\pi r^4}$

$$= \frac{(\pi r^2)^2}{3\pi r^4} = \frac{\pi}{3}$$

$$\text{Flexural rigidity ratio} = \frac{\pi}{3}$$

Example 6.38

A square plate of dimension $L \times L$ is subjected to a uniform pressure load $p = 250$ MPa on its edges as shown in the figure. Assume plane stress conditions. The Young's modulus $E = 200$ GPa.

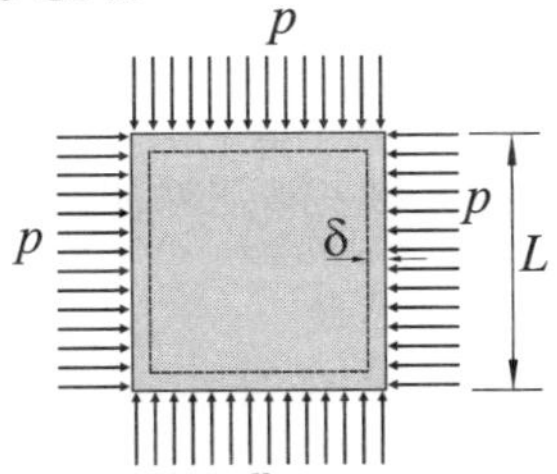

The deformed shape is a square of dimension $L - 2\delta$. If $L = 2$ m and $\delta = 0.001$ m, the Poisson's ratio of the plate material is_______.

GATE 2016

Solution

Strain of side; $\frac{2\delta}{L}$ = Strain in x - direction due to σ_x

– Strain in x - direction due to σ_y

$$\frac{2\delta}{L} = \frac{\sigma_x}{E} - \nu\frac{\sigma_y}{E}$$

Substituting $\sigma_x = \sigma_y = p$, we have

$$\frac{2\delta}{L} = \frac{p}{E} - \nu\frac{p}{E}$$

or $$\nu = 1 - \frac{2\delta E}{pL} = 1 - \frac{2 \times 0.001 \times 200 \times 10^9}{250 \times 10^6 \times 2}$$

$$\text{Poisson ratio } \nu = 0.2$$

Example 6.39

Two circular shafts made of same material, one solid (S) and one hollow (H), have the same length and polar moment of inertia. Both are subjected to same torque. Here, θ_S is the twist and τ_S is the maximum shear stress in the solid shaft, whereas θ_H is the twist and τ_H is the maximum shear stress in the hollow shaft. Which one of the following is TRUE?

(A) $\theta_S = \theta_H$ and $\tau_S = \tau_H$ (B) $\theta_S > \theta_H$ and $\tau_S > \tau_H$

(C) $\theta_S < \theta_H$ and $\tau_S < \tau_H$ (D) $\theta_S = \theta_H$ and $\tau_S < \tau_H$

GATE 2016

Solution

Torsion formula $\frac{T}{J} = \frac{\tau}{r} = \frac{G\theta}{l}$

Shaft have the same length, same polar moment of inertia, and same torque.

$$\frac{T}{J} = \frac{\tau_H}{r_H} = \frac{G\theta_H}{l} = \frac{\tau_S}{r_S} = \frac{G\theta_S}{l}$$

From which, we get

$$\theta_H = \theta_S$$

and $$\tau_H = \frac{r_H}{r_S}\tau_S \quad \left[\text{For } J_H = J_S;\ \frac{r_H}{r_S} > 1\right]$$

$$\tau_H > \tau_S$$

Example 6.40

A beam of length L is carrying a uniformly distributed load ω per unit length. The flexural rigidity of the beam is EI. The reaction at the simple support at the right end is

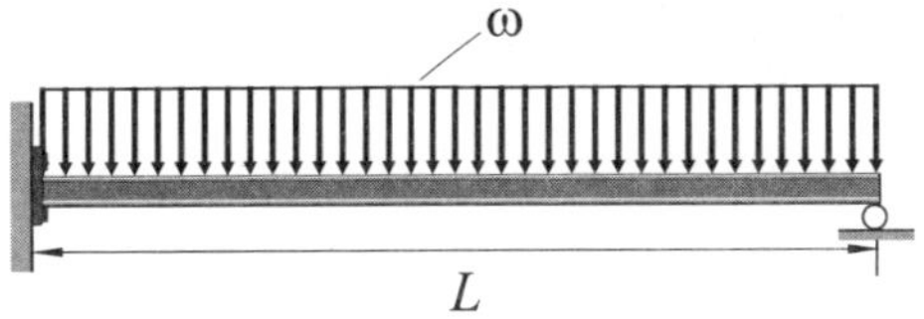

(A) $\frac{\omega L}{2}$ (B) $\frac{3\omega L}{8}$ (C) $\frac{\omega L}{4}$ (D) $\frac{\omega L}{8}$

GATE 2016

Solution

Let R_B be the reaction of roller support. Net deflection of roller support is zero.

Deflection at B = Deflection at B due uniformly distributed load (↓) – Deflection at B due to point load $R_B = 0$

Deflection of beam at B, $\frac{\omega L^4}{8EI} - \frac{R_B L^3}{3EI} = 0$

$$R_B = \frac{3}{8}\omega L$$

Example 6.41

The Poisson's ratio for a perfectly incompressible linear elastic material is

(A) 1 (B) 0.5 (C) 0 (D) infinity

GATE 2017

Solution

Consider a cylinder of incompressible material.

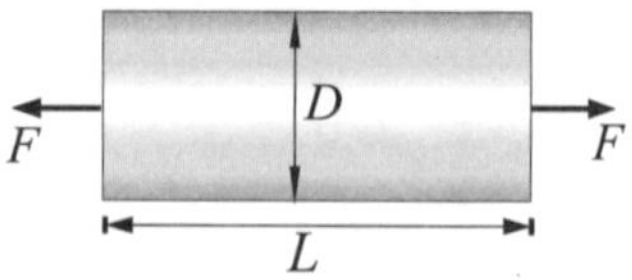

Volume $V = \frac{\pi}{4} D^2 L$

$$\frac{dV}{V} = 2\frac{dD}{D} + \frac{dL}{L}$$

For incompressible material; $\frac{dV}{V} = 0 \Rightarrow 2\frac{dD}{D} + \frac{dL}{L} = 0$

or $2\varepsilon_{\text{trans}} + \varepsilon_{\text{long}} = 0 \quad \Rightarrow \quad \frac{\varepsilon_{\text{trans}}}{\varepsilon_{\text{long}}} = -\frac{1}{2}$

Poisson's ratio $\nu = -\frac{\varepsilon_{\text{trans}}}{\varepsilon_{\text{long}}} = -\left(-\frac{1}{2}\right)$

$$\text{Poisson's ratio } \nu = 0.5$$

Example 6.42

Consider a beam with circular cross-section of diameter *d*. The ratio of the second moment of area about the neutral axis to the section modulus of the area is.

(A) $\frac{d}{2}$ (B) $\frac{\pi d}{2}$ (C) d (D) πd

GATE 2017

Solution

Second moment of area, $I = \frac{\pi d^4}{64}$

Section modulus, $Z = \frac{I}{y} = \frac{\pi d^4/64}{d/2} = \frac{\pi d^3}{32}$

$$\frac{I}{Z} = \frac{\pi d^4/64}{\pi d^4/32} = \frac{d}{2}$$

$$\frac{I}{Z} = \frac{d}{2}$$

Example 6.43

In the engineering stress-strain curve for mild steel, the Ultimate Tensile Strength (UTS) refers to

(A) Yield stress (B) Proportional limit

(C) Maximum stress (D) Fracture stress

GATE 2017

Solution

Ultimate Tensile Strength (UTS) refers to maximum stress

Example 6.44

An initially stress-free massless elastic beam of length *L* and circular cross-section with diameter *d* ($d << L$) is held fixed between two walls as shown. The beam material has Young's modulus *E* and coefficient of thermal expansion α.

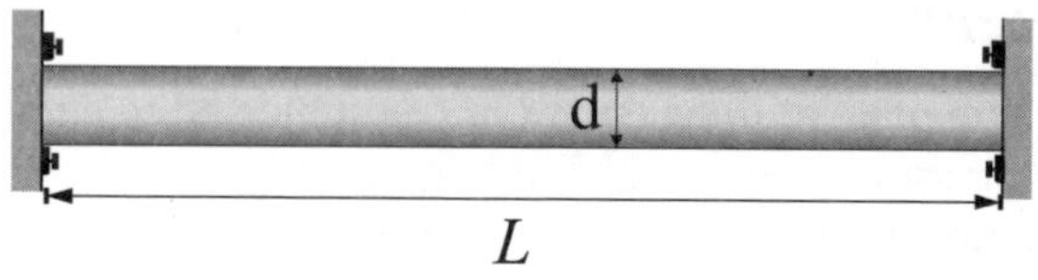

If the beam is slowly and uniformly heated, the temperature rise required to cause the beam to buckle is proportional to

(A) d (B) d^2 (C) d^3 (D) d^4

GATE 2017

Solution

Thermal strain $\frac{dL}{L} = \alpha\, \Delta T$

Stress developed in the beam $\sigma = E\varepsilon = E\alpha\Delta T$

Compressive force $F = \sigma A = EA\alpha\Delta T$ (i)

Critical load(Euler load) for the column(beam)

$$P_{cr} = \frac{\pi^2 EI}{l_e^2} \quad \text{(ii)}$$

From Equations (i) and (ii), we have

$$P = P_{cr} \Rightarrow EA\alpha\Delta T = \frac{\pi^2 EI}{l_e^2}$$

$$\Delta T = \frac{\pi^2 EI}{EA\alpha l_e^2} = \frac{\pi^2 E}{E\alpha l_e^2}\frac{\frac{\pi d^4}{64}}{\frac{\pi d^2}{4}} = \left(\frac{\pi^2 E}{16E\alpha l_e^2}\right)d^2$$

$$\Delta T \propto d^2$$

Example 6.45

A point mass of 100 kg is dropped onto a massless elastic bar (cross-sectional area = 100 mm^2, length = 1m, Young's modulus = 100 GPa) from a height h of 10 mm as shown

(Figure is not to scale). If g = 10 m/s^2, the maximum compression of the elastic bar is ________mm.

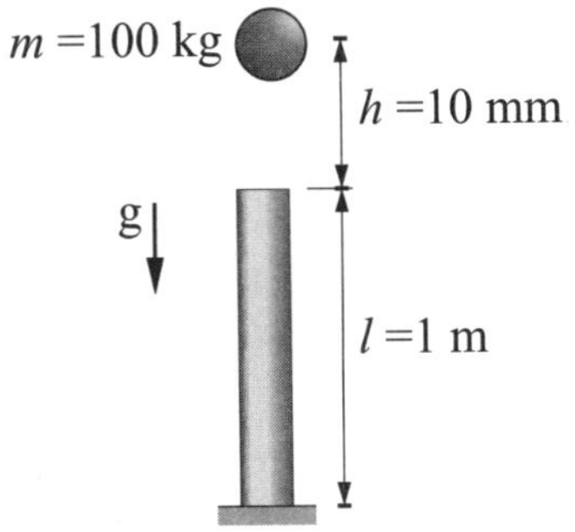

GATE 2017

Solution

Let σ be the stress induced in the bar.

Potential energy lost by the weight = strain energy stored in the beam

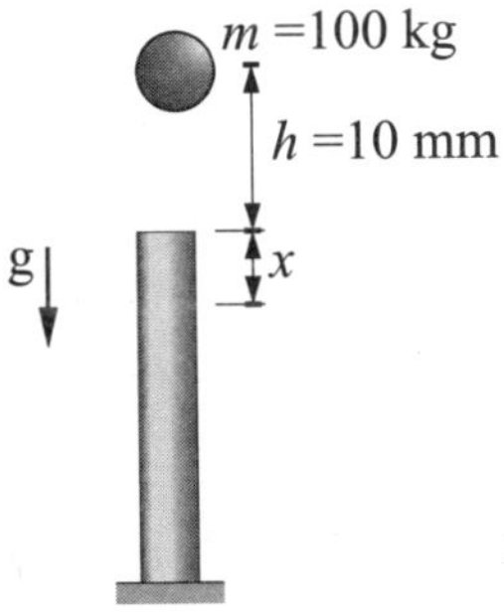

$$mg(h+x)=\frac{1}{2}\sigma Ax$$

$$mg\left(h+\frac{\sigma l}{E}\right)=\frac{1}{2}\sigma A\left(\frac{\sigma l}{E}\right)$$

$$\sigma^2\left(\frac{Al}{2E}\right)-\sigma\left(\frac{mgl}{E}\right)-mgh=0$$

$$\sigma=\frac{\frac{mgl}{E}\pm\sqrt{\left(\frac{mgl}{E}\right)^2+4\left(\frac{Al}{2E}\right)mgh}}{2\left(\frac{Al}{2E}\right)}$$

$$\sigma=\frac{mg}{A}\left[1+\sqrt{1+\frac{2EAh}{mgl}}\right]$$

Substituting given values m =100 kg, A= 100 mm^2, l = 1m, E = 100 GPa, h =10 mm and g = 10 m/s^2, we obtain

$$\sigma=151.7\ \text{N/mm}^2$$

$$\text{Compression } \delta l=\frac{\sigma l}{E}=\frac{151.7\times 1000}{1\times 10^5}=1.517$$

$$\delta l=1.517\ \text{mm}$$

Example 6.46

A rectangular region in a solid is in a state of plane strain. The (x, y) coordinates of the corners of the undeformed rectangle are given by P(0, 0), Q(4, 0), R(4, 3) S(0, 3). The rectangle is subjected to uniform strains, $\varepsilon_{xx}=0.001$, $\varepsilon_{yy}=0.002$, $\gamma_{xy}=0.003$. The deformed length of the elongated diagonal, up to three decimal places, is ______ units.

GATE 2017

Solution

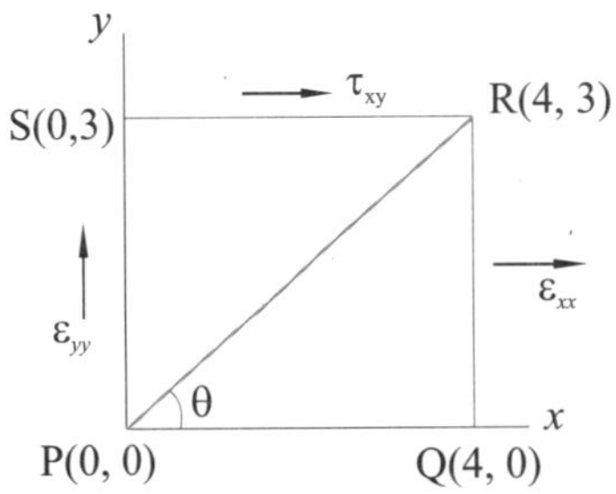

Given: $\varepsilon_{xx}=0.001, \varepsilon_{yy}=0.002, \gamma_{xy}=0.003$

$$\theta=\tan^{-1}\left(\frac{3}{4}\right)=40.96,\qquad \text{PR}=\sqrt{3^2+4^2}=5$$

$$\text{Strain}\quad \varepsilon_\theta=\frac{\varepsilon_{xx}+\varepsilon_{yy}}{2}+\frac{\varepsilon_{xx}-\varepsilon_{yy}}{2}\cos 2\theta+\frac{\gamma_{xy}}{2}\sin 2\theta$$

$$\varepsilon_\theta=\frac{0.001+0.002}{2}+\frac{0.001-0.002}{2}\cos 81.93+\frac{0.003}{2}\sin 81.93$$

$$\varepsilon_\theta=0.0028=\frac{\Delta(PR)}{PR}$$

$$\Delta(PR)=0.0028\times 5=0.014$$

Length of deformed diagonal = 5 + 0.014 = 5.014 mm

Example 6.47

A horizontal bar, fixed at one end ($x=0$), has a length of 1 m, and cross-sectional area of 100 mm^2. Its elastic modulus varies along its length as given by $E(x)=100\,e^{-x}$ GPa, where x is the length coordinate (in m) along the axis of the bar. An axial tensile load of 10 kN is applied at the free end ($x=1$). The axial displacement of the free end is________mm.

GATE 2017

Solution

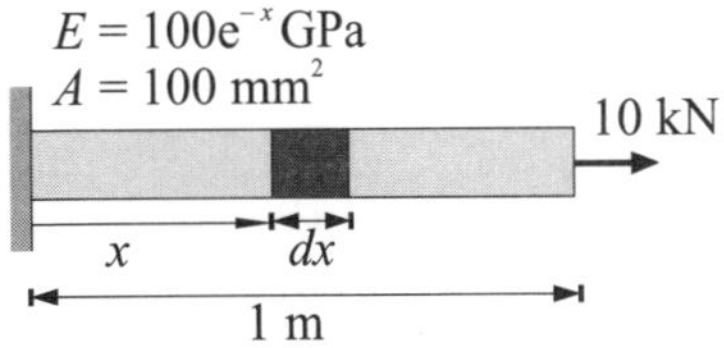

Consider an element of length dx.

$$\text{Strain of element}\qquad \frac{du}{dx}=\frac{P}{EA}$$

$$\text{Change in length } \Delta=\int_0^1\frac{Pdx}{EA}$$

$$\Delta = \int_0^1 \frac{10\times 10^3\, dx}{100\, e^{-x}\times 10^9 \times \dfrac{100}{1000\times 1000}}\ \text{m}$$

$$\Delta = \int_0^1 \frac{e^x\, dx}{1000} = [e^1 - 1]\ \text{mm}$$

$$\Delta = 1.718\ \text{mm}$$

Example 6.48

The state of stress at a point is $\sigma_x = \sigma_y = \sigma_z = \tau_{xz} = \tau_{zx} = \tau_{yz} = \tau_{zy} = 0$ and $\tau_{xy} = \tau_{yx} = 50$ MPa. The maximum normal stress (in MPa) at that point is ______.

GATE 2017

Solution

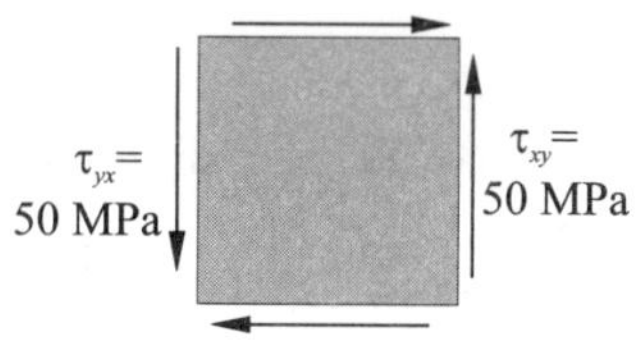

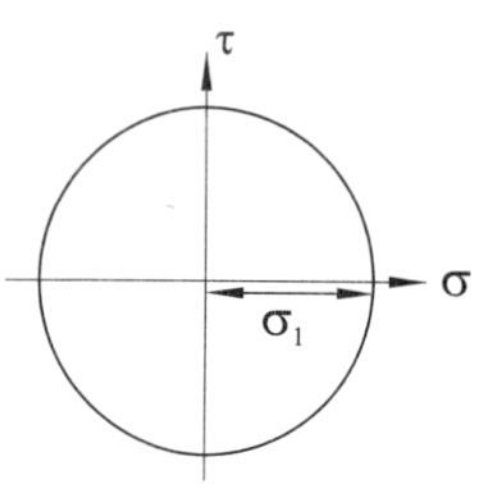

Mohr circle

It is pure shear stress in 2-dimensional.

Maximum normal stress $\sigma_1 = \tau_{xy} = 50$

$$\sigma = 50\ \text{MPa}$$

Example 6.49

For a loaded cantilever beam of uniform cross-section, the bending moment (in N.mm) along the length is $M(x) = 5x^2 + 10x$, where x is the distance (in mm) measured from the free end of the beam. The magnitude of shear force (in N) in the cross-section at $x = 10$ mm is______.

GATE 2017

Solution

Shear force $S = \dfrac{dM}{dx}$

$$S = \frac{d}{dx}(5x^2 + 10x) = 10x + 10$$

$$S_{x=10\text{mm}} = 10\times 10 + 10$$

$$\text{Shear force } S_{x=10\text{mm}} = 110\ \text{N}$$

Example 6.50

A cantilever beam of length L and flexural modulus EI is subjected to a point load P at the free end. The elastic strain energy stored in the beam due to bending (neglecting transverse shear) is

(A) $\dfrac{P^2L^3}{6EI}$ (B) $\dfrac{P^2L^3}{3EI}$ (C) $\dfrac{PL^3}{3EI}$ (D) $\dfrac{PL^3}{6EI}$

GATE 2017

Solution

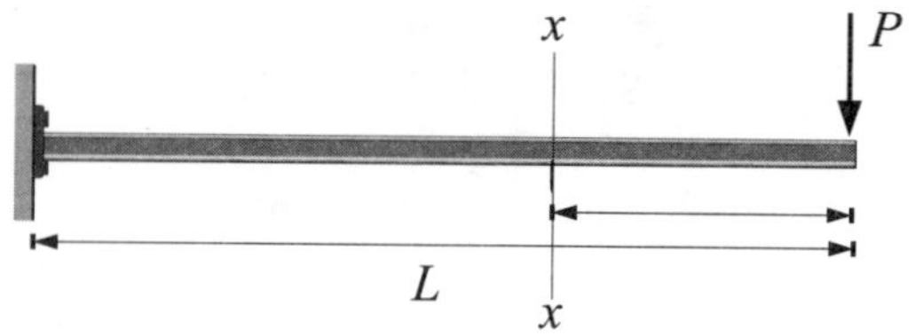

Bending moment at $x - x$, $M = Px$

Elastic strain energy in the beam due to bending is

$$U = \int_0^L \frac{M^2 dx}{2EI} = \int_0^L \frac{(Px)^2 dx}{2EI}$$

$$U = \frac{P^2L^3}{6EI}$$

Example 6.51

A steel bar is held by two fixed supports as shown in the figure and is subjected to an increases of temperature $\Delta T = 100°\text{C}$. If the coefficient of thermal expansion and Young's modulus of elasticity of steel are 11×10^{-6} /°C and 200 GPa, respectively, the magnitude of thermal stress (in MPa) induced in the bar is________.

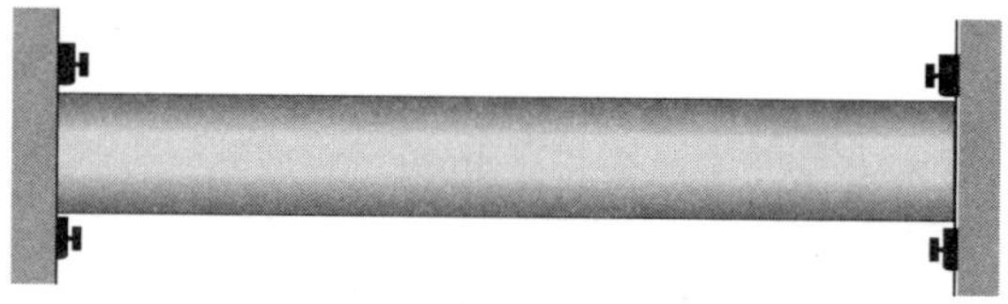

GATE 2017

Solution

Given: $\Delta T = 100°\text{C}$, $\alpha = 11\times 10^{-6}$ /°C and $E = 200$ GPa.

Thermal strain $\varepsilon = \dfrac{\Delta l}{l} = \alpha\Delta T$

Thermal stress $\sigma = E\varepsilon = E\alpha\Delta T$

$$\sigma = 200\times 11\times 10^{-6}\times 100\ \text{GPa}$$

$$\sigma = 220\ \text{MPa}$$

Example 6.52

A rod of length 20 mm is stretched to make a rod of length 40 mm. Subsequently, it is compressed to make a rod of final length 10 mm. Consider the longitudinal tensile strain as positive and compressive strain as negative. The total true longitudinal strain in the rod is

(A) –0.5 (B) –0.69 (C) –0.75 (D) –1.0

GATE 2017

Solution

Given: $l_1 = 20$ mm, $l_2 = 10$ mm

True strain $\varepsilon_{true} = \ln\left(\frac{l_2}{l_1}\right) = \ln\left(\frac{10}{20}\right)$

$$\varepsilon_{true} = -0.69$$

Example 6.53

If σ_1 and σ_3 are the algebraically largest and smallest principal stresses respectively, the value of the maximum shear stress is

(A) $\frac{\sigma_1 + \sigma_3}{2}$ (B) $\frac{\sigma_1 - \sigma_3}{2}$

(C) $\sqrt{\frac{\sigma_1 + \sigma_3}{2}}$ (D) $\sqrt{\frac{\sigma_1 - \sigma_3}{2}}$

GATE 2018

Solution

Maximum shear stress

$$= \frac{\text{Largest principal stress - Smallest Principal stress}}{2}$$

$$\text{Maximum shear stress} = \frac{\sigma_1 - \sigma_3}{2}$$

Example 6.54

A steel column of rectangular section (15 mm × 10 mm) and length 1.5 m is simply supported at both ends. Assuming modulus of elasticity, E = 200 GPa for steel, the critical axial load (in kN) is ____ .

GATE 2018

Solution

Critical axial load, $P_{cr} = \frac{\pi^2 EI_{min}}{l^2}$

Substituting $E = 200 \times 10^3$ MPa, $b = 15$ mm, $d = 10$ mm and $l = 1500$ mm.

$$P_{cr} = \frac{\pi^2 E \frac{bd^3}{12}}{l^2} = \frac{\pi^2 \times 200 \times 10^3 \times \frac{15 \times 10^3}{12}}{(1500)^2}$$

$$P_{cr} = 1096.62 \text{ N}$$

$$P_{cr} = 1.097 \text{ kN}$$

Example 6.55

The state of stress at a point, for a body in plane stress, is shown in the figure below. If the minimum principal stress is 10 kPa, then the normal stress σ_y (in kPa) is

(A) 9.45 (B) 18.88 (C) 37.78 (D) 75.50

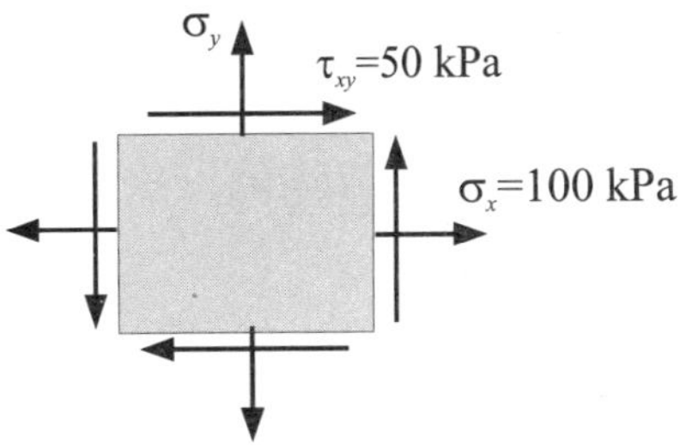

GATE 2018

Solution

Minimum principal stress

$$\sigma_2 = \frac{\sigma_x + \sigma_y}{2} - \sqrt{\left(\frac{\sigma_y - \sigma_x}{2}\right)^2 + \tau_{xy}^2}$$

Substituting $\sigma_2 = 10$ kPa, $\sigma_x = 100$ kPa and $\tau_{xy} = 50$ kPa

$$10 = \frac{100 + \sigma_y}{2} - \sqrt{\left(\frac{\sigma_y - 100}{2}\right)^2 + 50^2}$$

or $$\sqrt{\left(\frac{\sigma_y}{2} - 50\right)^2 + 50^2} = -\left(40 + \frac{\sigma_y}{2}\right)$$

or $$90\sigma_y = 3400$$

$$\sigma_y = 37.78 \text{ MPa}$$

Example 6.56

A simply supported beam of width 100 mm, height 200 mm and length 4 m is carrying a uniformly distributed load of intensity 10 kN/m. The maximum bending stress (in MPa) in the beam is _________ .

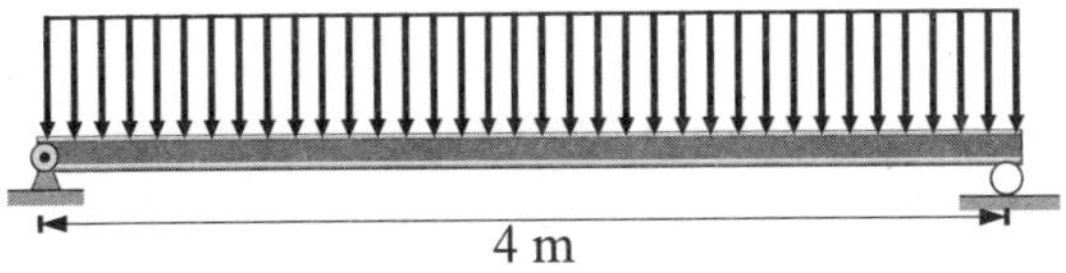

GATE 2018

Solution

Maximum bending moment (at centre)

$$M_{max} = \frac{\omega l^3}{8}$$

Maximum bending stress

$$\sigma_{max} = \frac{M_{max}}{I} y_{max} = \frac{\frac{\omega l^2}{8}}{\left(\frac{bd^3}{12}\right)} \times \frac{d}{2} = \frac{3}{4} \frac{\omega l^2}{bd^2}$$

$$\sigma_{max} = \frac{3}{4}\frac{10\times10^3\times4^2}{\frac{100}{1000}\times\left(\frac{200}{1000}\right)^2} = 30\times10^6 \text{ N/m}^2$$

$$\sigma_{max} = 30 \text{ MPa}$$

Example 6.57

The minimum axial compressive load, P, required to initiate buckling for a pinned-pinned slender column with bending stiffness EI and length L is

(A) $P = \frac{\pi^2 EI}{4L^2}$ (B) $P = \frac{\pi^2 EI}{L^2}$

(C) $P = \frac{3\pi^2 EI}{4L^2}$ (D) $P = \frac{4\pi^2 EI}{L^2}$

GATE 2018

Solution

Euler's formula for buckling load

$$P = \frac{\pi^2 EI}{l_{eq}^2}$$

$[\,l_{eq} = L$ for pinned-pinned column$]$

$$P = \frac{\pi^2 EI}{L^2}$$

Example 6.58

A bar of circular cross section is clamped at ends P and Q as shown in the figure. A torsional moment $T = 150$ Nm is applied at a distance of 100 mm from end P. The torsional reactions (T_P, T_Q) in Nm at the ends P and Q respectively are

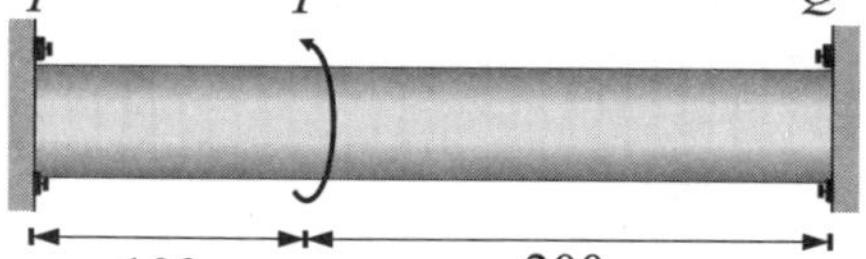

(A) (50, 100) (B) (75, 75)

(C) (100, 50) (D) (120, 30)

GATE 2018

Solution

Let T_P and T_Q be the torsional reactions at the end P and Q, respectively.

$$T_P + T_Q = 150 \quad \text{(i)}$$

Angle of twist $\theta = \frac{T_P\times100}{GJ} = \frac{T_Q\times200}{GJ}$

$$T_P = 2T_Q \quad \text{(ii)}$$

From Equations (i) and (ii), we obtain

$$T_P = 100 \text{ Nm and } T_Q = 50 \text{ Nm}$$

Example 6.59

A bimetallic cylindrical bar of cross sectional area 1 m^2 is made by bonding Steel (Young's modulus = 210 GPa) and Aluminium (Young's modulus = 70 GPa) as shown the figure. To maintain tensile axial strain of magnitude 10^{-6} in Steel bar and compressive axial strain of magnitude 10^{-6} in Aluminium bar, the magnitude of the required force P (in kN) along the indicated direction is

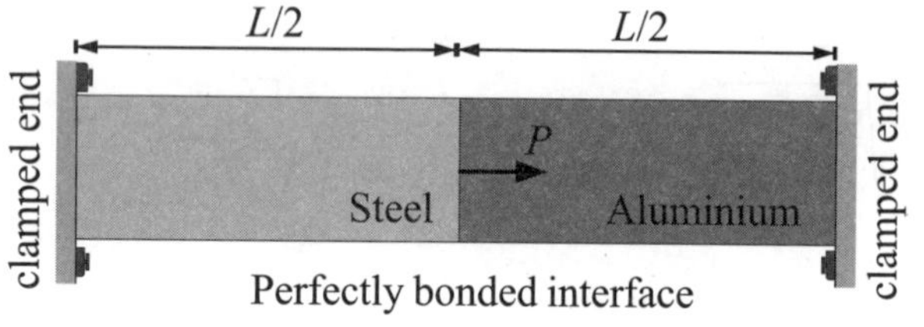

(A) 70 (B) 140 (C) 210 (D) 280

GATE 2018

Solution

Let R_{steel} and R_{Al} be the reactions at clamped ends.

$$R_{steel} + R_{Al} = P \quad \text{(i)}$$

Strain $\varepsilon = \frac{R_{steel}}{E_{steel}A} = \frac{R_{Al}}{E_{Al}A}$

$$R_{steel} = \frac{E_{steel}}{E_{Al}}R_{Al} = \frac{210}{70}R_{Al}$$

$$R_{steel} = 3R_{Al} \quad \text{(ii)}$$

From Equations (i) and (ii), we obtain

$$R_{steel} = \frac{3P}{4} \text{ and } R_{Al} = \frac{P}{4}$$

Axial strain $\varepsilon = \frac{\Delta L}{L} = 10^{-6} = \frac{R_{steel}}{E_{steel}A}$

$$10^{-6} = \frac{\frac{3P}{4}}{210\times10^9\times1}$$

$$P = \frac{4}{3}\times10^{-6}\times210\times10^9$$

$$P = 280 \text{ kN}$$

Example 6.60

A thin-walled cylindrical can with rigid end caps has a mean radius $R = 100$ mm and a wall thickness of $t = 5$ mm. The can is pressurized and an additional tensile stress of 50

MPa is imposed along the axial direction as shown in the figure. Assume that the state of stress in the wall is uniform along its length. If the magnitudes of axial and circumferential components of stress in the can are equal, the pressure (in MPa) inside the can is ____ .

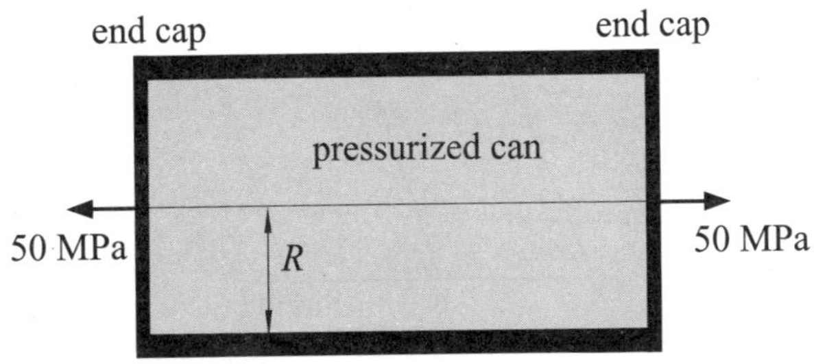

GATE 2018

Solution

Circumferential stress, $\sigma_\theta = \dfrac{pd}{2t}$

Resultant longitudinal stress, $\sigma = \dfrac{pd}{4t} + 50$

$$\sigma_\theta = \sigma \Rightarrow \frac{pd}{2t} = \frac{pd}{4t} + 50$$

or $$\frac{pd}{4t} = 50$$

$$\frac{p \times 200}{4 \times 5} = 50$$

$$p = 5 \text{ MPa}$$

Example 6.61

The true stress (in MPa) versus true strain relationship for a metal is given by

$$\sigma = 1020\varepsilon^{0.4}$$

The cross-sectional area at the start of a test (when the stress and strain values are equal to zero) is 100 mm^2. The cross-sectional area at the time of necking (in mm^2) is______ .

GATE 2018

Solution

Load $P = \sigma A \quad \Rightarrow dP = A\,d\sigma + \sigma\,dA$

At ultimate point, $dP = 0 \Rightarrow \quad \dfrac{d\sigma}{\sigma} = -\dfrac{dA}{A}$ (i)

Since $Al = \text{constant} \quad \Rightarrow \quad \dfrac{dl}{l} = -\dfrac{dA}{A} = d\varepsilon$ (ii)

From Equations (i) and (ii) we obtain

$$\frac{d\sigma}{\sigma} = d\varepsilon \quad \Rightarrow \quad \frac{d\sigma}{d\varepsilon} = \sigma$$

Substituting $\sigma = 1020\varepsilon^{0.4}$,

$$\frac{d}{d\varepsilon}1020\varepsilon^{0.4} = 1020\varepsilon^{0.4}$$

$\varepsilon = 0.4$ Neck formation start at ultimate point

$$\ln\left(\frac{A_o}{A_f}\right) = 0.4$$

$$A_f = \frac{A_o}{e^{0.4}} = \frac{100}{e^{0.4}} = 67.032$$

Cross-section area at the time of necking = 67.032 mm^2

Example 6.62

A cylindrical rod of diameter 10 mm and length 1.0 m is fixed at one end. The other end is twisted by an angle of $10°$ by applying a torque. If the maximum shear strain in the rod is $p \times 10^{-3}$, then p is equal to ______(round off to two decimal places).

GATE 2019

Solution

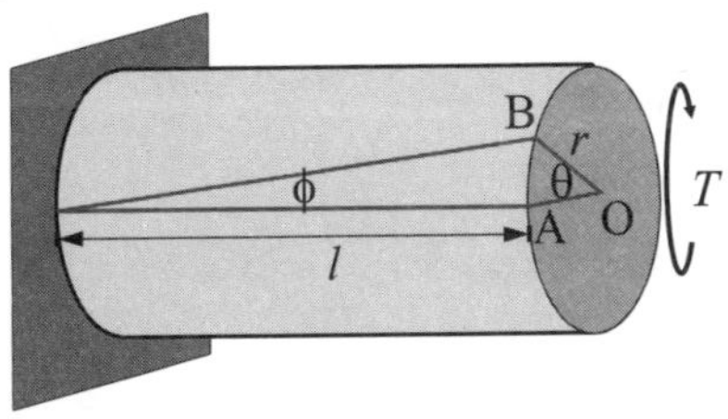

From the geometry of figure.

$$AB = l\phi = r\theta$$

or $$\phi = \frac{r\theta}{l}$$

Maximum shear strain, $\phi = \dfrac{r\theta}{l} = p \times 10^{-3}$

$$\frac{\dfrac{5}{1000} \times \dfrac{10\pi}{180}}{1} = p \times 10^{-3}$$

or $$p = \frac{5\pi}{18}$$

$$p = 0.8726$$

Example 6.63

A solid cube of side 1 m kept at a room temperature of 32°C. The coefficient of linear thermal expansion of the cube material is 1×10^{-5} /°C and the bulk modulus is 200 GPa. If the cube is constrained all around and heated uniformly to 42°, then the magnitude of volumetric (mean) stress (in MPa) induced due to heating is ______.

GATE 2019

Solution

Thermal strain of each side of cube

$$\frac{\Delta l}{l} = \alpha \Delta T \qquad \text{(i)}$$

Let σ be the stress developed in the cube.

$$\text{Strain} \quad \frac{\Delta l}{l} = \frac{\sigma}{E} - \nu\frac{\sigma}{E} - \nu\frac{\sigma}{E}$$

$$\frac{\Delta l}{l} = \frac{\sigma}{E}(1-2\nu) \qquad \text{(ii)}$$

From Equations (i) and (ii), we obtain

$$\alpha \Delta T = \frac{\sigma}{E}(1-2\nu) \quad \text{or} \quad \sigma = \frac{E\alpha\Delta T}{(1-2\nu)}$$

Substituting $E = 3K(1-2\nu)$

$$\sigma = 3K\alpha\Delta T \Rightarrow \sigma = 3\times 200\times 10^9 \times 1\times 10^{-5}\times(42-32)$$

$$\sigma = 60 \text{ MPa}$$

or

$$\text{Volume of cube } V = l^3 \Rightarrow \frac{dV}{V} = 3\frac{dl}{l}$$

$$\text{or} \quad \varepsilon_V = 3\varepsilon_l \Rightarrow \frac{\sigma}{K} = 3\alpha\,\Delta T$$

$$\sigma = 3K\alpha\,\Delta T = 3\times 200\times 10^9\times 1\times 10^{-5}\times(42-32)$$

$$\sigma = 60 \text{ MPa}$$

Example 6.64

Consider the stress-strain curve for an ideal elastic-plastic strain hardening metal as shown in the figure. The metal was loaded in uniaxial tension starting from O. Upon loading, the stress-stain curve passes through initial point at P, and then strain hardens to point Q, where the loading was stopped. From point Q, the specimen was unloaded to point R, where the stress is zero. If the same specimen is reloaded in tension from point R, the value of stress at which the material yields again is_____ MPa.

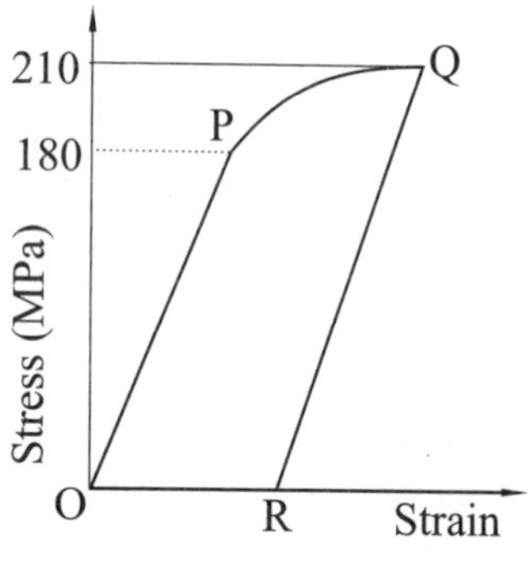

GATE 2019

Solution

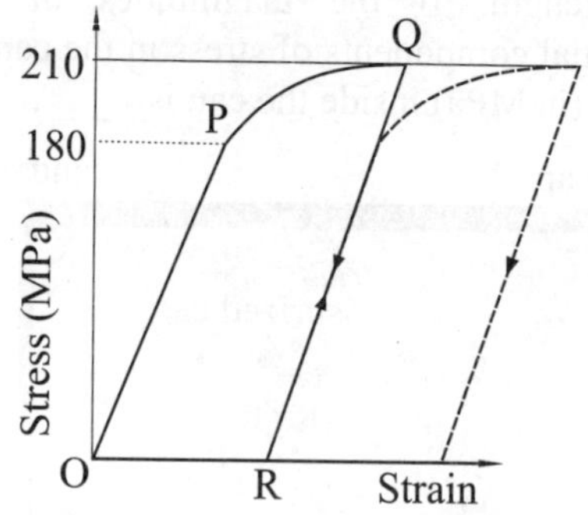

The value of stress at which the material yields again is 210 MPa.

Example 6.65

Consider an elastic straight beam of length $L = 10\pi$ m, with square cross-section of wide $a = 5$ mm, and Young's modulus $E = 200$ GPa. This straight beam was bent in such a way that the two ends meet, to form a circle of mean radius R. Assuming that Euler-Bernoulli beam theory is applicable to this bending problem, the maximum tensile bending stress in the bend beam is ______MPa.

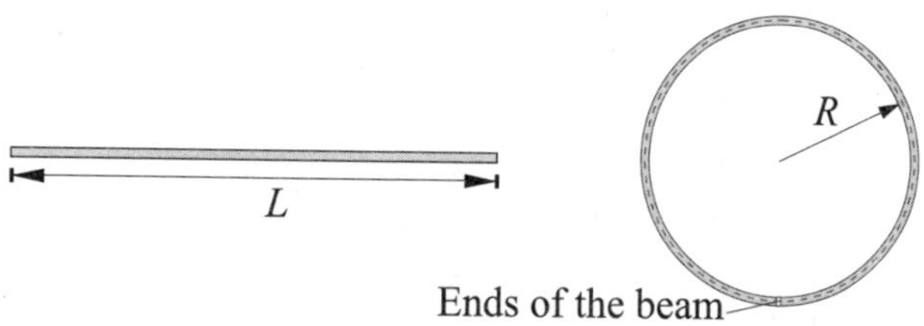

GATE 2019

Solution

$$\text{Bending formula,} \quad \frac{M}{I} = \frac{\sigma}{y} = \frac{E}{R}$$

$$\text{Maximum stress, } \sigma_{max} = \frac{E}{R}y_{max} = \frac{E}{R}\times\frac{a}{2}$$

Substituting $R = \frac{L}{2\pi} = \frac{10\pi}{2\pi} = 5$ m, $a = \frac{5}{1000}$ m and $E = 200\times 10^9$ N/m^2, we have

$$\sigma_{max} = \frac{200\times 10^9}{5}\times\frac{5}{2\times 1000} = 200\times 10^6$$

$$\sigma_{max} = 100 \text{ MPa}$$

Example 6.66

Consider a prismatic straight beam of length $L = \pi$ m, pinned at the two ends as shown in the figure. The beam has a square cross-section of side $p = 6$ mm. The Young's modulus $E = 200$ GPa, and the coefficient of thermal expansion $\alpha = 3\times10^{-6}\ K^{-1}$. The minimum temperature rise required to cause Euler buckling of beam is ______ K.

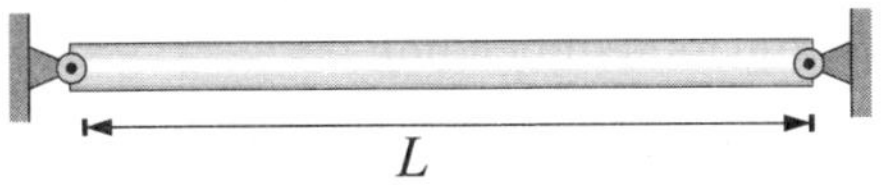

GATE 2019

Solution

Thermal strain $\frac{dL}{L} = \alpha\,\Delta T$

Stress developed in the beam $\sigma = E\varepsilon = E\alpha\Delta T$

Compressive force $F = \sigma A = EA\alpha\Delta T$ (i)

Critical load (Euler load) for the beam

$$P_{cr} = \frac{\pi^2 EI}{l_e^2} \quad \text{(ii)}$$

From Equations (i) and (ii), we have

$$P = P_{cr} \Rightarrow EA\alpha\Delta T = \frac{\pi^2 EI}{l_e^2}$$

$$\Delta T = \frac{\pi^2 I}{A\alpha l_e^2} = \frac{\pi^2}{\alpha l_e^2}\frac{\frac{a^4}{12}}{a^2}$$

$$\Delta T = \frac{\pi^2 a^2}{12\alpha\, l_e^2} = \frac{\pi^2\left(\frac{6}{1000}\right)^2}{12\times3\times10^{-6}\times\pi^2} = 1$$

$\Delta T = 1\,\text{K}$

Example 6.67

In a UTM experiment, a sample of length 100 mm, was loaded in tension until failure. The failure load was 40 kN. The displacement, measured using the cross-head motion, at failure, was 15 mm. The compliance of the UTM is constant and is given by 5×10^{-8} m/N. The strain at failure in the sample is ______ %.

GATE 2019

Solution

Load deflection cure for a specimen is shown in figure.

Sample length $l = 100$ mm

Failure load = 40 kN

Total strain $\frac{\Delta_{total}}{l} = \frac{15}{100} = 15\,\%$

Compliance of the UTM $= \frac{1}{\text{Stiffness}} = 5\times10^{-8}$ m / N

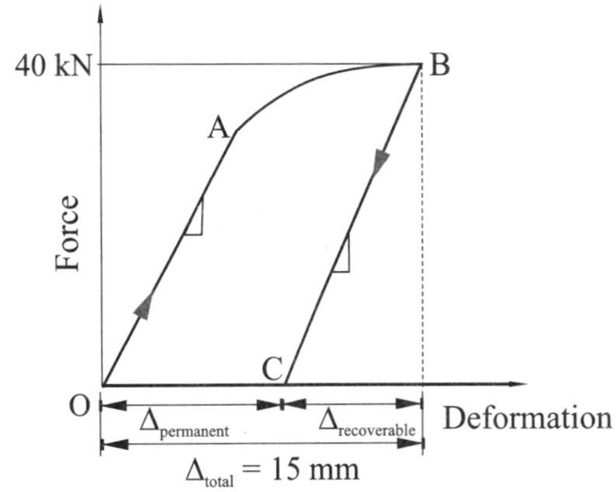

$$\text{Stiffness} = \frac{1}{5\times10^{-8}} = \frac{40\times1000}{\Delta_{recoverable}}$$

or $\Delta_{recoverable} = 40\times1000\times5\times10^{-8}\times1000$ mm

$\Delta_{recoverable} = 2$ mm

$\Delta_{permanent} = \Delta_{total} - \Delta_{recoverable} = 15 - 2 = 13$ mm

Permanent strain $= \frac{\Delta_{permanent}}{l} = \frac{13}{100}$

Permanent strain = 13 %

Example 6.68

The state of stress at a point in a component is represented by a Mohr's circle of radius 100 MPa centered at 200 MPa on the normal stress axis. On a plane passing through the same point, the normal stress is 260 MPa. The magnitude of the shear stress on the same plane at the same point is_____MPa.

GATE 2019

Solution

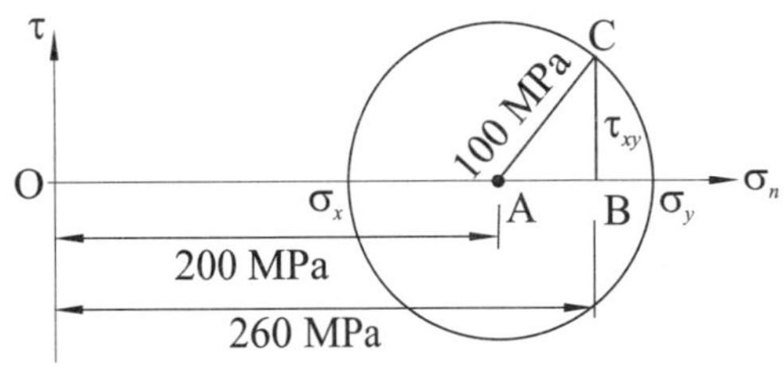

Mohr circle

Radius of Mohr's circle $r = \frac{\sigma_y - \sigma_x}{2} = 100$ MPa, Center of Mohr's circle $OA = \frac{\sigma_y + \sigma_x}{2} = 200$ MPa.

From the geometry of Mohr's circle; $AB^2 = AC^2 + BC^2$

$100^2 = 60^2 + \tau_{xy}^2$

$$\tau_{xy}^2 = 80^2$$

$$\tau_{xy} = 80 \text{ MPa}$$

Example 6.69

A wire of circular cross-section of diameter 1.0 mm is bent into a circular arc of radius 1.0 m by application of pure bending moments at its ends. The Young's modulus of the material of the wire is 100 GPa. The maximum tensile stress developed in the wire is _____ MPa.

GATE 2019

Solution

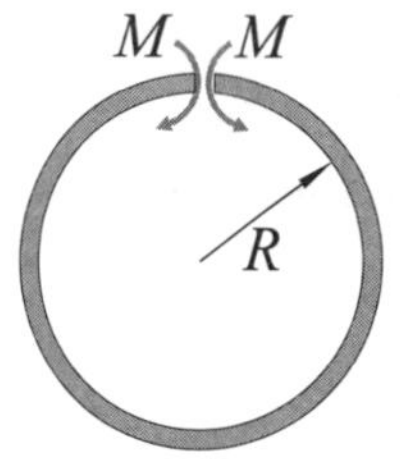

Bending formula,

$$\frac{M}{I} = \frac{\sigma}{y} = \frac{E}{R}$$

Maximum stress, $\sigma_{\max} = \frac{E}{R} y_{\max}$

$$\sigma_{\max} = \frac{E}{R} \times \frac{d}{2}$$

Substituting $R = 1$ m, $d = \frac{1}{1000}$ m and $E = 100 \times 10^9 \text{ N/m}^2$, we have

$$\sigma_{\max} = \frac{100 \times 10^9}{1} \times \frac{1}{2 \times 1000} = 50 \times 10^6$$

$$\sigma_{\max} = 50 \text{ MPa}$$

Example 6.70

A prismatic, straight, elastic, cantilever beam is subjected to a linearly distributed transverse load as shown below. If the beam length is L, Young's modulus E, and area moment of inertia I, the magnitude of the maximum deflection is

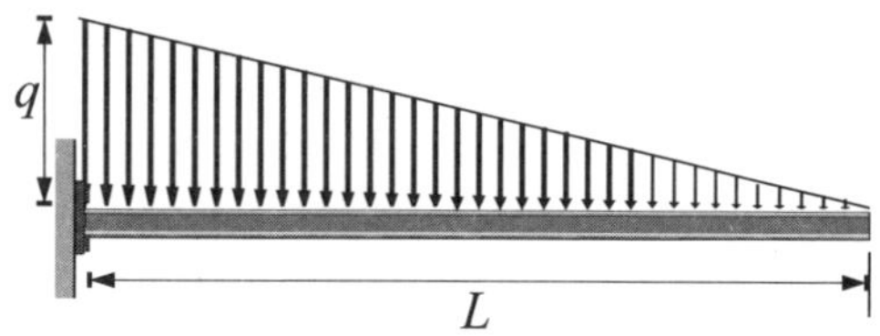

(A) $\frac{qL^4}{15EI}$ (B) $\frac{qL^4}{30EI}$ (C) $\frac{qL^4}{10EI}$ (D) $\frac{qL^4}{60EI}$

GATE 2019

Solution

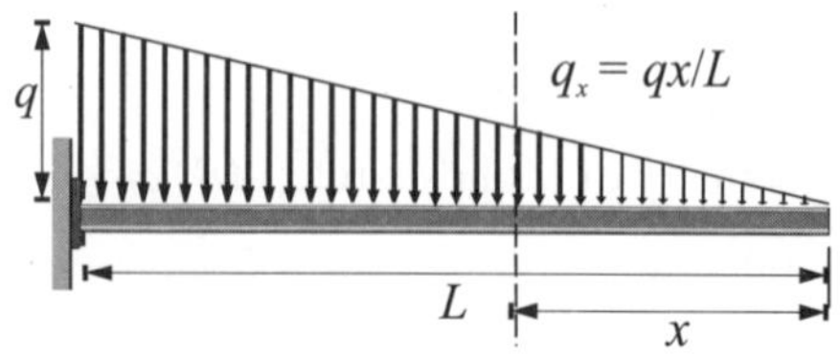

Bending moment at $M_x = \frac{qx^3}{6L}$

Differential equation of bending is

$$EI \frac{d^2y}{dx^2} = -M_x \quad \Rightarrow \quad \frac{d^2y}{dx^2} = -\frac{qx^3}{6EI\,L}$$

Integrating, we get

$$\frac{dy}{dx} = -\frac{qx^4}{4 \times 6EI\,L} + c_1 \qquad \text{(i)}$$

Integrating again, we get

$$y = -\frac{qx^5}{5 \times 4 \times 6EI\,L} + c_1 x + c_2 \qquad \text{(ii)}$$

At $x = L$, $y = 0$ and $\frac{dy}{dx} = 0$, we get

$$c_1 = \frac{qL^3}{24EI} \text{ and } c_2 = -\frac{qL^4}{30EI}$$

$$y = -\frac{qx^5}{120EI\,L} + \frac{qL^3}{24EI}x - \frac{qL^4}{30EI}$$

Maximum deflection at $x = 0$; $\quad y_{x=0} = \Delta = -\frac{qL^4}{30EI}$

$$\Delta = \frac{qL^4}{30EI}$$

Example 6.71

A horizontal cantilever beam of circular cross-section, length 1.0 m and flexural rigidity $EI = 200 \text{ N.m}^2$ is subjected to an applied moment $M_A = 1.0$ N.m at the free end as shown in the figure. The magnitude of the vertical deflection of the free end is ____ mm (round off to one decimal place).

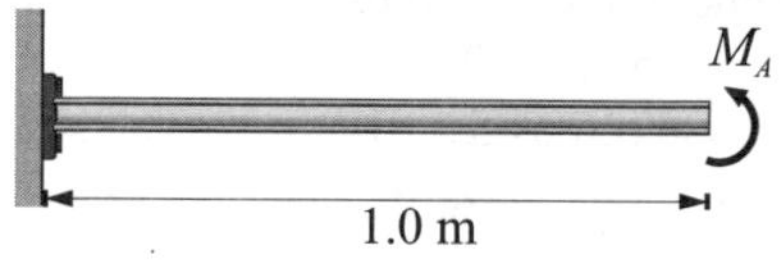

GATE 2019

Solution

Deflection at the end of cantilever due to uniform bending is

$$\Delta = \frac{ML^2}{2EI}$$

$$\Delta = \frac{1 \times 1^2}{2 \times 200} \text{ m} = \frac{1000}{400} \text{ mm}$$

$$\Delta = 2.5 \text{ mm}$$

6.3 PRACTICE PAPER

Time: 3 hours **Max. Marks:100**

Q.1 to Q.30 carry one mark each

Q.1 to Q.20 Multiple Choice Questions

Q.1 For the beam shown, which of the following are discontinuous at the mid span?

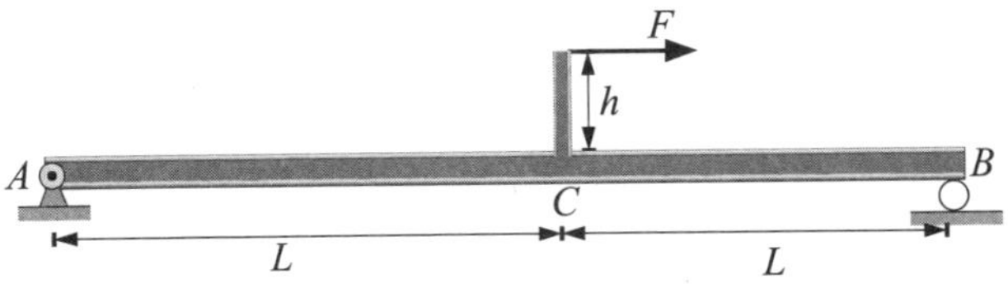

(A) Bending moment only

(B) Axial force and bending moment only

(C) Bending moment and shear force only

(D) Axial force, bending moment and shear force

Q.2 A beam is fixed at the left end and supported by a spring at the other end. The length of the beam is L and its flexural rigidity is EI. The spring constant is $k = \frac{3EI}{L^3}$. A vertical downward load P is applied at the right end. The deflection of the point under the load P is

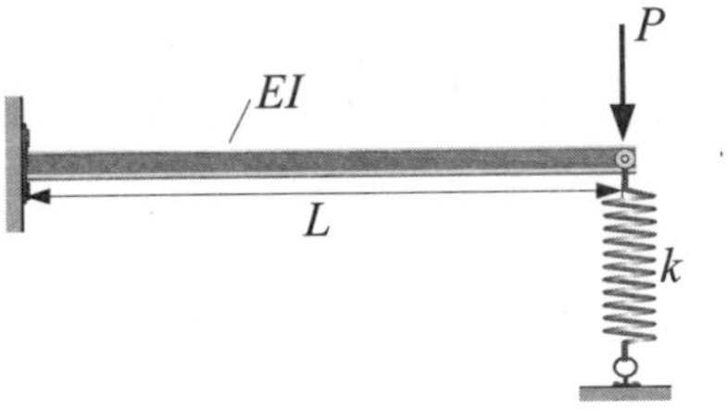

(A) $\frac{PL^3}{9EI}$ (B) $\frac{PL^3}{6EI}$ (C) $\frac{2PL^3}{9EI}$ (D) $\frac{5PL^3}{9EI}$

Q.3 The diameter of a shaft is increased from 30 mm to 60 mm, all other conditions remaining unchanged. How many times is its torque carrying capacity increased?

(A) 2 times (B) 4 times (C) 8 times (D) 16 times

Q.4 When a steel tyre of internal diameter of 'd' is shrinked over a wheel of external diameter of 'D' and if E be the Young's modulus of steel, then hoop stress in tyre is

(A) $\frac{E(D-d)}{d}$ (B) $E\frac{D}{d}$ (C) $E\left(\frac{D-d}{D}\right)^2$ (D) 0

Q.5 A simply supported beam is subjected to a distributed loading as shown in the diagram given below. What is the maximum shear force in the beam?

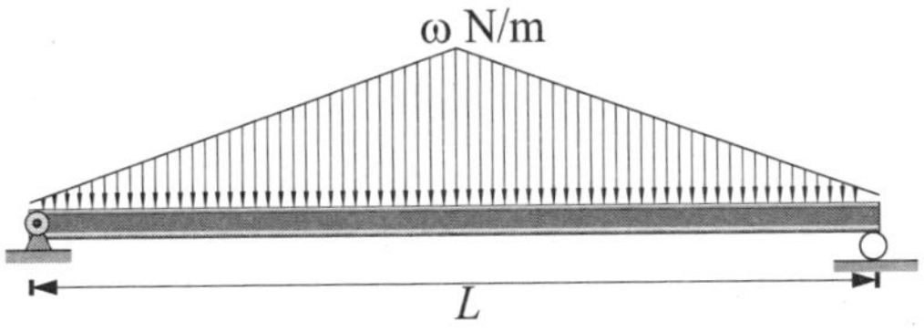

(A) $\frac{\omega L}{4}$ (B) $\frac{\omega L}{2}$ (C) $\frac{\omega L}{3}$ (D) $\frac{\omega L}{6}$

Q.6 A beam AB is pinned at A and supported by spring of stiffness k at the other end. The flexural rigidity of the beam is EI. The deflection at the center of beam is

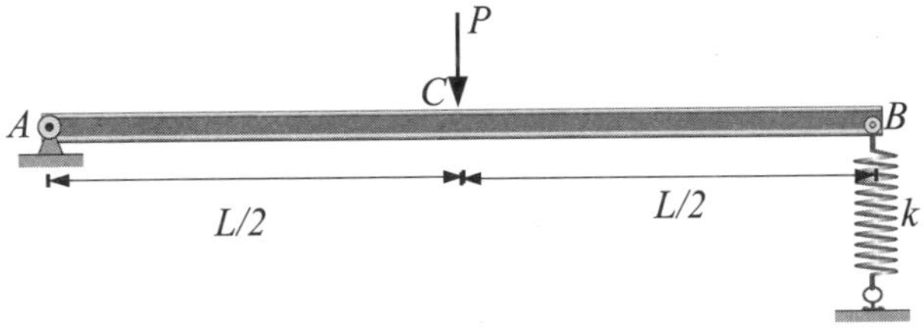

(A) $\frac{P}{2k}$ (B) $\frac{PL^3}{48EI}+\frac{P}{4k}$

(C) $\frac{PL^3}{48EI}+\frac{P}{2k}$ (D) $\frac{PL^3}{3EI}+\frac{P}{2k}$

Q.7 A cantilever beam is constructed by two beams (with flexural rigidity EI and $2EI$) as shown in figure. The deflection under the load P is

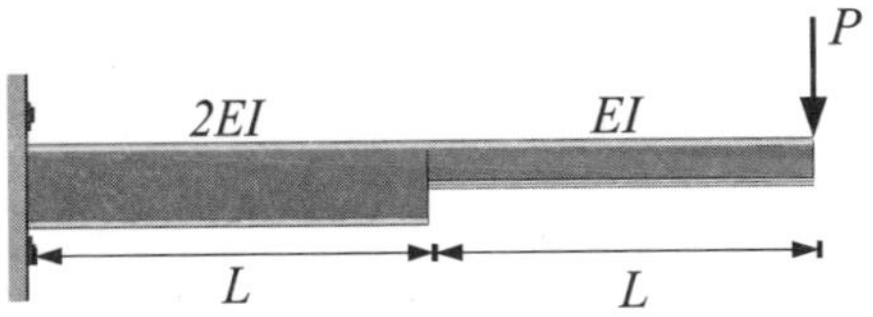

(A) $\frac{3}{2}\frac{PL^3}{EI}$ (B) $\frac{3}{7}\frac{PL^3}{EI}$

(C) $1.33\frac{PL^3}{EI}$ (D) None of these

Q.8 Circumferential and longitudinal strain of a cylinder boiler under steam pressure are ε_θ and ε_l respectively. The change in volume of boiler cylinder per unit volume will be

(A) $\varepsilon_\theta + 2\varepsilon_l$ (B) $\varepsilon_\theta + \varepsilon_l$ (C) $2\varepsilon_\theta + \varepsilon_l$ (D) $2\varepsilon_\theta \varepsilon_l$

Q.9 The two-dimensional state of stress at a point is given by the corresponding Mohr's circle is a

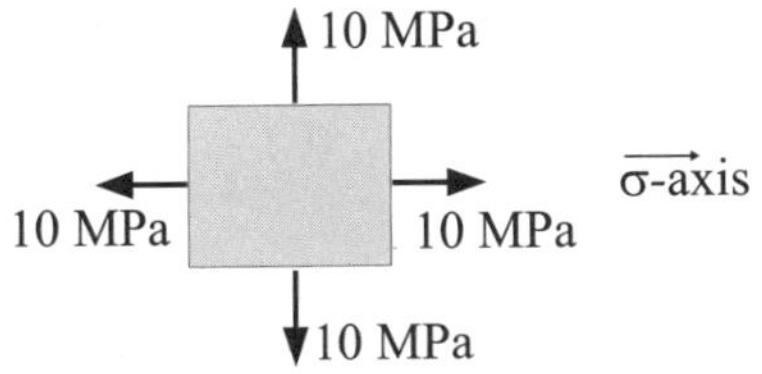

(A) Circle of radius 10 MPa with center at 10 MPa on the σ-axis.

(B) Circle of radius 10 MPa with center at −10 MPa on the σ-axis.

(C) Point on the positive σ-axis.

(D) Point on the negative σ-axis.

Q.10 Five rods of area of cross-section A, length L and Young's modulus E, are pinned jointed together as shown in figure. The vertical deflection of pin D is

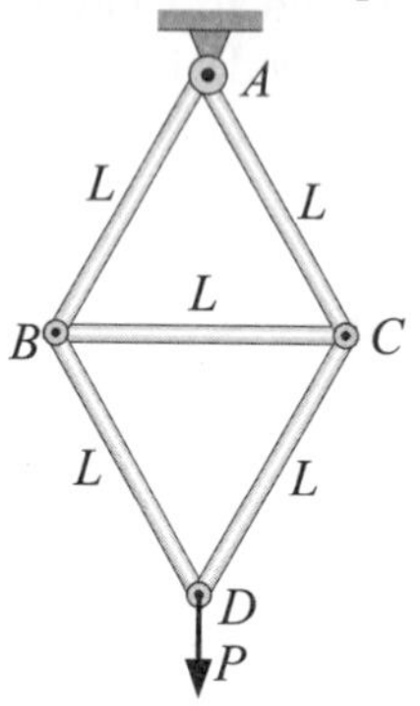

(A) $\frac{7}{2}\frac{PL}{EA}$ (B) $3\frac{PL}{EA}$ (C) $\frac{5}{3}\frac{PL}{EA}$ (D) None of these

Q.11 A frame of two arms of equal length L is shown in the following figure. The flexural rigidity of each arm of the frame is EI. The vertical deflection at the point of application of load P is

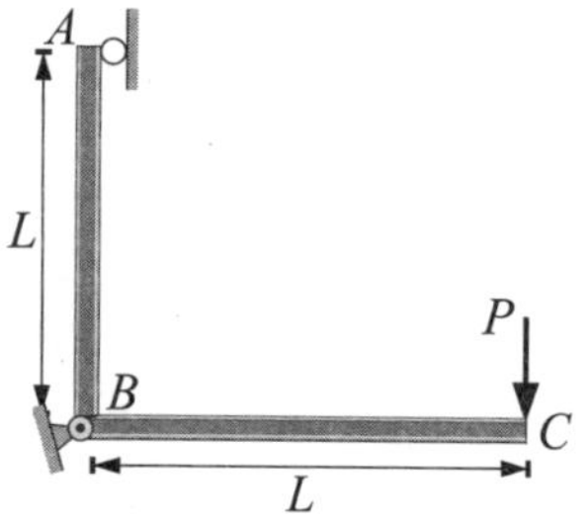

(A) $\frac{PL^3}{3EI}$ (B) $\frac{2PL^3}{3EI}$ (C) $\frac{PL^3}{EI}$ (D) $\frac{4PL^3}{3EI}$

Q.12 A simply supported beam of span L is subjected to a concentrated load P at mid-span. The cross-section of the beam is rectangular. The ratio of the shear stress at $\frac{1}{4}$th the depth of the beam to the shear stress at the center of the cross-section is

(A) $\frac{3}{8}$ (B) $\frac{1}{2}$ (C) $\frac{3}{4}$ (D) 2

Q.13 Figure shows the shear force diagram (SFD) of the beam. The maximum bending moment (by magnitude) in the beam is

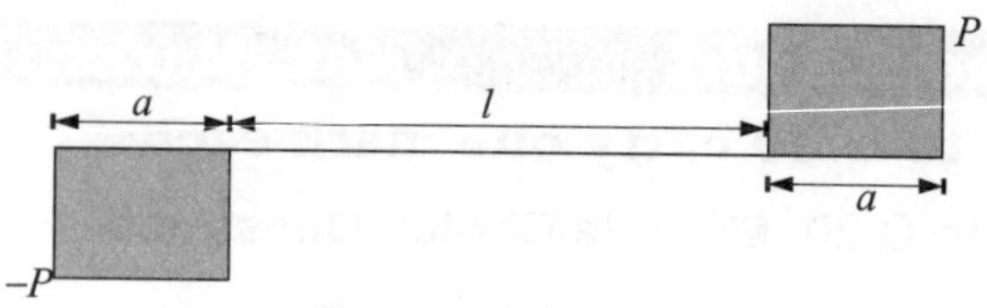

Shear force diagram

(A) Pa (B) $P\left(a+\frac{l}{2}\right)$ (C) Pl (D) 0

Q.14 If a fixed beam of length l is subjected to a load W at the mid span, then the bending moment under the load will be equal to

(A) $\frac{Wl}{2}$ (B) $\frac{Wl}{4}$ (C) $\frac{Wl}{8}$ (D) None of these

Q.15 Consider the following statements:

A simply supported beam is subjected to a couple some where in the span. It would produce

1. A rectangular shear force diagram
2. Parabolic bending moment diagram
3. Both +ve and -ve bending moment which are maximum at the point of application of the couple.

Of these statements, which are correct

(A) 1, 2 and 3 are correct (B) 1 and 2 are correct

(C) 2 and 3 are correct (D) 1 and 3 are correct

Q.16 Polar moment of inertia of a hollow tube of diameter 'd' and wall thickness 't' is

(A) $\frac{\pi d^3 t}{32}$ (B) $\frac{\pi d^3 t}{16}$ (C) $\frac{\pi d^3 t}{4}$ (D) $\frac{\pi d^4}{16}$

Q.17 A fixed beam of length l carrying uniformly distributed load ω, the location of zero bending moment from fixed end is

(A) $\frac{l}{2}$ (B) $\frac{l}{4}$ (C) $\frac{l}{8}$ (D) None of these

Q.18 A cube is subjected to three mutually perpendicular tensile stress σ, the volumetric strain of cube will be

(A) $\frac{3\sigma}{E}(1-2\nu)$ (B) $\frac{\sigma}{E}(1-2\nu)$

(C) $\frac{3\sigma}{E}(2-\nu)$ (D) None of these

Q.19 Thin cylindrical shell of diameter d, thickness t and Poisson's ratio ν is subjected to internal pressure P. The hoop strain (circumferential strain) is

(A) $\frac{Pd}{2tE}\left(1-\frac{\nu}{2}\right)$ (B) $\frac{Pd}{2tE}(1-2\nu)$

(C) $\frac{Pd}{2tE}(0.5-\nu)$ (D) None of these

Q.20 The strain energy stored in a simply supported beam as shown in figure, is

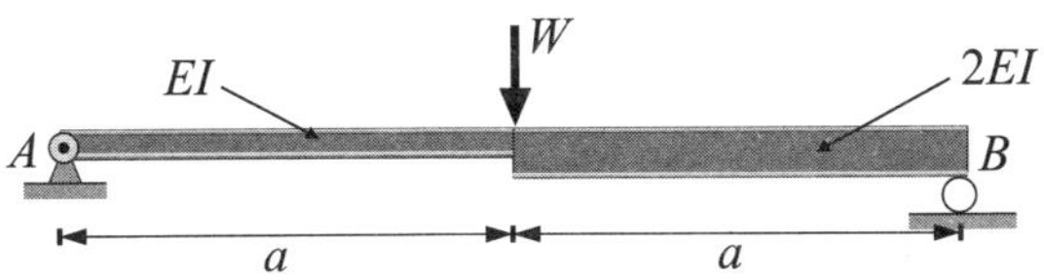

(A) $\frac{W^2a^3}{96EI}$ (B) $\frac{W^2a^3}{24EI}$ (C) $\frac{W^2a^3}{16EI}$ (D) 0

Q.21 to Q.30 Numerical Answer Questions

Q.21 The PQ of length 5 m with flexural rigidity 2×10^5 N is hinged at both ends. For what minimum force F (in N) is it expected to buckle? _______.

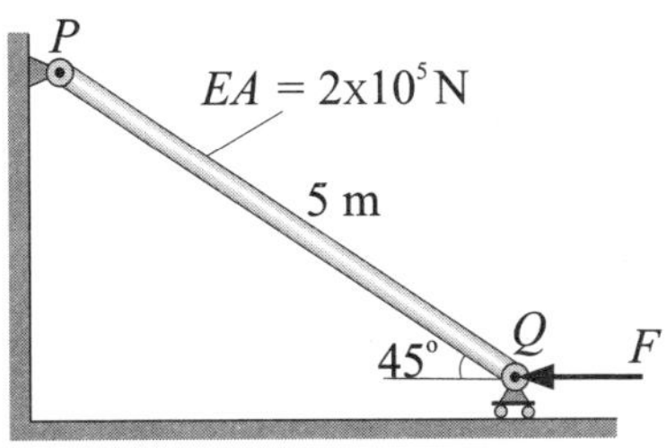

Q.22 At a point in a body subjected to plane stress, the state of stress is shown in the figure. One of the principal stresses is 180 MPa. The unknown shear stress τ (in MPa) is___.

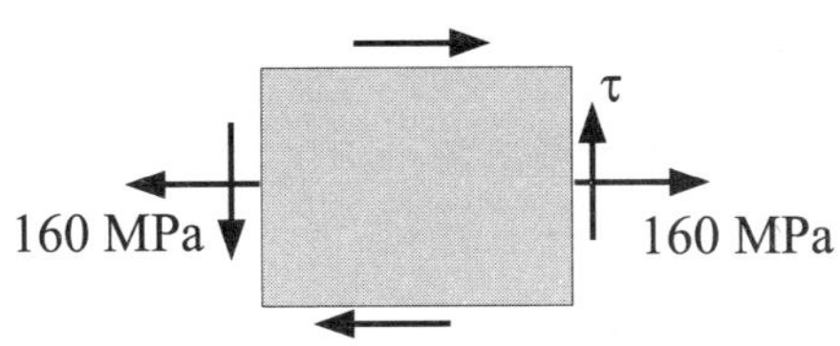

Q.23 A stepped circular shaft made of steel is rigidly fixed at two supports A and C as shown in the figure. A torque of 680 Nm is applied on the shaft at point B. The diameter of portion AB is twice that of portion BC. The magnitudes of torque reactions at supports A is_________.

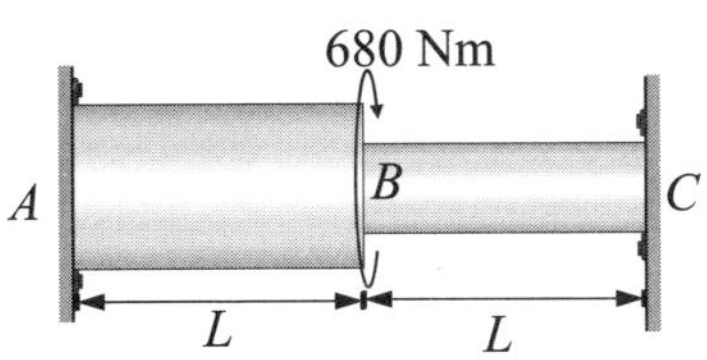

Q.24 A propped cantilever beam of span 4 m is subjected to a uniformly distributed load of 20 kN/m as shown in the figure. The reaction at the roller support is______.

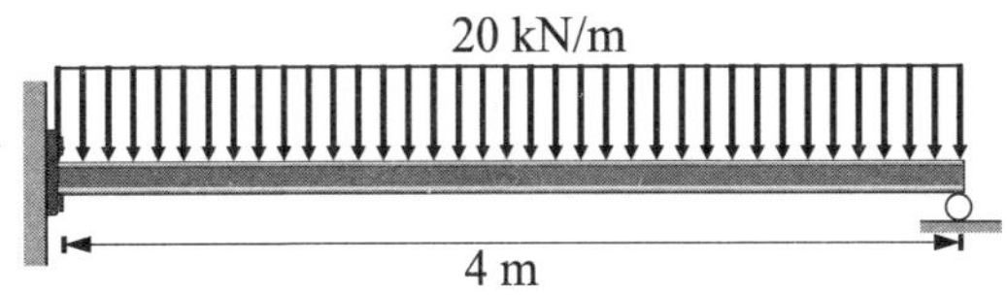

Q.25 A beam subjected to pure bending due to a moment M_0 has a radius of curvature $R = 5000$ cm as shown due to this moment. The moment of inertia of the cross-section is $I = 50\,\text{cm}^4$ and the Young's modulus of the beam material is $E = 200$ GPa. The bending moment M_0 (in kNm) is____.

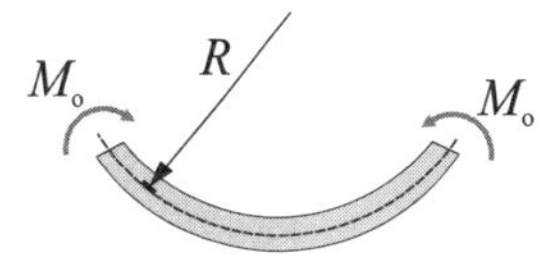

Q.26 A 100 mm thick steel rectangular plate of size 100 mm × 200 mm is subjected to biaxial stresses of $\sigma_x = 150$ MPa, $\sigma_y = 200$ MPa, as shown below. The Young's modulus and Poisson's ratio are 200 GPa and 0.3 respectively. The change in the thickness of the plate is___.

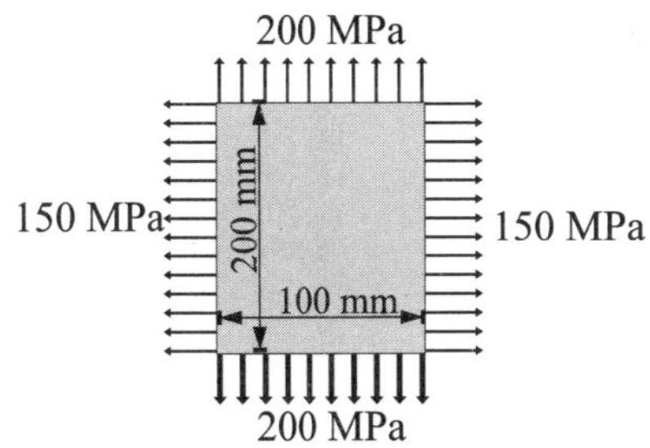

Q.27 A simply supported beam with an overhanging end is loaded as shown below. The maximum bending (in kNm) moment (by magnitude) in the beam is_________.

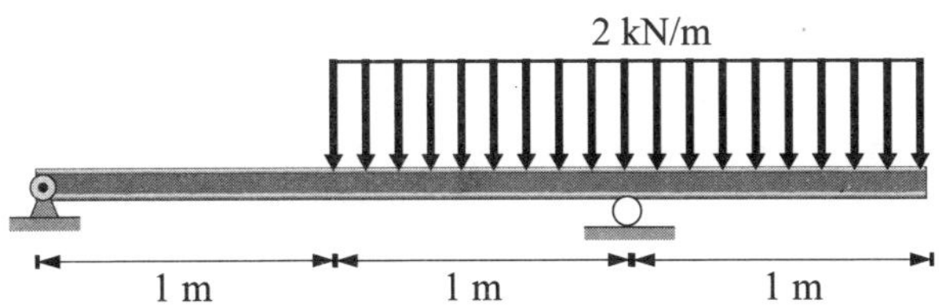

Q.28 A double overhanging beam is shown in the following figure. The minimum value of $\frac{a}{L}$ to ensure a pure negative moment all through the span is_________.

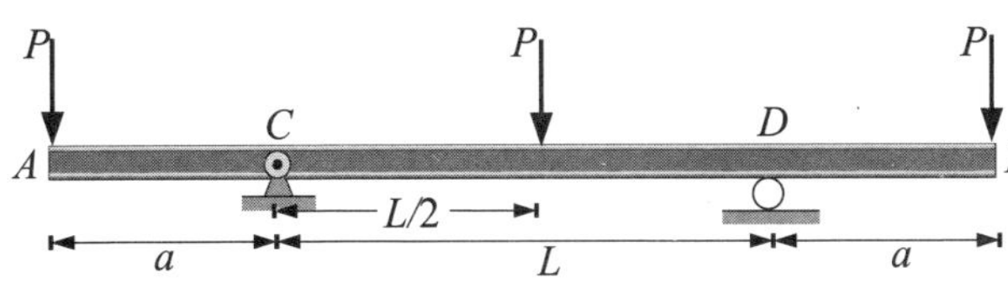

Q.29 An axial core of 100 mm is bored throughout the length of 200 mm diameter solid circular shaft. For the same maximum shear stress, the percentage torque carrying capacity lost by this operation is _______.

Q.30 The given figure (all dimensions are in mm) shows the I-section of the beam. The shear stress at point P (very close to the web) is 12 MPa. The stress at point Q in the web very close to the flange is _________.

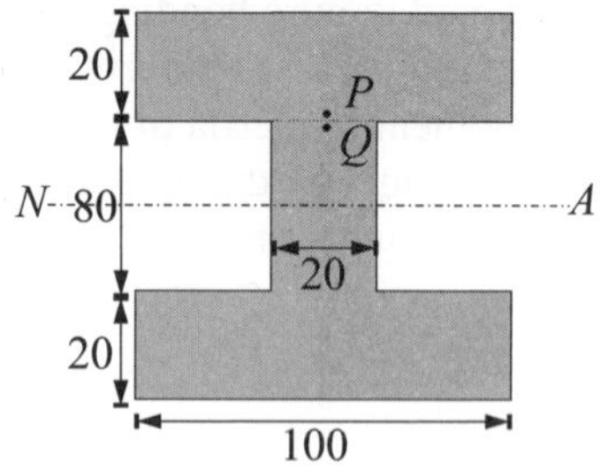

Q.31 to Q.65 carry two marks each

Q.31 to Q.50 Multiple Choice Questions

Q.31 A frame ABC is shown in the figure. Members AB and BC both have a length L, and Young's modulus E. Member AB and BC both have a square cross-section of side 'a'. A load P is applied at point C as shown in the figure. The maximum bending stress in the frame is

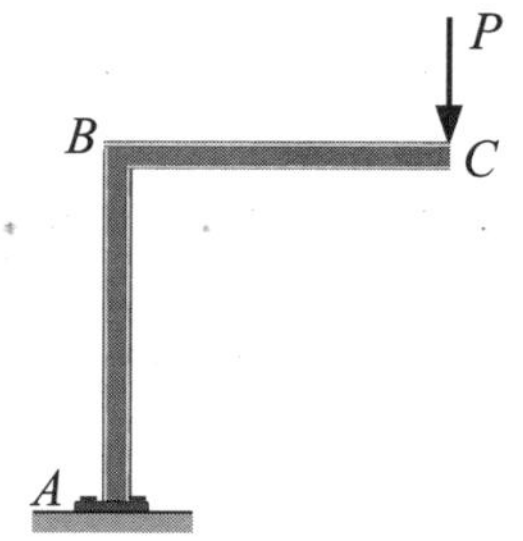

(A) $\dfrac{3PL}{a^3}$ (B) $\dfrac{6PL}{a^3}$ (C) $\dfrac{9PL}{a^3}$ (D) $\dfrac{12PL}{a^3}$

Q.32 A cantilever beam with a square bend at the end as shown is loaded with a force P. The cross-section of the beam is square with side a. The maximum flexural stress (σ_{max}) in the beam is

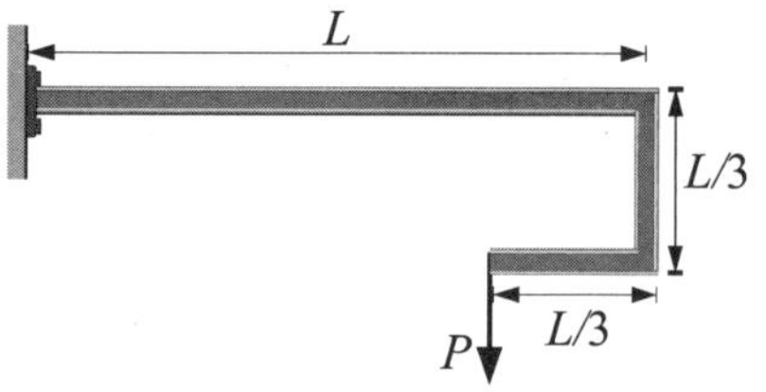

(A) $\dfrac{16Pl}{a^3}$ (B) $\dfrac{10Pl}{a^3}$ (C) $\dfrac{8Pl}{a^3}$ (D) None of these

Q.33 A solid circular shaft of diameter d and of total length $3L$ is held fixed at one end and load by a torque T_1 at B and T_2 at C as shown in figure. The angle of twist in the shaft at C is

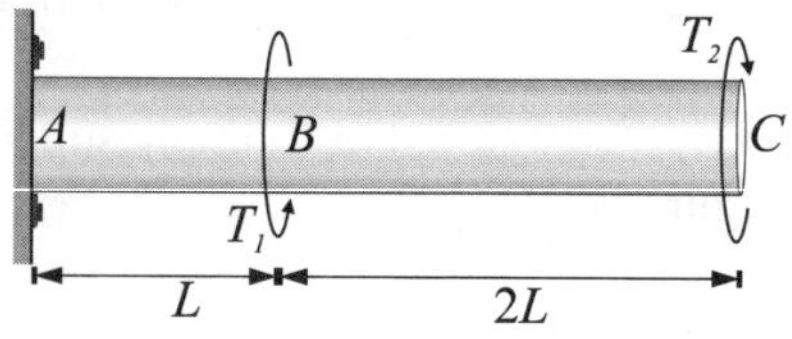

(A) $\dfrac{32(3T_2+T_1)L}{\pi Gd^4}$ (B) $\dfrac{32(3T_2-T_1)L}{\pi Gd^4}$

(C) $\dfrac{64(2T_2+T_1)L}{\pi Gd^4}$ (D) $\dfrac{64(2T_2-T_1)L}{\pi Gd^4}$

Q.34 Two shafts of the same material and equal length are subjected to the torque. The diameter of the first shaft is twice that of the second. The ratio of the strain energy of the first shaft to that of the second shaft is

(A) 16 : 1 (B) 1 : 16 (C) 1 : 2 (D) 2 : 1

Q.35 Two bars of length L are joined together to form a structural system that is fixed at top and bottom as shown. The bottom part BC of the structure has a cross-sectional area twice that of the top part AB. Both bars are made of the same elastic material. What is the stress in the top part AB of this structural system if a load P acts at B as shown in figure. Neglect the self weight of the system

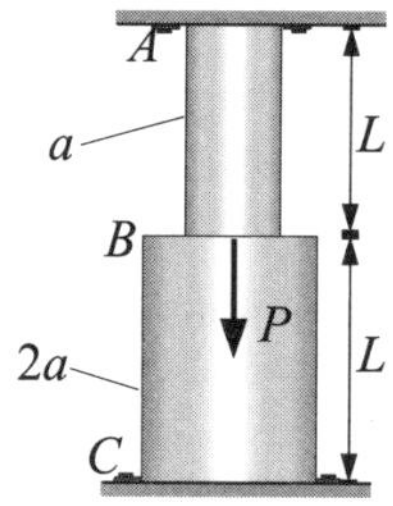

(A) $\dfrac{P}{3a}$ (B) $\dfrac{P}{2a}$ (C) $\dfrac{2P}{a}$ (D) $\dfrac{P}{4a}$

Q.36 A L-shaped bar of square cross-section with sides 'b' is loaded as shown in figure. If the value of the stress component σ_x at point P is zero, the distance a of the force F from the x-axis should be

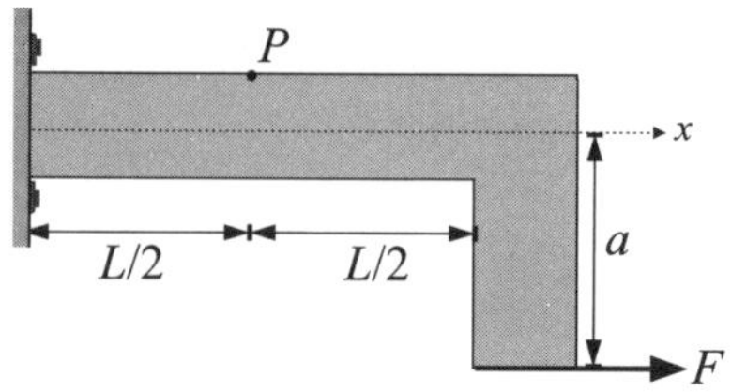

(A) b (B) $\dfrac{b}{2}$ (C) $\dfrac{b}{3}$ (D) $\dfrac{b}{6}$

Q.37 A stepped shaft PQR is fixed at both ends as shown in the figure. A torque T is applied at point Q. The polar moment of inertia of the shafts PQ and QR are J_1 and J_2 respectively. Modulus of rigidity is G. The angle of twist at point Q due to torque T, is given by (in radians)

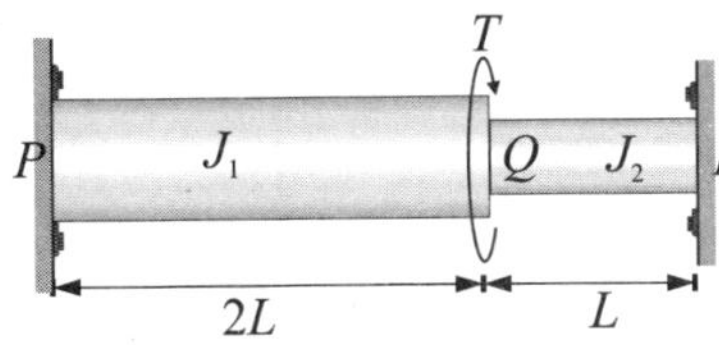

(A) $\frac{2}{J_1}\left(\frac{TL}{G}\right)$ (B) $\frac{1}{J_2}\left(\frac{TL}{G}\right)$

(C) $\left(\frac{2}{J_1}+\frac{1}{J_2}\right)\left(\frac{TL}{G}\right)$ (D) $\left(\frac{2}{J_1+2J_2}\right)\left(\frac{TL}{G}\right)$

Q.38 Two bars of different Young's modulus, E_1 and E_2, but with the same cross-sectional area, A and coefficient of thermal expansion, α , are attached together at one end and fixed at the other as shown in the figure. The construction of this setup was carried out at an ambient temperature of 25°C. The stress in the bars when the temperature is uniformly increased by 10°C is

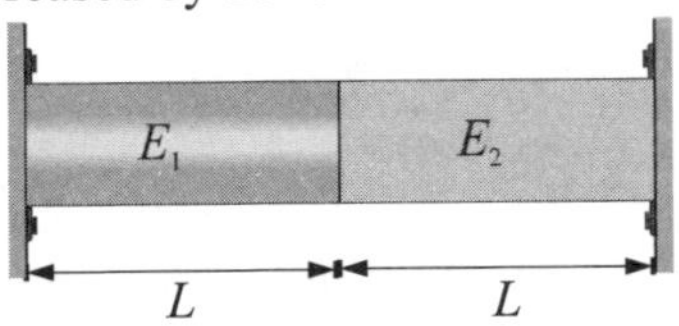

(A) $\sigma=10\alpha\,(E_1+E_2)$ (B) $\sigma=20\alpha\,(E_1+E_2)$

(C) $\sigma=20\alpha\left(\frac{E_1E_2}{E_1+E_2}\right)$ (D) $\sigma=10\alpha\left(\frac{E_1E_2}{E_1+E_2}\right)$

Q.39 At a point in a body in plane stress, is subjected to two different condition (a) an equibiaxial stress $\sigma_{xx}=\sigma_{yy}=\sigma$, and (b) a pure shear stress $\tau_{xy}=\sigma$. The magnitude of the maximum– principal stress in each of these cases, are

(A) $\sigma_{max}=\sigma$, $\sigma_{max}=\sigma$ (B) $\sigma_{max}=0$, $\sigma_{max}=\sigma$

(C) $\sigma_{max}=\sigma$, $\sigma_{max}=0$ (D) $\sigma_{max}=0$, $\sigma_{max}=0$

Q.40 Consider the following statements with reference to a continuous beam supported at A, C and E for which the shear force diagram is shown in figure.

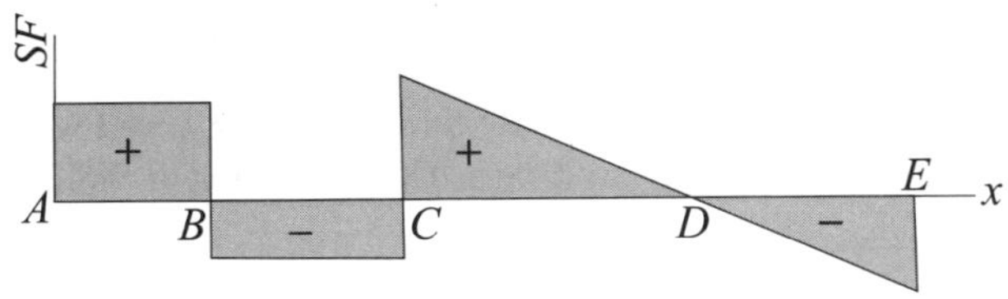

There is a

(1) Concentrated load acting at point B

(2) Concentrated load acting at point D

(3) Uniformly distributed load acting on the portion CE

Of these statements

(A) 1, 2 and 3 are correct (B) 1and 2 are correct

(C) 2 and 3 are correct (D) 1and 3 are correct

Q.41 Maximum stress (σ_{max}) induced in a bar of length L and density ρ, rotating at an angular velocity ω about its one end is given by

(A) $\rho\omega^2L^2$ (B) $\frac{\rho\omega^2L^2}{2}$ (C) $\frac{\rho\omega^2L^2}{8}$ (D) None of these

Q.42 A uniform rod of length L cross-section area A and modulus of elasticity E is held rigidly by fixed supports at the ends and an axial load P is applied at mid length of the rod. The strain energy stored is

(A) $\frac{P^2L}{EA}$ (B) $\frac{P^2L}{4EA}$ (C) $\frac{P^2L}{8EA}$ (D) None of these

Q.43 Two beams AB and BC are jointed at B and loaded as shown in figure. The bending moment at fixed support A is

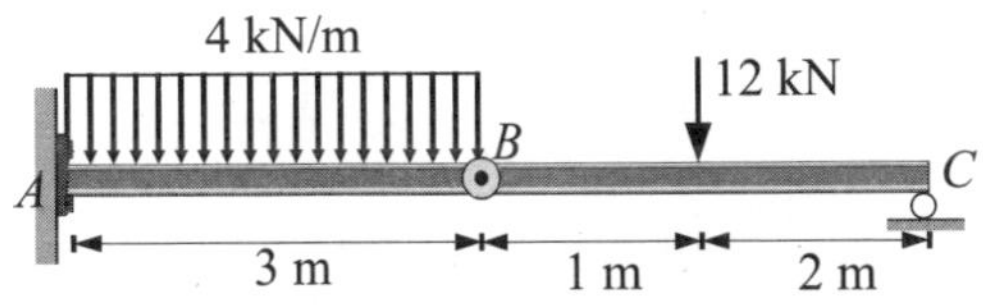

(A) 42 kNm (B) 21 kNm (C) 24 kNm (D) 18 kNm

Q.44 Deflection of the free end of a cantilever beam (See figure) is subjected to a concentrated load at the middle of its span is given by

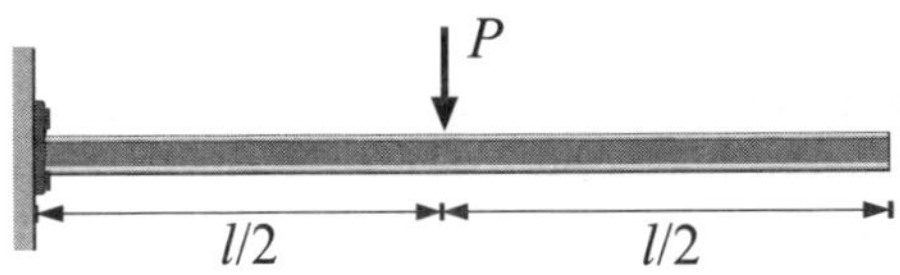

(A) $\frac{5Pl^3}{48EI}$ (B) $\frac{Pl^3}{8EI}$ (C) $\frac{Pl^3}{3EI}$ (D) $\frac{Pl^3}{6EI}$

Q.45 The maximum eccentricity e of compressive load acting on a short strut of diameter d without producing tension at the base section is

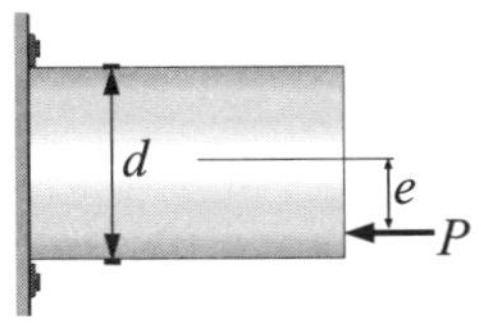

(A) $e=\frac{d}{2}$ (B) $e=\frac{d}{4}$ (C) $e=\frac{d}{8}$ (D) $e=\frac{d}{\sqrt{2}}$

Q.46 The compound shaft shown in figure is fixed at the two ends. It is subjected to a twisting moment T at the middle. The ratio of reaction torque T_1/T_2 is

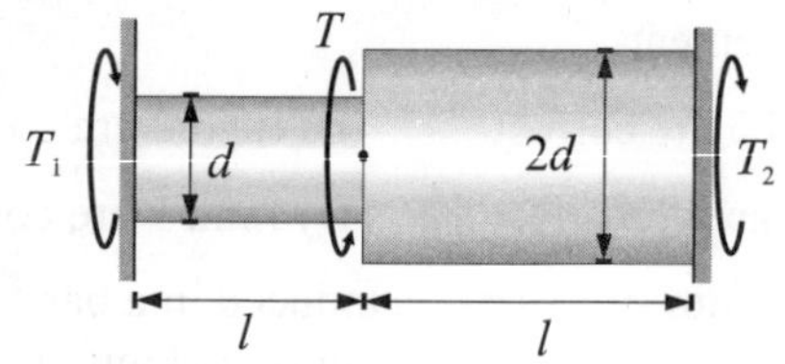

(A) $\frac{1}{8}$ (B) $\frac{1}{16}$ (C) $\frac{3}{16}$ (D) None of these.

Q.47 A rectangular section beam subjected to a bending moment M varying along its length is required to develop same maximum bending stress at any cross-section. If the depth of the section is constant, then its width will very as

(A) M (B) $\sqrt{M}$ (C) M^2 (D) $1/M$

Q.48 A continuous frame $ABCD$ built-in at A is loaded as shown in figure. All members have same length L and same flexural rigidity EI. Considering only bending effect, the vertical deflection of point D is

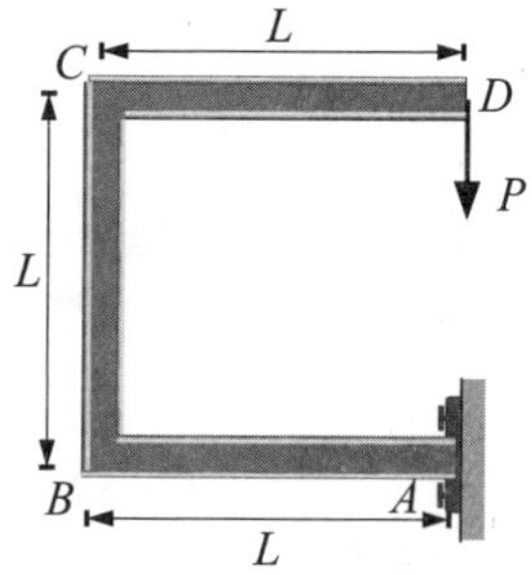

(A) $\frac{PL^3}{3EI}$ (B) $\frac{4PL^3}{3EI}$ (C) $\frac{5PL^3}{3EI}$ (D) $\frac{2PL^3}{3EI}$

Q.49 A long rod of length L, cross-section area a, density ρ and modulus of elasticity E hangs vertically from a roof. The maximum longitudinal strain in the rod is

(A) $\frac{\rho g L^2}{E}$ (B) $\frac{\rho g L^2}{2E}$ (C) $\frac{2\rho g L^2}{E}$ (D) 0

Q.50 A rectangular strain rosette, shown in figure, gives following readings in a strain measurement task $\varepsilon_1 = 1000\times10^{-6}$, $\varepsilon_2 = 800\times10^{-6}$ and $\varepsilon_3 = 600\times10^{-6}$. The direction of the major principal strain with respect to gauge 1 is

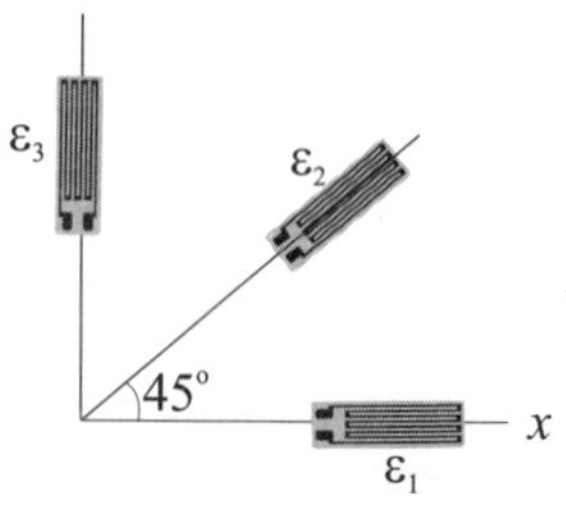

(A) 45° (B) 30° (C) 15° (D) 0°

Q.50 to Q.65 Numerical Answer Questions

Q.51 The maximum bending moment (magnitude wise in kNm) for the beam shown in figure, is________.

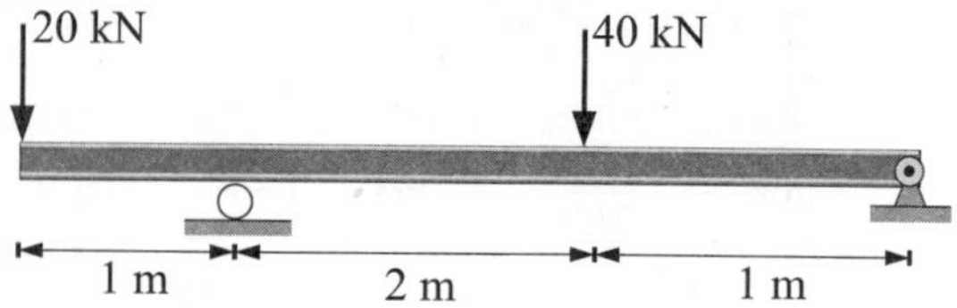

Q.52 At a point in an object subjected to a plane stress conditions, the state of stress is as shown in the figure. The normal stress on the plane AB (in MPa) is_______.

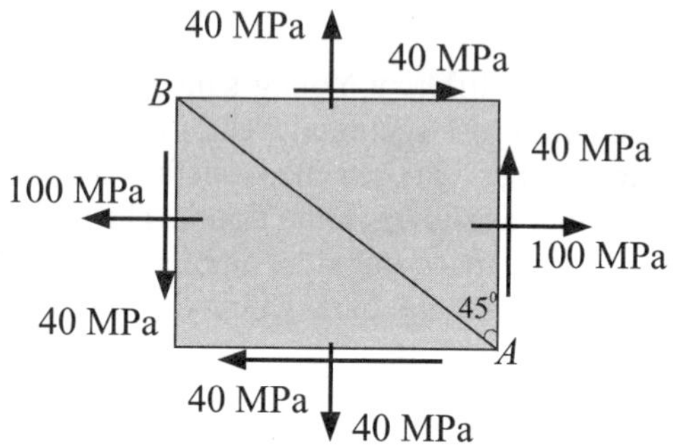

Q.53 For the truss shown in the figure, both the members have a cross-sectional area A and Young's modulus E. The vertical deflection of point B is________.

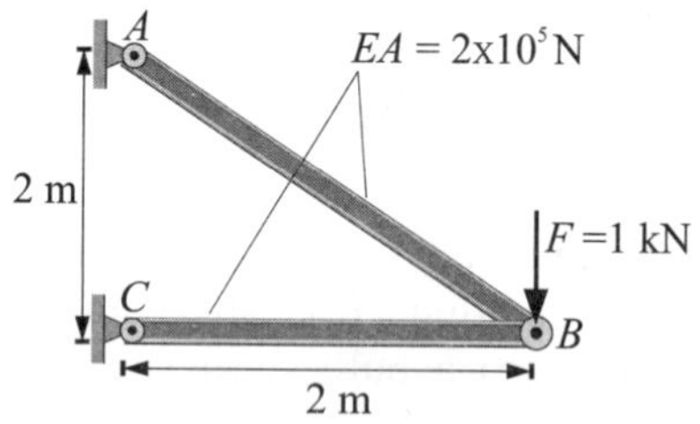

Q.54 Figure shows the dimensions as well as loading on a simply supported beam. The distance (in m) from end A, of the point where maximum bending moment occurs, is___.

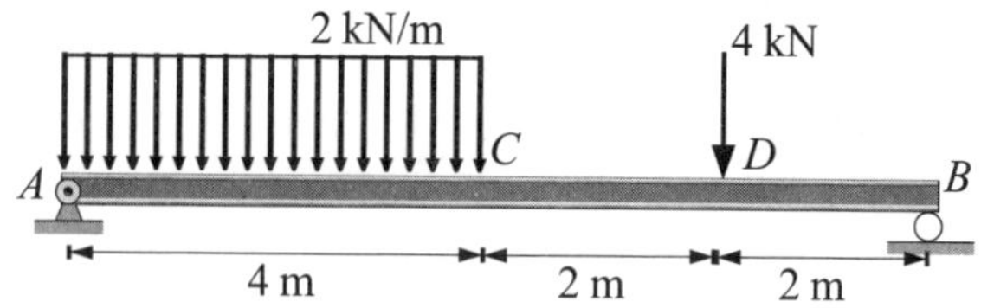

Q.55 A cantilever beam of flexural rigidity $EI = 81$ MN/m^2 is loaded as shown in figure. The deflection at the free end is________.

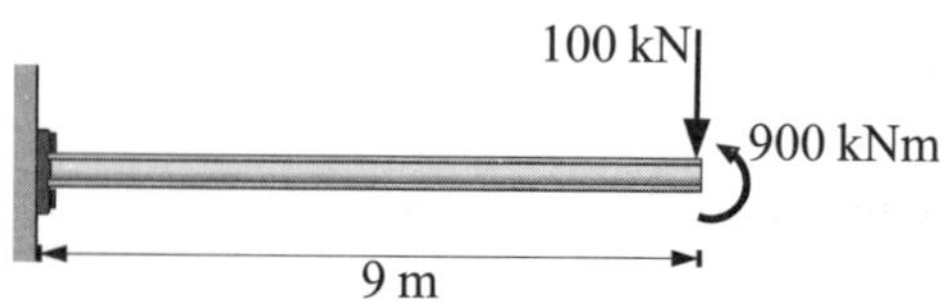

Q.56 A steel plate is subjected to stresses 400 MPa (tension) and 200 MPa (compression) as shown in figure. The normal stress σ_n(in MPa) on the plane AC is_____.

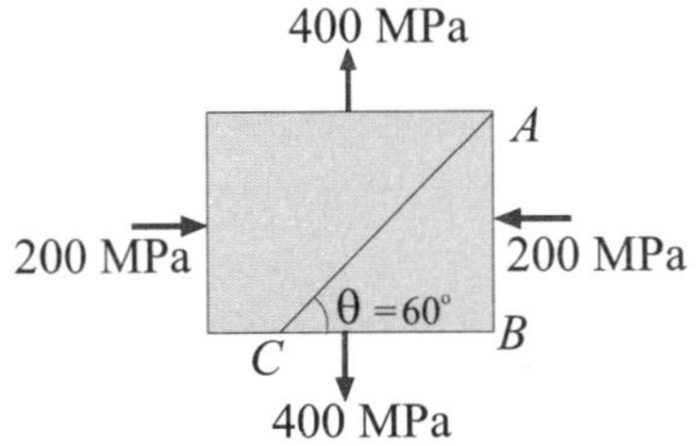

Q.57 There are two cantilever beams with the same flexural rigidity of EI and length of 2 m. First beam is subjected to a uniformly distributed load of 6 N/m and the second beam is subjected to concentrated point load of 2 N at the free-end. The ratio of strain energies due to bending of first beam to second beam is____.

Q.58 A uniformly distributed load ω (in kN/m) is acting over the entire length of a 3 m long cantilever beam. If the shear force of the midpoint of cantilever is 6 kN, what is the value of ω ?_________.

Q.59 A beam $ABCD$ with simple supports at A, B and D and an internal hinge at C is subjected to loads as shown in the figure. The reaction at middle support B, is _________.

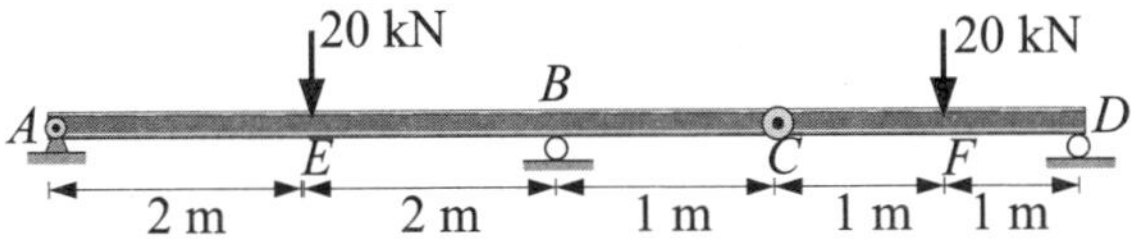

Q.60 A beam of rectangular cross-section is subjected to transverse loads. In a section where the shear stress at (1/4)th of the beam depth is 120 MPa, the maximum shear stress (in MPa) is_________.

Q.61 A circular log of timber has diameter d. The ratio of depth to breadth of rectangular beam that can be cut from a circular log for the strongest section in bending, is ___.

Q.62 A solid circular steel shaft of 50 mm diameter, fixed at one end, is subjected to torques as shown below. The shearing modulus of the material is 80 GPa. The rotation (in radians) of the free end S due to torsion is_______.

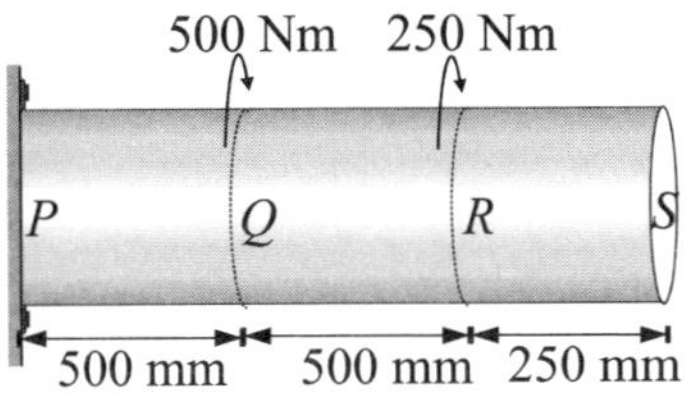

Q.63 The principal stresses at a point on body subjected to a state of plane stress are 10 MPa and 20 MPa. The magnitude of shear stress on a plane in which the normal stress is 12 MPa is_________.

Q.64 A 0.2 mm thick tape goes over a frictional pulley of 25 cm diameter. If modulus of elasticity E of material is 100 GPa, then the maximum stress induced in the tape is_.

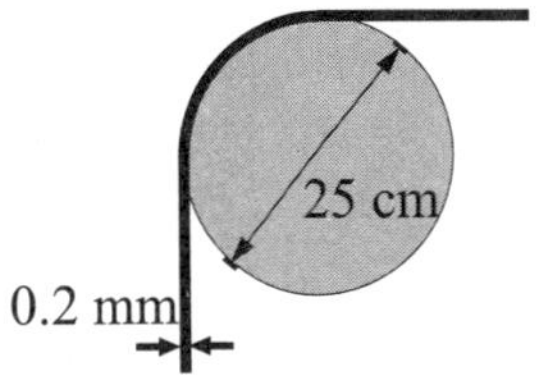

Q.65 Shear force diagram of simply supported beam is shown in figure. The value of maximum bending (in kNm) moment in the beam is_________.

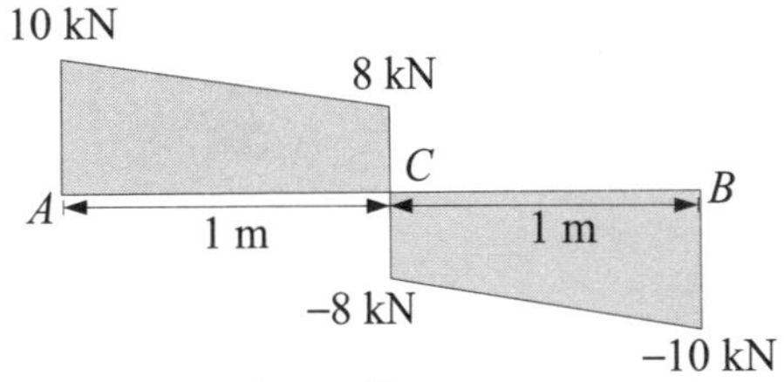

Shear force diagram

6.4 SOLUTION TO PRACTICE PAPER

Q.1 Ans:(B)

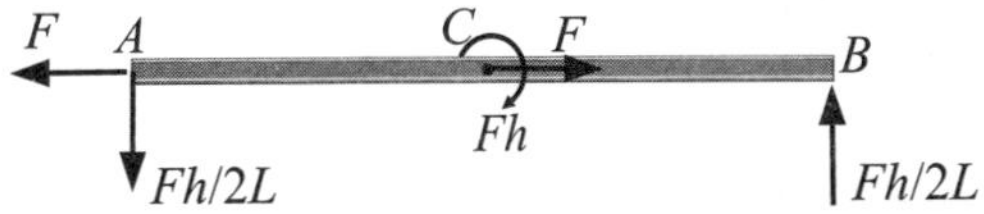

Free-body diagram of beam

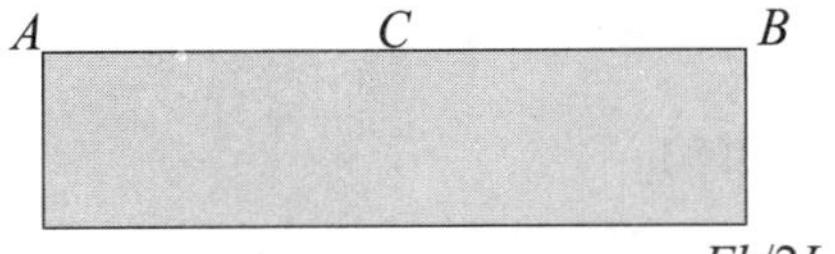

Shear force diagram

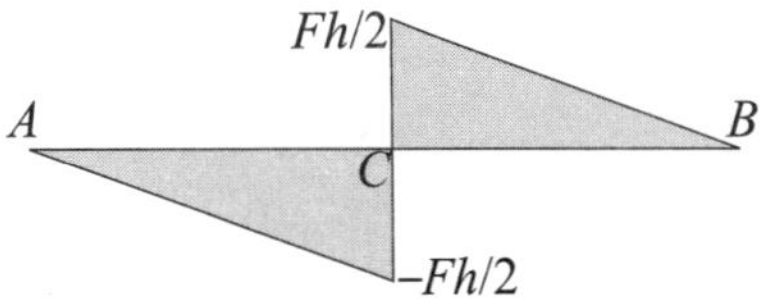

Bending moment diagram

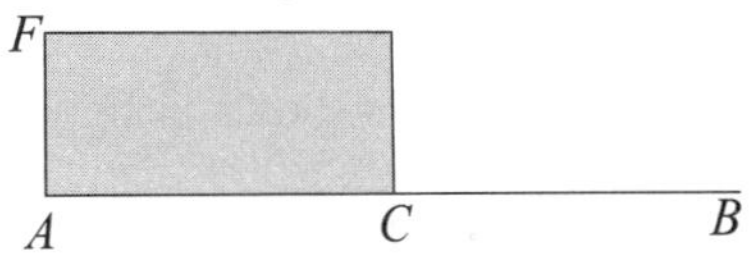

Axial force diagram

Force F is transferred at C by a force F and moment Fh. Free-body diagram of beam, shear force, bending moment and axial force diagram are shown in figure.

Q.2 Ans:(B)

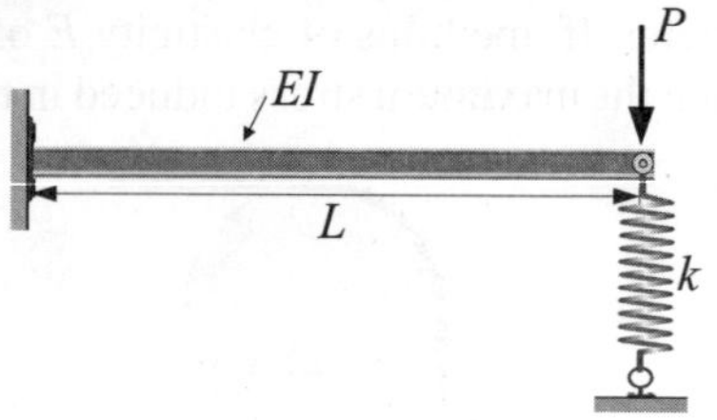

Stiffness of cantilever $k_c = \frac{P}{\Delta} = \frac{3EI}{L^3}$

Figure shows the equivalent diagram of given cantilever beam with spring supported end.

$$\Delta = \frac{P}{k_{eq}} = \frac{P}{k_c + k_{\text{spring}}} = \frac{P}{\frac{3EI}{L^3} + \frac{3EI}{L^3}}$$

which gives

$$\Delta = \frac{PL^3}{6EI}$$

Q.3 Ans:(B)

Torsion formula $\frac{T}{J} = \frac{\tau}{r} = \frac{G\theta}{l} \quad \Rightarrow \quad T = J\frac{\tau}{r}$

or $\quad T = \frac{\pi d^3}{16}\tau$

$$\frac{T_2}{T_1} = \left(\frac{d_2}{d_1}\right)^3 = \left(\frac{60}{30}\right)^3$$

$$\frac{T_2}{T_1} = 8$$

Q.4 Ans:(B)(A)

Hoop strain $\varepsilon_\theta = \frac{\pi D - \pi d}{\pi d} = \frac{D-d}{d}$

Hoop stress $\sigma_\theta = E\,\varepsilon_\theta = E\left(\frac{D-d}{d}\right)$

$$\sigma_\theta = \frac{E(D-d)}{d}$$

Q.5 Ans:(A)

Shear force diagram of beam is shown in figure.

Maximum shear force is at supports.

Reaction at support A, $\quad R_A = \frac{\frac{1}{2}\omega L}{2} = \frac{\omega L}{4}$

Therefore,

$$\text{Maximum shear force} = \frac{\omega L}{4}$$

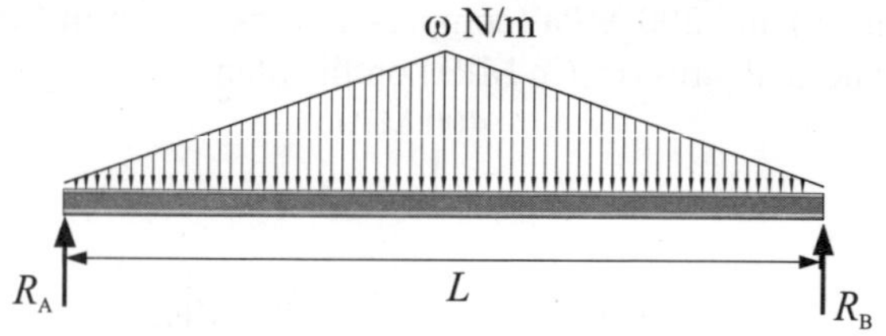

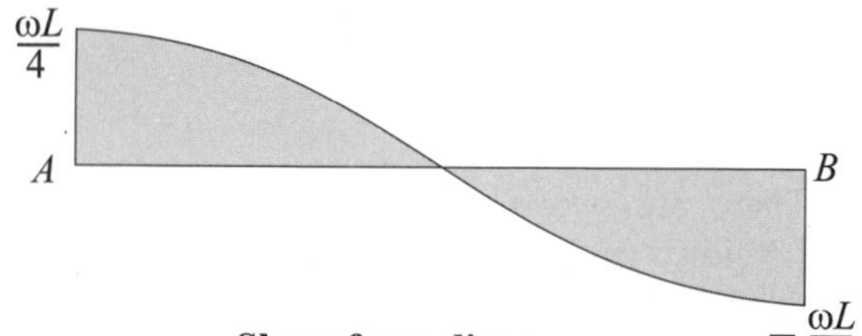

Shear force diagram

Q.6 Ans:(B)

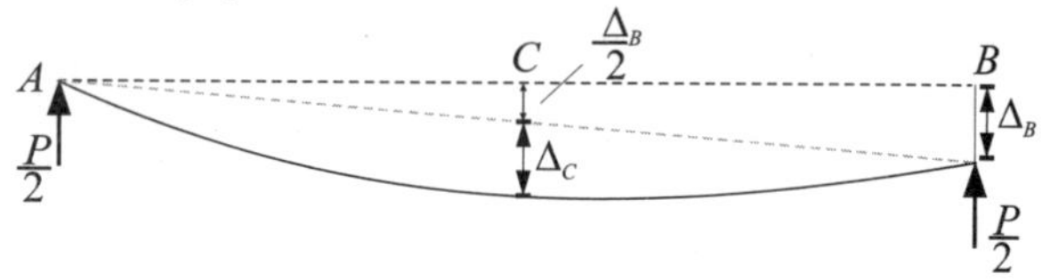

Support reactions $R_A = R_B = \frac{P}{2}$

Deflection of spring support $\Delta_B = \frac{P}{2k}$

Deflection of beam at center when supports are rigid

$$\Delta_C = \frac{PL^3}{48EI}$$

Resultant deflection of beam at centre $\Delta = \Delta_C + \frac{\Delta_B}{2}$

$$\Delta = \frac{PL^3}{48EI} + \frac{P}{4k}$$

Q.7 Ans:(A)

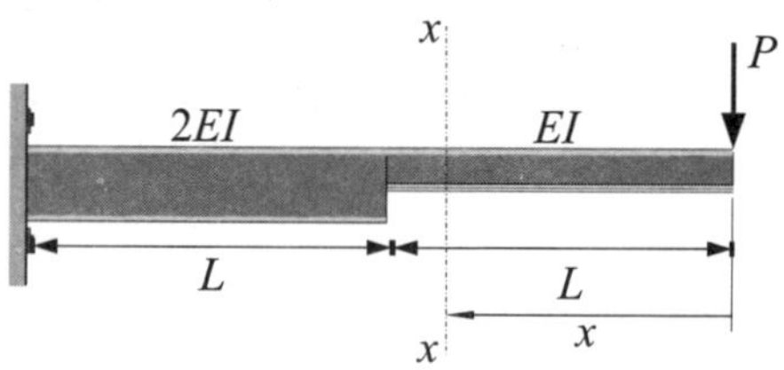

Bending moment at x-x, $\quad M_x = Px$

Strain energy of cantilever beam

$$U = \int_0^L \frac{M^2 dx}{2EI} + \int_L^{2L} \frac{M^2 dx}{2 \times 2EI}$$

or $\quad U = \int_0^L \frac{(Px)^2 dx}{2EI} + \int_L^{2L} \frac{(Px)^2 dx}{2 \times 2EI}$

which gives $U = \frac{3}{4}\frac{P^2L^3}{EI}$

Deflection of free end (by Castigliano's theorem)

$$\Delta = \frac{\partial U}{\partial P} = \frac{3}{2}\frac{PL^3}{EI}$$

$$\Delta = \frac{3}{2}\frac{PL^3}{EI}$$

Q.8 Ans:(C)

Volume of boiler

$$V = \pi r^2 l \quad \Rightarrow \quad \log V = \log \pi + 2\log r + \log l$$

Differential form $\frac{dV}{V} = 2\frac{dr}{r} + \frac{dl}{l}$

Substituting $\varepsilon_\theta = \frac{dr}{r}$ and $\varepsilon_l = \frac{dl}{l}$

which gives

$$\varepsilon_v = 2\varepsilon_\theta + \varepsilon_l$$

Q.9 Ans:(C)

Given: $\sigma_x = 10$ MPa, $\sigma_y = 10$ MPa and $\tau_{xy} = 0$

Radius of Mohr's circle, $r = \sqrt{\left(\frac{\sigma_y - \sigma_x}{2}\right)^2 + \tau_{xy}^2}$

or $r = \sqrt{\left(\frac{10-10}{2}\right)^2 + 0^2} = 0$

Coordinate of center of Mohr's circle

$$= \left(\frac{\sigma_y + \sigma_x}{2}, 0\right) = (10, 0)$$

Q.10 Ans:(C)

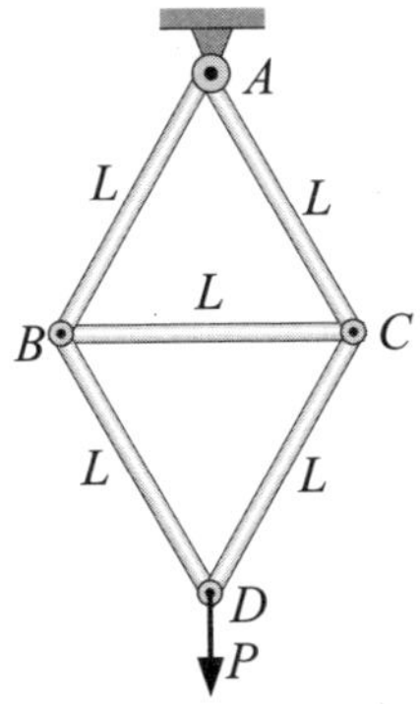

Consider the joint D. From the equilibrium equations

$$\sum F_y = 0; \quad F_{BD}\cos 30 + F_{CD}\cos 30 - P = 0$$

$$\sum F_x = 0; \quad -F_{BD}\sin 30 + F_{CD}\sin 30 = 0$$

which gives $F_{BD} = F_{CD} = \frac{P}{\sqrt{3}}$

Similarly for joint B; $\quad F_{AB} = F_{BC} = \frac{P}{\sqrt{3}}$

$$F_{AB} = F_{BD} = F_{DC} = F_{BC} = F_{AC} = \frac{P}{\sqrt{3}}$$

Strain energy of frame

$$U = \sum \frac{F^2L}{2EA} = 5 \times \frac{\left(\frac{P}{\sqrt{3}}\right)^2 L}{2EA} = \frac{5}{6}\frac{P^2L}{EA}$$

Deflection of joint D (by Castigliano's theorem)

$$\Delta = \frac{\partial U}{\partial P} = \frac{\partial}{\partial P}\left(\frac{5}{6}\frac{P^2L}{EA}\right) = \frac{5PL}{3EA}$$

$$\Delta = \frac{5PL}{3EA}$$

Q.11 Ans:(B)

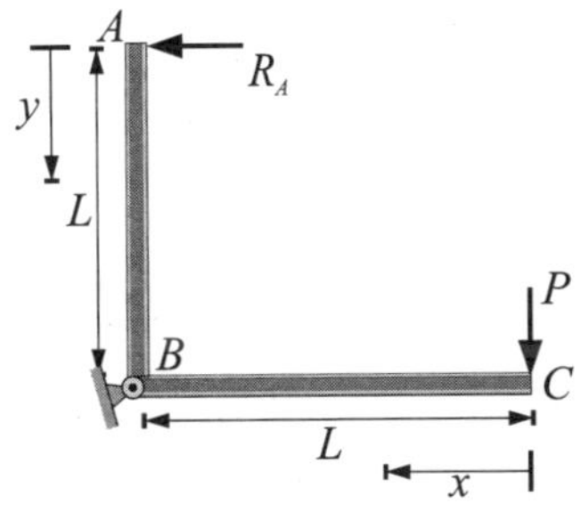

Reaction at support A, $\quad R_A = P$

Bending moment at x, $\quad M_x = Px$

Bending moment at y, $\quad M_y = Py$

Strain energy, $\quad U = \int_0^L \frac{M_x^2 dx}{2EI} + \int_0^L \frac{M_y^2 dy}{2EI}$

or $\quad U = \int_0^L \frac{(Px)^2 dx}{2EI} + \int_0^L \frac{(Py)^2 dy}{2EI}$

or $\quad U = \frac{P^2L^3}{3EI}$

Deflection of C (by Castigalaneo theorem)

$$\Delta = \frac{\partial}{\partial P}\left(\frac{P^2L^3}{3EI}\right)$$

$$\Delta = \frac{2PL^3}{3EI}$$

Q.12 Ans:(C)

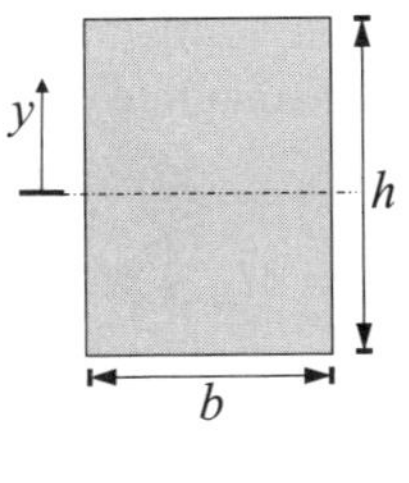

Shear stress at y from neutral axis in rectangular cross section beam is given by

$$\tau = \frac{6F}{bh^3}\left(\frac{h^2}{4} - y^2\right)$$

Shear stress at center of the cross-section $y = 0$;

$$\tau_{y=0} = \frac{6F}{bh^3}\left(\frac{h^2}{4}\right)$$

Shear stress at $\frac{1}{4}$th the depth of beam $y = \frac{h}{2} - \frac{h}{4} = \frac{h}{4}$;

$$\tau_{y=h/4} = \frac{6F}{bh^3}\left[\frac{h^2}{4} - \left(\frac{h}{4}\right)^2\right]$$

from which $$\frac{\tau_{y=h/4}}{\tau_{y=0}} = \frac{6F}{bh^3}\left[\frac{h^2}{4} - \left(\frac{h}{4}\right)^2\right] \Big/ \frac{6F}{bh^3}\left(\frac{h^2}{4}\right)$$

$$\frac{\tau_{y=h/4}}{\tau_{y=0}} = \frac{3}{4}$$

Q.13 Ans:(A)

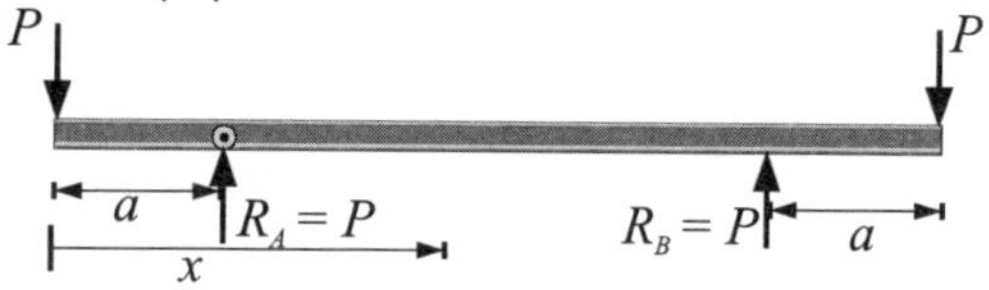

Free body diagram of beam

Bending moment diagram

Figure shows free body and bending moment diagram of beam from given SFD.

Maximum bending moment diagram (by magnitude)

$$M_{max} = Pa$$

Q.14 Ans:(C)

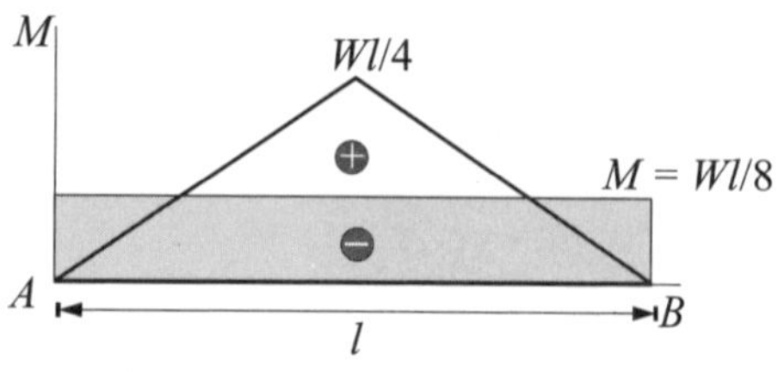

Area of fixing moment diagram (+) = Area of bending moment diagram (–)

Due to symmetry $M_A = M_B = M$; $M \times l = \frac{1}{2} \times \frac{Wl}{4} \times l$

or $$M = \frac{Wl}{8}$$

Bending moment at the mid-span, $M_C = \frac{Wl}{4} - \frac{Wl}{8}$

$$M_C = \frac{Wl}{8}$$

Q.15 Ans:(D)

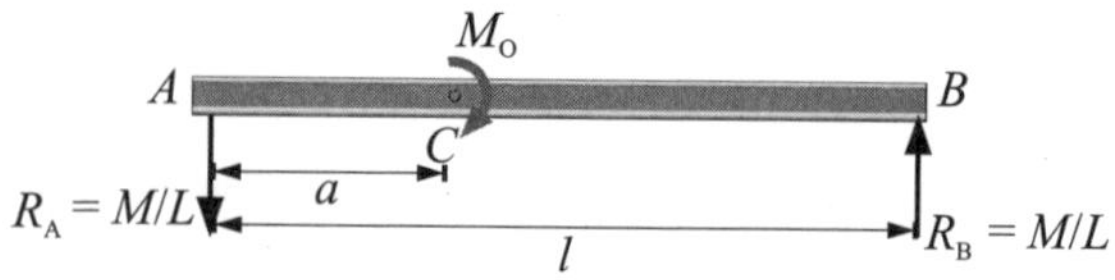

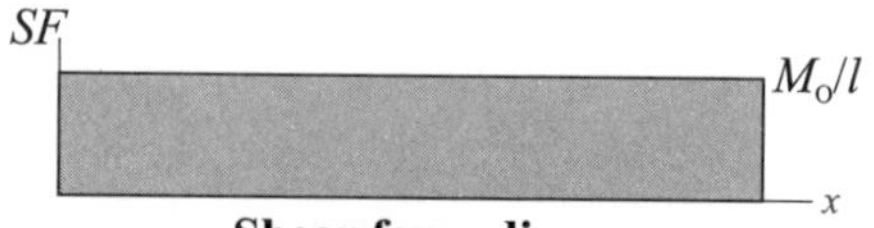

Shear force diagram

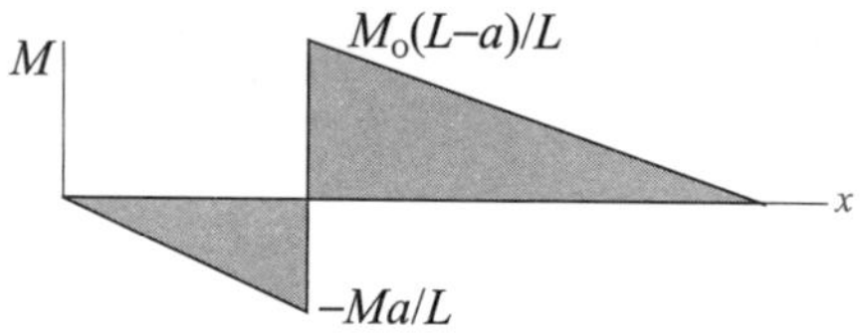

Bending moment diagram

Option# 1. A rectangular shear force diagram.

Option# 3. Both +ve and – ve bending moment which are maximum at the point of application of the couple.

Q.16 Ans:(C)

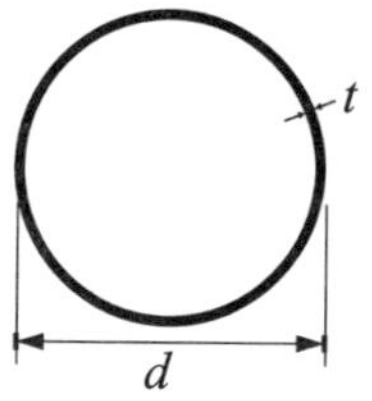

Polar moment of inertia of hollow tube

$$I = \frac{\pi}{32}d^4 - \frac{\pi}{32}(d-2t)^4$$

$$I = \frac{\pi}{32}d^4\left[1 - \left(1 - \frac{2t}{d}\right)^4\right]$$

or $$I = \frac{\pi d^4}{32}\left[1 - \left(1 - 4\times\frac{2t}{d} + \ldots\right)\right]$$

or $$I = \frac{\pi d^4}{32} \times \frac{8t}{d} = \frac{\pi d^3 t}{4}$$

$$I = \frac{\pi d^3 t}{4}$$

Q.17 Ans:(D)

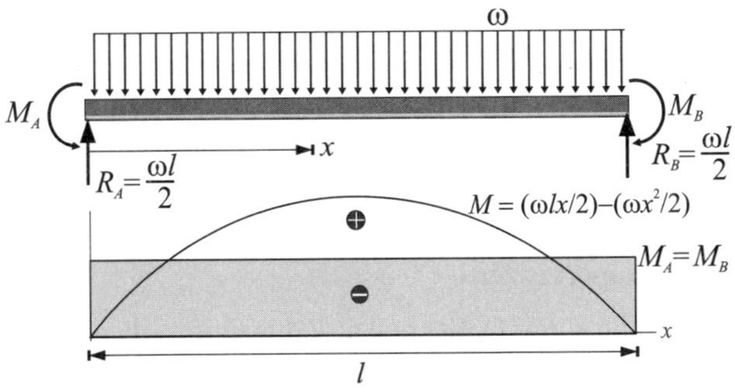

Free moment and fixing moment diagram

Due to symmetrical loading

$$M_A = M_B$$

Area of fixing moment diagram

$$A_1 = -M_A \times l$$

and area of free-moment diagram

$$A_2 = \frac{\omega l^2}{8} \times \frac{2}{3} l = \frac{\omega l^3}{12}$$

But $A_1 + A_2 = 0$

or $$\frac{\omega l^3}{12} - M_A \times l = 0$$

$$M_A = \frac{\omega l^2}{12}$$

Bending moment at x, $$M_x = \frac{\omega l}{2} x - \frac{\omega x^2}{2} - \frac{\omega l^2}{12} = 0$$

or $$6x^2 - 6lx - l^2 = 0$$

Solving for x, we get

$$x = 0.211\,l \text{ and } 0.789\,l$$

Q.18 Ans:(A)

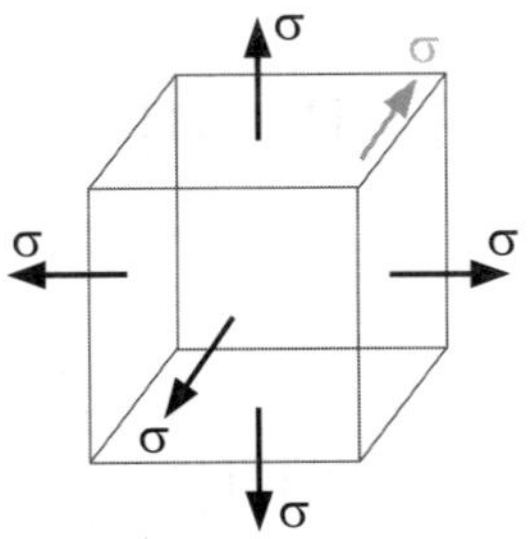

Strain of side $\varepsilon_l = \frac{\sigma}{E} - \nu\frac{\sigma}{E} - \nu\frac{\sigma}{E}$

or $$\varepsilon_l = \frac{\sigma}{E}(1-2\nu)$$

Volume of cube $V = a^3$

Differential form $$\frac{dV}{V} = 3\frac{d\,a}{a}$$

or $$\varepsilon_V = 3\varepsilon_l$$

$$\text{Volumetric strain } \varepsilon_V = \frac{3\sigma}{E}(1-2\nu)$$

Q.19 Ans:(A)

Hoop stress $\sigma_\theta = \frac{Pd}{2t}$

Longitudinal stress $\sigma_l = \frac{Pd}{4t}$

Hoop strain $\varepsilon_\theta = \frac{\sigma_\theta}{E} - \nu\frac{\sigma_l}{E}$

$$\varepsilon_\theta = \frac{1}{E}\left(\frac{Pd}{2t} - \nu\frac{Pd}{4t}\right) = \frac{Pd}{2tE}\left(1 - \frac{\nu}{2}\right)$$

$$\varepsilon_\theta = \frac{Pd}{2tE}\left(1-\frac{\nu}{2}\right)$$

Q.20 Ans:(C)

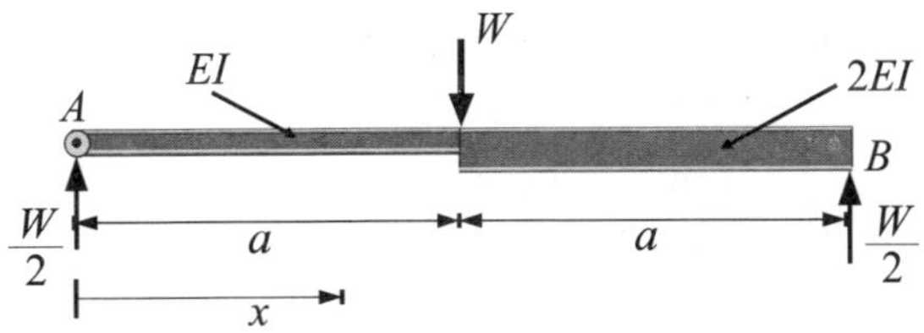

Bending moment:

$$M_x = \frac{W}{2}x; \qquad 0 < x \le a$$

$$M_x = \frac{W}{2}x - W(x-a) = W\left(\frac{2a-x}{2}\right); \qquad a < x \le 2a$$

Strain energy of beam:

$$U = \int_0^a \frac{\left(\frac{W}{2}x\right)^2 dx}{2EI} + \int_a^{2a} \frac{\left(\frac{W(2a-x)}{2}\right)^2 dx}{2 \times 2EI}$$

which gives

$$U = \frac{W^2 a^3}{16EI}$$

Q.21 Ans:[55.83]

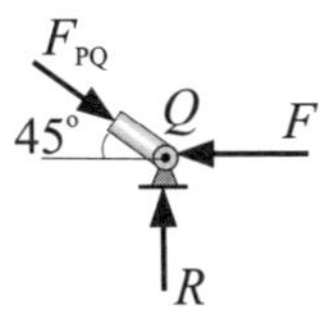

Consider the joint Q.

$$\sum F_x = 0 \Rightarrow F_{PQ}\cos 45 = F$$

$$F_{PQ} = \frac{F}{\cos 45} = \sqrt{2}F$$

Compressive force in rod PQ is $F_{PQ} = \sqrt{2}F$

Critical buckling load for pinned ended joint $P_{cr} = \dfrac{\pi^2 EI}{L^2}$

$$\sqrt{2}F = \frac{\pi^2 \times 2\times 10^5}{5^2}$$

or $$F = \frac{\pi^2 \times 2\times 10^5}{\sqrt{2}\times 5^2}$$

or $$F = \frac{\pi^2 \times 2\times 10^5}{\sqrt{2}\times 5^2}$$

$$F = 55.83 \text{ kN}$$

Q.22 Ans:[60]

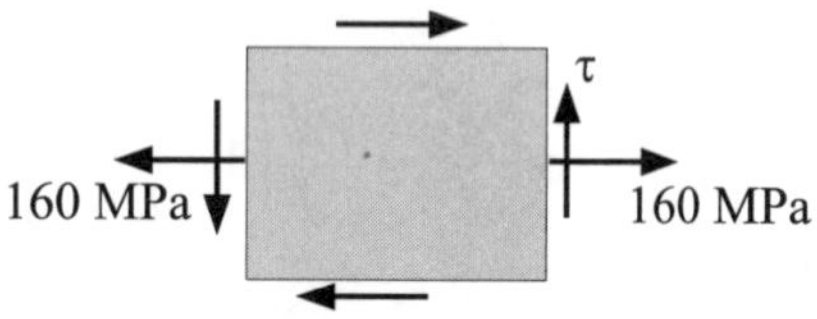

Principle stress, $\sigma_1 = \dfrac{\sigma_x}{2} + \sqrt{\left(\dfrac{\sigma_x}{2}\right)^2 + \tau_{xy}^2}$

substituting $\sigma_x = 160$ MPa and $\sigma_1 = 180$ MPa in above equation, we have

$$180 = \frac{160}{2} + \sqrt{\left(\frac{160}{2}\right)^2 + \tau^2}$$

from which,

$$\tau = 60 \text{ MPa}$$

Q.23 Ans:[640]

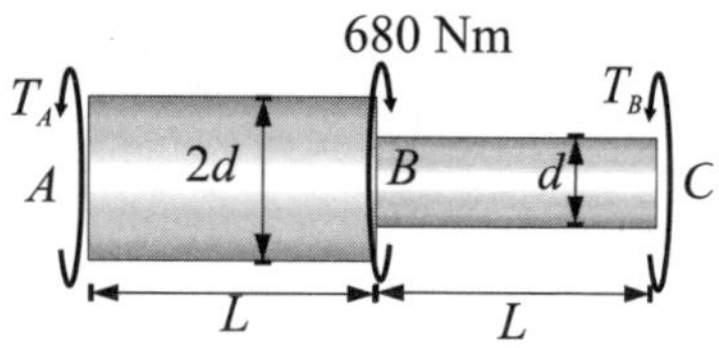

Let T_A and T_C be the torque reactions at supports A and C respectively.

$$\sum T = 0 \quad \Rightarrow T_A + T_C = 680 \qquad \text{(i)}$$

Angle of twist at B; $\theta_B = \dfrac{T_A L}{GJ_A} = \dfrac{T_C L}{GJ_C}$

Substituting $J_A = \dfrac{\pi(2d)^4}{32}$ and $J_C = \dfrac{\pi d^4}{32}$, we have

$$\frac{T_A}{2^4} = T_C \qquad \text{(ii)}$$

Solving for T_A from Equations (i) and (ii), we get

$$T_A = 640 \text{ Nm}$$

Q.24 Ans:[30]

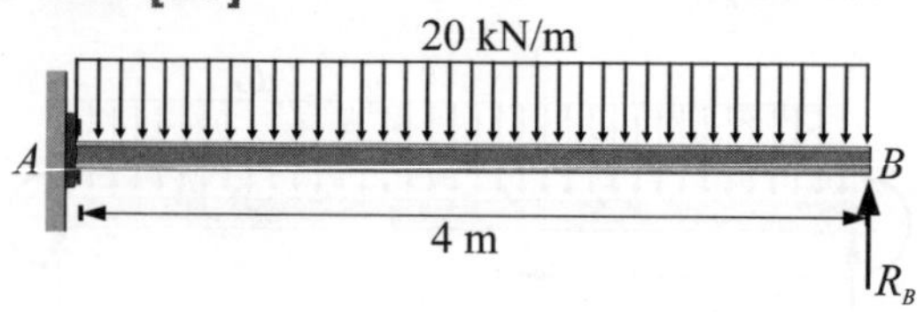

Let R_B be the reaction of roller support. Net deflection of roller support is zero.

Deflection at B = Deflection at B due uniformly distributed load (↓) – Deflection at B due to point load $R_B = 0$

Deflection of beam at B, $\dfrac{\omega l^4}{8EI} - \dfrac{R_B l^3}{3EI} = 0$

$$R_B = \frac{3}{8}\omega l = \frac{3}{8}\times 20\times 4$$

$$R_B = 30 \text{ kN}$$

Q.25 Ans:[2]

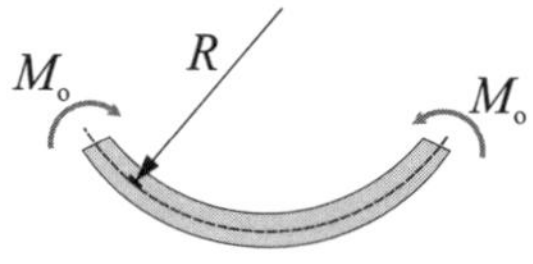

Bending formula, $\dfrac{M}{I} = \dfrac{\sigma}{y} = \dfrac{E}{R}$

Bending moment, $M = \dfrac{EI}{R}$

Substituting $R = 50$ m, $I = 50\times 10^{-8}$ m^4 and $E = 200\times 10^9$ N/m^2, we have

$$M_0 = \frac{200\times 10^9 \times 50\times 10^{-8}}{50} = 2000$$

$$M_0 = 2 \text{ kNm}$$

Q.26 Ans:[0.0523]

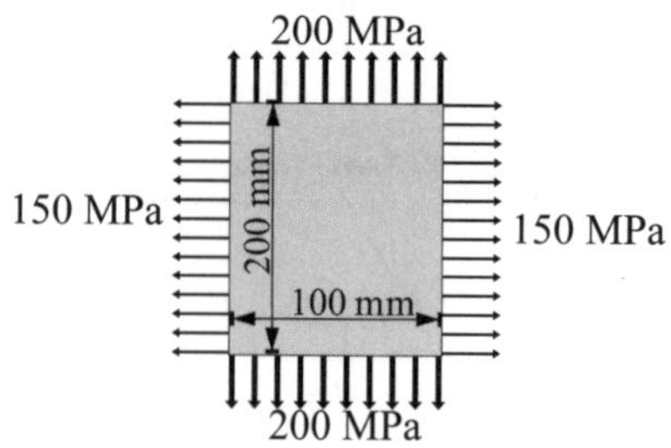

Strain of thickness, $\varepsilon_z = \dfrac{\Delta t}{t} = \dfrac{\sigma_z}{E} - \nu\dfrac{\sigma_x}{E} - \nu\dfrac{\sigma_y}{E}$

Substituting $\sigma_z = 0$, $\sigma_x = 150$ MPa, $\sigma_y = 200$ MPa, $E = 200\times 10^9$ N/m^2 and $\nu = 0.3$, we have

$$\frac{\Delta t}{100} = \frac{0}{E} - \frac{0.3}{200 \times 10^9}(150 + 200) \times 10^6$$

$$\Delta t = 0.0523 \text{ mm}$$

Q.27 Ans:[1]

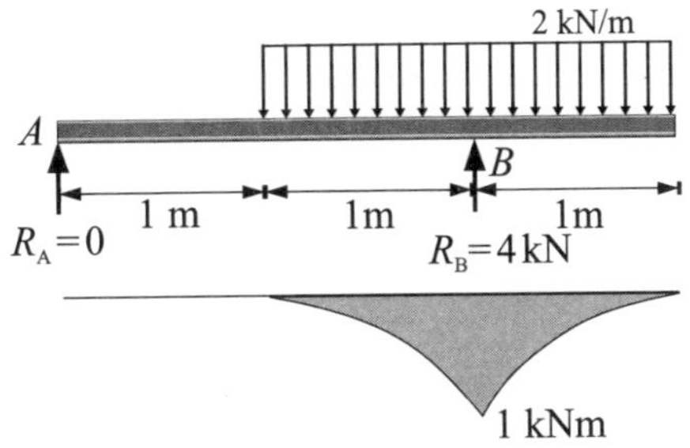

Bending moment diagram

Free body and bending moment diagrams of beam is shown in figure.

Reactions at supports are $R_A = 0$ and $R_B = 4$ kN.

Maximum bending moment is at B, is

$$M_{max} = \frac{2 \times 1^2}{2}$$

$$1 \text{ kNm}$$

Q.28 Ans:[0.25]

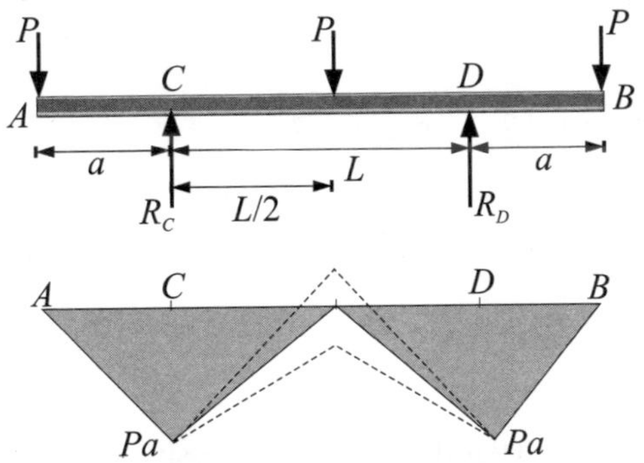

Bending moment diagram

Free-body diagram of overhang beam is shown in figure.

Reaction of supports are $R_C = R_D = \frac{3P}{2}$

Bending moments at center $x = a + \frac{L}{2}$ is (negative)

$$M_{center} = \frac{P}{2}\left(a + \frac{L}{2}\right) - \frac{3P}{2}a < 0$$

from which $\frac{a}{L} > \frac{1}{4}$

$$\frac{a}{L} > 0.25$$

Q.29 Ans:[6.25]

Torsion formula; $\frac{T}{J} = \frac{\tau}{r} \Rightarrow T = \tau\frac{J}{r}$

For solid shaft; $$T_{solid} = \left(\frac{\tau}{D/2}\right)\frac{\pi D^4}{32} \qquad \text{(i)}$$

For hollow shaft; $$T_{hollow} = \left(\frac{\tau}{D/2}\right)\frac{\pi}{32}(D^4 - d^4) \qquad \text{(ii)}$$

From Equations (i) and (ii), we have

% torque carrying capacity lost

$$= \frac{T_{solid} - T_{hollow}}{T_{solid}} \times 100 = \left(\frac{d}{D}\right)^4 \times 100$$

$$= \left(\frac{100}{200}\right)^4 \times 100 = \frac{25}{4} \%$$

Torque carrying capacity lost 6.25 %

Q.30 Ans:[60]

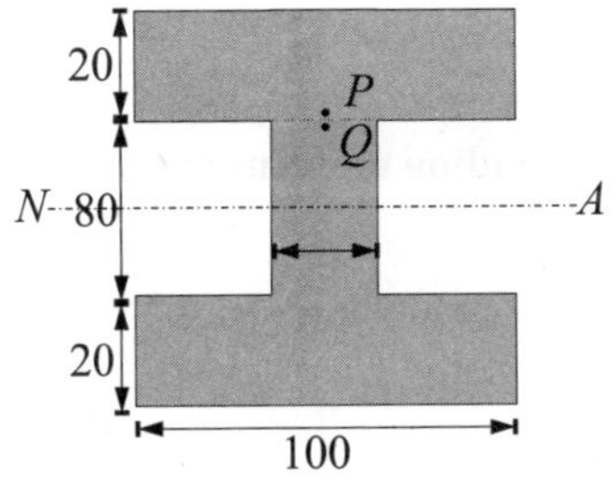

Shear stress, $\tau = \frac{FA\bar{y}}{Ib}$

Shear stress at, $P\ (b = 100)$; $\tau_P = \frac{FA\bar{y}}{I \times 100} = 12$

Shear stress at, $Q\ (b = 20)$; $\tau_Q = \frac{FA\bar{y}}{I \times 20}$

which gives

$$\tau_Q = 60 \text{ MPa}$$

Q.31 Ans:(B)

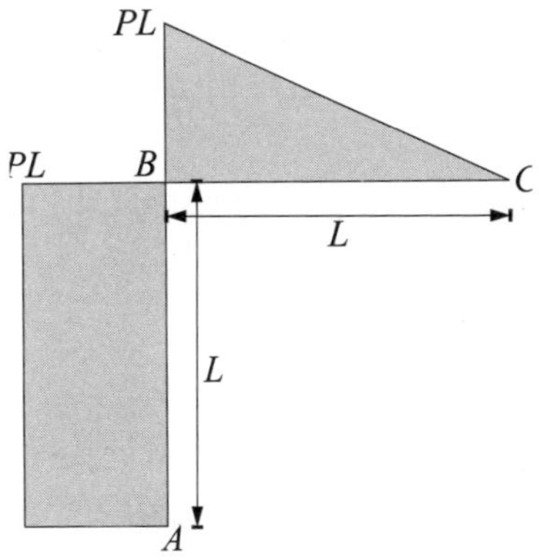

Bending moment diagram

Bending moment diagram of beam is shown in figure.

Maximum bending moment $M_{max} = PL$ (constant from B to A)

Maximum bending stress $\sigma_{max} = \frac{M_{max}}{I} y_{max}$

$$\sigma_{max} = \frac{PL}{\left(\frac{a^4}{12}\right)} \times \frac{a}{2}$$

$$\sigma_{max} = \frac{6PL}{a^3}$$

Q.32 Ans:(D)

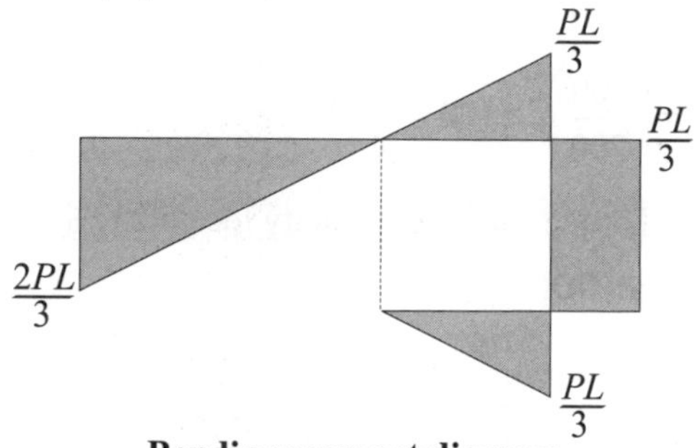

Bending moment diagram

Maximum bending moment, $M_{max} = \frac{2PL}{3}$

Maximum bending stress, $\sigma_{max} = \frac{M_{max}}{I} y$

$$\sigma_{max} = \frac{\frac{2PL}{3}}{\frac{a^4}{12}} \times \frac{a}{2}$$

$$\sigma_{max} = \frac{4PL}{a^3}$$

Q.33 Ans:(B)

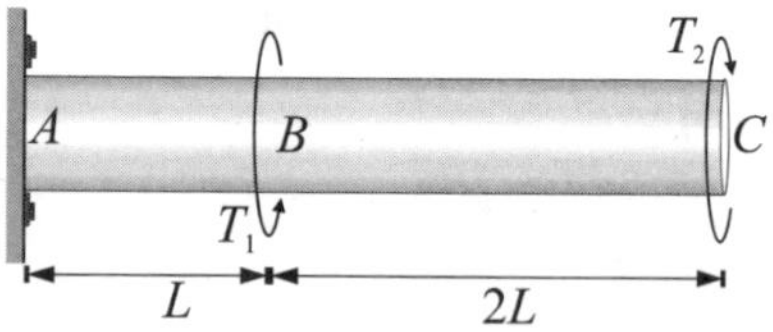

Angle of twist at C = Angle of twist at C by torque $T_2(+)$ – Angle of twist at C by torque $T_1(-)$

$$\theta_C = \frac{T_2 \times 3L}{G\left(\frac{\pi d^4}{32}\right)} - \frac{T_1 \times L}{G\left(\frac{\pi d^4}{32}\right)}$$

$$\theta_C = \frac{32(3T_2 - T_1)L}{G\pi d^4}$$

Q.34 Ans:(B)

Strain energy of shaft of diameter $2d$;

$$U_1 = \frac{T^2 L}{G\frac{\pi(2d)^4}{32}} = \frac{32T^2 L}{16G\pi d^4}$$

Strain energy of shaft of diameter d;

$$U_2 = \frac{T^2 L}{G\frac{\pi d^4}{32}} = \frac{32T^2 L}{G\pi d^4}$$

from which

$$\frac{U_1}{U_2} = \frac{1}{16}$$

Q.35 Ans:(A)

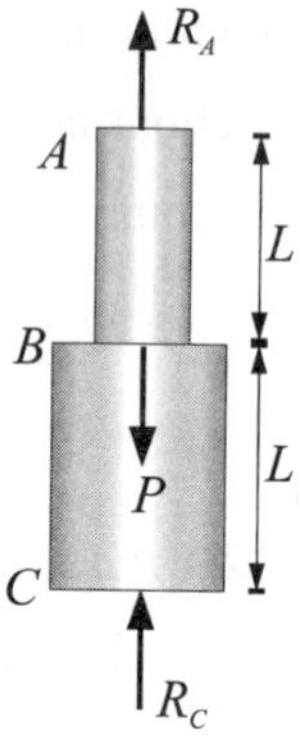

Let R_A and R_C be the reactions at the ends A and C respectively. Equilibrium equation

$$R_A + R_C = P \quad \text{(i)}$$

Deflection of B, $\Delta_B = \frac{R_A L}{EA} = \frac{R_C L}{E2A}$

$$R_C = 2R_A \quad \text{(ii)}$$

which yields $R_A = \frac{P}{3}$

Stress in part AB, $\sigma_{AB} = \frac{R_A}{A}$

$$\sigma_{AB} = \frac{P}{3A}$$

Q.36 Ans:(D)

Resultant stress at point P,

$$\sigma = \sigma_d(\text{tensile}) - \sigma_b(\text{compressive})$$

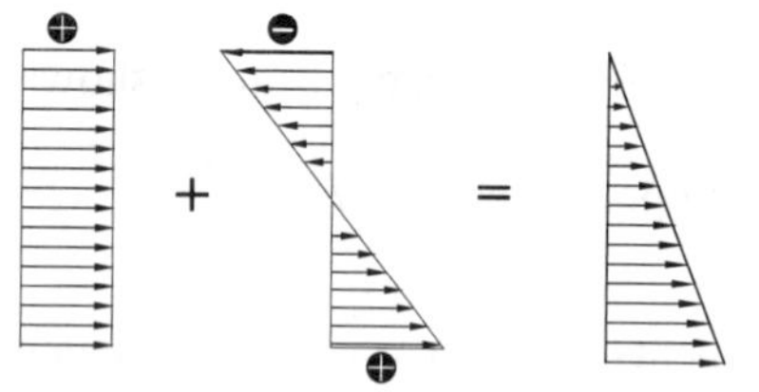

Direct stress, $\sigma_d = \frac{F}{b^2}$ and

Bending stress, $\sigma_b = \frac{M}{I} y = \frac{Fa}{\left(\frac{b^4}{12}\right)} \times \frac{b}{2} = \frac{6Fa}{b^3}$

Resultant stress at point P, $\sigma = \dfrac{F}{b^2} - \dfrac{6Fa}{b^3} = 0$

which yields

$$a = \frac{b}{6}$$

Q.37 Ans:(D)

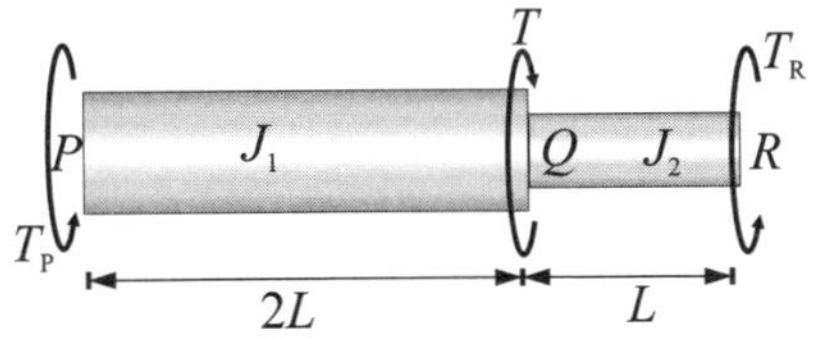

Let T_P and T_R be the torque reactions at fixed supports P and Q respectively.

$$T_P + T_R = T \quad \text{(i)}$$

Angle of twist at Q, $\theta = \dfrac{T_P \times 2L}{GJ_1} = \dfrac{T_R \times L}{GJ_2}$

$$\frac{2T_P}{J_1} = \frac{T_R}{J_2} \quad \text{(ii)}$$

Thus, the support torque reaction at P is

$$T_P = T\left(\frac{J_1}{J_1 + 2J_2}\right)$$

Angle of twist at Q,

$$\theta = \frac{T_P \times 2L}{GJ_1} = T\left(\frac{J_1}{J_1 + 2J_2}\right) \times \frac{2L}{GJ_1}$$

$$\theta = \frac{2TL}{G(J_1 + 2J_2)}$$

Q.38 Ans:(C)

Let P be the compressive force developed in the bar.

Strain of bars, $\varepsilon_1 = \dfrac{\Delta L}{L} = \dfrac{P}{E_1 A}$ and $\varepsilon_2 = \dfrac{\Delta L}{L} = \dfrac{P}{E_2 A}$

Change of length, $\Delta = \dfrac{PL}{E_1 A} + \dfrac{PL}{E_2 A}$ (i)

Thermal strain, $\varepsilon_{t_1} = \varepsilon_{t_1} = \dfrac{\Delta L}{L} = \alpha \Delta T = 10\alpha$

Change of length, $\Delta = 10\alpha L + 10\alpha L = 20\alpha L$ (ii)

Net change in length, $\Delta = 0 = \dfrac{PL}{E_1 A} + \dfrac{PL}{E_2 A} = 20\alpha\, L$

$$P = \frac{20\alpha\, E_1 E_2 A}{E_1 + E_2}$$

$$\text{Stress, } \sigma = 20\alpha\left(\frac{E_1 E_2}{E_1 + E_2}\right)$$

Q.39 Ans:(A)

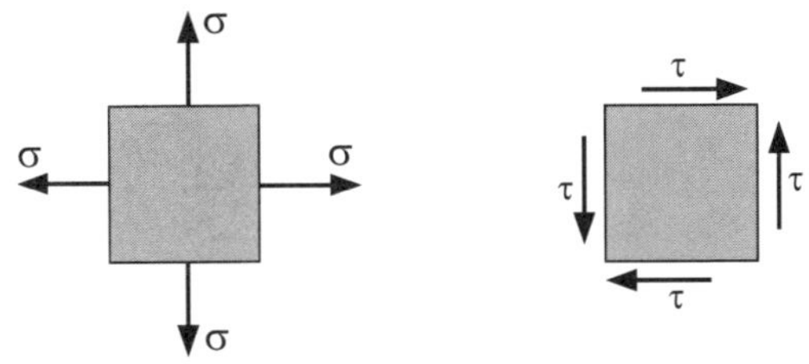

$\sigma_{max} = \sigma$ $\sigma_{max} = \sigma$

Q.40 Ans:(D)

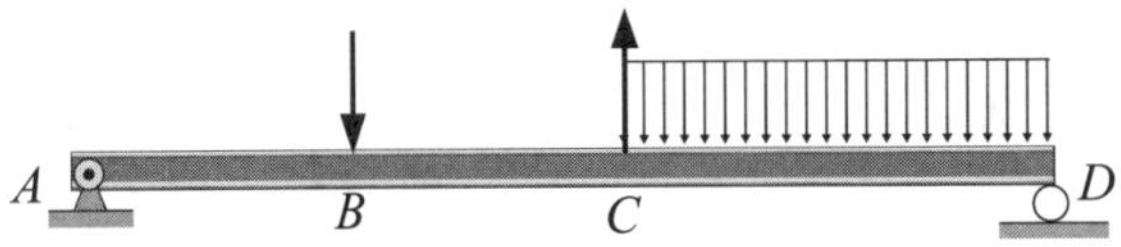

Figure shows the loading diagram of given shear force diagram.

From which

1. A concentrated load acting at point B
3. A uniformly distributed load acting on the portion CE

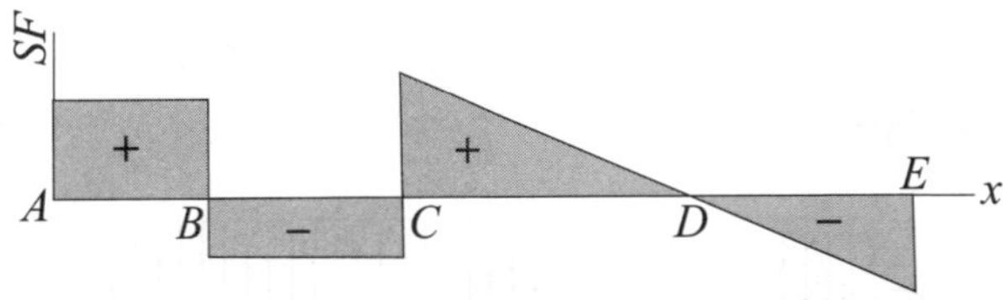

Q.41 Ans:(B)

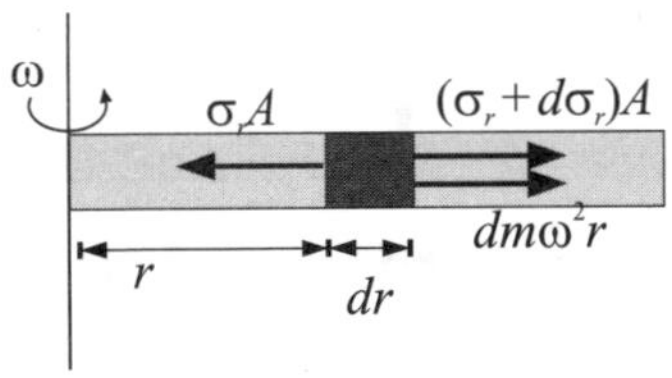

Consider an element of length dr at radius, r as shown in figure.

$\sum F_r = 0 \Rightarrow (\sigma_r + d\sigma_r)A + dm\omega^2 r - \sigma_r A = 0$

or $\quad d\sigma_r A = -\rho A dr \omega^2 r$

or $\quad \displaystyle\int_{\sigma_{max}}^{0} d\sigma_r = -\rho\omega^2 \int_0^L r\,dr$

or $\quad \displaystyle\int_{\sigma_{max}}^{0} d\sigma_r = -\rho\omega^2 \int_0^L r\,dr$

$$\sigma_{max} = \frac{\rho\omega^2 L^2}{2}$$

Q.42 Ans:(C)

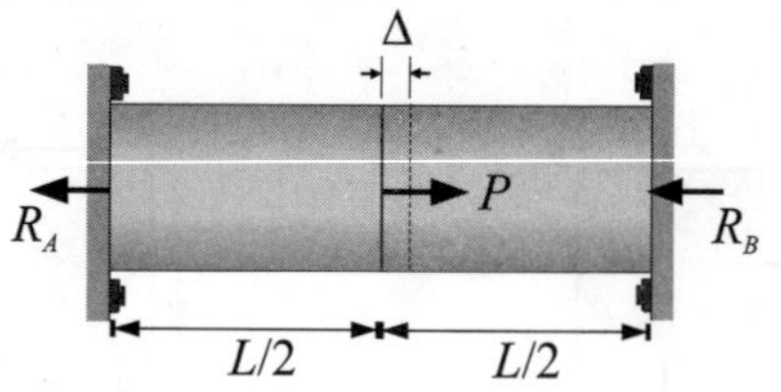

Let R_A and R_B be reaction at A and B,

$$R_A + R_B = P \qquad \text{(i)}$$

Deflection of center,

$$\Delta = \frac{R_A\left(\frac{L}{2}\right)}{EA} = \frac{R_B\left(\frac{L}{2}\right)}{EA} \qquad \text{(ii)}$$

From Equations (i) and (ii), we have $R_A = R_B = \frac{P}{2}$

Strain energy stored

$$U = \sum \frac{F^2 l}{2EA} = \frac{\left(\frac{P}{2}\right)^2 \times \frac{L}{2}}{2EA} + \frac{\left(\frac{P}{2}\right)^2 \times \frac{L}{2}}{2EA}$$

$$U = \frac{P^2 L}{8EA}$$

Q.43 Ans:(A)

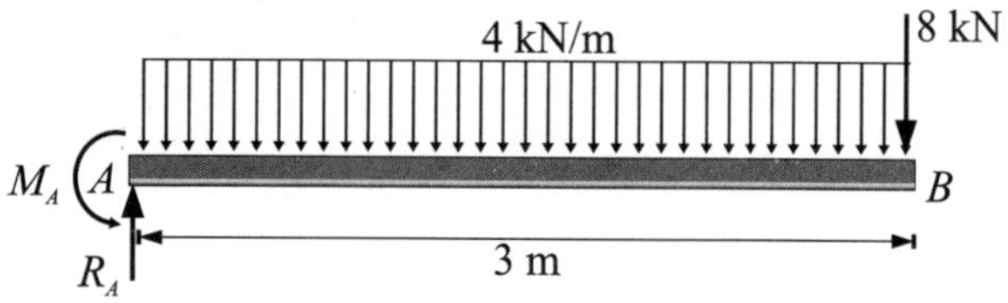

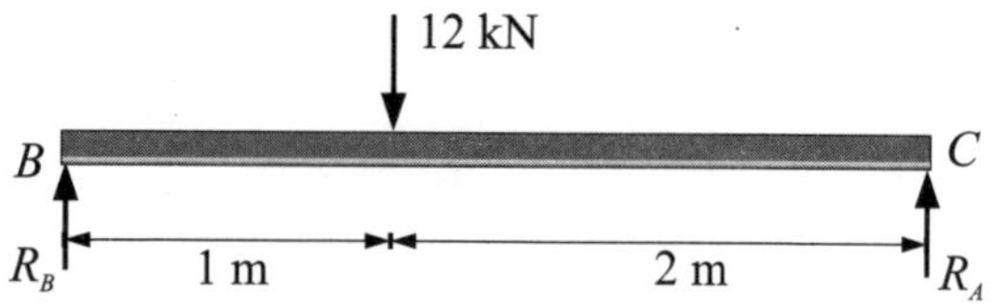

Consider the beam BC,

Taking moment about C,

$$\sum M_C = 0 \Rightarrow R_B \times 3 - 12 \times 2 = 0$$

$$R_B = 8\,\text{kN}$$

Now consider the beam AB

Bending moment at A

$$M_A = 8 \times 3 + \frac{4 \times 3^2}{2}$$

$$M_A = 42\,\text{kNm}$$

Q.44 Ans:(A)

Deflection of free end $\Delta = \Delta_1 + \Delta_2$

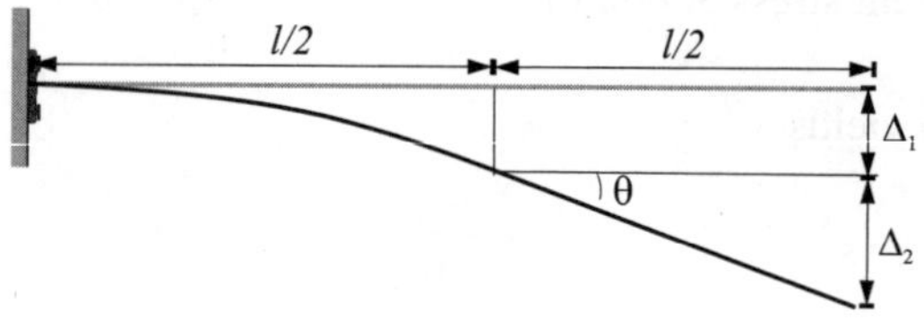

where $\Delta_1 = \frac{P\left(\frac{l}{2}\right)^3}{3EI}$

and $\Delta_2 = \frac{l}{2} \times \theta = \frac{l}{2} \times \frac{P\left(\frac{l}{2}\right)^2}{2EI} = \frac{P\left(\frac{l}{2}\right)^3}{2EI}$

$$\Delta = \frac{P\left(\frac{l}{2}\right)^3}{3EI} + \frac{P\left(\frac{l}{2}\right)^3}{2EI} = \frac{5}{6} \times \frac{Pl^3}{8EI}$$

$$\Delta = \frac{5Pl^3}{48EI}$$

Q.45 Ans:(C)

Maximum stress, $\sigma = \sigma_d \pm \sigma_b$

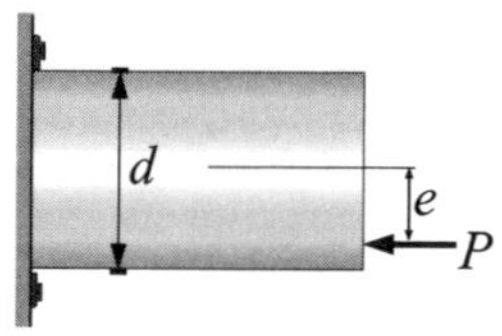

$$\sigma = \frac{P}{A} \pm \frac{M}{I} y = \frac{P}{\frac{\pi d^2}{4}} \pm \frac{Pe \times \frac{d}{2}}{\frac{\pi d^4}{64}}$$

$$\sigma = \frac{4P}{\pi d^2} - \frac{32Pe}{\pi d^3} = 0$$

$$e = \frac{d}{8}$$

Q.46 Ans:(B)

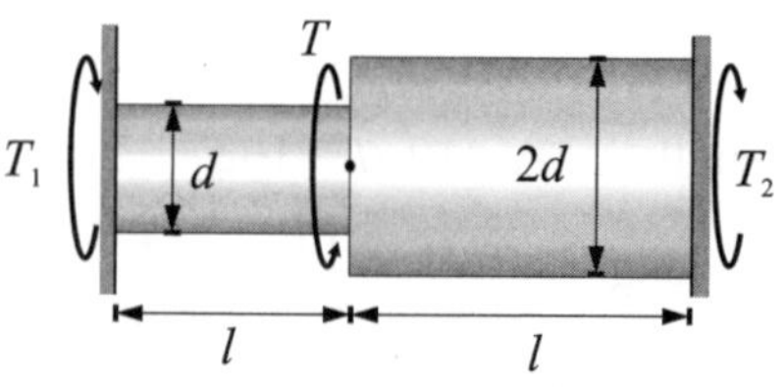

Angle of twist, $\theta = \frac{T_1 l}{GJ_1} = \frac{T_2 l}{GJ_2}$

$$\frac{T_1}{T_2} = \frac{J_1}{J_2} = \frac{\frac{\pi d^4}{32}}{\frac{\pi (2d)^4}{32}}$$

$$\frac{T_1}{T_2} = \frac{1}{16}$$

Q.47 Ans:(B)

Bending stress, $\sigma = \frac{M}{I} y$

$$\sigma = \frac{M}{\frac{bd^3}{12}} \times \frac{d}{2} = \frac{6M}{bd^2}$$

or $d^2 = \left(\frac{6}{b\sigma}\right) M$

$$d \propto \sqrt{M}$$

Q.48 Ans:(C)

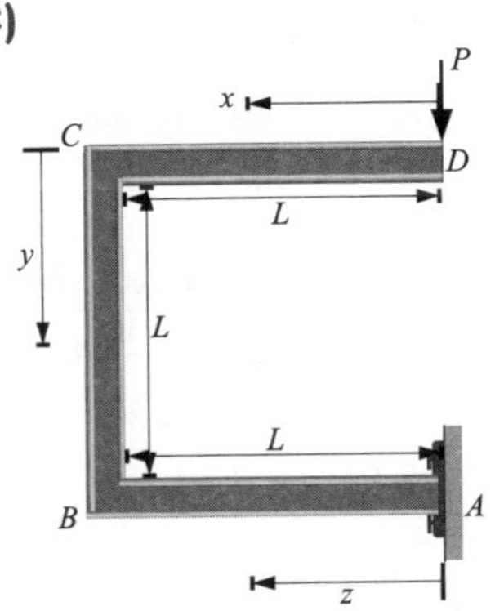

Bending moment at x, $M_x = Px$

Bending moment at y, $M_y = PL$

Bending moment at z, $M_z = Pz$

Strain energy, $U = U_{CD} + U_{CB} + U_{BA}$

$$U = \int_0^L \frac{M_x^2 dx}{2EI} + \int_0^L \frac{M_y^2 dy}{2EI} + \int_0^L \frac{M_z^2 dz}{2EI}$$

$$U = \frac{1}{2EI}\left(\int_0^L (Px)^2 dx + \int_0^L (PL)^2 dy + \int_0^L (Pz)^2 dz\right)$$

$$U = \frac{5}{6}\frac{P^2L^3}{EI}$$

Deflection of D (by Castigalaneo theorem)

$$\Delta = \frac{\partial}{\partial P}\left(\frac{5}{6}\frac{P^2L^3}{EI}\right)$$

$$\Delta = \frac{5}{3}\frac{P^2L^3}{EI}$$

Q.49 Ans:(B)

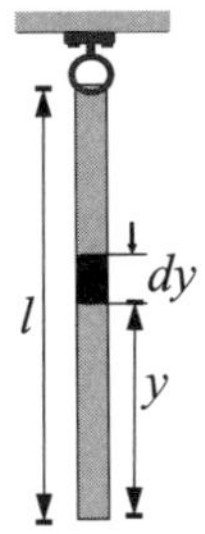

Stress (at y), $\sigma = \frac{mg}{a} = \frac{\rho a y g}{a}$

or $\sigma = \rho g y$

Strain of element of length dy, $\varepsilon = \frac{du}{dy}$

$$\sigma = E\varepsilon \Rightarrow \rho g y = E\frac{du}{dy}$$

$$du = \frac{\rho g}{E} y dy$$

Total elongation $\int du = \frac{\rho g}{E}\int_0^l y dy$

$$\Delta = \frac{\rho g l^2}{2E}$$

Q.50 Ans:(D)

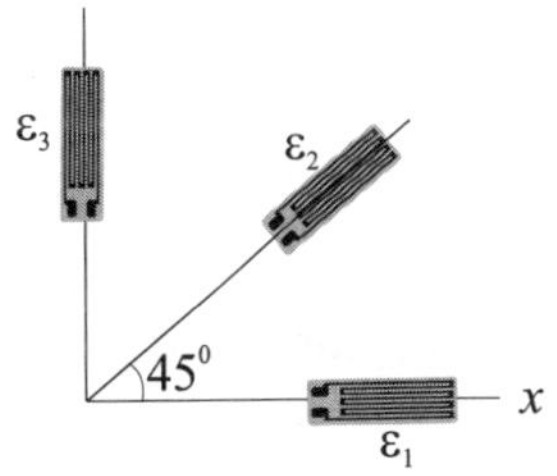

From given rosette; $\varepsilon_1 = \varepsilon_x = 1000 \times 10^{-6}$, $\varepsilon_3 = \varepsilon_y = 600 \times 10^{-6}$ and $\varepsilon_{45^\circ} = \varepsilon_2 = 800 \times 10^{-6}$

Strain at 45° ;

$\varepsilon_{45^0} = \varepsilon_2 = 800 \times 10^{-6}$

$$= \frac{\varepsilon_x + \varepsilon_y}{2} + \frac{\varepsilon_x - \varepsilon_y}{2}\cos 2\times 45 + \frac{\gamma_{xy}}{2}\cos 2\times 45$$

$$= \frac{1000\times10^{-6} + 600\times10^{-6}}{2} + \frac{1000\times10^{-6} - 600\times10^{-6}}{2}\cos 90 + \frac{\gamma_{xy}}{2}\cos 90$$

$$\gamma_{xy} = 0$$

Direction of the major principle strain

$$\theta = \frac{1}{2}\tan^{-1}\left(\frac{\gamma_{xy}}{\varepsilon_x - \varepsilon_y}\right) = \frac{1}{2}\tan^{-1}\left(\frac{0}{\varepsilon_x - \varepsilon_y}\right) = 0$$

$$\theta = 0^\circ$$

Q.51 Ans:[20]

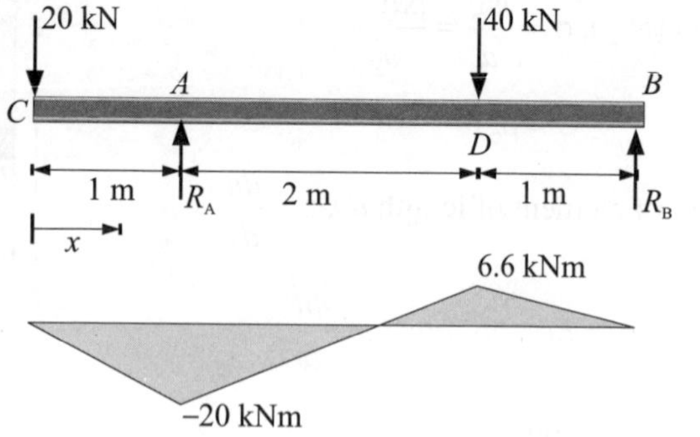

Bending moment diagram

A free-body diagram for the complete beam is shown in figure. The equations of equilibrium give

$R_A \times 3 - 20 \times 4 - 20 \times 1 = 0$ or $R_A = \dfrac{100}{3}$ kN

Bending moments,

$$M_{x=0} = 0$$

$$M_{x=1} = -20 \text{ kNm}$$

$$M_{x=3} = -20 \times 3 + \frac{100}{3} \times 2 = 6.6 \text{ kNm}$$

Maximum bending moment $M_{max} = 20$ kNm at A

Q.52 Ans:[110]

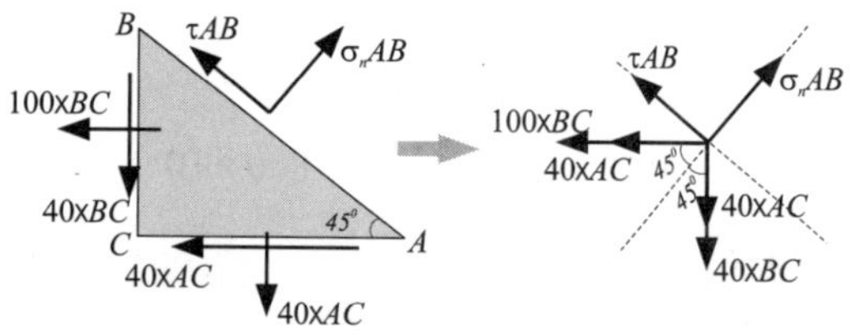

Free body diagram

Figure shows the free-body diagram of left part of block. Resolving the forces along normal to the plane AB.

$$\sigma_n AB = 100BC\cos 45 + 40AC\cos 45 + 40BC\cos 45 + 40AC\cos 45$$

$$\sigma_n = 100\frac{BC}{AB}\cos 45 + 40\frac{AC}{AB}\cos 45 + 40\frac{BC}{AB}\cos 45 + 40\frac{AC}{AB}\cos 45$$

$$\sigma_n = 100\sin 45\cos 45 + 100\cos 45\cos 45 + 40\sin 45\cos 45 + 40\cos 45\cos 45 = 220\left(\frac{1}{\sqrt{2}}\right)^2$$

$$\sigma_n = 110 \text{ MPa}$$

Q.53 Ans:[38.28]

Consider the joint B

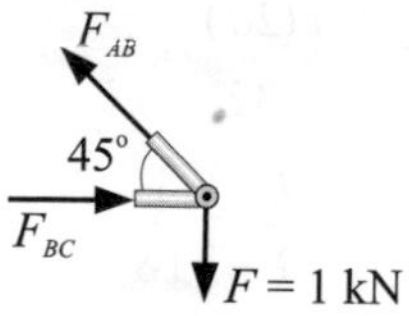

$$\sum F_y = 0 \Rightarrow F_{AB}\sin 45 - F = 0$$

$$F_{AB} = \sqrt{2}F$$

$$\sum F_x = 0 \Rightarrow F_{BC} - F_{AB}\cos 45 = 0$$

$$F_{BC} = \frac{F_{AB}}{\sqrt{2}} = F$$

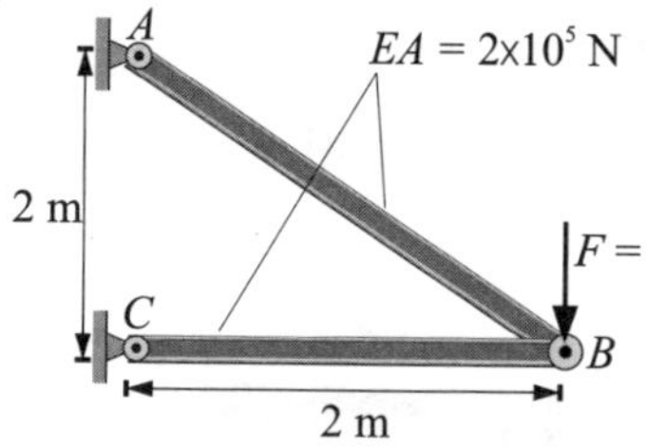

Strain energy, $U = \dfrac{F_{BC}^2 \times BC}{2EA} + \dfrac{F_{AB}^2 \times AB}{2EA}$

or $U = \dfrac{F^2 \times 2}{2EA} + \dfrac{2F^2 \times \sqrt{8}}{2EA}$

or $U = \dfrac{F^2}{EA}(1 + \sqrt{8})$

Vertical deflection of B, $\Delta = \dfrac{\partial U}{\partial P} = \dfrac{2F}{EA}(1 + \sqrt{8})$

$$\Delta = \frac{2 \times 1 \times 10^3}{2 \times 10^5}(1 + \sqrt{8}) = 0.03828$$

$$\Delta = 38.28 \text{ mm}$$

Q.54 Ans:[3.5]

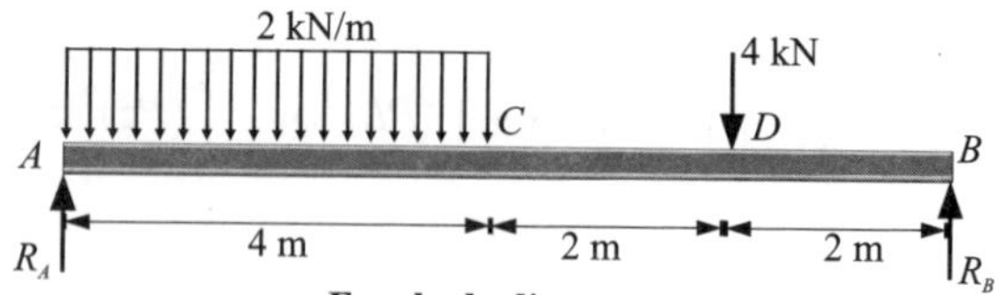

Free body diagram

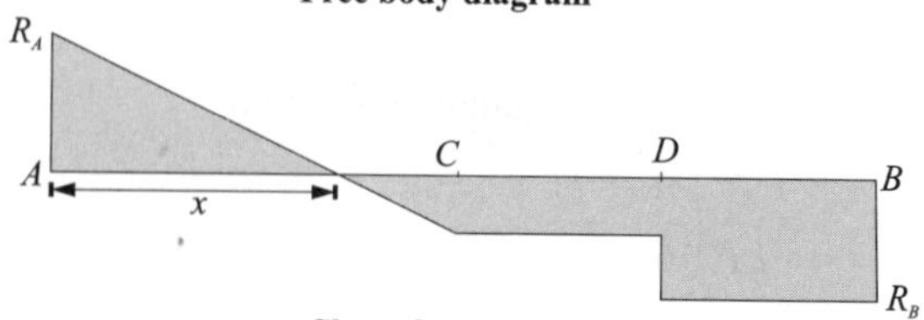

Shear force diagram

A free body diagram for the complete beam is shown in

figure.The equations of equilibrium give

$$\sum M_A = 2\times4\times2+4\times6-R_B\times8=0$$

$R_B = 5\,\text{kN}$ and $R_A = 8+4-5 = 7\,\text{kN}$

Equation of shear force in portion AC,

$$S_x = R_A - \omega x = 7-2x$$

Maximum bending occurs where shear force is zero.

$$S_x = 7-2x = 0$$

$$x = 3.5\,\text{m}$$

Q.55 Ans:[0.15]

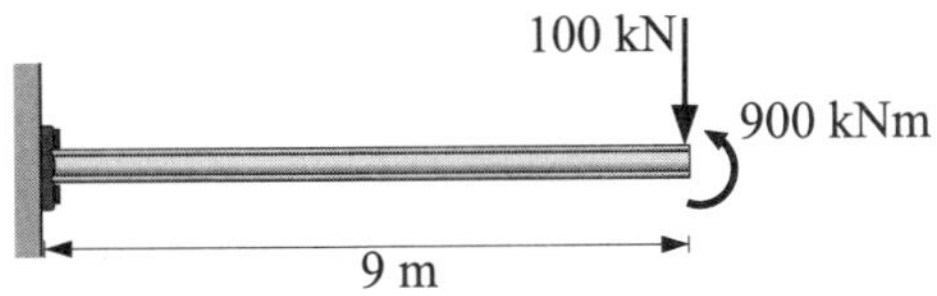

Deflection at free end Δ = Deflection at free end due to point load + Deflection at free end due to moment.

$$\Delta = \frac{PL^3}{3EI} - \frac{ML^2}{2EI} = \frac{100\times10^3\times9^3}{3\times81\times0^6} - \frac{900\times10^3\times9^2}{3\times81\times0^6}$$

$$\Delta = 0.15\,\text{m}$$

Q.56 Ans:[-50]

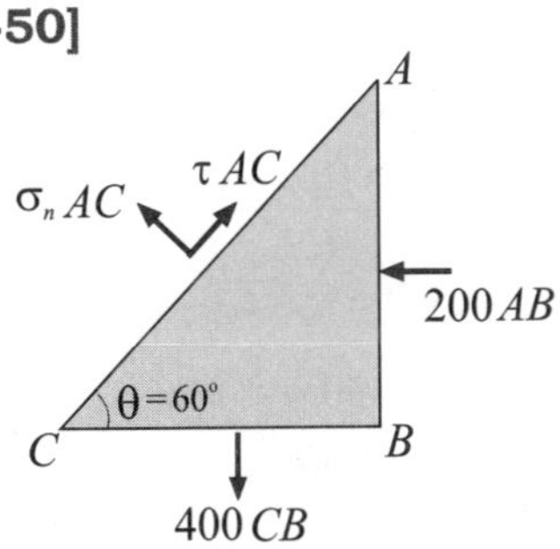

Normal stress on plane AC is given by

$$\sigma_n = \frac{\sigma_x+\sigma_y}{2} + \frac{\sigma_y-\sigma_x}{2}\cos2\theta$$

or $$\sigma_n = \frac{-200+400}{2} + \frac{400+200}{2}\cos2\theta$$

or $$\sigma_n = 100+300\cos2\theta = 100+300\cos2\times60$$

$$\sigma_n = -50\,\text{MPa}$$

Q.57 Ans:[5.4]

Consider cantilever beam of uniformly distributed load.

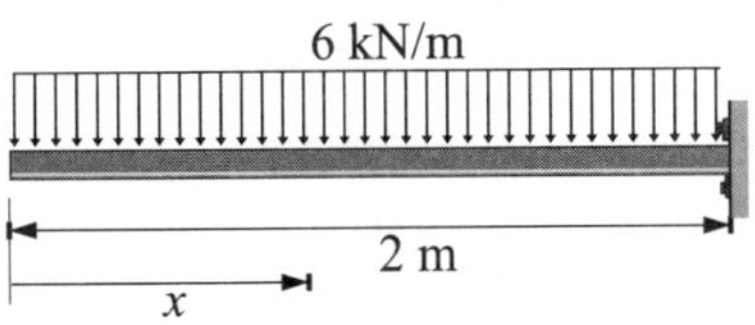

Bending moment at x,

$$M_x = \frac{\omega x^2}{2} = \frac{6x^2}{2} = 3x^2$$

Strain energy $$U_1 = \int_0^2 \frac{M_x^2\,dx}{2EI} = \frac{1}{2EI}\int_0^2 (3x^2)^2\,dx$$

$$U_1 = \frac{1}{2EI}\times\frac{9}{5}\times2^5 \qquad \text{(i)}$$

Consider cantilever beam of point load at the free end.

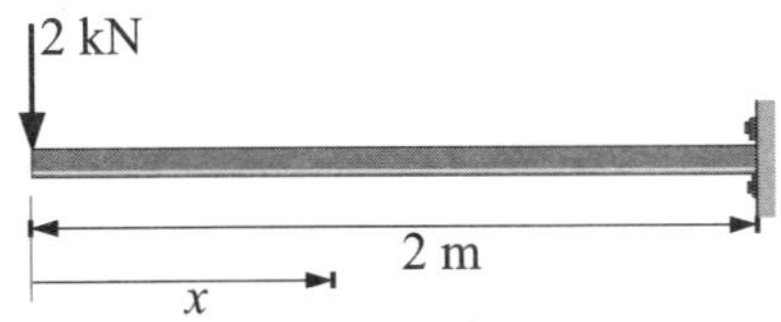

Bending moment at x, $\qquad M_x = 2x$

Strain energy, $$U_2 = \int_0^2 \frac{M_x^2\,dx}{2EI} = \frac{1}{2EI}\int_0^2 (2x)^2\,dx$$

$$U_2 = \frac{1}{2EI}\times\frac{4}{3}\times2^3 \qquad \text{(ii)}$$

From Equations (i) and (ii), we have

$$\frac{U_1}{U_2} = \frac{\frac{9}{5}\times2^5}{\frac{4}{3}\times2^3}$$

$$\frac{U_1}{U_2} = 5.4$$

Q.58 Ans:[4]

Shear force $= \omega x$

Shear force at mid-point $= \omega\times\frac{3}{2} = 6$

$$\omega = 4\,\text{kN/m}$$

Q.59 Ans:[22.5]

Consider beam CD

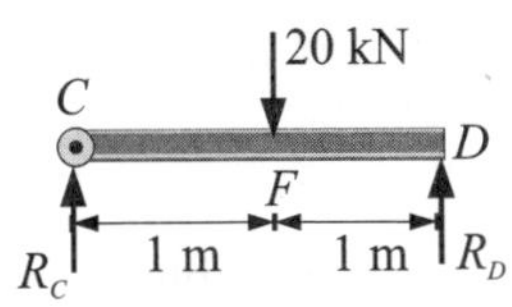

Free body diagram of beam CD

Taking moment about D

$$R_C\times2-20\times1=0$$

$$R_C = 10\,\text{kN}$$

Now, consider beam AC

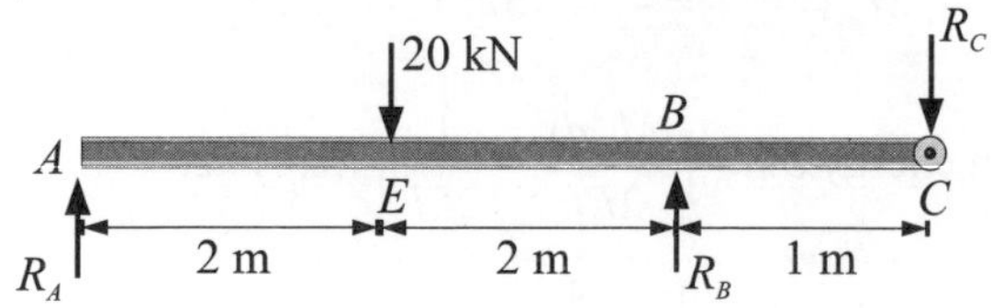

Free body diagram of beam AC

Taking moment about A

$$20 \times 2 + R_C \times 5 - R_B \times 4 = 0$$

$$20 \times 2 + 10 \times 5 - R_B \times 4 = 0$$

$$R_B = 22.5 \text{ kN}$$

Q.60 Ans:[160]

Shear stress in rectangular cross-section beam at y from neutral axis

$$\tau = \frac{6F}{bh^3}\left(\frac{h^2}{4} - y^2\right)$$

at $y = \left(\frac{h}{2} - \frac{h}{4}\right) = \frac{h}{4}$; $\tau = \frac{6F}{bh^3}\left[\frac{h^2}{4} - \left(\frac{h}{4}\right)^2\right] = 120$

$$\frac{F}{bh} = \frac{120 \times 16}{3 \times 6} \quad \text{(i)}$$

Maximum stress ($y = 0$)

$$\tau_{max} = \frac{6F}{bh^3}\left(\frac{h^2}{4}\right) = \frac{3F}{2bh} \quad \text{(ii)}$$

From Equations (i) and (ii), we have

$$\tau_{max} = \frac{3}{2} \times \frac{120 \times 16}{3 \times 6}$$

$$\tau_{max} = 160 \text{ MPa}$$

Q.61 Ans:[1.414]

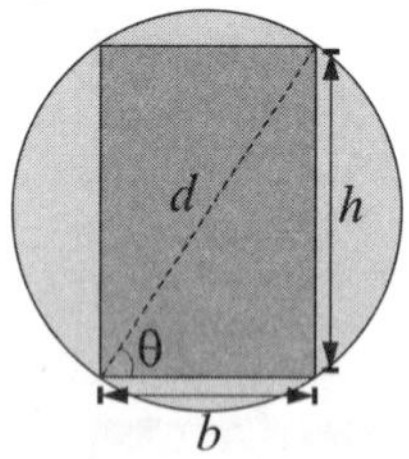

Let h and b be the depth and breadth of rectangular cross-section beam.

$$b = d\cos\theta \text{ and } h = d\sin\theta$$

Section modulus,

$$Z = \frac{d\cos\theta \times (d\sin\theta)^2}{6} = \frac{d^3}{6}\cos\theta \times (1 - \cos^2\theta)$$

Condition for optimum Z; $\frac{d}{d\theta}Z = 0$

$$\frac{d^3}{6}(-\sin\theta + 3\cos^2\theta\sin\theta) = 0$$

from which

$$\cos^2\theta = \frac{1}{3} \quad \text{or} \quad \sin^2\theta = \frac{2}{3}$$

The ratio of depth to breadth of rectangular beam

$$\frac{h}{b} = \frac{d\sin\theta}{d\cos\theta} = \frac{\frac{\sqrt{2}}{\sqrt{3}}}{\frac{1}{\sqrt{3}}} = \sqrt{2}$$

$$\frac{b}{h} = 1.414$$

Q.62 Ans:[0.010]

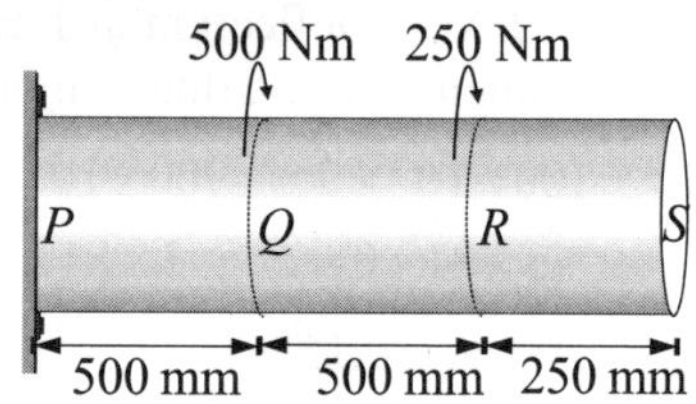

Angle of twist θ at S = Angle of twist at S due to 500 Nm + Angle of twist at S due to 250 Nm.

$$\theta = \frac{500 \times 0.5}{GJ} + \frac{250 \times (0.5 + 0.5)}{GJ} = \frac{500}{GJ}$$

$$\theta = \frac{500}{80 \times 10^9 \times \dfrac{\pi \times \left(\dfrac{50}{1000}\right)^4}{32}} = 0.01018$$

$$\theta = 0.0101 \text{ rad}$$

Q.63 Ans:[4]

Normal stress, $\sigma_n = \frac{\sigma_x + \sigma_y}{2} + \frac{\sigma_y - \sigma_x}{2}\cos 2\theta$

Substituting $\sigma_x = 10$ MPa, $\sigma_y = 20$ MPa and $\sigma_n = 12$ MPa, we have

$$12 = \frac{10 + 20}{2} + \frac{20 - 10}{2}\cos 2\theta$$

$$\Rightarrow \cos 2\theta = -\frac{3}{5}$$

Shear stress $\tau = \frac{\sigma_y - \sigma_x}{2}\sin 2\theta$

$$= \frac{20 - 10}{2}\sqrt{1 - \left(-\frac{3}{5}\right)^2}$$

$$\tau = 4 \text{ MPa}$$

Q.64 Ans:[80]

Bending formula,

$$\frac{M}{I} = \frac{\sigma}{y} = \frac{E}{R}$$

$$\sigma_{max} = \frac{E}{R}(y_{max})$$

$$= \frac{100 \times 10^9}{\frac{25}{2 \times 100}} \times \frac{\frac{0.2}{2}}{1000}$$

$$\sigma_{max} = 8 \times 10^7$$

$$\sigma_{max} = 80\,\text{MPa}$$

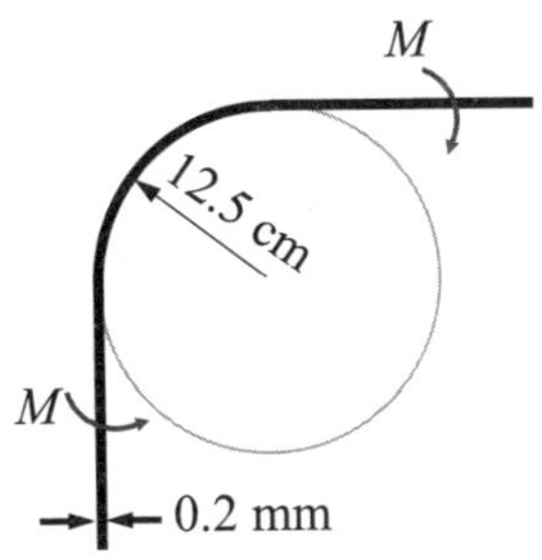

Q.65 Ans:[9]

Free body diagram and bending moment diagram of beam

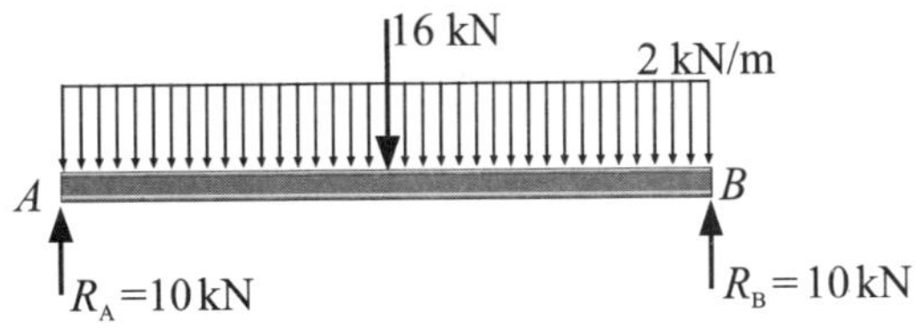

Loading diagram

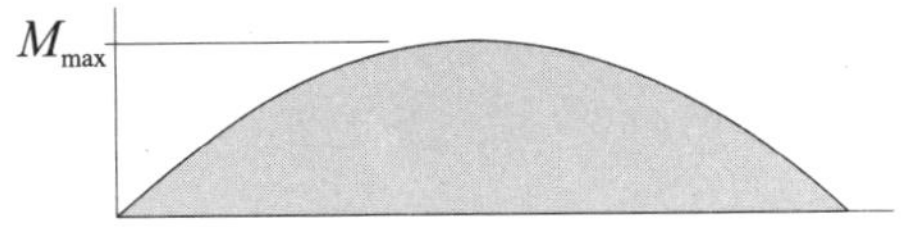

Bending moment diagram

is drawn from given shear force diagram.

Maximum bending moment, $M_{max} = \left[10x - \frac{\omega x^2}{2}\right]_{x=1m}$

$$M_{max} = 9\,\text{kNm}$$

7 Theory of Machines

GATE Syllabus

Displacement, velocity and acceleration analysis of plane mechanisms; Dynamic analysis of linkages; Cams; Gears and gear trains; Flywheels and governors; Balancing of reciprocating and rotating masses; Gyroscope.

Chapter Outline

7.1 KEY CONCEPTS AND FORMULAS

Plane Mechanisms

Theory of machines is the branch of engineering which deals with the relative motion and forces between various machine elements. It is divided into two parts, i.e., Kinematics of Machines and Dynamics of Machines.

Link or element: It is the part of a machine which has motion relative to some other parts. Links can be classified as: binary ternary, quaternary, etc. depending upon its ends on which revolute or turning pairs can be placed. There are three types of links, i.e., Rigid link, Flexible link and Fluid link.

Types of constrained motion

1. **Completely constrained motion**: This motion is in a definite direction, e.g., square bar moving in a square hole and a shaft with collars at its ends rotate in a round hole.

2. **Incompletely constrained motion**: This type of motion takes place in more than one direction, e.g., a circular bar moving in a circular hole may have two motions rotary and reciprocating and both motions are independent.

3. **Partially (or successfully) constrained motion**: When the constrained motion between a pair is not completed by itself but by some other means, e.g., the motion of shaft in a footstep bearing.

Kinematic pair: It has two elements or links together which have relative motion between them. It can be classified on the basis of (a) Types of contact: (i) Lower pair and (ii) Higher pair,

(b) Type of constraint: (i) Closed pair and (ii) Unclosed pair,

(c) Type of relative motion (i) Sliding pair (ii) Turning pair (iii) rolling pair (iv) Screw pair and (v) Spherical pair.

Kinematic chain: A kinematic chain is the combination of kinematic pairs joined in such a way that the relative motion between them is completely constrained. The relations between number of links 'L', number of pairs 'P' and number of joint 'J' for lower pair kinematic chain are:

$$L = 2P - 4 \quad \text{and} \quad L = \frac{2}{3}(J+2)$$

Grashof's Law

This law states that in a four-bar mechanism, the sum of the lengths of the shortest and the largest links should be less than the sum of the lengths of the other link, i.e.,

$(l+s) < (p+q)$, where l = length of longest link, s = length of shortest link and p, q = length of other links

Gruebler's Criteria

An equation to determine the degree of freedom of a mechanism is $F = 3(n-1) - 2p - h$

where F = degree of freedom, n = number of links, p = number of lower pairs and h = number of higher pairs.

Mechanism

When one link of a kinematic chain is fixed, it is known as mechanism. It is used to transmit motion. A mechanism can be of two types, simple and compound. A simple mechanism has four links and a compound mechanism has more than four links.

Inversion of Mechanism

Mechanism obtained by fixing the different links of the same kinematic chain is called inversion of mechanism.

Kinematic Chain →
- Four-bar chain (All four turning pairs)
- Slider-crank chain (Three turning and one sliding pair)
- Double-slider crank chain (Two turning and two sliding pairs)

Four-bar Chain

This is also known as *quadric cycle chain*. It has four links and four turning pairs.

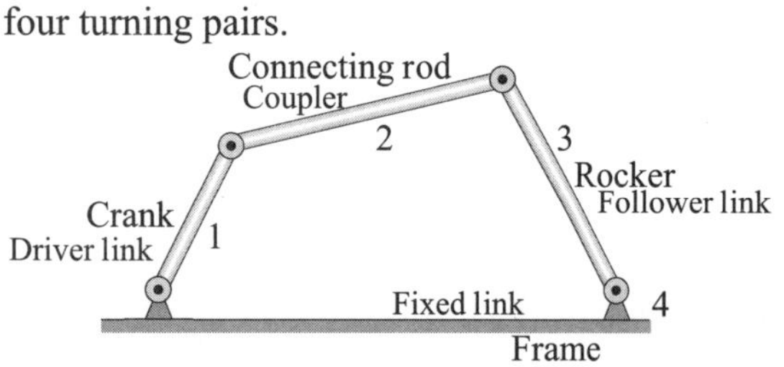

Four-Bar chain

Inversion of Four-Bar Chain

Coupled wheels of locomotive, Beam engine, Watt's Indicator, Pantograph

Inversion of Slider-crank Chain

Pendulum pump, Oscillating cylinder engine, Crank and slotted lever quick return motion mechanism, Whirworth quick return motion mechanism,Toggle mechanism, Rotary internal combustion engine (Gnome Engines)

Double-slider Crank Chain

Scotch Yoke mechanism, Elliptical trammel, Oldham's coupling

Instantaneous centre: A link or rigid body as a whole may be considered to be rotating about an imaginary centre at a given instant which has zero velocity.

Klein's construction: It is a graphical procedure of drawing the acceleration diagram for a slider-crank mechanism.

Coriolis Acceleration

If the distance between the two points does not remain fixed and the second point slides, the total acceleration will contain an additional component of acceleration, known as *coriolis acceleration*.

Coriolis acceleration, $a_{cc} = 2v.\omega$

Straight Line Motion

Accurate Straight line Mechanism

Peaucellier mechanism, Hart mechanism, Scott-Russel mechanism

Approximate Straight Line motion

Grasshopper mechanism, Watt mechanism, Tchebicheff Mechanism

Slider-crank Mechanism

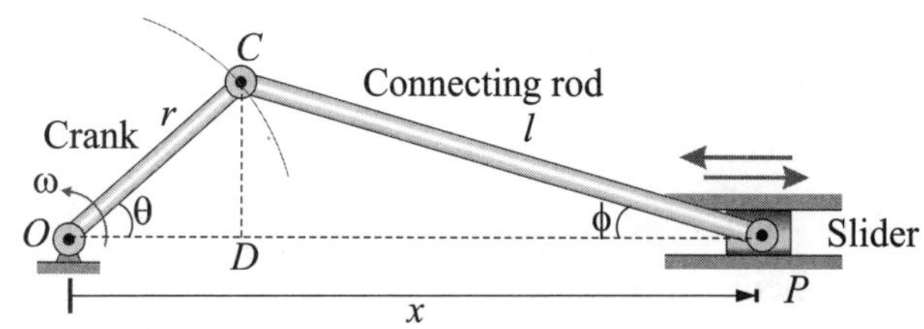

From geometry in figure,

$$x = r\cos\theta + l\cos\phi \quad \text{and} \quad \sin\phi = \frac{\sin\theta}{l/r} = \frac{\sin\theta}{n}$$

Velocity of slider, $$v = \omega r\left(\sin\theta + \frac{\sin 2\theta}{2\sqrt{n^2 - \sin^2\theta}}\right)$$

or $$v \approx \omega r\left(\sin\theta + \frac{\sin 2\theta}{2n}\right)$$

Acceleration of slider, $$a = \omega^2 r\left(\cos\theta + \frac{\cos 2\theta}{n}\right)$$

Angular velocity of connecting rod, $$\omega_r = \frac{\omega\cos\theta}{\sqrt{n^2 - \sin^2\theta}}$$

Cams

A cam is a mechanical element used to drive another element, called the follower, through a specified motion by direct contact.

Types of cams and followers are as follows:

Cams

- Disc cam
- Wedge cam
- Cylindrical cam or barrel cam
- End cam or face cam

Follower

- Knife edge follower
- Flat-face follower
- Roller follower
- Spherical-face follower

Displacement Diagram

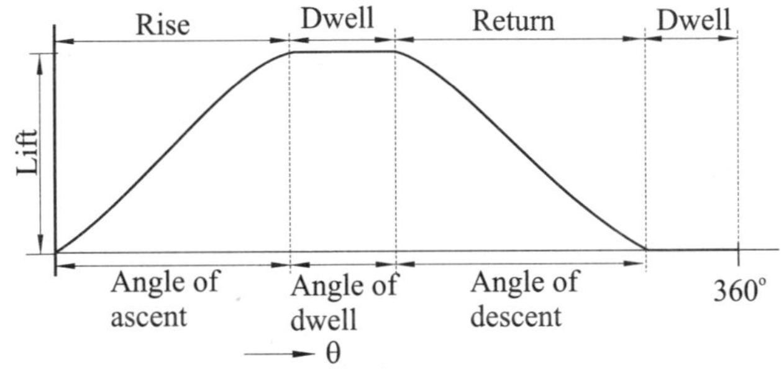

The displacement diagram for uniform motion is a straight line with a constant slope.

Types of motion are: (a) uniform motion, (b) simple harmonic motion, (c) cycloidal motion, and (d) uniformly acceleration and deceleration.

Graphical Layout of Cam Profile

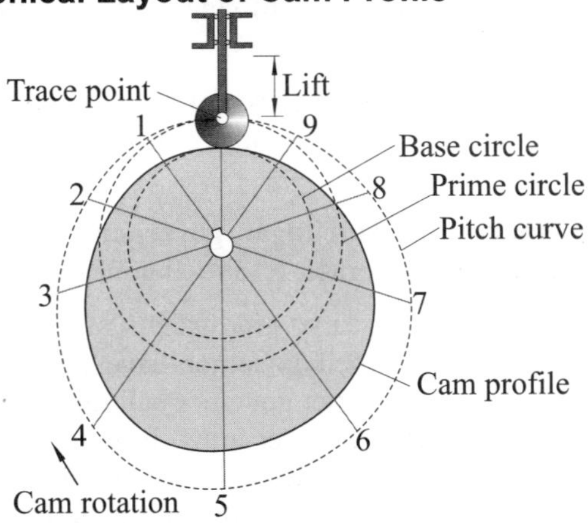

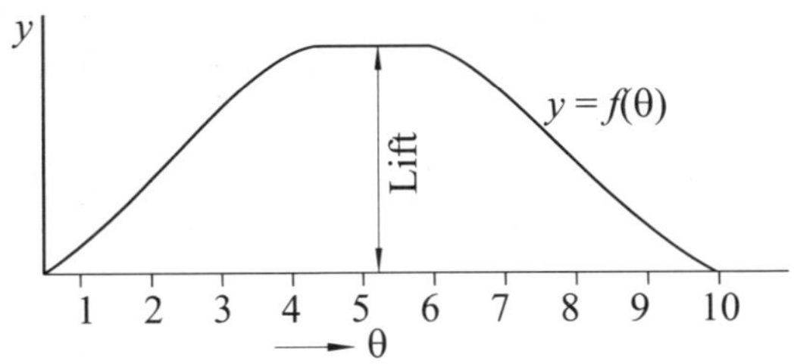

Gear Trains

A gear train is composed of two or more gears in mesh for the purpose of transmitting motion from one shaft to another.

Train Value: It is the ratio of the angular speed of follower or driven gear to that of the driver.

Types of gear trains

Simple gear train

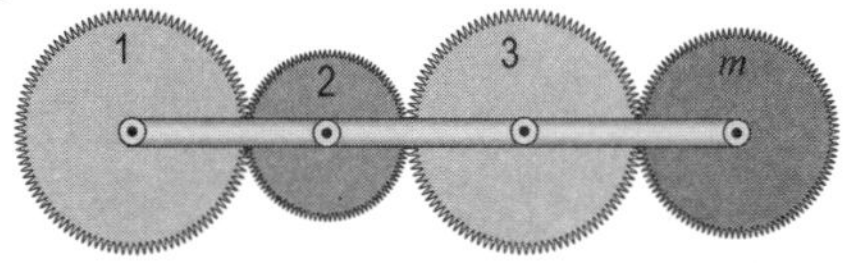

$$\frac{N_m}{N_1} = \frac{T_1}{T_m}$$

Compound Gear Train

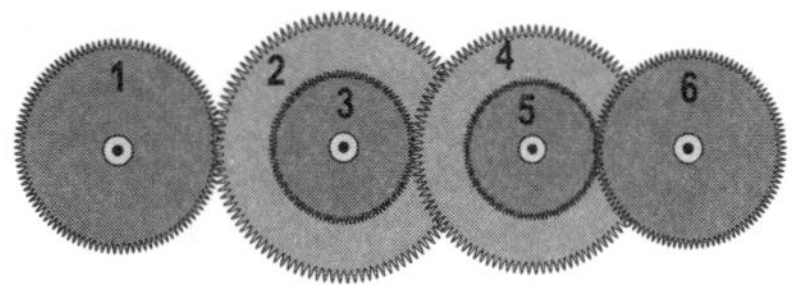

$$\frac{N_m}{N_1} = \frac{T_1}{T_2} \times \frac{T_3}{T_4} \times \frac{T_5}{T_6} \ldots$$

Reverted Gear Train

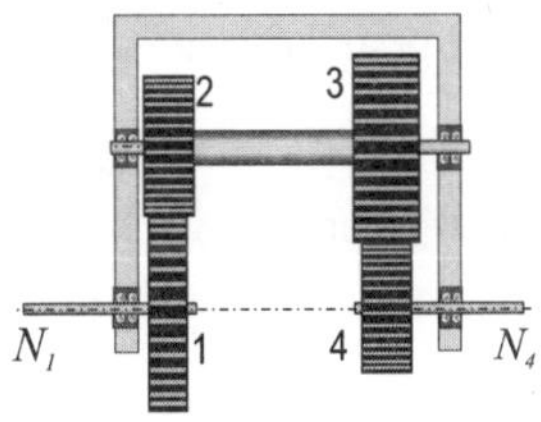

Centre distance, $C = \frac{1}{2}(d_1 + d_2) = \frac{1}{2}(d_3 + d_4)$

and $\quad T_1 + T_2 = T_3 + T_4$

$$\frac{N_4}{N_1} = \frac{T_1}{T_2} \times \frac{T_3}{T_4}$$

Planetary Gear Train/Epicyclic Gear Train

Speed ratio can be determine by

(i) Relative velocity

(ii) Algebraic or tabular method.

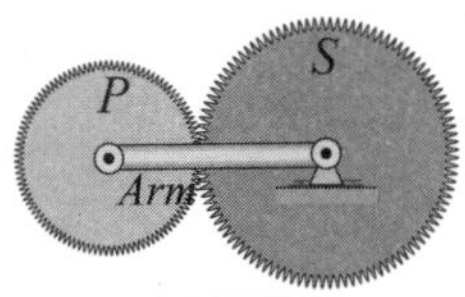

Operation	Gear S	Gear P	Arm
+1 revolution of gear S	1	$-\frac{T_s}{T_P}$	0
Multiply by x	x	$-\frac{T_s}{T_P}x$	0
Add y	$x+y$	$y-\frac{T_s}{T_P}x$	y

Revolution of gear $S = x + y$

Revolution of gear $P = y - \frac{T_s}{T_P} x$

Revolution of arm $= y$

Sun and Planet Gear

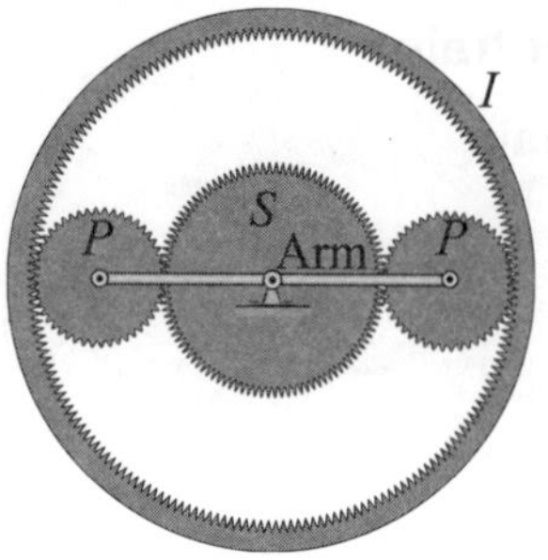

Operation	Arm A	Sun gear S	Planet gear P	Annular gear I
+1 revolution of Gear S	0	1	$-\frac{T_S}{T_P}$	$-\frac{T_S}{T_I}$
Multiply by x	0	x	$-\frac{T_S}{T_P}x$	$-\frac{T_S}{T_I}x$
Add y	y	$x+y$	$y-\frac{T_S}{T_P}x$	$y-\frac{T_S}{T_I}x$

Revolution of sun gear, $S = x + y$

Revolution of planet gear, $P = y - \frac{T_s}{T_P} x$

Revolution of annular gear, $I = y - \frac{T_s}{T_I} x$

Revolution of arm $= y$

Flywheel

A flywheel is an energy storage device. It absorbs mechanical energy by increasing its angular velocity and delivers energy by decreasing its angular velocity. Commonly, the flywheel controls the fluctuation of speed of the prime mover during each cycle of operation.

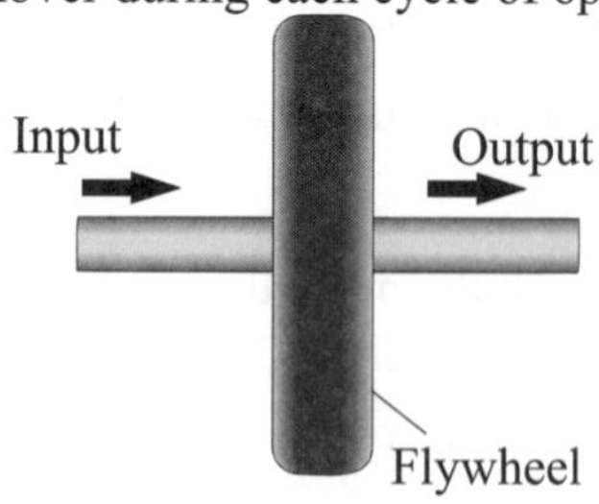

Mathematical representation of a flywheel is shown in figure.

Let ω_{max} and ω_{min} be the maximum and minimum angular velocities of flywheel, respectively.

Maximum kinetic energy of the flywheel, $E_{max} = \frac{1}{2} I\omega_{max}^2$

Minimum kinetic energy of the flywheel, $E_{min} = \frac{1}{2} I\omega_{min}^2$

Fluctuation of energy, $E_f = E_{max} - E_{min}$

or $E_f = \frac{1}{2} I\omega_{max}^2 - \frac{1}{2} I\omega_{min}^2$

or $E_f = I(\omega_{max} - \omega_{min}) \frac{(\omega_{max} + \omega_{min})}{2}$

or $E_f = I\,\Delta\omega\omega_m$ or $E_f = I\left(\frac{\Delta\omega}{\omega_m}\right)\omega_m^2$

or $E_f = I\,K_s\omega_m^2$

K_s = Coefficient of fluctuation of speed $= \frac{\omega_{max} - \omega_{min}}{\left(\frac{\omega_{max} + \omega_{min}}{2}\right)}$

Governor

The governors are control mechanisms and they work on the principle of feedback control. Their basic function is to control the speed within limits when the load on the prime mover changes. They have no control over the change is speed within the cycle. The speed control within the cycle is done by the flywheel.

Classification of Governors

The broad classification of governor can be made depending on their operation.

(a) Centrifugal governors, (b) Inertia and flywheel governors, (c) Pickering governors.

Types of centrifugal governors: (a) Gravity controlled centrifugal governors, and (b)Spring controlled centrifugal governors.

Gravity controlled centrifugal governors: (a) Watt governor, (b) Porter governor, (c) Proell governor.

Watt governor does not carry dead weight at the sleeve. Porter governor and Proell governor have heavy dead weight at the sleeve. In Porter governor balls are placed at the junction of upper and lower arms. In case of Proell governor, the balls are placed at the extension of lower arms. The sensitiveness of Watt governor is poor at high speed and this limits its field of application. Porter governor is more sensitive than Watt governor. The Proell governor is most sensitive out of these three.

Spring controlled centrifugal governors: (a) Hartnell governor, (b) Wilson-Hartnell governor, (c) Hartung governor.

Height of Governor

Height of Watt governor, $h = \dfrac{g}{\omega^2}$ (weightless of arms)

Height of Watt governor, $h = \dfrac{g}{\omega^2}\left(\dfrac{w + \dfrac{W_1}{2}}{w + \dfrac{W_1}{3}}\right)$

where W_1 = Weight of arm and w = Weight of ball

Height of Porter governor, $h = \dfrac{g}{\omega^2}\left(\dfrac{w+W}{w}\right)$

Height of Proell governor, $h = \dfrac{g}{\omega^2}\left(\dfrac{w+W}{w}\right)\dfrac{AB}{AC}$

Governor Effort and Power

Effort: The effort of a governor is the force with which it can exert at the sleeve on the mechanism which controls the supply of fuel to the engine.

Power: The power of a governor is defined as the work done at the sleeve for a given percentage change of speed.

Power = Effort × Displacement of sleeve

Controlling Force: A single force replacing all the forces which tries to pull the ball in a raidally inwards direction is known as the *controlling force*.

Characteristics of Governors

Stability: A governor is said to stable when for each speed within the working range, there is only one radius of rotation of the governor balls at which the governor is in equilibrium.

For spring controlled governor,

Controlling force $F = Ar + B$

Sensitiveness:

$$\text{Sensitiveness} = \frac{\text{Range of speed}}{\text{Mean speed}} = \frac{2(N_{max} - N_{min})}{(N_{max} + N_{min})}$$

Isochronism: A governor is said to be isochronous if equilibrium speed is constant for all the radii of rotation in the working range. Therefore, for an isochronous governor, the speed range is zero and this type of governor shall maintain constant speed.

Hunting: It is a condition in which the speed of the engine controlled by the governor fluctuates continuous above and below the mean speed.

Balancing

Balancing is the method of correcting or eliminating unwanted inertia forces and moment in rotating machinery.

Balancing of Rotating Masses

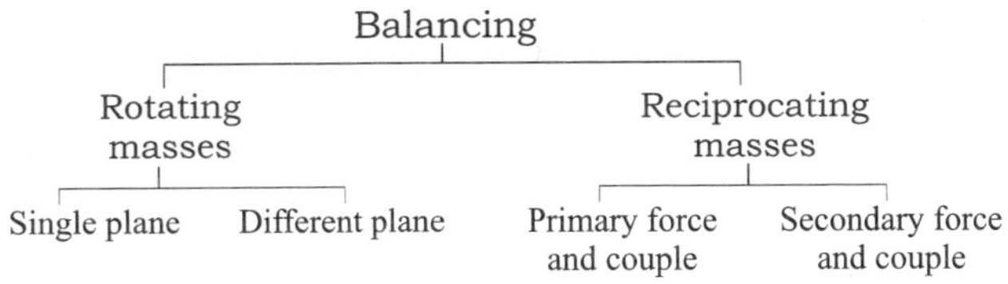

Balancing of rotating mass in single plane:

$\sum F = 0 \Rightarrow M\omega^2 r = B\omega^2 b$ or $Mr = Bb$

Balancing of a number of rotating masses in single plane:

$\sum F = 0 \Rightarrow \sum F_x = 0$ or $\sum mr\cos\theta = 0$

and $\sum F_y = 0$ or $\sum mr\sin\theta = 0$

Balancing of a number of rotating masses in different plane: $\sum F = 0$ [Force polygon]

$\sum M = 0$ [Moment polygon]

Balancing of Reciprocating Masses

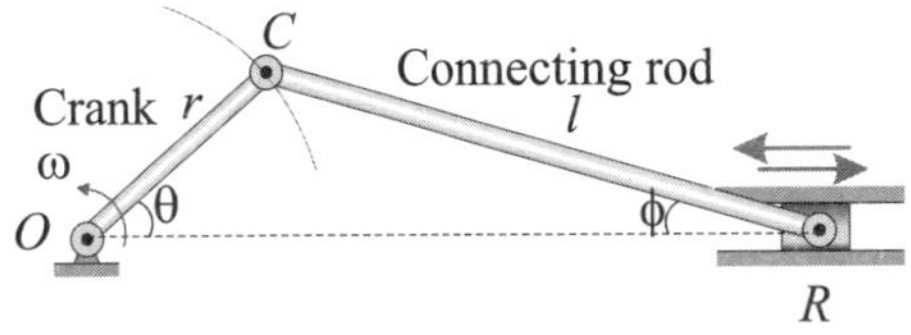

If R is the mass of the reciprocating parts, then the accelerating force and the opposing inertia force, acting always along the line of stroke,

$$F_i = R\omega^2 r\left(\cos\theta + \frac{\cos 2\theta}{n}\right); \quad \text{where } n = \frac{l}{r}$$

$$F_i = \underbrace{R\omega^2 r\cos\theta}_{\text{Primary force}} + \underbrace{R\omega^2 r\frac{\cos 2\theta}{n}}_{\text{Secondary force}}$$

Partial Balancing of Primary Forces

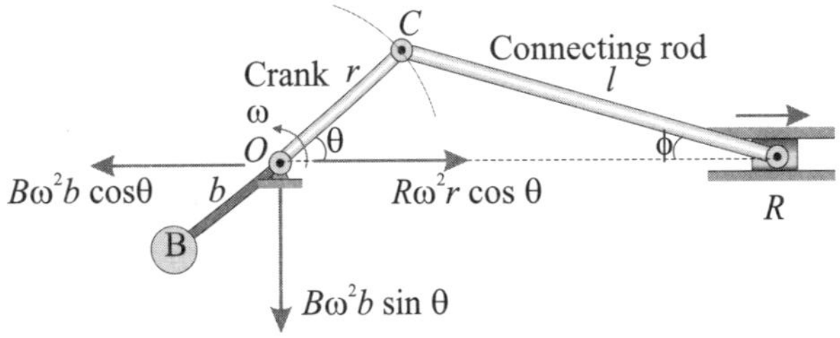

Unbalanced force along line of stroke

$= R\omega^2 r\cos\theta - B\omega^2 b\cos\theta = (Rr - Bb)\omega^2\cos\theta$

Unbalanced force along line of stroke

$= R(1-c)\omega^2\cos\theta$; where $Bb = cRr$

Unbalanced force perpendicular to the line of stroke

$= B\omega^2 b\sin\theta = cR\omega^2 r\sin\theta$

Resultant unbalance force

$$= \sqrt{(1-c)^2 \cos^2\theta + c^2 \sin^2\theta} \times \omega^2 r$$

Hammer blow: The unbalanced force perpendicular to the line of stroke due to balance mass B at radius b to balance the reciprocating parts only is equal to $B\omega^2 b \sin\theta$.

$$\text{Hammer blow} = B\omega^2 b \sin\theta$$

Gyroscope

Gyroscopic couple, $C = I\omega\omega_p$

where I = moment of inertia of body, ω = angular velocity, ω_p = angular velocity of precession.

7.2 SOLVED EXAMPLES

Previous Years GATE Questions

Example 7.1

The number of degrees of freedom of the planetary gear train shown in the figure is

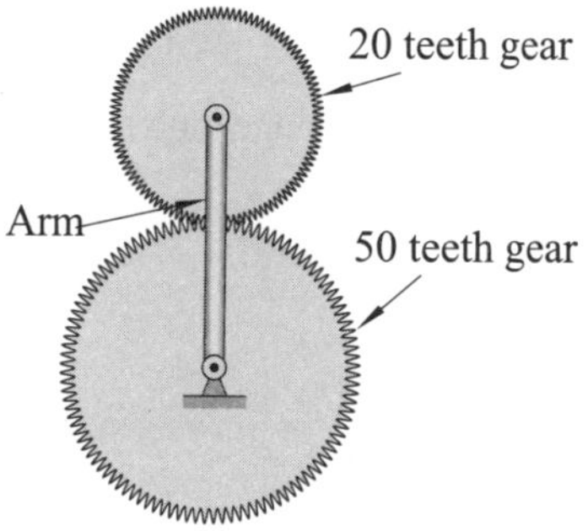

(A) 0 (B) 1 (C) 2 (D) 3

GATE 2015

Solution

Degree of freedom is given by

$$F = 3(n-1) - 2p - h$$

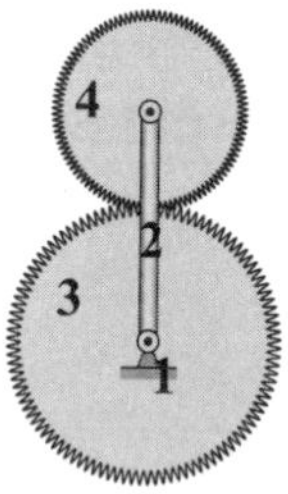

Substituting n = Number of links = 4

p = Number of lower pair(revolute) = 3

h = Number of higher pairs (gear pair) = 1

Degree of freedom, $F = 3(4-1) - 2\times 3 - 1$

$$\text{Degree of freedom } F = 2$$

Example 7.2

A rope brake dynamometer attached to the crank shaft of an IC engine measures a brake power of 10 kW when the speed of rotation of the shaft is 400 rad/s. The shaft torque (in N-m) sensed by the dynamometer is_____.

GATE 2015

Solution

Brake power, $P = \tau \times \omega$

Shaft torque, $\tau = \dfrac{10\times 10^3}{400}$

$$\tau = 25 \text{ Nm}$$

Example 7.3

In a certain slider crank mechanism, lengths of crank and connecting rod are equal. If the crank rotates with a uniform angular speed of 14 rad/s and the crank length is 300 mm, the maximum acceleration of the slider (in m/s^2) is______.

GATE 2015

Solution

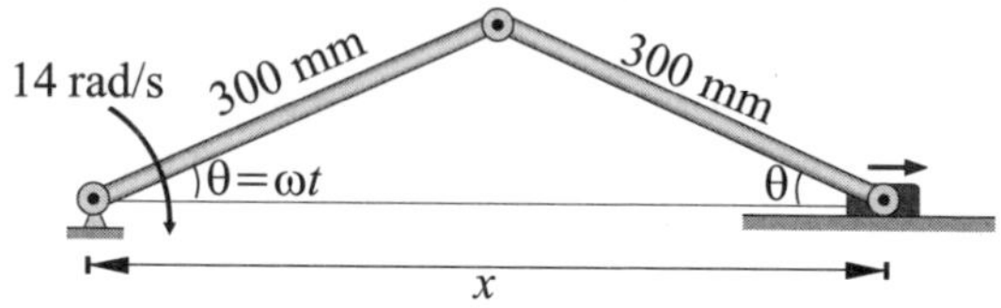

Position of slider from crank pin, $x = 2\times 300\cos\omega t$

Acceleration of slider, $a = \dfrac{d^2x}{dt^2} = -600\omega^2\cos\omega t$

Maximum acceleration of slider, $a_{max} = -\dfrac{600}{1000}\times 14^2$

$$a_{max} = 117.6 \text{ m/s}^2$$

Example 7.4

In the figure, link 2 rotates with constant angular velocity ω_2. A slider link 3 moves outwards with a constant relative velocity $V_{Q/P}$, where Q is a point on slider 3 and P is point on link 2. The magnitude and direction of Coriolis component of acceleration is given by

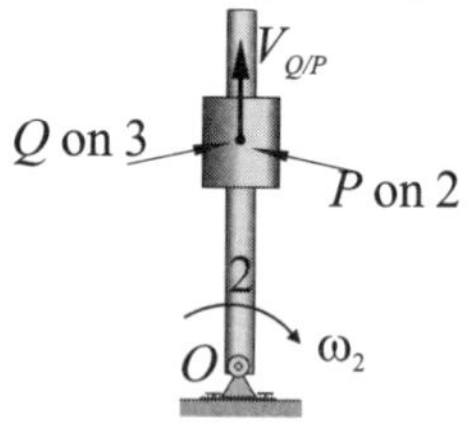

(A) $2\omega_2 V_{Q/P}$ direction of $V_{Q/P}$ rotated by 90° in the direction of ω_2

(B) $\omega_2 V_{Q/P}$ direction of $V_{Q/P}$ rotated by 90° in the direction of ω_2

(C) $2\omega_2 V_{Q/P}$ direction of $V_{Q/P}$ rotated by 90° opposite to the direction of ω_2

(D) $\omega_2 V_{Q/P}$ direction of $V_{Q/P}$ rotated by 90° opposite to the direction of ω_2

GATE 2015

Solution

Magnitude of coriolis acceleration is $a_{cc} = 2\omega_2 V_{Q/P}$

Direction of coriolis acceleration is direction of $V_{Q/P}$ rotated by $90°$ in the direction of ω_2.

Example 7.5

A gear train is made up of five spur gears as shown in the figure. Gear 2 is driver and gear 6 is driven member. N_2, N_3, N_4, N_5 and N_6 represent number of teeth on gears 2, 3, 4, 5 and 6 respectively. The gear(s) which act(s) as idler(s) is /are

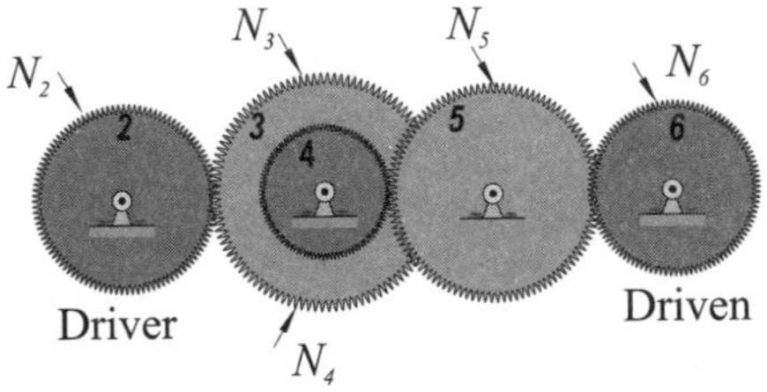

(A) Only 3 (B) Only 4 (C) Only 5 (D) Both 3 and 5

GATE 2015

Solution

Gear 5 acts as idler.

Example 7.6

The number of degree of freedom of the linkage shown in figure is

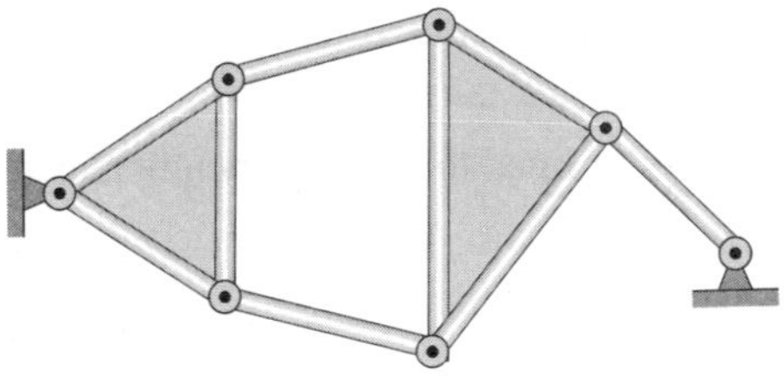

(A) –3 (B) 0 (C) 1 (D) 2

GATE 2015

Solution

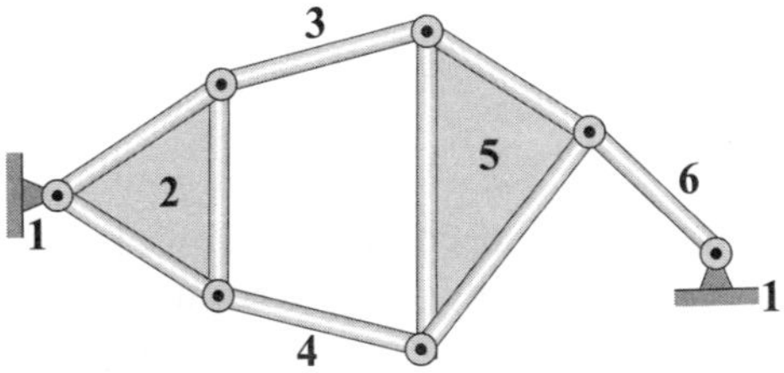

Degree of freedom is given by

$$F = 3(n-1) - 2p - h$$

Substituting n = Number of links = 6

p = Number of lower pair(revolute) = 7

h = Number of higher pairs (gear pair) = 0

Degree of freedom, $F = 3(6-1) - 2\times 7 - 0$

Degree of freedom, $F = 1$

Example 7.7

The torque (in N-m) exerted on the crank shaft of a two-stroke engine can be described as $T = 10000 + 1000\sin 2\theta - 1200\cos\theta$, where θ is the crank angle as measured from inner dead center position. Assuming the resisting torque to be constant, the power (in kW) developed by the engine at 100 rpm is _______.

GATE 2015

Solution

Average torque $T_{avg} = \frac{1}{2\pi}\int_0^{2\pi} T d\theta$

$$T_{avg} = \frac{\int_0^{2\pi}(10000 + 1000\sin 2\theta - 1200\cos\theta)d\theta}{2\pi}$$

$$T_{avg} = 10000 \text{ Nm}$$

Power developed by the engine, $P = \frac{2\pi NT}{60}$

$$P = \frac{2\pi\times 100\times 1000}{60}$$

$$P = 104.32 \text{ kW}$$

Example 7.8

A pinion with radius r_1, and inertia I_1 is driving a gear with radius r_2 and inertia I_2. Torque τ_1 is applied on pinion. The following are free body diagrams of pinion and gear showing important force (F_1 and F_2) of interaction. Which of the following relations hold true?

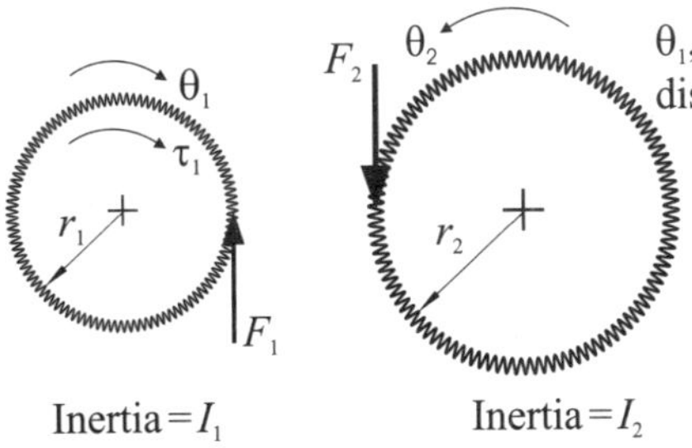

(A) $F_1 \neq F_2;\ \tau_1 = I_1\ddot{\theta}_1;\ F_2 = I_2\frac{r_1}{r_2}\ddot{\theta}_1$

(B) $F_1 = F_2;\ \tau_1 = \left[I_1 + I_2\left(\frac{r_1}{r_2}\right)^2\right]\ddot{\theta}_1;\ F_2 = I_2\frac{r_1}{r_2}\ddot{\theta}_1$

(C) $F_1 = F_2;\ \tau_1 = I_1\ddot{\theta}_1;\ F_2 = I_2\frac{1}{r_2}\ddot{\theta}_2$

(D) $F_1 \neq F_2;\ \tau_1 = \left[I_1 + I_2\left(\frac{r_1}{r_2}\right)^2\right]\ddot{\theta}_1;\ F_2 = I_2\frac{1}{r_2}\ddot{\theta}_2$

GATE 2015

Solution

From free body diagram

$$F_1 = F_2$$

Consider the motion of pinion

$$\sum \tau = \tau_1 - F_1 r_1 = I_1\ddot{\theta}_1$$

or $$\frac{\tau_1}{r_1} - F_1 = \frac{I_1}{r_1}\ddot{\theta}_1 \quad \text{(i)}$$

Consider the motion of gear

$$F_2 r_2 = I_2\ddot{\theta}_2$$

$$F_2 = \frac{I_2}{r_2}\ddot{\theta}_2 \quad \text{(ii)}$$

From Equations (i) and (ii), we obtain

$$\frac{\tau_1}{r_1} = \frac{I_1}{r_1}\ddot{\theta}_1 + \frac{I_2}{r_2}\ddot{\theta}_2$$

$$\tau_1 = I_1\ddot{\theta}_1 + \frac{r_1}{r_2}I_2\ddot{\theta}_2$$

Relation between $\ddot{\theta}_1$ and $\ddot{\theta}_2$;

$$r_1\ddot{\theta}_1 = r_2\ddot{\theta}_2 \quad \text{(iii)}$$

$$\tau_1 = I_1\ddot{\theta}_1 + \frac{r_1}{r_2}I_2 \times \frac{r_1}{r_2}\ddot{\theta}_1$$

$$\tau_1 = \left[I_1 + \left(\frac{r_1}{r_2}\right)^2 I_2\right]\ddot{\theta}_1$$

From Equations (ii) and (iii), we have

$$F_2 = \frac{I_2}{r_2}\ddot{\theta}_2 = \frac{I_2}{r_2} \times \frac{r_1\ddot{\theta}_1}{r_2}$$

$$F_2 = I_2\frac{r_1}{r_2^2}\ddot{\theta}_1$$

Example 7.9

The input link O_2P of a four-bar linkage is rotated at 2 rad/s counter clockwise direction as shown in the figure. The angular velocity of the coupler PQ in rad/s, at an instant when $\angle O_4O_2P = 180°$, is

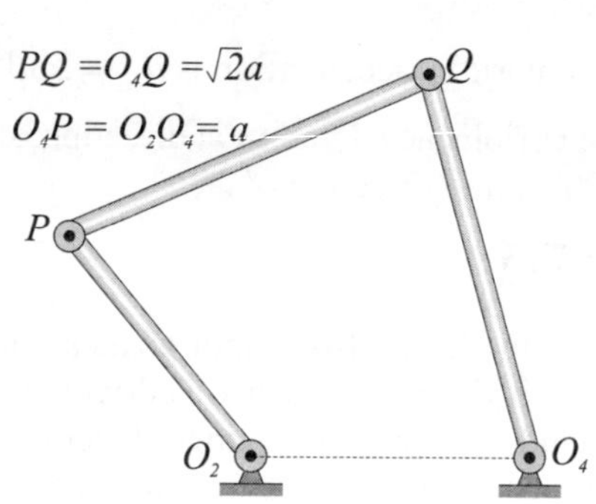

(A) 4 (B) $2\sqrt{2}$ (C) 1 (D) $\frac{1}{\sqrt{2}}$

GATE 2007

Solution

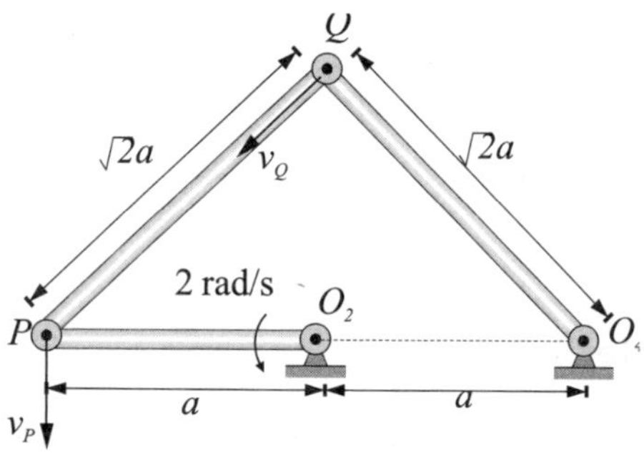

Let ω be the angular velocity of coupler PQ.

The instantaneous center of coupler PQ is located at the intersection of the lines that are perpendicular to v_P and v_Q, that is O_4.

Angular velocity of coupler PQ is

$$\omega = \frac{v_P}{PO_4} = \frac{v_Q}{QO_4}$$

or $$\omega = \frac{2 \times PO_2}{PO_4} = \frac{2 \times a}{2a}$$

$$\omega = 1\ \text{rad/s}$$

Example 7.10

An offset slider-crank mechanism is shown in the figure at an instant. Conventionally, the quick return ratio(QRR) is considered to be greater than one. The value of QRR is__.

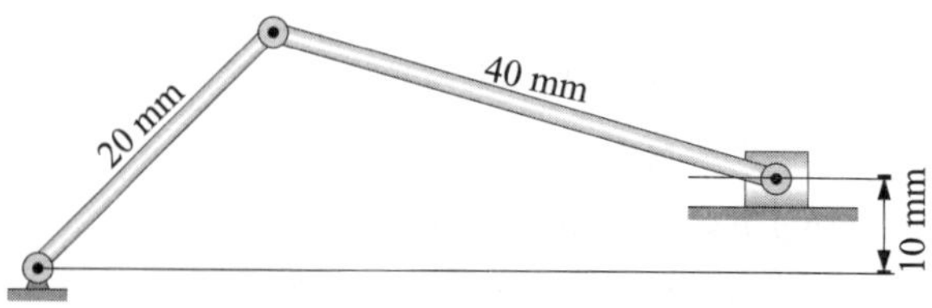

GATE 2014

Solution

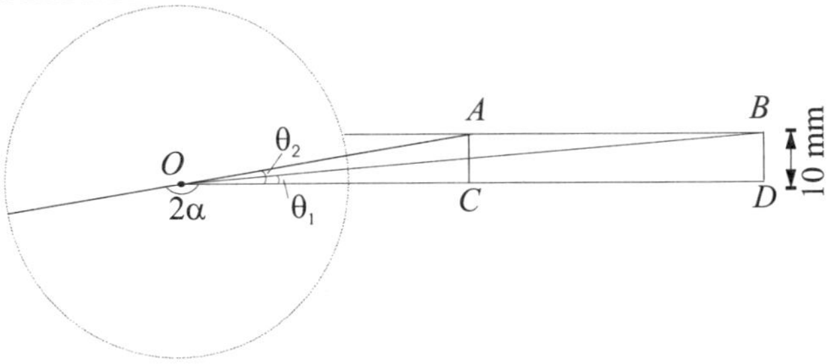

From the geometry of figure

In triangle OBD, $\sin\theta_1 = \frac{BD}{OB} = \frac{10}{20+40}$

From which $\theta_1 = 9.59°$

In triangle OAC, $\sin\theta_2 = \frac{AC}{OA} = \frac{10}{40-20}$

From which $\theta_2 = 30°$

$$2\alpha = 180 - (30 - 9.59)$$

Angle of return stroke $2\alpha = 159.59$

Therefore,

$$\text{Quick return ratio (QRR)} = \frac{360 - 2\alpha}{2\alpha}$$

$$\text{QRR} = \frac{360 - 159.59}{159.59}$$

$$\text{QRR} = 1.25$$

Example 7.11

A slider crank mechanism has slider mass of 10 kg, stroke of 0.2 m and rotates with a uniform angular velocity of 10 rad/s. The primary inertia force of the slider are partially balanced by a revolving mass of 6 kg at the crank, placed at a distance equal to crank radius. Neglect the mass of connected rod and crank. When the crank angle (with respect to slider axis) is 30°, the unbalanced force (in newton) normal to the slider axis is _____.

GATE 2014

Solution

Slider crank mechanism is shown in figure.

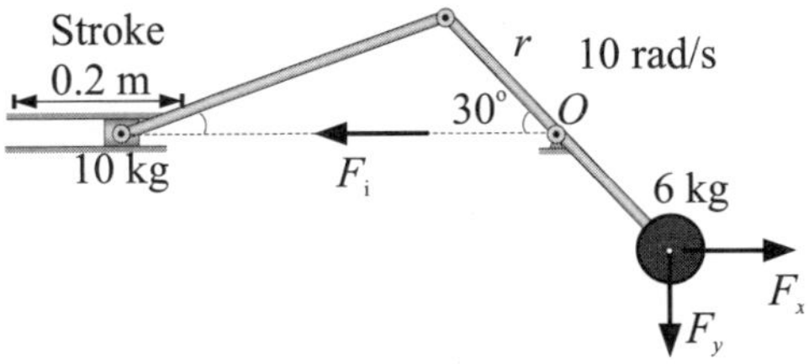

$$\text{Crank radius} = \frac{\text{Stroke}}{2}$$

$$\text{Crank radius } r = \frac{0.2}{2} = 0.1 \text{ m}$$

Unbalanced force normal to the slider axis is

$$F_y = m\omega^2 r\sin\theta$$

or $$F_y = 6\times 10^2 \times 0.1\sin 30$$

$$F_y = 30\text{ N}$$

Example 7.12

Common Data Questions

A quick return mechanism is shown below. The crank OS is driven at 2 rev/s in counterclockwise direction.

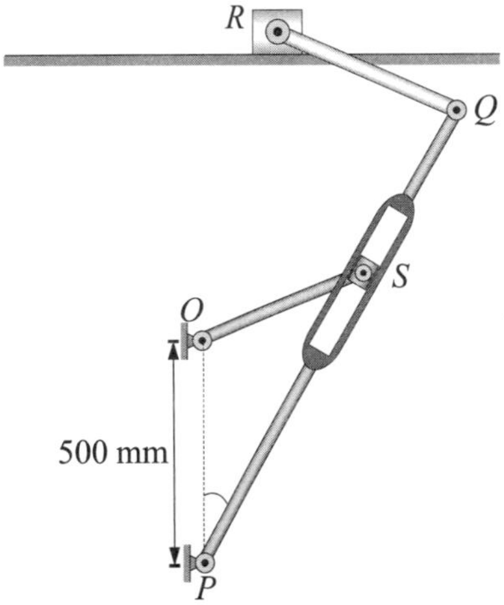

(a) If the quick return ratio is 1:2, then the length of the crank in mm is

(A) 250 (B) $250\sqrt{3}$ (C) 500 (D) $500\sqrt{3}$

(b) The angular speed of PQ in rad/s when the block R attains maximum speed during forward stroke (stroke with slower speed) is

(A) $\frac{1}{3}$ (B) $\frac{2}{3}$ (C) 2 (D) 3

GATE 2007

Solution

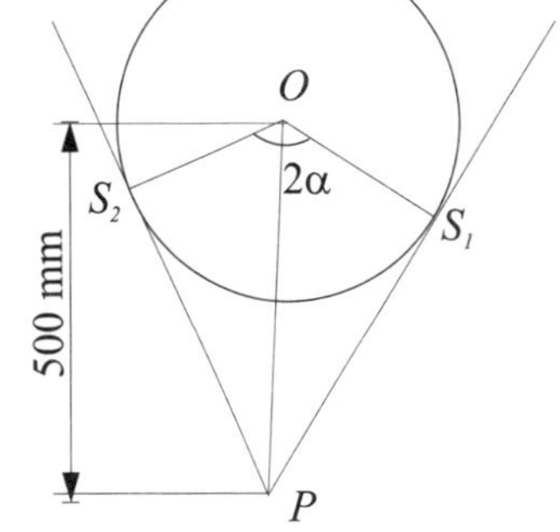

(a) Let 2α be $\angle S_1OS_2$ in extreme points as shown in figure.

Quick return ratio $= \frac{1}{2} = \frac{2\alpha}{360 - 2\alpha}$

From which $\alpha = 60°$

In the triangle S_1OP, $\cos\alpha = \frac{OS_1}{OP}$

$$\cos 60 = \frac{r}{500}$$

From which

$$\text{Crank radius } r = 250 \text{ mm}$$

(b) Maximum speed in forward stroke will occur when PQ and OS are in the same vertical line.

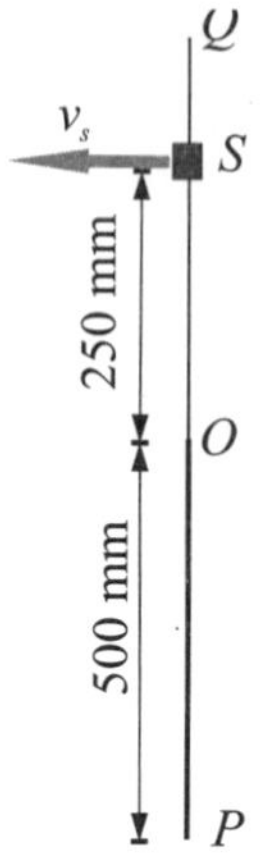

The velocity of point S on link OS is

$$v_S = 2 \times 250$$

or $$v_S = 500 \text{ mm/s}$$

For PQ, P acts as instantaneous center, Angular velocity of PQ is

$$\omega_{PQ} = \frac{v_S}{PQ} = \frac{500}{500 + 250}$$

$$\omega_{PQ} = \frac{2}{3} \text{ rad/s}$$

Example 7.13

The sun gear in the figure is driven clockwise at 100 rpm. The ring gear is held stationery. For the number of teeth shown on the gears, the arm rotates at

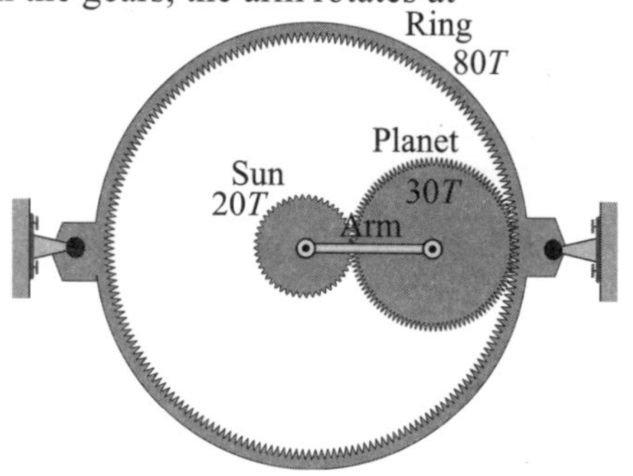

(A) 0 rpm (B) 20 rpm (C) 33.33 rpm (D) 66.67 rpm

GATE 2001

Solution

Operations	Sun gear (rpm)	Planet gear (rpm)	Ring (rpm)	Arm (rpm)
1 rpm of sun gear	1	$-\frac{20}{30}$	$-\frac{20}{80}$	0
x rpm of sun gear (multiply by x)	x	$-\frac{20}{30}x$	$-\frac{20}{80}x$	0
y rpm of arm(add y)	$x + y$	$y - \frac{20}{30}x$	$y - \frac{20}{80}x$	y

Given that ring is stationery, $y - \frac{20}{80}x = 0$ (i)

Speed of sun gear is 100 rpm; $x + y = 100$ rpm (ii)

From Equations (i) and (ii), we obtain

$$x = 80 \text{ and } y = 20$$

$$\text{Speed of arm } y = 20 \text{ rpm}$$

Example 7.14

A compound gear train with gears P, Q, R and S has number of teeth 20, 40, 15 and 20, respectively. Gear Q and R are mounted on the same shaft as shown in the figure below. The diameter of the gear Q is twice that of the gear R. If the module of gear R is 2 mm, the center distance in mm between gear P and S is

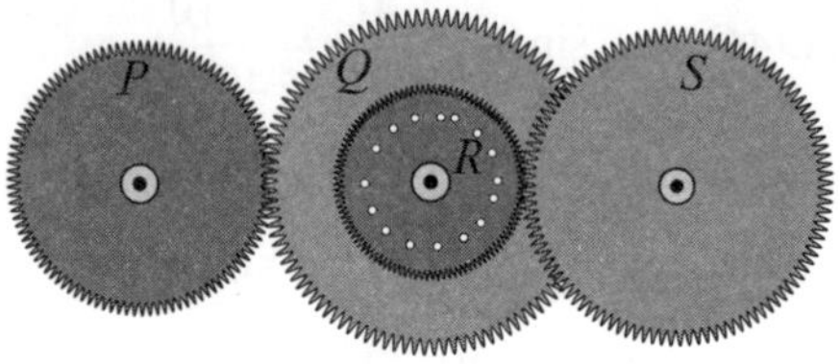

(A) 40 (B) 80 (C) 120 (D) 160

GATE 2013

Solution

The module of gear is given by $m = \frac{D}{T}$

The diameter of gear RR is $D_R = mT_R$

$$D_R = 2 \times 15 = 30 \text{ mm}$$

The diameter of gear S is $D_S = mT_S$

$$D_S = 2 \times 20 = 40 \text{ mm}$$

The diameter of gear Q is $D_Q = 2D_R$

$$D_Q = 2 \times 30 = 60 \text{ mm}$$

The diameter of gear P is determined by

$$\frac{D_P}{D_Q} = \frac{T_P}{T_Q} \Rightarrow D_P = \frac{T_P}{T_Q} \times D_Q = \frac{20}{40} \times 60$$

$$D_P = 30 \text{ mm}$$

The center distance between gears P and S is

$$C = \frac{D_P}{2} + \frac{D_Q}{2} + \frac{D_R}{2} + \frac{D_S}{2}$$

or $$C = \frac{30}{2} + \frac{60}{2} + \frac{30}{2} + \frac{40}{2}$$

$$\text{Center distance } C = 80 \text{ mm}$$

Example 7.15

For the epicyclic gear arrangement shown in the figure,

$\omega_2 = 100$ rad/s clockwise (cw) and $\omega_{arm} = 80$ rad/s counter clockwise (ccw). The angular velocity ω_5 (in rad/s) is

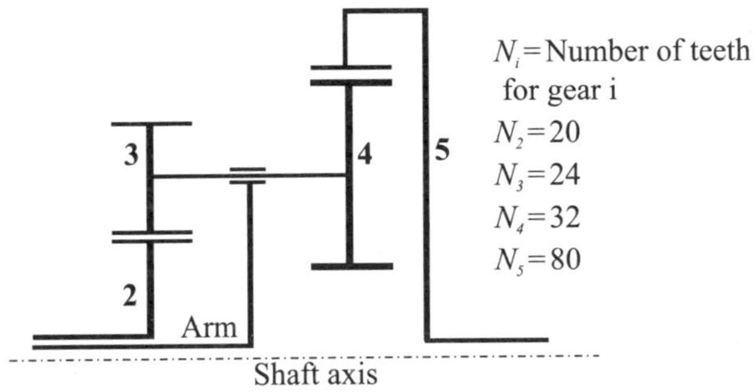

(A) 0 (B) 70 cw (C) 140 ccw (D) 140 cw

GATE 2010

Solution

Operations	Gear 2 (rad/s)	Gear 3 (rad/s)	Gear 4 (rad/s)	Gear 5 (rad/s)	Arm (rad/s)
1 rad/s of gear 2	1	$-\frac{20}{24}$	$-\frac{20}{24}$	$-\frac{20}{24}\times\frac{32}{80}$	0
x rad/s of gear 2	x	$-\frac{20}{24}x$	$-\frac{20}{24}x$	$-\frac{20}{24}\times\frac{32}{80}x$	0
y rad/s of arm (add y)	$x+y$	$y-\frac{20}{24}x$	$y-\frac{20}{24}x$	$y-\frac{20}{24}\times\frac{32}{80}x$	y

Given that angular velocity of gear 2, $\omega_2 = 100$ rad/s

$$x + y = 100 \text{ rad/s}$$

and $\omega_{arm} = 80$ rad/s(ccw); $y = -80$ rad/s

From which $x = 180$ rad/s

Angular velocity of gear 5, $\omega_5 = y - \frac{20}{24}\times\frac{32}{80}x$

or $\omega_5 = -80 - \frac{20}{24}\times\frac{32}{80}\times 180$

or $\omega_5 = -140$

$$\omega_5 = 140 \text{ ccw}$$

Example 7.16

A planetary gear train is shown in figure. Internal gear (1) has 104 teeth and is held fixed and planet gear (2) has 96 teeth. How much does the planet gear rotate for sixty revolutions of the planet carrier (3) in clockwise direction?

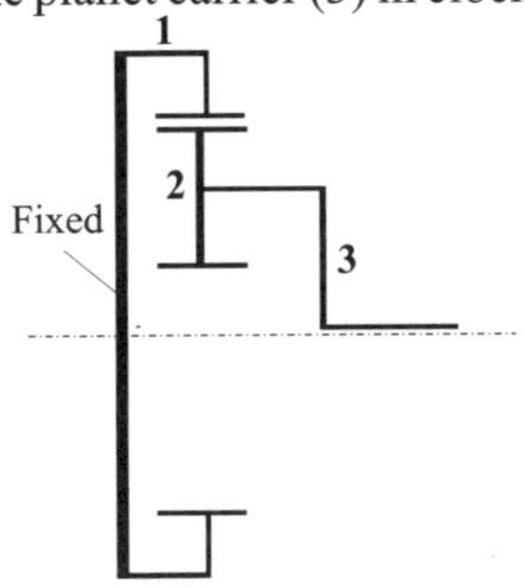

GATE 1999

Solution

Operations	Gear 2 (Planet)	Gear 1	Carrier 3
1 revolution of gear 2	1	$\frac{96}{104}$	0
x revolution of gear 2 (multiply by x)	x	$\frac{96}{104}x$	0
y revolution of carrier (add y)	$x+y$	$y+\frac{96}{104}x$	y

Given that gear 1 is fixed; $y + \frac{96}{104}x = 0$

Carrier 3 rotates sixty revolution; $y = 60$

From which $x = -65$

Planet (gear 2) rotates $= x + y = -65 + 60 = -5$

Planet (gear 2) rotates = 5 revolutions

Example 7.17

An epicyclic gear train is shown schematically in the given figure.

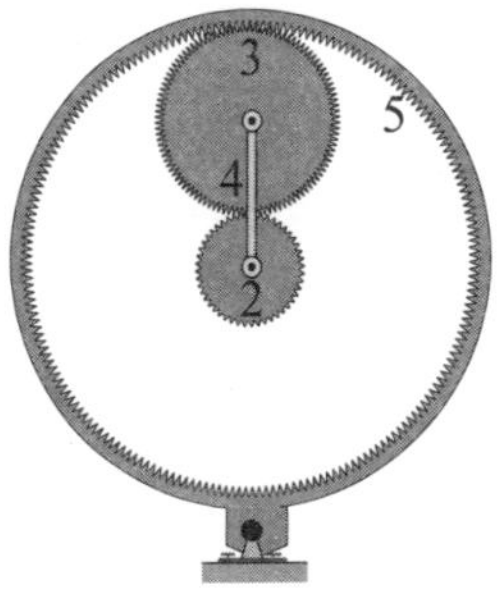

The sun gear 2 on the input shaft is a 20 teeth external gear. The planet gear 3 is a 40 teeth external gear. The ring gear 5 is a 100 teeth internal gear. The ring gear 5 is fixed and gear 2 is rotating at 60 rpm ccw (ccw = counter clockwise and cw = clockwise). The arm 4 attached to the output shaft will rotate at

(A) 10 rpm ccw (B) 10 rpm cw

(C) 12 rpm cw (D) 12 rpm ccw

GATE 2009

Solution

Operations	Sun gear 2	Planet gear 3	Ring gear 5	Arm 4
1 rotation of sun gear 2	1	$-\frac{20}{40}$	$-\frac{20}{100}$	0
x rotations of sun gear 2 (multiply by x)	x	$-\frac{1}{2}x$	$-\frac{1}{5}x$	0
y rotations of arm 4 (add y)	$x+y$	$y-\frac{1}{2}x$	$y-\frac{1}{5}x$	y

Given that ring gear 5 is fixed ; $y-\frac{1}{5}x=0$

Gear 2 is rotating at 60 rpm; $x+y=-60$

From which $y=-10, x=-50$

Thus,

$$\text{Speed of arm } y=10 \text{ rpm ccw}$$

Example 7.18

A simple quick return mechanism is shown in the figure. The forward to return ratio of the quick return mechanism is 2:1. If the radius of the crank O_1P is 125 mm, then the distance 'd' (in mm) between the crank centre to lever pivot center point should be

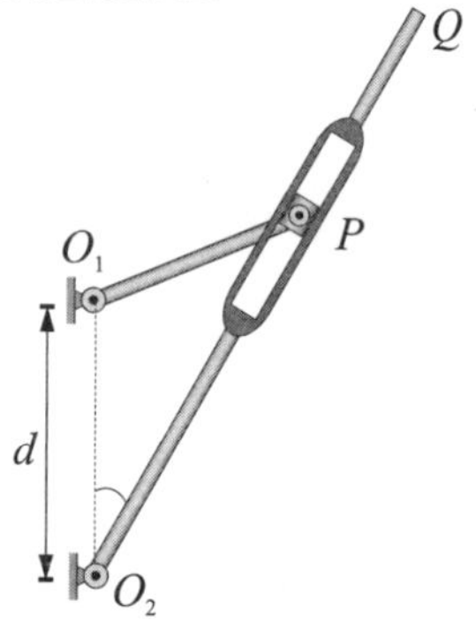

(A) 144.3 (B) 216.5 (C) 240.0 (D) 250.0

GATE 2009

Solution

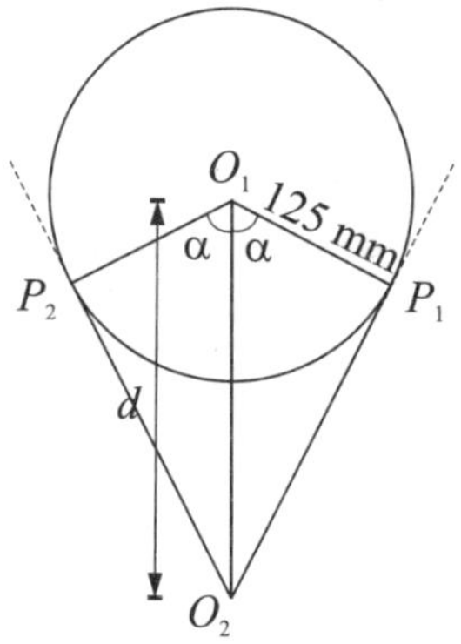

Let 2α be $\angle P_1OP_2$ in extreme point as shown in figure.

Forward to return ratio $=\dfrac{360-2\alpha}{2\alpha}$

$$2=\frac{360-2\alpha}{2\alpha}$$

or $\alpha=60°$

In the triangle $O_1P_1O_2$, $\cos\alpha=\dfrac{O_1P_1}{O_1O_2}$

or $\cos 60=\dfrac{125}{d}$

From which

$$d=250 \text{ mm}$$

Example 7.19

Common Data Questions

A planetary gear train has four gears and one carrier angular velocities of the gears are ω_1, ω_2, ω_3 and ω_4, respectively. The carrier rotates with angular velocity ω_5.

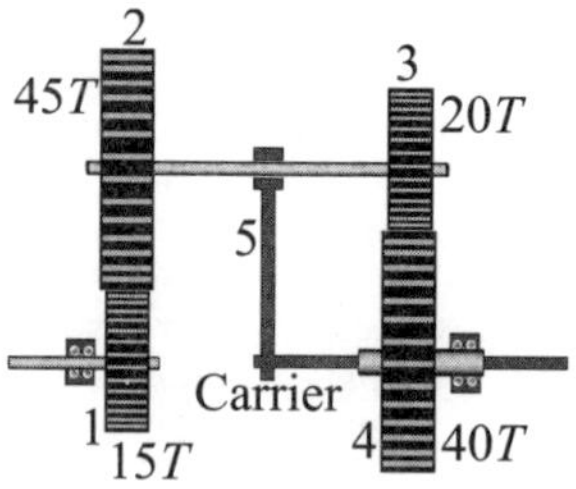

(a) What is the relation between the angular velocities of gear 1 and gear 4?

(A) $\dfrac{\omega_1-\omega_5}{\omega_4-\omega_5}=6$ (B) $\dfrac{\omega_4-\omega_5}{\omega_1-\omega_5}=6$

(C) $\dfrac{\omega_1-\omega_2}{\omega_4-\omega_3}=\dfrac{2}{3}$ (D) $\dfrac{\omega_2-\omega_5}{\omega_4-\omega_5}=\dfrac{8}{9}$

(b) For $\omega_1=60$ rpm clockwise (cw) when looked from the left, what is the angular velocity of the carrier and its direction so that gear 4 rotates in counter clockwise (ccw) direction at twice the angular velocity of gear 1 when looked from the left?

(A) 130 rpm, cw (B) 223 rpm, ccw

(C) 256 rpm, cw (D) 156 rpm, ccw

GATE 2006

Solution

(a)

Operations	Gear 1	Gear 2	Gear 3	Gear 4	Carrier 5
1 rotation of Gear 1	1	$-\frac{15}{45}$	$-\frac{15}{45}$	$\frac{15}{45}\times\frac{20}{40}$	0
x rotations of Gear 1 (multiply by x)	x	$-\frac{1}{3}x$	$-\frac{1}{3}x$	$\frac{1}{6}x$	0
y rotations of Carrier 5 (add y)	$x+y$	$y-\frac{1}{3}x$	$y-\frac{1}{3}x$	$y+\frac{1}{6}x$	y
	$=\omega_1$	$=\omega_2$	$=\omega_3$	$=\omega_4$	$=\omega_5$

From table,

$$\frac{\omega_1 - \omega_5}{\omega_4 - \omega_5} = \frac{x + y - y}{x + \frac{1}{6}x - y} = 6,$$

$$\frac{\omega_4 - \omega_5}{\omega_1 - \omega_5} = \frac{x + \frac{1}{6}x - y}{x + y - y} = \frac{1}{6}$$

$$\frac{\omega_1 - \omega_2}{\omega_4 - \omega_3} = \frac{x + y - y + \frac{1}{3}x}{y + \frac{1}{6}x - y + \frac{1}{3}x} = \frac{8}{3}$$

and
$$\frac{\omega_2 - \omega_5}{\omega_4 - \omega_5} = \frac{y - \frac{1}{3}x - y}{y + \frac{1}{6}x - y} = -2$$

(*b*) Given that angular velocity of gear 1;

$$\omega_1 = x + y = 60$$

Angular velocity of gear 4; $\omega_4 = y + \frac{1}{6}x = -120$

From which

$$x = 216 \text{ and } y = -156$$

Angular velocity of carrier 5; $y = 156$ rpm, ccw

Example 7.20

A flywheel connected to a punching machine has to supply energy of 400 Nm while running a mean angular speed of 20 rad/s. If the total fluctuation of speed is not to exceed $\pm 2\%$, the mass moment of inertia of the flywheel in kg m^2 is

(A) 25 (B) 50 (C) 100 (D) 125

GATE 2013

Solution

Fluctuation of energy is given by $E_f = E_{max} - E_{min}$

or
$$E_f = \frac{1}{2} I (\omega_{max}^2 - \omega_{min}^2)$$

or
$$E_f = I \left(\frac{\Delta\omega}{\omega_m} \right) \omega_m^2$$

Substituting $E_f = 400$ Nm, $\omega_m = 20$ rad/s and $\left(\frac{\Delta\omega}{\omega_m} \right) = \frac{2 - (-2)}{100} = \frac{4}{100}$, we obtain

$$400 = I \times \left(\frac{4}{100} \right) \times 20^2$$

From which

Mass moment of inertia, $I = 25$ kgm^2

Example 7.21

A punch press, fitted with a flywheel having a radius of gyration of 0.5 m, runs at 260 rev/min. The press is capable of punching 600 holes per hour. Each punching operation takes 1.5 s and requires a work of 10000 Nm. The rating of the electric motor used is 2 kW. Determine the mass of the flywheel, if the speed of the flywheel should not drop below 240 rev/min.

GATE 2000

Solution

Energy absorbed during one punching operation which takes 1.5 seconds = 10,000 Nm

Energy required, $E_1 = \frac{10000}{1.5} = 6666.67$ Nm/s

Motor power supplied, $E_2 = 2000$ Nm/s

Maximum fluctuation of energy per second

$$E_f = (6666.67 - 2000) \text{ Nm/s}$$

$$E_f = 4666.67 \text{ Nm/s}$$

Maximum fluctuation of energy, $E_f = \frac{1}{2} I (\omega_1^2 - \omega_2^2)$

$$E_f = \frac{1}{2} mk^2 \left[\left(\frac{2\pi N_1}{60} \right)^2 - \left(\frac{2\pi N_2}{60} \right)^2 \right]$$

Substituting given data

$$4666.67 = \frac{1}{2} m (0.5)^2 \left[\left(\frac{2\pi \times 260}{60} \right)^2 - \left(\frac{2\pi \times 240}{60} \right)^2 \right]$$

From which

$$m = 340 \text{ kg}$$

Example 7.22

A pair of spur gears with module 5 mm and a centre distance of 450 mm is used for a speed reduction of 5:1. The number of teeth on pinion is______.

GATE 2014

Solution

Let d and T be diameter and number of teeth of pinion.

Diameter of gear $D = 5d$

Center distance, $C = \frac{D}{2} + \frac{d}{2}$ or $C = \frac{5d}{2} + \frac{d}{2} = 3d$

Module of gear, $m = \frac{d}{T}$

$$C = 3mT$$

Substituting given data

$$450 = 3 \times 5 \times T$$

$$T = 30$$

Example 7.23

For the configuration shown, the angular velocity of link AB is 10 rad/s counter clockwise. The magnitude of the relative sliding velocity (in m/s) of slider B with respect to rigid link CD is

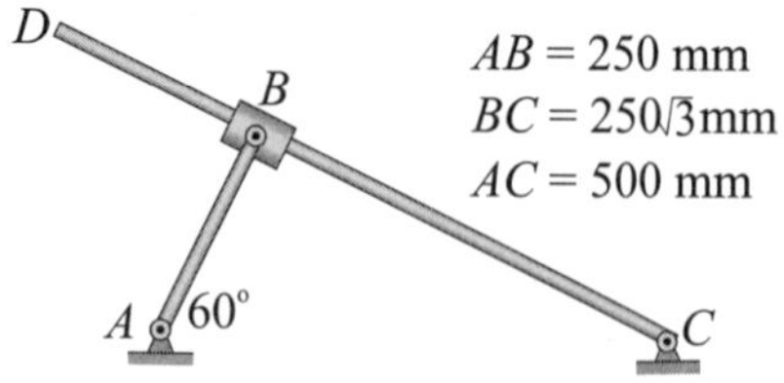

(A) 0 (B) 0.86 (C) 1.25 (D) 2.50

GATE 2010

Solution

In the triangle ABC, $AC^2 = AB^2 + BC^2$

Therefore, AB is perpendicular to BC

Thus, relative velocity of the slider with respect to rigid link CD is

$$v = \omega \times AB$$

$$v = 10 \times 250 = 2500 \text{ mm/s}$$

$$v = 2.5 \text{ m/s}$$

Example 7.24

A rigid link PQ is 2 m long and oriented at 20° to the horizontal as shown in the figure. The magnitude and direction of velocity v_Q and the direction of velocity v_P are given. The magnitude of v_P(in m/s) at this instant is

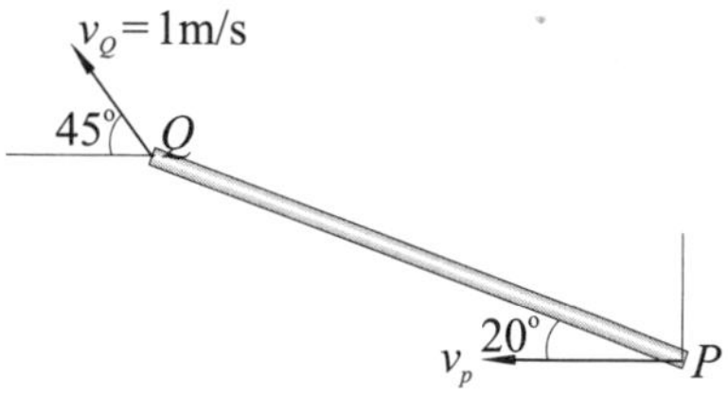

(A) 2.14 (B) 1.89 (C) 1.21 (D) 0.96

GATE 2014

Solution

We first locate the instantaneous center I of link PQ, it is located at the point of intersection of the lines that are perpendicular to the velocity vector of P and Q.

Let ω be the angular velocity of PQ.

Angular velocity of link PQ is

$$\omega = \frac{v_P}{IP} = \frac{v_Q}{IQ} \quad \text{or} \quad v_P = \frac{IP}{IQ} v_Q$$

Using sine law for triangle PQI

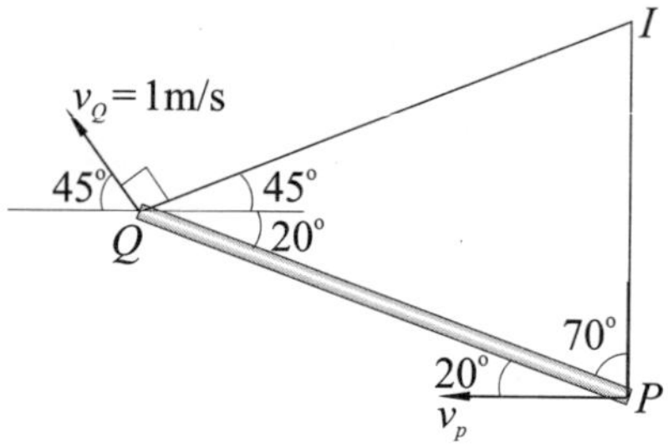

$$\frac{IP}{\sin(20+45)} = \frac{IQ}{\sin(70)}$$

or $$\frac{IP}{IQ} = \frac{\sin(20+45)}{\sin(70)}$$

Therefore $$v_P = \frac{IP}{IQ} v_Q = \frac{\sin(20+45)}{\sin(70)} v_Q$$

or $$v_P = \frac{\sin(20+45)}{\sin(70)} \times 1$$

$$v_P = 0.96 \text{ m/s}$$

Example 7.25

One tooth of a gear having 4 module and 32 teeth is shown in the figure. Assume that the gear tooth and the corresponding tooth space make equal intercepts on the pitch circumference. The dimensions 'a' and 'b', respectively, are closest to

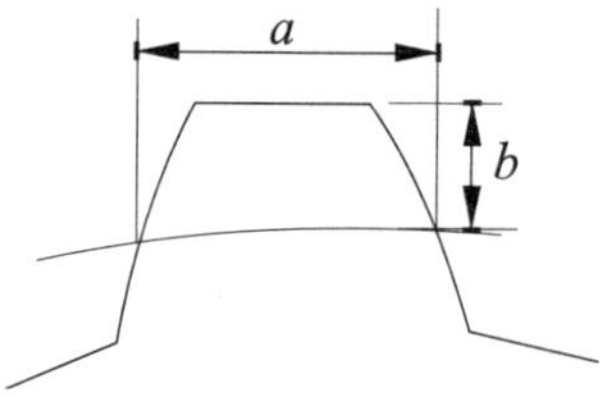

(A) 6.08 mm, 4 mm (B) 6.48 mm, 4.2 mm

(C) 6.28 mm, 4.3 m (D) 6.28 mm, 4.1 mm

GATE 2008

Solution

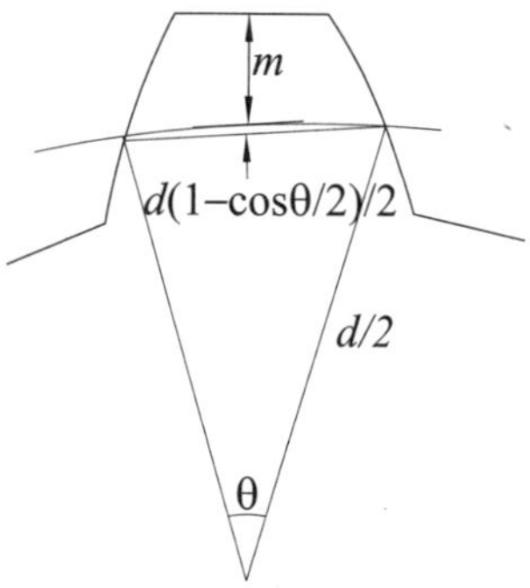

Module of gear is

$$m = \frac{d}{T}$$

Pitch circle diameter,

$$d = mT = 4 \times 32$$

or $d = 128$ mm

Circular pitch,

$$P_c = \frac{\pi d}{T} = \frac{\pi \times 128}{32}$$

or $P_c = 12.56$

Tooth thickness $= \frac{P_c}{2}$

Tooth thickness, $a = 6.28$ mm

From the geometry of tooth

$$\theta = \frac{\text{arc}}{d/2} = \frac{2 \times 6.28}{128} = 0.09812 \text{ rad} = 5.6^\circ$$

and $$b = 1 \text{ module} + \frac{d}{2}\left(1 - \cos\frac{\theta}{2}\right)$$

or $$b = 4 + \frac{128}{2}\left(1 - \cos\frac{5.6}{2}\right)$$

$$b \approx 4.1 \text{ mm}$$

Example 7.26

A car is moving on a curved horizontal road of radius 100 m with a speed of 20 m/s. The rotating masses of the engine have an angular speed of 100 rad/s in clockwise direction when viewed from the front of the car. The combined moment of inertia of the rotating masses is 10 kg · m^2. The magnitude of the gyroscopic moment (in Nm) is _____.

GATE 2016

Solution

Gyroscopic moment $= I\,\omega\omega_p$

Substituting $I = 10$ kg.m^2, $\omega = 100$ rad/s

Precision angular velocity, $\omega_p = \frac{v}{r} = \frac{20}{100}$ rad/s

Gyroscopic moment $= 10 \times 100 \times \frac{20}{100} = 200$ Nm

$$\text{Gyroscopic moment} = 200 \text{ Nm}$$

Example 7.27

A slider-crank mechanism with crank radius 200 mm and connecting rod length 800 mm is shown. The crank is rotating at 600 rpm in the counter clockwise direction. In the configuration shown, the crank makes an angle of 90° with the sliding direction of the slider, and a force of 5 kN is acting on the slider. Neglecting the inertia forces, the turning moment on the crank (in kN-m) is _________.

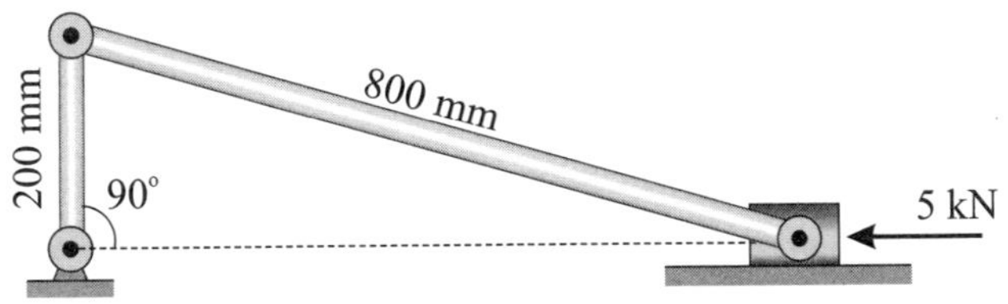

GATE 2016

Solution

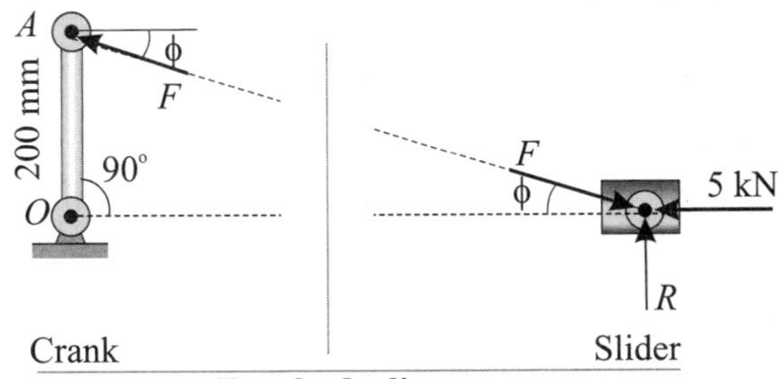

Free body digrams

Consider the slider

$$\sum F_x = 0 \Rightarrow F\cos\phi - 5 = 0$$

or $$F = \frac{5}{\cos\phi} \text{ kN}$$

Now, consider crank OA,

Turning moment $= F\cos\phi \times OA$

Turning moment $= \frac{5}{\cos\phi} \times \cos\phi \times \frac{200}{1000}$

$$\text{Turning moment} = 1 \text{ kNm}$$

Example 7.28

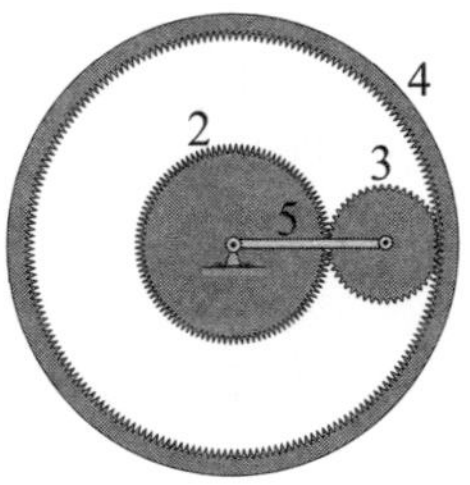

In the gear train shown, gear 3 is carried on arm 5. Gear 3 meshes with gear 2 and gear 4. The number of teeth on gear 2, 3, and 4 are 60, 20, and 100, respectively. If gear 2 is fixed and gear 4 rotates with an angular velocity of 100 rpm in the counter clockwise direction, the angular speed of arm 5 (in rpm) is

(A) 166.7 counter clockwise (B) 166.7 clockwise

(C) 62.5 counter clockwise (D) 62.5 clockwise

GATE 2016

Solution

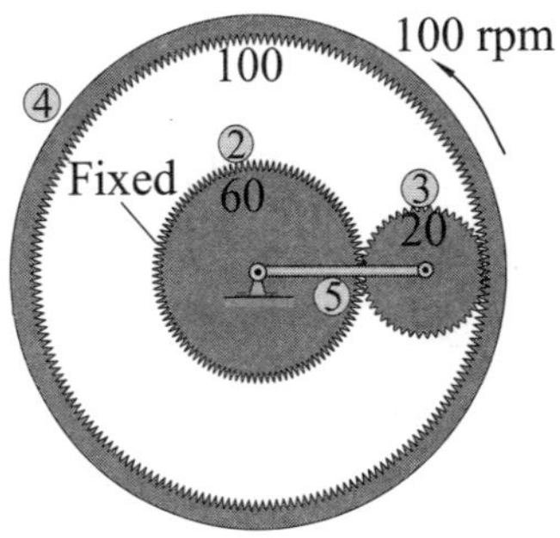

Operations	Gear 2	Gear 3	Gear 4	Gear 5
1 rpm of gear 2	1	$-\frac{60}{20}$	$-\frac{60}{100}$	0
x rpm of gear 2	x	$-\frac{60}{20}x$	$-\frac{60}{100}x$	0
y rpm of arm (add y)	$x+y$	$y-\frac{60}{20}x$	$y-\frac{60}{100}x$	y
	$=0$		$=-100$	

Gear 2 is fixed; $x+y=0$

Gear 4 is rotated at 100 (counter clockwise) ;

$$y-\frac{60}{100}x=-100$$

From which we get, $y=-\frac{1000}{16}=-62.5$ rpm

Speed of arm $y=62.5$ rpm (counter clockwise)

Example 7.29

The rod AB, of length 1 m, shown in the figure is connected to two sliders at each end through pins. The sliders can slide along QP and QR. If the velocity V_A of the slider at A is 2 m/s, the velocity of the midpoint of the rod at this instant is____ m/s.

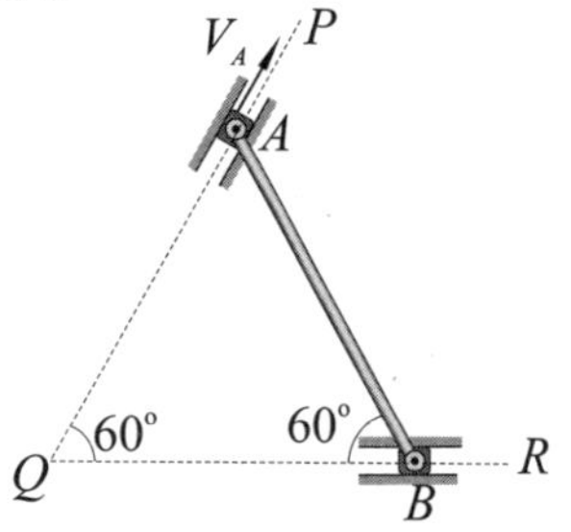

GATE 2016

Solution

The velocity triangle of given system is drawn as shown in figure.

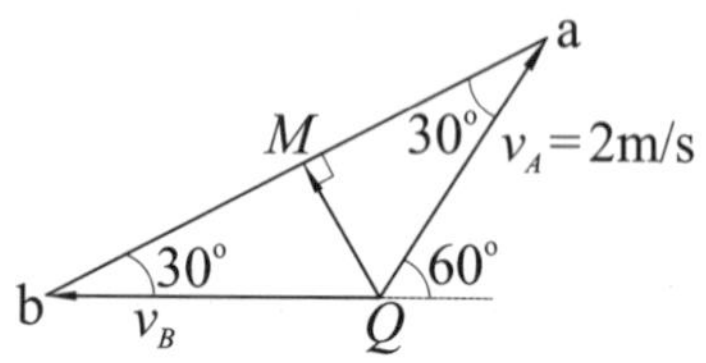

From the geometry of figure, velocity of the mid-point M

$$v_M=v_A\sin 30$$

$$v_M=2\sin 30=1$$

$$v_M=1\text{ m / s}$$

Example 7.30

A rigid link PQ is undergoing plane motion as shown in the figure (V_P and V_Q are non-zero). V_{QP} is the relative velocity of point Q with respect to point P.

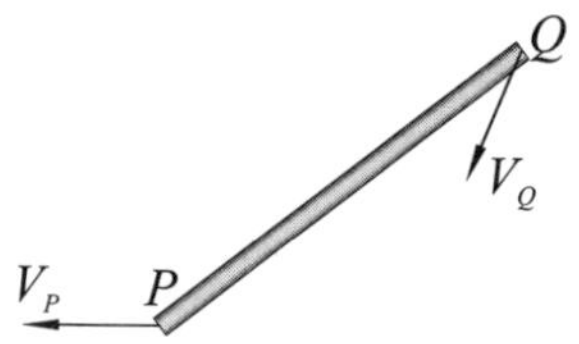

Which one of the following is TRUE?

(A) V_{QP} has components along and perpendicular to PQ

(B) V_{QP} has only one component directed from P to Q

(C) V_{QP} has only one component directed from Q to P

(D) V_{QP} has only one component perpendicular to PQ

GATE 2016

Solution

Velocity triangle of rigid link PQ is shown in figure.

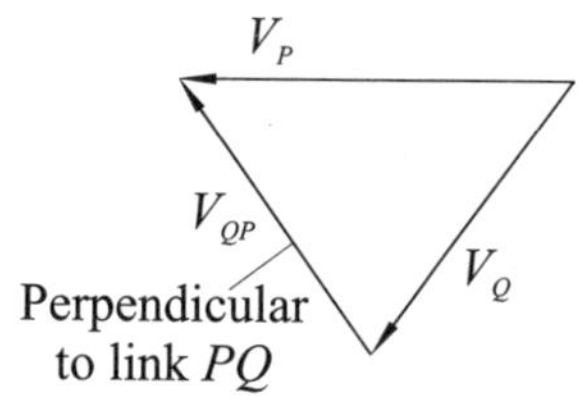

Direction of v_{QP} is perpendicular to PQ.

Example 7.31

The number of degrees of freedom in a planar mechanism having n links and j simple hinge joints is

(A) $3(n-3)-2j$ (B) $3(n-1)-2j$

(C) $3n-2j$ (D) $2j-3n+4$

GATE 2016

Solution

Gruebler's criteria, $F=3(n-1)-2p-h$

For planer mechanism $h=0$ and number of joint $p=j$,

$$F=3(n-1)-2j$$

Example 7.32

A rigid rod (AB) of length $L=\sqrt{2}$ m is undergoing translational as well as rotational motion in the xy plane (see the figure). The point A has the velocity $V_1=i+2j$ m/s. The end B is constrained to move only along the x direction.

The magnitude of the velocity V_2 (in m/s) at the end B is __.

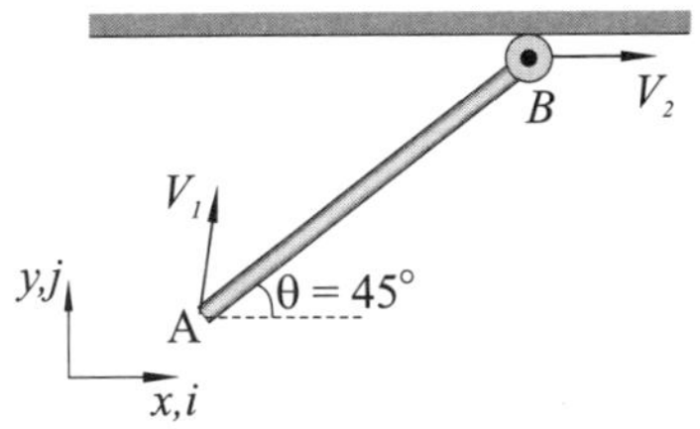

GATE 2016

Solution

Velocity triangle of rigid rod AB is constructed as shown in figure.

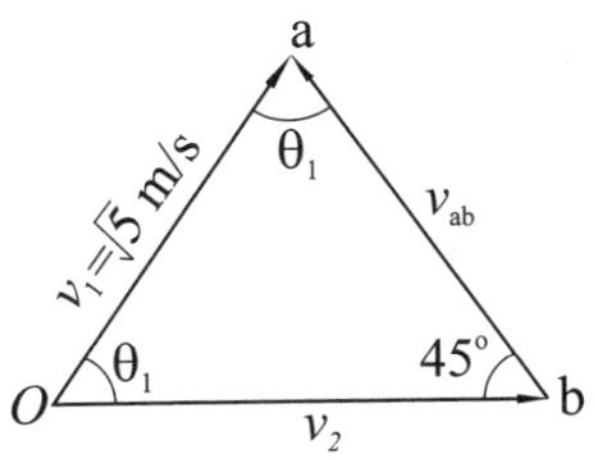

$$\tan\theta_1 = \frac{2}{1} \Rightarrow \theta_1 = 63.43°$$

$$\theta_2 = 180 - 45 - 63.43° = 71.56°$$

Using the law of sines, we have

$$\frac{v_2}{\sin 71.56} = \frac{\sqrt{5}}{\sin 45} = \frac{v_{ab}}{\sin 63.43}$$

Velocity, $$v_2 = \frac{\sqrt{5}}{\sin 45}\sin 71.56$$

$$v_2 = 3 \text{ m/s}$$

Example 7.33

Two masses m are attached to opposite sides of a rigid rotating shaft in the vertical plane. Another pair of equal mass m_1 is attached to the opposite sides of the shaft in the vertical plane as shown in figure. Consider $m = 1$ kg, $e = 50$ mm, $e_1 = 20\,\text{mm}$, $b = 0.3\,\text{m}$, $a = 2\,\text{m}$ and $a_1 = 2.5\,\text{m}$. For the system to be dynamically balanced, m_1 should be ____kg.

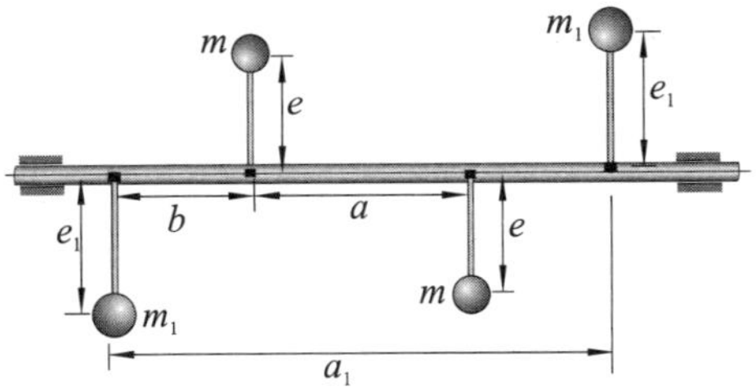

GATE 2016

Solution

The system is dynamically balanced ; $\sum M = 0$

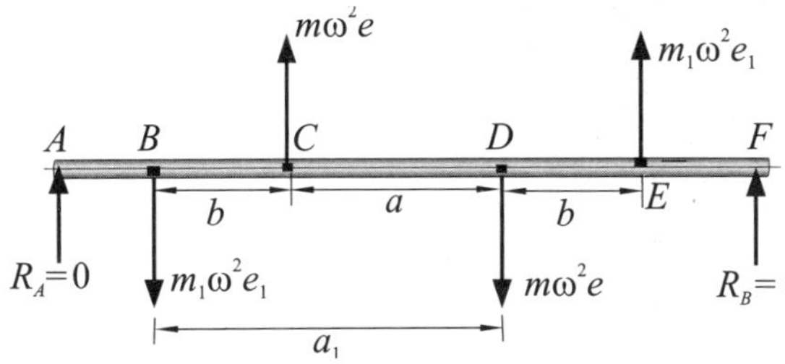

Moment about B,

$$\sum M = 0,\; m\omega^2 e \times b - m\omega^2 e \times (a+b) + m_1\,\omega^2 e_1 \times a_1 = 0$$

or $$m\,eb - m\,e \times (a+b) + m_1\,e_1 a_1$$

or $$m_1 = m \times \frac{e}{e_1} \times \frac{a}{a_1}$$

$$m_1 = 1 \times \frac{50}{20} \times \frac{2}{2.5}$$

$$m_1 = 2\,\text{kg}$$

Example 7.34

In an epicyclic gear train, shown in the figure, the outer ring gear is fixed, while the sun gear rotates counterclockwise at 100 rpm. Let the number of teeth on the sun, planet and outer gears to be 50, 25, and 100, respectively. The ratio of magnitudes of angular velocity of the planet gear to the angular velocity of the carrier arm is ________.

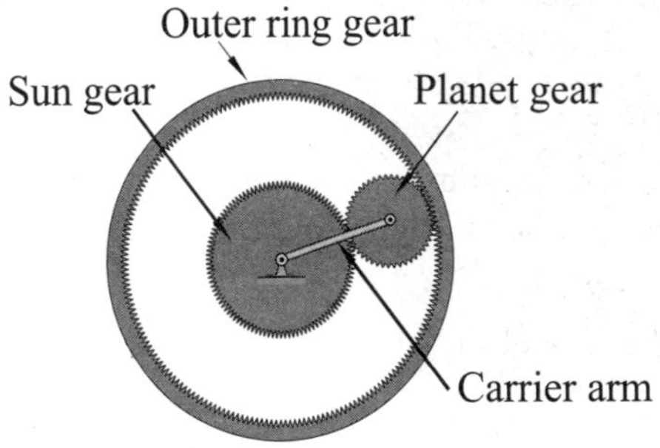

GATE 2017

Solution

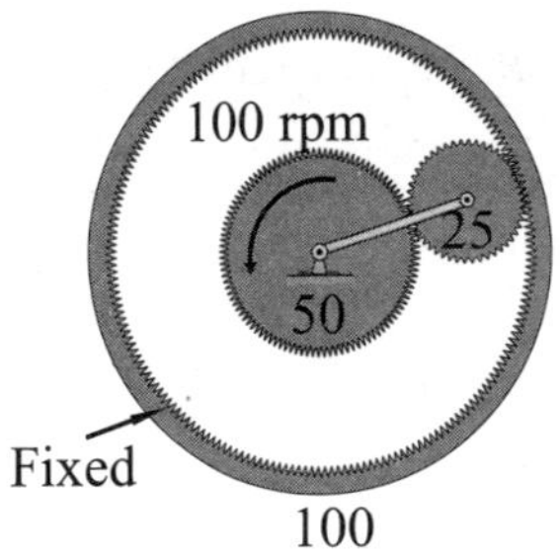

Operations	Sun gear	Planet gear	Outer ring	Carrier arm
1 rpm of sun gear	1	$-\frac{50}{25}$	$-\frac{50}{100}$	0
x rpm of sun gear (multiply by x)	x	$-2x$	$-\frac{x}{2}$	0
y rpm of arm (Add by y)	$x+y$	$y-2x$	$y-\frac{x}{2}$	y

Sun gear; $x + y = -100$ (i)

Outer ring; $y - \frac{x}{2} = 0$ (ii)

From equations (i) and (ii), we obtain

$$x = -\frac{200}{3},\ y = -\frac{100}{3}$$

$$\text{Planet gear} = y - 2x = -\frac{100}{3} - 2 \times -\frac{200}{3} = 100$$

Ratio of magnitudes of angular velocity of the planet gear to the angular velocity of the carrier arm is

$$= \frac{100}{100/3} = 3$$

Example 7.35

For an inline slider-crank mechanism, the lengths of the crank and connecting rod are 3 m and 4 m, respectively. At the instant when the connecting rod is perpendicular to the crank, if the velocity of the slider is 1 m/s, the magnitude of angular velocity (upto 3 decimal points accuracy) of the crank is_______radian/s.

GATE 2017

Solution

The velocity diagram of slider-crank mechanism is constructed as shown in figure.

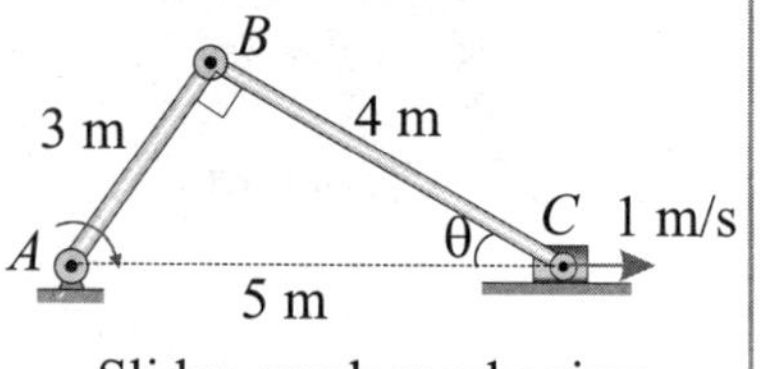

Slider-crank mechanism

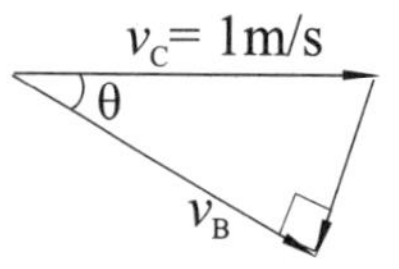

Velocity diagram

Velocity of point B, $v_B = v_C \cos\theta = 1 \times \frac{4}{5}$

Angular velocity of crank, $\omega_{AB} = \frac{v_B}{AB} = \frac{4}{5} \times \frac{1}{3} = \frac{4}{15}$

$$\omega_{AB} = 0.266 \text{ rad/s}$$

Example 7.36

In a slider-crank mechanism, the lengths of the crank and the connecting rod are 100 mm and 160 mm, respectively. The crank is rotating with an angular velocity of 10 radian/s counter- clockwise. The magnitude of linear velocity (in m/s) of the piston at the instant corresponding to the configuration shown in the figure is______.

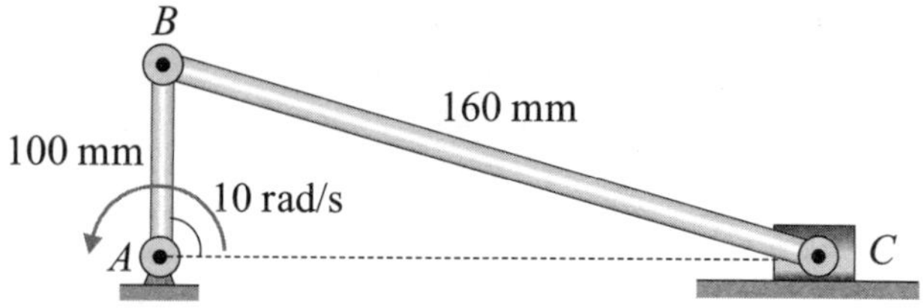

GATE 2017

Solution

Given: $r = 100$ mm, $l = 160$ mm and $\omega = 10$ rad/s

Velocity of slider, $v = \omega r\left(\sin\theta + \frac{\sin 2\theta}{n}\right)$

$$v = 10 \times \frac{100}{1000} \times \left(\sin 90 + \frac{\sin 2 \times 90}{(160/100)}\right)$$

$$v = 1 \text{ m/s}$$

Example 7.37

Block 2 slides outward on link 1 at a uniform velocity of 6 m/s as shown in the figure. Link 1 is rotating at a constant angular velocity of 20 radian/s counterclockwise. The magnitude of the total acceleration (in m/s^2) of point P of the block with respect to fixed point O is _______.

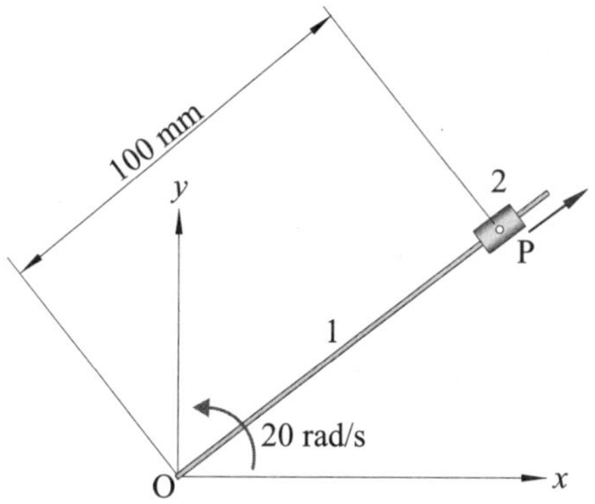

GATE 2017

Solution

Coriolis acceleration, $a_{cor} = 2v\omega$

Radial acceleration, $a_r = \omega^2 r$

Total acceleration,

$$a = \sqrt{a_r^2 + a_{cor}^2}$$

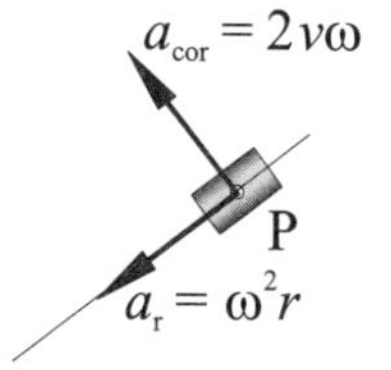

$$a = \sqrt{\left(20^2 \times \frac{100}{1000}\right)^2 + (2 \times 6 \times 20)^2}$$

$$a = 243.3 \text{ m/s}$$

Example 7.38

A gear train shown in the figure consists of gears P, Q, R and S. Gear Q and gear R are mounted on the same shaft. All the gears are mounted on parallel shafts and the number of teeth of P, Q, R and S are 24, 45, 30 and 80, respectively. Gear P is rotating at 400 rpm. The speed (in rpm) of the gear S is____.

GATE 2017

Solution

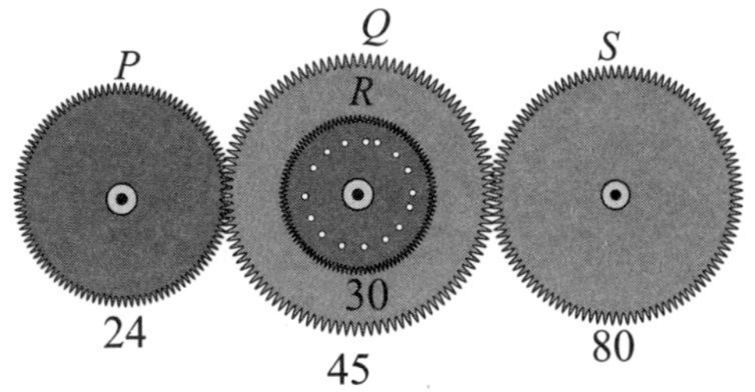

$$\frac{N_P}{N_Q} = \frac{T_Q}{T_P} \quad \text{(i)}$$

$$\frac{N_Q}{N_S} = \frac{T_S}{T_Q} \quad \text{(ii)}$$

From equations (i) and (ii) we obtain

$$\frac{N_P}{N_S} = \frac{T_S}{T_P} \Rightarrow \frac{400}{N_S} = \frac{80}{24}$$

$$N_S = 120 \text{ rpm}$$

Example 7.39

Three masses are connected to a rotating shaft supported on bearings A and B as shown in the figure. The system is in a space where the gravitational effect is absent. Neglect the mass of shaft and rods connecting the masses. For $m_1 = 10$ kg, $m_2 = 5$ kg and $m_3 = 2.5$ kg and for a shaft angular speed of 1000 radian/s, the magnitude of the bearing reaction (in N) at location B is______.

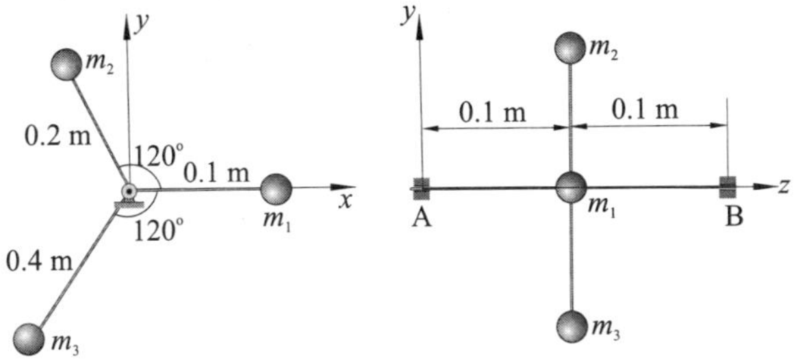

GATE 2017

Solution

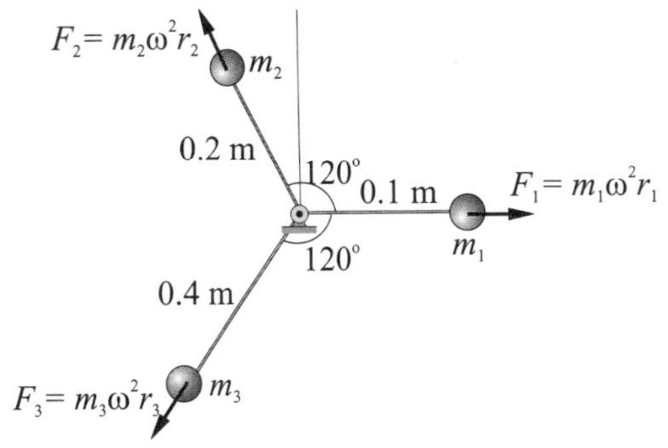

Resultant of x – components of centrifugal forces

$$\sum F_x = m_1\omega^2 r_1 - m_2\omega^2 r_2 \cos 60 - m_3\omega^2 r_3 \cos 60$$

$$\sum F_x = \omega^2 (m_1 r_1 - m_2 r_2 \cos 60 - m_3 r_3 \cos 60)$$

$$\sum F_x = \omega^2\left(10 \times 0.1 - \frac{5 \times 0.2}{2} - \frac{2.5 \times 0.4}{2}\right) = 0$$

Resultant of y – components of centrifugal forces

$$\sum F_y = +m_2\omega^2 r_2 \sin 60 - m_3\omega^2 r_3 \sin 60$$

$$\sum F_y = \omega^2\left(m_2 r_2 \frac{\sqrt{3}}{2} - m_3 r_3 \frac{\sqrt{3}}{2}\right)$$

$$\sum F_y = \omega^2\left(\frac{5 \times 0.2 \times \sqrt{3}}{2} - \frac{2.5 \times 0.4 \times \sqrt{3}}{2}\right) = 0$$

$$\text{Resultant force} = \sqrt{F_x^2 + F_y^2} = \sqrt{0^2 + 0^2} = 0$$

Therefore,

$$\text{Reaction at A and B} = 0$$

Example 7.40

For an Oldham coupling used between two shafts, which among the following statements are correct?

I. Torsional load is transferred along shaft axis.

II. A velocity ratio of 1:2 between shafts is obtained without using gears.

III. Bending load is transferred transverse to shaft axis.

IV. Rotation is transferred along shaft axis.

(A) I and III (B) I and IV (C) II and III (D) II and IV

GATE 2018

Solution

Correct statement for Oldham coupling

I. Torsional load is transferred along shaft axis.

IV. Rotation is transferred along shaft axis.

Example 7.41

A four bar mechanism is made up of links of length 100, 200, 300 and 350 mm. If the 350 mm link is fixed, the number of links that can rotate fully is ________.

GATE 2018

Solution

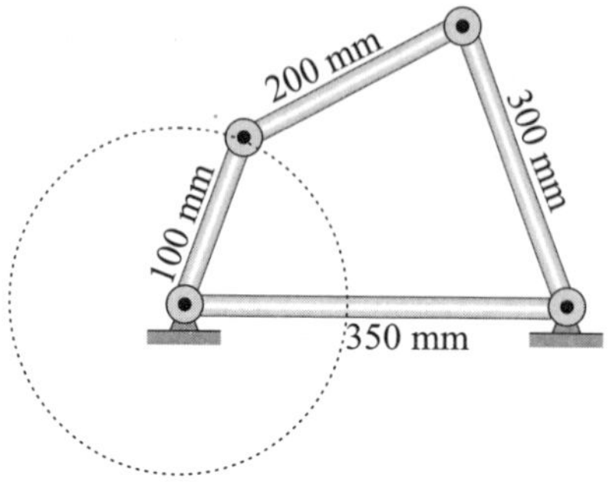

Given: $l = 350$ mm, $s = 100$ mm, $p = 200$ mm, and $q = 300$ mm

$p + q > l + s \Rightarrow 500 > 450$ Grashof's law satisfied

One shortest link $s = 100$ mm can rotate fully.

Number of link = 1

Example 7.42

An epicyclic gear train is shown in the figure below. The number of teeth on the gears A, B and D are 20, 30 and 20, respectively. Gear C has 80 teeth on the inner surface and 100 teeth on the outer surface. If the carrier arm AB is fixed and the sun gear A rotates at 300 rpm in the clockwise direction, then the rpm of D in the clockwise direction is

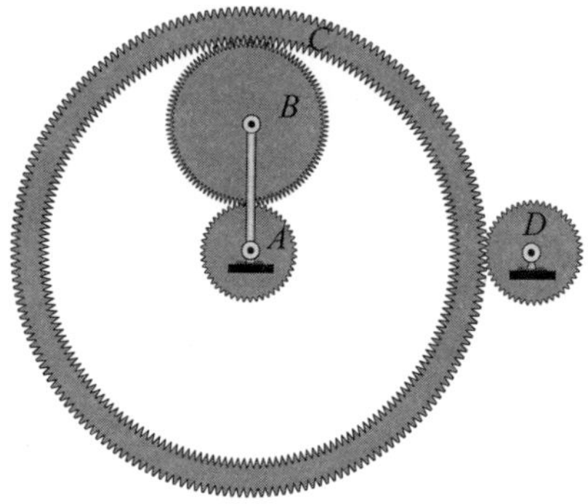

(A) 240 (B) –240 (C) 375 (D) –375

GATE 2018

Solution

Given that carrier arm AB is fixed

$$T_A N_A = T_B N_B \quad (1)$$

$$(T_C)_{\text{inner}} N_C = T_B N_B \quad (2)$$

$$(T_C)_{\text{outer}} N_C = T_D N_D \quad (3)$$

From equations (1), (2) and (3), we have

$$\frac{(T_C)_{\text{inner}}}{(T_C)_{\text{outer}}} = \frac{T_B N_B}{T_D N_D}$$

$$\frac{(T_C)_{\text{inner}}}{(T_C)_{\text{outer}}} = \frac{T_B}{T_D N_D} \times \frac{T_A N_A}{T_B}$$

$$N_D = \frac{(T_C)_{\text{outer}}}{(T_C)_{\text{inner}}} \times \frac{T_A}{T_D} \times N_A$$

Substituting $T_A = 20$, $T_D = 20$, $(T_C)_{\text{inner}} = 80$, $(T_C)_{\text{outer}} = 100$ and $N_A = 300$ rpm.

$$N_D = \frac{100}{80} \times \frac{20}{20} \times 300$$

$N_D = 375$ rpm clockwise

Example 7.43

A slider crank mechanism is shown in the figure. At some instant, the crank angle is $45°$ and a force of 40 N is acting towards the left on the slider. The length of the crank is 30 mm and the connecting rod is 70 mm. Ignoring the effect of gravity, friction and inertial forces, the magnitude of the crankshaft torque (in Nm) needed to keep the mechanism in equilibrium is ________.

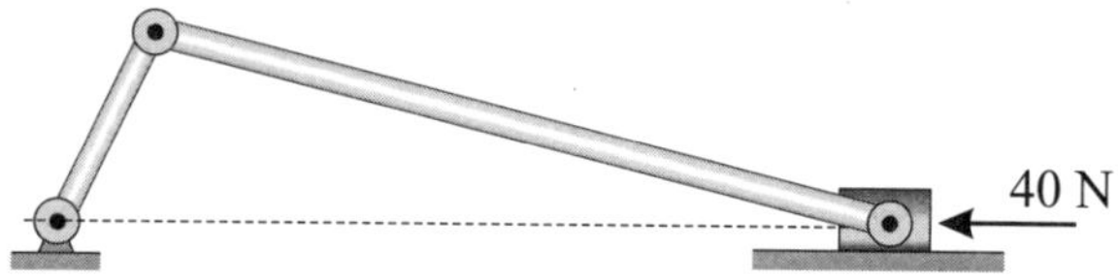

GATE 2018

Solution

From geometry of figure,

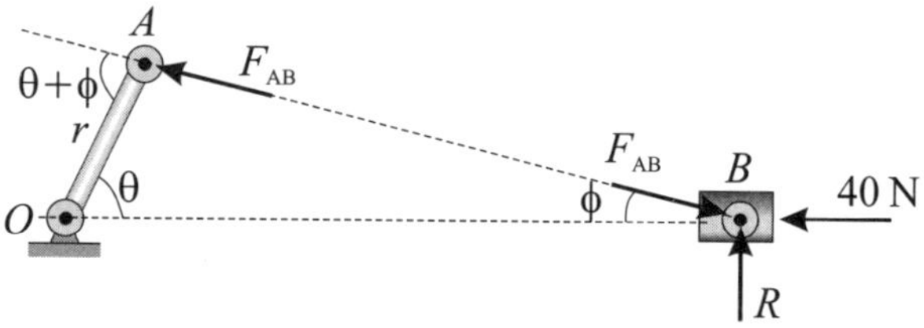

$$30 \sin 45 = 70 \sin \phi$$

$$\phi = \sin^{-1}\left(\frac{30 \sin 45}{70}\right)$$

$$\phi = 17.64 \qquad F_{AB} \cos\phi = 40 \Rightarrow F_{AB} = \frac{40}{\cos\phi}$$

Crankshaft torque,

$$M = F_{AB} \sin(\theta + \phi) \times r = \frac{40}{\cos\phi} \times \sin(\theta + \phi) \times r$$

$$M = \frac{40}{\cos 17.64} \times \sin(45 + 17.64) \times \frac{30}{1000}$$

$$M = 1.12\ \text{Nm}$$

Example 7.44

A frictionless gear train is shown in the figure. The leftmost 12-teeth gear is given a torque of 100 N-m. The output torque from the 60-teeth gear on the right in N-m is

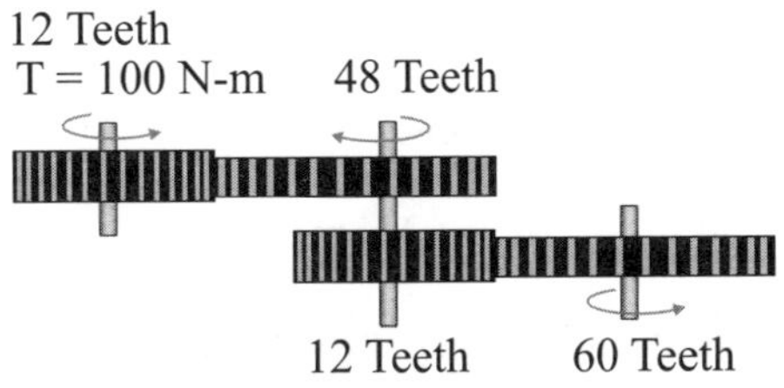

(A) 5 (B) 20 (C) 500 (D) 2000

GATE 2018

Solution

For gear 1 and gear 2 $\quad N_1T_1 = N_2T_2 \quad$ (i)

For gear 3 and gear 4 $\quad N_3T_3 = N_4T_4$

Substituting $N_3 = N_2$

$$N_2T_3 = N_4T_4 \quad \text{(ii)}$$

From equations (i) and (ii), we obtained

$$\frac{N_1T_1}{T_2} = \frac{N_4T_4}{T_3} \Rightarrow \frac{N_1}{N_4} = \frac{T_2 \times T_4}{T_1 \times T_3}$$

$$\frac{N_1}{N_4} = \frac{48 \times 60}{12 \times 12}$$

$$\frac{N_1}{N_4} = 20$$

Power transmitted, $\quad P = \dfrac{2\pi N_1 M_1}{60} = \dfrac{2\pi N_4 M_4}{60}$

$$M_4 = \frac{N_1}{N_4} M_1 = 20 \times 100$$

$$M_4 = 2000\ \text{Nm}$$

Example 7.45

A rigid rod of length 1 m is resting at an angle $\theta = 45°$ as shown in the figure. The end P is dragged with a velocity of $U = 5$ m/s to the right. At the instant shown, the magnitude of the velocity V (in m/s) of point Q as it moves along the wall without losing contact is

A) 5 (B) 6 (C) 8 (D) 10

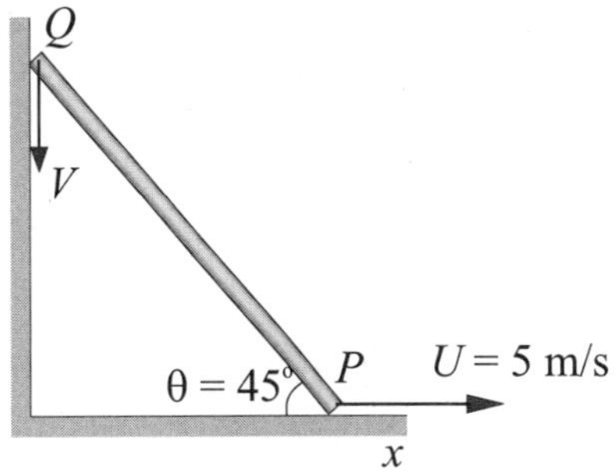

GATE 2018

Solution

Let ω be the angular velocity of rod PQ and I be the instantaneous centre.

Angular velocity of rod PQ,

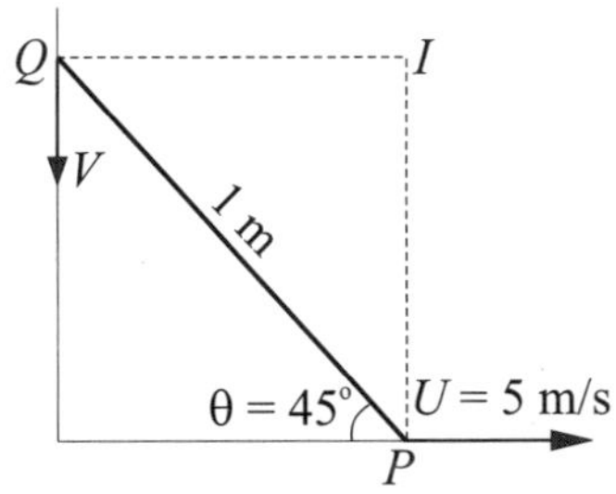

$$\omega = \frac{v_P}{IP} = \frac{v_Q}{IQ}$$

or

$$\frac{5}{1 \times \sin 45} = \frac{V}{1 \times \cos 45}$$

$$V = 5\ \text{m/s}$$

Example 7.46

In a cam-follower, the follower rises by h as the cam rotates by δ (radians) at constant angular velocity ω (radians/s). The follower is uniformly accelerating during the first half of the rise period and it is uniformly decelerating in the latter half of the rise period. Assuming that the magnitudes of the acceleration and deceleration are same, the maximum velocity of the follower is

(A) $\dfrac{4h\omega}{\delta}$ (B) $h\omega$ (C) $\dfrac{2h\omega}{\delta}$ (D) $2h\omega$

GATE 2018

Solution

Equation of motion of follower

$$S = ut + \frac{1}{2}ft^2 \Rightarrow \frac{h}{2} = 0 \times \frac{T}{2} + \frac{1}{2}f\left(\frac{T}{2}\right)^2$$

Substituting $T = \dfrac{\delta}{\omega}$, we obtain

$$f = \frac{4h}{T^2} == \frac{4h}{(\delta/\omega)^2} \quad \text{or} \quad f = \frac{4h\omega^2}{\delta^2}$$

Maximum velocity, $\quad v_{max} = f\dfrac{T}{2} = \dfrac{4h\omega^2}{\delta^2} \times \dfrac{\delta}{2\omega}$

$$v_{max} = \frac{2h\omega}{\delta}$$

Example 7.47

A flat-faced follower is driven using a circular eccentric cam rotating at a constant angular velocity ω. At time $t = 0$, the vertical position of the follower is $y(0) = 0$, and the system is in the configuration shown below.

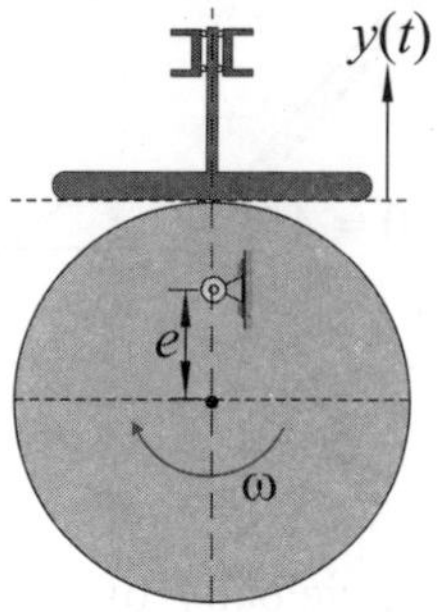

The vertical position of the follower face, $y(t)$ is given by

(A) $e \sin \omega t$ (B) $e(1+\cos 2\omega t)$

(C) $e(1-\cos \omega t)$ (D) $e \sin 2\omega t$

GATE 2019

Solution

Displaced position diagram of cam and follower is shown in figure.

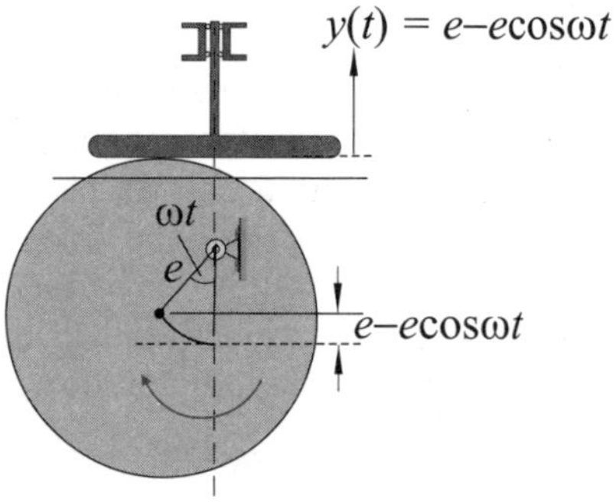

Vertical position of the follower face; $y(t) = e - e\cos \omega t$

$$y(t) = e(1-\cos \omega t)$$

Example 7.48

The rotor of a turbojet engine of an aircraft has a mass 180 kg and polar moment of inertia 10 kg.m^2 about the rotor axis. The rotor rotates at a constant speed of 1100 rad/s in the clockwise direction when viewed from the front of the aircraft. The aircraft while flying at a speed of 800 km per hour takes a turn with a radius of 1.5 km to the left. The gyroscopic moment exerted by the rotor on the aircraft structure and the direction of motion of the nose when the aircraft turns, are

(A) 1629.6 N.m and the nose goes up

(B) 1629.6 N.m and the nose goes down

(C) 162.9 N.m and the nose goes up

(D) 162.9 N.m and the nose goes down

GATE 2019

Solution

Given: $m = 180$, $I = 10$ kg.m^2, $\omega = 1100$ rad/s, $v = 800$ km/hr, $r = 1.5$ km.

Angular velocity of precession; $\omega_p = \dfrac{v}{r} = \dfrac{800}{1.5} \times \dfrac{1}{3600}$ rad/s

$$\omega_p = \frac{4}{27} \text{ rad/s}$$

Gyroscopic couple, $C = I\,\omega\omega_p$

$$C = 10 \times 1100 \times \frac{4}{27} = 1629.62 \text{ N.m}$$

C =1629.6 N.m and the nose goes down

Example 7.49

In a four bar planar mechanism shown in the figure, $AB = 5$ cm, $AD = 4$ cm and $DC = 2$ cm. In the configuration shown, both AB and DC are perpendicular to AD. The bar AB rotates with an angular velocity of 10 rad/s. The magnintude of angular velocity (in rad/s) of bar DC at this instant is

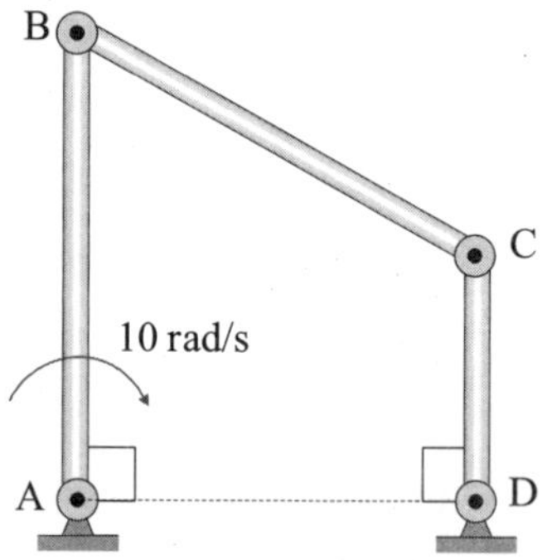

(A) 0 (B) 10 (C)15 (D)25

GATE 2019

Solution

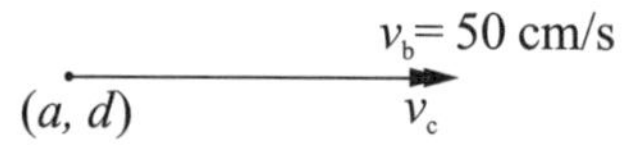

Velocity Diagram

Velocity of point B; $v_B = \omega \times AB = 10 \times 5 = 50$ cm/s

Velocity of point C; $v_B = v_C = 50$ cm/s [since $v_{ab} = 0$]

Angular velocity of link CD; $\omega_{CD} = \dfrac{v_C}{CD} = \dfrac{50}{2}$

$$\omega_{CD} = 25 \text{ rad/s}$$

Example 7.50

A rigid triangular body, PQR, with sides of equal length of 1 unit moves on a flat plane. At the instant shown, edge QR is parallel to the x-axis, and the body moves such that velocities of points P and R are V_P and V_R, in the x and y directions, respectively. The magnitude of the angular velocity of the body is

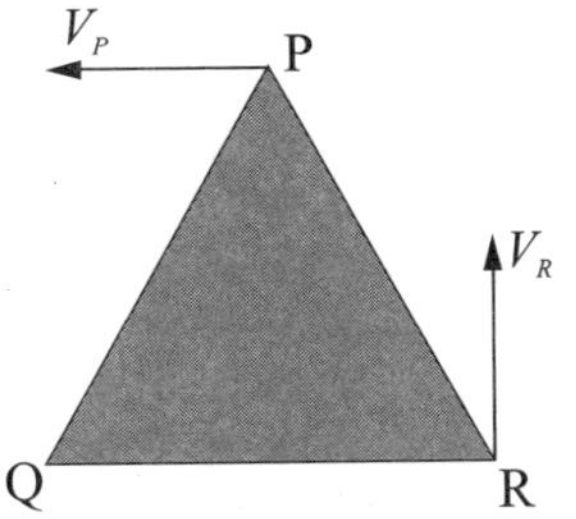

(A) $2V_R$ (B) $2V_P$ (C) $\frac{V_R}{\sqrt{3}}$ (D) $\frac{V_P}{\sqrt{3}}$

GATE 2019

Solution

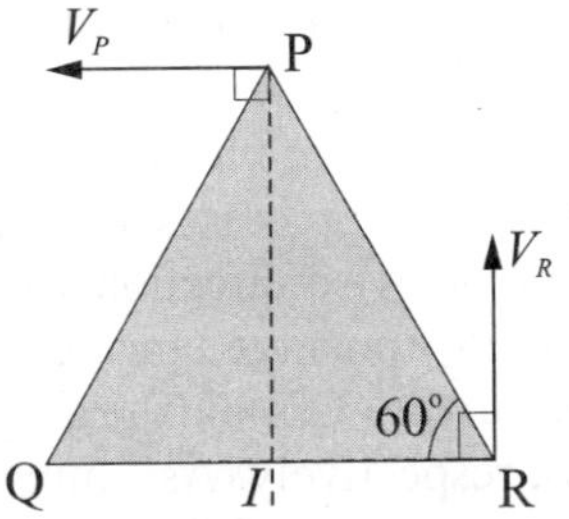

We first locate the instantaneous center I of body PQR, it is located at the point of intersection of lines that are perpendicular to the velocity vector of V_R and V_P.

Angular velocity of body PQR;

$$\omega = \frac{V_P}{IP} = \frac{V_R}{IR}$$

$$\omega = \frac{V_P}{\sqrt{3}/2} = \frac{V_R}{1/2} \quad \Rightarrow \quad \omega = \frac{2V_P}{\sqrt{3}} = 2V_R$$

$$\omega = 2V_R$$

Example 7.51

A spur gear has pitch circle diameter D and number of teeth T. The circular pitch of the gear is

(A) $\frac{\pi D}{T}$ (B) $\frac{T}{D}$ (C) $\frac{D}{T}$ (D) $\frac{2\pi D}{T}$

GATE 2019

Solution

$$\text{Circular pitch} = \frac{\pi D}{T}$$

Example 7.52

The crank of a slider-crank mechanism rotates counter-clocwise (CCW) with a constant angular velocity ω, as shown. Assume the length of the crank to be r.

Using exact analysis, the acceleration of the slider in the

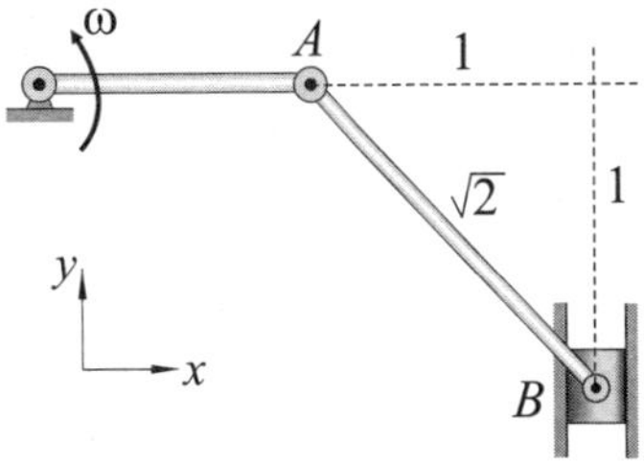

y-direction, at the instant shown, where the crank is parallel to x-axis, is given by

(A) $-\omega^2 r$ (B) $2\omega^2 r$ (C) $\omega^2 r$ (D) $-2\omega^2 r$

GATE 2019

Solution

Velocity and acceleration diagrams of slider-crank mechanism are drawn as shown in figure.

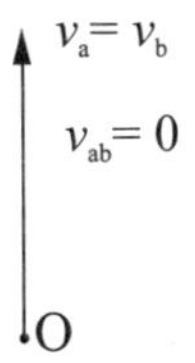

Velocity Diagram

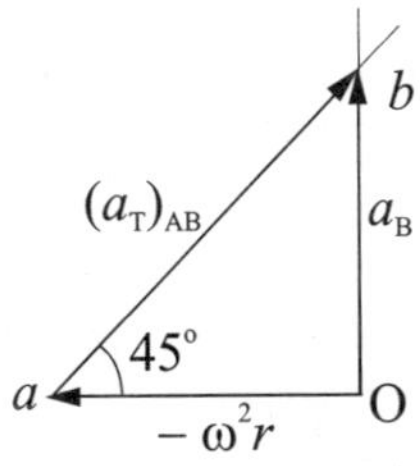

Acceleration Diagram

Radial acceleration of A, $(a_r)_A = -\omega^2 r$ [toward O]

Acceleration diagram of slider $a_B = \omega^2 r$

Example 7.53

Two masses A and B having mass m_a and m_b, respectively, lying in the plane of the figure shown, are rigidly attached to a shaft which revolves about an axis through O perpendicular to the plane of the figure. The radii of rotation of the masses m_a and m_b are r_a and r_b, respectively. The angle between lines OA and OB is 90°. If $m_a = 10$ kg, $m_b = 20$ kg, $r_a = 200$ mm and $r_b = 400$ mm, then the balance mass to be placed at a radius of 200 mm is _____ kg (round off to two decimal places).

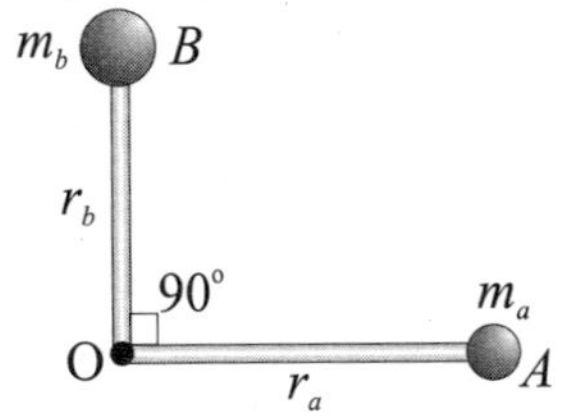

GATE 2019

Solution

Let m be the mass of balance weight.

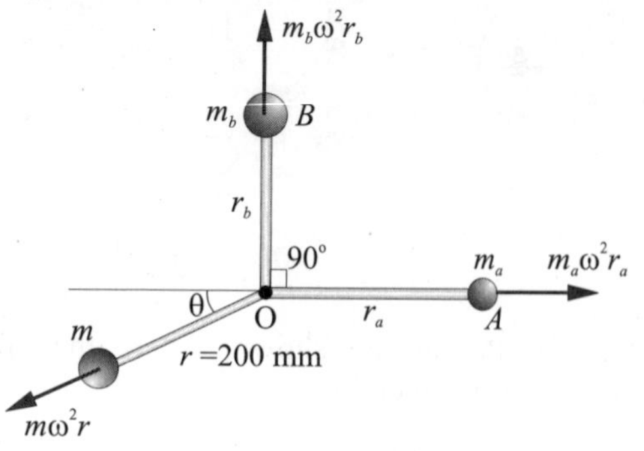

$$\sum F_x = 0 \quad \Rightarrow \quad m_a\omega^2 r_a - m\omega^2 r\cos\theta = 0$$

or $\quad mr\cos\theta = m_a r_a \quad$ (i)

$$\sum F_y = 0 \quad \Rightarrow \quad m_b\omega^2 r_b - m\omega^2 r\sin\theta = 0$$

or $\quad mr\sin\theta = m_b r_b \quad$ (ii)

From Equations (i) and (ii), we have

$$m = \sqrt{\frac{(m_a r_a)^2 + (m_b r_b)^2}{r^2}} = \sqrt{\frac{(10\times 200)^2 + (20\times 400)^2}{200^2}}$$

$$m = 41.23 \text{ kg}$$

Example 7.54

A four bar mechanism is shown in the figure. The link numbers are mentioned near the links. Input link 2 is rotating anticlockwise with a constant angular speed ω_2. Length of different links are:

$$O_2O_4 = O_2A = L,$$

$$AB = O_4B = \sqrt{2}L.$$

The magnitude of the angular speed of the output link 4 is ω_4 at the instant when link 2 makes an angle of 90° with O_2O_4 as shown. The ratio $\frac{\omega_4}{\omega_2}$ is _______ (round off to two decimal places).

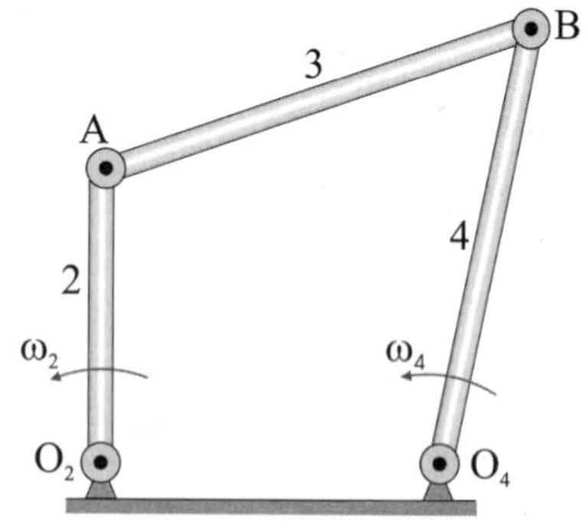

GATE 2019

Solution

First we locate instantaneous center of links 2 and 4.

Relation between ω_4 and ω_2 is given by

$$\omega_4 I_{24}O_4 = \omega_2 I_{24}O_2$$

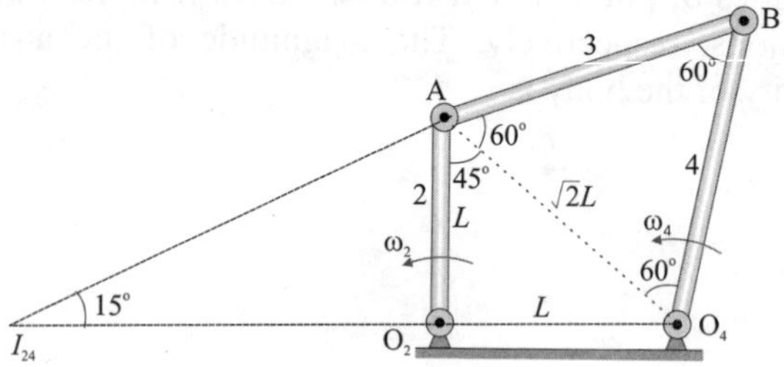

$$\frac{\omega_4}{\omega_2} = \frac{I_{24}O_2}{I_{24}O_4} = \frac{L\cot 15}{L + L\cot 15} = 0.788$$

$$\frac{\omega_4}{\omega_2} = 0.788$$

Example 7.55

A uniform disc with radius r and a mass of m kg is mounted centrally on a horizontal axle of negligible mass and length of $1.5r$. The disc spins counter-clockwise about the axle with angular speed ω, when viewed from the right-hand side bearing, Q. The axle precesses about a vertical axis at $\omega_p = \omega/10$ in the clockwise direction when viewed from above. Let R_P and R_Q (positive upwards) be the resultant reaction forces due to the mass and the gyroscopic effect, at bearings P and Q, respectively. Assuming $\omega^2 r = 300$ m/s^2 and $g = 10$ m/s^2, the ratio of the larger to the smaller bearing reaction force (considering appropriate signs) is _____.

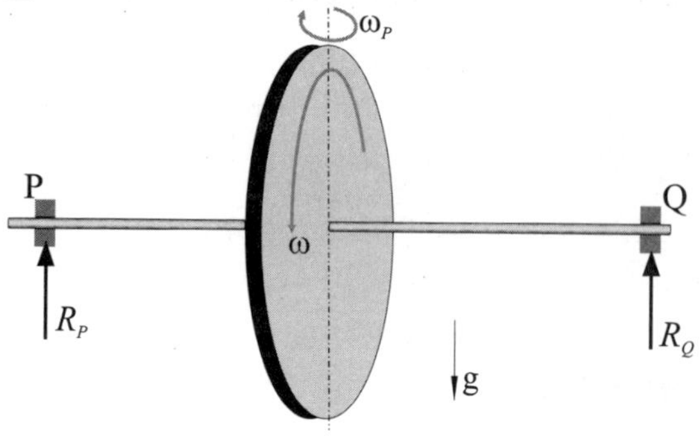

GATE 2019

Solution

Gyroscopic couple, $C = I\omega\omega_p$

$$C = I\omega\omega_p = \frac{1}{2}mr^2 \times \omega \times \frac{\omega}{10} = \frac{m\omega^2 r^2}{20}$$

Free-body diagram of axle is shown in figure.

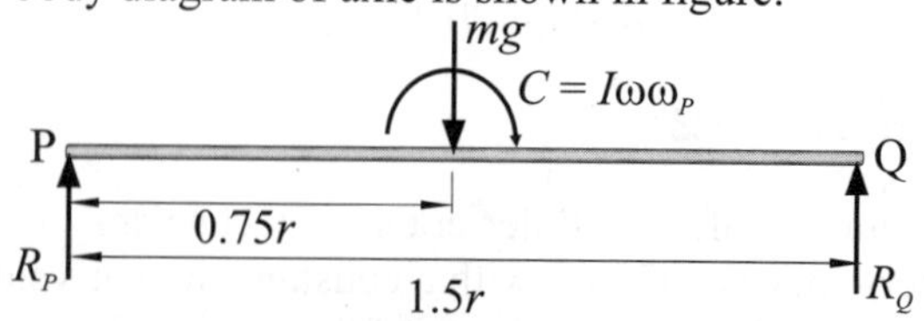

Equilibrium equations

$$\sum M_P = 0 \quad \Rightarrow \quad R_Q \times 1.5r = mg \times \frac{1.5r}{2} + \frac{m\omega^2 r^2}{20}$$

$$R_Q = \frac{mg}{2} + \frac{m\omega^2 r^2}{30}$$

$$\sum F_y = 0 \quad \Rightarrow \quad R_P + R_Q = mg \quad \text{or}$$

$$R_P + \frac{mg}{2} + \frac{m\omega^2 r^2}{30} = mg \quad \Rightarrow \quad R_P = \frac{mg}{2} - \frac{m\omega^2 r^2}{30}$$

Ratio of the larger to the smaller bearing reaction force;

$$R_Q / R_P = \left(\frac{mg}{2} + \frac{m\omega^2 r^2}{30}\right) \Big/ \left(\frac{mg}{2} - \frac{m\omega^2 r^2}{30}\right)$$

[Substituting $\omega^2 r = 300\ \text{m/s}^2$ and $g = 10\ \text{m/s}^2$]

$$\frac{R_Q}{R_P} = \frac{\frac{10}{2} + \frac{300}{30}}{\frac{10}{2} - \frac{300}{30}} = -3$$

$$\boxed{\frac{R_Q}{R_P} = -3}$$

7.3 PRACTICE PAPER

Time: 3 hours | **Max. Marks: 100**

Q.1 to Q.30 carry one mark each

Q.1 to Q.20 Multiple Choice Questions

Q.1 Degree of freedom of the linkage shown in figure, is

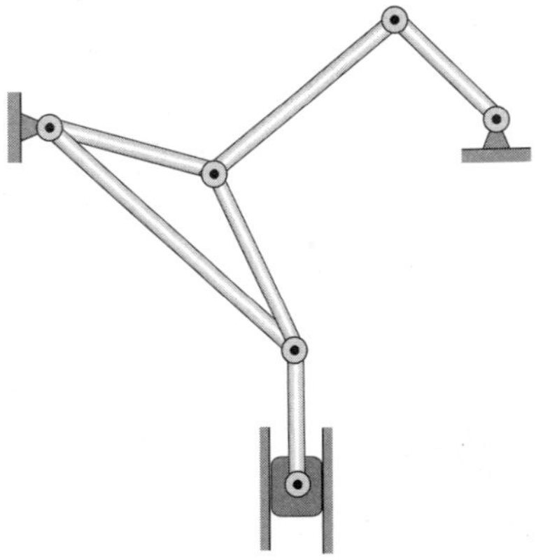

(A) 1 (B) 2 (C) 3 (D) 0

Q.2 In an elliptic trammel, the length of the link connecting the two sliders is 100 mm. The tracing pen is placed on 150 mm extension of this link. The major and minor axes of the ellipse traced by the mechanism would be

(A) 250 mm and 150 mm (B) 250 mm and 100 mm

(C) 500 mm and 300 mm (D) 500 mm and 200 mm

Q.3 Match List-I (Mechanism) with List-II (Motion) and select the correct answer:

List-I (Mechanism)	List-II (Motion)
(a) Hart mechanism	(1) Quick return motion
(b) Pantograph	(2) Copying mechanism
(c) Whit worth mechanism	(3) Exact straight line motion
(d) Scotch yoke	(4) Simple harmonic motion
	(5) Approximate straight live motion

(A) a-5, b-1, c-2, d-3 (B) a-3, b-2, c-1, d-4

(C) a-5, b-2, c-1, d-3 (D) a-3, b-1, c-2, d-4

Q.4 The kinematic chain shown in the figure is a

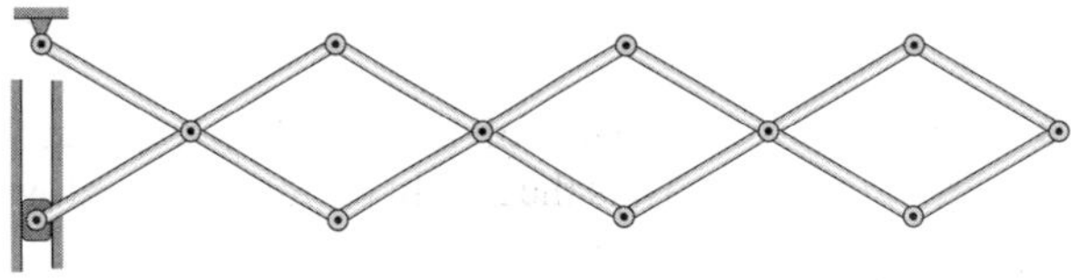

(A) Structure

(B) Mechanism with one degree of freedom

(C) Mechanism with two degree of freedom

(D) Mechanism with more than two degrees of freedom

Q.5 The given figure shows a cam with a circular profile, rotating with a uniform angular velocity of ω rad/s. What is the nature of displacement of the follower ?

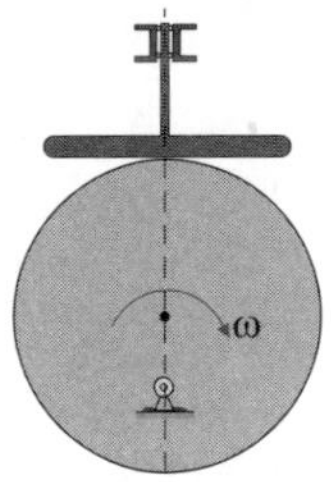

(A) Uniform (B) Parabolic

(C) Simple harmonic (D) Cycloidal

Q.6 The speed of an engine varies from 210 rad/s to 190 rad/s. During a cycle of operation, the change in kinetic energy is found to be 400 Nm. The inertia of flywheel (in kgm^2) is

(A) 0.1 (B) 20 (C) 30 (D) 40

Q.7 Match List-I with List-II and select the correct answer using the codes given below the lists:

List-I	List-II
(a) Flywheel	(1) Dunkerley method
(b) Governor	(2) Turning moment
(c) Critical speed	(3) d' Alembert principle
(d) Inertia force	(4) Speed control on prime mover with load

(A) a-4, b-2, c-3, d-1 (B) a-4, b-2, c-1, d-3

(C) a-2, b-4, c-1, d-3 (D) a-2, b-4, c-3, d-1

Q.8 Masses B_1, B_2 and 9 kg are attached to a shaft in parallel planes as shown in the figure. If the shaft is rotating at 100 rpm, the masses B_1 and B_2 are, respectively

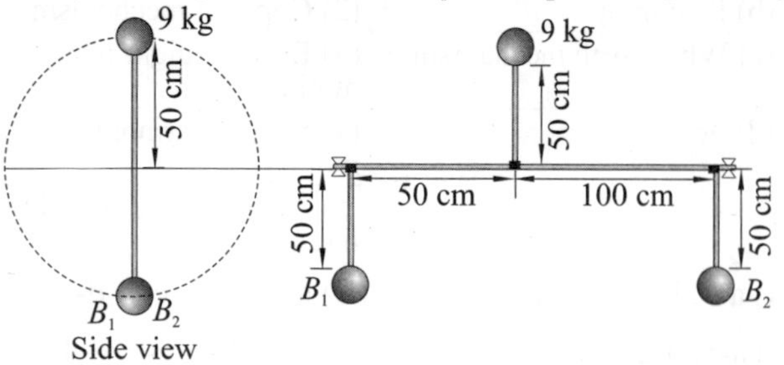

(A) 3 kg, 6 kg (B) 6 kg, 3 kg

(C) 5 kg, 9 kg (D) 9 kg, 5 kg

Q.9 The sensitivity dh/dN of a given Porter governor shown in figure, where h is the height of governor and N is the rpm, is proportional to

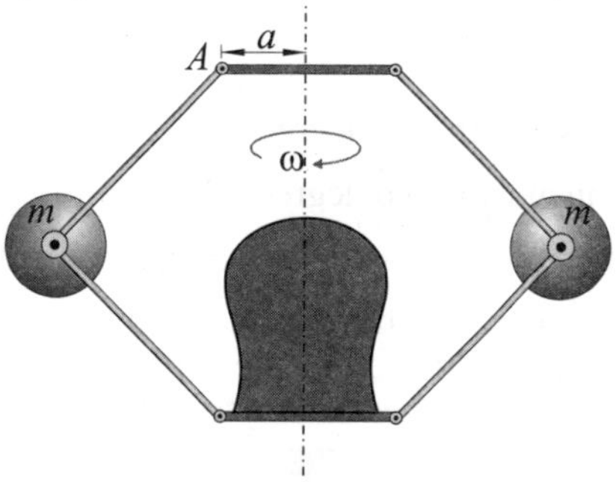

(A) $\frac{1}{N^3}$ (B) N^3 (C) $\frac{1}{N^2}$ (D) N^2

Q.10 A wheel is rolling on a straight level track with a uniform velocity 'v'. The instantaneous velocity of a point on the wheel lying at the mid-point of a radius

(A) Varies between $\frac{3}{2}v$ and $-\frac{1}{2}v$

(B) Varies between $\frac{1}{2}v$ and $-\frac{1}{2}v$

(C) Varies between $\frac{3}{2}v$ and $\frac{1}{2}v$

(D) Does not vary and equal to v

Q.11 If C_f is the coefficient of speed fluctuation of a flywheel then the ratio of $\frac{\omega_{max}}{\omega_{min}}$ will be

(A) $\frac{1-2C_f}{1+2C_f}$ (B) $\frac{2-C_f}{2+2C_f}$

(C) $\frac{1+2C_f}{1-2C_f}$ (D) $\frac{2+C_f}{2-C_f}$

Q.12 A wheel of radius R is rolling without slipping with clockwise angular velocity ω, as shown in figure. The speed of point A is

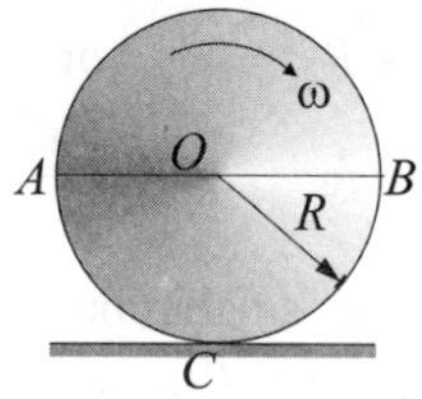

(A) ωR (B) $\sqrt{2}\,\omega R$ (C) $2\omega R$ (D) $\sqrt{3}\,\omega R$

Q.13 Figure shown Klen's construction for slider-crank mechanism, OCD drawn to full scale. What velocity does CD represent?

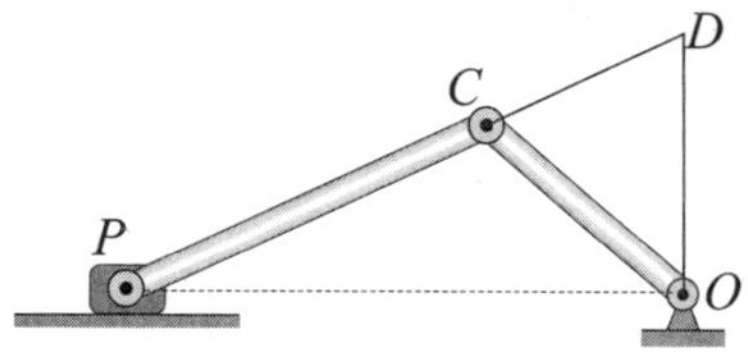

(A) Velocity of the crank pin

(B) Velocity of the piston

(C) Velocity of the piston with respect to crank pin

(D) Angular velocity of the connecting rod

Q.14 Figure shows the Scotch-Yoke mechanism. The velocity of point B in the position shown, is

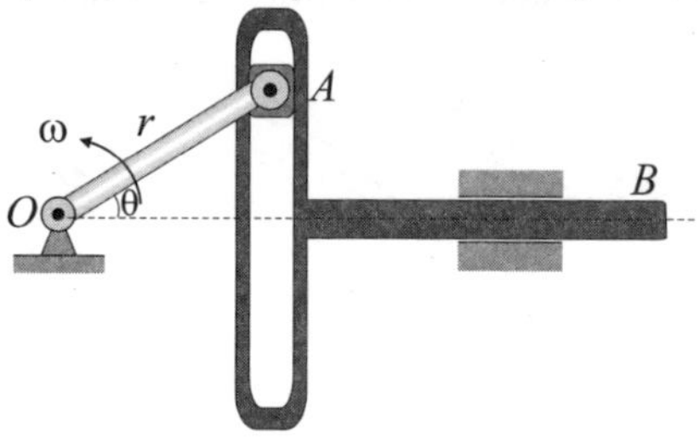

(A) $\omega r\cos\theta$ (B) $\omega r\sin\theta$

(C) $\omega r(\cos\theta + \sqrt{1-\cos\theta})$ (D) None of these

Q.15 The wheel of radius r is rolling without slipping. At the instant shown, its angular velocity and angular acceleration are ω and α, both clockwise. The acceleration of point A is

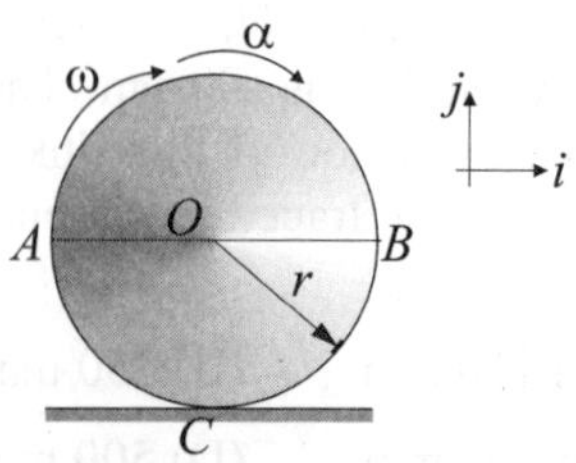

(A) $(r\alpha + \omega^2 r)i + r\alpha\ j$ (B) $\omega^2 r\, i + r\alpha\ j$

(C) $\omega^2 r\, i$ (D) $r\alpha\ j$

Q.16 Match List-I and List-II and select the correct answer using the codes given below the list:

List-I	List-II
(a) Compound train	1. Hart mechanism
(b) Quick return mechanism	2. Coriolis force
(c) Exact straight line motion	3. Transmission of motion around bends and corners
(d) Approximate straight line motion	4. Watt mechanism

(A) a-1, b-2, c-3, d-4 (B) a-3, b-2, c-1, d-4

(C) a-3, b-4, c-1, d-2 (D) a-1, b-4, c-3, d-2

Q.17 The Whitworth quick return mechanism is formed in a slider-crank chain when the

(A) Coupler link is fixed (B) Longest link is a fixed link

(C) Slider is a fixed link (D) Smallest link is a fixed link

Q.18 Which of the following are the inversions of double slider crank mechanism?

1. Oldham coupling
2. Whitworth quick return mechanism
3. Beam engine mechanism
4. Elliptical trammel mechanism

Select the correct answer from the codes given below:

(A) 1 and 2 (B) 1 and 4

(C) 1, 2 and 3 (D) 2, 3 and 4

Q.19 The mechanism shown in figure represents

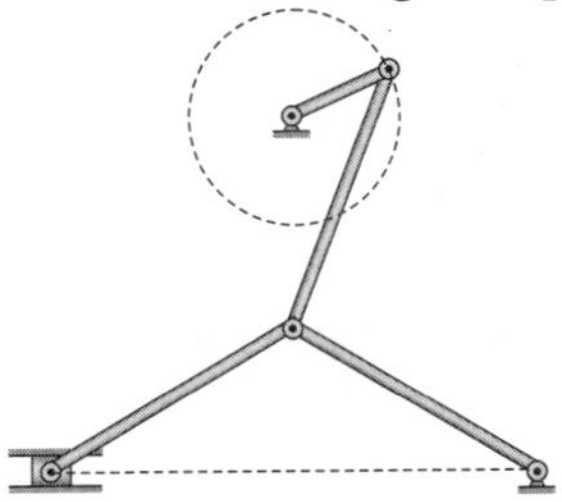

(A) Hart's mechanism (B) Toggle mechanism

(C) Watt's mechanism (D) Beam engine mechanism

Q.20 $ABCD$ is a mechanism with link lengths $AB = 200$ mm, $BC = 300$ mm, $CD = 400$ mm and $DA = 350$ mm. Which one of the following links should be fixed for the resulting mechanism to be a double crank mechanism?

(A) AB (B) BC (C) CD (D) DA

Q.21 to Q.30 Numerical Answer Questions

Q.21 Link OA in the figure has an angular velocity of $\omega = 100$ rad/s and an angular acceleration of 5000 rad/s^2 at the instant shown. The magnitude of absolute acceleration (in m/s^2) of point A is________.

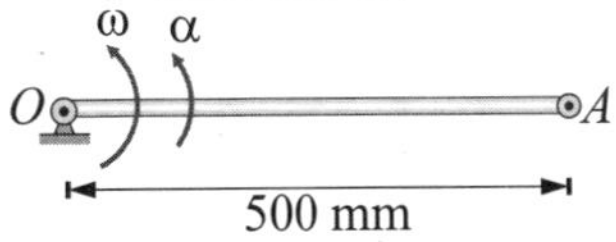

Q.22 An external gear with 60 teeth meshes with a pinion of 20 teeth, module being 6 mm. What is the centre distance in mm ?_____.

Q.23 The figure as shown below is a rigid body undergoes planar motion. The absolute tangential acceleration of the points R and S on the body are 150 mm/s^2 and 300 mm/s^2 respectively in the directions shown. What is the angular acceleration of the rigid body?____.

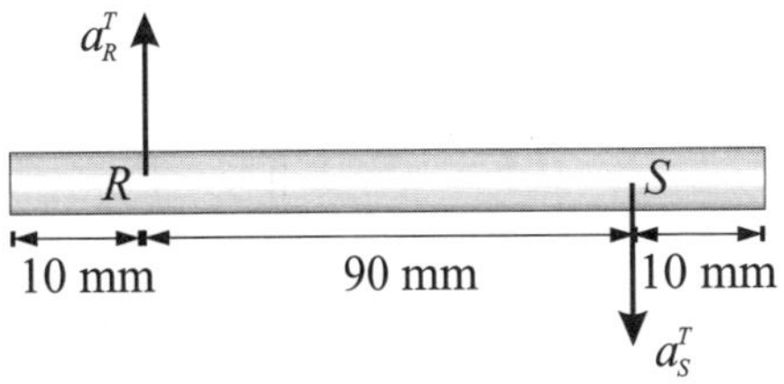

Q.24 If the annular wheel of an epicyclic gear train has 100 teeth and the planet wheel has 20 teeth, the number of teeth on the sun wheel is___________.

Q.25 Consider a four bar mechanism shown in the given figure. The driving link AB is rotating uniformly at a speed of 100 rpm clockwise. The velocity of B will be_______.

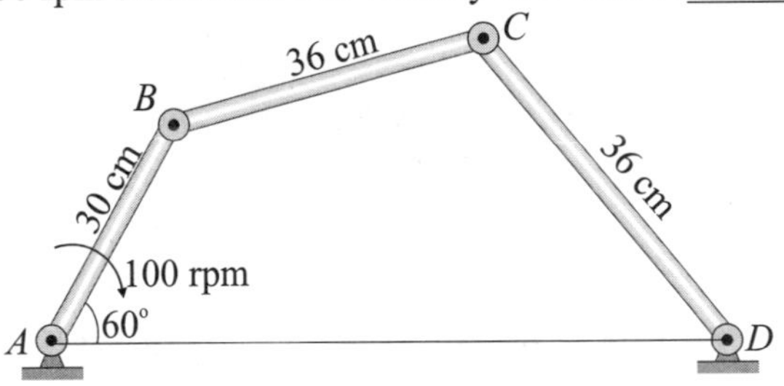

Q.26 The degree of freedom of the linkage shown in figure is________.

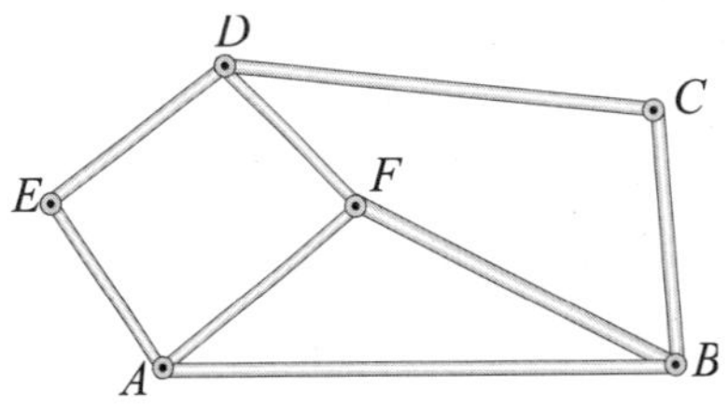

Q.27 A flywheel of moment of inertia 9.8 kg·m^2 fluctuates by 30 rpm for a fluctuation of energy of 1936 J. The mean speed (in rpm) of the flywheel is______.

Q.28 Slider C of the slider-crank mechanism shown in figure is moving with a constant velocity 1 m/s. The angular velocity of crank AB in this position is______.

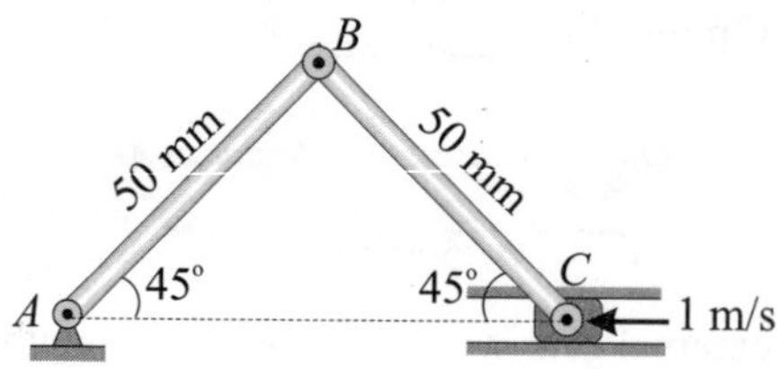

Q.29 In the given figure *ABCD* is a four bar mechanism. At the instant shown, *AB* and *CD* are vertical and *BC* is horizontal. *AB* is shorter than *CD* by 300 mm. *AB* is rotating at 5 rad/s and *CD* is rotating at 2 rad/s. The length(in mm) of *AB* is__________.

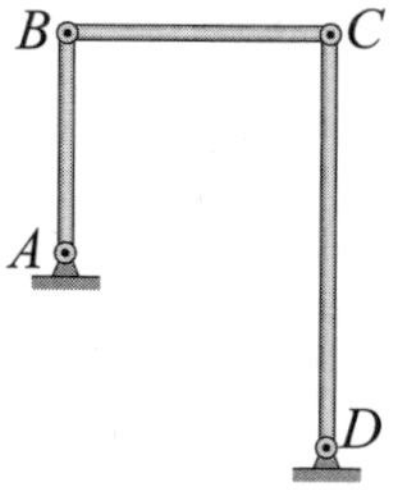

Q.30 In the mechanism given below, if the angular velocity of the eccentric circular disc is 1.0 rad/s, the angular velocity (rad/s) of the follower link for the instant shown in the figure is__________.

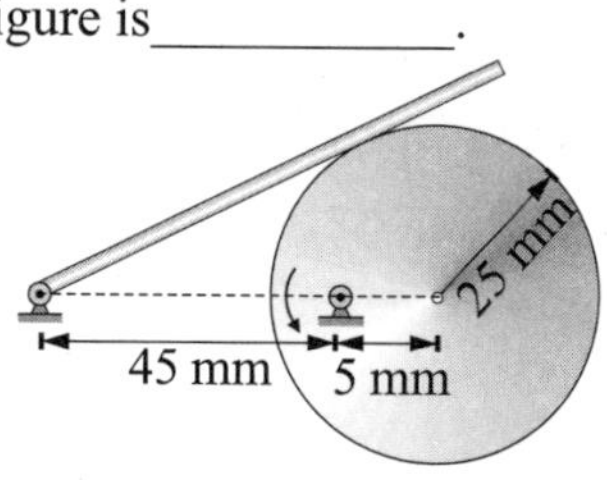

GATE 2012

Q.31 to Q.65 carry two marks each.

Q.31 to Q.50 Multiple Choice Questions

Q.31 In the slider crank mechanism, when does the connecting rod has zero angular velocity?

(A) When the crank angle = 0°

(B) When the crank angle = 90°

(C) When the crank angle = 45°

(D) Never

Q.32 The cross head velocity in the slider crank mechanism for the position shown in figure is

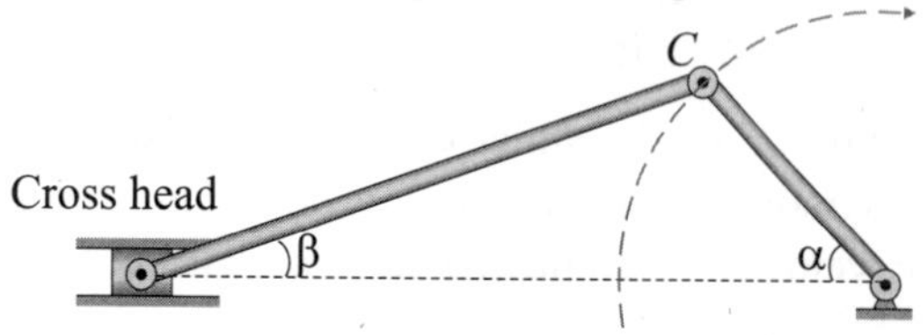

(A) $v_c \cos[90 - (\alpha + \beta)]\cos\beta$

(B) $v_c \cos[90 - (\alpha + \beta)]\sec\beta$

(C) $v_c \cos[90 - (\alpha - \beta)]\cos\beta$

(D) $v_c \cos[90 - (\alpha - \beta)]\sec\beta$

Q.33 An epicyclic gear train has 3 shafts *A*, *B* and *C*. *A* is an input shaft running at 100 rpm clockwise. *B* is an output shaft running at 250 rpm clockwise. Torque on *A* is 50 kNm (clockwise). *C* is fixed shaft. The torque to fixed shaft *C* is

(A) 20 kNm (anti-clockwise)

(B) 30 kNm (anti-clockwise)

(C) 30 kNm (clockwise)

(D) Cannot be determined as the data is insufficient

Q.34 For a slider-crank mechanism with radius of crank *r*, length of connecting rod *l*, obliquity ratio *n*, crank rotating at an angular velocity ω ; for any angle θ of the crank, Match List-I (Kinematic variable) with List-II (Equation) and select the correct answer using the codes given below the lists:

List-I (Kinematic variable)	List-II (Equation)
(a) Velocity of piston	(1) $\frac{\omega}{n}\cos\theta$
(b) Acceleration of piston	(2) $\omega^2 r\left(\cos\theta + \frac{\cos 2\theta}{n}\right)$
(c) Angular velocity of connecting rod	(3) $-\frac{\omega^2}{n}\sin\theta$
(d) Angular acceleration of connecting rod	(4) $\omega r\left(\sin\theta + \frac{\sin 2\theta}{2n}\right)$

(A) a-4, b-2, c-3, d-1 (B) a-2, b-4, c-3, d-1

(C) a-4, b-2,c-1, d-3 (D) a-2, b-4, c-1, d-3

Q.35 Slider *C* gives a constant linear acceleration '*a*' to the right starting from rest with *x* essentially zero. The angular velocity of the link *AB* is

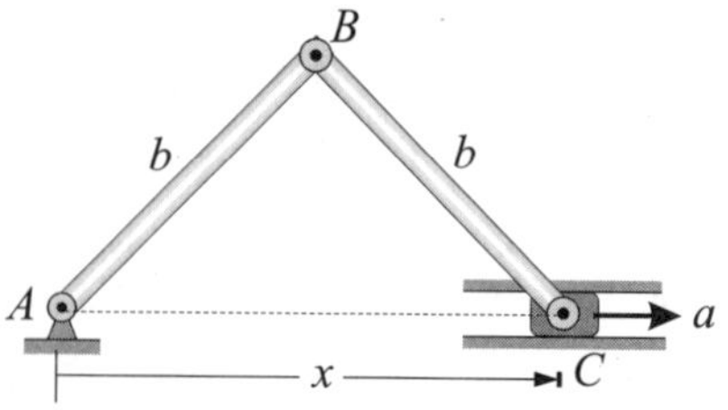

(A) $\frac{\sqrt{2ax}}{\sqrt{b^2 - x^2}}$ (B) $\frac{\sqrt{2ax}}{\sqrt{(2b)^2 - x^2}}$

(C) $\frac{\sqrt{2ax}}{b}$ (D) None of these

Q.36 Gear S of the planetary gear train is rotating clockwise at $\omega_s = 10$ rad/s as shown in figure. The angular velocity of gear P is (annular wheel A is stationery)

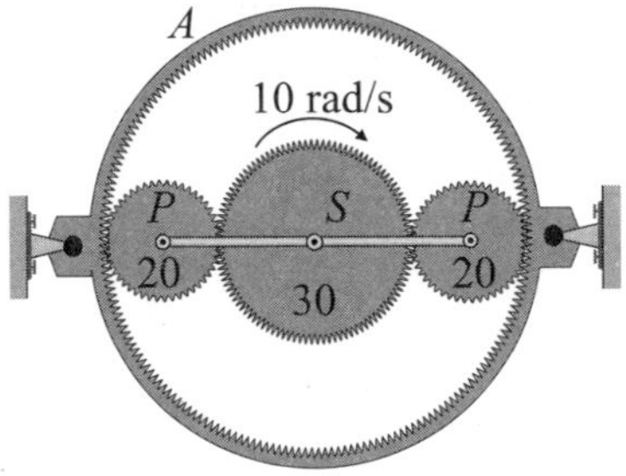

(A) 3 rad/s (B) 7 rad/s (C) 3.5 rad/s (D) 7.5 rad/s

Q.37 The velocity of point B is controlled by slider C as shown in mechanism. The velocity of point B in the position shown is

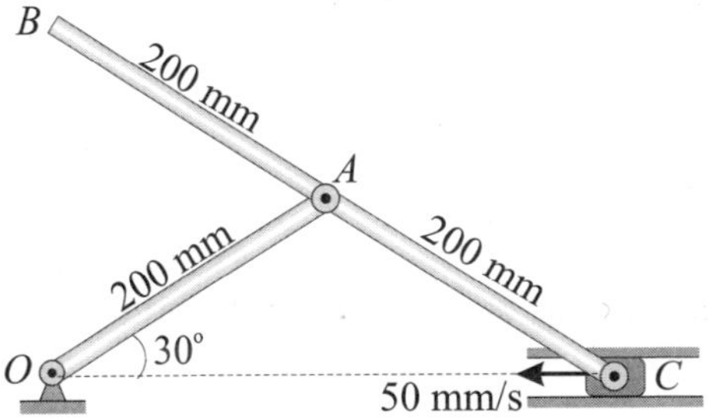

(A) 86.6 mm/s ↑ (B) 50 mm/s ↑

(C) 28.86 mm/s ↑ (D) 50 mm/s ↑

Q.38 The arm connected between the centers of gears A and B is rotating counter clockwise angular velocity of 4.8 rad/s. At the same time, gear A is rotating at 24 rad/s, also counter clockwise. The angular velocity of gear B is

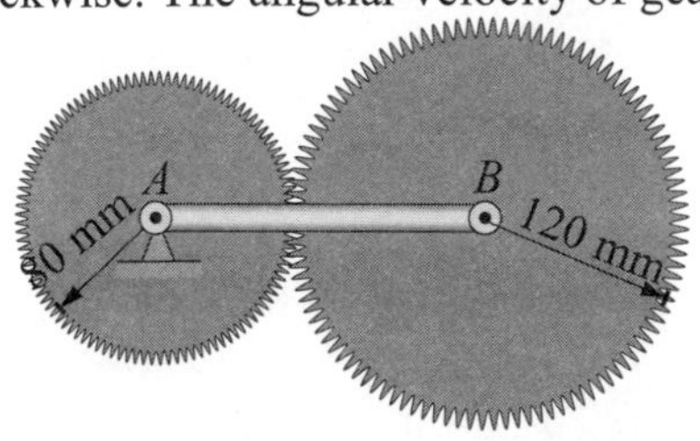

(A) 4 rad/s (counter clockwise) (B) 8 rad/s (clockwise)

(C) 3.2 rad/s (clockwise) (D) None of these

Q.39 Consider the following statements.

In petrol engine mechanism, the piston is at its dead centre position when piston's

1. Acceleration is zero 2. Acceleration is maximum

3. Velocity is zero 4. Velocity is infinity

Which of these statements are correct?

(A) 1 and 4 (B) 1 and 3 (C) 2 and 3 (D) 2 and 4

Q.40 Two wheels connected by link AB rolls without slipping with angular velocity ω. The coordinates of the instantaneous centre for the velocity of link AB is

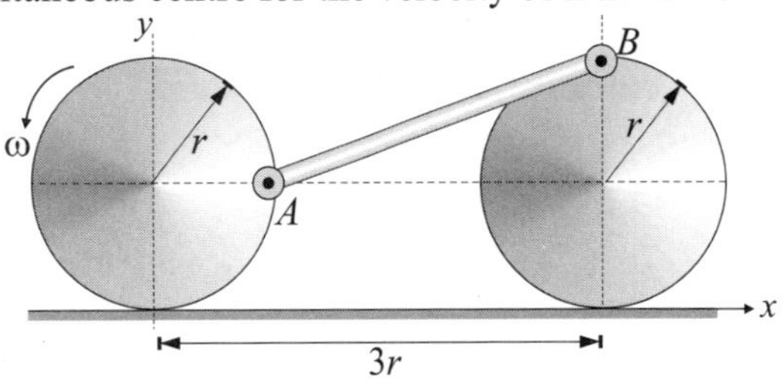

(A) $(3r, r)$ (B) $(0, r)$ (C) $(3r, 2r)$ (D) $(\sqrt{2}\,r, r)$

Q.41 The three gears P, Q and R of equal number of teeth are mounted on a rotating arm as shown. Arm OA rotates clockwise about O at the angular velocity of 4 rad/s, while gear P rotates independently at the counter clockwise rate of 8 rad/s. The angular velocity of gear R is

(A) 4 rad/s (counter clockwise)

(B) 2 rad/s (counter clockwise)

(C) 4 rad/s (clockwise)

(D) 8 rad/s (counter clockwise)

Q.42 End A of bar AB is pushed to the right with constant the constant velocity $v_A = 0.6$ m/s. The angular velocity (in rad/s) of bar AB as a function of θ, is

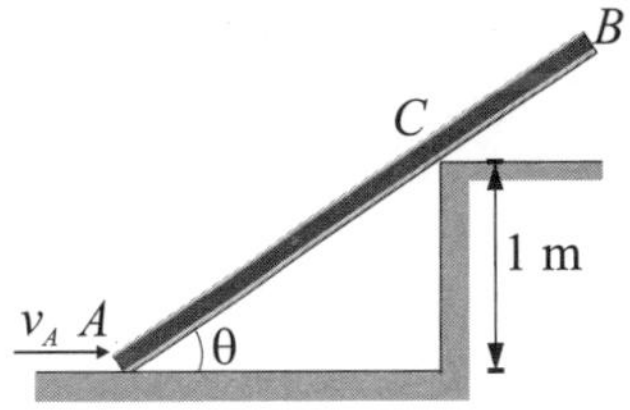

(A) $0.6 \sin^2\theta$ (B) $0.6 \cos\theta$ (C) $0.6 \sin\theta$ (D) $0.6 \tan\theta$

Q.43 The maximum fluctuation of energy E_f during a cycle for a flywheel is

(A) $I(\omega_{max}^2 - \omega_{min}^2)$ (B) $\frac{1}{2} I\omega_{av}(\omega_{max} - \omega_{min})$

(C) $\frac{1}{2} I K_s \omega_{av}$ (D) $I\omega_{av}^2 K_s$

(where I = moment of inertia of the flywheel, ω_{av} = average rotational speed, K_s = coefficient of fluctuation of speed)

Q.44 The pinion gear meshes with the two racks A and B as shown in figure. If the racks are moving with the velocities 0.6 m/s and 0.8 m/s shown in figure. The velocity of gear at its center C is

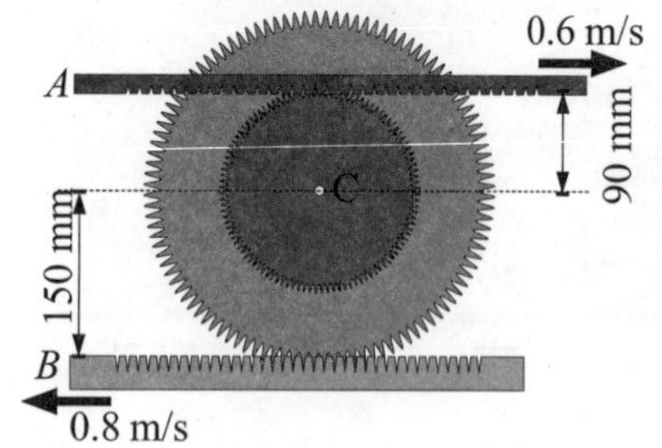

(A) 0.2 m/s ←
(B) 0.2 m/s →
(C) 0.075 m/s →
(D) 0.7 m/s →

Q.45 Figure shows an offset slider crank mechanism. The quick return ratio when the crank rotates at a constant angular speed is

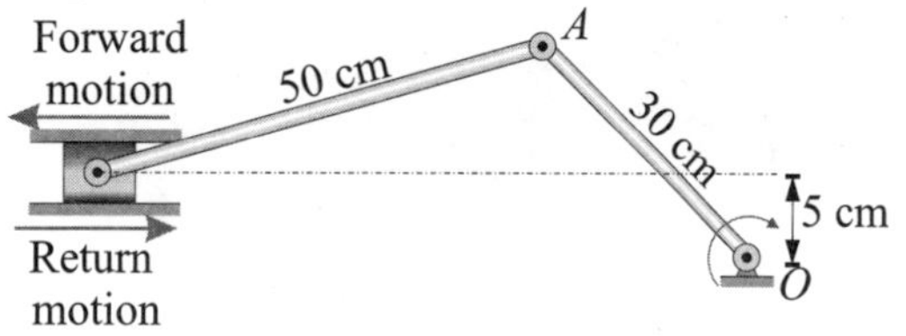

(A) 2.0 (B) 2.5 (C) 3.5 (D) 1.14

Q.46 When the linkage in figure is in the position shown the angular velocity of bar AB is 2 rad/s clockwise. For this position, the velocity of C is

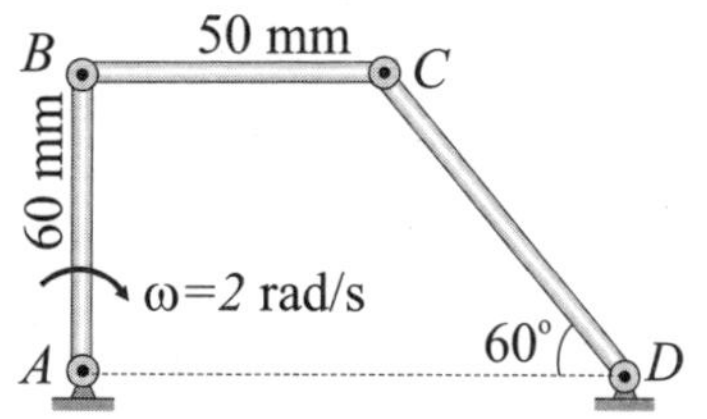

(A) 134.6 mm/s
(B) 102.4 mm/s
(C) 62.2 mm/s
(D) None of these

Q.47 A slider-crank mechanism is shown in given figure

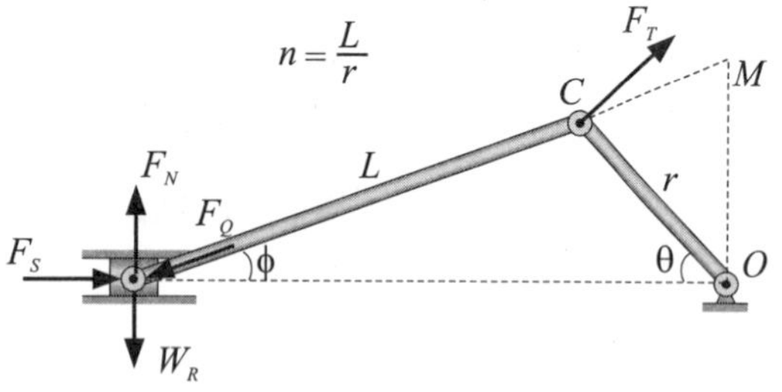

Which of the following expressions stand for crank effort?

1. $F_Q \sin(\theta + \phi)$
2. $F_s.r\left(\sin\theta + \dfrac{\sin 2\theta}{n}\right)$
3. $F_s.OM$
4. $F_T.r$

Select the correct answer using the codes given code:

(A) 1 and 3
(B) 1, 2 and 4
(C) 1, 2 and 3
(D) 2, 3 and 4

Q.48 The crank and slotted lever quick-return motion mechanism is shown in figure. The length of links O_1O_2, O_1C and O_2A are 10 cm, 20 cm and 5 cm respectively. The ratio of time for forward motion to that for return motion is

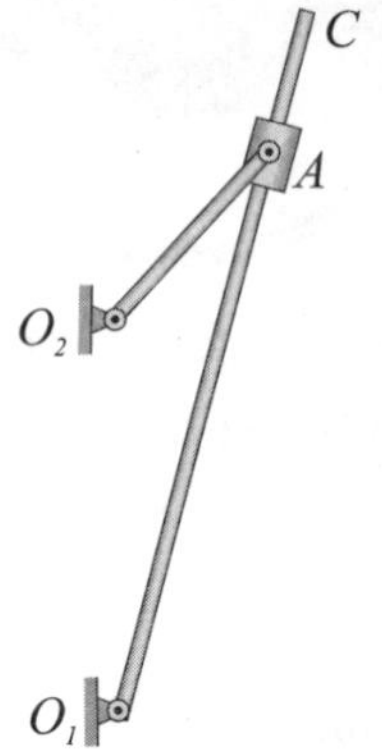

(A) 3.0 (B) 2.75 (C) 2.5 (D) 2.0

Q.49 In the figure, the link 2 rotates at an angular velocity of 2 rad/s. What is the magnitude of Coriolis acceleration (in m/s^2) experienced by the link 4?

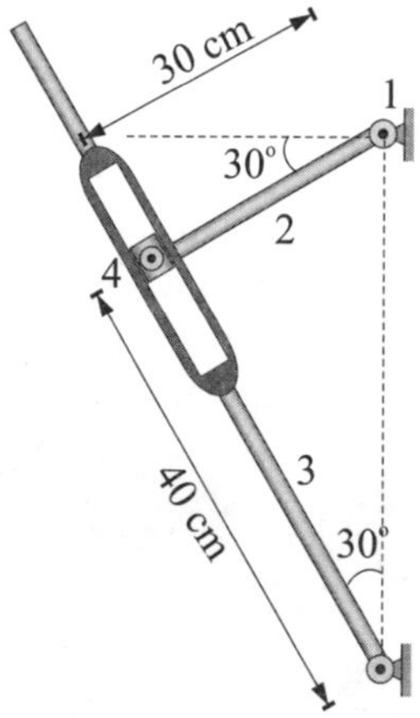

(A) 0 (B) 0.8 (C) 0.24 (D) 0.32

Q.50 Two gears having an angular velocity ratio 3:1 are mounted on shaft whose centers are 136 mm apart. If the module of the gear is 4 mm. The number of teeth on smaller gear is

(A) 12 (B) 36 (C) 51 (D) 17

Q.51 to Q.65 Numerical Answer Questions

Q.51 The figure shows the turning moment diagram of an engine. The mean speed of prime mover is 2π rad/s and moment of inertia is 0.1 kg·m^2. What is the coefficient of fluctuation of energy (in %) ?________

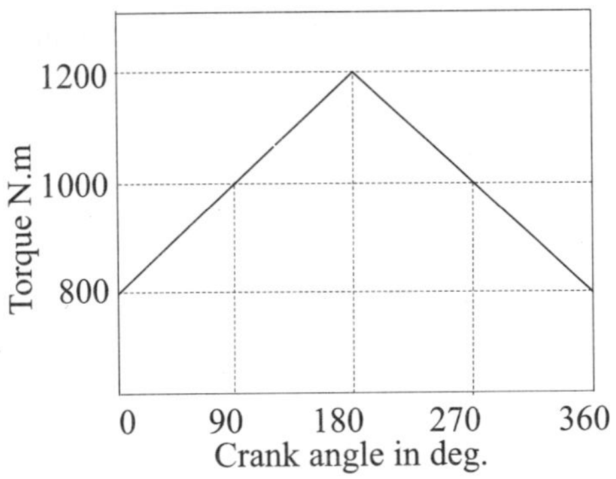

Q.52 In a Hartnell governor, the mass of each ball is 2.5 kg. Maximum and minimum speeds of rotation are 10 rad/s and 8 rad/s respectively. Maximum and minimum radii of rotation are 20 cm and 14 cm respectively. The lengths of horizontal and vertical arms of bell crank levers are 10 cm and 20 cm respectively. Neglecting obliquity and gravitational effects, the lift (in cm) of the sleeve is____.

Q.53 The gear D rotates counter clockwise about O with constant angular velocity of 15 rpm. A straight rack rests on a gear and is attached to a block B. The velocity of block B in the position ($\theta = 20^\circ$) shown is_________.

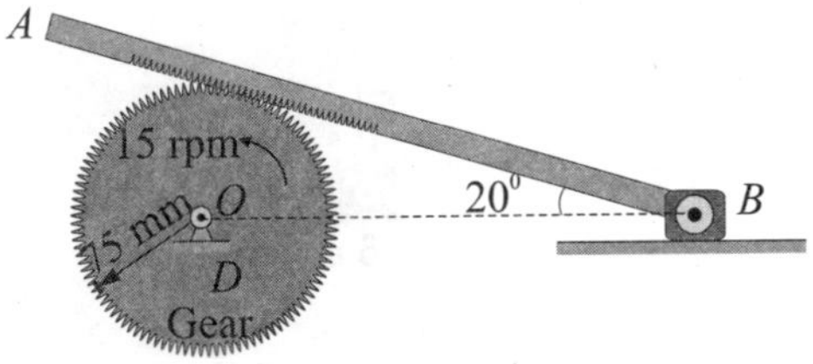

Q.54 A simplified turning moment diagram of a four-stroke engine is shown in given figure. If the mean torque 'T_m' is 10 Nm, the estimated peak torque T_p will be (assuming negative torque demand in negligible)._____.

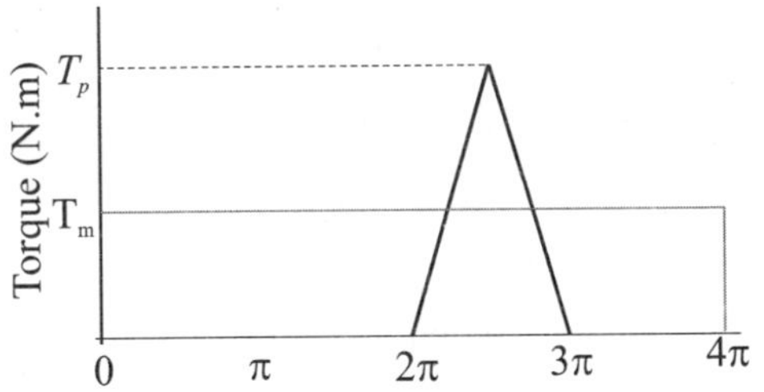

Q.55 Figure shown the reverted gear train. The number of teeth on gear A, B and C are 30, 20 and 30 respectively. If gear A rotates with speed 300 rpm, then the speed of gear D is_________.

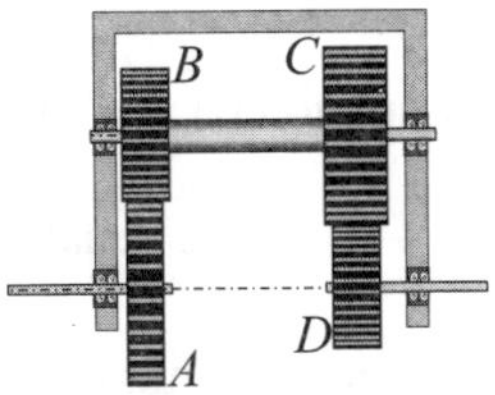

Q.56 The link AB rotates with the constant angular velocity of 6 rad/s. The angular velocity (rad/s) of link BC in the position shown is_________.

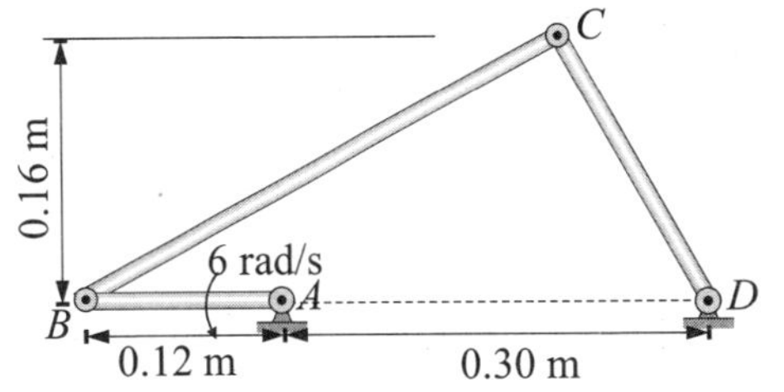

Q.57 In a Hartnell governor, the mass of each ball is 2.5 kg. Maximum and minimum centrifugal forces on the balls are 2000 N and 100 N corresponding to radii 20 cm and 15 cm respectively. Lengths of vertical and horizontal arms of the bell-crank levers are the same, then what is the spring stiffness (in N/cm) is_________.

Q.58 Figure shows a four-bar mechanism. If the crank AB rotates with an angular velocity of 150 rpm in the clockwise direction, then the velocity(in cm/s) of end C is_____ .

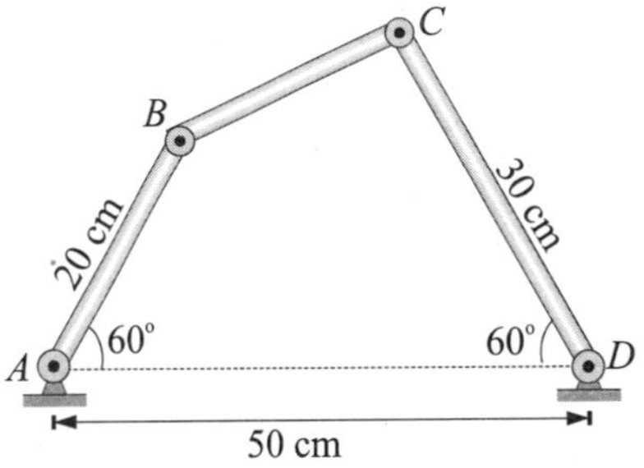

Q.59 The crank of slider-crank punching press has a mass-moment of inertia of 1.0 kg m^2. The figure shows the torque demand per revolution for a punching operation. If the speed of the crank is found to drop from 30 rad/s to 20 rad/s during punching, the maximum torque (in Nm) demand during the punching operation is ______.

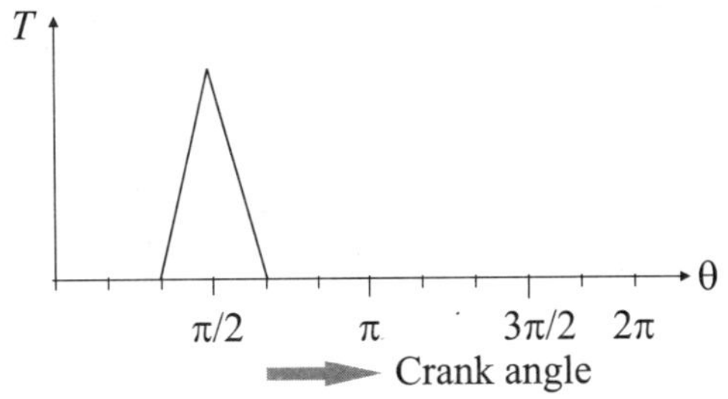

Q.60 The slider C is moving up in the slot with the constant speed of 1.2 m/s. The angular velocity of bar AB is_______.

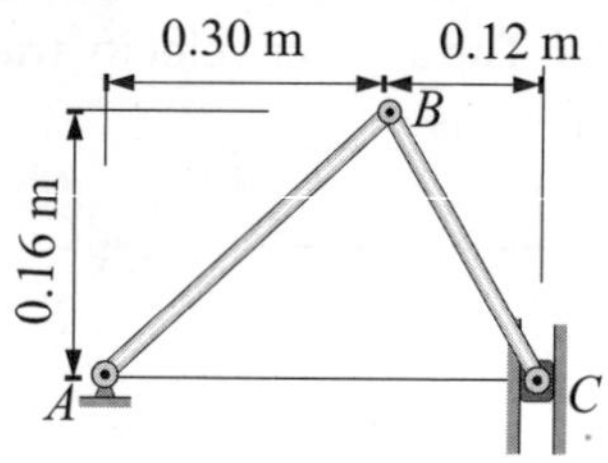

Q.61 A wheel rolls without slipping as shown in figure. The vertical component of the velocity of point B (for this position) is 9 m/s directed upward. The velocity (in m/s) of its centre C is______.

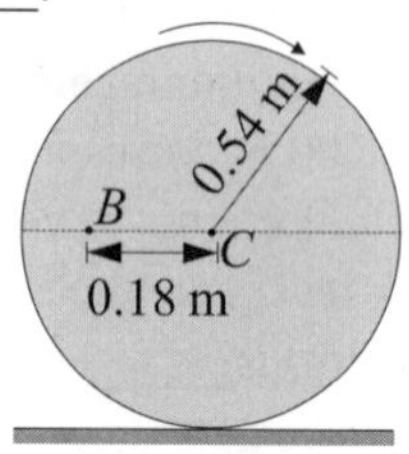

Q.62 A rod of length 1 m is sliding in a corner as shown in figure. At an instant when the rod makes an angle of 60°with the horizontal plane, the velocity of point A on the rod is 1 m/s. The angular velocity of the rod at this instant is_____.

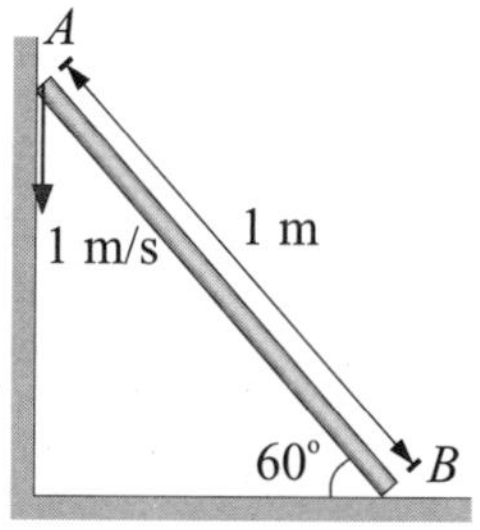

Q.63 Figure shows slider-crank mechanism. Turning moment about O is____________.

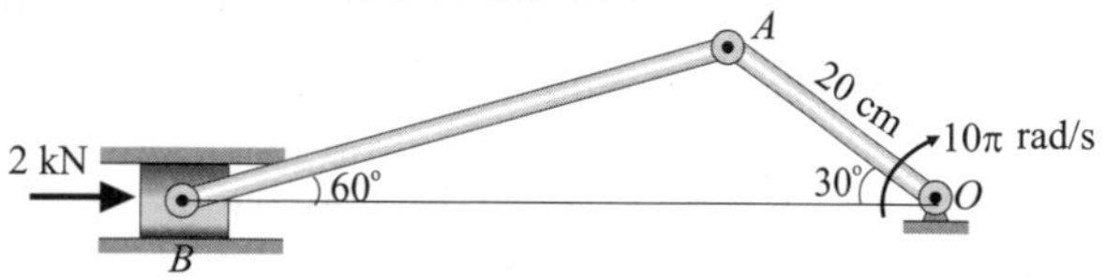

Q.64 For the triangular plate undergoing plane motion, velocity of corner v_A and the direction of v_B are known as shown in figure. The angular velocity (in rad/s) of plate is_____.

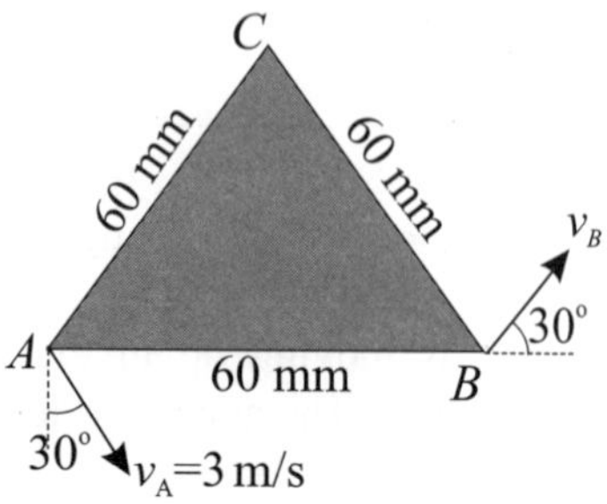

Q.65 Crank AB of the mechanism rotates at the constant angular velocity 8 rad/s clockwise. For the position shown the angular velocity of rod BE is___________.

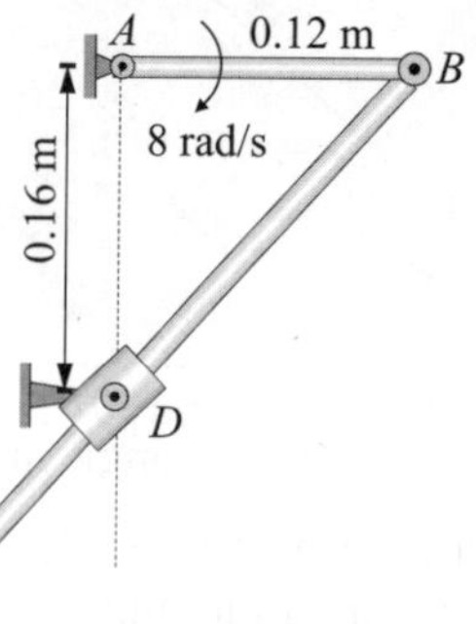

7.4 SOLUTION TO PRACTICE PAPER

Q.1 Ans:(A)

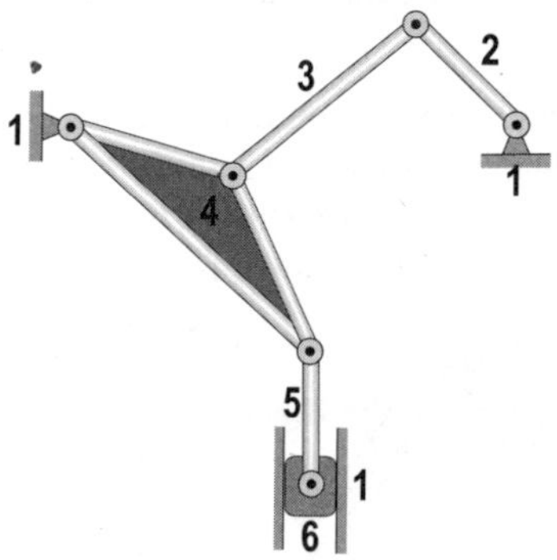

Number of links, $n = 6$

Number of pairs (turning + sliding), $p = 6 + 1$

or $\quad p = 7$

Number of higher pair, $h = 0$

Degree of freedom is given by, $F = 3(n-1) - 2p - h$

or $\quad F = 3(6-1) - 2\times 7 - 0$

$$F = 1$$

Q.2 Ans:(C)

Elliptical trammel is shown in figure.

x - coordinate of tracing pen P is

$x = 150\cos\theta \qquad$ (i)

y - coordinate of tracing pen P is

$y = 250\sin\theta \qquad$ (ii)

Elimination θ from Equation (i) and (ii), we obtain

$$\frac{x^2}{150^2} + \frac{y^2}{250^2} = 1 \leftarrow \text{This the equation of ellipse}$$

Major axis $(2a) = 500$ mm and minor axis $(2b) = 300$ mm

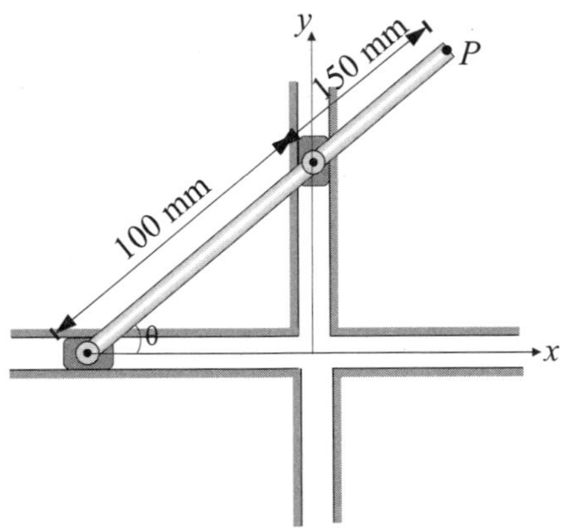

Q.3 Ans:(B)

Correct match:

(a) Hart mechanism (3) Exact straight line motion

(b) Pantograph (2) Copying mechanism

(c) Whit worth mechanism (1) Quick return motion

(d) Scotch yoke (4) Simple harmonic motion

Q.4 Ans:(B)

Kinematic chain is mechanism with one degree of freedom.

Q.5 Ans:(C)

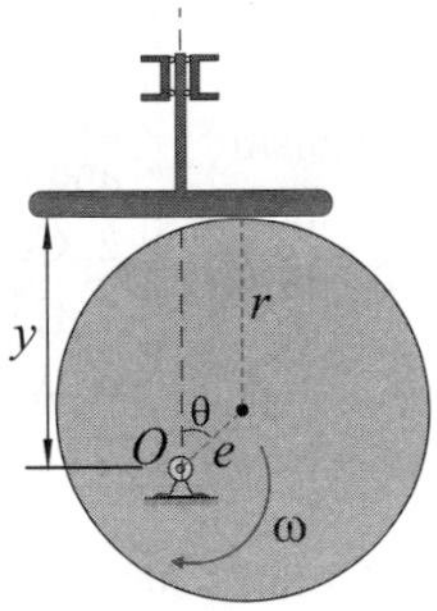

Let e be the eccentricity and r be the radius of circular cam.

Position of follower $y = r + e\cos\theta$

Velocity of follower $v = -\omega e \cos\omega t$

Hence, it is the equation of simple harmonic motion.

Q.6 Ans:(A)

Change in kinetic energy, $\Delta E = \frac{1}{2}I\omega_2^2 - \frac{1}{2}I\omega_1^2$

Moment of inertia of flywheel,

$$I = \frac{2\Delta E}{\omega_2^2 - \omega_1^2} = \frac{2\times 400}{210^2 - 190^2}$$

or $$I = \frac{2\Delta E}{\omega_2^2 - \omega_1^2} = \frac{2\times 400}{210^2 - 190^2}$$

$$I = 0.1 \text{ kg}\cdot\text{m}^2$$

Q.7 Ans:(C)

Correct option

(a) Flywheel → (2)Turning Moment

(b) Governor → (4) Speed control on prime mover with load

(c) Critical speed → (1) Dunkerley Method

(d) Inertia force → (3) d' Alembert principle

Q.8 Ans:(B)

The system is under equilibrium , if $\sum F = 0, \sum M = 0$

$$\sum F = 0 \Rightarrow \quad 9\omega^2\times 50 - B_1\omega^2\times 50 - B_2\omega^2\times 50 = 0$$

$$B_1 + B_2 = 9 \text{ kg} \quad \text{(i)}$$

$$\sum M = 0 \Rightarrow (9\omega^2\times 50)\times 50 - (B_2\omega^2\times 50)\times 150 = 0$$

$$B_2 = 3 \text{ kg} \quad \text{(ii)}$$

Equations (i) and (ii) gives

$$B_1 = 6 \text{ kg}, B_2 = 3 \text{ kg}$$

Q.9(A)

Height of Porter governor

$$h = \frac{g}{\omega^2}\left(\frac{m+M}{m}\right)$$

where m = mass of ball, M = mass of sleeve.

or $$h = \left(\frac{60}{2\pi}\right)^2 \frac{g}{N^2}\left(\frac{m+M}{m}\right)$$

Differentiation with respect to N, we get

$$\frac{dh}{dN} = -2\left(\frac{60}{2\pi}\right)^2 \frac{g}{N^3}\left(\frac{m+M}{m}\right)$$

$$\frac{dh}{dN} \propto \frac{1}{N^3}$$

Q.10 Ans:(C)

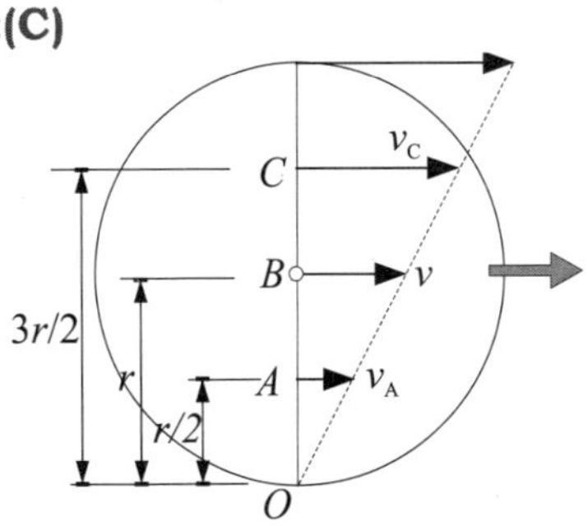

Let v be the velocity of wheel,

$$\frac{v}{OB} = \frac{v_A}{OA} = \frac{v_C}{OC} \quad \text{or} \quad \frac{v}{r} = \frac{v_A}{r/2} = \frac{v_C}{3r/2}$$

Minimum velocity of point A, $v_A = \frac{v}{2}$

Maximum velocity of point C, $v_C = \frac{3}{2}v$

Velocity varies between $\frac{3}{2}v$ and $\frac{1}{2}v$

Q.11 Ans:(D)

Coefficient of speed $C_f = \frac{\omega_{max} - \omega_{min}}{\omega_m}$

or $$C_f = \frac{\omega_{max} - \omega_{min}}{\left(\frac{\omega_{max} + \omega_{min}}{2}\right)}$$

or $$\frac{C_f}{2} = \frac{\omega_{max} - \omega_{min}}{\omega_{max} + \omega_{min}}$$

or $$\frac{C_f + 2}{C_f - 2} = \frac{2\omega_{max}}{-2\omega_{min}}$$

$$\frac{\omega_{max}}{\omega_{min}} = \frac{2 + C_f}{2 - C_f}$$

Q.12 Ans:(B)

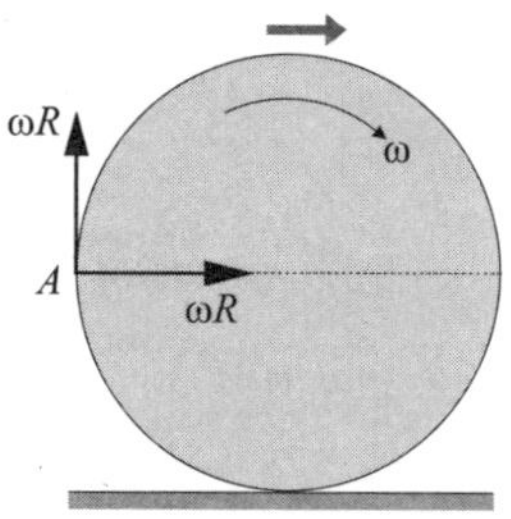

Components of velocity of point A are shown in figure.

ωR in horizontal direction and ωR in vertical direction

Resultant velocity of point A

$$V_A = \sqrt{(\omega R)^2 + (\omega R)^2}$$

$$V_A = \sqrt{2}\,\omega R$$

Q.13 Ans:(A)

CD represent the velocity of crank pin C with respect to slider P

Q.14 Ans:(B)

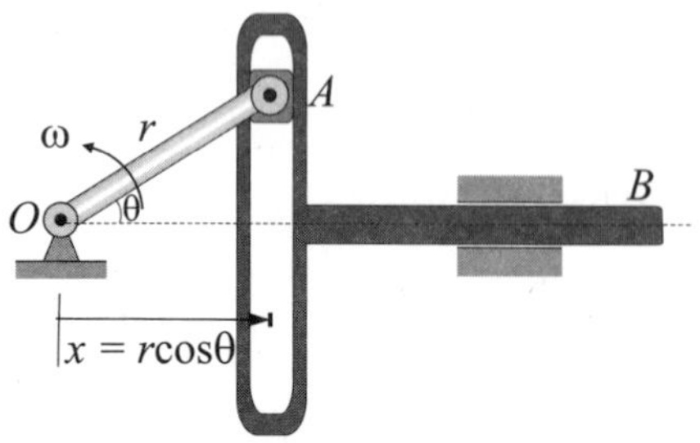

From the geometry of figure,

x-coordinate of slider is $x = r\cos\theta$

Differentiate with respect to t, we obtain

$$\frac{dx}{dt} = -r\sin\theta\frac{d\theta}{dt} = -r\sin\theta(-\omega)$$

Velocity of point B, $v_B = \omega r\sin\theta$

Q.15 Ans:(A)

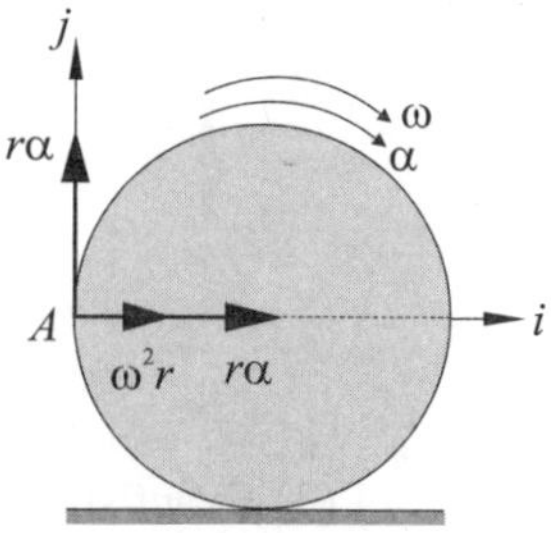

Acceleration along x-direction, $a_x = \omega^2 r + r\alpha$

Acceleration along y-direction, $a_y = r\alpha$

Acceleration of point A, $a = a_x i + a_y j$

$$a = (\omega^2 r + r\alpha)i + r\alpha\, j$$

Q.16 Ans:(B)

Correct match:

(a) Compound train	3. Transmission of motion around bends and corners
(b) Quick return mechanism	2. Coriolis force
(c) Exact straight line motion	1. Hart mechanism
(d) Approximate straight line motion	4. Watt mechanism

Q.17 Ans:(D)

The Whitworth quick return mechanism is formed in a slider-crank chain when the

Smallest link(crank) is a fixed link

Q.18 Ans:(B)

Following are the inversions of double slider-crank mechanism.

Oldham coupling and Elliptical trammel mechanism

Q.19 Ans:(B)

The mechanism shown in figure represents Toggle mechanism.

Q.20 Ans:(A)

Link AB should be fixed for double crank mechanism.

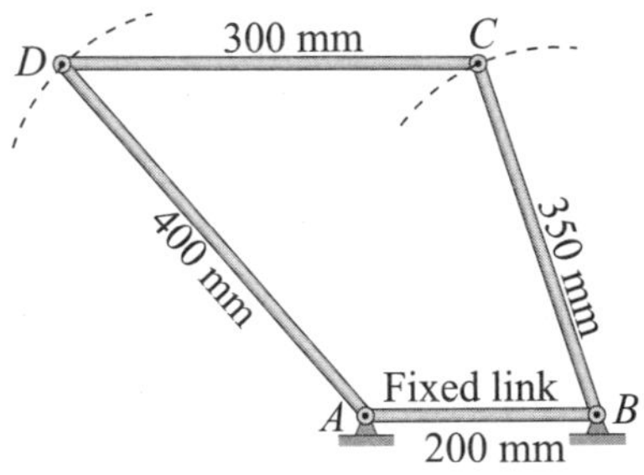

Q.21 Ans:[5590]

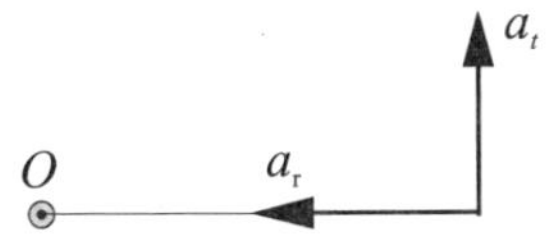

Radial acceleration, $a_r = \omega^2 r$

$$a_r = 100^2 \times \frac{500}{1000} = 5000 \text{ m/s}^2$$

Tangential acceleration, $a_t = r\alpha$

$$a_t = r\alpha = \frac{500}{1000} \times 5000 = \frac{5000}{2} \text{ m/s}^2$$

Resultant absolute acceleration,

$$a = \sqrt{5000^2 + \left(\frac{5000}{2}\right)^2}$$

$$a = 5590 \text{ m/s}^2$$

Q.22 Ans:[240]

Center distance, $C = \frac{d_1}{2} + \frac{d_2}{2} = \frac{1}{2}(d_1 + d_2)$

Substituting $d_1 = mT_1$ and $d_2 = mT_2$, we obtain

$$C = \frac{m}{2}(T_1 + T_2) = \frac{6}{2}(60 + 20)$$

Center distance $C = 240$ mm

Q.23 Ans:[1.66]

Angular acceleration, $\alpha = \frac{a}{r} = \frac{a_S^T - a_R^T}{RS} = \frac{300 - 150}{90}$

$$\alpha = 1.66 \text{ rad/s}^2$$

Q.24 Ans:[60]

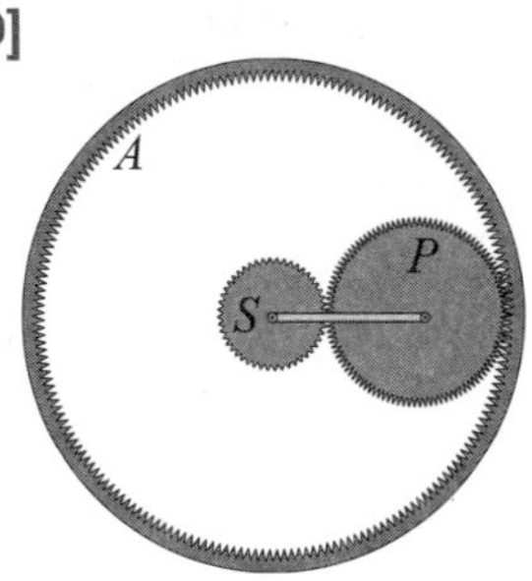

Let T_P be the number of teeth on planet wheel.

$$\frac{D_A}{2} = \frac{D_s}{2} + D_P$$

Substituting $d = mT$, we have

$$\frac{mT_A}{2} = \frac{mT_S}{2} + mT_P \quad \text{or} \quad T_A = T_S + 2T_P$$

or $\quad 100 = T_S + 2 \times 20$

Number of teeth on sun wheel, $T_S = 60$

Q.25 Ans:[3.14]

Velocity of B, $\quad V_B = \omega_{AB} \times AB$

$$V_B = \frac{2\pi \times 100}{60} \times \frac{30}{100}$$

$$V_B = 3.14 \text{ m/s}$$

Q.26 Ans:[1]

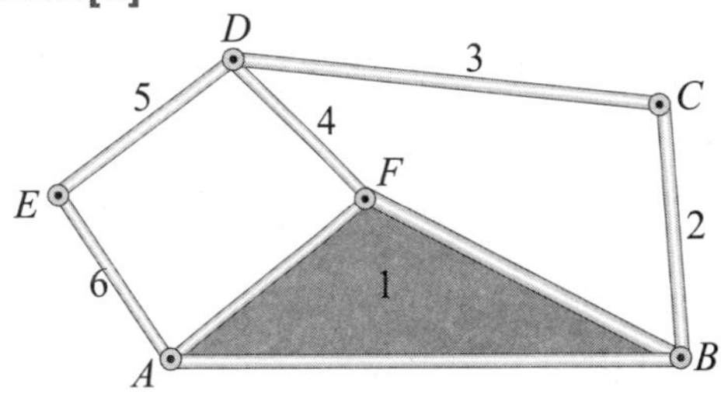

ABF is a ternary link, BC, CD, DF, DE and EA are binary links

Number of links, $n = 6$

At joint D, three links join, so it is equal to two revolute pairs.

Total number of revolute pairs, $p = 7$

The degree of freedom F is given by

$$F = 3(n-1) - 2p - h$$

or $\quad F = 3(6-1) - 2 \times 7 - 0$

$$F = 1$$

Q.27 Ans:[600]

Fluctuation energy

$$\Delta E = \frac{1}{2} I(\omega_2^2 - \omega_1^2) = I\left(\frac{\omega_2 + \omega_1}{2}\right)(\omega_2 - \omega_1)$$

or $\quad \Delta E = I\,\omega_{mean}\Delta\omega$

or $\quad \Delta E = I\left(\frac{2\pi}{60}\right)^2 N_{\text{mean}}\,\Delta N$

or $\quad N_{\text{mean}} = \frac{\Delta E}{I\left(\frac{2\pi}{60}\right)^2 \Delta N} = \frac{1936}{9.8 \times \left(\frac{2\pi}{60}\right)^2 \times 30}$

$$N_{\text{mean}} = 600 \text{ rpm}$$

Q.28 Ans:[14.14]

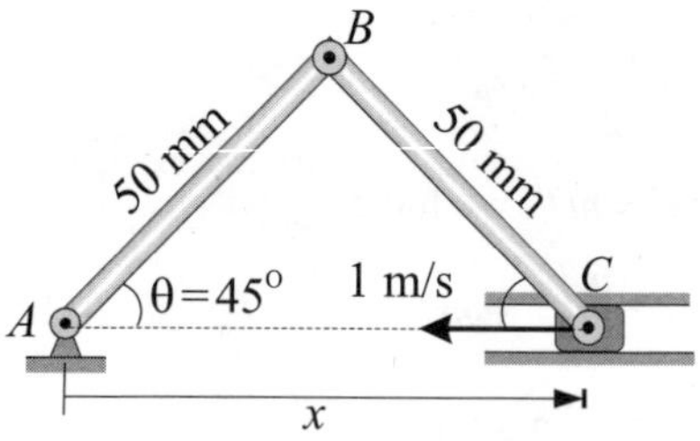

From the geometry of figure,

$$AC = 2AB\cos\theta$$

or $$x = 2\times\frac{50}{1000}\cos\theta$$

Differentiate with respect to t, we have

$$\frac{dx}{dt} = -0.1\sin\theta\,\frac{d\theta}{dt}$$

Substituting $\frac{dx}{dt} = -1.0$ m/s and $\theta = 45°$, we obtain

Angular velocity of crank $\frac{d\theta}{dt} = \frac{1}{-0.1\sin 45}(-1) = 10\sqrt{2}$

Angular velocity of crank, $\omega_{AB} = 14.14$ rad/s

Q.29 Ans:[200]

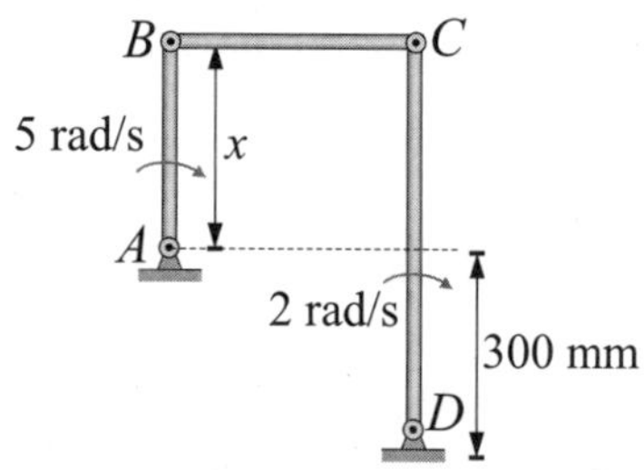

Let x be the length of AB

Velocity of B = Velocity of C

$$\omega_{AB}\times AB = \omega_{CD}\times CD$$

$$5\times x = 2\times(300+x)$$

Length of AB $x = 200$ mm

Q.30 Ans:[0.1]

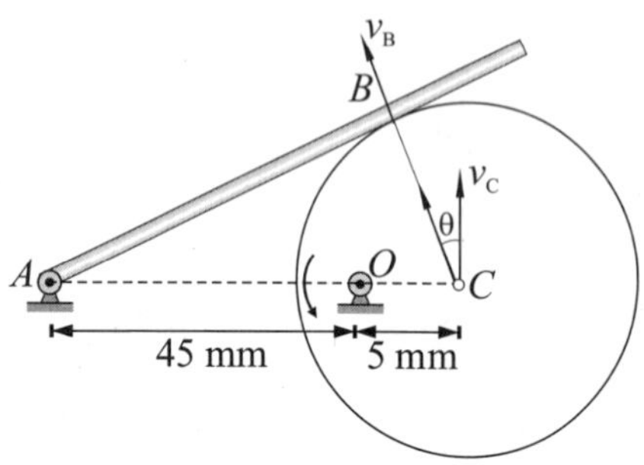

From the geometry of figure,

$$AB = \sqrt{AC^2 - BC^2}$$

$$AB = \sqrt{(45+5)^2 - 25^2}$$

$$AB = 43.3 \text{ mm}$$

In triangle ACB

$$\cos(90-\theta) = \frac{BC}{AC}$$

$$\sin\theta = \frac{25}{50} \Rightarrow \theta = 30°$$

Velocity of point C is $v_C = 1\times OC = 1\times 5$

$$v_C = 5 \text{ mm/s}$$

Velocity of point B, $v_B = v_C\cos\theta$

$$v_B = 5\times\cos 30$$

Angular velocity of the follower link, $\omega = \frac{v_B}{AB}$

$$\omega = \frac{5\times\cos 30}{43.3}$$

Angular velocity of follower link, $\omega = 0.1$ rad/s

Q.31 Ans:(B)

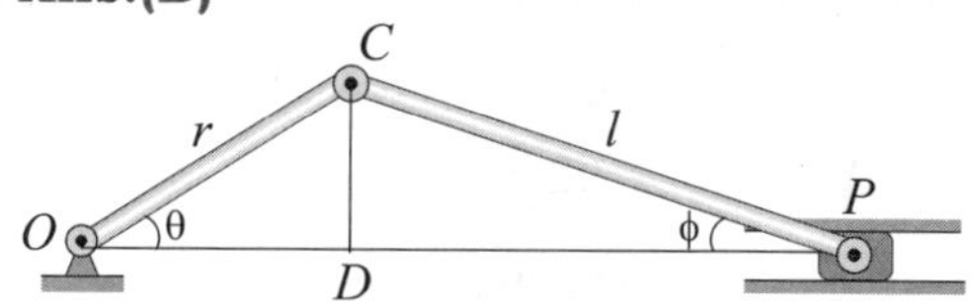

From the geometry of figure,

$$CD = r\sin\theta = l\sin\phi \quad\text{or}\quad \sin\phi = \frac{r\sin\theta}{l}$$

Differentiate with respect to t, we have

$$\cos\phi\,\frac{d\phi}{dt} = \frac{r\cos\theta}{l}\frac{d\theta}{dt}$$

Angular velocity of connecting rod, $\frac{d\phi}{dt} = \frac{\omega r\cos\theta}{l\cos\phi}$

Angular velocity of connecting rod $\frac{d\phi}{dt} = 0$ at crank angle $\theta = 90°$.

Q.32 Ans:(B)

Let v_d be the velocity of cross head

In triangle Δcad, $ad = v_c\cos\angle cad$

or $ad = v_c\cos[90-(\alpha+\beta)]$

In triangle Δbad, $ab\cos\beta = ad$

$$v_b\cos\beta = ad$$

or $$v_b\cos\beta = v_c\cos[90-(\alpha+\beta)]$$

$v_b = v_c\cos[90-(\alpha+\beta)]\sec\beta$

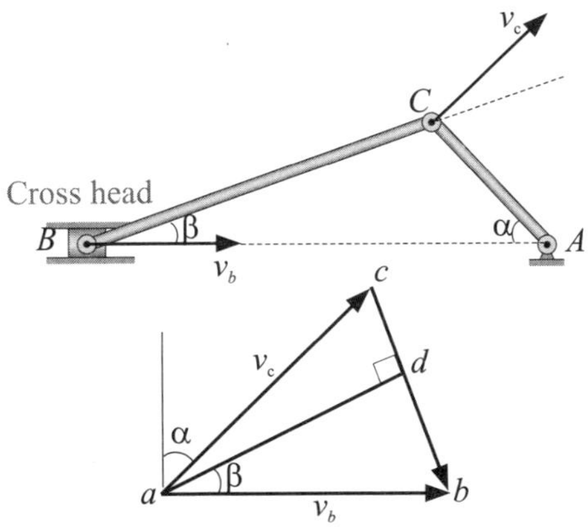

Velocity diagram

Q.33 Ans:(B)

$\sum T\omega = 0 \quad \Rightarrow \quad T_A\omega_A + T_B\omega_B + T_C\omega_C = 0$

or $\quad T_A N_A + T_B N_B + T_C N_C = 0$

Substituting $T_A = 50$ kNm, $N_A = 100$ rpm, $N_B = 250$ rpm and $N_C = 0$, we have

$$50 \times 100 + T_B \times 250 + T_C \times 0 = 0$$

$$T_B = -20 \text{ kNm}$$

$\sum T = 0 \Rightarrow \quad 50 - 20 + T_C = 0$

or $\quad T_C = -30 \text{ kNm}$

$$T_C = 30 \text{ kNm (counter clockwise)}$$

Q.34 Ans:(C)

Correct match:

(a) Velocity of piston $\quad$ (4) $\omega r\left(\sin\theta + \dfrac{\sin 2\theta}{2n}\right)$

(b) Acceleration of piston (2) $\omega^2 r\left(\cos\theta + \dfrac{\cos 2\theta}{n}\right)$

(c) Angular velocity of connecting rod $\quad$ (1) $\dfrac{\omega}{n}\cos\theta$

(d) Angular acceleration of connecting rod (3) $-\dfrac{\omega^2}{n}\sin\theta$

Q.35 Ans:(B)

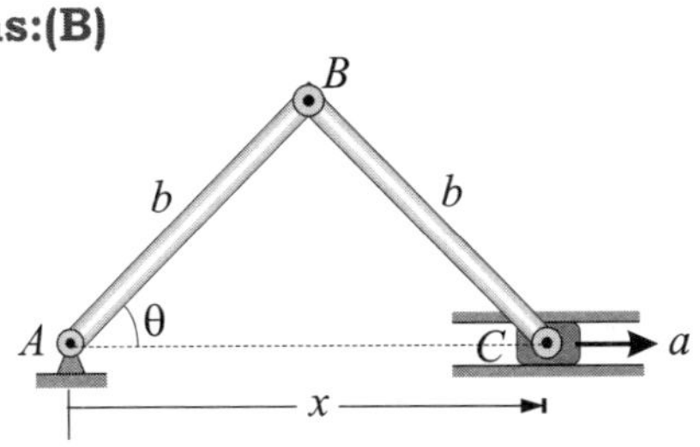

From the geometry of figure, $\quad x = 2b\cos\theta$

Differentiate with respect to t, we have

$$\frac{dx}{dt} = -2b\sin\theta\frac{d\theta}{dt} \qquad \text{or} \qquad v = -2b\sin\theta\frac{d\theta}{dt}$$

Angular velocity of the link AB,

$$\frac{d\theta}{dt} = \frac{v}{2b\sin\theta} = \frac{v}{2b\sqrt{1-\cos^2\theta}} \text{ (clockwise)}$$

Substituting, $\cos\theta = \dfrac{x}{2b}$ and $v = \sqrt{2ax}$, we obtain

$$\frac{d\theta}{dt} = \frac{\sqrt{2ax}}{\sqrt{(2b)^2 - x^2}}$$

Q.36 Ans:(D)

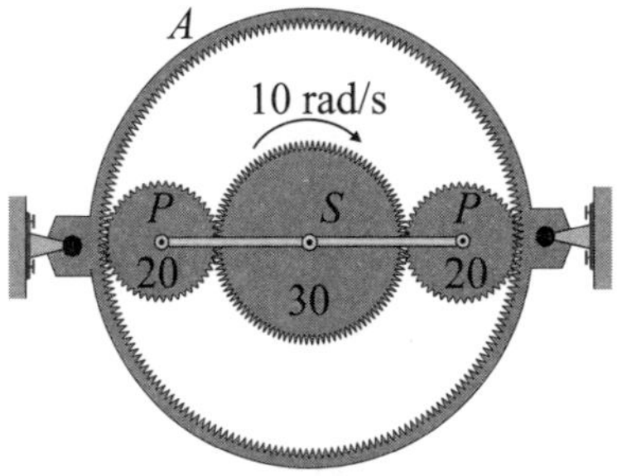

Let m be the module of gear.

Diameter of annular gear is

$$d_A = d_P + d_S + d_P \Rightarrow mT_A = mT_P + mT_S + mT_P$$

or $\quad T_A = T_P + T_S + T_P$

or $\quad T_A = 20 + 30 + 20$

Number of teeth on annular gear $T_A = 70$

Operation	Sun gear S	Planetary gear P	Annular gear A	Arm
1 Rotation of gear S	1	$-\dfrac{30}{20}$	$-\dfrac{30}{70}$	0
Multiply by x	x	$-\dfrac{30}{20}x$	$-\dfrac{30}{70}x$	0
Add y	$x+y$	$y-\dfrac{30}{20}x$	$y-\dfrac{30}{70}x$	y

Given: Angular velocity of sun gear $\quad x + y = 10$

and angular velocity of annular wheel $\quad y - \dfrac{30}{70}x = 0$

From which $y = 3$ and $x = 7$

Angular velocity of planetary gear $P \quad y - \dfrac{30}{20}x = 3 - \dfrac{30}{20}\times 7$

Angular velocity of planetary gear $P = -7.5$ rad/s (7.5 rad/s counter clockwise)

Q.37 Ans:(A)

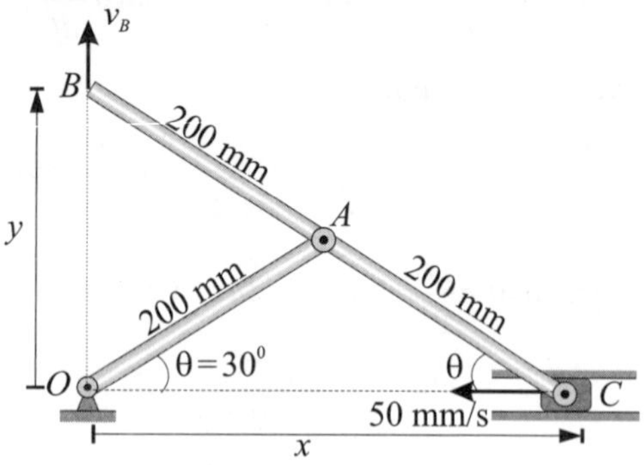

From the geometry of figure,

$$x = 400\cos\theta \text{ and } y = 400\sin\theta$$

Eliminating θ, we have $x^2 + y^2 = 400^2$

Differentiate with respect to *t*, we have

$$x\frac{dx}{dt} + y\frac{dy}{dt} = 0$$

or $\quad x(-v_C) + y(v_B) = 0$

or $\quad v_B = v_C \dfrac{x}{y} = v_C \dfrac{400\cos\theta}{400\sin\theta} = v_C \dfrac{\cos\theta}{\sin\theta}$

$$v_B = 50\frac{\cos 30}{\sin 30} = 50\sqrt{3}$$

$$v_b = 86.6 \text{ mm/s}$$

Q.38 Ans:(B)

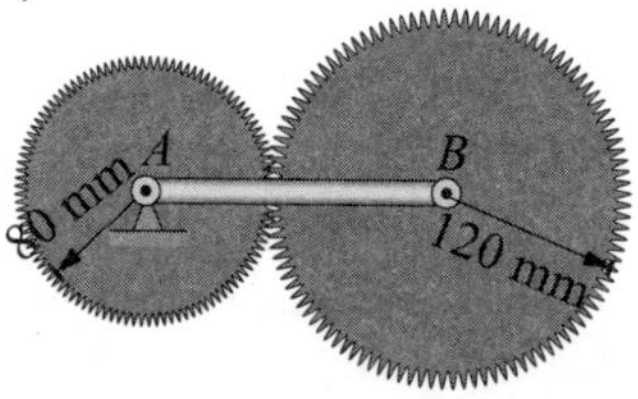

Operation	Gear A	Gear B	Arm
1 Rotation of gear A	1	$-\dfrac{80}{120}$	0
Multiply by x	x	$-\dfrac{2}{3}x$	0
Add y	$x+y$	$y-\dfrac{2}{3}x$	y

Angular velocity of arm, $y = 4.8$ rad/s (counter clockwise)

Angular velocity of A, $x + y = 24$ rad/s (counter clockwise)

From which, $x = 19.2$

Angular velocity of gear B; $\omega_B = y - \dfrac{2}{3}x$

or $\quad \omega_B = 4.8 - \dfrac{2}{3}\times 19.2$

$$\omega_B = 8 \text{ rad/s (clockwise)}$$

Q.39 Ans:(C)

Acceleration is maximum and velocity is zero at dead centers.

Q.40 Ans:(A)

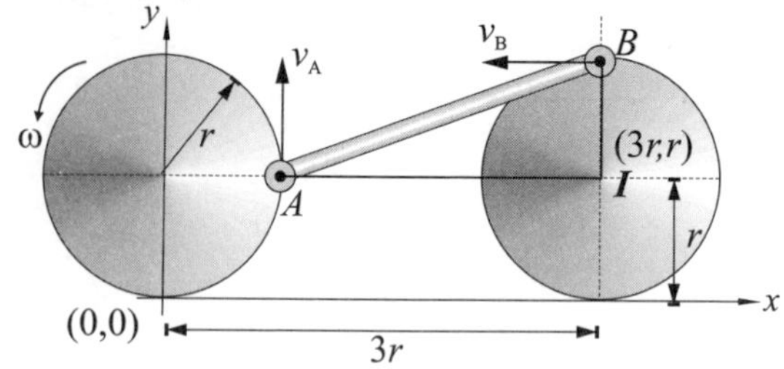

The instant centre of link AB, labeled I in figure, is located at the intersection of the lines that are perpendicular to v_A and v_B.

Coordinate of instant center is $(3r, r)$

Q.41 Ans:(D)

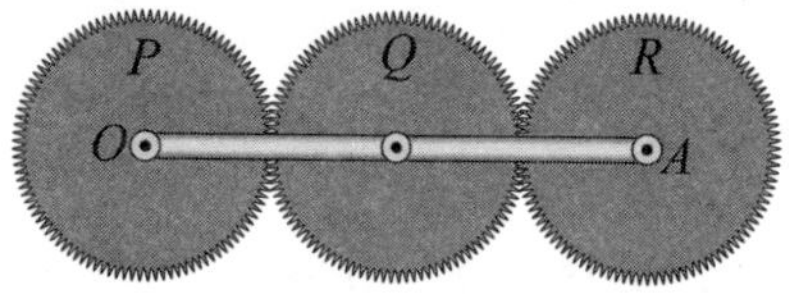

Operation	Gear P	Gear Q	Gear R	Arm OA
1 Rotation of gear P	1	−1	1	0
Multiply by x	x	$-x$	x	0
Add y	$x+y$	$y-x$	$x+y$	y

Given: $y = 4$ rad/s and $x + y = -8$ rad/s

From which $x = -12$ rad/s

Angular velocity of gear R

$\omega_R = x + y = -12 + 4 = -8$ rad/s

$$\omega_R = 8 \text{ rad/s counter clockwise}$$

Q.42 Ans:(A)

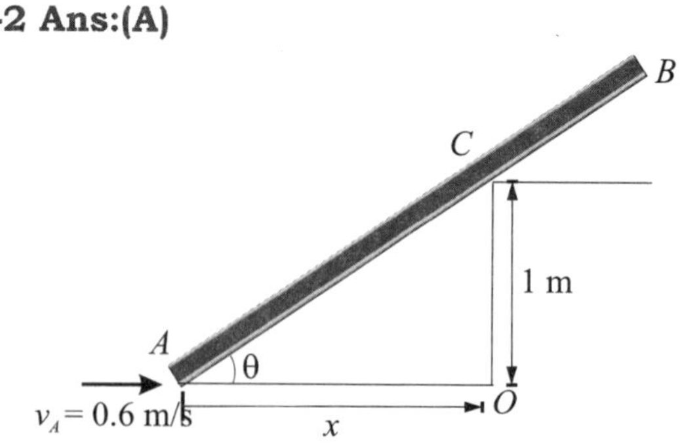

In ΔOAC, $\qquad x = \cot\theta$

Differentiate with respect to *t*, we have

$$\frac{dx}{dt} = -\text{cosec}^2\theta\frac{d\theta}{dt}$$

Angular velocity of AB,

$$\frac{d\theta}{dt} = -\sin^2\theta\frac{dx}{dt} = -\sin^2\theta(-0.6)$$

$$\frac{d\theta}{dt} = 0.6\sin^2\theta \text{ rad/s}$$

Q.43 Ans:(D)

Maximum fluctuation of energy $E_f = E_{max} - E_{min}$

or $$E_f = \frac{1}{2}I\omega^2_{max} - \frac{1}{2}I\omega^2_{min}$$

or $$E_f = I(\omega_{max} - \omega_{min})\frac{(\omega_{max} + \omega_{min})}{2}$$

$$= I(\omega_{max} - \omega_{min})\omega_{av}$$

or $$E_f = I\frac{(\omega_{max} - \omega_{min})}{\omega_{av}}\omega^2_{av} = I\omega^2_{av}K_s$$

$$E_f = I\omega^2_{av}K_s$$

Q.44 Ans:(C)

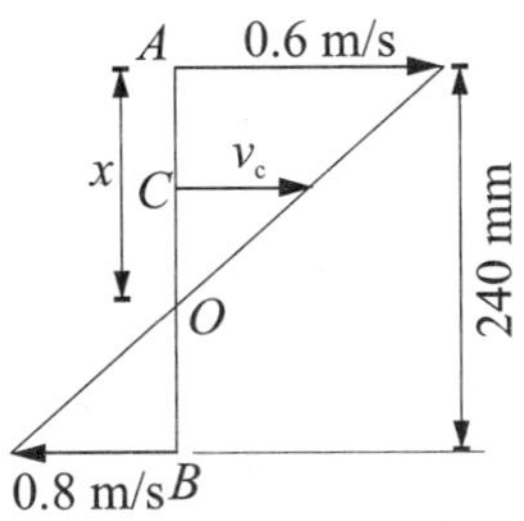

From the geometry in figure,

$$\frac{0.6}{x} = \frac{0.8}{240 - x} \Rightarrow x = 102.85 \text{ mm}$$

and $$\frac{0.6}{x} = \frac{v_c}{OC} \Rightarrow \frac{0.6}{102.85} = \frac{v_c}{102.85 - 90}$$

$$v_c = 0.075 \text{ m/s} \rightarrow$$

Q.45 Ans:(D)

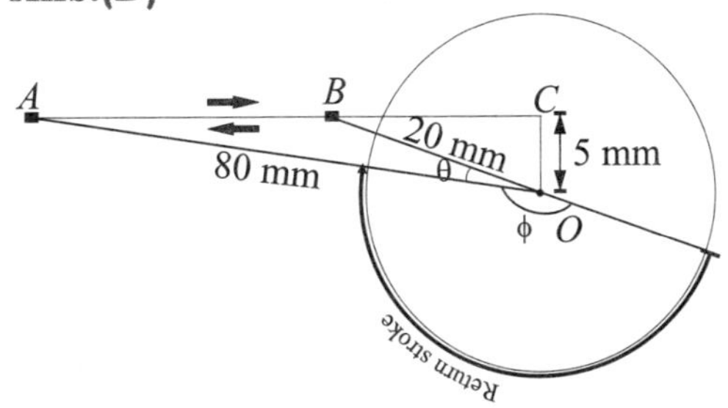

From the geometry of figure,

$$\theta = \cos^{-1}\left(\frac{5}{80}\right) - \cos^{-1}\left(\frac{5}{20}\right)$$

$$\theta = 12.108°$$

Return stroke angle $\phi = 180 - \theta$

or $$\phi = 180 - 12.108 = 167.89$$

Quick return ratio $= \dfrac{360 - \phi}{\phi} = \dfrac{360 - 167.89}{167.89}$

Quick return ratio = 1.14

Q.46 Ans:(A)

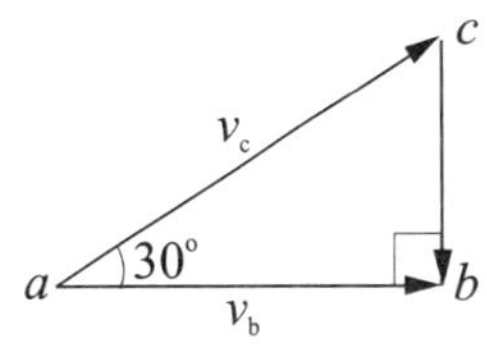

Velocity diagram is shown in figure.

Velocity of joint B, $v_b = \omega_{AB} \times AB = 2 \times 60 = 120$ mm

$$v_c\cos 30 = v_b$$

Velocity of joint C, $v_c = \dfrac{v_b}{\cos 30} = \dfrac{120}{\cos 30}$

$$v_c = 134.67 \text{ mm/s}$$

Q.47 Ans:(D)

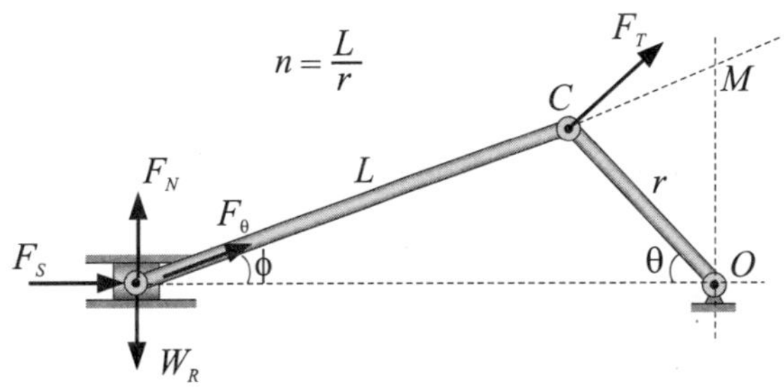

Crank effort $M = F_T \times OC = F_T \times r$ (Option 4 is correct)

where $F_T = F_Q\sin(\theta + \phi)$

$$M = F_Q\sin(\theta + \phi) \times OC = F_Q r\sin(\theta + \phi)$$

From the geometry of figure, $r\sin(\theta + \phi) = OM\cos\phi$

$$M = F_Q\ OM\cos\phi$$

$M = F_Q\cos\phi\ OM = F_S OM$ (Option 3 is correct)

$$M = F_S OM \quad \text{or} \quad M = F_S\frac{r\sin(\theta + \phi)}{\cos\phi}$$

$$M = F_S r\left(\sin\theta + \cos\theta\frac{\sin\phi}{\cos\phi}\right)$$

Substituting $\sin\phi = \dfrac{\sin\theta}{n}$ and $\cos\phi = \sqrt{1 - \sin^2\phi}$

$[\ l\sin\phi = r\sin\theta]$

$M = F_S r\left(\sin\theta + \dfrac{\sin 2\theta}{n}\right)$ (Option 2 is correct)

Q.48 Ans:(D)

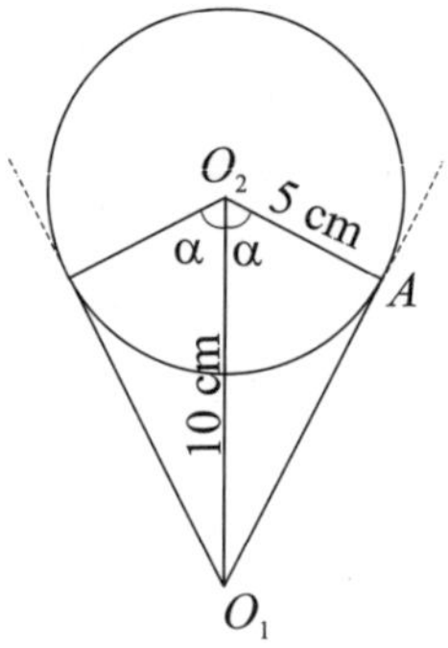

In triangle O_1O_2A,

$$\cos\alpha = \frac{O_2A}{O_1O_2} = \frac{5}{10} \Rightarrow \alpha = 60^\circ$$

$$\text{Quick return ratio} = \frac{360-2\alpha}{2\alpha} = \frac{360-120}{120}$$

$$\text{Quick return ratio} = 2$$

Q.49 Ans:(A)

Linear velocity of link (slider) $v = \omega \times r$

$$v = 2\times\frac{30}{100} = 0.6\text{ m/s}$$

At this instant angular velocity of slotted lever (3), $\omega_3 = 0$

Coriolis acceleration $= 2v\omega = 2\times0.6\times0$

$$\text{Coriolis acceleration} = 0$$

Q.50 Ans:(D)

Let T be the number of teeth on smaller gear.

Number of teeth on bigger gear $= 3T$

Center distance, $C = \frac{1}{2}(d_1+d_2) = \frac{1}{2}(mT_1+mT_2)$

or $C = \frac{m}{2}(T_1+T_2) = \frac{m}{2}(T+3T) = 2mT$

or $136 = 2\times4\times T$

$$T = 17$$

Q.51 Ans:[5]

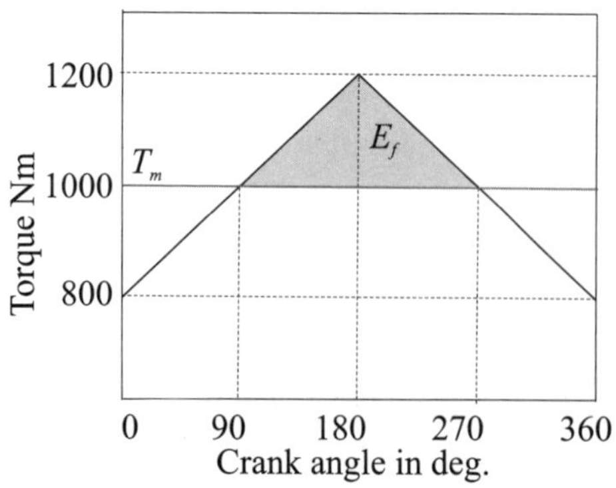

Mean torque,

$$T_m = \frac{\frac{1}{2}(1200-800)(2\pi-0)+800(2\pi-0)}{(2\pi-0)}$$

$$T_m = 1000\text{ Nm}$$

Mean energy, $E_m = T_m\times2\pi = 1000\times2\pi$

Fluctuation energy

$$E_f = \frac{1}{2}(1200-1000)\left(\frac{3}{2}\pi-\frac{1}{2}\pi\right)$$

or $E_f = 100\pi$

Coefficient of fluctuation of energy

$$\frac{E_f}{E_m}\times100 = \frac{100\times\pi}{1000\times2\pi}\times100$$

Coefficient of fluctuation of energy $= 5\%$

Q.52 Ans:[3]

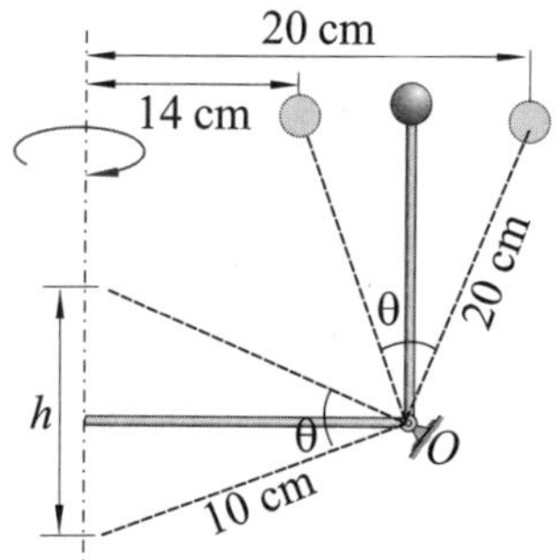

From the geometry of figure,

$$\theta = \frac{h}{10} = \frac{20-14}{20}$$

$$\text{Lift } h = \frac{10}{20}(20-14)$$

$$h = 3.0\text{ cm}$$

Q.53 Ans:[0.1254]

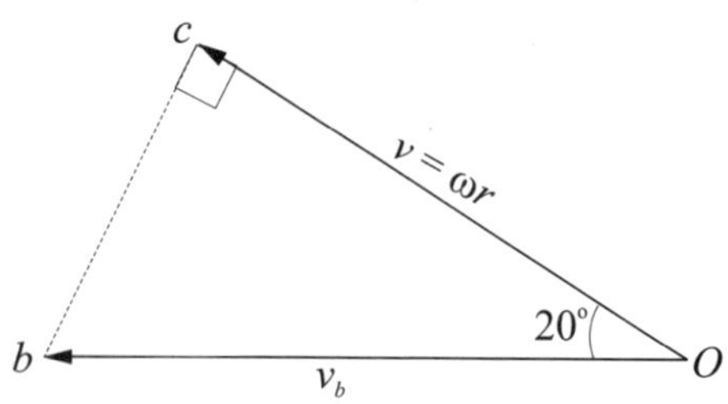

Velocity diagram is shown in figure.

$v_b\cos20 = v = \omega r$

Velocity of block B

$$v_b = \frac{\omega r}{\cos 20} = \frac{2\pi\left(\frac{15}{60}\right)\times\frac{75}{1000}}{\cos 20}$$

$$v_b = 0.1254 \text{ m/s}$$

Q.54 Ans:[80]

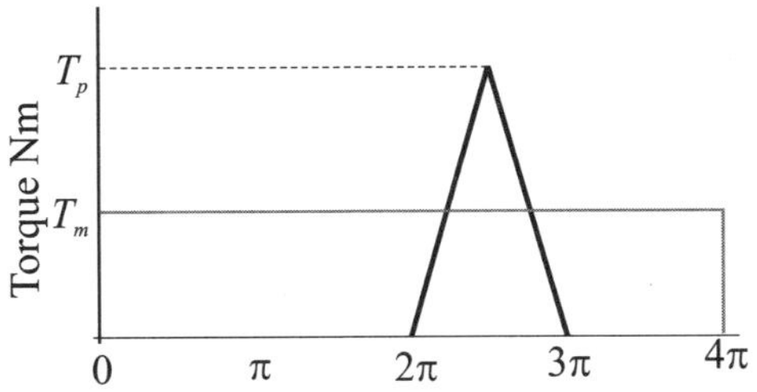

$$\text{Area of triangle} = \frac{1}{2}T_P(3\pi - 2\pi)$$

$$\text{Area of rectangle} = T_m(4\pi - 0) = 10\times 4\pi$$

$$\text{From which } \frac{1}{2}T_P(3\pi - 2\pi) = 10\times 4\pi$$

$$T_P = 80 \text{ Nm}$$

Q.55 Ans:[675]

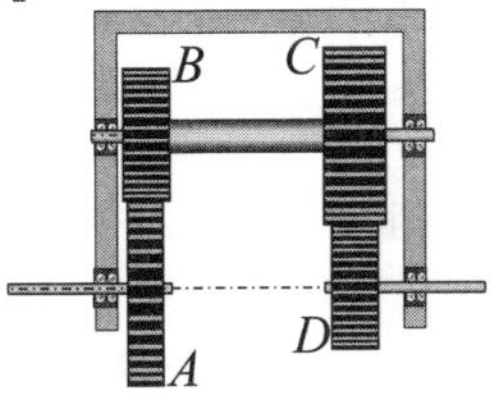

Let T_D be the number of teeth on gear D.

$$T_A + T_B = T_C + T_D \quad \text{or} \quad 30+20 = 30+T_D \Rightarrow T_D = 20$$

$$\frac{N_B}{N_A} = \frac{T_A}{T_B},\ \frac{N_C}{N_D} = \frac{T_D}{T_C} \text{ and } N_B = N_C$$

$$\text{From which } N_D = N_A\left(\frac{T_A}{T_B}\right)\left(\frac{T_C}{T_D}\right)$$

$$N_D = 300\left(\frac{30}{20}\right)\left(\frac{30}{20}\right)$$

$$N_D = 675$$

Q.56 Ans:[1.714]

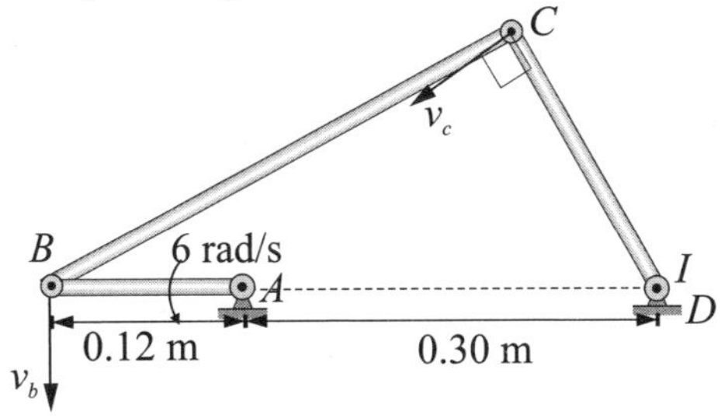

We first locate the instantaneous center ***I*** of link BC, it is located at the point of intersection of the lines that are perpendicular to the velocity vector of B and C.

Let ω be the angular velocity of BC.

$$\omega = \frac{v_B}{IB} = \frac{v_C}{IC}$$

$$\omega = \frac{v_B}{IB} = \frac{\omega\times AB}{IB}$$

$$= \frac{6\times 0.12}{(0.12+0.30)} = \frac{6\times 0.12}{0.42}$$

$$\omega = 1.714 \text{ rad/s}$$

Q.57 Ans:[380]

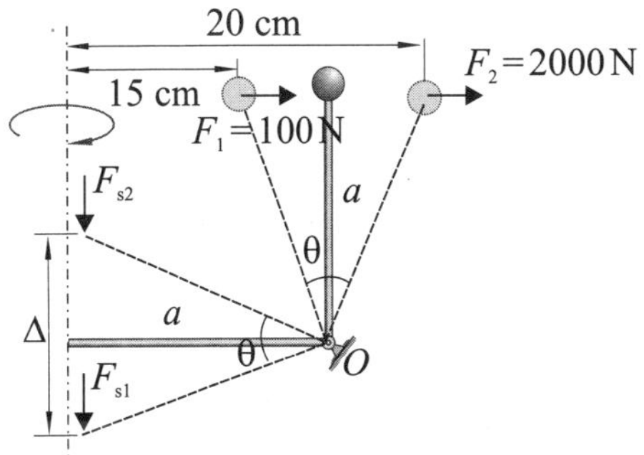

Let a be the length of vertical and horizontal arms.

From the geometry of the figure,

$$\frac{\Delta}{a} = \frac{r_2 - r_1}{a}$$

Extension of spring

$$\Delta = r_2 - r_1 = (20-15) = 5 \text{cm}$$

Moment about O; $\quad F_2 \times a = F_{s2}\times a$

or $\quad F_{s2} = F_2 = 2000\text{N}$ and $F_{s1} = F_1 = 100\text{N}$

$$\text{Spring stiffness, } k = \frac{F_{s2} - F_{s1}}{\Delta}$$

$$= \frac{2000-100}{5} \text{ N/cm}$$

$$k = 380 \text{ N/cm}$$

Q.58 Ans:[209.4]

From the geometry of figure,

$$(20+a)\sin 60 = (30+b)\sin 60$$

$$a = 10 + b \qquad \text{(i)}$$

$$(20+a)\cos 60 + (30+b)\cos 60 = 50$$

$$a + b = 50 \qquad \text{(ii)}$$

From which $a = 30$ and $b = 20$

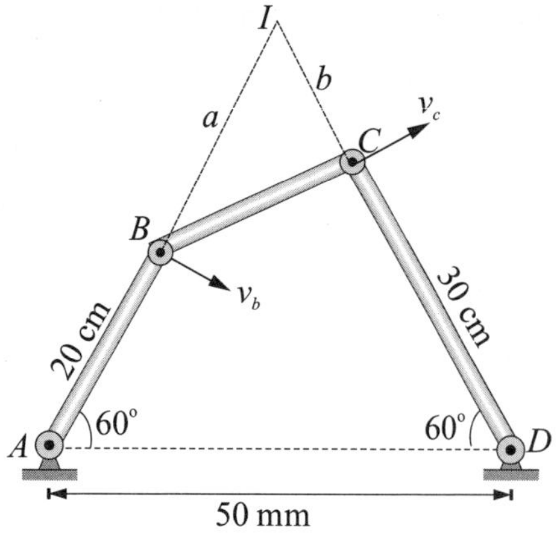

$$\omega = \frac{v_b}{IB} = \frac{v_c}{IC} \Rightarrow \frac{2\pi\frac{150}{60}}{30} = \frac{v_c}{20}$$

$$v_c = 209.4 \text{ cm/s}$$

Q.59 Ans:[477.46]

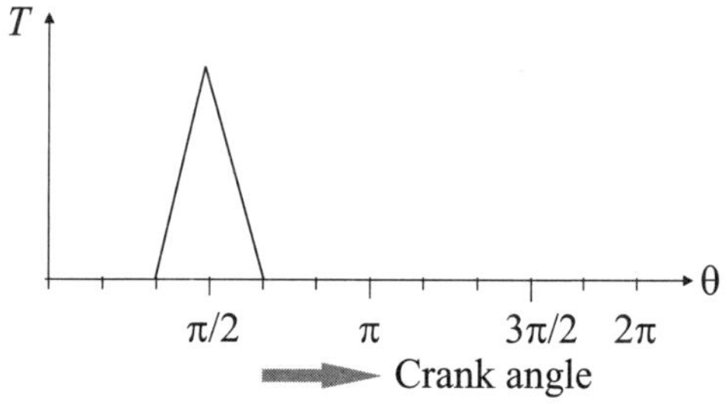

ΔE = Area of triagle = Fluctuation of energy

$$\frac{1}{2}I(\omega_2^2 - \omega_1^2) = \frac{1}{2}T\Delta\theta$$

Substituting $I = 1 \text{ kg}\cdot\text{m}^2, \omega_1 = 20 \text{ rad/s}, \text{and } \omega_2 = 30 \text{ rad/s}$, we have

$$\frac{1}{2}\times 1(30^2 - 20^2) = \frac{1}{2}T\times\frac{\pi}{3}$$

or $$T = \frac{1500}{\pi} \text{ Nm}$$

$$T = 477.46 \text{ Nm}$$

Q.60 Ans:[2.85]

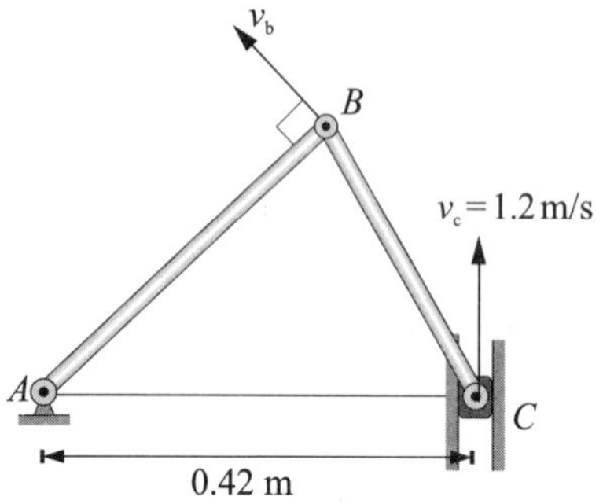

The instantaneous center for bar BC, labeled A in figure, is located at the point of intersection of the lines that are perpendicular to the velocity vector of B and C.

$$\omega_{BC} = \frac{v_c}{AC} = \frac{v_B}{AB}$$

or $$\omega_{BC} = \frac{1.2}{0.3 + 0.12}$$

$$\omega_{BC} = 2.857 \text{ rad/s}$$

Q.61 Ans:[27]

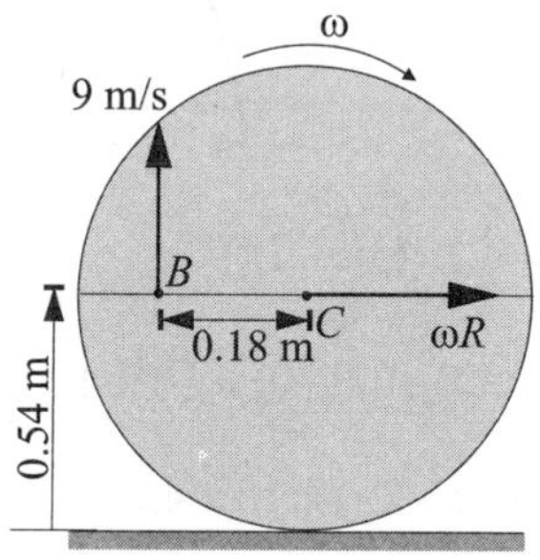

Let ω be the angular velocity of wheel.

Vertical component of the velocity of point B is

$$v_B \uparrow = 9 = \omega \times BC$$

$$\omega = \frac{9}{BC} = \frac{9}{0.18} \text{ rad/s}$$

Velocity of center C, $v = \omega R = \frac{9}{0.18}\times 0.54$

$$v = 27 \text{ m/s}$$

Q.62 Ans:[2]

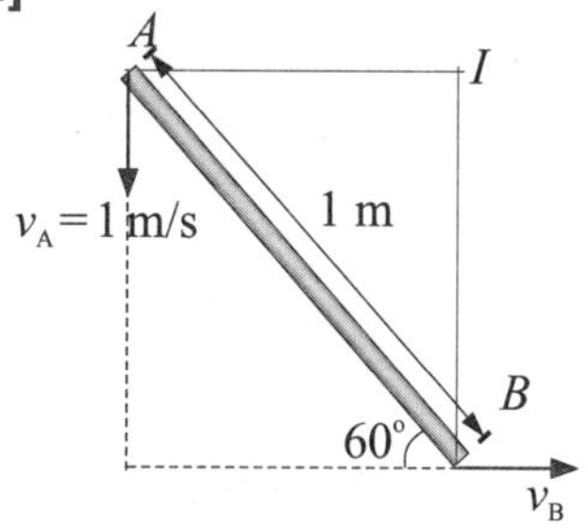

Let ω be the angular velocity of rod AB and I be the Instantaneous center.

Angular velocity rod AB $\omega = \frac{v_A}{IA} = \frac{v_B}{IB}$

$$\omega = \frac{v_A}{IA} = \frac{1}{1\cos 60} = 2$$

$$\omega = 2 \text{ rad/s}$$

Q.63 Ans:[800]

Consider joint B,

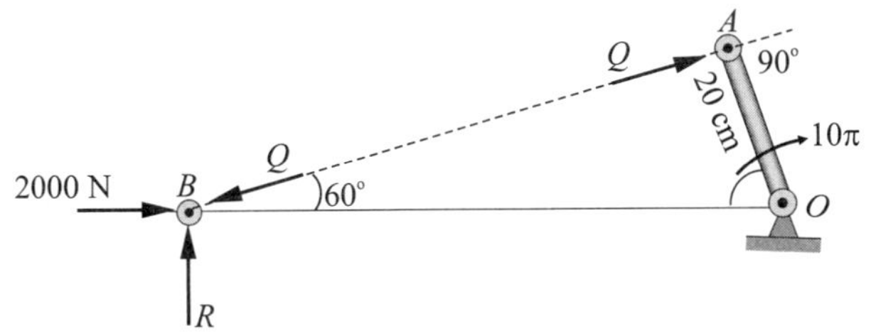

$$\left(\sum F_x\right)_B = 0 \quad \Rightarrow \quad Q\cos 60 = 2000$$

$$\Rightarrow \quad Q = \frac{2000}{\cos 60} = \frac{2000}{1/2} = 4000\,\text{N}$$

Turning moment about O, $\quad M_O = Q \times OA$

or $\quad M_O = 4000 \times 0.2 = 800$

Turning moment about O is 800 N m

Q.64 Ans:[57.73]

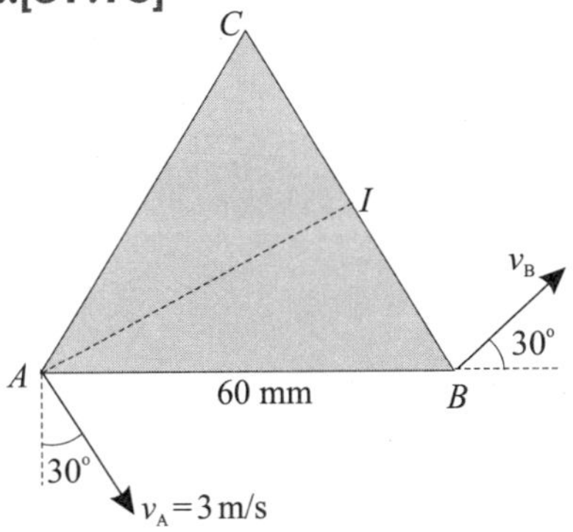

First we locate instantaneous center I.

$$\omega = \frac{v_A}{IA} = \frac{v_B}{IB}$$

or $$\omega = \frac{3}{\frac{60}{1000} \times \frac{\sqrt{3}}{2}}$$

$$\omega = 57.73\ \text{rad/s}$$

Q.65 Ans:[2.88]

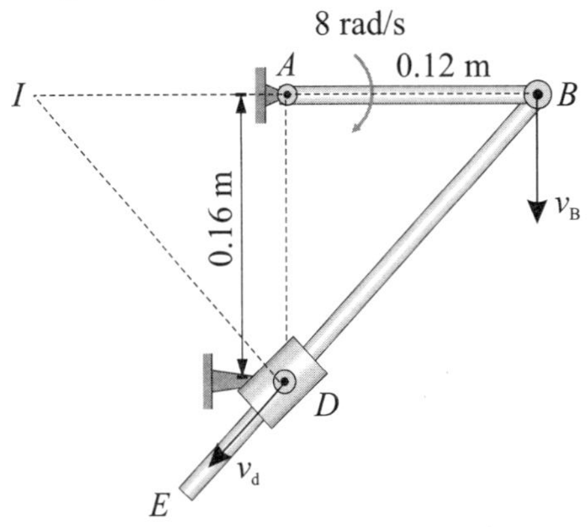

From the geometry of figure,

$$BD = \sqrt{0.12^2 + 0.16^2} = 0.20\,\text{m}$$

I is the instantaneous center

$$\frac{BD}{IB} = \cos\theta$$

or $$IB = \frac{BD}{\cos\theta} = \frac{0.20}{\left(\frac{0.12}{0.20}\right)} = 0.333\ \text{m}$$

Angular velocity of BD, $\quad \omega = \frac{v_B}{IB} = \frac{8 \times 0.12}{0.333}$

$$\omega = 2.88\ \text{rad/s}$$

GATE Syllabus

Free and forced vibration of single degree of freedom systems, Effect of damping; Vibration isolation; Resonance; Critical speeds of shafts.

Chapter Outline

8.1 KEY CONCEPTS AND FORMULAS

Undamped Free Vibrations

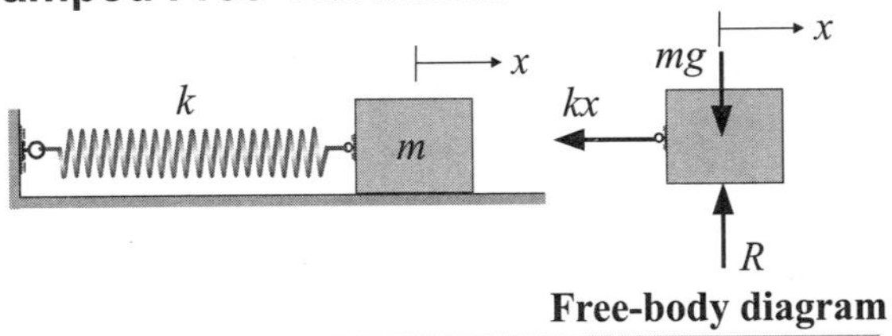

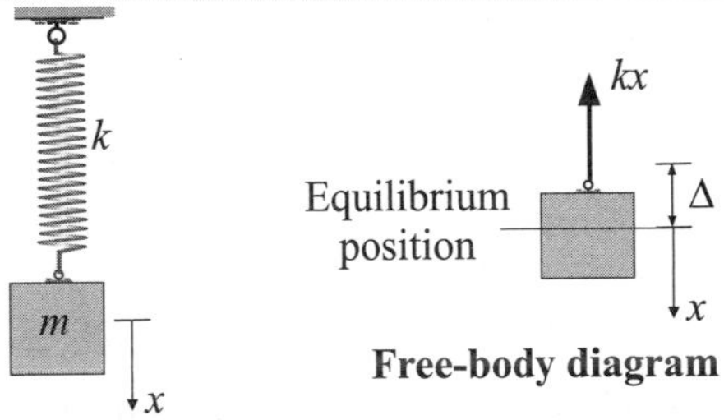

Spring-mass System

Free-body diagram is drawn for arbitrary positive displacement x from equilibrium position. From free-body diagram, Newton's second law gives

$$-kx = m\frac{d^2x}{dt^2}$$

or

$$\frac{d^2x}{dt^2} + \frac{k}{m}x = 0$$

Natural circular frequency, $\omega_n = \sqrt{\frac{k}{m}}$

Frequency, $f_n = \frac{1}{2\pi}\sqrt{\frac{k}{m}}$ Hz

Simple Pendulum

Figure shows the free-body diagram of mass (bob). The tangential component of the weight, $mg\sin\theta$, always acts toward O, opposite to the displacement.

Therefore, the tangential force is a restoring force, and we can write the equation of motion in the tangential direction

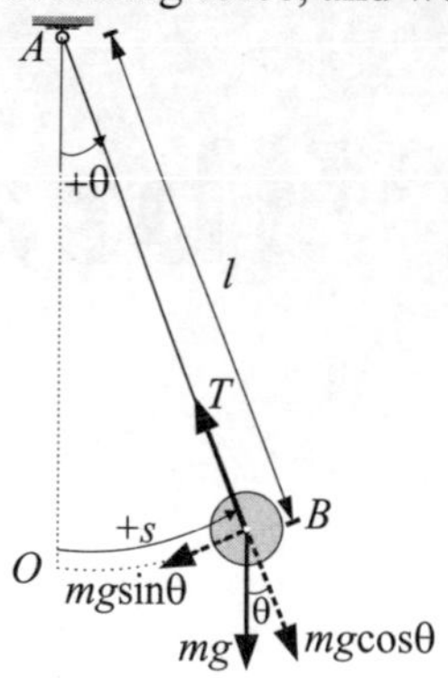

$$-mg\sin\theta = m\frac{d^2s}{dt^2}$$

Since $s = l\theta$ and θ is small, this equation reduces to:

$$\frac{d^2\theta}{dt^2} + \frac{g}{l}\theta = 0$$

Natural frequency, $\omega_n = \sqrt{\frac{g}{l}}$

Period of the motion, $T = \frac{2\pi}{\omega_n} = 2\pi\sqrt{\frac{g}{l}}$

Compound Pendulum

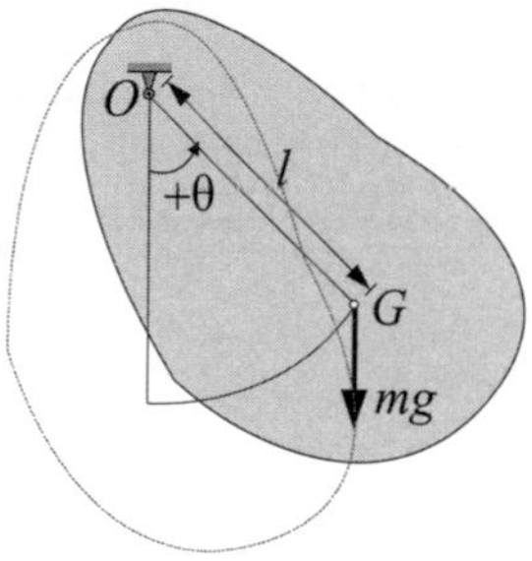

A compound pendulum consists of any rigid body suspended from a fixed axis that does not pass through the body's center of gravity. The restoring torque about O is provided by the force of gravity (mg), and its magnitude is $(mg\sin\theta)l$. Therefore, we can write the equation of motion:

$$[M = I\ddot{\theta}] \quad \Rightarrow -(mg\sin\theta)l = I_O\frac{d^2\theta}{dt^2}$$

where I_O is the moment of inertia of body about O. Since θ is small; $\frac{d^2\theta}{dt^2} + \frac{mgl}{I_O}\theta = 0$

Natural frequency, $\omega_n = \sqrt{\frac{mgl}{I_O}}$

Period of the motion, $T = 2\pi\sqrt{\frac{l + \frac{k^2}{l}}{g}}$

Torsional Pendulum

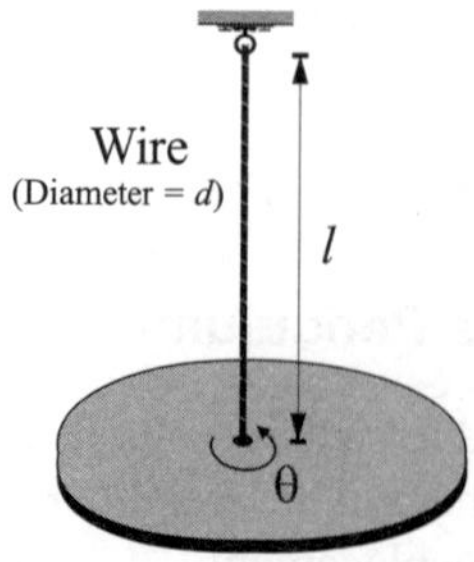

Figure shows a rigid body suspended by a wire attached at the top to a fixed support. When the body is twisted through some small angle θ, the twisted wire exerts a restoring torque on the body proportional to the angular displacement. That is

$$M = -k_\theta\theta$$

Where k_θ is torsional constant of the wire $\left[k_\theta = \frac{T}{\theta} = \frac{GJ}{l}\right]$.

Newton's second law for rotational motion gives

$$-k_\theta\theta = I\frac{d^2\theta}{dt^2} \quad \text{or} \quad \frac{d^2\theta}{dt^2} + \frac{k_\theta}{I}\theta = 0$$

Circular frequency, $\omega_n = \sqrt{\frac{k_\theta}{I}}$

or $\omega_n = \sqrt{\frac{GJ}{Il}}$

Damped Free Vibrations

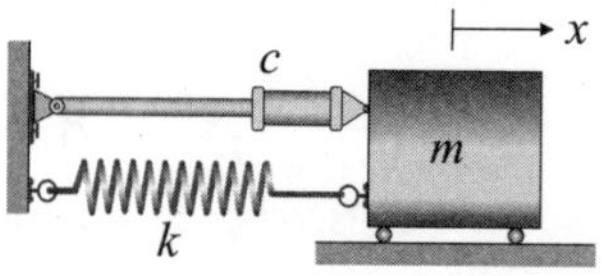

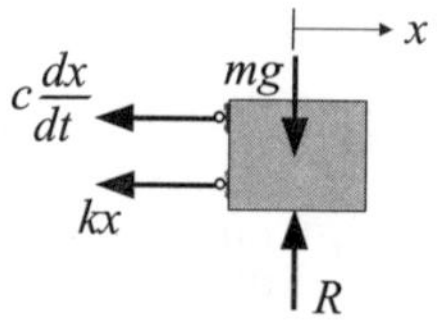

Free-body diagram

The equation of motion for the body with damping is determine from the free-body diagram as shown in figure. Netwon's second law gives

$$m\frac{d^2x}{dt^2} = -kx - c\frac{dx}{dt}$$

or
$$\frac{d^2x}{dt^2} + \frac{c}{m}\frac{dx}{dt} + \frac{k}{m}x = 0$$

Damping factor $\zeta = \frac{c}{2m\omega_n}$ and $\omega_n = \sqrt{\frac{k}{m}}$

$$\frac{d^2x}{dt^2} + 2\zeta\omega_n\frac{dx}{dt} + \omega_n^2x = 0$$

Roots are $(-\zeta + \sqrt{\zeta^2 - 1})\omega_n$ and $(-\zeta - \sqrt{\zeta^2 - 1})\omega_n$

Solution of above differential equation is

$$x = c_1e^{(-\zeta+\sqrt{\zeta^2-1})\omega_n t} + c_2e^{(-\zeta-\sqrt{\zeta^2-1})\omega_n t}; \quad \text{For } \zeta > 1$$

$$x = (c_1 + c_2t)e^{-\omega_n t}; \quad \text{For } \zeta = 1$$

$$x = x_0e^{-\zeta\omega_n t}\cos(\sqrt{1-\zeta^2}\,\omega_n t + \phi); \quad \text{For } \zeta < 1$$

Categories of damped motion

1. $\zeta > 1$ (over damped); There is no oscillation.
2. $\zeta = 1$ (critically damped); The motion is non-periodic.
3. $\zeta < 1$ (under damped); The motion is periodic.

$$x = ce^{-\zeta\omega_n t}\sin[\sqrt{1-\zeta^2}\,\omega_n t + \phi]$$

Damped natural frequency, $\omega_d = \omega_n\sqrt{1-\zeta^2}$

Damped period, $t_d = \frac{2\pi}{\omega_d} = \frac{2\pi}{\omega_n\sqrt{1-\zeta^2}}$

Logarithmic decrement δ: It is the logarithm of the ratio of any two successive amplitudes,

$$\delta = \ln\frac{x_1}{x_2} = \zeta\omega_n t_d = \frac{2\pi\zeta}{\sqrt{1-\zeta^2}}$$

$$\delta = \frac{2\pi\zeta}{\sqrt{1-\zeta^2}}$$

or $$\zeta = \frac{\delta}{\sqrt{4\pi^2+\delta^2}}$$

Undamped Forced Vibration

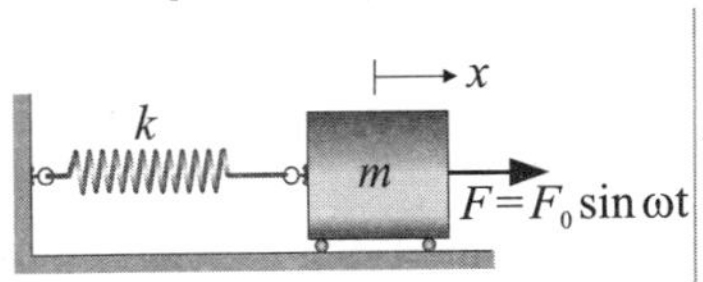

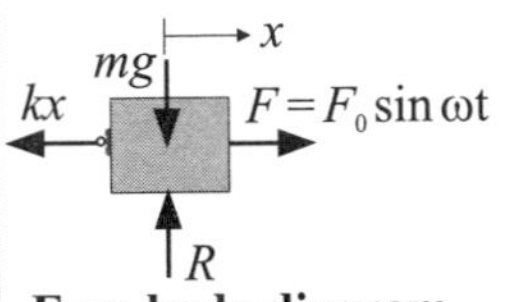

Free-body diagram

The equation of motion for the body of figure is obtained by first drawing its free-body diagram. Newton's second law gives

$$-kx + F_0\sin\omega t = m\frac{d^2x}{dt^2}$$

or $$\frac{d^2x}{dt^2} + \frac{k}{m}x = \frac{F_0}{m}\sin\omega t$$

Amplitude of periodic vibration,

$$X = \frac{\frac{F_0}{m}}{\frac{k}{m}-\omega^2} = \frac{\frac{F_0}{k}}{1-\frac{\omega^2}{k/m}} = \frac{X_{st}}{1-\frac{\omega^2}{\omega_n^2}}$$

Magnification factor (Amplitude ratio) $\frac{X}{X_{st}} = \frac{1}{1-\left(\frac{\omega}{\omega_n}\right)^2}$

Damped Forced Vibrations

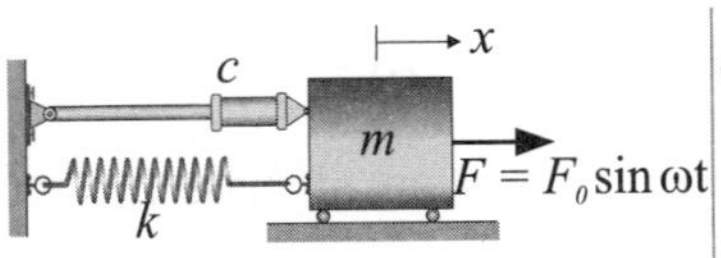

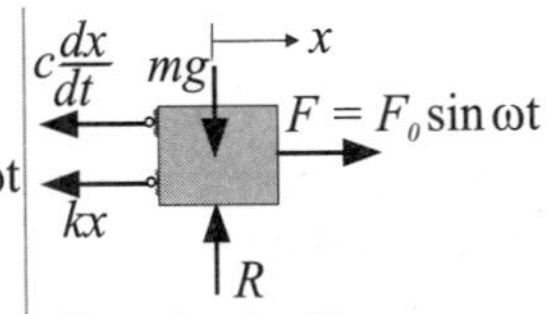

Free-body diagram

From the free-body diagram, Newton's second law gives

$$-kx - c\frac{dx}{dt} + F_0\sin\omega t = m\frac{d^2x}{dt^2}$$

or $$\frac{d^2x}{dt^2} + c\frac{dx}{dt} + \frac{k}{m}x = \frac{F_0}{m}\sin\omega t$$

Amplitude, $X = \frac{F_0}{\sqrt{(k-m\omega^2)^2+(c\omega)^2}}$

$$X = \frac{F_0/k}{\sqrt{\left(1-\frac{\omega^2}{k/m}\right)^2+\left(\frac{c\omega}{k}\right)^2}}$$

$$\frac{X}{X_{st}} = \frac{1}{\sqrt{\left(1-\left(\frac{\omega}{\omega_n}\right)^2\right)^2+\left[2\zeta\left(\frac{\omega}{\omega_n}\right)\right]^2}}$$

Phase of displacement, $\phi = \tan^{-1}\frac{c\omega}{k-m\omega^2}$

$$\phi = \tan^{-1}\frac{\frac{c\omega}{k}}{1-\frac{\omega^2}{k/m}} \quad \text{or} \quad \phi = \tan^{-1}\frac{2\zeta\left(\frac{\omega}{\omega_n}\right)}{1-\left(\frac{\omega}{\omega_n}\right)^2}$$

where $\zeta = \frac{c}{2m\omega_n}$

Energy Method

If all of the forces that act on a mechanical system are conservative, the total mechanical energy of the system is conserved. That is

$$\text{KE} + \text{PE} = \text{constant}$$

or $$\frac{d}{dt}[\text{KE} + \text{PE}] = 0$$

We obtain the equation of motion:

$$\frac{d^2x}{dt^2} + \omega_n^2 x = 0$$

Vibration Isolation

Vibratory force of a machine or structure will be transmitted to its supporting structure. These transmitted forces produce undesirable effect. To prevent these vibrations or minimise their effect, such machine are mounted on spring or vibration isolation material.

To measure effectiveness of vibration isolation material, the term transmissibility is used. It is defined as the ratio of force transmitted to the impressed force.

The force to be isolated is transmitted through the spring and damper as shown in figure.

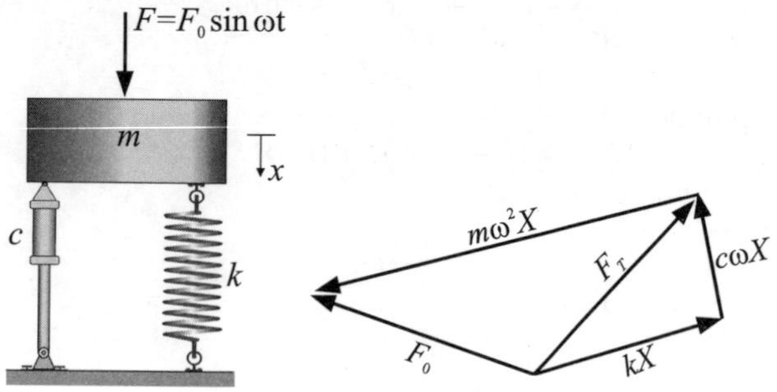

$$F_T = \sqrt{(kX)^2 + (c\omega X)^2}$$

$$= kX\sqrt{1+\left(\frac{c\omega}{k}\right)^2} = kX\sqrt{1+\left(2\zeta\frac{\omega}{\omega_n}\right)^2}$$

Substituting $X = \dfrac{F_0/k}{\sqrt{\left(1-\left(\frac{\omega}{\omega_n}\right)^2\right)^2+\left[2\zeta\left(\frac{\omega}{\omega_n}\right)\right]^2}}$,

$$F_T = \frac{F_0\sqrt{1+\left(2\zeta\frac{\omega}{\omega_n}\right)^2}}{\sqrt{\left(1-\left(\frac{\omega}{\omega_n}\right)^2\right)^2+\left[2\zeta\left(\frac{\omega}{\omega_n}\right)\right]^2}}$$

Transmissibility,

$$TR = \left|\frac{F_T}{F_0}\right| = \frac{\sqrt{1+\left(2\zeta\frac{\omega}{\omega_n}\right)^2}}{\sqrt{\left(1-\left(\frac{\omega}{\omega_n}\right)^2\right)^2+\left[2\zeta\left(\frac{\omega}{\omega_n}\right)\right]^2}}$$

When the damping is negligible, the transmissibility equation reduce to:

$$TR = \frac{1}{\left(\frac{\omega}{\omega_n}\right)^2 - 1}$$

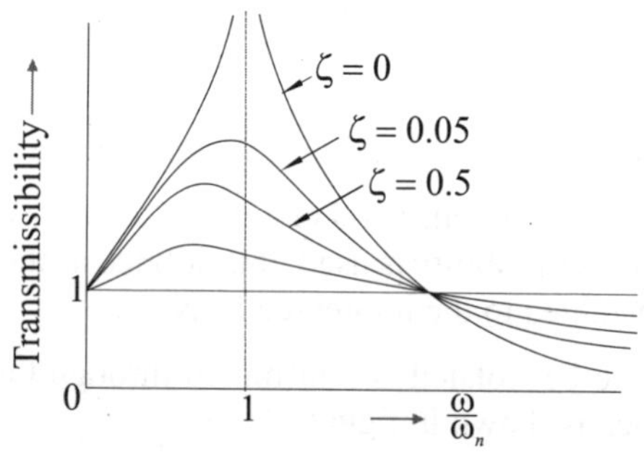

Critical Speed of Shaft

A critical speed (whirling speed) of a rotating shaft is the speed at which the shaft starts to vibrate violently in the transverse direction.

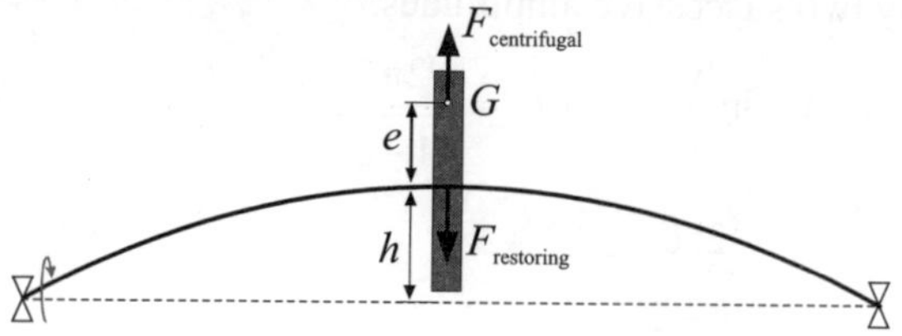

Under equilibrium:

Centrifugal force = Restoring force

$$m\omega^2(h+e) = kh$$

which gives

$$h = \frac{m\omega^2 e}{k - m\omega^2} = \frac{\omega^2 e}{\frac{k}{m} - \omega^2} = \frac{\omega^2 e}{\omega_n^2 - \omega^2}$$

$h = \dfrac{\left(\frac{\omega}{\omega_n}\right)^2 e}{1-\left(\frac{\omega}{\omega_n}\right)^2}$, where ω_n is the natural frequency of the lateral vibration of the shaft.

8.2 SOLVED EXAMPLES

Previous Years GATE Questions

Example 8.1

In a spring-mass system, the mass is m and the spring constant is k. The critical damping coefficient of the system is 0.1 kg/s. In another spring-mass system, the mass is 2 m and the spring constant is $8k$. The critical damping coefficient (in kg/s) of this system is ______.

GATE 2015

Solution

Critical damping coefficient of system of mass m and spring constant k is

$$c_c = \sqrt{2mk} = 0.1 \quad \text{(i)}$$

Critical damping coefficient of system of mass $2m$ and spring constant $8k$ is

$$c_c' = \sqrt{2\times 2m \times 8k} = 4\sqrt{2mk} \quad \text{(ii)}$$

From Equations (i) and (ii), we have

$$c_c' = 4\times 0.1$$

$$c_c' = 0.4$$

Example 8.2

A single degree freedom of spring-mass is subjected to a sinusoidal force of 10 N amplitude and frequency ω along the axis of the spring. The stiffness of the spring is 150 N/m, damping factor is 0.2 and undamped natural frequency is 10ω. At steady state, the amplitude of vibration (in m) is approximately

(A) 0.05 (B) 0.07 (C) 0.70 (D) 0.90

GATE 2015

Solution

Figure shows the equivalent diagram.

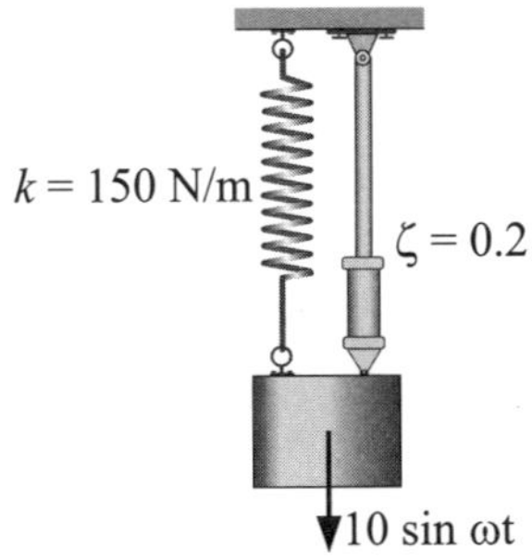

Amplitude of vibration(shown in figure) is given by

$$X = \frac{F_0 / k}{\sqrt{\left(1-\left(\frac{\omega}{\omega_n}\right)^2\right)^2 + \left[2\zeta\left(\frac{\omega}{\omega_n}\right)\right]^2}}$$

$$X = \frac{10/150}{\sqrt{\left(1-\left(\frac{\omega}{10\omega}\right)^2\right)^2 + \left[2\times 0.2\left(\frac{\omega}{10\omega}\right)\right]^2}}$$

$$X = \frac{10/150}{\sqrt{\left(\frac{99}{100}\right)^2 + \left(\frac{0.4}{10}\right)^2}}$$

$$X = 0.067\text{ m}$$

Example 8.3

Figure shows a single degree of freedom system. The system consists of a mass less rigid bar OP hinged at O and a mass m at end P. The natural frequency of vibration of the system is

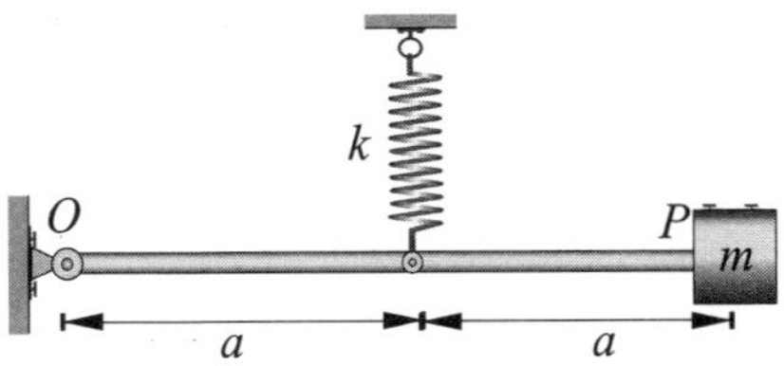

(A) $f_n = \frac{1}{2\pi}\sqrt{\frac{k}{4m}}$ (B) $f_n = \frac{1}{2\pi}\sqrt{\frac{k}{2m}}$

(C) $f_n = \frac{1}{2\pi}\sqrt{\frac{k}{m}}$ (D) $f_n = \frac{1}{2\pi}\sqrt{\frac{2k}{m}}$

GATE 2015

Solution

The free-body diagram of system is constructed for an arbitrary displacement θ from mean position as shown in figure.

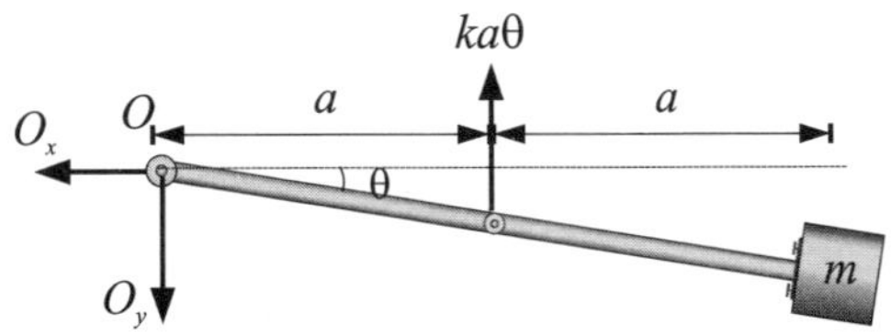

Moment equation about hinge O; $I_O \frac{d^2\theta}{dt^2} = -ka\theta \times a$

or $\frac{d^2\theta}{dt^2} + \frac{ka^2}{I_O}\theta = 0$

Substituting $I_O = m(2a)^2 = 4ma^2$

$$\frac{d^2\theta}{dt^2} + \frac{ka^2}{4ma^2}\theta = 0$$

From which

Natural frequency, $\omega_n = \sqrt{\frac{ka^2}{4ma^2}}$

$$2\pi f_n = \sqrt{\frac{ka^2}{4ma^2}}$$

$$f_n = \frac{1}{2\pi}\sqrt{\frac{k}{4m}}$$

Example 8.4

Considering massless rigid rod and small oscillations, the natural frequency (in rad/s) of vibration of the system shown in the figure is

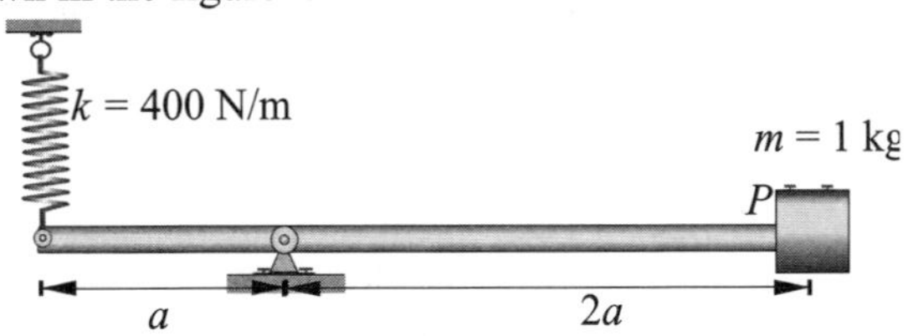

(A) $\sqrt{\frac{400}{1}}$ (B) $\sqrt{\frac{400}{2}}$ (C) $\sqrt{\frac{400}{3}}$ (D) $\sqrt{\frac{400}{4}}$

GATE 2015

Solution

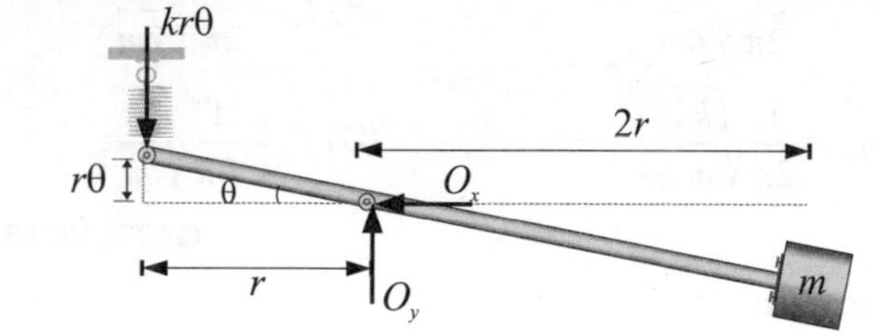

The rod is displaced by small angular displacement θ from equilibrium position as shown in figure. Moment equation about hinge O is

$$I_O \frac{d^2\theta}{dt^2} = -k\,r\theta \times 2r$$

or
$$\frac{d^2\theta}{dt^2} + \frac{2k\,r^2}{I_O}\theta = 0$$

Substituting moment of inertia O; $I_O = m(2r)^2 = 4mr^2$

$$\frac{d^2\theta}{dt^2} + \frac{2k\,r^2}{4m\,r^2}\theta = 0$$

Thus, the natural frequency, $\omega_n = \sqrt{\frac{k}{4m}} = \sqrt{\frac{400}{4\times 1}}$

$$\omega_n = \sqrt{\frac{400}{4}}$$

Example 8.5

A concentrated mass m is attached at the centre of a rod of length $2L$ as shown in the figure. The rod is kept in a horizontal equilibrium position by a spring of stiffness k. For very small amplitude of vibration, neglecting the weights of the rod and spring, the undamped natural frequency of the system is

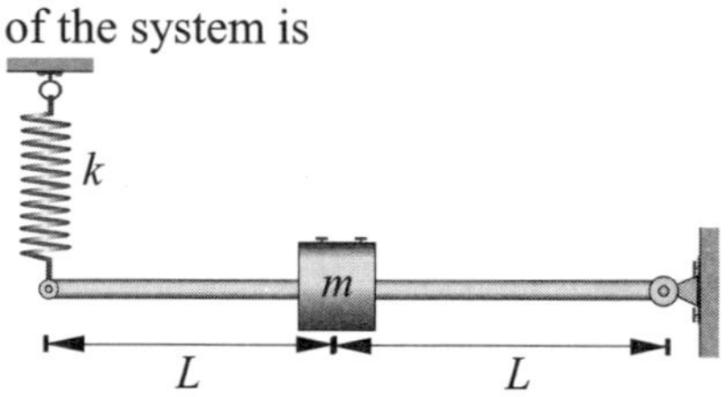

(A) $\sqrt{\frac{k}{m}}$ (B) $\sqrt{\frac{k}{2m}}$ (C) $\sqrt{\frac{2k}{m}}$ (D) $\sqrt{\frac{4k}{m}}$

GATE 2012

Solution

The rod is displaced by a small angular displacement θ from the equilibrium position shown in figure.

The moment equation $\sum M_O = I_O\ddot{\theta}$, applied to the free body diagram, gives

$$\sum M_O = I_O\ddot{\theta} \quad \Rightarrow \quad -2kL\theta \times 2L = I_O\ddot{\theta}$$

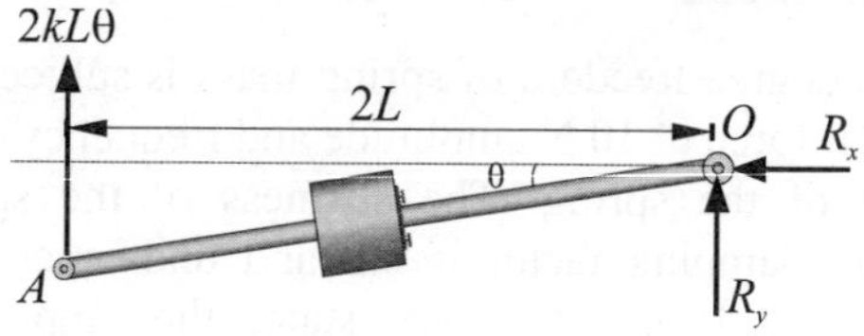

or
$$I_O\ddot{\theta} + 4kL^2\theta = 0$$

or
$$\ddot{\theta} + \frac{4kL^2}{I_O}\theta = 0$$

Substituting moment of inertia of mass about O, $I_O = mL^2$

$$\ddot{\theta} + \frac{4kL^2}{mL^2}\theta = 0$$

or
$$\ddot{\theta} + \frac{4k}{m}\theta = 0$$

Hence, the natural frequency of vibration,

$$\omega_n = \sqrt{\frac{4k}{m}}$$

Example 8.6

A rigid uniform rod AB of length L and mass m is hinged at C such that $AC = \frac{L}{3}$, $CB = \frac{2L}{3}$. Ends A and B are supported by springs of spring constant k. The natural frequency of the system is given by

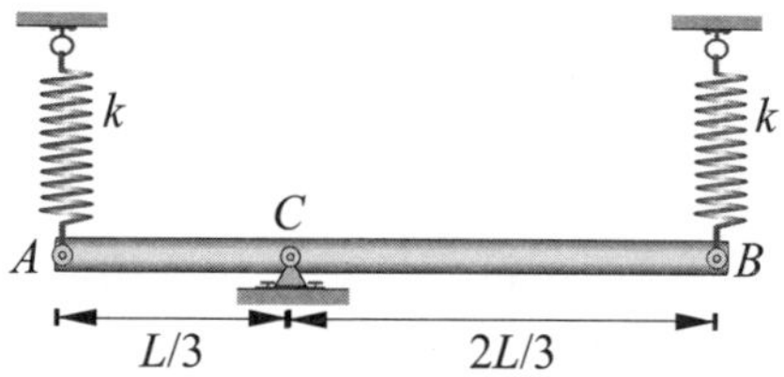

(A) $\sqrt{\frac{k}{2m}}$ (B) $\sqrt{\frac{k}{m}}$ (C) $\sqrt{\frac{2k}{m}}$ (D) $\sqrt{\frac{5k}{m}}$

GATE 2014

Solution

The moment of inertia of the rod about C is

$$I_C = I_G + md^2$$

or
$$I_C = \frac{mL^2}{12} + m\left(\frac{L}{2} - \frac{L}{3}\right)^2$$

or
$$I_C = \frac{mL^2}{9}$$

Let the rod be displaced through a small angle θ, as shown in figure.

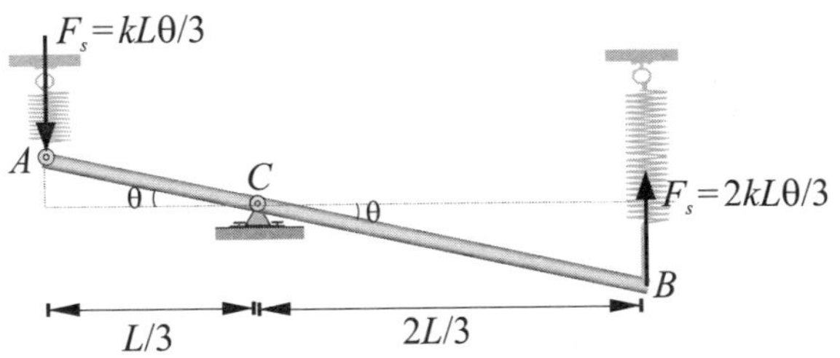

Restoring moment about C is

$$M_C = F_{s1} \times \frac{L}{3} + F_{s2} \times \frac{2L}{3}$$

or $$M_C = k\frac{L}{3}\theta \times \frac{L}{3} + k\frac{2L}{3}\theta \times \frac{2L}{3} = \frac{5kL^2}{9}\theta$$

or $$M_C = \frac{5kL^2}{9}\theta$$

Therefore, the equation of motion is

$$I_C \frac{d^2\theta}{dt^2} = -M_C \quad \Rightarrow \quad \frac{mL^2}{9}\frac{d^2\theta}{dt^2} = -\frac{5kL^2}{9}\theta$$

or $$\frac{d^2\theta}{dt^2} + \frac{5k}{m}\theta$$

Hence,

$$\omega_n = \sqrt{\frac{5k}{m}}$$

Example 8.7

The assembly shown in the figure is composed of two massless rod of length l with two particles, each of mass m. The natural frequency of this assembly for mass oscillations is

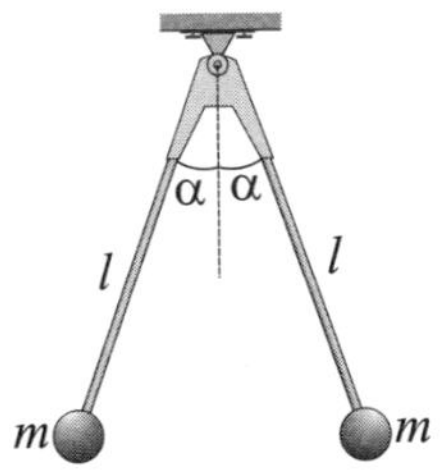

(A) $\sqrt{\frac{g}{l}}$ (B) $\sqrt{\frac{2g}{l\cos\alpha}}$

(C) $\sqrt{\frac{g}{l\cos\alpha}}$ (D) $\sqrt{\frac{g\cos\alpha}{l}}$

GATE 2001

Solution

The moment of inertia of the system about O is

$$I_O = ml^2 + ml^2 = 2ml^2$$

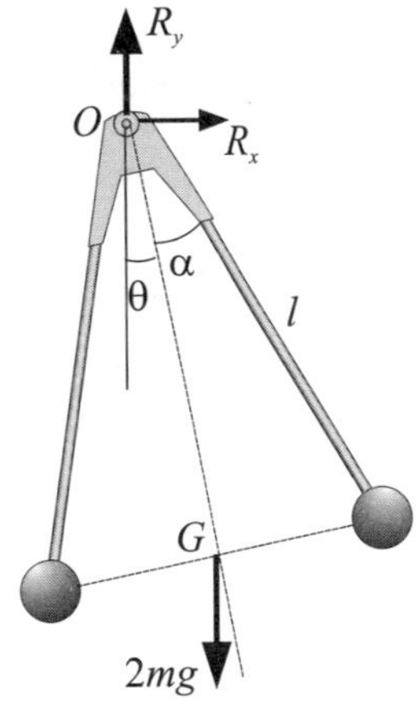

Let the system be displaced through a small angle θ, as shown in figure. Then

The restoring moment about O is

$$M_O = 2mg\sin\theta \times OG$$

or $$M_O = 2mg\sin\theta \times l\cos\alpha = 2mgl\cos\alpha\,\sin\theta$$

Since θ is small, $M_O = 2mgl\cos\alpha\,\theta$

Therefore, the equation of motion is

$$I_O \frac{d^2\theta}{dt^2} = -M_O \quad \Rightarrow \quad 2ml^2\frac{d^2\theta}{dt^2} = -2mgl\cos\alpha\theta$$

or $$\frac{d^2\theta}{dt^2} + \frac{g\cos\alpha}{l}\theta = 0$$

Hence, the natural frequency of the system is

$$\omega_n = \sqrt{\frac{g\cos\alpha}{l}}$$

Example 8.8

A disc of mass m is attached to a spring of stiffness k as shown in the figure. The disc rolls without slipping on a horizontal surface. The natural frequency of vibration of the system is

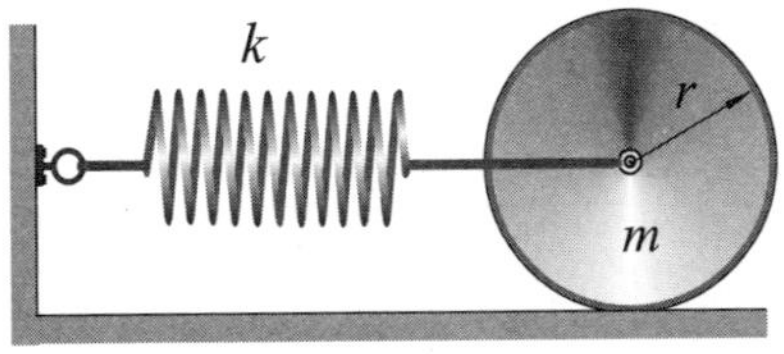

(A) $\frac{1}{2\pi}\sqrt{\frac{k}{m}}$ (B) $\frac{1}{2\pi}\sqrt{\frac{2k}{3m}}$

(C) $\frac{1}{2\pi}\sqrt{\frac{2k}{m}}$ (D) $\frac{1}{2\pi}\sqrt{\frac{3k}{2m}}$

GATE 2011

Solution

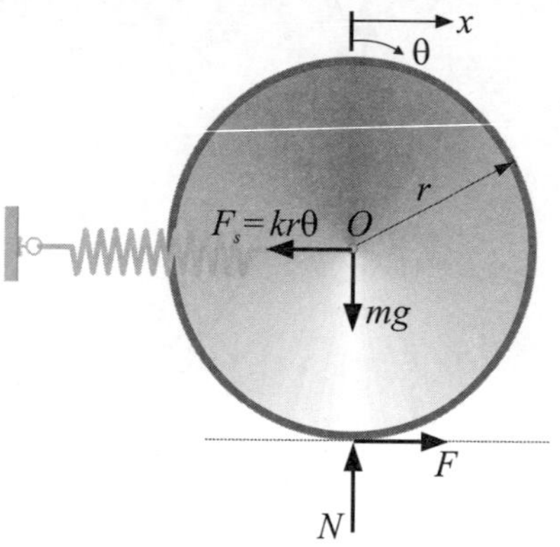

The free-body diagram of the cylinder is constructed for an arbitrary displacement x from the equilibrium position as shown in figure. The forces acting on the cylinder are its weight mg, reaction N, friction force F, and spring force $kx\,(=kr\theta)$.

The governing equations are:

$$\sum F_x = ma_x \quad \Rightarrow \quad -kx + F = m\ddot{x}$$

$$\sum F_y = 0 \quad \Rightarrow \quad mg = N$$

$$\sum M_o = I_o\ddot{\theta} \quad \Rightarrow \quad -Fr = I_o\ddot{\theta}$$

Eliminating F from above equations, we have

$$-kx + \frac{-I_o\ddot{\theta}}{r} = m\ddot{x}$$

or
$$-kr\theta + \frac{-I_o\ddot{\theta}}{r} = mr\ddot{\theta} \quad [x = r\theta]$$

On rearranging the terms, the equation becomes

$$\ddot{\theta} + \frac{kr^2}{(mr^2 + I_o)}\theta = 0$$

The natural frequency is determined from differential equation as:

$$\omega_n = \sqrt{\frac{kr^2}{(mr^2 + I_o)}}$$

or
$$\omega_n = \sqrt{\frac{kr^2}{mr^2 + \frac{1}{2}mr^2}} = \sqrt{\frac{2k}{3m}} \qquad \left[I_o = \frac{1}{2}mr^2\right]$$

$$\omega_n = \sqrt{\frac{2k}{3m}}$$

Energy Method

The figure shows the cylinder when it is displaced a small angle θ from the equilibrium. The kinetic energy and potential energy of the cylinder may be written as

$$\text{KE} = \frac{1}{2}m\dot{x}^2 + \frac{1}{2}I_o\dot{\theta}^2 \text{ and PE} = \frac{1}{2}kx^2$$

Total energy of the system is

$$\text{KE} + \text{PE} = \frac{1}{2}m\dot{x}^2 + \frac{1}{2}I_o\dot{\theta}^2 + \frac{1}{2}kx^2$$

Total energy of the system remains constant;

$$\frac{d}{dt}(\text{KE} + \text{PE}) = 0,$$

$$\frac{\text{d}}{\text{dt}}\left(\frac{1}{2}m\dot{x}^2 + \frac{1}{2}I_o\dot{\theta}^2 + \frac{1}{2}kx^2\right) = 0$$

or
$$m\dot{x}\ddot{x} + I_o\dot{\theta}\ddot{\theta} + kx\dot{x} = 0$$

x may be related by equation $x = r\theta$, so that $\dot{x} = r\dot{\theta}$ and $\ddot{x} = r\ddot{\theta}$. Hence above equation is reduced to the form:

$$mr^2\dot{\theta}\ddot{\theta} + I_o\dot{\theta}\ddot{\theta} + kr^2\theta\dot{\theta} = 0$$

or
$$\dot{\theta}\{(mr^2 + I_o)\ddot{\theta} + kr^2\theta\} = 0$$

Since the angular velocity $\dot{\theta}$ is not always zero,

$$(mr^2 + I_o)\ddot{\theta} + kr^2\theta = 0$$

or
$$\ddot{\theta} + \frac{kr^2}{mr^2 + I_o}\theta = 0$$

Hence,

$$\omega_n = \sqrt{\frac{kr^2}{mr^2 + I_o}} = \sqrt{\frac{kr^2}{mr^2 + \frac{1}{2}mr^2}} \qquad \left[I_o = \frac{1}{2}mr^2\right]$$

$$\omega_n = \sqrt{\frac{2k}{3m}}$$

Example 8.9

Consider a cantilever beam, having negligible mass and uniform flexural rigidity, with length 0.01 m. The frequency of vibration of the beam, with a 0.5 kg mass attached at the free tip, is 100 Hz. The flexural rigidity (in $\text{N} \cdot \text{m}^2$) of beam is ________.

GATE 2014

Solution

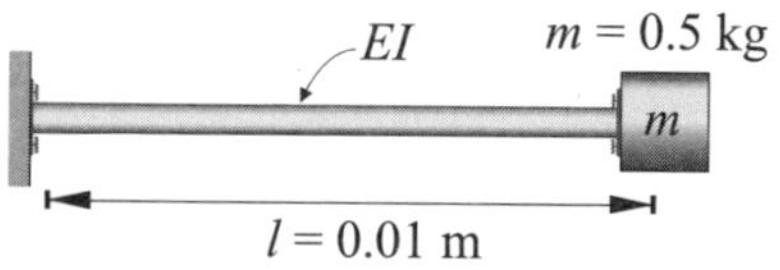

The deflection of cantilever at free end is given by

$$\Delta = \frac{Wl^3}{3EI}$$

Stiffness of cantilever beam is $k = \frac{W}{\Delta} = \frac{3EI}{l^3}$

Natural frequency of cantilever beam

$$\omega_n = \sqrt{\frac{k}{m}} = \sqrt{\frac{3EI}{ml^3}}$$

Flexural rigidity, $EI = \omega_n^2 \frac{ml^3}{3} = (2\pi f_n)^2 \frac{ml^3}{3}$

Substituting given data, gives

$$EI = (2\pi \times 100)^2 \times \frac{0.5 \times (0.01)^3}{3}$$

$$\text{Flexural rigidity, } EI = 0.0658 \text{ N}\cdot\text{m}^2$$

Example 8.10

Consider the system of two wagons shown in figure. The natural frequencies of this system are:

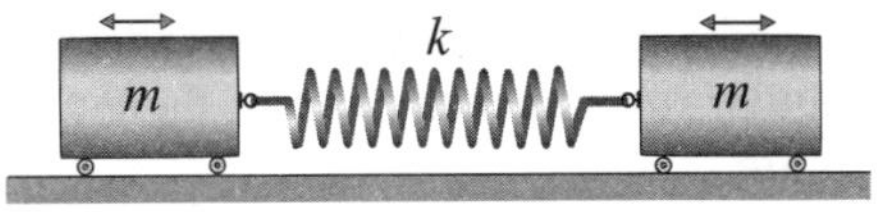

(A) $0, \sqrt{\frac{2k}{m}}$ (B) $\sqrt{\frac{k}{m}}, \sqrt{\frac{2k}{m}}$

(C) $\sqrt{\frac{k}{m}}, \sqrt{\frac{k}{2m}}$ (D) $0, \sqrt{\frac{k}{2m}}$

GATE 1999

Solution

Let l be the normal length of spring and let at any given instant the coordinate of the wagons be x_1 and x_2. Then the extension of spring,

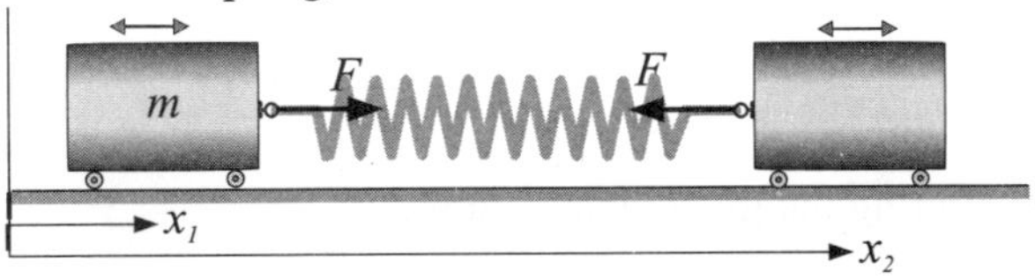

$$x = (x_2 - x_1) - l$$

The force F exerted by the spring on the two bodies are obviously equal in magnitude but opposite in sign, as indicated in the figure. magnitude of each being kx.

The equation of motions for the wagons A and B, respectively

$$\sum F = m\ddot{x}_1 \Rightarrow \text{F} = m\ddot{x}_1$$

or $kx = m\ddot{x}_1$ (i)

$$\sum F = m\ddot{x}_2 \Rightarrow F = m\ddot{x}_2$$

or $-kx = m\ddot{x}_2$ (ii)

Subtracting Equation (i) by equation (ii), we have

$$m(\ddot{x}_2 - \ddot{x}_1) = -2kx$$

or $(\ddot{x}_2 - \ddot{x}_1) + \frac{2k}{m}x = 0$

$[\text{since } x = (x_2 - x_1) - l \Rightarrow \ddot{x} = (\ddot{x}_2 - \ddot{x}_1)]$

or $\ddot{x} + \frac{2k}{m}x = 0$

This is single degree of freedom, therefore,

$$\omega_n = 0, \sqrt{\frac{2k}{m}}$$

Example 8.11

A mass M of 20 kg is attached to the free end of a steel cantilever beam of length 1000 mm having cross-section of $25 \times 25 \text{ mm}^2$. Assume the mass of the cantilever to be negligible and $E_{\text{steel}} = 200$ GPa. If the lateral vibration of this system is critically damped using a viscous damper, then damping coefficient of the damper is

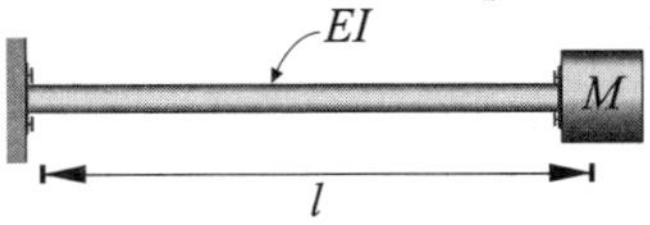

(A) 1250 Ns/m (B) 625 Ns/m

(C) 312.5 Ns/m (D) 156.25 Ns/m

GATE 2004

Solution

The deflection of the cantilever beam under a concentrated end force P is

$$\Delta = \frac{Pl^3}{3EI} = \frac{P}{k}$$

Where EI is the flexural rigidity. Thus the stiffness of the beam is $k = \frac{3EI}{l^3}$.

Figure shows the equivalent diagram of cantilever beam with viscous damping.

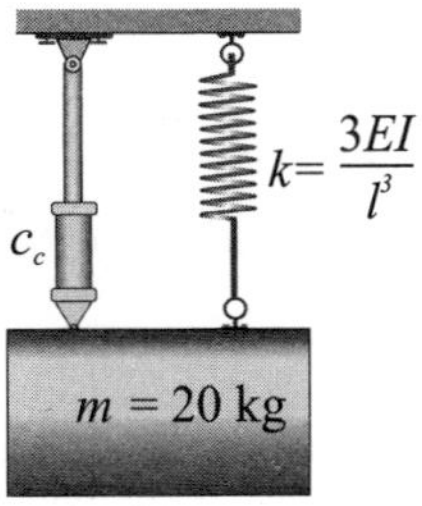

Critical damping coefficient

$$c_c = 2m\sqrt{\frac{k}{m}} = 2m\omega_n = 2\sqrt{km}$$

or $$c_c = 2\sqrt{\frac{3EI}{l^3}m} = \sqrt{\frac{Ebd^3m}{l^3}} \qquad \left[I = \frac{bd^3}{12}\right]$$

or $$c_c = \sqrt{\frac{200\times 10^9 \times \frac{25}{1000}\left(\frac{25}{1000}\right)^3 \times 20}{\left(\frac{1000}{1000}\right)^3}}$$

$$c_c = 1250 \text{ Ns/m}$$

Example 8.12

The differential equation governing the vibrating system is

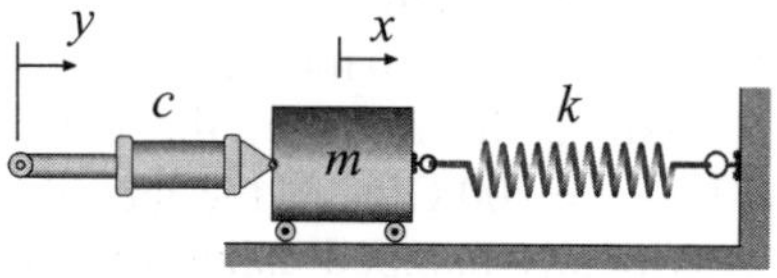

(A) $m\ddot{x} + c\dot{x} + k(x - y) = 0$

(B) $m(\ddot{x} - \ddot{y}) + c(\dot{x} - \dot{y}) + kx = 0$

(C) $m\ddot{x} + c(\dot{x} - \dot{y}) + kx = 0$

(D) $m(\ddot{x} - \ddot{y}) + c(\dot{x} - \dot{y}) + k(x - y) = 0$

GATE 2006

Solution

The free body diagram of mass when it is displaced by an arbitrary distance x is shown in figure.

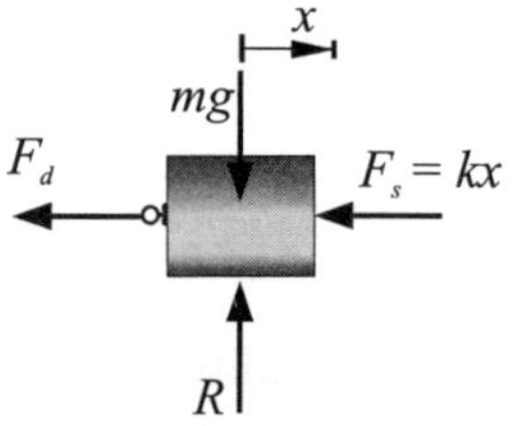

The equation of motion $\sum F = m\ddot{x}$, applied to the free body diagram, gives $m\ddot{x} = -F_s - F_d$;

Where spring force, $F_s = kx$ and damping force, $F_d = c(\dot{x} - \dot{y})$

From which

$$m\ddot{x} = -kx - c(\dot{x} - \dot{y})$$

$$m\ddot{x} + c(\dot{x} - \dot{y}) + kx = 0$$

Example 8.13

A uniform rigid slender bar of mass 10 kg, hinged at the left end is suspended with the help of spring and damper arrangement as shown in the figure. Where $k = 2$ kN/m, $c = 500$ Ns/m, and the stiffness of the torsional spring k_θ is 1.0 kN/m/rad. Ignore the hinge dimensions.

(a) The undamped natural frequency of oscillations of the bar about the hinge point is

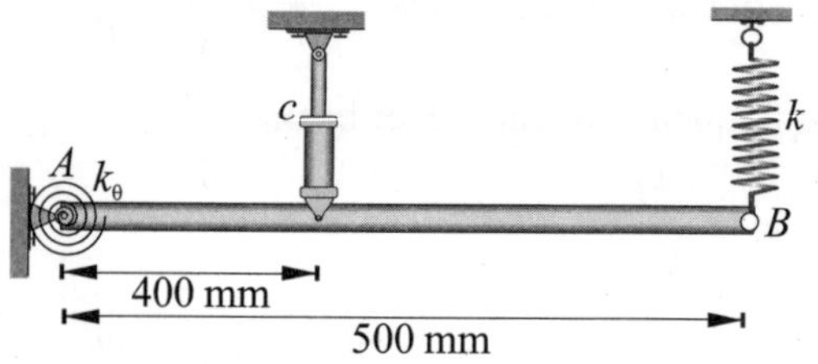

(A) 42.43 rad/s (B) 30 rad/s

(C) 17.32 rad/s (D) 14.14 rad/s

(b) The damping coefficient in the vibration equation is given by

(A) 500 Nms/rad (B) 500 N/ms

(C) 80 Nms/rad (D) 80 N/m/s

GATE 2003

Solution

(a) The free-body diagram of the rod is constructed for an arbitrary angular displacement θ from the equilibrium as shown in figure.

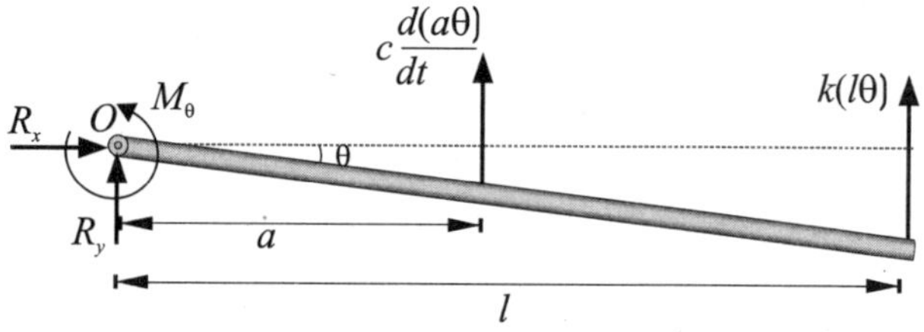

Summing moment about O; $\sum M_o = I_o\ddot{\theta}$

$$\frac{ml^2}{3}\frac{d^2\theta}{dt^2} = -kl\theta \times l - c\frac{d(a\theta)}{dt}a - k_\theta\theta$$

or $$\frac{d^2\theta}{dt^2} + \frac{3ca^2}{ml^2}\frac{d\theta}{dt} + \frac{3kl^2}{ml^2}\theta + \frac{3k_\theta}{ml^2}\theta = 0$$

Substituting the given data yields

$$\frac{d^2\theta}{dt^2} + \frac{3\times 500}{10}\times\left(\frac{400}{500}\right)^2\frac{d\theta}{dt} + \frac{3\times 2000}{10}\theta + \frac{3\times 1000}{10\times 0.5^2}\theta = 0$$

or $$\frac{d^2\theta}{dt^2} + 96\frac{d\theta}{dt} + 1800\,\theta = 0$$

From which

Undamped natural frequency, $\omega_n = \sqrt{1800}$

$$\omega_n = 42.42 \text{ rad/s}$$

(b) Summing moment about O, $\sum M_o = I_o\ddot{\theta}$

$$I_O\frac{d^2\theta}{dt^2} = -kl\theta \times l - c\frac{d(a\theta)}{dt}a - k_\theta\theta$$

or $$I_O \frac{d^2\theta}{dt^2} + ca^2\frac{d\theta}{dt} + (kl^2 + k_\theta)\theta = 0$$

Damping coefficient in the vibrating equation is given by

$$c_{eq} = ca^2$$

or $$c_{eq} = 500 \times 0.4^2$$

$$c_{eq} = 80 \text{ Nms/rad}$$

Example 8.14

In a spring-mass system, the mass is 0.1 kg and the stiffness of the spring is 1.0 kN/m. By introducing a damper, the frequency of oscillation is found to be 90% of the original value. What is the damping coefficient of the damper?

(A) 1.2 Ns/m (B) 3.4 Ns/m

(C) 8.7 Ns/m (D) 12.0 Ns/m

GATE 2005

Solution

Natural frequency is of spring-mass system is given by

$$\omega_n = \sqrt{\frac{k}{m}} \quad \text{or} \quad \omega_n = \sqrt{\frac{1000}{0.1}}$$

$$\omega_n = 100 \text{ rad/s}$$

Damped frequency of spring-mass damper system is given by

$$\omega_d = \omega_n\sqrt{1-\zeta^2}$$

or $$0.9\omega_n = \omega_n\sqrt{1-\zeta^2}$$

$$\zeta = 0.435$$

Damping ratio, $\zeta = \frac{c}{c_c} = \frac{c}{2\sqrt{mk}}$

$$\frac{c}{2\sqrt{0.1\times 1000}} = 0.435$$

From which

Damping coefficient, $c = 8.717$ Ns/m

Example 8.15

A vibrating system consists of a mass 12.5 kg, spring of stiffness 1000 Ns/m, and a dashpot with damping coefficient of 15 Ns/m.

(a) The value of critical damping of the system is

(A) 0.223 Ns/m (B) 17.88 Ns/m

(C) 71.4 Ns/m (D) 223.6 Ns/m

(b) The value of logarithmic decrement is

(A) 1.35 (B) 1.32 (C) 0.68 (D) 0.42

GATE 2006

Solution

(a) The critical damping coefficient is given by

$$c_c = 2\sqrt{mk}$$

Substituting given data yields, $c_c = 2\sqrt{12.5\times 1000}$

$$c_c = 223.6 \text{ Ns/m}$$

(b) Logarithmic decrement δ is

$$\delta = \ln\frac{x_1}{x_2} = \zeta\omega_n t_d$$

$$= \zeta\omega_n \times \frac{2\pi}{\omega_n\sqrt{1-\zeta^2}}$$

or $$\delta = \frac{2\pi\zeta}{\sqrt{1-\zeta^2}}$$

Substituting the value of damping factor,

$$\zeta = \frac{c}{2\sqrt{mk}} = \frac{15}{2\sqrt{12.5\times 1000}} = 0.06708, \text{ we have}$$

$$\delta = \frac{2\pi\times 0.06708}{\sqrt{1-0.06708^2}}$$

$$\delta = 0.422$$

Example 8.16

The equation of motion of a harmonic oscillator is given by

$$\frac{d^2x}{dt^2} + 2\zeta\omega_n\frac{dx}{dt} + \omega_n^2 x = 0$$

and the initial conditions at $t = 0$ are $x(0) = X$, $\frac{dx}{dt}(0) = 0$.

The amplitude of $x(t)$ after n complete cycle is

(A) $Xe^{-2\pi n\frac{\zeta}{\sqrt{1-\zeta^2}}}$ (B) $Xe^{2\pi n\frac{\zeta}{\sqrt{1-\zeta^2}}}$

(C) $Xe^{-2\pi n\frac{\sqrt{1-\zeta^2}}{\zeta}}$ (D) $Xe^{2\pi n\frac{\sqrt{1-\zeta^2}}{\zeta}}$

GATE 2007

Solution

Equation of motion of a harmonic oscillator is

$$\frac{d^2x}{dt^2} + 2\zeta\omega_n\frac{dx}{dt} + \omega_n^2 x = 0$$

Solution of above equation

$$x = ce^{-\zeta\omega_n t}\sin(\sqrt{1-\zeta^2}\,\omega_n t + \phi)$$

Applying initial conditions: (i) $t = 0$, $x(0) = X$, and (ii) $t = 0$, $\frac{dx}{dt} = 0$, we obtain

$$x = Xe^{-\zeta\omega_n t}\sin(\sqrt{1-\zeta^2}\,\omega_n t)$$

If x_1 and x_2 are amplitude of first and second oscillations, then

$$\frac{x_1}{x_2} = \frac{Xe^{-\zeta\omega_n t}\sin(\sqrt{1-\zeta^2}\,\omega_n t)}{Xe^{-\zeta\omega_n (t+t_p)}\sin\{\sqrt{1-\zeta^2}\,\omega_n (t+t_p)\}}$$

where $t_p = \dfrac{2\pi}{\omega_n\sqrt{1-\zeta^2}}$

or $\dfrac{x_1}{x_2} = e^{\zeta\omega_n t_p}$

Similarly, $\dfrac{x_1}{x_2} = \dfrac{x_2}{x_3} = \dfrac{x_3}{x_4} = \ldots = \dfrac{x_n}{x_{n+1}} = e^{\zeta\omega_n t_p}$

Therefore, $\dfrac{x_1}{x_{n+1}} = e^{\zeta\omega_n t_p n} = e^{\zeta\omega_n \frac{2\pi}{\omega_n\sqrt{1-\zeta^2}} n}$

$$x_{n+1} = x_1 e^{-\frac{2\pi\zeta n}{\sqrt{1-\zeta^2}}}$$

Thus, the amplitude of $x(t)$ after n complete cycle is

$$x(t) = \mathrm{X}\,e^{-\frac{2\pi\zeta n}{\sqrt{1-\zeta^2}}}$$

Example 8.17

A vehicle suspension system consists of a spring and a damper. The stiffness of the spring is 3.6 kN/m and the damping constant of the damper is 400 Ns/m. If the mass is 50 kg, the damping factor ζ and damped natural frequency (f_n), respectively, are:

(A) 0.471 and 1.19 Hz (B) 0.471 and 7.48 Hz

(C) 0.666 and 1.35 Hz (D) 0.666 and 8.50 Hz

GATE 2009

Solution

The damping factor is

$$\zeta = \frac{c}{2\sqrt{mk}}$$

Substituting given values, $\zeta = \dfrac{c}{c_c} = \dfrac{400}{2\sqrt{50\times 3.6\times 10^3}}$

or $\zeta = 0.471$

Damped natural frequency, $\omega_d = \sqrt{\dfrac{k}{m}}\sqrt{1-\zeta^2}$

or $\omega_d = \sqrt{\dfrac{3.6\times 10^3}{50}}\sqrt{1-(0.471)^2}$

or $\omega_d = 2\pi f_d = 7.48$ rad/s

From which

$$f_d = 1.19\text{ Hz}$$

Example 8.18

A mass m attached to a spring is subjected to a harmonic force as shown in figure. The amplitude of the forced motion is observed to be 50 mm. The value of m (in kg) is

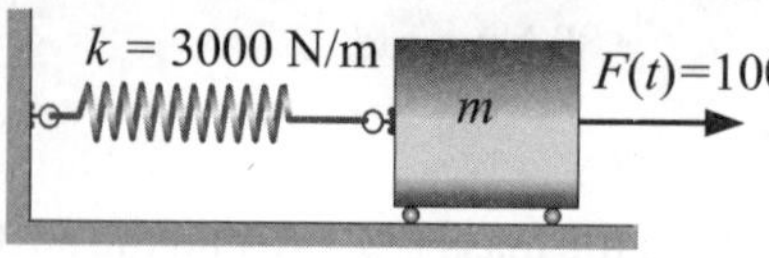

(A) 0.1 (B) 1.0 (C) 0.3 (D) 0.5

GATE 2010

Solution

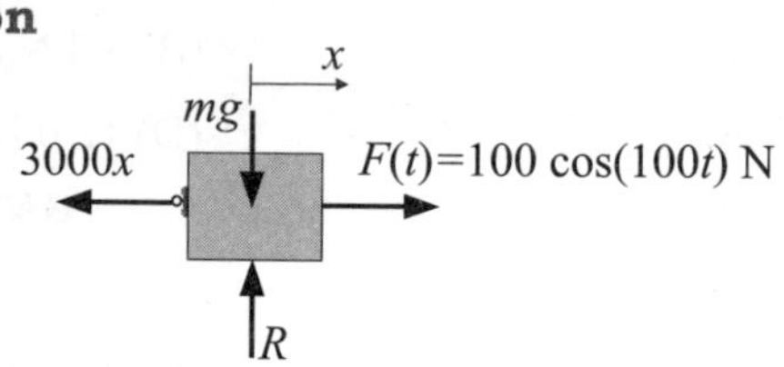

The equation of motion for the body of figure is obtained by first drawing its free body diagram. Newton's second law gives:

$$-3000x + 100\cos(100t) = m\frac{d^2x}{dt^2}$$

or $\dfrac{d^2x}{dt^2} + \dfrac{3000}{m}x = \dfrac{100}{m}\cos(100t)$

Amplitude of periodic vibration, $X = \dfrac{\frac{100}{m}}{\frac{3000}{m} - 100^2}$

Substituting, $X = \dfrac{50}{1000}$ m, gives

$$\frac{50}{1000} = \frac{\frac{100}{m}}{\frac{3000}{m} - 100^2}$$

From which

$$m = 0.1\text{ kg}$$

Example 8.19

A machine of 250 kg mass is supported on springs of total stiffness 100 kN/m. Machine has an unbalanced rotating force of 350 N at speed of 3600 rpm. Assuming a damping factor of 0.15, the value of transmissibility ratio is

(A) 0.0531 (B) 0.9922 (C) 0.0162 (D) 0.0028

GATE 2006

Solution

The transmissibility ratio is given by

$$TR = \left|\frac{F_T}{F_0}\right| = \frac{\sqrt{1+\left(2\zeta\frac{\omega}{\omega_n}\right)^2}}{\sqrt{\left(1-\left(\frac{\omega}{\omega_n}\right)^2\right)^2+\left[2\zeta\left(\frac{\omega}{\omega_n}\right)\right]^2}}$$

Substituting $\zeta = 0.15$, $\omega_n = \sqrt{\frac{k}{m}} = \sqrt{\frac{100\times10^3}{250}} = 20$ and $\omega = \frac{2\pi\times3600}{60} = 376.99$, gives

Transmissibility ratio,

$$TR = \frac{\sqrt{1+\left(2\times0.15\times\frac{376.99}{20}\right)^2}}{\sqrt{\left(1-\left(\frac{376.99}{20}\right)^2\right)^2+\left[2\times0.15\times\left(\frac{376.99}{20}\right)\right]^2}}$$

$$TR = 0.0162$$

Example 8.20

A proper base isolation is to be designed for mounting a sensitive instrument as shown in the figure. At the point of mounting, the base vibration due to other disturbances is indicated in the figure. If the permitted absolute displacement amplitude on the rigid mounting pad is 0.001 mm, find the stiffness of the spring. Assume the total mass of the mounting pad and the instrument is 50 kg.

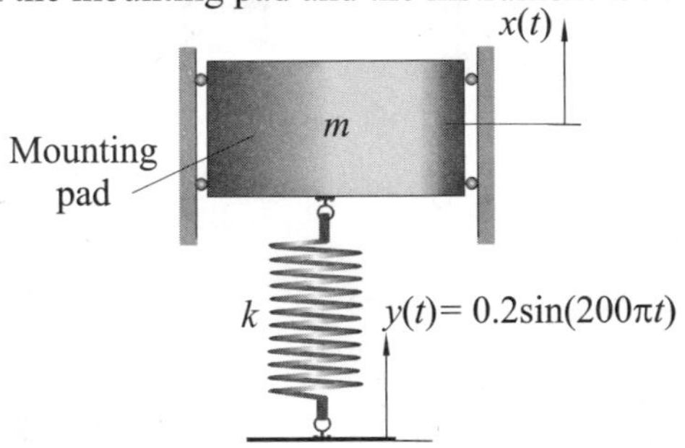

GATE 1999

Solution

The equation of motion for the body

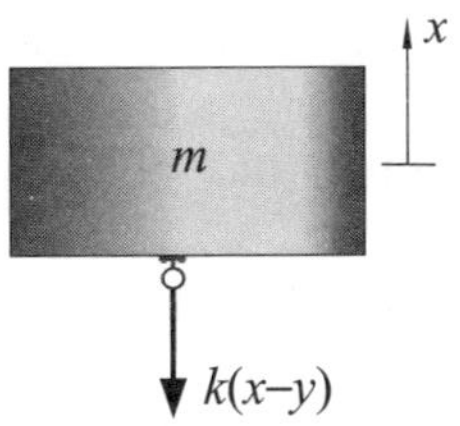

$$m\frac{d^2x}{dt^2} = -k(x-y)$$

or $$\frac{d^2x}{dt^2} + \frac{k}{m}x = \frac{k}{m}y$$

or $$\frac{d^2x}{dt^2} + \frac{k}{m}x = \frac{k}{m}0.2\sin(200\pi t)$$

The amplitude of periodic vibrations is

$$X = \frac{\frac{k}{m}\times\frac{0.2}{1000}}{\frac{k}{m}-(200\pi)^2}$$

or $$\frac{0.001}{1000} = \frac{\frac{k}{50}\times\frac{0.2}{1000}}{\frac{k}{50}-(200\pi)^2}$$

From which

$$k = 99.19\text{ kN/m}$$

Example 8.21

A single degree of freedom spring mass system with viscous damping has a spring constant of 10 kN/m. The system is excited by a sinusoidal force of amplitude 100 N. If the damping factor (ratio) is 0.25, the amplitude of steady state oscillation at resonance is ____mm.

GATE 2016

Solution

Amplitude of forced-damped vibration is given by

$$X = \frac{F_0/k}{\sqrt{\left(1-\left(\frac{\omega}{\omega_n}\right)^2\right)^2+\left[2\zeta\left(\frac{\omega}{\omega_n}\right)\right]^2}}$$

At resonance, $\omega = \omega_n$;

$$X = \frac{F_0/k}{2\zeta} = \frac{100/10\times10^3}{2\times0.25} = 0.02\text{ m}$$

$$X = 20\text{ mm}$$

Example 8.22

A solid disc with radius a is connected to a spring at a point d above the center of the disk. The other end of the spring is fixed to the vertical wall. The disc is free to roll without slipping on the ground. The mass of the disc is M and the spring constant is k. The polar moment of inertia for the disc about its centre is $J = \frac{Ma^2}{2}$. The natural frequency of this system in rad/s is given by

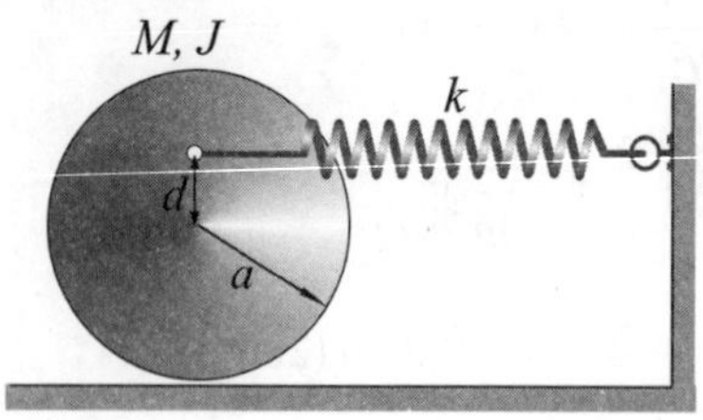

(A) $\sqrt{\dfrac{2k(a+d)^2}{3Ma^2}}$ (B) $\sqrt{\dfrac{2k}{3M}}$

(C) $\sqrt{\dfrac{2k(a+d)^2}{Ma^2}}$ (D) $\sqrt{\dfrac{k(a+d)^2}{Ma^2}}$

GATE 2016

Solution

Figure shows the free-body diagram of disc when it is displaced θ from equilibrium. Moment equation about O is

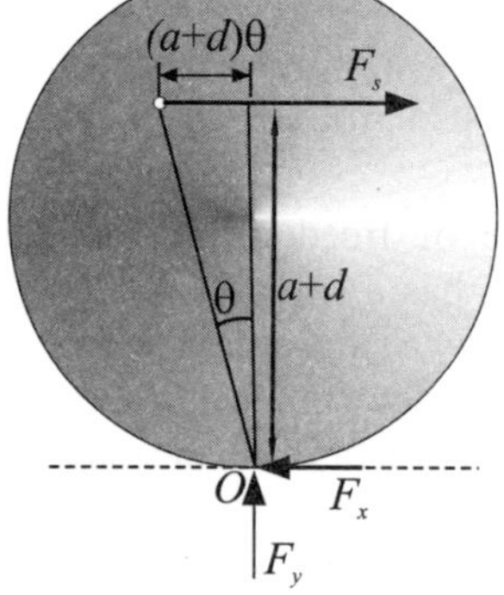

$$I_O \frac{d^2\theta}{dt^2} = -F_s \times (a+d)$$

or $$I_O \frac{d^2\theta}{dt^2} = -k(a+d)\theta \times (a+d)$$

or $$\frac{d^2\theta}{dt^2} + \frac{k(a+d)^2}{I_O}\theta = 0$$

Natural frequency,

$$\omega_n = \sqrt{\frac{k(a+d)^2}{I_O}} = \sqrt{\frac{k(a+d)^2}{\frac{1}{2}Ma^2}}$$

$$\omega_n = \sqrt{\frac{2k(a+d)^2}{Ma^2}}$$

Example 8.23

A single degree of freedom mass-spring-viscous damper system with mass m, spring constant k and viscous damping coefficient c is critically damped. The correct relation among m, k, and c is

(A) $c = \sqrt{2km}$ (B) $c = 2\sqrt{km}$

(C) $c = \sqrt{\dfrac{2k}{m}}$ (D) $c = 2\sqrt{\dfrac{k}{m}}$

GATE 2016

Solution

Damping factor, $$\zeta = \frac{c}{2m\omega_n}$$

Critically damped, $$\zeta = 1 \Rightarrow \frac{c}{2m\omega_n} = 1$$

or $$c = 2m\omega_n = 2m\sqrt{\frac{k}{m}}$$

$$c = 2\sqrt{mk}$$

Example 8.24

The system shown in the figure consists of block A of mass 5 kg connected to a spring through a massless rope passing over pulley B of radius r and mass 20 kg. The spring constant k is 1500 N/m. If there is no slipping of the rope over the pulley, the natural frequency of the system is_____ rad/s.

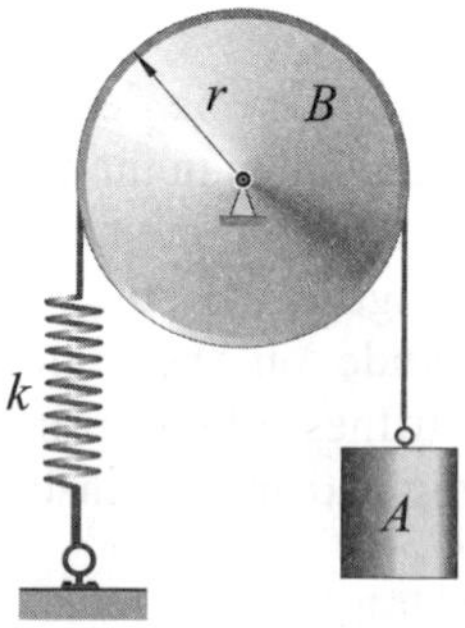

GATE 2016

Solution

Let T be the tension in the rope and x and θ be the displacements of the mass and pulley respectively from the static equilibrium position as shown in figure.

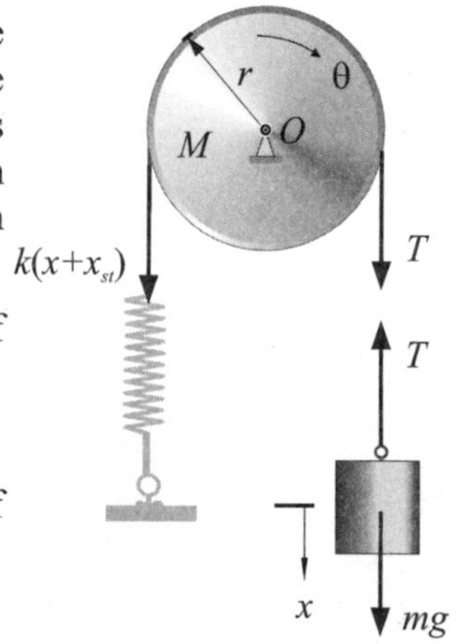

The equation of motion of the mass is

$$mg - T = m\ddot{x}$$

The equation of motion of the pulley is

$$Tr - k(x + x_{st})r = I_O\ddot{\theta}$$

Eliminating T from above equations, we have

$$mg - k(x + x_{st}) = \frac{I_O}{r}\ddot{\theta} + m\ddot{x}$$

or $$mg - k(x + x_{st}) = \frac{I_O}{r^2}\ddot{x} + m\ddot{x} \qquad \left[\ddot{\theta} = \frac{\ddot{x}}{r}\right]$$

Under the static equilibrium; $mg = kx_{st}$, the equation reduces to:

$$\left(\frac{I_O}{r^2} + m\right)\ddot{x} = -kx$$

or $$\ddot{x} + \frac{k}{\left(\frac{I_O}{r^2} + m\right)}x = 0$$

So that

$$\omega_n = \sqrt{\frac{k}{\left(\frac{I_O}{r^2} + m\right)}} = \sqrt{\frac{2k}{(M + 2m)}} \qquad \left[I_O = \frac{1}{2}Mr^2\right]$$

Substituting $k = 1500$ N/m, $m = 5$ kg, $M = 20$ kg, we get

$$\omega_n == \sqrt{\frac{2 \times 1500}{(20 + 2 \times 5)}} = 10$$

$$\omega_n = 10 \text{ rad/s}$$

Example 8.25

The static deflection of a spring under gravity, when a mass of 1 kg is suspended from it, is 1 mm. Assume the acceleration due to gravity g = 10 m/s^2. The natural frequency of this spring-mass system (in rad/s) is_____.

GATE 2016

Solution

Natural frequency of spring mass system is

$$\omega_n = \sqrt{\frac{k}{m}}$$

Under static equilibrium;

$$mg = k\Delta \qquad \text{or} \qquad \frac{k}{m} = \frac{g}{\Delta}$$

$$\omega_n = \sqrt{\frac{k}{m}} = \sqrt{\frac{g}{\Delta}} = \sqrt{\frac{10}{1/1000}}$$

$$\omega_n = 100 \text{ rad/s}$$

Example 8.26

A single degree of freedom spring-mass system is subjected to a harmonic force of constant amplitude. For an excitation frequency of $\sqrt{\frac{3k}{m}}$, the ratio of the amplitude of steady state response to the static deflection of the spring is___.

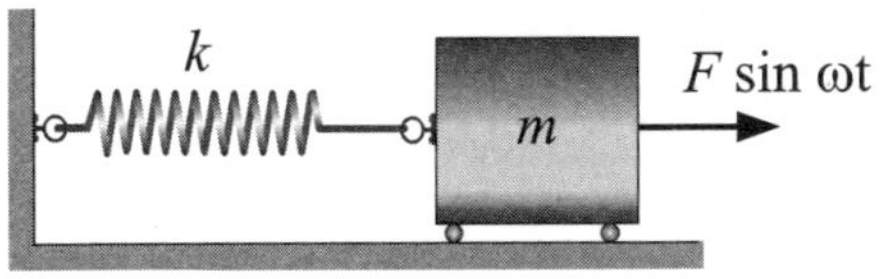

GATE 2016

Solution

The equation of motion for the body of figure is obtained by first drawing its free body diagram. Newton's second law gives

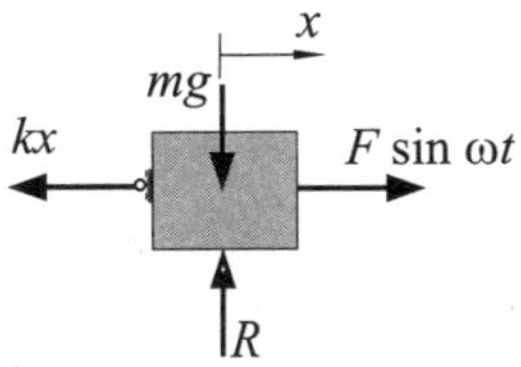

$$m\frac{d^2x}{dt^2} = -kx + F\sin\omega t$$

or $$\frac{d^2x}{dt^2} + \frac{k}{m}x = \frac{F}{m}\sin\omega t)$$

Amplitude of periodic vibration, $X = \left|\frac{\frac{F}{m}}{\frac{k}{m} - \omega^2}\right|$

Substituting excitation frequency, $\omega = \sqrt{\frac{3k}{m}}$ and

$$X = \left|\frac{\frac{F}{m}}{\frac{k}{m} - \left(\sqrt{\frac{3k}{m}}\right)^2}\right|$$

or $$X = 0.5\left(\frac{F}{k}\right)$$

or $$X = 0.5\,X_{st}$$

$$\frac{X}{X_{st}} = 0.5$$

Example 8.27

The damping ratio for a viscously damped spring mass system, governed by the relationship $m\frac{d^2x}{dt^2} + c\frac{dx}{dt} + kx = F(t)$, is given by

(A) $\sqrt{\frac{c}{mk}}$ (B) $\frac{c}{2\sqrt{mk}}$ (C) $\frac{c}{\sqrt{mk}}$ (D) $\frac{c}{\sqrt{2mk}}$

GATE 2017

Solution

Damping ratio $\zeta = \frac{c}{c_c} = \frac{c}{2\sqrt{mk}}$

$$\zeta = \frac{c}{2\sqrt{mk}}$$

Example 8.28

A thin uniform rigid bar of length L and mass M is hinged at point O, located at a distance of $\frac{L}{3}$ from one of its ends. The bar is further supported using springs, each of stiffness k, located at the two ends. A particle of mass $m = \frac{M}{4}$ is fixed at one end of the bar, as shown in the figure. For small rotations of the bar about O, the natural frequency of the systems is

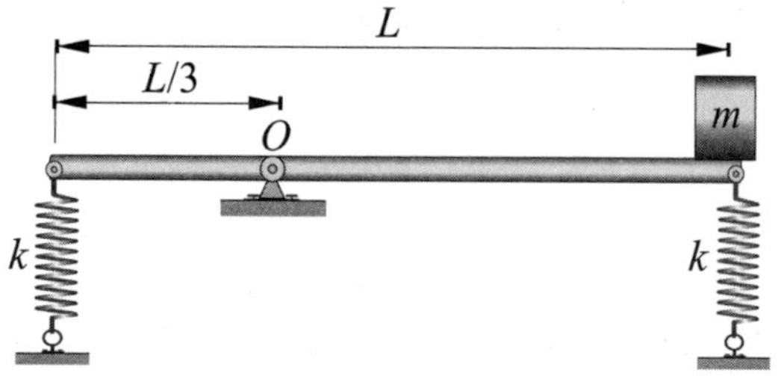

(A) $\sqrt{\frac{5k}{M}}$ (B) $\sqrt{\frac{5k}{2M}}$ (C) $\sqrt{\frac{3k}{2M}}$ (D) $\sqrt{\frac{3k}{M}}$

GATE 2017

Solution

Moment of inertia of system (rod and particle) about O

$$I_o = [I_G + Mh^2] + m\left(\frac{2L}{3}\right)^2$$

or $$I_o = \left[\frac{ML^2}{12} + M\left(\frac{L}{2} - \frac{L}{3}\right)^2\right] + \frac{M}{4}\left(\frac{2L}{3}\right)^2$$

$$I_o = \frac{2ML^2}{9}$$

The rod is displaced by a small angular displacement θ from the equilibrium position shown in figure.

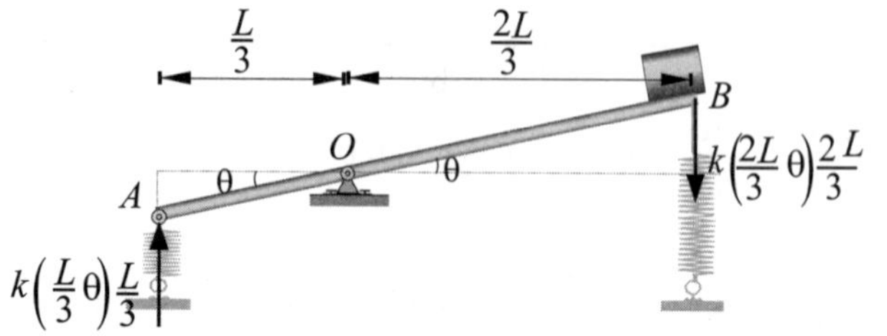

Moment equation about O is

$$\frac{2ML^2}{9}\frac{d^2\theta}{dt^2} = -k\left(\frac{L}{3}\theta\right)\frac{L}{3} - k\left(\frac{2L}{3}\theta\right)\frac{2L}{3}$$

$$\frac{d^2\theta}{dt^2} + \frac{5k}{2M}\theta = 0$$

Thus, the natural frequency

$$\omega_n = \sqrt{\frac{5k}{2M}}$$

Example 8.29

A mass m is attached to two identical springs having spring constant k as shown in the figure. The natural frequency ω of this single degree of freedom system is

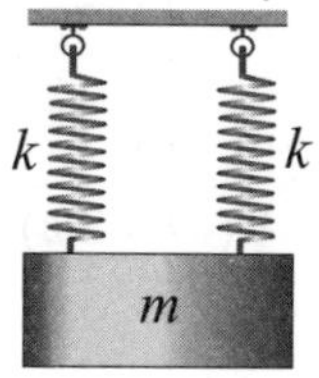

(A) $\sqrt{\frac{2k}{m}}$ (B) $\sqrt{\frac{k}{m}}$ (C) $\sqrt{\frac{k}{2m}}$ (D) $\sqrt{\frac{4k}{m}}$

GATE 2017

Solution

Equivalent stiffness $k_{eq} = k + k = 2k$

Natural frequency $\omega = \sqrt{\frac{k_{eq}}{m}}$

$$\omega = \sqrt{\frac{2k}{m}}$$

Example 8.30

The radius of gyration of a compound pendulum about the point of suspension is 100 mm. The distance between the point of suspension and the centre of mass is 250 mm. Considering the acceleration due to gravity as 9.81 m/s^2, the natural frequency (in radian/s) of the compound pendulum is______.

GATE 2017

Solution

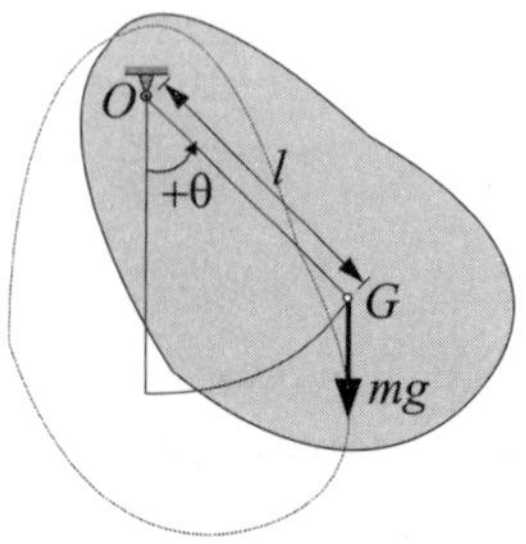

Natural frequency of compound pendulum,

$$\omega = \sqrt{\frac{mgl}{I_o}} = \sqrt{\frac{mgl}{I_G + ml^2}} = \sqrt{\frac{mgl}{mk^2 + ml^2}}$$

Substituting $k = 0.1$ m, $l = 0.250$ m and $g = 9.81$ m/s^2

$$\omega = \sqrt{\frac{g}{\frac{k^2}{l} + l}} = \sqrt{\frac{9.81}{\frac{0.1^2}{0.250} + 0.250}} = 5.81$$

$$\omega = 5.81 \text{ rad/s}$$

Example 8.31

The equation of motion for a spring-mass system excited by a harmonic force is

$$m\ddot{x} + kx = F\cos(\omega t)$$

where m is the mass, k is the spring stiffness, F is the force amplitude and ω is the angular frequency of excitation. Resonance occurs when ω is equal to

(A) $\sqrt{\frac{m}{k}}$ (B) $\frac{1}{2\pi}\sqrt{\frac{k}{m}}$ (C) $2\pi\sqrt{\frac{k}{m}}$ (D) $\sqrt{\frac{k}{m}}$

GATE 2018

Solution

Natural frequency of given system $\omega_n = \sqrt{\frac{k}{m}}$

Resonance occurs at frequency $\omega = \omega_n$

$$\omega = \sqrt{\frac{k}{m}}$$

Example 8.32

A machine of mass $m = 200$ kg is supported on two mounts, each of stiffness $k = 10$ kN/m. The machine is subjected to an external force (in N) $F(t) = 50\cos 5t$. Assuming only vertical translatory motion, the magnitude of the dynamic force (in N) transmitted from each mount to the ground is______.

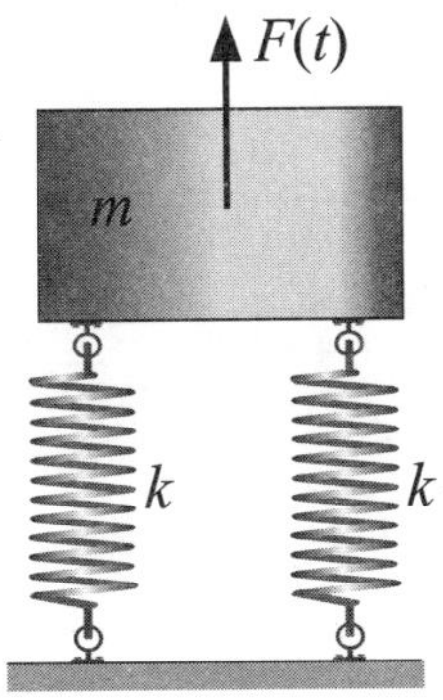

GATE 2018

Solution

Transmissibility, $$\frac{F_T}{F_o} = \frac{\sqrt{1 + \left(2\zeta\frac{\omega}{\omega_n}\right)^2}}{\sqrt{\left[1 - \left(\frac{\omega}{\omega_n}\right)^2\right]^2 + \left(2\zeta\frac{\omega}{\omega_n}\right)^2}}$$

Substituting $\omega = 5$ rad/s, $\zeta = 0\,(c = 0)$, $F_0 = 50$ N and Natural frequency $\omega_n = \sqrt{\frac{k_{eq}}{m}} = \sqrt{\frac{(10+10)\times 1000}{200}} = 10$ rad/s.

Transmissibility, $$\frac{F_T}{50} = \frac{1}{1 - \left(\frac{5}{10}\right)^2}$$

or $F_T = 66.6$ N

Force transmitted from each mount $\frac{F_T}{2} = 33.3$ N

Example 8.33

In a single degree of freedom underdamped spring-mass -damper system as shown in the figure, an additional damper is added in parallel such that the system still remains underdamped. Which one of the following statements is ALWAYS true?

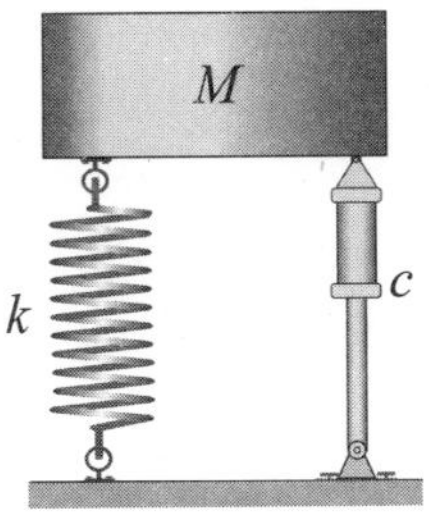

(A) Transmissibility will increase.

(B) Transmissibility will decrease.

(C) Time period of free oscillations will increase.

(D) Time period of free oscillations will decrease.

GATE 2018

Solution

Given system is damped free vibration. Transmissibility will neither increase nor decrease.

Time period $T_d = \frac{2\pi}{\omega_d} = \frac{2\pi}{\omega_n\sqrt{1-\zeta^2}}$, where $\zeta = \frac{c}{c_c}$

Additional damper is added into parallel.

Then damping coefficient (c) will increase, but it is still under damped ($\zeta < 1$).

As ζ increases then $\omega_n\sqrt{1-\zeta^2}$ will decrease.

Time period $T_d = \dfrac{2\pi}{\omega_n\sqrt{1-\zeta^2}}$ will increase.

Example 8.34

The natural frequencies corresponding to the spring-mass systems I and II are ω_I and ω_{II}, respectively. The ratio $\dfrac{\omega_I}{\omega_{II}}$ is

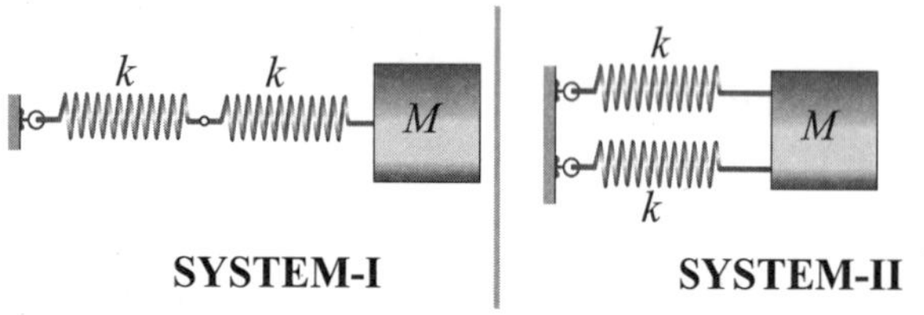

(A) $\dfrac{1}{4}$ (B) $\dfrac{1}{2}$ (C) 2 (D) 4

GATE 2019

Solution

Equivalent spring coefficient of system-I and system-II;

$$k_I = \frac{kk}{k+k} = \frac{k}{2} \text{ and } k_{II} = k + k = 2k$$

Natural frequency of system-I; $\omega_I = \sqrt{\dfrac{k_I}{m}} = \sqrt{\dfrac{k}{2m}}$

Natural frequency of system-II; $\omega_{II} = \sqrt{\dfrac{k_{II}}{m}} = \sqrt{\dfrac{2k}{m}}$

Thus, natural frequencies ratio; $\dfrac{\omega_I}{\omega_{II}} = \sqrt{\dfrac{k}{2m}} \times \sqrt{\dfrac{m}{2k}} = \dfrac{1}{\sqrt{4}}$

$$\frac{\omega_I}{\omega_{II}} = \frac{1}{2}$$

Example 8.35

A uniform thin disk of mass 1 kg and radius 0.1 m is kept on a surface as shown in the figure. A spring of stiffness $k_1 = 400$ N/m is connected to the disk center A and another spring of stiffness $k_2 = 100$ N/m is connected at point B just above point A on the circumference of the disk. Initially, both the springs are unstretched. Assume pure rolling of the disk. For small disturbance from the equilibrium, the natural frequency of vibration of the system is ______ rad/s (round off to one decimal place)

GATE 2019

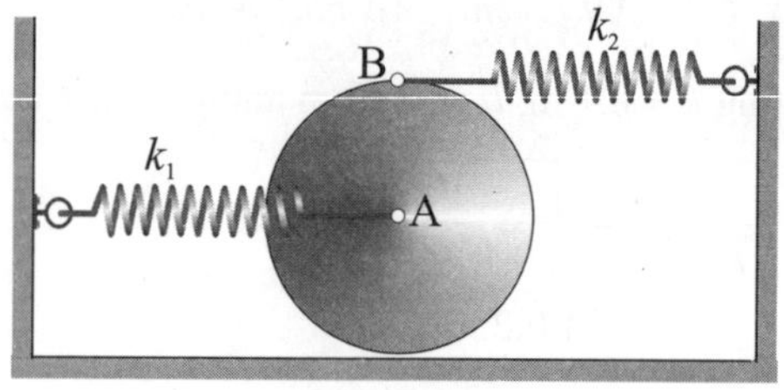

Solution

The disc is displaced by small angular displacement θ from equilibrium position as shown in figure.

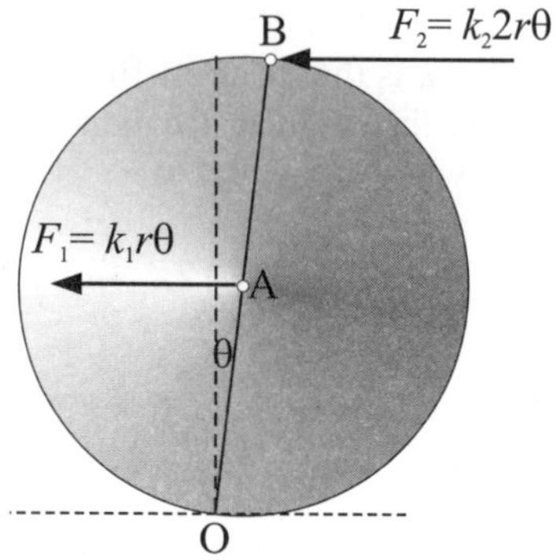

Moment equation about O is

$$I_o \frac{d^2\theta}{dt^2} = -F_1 \times r - F_2 \times 2r$$

$$\left[\frac{3}{2}mr^2\right]\frac{d^2\theta}{dt^2} = -k_1 r\theta \times r - k_2 2r\theta \times 2r$$

or $$\left[\frac{3}{2}mr^2\right]\frac{d^2\theta}{dt^2} = -(k_1 + 4k_2)r^2\theta$$

or $$\frac{d^2\theta}{dt^2} + \frac{2(k_1 + 4k_2)}{3m}\theta = 0$$

Natural frequency, $\omega_n = \sqrt{\dfrac{2(k_1 + 4k_2)}{3m}}$

$$\omega_n = \sqrt{\frac{2(400 + 4 \times 100)}{3 \times 1}} = 23.1$$

$$\omega_n = 23.1 \text{ rad/s}$$

Example 8.36

A slender uniform rigid bar of mass m is hinged at O and supported by two springs, with stiffness $3k$ and k, and a damper with damping coefficient c, as shown in the figure.

For the system to be critically damped, the ratio $c/\sqrt{km}$ should be

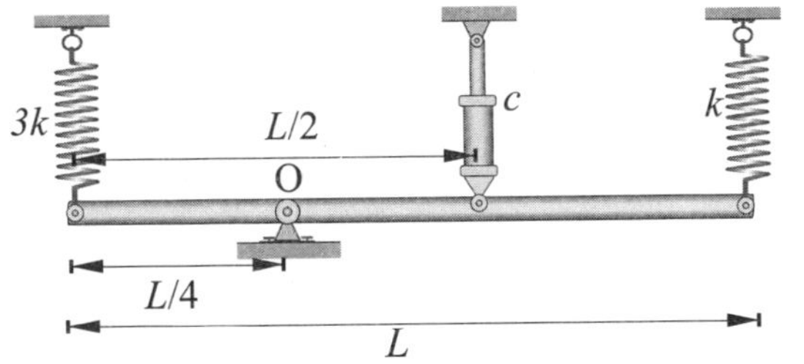

(A) 2 (B) 4 (C) $2\sqrt{7}$ (D) $4\sqrt{7}$

GATE 2019

Solution

The free body diagram of the rod is constructed for an arbitrary angular displacement θ from the equilibrium as shown in figure.

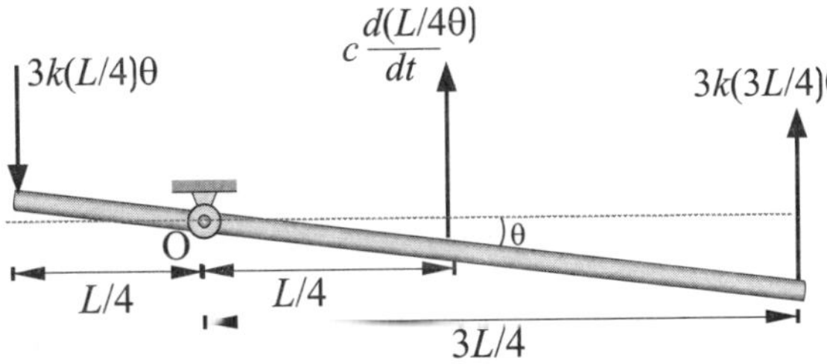

Moment equation about O is

$$I_o \frac{d^2\theta}{dt^2} = -3k\left(\frac{L}{4}\theta\right)\times\frac{L}{4} - c\frac{d}{dt}\left(\frac{L}{4}\theta\right)\times\frac{L}{4} - k\left(\frac{3L}{4}\theta\right)\times\frac{3L}{4}$$

or $$\frac{7}{48}mL^2\frac{d^2\theta}{dt^2} = -\frac{3kL^2}{4\times4}\theta - c\frac{d\theta}{dt}\times\frac{L^2}{4\times4} - \frac{9kL^2}{4\times4}\theta$$

or $$m\frac{d^2\theta}{dt^2} + \frac{3}{7}c\frac{d\theta}{dt} + \frac{36}{7}k\theta = 0$$

For critically damped system $[b^2 - 4ac = 0]$

$$\left(\frac{3}{7}c\right)^2 = 4m\times\frac{36}{7}k \Rightarrow \frac{c}{\sqrt{mk}} = \sqrt{\frac{4\times36}{7}\times\left(\frac{7}{3}\right)^2} = 4\sqrt{7}$$

$$\frac{c}{\sqrt{mk}} = 4\sqrt{7}$$

8.3 PRACTICE PAPER

Time: 3 hours **Max. Marks:100**

Q.1 to Q.30 carry one mark each

Q.1 to Q.20 Multiple Choice Questions

Q.1 A particle oscillates on the x-axis according to the equation $x = a + b\sin\omega t$. The amplitude of motion is

(A) a (B) b (C) $a+b$ (D) $\sqrt{a^2+b^2}$

Q.2 Displacement of body (in free damped system) from mean position is given by $x = 0.02e^{-5t}\sin(25t + \pi/3)$. Damping factor of system is

(A) 0.19 (B) 0.29 (C) 0.39 (D) None of these

Q.3 A block of 10 kg mass is suspended from spring with spring constant 1 kN/m. The block is pulled down by 10 cm and released. The maximum velocity (in m/s) of block is

(A) 0.2 (B) 1 (C) 5 (D) 10

Q.4 For small oscillations, the natural frequency of the system in terms of k, a, b and m is (assuming ideal joints and mass-less rigid rod ABC)

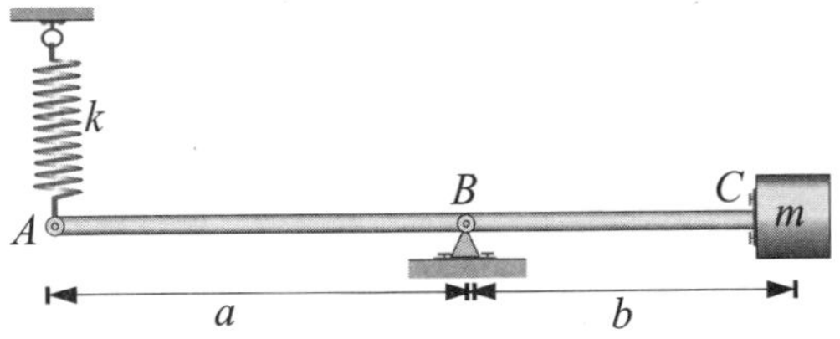

(A) $\sqrt{\frac{k}{m}}$ (B) $\sqrt{\frac{ka}{mb}}$ (C) $\sqrt{\frac{kb^2}{ma^2}}$ (D) $\sqrt{\frac{ka^2}{mb^2}}$

Q.5 The differential equation of motion for the system shown in the figure is

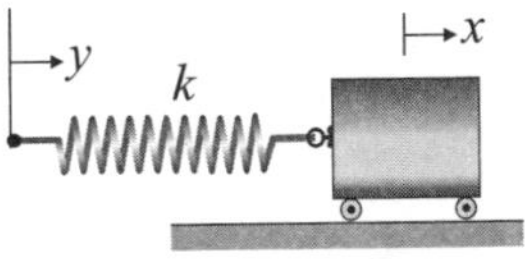

(A) $m\frac{d^2x}{dt^2} + kx = ky$ (B) $m\left(\frac{d^2x}{dt^2} - \frac{d^2y}{dt^2}\right) + kx = 0$

(C) $m\frac{d^2x}{dt^2} + ky = 0$ (D) $m\frac{d^2x}{dt^2} + kx = 0$

Q.6 A free damped vibration system with viscous damping consists of a mass m, spring stiffness k and a damper with a damping coefficient which can be varied. The natural frequency of the system is ω_n. For the system to be critically damped, the damping coefficient c_c is

(A) $2m\omega_n$ (B) $m\omega_n$ (C) $\sqrt{2}\,m\omega_n$ (D) $\frac{1}{\sqrt{2}}m\omega_n$

Q.7 The ratio of the maximum dynamic displacement due to dynamic force to the deflection due to the static force of the same magnitude is called

(A) Displacement ratio (B) Deflection ratio

(C) Force factor (D) Magnification factor

Q.8 For effective vibration isolation, the natural frequency ω_n of the system must be (ω is the forcing frequency)

(A) $\frac{\omega}{4}$ (B) ω (C) 4ω (D) 10ω

Q.9 Consider the following statements.

The critical speed of a shaft is affected by the

1. Eccentricity of the shaft
2. Span of the shaft
3. Diameter of the shaft

Of the statements:

(A) 1 and 2 are correct (B) 1 and 3 are correct

(C) 2 and 3 are correct (D) 1, 2 and 3 are correct

Q.10 Whirling speed of a shaft coincides with the natural frequency of its

(A) Longitudinal vibration (B) Transverse vibration

(C) Torsional vibration

(D) Coupled bending torsional vibration

Q.11 Two heavy rotating masses are connected by a shaft of length l_1, l_2 and l_3 and the corresponding diameter are d_1, d_2 and d_3. This system is reduced to a torsionally equivalent system having uniform diameter d_1 of the shaft. The equivalent length of the shaft is equal to:

(A) $l_1 + l_2 + l_3$ (B) $\frac{l_1 + l_2 + l_3}{3}$

(C) $l_1 + l_2\left(\frac{d_1}{d_2}\right)^3 + l_3\left(\frac{d_1}{d_3}\right)^3$ (D) $l_1 + l_2\left(\frac{d_1}{d_2}\right)^4 + l_3\left(\frac{d_1}{d_3}\right)^4$

Q.12 In a forced vibration with viscous damping, maximum amplitude occurs when forced frequency is

(A) Equal to natural frequency

(B) Slightly less than natural frequency

(C) Slightly greater than natural frequency

(D) Zero

Q.13 Figure shows spring loaded inverted pendulum is in its equilibrium position. The minimum value of spring constant k for which such oscillations will occur is

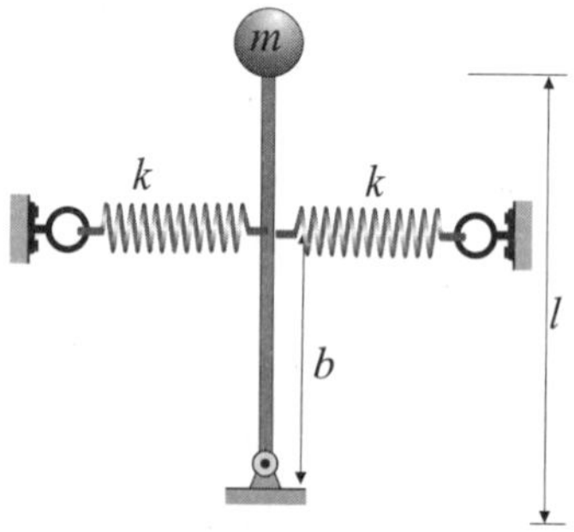

(A) $\frac{mg}{b}$ (B) $\frac{mgl}{2b^2}$ (C) $\frac{mgl}{b^2}$ (D) 0

Q.14 Match List-I and List-II and select the correct answer using the codes given below the list:

List-I	List-II
(a) Node and mode	1. Geared vibration
(b) Equivalent inertia	2. Damped free-vibration
(c) Log decrement	3. Forced vibration
(d) Resonance	4. Multi-rotor vibration

(A) a-1 b-4 c-3 d-2 (B) a-4 b-1 c-2 d-3

(C) a-1 b-4 c-2 d-3 (D) a-4 b-1 c-3 d-2

Q.15 A rigid massless rod is restrained to oscillate in the vertical plane as shown in figure. The equivalent stiffness (k_{eq}) of the system is

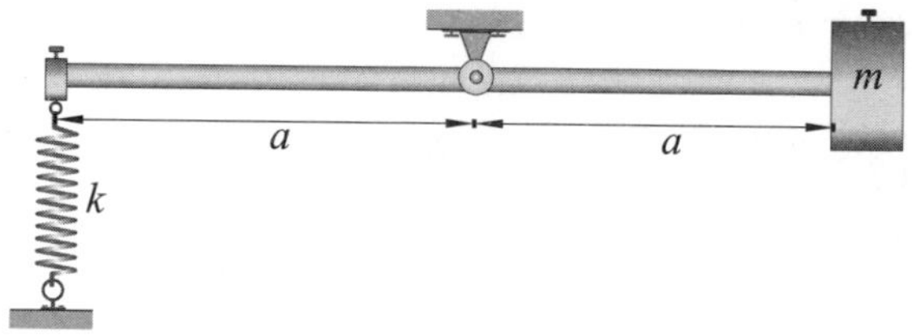

(A) k (B) $\frac{k}{4}$ (C) $4k$ (D) $2k$

Q.16 A machine mounted on a single coil spring has a period of free vibration of T. If the spring is cut into four equal parts and placed in parallel and the machine is mounted on them, then the period of free vibration of the new system will become

(A) $16T$ (B) $4T$ (C) $\frac{T}{4}$ (D) $\frac{T}{16}$

Q.17 A rigid massless rod is restrained to oscillate in the vertical plane as shown in figure.

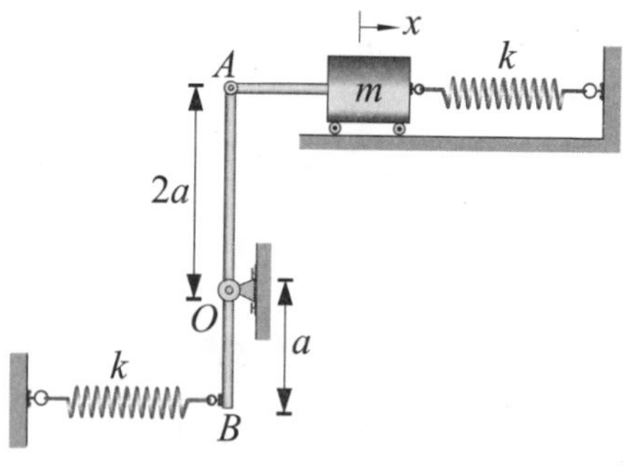

The equation of motion for the system is given by $m\frac{d^2x}{dt^2} + k_{eq}x = 0$. Equivalent spring stiffness (k_{eq}) is

(A) $\frac{5}{4}k$ (B) $\frac{3}{2}k$ (C) k (D) $2k$

Q.18 A cylinder of mass m and radius r is free to roll without slipping but is restrained by the spring k as shown in figure. The natural frequency (ω_n) of oscillation is

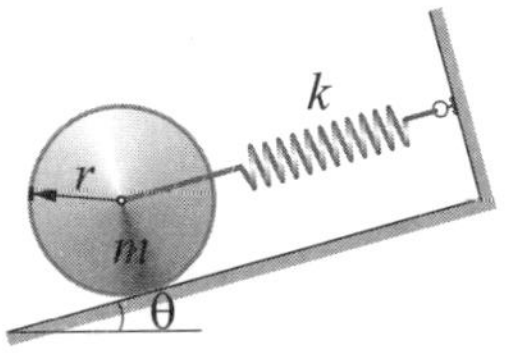

(A) $\sqrt{\dfrac{2k\cos\theta}{3m}}$ (B) $\sqrt{\dfrac{2k}{3m}}$

(C) $\sqrt{\dfrac{2k\cos^2\theta}{3m}}$ (D) $\sqrt{\dfrac{2k\sin\theta}{3m}}$

Q.19 The governing differential equation of motion for the system shown in figure is

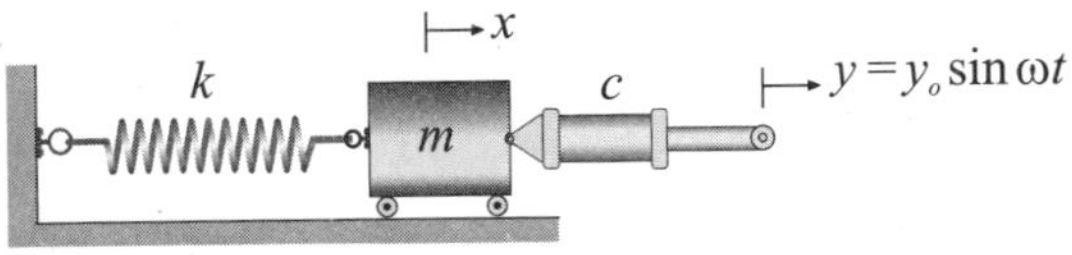

(A) $m\dfrac{d^2x}{dt^2}+c\dfrac{dx}{dt}+kx=c\omega y_o\sin\omega t$

(B) $m\dfrac{d^2x}{dt^2}+c\dfrac{dx}{dt}+kx=c\omega y_o\cos\omega t$

(C) $m\dfrac{d^2x}{dt^2}+c\dfrac{dx}{dt}+kx=\omega^2 y_o\sin\omega t$

(D) None of these

Q.20 The vibrating system is shown in figure.

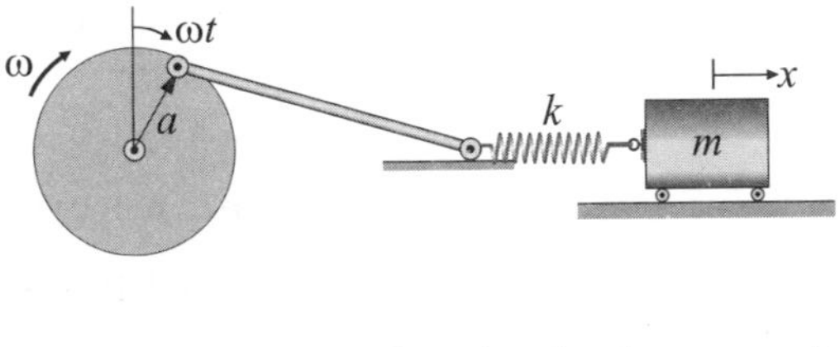

The differential equation of motion for the system is

(A) $m\dfrac{d^2x}{dt^2}+kx=ka\sin\omega t$ (B) $m\dfrac{d^2x}{dt^2}+kx=a\sin\omega t$

(C) $m\dfrac{d^2x}{dt^2}+kx=a\cos\omega t$ (D) None of these

Q.21 to Q.30 Numerical Answer Questions

Q.21 A weight of 50 N is suspended from a spring of stiffness 5 kN/m and is subjected to a harmonic force of amplitude 40 N and frequency of 4 Hz. The amplitude (in m) of the forced motion of the weight is_____.

Q.22 A simple mass-spring system shown has a natural frequency of 5 Hz. The static deflection (in m) of the spring due to the mass is (mass of the spring is negligible) ___.

Q.23 A damped spring-mass system shown in figure is critically damped. The value of damping coefficient c (in Ns/m) is__________.

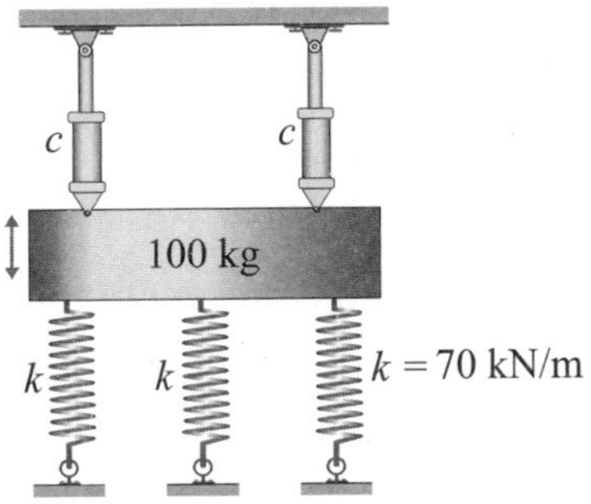

Q.24 The equation of motion for a single degree of freedom system with viscous damping is

$$16\frac{d^2x}{dt^2}+5\frac{dx}{dt}+4x=0$$

The damping ratio of the system is__________.

Q.25 Two heavy rotating masses are connected by shaft of length 1.5 m, 2.0 m and 1.5 m and the corresponding diameters are 20 cm, 25 cm and 30 cm. The system is reduced to torsionally equivalent system having uniform diameter 15 cm of the shaft. The equivalent length of the shaft is_______.

Q.26 The figure shows, two rotors connected by an elastic shaft undergoing torsional vibration. The rotor A has a mass of 2 kg and a diameter of 60 cm, while the rotor B has a mass of 1 kg and a diameter of 20 cm. What is the distance x at which the node vibration of torsional vibration occurs? ____.

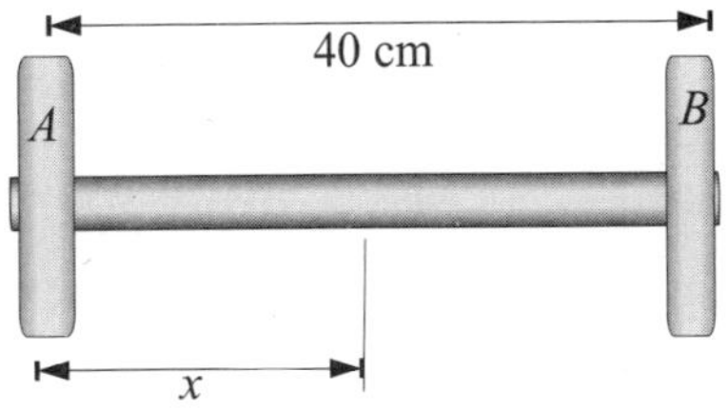

Q.27 The equation of motion for a damped viscous vibration is $3\dfrac{d^2x}{dt^2}+9\dfrac{dx}{dt}+27x=0$. The damped frequency ($\omega_d$) is _____.

Q.28 The potential energy of a linear mass-spring system is given in Ns by $81x^2$, where x is the displacement in m from neutral equilibrium position. The kinetic energy of the system is given in Ns by $9\left(\frac{dx}{dt}\right)^2$. Period of its oscillation is______.

Q.29 A reciprocating engine running at 80 rad/s is supported on springs. The static deflection of the spring is 1mm and $g = 10\ \text{m/s}^2$. When the engine runs, what will be the frequency of vibrations of the system?________.

Q.30 A 50 kg mass is hanging from a spring of stiffness 50 kN/m. A harmonic force of magnitude 100 N and frequency 100 rad/s is applied to the system. The amplitude (in mm) of the forced respond is ______.

Q.31 to Q.65 carry two marks each.

Q.31 to Q.50 Multiple Choice Questions

Q.31 One end of the L-shaped body is connected to the block of mass m, while the other end is attached to the linear spring. The mass of the body can be neglected. What is the range values of the spring constant k for which the oscillations will be stable?

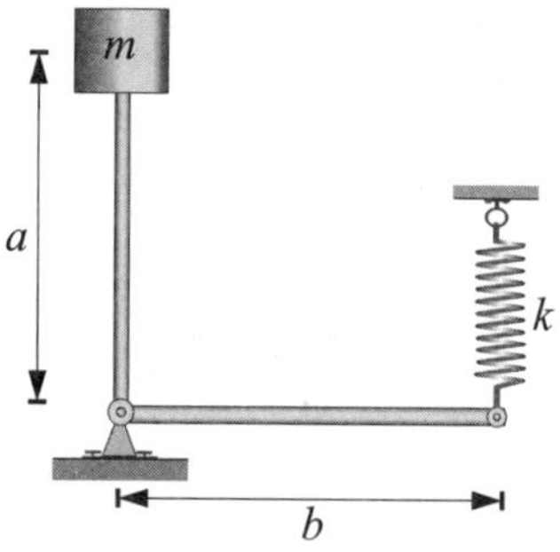

(A) $k > \frac{mga}{b^2}$

(B) $k > \frac{mg}{b}$

(C) $k < \frac{mg}{b}$

(D) None of these

Q.32 The differential equation governing the vibrating system is

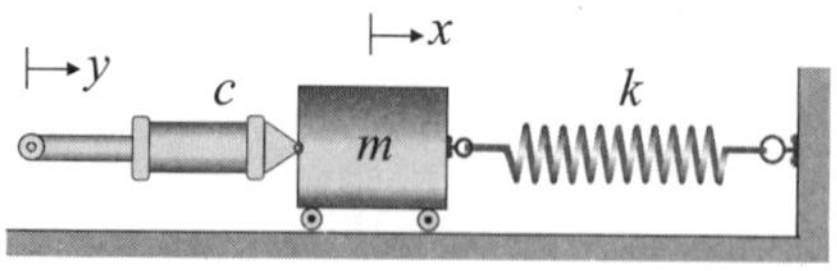

(A) $m\frac{d^2x}{dt^2} + cx + k(x - y) = 0$

(B) $m\left(\frac{d^2x}{dt^2} - \frac{d^2y}{dt^2}\right) + c\left(\frac{dx}{dt^2} - \frac{dy}{dt^2}\right) + kx = 0$

(C) $m\frac{d^2x}{dt^2} + c\left(\frac{dx}{dt} - \frac{dy}{dt}\right) + kx = 0$

(D) $m\left(\frac{d^2x}{dt^2} - \frac{d^2y}{dt^2}\right) + c\left(\frac{dx}{dt^2} - \frac{dy}{dt^2}\right) + k(x - y) = 0$

Q.33 Neglecting the mass of links and lever, the natural frequency of system shown in figure is

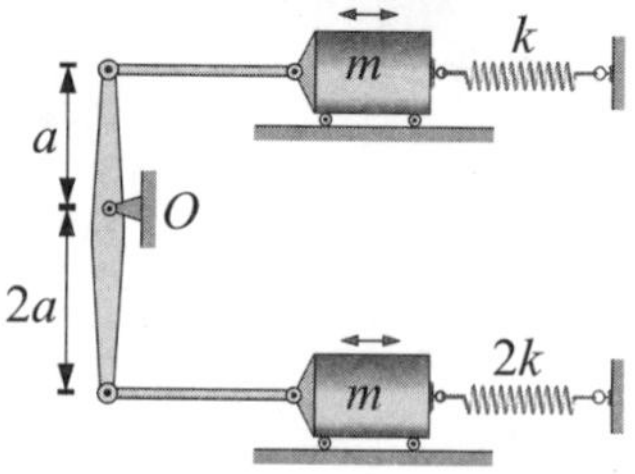

(A) $\omega_n = \sqrt{\frac{k}{2m}}$

(B) $\omega_n = \sqrt{\frac{9k}{5m}}$

(C) $\omega_n = \sqrt{\frac{9k}{m}}$

(D) $\omega_n = \sqrt{\frac{5k}{9m}}$

Q.34 Match List-I and List-II and select the correct answer using the codes given below:

List-I	List-II
(a) $\frac{d^2x}{dt^2} + bx = 0$	1. Undamped forced vibrations
(b) $\frac{d^2x}{dt^2} + bx = c\sin\omega t$	2. Damped forced vibrations
(c) $\frac{d^2x}{dt^2} + a\frac{dx}{dt} + bx = 0$	3. Undamped free vibrations
(d) $\frac{d^2x}{dt^2} + a\frac{dx}{dt} + bx = c\sin\omega t$	4. Damped free vibrations

(A) a-4, b-1, c-3, d-2

(B) a-3, b-1, c-4, d-2

(C) a-3, b-2, c-4, d-1

(D) a-2, b-1, c-4, d-3

Q.35 The equation of motion for the system shown in figure is

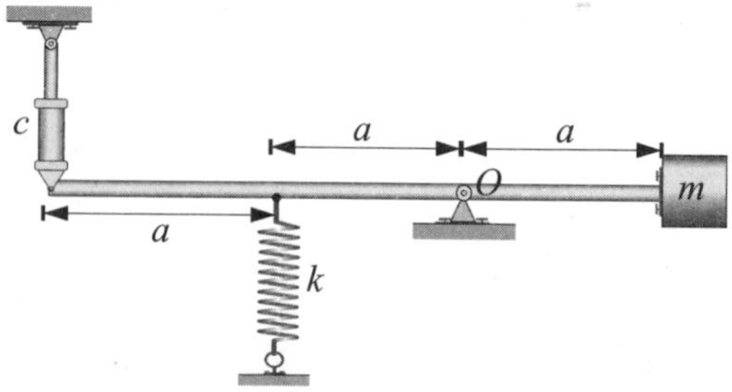

(A) $\frac{d^2\theta}{dt^2} + \frac{4c}{m}\frac{d\theta}{dt} + \frac{k}{m}\theta = 0$

(B) $\frac{d^2\theta}{dt^2} + \frac{2ca^2}{m}\frac{d\theta}{dt} + \frac{k}{m}\theta = 0$

(C) $\frac{d^2\theta}{dt^2} + \frac{2c}{4m}\frac{d\theta}{dt} + \frac{k}{4m}\theta = 0$

(D) None of these

Q.36 A mass m is fixed on spring and the end of cantilever beam of negligible mass as shown in figure. The natural frequency (ω_n) of the system is

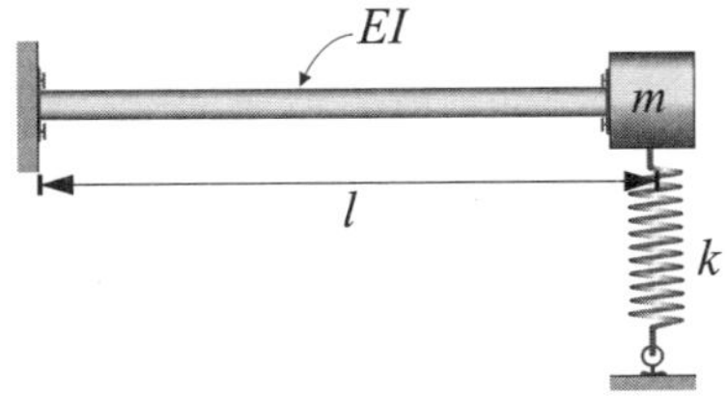

(A) $\sqrt{\frac{3EI + kl^3}{ml^3}}$ (B) $\sqrt{\frac{2EI + kl^3}{ml^3}}$

(C) $\sqrt{\frac{EI + kl^3}{ml^3}}$ (D) None of these

Q.37 A system of rack-pinion-spring is shown in figure. The governing differential equation of the system (considering the pinion to be a thin circular disc) is

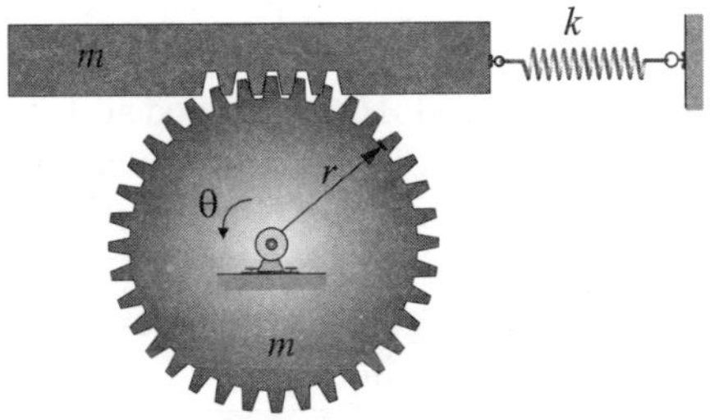

(A) $\frac{d^2\theta}{dt^2} + \frac{2k}{3m}\theta = 0$ (B) $\frac{d^2\theta}{dt^2} + \frac{2k}{m}\theta = 0$

(C) $\frac{d^2\theta}{dt^2} + \frac{5k}{3m}\theta = 0$ (D) $\frac{d^2\theta}{dt^2} + \frac{k}{m}\theta = 0$

Q.38 A torsional system with discs of moment of inertia I_A and I_B shown in the given figure, is gear driven such that the ratio of the speed of shaft B to A is 'n'. Neglecting the inertia of gears, the equivalent inertia of disc of B at the speed of shaft A is equal to

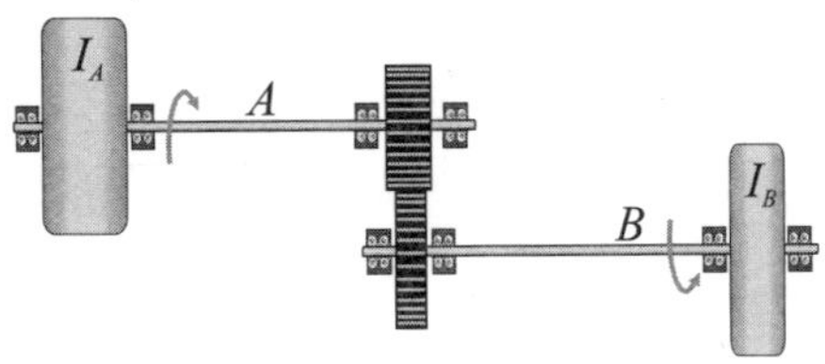

(A) nI_B (B) $n^2 I_B$ (C) $\frac{I_B}{n^2}$ (D) $\frac{I_B}{n}$

Q.39 The natural frequency (ω_n) of spring-mass system shown in figure is

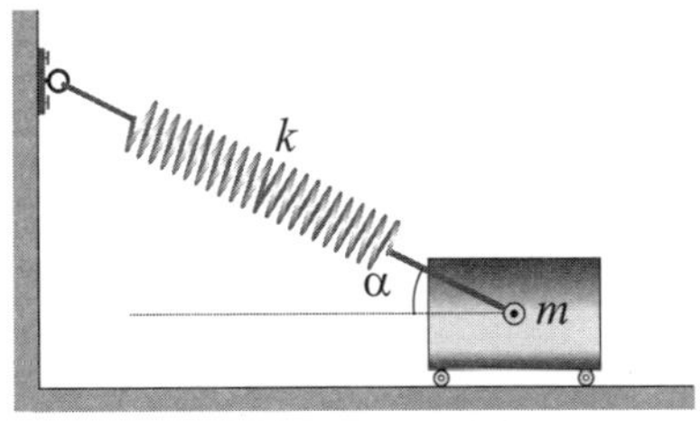

(A) $\sqrt{\frac{k\cos\alpha}{m}}$ (B) $\sqrt{\frac{k\cos^2\alpha}{m}}$

(C) $\sqrt{\frac{k}{m}}$ (D) $\sqrt{\frac{k\tan\alpha}{m}}$

Q.40 The natural frequency (ω_n) of the system shown in figure is

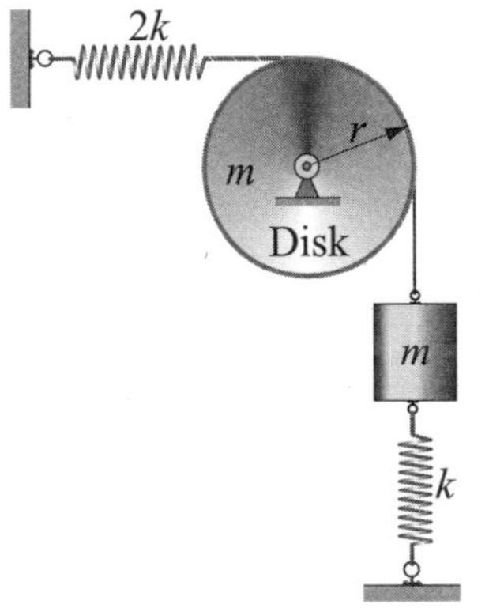

(A) $\sqrt{\frac{2k}{m}}$ (B) $\sqrt{\frac{3k}{2m}}$ (C) $\sqrt{\frac{4k}{3m}}$ (D) None of these

Q.41 A spring-mass system shown in figure is vibrating with very small amplitude. The natural frequency of the system is

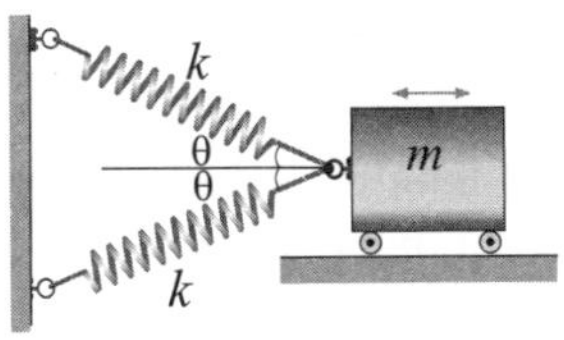

(A) $\sqrt{\frac{k}{m}}$ (B) $\sqrt{\frac{2k}{m}}$

(C) $\sqrt{\frac{2k\cos\theta}{m}}$ (D) $\sqrt{\frac{2k\cos^2\theta}{m}}$

Q.42 A glass tube bent into a circle of radius R is rigidly fixed in the vertical plane with the top ends open to the atmosphere. A liquid of density ρ is filled in the tube so that the liquid column forms a semi-circle. If the liquid is disturbed slightly, time period of oscillations will be

(A) $\sqrt{\frac{4\pi^3 R}{g}}$ (B) $\sqrt{\frac{3\pi^3 R}{g}}$ (C) $\sqrt{\frac{\pi R}{g}}$ (D) $\sqrt{\frac{2\pi^3 R}{g}}$

Q.43 A disc of mass m and radius r is attached to a spring and viscous damper as shown in figure. The governing differential equation of motion of disc is

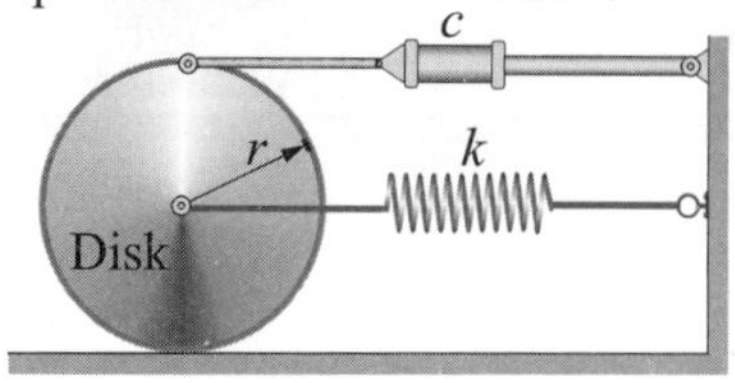

(A) $\frac{d^2\theta}{dt^2} + \frac{c}{m}\frac{d\theta}{dt} + \frac{k}{m}\theta = 0$

(B) $\frac{d^2\theta}{dt^2} + \frac{8c}{3m}\frac{d\theta}{dt} + \frac{2k}{3m}\theta = 0$

(C) $\frac{d^2\theta}{dt^2} + \frac{2c}{3m}\frac{d\theta}{dt} + \frac{2k}{3m}\theta = 0$

(D) None of these

Q.44 Two uniform disks of mass m each are attached to massless rod and spring of constant k is attached to the rod as shown in figure. The disks roll without sliding, the frequency of vibration of the system is

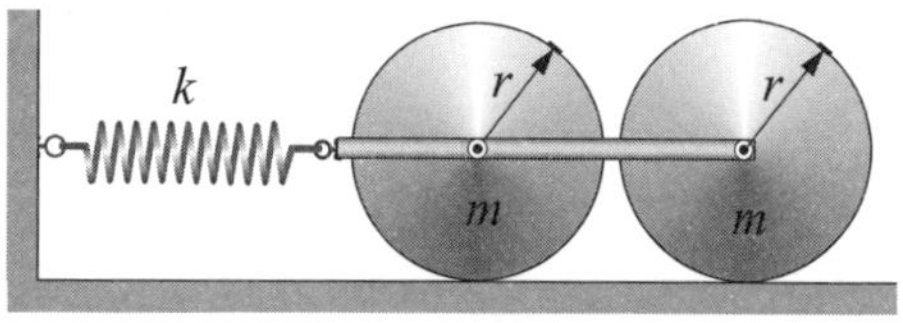

(A) $\omega_n = \sqrt{\frac{k}{7m}}$ (B) $\omega_n = \sqrt{\frac{k}{3m}}$

(C) $\omega_n = \sqrt{\frac{k}{\sqrt{3}\, m}}$ (D) None of these

Q.45 A thin rod of length l and area of cross-section A is pivoted at its lowest point O inside a non-viscous liquid as shown in figure. The rod is free to rotate in a vertical plane about a horizontal axis passing through O. The density ρ_1 of the material of the rod is smaller than the density ρ_2 of liquid. The rod is displaced by a small angle θ from its equilibrium position and then released, and starts oscillating. Determine the natural frequency.

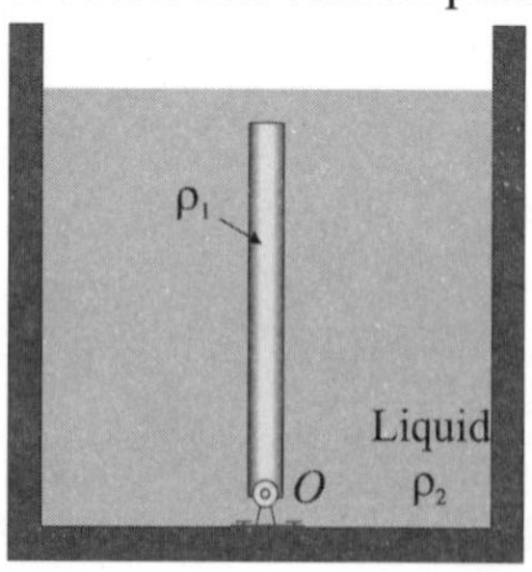

(A) $\omega_n = \sqrt{\frac{3(\rho_2 - \rho_1)g}{2\rho_1 l}}$ (B) $\omega_n = \sqrt{\frac{3(\rho_2 + \rho_1)g}{2\rho_1 l}}$

(C) $\omega_n = \sqrt{\frac{3\rho_2 g}{2l}}$ (D) None of these

Q.46 A small mass m is attached to the end of the L-shaped rod of negligible mass. The spring tension is adjusted so that the system is in equilibrium in the position shown in figure. Moment of inertia of the system about O is I_O. The system becomes unstable (does not vibrate), if

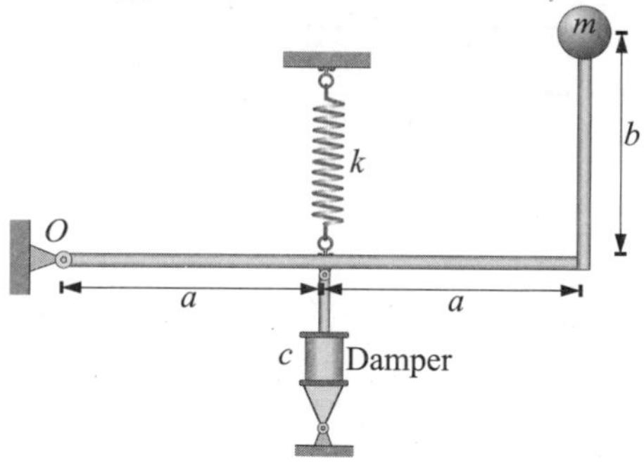

(A) $a > \sqrt{\frac{mgb}{k}}$ (B) $ka^2 - mgb < I_O$

(C) $ka^2 > I_O$ (D) $b > \frac{ka^2}{mg}$

Q.47 A rigid massless rod ABC is hinged at A and carries a point mass m (in kg) at C. Point B is connected to a linear spring with spring constant k (in N/m) as shown in figure. The length AB and AC are a and l, respectively. Considering the effect of gravity, the natural frequency ω_n of this spring-mass system in rad/s is

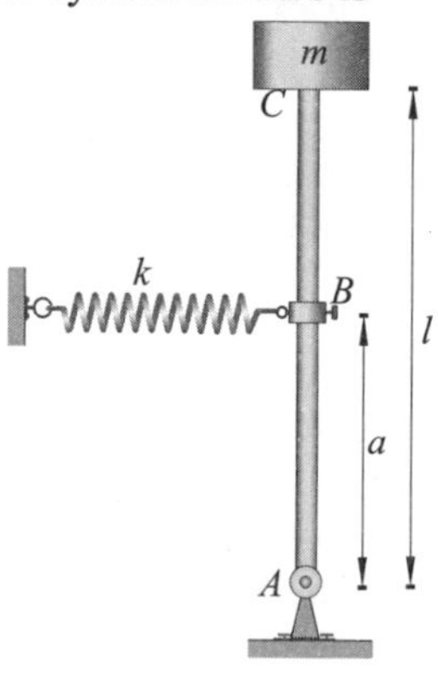

(A) $\sqrt{\frac{kL^2 - mgl}{ma^2}}$ (B) $\sqrt{\frac{ka^2 - mgl}{ml^2}}$

(C) $\sqrt{\frac{kL - mg}{ma}}$ (D) $\sqrt{\frac{ka - ml}{ml}}$

Q.48 A damped spring-mass pulley system is shown in figure. The mass and friction of the pulleys are negligible, and cable remains taut at all times. Equation of motion for the system is

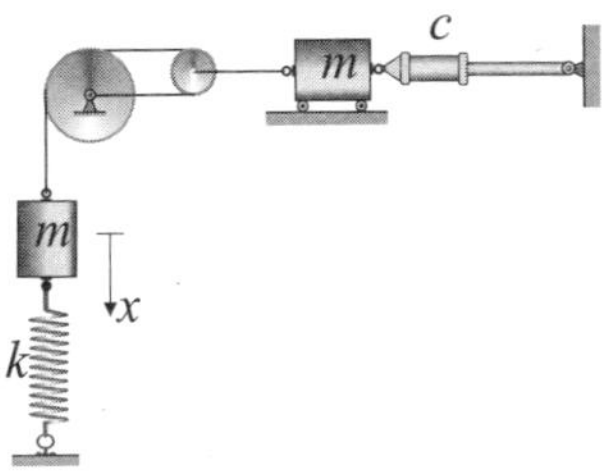

(A) $2m\frac{d^2x}{dt^2}+c\frac{dx}{dt}+kx=0$ (B) $5m\frac{d^2x}{dt^2}+c\frac{dx}{dt}+4kx=0$

(C) $3m\frac{d^2x}{dt^2}+\frac{c}{2}\frac{dx}{dt}+kx=0$ (D) $2m\frac{d^2x}{dt^2}+c\frac{dx}{dt}+2kx=0$

Q.49 A block of mass m is attached to a hinged rod of negligible mass as shown in figure. The natural frequency (ω_n) of the system is

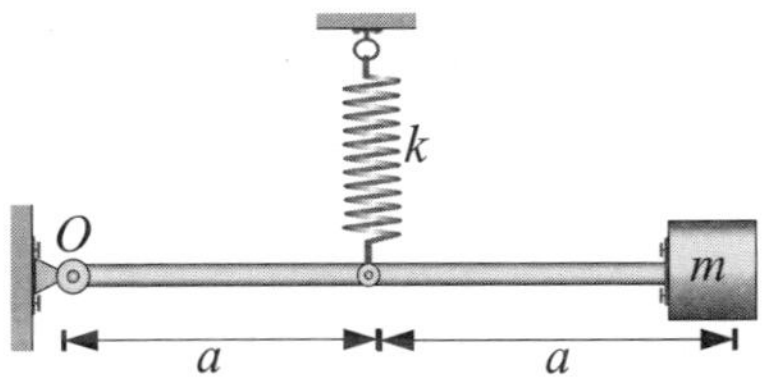

(A) $\sqrt{\frac{k}{m}}$ (B) $\sqrt{\frac{k}{2m}}$ (C) $\sqrt{\frac{k}{4m}}$ (D) $\sqrt{\frac{k}{8m}}$

Q.50 The figure shows a critically damped spring mass system undergoing single degree of free vibrations. If $m=5$ kg and $k=20$ N/m, the value of viscous damping coefficient (in Ns/m) is

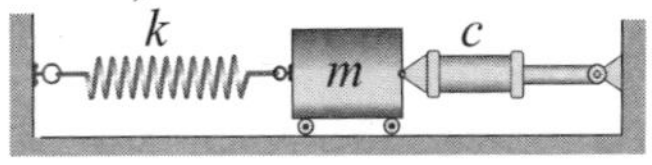

(A) 1.5 (B) 4.8 (C) 12.3 (D) 20.0

Q.51 to Q.65 Numerical Answer Questions

Q.51 The natural frequency (ω_n) of vibration of the system shown in figure is $\omega_n=\sqrt{\frac{k_{eq}}{m}}$. Bar AB is rigid and massless. The equivalent spring stiffness k_{eq} (in kN/m) is____.

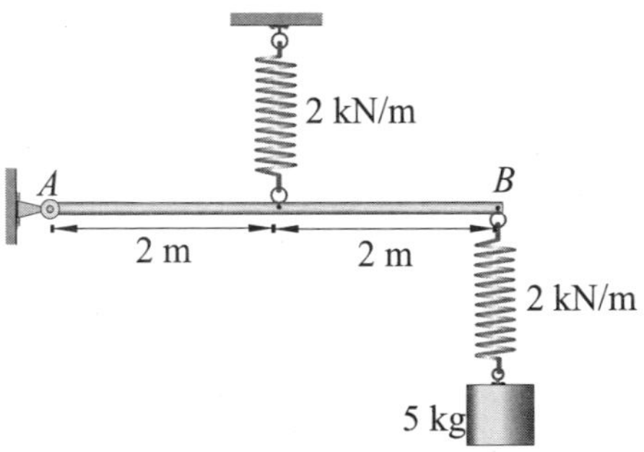

Q.52 The system shown is critically damped. The damping factor ζ is__________.

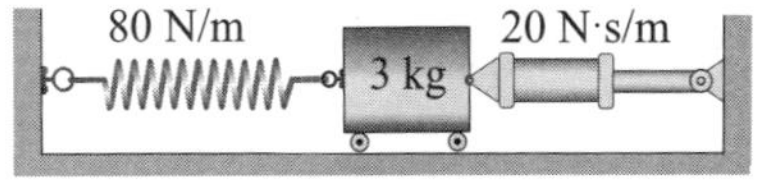

Q.53 Neglecting mass of pulleys, natural frequency (ω_n) of vibration of system(See figure) is___________.

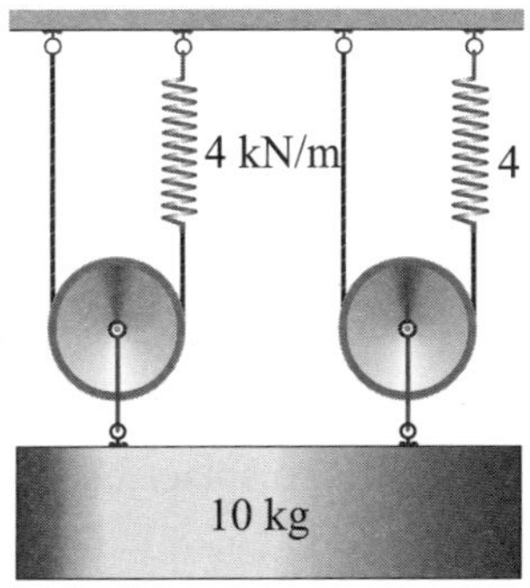

Q.54 The pendulum of length 0.1 m is suspended from a sliding collar as shown in Figure. If the horizontal displacement $y=0.01\sin(6t)$, where y in m, is imposed on the collar. The steady state angular amplitude (θ_{max}) in degree, of pendulum is ______.

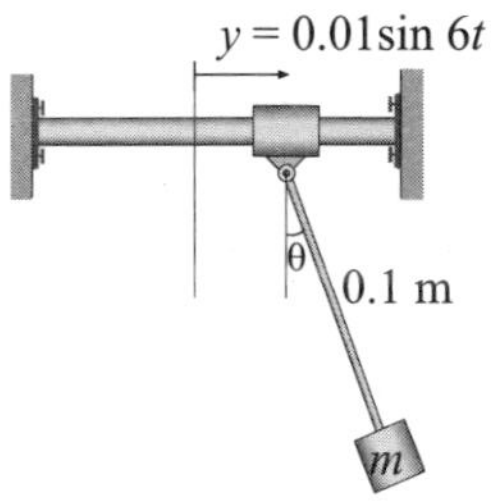

Q.55 If $\frac{\omega}{\omega_n}=\sqrt{2}$, where ω is the frequency of excitation and ω_n is the natural frequency of vibrations, then the transmissibility of forced undamped vibration will be __.

Q.56 A rigid bar AB of mass 24 kg is in equilibrium in the position shown. If the system is critically damped, then the value of damping coefficient (in Ns/m) c is__________.

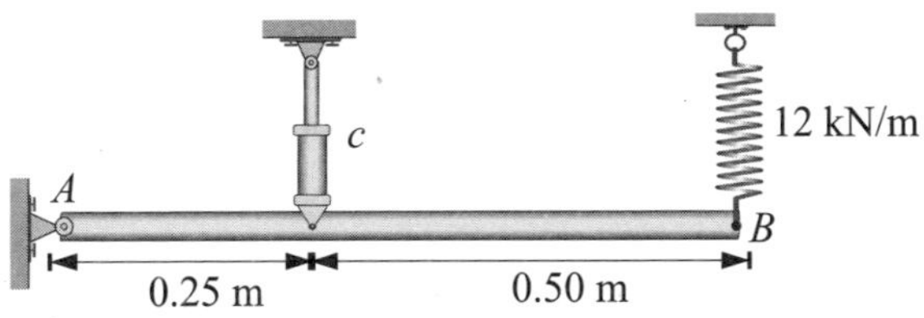

Q.57 A uniform bar of length 3 m oscillates about O located at a distance x from the mass center G of the bar as shown in figure. The distance c (in m) for which the period of oscillation is minimum, will be_______.

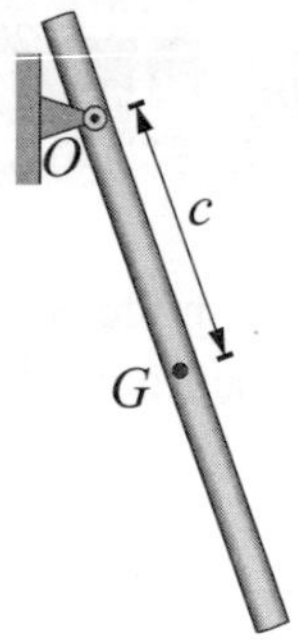

Q.58 A spring-mass damped system is released from the rest from a positive initial displacement x_o. If the succeeding maximum positive displacement is $\frac{x_o}{2}$, then the damping ratio ξ of the system is____.

Q.59 A block of mass m attached to a spring is subjected to a harmonic force as shown in figure. The amplitude of the forced motion is observed to be 50 mm. The value of m (in kg) is__________.

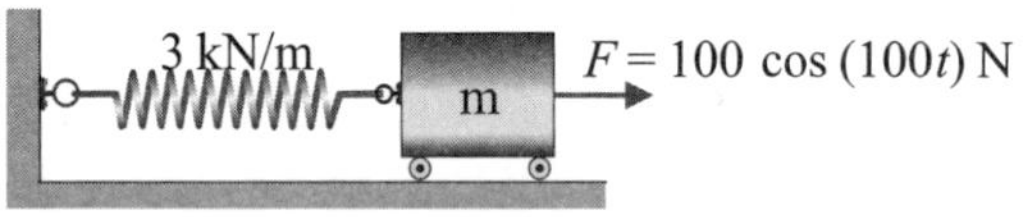

Q.60 A shaft of 50 mm diameter and 1.0 m length carries a disc which has mass eccentricity equal to 190 microns. At a speed which is 90% of critical speed, what will be the displacement of the shaft in microns?__________.

Q.61 A uniform disk of moment of inertia 15 $kg \cdot m^2$ is welded at its center to two shafts of equal diameter 40 mm, length 1.0 m and modulus of rigidity (G) of 85 GN/m^2. The frequency (in Hz) of torsional vibrations of the disk is___.

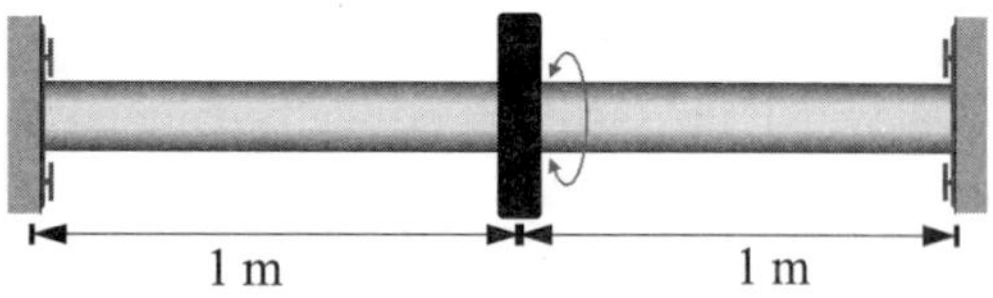

Q.62 A motor of mass 200 kg is supported by six springs, each having a spring constant $k = 100$ kN/m. The unbalance of the rotor is equivalent to a mass of 30g located 150 mm from the axis of rotation. Motor is constrained to move vertically. The resonance will occur at the speed (r.p.m.)_________.

Q.63 A system of cylinder-spring-damper is shown in figure. The cylinder rolls without slipping. The damping ratio of system is__________.

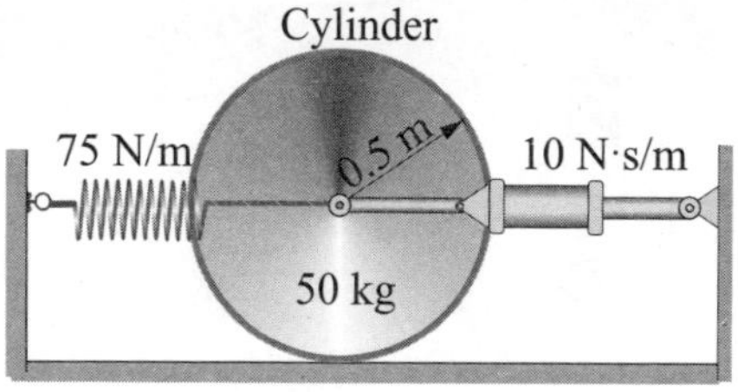

Q.64 A cylinder of mass 4 kg and cross-sectional area $0.01\,m^2$ floats in water of density 1000 kg/m^3 as shown in figure. What will be the frequency (in Hz) of oscillation if the cylinder is depressed some what and released. (Neglect the damping effect of the liquid)________.

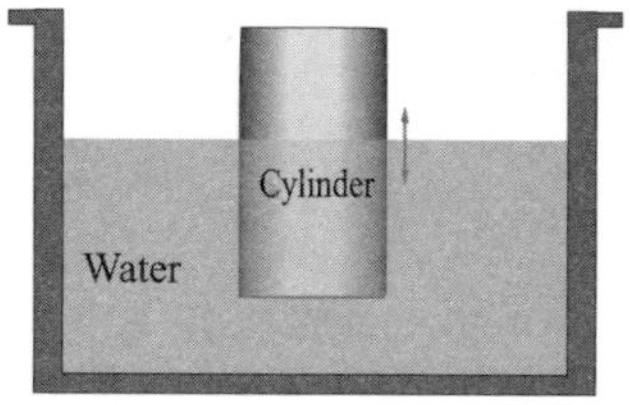

Q.65 The system shown in figure is under damped with a damped period of t_d. When the damper is removed, the period changes to $0.2t_d$. The damping coefficient c (in Ns/m) is__________.

8.4 SOLUTION TO PRACTICE PAPER

Q.1 Ans:(B)

Amplitude of particle $A = \frac{x_{max} - x_{min}}{2}$

$$A = \frac{(a+b)-(a-b)}{2}$$

$$\text{Amplitude, } A = b$$

Q.2 Ans:(A)

Compare the given equation $x = 0.02e^{-5t}\sin(25t + \pi/3)$ with standard equation

$$x = x_0 e^{-\zeta\omega_n t}\cos(\sqrt{1-\zeta^2})\omega_n t + \phi)$$

$$\zeta\omega_n = 5 \text{ and } (\sqrt{1-\zeta^2})\omega_n = 25$$

From which

The damping factor ζ of system is 0.19

Q.3 Ans:(B)

Natural frequency, $\omega_n = \sqrt{\frac{k}{m}} = \sqrt{\frac{1000}{10}} = 10$

Maximum velocity, $v_{max} = A\omega = \frac{10}{1000} \times 10$ m/s

$$v_{max} = 1$$

Q.4 Ans:(D)

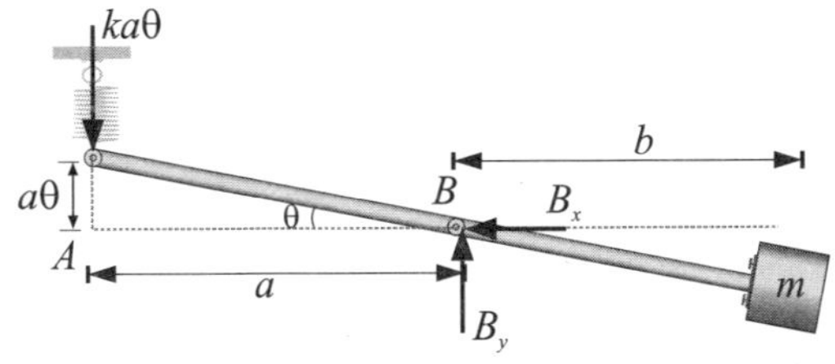

The free-body diagram of the bar is constructed for an arbitrary angular displacement θ from equilibrium position as shown in figure. Moment equation about B gives

$$mb^2 \frac{d^2\theta}{dt^2} = -ka\theta \times a$$

or $$\frac{d^2\theta}{dt^2} + \frac{ka^2}{mb^2}\theta = 0$$

From which

$$\omega_n = \sqrt{\frac{ka^2}{mb^2}}$$

Q.5 Ans:(A)

From the free-body diagram of figure, we may apply Newton's second law to obtain

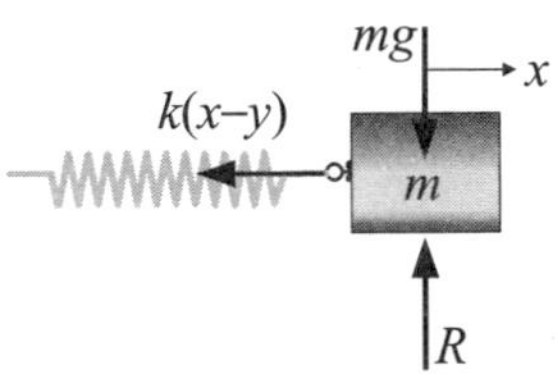

$$m\frac{d^2x}{dt^2} = -k(x-y)$$

$$m\frac{d^2x}{dt^2} + kx = ky$$

Q.6 Ans:(A)

Critical damping coefficient, $c_c = 2\sqrt{mk}$

or $$c_c = 2\sqrt{m^2\frac{k}{m}} = 2m\sqrt{\frac{k}{m}} = 2m\omega_n$$

$$c_c = 2m\omega_n$$

Q.7 Ans:(B)

$$\text{Magnification factor (MF)} = \frac{X}{X_{st}}$$

Q.8 Ans:(A)

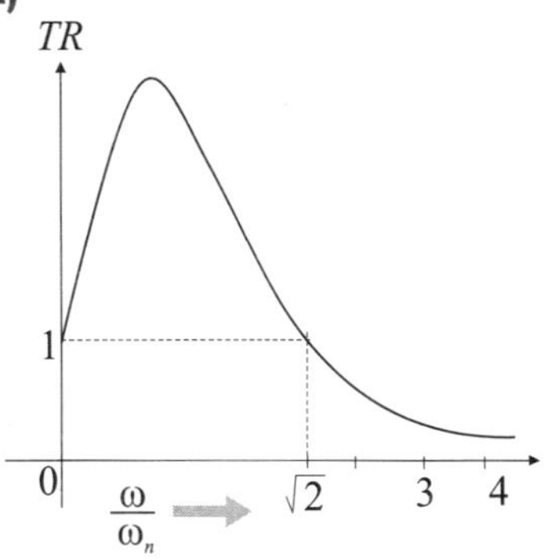

Transmissibility, $TR = \left|\frac{F_T}{F_o}\right|$

$$TR = \sqrt{\frac{1 + \left(2\zeta\frac{\omega}{\omega_n}\right)^2}{\sqrt{\left[1 - \left(\frac{\omega}{\omega_n}\right)^2\right]^2 + \left(2\zeta\frac{\omega}{\omega_n}\right)^2}}}$$

For effective vibration isolation $\frac{\omega}{\omega_n} >> \sqrt{2}$

$$\omega_n = \frac{\omega}{4}$$

Q.9 Ans:(C)

Critical speed of shaft $= \sqrt{\frac{48EI}{l^3 m}} = \sqrt{\frac{48E \times \frac{\pi d^4}{64}}{l^3 m}}$

The critical speed of a shaft depends on l and d.

Span(l) of the shaft and diameter(d) of the shaft

Q.10 Ans:(B)

Natural frequency $= \frac{48EI}{l^3}$ ← (Transverse vibration)

Transverse vibration

Q.11 Ans:(D)

Torsion formula $\frac{T}{J} = \frac{G\theta}{l} \Rightarrow \theta = \frac{Tl}{GJ} = \frac{32Tl}{G\pi d^4}$

Angle of twist $\theta = \theta_1 + \theta_2 + \theta_3$

or $$\frac{32Tl}{G\pi d^4} = \frac{32Tl_1}{G\pi d_1^4} + \frac{32Tl_2}{G\pi d_2^4} + \frac{32Tl_3}{G\pi d_3^4}$$

or $$l = l_1\frac{d^4}{d_1^4} + l_2\frac{d^4}{d_2^4} + l_3\frac{d^4}{d_3^4}$$

Equivalent length for diameter $d = d_1$.

$$l_{eq} = l_1 + l_2\left(\frac{d_1}{d_2}\right)^4 + l_3\left(\frac{d_1}{d_3}\right)^4$$

Q.12 Ans:(B)

Maximum amplitude occurs when forced frequency is slightly less than natural frequency.

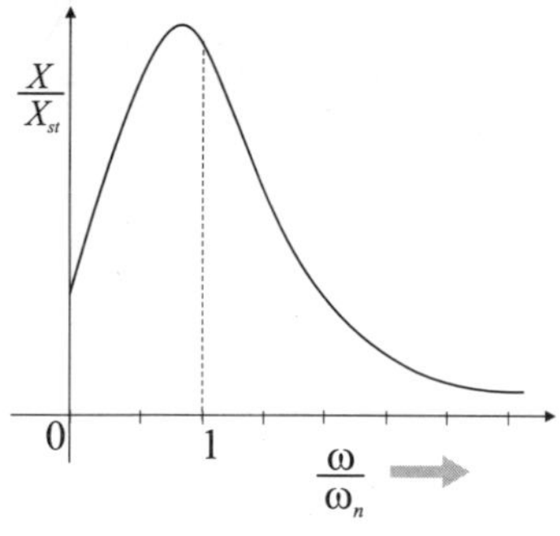

Q.13 Ans:(C)

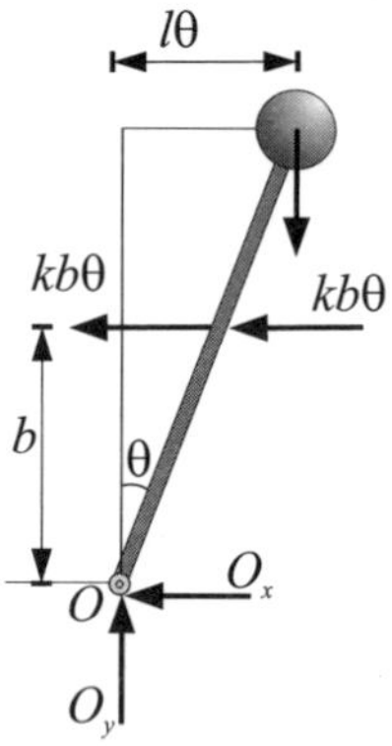

Figure shows the free-body diagram of inverted pendulum when it is displaced θ from equilibrium.

Inverted pendulum oscillates if $2kb\theta \times b > mg \times l\theta$

$$k > \frac{mgl}{b^2}$$

Q.14 Ans:(B)

(a) Node and mode → 4. Multi-rotor vibration

(b) Equivalent inertia → 1. Geared vibration

(c) Log decrement → 2. Damped free-vibration

(d) Resonance → 3. Forced vibration

Q.15 Ans:(A)

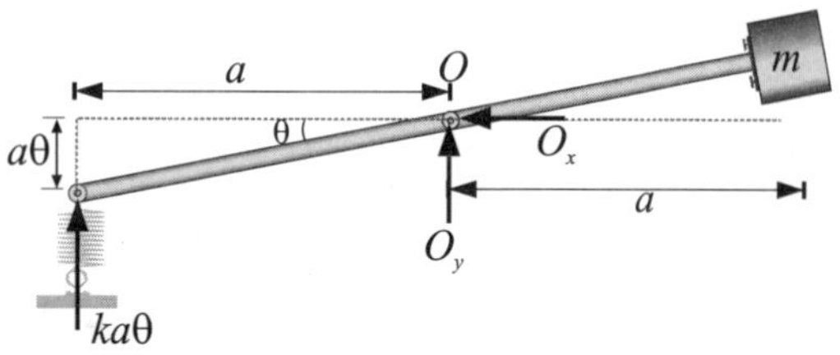

From the free-body diagram, moment equation about O gives, $ma^2\dfrac{d^2\theta}{dt^2} = -ka\theta \times a$

or $$m\frac{d^2\theta}{dt^2} + k\theta = 0$$

Compare with standard form $m_{eq}\dfrac{d^2\theta}{dt^2} + k_{eq}\theta = 0,$

we have

$$k_{eq} = k$$

Q.16 Ans:(C)

Let n be the number of coils and k be the stiffness of spring.

$$k = \frac{Gd^4}{8D^3 n} = \frac{c_1}{n} \text{ and } T = 2\pi\sqrt{\frac{M}{k}}$$

Stiffness of new spring $\left(n' = \dfrac{n}{4}\right)$, $k' = \dfrac{c_1}{n/4} = 4\dfrac{c_1}{n} = 4k$

Four spring are connected in parallel,

$$k_{eq} = 4k' = 4 \times 4k = 16k$$

$$T' = 2\pi\sqrt{\frac{M}{k_{eq}}}$$

or $$T = 2\pi\sqrt{\frac{M}{16k}} = \frac{1}{4}\left[2\pi\sqrt{\frac{M}{k}}\right] = \frac{T}{4}$$

$$T' = \frac{T}{4}$$

Q.17 Ans:(A)

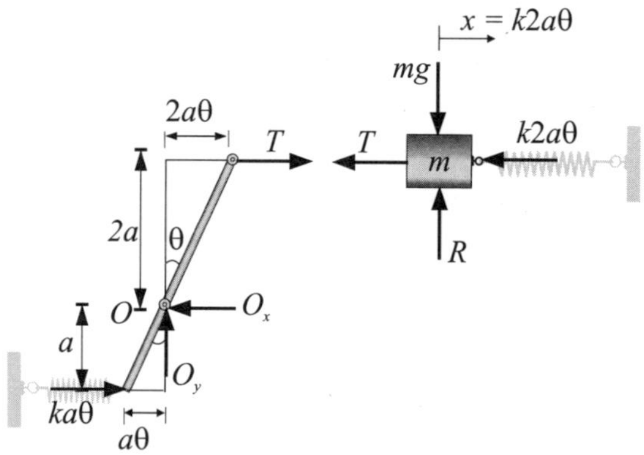

The equation of motion for the body of figure is obtained by first drawing its free-body diagram. The governing equations are:

Equation of motion of the mass for a angular

$$m\frac{d^2x}{dt^2} = -T - kx \qquad \text{(i)}$$

$$\sum M_o = 0 \Rightarrow T \times 2a = \frac{kx}{2} \times a$$

or $$T = \frac{kx}{4} \qquad \text{(ii)}$$

Eliminating T from Equations (i) and (ii), we have

$$m\frac{d^2x}{dt^2} = \frac{-5k}{4}\theta \quad \text{or} \quad m\frac{d^2\theta}{dt^2} + \frac{5k}{4}\theta$$

$$\text{Equivalent spring stiffness, } k_{eq} = \frac{5}{4}k$$

Q.18 Ans:(B)

From free-body diagram of cylinder, we may apply moment equation about A to obtain

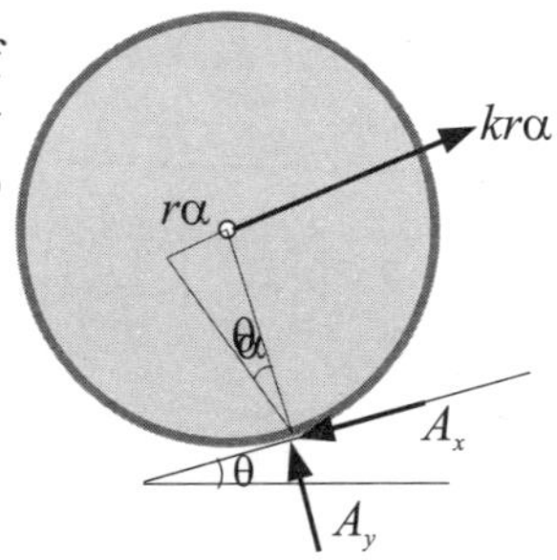

$$I_A\frac{d^2\alpha}{dt^2} = -kr\alpha \times r$$

or $$\frac{d^2\alpha}{dt^2} + \frac{kr^2}{I_A}\alpha = 0$$

Substituting $I_A = \frac{3}{2}mr^2$, we have $\frac{d^2\alpha}{dt^2} + \frac{2k}{3m}\alpha = 0$

$$\omega_n = \sqrt{\frac{2k}{3m}}$$

Q.19 Ans:(B)

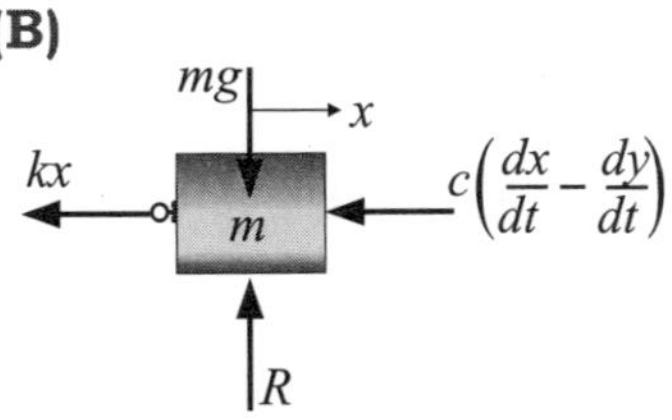

The equation of motion for the body is determined from the free-body diagram as shown in figure. Newton's second law gives

$$m\frac{d^2x}{dt^2} = -kx - c\left(\frac{dx}{dt} - \frac{dy}{dt}\right)$$

or $$m\frac{d^2x}{dt^2} + c\frac{dx}{dt} + kx = c\frac{d}{dt}(y_o \sin\omega t)$$

$$m\frac{d^2x}{dt^2} + c\frac{dx}{dt} + kx = cy_o\omega \cos\omega t$$

Q.20 Ans:(A)

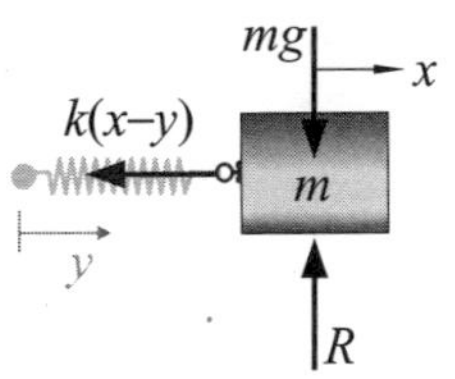

The displacement of one end of spring is $y = a\sin\omega t$. Spring force acting on the body $F_s = k(x - y)$. Applying the Newton's second law $m\frac{d^2x}{dt^2} = -F_s$.

$$m\frac{d^2x}{dt^2} = -k(x - y)$$

or $$m\frac{d^2x}{dt^2} = -k(x - a\sin\omega t)$$

$$m\frac{d^2x}{dt^2} + kx = ka\sin\omega t$$

Q.21 Ans:[0.0225]

Given: $W = 50$ N, $k = 5000$ N/m, $f = 4$ Hz and $F_o = 40$ N

$$f_n = \frac{1}{2\pi}\sqrt{\frac{k}{m}} = \frac{1}{2\pi}\sqrt{\frac{kg}{W}} = \frac{1}{2\pi}\sqrt{\frac{5000 \times 9.81}{50}} = 4.98 \text{ Hz}$$

Static deflection, $$X_{st} = \frac{F_o}{k} = \frac{40}{5000} = 8 \times 10^{-3} \text{ m}$$

Magnification factor, $$\frac{X}{X_{st}} = \frac{1}{1 - \left(\frac{f}{f_n}\right)^2}$$

or $$\frac{X}{8 \times 10^{-3}} = \frac{1}{1 - \left(\frac{4}{4.98}\right)^2}$$

$$X = 0.0225 \text{ m}$$

Q.22 Ans:[0.01]

Natural frequency $$f_n = \frac{1}{2\pi}\sqrt{\frac{k}{m}} = 5$$

or $$\sqrt{\frac{k}{m}} = 10\pi$$

or $$\sqrt{\frac{kg}{mg}} = \sqrt{\frac{kg}{k\Delta}} = 10\pi$$

From which

$$\text{Static deflection, } \Delta = 0.01 \text{ m}$$

Q.23 Ans:[4582.5]

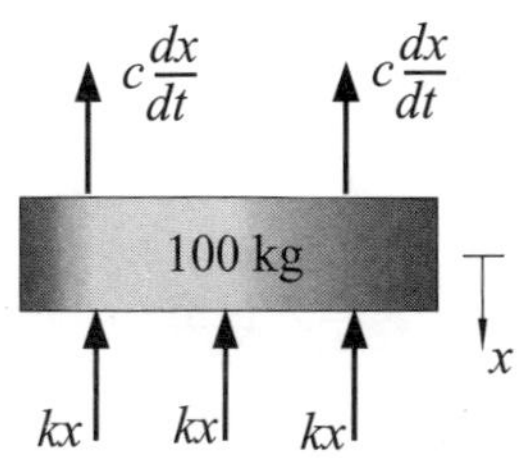

From the free-body diagram of figure, Newton's second law gives $$m\frac{d^2x}{dt^2} = -2c\frac{dx}{dt} - 3kx$$

or $$\frac{d^2x}{dt^2} + \frac{2c}{m}\frac{dx}{dt} + \frac{3k}{m}x = 0$$

Condition for critically damped system;

$$\left(\frac{2c}{m}\right)^2 = 4\times\frac{3k}{m}$$

$$c=\sqrt{3mk}=\sqrt{3\times 100\times 70000}$$

$$c = 4582.5 \text{ Ns/m}$$

Q.24 Ans:[0.3125]

Equation of motion $16\frac{d^2x}{dt^2}+5\frac{dx}{dt}+4x=0$

Damping ratio, $\zeta=\frac{c}{c_c}=\frac{c}{\sqrt{4mk}}=\frac{5}{\sqrt{4\times16\times4}}=\frac{5}{16}$

$$\zeta = 0.3125$$

Q.25 Ans:[0.827]

Equivalent length $l=l_1\left(\frac{d}{d_1}\right)^4+l_2\left(\frac{d}{d_2}\right)^4+l_3\left(\frac{d}{d_3}\right)^4$

$$l=1.5\times\left(\frac{15}{20}\right)^4+2.0\times\left(\frac{15}{25}\right)^4+1.5\times\left(\frac{15}{30}\right)^4$$

$$l=0.827 \text{ m}$$

Q.26 Ans:[2.1]

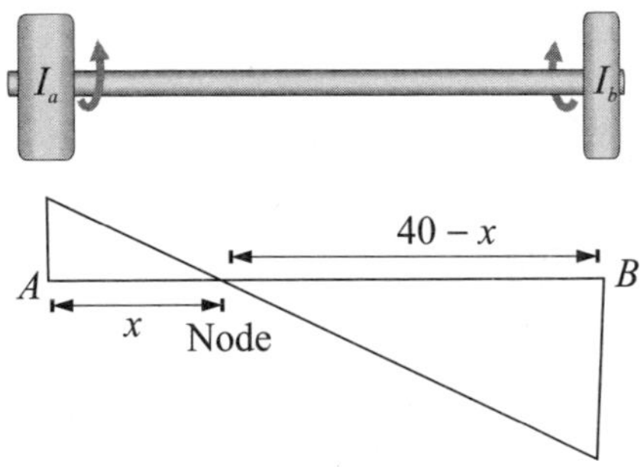

Torsional frequency about node, $\omega=\sqrt{\frac{GJ}{I_a l_a}}=\sqrt{\frac{GJ}{I_b l_b}}$

or $\quad I_a l_a = I_b l_b$

or $\quad \frac{1}{2}\times2\times30^2x=\frac{1}{2}\times1\times10^2(40-x)$

From which

$$x = 2.1 \text{ cm}$$

Q.27 Ans:[2.59]

Damped frequency, $\omega_d=\omega_n\sqrt{1-\zeta^2}$

Substituting $\omega_n=\sqrt{\frac{k}{m}}=\sqrt{\frac{27}{3}}=3$ and

$$\zeta=\frac{c}{c_c}=\frac{c}{2\sqrt{mk}}=\frac{9}{2\sqrt{3\times27}}=0.5$$

$$\omega_d=3\sqrt{1-0.5^2}$$

$$\omega_d = 2.59 \text{ rad/s}$$

Q.28 Ans:[2.09]

Total energy of system $\quad 9\left(\frac{dx}{dt}\right)^2+81x^2=\text{constant}$

$$\frac{d}{dt}\left[9\left(\frac{dx}{dt}\right)^2+81x^2\right]=0$$

$$2\times9\left(\frac{dx}{dt}\right)\left(\frac{d^2x}{dt^2}\right)+81\times2x\left(\frac{dx}{dt}\right)=0$$

or $\quad \frac{d^2x}{dt^2}+9x=0$

$$\omega_n=3=\frac{2\pi}{T}$$

$$T = 2.09 \text{ s}$$

Q.29 Ans:[100]

Natural frequency, $\omega_n=\sqrt{\frac{g}{\Delta}}=\sqrt{\frac{10}{\frac{1}{1000}}}$

$$\omega_n = 100 \text{ rad/s}$$

Q.30 Ans:[0.222]

Given: $m=50$ kg, $k=50$ kN/m, $F_0=100$ N and $\omega=100$ rad/s

$$\omega_n=\sqrt{\frac{k}{m}}=\sqrt{\frac{50\times1000}{50}}=31.62 \text{ rad/s}$$

Amplitude ratio, $\quad \frac{X}{X_{st}}=\frac{1}{1-\left(\frac{\omega}{\omega_n}\right)^2}$

or $\quad \frac{X}{F_o/k}=\frac{1}{1-\left(\frac{\omega}{\omega_n}\right)^2}$

$$X=\frac{100/50000}{1-\left(\frac{100}{31.62}\right)^2}=2.22\times10^{-4}\text{ m}$$

$$X = 0.222 \text{ mm}$$

Q.31 Ans:(A)

The free-body diagram of system is constructed for an arbitrary displacement θ from mean position as shown in figure. Moment equation about hinge O,

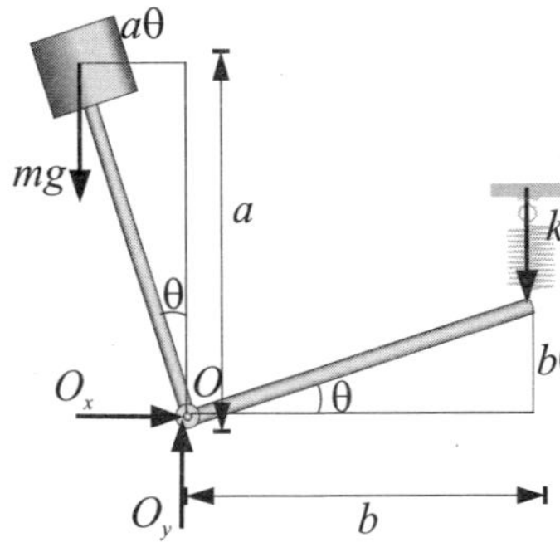

$$ma^2 \frac{d^2\theta}{dt^2} = -kb\theta \times b + mg \times a\theta$$

or $$\frac{d^2\theta}{dt^2} + \frac{(kb^2 - mga)}{ma^2}\theta = 0$$

Oscillations occurs if $kb^2 - mga > 0$

$$k > \frac{mga}{b^2}$$

Q.32 Ans:(C)

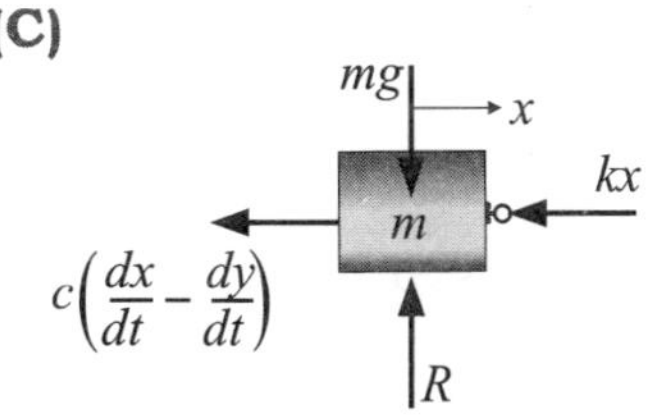

From the free-body diagram of figure, Newton second law gives

$$m\frac{d^2x}{dt^2} = -kx - c\left(\frac{dx}{dt} - \frac{dy}{dt}\right)$$

$$m\frac{d^2x}{dt^2} + c\left(\frac{dx}{dt} - \frac{dy}{dt}\right) + kx = 0$$

Q.33 Ans:(B)

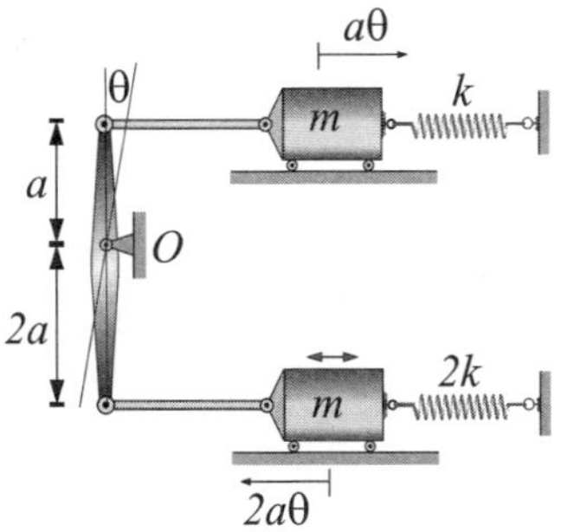

Applying moment about O,

$$ma^2 \frac{d^2\theta}{dt^2} + m(2a)^2 \frac{d^2\theta}{dt^2} = -ka\theta \times a - 2k(2a\theta) \times 2a$$

or $$5ma^2 \frac{d^2\theta}{dt^2} = -9ka^2\theta$$

or $$\frac{d^2\theta}{dt^2} + \frac{9k}{5m}\theta = 0$$

From which

$$\omega_n = \sqrt{\frac{9k}{5m}}$$

Q.34 Ans:(B)

(a) $\frac{d^2x}{dt^2} + bx = 0$ $\rightarrow$ 3. Undamped free vibrations

(b) $\frac{d^2x}{dt^2} + bx = c\sin\omega t$ $\rightarrow$ 1. Undamped forced vibrations

(c) $\frac{d^2x}{dt^2} + a\frac{dx}{dt} + bx = 0$ $\rightarrow$ 4. Damped free vibrations

(d) $\frac{d^2x}{dt^2} + a\frac{dx}{dt} + bx = c\sin\omega t$ $\rightarrow$ 2. Damped forced vibrations

Q.35 Ans:(A)

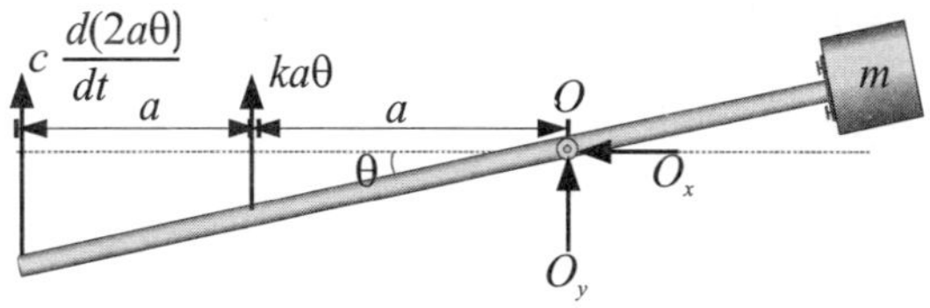

From the free body diagram of figure, we may apply moment equation about O to obtain

$$ma^2 \frac{d^2\theta}{dt^2} = -ka\theta \times a - c\frac{d(2a\theta)}{dt} \times 2a$$

or $$ma^2 \frac{d^2\theta}{dt^2} + 4a^2c\frac{d\theta}{dt} + ka^2\theta = 0$$

$$\frac{d^2\theta}{dt^2} + \frac{4c}{m}\frac{d\theta}{dt} + \frac{k}{m}\theta = 0$$

Q.36 Ans:(A)

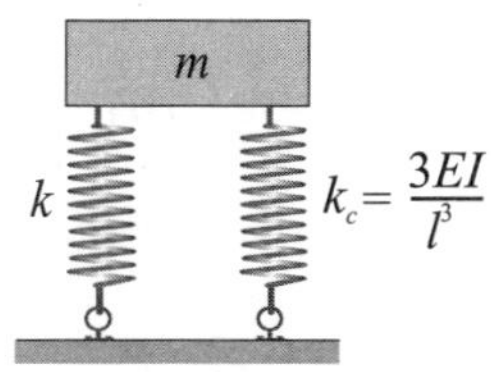

Equivalent diagram

Spring stiffness of cantilever beam, $k_c = \frac{P}{\Delta} = \frac{3EI}{l^3}$

Equivalent stiffness, $k_{eq} = k_c + k = \frac{3EI}{l^3} + k$

or $$k_{eq} = \frac{3EI + kl^3}{l^3}$$

Natural frequency, $$\omega_n = \sqrt{\frac{k_{eq}}{m}} = \sqrt{\frac{3EI + kl^3}{ml^3}}$$

$$\omega_n = \sqrt{\frac{3EI + kl^3}{ml^3}}$$

Q.37 Ans:(A)

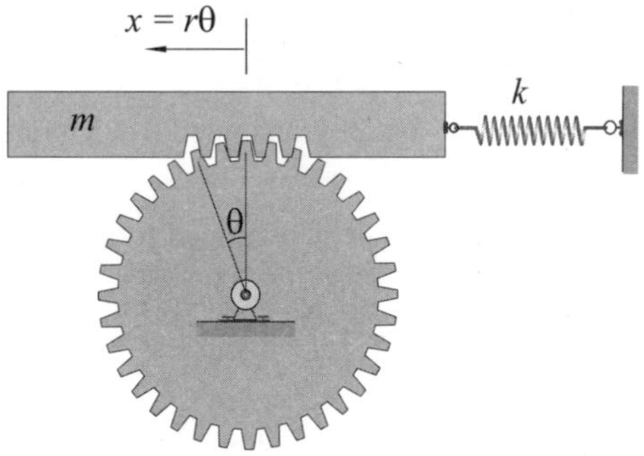

A diagram of rack-pinion-spring when rack is displaced by x from the equilibrium position is shown in the figure. Since $x = r\theta$, the kinetic energy of the system is

$$\text{KE} = \frac{1}{2}m\left(\frac{dx}{dt}\right)^2 + \frac{1}{2}I\left(\frac{d\theta}{dt}\right)^2$$

$$\text{KE} = \frac{1}{2}m\left(\frac{d(r\theta)}{dt}\right)^2 + \frac{1}{2}\times\frac{1}{2}mr^2\left(\frac{d\theta}{dt}\right)^2$$

$$= \frac{3}{4}mr^2\left(\frac{d\theta}{dt}\right)^2$$

Potential energy, $\text{PE} = \frac{1}{2}kx^2 = \frac{1}{2}k(r\theta)^2$

Total energy of the system,

$$\text{KE} + \text{PE} = \frac{3}{4}mr^2\left(\frac{d\theta}{dt}\right)^2 + \frac{1}{2}k(r\theta)^2$$

Total energy of the system remains constant

$$\frac{d}{dt}\left[\frac{3}{4}mr^2\left(\frac{d\theta}{dt}\right)^2 + \frac{1}{2}k(r\theta)^2\right] = 0$$

From which

$$\frac{d^2\theta}{dt^2} + \frac{2k}{3m} = 0$$

Q.38 Ans:(B)

Kinetic energy of the system, $\text{KE} = \frac{1}{2}I_A\omega_A^2 + \frac{1}{2}I_B\omega_B^2$

Substituting $\omega_B = n\omega_A$, we have

$$\text{KE} = \frac{1}{2}I_A\omega_A^2 + \frac{1}{2}I_B(n\omega_A)^2$$

or $$\text{KE} = \frac{1}{2}(I_A + n^2 I_B)\omega_A^2$$

Equivalent moment of inertia of disk B at the speed of shaft A is equal to $n^2 I_B$.

Q.39 Ans:(B)

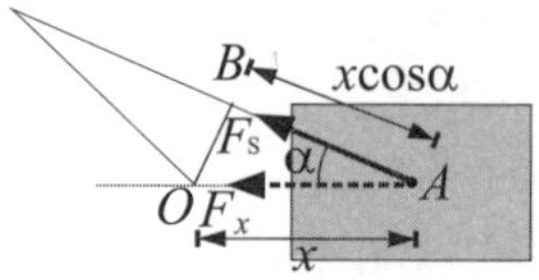

Free body diagram of the mass is constructed for an arbitrary displacement x from equilibrium position as shown in figure. The spring is deformed by an amount $AB = x\cos\alpha$ along its axis.

Spring force along spring axis is $F_s = k(x\cos\alpha)$

The component of F_S along the direction of motion of mass is $F_x = F_s\cos\alpha = kx\cos^2\alpha$

The equation of motion of the mass m is $m\frac{d^2x}{dt^2} = -F_x$

or $$m\frac{d^2x}{dt^2} = -kx\cos^2\alpha$$

or $$\frac{d^2x}{dt^2} + \frac{k\cos^2\alpha}{m}x = 0$$

$$\omega_n = \sqrt{\frac{k\cos^2\alpha}{m}}$$

Q.40 Ans:(A)

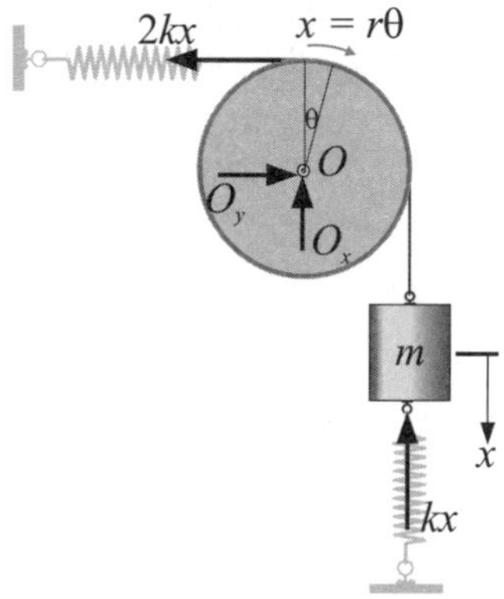

Free-body diagram of the system, which includes the block of mass m and pulley(disk), at an arbitrary instant is shown in figure. The governing equation is:

$$m\frac{d^2x}{dt^2}\times r + I\frac{d^2\theta}{dt^2} = -kx\times r - 2kx\times r$$

Substituting $x = r\theta$ and $I = \frac{1}{2}mr^2$

$$m\frac{d^2(r\theta)}{dt^2} \times r + \frac{1}{2}mr^2\frac{d^2\theta}{dt^2} = -kr\theta \times r - 2kr\theta \times r$$

or $$\frac{d^2\theta}{dt^2} + \frac{2k}{m}\theta = 0$$

From which

$$\omega_n = \sqrt{\frac{2k}{m}}$$

Q.41 Ans:(D)

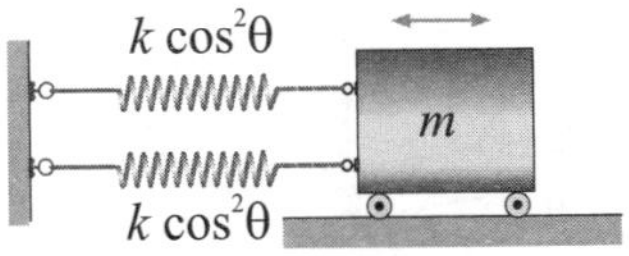

Equivalent diagram

Equivalent spring constant along the direction of motion:

$$k_{eq} = k\cos^2\theta + k\cos^2\theta = 2k\cos^2\theta$$

Natural frequency, $$\omega_n = \sqrt{\frac{k_{eq}}{m}} = \sqrt{\frac{2k\cos^2\theta}{m}}$$

$$\omega_n = \sqrt{\frac{2k\cos^2\theta}{m}}$$

Q.42 Ans:(D)

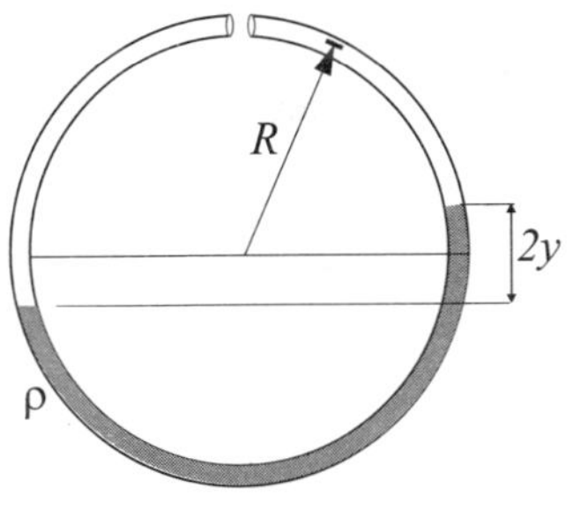

Let a be the cross-sectional area of glass tube, ρ be the density of fluid and R be the radius of the tube. Then the total mass of manometric fluid undergoing motion is $m = \rho\pi Ra$. If the column of liquid is displaced vertically by a distance of y, then the restoring force acting on the liquid mass tending to bring it to the equilibrium.

Restoring force, $F = \rho g 2ya$

Governing equation, $$m\frac{d^2y}{dt^2} = -F$$

$$\rho\pi Ra\frac{d^2y}{dt^2} = -\rho g2ya$$

or $$\frac{d^2y}{dt^2} + \frac{2g}{\pi R}y = 0$$

From which

$$\omega_n = \sqrt{\frac{2g}{\pi R}} = \frac{2\pi}{T}$$

$$T = \sqrt{\frac{2\pi^3 R}{g}}$$

Q.43 Ans:(B)

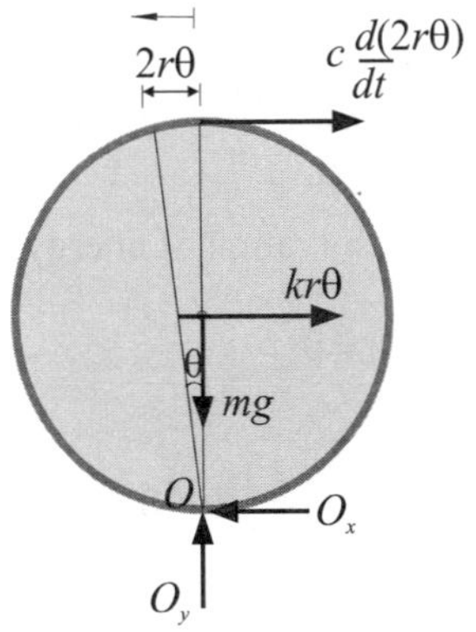

The equation of motion for the body with damping is determined from the free-body diagram as shown in figure.

$$I_O\frac{d^2\theta}{dt^2} = -\sum M_O$$

or $$\frac{3}{2}mr^2\frac{d^2\theta}{dt^2} = -kr\theta \times r - c\frac{d(2r\theta)}{dt} \times 2r$$

or $$\frac{3}{2}mr^2\frac{d^2\theta}{dt^2} + 4cr^2\frac{d\theta}{dt} + kr^2\theta = 0$$

$$\frac{d^2\theta}{dt^2} + \frac{8c}{3m}\frac{d\theta}{dt} + \frac{2k}{3m}\theta = 0$$

Q.44 Ans:(B)

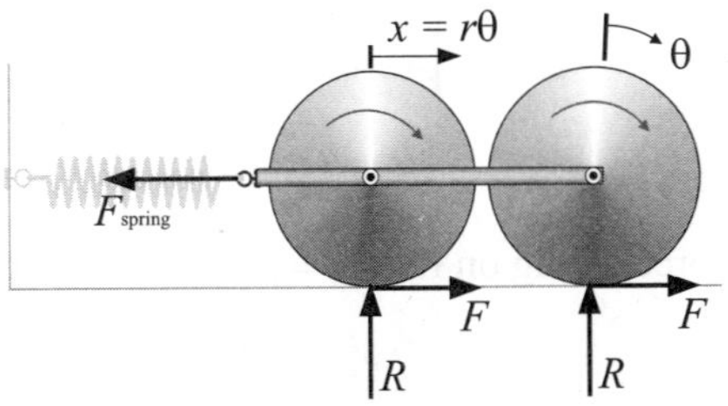

A diagram of the rod and disks when they are displaced by x from the equilibrium position is shown in figure. Since $x = r\theta$, the kinetic energy of the system is

$$\text{KE} = 2\left[\frac{1}{2}I\left(\frac{d\theta}{dt}\right)^2 + \frac{1}{2}m\left(\frac{dx}{dt}\right)^2\right]$$

$$= 2\left[\frac{1}{2}\times\frac{1}{2}mr^2\left(\frac{d\theta}{dt}\right)^2 + \frac{1}{2}m\left(\frac{d(r\theta)}{dt}\right)^2\right]$$

$$= \frac{3}{2}mr^2\left(\frac{d\theta}{dt}\right)^2$$

Potential energy of the system is

$$\text{PE} = \frac{1}{2}kx^2 = \frac{1}{2}kr^2\theta^2 \qquad [x = r\theta]$$

Total energy for the system is

$$\text{KE} + \text{PE} = \frac{3}{2}mr^2\left(\frac{d\theta}{dt}\right)^2 + \frac{1}{2}kr^2\theta^2$$

The condition for conservation of energy,

$$\frac{d}{dt}(\text{KE} + \text{PE}) = 0$$

$$\frac{d}{dt}\left[\frac{3}{2}mr^2\left(\frac{d\theta}{dt}\right)^2 + \frac{1}{2}kr^2\theta^2\right] = 0$$

or $$\left(\frac{d^2\theta}{dt^2}\right) + \frac{k}{3m}\theta = 0$$

$$\omega_n = \sqrt{\frac{k}{3m}}$$

Q.45 Ans:(A)

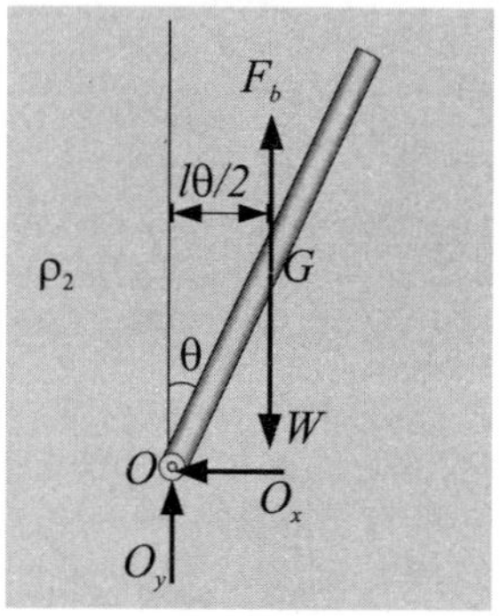

Buoyant force acting on rod $F_b = \rho_2 gAl$ and weight of rod $W = \rho_1 gAl$

Restoring moment, $M = (F_b - W)\frac{l}{2}\theta$

Governing equation of motion, $I_O\frac{d^2\theta}{dt^2} = -(F_b - W)\frac{l}{2}\theta$

$$\frac{d^2\theta}{dt^2} + \frac{(F_b - W)l}{2I_O}\theta = 0$$

or $$\frac{d^2\theta}{dt^2} + \frac{(\rho_2 gAl - \rho_1 gAl)l}{2\times\frac{1}{3}\rho_1 Al\times l^2}\theta = 0$$

$$\omega_n = \sqrt{\frac{3(\rho_2 - \rho_1)g}{2\rho_1 l}}$$

Q.46 Ans:(D)

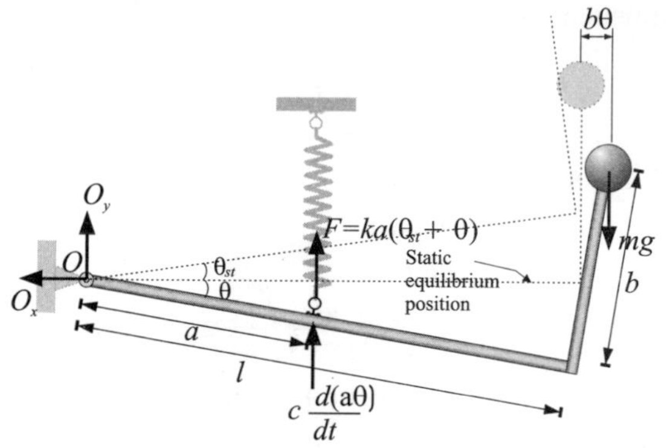

The free-body diagram of the rod is constructed for an arbitrary displacement θ from equilibrium position as shown in figure. The moment equation is

$$I_O\frac{d^2\theta}{dt^2} = -ka\theta\times a - c\frac{d(a\theta)}{dt}\times a + mgb\theta$$

or $$\frac{d^2\theta}{dt^2} + \frac{ca^2}{I_O}\frac{d\theta}{dt} + \left(\frac{ka^2 - mgb}{I_O}\right)\theta = 0$$

The system becomes unstable (does not vibrate), if

$$\left(\frac{ka^2 - mgb}{I_O}\right) < 0 \text{ (negative)}$$

$$b > \frac{ka^2}{mg}$$

Q.47 Ans:(B)

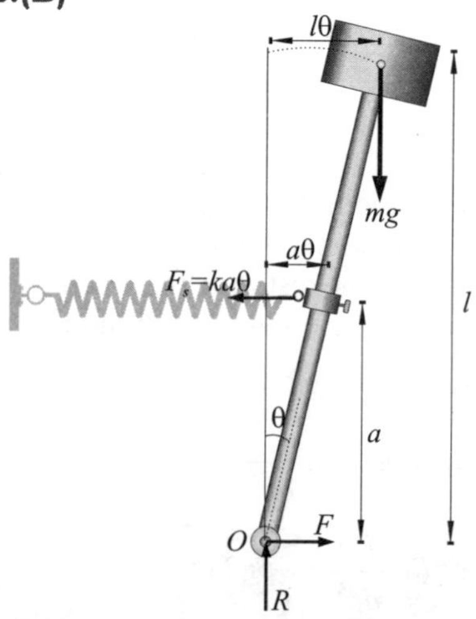

Figure shows the free-body diagram of system when it is displaced a small angle θ from the vertical equilibrium position. Moment equation about O.

$$-ka\theta \times a + mg \times l\theta = I_O \frac{d^2\theta}{dt^2}$$

$$I_O \frac{d^2\theta}{dt^2} + (ka^2 - mgl)\theta = 0$$

or
$$\frac{d^2\theta}{dt^2} + \frac{(ka^2 - mgl)}{I_O}\theta = 0$$

Hence

$$\omega_n = \sqrt{\frac{ka^2 - mgl}{I_O}}$$

Q.48 Ans:(B)

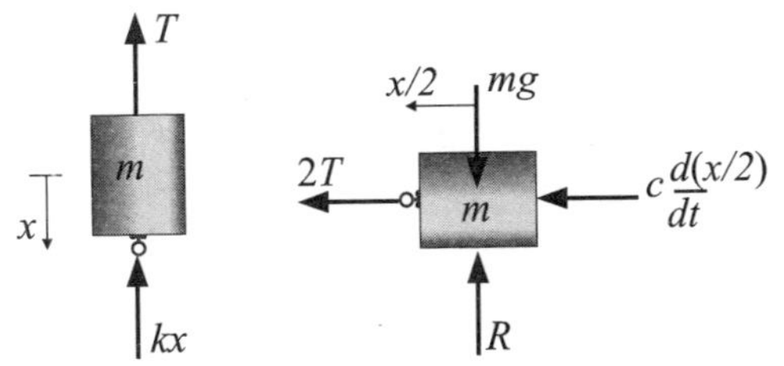

Let T be the tension of cable. From the free-body diagram of figure, Newton's second law gives

$$m\frac{d^2x}{dt^2} = -kx - T \qquad \text{(i)}$$

$$m\frac{d^2(x/2)}{dt^2} = -c\frac{d(x/2)}{dt} + 2T \qquad \text{(ii)}$$

Eliminating T from Equation (i) and (ii), we obtain

$$5m\frac{d^2x}{dt^2} + c\frac{dx}{dt} + 4kx = 0$$

Q.49 Ans:(C)

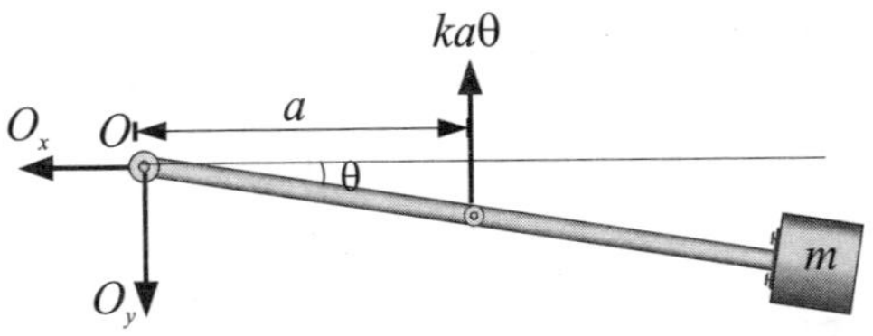

From the free-body diagram, moment equation gives

$$m(2a)^2\frac{d^2\theta}{dt^2} = -ka\theta \times a$$

or
$$\frac{d^2\theta}{dt^2} + \frac{ka^2}{4ma^2}\theta = 0$$

$$\omega_n = \sqrt{\frac{k}{4m}}$$

Q.50 Ans:(D)

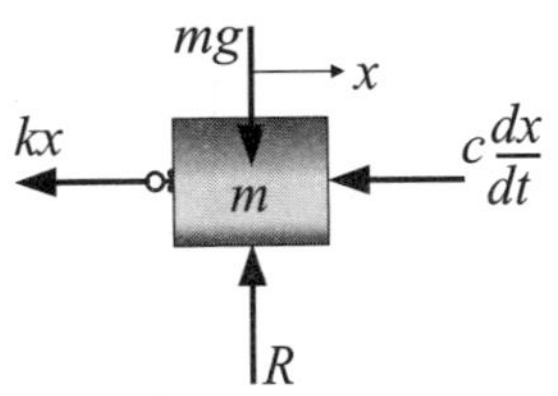

From the free-body diagram, Newton's second law gives

$$m\frac{d^2x}{dt^2} = -kx - c\frac{dx}{dt}$$

or
$$m\frac{d^2x}{dt^2} + c\frac{dx}{dt} + kx = 0$$

Condition of critically damped system,

$$c^2 = \sqrt{4mk} = \sqrt{4 \times 5 \times 20}$$

$$c = 20 \text{ Ns/m}$$

Q.51 Ans:[0.4]

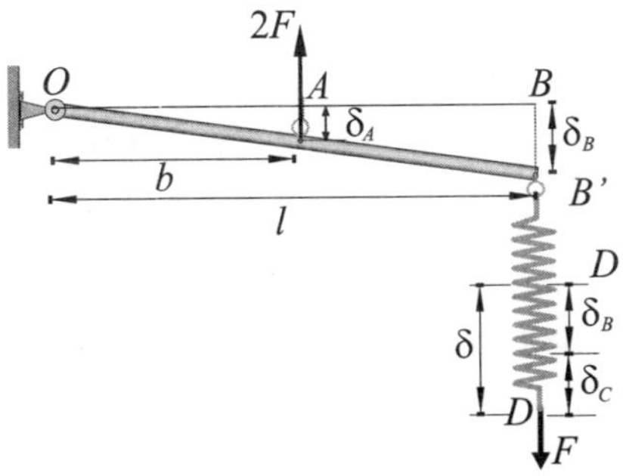

Figure shows method for calculating the equivalent spring stiffness. First, vertical force F is applied at B, and the vertical moment δ is computed, the equivalent spring stiffness $k_{eq} = \frac{F}{\delta}$.

$$\delta = \frac{4F}{k} + \frac{F}{k} = \frac{5F}{k}$$

or
$$k_{eq} = \frac{F}{\delta} = \frac{k}{5} = \frac{2}{5} \text{ kN/m}$$

$$k_{eq} = 0.4 \text{ kN/m}$$

Q.52 Ans:[0.64]

Damping factor $\zeta = \frac{c}{c_c} = \frac{c}{2\sqrt{mk}}$

$$= \frac{20}{2\sqrt{3 \times 80}}$$

$$\zeta = 0.64$$

Q.53 Ans:[56.5]

Figure shows a method for calculating the equivalent spring stiffness. Vertical force F is applied at mass and the vertical deflection δ is calculated.

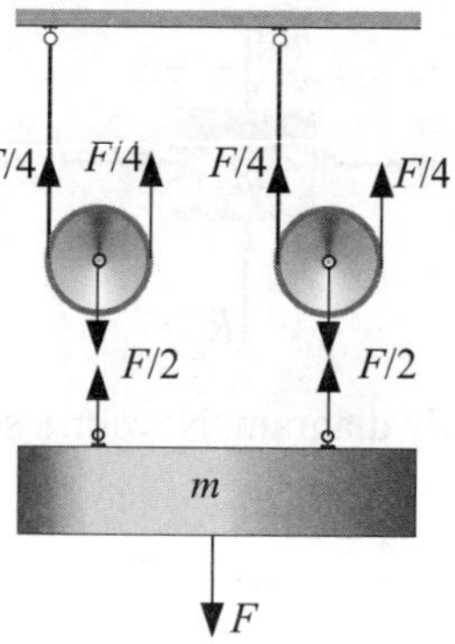

$$k_{eq} = \frac{F}{\delta}$$

Force in each spring is $\frac{F}{4}$ and deflection of spring is $\frac{F}{4k}$, the displacement of center of pulley is $\frac{F}{8k}$. Therefore,

$$\delta = \frac{F}{8k} \Rightarrow k_{eq} = \frac{F}{\delta} = 8k = 8 \times 4000$$

Natural frequency, $\omega_n = \sqrt{\frac{k_{eq}}{m}} = \sqrt{\frac{8 \times 4000}{10}}$

$$\omega_n = 56.5 \text{ rad/s}$$

Q.54 Ans:[3.32]

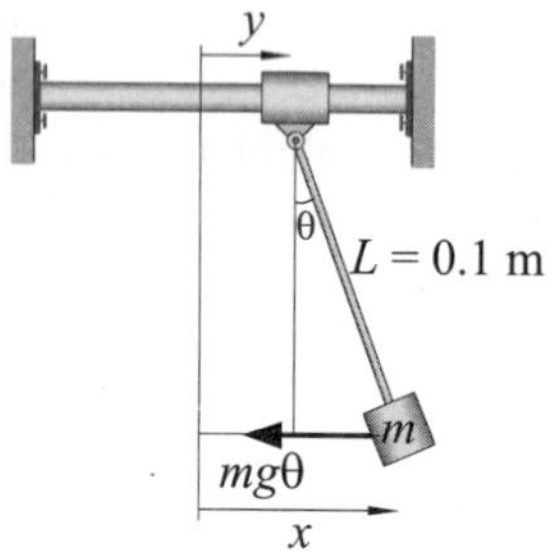

Applying Newton's second law along x-axis,

$$m\frac{d^2x}{dt^2} = -mg\theta$$

or $$\frac{d^2x}{dt^2} + g\theta = 0$$

Substituting $\theta = \frac{x-y}{L}$; $\frac{d^2x}{dt^2} + g\left(\frac{x-y}{L}\right) = 0$

$$\frac{d^2x}{dt^2} + \frac{g}{L}x = \frac{g}{L} \times 0.01\sin(6t)$$

Steady state amplitude,

$$X = \frac{\frac{g}{L} \times 0.01}{\frac{g}{L} - 6^2} = \frac{\frac{9.81}{0.1} \times 0.01}{\frac{9.81}{0.1} - 6^2} = 0.0158 \text{ and } Y = 0.01$$

Angular amplitude, $\theta_{max} = \frac{X - Y}{L} = \frac{0.0158 - 0.01}{0.1}$

$$\theta_{max} = \frac{6^2 \times 0.01}{9.81 - 6^2 \times 0.1} = 0.057 \text{ rad}$$

$$\theta_{max} = 3.32^\circ$$

Q.55 Ans:[1]

Transmissibility, $TR = \frac{1}{1 - \left(\frac{\omega}{\omega_n}\right)^2} = \frac{1}{1 - (\sqrt{2})^2}$

$$TR = 1$$

Q.56 Ans:[5577]

From the free-body diagram, moment equation gives

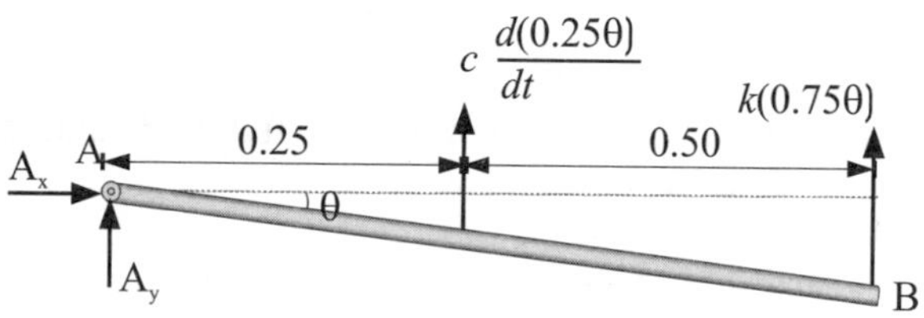

$$I_A\frac{d^2\theta}{dt^2} = -c\frac{d(0.25\theta)}{dt} \times 0.25 - k \times 0.75\theta \times 0.75 = 0$$

or $$\frac{1}{3}m(0.75)^2\frac{d^2\theta}{dt^2} + c(0.25)^2\frac{d\theta}{dt} + k(0.75)^2\theta = 0$$

or $$\frac{d^2\theta}{dt^2} + \left(\frac{c}{3m}\right)\frac{d\theta}{dt} + \frac{3k}{m}\theta = 0$$

System is critically damped; $\left(\frac{c}{3m}\right)^2 = 4 \times \frac{3k}{m}$

or $$c = 6\sqrt{3mk} = 6\sqrt{3 \times 24 \times 12000}$$

$$c = 5577 \text{ Ns/m}$$

Q.57 Ans:[0.866]

The moment of inertia of bar about O, $I_O = m\left(\frac{l^2}{12} + c^2\right)$

Let the bar be displaced through a small angle θ from vertical equilibrium position as shown in figure.

Then restoring moment,

$$M_O = -mg\sin\theta \times OG$$

or $M_O = -mg\theta \times OG$ (since θ is small)

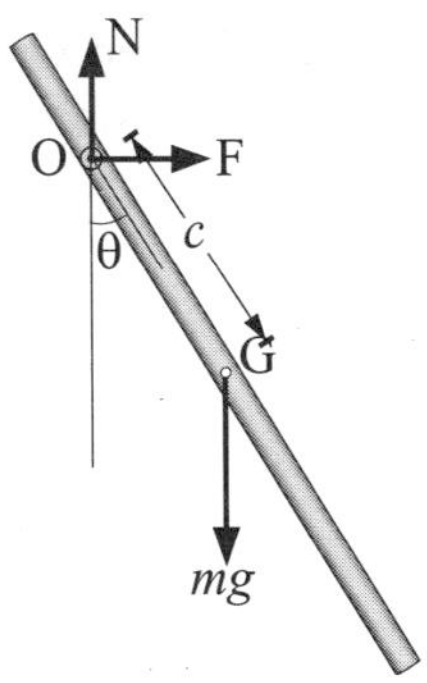

Therefore, the equation of motion for bar is

$$I_O \frac{d^2\theta}{dt^2} = -mg\theta \times OG$$

or $$m\left(\frac{l^2}{12}+c^2\right)\frac{d^2\theta}{dt^2} + mg\theta \times c = 0$$

or $$\frac{d^2\theta}{dt^2} + \frac{g}{\left(\frac{l^2}{12c}+c\right)}\theta = 0$$

Period of oscillation, $T = 2\pi\sqrt{\dfrac{\left(\frac{l^2}{12c}+c\right)}{g}}$

For minimum period of oscillation, $\dfrac{dT}{dc} = 0$

From which $c = \dfrac{l}{\sqrt{12}} = \dfrac{3}{\sqrt{12}}$

$$c = 0.866\,\text{m}$$

Q.58 Ans:[0.110]

Ratio of successive amplitude, $\dfrac{x_i}{x_{i+1}} = \dfrac{x_0}{x_0/2} = 2$

Logarithmic decrement, $\delta = \ln\left(\dfrac{x_i}{x_{i+1}}\right) = \ln 2 = 0.693$

$$\delta = \frac{2\pi}{\sqrt{1-\zeta^2}}$$

or $$\zeta = \frac{\delta}{\sqrt{(2\pi)^2+\delta^2}} = \frac{0.693}{\sqrt{(2\pi)^2+0.693^2}}$$

Damping ratio, $\zeta = 0.110$

Q.59 Ans:[0.1]

Amplitude ratio of undamped forced vibration,

$$\frac{X}{X_{st}} = \frac{1}{1-\left(\frac{\omega}{\omega_n}\right)^2}$$

or $$\frac{X}{(F_o/k)} = \frac{1}{1-\left(\frac{\omega}{\omega_n}\right)^2}$$

Substituting $F_o = 100$ N, $k = 3000$ N/m, $X = \dfrac{50}{1000}$ m and $\omega = 100$ rad/s

$$\frac{\frac{50}{1000}}{\frac{100}{3000}} = \frac{1}{1-\left(\frac{100}{\omega_n}\right)^2}$$

From which

$$\omega_n = 173.2 = \sqrt{\frac{k}{m}} \quad \text{or} \quad \sqrt{\frac{3000}{m}} = 173.2$$

$$m = 0.1\,\text{kg}$$

Q.60 Ans:[810]

Deflection of shaft, $h = \dfrac{\left(\frac{\omega}{\omega_n}\right)^2 e}{1-\left(\frac{\omega}{\omega_n}\right)^2}$

Substituting $\dfrac{\omega}{\omega_n} = 0.9$ and $e = 190$ microns, we have

$$h = \frac{0.9^2 \times 190}{1-0.9^2}$$

$$h = 810\,\text{microns}$$

Q.61 Ans:[8.49]

Frequency of torsional vibration, $f_n = \dfrac{1}{2\pi}\sqrt{\dfrac{k_t}{I}}$

Substituting $I = 15.\,\text{kg·m}^2$ and $k_t = 2 \times \dfrac{GJ}{l} = \dfrac{G\pi d^4}{16l}$

$$k_t = \frac{85\times10^9 \times \pi \times \left(\frac{40}{1000}\right)^4}{16\times1} = 42725.66$$

$$f_n = \frac{1}{2\pi}\sqrt{\frac{42725.66}{15}}$$

$$f_n = 8.49\,\text{Hz}$$

Q.62 Ans:[427]

Equivalent spring constant, $k_{eq} = 4k = 4 \times 100 \times 1000$

$$\omega_n = \sqrt{\frac{k_{eq}}{m}} = \sqrt{\frac{4 \times 10^5}{200}} = 44.72$$

or $$\frac{2\pi N}{60} = 44.72$$

Resonance occurs at $N = 427$ rpm

Q.63 Ans:[0.066]

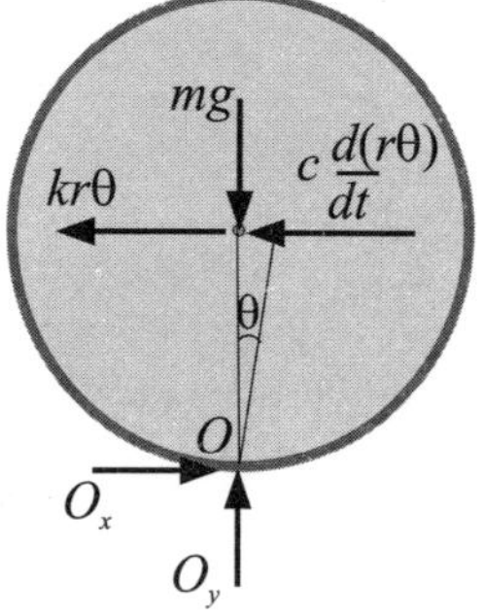

From the free-body diagram, moment equation about O gives

$$I_O \frac{d^2\theta}{dt^2} = -kr\theta \times r - c\frac{d(r\theta)}{dt} \times r$$

or $$\frac{3}{2}mr^2 \frac{d^2\theta}{dt^2} + cr^2 \frac{d\theta}{dt} + kr^2\theta = 0$$

or $$\frac{3}{2}m\frac{d^2\theta}{dt^2} + c\frac{d\theta}{dt} + k\theta = 0$$

Damping ratio, $$\zeta = \frac{c}{c_c} = \frac{c}{2\sqrt{\frac{3}{2}mk}}$$

$$\zeta = \frac{c}{\sqrt{6mk}} = \frac{10}{\sqrt{6 \times 50 \times 75}}$$

$$\zeta = 0.066$$

Q.64 Ans:[0.788]

Free-body diagram of the cylinder when it is displaced an arbitrary distance x below its equilibrium position is shown in figure. From the free-body diagram, Newton second law gives

$$m\frac{d^2x}{dt^2} = -F_b$$

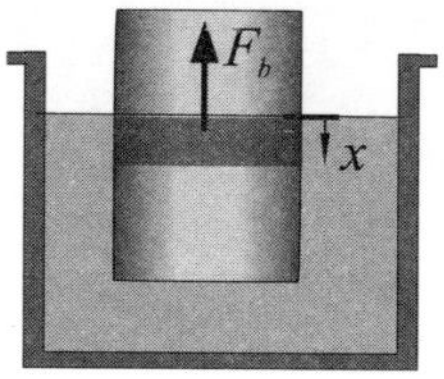

or $$\frac{d^2x}{dt^2} + \frac{F_b}{m} = 0$$

or $$\frac{d^2x}{dt^2} + \frac{\rho A g}{m}x = 0$$

Hence, the natural frequency of the system is

$$f_n = \frac{1}{2\pi}\sqrt{\frac{\rho A g}{m}} = \frac{1}{2\pi}\sqrt{\frac{1000 \times 0.01 \times 9.81}{4}}$$

$$f_n = 0.788 \text{ Hz}$$

Q.65 Ans:[43.81]

Damped frequency, $\omega_d = \omega_n\sqrt{1-\zeta^2}$

or damped period, $$T_d = \frac{T}{\sqrt{1-\zeta^2}}$$

Substituting $T = 0.2T_d$, we get

$$T_d = \frac{0.2T_d}{\sqrt{1-\zeta^2}}$$

We obtain, $\zeta = 0.979$

or $$\zeta = \frac{c}{2\sqrt{mk}} = \frac{c}{2\sqrt{5 \times 100}} = 0.979$$

$$c = 43.81 \text{ Ns/m}$$

GATE Syllabus

Design for static and dynamic loading; Failure theories; Fatigue strength and the S-N diagram; Principles of the design of machine elements such as bolted, riveted and welded joints; Shafts, gears, rolling, sliding contact bearings, brakes and clutches, and springs.

Chapter Outline

9.1 KEY CONCEPTS AND FORMULAS

Design for Static and Dynamic Loading

A static load is defined as a force, which is gradually applied to a mechanical component and which does not change its magnitude or direction with respect to time.

Factor of safety (FS)

The factor of safety is defined as: $\text{FS} = \dfrac{\text{Failure stress}}{\text{Allowable stress}}$

or $$\text{FS} = \frac{\text{Failure load}}{\text{Working stress}}$$

The allowable stress is the stress value, which is used in design to determine the dimensions of the components.

Allowable stress

$$\sigma = \frac{\sigma_{yt}}{\text{FS}} \text{ (for ductile materials)}$$

$$\sigma = \frac{\sigma_{ut}}{\text{FS}} \text{ (for brittle materials)}$$

Relation between Stress and Strain

The internal resisting force per unit area of the component is called *stress*, $\sigma = \dfrac{P}{A}$

$1 \text{ MPa} = 10^6 \text{ Pa} = 1 \text{ N/mm}^2$

The strain is deformation per unit length. It is given by $\varepsilon = \dfrac{\delta}{l}$.

According to Hooke's law; the stress is directly proportional to the strain within elastic limit.

$$\sigma = E\varepsilon$$

Modulus of elasticity, $E = 207\text{GPa}$ (Carbon steel), $E = 100\text{GPa}$ (Grey cast steel)

Shear stress-strain relationship, $\tau = G\gamma$

The relationship between the modulus of elasticity E, modulus of rigidity G, $E = 2G(1+\mu)$

The permissible shear stress, $\tau = \frac{\tau_{ys}}{FS}$

According to principal shear stress theory of failure, $\tau_{ys} = \frac{\sigma_{yt}}{2}$

Stresses due to Bending and Torsional Moment

Bending stress, $\sigma_b = \frac{M_b}{I} y$

For a rectangular cross-section, $I = \frac{b d^3}{12}$

For a circular cross-section, $I = \frac{\pi d^4}{64}$

Torsional shear stress, $\tau = \frac{T}{J} r$, Angle of twist, $\theta = \frac{TL}{GJ}$

For a circular cross-section, $J = \frac{\pi d^4}{32}$

For a hollow circular cross-section, $J = \frac{\pi(d_o^4 - d_i^4)}{32}$

Principal Stresses

Maximum and minimum normal stress:

$$\sigma_{1,2} = \frac{\sigma_x + \sigma_y}{2} \pm \sqrt{\left(\frac{\sigma_x - \sigma_y}{2}\right)^2 + \tau_{xy}^2}$$

Principle shear stress, $\tau_{max} = \sqrt{\left(\frac{\sigma_x - \sigma_y}{2}\right)^2 + \tau_{xy}^2}$

Failure Theories

Maximum Normal Stress Theory (Rankine's theory)

The theory states that the failure of the mechanical component subjected to bi-axial or tri-axial stresses occurs when the maximum principal stress reaches the yield or ultimate strength of the material.

If σ_1, σ_2 and σ_3 are the three principal stresses at a point on the component and $\sigma_1 > \sigma_2 > \sigma_3$ then according to this theory, the failure occurs whenever $\sigma_1 = \sigma_{yt}$ or $\sigma_1 = \sigma_{ut}$ whichever is applicable.

The dimensions of the component are determined by using a factor of safety.

For tensile stresses, $\sigma_1 = \frac{\sigma_{yt}}{FS}$ or $\sigma_1 = \frac{\sigma_{ut}}{FS}$

For compressive stresses, $\sigma_1 = \frac{\sigma_{yc}}{FS}$ or $\sigma_1 = \frac{\sigma_{uc}}{FS}$

Maximum Shear Stress Theory (Tresca-Guest theory)

The theory states that the failure of a mechanical component subjected to bi-axial or tri-axial stresses occurs when the maximum shear stress at any point in the component becomes equal to the maximum shear stress in the standard specimen of the tension test, when yielding starts.

Suppose σ_1, σ_2 and σ_3 are the three principal stresses at a point on the component, the shear stresses on three different planes are given by $\tau_{12} = \frac{\sigma_1 - \sigma_2}{2}$, $\tau_{23} = \frac{\sigma_2 - \sigma_3}{2}$ and $\tau_{31} = \frac{\sigma_3 - \sigma_1}{2}$.

The largest of these stresses is equated to τ_{max} or $\frac{\sigma_{yt}}{2}$.

Considering factor of safety, $\sigma_1 - \sigma_2 = \frac{\sigma_{yt}}{FS}$,

$$\sigma_2 - \sigma_3 = \frac{\sigma_{yt}}{FS}, \quad \sigma_3 - \sigma_1 = \frac{\sigma_{yt}}{FS}$$

Distortion Energy Theory (Huber Mises-Hencky theory)

The theory states that the failure of the mechanical component subjected to bi-axial or tri-axial stresses occurs when the strain energy of distortion per unit volume at any point in the component, becomes equal to the strain energy of distortion per unit volume in the standard specimen of tension test when yielding starts.

$$\frac{\sigma_{yt}}{FS} = \sqrt{\frac{1}{2}[(\sigma_1 - \sigma_1)^2 + (\sigma_2 - \sigma_3)^2 + (\sigma_3 - \sigma_1)^2]}$$

For bi-axial stresses, $\frac{\sigma_{yt}}{FS} = \sqrt{\sigma_1^2 - \sigma_1\sigma_2 + \sigma_2^2}$

Stress Concentration

Stress concentration is defined as the localisation of high stresses due to the irregularities present in the component and abrupt changes of the cross-section.

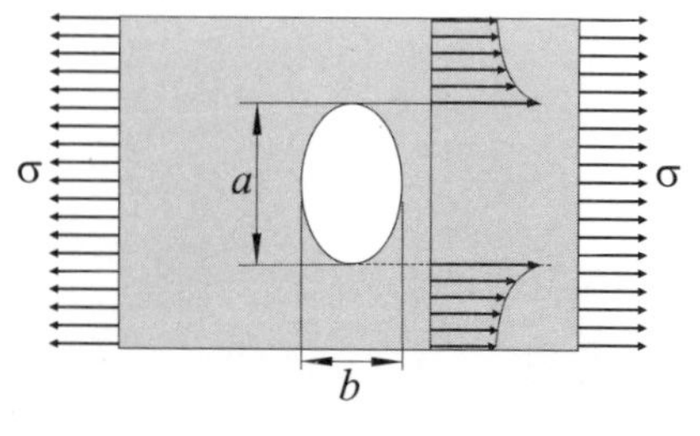

Stress concentration factor,

$$K_t = \frac{\text{Highest value of actual stress near discontinuity}}{\text{Nominal stress}}$$

Stress concentration due to elliptical hole, $K_t = 1 + 2\left(\frac{a}{b}\right)$

Fluctuating Stresses

The components subjected to loads or stresses which are not static, but vary in magnitude with respect to time are said to undergo fluctuating stresses.

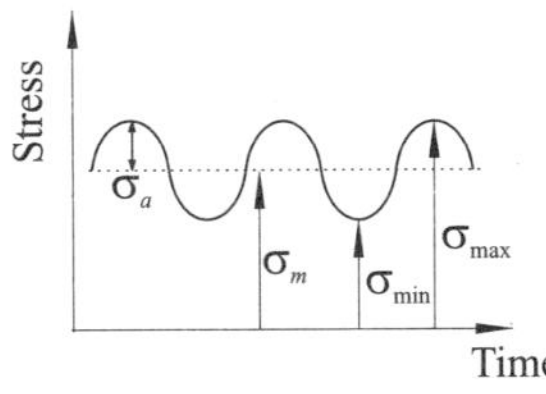

(i) Fluctuting stresses

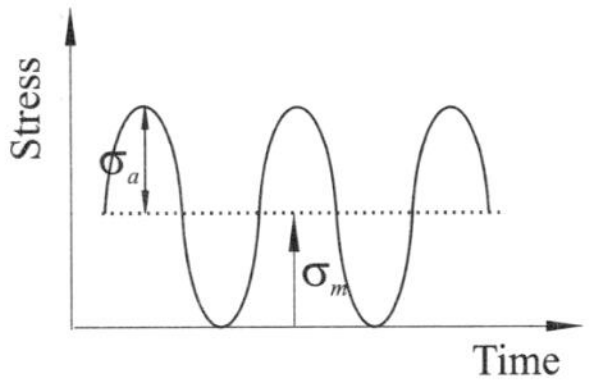

(ii) Repeated stresses

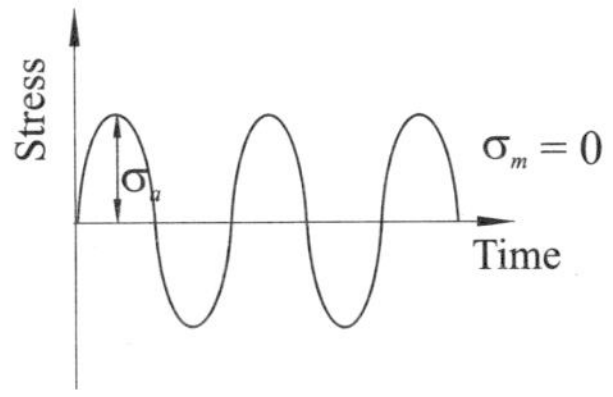

(iii) Reversed stresses

Mean stress, $\sigma_m = \frac{\sigma_{max} + \sigma_{min}}{2}$

Stress amplitude, $\sigma_a = \frac{\sigma_{max} - \sigma_{min}}{2}$

Endurance Limit

The fatigue or endurance limit of a material is defined as the maximum amplitude of completely reversed stress that the standard specimen can sustain for an unlimited number of cycles without fatigue failure.

The fatigue life is defined as the number of stress cycles that the standard specimen can complete during the test before the appearance of the first fatigue crack.

Notch Sensitivity

Fatigue stress concentration factor,

$$K_f = \frac{\text{Endurance limit of the notch free specimen}}{\text{Endurance limit of the notched specimen}}$$

S-N diagram

S-N curve is the graphical representation of stress amplitude (S_f) versus the number of stress cycles (N) before the fatigue failure on a log-log scale.

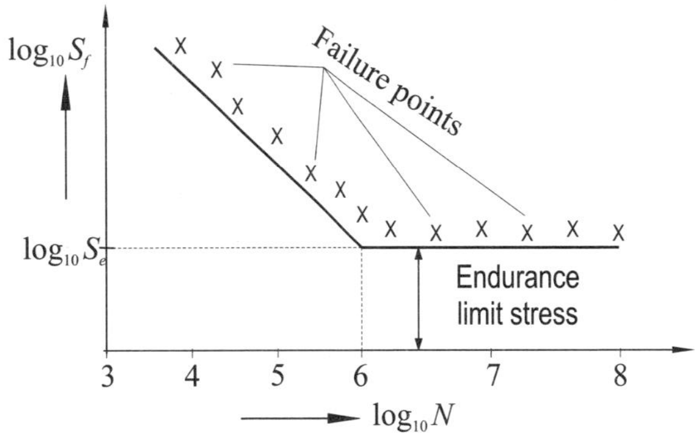

Endurance Limit: Approximate Estimation

For steel, $\sigma'_e = 0.5\,\sigma_{ut}$,

For cast iron and cast steel, $\sigma'_e = 0.4\,\sigma_{ut}$

For wrought aluminum alloys, $\sigma'_e = 0.4\,\sigma_{ut}$

$$\sigma_e = K_a K_b K_c K_d \sigma'_e$$

where K_a = Surface finish factor, K_b = Size factor, K_c = Reliability factor and K_d = Modifying factor to account for stress concentration.

Cumulative Fatigue Damage: Miner's Equation

Suppose that a component is subjected to completely reversed stresses (σ_1) for n_1 cycles, (σ_2) for n_2 cycles and so on. Let N_1 be the number of stress cycles before fatigue failure, if only the alternating stress (σ_1) is acting.

$$\frac{n_1}{N_1} + \frac{n_2}{N_2} + \ldots + \frac{n_x}{N_x} = 1$$

Fatigue Failure Criterion

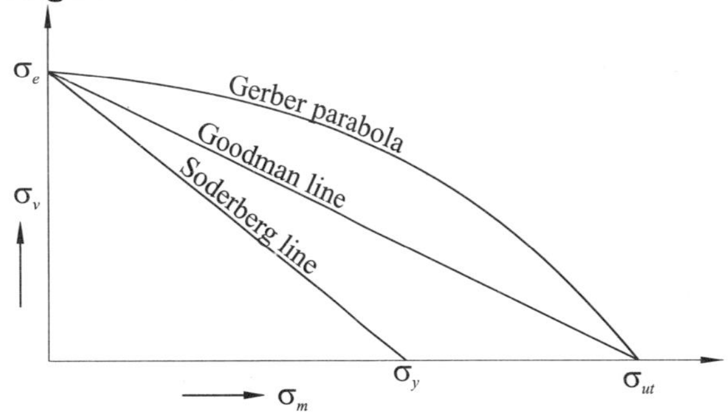

Soderberg Line : $\frac{\sigma_m}{\sigma_y} + \frac{k_f \sigma_v}{\sigma_e} = \frac{1}{\text{FS}}$

Goodman Line : $\frac{\sigma_m}{\sigma_{ut}} + \frac{k_f \sigma_v}{\sigma_e} = \frac{1}{\text{FS}}$

Gerber Parabola: $\left(\text{FS}\frac{\sigma_m}{\sigma_{ut}}\right)^2 + \text{FS}\frac{k_f \sigma_v}{\sigma_e} = 1$

Design of Bolt

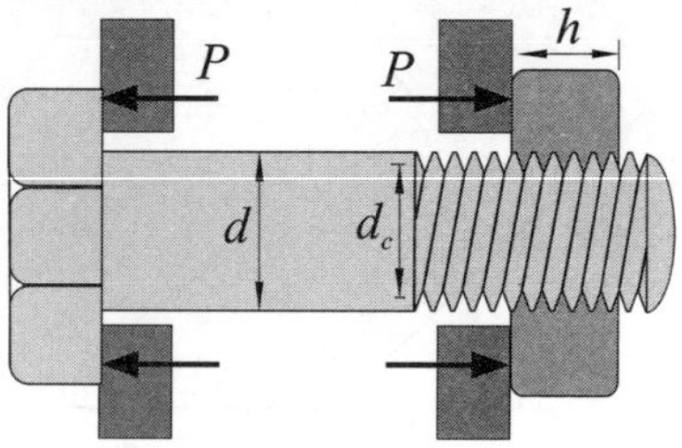

Maximum tensile stress in the bolt, $\sigma_t = \dfrac{P}{\frac{\pi}{4} d_c^2} = \dfrac{\sigma_{yt}}{\text{FS}}$

Maximum shear stress in the bolt, $\tau = \dfrac{P}{\pi d_c h} = \dfrac{\sigma_{st}}{\text{FS}} = \dfrac{\sigma_{yt}}{2\,\text{FS}}$

Design of Riveted Joints

Types of fastenings: (i) Temporary fastenings like bolts, cotter, pins, etc. (ii) Permanent fastening-like rivets and welds.

Types of Riveted Joints

Riveted Joints

- Lap joint
- Butt joint
  - Single cover plate
  - Double cover plate
- Lozenge or diamond joint
  - Lap joint
  - Butt joint
    - Single cover plate
    - Double cover plate

Strength Equations

The strength of riveted joint is defined as the force that the joint can withstand without causing failure.

Types of failure: (a) Shear failure of the rivets, (b) Tensile failure of the plate between rivets, (c) Crushing failure of the plate.

Rivets Under Eccentric Loading

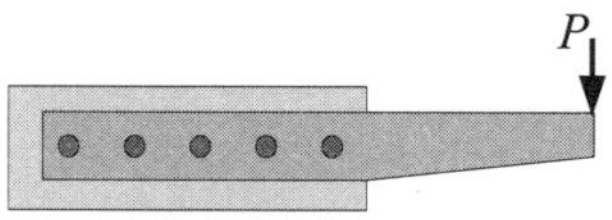

Horizontal group

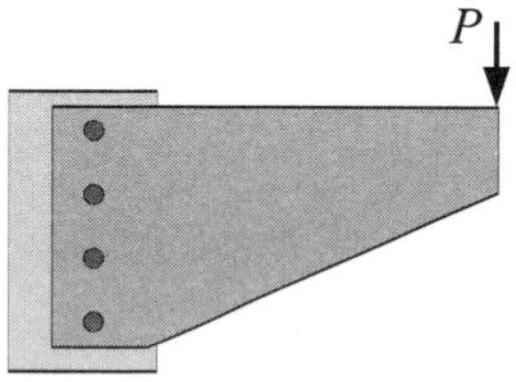

Vertical group

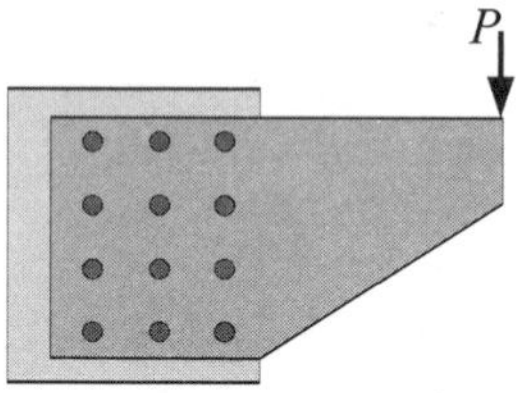

Compound group

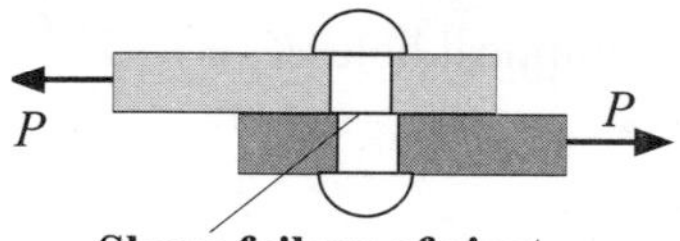

Shear failure of rivet

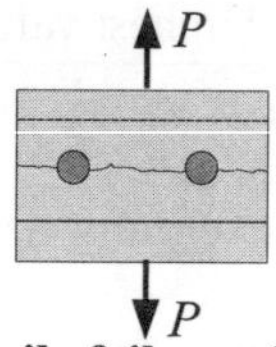

Tensile failure of plate between rivets

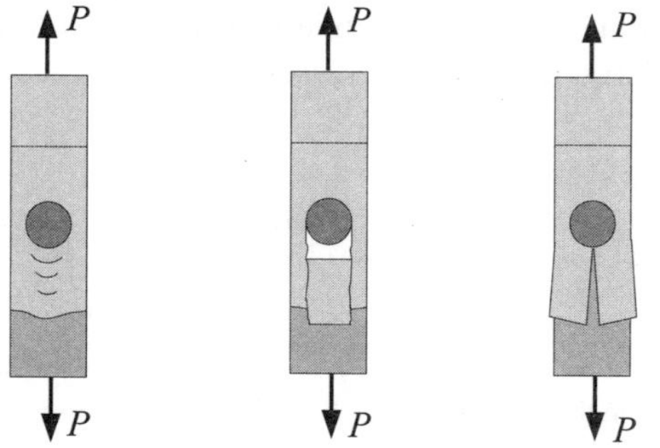

Crushing failure of plate by rivet | **Shear failure of plate by rivet** | **Tearing of plate**

Design of Welded Joints

Types of welded joints

(i) Butt weld (ii) Lap weld (iii) Edge weld (iv) Corner weld (v) Tee weld

Strength of Welds

Butt weld

Tensile stress, $\sigma_t = \dfrac{P}{hl}$

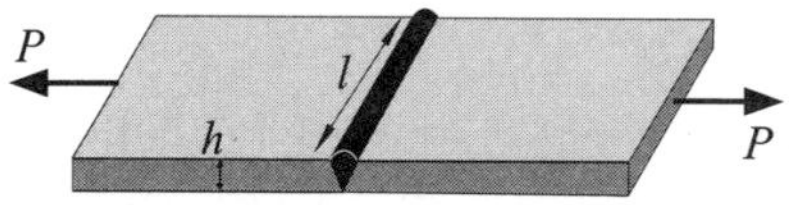

Parallel fillet weld

Shear stress, $\tau = \dfrac{P}{tl} = \dfrac{P}{h \cos 45 l}$

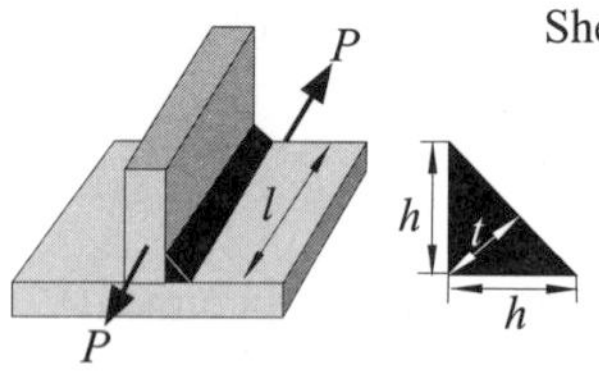

Transverse fillet weld

Tensile stress, $\sigma_t = \dfrac{P}{2(tl)}$

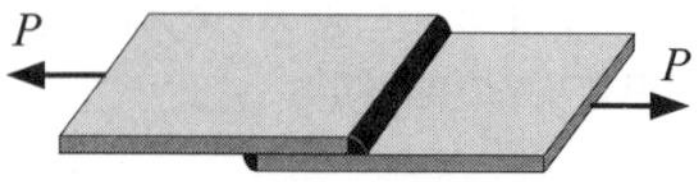

Welds under Eccentric Loading

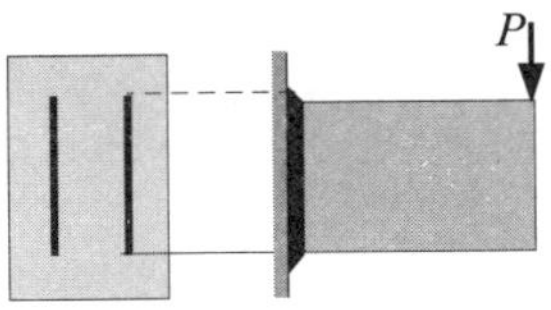

Load parallel to the weld

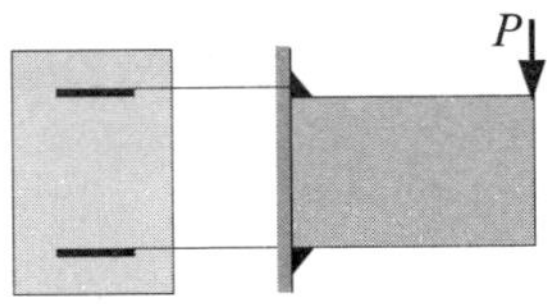

Load perpendicular to the weld

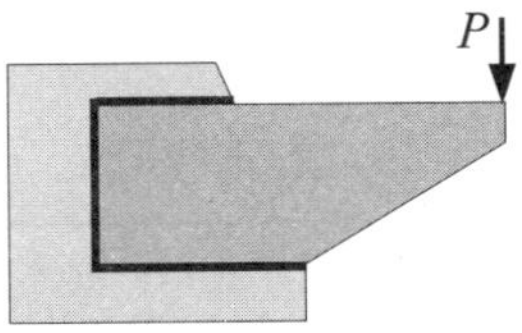

Weld parallel and perpendicular to the weld

Shafts

A shaft is a rotating elements which is used to transmit power from one place to another.

Pure Torsion

Shear stress, $\tau = \dfrac{16T}{\pi d^3}$ (for solid shaft),

$$\tau = \frac{16T}{\pi d_o^3\left[1-\left(\dfrac{d_i}{d_o}\right)^4\right]} \text{ (for hollow shaft)}$$

Pure Bending

Bending stress, $\sigma_b = \dfrac{32M}{\pi d^3}$ (for solid shaft),

$$\sigma_b = \frac{32M}{\pi d_o^3\left[1-\left(\dfrac{d_i}{d_o}\right)^4\right]} \text{ (for hollow shaft)}$$

Combined Bending and Torsion

Maximum shear stress, $\tau_{max} = \dfrac{1}{2}\sqrt{\sigma_b^2 + 4\tau^2}$

or $\tau_{max} = \dfrac{16}{\pi d^3}\sqrt{M^2+T^2}$

Equivalent torque, $T_{eq} = \sqrt{M^2+T^2}$

Maximum normal stress,

$$\sigma_{max} = \frac{1}{2}\sigma_b + \frac{1}{2}\sqrt{\sigma_b^2+4\tau^2}$$

or $\sigma_{max} = \dfrac{32}{\pi d^3}\times\dfrac{1}{2}(M+\sqrt{M^2+T^2})$

Equivalent bending moment, $M_{eq} = \dfrac{1}{2}(M+\sqrt{M^2+T^2})$

Shaft subjected to fluctuating loads:

Equivalent torque, $T_{eq} = \sqrt{(k_m M)^2 + (k_t T)^2}$

Equivalent bending moment,

$$M_{eq} = \frac{1}{2}[k_m M + \sqrt{(k_m M)^2 + (k_t T)^2}]$$

Gears

Gears are defined as toothed members transmitting rotary motion from one shaft to another.

Classifications of Gears

Shaft	Gear
Parallel axis shaft	Spur gear Helical gear Herringbone
Non-parallel and non-intersecting shaft	Spiral gear
Non-intersecting and at right angle shaft	Worm gear
Intersecting axis and in one plane shaft	Bevel gear

Geometry and Nomenclature

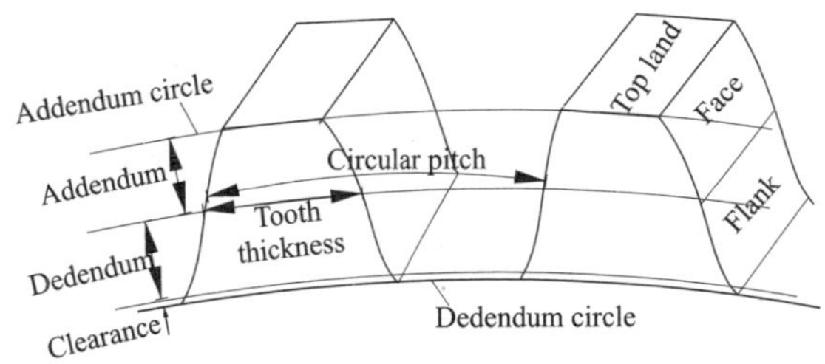

Circular pitch, $p_c = \dfrac{\pi D}{T}$

Diametral pitch, $p_d = \dfrac{T}{D}$

Module, $m = \dfrac{D}{T}$, Addendum = 1 module

Dedendum $= \left(1+\dfrac{\pi}{20}\right)$ module

Clearance = Addendum − Dedendum $= \dfrac{\pi}{20}$ module

Minimum Number of Teeth

Minimum number of teeth on wheel:

$$T = \frac{2a_w G}{\sqrt{G^2+(1+2G)\sin^2\phi} - G}$$

Minimum number of teeth on pinion:

$$t = \frac{2a_w}{\sqrt{1+G(G+2)\sin^2\phi} - 1}, \text{ where } G = \text{gear ratio} = \frac{T}{t}$$

Strength of Gear Teeth-Lewis Equation

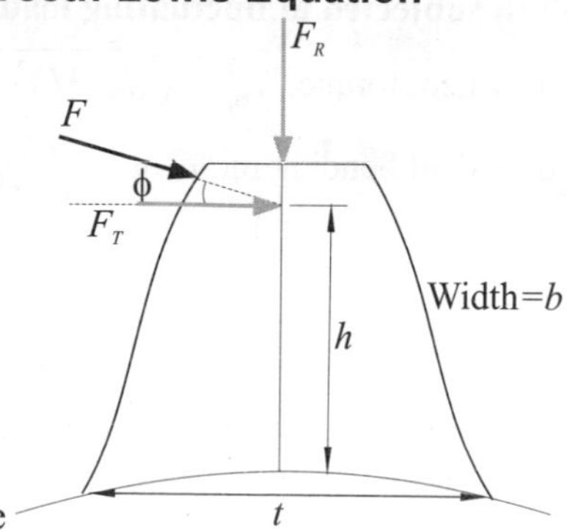

Maximum bending stress,

$$\sigma_b = \frac{M}{Z} = \frac{6 F_T h}{b t^2}$$

or

$$F_T = \sigma_b b \left(\frac{t^2}{6h} \right)$$

The t and h are dependent on the size of tooth,

(Let $t = x\, p_c$ and $h = k\, p_c$), then

$$F_T = \sigma_b b \left(\frac{x^2}{6k} \right) p_c = \sigma_b b\, p_c y$$

or $\quad F_T = \sigma_b b \pi m y$; where y is Lewis form factor

$$F_T = \sigma_b b \frac{\pi}{p_d} y$$

$$F_T = \frac{\sigma_b b Y}{p_d}; \text{ where } Y = \text{another form factor}$$

Consider velocity factor and stress-concentration factor,

$$F_T = \frac{\sigma_b C_v}{k_f} b\, p_c y$$

Sliding Contact Bearing

A bearing is a machine element which supports another moving machine element (known as *journal*). It permits a relative motion between the contact surfaces of the members, while carrying the load.

Classification of Bearings

1. Depending upon the direction of load to be supported: (a) Radial bearings, and (b) Thrust bearings.

2. Depending upon the nature of contact: (a) Sliding contact bearings, and (b) Rolling contact bearings.

Types of Sliding Contact Bearings

Thick film bearings: The thick film bearings are those in which the working surfaces are completely separated from each other by the lubricant. Such type of bearings are also called as *hydrodynamic lubricated bearings*.

Thin film bearings: The thin film bearings are those in which, although lubricant is present, the working surfaces partially contact each other at least part of the time. Such type of bearings are also called *boundary lubricated bearings*.

Zero film bearings: The zero film bearings are those which operate without any lubricant present.

Hydrostatic or externally pressurized lubricated bearings: The hydrostatic bearings are those which can support steady loads without any relative motion between the journal and the bearing. This is achieved by forcing externally pressurized lubricant between the members.

Basic Concepts of Hydrodynamic Lubrication

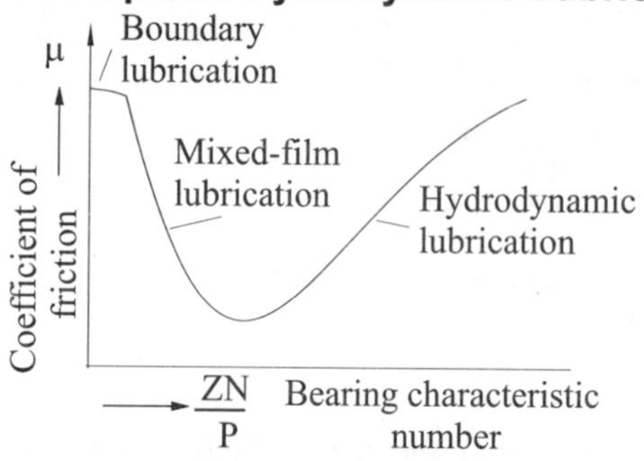

Terms used in Hydrodynamic Journal Bearings

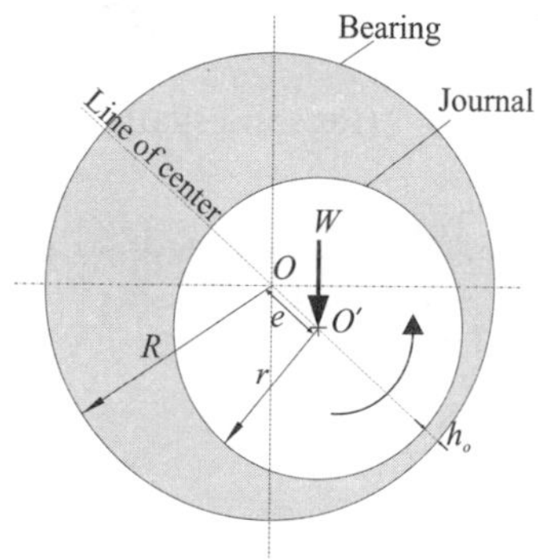

A hydrodynamic journal bearing is shown in figure.

D = Diameter of the bearing, d = Diameter of the journal, l = Length of the bearing.

Diametral clearance, $c = D - d$

Radial clearance, $c_r = \frac{D-d}{2}$

Eccentricity ratio, $\varepsilon = \frac{e}{\left(\frac{D-d}{2}\right)}$

Rolling Bearing

Rolling contact bearings are also called anti-friction bearing due to its low friction characteristics. These bearings are used for radial load, thrust load and combination of thrust and radial load.

Most rolling bearings consist of rings with raceway (inner ring and outer ring), rolling elements (either balls or rollers) and cage. The cage separates the rolling elements at regular intervals, holds them in place within the inner and outer raceways, and allows them to rotate freely.

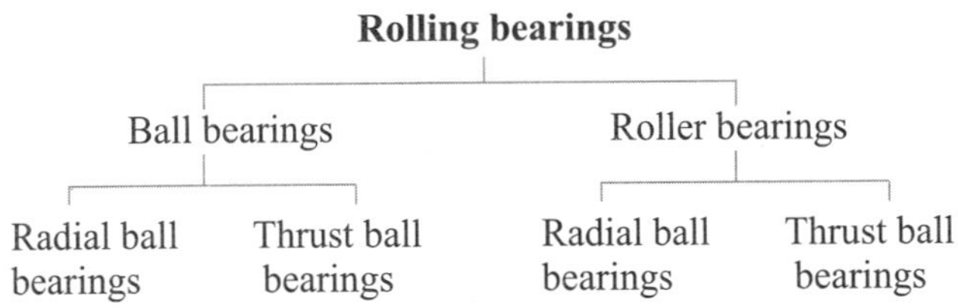

Equivalent Bearing load

It is constant radial load in radial bearing (or thrust load in thrust bearing), which if applied to the bearing would give same life as that the bearing will attain under actual condition of forces.

Dynamic load, $P = XVF_r + YF_a$

Where F_r is radial load (N), F_a is axial or thrust load (N). and V is race-rotation factor, X and Y are radial and thrust factors respectively.

$V = 1$: When the inner race rotates while the outer race is held stationary.

$V = 1.2$: When the outer race rotates while the inner race is held stationary.

$P = F_r$ (Pure radial load) and $P = F_a$ (Pure thrust load)

Load-Life Relationship

The relationship between dynamic load, equivalent dynamic load and bearing life is given by

$$L = \left(\frac{C}{P}\right)^p$$

$p = 3$ for ball bearing, $p = 3.33$ for roller bearing

Where $L =$ Rated bearing life (in million revolutions), $C =$ Dynamic load capacity (N), and $P =$ Equivalent load (N)

The relationship between life in million revolutions and life in working hours is given by

$$L = \frac{60n\,L_H}{10^6}$$

Where $L =$ Rated bearing life (in millian revolutions), $L_H =$ Rated bearing life in hours, and $n =$ speed of rotations.

Brakes and Clutches

The function of a clutch is to permit smooth, gradual connection and disconnection of two members having a common axis of rotation. A brake acts similarly except that one of the member is fixed.

Energy absorption: The basis function of a brake is to absorb energy, that is, to convert kinetic and potential energy into friction heat.

Source of energy to be absorbed are kinetic and potential energy.

Kinetic energy of translation, $\text{KE} = \frac{1}{2}mv^2$

Kinetic energy of rotation, $\text{KE} = \frac{1}{2}\text{I}\omega^2$

Potential energy, $\text{PE} = mgh$

Basic heat transfer rate, $Q = UA(T_s - T_a)$

Basic Analysis of Brakes

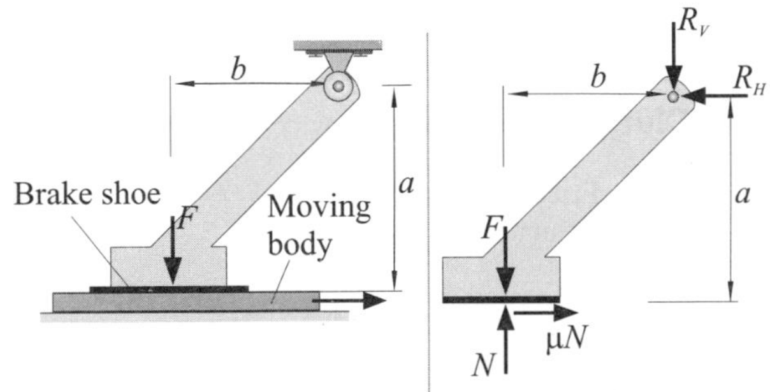

Free body diagram

Normal force $N = p_{max}A$, where p_{max} = maximum pressure and A = contact area of surface.

$$\sum M = 0 \Rightarrow Fb - Nb + \mu Na = 0$$

Actuating force, $F = \frac{N}{b}(\mu a - b)$

or $\quad F = \frac{p_{max}A}{b}(\mu a - b)$

Condition of self locking/self-energising; $(\mu a - b) \le 0$.

Disk Clutch and Brake

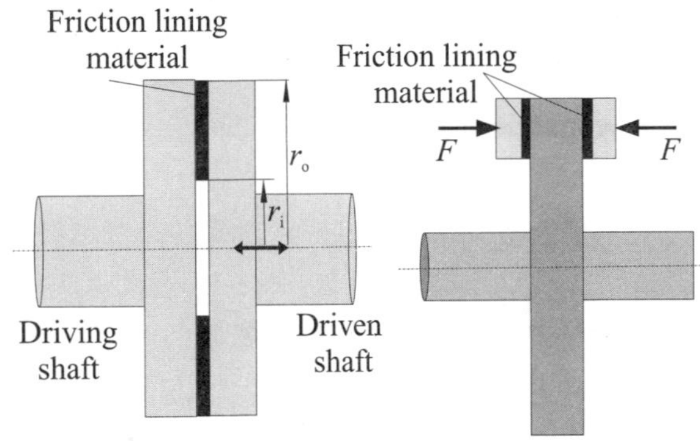

Disk clutch **Disk brake**

Uniform pressure theory

Axial force, $F = \pi p(r_o^2 - r_i^2)$; where p = interface pressure.

Total torque, $T = \frac{2}{3}\mu\, p\pi\,(r_o^3 - r_i^3)$

$$T = \frac{2}{3}\mu F\left(\frac{r_o^3 - r_i^3}{r_o^2 - r_i^2}\right)$$

Uniform wear theory

$pr = \text{constant} \Rightarrow pr = p_{\max}\, r_i$

Axial force, $F = 2\pi\, p_{\max}\, r_i\,(r_o - r_i)$

Total torque, $T = \mu\, p_{\max}\, \pi\, r_i\,(r_o^2 - r_i^2)$

$$T = \mu F \left(\frac{r_i + r_o}{2}\right)$$

Disk brake: A disk brake is similar to a plate clutch, except that one of the shafts is replaced by a fixed member.

Cone Clutch and Brake

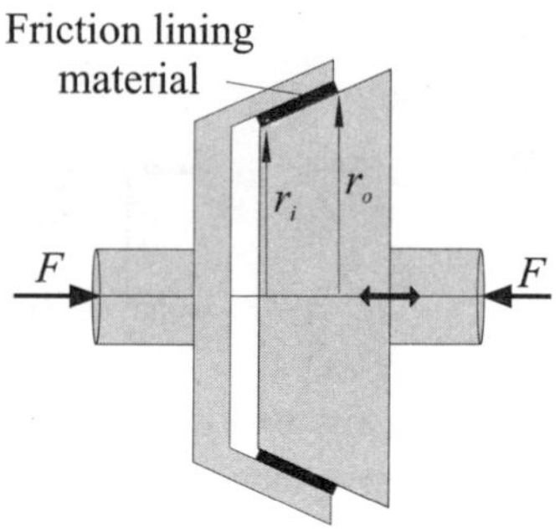

Uniform pressure theory

Axial force, $F = \pi\, p\,(r_o^2 - r_i^2)$; where p = interface pressure

Total torque, $T = \dfrac{2}{3}\dfrac{\mu}{\sin\alpha}\, p\,\pi\,(r_o^3 - r_i^3)$

$$T = \frac{2}{3}\frac{\mu}{\sin\alpha}\, F\left(\frac{r_o^3 - r_i^3}{r_o^2 - r_i^2}\right)$$

Uniform wear theory

$pr = \text{constant} \Rightarrow pr = p_{\max}\, r_i$

Axial force, $F = 2\pi\, p_{\max}\, r_i\,(r_o - r_i)$

Total torque, $T = \dfrac{\mu}{\sin\alpha}\, p_{\max}\, \pi\, r_i\,(r_o^2 - r_i^2)$

$$T = \frac{\mu}{\sin\alpha}\, F\left(\frac{r_i + r_o}{2}\right)$$

Rim (Drum) Brakes with short shoes

Braking torque, $M = \mu N r$

Actuating force, $F = \dfrac{N}{a}(b - \mu c)$

Condition for self-locking/self energizing, $b - \mu c \le 0$.

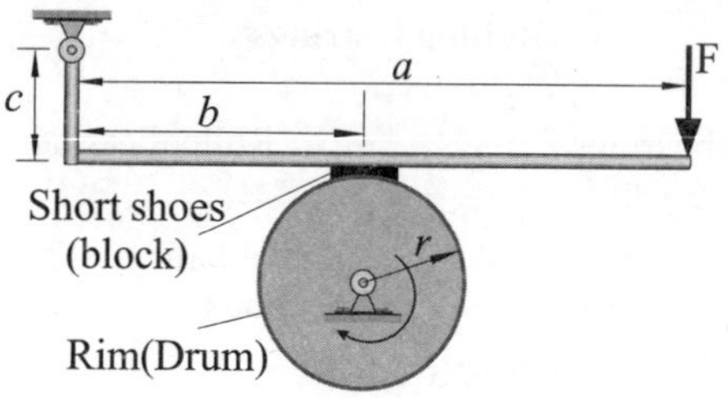

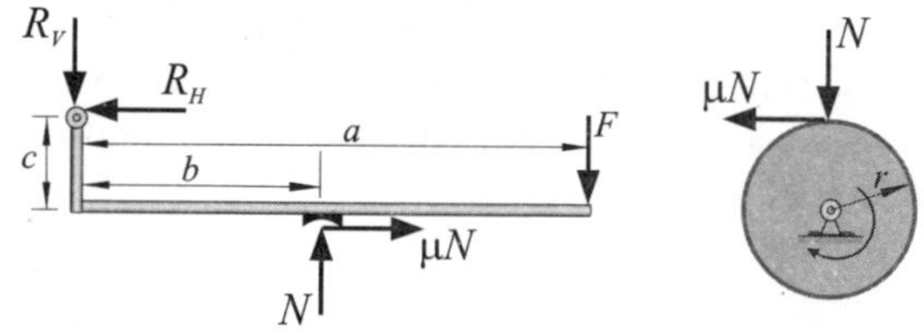

Free body diagrams

Block Brake

Equivalent coefficient of friction,

$$\mu' = \frac{4\mu \sin\theta}{2\theta + \sin 2\theta}$$

Breaking torque,

$$M = \frac{4\mu \sin\theta}{2\theta + \sin 2\theta}\, Nr$$

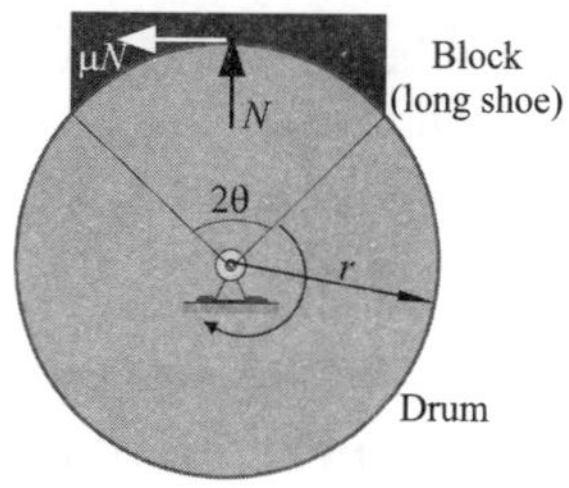

Band Brake

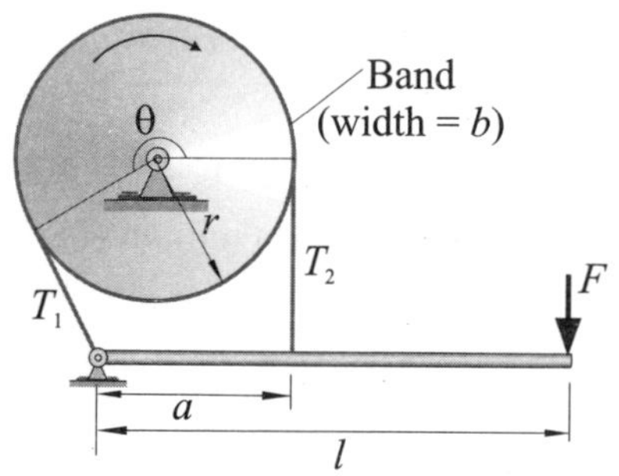

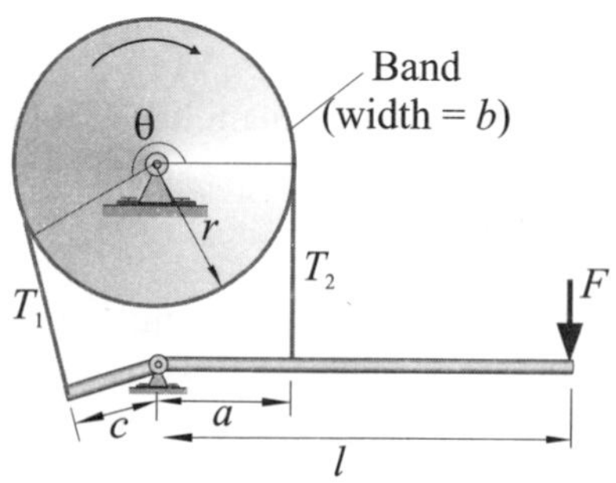

Differential band brake

Tension ratio, $\dfrac{T_1}{T_2} = e^{\mu\theta}$

Pressure at any point in the arc of contact, $p = \frac{T}{b\,r}$, where

T = Tensile force in the band.

Maximum pressure, $p_{max} = \frac{T_1}{b\,r} = \frac{T_2}{b\,r} e^{\mu\theta}$

Breaking torque, $M = (T_1 - T_2)r = p_{max}\,br^2(1 - e^{-\mu\theta})$

Springs

Springs is an elastic member whose primary function is to deflect or distort under load and thus absorbs energy. Springs can be classified according to their shape and the nature of stress introduced in them.

Type of springs: (i) Helical tension or compression springs, (ii) Helical torsion springs, (iii) Leaf springs, (iv) Belliville springs.

Helical Spring

A helical spring is a piece of wire coiled in the form of helix. If the slope of the helix of the coil is so small that bending effects can be neglected, then the spring is called a close-coiled spring.

Closed-Coiled Helical Spring – Axial load

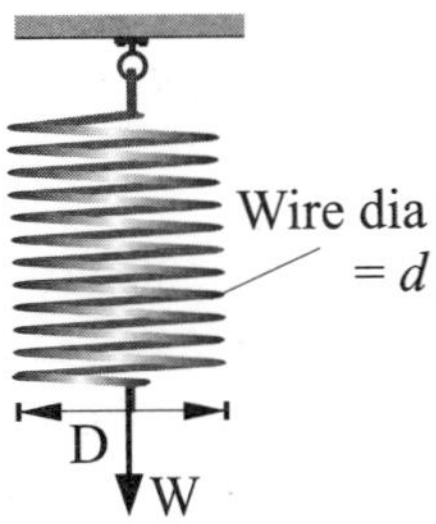

Torque on the spring, $T = \frac{WD}{2}$

Shear stress, $\tau = \frac{8WD}{\pi d^3}$

Angle of twist, $\theta = \frac{16\,WD^2 n}{G\,d^4}$

Deflection, $\delta = \frac{8WD^3 n}{G\,d^4}$

Stiffness, $k = \frac{G\,d^4}{8\,D^3 n}$

Direct shear stress, $\tau_d = \frac{4W}{\pi\,d^2}$

Strain energy, $U = \frac{\tau^2}{4G} \times \text{Volume}$

Maximum resultant shear stress, $\tau_{max} = \frac{8WD}{\pi\,d^3} + \frac{4W}{\pi\,d^2}$

$$\tau_{max} = \frac{8WD}{\pi d^3} k_w$$

where k_w = Wahl factor $= \frac{4C - 1}{4C - 4} + \frac{0.615}{C}$

Spring index, $C = \frac{D}{d}$

Closed-Coiled Helical Spring – Axial torque

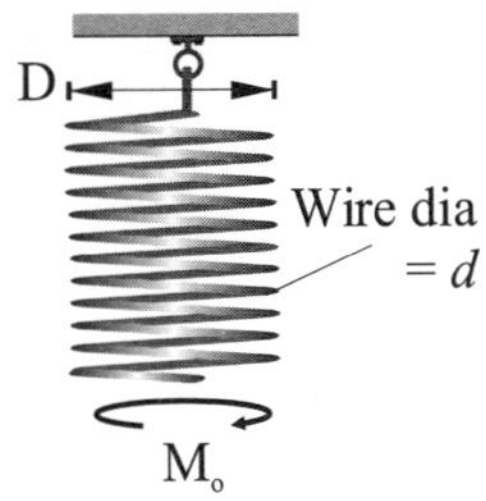

Change of curvature,

$$= \frac{1}{R_2} - \frac{1}{R_1} = \frac{M_o}{EI}$$

Axial torque,

$$M_o = \frac{2\pi\,EI}{l}(n_2 - n_1)$$

Angle of rotation(wind up angle), $\phi = 2\pi(n_2 - n_1)$

$$\phi = \frac{M_0 l}{EI} = \frac{2\pi R_1 n_1 M_0}{EI} = \frac{64D\,n_1 M_0}{E\,d^4}$$

Bending stress, $\sigma_b = \frac{32M_0}{\pi d^3}$

Strain energy, $U = \frac{\sigma_b^2}{8E} \times \text{Volume}$

Open-Coiled Helical Spring – Axial load

Length of spring wire, $l = 2\pi R\,n \sec\alpha$

Helix angle, $\alpha = \frac{\text{Pitch}\,(p)}{2\pi\,R}$

Torque, $T = \frac{WD}{2}\cos\alpha$

Bending moment, $M = \frac{WD}{2}\sin\alpha$

Strain energy, $U = \frac{T^2 l}{2G\,J} + \frac{M^2 l}{2EI}$

$$U = \frac{8W\,D^3 n \sec\alpha}{d^4}\left(\frac{\cos^2\alpha}{G} + \frac{2\sin^2\alpha}{E}\right)$$

Shear stress, $\tau = \frac{8\,W\,D}{\pi d^3}\cos\alpha$

Bending stress, $\sigma = \frac{16\,W\,D}{\pi d^3}\sin\alpha$

Principal stress, $\sigma_{1,2} = \frac{16\,W\,D}{\pi d^3}(\sin\alpha \pm 1)$

Maximum shear stress, $\tau_{max} = \frac{8\,W\,D}{\pi d^3}$

Concentric or Cluster Springs

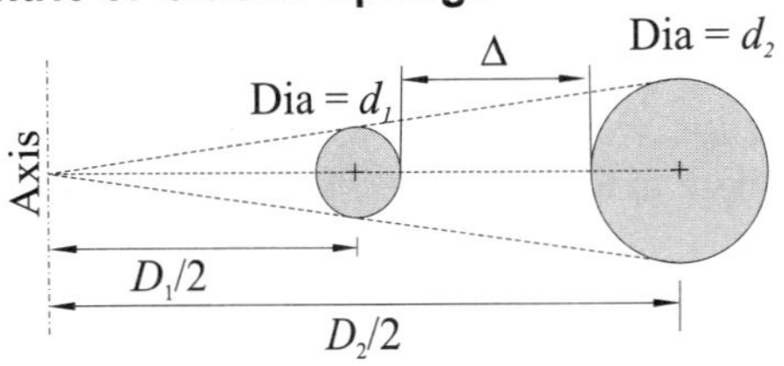

Clearance, $\Delta = \left(\frac{D_2 - D_1}{2}\right) - \left(\frac{d_1 + d_2}{2}\right)$

$$\tau_1 = \tau_2 \Rightarrow \frac{8W_1 D_1}{\pi d_1^3} = \frac{8W_2 D_2}{\pi d_2^3} \text{ and } W_1 + W_2 = W$$

Deflection, $\frac{8W_1 D_1^3 n_1}{G_1 d_1^4} = \frac{8W_2 D_2^3 n_2}{G_2 d_2^4}$

Solid length $n_1 d_1 = n_2 d_2$

Leaf Spring

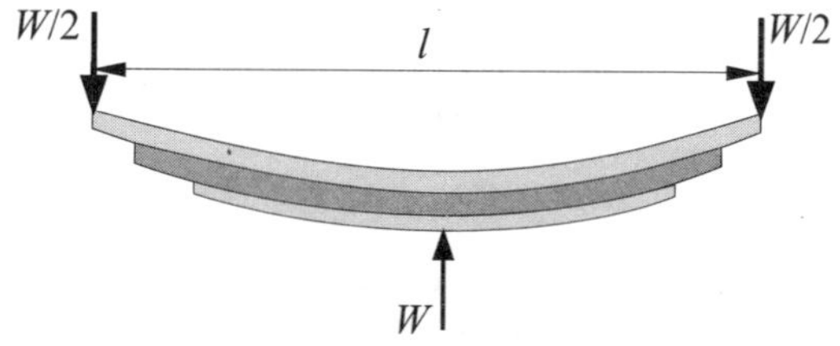

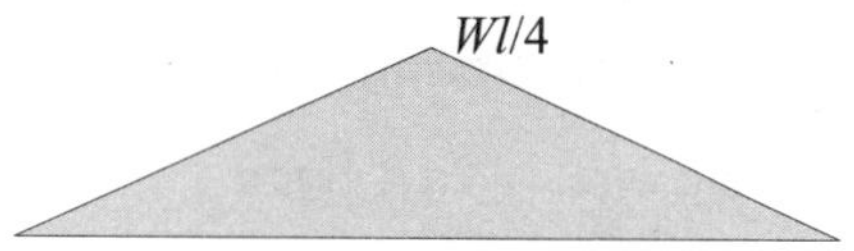

Bending moment diagram

A leaf spring is a beam of uniform strength supported at the center and loaded at the ends.

Bending moment for each plate, $M = \frac{Wl}{4n}$

Bending stress, $\sigma = \frac{Wl}{4n} \times \frac{6}{bd^2} = \frac{3}{2}\frac{Wl}{nbd^2}$

Deflection at center, $\delta = \frac{3}{8}\frac{Wl^3}{nEbd^2}$

9.2 SOLVED EXAMPLES

Previous Years GATE Questions

Example 9.1

At uniaxial yield stress of a material is 300 MPa. According to Von Mises criterion, the shear yield stress (in MPa) of the material is ___________.

GATE 2015

Solution

According to the distortion energy theory (Von Misses criterion), the yield strength in shear is 0.577 times the yield strength in tension. Therefore,

Shear yield stress, $\sigma_{sy} = \frac{\sigma_{yt}}{\sqrt{3}} = 0.577\sigma_{yt}$

or $\sigma_{sy} = \frac{300}{\sqrt{3}}$

$$\sigma_{sy} = 173.2 \text{ MPa}$$

Example 9.2

A hollow shaft ($d_0 = 2d_i$, where d_0 and d_i are the outer and inner diameter respectively) needs to transmit 20 kW power at 3000 rpm. If the maximum permissible shear stress is 30 MPa, the outer diameter d_0 is

(A) 11.29 mm (B) 22.58 mm

(C) 33.87 mm (D) 45.16 mm

GATE 2015

Solution

Using the relation, $T = \frac{60P}{2\pi N}$

We get, $T = \frac{60 \times 20 \times 10^3}{2\pi \times 3000} = \frac{200}{\pi}$ Nm

Maximum shear stress, $\tau = \frac{T}{J} \times \frac{d_o}{2} = \frac{16T d_o}{\pi(d_o^4 - d_i^4)}$

Substituting $d_0 = 2d_i$; $\tau = \frac{16T \times 2d_i}{\pi[(2d_i)^4 - d_i^4]} = \frac{32T}{15\pi d_i^3}$

or $30 \times 10^6 = \frac{32}{15\pi d_i^3} \times \frac{200}{\pi}$

This gives,

Inner diameter $d_i = 11.30 \times 10^{-3}$ m

Outer diameter, $d_o = 22.60$ mm

Example 9.3

A hollow shaft of 1m length is designed to transmit a power of 30 kW at 700 rpm. The maximum permissible angle of twist in the shaft is 1°. The inner diameter of the shaft is 0.7 times the outer diameter. The modulus of rigidity is 80 GPa. The outside diameter (in mm) of the shaft is________.

GATE 2015

Solution

Torque transmitted by the shaft, $T = \frac{60P}{2\pi N}$

$$T = \frac{60 \times 30 \times 10^3}{2\pi \times 700} = 409.25 \text{ Nm}$$

Torsion formula, $\frac{T}{J}=\frac{G\theta}{l}=\frac{\tau}{r}$

$$\frac{T}{\frac{\pi}{32}(d_o^4-d_i^4)}=\frac{G\theta}{l}$$

$$\frac{409.25}{\frac{\pi}{32}[d_o^4-(0.8d_o)^4]}=\frac{80\times10^9\times\frac{\pi}{180}}{1}$$

or $\quad d_o=0.0474\,\text{m}$

$$d_o=47.4\,\text{mm}$$

Example 9.4

For the given fluctuating fatigue load, the value of stress amplitude and stress ratio are respectively,

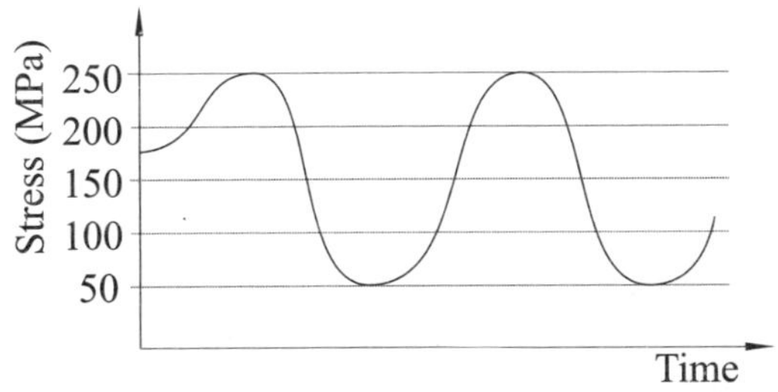

(A) 100 MPa and 5 (B) 250 MPa and 5

(C) 100 MPa and 0.20 (D) 250 MPa and 0.20

GATE 2015

Solution

From the graph, $\sigma_{max}=250$ and $\sigma_{min}=50$

Stress amplitude, $\sigma_a=\sigma_{max}-\sigma_m$

or $\quad \sigma_a=250-\left(\frac{250+50}{2}\right)$

Stress amplitude, $\sigma_{amp}=100$

Stress ratio $=\frac{\sigma_{max}}{\sigma_{min}}=\frac{250}{50}$

Stress ratio = 5

Example 9.5

A cantilever bracket is bolted to a column using three $M12\times1.75$ bolts P, Q and R. The value of maximum shear stress developed in the bolt P (in MPa) is _______.

GATE 2015

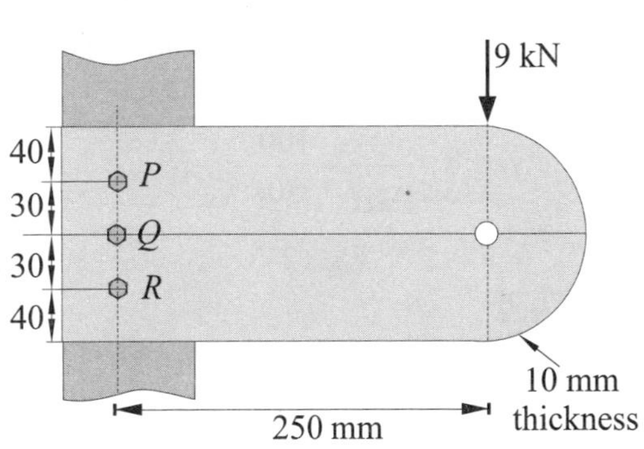

Solution

The primary and secondary forces are shown in figure.

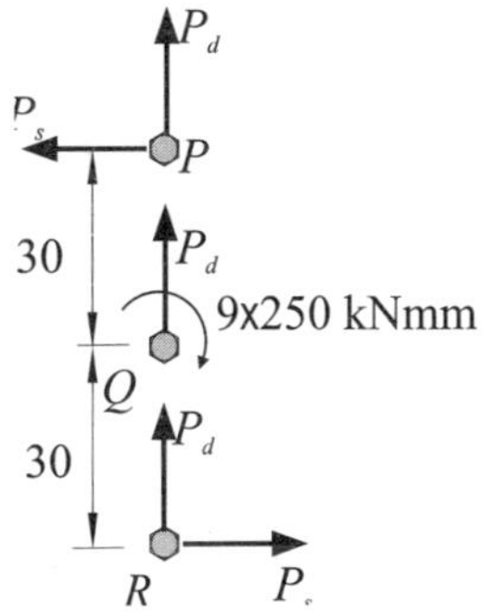

Direct (primary) shear force on each bolt,

$$P_d=\frac{9000}{3}=3000\,\text{N}$$

Equating the turning and resisting moment about centroid of bolts area Q, we get

$$P_s\times30+P_s\times30=9000\times250$$

or $\quad P_s=37500\,\text{N}$

Resultant of Primary shear force (P_d) and secondary shear force (P_s) is same in bolts P and R.

$$R=\sqrt{P_d^2+P_s^2}$$

$$=\sqrt{3000^2+37500^2}$$

or $\quad R=37619.8\,\text{N}$

Maximum shear stress, $\tau=\frac{37619.8}{\frac{\pi}{4}\times\left(\frac{12}{1000}\right)^2}$;

Diameter of bolt $M12\times1.75$ is 12 mm

$$\tau=332.6\,\text{MPa}$$

Example 9.6

A machine element is subjected to the following bi-axial state of stress; $\sigma_x=80\,\text{MPa}$, $\sigma_y=20\,\text{MPa}$, $\tau_{xy}=40\,\text{MPa}$. If the shear strength of the material is 100 MPa, the factor of safety as per Tresca's maximum shear stress theory is

(A) 1.0 (B) 2.0 (C) 2.5 (D) 3.3

GATE 2015

Solution

Maximum shear stress, $\tau_{max}=\sqrt{\left(\frac{\sigma_x-\sigma_y}{2}\right)^2+\tau_{xy}^2}$

$$\tau_{max} = \sqrt{\left(\frac{80-20}{2}\right)^2 + 40^2} = 50\,\text{MPa}$$

Factor of safety, $FS = \frac{\tau}{\tau_{max}} = \frac{100}{50}$

$$FS = 2$$

Example 9.7

A horizontal plate has been joined to a vertical post using four rivets arranged as shown in the figure. The magnitude of load on the worst loaded rivet (in N) is___.

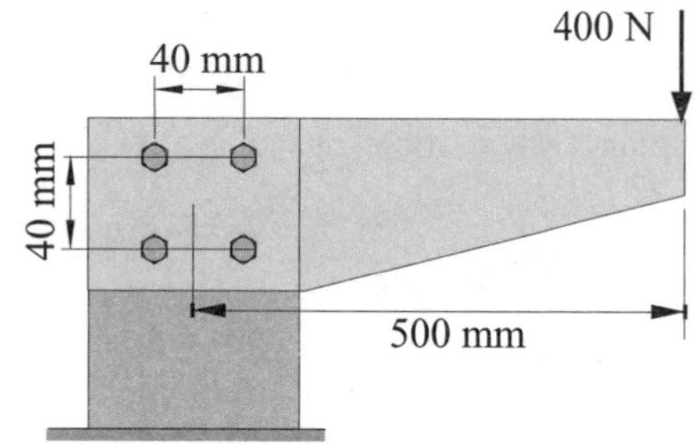

GATE 2015

Solution

The primary and secondary forces are shown in figure.

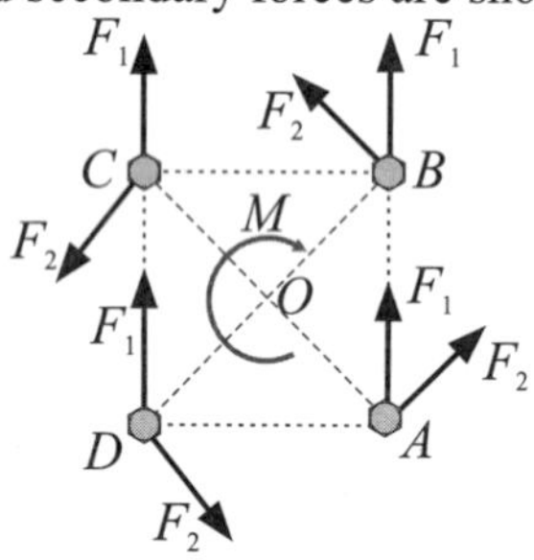

Direct shear force on each bolt, $F_1 = \frac{400}{4} = 100\,\text{N}$

Equating the turning and resisting moment about centroid of bolts area O, we get

$$4 \times F_2 \times OA = 400 \times \frac{500}{1000}$$

or $\quad F_2 = \frac{2500}{\sqrt{2}}\,\text{N}$

Resultant of primary shear force (F_1) and secondary shear force (F_2) at bolt A and B are maximum and equal.

$$R = \sqrt{F_1^2 + F_2^2 + 2F_1F_2\cos 45}$$

$$R = \sqrt{100^2 + \left(\frac{2500}{\sqrt{2}}\right)^2 + 2\times 100 \times \frac{2500}{\sqrt{2}} \times \cos 45}$$

$$R = 1839.8\,\text{N}$$

Example 9.8

A hydrodynamic journal bearing is subject to 2000 N load at a rotational speed of 2000 rpm. Both bearing bore diameter and length are 40 mm. If radial clearance is 20 μm and bearing is lubricated with an oil having viscosity 0.03 Pa.s, the Sommerfeld number of the bearing is____.

GATE 2014

Solution

Sommerfeld number $= \frac{\mu N}{P} \times \left(\frac{r}{c}\right)^2$

Substituting given value $r = 20\,\text{mm}$, $c = 20 \times 10^{-3}\,\text{mm}$,

$\mu = 0.03\,\text{Pa.s}$, $N = \frac{2000}{60}$ rps and

$$P = \frac{F}{Ld} = \frac{2000}{40\times 10^{-3} \times 40 \times 10^{-3}}$$

Sommerfeld number

$$= \frac{0.03 \times \frac{2000}{60}}{\frac{2000}{40\times10^{-3}\times 40\times 10^{-3}}} \times \left(\frac{20}{20\times 10^{-3}}\right)^2$$

$$\text{Sommerfeld number} = 0.8$$

Example 9.9

Two threaded bolts A and B of same material and length are subjected to identical tensile load. If the elastic strain energy stored in bolt A is 4 times that of bolt B and the mean diameter of bolt A is 12 mm, the mean diameter of bolt B (in mm) is

(A)16 (B) 24 (C) 36 (D) 48

GATE 2013

Solution

Elastic strain energy stored in bolt A; $U_1 = \frac{P^2L}{2EA_1}$

Elastic strain energy stored in bolt B; $U_2 = \frac{P^2L}{2EA_2}$

$$U_1 = 4U_2 \Rightarrow \frac{P^2L}{2EA_1} = 4\frac{P^2L}{2EA_2}$$

or $\quad A_2 = 4A_1$

or $\quad \frac{\pi}{4}d_2^2 = 4 \times \frac{\pi}{4}d_2^2$

or $\quad d_2 = 2d_1 = 2 \times 12$

$$d_2 = 24\,\text{mm}$$

Example 9.10

A bar is subjected to fluctuating tensile load from 20 kN to 100 kN. The material has yield strength of 240 MPa and endurance limit in reversed bending is 160 MPa. According to the Soderberg principle, the area of cross-section (in mm^2) of the bar for a factor of safety of 2 is

(A) 400 (B) 600 (C) 750 (D) 1000

GATE 2013

Solution

Given: $F_{\min} = 20$ kN, $F_{\max} = 100$ kN, $\sigma_y = 240$ MPa, $\sigma_e = 160$ MPa and FS = 2

Let A be the area of cross-section in mm^2

$$\sigma_m = \frac{F_{\max} + F_{\min}}{2A} = \frac{60}{A}$$

and $$\sigma_v = \frac{F_{\max} - F_{\min}}{2A} = \frac{40}{A}$$

Using Soderberg criteria,

$$\left(\frac{60\times10^3}{A}\right)\frac{1}{240} + \left(\frac{40\times10^3}{A}\right)\frac{1}{160} = \frac{1}{2}$$

$$A = 1000 \text{ mm}^2$$

Example 9.11

Common Data Questions

A single riveted lap joint of two similar plates as shown in the figure below has the following geometrical and material details

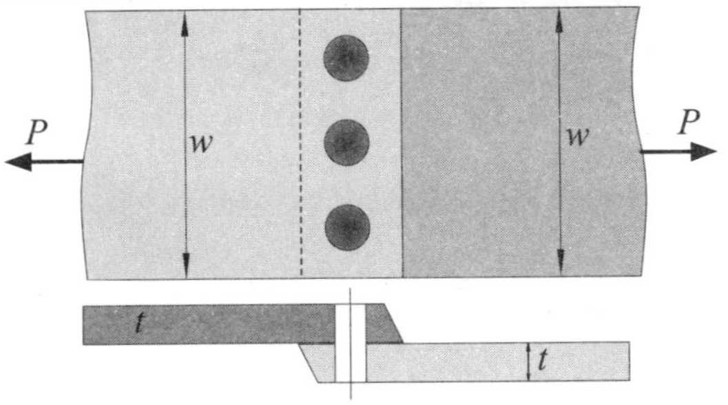

Width of plate, $w = 200$ mm

Thickness of the plate, $t = 5$ mm

Number of rivets, $n = 3$

Diameter of the rivet, $d_r = 10$ mm

Diameter of the rivet hole, $d_h = 11$ mm

Allowable tensile stress of the plate, $\sigma_p = 200$ MPa

Allowable shear stress of the rivet, $\sigma_s = 100$ MPa

Allowable bearing stress of the rivet, $\sigma_c = 150$ MPa.

Q(a) If the rivets are to be designed to avoid crushing failure, the maximum permissible load P (in kN) is

(A) 7.50 (B) 15.00 (C) 22.50 (D) 30.00

Q(b) If the plates are to be designed to avoid tearing failure, the maximum permissible load P (in kN) is

(A) 83 (B) 125 (C) 167 (D) 501

GATE 2013

Solution

(a) The maximum permissible load P to avoid crushing of the rivets is

$$P = n\,d\,t\sigma_c = 3\times10\times5\times150 \text{ N}$$

$$P = 22.5 \text{N}$$

(b) The maximum permissible load P to avoid tearing of the plate is

$$P = (w - n d_c)t\sigma_t = (200 - 3\times11)\times5\times200 \text{ N}$$

$$P = 167 \text{ kN}$$

Example 9.12

A fillet welded joint is subjected to transverse loading F as shown in the figure. Both legs of the fillets are of 10 mm size and the weld length is 30 mm. If the allowable shear stress of the weld is 94 MPa, considering the minimum throat area of the weld, the maximum allowable transverse load (in kN) is

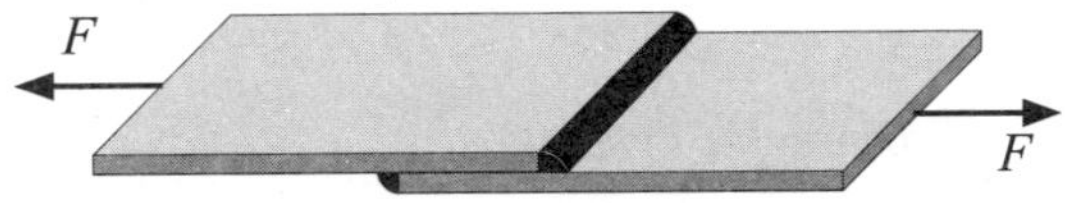

(A) 14.44 (B) 19.93 (C) 17.92 (D) 22.16

GATE 2012

Solution

Given: $h = 10$ mm, $l = 30$ mm and $\sigma_s = 94$ MPa

Minimum transverse load, $F = t l \sigma_s$

or $$F = \frac{h}{\sqrt{2}} l\sigma_s$$

$$F = \frac{10}{\sqrt{2}\times1000}\times\frac{30}{1000}\times94\times10^6 \text{ N}$$

$$F = 19.940 \text{ N}$$

Example 9.13

A solid circular shaft needs to be designed to transmit a torque of 50 Nm. If the allowable shear stress of the material is 140 MPa, assuming a factor of safety of 2, the minimum allowable design diameter (in mm) is

(A) 8 (B) 24 (C) 16 (D) 32

GATE 2012

Solution

Given: $T = 50$ Nm, $\tau_{allow} = 140$ MPa and FS $= 2$

Let d be the diameter of shaft.

Torsion formula, $\frac{T}{J} = \frac{\tau}{r} = \frac{G\theta}{l}$

or $\frac{T}{\frac{\pi}{32}d^4} = \frac{\tau_{max}}{\frac{d}{2}}$

or $d = \left(\frac{16T}{\pi\tau_{max}}\right)^{\frac{1}{3}} = \left(\frac{16T}{\pi\frac{\tau_{allow}}{FS}}\right)^{\frac{1}{3}} = \left(\frac{16\times 50}{\pi\times\frac{140}{2}\times 10^6}\right)^{\frac{1}{3}}$

or $d = 0.0153797$ m

$d = 15.37$ mm

Example 9.14

Two identical ball bearings P and Q are operating at loads 30 kN and 45 kN respectively. The ratio of the life of bearing P to the life of bearing Q is

(A) $\frac{81}{16}$ (B) $\frac{9}{4}$ (C) $\frac{27}{8}$ (D) $\frac{3}{2}$

GATE 2011

Solution

Life of ball bearing is given by

$$L = \left(\frac{C}{W}\right)^3$$

$$\frac{L_P}{L_Q} = \left(\frac{W_Q}{W_P}\right)^3$$

or $\frac{L_P}{L_Q} = \left(\frac{45}{30}\right)^3$

$$\frac{L_P}{L_Q} = \frac{27}{8}$$

Example 9.15

A band brake having band-width of 80 mm, drum diameter of 250 mm, coefficient of friction of 0.25 and angle of wrap of 270° is required to exert a friction torque of 1000 Nm. The maximum tension (in kN) developed in the band is

(A) 1.88 (B) 3.56 (C) 6.12 (D) 11.56

GATE 2010

Solution

Given: Diameter $d = 250$ mm, $\mu = 0.25$, $\theta = 270^0$ and Torque $M_t = 1000$ Nm

Tension ratio of belt $\frac{T_1}{T_2} = e^{\mu\theta}$

or $\frac{T_1}{T_2} = e^{0.25\times\left(\frac{\pi}{180}\times 270\right)} = 3.24$

Torque, $M_t = (T_1 - T_2)\times r$

or $1000 = \left(T_1 - \frac{T_1}{324}\right)\times\frac{250}{2\times 1000}$

This gives $T_1 = 11550$ N

Maximum tension, $T_1 = 11.55$ kN

Example 9.16

A bracket (shown in figure) is rigidly mounted on wall using four rivets. Each rivet is 6 mm in diameter and has an effective length of 12 mm.

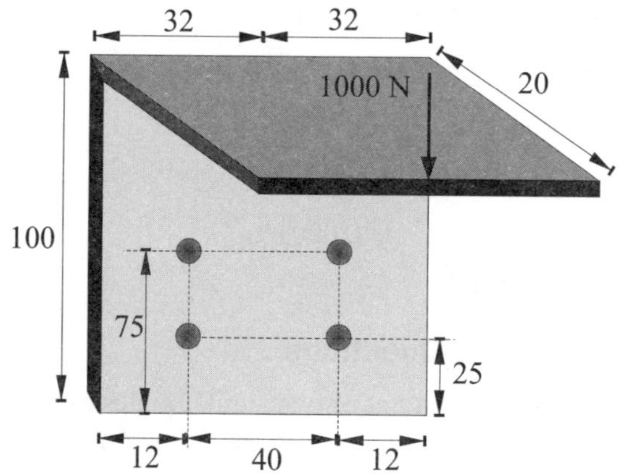

Direct shear stress (in MPa) in the most heavily loaded rivet is

(A) 4.4 (B) 8.8 (C) 17.6 (D) 35.2

GATE 2010

Solution

Direct shear stress, $\tau = \frac{P/4}{A} = \frac{P}{4A\times\frac{\pi}{4}d^2}$

$$\tau = \frac{1000}{4\times\frac{\pi}{4}\times\left(\frac{6}{1000}\right)^2} = 8.8\times 10^6 \text{ N/m}^2$$

$\tau = 8.8$ MPa

Example 9.17

A lightly loaded full journal bearing has journal diameter of 50 mm, bush bore of 50.05 mm and bush length of 20 mm. If rotational speed of journal is 120 rpm and average viscosity of liquid lubricant is 0.03 Pa.s, the power loss (in W) will be

(A) 0.37 (B) 74 (C) 118 (D) 237

GATE 2010

Solution

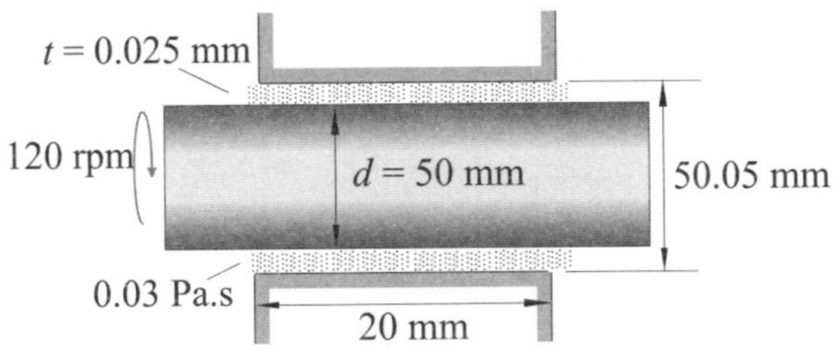

Viscous force, $F = \tau A$

or $F = \mu \frac{V}{t} A = \mu \frac{\omega r}{t} A$

Torque due to viscous force, $T = Fr$ or $T = \frac{\mu \omega r^2 A}{t}$

Power loss, $P = T \times \omega$

or $P = \frac{\mu \omega r^2 (2\pi r L)}{t} \times \omega$

or $P = \frac{2\pi \mu \omega^2 r^3 L}{t}$

or $$P = \frac{2\pi \times 0.03 \times \left(\frac{2\pi \times 120}{60}\right)^2 \left(\frac{25}{1000}\right)^3 \left(\frac{20}{1000}\right)}{\frac{0.025}{1000}}$$

$$P = 0.37\,\text{W}$$

Example 9.18

A solid circular shaft of diameter d is subjected to a combined bending moment M and torque T. The material property to be used for designing the shaft using the relation $\frac{16}{\pi d^3}\sqrt{M^2 + T^2}$ is

(A) Ultimate tensile strength (S_u)

(B) Tensile yield strength (S_y)

(C) Torsional yield strength (S_{sy})

(D) Endurance strength (S_e)

GATE 2009

Solution

Torsion formula, $\frac{T}{J} = \frac{\tau}{r} = \frac{G\theta}{l}$

or $$\frac{T}{\frac{\pi}{32} d^4} = \frac{\tau_{max}}{\frac{d}{2}}$$

or $$\tau_{max} = \frac{16\,T}{\pi d^3}$$

$$\tau_{max} = \frac{16}{\pi d^3}\sqrt{M^2 + T^2} = \text{Torsonal yield strength } (S_{sy})$$

Example 9.19

A forged steel link with uniform diameter of 30 mm at the centre is subjected to an axial force that varies from 40 kN in compression to 160 kN in tension. The tensile (σ_u), yield (σ_y) and corrected endurance (σ_e) strengths of the steel material are 600 MPa, 420 MPa and 240 MPa respectively. The factor of safety against fatigue endurance as per Soderberg's criterion is

(A) 1.26 (B) 1.37 (C) 1.45 (D) 2.00

GATE 2009

Solution

Mean stress, $\sigma_m = \frac{(F_{max} + F_{min})/2}{\pi d^2/4}$

$$\sigma_m = \frac{(160 - 40)/2}{\pi \times 30^2/4} = 84.88\,\text{MPa}$$

Variable stress, $\sigma_v = \frac{(F_{max} - F_{min})/2}{\pi d^2/4}$

$$\sigma_v = \frac{(160 + 40)/2}{\pi \times 30^2/4} = 141.47\,\text{MPa}$$

Applying Soderberg criterion, $\frac{1}{\text{FS}} = \frac{\sigma_m}{\sigma_y} + \frac{\sigma_v}{\sigma_e}$

or $\frac{1}{\text{FS}} = \frac{84.88}{420} + \frac{141.47}{240}$

This gives

$$\text{FS} = 1.26$$

Example 9.20

Linked Answer Questions

A 20° full depth involute spur pinion of 4 mm module and 21 teeth is to transmit 15 kW at 960 rpm. Its face width is 25 mm.

Q(a) The tangential force transmitted (in N) is

(A) 3552 (B) 2611 (C) 1776 (D) 1305

Q(b) Given that the tooth geometry factor is 0.32 and the combined effect of dynamic load and allied factors intensifying the stress is 1.5; the minimum allowable stress (in MPa) for the gear material is

(A) 242.0 (B) 166.5 (C) 121.0 (D) 74.0

GATE 2009

Solution

Given: $\phi = 20^0$, $P = 15\times10^3$ W, $m = 4$ mm, $T = 21$ teeth, $N = 960$ rpm, $b = 25$ mm

(a) Pitch circle diameter $d = mT$

$$d = 4\times21 = 84 \text{ mm}$$

Power transmitted, $P = F_T\, v = F_T \times\left(\omega\times\frac{d}{2}\right)$

Tangential force, $$F_T = \frac{P}{\omega\times\frac{d}{2}} = \frac{15\times10^3}{\frac{2\pi\times960}{60}\times\frac{84}{2\times1000}}$$

$$F_T = 3552.57 \text{ N}$$

(b) Given: $Y = 0.32$, $k_f = 1.5$

Using Levis equation,

Minimum allowable stress is $\sigma = \frac{F_T\times k_f}{m\,b\,Y}$

or $$\sigma = \frac{3552.57\times1.5}{\frac{4}{1000}\times\frac{25}{1000}\times0.32}$$

$$\sigma = 166.52 \text{ MPa}$$

Example 9.21

A journal bearing has shaft diameter of 40 mm and a length of 40 mm. The shaft is rotating at 20 rad/s and the viscosity of the lubricant is 20 mPa.s. The clearance is 0.020 mm. The loss of torque (in Nm) due to the viscosity of the lubricant is approximately

(A) 0.040 (B) 0.252 (C) 0.400 (D) 0.652

GATE 2008

Solution

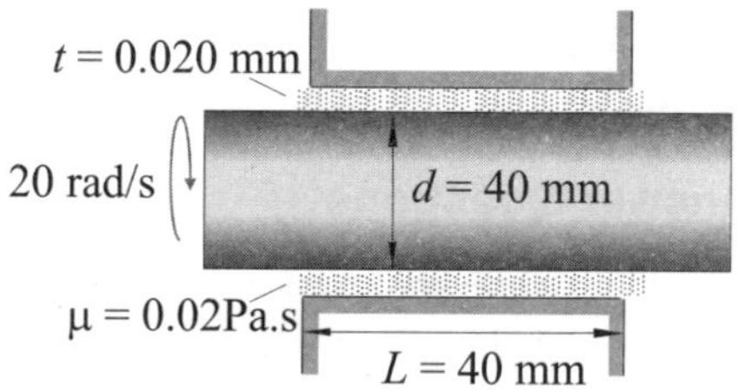

Viscous force, $F = \tau A$

or $$F = \mu\frac{V}{t}\pi d\,L$$

Torque due to viscous force, $T = F\times\frac{d}{2} = \mu\frac{V}{t}\pi d\,L\times\frac{d}{2}$

or $$T = \mu\frac{\omega\times\frac{d}{2}}{t}\pi d\,L\times\frac{d}{2}$$

or $$T = \frac{\mu\omega d^3\pi L}{4t}$$

or $$T = \frac{20\times10^{-3}\times20\times\left(\frac{40}{1000}\right)^3\times\pi\times\frac{40}{1000}}{4\times\frac{0.02}{1000}}$$

$$T = 0.040 \text{ Nm}$$

Example 9.22

A clutch has outer and inner diameters 100 mm and 40 mm respectively. Assuming a uniform pressure of 2 MPa and coefficient of friction of liner material 0.4, the torque carrying capacity of the clutch is

(A) 148 Nm (B) 196 Nm

(C) 375 Nm (D) 490 Nm

GATE 2008

Solution

Given: $r_o = \frac{100}{2}$ mm, $r_i = \frac{40}{2}$ mm, $p = 2$ MPa and $\mu = 0.4$

Torque carrying capacity,

$$T = \frac{2}{3}\mu W\left(\frac{r_o^3 - r_i^3}{r_o^2 - r_i^2}\right) \quad \text{[uniform pressure]}$$

or $$T = \frac{2}{3}\mu\times\frac{W}{\pi(r_o^2 - r_i^2)}\times\pi(r_o^3 - r_i^3)$$

or $$T = \frac{2}{3}\mu p\times\pi(r_o^3 - r_i^3)$$

Where uniform pressure, $p = \frac{W}{\pi(r_o^2 - r_i^2)}$

or $$T = \frac{2}{3}\times0.4\times2\times10^6\times\pi\left[\left(\frac{50}{1000}\right)^3 - \left(\frac{20}{1000}\right)^3\right]$$

$$T = 196.03 \text{ Nm}$$

Example 9.23

A spur gear has a module of 3 mm, number of teeth 16, a face width of 36 mm and a pressure angle of 20°. It is transmitting a power of 3kW at 20 rev/s. Taking a velocity factor of 1.5, and a form factor of 0.3, the stress in the gear tooth is

(A) 32 MPa (B) 46 MPa (C) 58 MPa (D) 70 MPa

GATE 2008

Solution

Given: $m = 3$ mm, $T = 16$ teeth, $b = 36$ mm, $\phi = 20°$, $P = 3$ kW, $N = 20$ rps, $k_f = 1.5$ and $Y = 0.3$.

Pitch circle diameter, $d = mT = 3 \times 16$

$$d = 48 \text{ mm}$$

Pitch circle velocity, $v = \omega \times \frac{d}{2} = 2\pi N \times \frac{d}{2}$

or $$v = 2\pi \times 20 \times \frac{48}{2 \times 1000} = 3.01 \text{ m/s}$$

Tangential load, $F_T = \frac{P}{v} = \frac{3 \times 10^3}{3.01} = 994.7 \text{ N}$

Using Lewis equation, $\sigma = \frac{F_T \times k_f}{m\, b\, Y}$

$$\sigma = \frac{994.7 \times 1.5}{\frac{3}{1000} \times \frac{36}{1000} \times 0.3}$$

$$\sigma = 46.05 \text{ MPa}$$

Example 9.24

A ball bearing operating at a load F has 8000 h of life. The life of the bearing in hours, when the load is doubled to $2F$ is

(A) 8000 (B) 6000 (C) 4000 (D) 1000

GATE 2007

Solution

Life of ball bearing is given by $L = \left(\frac{C}{W}\right)^3$

or $\frac{L_1}{L_2} = \left(\frac{W_2}{W_1}\right)^3$ or $\frac{8000}{L_2} = \left(\frac{2F}{F}\right)^3$

$$L_2 = 1000 \text{ h}$$

Example 9.25

A thin spherical pressure vessel of 200 mm diameter and 1 mm thickness is subjected to an internal pressure varying from 4 MPa to 8 MPa. Assume that the yield, ultimate, and endurance strength of material are 600 MPa, 800 MPa and 400 MPa respectively. The factor of safety as per Goodman's relation is

(A) 2.0 (B) 2.5 (C) 3 (D) 3.5

GATE 2007

Solution

Given: $d = 200$ mm, $t = 1$ mm, $P_{min} = 4$ MPa, $P_{max} = 8$ MPa, $\sigma_y = 600$ MPa, $\sigma_{ut} = 800$ MPa and $\sigma_{en} = 400$ MPa.

Hoop stress, $\sigma = \frac{pd}{4t}$

Minimum hoop stress, $\sigma_{min} = \frac{4 \times 200}{4 \times 1}$

or $$\sigma_{min} = 200 \text{ MPa}$$

Maximum hoop stress, $\sigma_{max} = \frac{8 \times 200}{4 \times 1} = 400$ MPa

Mean stress, $\sigma_m = \frac{\sigma_{max} + \sigma_{min}}{2} = \frac{400 + 200}{2} = 300$ MPa

Variable stress,

$$\sigma_v = \frac{\sigma_{max} - \sigma_{min}}{2} = \frac{400 - 200}{2} = 100 \text{ MPa}$$

Applying Goodman's criteria, $\frac{1}{FS} = \frac{\sigma_m}{\sigma_{ut}} + \frac{\sigma_v}{\sigma_e}$

$$\frac{1}{FS} = \frac{300}{800} + \frac{100}{400}$$

Factor of safety, FS = 1.6

Example 9.26

A natural feed journal bearing of diameter 50 mm and length 50 mm operating at 20 revolution/s carries a load of 2.0 kN. The lubricant used has a viscosity of 20 mPa.s. The radial clearance is 50 μm. The Sommerfeld number for the bearing is

(A) 0.062 (B) 0.125 (C) 0.250 (D) 0.785

GATE 2007

Solution

Sommerfeld number $= \frac{\mu N}{P} \times \left(\frac{r}{c}\right)^2$

Substituting given value $d = 50$ mm, $l = 50$ mm, $N = 20$ rps, $W = 2.0$ kW, $\mu = 20 \times 10^{-3}$ Pa.s, $c = 50 \times 10^{-3}$ mm and

$$P = \frac{W}{l\,d} = \frac{2 \times 10^3}{\frac{50}{1000} \times \frac{50}{1000}} = 8 \times 10^5 \text{ N/m}^2$$

Sommerfeld number $= \frac{20 \times 10^{-3} \times 20}{8 \times 10^5} \times \left(\frac{25}{50 \times 10^{-3}}\right)^2$

Sommerfeld number = 0.125

Example 9.27

A bolted joint is shown in the figure. The maximum shear stress, in MPa, in the bolts at A and B, respectively are

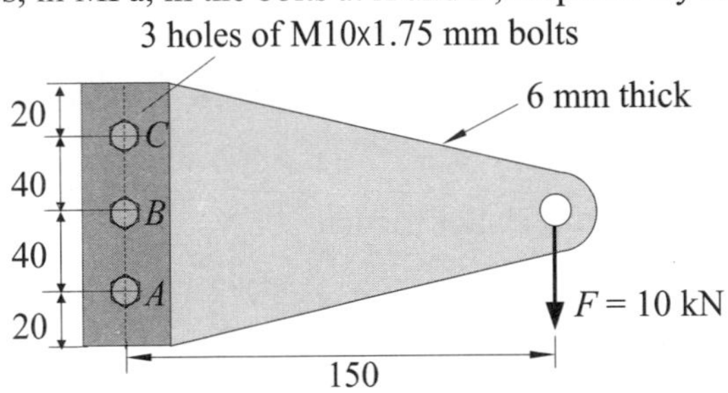

(all dimensions are in mm)

(A) 242.6, 42.5 (B) 42.5, 242.6
(C) 42.5, 42.5 (D) 242.6, 242.6

GATE 2007

Solution

Direct shear stress,

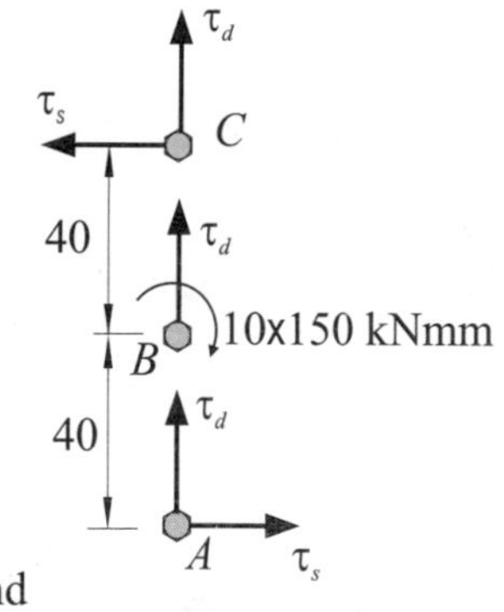

$$\tau_d = \frac{\frac{10}{3}\times 10^3}{\frac{\pi}{4}\times\left(\frac{10}{1000}\right)^2}$$

or $\tau_d = 4.24\times 10^7 \text{N/m}^2$

or $\tau_d = 42.4\,\text{MPa}$

Equating the turning and resisting moment about centroid of bolt B, we get

$$2\times P_s \times 40 = 10\times 10^3 \times 150$$

or $P_s = 18750\,\text{N}$

Secondary shear stress, $\tau_s = \dfrac{18750}{\frac{\pi}{4}\times\left(\frac{10}{1000}\right)^2} = 238.7\,\text{MPa}$

Shear stress in bolt A;

$$(\tau)_A = \sqrt{\tau_d^2 + \tau_s^2} = \sqrt{42.4^2 + 238.7^2}$$

$$(\tau)_A = 242.43\,\text{MPa}$$

Shear stress in bolt B; $(\tau)_B = \tau_d = 42.4\,\text{MPa}$

$$(\tau)_B = 42.4\,\text{MPa}$$

Example 9.28

A block-brake shown in figure has a face width of 300 mm and a mean coefficient of friction of 0.25. For an activating force of 400 N, the braking torque in Nm is

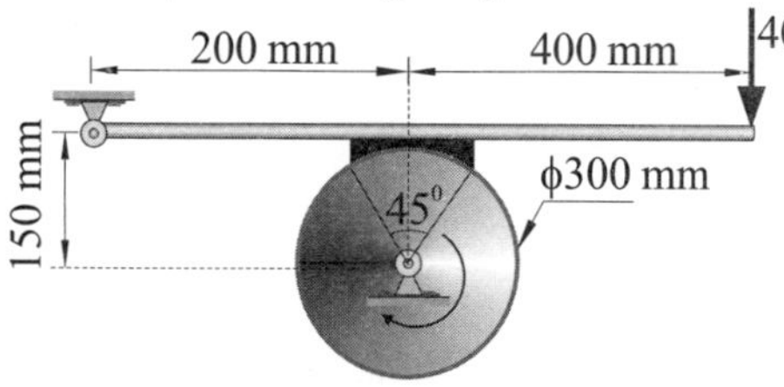

(A) 30 (B) 40 (C) 45 (D) 60

GATE 2007

Solution

Equivalent coefficient of friction,

$$\mu' = \mu\frac{4\sin\theta}{2\theta + \sin 2\theta} = 0.25\frac{4\sin\left(\frac{45}{2}\right)}{\frac{\pi}{4} + \sin 45}$$

or $\mu' = 0.256$

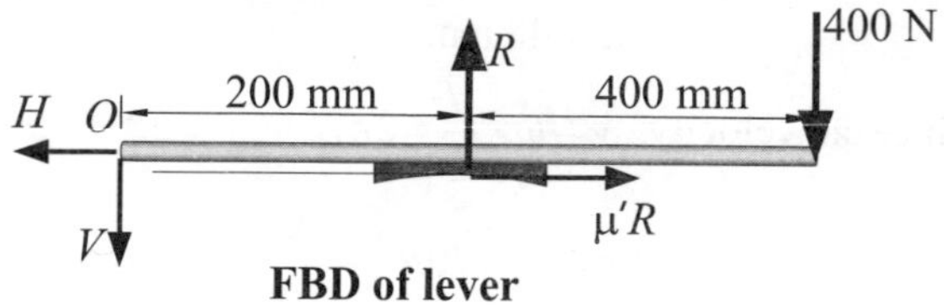

FBD of lever

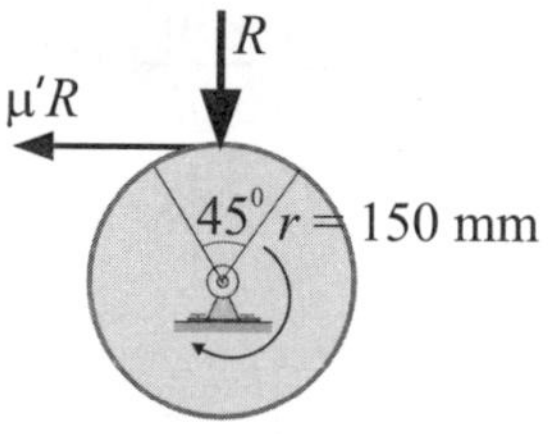

FBD of drum

Taking moment about O,

$$400\times(200+400) - R\times 200 = 0$$

or $R = 1200\,\text{N}$

Breaking torque, $M_t = \mu' R \times r$

$$M_t = 0.256\times 1200\times\frac{150}{1000}$$

$$M_t = 46\,\text{Nm}$$

Example 9.29

Common Data Questions

A gear set has a pinion with 20 teeth and a gear with 40 teeth. The pinion runs at 30 rev/s and transmits a power of 20 kW. The teeth are on the 20° full-depth system and have a module of 5 mm. The length of the line of action is 19 mm.

Q(a) The center distance for the above gear set in mm is

(A) 140 (B) 150 (C) 160 (D) 170

Q(b) The contact ratio of the contacting tooth is

(A) 1.21 (B) 1.25 (C) 1.29 (D) 1.33

Q(c) The resultant force on the contacting gear tooth in N is

(A) 77.23 (B) 2122.0 (C) 225.80 (D) 289.43

GATE 2007

Solution

Given: $T_P = 20$ teeth, $T_G = 40$ teeth, $N_G = 30$ rev/s, $P = 20\,\text{kW}$, $\phi = 20^0$ and $m = 5\,\text{mm}$.

(a) Center distance, $C = \dfrac{mT_P}{2} + \dfrac{mT_G}{2}$

$$C = \frac{m}{2}(T_P + T_G) = \frac{5}{2}(20+40)$$

$$C = 150\,\text{mm}$$

(b) Contact ratio, $\quad CR = \dfrac{\text{Arc of contact}}{\text{Circular pitch}}$

$$\text{Arc of contact} = \frac{\text{Path of contact}}{\cos\phi}$$

$$CR = \frac{\text{Path of contact}}{\text{Circular pitch} \times \cos\phi} = \frac{19}{\pi m \times \cos\phi} = \frac{19}{\pi \times 5 \times \cos 20}$$

$$CR = 1.287$$

(c) Tangential force, $F_t = \dfrac{T}{r_p} = \dfrac{P/\omega}{r_p} = \dfrac{P}{2\pi N r_p}$

$$F_t = \frac{20 \times 10^3}{2\pi \times 30 \times \left(\frac{50}{1000}\right)}$$

where $\quad r_p = \dfrac{mT_p}{2} = \dfrac{5 \times 20}{2} = 50\,\text{mm}$

$$F_t = 2122.06\,\text{N}$$

Example 9.30

A disk clutch is required to transmit 5 kW at 2000 rpm. The disk has a friction lining with coefficient of friction equal to 0.25. Bore radius of friction lining is equal to 25 mm. Assume uniform contact pressure of 1 MPa. The value of outside radius of the friction lining is

(A) 39.4 mm (B) 49.5 mm (C) 97.9 mm (D)142.9 mm

GATE 2006

Solution

Torque, $T = \dfrac{P}{\omega}$

Frictional torque, $\quad T = \mu \dfrac{2}{3} p\pi(r_o^3 - r_i^3)$

Therefore, $\quad \mu \dfrac{2}{3} p\pi(r_o^3 - r_i^3) = \dfrac{P}{\omega}$

Substituting $P = 5\,\text{kW}$, $N = 2000\,\text{rpm}$, $\mu = 0.25$, $r_i = 25\,\text{mm}$ and $p = 1\,\text{MPa}$, we have

$$0.25 \times \frac{2}{3} \times 1 \times 10^6 \times \pi \left[r_o^3 - \left(\frac{25}{1000}\right)^3 \right] = \frac{5 \times 10^3}{\frac{2\pi \times 2000}{60}}$$

This gives

$$r_o = 39.4\,\text{mm}$$

Example 9.31

Twenty degree full depth involute profiled 19-teeth pinion and 37-teeth gear are in mesh. If the module is 5 mm, the centre distance between the gear pair will be

(A) 140 mm (B) 150 mm (C) 280 mm (D) 300 mm

GATE 2006

Solution

Center distance $\quad C = \dfrac{d_p}{2} + \dfrac{d_G}{2} = \dfrac{mT_p}{2} + \dfrac{mT_G}{2}$

or $\quad C = \dfrac{m}{2}(T_p + T_G)$

or $\quad C = \dfrac{5}{2}(19 + 37)$

$$C = 140\,\text{mm}$$

Example 9.32

A cylindrical shaft is subjected to an alternating stress of 100 MPa. Fatigue strength to sustain 1000 cycles is 490 MPa. If the corrected endurance strength is 70 MPa, estimated shaft life (in cycles) will be

(A) 1071 (B) 15000 (C) 281914 (D) 928643

GATE 2006

Solution

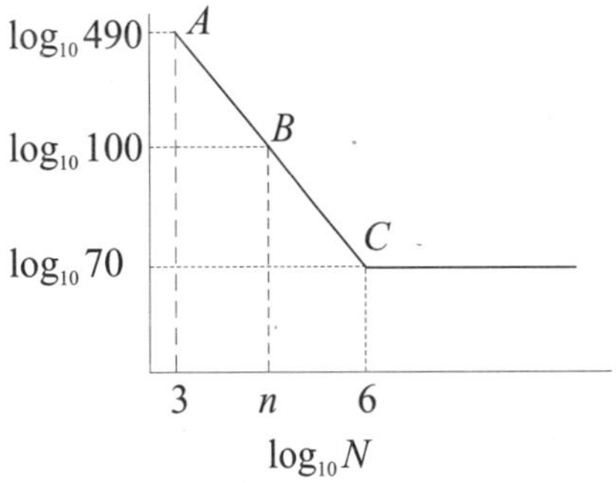

Given: For 10^6 cycles, $\sigma_e = 70\,\text{MPa}$

Graph between $\log_{10}\sigma_e$ v/s $\log_{10} N$ is shown in figure.

Equation of line AB:

$$\frac{\log_{10} 490 - \log_{10} 70}{6 - 3} = \frac{\log_{10} 100 - \log_{10} 70}{n - 3}$$

or $\quad n = 6 - 3 \times \dfrac{\log_{10} \frac{100}{70}}{\log_{10} 7}$

or $\quad n = \log_{10} N = 5.450116$

$$N = 281913.5$$

Example 9.33

A 60 mm long and 6 mm thick fillet weld carries a steady load of 15 kN along the weld. The shear strength of the weld material is equal to 200 MPa. The factor of safety is

(A) 2.4 (B) 3.4 (C) 4.8 (D) 6.8

GATE 2006

Solution

$$\text{Factor of safety, FS} = \frac{\text{Shear strength of weld}}{\text{Working shear stress}}$$

or
$$FS = \frac{200}{\dfrac{15\times10^3}{60\times\dfrac{6}{\sqrt{2}}}}$$

$$FS = 3.39$$

$$\text{Factor of safety, FS} = 3.39$$

Example 9.34

Linked Answer Questions

A band brake consists of a lever attached to one end of the band. The other end of the band is fixed to the ground. The wheel has a radius of 200 mm and the wrap angle of the band is 270°. The braking force applied to the lever is limited to 100 Nm, and the coefficient of friction between the band and the wheel is 0.5. No other information is given.

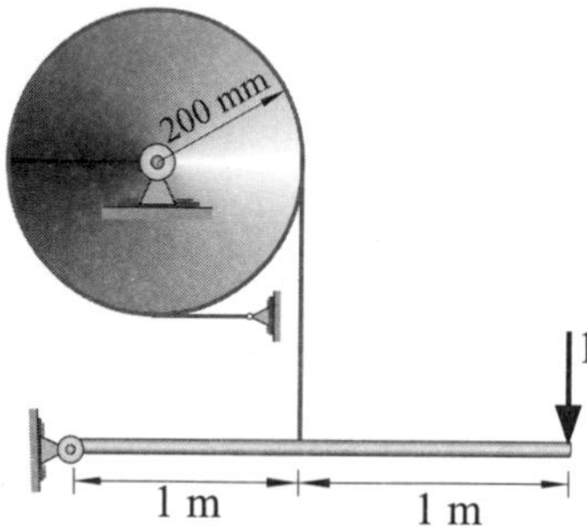

Q(a) The maximum tension that can be generated in the band during braking is

(A) 1200 N (B) 2110 N (C) 3224 N (D) 4420 N

Q(b) The maximum wheel torque that can be completely braked is

(A) 200 Nm (B) 382 Nm (C) 604 Nm (D) 844 Nm

GATE 2005

Solution

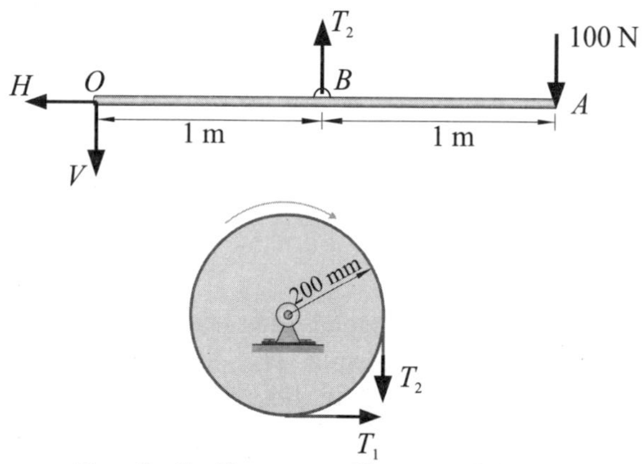

Free body diagrams of lever and drum

Free-body diagrams of drum and lever are shown in figure.

Taking moment about O; $100\times2 - T_2\times1 = 0$

This gives $T_2 = 200\,\text{N}$

Tension ratio $\dfrac{T_1}{T_2} = e^{\mu\theta} \Rightarrow \dfrac{T_1}{200} = e^{0.5\times\left(\frac{\pi}{180}\times270\right)}$

$$T_1 = 2110\,\text{N}$$

(b) Maximum wheel torque,

$$M_t = (T_1 - T_2)r = (2110-200)\times\frac{200}{1000}$$

$$M_t = 382\,\text{Nm}$$

Example 9.35

The spring constant of a helical compression spring DOES NOT depend on

(A) Coil diameter (B) Material strength

(C) Number of active turns (D) Wire diameter

GATE 2016

Solution

The spring constant of a helical spring is given by

$$k = \frac{G d^4}{8D^3 n}$$

The spring constant of a helical compression spring DOES NOT depend on material strength.

Example 9.36

The principal stresses at a point inside a solid object are $\sigma_1 = 100$ MPa, $\sigma_2 = 100$ MPa and $\sigma_3 = 0$. The yield strength of the material is 200 MPa. The factor of safety calculated using Tresca (maximum shear stress) theory is n_T and the factor of safety calculated using Von Mises (maximum distortional energy) theory is n_V. Which one of the following relations is TRUE?

(A) $n_T = \dfrac{\sqrt{3}}{2}n_V$ (B) $n_T = \sqrt{3}\,n_V$

(C) $n_T = n_V$ (D) $n_V = \sqrt{3}\,n_T$

GATE 2016

Solution

Given: $\sigma_1 = 100$ MPa, $\sigma_2 = 100$ MPa, $\sigma_3 = 0$ MPa and $\sigma_{yt} = 200$ MPa

According to Maximum shear stress theory (Tresca-Guest theory),

$$\tau_{max} = \text{Maximum of}\left\{\left|\frac{(\sigma_1-\sigma_2)}{2}\right|, \left|\frac{(\sigma_2-\sigma_3)}{2}\right|, \left|\frac{(\sigma_1-\sigma_3)}{2}\right|\right\}$$

or $\tau_{max} = \frac{(100-0)}{2} = 50\text{ MPa}$

or $\tau_{max} = \frac{\sigma_{yt}/2}{\eta_T} = \frac{200/2}{\eta_T} = 50\text{ MPa}$

$\eta_T = 2$

According to maximum distortion theory

$$\frac{\sigma_{yt}}{\eta_V} = \sqrt{\frac{1}{2}[(\sigma_1-\sigma_2)^2+(\sigma_2-\sigma_3)^2+(\sigma_3-\sigma_1)^2]}$$

or $$\frac{200}{\eta_V} = \sqrt{\frac{1}{2}[(100-100)^2+(100-0)^2+(0-100)^2]}$$

$\eta_V = 2$

$$\eta_T = \eta_V = 2$$

Example 9.37

For the brake shown in the figure, which one of the following is TRUE?

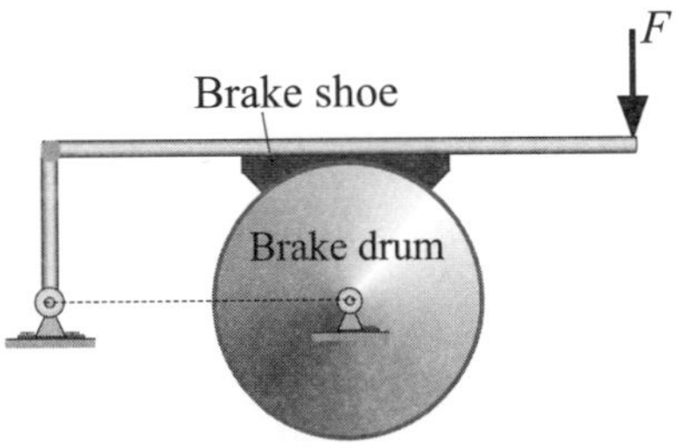

(A) Self energising for clockwise rotation of the drum

(B) Self energising for anti-clockwise rotation of the drum

(C) Self energising for rotation in either direction of the drum

(D) Not of the self energising type

GATE 2016

Solution

Self energising when drum rotates clockwise.

Example 9.38

In a structural member under fatigue loading, the minimum and maximum stresses developed at the critical point are 50 MPa and 150 MPa, respectively. The endurance, yield, and the ultimate strengths of the material are 200 MPa, 300 MPa and 400 MPa, respectively. The factor of safety using modified Goodman criterion is

(A) $\frac{3}{2}$ (B) $\frac{8}{5}$ (C) $\frac{12}{7}$ (D) 2

GATE 2016

Solution

Given: $\sigma_{min} = 50\text{ MPa}$, $\sigma_{max} = 150\text{ MPa}$, $\sigma_e = 200\text{ MPa}$, $\sigma_y = 300\text{ MPa}$ and $\sigma_{ut} = 400\text{ MPa}$.

Mean stress, $\sigma_m = \frac{\sigma_{min}+\sigma_{max}}{2} = \frac{50+150}{2} = 100\text{ MPa}$

Variable stress, $\sigma_v = \frac{\sigma_{max}-\sigma_{min}}{2} = \frac{150-50}{2} = 50\text{ MPa}$

Equation of Goodman line, $\frac{\sigma_m}{\sigma_{ut}} + \frac{\sigma_v}{\sigma_e} = \frac{1}{FS}$

$$\frac{100}{400} + \frac{50}{200} = \frac{1}{FS}$$

Factor of safety, $FS = 2$

Example 9.39

The forces F_1 and F_2 in a brake band and the direction of rotation of the drum are as shown in the figure. The coefficient of friction is 0.25. The angle of wrap is $\frac{3\pi}{2}$ radians. It is given that $R = 1$ m and $F_2 = 1$ N. The torque (in N-m) exerted on the drum is ________.

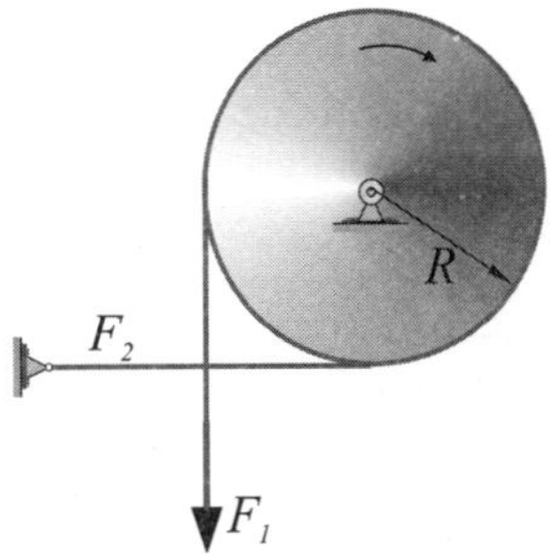

GATE 2016

Solution

Tension ratio of belt, $\frac{F_1}{F_2} = e^{\mu\theta}$

$$\frac{F_1}{1} = e^{0.25\times\frac{3}{2}\pi}$$

$F_1 = 3.24\text{ N}$

Torque exerted on the drum,

$$M = (F_1 - F_2)r = (3.24-1)\times 1$$

$M = 2.24\text{ Nm}$

Example 9.40

Which of the bearings given below SHOULD NOT be subjected to a thrust load?

(A) Deep groove ball bearing

(B) Angular contact ball bearing

(C) Cylindrical (straight) roller bearing

(D) Single row tapered roller bearing

GATE 2016

Solution

Cylindrical (straight) roller bearing is not used for thrust load.

Example 9.41

A bolted joint has four bolts arranged as shown in figure. The cross-sectional area of each bolt is 25 mm^2. A torque $T = 200$ N-m is acting on the joint. Neglecting friction due to clamping force, maximum shear stress in a bolt is___ MPa.

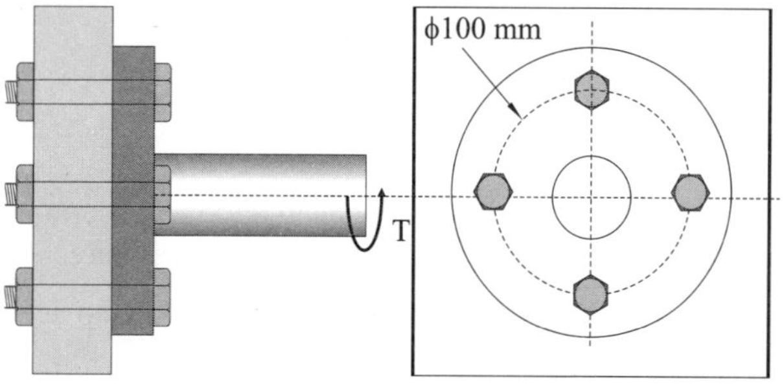

GATE 2016

Solution

Let F be the shear force on each bolt.

Torque, $T = 4F \times \frac{d}{2}$

Shear force, $F = \frac{T}{2d} = \frac{200}{2 \times \frac{100}{1000}} = 1000\,\text{N}$

Maximum shear stress, $\tau_{max} = \frac{F}{A} = \frac{1000}{25 \times 10^{-6}}$

$$\tau_{max} = 40 \times 10^6\ \text{N/m}^2$$

$$\tau_{max} = 40\,\text{MPa}$$

Example 9.42

A motor driving a solid circular steel shaft transmits 40 kW of power at 500 rpm. If the diameter of the shaft is 40 mm, the maximum shear stress in the shaft is____MPa.

GATE 2017

Solution

Torsion formula $\frac{T}{J} = \frac{\tau}{r} = \frac{G\theta}{l} \Rightarrow \tau_{max} = \frac{16T}{\pi d^3}$

Power $P = \frac{2\pi NT}{60} \Rightarrow T = \frac{60P}{2\pi N}$

or $\tau_{max} = \frac{16}{\pi d^3} \times \frac{60P}{2\pi N}$

Substituting $P = 40 \times 10^3$W, $N = 500$ rpm and $d = \frac{40}{1000}$ m

$$\tau_{max} = \frac{16}{\pi(40/1000)^3} \times \frac{60 \times 40 \times 10^3}{2\pi \times 500}$$

$$\tau_{max} = 60.79\ \text{MPa}$$

Example 9.43

Consider the schematic of a riveted lap joint subjected to tensile load F, as shown below. Let d be the diameter of the rivets, and S_f be the maximum permissible tensile stress in the plates. What should be the minimum value for the thickness of the plates to guard against tensile failure of the plates? Assume the plates to be identical.

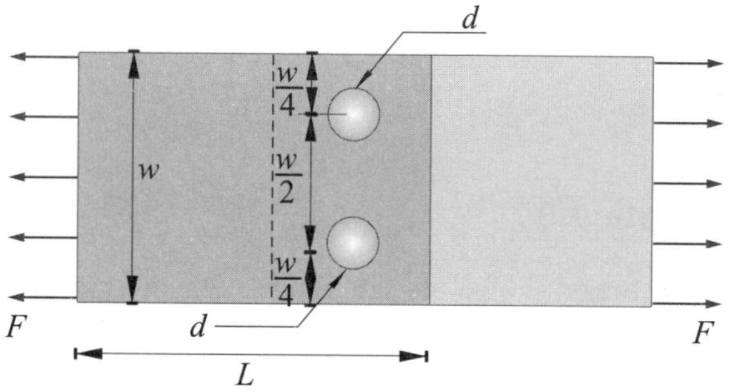

(A) $\frac{F}{S_f(w-2d)}$ (B) $\frac{F}{S_f w}$ (C) $\frac{F}{S_f(w-d)}$ (D) $\frac{2F}{S_f w}$

GATE 2017

Solution

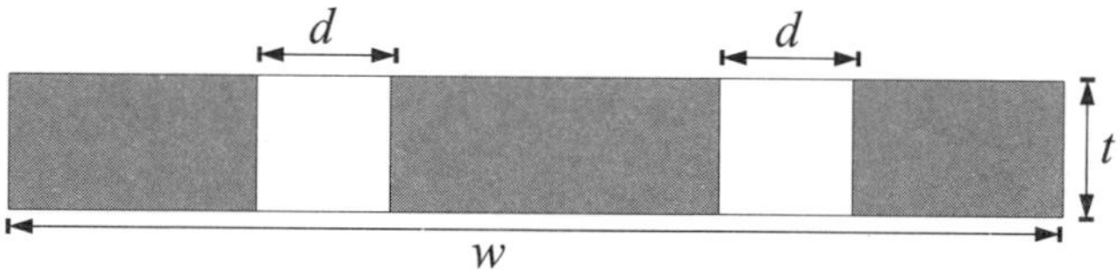

Maximum permissible tensile stress $S_f = \frac{F}{A_{min}}$

$$S_f = \frac{F}{wt - dt - dt} = \frac{F}{(w-2d)t}$$

Minimum thickness of plate $t = \frac{F}{(w-2d)S_f}$

$$t = \frac{F}{(w-2d)S_f}$$

Example 9.44

In a metal forming operation when the material has just started yielding, the principal stresses are $\sigma_1 = +180$ MPa, $\sigma_2 = -100$ MPa, $\sigma_3 = 0$. Following von- Mises' criterion, the yield stress is ______ MPa.

GATE 2017

Solution

Von-Mises criterion rule

$$2\sigma_m^2 = (\sigma_1 - \sigma_2)^2 + (\sigma_2 - \sigma_3)^2 + (\sigma_3 - \sigma_1)^2$$

$$2\sigma_m^2 = [180 - (-100)]^2 + (-100 - 0)^2 + (0 - 180)^2$$

$$\sigma_m = \sqrt{\frac{280^2 + 100^2 + 180^2}{2}}$$

$$\sigma_m = 245.76 \text{ MPa}$$

Example 9.45

A machine element has an ultimate strength (σ_u) of 600 N/mm^2, and endurance limit (σ_{en}) of 250 N/mm^2. The fatigue curve for the element on a **log-log** plot is shown below. If the element is to be designed for a finite life of 10000 cycles, the maximum amplitude of a completely reversed operating stress is __________ N/mm^2.

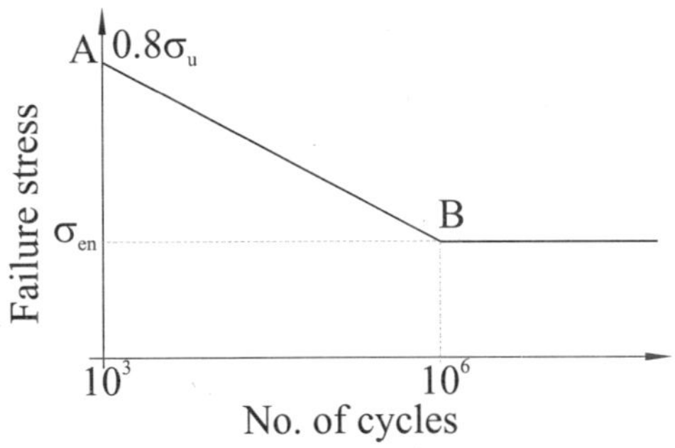

GATE 2017

Solution

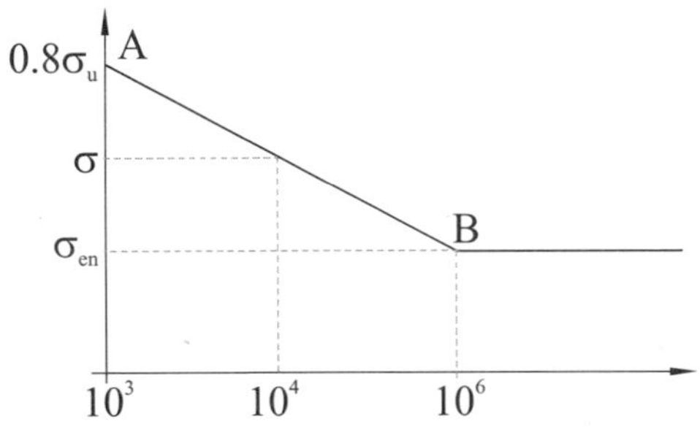

Given: $\sigma_u = 600$ N/mm^2, $\sigma_{en} = 250$ N/mm^2 and $N = 10^4$ cycle

$$\frac{\log 0.8\sigma_u - \log \sigma_{eu}}{6-3} = \frac{\log \sigma - \log 0.8\sigma_u}{4-3}$$

or $$\frac{\log 0.8 \times 600 - \log 250}{3} = \frac{\log \sigma - \log 0.8 \times 600}{1}$$

or $$\log \sigma = \log 480 + \frac{\log 480 - \log 250}{3}$$

$$\sigma = 386.19 \text{ MPa}$$

Example 9.46

A machine component made of a ductile material is subjected to a variable loading with $\sigma_{min} = -50$ MPa and $\sigma_{max} = 50$ MPa. If the corrected endurance limit and the yield strength for the material are $\sigma_e' = 100$ MPa and $\sigma_y = 300$ MPa, respectively the factor of safety is_______.

GATE 2017

Solution

Given: $\sigma_{min} = -50$ MPa, $\sigma_{max} = 50$ MPa, $\sigma_e = 100$ MPa and $\sigma_y = 300$ MPa.

$$\sigma_m = \frac{50 - 50}{2} = 0, \sigma_v = \frac{50 - (-50)}{2} = 50 \text{ MPa}$$

Applying the Soderberge line fatigue failure criterion

$$\frac{\sigma_m}{\sigma_y} + \frac{\sigma_v}{\sigma_e} = \frac{1}{FS}$$

$$\frac{0}{300} + \frac{50}{100} = \frac{1}{FS}$$

$$FS = 2$$

Example 9.47

A steel plate, connected to a fixed channel using three identical bolts A, B and C, carries a load of 6 kN as shown in the figure. Considering the effect of direct load and moment, the magnitude of resultant shear force (in kN) on bolt C is

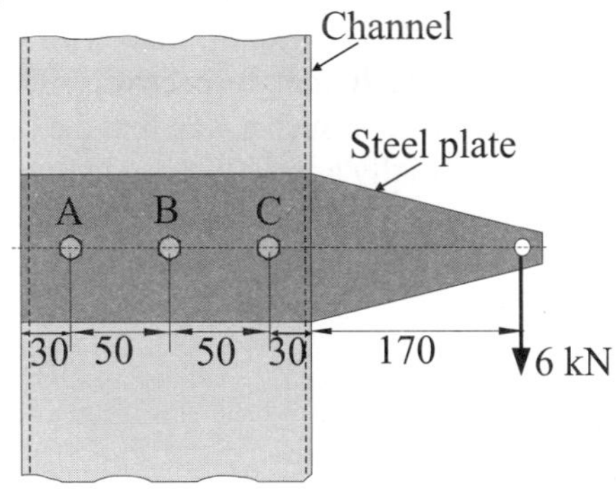

All dimensions are in mm

(A) 13 (B)15 (C) 17 (D)30

GATE 2017

Solution

Direct shear force $F_d = \frac{6}{3} = 2$ kN

Equating the turning resisting moment about centroid of bolts (bolt B).

$$F_A \times 50 + F_C \times 50 = 6 \times (170 + 30 + 50) \qquad [F_A = F_C]$$

$$F_A = F_C = 15$$

Resultant shear force on bolt C, $F_d + F_C = 2 + 15 = 17$

Resultant shear force on bolt C = 17 kN

Example 9.48

A helical compression spring made of wire of circular cross-section is subjected to a compressive load. The maximum shear stress induced in the cross-section of the wire is 24 MPa. For the same compressive load, if both the wire diameter and the mean coil diameter are doubled, the maximum shear stress (in MPa) induced in the cross-section of the wire is_____.

GATE 2017

Solution

Shear stress $\tau_{max} = \frac{8WD}{\pi d^3}$ [Neglected direct stress]

$$24 = \frac{8WD}{\pi d^3} \quad \text{(i)}$$

$$\tau = \frac{8W(2D)}{\pi(2d)^3} = \frac{1}{4}\frac{8WD}{\pi d^3} \quad \text{(ii)}$$

From Equations (i) and (ii), we obtain

$$\tau = \frac{24}{4} = 6$$

$$\tau = 6 \text{ MPa}$$

Example 9.49

A single-plate clutch has a friction disc with inner and outer radii of 20 mm and 40 mm, respectively. The friction lining in the disc is made in such a way that the coefficient of friction μ varies radially as $\mu = 0.01r$, where r is in mm. The clutch needs to transmit a friction torque of 18.85 kN.mm. As per uniform pressure theory, the pressure (in MPa) on the disc is______.

GATE 2017

Solution

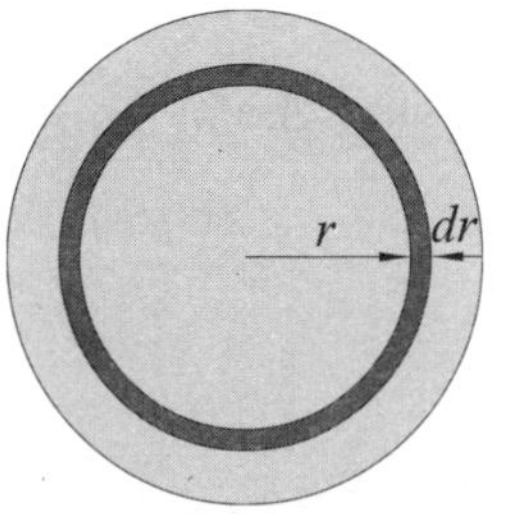

Let p = uniform pressure

Consider an element of radius r and thickness dr.

Friction force $dF = \mu p \times 2\pi r dr$

Frictional torque $dT = r \times dF = \mu p \times 2\pi r^2 dr$

$$dT = 0.01r \times p 2\pi r^2 dr = p \times 2\pi \times 0.01 \times r^3 dr$$

$$T = p \times 2\pi \times 0.01 \times \int_{20}^{40} r^3 dr = \frac{p \times 2\pi \times 0.01}{4}(40^4 - 20^4)$$

$$18.85 = 0.0628 p(40^4 - 20^4)$$

$$p = 0.5 \text{ MPa}$$

Example 9.50

The principal stresses at a point in a critical section of a machine component are $\sigma_1 = 60$ MPa, $\sigma_2 = 5$ MPa and $\sigma_3 = -40$ MPa. For the material of the component, the tensile yield strength is $\sigma_y = 200$ MPa. According to the maximum shear stress theory, the factor of safety is

(A) 1.67 (B) 2.00 (C) 3.60 (D) 4.00

GATE 2017

Solution

Given: $\sigma_1 = 60$ MPa, $\sigma_2 = 5$ MPa, $\sigma_3 = -40$ MPa and $\sigma_y = 200$ MPa

According to the maximum shear stress theory

$$\text{Maximum of } \left[\sigma_1 - \sigma_2 = \frac{\sigma_y}{FS}, \quad \sigma_2 - \sigma_3 = \frac{\sigma_y}{FS}, \quad \sigma_3 - \sigma_1 = \frac{\sigma_y}{FS}\right]$$

$$\sigma_1 - \sigma_2 = 55, \sigma_2 - \sigma_3 = 45, \sigma_3 - \sigma_1 = 100$$

Thus,

$$100 = \frac{200}{FS}$$

$$FS = 2$$

Example 9.51

If the wire diameter of a compressive helical spring is increased by 2%, the change in spring stiffness (in %) is_____.

GATE 2018

Solution

Stiffness of spring $k = \frac{Gd^4}{8D^3 n}$

$$k' = \frac{G(1.02d)^4}{8D^3 n} = 1.0824 \frac{Gd^4}{8D^3 n}$$

$$k' = 1.0824k$$

$$\% \text{ increase in stiffness} = \frac{k' - k}{k} \times 100 = 8.24$$

% increase in stiffness = 8.24%

Example 9.52

A carpenter glues a pair of cylindrical wooden logs by bonding their end faces at an angle of 30° as shown in the figure.

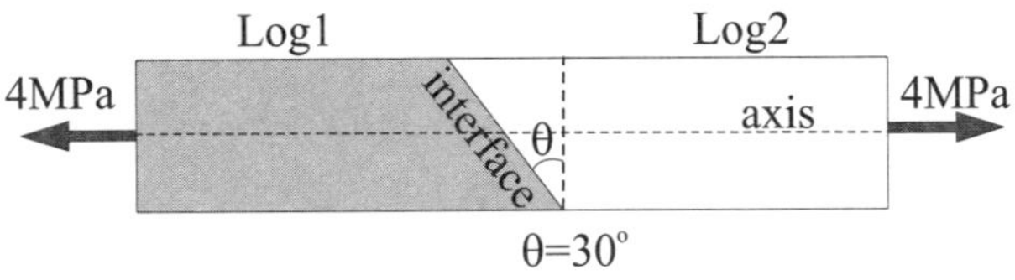

The glue used at the interface fails if

Criterion 1: the maximum normal stress exceeds 2.5 MPa.

Criterion 2: the maximum shear stress exceeds 1.5 MPa.

Assume that the interface fails before the logs fail. When a uniform tensile stress of 4 MPa is applied, the interface

(A) fails only because of criterion 1

(B) fails only because of criterion 2

(C) fails because of both criteria 1 and 2

(D) does not fail

GATE 2018

Solution

Let σ_n be normal stress and τ be shear stress.

Figure shows the free-body diagram of element ABC.

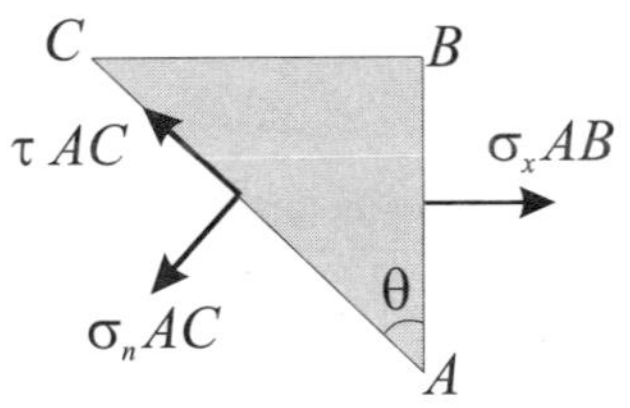

Resolving the forces along and normal to plane AC.

$$\sigma_x AB\cos\theta = \sigma_n AC$$

$$\sigma_n = \sigma_x \frac{AB}{AC}\cos\theta = \sigma_x \cos^2\theta$$

Normal stress $\sigma_n = 4\cos^2 30 = 3$

$$\sigma_n = 3 \text{ MPa}$$

$$\sigma_x AB\sin\theta = \tau AC$$

$$\tau = \sigma_x \frac{AB}{AC}\sin\theta = \frac{\sigma_x \sin 2\theta}{2}$$

Shear stress $\tau = \dfrac{2\sin(2\times 30)}{2} = 1.73$

$$\tau = 1.73 \text{ MPa}$$

Example 9.53

A self-aligning ball bearing has a basic dynamic load rating (C_{10}, for 10^6 revolutions) of 35 kN. If the equivalent radial load on the bearing is 45 kN, the expected life (in 10^6 revolutions) is

(A) below 0.5 (B) 0.5 to 0.8

(C) 0.8 to 1.0 (D) above 1.0

GATE 2018

Solution

Load-life relation for ball bearing, $L = \left(\dfrac{C}{P}\right)^3$

Substituting dynamic load capacity $C = 35$ kN, equivalent radial load $P = 45$ kN. We have

$$L = \left(\frac{35}{45}\right)^3$$

$$L = 0.4705$$

Example 9.54

Pre-tensioning of a bolted joint is used to

(A) strain harden the bolt head

(B) decrease stiffness of the bolted joint

(C) increase stiffness of the bolted joint

(D) prevent yielding of the thread root

GATE 2018

Solution

Pre-tensioning of a bolted joint is used to increase stiffness of the bolted joint.

Example 9.55

A hollow circular shaft of inner radius 10 mm, outer radius 20 mm and length 1 m is to be used as a torsional spring. If the shear modulus of the material of the shaft is 150 GPa, the torsional stiffness of the shaft (in kN-m/rad) is ____ .

GATE 2018

Solution

Torsional stiffness $k_\theta = \dfrac{T}{\theta} = \dfrac{GJ}{l}$

$$k_\theta = \frac{150\times 10^9 \times \frac{\pi}{32}\left[\left(\frac{40}{1000}\right)^4 - \left(\frac{20}{1000}\right)^4\right]}{1}$$

$$k_\theta = 35343 \text{ Nm/rad}$$

$$k_\theta = 35.3 \text{ kNm/rad}$$

Example 9.56

Fatigue life of a material for a fully reversed loading condition is estimated from

$$\sigma_a = 1100N^{-0.15}$$

where σ_a is the stress amplitude in MPa and N is the failure life in cycles. The maximum allowable stress amplitude (in MPa) for a life of 1×10^5 cycles under the same loading condition is ________ .

GATE 2018

Solution

Stress amplitude $\sigma_a = \dfrac{\sigma_{max} - \sigma_{min}}{2} = 1100N^{-0.15}$

Fully reversed loading, $\sigma_{min} = -\sigma_{max}$

$$\frac{\sigma_{max} - (-\sigma_{max})}{2} = 1100N^{-0.15}$$

$$\sigma_{max} = 1100\,N^{-0.15}$$

or $\sigma_{max} = 1100 \times (1\times10^5)^{-0.15}$

$$\sigma_{max} = 195.61\,\text{MPa}$$

Example 9.57

A bar is subjected to a combination of a steady load of 60 kN and a load fluctuating between –10 kN and 90 kN. The corrected endurance limit of the bar is 150 MPa, the yield strength of the material is 480 MPa and the ultimate strength of the material is 600 MPa. The bar cross-section is square with side *a*. If the factor of safety is 2, the value of *a* (in mm), according to the modified Goodman's criterion, is ________ .

GATE 2018

Solution

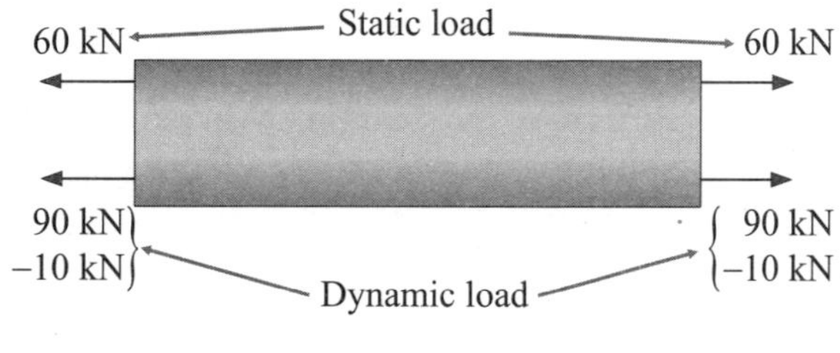

Mean stress $\sigma_m = \dfrac{\sigma_{max} + \sigma_{min}}{2} = \dfrac{P_{max} + P_{min}}{2a^2}$

$$\sigma_m = \frac{150 + 50}{2a^2} = \frac{100}{a^2}\ \text{MPa}$$

Variable stress $\sigma_v = \dfrac{P_{max} - P_{min}}{2a^2}$

$$\sigma_v = \frac{150 - 50}{2a^2} = \frac{50}{a^2}\ \text{MPa}$$

Goodman equation $\dfrac{\sigma_m}{\sigma_{ut}} + \dfrac{\sigma_v}{\sigma_e} = \dfrac{1}{N}$

$$100\left(\frac{100}{a^2\times600} + \frac{50}{a^2\times150}\right) = \frac{1}{2}$$

or $a^2 = 1000$

$$a = 31.62\ \text{mm}$$

Example 9.58

A spur gear with 20° full depth teeth is transmitting 20 kW at 200 rad/s. The pitch circle diameter of the gear is 100 mm. The magnitude of the force applied on the gear in the radial direction is

(A) 0.36 kN (B) 0.36 kN (C) 0.36 kN (D) 0.36 kN

GATE 2019

Solution

Given: $\phi = 20°, P = 20\,\text{kW}, \omega = 200\,\text{rad/s, and}\ d = 100\,\text{mm}.$

Torque transmitted, $T = \dfrac{P}{\omega} = \dfrac{20\times10^3}{200}$

$$T = 100\ \text{Nm}$$

Tangential force on tooth, $F_t = \dfrac{T}{d/2} = \dfrac{100}{(100/2\times1000)}$

$$F_t = 2000\ \text{N}$$

$$\frac{F_r}{F_t} = \tan\phi \Rightarrow F_r = F_t\tan\phi$$

Radial force, $F_r = 2000\tan 20 = 727.9\ \text{N}$

$$F_r = 0.73\ \text{kN}$$

Example 9.59

During a high cycle fatigue test, a metallic specimen is subjected to cyclic loading with a mean stress of +140 MPa, and a minimum stress of –70 MPa. The *R*- ratio (minimum stress to maximum stress) for this cyclic loading is _______ (round off to one decimal place)

GATE 2019

Solution

Given: $\sigma_{mean} = 140$ MPa and $\sigma_{min} = -70$ MPa

Mean stress, $\sigma_{mean} = \dfrac{\sigma_{max} + \sigma_{min}}{2} = 140$

$$\frac{\sigma_{max} - 70}{2} = 140 \Rightarrow \quad \sigma_{max} = 350\ \text{MPa}$$

Thus,

$$R\text{-ratio} = \frac{\sigma_{min}}{\sigma_{max}} = -\frac{70}{350} = -0.2$$

$$R\text{-ratio} = -0.2$$

Example 9.60

At a critical point in a component, the state of stress is given as $\sigma_{xx} = 100$ MPa, $\sigma_{yy} = 220$ MPa, $\sigma_{xy} = \sigma_{yx} = 80$ MPa and all other stress components are zero. The yield strength of the material is 468 MPa. The factor of safety on the basis of maximum shear stress theory is _______ (round off to one decimal place).

GATE 2019

Solution

Given: $\sigma_x = 100$ MPa, $\sigma_y = 220$ MPa, $\tau_{xy} = 80$ MPa

Principal stresses;

$$\sigma_{1,2} = \frac{100+220}{2} \pm \sqrt{\left(\frac{220-100}{2}\right)^2 + 80^2}$$

$$\sigma_1 = 260 \text{ MPa}, \sigma_2 = 60 \text{ MPa}$$

Maximum shear stress theory;

$$\tau_{max} = \frac{\sigma_{yt}}{2\times \text{FS}} = \text{Max}\left[\left|\frac{\sigma_1 - \sigma_2}{2}\right|, \left|\frac{\sigma_1}{2}\right|, \left|\frac{\sigma_2}{2}\right|\right]$$

$$\frac{468}{2\times \text{FS}} = \text{Max}\left[\left|\frac{260-60}{2}\right|, \left|\frac{260}{2}\right|, \left|\frac{60}{2}\right|\right] = 130$$

$$\text{FS} = \frac{468}{2\times 130} = 1.8$$

$$\text{FS} = 1.8$$

Example 9.61

A single block brake with a short shoe and torque capacity of 250 Nm is shown. The cylindrical brake drum rotates anticlockwise at 100 rpm and the coefficient of friction is 0.25. The value of a, in mm (round off to one decimal place), such that the maximum actuating force P is 2000 N, is __________.

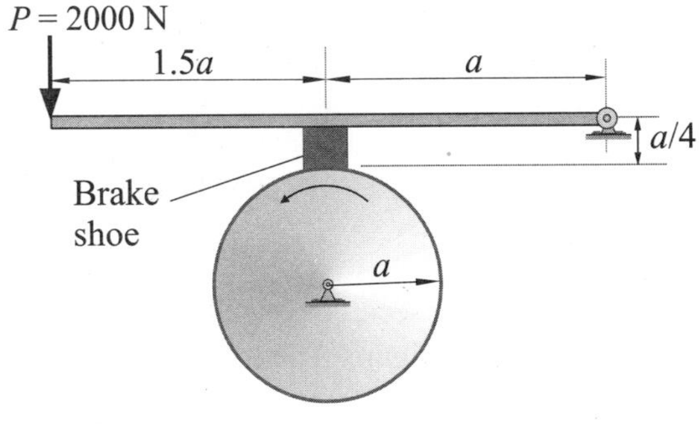

GATE 2019

Solution

Free-body diagram of lever is shown in figure.

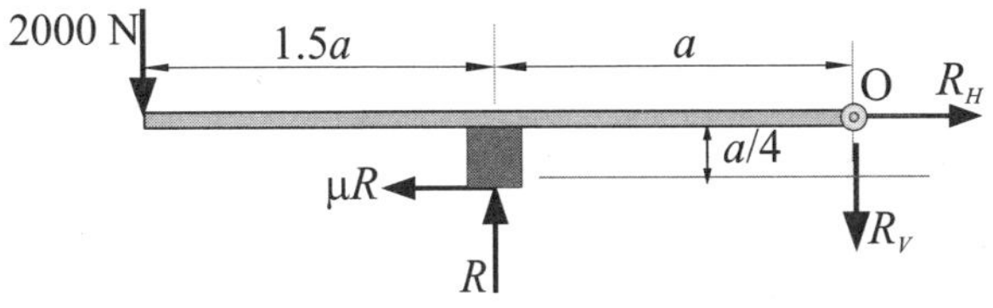

Frictional torque, $T = \mu R \times r$

$$250 = 0.25R \times a$$

or $$R = \frac{250}{0.25a}$$

Taking moment about O;

$$2000 \times 2.5a - 0.25R \times \frac{a}{4} - R \times a = 0$$

Substituting $R = \dfrac{250}{0.25a}$, we have

$$2000 \times 2.5a - 0.25 \times \frac{250}{0.25a} \times \frac{a}{4} - \frac{250}{0.25a} \times a = 0$$

$$a = 212.5 \text{ mm}$$

Example 9.62

Endurance limit of a beam subjected to pure bending decreases with

(A) decrease in the surface roughness and decrease in the size of the beam

(B) increase in the surface roughness and decrease in the size of the beam

(C) increase in the surface roughness and increase in the size of the beam

(D) decrease in the surface roughness and increase in the size of the beam

GATE 2019

Solution

Endurance limit of a beam subjected to pure bending decreases with increase in the surface roughness and increase in the size of the beam.

Example 9.63

A short shoe external drum brake is shown in the figure. The diameter of the brake drum is 500 mm. The dimensions $a = 1000$ mm, $b = 500$ mm and $c = 200$ mm. The coefficient of friction between the drum and the shoe is 0.35. The force applied on the lever $F = 100$ N as shown in the figure. The drum is rotating anti-clockwise. The braking torque on the drum is ________ Nm (round off to two decimal places)

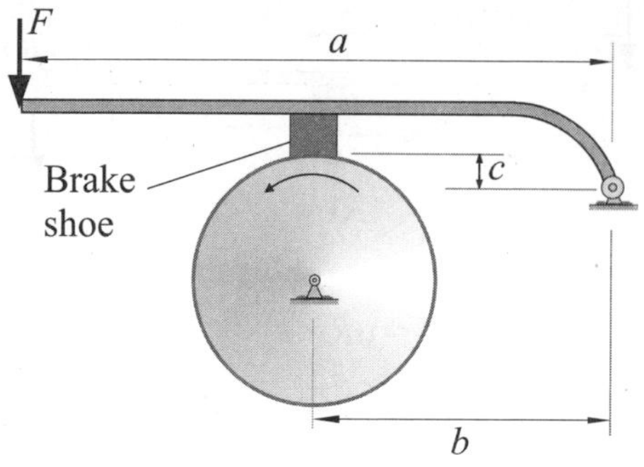

GATE 2019

Solution

Free-body diagram of lever is shown in figure.

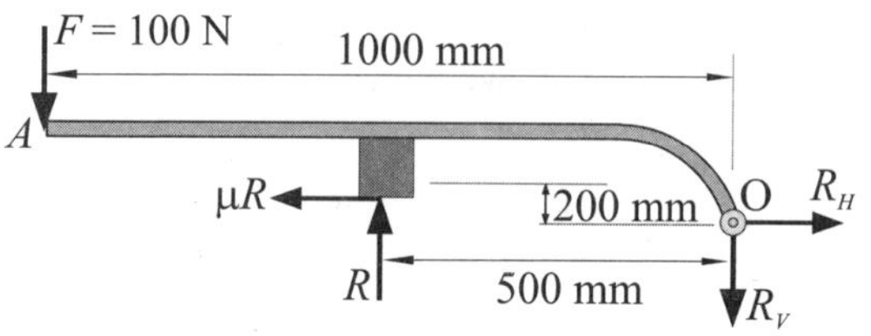

Taking moment about O;

$$100 \times 1000 + 0.35R \times 200 - R \times 500 = 0$$

or $$R = \frac{100 \times 1000}{500 - 0.35 \times 200} = 232.55\text{ N}$$

Braking torque, $$T = \mu R \times r = 0.35 \times 232.55 \times \frac{500}{2 \times 1000}$$

$$T = 20.34\text{ Nm}$$

9.3 PRACTICE PAPER

Time: 3 hours **Max. Marks: 100**

Q.1 to Q.30 carry one mark each

Q.1 to Q.20 Multiple Choice Questions

Q.1 A helical spring has N turns of coil of diameter D, and a second spring, made of same wire diameter and of same material, has $N/2$ turns of coils of diameter $2D$. If the stiffness of the first spring is k, then the stiffness of the second spring will be

(A) $2k$ (B) $k/2$ (C) $k/4$ (D) $4k$

Q.2 A full journal bearing having clearance to radius ratio of $\frac{1}{100}$, using a lubricant with $\mu = 28 \times 10^{-3}$ Pa.s supports the shaft journal running at $N = 2400$ rpm. If bearing pressure is 1.4 MPa, the Sommerfeld number is

(A) 8×10^{-3} (B) 8×10^{-5}

(C) 0.48 (D) 0.48×10^{-2}

Q.3 A shaft is subjected to the combined action of bending moment 400 Nm and torque 300 Nm. What, respectively are the equivalent bending moment and equivalent torque ?

(A) 450 Nm and 500 Nm (B) 900 Nm and 350 Nm

(C) 900 Nm and 500 Nm (D) 400 Nm and 500 Nm

Q.4 The module and the pitch diameter of a 40 teeth gear whose circular pitch is 88 mm/tooth, are (respectively)

(A) 88, 3520 (B) 28, 1120

(C) 44, 1760 (D) None of these

Q.5 If the load on a ball bearing is halved, its life

(A) Remains unchanged (B) Increases two times

(C) Increases four times (D) Increases eight times

Q.6 Match List-I with List-II and select the correct answer using the codes given below the lists

List-I	List-II
(a) Under cutting	(1) Beam strength
(b) Addendum	(2) Interference
(c) Lewis equation	(3) Large speed reduction
(d) Worm and wheel	(4) Intersection axes
	(5) Module

(A) a–2, b–5, c–1, d–3 (B) a–1, b–5, c–4, d–3

(C) a–1, b–3, c–4, d–5 (D) a–2, b–3 c–1, d–5

Q.7 An eccentrically loaded riveted joint is shown with 4 rivets at P, Q, R and S. Which of the rivets are the most loaded?

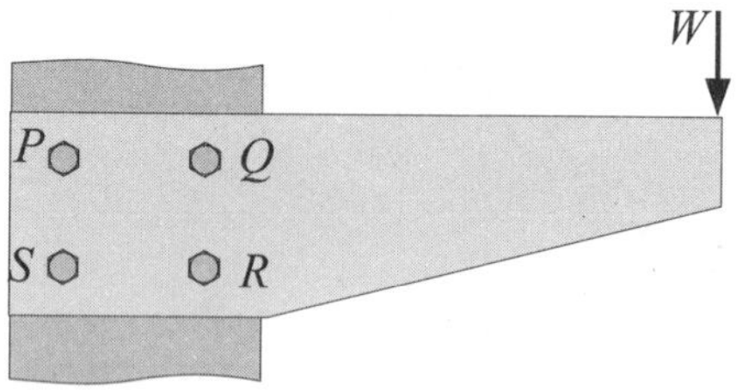

(A) R and Q (B) Q and R

(C) R and S (D) S and P

Q.8 A steel bracket is secured to wall by means of four steel bolts as shown in figure. The load on the bracket is 15 kN which acts at a distance of 175 mm from the wall.

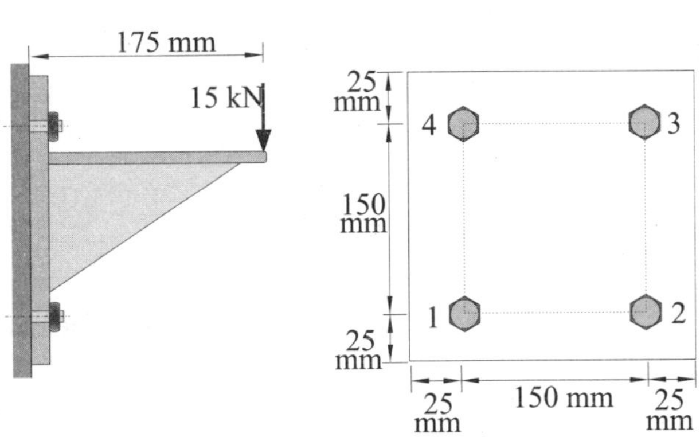

The primary shear force in bolt (number 3) is

(A) 8.9 kN (B) 3.75 kN (C) 7.35 kN (D) None of these

Q.9 It is seen from the curve that there is a minimum value of the coefficient of friction μ for a particular value of the bearing characteristic number denoted by α. What is this value of the bearing characteristic number called?

(A) Mckee number (B) Reynolds number

(C) Bearing modulus (D) Sommerfeld number

Q.10 Life of the roller bearing is given in million numbers of cycles by

(A) $\left(\frac{C}{P}\right)^{3}$ (B) $\left(\frac{C}{P}\right)^{\frac{10}{3}}$ (C) $\left(\frac{C}{P}\right)^{2.5}$ (D) $\left(\frac{C}{P}\right)^{4}$

Q.11 The single block-type hand brake shown in figure has mean coefficient of friction of 0.35. The equivalent coefficient of friction is

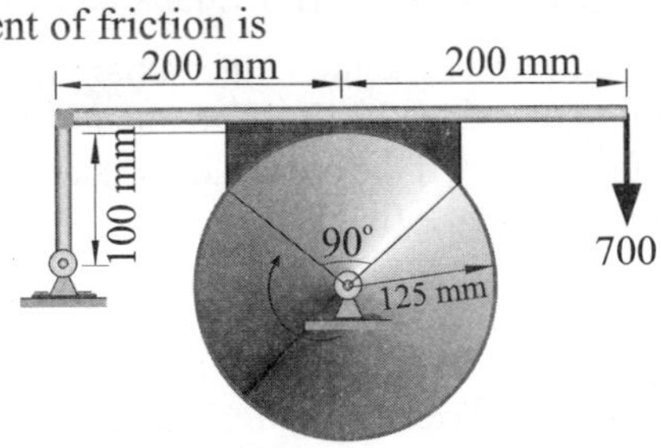

(A) 0.385 (B) 0.295 (C) 0.300 (D) None of these

Q.12 A small element at the critical section of a component is in a bi-axial state of stress with the two principal stresses being 360 MPa and 140 MPa. The maximum working stress according to distortion energy theory is

(A) 220 MPa (B) 110 MPa

(C) 314 MPa (D) 330 MPa

Q.13 A large uniform plate of 100 mm width containing a rivet-hole of size 5 mm is subjected to uniform uni-axial tension of 120 MPa. The maximum stress (in MPa) in the plate is

(A) 120 (B) 150 (C) 160 (D) 360

Q.14 From a tension test, the yield strength of steel is found to be 200 N/mm^2. Using a factor of safety of 2 and applying maximum principle stress theory of failure, the permissible stress (in N/mm^2) in the steel shaft subjected to torque will be

(A) 50 (B) 57.7 (C) 86.6 (D) 100

Q.15 The permissible stress in a filled weld is 100 N/mm^2. The fillet weld has equal leg length of 15 mm each. The allowable shearing load on weld per cm length of the weld is

(A) 22.5 N (B) 15.0 N (C) 10.6N (D) 7.5 kN

Q.16 Eight bolts are to be selected for fixing the cover plate of a cylinder subjected to a maximum load of 980 kN. If the design stress for the bolt material is 315 N/mm^2, what is the diameter of each bolt?

(A) 10 mm (B) 22 mm (C) 30 mm (D) 36 mm

Q.17 A shaft of diameter 60 mm is subjected to shear stress of 40 MPa and has an angle of twist equal to 0.01 radian. Modulus of rigidity $G = 0.8 \times 10^5$ MPa. The length of shaft is

(A) 600 mm (B) 400 mm (C) 100 mm (D) 200 mm

Q.18 A pull of 100 kN is transmitted from a bar A to the bar B through a pin as shown in figure. The maximum permissible tensile stress in the bar is 100 N/mm^2 and the permissible shear stress in the pin is 80 N/mm^2. The diameter d (in mm) of the pin is

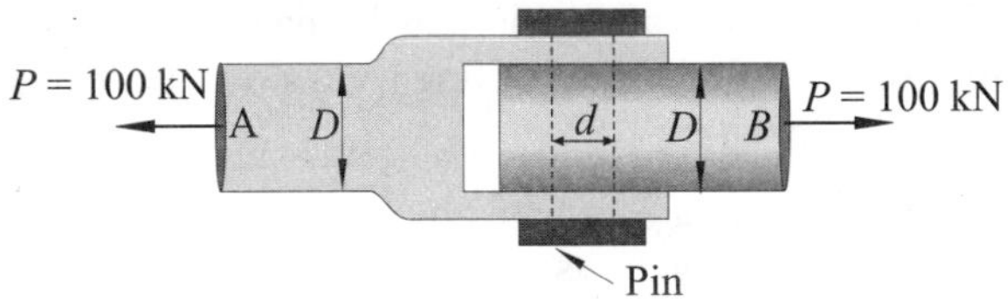

(A) 35.68 (B) 28.2 (C) 17.32 (D) 14.1

Q.19 A square section bar is welded to a bracket by means of a fillet weld as shown in figure. The size of weld is 3 mm. The direct shear stress is

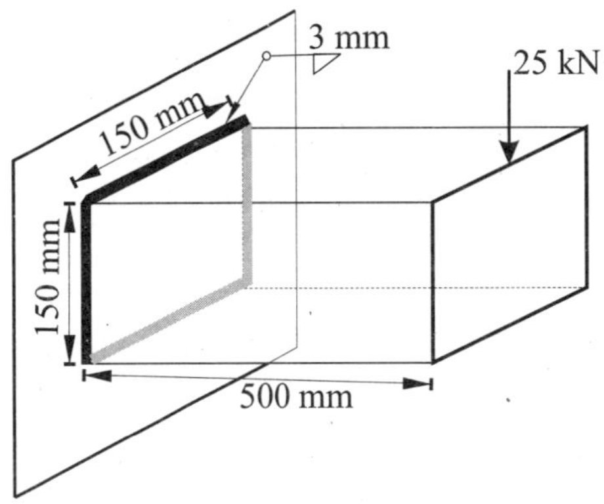

(A) 20.67 MPa (B) 196.41 MPa

(C) 19.64 MPa (D) None of these

Q.20 For a power transmission shaft transmitting power P at N rpm, its diameter is proportional to

(A) $\left(\frac{P}{N}\right)^{\frac{1}{3}}$ (B) $\left(\frac{P}{N}\right)^{\frac{1}{2}}$ (C) $\left(\frac{P}{N}\right)^{\frac{2}{3}}$ (D) $\frac{P}{N}$

Q.21 to Q.30 Numerical Answer Questions

Q.21 A single plate clutch is designed to transmit 10 kW power at 2000 rpm as shown in figure. The equivalent mass and radius of gyration of input and output shaft are 20 kg, 75 mm and 35 kg, 125 mm respectively. The heat generated (in J) during the clutching operation is __.

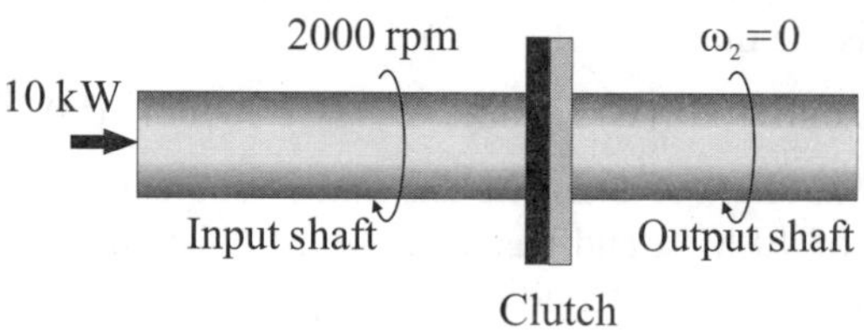

Q.22 A close coiled helical spring is made of 5 mm diameter wire coiled to 50 mm mean diameter. Maximum shear stress in the spring under the action of an axial force is 20 N/mm^2. The maximum shear stress in a spring made of 3 mm diameter wire coiled to 30 mm mean diameter, under the action of the same force will be (in N/mm^2) nearly ________.

Q.23 What is the safe static tensile load (in kN) for a M36 × 4C bolt of mild steel having yield stress of 280 MPa and a factor of safety 1.5?________.

Q.24 Two plates are fastened by means of two bolts as shown in figure. The bolts are made of plain carbon steel (σ_{yt} = 400 N/mm^2) and the factor of safety is 5. The size (diameter d in mm) of bolt is ________.

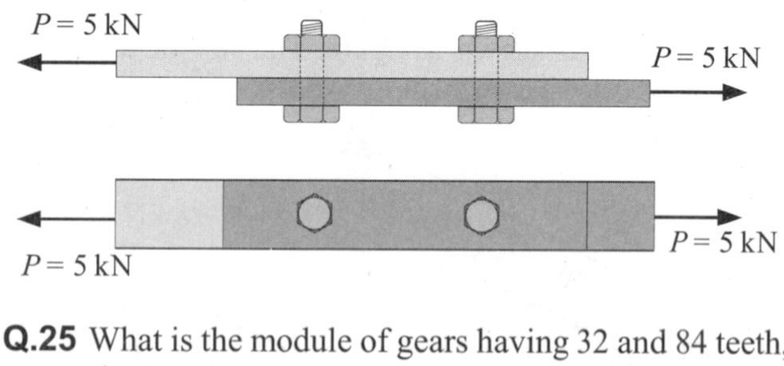

Q.25 What is the module of gears having 32 and 84 teeth, respectively, whose centre distance is 92 mm?_________.

Q.26 A pull of 100 kN is transmitted from a bar A to the bar B through a pin as shown in figure. The maximum permissible tensile stress in the bar is 100 N/mm^2 and the permissible shear stress in the pin is 80 N/mm^2. The diameter D (in mm) of bar is_________.

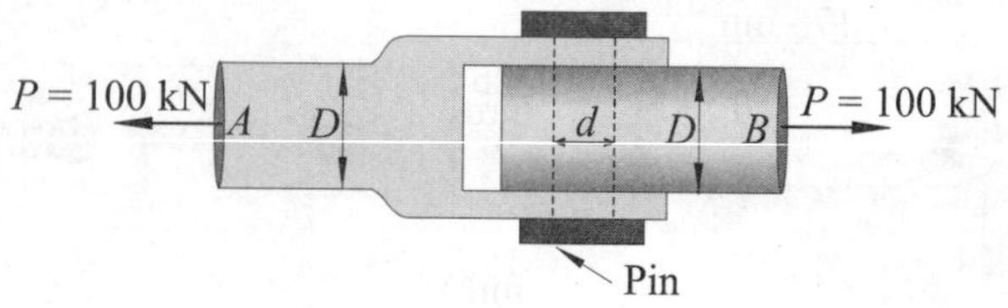

Q.27 The involute function of 20° is_________.

Q.28 The thickness of a boiler plate is 25 mm. The rivet diameter (in mm) will be_________.

Q.29 A flat and foot-step bearing supports a vertical shaft of 150 mm diameter rotating at 10 rad/s. The shaft carries a vertical load of 20 kN. Assuming uniform pressure distribution and coefficient of friction equal to 0.5, the power lost (in W) in friction is_________.

Q.30 A taper roller bearing has a dynamic load capacity of 20 kN. The desired life for 90% of the bearing is 10,000 hours and the speed is 300 rpm. The bearing life (in million revolution) is ______.

Q.31 to Q.65 carry two marks each.

Q.31 to Q.50 Multiple Choice Questions

Q.31 A spur gear transmits 10 kW at a pitch line velocity of 10 m/s; driving gear has a diameter of 1.0 m. Find the tangential force between the driver and the follower, and the transmitted torque respectively.

(A) 1.0 kN and 0.5 kN-m (B) 10.0 kN and 5.0 kN-m

(C) 0.5 kN and 0.25 kN-m (D) 1.0 kN and 1.0 kN-m

Q.32 In a multiple-disc clutch, the axial intensity of pressure is not to exceed 0.2 MPa. The inner radius of the discs is 100 mm and is half the outer radius. The axial force per pair of contact surface (in N) is

(A) 2000π (B) 3000π (C) 4000π (D) 6000π

Q.33 A single plate clutch is designed to transmit 10 kW power at 2000 rpm as shown in figure. The equivalent mass and radius of gyration of input and output shaft are 20 kg, 75 mm and 35 kg, 125 mm respectively. The time (in seconds) required to bring the output shaft to the rated speed from rest is

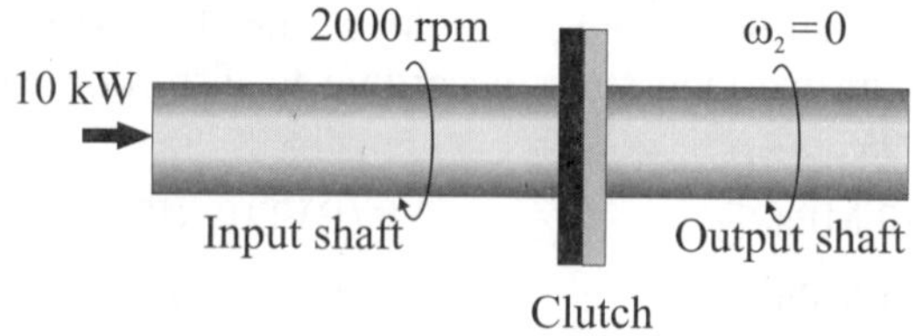

(A) 0.852 (B) 0.409 (C) 0.685 (D) 0.125

Q.34 A riveted joint has been designed to support an eccentric load P. The load generates value of F_1 equal to 4 kN and F_2 equal to 3 kN. The cross-sectional area rivet is

500 mm^2. Consider the following statements:

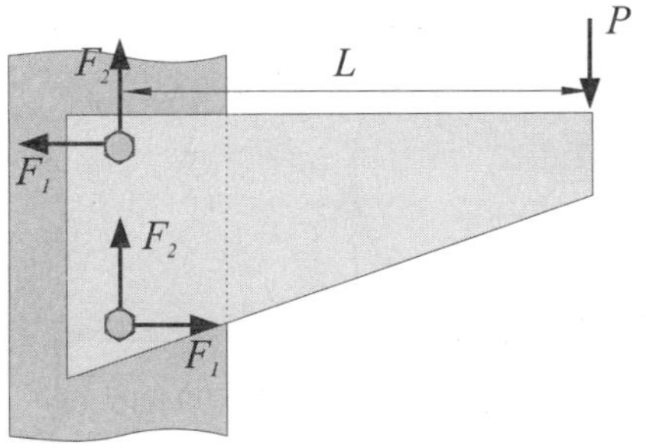

1. The stress in the rivet is 10 N/mm^2
2. The value of eccentricity L is 100 mm
3. The value of load P is 6 kN
4. The resultant force in each rivet is 6 kN

Which of these statements are correct?

(A) 1 and 2 (B) 2 and 3 (C) 3 and 4 (D) 1 and 3

Q.35 A hollow shaft of the same cross-sectional area and material as that of a solid shaft, transmits

(A) Same torque

(B) Lesser torque

(C) More torque

(D) Cannot be predicted without more data

Q.36 For obtaining the maximum shear stress induced in the shaft shown in the given figure, the torque should be equal to

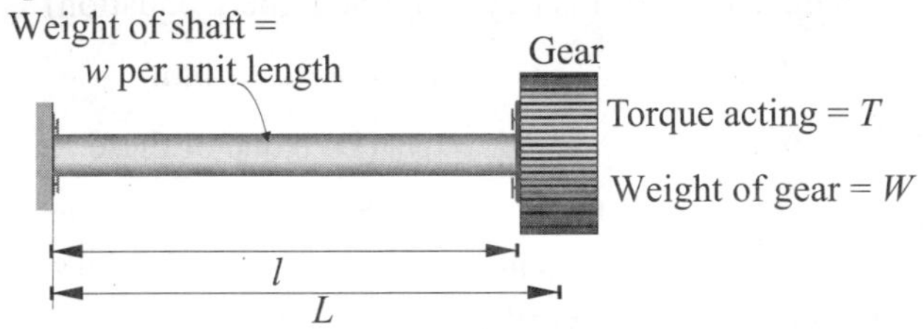

(A) T (B) $Wl + T$

(C) $\sqrt{Wl + \left(\frac{WL}{2}\right)^2}$ (D) $\sqrt{\left(WL + \frac{1}{2}wl^2\right)^2 + T^2}$

Q.37 A spring with 25 active coil cannot be accommodated within a given space. Hence, 5 coils of the spring are cut. What is the stiffness of the new spring?

(A) Same as the original spring

(B) 0.8 times the original spring

(C) 1.25 times the original spring

(D) 0.5 times the original spring

Q.38 A compacting machine shown in the figure below is used to crate a desired thrust force by using a rack and pinion arrangement. The input gear is mounted on the motor shaft. The gear have involute teeth of 2 mm module. If the drive efficiency is 80%, then torque required on the input shaft to create 1000 N output thrust is

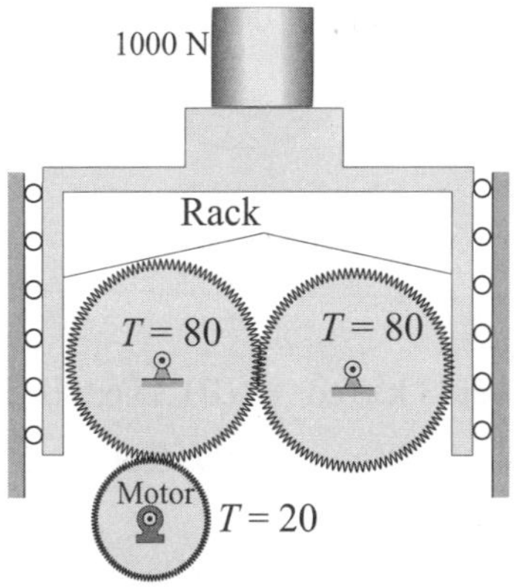

(A) 20 Nm (B) 25 Nm (C) 32 Nm (D) 50 Nm

Q.39 A circular shaft of diameter 50 mm is welded to the support by means of circumferential fillet weld as shown in figure. It is subjected to torsional moment of 2500 Nm. If the permissible shear stress in the weld is limited to 140 N/mm^2, then the size of weld is

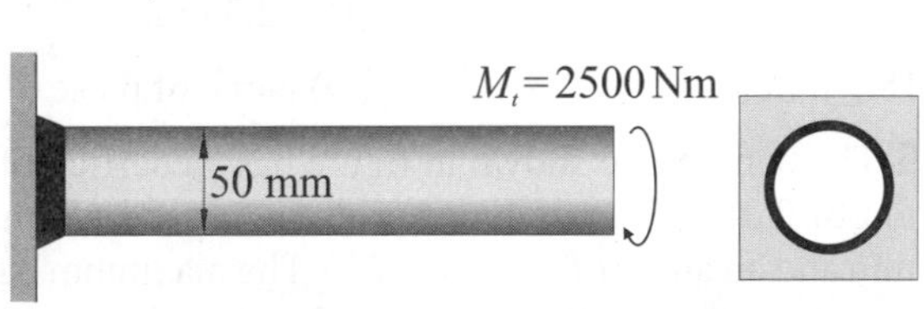

(A) 6.2 mm (B) 4.5 mm (C) 6.3 mm (D) 3.8 mm

Q.40 A circular rod of diameter d is welded to a flat plate along its circumference by fillet weld of thickness t. Assuming τ_w as the allowable shear stress for the weld material, what is the value of the safe torque that can be transmitted ?

(A) $\pi d^2 t \tau_w$ (B) $\frac{\pi d^2 t}{2} \tau_w$

(C) $\frac{\pi d^2 t}{2\sqrt{2}} \tau_w$ (D) $\frac{\pi d^2 t}{\sqrt{2}} \tau_w$

Q.41 The radial load acting on a ball bearing is 5 kN and the expected life for 90% of the bearing is 10,000 hours. The dynamic load (in N) carrying capacity of bearing, when shaft rotates at 1500 rpm, is

(A) 4500 N (B) 78003 N (C) 84362 N (D) 48263 N

Q.42 A mass of 3000 kg attached to a string is lowered at a velocity of 2.0 m/s from a drum of diameter 2 m and mass 100 kg. Radius of gyration of the drum is 1.0 m. On applying the brake, the mass is brought to rest in a distance of 1.0 m.The energy absorbed by the brake and torque

capacity are respectively

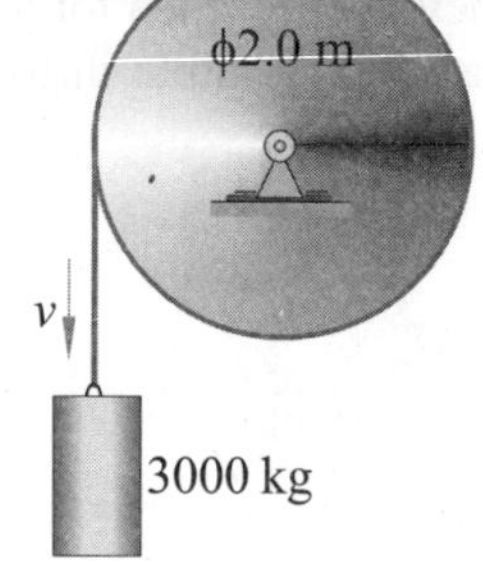

(A) 55.63 kJ, 45.73 kJ/rad (B) 35.63 kJ, 35.63 kJ/rad

(C) 78.33 kJ, 15.23 kJ/rad (D) 5.60 kJ, 55.63 kJ/rad

Q.43 The principal stresses σ_1, σ_2 and σ_3 at a point respectively are 80 MPa, 30 MPa and –40 MPa. The maximum shear stress(in MPa) is

(A) 25 (B) 35 (C) 55 (D) 60

Q.44 A bolt of C15 having 200 N/mm^2 yield strength is subjected to a direct load of 25 kN and shear load of 15 kN. Taking factor of safety 2, the size '*d*' of bolt by maximum shear stress theory is

(A) 15.7 mm (B) 22.3 mm

(C) 18.7 mm (D) None of these

Q.45 The band brake shown in figure has a coefficient of friction of 0.25, 350 mm diameter drum, a band width of 100 mm and an angle of wrap of 270°. The maximum band interface pressure on the brake is 620 kPa. The braking torque is

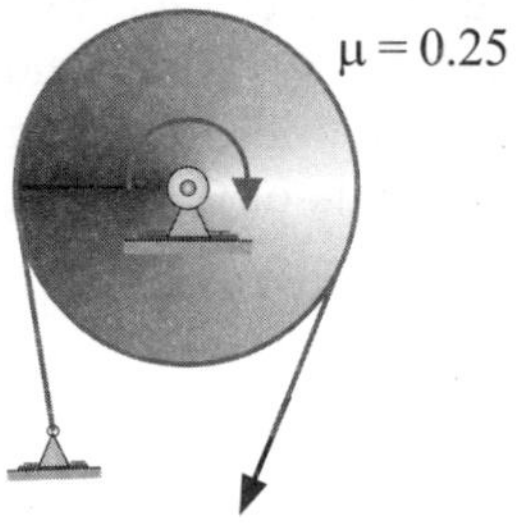

(A) 2.621 kNm (B) 10.852 kNm

(C) 1.314 kNm (D) None of these

Q.46 The band brake shown in figure is part of a hoisting machine. What size '*d*' shaft should be used to transmit the resisting torque developed by the brake to the machine if the shaft is to be made of a steel with an allowable shearing stress of 55 MPa?

(A) 35.2 mm (B) 61.3 mm

(C) 12.6 mm (D) None of these

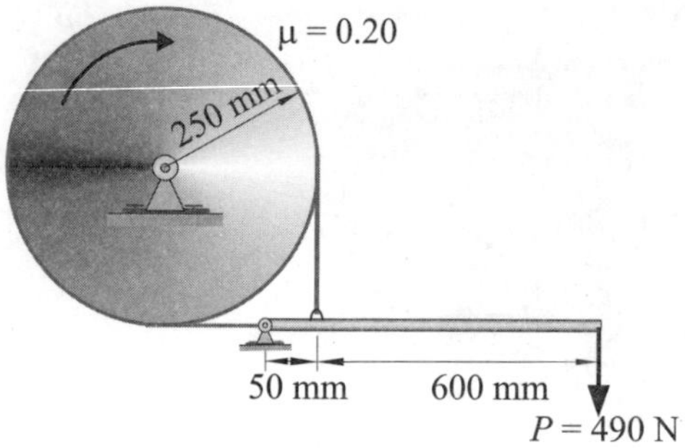

Q.47 The plate shown in figure is subjected to a completely reversible load of 16000 N, $\sigma_u = 440$ MPa, $q = 0.8$, surface finish factor = 0.67, size factor = 0.85, reliability factor = 0.897, $k_t = 2.35$ and FS = 1.5. The thickness of plate for infinite life is

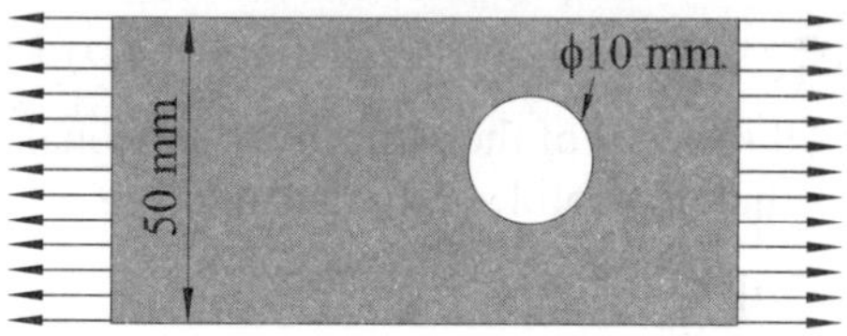

(A) 6.8 mm (B) 9.2 mm (C) 11.1 mm (D) 6.3 mm

Q.48 A shaft is subjected to a torque varying between 100 Nm to 500 Nm. k_r due to keyway is 1.5, FOS = 2, $\sigma_y = 300$ MPa, $\sigma_e = 300$ MPa, correction factor for torsion = 0.6, surface finish factor = 0.85 and size factor = 0.82. The diameter of shaft is (By using Soderberg equation)

(A) 33.18 mm (B) 30.12 mm

(C) 28.26 mm (D) None of these

Q.49 A bracket is fitted to the channel with 4 bolts as shown in figure. Permissible shear stress for bolt is 37.5 MPa. The diameter of bolt is

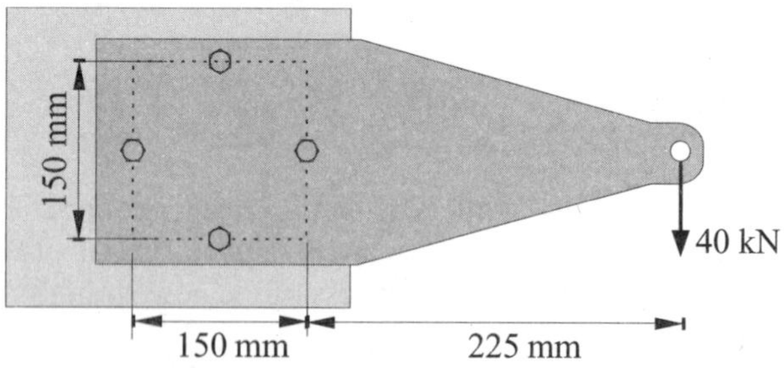

(A) 30.2 mm (B) 35.6 mm

(C) 38.4 mm (D) 41.20 mm

Q.50 A beam is welded to the vertical plate by means of two fillet welds as shown in figure. The permissible shear stress of weld is 70 N/mm^2. The size of weld is

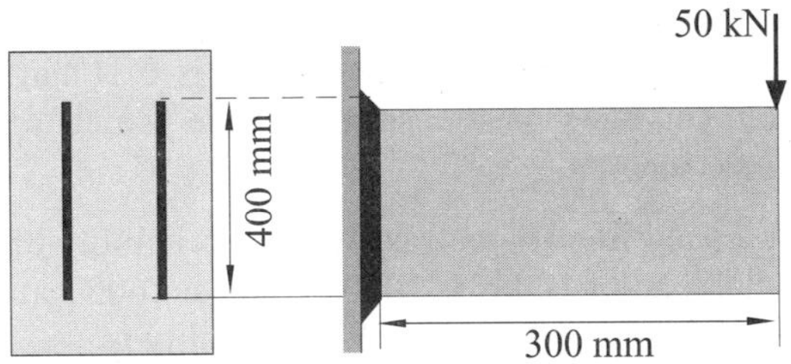

(A) 3.1 mm (B) 4.6 mm (C) 5.8 mm (D) 6.2 mm

Q.51 to Q.65 Numerical Answer Questions

Q.51 A square section bar is welded to a bracket by means of a fillet weld as shown in figure. The size of weld is 3 mm. The maximum bending stress (in MPa) is _____.

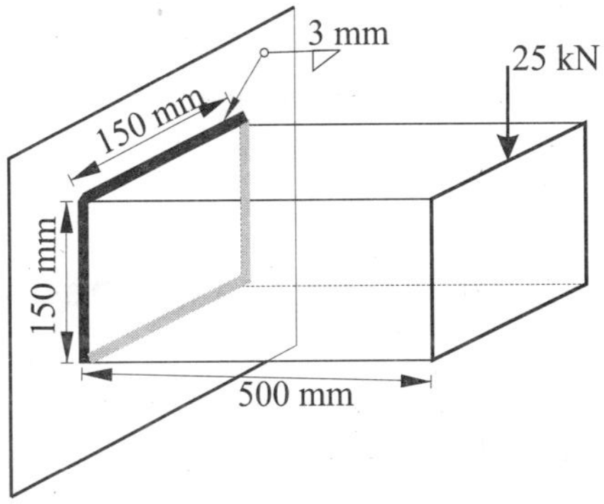

Q.52 The single block-type hand brake shown in figure has mean coefficient of friction of 0.35. The braking torque (in Nm) is________.

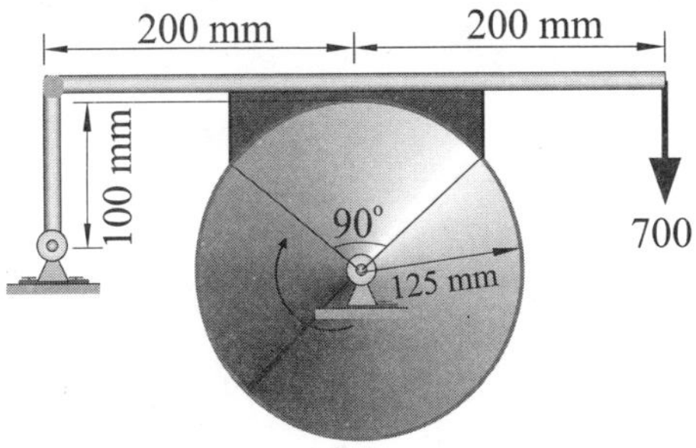

Q.53 A steel bracket is secured to wall by means of four steel bolts as shown in figure. The load on the bracket is 15 kN which acts at a distance of 175 mm from the wall. The equivalent tensile force (in kN) in bolt (number 3) is______ .

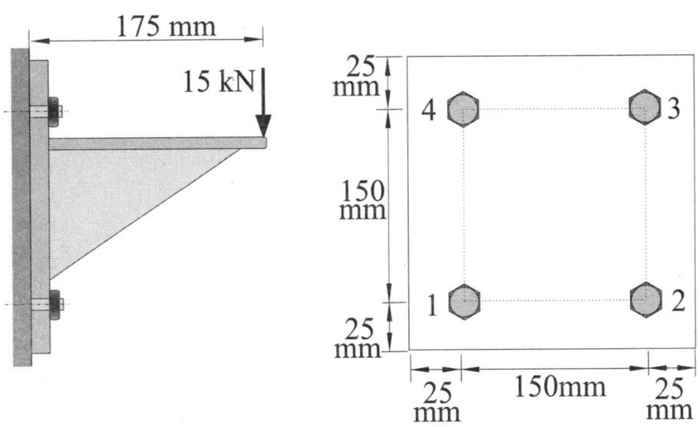

Q.54 A column of square section 40 mm × 40 mm, fixed to the ground carries an eccentric load P of 1600 N as shown in figure.

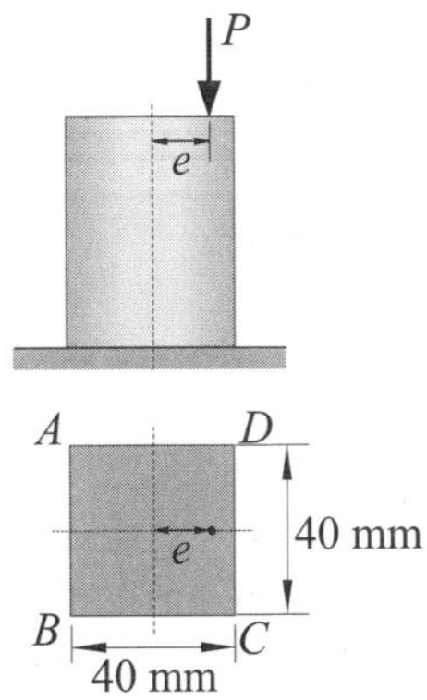

If the stress developed along the edge CD is -1.2 N/mm^2, the stress (in N/mm^2) along the edge AB will be_______.

Q.55 A circular solid shaft is subjected to a bending moment of 400 kNm and twisting moment of 300 kNm. On the basis of the maximum principal stress theory, the direct stress is σ and according to the maximum shear stress theory, the shear stress is τ. The ratio $\frac{\sigma}{\tau}$ is________.

Q.56 A steel bar of rectangular cross-section 10 mm × 50 mm is attached to a support by means of round pin of diameter 20 mm as shown in the figure.

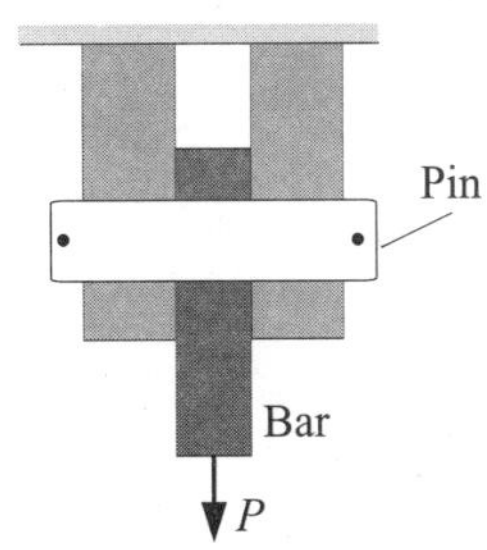

The allowable stresses for the bar in tension and the pin in shear are 150 MPa and 80 MPa, respectively. What is the maximum permissible value of tensile load that the bar can carry?______.

Q.57 A ductile component is subjected to dynamic stres varying between 150 MPa and 250 MPa. The ultimate tensile strength of the material is 450 MPa, yield point in tension is 350 MPa, and endurance limit for reversed bending is 250 MPa. Determine the factor of safety for the design of the component.________.

Q.58 A shaft is subjected to torque 1500 Nm and bending moment 75 Nm. The combined shock and fatigue factor for bending is 1.5 and for torsion is 2. The equivalent twisting moment for the shaft is ________.

Q.59 A cantilever beam of rectangular cross-section is used to support a static load of 15 kN attached to a string passing through a pulley of radius 0.5 m. The ratio of depth to width of the cross-section is 3.

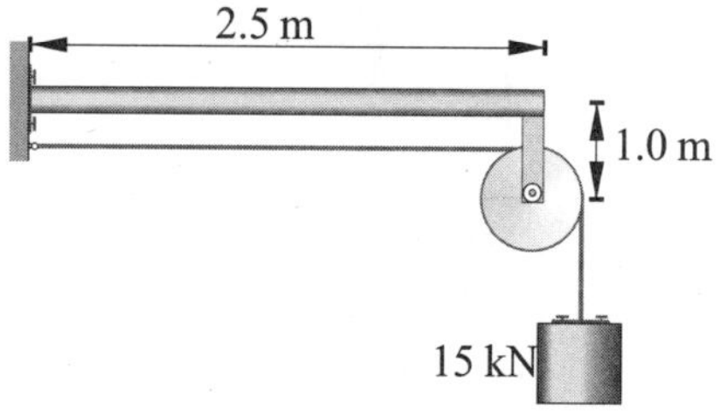

The yield strength of the beam material is 250 N/mm^2. Using the maximum normal stress theory of failure, determine the width (in mm) of the cross-section of the beam for factor of safety 2.5. Weight of the beam material can be ignored.________.

Q.60 A 26-teeth of 5 mm module and 20° full depth pinion receives 5.1 kW at 750 rpm. The tangential force (in N) on the gear is__________.

Q.61 A steel cantilever of cross-section 20 mm × 60 mm is bolted to a frame with two M16 bolts (B_1 and B_2). It is used to support a load of 5 kN attached to a string passing through two pulleys as shown in the figure.

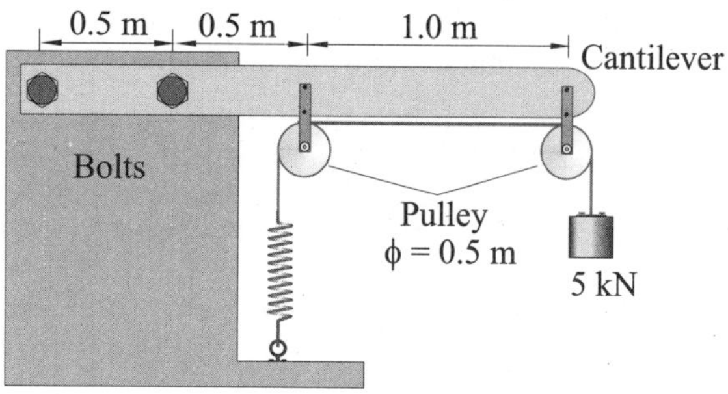

The maximum resultant shear stress (in MPa) on the bolts is _______.

Q.62 A plate is welded to another plate by a fillet weld as shown in the following figure. Total length of weld is 50 cm. The length l_1 (in cm) of weld is__________.

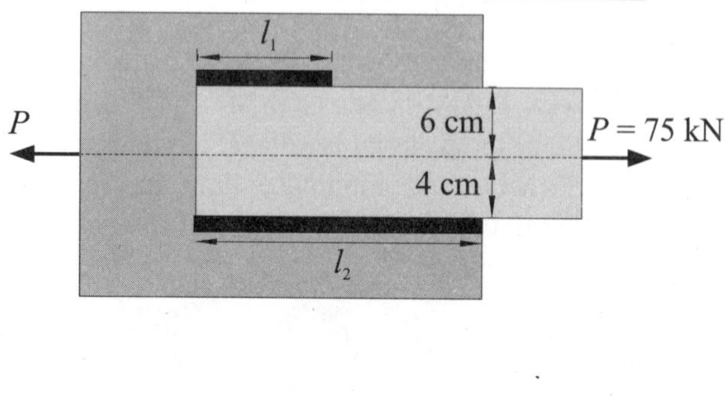

Q.63 A hole is to be punched in a 15 mm thick plate having an ultimate shear strength of 3 N/mm^2. If the allowable crushing stress in the punch is 6 N/mm^2, the diameter (in mm) of the smallest hole which can be punched is equal to_______.

Q.64 Desired life of a ball bearing for reliability of 99% and radial load of 10 kN is 10000 hours at 1600 rpm. The life of bearing in millions for 99% reliability is_____.

Q.65 A shaft of diameter 60 mm is welded by a ring of fillet weld bead to support an eccentric load of 15 kN.

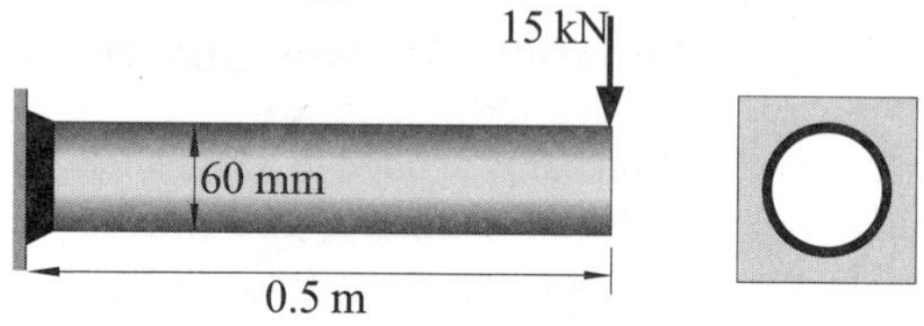

The permissible shear stress for the weld is 150 N/mm^2. Note that the moment of inertia about diametral axis of a circular ring of thickness t and radius r is $\pi t r^3$. The size (in mm) of the weld is_________.

9.4 SOLUTION TO PRACTICE PAPER

Q.1 Ans:(C)

Stiffness of first spring is

$$k = \frac{G d^4}{8 D^3 N} \qquad \text{(i)}$$

Stiffness of second spring is

$$k' = \frac{G d^4}{8 (2D)^3 \times \frac{N}{2}} \qquad \text{(ii)}$$

Equations (i) and (ii) gives

$$k' = \frac{k}{4}$$

Q.2 Ans:(A)

$$\text{Sommerfeld number} = \frac{\mu N}{P} \times \left(\frac{r}{c}\right)^2$$

Substituting given values $\frac{c}{r} = \frac{1}{100}$, $\mu = 28 \times 10^{-3}$ Pa.s, $N = \frac{2400}{60}$ rps and $P = 1.4$ MPa

$$\text{Sommerfeld number} = \frac{28 \times 10^{-3} \times \left(\frac{2400}{60}\right) \times 100^2}{1.4 \times 10^6}$$

$$\text{Sommerfeld number} = 8 \times 10^{-3}$$

Q.3 Ans:(A)

Equivalent bending moment, $M_{eq} = \frac{1}{2}(M + \sqrt{M^2 + T^2})$

$$M_{eq} = \frac{1}{2}(400 + \sqrt{400^2 + 300^2})$$

$$M_{eq} = 450\,\text{Nm}$$

Equivalent torque, $T_{eq} = \sqrt{M^2 + T^2}$

$$T_{eq} = \sqrt{400^2 + 300^2}$$

$$T_{eq} = 500\,\text{Nm}$$

Q.4 Ans:(B)

Circular pitch, $P_c = \frac{\pi d}{T} \Rightarrow 88 = \frac{\pi d}{40}$

$$d = 1120\,\text{mm}$$

Module, $m = \frac{d}{T} = \frac{1120}{40}$

$$m = 28$$

Q.5 Ans:(D)

Life of bearing life is given by

$$L = \left(\frac{C}{W}\right)^p; \quad p = 3 \text{ for ball bearing}$$

or $$L_2 = L_1\left(\frac{W_1}{W_2}\right)^3$$

Substituting given load $W_2 = \frac{W_1}{2}$, we get

$$L_2 = L_1\left(\frac{W_1}{W_1/2}\right)^3 = L_1 \times 2^3$$

$$L_2 = 8L_1$$

Q.6 Ans:(A)

Correct match:

(a) Under cutting ← (2) Interference

(b) Addendum ← (5) Module

(c) Lewis equation ← (1) Beam strength

(d) Worm and wheel ← (3) Large speed reduction

Q.7 Ans:(B)

The primary force (F_1) and secondary forces (F_2) are shown in the figure of free-body diagram.

Primary forces (F_1) and secondary forces (F_2) are same on all bolts.

Resultant of primary force and secondary force F_2 on bolt Q and R is maximum.

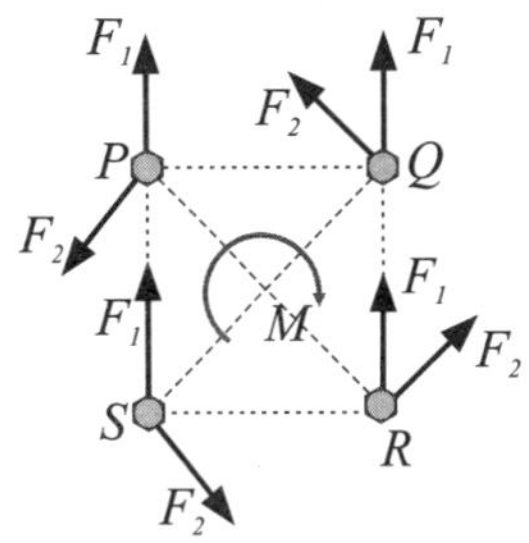

Q.8 Ans:(B)

Number of bolts, $n = 4$

Primary shear load on each bolt

$$F_s = \frac{\text{Total force}}{\text{Number of bolts}} = \frac{15}{4}\ \text{kN}$$

$$F_s = 3.75\,\text{kN}$$

Q.9 Ans:(C)

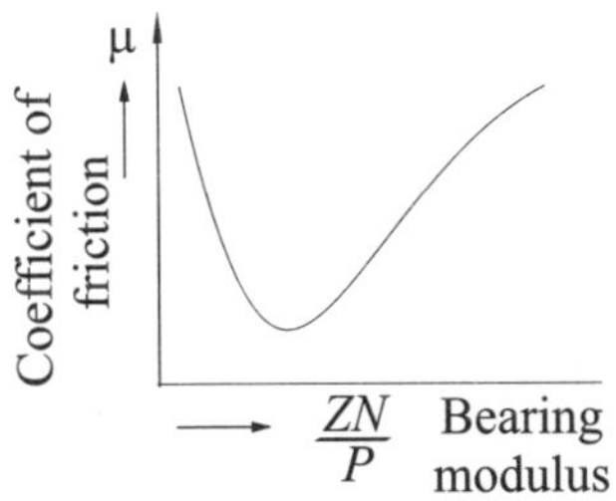

$\frac{ZN}{P}$ is called bearing modulus or bearing characteristic number.

Q.10 Ans:(B)

Bearing life (in million revolution) of roller bearing is given by

$$L = \left(\frac{C}{P}\right)^{\frac{10}{3}}$$

Q.11 Ans:(A)

The equivalent coefficient of friction is

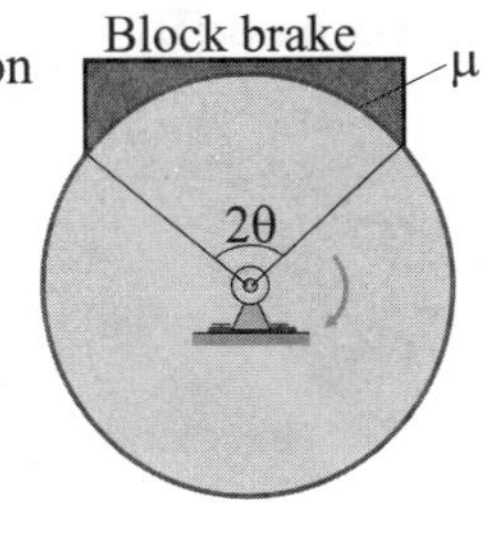

$$\mu' = \mu\frac{4\sin\theta}{2\theta + \sin 2\theta}$$

or $$\mu' = 035\frac{4\sin 45}{2 \times \frac{\pi}{4} + \sin 90}$$

$$\mu' = 0.385$$

Q.12 Ans:(C)

According to distortion energy theory, the maximum stress is

$$\sigma = \sqrt{\sigma_1^2 + \sigma_2^2 - \sigma_1\sigma_2}$$

Substituting $\sigma_1 = 360$ MPa and $\sigma_2 = 140$ MPa, we get

$$\sigma = \sqrt{360^2 + 140^2 - 360 \times 140}$$

$$\sigma = 314.32 \text{ MPa}$$

Q.13 Ans:(D)

Maximum stress is given by $\sigma_{max} = \sigma\left(1 + 2\frac{b}{a}\right)$

For circular hole $a = b$; $\sigma_{max} = \sigma(1 + 2 \times 1)$

or $\sigma_{max} = 3\sigma = 3 \times 120$

$$\sigma_{max} = 360 \text{ MPa}$$

Q.14 Ans:(A)

According maximum stress theory, permissible shear stress in the steel shaft is

$$\tau = \frac{\frac{\sigma_{yt}}{2}}{FS} = \frac{\frac{200}{2}}{2}$$

$$\tau = 50 \text{ N/mm}^2$$

Q.15 Ans:(C)

Shearing strength of weld

$$= \tau_{max}(l \times t) = \tau_{max}\left(l \times \frac{h}{\sqrt{2}}\right)$$

Equating this to allowable shearing load (F) gives

$$F = \tau_{max}\left(l \times \frac{h}{\sqrt{2}}\right)$$

or $$F = 100\left(10 \times \frac{15}{\sqrt{2}}\right) = 10606.6 \text{ N}$$

$$F = 10.6 \text{ kN}$$

Q.16 Ans:(B)

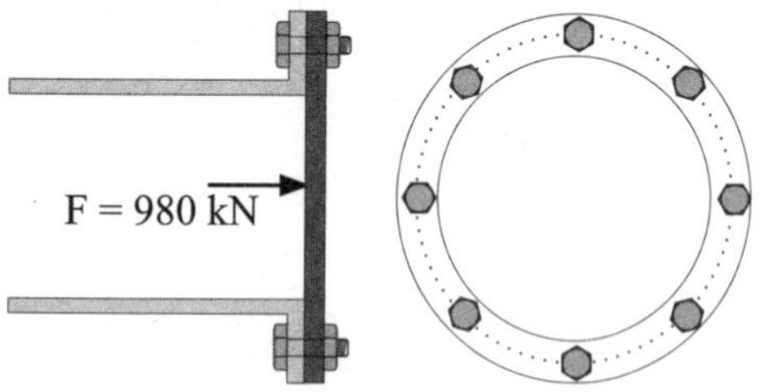

Let d be the diameter of each bolt.

Tensile strength of bolts $= \sigma \times \left(\frac{\pi}{4}d^2 \times 8\right)$

Equating this to load $F = 980$ kN gives

$$\sigma \times \left(\frac{\pi}{4}d^2 \times 8\right) = F$$

$$d = \sqrt{\frac{F}{2\pi\sigma}} = \sqrt{\frac{980 \times 10^3}{2\pi \times 315}}$$

$$d = 22.2 \text{ mm}$$

Q.17 Ans:(A)

Torsion formula, $\frac{T}{J} = \frac{\tau}{r} = \frac{G\theta}{l}$

Length of shaft, $l = \frac{G\theta}{\tau}r$

$$l = \frac{0.8 \times 10^5 \times 10^6 \times 0.01}{40 \times 10^6} \times \frac{60}{2 \times 1000}$$

$$l = 0.6 \text{ m}$$

$$l = 600 \text{ mm}$$

Q.18 Ans:(B)

Given: $P = 100$ kN, $\sigma_t = 100$ N/mm^2 and $\tau = 80$ N/mm^2.

Let d be the diameter of pin.

Shear area, $A = 2 \times \frac{\pi}{4}d^2$

Permissible shear stress, $\tau = \frac{P}{A}$

$$80 = \frac{100 \times 10^3}{2 \times \frac{\pi}{4}d^2}$$

This gives

Diameter of pin, $d = 28.2$ mm

Q.19 Ans:(C)

Length of weld, $l = 2(150 + 150) = 600$ mm

Thickness of weld at throat, $t = \frac{h}{\sqrt{2}} = \frac{3}{\sqrt{2}}$ mm

Area of weld, $A = l \times t = 600 \times \frac{3}{\sqrt{2}}$ mm^2

Direct shear stress, $\sigma_d = \frac{F}{A} = \frac{25}{600 \times \frac{3}{\sqrt{2}}}$ kN/mm^2

$$\sigma_d = 0.01964 \text{ kN/mm}^2$$

$$\sigma_d = 19.64 \text{ MPa}$$

Q.20 Ans:(A)

If d is the diameter of shaft, then

$$T = \frac{\pi}{16} d^3 \tau$$

Power transmitted by shaft, $P = T\omega$

$$P = \frac{\pi}{16} d^3 \tau \omega$$

or $$P = \frac{\pi}{16} d^3 \tau \frac{2\pi N}{60}$$

or $$d^3 = \frac{480}{\pi \tau} \frac{P}{N}$$

$$d \propto \left(\frac{P}{N}\right)^{\frac{1}{3}}$$

Q.21 Ans:[2046.45]

Given: $P = 10 \times 10^3$ W, $N = 2000$ rpm, $m_1 = 20$ kg, $k_1 = 75$ mm, $m_2 = 35$ kg and $k_2 = 125$ mm

Heat generated = Loss of kinetic energy

Heat generated, $Q = \frac{1}{2} I_{eq} (\omega_1 - \omega_2)^2$

$$Q = \frac{1}{2}\left(\frac{I_1 I_2}{I_1 + I_2}\right)(\omega_1 - \omega_2)^2$$

or $$Q = \frac{1}{2}\left(\frac{20(0.075)^2 \times 35(0.125)^2}{20(0.075)^2 + 35(0.125)^2}\right)\left(\frac{2\pi \times 2000}{60} - 0\right)^2$$

$$Q = 2046.45 \text{ J}$$

Q.22 Ans:[55.55]

Maximum shear stress in the spring under an axial force is given by

$$\tau = \frac{8WD}{\pi d^3}$$

Shear stress ratio $\frac{\tau_1}{\tau_2} = \frac{W_1}{W_2} \times \frac{D_1}{D_2} \times \left(\frac{d_2}{d_1}\right)^3$

Substituting given values $d_1 = 5$ mm, $D_1 = 50$ mm, $\tau_1 =$ 20 N/mm^2, $d_2 = 3$ mm, $D_2 = 30$ mm, $W_1 = W_2$.

$$\frac{20}{\tau_2} = \frac{W_2}{W_2} \times \frac{50}{30} \times \left(\frac{3}{5}\right)^3$$

or $$\tau_2 = 20 \times \left(\frac{5}{3}\right)^3$$

$$\tau_2 = 55.55 \text{ N/mm}^2$$

Q.23 Ans:[190]

Tensile strength of the bolt $= \sigma_y \times \frac{\pi}{4} d^2$

Safe static tensile load, $P_{safe} = \frac{\sigma_y \times \frac{\pi}{4} d^2}{FS}$

Substituting diameter of bolt (M36 × 4C) $d = 36$ mm, yield stress $\sigma_y = 280 \times 10^6$ N/mm^2 and factor of safety FS = 1.5.

or $$P_{safe} = \frac{280 \times 10^6 \times \frac{\pi}{4}\left(\frac{36}{1000}\right)^2}{1.5}$$

$$P_{safe} = 190 \times 10^3 \text{ N}$$

$$P_{safe} = 190 \text{ kN}$$

Q.24 Ans:[8.92]

Let d be the diameter of bolt.

Permissible shear stress, $\tau = \frac{\sigma_{sy}}{FS} = \frac{\sigma_{yt}/2}{FS} = \frac{400/2}{5}$

$$\tau = 40 \text{ N/mm}^2$$

Load $P = \tau \times$ Shear area

$$P = \tau \times \left(2 \times \frac{\pi}{4} d^2\right)$$

or $$d = \sqrt{\frac{2P}{\tau \pi}} = \sqrt{\frac{2 \times 5 \times 10^3}{40\pi}}$$

$$d = 8.92 \text{ mm}$$

Q.25 Ans:[1.586]

Given: $T_1 = 32$ teeth, $T_2 = 84$ teeth and $C = 92$ mm

Let m be the module of gears.

Module, $m = \frac{d}{T} \Rightarrow d = mT$

Pitch circle diameters; $d_1 = m \times 32$ and $d_2 = m \times 84$

Center distance, $C = \frac{d_1}{2} + \frac{d_2}{2}$

or $$C = \frac{m \times 32}{2} + \frac{m \times 82}{2} = 92 \text{ mm}$$

$$m = 1.586$$

Q.26 Ans:[35.68]

Given: $P = 100$ kN, $\sigma_t = 100$ N/mm^2 and $\tau = 80$ N/mm^2.

Let D be the diameter of bar.

Cross-sectional area of bars, $A = \frac{\pi}{4} D^2$

Tensile stress, $\sigma = \frac{P}{A} \Rightarrow 100 = \frac{100 \times 10^3}{\frac{\pi}{4} D^2}$

This gives

$$\text{Diameter of bar } D = 35.68\,\text{mm}$$

Q.27 Ans:[0.0149]

Involute function of ϕ is given by

$$\text{Inv}\,\phi = \tan\phi - \phi$$

$$\text{Inv}\,20 = \tan 20 - \left(\frac{\pi}{180}\times 20\right)$$

$$\text{Inv}\,20 = 0.0149$$

Q.28 Ans:[30]

Given: Thickness of plate, $t = 25$ mm

Diameter of rivet, $d = 6.01\sqrt{t}$

[Unwin's empirical formula for $t > 8$ mm]

$$d = 6.01\sqrt{25}$$

$$d = 30\,\text{mm}$$

Q.29 Ans:[5000]

Assuming uniform pressure distribution, friction torque is

$$T = \frac{2}{3}\mu W r = \frac{2}{3}\times 0.5\times 20\times 10^3\times\frac{150}{2\times 1000}\,\text{Nm}$$

Power lost, $P = T\omega$

or $$P = \frac{2}{3}\times 0.5\times 20\times 10^3\times\frac{150}{2\times 1000}\times 10$$

$$P = 5000\,\text{W}$$

Q.30 Ans:[180]

Given: $C = 20\,\text{kN}$, $L_H = 10{,}000\,\text{h}$ and $n = 300$ rpm.

Bearing life (in million revolution) is given by

$$L = \frac{60\,n\,L_H}{10^6} = \frac{60\times 300\times 10000}{10^6}$$

$$L = 180\,\text{million revolutions}$$

Q.31 Ans:(A)

Given: $P = 10\,\text{kW}$, $v = 10$ m/s and $d = 1.0\,\text{m}$

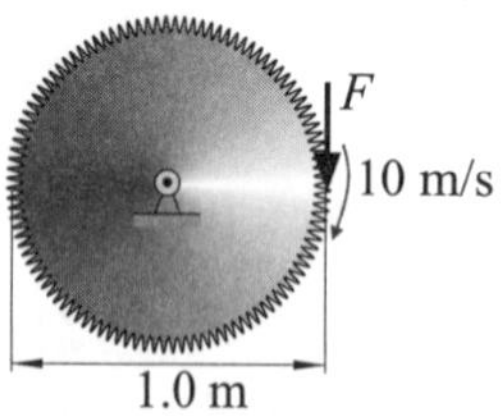

Power, $P = Fv$

Tangential force, $F = \frac{P}{v} = \frac{10}{10}$

$$F = 1.0\,\text{kN}$$

Transmitted torque, $\tau = F\times\frac{d}{2}$

$$\tau = 1.0\times\frac{1}{2}$$

$$\tau = 0.5\,\text{kNm}$$

Q.32 Ans:(D)

Given: $p = 0.2\,\text{MPa}$, $r_i = 100\,\text{mm}$ and $r_o = 2r_i = 200\,\text{mm}$

Axial force is given by $F = p\pi(r_o^2 - r_i^2)$

$$F = 0.2\times 10^6\times\pi\left[\left(\frac{200}{1000}\right)^2 - \left(\frac{100}{1000}\right)^2\right]$$

$$\text{F} = 6000\pi\,\text{N}$$

Q.33 Ans:(B)

Given: $P = 10\times 10^3\,\text{W}$, $N = 2000$ rpm, $m_1 = 20\,\text{kg}$, $k_1 = 75\,\text{mm}$, $m_2 = 35\,\text{kg}$ and $k_2 = 125\,\text{mm}$.

Using the relation, $P = \frac{2\pi N T}{60}$

Torque, $T = \frac{60P}{2\pi N}$

$$T = \frac{60\times 10\times 10^3}{2\pi\times 2000} = 47.74\,\text{Nm}$$

Using the impulse-angular momentum relation,

$$T\times\Delta t = I_{eq}\Delta\omega$$

$$\Delta t = \frac{I_{eq}\Delta\omega}{T} = \frac{I_1 I_2}{I_1 + I_2}\left(\frac{\omega_1 - \omega_2}{T}\right)$$

or $$\Delta t = \frac{20(0.075)^2\times 35(0.125)^2}{20(0.075)^2 + 35(0.125)^2}\left(\frac{\frac{2\pi\times 2000}{60} - 0}{47.74}\right)$$

$$\Delta t = 0.409\,\text{s}$$

Q.34 Ans:(D)

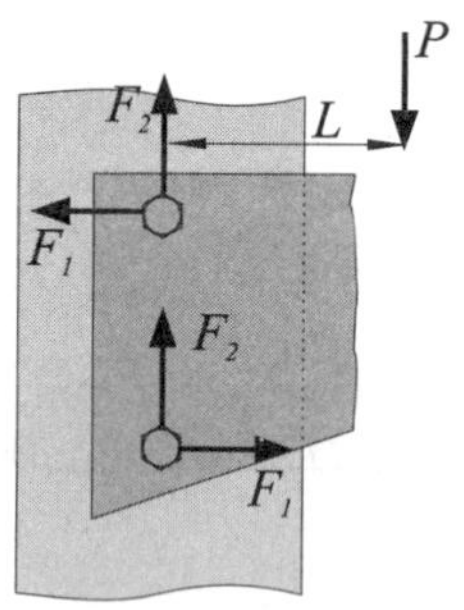

Resultant of F_1 and F_2 is,

$$R = \sqrt{F_1^2 + F_2^2} = \sqrt{4^2 + 3^2}$$

$$R = 5\text{ kN}$$

Stress in the rivet, $\sigma = \frac{R}{A} = \frac{5000}{500}$

$$\sigma = 10\,\text{N/mm}^2 \quad \text{(Statement 1 is correct)}$$

Direct load, $F_2 = \dfrac{P}{n} = \dfrac{P}{2}$

$$3 = \frac{P}{2}$$

$P = 6\,\text{kN}$ (Statement 3 is correct)

Q.35 Ans:(C)

Torsion formula, $\dfrac{T}{J} = \dfrac{\tau}{r} = \dfrac{G\theta}{l} \quad \Rightarrow \quad T = \dfrac{\tau}{r} J$

$$T_1 = \frac{\tau}{D/2}\left(\frac{\pi D^4 - \pi d^4}{32}\right) = \frac{\tau\pi}{16\text{D}}(D^4 - d^4)$$

For hollow shaft, $T_1 = \dfrac{\tau\,\pi}{16D}(D^4 - d^4)$

For solid shaft, $T_2 = \dfrac{\tau\,\pi}{16} d'^3$

From which

$$\frac{T_1}{T_2} = \frac{D^4 - d^4}{d'^3 D}$$

For same cross-section area, $\dfrac{\pi}{4}(D^2 - d^2) = \dfrac{\pi}{4} d'^2$

or $$\frac{T_1}{T_2} = \frac{(D^2 - d^2)(D^2 + d^2)}{d'^2\, d'\, D} = \frac{D^2 + d^2}{d'\, D}$$

or $$\frac{T_1}{T_2} = \frac{D^2 + d^2}{\sqrt{D^2 - d^2}\, D} = \frac{\left(\dfrac{D}{d}\right)^2 + 1}{\dfrac{D}{d}\sqrt{\left(\dfrac{D}{d}\right)^2 - 1}} > 1$$

$$\frac{T_1}{T_2} > 1$$

For same cross-section area; the hollow shaft transmits more torque than solid shaft.

Q.36 Ans:(D)

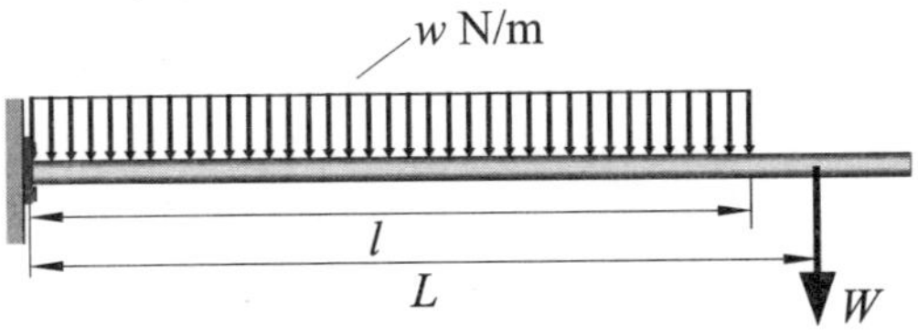

Equivalent diagram of beam is shown in figure.

Bending moment at support, $M = wl \times \dfrac{l}{2} + WL$

or $$M = \left(WL + \frac{wl^2}{2}\right)$$

Equivalent torque, $T_{eq} = \sqrt{M^2 + T^2}$

$$T_{eq} = \sqrt{\left(WL + \frac{wl^2}{2}\right)^2 + T^2}$$

Q.37 Ans:(C)

Stiffness of closed-coiled helical spring is given by

$$k = \frac{G\,d^4}{8D^3 N}$$

Stiffness of spring of 25 active coil is

$$k_1 = \frac{G\,d^4}{8D^3 \times 25} \qquad \text{(i)}$$

Stiffness of spring of 20 active coil is

$$k_2 = \frac{G\,d^4}{8D^3 \times 20} \qquad \text{(ii)}$$

Equations (i) and (ii) give

$$\frac{k_2}{k_1} = \frac{25}{20} = 1.25$$

$$k_{\text{new spring}} = 1.25 \times k_{\text{original spring}}$$

Q.38 Ans:(B)

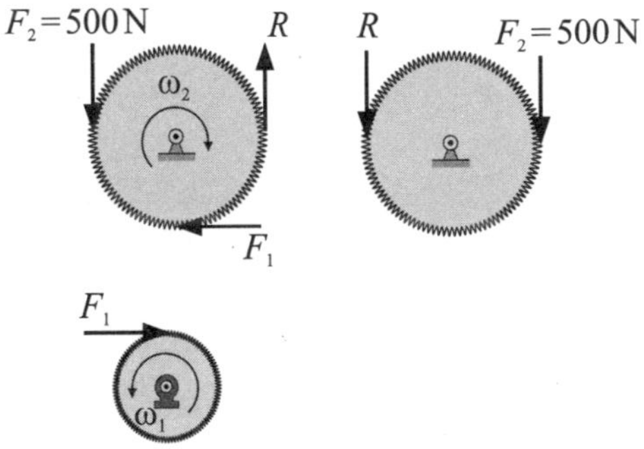

Free-body diagram of gears and pinion is shown in the figure.

Tangential force on gear, $F_2 = \dfrac{1000}{2} = 500\,\text{N}$

Diameter of pinion, $D = mT$

$$D = 2 \times 80 = 160\,\text{mm}$$

Diameter of inlet gear, $d = mT$

$$d = 2 \times 20 = 40\,\text{mm}$$

Drive efficiency, $\eta = \dfrac{\text{Output power}}{\text{Input power}} = \dfrac{\tau_2\omega_2}{\tau_1\omega_1}$

$$0.8 = \frac{\left(F_2 \times \dfrac{80}{1000} + R \times \dfrac{80}{1000}\right)}{\tau_1} \times \frac{T_1}{T_2}$$

or $$0.8=\frac{\left(F_2\times\frac{80}{1000}+R\times\frac{80}{1000}\right)}{\tau_1}\times\frac{20}{80}$$

$$\text{Input torque } \tau_1=25\text{ Nm}$$

Q.39 Ans:(C)

Let t be the thickness at throat of weld.

Torsional moment, $M_t=J\frac{\tau}{r}$

or $$M_t=\frac{\pi}{32}[d^4-(d-2t)^4]\frac{\tau}{d/2}=\frac{\pi d^2 t\,\tau}{2}$$

or $$t=\frac{2M_t}{\pi\tau d^2}$$

or $$t=\frac{2\times2500}{\pi\times140\times10^6\times\left(\frac{50}{1000}\right)^2}=4.5\times10^{-3}\text{ m}$$

Size of weld, $h=4.5\times10^{-3}\times\sqrt{2}=6.36\times10^{-3}\text{ m}$

$$\text{Size of weld, } h=6.36\text{ mm}$$

Q.40 Ans:(C)

Shear area of weld, $A=\pi d\times\frac{t}{\sqrt{2}}$

Safe torque, $T=\tau_w A\times\frac{d}{2}$

$$T=\tau_w\times\pi d\times\frac{t}{\sqrt{2}}\times\frac{d}{2}$$

$$T=\frac{\pi d^2 t}{2\sqrt{2}}\tau_w$$

Q.41 Ans:(D)

Given: $F_r=5\text{ kN}$, $L_H=10{,}000$ hours and $n=1500$ rpm

Bearing life (in million revolution) is given by

$$L=\frac{60\,n\,L_H}{10^6}=\frac{60\times1500\times10000}{10^6}$$

$$L=900\text{ million revolutions}$$

Dynamic load capacity $C=P\,L^{\frac{1}{n}}$

Substituting $n=3$ for ball bearing, $P=F_r=5000\text{ N}$ and $L=900$, we have

$$C=5000\times(900)^{\frac{1}{3}}$$

$$\text{Dynamic load capacity, } C=48263\text{ N}$$

Q.42 Ans:(B)

Kinetic energy of mass 3000 kg;

$$E_1=\frac{1}{2}mv^2=\frac{1}{2}\times3000\times2^2=6000\text{ Nm}$$

Kinetic energy of drum, $E_2=\frac{1}{2}I\omega^2$

$$E_2=\frac{1}{2}\times(100\times1^2)\times\left(\frac{2}{1}\right)^2=200\text{ Nm}$$

Potential energy,

$$E_3=mgh=3000\times9.81\times1=29430\text{ Nm}$$

The energy absorbed by the brake, $E=E_1+E_2+E_3$

$$E=6000+200+29430$$

$$E=35.63\text{ kNm}$$

Angle turned by the drum is $\theta=\frac{h}{r}=\frac{1}{1}=1$ radian

Energy, $E=T\times\theta$

Torque capacity, $T=\frac{E}{\theta}$

$$T=\frac{35.63}{1}$$

$$T=35.63\text{ kNm}$$

Q.43 Ans:(D)

Given: $\sigma_1=80\text{ MPa}$, $\sigma_2=30\text{ MPa}$ and $\sigma_3=-40\text{ MPa}$

Maximum shear stress,

$$\tau_{max}=\text{Maximum of}\begin{cases}\frac{\sigma_1-\sigma_2}{2}=\frac{80-30}{2}=25\text{ MPa}\\ \frac{\sigma_1-\sigma_2}{2}=\frac{80+40}{2}=60\text{ MPa}\\ \frac{\sigma_1-\sigma_2}{2}=\frac{30+40}{2}=35\text{ MPa}\end{cases}$$

This gives

$$\tau_{max}=60\text{ MPa}$$

Q.44 Ans:(A)

Given: $\sigma_y=200\text{ N/mm}^2$, direct load $P=25\text{ kN}$, shear load $=15\text{ kN}$ and FS $=2$.

Direct stress, $$\sigma_d=\frac{P}{\frac{\pi}{4}d^2}=\frac{25\times10^3}{\frac{\pi}{4}d^2}$$

Shear stress, $$\tau=\frac{F}{\frac{\pi}{4}d^2}=\frac{15\times10^3}{\frac{\pi}{4}d^2}$$

Maximum shear stress, $$\tau_{max}=\frac{1}{4}\sqrt{\sigma^2+4\tau^2}$$

or $$\frac{\sigma_y}{2\times \text{FS}}=\frac{1}{4}\sqrt{\sigma^2+4\tau^2}$$

$$\frac{200}{2\times 2}=\frac{1}{4}\sqrt{\left(\frac{25\times 10^3}{\frac{\pi}{4}d^2}\right)^2+4\left(\frac{15\times 10^3}{\frac{\pi}{4}d^2}\right)^2}$$

This gives

$$d=15.76\,\text{mm}$$

Q.45 Ans:(C)

Given: $\mu=0.25$, $d=350$ mm, $b=100$ mm, $P_{max}=620$ kPa and $\theta=\frac{\pi}{180}\times 270$ radians

$$P_{max}=\frac{2T_1}{bd}=\frac{2T_1}{\frac{100}{1000}\times\frac{350}{1000}}=620\,\text{kPa}$$

$$T_1=10.85\,\text{kN}$$

Tension ratio $\frac{T_1}{T_2}=e^{\mu\theta}$

or $$\frac{10.85}{T_2}=e^{0.25\left(\frac{\pi}{180}\times 270\right)}$$

$$T_2=3.34\,\text{kN}$$

Breaking torque, $M_t=(T_1-T_2)\frac{d}{2}$

$$M_t=(10.85-3.34)\frac{350}{2\times 1000}\,\text{kNm}$$

$$M_t=1.314\,\text{kNm}$$

Q.46 Ans:(B)

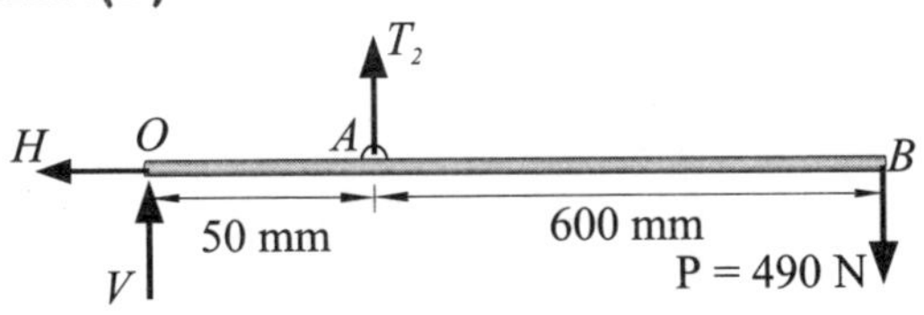

Free body diagram of lever is shown in the figure.

Let T_1 and T_2 be the tensions of belt.

Taking moment about O, $T_2\times 50-490(50+600)=0$

$$T_2=6370\,\text{N}$$

Tension ratio $\frac{T_1}{T_2}=e^{\mu\theta}$ or $\frac{T_1}{6370}=e^{0.25\left(\frac{\pi}{180}\times 270\right)}$

$$T_1=16347.5\,\text{N}$$

Torque, $M_t=(T_1-T_2)r=(16347.5-6370)\frac{250}{1000}$ Nm

$$M_t=2494.3\,\text{Nm}$$

If d is the diameter of the shaft, then

Torque transmitted, $M_t=\tau\times\frac{\pi d^3}{16}$

$$24943=55\times 10^6\times\frac{\pi d^3}{16}$$

This gives $d=0.061$ m

$$d=61.3\,\text{mm}$$

Q.47 Ans:(C)

Given: $P=16000$ N, $\sigma_u=440$ MPa, $q=0.8$, $k_a=0.67$, $k_b=0.85$, $k_c=0.897$, $k_t=2.35$, and FS $=1.5$.

$$k_f=1+q(k_t-1)=1+0.8(2.35-1)=2.08$$

Permissible stress, $\sigma=\frac{0.5\sigma_u k_a k_b k_c}{k_f\times \text{FS}}$

or $$\sigma=\frac{0.5\times 440\times 0.67\times 0.85\times 0.897}{2.08\times 1.5}$$

or $$\sigma=36.02\,\text{MPa}$$

$$\sigma=\frac{P}{A}\Rightarrow\sigma=\frac{16000}{\frac{(50-10)t}{1000\times 1000}}=36.02\times 10^6$$

$$t=11.1\,\text{mm}$$

Q.48 Ans:(A)

Mean torque, $T_m=\frac{T_{max}+T_{min}}{2}=\frac{500+100}{2}=300$ Nm

Variable torque, $T_v=\frac{T_{max}-T_{min}}{2}=\frac{500-100}{2}=200$ Nm

Mean shear stress, $\sigma_{ms}=\tau_m=\frac{16}{\pi d^3}T_m=\frac{16}{\pi d^3}\times 300$

Variable shear stress, $\sigma_{vs}=\tau_v=\frac{16}{\pi d^3}T_v=\frac{16}{\pi d^3}\times 200$

$$\sigma_{ys}=0.5\sigma_y=0.5\times 300=150$$

$$\sigma_e=\sigma_e'\times 0.6\times 0.85\times 0.82$$

$$=0.4182\sigma_e'=0.4182\times 300$$

$$\sigma_e=125.46$$

Applying the Soderberg equation, $\frac{1}{\text{FS}}=\frac{\sigma_{ms}}{\sigma_{ms}}+\frac{\sigma_{vs}}{\sigma_e'}$

or $$\frac{1}{2}=\frac{\frac{16}{\pi d^3}\times 300}{150}+\frac{\frac{16}{\pi d^3}\times 200}{125.46}$$

or $\quad d = 33.18 \times 10^{-3}\,\text{m}$

$$d = 33.18\ \text{mm}$$

Q.49 Ans:(D)

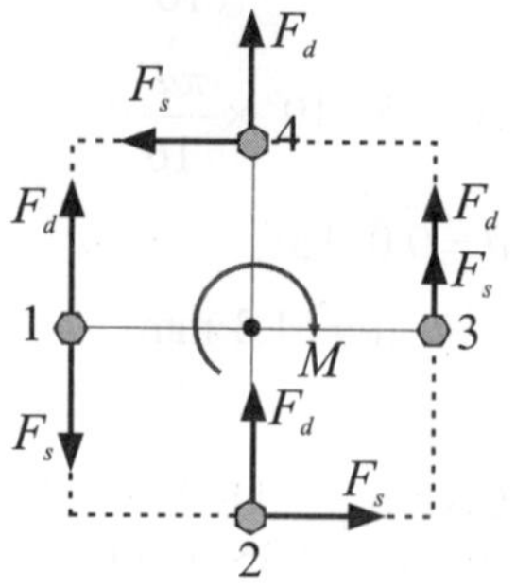

Let F_d and F_s be the primary and secondary shear forces on the bolts as shown in the figure.

Primary shear force, $P_d = \dfrac{40}{4} = 10\,\text{kN}$

Equating the turning moment due to eccentricity of the load to resisting moment of bolts.

$$40 \times 1000 \times \frac{(225+75)}{1000} = 4P_s \times \frac{150}{2}$$

Since the secondary forces are proportional to their radial distance from the center, therefore

$$P_s = \lambda \frac{150}{2}, \text{ we have}$$

$$40 \times 1000 \times \frac{(225+75)}{1000} = 4\lambda \times \left(\frac{150}{2}\right)^2$$

$$\lambda = 533.33\ \text{N/mm}$$

Therefore, $P_s = 533.33 \times \dfrac{150}{2} = 40000\,\text{N}$

Resultant of primary shear force P_d and secondary shear force P_s in bolt 3 is maximum.

Resultant shear stress in bolt 3, $\quad \tau = \dfrac{P_d}{A} + \dfrac{P_s}{A}$

or $\quad 37.5 \times 10^6 = \dfrac{10 \times 10^3}{\frac{\pi}{4} d^2} + \dfrac{4000}{\frac{\pi}{4} d^2}$

or $\quad d = \sqrt{\dfrac{4}{\pi} \times \dfrac{14000}{37.5 \times 10^6}}$

$$d = 41.2\ \text{mm}$$

Q.50 Ans:(A)

Let t be the thickness of throat,

Primary shear stress, $\tau_1 = \dfrac{P}{A} = \dfrac{50 \times 10^3}{2 \times 400t} = \dfrac{625}{t}\ \text{N/mm}^2$

Bending stress, $\sigma_b = \dfrac{M}{I} y = \dfrac{50 \times 10^3 \times 300}{2 \times \dfrac{t \times 400^3}{12}} \times \dfrac{400}{2}$

$$\sigma_b = \frac{281.16}{t}\ \text{N/mm}^2$$

Maximum principal shear stress

$$\tau = \sqrt{\left(\frac{\sigma_b}{2}\right)^2 + \tau_1^2} = \sqrt{\left(\frac{281.16}{2t}\right)^2 + \left(\frac{62.5}{t}\right)^2}$$

$$\tau = \frac{153.85}{t}$$

The permissible shear stress in the weld is 70 N/mm^2. Therefore

$$\tau = \frac{153.85}{t} = 70 \quad \text{or} \quad t = 2.2\,\text{mm}$$

Size of weld, $\quad h = \sqrt{2}\,t = \sqrt{2} \times 2.2$

Size of weld, $h = 3.1\,\text{mm}$

Q.51 Ans:[196.41]

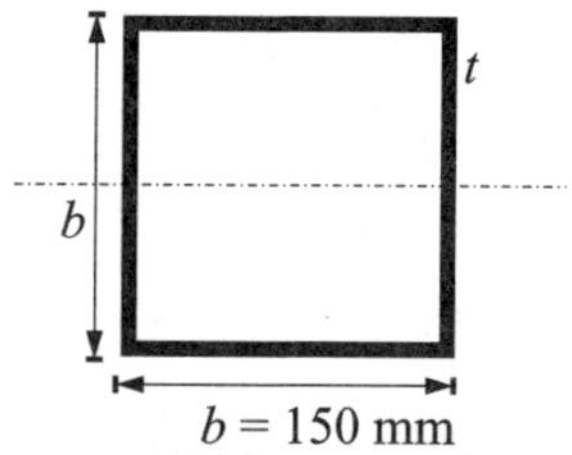

Let t be the throat thickness of weld.

Section modulus,

$$Z = \frac{I}{(b/2)} = 2\left[\frac{tb^3}{12} + \frac{bt^3}{12} + bt\left(\frac{b}{2}\right)^2\right] \times \frac{2}{b}$$

or $\quad Z = \dfrac{t}{3}(4b^2 + t^2) \approx \dfrac{4}{3} b^2 t$

Bending stress, $\sigma_b = \dfrac{M}{Z} = \dfrac{Pe}{\frac{4}{3} b^2 t} = \dfrac{3Pe}{4b^2 t}$

$$\sigma_b = \frac{3 \times 25 \times 10^3 \times 500}{4 \times 150^2 \times \frac{3}{\sqrt{2}}}\ \text{N/mm}^2$$

$$\sigma_b = 196.41\,\text{MPa}$$

Q.52 Ans:[83.43]

Equivalent coefficient of friction

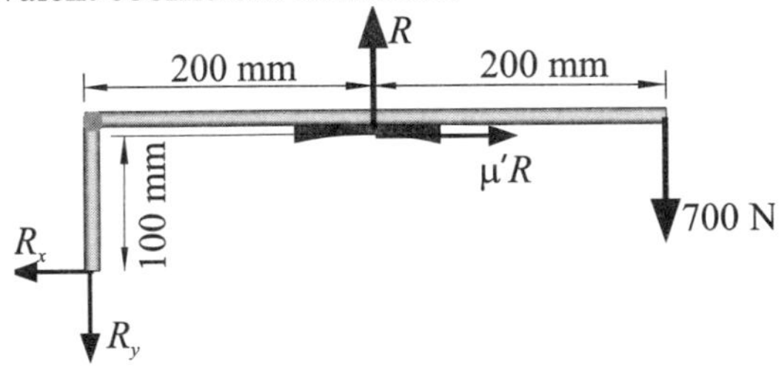

$$\mu' = \mu\left(\frac{4\sin\theta}{2\theta + \sin 2\theta}\right)$$

or $$\mu' = 0.35 \times \frac{4\sin 45}{\frac{\pi}{180} \times 90 + \sin 90}$$

$$\mu' = 0.385$$

Free-body diagram of lever is shown in figure.

Taking moment about hinged point.

$$700 \times (200 + 200) + \mu' R \times 100 - R \times 200 = 0$$

or $$R = \frac{700 \times 400}{200 - 0.385 \times 100} = 1733.7\text{ N}$$

Breaking torque, $T = \mu' R \times r = 0.385 \times 1733.7 \times \frac{125}{1000}$

$$T = 83.43\text{ Nm}$$

Q.53 Ans:[8.92]

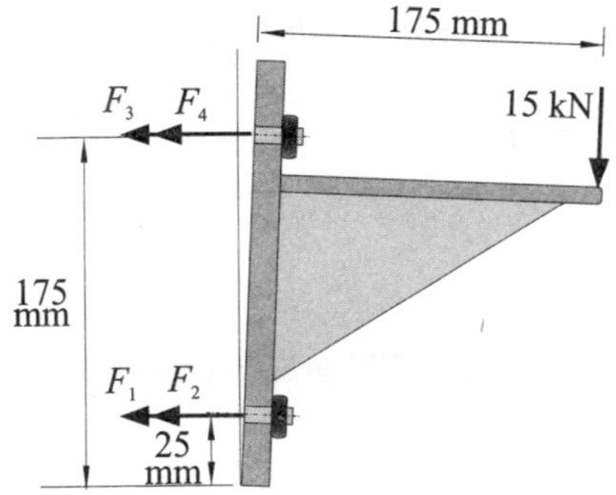

Direct shear load on each bolt, $F_s = \frac{15}{4} = 3.75\text{ kN}$

Turning moment produced by the load 15 kN due to eccentricity 175 mm $= 15 \times 175$

This turning moment is resisted by four bolts as shown in figure.

$$F_1 \times 25 + F_2 \times 25 + F_3 \times 175 + F_4 \times 175 = 15 \times 175$$

Since $F_1 = F_2$ and $F_3 = F_4$,

$$F_1 \times 25 + F_3 \times 175 = \frac{15 \times 175}{2}$$

Substituting $F_1 = \lambda \times 25$, $F_2 = \lambda \times 25$, $F_3 = \lambda \times 175$ and $F_4 = \lambda \times 175$

$$\lambda \times 25^2 + \lambda \times 175^2 = \frac{15 \times 175}{2}$$

$$\lambda = 0.042$$

Thus, $F_3 = \lambda \times 175 = 0.042 \times 175 = 7.35\text{ kN}$ (Tensile)

Equivalent tensile force in bolt (3),

$$F_{eq} = \frac{1}{2}[F_3 + \sqrt{F_3^2 + 4F_s^2}]$$

or $$F_{eq} = \frac{1}{2}[7.35 + \sqrt{7.35^2 + 4 \times 3.75^2}]$$

$$F_{eq} = 8.92\text{ kN}$$

Q.54 Ans:[-0.8]

Direct stress, $\sigma_d = \frac{P}{A} = \frac{1600}{40 \times 40}$

$$\sigma_d = 1\text{ N/mm}^2 \quad \text{(compressive)}$$

Bending stress, $\sigma_b = \frac{M}{I} y = \frac{1600\,e}{\frac{40 \times 40^3}{12}} \times \left(\frac{40}{2}\right)$

$$\sigma_b = \frac{6 \times 1600e}{40^3}$$

Stress along CD, $\sigma_{CD} = -\frac{6 \times 1600e}{40^3} - 1 = -1.2$

$$\Rightarrow \quad \frac{6 \times 1600e}{40^3} = 0.2$$

Stress along AB, $\sigma_{AB} = \frac{6 \times 1600e}{40^3} - 1$

or $$\sigma_{AB} = 0.2 - 1 = -0.8$$

Stress along AB, $\sigma_{AB} = -0.8\text{ N/mm}^2$

Q.55 Ans:[1.8]

Equivalent bending moment, $M_{eq} = \frac{1}{2}[M + \sqrt{M^2 + T^2}]$

$$M_{eq} = \frac{1}{2}[400 + \sqrt{400^2 + 300^2}]$$

$$M_{eq} = 450\text{ kNm}$$

Equivalent torque, $T_{eq} = \sqrt{M^2 + T^2}$

$$T_{eq} = \sqrt{400^2 + 300^2}$$

$$T_{eq} = 500\text{ kNm}$$

Maximum bending stress, $\sigma = \frac{M}{I} y = \frac{450}{\frac{\pi d^4}{64}} \times \frac{d}{2}$

$$\sigma = \frac{M}{I} y = \frac{32 \times 450}{\pi d^3} \quad \text{(i)}$$

Shear stress, $\tau = \frac{T}{J} r = \frac{500}{\frac{\pi d^4}{32}} \times \frac{d}{2}$

Maximum shear stress, $\tau = \frac{16 \times 500}{\pi d^3}$ (ii)

From Equations (i) and (ii), we get

$$\frac{\sigma}{\tau} = \frac{32 \times 450}{\pi d^3} \times \frac{\pi d^3}{16 \times 500}$$

$$\frac{\sigma}{\tau} = \frac{9}{5} = 1.8$$

Q.56 Ans:[45]

Width of bar at minimum cross-section,

$$b = 50 - 20 = 30 \text{ mm}$$

Allowable tensile load for safe tensile stress

$$F_1 = \sigma_t A = 150 \times 10^6 \times \left(\frac{30}{1000} \times \frac{10}{1000} \right)$$

$$F_1 = 45 \text{ kN}$$

Shear area of pin, $A = 2 \times \frac{\pi}{4} d^2$

Allowable load for safe shear stress in the pin

$$F_2 = \tau A = 80 \times 10^6 \times 2 \left(\frac{\pi}{4} \times 20^2 \right)$$

$$F_2 = 50.26 \text{ kN}$$

Therefore,

Safe load is $F_1 = 45$ kN

Q.57 Ans:[1.29]

Given: $\sigma_{max} = 250$ MPa, $\sigma_{min} = 150$ MPa, $\sigma_{ut} = 450$ MPa, $\sigma_{yt} = 350$ MPa and $\sigma_e = 250$ MPa

Mean stress, $\sigma_m = \frac{250 + 150}{2} = 200$ MPa

Variable stress, $\sigma_v = \frac{250 - 150}{2} = 50$ MPa

Using Soderberg criteria for ductile materials,

$$\frac{1}{\text{FS}} = \frac{\sigma_m}{\sigma_{yt}} + \frac{\sigma_v}{\sigma_e} = \frac{200}{350} + \frac{50}{250}$$

$$\text{FS} = 1.29$$

Q.58 Ans:[3204]

Given: $T = 1500$ Nm, $M = 750$ Nm, $k_m = 1.5$ and $k_t = 2$

Equivalent twisting moment

$$T_{eq} = \sqrt{(k_m M)^2 + (k_t T)^2}$$

$$T_{eq} = \sqrt{(1.5 \times 750)^2 + (2 \times 1500)^2}$$

$$T_{eq} = 3204 \text{ Nm}$$

Q.59 Ans:[70.4]

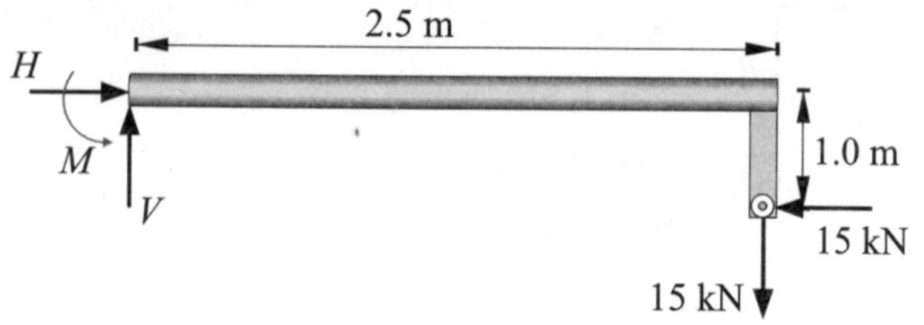

Free-body diagram of beam is shown in figure.

Maximum bending is at the fixed end

$$M = 15 \times 2.5 + 15 \times 1 = 52.5 \text{ kNm}$$

The allowable bending stress in the material is

$$\sigma_b = \frac{250}{2.5} = 100 \text{ N/mm}^2$$

$$\sigma_b = \frac{M}{Z} = \frac{M}{\frac{bd^2}{6}} = \frac{6M}{bd^2}$$

Substituting $d = 3b$,

$$\sigma_b = \frac{6M}{b(3b)^2} = \frac{2M}{3b^3}$$

or $b = \left(\frac{2M}{3\sigma_b} \right)^{\frac{1}{3}} = \left(\frac{2 \times 52.5 \times 10^3}{3 \times 100 \times (10^3)^2} \right)^{\frac{1}{3}}$

$$b = 0.070 \text{ m}$$

Width, $b = 70.4$ mm

Q.60 Ans:[1]

Given: $T = 26$ teeth, $m = 5$ mm, $\phi = 20^0$, $P = 5.1$ kW and $N = 750$ rpm.

Velocity of pinion at pitch circle, $V = \frac{\pi d N}{60}$

Substituting diameter, $d = mT$

$$V = \frac{\pi m T N}{60} = \frac{\pi \times \frac{5}{1000} \times 26 \times 750}{60}$$

$$V = 5.1 \text{ m/s}$$

Power transmitted, $P = F_t \times V$

Tangential force, $F_t = \frac{P}{V} = \frac{5.1}{5.1}$

$$F_t = 1\text{ kN}$$

Q.61 Ans:[149.2]

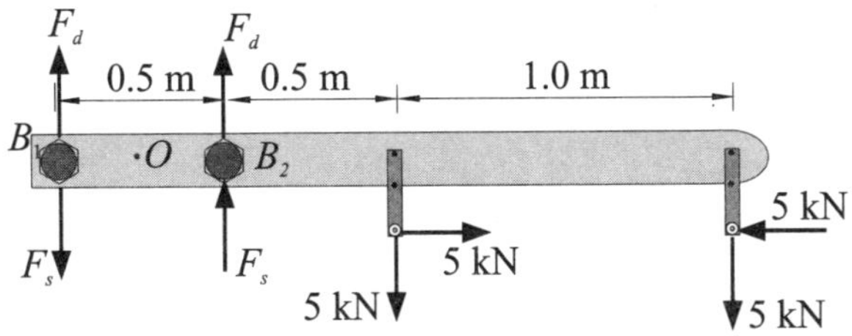

Free-body diagram of beam is shown in figure.

Direct shear force in each bolt, $F_d = \frac{5+5}{2} = 5\text{ kN}$

Let F_s be the secondary force in each bolt.

$$F_s \times \frac{05}{2} + F_s \times \frac{0.5}{2} = 5 \times (0.5 + 0.25) + 5(1 + 0.5 + 0.25)$$

$$F_s = 25\text{ kN}$$

Resultant force in bolt B_2 is maximum. That is,

$$R = F_d + F_s = 5 + 25 = 30\text{ kN}$$

Maximum shear stress,

$$\tau = \frac{R}{A} = \frac{30 \times 10^3}{\frac{\pi}{4} \times \left(\frac{16}{1000}\right)^2}\text{ N/m}^2$$

[where diameter of bolt M16 is 16 mm]

$$\tau = 149.2\text{ MPa}$$

Q.62 Ans:[20]

Free-body diagram of welded plate is shown in the figure.

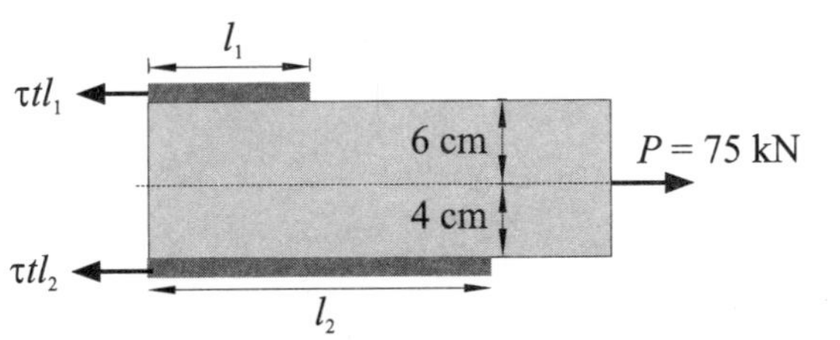

Total length of weld,

$$l = l_1 + l_2 = 50\text{ cm} \quad \text{(i)}$$

Moment of the top weld about the axis

$$= \tau\, t\, l_1 \times 6 \quad \text{(ii)}$$

Moment of the bottom weld about the axis

$$= \tau\, t\, l_2 \times 4 \quad \text{(iii)}$$

Equating Equations (ii) and (iii), we get

$$3l_1 = 2l_2 \quad \text{(iv)}$$

From Equations (i) and (iv), we obtain

$$l_1 = 20\text{ cm}$$

Q.63 Ans:[30]

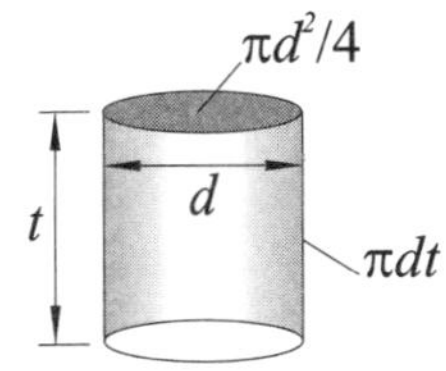

Given: $t = 15\text{ mm}$, $\sigma_{ys} = 3\text{ N/mm}^2$ and $\sigma_{cr} = 6\text{ N/mm}^2$

Let d be the diameter of hole.

Safe load, $P = \pi d\, t\, \sigma_{ys} = \frac{\pi}{4} d^2 \sigma_{cr}$

$$d = \frac{4t\sigma_{ys}}{\sigma_{cr}} = \frac{4 \times 15 \times 3}{6}$$

$$d = 30\text{ mm}$$

Q.64 Ans:[960]

The relationship between life in million revolution and life in working hours is given by

$$L = \frac{60\, N\, L_H}{10^6}$$

where L_H = bearing life(hours) and N = speed of rotation.

The revolution in million for 90% reliability is

$$L_{99} = \frac{60 \times 1600 \times 10000}{10^6}$$

$$L_{99} = 960$$

Q.65 Ans:[8.84]

Let t be the thickness of throat of weld.

Total area of the weld;

$$A = \pi dt = \pi \times 60 \times t$$

$$A = 188.49 \times t\ \text{mm}^2$$

Primary shear stress, $\tau_1 = \frac{P}{A} = \frac{15 \times 10^3}{188.49 \times t} = \frac{53.05}{t}\text{ N/mm}^2$

Bending stress at the top weld, $\sigma_b = \frac{M}{Z} = \frac{M}{\pi t r^2}$

$$\sigma_b = \frac{15 \times 10^3 \times 0.5}{\pi t \left(\frac{30}{1000}\right)^2} = \frac{2652.58}{t} \text{ N/mm}^2$$

Maximum shear stress in the weld is

$$\tau_{max} = \sqrt{\left(\frac{\sigma_b}{2}\right)^2 + \tau_1^2}$$

Permissible shear stress,

$$150 = \sqrt{\left(\frac{2652.58}{2t}\right)^2 + \left(\frac{53.05}{t}\right)^2}$$

This gives

$$t = 8.84 \text{ mm}$$

10 Fluid Mechanics and Turbo-machinery

GATE Mechanical Engg.

GATE Syllabus

Fluid properties; Fluid statics, Manometry, Buoyancy, Forces on submerged bodies, Stability of floating bodies; Control-volume analysis of mass, Momentum and energy; Fluid acceleration; Differential equations of continuity and momentum; Bernoulli's equation; Dimensional analysis; Viscous flow of incompressible fluids; Boundary layer, Elementary turbulent flow, Flow through pipes, Head losses in pipes, Bends and fittings.

Turbo-machinery: Impulse and reaction principles, Velocity diagrams, Pelton-wheel, Francis and Kaplan turbines.

Chapter Outline

10.1 KEY CONCEPTS AND FORMULAS

Properties of Fluids

Fluid

A fluid is a substance that deforms continuously when subjected to a shear stress, no matter how small that shear stress may be.

Density and Specific Gravity

Density 'ρ' is defined as mass per unit volume,

$$\rho = \frac{m}{V} \quad (\text{kg/m}^3).$$

Specific gravity or relative density 'S' is defined as the ratio of the density of a substance to the density of some standard substance at a specified temperature (usually water at 4°C, $\rho_{\text{water}} = 1000\,\text{kg/m}^3$)

Specific gravity: $S = \dfrac{\rho}{\rho_{\text{water}}}$

Specific weight 'w' is the weight of a unit volume of a substance.

Specific weight, $w = \dfrac{mg}{V} = \rho g$

Viscosity

Viscosity of a fluid is a measure of its resistance to flow.

Newton's law of viscosity:

Shear stress, $\tau = \mu \dfrac{du}{dy}$

Kinematic viscosity, $\nu = \dfrac{\mu}{\rho}$ (m^2/s) (1 stoke = 1 cm^2/s).

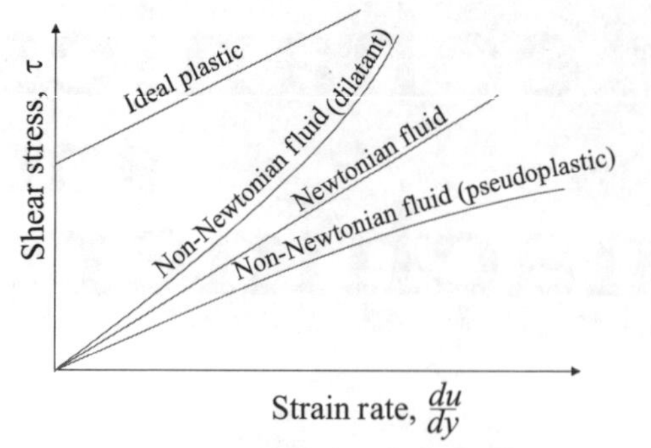

Surface Tension and Capillary Effect

The pulling effect on the liquid molecules at an interface caused by the attractive forces of molecules per unit length is called *surface tension*, σ_s.

Pressure difference inside and outside:

$\Delta P = \frac{4\sigma_s}{d}$ (in droplet), $\Delta P = \frac{8\sigma_s}{d}$ (in bubble), $\Delta P = \frac{2\sigma_s}{d}$ (in liquid jet)

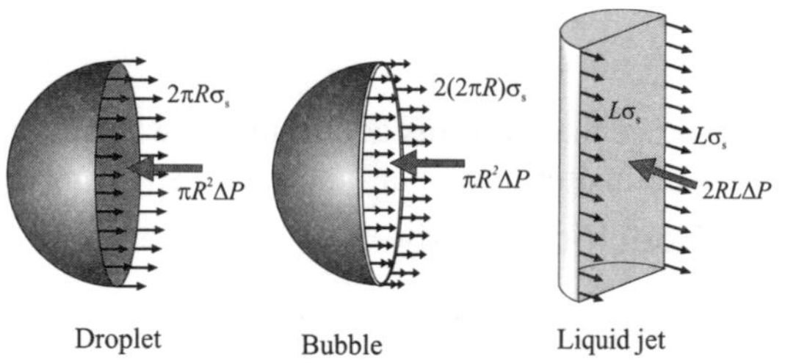

Free body diagrams

The rise or fall of a liquid in a small-diameter tube inserted into the liquid due to surface tension is called the *capillary effect*. The capillary rise or drop is given by:

$$h = \frac{4\sigma_s \cos\theta}{\rho \times g \times d}$$

Fluid Statics

Pressure

Pressure is defined as a normal force exerted by a fluid per unit area. The unit of pressure is pascal (Pa). That is,

$1\,\text{Pa} = 1\ \text{N/m}^2$, $1\,\text{bar} = 10^5\,\text{Pa}$ and $1\,\text{atm} = 1.01325$ bars.

$$P_{\text{gauge}} = P_{\text{abs}} - P_{\text{atm}} \text{ and } P_{\text{vacuum}} = P_{\text{atm}} - P_{\text{abs}}$$

Pascal Law

The pressure at a point in a fluid has the same magnitude in all directions, $P = P_x = P_y = P_z$.

Variation of pressure with depth

Hydrostatic law, $\frac{dp}{dz} = \rho g$

Manometers: Manometers are instruments that use columns of liquids to measure pressures.

Hydrostatic Forces on Submerged Plane Surfaces

Hydrostatic force on submerged plane surface, $F = wA\bar{h}$

where $\bar{h}$ is the vertical distance of centroid of plane surface from free surface of liquid. Hydrostatic force always acts normal to the plane surface.

Center of pressure (h^*): It is defined as the point of application of the hydrostatic forces.

Vertical plane surface: $h^* = \bar{h} + \frac{I_G}{A\bar{h}}$

Horizontal plane surface: $h^* = \bar{h}$

Inclined plane surface: $h^* = \bar{h} + \frac{I_G \sin^2\theta}{A\bar{h}}$

Hydrostatic Forces on Submerged Curved Surfaces

1. The horizontal component F_H of the hydrostatic force acting on a curved surface is equal (in both magnitude and the line of action) to the hydrostatic force acting on the vertical projection of the curved surface.

2. The vertical component F_V of the hydrostatic force acting on a curved surface is equal to the hydrostatic force acting on the horizontal projection of the curve surface.

Resultant hydrostatic force is $F = \sqrt{F_H^2 + F_V^2}$

Buoyancy

Buoyant Force

The upward force exerted by a fluid on a body when the body is immersed in the fluid is known as *buoyant force*, $F_B \uparrow$.

$$F_B \uparrow = \rho_f g \forall$$

Archimedes principle: Buoyant force F_B acting on a body immersed in a fluid is equal to the weight of the fluid displaced by the body; it acts upward ↑ through the centroid of the displaced volume.

Centre of buoyancy (B): It is the point through which buoyant force is supposed to act.

Meta-centre (M): This is the point about which a body start oscillating when it is tilted.

Meta-centric height (GM): It is the distance between the meta-center and centre of gravity.

$$GM = \frac{I}{\forall} - BG$$

Stability of immersed body

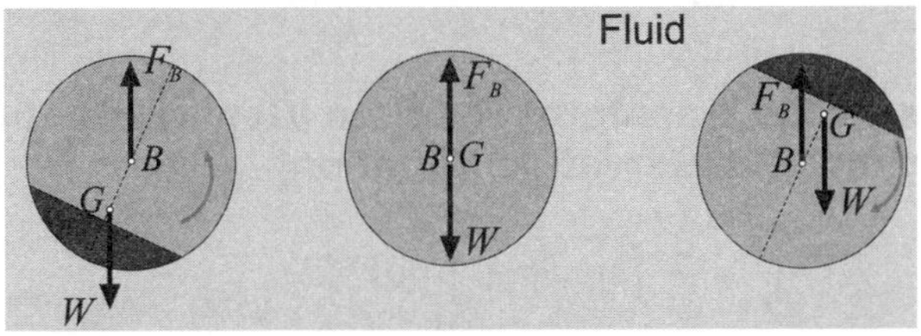

Stable Neutrally stable Unstable

Stability of Floating Body

Measure of stability for floating body is the meta-centric height GM.

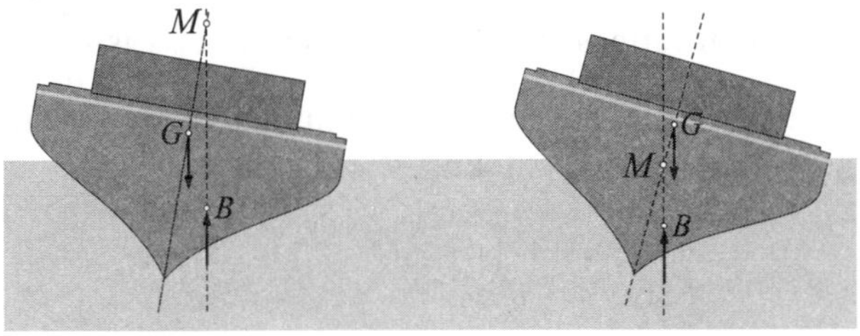

Stable Unstable

A floating is stable if point M is above point G, and thus GM is positive, and unstable if point M is below point G, and thus GM is negative.

Linearly Accelerating Container with Fluid

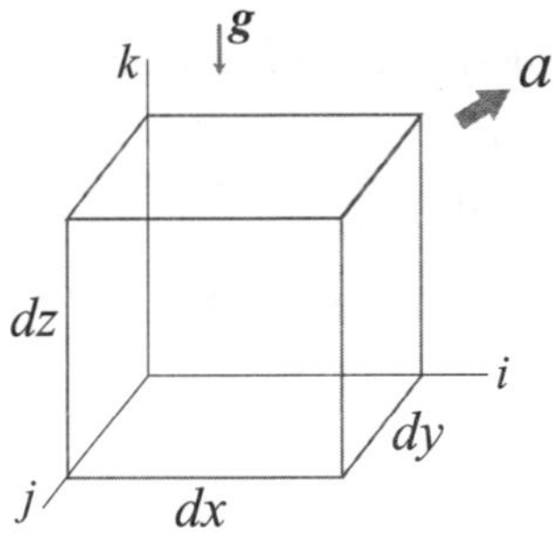

Equation of motion, $\delta F = \delta m \cdot a$

$$\nabla P + \rho g\, k = -\rho\, a$$

Accelerating fluids:

$$\frac{\partial P}{\partial x} = -\rho a_x,\ \frac{\partial P}{\partial y} = -\rho a_y \text{ and } \frac{\partial P}{\partial z} = -\rho(g + a_z)$$

(i) Fluid at rest:

$$\frac{\partial P}{\partial x} = 0,\ \frac{\partial P}{\partial y} = 0 \quad \text{and} \quad \frac{\partial P}{\partial z} = -\rho g$$

(ii) Free fall of a fluid body:

$$\frac{\partial P}{\partial x} = 0,\ \frac{\partial P}{\partial y} = 0 \quad \text{and} \quad \frac{\partial P}{\partial z} = 0$$

(iii) Acceleration on a straight path (x-axis):

$$\frac{\partial P}{\partial x} = -\rho a_x,\ \frac{\partial P}{\partial y} = 0 \text{ and } \frac{\partial P}{\partial z} = -\rho g$$

$$dP = \frac{\partial P}{\partial x} dx + \frac{\partial P}{\partial z} dz \Rightarrow dP = -\rho a_x dx - \rho g dz$$

$$P_2 - P_1 = -\rho a_x (x_2 - x_1) - \rho g (z_2 - z_1)$$

Rotating Containers

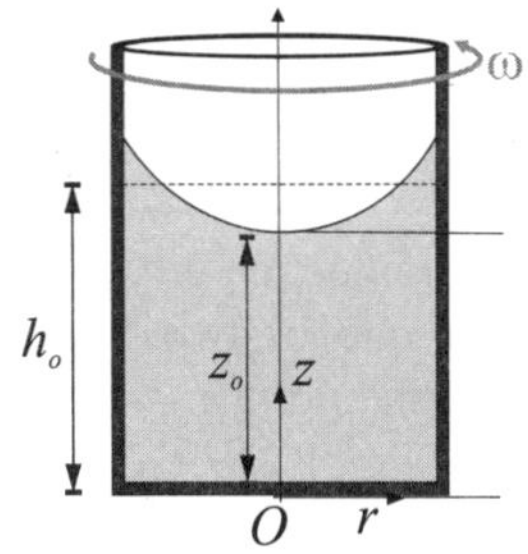

Pressure, $P = f(r, z) \quad \Rightarrow dP = \frac{\partial P}{\partial r} dr + \frac{\partial P}{\partial z} dz$

Where $\frac{\partial P}{\partial r} = \rho r \omega^2$ and $\frac{\partial P}{\partial z} = -\rho g$

$dP = \rho r \omega^2 dr - \rho g dz$

At free surface $dP = 0$; $\frac{dz}{dr} = \frac{r\omega^2}{g}$ and $z = z_o + \frac{1}{2}\frac{\omega^2 r^2}{g}$

Fluid Kinematics

Types of fluid flow: (i) Steady and unsteady flows, (ii) Uniform and non-uniform flows, (iii) Laminar and turbulent flows, (iv) Compressible and incompressible flows, (v) Rotational and irrotational flows, and (vi) One, two and three-dimensional flows.

Velocity of fluid particle $V = ui + vj + wk$, where $u = f_1(x, y, z, t)$, $v = f_2(x, y, z, t)$, $w = f_3(x, y, z, t)$

Acceleration of Fluid Particle

$$a = \frac{dV}{dt} = \frac{\partial V}{\partial t}\frac{dt}{dt} + \frac{\partial V}{\partial x}\frac{dx}{dt} + \frac{\partial V}{\partial y}\frac{dy}{dt} + \frac{\partial V}{\partial z}\frac{dz}{dt}$$

$$a = \frac{\partial V}{\partial t} + u\frac{\partial V}{\partial x} + v\frac{\partial V}{\partial y} + w\frac{\partial V}{\partial z}$$

$$a = \frac{\partial V}{\partial t} + (V \cdot \nabla)V$$

$\frac{D}{Dt} = \frac{\partial}{\partial t} + u\frac{\partial}{\partial x} + v\frac{\partial}{\partial y} + w\frac{\partial}{\partial z} \leftarrow$ This derivative is called material derivative.

$$a_x = \frac{\partial u}{\partial t} + u\frac{\partial u}{\partial x} + v\frac{\partial u}{\partial y} + w\frac{\partial u}{\partial z},\ a_y = \frac{\partial v}{\partial t} + u\frac{\partial v}{\partial x} + v\frac{\partial v}{\partial y} + w\frac{\partial v}{\partial z}$$

$$a_z = \frac{\partial w}{\partial t} + u\frac{\partial w}{\partial x} + v\frac{\partial w}{\partial y} + w\frac{\partial w}{\partial z}$$

Streamlines, Pathlines and Steaklines

Streamline: It is a curve that is everywhere tangent to the instantaneous local velocity vector.

Equation for a streamline: $\frac{dr}{V}=\frac{dx}{u}=\frac{dy}{v}=\frac{dz}{w}$

Pathline: It is the actual path travelled by a individual fluid particle over some time period.

Streakline: It is the locus of fluid particles that have passed sequentially through a prescribed point in the flow.

Angular velocity: Angular velocity at a point is defined as the average rotation rate of two initially perpendicular lines that intersect at that point.

Angular velocity, $\omega_x=\frac{1}{2}\left(\frac{\partial w}{\partial y}-\frac{\partial v}{\partial z}\right)$, $\omega_y=\frac{1}{2}\left(\frac{\partial u}{\partial z}-\frac{\partial w}{\partial x}\right)$

and $\omega_z=\frac{1}{2}\left(\frac{\partial v}{\partial x}-\frac{\partial u}{\partial y}\right)$

Vorticity: It is a measure of rotation of a fluid particle. It is a property of fluid flows that indicates the rotationality of fluid particles.

Vorticity, $\zeta=2\omega=\nabla\times V$

$u=-\frac{\partial\phi}{\partial x}$, $v=-\frac{\partial\phi}{\partial y}$ and $w=-\frac{\partial\phi}{\partial z}$, $u_r=\frac{\partial\phi}{\partial r}$, $u_\theta=\frac{\partial\phi}{r\partial\theta}$,

where ϕ is velocity potential function.

$$\frac{\partial\psi}{\partial x}=v,\ \frac{\partial\psi}{\partial y}=-u,\ \frac{1}{r}\frac{\partial\psi}{\partial\theta}=u_r,\ -\frac{\partial\psi}{\partial r}=u_\theta$$

where ψ is stream function.

Three Basic Laws

1. **Conservation of mass**: The mass of a system remains constant, $\frac{d}{dt}\int_{Sys}\rho d\forall=0$

2. **First law of thermodynamics**: The rate of heat transfer to a system minus the rate at which the system does work equals the rate at which the energy of the system of the system is changing.

3. **Newton's second law**: The resultant force acting on a system equals the rate at which the momentum of the system is changing.

$$\sum F=\frac{d}{dt}\int_{Sys}V\rho d\forall$$

Moment of Momentum Equation

The resultant moment acting on a system equals the rate of change of the angular momentum of the system.

$$\sum M=\frac{d}{dt}\int_{Sys}r\times V\rho d\forall$$

Reynolds Transform Theorem (General Control Volume Conservation Equation)

$$\frac{dN}{dt}=\frac{\partial}{\partial t}\int_{C.V}\eta\rho d\forall+\int_{C.S}\eta\rho V\cdot dA$$

Where N is the total amount of some property (e.g., mass, energy, or momentum) and η is the amount of this property, per unit mass.

Conservation of Mass

The system form of the conservation of mass is $\frac{dm}{dt}=0$, which states that the mass m within the system remains constant in time. Substituting $N=m$, then $\eta=1$.

$$0=\frac{\partial}{\partial t}\int_{C.V}\rho d\forall+\int_{C.S}\rho V\cdot dA$$

If the flow is steady $\int_{C.S}\rho V\cdot dA=0$, and for a uniform flow with one entrance and one exit $\rho_2A_2V_2=\rho_1A_1V_1$.

Continuity Equation in 3-Dimensions

$$\frac{\partial}{\partial x}(\rho u)+\frac{\partial}{\partial y}(\rho v)+\frac{\partial}{\partial z}(\rho w)+\frac{\partial\rho}{\partial t}=0,\ \text{(for steady flow }\frac{\partial\rho}{\partial t}=0)$$

Continuity equation in cylindrical polar coordinates:

$$\rho\left[\frac{u_r}{r}+\frac{\partial u_r}{\partial r}\right]+\rho\frac{\partial u_\theta}{r\partial\theta}+\frac{\partial\rho}{\partial t}=0,\ \text{(for steady flow }\frac{\partial\rho}{\partial t}=0)$$

Linear Momentum Equation

Substituting $N=mV$ and $\eta=V$ in (Reynolds transform theorem), we obtain

$$\sum F=\frac{d\,mV}{dt}=\frac{\partial}{\partial t}\int_{C.V}V\rho d\forall+\int_{C.S}\rho V(V_r\cdot dA)$$

Energy Equations

Mechanical energy: The energy that can be converted to mechanical work completely and directly by an ideal mechanical device such as an ideal turbine.

Mechanical energy per unit mass of a flowing fluid is

$$e_{mech}=\frac{P}{\rho}+\frac{V^2}{2}+gz$$

where $\frac{P}{\rho}$ is the flow energy, $\frac{V^2}{2}$ is the kinetic energy and gz is the potential energy of the fluid, all per unit mass.

$$\Delta e_{mech} = \frac{P_2 - P_1}{\rho} + \frac{V_2^2 - V_1^2}{2} + g(z_2 - z_1)$$

Work supplied to fluid if $\Delta e_{mech} > 0$, and work extracted from fluid if $\Delta e_{mech} < 0$.

Bernoulli's Equation

The sum of the kinetic, potential, and flow energies of a fluid particle is constant along a streamline during steady flow when the compressibility and frictional effect are negligible.

$$\frac{P}{\rho g} + \frac{V^2}{2g} + z = \text{constant}$$

or $$\frac{P}{\rho g} + \frac{V^2}{2g} + z = H = \text{constant}$$

where $\frac{P}{\rho g}$ is the pressure head, $\frac{V^2}{2g}$ is the velocity head, z is the elevation head and H is total head.

Multiplying the Bernoulli Equation by ρg, $P + \rho\frac{V^2}{2} + \rho g z = \text{constant}$. Each term in this equation has pressure units. P is the static pressure, $\rho\frac{V^2}{2}$ is the dynamic pressure and $\rho g z$ is the hydrostatic pressure.

Sum of the static and dynamic pressures is called the *stagnation pressure.*

$$P_{stag} = P + \rho\frac{V^2}{2}$$

The line that represents the sum of the static pressure and the elevation heads, $\frac{P}{\rho g} + z$ is called the *hydraulic grade line* (HGL), and the line that represents the total head of the fluid $\frac{P}{\rho g} + \frac{V^2}{2g} + z$, is called the *energy grade line* (EGL).

Viscous Flow of Incompressible Fluids

A flow is said to be viscous if the Reynolds number in pipe is less than 2000, or fluid flows in layers.

Viscous Flow through Circular Pipes

Shear stress, $\tau = -\frac{r}{2}\frac{\partial p}{\partial r}$

Velocity, $u = -\frac{1}{4\mu}\frac{\partial p}{\partial r}(R^2 - r^2)$

Maximum velocity, $u_{max} = -\frac{1}{4\mu}\frac{\partial p}{\partial r}R^2$

$$\frac{u_{max}}{\bar{u}} = 2$$

Loss of pressure head $\frac{P_2 - P_1}{\rho g} = h_f = \frac{32\mu\bar{u}L}{\rho g D^2}$

Viscous Flow between Two Parallel Plates

Shear stress, $\tau = -\frac{1}{2}\frac{\partial p}{\partial x}(t - 2y)$

Velocity, $u = -\frac{1}{2\mu}\frac{\partial p}{\partial x}(ty - y^2)$

Maximum velocity, $u_{max} = -\frac{1}{8\mu}\frac{\partial p}{\partial x}t^2$

or $$\frac{u_{max}}{\bar{u}} = \frac{3}{2}$$

Loss of pressure head $\frac{P_2 - P_1}{\rho g} = h_f = \frac{12\mu\bar{u}L}{\rho g t^2}$

Boundary Layer

When a solid body is immersed in a flowing fluid, there is narrow region of the fluid in the neighborhood of the solid body, where the velocity of fluid varies from zero to free-stream velocity. This narrow region of fluid is called *boundary layer.*

Laminar boundary layer if Reynold's number,

$$R_e = \frac{\rho U x}{\mu} < 5 \times 10^5$$

Turbulent boundary layer if Reynold's number,

$$R_e = \frac{\rho U x}{\mu} > 5 \times 10^5$$

Boundary Layer Thickness

The distance from the surface of the solid body in the direction perpendicular to flow, where the velocity of fluid is approximately equal to 0.99 times the free-stream velocity is called *boundary layer thickness.*

Displacement thickness, $\delta^* = \int_0^\delta \left(1 - \frac{u}{U}\right)dy$

Momentum thickness, $\theta = \int_0^\delta \frac{u}{U}\left(1 - \frac{u}{U}\right)dy$

Energy thickness, $\delta^{**} = \int_0^\delta \frac{u}{U}\left(1 - \frac{u^2}{U^2}\right)dy$

Von-Karman Momentum Integral Equation

$$\frac{\tau}{\rho U^2} = \frac{\partial\theta}{\partial x}$$

Laminar boundary layer thickness, $\delta = \frac{4.91x}{\sqrt{R_{e_x}}}$

Coefficient of drag, $C_D = \frac{1.328}{\sqrt{R_{e_L}}}$

Turbulent Flow

Shear stress $\tau = \tau_V + \tau_t$ where τ_V = shear stress due to viscosity, τ_t = shear stress due to turbulence.

$$\tau = \mu \frac{d\bar{u}}{dy} + \eta \frac{d\bar{u}}{dy}$$

Turbulent shear stress $\tau = \rho u' v'$ (by Reynolds) where u' and v' = fluctuating component of velocity.

$\bar{\tau} = \rho l^2 \left(\frac{du}{dy}\right)^2$, where l = mixing length (by Prandtl mixing theory)

Velocity distribution in the turbulent flow of pipe:

$$u = u_{max} + 2.5u^* \log_e (y/R)$$

Flow through Pipes

- Loss of energy in pipes (head losses in pipe)

1. Major energy (head) losses

This is due to friction and it is calculated by Darcy-Weisbach formula, $h_f = \frac{4fLV^2}{d2g}$

2. Minor energy (head) losses

(a) Loss of head due to sudden enlargement of pipe,

$$h_e = \frac{(V_1 - V_2)^2}{2g}$$

(b) Loss of head due to sudden contraction of pipe,

$$h_c = 0.375 \frac{V_2^2}{2g} \quad \text{or} \quad \left(h_c = 0.5 \frac{V_2^2}{2g}\right)$$

(c) Loss of head at the entrance of pipe, $h_i = 0.5 \frac{V^2}{2g}$

(d) Loss of head at the exit of a pipe, $h_o = \frac{V^2}{2g}$

(e) Loss of head due to obstruction/bend/various fittings,

$$h = k \frac{V^2}{2g}$$

- Hydraulic gradient line (HGL): Line which gives $\left(\frac{p}{\rho g} + z\right)$
- Total energy line (TEL): Line which gives $\left(\frac{p}{\rho g} + \frac{V^2}{2g} + z\right)$
- Dupuit's equation, $\frac{L}{d^5} = \frac{L_1}{d_1^5} + \frac{L_2}{d_2^5} + \frac{L_3}{d_3^5} + \ldots$ (pipe in series)
- Power transmitted through pipe, $P = \dot{m}g(H - h_f)$

  where $\dot{m} = \rho g \times \frac{\pi}{4} d^2 \times V$, $h_f = \frac{4fLV^2}{d2g}$
- Efficiency of power transmission, $\eta = \frac{H - h_f}{H}$
- Condition for maximum transmission of power, $h_f = \frac{H}{3}$,

  $\eta_{max} = 66.66\%$

Dimensional Analysis

Dimensional analysis is a powerful tool that reduces the number of variables influencing the flow to a great extent.

Methods of dimensional analysis: (1) Rayleigh's method (2) Buckingham's π theorem.

Buckingham's π-theorem

When a physical phenomenon is described by n number of variables (both independent and dependent) having m fundamental dimensions, according the Buckingham's π- theorem the phenomenon can be described by $(n - m)$ number of independent dimensionless group called as π-terms.

Model Analysis

The study of models of actual machines or structures is called the *model analysis*. The actual machine or structure is called the *prototype*. The model is the replica of the actual machine or structure on which testing are executed.

Similitude

Similitude is the study of predicting prototype behaviour from model observations. The different types of similarities that must exist between a model and a prototype are: (i) Geometric similarity, (ii) Kinematic similarity, (iii) Dynamic similarity.

Dimensionless Numbers

Reynold number, $Re = \frac{\text{Inertia force}}{\text{Viscous force}} = \frac{\rho VL}{\mu}$

Froude number, $Fr = \sqrt{\dfrac{\text{Inertia force}}{\text{Gravity force}}} = \dfrac{V}{\sqrt{gL}}$

Euler number, $Eu = \sqrt{\dfrac{\text{Inertia force}}{\text{Pressure force}}} = \dfrac{V}{\sqrt{\dfrac{\Delta P}{\rho}}}$

Mach number, $M = \sqrt{\dfrac{\text{Inertia force}}{\text{Elastic force}}} = \dfrac{V}{\sqrt{\dfrac{K}{\rho}}}$

Weber number, $W = \sqrt{\dfrac{\text{Inertia force}}{\text{Surface tension force}}} = \dfrac{V}{\sqrt{\dfrac{\sigma}{\rho L}}}$

Model Laws

Different model laws are:

(i) Reynolds model law, (ii) Froude model law, (iii) Euler model law, (iv) Mach model law, (v) Weber model law.

Turbo-machinery

Classifications of Turbines

1. *According to type of energy available at inlet*:

(a) Impulse turbine: The entire available energy of the water is converted into kinetic energy.

(b) Reaction turbine: Only a portion of the fluid energy is converted into kinetic energy before the fluid enters the turbine runner.

2. *According to direction of flow of water through runner*:

(a) Tangential flow

(b) Radial flow: (i) Inward flow turbine (ii) Outward flow turbine

(c) Axial flow

(d) Mixed flow

3. *According to position of turbine shaft*:

(a) Horizontal shaft turbine (b) Vertical shaft turbine.

4. *According head*:

(a) High head turbine (from 150 m to 2000 m or even more)

(b) Medium head turbine (from 30 m to 150 m)

(c) Low head turbine (less than 30 m).

5. *According to specific speed*:

(a) Low specific speed turbine: (Specific speed less than 50). For example, Pelton wheel turbine

(b) Medium specific turbine: (Specific speed from 50 to 250). For example Francis turbine

(c) High specific speed turbine: (Specific speed more than 250). For example Kaplan turbine

Heads, Head Loss and Efficiencies

Gross head (H_g): The difference between the head race level and tail race level when no water is flowing.

Net head or effective head (H): It is defined as the head available at the inlet of the turbine. It is also called *effective head*, $H = H_g - h_f$.

Head loss due to friction (h_f); $h_f = \dfrac{4f\,lV^2}{d.2g}$

Hydraulic efficiency (η_h): It is defined as the ratio of power delivered to the runner to the the power supplied at inlet, (i.e., water power):

$$\eta_h = \frac{\text{Power delivered to the runner of the turbine}}{\text{Water power}} = \frac{\text{RP}}{\text{WP}}$$

where, runner power (RP) $= \rho Q(V_{w1} \pm V_{w2})u$ and water power (WP)= ρgQH

$$\eta_h = \frac{(V_{w1} \pm V_{w2})u}{gH}$$

Mechanical efficiency (η_m): It is defined as the ratio of the power available at the shaft of the turbine to the power delivered to the runner.

$$\eta_m = \frac{\text{Power available at the turbine shaft}}{\text{Power delivered to the runner of the turbine}} = \frac{\text{SP}}{\text{RP}}$$

or $$\eta_m = \frac{\text{SP}}{\rho Q(V_{w1} \pm V_{w2})u}$$

Volumetric efficiency (η_v): It is defined as the ratio of the volume of the water actually striking the runner to the volume of water supplied to the turbine.

Overall efficiency (η_0): It is defined as the ratio of power available at the turbine shaft to the power available from the water jet.

$$\eta_0 = \frac{\text{Shaft power}}{\text{Water power}} = \frac{\text{SP}}{\text{WP}}$$

or $$\eta_0 = \frac{\text{SP}}{\text{RP}} \times \frac{\text{RP}}{\text{WP}}$$

$$\eta_0 = \eta_m \times \eta_h$$

Pelton Wheel

The Pelton wheel or Pelton turbine is a tangential flow, high head impulse turbine.

General layout of a hydroelectric power plant:

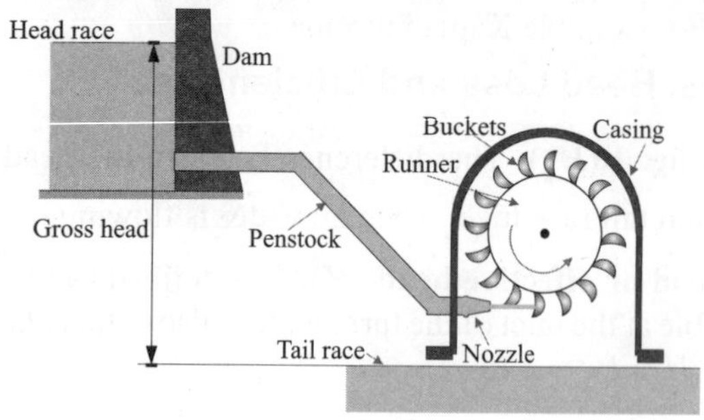

Velocity Triangle, Work Done and Efficiency of Pelton Wheel

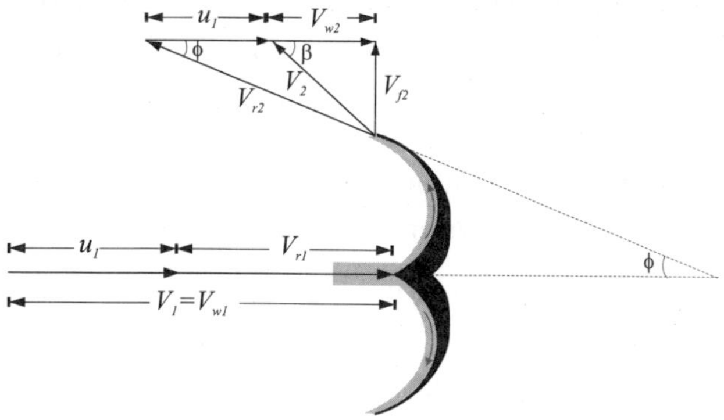

Velocity of jet, $V_1 = c_v\sqrt{2gH}$

Bucket velocity (at inlet and outlet tip), $u_1 = u_2 = \dfrac{\pi DN}{60}$

Force exerted by the jet of water in the direction of motion,

$$F_x = \rho Q(V_{w1} \pm V_{w2})$$

Work done by the jet on the runner per second

$$WD = F_x u = \rho Q(V_{w1} \pm V_{w2})u$$

Work done by the jet per unit weight of water

$$= \frac{(V_{w1} \pm V_{w2})u}{g}$$

Kinetic energy of jet, $\quad \text{KE} = \dfrac{1}{2}\rho Q V_1^2$

Hydraulic efficiency of the Pelton wheel,

$$\eta_h = \frac{\rho Q(V_{w1} \pm V_{w2})u}{\frac{1}{2}\rho Q V_1^2}$$

$$\eta_h = \frac{2u(V_{w1} \pm V_{w2})}{V_1^2}$$

or $$\eta_h = \frac{2u(V_1 - u)(1 + k\cos\phi)}{V_1^2}$$

$$(\eta_h)_{\max} = \frac{1 + k\cos\phi}{2} \quad \text{at} \quad \frac{u}{V_1} = \frac{1}{2}$$

Working Proportion of a Pelton Wheel

The velocity of jet at inlet, $\quad V_1 = c_v\sqrt{2gH}$

Coefficient of velocity c_v varies from 0.97 to 0.99

The velocity of wheel, $\quad u = \phi\sqrt{2gH}$

Speed ratio ϕ varies from 0.43 to 0.47

Pitch diameter, $\quad D = \dfrac{60u}{\pi N}$

Jet ratio, $\quad m = \dfrac{D}{d} \quad (10 < m < 14)$

Number of buckets on the runner, $\quad Z = 15 + \dfrac{D}{2d}$

Angle of deflection $180 - \phi$, it is around $165°$.

Francis Turbine

Francis turbine is a mixed flow, medium head reaction turbine.

Main Parts and Velocity Triangles of Inward Flow Reaction Turbine

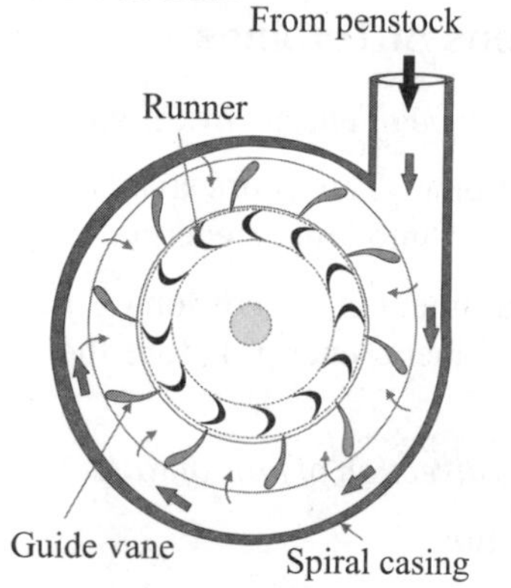

Components of Francis turbine

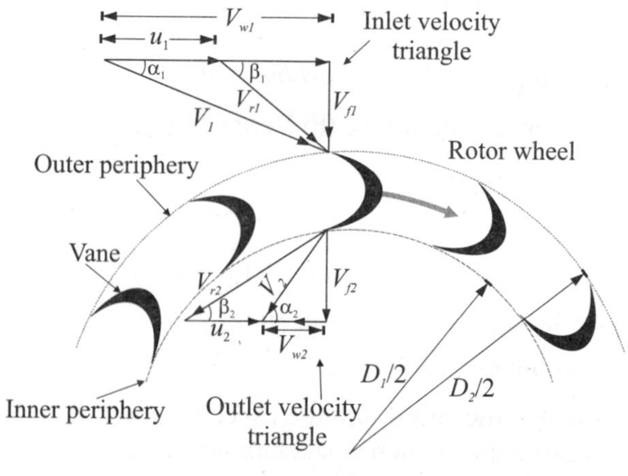

Velocity triangles of Francis Turbine

Work done by runner, $WD = \rho Q (V_{w1}u_1 \pm V_{w2}u_2)$

For maximum output, the runner is so designed that a radial discharge occurs at the outlet tip. Then $V_{w2} = 0$ and therefore,

$$WD = \rho Q V_{w1} u_1$$

Hydraulic efficiency, $\eta_h = \dfrac{\rho Q (V_{w1}u_1 \pm V_{w2}u_2)}{\rho Q g H}$

or $$\eta_h = \frac{V_{w1}u_1 \pm V_{w2}u_2}{gH}$$

For radially inward flow reaction turbine:

$$\eta_h = \frac{V_{w1}u_1}{gH} \text{ (Francis turbine } V_{w2} = 0)$$

Discharge of the turbine, $Q = \pi D_1 B_1 \times V_{f1} = \pi D_2 B_2 \times V_{f2}$

Working proportions:

1. Ratio of width to diameter $\dfrac{b_1}{D_1}$: Its value ranges from 0.1 to 0.45.

2. Speed ratio, $K_u = \dfrac{u_1}{\sqrt{2gH}}$; $K_u \approx 0.6$ to 0.9

3. Flow ratio, $K_f = \dfrac{V_{f1}}{\sqrt{2gH}}$; $K_f \approx 0.15$ to 0.30

Axial Flow Reaction Turbine (Propeller and Kaplan Turbine)

Main parts and velocity triangle of axial flow reaction turbine:

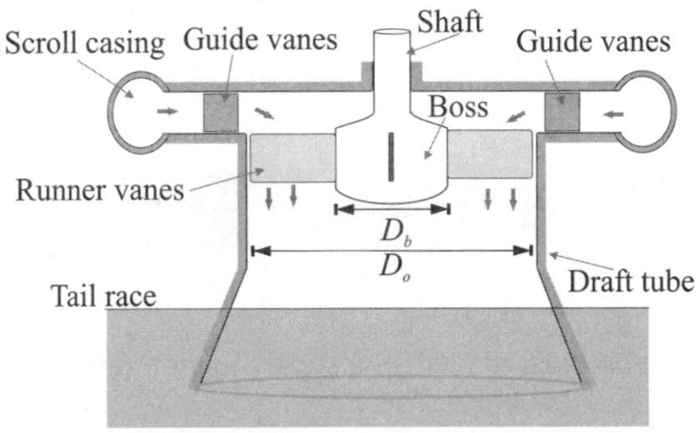

Components of axial flow reaction turbine

Discharge through the runner, $Q = V_{f1} \times \dfrac{\pi}{4}(D_o^2 - D_b^2)$

Peripheral velocity at inlet and outlet are equal, that is,

$$u_1 = \frac{\pi D N}{60} = u_2$$

Velocity of flow at inlet and outlet is equal, that is,

$$V_{f1} = V_{f2}$$

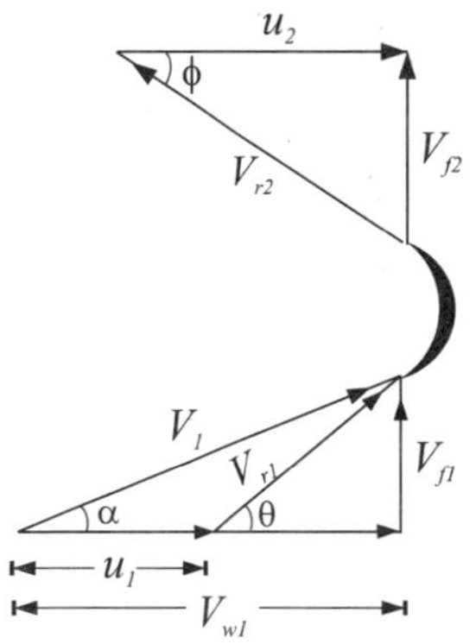

Velocity triagles of axial flow reaction turbine

Draft Tube

The diverging passage which connects the runner exits to the tail race is known as *draft tube*. The functions of draft tube are: (a) decrease the pressure at the runner exit to a value less than atmospheric pressure and thereby increase the working head, and (b) recover a portion of the exit kinetic energy which otherwise goes waste to the tail race.

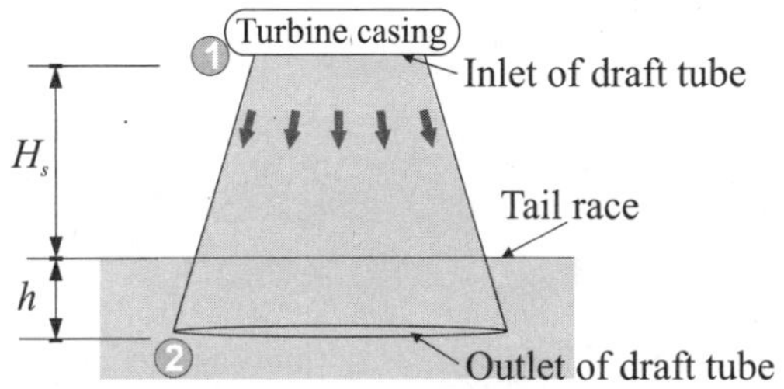

Types of draft tube: (a) Conical draft tube, (b) Simple elbow tube, (c) Moody spread tube, (d) Draft tube with circular inlet and rectangular outlet.

Draft Tube Theory

Energy equation between 1 and 2:

$$\frac{P_1}{\rho g} + \frac{V_1^2}{2g} + z_1 = \frac{P_2}{\rho g} + \frac{V_2^2}{2g} + z_2 + h_f$$

$$\frac{P_1}{\rho g} + \frac{V_1^2}{2g} + H_s + h = \frac{P_{atm}}{\rho g} + h + \frac{V_2^2}{2g} + 0 + h_f$$

$$\frac{P_1}{\rho g} = \frac{P_{atm}}{rg} - H_s - \left(\frac{V_1^2}{2g} - \frac{V_2^2}{2g} - h_f\right)$$

Efficiency of draft tube: It is the ratio of actual conversion of kinetic energy into pressure energy in the draft tube to the kinetic energy available at the inlet to the draft tube. Mathematically,

$$\eta_d = \frac{\frac{V_1^2}{2g} - \frac{V_2^2}{2g} - h_f}{\frac{V_1^2}{2g}}$$

Unit Quantities and Specific Speed

Unit Quantities

Unit speed N_u: The speed of turbine working under unit head (1 m) is known as *unit speed* of the turbine.

$$N_u = \frac{N}{\sqrt{H}}$$

Unit Power P_u: The power developed by turbine working under unit head (1 m) is known as *unit power* of the turbine.

$$P_u = \frac{P}{H^{\frac{3}{2}}}$$

Unit Discharge Q_u: The discharge of the turbine working under unit head (1 m) is known as *unit discharge* of the turbine.

$$Q_u = \frac{Q}{\sqrt{H}}$$

Specific Speed

Specific Speed of a turbine is defined as the speed of the turbine which produces unit power at unit head.

Specific speed, $$N_s = \frac{N\sqrt{P}}{H^{\frac{5}{4}}}$$

Similarity Ratios of Turbines

Power developed by turbine depends upon diameter of the runner D, rotational speed N, specific energy gH, discharge through turbine Q, density of water ρ and viscosity μ.

By using the dimensional analysis (Buckingham π- theorem)

$$\frac{P}{\rho N^3 D^5} = f\left(\frac{gH}{N^2 D^2}, \frac{Q}{ND^3}, \frac{\rho ND^2}{\mu}\right)$$

Similarity between model and prototype:

$$\left[\frac{P}{\rho N^3 D^5}\right]_m = \left[\frac{P}{\rho N^3 D^5}\right]_p,$$

$$\left[\frac{gH}{N^2 D^2}\right]_m = \left[\frac{gH}{N^2 D^2}\right]_p$$

$$\left[\frac{Q}{ND^3}\right]_m = \left[\frac{Q}{ND^3}\right]_p, \quad g \text{ and } \rho \text{ are same}$$

$$\left[\frac{P}{N^3 D^5}\right]_m = \left[\frac{P}{N^3 D^5}\right]_p,$$

$$\left[\frac{H}{N^2 D^2}\right]_m = \left[\frac{H}{N^2 D^2}\right]_p$$

$$\left[\frac{Q}{ND^3}\right]_m = \left[\frac{Q}{ND^3}\right]_p$$

10.2 SOLVED EXAMPLES

Previous Years GATE Questions

Example 10.1

If the fluid velocity for a potential flow is given by $V(x, y) = u(x, y)i + v(x, y)j$ with usual notation, then the slope of potential line at (x, y) is

(A) $\frac{v}{u}$ (B) $-\frac{u}{v}$ (C) $\frac{v^2}{u^2}$ (D) $\frac{u}{v}$

GATE 2015

Solution

Velocity potential is expressed as $\phi = \phi(x, y)$

From chain rule, we have

$$d\phi = \frac{\partial \phi}{\partial x} dx + \frac{\partial \phi}{\partial y} dy$$

or $$d\phi = u\,dx + v\,dy$$

For constant velocity potential, $\phi = 0$

$$0 = u\,dx + v\,dy \quad \text{or} \quad \frac{dy}{dx} = -\frac{u}{v}$$

Slope of potential line $\frac{dy}{dx} = -\frac{u}{v}$

Example 10.2

Within a boundary layer for a steady incompressible flow, the Bernoulli equation

(A) Holds because the flow is steady

(B) Holds because the flow is incompressible

(C) Holds because the flow is transitional

(D) Does not hold because the flow is frictional

GATE 2015

Solution

Within a boundary layer for a steady incompressible flow, the Bernoulli equation does not hold because the flow is frictional (viscous).

Example 10.3

For a fully developed laminar flow of water (dynamic viscosity 0.001 Pa.s) through a pipe of radius 5 cm, the axial pressure gradient is 10 Pa/m. The magnitude of axial velocity (in m/s) at a radial location of 0.2 cm is _____.

GATE 2015

Solution

The velocity distribution is given by

$$u = -\frac{1}{4\mu}\frac{dp}{dx}(R^2 - r^2)$$

Substituting $\mu = 0.001$ Pa.s, $-\frac{dp}{dx} = 10$ Pa/m, $R = \frac{5}{100}$ m and $r = \frac{0.2}{100}$ m

Velocity at $r = \frac{0.2}{100}$ m,

$$u = -\frac{1}{4\times 0.001}(-10)\left[\left(\frac{5}{100}\right)^2 - \left(\frac{0.2}{100}\right)^2\right]$$

$$u = 6.24 \text{ m/s}$$

Example 10.4

The head loss for a laminar incompressible flow through a horizontal circular pipe is h_1. Pipe length and fluid remaining the same, if the average flow velocity doubles and the pipe diameter reduces to half its previous value, the head loss is h_2. The ratio $\frac{h_2}{h_1}$ is

(A) 1 (B) 4 (C) 8 (D) 16

GATE 2015

Solution

The loss of head due to friction is given by

$$h_f = \frac{4f\,lv^2}{d\cdot 2g}$$

$$h_1 = \frac{4f\,lv^2}{d\cdot 2g} \quad \text{(i)}$$

$$h_2 = \frac{4f\,l(2v)^2}{(d/2)\cdot 2g} = 8\times\frac{4f\,lv^2}{d\cdot 2g} \quad \text{(ii)}$$

From Equations (i) and (ii), we obtain

$$h_2 = 8\times h_1$$

$$\frac{h_2}{h_1} = 8$$

Example 10.5

Three parallel pipes connected at the two ends have flow-rates Q_1, Q_2 and Q_3 respectively, and the corresponding frictional head losses are h_{L1}, h_{L2} and h_{L3} respectively. The correct expression for total flow rate (Q) and frictional head loss across the two ends (h_L) are

(A) $Q = Q_1 + Q_2 + Q_3$; $h_L = h_{L1} + h_{L2} + h_{L3}$

(B) $Q = Q_1 + Q_2 + Q_3$; $h_L = h_{L1} = h_{L2} = h_{L3}$

(C) $Q = Q_1 = Q_2 = Q_3$; $h_L = h_{L1} + h_{L2} + h_{L3}$

(D) $Q = Q_1 = Q_2 = Q_3$; $h_L = h_{L1} = h_{L2} = h_{L3}$

GATE 2015

Solution

In parallel connected pipes

Head loss, $h_L = h_{L1} = h_{L2} = h_{L3}$

Total flow rate, $Q = Q_1 + Q_2 + Q_3$

Example 10.6

Couette flow is characterised by

(A) Steady, incompressible, laminar flow through a straight circular pipe

(B) Fully developed turbulent flow through a straight circular pipe

(C) Steady, incompressible, laminar flow between two fixed parallel plates

(D) Steady, incompressible, laminar flow between one fixed plate and the other moving with a constant velocity

GATE 2015

Solution

Couette flow is steady, incompressible, laminar flow between one fixed plate and the other moving with a constant velocity

Example 10.7

A Prandtl tube (Pitot-static tube with $c_v = 1$) is used to measure the velocity of water. The differential manometer reading is 10 mm of liquid column with a relative density of 10. Assuming $g = 9.8\text{ m/s}^2$, the velocity of water (in m/s) is _____.

GATE 2015

Solution

Velocity of fluid by Pitot tube is given by

$$V = c_v\sqrt{2g\frac{P_2 - P_1}{\rho g}}$$

Substituting $\left[\dfrac{P_2 - P_1}{\rho g} = h_m\left(\dfrac{\rho_m}{\rho} - 1\right)\right]$

or $$V = 1 \times \sqrt{2 \times 9.8 \times \frac{10}{1000}(10-1)}$$

$$V = 1.32 \text{ m/s}$$

Example 10.8

Consider fully developed flow in a circular pipe with negligible entrance length effects. Assuming the mass flow rate, density and friction factor to be constant, if the length of the pipe is doubled and the diameter is halved, the head loss due to friction will increase by a factor of

(A) 4 (B) 16 (C) 32 (D) 64

GATE 2015

Solution

The loss of head due to friction is given by

$$h_f = \frac{4f\,l v^2}{d \cdot 2g}$$

$$h_1 = \frac{4f\,l_1 v_1^2}{d_1 \cdot 2g} \quad \text{(i)}$$

and $$h_2 = \frac{4f\,l_2 v_2^2}{d_2 \cdot 2g} \quad \text{(ii)}$$

From Equations (i) and (ii), we have

$$\frac{h_2}{h_1} = \frac{l_2}{l_1}\left(\frac{v_2}{v_1}\right)^2 \frac{d_1}{d_2}$$

Substituting $d_2 = \dfrac{d_1}{2}$, $l_2 = 2l_1$,

$$\dot{m} = \rho\left(\frac{\pi}{4}d_1^2\right)v_1 = \rho\left(\frac{\pi}{4}d_2^2\right)v_2$$

or $$d_1^2 v_1 = d_2^2 v_2$$

$$\frac{h_2}{h_1} = \frac{2l_1}{l_1}\left(\frac{d_1^2}{(d_1/2)^2}\right)^2 \frac{d_1}{d_1/2}$$

or $$\frac{h_2}{h_1} = 2 \times 2^4 \times 2$$

$$\frac{h_2}{h_1} = 64$$

Example 10.9

Match the following pairs:

	Product		Process
P	$\nabla \times \mathbf{V} = 0$	I	Incompressible continuity equation
Q	$\nabla \cdot \mathbf{V} = 0$	II	Steady flow
R	$\dfrac{D\mathbf{V}}{Dt} = 0$	III	Irrotational flow
S	$\dfrac{\partial \mathbf{V}}{\partial t} = 0$	IV	Zero acceleration of fluid particle

(A) P-IV, Q-I, R-II, S-III (B) P-IV, Q-III, R-I, S-II

(C) P-III, Q-I, R-IV, S-II (D) P-III, Q-I, R-II, S-IV

GATE 2015

Solution

$\nabla \times \mathbf{V} = 0$ ← Irrotational flow

$\nabla \cdot \mathbf{V} = 0$ ← Incompressible continuity equation

$\dfrac{D\mathbf{V}}{Dt} = 0$ ← Zero acceleration of fluid particle

$\dfrac{\partial \mathbf{V}}{\partial t} = 0$ ← Steady flow

Example 10.10

The velocity field on an incompressible flow is given by

$$V = (a_1 x + a_2 y + a_3 z)i + (b_1 x + b_2 y + b_3 z)j + (c_1 x + c_2 y + c_3 z)k$$

where $a_1 = 2$ and $c_3 = -4$. The value of b_2 is_______.

GATE 2015

Solution

Condition for incompressible flow is $\nabla \cdot V = 0$

$$\nabla \cdot [(a_1 x + a_2 y + a_3 z)i + (b_1 x + b_2 y + b_3 z)j + (c_1 x + c_2 y + c_3 z)k] = 0$$

or $$a_1 + b_2 + c_3 = 0$$

or $$2 + b_2 - 4 = 0$$

$$b_2 = 2$$

Example 10.11

Air ($\rho = 1.2\,\text{kg/m}^3$) and kinematic viscosity, $\nu = 2 \times 10^{-5}\,\text{m}^2/\text{s}$ with a velocity of 2 m/s flows over the top surface of a flat plate of length 2.5 m. If the average value of friction coefficient is $C_f = \dfrac{1328}{\sqrt{\text{Re}_x}}$, the total drag force (in N) per unit width of the plate is _______.

GATE 2015

Solution

Total drag force on body is given by

$$F_D = C_D A \frac{1}{2}\rho u^2$$

or $$F_D = \frac{1328}{\sqrt{\text{Re}_l}}(l \times b)\frac{1}{2}\rho u^2$$

Total drag force per unit width, $F_D = \frac{1328}{\sqrt{\text{Re}_l}} \times l \frac{1}{2}\rho u^2$

or $$F_D = \frac{1.328}{\sqrt{\frac{ul}{\nu}}} \times l \frac{1}{2}\rho u^2$$

$$F_D = \frac{1.328}{\sqrt{\frac{2 \times 2.5}{2 \times 10^{-5}}}} \times 2.5 \times \frac{1}{2} \times 1.2 \times 2^2$$

$$F_D = 0.016 \text{ m/s}$$

Example 10.12

Water ($\rho = 1000 \text{ kg/m}^3$) flows through a venturimeter with inlet diameter 80 mm and throat diameter 40 mm. The inlet and throat gauge pressures are measured to be 400 kPa and 130 kPa respectively. Assuming the venturimeter to be horizontal and neglecting friction, the inlet velocity (in m/s) is ______.

GATE 2015

Solution

Flow through venturimeter is given by

$$Q = \frac{a_1 a_2}{\sqrt{a_2^2 - a_1^2}}\sqrt{2g\left(\frac{P_2 - P_1}{\rho g}\right)}$$

Velocity of fluid at inlet,

$$V_1 = \frac{Q}{a_1} = \frac{a_2}{\sqrt{a_2^2 - a_1^2}}\sqrt{2g\left(\frac{P_2 - P_1}{\rho g}\right)}$$

or $$V_1 = \frac{\frac{\pi}{4}d_2^2}{\sqrt{\left(\frac{\pi}{4}d_1^2\right)^2 - \left(\frac{\pi}{4}d_2^2\right)^2}}\sqrt{2g\left(\frac{P_2 - P_1}{\rho g}\right)}$$

or $$V_1 = \frac{d_2^2}{\sqrt{d_1^4 - d_2^4}}\sqrt{2g\left(\frac{P_2 - P_1}{\rho g}\right)}$$

or $$V_1 = \frac{0.04^2}{\sqrt{0.08^4 - 0.04^4}}\sqrt{2 \times 9.81 \times \left(\frac{(400 - 130) \times 10^3}{1000 \times 9.81}\right)}$$

$$V_1 = 6 \text{ N/m}$$

Example 10.13

For a fluid flow through a divergent pipe of length L having inlet and outlet radii R_1 and R_2 respectively and a constant flow rate of Q. Assuming the velocity to be axial and uniform at any cross-section, determine the acceleration at the exit of pipe.

(A) $\frac{2Q(R_1 - R_2)}{\pi L R_2^3}$ (B) $\frac{2Q^2(R_1 - R_2)}{\pi L R_2^3}$

(C) $\frac{2Q^2(R_1 - R_2)}{\pi^2 L R_2^5}$ (D) $\frac{2Q^2(R_2 - R_1)}{\pi^2 L R_2^5}$

GATE 2004

Solution

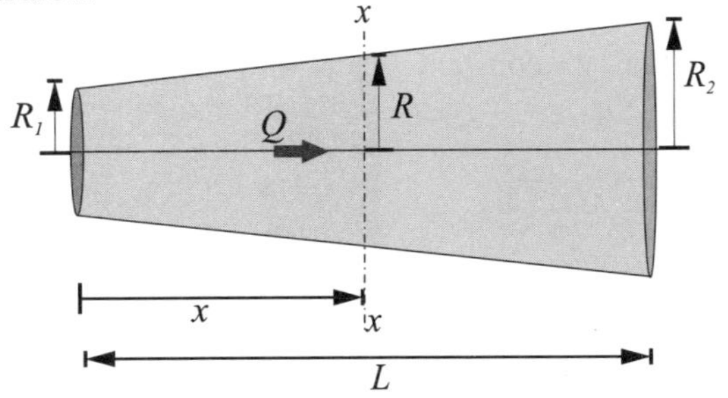

Let R be the radius of pipe at plane x-x.

$$R = R_1 + \frac{R_2 - R_1}{L}x$$

Flow rate, $Q = av$

Velocity of fluid at x-x, $v = \frac{Q}{a} = \frac{Q}{\pi R^2}$

or $$v = \frac{Q}{\pi\left(R_1 + \frac{R_2 - R_1}{L}x\right)^2}$$

Acceleration of fluid at x-x, $a = \frac{dv}{dt} = v\frac{dv}{dx}$

$$a = \frac{Q}{\pi\left(R_1 + \frac{R_2 - R_1}{L}x\right)^2}\frac{d}{dx}\frac{Q}{\pi\left(R_1 + \frac{R_2 - R_1}{L}x\right)^2}$$

Acceleration of fluid at exit of pipe ($x = L$),

$$a_{\text{exit}} = v\frac{dv}{dx} = \frac{Q^2}{\pi^2 R_2^2} \times \frac{-2(R_2 - R_1)}{L R_2^3}$$

$$a_{\text{exit}} = \frac{2Q^2(R_1 - R_2)}{\pi^2 L R_2^5}$$

Example 10.14

A two-dimensional flow field has velocities along the x and y directions given by $u = x^2 t$ and $v = -2xyt$ respectively, where t is time. The equation of streamlines is

(A) $x^2 y = \text{constant}$ (B) $y^2 x = \text{constant}$

(C) $xy = \text{constant}$ (D) Not possible to determine

GATE 2006

Solution

The streamline is represented as

$$\frac{dx}{u} = \frac{dy}{v}$$

Substituting $u = x^2 t$ and $v = -2xyt$, we have

$$\frac{dx}{x^2 t} = \frac{dy}{-2xyt} \quad \text{or} \quad 2\frac{dx}{x} + \frac{dy}{y} = 0$$

Integrating both sides, we get

$$\ln y + \ln x^2 = \text{constant}$$

or $$\ln x^2 y = \text{constant}$$

$$x^2 y = \text{constant}$$

Example 10.15

A hinged gate of length 5 m, inclined at 30° with the horizontal and with water mass on its left, is shown in the figure below. Density of water is 1000 kg/m^3. The minimum mass of the gate in kg per unit width (perpendicular to the plane of paper) required to keep it closed is

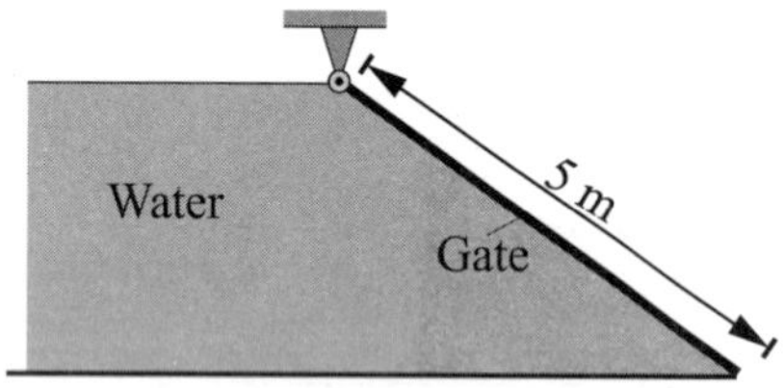

(A) 5000 (B) 6600 (C) 7546 (D) 9623

GATE 2013

Solution

Figure shows the free-body diagram of gate.

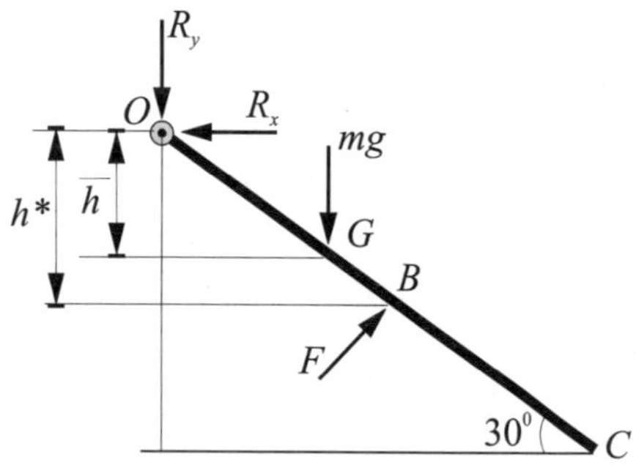

Total hydrostatic force, $F = \rho g A\bar{h}$

$$F = 1000 \times 9.81 \times 5 \times 1 \times \frac{5}{2} \times \sin 30$$

$$F = 61312.5 \text{ N}$$

Vertical depth of center of pressure, $h^* = \bar{h} + \dfrac{I_G \sin^2\theta}{A\bar{h}}$

$$h^* = \frac{5}{2}\sin 30 + \frac{\dfrac{1\times 5^3}{12}\sin^2 30}{5\times 1\times \dfrac{5}{2}\sin 30}$$

$$h^* = 1.667 \text{ m}$$

Taking moment about hinge O,

$$mg\frac{5}{2}\cos 30 = F \times \frac{h^*}{\sin 30}$$

or $$m \times 9.81 \times \frac{5}{2} \times \cos 30 = 61312.5 \times \frac{1.667}{\sin 30}$$

$$m = 9624.4 \text{ kg}$$

Example 10.16

A U-tube manometer with a small quantity of mercury is used to measure the static pressure difference between two location A and B in a conical section through which an incompressible fluid (water) flow. At a particular flow rate, the mercury column appears as shown in the figure. The density of mercury is 13600 kg/m^3 and $g = 9.81$ m/s^2. Which of the following is correct?

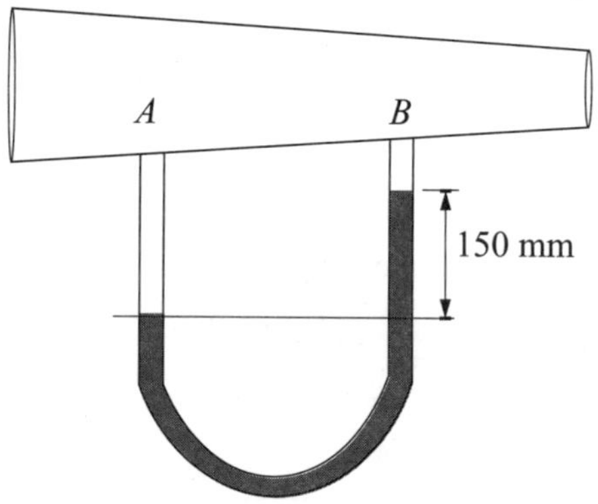

(A) Flow direction is A to B and $P_A - P_B = 18.5$ kPa
(B) Flow direction is B to A and $P_A - P_B = 1.4$ kPa
(C) Flow direction is A to B and $P_B - P_A = 20$ kPa
(D) Flow direction is B to A and $P_B - P_A = 1.4$ kPa

GATE 2005

Solution

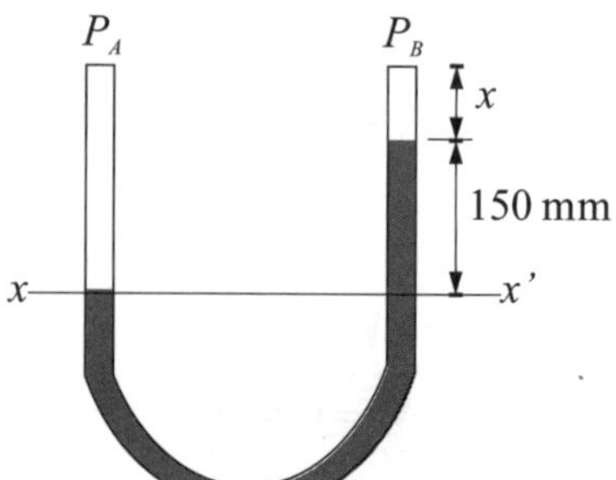

Equating the pressures on both the limbs along the horizontal plane x-x.

$$P_A + \rho g(x+0.15) = P_B + \rho g x + \rho_{Hg} g \times 0.15$$

or $$P_A - P_B = (\rho_{Hg} - \rho) g \times 0.15$$

or $$P_A - P_B = (13600 - 1000) 9.81 \times 0.15$$

$$P_A - P_B = 18.5\,\text{kPa}$$

Since $P_A > P_B$

Direction of flow is from A to B

Example 10.17

Consider steady, incompressible and irrotational flow through a reducer in a horizontal pipe where the diameter is reduced from 20 cm to 10 cm. The pressure in the 20 cm pipe just upstream of the reducer is 150 kPa. The fluid has a vapour pressure of 50 kPa and a specific weight of $5\,\text{kN/m}^3$. Neglecting frictional effects, the maximum discharge (in $\text{m}^3\text{/s}$) that can pass through the reducer without causing cavitation is

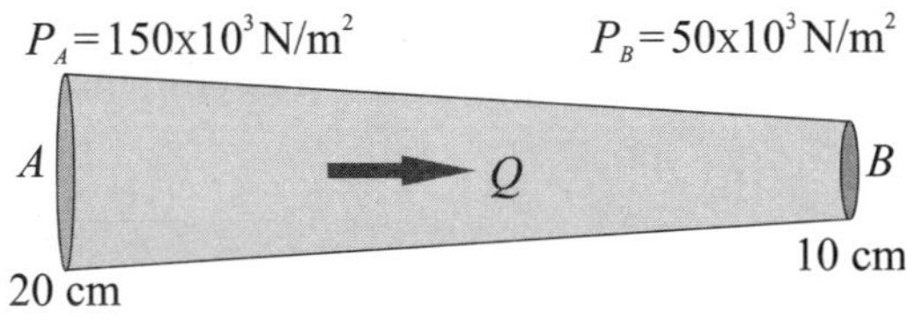

(A) 0.05 (B) 0.16 (C) 0.27 (D) 0.38

GATE 2009

Solution

Let v_A and v_B be the velocities of fluid at A and B respectively.

Applying Bernoulli's equation,

$$\frac{P_A}{\rho g} + \frac{v_A^2}{2g} + z_A = \frac{P_B}{\rho g} + \frac{v_B^2}{2g} + z_B$$

Since $z_A = z_B$; $$\frac{P_A}{\rho g} + \frac{v_A^2}{2g} = \frac{P_B}{\rho g} + \frac{v_B^2}{2g}$$

Substituting $P_A = 150 \times 10^3\ \text{N/m}^2$, $P_B = 50 \times 10^3\ \text{N/m}^2$ and $\rho g = 5 \times 10^3\ \text{N/m}^3$, we have

$$\frac{150 \times 10^3}{5 \times 10^3} + \frac{v_A^2}{2g} = \frac{50 \times 10^3}{5 \times 10^3} + \frac{v_B^2}{2g}$$

or $$\frac{v_B^2 - v_A^2}{2g} = 20$$

Using continuity equation for incompressible fluid,

$$v_A = \frac{\frac{p}{4} \times 10^2}{\frac{p}{4} \times 20^2} v_B = \frac{v_B}{4}$$

$$\frac{v_B^2 - v_A^2}{2g} = 20 \quad \Rightarrow \quad \frac{v_B^2 - \left(\frac{v_B}{4}\right)^2}{2g} = 20$$

or $$v_B = 20.458\ \text{m/s}$$

$\therefore$ Discharge, $$Q = A_B v_B = \frac{\pi}{4}\left(\frac{10}{100}\right)^2 \times 20.458$$

$$Q = 0.1606\,\text{m}^3\text{/s}$$

Example 10.18

Water flows through a vertical contraction from a pipe of diameter d to another of diameter $\frac{d}{2}$ (see figure). The flow velocity at the inlet to the contraction is 2 m/s and pressure $200\,\text{kN/m}^2$. If the height of the contraction is 2 m, then the pressure at the exit of the contraction will be very nearly

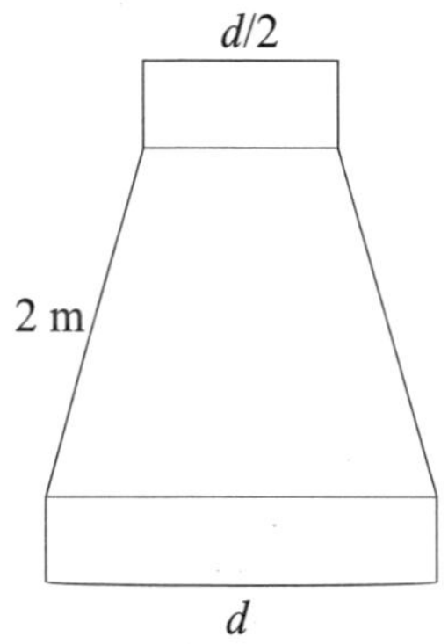

(A) $168\,\text{kN/m}^2$ (B) $192\,\text{kN/m}^2$

(C) $150\,\text{kN/m}^2$ (D) $174\,\text{kN/m}^2$

GATE 1999

Solution

Let v_1 and v_2 be the velocities of fluid at 1 and 2 respectively.

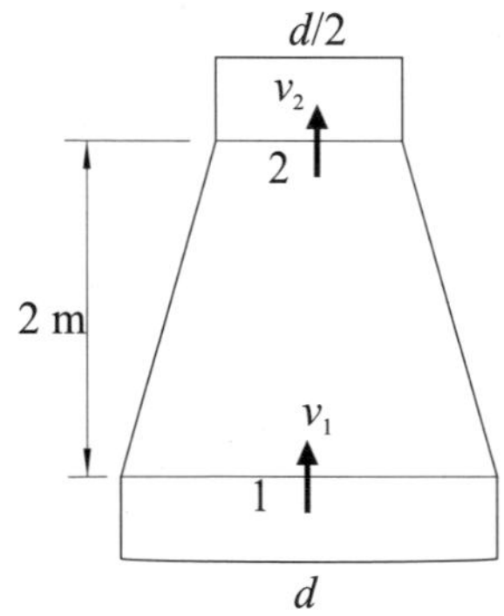

Applying Bernoulli's equation,

$$\frac{P_1}{\rho g} + \frac{v_1^2}{2g} + z_1 = \frac{P_2}{\rho g} + \frac{v_2^2}{2g} + z_2 \qquad \text{(i)}$$

Using continuity equation,

$$\rho_1 A_1 v_1 = \rho_2 A_2 v_2$$

$$\rho_1 = \rho_2; \quad \frac{\pi}{4} d^2 v_1 = \frac{\pi}{4}\left(\frac{d}{2}\right)^2 v_2$$

$$v_2 = 4v_1 \qquad \text{(ii)}$$

From Equations (i) and (ii), we have

$$\frac{P_1}{\rho g} + \frac{v_1^2}{2g} + z_1 = \frac{P_2}{\rho g} + \frac{(4v_1)^2}{2g} + z_2$$

$$\frac{P_2}{\rho g} = \frac{P_1}{\rho g} - 15\frac{v_1^2}{2g} - (z_2 - z_1)$$

Substituting $P_1 = 200 \times 10^3$ N/m^2, $v_1 = 2$ m/s and $z_2 - z_1 = 2\,\text{m}$, we have

$$\frac{P_2}{1000 \times 9.81} = \frac{200 \times 10^3}{1000 \times 9.81} - 15\frac{2^2}{2 \times 9.81} - 2$$

or $\quad P_2 = 150.3 \times 10^3\ \text{N/m}^2$

$$P_2 = 150\ \text{kN/m}^2$$

Example 10.19

Water ($\rho = 1000\ \text{kg/m}^3$) flows horizontal through a nozzle into the atmosphere under the conditions given below (Assume steady state flow).

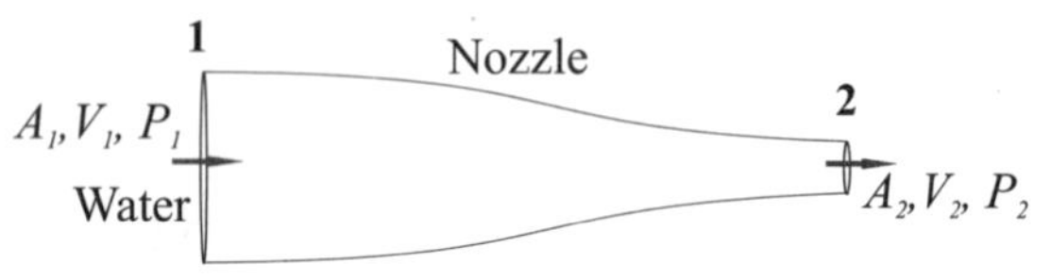

At inlet; $A_1 = 10^{-3}\ \text{m}^2$, $V_1 = 2$ m/s and $P_1 = 3 \times 10^5$Pa

At outlet; $A_2 = 10^{-4}\text{m}^2$ and $P_2 = P_{atm}$

Determine the external horizontal force needed to keep the nozzle in place.

GATE 2001

Solution

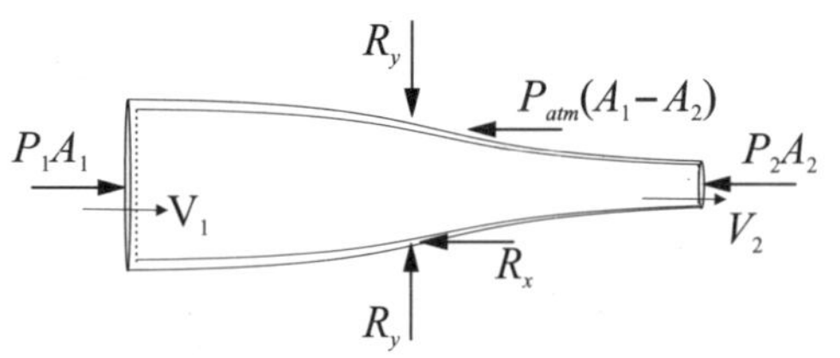

Consider the control volume as shown by dotted line in figure.

Using continuity equation, $\quad A_1V_1 = A_2V_2$

$$V_2 = \frac{A_1}{A_2}V_1 = \frac{10^{-3}}{10^{-4}} \times 2$$

$$V_2 = 20\ \text{m/s}$$

Applying momentum equation in x-direction,

$$P_1A_1 - R_x - P_2A_2 - P_{atm}(A_1 - A_2) = \rho Q(V_2 - V_1)$$

or $\quad R_x = P_1A_1 - P_{atm}A_2 - P_{atm}(A_1 - A_2) - \rho A_2V_2V_2 + \rho A_1V_1V_1$

or $\quad R_x = (P_1 - P_{atm})A_1 - \rho A_2V_2^2 + \rho A_1V_1^2$

Substituting $P_1 - P_{atm} = 3 \times 10^5$ Pa, $A_1 = 10^{-3}\text{m}^2$, $V_1 = 2$ m/s, $V_2 = 20$ m/s and $A_2 = 10^{-4}\text{m}^2$, we obtain

$$R_x = 3 \times 10^5 \times 10^{-3} - 40 + 4$$

$$R_x = 264\ \text{N}$$

Example 10.20

The velocity profile in fully developed laminar flow in a pipe of diameter D is given by $u = u_o\left(1 - \frac{4r^2}{D^2}\right)$, where r is the radial distance from the center. If the viscosity of the fluid is μ, the pressure drop across a length L of the pipe is

(A) $\frac{\mu u_o L}{D^2}$ (B) $\frac{4\mu u_o L}{D^2}$ (C) $\frac{8\mu u_o L}{D^2}$ (D) $\frac{16\mu u_o L}{D^2}$

GATE 2006

Solution

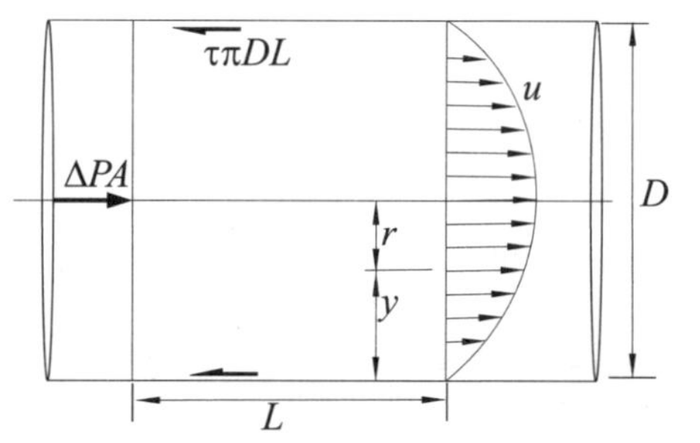

Velocity of fluid at radial distance r from center of pipe,

$$u = u_o\left(1 - \frac{4r^2}{D^2}\right)$$

Shear stress (at surface $y = 0$), $\quad \tau = \mu\left(\frac{du}{dy}\right)_{y=0}$

Let $\quad y + r = \frac{D}{2} \quad \Rightarrow \quad dy = -dr$

Shear stress (at surface $y = 0$)

$$\tau = -\mu\left(\frac{du}{dr}\right)_{r=\frac{D}{2}} = -\mu\left[\frac{d}{dr}u_o\left(1 - \frac{4r^2}{D^2}\right)\right]_{r=\frac{D}{2}}$$

or $\quad \tau = \frac{4\mu u_o}{D}$

Shear force, $F = \tau \times \pi DL = \frac{4\mu u_o}{D} \times \pi DL$

or $F = 4\pi\mu u_o L$

Shear force, F = Force due to pressure difference

$$4\pi\mu u_o L = \Delta P \frac{\pi}{4} D^2$$

$$\Delta P = \frac{16\mu u_o L}{D^2}$$

Example 10.21

A centrifugal pump is required to pump water to an open tank situated 4 km away from the location of the pump through a pipe of diameter 0.2 m having Darcy's friction factor of 0.01. The average speed of water in the pipe is 2 m/s. If it is to maintain a constant head of 5 m in the tank, neglecting other minor losses, then absolute discharge pressure at the pump exit is

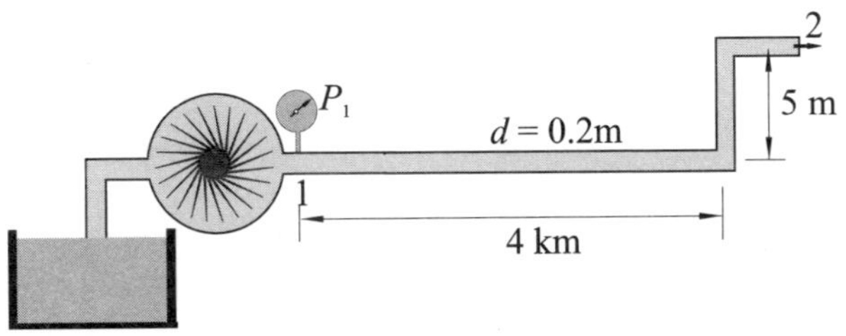

(A) 0.449 bar (B) 5.503 bar

(C) 44.911 bar (D) 55.203 bar

GATE 2004

Solution

Let P_1 be the pressure at the exit of pump.

Applying Bernoulli's equation between exit and inlet of pump.

$$\frac{P_1}{\rho g} + \frac{v_1^2}{2g} + z_1 = \frac{P_2}{\rho g} + \frac{v_2^2}{2g} + z_2 + h_{\text{losses}}$$

or $$\frac{P_1}{\rho g} + \frac{v_1^2}{2g} + z_1 = \frac{P_2}{\rho g} + \frac{v_2^2}{2g} + z_2 + \frac{f\, l v^2}{d \cdot 2g}$$

Substituting $v_1 = v_2 = v = 2$ m/s, $l = 4000$ m, $d = 0.2$ m, $f = 0.01$, $P_2 = 1 \times 10^5$ N/m^2 and $z_2 - z_1 = 5$ m, we have

$$\frac{P_1}{1000 \times 9.81} + \frac{2^2}{2 \times 9.81} = \frac{1 \times 10^5}{1000 \times 9.81} + \frac{2^2}{2 \times 9.81} + 5 + \frac{0.01 \times 4000 \times 2^2}{0.2 \times 2 \times 9.81}$$

From which $P_1 = 5.503 \times 10^5$ N/m^2

$$P_1 = 5.503 \text{ bar}$$

Example 10.22

A syringe with a frictionless plunger contains water and has at its end a 100 mm long needle of 1 mm diameter. The internal diameter of the syringe is 10 mm. Water density is 1000 kg/m^3. The plunger is pushed at 10 mm/s and the water comes out as a jet.

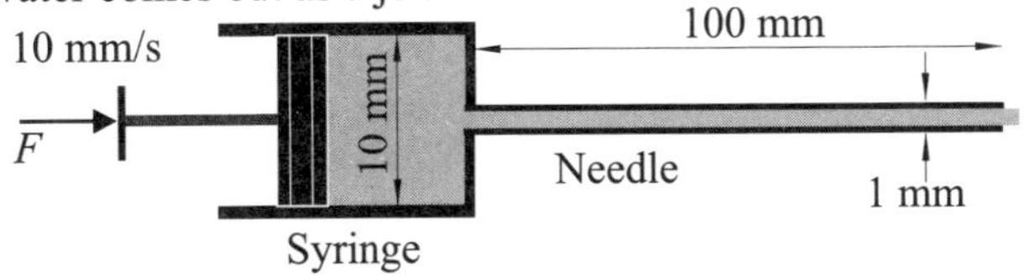

Q(a) Assuming ideal flow, the force F (in N) required on the plunger to push out the water is

(A) 0 (B) 0.04 (C) 0.13 (D) 1.15

Q(b) Neglect losses in the cylinder and assume fully developed laminar viscous flow throughout the needle; the Darcy friction factor is $f = 64/Re$. Where Re is the Reynold number. Given that the viscosity of water is 1.0×10^{-3} kg/m.s, the force F in newton required on the plunger is

(A) 0.13 (B) 0.16 (C) 0.3 (D) 4.4

GATE 2003

Solution

(a) Let v_2 be the velocity of water in needle.

Applying continuity equation $a_1 v_1 = a_2 v_2$,

$$v_2 = \frac{a_1}{a_2} v_1 = \frac{d_1^2}{d_2^2} v_1 = \left(\frac{10}{1}\right)^2 \times 10$$

$$v_2 = 1000 \text{ mm/s} = 1.0 \text{ m/s}$$

Applying Bernoulli's equation between syringe and exit of needle,

$$\frac{P_1}{\rho g} + \frac{v_1^2}{2g} + z_1 = \frac{P_2}{\rho g} + \frac{v_2^2}{2g} + z_2$$

or $$\frac{P_1}{\rho g} = \frac{0}{\rho g} + \frac{v_2^2 - v_1^2}{2g}$$

or $$P_1 = \frac{\rho}{2}(v_2^2 - v_1^2)$$

or $$P_1 = \frac{1000}{2}(1^2 - 0.01^2)$$

or $$P_1 = 499.95 \text{ N/m}^2$$

Force required $F = P_1 A$

$$F = 499.95 \times \frac{\pi}{4} \times \left(\frac{10}{1000}\right)^2$$

$$F = 0.039 \text{ N}$$

(b) Reynolds number in needle,

$$Re = \frac{\rho v_2 d_2}{\mu} = \frac{1000 \times 1 \times \frac{1}{1000}}{1 \times 10^{-3}}$$

$$Re = 1000$$

Darcy friction factor, $f = \frac{64}{Re} = \frac{64}{1000}$

$$f = 0.064$$

Frictional head loss

$$h_f = \frac{4f\, l_2 v_2^2}{d_2 \cdot 2g} = \frac{4 \times 0.064 \times \frac{100}{1000} \times 1^2}{\frac{1}{1000} \times 2 \times 9.81}$$

$$h_f = 0.326\text{ m}$$

Using Bernoulli's equation,

$$\frac{P_1}{\rho g} + \frac{v_1^2}{2g} + z_1 = \frac{P_2}{\rho g} + \frac{v_2^2}{2g} + z_2 + h_f$$

or $$\frac{P_1}{1000 \times 9.81} + \frac{0.01^2}{2 \times 9.81} = \frac{0}{1000 \times 9.81} + \frac{1^2}{2 \times 9.81} + 0.326$$

$$P_1 = 3697.06\ \text{N/m}^2$$

Force required $F = P_1 A$

$$F = 3697.06 \times \frac{\pi}{4} \times \left(\frac{10}{1000}\right)^2$$

$$F = 0.29\,\text{N}$$

Example 10.23

Air flows through a venturi and into atmosphere. Air density is ρ; atmospheric pressure is P_a; throat diameter is D_t; exit diameter is D and exit velocity u. The throat is connected to a spring. The spring constant is k. The bottom surface of the piston is exposed to atmosphere. Due to the flow, the piston moves by distance x. Assuming flow is incompressible and frictionless flow, x is

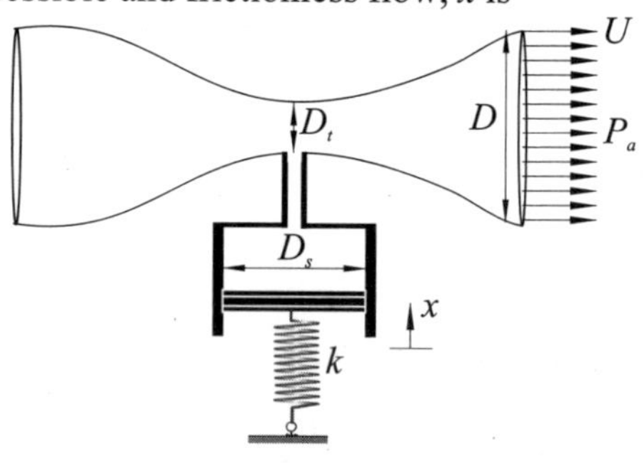

(A) $\frac{\rho u^2}{2k}\pi D_s^2$

(B) $\frac{\rho u^2}{8k}\left(\frac{D^2}{D_t^2} - 1\right)\pi D_s^2$

(C) $\frac{\rho u^2}{2k}\left(\frac{D^2}{D_t^2} - 1\right)\pi D_s^2$

(D) $\frac{\rho u^2}{8k}\left(\frac{D^4}{D_t^4} - 1\right)\pi D_s^2$

GATE 2003

Solution

Let P_t be the pressure at throat.

Applying Bernoulli's equation between throat and exit of pipe,

$$\frac{P_t}{\rho g} + \frac{v_t^2}{2g} + z_t = \frac{P_a}{\rho g} + \frac{v_a^2}{2g} + z_a$$

Since $z_t = z_a$,

$$\frac{P_a - P_t}{\rho g} = \frac{v_t^2 - u^2}{2g} \qquad \text{(i)}$$

Applying continuity equation for incompressible fluid; $A_t v_t = A_a u$

or $$v_t = \frac{A_a}{A_t} u = \frac{\frac{\pi}{4} D^2}{\frac{\pi}{4} D_t^2} u = \left(\frac{D}{D_t}\right)^2 u \qquad \text{(ii)}$$

From Equation (i) and (ii), we obtain

$$\frac{P_a - P_t}{\rho g} = \frac{\left[\left(\frac{D}{D_t}\right)^2 u\right]^2 - u^2}{2g}$$

$$\frac{P_a - P_t}{\rho g} = \frac{\left[\left(\frac{D}{D_t}\right)^4 - 1\right] u^2}{2g} \qquad \text{(iii)}$$

Now consider piston.

Net force on piston due to pressure difference,

$$P_a \frac{\pi}{4} D_s^2 - P_s \frac{\pi}{4} D_s^2 = kx$$

$$x = \frac{(P_a - P_s)}{k} \frac{\pi}{4} D_s^2 \qquad \text{(iv)}$$

From Equation (iii) and (iv), we have

$$x = \frac{\rho\left[\left(\frac{D}{D_t}\right)^4 - 1\right] u^2}{2k} \frac{\pi}{4} D_s^2$$

$$x = \frac{\rho u^2}{8k}\left[\frac{D^4}{D_t^4} - 1\right]\pi D_s^2$$

Example 10.24

For air flow over a flat plate, velocity U and boundary layer thickness (δ) can be expressed respectively.

$$\frac{u}{U_\infty}=\frac{3}{2}\left(\frac{y}{\delta}\right)-\frac{1}{2}\left(\frac{y}{\delta}\right)^3; \quad \delta=\frac{4.64x}{\sqrt{Re_x}}$$

If the free stream velocity is 2 m/s, and air has kinematic viscosity of $1.5\times10^{-5}\ \text{m}^2/\text{s}$ and density of $1.23\ \text{kg/m}^3$, then wall shear stress at $x=1\ \text{m}$, is

(A) $2.36\times10^{2}\ \text{N/m}^2$ (B) $43.6\times10^{-3}\ \text{N/m}^2$

(C) $4.36\times10^{-3}\ \text{N/m}^2$ (D) $2.18\times10^{-3}\ \text{N/m}^2$

GATE 2004

Solution

Boundary layer thickness at $x=1$,

$$\delta=\left[\frac{4.64x}{\sqrt{Re_x}}\right]_{x=1}=\left[\frac{4.64x}{\sqrt{\rho v x/\mu}}\right]_{x=1}=\left[4.64\sqrt{\frac{\mu x}{\rho v}}\right]_{x=1}$$

or $$\delta=\left[4.64\sqrt{\frac{\nu x}{v}}\right]_{x=1}$$

or $$\delta=4.64\sqrt{\frac{1.5\times10^{-5}\times1}{2}}$$

$$\delta=0.012707\ \text{m}$$

Wall shear stress at $x=1$; $\tau=\mu\left[\frac{du}{dy}\right]_{y=0}$

$$\tau=\mu\left[\frac{d}{dy}U_\infty\left\{\frac{3}{2}\left(\frac{y}{\delta}\right)-\frac{1}{2}\left(\frac{y}{\delta}\right)^3\right\}\right]_{y=0}$$

or $$\tau=\mu\frac{3U_\infty}{2\delta}=\rho\nu\times\frac{3U_\infty}{2\delta}$$

or $$\tau=\mu\frac{3U_\infty}{2\delta}=\rho\nu\times\frac{3U_\infty}{2\delta}$$

or $$\tau=1.23\times1.5\times10^{-5}\times\frac{3\times2}{2\times0.012707}$$

$$\tau=4.36\times10^{-3}\ \text{N/m}^2$$

Example 10.25

A smooth flat plate with a sharp leading edge is placed along a gas stream flowing at $U=10$ m/s. The thickness of the boundary layer at section r - s is 10 mm, the breadth of the plate is 1 m (into the paper) and the density of the gas $\rho=1.0\ \text{kg/m}^3$. Assume that the boundary layer is thin, two-dimensional, and follows a linear velocity distribution, $u=U\left(\frac{y}{\delta}\right)$, at the section r - s, where y is the height from the plate. The mass flow rate across the section q - r is

(A) Zero (B) 0.05 (C) 0.10 (D) 0.15

GATE 2006

Solution

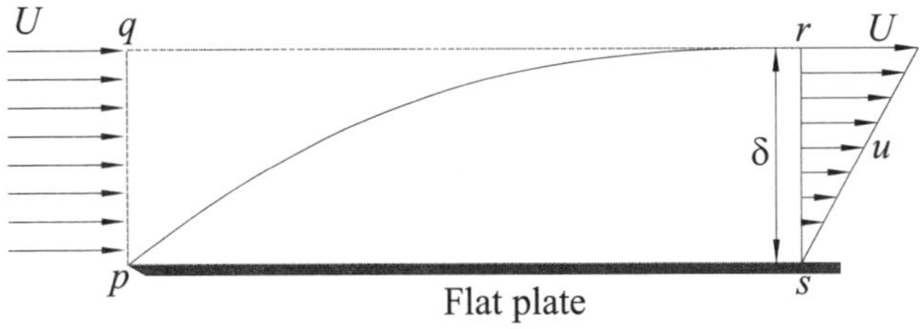

Mass flow rate across r - s,

$$m_{r-s}=\int_0^\delta u\,dy\times1=\int_0^\delta U\left(\frac{y}{\delta}\right)dy\times1$$

or $$m_{r-s}=\frac{U\delta}{2}=\frac{10\times\frac{10}{1000}}{2}$$

$$m_{r-s}=0.05\ \text{kg/s}$$

Mass flow rate across q - p,

$$m_{q-p}=u\times\delta\times1=10\times\frac{10}{1000}\times1$$

$$m_{q-p}=0.1\ \text{kg/s}$$

Mass flow rate across flat plate p - s; $m_{p-s}=0$

Applying the principle of conservation of mass,

$$\sum m=0; \qquad m_{p-q}=m_{p-s}+m_{r-s}+m_{q-r}$$

or $$0.1=0+0.05+m_{q-r}$$

$$m_{q-r}=0.05\ \text{kg/s}$$

Example 10.26

Consider a steady incompressible flow through channel as shown in figure.

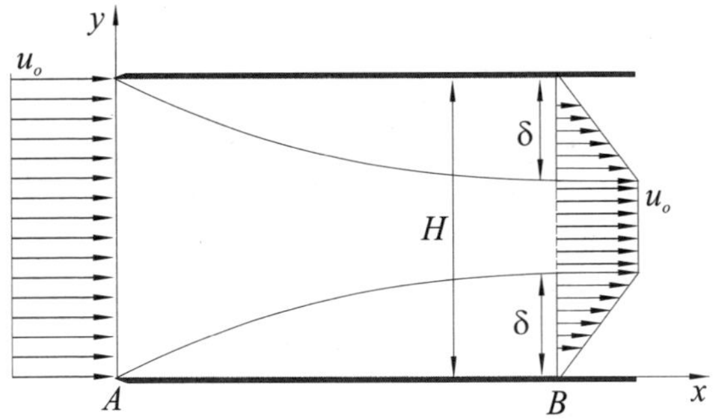

The velocity profile is uniform with a value of u_o at the inlet section A. The velocity profile at section B downstream is

$$u = \begin{cases} V_m\left(\dfrac{y}{\delta}\right) & 0 \le y \le \delta \\ V_m & \delta \le y \le H-\delta \\ V_m\left(\dfrac{H-y}{\delta}\right) & H-\delta \le y \le H \end{cases}$$

Q(a) The ratio $\dfrac{V_m}{u_o}$ is

(A) $\left(1-\dfrac{2\delta}{H}\right)^{-1}$ (B) $\left(1+\dfrac{2\delta}{H}\right)^{-1}$

(C) $\left(1-\dfrac{\delta}{H}\right)^{-1}$ (D) $\left(1+\dfrac{\delta}{H}\right)^{-1}$

Q(b) The ratio $\dfrac{P_A-P_B}{\frac{1}{2}\rho u_o^2}$ (where P_A and P_B are the pressures at sections A and B, respectively, and ρ is the density of the fluid) is

(A) $\left(1-\dfrac{\delta}{H}\right)^{-2}-1$ (B) $\left(1-\dfrac{\delta}{H}\right)^{-2}$

(C) $\left(1-\dfrac{2\delta}{H}\right)^{-2}-1$ (D) $\left(1-\dfrac{\delta}{H}\right)^{-1}$

GATE 2007

Solution

(a) Applying continuity equation between sections A and B,

$$u_o \times H = \int_0^{\delta} V_m\left(\frac{y}{\delta}\right)dy + V_m\,(H-2\delta) + \int_{H-\delta}^{H} V_m\left(\frac{H-y}{\delta}\right)dy$$

or $$u_o \times H = \frac{V_m\delta}{2} + V_m(H-2\delta) + \frac{V_m\delta}{2}$$

or $$u_o \times H = V_m(H-\delta)$$

$$\frac{V_m}{u_o} = \frac{H}{H-\delta}$$

(b) Applying the Bernoull's equation between A and B,

$$\frac{P_A}{\rho g} + \frac{v_A^2}{2g} + z_A = \frac{P_B}{\rho g} + \frac{v_B^2}{2g} + z_B \Rightarrow \frac{P_A-P_B}{\rho g} = \frac{v_B^2 - v_A^2}{2g}$$

Substituting $v_A = u_o$ and $v_B = v_m = u_o\dfrac{H}{H-\delta}$,

$$\frac{P_A-P_B}{\rho g} = \frac{\left(u_o\dfrac{H}{H-\delta}\right)^2 - u_o^2}{2g}$$

or $$\frac{P_A-P_B}{\frac{1}{2}\rho u_o^2} = \left(\frac{H}{H-\delta}\right)^2 - 1$$

$$\frac{P_A-P_B}{\frac{1}{2}\rho u_o^2} = \left[\left(1-\frac{\delta}{H}\right)^{-2} - 1\right]$$

Example 10.27

A large hydraulic turbine is to generate 300 kW at 1000 rpm under a head of 40 m. For initial testing, a 1:4 scale model of the turbine operates under a head of 10 m. The power (in kW) will be

(A) 2.34 (B) 4.68 (C) 9.38 (D) 18.75

GATE 2006

Solution

Given:

Fullscale (Prototype)	**Model**
$P_p = 300\,\text{kW}$	$P_m = ?$
$N_p = 1000\,\text{rpm}$	$H_m = 10\,\text{m}$
$H_p = 40\,\text{m}$	

For similar turbine, each of the dimensions parameters; Head coefficient $= \dfrac{H}{N^2D^2}$; Flow coefficient $= \dfrac{Q}{ND^3}$; and Power coefficient $= \dfrac{P}{N^3D^5}$ must be same for both model and the prototype.

Head coefficient, $$\left(\frac{H}{N^2D^2}\right)_m = \left(\frac{H}{N^2D^2}\right)_p$$

$$\Rightarrow \quad \frac{10}{N_m^2D_m^2} = \frac{40}{N_m^2D_p^2}$$

$$\frac{D_p}{D_m}\frac{N_p}{N_m} = 2$$

Substituting scale 1:4, $$\frac{D_p}{D_m} = 4$$

or $$4 \times \frac{1000}{N_m} = 2$$

$$N_m = 2000\text{ rpm}$$

Power coefficient, $$\left(\frac{P}{N^3D^5}\right)_m = \left(\frac{P}{N^3D^5}\right)_p$$

Power developed by the model,

$$P_m = P_p\left(\frac{N_m}{N_p}\right)^3\left(\frac{D_m}{D_p}\right)^5$$

$$P_m = 300\left(\frac{2000}{1000}\right)^3\left(\frac{1}{4}\right)^5$$

$$P_m = 2.34\,\text{kW}$$

Example 10.28

A Francis turbine running at 200 rpm develops a power of 5000 kW under a head 25 m. Determine the power output under a head of 100 m.

GATE 2001

Solution

Since we are concerned with the same machine, we equate the relations for unit speed, unit discharge and unit power.

Equating unit power ; $\dfrac{P_1}{H_1^{3/2}} = \dfrac{P_2}{H_2^{3/2}}$

or $\quad P_2 = P_1\dfrac{H_2^{3/2}}{H_1^{3/2}}$

$$P_2 = 5000\left(\frac{100}{25}\right)^{3/2}$$

$$P_2 = 40000\,\text{kW}$$

Example 10.29

The instantaneous stream-wise velocity of a turbulent flow is given as follows:

$$u(x, y, z, t) = \bar{u}(x, y, z) + u'(x, y, z, t)$$

The time-average of the fluctuating velocity $u'(x, y, z, t)$ is

(A) $\dfrac{u'}{2}$ (B) $-\dfrac{\bar{u}}{2}$ (C) Zero (D) $\dfrac{\bar{u}}{2}$

GATE 2016

Solution

$$\bar{u}'(x, y, z, t) = \frac{1}{T}\int_0^T u'\,dt = 0$$

The time-average of the fluctuating velocity $u'(x, y, z, t)$ is zero.

Example 10.30

For a floating body, buoyant force acts at the

(A) Centroid of the floating body

(B) Centre of gravity of the body

(C) Centroid of the fluid vertically below the body

(D) Centroid of the displaced fluid

GATE 2016

Solution

For a floating body, buoyant force acts at the centroid of the displaced fluid.

Example 10.31

Consider two hydraulic turbines having identical specific speed and effective head at the inlet. If the speed ratio (N_1/N_2) of the two turbines is 2, then the respective power ratio (P_1/P_2) is__________.

GATE 2016

Solution

Specific speed of turbine is given by

$$N_s = \frac{N\sqrt{P}}{H^{5/4}}$$

Substituting $(N_s)_1 = (N_s)_2$ and $H_1 = H_2$

$$\frac{N_1\sqrt{P_1}}{H^{5/4}} = \frac{N_2\sqrt{P_2}}{H^{5/4}} \quad \text{or} \quad \frac{P_1}{P_2} = \left(\frac{N_2}{N_1}\right)^2$$

$$\frac{P_1}{P_2} = \left(\frac{1}{2}\right)^2$$

$$\frac{P_1}{P_2} = 0.25$$

Example 10.32

An inverted U-tube manometer is used to measure the pressure difference between two pipes A and B, as shown in the figure. Pipe A is carrying oil (specific gravity = 0.8) and pipe B is carrying water. The densities of air and water are 1.16 kg/m^3 and 1000 kg/m^3, respectively. The pressure difference between pipes A and B is _____ kPa.

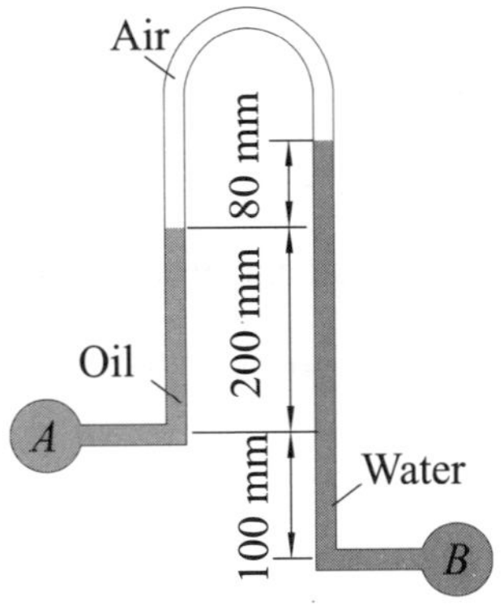

Acceleration due to gravity, $g = 10$ m^2/s.

GATE 2016

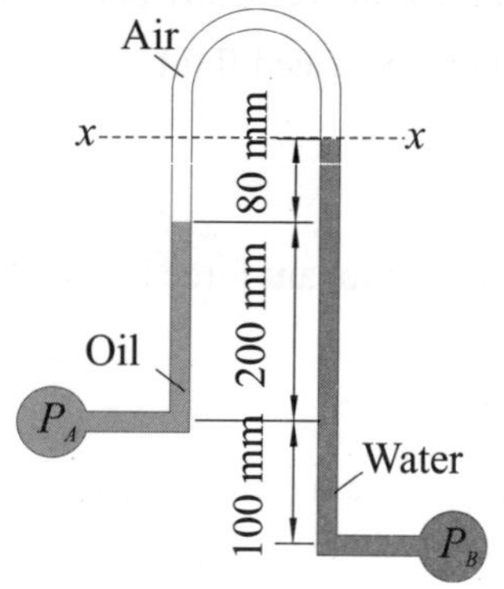

Solution

Equating the pressures of the limb along the horizontal plane x - x, we have

$$(P_{x-x})_{\text{left limb}} = (P_{x-x})_{\text{right limb}}$$

$$P_A - \rho_{\text{oil}} g \times \frac{200}{1000} - \rho_{\text{air}} g \times \frac{80}{1000} = P_B - \rho_{\text{water}} g \times \frac{380}{1000}$$

$$P_A - P_B = \left(\rho_{\text{oil}} \times \frac{200}{1000} + \rho_{\text{air}} \times \frac{80}{1000} - \rho_{\text{water}} \times \frac{380}{1000}\right) g$$

$$P_A - P_B = \left(800 \times \frac{200}{1000} + 1.16 \times \frac{80}{1000} - 1000 \times \frac{380}{1000}\right) \times 10$$

$$P_A - P_B = -2.199 \text{ kPa}$$

Example 10.33

Oil (kinematic viscosity, $\nu_{\text{oil}} = 1.0 \times 10^{-5}$ m^2/s flows through a pipe of 0.5 m diameter with a velocity of 10 m/s. Water (kinematic viscosity, $\nu_w = 0.89 \times 10^{-6}$ m^2/s is flowing through a model pipe of diameter 20 mm. For satisfying the dynamic similarity, the velocity of water (in m/s) is ______.

GATE 2016

Solution

Given: $\nu_{\text{oil}} = 1.0 \times 10^{-5}$ m^2/s, $\nu_w = 0.89 \times 10^{-6}$ m^2/s,

$V_{\text{oil}} = 10$ m/s, $d_{\text{oil}} = 0.5$ m and $d_{\text{water}} = \frac{20}{1000}$ m

Similarity between model and prototype.

Reynold's number, $(Re)_{\text{oil}} = (Re)_{\text{water}}$

or $$\left(\frac{Vd}{\nu}\right)_{\text{oil}} = \left(\frac{Vd}{\nu}\right)_{\text{water}}$$

or $$\frac{10 \times 0.5}{1.0 \times 10^{-5}} = \frac{V_{\text{water}} \times \frac{20}{1000}}{0.89 \times 10^{-6}}$$

$$V_{\text{water}} = 22.25 \text{ m/s}$$

Example 10.34

A steady laminar boundary layer is formed over a flat plate as shown in the figure.

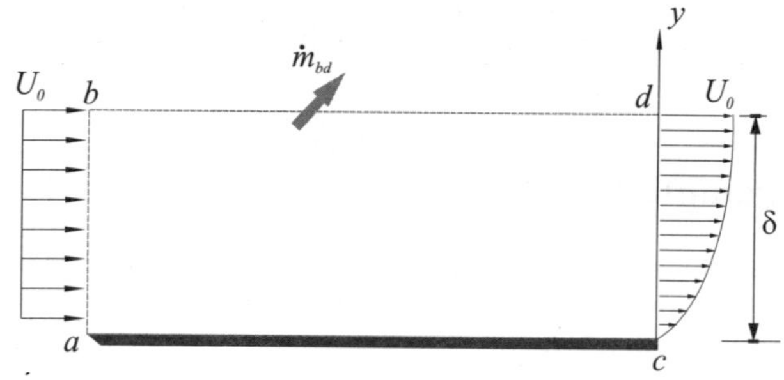

The free stream velocity of the fluid is U_0. The velocity profile at the inlet a-b is uniform, while that at a downstream location c-d is given by

$$u = U_0 \left\{ 2\left(\frac{y}{\delta}\right) - \left(\frac{y}{\delta}\right)^2 \right\}$$

The ratio of the mass flow rate, $\dot{m}_{bd}$, leaving through the horizontal section b-d to that entering through the vertical section a-b is __________.

GATE 2016

Solution

Applying the continuity equation,

$$\dot{m}_{ab} = \dot{m}_{bd} + \dot{m}_{cd}$$

or $$\rho U_0 \delta = \dot{m}_{bd} + \rho \int_0^\delta u\, dy$$

or $$\rho U_0 \delta = \dot{m}_{bd} + \rho \int_0^\delta U_0 \left\{ 2\left(\frac{y}{\delta}\right) - \left(\frac{y}{\delta}\right)^2 \right\} dy$$

or $$\dot{m}_{bd} = \rho U_0 \delta - \rho \int_0^\delta U_0 \left\{ 2\left(\frac{y}{\delta}\right) - \left(\frac{y}{\delta}\right)^2 \right\} dy$$

or $$\dot{m}_{bd} = \frac{1}{3} \rho U_0 \delta$$

$$\frac{\dot{m}_{bd}}{\dot{m}_{ab}} = \frac{\frac{1}{3}\rho U_0 \delta}{\rho U_0 \delta} = \frac{1}{3}$$

$$\frac{\dot{m}_{bd}}{\dot{m}_{ab}} = \frac{1}{3}$$

Example 10.35

The volumetric flow rate (per unit depth) between two streamlines having stream functions ψ_1 and ψ_2 is

(A) $|\psi_1 + \psi_2|$ (B) $\psi_1 \psi_2$ (C) $\frac{\psi_1}{\psi_2}$ (D) $|\psi_1 - \psi_2|$

GATE 2016

Solution

Stream function, $u = \frac{\partial\psi}{\partial y} \Rightarrow \partial\psi = u\partial y$

Volumetric flow rate (per unit depth) $= \int u\partial y \times 1$

$= |\psi_1 - \psi_2|$

Example 10.36

Assuming constant temperature condition and air to be an ideal gas, the variation in atmospheric pressure with height calculated from fluid statics is

(A) Linear (B) Exponential (C) Quadratic (D) Cubic

GATE 2016

Solution

Characteristic gas equation, $\frac{P}{\rho} = RT$

Hydrostatic equation, $\frac{dP}{dz} = -\rho g$

or $\frac{dP}{dz} = -\frac{P}{RT} g$

or $\frac{dP}{P} = -\frac{g}{RT_0} dz$

Here, T_0 = constant (constant temperature)

Integrating $\int_{P_0}^{P} \frac{dP}{P} = -\int_0^z \frac{g}{RT_0} dz$

$$P = P_0 e^{-\frac{g}{RT_0}z}$$

Variation in atmospheric pressure with height is exponential.

Example 10.37

The large vessel shown in the figure contains oil and water. A body is submerged at the interface of oil and water such that 45% of its volume is in oil while the rest is in water. The density of the body is _ _____ kg/m^3.

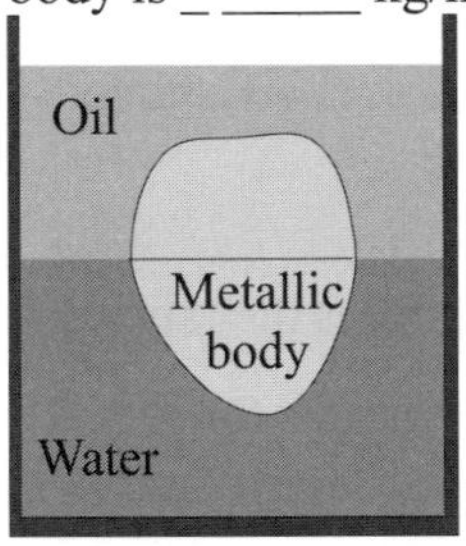

The specific gravity of oil is 0.7 and density of water is 1000 kg/m^3. Acceleration due to gravity g = 10 m/s^2.

GATE 2016

Solution

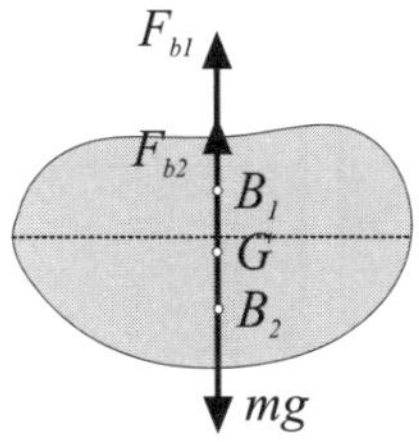

Let V be the volume of body.

Equilibrium equation

$\sum F_v = 0 \Rightarrow F_{b_1} + F_{b_2} - mg = 0$

or $\rho_{oil}\, g \times 0.45V + \rho_{water}\, g \times 0.55V - \rho_b g \times V = 0$

or $700\, g \times 0.45V + 1000\, g \times 0.55V - \rho_b g\, V = 0$

$$\rho_b = 865 \text{ kg/m}^3$$

Example 10.38

Consider fluid flow between two infinite horizontal plates which are parallel (the gap between them being 50 mm). The top plate is sliding parallel to the stationary bottom plate at a speed of 3 m/s. The flow between the plates is solely due to the motion of the top plate. The force per unit area (magnitude) required to maintain the bottom plate stationary is_________ N/m^2.

Viscosity of the fluid μ = 0.44 kg/m-s and density ρ = 888 kg/m^3.

GATE 2016

Solution

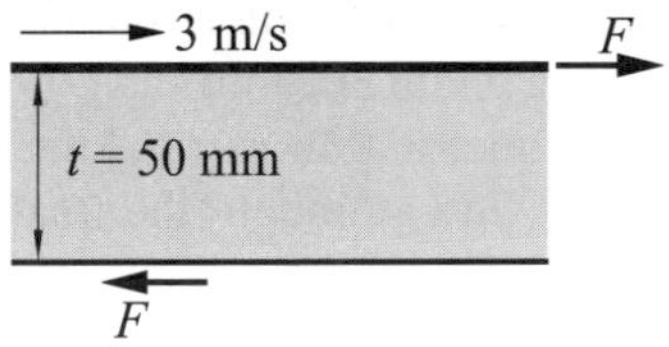

Viscous force, $F = \left(\mu \frac{V}{t}\right) A$

Force per unit area, $\frac{F}{A} = \mu \frac{V}{t} = 0.44 \times \frac{3}{\left(\frac{50}{1000}\right)}$

Force per unit area = 26.4 N/mm^2

Example 10.39

Consider a frictionless, massless and leak-proof plug blocking a rectangular hole of dimensions $2R \times L$ at the bottom of an open tank as shown in the figure. The head of the plug has the shape of a semi-cylinder of radius R. The tank is filled with a liquid of density ρ up to the tip of the plug. The gravitational acceleration is g. Neglect the effect of the atmospheric pressure.

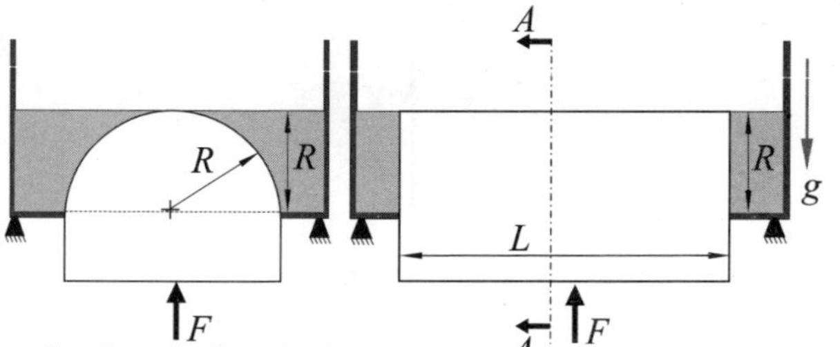

Sectional view A-A

The force F required to hold the plug in its position is

(A) $2\rho R^2 g L\left(1-\frac{\pi}{4}\right)$ (B) $2\rho R^2 g L\left(1+\frac{\pi}{4}\right)$

(C) $\pi R^2 \rho g L$ (D) $\frac{\pi}{2} R^2 \rho g L$

GATE 2016

Solution

The force required to hold the plug in its position,

F = Weight of fluid above the curved surface

$$F = \rho g\left(2R \times R \times L - \frac{\pi R^2}{2} \times L\right)$$

$$F = 2\rho R^2 gL\left(1-\frac{\pi}{4}\right)$$

Example 10.40

A channel of width 450 mm branches into two sub-channels having width 300 mm and 200 mm as shown in figure. If the volumetric flow rate (taking unit depth) of an incompressible flow through the main channel is 0.9 m^3/s and the velocity in the sub-channel of width 200 mm is 3 m/s, the velocity in the sub-channel of width 300 mm is______m/s.

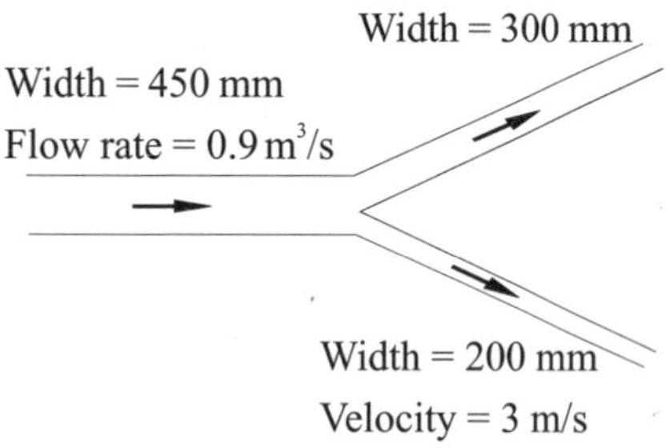

Assume both inlet and outlet to be at the same elevation.

GATE 2016

Solution

Velocity of fluid at section 1-1;

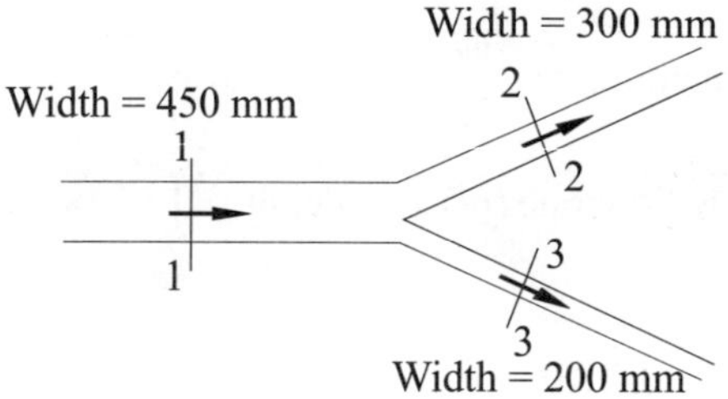

$$v_1 = \frac{Q}{A_1} = \frac{0.9}{\left(\frac{450}{1000}\right)} = 2 \text{ m/s}$$

Applying the continuity equation,

$$A_1 v_1 = A_2 v_2 + A_3 v_3$$

$$\frac{450}{1000} \times 1 \times 2 = \frac{300}{1000} \times 1 \times v_2 + \frac{200}{1000} \times 1 \times 3$$

$$v_2 = 1 \text{ m/s}$$

Example 10.41

For a certain two-dimensional incompressible flow, velocity field is given by $2xy\,i - y^2 j$. The streamlines for this flow are given by the family of curves

(A) $x^2 y^2$ = Constant (B) xy^2 = Constant

(C) $2xy - y^2$ = Constant (D) xy = Constant

GATE 2016

Solution

Velocity, $V = 2xy\,i - y^2 j = u\,i + v\,j$

where $u = 2xy, v = -y^2$

Equation of streamline, $\frac{dx}{u} = \frac{dy}{v} = \frac{dz}{w}$

$$\frac{dx}{2xy} = \frac{dy}{-y^2} \quad \text{or} \quad \frac{dx}{x} + 2\frac{dy}{y} = 0$$

Integrating $\int \frac{dx}{x} + 2\int \frac{dy}{y}$ = Constant

$$x\,y^2 = \text{Constant}$$

Example 10.42

Grashof number signifies the ratio of

(A) Inertia force to viscous force

(B) Buoyancy force to viscous force

(C) Buoyancy force to inertia force

(D) Inertia force to surface tension force

Solution

Grashof number, $Gr = \dfrac{\text{Inertia force} \times \text{Buoyancy force}}{(\text{Viscous force})^2}$

Grashof number signifies the ratio of buoyancy force to viscous force

Example 10.43

The blade and fluid velocities for an axial turbine are as shown in the figure.

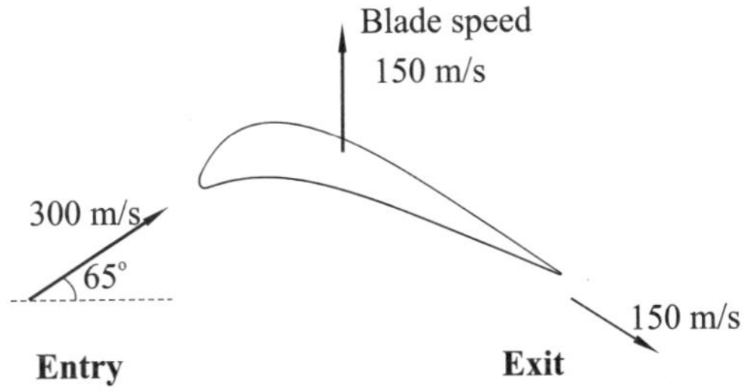

The magnitude of absolute velocity at entry is 300 m/s at an angle of 65° to the axial direction, while the magnitude of the absolute velocity at exit is 150 m/s. The exit velocity vector has a component in the downward direction. Given that the axial (horizontal) velocity is the same at entry and exit, the specific work (in kJ/kg) is__________.

GATE 2016

Solution

Inlet and exit velocity triangle are shown in figure.

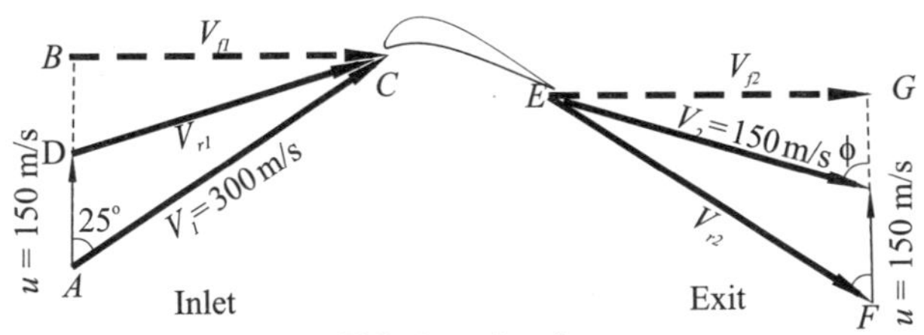

Velocity triangles

From inlet velocity triangle, $V_{f1} = V_1 \sin 25$

$$V_{f1} = 300 \sin 25 = 126.78 \text{ m/s}$$

Inlet whirl velocity, $V_{w1} = V_1 \cos 25$

$$V_{w1} = 300 \times \cos 25 = 271.9 \text{ m/s}$$

Given: $V_{f1} = V_{f2} = 126.78$ m/s

From inlet velocity triangle, $V_{f2} = V_2 \sin \phi$

or $$\phi = \sin^{-1}\left(\frac{V_{f2}}{V_2}\right) = \sin^{-1}\left(\frac{126.78}{150}\right)$$

$$\phi = 57.69°$$

Exit Whirl velocity, $V_{w2} = V_2 \cos 57.69$

$$V_{w1} = 150 \times \cos 57.69 = 80.17 \text{ m/s}$$

Specific work $= (V_{w1}u_1 + V_{w2}u_2)$

Specific work $= (271.9 \times 150 + 80.17 \times 150)$

$$= 52810.5 \text{ J/kg}$$

$$\text{Specific work} = 52.81 \text{ J/kg}$$

Example 10.44

Consider a fully developed steady laminar flow of an incompressible fluid with viscosity μ through a circular pipe of radius R. Given that the velocity at a radial location of $R/2$ from the centerline of the pipe is U_1, the shear stress at the wall is $K\mu \dfrac{U_1}{R}$, where K is________.

GATE 2016

Solution

Velocity of fluid in pipe is given by

$$u = -\frac{1}{4\mu}\frac{\partial P}{\partial r}(R^2 - r^2)$$

Velocity $u = U_1$ at $r = \dfrac{R}{2}$;

$$U_1 = -\frac{1}{4\mu}\frac{\partial P}{\partial r}\left[R^2 - \left(\frac{R}{2}\right)^2\right]$$

$$U_1 = -\frac{3}{4}\frac{1}{4\mu}\frac{\partial P}{\partial r}R^2 \quad \text{(i)}$$

Shear stress is given by $\tau = -\dfrac{r}{2}\dfrac{\partial P}{\partial x}$

Shear stress at the wall $r = R$;

$$\tau_{r=R} = -\frac{R}{2}\frac{\partial P}{\partial x} = K\mu\frac{U_1}{R} \quad \text{(ii)}$$

From Equations (i) and (ii), we have

$$U_1 = -\frac{3}{4}\frac{1}{4\mu}\left(-\frac{2}{R}K\mu\frac{U_1}{R}\right)R^2$$

$$K = \frac{8}{3}$$

Example 10.45

The water jet exiting from a stationary tank through a circular opening of diameter 300 mm impinges on a rigid wall as shown in the figure. Neglect all minor losses and assume the water level in the tank to remain constant. The net horizontal force experienced by the wall is______ kN.

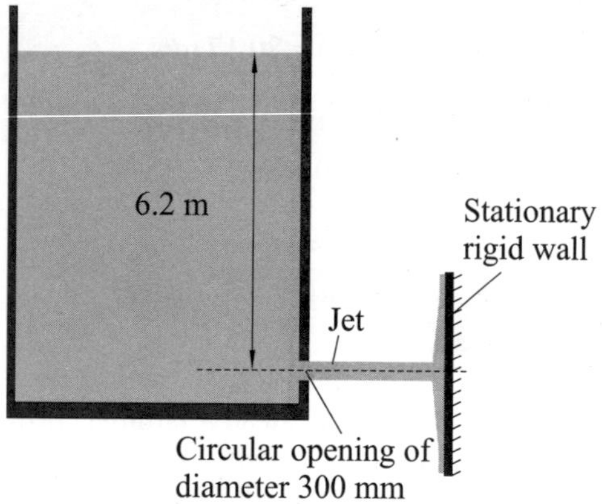

Density of water is 1000 kg/m^3.

Acceleration due to gravity $g = 10$ m/s^2.

GATE 2016

Solution

Velocity of jet, $V = \sqrt{2gh} = \sqrt{2 \times 10 \times 6.2}$

$$V = 11.13 \text{ m/s}$$

Net horizontal force, $F = \dot{m}(V - 0)$

$$F = \rho a V(V-0) = \rho a V^2$$

$$F = 1000 \times \frac{\pi}{4} \times \left(\frac{300}{1000}\right)^2 \times 11.13^2 = 8756.34 \text{ N}$$

$$F = 8.75 \text{ kN}$$

Example 10.46

Consider the two-dimensional velocity field given by $\mathbf{V} = (5 + a_1 x + b_1 y)\mathbf{i} + (4 + a_2 x + b_2 y)\mathbf{j}$, where a_1, b_1, a_2 and b_2 are constants. Which one of the following conditions needs to be satisfied for the flow to be incompressible?

(A) $a_1 + b_1 = 0$ (B) $a_1 + b_2 = 0$

(C) $a_2 + b_2 = 0$ (D) $a_2 + b_1 = 0$

GATE 2017

Solution

Given: $\mathbf{V} = (5 + a_1 x + b_1 y)\mathbf{i} + (4 + a_2 x + b_2 y)\mathbf{j}$

For incompressible flow, $\nabla \mathbf{V} = 0 \Rightarrow \frac{\partial u}{\partial x} + \frac{\partial v}{\partial y} = 0$

or $$\frac{\partial}{\partial x}(5 + a_1 x + b_1 y) + \frac{\partial}{\partial y}(4 + a_2 x + b_2 y) = 0$$

$$a_1 + b_1 = 0$$

Example 10.47

Water (density =1000 kg/m^3) at ambient temperature flows through a horizontal pipe of uniform cross section at the rate of 1 kg/s. If the pressure drop across the pipe is 100 kPa, the minimum power required to pump the water across the pipe, in watts, is________.

GATE 2017

Solution

Given: $\rho = 1000$ kg/m^3, $\dot{m} = 1$ kg/s, $\Delta p = 100$ kPa

Minimum power required to pump $P = \dot{m}gh$

or $$P = \dot{m}g\left(\frac{\Delta p}{\rho g}\right) = \dot{m}\left(\frac{\Delta p}{\rho}\right)$$

$$P = 1 \times \left(\frac{100 \times 10^3}{1000}\right)$$

$$P = 100 \text{ W}$$

Example 10.48

The velocity profile inside the boundary layer for flow over a flat plate is given as $\frac{u}{U_\infty} = \sin\left(\frac{\pi}{2}\frac{y}{\delta}\right)$, where U_∞ is the free stream velocity and δ is the local boundary layer thickness. If δ^* is the local displacement thickness, the value of $\frac{\delta^*}{\delta}$ is

(A) $\frac{2}{\pi}$ (B) $1 - \frac{2}{\pi}$ (C) $1 + \frac{2}{\pi}$ (D) 0

GATE 2017

Solution

Given velocity profile $$\frac{u}{U_\infty} = \sin\left(\frac{\pi}{2}\frac{y}{\delta}\right)$$

Displacement thickness $$\delta^* = \int_0^\delta \left(1 - \frac{u}{U_\infty}\right) dy$$

$$\delta^* = \int_0^\delta \left(1 - \sin\left(\frac{\pi}{2}\frac{y}{\delta}\right)\right) dy = \delta + \left[\frac{2\delta}{\pi}\cos\left(\frac{\pi}{2}\frac{y}{\delta}\right)\right]_0^\delta$$

$$\delta^* = \delta - \frac{2\delta}{\pi}$$

$$\frac{\delta^*}{\delta} = 1 - \frac{2}{\pi}$$

Example 10.49

Consider steady flow of an incompressible fluid through two long and straight pipes of diameters d_1 and d_2 arranged in series. Both pipes are of equal length and the flow is turbulent in both pipes. The friction factor for turbulent flow though pipes is of the form, $f = K(\text{Re})^{-n}$, where K and n are known positive constants and Re is the Reynolds number. Neglecting minor losses, the ratio of the frictional pressure drop in pipe 1 to that in pipe 2, $\left(\dfrac{\Delta P_1}{\Delta P_2}\right)$ is given by

(A) $\left(\dfrac{d_2}{d_1}\right)^{(5-n)}$ (B) $\left(\dfrac{d_2}{d_1}\right)^{5}$ (C) $\left(\dfrac{d_2}{d_1}\right)^{(3-n)}$ (D) $\left(\dfrac{d_2}{d_1}\right)^{(5+n)}$

GATE 2017

Solution

Frictional pressure head drop $\dfrac{\Delta p}{\rho g} = \dfrac{4fLV^2}{d2g}$

$$\Delta p = \frac{4fLV^2}{d2g}\cdot \rho g$$

Substituting $V = \dfrac{Q}{\frac{\pi}{4}d^2} = \dfrac{4Q}{\pi d^2}$ and

$$f = \frac{K}{(\text{Re})^n} = K\left(\frac{\mu}{\rho V d}\right)^n = K(\mu\pi d/\rho 4Q)^n$$

$$\Delta p = \frac{4K(\mu\pi d/\rho 4Q)^n L(4Q/\pi d^2)^2}{d2g}\cdot \rho g$$

$$\Delta p = \frac{4K(\mu\pi/\rho 4Q)^n L(4Q/\pi)^2}{2g}\cdot \rho g\, d^{n-5}$$

$$\frac{\Delta p_1}{\Delta p_2} = \frac{d_1^{\,n-5}}{d_2^{\,n-5}}$$

$$\frac{\Delta p_1}{\Delta p_2} = \left(\frac{d_2}{d_1}\right)^{5-n}$$

Example 10.50

For a steady flow, the velocity field is $\mathbf{V} = (-x^2 + 3y)\,\mathbf{i} + (2xy)\,\mathbf{j}$. The magnitude of the acceleration of a particle at (1, –1) is

(A) 2 (B) 1 (C) $2\sqrt{5}$ (D) 0

GATE 2017

Solution

Let $\mathbf{V} = (-x^2 + 3y)\,\mathbf{i} + (2xy)\,\mathbf{j} = u\,\mathbf{i} + v\,\mathbf{j}$

Acceleration $a_x = \dfrac{\partial u}{\partial t} + u\dfrac{\partial u}{\partial x} + v\dfrac{\partial u}{\partial y}$, $a_y = \dfrac{\partial v}{\partial t} + u\dfrac{\partial v}{\partial x} + v\dfrac{\partial v}{\partial y}$

$a_x = (-x^2 + 3y)(-2x) + 2xy \times 3$; Steady state $\dfrac{\partial u}{\partial t} = 0$

$[a_x]_{(1,-1)} = 2$

$a_y = (-x^2 + 3y)2y + 2xy \times 2x$; Steady state $\dfrac{\partial u}{\partial t} = 0$

$[a_y]_{(1,-1)} = 4$

Magnitude of acceleration $a = \sqrt{a_x^2 + a_y^2} = \sqrt{2^2 + 4^2}$

$$a = 2\sqrt{5}$$

Example 10.51

Which one of the following statement is TRUE?

(A) Both Pelton and Francis turbines are impulse turbines.

(B) Francis turbine is a reaction turbine but Kaplan turbine is an impulse turbine.

(C) Francis turbine is an axial-flow reaction turbine.

(D) Kaplan turbine is an axial-flow reaction turbine.

GATE 2017

Solution

(D) Kaplan turbine is an axial-flow reaction turbine.

Example 10.52

For the stability of a floating body the

(A) centre of buoyancy must coincide with the centre of gravity

(B) centre of buoyancy must be above the centre of gravity

(C) centre of gravity must be above the centre of buoyancy

(D) metacentre must be above the centre of gravity

GATE 2017

Solution

(D) metacentre must be above the centre of gravity

Example 10.53

The arrangement shown in the figure measures the velocity V of a gas of density 1 kg/m^3 flowing through a pipe. The acceleration due to gravity is 9.81 m/s^2. If the manometric fluid is water (density 1000 kg/m^3) and the velocity V is 20 m/s, the differential head h (in mm) between the two arms of the manometer is_______.

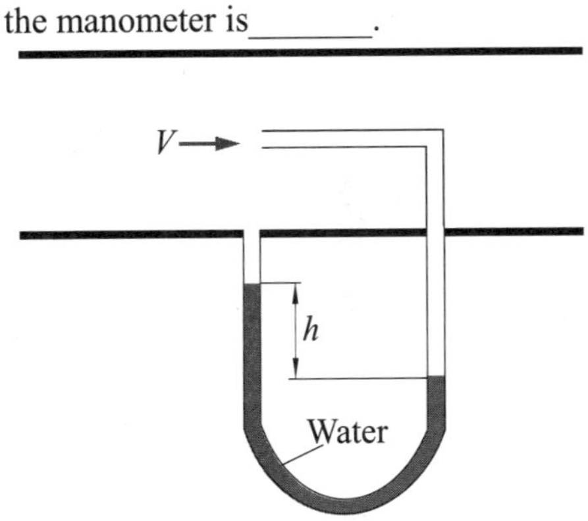

GATE 2017

Solution

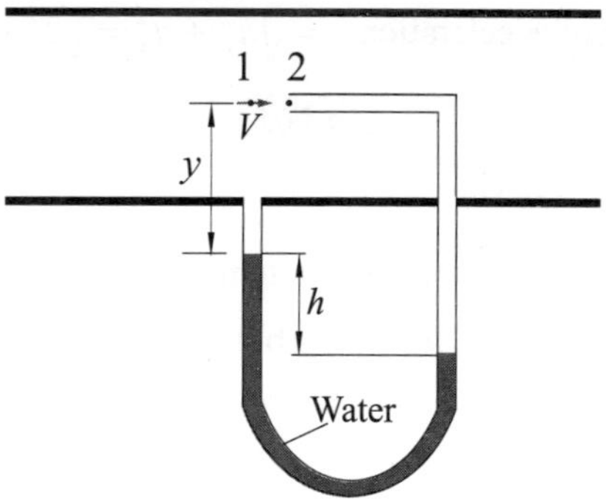

Applying Bernoulli's theorem

$$\frac{p_1}{\rho g}+\frac{v_1^2}{2g}+z_1=\frac{p_2}{\rho g}+\frac{v_2^2}{2g}+z_2; \qquad [z_1=z_2,\ v_2=0]$$

$$v_1=\sqrt{2g\frac{p_2-p_1}{\rho g}} \qquad \text{(i)}$$

Equating the pressure on the limbs along the horizontal plane $x-x$, we obtain

$$p_1+\rho gy+\rho_w gh=p_2+\rho gy+\rho g(y+h)$$

$$\frac{p_2-p_1}{\rho g}=\left(\frac{\rho_w}{\rho}-1\right)h \qquad \text{(ii)}$$

From equations (i) and (ii), we obtain

$$v_1=\sqrt{2g\left(\frac{\rho_w}{\rho}-1\right)h}$$

$$20=\sqrt{2\times 9.81\left(\frac{1000}{1}-1\right)\frac{h}{1000}}$$

$$h=20.38\text{ mm}$$

Example 10.54

A 60 mm-diameter water jet strikes a plate containing a hole of 40 mm diameter as shown in the figure. Part of the jet passes through the hole horizontally, and the remaining is deflected vertically. The density of water is 1000 kg/m^3. If velocities are as indicated in the figure, the magnitude of horizontal force (in N) required to hold the plate is ____.

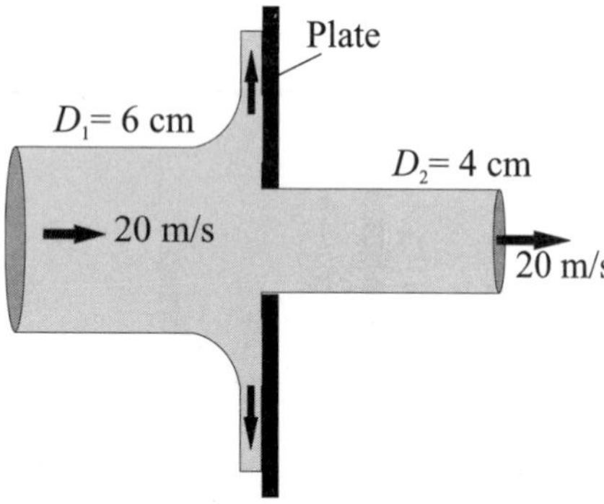

Solution

Horizontal force required to hold the plate

$$F_x=(\text{Initial momentum}-\text{Final momentum})_{x\text{-direction}}$$

$$F_x=\dot m_1 v_1-\dot m_2 v_2=\rho a_1 v_1 v_1-\rho a_2 v_2 v_2; \qquad v_1=v_2=v$$

$$F_x=\rho v^2(a_1-a_2)$$

$$=1000\times 20^2\times\left[\frac{\pi}{4}\left(\frac{6}{100}\right)^2-\frac{\pi}{4}\left(\frac{4}{100}\right)^2\right]$$

$$F_x=628.32\text{ N}$$

Example 10.55

For the laminar flow of water over a sphere, the drag coefficient C_F is defined as $C_F=F/\rho U^2D^2$, where F is the drag force, ρ is the fluid density, U is the fluid velocity and D is the diameter of the sphere. The density of water is 1000 kg/m^3. When the diameter of the sphere is 100 mm and the fluid velocity is 2 m/s, the drag coefficient is 0.5. If water now flows over another sphere of diameter 200 mm under dynamically similar conditions, the drag force (in N) on this sphere is_____.

GATE 2017

Solution

Given: $C_F=F/\rho U^2D^2$, $\rho=1000$ kg/m^3, $D=100$ mm, $U=2$ m/s, $C_F=0.5$.

Given that the condition is dynamic similarity, and in the given condition, inertia and viscous force plays major role, hence Reynold's number should be same for both model and prototype.

$$(\text{Re})_1=(\text{Re})_2 \quad\Rightarrow\quad \frac{\rho_1U_1D_1}{\mu_1}=\frac{\rho_2U_2D_2}{\mu_2}$$

Same fluid (water) is flowing on both sphere, $\rho_1=\rho_2$, $\mu_1=\mu_2$

$$U_1D_1=U_2D_2 \quad\Rightarrow\quad 2\times 100=U_2\times 200$$

$$U_2=1\text{ m/s}$$

$$\text{Drag force } F_2=C_F\rho U_2^2D_2^2=0.5\times 1000\times 1^2\times\frac{200}{1000}$$

$$F_2=20\text{ N}$$

Example 10.56

For a two-dimensional incompressible flow field given by $\mathbf{u}=A(x\,\mathbf{i}-y\,\mathbf{j})$, where $A>0$, which one of the following statements is FALSE?

(A) It satisfies continuity equation.

(B) It is unidirectional when $x\to 0$ and $y\to\infty$.

(C) Its streamlines are given by $x=y$.

(D) It is irrotational.

GATE 2018

Solution

The equation of a streamline in two-dimensional flow is

$$\frac{dx}{Ax} = \frac{dy}{-Ay} \Rightarrow \int \frac{dx}{x} + \int \frac{dy}{y} = c$$

$$\ln x + \ln y = c$$

Streamline equation $xy = C$ Option (C) is FALSE

Example 10.57

A flat plate of width $L = 1\,\text{m}$ is pushed down with a velocity $U = 0.01$ m/s towards a wall resulting in the drainage of the fluid between the plate and the wall as shown in the figure. Assume two-dimensional incompressible flow and that the plate remains parallel to the wall. The average velocity, u_{avg} of the fluid (in m/s) draining out at the instant shown in the figure is ______.

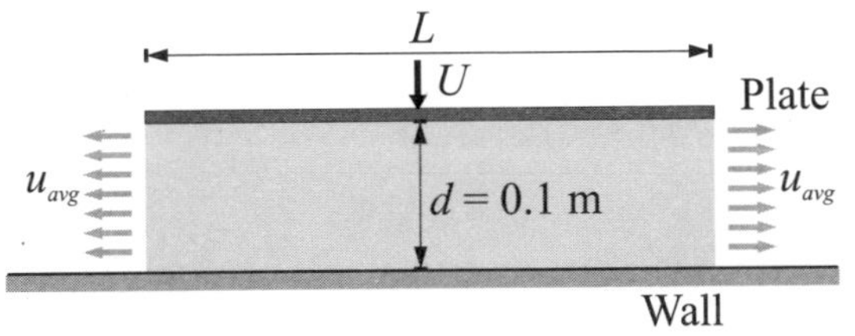

GATE 2018

Solution

Let B be the width of plate.

Applying continuity equation

$$L \times B \times U = 2d \times B \times u_{avg}$$

$$u_{avg} = \frac{LU}{2d} = \frac{1 \times 0.01}{2 \times 0.1}$$

$$u_{avg} = 0.05 \text{ m/s}$$

Example 10.58

For a Pelton wheel with a given water jet velocity, the maximum output power from the Pelton wheel is obtained when the ratio of the bucket speed to the water jet speed is_______ .

GATE 2018

Solution

Output Power, $P = \rho Q(V_{w1} + V_{w2})u$

or $P = \rho Q(V_1 - u)u(1 + k\cos\phi)$

For maximum efficiency $\frac{dP}{du} = 0 \Rightarrow V_1 - 2u = 0$

or $\frac{u}{V_1} = \frac{1}{2}$

$$\frac{u}{V_1} = 0.5$$

Example 10.59

A tank open at the top with a water level of 1 m, as shown in the figure, has a hole at a height of 0.5 m. A free jet leaves horizontally from the smooth hole. The distance X (in m) where the jet strikes the floor is

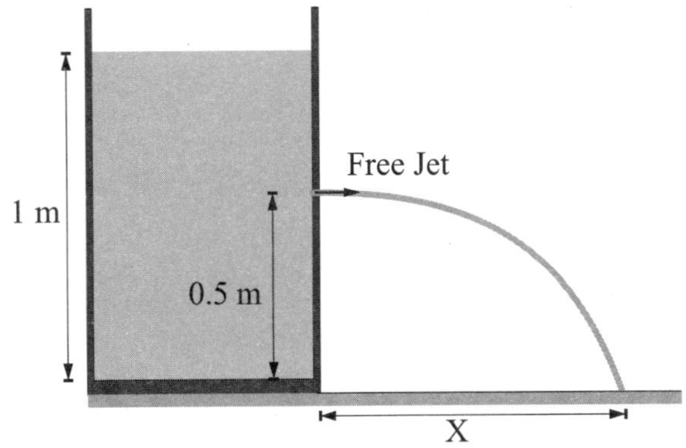

GATE 2018

(A) 0.5 (B) 1.0 (C) 2.0 (D) 4.0

Solution

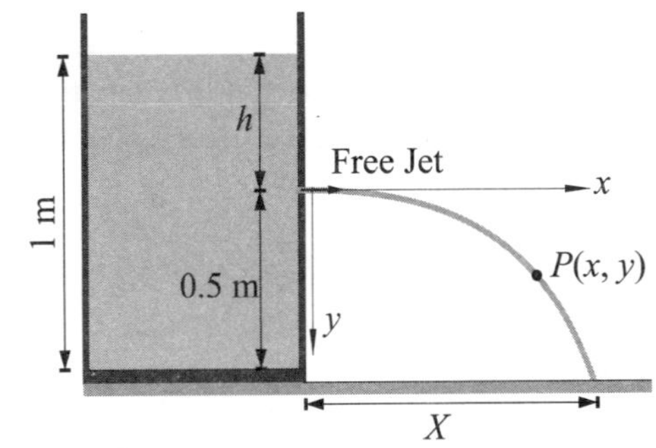

Velocity of jet at hole, $v = \sqrt{2gh}$

Applying equations of motion.

$$x = vt \qquad \text{(i)}$$

$$-y = 0 \times t - \frac{1}{2}gt^2 \qquad \text{(ii)}$$

Eliminating t from Equations (i) and (ii), we have

$$x = v \times \sqrt{\frac{2y}{g}} = \sqrt{2gh} \times \sqrt{\frac{2y}{g}}$$

$$x = \sqrt{4yh}$$

Substituting $y = 0.5$ m, $h = 0.5$ m and $x = X$

$$X = \sqrt{4 \times 0.5 \times 0.5}$$

$$X = 1\,\text{m}$$

Example 10.60

In a Lagrangian system, the position of a fluid particle in a flow is described as $x = x_0 e^{-kt}$ and $y = y_0 e^{kt}$ where t is the time while x_o, y_o and k are constants. The flow is

(A) unsteady and one-dimensional

(B) steady and two-dimensional

(C) steady and one-dimensional

(D) unsteady and two-dimensional

GATE 2018

Solution

Position of fluid particle, $x = x_o e^{-kt}$ and $y = y_o e^{kt}$

$$u = \frac{\partial x}{\partial t} = \frac{\partial}{\partial t}(x_o e^{-kt}) = -kx_o e^{-kt}$$

$$v = \frac{\partial y}{\partial t} = \frac{\partial}{\partial t}(y_o e^{kt}) = ky_o e^{kt}$$

$$\mathbf{V} = u\,\mathbf{i} + v\,\mathbf{j} = -kx_o e^{-kt}\,\mathbf{i} + ky_o e^{kt}\,\mathbf{j}$$

u and v are non-zero scalar, $t \geq 0$, so it is 2D flow.

$$\frac{\partial u}{\partial x} + \frac{\partial v}{\partial y} = 0 + 0$$

$$\frac{\partial u}{\partial x} + \frac{\partial v}{\partial y} = 0, \text{ Continuity equation satisfy}$$

$$\frac{\partial u}{\partial t} = k^2 x_o e^{-kt} \neq 0$$

$$\frac{\partial v}{\partial t} = k^2 y_o e^{kt} \neq 0$$

$$\frac{\partial u}{\partial t} \neq 0 \text{ and } \frac{\partial v}{\partial t} \neq 0, \text{ Flow is unsteady}$$

Example 10.61

A sprinkler shown in the figure rotates about its hinge point in a horizontal plane due to water flow discharged through its two exit nozzles. The total flow rate Q through the sprinkler is 1 litre/sec and the cross-sectional area of each exit nozzle is 1 cm^2. Assuming equal flow rate through both arms and a frictionless hinge, the steady state angular speed of rotation (in rad/s) of the sprinkler is_________.

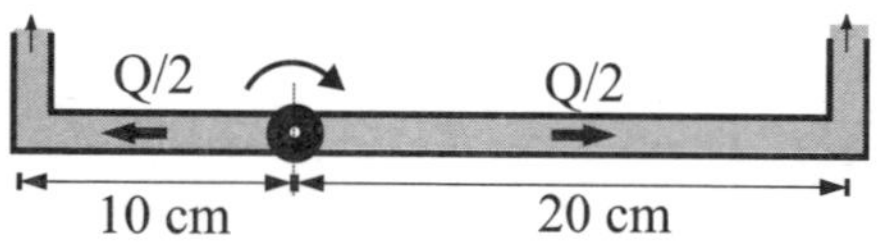

GATE 2018

Solution

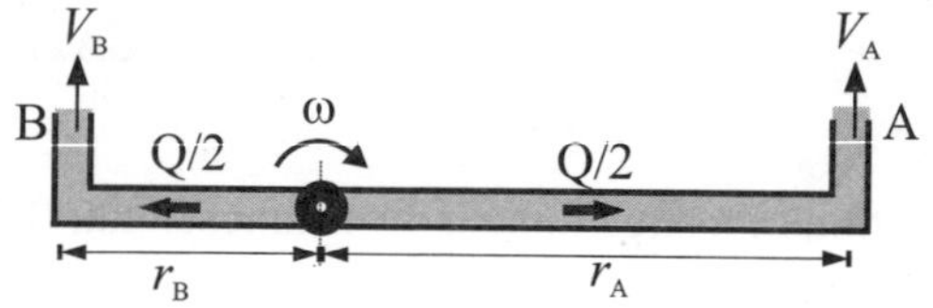

Relative velocity of water with sprinkler.

$$V_A = V_B = \frac{Q/2}{A} = \frac{1 \times 10^{-3}/2}{1 \times 10^{-4}} = 5$$

$$V_A = V_B = 5 \text{ m/s}$$

Absolute velocity of water at B, $(V_B)_{abs} = V_B + \omega \times r_B$

$$(V_B)_{abs} = 5 + 0.1\omega$$

Absolute velocity of water at A, $(V_A)_{abs} = V_A - \omega \times r_A$

$$(V_A)_{abs} = 5 - 0.2\omega$$

External torque to the sprinkler is zero.

$$m_A (V_A)_{abs} r_A - m_B (V_B)_{abs} r_B = 0$$

$$\rho \frac{Q}{2}(5 - 0.2\omega) \times 0.2 - \rho \frac{Q}{2}(5 + 0.1\omega) \times 0.1 = 0$$

$$1 - 0.02\omega - 0.5 - 0.01\omega = 0$$

$$\omega = 10 \text{ rad/s}$$

Example 10.62

A solid block of 2.0 kg mass slides steadily at a velocity v along a vertical wall as shown in the figure below. A thin oil film of thickness h = 0.15 mm provides lubrication between the block and the wall. The surface area of the face of the block in contact with the oil film is 0.04 m^2. The velocity distribution within the oil film gap is linear as shown in the figure. Take dynamic viscosity of oil as 7×10^{-3} Pa-s and acceleration due to gravity as 10 m/s^2. Neglect weight of the oil. The terminal velocity v (in m/s) of the block is _________ .

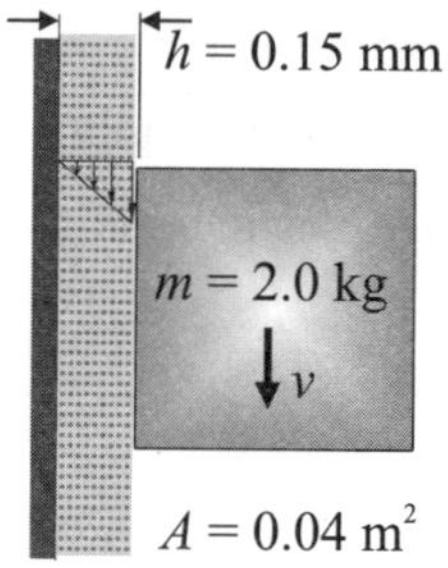

GATE 2018

Solution

Under steady state at terminal velocity of block.

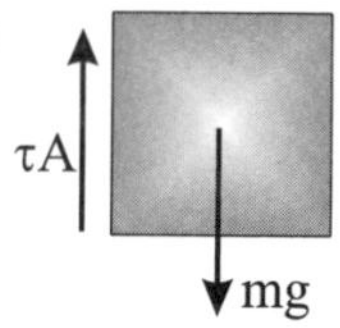

$$\sum F_y = 0 \quad \Rightarrow \quad mg - \tau A = 0$$

or $$mg - \mu \frac{v}{h} A = 0$$

$$2.0 \times 10 - 7 \times 10^{-3} \times \frac{v}{(0.15/1000)} \times 0.04 = 0$$

$$v = 10.714 \text{ m/s}$$

Example 10.63

The viscous laminar flow of air over a flat plate results in the formation of a boundary layer. The boundary layer thickness at the end of the plate of length L is δ_L. When the plate length is increased to twice its original length, the percentage change in laminar boundary layer thickness at the end of the plate (with respect to δ_L) is ___ .

GATE 2018

Solution

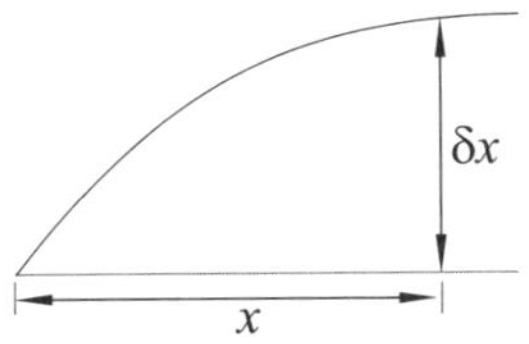

Laminar Boundary layer thickness

$$\delta_x = \frac{5x}{\sqrt{Re_x}} = \frac{5x}{\sqrt{\frac{\rho v x}{\mu}}} = 5\sqrt{\frac{\mu x}{\rho v}}$$

$$\delta_x \propto \sqrt{x}$$

$$\frac{\delta_{2L}}{\delta_L} = \sqrt{2}$$

% change in laminar boundary layer thickness

$$= \frac{\delta_{2L} - \delta_L}{\delta_L} \times 100$$

$$= (\sqrt{2} - 1)100$$

% change in laminar boundary layer thickness = 41.42%

Example 10.64

Air flows at the rate of 1.5 m^3/s through a horizontal pipe with a gradually reducing cross-section as shown in the figure. The two cross-sections of the pipe have diameters of 400 mm and 200 mm. Take the air density as 1.2 kg/m^3 and assume inviscid incompressible flow. The change in pressure $(p_2 - p_1)$ (in kPa) between sections 1 and 2 is

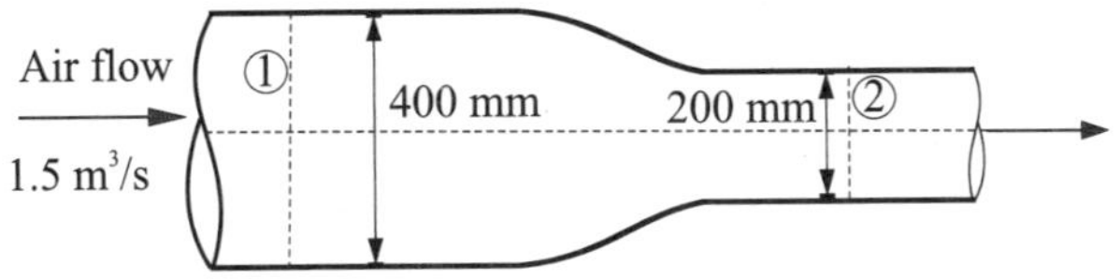

(A) – 1.28 (B) 2.56 (C) – 2.13 (D) 1.28

GATE 2018

Solution

Given that $Q = 1.5\ m^3/s$, $d_1 = 400$ mm, $d_2 = 200$ mm, ρ = 1.2 kg/m^3 and fluid is inviscid incompressible flow.

$$v_1 = \frac{4Q}{\pi d_1^2} = \frac{4 \times 1.5}{\pi (0.4)^2} = 11.93\ m/s$$

$$v_2 = \frac{4Q}{\pi d_2^2} = \frac{4 \times 1.5}{\pi (0.2)^2} = 47.74\ m/s$$

Applying Bernoulli's equation

$$\frac{p_1}{\rho g} + \frac{v_1^2}{2g} + z_1 = \frac{p_2}{\rho g} + \frac{v_2^2}{2g} + z_2$$

or $$p_2 - p_1 = \frac{\rho}{2}(v_1^2 - v_2^2)$$

$$p_2 - p_1 = \frac{1.2}{2}(11.93^2 - 47.74^2) = -1282.06$$

$$p_2 - p_1 = -1.28\ kPa$$

Example 10.65

A frictionless circular piston of area $10^{-2}\ m^2$ and mass 100 kg sinks into a cylindrical container of the same area filled with water of density 1000 kg/m^3 as shown in the figure. The container has a hole of area $10^{-3}\ m^2$ at the bottom that is open to the atmosphere. Assuming there is no leakage from the edges of the piston and considering water to be incompressible, the magnitude of the piston velocity (in m/s) at the instant shown is _____.

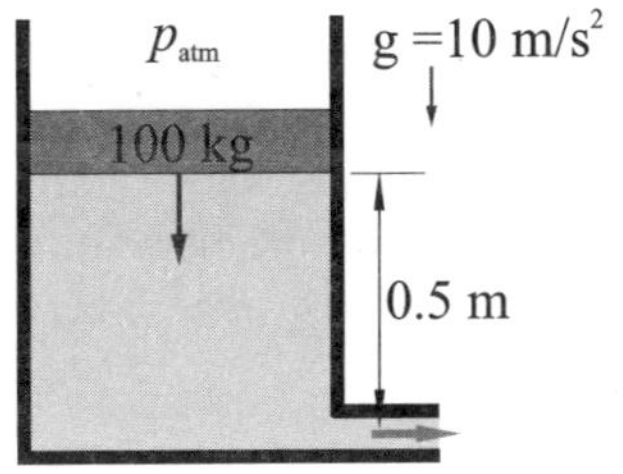

GATE 2018

Solution

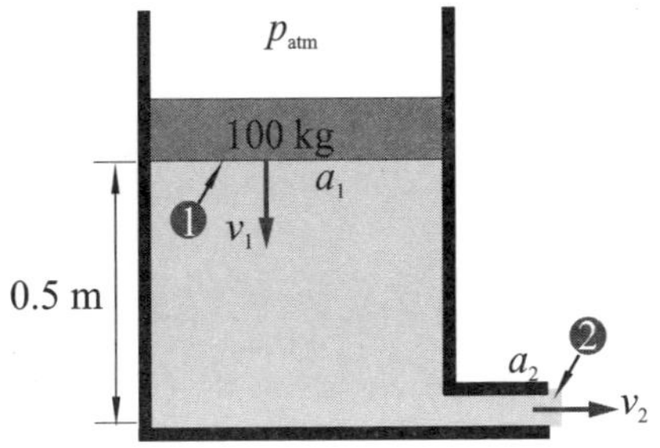

Continuity equation, $a_1 v_1 = a_2 v_2$

$$10^{-2} v_1 = 10^{-3} v_2 \quad \Rightarrow \quad v_2 = 10 v_1$$

Applying Bernoulli's equation

$$\frac{p_1}{\rho g}+\frac{v_1^2}{2g}+z_1=\frac{p_2}{\rho g}+\frac{v_2^2}{2g}+z_2$$

Substituting $v_2=10v_1$, $p_1=p_{atm}+\dfrac{100\times 9.81}{10^{-2}}$, $p_2=p_{atm}$, $z_1=0.5$ m and $z_2=0$.

$$\frac{\left(p_{atm}+\dfrac{100\times 9.81}{10^{-2}}\right)}{\rho g}+\frac{v_1^2}{2g}+0.5=\frac{p_{atm}}{\rho g}+\frac{(10v_1)^2}{2g}+0$$

or
$$\frac{99v_1^2}{2\times 9.81}=10.5$$

$$v_1=1.456 \text{ m/s}$$

Example 10.66

As per common design practice, the three types of hydraulic turbines, in descending order of flow rate, are

(A) Kaplan, Francis, Pelton (B) Pelton, Francis, Kaplan

(C) Francis, Kaplan, Pelton (D) Pelton, Kaplan, Francis

GATE 2019

Solution

(A) Kaplan, Francis, Pelton

Example 10.67

Water flows through a pipe with a velocity given by $\vec{V}=\left(\dfrac{4}{t}+x+y\right)j$ m/s, where j is the unit vector in the y direction, t (>0) is in seconds, and x and y are in meters. The magnitude of total acceleration at the point $(x, y)=(1,1)$ at $t=2$ s is ______ m/s^2.

GATE 2019

Solution

For given fluid flow field $\mathbf{V}=\left(\dfrac{4}{t}+x+y\right)j \Rightarrow u=0$, $v=\dfrac{4}{t}+x+y$, $w=0$

Acceleration of fluid; $$\boldsymbol{a}=\frac{\partial \mathbf{V}}{\partial t}+u\frac{\partial \mathbf{V}}{\partial x}+v\frac{\partial \mathbf{V}}{\partial y}+w\frac{\partial \mathbf{V}}{\partial z}$$

$$\boldsymbol{a}=-\frac{4}{t^2}j+0+\left(\frac{4}{t}+x+y\right)j+0=\left(-\frac{4}{t^2}+\frac{4}{t}+x+y\right)j$$

Total acceleration at the point $(x, y)=(1,1)$ at $t=2$ s is

$$\boldsymbol{a}=\left(-\frac{4}{2^2}+\frac{4}{2}+1+1\right)j=3j$$

$$a=3$$

Example 10.68

Two immiscible, incompressible, viscous fluids having same densities but different viscosities are contained between two infinite horizontal parallel plates, 2 m apart as shown below. The bottom plate is fixed and the upper plate move to the right with a constant velocity of 3 m/s. With the assumptions of Newtonian fluid, steady, and fully developed laminar flow with zero pressure gradient in all directions, the momentum equations simplify to

$$\frac{d^2u}{dx^2}=0.$$

If the dynamic viscosity of the lower fluid, μ_2, is twice that of the upper fluid, μ_1, then the velocity at the interface (round off to two decimal places) is ________ m/s.

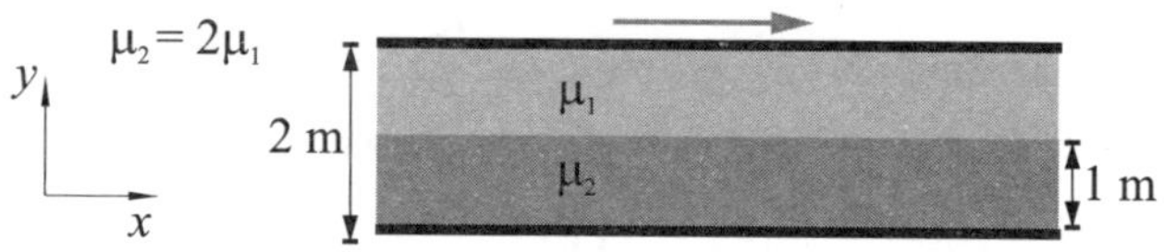

GATE 2019

Solution

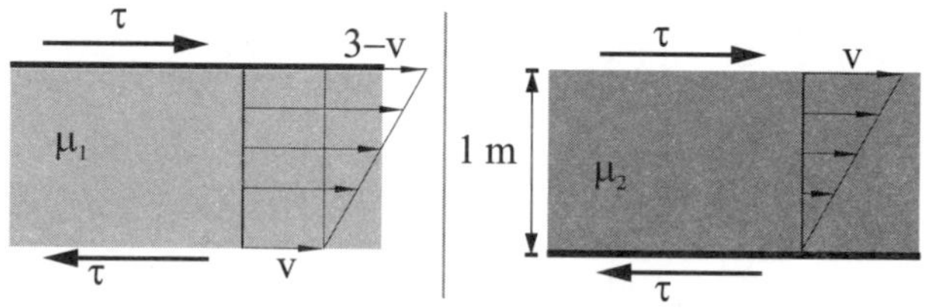

Free-body diagram and velocity profile of fluid 1 and flud 2 are shown in figure.

Given: $\dfrac{d^2u}{dx^2}=0 \Rightarrow \dfrac{du}{dx}=c_1$ and $u=c_1x+c_2$

Shear stress, $$\tau=\mu_1\frac{3-v}{1}=\mu_2\frac{v-0}{1}$$

Substituting $\mu_2=2\mu_1$, we have

$$\mu_1(3-v)=2\mu_1 v$$

$$v=1 \text{ m/s}$$

Example 10.69

A cube of side 100 mm is placed at the bottom of an empty container on one of its faces. The density of the material of the cube is 800 kg/m^3. Liquid of density 1000 kg/m^3 is now poured into the container. The minimum height to which the liquid needs to be poured into the container for the cube to just lift up is _______ mm.

GATE 2019

Solution

Free-body diagram of floating body is shown in figure.

Let h be the height of fluid.

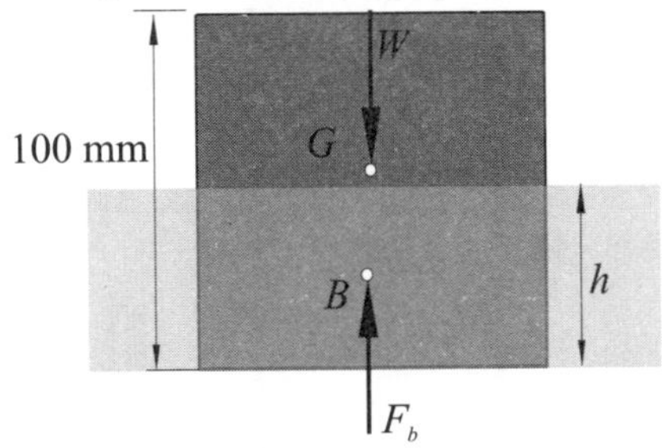

Cube is just about to lift, when

Weight of body = Buoyant force

$F_B \uparrow = W \downarrow \Rightarrow \rho_f g V = \rho_b g V$

$1000 \times 100 \times 100 \times h = 800 \times 100 \times 100 \times 100$

$$h = 80\,\text{mm}$$

Example 10.70

A two-dimensional incompressible frictionless flow field is given by $\vec{u} = x\,i - y\,j$. If ρ is the density of the fluid, the expression for pressure gradient vector at any point in the flow field is given as

(A) $\rho(x\,i + y\,j)$ (B) $-\rho(x\,i + y\,j)$

(C) $\rho(x\,i - y\,j)$ (D) $-\rho(x^2\,i + y^2\,j)$

GATE 2019

Solution

For given flow field $u = x,\ v = -y,\ w = 0$

Euler's equation of motion in x and y- directions are

$$X - \frac{1}{\rho}\frac{\partial p}{\partial x} = \frac{\partial u}{\partial t} + u\frac{\partial u}{\partial x} + v\frac{\partial u}{\partial y} + w\frac{\partial u}{\partial z}$$

$$0 - \frac{1}{\rho}\frac{\partial p}{\partial x} = 0 + x \times 1 + 0 + 0 \qquad [\text{External force } X = 0]$$

$$\frac{\partial p}{\partial x} = -\rho x$$

$$Y - \frac{1}{\rho}\frac{\partial p}{\partial y} = \frac{\partial v}{\partial t} + u\frac{\partial v}{\partial x} + v\frac{\partial v}{\partial y} + w\frac{\partial v}{\partial z}$$

$$0 - \frac{1}{\rho}\frac{\partial p}{\partial y} = 0 + 0 + y + 0 \qquad [\text{External force } Y = 0]$$

$$\frac{\partial p}{\partial y} = -\rho y$$

Pressure gradient vector $\dfrac{\partial p}{\partial x}i + \dfrac{\partial p}{\partial y}j = -\rho x\,i - \rho y\,j$

Pressure gradient vector $= -\rho(x\,i + y\,j)$

Example 10.71

Water enters a circular pipe of length $L = 5.0$ m and diameter $D = 0.20$ m with Reynolds number $Re_D = 500$. The velocity profile at the inlet of the pipe is uniform while it is parabolic at the exit. The Reynolds number at the exit of the pipe is ________.

GATE 2019

Solution

Reynold's number $Re_D = \dfrac{\rho V d}{\mu}$; Where V = Average velocity of fluid in pipe.

$$(Re_D)_{\text{inlet}} = (Re_D)_{\text{Exit}} = 500$$

Example 10.72

Water flows through two different pipes **A** and **B** of the same circular cross-section but at different flow rates. The length of pipe **A** is 1.0 m and that of pipe **B** is 2.0 m. The flow in both the pipes is laminar and fully developed. If the frictional head loss across the length of the pipes is same, the ratio of volume flow rates Q_B / Q_A is ______ (round off to two decimal places).

GATE 2019

Solution

Head loss in pipe; $h_{loss} = \dfrac{32\mu u L}{\rho g d^2}$

$(h_{loss})_A = (h_{loss})_B \Rightarrow \dfrac{32\mu u_A L_A}{\rho g d^2} = \dfrac{32\mu u_B L_B}{\rho g d^2}$

$u_A L_A = u_B L_B \Rightarrow u_A \times 1 = u_B \times 2$

Flow rate ratio; $\dfrac{Q_B}{Q_A} = \dfrac{\pi d^2 u_B / 4}{\pi d^2 u_A / 4}$

$$\frac{Q_B}{Q_A} = \frac{u_B}{u_A} = \frac{u_B}{2u_B} = 0.5$$

$$Q_B / Q_A = 0.5$$

Example 10.73

The aerodynamic drag on a sports car depends on its shape. The car has a drag coefficient of 0.1 with the windows and the roof closed. With the windows and the roof open, the drag coefficient becomes 0.8. The car travels at 44 km/h with the windows and roof closed. For the same amount of power needed to overcome the aerodynamic drag, the speed of the car with the windows and roof open (round off to two decimal places), is _____ km/h (The density of air and the frontal area may be assumed to be constant).

GATE 2019

Solution

Drag force $F_D = \dfrac{1}{2}C_d \rho A u^2$

Power required $P = F_D u = \dfrac{1}{2}C_d\,\rho\,A u^3$

$$P_{Closed} = P_{Open}$$

$$\frac{1}{2}(C_d)_{closed}\, \rho\, A(u^3)_{closed} = \frac{1}{2}(C_d)_{open}\, \rho\, A(u^3)_{open}$$

$$0.1 \times 44^3 = 0.8 \times (u^3)_{Open} \quad \text{or} \quad u_{Open} = \left(\frac{0.1}{0.8}\right)^{1/3} \times 44 = 22$$

$$u_{Open} = 22 \text{ km/h}$$

Example 10.74

An idealized centrifugal pump (blade outer radius of 50 mm) consumes 2 kW power while running at 3000 rpm. The entry of the liquid into the pump is axial and exit from the pump is radial with respect to impeller. If the losses are neglected, then the mass flow rate of the liquid through the pump is ____ kg/s (round off to two decimal places).

GATE 2019

Solution

Power required to drive the pump $P = \dot{m}gh_m$

Where $h_m = \dfrac{V_{w2}u_2 - V_{w1}u_1}{g} = \dfrac{u_2^2}{g}$, $\quad [V_{w2} = u_2,\ V_{w1} = 0]$

$$P = \dot{m}g\left(\frac{u_2^2}{g}\right) = \dot{m}u_2^2; \left[u_2 = \frac{\pi dn}{60} = \frac{\pi \times 2 \times 100 \times 3000}{1000 \times 60} = 5\pi\right]$$

$$\dot{m} = \frac{P}{u_2^2} = \frac{2000}{(5\pi)^2} = 8.11$$

$$\dot{m} = 8.11 \text{ kg/s}$$

10.3 PRACTICE PAPER

Max. Marks:100 **Time: 3 hours**

Q.1 to Q.30 carry one mark each

Q.1 to Q.20 Multiple Choice Questions

Q.1 Which one of the following equations represents the continuity equation for steady compressible fluid flow?

(A) $\nabla \rho V + \dfrac{\partial \rho}{\partial t} = 0$ (B) $\nabla \rho V - \dfrac{\partial \rho}{\partial t} = 0$

(C) $\nabla \cdot V = 0$ (D) $\nabla \cdot \rho V = 0$

Q.2 The pressure variation along the radial direction for vortex flow along a horizontal plane is given as

(A) $\dfrac{\partial P}{\partial r} = -\rho\omega^2 r$ (B) $\dfrac{\partial P}{\partial r} = \dfrac{\rho\omega}{r}$

(C) $\dfrac{\partial P}{\partial r} = \rho\omega^2 r$ (D) $\dfrac{\partial P}{\partial r} = \text{Constant}$

Q.3 Three immiscible liquids of specific density ρ, 2ρ and 3ρ are kept in a jar. The height of the liquids in the jar and at the piezometer fitted to the bottom of the jar are as shown in the given figure. The ratio of $\dfrac{H}{h}$ is

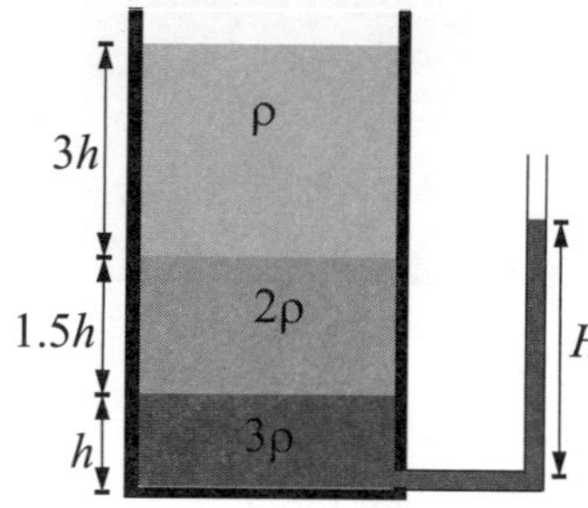

(A) 4 (B) 3.5 (C) 3 (D) 2.5

Q.4 A thin layer of oil of thickness $h = 1$ mm flows steadily down an inclined plane as shown in figure. The oil has a density of 900 kg/m^3. The wall shear stress which can be determined from equilibrium consideration of a fluid element, is

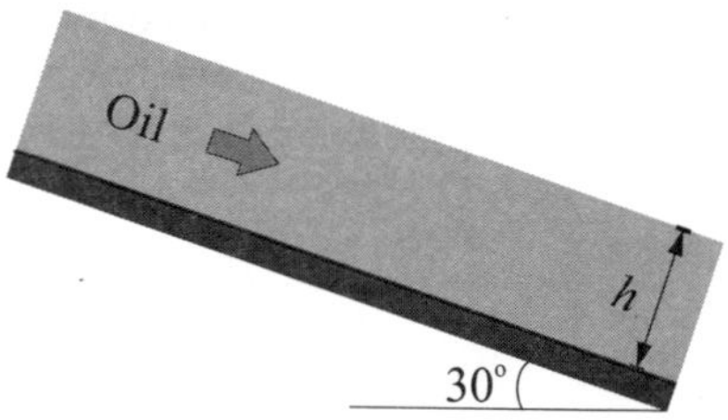

(A) 8.82 N/m^2 (B) 4.41 N/m^2

(C) 2.20 N/m^2 (D) 13.23 N/m^2

Q.5 While water passes through a given pipe at a mean velocity V, the flow is found to change from laminar to turbulent. If another fluid of specific gravity 0.8 and coefficient of viscosity 20% of that of water, is passed through the same pipe, the transition of flow from laminar to turbulent is expected if the flow velocity is

(A) $2V$ (B) V (C) $\dfrac{V}{2}$ (D) $\dfrac{V}{4}$

Q.6 Consider incompressible flow through a two-dimensional open channel. At a certain section *A-A*, the velocity profile is parabolic. Neglecting air resistance at the free surface, find the volume flow rate (in m^3/s) per unit width of the channel.

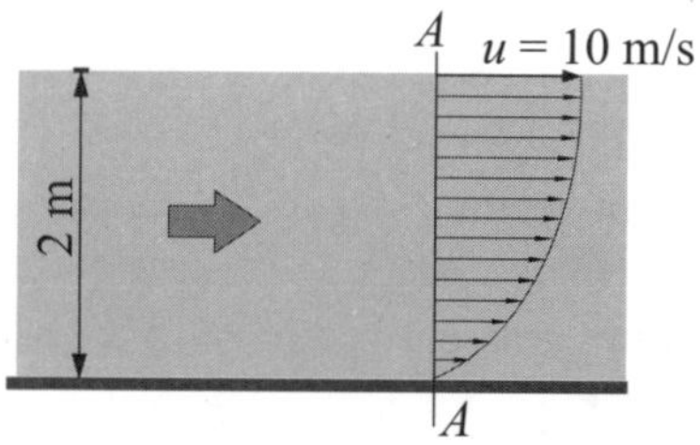

(A) 10 (B) 13.33 (C) 20 (D) 33.33

Q.7 Water is supplied to a tank at the rate of 0.02 m^3/s, as shown in the figure below. The cross-sectional area of the tank is 1 m^2 and the inner diameter of the outlet pipe is 60 mm. At a time when the water level in the tank is increasing at the rate of 5 mm/s, the average velocity (in m/s) of water in the outlet pipe is approximately

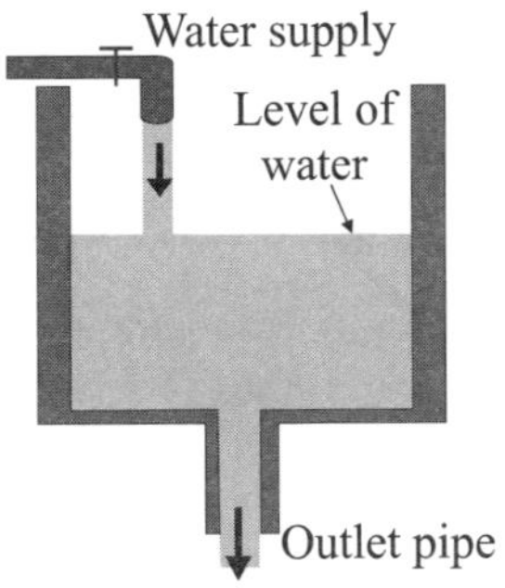

(A) 0.005 (B) 0.06 (C) 5.3 (D) 20

Q.8 A U-tube with both limbs open to atmosphere contains two immiscible liquids of densities ρ_1 and ρ_2 (Figure). Under equilibrium the height h is given by

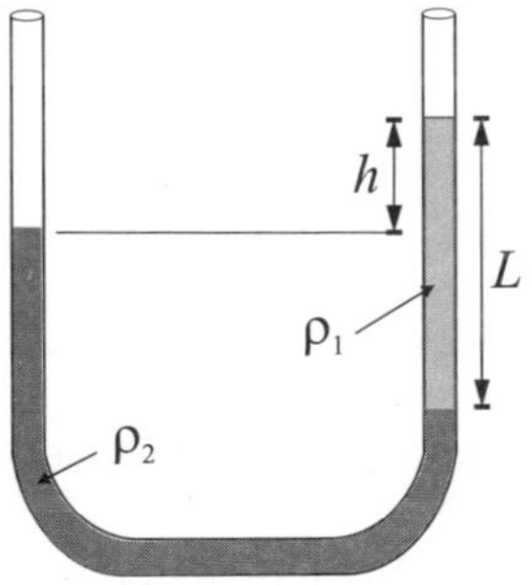

(A) $h = L\left(1 - \frac{\rho_1}{\rho_2}\right)$ (B) $h = L\left(\frac{\rho_2}{\rho_1} - 1\right)$

(C) $h = L\frac{\rho_2}{\rho_1}$ (D) $h = 0$

Q.9 Water enters a large tank at the rate of 5×10^{-2} m^3/s. The liquid from the tank is drawn by a siphon of 10^{-2} m^2 in cross-section as shown in figure. The siphon discharge is at the same level as the box of the tank. Neglecting friction and other minor losses, the steady state height h of water in the tank is

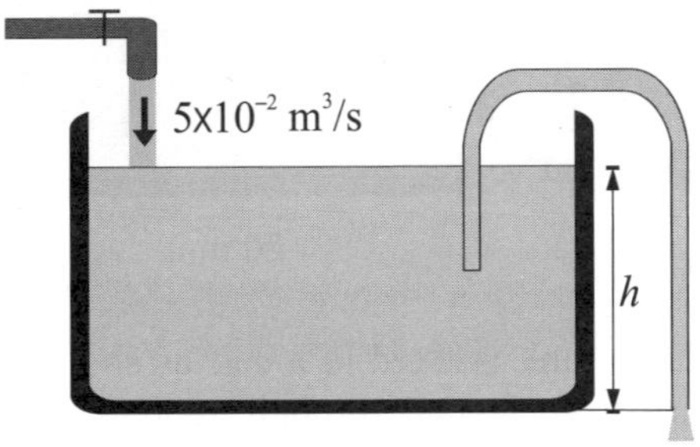

(A) 2.63 m (B) 1.89 m (C) 1.61 m (D) 1.27 m

Q.10 A jet of water with 20 mm diameter nozzle leaves the nozzle tip with 15 m/s and is directed vertically upwards. Assume that jet remains circular and no losses of energy. The diameter of jet above 5 m above nozzle tip is

(A) 23.08 mm (B) 21.34 mm

(C) 22.16 mm (D) None of these

Q.11 A jet of water, issuing horizontality from a stationary nozzle with a velocity of 100 m/s, impinges on a vertical plane which is moving away from the jet with a velocity of 50 m/s. If the jet diameter is 0.1 m, the force on the plate is

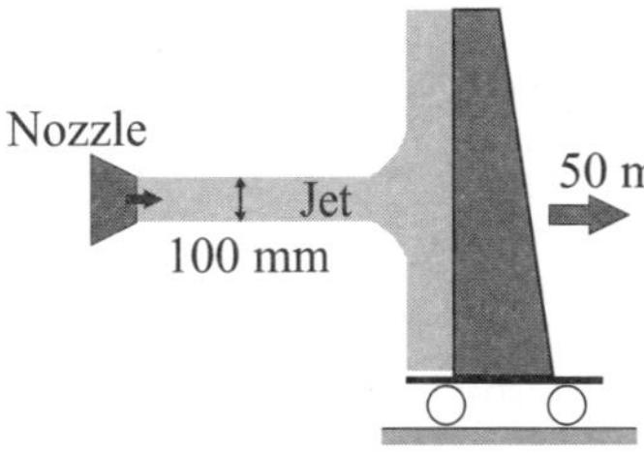

(A) 78.5 kN (B) 19.6 kN (C) 39.3 kN (D) 118 kN

Q.12 A U-tube manometer is placed on a truck that is moving at a velocity v and accelerating at a constant rate a. The distance between the two limbs of the monometer is L and the difference in the level of water in the two lambs is h. The densities of water and air are ρ_w and ρ_a respectively. The acceleration a is given by

(A) $\frac{\rho_w hv^2}{\rho_a L^2}$ (B) $\frac{hv^2}{L^2}$ (C) $g\frac{h}{L}$ (D) $\frac{\rho_w hg}{\rho_a L}$

Q.13 A differential U-tube manometer with mercury as the manometer fluid is used to measure the pressure difference between two section A and B in a horizontal pipe carrying water at steady state as shown in the figure. If the difference in mercury levels in the two limbs of the manometer is 0.75 m, the difference in pressure (kPa) between section A and B is

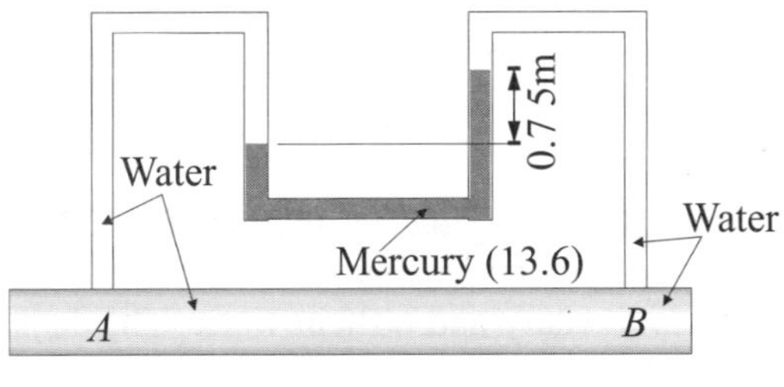

(A) 49.2 (B) 92.7 (C) 9.4 (D) 492.7

Q.14 Water steadily flowing from a 100 mm diameter pipe abruptly enters a 200 mm diameter pipe. If the velocity in the 100 mm dia pipe is 5 m/s, the head loss due to abrupt expansion in terms of height of water is

(A) 1.276 m (B) 0.717 m (C) 0.562 m (D) 1.5 m

Q.15 The metacentric height for a floating spherical ball of radius R and depth of immersion also equal to R is

(A) R (B) $\sqrt{1+R^2}$ (C) $\frac{6}{5}R$ (D) 0

Q.16 If H is the head available for a hydraulic turbine, the power, speed and discharge, respectively are proportional to

(A) $H^{\frac{1}{2}}, H^{\frac{1}{2}}, H^{\frac{3}{2}}$ (B) $H^{\frac{3}{2}}, H^{\frac{1}{2}}, H^{\frac{1}{2}}$

(C) $H^{\frac{1}{2}}, H^{\frac{3}{2}}, H^{\frac{1}{2}}$ (D) $H^{\frac{3}{2}}, H^{\frac{1}{2}}, H$

Q.17 The velocity field is given by
$\mathbf{V} = (axy - z^3)i + (a-2)x^2 j + (1-a)xz^2 k$ is irrotational. The value of a is

(A) 4 (B) 2 (C) 3 (D) 1

Q.18 A Francis turbine has a runner of 4.0 m outer diameter. The breadth at the inlet and also at outlet is 0.8 m and the velocity of flow is constant at 3.0 m/s. The discharge through the turbine is

(A) 15.08 m^3/s (B) 28.28 m^3/s

(C) 30.16 m^3/s (D) 37.70 m^3/s

Q.19 The level of runner exit is 5 m above the tail race, and atmospheric pressure is 10.3 m. The pressure at the exit of the runner for a divergent draft tube can be

(A) 5 m (B) 5.3 m (C) 10 m (D) 10.3 m

Q.20 The gross head on a turbine is 300 m. The length of penstock supplying water from reservoir to the turbine is 400 m. The diameter of the penstock is 1 m and velocity of water through penstock is 5 m/s. If Darcy's friction factor is 0.0098, the net heat on the turbine would be, nearly

(A) 310 m (B) 295 m (C) 200 m (D) 150 m

Q.21 to Q.30 Numerical Answer Questions

Q.21 The speed ratio of a Pelton-wheel operating under a head of 900 m is 0.45. What is the peripheral velocity of the turbine wheel? ____.

Q.22 A metallic body floats at the interface of mercury (13.6) and water in such a way that 40% of its volume in submerged in mercury and 60% in water. The density (in kg/m^3) of metallic body is____________.

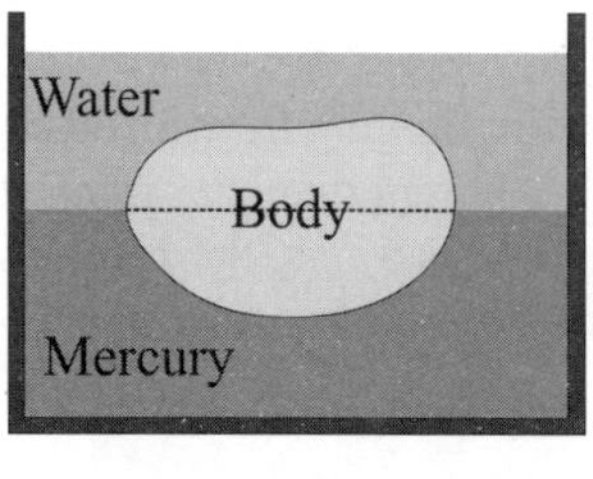

Q.23 A symmetrical stationary vane experience a force F of 100 N as shown in figure, when the mass flow rate of water over the vane is 5 kg/s with a velocity 20 m/s without friction. The angle α (in degree) of the vane is ___.

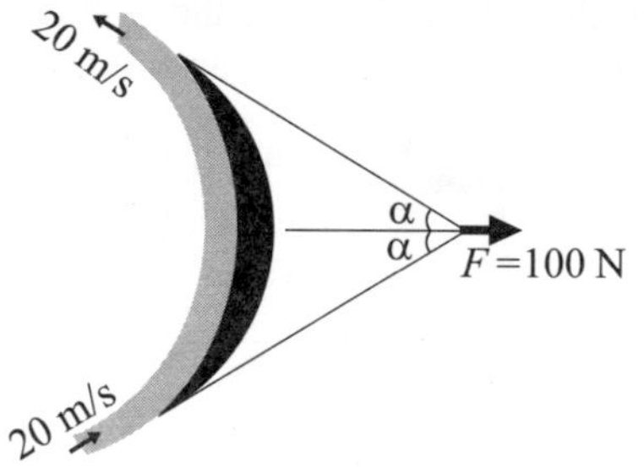

Q.24 The pressure drop for a relatively low Reynolds number flow in a 600 mm diameter, 30 m long pipeline is 70 kPa. What is the wall shear stress(in N/m^2)? ______.

Q.25 A cylindrical gate is holding water on one side shown in the given figure. The resultant vertical component force (in N/m) of water per metre width of gate will be __________.

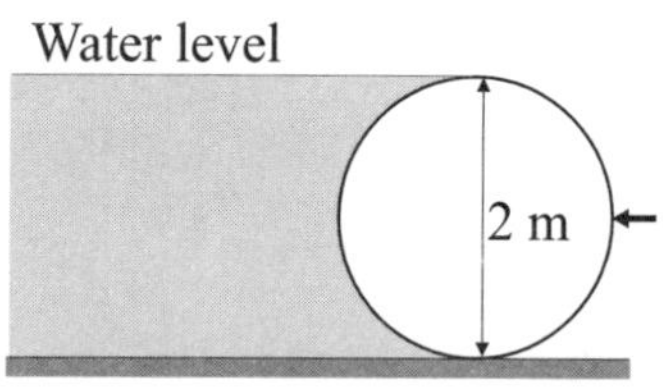

Q.26 A U-tube open at both ends and made of 8 mm diameter glass tube has mercury up to a height of 10 cm in the both the limbs. If 19 cm^3 of water is added to one of the limbs, the difference (in cm) in mercury levels in the two limbs at equilibrium is____________.

Q.27 Electric wire is to be coated with varnish for insulation by drawing it through a circular die of 0.9 mm diameter. The wire diameter is 0.8 mm and it is centered in the die. The varnish ($\mu = 0.02$ N.s/m^2) completely fills the space between the wire and the die for a length of 20 mm. The wire is drawn through the die at a speed of 50 m/s (See figure). The force (in N) required to pull the wire is_____.

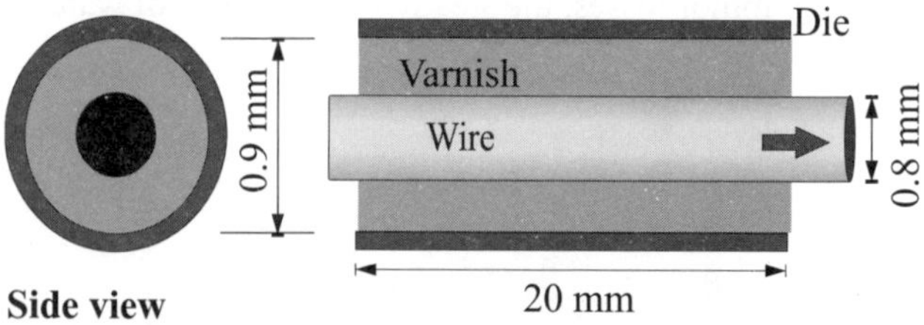

Q.28 A large tank is fixed to a cart as shown in figure. Water spurts from the tank through a 600 mm^2 nozzle at a velocity of 10 m/s. The water level in the tank is maintained constant by adding water through a vertical pipe. The tension (in N) in the wire holding the car stationary is______.

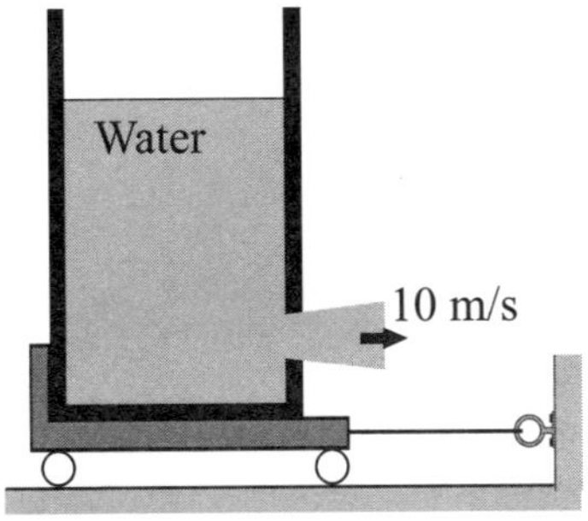

Q.29 A Pelton wheel with single jet rotates at 600 rpm. The velocity of the jet from the nozzle is 100 m/s. If the ratio of the vane velocity to jet velocity is 0.44, then the diameter(in m) of the Pelton wheel is____________.

Q.30 A hydraulic reaction turbine working under a head of 16 m develops 640 kW of power. The unit power (in kW) of the turbine is____________.

Q.31 to Q.65 carry two marks each

Q.31 to Q.50 Multiple Choice Questions

Q.31 A spherical water (surface tension $=0.7$ N/m) droplet of 1.2 mm in diameter splits up in air into 64 smaller droplets of equal size. The work required in splitting up the droplet is

(A) 7.6×10^{-6} J (B) 3.8×10^{-5} J

(C) 9.5×10^{-6} J (D) None of these

Q.32 The loss of head in a pipe of certain length carrying a rate of flow of Q is found to be H. If a pipe of twice the diameter but of the same length is to carry a flow rate of $2Q$, then the head loss will be

(A) H (B) $\frac{H}{2}$ (C) $\frac{H}{4}$ (D) $\frac{H}{8}$

Q.33 A fluid of constant density ρ flows steadily past a porous plate with a uniform free stream velocity U_∞ as shown in the figure. Fluid is sucked through the porous section with a velocity of $0.1U_\infty$ velocity distribution at section CD is given by $\frac{u}{U_\infty}=\frac{3}{2}\left(\frac{y}{\delta}\right)-\frac{1}{2}\left(\frac{y}{\delta}\right)^3$.

Mass flow rate per unit width of the plate, perpendicular to the plane of the figure across the section BC is

(A) $\rho U_\infty \frac{3}{8}\delta$ (B) $\rho U_\infty\left(\frac{3}{8}\delta+0.1L\right)$

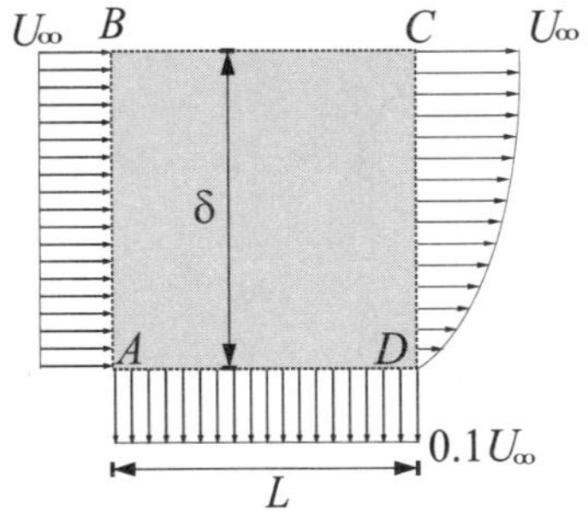

(C) $\rho U_\infty\left(\frac{3}{2}\delta-0.1L\right)$ (D) $\rho U_\infty\left(\frac{3}{8}\delta-0.1L\right)$

Q.34 The hydrodynamic boundary layer over a flat plate is shown in the figure. The velocity in the x-direction is approximated as $u=a+by+cy^2$, where a, b and c are constants, U is the free stream velocity and δ is the boundary layer thickness at any point x on the plate. The dimensionless velocity profile is

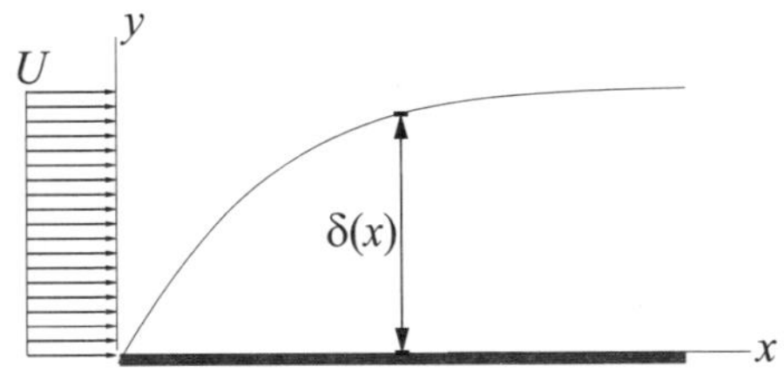

(A) $\frac{u}{U}=2\left(\frac{y}{\delta}\right)-\left(\frac{y}{\delta}\right)^2$

(B) $\frac{u}{U}=2\left(\frac{y}{\delta}\right)+\left(\frac{y}{\delta}\right)^2$

(C) $\frac{u}{U}=1.5\left(\frac{y}{\delta}\right)-0.5\left(\frac{y}{\delta}\right)^2$

(D) $\frac{u}{U}=1.5\left(\frac{y}{\delta}\right)+0.5\left(\frac{y}{\delta}\right)^2$

Q.35 Two pipe lines of equal lengths are connected in series. The diameter of the second pipe is two times that of the first pipe. The ratio of frictional head losses between the first pipe and the second pipe is

(A) 1:32 (B) 1:16 (C) 1:8 (D) 1:4

Q.36 A vertical shaft has a hemispherical bottom of radius of radius R which rotates inside a bearing of identical shape at its end as shown in figure. An oil film of thickness t and viscosity μ is maintained in bearing. The torque required to rotate the shaft at constant angular velocity ω is

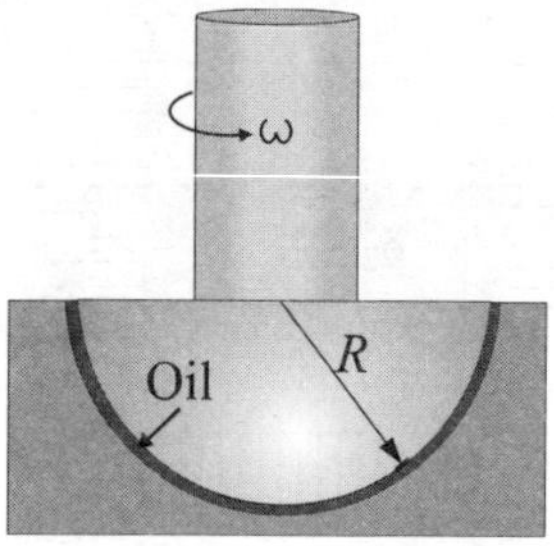

(A) $T = \dfrac{4\pi\mu\omega R^4}{3t}$ (B) $T = \dfrac{2\pi\mu\omega R^4}{t}$

(C) $T = \dfrac{\pi\mu\omega R^4}{2t}$ (D) None of these

Q.37 An open cubical tank was initially filled with water. When the tank was accelerated on a horizontal plane along one of its sides, it was found that one-third of the volume of water spilled out. The acceleration was

(A) $\dfrac{1}{3}g$ (B) $\dfrac{1}{2}g$ (C) $\dfrac{2}{3}g$ (D) None of these

Q.38 A horizontal tube AB of length l rotates with a constant angular velocity ω about vertical axis as shown in figure. The tube is filled with ideal fluid. The end A of the tube is open, the closed end B has very small orifice. The velocity of fluid relative to tube is

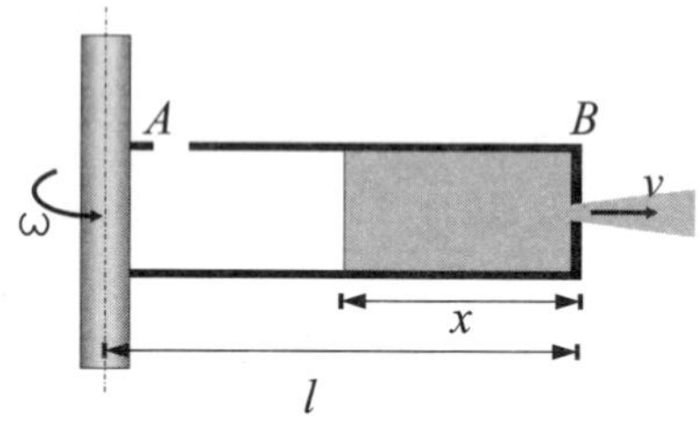

(A) $v = \omega\sqrt{2lx - x^2}$ (B) $v = \omega\sqrt{l^2 - x^2}$

(C) $v = \omega\sqrt{lx - x^2}$ (D) None of these

Q.39 A cube of side 10 cm and weight 5 N is immersed in a liquid of density 800 kg/m^3 contained in a rectangular tank of cross-sectional area $15\text{cm} \times 15\text{cm}$. If the tank contained liquid to a height of 8 cm before the immersion of cube, then the level of water after immersion of cube is

(A) 11.12 cm (B) 10.83 cm

(C) 12.93 cm (D) None of these

Q.40 A tank has a orifice 1 of diameter d_1 at depth h below the free surface. At the opposite side of orifice 1, another orifice 2 is proposed at depth $\dfrac{h}{2}$ as shown in figure. If the net horizontal force on the tank is zero, then the diameter of orifice d_2 is

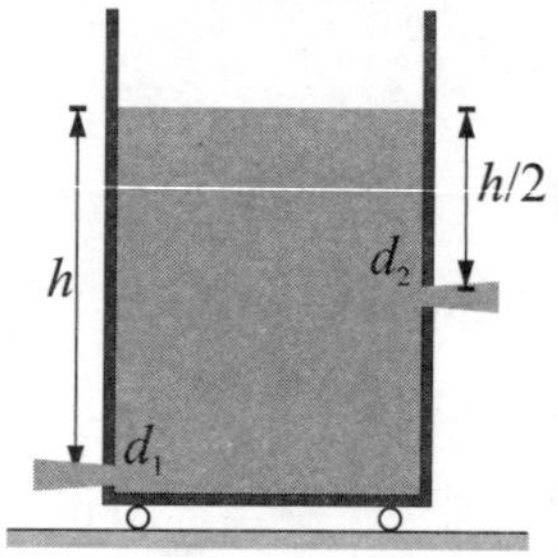

(A) $d_2 = 2d_1$ (B) $d_2 = \sqrt{2}d_1$

(C) $d_2 = \sqrt{3}d_1$ (D) None of these

Q.41 The Darcy-Weisbatch equation for bead loss through a pipe is given as $h = f\dfrac{L}{D}\dfrac{V^2}{2g}$. A reservoir, as shown in the figure, stores water to a height of 8 m. The entrance from the reservoir to the pipe (length 50 m, diameter 10 cm) is sharp, with a loss coefficient of 0.5, and the friction factor for the pipe is 0.017. What would be the discharge (in m^3/s) through the pipe?

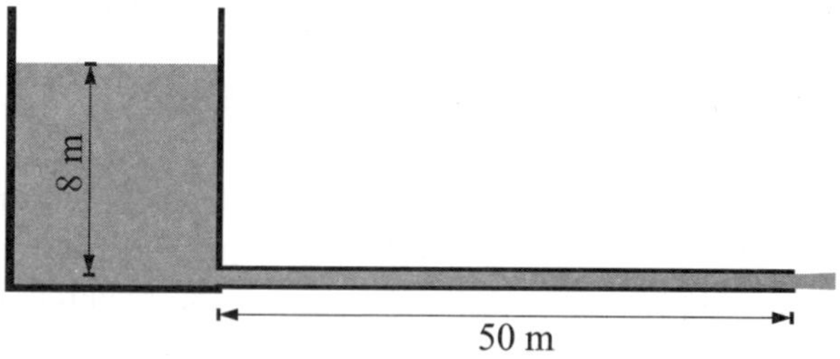

(A) 0.0341 (B) 0.0322 (C) 0.0331 (D) 0.0314

Q.42 The manometer shown in figure contains a liquid of density ρ and rotates at constant angular velocity ω about one of its vertical limbs. The difference in the level h of liquid is

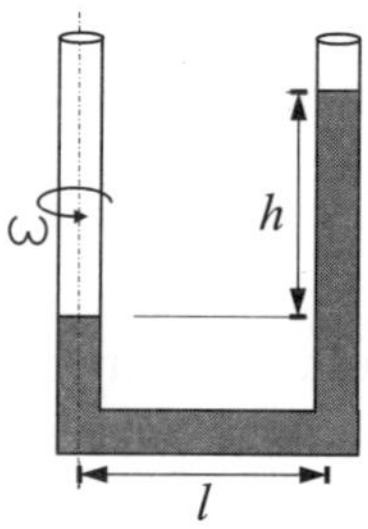

(A) $h = \dfrac{2}{3}\dfrac{\omega^2 l^2}{g}$ (B) $h = \dfrac{\omega^2 l^2}{2g}$ (C) $h = \dfrac{\omega^2 l^2}{3g}$ (D) 0

Q.43 If a cylindrical wooden pole, 20 cm in diameter and 1.0 m in height is placed in a pool of water in a vertical position (the specific gravity of wood is 0.6), then it will

(A) Float in stable equilibrium

(B) Float in unstable

(C) Float in neutral equilibrium

(D) Start moving horizontally

Q.44 An incompressible fluid is place between two horizontal large circular plates at distance d apart. If the bottom plate is fixed and the top plate is moved downwards at a constant velocity v_0 as shown in figure. The velocity of fluid at radial distance r is

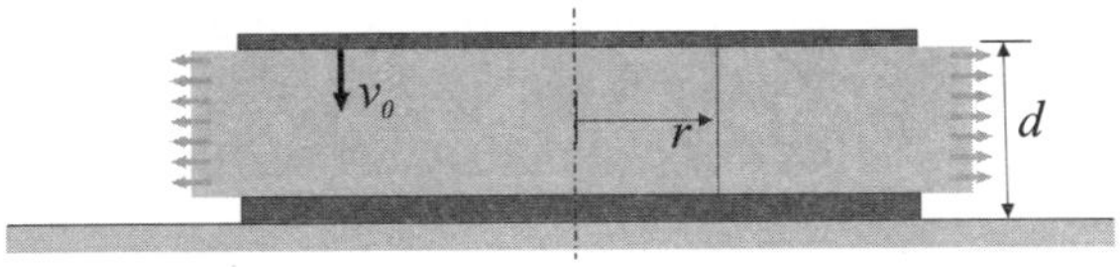

(A) $\frac{v_0 r}{d}$ (B) $\frac{v_0 r}{2d}$ (C) $\frac{v_0 r}{4d}$ (D) $\frac{v_0}{2}$

Q.45 In a flow condition where both viscous and gravity forces dominate and both the Froude number and the Reynolds number are the same in model and prototype; and the ratio of kinematic viscosity of model to that of the prototype is 0.0894. What is the model scale?

(A) 1: 3.3 (B) 3.3:1 (C) 5:1 (D) 1:5

Q.46 The dimensionless group formed by wavelength λ, density of fluid ρ, acceleration due to gravity g and surface tension σ, is

(A) $\frac{\rho}{\lambda^2 g\sigma}$ (B) $\frac{\sigma}{\lambda g^2 \rho}$ (C) $\frac{\sigma g}{\lambda^2 \rho}$ (D) $\frac{\sigma}{\lambda^2 g\rho}$

Q.47 In a Kaplan turbine working under a head of 35 m, the speed ratio is 2.0. If the outer diameter of the runner is 2.0 m and the bulb diameter is 0.6 m, the rotational speed is

(A) 500 (B) 760 (C) 1670 (D) 56

Q.48 A Pelton wheel with single jet rotates at 600 rpm. The velocity of the jet from the nozzle is 100 m/s. If the ratio of the bucket velocity to jet velocity is 0.44 and the speed ratio is 0.43, what is the coefficient of velocity of the nozzle?

(A) 0.87 m (B) 0.922 m (C) 0.95 m (D) 0.977 m

Q.49 Consider a one-dimensional incompressible flow of water through a duct of constant cross-sectional area $1\,m^2$ as shown in figure. A motor imports 1 MW power to the fluid via a fan. Neglect energy loss and assume that the fan does not swirl in the flow. The pressure P_2 is

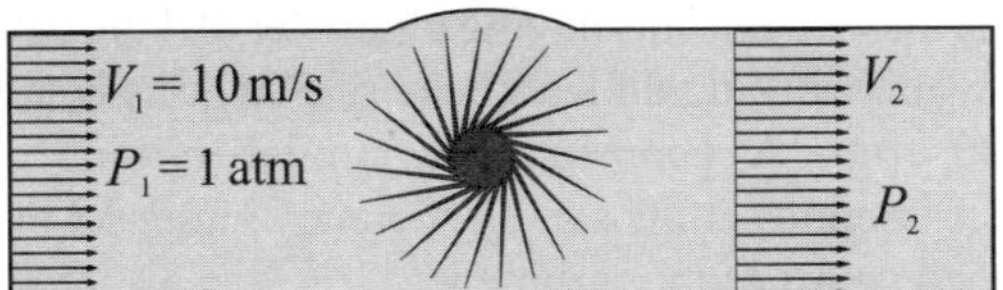

(A) 1 atm (B) 2 atm

(C) Insufficient data (D) More than 3 atm

Q.50 The weightless hinged L-shape gate shown in figure. When the water level rises above a certain value of h, the gate will open. The value of h is

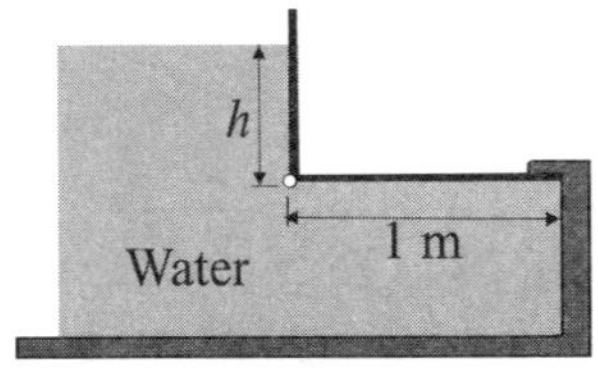

(A) 1.73 m (B) 1.41 m (C) 2.36 m (D) 2.80 m

Q.51 to Q.65 Numerical Answer Questions

Q.51 The velocity distribution in the boundary layer over the face of a high spillway found to have the following form:

$$\frac{u}{U_\infty} = \left(\frac{y}{\delta}\right)^{0.25}$$

In a certain section, the free stream velocity U_∞ was found to be 20 m/s and the boundary layer thickness was estimated to be 5 cm. The displacement thickness (in cm) is_____.

Q.52 A conical tank of diameter 2 m and height 1 m contains full of water. A small orifice is provided at the bottom of tank as shown in figure. The time (in seconds) required to completely emptying the tank is ____.

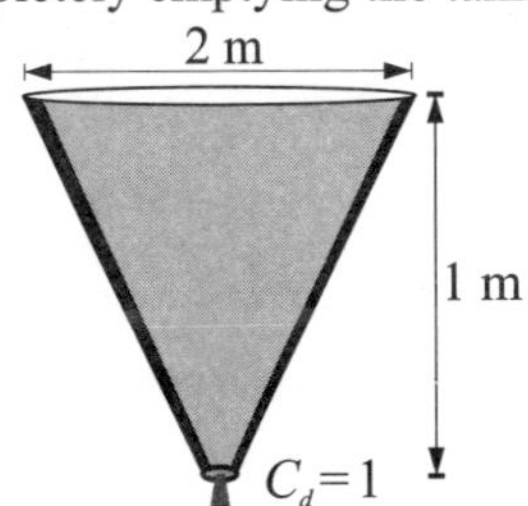

Orifice area = 5 cm^2

Q.53 A ship whose full length is 100 m is to travel at 10 m/s. For dynamic similarity, with that velocity (in m/s) should a 1:25 model of the ship to towed ___.

Q.54 A bent tube is lowered into a water stream as shown in figure. The closed upper end of the tube located at the height 10 cm has small orifice. The velocity of the stream relative to the tube is equal to $v = 4$ m/s. The height h (in cm) of the water jet spurt is_______.

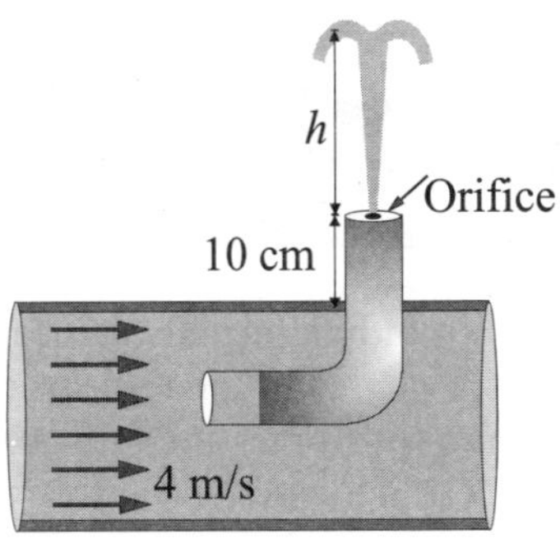

Q.55 Pump of flow rate 0.2 m^3/s is to increase the pressure from 300 kPa to 700 kPa as shown in figure. If pump is 85% efficient and inlet and exit area are equal. The power (in kW) required by pump is ______.

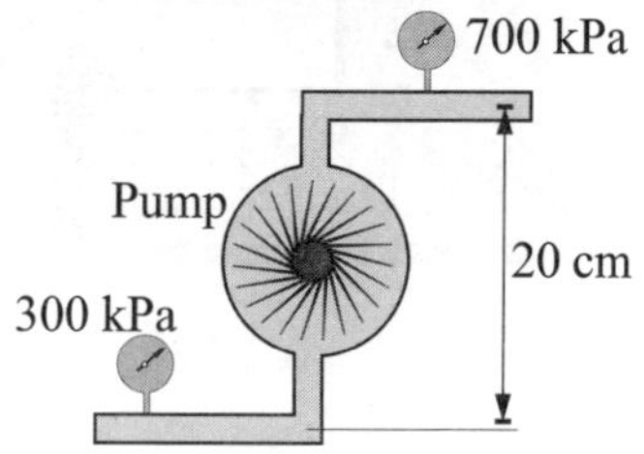

Q.56 The outlet at the side of a tank is so formed that the velocity of water at point A is 2.0 times the mean velocity within the outlet pipe B (See figure). Neglect all other losses, and atmospheric pressure is 95.48 kPa (absolute) and vapour pressure is 4.00 kPa (absolute). The maximum velocity (in m/s) of fluid at B without producing cavitation in pipe is ____.

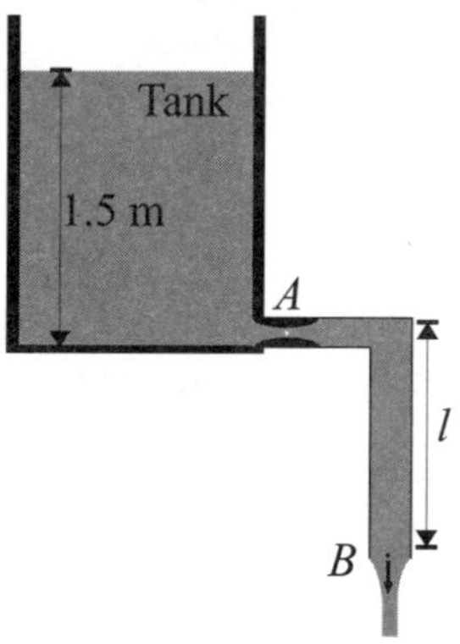

Q.57 Air inducted from atmosphere through a bell-mouthed duct by the application of suction at the other end. A glass tube with its lower end immersed into a vessel containing water is attached to the cylindrical part of the duct (see figure). If the liquid level in the glass tube rises by 25 mm above the free surface and the density of air is equal to 1.2 kg/m^3, the velocity (in m/s) of air in the cylindrical portion is___________.

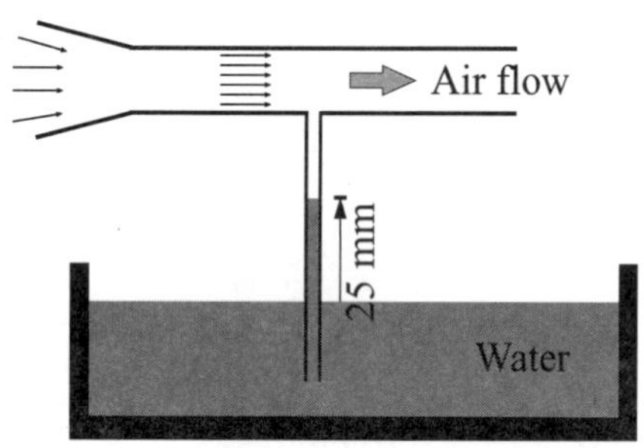

Q.58 Water enters a turbine steadily at the rate of 100 l/s with a pressure of 3×10^5 N/m^2 and a velocity of 100 m/s. It leaves the turbine with a pressure of 1×10^5 N/m^2 and a velocity of 50 m/s. If no losses occur, the power (in kW) produced by the turbine is___

Q.59 A pump is lifting water from a pond and delivering it to an overhead reservoir in which the level of water is 15 m above that in the pond. The flow rate through the pump is 180 m^3/h. If the head loss through the pump and piping system is 5 m water column and the efficiency of the pump is 50%, the power (in kW) required to drive the pump is__.

Q.60 Two streams of water at the same pressure P_1 but with velocities $v_1 = 25$ m/s and $v_2 = 5$ m/s enter a mixing chamber, and after complete mixing emerge as a simple stream with uniform properties. Assume that there are no losses in flow. Given $A_1 = 20\ cm^2$, $A_2 = 40\ cm^2$, $A_3 = 60\ cm^2$. The pressure difference $P_3 - P_1$ (in kN/m^2) is ____.

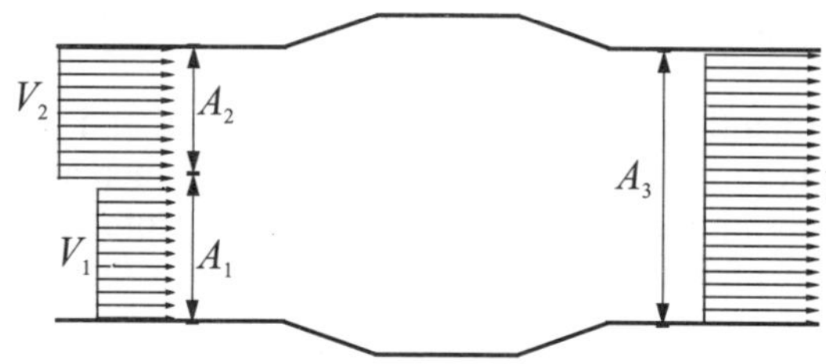

Q.61 The U-tube arrangement shown rotates about y-y' at $\frac{60}{\pi}$ rpm. Initially (before rotation) the level in the arms of the U-tube is 60 cm. The steady state difference in the levels of the two limbs (in cm) is___________.

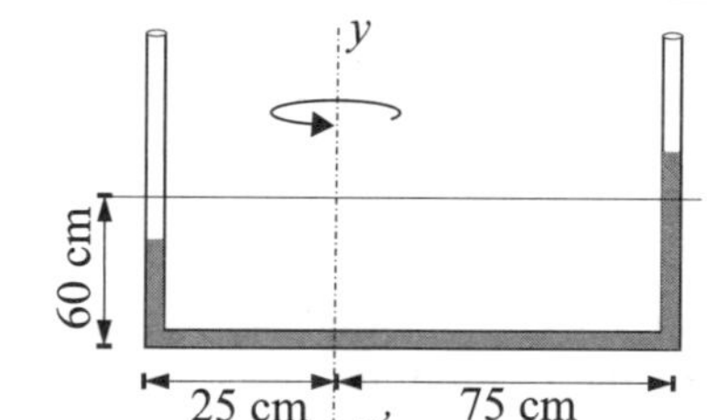

Q.62 If the full-scale turbine is required to work under a head of 30 m and to run at 428 rpm, then a quarter scale turbine model tested under a head of 10 m must run (in rpm) at______.

Q.63 The following data is related to the Pelton wheel:

Mean bucket speed = 10 m/s, Discharge = 0.7 m^3/s, Head = 30 m, Angle of deflection of jet = 160° and C_v = 0.98. The whirl velocity (in m/s) at outlet is_______.

Q.64 A model turbine having diameter 0.4 m develops 15 kW when working under a head of 5 m at its best speed of 1600 rpm. A geometrically similar turbine 1.6 m diameter operates at the same efficiency under 18 m head. The speed (rpm) of the turbine is _______.

Q.65 A turbine works at 20 m head and 500 rpm speed. If 1:2 scale model that is to be tested at a head of 20 m should have a rotational speed (in rpm) of nearly ________.

10.4 SOLUTION TO PRACTICE PAPER

Q.1 Ans:(A)

Continuity equation for compressible fluid

$$\frac{\partial}{\partial x}(\rho u)+\frac{\partial}{\partial y}(\rho v)+\frac{\partial}{\partial z}(\rho w)+\frac{\partial}{\partial t}\rho=0$$

or $$\left(\frac{\partial}{\partial x}+\frac{\partial}{\partial y}+\frac{\partial}{\partial z}\right)\rho(ui+vj+wk)+\frac{\partial}{\partial t}\rho=0$$

or $$\left(\frac{\partial}{\partial x}+\frac{\partial}{\partial y}+\frac{\partial}{\partial z}\right)\rho\vec{V}+\frac{\partial}{\partial t}\rho=0$$

where $V=ui+vj+wk$

$$\nabla.\rho V+\frac{\partial}{\partial t}\rho=0$$

Q.2 Ans:(C)

Figure shows the free-body diagram of element. Let t be thickness of fluid element.

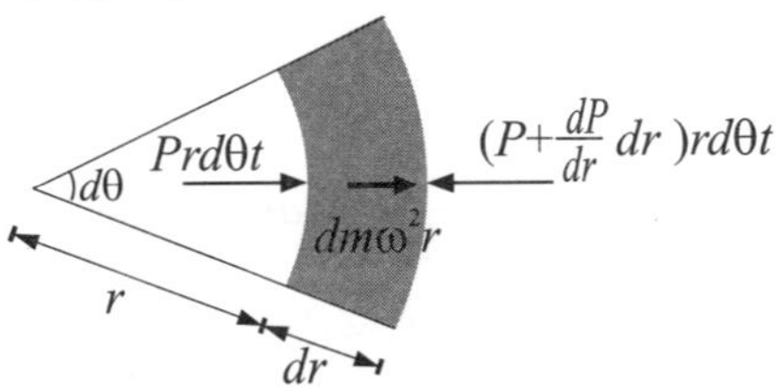

$$\sum F_r=0 \Rightarrow \quad prd\theta t+dm\frac{v^2}{r}-\left(p+\frac{\partial p}{\partial r}dr\right)rd\theta t=0$$

or $$\frac{\partial p}{\partial r}drrd\theta t=\rho rd\theta drt\frac{v^2}{r}$$

$$\frac{\partial P}{\partial r}=\frac{\rho v^2}{r}=\rho\omega^2 r$$

Q.3 Ans:(C)

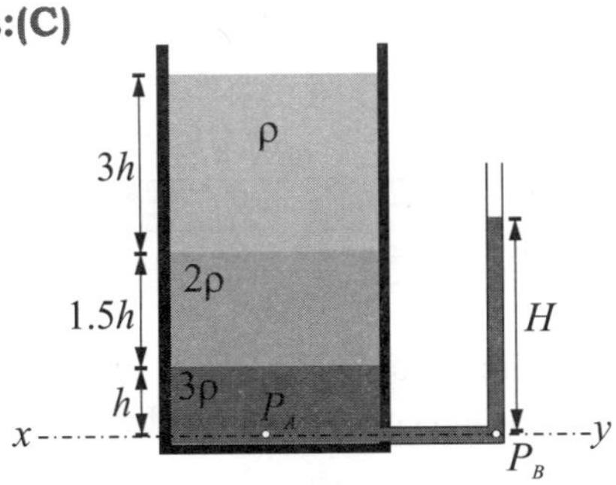

Pressure along plane x-y

Equating pressure at A and B; $P_A=P_B$

or $\rho g\times 3h+2\rho g\times 1.5h+3\rho g\times h=3\rho g\times H$

From which

$$\frac{H}{h}=3$$

Q.4 Ans:(B)

At the terminal condition, equilibrium occurs.

Viscous resistance = Component of weight along slope

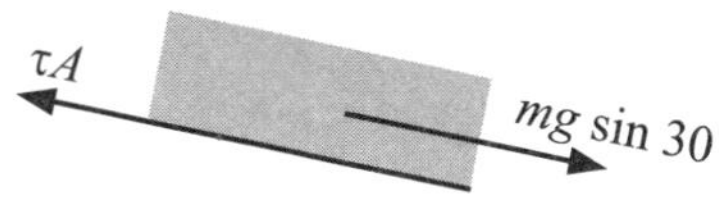

$$\tau A=mg\sin 30$$

or $$\tau=\frac{mg\sin 30}{A}=\frac{\rho Ahg\sin 30}{A}$$

or $$\tau=\rho hg\sin 30$$

or $$\tau=900\times\frac{1}{1000}\times 9.81\times\sin 30$$

$$\tau=4.41\ \text{N/m}^2$$

Q.5 Ans:(D)

Reynold's number, $Re=\frac{\rho_1 V_1 d_1}{\mu_1}=\frac{\rho_2 V_2 d_2}{\mu_2}$

or $$\frac{1000V\,d}{\mu}=\frac{800V_2\,d}{0.2\mu}$$

From which

$$V_2=\frac{V}{4}$$

Q.6 Ans:(B)

Let u be the velocity of fluid at y.

Velocity $u=a+by+cy^2$

Boundary conditions: (i) at $y=0, u=0$

(ii) at $y=2$ m, $u=10$ m/s and (iii) at $y=2$ m, $\frac{du}{dy}=0$

From which $a=0, b=10$ and $c=-\frac{5}{2}$

Velocity $$u=10y-\frac{5}{2}y^2$$

Volume flow rate, $$Q=\int_0^2 udy=\int_0^2(10y-\frac{5}{2}y^2)\,dy.$$

$$Q=13.33\ \text{m}^3/\text{s}$$

Q.7 Ans:(C)

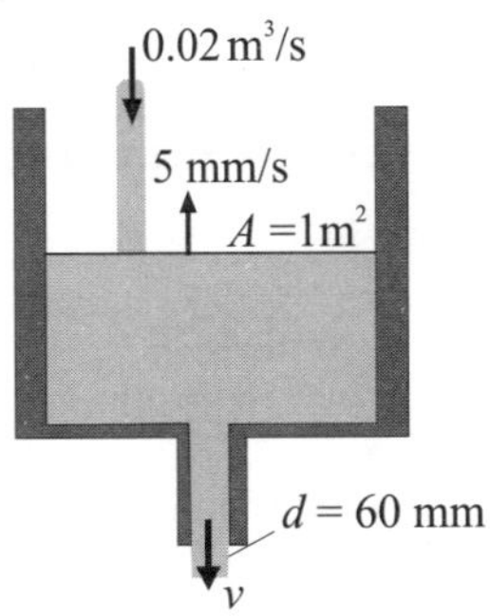

$$Q_{in} = 0.02\ \text{m}^3/\text{s}$$

$$\Delta Q + Q_{out} = 1 \times \frac{5}{1000} + \frac{\pi}{4}\left(\frac{60}{1000}\right)^2 v$$

Applying continuity equation, $Q_{in} = Q_{out}$

$$0.02 = 1 \times \frac{5}{1000} + \frac{\pi}{4}\left(\frac{60}{1000}\right)^2 v$$

or $\quad 0.02 = 0.005 + 0.0028\, v$

$$v = 5.35\ \text{m/s}$$

Q.8 Ans:(A)

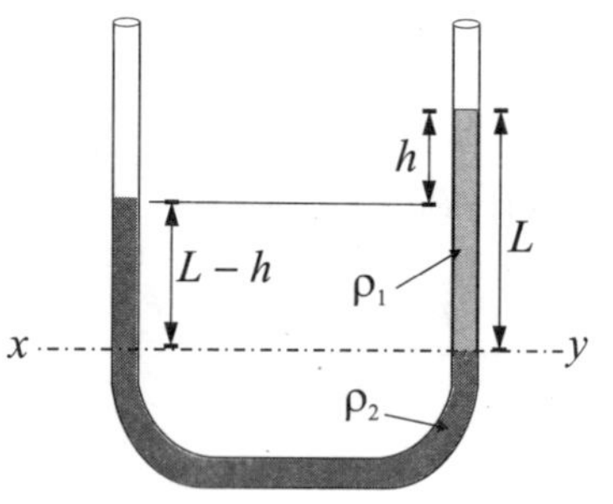

Equating the pressures of the limb along the horizontal plane *x*-*y*, we have

$$(P_{x-y})_{\text{left limb}} = (P_{x-y})_{\text{right limb}}$$

or $\quad \rho_2 g(L-h) = \rho_1 gL \Rightarrow L - h = \frac{\rho_1}{\rho_2} L$

or $\quad h = L - \frac{\rho_1}{\rho_2} L$

$$h = L\left(1 - \frac{\rho_1}{\rho_2}\right)$$

Q.9 Ans:(D)

Discharge through exit pipe, $Q_{out} = av$

$$Q_{out} = a\sqrt{2gh}$$

or $\quad Q_{out} = 10^{-2}\sqrt{2g \times h} \qquad$ (i)

Water supply to tank, $\quad Q_{in} = 5 \times 10^{-2} \qquad$ (ii)

Steady state condition, $\quad Q_{in} = Q_{out}$

$$5 \times 10^{-2} = 10^{-2} \times \sqrt{2 \times 9.81 \times h}$$

From which

$$h = 1.27\ \text{m}$$

Q.10 Ans:(A)

Let *D* and *V* be the diameter and velocity of jet above 5 m from nozzle.

Applying Bernoulli's theorem,

$$\frac{P_1}{\rho g} + \frac{u^2}{2g} + z_1 = \frac{P_2}{\rho g} + \frac{V^2}{2g} + z_2$$

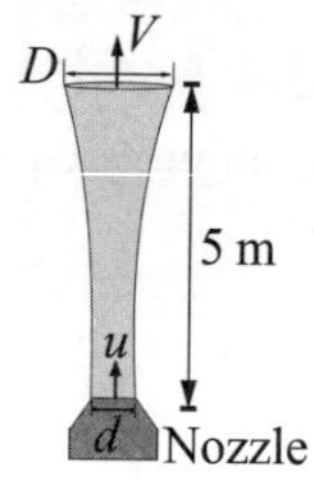

Since $\quad P_1 = P_2,\ z_1 - z_2 = 5$ m;

$$V = \sqrt{u^2 - 2g \times 5} = \sqrt{15^2 - 2 \times 9.81 \times 5}$$

$$V = 11.26\ \text{m/s}$$

Applying continuity equation, $a_1 u = a_2 V$

$$\frac{\pi}{4} d^2 u = \frac{\pi}{4} D^2 V$$

$$D = d\sqrt{\frac{u}{V}} = 20\sqrt{\frac{15}{11.26}}$$

$$D = 23.08\ \text{mm}$$

Q.11 Ans:(B)

Given: $V = 100$ m/s and $u = 50$ m/s

Force exerted by jet on the plate $F = \dot{m}(V - u)$, where mass flow rate $\dot{m} = \rho a(V - u)$.

$$F = \rho a(V-u)(V-u) = \rho a(V-u)^2$$

or $\quad F = 1000 \times \frac{\pi}{4} \times (0.1)^2 \times (100 - 50)^2 = 19634.9\ \text{N}$

$$F = 19.6\ \text{kN}$$

Q.12 Ans:(C)

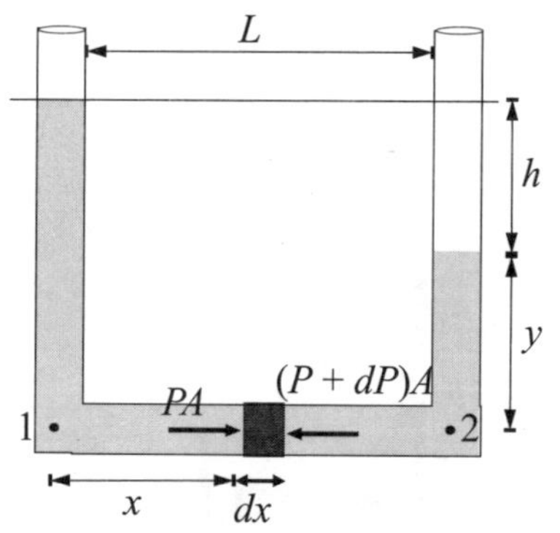

Consider an element of width *dx* at *x* from left limb. Applying equilibrium equation of on element.

$$\sum F = PA - (P + dP)A = \rho_w A dx a$$

or $\quad dP = -\rho_w dx a \Rightarrow \int_1^2 dP = -\rho_w a \int_0^L dx$

or $\quad P_1 - P_2 = \rho_w aL$

$$\rho_w g(h + y) - \rho_w gy = \rho_w aL$$

$$a = g\frac{h}{L}$$

Q.13 Ans:(B)

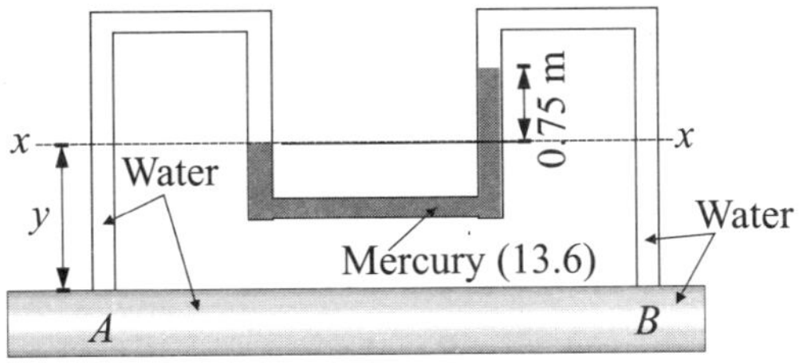

Equating Pressure along plane *x-x*,

$$P_A - \rho_w g y = P_B - \rho_w g(y+0.75) + \rho_{Hg} g \times 0.75$$

$$P_A - P_B = \rho_w g y - \rho_w g(y+0.75) + \rho_{Hg} g \times 0.75$$

$$= \rho_{Hg} g \times 0.75 - \rho_w g \times 0.75$$

or $$P_A - P_B = 13600 \times 9.81 \times 0.75 - 1000 \times 9.81 \times 0.75$$

$$P_A - P_B = 92.7\,\text{kPa}$$

Q.14 Ans:(B)

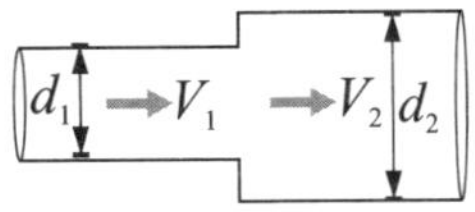

Given: $d_1 = 100\,\text{mm}$, $d_2 = 200\,\text{mm}$ and $v_1 = 5\,\text{m/s}$

Flow rate, $Q = a_1 v_1 = a_2 v_2$

$$v_2 = \frac{a_1}{a_2} v_1 = \frac{d_1^2 v_1}{d_2^2} = \frac{1}{4} \times 5 = \frac{5}{4}$$

Head loss, $$h = \frac{(v_1 - v_2)^2}{2g} = \frac{\left(5 - \frac{5}{4}\right)^2}{2g} = \frac{225}{16 \times 2 \times 9.81}$$

$$h = 0.716\,\text{m}$$

Q.15 Ans:(D)

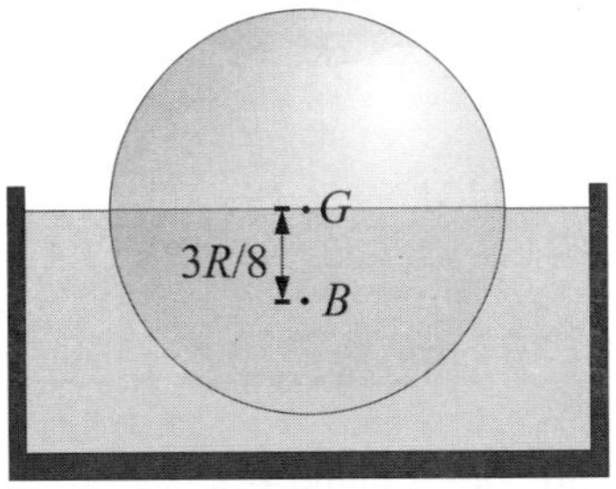

Metacentric height is given by $MG = \frac{I}{\forall} - BG$

Where, $$I = \frac{\pi d^4}{64} = \frac{\pi (2R)^4}{64} = \frac{\pi R^4}{4}$$

$$\forall = \frac{2}{3}\pi R^3 \text{ and } BG = \frac{3R}{8}$$

$$MG = \frac{\frac{1}{4}\pi R^4}{\frac{2}{3}\pi R^3} - \frac{3R}{8} = \frac{3R}{8} - \frac{3R}{8} = 0$$

$$MG = 0$$

Q.16 Ans:(B)

Unit power, $P_u = \frac{P}{H^{3/2}}$ or $P \propto H^{3/2}$

Unit speed, $N_u = \frac{N}{\sqrt{H}}$ or $N \propto H^{1/2}$

Unit discharge, $Q_u = \frac{Q}{\sqrt{H}}$ or $Q \propto H^{1/2}$

Q.17 Ans:(A)

Given: Flow field

$V = (axy - z^3)i + (a-2)x^2 j + (1-a)xz^2 k$ is irrotational.

For irrotational flow, $\text{curl}\,\mathbf{V} = 0 \Rightarrow \nabla \times \mathbf{V} = 0$

$$\nabla \times \mathbf{V} = \begin{vmatrix} i & j & k \\ \frac{\partial}{\partial x} & \frac{\partial}{\partial y} & \frac{\partial}{\partial z} \\ (axy - z^3) & i + (a-2)x^2 & (1-a)xz^2 \end{vmatrix} = 0$$

From which

$$a = 4$$

Q.18 Ans:(C)

Given: $D = 4.0$ m, $B = 0.8$ m and $V_{f_1} = 3$ m/s

Discharge through turbine, $Q = \pi D B V_{f_1}$

or $$Q = \pi \times 4 \times 0.8 \times 3$$

$$Q = 30.16\,\text{m}^3/\text{s}$$

Q.19 Ans:(B)

Applying Bernoulli's equation between 1 and 2,

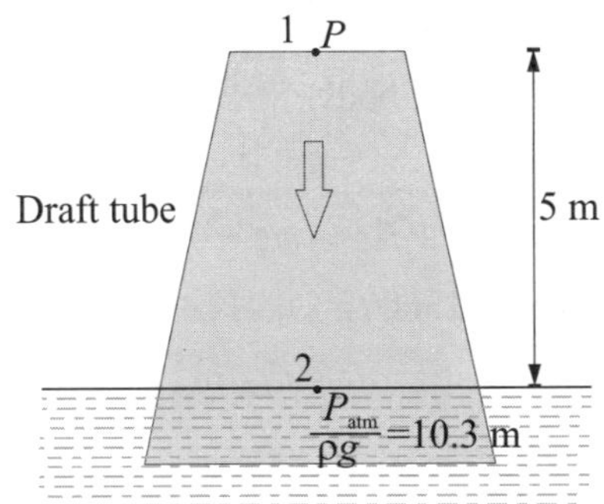

$$\frac{P_1}{\rho g} + \frac{V_1^2}{2g} + z_1 = \frac{P_{atm}}{\rho g} + \frac{V_2^2}{2g} + z_2$$

$$\frac{P_1}{\rho g}+0+5=10.3+0+0$$

$$\frac{P_1}{\rho g}=10.3-5=5.3$$

$$\frac{P}{\rho g}=5.3\text{ m}$$

Q.20 Ans:(B)

Given: $H_g=300\text{ m}$, $L=400\text{ m}$, $d=1\text{ m}$, $v=5$ m/s and $f=0.0098$.

Head loss due to friction in pipe is given by

$$h_f=\frac{fLv^2}{d2g}=\frac{0.0098\times 400\times 5^2}{1\times 2\times 9.81}$$

$$h_f=4.9925$$

Net head, $H=H_g-h_f=300-4.9925$

$$H=295\text{ m}$$

Q.21 Ans:[59.79]

Given: Speed ratio = 0.45 and $H=900$ m

$$\text{Speed ratio}=\frac{u}{\sqrt{2gH}}=0.45$$

$$u=0.45\sqrt{2gH}$$

or $u=0.45\times\sqrt{2g\times 900}$

$$u=59.79\text{ m/s}$$

Q.22 Ans:[6040]

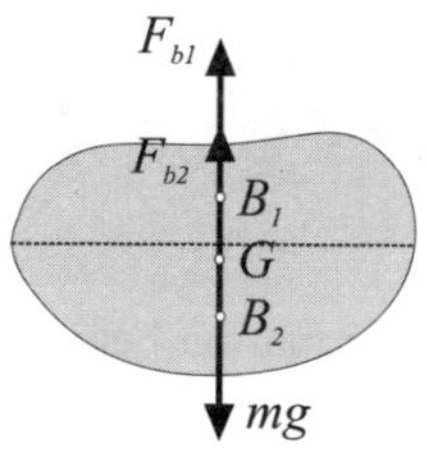

Let V be the volume of body.

Equilibrium equation

$$\sum F_v=0 \quad\Rightarrow F_{b_1}+F_{b_2}-mg=0$$

$$1000g\times 0.6V+13600g\times 0.4V-\rho_b gV=0$$

$$\rho_b=6040\text{ kg/m}^3$$

Q.23 Ans:[60]

Force exerted by jet on stationary vane

$$F_x=\dot{m}(V_{1x}-V_{2x})$$

or $F_x=100=5\times[20\cos\alpha-(-20\cos\alpha)]$

or $\cos\alpha=\dfrac{100}{5\times 2\times 20}=\dfrac{1}{2}$

$$\alpha=60^\circ$$

Q.24 Ans:[350]

Shear stress, $\tau=-\dfrac{r}{2}\dfrac{\partial p}{\partial x}$

Shear stress at wall, $\tau=\dfrac{R}{2}\times\dfrac{\Delta p}{\Delta x}$

or $\tau=\dfrac{0.3}{2}\times\dfrac{70\times 10^3}{30}$

$$\tau=350\text{ N/m}^2$$

Q.25 Ans:[15.4]

Vertical force F_y = Weight of water enclosed by curved surface ABC per unit width

$$F_y=\rho g\frac{\pi}{2}R^2\times 1$$

or $F_y=1000\times 9.81\times\dfrac{\pi}{2}1^2\times 1=15409.5$

$$F_y=15.4\text{ N/m}$$

Q.26 Ans:[2.77]

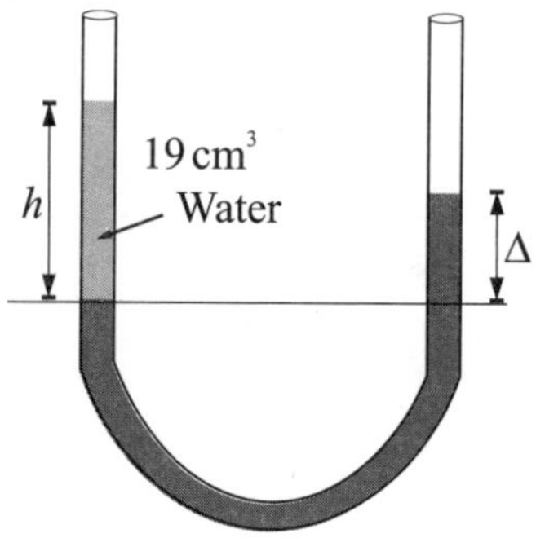

Volume of water added, $19=\dfrac{\pi}{4}\left(\dfrac{8}{10}\right)^2 h$

or $h=\dfrac{19\times 25}{4\pi}$ cm

Equating pressure along plane x-y,

$$1000g\times\frac{19\times 25}{4\pi}=13600g\times\Delta$$

From which

$$\Delta=2.77\text{ cm}$$

Q.27 Ans:[1.005]

Force, F = Shear force, τA

$$F = \mu \frac{V}{t} A = \mu \frac{V}{t} \pi d L$$

$$= \frac{20 \times 10^{-3} \times 50 \times \pi \times \frac{0.8}{1000} \times \frac{20}{1000}}{\left(\frac{0.1}{2 \times 1000}\right)}$$

$$F = 1.005 \text{ N}$$

Q.28 Ans:[60]

Tension of wire, T = Reaction by jet

$$T = \dot{m}(V - 0) = \rho Q V = \rho a V \times V$$

or $$T = \rho a V^2 = 1000 \times \frac{600}{1000 \times 1000} \times 10^2$$

$$T = 60 \text{ N}$$

Q.29 Ans:[1.4]

Given: $N = 600$ rpm, $V = 100$ m/s, $\frac{u}{V} = 0.44$

Bucket velocity, $u = \frac{\pi D N}{60}$

or $$0.44V = \frac{\pi D N}{60}$$

$$0.44 \times 100 = \frac{\pi D \times 600}{60}$$

From which

$$D = 1.4 \text{ m}$$

Q.30 Ans:[10]

Unit power, $P_u = \frac{P}{H^{3/2}} = \frac{640}{16^{3/2}}$

$$P_u = 10 \text{ kW}$$

Q.31 Ans:(C)

Work against surface tension, $W = \sigma \times \Delta A$

or $$W = \sigma \times (n 4\pi r^2 - 4\pi R^2)$$

or $$W = \sigma \times 4\pi(nr^2 - R^2) \quad \text{(i)}$$

Volume of water $= \frac{4}{3}\pi r^3 n = \frac{4}{3}\pi R^3$

$$r^3 = \frac{R^3}{n} = \frac{R^3}{64} \quad \text{or} \quad r = \frac{R}{4}$$

$$W = \sigma \times 4\pi\left[64 \times \left(\frac{R^2}{16}\right) - R^2\right]$$

$$W = 12\pi\sigma R^2 = 12\pi \times 0.7 \times \left(\frac{0.6}{1000}\right)^2$$

$$W = 9.5 \times 10^{-6} \text{ J}$$

Q.32 Ans:(D)

Head loss due to friction in pipe is given by

$$h_f = \frac{4f\,lV^2}{d2g} = \frac{4f\,l}{d2g}\left(\frac{Q}{\frac{\pi}{4}d^2}\right)^2$$

or $$h_f = \frac{64 f\,lQ^2}{\pi^2 d^5 2g}$$

$h_f = H$ when flow rate Q;

$$H = \frac{64 f\,LQ^2}{\pi^2 D^5 2g} \quad \text{(i)}$$

$h_f = H'$ when flow rate Q;

$$H' = \frac{64 f\,L(2Q)^2}{\pi^2 (2D)^5 2g} \quad \text{(ii)}$$

From Equations (i) and (ii), we have

$$H' = \frac{H}{8}$$

Q.33 Ans:(D)

Applying the continuity equation,

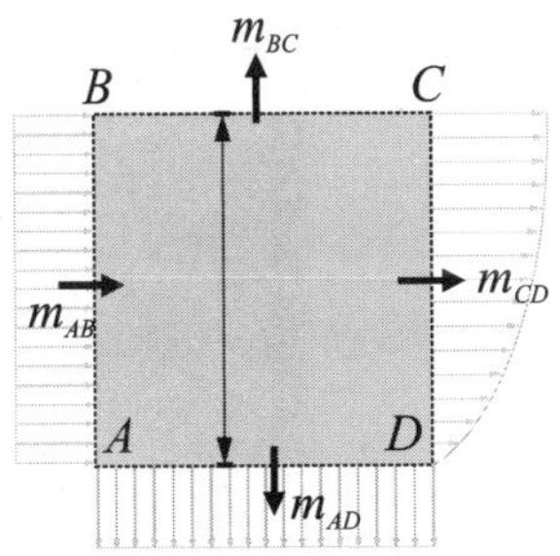

$$m_{AB} = m_{AD} + m_{CD} + m_{BC}$$

or $$m_{BC} = m_{AB} - m_{AD} - m_{CD}$$

or $$m_{BC} = \rho U_\infty AB - \rho \times 0.1 U_\infty AD - \rho\int_0^\delta u\,dy$$

or $$m_{BC} = \rho\left[U_\infty AB - 0.1U_\infty L - \int_0^\delta U_\infty\left\{\frac{3}{2}\frac{y}{\delta} - \frac{1}{2}\left(\frac{y}{\delta}\right)^3\right\}\right]dy$$

or $$m_{BC} = \rho\left[U_\infty \delta - 0.1U_\infty L - \frac{3}{4}U_\infty \delta + \frac{U_\infty \delta}{8}\right]$$

$$m_{BC} = \rho U_\infty\left(\frac{3}{8}\delta - 0.1L\right)$$

Q.34 Ans:(A)

Velocity of fluid $u = a + by + cy^2$

Boundary conditions: (i) at $y = 0, u = 0 \Rightarrow a = 0$

(ii) at $y=\delta, \dfrac{du}{dy}=0 \Rightarrow b=2c\delta=0 \Rightarrow b=-2c\delta$

(iii) at $y=\delta, u=U \Rightarrow b\delta+c\delta^2=U$

From which

$$c=-\frac{U}{\delta^2} \text{ and } b=-c\delta=\frac{2U}{\delta}$$

$$u=\frac{2U}{\delta}y-\frac{U}{\delta^2}y^2$$

$$\frac{u}{U}=2\left(\frac{y}{\delta}\right)-\left(\frac{y}{\delta}\right)^2$$

Q.35 Ans:(A)

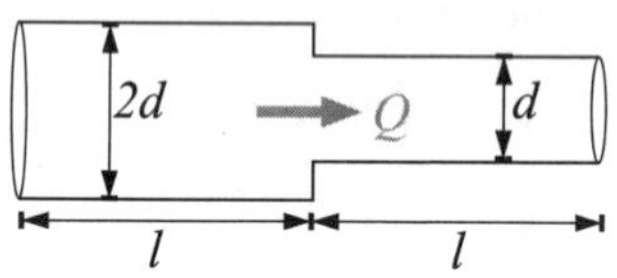

Flow rate, $Q=\dfrac{\pi}{4}(2d)^2v_1=\dfrac{\pi}{4}d^2v_2 \Rightarrow 4v_1=v_2$

Ratio of frictional head losses between first pipe and second pipe is

$$\frac{h_{f1}}{h_{f2}}=\frac{\dfrac{4f\,lv_1^2}{2d2g}}{\dfrac{4f\,lv_2^2}{d2g}}=\frac{v_1^2}{2v_2^2}=\frac{1}{2}\times\frac{1}{16}$$

or $$\frac{h_{f1}}{h_{f2}}=\frac{1}{2}\times\frac{1}{16}$$

$$\frac{h_{f1}}{h_{f2}}=\frac{1}{32}$$

Q.36 Ans:(A)

Consider an element of fluid of angular thickness $d\theta$ at angle θ as shown in figure.

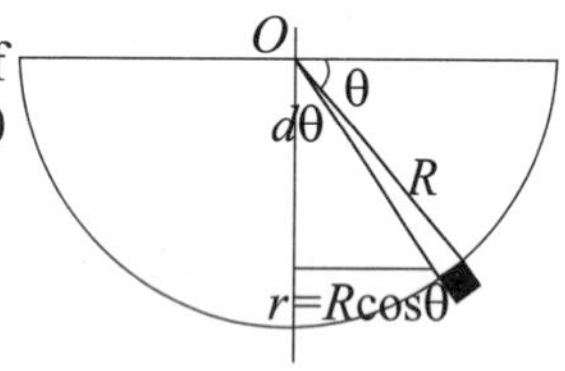

Shear force, $dF=\tau dA$

Torque, $dT=dF\times r$

where $\tau=\mu\dfrac{V}{t}$

Substituting $V=\omega R\cos\theta$, and

$$dA=2\pi rRd\theta=2\pi R\cos\theta Rd\theta$$

$$dT=\frac{\mu\omega R\cos\theta}{t}\times 2\pi R\cos\theta Rd\theta\times R\cos\theta$$

or $$\int dT=\int\frac{2\pi\mu\omega R^4\cos^3\theta}{t}d\theta$$

or $$T=\frac{2\pi\mu\omega R^4}{t}\int_0^{\pi/2}\cos^3\theta d\theta$$

$$T=\frac{4\pi\mu\omega R^4}{3t}$$

Q.37 Ans:(C)

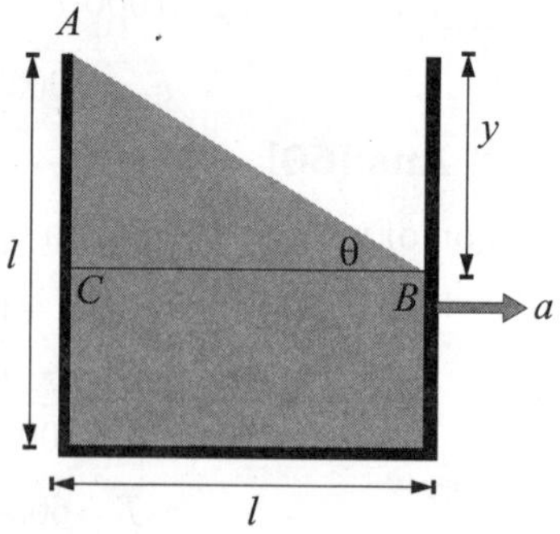

Volume of ABC

$$=\frac{1}{2}yl\times l=\frac{l^3}{3}$$

or $$y=\frac{2}{3}l$$

$$\tan\theta=\frac{y}{l}=\frac{\frac{2}{3}l}{l}=\frac{2}{3} \text{ and}$$

$$\tan\theta=\frac{a}{g}=\frac{2}{3}$$

$$a=\frac{2}{3}g$$

Q.38 Ans:(A)

Applying equilibrium equation,

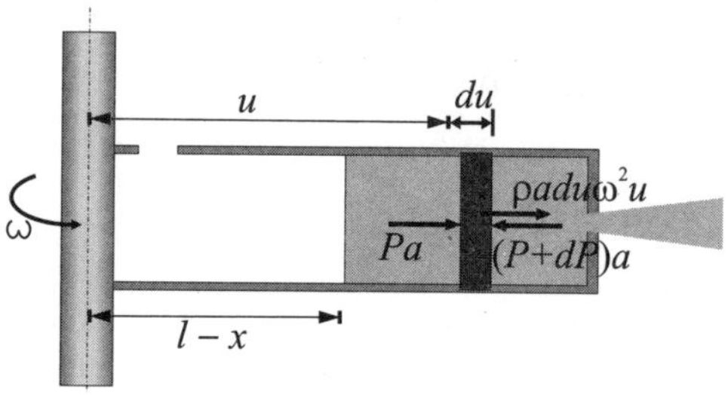

$$Pa+\rho adu\omega^2u-(P+dP)a=0$$

or $$dP=\rho\omega^2udu$$

Integrating $$\int_0^P dP=\rho\omega^2\int_{l-x}^{l}udu$$

or $$P=\frac{\rho\omega^2}{2}\left[l^2-(l-x)^2\right]$$

or $$P=\frac{\rho\omega^2}{2}(2lx-x^2)$$

Now, applying conservation of energy,

$$\frac{P}{\rho g}=\frac{v^2}{2g} \Rightarrow v=\sqrt{\frac{2P}{\rho}}$$

or $$v=\sqrt{\frac{2}{\rho}\left(\frac{\rho\omega^2}{2}(2lx-x^2)\right)}$$

$$v=\omega\sqrt{(2lx-x^2)}$$

Q.39 Ans:(B)

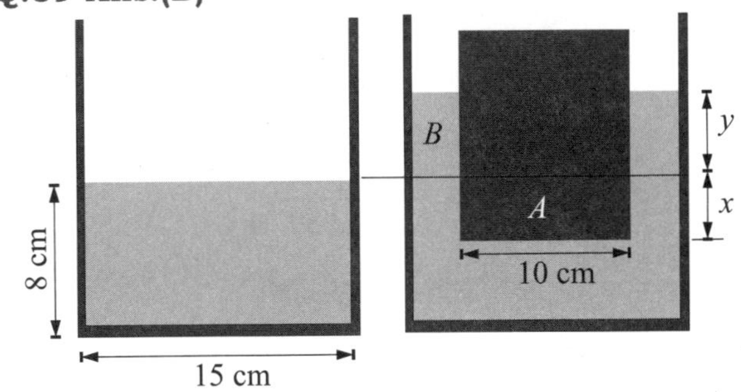

Volume of A = Volume of B,

$$10 \times 10 \times x = 15^2 y - 10^2 y$$

$$x = 1.25y \quad \text{(i)}$$

Weight of cube = Buoyant force

$$5 = \frac{10 \times 10(x+y)}{10^6} \times 800 \times 9.81$$

or $$5 = 0.784(x+y) \quad \text{(ii)}$$

From Equations (i) and (ii), we get

$$y = 2.83 \text{ cm and } x = 3.54 \text{ cm}$$

Level of water after immersion $= 8 + y = 8 + 2.83$

$$10.83 \text{ cm}$$

Q.40 Ans:(B)

Mass flow rate through orifice $\dot{m} = \rho AV$, where $V = \sqrt{2gH}$ and $A = \frac{\pi}{4}D^2$

Reaction on the tank by jet ;

$$F = \dot{m}(V-0) = \rho AV(V-0) = \rho AV^2$$

For first orifice, $F_1 = \rho \frac{\pi}{4} d_1^2 \left(\sqrt{2gh}\right)^2$

For second orifice, $F_2 = \rho \frac{\pi}{4} d_2^2 \left(\sqrt{2g\frac{h}{2}}\right)^2$

Given: $F_1 = F_2$

or $$\rho \frac{\pi}{4} d_1^2 \left(\sqrt{2gh}\right)^2 = \rho \frac{\pi}{4} d_2^2 \left(\sqrt{2g\frac{h}{2}}\right)^2$$

$$d_2 = \sqrt{2}d_1$$

Q.41 Ans:(D)

Applying Bernoulli's theorem between 1 and 2,

$$\frac{P_1}{\rho g} + \frac{V_1^2}{2g} + z_1 = \frac{P_2}{\rho g} + \frac{V_2^2}{2g} + z_2 + h_{\text{losses}}$$

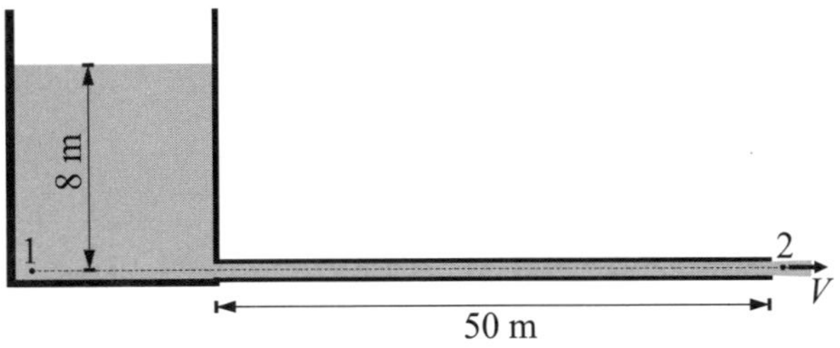

or $$0 + 0 + 8 = 0 + \frac{V^2}{2g} + 0 + h_i + h_f$$

or $$8 = \frac{V^2}{2g} + \frac{0.5V^2}{2g} + \frac{0.017 \times 50 \times V^2}{0.1 \times 2 \times g}$$

$$\frac{V^2}{2g}\left[1 + 0.5 + \frac{0.017 \times 50}{0.1}\right] = 8$$

$$V = 3.96 \text{ m/s}$$

Discharge, $Q = AV = \frac{\pi}{4}d^2V = \frac{\pi}{4} \times 0.1^2 \times 3.96$

$$Q = 0.0311 \text{ m}^3/\text{s}$$

Q.42 Ans:(B)

Pressure difference, $P_2 - P_1 = \rho g(h+a) - \rho ga$

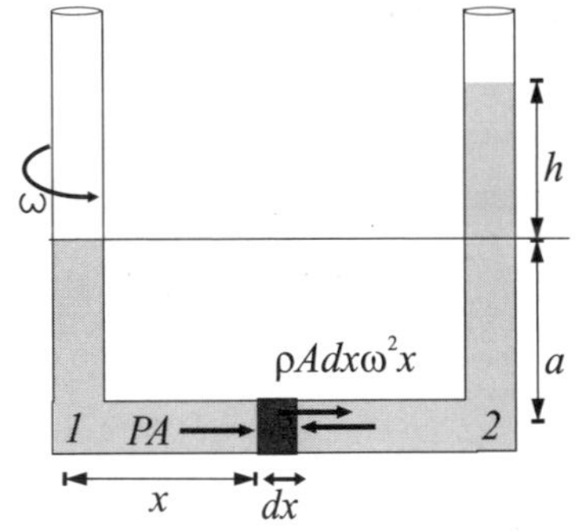

or $$P_2 - P_1 = \rho gh \quad \text{(i)}$$

Consider an small element at x from rotational limb. Equilibrium equation,

$$PA + \rho A dx \omega^2 x - (P + dP)A = 0$$

or $$\int_{P_1}^{P_2} dP = \rho\omega^2 \int_0^l x\,dx$$

or $$P_2 - P_1 = \frac{\rho\omega^2 l^2}{2} \quad \text{(ii)}$$

From Equation (i) and (ii), we have $\rho gh = \frac{\rho\omega^2 l^2}{2}$

$$h = \frac{\omega^2 l^2}{2g}$$

Q.43 Ans:(B)

Let h be the depth of immersion

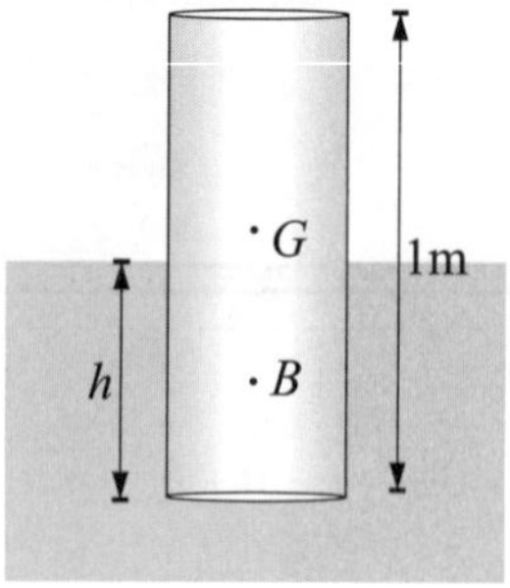

$$mg = F_B$$

or $$600g \times \frac{\pi}{4}d^2 \times 1 = 1000g \times \frac{\pi}{4}d^2 \times h$$

$$h = 0.6\,\text{m}$$

$$BG = \frac{1}{2} - \frac{h}{2} = \frac{1}{2} - \frac{0.6}{2} \Rightarrow BG = 0.2\,\text{m}$$

$$\frac{I}{\forall} = \frac{\frac{\pi d^4}{64}}{\frac{\pi}{4}d^2 h} = \frac{d^2}{16h} = \frac{0.2^2}{16 \times 0.6} = 0.0041\,\text{m}$$

Metacentric height, $MG = \frac{I}{\forall} - BG = 0.0042 - 0.2$

$$MG = -0.195$$

Negative sign means that the Metacenter M is below the center of gravity G.

Thus, the cylinder float unstable equilibrium.

Q.44 Ans:(B)

Volume of fluid displaced by upper plate in time Δt is

$$= v_0 \pi r^2 = \text{Radial out flow} = v_r 2\pi r d$$

or $$v_r = \frac{v_0 \pi r^2}{2\pi r d} = \frac{v_0 r}{2d}$$

$$\text{Radial velocity, } v_r = \frac{v_0 r}{2d}$$

Q.45 Ans:(C)

Given: $(F_r)_m = (F_r)_p$, $(Re)_m = (Re)_p$ and $\frac{\nu_m}{\nu_p} = 0.0894$

$$(F_r)_m = (F_r)_p \Rightarrow \left(\frac{V}{\sqrt{gL}}\right)_m = \left(\frac{V}{\sqrt{gL}}\right)_p \quad \text{(i)}$$

$$(Re)_m = (Re)_p \Rightarrow \left(\frac{VL}{\nu}\right)_m = \left(\frac{VL}{\nu}\right)_p \quad \text{(ii)}$$

From Equations (i) and (ii), we obtain

$$\left(\frac{\nu}{L^{3/2}}\right)_m = \left(\frac{\nu}{L^{3/2}}\right)_p$$

$$\text{Model scale} = \frac{L_p}{L_m} = \left(\frac{\nu_p}{\nu_p}\right)^{2/3} = \left(\frac{1}{0.0894}\right)^{2/3} = 5$$

$$\text{Model scale} = 5:1$$

Q.46 Ans:(D)

Number of variables $= 4\,(\lambda, \rho, g \text{ and } \sigma)$

Number of π - terms $= 4 - 3 = 1$

Therefore, $\pi_1 = \lambda^a \rho^b g^c \sigma$

$$\pi_1 = L^a M^b L^{-3b} L^c T^{-2c} M T^{-2}$$

or $$M^0 L^0 T^0 = M^{b+1} L^{a-3b+c} T^{-2c-2}$$

From which $b = -1, c = -1, a = -2$

$$\pi_1 = \frac{\sigma}{\lambda^2 g \rho}$$

Q.47 Ans:(A)

Given: H = 35 m; Speed ratio, $K_u = 2.0$; $D_0 = 2.0$ m and $D_b = 0.6$ m.

Speed ratio, $K_u = 2 = \frac{u_1}{\sqrt{2gH}}$

or $$u_1 = 2 \times \sqrt{2 \times 9.81 \times 35}$$

$$u_1 = 52.41\,\text{m/s}$$

Speed of runner, $N = \frac{60u_1}{\pi D_0} = \frac{60 \times 52.41}{\pi \times 2}$

$$N = 500\,\text{rpm}$$

Q.48 Ans:(D)

Given: N = 600 rpm; V=100 m/s; $\frac{u}{V} = 0.44$ and Speed ratio, $K_v = \frac{u}{\sqrt{2gH}} = 0.43$

$$u = 0.44 \times 100 = 44\,\text{m/s}$$

$$\frac{44}{\sqrt{2gH}} = 0.43 \Rightarrow \sqrt{2gH} = 10232$$

Coefficient of velocity,

$$C_v = \frac{\text{Actual velocity}}{\text{Theoretical velocity}} = \frac{100}{102.32}$$

$$C_v = 0.977$$

Q.49 Ans:(B)

Applying principle of conservation of energy,

Power supply = Increase in total energy

$$\text{Power, } P = \frac{(P_2 - P_1)}{\rho g}\dot{m}g + \frac{V_2^2 - V_1^2}{2g}\dot{m}g + (z_2 - z_1)\dot{m}g$$

Since $V_2 = V_1$, $z_2 = z_1$ and $\dot{m} = \rho Q$

$$\text{Power } P = \frac{(P_2 - P_1)}{\rho g}\dot{m}g = \frac{(P_2 - P_1)}{\rho g}\rho Q g$$

or $\quad P = (P_2 - P_1)Q$

or $\quad P = (P_2 - P_1)AV$

$$1\times 10^6 = (P_2 - 1.01\times 10^5)1\times 10$$

$$P_2 = 2.01\times 10^5 \text{ N/m}^2$$

$$P_2 = 2 \text{ atm}$$

Q.50 Ans:(A)

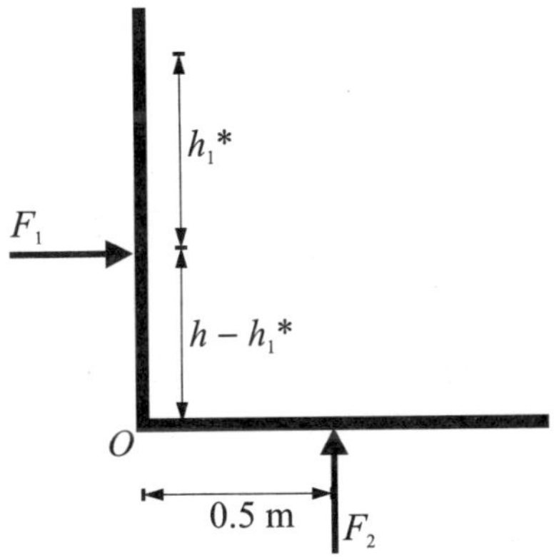

Moment about hinged point O,

$$F_1 \times (h - h_1^*) = F_2 \times 0.5 \qquad \text{(i)}$$

where $F_2 = wA\bar{h} = \rho g b \times 1 \times h = \rho g b h$,

$$h_1^* = \frac{I_G}{A\bar{h}} + \bar{h} = \frac{\frac{bh^3}{12}}{bh \times \frac{h}{2}} + \frac{h}{2} = \frac{2}{3}h$$

and $F_1 = wA\bar{h} = \rho g b h \times \dfrac{h}{2} = \dfrac{\rho g b h^2}{2}$

From Equation (i), we have

$$\frac{\rho g b h^2}{2} \times \left(h - \frac{2}{3}h\right) = \rho g b h \times 0.5$$

or $\quad h^2 = 3$

$$h = 1.73 \text{ m}$$

Q.51 Ans:[1]

Velocity distribution $\dfrac{u}{U_\infty} = \left(\dfrac{y}{\delta}\right)^{0.25}$ where $U_\infty = 20$ m/s and $\delta = 5$ cm

$$\text{Displacement thickness, } \delta^* = \int_0^\delta \left(1 - \frac{u}{U_\infty}\right) dy$$

$$\delta^* = \int_0^\delta \left[1 - \left(\frac{y}{5}\right)^{0.25}\right] dy = \left[y - \frac{1}{5^{0.25}}\frac{y^{1.25}}{1.25}\right]_0^5$$

or $\quad \delta^* = 5 - \dfrac{5}{1.25}$

$$\delta^* = 1 \text{ cm}$$

Q.52 Ans:[567]

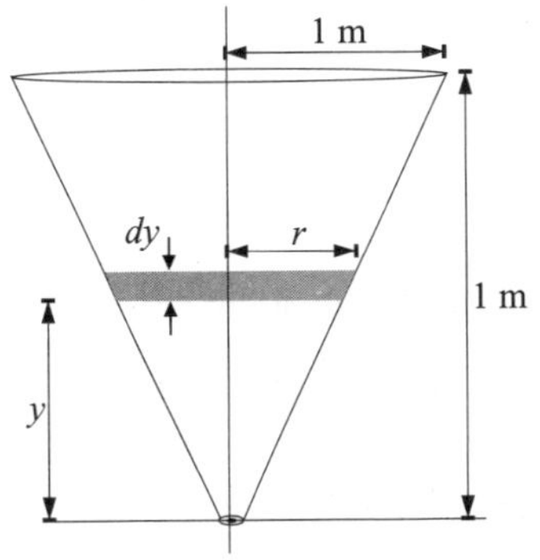

Let any time, the height of liquid from orifice is y and let the liquid surface fall by a small height dy in time dt. Then volume of liquid leaving the tank = Volume of liquid flowing through orifice in time dt

$$\pi r^2 dy = a\sqrt{2gy}adt$$

From geometry of figure $\dfrac{1}{1} = \dfrac{r}{y} \Rightarrow r = y$

$$\pi \frac{y^2}{\sqrt{y}} dy = a\sqrt{2g}\, dt,$$

$$\text{Integrating } \int_0^H \pi y^{3/2} dy = \sqrt{2g}a \int_0^T dt$$

$$T = \frac{2\pi H^{5/2}}{5a\sqrt{2g}} = \frac{2\pi \times 1^{5/2}}{5 \times \frac{5}{10000}\sqrt{2g}}$$

$$T = 567 \text{ s}$$

Q.53 Ans:[2]

For dynamic similarity, Froude number be same for model and prototype.

$$\left(\frac{V}{\sqrt{gL}}\right)_m = \left(\frac{V}{\sqrt{gL}}\right)_p$$

$$V_m = V_p\sqrt{\frac{L_m}{L_p}}$$

or $$V_m = 10\times\sqrt{\frac{1}{25}}$$

$$V_m = 2\,\text{m/s}$$

Q.54 Ans:[71.5]

Kinetic head = Potential head

$$\frac{v^2}{2g} = h + 0.1$$

or $$h = \frac{v^2}{2g} - 0.1 = \frac{4^2}{2\times 9.81} - 0.1$$

or $$h = 0.715\,\text{m}$$

$$h = 71.5\,\text{cm}$$

Q.55 Ans:[94.57]

Applying energy equation at inlet and exit of pump,

$$\frac{P_1}{\rho g} + \frac{V_1^2}{2g} + z_1 + h = \frac{P_2}{\rho g} + \frac{V_2^2}{2g} + z_2$$

and $\rho A V_1 = \rho A V_2 \Rightarrow V_1 = V_2$

or $$h = \frac{P_2 - P_1}{\rho g} + z_2 - z_1 = \frac{(700-300)\times 10^3}{1000\times 9.81g} + 0.2$$

or $$h = 40.97$$

Power required by pump, $P = \dfrac{\rho Q g h}{\eta}$

$$P = \frac{1000\times 0.2\times 9.81\times 40.97}{0.85}$$

$$P = 94.57\,\text{kW}$$

Q.56 Ans:[7.28]

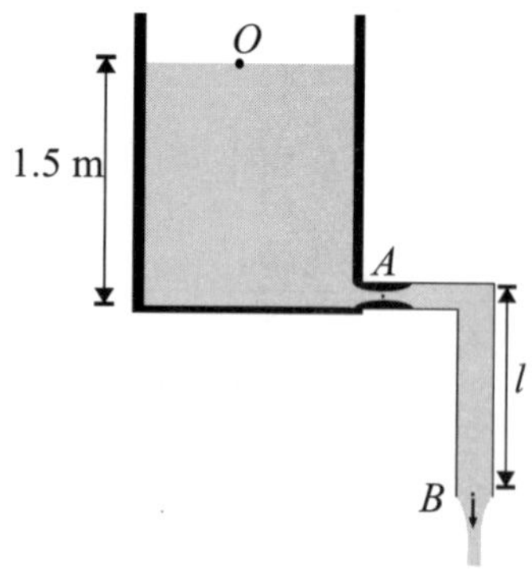

Applying Bernoulli's equation between free surface and at A,

$$\frac{P_0}{\rho g} + \frac{V_0^2}{2g} + z_0 = \frac{P_A}{\rho g} + \frac{V_A^2}{2g} + z_A$$

or $$\frac{95.48\times 10^3}{1000\times 9.81} + 0 + 1.5 = \frac{4\times 10^3}{1000\times 9.81} + \frac{V_A^2}{2g} + 0$$

$$V_A = 14.57\ \text{m/s and } V_B = \frac{V_A}{2} = 7.28\,\text{m/s}$$

Velocity at B, $V_B = 7.28\,\text{m/s}$

Q.57 Ans:[20.2]

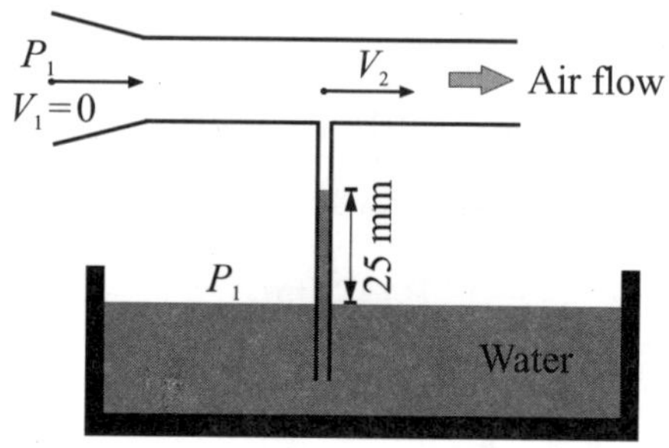

Applying Bernoulli's equation between 1 and 2,

$$\frac{P_1}{\rho g} + \frac{V_1^2}{2g} + z_1 = \frac{P_2}{\rho g} + \frac{V_2^2}{2g} + z_2$$

since $z_1 = z_2$ and $V_1 = 0$, we have

$$V_2 = \sqrt{2g\frac{P_1 - P_2}{\rho g}}$$

Pressure at point 2,

$$P_2 = P_1 - \rho_w g\times\frac{25}{1000} \Rightarrow P_2 = P_1 - 1000g\times\frac{25}{1000}$$

$$P_1 - P_2 = 25g$$

$$V_2 = \sqrt{2g\times\frac{25g}{\rho g}} = \sqrt{\frac{2\times 25\times 9.81}{1.2}}$$

$$V_2 = 20.2\,\text{m/s}$$

Q.58 Ans:[395]

Given: $Q = 100$ l/s, $P_1 = 3\times 10^5$ N/m^2, $V_1 = 100$ m/s, $P_2 = 1\times 10^5$ N/m^2 and $V_2 = 50$ m/s

Applying energy equation,

$$mg\left(\frac{P_1}{\rho g} + \frac{V_1^2}{2g} + z_1\right) = mg\left(\frac{P_2}{rg} + \frac{V_2^2}{2g} + z_2\right) + \text{Power } P$$

or $$\text{Power } P = \left(\frac{P_1 - P_2}{\rho}\right)m + \left(\frac{V_1^2 - V_2^2}{2}\right)m + m(z_1 - z_2)$$

$$P = \left(\frac{3\times10^5 - 1\times10^5}{\rho}\right)\rho\times100\times10^{-3}$$

$$+\left(\frac{100^2 - 50^2}{2}\right)1000\times100\times10^{-3}$$

or $P = 20000 + 375000 = 395000\text{ W}$

$$P = 395\text{ kW}$$

Q.59 Ans:[19.6]

Net head, $h = 15 + 5 = 20\text{ m}$

Flow rate, $Q = 180\text{ m}^3/\text{h} = \frac{1}{20}\text{ m}^3/\text{s}$

Power required, $P = \frac{\rho Q g h}{\eta} = \frac{1000\times\frac{1}{20}9.81\times20}{0.5}$

$$P = 19.6\text{ kW}$$

Q.60 Ans:[158.72]

Applying the principle of conservation of energy,

$$\dot{m}_1 g\left(\frac{P_1}{\rho g} + \frac{V_1^2}{2g}\right) + \dot{m}_2 g\left(\frac{P_2}{rg} + \frac{V_2^2}{2g}\right) = \dot{m}_3 g\left(\frac{P_3}{rg} + \frac{V_3^2}{2g}\right)$$

or $\dot{m}_1\frac{V_1^2}{2g} + \dot{m}_2\frac{V_2^2}{2g} - \dot{m}_3\frac{V_3^2}{2g} = \dot{m}_3\frac{P_3}{\rho g} - \dot{m}_1\frac{P_1}{\rho g} - \dot{m}_2\frac{P_2}{\rho g}$

Since $P_1 = P_2$,

$$P_3 - P_1 = \frac{\rho}{2}\left[\left(\frac{\dot{m}_1}{\dot{m}_2}\right)V_1^2 + \left(\frac{\dot{m}_2}{\dot{m}_3}\right)V_2^2 - V_3^2\right]$$

Applying continuity equation,

$$A_1V_1 + A_2V_2 = A_3V_3 \Rightarrow \quad 20\times25 + 40\times5 = 60V_3$$

$$V_3 = \frac{70}{6} = 11.67\text{ m/s}$$

$$\dot{m}_1 = 1000\times\frac{20}{10^4}\times25 = 50\text{ kg/s}$$

$$\dot{m}_2 = 1000\times\frac{40}{10^4}\times5 = 20\text{ kg/s}$$

$$\dot{m}_3 = \dot{m}_1 + \dot{m}_2 = 70\text{ kg/s}$$

From which

$$P_3 - P_1 = \frac{1000}{2}\left[\left(\frac{50}{70}\right)\times25^2 + \left(\frac{20}{70}\right)\times5^2 - \left(\frac{70}{6}\right)^2\right]$$

$$P_3 - P_1 = 158.72\text{ kN/m}^2$$

Q.61 Ans:[10.1]

Consider an element of thickness dr at distance r from rotational axis.

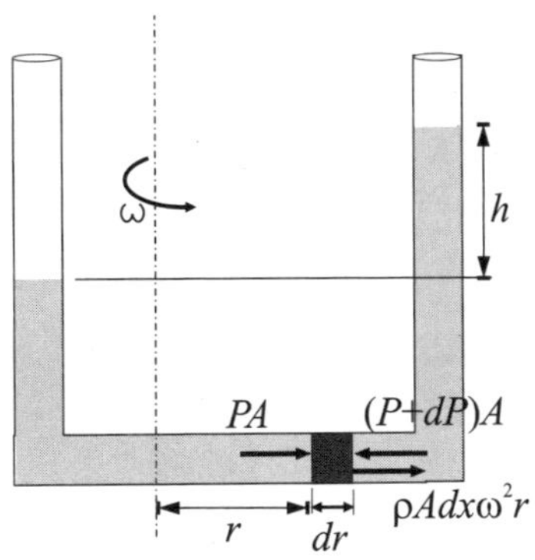

$$\Sigma F = 0 \Rightarrow PA + dm\omega^2 r - (P + dP)A = 0$$

or $dPA = dm\omega^2 r = \rho A dr\omega^2 r$

$$\int_1^2 dP = \int_{-r_1}^{r_2}\rho\omega^2 r dr \Rightarrow (P_2 - P_1) = \frac{\rho\omega^2}{2}(r_2^2 - r_1^2)$$

Substituting $P_2 - P_1 = \rho g h$, we have

$$\rho g h = \frac{\rho\omega^2}{2}(r_2^2 - r_1^2) \Rightarrow h = \frac{\omega^2}{2g}(r_2^2 - r_1^2)$$

or $h = \frac{1}{2\times9.81}\times\left(\frac{2\pi\times60}{\pi\times60}\right)^2\times\left[\frac{75^2 - 25^2}{100^2}\right]$

or $h = 0.101\text{ m}$

$$h = 10.1\text{ cm}$$

Q.62 Ans:[988.4]

Given:

Full scale	Model
$H_p = 30$	$H_m = 10\text{ m}$
$N_p = 428$	$N_m = ?$
Diameter $= D_p$	$D_m = \frac{D_p}{4}$

Blade velocity of turbine $u \propto$ velocity of water (V)

$$\frac{\pi DN}{60} \propto \sqrt{2gH} \quad \Rightarrow \quad DN \propto \sqrt{H}$$

or $\frac{D_m N_m}{D_p N_p} = \frac{\sqrt{H_m}}{\sqrt{H_p}}$

or $\frac{\frac{D_p}{4}}{D_p}\times\frac{N_m}{428} = \sqrt{\frac{10}{30}}$

or $N_m = \frac{428\times4}{\sqrt{3}}$

$$N_m = 988.4\text{ rpm}$$

Q.63 Ans:[2.93]

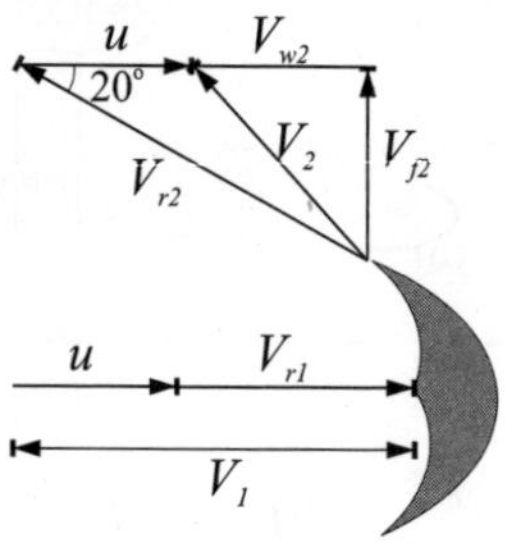

Given: $u = 10$ m/s; $Q = 0.7\ \text{m}^3/\text{s}$; $H = 30$ m;
$\phi = 180 - 160 = 20°$ and $C_v = 0.98$

$V_1 = C_v\sqrt{2gH} = 0.98\sqrt{2\times 9.81\times 30} = 23.77$ m/s

From velocity triangle,

$$V_{r_1} = V_1 - u = 23.77 - 10 = 13.77 \text{ m/s}$$

Whirl velocity at outlet,

$$V_{w_2} = V_{r2}\cos 20 - u = V_{r1}\cos 20 - u$$

$$V_{w_2} = 13.77\cos 20 - 10$$

$$V_{w_2} = 2.93 \text{ m/s}$$

Q.64 Ans:[758.94]

Given: $D_m = 0.4$ m, $P_m = 15$ kW, $H_m = 5$ m, $N_m = 1600$ rpm, $D_P = 1.6$ m and $H_P = 18$ m

Similarity between model and prototype,

$$\frac{H_m}{N_m^2 D_m^2} = \frac{H_P}{N_P^2 D_P^2}$$

or $$N_P^2 = \frac{H_P}{H_m}\times\frac{D_m^2}{D_P^2}N_m^2$$

or $$N_P^2 = \frac{18}{5}\times\left(\frac{0.4}{1.6}\right)^2\times 1600^2$$

$$N_P = 758.94 \text{ rpm}$$

Q.65 Ans:[1000]

Given: $H_P = 20$ m; $N_P = 500$ rpm; scale $= 1:2$ and $H_m = 20$ m

Similarity between model and prototype,

$$\frac{N_m D_m}{\sqrt{H_m}} = \frac{N_P D_P}{\sqrt{H_p}}$$

or $$N_m = \frac{D_P}{D_M}\times\sqrt{\frac{H_m}{H_p}}\times N_P$$

or $$N_m = 2\times\sqrt{\frac{20}{20}}\times 500$$

$$N_m = 1000 \text{ rpm}$$

11 Heat Transfer

GATE Mechanical Engg.

GATE Syllabus

Modes of heat transfer; One-dimensional heat conduction, resistance concept and electrical analogy, heat transfer through fins; Unsteady heat conduction, lumped parameter system, Heisler's charts; Thermal boundary layer, dimensionless parameters in free and forced convective heat transfer, heat transfer correlations for flow over flat plates and through pipes, effect of turbulence; Heat exchanger performance, LMTD and NTU methods; Radiative heat transfer, Stefan-Boltzmann law, Wien's displacement law, black and grey surfaces, view factors, radiation network analysis.

Chapter Outline

11.1 KEY CONCEPTS AND FORMULAS

Modes of Heat Transfer

1. Conduction, 2. Convection, and 3. Radiation. All modes of heat transfer require the existence of a temperature difference.

Conduction

In conduction, the energy exchange takes place from the region of high temperature to that of low temperature by the kinetic motion or direct impact of molecules, as in the case of fluid at rest and by the drift of electrons, as in case of metals.

The empirical law of heat conduction based on experimental observations by Fourier.

Fourier's law of heat conduction $Q = -kA\dfrac{dT}{dx}$ (W), where k is the thermal conductivity of material.

Heat flux,

$$q = \frac{Q}{A} = -k\frac{dT}{dx} \text{ W/m}^2$$

$$\text{Thermal diffusivity, } \alpha = \frac{\text{Heat conduction}}{\text{Heat storage}} = \frac{k}{\rho c_p} \ (\text{m}^2/\text{s})$$

The physical significance of thermal diffusivity is associate with the propagation of heat into the medium during changes of temperature with time.

Conduction-basic Equations

One-dimensional Heat Conduction Equation

$$\frac{1}{A}\frac{\partial}{\partial x}\left(kA\frac{\partial T}{\partial x}\right) + q_g = \rho c_p \frac{\partial T}{\partial t}$$

Rectangular coordinates:

$$\frac{\partial}{\partial x}\left(k\frac{\partial T}{\partial x}\right)+q_g=\rho c_p\frac{\partial T}{\partial t} \leftarrow A=\text{constant}$$

Cylindrical coordinates:

$$\frac{1}{r}\frac{\partial}{\partial r}\left(rk\frac{\partial T}{\partial r}\right)+q_g=\rho c_p\frac{\partial T}{\partial t}$$

Spherical coordinates:

$$\frac{1}{r^2}\frac{\partial}{\partial r}\left(r^2k\frac{\partial T}{\partial r}\right)+q_g=\rho c_p\frac{\partial T}{\partial t}$$

$$\frac{1}{r^n}\frac{\partial}{\partial x}\left(r^nk\frac{\partial T}{\partial r}\right)+q_g=\rho c_p\frac{\partial T}{\partial t},\quad n=\begin{cases}0 & \text{for rectangular coordinates}\\ 1 & \text{for cylindrical coordinates}\\ 2 & \text{for spherical coordinates}\end{cases}$$

Three-dimensional Heat Conduction Equation

Rectangular coordinate system:

$$\frac{\partial^2T}{\partial x^2}+\frac{\partial^2T}{\partial y^2}+\frac{\partial^2T}{\partial z^2}+\frac{q_g}{k}=\frac{1}{\alpha}\frac{\partial T}{\partial t}$$

Cylindrical coordinate system:

$$\frac{1}{r}\frac{\partial}{\partial r}\left(r\frac{\partial T}{\partial r}\right)+\frac{1}{r^2}\frac{\partial^2T}{\partial\phi^2}+\frac{\partial^2T}{\partial z^2}+\frac{q_g}{k}=\frac{1}{\alpha}\frac{\partial T}{\partial t}$$

Spherical coordinate system:

$$\frac{1}{r^2}\frac{\partial}{\partial r}\left(r^2\frac{\partial T}{\partial r}\right)+\frac{1}{r^2\sin\theta}\frac{\partial}{\partial\theta}\left(\sin\theta\frac{\partial T}{\partial\theta}\right)+\frac{1}{r^2\sin^2\theta}\frac{\partial^2T}{\partial\phi^2}+\frac{q_g}{k}=\frac{1}{\alpha}\frac{\partial T}{\partial t}$$

One-dimensional steady-state Heat Conduction

The Slab

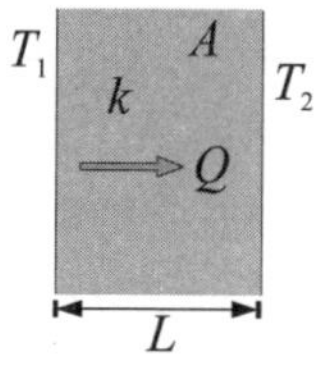

$$\frac{d^2T}{dx^2}+\frac{q_g}{k}=0;$$

Solution: $T=-\frac{q_o}{2k}x^2+c_1x+c_2$

Two boundary conditions are needed to determine c_1 and c_2.

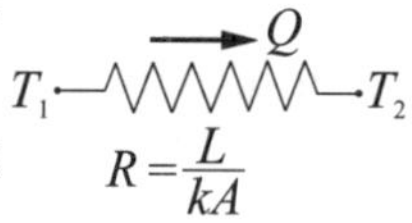

Figure shows a slab without heat generation ($q_g=0$),

Governing equation, $\frac{d^2T}{dx^2}=0$

Boundary conditions (i) $T=T_1$ at $x=0$ and (ii) $T=T_2$ at $x=L$

Solution: $T=T_1-\frac{T_1-T_2}{L}x$

$$Q=-kA\frac{d}{dx}\left(T_1-\frac{T_1-T_2}{L}x\right)=\frac{kA(T_1-T_2)}{L}$$

$$Q=\frac{T_1-T_2}{\left(\frac{L}{kA}\right)}=\frac{T_1-T_2}{R}$$

Where R is the thermal resistance, $\left[R=\frac{L}{kA}\text{ for slab}\right]$.

The Cylinder

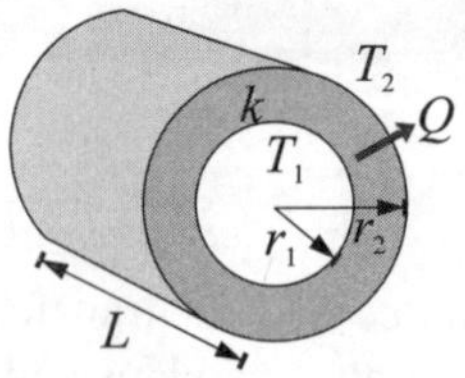

$$\frac{1}{r}\frac{d}{dr}\left(r\frac{dT}{dr}\right)+\frac{q_g}{k}=0;$$

Solution: $T=-\frac{q_o}{4k}r^2+c_1\ln r+c_2$

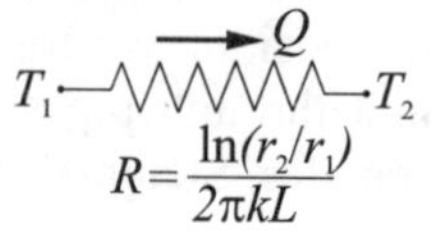

Figure shows a hollow cylinder without heat generation ($q_g=0$), Governing equation:

$$\frac{d}{dr}\left(r\frac{dT}{dr}\right)=0;$$

Boundary conditions: (i) $T=T_1$ at $r=r_1$ and (ii) $T=T_2$ at $r=r_2$

Solution: $$T=T_1+\frac{\ln(r/r_1)}{\ln(r_2/r_1)}(T_2-T_1)$$

$$Q=-k2\pi rL\frac{d}{dx}\left(T_1+\frac{\ln(r/r_1)}{\ln(r_2/r_1)}(T_2-T_1)\right)$$

$$Q=\frac{(T_1-T_2)}{\frac{\ln(r_2/r_1)}{2\pi kL}}=\frac{T_1-T_2}{R};$$ where R is the thermal resistance.

The Sphere

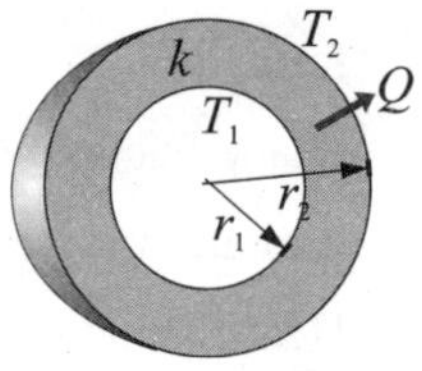

$$\frac{1}{r^2}\frac{d}{dr}\left(r^2\frac{dT}{dr}\right)+\frac{q_g}{k}=0;$$

Solution: $T=-\frac{q_o}{6k}r^2-\frac{c_1}{r}+c_2$

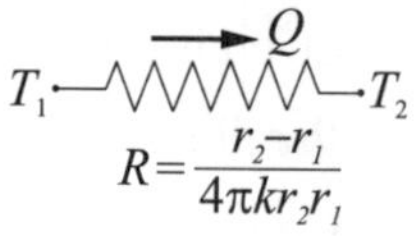

Figure shows a hollow sphere without heat generation ($q_g=0$).

Governing equation:

$$\frac{1}{r^2}\frac{d}{dr}\left(r^2\frac{dT}{dr}\right)=0$$

Boundary conditions: (i) $T=T_1$ at $r=r_1$ and (ii) $T=T_2$ at $r=r_2$

Solution: $$T=\frac{r_1}{r}\left(\frac{r_2-r}{r_2-r_1}\right)T_1+\frac{r_2}{r}\left(\frac{r_2-r_1}{r_2-r_1}\right)T_2$$

$$Q=-k4\pi r^2\frac{d}{dx}\left(\frac{r_1}{r}\left(\frac{r_2-r}{r_2-r_1}\right)T_1+\frac{r_2}{r}\left(\frac{r_2-r_1}{r_2-r_1}\right)T_2\right)$$

$$Q = \frac{(T_1 - T_2)}{\frac{r_2 - r_1}{4\pi k r_1 r_2}} = \frac{T_1 - T_2}{R}$$

Composite Medium

Composite Slab (in series)

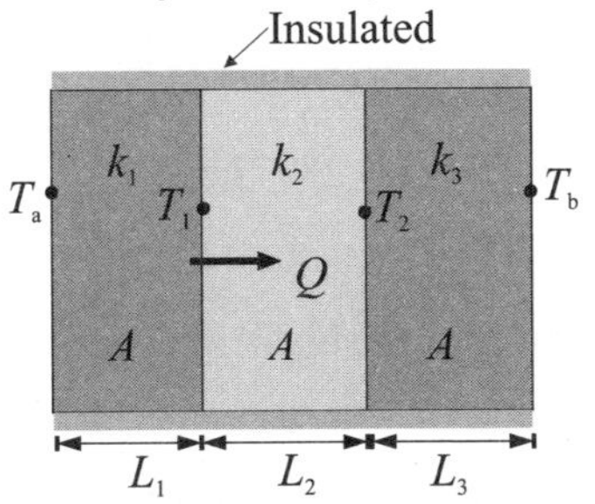

A composite of three walls in series

$$R_1 = \frac{L_1}{K_1 A}; \quad R_2 = \frac{L_2}{K_2 A}; \quad R_3 = \frac{L_3}{k_3 A}$$

Equivalent thermal resistance network

Heat transfer rate, $Q = \frac{T_a - T_1}{R_1} = \frac{T_1 - T_2}{R_2} = \frac{T_2 - T_3}{R_3}$

or $\quad Q = \frac{T_a - T_b}{R_1 + R_2 + R_3}$

Critical Radius of Insulation

Adding the insulation to a cylinder or sphere increases the rate of heat transfer if the outer radius of the insulation is less than the critical radius r_c of insulation, defined as

$$r_c = \frac{k}{h} \text{ (cylinder)} \quad \text{and} \quad r_c = \frac{2k}{h} \text{ (sphere)}$$

Finned Surfaces

Fins enhance heat transfer from a surface by exposing a larger surface area to convection.

Governing differential equation of fin:

$$\frac{d^2T}{d^2x} - \frac{hP}{kA_c}(T - T_\infty) = 0$$

or $\quad \frac{d^2\theta}{d^2x} - m^2\theta = 0 \quad$ where, $m = \sqrt{\frac{hP}{kA_c}}$ and $\theta = T - T_\infty$

The temperature distribution along the fin are given by

$$\frac{T - T_\infty}{T_o - T_\infty} = e^{-mx} \qquad \text{(very long fin)}$$

$$\frac{T - T_\infty}{T_o - T_\infty} = \frac{\cosh m(L - x)}{\cosh mL} \qquad \text{(insulated fin tip)}$$

The rate of heat transfer from fin are given by

$Q = -kA_c\left(\frac{dT}{dx}\right)_{x=0} = \sqrt{hpkA_c}(T_o - T_\infty)$; very long fin

$Q = -kA_c\left(\frac{dT}{dx}\right)_{x=0} = \sqrt{hpkA_c}(T_o - T_\infty)\tanh mL$; Insulated fin tip

Effectiveness of fin,

$$\varepsilon = \frac{\text{Heat transfer from fin}}{\text{Heat transfer without fin from same base area}}$$

or $\quad \varepsilon = \sqrt{\frac{hP}{kA_c}}$ (very long fin)

Efficiency of fin

$$\eta = \frac{\text{Heat transfer from fin}}{\text{Heat transfer from fin if the entire fin were at base temperature}}$$

Fin efficiency and fin effectiveness are related to each other by $\varepsilon = \frac{A_{fin}}{A_o}\eta$

Convection

In convection, the energy transfer takes place between a solid surface and the adjacent liquid or gas that is in motion, and it involves the combined effects of conduction and fluid motion.

Heat transfer rate, $Q = hA(T_S - T_\infty) \leftarrow$ Newton's law of cooling

Convection heat transfer coefficient, $h = \frac{-k_{\text{fluid}}\left(\frac{\partial T}{\partial y}\right)_{y=0}}{T_s - T_\infty}$

Nusselt number, $Nu = \frac{hL_c}{k}$

Prandtl number, $Pr = \frac{\mu c_p}{k}$

Reynold number, $Re = \frac{\rho V x}{\mu}$

Grashof number, $Gr = \frac{\beta g \Delta T L_c^3}{(\mu/\rho)^2}$

Transient Heat Conduction

Lumped System

Lumped system in which the temperature varies with time but remains uniform throughout the system at any time.

$$\frac{T - T_\infty}{T_i - T_\infty} = e^{-\frac{hA}{\rho V c_p}t}$$

or $$\frac{T - T_\infty}{T_i - T_\infty} = e^{-\frac{hL_c}{k} \times \frac{k}{\rho c_p L_c^2} t} = e^{-\left(\frac{hL_c}{k}\right) \times \left(\frac{\alpha t}{L_c^2}\right)}$$

$$\frac{T - T_\infty}{T_i - T_\infty} = e^{-Bi \times Fo}$$

Biot number, $Bi = \frac{hL_c}{k}$; Fourier number, $F_o = \frac{\alpha t}{L_c^2}$;

Characteristic length, $L_c = \frac{V}{A}$.

Thermal Boundary Layer

Thermal Boundary Thickness

It is the distance from the surface at which the temperature difference $T - T_\infty$ equals $0.99 (T_s - T_\infty)$.

Thermal boundary thickness,

$$\delta_t = \frac{4.91x}{Pr^{\frac{1}{3}} \sqrt{Re_x}} \text{ (for flat plate and laminar flow)}$$

Local Nusselt number, $Nu_x = \frac{h_x x}{k} = 0332 \, Pr^{\frac{1}{3}} Re_x^{\frac{1}{2}}$ (for flat plate and laminar flow)

Velocity Boundary Thickness

It is the distance from the surface at which $u = 0.99U$.

Velocity boundary thickness $\delta = \frac{4.91x}{\sqrt{\text{Re}_x}}$ (for flat plate)

Radiation

Radiation is the process in which energy emitted by matter in the form of electromagnetic waves (or photons) as a result of the changes in the electronic configurations of the atoms or molecules.

Heat transfer from black body,

$$Q = \sigma A T^4 \leftarrow \text{Stefan-Boltzmann law}$$

Stefan-Boltzmann constant $\sigma = 5.6697 \times 10^{-8}$ W/m^2 K^4

Heat transfer from real body, $Q = \varepsilon \sigma A T^4$, where ε is the emissivity of the surface, $0 \le \varepsilon \le 1$.

Emissive Power

The *emissive power* (E_b) of a body is defined as the amount of thermal energy emitted by radiation from a surface in all directions and at all wavelengths per unit surface area. The amount of radiation emitted per unit wavelength is called *monochromatic emission power* ($E_{b\lambda}$).

Plank's Law

Emissive power of a black body at a given temperature is

$$E_{b\lambda} = \frac{C_1}{\lambda^5 (e^{C_2/\lambda T} - 1)}$$

Wien's Displacement Law

Relationship between the wavelength at which emissive power is maximum and the absolute temperature.

$$\frac{d}{d\lambda} E_{b\lambda} = 0 \Rightarrow \frac{d}{d\lambda}\left[\frac{C_1}{\lambda^5 (e^{C_2/\lambda T} - 1)}\right] = 0$$

$$\lambda_m T = b = 2897 \, \mu\text{m.K}$$

Stefan-Boltzman Law

Total emissive power of the black body for the wavelength 0 to ∞ is

$$E_b = \int_0^\infty E_{b\lambda} d\lambda = \sigma T^4 \text{ W/m}^2; \quad \sigma = 5.67 \times 10^{-8} \text{ W/m}^2 \cdot \text{K}^4$$

Black body radiation function, $f_{0-\lambda} = \frac{\int_0^\lambda E_{b\lambda} d\lambda}{\int_0^\infty E_{b\lambda} d\lambda}$

Shape Factor (View Factor)

The view factor from surface i to a surface j is denoted by F_{i-j} is defined as the fraction of the radiation leaving surface i that strikes surface j directly.

$$F_{i-j} = \frac{1}{A_1} \int_{A_1} \int_{A_2} \frac{\cos\theta_1 \cos\theta_1}{\pi r^2} dA_1 dA_2$$

View Factor Relations

1. Reciprocity relation, $A_i F_{i-j} = A_j F_{j-i}$
2. Summation rule, $\sum_{j=1}^{N} F_{i-j} = 1$ (For enclosure)
3. Superposition rule, $F_{1-(2,3)} = F_{1-2} + F_{1-3}$
4. The shape factor for convex and plane surfaces is equal to zero.

Radiation Heat Transfer: Black Surfaces

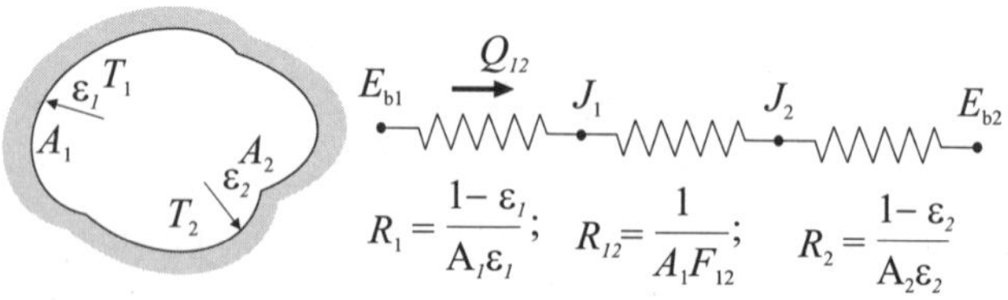

Two surface enclosure **Radiation network**

$$Q_{1-2} = A_1 F_{1-2} \sigma (T_1^4 - T_2^4)$$

Radiation heat transfer in Two surfaces enclosures:

$$Q_{1-2} = \frac{E_{b1} - E_{b2}}{R_1 + R_{12} + R_2}$$

$$Q_{1-2} = \frac{\sigma(T_1^4 - T_2^4)}{\dfrac{1-\varepsilon_1}{A_1\varepsilon_1} + \dfrac{1}{A_1F_{1-2}} + \dfrac{1-\varepsilon_2}{A_2\varepsilon_2}}$$

Heat Exchangers

Classification of Heat Exchangers

Classification by transfer process: 1. Direct contact, and 2. Indirect contact.

Classification according to compactness: The ratio of the heat transfer surface area on one side of the heat exchanger to the volume can be used as a measure of the compactness of heat exchanger.

Classification by construction type: 1.Tubular heat exchanger, 2. Plate heat exchangers, 3. Plate-fin heat exchanger, 4. Tube-fin heat exchanger, and 5. Regenerative heat exchanger.

Classification by flow arrangement: 1. Parallel-flow, 2. Counter-flow, 3. Cross-flow, and 4. Multipass flow.

Classification by heat transfer mechanism: (i) Single-phase forced or free convection, (ii) Phase change (boiling or condensation, and (iii) Radiation or combined convection and radiation.

Temperature Distribution In Heat-exchangers

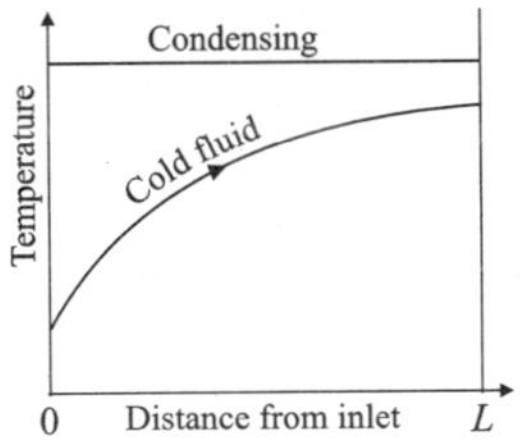

Condesors

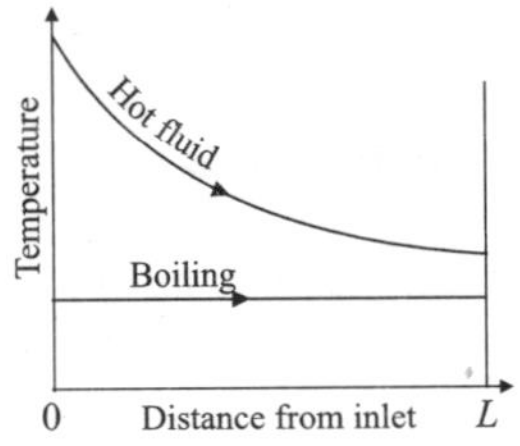

Evaporator

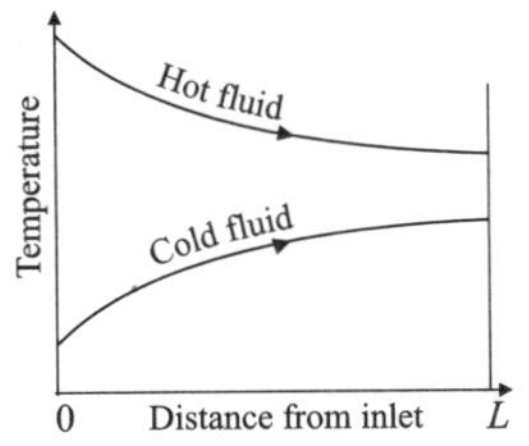

Parallel flow heat exchanger

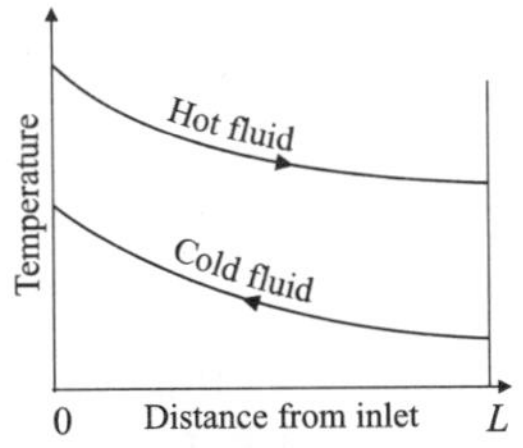

Counter flow heat exchanger

Overall Heat Transfer Coefficient

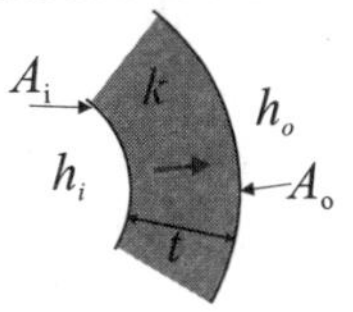

Thermal resistance, R to heat flow across a tube, between the inside and the outside flow, is composed of the following thermal resistance:

$$R = \begin{pmatrix}\text{thermal}\\ \text{resistance}\\ \text{of inside}\\ \text{flow}\end{pmatrix} + \begin{pmatrix}\text{thermal}\\ \text{resistance}\\ \text{of tube}\\ \text{material}\end{pmatrix} + \begin{pmatrix}\text{thermal}\\ \text{resistance}\\ \text{of outside}\\ \text{flow}\end{pmatrix}$$

or $$R = \frac{1}{A_ih_i} + \frac{t}{A_mk} + \frac{1}{A_oh_o}$$

where $A_m = \dfrac{A_o - A_i}{\ln(A_o/A_i)}$ = logarithmic mean area, m^2

Thermal resistance, R can be expressed as an overall heat transfer coefficient based on either the inside or the outside surface of the tube.

The overall heat transfer coefficient U_o based on the outside (or inside or specified) surface of the tube is

$$R = \frac{1}{U_oA_o} = \frac{1}{A_ih_i} + \frac{t}{A_mk} + \frac{1}{A_oh_o}$$

$$U_o = \frac{1}{\dfrac{A_o}{A_i}\cdot\dfrac{1}{h_i} + \dfrac{A_o}{A_m}\cdot\dfrac{t}{k} + \dfrac{1}{h_o}}$$

$$R = \frac{1}{U_oA_o} = \frac{1}{A_ih_i} + \frac{F_i}{A_i} + \frac{t}{A_mk} + \frac{1}{A_oh_o},$$

where F_i is fouling factor

Parallel Flow Heat Exchanger

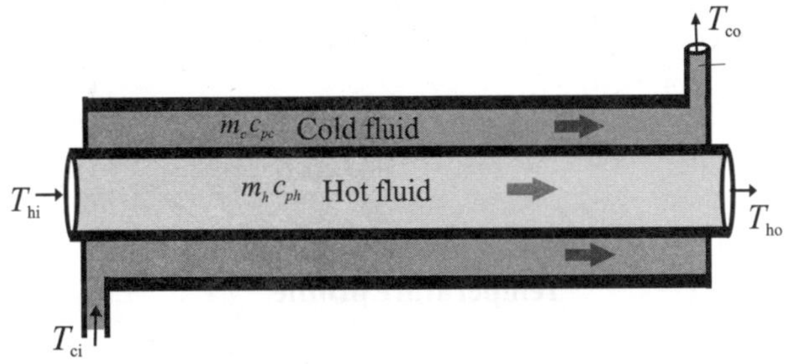

Parallel flow heat exchanger

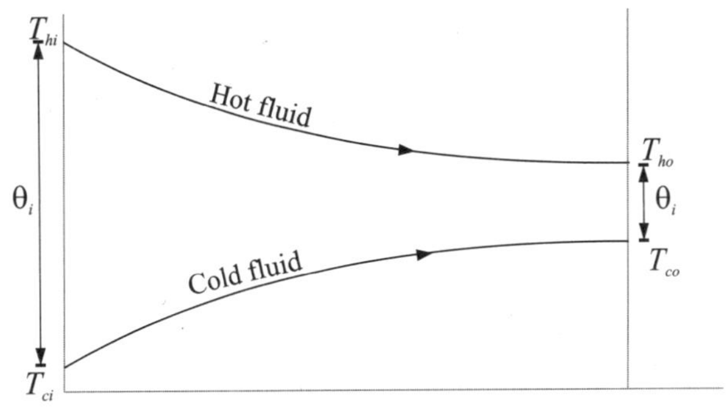

Temperature profile

Heat transfer rate, $Q = m_hc_{ph}(T_{hi} - T_{ho}) = m_cc_{ch}(T_{co} - T_{ci})$

$$Q = UA\,(\text{LMTD})$$

$$\text{LMTD} = \frac{\theta_i - \theta_o}{\ln(\theta_i/\theta_o)}$$

$$\text{Effectiveness, } \varepsilon = \frac{Q}{Q_{max}}$$

$$Q_{max} = (mc)_{min}(T_{hi} - T_{ci})$$

$(mc)_{min}$ is the small of $m_h c_{ph}$ and $m_c c_{ch}$.

$$\varepsilon = \frac{1 - e^{-\text{NTU}(1+C)}}{1+C}$$

where $C = \dfrac{C_{min}}{C_{max}}$ and $\text{NTU} = \dfrac{UA}{C_{min}}$

Counter Flow Heat Exchanger

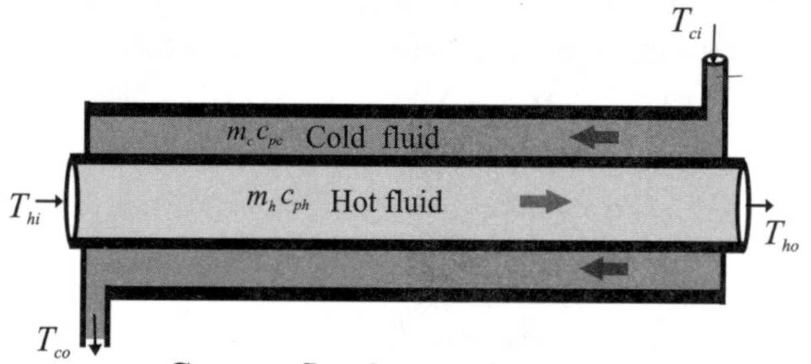

Counter flow heat exchanger

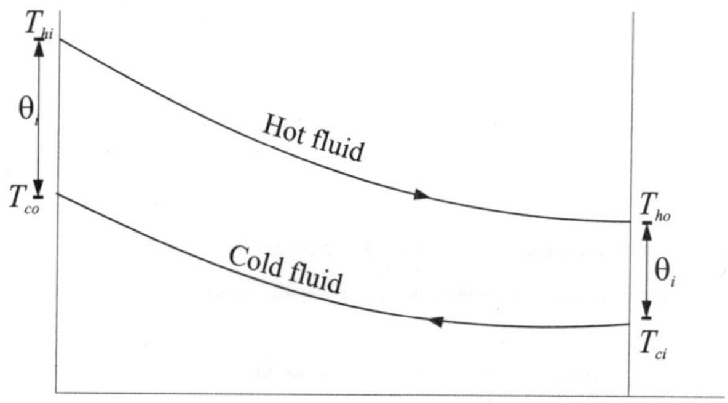

Temperature profile

Heat transfer rate, $Q = m_h c_{ph}(T_{hi} - T_{ho}) = m_c c_{ch}(T_{co} - T_{ci})$

$$Q = UA\,(\text{LMTD})$$

$$\text{LMTD} = \frac{\theta_i - \theta_o}{\ln(\theta_i/\theta_o)}$$

$$\text{Effectiveness, } \varepsilon = \frac{Q}{Q_{max}}$$

$$Q_{max} = (mc)_{min}(T_{hi} - T_{ci})$$

$(mc)_{min}$ is the small of $m_h c_{ph}$ and $m_c c_{ch}$.

$$\varepsilon = \frac{1 - e^{-\text{NTU}(1-C)}}{1 - C\,e^{-\text{NTU}(1-C)}}$$

11.2 SOLVED EXAMPLES

Previous Years GATE Questions

Example 11.1

If a foam insulation is added to a 4 cm outer diameter pipe as shown in figure, the critical radius of insulation (in cm) is______

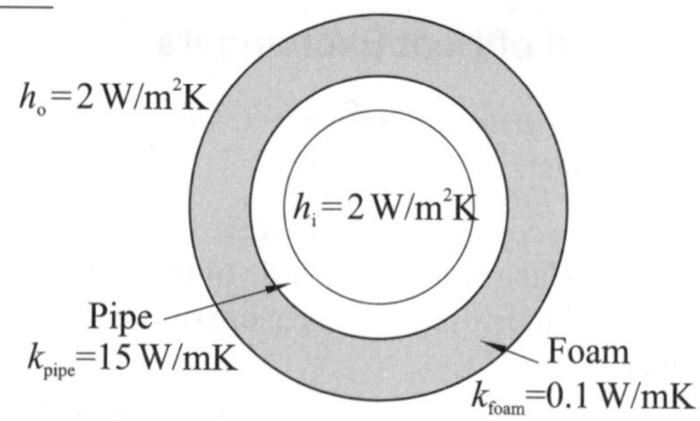

GATE 2015

Solution

The critical radius of insulation for cylinder is

$$r_c = \frac{k}{h}$$

Substituting given data, $k_{foam} = 0.1$ W/m.K and $h_o = 2$ W/m^2·K, we have

$$r_c = \frac{0.1}{2}$$

$$r_c = 5 \text{ cm}$$

Example 11.2

In laminar flow of air ($Pr = 0.7$) over a heated plate, if δ and δ_T denote, respectively the hydrodynamic and thermal boundary layer thickness, then

(A) $\delta = \delta_T$ (B) $\delta > \delta_T$ (C) $\delta < \delta_T$ (D) $\delta = 0$ but $\delta_T \neq 0$

GATE 2015

Solution

If $Pr = 1$ then $\delta = \delta_T$

If $Pr > 1$ then $\delta > \delta_T$

If $Pr < 1\,(0.7)$ then $\delta < \delta_T$

Example 11.3

A cylindrical uranium fuel rod of radius 5 mm in a nuclear reactor is generating heat at the rate of 4×10^7 W/m^3. The rod is cooled by a liquid (convective heat transfer coefficient 1000 W/m^2·K) at 25°C at steady state, the surface temperature (in K) of the rod is

(A) 308 (B) 398 (C) 418 (D) 448

GATE 2015

Solution

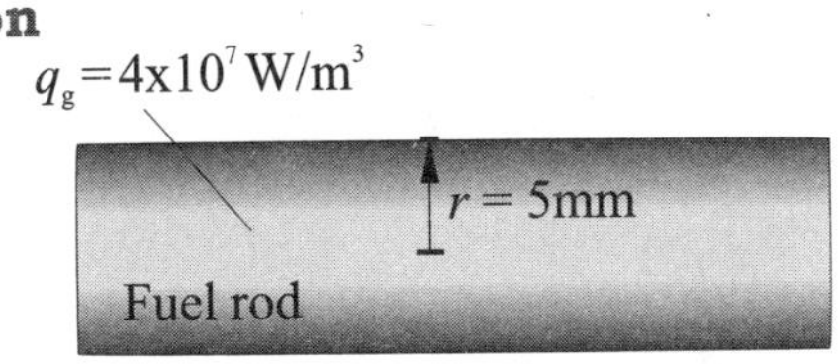

$$h = 1000\ \text{W/m}^2\text{K}$$
$$T_a = 273 + 25 = 298\ \text{K}$$

Total heat generated $Q_g = q_g \times$ Volume of fuel rod

$$Q_g = q_g \times \pi r^2 L \qquad \text{(i)}$$

Heat transfer from surface of fuel rod

$$Q_{\text{conv}} = hA(T - T_a)$$
$$Q_{\text{conv}} = h2\pi rL(T - T_a) \qquad \text{(ii)}$$

Under steady state condition, equating Equations (i) and (ii), we have $Q_g = Q_{\text{conv}}$

$$q_g \times \pi r^2 L = h2\pi rL(T - T_a)$$

or $$T - T_a = \frac{q_g r}{2h}$$

$$T - 298 = \frac{4 \times 10^7 \times \frac{5}{1000}}{2 \times 1000}$$

$$T = 398\ \text{K}$$

Example 11.4

The total emissive power of a surface is 500 W/m^2 at temperature T_1 and 1200 W/m^2 at a temperature T_2, where the temperature are in Kelvin. Assuming the emissivity of the surface to be constant, the ratio of the temperature $\frac{T_1}{T_2}$ is

(A) 0.308 (B) 0.416 (C) 0.803 (D) 0.874

GATE 2015

Solution

Total emissive power is $Q = \sigma A T^4$

or $$\frac{Q_1}{Q_2} = \frac{\sigma A T_1^4}{\sigma A T_2^4}$$

or $$\frac{T_1}{T_2} = \left(\frac{Q_1}{Q_2}\right)^{\frac{1}{4}} = \left(\frac{500}{1200}\right)^{\frac{1}{4}}$$

$$\frac{T_1}{T_2} = 0.803$$

Example 11.5

The ratio of momentum diffusivity (ν) to thermal diffusivity (α), is called

(A) Prandtl number (B) Nusselt number

(C) Biot number (D) Lewis number

GATE 2015

Solution

Prandtl number, $Pr = \frac{\mu c_p}{k}$

$$Pr = \frac{\mu}{\frac{k}{c_p}} = \frac{\left(\frac{\mu}{\rho}\right)}{\left(\frac{k}{\rho c_p}\right)} = \frac{\nu \leftarrow \text{momentum diffusivity}}{\alpha \leftarrow \text{thermal diffusivity}}$$

Example 11.6

Saturated vapour is condensed to saturated liquid is a condenser. The heat capacity ratio is $C_r = \frac{C_{\min}}{C_{\max}}$. The effectiveness ($\varepsilon$) of the condenser is

(A) $\frac{1 - \exp[-\text{NTU}(1 + C_r)]}{1 + C_r}$

(B) $\frac{1 - \exp[-\text{NTU}(1 - C_r)]}{1 - C_r \exp[-\text{NTU}(1 - C_r)]}$

(C) $\frac{\text{NTU}}{1 + \text{NTU}}$

(D) $1 - \exp(-\text{NTU})$

GATE 2015

Solution

Effectiveness of heat of exchanger,

$$\varepsilon = \frac{1 - e^{-\text{NTU}(1+C)}}{1 + C} \qquad \text{(Parallel flow heat exchanger)}$$

$$\varepsilon = \frac{1 - e^{-\text{NTU}(1-C)}}{1 - Ce^{-\text{NTU}(1-C)}} \qquad \text{(Counter flow heat exchanger)}$$

Heat capacity ratio for condenser is $C = C_r = \frac{C_{\min}}{C_{\max}} = 0$

$$\varepsilon = 1 - e^{-\text{NTU}}$$

Example 11.7

A brick wall ($k = 0.9$ W/mK) of thickness 0.18 m separated the warm air in a room from the cold ambient air. On a particular winter day, the outside air temperature is $-5°$C and the room needs to be maintained at 27°C. The heat transfer coefficient associated with outside air is $h = 20$ W/m^2 K. Neglecting the convective resistance of the air inside the room, the heat loss (in W/m^2) is

(A) 88 (B) 110 (C) 128 (D) 160

GATE 2015

Solution

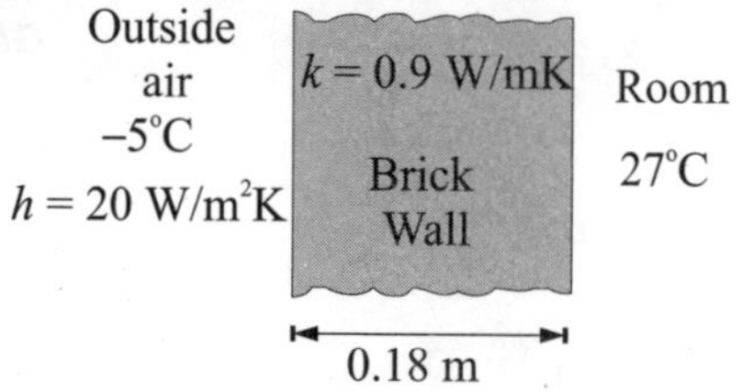

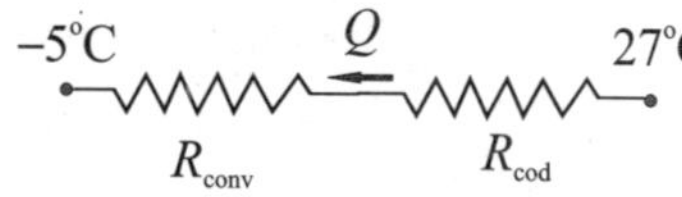

Equivalent electric circuit

Heat loss, $$Q = \frac{T_1 - T_2}{R_{\text{conv}} + R_{\text{cond}}}$$

Heat loss per unit surface area, $$q = \frac{T_1 - T_2}{\frac{1}{h} + \frac{L}{k}}$$

Substituting given values, we have

$$q = \frac{27-(-5)}{\frac{1}{20} + \frac{0.18}{0.9}}$$

$$q = 128 \text{ W/m}^2$$

Example 11.8

A solid sphere 1 of radius r is placed inside a hollow, closed hemispherical surface 2 of radius $4r$. The shape factor F_{2-1} is

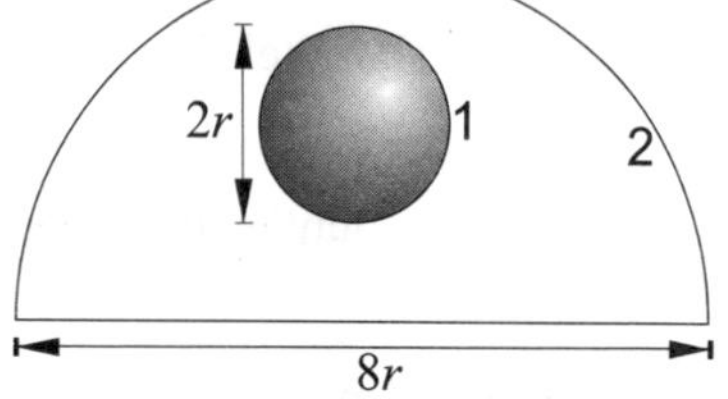

(A) $\frac{1}{12}$ (B) $\frac{1}{2}$ (C) 2 (D) 12

GATE 2015

Solution

Applying the summation rule to surface 1, yields

$$F_{1-1} + F_{1-2} = 1$$

For surface (sphere) 1; $F_{1-1} = 0$

$$F_{1-2} = 1$$

Applying the reciprocity relation to surface 1 and 2, we have

$$A_1 F_{1-2} = A_2 F_{2-1}$$

or $$F_{2-1} = \frac{A_1}{A_2} F_{1-2}$$

or $$F_{2-1} = \frac{A_1}{A_2} \times 1 = \frac{4\pi(r)^2}{\frac{4\pi(4r)^2}{2} + \pi(4r)^2}$$

$$F_{2-1} = \frac{1}{12}$$

Example 11.9

A 10 mm diameter electrical conductor is covered by an insulation of 2 mm thickness. The conductivity of the insulation is 0.08 W/mK and the convection coefficient at the insulation surface is 10 W/m²K. Addition of further insulation of the same material will

(A) Increase heat loss continuously

(B) Decrease heat loss continuously

(C) Increase heat loss to a maximum and then decrease heat loss

(D) Decrease heat loss to a minimum and then increase heat loss

GATE 2015

Solution

Critical radius of insulation, $$r_c = \frac{h}{k}$$

or $$r_c = \frac{0.08}{10} \text{ m} = 8 \text{ mm}$$

Thickness of critical insulation = 8 – 5 = 3 mm

The heat flow for various radius is shown in figure.

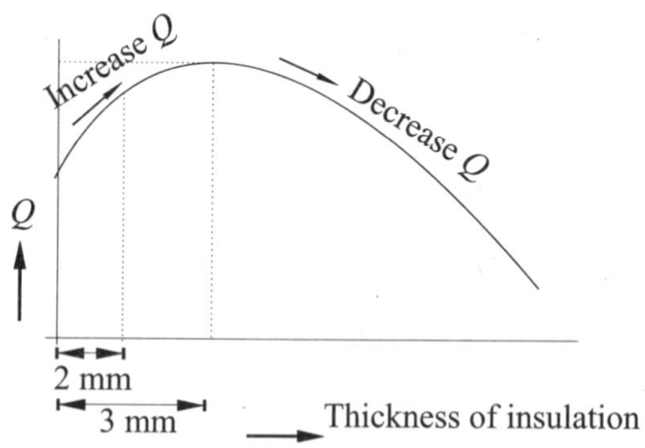

Heat loss will increase up to thickness 3 mm of insulation then decrease.

Addition of further insulation of the same material will increase heat loss to a maximum and then decrease heat loss.

Example 11.10

For flow through a pipe of radius R, the velocity and temperature distribution are as follows:

$U(r,x) = C_1$ and $T(r,x) = C_2\left[1-\left(\frac{r}{R}\right)^3\right]$; where C_1 and C_2 are constants. The bulk mean temperature is given by

$T_m = \frac{2}{U_m R^2}\int_0^R U(r,x)T(r,x)\,rdr$, with U_m being the mean velocity of flow. The value of T_m is

(A) $\frac{0.5C_2}{U_m}$ (B) $0.5C_2$ (C) $0.6C_2$ (D) $\frac{0.6C_2}{U_m}$

GATE 2015

Solution

Mean velocity of fluid

$$U_m = \frac{\int dQ}{\pi R^2} = \frac{\int_0^R U\,2\pi r dr}{\pi R^2} = \frac{\int_0^R C_1 2\pi r dr}{\pi R^2} = C_1$$

or $U_m = C_1$

Now $T_m = \frac{2}{U_m R^2}\int_0^R U(r,x)T(r,x)\,rdr$

or $T_m = \frac{2}{U_m R^2}\int_0^R C_1 \times C_2\left[1-\left(\frac{r}{R}\right)^3\right] rdr$

or $T_m = \frac{2U_m C_2}{U_m R^2}\times\frac{3}{10}R^2$

$$T_m = 0.6C_2$$

Example 11.11

Consider one dimensional steady state heat conduction across a wall (as shown in figure below) of thickness 30 mm and thermal conductivity 15 W/mK. At $x = 0$, a constant heat flux, $q'' = 1\times10^5$ W/m^2 is applied. On the other side of the wall, heat is removed from the wall by convection with a fluid at 25°C and heat transfer coefficient of 250 W/m^2 K. The temperature (in °C), at $x = 0$ is _____

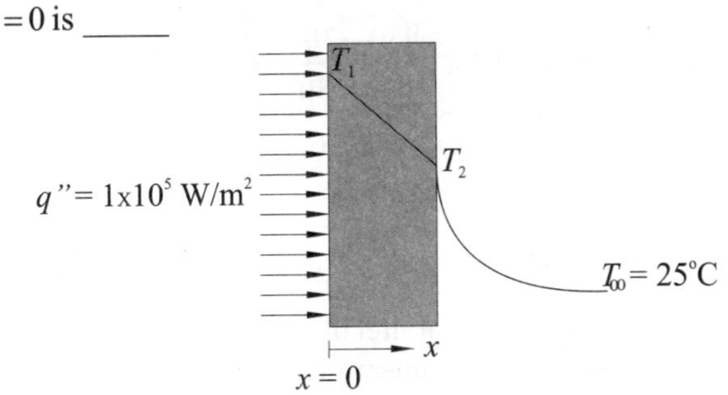

GATE 2014

Solution

The thermal resistance network for this problem involves two resistances in series and is given in figure.

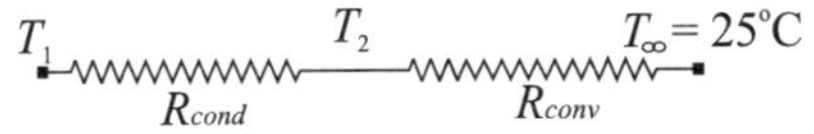

Conductive thermal resistance, $R_{cond} = \frac{L}{kA}$

Convective thermal resistance, $R_{conv} = \frac{1}{hA}$

Rate of heat transfer, $Q = \frac{\Delta T}{\sum R}$

or $Q = \frac{T_1 - T_\infty}{R_{cond} + R_{conv}}$

or $Q = \frac{T_1 - T_\infty}{\frac{L}{kA} + \frac{1}{hA}}$

Heat flux, $q'' = \frac{T_1 - T_\infty}{\left(\frac{L}{k} + \frac{1}{h}\right)}$

Substituting given data $L = \frac{30}{1000}$ m, $k = 15$ W/m, $h = 250$ W/m^2 K, $T_\infty = 25$°C and $q'' = 1\times10^5$, we have

$$1\times10^5 = \frac{T_1 - 25}{\left(\frac{0.03}{15} + \frac{1}{250}\right)}$$

From which

$$T_1 = 625°C$$

Example 11.12

A fin has 5 mm diameter and 100 mm length. The thermal conductivity of fin material is 400 W/mK. One end of the fin is maintained at 130°C and its remaining surface is exposed to ambient are at 30°C. If the convective heat transfer coefficient is 40 W/m^2 K, the heat loss (in W) from the fin is

(A) 0.08 (B) 5.0 (C) 7.0 (D) 7.8

GATE 2010

Solution

Heat transfer from fin is

$$Q_{fin} = \sqrt{hPkA}(T_o - T_a)\frac{\sinh mL + (h/mk)\cosh mL}{\cosh mL + (h/mk)\sinh mL}$$

Substituting $d = \frac{5}{1000}$ m, $L = \frac{100}{1000}$m, $k = 400$ W/mK, $T_o = 130°C$, $T_a = 30°C$, $h = 40$ W/m^2 K and

$$m = \sqrt{\frac{4h}{kd}} = \sqrt{\frac{4\times 40}{400\times 5}} = 8.94$$

$$Q_{\text{fin}} = \left[\sqrt{40\times\pi\times\frac{5}{1000}\times 400\times\frac{\pi}{4}\times\left(\frac{5}{1000}\right)^2}\right](130-30)$$

$$\times\frac{\sinh(8.9\times 0.1)+(40/8.9\times 400)\cosh(8.9\times 0.1)}{\cosh(8.9\times 0.1)+(40/8.9\times 400)\sinh(8.9\times 0.1)}$$

$$Q_{\text{fin}} = 7.02 \text{ W}$$

Example 11.13

The non-dimensional fluid temperature profile near the surface of a convectively cooled flat plate is given by $\frac{T_w - T}{T_w - T_\infty} = a + b\left(\frac{y}{L}\right) + c\left(\frac{y}{L}\right)^2$, where y is measured perpendicular to the plate, L is the plate length, and a, b and c are arbitrary constants. T_w and T_∞ are wall and ambient temperatures, respectively. If the thermal conductivity of the fluid is k and the wall heat flux is q'', the Nusselt number, $Nu = \frac{q''}{T_w - T_\infty}\frac{L}{k}$ is equal to

(A) a (B) b (C) $2c$ (D) $b + 2c$

GATE 2014

Solution

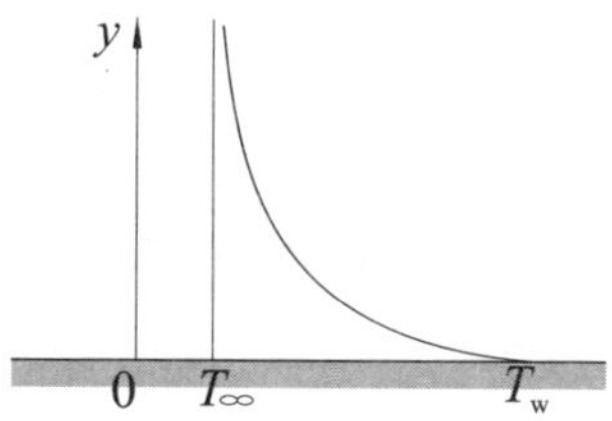

Wall heat flux is given by

$$q'' = -k\left(\frac{dT}{dy}\right)_{y=0}$$

Substituting given temperature,

$$T = T_w - (T_w - T_\infty)\left[a + b\left(\frac{y}{L}\right) + c\left(\frac{y}{L}\right)^2\right]$$

$$q'' = -k\left(\frac{d}{dy}\left[T_w - (T_w - T_\infty)\left\{a + b\left(\frac{y}{L}\right) + c\left(\frac{y}{L}\right)^2\right\}\right]\right)_{y=0}$$

or $$q'' = \frac{k(T_w - T_\infty)b}{L}$$

Nusselt number, $$Nu = \frac{q''}{T_w - T_\infty}\times\frac{L}{k}$$

or $$Nu = \frac{1}{T_w - T_\infty}\times\frac{k(T_w - T_\infty)b}{L}\times\frac{L}{k}$$

$$Nu = b$$

Example 11.14

A steel ball of diameter 60 mm is initially in thermal equilibrium at 1030 °C in a furnace. It is suddenly removed from the furnace and cooled in ambient air at 30 °C, with convective heat transfer coefficient $h = 20$ W/m^2 K. The thermo-physical properties of steel are: density $\rho = 7800$ Kg/m^3, conductivity $k = 40$ W/mK and specific heat $c = 600$ J/kgK. The time required in seconds to cool the steel ball in air from 1030 °C to 430 °C is

(A) 519 (B) 931 (C) 1195 (D) 2144

GATE 2013

Solution

Given that $d = 60$ mm, $T_i = 1030°C$, $T_a = 30°C$, $h = 20$ W/m^{2}K, $\rho = 7800$ kg/m^3, $k = 40$ W/mK, $c = 600$ J/kgK and $T = 430°C$.

The characteristic length of the steel ball

$$l = \frac{V}{A} = \frac{\frac{4}{3}\pi r^3}{4\pi r^2} = \frac{r}{3} = \frac{d}{6}$$

$$l = \frac{60}{6} = 10 \text{ mm}$$

Biot number, $Bi = \frac{hl}{k} = \frac{20}{40}\times\frac{10}{1000} = 0.005$, which is less than 0.1, hence the lumped heat capacity system analysis may be applied.

The temperature distribution in a body at time t during a Newtonian heating or cooling is given by

$$\frac{T - T_a}{T_i - T_a} = e^{-\frac{hA}{\rho Vc}t}$$

Substituting given data; $$\frac{430-30}{1030-30} = e^{-\frac{20}{7800\times\frac{10}{1000}\times 600}t}$$

From which

$$t = 2144 \text{ s}$$

Example 11.15

Two large diffuse gray parallel plates, separated by a small distance, have surface temperatures of 400 K and 300 K. If the emissivities of the surfaces are 0.8 and the Stefan Boltzmann constant is 5.67×10^{-8} W/m^{2}K^4, the net radiation heat exchange rate in kW/m^2 between the two plates is

(A) 0.66 (B) 0.79 (C) 0.99 (D) 3.96

GATE 2013

Solution

The radiation heat exchange between two large parallel grey plates kept at temperatures T_1 and T_2, is

$$Q_{1-2} = \frac{\sigma A(T_1^4 - T_2^4)}{\left(\frac{1}{\varepsilon_1} + \frac{1}{\varepsilon_2} - 1\right)}$$

Substituting given data

$$q_{1-2} = \frac{Q_{1-2}}{A} = \frac{5.67\times10^{-8}(400^4 - 300^4)}{\left(\frac{1}{0.8}+\frac{1}{0.8}-1\right)}$$

or $$q_{1-2} = 661.5 \text{ W/m}^2$$

$$q_{1-2} = 0.661 \text{ kW/m}^2$$

Example 11.16

Common Data Questions

Water (specific heat $c_P = 4.18$ kJ/kgK) enters a pipe at a rate of 0.01 kg/s and a temperature of 20°C. The pipe of diameter 50 mm and length 3 m, is subjected to a wall heat flux q_w'' in W/m^2.

Q(a) If $q_w'' = 2500x$, where x is in meter and in the direction of flow ($x = 0$ at the inlet), the bulk mean temperature of the water leaving the pipe in °C is

(A) 42 (B) 62 (C) 74 (D) 104

Q(b) If $q_w'' = 5000$, and the convection heat transfer coefficient at the pipe outlet is 1000 W/m^2K, the temperature in °C at the inner surface of the pipe at the outlet is

(A) 71 (B) 76 (C) 79 (D) 81

GATE 2013

Solution

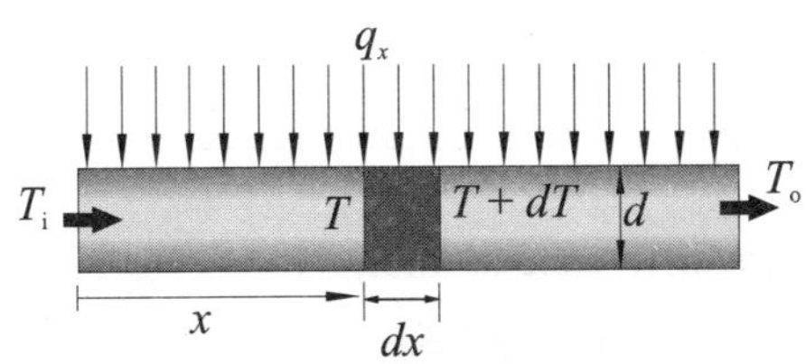

(a) Let T_o be the mean bulk temperature of the water leaving the pipe.

Consider an small volume of fluid of length dx

Heat transfer through wall = Heat gain by fluid

$$q_x \pi d \times dx = mc\,dT$$

or $$2500x\pi d \times dx = mc\,dT$$

or $$2500\pi d\int_0^L x\times dx = mc\int_{T_i}^{T_o} dT$$

$$T_o = T_i + \frac{2500\pi d}{mc}\frac{L^2}{2}$$

Substituting given data

$$T_o = 20 + \frac{2500\pi\times\frac{50}{1000}}{0.01\times4.18}\times\frac{3^2}{2}$$

$$T_o = 62.27\ °C$$

(b) Consider an small element of length dx

Heat transfer through wall = Heat gain by fluid

$$q_x \pi d\times dx = mc\,dT$$

or $$5000\pi d\times dx = mc\,dT$$

or $$5000\pi d\int_0^L dx = mc\int_{T_i}^{T_o} dT$$

or $$T_o = T_i + \frac{5000\pi dL}{mc}$$

Substituting given data

$$T_o = 20 + \frac{5000\pi\times\frac{50}{1000}\times3}{0.01\times4.18}$$

$$T_o = 76.37°C$$

Let T_e be the temperature of inner surface of the pipe at exit.

Heat flux $q_x = h(T_e - T_o)$

$$T_e = T_o + \frac{q_x}{h}$$

or $$T_e = 76.37 + \frac{5000}{1\times1000}$$

$$T_e = 81.37°C$$

Example 11.17

Consider two infinitely long thin concentric tubes of circular cross-section as shown in the figure. If D_1 and D_2 are the diameters of the inner and outer tubes respectively, then the view factor F_{22} is given by

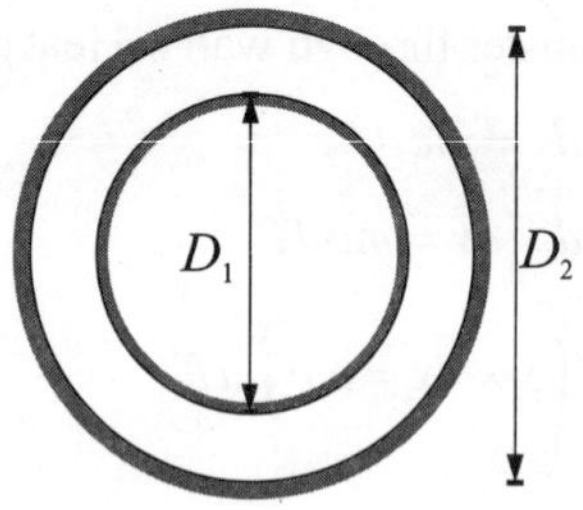

(A) $\frac{D_2}{D_1}-1$ (B) $\left(\frac{D_1}{D_2}\right)$ (C) zero (D) $1-\left(\frac{D_1}{D_2}\right)$

GATE 2012

Solution

Applying summing rule to outer tube 2,

$$F_{2-2}+F_{2-1}=1$$

or $$F_{2-2}=1-F_{2-1} \quad \text{(i)}$$

Applying the reciprocity relation,

$$A_1F_{1-2}=A_2F_{2-1} \quad \text{or} \quad F_{2-1}=\frac{A_1}{A_2}F_{1-2} \quad \text{(ii)}$$

From Equation (i) and (ii), we have

$$F_{2-2}=1-\frac{A_1}{A_2}F_{1-2}$$

Since $F_{1-2}=1$; $F_{2-2}=1-\frac{\pi D_1 L}{\pi D_2 L}\times 1$

$$F_{2-2}=1-\frac{D_1}{D_2}$$

Example 11.18

Water ($c_P=4.18$ kJ/kgK) at 80 °C enters a counter flow heat exchanger with a mass flow rate of 0.5 kg/s. Air ($c_P=1$ kJ/kgK) enters at 30 °C with a mass flow rate of 2.09 kg/s. If the effectiveness of the heat exchanger is 0.8, the LMTD (in °C) is

(A) 40 (B) 10 (C) 20 (D) 5

GATE 2012

Solution

Effectiveness of heat exchanger is given by $\varepsilon=\frac{Q_{act}}{Q_{max}}$

or $$\varepsilon=\frac{m_h c_{ph}(T_{hi}-T_{ho})}{(mc)_{min}(T_{hi}-T_{ci})}$$

$$0.8=\frac{0.5\times 4.18(80-T_{ho})}{2.09\times 1(80-30)}$$

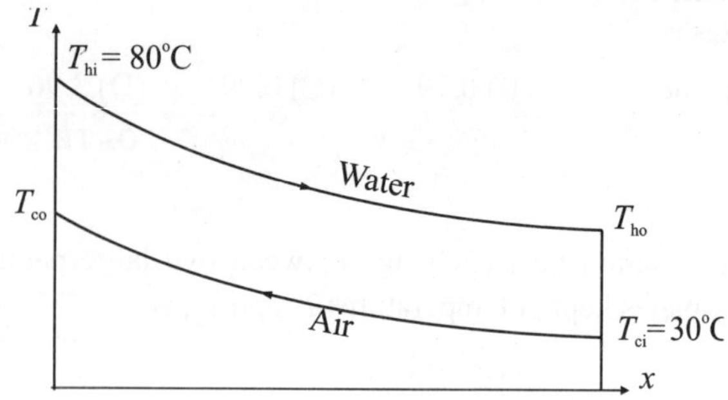

From which

$$T_{ho}=40°C$$

Heat balance equation:

Heat loss by water = Heat gain by air

$$0.5\times 4.18(80-40)=2.09\times 1(T_{co}-30)$$

$$T_{co}=70°C$$

Temperature differences $\theta_i=80-70=10°C$ and $\theta_o=40-30=10°C$

$$\text{LMTD}=\theta_i=\theta_o=10$$

$$\text{LMTD}=10°C$$

Example 11.19

In a condenser of a power plant, the steam condenses at a temperature of 60 °C. The cooling water enters at 30 °C and leaves 45 °C. The logarithmic mean temperature difference (LMTD) of the condenser is

(A) 16.2 °C (B) 30 °C (C) 21.6 °C (D) 37.5 °C

GATE 2011

Solution

The temperature distribution graph of condenser is shown in figure.

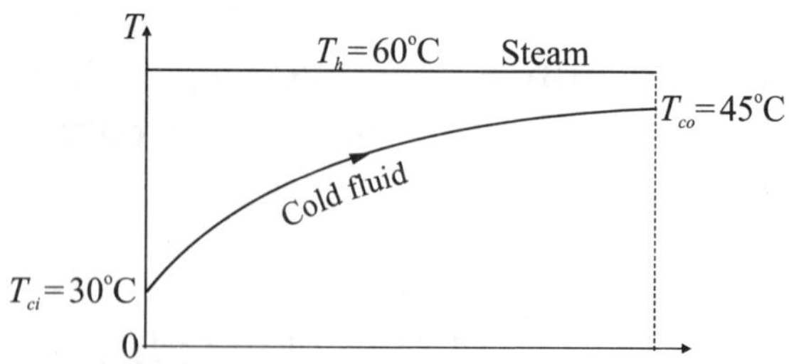

Temperature difference at inlet,

$$\theta_i=T_h-T_{ci}=60-30=30°C$$

Temperature difference at exit,

$$\theta_0=T_h-T_{co}=60-45=15°C$$

$$\text{LMTD} = \frac{\theta_i - \theta_o}{\ln\frac{\theta_i}{\theta_o}} = \frac{30-15}{\ln\frac{30}{15}}$$

From which

$$\text{LMTD} = 21.64°\text{C}$$

Example 11.20

The ratio of the laminar hydrodynamic boundary layer thickness to thermal boundary layer thickness of flows of two fluids P and Q on a flat plate are $\frac{1}{2}$ and 2 respectively. The Reynolds number based on the plate length for both the flows is 10^4. The Prandtl and Nusselt numbers for P are $\frac{1}{8}$ and 35 respectively. The Prandtl and Nusselt numbers for Q are respectively

(A) 8 and 140 (B) 4 and 70
(C) 8 and 70 (D) 4 and 35

GATE 2011

Solution

The ratio of laminar hydrodynamic boundary layer thickness (δ) to thermal boundary layer thickness (δ_t) is

$$\frac{\delta}{\delta_t} = Pr^{1/3} \quad \text{or} \quad Pr = \left(\frac{\delta}{\delta_t}\right)^3$$

Prandlt number of fluid P is $(Pr)_P = \left(\frac{1}{2}\right)^3 = \frac{1}{8}$

Prandlt number of fluid Q is $(Pr)_Q = (2)^3 = 8$

Nusselt number is given by (empirical relation)

$$Nu = C_1 (Re)^m (Pr)^{1/3}$$

$$\frac{(Nu)_Q}{(Nu)_P} = \frac{C_1 (Re)^m}{C_1 (Re)^m} \times \frac{(Pr)_Q^{1/3}}{(Pr)_P^{1/3}}$$

or $$\frac{(Nu)_Q}{35} = \frac{(8)^{1/3}}{(1/8)^{1/3}}$$

or $$(Nu)_Q = 4 \times 35$$

$$(Nu)_Q = 140$$

Example 11.21

A coolant fluid at 30°C flows over a heated flat plate maintained at a constant temperature of 100°C. The boundary layer temperature distribution at a given location on the plate may be approximated as $T = 30 + 70\exp(-y)$ where y (in m) is the distance normal to the plate and T is in °C. If thermal conductivity of the fluid is 1.0 W/mK, the local convective heat transfer coefficient (in W/m^{2}K) at that location will be

(A) 0.2 (B) 1 (C) 5 (D) 10

GATE 2009

Solution

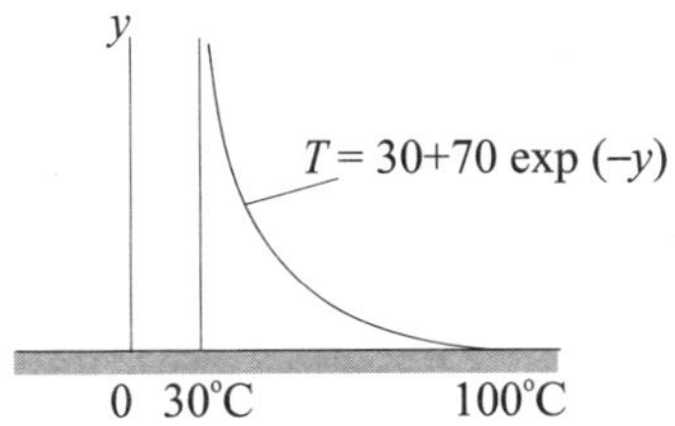

Heat transfer from surface of plate by conduction = Heat transfer by convection

$$-kA\left(\frac{dT}{dy}\right)_{y=0} = hA(T_s - T_\infty)$$

Substituting given data

$$-1 \times \left[\frac{d}{dy}\{30 + 70\exp(-y)\}\right]_{y=0} = h(100-30)$$

or $$-1 \times -70 = h \times 70$$

$$h = 1.0\ \text{W/m}^2\text{K}$$

Example 11.22

In a parallel flow heat exchanger operating under steady state, the heat capacity rates (product of specific heat at constant pressure and mass flow rate) of the hot and cold fluid are equal. The hot fluid, flowing at 1 kg/s with $c_P = 4$ kJ/kgK, enters the heat exchanger at 102 °C while the cold fluid has an inlet temperature of 15 °C. The overall heat transfer coefficient for the heat exchanger is estimated to be 1 kW/m^{2}K and the corresponding heat transfer surface area is 5 m^2. Neglect heat transfer between the heat exchanger and the ambient. The heat exchanger is characterised by the following relation:

$$2\varepsilon = 1 - \exp(-2\,\text{NTU})$$

The exit temperature (in °C) for the cold fluid is

(A) 45 (B) 55 (C) 65 (D) 75

GATE 2009

Solution

Given that $m_h c_{ph} = m_c c_{pc} \Rightarrow C_h = C_C$, $m_h = 1$ kg/s, $c_{ph} = 4$ kJ/kgK, $T_{hi} = 102$°C, $T_{ci} = 15$°C, $U = 1$ kW/m^{2}K, $A = 5$ m^2 and $2\varepsilon = 1 - \exp(-2\,\text{NTU})$

$$\text{NTU} = \frac{UA}{C_{min}} = \frac{UA}{m_h c_{ph}}$$

$$\text{NTU} = \frac{1000 \times 5}{1 \times 4000}$$

$$\text{NTU} = 1.25$$

Effectiveness of heat exchanger,

$$\varepsilon = \frac{1 - \exp(-2\,\text{NTU})}{2}$$

or $$\varepsilon = \frac{1 - \exp(-2 \times 1.25)}{2}$$

or $$\varepsilon = 0.4589$$

Effectiveness of heat exchanger,

$$\varepsilon = \frac{Q_{\text{act}}}{Q_{\max}} = \frac{m_c c_{pc}(T_{co} - T_{ci})}{(mc)_{\min}(T_{hi} - T_{ci})}$$

or $$\varepsilon = \frac{T_{co} - T_{ci}}{T_{hi} - T_{ci}}$$

$$0.4589 = \frac{T_{co} - 15}{102 - 15}$$

From which

$$T_{co} = 54.92°\text{C}$$

Example 11.23

Consider steady-state heat conduction across the thickness in a plane composite wall (as shown in the figure) exposed to convection conditions on both sides.

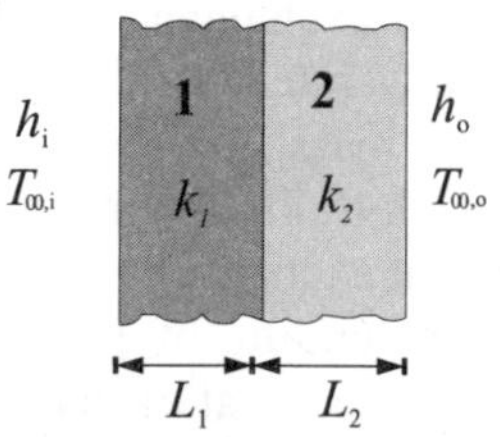

Given: $h_1 = 20\ \text{W/m}^2\text{K}$; $h_o = 50\ \text{W/m}^2\text{K}$; $T_{\infty,i} = 20°\text{C}$; $T_{\infty,o} = -2°\text{C}$; $k_1 = 20\ \text{W/mK}$; $k_2 = 50\ \text{W/mK}$; $L_1 = 0.30\ \text{m}$ and $L_2 = 0.15\ \text{m}$. Assuming negligible contact resistance between the wall surfaces, the interface temperature, T (in °C), of the two walls will be

(A) −0.50 (B) 2 .75 (C) 3.75 (D) 4.50

GATE 2009

Solution

The thermal resistance network for this problem involves four resistance in series and is given in figure.

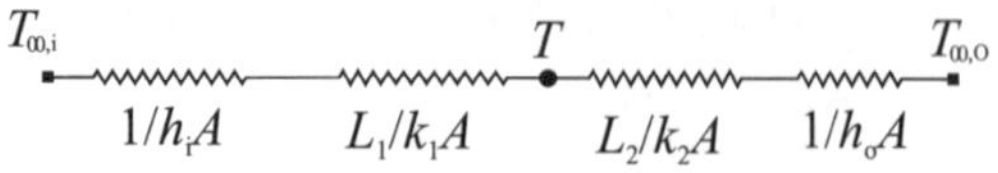

Total thermal resistance,

$$R_{th} = \frac{1}{h_i A} + \frac{L_1}{k_1 A} + \frac{L_2}{k_2 A} + \frac{1}{h_o A}$$

$$R_{th} = \frac{1}{20 \times 1} + \frac{0.3}{20 \times 1} + \frac{0.15}{50 \times 1} + \frac{1}{50 \times 1} \quad [\text{Let } A = 1\,\text{m}^2]$$

$$R_{th} = 0.088$$

Heat transfer,

$$Q = \frac{T_{\infty,i} - T}{\left(\dfrac{1}{h_i A} + \dfrac{L_1}{k_1 A}\right)} = \frac{T_{\infty,i} - T_{\infty,o}}{\left(\dfrac{1}{h_i A} + \dfrac{L_1}{k_1 A} + \dfrac{L_2}{k_2 A} + \dfrac{1}{h_o A}\right)}$$

or $$Q = \frac{20 - T}{\left(\dfrac{1}{20 \times 1} + \dfrac{03}{20 \times 1}\right)} = \frac{20 - (-2)}{0.088}$$

From which

$$T = 3.75°\text{C}$$

Example 11.24

For flow of fluid over a heated plate, the following fluid properties are known:

Viscosity = 0.001 Pa.s

Specific heat at constant pressure, $c_p = 1\ \text{kJ/kgK}$

Thermal conductivity, $k = 1\ \text{W/mK}$

The hydrodynamic boundary layer thickness at a specified location on the plate is 1 mm. The thermal boundary layer thickness at the same location is

(A) 0.0001 mm (B) 0.01mm (C) 1mm (D)1000 mm

GATE 2008

Solution

The ratio of laminar boundary layer thickness δ to thermal boundary layer thickness δ_t is

$$\frac{\delta}{\delta_t} = (Pr)^{1/3}$$

or $$\delta_t = \frac{\delta}{(Pr)^{1/3}}$$

Prandtl number, $$Pr = \frac{\mu c_p}{k}$$

$$Pr = \frac{0.001 \times 1 \times 1000}{1} = 1$$

or $$\delta_t = \frac{1}{(1)^{1/3}}$$

$$\delta_t = 1\,\text{mm}$$

Example 11.25

For the three-dimensional object shown in the figure, five faces are insulated. The sixth face (*PQRS*), which is not insulated, interacts thermally with the ambient, with a convective heat transfer coefficient of 10 W/m^{2}K. The ambient temperature is 30 °C. Heat is uniformly generated inside the object at the rate of 100 W/m^3. Assuming the face *PQRS* to be at uniform temperature, its steady state temperature is

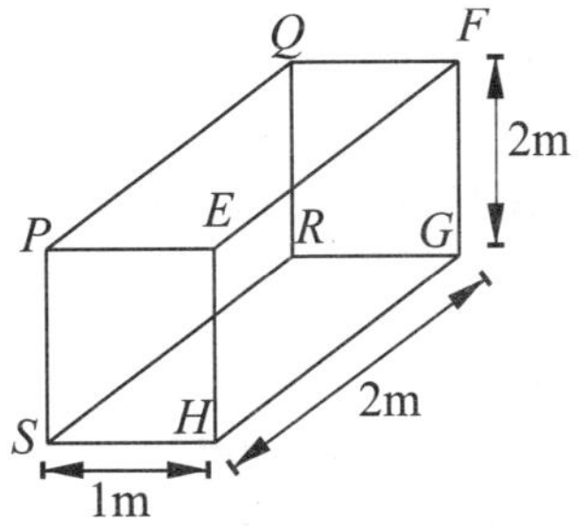

(A) 10 °C (B) 20 °C (C) 30 °C (D) 40 °C

GATE 2008

Solution

Let T_s be the surface temperature of face *PQRS*.

Heat generated = Heat convected from face *PQRS*

$$q_g \times \text{Volume of } PQRS = hA\,(T_s - T_a)$$

$$100 \times 1 \times 2 \times 2 = 10 \times (2 \times 2)(T_s - 30)$$

From which

$$T_s = 40°\text{C}$$

Example 11.26

A hollow enclosure is formed between two infinitely long concentric cylinders of radii 1 m and 2 m, respectively. Radiative heat exchange takes place between the inner surface of the larger cylinder (surface -2) and the outer surface of the smaller cylinder (surface -1). The radiating surfaces are diffuse and the medium in the enclosure is non-participating. The fraction of the thermal radiation leaving the larger surface and striking itself is

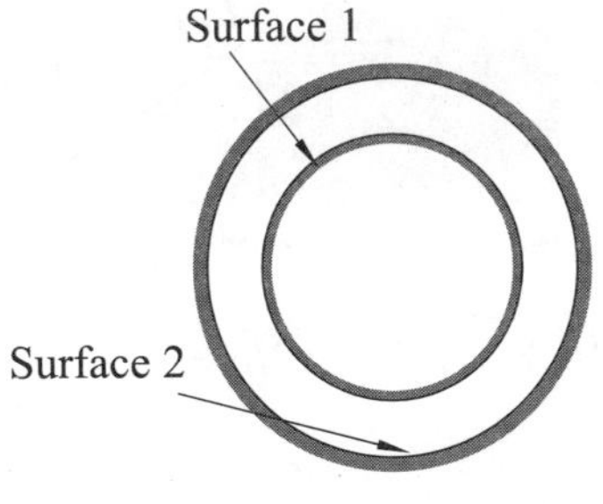

(A) 0.25 (B) 0.5 (C) 0.75 (D) 1

GATE 2008

Solution

For surface 1 (concave surface); $F_{1-1} = 0$

Applying summing rule to inner surface,

$$F_{1-1} + F_{1-2} = 1 \quad \Rightarrow \quad 0 + F_{1-2} = 1$$

$$F_{1-2} = 1$$

Applying the reciprocity relation:

For surface 1; $A_1 F_{1-2} = A_2 F_{2-1}$

or $F_{2-1} = \dfrac{A_1}{A_2} F_{1-2}$

or $F_{2-1} = \dfrac{\pi D_1 L}{\pi D_2 L} \times 1 = \dfrac{D_1}{D_2}$

or $F_{2-1} = \dfrac{1}{2}$

For surface 2; $F_{2-2} + F_{2-1} = 1$

or $F_{2-2} + \dfrac{1}{2} = 1$

$$F_{2-2} = 05$$

Example 11.27

Steady two-dimensional heat conduction takes place in the body shown in the figure. The normal temperature

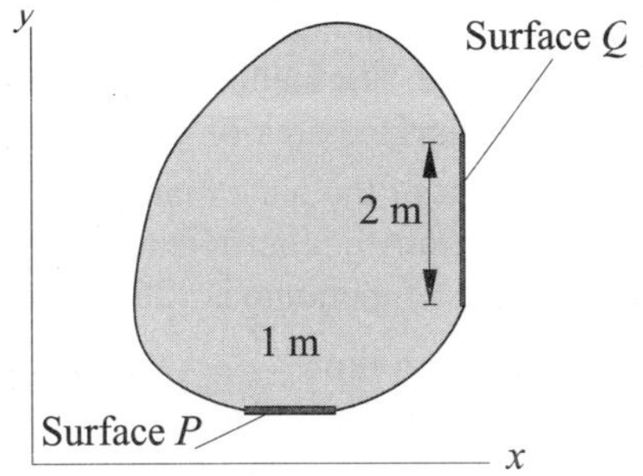

gradients over surfaces *P* and *Q* can be considered to be uniform. The temperature gradient $\dfrac{\partial T}{\partial x}$ at surface *Q* is equal to 10 K/m. Surfaces *P* and *Q* are maintained at constant temperature as shown in the figure, while the remaining part of the boundary is insulated. The body has a constant thermal conductivity of 0.1 W/mK. The values of $\dfrac{\partial T}{\partial x}$ and $\dfrac{\partial T}{\partial y}$ at surface *P* are:

(A) $\dfrac{\partial T}{\partial x} = 20$ K/m and $\dfrac{\partial T}{\partial y} = 0$ K/m

(B) $\dfrac{\partial T}{\partial x} = 0$ K/m and $\dfrac{\partial T}{\partial y} = 10$ K/m

(C) $\dfrac{\partial T}{\partial x} = 10$ K/m and $\dfrac{\partial T}{\partial y} = 10$ K/m

(D) $\dfrac{\partial T}{\partial x} = 0$ K/m and $\dfrac{\partial T}{\partial y} = 20$ K/m

GATE 2008

Solution

Given that $\left(\frac{\partial T}{\partial x}\right)_Q = 10\text{ K/m}$

Heat transfer takes place at P and Q only, therefore,

Heat transfer from P = Heat transfer from Q

$$-kA_P\left(\frac{\partial T}{\partial y}\right)_P = -kA_Q\left(\frac{\partial T}{\partial x}\right)_Q$$

or $$1\times\left(\frac{\partial T}{\partial y}\right)_P = 2\times 10$$

$$\left(\frac{\partial T}{\partial y}\right)_P = 20\text{ K/m and }\left(\frac{\partial T}{\partial x}\right)_P = 0\text{ K/m}$$

Example 11.28

The average heat transfer coefficient on a thin hot vertical plate suspended in still air can be determined from observations of the change in plate temperature with time as it cools. Assume the plate temperature to be uniform at any instant of time and radiation heat exchange with the surroundings negligible. The ambient temperature is $25\,^{\circ}\text{C}$, the plate has a total surface area of $0.1\,\text{m}^2$ and a mass of 4 kg. The specific heat of the plate material is 2.5 kJ/kgK. The convective heat transfer coefficient in $\text{W/m}^2\text{K}$, at the instant when the plate temperature is $225\,^{\circ}\text{C}$ and the change in plate temperature with time $\frac{dT}{dt} = -0.02$ K/s, is

(A) 200 (B) 20 (C) 15 (D) 10

GATE 2007

Solution

Given that $T_a = 25°\text{C}$, $A = 0.1\,\text{m}^2$, $m = 4$ kg, $c = 2.5$ kJ/kgK, $T = 225°\text{C}$ and $\frac{dT}{dt} = -0.02$ K/s

In absence of any temperature gradient in plate, the energy balance for element is

The rate of heat flow out of plate through the boundary surface = The rate of decrease of internal energy of plate

$$hA(T - T_a) = -mc\frac{dT}{dt}$$

Substituting given data

$$h\times 0.1(225-25) = -4\times 2.5\times 10^3\times -0.02$$

From which

$$h = 10\text{ W/m}^2\text{K}$$

Example 11.29

A spherical thermocouple junction of diameter 0.706 mm is to be used for the measurement of temperature to a gas stream. The convective heat transfer coefficient of the bead surface is 400 $\text{W/m}^2\text{K}$. Thermo-physical properties of thermocouple material are $k = 20$ W/mK, $C = 400$ J/kgK and $\rho = 8500\,\text{kg/m}^3$. If the thermocouple initially at $30\,^{\circ}\text{C}$ is placed in a hot stream of $300\,^{\circ}\text{C}$, then time taken by the bead to reach $298\,^{\circ}\text{C}$, is

(A) 2.35s (B) 4.9s (C) 14.7s (D) 29.4s

GATE 2004

Solution

Given that $d = 0.706$ mm, $h = 400\text{ W/m}^2\text{K}$, $k = 20$ W/mK, $c = 400$ J/kgK, $\rho = 8500\text{ kg/m}^3$, $T_i = 30°\text{C}$, $T_a = 300°\text{C}$ and $T = 298°\text{C}$.

The temperature distribution within the solid is

$$\frac{T - T_a}{T_i - T_a} = e^{-\frac{hA}{\rho Vc}t}$$

or $$\frac{298-300}{30-300} = e^{-\frac{400\times 6}{8500\times\frac{0.706}{1000}\times 400}t}$$

or $$135 = e^{0.999t}$$

$$t = 4.98\,\text{s}$$

Example 11.30

In a composite slab, the temperature at the interface (Timber) between two materials is equal to the average of the temperatures at the two ends. Assuming steady one-dimensional heat conduction, which of the following statements is true about the respective thermal conductivities?

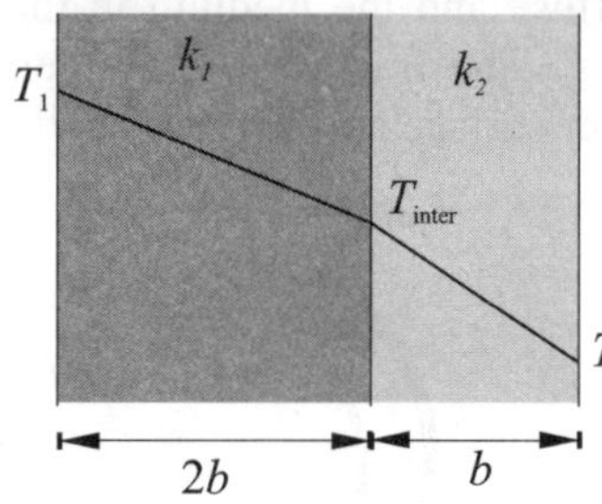

(A) $2k_1 = k_2$ (B) $k_1 = k_2$ (C) $2k_1 = 3k_2$ (D) $k_1 = 2k_2$

GATE 2006

Solution

Given that:

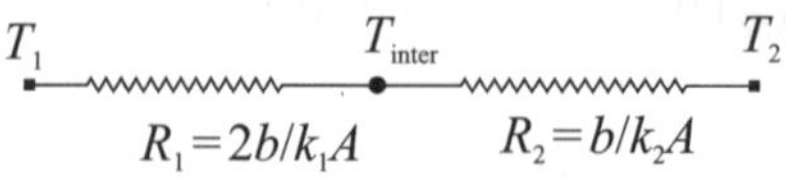

$$T_{inter} = \frac{T_1 + T_2}{2}$$

Heat transfer rate, $$Q = \frac{T_1 - T_{inter}}{R_1} = \frac{T_{inter} - T_2}{R_2}$$

$$Q = \frac{T_1 - \frac{T_1 + T_2}{2}}{\frac{2b}{k_1 A}} = \frac{\frac{T_1 + T_2}{2} - T_2}{\frac{b}{k_2 A}}$$

From which

$$k_1 = 2k_2$$

Example 11.31

Heat flows through a composite slab, as shown. The depth of the slab is 1 m. The k values are W/mK. The overall thermal resistance in K/W is

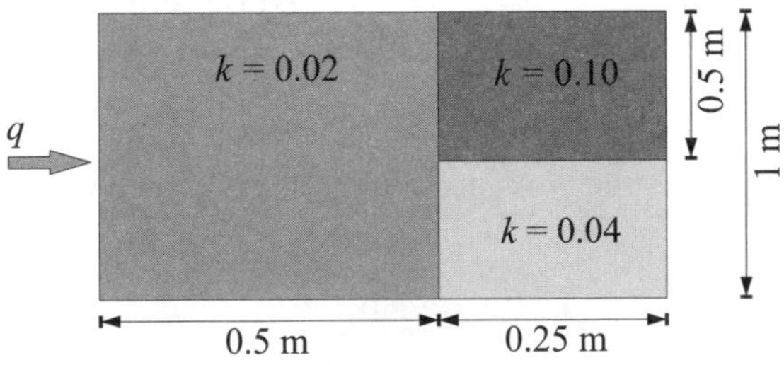

(A) 17.2 (B) 21.9 (C) 28.6 (D) 39.2

GATE 2005

Solution

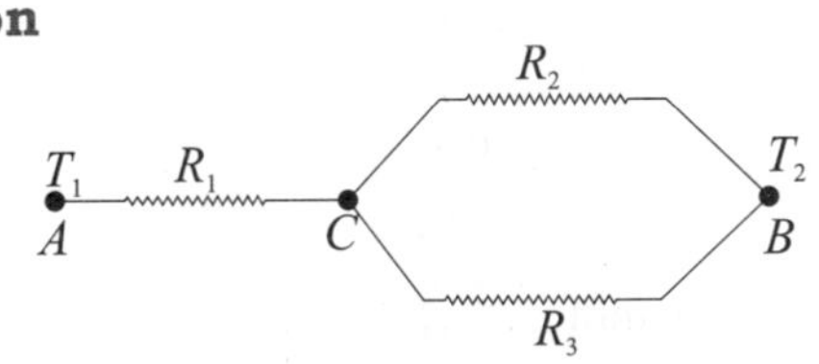

The thermal resistance network for the representative sections of slab becomes as shown in figure. Then the individual thermal resistance become

$$R_1 = \frac{0.5}{0.02 \times (1 \times 1)} = 25, \quad R_2 = \frac{0.25}{0.10 \times (0.5 \times 1)} = 5 \quad \text{and}$$

$$R_3 = \frac{0.25}{0.04 \times (0.5 \times 1)} = 12.5$$

Equivalent thermal resistance between C and B,

$$R_{BC} = \frac{R_2 R_3}{R_2 + R_3} = \frac{5 \times 12.5}{5 + 12.5}$$

$$R_{BC} = 3.57$$

Equivalent thermal resistance between A and B,

$$R = R_1 + R_{BC} = 25 + 3.57$$

$$R = 28.57 \text{ K/W}$$

Example 11.32

A small copper ball of 5 mm diameter at 500 K is dropped into an oil bath whose temperature is 300 K. The internal conductivity of copper is 400 W/mK, its density 9000 kg/m^3 and its specific heat 385 J/kgK. If the heat transfer coefficient is 250 W/m^{2}K and lumped analysis is assumed to be valid, the rate of fall of the temperature of the ball at the beginning of cooling will be (in K/s)

(A) 8.7 (B) 13.9 (C)17.3 (D)27.7

GATE 2005

Solution

Given that $d = 5$ mm, $T_i = 500$ K, $T_a = 300$ K, $k = 400$ W/mK, $\rho = 9000$ kg/m^3, $c = 385$ J/kgK, $h = 250$ W/m^{2}K.

Rate of heat convected from ball = Rate of change of internal energy

$$hA(T - T_a) = -mc\frac{dT}{dt}$$

Rate of fall of the temperature, $\frac{dT}{dt} = -\frac{hA(T - T_a)}{mc}$

or

$$\frac{dT}{dt} = -\frac{250 \times 4\pi\left(\frac{5}{2 \times 1000}\right)^2 (500 - 300)}{\frac{4}{3}\pi\left(\frac{5}{2 \times 1000}\right)^3 \times 9000 \times 385}$$

Rate of fall of the temperature, $\frac{dT}{dt} = -17.31°\text{C/s}$

Example 11.33

A solid cylinder (Surface-2) is located at the centre of a hollow sphere (Surface-1). The diameter of the sphere is 1 m, while the cylinder has a diameter and length of 0.5 m each. The radiation configuration factor F_{11} is

(A) 0.375 (B) 0.625 (C) 0.75 (D) 1

GATE 2005

Solution

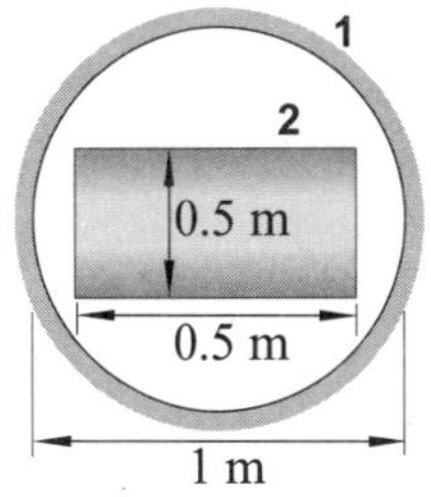

Given that $d_1 = 1$ m, $d_2 = 0.5$ m and $l_2 = 0.5$ m

Surface area of cylinder is

$$A_2 = \pi d_2 l_2 + 2\frac{\pi}{4}d_2^2$$

Surface area of sphere is $A_1 = 4\pi\left(\frac{d_1}{2}\right)^2 = \pi d_1^2$

Applying property of view factor, $F_{2-2} = 0$

Summing rule: $F_{2-1} + F_{2-2} = 1 \Rightarrow F_{2-1} = 1$

Reciprocity relation:

$$A_1 F_{1-2} = A_2 F_{2-1} \Rightarrow F_{1-2} = \frac{A_2}{A_1} \times 1$$

Summing rule; $F_{1-1} + F_{1-2} = 1 \Rightarrow F_{1-1} = 1 - F_{1-2}$

or $$F_{1-1} = 1 - \frac{A_2}{A_1}$$

or $$F_{1-1} = 1 - \frac{\pi d_2 l_2 + 2\frac{\pi}{4} d_2^2}{\pi d_1^2} = 1 - \frac{0.5 \times 0.5 + \frac{0.5^2}{2}}{1}$$

$$F_{1-1} = 0.625$$

Example 11.34

In a condenser, water enters at 30°C and flows at the rate 1500 kg/h. The condensing steam is at a temperature of 120°C and cooling water leaves the condenser at 80°C. Specific heat of water is 4.187 kJ/kgK. If the overall heat transfer coefficient is 2000 W/m^{2}K, then heat transfer area is

(A) 0.707 m^2 (B) 7.07 m^2 (C) 70.7 m^2 (D) 141.4 m^2

GATE 2004

Solution

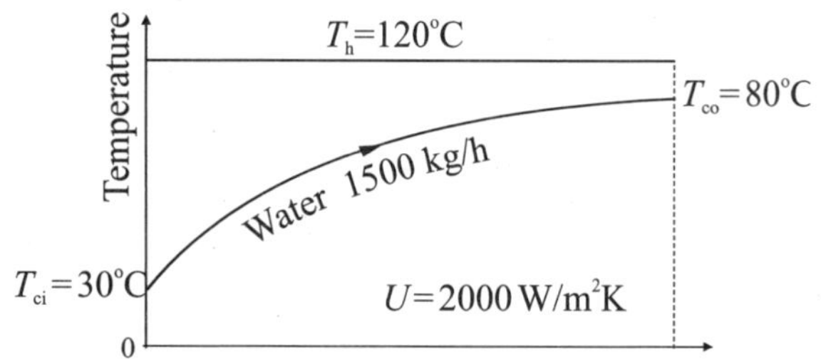

Heat transfer

$$Q = UA(\text{LMTD})$$

Heat transfer area, $$A = \frac{Q}{U(\text{LMTD})}$$

or $$A = \frac{m_h c_{ph}(T_{co} - T_{ci})}{U \times \frac{[(T_h - T_{ci}) - (T_h - T_{co})]}{\ln\left(\frac{T_h - T_{ci}}{T_h - T_{co}}\right)}}$$

Substituting given data:

$$A = \frac{\frac{1500}{60 \times 60} \times 4.187 \times 10^3 (80 - 30)}{2000 \times \frac{[(120-30) - (120-80)]}{\ln\left(\frac{120-30}{120-80}\right)}}$$

From which

$$A = 0.707\ \text{m}^2$$

Example 11.35

A plastic sleeve of outer radius $r_o = 1$ mm covers a wire (radius $r = 0.5$ mm) carrying electric current. Thermal conductivity of the plastic is 0.15W/mK. The heat transfer coefficient on the outer surface of the sleeve exposed to air is 25 W/m^{2}K. Due to the addition of the plastic cover, the heat transfer from the wire to the ambient will

(A) Increase (B) Remain the same

(C) Decrease (D) Be zero

GATE 2016

Solution

Figure shows the cross-section of plastic coated wire.

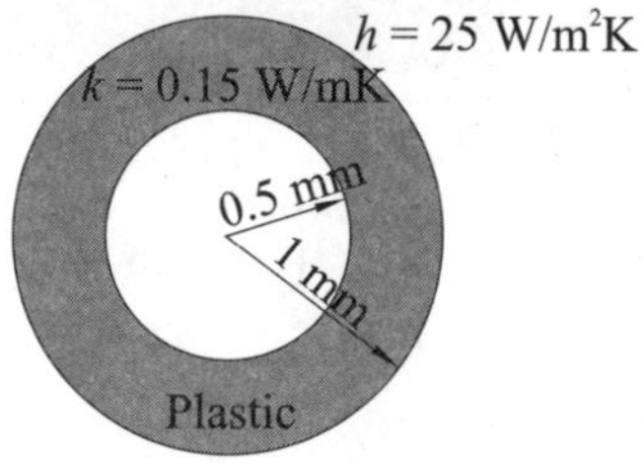

Critical radius, $$r_c = \frac{k}{h} = \frac{0.15}{25}\ \text{m}$$

$$r_c = 6\ \text{mm}$$

Radius of coating ($r_o = 1$ mm) is less than critical radius ($r_c = 6$ mm).

Therefore, addition of plastic sleeve will increase the heat transfer.

Example 11.36

A steel ball of 10 mm diameter at 1000 K is required to be cooled to 350 K by immersing it in a water environment at 300 K. The convective heat transfer coefficient is 1000 W/m^{2}K. Thermal conductivity of steel is 40 W/mK. The time constant for the cooling process τ is 16 s. The time required (in s) to reach the final temperature is ___.

GATE 2016

Solution

Given: $d = 10$ mm, $T_i = 1000$ K, $T = 350$ K, $T_a = 300$ K, $h = 1000$ W/m^{2}K, $k = 40$ W/mK and $t_c = 16$ s.

The characteristic length of the steel ball,

$$l = \frac{V}{A} = \frac{\frac{4}{3}\pi r^3}{4\pi r^2} = \frac{r}{3} = \frac{d}{6}$$

$$l = \frac{10}{6} = \frac{1.67}{1000}\,\text{m}$$

Biot number, $Bi = \frac{hl}{k} = \frac{1000}{40} \times \frac{1.67}{1000} = 0.041$, which is less than 0.1, hence the lumped heat capacity system analysis may be applied.

The temperature distribution in a body at time t during a Newtonian heating or cooling is given by

$$\frac{T - T_a}{T_i - T_a} = e^{-\frac{hA}{\rho Vc}t}$$

Substituting given data; $\frac{430-30}{1030-30} = e^{-\frac{20}{7800 \times \frac{10}{1000} \times 600}t}$

From which, we get

$$t = 42.22\ \text{s}$$

Example 11.37

An infinitely long furnace of 0.5 m × 0.4 m cross-section is shown in the figure. Consider all surfaces of the furnace to be black. The top and bottom walls are maintained at temperature $T_1 = T_3 = 927°\text{C}$ while the side walls are at temperature $T_2 = T_4 = 527°\text{C}$. The view factor, F_{1-2} is 0.26. The net radiation heat loss or gain on side 1 is___ W/m.

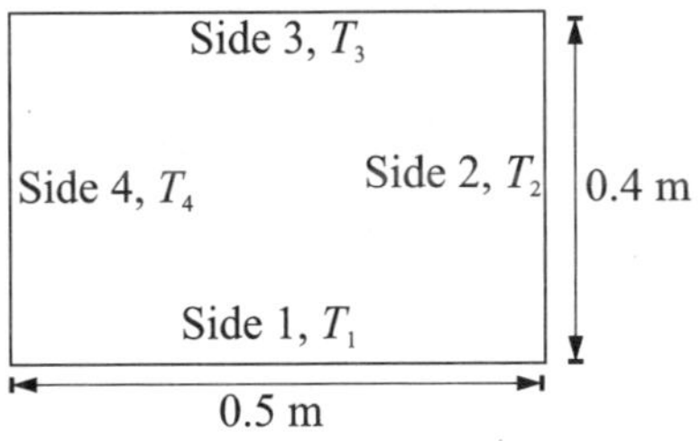

Stefan-Boltzmann constant = 5.67×10^{-8} W/m^{2}K^4

GATE 2016

Solution

Given: $T_1 = T_3 = 273 + 927 = 1200$ K,
$T_2 = T_4 = 273 + 527 = 800$ K and $F_{1-2} = 0.26$

Applying property of view factor

Summing rule: $F_{1-1} + F_{1-2} + F_{1-3} + F_{1-4} = 1$

Substituting $F_{1-1} = 0, F_{1-2} = F_{1-4} = 0.26$, we have

$$F_{1-3} = 1 - 0.26 - 0.26 = 0.48$$

Net heat radiation on side 1,

$$Q_1 = Q_{1-2} + Q_{1-4} + Q_{1-3}$$

$$Q_1 = \sigma A_1 F_{1-2}(T_1^4 - T_2^4) + \sigma A_1 F_{1-4}(T_1^4 - T_4^4) + \sigma A_1 F_{1-3}(T_1^4 - T_3^4)$$

But $T_1 = T_3, F_{1-2} = F_{1-4} = 0.26$ and $T_2 = T_4$

$$Q_1 = 2\sigma A_1 F_{1-2}(T_1^4 - T_2^4)$$

$$Q_1 = 2 \times 5.67 \times 10^{-8} \times 0.5 \times 0.26 \times (1200^4 - 800^4)$$

$$Q_1 = 24530\ \text{W/m}$$

Example 11.38

A fluid (Prandtl number, $Pr = 1$) at 500 K flows over a flat plate of 1.5 m length, maintained at 300 K. The velocity of the fluid is 10 m/s. Assuming kinematic viscosity, $\nu = 30 \times 10^{-6}\,\text{m}^2/\text{s}$, the thermal boundary layer thickness (in mm) at 0.5 m from the leading edge is ________.

GATE 2016

Solution

Given: $Pr = 1$, $u = 10$ m/s, $\nu = 30 \times 10^{-6}\,\text{m}^2/\text{s}$ and $x = 0.5$ m.

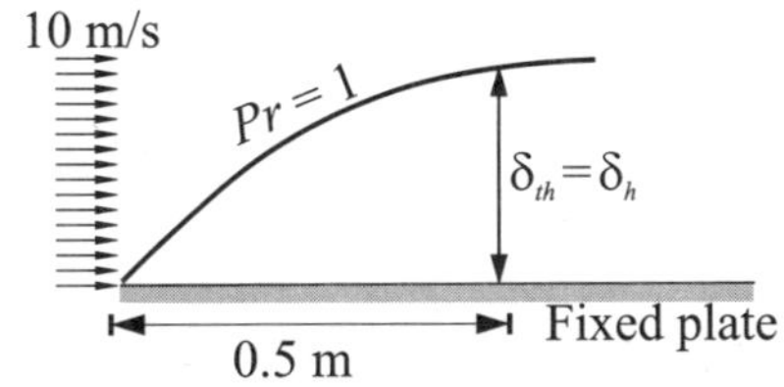

$$Re_x = \frac{ux}{\nu} = \frac{5 \times 0.5}{30 \times 10^{-6}} = 1.67 \times 10^5$$

Hydrodynamic boundary layer thickness is given by

$$\delta_h = \frac{5x}{\sqrt{Re_x}}$$

$$\delta_h = \frac{5 \times 0.5}{\sqrt{1.67 \times 10^5}} = 6.11 \times 10^{-3}\,\text{m}$$

Prandtl number, $Pr = 1 \Rightarrow \delta_h = \delta_{th} = 6.11 \times 10^{-3}$ m

Thermal boundary layer thickness, $\delta_{th} = 6.11$ mm

Example 11.39

A hollow cylinder has length L, inner radius r_1, outer radius r_2, and thermal conductivity k. The thermal resistance of the cylinder for radial conduction is

(A) $\frac{\ln\left(\frac{r_2}{r_1}\right)}{2\pi k L}$ (B) $\frac{\ln\left(\frac{r_1}{r_2}\right)}{2\pi k L}$

(C) $\frac{2\pi k L}{\ln\left(\frac{r_2}{r_1}\right)}$ (D) $\frac{2\pi k L}{\ln\left(\frac{r_1}{r_2}\right)}$

GATE 2016

Solution

Heat transfer through hollow cylinder is given by

$$Q = \frac{(T_1 - T_2)}{\dfrac{\ln\left(\dfrac{r_2}{r_1}\right)}{2\pi kL}} = \frac{T_1 - T_2}{R}$$

or $$Q = \frac{T_1 - T_2}{R_{th}}$$

The thermal resistance of the cylinder is

$$R_{th} = \frac{\ln\left(\dfrac{r_2}{r_1}\right)}{2\pi kL}$$

Example 11.40

Consider the radiation heat exchange inside an annulus between two very long concentric cylinders. The radius of the outer cylinder is R_o and that of the inner cylinder is R_i. The radiation view factor of the outer cylinder onto itself is

(A) $1 - \sqrt{\dfrac{R_i}{R_o}}$ (B) $\sqrt{1 - \dfrac{R_i}{R_o}}$

(C) $1 - \left(\dfrac{R_i}{R_o}\right)^{\frac{1}{3}}$ (D) $1 - \dfrac{R_i}{R_o}$

GATE 2016

Solution

Applying the summation rule to surface 2:

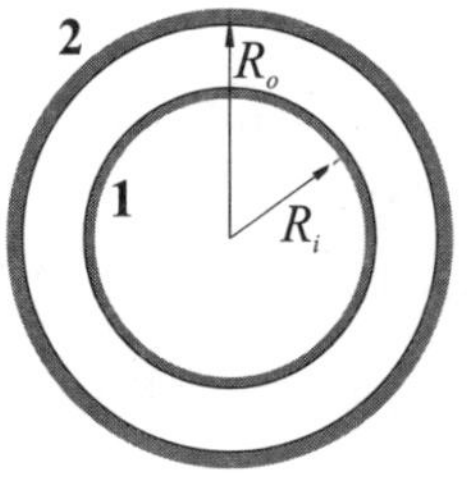

$$F_{2\text{-}2} + F_{2\text{-}1} = 1 \quad \text{or} \quad F_{2\text{-}2} = 1 - F_{2\text{-}1} \qquad \text{(i)}$$

Applying the reciprocity relation to surface 1 and 2,

$$A_1 F_{1\text{-}2} = A_2 F_{2\text{-}1}$$

or $$F_{2\text{-}1} = \frac{A_1}{A_2} F_{1\text{-}2} \qquad \text{(ii)}$$

From Equation (i) and (ii), we have

$$F_{2\text{-}2} = 1 - \frac{A_1}{A_2} F_{1\text{-}2}$$

Since $F_{1\text{-}2} = 1$; $F_{2\text{-}2} = 1 - \dfrac{A_1}{A_2} = 1 - \dfrac{2\pi R_i L}{2\pi R_o L} = 1 - \dfrac{R_i}{R_o}$

$$F_{2\text{-}2} = 1 - \frac{R_i}{R_o}$$

Example 11.41

Consider a parallel-flow heat exchanger with area A_p and a counter-flow heat exchanger with area A_c. In both the heat exchangers, the hot stream flowing at 1 kg/s cools from 80°C to 50°C. For the cold stream in both the heat exchangers, the flow rate and the inlet temperature are 2 kg/s and 10°C, respectively. The hot and cold streams in both the heat exchangers are of the same fluid. Also, both the heat exchangers have the same overall heat transfer coefficient. The ratio $\dfrac{A_c}{A_p}$ is ________.

GATE 2016

Solution

Temperature distribution diagrams of parallel flow and counter-flow heat exchanger.

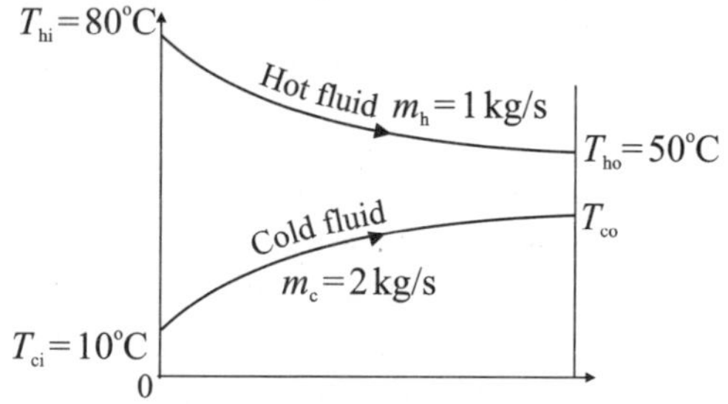

Parallel flow heat exchanger

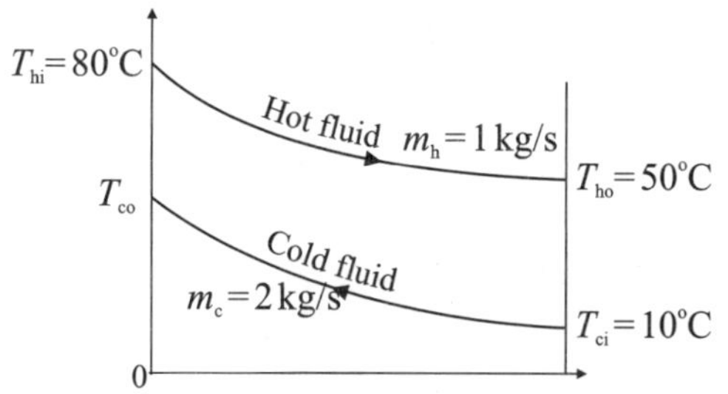

Counter flow heat exchanger

Heat transfer, $Q = m_h c_{ph}(T_{hi} - T_{ho}) = m_c c_{pc}(T_{co} - T_{ci})$

Same fluid $c_{ph} = c_{pc}$; $1 \times (80 - 50) = 2 \times (T_{co} - 10)$

$$T_{co} = 25°C$$

$$Q = UA_c(\text{LMTD})_{\text{count}} = UA_P(\text{LMTD})_{\text{parallel}}$$

or $$\frac{A_c}{A_P} = \frac{(\text{LMTD})_{\text{parallel}}}{(\text{LMTD})_{\text{count}}}$$

$$\frac{A_c}{A_P} = \frac{\dfrac{(80-0)-(50-25)}{\ln\left(\dfrac{80-0}{50-25}\right)}}{\dfrac{(80-25)-(50-10)}{\ln\left(\dfrac{80-25}{50-10}\right)}} = 0.927$$

$$\frac{A_c}{A_P} = 0.927$$

Example 11.42

Two cylindrical shafts A and B at the same initial temperature are simultaneously placed in a furnace. The surfaces of the shafts remain at the furnace gas temperature at all times after they are introduced into the furnace. The temperature variation in the axial direction of the shafts can be assumed to be negligible. The data related to shafts A and B is given in the following table:

Quantity	Shaft A	Shaft B
Diameter (m)	0.4	0.1
Thermal conductivity (W/mK)	40	20
Volumetric heat capacity (J/m^{3}K)	2×10^6	2×10^7

The temperature at the centerline of the shaft A reaches 400°C after two hours. The time required (in hours) for the centerline of the shaft B to attain the temperature of 400°C is ______.

GATE 2016

Solution

The temperature distribution within the solid is given by

$$\frac{T - T_a}{T_i - T_a} = e^{-\frac{hA}{\rho Vc}t}$$

Same temperature reaches

$$\frac{T - T_a}{T_i - T_a} = e^{-\left(\frac{hA}{\rho Vc}t\right)_A} = e^{-\left(\frac{hA}{\rho Vc}t\right)_B}$$

or

$$\left(\frac{hA}{\rho Vc}t\right)_A = \left(\frac{hA}{\rho Vc}t\right)_B$$

or

$$\frac{ht_A}{\left(\frac{V}{A}\right)_A (\rho c)_A} = \frac{ht_B}{\left(\frac{V}{A}\right)_B (\rho c)_B}$$

Substituting given values

$$\frac{2}{\frac{0.4}{6} \times 2 \times 10^6} = \frac{t_B}{\frac{0.1}{6} \times 2 \times 10^7}$$

$$t_B = 5\text{ h}$$

Example 11.43

Steady one-dimensional heat conduction takes place across the faces 1 and 3 of a composite slab consisting of slabs A and B in perfect contact as shown in the figure, where k_A, k_B denote the respective thermal conductivities. Using the data as given in the figure, the interface temperature T_2 (in °C) is ____ .

GATE 2016

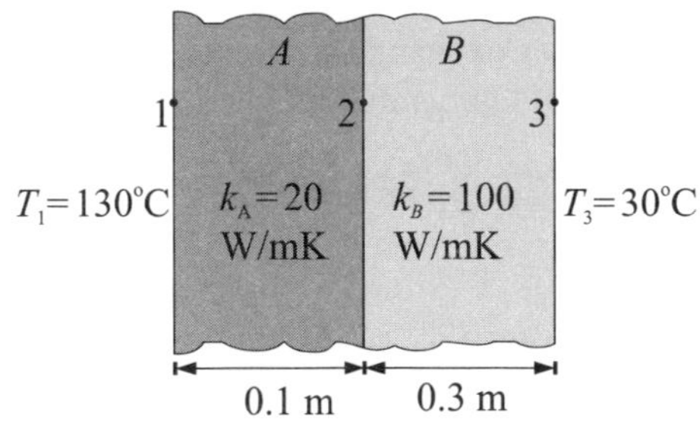

Solution

The thermal resistance network for the representative sections of slab becomes as shown in figure. Then the individual thermal resistance become

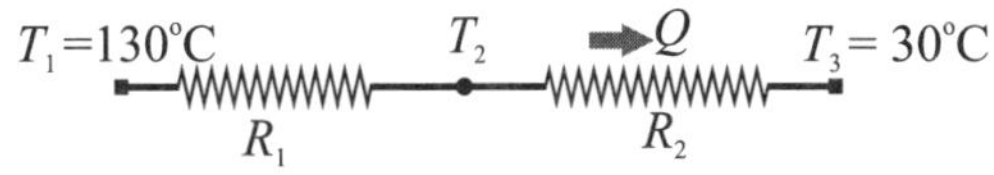

$$R_1 = \frac{0.1}{20A} \text{ and } R_2 = \frac{0.3}{100A}$$

Heat transfer,
$$Q = \frac{T_1 - T_3}{R_1 + R_3} = \frac{T_1 - T_2}{R_1}$$

$$Q = \frac{130 - 30}{\frac{0.1}{20A} + \frac{0.3}{100A}} = \frac{130 - T_2}{\frac{0.1}{20A}}$$

From which, we get

$$T_2 = 67.5°\text{C}$$

Example 11.44

For a heat exchanger, ΔT_{max} is the maximum temperature difference and ΔT_{min} is the minimum temperature difference between the two fluids. LMTD is the log mean temperature difference. C_{min} and C_{max} are the minimum and the maximum heat capacity rates. The maximum possible heat transfer (Q_{max}) between the two fluids is

(A) C_{min} LMTD (B) $C_{min}\ \Delta T_{max}$

(C) $C_{max}\ \Delta T_{max}$ (D) $C_{max}\ \Delta T_{min}$

GATE 2016

Solution

Maximum possible heat transfer

$$Q_{max} = (mc)_{min}\ \Delta T_{max}$$

$$Q_{max} = C_{min}\ \Delta T_{max}$$

Example 11.45

Two large parallel plates having a gap of 10 mm in between them are maintained at temperatures $T_1 = 1000$ K and $T_2 = 400$ K. Given emissivity values, $\varepsilon_1 = 0.5, \varepsilon_2 = 0.25$ and Stefan-Boltzmann constant $\sigma = 5.67 \times 10^{-8}$ W/m^{2}K^4, the heat transfer between the plates (in kW/m^2) is _____.

GATE 2016

Solution

The radiation heat exchange between two large parallel grey plates kept at temperatures T_1 and T_2, is

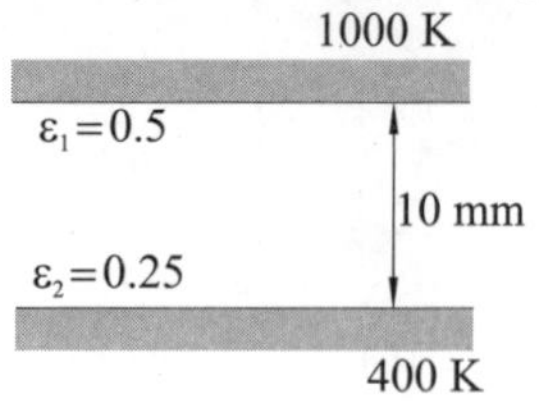

$$\dot{Q}_{1-2} = \frac{\sigma A(T_1^4 - T_2^4)}{\left(\frac{1}{\varepsilon_1} + \frac{1}{\varepsilon_2} - 1\right)}$$

Substituting given data:

$$q_{1-2} = \frac{Q_{1-2}}{A} = \frac{5.67 \times 10^{-8}(1000^4 - 400^4)}{\left(\frac{1}{0.5} + \frac{1}{0.25} - 1\right)}$$

$$q_{1-2} = 11.049 \text{ W/m}^2$$

Example 11.46

A cylindrical steel rod, 0.01 m in diameter and 0.2 m in length is first heated to 750 °C and then immersed in a water bath at 100 °C. The heat transfer coefficient is 250 W/m^{2}K. The density, specific heat and thermal conductivity of steel are $\rho = 7801$ kg/m^3, $c = 473$ J/kgK, and $k = 43$ W/mK, respectively. The time required for the rod to reach 300 °C is ________ s.

GATE 2016

Solution

First, we calculate the Biot number,

$$Bi = \frac{hl_c}{k} = \frac{h \times \left(\frac{V}{A}\right)}{k} = \frac{h \times \frac{\frac{4}{3}\pi R^3}{4\pi R^2}}{k} = \frac{h}{k} \times \frac{R}{3}$$

or $$Bi = \frac{250}{43} \times \frac{0.005}{3} = 0.014$$

Since $Bi < 0.1$, lumped system analysis is applicable. Temperature-time equation is given by

$$\frac{T - T_\infty}{T_i - T_\infty} = e^{-\frac{hA}{\rho V c_p}t} = e^{-\frac{h \times 3}{\rho r c_p}t}$$

$$\frac{300 - 100}{750 - 100} = e^{-\frac{250 \times 3}{7801 \times 0.005 \times 473}t}$$

From which, we get

$$t = 41.75 \text{ s}$$

Example 11.47

Saturated steam at 100 °C condenses on the outside of a tube. Cold fluid enters the tube at 20 °C and exists at 50 °C. The value of the Log Mean Temperature Difference (LMTD) is_______ °C.

GATE 2017

Solution

The temperature distribution graph of condenser is shown in figure.

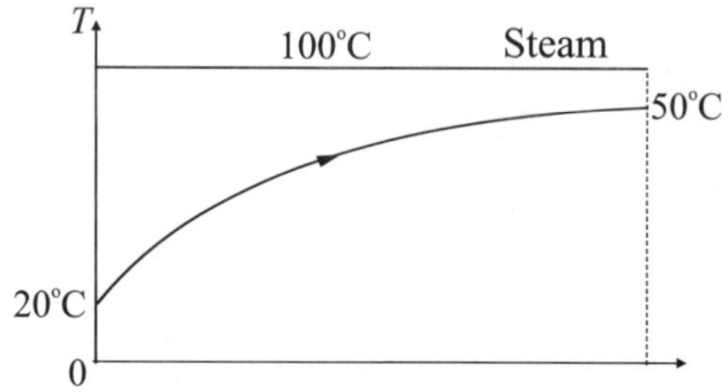

Temperature difference at inlet $\theta_i = 100 - 20 = 80°C$

Temperature difference at outlet $\theta_o = 100 - 50 = 50°C$

$$\text{LMTD} = \frac{\theta_i - \theta_o}{\ln\left(\frac{\theta_i}{\theta_o}\right)}$$

$$\text{LMTD} = \frac{80 - 50}{\ln\left(\frac{80}{50}\right)}$$

$$\text{LMTD} = 63.82°C$$

Example 11.48

Two black surfaces, AB and BC, of lengths 5 m and 6 m, respectively, are oriented as shown. Both surfaces extend infinitely into the third dimension. Given that view factor $F_{12} = 0.5$, $T_1 = 800$ K, $T_2 = 600$ K, $T_{surrounding} = 300$ K and Stefan Boltzmann constant, $\sigma = 5.67 \times 10^{-8}$ W/(m^{2}K^4), the heat transfer rate from surface 2 to the surrounding environment is ______ kW/m.

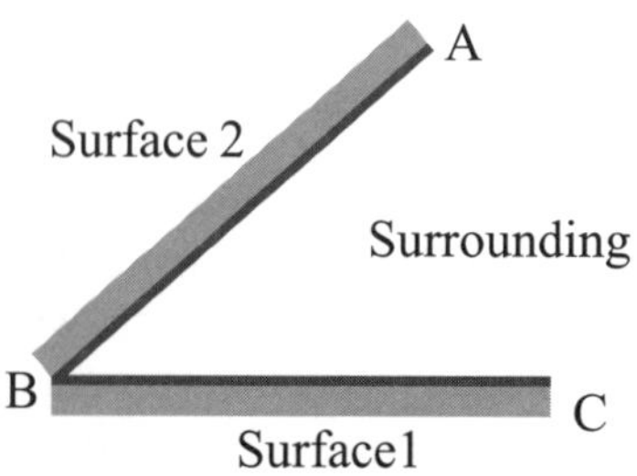

GATE 2017

Solution

Heat transfer rate from surface 2 to the surrounding environment

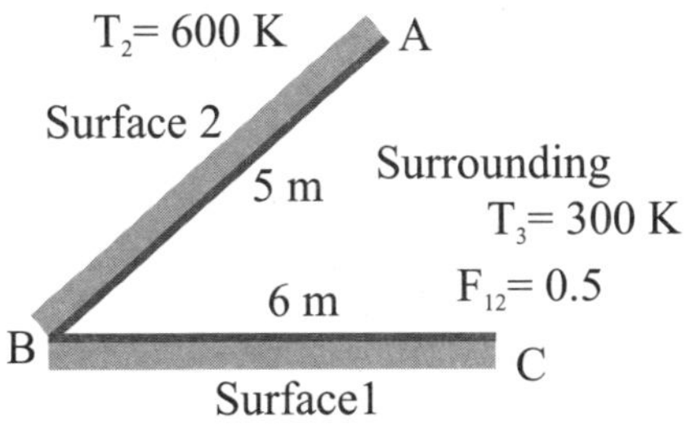

$$Q_{23} = \sigma A_2 F_{23}(T_2^4 - T_3^4)$$

$$F_{11} = F_{22} = 0 \quad \text{[for flat surfaces 1 and 2]}$$

Applying the reciprocity relation, $A_1 F_{12} = A_2 F_{21}$

$$F_{21} = \frac{A_1}{A_2} F_{12} = \frac{6\times 1}{5\times 1}\times 0.5 = \frac{3}{5}$$

Applying summing rule, $F_{22} + F_{23} + F_{21} = 1$

$$0 + F_{23} + \frac{3}{5} = 1$$

$$F_{23} = \frac{2}{5}$$

$$Q_{23} = 5.67\times 10^{-8}\times 5\times 1\times \frac{2}{5}(600^4 - 300^4)$$

$$Q_{23} = 13.778 \text{ kW/m}$$

Example 11.49

Heat is generated uniformly in a long solid cylindrical rod (diameter = 10 mm) at the rate of $4\times 10^7 \text{ W/m}^3$. The thermal conductivity of the rod material is 25 W/m.K. Under steady state conditions, the temperature difference between the centre and the surface of the rod is_____°C.

GATE 2017

Solution

Given: $q_g = 4\times 10^7 \text{ W/m}^3$, $k = 25$ W/mK, $d = 10$ mm.

Steady state one-dimensional heat conduction in cylindrical coordinates

$$\frac{1}{r}\frac{d}{dr}\left(rk\frac{dT}{dr}\right) + q_g = 0$$

$$\frac{dT}{dr} + \frac{q_g r}{2k} = \frac{c_1}{r} \qquad \text{(i)}$$

$$T + \frac{q_g r^2}{4k} = c_1 \ln r + c_2 \qquad \text{(ii)}$$

Applying boundary conditions (i) $\frac{dT}{dr} = 0$ at $r = 0$ and (ii) $T = T_{\max}$ at $r = 0$

We obtain $c_1 = 0$ and $c_2 = T_{\max}$

$$T + \frac{q_g r^2}{4k} = T_{\max}$$

Temperature at surface $r = r_0$, $\quad T_s = T_{\max} - \frac{q_g r_0^2}{4k}$

$$T_{\max} - T_s = \frac{q_g r_0^2}{4k} = \frac{4\times 10^7\times\left(\frac{5}{1000}\right)^2}{4\times 25}$$

$$T_{\max} - T_s = 10^0\text{C}$$

Example 11.50

The heat loss from a fin is 6 W. The effectiveness and efficiency of the fin are 3 and 0.75, respectively. The heat loss (in W) from the fin, keeping the entire fin surface at base temperature, is______.

GATE 2017

Solution

Given: $Q_{fin} = 6$ W, $\varepsilon = 3$, $\eta = 0.75$

Efficiency of fin $\eta = \frac{Q_{fin}}{Q_{max}}$

$$0.75 = \frac{6}{Q_{max}}$$

$$Q_{max} = \frac{6}{0.75} = 8$$

$$Q_{max} = 8 \text{ W}$$

Example 11.51

The emissive power of a black body is *P*. If its absolute temperature is doubled, the emissive power becomes.

(A) 2*P* (B) 4*P* (C) 8*P* (D) 16*P*

GATE 2017

Solution

Emissive power, $\quad E_b = \sigma T^4$

$$(E_b)_1 = \sigma T_1^4 = P$$

$$(E_b)_2 = \sigma(2T_1)^4 = 16\sigma T_1^4$$

$$(E_b)_2 = \sigma(2T_1)^4 = 16P$$

Example 11.52

A metal ball of diameter 60 mm is initially at 220 °C. The ball is suddenly cooled by an air jet of 20°C. The heat transfer coefficient is 200 W/m^2.K. The specific heat, thermal conductivity and density of metal ball are 400 J/kg.K, 400 W/mK and 9000 kg/m^3, respectively. The ball temperature (in °C) after 90 seconds will be approximately.

(A) 141 (B) 163 (C) 189 (D) 210

GATE 2017

Solution

The temperature distribution within the body is given by

$$\frac{T-T_a}{T_i-T_a}=e^{-\frac{hA}{\rho Vc}t};$$

Substituting $\frac{A}{V}=\frac{4\pi r^2}{4\pi r^3/3}=\frac{3}{r}=\frac{6}{d}$

$$\frac{T-T_a}{T_i-T_a}=e^{-\frac{h6}{\rho dc}t}$$

$$\frac{T-20}{220-20}=e^{-\frac{200}{9000\times400}\times\frac{6}{(60/1000)}\times90}$$

$$T=141.3°\text{C}$$

Example 11.53

A plane slab of thickness L and thermal conductivity k is heated with a fluid on one side (P), and the other side (Q) is maintained at a constant temperature, T_Q of 25°C, as shown in the figure. The fluid is at 45°C and the surface heat transfer coefficient, h, is 10 W/m^{2}K. The steady state temperature, T_P, (in °C) of the side which is exposed to the fluid is _______.

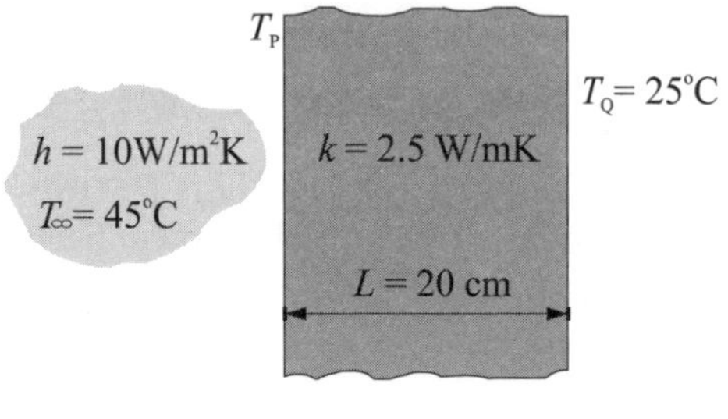

GATE 2018

Solution

The thermal resistance network for this problem involves two resistance in series and is given in figure.

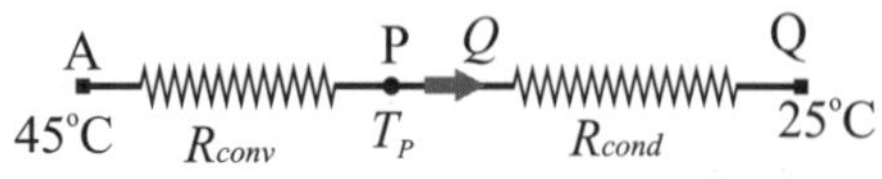

Heat transfer, $Q=\frac{45-T_P}{\frac{1}{hA}}=\frac{T_P-25}{\frac{L}{kA}}$

$$45-T_P=\frac{k}{hL}(T_P-25)$$

or $$45-T_P=\frac{2.5}{10\times0.2}(T_P-25)$$

$$T_P=33.88°\text{C}$$

Example 11.54

The peak wavelength of radiation emitted by a black body at a temperature of 2000 K is 1.45 μm. If the peak wavelength of emitted radiation changes to 2.90 μm, then the temperature (in K) of the black body is

(A) 500 (B) 1000 (C) 4000 (D) 8000

GATE 2018

Solution

Applying Wein's Law $\lambda T=b$

$$\lambda_1T_1=\lambda_2T_2$$

$$1.45\times2000=2.90\times T_2$$

$$T_2=1000\text{ K}$$

Example 11.55

A 0.2 m thick infinite black plate having a thermal conductivity of 3.96 W/m-K is exposed to two infinite black surfaces at 300 K and 400 K as shown in the figure. At steady state, the surface temperature of the plate facing the cold side is 350 K. The value of Stefan Boltzmann constant, σ, is 5.67 × 10^{-8} W/m^2 K^4. Assuming 1-D heat conduction, the magnitude of heat flux through the plate (in W/m^2) is _______.

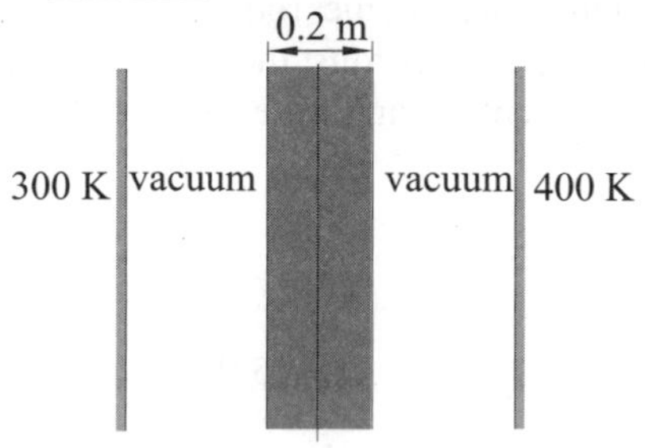

GATE 2018

Solution

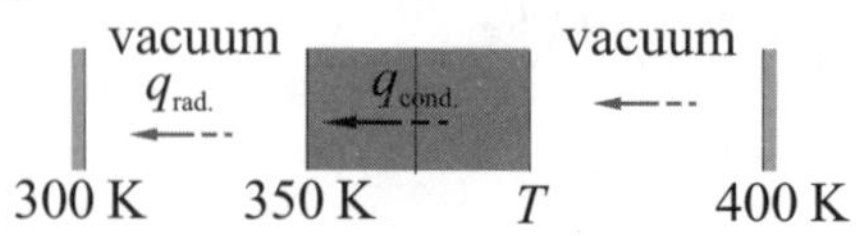

Under steady state condition,

Heat flux through wall q = flux from wall to surface at

300 K

$$q = 5.67 \times 10^{-8}(350^4 - 300^4)$$

$$q = 391.612 \text{ W/m}^2$$

Example 11.56

Steam in the condenser of a thermal power plant is to be condensed at a temperature of 30 °C with cooling water which enters the tubes of the condenser at 14 °C and exits at 22 °C. The total surface area of the tubes is 50 m^2, and the overall heat transfer coefficient is 2000 W/m^2 K. The heat transfer (in MW) to the condenser is ______ .

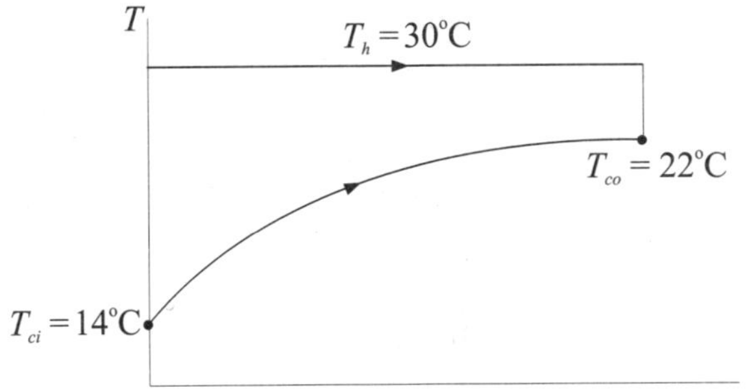

Temperature Distribution Diagram

GATE 2018

Solution

LMTD for condenser

$$\text{LMTD} = \frac{\theta_i - \theta_o}{\ln\left(\frac{\theta_i}{\theta_o}\right)} = \frac{(T_h - T_{ci}) - (T_h - T_{co})}{\ln\left(\frac{T_h - T_{ci}}{T_h - T_{co}}\right)}$$

Substituting $T_h = 30°\text{C}$, $T_{ci} = 14°\text{C}$ and $T_{co} = 22°\text{C}$.

$$\text{LMTD} = \frac{(30-14)-(30-22)}{\ln\left(\frac{30-14}{30-22}\right)} = 11.84°\text{C}$$

Heat transfer $Q = UA(LMTD)$

$$Q = 2000 \times 50 \times 11.84 = 11.54 \times 10^5 \text{W}$$

$$Q = 1.154 \text{ MW}$$

Example 11.57

A slender rod of length L, diameter d ($L >> d$) and thermal conductivity k_1 is joined with another rod of identical dimensions, but of thermal conductivity k_2, to form a composite cylindrical rod of length $2L$. The heat transfer in radial direction and contact resistance are negligible. The effective thermal conductivity of the composite rod is

(A) $k_1 + k_2$ (B) $\sqrt{k_1 k_2}$ (C) $\frac{k_1 k_2}{k_1 + k_2}$ (D) $\frac{2k_1 k_2}{k_1 + k_2}$

GATE 2019

Solution

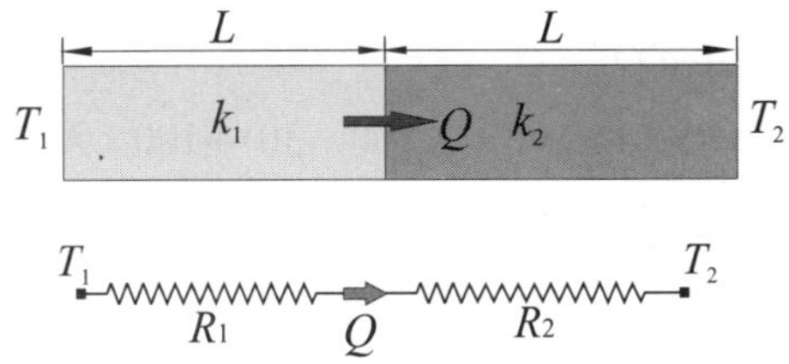

Thermal resistance of rods are $R_1 = \frac{L}{k_1 A}$ and $R_2 = \frac{L}{k_2 A}$

Heat transfer rate, $$Q = \frac{T_1 - T_2}{R_1 + R_2} = \frac{T_1 - T_2}{R}$$

or $$Q = \frac{T_1 - T_2}{\frac{L}{k_1 A} + \frac{L}{k_2 A}} = \frac{T_1 - T_2}{\frac{2L}{k_{eq} A}}$$

we obtain

$$k_{eq} = \frac{2k_1 k_2}{k_1 + k_2}$$

Example 11.58

Three slabs are joined together as shown in the figure. There is no thermal contact resistance at the interfaces. The center slab experiences a non-uniform internal heat generation with an average value equal to 10000 W/m^3, while the left and right slabs have no internal heat generation. All slabs have thickness equal to 1 m and thermal conductivity of each slab is equal to 5 W/mK. The two extreme faces are exposed to fluid with heat transfer coefficient 100 W/m^{2}K and bulk temperature 30 °C as shown. The heat transfer in the slabs is assumed to be one dimensional and steady, and all properties are constant. If the left extreme face temperature T_1 is measured to be 100 °C, the right extreme face temperature T_2 is ____ °C.

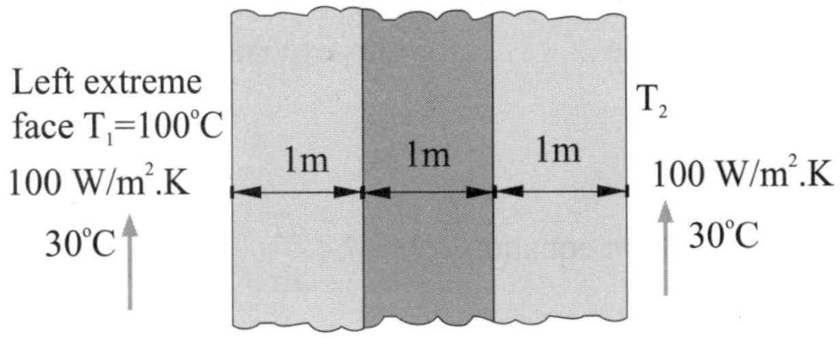

GATE 2019

Solution

Heat generated $Q_g = 10000 \times \text{A} \times 1 \text{ W}$

Heat transfer from left surface $Q_1 = 100 \times \text{A}(100 - 30) \text{ W}$

Heat transfer from right surface $Q_2 = 100 \times \text{A}(T_2 - 30) \text{ W}$

Under steady state condition

Heat generated $Q_g = Q_1 + Q_2$

$$10000 \times A \times 1 = 100 \times A(100 - 30) + 100 \times A(T_2 - 30)$$

or $100 = (100 - 30) + (T_2 - 30)$

$$T_2 = 60\ °C$$

Example 11.59

Sphere **1** with a diameter of 0.1 m is completely enclosed by another sphere **2** of diameter 0.4 m. The view factor $\mathbf{F}_{12}$ is

(A) 0.0625 (B) 0.25 (C) 0.5 (D)1.0

GATE 2019

Solution

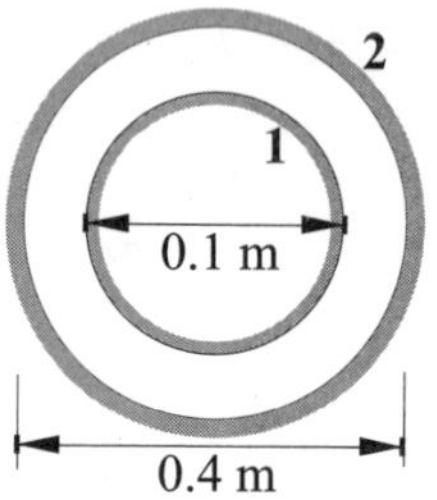

Applying the summation rule to surface 1, yields

$$F_{1-1} + F_{1-2} = 1$$

Substituting $F_{1-1} = 0$, we have

$$F_{1-2} = 1$$

Example 11.60

One-dimensional steady state heat conduction takes place through a solid whose cross-sectional area varies lineally in the direction of heat transfer. Assume there is no heat generation in the solid and the thermal conductivity of the material is constant and independent of temperature. The temperature distribution in the solid is

(A) Linear (B) Quadratic

(C) Logarithmic (D) Exponential

GATE 2019

Solution

Heat conduction equation, $Q = -kA\dfrac{dT}{dx}$

or $$Q\int \frac{dx}{A} = -k\int dT$$

Substituting cross-sectional area, $A = c_1x + c_2$

$$Q\int_0^x \frac{dx}{c_1x + c_2} = -k\int_{T_1}^{T} dT$$

$$\frac{Q}{c_1}\ln\left(\frac{c_1x + c_2}{c_2}\right) = k(T_1 - T)$$

$$T = T_1 - \frac{Q}{c_1k}\ln\left(\frac{c_1x + c_2}{c_2}\right)$$

Temperature distribution in the solid is Logarithmic.

Example 11.60

A thin vertical flat plate of height L, and infinite width perpendicular to the plane of the figure, is losing heat to the surrounding by natural convection. The temperature of the plate and the surroundings, and the properties of the surrounding fluid, are constant. The relationship between the average Nusselt and Rayleigh numbers is given by $Nu = K\,Ra^{1/4}$, where K is a constant. The length scales for Nusselt and Rayleigh numbers are the height of the plate. The height of the plate is increased to $16L$ keeping all other factors constant.

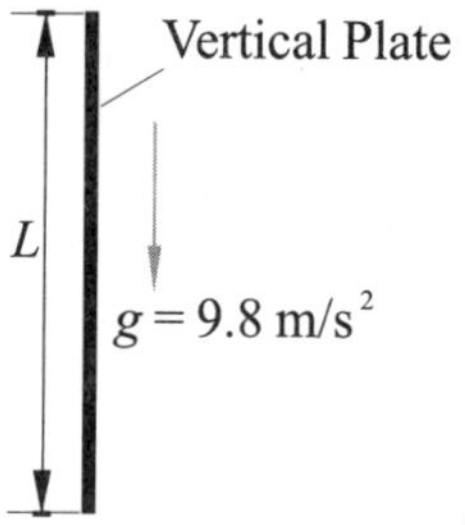

If the average heat transfer coefficient for the first plate is h_1 and that for the second plate is h_2, the value of the ratio h_1 / h_2 is ______.

GATE 2019

Solution

Given: Nusselt number $Nu = K\,Ra^{1/4}$

or $Nu = K\,(\mathrm{Gr} \times \mathrm{Pr})^{1/4}$

or $Nu = K\,\mathrm{Gr}^{1/4} \times \mathrm{Pr}^{1/4}$

or $$\frac{hL}{k} = K\left(\frac{\beta g \Delta T L^3}{\nu^2}\right)^{1/4} \times \left(\frac{\mu c_p}{k}\right)^{1/4}$$

or $h \propto L^{-1/4}$

$$\frac{h_1}{h_2} = \left(\frac{L_2}{L_1}\right)^{1/4} = \left(\frac{16L_1}{L_1}\right)^{1/4}$$

$$\frac{h_1}{h_2} = 2$$

Example 11.61

Three sets of parallel plates LM, NR and PQ are given in Figures 1, 2 and 3. The view factor F_{IJ} is defined as the fraction of radiation leaving plate I that is intercepted by plate J. Assume that the values of F_{LM} and F_{NR} are 0.8 and

0.4, respectively. The value of F_{PQ} (round off to one decimal place) is ________.

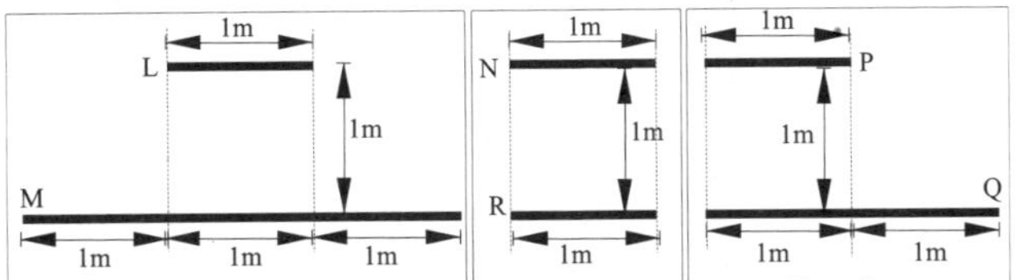

Figure 1 Figure 2 Figure 3

GATE 2019

Solution

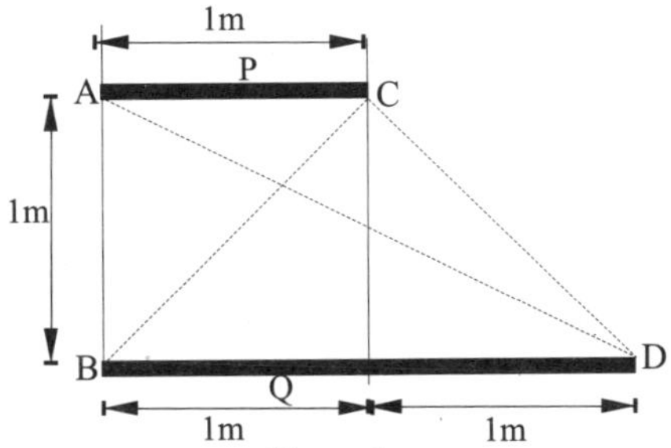

Figure 3

View factor

$$F_{i-j} = \frac{\sum(\text{Crossed strings}) - \sum(\text{Uncrossed strings})}{2 \times \text{string on surface}}$$

$$F_{PQ} = \frac{(AD + BC) - (AB + CD)}{2 \times AC}$$

$$F_{PQ} = \frac{(\sqrt{5} + \sqrt{2}) - (1 + \sqrt{2})}{2 \times 1}$$

$$F_{PQ} = 0.6$$

Example 11.62

Hot and cold fluids enter a parallel flow double tube heat exchanger at 100°C and 15°C, respectively. The heat capacity rates of hot and cold fluids are $C_h = 2000$ W/h and $C_c = 1200$ W/h, respectively. If the outlet temperature of the cold fluid is 45°C, the log mean temperature difference (LMTD) of the heat exchanger is ____ K (round off to two decimal places).

GATE 2019

Solution

Heat transfer, $Q = C_h(T_{hi} - T_{ho}) = C_c(T_{co} - T_{ci})$

$2000 \times (1000 - T_{ho}) = 1200 \times (45 - 15) \quad \Rightarrow T_{ho} = 82°C$

Temperature difference at inlet, $\theta_i = 100 - 15 = 85°C$

Temperature difference at outlet, $\theta_o = 82 - 15 = 37°C$

$$LMTD = \frac{\theta_i - \theta_o}{\ln\left(\frac{\theta_i}{\theta_o}\right)} = \frac{85 - 37}{\ln\left(\frac{85}{37}\right)} = 57.71$$

$$LMTD = 57.71$$

11.3 PRACTICE PAPER

Time: 3 hours **Max. Marks: 100**

Q.1 to Q.30 carry one mark each

Q.1 to Q.20 Multiple Choice Questions

Q.1 A composite wall consists of two layers of different materials having conductivity k_1 and k_2. For equal thickness of the two layers, the equivalent thermal conductivity of the slab will be

(A) $k_1 + k_2$ (B) $\frac{2k_1k_2}{k_1 + k_2}$

(C) $\sqrt{k_1k_2}$ (D) $\frac{k_1k_2}{k_1 + k_2}$

Q.2 Lumped system analysis of transient heat conduction situation is valid when the Biot number is

(A) Very small (B) Very large

(C) Approximately one

(D) Cannot say unless the Fourier number is also know

Q.3 In a long cylindrical rod of radius r and a surface heat flux of q_0, the uniform internal heat generation rate is

(A) $\frac{2q_0}{r}$ (B) $2q_0$ (C) $\frac{q_0}{r}$ (D) $\frac{q_0}{r^2}$

Q.4 The wave length at which the black body emissive power reaches its maximum value at 300 K is

(A) 9.6 μm (B) 15.5 μm (C) 5.1 μm (D) 38.0 μm

Q.5 The equation of effectiveness $\varepsilon = 1 - e^{-NTU}$ of a heat exchanger is valid in the case of

(A) Boiler and condenser for parallel flow

(B) Boiler and condenser counter flow

(C) Boiler and condenser for both parallel flow and counter-flow

(D) Gas turbine for both parallel flow and counter-flow

Q.6 Match List-I with List-II and select correct answer using the codes given below the lists (notations have their usual meaning).

List-I	List-II
(a) Fins	1. $\frac{UA}{C_{min}}$
(b) Heat exchanger	2. $\frac{x}{2\sqrt{\alpha\tau}}$
(c) Transient conduction	3. $\sqrt{\frac{hP}{kA}}$

(d) Heisler chart 4. $\frac{hl}{k}$

(A) a-3, b-1, c-2, d-4 (B) a-2, b-1, c-3, d-4

(C) a-3, b-4, c-2, d-1 (D) a- 2, b-4, c-3, d-1

Q.7 Match List-I (governing equations of heat transfer) with List-II (specific cases of heat transfer) and select correct answer using the codes given below the lists.

List-I	List-II
(a) $\frac{d^2T}{dr^2}+\frac{2}{r}\frac{dT}{dr}=0$	1. Pin-fin 1-D case
(b) $\frac{\partial^2 T}{\partial x^2}=\frac{1}{\alpha}\frac{\partial T}{\partial t}$	2. 1-D conduction in cylinder
(c) $\frac{d^2T}{dr^2}+\frac{1}{r}\frac{dT}{dr}=0$	3. 1-D conduction in sphere
(d) $\frac{d^2\theta}{dx^2}-m^2\theta=0$	4. Plane slab

Symbols have their usual meanings

(A) a-2, b-4, c-3, d-1 (B) a-3, b-1, c-2, d- 4

(C) a-2, b-1, c-3, d-4 (D) a-3, b-4, c-2, d-1

Q.8 A cross flow type air heater has an area of $50\,m^2$. The overall heat transfer coefficient is 100 W/m^{2}K and heat capacity of both hot and cold stream is 1000 W/K. The value of NTU is

(A) 0 (B)1 (C) 5 (D) 100

Q.9 The Biot number is given by $Bi=\frac{hL_c}{k}$. The characteristic length L_c of a steel ball of diameter 12 cm is

(A) 2 cm (B) 6 cm (C) 3 cm (D) 4 cm

Q.10 The heat flow equation through a cylinder of inner radius r_1 and outer radius r_2 is desired in the same form as that for heat flow through a plane wall. The equivalent area A_m is given by

(A) $\frac{A_1+A_2}{\log_e\left(\frac{A_2}{A_1}\right)}$ (B) $\frac{A_1+A_2}{2\log_e\left(\frac{A_2}{A_1}\right)}$

(C) $\frac{A_2-A_1}{2\log_e\left(\frac{A_2}{A_1}\right)}$ (D) $\frac{A_2-A_1}{\log_e\left(\frac{A_2}{A_1}\right)}$

Q.11 A plane wall of thickness $2l$ has a uniform volumetric heat source q_g(W/m^3). It is exposed to local ambient temperature T_∞ at both the ends ($x=\pm l$). The surface temperature T_s of the wall under steady-state condition (where h and k have their usual meaning) is given by

(A) $T_s=T_\infty+\frac{q_g l}{h}$ (B) $T_s=T_\infty+\frac{q_g l^2}{2k}$

(C) $T_s=T_\infty+\frac{q_g l^2}{h}$ (D) $T_s=T_\infty+\frac{q_g l^3}{2k}$

Q.12 Which one is the correct expression for one-dimensional, steady state, constant thermal conductivity heat conduction equation for a cylinder with heat generation?

(A) $\frac{d}{dr}\left(r\frac{dT}{dr}\right)=0$ (B) $\frac{1}{r}\frac{d}{dr}\left(r\frac{dT}{dr}\right)+\frac{q_g}{k}=0$

(C) $\frac{1}{r}\frac{\partial}{\partial r}\left(r\frac{\partial T}{\partial r}\right)=\frac{1}{\alpha}\frac{\partial T}{\partial t}$ (D) $\frac{1}{r}\frac{\partial}{\partial r}\left(r\frac{\partial T}{\partial r}\right)+\frac{q_g}{k}=\frac{1}{\alpha}\frac{\partial T}{\partial t}$

Q.13 The Biot number is the ratio of

(A) The conduction thermal resistance to the convection thermal resistance

(B) The convection thermal resistance to the conduction thermal resistance

(C) The thermal energy storage capacity to the conduction thermal resistance

(D) The thermal energy storage capacity to the convection thermal resistance

Q.14 Heat transfer rate from the circular tube of inner radius r_i, outer radius r_o and thermal conductivity k is given by $Q=\frac{2\pi(T_i-T_o)}{\frac{\ln(r_o/r_i)}{k}+\frac{1}{r_o h}}$

Increasing r_o will reduce the heat transfer as long as

(A) $r_o<\frac{k}{h}$ (B) $r_o>\frac{k}{h}$ (C) $r_o>\frac{2k}{h}$

(D) Increasing r_o will always reduce the heat transfer

Q.15 In transient heat conduction, the two significant dimensionless parameters are___number and____number.

(A) Fourier, Reynolds (B) Reynolds, Prandtl

(C) Biot, Fourier (D) Reynolds, Biot

Q.16 The heat conduction equation

$$\frac{\partial^2 T}{\partial x^2}+\frac{\partial^2 T}{\partial y^2}+\frac{\partial^2 T}{\partial z^2}=\frac{1}{\alpha}\frac{\partial T}{\partial t}$$ is known as

(A) Poisson equation (B) Diffusion equation

(C) Laplace equation (D) Fourier equation

Q.17 Sun's surface at 5800 K emits radiation at a wave length of 0.5μ. A furnace at 300°C will emit through a small opening, radiation at a wavelength of nearly

(A) $10\,\mu m$ (B) $5\,\mu m$ (C) $0.25\,\mu m$ (D) $0.025\,\mu m$

Q.18 A fin will be necessary and effective only when

(A) k is small and h is large

(B) k is large and h is also large

(C) k is small and h is also small

(D) k is large and h is small

Q.19 For same initial conditions, one can expect the laminar thermal and velocity boundary layer on a flat plate to have the same thickness when the Prandtl number of the flowing fluid is

(A) 1 (B) 0 (C) 2 (D) 10

Q.20 In a heat exchanger, the hot gases enter with a temperature of $150\,°C$ and leave at $75\,°C$. The cold fluid enters at $25\,°C$ and leaves at $125\,°C$. The capacity ratio of the exchanger is

(A) 0.65 (B) 0.75 (C) 0.85 (D) 0.95

Q.21 to Q.30 Numerical Answer Questions

Q.21 The spectral emissive power E_λ for a diffusely emitting surface is

$E_\lambda = 0$ for $\lambda < 3\,\mu m$

$E_\lambda = 150\ W/m^2\,\mu m$ for $3 < \lambda < 12\,\mu m$

$E_\lambda = 300\ W/m^2\,\mu m$ for $12 < \lambda < 25\,\mu m$

$E_\lambda = 0$ for $\lambda < 25\,\mu m$

The total emissive power of the surface over the entire spectrum is________.

Q.22 A cylindrical rod of diameter 4 cm and length 6 cm is at 1200 K. If the emissivity of the rod surface is 0.75, the total amount of radiation (in kJ) emitted by all surfaces of the rod in 20 min is________.

Q.23 Consider an infinitely long three-sided triangular enclosure with side length 5 cm, 3 cm and 4 cm. The view factor from the 5 cm side to the 4 cm side is________.

Q.24 6.0 kJ of conduction heat transfer has to take place in 10 minutes from one end to other end of a metallic cylinder of 10 cm^2 cross-sectional area, length 1 m and thermal conductivity as 100 W/mK. What is the temperature difference between the two ends of the cylindrical bar?________.

Q.25 Heat is lost from a 100 mm diameter steam pipe placed horizontally in ambient at 30°C. If the Nusselt number is 25 and thermal conductivity of air is 0.03 W/mK, then the heat transfer coefficient (W/m^2K) will be ____.

Q.26 Water enters a 4 cm diameter and 6 m long tube whose walls are maintained at $100\,°C$. The water enters this tube with a bulk temperature of $25\,°C$ and a volume flow rate of 3 m^3/h. The Reynolds number for this internal flow is___.

(For water, use $k = 0.607$ W/mK, $\mu = 9.0 \times 10^{-4}$ kg/ms, $\rho = 1000\ kg/m^3$)

Q.27 The NTU of condenser of boiler is 0.6. The effectiveness of condenser is________.

Q.28 A furnace has a 20 cm thick wall with thermal conductivity 0.8 W/mK. For the same heat loss from the furnace, what will be the thickness of the wall if the thermal conductivity of the material is 0.16 W/mK? ____.

Q.29 A 3 m high, 4 m wide and 25 cm thick wall of a house has a thermal resistance of $0.04\,°C/W$. Thermal conductivity of the wall is______.

Q.30 In an evaporator, evaporates at $100\,°C$ taking heat from hot air entering at $260\,°C$ and leaving at $150\,°C$. The LMTD is ____.

Q.31 to Q.65 carry two marks each.

Q.31 to Q.50 Multiple Choice Questions

Q.31 In a double-pipe counter flow heat exchanger, 1000 kg/h of oil having a specific heat 20 J/kgK is cooled from $150\,°C$ to $125\,°C$ by 1250 kg/h of fluid of specific heat 16 J/kgK. The fluid leaves the heat exchanger at 75°C. In such case, the temperature at which the cooling fluid is entering the heat exchanger and LMTD will be

(A) 25°C and 50°C (B) 50°C and 50°C

(C) 50°C and 75°C (D) 75°C and 50°C

Q.32 A 0.5 m thick large plane wall has its two surfaces kept at $300\,°C$ and $200\,°C$. Thermal conductivity of the wall varies linearly with temperature and its values at $300\,°C$ and $200\,°C$ are 25 W/mK and 15 W/mK, respectively. Then the steady heat flux through the wall is

(A) 8 kW/m^2 (B) 5 kW/m^2 (C) 4 kW/m^2 (D) 3 kW/m^2

Q.33 For laminar flow over a flat plate, the local heat transfer coefficient h_x varies as $x^{-\frac{1}{2}}$, where x is the distance from the leading edge ($x = 0$) of the plate. The ratio of the average coefficient h_x between the leading edge and some location A at $x = x$ on the plate to the local heat transfer coefficient h_x at A is

(A) 1 (B) 2 (C) 4 (D) 8

Q.34 Consider a wall of cross-section area 1 m^2 and thickness 3 m shown in figure. The left and right surfaces of the wall are maintained at uniform temperature of $100\,°C$ and $20\,°C$ respectively assuming heat transfer through the wall to be one-dimensional. Heat transfer rate Q through the wall is

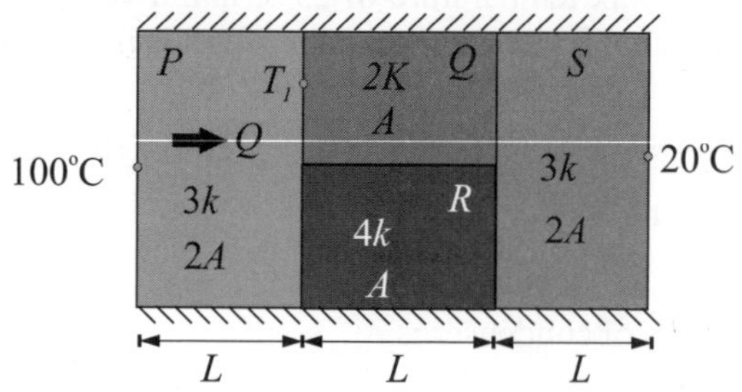

Where $A = 0.5$ m²; $L = 1$m; $k = 100$ W/mK

(A) 4 kW (B) 8 kW

(C) 3.66 kW (D) None of these

Q.35 A large concrete slab 1 m thick has one-dimensional temperature distribution $T(x) = 4 - 10x + 20x^2 + 10x^3$, where T is temperature and x is distance from one face towards other face of wall. If the slab material has thermal diffusivity of 2×10^{-3} m²/h, what is the rate of change of temperature at the other face of the wall?

(A) 0.1 °C/h (B) 0.2 °C/h (C) 0.3 °C/h (D) 0.4 °C/h

Q.36 The radiative heat transfer rate per unit area (W/m²) between two plane parallel grey surfaces whose emissivity is 0.9 and maintained at 400 K and 300 K is

(A) 992 (B) 812 (C) 567 (D) 464

Q.37 What will be the view factor F_{21} for the geometry as shown in the figure (sphere within a cube)?

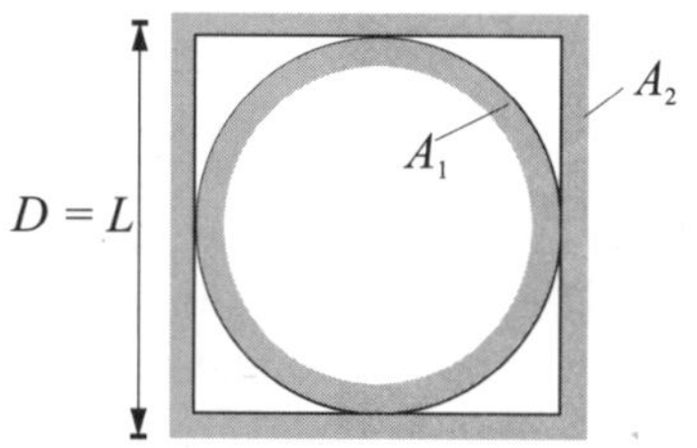

(A) $\frac{\pi}{2}$ (B) $\frac{\pi}{4}$ (C) $\frac{\pi}{3}$ (D) $\frac{\pi}{6}$

Q.38 A flat plate has thickness 5 cm, thermal conductivity 1 W/mK, convective heat transfer coefficients on its two flat faces of 10 W/m²K and 20 W/m²K. The overall heat transfer coefficient (in W/m²K) for such a flat plate is

(A) 5 (B) 6.33 (C) 20 (D) 30

Q.39 A hot plane surface at 250 °C is exposed to air at 25 °C with a combined heat transfer coefficient of 25 W/m² K. The heat loss from the surface is to be reduced by half by covering it with sufficient insulation with a thermal conductivity of 0.25 W/mK. Assuming the heat transfer coefficient to remain constant, the required thickness of insulation is

(A) 1 cm (B) 10 cm (C) 20 cm (D) 0.1 cm

Q.40 A very long 25 mm diameter copper rod $k = 380$ W/mK extends horizontally from a plane heated wall at 125 °C. The temperature of the surrounding air is 25 °C and convective heat transfer coefficient is 9.0 W/m²K. Temperature of rod at distance x from the heated wall is

(A) $25 + 100e^{-1.946x}$ (B) $100e^{-1.946x}$

(C) $25 - e^{-1.946x}$ (D) None of these

Q.41 In a parallel flow heat exchanger, the NTU is calculated to be 3. The lowest possible effectiveness for this heat exchange is

(A) 10% (B) 27% (C) 41% (D) 50%

Q.42 A fin of diameter 1 cm, length 30 cm and conductivity 237 W/mK is attached to a surface at 80°C. The surface is exposed to ambient air at 22°C with a heat transfer coefficient of 18 W/m²K. If the fin can be assumed to be very long, the rate of heat transfer from the fin is

(A) 2.0 W (B) 5.95 W (C) 3.0 W (D) None of these

Q.43 A heat exchanger is used to heat cold water ($C_p = 4.18$ kJ/kgK) entering at 12 °C at a rate of 1.2 kg/s by hot air ($C_p = 1.0$ kJ/kgK) at 90 °C at rate of 2.5 kg/s. The highest rate of heat transfer in the heat exchanger is

(A) 82 kW (B) 195 kW (C) 391 kW (D) None of these

Q.44 A cylindrical pin fin of diameter 0.5 cm and length of 4 cm with negligible heat loss from the tip has an efficiency of 0.7. The effectiveness of this fin is

(A) 0.6 (B) 22.4 (C) 0.8 (D) 1.6

Q.45 Heat is generated in spherical shape ($d = 10$ cm) radioactive material whose thermal conductivity is 25 W/mK uniformly at a rate of 15 W/cm³. If the surface temperature of the material is measured to be 120 °C, the centre temperature of the material during steady operation is

(A) 160 °C (B) 205 °C (C) 280 °C (D) 370 °C

Q.46 Figure shows the wall consists of two layers A and B with the following values; K_A = 1.2 W/mK, L_A = 8 cm, K_B = 0.2 W/mK, L_B = 5 cm. If the temperature drops across the wall is 18 °C, the rate of heat transfer through the wall per unit area of the wall is

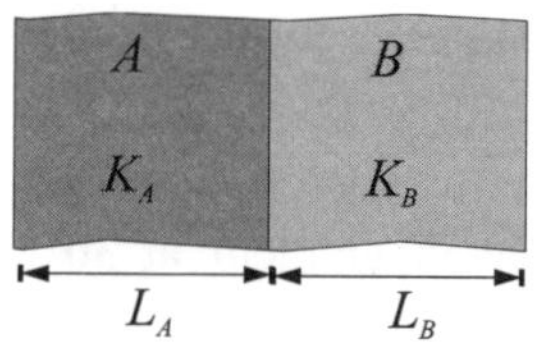

(A) 56.8 W/m² (B) 72.1 W/m²

(C) 114 W/m² (D) 201 W/m²

Q.47 Two concentric spheres are maintained at temperatures T_1 = 30°C and T_2 = 300°C and have emissivity's $\varepsilon_1 = 0.25$ and $\varepsilon_2 = 0.75$, respectively. If the ratio of the diameters is $\frac{D_1}{D_2} = 0.3$, the net rate of radiation heat transfer between the two spheres per unit surface area of the inner sphere is

(A) -1413 W/m^2 (B) -721 W/m^2

(C) 2107 W/m^2 (D) None of these

Q.48 Consider air flow at $T_\infty = 20$°C over a plate surface maintained at a constant temperature of $T_s = 160$°C, temperature profile within air layer over the plate is $T(y) = T_\infty + (T_s - T_\infty)e^{-3200y}$, where y is the vertical distance from the plate surface in metre. Thermal conductivity of air at 90°C is 0.03024 W/mK. Heat flux on the plate surface is

(A) 3.25×10^3 W/m^2 (B) 1.35×10^4 W/m^2

(C) 3207 W/m^2 (D) None of these

Q.49 A cubical furnace shown in figure, whose surfaces closely approximate black surfaces. The base, top and side surfaces of furnace are maintained at 800 K, 1500 K and 500 K, respectively. Given $F_{1-2} = 0.2$. The net rate of radiation heat transfer between the base and the top surface is

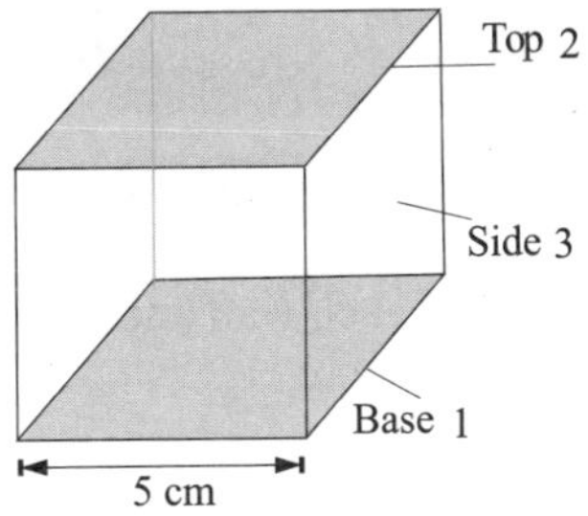

(A) -131.9 W (B) -236 W

(C) -1036.9 W (D) -504 W

Q.50 A counter flow shell and tube heat exchanger is used to heat water at a rate of $m = 0.8$ kg/s from T_i = 30°C to $T_o = 80$°C with hot oil entering at 120°C and leaving at 85°C. The overall heat transfer coefficient is $U = 125$ W/m^{2}K. The heat transfer area is

(A) 121.4m^2 (B) 48.6m^2 (C) 183.4m^2 (D) 28.4m^2

Q.51 to Q.65 Numerical Answer Questions

Q.51 Water at 20°C ($\rho = 998$ kg/m^3) and ($\mu = 1.002 \times 10^{-3}$ kg/ms) is flowing with a velocity of 0.5 m/s between two parallel flat plate placed 1 cm apart as shown in figure. The distance (in m) from entrance at which the velocity boundary layers meet is______.

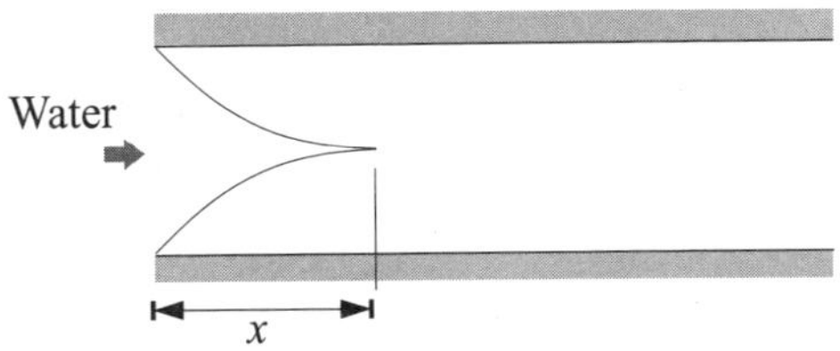

Q.52 A copper ball (C_p = 385 J/kgK, k = 401 W/mK, ρ = 8933 kg/m^3, $\alpha = 1.166 \times 10^{-4}$ m^2/s) initially at 200°C is allowed to cool in air at 30°C for a period of 2 minutes. If the ball has diameter of 2 cm and the heat transfer coefficient is 80 W/m^{2}K, the center temperature of the ball at the end of cooling is________.

Q.53 Water is boiled at 150°C in a boiler by hot exhaust gases (C_p = 1.05 kJ/kgK) that enter the boiler at 550°C at a rate of 0.5 kg/s and leaves at 200°C. The surface area of the heat exchanger is 0.64 m^2. The overall heat transfer coefficient U (in kW/m^{2}K) of heat exchanger is____.

Q.54 Two large parallel plates, as shown in figure with equal emissivities $\varepsilon = 0.4$ exchange heat by radiation. If a polished aluminum radiation shield $\varepsilon = 0.05$ is placed between them, then the percentage reduction in heat transfer is________%.

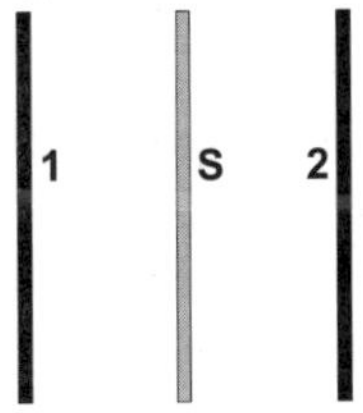

Q.55 Heat generation rate in a cylindrical heater of diameter 3 mm is 0.18 W/mm^3. The heat flux (in W/mm^2) at the surface of the heater is steady-state condition is ___.

Q.56 The view factor of black hemispherical cavity of radius R with respect to it self is______.

Q.57 Two large parallel grey plates with a small gap, exchange radiation at the rate of 1000 W/m^2 when their emissivities are 0.5 each. By coating one plate, its emissivity is reduced to 0.25. Temperatures remain unchanged. The new rate of heat exchange shall become___.

Q.58 A cubical furnace shown in figure, whose surfaces closely approximate black surfaces. The base, top and side surfaces of furnace are maintained at 800 K, 1500 K and 500 K, respectively. Given $F_{1-2} = 0.2$. The net rate of radiation heat transfer(in kW) between the base and the side surfaces is________.

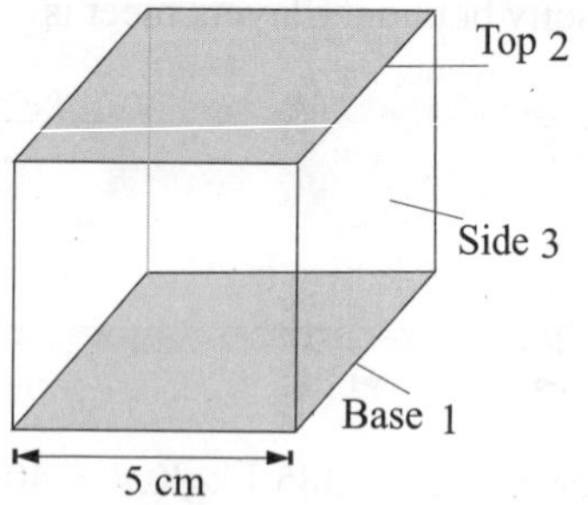

Q.59 Two very large parallel plates are maintained at uniform temperatures $T_1 = 800$ K and $T_2 = 500$ K and have emissivities $\varepsilon_1 = 0.2$ and $\varepsilon_2 = 0.7$, respectively. The net rate of radiation heat transfer (in kW/m^2) between two surfaces per unit surface area of the plates is________.

Q.60 Water at $20°C(\rho = 998\ kg/m^3, \mu = 1.002 \times 10^{-3}$ kg/ms and $c_p = 4182$ J/kgK) is flowing with a velocity of 0.5 m/s between two parallel flat plate placed 1 cm apart as shown in figure. The distance (in m) from entrance at which the thermal boundary layers meet is_______.

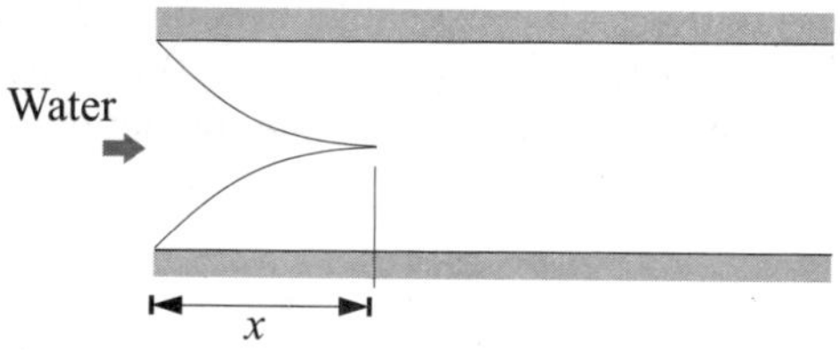

Q.61 Consider two infinitely long black body concentric cylinders with a diameter ratio $\frac{D_2}{D_1} = 3$. The shape factor for the outer cylinder with itself will be_______.

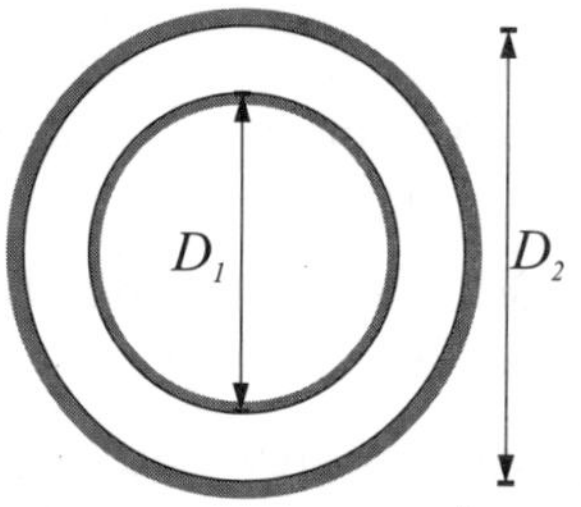

Q.62 An enclosure consists of four surfaces 1, 2, 3 and 4. The view factors for radiation heat transfer (where the subscripts 1, 2, 3, 4 refer to the respective surfaces) are $F_{11} = 0.1, F_{12} = 0.4$ and $F_{13} = 0.25$. The surface areas A_1 and A_4 are 4 m^2 and 2 m^2 respectively. The view factor F_{41} is__________.

Q.63 Figure shows the pyramid of base is square and its side surfaces are isosceles triangle. The view factor from base to side surface is________.

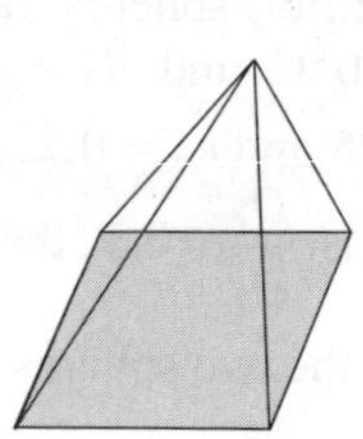

Q.64 Consider air flow at $T_\infty = 20°C$ over a plate surface maintained at a constant temperature of $T_s = 160°C$, temperature profile within air layer over the plate is $T(y) = T_\infty + (T_s - T_\infty)e^{-3200y}$, where y is the vertical distance from the plate surface in metre. Thermal conductivity of air at 90°C is 0.03024 W/mK. The convective heat transfer coefficient of the air flow is ___.

Q.65 Cold water ($C_p = 4.18$ kJ/kgK) enters a counter flow heat exchanger at 10°C at a rate of 0.31 kg/s, where it is heated by hot exhaust air ($C_p = 1.0$ kJ/kgK) that enters the heat exchanger at 50°C at a rate of 1.4 kg/s and leaves at 25°C. The effectiveness of this heat exchanger is_____.

11.4 SOLUTION TO PRACTICE PAPER

Q.1 Ans:(B)

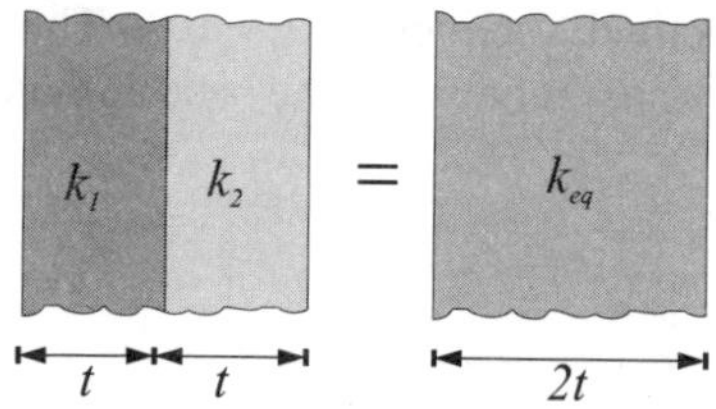

Let t be the thickness of each wall and A be the area

Heat transfer rate, $$Q = \frac{T_1 - T_2}{R_1 + R_2} = \frac{T_1 - T_2}{R}$$

or $$Q = \frac{T_1 - T_2}{\frac{t}{k_1 A} + \frac{t}{k_2 A}} = \frac{T_1 - T_2}{\frac{2t}{k_{eq} A}}$$

we obtain

$$k_{eq} = \frac{2k_1 k_2}{k_1 + k_2}$$

Q.2 Ans:(A)

Lumped system analysis of transient heat conduction is valid for $B_i < 0.1$ (very small)

Q.3 Ans:(A)

Let q_g be the heat generation rate.

Heat generation $= q_g \pi r^2 l$ and Heat transfer rate $= q_0 2\pi r l$

Heat generation = Heat transfer rate

$$q_g \pi r^2 l = q_0 2\pi r l$$

$$q_g = \frac{2q_0}{r}$$

Q.4(A)

Wein's displacement law $\lambda_m T = b = 2.9\times10^{-3}\,\text{mK}$

$$\lambda_m \times 300 = 2.9\times10^{-3}$$

or $$\lambda_m = \frac{2.9\times10^{-3}}{300} = 9.6\times10^{-6}\ \text{m}$$

$$\lambda_m = 9.6\,\mu\text{m}$$

Q.5(C)

Effectiveness of parallel flow heat exchanger,

$$\varepsilon_{\text{par}} = \frac{1-e^{-\text{NTU}(1+C)}}{1+C}$$

Effectiveness of counter flow heat exchanger,

$$\varepsilon_{\text{count}} = \frac{1-e^{-\text{NTU}(1+C)}}{1-Ce^{-\text{NTU}(1+C)}}$$

For boiler and condenser, $C = 0$,

$$\varepsilon_{\text{par}} = \varepsilon_{\text{count}} = 1-e^{-\text{NTU}}$$

$\varepsilon = 1-e^{-\text{NTU}}$ is valid for boiler and condenser for parallel and counter flow heat exchanger.

Q.6(A)

Correct match:

(a) Fins → (3) $\sqrt{\dfrac{hP}{kA}}$

(b) Heat exchanger → (1) $\dfrac{UA}{C_{\min}}$

(c) Transient conduction → (2) $\dfrac{x}{2\sqrt{\alpha\tau}}$

(d) Heisler chart → (4) $\dfrac{hl}{k}$

Q.7 Ans:(D)

Correct match:

(a) $\dfrac{d^2T}{dr^2} + \dfrac{2}{r}\dfrac{dT}{dr} = 0$ → (3) 1-D conduction in sphere

(b) $\dfrac{\partial^2 T}{\partial x^2} = \dfrac{1}{\alpha}\dfrac{\partial T}{\partial t}$ → (4) Plane slab

(c) $\dfrac{d^2T}{dr^2} + \dfrac{1}{r}\dfrac{dT}{dr} = 0$ → (2) 1-D conduction in cylinder

(d) $\dfrac{d^2\theta}{dx^2} - m^2\theta = 0$ → (1) Pin-fin 1-D case

Q.8 Ans:(C)

NTU is given by $\dfrac{AU}{C_{\min}}$

Substituting $A = 50\,\text{m}^2, U = 100\ \text{W/m}^2\text{K}$ and $C = 1000\ \text{W/K}$, we have

$$\text{NTU} = \frac{50\times100}{1000}$$

$$\text{NTU} = 5$$

Q.9 Ans:(A)

Characteristic length of ball, $L_c = \dfrac{V}{A} = \dfrac{\frac{4}{3}\pi R^3}{4\pi R^3} = \dfrac{R}{3} = \dfrac{6}{3}$

$$L_c = 2\ \text{cm}$$

Q.10 Ans:(D)

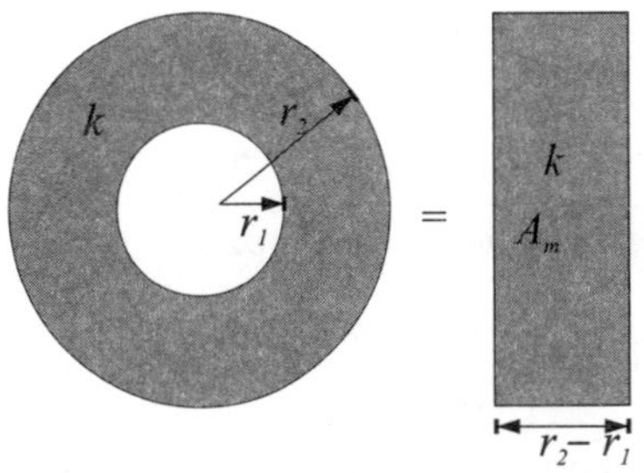

Heat transfer through cylinder

$$Q = \frac{T_1 - T_2}{\dfrac{\log\frac{r_2}{r_2}}{2\pi kL}} \qquad \text{(i)}$$

Heat transfer through plane wall,

$$Q = \frac{T_1 - T_2}{\dfrac{L}{kA}} = \frac{T_1 - T_2}{\dfrac{r_2 - r_1}{kA_m}} \qquad \text{(ii)}$$

From Equations (i) and (ii), we have

$$\frac{T_1 - T_2}{\dfrac{r_2 - r_1}{kA_m}} = \frac{T_1 - T_2}{\dfrac{\log\frac{r_2}{r_1}}{2\pi kL}}$$

or $$A_m = \frac{2\pi L(r_2 - r_1)}{\log\dfrac{r_2}{r_1}} = \frac{2\pi L r_2 - 2\pi L r_1}{\log\dfrac{2\pi r_2 L}{2\pi r_1 L}}$$

$$A_m = \frac{A_2 - A_1}{\log_e\left(\frac{A_2}{A_1}\right)}$$

Q.11(A)

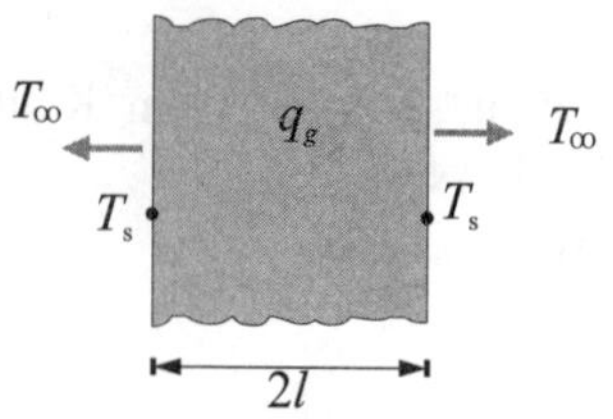

Under steady-state condition,

Heat generated = Heat convected from both surfaces

$$q_g A 2l = 2hA(T_s - T_\infty)$$

$$T_s = T_\infty + \frac{q_g l}{h}$$

Q.12 Ans:(B)

General heat conduction equation in cylindrical coordinates,

$$\frac{1}{r}\frac{\partial}{\partial r}\left(kr\frac{\partial T}{\partial r}\right) + \frac{1}{r^2}\frac{\partial}{\partial \phi}\left(k\frac{\partial T}{\partial \phi}\right) + \frac{\partial}{\partial z}\left(k\frac{\partial T}{\partial z}\right) + q_g = \rho c\frac{\partial T}{\partial t}$$

One-dimensional $\left(\frac{\partial T}{\partial \phi} = 0, \frac{\partial T}{\partial z} = 0\right)$, steady-state $\left(\frac{\partial T}{\partial t} = 0\right)$, and constant thermal conductivity (k = constant) with heat generation ($q_g \neq 0$) conduction equation is

$$\frac{1}{r}\frac{\partial}{\partial r}\left(r\frac{\partial T}{\partial r}\right) + \frac{q_g}{k} = 0$$

Q.13 Ans:(A)

Biot number, $B_i = \frac{hl}{k} = \frac{\frac{l}{kA}}{\frac{1}{hA}} = \frac{R_{\text{cond}}}{R_{\text{conv}}}$

$$B_i = \frac{\text{Conduction thermal resistance}}{\text{Convection thermal resistance}}$$

Q.14 Ans:(B)

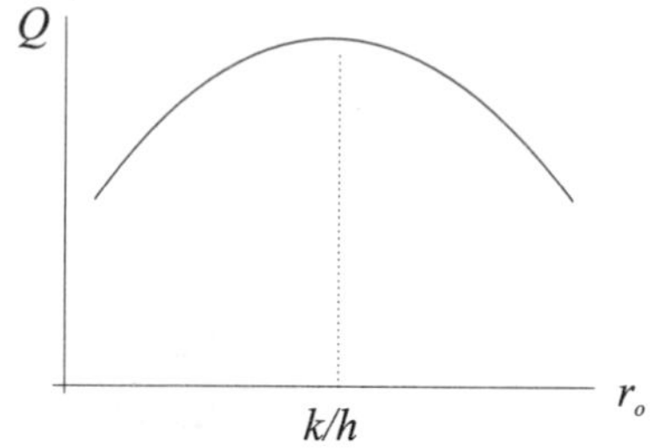

Figure shows the graph between Q and r_o.

Heat transfer rate Q decreases with increases $r_o > \frac{k}{h}$

Q.15 Ans:(C)

Biot number and Fourier number

Q.16 Ans:(B)

$$\frac{\partial^2 T}{\partial x^2} + \frac{\partial^2 T}{\partial y^2} + \frac{\partial^2 T}{\partial z^2} = \frac{1}{\alpha}\frac{\partial T}{\partial t}$$

$$\nabla^2 T = \frac{1}{\alpha}\frac{\partial T}{\partial t} \leftarrow \text{Diffusion equation}$$

Q.17 Ans:(B)

Wein's displacement law $\lambda_m T = b = \text{constant}$

$$0.5 \times 5800 = \lambda \times (273 + 300)$$

or $$\lambda = \frac{0.5 \times 5800}{(273 + 300)}$$

$$\lambda = 5\,\mu\text{m}$$

Q.18 Ans:(D)

Effectiveness of long fin is given by $\varepsilon = \sqrt{\frac{hP}{kA}}$

Fin is effective when k is large and h is small.

Q.19 Ans:(A)

Thermal boundary and velocity boundary thickness are same at Prandtl number, $Pr = 1$.

Q.20 Ans:(B)

Let C_h and C_c be the heat capacity of hot and cold fluid, respectively.

Heat transfer $Q = C_h(T_{hi} - T_{ho}) = C_c(T_{co} - T_{ci})$

or $$C_h(150 - 75) = C_c(125 - 25)$$

Capacity ratio, $C = \frac{C_{\min}}{C_{\max}} = \frac{C_c}{C_h} = \frac{(150-75)}{(125-25)} = \frac{75}{100}$

Capacity ratio, $C = 0.75$

Q.21 Ans:[5250]

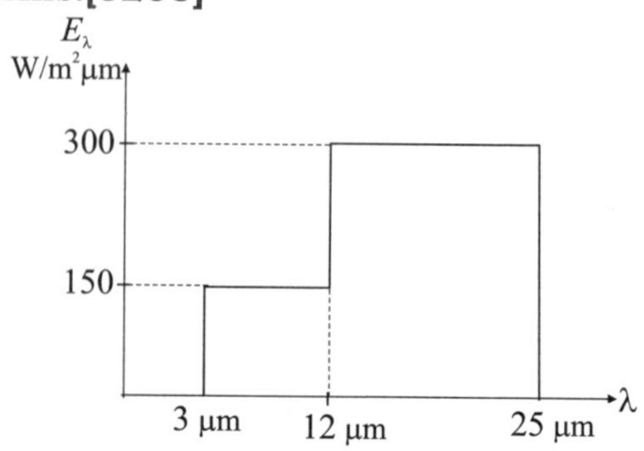

Emissive Power $= \int_0^\infty E_\lambda d\lambda$

$$E = 0\times(3-0)+150\times(12-3)+300\times(25-12)+0\times(\infty-25)$$

$$E = 5250\ \text{W/m}^2$$

Q.22 Ans:[1064]

Total area, $A = 2\times\frac{\pi}{4}d^2 + \pi dl$

$$A = \frac{\pi}{2}4^2 + \pi\times4\times6 = 100.53\ \text{cm}^2$$

Radiation heat transfer, $Q = \sigma A\varepsilon T^4$

$$Q = 5.67\times10^{-8}\times100.53\times10^{-4}\times0.75\times1200^4$$

$$Q = 886.47\ \text{W}$$

Radiation emitted in 20 min

$$Q_{\text{total}} = 886.47\times20\times60\ \text{J}$$

$$Q_{\text{total}} = 1064\ \text{J}$$

Q.23 Ans:[0.6]

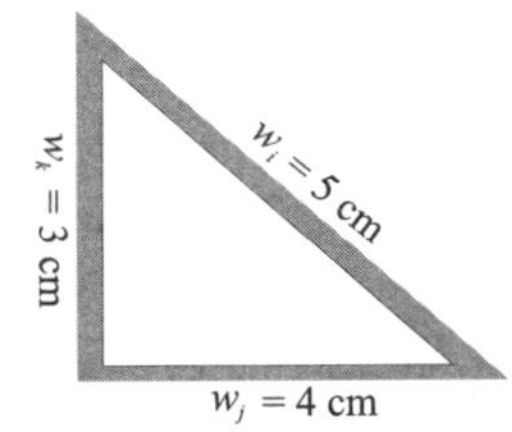

View factor, $F_{i-j} = \frac{w_i + w_j - w_k}{2w_i}$

or $F_{5-4} = \frac{5+4-3}{2\times5} = \frac{6}{10}$

$$F_{5-4} = 0.6$$

Q.24 Ans:[100]

Heat transfer rate, $Q = \frac{6}{10}\text{kJ/min} = 10\ \text{J/s}$

$$Q = \frac{kA(T_1-T_2)}{L} \Rightarrow 10 = \frac{100\times10\times10^{-4}\times(T_1-T_2)}{1}$$

Temperature difference $(T_1 - T_2) = 100°\text{C}$

Q.25 Ans:[7.5]

Nussult number, $Nu = \frac{hd}{k}$

or $\frac{h\times\frac{100}{1000}}{0.03} = 25$

$$h = 7.5\ \text{W/m}^2\text{K}$$

Q.26 Ans:[29473]

Reynolds Number, $Re = \frac{\rho Vd}{\mu} = \frac{\rho\left(\frac{Q}{\pi d^2/4}\right)d}{\mu}$

$$Re = \frac{4\rho Q}{\pi d\mu} = \frac{4\times1000\times(3/60\times60)}{\pi(4/100)\times9\times10^{-4}}$$

$$Re = 29473$$

Q.27 Ans:[0.451]

Effectiveness of condenser, $\varepsilon = 1 - e^{-\text{NTU}}$

or $\varepsilon = 1 - e^{-0.6}$

$$\varepsilon = 0.451$$

Q.28 Ans:[4]

For same heat loss $(R_{th})_1 = (R_{th})_2$

$$\frac{L_1}{k_1A_1} = \frac{L_2}{k_2A_2}$$

or $\frac{0.2}{0.8A} = \frac{L_2}{0.16A} \Rightarrow L_2 = 0.04$

Thickness = 4 cm

Q.29 Ans:[0.52]

Thermal resistance, $R_{th} = \frac{L}{kA}$

or $0.04 = \frac{025}{k(3\times4)}$

Thermal conductivity, $k = 0.52\ \text{W/m}^2\text{K}$

Q.30 Ans:[94.5]

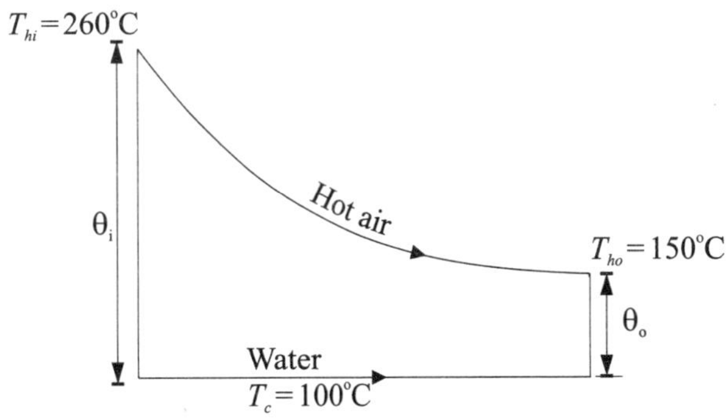

Inlet temperature difference, $\theta_i = 260 - 100 = 160°\text{C}$

Outlet temperature difference, $\theta_o = 150 - 100 = 50°\text{C}$

$$\text{LMTD} = \frac{\theta_i - \theta_o}{\ln\frac{\theta_i}{\theta_o}} = \frac{160-50}{\ln\frac{160}{50}} = \frac{110}{\ln 3.2}$$

$$\text{LMTD} = 94.5°\text{C}$$

Q.31 Ans:(C)

Heat gain by cold fluid = Heat loss by hot fluid

$$m_c c_{pc}(T_{co} - T_{ci}) = m_h c_{ph}(T_{hi} - T_{ho})$$

or $$1250 \times 16(75 - T_{ci}) = 1000 \times 20(150 - 125)$$

$$T_{ci} = 50°\text{C}$$

$$\theta_i = T_{hi} - T_{co} = 150 - 75 = 75$$

$$\theta_o = T_{ho} - T_{ci} = 125 - 50 = 75$$

$$\text{LMTD}_{\theta_i - \theta_o} = \frac{\theta_i - \theta_o}{\ln\frac{\theta_i}{\theta_o}} = \theta_i = 75$$

$$\text{LMTD} = 75$$

Q.32 Ans:(C)

Thermal conductivity k of the wall at temperature T is given by the relation

$$k = \frac{T}{10} - 5 \leftarrow \left[\frac{25-15}{300-200} = \frac{25-k}{300-T}\right]$$

Fourier conduction equation,

$$q = -k\frac{dT}{dx}$$

or $$q\int_0^L dx = -\int_{T_1}^{T_2} kdT$$

$$q\int_0^L dx = -\int_{T_1}^{T_2}\left(\frac{T}{10} - 5\right)dT$$

or $$q = \frac{T_1 - T_2}{L}\left[\frac{T_1 + T_2}{20} - 5\right]$$

or $$q = \frac{300-200}{2 \times 0.5} \times \left[\frac{300+200}{20} - 5\right]$$

$$q = 4\,\text{kW/m}^2$$

Q.33 Ans:(B)

Average heat transfer, $\bar{h} = \frac{1}{x}\int_0^x h_x dx$

Ratio of $\bar{h}$ and h_x is

$$\frac{\bar{h}}{h_x} = \frac{\frac{1}{x}\int_0^x h_x dx}{h_x} = \frac{\frac{1}{x}\int_0^x x^{-\frac{1}{2}}dx}{x^{-\frac{1}{2}}} = \frac{2}{x} \times \frac{x^{\frac{1}{2}}}{x^{-\frac{1}{2}}}$$

$$\frac{\bar{h}}{h_x} = 2$$

Q.34 Ans:(B)

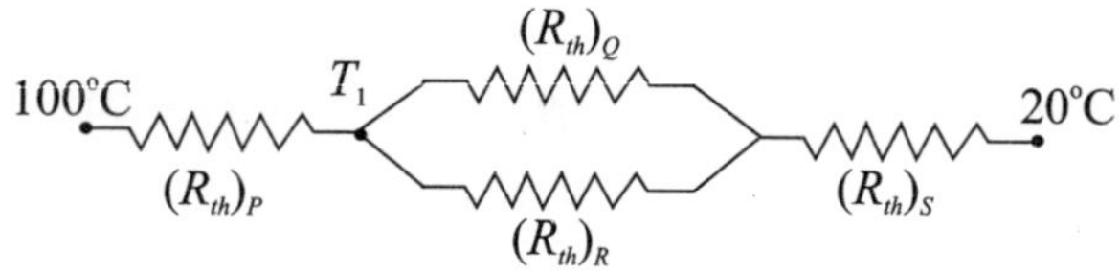

$$(R_{th})_P = \frac{L}{3k \times 2A} = \frac{L}{6kA} = \frac{1}{6 \times 100 \times 0.5} = \frac{1}{300}$$

$$(R_{th})_Q = \frac{L}{2k \times A} = \frac{L}{2kA} = \frac{1}{2 \times 100 \times 0.5} = \frac{1}{100}$$

$$(R_{th})_R = \frac{L}{4k \times A} = \frac{L}{4kA} = \frac{1}{4 \times 100 \times 0.5} = \frac{1}{200}$$

$$(R_{th})_S = \frac{L}{3k \times 2A} = \frac{L}{6kA} = \frac{1}{6 \times 100 \times 0.5} = \frac{1}{300}$$

Total thermal resistance

$$\sum R_{th} = (R_{th})_P + (R_{th})_S + \frac{(R_{th})_R \times (R_{th})_Q}{(R_{th})_R + (R_{th})_Q}$$

$$\sum R_{th} = \frac{1}{300} + \frac{1}{300} + \frac{\frac{1}{100} \times \frac{1}{200}}{\frac{1}{100} + \frac{1}{200}}$$

or $$\sum R_{th} = \frac{1}{100}$$

Rate of heat transfer, $Q = \frac{100-20}{\frac{1}{100}} = 8000$

$$Q = 8\,\text{kW}$$

Q.35 Ans:(B)

One-dimensional without heat generation heat equation is

$$\frac{d^2T}{dx^2} = \frac{1}{\alpha}\frac{dT}{dt}$$

Rate of change of temperature at the other face,

$$\frac{dT}{dt} = \alpha\frac{d^2T}{dx^2}$$

$$\frac{dT}{dt} = 2 \times 10^{-3}\left[\frac{d^2}{dx^2}(4 - 10x + 20x^2 + 10x^3)\right]_{x=1}$$

$$\frac{dT}{dt} = 0.2\ °\text{C/h}$$

Q.36 Ans:(D)

Radiative heat transfer per unit area between grey surfaces,

$$q = \frac{Q_{1-2}}{A} = \frac{\sigma(T_1^4 - T_2^4)}{\left(\frac{1}{\varepsilon_1} + \frac{1}{\varepsilon_2} - 1\right)}$$

$$\varepsilon_1 = \varepsilon_2;\ q = \frac{\varepsilon}{2-\varepsilon}\sigma(T_1^4 - T_2^4)$$

or $$q = \frac{0.9}{2-0.9} \times 5.6 \times 10^{-8}(400^4 - 300^4)$$

$$q = 464\ \text{W/m}^2$$

Q.37 Ans:(D)

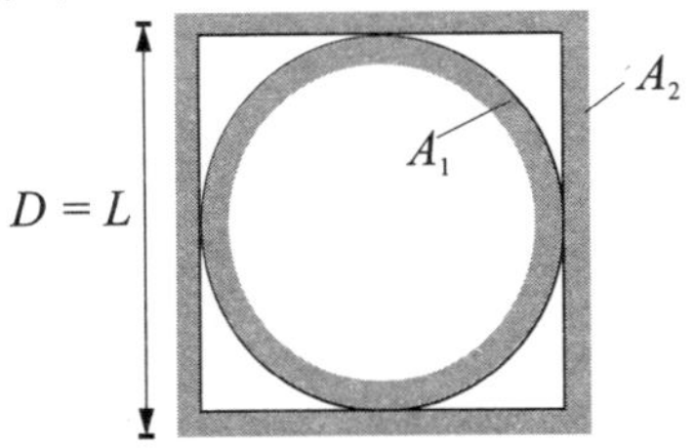

Applying the summation rule to surface 1, yields

$$F_{1-1} + F_{1-2} = 1$$

Substituting $F_{1-1} = 0$, we have

$$F_{1-2} = 1$$

Applying the reciprocity relation to surfaces 1 and 2,

$$A_1F_{1-2} = A_2F_{2-1}$$

or $$F_{2-1} = \frac{A_1}{A_2}F_{1-2} = \frac{A_1}{A_2} = \frac{4\pi\left(\frac{D}{2}\right)^2}{6D^2}$$

$$F_{2-1} = \frac{\pi}{6}$$

Q.38 Ans:(A)

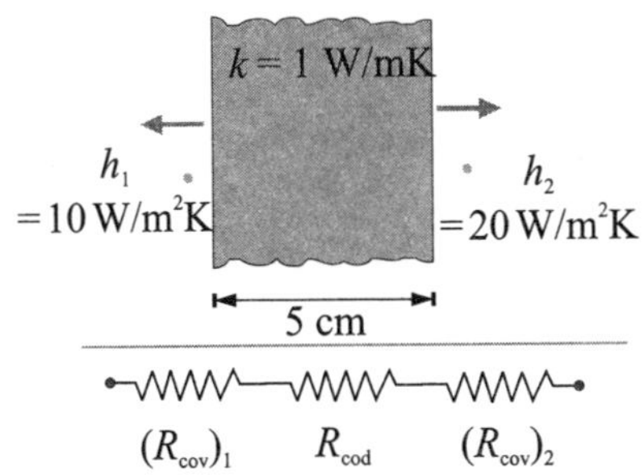

Equivalent electric circuit

$$(R_{cov})_1 = \frac{1}{h_1A} = \frac{1}{10A},\ R_{con} = \frac{L}{kA} = \frac{0.05}{A},$$

$$(R_{cov})_2 = \frac{1}{h_2A} = \frac{1}{20A}$$

$$\frac{1}{UA} = \sum R = \frac{1}{10A} + \frac{0.05}{A} + \frac{1}{20A} = \frac{1}{5A}$$

$$U = 5\ \text{W/m}^2\text{K}$$

Q.39 Ans:(A)

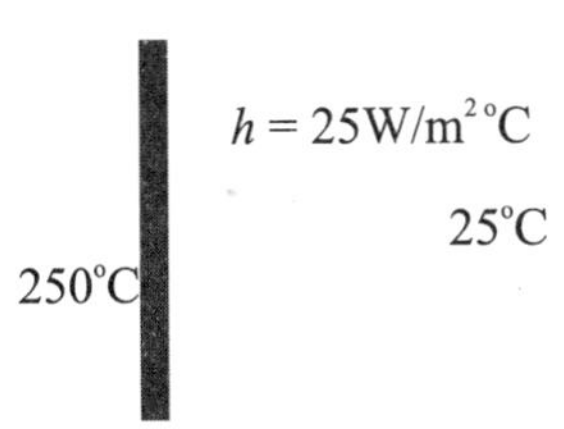

Without insulation

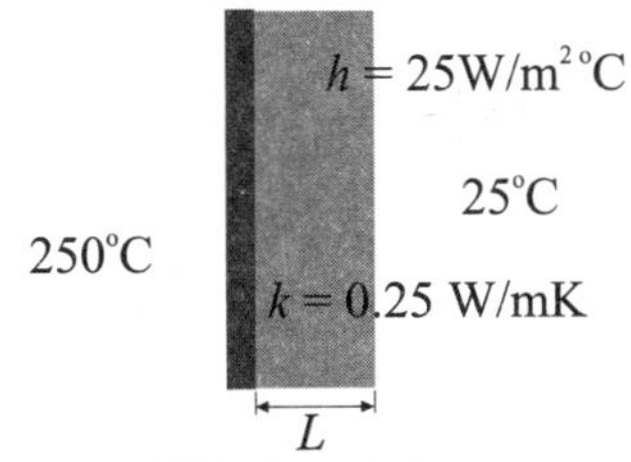

With insulation

Without insulation heat flux,

$$q_1 = \frac{Q_1}{A} = h(T_s - T_\infty) \qquad \text{(i)}$$

With insulation heat flux,

$$q_2 = \frac{Q_2}{A} = \frac{T_s - T_\infty}{\frac{1}{h} + \frac{L}{k}} \qquad \text{(ii)}$$

From Equations (i) and (ii), we have

$$q_2 = \frac{q_1}{2} \Rightarrow \frac{T_s - T_\infty}{\frac{1}{h} + \frac{L}{k}} = \frac{1}{2}h(T_s - T_\infty)$$

or $$L = \frac{k}{h} = \frac{0.25}{25}\ \text{m}$$

$$L = 1\ \text{cm}$$

Q.40 Ans:(A)

Temperature difference, $\theta = \theta_0 e^{-mx}$ for very long rod.

or $$T - T_\infty = (T_0 - T_\infty)e^{-\sqrt{\frac{hp}{kA}}x}$$

or $$T = T_\infty + (T_0 - T_\infty)e^{-\sqrt{\frac{h\times 4}{kd}}x}$$

or $$T = 25 + (125 - 25)e^{-\sqrt{\frac{9\times 4}{380\times 0.025}}x}$$

$$T = 25 + 100e^{-1.946x}$$

Q.41 Ans:(D)

Effectiveness, $\varepsilon = \dfrac{1 - e^{-\text{NTU}(1+C)}}{1+C}$

Substituting NTU = 3, we have $\varepsilon = \dfrac{1 - e^{-3(1+C)}}{1+C}$

Minimum value of ε is at $C = 1$; $\varepsilon_{min} = \dfrac{1 - e^{-6}}{2}$

$$\varepsilon_{min} = 50\%$$

Q.42 Ans:(B)

Heat transfer from fin, $Q = \left[-kA \dfrac{d\theta}{dx} \right]_{x=0}$

For long fin, substituting $\theta = \theta_0 e^{-mx}$

$$Q = \left[-kA \frac{d}{dx} (\theta_0 e^{-mx}) \right]_{x=0}$$

$$Q = mkA\theta_0 = \sqrt{\frac{hP}{kA}} kA\theta_0 = \sqrt{hPkA}\,\theta_0$$

$$Q = \left(\sqrt{18 \times \pi \times \left(\frac{1}{100}\right) \times 237 \times \frac{\pi}{4} \times \left(\frac{1}{100}\right)^2} \right) (80-22)$$

$$Q = 5.95\text{ W}$$

Q.43 Ans:(B)

Heat capacity of cold fluid,

$$C_c = m_c c_{pc} = 1.2 \times 4.18 = 5.016 \quad \leftarrow C_{max}$$

Heat capacity of hot fluid,

$$C_h = m_h c_{ph} = 2.5 \times 1.00 = 2.50 \quad \leftarrow C_{min}$$

Highest rate of heat transfer, $Q_{max} = C_{min}(T_{hi} - T_{ci})$

$$Q_{max} = 2.5 \times (90 - 12)$$

$$Q_{max} = 195\text{ kW}$$

Q.44 Ans:(B)

Fin efficiency and fin effectiveness are related to each other by

$$\varepsilon = \frac{A_{fin}}{A_b}\eta = \frac{\pi dL}{\frac{\pi}{5}d^2}\eta = \frac{4L}{d}\eta$$

or $$\varepsilon = \frac{4 \times \frac{4}{100}}{\frac{0.5}{100}} \times 0.7$$

$$\varepsilon = 22.4$$

Q.45 Ans:(D)

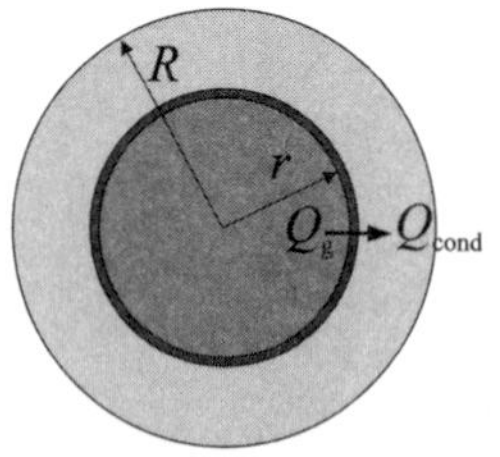

Consider a sphere of radius r.

Heat transfer from surface of sphere r = Heat generated in sphere.

$$Q_{cond} = Q_g$$

$$-k4\pi r^2 \frac{dT}{dr} = q_g \frac{4}{3}\pi r^3$$

or $$\int_{T_{max}}^{T_s} dT = -\frac{q_g}{3k}\int_0^R r\,dr$$

or $$T_s - T_{max} = -\frac{q_g}{6k}R^2$$

or $$T_{max} = T_s + \frac{q_g}{6k}R^2$$

or $$T_{max} = 120 + \frac{15 \times 10^6}{6 \times 25}\left(\frac{5}{100}\right)^2$$

$$T_{max} = 370°\text{C}$$

Q.46 Ans:(A)

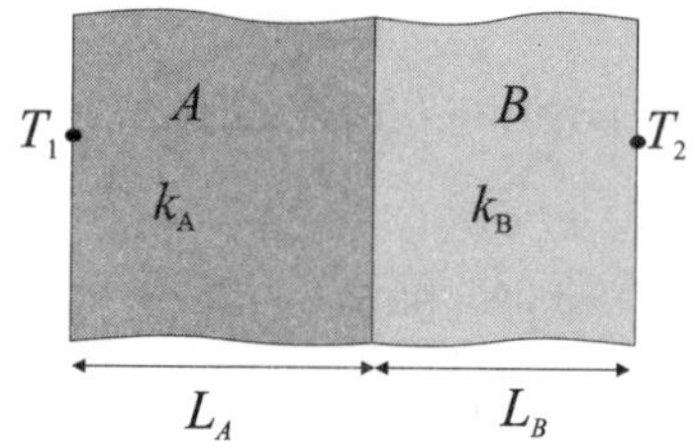

Heat transfer rate, $Q = \dfrac{T_1 - T_2}{\dfrac{L_A}{k_A A} + \dfrac{L_B}{k_B A}}$

$$q = \frac{Q}{A} = \frac{T_1 - T_2}{\frac{L_A}{k_A} + \frac{L_B}{k_B}} = \frac{18}{\frac{0.08}{1.2} + \frac{0.05}{0.2}}$$

$$q = 56.8\text{ W/m}^2$$

Q.47 Ans:(A)

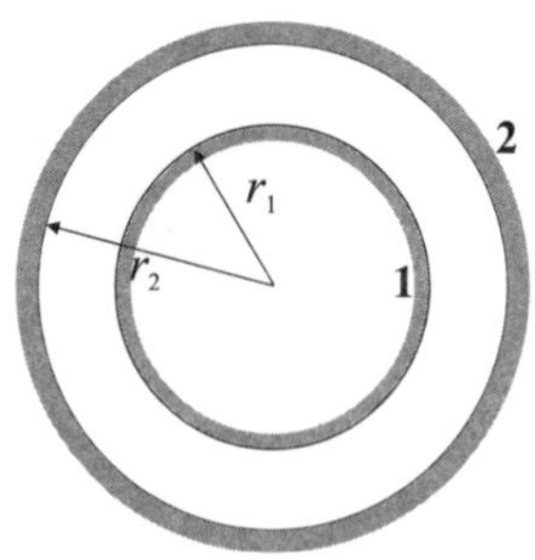

$$Q_{1-2} = \frac{A_1\sigma(T_1^4 - T_2^4)}{\frac{1}{\varepsilon_1} + \left(\frac{1}{\varepsilon_2} - 1\right)\left(\frac{r_1}{r_2}\right)^2}$$

$$q_{1-2}=\frac{Q_{1-2}}{A_1}=\frac{\sigma(T_1^4-T_2^4)}{\frac{1}{\varepsilon_1}+\left(\frac{1}{\varepsilon_2}-1\right)\left(\frac{r_1}{r_2}\right)^2}$$

$$q_{1-2}=\frac{5.67\times10^{-8}(293^4-573^4)}{\frac{1}{0.25}+\left(\frac{1}{0.75}-1\right)\times0.3^2}$$

$$q_{1-2}=-1413\text{ W/m}^2$$

Q.48 Ans:(B)

Heat flux, $q=-k_{\text{air}}\left(\frac{dT}{dy}\right)_{y=0}$

or $\quad q=-k_{\text{air}}\left(\frac{d}{dy}T_\infty+(T_s-T_\infty)e^{-3200y}\right)_{y=0}$

or $\quad q=k_{\text{air}}\times3200(T_s-T_\infty)$

or $\quad q=0.03024\times3200(160-20)$

$$q=1.35\times10^4\text{ W/m}^2$$

Q.49 Ans:(A)

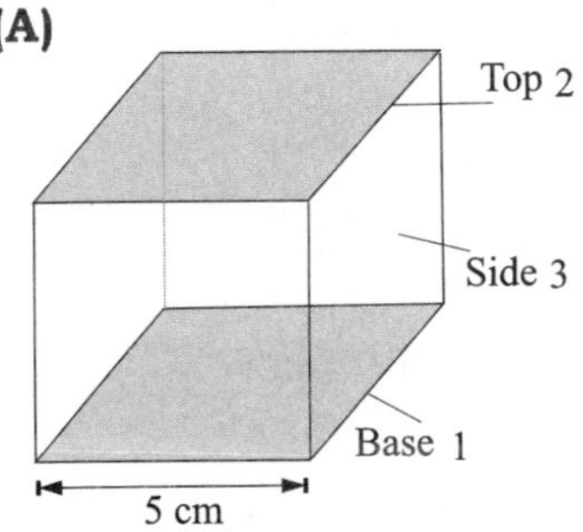

Heat transfer from base to top,

$$Q_{1-2}=A_1F_{1-2}\sigma(T_1^4-T_2^4)$$

$$Q_{1-2}=\frac{5\times5}{100\times100}\times0.2\times5.67\times10^{-8}(800^4-1500^4)$$

$$Q_{1-2}=-131.9\text{ W}$$

Q.50 Ans:(D)

Heat transfer, $\quad Q=m_cc_{pc}(T_{co}-T_{ci})=UA(\text{LMTD})$

Area, $\quad A=\frac{m_cc_{pc}(T_{co}-T_{ci})}{U(\text{LMTD})}=\frac{m_cc_{pc}(T_{co}-T_{ci})}{U\frac{\theta_i-\theta_o}{\ln\frac{\theta_i}{\theta_o}}}$

or $\quad A=\frac{0.8\times4.18\times10^3\times(80-30)}{125\times\frac{(120-80)-(85-30)}{\ln\frac{(120-80)}{(85-30)}}}$

$$A=28.4\text{ m}^2$$

Q.51 Ans:[0.516]

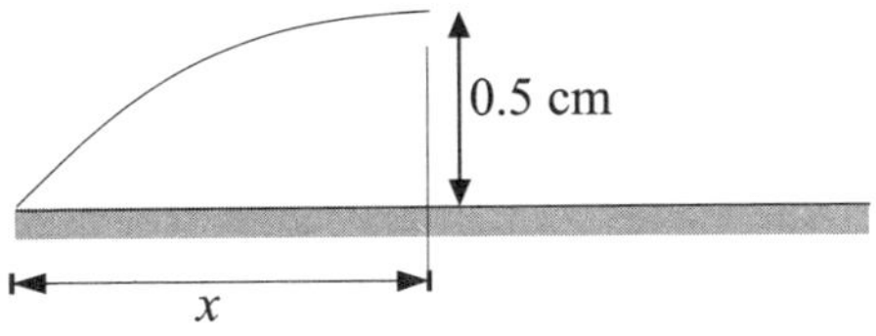

Let x be the distance from entrance where both velocity boundary layers thickness meet.

Velocity boundary layer thickness is given by

$$\delta=\frac{4.91x}{\sqrt{Re}}=\frac{4.91x}{\sqrt{\frac{\rho Vx}{\mu}}}$$

Substituting the value of velocity boundary thickness $\delta=\frac{0.5}{100}$ m, $\rho=998$ kg/m^3, $\mu=1.002\times10^{-3}$ kg/ms and $V=0.5$ m/s, we have

or $\quad \frac{0.5}{100}=\frac{4.91x}{\sqrt{\frac{998\times0.5x}{1.002\times10^{-3}}}}$

or $\quad \sqrt{x}=\frac{0.5}{100}\times\frac{1}{4.91}\sqrt{\frac{998\times0.5}{1.002\times10^{-3}}}$

$$x=0.516\text{ m}$$

Q.52 Ans:[103.58]

First, calculate the Biot number,

$$Bi=\frac{hl_c}{k}=\frac{h\times\left(\frac{V}{A}\right)}{k}=\frac{h\times\frac{\frac{4}{3}\pi R^3}{4\pi R^2}}{k}=\frac{h}{k}\times\frac{R}{3}$$

or $\quad Bi=\frac{80}{401}\times\frac{1/100}{3}=0.00066$

Since $Bi<0.1$, lumped system analysis is applicable. Temperature-time equation is given by

$$\frac{T-T_\infty}{T_i-T_\infty}=e^{-\frac{hA}{\rho Vc_p}t}$$

or $\quad \frac{T-T_\infty}{T_i-T_\infty}=e^{-\frac{h\times3}{\rho rc_p}t}$

or $\quad \frac{T-30}{200-30}=e^{-\frac{80\times3\times2\times60}{8933\times\frac{1}{100}\times385}}$

$$T=103.58^\circ\text{C}$$

Q.53 Ans:[1.705]

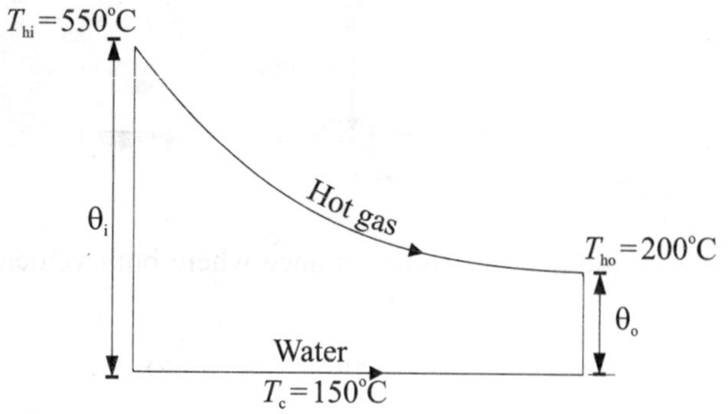

Heat transfer, $Q = UA(\text{LMTD})$

or $Q = m_h c_{ph}(T_{hi} - T_{ho}) = UA(\text{LMTD})$

Overall heat transfer coefficient

$$U = \frac{m_h c_{ph}(T_{hi} - T_{ho})}{A(\text{LMTD})} = \frac{m_h c_{ph}(T_{hi} - T_{ho})}{A \times \dfrac{(T_{hi} - T_c) - (T_{ho} - T_c)}{\ln\left(\dfrac{T_{hi} - T_c}{T_{ho} - T_c}\right)}}$$

Overall heat transfer coefficient,

$$U = \frac{0.5 \times 1.05 \times 10^3 (550 - 200)}{0.64 \times \dfrac{(550 - 150) - (200 - 150)}{\ln\left(\dfrac{550 - 150}{200 - 150}\right)}}$$

$$U = 1.705\ \text{kW/m}^2\,°\text{C}$$

Q.54 Ans:[90.6]

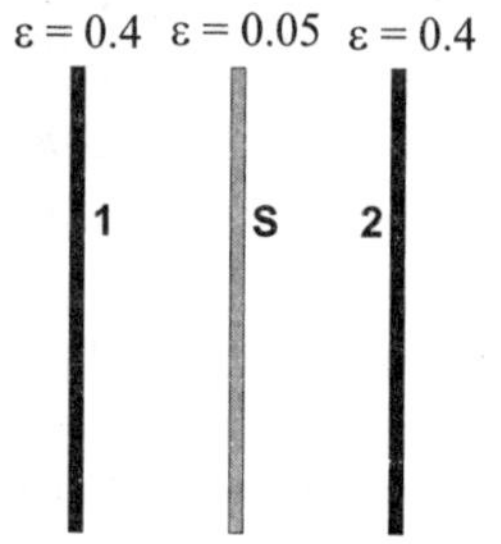

Let T_1 and T_2 be the temperature of plates.

Heat transfer without shield,

$$Q_1 = \frac{\sigma A(T_1^4 - T_1^4)}{\dfrac{1}{\varepsilon_1} + \dfrac{1}{\varepsilon_2} - 1} = \frac{\sigma A(T_1^4 - T_1^4)}{\dfrac{1}{0.4} + \dfrac{1}{0.4} - 1}$$

$$Q_1 = \frac{\sigma A(T_1^4 - T_1^4)}{4}$$

Heat transfer with shield,

$$Q_2 = \frac{\sigma A(T_1^4 - T_1^4)}{\dfrac{1-\varepsilon_1}{\varepsilon_1} + \dfrac{1}{F_{1-s}} + \dfrac{1-\varepsilon_s}{\varepsilon_s} + \dfrac{1-\varepsilon_s}{\varepsilon_s} + \dfrac{1}{F_{s-2}} + \dfrac{1-\varepsilon_2}{\varepsilon_2}}$$

$$Q_2 = \frac{\sigma A(T_1^4 - T_1^4)}{\dfrac{1-0.4}{0.4} + \dfrac{1}{1} + \dfrac{1-0.05}{0.05} + \dfrac{1-0.05}{0.05} + \dfrac{1}{1} + \dfrac{1-0.4}{0.4}}$$

$$Q_2 = \frac{\sigma A(T_1^4 - T_1^4)}{43}$$

Percentage reduction in heat transfer,

$$\frac{Q_1 - Q_2}{Q_1} \times 100 = \frac{\dfrac{1}{4} - \dfrac{1}{43}}{\dfrac{1}{4}} \times 100$$

Percentage reduction in heat transfer = 90.6

Q.55 Ans:[0.135]

Let q_g be the heat generation rate.

Heat generation = $q_g \pi r^2 l$, and Heat transfer rate = $q_o 2\pi r l$.

Heat generation = Heat transfer rate

$$q_g \pi r^2 l = q_o 2\pi r l$$

or $$q_o = \frac{q_g r}{2} = \frac{q_g d}{4} = \frac{0.18 \times 3}{4}$$

$$q_o = 0.135\ \text{W/m}^2$$

Q.56 Ans:[0.5]

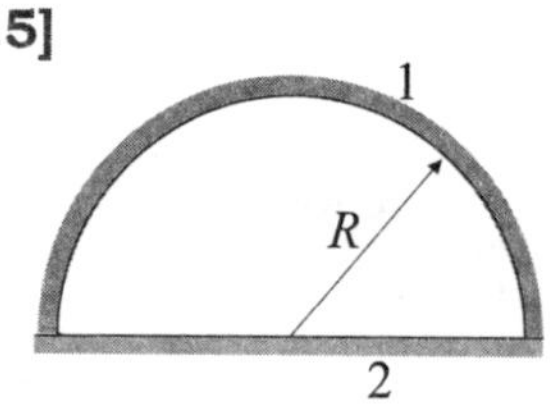

For surface $F_{2-1} = 1$

Applying the reciprocity relation to surfaces 1 and 2

$$A_1 F_{1-2} = A_2 F_{2-1}$$

or $$F_{1-2} = \frac{A_2}{A_1} \times 1 = \frac{\pi R^2}{2\pi R^2} = 0.5$$

and $F_{1-1} + F_{1-2} = 1$

$\Rightarrow F_{1-1} = 1 - F_{1-2} = 1 - 0.5$

$$F_{1-1} = 0.5$$

Q.57 Ans:[428.5]

Heat flux, $$q = \frac{\sigma(T_1^4 - T_2^4)}{\dfrac{1}{\varepsilon_1} + \dfrac{1}{\varepsilon_2} - 1}$$

Substituting $\varepsilon_1 = \varepsilon_2 = 0.5$,

$$q_1 = \frac{\sigma(T_1^4 - T_2^4)}{\frac{1}{0.5} + \frac{1}{0.5} - 1} = \frac{\sigma(T_1^4 - T_2^4)}{3} = 1000 \qquad \text{(i)}$$

Substituting $\varepsilon_1 = 0.5$, $\varepsilon_2 = 0.25$,

$$q_2 = \frac{\sigma(T_1^4 - T_2^4)}{\frac{1}{0.5} + \frac{1}{0.25} - 1} = \frac{\sigma(T_1^4 - T_2^4)}{7} \qquad \text{(ii)}$$

From Equations (i) and (ii), we obtain

$$q_2 = \frac{3}{7} \times 1000$$

$$q_2 = 428.5 \text{ W/m}^2$$

Q.58 Ans:[39.36]

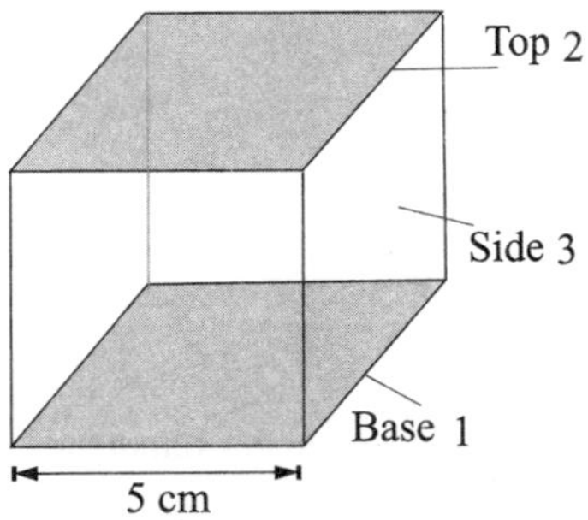

Applying the summation rule to surface 1 yields,

$$F_{1-1} + F_{1-2} + F_{1-3} = 1$$

or $$F_{1-3} = 1 - F_{1-1} - F_{1-2} = 1 - 0 - 0.2$$

$$F_{1-3} = 0.8$$

Heat transfer from base 1 to side 3,

$$Q_{1-3} = A_1 F_{1-3} \sigma(T_1^4 - T_1^4)$$

or $$Q_{1-3} = (5 \times 10^{-2})^2 \times 0.8 \times 5.67 \times 10^{-8} (800^4 - 500^4)$$

$$Q_{1-3} = 39.36 \text{ W}$$

Q.59 Ans:[3.6]

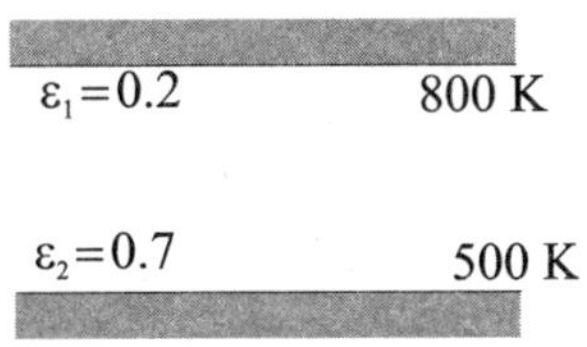

Heat transfer, $$Q_{1-2} = \frac{A\sigma(T_1^4 - T_1^4)}{\left(\frac{1}{\varepsilon_1} + \frac{1}{\varepsilon_2} - 1\right)}$$

Heat transfer per unit area,

$$q = \frac{Q_{1-2}}{A} = \frac{5.67 \times 10^{-8} (800^4 - 500^4)}{\left(\frac{1}{0.2} + \frac{1}{0.7} - 1\right)} = 3625.7 \text{ W/m}^2$$

$$q = 3.6 \text{ kW/m}^2$$

Q.60 Ans:[1.89]

Let x be the distance from entrance where both thermal boundary layer thickness meet.

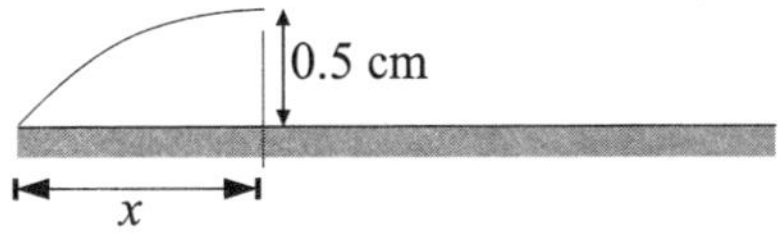

Thermal boundary layer thickness is given by

$$\delta_t = \frac{4.91x}{Pr^{\frac{1}{3}}\sqrt{Re}} = \frac{4.91x}{Pr^{\frac{1}{3}}\sqrt{\frac{\rho V x}{\mu}}}$$

Substituting the value of thermal boundary thickness,

$\delta_t = \frac{0.5}{100}$ m, $Pr = \frac{\mu c_p}{k} = \frac{1.002 \times 10^{-3} \times 4182}{0.598} = 7.01$,

$\rho = 998 \text{ kg/m}^3$, $\mu = 1.002 \times 10^{-3}$ kg/ms and $V = 0.5$ m/s, we have

or $$\frac{0.5}{100} = \frac{4.91x}{7.01^{\frac{1}{3}}\sqrt{\frac{998 \times 0.5x}{1.002 \times 10^{-3}}}}$$

or $$\sqrt{x} = \frac{0.5}{100} \times \frac{7.01^{\frac{1}{3}}}{4.91}\sqrt{\frac{998 \times 0.5}{1.002 \times 10^{-3}}}$$

$$x = 1.89$$

Q.61 Ans:[0.66]

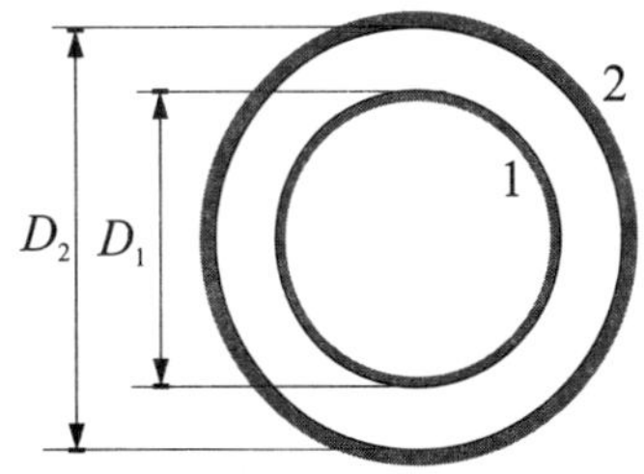

Applying the summation rule to surface 2,

$$F_{2-2} + F_{2-1} = 1$$

or $$F_{2-2} = 1 - F_{2-1} \qquad \text{(i)}$$

Applying the reciprocity relation to surfaces 1 and 2,

$$A_1 F_{1-2} = A_2 F_{2-1}$$

or $$F_{2-1} = \frac{A_1}{A_2} F_{1-2} \qquad \text{(ii)}$$

From Equations (i) and (ii), we have

$$F_{2-2} = 1 - \frac{A_1}{A_2} F_{1-2}$$

Since $F_{1-2} = 1$; $F_{2-2} = 1 - \frac{A_1}{A_2} = 1 - \frac{\pi D_1 L}{\pi D_2 L} = 1 - \frac{D_1}{D_2}$

$$F_{2-2} = 1 - \frac{D_1}{D_2} = 1 - \frac{1}{3} = \frac{2}{3}$$

$$F_{2-2} = 0.66$$

Q.62 Ans:[0.5]

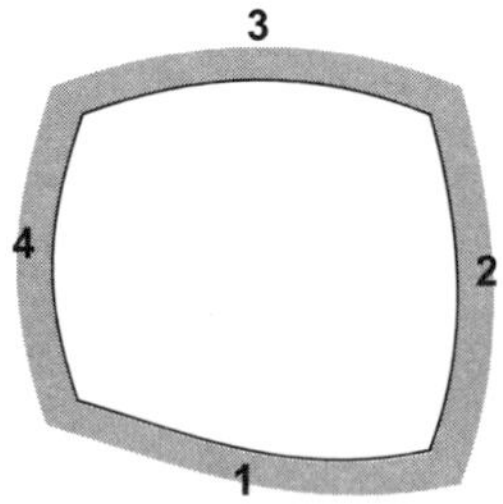

Applying the summation rule to surface 1 of the four surface enclosure yields,

$$F_{1-1} + F_{1-2} + F_{1-3} + F_{1-4} = 1$$

or $$0.1 + 0.4 + 0.25 + F_{1-4} = 1$$

$$F_{1-4} = 0.25$$

Applying the reciprocity relation to surface 1 and 4,

$$A_1 F_{1-4} = A_4 F_{4-1}$$

$$F_{4-1} = \frac{A_1}{A_4} F_{1-4}$$

or $$F_{4-1} = \frac{4}{2} \times 0.25$$

$$F_{4-1} = 0.5$$

Q.63 Ans:[0.25]

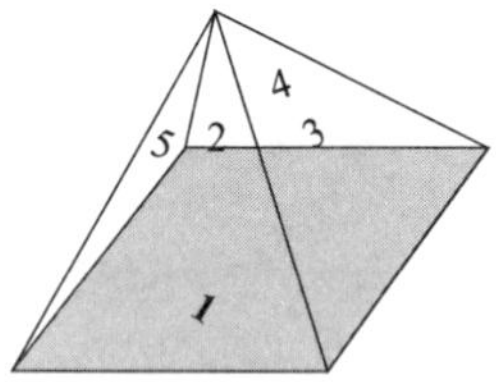

Applying the summation rule to surface 1 yields,

$$F_{1-1} + F_{1-2} + F_{1-3} + F_{1-4} + F_{1-5} = 1$$

Substituting $F_{1-1} = 0$ and $F_{1-2} = F_{1-3} = F_{1-4} = F_{1-5}$, we obtain

$$F_{1-2} = 0.25$$

Q.64 Ans:[96.76]

Heat transfer from surface (by conduction) = Heat convected

$$-k_{air} A \left(\frac{dT}{dy}\right)_{y=0} = hA(T_s - T_\infty)$$

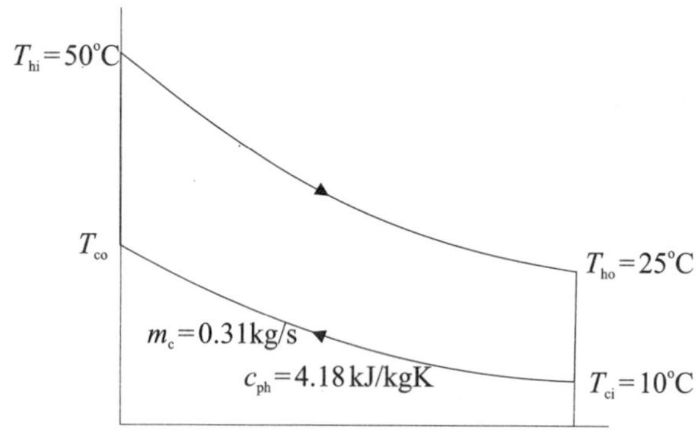

Counter flow heat exchanger

or $$-0.03024 \left(\frac{d}{dy} T_\infty + (T_s - T_\infty) e^{-3200y}\right)_{y=0} = h(T_s - T_\infty)$$

or $$-0.03024 \times 3200 \times (T_s - T_\infty) = h(T_s - T_\infty)$$

$$h = 96.76 \text{ W/m}^2\text{K}$$

Q.65 Ans:[0.67]

Heat capacity of hot fluid,

$$C_h = m_h c_{ph} = 1.4 \times 1.0 = 1.4$$

Heat capacity of cold fluid,

$$C_c = m_c c_{pc} = 0.31 \times 4.18 = 1.2958 \leftarrow C_{min}$$

Effectiveness, $$\varepsilon = \frac{Q_{act}}{Q_{max}} = \frac{Q_{act}}{(mc)_{min}(50-10)}$$

or $$\varepsilon = \frac{1.4 \times 1(50-25)}{1.2958 \times (50-10)} = \frac{35}{51.832}$$

$$\varepsilon = 0.67$$

12 Thermodynamics

GATE Mechanical Engg.

GATE Syllabus

Thermodynamic systems and processes; Properties of pure substances; Behaviour of ideal and real gases; Zeroth and first laws of thermodynamics; Calculation of work and heat in various processes; Second law of thermodynamics; Thermodynamic property charts and tables; Availability and irreversibility; Thermodynamic relations.

Chapter Outline

12.1 KEY CONCEPTS AND FORMULAS

Thermodynamic Systems

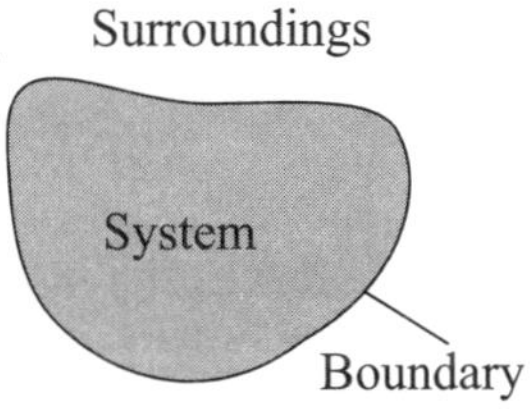

System: A system is a finite quantity of matter, or a prescribed region of space, which is under the thermodynamic study.

Boundary: The actual or hypothetical envelope enclosing a system is the boundary of the system. The boundary may be real or hypothetical.

Surroundings: Everything outside a system boundary is termed as surroundings.

System + Surroundings = Universe

Closed, Isolated and Open System

Closed system can exchange energy (as heat or work) but not matter, with its surroundings. An isolated system cannot exchange any heat, work, or matter with the surroundings, while an open system can exchange all heat, work and matter.

Control Volume

If the volume of a system under study remains constant, then this is called the *control volume* (CV). The control volume is bounded by the control surface (CS).

System Properties

Intensive properties: These are the properties that do not depend on the mass of system, e.g., temperature, pressure, and density.

Extensive properties: These properties essentially depend on the mass of a system, e.g., volume, entropy, and enthalpy.

Extensive properties per unit mass are intensive properties, e.g. specific volume, specific enthalpy, specific entropy and density.

State: The condition or state of a system is specified by the values of its properties.

A system is in an equilibrium state (or in equilibrium) if no changes can occur in the state of the system without the aid of an external stimulus.

Process and path: A change of a system from one state to another is called a *process*. The path of the process is the series of states through which the system passes during the process.

If the path is completely specified, it is called a process. It may be a

1. Constant pressure (isobaric) process, 2. Constant volume (isochoric) process, 3. Consant temperature (isothermal) process, 4. Constant entropy (isentropic) process, 5. Adiabatic process.

Cyclic process: If a system undergoes a series of processes and is returned to its original state, it is said to have undergone a cycle or cyclic process.

Non-flow process: A process may be a non-flow process in which no mass transfer occurs across the system boundary while the system is undergoing a change of state.

Flow process: A process may be a flow process if mass enters or leaves the system boundary. This is feasible in open system only.

Reversible Process: A reversible process is defined as a process that once having taken place in a direction, can be reversed without leaving any trace on either system or surroundings.

Quasi-equilibrium: If during a process, a system passes through series of only equilibrium states, so that the system at any instant is in equilibrium close to being equilibrium, the process is called a *quasi-equilibrium process*.

Point function: Thermodynamic properties are the point function for a given state where there is one and only one value for each property.

Path function: There are certain quantities which cannot be located on a graph by a point but are given by the area under the graph. Such quantities are called path functions. Heat and work are path functions.

Zeroth Law of Thermodynamics

It states that if two bodies are in thermal equilibrium with a third body, they are also in thermal equilibrium with each other.

Temperature scales, $T\,(\text{K}) = T\,(^\circ\text{C}) + 273.15$

Heat and Work Transfer

Forms of Energy

Potential energy, $\text{PE} = mgz$

Kinetic energy, $\text{KE} = \frac{1}{2}mv^2$

Internal energy U: The sum of all the microscopic forms of energy is called *internal energy*.

$U = K + P$, where K = internal energy of molecules and P = internal potential energy of molecules.

Mechanical energy: It can be defined as a form of energy that can be converted directly and completely into mechanical work by an ideal mechanical device such as an ideal turbine or pump. Thermal (heat) energy is not a form of mechanical energy.

Mechanical energy of a flowing fluid:

$$\dot{E}_{\text{mech}} = \dot{m}\left(pv + \frac{V^2}{2} + gz\right)$$

Enthalpy

The sum of the internal energy U and the product of pressure P and volume V.

Enthalpy, $H = U + PV$ (kJ)

Specific enthalpy, $h = u + Pv$ (kJ/kg)

Heat

It is a transfer form of energy that flows between two system (or a system and its surroundings) by virtue of the temperature difference between them, $q = \frac{Q}{m}$ (kJ/kg).

Heat capacity: The product of mass and specific heat is defined as heat capacity of the system.

Work

Work like heat is also a form of energy in transit. Energy can cross the boundary of the system as heat or work.

Sign convention for work transfer: Work done by system is considered as positive. Work done on system is considered as negative.

Forms of Work Transfer

1. Electric work, $W_E = VI\,\Delta t$,
2. Mechanical work, $W = \int PdV$
3. Flow work, $W = pv$
4. Gravitational work, $\Delta\text{PE} = mg(z_2 - z_1)$
5. Acceleration work, $\Delta\text{KE} = \frac{1}{2}m(V_2^2 - V_1^2)$
6. Shaft work, $W_s = 2\pi nT$
7. Spring work, $W_{\text{spring}} = \frac{1}{2}k(x_2^2 - x_1^2)$

First Law of Thermodynamics

First law of thermodynamics states that energy can be neither created nor destroyed. However, energy can change forms, and energy can flow from one place to another. The total energy of an isolated system remains the same.

$$Q = \Delta U + W$$

where Q is the energy entering a system causing an increase in the system's internal energy by ΔU and producing some external work W.

In differential form $\delta Q = dU + PdV$, and in the internal form, $Q = \Delta U + \int PdV$

Application of the First Law of Thermodynamics

Isolated system: $\Delta U = 0, W = 0, Q = 0$

Isobaric process: $\Delta U = mc_v(T_2 - T_1)$

$$W = \int_1^2 PdV = P(V_2 - V_1)$$

$$Q = m\frac{\gamma R}{\gamma - 1}(T_2 - T_1) = mc_p(T_2 - T_1)$$

Isochoric process: $\Delta U = mc_v(T_2 - T_1)$

$$W = \int_1^2 PdV = 0$$

$$Q = mc_v(T_2 - T_1)$$

Isothermal process: $\Delta U = 0$

$$W = \int_1^2 PdV = P_1V_1 \log_e\left(\frac{V_2}{V_1}\right)$$

$$Q = P_1V_1 \log_e\left(\frac{V_2}{V_1}\right)$$

Adiabatic process: $Q = 0$

$$\Delta U + W = 0, W = -\Delta U = \frac{P_1V_1 - P_2V_2}{\gamma - 1}$$

Polytropic process: $Q = \Delta U + W$

$$Q = mc_v(T_2 - T_1) + \frac{P_1V_1 - P_2V_2}{n - 1}$$

$$Q = mc_v(T_2 - T_1)\left(\frac{n - \gamma}{n - 1}\right)$$

Steady Flow Process

In a steady flow process, the mass flow rate and energy flow rate across the system boundary are constant. During a steady-state flow, there is neither any accumulation of mass nor energy.

$$(\sum \text{Energy})_{\text{in}} = (\sum \text{Energy})_{\text{out}}$$

Steady flow energy equation (SFEE)

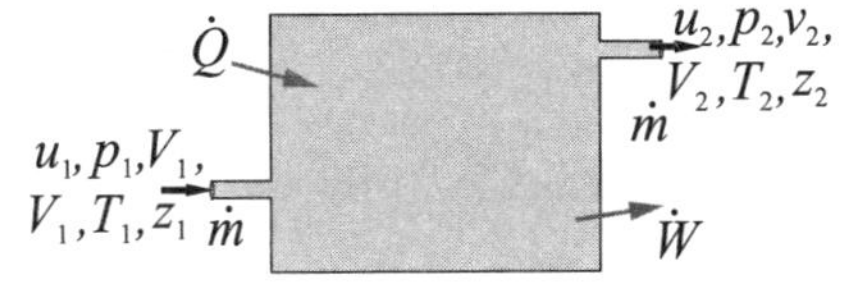

$$\dot{Q} - \dot{W} = \dot{m}\left[(u_2 - u_1) + (p_2v_2 - p_1v_1) + \frac{1}{2}(V_2^2 - V_1^2) + (z_2 - z_1)g\right] \text{(J/s)}$$

or $$\dot{q} - \dot{w} = (h_2 - h_1) + \frac{1}{2}(V_2^2 - V_1^2) + (z_2 - z_1)g \quad \text{(J/kg)}$$

Steady flow energy equation is applied to 1. Steam turbine, 2. Pump, 3. Nozzle, 4. Boiler, 5. Compressor, 6. Throttling, 7. Adiabatic mixing, etc.

Second Law of Thermodynamics

The second law of thermodynamics states that the total entropy of an isolated system always increases over time, or remains constant in ideal cases where the system is in a steady-state or undergoing a reversible process.

Heat Reservoir

A thermal reservoir is a heat source or heat sink that remains at a constant temperature, regardless of energy interaction.

Heat Engine

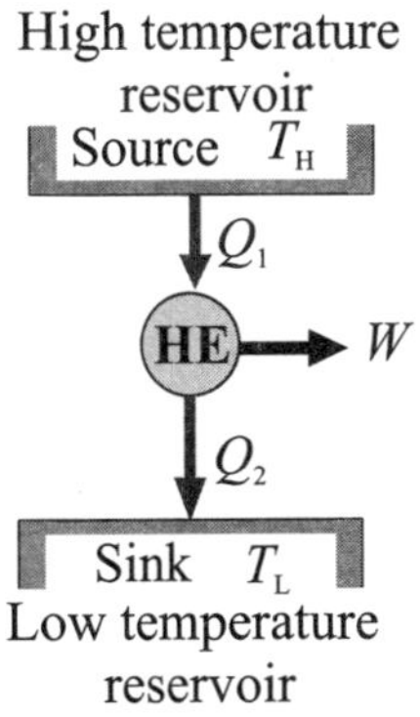

A heat engine is a device that converts heat into work.

Heat input $= Q_1$

Heat rejected to the sink $= Q_2$

Net heat converted to work, $Q_{\text{net}} = W_{\text{net}} = Q_1 - Q_2$

Efficiency of the heat engine, $\eta = \frac{W_{\text{net}}}{Q_1}$ or $\eta = 1 - \frac{Q_2}{Q_1}$

or $$\eta = 1 - \frac{T_2}{T_1}$$

Steam power plant: It is a typical heat engine in which low grade energy (heat) is converted to high grade energy (mechanical work).

Heat Pump

A heat pump is a reversed heat engine. It receives heat from a low temperature reservoir (source) and rejects it to a high temperature reservoir (sink).

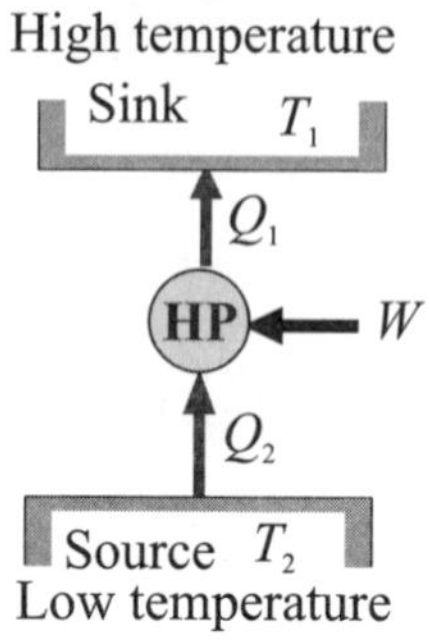

A heat pump extract, Q_2 amount of heat from the low temperature (T_2) source and delivers Q_1 amount of heat to the high temperature (T_1) sink by consuming W amount of external work.

$$\text{Coefficient of performance (COP)} = \frac{\text{Desired effect}}{\text{Work input}}$$

$$(\text{COP})_{\text{HP}} = \frac{Q_1}{W}$$

or $$(\text{COP})_{\text{HP}} = \frac{Q_1}{W} = \frac{Q_1}{Q_1 - Q_2}$$

Refrigerator

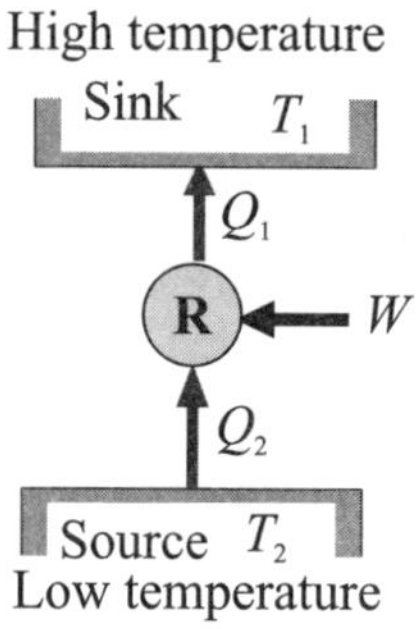

A refrigerator is a device, operating in a cycle, that maintains a body at lower temperature than its surroundings. A refrigerator extracts heat continuously from a controlled space, and thus it is maintained at a lower temperature than its surroundings.

The desired effect of a refrigerator is to remove Q_2 heat from refrigerated space at temperature T_2. The work input to the compressor is W and heat rejected at the condenser is Q_1.

$$\text{Coefficient of performance (COP)} = \frac{\text{Desired effect}}{\text{Work input}}$$

$$(\text{COP})_{\text{Ref}} = \frac{Q_2}{W}$$

or $$(\text{COP})_{\text{Ref}} = \frac{Q_2}{W} = \frac{Q_2}{Q_1 - Q_2}$$

Statement of the Second Law

There are two classical statements of the second law of thermodynamics:

Clausius Statement

It is impossible to construct a device that will produce no effect other than the transfer of heat from a low temperature body to a high temperature body while operating in a cycle.

Kelvin-Plank Statement

No heat engine, operating in cycle, can convert entire heat into work. It is impossible to build a heat engine that can register 100% efficiency.

Perpetual motion machine of second kind (PMM II): PMM II is a hypothetical machine that will continuously transfer heat from a low temperature reservoir to a high temperature without taking up any input work energy from its surrounding.

Carnot Cycle

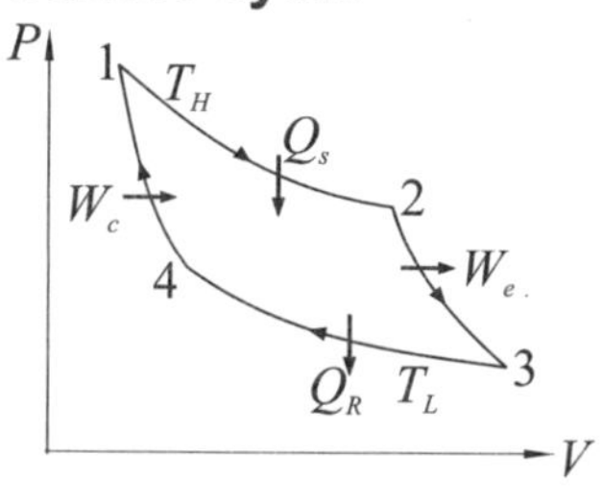

P-V diagram

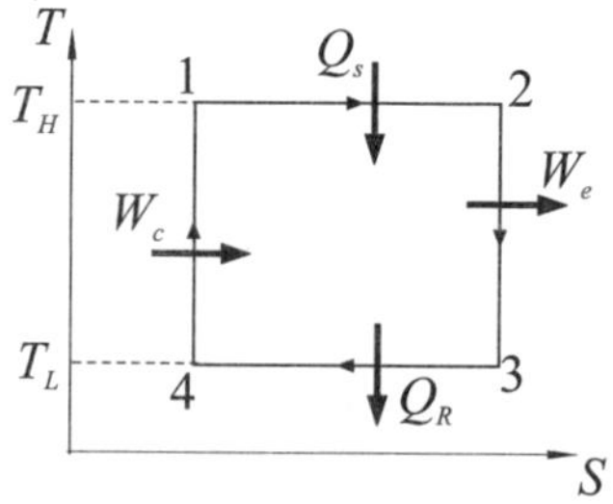

T-S diagram

It is theoretically a heat engine that converts the maximum amount of energy into mechanical work. The Carnot cycle, also called *reversible cycle*, comprises of four reversible processes as given:

1. Reversible isothermal expansion
2. Reversible adiabatic (isentropic) expansion
3. Reversible isothermal compression
4. Reversible adiabatic (isentropicc) compression

$$\text{Heat supplied, } Q_s = RT_H \ln\left(\frac{V_2}{V_1}\right)$$

$$\text{Heat rejected, } Q_R = RT_L \ln\left(\frac{V_3}{V_4}\right)$$

$$\text{Net work done, } W_{\text{net}} = Q_s - Q_R = (T_H - T_L)R \ln\left(\frac{V_2}{V_1}\right)$$

Thermal efficiency of Carnot heat engine,

$$\eta = \frac{W_{\text{net}}}{Q_S} = \frac{Q_S - Q_R}{Q_S} = 1 - \frac{T_L}{T_H}$$

Clasusis Inequiality

$\oint \frac{dQ}{T} = 0$; for a reversible process

$\oint \frac{dQ}{T} < 0$; for a irreversible process

$\oint \frac{dQ}{T} > 0$; for a process that is impossible

Entropy

Entropy is an abstract property. It is the quantitative measure of molecular disorder within a system. The entropy change dS is defined as:

$$S_2 - S_1 = \int dS = \int \frac{dQ}{T}$$

Thermodynamic relations:

$$\left.\begin{aligned} Tds &= du + pdv \\ Tds &= dh - vdp \end{aligned}\right\} \text{For closed system}$$

Entropy change in ideal gas:

$$\Delta s = c_v \ln\left(\frac{T_2}{T_1}\right) + R \ln\left(\frac{V_2}{V_1}\right)$$

$$\Delta s = c_p \ln\left(\frac{T_2}{T_1}\right) - R \ln\left(\frac{p_2}{p_1}\right)$$

For solids and incompressible liquids, $\Delta s = c \ln\left(\frac{T_2}{T_1}\right)$

Availability

The available energy is that portion of heat energy applied to a reversible engine, which could be converted into useful work.

The maximum useful work potetial of a system at the specified state is called *availability*.

Pure Substances

A substance that has fixed chemical composition throughout is called a *pure substance*.

Phases of a pure substance: (a) Solid, (b) Liquid, (c) Gas

Properties of Steam

Dryness fraction: It is a parameter that defines the quality of wet steam. It is the ratio of the mass of dry steam (m_g) to the mass of wet steam ($m_g + m_f$).

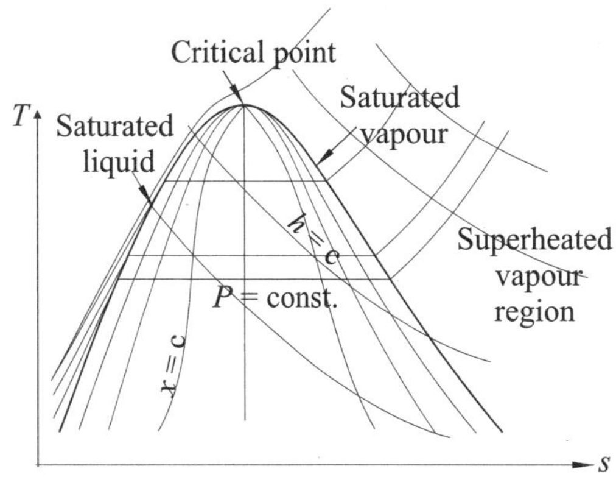

Thermodynamic properties chart

Dryness fraction, $x = \frac{m_g}{m_g + m_f}$

$$\begin{cases} m_g = \text{Mass of dry steam} \\ m_f = \text{Mass of wet steam} \end{cases}$$

Specific volume of wet steam, $v = v_f + x\, v_{fg}$

where $v_{fg} = v_g - v_f$

Enthalpy of wet steam, $h = h_f + x\, h_{fg}$

Internal energy of wet steam, $u = u_f + x\, u_{fg}$

Entropy of wet steam, $s = s_f + x\, s_{fg}$

Specific volume of superheated steam, $v_{\text{sup}} = v_g \frac{T_{\text{sup}}}{T_g}$

Specific enthalpy of superheated steam,

$$h_{\text{sup}} = h_g + c_p (T_{\text{sup}} - T_g)$$

Entropy of superheated steam, $s_{\text{sup}} = s_g + c_p \ln\left(\frac{T_{\text{sup}}}{T_g}\right)$

Internal energy of superheated steam,

$$u_{\text{sup}} = h_g + c_p (T_{\text{sup}} - T_g) - Pv_{\text{sup}}$$

Ideal Gas and Real Gas

Equation of state: Any equation that relates the pressure, temperature and specific volume of a substance is called an *equation of state*.

Ideal gas relation: $PV = mRT$

$$PV = m\frac{\bar{R}}{\mu}T;\ R = \frac{\bar{R} = 8.3144}{\mu \leftarrow \text{Molecular weight}}\ \text{kJ/kmolK}$$

Relation between specific heats: $c_p - c_v = R$

where $c_p = \frac{\gamma}{\gamma - 1}R$, $c_v = \frac{R}{\gamma - 1}$

Real gas relation:

$$\left(P+\frac{a}{v^2}\right)(v-b)=RT \quad \text{(van der Waals equation)}$$

$$\left(P+\frac{a}{Tv^2}\right)(v-b)=RT \quad \text{[Berthelot]}$$

Compressibility factor, $Z=\frac{Pv}{RT}$

Dalton's law of partial pressures,

$$P=P_A+P_B+P_C+\ldots$$

Density of gas mixture, $\rho=\rho_A+\rho_B+\rho_C+\ldots$

Thermodynamics Relations

Maxwell Relations

$$\left(\frac{\partial T}{\partial V}\right)_S=-\left(\frac{\partial P}{\partial S}\right)_V \quad \text{First relation}$$

$$\left(\frac{\partial T}{\partial P}\right)_S=\left(\frac{\partial V}{\partial S}\right)_P \quad \text{Second relation}$$

$$\left(\frac{\partial P}{\partial T}\right)_V=\left(\frac{\partial S}{\partial V}\right)_T \quad \text{Third relation}$$

$$\left(\frac{\partial V}{\partial T}\right)_P=-\left(\frac{\partial S}{\partial P}\right)_T \quad \text{Fourth relation}$$

Thermodynamic Relation

$$c_p=\left(\frac{\partial S}{\partial T}\right)_P, c_v=\left(\frac{\partial S}{\partial T}\right)_v$$

$$TdS=c_v dT+T\left(\frac{\partial P}{\partial T}\right)_V dV$$

$$TdS=c_p dT-T\left(\frac{\partial V}{\partial T}\right)_P dP$$

$$c_p-c_v=-T\left(\frac{\partial P}{\partial V}\right)_T\left(\frac{\partial V}{\partial T}\right)_P^2$$

$$dh=TdS+VdP=c_p dT+\left[V-T\left(\frac{\partial V}{\partial T}\right)_P\right]dP$$

$$du=TdS-PdV=c_v dT+\left[T\left(\frac{\partial P}{\partial T}\right)_V-P\right]dV$$

Joule-Thomson Coefficient

$$\mu_j=\left(\frac{\partial T}{\partial P}\right)_h=\frac{1}{c_p}\left[T\left(\frac{\partial V}{\partial T}\right)_P-V\right]$$

Clausius-Clapeyron Equation

$$\frac{dP}{dT}=\frac{L}{T\Delta V} \quad \text{(where } L \text{ is latent heat)}$$

12.2 SOLVED EXAMPLES

Previous Years GATE Questions

Example 12.1

The van der Waals equation of state is $\left(P+\frac{a}{v^2}\right)(v-b)=RT$, where P is pressure, v is specific volume, T is temperature and R is characteristic gas constant. The SI unit of a is

(A) J/kgK (B) m^3/kg

(C) $m^5/kg\,s^2$ (D) Pa/kg

GATE 2015

Solution

The unit of term $\frac{a}{v^2}$ is N/m^2 (unit of pressure)

Thus, the unit of a, $\frac{N}{m^2}\times\left(\frac{m^3}{kg}\right)^2$

or $\frac{kg\,m/s^2}{m^2}\times\left(\frac{m^3}{kg}\right)^2$

Unit of a is $\frac{m^5}{kgs^2}$

Example 12.2

The COP of a Carnot heat pump operating between 6°C and 37°C is________.

GATE 2015

Solution

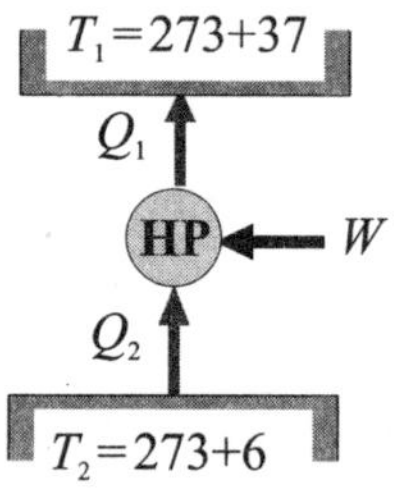

COP of Carnot heat pump is given by $COP=\frac{T_1}{T_1-T_2}$

$$COP=\frac{273+37}{(273+37)-(273+6)}$$

$$COP=10$$

Example 12.3

Work is done on a adiabatic system due to which its velocity changes from 10 m/s to 20 m/s, elevation increases by 20 m and temperature increases by 1K. The mass of the system is 10 kg, $c_v = 100$ J/kgK and gravitational acceleration is $10\ \text{m/s}^2$. If there is no change in any other component of the energy of the system, the magnitude of total work (in kJ) on the system is _______.

GATE 2015

Solution

Applying energy equation for adiabatic and non-flow system,

$$\frac{1}{2}mv_1^2 + mgh_1 + mc_vT_1 = \frac{1}{2}mv_2^2 + mgh_2 + mc_vT_2 + W$$

Work done by the system,

$$W = \frac{1}{2}m(v_1^2 - v_2^2) + mg(h_1 - h_2) + mc_v(T_1 - T_2)$$

Work done on the system,

$$W = \frac{1}{2}m(v_2^2 - v_1^2) + mg(h_2 - h_1) + mc_v(T_2 - T_1)$$

or $$W = \frac{1}{2}10 \times (20^2 - 10^2) + 10 \times 10 \times 20 + 10 \times 100 \times 1$$

Work done on the system, $W = 4.5$ kJ

Example 12.4

One kg of air ($R = 287$ J/kgK) undergoes irreversible process between equilibrium state 1 (20°C, 0.9 m^3) and equilibrium state 2 (20°C, 0.6 m^3). The change in entropy $s_2 - s_1$ (in J/kgK) is_________.

GATE 2015

Solution

Change of entropy $$s_2 - s_1 = \int \frac{dQ}{T} = \int \frac{du + PdV}{T}$$

For constant temperature process, $du = 0$

$$s_2 - s_1 = \int \frac{PdV}{T} = mR\int_{V_1}^{V_2} \frac{dV}{V}$$

or $$s_2 - s_1 = mR\ln\left(\frac{V_2}{V_1}\right)$$

or $$s_2 - s_1 = 1 \times 287 \times \ln\left(\frac{0.6}{0.9}\right)$$

$s_2 - s_1 = -116.36$ J/kgK

Example 12.5

Steam enters a turbine at 30 bar, 300°C ($u = 2750$ kJ/kg, $h = 2993$ kJ/kg) and exits the turbine as saturated liquid at 15 kPa ($u = 225$ kJ/g, $h = 226$ kJ/kg). Heat loss to the surrounding is 50 kJ/kg of steam flowing through the turbine. Neglecting changes in kinetic energy and potential energy, the work output of the turbine (in kJ/kg of steam) is____.

GATE 2015

Solution

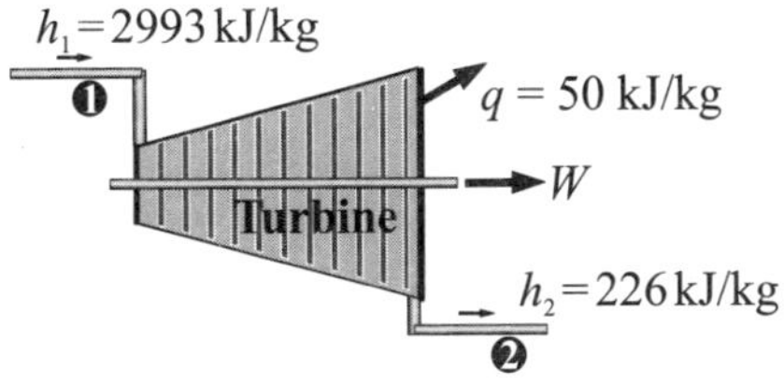

Neglecting the kinetic and potential energy, the energy equation takes the form:

$$h_1 + q = h_2 + W$$

or $$2993 + (-50) = 226 + W$$

Work output of the turbine, $W = 2717$ kJ/kg

Example 12.6

A mixture of ideal gases has the following composition by mass:

N_2	O_2	CO_2
60%	30%	10%

If the universal gas constant is 8314 J/kmolK, the characteristic gas constant of the mixture (in J/kgK) is__.

GATE 2015

Solution

Let m be the mass of mixture and V be the volume.

Mass of N_2, $m_{N_2} = 0.6m$ and molecular weight $\mu_{N_2} = 28$

Mass of O_2, $m_{O_2} = 0.3m$ and molecular weight $\mu_{O_2} = 32$

Mass of CO_2, $m_{CO_2} = 0.1m$ and molecular weight $\mu_{CO_2} = 44$

Equation of state,

$$P_{N_2}V = m_{N_2}\frac{\bar{R}}{\mu_{N_2}}T,\quad P_{O_2}V = m_{O_2}\frac{\bar{R}}{\mu_{O_2}}T$$

and $$P_{CO_2}V = m_{CO_2}\frac{\bar{R}}{\mu_{CO_2}}T$$

From which

$$(P_{N_2} + P_{O_2} + P_{CO_2})V = \left(\frac{m_{N_2}}{\mu_{N_2}} + \frac{m_{O_2}}{\mu_{O_2}} + \frac{m_{CO_2}}{\mu_{CO_2}}\right)\bar{R}T = mRT$$

or $$R = \left(\frac{1}{\mu_{N_2}}\frac{m_{N_2}}{m} + \frac{1}{\mu_{O_2}}\frac{m_{O_2}}{m} + \frac{1}{\mu_{CO_2}}\frac{m_{CO_2}}{m}\right)\bar{R}$$

or $$R = \left(\frac{1}{28}\times 0.6 + \frac{1}{32}\times 0.3 + \frac{1}{44}\times 0.1\right)8314$$

$R = 274.9$ J/kgK

Example 12.7

For an ideal gas with constant values of specific heats, for calculation of the specific enthalpy,

(A) It is sufficient to know only the temperature

(B) Both temperature and pressure are required to be known

(C) Both temperature and volume are required to be known

(D) Both temperature and mass are required to be known

GATE 2015

Solution

Specific enthalpy, $h = c_p T$

For calculation of the specific enthalpy, it is sufficient to know only the temperature.

Example 12.8

A Carnot engine (CE-1) works between two temperature reservoirs A and B, where $T_A = 900\,\text{K}$ and $T_B = 500\,\text{K}$. A second Carnot engine (CE-2) works between temperature reservoirs B and C, where $T_C = 300\,\text{K}$. In each cycle of CE-1 and CE-2, all the heat rejected by CE-1 to reservoir B is used by CE-2. For one cycle operation, if the net Q absorbed by CE-1 from reservoir A is 150 MJ, the net heat rejected to reservoir C by CE-2 (in MJ) is _______.

GATE 2015

Solution

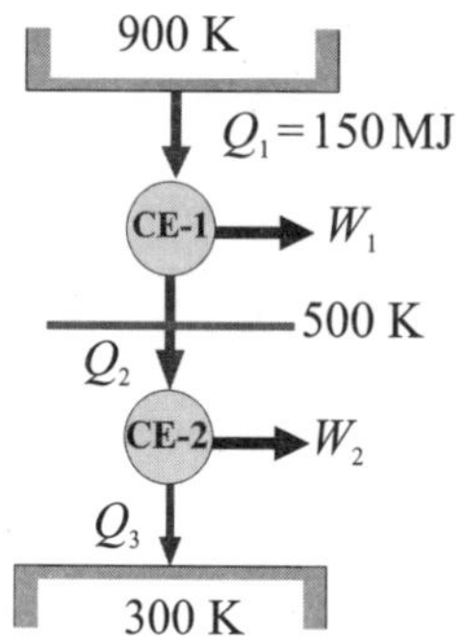

For reversible engine CE-1,

$$\frac{150}{900} = \frac{Q_2}{500}$$

For reversible engine CE-2,

$$\frac{Q_2}{500} = \frac{Q_3}{300}$$

From which $\dfrac{150}{900} = \dfrac{Q_2}{500} = \dfrac{Q_3}{300}$

Heat rejected by CE-2,

$$Q_3 = \frac{150}{900} \times 300$$

$$Q_3 = 50\,\text{MJ}$$

Example 12.9

Temperature of nitrogen in a vessel of volume 2 m^3 is 288 K. A U-tube manometer connected to the vessel shows a reading of 70 cm of mercury (level higher in the end open to atmosphere). The universal gas constant is 8314 J/kmolK, atmospheric pressure is 1.01325 bar, acceleration due to gravity is 9.81 m/s^2 and density of mercury is 13600 kg/m^3. The mass of nitrogen (in kg) in the vessel is _______.

GATE 2015

Solution

Pressure of vessel $P = P_{atm} + \rho g h$

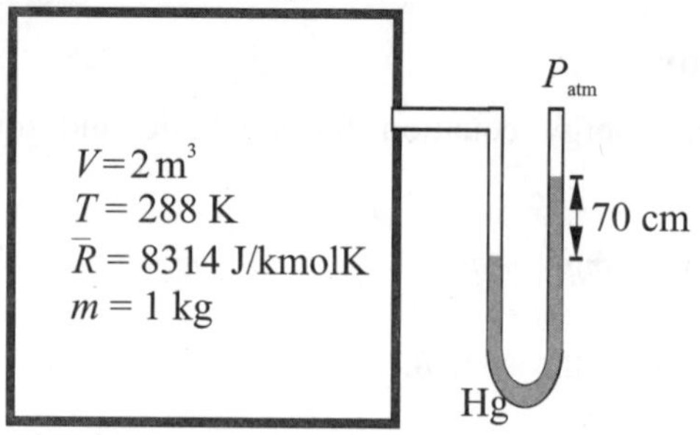

$$P = 1.01325 \times 10^5 + 13600 \times 9.81 \times \frac{70}{100}$$

$$P = 194716\,\text{N/m}^2$$

Equation of state, $PV = m\dfrac{\bar{R}}{\mu}T$

Mass of nitrogen, $m = \dfrac{PV}{\dfrac{\bar{R}}{\mu}T} = \dfrac{194716 \times 2}{\dfrac{8314}{28} \times 288}$

Mass of nitrogen, $m = 4.56\,\text{kg}$

Example 12.10

A well insulated rigid container of volume 1.0 m^3 contains 1.0 kg of an ideal gas $c_P = 1000$ J/kgK and $c_v = 800$ J/kgK at a pressure of 10^5 Pa. A stirrer is rotated at constant rpm in the container for 1000 rotations and the applied torque is 100 Nm. The final temperature of the gas (in K) is_______.

GATE 2015

Solution

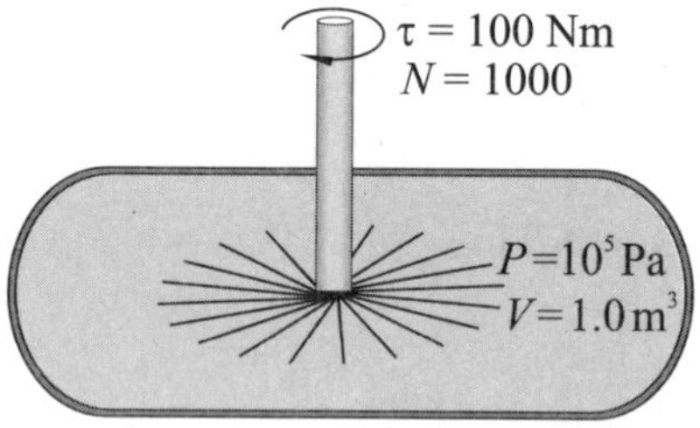

Given: $V = 1.0\,\text{m}^3$, $m = 1$ kg, $c_P = 1000$ J/kgK, $c_v = 800$ J/kgK, $P = 10^5$ Pa, Torque $\tau = 100$ Nm and N = 1000 rotations

To find initial temperature of gas, we use the ideal gas equation. It gives us

$$T_1 = \frac{PV}{mR} = \frac{PV}{m(c_P - c_v)} = \frac{10^5 \times 1}{1 \times (1000 - 800)}$$

$$T_1 = 500\,\text{K}$$

Work done on system at constant volume,

$$W = \tau\omega = mc_v(T_2 - T_1)$$

or $$T_2 = T_1 + \frac{\tau\omega}{mc_v}$$

$$T_2 = 500 + \frac{100 \times 2\pi 1000}{1 \times 800}$$

$$T_2 = 1285.3\,\text{K}$$

Example 12.11

Steam enters an adiabatic turbine operating at steady state with an enthalpy of 3251.0 kJ/kg and leaves as a saturated mixture at 15 kPa with quality (dryness fraction) 0.9. The enthalpies of the saturated liquid and vapour at 15 kPa are $h_f = 225.94$ kJ/kg and $h_g = 2598.3$ kJ/kg respectively. The mass flow rate of steam is 10 kg/s. Kinetic and potential energy changes are negligible. The power output of the turbine in MW is

(A) 6.5 (B) 9.1 (C) 8.9 (D) 27.0

GATE 2012

Solution

Power output of turbine is

$$P = m(h_1 - h_2)$$

Substituting:

Mass flow rate of steam, $m = 10$ kg/s

Enthalpy of steam at inlet, $h_1 = 3251.0$ kJ/kg

Enthalpy of steam at exit,

$$h_2 = h_f + x(h_g - h_f) = 225.94 + 0.9(2598.3 - 225.9$$

$$h_2 = 2361.1\,\text{kJ/kg}$$

$$P = 10 \times (3251.0 - 2361.1)\,\text{kJ/s}$$

$$P = 8.9\,\text{MW}$$

Example 12.12

A cylinder contains 5 m^3 of an ideal gas at a pressure of 1 bar. This gas is compressed in a reversible isothermal process till its pressure increases to 5 bar. The work in kJ required for this process is

(A) 804.7 (B) 953.2 (C) 981.7 (D) 1012.2

GATE 2013

Solution

Work in isothermal compression is

$$W = P_1V_1 \ln\left(\frac{P_2}{P_1}\right)$$

Substituting given data $P_1 = 1 \times 10^5$ N/m^2, $V_1 = 5$ m^3 and $P_1 = 5 \times 10^5$ N/m^2

$$W = 1 \times 10^5 \times 5 \ln\left(\frac{5 \times 10^5}{1 \times 10^5}\right)$$

$$W = 804.7\,\text{kJ}$$

Example 12.13

1.5 kg of water is in saturated liquid state at 2 bar ($v_f = 0.001061$ m^3/kg, $u_f = 504.0$ kJ/kg, $h_f = 505.0$ kJ/kg). Heat is added in a constant pressure process till the temperature of water reaches 400°C ($v = 1.5493$ m^3/kg, $u = 2967.0$ kJ/kg, $h = 3277.0$ kJ/kg). The heat added (in kJ) in the process is ____.

GATE 2014

Solution

Applying first law of thermodynamics,

$$dQ = du + PdV$$

or $$dQ = dh - V\,dP$$

For constant pressure process ($dP = 0$); $\int dQ = \int dh - 0$

Heat added, $$Q_{\text{add}} = m(h_2 - h_1)$$

$$Q_{\text{add}} = 1.5 \times (3277.0 - 505)$$

$$Q_{\text{add}} = 4158\,\text{kJ}$$

Example 12.14

A reversible heat engine receives 2 kJ of heat from a reservoir at 1000 K and a certain amount of heat from a reservoir at 800 K. It rejects 1 kJ of heat to a reservoir at 400 K. The net work output (in kJ) of the cycle is

(A) 0.8 (B) 1.0 (C) 1.4 (D) 2.0

GATE 2014

Solution

For reversible engine

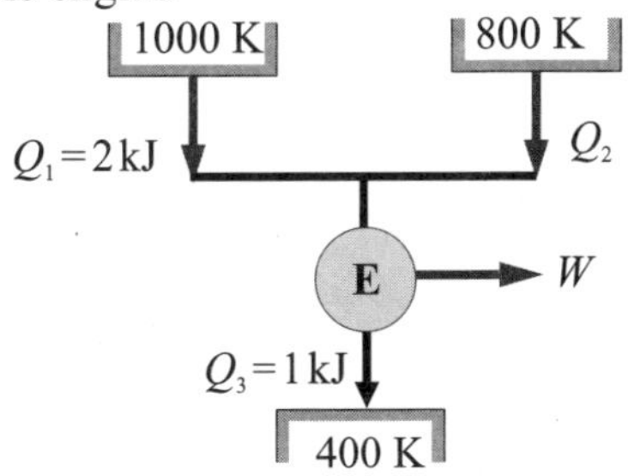

Change in entropy $\Delta S = 0$

$$\left(\frac{Q_1}{T_1} + \frac{Q_2}{T_2}\right) - \frac{Q_3}{T_3} = 0$$

$$\left(\frac{2}{1000}+\frac{Q_2}{800}\right)-\frac{1}{400}=0$$

From which

$$Q_2=0.4\,\text{kJ}$$

Net work output, $W=(Q_1+Q_2)-Q_3$

$$W=(2+0.4)-1$$

$$W=1.4\text{ kJ}$$

Example 12.15

Specific enthalpy and velocity of steam at inlet and exit of a steam turbine, running under steady state, are given below

	Specific enthalpy (kJ/kg)	Velocity (m/s)
Inlet steam condition	3250	180
Exit steam condition	2360	5

The rate of heat loss from the turbine per kg of steam flow rate is 5 kW. Neglecting changes potential energy of steam, the power developed in kW by the steam turbine per kg of steam flow rate, is

(A) 901.2 (B) 911.2 (C)17072.5 (D) 17082.5

GATE 2013

Solution

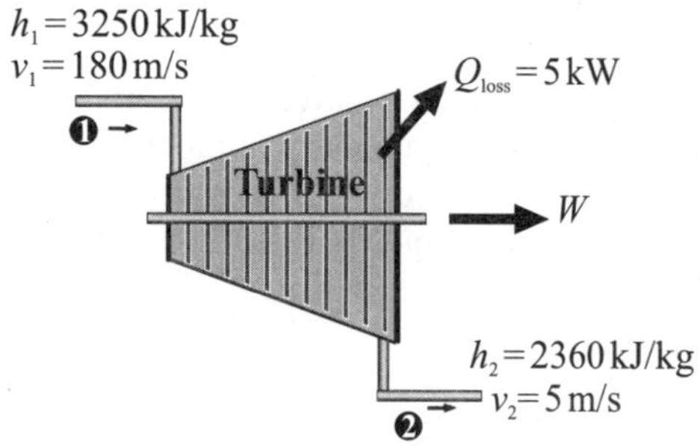

Applying steady flow energy equation

$$h_1+\frac{v_1^2}{2}=h_2+\frac{v_2^2}{2}+Q+W$$

Substituting given data: $h_1=3250\times10^3$ J/kg, $v_1=180$ m/s, $h_2=2360\times10^3$ J/kg, $v_2=5$ m/s and $Q=5\times10^3$ W, we have

$$3250\times10^3+\frac{180^2}{2}=2360\times10^3+\frac{5^2}{2}+5\times10^3+W$$

$$W=901.2\,\text{kW}$$

Example 12.16

A mono-atomic ideal gas ($\gamma=1.67$, molecular weight = 40) is compressed adiabatically from 0.1 MPa, 300 K to 0.2 MPa. The universal gas constant is 8.314 kJ/kmolK. The work of compression of the gas (in kJ/kg) is

(A) 29.7 (B) 19.9 (C) 13.3 (D) 0

GATE 2010

Solution

Temperature at the end of adiabatic compression is

$$T_2=T_1\left(\frac{P_2}{P_1}\right)^{\frac{\gamma-1}{\gamma}}$$

or $$T_2=300\times\left(\frac{0.2}{0.1}\right)^{\frac{1.67-1}{1.67}}$$

$$T_2=396.18\,\text{K}$$

Gas constant for mono-atomic ideal gas is

$$R=\frac{8.314}{40}=0.2078\,\text{kJ/kgK}$$

Work done in adiabatic process per kg is

$$W=\frac{R(T_2-T_1)}{\gamma-1}$$

$$W=\frac{0.2078\times(396.18-300)}{1.67-1}$$

$$W=29.83\,\text{kJ/kg}$$

Example 12.17

A small steam whistle (perfectly insulated and doing no shaft work) causes a drop of 0.8 kJ/kg in the enthalpy of steam from entry to exit. If the kinetic energy of the steam at entry is negligible, the velocity of the steam at exit is

(A) 4 m/s (B) 40 m/s (C) 80 m/s (D) 120 m/s

GATE 2001

Solution

Applying steady flow energy equation at inlet and exit of whistle

$$h_1+\frac{v_1^2}{2}=h_2+\frac{v_2^2}{2}$$

or $$v_2=\sqrt{2(h_1-h_2)+v_1^2}$$

Substituting $h_1-h_2=0.8\times10^3$ J/kg and $v_1=0$;

$$v_2=\sqrt{2\times0.8\times10^3+0}$$

Velocity of the steam at exit, $v_2=40$ m/s

Example 12.18

An ideal gas of mass m and temperature T_1 undergoes a reversible isothermal process from an initial pressure P_1 to final pressure P_2. The heat loss during the process is Q. The entropy change ΔS of gas is

(A) $mR\ \ln\left(\frac{P_2}{P_1}\right)$ (B) $mR\ \ln\left(\frac{P_2}{P_1}\right)-\frac{Q}{T_1}$

(C) $mR\ \ln\left(\frac{P_1}{P_2}\right)$ (D) Zero

GATE 2012

Solution

Applying first law of thermodynamics for isothermal process $[du=0]$;

$$dQ = 0 + PdV$$

Entropy change, $\Delta S = \int \frac{dQ}{T}$

or $$\Delta S = \int \frac{PdV}{T} = mR\int_{V_1}^{V_2} \frac{dV}{V}$$

or $$\Delta S = mR\ \ln\left(\frac{V_2}{V_1}\right)$$

[Isothermal process, $P_1V_1 = P_2V_2 = RT$]

$$\Delta S = mR\ \ln\left(\frac{P_1}{P_2}\right)$$

Example 12.19

Linked Answer Questions

Air enters an adiabatic nozzle at 300 kPa, 500 K with a velocity of 10 m/s. It leaves the nozzle at 100 kPa with a velocity of 180 m/s. The inlet area is 80 cm^2. The specific heat of air c_p is 1008 J/kgK.

Q(a) The exit temperature of the air is

(A) 516 K (B) 484 K (C) 532 K (D) 468 K

Q(b) The exit area of the nozzle in cm^2 is

(A) 90.1 (B) 4.4 (C) 56.3 (D) 12.9

GATE 2012

Solution

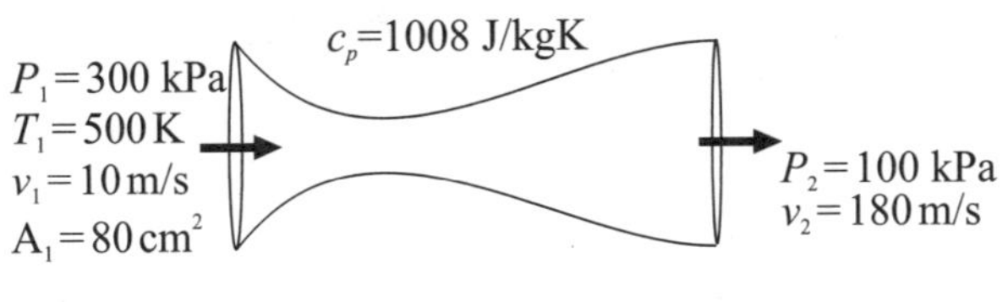

(a) Applying steady flow energy equation for nozzle

$$h_1 + \frac{v_1^2}{2} = h_2 + \frac{v_2^2}{2}$$

or $$c_pT_1 + \frac{v_1^2}{2} = c_pT_2 + \frac{v_2^2}{2}$$

or $$T_2 = T_1 + \frac{1}{2c_p}(v_1^2 - v_2^2)$$

or $$T_2 = 500 + \frac{1}{2\times 1008}(10^2 - 180^2)$$

$$T_2 = 483.97\ \text{K}$$

(b) Applying continuity equation; $\rho_1 A_1 V_1 = \rho_2 A_2 V_2$

Substituting, $\rho_1 = \frac{P_1}{RT_1}$ and $\rho_2 = \frac{P_2}{RT_2}$, we have

$$\frac{P_1}{RT_1}A_1V_1 = \frac{P_2}{RT_2}A_2V_2$$

or $$A_2 = \frac{P_1}{P_2}\times\frac{T_2}{T_1}\times\frac{V_1}{V_2}\times A_1$$

or $$A_2 = \frac{300}{100}\times\frac{483.97}{500}\times\frac{10}{180}\times 80$$

$$A_2 = 12.9\ \text{cm}^2$$

Example 12.20

Common Data Questions

In an experimental set-up, air flows between two stations P and Q adiabatically. The direction of flow depends on the pressure and temperature conditions maintained at P and Q. The conditions at stations P are 150 kPa and 350 K. The temperature at station Q is 300 K.

The following are the properties and relations pertaining to air:

Specific heat at constant pressure, $c_p = 1.005$ kJ/kgK

Specific heat at constant volume, $c_v = 0.718$ kJ/kgK

Characteristic gas constant, $R = 0.287$ kJ/kgK

Enthalpy, $h = c_pT$

Internal energy, $u = c_vT$

Q(a) If the pressure at station Q is 50 kPa, the change in entropy $(s_Q - s_P)$ in kJ/kgK is

(A) –0.155 (B) 0.160 (C) 0 (D) 0.355

Q(b) If the air has to flow from station P to station Q, the maximum possible value of pressure in kPa at station Q is close to

(A) 50 (B) 128 (C) 87 (D) 150

GATE 2011

Solution

(a) Entropy change,

$$s_Q - s_P = \int ds = \int \frac{dQ}{T}$$

or $$s_Q - s_P = \int \frac{dh - VdP}{T}$$

or $$s_Q - s_P = c_p \int_{T_1}^{T_2} \frac{dT}{T} - R\int_{P_1}^{P_2} \frac{dP}{P} = c_p \ln\frac{T_2}{T_1} - R\ln\frac{P_2}{P_1}$$

or $$s_Q - s_P = 1.005 \ln\frac{300}{350} - 0.287\ln\frac{50}{150}$$

$$s_Q - s_P = 0.1604 \text{ kJ/kgK}$$

(b) If the process is isentropic then we get maximum pressure at station Q.

$$s_Q - s_P = 0 \Rightarrow c_p \ln\frac{T_2}{T_1} - R\ln\frac{P_2}{P_1} = 0$$

or $$1.005 \times \ln\frac{300}{350} - 0.287 \times \ln\frac{P_2}{150} = 0$$

From which

$$P_2 = 87.43 \text{ kPa}$$

Example 12.21

A 100 W electric bulb was switched on in a $2.5\,\text{m} \times 3\,\text{m} \times 3\,\text{m}$ size thermally insulated room having a temperature of 20°C. The room temperature at the end of 24 hours will be

(A) 321°C (B) 341°C (C) 450°C (D) 470°C

GATE 2006

Solution

Let t_2 be the temperature of room after 24 hours.

Heat generated by electric bulb $Q_s = mc_v(t_2 - t_1)$

$$t_2 = t_1 + \frac{Q_s}{m\, c_v}$$

or $$t_2 = t_1 + \frac{Q_s}{\rho V c_v}$$

Substituting, $Q_s = 100 \times 24 \times 60 \times 60$ J, $V = 2.5 \times 3 \times 3\,\text{m}^3$, $c_v = 0.718 \times 10^3$ J/kgK and

$$\rho = \frac{m}{V} = \frac{P}{RT} = \frac{1 \times 10^5}{0.287 \times 10^3 \times (273 + 20)} = 1.1891 \text{ kg/m}^3$$

$$t_2 = 20 + \frac{100 \times 24 \times 60 \times 60}{1.1891 \times 2.5 \times 3 \times 3 \times 0.718 \times 10^3}$$

$$t_2 = 469.73\text{°C}$$

Example 12.22

Linked Answer Questions

The temperature and pressure of air in a large reservoir are 400 K and 3 bar respectively. A converging-diverging nozzle of exit is 0.005 m^2 is fitted to the wall of the reservoir as shown in the figure. The static pressure of air at the exit section or isentropic flow through the nozzle is 50 kPa. The characteristic gas constant and the ratio of specific heats of air are 0.287 kJ/kgK and 1.4 respectively.

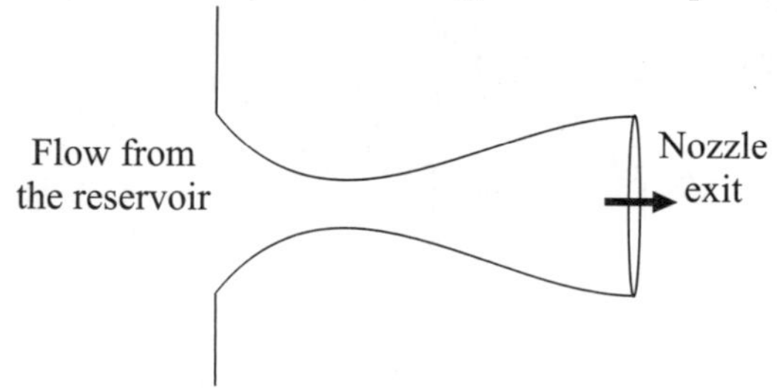

Q (a) The density of air in kg/m^3 at the nozzle exit is

(A) 0.560 (B) 0.727 (C) 0.600 (D) 0.800

Q (b) The mass flow rate of air through the nozzle in kg/s is

(A) 1.30 (B) 1.85 (C) 1.77 (D) 2.06

GATE 2011

Solution

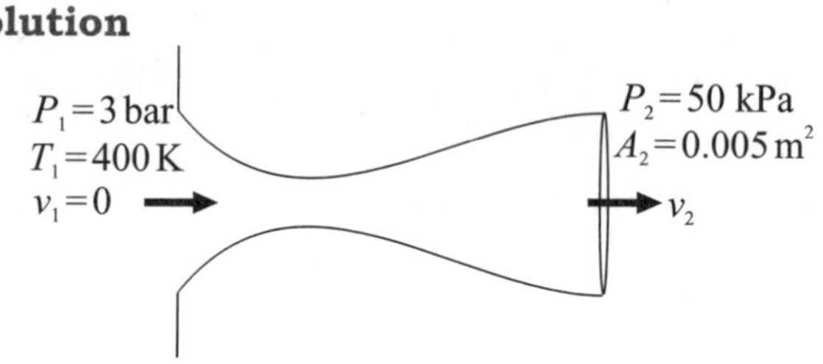

For isentropic flow, $$\frac{T_2}{T_1} = \left(\frac{P_2}{P_1}\right)^{\frac{\gamma-1}{\gamma}}$$

Temperature at exit is, $$T_2 = T_1\left(\frac{P_2}{P_1}\right)^{\frac{\gamma-1}{\gamma}}$$

or $$T_2 = 400 \times \left(\frac{50}{300}\right)^{\frac{1.4-1}{1.4}}$$

or $$T_2 = 239.7\,\text{K}$$

The density of air at the exit of nozzle is $\rho_2 = \dfrac{P_2}{RT_2}$

or $$\rho_2 = \frac{50\times10^3}{0.287\times10^3\times239.7}$$

$$\rho_2 = 0.726\ \text{kg/m}^3$$

(b) Applying steady flow energy equation

$$h_1 + \frac{v_1^2}{2} = h_2 + \frac{v_2^2}{2}$$

or $$v_2 = \sqrt{2(h_1 - h_2)} = \sqrt{2c_p(T_1 - T_2)}$$

or $$v_2 = \sqrt{2\frac{\gamma R}{\gamma-1}(T_1 - T_2)}$$

or $$v_2 = \sqrt{2\times\frac{1.4\times0.287\times10^3}{1.4-1}(400-239.7)}$$

or $$v_2 = 567.4\ \text{m/s}$$

Mass flow rate, $m = \rho_2 A_2 v_2$

$$m = 0.726\times0.005\times567.4$$

$$m = 2.06\ \text{kg/s}$$

Example 12.23

Common Data Questions

The inlet and the outlet conditions of steam for an adiabatic steam turbine are as indicated in the figure.

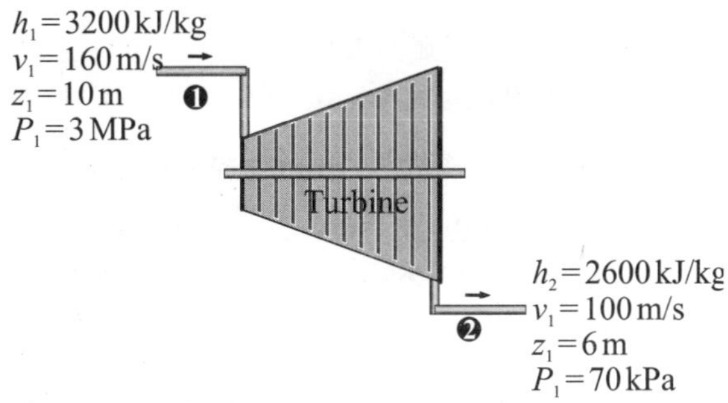

The notation are as usually followed.

Q(a) If mass of steam through the turbine is 20 kg/s, the power output of the turbine (in MW) is

(A) 12.157 (B) 12.941 (C) 168.001 (D) 168.785

Q(b) Assume the above turbine to be part of a simple Rankine cycle. The density of water at the inlet to the pump is 1000 kg/m^3. Ignore kinetic and potential energy effects, the specific work (in kJ/kg) supplied to the pump is

(A) 0.293 (B) 0.351 (C) 2.930 (D) 3.510

GATE 2009

Solution

(a) Applying steady flow energy equation,

$$W_T = m\left(h_1 + \frac{v_1^2}{2} + gz_1\right) - m\left(h_2 + \frac{v_2^2}{2} + gz_2\right)$$

or $$W_T = m(h_1 - h_2) + m\left(+\frac{v_1^2 - v_2^2}{2}\right) + mg(z_1 - z_2)$$

Substituting given data,

$$W_T = 20\times(3200-2600)\times10^3 + 20\left(\frac{160^2 - 100^2}{2}\right) + 20\times9.81\,(10-6)$$

$$W_T = 12.157\ \text{MW}$$

(b) Pump work is

$$W_p = (P_2 - P_1)v = (3\times10^6 - 70\times10^3)\times\frac{1}{1000}$$

or $$W_p = 2970\ \text{J/kg}$$

$$W_p = 2.970\ \text{J/kg}$$

Example 12.24

A heat transformer is a device that transfers a part of the heat, supplied to it at an intermediate temperature, to a high temperature reservoir while rejecting the remaining part to a low temperature heat sink. In such a heat transformer, 100 kJ of heat is supplied at 350 K. The maximum amount of heat in kJ that can be transferred to 400 K, when the rest is rejected to a heat sink at 300 K is

(A) 12.50 (B) 14.29 (C) 33.33 (D) 57.14

GATE 2007

Solution

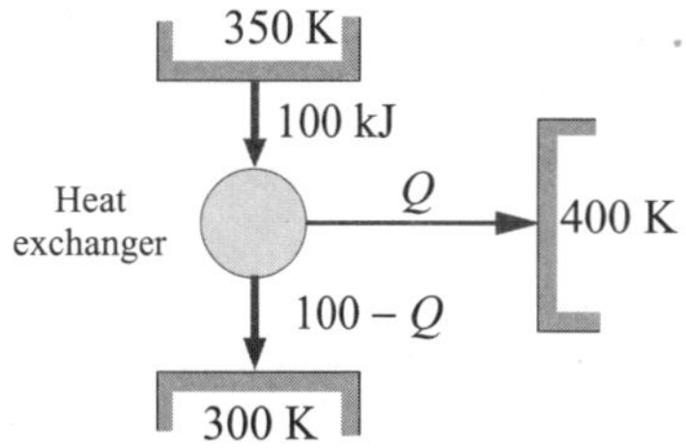

Let Q be the heat supplied at 400 K.

Condition for maximum heat supplied Q; $\Delta S = 0$ [Reversible process]

$$\frac{100}{350} - \frac{Q}{400} - \frac{100-Q}{300} = 0$$

From which

$$Q = 57.14\ \text{kJ}$$

Example 12.25

Common Data Questions

A thermodynamic cycle with an ideal gas as working fluid is shown in the figure.

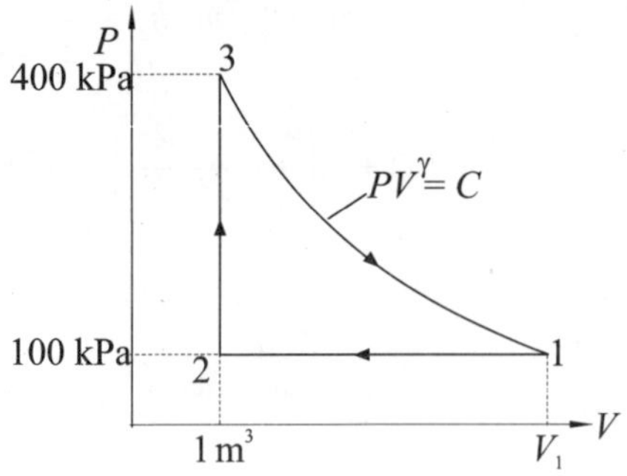

Q(a) The above cycle is represented on T - S plane by

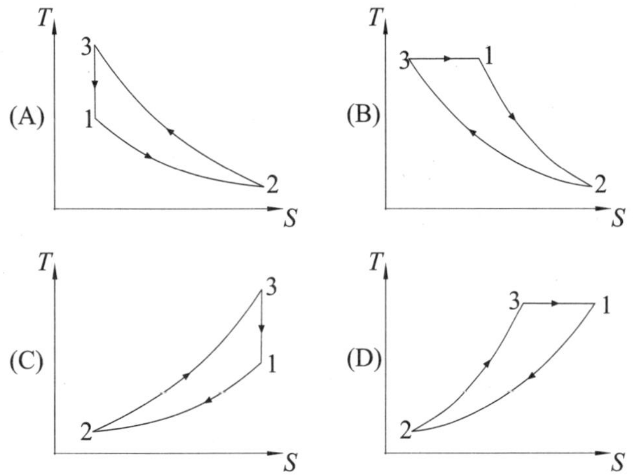

Q(b) If the specific heat of the working fluid is constant and the value of specific heat ratio γ is 1.4, the thermal efficiency (%) of the cycle is

(A) 21 (B) 40.9 (C) 42.6 (D) 59.7

GATE 2007

Solution

(a)

(i) Process 3-1 is isentropic expansion; Temperature decreases and entropy remains constant.

(ii) Process 1-2 is constant pressure heat rejection; Temperature and entropy are decreased.

(iii) Process 2-3 is constant volume heat addition; Temperature and entropy are increased.

Therefore, correct T - S diagram is shown in figure

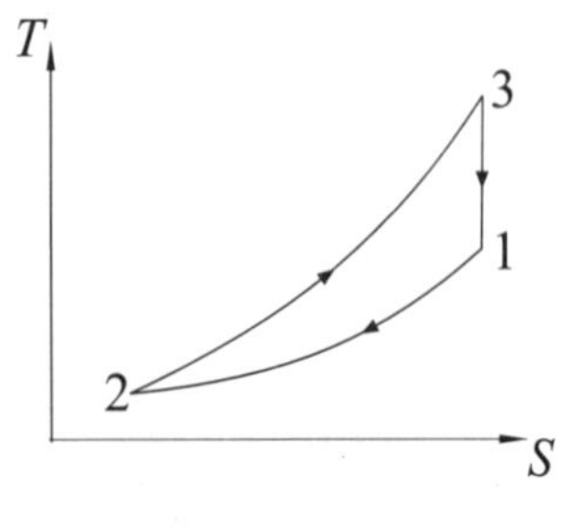

(b) For process 3-1; $P_3V_3^{\gamma} = P_1V_1^{\gamma}$

$$V_1 = V_3\left(\frac{P_3}{P_1}\right)^{\frac{1}{\gamma}} = 1\times\left(\frac{400}{100}\right)^{\frac{1}{1.4}}$$

$$V_1 = 2.69 \text{ m}^3$$

Heat supplied, $Q_s = Q_{2-3} = c_v(T_3 - T_2) = \dfrac{R}{\gamma - 1}(T_3 - T_2)$

or $$Q_s = \frac{(P_3V_3 - P_2V_2)}{\gamma - 1} = \frac{(P_3 - P_2)V_2}{\gamma - 1}$$

Heat rejected, $Q_r = Q_{1-2} = c_P(T_1 - T_2) = \dfrac{\gamma R}{\gamma - 1}(T_1 - T_2)$

or $$Q_r = \frac{\gamma}{\gamma - 1}(P_1V_1 - P_2V_2) = \frac{\gamma(V_1 - V_2)P_1}{\gamma - 1}$$

Therefore, the efficiency of cycle,

$$\eta = 1 - \frac{Q_r}{Q_s} = 1 - \frac{\dfrac{\gamma(V_1 - V_2)P_1}{\gamma - 1}}{\dfrac{(P_3 - P_2)V_2}{\gamma - 1}}$$

or $$\eta = 1 - \frac{\gamma(V_1 - V_2)P_1}{(P_3 - P_2)V_2}$$

or $$\eta = 1 - \frac{1.4\times(2.69 - 1)100\times 10^3}{(400 - 100)\times 1}$$

$$\eta = 21.1\%$$

Example 12.26

Data given below is extracted from steam table

T (°C)	P_{atm} (bar)	Specific volume (m³/kg)		Enthalpy (kJ/kg)	
		Saturated liquid	Saturated vapour	Saturated liquid	Saturated vapour
45	0.09593	0.001010	15.26	188.45	2394.8
342.24	150	0.001658	0.010337	1610.5	2610.5

Specific enthalpy of water in kJ/kg at 150 bar and 45 °C is

(A) 203.60 (B) 200.53 (C) 196.38 (D) 188.45

GATE 2006

Solution

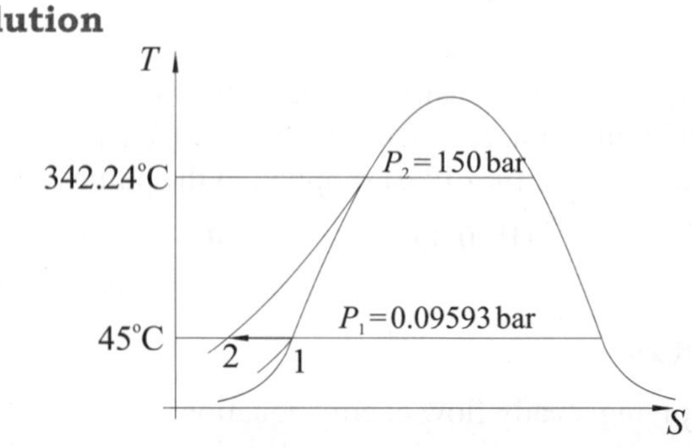

From given steam table,

$$h_1 = 188.45 \text{ kJ/kg}, \ v_1 = 0.001010 \text{ m}^3\text{/kg}$$

Specific enthalpy at point 2, (150 bar and 45°C) is

$$h_2 = h_1 + W_p$$

or $$h_2 = h_1 + (P_2 - P_1)v_1$$

$$h_2 = 188.45 \times 10^3 + (150 - 0.09593) \times 10^5 \times 0.001010 \text{ J}$$

$$h_2 = 203.59 \text{ kJ/kg}$$

Example 12.27

Linked Answer Questions

A football was inflated to a gauge pressure of 1 bar when the ambient temperature was 15 °C. When the game started next day, the air temperature at the stadium was 5 °C.

Assume that the volume of the football remains constant at 2500 cm^3.

Q(a) The amount of heat lost by the air in the football and the gauge pressure of air in the football at the stadium respectively equal

(A) 30.6 J, 1.94 bar (B) 21.8 J, 0.93 bar

(C) 61.1 J, 1.94 bar (D) 43.7 J, 0.93 bar

Q(b) Gauge pressure of air to which the ball must have been originally inflated so that it would equal 1 bar gauge at the stadium is

(A) 2.23 bar (B) 1.94 bar

(C) 1.07 bar (D) 1.00 bar

GATE 2006

Solution

Given that

$P_1 = P_{atm} + P_{gauge} = 1 + 1 = 2$ bar (absolute),
$T_1 = 273 + 15 = 288$ K and $V_1 = V_2 = 2500$ cm^3.

Mass of the air in the football is

$$m = \frac{P_1V_1}{RT_1} = \frac{2 \times 10^5 \times 2500 \times 10^{-6}}{287 \times 288}$$

$$m = 0.006049 \text{ kg}$$

Heat transfer is constant volume process,

$$Q = mc_v\Delta T = 0.006049 \times 0.718 \times 10 \text{ kJ}$$

$$Q = 43.43 \text{ J}$$

Absolute pressure in the football at temperature 5°C is

$$(P_2)_{abs} = P_1 \times \frac{T_2}{T_1} = 2 \times 10^5 \times \left(\frac{5 + 273}{5 + 273}\right)$$

$$(P_2)_{abs} = 1.9305 \text{ bar}$$

Gauge pressure in the football,

$$P_2 = (P_2)_{abs} - P_{atm} = 1.9305 - 1$$

$$P_2 = 0.9305 \text{ bar (gauge)}$$

(b) Initial gauge pressure to get 1 bar gauge pressure (or 2 bar absolute) at the stadium is

$$P_1 = P_2 \times \frac{T_1}{T_2} - P_{atm} \text{ (gauge)}$$

$$P_1 = 2 \times \frac{(273 + 15)}{(273 + 5)} - 1$$

$$P_1 = 1.07 \text{ bar}$$

Example 12.28

A vapour absorption refrigeration system is a heat pump with three thermal reservoirs as shown in figure. A refrigeration effect of 100 W is required at 250 K when the heat source available is at 400 K. Heat rejection occurs at 300 K. The minimum value of heat required (in W) is

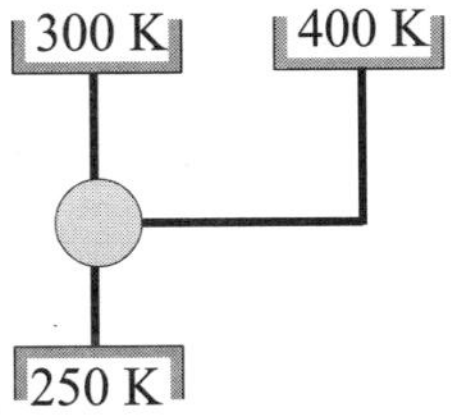

(A) 167 (B) 100 (C) 80 (D) 20

GATE 2005

Solution

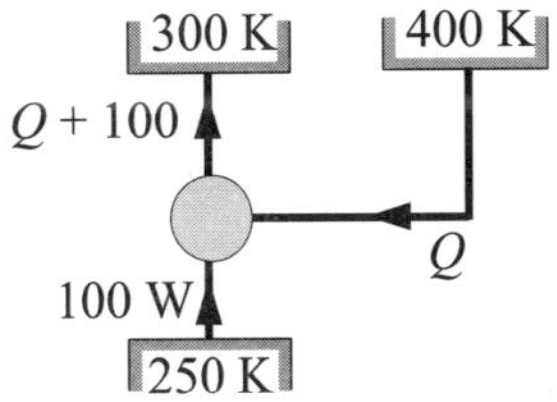

Let Q be the heat required from heat source.

For reversible heat pump; $\Delta S = 0$

$$\frac{100}{250} + \frac{Q}{400} - \frac{Q + 100}{300} = 0$$

From which

$$Q = 80 \text{ W}$$

Example 12.29

A gas contained in a cylinder is compressed, the work required for compression being 5000 kJ. During the process, heat interaction of 2000 kJ causes the surroundings to the heated. The change in internal energy of the gas during the process is

(A) – 7000 kJ (B) – 3000 kJ

(C) + 3000 kJ (D) + 7000 kJ

GATE 2004

Solution

Work required for compression, $W = -5000\,\text{kJ}$

Heat interaction, $Q = -2000\,\text{kJ}$ (Heat rejected)

Using first law of thermodynamics, $Q = \Delta U + W$

Change in internal energy, $\Delta U = Q - W$

$$\Delta U = -2000 - (-5000)$$

$$\Delta U = 3000\ \text{kJ}$$

Example 12.30

A heat engine having an efficiency of 70% is used to drive a refrigerator having a coefficient of performance of 5. The energy absorbed from low temperature reservoir by the refrigerator for each kJ of energy absorbed from high temperature source by the engine is

(A) 0.14 kJ (B) 0.71 kJ (C) 3.5 kJ (D) 7.1 kJ

GATE 2004

Solution

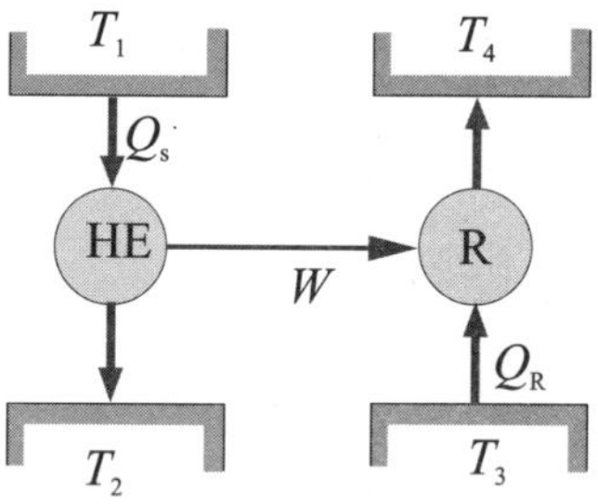

Consider heat engine

Efficiency of engine, $\eta = \dfrac{W}{Q_s}$

$$0.7 = \frac{W}{Q_s} \quad \text{(i)}$$

Consider refrigerator, $\text{COP} = \dfrac{Q_R}{W}$

$$5 = \frac{Q_R}{W} \quad \text{(ii)}$$

From Equations (i) and (ii), we have $5 = \dfrac{Q_R}{0.7Q_S}$

$$\frac{Q_R}{Q_S} = 3.5$$

Example 12.31

A solar collector receiving solar radiation at the rate of $0.6\,\text{kW/m}^2$ transforms it to the internal energy of a fluid at an overall efficiency of 50%. The fluid heated to 350 K is used to run a heat engine which rejects heat at 313 K. If the heat engine is to deliver 2.5 kW power, then minimum area of the solar collector required would be

(A) $8.33\ \text{m}^2$ (B) $16.66\ \text{m}^2$ (C) $39.68\ \text{m}^2$ (D) $79.36\ \text{m}^2$

GATE 2004

Solution

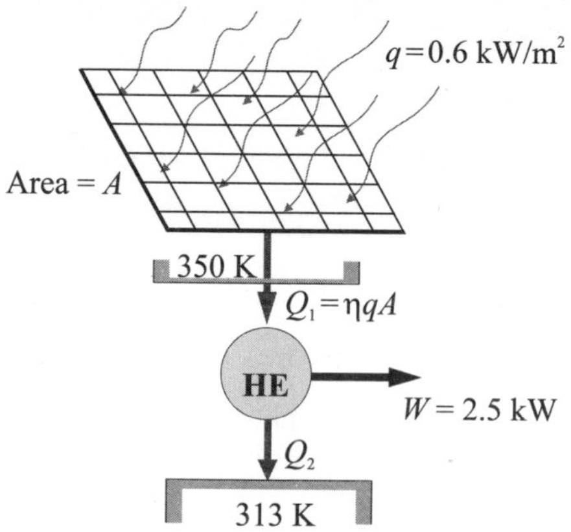

Schematic diagram of solar collector heat engine is shown in figure.

For reversible heat engine, $\dfrac{Q_1}{T_1} = \dfrac{Q_2}{T_2} = \dfrac{W}{T_1 - T_2}$

or $$\frac{qA\eta}{T_1} = \frac{W}{T_1 - T_2}$$

or $$A = \frac{W}{q\eta}\frac{T_1}{T_1 - T_2}$$

or $$A = \frac{2.5\times 10^3}{0.6\times 10^3 \times 0.5}\left(\frac{350}{350-313}\right)$$

$$A = 78.82\,\text{m}^2$$

Example 12.32

A steel billet of 2000 kg mass is to be cooled from 1250 K to 450 K. The heat released during this process is to be used as source of energy. The ambient temperature is 303 K and specific heat of steel is 0.5 kJ/kgK. The available energy (in MJ) of this billet is

(A) 490.44 (B) 30.95 (C) 10.35 (D) 0.10

GATE 2004

Solution

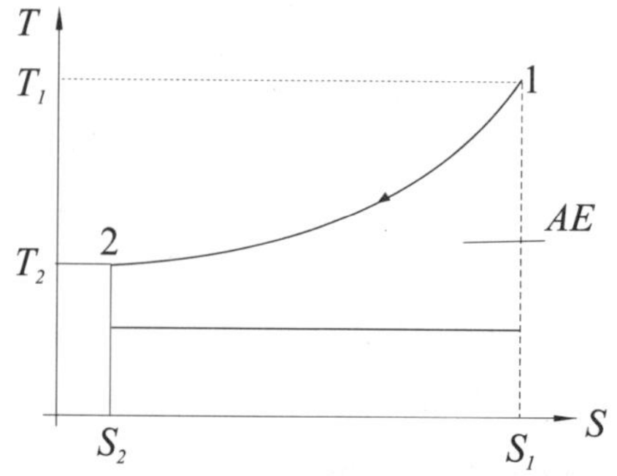

Given that $m = 2000$ kg, $T_1 = 1250$ K, $T_2 = 450$ K, $T_0 = 303$ K and $c = 0.5$ kJ/kgK

Change in entropy of billet, $\Delta S = \int \frac{dQ}{T} = mc\int \frac{dT}{T}$

$$S_1 - S_2 = mc\ln\left(\frac{T_1}{T_2}\right) = 2000 \times 0.5 \ln\left(\frac{1250}{450}\right)$$

$$S_1 - S_2 = 1021.65 \text{ kJ/K}$$

Change in internal energy of billet,

$$Q_1 = mc(T_1 - T_2) = 2000 \times 0.5 \times (1250 - 450)$$

$$Q_1 = 8 \times 10^5 \text{ kJ}$$

Available energy (or availability),

$$AE = Q_1 - T_o(S_1 - S_2)$$

$$AE = 8 \times 10^5 - 303 \times 1021.65$$

$$AE = 490.4 \text{ MJ}$$

Example 12.33

In a gas turbine, hot combustion products with the specific heat $c_p = 0.98$ kJ/kgK, and $c_v = 0.7538$ kJ/kgK enter the turbine at 20 bar, 1500 K and exit at 1 bar. The isentropic efficiency of the turbine is 0.94. The work developed by the turbine per kg of gas flow is

(A) 689.64 kJ/kg (B) 794.66 kJ/kg

(C)1009.72 kJ/kg (D) 1312.00 kJ/kg

GATE 2003

Solution

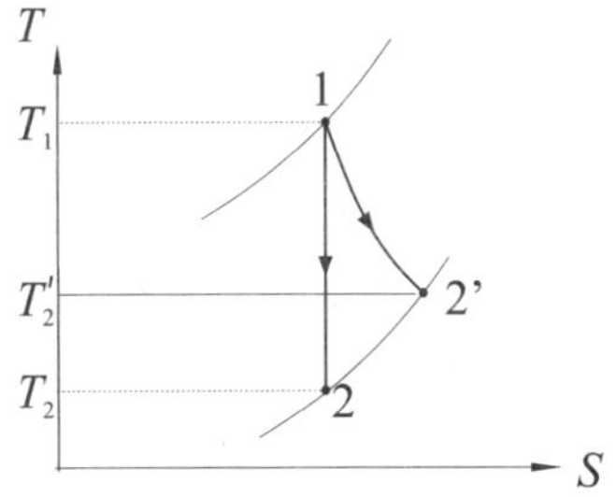

Given that $c_p = 0.98$ kJ/kgK, $c_v = 0.7538$ kJ/kgK, $P_2 = 20$ bar, $P_2 = 1$ bar, $T_1 = 1500$ K and $\eta = 0.94$.

Ratio of specific heats, $\gamma = \frac{c_p}{c_v} = \frac{0.98}{0.7538}$

$$\gamma = 1.30008$$

Temperature after isentropic expansion is

$$T_2 = \frac{T_1}{\left(\frac{P_2}{P_1}\right)^{\frac{\gamma-1}{\gamma}}} = \frac{1500}{\left(\frac{20}{1}\right)^{\frac{1.30008-1}{1.30008}}}$$

$$T_2 = 751.27 \text{ K}$$

Efficiency of turbine, $\eta_T = \frac{T_1 - T_2'}{T_1 - T_2}$

$$0.94 = \frac{1500 - T_2'}{1500 - 751.27}$$

$$T_2' = 796.2 \text{ K}$$

Therefore, turbine work, $W_T = (h_1 - h_2') = c_p(T_1 - T_2')$

$$W_T = 0.98 \times (1500 - 796.2)$$

$$W_T = 689.7 \text{ kJ/kg}$$

Example 12.34

Which of the following statements are TRUE with respect to heat and work?

(i) They are boundary phenomena

(ii) They are exact differentials

(iii) They are path functions

(A) Both (i) and (ii) (B) Both (i) and (iii)

(C) Both (ii) and (iii) (D) Only (iii)

GATE 2016

Solution

Heat and work are path functions and boundary phenomena.

Example 12.35

Propane (C_3H_8) is burned in an oxygen atmosphere with 10% deficit oxygen with respect to the stoichiometric requirement. Assuming no hydrocarbons in the products, the volume percentage of CO in the products is ________.

GATE 2016

Solution

Chemical reaction, $2C_3H_8 + 10O_2 = 8H_2O + 6CO_2$

Chemical reaction at 10% deficit oxygen,

$$2C_3H_8 + 9O_2 = 8H_2O + 4CO_2 + 2CO$$

From which, we get

Volume percentage of CO $= \frac{2}{8+4+2} \times 100$

Volume percentage of CO = 14.28 %

Example 12.36

For water at 25°C, $\frac{dP_s}{dT_s} = 0.189$ kPa/kg (P_s is the saturation pressure in kPa and T_s is the saturation temperature in K) and the specific volume of dry saturated vapour is $43.38\ m^3/kg$. Assume that the specific volume of liquid is negligible in comparison with that of vapour. Using the Clausius-Clapeyron equation, an estimate of the enthalpy of evaporation of water at 25°C (in kJ/kg) is ________.

GATE 2016

Solution

Clausius-Clapeyron equation, $\frac{dP_s}{dT_s} = \frac{h_{fg}}{T_s(V_g - V_f)}$

Substituting given values $\frac{dP_s}{dT_s} = 0.189$ kPa/K,

$T_s = 273 + 25 = 298$ K, $V_g = 43.38\ m^3/kg$ and $V_f = 0$, we get

$$0.189 = \frac{h_{fg}}{298 \times (43.38 - 0)}$$

$$h_{fg} = 2443.248 \text{ kJ/kg}$$

Example 12.37

An ideal gas undergoes a reversible process in which the pressure varies linearly with volume. The conditions at the start (subscript 1) and at the end (subscript 2) of the process with usual notation are: $P_1 = 100$ kPa, $V_1 = 0.2\ m^3$ and $P_2 = 200$ kPa, $V_2 = 0.1\ m^3$ and the gas constant, $R = 0.275$ kJ/kgK. The magnitude of the work required for the process (in kJ) is______.

GATE 2016

Solution

The process is shown in figure.

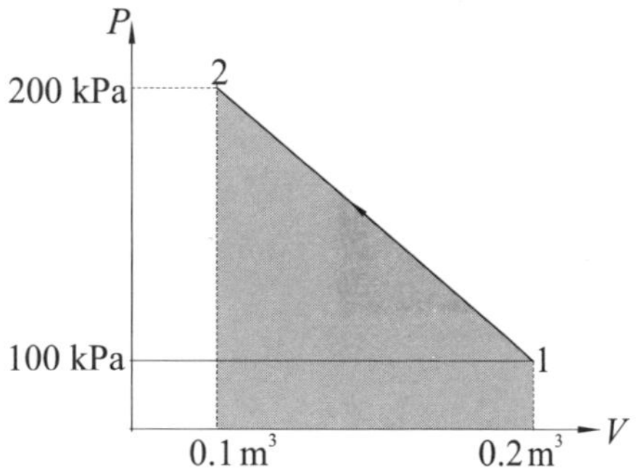

Work required for this process is

$$W = -\text{Area under the line 1-2}$$

$$W = -\frac{1}{2}(200 + 100)(0.2 - 0.1) \text{ kJ}$$

$$W = -15 \text{ kJ}$$

Example 12.38

Heat is removed from a molten metal of mass 2 kg at a constant rate of 10 kW till it is completely solidified. The cooling curve is shown in the figure.

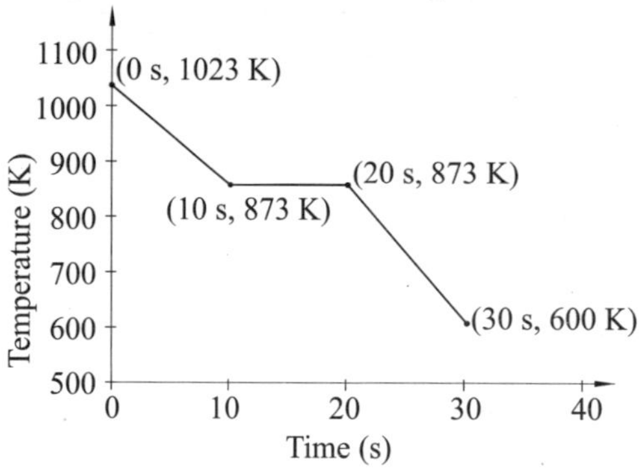

Assuming uniform temperature throughout the volume of the metal during solidification, the latent heat of fusion of the metal (in kJ/kg) is ________.

GATE 2016

Solution

Latent heat of fusion

$$L = \frac{\text{Heat removed at constant temperature (solidification)}}{m}$$

$$L = \frac{Q \times \Delta\tau}{m} = \frac{10 \times (20 - 10)}{2}$$

Latent heat of fusion, $L = 50$ kJ / kg

Example 12.39

The internal energy of an ideal gas is a function of

(A) Temperature and pressure (B) Volume and pressure

(C) Entropy and pressure (D) Temperature only

GATE 2016

Solution

The internal energy of an ideal gas is a function of temperature only.

Example 12.40

A piston-cylinder device initially contains $0.4\ m^3$ of air (to be treated as an ideal gas) at 100 kPa and 80°C. The air is now isothermally compressed to $0.1\ m^3$. The work done during this process is _______ kJ.

(Take the sign convention such that work done on the system is negative)

GATE 2016

Solution

The work done during isothermal compression is

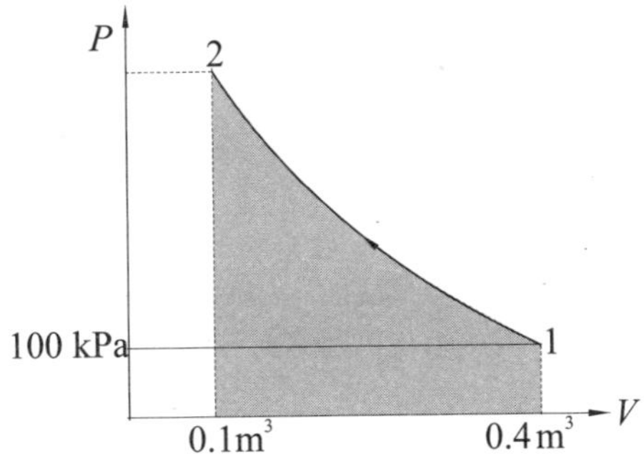

$$W = -P_1 V_1 \ln\left(\frac{V_2}{V_1}\right)$$

$$W = -100 \times 0.4 \ln\left(\frac{0.4}{0.1}\right)$$

$$W = -55.45 \text{ kJ}$$

Example 12.41

A reversible cycle receives 40 kJ of heat from one heat source at a temperature of 127°C and 37 kJ from another heat source at 97°C. The heat rejected (in kJ) to the heat sink at 47°C is________.

GATE 2016

Solution

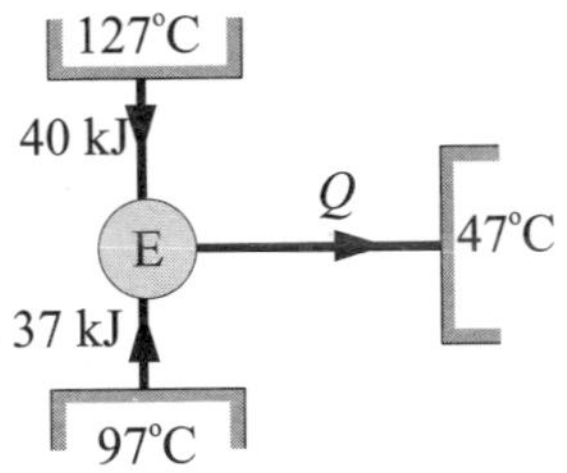

For reversible engine,

$$\sum \frac{Q}{T} = 0$$

or $$\frac{40}{(273+127)} + \frac{37}{(273+97)} - \frac{Q}{(273+47)} = 0$$

or $$\frac{40}{400} + \frac{37}{370} - \frac{Q}{320} = 0$$

$$Q = 64 \text{ kJ}$$

Example 12.42

Steam at an initial enthalpy of 100 kJ/kg and inlet velocity of 100 m/s, enters an insulated horizontal nozzle. It leaves the nozzle at 200 m/s. The exit enthalpy (in kJ/kg) is________.

GATE 2016

Solution

Using steady flow energy equation for nozzle,

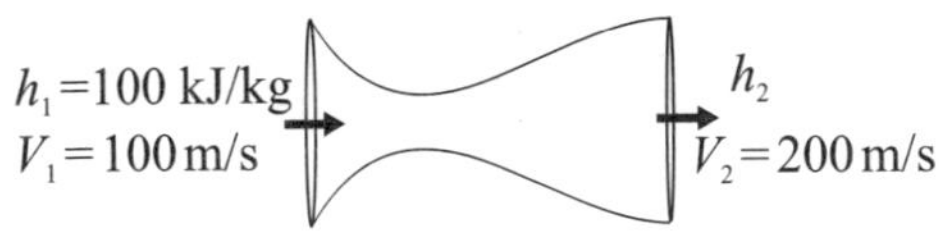

$$h_1 + \frac{V_1^2}{2} = h_2 + \frac{V_2^2}{2}$$

Substituting given values $h_1 = 100$ kJ/kg, $V_1 = 100$ m/s and $V_2 = 200$ m/s, we have

$$100 \times 10^3 + \frac{100^2}{2} = h_2 + \frac{200^2}{2}$$

From which, we get

$$h_2 = 85 \text{ kJ/kg}$$

Example 12.43

The molar specific heat at constant volume of an ideal gas is equal to 2.5 times the universal gas constant (8.314 J/mol ·K). When the temperature increases by 100 K, the change in molar specific enthalpy is ____ J/mol.

GATE 2017

Solution

Change in molar specific enthalpy $\Delta H = c_p \Delta T$

$$\Delta H = (R + c_v)\Delta T = (R + 2.5R)\Delta T$$

$$\Delta H = 3.5R\Delta T = 3.5 \times 8.314 \times 100$$

$$\Delta H = 2909.9 \text{ J/mole}$$

Example 12.44

A heat pump absorbs 10 kW of heat from outside environment at 250 K while absorbing 15 kW of work. It delivers the heat to a room that must be kept warm at 300 K. The Coefficient of Performance (COP) of the heat pump is______.

GATE 2017

Solution

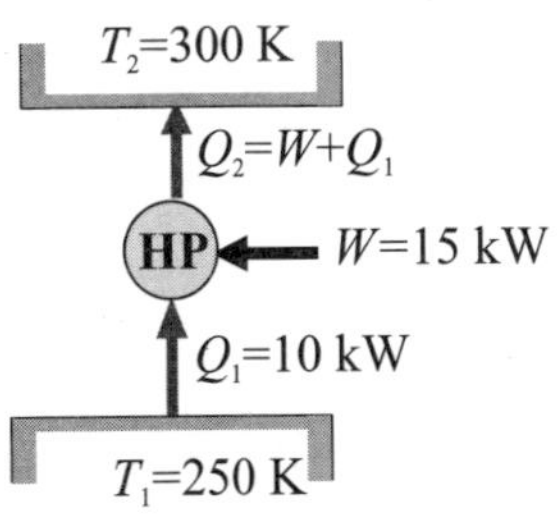

$$\text{COP of the heat pump} = \frac{Q_2}{W} = \frac{W + Q_1}{W} = \frac{15+10}{15} = 1.66$$

$$\text{COP of the heat pump} = 1.66$$

Example 12.45

One kg of an ideal gas (gas constant, R = 400 J/kg.K;

specific heat at constant volume, c_v=1000 J/kg.K) at 1 bar, and 300 K is contained in a sealed rigid cylinder. During an adiabatic process, 100 kJ of work is done on the system by a stirrer. The increase in entropy of the system is____J/K.

GATE 2017

Solution

Given: $m = 1\text{kg}, R = 400\,\text{J/kgK}, c_v = 1000\,\text{J/kgK}, P_1 = 1\,\text{bar}$, and $T_1 = 300\,\text{K}$.

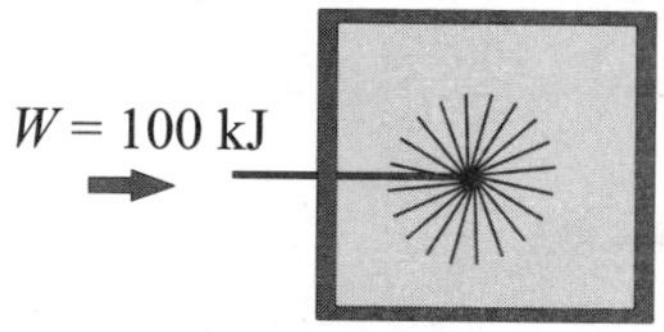

Applying first law of thermodynamics for sealed rigid cylinder)

$$Q = 0 = \Delta u + W$$

or $$mc_v(T_2 - T_1) + W = 0$$

$$1\times 1000(T_2 - 300) - 100\times 10^3 = 0$$

$$T_2 = 400\,\text{K}$$

Now $$TdS = du + PdV$$

$$dS = mc_v\frac{dT}{T} + \frac{P}{T}dV$$

or $$\Delta S = mc_v\int_{T_1}^{T_2}\frac{dT}{T} + 0 \quad [\text{Constant volume } dV = 0]$$

or $$\Delta S = mc_v \ln\left(\frac{T_2}{T_1}\right) = 1\times 1000\ln\left(\frac{400}{300}\right)$$

Change in entropy $\Delta S = 287.682\,\text{J/K}$

Example 12.46

Air contains 79% N_2 and 21% O_2 on a molar basis. Methane (CH_4) is burned with 50% excess air than required stoichiometrically. Assuming complete combustion of methane, the molar percentage of N_2 in the products is _________.

GATE 2017

Solution

Stoichiometric reaction

$$CH_4 + 2\left(O_2 + \frac{79}{21}N_2\right) \rightarrow 2H_2O + CO_2 + 2\times\frac{79}{21}N_2$$

50% excess air

$$CH_4 + 3\left(O_2 + \frac{79}{21}N_2\right) \rightarrow 2H_2O + CO_2 + 3\times\frac{79}{21}N_2 + O_2$$

$$\text{Percentage } N_2 = \frac{3\times\frac{79}{21}}{2+1+3+1}\times 100 = 73.83\,\%$$

Percentage $N_2 = 73.83\,\%$

Example 12.47

A mass m of a perfect gas at pressure p_1 and volume V_1 undergoes an isothermal process. The final pressure is p_2 and volume is V_2. The work done on the system is considered positive. If R is the gas constant and T is the temperature, then the work done in the process is

(A) $p_1V_1 \ln\frac{V_2}{V_1}$ (B) $-p_1V_1 \ln\frac{p_1}{p_2}$

(C) $RT \ln\frac{V_2}{V_1}$ (D) $-mRT \ln\frac{p_2}{p_1}$

GATE 2017

Solution

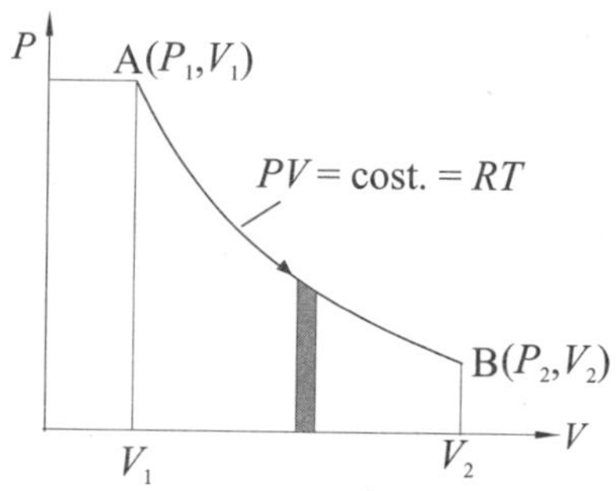

Work done W = Area under the curve AB

$$W = \int_{V_1}^{V_2} pdV = p_1V_1 \ln\left(\frac{V_2}{V_1}\right) = mRT \ln\left(\frac{V_2}{V_1}\right)$$

$$= p_1V_1 \ln\left(\frac{P_1}{P_2}\right) = mRT \ln\left(\frac{P_1}{P_2}\right); \quad [\text{For isothermal process}]$$

Given: The work done on the system is consider positive.

Workdone in the process $W = -p_1V_1 \ln\left(\frac{P_1}{P_2}\right)$

Example 12.48

A calorically perfect gas (specific heat at constant pressure 1000 J/kg.K) enters and leaves a gas turbine with the same velocity. The temperatures of the gas at turbine entry and exit are 1100 K and 400 K. respectively. The power produced is 4.6 MW and heat escapes at the rate of 300 kJ/s through the turbine casing. The mass flow rate of the gas (in kg/s) through the turbine is.

(A) 6.14 (B) 7.00 (C) 7.50 (D) 8.00

GATE 2017

Solution

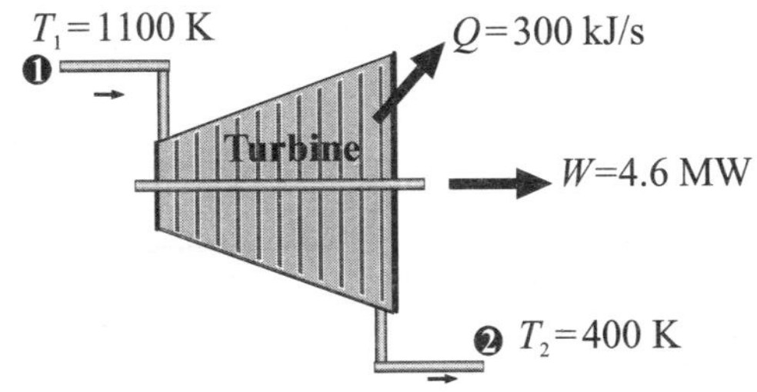

Using the steady flow energy equation

$$h_1 + \frac{v_1^2}{2} + gz_1 + \frac{Q}{\dot{m}} = h_2 + \frac{v_2^2}{2} + gz_2 + \frac{W}{\dot{m}}$$

$$c_p T_1 + \frac{v_1^2}{2} + gz_1 + \frac{Q}{\dot{m}} = c_p T_2 + \frac{v_2^2}{2} + gz_2 + \frac{W}{\dot{m}}$$

$$1000 \times 1100 + 0 + 0 + \frac{300 \times 10^3}{\dot{m}}$$

$$= 1000 \times 400 + 0 + 0 + \frac{4.6 \times 10^6}{\dot{m}}$$

$$\dot{m} = 7 \text{ kg/s}$$

Example 12.49

One kg of an ideal gas (gas constant $R = 287$ J/kg.K) undergoes an irreversible process from state-1 (1 bar, 300 K) to state-2 (2 bar, 300 K). The change in specific entropy $(s_2 - s_1)$ of the gas (in J/kg. K) in the process is_______.

GATE 2017

Solution

Given: $m = 1$ kg, $R = 287$ J/kgK, $p_1 = 1$ bar, $T_1 = 300$ K, $p_2 = 2$ bar, $T_2 = 300$ K.

Thermodynamic relation $TdS = dh - vdp$

$$dS = c_p \frac{dT}{T} - \frac{v}{T} dp \Rightarrow S_2 - S_1 = c_p \int_{T_1}^{T_2} \frac{dT}{T} - R \int_{p_1}^{p_2} \frac{dp}{p}$$

$$S_2 - S_1 = c_p \ln\left(\frac{T_2}{T_1}\right) - R \ln\left(\frac{p_2}{p_1}\right)$$

$$S_2 - S_1 = 0 - 287 \ln\left(\frac{2}{2}\right) = -198.93$$

$$S_2 - S_1 = -198.93 \text{ J/kgK}$$

Example 12.50

The volume and temperature of air (assumed to be an ideal gas) in a closed vessel is 2.87 m^3 and 300 K, respectively. The gauge pressure indicated by a manometer fitted to the wall of the vessel is 0.5 bar. If the gas constant of air is $R = 287$ J/kg.K and the atmospheric pressure is 1 bar, the mass of air (in kg) in the vessel is

(A) 1.67 (B) 3.33 (C) 5.00 (D) 6.66

GATE 2017

Solution

P_{atm} = 1 bar

V = 2.87 m^3
T = 300 K
P_{gauge} = 0.5 bar
R = 287 J/kgK

Absolute pressure $p = p_{atm} + p_{gauge}$

$$pV = mRT$$

$$m = \frac{pV}{RT} = \frac{1.5 \times 10^5 \times 2.87}{287 \times 300}$$

$$m = 5 \text{ kg}$$

Example 12.51

Which one of the following statements is correct for a superheated vapour?

(A) Its pressure is less than the saturation pressure at a given temperature.

(B) Its temperature is less than the saturation temperature at a given pressure.

(C) Its volume is less than the volume of the saturated vapour at a given temperature.

(D) Its enthalpy is less than the enthalpy of the saturated vapour at a given pressure.

GATE 2018

Solution

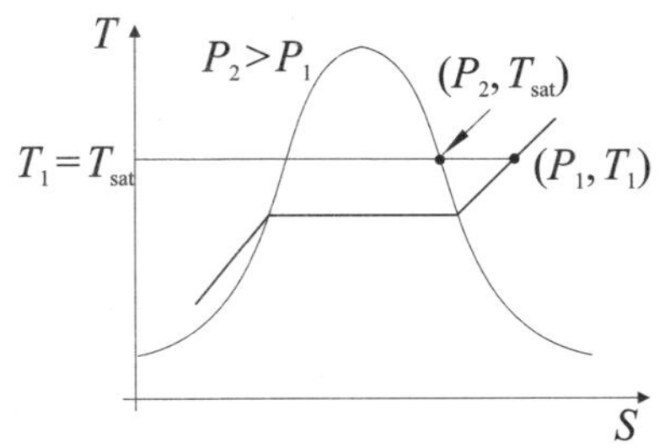

Superheated vapour ⇒ Its pressure is less than the saturation pressure at a given temperature.

Example 12.51

An ideal gas undergoes a process from state 1 ($T_1 = 300$ K, $p_1 = 100$ kPa) to state 2 ($T_2 = 600$ K, $p_2 = 500$ kPa). The specific heats of the ideal are : $c_p = 1$ kJ/kg-K and $c_v = 0.7$ kJ/kg-K. The change in specific entropy of the ideal gas from state 1 to state 2 (in kJ/kg-K) is ___________.

GATE 2018

Solution

Change in entropy, $s_2 - s_1 = c_p \ln\left(\frac{T_2}{T_1}\right) - R \ln\left(\frac{p_2}{p_1}\right)$

$$s_2 - s_1 = c_p \ln\left(\frac{T_2}{T_1}\right) - (c_p - c_v)\ln\left(\frac{p_2}{p_1}\right)$$

$$s_2 - s_1 = 1\times \ln\left(\frac{600}{300}\right) - (1-0.7)\ln\left(\frac{500}{100}\right)$$

$$s_2 - s_1 = 0.21\,\text{kJ/kg.K}$$

Example 12.52

A tank of volume 0.05 m^3 contains a mixture of saturated water and saturated steam at 200 °C. The mass of the liquid present is 8 kg. The entropy (in kJ/kg K) of the mixture is ________.

Property data for saturated steam and water are:

At 200 °C, $p_{sat} = 1.5538$ MPa

$v_f = 0.001157\ \text{m}^3/\text{kg}$, $v_g = 0.12736\ \text{m}^3/\text{kg}$

$s_{fg} = 4.1014$ kJ/kg K, $s_f = 2.3309$ kJ/kg K

GATE 2018

Solution

Let V_l and V_g be the volume of water and steam at 200 °C respectively.

$$V = V_l + V_g \Rightarrow 0.05 = 8\times 0.001157 + V_g$$

$$V_g = 0.0474\ \text{m}^3$$

Mass of steam, $m_g = \dfrac{V_g}{v_g} = \dfrac{0.0474}{0.12736} = 0.3198$ kg

Dryness fraction, $x = \dfrac{m_g}{m_g + m_l} = \dfrac{0.3198}{0.3198+8}$

$$x = 0.0384$$

Specific entropy of mixture, $s = s_f + x\, s_{fg}$

$$s = 2.3309 + 0.0384\times 4.1014$$

$$s = 2.4884\ \text{kJ/kgK}$$

Example 12.53

Steam flows through a nozzle at a mass flow rate of $\dot m = 0.1$ kg/s with a heat loss of 5 kW. The enthalpies at inlet and exit are 2500 kJ/kg and 2350 kJ/kg, respectively. Assuming negligible velocity at inlet ($C_1 = 0$), the velocity (C_2) of steam (in m/s) at the nozzle exit is ________.

GATE 2018

Solution

Applying steady flow energy equation.

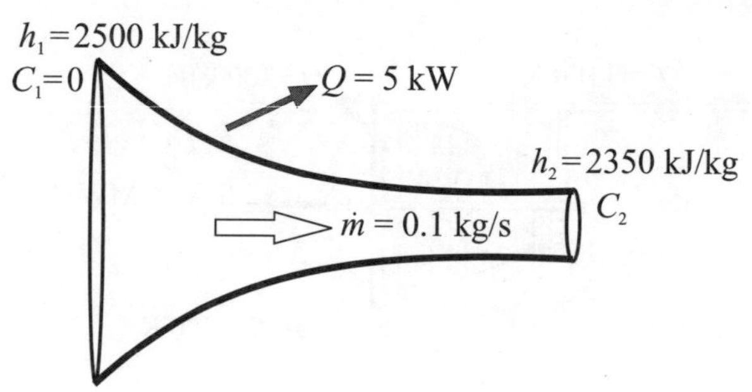

$$\dot m\left(h_1 + \frac{C_1^2}{2} + gz_1\right) + Q = \dot m\left(h_2 + \frac{C_2^2}{2} + gz_2\right) + W$$

$$\dot m h_1 + Q = \dot m h_2 + \dot m\frac{C_2^2}{2}$$

$$C_2 = \sqrt{2(h_1 - h_2) + 2\frac{Q}{\dot m}}$$

Substituting given values $\dot m = 0.1$ kg/s, $Q = 5$ kW, $h_1 = 2500$ kJ/kg, $h_2 = 2350$ kJ/kg and $C_1 \approx 0$.

$$C_2 = \sqrt{\left[2(2500-2350) + 2\times\frac{5}{0.1}\right]\times 10^3}$$

$$C_2 = 447.213\ \text{m/s}$$

Example 12.54

For an ideal gas with constant properties undergoing a quasi-static process, which one of the following represents the change of entropy (Δs) from state 1 to 2?

(A) $\Delta s = C_p \ln\left(\frac{T_2}{T_1}\right) - R\ln\left(\frac{P_2}{P_1}\right)$

(B) $\Delta s = C_V \ln\left(\frac{T_2}{T_1}\right) - C_p\ln\left(\frac{V_2}{V_1}\right)$

(C) $\Delta s = C_p \ln\left(\frac{T_2}{T_1}\right) - C_v\ln\left(\frac{P_2}{P_1}\right)$

(D) $\Delta s = C_v \ln\left(\frac{T_2}{T_1}\right) + R\ln\left(\frac{V_1}{V_2}\right)$

GATE 2018

Solution

Change of entropy, $ds = \dfrac{dQ}{T} = \dfrac{dh - vdP}{T}$

or $$ds = \frac{dh}{T} - v\frac{dP}{T}$$

or $$\Delta s = \int_{T_1}^{T_2}\frac{dh}{T} - \int_{P_1}^{P_2}\frac{v}{T}dP$$

or $$\Delta s = C_p \int_{T_1}^{T_2} \frac{dT}{T} - R \int_{P_1}^{P_2} \frac{dP}{P}$$

$$\Delta s = C_p \ln\left(\frac{T_2}{T_1}\right) - R \ln\left(\frac{P_2}{P_1}\right)$$

Example 12.55

An engine operates on the reversible cycle as shown in the figure. The work output from the engine (in kJ/cycle) is_____.

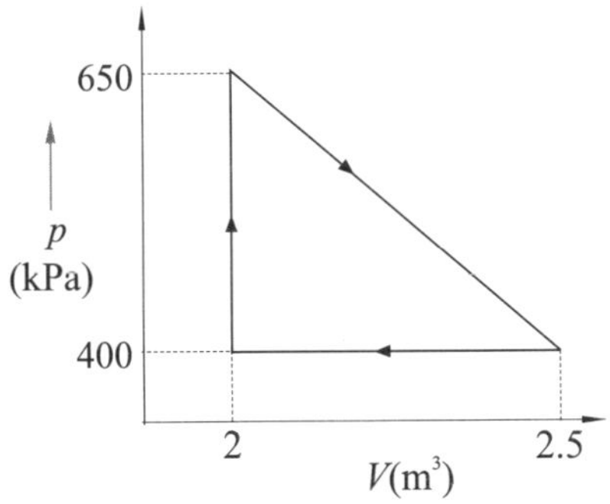

GATE 2018

Solution

Work output = Area enclosed of $p - V$ diagram

Work output $W = \frac{1}{2}(2.5-2)(650-400)$

$$W = 62.5 \text{ kJ/cycle}$$

Example 12.56

Air is held inside a non-insulated cylinder using a piston (mass $M = 25$ kg and area $A = 100\text{ cm}^2$) and stoppers (of negligible area), as shown in the figure. The initial pressure P_i and temperature T_i of air inside the cylinder are 200 kPa and 400 °C, respectively. The ambient pressure P_∞ and temperature T_∞ are 100 kPa and 27 °C, respectively. The temperature of the air inside the cylinder (°C) at which the piston will begin to move is _________.

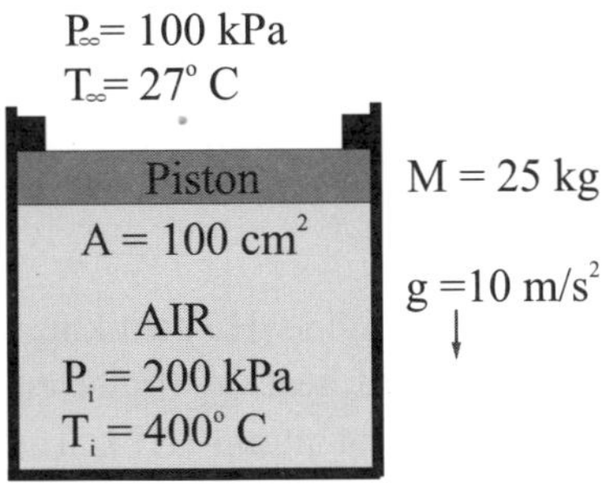

GATE 2018

Solution

Figure shows the free body diagram of piston at which piston is about to move.

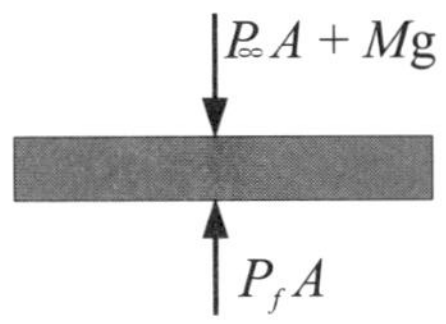

$$p_\infty A + Mg = p_f A$$

$$p_f = p_\infty + \frac{Mg}{A} = 100 \times 10^3 + \frac{25 \times 9.81}{100/100^2} \text{ Pa}$$

$$p_f = 124.5 \text{ kPa}$$

Mass in two state is conserved, $m_i = m_f$

$$\frac{p_i V_i}{R T_i} = \frac{p_f V_f}{R T_f} \qquad [V_i = V_f]$$

$$T_f = \frac{p_f}{p_i} T_i = \frac{124.5}{200} \times 673$$

$$T_f = 146.026 °\text{C}$$

Example 12.57

During a non-flow thermodynamic process (1-2) executed by a perfect gas, the heat interaction is equal to the work interaction ($Q_{1-2} = W_{1-2}$) when the process is

(A) Isentropic (B) Polytropic

(C) Isothermal (D) Adiabatic

GATE 2019

Solution

First law of thermodynamics for process 1-2;

$$Q_{1-2} = \Delta U + W_{1-2}$$

$$Q_{1-2} = W_{1-2} \qquad \text{when } \Delta U = 0 \Rightarrow T_1 = T_2 \text{(isothermal)}$$

Process 1-2 is isothermal.

Example 12.58

Air of mass 1 kg, initially at 300 K and 10 bar, is allowed to expand isothermally till it reaches a pressure of 1 bar. Assuming air as an ideal gas with gas constant of 0.287 kJ/kg.K, The change in entropy of air (in kJ/kg.K, round off to two decimal places) is ________.

GATE 2019

Solution

Entropy change,

$$\Delta S = \int ds = \int \frac{dQ}{T} = \int \frac{dh - VdP}{T}$$

or $$\Delta S = m\left(c_p \ln\frac{T_2}{T_1} - R\ln\frac{P_2}{P_1}\right)$$

Substituting $m = 1$ kg/s, $T_1 = T_2 = 300$ K, $P_1 = 10$ bar, $P_2 = 1$ bar and $R = 0.287$ kJ/kg.K.

$$\Delta S = 1\times\left(c_p \ln\frac{300}{300} - 0.287\ln\frac{1}{10}\right)$$

$$\Delta S = 0.66 \text{ kJ/kg.K}$$

Example 12.59

A gas is heated in a duct as it flows over a resistance heater. Consider a 101 kW electric heating system. The gas enters the heating section of the duct at 100 kPa and 27 °C with a volume flow rate of 15 m^3/s. If heat is lost from the gas in the duct to the surroundings at a rate of 51 kW, the exit temperature of the gas is

(Assume constant pressure, ideal gas, negligible change in kinetic and potential energies and constant specific heat; $C_p = 1$ kJ/kg.K; $R = 0.5$ kJ/kg.K)

(A) 32 °C (B) 37 °C (C) 53 °C (D) 76 °C

GATE 2019

Solution

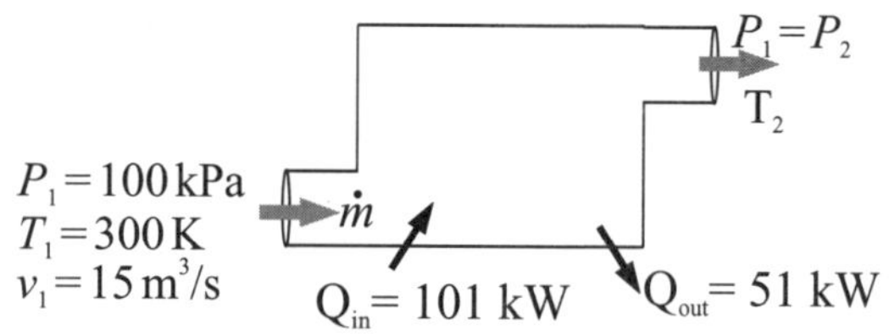

Mass flow rate $m = \dfrac{P_1 v_1}{RT_1} = \dfrac{100\times 15}{0.5\times 300} = 10$ kg/s

Applying steady flow energy equation

$$\dot{m}h_1 + Q_{in} - Q_{out} = \dot{m}h_2$$

or $$\dot{m}c_pT_1 + Q_{in} - Q_{out} = \dot{m}c_pT_2$$

$$10\times1\times300 + 101 - 51 = 10\times1\times T_2$$

$$T_2 = 305 \text{ K}$$

$$T_2 = 32 \text{°C}$$

Example 12.60

If one mole of H_2 gas occupies a rigid container with a capacity of 1000 litres and the temperature is raised from 27 °C to 37 °C, the change in pressure of the contained gas (round off to two decimal places), assuming ideal gas behavior, is _____ Pa. ($R = 8.314$ J/mole.K)

GATE 2019

Solution

$n = 1$ mole
$V_1 = 1.0$ m^3
$T_1 = 300$ K $T_2 = 310$ K

Given: $V_1 = V_2 = 1.0\,\text{m}^3, T_1 = 273 + 27 = 300\,\text{K}, T_2 = 310\,\text{K}$, $n = 1$ mole and $\overline{R} = 8.314$ J/mole.K.

$$P_1 = \frac{n\overline{R}T_1}{V_1} = \frac{1\times\overline{R}\times300}{1} = 300\overline{R}$$

Using equation of state $\dfrac{P_1V_1}{T_1} = \dfrac{P_2V_2}{T_2} \Rightarrow \dfrac{300\overline{R}}{300} = \dfrac{P_2}{310}$

$$P_2 = 310\overline{R}$$

Change in pressure; $\Delta P = P_2 - P_1 = 310\overline{R} - 300\overline{R}$

$$\Delta P = 10\times8.314 = 83.14$$

$$\Delta P = 83.14 \text{ Pa}$$

Example 12.61

For a simple compressible system, v, s, p and T are specific volume, specific entropy, pressure and temperature, respectively. As per Maxwell's relations, $\left(\dfrac{\partial v}{\partial s}\right)_p$ is equal to

(A) $\left(\dfrac{\partial s}{\partial T}\right)_p$ (B) $\left(\dfrac{\partial p}{\partial v}\right)_T$

(C) $-\left(\dfrac{\partial T}{\partial v}\right)_p$ (D) $\left(\dfrac{\partial T}{\partial p}\right)_s$

GATE 2019

Solution

Maxwell's relations,

$$\left(\frac{\partial v}{\partial s}\right)_p = \left(\frac{\partial T}{\partial p}\right)_s$$

Example 12.62

The figure shows a heat engine (HE) working between two reservoirs. The amount of heat (Q_2) rejected by the heat engine is drawn by a heat pump (HP). The heat pump receives the entire work output (W) of the heat engine. If temperature, $T_1 > T_3 > T_2$, then the relation between the efficiency (η) of the heat engine and the coefficient of performance (COP) of the heat pump is

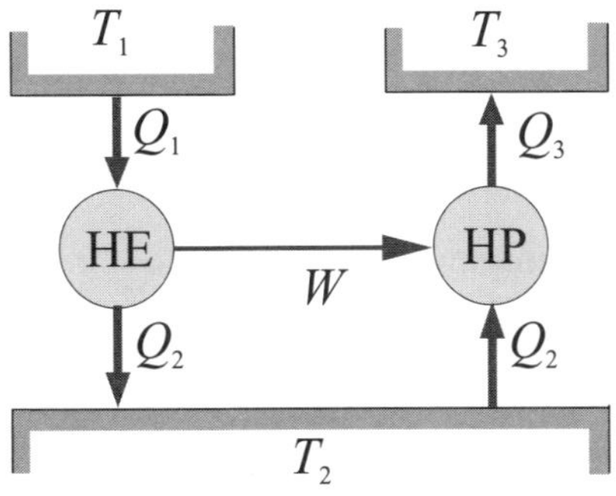

(A) $\text{COP} = \eta$ (B) $\text{COP} = 1 + \eta$

(C) $\text{COP} = \eta^{-1}$ (D) $\text{COP} = \eta^{-1} - 1$

GATE 2019

Solution

Coefficient of performance of Heat pump,

$$COP = \frac{Q_3}{W}$$

Substituting $Q_3 = W + Q_2$;

$$COP = \frac{W + Q_2}{W} \quad \text{(i)}$$

Efficiency of Heat engine,

$$\eta = \frac{W}{Q_1}$$

Substituting $Q_1 = W + Q_2$;

$$\eta = \frac{W}{W + Q_2} \quad \text{(ii)}$$

From Equations (i) and (ii), we have

$$COP \times \eta = 1$$

$$COP = \eta^{-1}$$

Example 12.63

Water flowing at the rate of 1 kg/s through a system is heated using an electric heater such that the specific enthalpy of the water increses by 2.50 kJ/kg and the specific entropy increases by 0.007 kJ/kg.K. The power input to the electric heater is 2.50 kW. There is no other work or heat interaction between the system and the surroundings. Assuming an ambient temperature of 300 K, the irreversibility rate of the system is ________kW (round off to two decimal places).

GATE 2019

Solution

Given: $m = 1$ kg/s, $h_2 - h_1 = 2.5$ kJ/kg, $s_2 - s_1 = 0.007$ kJ/kg.K and $T_o = 300$ K.

Irreversibility $I = mT_o(\Delta s)$

$$I = 1 \times 300 \times 0.007$$

$$I = 2.1\,\text{kW}$$

12.3 PRACTICE PAPER

Time: 3 hours Max. Marks: 100

Q.1 to Q.30 carry one mark each

Q.1 to Q.20 Multiple Choice Questions

Q.1 The thermal efficiency of a reversible heat engine operating between two thermal reservoirs is η_{max}. The coefficient of performance of a reversible refrigeration cycle operating between the same two reservoirs is

(A) $\left(\frac{1}{\eta_{max}}\right) - 1$ (B) $\left(\frac{1}{\eta_{max}}\right) + 1$

(C) $\left(\frac{1}{\eta_{max}}\right)$ (D) $1 - \left(\frac{1}{\eta_{max}}\right)$

Q.2 An air standard Otto cycle has the following shape on a thermodynamic property plane.

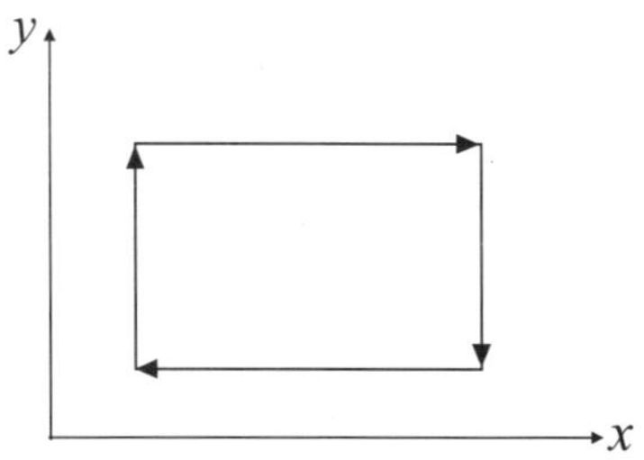

The x and y coordinates, respectively are:

(A) V and P (B) S and V

(C) V and T (D) S and P

Q.3 For an ideal gas as a working fluid for a given heat input Q, the process that gives the maximum work among the following four processes is:

(A) Isothermal (B) Constant volume

(C) Constant pressure (D) Isentropic

Q.4 Air enters an insulated diffuser operating at steady state with a pressure of 0.7 bar, a temperature of 57°C and a velocity of 200 m/s. The inlet area is 0.4 m^2. At the exit, the pressure is 1 bar and the area is 0.6 m^2. Potential energy changes can be neglected. Assume ideal gas behaviour for air. The mass flow rate of air entering the diffuser in kg/s is

(A) 59.1 (B) 72.3 (C) 44.8 (D) 36.2

Q.5 In a cyclic heat engine operating between a source temperature of 600°C and a sink temperature of 20°C, the least rate of heat rejection per kW net output of the engine is

(A) 0.460 kW (B) 0.505 kW

(C) 0.588 kW (D) 0.650 kW

Q.6 Consider the following thermodynamics relations:

1. $Tds = du + PdV$
2. $Tds = du - PdV$
3. $Tds = dh + VdP$
4. $Tds = dh - VdP$

Which of these thermodynamic relations are correct?

(A) 1 and 3 (B) 1 and 4

(C) 2 and 3 (D) 2 and 4

Q.7 When a system is taken from state A to state B along the path A-C-B, 180 kJ of heat flows into the system and it does 130 kJ of work. (see figure) How much heat will flow into the system along the path A-D-B if the work done by it along the path is 40 kJ.

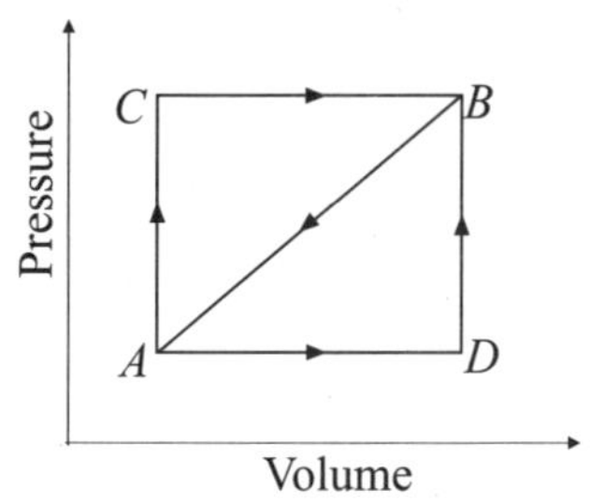

(A) 40 kJ (B) 60 kJ (C) 90 kJ (D) 135 kJ

Q.8 Consider an engine executing a reversible cycle such that it has heat interaction with three reservoirs and delivering work as shown in figure. The value of heat Q_1 and W respectively are:

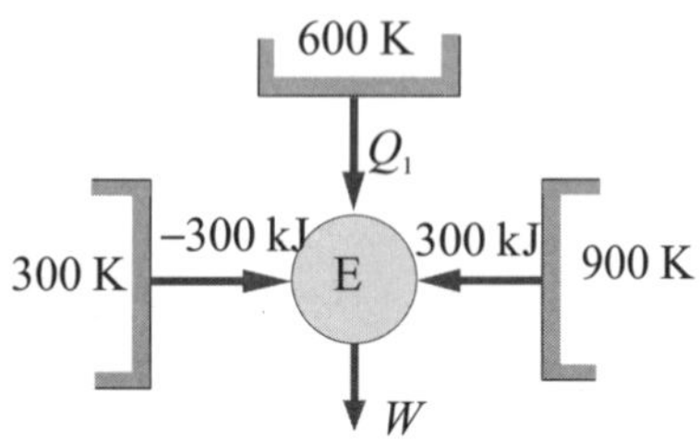

(A) 300 kJ, 300 kJ (B) 400 kJ, 400 kJ

(C) 500 kJ, 500 kJ (D) 350 kJ, 350 kJ

Q.9 When ice melts at one atmosphere pressure and 0°C, which of the following is true?

(A) Change in enthalpy is zero

(B) Change in interval energy is zero

(C) Change in entropy is zero

(D) Change in free energy is zero

Q.10 The coefficient of performance (COP) of a Carnot refrigerator is 5. If the refrigerator, operating between the same two thermal reservoirs, is used as a Carnot heat pump, the COP of the heat pump will be

(A) 4 (B) 5 (C) 6 (D) 8

Q.11 When a closed system containing ideal gas undergoes reversible isothermal compression, its entropy

(A) Always increases (B) Always decreases

(C) May increase or decrease (D) Remains constant

Q.12 A carnot heat engine is operated between two temperatures T_1 and T_2 ($T_1 > T_2$ and T in kelvin). The efficiency of the engine can be increased by

(A) Decreasing T_2 at constant T_1

(B) Decreasing both T_1 and T_2

(C) Increasing both T_1 and T_2

(D) None of these

Q.13 The efficiency of a reversible cyclic process undergone by a substance as shown in the given diagram is

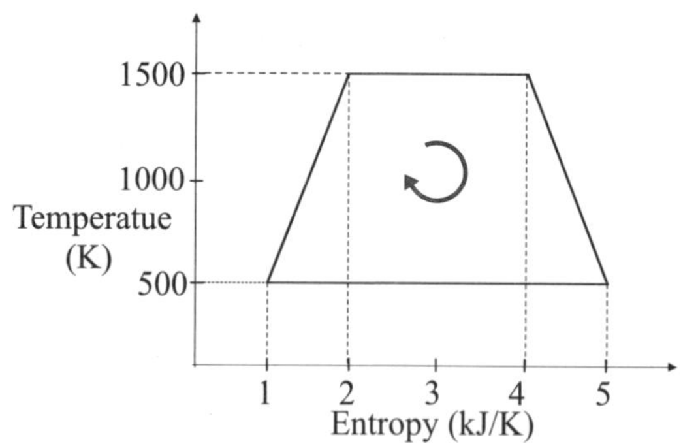

(A) 0.40 (B) 0.55 (C) 0.60 (D) None of theses

Q.14 An ideal gas ($\gamma = 1.67$) at a pressure of 2 bar expands twice its volume quasi statically by a polytropic process PV^n = constant. Maximum work is done by the gas when

(A) n = 1.67 (B) n = 1 (C) n = 1.2 (D) n = 1.13

Q.15 Match Group I with Group II

Group I	Group II
P. Work done	1. Point function
Q. Thermal equilibrium	2. Path function
R. Internal energy	3. Isolated system
S. No work and heat interaction	4. Equality of temperature

(A) P-2, Q-4, R-1, S-3 (B) P-2, Q-3, R-4, S-2

(C) P-4, Q-2, R-3, S-1 (D) P-3, Q-1, R-2, S-4

Q.16 For the cyclic process shown in figure, 1-2 is a reversible adiabatic process, 2-3 is an irreversible adiabatic process and 3-1 is an internally reversible constant pressure process. State whether the net output for the cycle is:

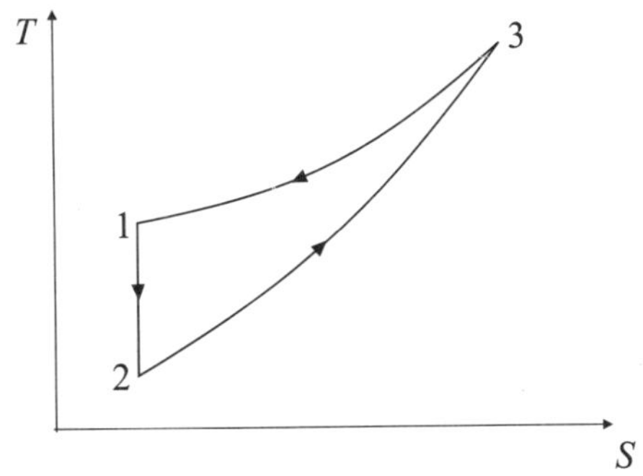

(A) zero (B) Positive

(C) Negative (D) Indeterminate

Q.17 A heat engine operates between two thermal reservoirs, one at 100°C and another at 20°C. 373 J of energy is removed from the hot reservoir. The change in entropy of the hot reservoir in J/K is:

(A) –1.27 (B) 1.0 (C) –1.0 (D) 1.27

Q.18 A reversible heat engine operates with four thermal reservoirs. If it receives 300 kJ and 1000 kJ energy as heat from the reservoirs at 300 K and 1000 K respectively and rejects 400 kJ energy as heat to a reservoir at 400 K, the net work delivered and the heat interaction with the reservoir at 600 K are, respectively.

(A) 300 kJ and –600 kJ (B) 600 kJ and –300 kJ

(C) 400 kJ and –800 kJ (D) 800 kJ and –400 kJ

Q.19 The figure shown below corresponds to a reversible heat engine cycle on a temperature entropy chart. The temperatures shown are in kelvin. The thermal efficiency of the heat engine is

(A) $\frac{3}{5}$ (B) $\frac{2}{5}$ (C) $\frac{1}{2}$ (D) $\frac{3}{4}$

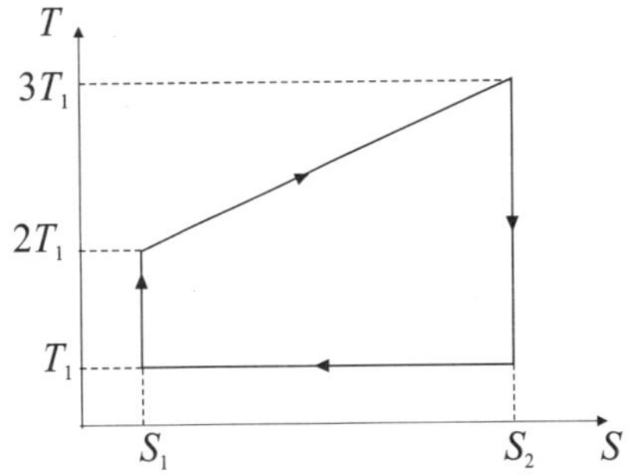

Q.20 When air is compressed, the enthalpy is increased from 100 to 200 kJ/kg. Heat lost during this compression is 50 kJ/kg. Neglecting kinetic and potential energies, the power required for a mass flow of 2 kg/s of air through the compressor will be

(A) 300 kW (B) 200 kW (C) 100 kW (D) 50 kW

Q.21 to Q.30 Numerical Answer Questions

Q.21 The thermal efficiency (in %) of the hypothetical heat engine cycle shown in the given figure is___.

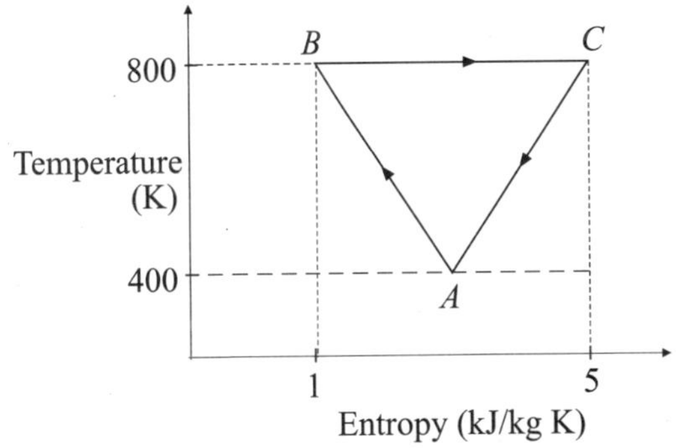

Q.22 The figure shows a reversible cycle comprising three processes (1-2, 2-3 and 3-1) executed by 0.5 kg of a gas. The net heat transfer (in kJ) of the cycle is__________.

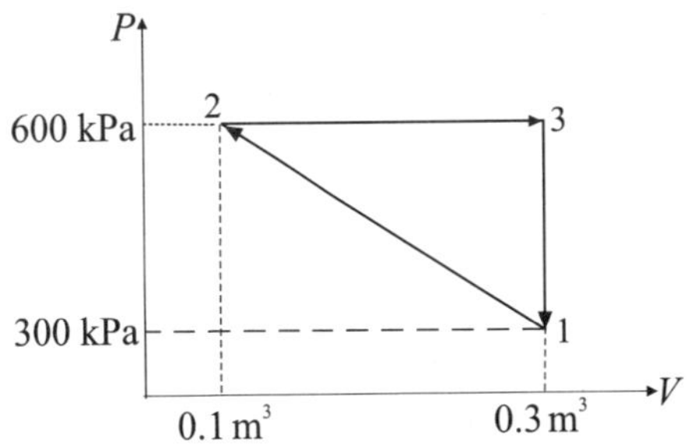

Q.23 A frictionless piston-cylinder device contains 1 kg of a gas, having a specific gas constant of 0.5 kJ/kgK. Assume 1.5 to be the specific heat ratio of the gas. The piston is free to move. Heat is added to the gas until the temperature rises by 10°C. The amount of heat added (in kJ) is______.

Q.24 An ideal gas is known to obey following relationships: $u = 200 + 0.718T$ and $PV = 0.287(T + 273)$, where u is specific internal energy (kJ/kg), T is temperature (°C), P is pressure (kPa) and V is specific volume (m^3/kg). Specific heat (in kJ/kgK) at constant pressure is______.

Q.25 Air at 10 bar and 400 K is flowing with a velocity of 20 m/s through a pipe of uniform cross-sectional area of 20 cm^2. The mass flow rate of air in the pipe is approximately_______.

Q.26 A Carnot engine having efficiency $\eta = 0.5$ drives a Carnot refrigerator with COP = 4. The energy absorbed by the refrigerator from the cold body for each kJ of energy absorbed from the source by the Carnot engine is_____.

Q.27 A car engine burns 5 kg of fuel (with a heating value of 40 MJ/kg) at 1500 K and rejects energy to the radiator and the exhaust gas at an average temperature of 750 K. The maximum amount of work (in MJ) the engine can provide is____.

Q.28 The network output for the cycle 1-2-3-4-5-6-1 shown in the figure is________.

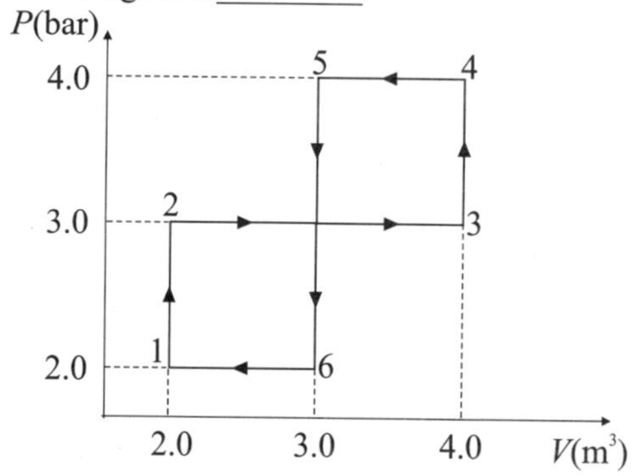

Q.29 A reversible engine operates between temperatures T_1 = 1000 K and T_2 = 400 K. The engine drives a refrigerator which operates between T_2 = 400 K and T_3 = 200 K. The energy transfer to the engine is 2000 kJ and the net work output of the combined engine and refrigerator is 300 kJ. The energy transferred to the refrigerator is____.

Q.30 A large furnace can supply heat at a temperature of 1200 K at a steady rate of 3200 kW. The ambient temperature is 27°C. The availability of this energy is __.

Q.31 to Q.65 carry two marks each

Q.31 to Q.49 Multiple Choice Questions

Q.31 In a process industry, two different streams of water (to be considered incompressible) as available at 10°C and 90°C as shown in the figure. Mass flow rates of both the streams are 1.0 kg/s. Rather than wasting these resources, it is desired to connect a reversible Carnot engine that will continuously extract heat from the hot stream and supply part of it to the cold stream such that the exit temperature of both the stream T_f is identical. Heat capacity of water is 4.18 kJ/kgK. The temperature T_f and work output W are, respectively

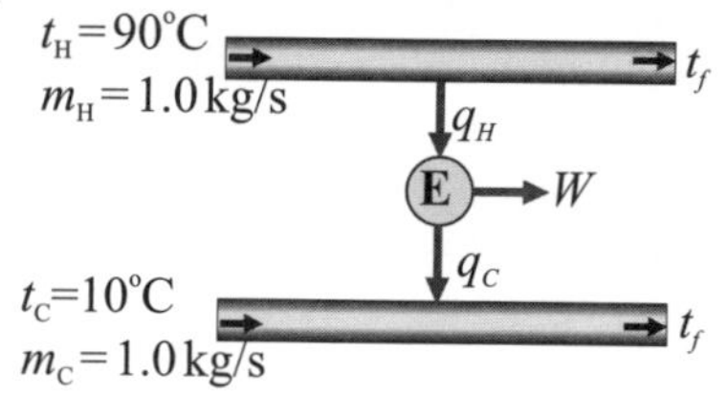

(A) 30°C, 167 kW (B) 42.5°C, 42.5 kW

(C) 47.5°C, 20.9 kW (D) 50°C, 63 kW

Q.32 Carnot engine A operates between two thermal reservoirs with temperature T_1 and T_2 (where $T_1 > T_2$). A second Carnot engine B operates between two thermal reservoirs with temperatures T_2 and T_3 (where $T_2 > T_3$). The engine B absorbs the same amount of energy as rejected by the engine A. If the work delivered by the engines are same, then T_1, T_2 and T_3 are related as:

(A) $T_1 - T_3 = T_2$ (B) $T_2^2 = T_1T_3$

(C) $T_1 + T_2 = 4T_3$ (D) $T_1 + T_3 = 2T_2$

Q.33 A person starts a 60 W table fan in an insulated room of volume 86.4 m^3. The person expects to cool the room from 32°C (Pressure = 100 kPa) and allows the fan to rotate for 4 hours. If the specific heat at constant volume of the room air is 0.718 kJ/kgK and characteristic gas constant is 0.287 kJ/kgK, after 4 hours, the person will find that the room is

(A) Hotter by approximately 12°C

(B) Cooler by approximately 10°C

(C) At the same temperature

(D) Hotter by approximately 8°C

Q.34 Air enters an adiabatic nozzle at 400 kPa and 900 K with negligible velocity. If the flow is ideal and exit pressure is 100 kPa, the exit temperature in kelvin and the exit velocity in m/s are respectively

(A) 605.7, 769.1 (B) 225, 1164.8

(C) 516.9, 877.5 (D) 129.2, 880.1

Q.35 A reversible engine (modified Carnot engine) as shown in figure receives 100 kJ of heat at 500 K and another 40 kJ at 400 K. Heat rejected at 300 K. The work output is equal to

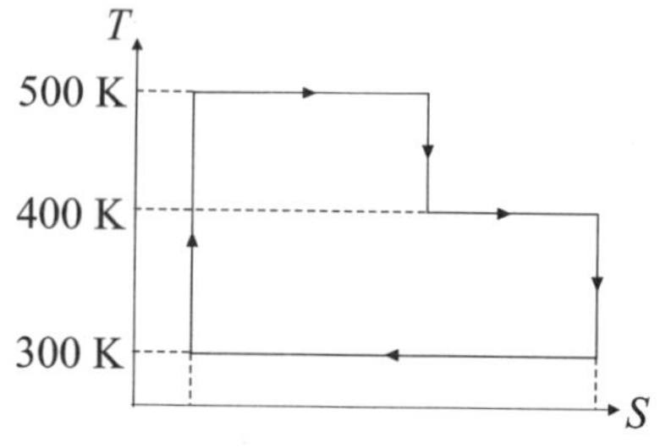

(A) 140 kJ (B) 90 kJ (C) 60 kJ (D) 50 kJ

Q.36 Two copper blocks, each of mass m and specific heat c, are used as heat source and sink to drive a reversible heat engine. The initial temperature of the source and sink are T_H and T_L respectively. The engine keeps producing work till the two blocks achieve the same temperature. The total work output of the engine is:

(A) $mc(T_H + T_L - \sqrt{T_H T_L})$ (B) 0

(C) $mc(T_H + T_L - 2\sqrt{T_H T_L})$ (D) $mc(T_H + T_L)$

Q.37 A metallic object cools from temperature T_1 to temperature T_2. The specific heat of the object varies as $c = a + b\,T^2$(where T is in kelvin). The change in specific entropy of the object during the cooling process is

(A) $a \ln\left(\frac{T_2}{T_1}\right) + 0.5b(T_2^2 - T_1^2)$ (B) $a \ln\left(\frac{T_2}{T_1}\right)$

(C) $a \ln(T_1 + T_2) + 0.5b(T_2^2 - T_1^2)$ (D) $a \ln\left[a + b\frac{(T_1 + T_2)}{2}\right]$

Q.38 A reversible heat engine receives heat inputs of 300 kJ and 200 kJ from two thermal reservoir at 1000 K and 800 K, respectively. The engine rejects heat Q to a reservoir at 300 K. The work delivered by the engine and the value of Q are respectively

(A) 35 kJ, 65 kJ (B) 135 kJ, 165 kJ

(C) 235 kJ, 100 kJ (D) 335 kJ, 165 kJ

Q.39 An ideal gas is taken through three processes as a result of which the final state is identical with the initial state. The nature of the processes, work done and heat transferred during the processes are as follows:

(i) 1-2 is a constant volume process with a heat input of 50 kJ.

(ii) 2-3 is an isothermal expansion process and the work done by the system is 500 kJ

(iii) 3-1 is a constant pressure process and the work done on the system is 200 kJ

The heat transferred and the change in internal energy in kJ during the process 3-1 are respectively.

(A) 250, 50 (B) 250, –50

(C) –250, 50 (D) –250, –50

Q.40 Two reversible heat engines work between three thermal reservoirs at temperatures T_1, T_2 and T_3 respectively. Engine E_1 receives heat from the reservoir at temperature T_1 and rejects heat to the reservoir at temperature T_2. Engine E_2 receives heat from the reservoir at temperature T_2 and rejects heat to the reservoir at temperature T_3. Assume that the heat rejected by engine E_1 is equal to the heat input to engine E_2. All temperatures are in kelvin. If the efficiencies of engine E_1 and E_2 are same, the reservoir temperature T_2 can be expressed as:

(A) $T_2 = \sqrt{T_1 T_3}$ (B) $T_2 = \frac{T_1 + T_3}{2}$

(C) $T_2 = \frac{T_1 - T_3}{2}$ (D) $T_2 = \sqrt{2T_1 T_3}$

Q.41 An ideal cycle is shown in the figure. Its thermal efficiency is given by

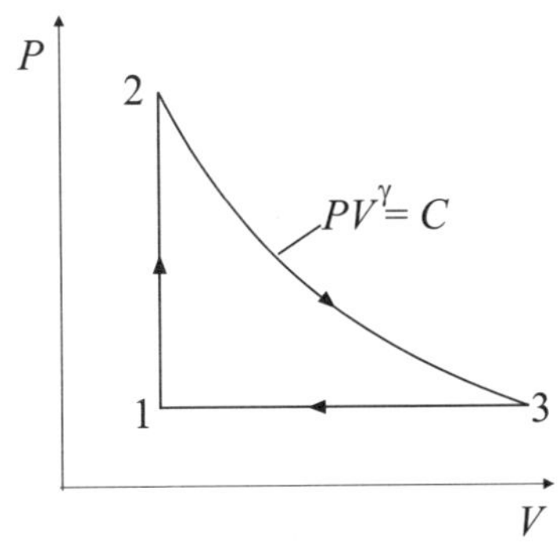

(A) $1 - \frac{\left(\frac{v_3}{v_1} - 1\right)}{\left(\frac{p_2}{p_1} - 1\right)}$ (B) $1 - \frac{1}{\gamma}\frac{\left(\frac{v_3}{v_1} - 1\right)}{\left(\frac{p_2}{p_1} - 1\right)}$

(C) $1 - \gamma\frac{(v_3 - v_1)}{(p_2 - p_1)}\frac{p_1}{v_1}$ (D) $1 - \frac{1}{\gamma}\frac{(p_2 - p_1)}{(v_3 - v_1)}\frac{v_1}{p_1}$

Q.42 The heat absorbed or rejected during a polytropic process is equal to

(A) $\left(\frac{\gamma - n}{\gamma - 1}\right)^{0.5} \times$ Work done (B) $\left(\frac{\gamma - n}{n - 1}\right) \times$ Work done

(C) $\left(\frac{\gamma - n}{\gamma - 1}\right) \times$ Work done (D) $\left(\frac{\gamma - n}{\gamma - 1}\right)^2 \times$ Work done

Q.43 A vapour pressure of liquid ammonia (in atmosphere) in the vicinity of the triple point can be expressed as $\ln P + \frac{3063}{T} = 15.16$; where temperature T is expressed in kelvin.

In a similar manner, the vapour pressure of solid ammonia can be expressed as $\ln P + \frac{3754}{T} = 18.7$

Take the molecular mass of ammonia to be 17 kg/K mole

The temperature and pressure at the triple point are:

(A) 295.2 K, 0.69 atm (B) 295.2 K, 0.59 atm

(C) 195.2 K, 0.69 atm (D) 195.2 K, 0.59 atm

Q.44 1.0 kg/s of saturated water at 50 bar and 2 kg/s of dry saturated steam at 50 bar enter an adiabatic mixing chamber operating under steady state conditions and leave as a single stream. The pressure remains constant throughout. Neglecting potential and kinetic energy changes, the quality of the steam leaving the vessel is

Steam property data								
P (bar)	v_f (m³/kg)	v_g (m³/kg)	u_f (kJ/kg)	u_g (kJ/kg)	h_f (kJ/kg)	h_g (kJ/kg)	s_f (kJ/kgK)	s_g (kJ/kgK)
50	0.001286	0.03944	1147.8	2597.1	1154.2	2794.2	2.9202	5.9734

(A) 0.55 (B) 0.67 (C) 0.75 (D) 0.32

Q.45 A Carnot engine E_1 operates between the temperature limits of 1000 K and 900 K. A second Carnot engine E_2 operates between the temperature limits of 500 K and 450 K. Both the engines produce the same amount of work. Which one of the following statements is true regarding the efficiency η and the heat rejected QR (subscripts 1 and 2 are used to denote the respective engines)?

(A) $\eta_1 > \eta_2$ and $QR_1 > QR_2$ (B) $\eta_1 > \eta_2$ and $QR_1 < QR_2$

(C) $\eta_1 = \eta_2$ and $QR_1 < QR_2$ (D) $\eta_1 = \eta_2$ and $QR_1 = QR_2$

Q.46 A Carnot heat engine is used to drive a Carnot heat pump. The arrangement, along with the pertinent temperatures, is indicated in the figure. The COP of the heat pump and Q_3 in kJ are, respectively

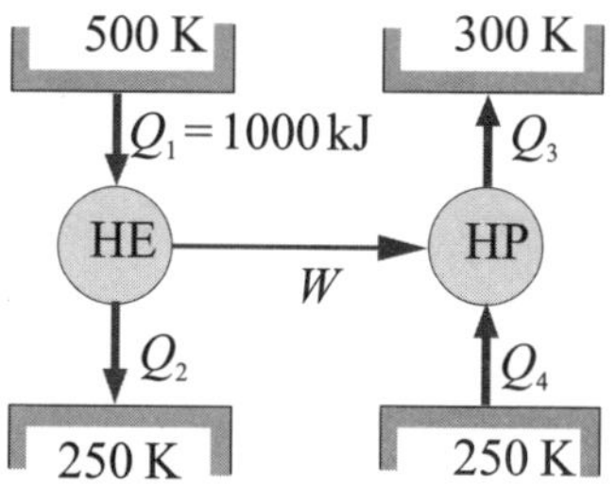

(A) 4, 1000 (B) 6, 500 (C) 6, 3000 (D) 2, 2500

Q.47 A liquid of mass m at temperature T_1 is mixed with an equal amount of the same liquid at temperature T_2. The specific heat of the liquid is c. The total entropy change due to the mixing process is:

(A) $2mc\ln\left(\frac{T_2}{T_1}\right)$ (B) $2mc\ln\left(\frac{T_1+T_2}{2\sqrt{T_1T_2}}\right)$

(C) $2mc\ln\left(\frac{T_1}{T_2}\right)$ (D) $2mc\ln\left(\frac{2\sqrt{T_1T_2}}{T_1+T_2}\right)$

Q.48 On a T-S diagram, the slope of the constant-volume line for an ideal gas is

(A) Less than that of constant pressure line

(B) More than that of constant pressure line

(C) Less than that of constant enthalpy line

(D) Equal to that of constant enthalpy line

Q.49 A thermodynamics cycle operates between one source at a temperature of 600 K, another source at a temperature of 300 K and a sink at a temperature T as shown in the figure.

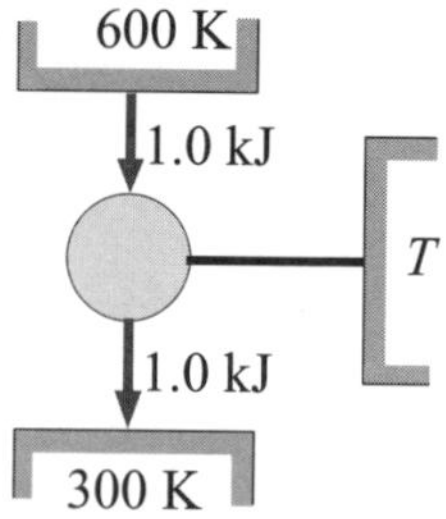

If the first and second laws of thermodynamics are not violated, what should be the value of T in kelvin.

(A) 400 (B) 200 (C) 50 (D) 25

Q.50 For an ideal gas, the slope of a constant pressure line on a T-S diagram at a state (T_0, S_0) is

(A) $\frac{(\gamma-1)T_0}{\gamma R}$ (B) $\frac{\gamma R}{(\gamma-1)T_0}$

(C) $\frac{R}{(\gamma-1)T_0}$ (D) $\frac{\gamma T_0}{(\gamma-1)R}$

Q.50 to Q.65 Numerical Answer Questions

Q.51 A stationary insulated rigid tank contains 1.0 kg of an ideal gas with constant specific heat (c_v = 0.7 kJ/kgK and c_p = 1.0 kJ/kgK) at 27°C and 300 kPa. A paddle wheel with a power capacity of 20 W is operated inside the tank for 15 minutes. The final pressure of air (in kPa) in the tank will be ______.

Q.52 A well-insulated rigid hot water tank receives steady flow of water from two sources as shown in figure. There is no accumulation of water in the tank. A back-up heater is provided to ensure a constant outflow temperature of water at 60°C from the tank under steady state. What is the required capacity (in kW) of back-up beater ?______.

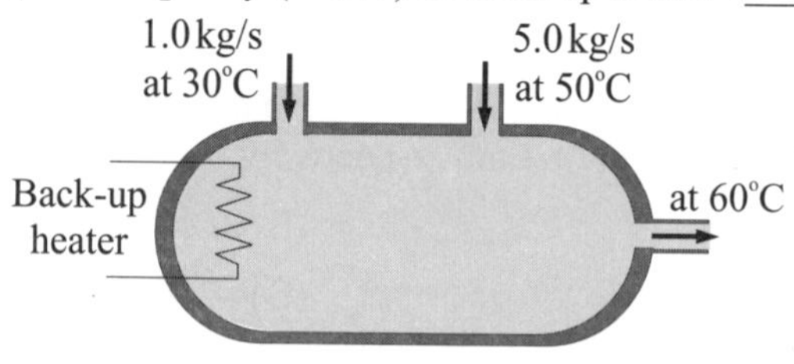

Q.53 A block of hot metal of mass 1 kg and specific heat of 1 kJ/kgK, initially at 600°C is allowed to cool down to room temperature of 30°C. The change in entropy(in kJ/K) of the metal is______.

Q.54 2 kg of water at 60°C is mixed thoroughly with 4 kg of water at 30°C in a perfectly insulated tank. Assuming the specific heat of water to be constant (= 4.18 kJ/kgK), the entropy generated (in J/K) during this process is___.

Q.55 It is proposed that a solar powered engine will operate on the Carnot cycle using ammonia as the working fluid. Heat addition is to occur at 50°C (transforming saturated liquid to dry saturated vapour) with heat rejection at 20°C. Given specific entropy data in kJ/kgK; s_g at 50°C = 4.761; at 20°C, s_f = 1.041 and s_g = 5.086; Enthalpy values: at 50°C, h_f = 421.5 kJ/kg and h_g= 1471.6 kJ/kg. The net work output of the cycle in kJ/kg is________.

Q.56 Saturated property data for NH_3 is given below

P (bar)	T (°C)	v_f (m³/kg)	v_g (m³/kg)
0.4	−50.4	1.424×10^{-3}	2.680
0.4	−46.5	1.433×10^{-3}	2.175
0.6	−43.3	1.441×10^{-3}	1.835

The latent heat of vaporization of NH_3 (in kJ/kg) at 0.5 bar is____.

Q.57 A system undergoes a process during which the heat transfer to the system per degree increase in temperature is given by $\dfrac{dQ}{dT} = 2\text{ kJ/°C}$.

The work done by the system per degree increase in temperature is given by $\dfrac{dW}{dT} = 2 - 0.1\,T$.

If the temperature of water during the process varies from 100ºC to 150ºC, what will be the change in internal energy?________.

Q.58 Air at a flow rate of 1.0 kg/s enters the nozzle of a jet engine at a temperature of 800 K, pressure of 200 kPa and a velocity of 50 m/s. It leaves the nozzle at a temperature of 650 K and a pressure of 100 kPa. Heat loss at a constant rate of 25 kW takes place from the nozzle to the surroundings. Assuming air to behave as on ideal gas with constant c_P value of 1.005 kJ/kg K and neglecting potential energy changes, the exit velocity of the air in m/s is________.

Q.59 1.0 kg of air in an insulated rigid tank of volume $1.0\,\text{m}^3$ is churned with a frictionless fan of 600 W capacity for 10 minutes. The fan efficiency is 100%. Treating air as an ideal gas and neglecting kinetic and potential energy changes, what is the increase of pressure to the nearest kPa?_____.

Q.60 Air at a mass flow rate of 2 kg/s enters a turbine at 0.5 MPa and 1200 K and with a velocity of 20 m/s. It is expanded in the turbine to a pressure of 0.1 MPa and temperature 800 K. The velocity at the exit of the turbine is 80 m/s. Heat loss to the surroundings is 50 kW. The power output of the turbine in kW is______.

Q.61 Consider steady flow of air (c_P= 1.005 kJ/kgK) in an adiabatic passage. Air enters the passage at 100 kPa, 500 K at a velocity of 150 m/s and exits the passage at 510 K. Assume air to be an ideal gas neglect gravitational effects. The velocity(in m/s) at the exit is _________.

Q.62 A system undergoes these quasi-state process sequentially as indicated in the figure. 1-2 is an isobaric process, 2-3 is a polytropic process with $n = 1.4$ and 3-1 is a process in which PV = constant. The following data may be made use of $P_1 = P_2 = 4\,\text{bar}$, $P_3 = 1.0\,\text{bar}$ and $V_1 = 1.0\,\text{m}^3$. The net heat interaction for the cycle in kJ is_ .

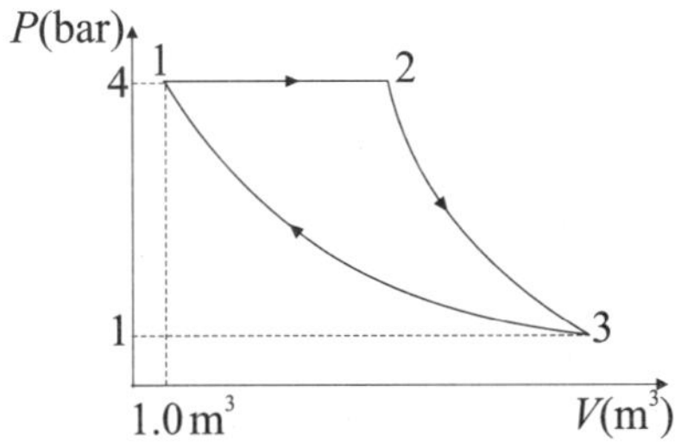

Q.63 Air is compressed via a quasi-static process in a piston cylinder assembly. The initial temperature and pressure of the air are 27°C and 0.1 MPa, respectively and it occupies a volume of $1\times10^{-3}\,\text{m}^3$. The compression process follows the law $PV^{1.3}$ = constant and the final pressure is 2 MPa. The work done on air during the compression in joule is_______.

Q.64 It is proposed that the solar energy be used to heat a large collector plate. The energy is turn be transferred as heat to a fluid within a heat engine, and the engine would reject energy as heat to the atmosphere. Experiments indicate that 0.5 kW/m² of energy can be collected at the operating temperature of the plate and the maximum efficiency of the engine is 0.2. The minimum collector area (in m²) that would be required for a plant to produce 1 kW of useful shaft power is________.

Q.65 The air with enthalpy of 100 kJ/kg is compressed by an air compressor to a pressure and temperature at which its enthalpy becomes 200 kJ/kg. The loss of heat is 40 kJ/kg from the compressor as the air passes through it. Neglecting kinetic and potential energies, the power required for an air mass flow of 0.5 kg/s is_________.

12.4 SOLUTION TO PRACTICE PAPER

Q.1 Ans:(A)

The efficiency of a reversible heat engine is given by

$$\eta_{max} = \frac{T_1 - T_2}{T_1} \qquad \text{or} \qquad \frac{T_2}{T_1} = 1 - \eta_{max}$$

COP of refrigeration cycle is given by

$$\text{COP} = \frac{T_2}{T_1 - T_2}$$

or $$\text{COP} = \frac{T_2/T_1}{1-(T_2/T_1)} = \frac{1-\eta_{max}}{1-(1-\eta_{max})}$$

$$\text{COP} = \left(\frac{1}{\eta_{max}}\right) - 1$$

Q.2 Ans:(B)

Graph of Otto cycle is drawn on S-V.

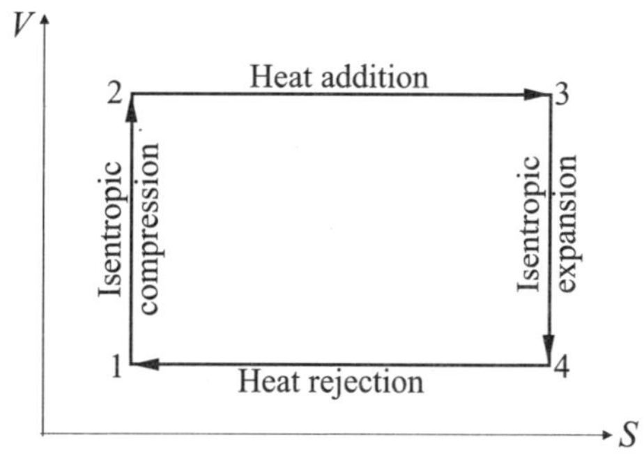

Q.3 Ans:(A)

From the first law, $Q = \Delta u + W$

$$Q = W_{max} \text{ ; when } \Delta u = 0$$

$$\Delta u = 0 \text{ in isothermal process}$$

Q.4 Ans:(A)

The mass flow rate $\dot{m} = \rho AV = \dfrac{P}{RT} AV$

Substituting $P = 0.7 \times 10^5$ N/m^2, $A = 0.4\,\text{m}^2$, $V = 200$ m/s, $R = 0.287 \times 10^3$ J/kgK and $T = 330$ K, we have

$$\dot{m} = \frac{0.7 \times 10^5 \times 0.4 \times 200}{0.287 \times 10^3 \times 330}$$

$$\dot{m} = 59.1\,\text{kg/s}$$

Q.5 Ans:(B)

The efficiency of the reversible heat engine is given by

$$\eta = \frac{T_1 - T_2}{T_1} = \frac{W}{Q_1}$$

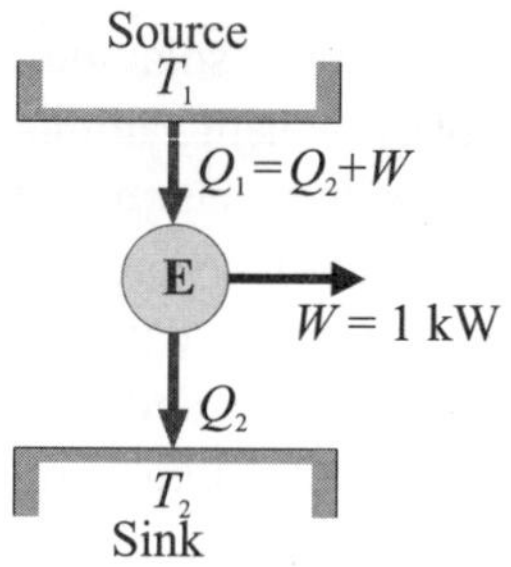

or $$\frac{(273+600)-(273+20)}{273+600} = \frac{W}{Q_1} = \frac{W}{Q_2 + W}$$

Substituting $W = 1$ kW, we have

$$\frac{580}{873} = \frac{1}{Q_2 + 1}$$

$$\text{Heat rejection, } Q_2 = 0.505\,\text{kW}$$

Q.6 Ans:(B)

First law of thermodynamics, $dQ = du + dW$, Substituting $dQ = TdS$ and $dW = PdV$,

$$Tds = du + PdV$$

Enthalpy $h = u + PV \Rightarrow dh = du + PdV + VdP$

or $$dh = TdS + VdP$$

$$Tds = dh - VdP$$

Correct options are (1) and (4)

Q.7 Ans:(C)

Let u_A and u_B be the internal energy at state A and state B respectively.

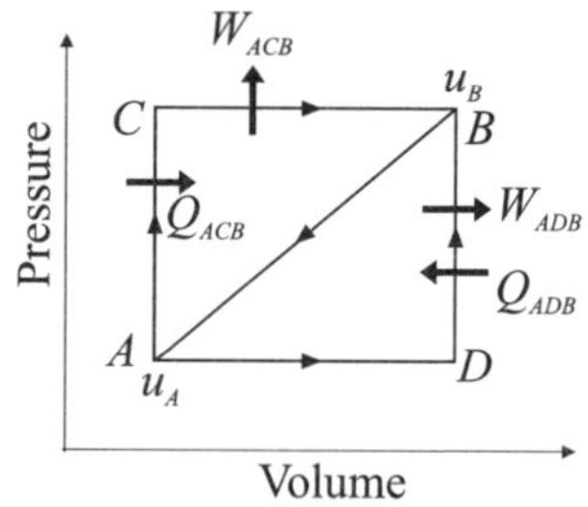

Using first law for A-C-B, we have

$$Q_{ACB} = (u_B - u_A) + W_{ACB}$$

or $$180 = (u_B - u_A) + 130$$

or $$u_B - u_A = 50$$

Using first law for A-D-B, we have

$$Q_{ADB} = (u_B - u_A) + W_{ADB}$$

or $$Q_{ADB} = 50 + 40$$

$$Q_{ADB} = 90\,\text{kJ}$$

Q.8 Ans:(B)

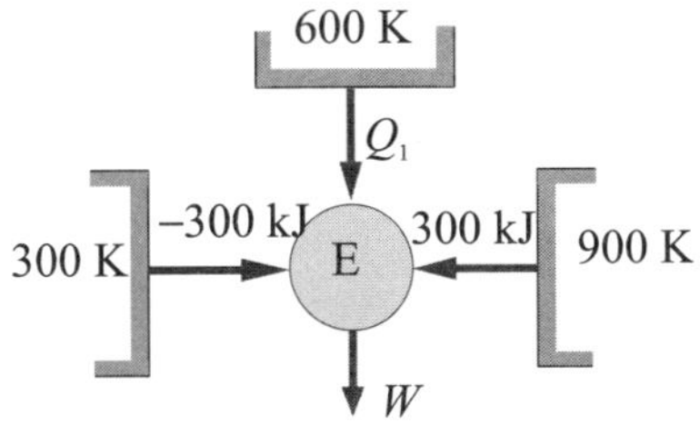

For the reversible cycle, $\sum \frac{Q}{T} = 0$

or $$\frac{Q_1}{600} - \frac{300}{300} + \frac{300}{900} = 0$$

$$Q_1 = 400 \text{ kJ}$$

and $$\sum Q = \sum W$$

or $$Q_1 - 300 + 300 = W$$

or $$400 - 300 + 300 = W$$

$$W = 400 \text{ kJ}$$

Q.9 Ans:(B)

Temperature of ice remains constant during melting of ice.

Change in internal energy is zero.

Q.10 Ans:(C)

Let T_1 and T_2 be the operating temperatures of Carnot refrigerator.

COP of refrigerator is given by

$$\text{COP} = 5 = \frac{T_2}{T_1 - T_2} \Rightarrow \frac{T_1}{T_2} = \frac{6}{5}$$

COP of heat pump is given by

$$\text{COP} = \frac{T_1}{T_1 - T_2} = \frac{T_1/T_2}{(T_1/T_2) - 1}$$

or $$\text{COP} = \frac{6/5}{(6/5) - 1}$$

COP of heat pump = 6

Q.11 Ans:(B)

In the isothermal compression, work done on system $W = -Q$

Change in entropy, $\Delta S = \frac{-Q}{T} = -\left(\frac{Q}{T}\right)$

Entropy decreases in isothermal compression.

Q.12 Ans:(A)

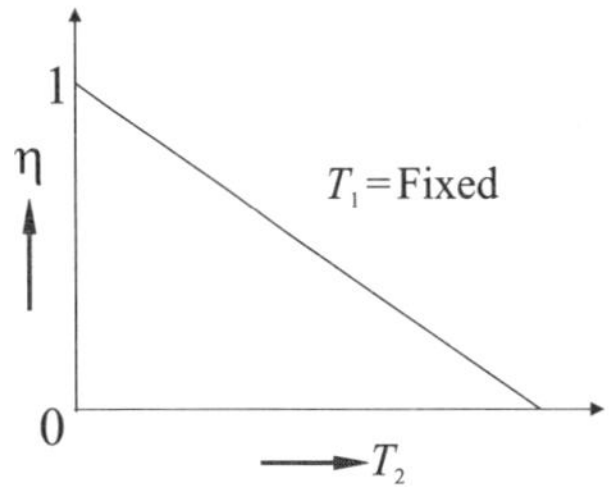

Efficiency of heat engine, $\eta = \frac{T_1 - T_2}{T_1}$

or $$\eta = 1 - \left(\frac{T_2}{T_1}\right)$$

Efficiency of heat engine is increased by decreasing $\left(\frac{T_2}{T_1}\right)$.

Efficiency of heat engine increases with decreasing T_2 at constant T_1.

Q.13 Ans:(C)

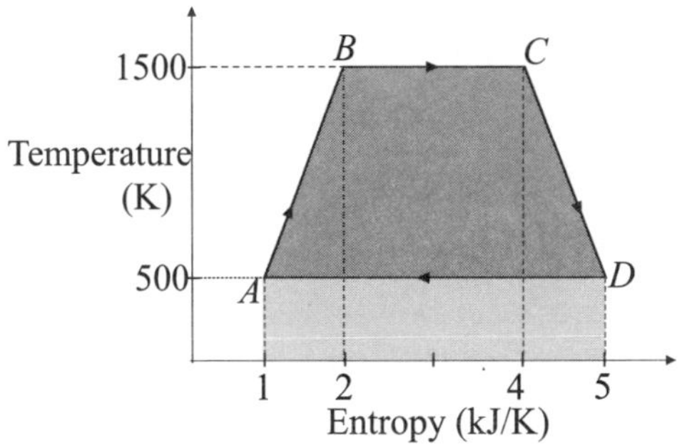

$$W = \text{Area of closed path } ABCDA$$

$$W = 2 \times \left[\frac{1}{2} \times (2-1) \times (1500-500)\right] + (1500-500) \times (4-2)$$

$$W = 1000 + 2000 = 3000 \text{ kJ}$$

Heat supplied Q_1 = area under $ABCD = \int_A^D TdS$

$$Q_1 = \text{Area under } ABCDA + \text{Area under } 1AD5$$

$$Q_1 = 3000 + 500 \times (5-1) = 5000$$

Efficiency of cycle,

$$\eta = \frac{W}{Q_1} = \frac{3000}{5000}$$

$$\eta = 0.60$$

Q.14 Ans:(B)

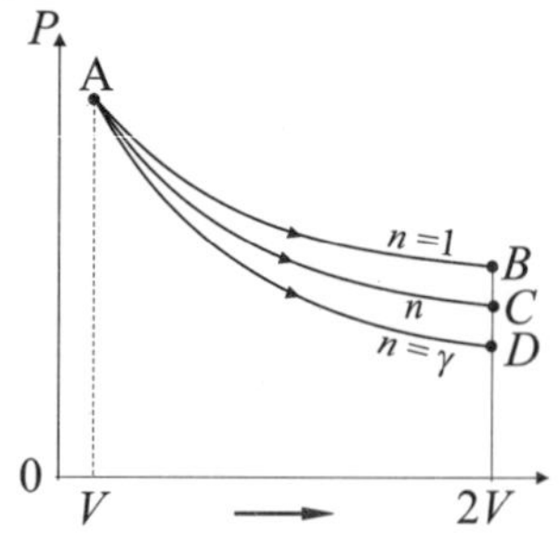

Work done = Area under the curve on P-V

Maximum work done = Maximum area under curve

Maximum work done = Area under curve AB which is isothermal process ($n = 1$)

Q.15 Ans:(A)

P. Work done	2. Path function
Q. Thermal equilibrium	4. Equality of temperature
R. Internal energy	1. Point function
S. No work and heat interaction	3. Isolated system

Q.16 Ans:(C)

Direction of cyclic process is anti-clockwise.

Work output of the cycle is negative

Q.17 Ans:(C)

Change in entropy of hot reservoir

$$\Delta S = -\frac{Q_1}{T_1} = -\left(\frac{373}{273+100}\right)$$

$$\Delta S = -1.0 \text{ J/K}$$

Q.18 Ans:(A)

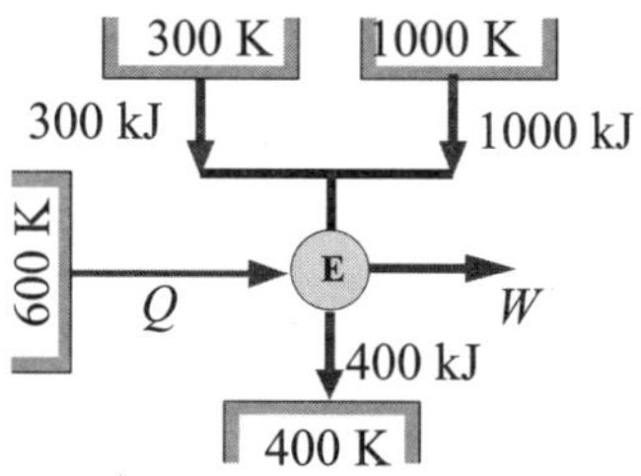

For the reversible heat engine,

$$\sum \frac{Q}{T} = 0$$

or $$\frac{300}{300} + \frac{1000}{1000} - \frac{400}{400} + \frac{Q}{600} = 0$$

$$Q = -600 \text{ kJ}$$

$$\sum Q = \sum W$$

$$300 + 1000 - 600 - 400 = W$$

$$W = 300$$

Q.19 Ans:(A)

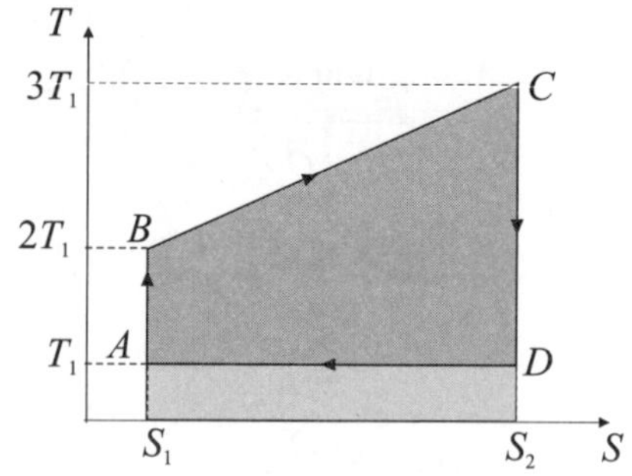

The thermal efficiency of the heat engine is

$$\eta = \frac{W}{Q} = \frac{\text{Area of } ABCDA}{\text{Area under } ABCD}$$

or $$\eta = \frac{(2.5T_1 - T_1)(S_2 - S_1)}{2.5T_1(S_2 - S_1)}$$

$$\eta = \frac{3}{5}$$

Q.20 Ans:(A)

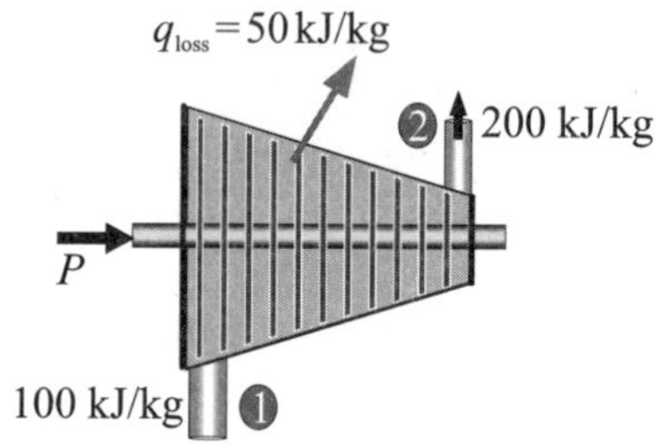

Neglecting the kinetic and potential energy, the energy equation takes the form

$$h_1 + q = h_2 + w$$

or $$100 - 50 = 200 + w$$

or $$w = -150 \text{ kJ/kg}$$

Power required for mass flow of 2 kg/s is

$$P = \dot{m} \times w = 2 \times 150$$

$$P = 300 \text{ kW}$$

Q.21 Ans:[25]

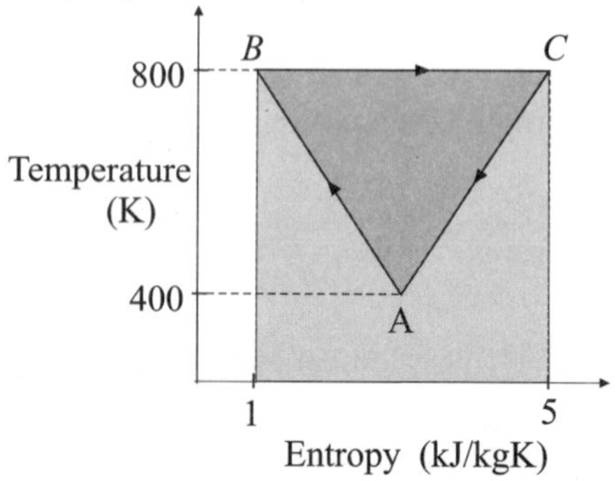

Thermal efficiency, $\eta = \frac{W}{Q} = \frac{\text{Area of } ABC}{\text{Area under } BC}$

$$\eta = \frac{\frac{1}{2} \times (800-400) \times (5-1)}{800 \times (5-1)}$$

$$\eta = 25\%$$

Q.22 Ans:[30]

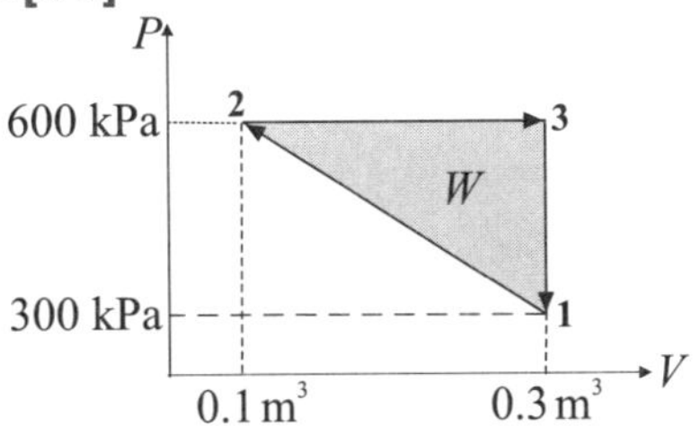

For closed cycle, $\sum Q = \sum W$

or $\sum Q =$ Area of 1231

or $\sum Q = \frac{1}{2}(0.3-0.1)(600-300)$

$$\text{Net heat transfer } \sum Q = 30\,\text{kJ}$$

Q.23 Ans:[15]

For the constant-pressure process, heat added $Q = mc_P \Delta T$

Substituting $c_p = \frac{\gamma}{\gamma - 1}R$, we have

$$Q = m\frac{\gamma}{\gamma-1}R\Delta T$$

or $Q = \frac{1 \times 1.5 \times 0.5 \times 10}{1.5 - 1}$

$$Q = 15\,\text{kJ}$$

Q.24 Ans:[1.005]

Specific heat at constant pressure, $c_p = \frac{dh}{dT}$

Substituting $h = u + PV$, we have

$$c_p = \frac{d(u+PV)}{dT} = \frac{du}{dT} + \frac{d(PV)}{dT}$$

or $c_p = \frac{d}{dT}(200 + 0.718T) + \frac{d}{dT}[0.287(T+273)]$

$$c_p = 1.005\ \text{kJ/kg}$$

Q.25 Ans:[0.35]

The mass flow rate, $\dot{m} = \rho AV = \frac{P}{RT}AV$

Substituting, $P = 10 \times 10^5\ \text{N/m}^2$, $A = \frac{20}{10000}\,\text{m}^2$, $V = 20\,\text{m/s}$, $R = 0.287 \times 10^3\,\text{J/kgK}$ and $T = 400\,\text{K}$, we have

$$\dot{m} = \frac{10 \times 10^5 \times \frac{20}{10000} \times 20}{0.287 \times 10^3 \times 400}$$

$$\dot{m} = 0.35\,\text{kg/s}$$

Q.26 Ans:[2]

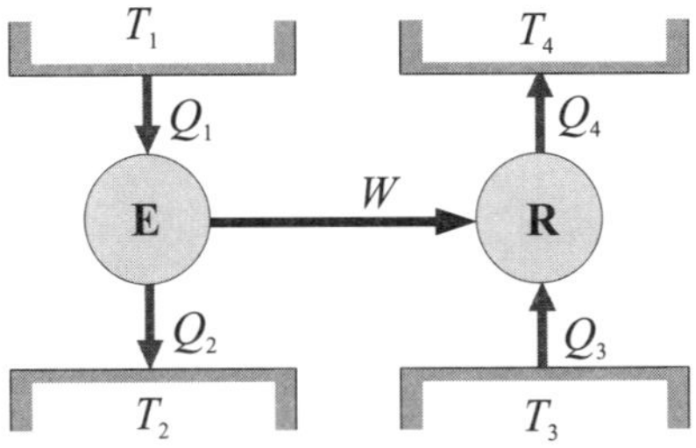

Efficiency of the Carnot engine,

$$\eta = \frac{Q_1 - Q_2}{Q_1} = 0.5$$

or $Q_2 = 0.5Q_1$

COP of refrigerator, $\frac{Q_3}{W} = 4$

or $\frac{Q_3}{Q_1 - Q_2} = 4$

From which

$$\frac{Q_3}{Q_1 - 05Q_1} = 4 \qquad \text{or} \qquad Q_3 = 2Q_1$$

Substituting $Q_1 = 1$ kJ, we have

$$Q_3 = 2\,\text{kJ}$$

Q.27 Ans:[100]

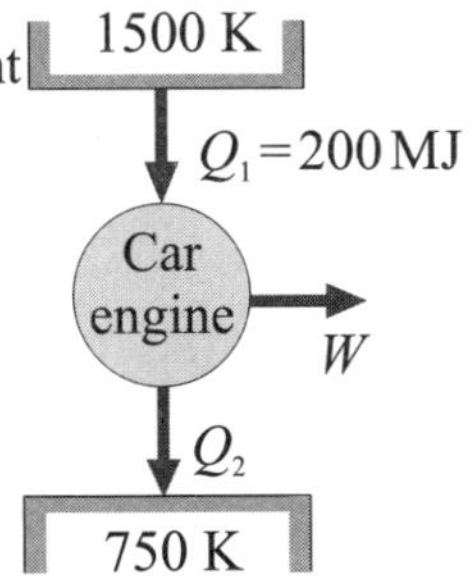

Heat supplied Q at constant temperature 1500 K is

$$Q_1 = 5 \times 40 = 200\,\text{MJ}$$

For the Carnot engine, $\frac{Q_1}{T_1} = \frac{Q_2}{T_2}$

$$Q_2 = Q_1\frac{T_2}{T_1} = 200 \times \frac{750}{1500} = 100\,\text{MJ}$$

Maximum amount of work, $W = Q_1 - Q_2 = 200 - 100$

$$W = 100\ \text{MJ}$$

Q.28 Ans:[0]

Net work output = Area of closed curve

Net work output $W = 1$(clockwise) $- 1$(anti - clockwise)

$$W = 0$$

Q.29 Ans:[900]

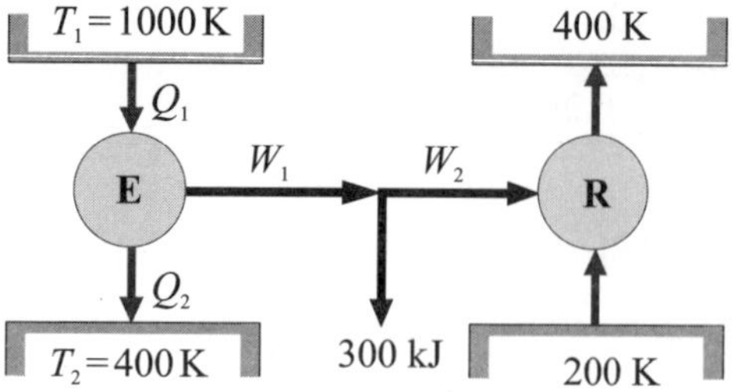

Efficiency of engine, $\eta = \dfrac{T_1 - T_2}{T_1} = \dfrac{W_1}{Q_1}$

or $\dfrac{1000 - 400}{1000} = \dfrac{W_1}{2000}$

or $W_1 = 1200$ kJ

Energy transfer to the refrigerator,

$$W_2 = W_1 - 300 = 1200 - 300$$

$$W_2 = 900 \text{ kJ}$$

Q.30 Ans:[2400]

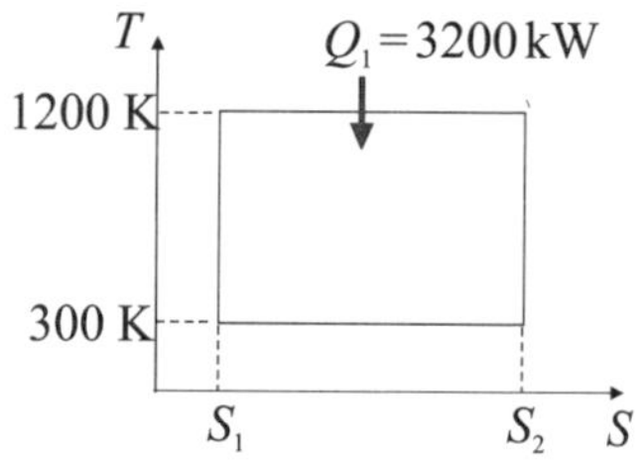

Available energy

$$AE = (1200 - 300)(S_2 - S_1)$$

$$AE = 900(S_2 - S_1)$$

and $S_2 - S_1 = \dfrac{3200}{1200} = \dfrac{8}{3}$

Availability $= 900 \times \dfrac{8}{3}$

$$\text{Availability} = 2400 \text{ kW}$$

Q.31 Ans:(C)

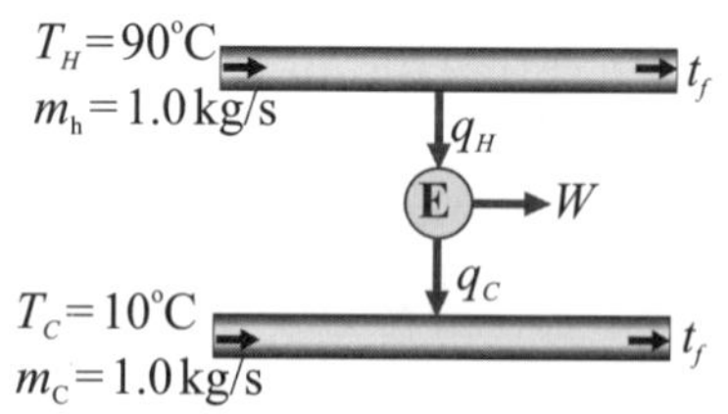

For reversible Carnot cycle, $\displaystyle\int \frac{dQ}{T} = 0$

$$m_h c \int_{273+90}^{T_f} \frac{dT}{T} + m_c c \int_{273+10}^{T_f} \frac{dT}{T} = 0$$

Substituting $m_h = m_c = 1$ kg/s, we have

$$\ln\left(\frac{T_f^2}{363 \times 283}\right) = 0 \quad \Rightarrow \quad T_f = 3205 \text{ K}$$

$$t_f = 47.5°\text{C}$$

Work output

$$W = q_H - q_C = m_h c(90 - 47.5) - m_c c(47.5 - 10)$$

$$W = 1 \times 4.18 \times (90 - 47.5) - 1 \times 4.18 \times (47.5 - 10)$$

$$W = 20.9 \text{ kW}$$

Q.32 Ans:(D)

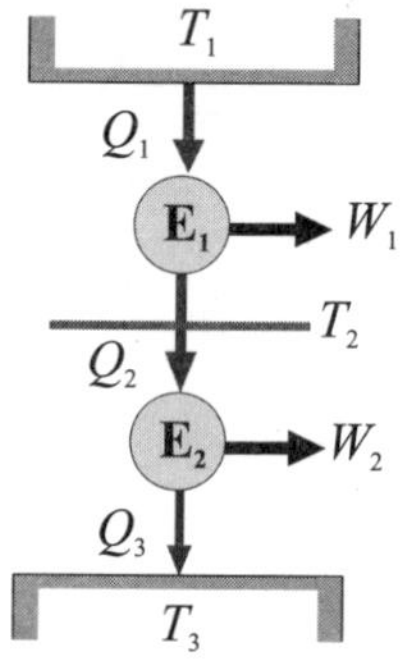

For the reversible engine,

$$\frac{Q_1}{T_1} = \frac{Q_2}{T_2} = \frac{Q_3}{T_3}$$

Given $W_1 = W_2$

or $Q_1 - Q_2 = Q_2 - Q_3$

or $T_1 - T_2 = T_2 - T_3$

$$T_1 + T_3 = 2T_2$$

Q.33 Ans:(A)

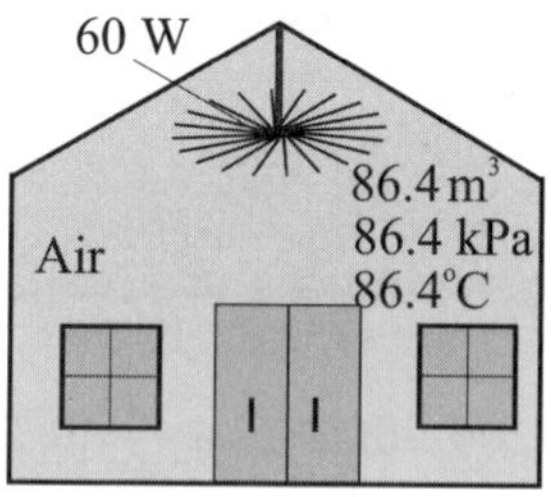

To find *m*, we use the ideal gas equation. It gives us

$$m = \frac{PV}{RT} = \frac{100 \times 10^3 \times 86.4}{0.287 \times 10^3 \times (273 + 32)}$$

$$m = 98.70 \text{ kg}$$

Work input, $W = 60 \times 4 \times 60 \times 60 = mc\Delta T$

$$\Delta T = \frac{60 \times 4 \times 60 \times 60}{mc} = \frac{60 \times 4 \times 60 \times 60}{98.70 \times 0.718 \times 10^3} = 12.19$$

Temperature increase, $\Delta T = 12°\text{C}$

Q.34 Ans:(A)

The final temperature T_2 is found for the adiabatic quasi-equilibrium process from 1 to 2, it is

$$\frac{T_1^\gamma}{P_1^{\gamma-1}} = \frac{T_2^\gamma}{P_2^{\gamma-1}}$$

$$T_2 = T_1\left(\frac{P_2}{P_1}\right)^{\frac{\gamma-1}{\gamma}} = 900\left(\frac{100}{400}\right)^{\frac{1.4-1}{1.4}}$$

$$T_2 = 605.7\,\text{K}$$

Neglecting the potential energy changes and zero heat transfer, energy equation takes the form

$$h_1 + \frac{v_1^2}{2} = h_2 + \frac{v_2^2}{2}$$

$$v_2 = \sqrt{2c_p(T_1 - T_2) + v_1^2}$$

$$v_2 = \sqrt{2 \times 1.005 \times 10^3 (900 - 605.7) + 0^2}$$

$$v_2 = 769.1\,\text{m/s}$$

Q.35 Ans:(D)

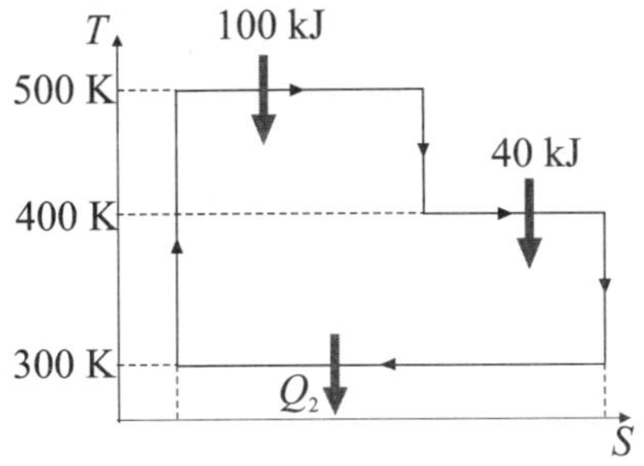

Let Q_2 be the heat rejection.

$$\frac{100}{500} + \frac{40}{400} - \frac{Q_2}{300} = 0$$

$$Q_2 = 90\,\text{kJ}$$

Work output, $W = 100 + 40 - 90$

$$W = 50\,\text{kJ}$$

Q.36 Ans:(C)

For the reversible heat engine, $\oint \frac{dQ}{T} = 0$

or $$mc\int_{T_H}^{T_f} \frac{dT}{T} + mc\int_{T_L}^{T_f} \frac{dT}{T} = 0$$

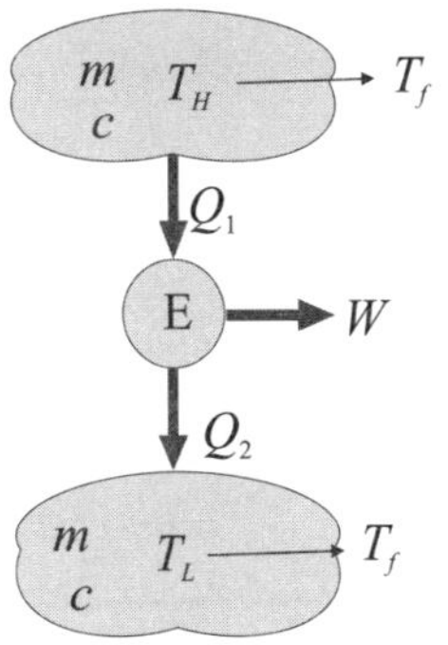

or $$\ln\left(\frac{T_f}{T_H}\right) + \ln\left(\frac{T_f}{T_L}\right) = 0$$

or $$\ln\left(\frac{T_f^2}{T_H T_L}\right) = 0$$

or $$T_f = \sqrt{T_H T_L}$$

Total work output,

$$W = Q_1 - Q_2 = mc(T_H - T_f) - mc(T_f - T_L)$$

$$W = mc(T_H + T_L - 2T_f)$$

Substituting $T_f = \sqrt{T_H T_L}$, we have

$$W = mc(T_H + T_L - 2\sqrt{T_H T_L})$$

Q.37 Ans:(A)

Change in entropy, $\Delta S = \int \frac{dQ}{T}$

$$\Delta S = \int_{T_1}^{T_2} 1 \times c\frac{dT}{T} = \int_{T_1}^{T_2} 1 \times (a + bT^2)\frac{dT}{T}$$

From which

$$\Delta S = a\ln\left(\frac{T_2}{T_1}\right) + 0.5b(T_2^2 - T_1^2)$$

Q.38 Ans:(D)

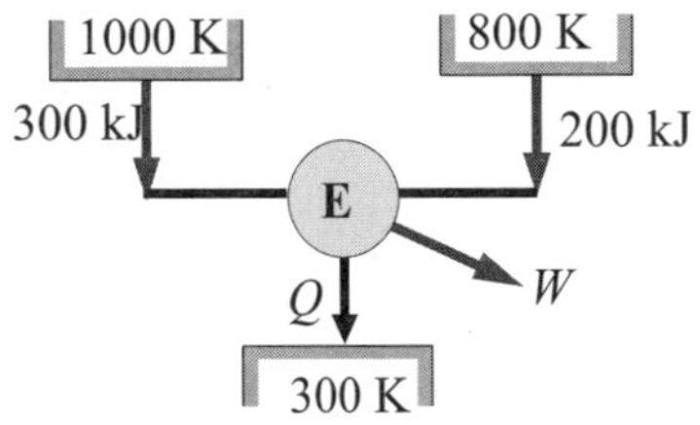

For the reversible heat engine,

$$\frac{300}{1000} + \frac{200}{800} - \frac{Q}{300} = 0$$

$$Q = 165\,\text{kJ}$$

$$W = 300 + 200 - 165$$

$$W = 335 \text{ kJ}$$

Q.39 Ans:(D)

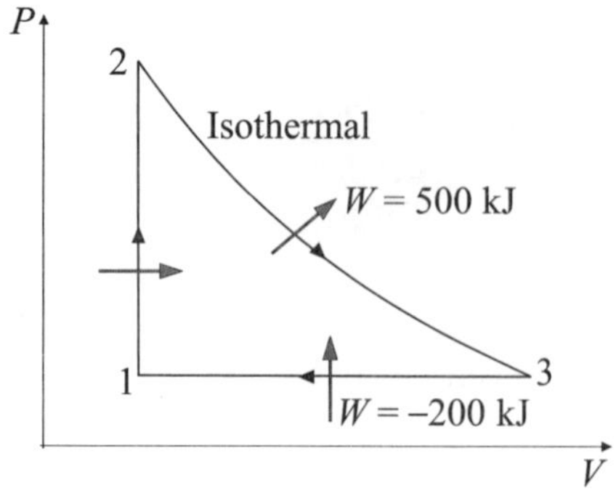

Given: For process 1-2; $Q_{1-2} = 50 \text{ kJ}$, $W_{1-2} = 0$

For process 2-3; $Q_{2-3} = 500 \text{ kJ}$, $W_{2-3} = 500 \text{ kJ}$

For process 3-1; $W_{3-1} = -200 \text{ kJ}$,

For cyclic process, $\sum Q = \sum W$

or $50 + 500 + Q_{3-1} = 0 + 500 - 200$

$$Q_{3-1} = -250 \text{ kJ}$$

For process 3-1; $Q_{3-1} = u_1 - u_3 + W_{3-1}$

$$-250 = u_1 - u_3 - 200$$

$$u_1 - u_3 = -50$$

Q.40 Ans:(A)

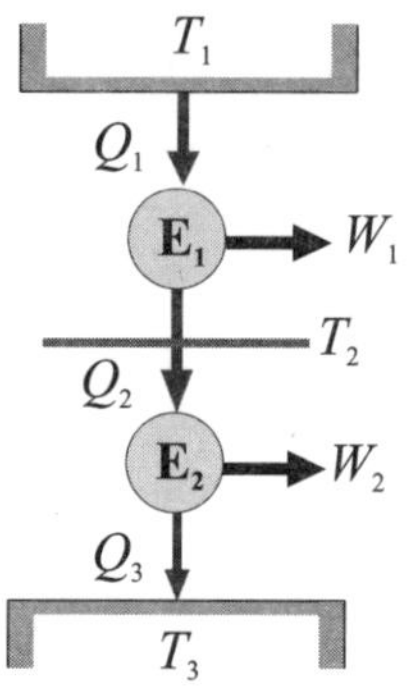

For the reversible engine,

$$\frac{Q_1}{T_1} = \frac{Q_2}{T_2} = \frac{Q_3}{T_3}$$

Efficiency of engine E_1, $\eta_1 = \frac{W_1}{Q_1} = \frac{Q_1 - Q_2}{Q_1} = 1 - \frac{Q_2}{Q_1}$

Efficiency of engine E_2, $\eta_2 = \frac{W_2}{Q_2} = \frac{Q_2 - Q_3}{Q_2} = 1 - \frac{Q_3}{Q_2}$

Efficiency of engine are same, $\eta_1 = \eta_2$

or $1 - \frac{Q_2}{Q_1} = 1 - \frac{Q_3}{Q_2} \Rightarrow Q_2^2 = Q_1 Q_3$

or $T_2^2 = T_1 T_3$

$$T_2 = \sqrt{T_1 T_3}$$

Q.41 Ans:(B)

Heat supplied, $Q_s = Q_{1\text{-}2} = c_p (T_2 - T_1)$

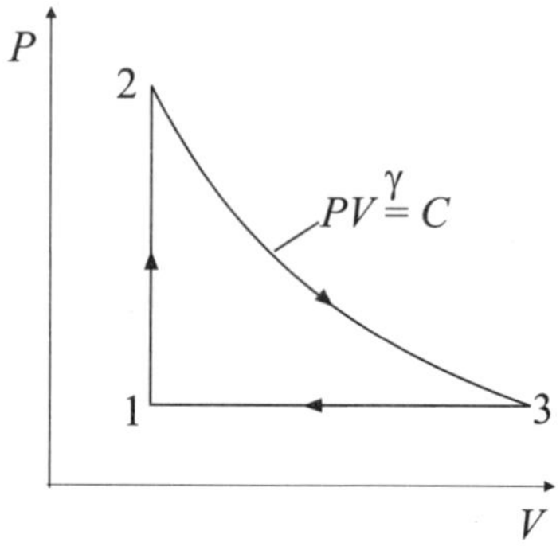

Heat rejected, $Q_r = Q_{3\text{-}1} = c_v (T_3 - T_1)$

$$Q_{2\text{-}3} = 0$$

Efficiency of cycle, $\eta = 1 - \frac{Q_r}{Q_s} = 1 - \frac{c_v (T_3 - T_1)}{c_p (T_2 - T_1)}$

$$\eta = 1 - \frac{1}{\gamma} \frac{(T_3 - T_1)}{(T_2 - T_1)} = 1 - \frac{1}{\gamma} \frac{\left(\frac{T_3}{T_1} - 1\right)}{\left(\frac{T_2}{T_1} - 1\right)}$$

Equation of state 1-3, $\frac{P_1 V_1}{T_1} = \frac{P_3 V_3}{T_3}$

$$\frac{T_3}{T_1} = \frac{P_3 V_3}{P_1 V_1} \quad \text{or} \quad \frac{T_3}{T_1} = \frac{V_3}{V_1}$$

Equation of state 2-1, $\frac{P_2 V_2}{T_2} = \frac{P_1 V_1}{T_1}$

$$\frac{T_2}{T_1} = \frac{P_2 V_2}{P_1 V_1} \quad \text{or} \quad \frac{T_2}{T_1} = \frac{P_2}{P_1}$$

From which

$$\eta = 1 - \frac{1}{\gamma} \frac{\left(\frac{v_3}{v_1} - 1\right)}{\left(\frac{p_2}{p_1} - 1\right)}$$

Q.42 Ans:(C)

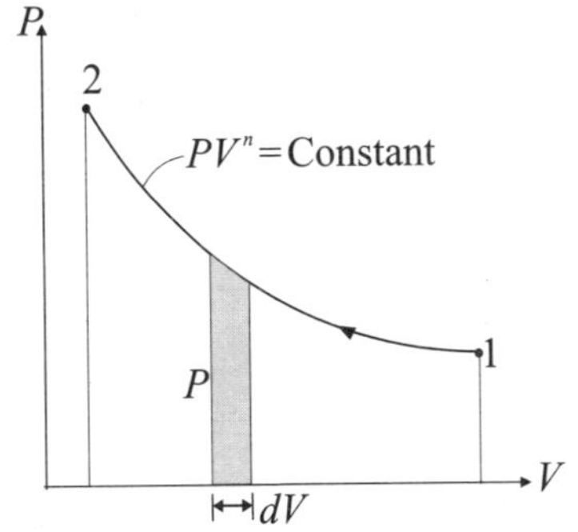

Work done in polytropic process,

$$W = \int_1^2 PdV = \int_1^2 \frac{C}{V^n} dV = \frac{C}{-n+1}[V^{-n+1}]_{V_1}^{V_2}$$

$$W = \frac{1}{1-n}\left[\frac{CV_2}{V_2^n} - \frac{CV_1}{V_1^n}\right] = \frac{P_2V_2 - P_1V_1}{1-n}$$

$$W = \frac{P_1V_1 - P_2V_2}{n-1}$$

Change in internal energy, $\Delta u = u_2 - u_1 = c_v(T_2 - T_1)$

Substituting $c_v = \frac{R}{\gamma - 1}$, we have

$$\Delta u = \frac{R}{\gamma-1}(T_2 - T_1) = \frac{RT_2 - RT_2}{\gamma - 1} = \frac{P_2V_2 - P_1V_1}{\gamma - 1}$$

From first law,

$$Q = \Delta u + W = \frac{P_2V_2 - P_1V_1}{\gamma-1} + \frac{P_1V_1 - P_2V_2}{n-1}$$

$$Q = \frac{\gamma - n}{\gamma - 1} \times \left(\frac{P_1V_1 - P_2V_2}{n-1}\right) = \frac{\gamma - n}{\gamma - 1} \times W$$

$$Q = \left(\frac{\gamma - n}{\gamma - 1}\right) \times \text{Work done}$$

Q.43 Ans:(D)

Let T_C and P_C be the critical temperature and critical pressure at triple point.

$$\ln P_C + \frac{3063}{T_C} = 15.16 \qquad \text{(i)}$$

$$\ln P_C + \frac{3754}{T_C} = 18.7 \qquad \text{(ii)}$$

From Equations (i) and (ii), $\frac{3754 - 3063}{T_C} = 3.54$

$$T_C = 195.2 \text{ K}$$

and $\ln P_C + \frac{3063}{1952} = 15.16$

$$P_C = 0.587 \text{ atm}$$

Q.44 Ans:(B)

By energy balance,

$$m_f h_f + m_g h_g = (m_f + m_g)h$$

or $1 \times 1154.2 + 2 \times 2794.2 = (1+2)h$

or $h = 2247.53$ kJ/kg

or $h = h_f + xh_{fg} = 2247.53$

or $1154.2 + x(2794.2 - 1154.2) = 2247.53$

$$x = 0.67$$

Q.45 Ans:(D)

Efficiency of Carnot engine E_1,

$$\eta_1 = \frac{1000 - 900}{1000} \quad \text{or} \quad \eta_1 = 0.1$$

Efficiency of Carnot engine E_2,

$$\eta_2 = \frac{500 - 450}{500} \quad \text{or} \quad \eta_2 = 0.1$$

$$\eta_1 = \eta_2 = 0.1$$

$$W_1 = W_2 \text{ and } \eta_1 = \eta_2 = \frac{W_1}{Q_1} = \frac{W_2}{Q_1'}$$

or $Q_1 = Q_1' \Rightarrow W_1 + QR_1 = W_2 + QR_2$

$$QR_1 = QR_2$$

Q.46 Ans:(C)

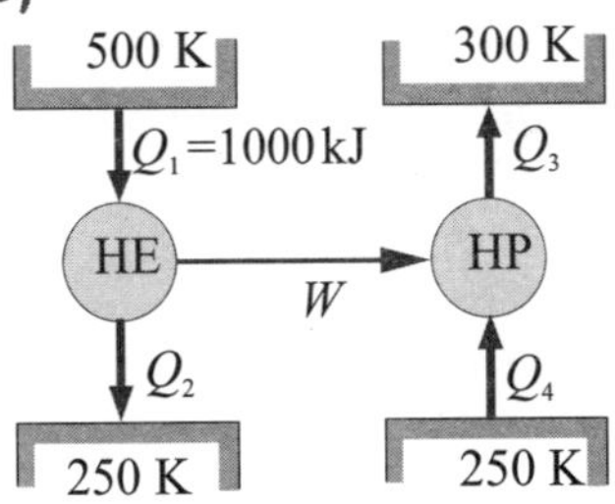

For the Carnot heat engine,

$$\frac{Q_1}{500} = \frac{Q_2}{250} = \frac{Q_1 - Q_2}{500 - 250}$$

or $\frac{1000}{500} = \frac{Q_2}{250} = \frac{W}{500 - 250}$

$$W = 500 \text{ kJ}$$

For the heat pump, $\frac{Q_4}{250} = \frac{Q_3}{300}$

or $\frac{Q_3 - W}{250} = \frac{Q_3}{300} = \frac{Q_3 - (Q_3 - W)}{300 - 250}$

$$\frac{Q_3}{300} = \frac{W}{50} = \frac{500}{50}$$

$$Q_3 = 3000 \text{ kJ}$$

COP of heat pump $= \dfrac{Q_3}{W} = \dfrac{3000}{500}$

$$\text{COP} = 6$$

Q.47 Ans:(B)

Let T_f be the final temperature of mixed liquid.

Heat gain by cold liquid = Heat loss by hot liquid

$$mc(T_f - T_1) = mc(T_2 - T_f)$$

or $$T_f = \frac{T_1 + T_2}{2}$$

Total entropy change, $\Delta S = \int_{T_1}^{T_f} mc\frac{dT}{T} + \int_{T_2}^{T_f} mc\frac{dT}{T}$

or $$\Delta S = mc\ln\frac{T_f}{T_1} + mc\ln\frac{T_f}{T_2}$$

or $$\Delta S = mc\ln\frac{T_f^2}{T_1T_2}$$

Substituting $T_f = \dfrac{T_1 + T_2}{2}$, we have

$$\Delta S = 2mc\ln\left(\frac{T_1 + T_2}{2\sqrt{T_1T_2}}\right)$$

Q.48 Ans:(B)

Entropy $dS = \dfrac{dQ}{T}$

Substituting $dQ = du + PdV$ and $dQ = dh - VdP$, we have

$$dS = \frac{du + PdV}{T} \quad \text{and} \quad dS = \frac{dh - VdP}{T}$$

For constant-volume process (V = Constant)

$$dS = \frac{du}{T} = \frac{c_v dT}{T}$$

Slope of constant volume line $\left(\dfrac{dT}{dS}\right)_{V=\text{const}} = \dfrac{T}{c_v}$

For constant-pressure process (P = Constant)

$$dS = \frac{dh}{T} = \frac{c_p dT}{T}$$

Slope of constant-pressure line $\left(\dfrac{dT}{dS}\right)_{P=\text{const}} = \dfrac{T}{c_P}$

$c_p > c_v$;

$$\left(\frac{dT}{dS}\right)_{V=\text{const.}} > \left(\frac{dT}{dS}\right)_{P=\text{const.}}$$

Q.49 Ans:(A)

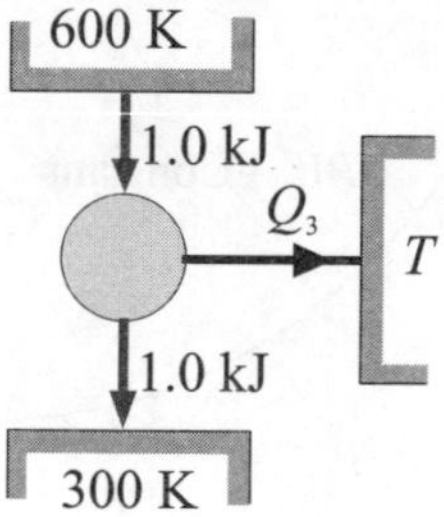

From the first law, $1 + 1 - Q_3 = 0$

$$Q_3 = 2 \text{ kJ}$$

For reversible cycle, $\sum \dfrac{Q}{T} = 0$

$$\frac{1}{600} + \frac{1}{300} - \frac{2}{T} = 0$$

$$T = 400 \text{ K}$$

Q.50 Ans:(A)

Enthalpy $h = u + PV$ or $dh = du + PdV + VdP$

Substituting $dQ = du + PdV$, we have

$$dh = dQ + VdP$$

or $$c_p dT = TdS + VdP$$

For constant pressure $dP = 0$; $c_p dT = TdS$

Slope of constant pressure curve $\dfrac{dT}{dS} = \dfrac{T}{c_p}$

Substituting $c_p = \dfrac{\gamma R}{\gamma - 1}$, we have

$$\left(\frac{dT}{dS}\right)_{(T_0,\, S_0)} = \frac{(\gamma - 1)T_0}{\gamma R}$$

Q.51 Ans:[325.7]

Heat supplied $Q = 20 \times 15 \times 60 = 18000$ J

$$Q = \Delta u + 0 \Rightarrow 18000 = 1 \times 0.7 \times 10^3 (t_2 - 27)$$

$$t_2 = 52.71°\text{C}$$

The pressure at state 2 is found using ideal-gas equation for constant-volume process,

$$\frac{P_1}{T_1} = \frac{P_2}{T_2} \Rightarrow P_2 = P_1\frac{T_2}{T_1}$$

or $$P_2 = 300 \times \frac{(273 + 52.71)}{(273 + 27)} = 325.71$$

$$P_2 = 325.71 \text{ kPa}$$

Q.52 Ans:[335]

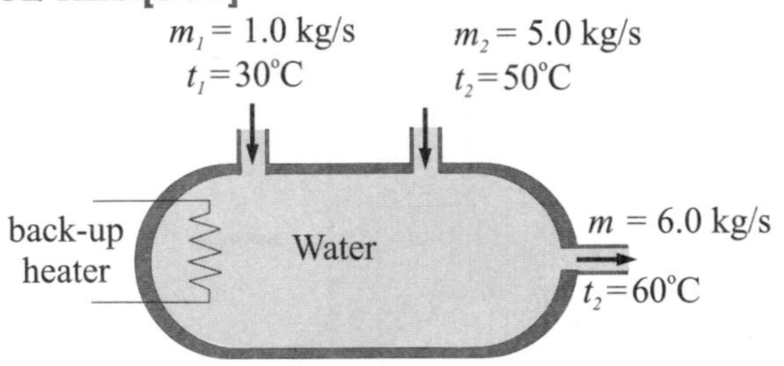

Neglecting kinetic and potential energy changes, the first law takes the form:

$$m_1h_1 + m_2h_2 + Q = (m_1 + m_3)h_3$$
$$Q = (m_1 + m_3)h_3 - m_1h_1 - m_2h_2$$
$$= (m_1 + m_3)ct_3 - m_1ct_1 - m_2ct_2$$

or $Q = (1+5)\times 4.18\times 60 - 1\times 4.18\times 30 - 5\times 4.18\times 50$

$$Q = 335 \text{ kW}$$

Q.53 Ans:[–1.058]

Change in entropy of metal, $\Delta S = \int_{T_1}^{T_2} mc\frac{dT}{T}$

$$\Delta S = mc\ln\left(\frac{T_2}{T_1}\right) = 1\times 1\times \ln\left(\frac{273+30}{273+600}\right)$$

$$\Delta S = -1.058 \text{ kJ/K}$$

Q.54 Ans:[25.10]

Final temperature of mixed water,

$$t_f = \frac{m_1t_1 + m_2t_2}{m_1 + m_2} = \frac{2\times 60 + 4\times 30}{2+4}$$

$$t_f = 40°\text{C}$$

Entropy generated, $\Delta S = m_1c_1\int_{T_1}^{T_f}\frac{dT}{T} + m_2c_2\int_{T_2}^{T_f}\frac{dT}{T}$

$$\Delta S = m_1c_1 \ln\left(\frac{T_f}{T_1}\right) + m_2c_2 \ln\left(\frac{T_f}{T_2}\right)$$

or $\Delta S = 2\times 4.18 \ln\left(\frac{273+40}{273+60}\right) + 4\times 4.18\ln\left(\frac{273+40}{273+30}\right)$

From which

$$\Delta S = 25.10 \text{ J/K}$$

Q.55 Ans:[97.5]

Heat supplied to engine, $Q_1 = (h_g - h_f)_{t_1=50°\text{C}}$

$$Q_1 = (1471.6 - 421.5) = 1050.1 \text{ kJ/kg}$$

$$\frac{Q_1}{T_1} = \frac{Q_2}{T_2} = \frac{W}{T_1 - T_2}$$

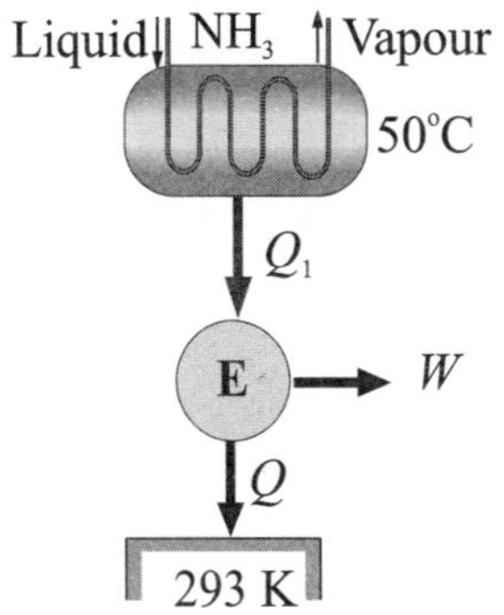

$$\Rightarrow \quad W = \frac{T_1 - T_2}{T_1}Q_1$$

$$W = \left(\frac{323-293}{323}\right)\times 1050.1$$

$$W = 97.5 \text{ kJ/kg}$$

Q.56 Ans:[1386.3]

Using Clausius-Clapeyron equation,

$$\frac{dP}{dT} = \frac{l}{T(V_f - V_g)}$$

or $$\frac{P_2 - P_1}{T_2 - T_1} = \frac{l}{T_o(V_{fo} - V_{go})}$$

At pressure 0.5 bar

$$\frac{(0.6-0.4)\times 10^5}{-43.3-(-50.4)} = \frac{l}{[273+(-46.5)][2.175-1.433\times 10^{-3}]}$$

Latent heat, $l = 13.86\times 10^5$

Latent heat, $l = 1386.3$ kJ/kg

Q.57 Ans:[625]

Using the first law, we have

$$dQ = du + dW$$

Dividing by dT, we have $\frac{dQ}{dT} = \frac{du}{dT} + \frac{dW}{dT}$

$$2 = \frac{du}{dT} + 2 - 01T$$

or $$\frac{du}{dT} = 01T$$

Change in internal energy,

$$\Delta u = \int_{T_1}^{T_2} 0.1T\,dT = 0.05(T_2^2 - T_1^2)$$

or $$\Delta u = 0.05(150^2 - 100^2)$$

$$\Delta u = 625 \text{ kJ}$$

Q.58 Ans:[504]

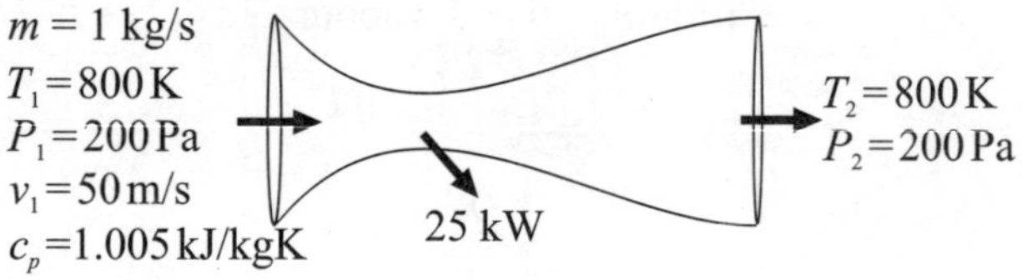

Neglecting the potential energy changes, energy equation takes the form:

$$h_1 + \frac{v_1^2}{2} + \frac{Q}{m} = h_2 + \frac{v_2^2}{2}$$

or $$c_p T_1 + \frac{v_1^2}{2} + \frac{Q}{m} = c_p T_2 + \frac{v_2^2}{2}$$

or $$v_2 = \sqrt{2c_p(T_1 - T_2) + v_1^2 + \frac{2Q}{m}}$$

or $$v_2 = \sqrt{2 \times 1.005 \times 10^3 (800 - 650) + 50^2 - \frac{2 \times 25 \times 10^3}{1}}$$

$$v_2 = 504 \text{ m/s}$$

Q.59 Ans:[144]

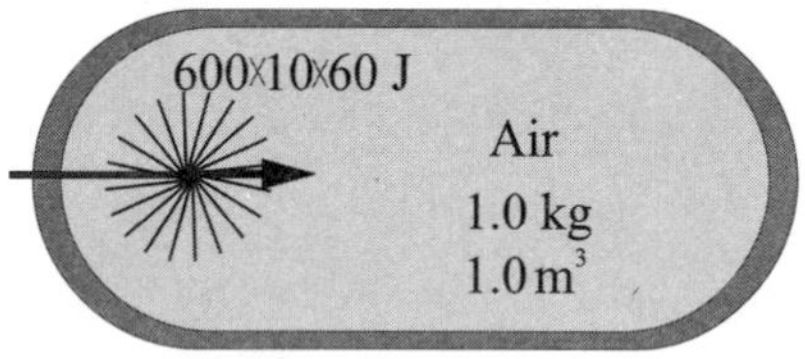

Heat added at constant volume,

$$Q = \Delta u = mc_v(T_2 - T_1)$$

or $$Q = mc_v T_1\left(\frac{T_2}{T_1} - 1\right) = mc_v T_1\left(\frac{P_2}{P_1} - 1\right)$$

or $$Q = mc_v \frac{(P_2 - P_1)}{\left(\frac{P_1}{T_1}\right)} = mc_v \frac{\Delta P}{\left(\frac{R}{V_1}\right)}$$

or $$Q = mV_1 \frac{c_v}{R}\Delta P = mV_1 \frac{\Delta P}{\gamma - 1}$$

$$\Delta P = \frac{(\gamma - 1)}{mV_1} Q$$

$$= \frac{(1.4 - 1)}{1 \times 1} 600 \times 10 \times 60 = 144000 \text{ Pa}$$

$$\Delta \text{P} = 144 \text{ kPa}$$

Q.60 Ans:[848]

Writing steady flow energy equation,

$$h_1 + \frac{v_1^2}{2} + gz_1 + \frac{Q}{m} = h_2 + \frac{v_2^2}{2} + gz_2 + \frac{W}{m}$$

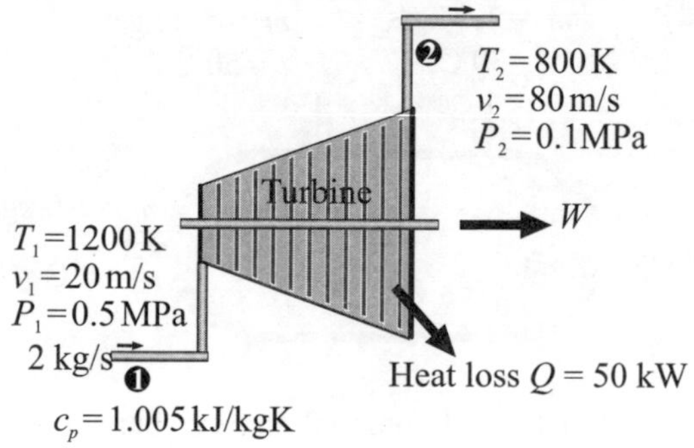

or $$W = m(h_1 - h_2) + \frac{m}{2}(v_1^2 - v_2^2) + Q$$

or $$W = mc_p(T_1 - T_2) + \frac{m}{2}(v_1^2 - v_2^2) + Q$$

or $$W = 2 \times 1.005 \times 10^3 (1200 - 800) + \frac{2}{2}(20^2 - 80^2) - 50 \times 10^3$$

$$W = 848 \text{ kW}$$

Q.61 Ans:[48.9]

Using the steady flow energy equation,

$$h_1 + \frac{v_1^2}{2} + gz_1 + \frac{Q}{\dot{m}} = h_2 + \frac{v_2^2}{2} + gz_2 + \frac{W}{\dot{m}}$$

or $$c_p T_1 + \frac{v_1^2}{2} + 0 + 0 = c_p T_2 + \frac{v_2^2}{2} + 0 + 0$$

$$v_2 = \sqrt{2c_p(T_1 - T_2) + v_1^2}$$

or $$v_2 = \sqrt{2 \times 1.005 \times 10^3 (500 - 510) + 150^2}$$

$$v_2 = 48.9 \text{ m/s}$$

Q.62 Ans:[126]

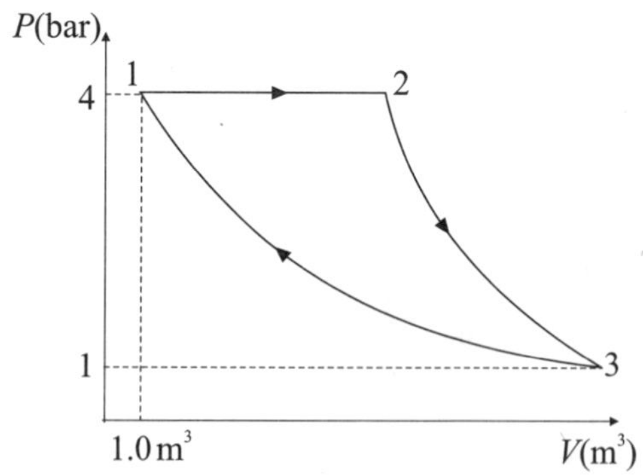

For closed cycle,

Net heat interaction, $\sum Q = \sum W =$ Area of 1231

Process 1-3; $P_1V_1 = P_3V_3$

or $$V_3 = V_1\left(\frac{P_1}{P_3}\right) = 1 \times \left(\frac{4}{1}\right) = 4 \text{ m}^3$$

Process 2-3; $P_2V_2^n = P_3V_3^n$

or $\quad 4\times V_2^{1.4} = 1\times 4^{1.4} \quad \Rightarrow \quad V_2 = 1.48\,\text{m}^3$

$$\sum Q = \sum W = \text{Area of } 1231$$

$$\sum Q = P_1(V_2 - V_1) + \frac{P_2V_2 - P_3V_3}{n-1} - P_1V_1\ln\left(\frac{V_3}{V_1}\right)$$

$$\sum Q = 4\times 10^5(1.48-1) + \frac{4\times10^5\times1.48 - 1\times10^5\times4}{1.4-1} - 1\times10^5\times4\ln\left(\frac{4}{1}\right)$$

$$\sum Q = 126\,\text{kJ}$$

Q.63 Ans:[57.8]

Work done, $W = \dfrac{P_2V_2 - P_1V_1}{n-1} = \dfrac{P_1V_1}{n-1}\left[\dfrac{P_2}{P_1}\left(\dfrac{V_2}{V_1}\right) - 1\right]$

or $\quad W = \dfrac{P_1V_1}{n-1}\left[\dfrac{P_2}{P_1}\left(\dfrac{P_1}{P_2}\right)^{\frac{1}{n}} - 1\right] = \dfrac{P_1V_1}{n-1}\left[\left(\dfrac{P_2}{P_1}\right)^{\frac{n-1}{n}} - 1\right]$

or $\quad W = \dfrac{0.1\times10^6\times1\times10^{-3}}{1.3-1}\left[\left(\dfrac{2}{1}\right)^{\frac{1.3-1}{1.3}} - 1\right]$

$$W = 57.80\,\text{J}$$

Q.64 Ans:[64]

Let A be the area of collector plat.

Energy collection per second $\quad Q_1 = 0.5A$ kW

Efficiency of engine,

$$\eta = \frac{W}{Q_1} = 0.2$$

or $\quad \dfrac{1}{Q_1} = 0.2$

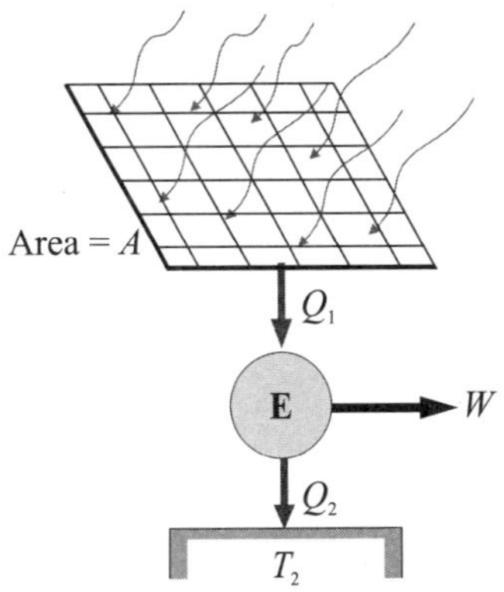

or $\quad \dfrac{1}{05A} = 02$

$$A = 10\,\text{m}^2$$

Q.65 Ans:[70]

Neglecting the kinetic and potential energy, the energy equation takes the form

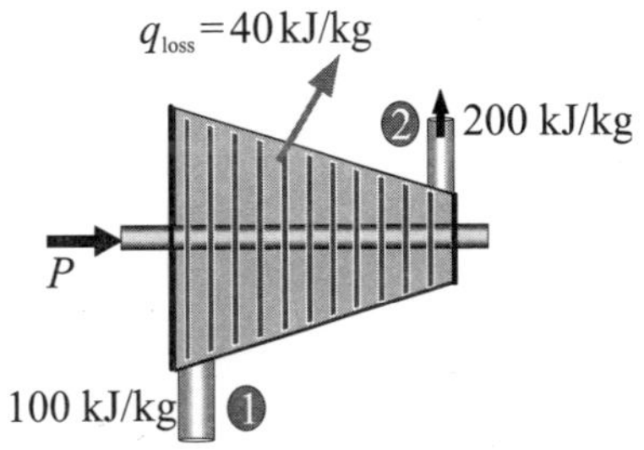

$$h_1 + q = h_2 + w$$

or $\quad 100 - 40 = 200 + w$

or $\quad w = -140\,\text{kJ/kg}$

Power required for mass flow of 0.5 kg/s is

$$P = \dot{m}\times w = 0.5\times140$$

$$P = 70\,\text{kW}$$

13 Thermodynamics Applications

GATE Mechanical Engg.

GATE Syllabus

Power Engineering: Air and gas compressors; Vapour and gas power cycles, Concepts of regeneration and reheat.

I.C. Engines: Air-standard Otto, Diesel and Dual cycles.

Refrigeration and air-conditioning: Vapour and gas refrigeration and heat pump cycles; Properties of moist air, psychrometric chart, basic psychrometric processes.

Chapter Outline

13.1 KEY CONCEPTS AND FORMULAS

Air and Gas Compressors

A gas compressor is a mechanical device that increases the pressure of a gas by reducing its volume.

Types of Compressors

Compressors
- Positive Displacement
  - Rotary
  - Reciprocating
- Dynamic
  - Centrifugal
  - Axial

Reciprocating Air compressor

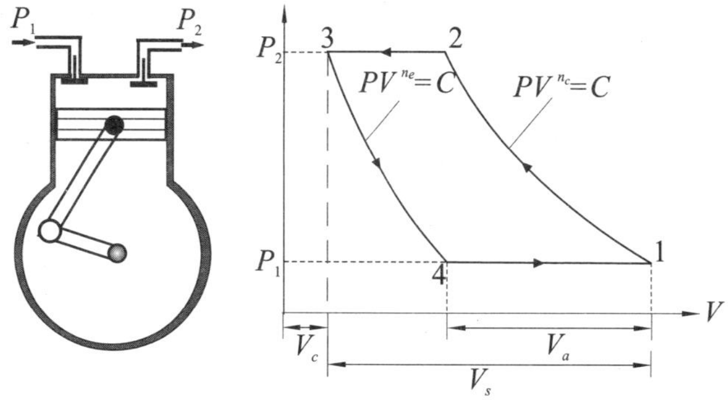

$$W_{comp} = W_{1-2} = \frac{n_c}{n_c - 1} P_1 V_1 \left[\left(\frac{P_2}{P_1} \right)^{\frac{n_c - 1}{n_c}} - 1 \right],$$

$$W_{exp} = W_{3\text{-}4} = \frac{n_e}{n_e - 1} P_1 V_4 \left[\left(\frac{P_2}{P_1} \right)^{\frac{n_e - 1}{n_e}} - 1 \right]$$

$$W_{net} = W_{comp} - W_{exp}$$

If $n_e = n_c = n$ then $W_{net} = \frac{n}{n-1} P_1 (V_1 - V_4)\left[\left(\frac{P_2}{P_1}\right)^{\frac{n-1}{n}} - 1\right]$

Volumetric efficiency:

$$\eta_{vol} = \frac{V_1 - V_4}{V_1 - V_3} = 1 + C - C\left(\frac{V_4}{V_3}\right)$$

$$\eta_{vol} = 1 - C\left[\left(\frac{P_2}{P_1}\right)^{\frac{1}{n}} - 1\right]; \text{ where } C = \frac{V_c}{V_s}$$

Condition for minimum compression work (multistage):

$$\frac{P_2}{P_1} = \frac{P_3}{P_2} = \frac{P_4}{P_3} = \ldots = \frac{P_{n+1}}{P_n}$$

$$r_p = \left(\frac{P_{n+1}}{P_1}\right)^{\frac{1}{n}}$$

Centrifugal Compressor

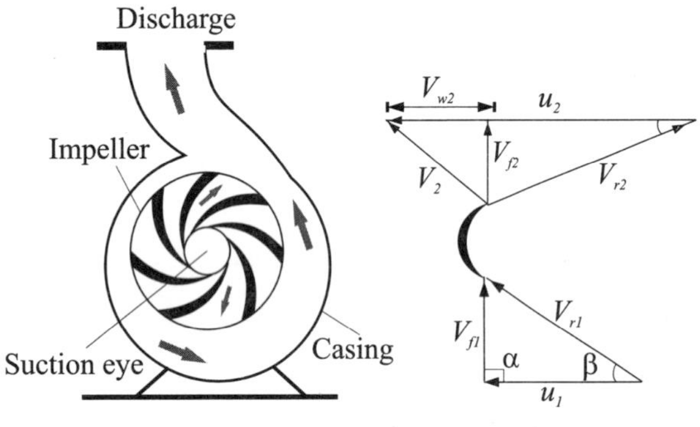

Centrifugal compressor **Velocity triangle**

Work input per kg of air $w = u_1 V_{w1} + u_2 V_{w2}$ (J/kg)

Fluid enters radially ($\alpha = 90°$); $V_{w1} = 0$

$$w = u_2 V_{w2} \text{ (J/kg)}$$

Power input to compressor, $P = \dot{m} u_2 V_{w2}$ (W)

Steady flow energy equation for compressor

$$w = \left(h_2 + \frac{V_2^2}{2}\right) - \left(h_1 + \frac{V_1^2}{2}\right)$$

$$w = h_{02} - h_{01} = c_p (T_{02} - T_{01}) = c_p T_{01}\left(\frac{T_{02}}{T_{01}} - 1\right)$$

$$w = c_p T_{01}\left[\left(\frac{T_{02}}{T_{01}}\right)^{\frac{\gamma-1}{\gamma}} - 1\right]$$

Degree of Reaction

The degree of reaction is defined as the ratio of static pressure rise in the impeller to the total static pressure rise in the compressor.

Slip: The difference between blade tip velocity u_2 and Whirl velocity V_{w2} is known as slip.

Slip factor $= \frac{V_{w2}}{u_2}$

Steam Tables

Steam is the vapour form of water and is invisible when pure and dry. It does not obey the laws of perfect gases, until it is perfectly dry.

The various properties of steam (such as specific volume, specific enthalpy and specific entropy) of dry saturated steam and superheated steam vary with the variations of temperature and pressure. These values are carefully determined by observations and calculations first in FPS system and are made available in a tabular form known as *steam table*. There are two important steam tables. One of them is based in terms of temperature and the other in terms of pressure.

Mollier Diagram

It is a graphical representation of steam tables, in which specific entropy is plotted along the ordinate (x-axis) and specific enthalpy along the abscissa (y-axis). A Mollier diagram has the following lines:

1. Dryness fraction lines, 2. Constant specific volume lines, 3. Constant pressure lines, 4. Constant temperature lines.

Rankine Cycle

Rankine cycle is composed of the four ideal processes shown on the T- S diagram.

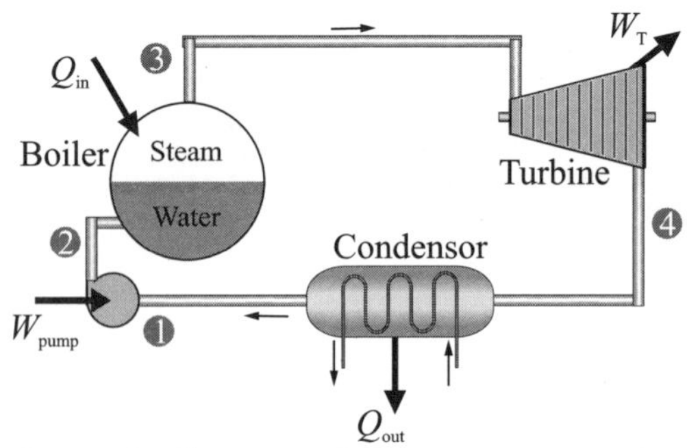

Schematic diagram of a steam power plant

It consists of four reversible processes: 1-2 Isentropic compression in a pump, 2-3 Constant pressure heat addition in a boiler, 3-4 Isentropic expansion in a Turbine, and 4-1 Constant pressure heat rejected in a condenser.

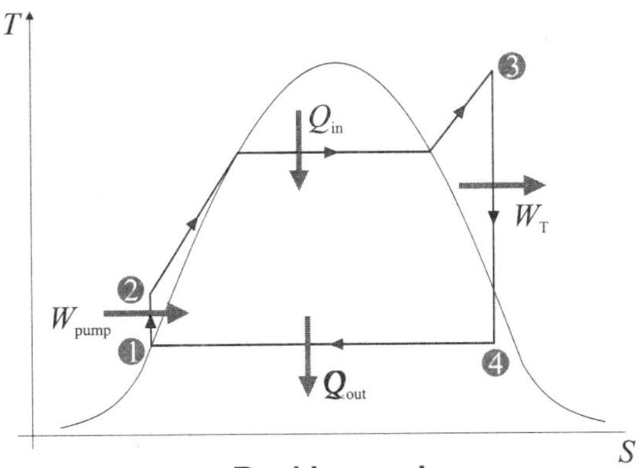

Rankine cycle

$$Q_{in} = \dot{m}(h_2 - h_1)$$
$$Q_{out} = \dot{m}(h_3 - h_4)$$
$$W_T = \dot{m}(h_2 - h_3)$$
$$W_p = \dot{m}(h_1 - h_4) \quad \text{or} \quad W_p = v(P_2 - P_1)$$
$$(\eta_{th})_{Rankine} = \frac{W_{net}}{Q_{in}} = \frac{W_T - W_P}{Q_{in}}$$

The efficiency of the Rankine cycle can be improved by: (a) lowering the condenser pressure, (b) Superheating the steam to high temperature, and (c) increasing the boiler pressure.

Brayton Cycle

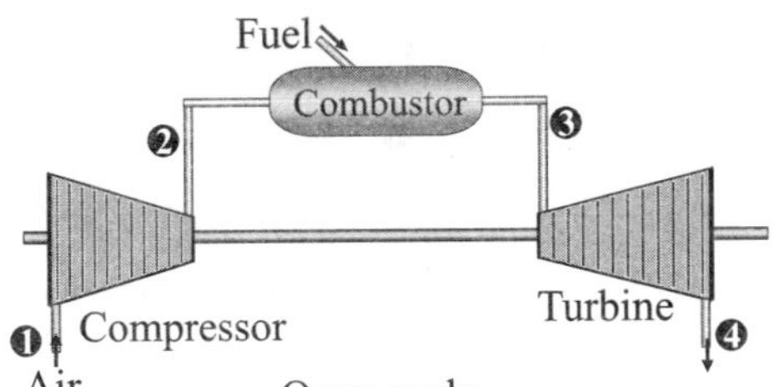

Open cycle

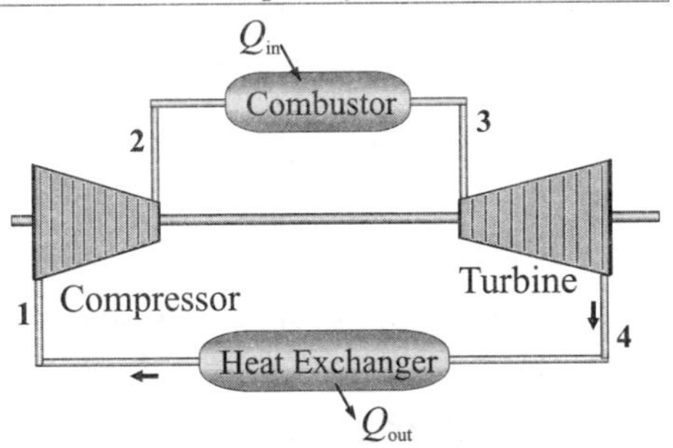

Closed cycle

Gas turbine cycles

The gas turbine may operate on open cycle when used in thermal power plants or airplane or on a closed cycle when used in a nuclear power plant.

$$Q_{in} = mc_p(T_3 - T_2); \qquad Q_{out} = mc_p(T_4 - T_1)$$

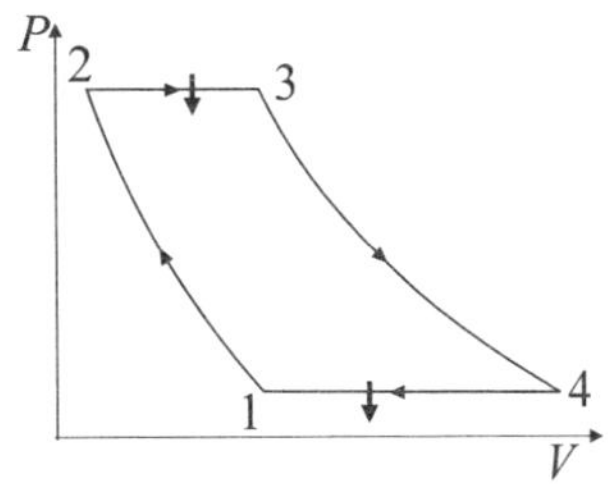

Brayton cycle on *P-V*

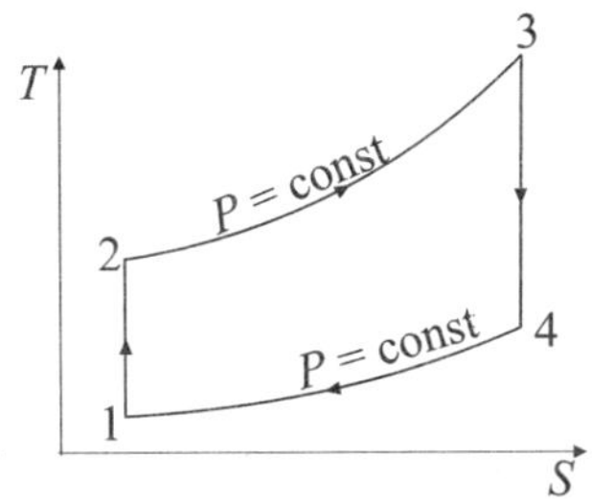

Brayton cycle on *T-S*

$$W_{compressor} = mc_p(T_2 - T_1); \quad W_{turbine} = mc_p(T_3 - T_4)$$

$$\text{Efficiency, } \eta = 1 - \frac{Q_{out}}{Q_{in}}$$

$$\text{or} \quad \eta = \frac{W_{turbine} - W_{compressor}}{Q_{in}} \quad \text{or} \quad \eta = 1 - \left(\frac{P_1}{P_2}\right)^{\frac{\gamma-1}{\gamma}},$$

$$\text{or} \quad \eta = 1 - \frac{1}{r_p^{(\gamma-1)/\gamma}}$$

$$\text{Back work ratio, BWR} = \frac{W_{compressor}}{W_{turbine}}$$

Brayton Cycle with Regeneration and Reheat

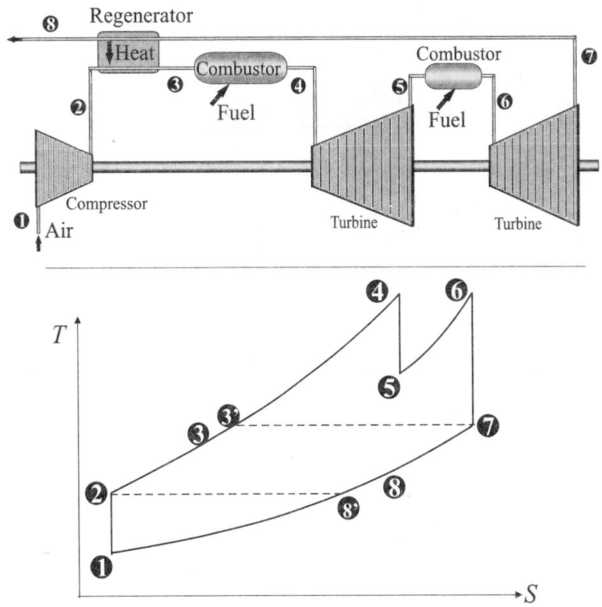

Brayton cycle with regeneration and reheat

I.C. Engines

Air-standard Assumptions:

(1) The working fluid is air and behaves as an ideal gas.

(2) All the processes in cycle are reversible.

(3) The combustion process is replaced by a heat addition

process from an external source.

(4) The exhaust process is replaced by a heat rejection process.

A cycle for which the air-standard assumptions are applicable is frequently referred to as an air-standard cycle.

Otto Cycle

The Otto cycle is the ideal cycle for spark-ignition reciprocating engine. It consists of four reversible processes: 1-2 Isentropic compression, 2-3 Constant-volume heat addition, 3-4 Isentropic expansion, and 4-1 Constant-volume heat rejection.

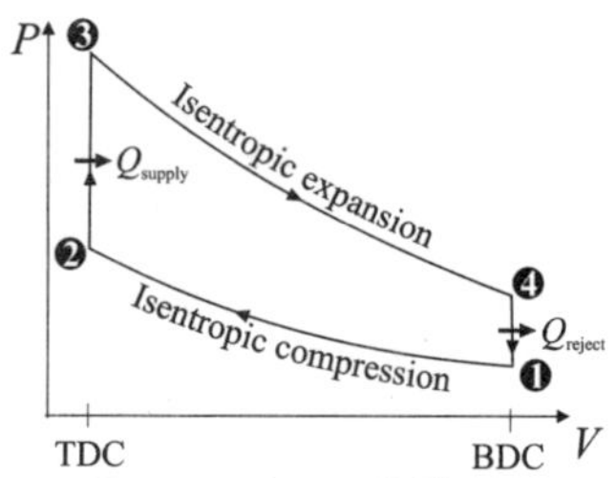

Otto cycle on *P-V*

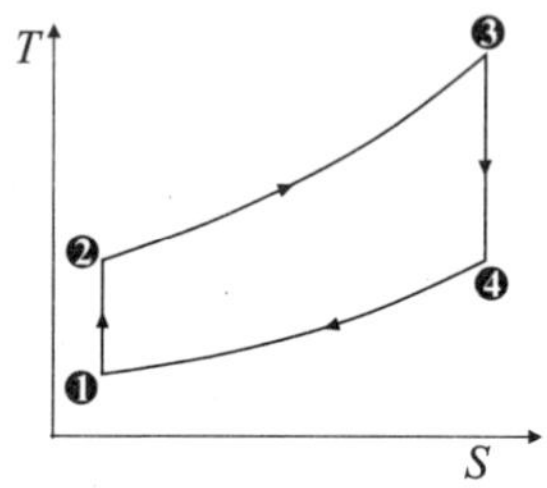

Otto cycle on *T-S*

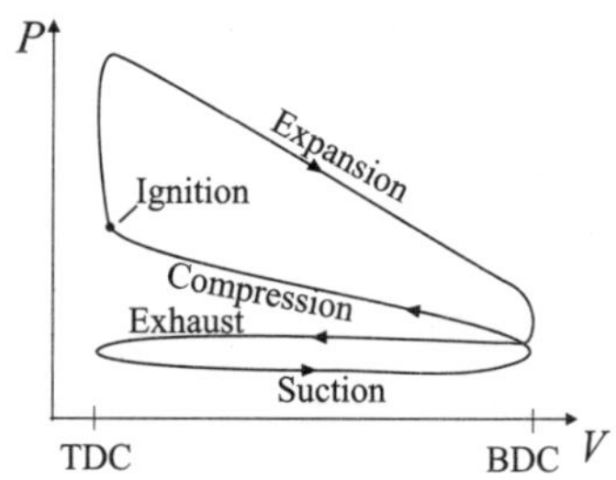

Actual four stroke spark ignition engine on *P-V*

Heat supplied, $Q_{in} = Q_{2-3} = mc_v(T_3 - T_2)$,

Heat rejected, $Q_{out} = Q_{4-1} = mc_v(T_4 - T_1)$

Efficiency, $\eta_{Otto} = 1 - \dfrac{Q_{out}}{Q_{in}}$

or $\eta_{Otto} = 1 - \dfrac{mc_v(T_4 - T_1)}{mc_v(T_3 - T_2)}$

or $\eta_{Otto} = 1 - \dfrac{1}{\left(\dfrac{V_1}{V_2}\right)^{\gamma-1}}$

$\eta_{otto} = 1 - \dfrac{1}{r^{\gamma-1}}$, where r is compression ratio.

The higher the compression ratio, the higher the efficiency.

Diesel Cycles

The diesel cycle is the ideal cycle for compression-ignition reciprocating engine. It consists of four reversible processes: 1-2 Isentropic compression, 2-3 Constant-pressure heat addition, 3-4 Isentropic expansion, and 4-1 Constant-volume heat rejection.

Heat supplied, $Q_{in} = Q_{2-3} = mc_p(T_3 - T_2)$,

Heat rejected, $Q_{out} = Q_{4-1} = mc_v(T_4 - T_1)$

Efficiency, $\eta_{diesel} = 1 - \dfrac{Q_{out}}{Q_{in}}$

or $\eta_{diesel} = 1 - \dfrac{mc_v(T_4 - T_1)}{mc_p(T_3 - T_2)}$

or $\eta_{diesel} = 1 - \dfrac{1}{\gamma}\dfrac{T_1\left(\dfrac{T_4}{T_1} - 1\right)}{T_2\left(\dfrac{T_3}{T_2} - 1\right)}$

$\eta_{diesel} = 1 - \dfrac{1}{r^{\gamma-1}}\left(\dfrac{r_c^{\gamma} - 1}{\gamma(r_c - 1)}\right)$, Where $r = \dfrac{V_1}{V_2}$ is compression ratio and $r_c = \dfrac{V_3}{V_2}$ is cut off-ratio.

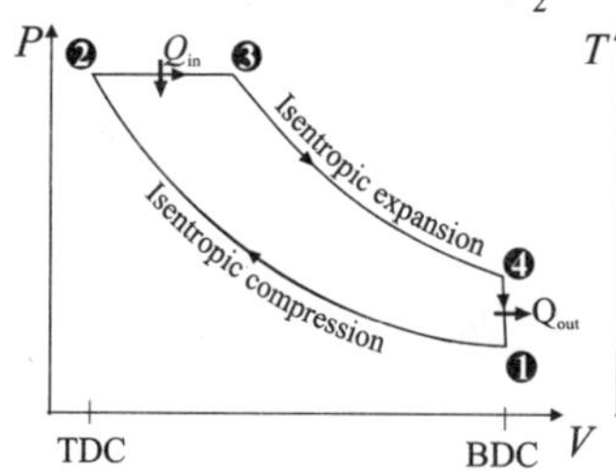

Diesel cycle on *P-V*

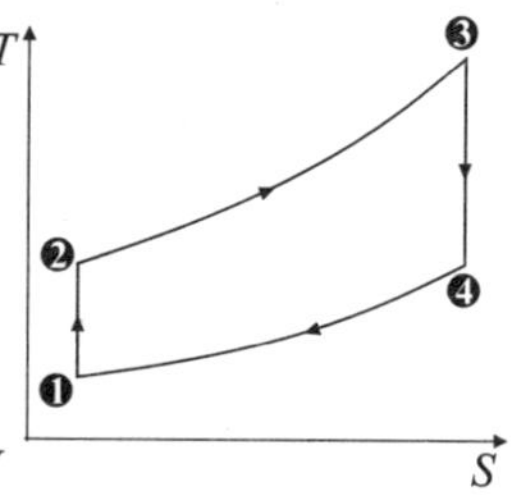

Diesel cycle on *T-S*

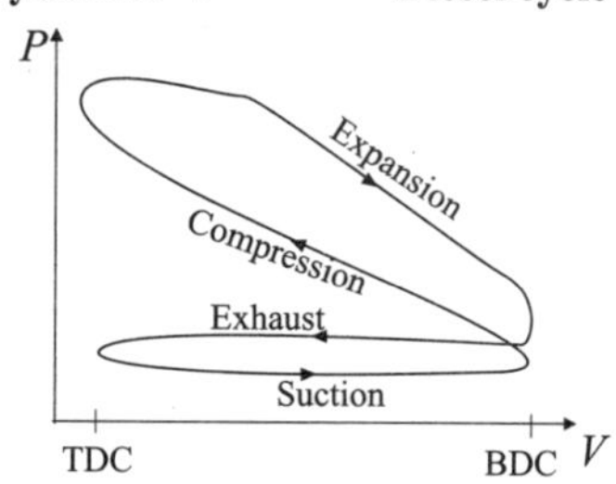

Actual four stroke compression ignition engine on *P-V*

Refrigerator and Heat Pump

Refrigerator and heat pump are the devices that transfer heat from a low-temperature medium to a high-temperature. Refrigerator and heat pump operate on the same cycle but differ in their objectives.

Unit of refrigeration (TR): A unit used in the field of refrigeration is known as *ton of refrigeration*.

A ton of refrigeration is defined as the quantity of heat required to be removed from one ton of ice within 24 hours when the initial condition of water is zero.

$$1\text{ TR} \approx \frac{1000 \times 80}{24} = 55.4\text{ kcal/min}$$

$$1\text{TR} \approx 50\text{ kcal/min} \quad \text{or} \quad 1\text{ TR} \approx 3.517\text{ kW}$$

Vapour-compression Refrigeration Cycle

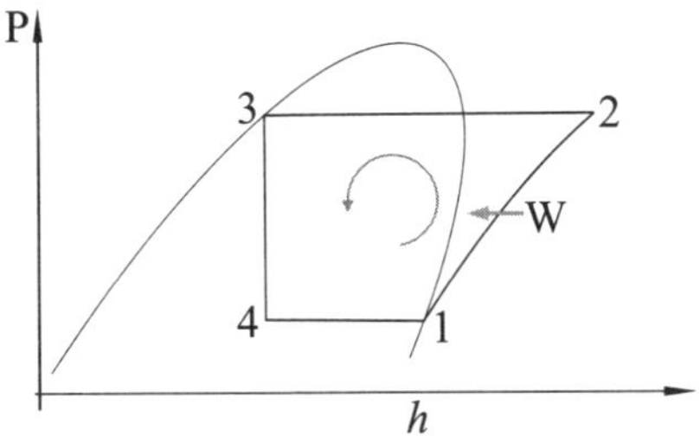

$$\text{COP} = \frac{Q_{4\text{-}1}}{W}$$

where $Q_{4\text{-}1} = m(h_1 - h_4)$ and $W = m(h_2 - h_1)$

$$\text{COP} = \frac{h_1 - h_4}{h_2 - h_1}$$

Reverse Brayton Cycle

Reverse Brayton cycle is also called Bell-Coleman cycle.

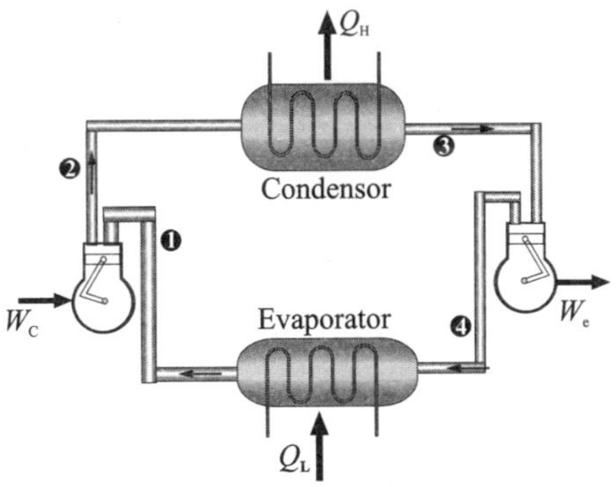

Schemetic flow diagram

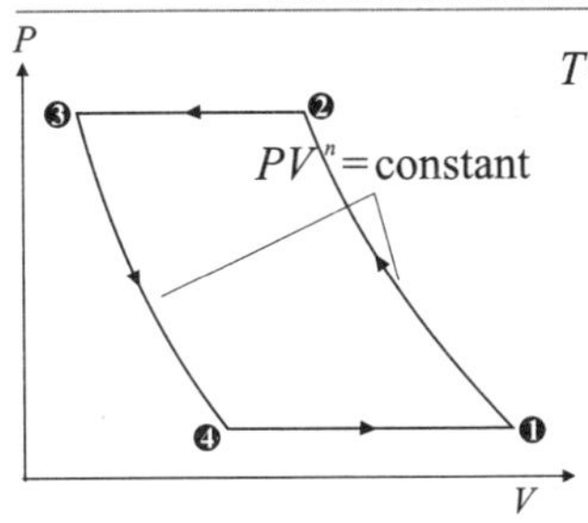

***P-V* diagram**

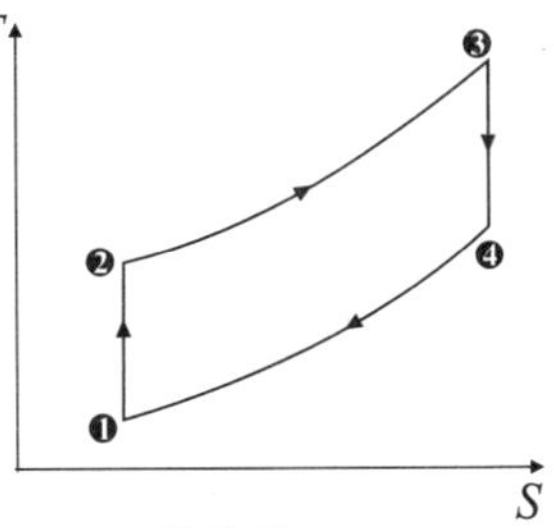

***T-S* diagram**

$$\text{COP} = \frac{Q_{4\text{-}1}}{W_C - W_e}, \text{ where } Q = c_p(T_1 - T_4)$$

$$W = \oint W = \oint Q = c_p(T_2 - T_3) - c_P(T_1 - T_4)$$

$$W = W_C - W_e$$

$$W = \frac{n}{n-1}(P_1V_1 - P_2V_2) - \frac{n}{n-1}(P_4V_4 - P_3V_3)$$

Refrigerant

The working fluid used in the refrigeration cycle is called a Refrigerant.

Selection of refrigerant depends on their: 1. availability, 2. cost, 3. toxicity, 4. COP (higher COP), 5. favourable thermodynamic and transport properties, 6. higher heat transfer coefficients, 7. ease of detectability in the event of a leakage, and 8. impact on the ozone layer.

Other desirable characteristics of a refrigerant are: 1. non-corrosive 2. non-inflammable 3. chemically stable 4. high enthalpy of evaporation, and 5. available at low cost.

Psychrometry and Psychrometric Properties

Dry air: Air is mixture of nitrogen, oxygen, carbon dioxide, argon and some other gases. When water vapour is not included it is called *dry air*.

Moist air: It is the mixture of dry air and water vapour.

Specific humidity (Humidity ratio): It is the ratio of the mass of water vapour to the mass of dry air in a given volume of air sample.

$$\text{Specific humidity, } \omega = \frac{m_{\text{vapour}}}{m_{\text{dry air}}} \quad \text{or } \omega = 0.622\left[\frac{P_v}{P - P_v}\right]$$

Relative humidity ϕ : It is the ratio of the actual mass of the water vapour in a given volume to that which it would have if it is saturated at the same temperature.

$$\text{Relative humidity, } \phi = \frac{m_v}{m_s} \quad \text{or} \quad \phi = \frac{P_v}{P_s}$$

Dry-bulb temperature: The temperature of air measured by ordinary thermometer is known as *dry-bulb temperature.*

Dew-point temperature t_{dp}: It is the temperature at which condensation begins, if air is cooled at constant pressure.

Wet-bulb temperature: The temperature measured by the thermometer when its bulb is covered with wet cloth and is exposed to a current of moving air is known as *wet-bulb temperature.*

Degree of saturation: It is the ratio of mass of water vapour associated with unit mass of dry air to mass of water vapour associated with saturated unit mass of dry air.

Enthalpy of moist air: The enthalpy of moist air is the sum of the enthalpy of dry air and the enthalpy of water vapour associated with the dry air.

Enthalpy of the moist air per unit mass of the dry air,

$$h = h_a + \omega h_v$$

Psychrometric Chart

Psychrometric chart shows the various properties (relative humidity, wet-bulb temperature, specific volume, specific enthalpy, etc.) plotted as a function of dry-bulb temperature and specific humidity (humidity ratio).

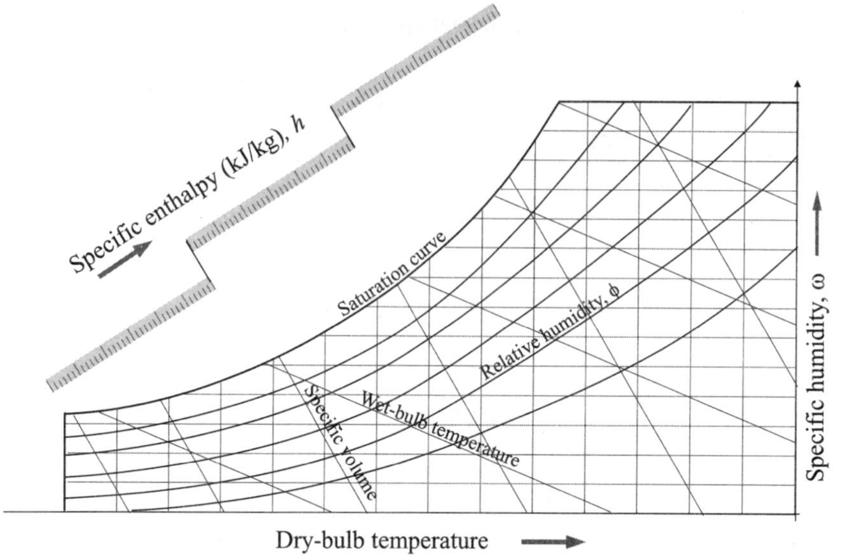

Psychrometric Chart

Psychrometric Processes

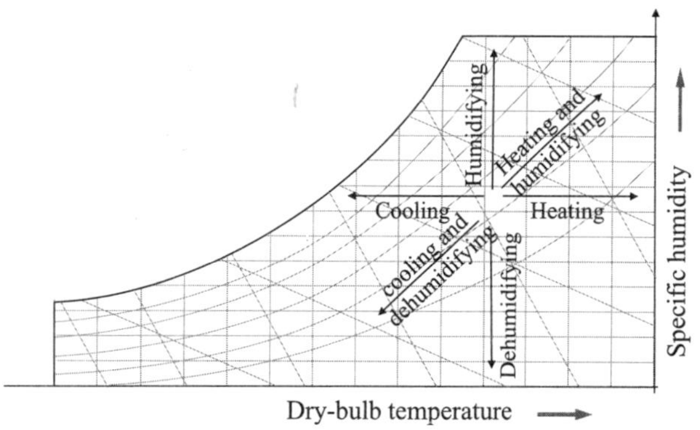

1. Sensible heating and cooling
2. Humidification and dehumidification
3. Cooling and adiabatic humidification
4. Cooling and humidification by water injection
5. Heating and humidification
6. Heating and humidification by steam injection
7. Adiabatic chemical dehumidification
8. Adiabatic mixing of air streams

Bypass Factor (BPF) of a Heating and Cooling Coils

When air is blown over a heating or a cooling coil, a part of it bypasses the coil unaffected, while the remaining part comes in a direct contact with coil and undergoes a temperature change. The degree of bypassing is measured in terms of bypass factor (BPF).

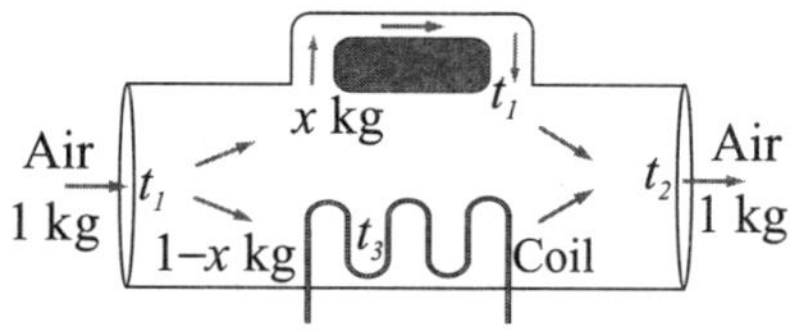

Using energy balance $x c_p t_1 + (1-x) c_p t_3 = x c_p t_2$

Bypass factor, BPF, $x = \dfrac{t_3 - t_2}{t_3 - t_1}$

$$\text{BPF} = \frac{t_3 - t_2}{t_3 - t_1} \text{ (for heating coil)}$$

$$\text{BPF} = \frac{t_2 - t_3}{t_1 - t_3} \text{ (for cooling coil)}$$

Efficiency of cooling or heating coil is $\eta = 1 - \text{BPF}$.

Sensible Heat Factor (SHF)

The heat added to moist air during a psychrometric process is made up of sensible heat and latent heat. The ratio of sensible heat to the total heat is known as *sensible heat factor*, SHF.

$$\text{SHF} = \frac{\text{SH}}{\text{SH} + \text{LH}}$$

where SH = Sensible heat, LH = Latent heat

13.2 SOLVED EXAMPLES

Previous Years GATE Questions

Example 13.1

Which of the following statements regarding a Rankine cycle with reheating are TRUE?

(i) Increase in average temperature of heat addition

(ii) Reduction in thermal efficiency

(iii) Drier steam at the turbine exit

(A) Only (i) and (ii) are correct

(B) Only (ii) and (iii) are correct

(C) Only (i) and (iii) are correct

(D) (i), (ii) and (iii) are correct

GATE 2015

Solution

By reheating in Rankine cycle,

(i) Increase in average temperature of heat addition

(iii) drier steam at the turbine exit

Example 13.2

In a Rankine cycle, the enthalpies at turbine entry and outlet are 3159 kJ/kg and 2187 kJ/kg respectively. If the specific pump work is 2 kJ/kg, the specific steam consumption (in kg/kW-h) of the cycle based on net output is ________.

GATE 2015

Solution

Turbine work output,

$$W_T = h_1 - h_2 = (3159 - 2187) \text{ kJ/kg}$$

$$W_T = 972 \text{ kJ/kg}$$

Specific steam consumption, $\dot{m} = \dfrac{1}{W_T - W_P} \dfrac{\text{kg}}{\text{kJ}}$

or $\dot{m} = \dfrac{3600}{W_T - W_P} \dfrac{\text{kg}}{\text{kW-h}}$

or $\dot{m} = \dfrac{3600}{972 - 2} \dfrac{\text{kg}}{\text{kW-h}}$

$$\dot{m} = 3.711 \frac{\text{kg}}{\text{kW-h}}$$

Example 13.3

For the same values of peak pressure, peak temperature and heat rejection, the correct order of efficiencies for Otto, Dual and Diesel cycles is

(A) $\eta_{\text{Otto}} > \eta_{\text{Dual}} > \eta_{\text{Diesel}}$

(B) $\eta_{\text{Diesel}} > \eta_{\text{Dual}} > \eta_{\text{Otto}}$

(C) $\eta_{\text{Dual}} > \eta_{\text{Diesel}} > \eta_{\text{Otto}}$

(D) $\eta_{\text{Diesel}} > \eta_{\text{Otto}} > \eta_{\text{Dual}}$

GATE 2015

Solution

Figure shows air standard cycles (Otto cycle 1-7-3-4-1, Dual cycle 1-5-6-3-4, Diesel cycle 1-2-3-4-1) for the same maximum pressure and temperature (state 3), the heat rejection being also the same.

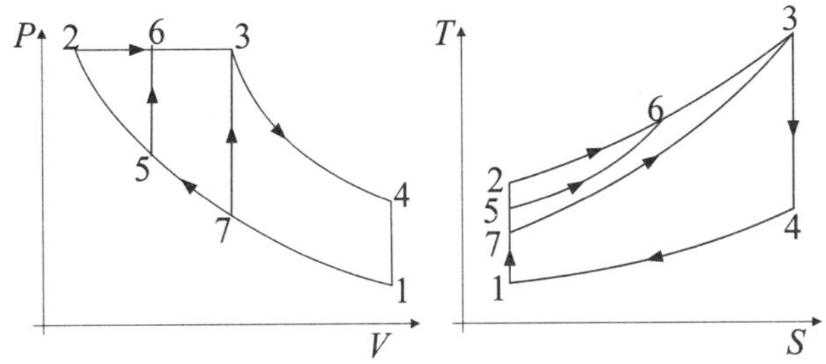

Heat supplied is represented by the area under 7-3 for the Otto cycle, by the area under 2-3 for diesel cycle and by the area under 5-6-3 for dual cycle in the *T-S* plot. Heat rejection being the same.

$$\eta_{\text{Diesel}} > \eta_{\text{Dual}} > \eta_{\text{Otto}}$$

Example 13.4

A rigid container of volume 0.5m^3 contains 1.0 kg of water at $120°\text{C}$ ($v_f = 0.00106 \text{ m}^3/\text{kg}$, $v_g = 0.8908 \text{ m}^3/\text{kg}$). The state of water is

(A) Compressed liquid

(B) Saturated liquid

(C) A mixture of saturated liquid and saturated vapour

(D) Superheated vapour

GATE 2015

Solution

Specific volume, $v = \dfrac{V}{m} = \dfrac{0.5}{1}$

$$v = 0.5 \text{ m}^3/\text{kg}$$

Specific volume, $v = v_f + x(v_g - v_f)$

$$0.5 = 0.00106 + x(0.8908 - 0.00106)$$

Dryness fraction $x = 0.56 \leftarrow$ mixutre of saturated liquied and saturated vapour.

Example 13.5

An air-standard Diesel cycle consists of the following process:

1-2: Air is compressed isentropically

2-3: Heat is added at constant pressure

3-4: Air expands isentropically to the original volume

4-5: Heat is rejected at constant volume

If γ and T denote the specific heat ratio and temperature, respectively, the efficiency of the cycle is

(A) $1-\frac{T_4-T_1}{T_3-T_2}$ (B) $1-\frac{T_4-T_1}{\gamma(T_3-T_2)}$

(C) $1-\frac{\gamma(T_4-T_1)}{T_3-T_2}$ (D) $1-\frac{(T_4-T_1)}{(\gamma-1)(T_3-T_2)}$

GATE 2015

Solution

Figure shows the Diesel cycle on P-V.

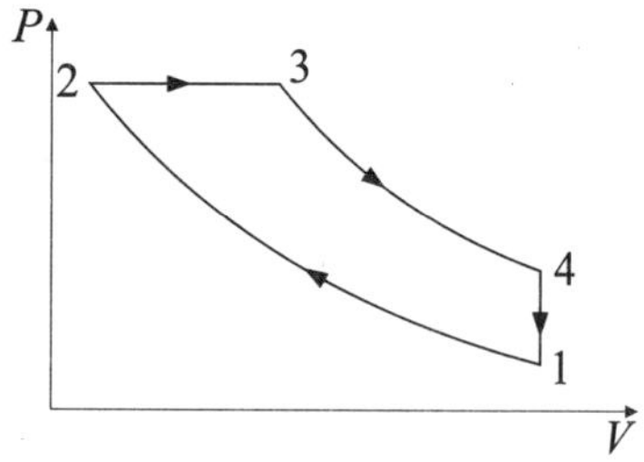

Heat supplied, $Q_1 = mc_p(T_3-T_2)$

Heat rejected, $Q_2 = mc_v(T_4-T_1)$

Efficiency of cycle, $\eta = 1-\frac{Q_2}{Q_1}$

or $$\eta = 1-\frac{mc_v(T_4-T_1)}{mc_p(T_3-T_2)}$$

or $$\eta = 1-\frac{T_4-T_1}{\frac{c_p}{c_v}(T_3-T_2)}$$

$$\eta = 1-\frac{T_4-T_1}{\gamma(T_3-T_2)}$$

Example 13.6

The thermodynamic cycle shown in figure (T- S diagram) indicates

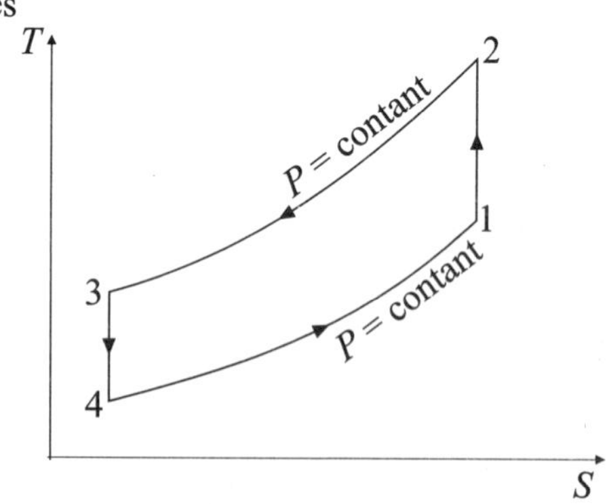

(A) Reversed Carnot cycle

(B) Reversed Brayton cycle

(C) Vapour compression cycle

(D) Vapour absorption cycle

GATE 2015

Solution

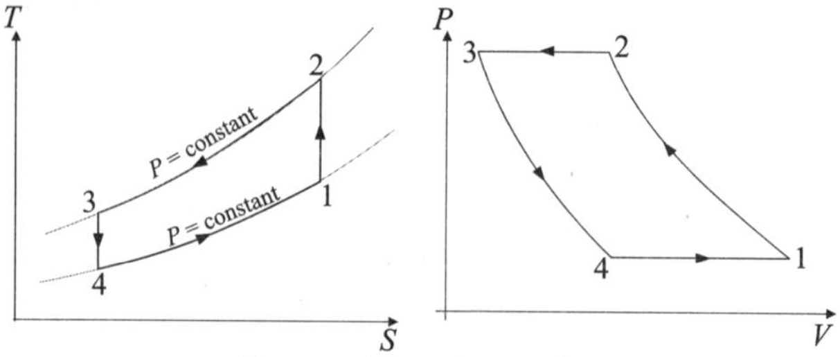

Reversed brayton cycle

4-1 ← Constant pressure heat addition

1-2 ← Isentropic compression

2-3 ← Constant pressure heat rejection

3-4 ← Isentropic expansion

The cycle is reversed Brayton cycle

Example 13.7

Refrigerant vapour enters into the compressor of a standard vapour compression cycle at $-10°C$ ($h = 402$ kJ/kg) and leaves the compressor at $50°C$ ($h = 432$ kJ/kg). It leaves the condenser at $30°C$ ($h = 237$ kJ/kg). The COP of the cycle is____.

GATE 2015

Solution

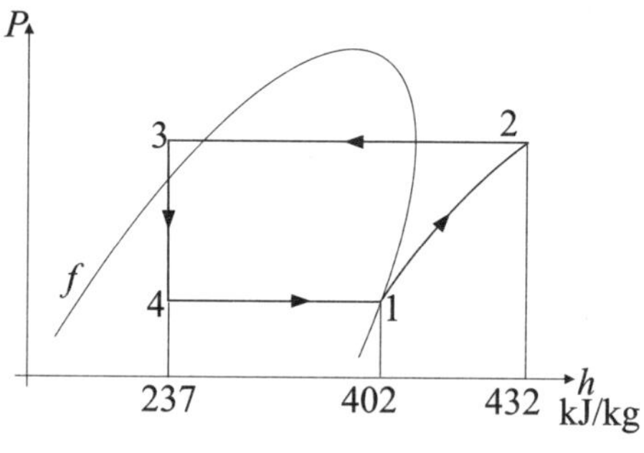

The P-h diagram of vapour refrigeration system is sketched for reference.

$$\text{COP} = \frac{\text{Desire effect}}{\text{Compressor work}} = \frac{h_1-h_4}{h_2-h_1}$$

$$\text{COP} = \frac{402-237}{432-402}$$

$$\text{COP} = 5.5$$

Example 13.8

Air in a room is at 35°C and 60% relative humidity (RH). The pressure in the room is 0.1 MPa. The saturation pressure of water at 35°C is 5.63 kPa. The humidity ratio of the air (in g/kg of dry air) is ________.

GATE 2015

Solution

Relative humidity, $\phi = \frac{P_v}{P_s}$

or $P_v = \phi P_s = 0.6 \times 5.63$

$P_v = 3.378$ kPa

Humidity ratio, $\phi = 0.622 \frac{P_v}{P - P_v} \frac{\text{kg}}{\text{kg of dry air}}$

$\phi = 0.622 \frac{3.378}{100 - 3.378} \frac{\text{kg}}{\text{kg of dry air}}$

or $\phi = 0.021745$ kg/kg of dry air

$\phi = 21.745$ g/kg of dry air

Example 13.9

Air enters a diesel engine with a density of 1.0 kg/m^3. The compression ratio is 21. At steady state, the air intake is 30×10^{-3} kg/s and the net work output is 15 kW. The mean effective pressure (in kPa) is _______.

GATE 2015

Solution

The P-V diagram of diesel cycle is sketched for reference.

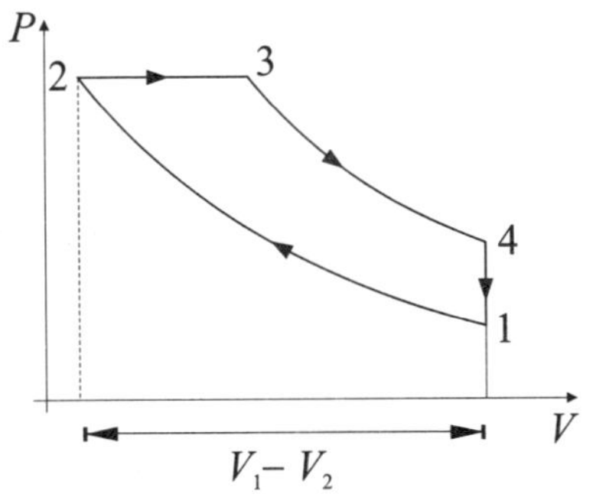

Given: $\dot{m} = 30 \times 10^{-3}$ kg/s, $\rho = 1.0$ kg/m^3, $r = 21$ and $W = 15$ kW

Volume flow rate at state 1, $V_1 = \frac{30 \times 10^{-3}}{1}$ m^3/s

Volume flow rate at state 2, $V_2 = \frac{V_1}{r} = \frac{30 \times 10^{-3}}{21}$ m^3/s

Mean effective pressure, $P_m = \frac{W}{V_1 - V_2}$

or $P_m = \frac{15}{30 \times 10^{-3} - \frac{30 \times 10^{-3}}{21}}$ N/m^2

$P_m = 525$ N/m^2

Example 13.10

A stream of moist air (mass flow rate = 10.1 kg/s) with humidity ratio of $0.01 \frac{\text{kg}}{\text{kg dry air}}$ mixes with a second stream of superheated water vapour flowing at 0.1 kg/s. Assuming proper and uniform mixing with no condensation, the humidity ratio of the final stream $\left(\text{in } \frac{\text{kg}}{\text{kg dry air}}\right)$ is _______.

GATE 2015

Solution

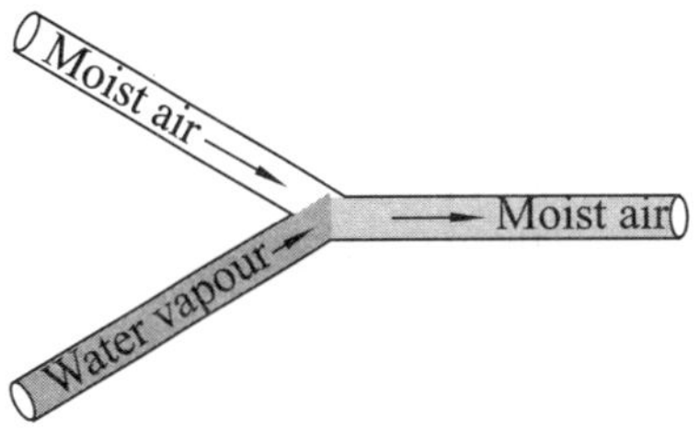

Humidity ratio, $\omega = \frac{m_v}{m_a}$

Mass flow rate of water vapour (first stream),

$(m_v)_1 = \omega \times m_a = 0.01 \times 10.1$

$(m_v)_1 = 0.101$ kg/s

Mass flow rate of water vapour in second stream,

$(m_v)_2 = 0.1$ kg/s (given)

Mass flow rate of water vapour after mixing first and second stream,

$m_v = (m_v)_1 + (m_v)_2$

or $m_v = 0.101 + 0.1 = 0.201$ kg/s

Humidity ratio after mixing, $\omega = \frac{m_v}{m_a} = \frac{0.201}{10.1}$

$\omega = 0.02$

Example 13.11

The pressure, dry bulb temperature and relative humidity of air in a room are 1 bar, 30°C and 70% respectively. If the saturated steam pressure at 30°C is 4.25 kPa, the specific humidity of the room air in kg water vapour/kg dry air is

(A) 0.0083 (B) 0.0101 (C) 0.0191 (D) 0.0232

GATE 2013

Solution

Specific humidity, $\omega = 0.622 \dfrac{P_v}{P - P_v}$

Relative humidity, $\phi = \dfrac{P_v}{P_s}$

Substituting $\phi = 0.7$, $P_s = 4.25 \times 10^3$ Pa and $P = 1.0 \times 10^5$ Pa, we have

$$\omega = 0.622 \frac{\phi P_s}{P - \phi P_s}$$

or $$\omega = 0.622 \times \frac{0.7 \times 4.25 \times 10^3}{1 \times 10^5 - 0.7 \times 4.25 \times 10^3}$$

$$\omega = 0.01907 \text{ kg/kg of dry air}$$

Example 13.12

In an air-standard Otto cycle, air is supplied at 0.1 MPa and 308 K. The ratio of the specific heats (γ) and the specific gas constant (R) of air are 1.4 and 288.8 J/kgK, respectively. If the compression ratio is 8 and the maximum temperature in the cycle is 2660 K, the heat (in kJ) supplied to the engine is _______

GATE 2014

Solution

The P-V diagram of Otto cycle is sketched for reference.

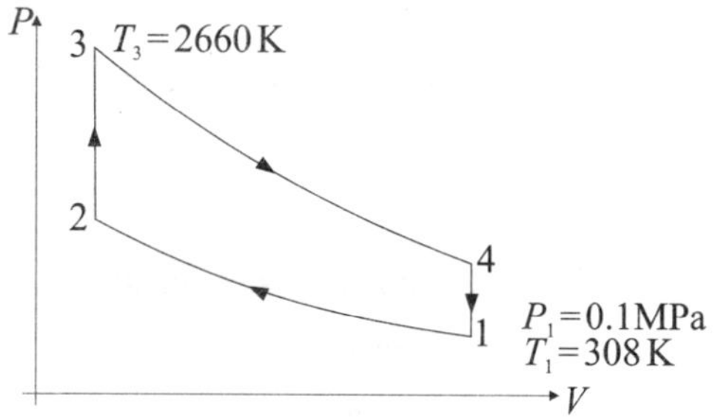

Given that:

$P_1 = 0.1$ MPa, $T_1 = 308$ K, $T_3 = 2660$ K, $r_k = 8$, $\gamma = 1.4$ and $R = 288.8$ J/kgK.

For isentropic process 1-2;

$$\frac{T_2}{T_1} = \left(\frac{V_1}{V_2}\right)^{\gamma-1} \quad \text{or} \quad \frac{T_2}{308} = 8^{1.4-1}$$

$$T_2 = 698.4 \text{ K}$$

For isochoric heat addition process 2-3;

$$Q_{\text{in}} = c_v (T_3 - T_2)$$

or $$Q_{\text{in}} = \frac{R}{\gamma - 1}(T_3 - T_2)$$

or $$Q_{\text{in}} = \frac{288.8}{1.4 - 1}(2660 - 698.4)$$

or $$Q_{\text{in}} = 1416275 \text{ J/kg}$$

$$Q_{\text{in}} = 1416.2 \text{ kJ/kg}$$

Example 13.13

A moist air sample has dry bulb temperature of 30°C and specific humidity of 11.5 g water vapour per kg dry air. Assume molecular weight of air as 28.93. If the saturation vapour pressure of water at 30°C is 4.24 kPa and the total pressure is 90 kPa, then the relative humidity (in %) of air sample is

(A) 50.5 (B)38.5 (C) 56.5 (D) 68.5

GATE 2010

Solution

Given that $\omega = \dfrac{11.5}{1000}$ kg/kg of dry air, $P_s = 4.24$ kPa, and $P = 90$ kPa.

Specific humidity, $\omega = 0.622 \times \dfrac{P_v}{P - P_v}$

$$\frac{11.5}{1000} = 0.622 \frac{P_v}{90 \times 10^3 - P_v}$$

From which $P_v = 1633.78$ Pa

Relative humidity, $\phi = \dfrac{P_v}{P_s} \times 100$

$$\phi = \frac{1633.78}{4.24 \times 10^3} \times 100$$

$$\phi = 38.53\%$$

Example 13.14

An ideal reheat Rankine cycle operates between the pressure limits of 10 kPa and 8 MPa, with reheat being done at 4 MPa. The temperature of steam at the inlets of both turbine is 500°C and the enthalpy of steam is 3185 kJ/kg at the exit of the high pressure turbine and 2247 kJ/kg at the exit of low pressure turbine. The enthalpy of water at the exit from the pump is 191 kJ/kg. Use the following table for relevant data.

Superheated steam temperature (°C)	Pressure (MPa)	v (m³/kg)	h (kJ/kg)	s (kJ/kgK)
500	4	0.08644	3446	7.0922
500	8	0.04177	3399	6.7266

Disregarding the pump work, the cycle efficiency (in percentage) is_______.

GATE 2014

Solution

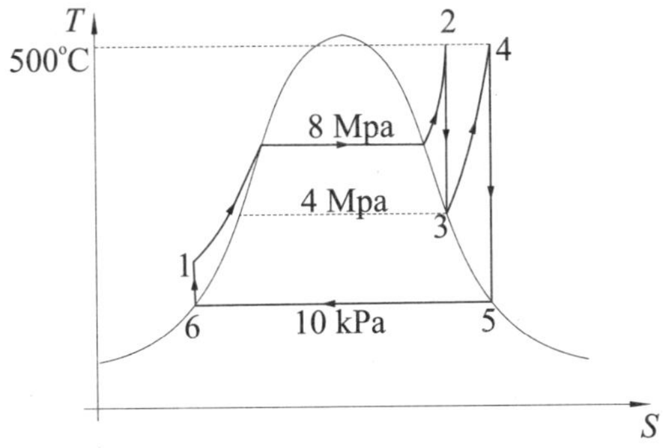

An ideal reheat Rankine cycle is shown in the figure.

Given that: $T_2 = T_4 = 500°\text{C}$, $h_3 = 3185$ kJ/kg, $h_5 = 2247$ kJ/kg, and $h_1 = 191$ kJ/kg.

From table:

$$h_2 = 3399 \text{ kJ/kg}, \; h_4 = 3446 \text{ kJ/kg}.$$

Work done by high pressure turbine,

$$W_{HP} = h_2 - h_3$$

Work done by low pressure turbine,

$$W_{LP} = h_4 - h_5$$

Heat added, $Q_s = (h_2 - h_1) + (h_4 - h_3)$

Efficiency of reheat Rankine cycle is

$$\eta = \frac{W_{net}}{Q_s} = \frac{W_{HP} + W_{LP}}{Q_s}$$

or $$\eta = \frac{(h_2 - h_3) + (h_4 - h_5)}{(h_2 - h_1) + (h_4 - h_3)}$$

Substituting given values,

$$\eta = \frac{(3399 - 3185) + (3446 - 2247)}{(3399 - 191) + (3446 - 3185)}$$

From which

$$\eta = 40.73\%$$

Example 13.15

Linked Answer Questions

In a simple Brayton cycle, the pressure ratio is 8 and temperatures at the entrance of compressor and turbine are 300 K and 1400 K respectively. Both compressor and gas turbine have isentropic efficiencies equal to 0.8. For the gas, assume a constant value of c_p (specific heat at constant pressure) equal to 1 kJ/kgK and ratio of specific heats is 1.4. Neglect changes in kinetic and potential energies.

Q(a) The power required by the compressor in kW/kg of gas flow rate is

(A) 194.7 (B) 243.4 (C) 304.3 (D) 378.5

Q(b) The thermal efficiency of the cycle in percentage (%) is

(A) 24.8 (B) 38.6 (C) 44.8 (D) 53.1

GATE 2013

Solution

(a) The Brayton cycle on T- S is sketched for reference.

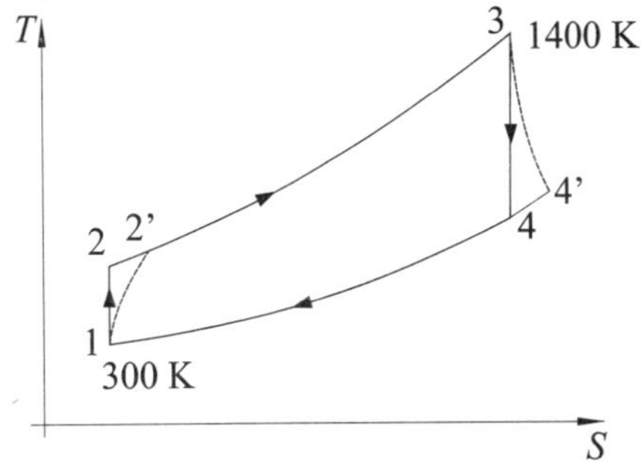

Given that: $T_1 = 300$ K, $T_3 = 1400$ K, pressure ratio $= 8$, $\eta_c = \eta_T = 0.8$, $c_p = 1$ kJ/kgK and $\gamma = 1.4$.

For isentropic process 1-2;

$$T_2 = T_1\left(\frac{P_2}{P_1}\right)^{\frac{\gamma-1}{\gamma}} = 300\,(8)^{\frac{1.4-1}{1.4}}$$

$$T_2 = 543.41 \text{ K}$$

Isentropic efficiency of compressor, $\eta_c = \dfrac{T_2 - T_1}{T_2' - T_1}$

$$0.8 = \frac{543.41 - 300}{T_2' - 300}$$

$$T_2' = 604.26 \text{ K}$$

Compressor work, $W_c = c_p(T_2' - T_1)$

$$W_c = 1 \times (604.26 - 300)$$

$$W_c = 304.3 \text{ kW/kg}$$

(b) For isentropic process 3-4;

$$T_4 = \frac{T_3}{\left(\frac{P_3}{P_4}\right)^{\frac{\gamma-1}{\gamma}}} = \frac{1400}{(8)^{\frac{1.4-1}{1.4}}}$$

$$T_4 = 772.8 \text{ K}$$

Isentropic efficiency of turbine, $\eta_T = \dfrac{T_3 - T_4'}{T_3 - T_4}$

$$0.8 = \frac{1400 - T_4'}{1400 - 772.8}$$

$$T_4' = 897.6 \text{ K}$$

Turbine work, $W_T = c_p(T_3 - T_4')$

$$W_T = 1\times(1400-897.6) = 502.4\text{ kW/kg}$$

Net work done, $W_{net} = W_T - W_C = 502.4 - 304.3$

$$W_{net} = 198.1\text{ kW/kg}$$

Heat supplied, $Q_s = c_p(T_3 - T_2')$

$$Q_s = 1\times(1400-604.26) = 795.74\text{ kW/kg}$$

Therefore, the thermal efficiency is $\eta = \dfrac{W_{net}}{Q_s}$

$$\eta = \frac{198.1}{795.74}$$

$$\eta = 24.89\%$$

Example 13.16

In a power plant, water (density $= 1000\text{ kg/m}^3$) is pumped from 80 kPa to 3 MPa. The pump has an isentropic efficiency of 0.85. Assuming that the temperature of the water remains the same, the specific work (in kJ/kg) supplied to the pump is

(A) 0.34 (B) 2.48 (C) 2.92 (D) 3.43

GATE 2014

Solution

Isentropic efficiency of pump is given by

$$\eta = \frac{\text{Isentropic compressor work }(W)}{\text{Actual compressor work }(W_{act})}$$

or Actual compressor work, $W_{act} = \dfrac{W}{\eta}$

or $$W_{act} = \frac{(P_2 - P_1)v}{\eta} = \frac{(P_2-P_1)\times\frac{1}{\rho}}{\eta}$$

or $$W_{act} = \frac{(3000-80)\times\frac{1}{1000}}{0.85}\text{ kJ/kg}$$

$$W_{act} = 3.43\text{ kJ/kg}$$

Example 13.17

The stroke and bore of a four stroke spark ignition engine are 250 mm and 200 mm respectively. The clearance volume is 0.001 m^3. If the specific heat ratio $\gamma = 1.4$, the air-standard cycle efficiency of the engine is

(A) 46.40% (B) 56.10% (C) 58.20% (D) 62.80%

GATE 2007

Solution

Swept volume, $V_s = \dfrac{\pi}{4}D^2L = \dfrac{\pi}{4}\left(\dfrac{200}{1000}\right)^2 \times \dfrac{250}{1000}$

$$V_s = 0.007854\text{ m}^3$$

Compression ratio, $r_k = \dfrac{V_c + V_s}{V_c} = \dfrac{0.001+0.007854}{0.001}$

$$r_k = 8.85$$

Air standard efficiency, $\eta_o = 1 - \dfrac{1}{r_k^{\gamma-1}}$

$$\eta_o = 1 - \frac{1}{(8.85)^{1.4-1}}$$

$$\eta_o = 58.19\%$$

Example 13.18

Common Data Questions

A refrigerator operates between 120 kPa and 800 kPa in an ideal vapour compression cycle with R-134a as the refrigerant. The refrigerant enters the compressor as saturated vapour and leaves the condenser as saturated liquid. The mass flow rate of the refrigerant is 0.2 kg/s. Properties for R-134a are as follow:

Saturated R-134a					
P (kPa)	T (°C)	h_f (kJ/kg)	h_g (kJ/kg)	s_f (kJ/kgK)	s_g (kJ/kgK)
120	−22.32	22.5	237	0.093	0.95
800	31.31	95.5	267.3	0.354	0.918

Superheated R-134a			
P (kPa)	T (°C)	h (kJ/kg)	s_f (kJ/kgK)
800	40	276.45	0.95

Q(a) The rate at which heat is extracted, in kJ/s from the refrigerated space is

(A) 28.3 (B) 34.4 (C) 42.9 (D)14.6

Q(b) The power required for the compressor in kW is

(A) 5.94 (B)7.9 (C)1.83 (D) 39.5

GATE 2012

Solution

The P - h diagram of vapour compression cycle is sketched for reference.

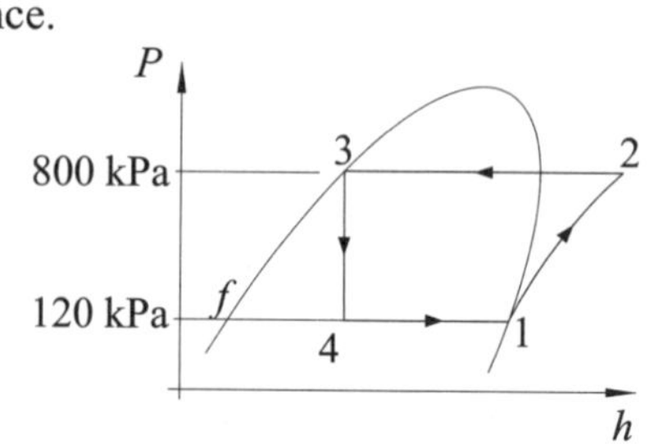

From table:

$h_1 = 237$ kJ/kg, $h_3 = 95.5$ kJ/kg $= h_4$, and $h_2 = 276.45$ kJ/kg.

(a) Heat extraction rate from refrigerated space is

$$Q_{extr} = m(h_1 - h_4)$$
$$Q_{extr} = 0.2 \times (237 - 95.5)$$
$$Q_{extr} = 28.3 \text{ kJ/s}$$

(b) Power required for the compressor is $P = m(h_2 - h_1)$

or $P = 0.2 \times (276.45 - 237)$

$$P = 7.89 \text{ kW}$$

Example 13.19

Common Data Questions

In a steam power plant operating on the Rankine cycle, steam enters the turbine at 4 MPa, 350°C and exits at a pressure of 15 kPa. Then it enters the condenser and exits as saturated water. Next, a pump feeds back the water to the boiler. The adiabatic efficiency of the turbine is 90%. The thermodynamic states of water and steam are given in table.

State	h (kJ/kg)		s (kJ/kgK)		v (m^3/kg)	
Steam 4 MPa, 350° C	3092.5		6.5821		0.06645	
Water 15 kPa	h_f	h_g	s_f	s_g	v_f	v_g
	225.94	2599.1	0.7549	8.0085	0.001014	10.02

h is specific enthalpy, *s* is specific entropy and *v* the specific volume; subscripts *f* and *g* denote saturated liquid state and saturated vapour state.

Q(a) The network output (kJ/kg) of the cycle is

(A) 498 (B) 775 (C) 860 (D) 957

Q(b) Heat supplied (kJ/kg) to the cycle is

(A) 2372 (B) 2576 (C) 2863 (D) 3092

GATE 2010

Solution

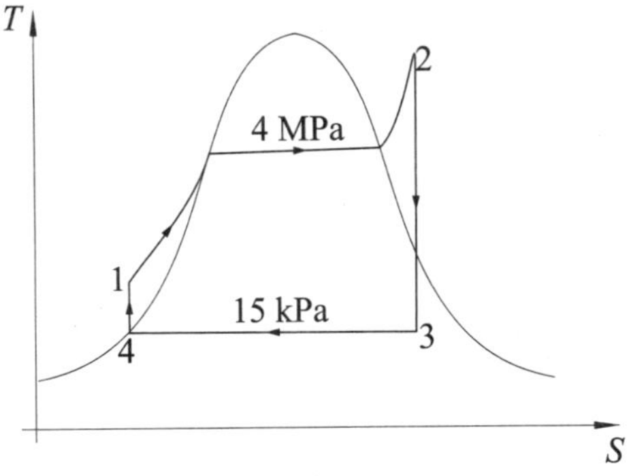

The *T-S* diagram of Rankine cycle is sketched for reference.

(a) Let x_3 be the quality of steam after expansion.

$$S_3 = S_2 = S_4 + x_3(S_g - S_4)$$
$$6.5821 = 0.7549 + x_3(8.0085 - 0.7549)$$
$$x_3 = 0.803$$

Enthalpy after expansion,

$$h_3 = 225.94 + 0.803 \times (2599.1 - 225.94)$$

From which $h_3 = 2131.58$ kJ/kg

Turbine work, $W_T = \eta(h_2 - h_3)$

$$W_T = 0.9 \times (3092.5 - 2131.58)$$
$$W_T = 864.8 \text{ kJ/kg}$$

Pump work, $W_P = (\Delta P)v_4$

$$W_P = (4000 - 15) \times 0.001014 = 4.04 \text{ kJ/kg}$$

Net work output, $W = W_T - W_P$

$$W = 864.8 - 4.04$$
$$W = 860 \text{ kJ/kg}$$

(b) Heat supplied to the boiler is $Q = h_2 - h_1$

$$Q = h_2 - (h_4 + W_P)$$
$$Q = 3092.5 - (225.94 + 4.04)$$
$$Q = 2863 \text{ kJ/kg}$$

Example 13.20

A ideal Brayton cycle, operating between the pressure limits of 1 bar and 6 bar, has minimum and maximum temperatures of 300 K and 1500 K. The ratio of specific heats of the working fluid is 1.4. The approximate final temperatures in kelvin at the end of the compression and expansion processes are respectively

(A) 500 and 900 (B) 500 and 500

(C) 900 and 500 (D) 900 and 900

GATE 2011

Solution

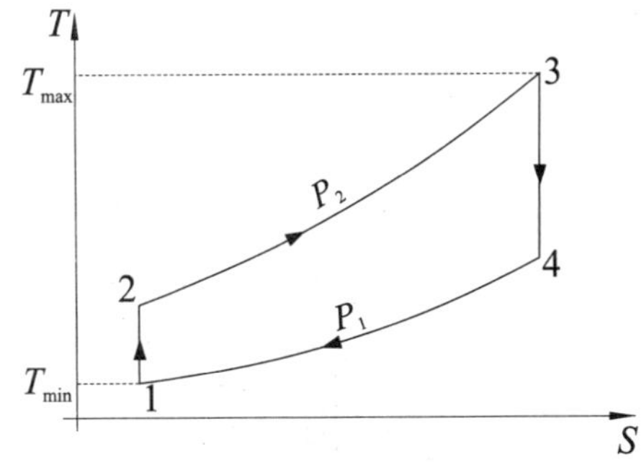

The *T-S* diagram of the Brayton cycle is sketched for reference.

Given that: $P_1 = 1$ bar, $P_2 = 6$ bar, $T_{min} = T_1 = 300$ K, $T_{max} = T_3 = 1500$ K and $\gamma = 1.4$.

For isentropic compression process 1-2;

$$\frac{T_2}{T_1} = \left(\frac{P_2}{P_1}\right)^{\frac{\gamma-1}{\gamma}} \quad \text{or} \quad \frac{T_2}{300} = \left(\frac{6}{1}\right)^{\frac{1.4-1}{1.4}}$$

The temperature at the end of compression, $T_2 = 500\,\text{K}$

For isentropic expansion 3-4; $\frac{T_3}{T_4} = \left(\frac{P_3}{P_4}\right)^{\frac{\gamma-1}{\gamma}}$

$$\frac{1500}{T_4} = \left(\frac{6}{1}\right)^{\frac{1.4-1}{1.4}}$$

The temperature at the end of expansion, $T_4 = 900\,\text{K}$

Example 13.21

A thermal power plant operates on a regenerative cycle with a single open feed water heater, as shown in figure. For the state points shown, the specific enthalpies are: $h_1 = 2800\,\text{kJ/kg}$, $h_2 = 200\,\text{kJ/kg}$. The bleed to the feed water heater is 20% of the boiler steam generation rate. The specific enthalpy at state 3 is

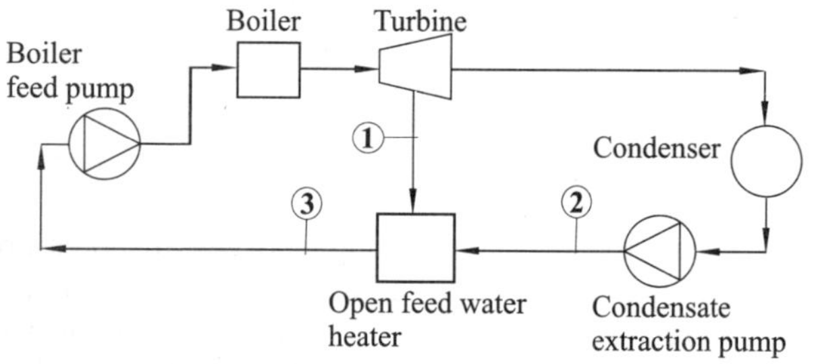

(A) 720 kJ/kg
(B) 2280 kJ/kg
(C)1500 kJ/kg
(D) 3000 kJ/kg

GATE 2008

Solution

Let m be the steam generation rate.

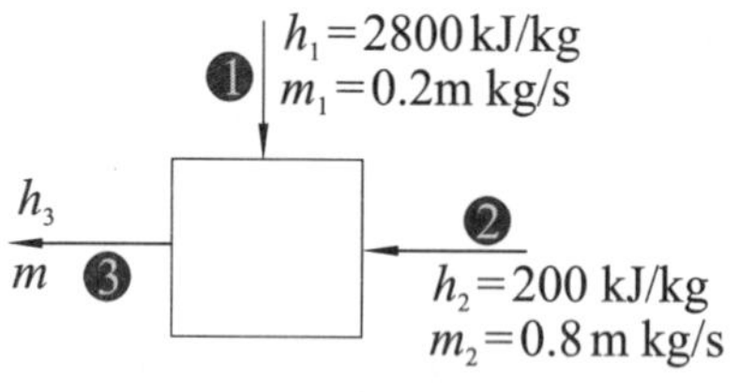

Applying heat balance equation,

$$m_1 h_1 + m_2 h_2 = (m_1 + m_2) h_3$$

$$0.2\,m \times 2800 + 0.8\,m \times 200 = m\,h_3$$

From which

$$h_3 = 720\,\text{kJ/kg}$$

Example 13.22

Common Data Questions

In two air standard cycles, one operating on the Otto and the other on the Brayton cycle. Air is isentropically compressed from 300 to 450 K. Heat is added to raise the temperature to 600 K in the Otto cycle and to 550 K in the Brayton cycle.

Q(a) If η_o and η_B are the efficiencies of the Otto and Brayton cycles, then

(A) $\eta_o = 0.25, \eta_B = 0.18$

(B) $\eta_o = \eta_B = 0.33$

(C) $\eta_o = 0.5, \eta_B = 0.45$

(D) It is not possible to calculate the efficiencies unless the temperature after the expansion is given

Q(b) If W_o and W_B are work outputs per unit mass, then

(A) $W_o > W_B$

(B) $W_o < W_B$

(C) $W_o = W_B$

(D) It is not possible to calculate the work outputs unless the temperature after the expansion is given

GATE 2005

Solution

The *T-S* diagram of Otto cycle and Brayton cycle are sketched for reference.

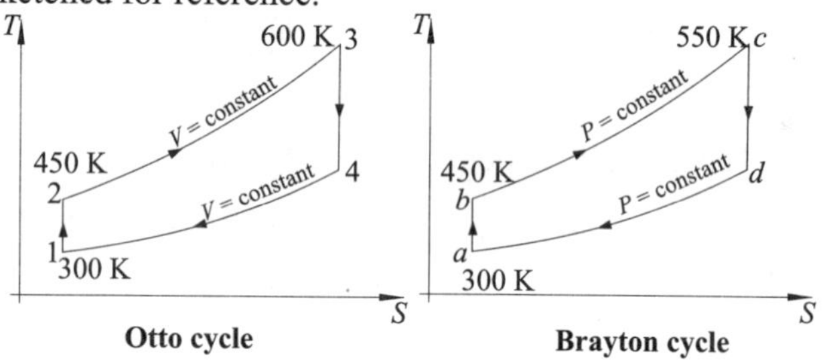

(a) For isentropic compression process 1-2 (Otto cycle);

$$\frac{V_1}{V_2} = \left(\frac{T_2}{T_1}\right)^{\frac{1}{\gamma-1}}$$

Compression ratio, $r_k = \frac{V_1}{V_2} = \left(\frac{450}{300}\right)^{\frac{1}{1.4-1}}$

$$r_k = 2.75$$

Efficiency of Otto cycle, $\eta_0 = 1 - \frac{1}{r_k^{\gamma-1}}$

$$\eta_0 = 1 - \frac{1}{(2.75)^{1.4-1}}$$

$$\eta_0 = 33.3\%$$

For isentropic compression process *a-b* (Brayton cycle),

$$\frac{P_2}{P_1} = \left(\frac{T_2}{T_1}\right)^{\frac{\gamma}{\gamma-1}}$$

Pressure ratio, $$r_p = \frac{P_2}{P_1} = \left(\frac{450}{300}\right)^{\frac{1.4}{1.4-1}}$$

$$r_p = 4.133$$

Efficiency of Brayton cycle, $$\eta_B = 1 - \frac{1}{(r_p)^{\frac{\gamma-1}{\gamma}}}$$

$$\eta_B = 1 - \frac{1}{(4.133)^{\frac{1.4-1}{1.4}}}$$

$$\eta_B = 33.3\%$$

Thus,

$$\eta_0 = \eta_B = 33.3\%$$

(b) Efficiency $$\eta = \frac{W}{Q_s}$$

Work output of Otto cycle $W_o = \eta_o[Q_s]_o$

$$W_o = 0.333\, c_v(T_3 - T_2)$$

$$W_o = 0.333 \times 0.718 \times (600 - 450)$$

$$W_o = 35.54 \text{ kJ}$$

Work output of Brayton cycle, $W_B = \eta_B[Q_s]_B$

$$W_B = 0.333\, c_P(T_c - T_b)$$

$$W_B = 0.333 \times 1.005 \times (550 - 450)$$

$$W_B = 33.16 \text{ kJ}$$

Therefore,

$$W_o > W_B$$

Example 13.23

For a typical sample of ambient air (at 35°C, 75% relative humidity and standard atmospheric pressure), the amount of moisture in kg per kg of dry air will be approximately

(A) 0.002 (B) 0.027 (C) 0.25 (D) 0.75

GATE 2005

Solution

Amount of moisture in kg per kg of dry air or specific humidity is given by

$$\omega = 0.622 \frac{P_v}{P - P_v}$$

Relative humidity, $$\phi = \frac{P_v}{P_s}$$

From which $$\omega = 0.622 \frac{\phi P_s}{P - \phi P_s}$$

Substituting $\phi = 0.75$, $P = 1$ bar and $P_s = 0.0562$ bar (at 35°C)

$$\omega = 0.622 \times \frac{0.75 \times 0.0562}{1.013 - 0.75 \times 0.0562}$$

$$\omega = 0.027 \text{ kg/kg of dry air}$$

Example 13.24

A building has to be maintained at 21°C (dry bulb) and 14.5°C (wet bulb). The dew point temperature under these conditions is 10.17°C. The outside temperature is −23°C (dry bulb) and the internal and external surface heat transfer coefficients are 8 W/m^{2}K and 23 W/m^{2}K respectively. If the building wall has a thermal conductivity of 1.2 W/mK, the minimum thickness (in m) of the wall required to prevent condensation is

(A) 0.471 (B) 0.407 (C) 0.321 (D) 0.125

GATE 2007

Solution

Let *t* be the thickness of wall.

Condensation starts when inner building wall surface temperature is reached at 10.17°C (Dew point).

The thermal resistance network for this problem involves three resistances in series and is given in figure.

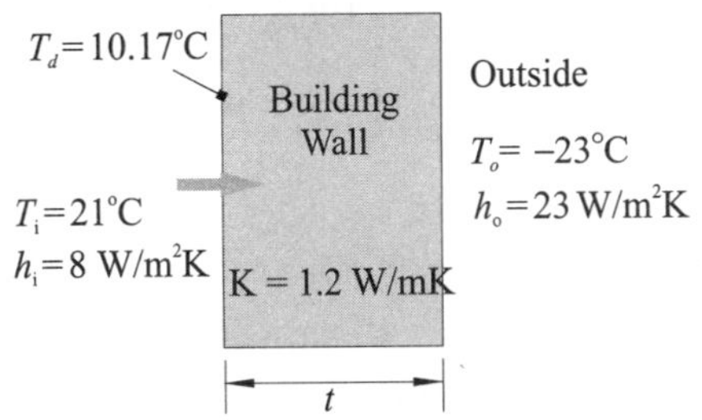

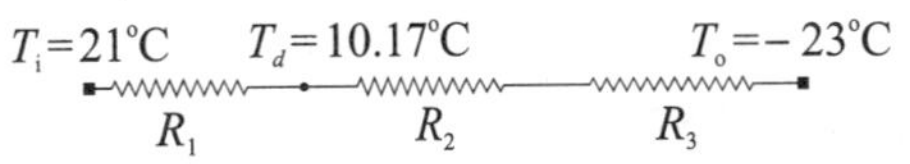

Equivalent electric circuit

For unit area, the thermal resistances are: $R_1 = \frac{1}{h_i A} = \frac{1}{8 \times 1}$,

$$R_2 = \frac{t}{kA} = \frac{t}{1.2 \times 1} \text{ and } R_3 = \frac{1}{h_o A} = \frac{1}{23 \times 1}$$

Rate of heat transfer, $$Q = \frac{T_i - T_d}{R_1} = \frac{T_i - T_o}{R_1 + R_2 + R_3}$$

$$\frac{21-10.17}{\frac{1}{8}}=\frac{21-(-23)}{\frac{1}{8}+\frac{t}{1.2}+\frac{1}{23}}$$

From which

$$\text{Wall thickness, } t=0.407 \text{ m}$$

Example 13.25

An engine working on air standard Otto cycle has cylinder diameter of 10 cm and stroke length of 15 cm. The ratio of specific heats for air is 1.4. If the clearance volume is 196.3 cc and the heat supplied per kg of air per cycle is 1800 kJ/kg, then work output per cycle per kg of air is

(A) 879.1 kJ (B) 890.2 kJ (C) 895.3kJ (D) 973.5 kJ

GATE 2004

Solution

Given that:

Diameter of cylinder, $D=10$ cm

Stroke length, $L=15$ cm

Clearance volume, $V_c=196.3$ cc

Heat supplied, $Q_s=1800$ kJ/kg

Swept volume, $V_s=\frac{\pi}{4}D^2L=\frac{\pi}{4}\times 10^2\times 15$

$$V_s=1178.09 \text{ cm}^3$$

Compression ratio,

$$r_k=\frac{V_s+V_c}{V_c}=\frac{1178.09+196.3}{196.3}=7$$

Air standard efficiency, $\eta=1-\frac{1}{r_k^{\gamma-1}}=1-\frac{1}{7^{1.4-1}}$

$$\eta=54.08\,\%$$

Workout put per cycle, $W=\eta\times Q_s$

$$W=0.5408\times 1800$$

$$W=973.44 \text{ kJ}$$

Example 13.26

Dew point temperature of air at one atmospheric pressure (1.013 bar) is 18°C. The air dry bulb temperature is 30°C. The saturation pressure of water at 18°C and 30°C are 0.02062 bar and 0.04241 bar respectively. The specific heat of air and water vapour respectively are 1.005 and 1.88 kJ/kgK and the latent heat of vaporisation of water at 0°C is 2500 kJ/kg. The specific humidity (kJ/kg of dry air) and enthalpy (kJ/kg of dry air) of this moist air respectively, are

(A) 0.01051, 52.64 (B) 0.01291, 63.15

(C) 0.01481, 78.60 (D) 0.01532, 81.40

GATE 2004

Solution

Given that: Dew point temperature, $T_{dp}=18$°C, dry bulb temperature, $T_{db}=30$°C, $P_v=0.02062$ bar, $c_a=1.005$ kJ/kgK, $c_v=1.88$ kJ/kgK, $h_{fg}=2500$ kJ/kgK.

Specific humidity is $\omega=0.622\frac{P_v}{P-P_v}$

or $$\omega=0.622\times\frac{0.02062}{1.013-0.02062}$$

$$\omega=0.01292 \text{ kg/kg of dry air}$$

Specific enthalpy of moist air,

$$h=c_aT_{db}+\omega h_{fg}+\omega c_v(T_{db}-T_{dp})$$

$$h=1.005\times 30+0.01292\times 2500+0.01292\times 1.88(30-18)$$

$$h=63.15 \text{ kJ/kg}$$

Example 13.27

For an engine operating on air standard Otto cycle, the clearance volume is 10% of the swept volume. The specific heat ratio of air is 1.4. The air standard cycle efficiency is

(A) 38.3% (B) 39.8% (C) 60.2% (D) 61.7%

GATE 2003

Solution

Compression ratio $r_k=\frac{V_c+V_s}{V_c}$

or $$r_k=\frac{0.1V_s+V_s}{0.1V_s}$$

or $$r_k=11$$

Efficiency of Otto cycle is $\eta_0=1-\frac{1}{r_k^{\gamma-1}}$

$$\eta_0=1-\frac{1}{11^{1.4-1}}$$

$$\eta_0=61.67\%$$

Example 13.28

A R-12 refrigerant reciprocating compressor operates between the condensing temperature of 30°C and evaporator temperature of –20°C. The clearance volume ratio of the compressor is 0.03. Specific heat ratio of the vapour is 1.15 and the specific volume at the suction is 0.1089 m^3/kg. Other properties at various states are given in the figure. To realise 2 tons of refrigeration, the actual volume displacement rate considering the effect of clearance is

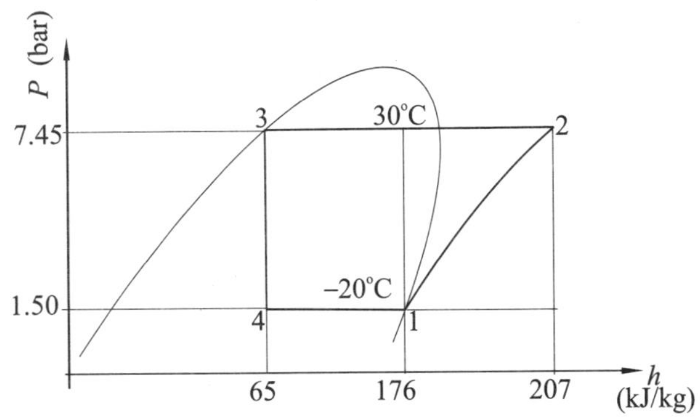

(A) 6.35×10^{-3} m^3/s (B) 63.5×10^{-3} m^3/s

(C) 635×10^{-3} m^3/s (D) 4.88×10^{-3} m^3/s

GATE 2004

Solution

Refrigeration effect, $Q_2 = 2$ tons

$$Q_2 = 2\times 3.516 \text{ kJ/s}$$

and $$Q_2 = \dot{m}(h_1 - h_4) = 2\times 3.516$$

or $$\dot{m} = \frac{2\times 3.516}{176-65} = 0.0633 \text{ kg/s}$$

Volumetric efficiency of compressor is

$$\eta_v = 1 - \frac{v_c}{v_s}\left[\left(\frac{P_2}{P_1}\right)^{\frac{1}{n}} - 1\right]$$

$$\eta_v = 1 - 0.03\times\left[\left(\frac{7.45}{1.5}\right)^{\frac{1}{1.15}} - 1\right]$$

$$\eta_v = 0.909$$

∴ Swept volume rate, $\dot{v}_s = \eta v_1 \times \dot{m}$

$$\dot{v}_s = 0.909\times 0.1089\times 0.0633$$

$$\dot{v}_s = 6.26\times10^{-3} \text{ m}^3/\text{s}$$

Example 13.29

In a spark ignition engine working on the ideal Otto cycle, the compression ratio is 5.5. The work output per cycle (i.e., area of the P - V diagram) is equal to $23.625\times10^5 V_c$ J, where V_c is the clearance volume in m^3. The indicated mean effective pressure is

(A) 4.295 bar (B) 5.250 bar

(C) 86.870 bar (D) 106.300 bar

GATE 2001

Solution

Given that: Compression ratio $r_k = \dfrac{V_s + V_c}{V_c} = 5.5$

or $$\frac{V_s}{V_c} = 4.5$$

Area of P - V diagram $= \oint PdV = 23.625\times10^5 V_c$

Indicated mean effective pressure is

$$P_m = \frac{\text{Net work output}}{\text{Swept volume}} = \frac{\text{Area of } P\text{-}V \text{ diagram}}{V_s}$$

or $$P_m = \frac{23.625\times10^5 V_c}{V_s}$$

Substituting $\dfrac{V_c}{V_s} = \dfrac{1}{4.5}$

$$P_m = 23.625\times10^5 \times \frac{1}{4.5} = 5.25\times10^5 \text{ N/m}^2$$

$$P_m = 5.25 \text{ bar}$$

Example 13.30

Common Data Questions

A refrigerator based on ideal vapour compression cycle operates between the temperature limits of −20°C and 40°C. The refrigerant enters the condenser as saturated vapour and leaves as saturated liquid. The enthalpy and entropy values for the saturated liquid and vapour at these temperatures are given in the table.

T (°C)	h_f (kJ/kg)	h_g (kJ/kg)	s_f (kJ/kgK)	s_g (kJ/kgK)
−20	20	180	0.07	0.7366
40	80	200	0.3	0.67

Q(a) If refrigerant circulation rate is 0.025 kg/s, the refrigeration effect is equal to

(A) 2.1 kW (B) 2.5 kW (C) 3.0 kW (D) 4.0 kW

Q(b) The COP of the refrigerator is

(A) 2.0 (B) 2.33 (C) 5.0 (D) 6.0

GATE 2003

Solution

The T-S and P-h diagrams of vapour compression refrigeration cycle are sketched for reference.

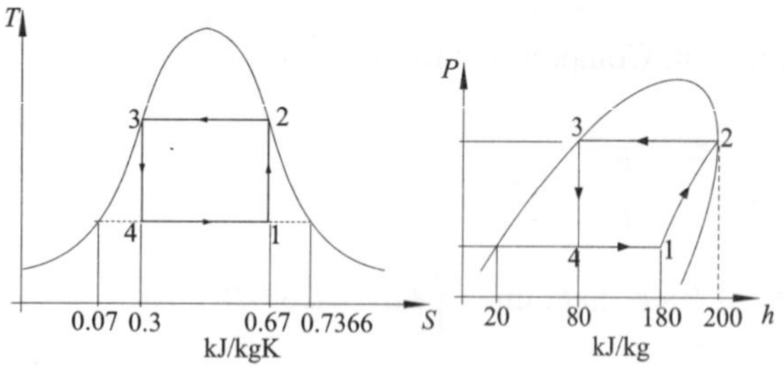

(a) Let x_1 be the moisture fraction at 1, then

$$s_1 = s_2 = s_{f1} + x_1(s_{g1} - s_{f1})$$

or $$0.67 = 0.07 + x_1(0.7366 - 0.07)$$

or $$x_1 = 0.9$$

Enthalpy at 1; $h_1 = 20 + 0.9(180 - 20)$

$$h_1 = 164 \text{ kJ/kg}$$

From given table $h_2 = 200$ kJ/kg, $h_3 = h_4 = 80$ kJ/kg

Refrigeration effect, $Q_R = m(h_1 - h_4)$

$$Q_R = 0.025 \times (164 - 80) = 2.1 \text{ kJ/s}$$

(b) Compressor work

$$W_c = m(h_2 - h_1) = 0.025(200 - 164)$$

$$W_c = 0.9 \text{ kJ/s}$$

Coefficient of performance of vapour compression cycle is

$$\text{COP} = \frac{Q_R}{W_C} = \frac{2.1}{0.9}$$

$$\text{COP} = 2.33$$

Example 13.31

Common Data Question

Consider a steam power plant using a reheat cycle as shown in the figure. Steam leaves the boiler and enters the turbine at 4 MPa, 350°C, ($h_3 = 3095$ kJ/kg). After expansion in the turbine to 400 kPa ($h_4 = 2609$ kJ/kg), the steam is reheated to 350°C ($h_5 = 3170$ kJ/kg), and then expanded in a low pressure turbine to 10 kPa ($h_6 = 2165$ kJ/kg).

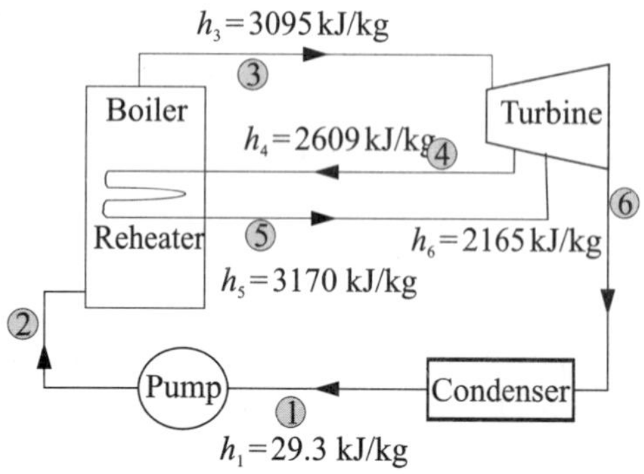

Q(a) The thermal efficiency of the plant neglecting pump work is

(A) 15.8% (B) 41.1% (C) 48.5% (D) 58.6%

Q(b) The enthalpy h_2 (in kJ/kg) at the pump discharge is

(A) 0.33 (B) 3.33 (C) 4.0 (D) 33.3

GATE 2004

Solution

(a) Turbine work, $W = W_1 + W_2$

or $$W = (h_3 - h_4) + (h_5 - h_6)$$

$$W = (3095 - 2609) + (3170 - 2165) = 1491 \text{ kJ/kg}$$

Heat input, $Q_s = (h_3 - h_1) + (h_5 - h_4)$

or $$Q_s = (3095 - 29.3) + (3170 - 2609)$$

$$Q_s = 3626.7 \text{ kJ/kg}$$

Thermal efficiency of the plant is

$$\eta = \frac{\text{Turbine work}}{\text{Heat input}} = \frac{1491}{3626.7}$$

$$\eta = 41.11\%$$

(b) Enthalpy at the pump discharge

$$h_2 = h_1 + v\Delta P = 29.3 + \frac{1}{1000}(4000 - 10)$$

$$h_2 = 33.3 \text{ kJ/kg}$$

Example 13.32

In a steam power plant operating on an ideal Rankine cycle, superheated steam enters the turbine at 3.0 MPa and 350°C. The condenser pressure is 75 kPa. The thermal efficiency of the cycle is ________%.

Given data:

For saturated liquid, at $P = 75$ kPa, $h_f = 384.39$ kJ/kg, $v_f = 0.001037 \text{ m}^3$/kg, and $s_f = 1.213$ kJ/kgK.

At 75 kPa, $h_{fg} = 2278.6$ kJ/kg, $s_{fg} = 6.2434$ kJ/kgK

At P = 3 MPa and T = 350°C (superheated steam), $h = 3115.3$ kJ/kg, $s = 6.7428$ kJ/kgK

GATE 2016

Solution

The T-S diagram of Rankine cycle is sketched for reference.

$h_1 = 384.39$ kJ/kg, $s_1 = 1.213$ kJ/kgK

$h_3 = 3115.3$ kJ/kg, $s_3 = 6.7428$ kJ/kgK

Let x_4 be the quality of steam after expansion.

$$s_3 = s_4 = s_1 + x_4 \times s_{fg}$$

or $$6.7428 = 1.213 + x_4 \times 6.2434$$

or $\quad x_4 = 0.885$

$$h_4 = h_1 + x_4 \times h_{fg}$$

$$h_4 = 384.39 + 0.885 \times 2278.6 = 2400.95 \text{ kJ/kg}$$

$$h_2 = h_1 + v\Delta P = 384.39 + 0.001037 \times (3000 - 75)$$

$$h_2 = 387.42 \text{ kJ/kg}$$

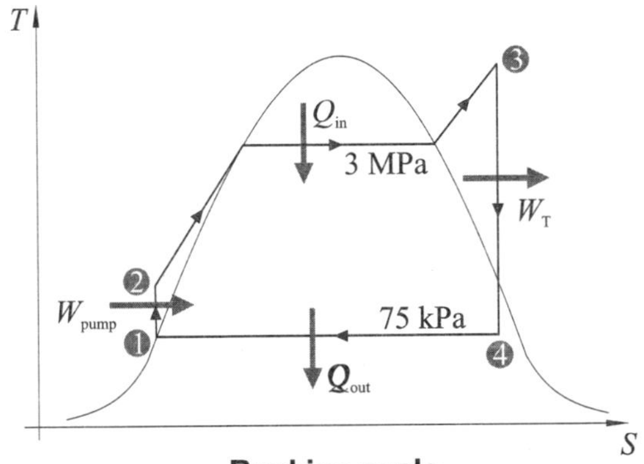

Rankine cycle

Thermal efficiency of cycle,

$$\eta = \frac{\text{Work output}}{\text{Heat supplied}} = \frac{W_T - W_P}{Q_1}$$

or
$$\eta = \frac{(h_3 - h_4) - (h_2 - h_1)}{(h_3 - h_2)}$$

$$\eta = \frac{(3115.3 - 2400.95) - (387.42 - 384.39)}{(3115.3 - 387.42)}$$

$$\eta = 26.07\%$$

Example 13.33

The heat removal rate from a refrigerated space and the power input to the compressor are 7.2 kW and 1.8 kW, respectively. The coefficient of performance (COP) of the refrigerator is ______.

GATE 2016

Solution

Coefficient of performance

$$\text{COP} = \frac{\text{Heat removal rate}}{\text{Power input}} = \frac{7.2}{1.8}$$

$$\text{COP} = 4$$

Example 13.34

Consider a simple gas turbine (Brayton) cycle and a gas turbine cycle with perfect regeneration. In both the cycles, the pressure ratio is 6 and the ratio of the specific heats of the working medium is 1.4. The ratio of minimum to maximum temperatures is 0.3 (with temperatures expressed in kelvin) in the regenerative cycle. The ratio of the thermal efficiency of the simple cycle to that of the regenerative cycle is _________.

GATE 2016

Solution

The efficiency of simple gas turbine (Brayton cycle) is given by $\eta_{\text{Brayton}} = 1 - \dfrac{1}{r_p^{\frac{\gamma-1}{\gamma}}}$

The efficiency of gas turbine cycle with regeneration is given by $\eta_{\text{regeneration}} = 1 - \dfrac{T_{\min}}{T_{\max}} r_p^{\frac{\gamma-1}{\gamma}}$

Substituting $r_p = 6$, $\gamma = 1.4$ and $\dfrac{T_{\min}}{T_{\max}} = 0.3$, we have

$$\eta_{\text{Brayton}} = 1 - \frac{1}{6^{\frac{0.4}{1.4}}} = 0.4006$$

$$\eta_{\text{regeneration}} = 1 - 0.3 \times 6^{\frac{0.4}{1.4}} = 0.4994$$

$$\frac{\eta_{\text{Brayton}}}{\eta_{\text{regeneration}}} = \frac{0.4006}{0.4994} = 0.8$$

$$\frac{\eta_{\text{Brayton}}}{\eta_{\text{regeneration}}} = 0.8$$

Example 13.35

A refrigerator uses R-134a as its refrigerant and operates on an ideal vapour-compression refrigeration cycle between 0.14 MPa and 0.8 MPa. If the mass flow rate of the refrigerant is 0.05 kg/s, the rate of heat rejection to the environment is _____ kW.

Given data:

At $P = 0.14$ MPa, $h = 236.04$ kJ/kg, $s = 0.9322$ kJ/kgK

At $P = 0.8$ MPa, $h = 272.05$ kJ/kg (superheated vapour)

At $P = 0.8$ MPa, $h = 93.42$ kJ/kg (saturated liquid)

GATE 2016

Solution

The P-h diagram of vapour compression refrigeration cycle is sketch for reference.

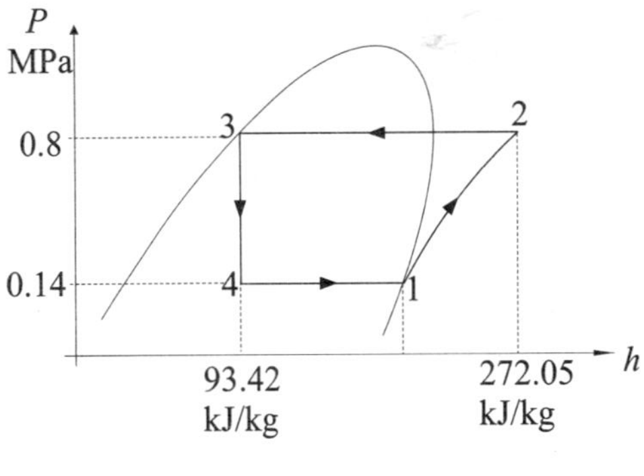

Rate of heat rejection to the environment is

$$Q_{rej} = m(h_2 - h_3)$$
$$Q_{rej} = 0.05 \times (272.05 - 93.42)\ \text{kW}$$
$$Q_{rej} = 8.93\ \text{kW}$$

Example 13.36

The partial pressure of water vapour in a moist air sample of relative humidity 70% is 1.6 kPa, the total pressure being 101.325 kPa. Moist air may be treated as an ideal gas mixture of water vapour and dry air. The relation between saturation temperature (T_s in K) and saturation pressure (P_s in kPa) for water is given by $\ln\left(\frac{P_s}{P_o}\right) = 14.317 - \frac{5304}{T_s}$, where P_o= 101.325 kPa. The dry bulb temperature of the moist air sample (in °C) is __________

GATE 2016

Solution

Relative humidity $\phi = \frac{P_v}{P_s} \quad \Rightarrow \quad 0.70 = \frac{1.6}{P_s}$

$$P_s = 2.28\ \text{kPa}$$

Substituting $P_s = 2.28$ kPa in the equation

$$\ln\left(\frac{P_s}{P_o}\right) = 14.317 - \frac{5304}{T_s}$$

$$\ln\left(\frac{2.28}{101.325}\right) = 14.317 - \frac{5304}{T_s}$$

$$T_s = 292.85\ \text{K}$$

$$T_s = 19.85\ °\text{C}$$

Example 13.37

In a mixture of dry air and water vapour at a total pressure of 750 mm of Hg, the partial pressure of water vapour is 20 mm of Hg. The humidity ratio of the air (in grams of water vapour per kg of dry air) is ______.

GATE 2016

Solution

Humidity ratio is given by $\omega = 0.622\left(\frac{P_v}{P - P_v}\right)$

$$\omega = 0.622\left(\frac{20}{750 - 20}\right)$$

or $$\omega = 0.01704\ \text{kg/kg of dry air}$$

$$\omega = 17.04\ \text{g/kg of dry air}$$

Example 13.38

In a 3-stage air compressor, the inlet pressure is P_1, discharge pressure is P_4 and the intermediate pressures are P_2 and P_3 ($P_2 < P_3$). The total pressure ratio of the compressor is 10 and the pressure ratios of the stages are equal. If P_1= 100 kPa, the value of the pressure P_3 (in kPa) is ____.

GATE 2016

Solution

Given: 3-stage air compressor, $P_1 = 100$ kPa and $\frac{P_4}{P_1} = 10$

Pressure ratio of each stage is equal; $\frac{P_2}{P_1} = \frac{P_3}{P_2} = \frac{P_4}{P_3} = \lambda$

$$\frac{P_2}{P_1} \times \frac{P_3}{P_2} \times \frac{P_4}{P_3} = \lambda^3 \quad \text{or} \quad \frac{P_4}{P_1} = 10 = \lambda^3$$

$$\lambda = 2.15$$

Now, $\frac{P_3}{P_1} = \lambda^2 \Rightarrow P_3 = 2.15^2 \times 100$

$$P_3 = 464.15\ \text{kPa}$$

Example 13.39

In the vapour compression cycle shown in the figure, the evaporating and condensing temperatures are 260 K and 310 K, respectively. The compressor takes in liquid vapour mixture (state-1) and isentropically compresses it to a dry saturated vapour condition (state 2). The specific heat of the liquid refrigerant is 4.8 kJ/kg and may be treated as constant. The enthalpy of evaporation for the refrigerant at 310 K is 1054 kJ/kg.

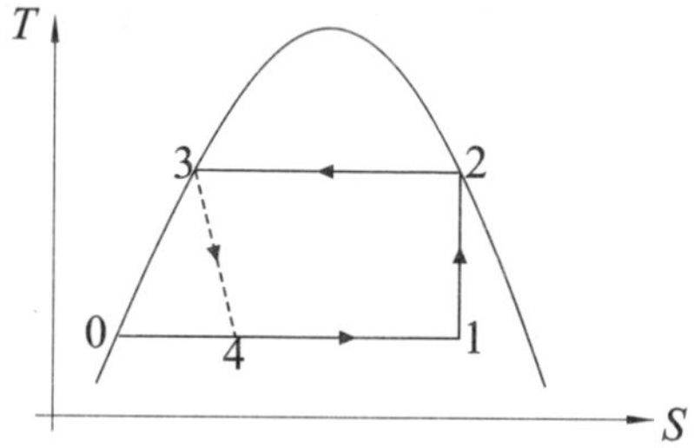

The difference between the enthalpies at state points 2 and 0 (in kJ/kg) is ____________

GATE 2016

Solution

Let h_o be the enthalpy at state 1.

$$h_3 = h_4$$

$$h_3 - h_0 = h_4 - h_0 = 4.8(310 - 260) = 240\ \text{kJ} \quad \text{(i)}$$

Enthalpy of evaporation at 310 K,

$$h_2 - h_3 = 1054 \text{ kJ/kg} \quad \text{(ii)}$$

From Equations (i) and (ii), we have

$$h_2 - h_0 = 1294 \text{ kJ/kg}$$

The difference between the enthalpies at state points 2 and 0 is 1294 kJ/kg.

Example 13.40

The Pressure ratio across a gas turbine (for air, specific heat at constant pressure, c_p = 1040 J / kg.K and ratio of specific heats, γ = 1.4) is 10. If the inlet temperature to the turbine is 1200 K and the isentropic efficiency is 0.9, the gas temperature at turbine exit is______ K.

GATE 2017

Solution

Given: $r_p = 10$, $c_p = 1040$ J/kgK, $\gamma = 1.4$, $T_3 = 1200$ K and $\eta_{\text{turbine}} = 0.9$.

The $T - S$ diagram of gas turbine is sketched for reference.

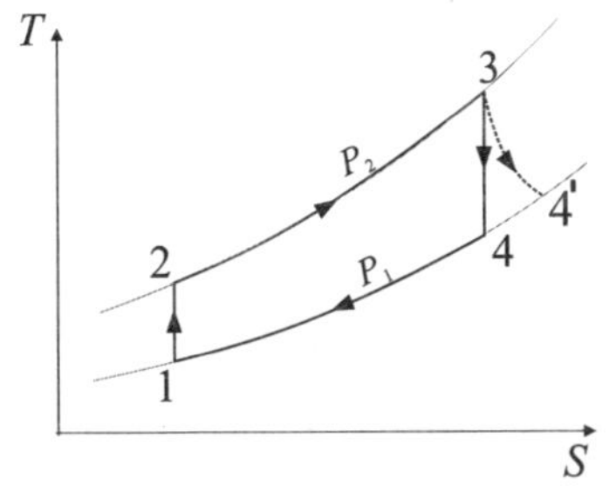

For isentropic process 3-4

$$\frac{T_3}{T_4} = \left(\frac{P_3}{P_4}\right)^{\frac{\gamma-1}{\gamma}} \Rightarrow \frac{1200}{T_4} = 10^{\frac{1.4-1}{1.4}}$$

$$T_4 = 621.5 \text{ K}$$

$$\text{Isentropic efficiency } \eta_{\text{turbine}} = \frac{T_3 - T_4'}{T_3 - T_4}$$

$$0.9 = \frac{1200 - T_4'}{1200 - 621.5}$$

$$T_4' = 679.38 \text{ K}$$

Example 13.41

Moist air is treated as an ideal gas mixture of water vapor and dry air (molecular weight of air = 28.84 and molecular weight of water = 18). At a location, the total pressure is 100 kPa, the temperature is 30°C and the relative humidity is 55%. Given that the saturation pressure of water at 30°C is 4246 Pa, the mass of water vapour per kg of dry air is _ _______ grams.

GATE 2017

Solution

Given $P = 100$ kPa, $T = 30°$C, $\phi = 55$ %, $P_s = 4246$ Pa

$$\text{Relative humidity, } \phi = \frac{m_v}{m_s} \quad \text{or} \quad \phi = \frac{P_v}{P_s}$$

$$0.55 = \frac{P_v}{4246} \quad \text{or} \quad P_v = 2335.3 \text{ Pa}$$

Specific humidity

$$\omega = 0.622\frac{P_v}{P - P_v} = 0.622\frac{2335.3}{100000 - 2335.3}$$

$$\omega = 0.01487 \text{ kg of water vapour/kg of dry air}$$

$$\omega = 14.87 \text{ gmkg of water vapour/kg of dry air}$$

Example 13.42

If a mass of moist air contained in a closed metallic vessel is heated, then its

(A) relative humidity decreases

(B) relative humidity increases

(C) specific humidity increases

(D) specific humidity decreases

GATE 2017

Solution

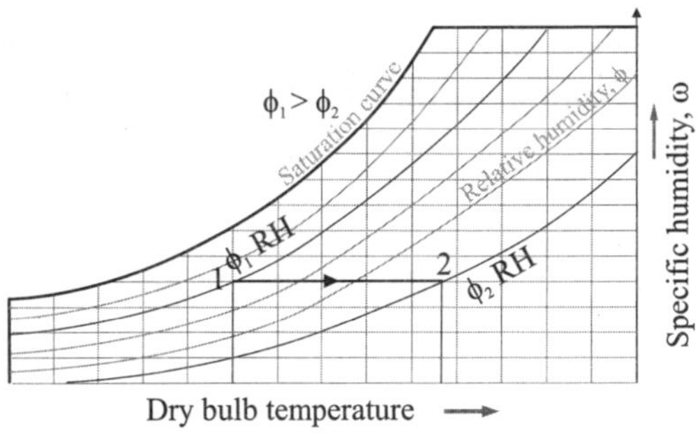

Psychrometric chart

If a mass of moist air contained in a closed metallic vessel is heated, then its relative humidity decreases

Example 13.43

In the Rankine cycle for a steam power plant the turbine entry and exit enthalpies are 2803 kJ/kg and 1800 kJ/kg, respectively. The enthalpies of water at pump entry and exit are 121 kJ/kg and 124 kJ/kg, respectively. The specific steam consumption (in kg/kW.h) of the cycle is________.

GATE 2017

Solution

The $T - s$ diagram of Rankine cycle is sketched for

reference.

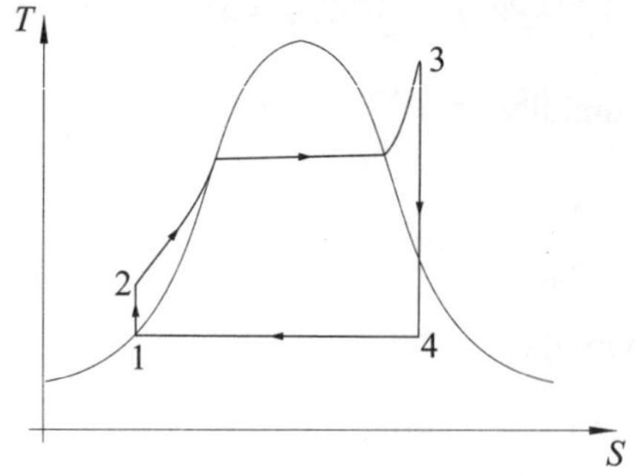

$h_3 = 2803$ kJ/kg, $h_4 = 1800$ kJ/kg, $h_1 = 121$ kJ/kg, $h_2 = 124$ kJ/kg

Turbine work $W_T = h_3 - h_4 = 2803 - 1800 = 1003$ kJ/kg

Pump work $W_P = h_2 - h_1 = 124 - 121 = 3$ kJ/kg

Network done $W_{net} = W_T - W_P = 1003 - 3 = 1000$ kJ/kg

$$\text{Specific steam consumption} = \frac{3600}{W_{net}} = \frac{3600}{1000} = 3.6$$

Specific steam consumption = 3.6 kg/kWh

Example 13.44

An engine working on air standard Otto cycle is supplied with air at 0.1 MPa and 35 °C. The compression ratio is 8. The heat supplied is 500 kJ/kg. Property data for air: c_p = 1.005 kJ/kg K, $c_v = 0.718$ kJ/kg K, $R = 0.287$ kJ/kgK. The maximum temperature (in K) of the cycle is_________ .

GATE 2018

Solution

The Otto cycle on $p - V$ is sketched for reference.

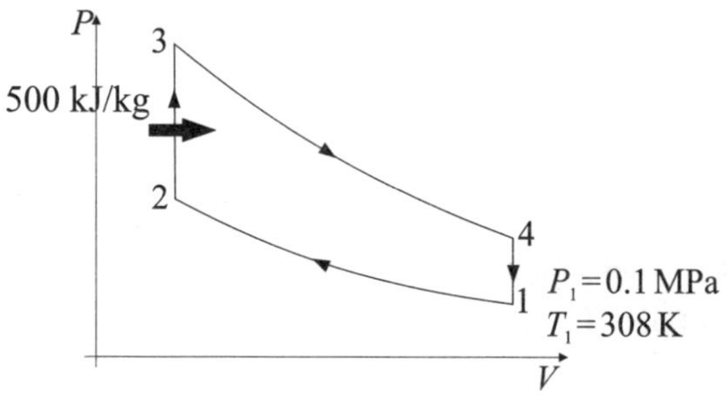

Given that: $p_1 = 0.1$ MPa, $T_1 = 308$ K, $Q_{2-3} = 500$ kJ/kg, $r = 8$, $c_p = 1.005$ kJ/kgK and $c_v = 0.718$ kJ/kgK.

$$\gamma = \frac{c_p}{c_v} = \frac{1.005}{0.718} = 1.399$$

For isentropic process 1-2, $\dfrac{T_2}{T_1} = \left(\dfrac{V_1}{V_2}\right)^{\gamma - 1}$

$$\frac{T_2}{308} = 8^{1.399-1}$$

$$T_2 = 707.6 \text{ K}$$

For the process 2-3, $Q_{2-3} = c_v(T_3 - T_2)$

$$500 = 0.718(T_3 - 707.6)$$

$$T_3 = 1403.9 \text{ K}$$

Maximum temperature $T_3 = 1403.9$ K

Example 13.45

A standard vapor compression refrigeration cycle operating with a condensing temperature of 35 °C and an evaporating temperature of −10°C develops 15 kW of cooling. The $p - h$ diagram shows the enthalpies at various states. If the isentropic efficiency of the compressor is 0.75, the magnitude of compressor power (in kW) is _______.

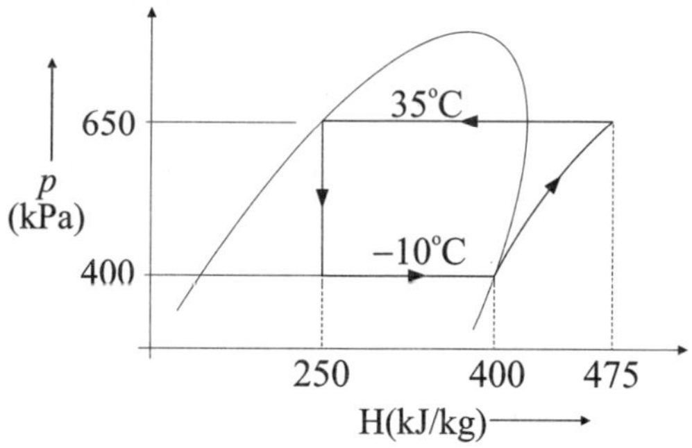

GATE 2018

Solution

Let $\dot{m}$ be the mass flow rate of refrigerant.

Cooling effect, $Q = \dot{m}(h_1 - h_2)$

$$15 = \dot{m}(400 - 250)$$

$$\dot{m} = 0.1 \text{ kg/s}$$

Compressor power $P = \dfrac{W_{\text{isentropic}}}{\eta}$

$$P = \frac{\dot{m}(h_2 - h_1)}{\eta} = \frac{0.1\,(475 - 400)}{0.75}$$

$P = 10$ kW

Example 13.46

Ambient air is at a pressure of 100 kPa, dry bulb temperature of 30 °C and 60% relative humidity. The saturation pressure of water at 30 °C is 4.24 kPa. The specific humidity of air (in g/kg of dry air) is ________ .

GATE 2018

Solution

Relative humidity $\phi = \frac{p_v}{p_{vs}} \Rightarrow 0.6 = \frac{p_v}{4.24}$

$$p_v = 2.544 \text{ kPa}$$

Specific humidity $\omega = 0.622 \frac{p_v}{p - p_v}$

$$\omega = 0.622 \times \frac{2.544}{100 - 2.544}$$

$$\omega = 16.24 \text{ kg/kg of dry air}$$

Example 13.47

A vehicle powered by a spark ignition engine follows air standard Otto cycle ($\gamma = 1.4$). The engine generates 70 kW while consuming 10.3 kg/hr of fuel. The calorific value of fuel is 44,000 kJ/kg. The compression ratio is _______ .

GATE 2018

Solution

Efficiency of cycle $\eta = \frac{W}{Q_{\text{in}}} = 1 - \frac{1}{r^{\gamma - 1}}$

Substituting $Q_{\text{in}} = \dot{m} \times CV = \frac{10.3}{60 \times 60} \times 44000 = 125.88 \text{ kW}$, $\gamma = 1.4$ and $W = 70$ kW.

$$\frac{70}{125.88} = 1 - \frac{1}{r^{1.4-1}}$$

or $r^{0.4} = 2.25$

Compression ratio $r = 7.61$

Example 13.48

Consider an ideal vapor compression refrigeration cycle. If the throttling process is replaced by an isentropic expansion process, keeping all the other processes unchanged, while one of the following statements is true for the modified cycle?

(A) Coefficient of performance is higher than that of the original cycle.

(B) Coefficient of performance is lower than that of the original cycle.

(C) Coefficient of performance is the same as that of the original cycle.

(D) Refrigerating effect is lower than that of the original cycle.

GATE 2019

Solution

From $T - s$ diagram of vapor compression refrigeration cycle

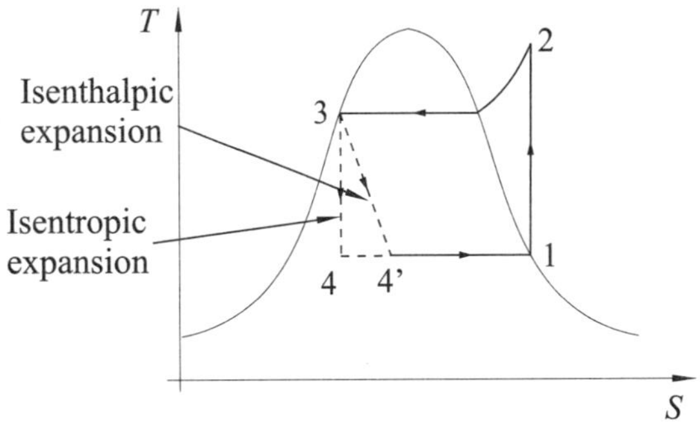

Refrigeration effect $h_1 - h_4 > h_1 - h_{4'}$

COP of isentropic expansion is more than isenthalpic expansion.

Example 13.49

A steam power cycle with regeneration as shown below the $T - s$ diagram employs a single open feedwater heater for efficiency improvement. The fluids mix with each other in an open feedwater heater. The turbine is isentropic and the input (bleed) to the feedwater heater from the turbine is at state 2 as shown in the figure. Process 3-4 occurs in the condenser. The pump work is negligible. The input to the boiler is at state 5. The following information is available from the steam table:

State	1	2	3	4	5	6
Enthaply (kJ/kg)	3350	2800	2300	175	700	1000

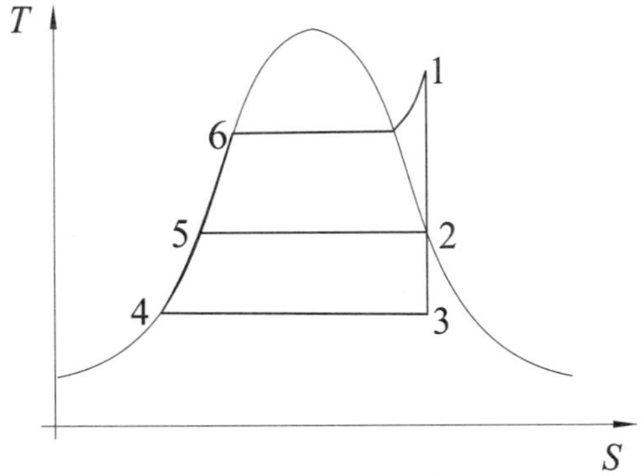

The mass flow rate of steam bled from the turbine as a percentage of the total mass flow rate as the inlet to the turbine at state 1 is _______.

GATE 2019

Solution

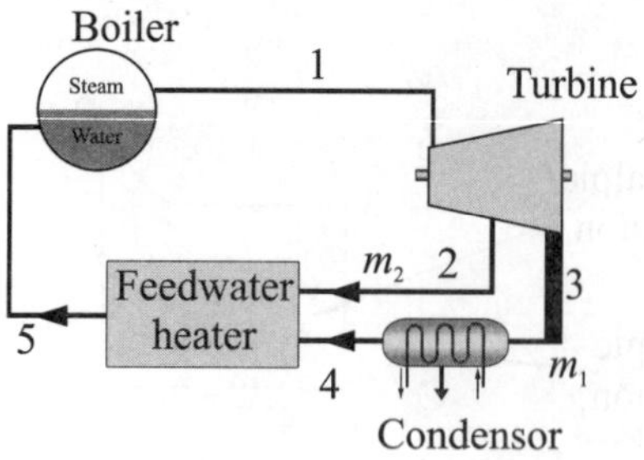

Let m_2 mass is bled at state 2 and m_1 goes to condenser.

Applying steady flow energy equation to mixing process

$$m_2 h_2 + m_1 h_4 = (m_1 + m_2) h_5$$

$$m_2 \times 2800 + m_1 \times 175 = (m_1 + m_2) \times 700$$

or $2100 m_2 = 525 m_1 \quad \Rightarrow \quad \frac{m_1}{m_2} = 0.25$

% Mass flow rate of steam bled from the turbine is

$$\frac{m_2}{m_1 + m_2} \times 100 = \frac{m_2 / m_1}{1 + (m_2 / m_1)} \times 100 = \frac{0.25}{1 + 0.25} \times 100$$

$$\frac{m_2}{m_1 + m_2} \times 100 = 20\%$$

Example 13.50

A gas turbine with air as the working fluid has an isentropic efficiency of 0.70 when operating at a pressure ratio of 3. Now, the pressure ratio of the turbine is increased to 5, while maintaining the same inlet conditions. Assume air as a perfect gas with specific heat ratio $\gamma = 1.4$. If the specific work output remains the same for both the cases, the isentropic efficiency of the turbine at the pressure ratio of 5 is ________ (round off to two decimal places)

GATE 2019

Solution

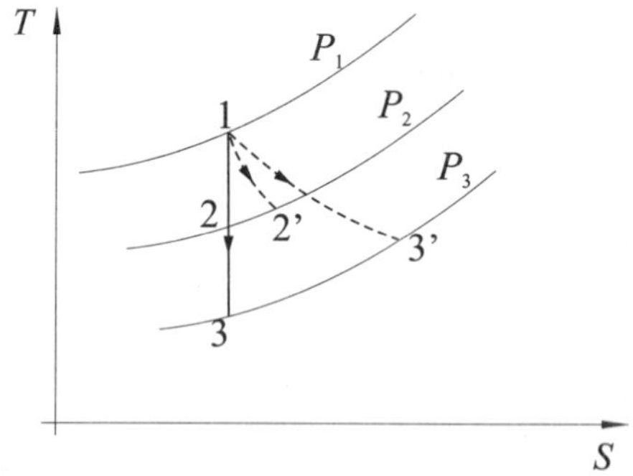

Work done by turbine 1; $WD_1 = c_p (T_1 - T_{2'})$

$$WD_1 = c_p \times \eta_1 \times (T_1 - T_2) \qquad \left[\frac{T_1}{T_2} = (r_{p1})^{\left(\frac{\gamma-1}{\gamma}\right)} \right]$$

$$WD_1 = c_p \times \eta_1 \times T_1 \left[1 - \frac{1}{(r_{p1})^{\left(\frac{\gamma-1}{\gamma}\right)}} \right]$$

Work done by turbine 2;

$$WD_2 = c_p \times \eta_2 \times T_1 \left[1 - \frac{1}{(r_{p2})^{\left(\frac{\gamma-1}{\gamma}\right)}} \right]$$

Since $WD_1 = WD_2$

$$c_p \times \eta_1 \times T_1 \left[1 - \frac{1}{(r_{p1})^{\left(\frac{\gamma-1}{\gamma}\right)}} \right] = c_p \times \eta_2 \times T_1 \left[1 - \frac{1}{(r_{p2})^{\left(\frac{\gamma-1}{\gamma}\right)}} \right]$$

or $0.7 \left[1 - \frac{1}{(3)^{\left(\frac{1.4-1}{1.4}\right)}} \right] = \eta_2 \left[1 - \frac{1}{(5)^{\left(\frac{1.4-1}{1.4}\right)}} \right]$

$$\eta_2 = 0.5115$$

Example 13.51

Which one of the following modifications of the simple ideal Rankine cycle increases the thermal efficiency and reduces the moister content of the steam at the turbine output?

(A) Increasing the boiler pressure.

(B) Decreasing the boiler pressure.

(C) Increasing the turbine inlet temperature.

(D) Decreasing the condenser pressure.

GATE 2019

Solution

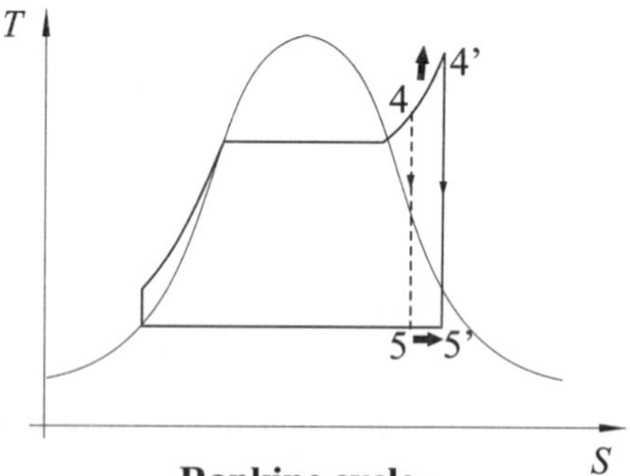

Rankine cycle

Increasing the inlet temperature to the turbine improves of quality of steam at the outlet of the turbine.

Example 13.52

An air standard Otto cycle has thermal efficiency of 0.5 and the mean effective pressure of the cycle is 1000 kPa. For air, assume specific heat ratio $\gamma = 1.4$ and specific gas constant $R = 0.287$ kJ/kg.K. If the pressure and temperature at the beginning of the compression stroke are 100 kPa and 300 K, respectively, then the specific net work output of the cycle is _____ kJ/kg (round off to two decimal places).

GATE 2019

Solution

The $P-V$ diagram of Otto cycle is sketched for reference.

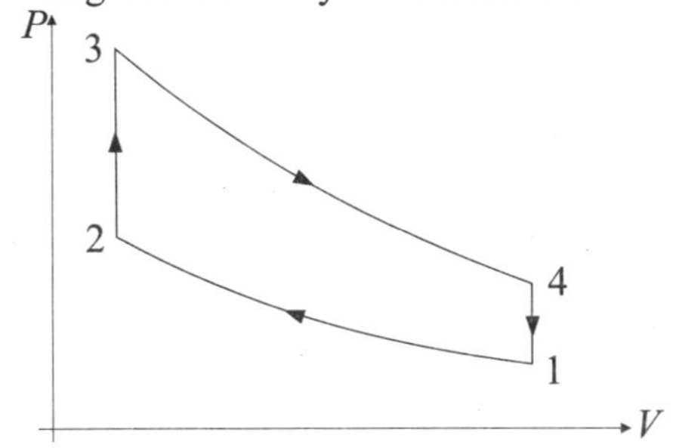

Given: $\eta_{\text{otto}} = 0.5$, $P_m = 1000$ kPa, $\gamma = 1.4$, $P_1 = 100$ kPa, $T_1 = 300$ K and $R = 0.287$ kJ/kg.K

$$\eta_{\text{otto}} = 1 - \frac{1}{r^{\gamma-1}} \quad \Rightarrow \quad 0.5 = 1 - \frac{1}{r^{1.4-1}}$$

$$r = \frac{V_1}{V_2} = 5.65$$

Substituting $V_1 = \dfrac{RT_1}{P_1} = \dfrac{0.287 \times 300}{100} = 0.861\ \text{m}^3/\text{kg}$

$$r = \frac{0.861}{V_2} = 5.65 \Rightarrow \qquad V_2 = 0.1524\ \text{m}^3/\text{kg}$$

Work done $WD = P_m(V_1 - V_2) = 1000(0.861 - 0.1524)$

$$WD = 708.6\ \text{kJ/kg}$$

13.3 PRACTICE PAPER

Time: 3 hours **Max. Marks: 100**

Q.1 to Q.30 carry one mark each

Q.1 to Q.20 Multiple Choice Questions

Q.1 The component of the Rankine cycle that leads to a relatively low cycle efficiency is

(A) Boiler (B) Pump (C) Turbine (D) Condenser

Q.2 Consider a simple ideal Rankine cycle with fixed boiler and condenser pressures. If the cycle is modified with reheating,

(A) The pump work input will decrease

(B) The amount of heat rejected will decrease

(C) The moisture content at turbine exit will decrease

(D) The turbine work output will decrease

Q.3 If P_a and P_v denote respectively the partial pressure of dry air and that of water vapour in moist air, the specific humidity of air is given by

(A) $\dfrac{P_a}{P_a + P_v}$ (B) $\dfrac{P_v}{P_a}$ (C) $0.622\dfrac{P_v}{P_a}$ (D) $0.622\dfrac{P_v}{P_a + P_v}$

Q.4 Which one of the thermodynamic cycles shown in the following figures represents that of Brayton cycle?

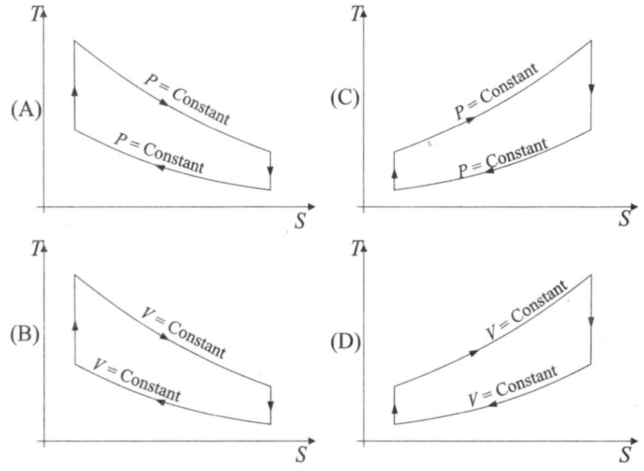

Q.5 In a Rankine cycle, with the maximum steam temperature being fixed from metallurgical consideration, as the boiler pressure increases,

(A) The condenser load will increase

(B) The quality of turbine exhaust will decrease

(C) The quality of turbine exhaust will increase

(D) The quality of turbine exhaust will remain unchanged

Q.6 A two-stage reciprocating compressor takes in air at 1.1 bar and discharge at 20 bar. For maximum efficiency, the intermediate pressure is

(A) 10.55 bar (B) 7.33 bar (C) 4.7 bar (D) 5.5 bar

Q.7 Consider the following processes:

1. Constant pressure heat addition

2. Adiabatic compression

3. Adiabatic expansion

4. Constant pressure heat rejection

The correct sequence of these processes in Rankine cycle is:

(A) 1-2-3-4 (B) 2 -1-4-3

(C) 2-1-3-4 (D) 1-2-4-3

Q.8 Consider the following statements:

When dry saturated steam is throttled from a higher pressure to a lower pressure, the

1. Pressure decreases and the volume increases
2. Temperature decreases and the steam becomes superheated.
3. Temperature and the dryness fraction increase
4. Entropy increases without any change in enthalpy

Which of these statements are correct?

(A) 1 and 4 (B) 1, 2 and 4 (C) 1 and 3 (D) 2 and 4

Q.9 In a psychometric process, the sensible heat added is 30 kW and latent heat added is 20 kW. The sensible heat factor (SHF) is

(A) 0.6 (B) 0.3 (C) 0.68 (D) 1.5

Q.10 Match List-I with List-II and select the correct answer using the codes given below the lists:

List-I Cycles operating between fixed temperature	List-II Characteristic of cycle efficiency 'η'
(P) Otto cycle	(1) η depends only upon temperature limits
(Q) Diesel cycle	(2) η depends only on pressure limits
(R) Carnot cycle	(3) η depends on volume compression ratio
(S) Brayton cycle	(4) η depends on cut-off ratio and volume compression ratio

(A) P-3, Q-4, R-1, S-2 (B) P-1, Q-4, R-3, S-2

(C) P-3, Q-2, R-1, S-4 (D) P-1, Q-2, R-3, S-2

Q.11 Air enters the compressor of an ideal gas-refrigeration cycle at 10°C and 80 kPa. The maximum and minimum temperatures in cycle are 250°C and –50°C. The compressor work is (nearest)

(A) 170 kJ/kg (B) 190 kJ/kg

(C) 241 kJ/kg (D) 220 kJ/kg

Q.12 The relation between $(COP)_{heat\ pump}$ and $(COP)_{refrigerator}$ working between same temperature range is given by

(A) $(COP)_{heat\ pump} = (COP)_{refrigerator} + 1$

(B) $(COP)_{heat\ pump} = (COP)_{refrigerator}$

(C) $(COP)_{heat\ pump} = (COP)_{refrigerator} - 1$

(D) None of these

Q.13 On the psychometric chart, a heating and humidification process appears as a line that is

(A) Diagonal upward to the right (NE direction)

(B) Diagonal upward to the left (NW direction)

(C) Diagonal downward to the right (SE direction)

(D) Horizontal to the right

Q.14 A refrigerator consumes 1 kW power and gives COP of 3.5, then its refrigeration capacity is

(A) 3.5 TR (B) 1.0 TR (C) 5.2 TR (D) 0.25 TR

Q.15 Which one is the ideal vapour-compression refrigeration cycle?

(A)

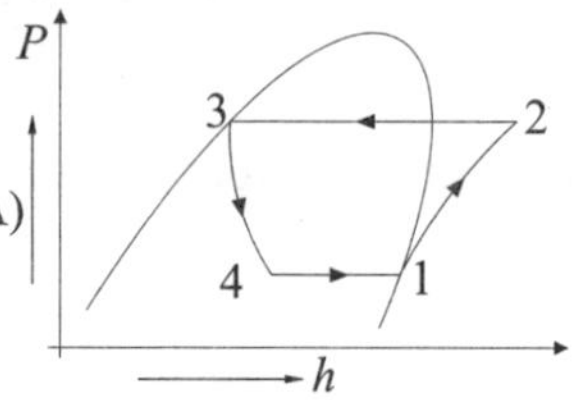

(B)

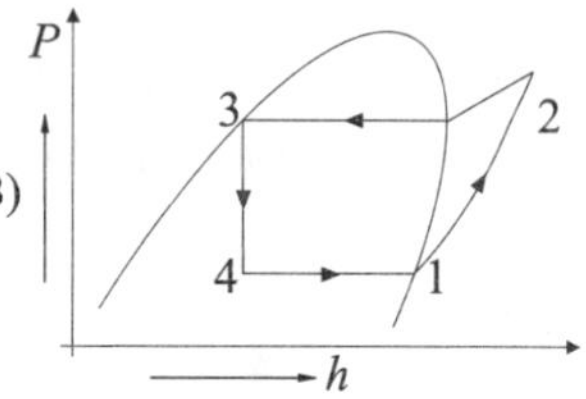

(C)

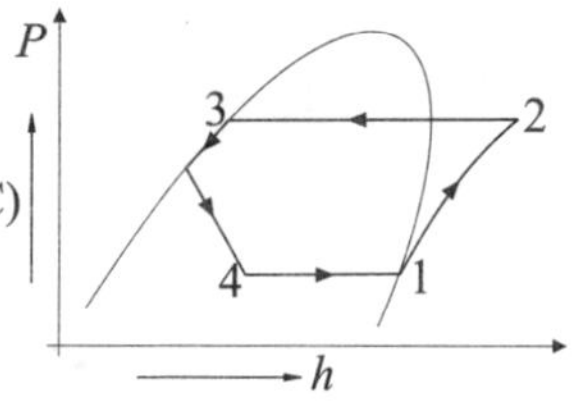

(D)

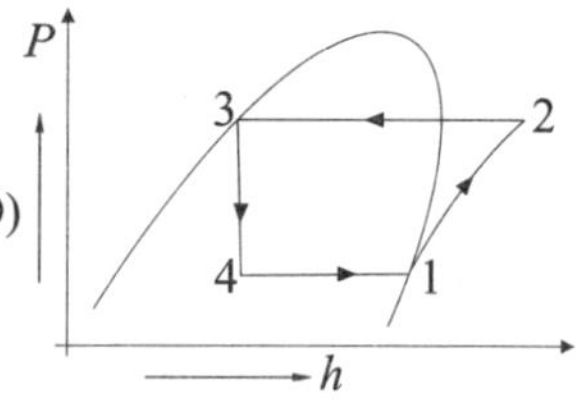

Q.16 In a simple vapour-compression refrigeration cycle, the enthalpies at different state points are given. Before compression = 375 kJ/kg. After compression = 425 kJ/kg. After throttling = 125 kJ/kg. The COP of refrigeration cycle is

(A) 3.5 (B) 6 (C) 5 (D) 2.8

Q.17 A simple ideal Brayton cycle with air as the working fluid has a pressure ratio of 10. The air enters the compressor at 27°C and the turbine at 827°C. The air temperature at the compressor exit is

(A) 306°C (B) 108°C (C) 248°C (D) 103°C

Q.18 A one ton capacity water cooler cools water steadily from 35°C to 20°C. The specific heat of water is 4.18 kJ/kgK. The water flow rate will be nearly

(A) 13.33 l/h (B) 123.13 l/h

(C) 120 l/h (D) 200 l/h

Q19 5 kg/s of dry saturated steam at a pressure of 50 bar expands in a turbine to a pressure of 5 bar. The exit steam has a quality of 90%. Neglect any changes in kinetic energy.

Properties of steam

P	v_f	v_g	u_f	u_g	h_f	h_g	s_f	s_g
(bar)	m³/kg	m³/kg	kJ/kg	kJ/kg	kJ/kg	kJ/kg	kJ/kgK	kJ/kgK
5	0.001093	0.3749	639.7	2561.2	640.2	2748.7	1.8607	6.8213
50	0.001286	0.03944	1147.8	2597.1	1154.2	2794.3	2.0202	5.9734

The actual power output of the turbine (in kW) is

(A) 2030 (B) 1493 (C) 4445 (D) 1282

Q.20 An open cycle constant pressure gas turbine uses a fuel of calorific value 40,000 kJ/kg, with air fuel ratio of 80:1 and develops a net output of 80 kJ/kg of air. What is the thermal efficiency (in%) of the cycle.

(A)16 (B) 8 (C) 40 (D) None of these

Q.21 to Q.30 Numerical Answer Question

Q.21 The latent heat load in an auditorium is 25% of sensible heat load. The value of sensible heat factor (SHF) is equal to________.

Q.22 A gas turbine power plant operates with air ($\gamma = 1.4$) between 1 bar and 20 bar. The maximum thermal efficiency (in %) for the corresponding air-standard cycle is________.

Q.23 Air at 5°C and 80% humidity is heated to 25°C in an enclosed room. The final humidity is (nearest) ____%.

Q.24 The flow rate of refrigerant R-12 in a refrigerator 0.03 kg/s. The refrigerant enters the compressor as saturated vapour at 150.9 kPa. After adiabatic compression, it enters the condenser as superheated vapour at 500 kPa and 100°C and leaves the condenser as saturated liquid at the same pressure. Use the following data to answer the questions.

Pressure (kPa)	Temperature (°C)	Specific enthalpy	
		h_f(kJ / kg)	h_g(kJ / kg)
150.9	–20	17.82	178.74
500	15.6	50.64	195.01
For the saturated vapour at 500 kPa and 100°C, $h = 252.05$ kJ/kg			

The refrigeration effect (in kW) is __________.

Q.25 A 3 m^3 rigid vessel contains steam at 4 MPa and 500°C. The mass (in kg) of the steam is (nearest) _____.

Q.26 A 100 m^3 rigid tank is filled with saturated liquid-vapour mixture of water at 200 kPa. If 20% of the mass is liquid and 80% of the mass is vapour, the total mass in the tank is___.

Q.27 An Otto cycle with air as the working fluid has bore of 250 mm, stroke of 300 mm and clearance volume 2500cc. the air standard efficiency (in %) of cycle is ___.

Q.28 In an ideal Otto cycle, air is compressed from 1.2 kg/m^3 and 2200 cc to 260 cc, and the net work output of the cycle is 440 kJ/kg. The mean effective pressure (in kPa) for this cycle is__________.

Q.29 A simple ideal Rankine cycle shown in figure operates between the pressure limits of 20 kPa and 6 MPa, with a turbine inlet temperature of 600°C. The pump work W_p (in kJ/kg) is_______.

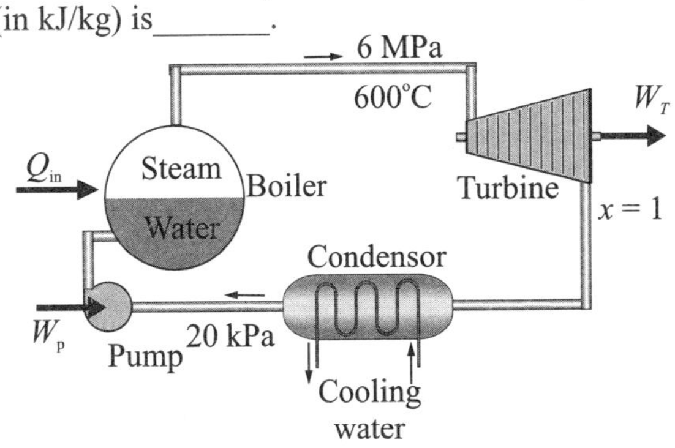

Steam power plant

Q.30 The compression ratio of an air-standard Otto cycle is 8. Prior to the isentropic compression process, the air is at 100 kPa, 27°C and 600 cm^3. The temperature at the end of the isentropic expansion process is 800 K. The highest temperature (in °C) in the cycle is_____.

Q.31 to Q.65 carry two marks each.

Q.31 to Q.50 Multiple Choice Questions

Q.31 In a thermal power plant operating on a Rankine cycle, steam having enthalpy $h = 2995.1$ kJ/kg and entropy $S = 6.5422$ kJ/kg°C is produced at 3 MPa and 300°C and is fed to a turbine where it expands to a condenser pressure of 5 kPa, where h_f = 137.77 kJ/kg, h_g = 2561.6 kJ/kg, S_f = 0.4763 kJ/kg°C and S_g = 8.3960 kJ/kg°C. At the entrance to the condenser, the quality and enthalpy (in kJ/kg) of steam, respectively are approximately.

(A) 0.77, 1994.42 (B) 0.68, 1795.67

(C) 0.79, 2055.02 (D) 0.79, 2055.02

Q.32 5 kg/s of dry saturated steam at a pressure of 50 bar expands in a turbine to a pressure of 5 bar. Neglect any changes in kinetic energy.

Properties of steam								
P	v_f	v_g	u_f	u_g	h_f	h_g	s_f	s_g
bar	m^3/kg	m^3/kg	kJ/kg	kJ/kg	kJ/kg	kJ/kg	kJ/kgK	kJ/kgK
5	0.001093	0.3749	639.7	2561.2	640.2	2748.7	1.8607	6.8213
50	0.001286	0.03944	1147.8	2597.1	1154.2	2794.3	2.0202	5.9734

The exit quality if the expansion to be reversible adiabatic, is

(A) 0.88 (B) 0.60 (C) 0.90 (D) 0.83

Q.33 A cold storage plant is used for storing 50 ton of apples in perforated plastic crates. During the storage apples are cooled down from 28°C to storage temperature of 2°C. (Specific heat of the apple = 0.874 kcal/kg°C). If the cooling is to be achieved in 8 hours, the power required (in hp) to operate the plant having a coefficient of performance (COP) of 2.5 will be

(A) 47 (B) 65 (C) 89 (D) 96

Q.34 A coal fired power plant, operating on a simple ideal Rankine cycle, has a boiler pressure of 32 bar and a condenser pressure of 0.75 bar. The exit state from the steam turbine is dry saturated vapour. Given saturated water properties:

Pressure (bar)	v_f (m^3/kg)	h_f (kJ/kg)	h_g (kJ/kg)	s_f (kJ/kgK)	s_g (kJ/kgK)
0.75	0.001037	384.36	2662.96	1.2129	7.4563
32	0.001224	1025	2803	2.678	6.160
Superheated steam properties at 32 bar and 592°C, h_g = 3663 kJ/kg, s_g = 7.4568 kJ/kgK.					

The specific heat-addition in the boiler (in kJ/kg) and the specific pump work input (in kJ/kg) would be

(A) 1778 and 3.24 (B) 2415.3 and 6.48

(C) 2638 and 641.64 (D) 3275.4 and 3.24

Q.35 In an air standard Diesel cycle, compression ratio is 14. At the beginning of compression of air ($R = 287$ J/kgK, $c_p = 1.005$ kJ/kgK and $\gamma = 1.4$), the temperature is 27°C and the pressure is 1 bar. If the specific volume after heat addition is two times the specific volume after compression, heat added (in kJ per kg of air) at constant pressure is:

(A) 555.5 (B) 622.7 (C) 622.7 (D) 866.4

Q.36 Atmospheric air at 100 kPa and 30°C has a relative humidity of 0.7. The saturation pressure for water vapour at 30°C is 4.25 kPa. The partial pressure (in kPa) of dry air in the atmospheric air, will be

(A) 70.0 (B) 74.25 (C) 95.75 (D) 96.98

Q.37 Match Group-I with Group-II

Group-I	Group-II
(P) Specific humidity	(1) $\dfrac{P_w}{P_s}$
(Q) Relative humidity	(2) $\dfrac{R_a}{R_W}\left(\dfrac{P_w}{P-P_s}\right)$
(R) Specific volume of dry air	(3) $\dfrac{P_w}{P_s}\left(\dfrac{P-P_s}{P-P_w}\right)$
	(4) $\dfrac{RT}{P-P_w}$

Here, the subscripts a, w and s refer to properties of air, water and saturation conditions

(A) P-1, Q-2, R-3 (B) P-2, Q-3, R-4

(C) P-2, Q-1, R-4 (D) P-4, Q-3, R-2

Q.38 A Brayton cycle operates with air entering the compressor at 100 kPa, 20°C, at a rate of 32.0 m^3/s, and air entering the turbine at 800 kPa, 1000°C. The power output of turbine is:

(A) 0.25 MW (B) 2.6 MW

(C) 21.8 MW (D) 11.8 MW

Q.39 Air enters the compressor of a simple gas turbine plant at 100 kPa, 27°C, at a rate of 2.2 kg/s. The compressor efficiency is 60%. Discharge pressure is 450 kPa. The amount of heat (kJ/kg) that must be added to provide a turbine inlet temperature of 650°C, is

(A) 784.2 kW (B) 1021.4 kW

(C) 510.7 kW (D) 110.7 kW

Q.40 An air-standard Otto cycle has a compression ratio of 8 and a maximum temperature of 1097°C. At the beginning of the compression stroke, the air is at 100 kPa, 27°C. The maximum pressure in the cycle is

(A) 653.8 kPa (B) 1837.9 kPa

(C) 3653 kPa (D) 4234 kPa

Q.41 A steam chest holds 500 kg at 10 bar and quality is 90% dryness. How much heat is to be added to make it 100% dry?

(A) 20.1 MJ (B) 48.6 MJ

(C) 80.1 MJ (D) 100.6 MJ

Q.42 A simple ideal Brayton cycle with air as the working fluid has a pressure ratio of 10. The air enters the compressor at 27°C and the turbine at 827°C. The back-work ratio is

(A) 0.81 (B) 0.73 (C) 0.52 (D) 0.43

Q.43 Air in an ideal Diesel cycle is compressed from 2 to 0.13 litres, and then it expands during the constant pressure heat addition process to 0.30 litre. The thermal efficiency of this cycle is:

(A) 59% (B) 34% (C) 64% (D) 19%

Q.44 Estimate the liters of water in the air in a $3\,m \times 10\,m \times 20\,m$ room if the temperature is 20°C and humidity is 70%.

(A) 7.5 litre (B) 6.2 litre (C) 5.1 litre (D) 4.0 litre

Q.45 In an open type of refrigerating installation, 1000 kg of atmospheric air are circulated per hour. The air is drawn from the cold chamber at temperature 7°C and 1 bar and then compressed isentropic to 5 bar. It is cooled at this pressure to 27°C and then led to the expansion where it expands isentropically down to atmospheric pressure and is discharged to cold chamber. Heat extracted (kW) from cold chamber is:

(A) 40 kW (B) 25.4 kW (C) 14.8 kW (D) 0

Q.46 A house contains air at 30°C and a total pressure of 96.0 kPa with a relative humidity of 75%. The partial pressure of dry air is:

(A) 82.0 kPa (B) 92.8 kPa

(C) 85.8 kPa (D) 90.6 kPa

Q.47 Air enters the compressor of an ideal gas-refrigeration cycle at 10 °C and 80 kPa. The maximum and minimum temperatures in cycle are 250 °C and –50 °C. The pressure ratio across the compressor in the cycle is (nearest)________.

(A) 8.6 (B) 8.0 (C) 7.8 (D) 7.4

Q.48 A simple vapour compressor refrigeration system using ammonia as refrigerant operates between an evaporator pressure of 119.5 kPa and a condenser pressure of 1554.9 kPa. The refrigerant is in a saturated condition at the exit of evaporator and condenser.

Saturated properties of ammonia					
P (kPa)	T (°C)	v_f (m^3/kg)	v_g (m^3/kg)	h_f (kJ/kg)	h_g (kJ/kg)
119.5	–30	0.001476	0.96339	44.26	1404.4
1554.9	40	0.001725	0.08313	371.43	1470.2

What is the dryness fraction (quality) of refrigerant at the inlet to the evaporator?

(A) 0.24 (B) 0.76 (C) 0.30 (D) 0.70

Q.49 Air at 35 °C and 70% humidity in a 3 m × 10 m × 20 m room is cooled to 25 °C and 40% humidity. How much (in kg) water is removed?

(A) 11.1 (B) 24.4 (C) 32.8 (D) 43

Q.50 Air enters the compressor of a simple gas-refrigeration cycle at –10 °C and 100 kPa. For a compression ratio of 10 and a turbine inlet temperature of 30 °C, the value of coefficient of performance is

(A) 2.54 (B) 1.86 (C) 1.08 (D) 3.55

Q.51 to Q.65 Numerical Answer Question

Q.51 The flow rate of refrigerant R-12 in a refrigerator 0.03 kg/s. The refrigerant enters the compressor as saturated vapour at 150.9 kPa. After adiabatic compression, it enters the condenser as superheated vapour at 500 kPa and 100 °C and leaves the condenser as saturated liquid at the same pressure. Use the following data to answer the question.

Pressure (kPa)	Temperature (°C)	Specific enthalpy	
		h_f (kJ/kg)	h_g (kJ/kg)
150.9	–20	17.82	178.74
500	15.6	50.64	195.01
For the saturated vapour at 500 kPa and 100° C, h = 252.05 kJ/kg			

The actual power input to the compressor (in kW) is ___.

Q.52 Air enters the compressor for an ideal air-standard Brayton cycle at 100 kPa, 300 K with a mass flow rate of 1.5 kg/s. The compressor pressure ratio is 10, and the heat addition during the cycle is 1237.5 kW. For air, assume constant c_p and c_v values of 1.005 kJ/kgK and 0.717 kJ/kgK, respectively. The turbine inlet temperature is __.

Q.53 A simple vapour compressor refrigeration system using ammonia as refrigerant operates between an evaporator pressure of 119.5 kPa and a condenser pressure of 1554.9 kPa. The refrigerant is in a saturated condition at the exit of evaporator and condenser.

Saturated properties of ammonia					
P (kPa)	T (°C)	v_f (m^3/kg)	v_g (m^3/kg)	h_f (kJ/kg)	h_g (kJ/kg)
119.5	–30	0.001476	0.96339	44.26	1404.4
1554.9	40	0.001725	0.08313	371.43	1470.2

At the inlet to the evaporator, what percent of the total volume is occupied by the vapour?_______.

Q.54 The specific volume of steam after expansion in a turbine is 12 m^3/kg. At this pressure, the saturated liquid and saturated vapour specific volumes are 0.001 m^3/kg and 15.25 m^3/kg respectively. The dryness fraction of steam is_____.

Q.55 A gas turbine operating on Brayton cycle has the maximum temperature of 1200 K and minimum temperature of 300 K. The cycle efficiency for the maximum work capacity will be_______.

Q.56 A cold storage plant is used for storing 50 tonnes of apples in perforated plastic crates. During the storage apples are cooled down from 28 °C to storage temperature of 2 °C. (Specific heat of the apple = 0.874 kcal/kg °C) If the required cooling is attained in 16 hours, the refrigeration plant capacity (in TR) is_______.

Q.57 A Diesel engine has a compression ratio of 16 and cut-off takes place at 8% of stroke. Assuming an air-standard cycle, the cut-off ratio is_______.

Q.58 A coal fired power plant operates on the Rankine cycle and has thermal efficiency of 30%. The heat input to the boiler is measured to be 500 MW. The pump input power is negligibly small. If the condenser is cooled by sea-water (c_p = 1.0 kJ/kgK) which is available at 20 °C, and if the measured exit temperature of the cooling water for the condenser is 30 °C, the mass flow rate (in kg/s) of sea-water required for the condenser (in kg/s) will be___.

Q.59 A saturated liquid-vapour mixture of refrigerant R-22 has a density of 36.12 kg/m^3 at –30 °C. If the densities of saturated liquid and saturated vapour at –30°C are 1377 kg/m^3 and 7.379 kg/m^3, respectively, the quality of the mixture is _______.

Q.60 A domestic refrigerator set at 2 °C handles on the average a thermal load of 8000 kJ per day. The ambient temperature is 30 °C. The COP of the refrigerator is equal to 0.15 times that of a carnot refrigerator. The daily electricity consumption (kWh) is_______.

Q.61 Saturated liquid at a high pressure P_1 having enthalpy of saturated liquid 1000 kJ/kg is throttled to a lower pressure P_2. At pressure P_2, enthalpy of saturated liquid and that of the saturated vapour are 800 kJ/kg and 2800 kJ/kg respectively. The dryness fraction of vapour after throttling process is _______.

Q.62 Water passes through four primary components as it traverses a cycle in a power plant: a turbine, a condenser, a pump, and a boiler. Estimate (in MJ/s) the heat rejected in condenser (if $Q_{\text{boiler}} = 55$ MW, $W_{\text{turbine}} = 18\times 10^6$ Nm/s and W_{pump} =100 hp). ______

Q.63 The ratio of the clearance volume to the displacement volume of a R-12 reciprocating compressor is 0.05. Specific volume at inlet and outlet of compressor are 0.04 and 0.02 m^3/kg respectively. The volumetric efficiency (in %) of the compressor is_______

Q.64 A simple ideal Rankine cycle shown in figure operates between the pressure limits of 20 kPa and 6 MPa, with a turbine inlet temperature of 600 °C. The cooling water is allowed a 10 °C increase. If $m_{\text{steam}} = 2$ kg/s, and the quality of the steam leaving the condenser is just 0.0, then the mass flow rate of cooling water is_______.

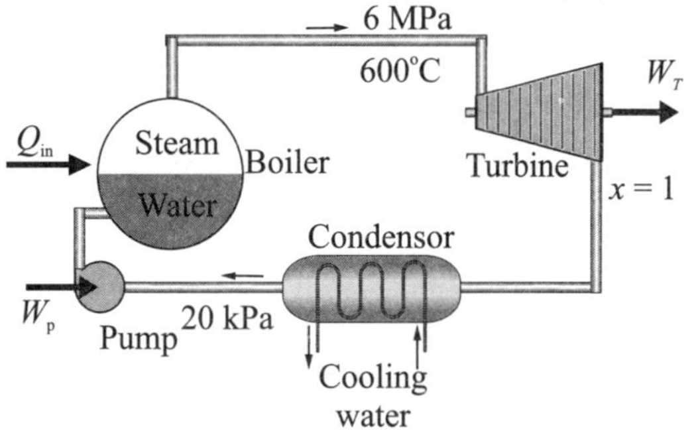

Steam power plant

Q.65 An ideal gas-refrigeration cycle operates between the pressure limits of 80 kPa and 280 kPa. Air is working fluid. Air is cooled to 35 °C before entering the turbine. The lowest temperature of this cycle is_______.

13.4 SOLUTION TO PRACTICE PAPER

Q.1 Ans:(D)

Efficiency of Rankine cycle, $\eta = \dfrac{Q_1 - Q_2}{Q_1}$

or $\eta = \dfrac{W_T - W_P}{Q_1}$

where Q_2 = Heat rejected (in condenser) and W_P = Pump work

$Q_2 > W_P \Rightarrow$ Heat rejected (in condenser) > Pump work

Relatively low cycle efficiency is due to condenser

Q.2 Ans:(C)

The T-S diagram (figure) is sketched of reheat cycle for reference.

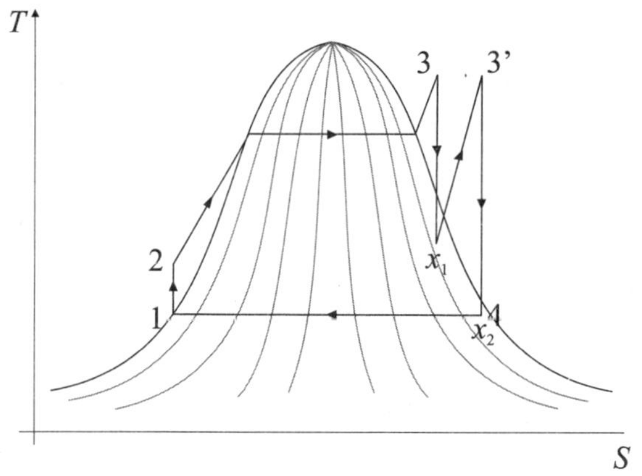

Reheat cycle

$x_2 > x_1$

The moisture content at the turbine exit will decrease by reheating.

Q.3 Ans:(C)

Specific humidity $\omega = \dfrac{m_v}{m_a} = \dfrac{\text{Mass of water vapour}}{\text{Mass of dry air}}$

or $\omega = \dfrac{\dfrac{P_vV}{R_vT}}{\dfrac{P_aV}{R_aT}} = \dfrac{R_a}{R_v}\dfrac{P_v}{P_a}$

or $\omega = \dfrac{0.287}{0.4615}\dfrac{P_v}{P_a}$

$$\omega = 0.622\frac{P_v}{P_a}$$

Q.4 Ans:(C)

Brayton cycle on T- S is shown in the figure.

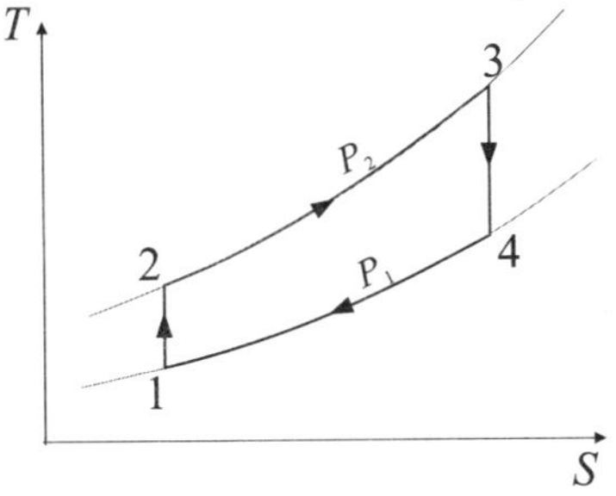

Q.5 Ans:(B)

The Rankine cycles on T- S at boiler pressure P_1 and P_2 is shown in figure.

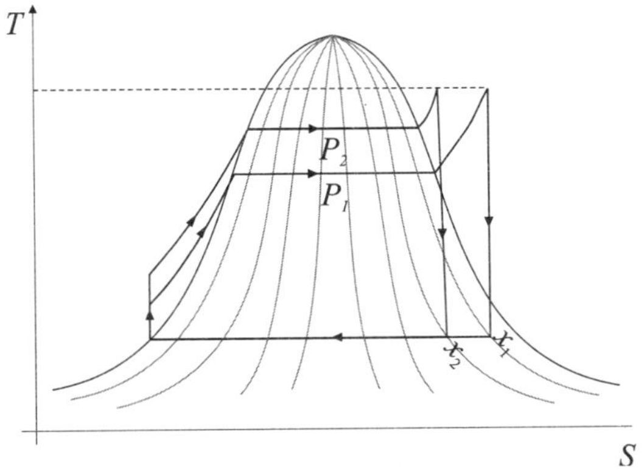

From figure $P_2 > P_1 \Rightarrow x_1 > x_2$

Boiler pressure increases, the quality of turbine exhaust will decrease.

Q.6 Ans:(C)

Condition for maximum efficiency;

$$\frac{P_2}{P_1} = \frac{P_3}{P_2} \quad \Rightarrow P_2 = \sqrt{P_1 P_3}$$

$$P_2 = \sqrt{1.1 \times 20} = 4.7$$

Intermediate pressure $P_2 = 4.7$ bars

Q.7(C)

Sequence of processes in Rankine cycle.

Aadiabatic compression $\rightarrow$ Constant pressure heat addition $\rightarrow$ Adiabatic expansion$\rightarrow$ Constant pressure heat rejection.

$$2 \rightarrow 1 \rightarrow 3 \rightarrow 4$$

Q.8 Ans:(A)

Dry saturated steam is throttled from a higher pressure to a lower pressure, the pressure decreases and the volume increases and entropy increases without any change in enthalpy.

Correct options are 1 and 4

Q.9 Ans:(A)

Sensible heat factor, $\text{SHF} = \dfrac{Q_s}{Q_s + Q_L}$

$$\text{SHF} = \frac{30}{30+20}$$

$$\text{SHF} = 0.6$$

Q.10 Ans:(A)

(P) $\eta_{\text{Otto}} = 1 - \dfrac{1}{r_k^{\gamma-1}}$	(3) η depends on volume compression ratio
(Q) $\eta_{\text{Diesel}} = 1 - \dfrac{1}{\gamma}\dfrac{1}{r_k^{\gamma-1}}\dfrac{r_c^{\gamma}-1}{r_c - 1}$	(4) η depends on cut-off ratio and volume compression ratio
(R) $\eta_{\text{Carnot}} = 1 - \dfrac{T_2}{T_1}$	(1) η depends only upon temperature limits
(S) $\eta_{\text{Brayton}} = 1 - \dfrac{1}{(r_p)^{\frac{\gamma-1}{\gamma}}}$	(2) η depends only on pressure limits

Q.11 Ans:(C)

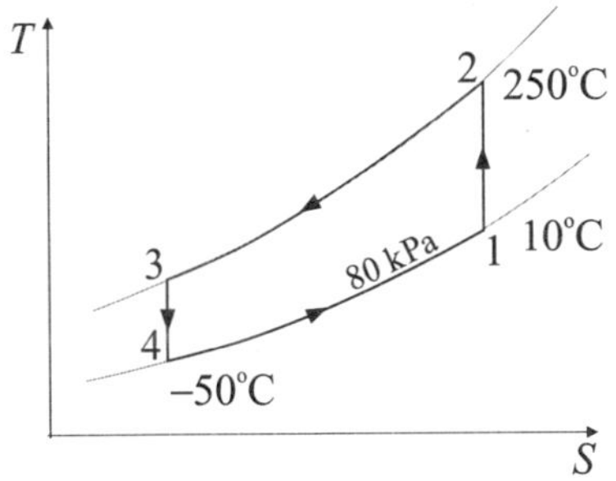

The T- S diagram of gas refrigeration cycle is sketched for reference.

Compressor work is given by $W_C = c_p (T_2 - T_1)$

or $\quad W_C = 1.005(250 - 10)$ kJ/kg

$$W_C = 241 \text{ kJ/kg}$$

Q.12 Ans:(A)

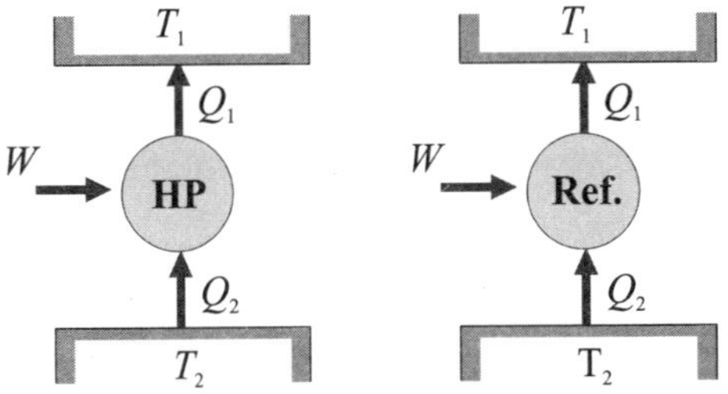

$$(\text{COP})_{\text{heat pump}} = \frac{Q_1}{W} = \frac{Q_1}{Q_1 - Q_2} \qquad \text{(i)}$$

$$(\text{COP})_{\text{refrigerator}} = \frac{Q_2}{Q_1 - Q_2} \qquad \text{(ii)}$$

From Equations (i) and (ii), we have

$$(\text{COP})_{\text{heat pump}} - (\text{COP})_{\text{refrigerator}} = 1$$

$$(\text{COP})_{\text{heat pump}} = 1 + (\text{COP})_{\text{refrigerator}}$$

Q.13 Ans:(A)

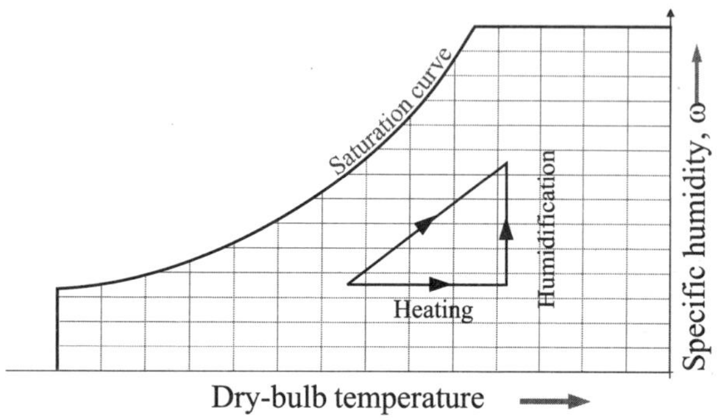

Q.14 Ans:(B)

$$\text{COP of refrigerator} = \frac{Q_2}{W}$$

or $$3.5 = \frac{Q_2}{1}$$

or $$Q_2 = 3.5\,\text{kW} \qquad [1\text{ TR} = 3.5\text{ kW}]$$

$$\text{Refrigeration capacity, } Q_2 = 1.0\text{ TR}$$

Q.15 Ans:(D)

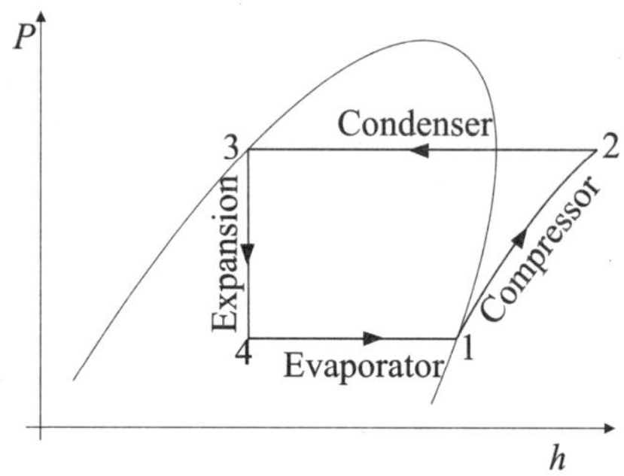

Q.16 Ans:(C)

The schematic diagram of vapour-compression refrigeration cycle is sketched for reference.

Given: $h_1 = 375$ kJ/kg, $h_2 = 425$ kJ/kg and $h_4 = 125$ kJ/kg

$$\text{COP} = \frac{\text{Desired effect}}{\text{Compressor work}}$$

$$\text{COP} = \frac{h_1 - h_4}{h_2 - h_1}$$

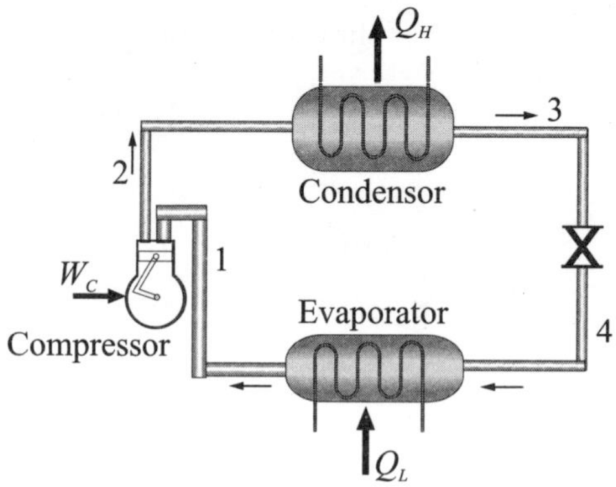

Vapour comresssion refrigeration cycle

or $$\text{COP} = \frac{375 - 125}{425 - 375}$$

$$\text{COP} = 5$$

Q.17 Ans:(A)

Pressure ratio $r_p = 10$

For the isentropic compression process 1-2 , we have

$$\frac{T_1^{\gamma}}{P_1^{\gamma-1}} = \frac{T_2^{\gamma}}{P_2^{\gamma-1}} \Rightarrow T_2 = T_1\left(\frac{P_2}{P_1}\right)^{\frac{\gamma-1}{\gamma}}$$

or $$T_2 = (273 + 27)(10)^{\frac{1.4-1}{1.4}}$$

or $$T_2 = 579.2\text{ K}$$

$$T_2 = 306°\text{C}$$

Q.18 Ans:(D)

The rate of refrigeration is $\qquad Q = \dot{m}c(t_2 - t_1)$

or $$\dot{m} \times 4.18(35 - 20) = 1\text{ TR}$$

or $$\dot{m} \times 4.18(35 - 20) = 1 \times 3.517$$

or $$\dot{m} = 0.05609\text{ kg/s} = 201.9\text{ kg/h}$$

$$\text{Water flow rate } \dot{m} \approx 200\text{ l/h}$$

Q.19 Ans:(D)

Power output of turbine, $W_T = m(h_1 - h_2)$

From properties of steam:

At 50 bar (steam is dry saturated), $h_1 = 2794.3$ kJ/kg

At 5 bar (steam quality is 90%),

$$h_2 = 640.2 + 0.9(2748.7 - 640.2)$$

or $$h_2 = 2537.85\text{ kJ/kg}$$

Now, $$W_T = m(h_1 - h_2) = 5 \times (2794.3 - 2537.85)$$

$$W_T = 1282\text{ kW}$$

Q.20 Ans:(A)

Let m_a and m_f be the mass flow rate of air and fuel respectively.

Air fuel ratio $\frac{m_a}{m_f} = 80$ or $m_a = 80m_f$

Heat supplied, $Q = CV \times m_f = 40000m_f$ kg/s

Work output, $W = 80m_a = 80 \times 80m_f$

Thermal efficiency of cycle, $\eta = \frac{W}{Q} = \frac{80 \times 80m_f}{40000m_f}$

$$\eta = 16\%$$

Q.21 Ans:[0.8]

Latent heat load $= 0.25 \times$ Sensible heat load

Sensible heat factor, $\text{SHF} = \frac{\text{SH}}{\text{SH} + \text{SL}}$

$$\text{SHF} = \frac{\text{SH}}{\text{SH} + 0.25\,\text{SH}} = \frac{1}{1.25}$$

$$\text{SHF} = 0.8$$

Q.22 Ans:[57.5]

Efficiency of Brayton cycle, $\eta_{\text{Brayton}} = 1 - \frac{1}{(r_p)^{\frac{\gamma-1}{\gamma}}}$

$$\eta_{\text{Brayton}} = 1 - \frac{1}{\left(\frac{P_2}{P_1}\right)^{\frac{\gamma-1}{\gamma}}} \quad \text{or} \quad \eta_{\text{Brayton}} = 1 - \frac{1}{\left(\frac{20}{1}\right)^{\frac{1.4-1}{1.4}}}$$

$$\eta_{\text{Brayton}} = 57.5\%$$

Q.23 Ans:[22]

Using the psychrometric chart, the intersection of constant specific humidity line and $T_{db} = 25°\text{C}$, gives

22 % relative humidity

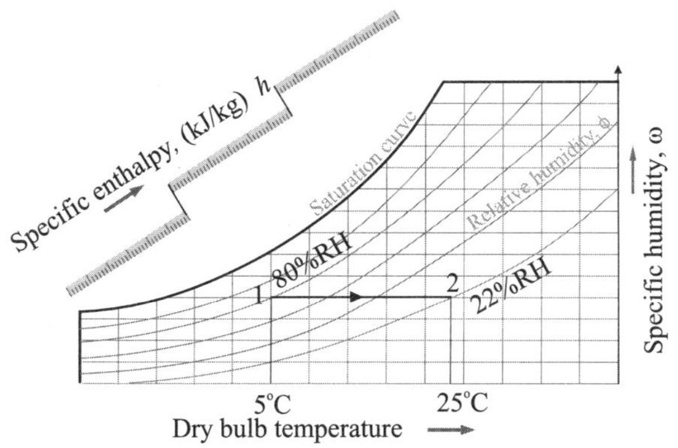

Psychrometric chart

Q.24 Ans:[3.84]

The P-h diagram is sketched for reference.

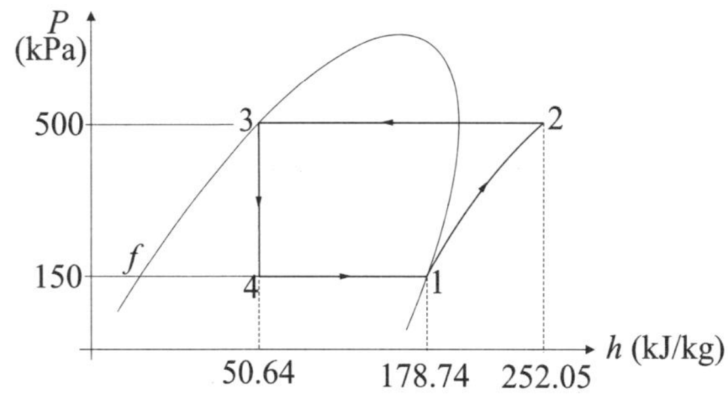

Refrigeration effect, $Q_r = m(h_1 - h_4)$

or $Q_r = 0.03 \times (178.74 - 50.64)$

$$Q_r = 3.84\text{ kW}$$

Q.25 Ans:[35]

From steam table:

At pressure 4 MPa (40 bar) and temperature $500°\text{C}$;

Specific volume, $v = 0.08634\ \text{m}^3/\text{kg}$

Mass of steam, $m = \frac{V}{v} = \frac{3}{0.08634} = 34.74$

$$m \approx 35\text{ kg}$$

Q.26 Ans:[562]

Dryness fraction, $x = 0.2$

From steam table (at 200 kPa):

$v_f = 0.001061\ \text{m}^3/\text{kg}$, $v_g = 0.88540\ \text{m}^3/\text{kg}$

Specific volume, $v = v_f + xv_{fg}$

$$v = 0.001061 + 0.2 \times (0.88540 - 0.001061)$$

or $v = 0.17792\ \text{m}^3/\text{kg}$

Total mass, $m = \frac{V}{v} = \frac{100}{0.17792}$

$$m = 562\text{ kg}$$

Q.27 Ans:[53.8]

Swept volume, $V_s = \frac{\pi}{4}D^2L$

$$V_s = \frac{\pi}{4} \times 25^2 \times 30$$

or $V_s = 14726.2\ \text{cm}^3$

Compression ratio,

$$r_k = \frac{V_c + V_s}{V_c} = \frac{2500 + 14726.2}{2500} = 6.89$$

Air standard efficiency, $\eta = 1 - \dfrac{1}{r_k^{\gamma-1}} = 1 - \dfrac{1}{6.89^{1.4-1}}$

$$\eta = 53.8\ \%$$

Q.28 Ans:[598.76]

Mass of air, $m = 1.2 \times 2200 \times 10^{-6} = 2.64 \times 10^{-3}\,\text{kg}$

$V_1 - V_2 = 2200 - 260 = 1940\,\text{cc} = 1940 \times 10^{-6}\ \text{m}^3$

Net work done, $W = 440 \times 2.64 \times 10^{-3}$ kJ

Mean effective pressure,

$$P_m = \frac{W}{V_1 - V_2} = \frac{440 \times 2.64 \times 10^{-3}}{1940 \times 10^{-6}}$$

$$P_m = 598.76\,\text{kPa}$$

Q.29 Ans:[6.34]

The *T-S* diagram (shown in figure) of Rankine cycle is sketched for reference.

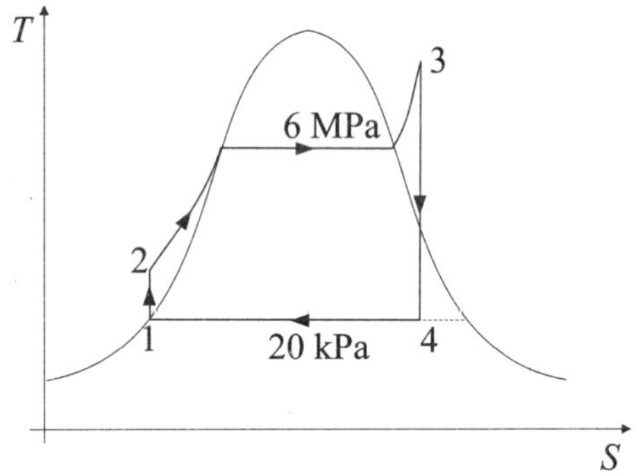

Specific volume of state 1,

$$v_1 = 0.001061\ \text{m}^3/\text{kg}$$

Pump work is given by

$$W_p = (P_2 - P_1)v_1$$

$$W_p = (6000 - 20) \times 0.001061\,\text{kNm/kg}$$

$$W_p = 6.34\,\text{kJ/kg}$$

Q.30 Ans:[1564]

The *P-V* diagram of Otto cycle is sketched for reference.

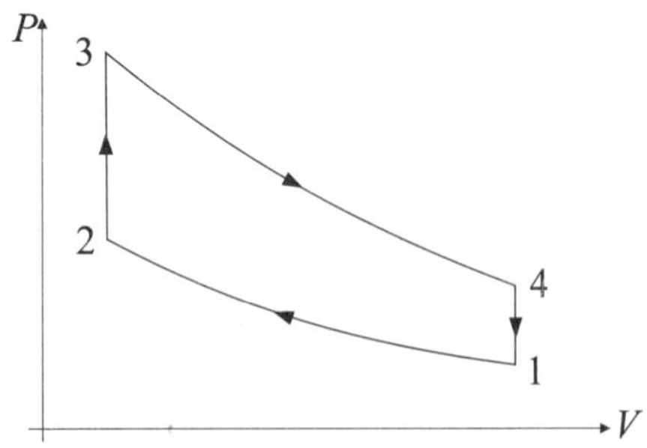

Compression ratio $\dfrac{V_1}{V_2} = 8$, $P_1 = 100$ kPa, $T_1 = 300\,\text{K}$,

$V_1 = 600\ \text{cm}^3$ and $T_4 = 800\,\text{K}$

For isentropic process 3-4,

$$T_3 = T_4\left(\frac{V_4}{V_3}\right)^{\gamma-1} = 800(8)^{1.4-1}$$

or $\quad T_3 = 1837\,\text{K} = T_{\text{max}}$

$$T_{\text{max}} = 1564^\circ\text{C}$$

Q.31 Ans:(A)

The *T-S* diagram of Rankine cycle is sketched for reference.

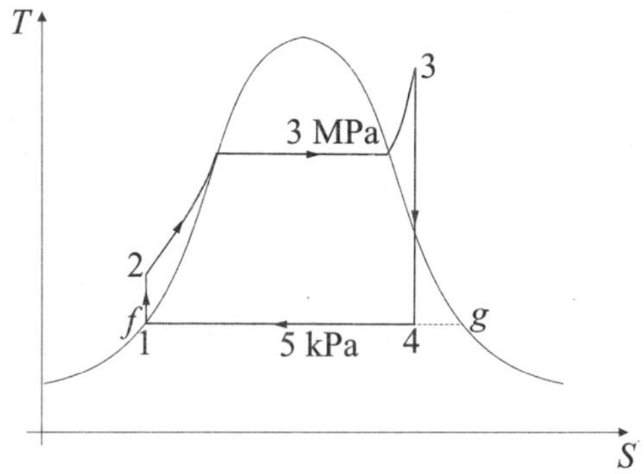

Given: at $P_3 = 3\,\text{MPa}$ and $T_3 = 300\,^\circ$;

$h_3 = 2995.1\,\text{kJ/kg}$, $S_3 = 6.5422$ kJ / kg°C and

$h_1 = h_f = 137.77$ kJ/kg, $h_g = 2561.6\,\text{kJ/kg}$

$s_f = 0.4763$ kJ/kg°C, $s_g = 8.3960\,\text{kJ/kg°C}$

Using $s_3 = s_4 \quad \Rightarrow \quad s_3 = s_f + x(s_g - s_f)$

$$x = \frac{s_3 - s_f}{s_g - s_f} = \frac{6.5422 - 0.4763}{8.3960 - 0.4763}$$

or $\quad x = 0.77$

Enthalpy at entrance of condenser, $h_4 = h_f + x(h_g - h_f)$

$$h_4 = 137.77 + 0.7659 \times (2561.6 - 137.77)$$

$$h_4 = 1994.18\,\text{kJ/kg}$$

Q.32 Ans:(D)

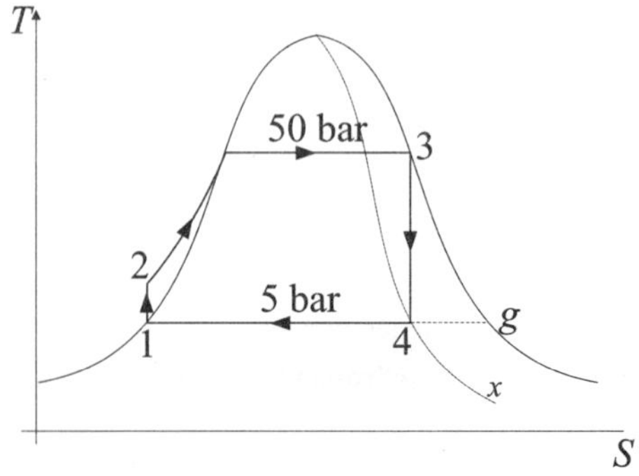

Using $S_3 = S_4$, the quality is found to be

$$\Rightarrow S_3 = S_4 = S_1 + x(S_g - S_1)$$

$$x = \frac{S_3 - S_1}{S_b - S_1}$$

or $$x = \frac{5.9734 - 1.8607}{6.8213 - 1.8607}$$

$$x = 0.83$$

Q.33 Ans:(C)

Heat removal rate, $$\dot{q} = \frac{Q}{t} = \frac{mc_p \Delta T}{t}$$

$$\dot{q} = \frac{50000 \times 0.874 \times (28 - 2)}{8 \times 60}$$

$$\dot{q} = 2367.08 \text{ kcal/min}$$

$$\text{COP} = \frac{\dot{q}}{W} \Rightarrow W = \frac{\dot{q}}{\text{COP}} = \frac{2367.08}{2.5}$$

$$W = 946.8 \text{ kcal/min} = 15.78 \text{ kcal/s}$$

$$[1 \text{ hp} = 736 \text{ J/s} = 0.176 \text{ kcal/s}]$$

or $$W = \frac{15.78}{0.176} \text{ hp} = 89 \text{ hp}$$

$$\text{Power} = 89 \text{ hp}$$

Q.34 Ans:(D)

The *T-S* diagram of Rankine cycle is sketched for referance.

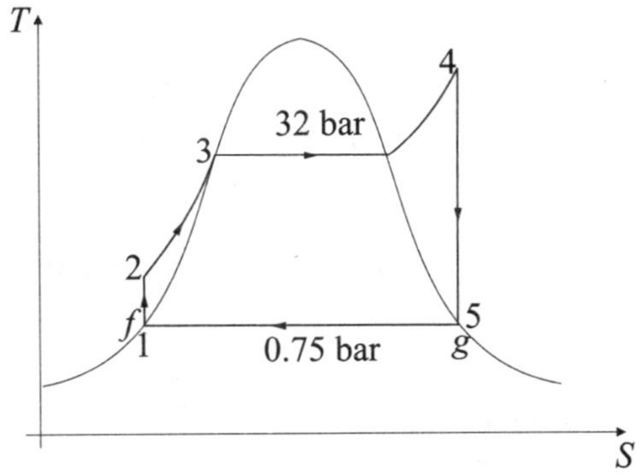

Pump work, $W_P = h_2 - h_1 = v_{f_1} \Delta P$

$$W_P = 0.00103 \times (32 - 0.75) \times 100 \text{ kJ/kg}$$

$$W_P = 3.24 \text{ kJ/kg}$$

Now $h_2 = h_1 + W_P = 384.36 + 3.24$

or $h_2 = 387.6 \text{ kJ/kg}$

Heat addition in boiler, $Q = h_4 - h_2$

or $Q = 3663 - 387.6$

$$Q = 3275.4 \text{ kJ/kg}$$

Q.35 Ans:(D)

The *P-V* diagram of Diesel cycle is sketched for reference.

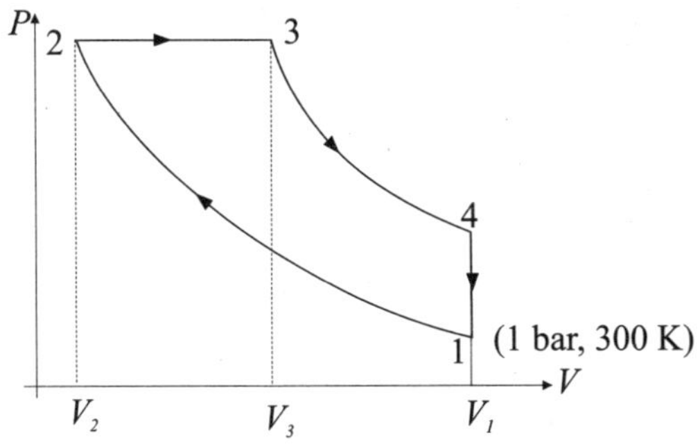

For the isentropic process 1-2, we have

$$T_2 = T_1 \left(\frac{V_1}{V_2} \right)^{\gamma - 1}$$

$$T_2 = 300(14)^{1.4-1} = 862.13 \text{ K}$$

For the process 2-3, we have $T_3 = T_2 \left(\frac{V_3}{V_2} \right)$

Given $\frac{V_1}{V_2} = 14$ and $\frac{V_3}{V_2} = 2$, from which $V_3 = \frac{V_1}{7}$

$$T_3 = 862.13 \left(\frac{V_1/7}{V_1/14} \right) = 1724.2 \text{ K}$$

Heat added,

$$Q = c_p (T_3 - T_2) = 1.005 \times (1724.2 - 862.13)$$

$$Q = 866.4 \text{ kJ/kg}$$

Q.36 Ans:(D)

Specific humidity, $$\omega = 0.622 \frac{P_v}{P - P_v}$$

and $$\omega_s = 0.622 \frac{P_s}{P - P_s}$$

Relative humidity,

$$\phi = \frac{\omega}{\omega_s} = \frac{0.622 \frac{P_v}{P - P_v}}{0.622 \frac{P_s}{P - P_s}} = \frac{P_v}{P - P_v} \times \frac{P - P_s}{P_s}$$

Substituting $P_v = P - P_a$, we have

$$\phi = \left(\frac{P}{P_a} - 1 \right) \times \left(\frac{P}{P_s} - 1 \right)$$

Now substituting,
$P = 100 \text{ kPa}, \phi = 0.7$ and $P_s = 4.25$ kPa, we have

$$0.7 = \left(\frac{100}{P_a} - 1\right) \times \left(\frac{100}{425} - 1\right)$$

$$P_a = 96.98 \text{ kPa}$$

Q.37 Ans:(C)

(P) Specific humidity (2) $\frac{R_a}{R_v}\left(\frac{P_v}{P - P_s}\right)$

(Q) Relative humidity (1) $\frac{P_v}{P_s}$

(R) Specific volume of dry air (4) $\frac{RT}{P - P_v}$

Q.38 Ans:(C)

The P-V diagram of Brayton cycle is sketched for reference.

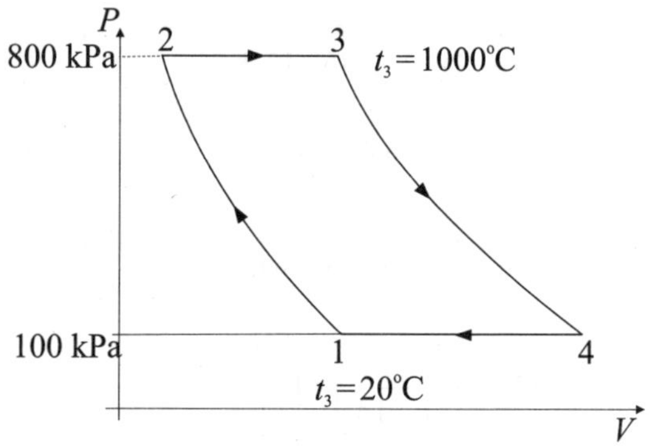

Pressure ratio $r_p = \frac{P_2}{P_1} = \frac{P_3}{P_4} = 8$

For the isentropic process 3-4,

$$T_4 = T_3\left(\frac{P_4}{P_3}\right)^{\frac{\gamma-1}{\gamma}} = \frac{1273}{(8)^{\frac{1.4-1}{1.4}}} = 702.7 \text{ K}$$

Air flow rate, $m = \frac{P_1 V_1}{RT_1}$

$$m = \frac{100 \times 32}{0.287 \times (273 + 20)} = 38.05 \text{ kg/s}$$

Power output of turbine, $W_T = mc_p(T_3 - T_4)$

$$W_T = 38.05 \times 1.005 \times (1273 - 702.7) = 21808.4 \text{ kW}$$

$$W_T = 21.8 \text{ MW}$$

Q.39 Ans:(A)

The T-S diagram of gas turbine plant is sketched for reference.

For the isentropic process 1-2,

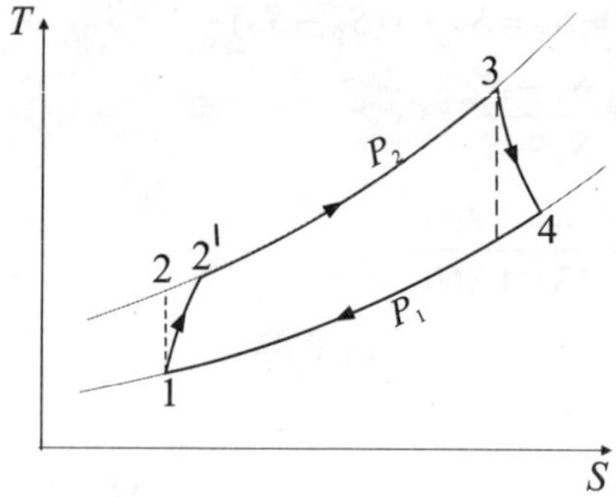

$$T_2 = T_1\left(\frac{P_2}{P_1}\right)^{\frac{\gamma-1}{\gamma}} = 300(4.5)^{\frac{1.4-1}{1.4}} = 461 \text{ K}$$

The efficiency of compressor, $\eta = \frac{T_2 - T_1}{T_2' - T_1}$

or $0.6 = \frac{461 - 300}{T_2' - 300}$

or $T_2' = 568.3 \text{ K}$

Heat added,

$$Q = mc_p(T_3 - T_2') = 2.2 \times 1.005 \times (923 - 568.3)$$

$$Q = 784.2 \text{ kW}$$

Q.40 Ans:(C)

The P-V diagram of Otto cycle is sketched for reference.

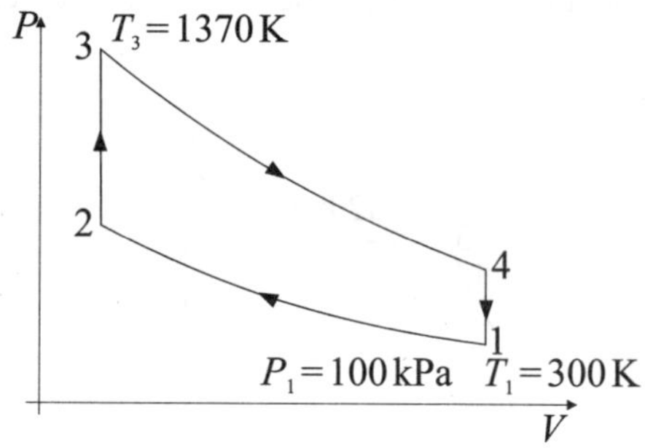

For isentropic process 1-2,

$$P_2 = P_1\left(\frac{V_1}{V_2}\right)^{\gamma} = 100(8)^{1.4} = 1837.9 \text{ kPa}$$

$$T_2 = T_1\left(\frac{V_1}{V_2}\right)^{\gamma-1} = 300(8)^{1.4-1} = 689.2 \text{ K}$$

For constant volume process 2-3,

$$P_3 = P_2\frac{T_3}{T_2} = 1837.9 \times \frac{1370}{689.2}$$

Maximum pressure in cycle, $P_3 = 3653$ kPa

Q.41 Ans:(D)

From the steam table:

At 10 bar; $h_f = 762.6$ kJ/kg and $h_g = 2776.2$ kJ/kg

Enthalpy of 90% dryness steam,

$$h_1 = h_f + x(h_g - h_f) = 762.6 + 0.9(2776.2 - 762.6)$$

$$h_1 = 2574.84 \text{ kJ/kg}$$

Enthalpy of 100% dryness steam,

$$h_2 = h_g = 2776.2 \text{ kJ/kg}$$

Heat added, $Q = m(h_2 - h_1) = 500 \times (2776.2 - 2574.84)$

$$Q = 100.6 \text{ MJ}$$

Q.42 Ans:(C)

The *P*-*V* diagram of Brayton cycle is sketched for reference.

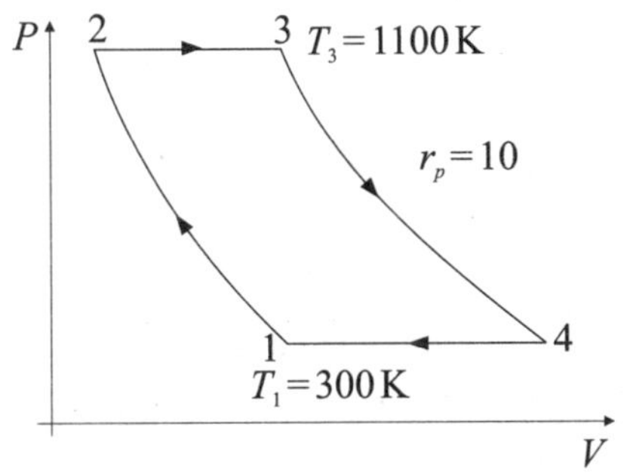

For the isentropic process 1-2,

$$T_2 = T_1\left(\frac{P_2}{P_1}\right)^{\frac{\gamma-1}{\gamma}} = 300(10)^{\frac{1.4-1}{1.4}} = 579.1 \text{ K}$$

For the isentropic process 3-4,

$$T_4 = T_3\left(\frac{P_4}{P_3}\right)^{\frac{\gamma-1}{\gamma}} = \frac{1100}{(10)^{\frac{1.4-1}{1.4}}} = 569.7 \text{ K}$$

$$\text{Back - work ratio} = \frac{\text{Compressor work}}{\text{Turbine work}} = \frac{W_C}{W_T}$$

$$\text{Back - work ratio} = \frac{mc_p(T_2 - T_1)}{mc_p(T_3 - T_4)}$$

$$\text{Back - work ratio} = \frac{579.1 - 300}{1100 - 569.7}$$

$$\text{Back - work ratio} = 0.52$$

Q.43 Ans:(A)

The *P*-*V* diagram of Diesel cycle is sketched for reference.

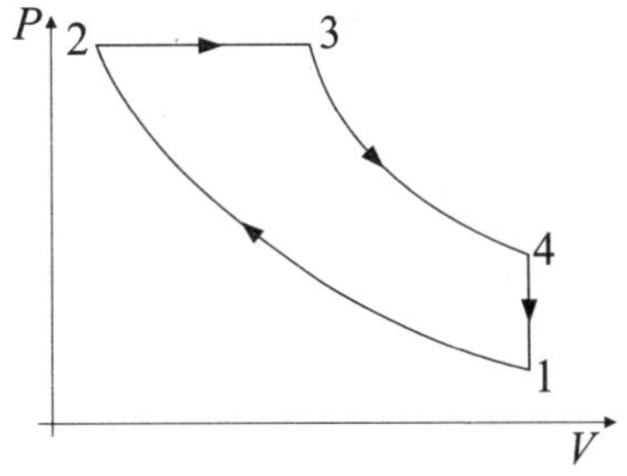

Given: $V_1 = 2$ litre, $V_2 = 0.13$ litre and $V_3 = 0.30$ litre

Compression ratio, $r_k = \frac{V_1}{V_2} = \frac{2}{0.13}$

$$r_k = 15.38$$

Expansion ratio, $r_e = \frac{V_4}{V_3} = \frac{V_1}{V_3} = \frac{2}{0.30}$

$$r_e = 6.66$$

Cut-off ratio, $r_c = \frac{V_3}{V_2} = \frac{0.30}{0.13}$

$$r_c = 2.3$$

Efficiency of Diesel cycle, $\eta_{\text{diesel}} = 1 - \frac{1}{r_k^{\gamma-1}}\left(\frac{r_c^{\gamma} - 1}{\gamma(r_c - 1)}\right)$

$$\eta_{\text{diesel}} = 1 - \frac{1}{(15.38)^{1.4-1}}\left(\frac{(2.3)^{1.4} - 1}{1.4(2.3 - 1)}\right) = 0.59$$

$$\eta_{\text{diesel}} = 59\ \%$$

Q.44 Ans:(A)

Volume of air $= 600 \text{ m}^3$

From properties of moist air (table) at 20°C; specific volume, $v = 0.8498 \text{ m}^3/\text{kg}$

Mass of air, $m = \frac{600}{0.8498} = 706.04$ kg

From psychrometric chart:

Specific humidity at 20°C and 70% RH;

$$\omega = 0.0107 \text{ kg/kg of dry air}$$

Mass of water, $m_w = 0.0107 \times 706.04$ kg

or $m_w = 7.5$ kg

$$m_w = 7.5 \text{ litre}$$

Q.45 Ans:(B)

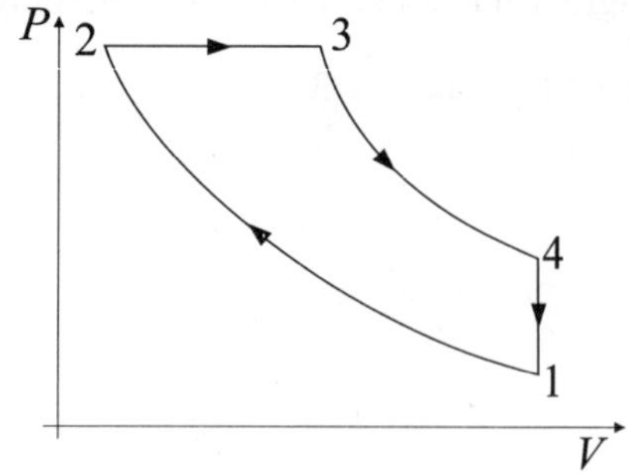

For isentropic process 3-4,

$$T_4 = T_3\left(\frac{P_4}{P_3}\right)^{\frac{\gamma-1}{\gamma}} = \frac{(273+27)}{5^{\frac{1.4-1}{1.4}}} = 189.6 \text{ K}$$

$$T_4 = -83.36°\text{C}$$

Heat extracted from cold chamber,

$$Q = mc_p(T_1 - T_4)$$

$$Q = \frac{1000}{60\times 60}\times 1.005(7+83.36)$$

$$Q = 25.4 \text{ kW}$$

Q.46 Ans:(B)

Relative humidity, $\phi = 0.75 = \frac{P_v}{P_g}$

$$0.75 = \frac{P - P_a}{P_g}$$

From properties of moist air table at, $t = 30°$C

$$P_g = 4.243$$

$$0.75 = \frac{96 - P_a}{4.243}$$

$$P_a = 92.8 \text{ kPa}$$

Q.47 Ans:(A)

The P-V diagram of gas refrigeration is sketched for reference.

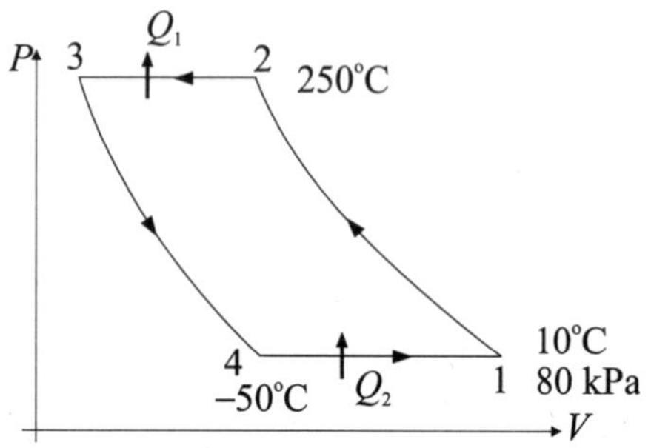

Maximum temperature, $T_{max} = T_2 = 273 + 250 = 523$ K

For isentropic process 1-2; $\frac{P_2}{P_1} = \left(\frac{T_2}{T_1}\right)^{\frac{\gamma}{\gamma-1}}$

Pressure ratio, $\frac{P_2}{P_1} = \left(\frac{523}{283}\right)^{\frac{1.4}{1.4-1}} = 8.58$

$$\frac{P_2}{P_1} = 8.6$$

Q.48 Ans:(A)

The P-h diagram of vapour refrigeration system is sketched for reference.

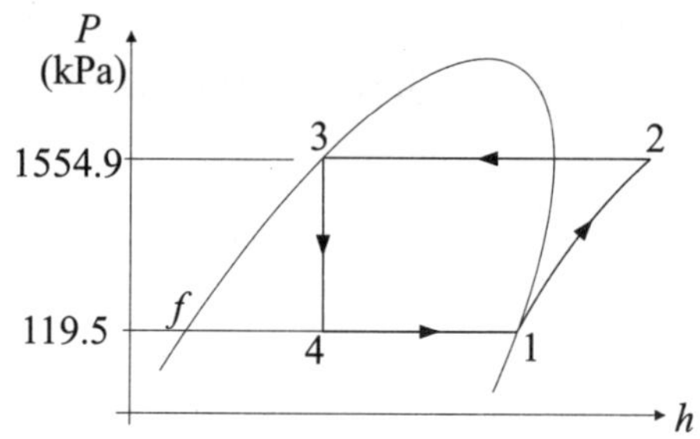

From properties of ammonia table:

$h_a = 44.26$ kJ/kg, $h_1 = 1404.4$ kJ/kg and $h_3 = h_4 = 371.43$ kJ/kg

Using $h_3 = h_4$, the quality is found to be

$$h_4 = h_f + x(h_1 - h_f)$$

or $$371.43 = 44.26 + x(1404.4 - 44.26)$$

or $$x = 0.24$$

Dryness fraction, $x = 0.24$

Q.49 Ans:(A)

From the psychrometric properties table:

Specific humidity at 35°C and 75% RH;

$$\omega_1 = 0.025 \text{ kg/kg of dry air}$$

Specific humidity at 25°C and 40% RH;

$$\omega_2 = 0.008 \text{ kg/kg of dry air}$$

Mass of dry air, $m_a = \frac{V}{v} = \frac{3\times 10\times 20}{0.92} = 652.17$ kg

Water removed, $m_w = (\omega_1 - \omega_2)\times m_a$

$$m_w = (0.025 - 0.008)\times 652.17$$

$$m_w = 11.1 \text{ kg}$$

Q.50 Ans:(C)

The P-V diagram of gas refrigeration cycle is sketched

for reference.

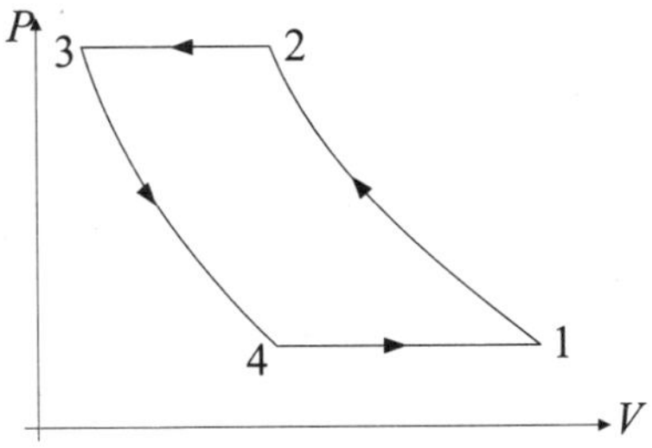

Given: $P_1 = P_4 = 100\,\text{kPa}$, $P_2 = P_3 = 10\times 100\,\text{kPa}$, $T_1 = 273 - 10 = 263\ \text{K}$ and $T_3 = 273 + 30 = 303\ \text{K}$

For isentropic process 1-2, we have

$$T_2 = T_1\left(\frac{P_2}{P_1}\right)^{\frac{\gamma-1}{\gamma}} = 263(10)^{\frac{1.4-1}{1.4}} = 507\ \text{K}$$

For isentropic process 3-4, we have

$$T_4 = \frac{T_3}{\left(\frac{P_3}{P_4}\right)^{\frac{\gamma-1}{\gamma}}} = \frac{303}{(10)^{\frac{1.4-1}{1.4}}} = 157\ \text{K}$$

$$\text{COP} = \frac{Q}{W} = \frac{c_p(T_1 - T_4)}{W} = \frac{c_p(T_1 - T_4)}{c_p(T_2 - T_1) - c_p(T_3 - T_4)}$$

$$\text{COP} = \frac{263 - 157}{(507 - 263) - (303 - 157)}$$

$$\text{COP} = 1.08$$

Q.51 Ans:[2.2]

The P- h diagram of vapour compression refrigeration system is sketched for referance.

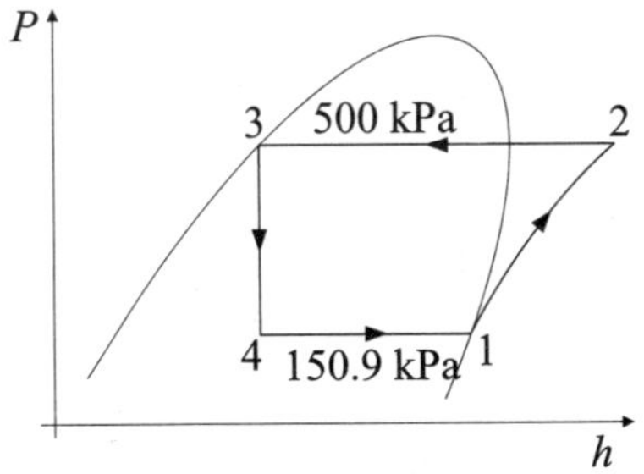

Given: $h_2 = 252.05$ kJ/kg and from table $h_1 = 178.74$ kJ/kg

Compressor work is given by

$$W_p = m(h_2 - h_1)$$

or $\quad W_p = 0.03(252.05 - 178.74)$

$$W_p = 2.2\ \text{kW}$$

Q.52 Ans:[1400]

The P- V diagram of Brayton cycle is sketched for reference.

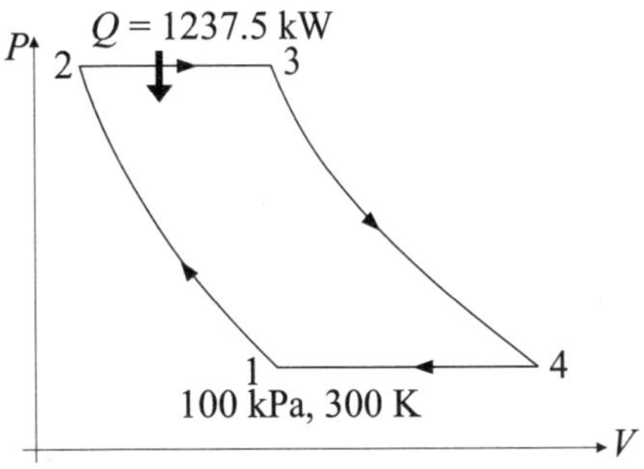

For the isentropic process 1-2,

$$T_2 = T_1\left(\frac{P_2}{P_1}\right)^{\frac{\gamma-1}{\gamma}} = 300(10)^{\frac{1.4-1}{1.4}} = 579.1\ \text{K}$$

Heat supplied, $Q = mc_p(T_3 - T_2)$

or $\quad 1237.5 = 1.5\times 1.005(T_3 - 579.19)$

or $\quad T_3 = 1400\,\text{K}$

Inlet temperature of turbine, $T_3 = 1400\,\text{K}$

Q.53 Ans:[76]

The P- h diagram of vapour compression refrigeration cycle is sketched for reference.

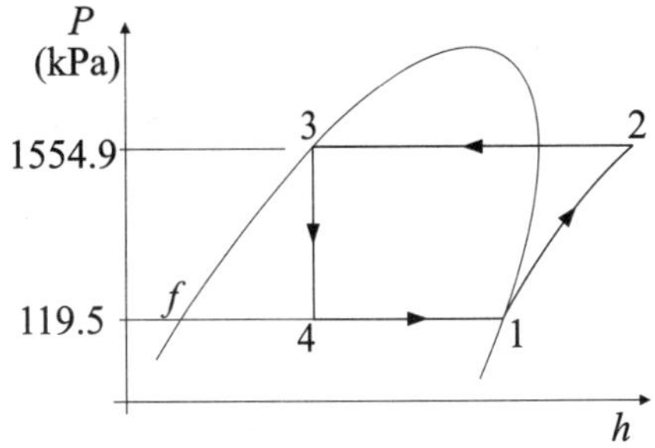

Using $h_3 = h_4$, the quality is found to be

$$h_3 = h_4 = h_f + x_4(h_1 - h_f)$$

or $\quad x_4 = \dfrac{h_3 - h_f}{h_1 - h_f}$

or $\quad x_4 = \dfrac{371.43 - 44.26}{1404.4 - 44.26}$

$$x_4 = 0.24$$

Volume of vapour $= (V_1 - V_4) = (V_1 - V_f) - x(V_1 - V_f)$
$= (1 - x)(V_1 - V_f)$

$$\%\ \text{volume of vapour} = \frac{(1-x)(V_1 - V_f)}{(V_1 - V_f)} \times 100$$

$= (1 - x)100 = (1 - 0.24)100$

$\%$ volume of vapour $= 76\%$

Q.54 Ans:[0.787]

$$v = v_f + x(v_g - v_f)$$

$$12 = 0.001 + x(15.25 - 0.001)$$

$$x = 0.787$$

Q.55 Ans:[50]

The T-S diagram of Brayton cycle is sketched for reference.

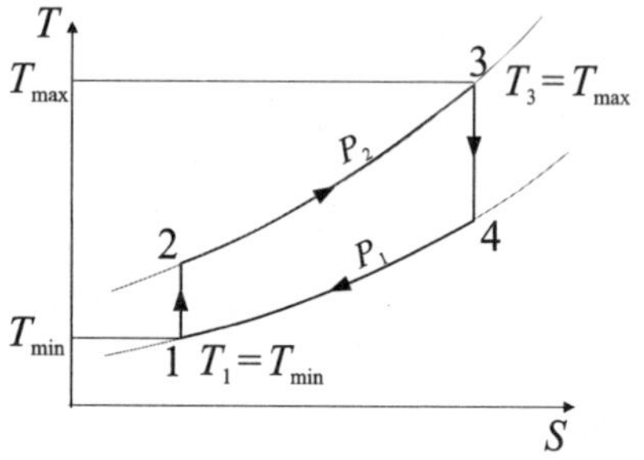

Net work output, $W_{net} = c_p(T_3 - T_4) - c_p(T_2 - T_1)$

where $T_3 = T_{max}$ and $T_1 = T_{min}$

Now, $\frac{T_3}{T_4} = r_p^{\frac{\gamma-1}{\gamma}}$ and $\frac{T_2}{T_1} = r_p^{\frac{\gamma-1}{\gamma}}$

$$W_{net} = c_p\left(T_3 - T_3 r_p^{-\left(\frac{\gamma-1}{\gamma}\right)}\right) - c_p\left(T_1 r_p^{\left(\frac{\gamma-1}{\gamma}\right)} - T_1\right)$$

$$W_{net} = c_p\left(T_{max} - T_{max} r_p^{-\left(\frac{\gamma-1}{\gamma}\right)}\right) - c_p\left(T_{min} r_p^{\left(\frac{\gamma-1}{\gamma}\right)} - T_{min}\right)$$

Condition for optimum work output $\frac{d}{dr_p}(W_{net}) = 0$, we obtain

$$r_p = \sqrt{\left(\frac{T_{max}}{T_{min}}\right)^{\frac{\gamma}{\gamma-1}}}$$

Efficiency of Brayton cycle, $\eta = 1 - \frac{1}{r_p^{\frac{\gamma-1}{\gamma}}}$

$$\eta_{opt} = 1 - \frac{1}{\sqrt{\frac{T_{max}}{T_{min}}}} = 1 - \frac{1}{\sqrt{\frac{1200}{300}}}$$

$$\eta_{opt} = 50\%$$

Q.56 Ans:[24]

Heat removal rate,

$$\dot{q} = \frac{Q}{t} = \frac{mc_p\Delta T}{t} = \frac{50 \times 1000 \times 0.874 \times (28 - 2)}{16 \times 60}$$

$$\dot{q} = 1183.5 \text{ kcal/min}$$

$$\text{Plant capacity} = \frac{1183.5}{50} = 23.67$$

$$\text{Plant capacity} = 24 \text{ TR}$$

Q.57 Ans:[2.2]

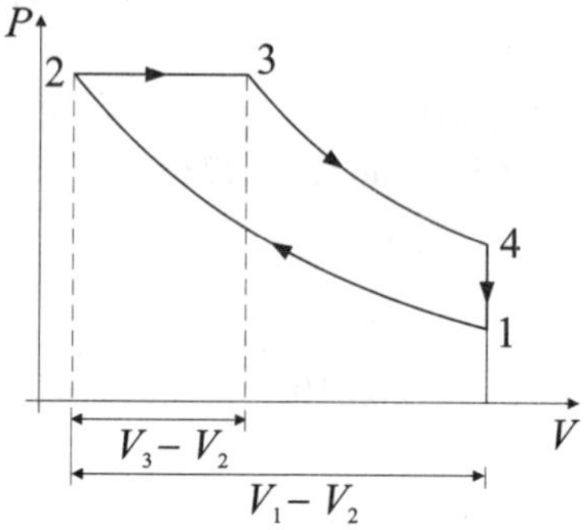

Given: Compression ratio $\frac{V_1}{V_2} = 16 \Rightarrow V_1 = 16V_2$

and $V_3 - V_2 = 0.08(V_1 - V_2)$

From which $V_3 - V_2 = 0.08(16V_2 - V_2)$

or $\frac{V_3}{V_2} = 2.2$

$$\text{Cut-off ratio} = \frac{V_3}{V_2} = 2.2$$

Q.58 Ans:[35000]

The efficiency of power plant, $\eta = \frac{Q_S - Q_R}{Q_S}$

or $0.3 = \frac{500 - Q_R}{500}$

$$Q_R = 350 \text{ MW}$$

$$350 \times 10^6 = m \times 1.0 \times 10^3 (30 - 20)$$

Mass flow rate of cooling water, $m = 35000$ kg/s

Q.59 Ans:[0.2]

Let x be quality of the mixture of refrigerant R-12.

Specific volume $v = v_f + x(v_g - v_f)$

Substituting $\rho = \frac{1}{v}, \rho_g = \frac{1}{v_g}$ and $\rho_f = \frac{1}{v_f}$, we have

$$\frac{1}{\rho} = \frac{1}{\rho_f} + x\left(\frac{1}{\rho_g} - \frac{1}{\rho_f}\right)$$

or $$\frac{1}{36.12} = \frac{1}{1377} + x\left(\frac{1}{7.379} - \frac{1}{1377}\right)$$

$$x = 0.2$$

Q.60 Ans:[1.5]

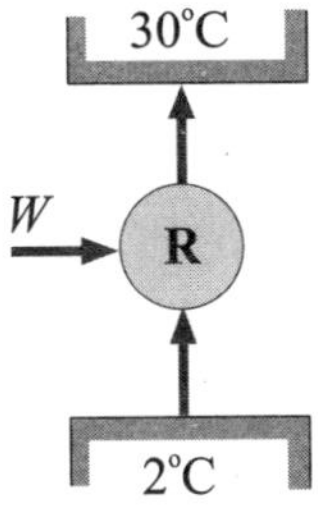

COP of Carnot refrigerator, $(\text{COP})_{\text{Carnot ref.}} = \frac{T_2}{T_1 - T_2}$

$$\text{COP} = \frac{273 + 2}{(273 + 30) - (273 + 2)}$$

$$\text{COP} = 9.82$$

COP of refrigerator,

$$(\text{COP})_{\text{ref.}} = 0.15 \times (\text{COP})_{\text{Carnot ref.}} = 0.15 \times 9.82 = 1.473$$

$$(\text{COP})_{\text{ref.}} = \frac{Q_2}{W} \Rightarrow \frac{8000}{W} = 1.473$$

$$W = 5431.09 \text{ kJ/day}$$

Daily electricity consumption, $W = 5431.09$ kJ

Substituting $1 \text{ kJ} = \frac{1}{3600} \text{ kWh}$

$$\text{Electricity consumption} = 1.5 \text{ kWh/day}$$

Q.61 Ans:[0.1]

In throttling process, $h_1 = h_2$

$$h_1 = h_f + x(h_g - h_f)$$

$$1000 = 800 + x(2800 - 800)$$

$$x = 0.1$$

Q.62 Ans:[37.07]

For any cyclic process, $\sum Q = \sum W$

$$Q_{\text{boiler}} - Q_{\text{condeser}} = W_{\text{turbine}} - W_{\text{pump}}$$

$$55 \times 10^6 - Q_{\text{condeser}} = 18 \times 10^6 - 100 \times 746$$

$$Q_{\text{condeser}} = 37.07 \text{ MJ/s}$$

Q.63 Ans:[95]

Given: $C = \frac{V_c}{V_s} = 0.05 V_1 = 0.04 \text{ m}^3/\text{kg}$ and $V_2 = 0.02 \text{ m}^3/\text{kg}$

Volumetric efficiency of the compressor is given by

$$\eta_{\text{vol}} = 1 + C - C\left(\frac{V_1}{V_2}\right)$$

$$\eta_{\text{vol}} = 1 + 0.05 - 0.05 \times \left(\frac{0.04}{0.02}\right)$$

$$\eta_{\text{vol}} = 0.95$$

$$\eta_{\text{vol}} = 95\%$$

Q.64 Ans:[113]

Let m be the mass flow rate of cooling water.

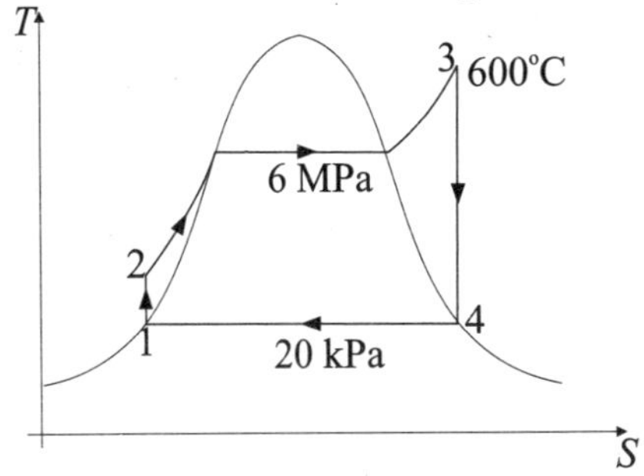

Heat rejected, $Q = mc_p(\Delta T)$

$$m_{\text{steam}}(h_4 - h_1) = mc_p(\Delta T)$$

or $$m = \frac{m_{\text{steam}}(h_4 - h_1)}{c_p(\Delta T)}$$

From steam table (at pressure 20 kPa):

$h_1 = 251.5$ kJ/kg and $h_4 = 2609.9$ kJ/kg

$$m_{\text{steam}} = \frac{2 \times (2609.9 - 251.5)}{4.18 \times 10}$$

$$m_{\text{steam}} = 113 \text{ kg/s}$$

Q.65 Ans:[-57.6]

The T-S diagram of gas refrigeration cycle is sketched for reference.

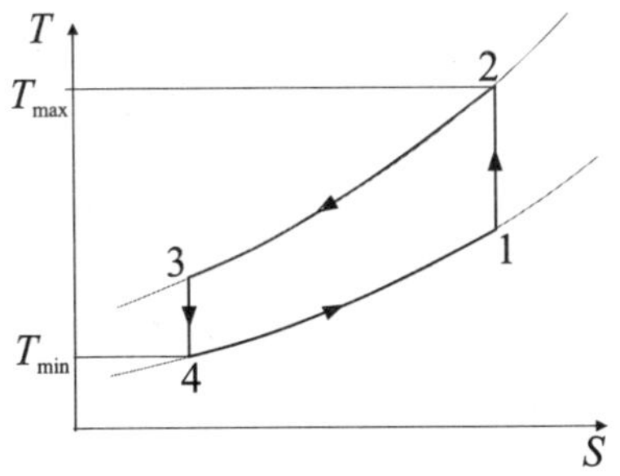

Given: $T_3 = 273 + 35 = 308$ K

For isentropic process 3-4, $\frac{T_4}{T_3} = \left(\frac{P_4}{P_3}\right)^{\frac{\gamma-1}{\gamma}}$

or $$T_4 = T_{\min} = \frac{308}{(3.5)^{\frac{1.4-1}{1.4}}} = 215.33 \text{ K}$$

$$T_{\min} = -57.6°\text{C}$$

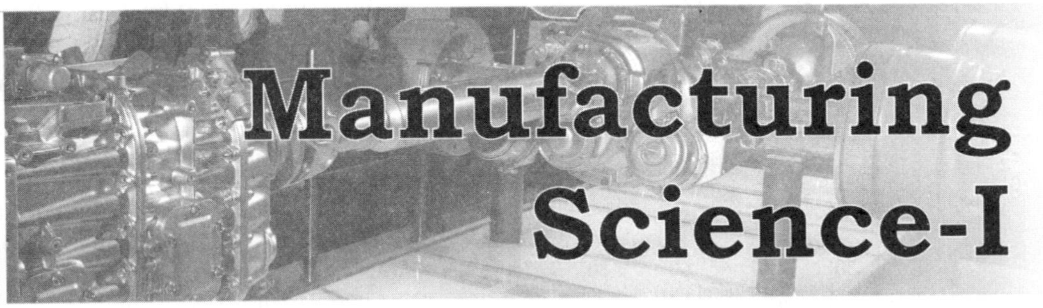

14 Manufacturing Science-I

GATE Mechanical Engg.

GATE Syllabus

Engineering Materials: Structure and properties of engineering materials, phase diagrams, heat treatment, stress-strain diagrams for engineering materials; Casting, Forming and Joining Processes: Different types of castings, design of patterns, moulds and cores; solidification and cooling; Riser and gating design. Plastic deformation and yield criteria; Fundamentals of hot and cold working processes; Load estimation for bulk (forging, rolling, extrusion, drawing) and sheet (shearing, deep drawing, bending) metal forming processes; Principles of powder metallurgy. Principles of welding, brazing, soldering and adhesive bonding.

Chapter Outline

14.1 KEY CONCEPTS AND FORMULAS

Engineering Materials

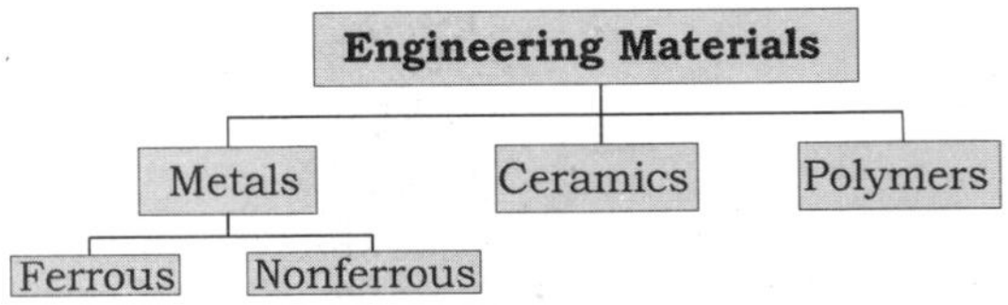

Crystalline Structures

Crystal structure: Body-centered cubic (BCC), face-centered cubic (FCC), and hexagonal close-packed (HCP).

$$\text{Atomic packing factor,} \quad APF = \frac{\text{Volume of atoms}}{\text{Volume of unit cell}}$$

APF of BCC is 0.68, FCC is 0.74 and HCP is 0.74

Defects (or imperfections) in crystals: Point defects, line defects and surface defects.

Metals properties: High stiffness, strength and hardness, toughness, good electrical conductivity and good thermal conductivity.

Alloys and Phase Diagrams

Alloys: Alloys is metal composed of two or more elements, at least one of which is metallic. Categories of alloys are (a) solid solutions and (b) intermediate phases.

Phase diagram: It is graphical representation of the combinations of temperature, pressure, composition, or other variables for which specific phases exist at equilibrium.

Phase diagram of copper-nickel alloy system is shown in figure.

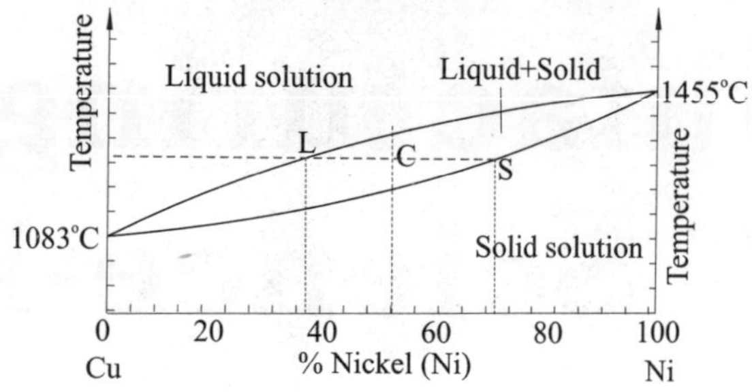

Phase diagram for the Copper-Nickel alloy system

Lever Rule

$$\text{L-phase proportion} = \frac{CS}{(CS + CL)}$$

$$\text{S-phase proportion } \frac{CL}{(CS + CL)}$$

Iron-Carbon Phase Diagram

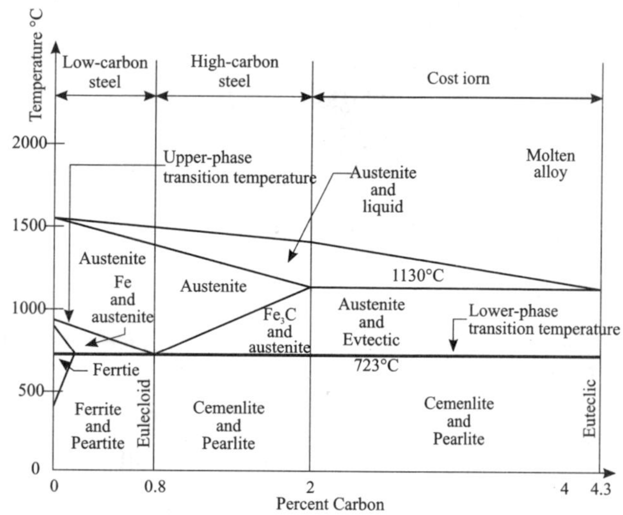

Steels

Steel is an alloy of iron that contains carbon ranging by weight between 0.02% and 2.11%. (Includes other alloys: manganese, chromium, nickel, molybdenum and vanadium).

Categories of steel: (i) Plain carbon steels, (ii) Low alloy steels, (iii) Stainless steels, and (iv) Tool steels.

Plain Carbon Steels

Plain carbon steels contain carbon as the principal alloying element with only small amount of other elements (about 0.5% manganese in normal).

It is specified by a four-digit number system: 10XX, where 10 indicates that steel is plain carbon, and XX indicates the % of carbon.

Low carbon steels contain carbon in amounts less than 0.20%.

Medium carbon steels range in carbon between 0.20% and 0.5%.

High carbon steels contain carbon in amounts greater than 0.50%.

Low Alloy Steels

Low alloy steels are iron-carbon alloys that contain additional alloying elements (chromium, manganese, molybdenum, nickel, and vanadium) in amounts totaling less than about 5% by weight.

Stainless Steels

Stainless steels are a group of highly alloyed steels designed to provide high corrosion resistance. The principal alloying element is chromium above 15%. Stainless steels are divided into three group: (i) Austenitic stainless, (ii) Ferritic stainless, (iii) Martensitic stainless.

Tool Steel

Tool steel are a highly alloyed steels designed for use as cutting tools and dies.

Types of tool steels: (i) High-speed tool steels, (ii) Hot-working tool steels, (iii) Cold-work tool steels, (iv) Water-hardening tool steels, (v) Shock-resistant tool steels, (vi) Mold steels, and (vii) Low alloy tool steels.

Cast Irons

Cast iron is an iron alloy containing from 2.1% to about 4% carbon and from 1% to 3% silicon.

Types of cast iron: (i) Gray cast iron, (ii) Ductile iron, (iii) White cast iron, (iv) Malleable iron, and (v) Alloy cast iron.

Other Alloys

Brasses: It is an alloy of copper and zinc.

Bronzes: It is an alloy of copper containing elements other than zinc, (Gunmetal 88% Cu, 10% Sn, and 2%Zn).

Heat Treatment of Steels

Heat treatment is a sequence of heating and cooling designed to get the desired combination of properties in the steel. The important principles of heat treatment: (i) Phase transformations during heating, (ii) Effect of cooling rate on structural changes during cooling, (iii) Effect of carbon content and alloying elements.

Heat Treatment Processes

Annealing: It is a process of heating the steel to austenite phase and then allowing it to cool down very slowly.

Normalizing: It is a process of heating the steel to austenite phase and then allowing it to cool in air.

Hardening and tempering: Hardening is process in which steel is heated to a temperature above the critical point, held at this temperature and quenched (rapidly cooled) in water, oil or molten salt baths.

Case hardening: It is a simple method of hardening steel. This techniques is used for steels with a low carbon content. Carbon is added to the outer surface of the steel, to a depth of approximately 0.03 mm. Methods of case hardening of steel: Carburizing, Nitriding, Carbonitriding, Cyaniding, Tuffride Process. Methods of surface hardening: Flame hardening, Induction hardening.

Time-Temperature-Transformation Diagram (TTTE Diagram)

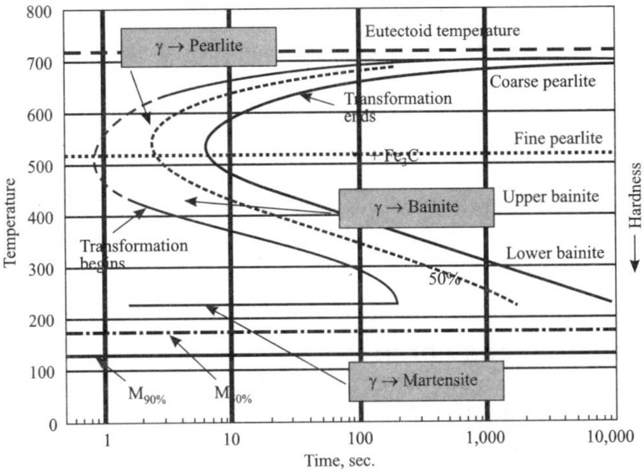

Metal Casting

Castings

It is a process in which molten metal flows by gravity or other force into a mold where it solidifies in the shape of the mold cavity.

Sand casting process: (i) Pattern making, (ii) Mould making, (iii) Core making, (iv) Melting of metal and pouring, (v) Cooling and solidification, (vi) Cleaning of castings and inspection.

Pattern Making

Pattern are the foundry man's mould forming tool. Pattern is used to form the mould cavity in which molten metal is poured.

Types of patterns: (i) Solid pattern, (ii) Split pattern, (iii) Loose-piece pattern, (iv) Gated pattern, (v) Match plate pattern, (vi) Sweep pattern.

Pattern materials:

Removable (permanent) category	Disposable category
Wooden pattens	Wax
Metallic patterns	Plystyrene
Plastic patterns	Styrofoam
Rubber patterns	

Pattern allowances: (i) Shrinkage allowance, (ii) Machining allowance, (iii) Draft or taper allowance, (iv) Distortion allowance, (v) Rapping or shake allowance.

Moulding Sand

Sand is the material used in the foundry for making mould. **Types of moulding sand**: (i) Green sand, (ii) Dry sand, (iii) Loam sand, (iv) Parting sand, (v) Core sand.

Properties of moulding sand: (i) Cohesiveness or strength, (ii) Chemical resistivity, (iii) Permeability, (iv) Flowabilitiy, (v) Adhesiveness, (vi) Refractoriness (vii) Collapsibility.

Moulding

Moulding is the process of making a mould with the desired cavity in sand to pour the molten metal.

Types of moulds: (i) Green sand mould, (ii) Dry sand mould, (iii) Loam mould, (iv) Metal mould.

Tools used in moulding: (i) Shovel, (ii) Riddle, (iii) Rammer, (iv) Trovel, (v) Sprue pin, (vi) Vent rod, (vii) Draw spike, (viii) Moulding boxes.

Gating System

Gating system refers to all the passages ways through which the molten metal passes to enter the mould cavity. Components of gating system shown in figure are:

(i) Pouring cup, (ii) Sprue, (iii) Sprue base, (iv) Runner,

(v) Gate, (vi) Riser.

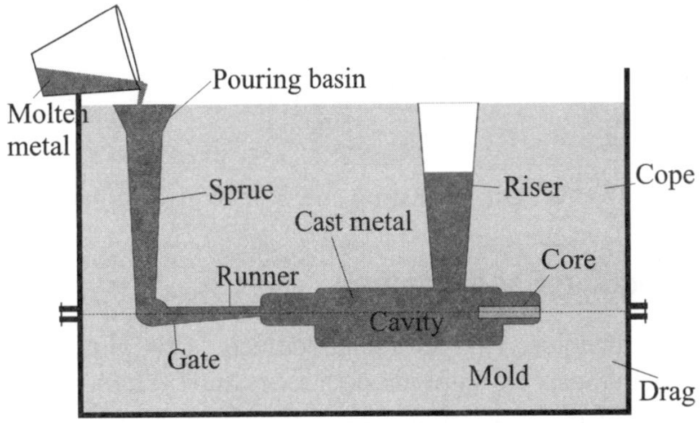

Flow through a gating system follows two laws of fluid dynamics:

(i) Continuity equation:

Volume flow rate $Q = A_1V_1 = A_2V_2$

Where, A = Area of cross-section, and V = Velocity of flow.

(ii) Bernoulli's equation: Total energy/unit weight of fluid = constant

$$\frac{P_1}{\rho g} + \frac{V_1^2}{2g} + h_1 = \frac{P_2}{\rho g} + \frac{V_2^2}{2g} + h_2$$

Design of Sprue

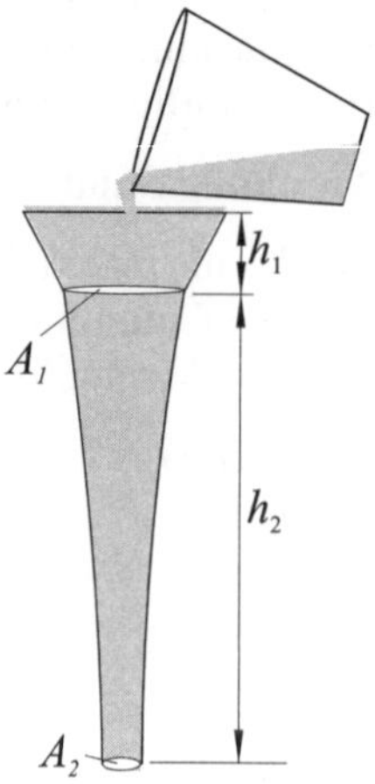

Sprue cross-section is given by

$$A_2 = A_1 \frac{V_1}{V_2} = A_1 \sqrt{\frac{h_1}{h_2}}$$

Casting weight, $W = A_{\text{choke}} V_{\text{choke}} \rho tc$,

Choke area, $A_{\text{choke}} = \dfrac{W}{\rho tc\sqrt{2gH}}$

where c is nozzle constant and t is pouring time.

Mold filling time,

$$\text{MFT} = \frac{\text{Volume of mold cavity}}{\text{Flow rate of molten metal}}$$

Solidification Time

Total solidification time is the time required for the casting to solidify after pouring. This time is depend on the size and shape of the casting by an empirical relationship known as *Chvorinov's rule*.

Total solidification time, $t = c_m \left(\dfrac{\text{Volume}}{\text{Surface area}}\right)^n$, where c_m is the mold constant and exponent $n \approx 2$.

Casting Yield

Casting yield is the ratio of casting mass to actual mass of the metal that has entered the mould cavity.

$$C_y = \frac{W_c}{W_c + W_g} \times 100$$

where W_c = Weight of casting and W_g = Weight of material in gating system.

Defects in Sand Casting

(i) Blowholes, (ii) Shrinkage defects, (iii) Hot tears, (iv) Misruns, cold shuts ans pour short, and (v) Inclusions.

Special Casting Processes

(i) Plaster mould casting process, (ii) Shell mould casting process, (iii) Permanent mould casting process, (iv) Die-casting process (hot chamber die-casting, cold chamber die-casting), (v) Continuous casting process, and (vi) Centrifugal casting process.

Metal Forming

The process in which the desired size and shape are obtained through the deformation of metals plastically under the action of externally applied forces.

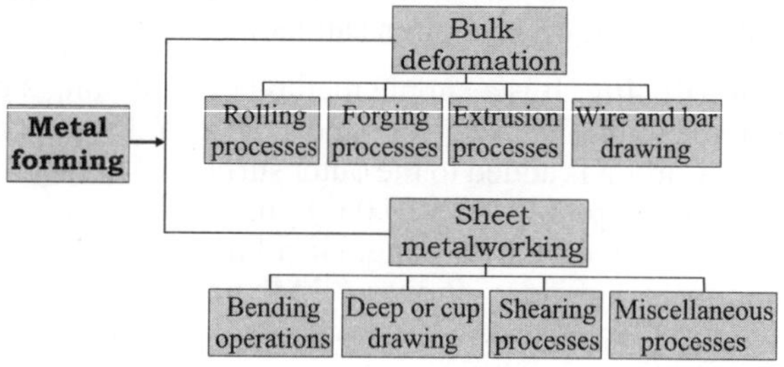

Plastic deformation processes: Operations that induce shape changes on the workpiece by plastic deformation under forces.

Bulk deformation process: These processes involve large amount of plastic deformation. The cross-section of workpiece changes without volume change. The ratio cross-section area/volume is small.

Sheet deformation processes: In sheet metal working operations, the cross-section of workpiece does not change the material is only subjected to shape changes. The ratio cross-section area/volume is very large.

Material behavior in Metal Forming

The relationship between true stress and true strain in the plastic region can be expressed as:

$\sigma = K\varepsilon^n$ (This equation is called the *flow curve*)

Here, K is called the strength coefficient and n is called the strain-hardening (work hardening) exponent.

Flow stress is the instantaneous value of stress required to continue deforming the material to keep the metal flowing.

$$\text{Flow stress, } \sigma_f = K\varepsilon^n$$

$$\text{The mean flow stress, } \quad \bar{\sigma}_f = \frac{K\varepsilon^n}{1+n}$$

The flow curve is valid for an ambient work temperature. For any material, strength coefficient K and n depend on temperature, and therefore material properties are changed with the work temperature.

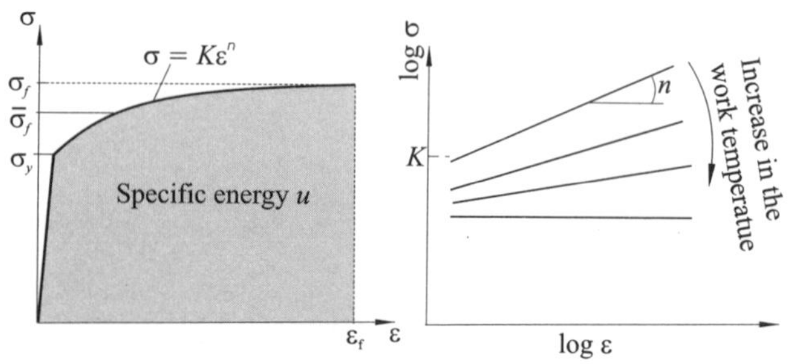

Temperature in Metal Forming

There are three temperature ranges: (i) Cold working temperature, (ii) Warm working temperature, and (iii) Hot working temperature.

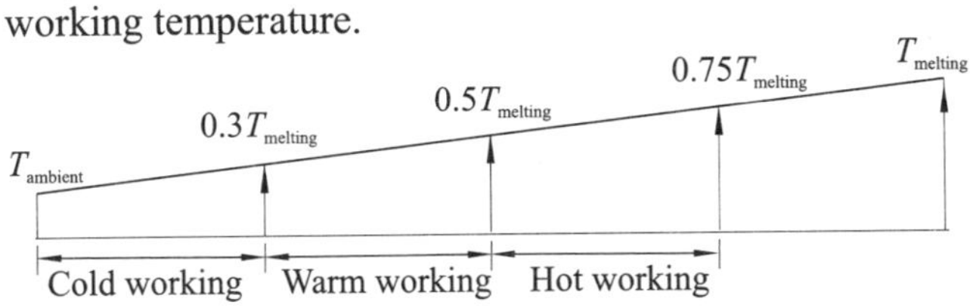

Classification of Metal Forming Processes

(i) Metal forming processes involving compressive stresses: (a) Forging, (b) Rolling, and (c) Extrusion.

(ii) Metal forming processes involving tensile stresses:

(a) Stretch forming, (b) Creep forming, and (c) Vacuum forming.

(iii) Metal forming processes involving shearing stresses: (a) Shearing, (b) Blanking, and (c) Fine blanking.

(iv) Metal forming processes involving the combination of tensile and compressive stresses: (a) Wire drawing, (b) Deep drawing, and (c) Ironing.

Rolling

Rolling is a deformation process in which the thickness of the work is reduced by compressive forces exerted by two opposing rolls.

Rolling mills: (a) Two high rolling mill, (b) Three high rolling mill, (c) Four high rolling mill, (d) Continuous rolling mill, (e) Planetary rolling mill, and (f) Universal rolling mill.

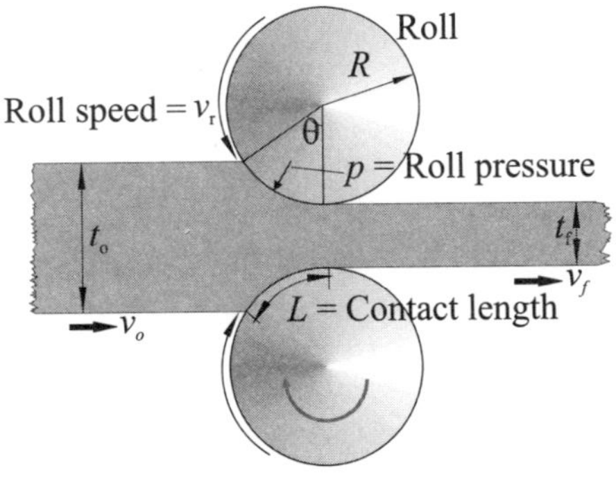

Flat rolling

Analysis of Flat Rolling

Draft $d = t_o - t_f$,

Reduction $r = \dfrac{d}{t_o}$

Volume of metal entering = Volume of metal exiting

or $\quad t_o w_o L_o = t_f w_f L_f$

or $\quad t_o w_o v_o = t_f w_f v_f$

Forward slip, $s = \dfrac{v_f - v_r}{v_r}$; where v_r = Roll speed

True strain, $\varepsilon = \ln \dfrac{t_o}{t_f}$,

Average flow stress, $\bar{\sigma}_f = \dfrac{K\varepsilon^n}{1+n}$

Maximum draft $d_{max} = \mu^2 R$; R = Roll radius and μ = coefficient of friction.

Rolling force F required to maintain separation between the two roll is

$F = w\int_0^L p\,dL$; where p = Roll pressure, w = Width of the work.

Rolling force, $F = \bar{\sigma}_f wL$,

Contact length $L = \sqrt{R(t_o - t_f)}$

Power required to drive each roll, $P = 2\pi NFL$

Forging

Forging is a deformation process in which the work is compressed two dies, using either impact or gradual pressure to form the part.

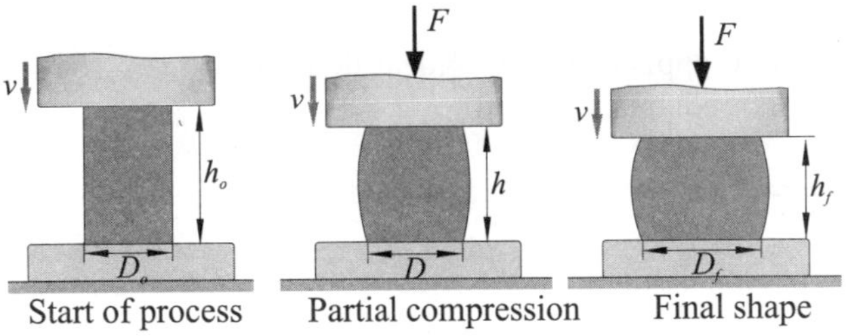

Open-die forging operation

Classification of forging operations:

(i) Open-die forging operation

(ii) Closed-die forging operation.

Forging operations: (i) Hand forging, (ii) Drop forging, (iii) Press forging, (iv) Machine or upset forging.

Analysis of Open-die Forging

True strain, $\varepsilon = \ln\left(\dfrac{h_o}{h}\right)$

Force require to continue the compression, $F = \sigma_f A$; where $\sigma_f = K\varepsilon^n$

Consider effect of friction and D/h ratio, $F = K_f \sigma_f A$

where forging shape factor, $K_f = 1 + \frac{0.4\mu D}{h}$

Forging operations: (i) Upsetting and Heading, (ii) Swaging and Radial forging, (iii) Roll forging, (iv) Orbital forging, and (v) Hobbing.

Extrusion

Extrusion is a compression forming process in which the work metal is forced to flow through a die opening to produce a desired cross-sectional shape.

Types of extrusion: (i) Direct extrusion (ii) Indirect extrusion (iii) Impact extrusion (iv) Side extrusion (v) Tube extrusion.

Analysis of Extrusion

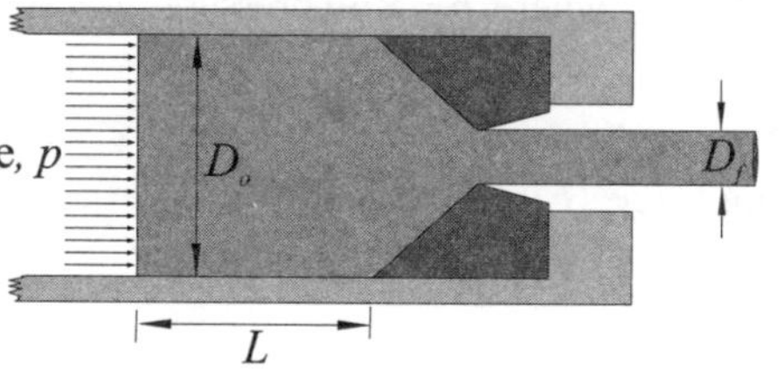

Direct extrusion

Reduction ratio (extrusion ratio); $r_x = \frac{A_o}{A_f}$

True strain, $\varepsilon = \ln r_x = \ln \frac{A_o}{A_f}$

Pressure applied by ram {ideal deformation (no friction and no redundant work)},

$p = \bar{\sigma}_f \ln r_x$; where $\bar{\sigma}_f$ = average flow stress $= \frac{K\varepsilon^n}{1+n}$

Extrusion strain, $\varepsilon_x = a + b \ln r_x$ (Johnson formula)

where $a = 0.8$ and $b = 1.2$ to 1.5.

In indirect extrusion, ram pressure, $p = \bar{\sigma}_f \varepsilon_x$; where $\bar{\sigma}_f$ is calculated based on ideal strain.

In direct extrusion, the effect of friction between the wall and the billet causes the ram pressure to be greater than for indirect extrusion.

$$p_f \frac{\pi}{4} D_o^2 = \mu p_c \pi D_o L = \sigma_{ys} \pi D_o L$$

where p_f = Additional pressure required to overcome friction and σ_{ys} = Shear yield stress $= \frac{\bar{\sigma}_f}{2}$.

$$p_f = \bar{\sigma}_f \frac{2L}{D_o}$$

ram pressure $= p + p_f = \bar{\sigma}_f \varepsilon_x + \bar{\sigma}_f \frac{2L}{D_o}$

$$p = \bar{\sigma}_f \left(\varepsilon_x + \frac{2L}{D_o} \right)$$

Ram force, $F = \bar{\sigma}_f \left(\varepsilon_x + \frac{2L}{D_o} \right) A$

Power required, $P = F v$

For shape other than round, ram pressure $p = K_x \bar{\sigma}_f$; where $K_x = 0.98 + 0.02 \left(\frac{C_x}{C_c} \right)^{2.25}$ and C_x = perimeter of the extruded cross section, C_c = perimeter of circle of the same area as the extruded shape.

$$p = K_x \bar{\sigma}_f \left(\varepsilon_x + \frac{2L}{D_o} \right)$$

Wire and Bar Drawing

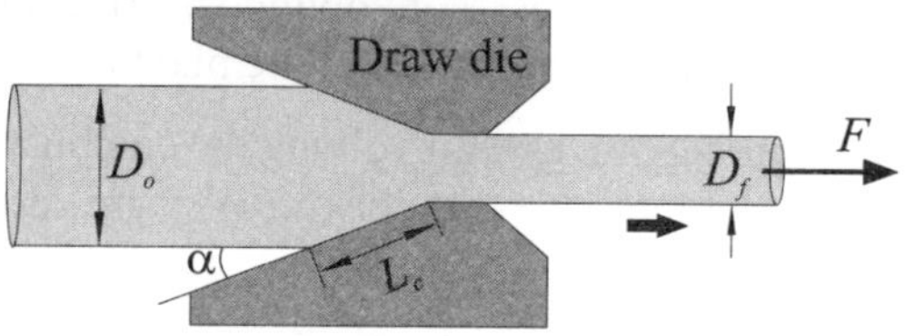

Drawing is an operation in which the cross-section of a bar, rod, or wire is reduced by pulling it through a die opening.

Analysis of Drawing

Area reduction, $r = \frac{A_o - A_f}{A_o}$, Draft $d = D_o - D_f$

True strain, $\varepsilon = \ln \left(\frac{A_o}{A_f} \right) = \ln \frac{1}{1-r}$

Drawing stress, $\sigma_d = \bar{\sigma}_f \varepsilon = \bar{\sigma}_f \ln \frac{A_o}{A_f}$; where $\bar{\sigma}_f = \frac{K\varepsilon^n}{1+n}$

Draw stress, $\sigma_d = \bar{\sigma}_f \left(1 + \frac{\mu}{\tan\alpha} \right) \phi \ln \frac{A_o}{A_f}$

Where $\phi = 0.88 + 0.12 \frac{D}{L_c}$, $D = \frac{D_o + D_f}{2}$ and

L_c = Contact length $= \frac{D_o - D_f}{2 \sin\alpha}$

Draw force, $F = A_f \sigma_d = A_f \bar{\sigma}_f \left(1 + \frac{\mu}{\tan\alpha} \right) \phi \ln \frac{A_o}{A_f}$

Maximum Reduction Per Pass

Maximum possible draw stress = Yield strength

$$\bar{\sigma}_f \ln \frac{A_o}{A_f} = \sigma \ln \frac{A_o}{A_f} = \sigma$$

or $\ln \frac{A_o}{A_f} = 1 \quad \Rightarrow \quad \ln \frac{1}{1-r} = 1$

$$r_{max} = \frac{e-1}{1} = 0.632$$

Maximum possible reduction $r_{max} = 0.632$.

Cutting Operations

Cutting of sheet metal accomplished by a shearing action between two sharp cutting edges.

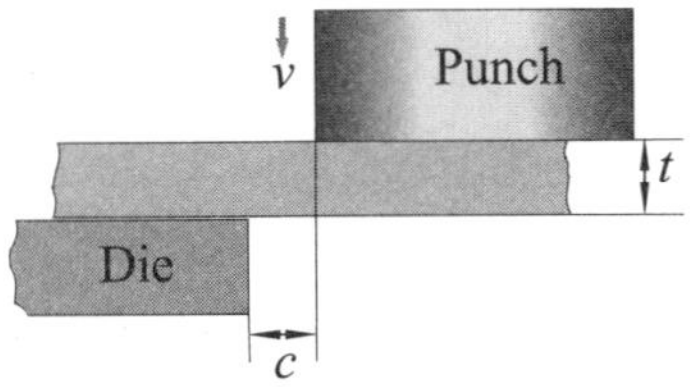

Blanking and Punching

If the part that is cut out is the desired product, the operation is called blanking and the product is called *blank*. If the remaining stock is the desired part, the operation is called *punching*.

Clearance c : It is the distance between the punch and die, as shown in figure. The range of clearance is between 4% to 8% of the sheet metal thickness t.

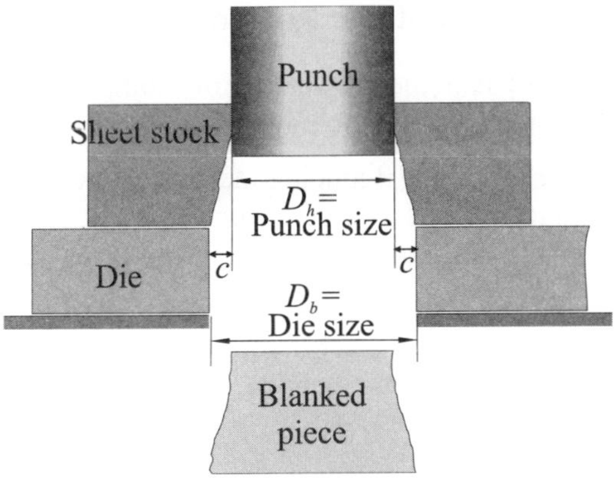

Clearance, $c = a\,t$

where a = Allowance and t = Stock thickness.

Allowance is determined according to type of metal. Punch and die sizes for a round blank of diameter D_b are determine as:

Blanking punch diameter $= D_b - 2c$

Blanking die diameter $= D_b$

Punch and die sizes for a round hole of diameter D_h are determine as:

Hole punch diameter $= D_h$

Hole die diameter $= D_h + 2c$

Cutting force, $F = \sigma_s\, t\, L = 0.7\sigma_{ut}\, t\, L$

Bending

It is defined as the straining of the metal around a straight axis, as shown in figure.

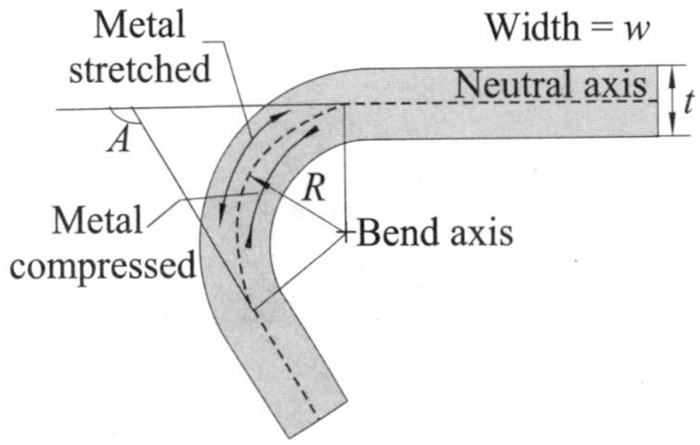

Bending allowance, $\text{BA} = 2\pi \frac{A}{360}(R + k_{ba} t)$;

$$k_{ba} = 0.33 \text{ if } R \le 2t$$

$$k_{ba} = 0.50 \text{ if } R \ge 2t$$

where A = Bend angle in degree, R = Bend radius, t = Stock thickness.

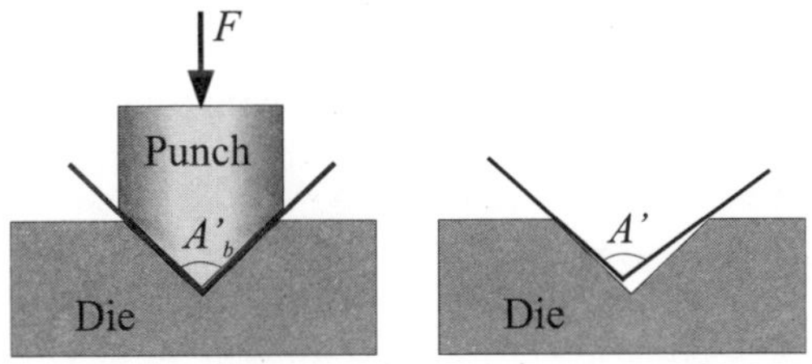

Spring back, $\text{SB} = \frac{A' - A_b'}{A_b'}$

Where A' = Included angle of the sheet metal part

A_b' = Included angle of the bending tool

Bending force, $F = \frac{k_{bf}\sigma_t w t^2}{D}$

where σ_t = Tensile strength, w = Width, t = Stock Thickness, D = Die opening dimension, and $k_{bf} = 1.33$ for V-bending, $k_{bf} = 0.33$ for edge bending.

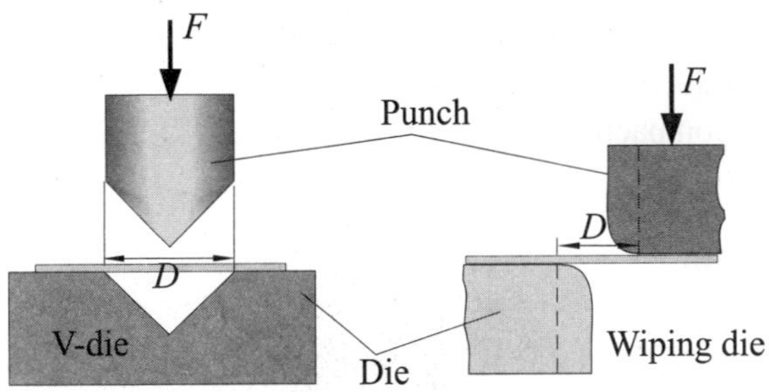

Die opening dimension, D

Drawing

Drawing is sheet-metal forming operation used to make cup-shaped, box-shaped, or other complex-curved, hollow-shaped parts.

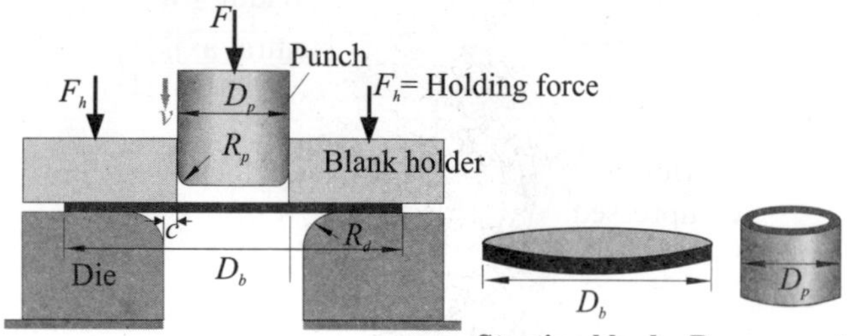

Clearance, $c = 1.1t$

Drawing ratio, $\text{DR} = \dfrac{D_b}{D_p} \le 2.0$

Reduction, $r = \dfrac{D_b - D_p}{D_b} \le 0.5$

Thickness-diameter ratio $= \dfrac{t}{D_b} > 1\%$

The $\dfrac{t}{D_b}$ decreases, the tendency for wrinkling increases.

Drawing force, $F = \pi D_p t \sigma_{yt}\left(\dfrac{D_b}{D_p} - 0.7\right)$

Holding force, $F_h = 0.015\sigma_y \pi\{D_b^2 - (D_p + 2.2t + 2R_d)^2\}$

where R_d = die corner radius.

$$\text{Volume} = \frac{\pi}{4}D_b^2 t = \frac{\pi}{4}D_p^2 t + \pi D_p t\, h$$

Size of blank, $D_b = \sqrt{D_p^2 + 4D_p h}$

Powder Metallurgy

Powder metallurgy is a manufacturing process where a desired shape is created from metal powder by compacting it in a die.

Powder metallurgy manufacturing process: (i) Production of metal powders, (ii) Mixing of powders, (iii) Compaction, (iv) Sintering, and (v) Secondary operations.

Powder

Particle size, $PS = \dfrac{1}{MC} - t_w$;

where, MC = Mesh count, opening per linear inch

t_w = Wire thichness of screen mesh (in inch)

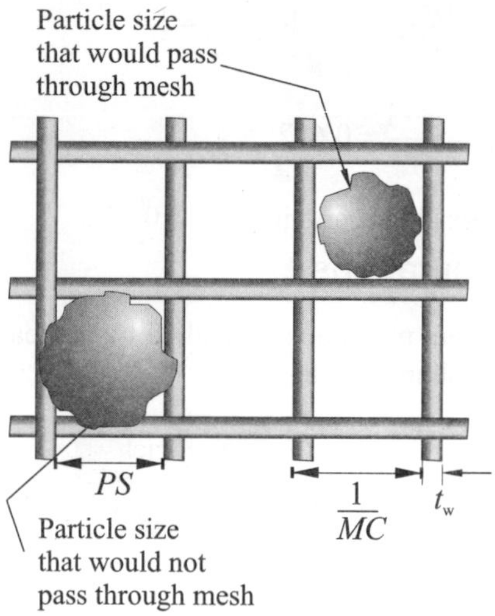

Shape factor, $K_s = \dfrac{A}{V}D$;

where V = Volume of particle, A = Surface area of particle, and D = Diameter of a sphere of equivalent volume as the non spherical particle.

Porosity + Packing factor = 1.0

$$\text{Aspect ratio} = \frac{\text{Maximum dimension}}{\text{Minimum dimension}}$$

Production of Metallic Powders

Atomization: It is the conversion of molten mental into droplets which solidify into powders.

Chemical reduction: Reducing metallic oxides by use of reducing agents which combine with the oxygen to free the metals in the form of powders is known as chemical reduction.

Electrolysis: Use of an electrolytic cell to deposit particles of the metal onto the cathode in the cell is called electrolysis.

Welding

Welding is the process of joining together two pieces of metal so that bonding takes place at their original boundary surfaces. When two parts to be joined are melted together, heat or pressure or both is applied and with or without added metal for formation of metallic bond.

Types of Welding Process

Fusion welding: (a) Arc welding, (b) Resistance welding (c) Oxyfuel gas welding, (d) Other fusion-welding.

Processes: (a) Electron beam welding, (b) Laser beam welding.

Solid state welding: (a) Diffusion welding, (b) Friction welding, (c) Ultrasonic welding.

Physics of Welding

Power density,

$$PD = \frac{\text{Power entering the surface}}{\text{Suface area over which the energy is entering}}$$

Heat require per unit volume to melt metal,

$$U_m = K T_m^2 \quad (\text{J/mm}^3)$$

Heat require to melt metal, $H_w = U_w V = K T_m^2 V$ (J)

where, T_m = Melting temperature of metal (in K),

V = Volume and constant, $K = 3.33 \times 10^{-6}$.

Heat energy available for welding, $H_w = f_1 f_2 H$

where, f_1 = Heat transfer efficiency, f_2 = Melting efficiency, and H = Total heat generated.

Rate of heat energy delivered to the operation,

$$HR_w = U_w(\text{WVR}) = f_1 f_2\, HR = U_m A_w v$$

where, WVR = volume rate of metal welded (mm^3/s), A_w = weld cross-section area, v = travel velocity of the weld and HR rate of input energy generated by the welding power source.

Welding Processes

Arc Welding

Consumable electrodes: (a) Gas metal arc welding, (b) Flux-cored arc welding, (c) Electro gas welding, and (d) Submerged arc welding.

Non-consumable electrodes: (a) Gas tungsten arc welding, (b) Plasma arc welding.

Power Source in Arc Welding

Both direct current (DC) and alternating current (AC) are used in arc welding.

Rate of heat energy delivered, $HR_w = f_1 f_2 VI = U_m A_w v$:

where, V = Voltage, I = Current.

Resistance Welding

(a) Resistance Spot Welding

(b) Resistance Seam Welding

(c) Resistance Projection Welding

(d) Other Resistance Welding: (i) Flash welding, (ii) Upset welding, (iii) Percussion welding, (iv) High-frequency resistance welding.

Power Source in Resistance Welding

Rate of heat energy delivered,

$$HR_w = f_1 f_2 I^2 R = U_m A_w v$$

where, V = Voltage, I = Current.

(i) Oxy-fuel Gas welding

(ii) Oxyacetylene welding

Alternative gases for oxy-fuel welding are fusion-welding processes. It includes: (a) Electron-beam welding

Power density, $PD = \dfrac{f_1\, VI}{A}$

(b) Laser beam welding

(c) Electroslag welding

(d) Thermit welding

[Chemical reaction $8\text{Al} + 3\text{Fe}_3\text{O}_4 = 9\,\text{Fe} + 4\text{Al}_2\text{O}_3$ + heat]

Solid-state Welding

(a) Forge welding, (b) Cold welding, (c) Roll welding, (d) Hot pressure welding, (e) Diffusion welding, (f) Explosion welding, (g) Friction welding, (h) Ultrasonic welding.

Brazing

Brazing is a joining process in which a filler metal is melted and distributed by capillary action between the faying surfaces of the metal part being joined.

Filler metal (brazing metal) has a melting temperature that is above 450°C but below the melting point of the base metal(s) to be joined.

Soldering

Soldering is a joining process in which a filler metal with melting point not exceeding 450°C is melted and distributed by capillary action between the faying surfaces of the metal part being joined.

Adhesive Bonding

Adhesive bonding is a joining process in which a filler material is used to hold two (or more) closely spaced parts together by surface attachment. The filler material that binds the parts together is the adhesive.

Adhesive type: (a) Natural, (b) Inorganic, (c) Synthetic.

14.2 SOLVED EXAMPLES

Previous Years GATE Questions

Example 14.1

A atomic packing factor for a material with body centered cubic structure is_______.

GATE 2015

Solution

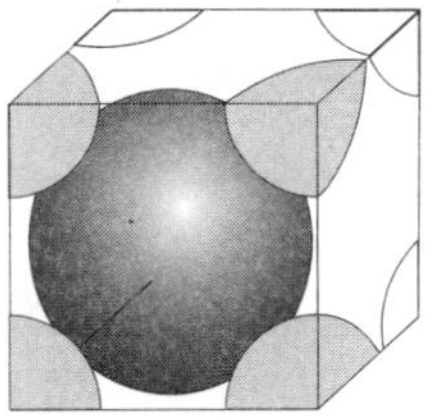

Unit cell

$$\text{Atomic packing factor} = \frac{\text{Volume of atom in unit cell}}{\text{Volume of unit cell}}$$

Let R be the radius of atom and a be the side of cube.

Volume of unit cell $= a^3$

$$\text{Number of atom in unit cell} = 1 + 8 \times \frac{1}{8} = 2$$

$$\text{Volume of atoms} = 2 \times \frac{4}{3}\pi R^3$$

$$\text{Diagonal of cell} = \sqrt{a^2 + a^2 + a^2} = R + 2R + R$$

$$R = \frac{\sqrt{3}}{4}\, a$$

Atomic packing factor

$$= \frac{2 \times \frac{4}{3}\pi R^3}{a^3} = \frac{8\pi}{3}\frac{R^3}{a^3} = \frac{8\pi}{3}\frac{\left(\frac{\sqrt{3}}{4}a\right)^3}{a^3}$$

$$\text{Atomic packing factor} = 0.68$$

Example 14.2

A cube and a sphere made of cast iron (each volume 1000 cm^3) were cast under identical conditions. The time taken for solidifying the cube was 4 s. The solidification time (in seconds) for the sphere is ______.

GATE 2015

Solution

Let a and r be the side of cube and radius of sphere respectively.

$$\text{Volume} = \frac{4}{3}\pi r^3 = a^3 = 1000 \text{ cm}^3$$

$$r = 6.20 \text{ cm} \quad \text{and} \quad a = 10 \text{ cm}$$

Solidification time is given by $t = c_m\left(\frac{V}{A}\right)^2$

For cube, $$t_{\text{cube}} = c_m\left(\frac{a}{6}\right)^2 = 4 \quad \text{(i)}$$

For sphere, $$t_{\text{sphere}} = c_m\left(\frac{r}{3}\right)^2 \quad \text{(ii)}$$

Equations (i) and (ii), gives

$$\frac{t_{\text{sphere}}}{4} = \left(2\frac{r}{a}\right)^2 = \left(2 \times \frac{6.20}{10}\right)^2 = 1.539$$

$$t_{\text{sphere}} = 6.15 \text{ s}$$

Example 14.3

In a two-stage wire drawing operation, the fractional reduction (ratio of change in cross-sectional area) in the first stage is 0.4. The fractional reduction in the second stage is 0.3. The overall fractional reduction in

(A) 0.24 (B) 0.58 (C) 0.60 (D) 1.00

GATE 2015

Solution

Let A_o, A_i and A_f be the cross-sectional area of wire at initial, intermediate and final stage respectively.

The fractional reduction in the first stage

$$= \frac{A_o - A_i}{A_o} = 0.4$$

or $$\frac{A_i}{A_o} = 0.6 \quad \text{(i)}$$

The fractional reduction in the second stage

$$= \frac{A_i - A_f}{A_i} = 0.3$$

or $$\frac{A_f}{A_i} = 0.7 \quad \text{(ii)}$$

Equations (i) and (ii) give $$\frac{A_f}{A_o} = 0.42$$

Overall fractional reduction

$$= \frac{A_o - A_f}{A_o} = 1 - \frac{A_f}{A_o} = 1 - 0.42$$

$$\text{Overall fractional reduction} = 0.58$$

Example 14.4

During a TIG welding process, the arc current and arc voltage are 50 A and 60 V, respectively, when the welding speed was 150 mm/min. In another process, the TIG welding is carried out at a welding speed of 120 mm/min at the same arc welding voltage and heat input to the material so that weld quality remains the same. The welding current (in A) for this process is

(A) 40.00 (B) 44.72 (C) 55.90 (D) 62.25

GATE 2015

Solution

Let u be the specific energy required for melting and η be the welding efficiency.

Heat supplied, $VI \times \eta = uAv$

For TIG welding process-I,

$$60 \times 50\eta = u\,A \times 150 \quad \text{(i)}$$

For TIG welding process -II;

$$60\times I\,\eta = u\,A\times 120 \qquad \text{(ii)}$$

Equations (i) and (ii), gives

$$\text{Current } I = 40\text{ A}$$

Example 14.5

The flowing stress (in MPa) of a material is given by

$\sigma = 500\varepsilon^{0.1}$, where ε is true strain.

The Young's modulus of elasticity of the material is 200 GPa. A block of thickness 100 mm made of this material is compressed to 95 mm thickness and then the load is removed. The final dimension of the block (in mm) is _____.

GATE 2015

Solution

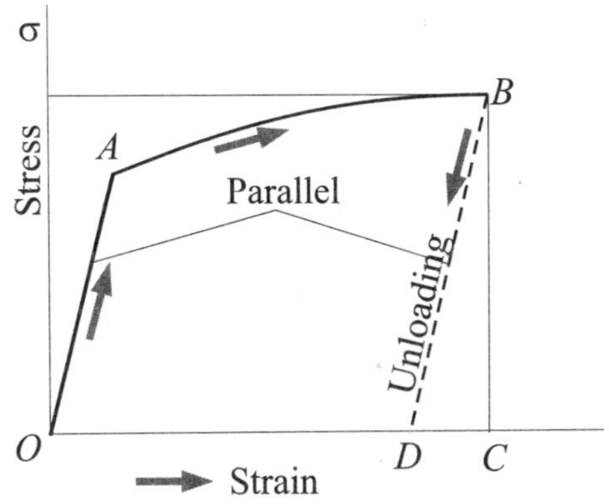

The stress-strain diagram is shown in figure.

The true strain at B is $\ln\dfrac{100}{95} = 0.05129$

The flow stress at B,

$$\sigma = 500(0.05129)^{0.1} = 371.51\text{ MPa}$$

Let x be the final dimension after load is removed.

Strain at D, $\varepsilon_D = \dfrac{100-x}{100}$

Strain at C, $\varepsilon_C = \dfrac{100-95}{100}$.

Slope of line OA = Slope of line BD

$$E = \frac{\sigma_B}{\varepsilon_C - \varepsilon_D}$$

or $$200\times 10^9 = \frac{371.51\times 10^6}{\dfrac{100-95}{100} - \dfrac{100-x}{100}}$$

$$x = 95.18\text{ mm}$$

Example 14.6

The dimensions of a cylindrical side riser (height = diameter) of a 25 cm ×15 cm × 5 cm steel casting are to be determined. For the tabulated shape factor values given below, the diameter of the riser (in cm) is________.

Shape factor	2	4	6	8	10	12
$\dfrac{\text{Riser volume}}{\text{Casting volume}}$	1.0	0.70	0.55	0.50	0.40	0.35

GATE 2015

Solution

$$\text{Shape factor} = \frac{\text{Length} + \text{Width}}{\text{Thickness}} = \frac{25+15}{5}$$

Shape factor = 8

From given table (for Shape factor = 8);

$$\frac{\text{Riser volume}}{\text{Casting volume}} = 0.5$$

$$\text{Riser volume} = 0.5\times\text{Casting volume}$$

or $$\text{Riser volume} = 0.5\times 25\times 15\times 5 = 937.5\text{ cm}^3$$

or $$\text{Riser volume} = \frac{\pi}{4}D^2\times D = 937.5\text{ cm}^3$$

or $$D^3 = 1193.6$$

$$\text{Diameter of riser, } D = 10.6\text{ cm}$$

Example 14.7

Ratio of solidification of a cylindrical casting (height = radius) to that of a cubic casting of side two times the height of cylindrical casting is __________

GATE 2015

Solution

Solidification time is given by $t = c_m\left(\dfrac{V}{A}\right)^2$

For cylindrical casting (height h = radius r) ;

$$t_{\text{cyl.}} = c_m\left(\frac{\pi r^2 h}{\pi r h + 2\pi r^2}\right)^2 = c_m\left(\frac{r}{3}\right)^2 \qquad \text{(i)}$$

For cubic casting (side $a = 2h = 2r$);

$$t_{\text{cube.}} = c_m\left(\frac{a^3}{6a^2}\right)^2 = c_m\left(\frac{a}{6}\right)^2 = c_m\left(\frac{2r}{6}\right)^2 \qquad \text{(ii)}$$

Equations (i) and (ii) give

$$\frac{t_{\text{cyl.}}}{t_{\text{cube}}} = 1$$

Example 14.8

In a rolling operation using rolls of diameter 500 mm, if a thick plate cannot be reduced to less than 20 mm in one pass, the coefficient of friction between the roll and the plate is _____

GATE 2015

Solution

Maximum possible draft for the given coefficient of friction is

$$d_{max} = \mu^2 R$$

Substituting given values $R = \frac{500}{2} = 250\,\text{mm}$ and $d_{max} = 20\,\text{mm}$, we have

$$20 = \mu^2 \times 250$$

or $$\mu = \sqrt{\frac{20}{250}}$$

$$\mu = 0.2828$$

Example 14.9

Match the following products with preferred manufacturing process:

Product	Process
P. Rails	1. Blow molding
Q. Engine crankshaft	2. Extrusion
R. Aluminum channels	3. Forging
S. PET water bottles	4. Rolling

(A) P-4, Q-3, R-1, S-2 (B) P-4, Q-3, R-2, S-1
(C) P-2, Q-4, R-3, S-1 (D) P-3, Q-4, R-2, S-1

GATE 2015

Solution

Correct matching P-4, Q-3, R-2, S-1

Example 14.10

A DC welding power source has a linear voltage-current (V - I) characteristic with open circuit voltage of 80 V and a short circuit current of 300 A. For maximum arc power, the current (in amperes) should be set as ______.

GATE 2015

Solution

Given: Open circuit voltage $V_o = 80\,\text{V}$, Short circuit current $I_s = 300\,\text{A}$

V-Icharacteristics of power source can be expressed in linear equation

$$V = V_o\left(1 - \frac{I}{I_s}\right)$$

$$V = 80\left(1 - \frac{I}{300}\right)$$

Power, $$P = VI = 80\left(1 - \frac{I}{300}\right) \times I$$

$$P = 80\left(I - \frac{I^2}{300}\right)$$

Thus, the current for maximum power can be determined using

$$\frac{dP}{dI} = 0 \Rightarrow \quad 80\left(1 - \frac{2I}{300}\right) = 0$$

$$I = 150\,\text{A}$$

Example 14.11

The solidification time of a casting is proportional to $\left(\frac{V}{A}\right)^2$, where V is the volume of the casting and A is the total casting surface area losing heat. Two cubes of same material and size are cast using sand casting process. The top face of one of the cubes is completely insulated. The ratio of the solidification time for the cube with top face insulated to that of the other cube is

(A) $\frac{25}{36}$ (B) $\frac{36}{25}$ (C) 1 (D) $\frac{6}{5}$

GATE 2015

Solution

Let x be the side of cube.

Volume of cube, $V = x^3$

Solidification time is given by

$$t = c_m\left(\frac{V}{A}\right)^2$$

For cube-1 (one face in insulated);

$$t_1 = c_m\left(\frac{x^3}{5x^2}\right)^2 = c_m\left(\frac{x}{5}\right)^2 \quad \text{(i)}$$

For cube-2;

$$t_2 = c_m\left(\frac{x^3}{6x^2}\right)^2 = c_m\left(\frac{x}{6}\right)^2 \quad \text{(ii)}$$

Equations (i) and (ii), give

$$\frac{t_1}{t_2} = \left(\frac{6}{5}\right)^2$$

$$\frac{t_1}{t_2} = \frac{36}{25}$$

Example 14.12

In a slab rolling operation, the maximum thickness reduction Δh_{max} is given by $\Delta h_{max} = \mu^2 R$, where R is the radius of the roll and μ is the coefficient of friction between the roll and the sheet. If $\mu = 0.1$, the maximum angle subtended by the deformation zone at the centre of the roll (bit angle in degree) is __________.

GATE 2015

Solution

$$\text{Angle of bite } '\alpha' = \tan^{-1}(\mu)$$

$$\alpha = \tan^{-1}(0.1)$$

$$\alpha = 5.7^\circ$$

Example 14.13

A metal rod of initial length L_o is subjected to a drawing process. The length of the rod at any instant is given by the expression, $L_t = L_o(1+t^2)$, where t is the time in minutes. The true strain rate (in min^{-1}) at the end of one minute is____.

GATE 2014

Solution

The true strain is $\varepsilon = \ln\left(\frac{l_t}{l_o}\right)$

The true strain rate is

$$\frac{d\varepsilon}{dt} = \frac{1}{l_t}\frac{dl_t}{dt} = \frac{1}{L_o(1+t^2)}\frac{dL_o(1+t^2)}{dt} = \frac{2t}{1+t^2}$$

The true strain rate at the end of one minute;

$$\frac{d\varepsilon}{dt} = \frac{2\times 1}{1+1^2} = 1$$

$$\frac{d\varepsilon}{dt} = 1$$

Example 14.14

An aluminum alloy (density 2600 kg/m^3) casting is to be produced. A cylindrical hole of 100 mm diameter and 100 mm length is made in the casting using sand core (density 1600 kg/m^3). The net buoyancy force (in newton) acting on the core is_________.

GATE 2014

Solution

Weight of sand core, $W\downarrow = mg = \rho_c \frac{\pi}{4} d^2 h g$

Buoyancy force, $F_B \uparrow = \rho_{al} \frac{\pi}{4} d^2 h g$

Net buoyancy force, $F\uparrow = F_B - W = (\rho_{al} - \rho_c)\frac{\pi}{4} d^2 h g$

$$F\uparrow = (2600-1600)\times\frac{\pi}{4}0.1^2\times 0.1\times 9.81$$

$$\text{Net buoyancy force, } F\uparrow = 7.704 \text{ N}$$

Example 14.15

A cube shaped casting solidifies in 5 min. The solidification time (in min) for a cube of the same material which is 8 times heavier than the original casting, will be

(A) 10 (B) 20 (C) 24 (D) 40

GATE 2013

Solution

Let x be the side of cube of original casting.

Solidification time is given by $t = c_m\left(\frac{V}{A}\right)^2$

For original casting (cube of side x); $t = c_m\left(\frac{x^3}{6x^2}\right)^2$

$$5 = c_m\left(\frac{x}{6}\right)^2 \qquad \text{(i)}$$

For 8 times heavier than original casting (cube of side $2x$);

$$t = c_m\left(\frac{8x^3}{6(2x)^2}\right)^2$$

or

$$t = c_m\left(\frac{2x}{6}\right)^2 \qquad \text{(ii)}$$

Equations (i) and (ii) give

$$\frac{t}{5} = 2^2$$

$$t = 40 \text{ min}$$

Example 14.16

A solid cylinder of diameter 100 mm and height 50 mm is forged between two frictionless flat dies to a height of 25 mm. The percentage change in diameter is

(A) 0 (B) 20.7 (C) 2.07 (D) 14.14

GATE 2012

Solution

Let D be the diameter of workpiece after forging.

During forging, workpiece volume remains constant.

$$\frac{\pi}{4}D^2\times 25 = \frac{\pi}{4}\times 100^2\times 50$$

or $D=\sqrt{\dfrac{100^2\times 50}{25}}=141.42\text{ mm}$

The percentage change in diameter is

$$=\frac{141.42-100}{100}\times 100=14.14\%$$

Example 14.17

In a DC arc welding operation, the voltage-arc length characteristic is obtained as $V_{\text{arc}}=20+5\,l$, where the arc length l was varied between 5 mm and 7 mm. Here V_{arc} denotes the arc voltage in volts. The arc current was varied from 400 A to 500 A. Assuming linear power source characteristic, the open circuit voltage and the short circuit current for the welding operation are:

(A) 45 V, 450 A (B) 95 V, 950 A

(C) 75 V, 750 A (D) 150 V, 1500 A

GATE 2012

Solution

For arc length $l=5$ mm; $V_{\text{arc}}=20+5\times 5=45$ V and current $I=500$ A

For arc length $l=7$ mm; $V_{\text{arc}}=20+5\times 7=55$ V and current $I=400$ A

Arc voltage and current are related to open circuit voltage V_o and short circuit current I_s as:

$$V_{\text{arc}}=V_o\left(1-\frac{I}{I_s}\right)$$

For $V_{\text{arc}}=45$ V and $I=500$ A;

$$45=V_o\left(1-\frac{500}{I_s}\right) \qquad \text{(i)}$$

For $V_{\text{arc}}=55$ V and $I=400$ A;

$$55=V_o\left(1-\frac{400}{I_s}\right) \qquad \text{(ii)}$$

Equations (i) and (ii) give

$$V_o=95\text{ V and } I_s=950\text{ A}$$

Example 14.18

In a single pass rolling process using 410 mm diameter steel rollers, a strip of width 140 mm and thickness 8 mm undergoes 10% reduction of thickness. The angle of bite (in radians) is

(A) 0.006 (B) 0.062 (C) 0.031 (D) 0.600

GATE 2012

Solution

Given: Roll radius, $R=\dfrac{410}{2}=205$ mm, initial thickness of plate $t_o=8$ mm and final thickness of plate $t_f=0.9\times 8=7.2$ mm

Maximum draft, $d_{\max}=\mu^2 R$

$$\mu=\sqrt{\frac{d_{\max}}{R}}=\sqrt{\frac{8-7.2}{205}}=0.0624$$

Angle of bite, $\alpha=\tan^{-1}\mu=\tan^{-1}(0.0624)$

$$\alpha=3.574^\circ$$

$$\alpha=0.0623\text{ radians}$$

Example 14.19

Calculate the punch size in mm, for a circular blanking operation for which details are given.

Size of the blank = 25 mm

Thickness of the sheet = 2 mm

Radial clearance between punch and die = 0.06 mm

Die allowance = 0.05 mm

(A) 24.83 (B) 25.01 (C) 24.89 (D) 25.17

GATE 2012

Solution

Punch diameter = Blank size − $2c$ − Die allowance

Punch diameter $=25-2\times 0.06-0.05$

Punch diameter = 24.83 mm

Example 14.20

The maximum possible draft in cold rolling of sheet increases with the

(A) Increase in coefficient of friction

(B) Decrease in roll radius

(C) Decrease in coefficient of friction

(D) Increase in roll velocity

GATE 2011

Solution

Maximum draft is given by

$$d_{\max}=\mu^2 R$$

Maximum draft $d_{\max}$ increases with increase coefficient μ and roll radius R.

Example 14.21

A cubic casting of 50 mm side undergoes volumetric solidification shrinkage and volumetric solid contraction of 4% and 6% respectively. No riser is used. Assume uniform cooling in all directions. The side of the cube after solidification and contraction is

(A) 48.32 mm (B) 49.94 mm

(C) 49.90 mm (D) 49.96 mm

GATE 2011

Solution

Let x be the side of cube after solidification and contraction.

$$x^3 = \left(1 - \frac{4}{100}\right)\left(1 - \frac{6}{100}\right) \times 50^3$$

or $$x^3 = 0.9024 \times 50^3$$

$$x = 48.317 \text{ mm}$$

Example 14.22

The shear strength of a sheet metal is 300 MPa. The blanking force required to produce a blank of 100 mm diameter from a 100 mm thick sheet is close to

(A) 45 kN (B) 141 kN (C) 70 kN (D) 3500 kN

GATE 2011

Solution

Blanking force, $F = \sigma_s A_s = \sigma_s \pi d t$

Substituting given values, $\sigma_s = 300$ MPa, $d = 100$ mm and $t = 1.5$ mm

$$F = 300 \times \pi \times 100 \times 1.5$$

$$F = 141.37 \text{ kN}$$

Example 14.23

Linked Answer Questions

In shear cutting operation, a sheet of 5 mm thickness is cut along a length of 200 mm. The cutting blade is 400 mm long (see figure) and zero-shear ($s = 0$) is provided on the edge. The ultimate shear strength of the sheet is 100 MPa and penetration to thickness ratio is 0.2. Neglect friction.

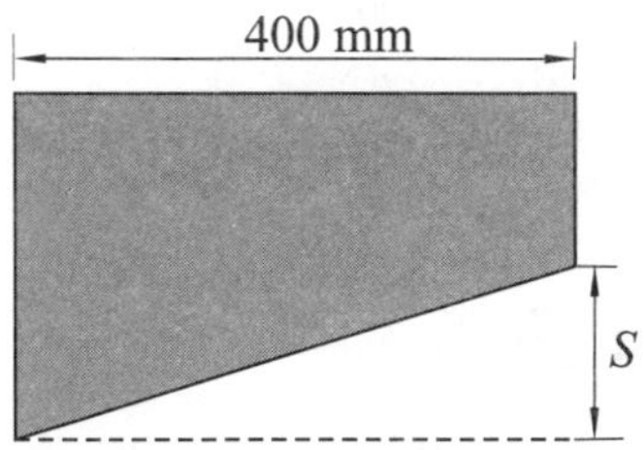

Q(a) Assuming force v/s displacement curve to be rectangular, the work done (in J) is

(A) 100 (B) 200 (C) 250 (D) 300

Q(b) A shear of 20 mm (s = 20 mm) is now provided on the blade. Assuming force vs displacement curve to be trapezoidal, the maximum force (in kN) exerted is

(A) 5 (B) 10 (C) 20 (D) 40

GATE 2010

Solution

Given: $t = 5$ mm, $l = 200$ mm, $\sigma_s = 100$ MPa and $p = 0.2$

(a) Shear force $F = \sigma_s l t$

$$F = 100 \times 200 \times 5 \text{ N}$$

$$F = 100 \text{ kN}$$

The punch needs to be displaced by pt distance, therefore,

$$\text{Work done } W = F \times pt = 100 \times 0.2 \times \frac{5}{1000} \text{ kJ}$$

$$W = 100 \text{ kJ}$$

(b) When shear of 20 mm is provided in the blade, it will be effective on the length of the sheet by $s = 10$ mm, and the punch need to be displaced total by $(pt + s)$.

Work done, $W = F \times (pt + s)$

Maximum force, $F = \dfrac{W}{(pt + s)} = \dfrac{100}{(0.2 \times 5 + 10)/1000}$

or $$F = 9090.9 \text{ N}$$

$$F \approx 10 \text{ kN}$$

Example 14.24

While cooling, a cubical casting of side 40 mm undergoes 3%, 4% and 5% volume shrinkage during the liquid state, phase transition and solid state, respectively. The volume of metal compensated from the riser is

(A) 2% (B) 7% (C) 8% (D) 9%

GATE 2008

Solution

Risers are used to compensate shrinkage before solidification (liquid state + phase transition). Therefore,

Volume of the metal compensated from the riser will be $3 + 4 = 7\%$.

Example 14.25

In a single pass rolling operation, a 20 mm thick plate with plate width of 100 mm, is reduced to 18 mm. The roller radius is 250 mm and rotational speed is 10 rpm. The average flow stress for the material is 300 MPa. The power required for the rolling operation (in kW) is closest to

(A) 15.2 (B) 82 (C) 31.4 (D) 45.6

GATE 2008

Solution

Given: Initial thickness $t_o = 20$ mm, $t_f = 18$ mm, $w = 100$ mm, $R = 250$ mm, $N = 100$ rpm and $\bar{\sigma}_f = 300$ MPa.

Contact length, $L = \sqrt{R(t_o - t_f)} = \sqrt{250 \times (20 - 18)}$

or $$L = 22.36 \text{ mm}$$

Roll force, $F = \bar{\sigma}_f wL = 300 \times 100 \times 22.36$

or $F = 670.82\,\text{kN}$

Power required for the rolling operation is

$$P = 2 \times 2\pi NFL$$

$$P = 2 \times 2\pi \times \frac{10}{60} \times 670.82 \times \frac{22.36}{1000}$$

$$P = 31.4\,\text{kW}$$

Example 14.26

In arc welding of a butt joint, the welding speed is to be selected such that the highest cooling rate is achieved. Melting efficiency and heat transfer efficiency are 0.5 and 0.7, respectively. The area of the weld cross-section is 5 mm^2 and the unit energy required to melt the metal is 10 J/mm^3. If welding power is 2 kW, welding speed in mm/s is closest to

(A) 4 (B) 14 (C) 24 (D) 34

GATE 2008

Solution

Given: Melting efficiency, $\eta_m = 0.5$, heat transfer efficiency, $\eta_h = 0.7$, weld cross-section area, $a = 5\,\text{mm}^2$, melting energy, $u = 10\,\text{J}/\text{mm}^3$ and welding power, $P = 2 \times 10^3\,\text{W}$.

Heat balance equation for welding speed v can be written as:

$$P \times \eta_m \times \eta_h = uva$$

Substituting given values

$$2 \times 10^3 \times 0.5 \times 0.7 = 10 \times v \times 5$$

$$v = 14\,\text{mm/s}$$

Example 14.27

A direct current welding machine with a linear power source characteristic provides open circuit voltage of 80 V and short circuit current of 800 A. During welding with the machine, the measured arc current is 500 A corresponding to an arc length of 5.0 mm and the measured arc current is 460 A corresponding to an arc length of 7.0 mm. The linear voltage (E)-arc length (L) characteristic of the welding arc can be given as (where E is in volt and L is in mm)

(A) $E = 20 + 2\,L$ (B) $E = 20 + 8\,L$

(C) $E = 80 + 2\,L$ (D) $E = 80 + 8\,L$

GATE 2007

Solution

Linear relation between I and arc length L is

$$I = a + bL$$

For given current, $I = 500$ A at arc length $L = 5.0$ mm;

$$500 = a + 5b \qquad \text{(i)}$$

For given current, $I = 460$ A at arc length $L = 7.0$ mm;

$$460 = a + 7b \qquad \text{(ii)}$$

Equations (i) and (ii) give

$$a = 600 \text{ and } b = -20$$

Therefore,

$$I = 600 - 20\,L$$

Voltage (E) – Current (I) relationship is:

$$E = E_o\left(1 - \frac{I}{I_s}\right)$$

$$E = 80\left(1 - \frac{600 - 20L}{800}\right)$$

$$E = 20 + 2\,L$$

Example 14.28

In open-die forging, a disc of diameter 200 mm and height 60 mm is compressed without any barreling effect. The final diameter of the disc is 400 mm. The true strain is

(A) 1.986 (B) 1.686 (C) 1.386 (D) 0.602

GATE 2007

Solution

Given: $d_o = 200\,\text{mm}$, $h_o = 60\,\text{mm}$ and $d_f = 400\,\text{mm}$

Workpiece volume, $V = \frac{\pi}{4} d_o^2 h_o = \frac{\pi}{4} d_f^2 h_f$

or $$h_f = \frac{d_o^2}{d_f^2} h_o = \left(\frac{200}{400}\right)^2 60$$

Final height, $h_f = 15\,\text{mm}$

The true stain, $\varepsilon = \ln\left(\frac{60}{15}\right)$

$$\varepsilon = 1.386$$

Example 14.29

The thickness of a metallic sheet is reduced from an initial value of 16 mm to a final value of 10 mm in one single pass rolling with a pair of cylindrical rollers each of diameter of 400 mm. The bite angle in degree will be

(A) 5.936 (B) 7.936 (C) 8.936 (D) 9.82

GATE 2007

Solution

Given: $t_o = 16\,\text{mm}$, $t_f = 10\,\text{mm}$ and $R = 200\,\text{mm}$.

Coefficient of friction for given maximum draft is

$$\mu = \sqrt{\frac{d_{max}}{R}} = \sqrt{\frac{t_o - t_f}{R}} = \sqrt{\frac{16-10}{200}}$$

$$\mu = 0.1732$$

Angle of bite, $\alpha = \tan^{-1}(0.1732)$

$$\text{Angle of bite, } \alpha = 9.82^\circ$$

Example 14.30

A 200 mm long down sprue has an area of cross-section of 650 mm^2 where the pouring basin meets the down sprue (i.e., at the beginning of the down sprue). A constant head of molten metal is maintained by the pouring basin. The molten metal flow rate is $6.5 \times 10^5 \text{mm}^3/\text{s}$. Considering the end of down sprue to be open to atmosphere and an acceleration due to gravity of 10^4 mm/s^2, the area of the down sprue (in mm^2) at its end (avoiding aspiration effect) should be

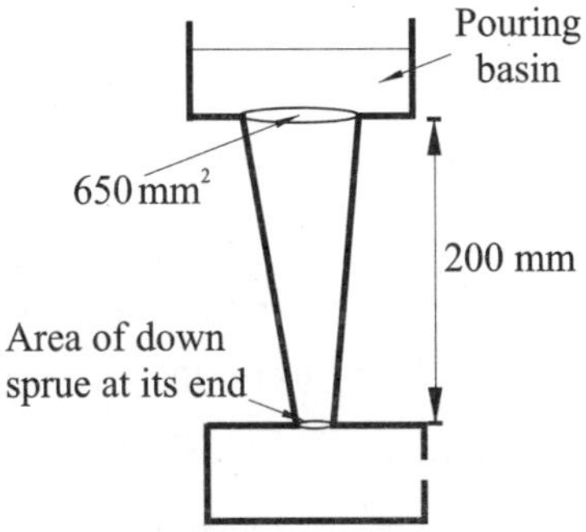

(A) 650.0 (B) 350.0 (C) 290.7 (D) 190.0

GATE 2007

Solution

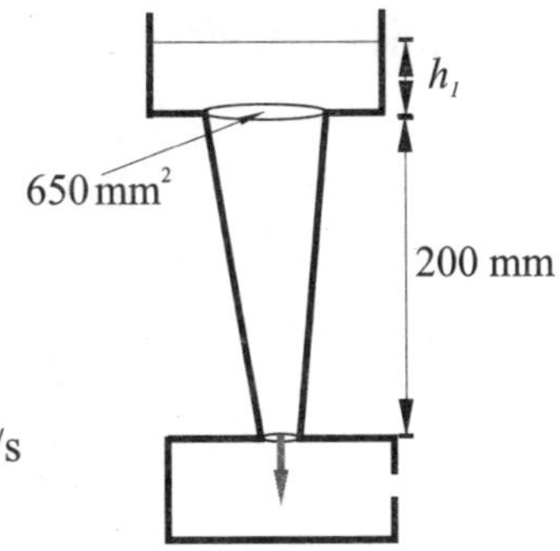

Flow rate, $Q = A_1 V_1$

Velocity of stream,

$$V_1 = \frac{Q}{A_1} = \frac{6.5 \times 10^5}{650}$$

$$V_1 = 1000 \text{ mm/s}$$

and $V_1 = \sqrt{2gh_1} = 1000 \text{mm/s}$

or $h_1 = \dfrac{1000^2}{2 \times 10^4} = 50 \text{ mm}$

Velocity at exit of the sprue, $V_2 = \sqrt{2g(h_1 + 200)}$

$$V_2 = \sqrt{2 \times 10^4 \times (50 + 200)} = 2236.06 \text{ mm/s}$$

Applying continuity equation, $Q = A_2 V_2$

$$A_2 = \frac{Q}{V_2} = \frac{6.5 \times 10^5}{2236.06}$$

$$A_2 = 290.68 \text{ mm}^2$$

Example 14.31

The force requirement in a blanking operation of low carbon steel sheet is 5.0 kN. The thickness of the sheet is t and diameter of the blanked part is d. For the same work material, if the diameter of the blanked part is increased to $1.5d$ and thickness is reduced to $0.4t$, the new blanking force in kN is

(A) 3.0 (B) 4.5 (C) 5.0 (D) 8.0

GATE 2007

Solution

Blanking force for the sheet of thickness t and diameter d is

$$F = \tau \pi dt$$

$$5 = \tau \pi dt \quad \text{(i)}$$

Blanking force for the sheet of thickness $0.4t$ and diameter $1.5\,d$ is

$$F = \tau \pi(1.5d)(0.4t) = 0.6\tau \pi dt \quad \text{(ii)}$$

Equations (i) and (ii), give

$$F = 3.0 \text{ kN}$$

Example 14.32

The ultimate tensile strength of a material is 400 MPa and the elongation up to maximum load is 35%. If the material obeys power law hardening, then the true stress-true strain relation (stress in MPa) in the plastic deformation range is

(A) $\sigma = 540\varepsilon^{0.30}$ (B) $\sigma = 775\varepsilon^{0.30}$

(C) $\sigma = 540\varepsilon^{0.35}$ (D) $\sigma = 775\varepsilon^{0.35}$

GATE 2006

Solution

Let A_o be the initial cross-sectional area.

The true strain at the elongation up to maximum load F is

$$\varepsilon = \ln\left(\frac{135}{100}\right) = 0.3$$

Therefore, the value of $n = 0.3$

and also $\varepsilon = \ln\left(\dfrac{A_o}{A}\right) = 0.3$

$$A = \frac{A_o}{e^{0.3}} = 0.74A_o$$

True ultimate strength is $\dfrac{F}{A} = \dfrac{400A_o}{0.74A_o} = 540 \text{ MPa}$

Therefore,

$$\text{True stress-true strain relation, } \sigma = 540\varepsilon^{0.3}$$

Example 14.33

A 4 mm thick sheet is rolled with 300 mm diameter rolls to reduce thickness without any charge in its width. The friction coefficient at the work-roll interface is 0.1. The minimum possible thickness of the sheet that can be produced in a single pass is

(A) 1.0 mm (B) 1.5 mm (C) 2.5 mm (D) 3.7 mm

GATE 2006

Solution

Given: $t_o = 4$ mm, $R = 150$ mm and $\mu = 0.1$

Maximum possible draft for the given coefficient of friction is

$$d_{máx} = \mu^2 R$$

or $$t_o - t_f = \mu^2 R$$

or $$4 - t_f = 0.1^2 \times 150$$

$$t_f = 2.5 \text{ mm}$$

Minimum possible thickness, $t_f = 2.5$ mm

Example 14.34

In a wire drawing operation, diameter of a steel wire is reduced from 10 mm to 8 mm. The mean flow stress of the material is 400 MPa. The ideal force required for drawing (ignoring friction and redundant work) is

(A) 4.48 kN (B) 8.97 kN

(C) 20.11 kN (D) 31.41 kN

GATE 2006

Solution

Given: $d_o = 10$ mm, $d_f = 8$ mm and $\bar{\sigma}_f = 400$ MPa

Drawing stress, $\sigma_d = \bar{\sigma}_f \varepsilon = \bar{\sigma}_f \ln\left(\frac{A_o}{A_f}\right)$

$$\sigma_d = 400 \ln\left(\frac{10}{8}\right)^2 = 178.51 \text{ MPa}$$

Drawing force, $F = \sigma_d \times \frac{\pi}{4} d_f^2 = 178.51 \times \frac{\pi}{4} \times 8^2$

$$F = 8.972 \text{ kN}$$

Example 14.35

In an arc welding process, the voltage and current are 25 V and 300 A respectively. The arc heat transfer efficiency is 0.85 and welding speed is 8 mm/s. The net heat input (in J/mm) is

(A) 64 (B) 797 (C) 1103 (D) 79700

GATE 2006

Solution

Heat generated, $Q_g = VI$

Heat transfer, $Q = \eta VI = 0.85 \times 25 \times 300$

$$Q = 6375 \text{ J/s}$$

Net heat input $q = \frac{Q}{v} = \frac{6375}{8}$ J/mm

$$q = 796.8 \text{ J/mm}$$

Example 14.36

A mold has a down sprue whose length is 20 cm and the cross-sectional area at the base of the down sprue is 1 cm^2. The down sprue feeds a horizontal runner leading into the mold cavity of volume 1000 cm^3. The time required to fill the mold cavity will be

(A) 4.05 s (B) 5.05 s (C) 6.05 s (D) 7.25 s

GATE 2005

Solution

Head available at base of sprue is

$$H = 20 \text{ cm}$$

Velocity of the stream entering the cavity is

$$v = \sqrt{2gH} = \sqrt{2 \times 981 \times 20}$$

or $$v = 198.09 \text{ cm/s}$$

Time required to fill the mold cavity,

$$T = \frac{\text{Volume of cavity}}{\text{Flow rate}} = \frac{V}{av} = \frac{1000}{1 \times 198.09}$$

$$T = 5.048 \text{ s}$$

Example 14.37

A 2 mm thick metal sheet is to be bent at an angle of one radian with a bend radius of 100 mm. If the stretch factor is 0.5, the bend allowance is

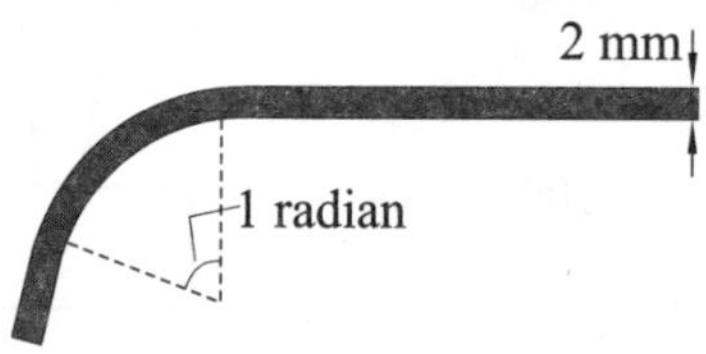

(A) 99 mm (B) 100 mm (C) 101 mm (D) 102 mm

GATE 2005

Solution

Given: $t = 2$ mm, $R = 100$ mm, $k_{ba} = 0.5$ and band angle $A = 1$ radian.

Bend allowance, $BA = \theta(R + k_{ba} t)$

$$BA = 1 \times (100 + 0.5 \times 2)$$

Bend allowance $BA = 101$ mm

Example 14.38

Spot welding of two 1 mm thick sheets of steel (density = 8000 kg/m^3) is carried out successfully by passing a certain amount of current for 0.1 s through the electrodes. The resultant weld nugget formed is 5 mm in diameter and 1.5 mm thick. If the latent heat of fusion of steel is 1400 kJ/kg and the effective resistance in the welding operation in 200 μΩ, the current passing through the electrodes is approximately.

(A) 1480 A (B) 3300 A (C) 4060 A (D) 9400 A

GATE 2005

Solution

Volume of nugget, $V = \frac{\pi}{4}d^2h = \frac{\pi}{4}5^2 \times 1.5$

$$V = 29.45 \text{ mm}^3$$

Mass of nugget, $\rho = 800 \times \frac{29.45}{(1000)^3} = 2.356 \times 10^{-4}$ kg

By heat balance equation,

Heat supplied = Heat gain

$$I^2Rt = mL$$

or $$I = \sqrt{\frac{mL}{Rt}} = \sqrt{\frac{2.356 \times 10^{-4} \times 1400 \times 10^3}{200 \times 10^{-6} \times 0.1}}$$

$$I = 4061 \text{ A}$$

Example 14.39

Two 1 mm thick steel sheets are to be spot welded at a current of 5000 A. Assuming effective resistance to be 200μΩ and current flow time of 0.2 s, heat generated during the process will be

(A) 0.2 J (B) 1 J (C) 5 J (D) 1000 J

GATE 2004

Solution

Heat generated, $Q = I^2Rt$

$$Q = 5000^2 \times 200 \times 10^{-6} \times 0.2$$

$$Q = 1000 \text{ J}$$

Example 14.40

10 mm diameter holes are to be punched in a steel sheet of 3 mm thickness. The shear strength of the material is 400 N/mm^2 and penetration is 40%. Shear provided on the punch is 2 mm. The blanking force during the operation will be

(A) 22.6 kN (B) 37.7 kN (C) 61.6 kN (D) 94.3 kN

GATE 2004

Solution

Given: $d = 10$ mm, $t = 3$mm, $\sigma_s = 400$ N/mm^2, $t_p = 0.4t$ and $t = 2$ mm.

Blanking force, $F = \sigma_s \pi dt\left(\frac{t_p}{t_s}\right)$

$$F = 400 \times \pi \times 10 \times 3 \times \left(\frac{0.4 \times 3}{2}\right)$$

$$F = 22.6 \text{ kN}$$

Example 14.41

Gray cast iron blocks $200 \times 100 \times 10$ mm^3 are to be cast in sand molds. Shrinkage allowance for pattern making is 1%. The ratio of the volume of pattern to that of the casting will be

(A) 0.97 (B) 0.99 (C) 1.01 (D) 1.03

GATE 2004

Solution

1% shrinkage allowance is given as addition to the each dimension of the casting.

Volume of pattern,

$$V_{\text{pattern}} = \left(1 + \frac{1}{100}\right)200 \times \left(1 + \frac{1}{100}\right)100 \times \left(1 + \frac{1}{100}\right)10$$

or $$V_{\text{pattern}} = \left(1 + \frac{1}{100}\right)^3 200 \times 100 \times 10$$

Volume of casting, $V_{\text{casting}} = 200 \times 100 \times 10$

The ratio of pattern volume to casting volume,

$$\frac{V_{\text{pattern}}}{V_{\text{casting}}} = \left(1 + \frac{1}{100}\right)^3$$

$$\frac{V_{\text{pattern}}}{V_{\text{casting}}} = 1.03$$

Example 14.42

In a rolling process, sheet of 25 mm thickness is rolled to 20 mm thickness. Roll is of diameter 600 mm and it rotates at 100 rpm. The roll strip contact length will be

(A) 5 mm (B) 39 mm (C) 78 mm (D) 120 mm

GATE 2004

Solution

Roll strip contact length is given by

$$L = \sqrt{R(t_o - t_f)}$$

Substituting $R = \frac{600}{2} = 300\,\text{mm}$, $t_o = 25$ mm and $t_f = 20\,\text{mm}$.

$$L = \sqrt{300(25-20)}$$

The roll strip contact length, $L = 38.72\,\text{mm}$

Example 14.43

From the lists given below, choose the most appropriate set of heat treatment process and corresponding process characteristic.

Process	Characteristics
P. Tempering	1. Austenite is converted into bainite
Q. Austempering	2. Austenite is converted into martensite
R. Martempering	3. Cementite is converted into globular structrure
	4. Both hardness and brittleness are reduced
	5. Carbon is absorbed into the metal

(A) P-3, Q-1, R-5 (B) P-4, Q-3, R-2

(C) P-4, Q-1, R-2 (D) P-1, Q-5, R-4

GATE 2004

Solution

P. Tempering→Both hardness and brittleness are reduced

Q. Austempering→ Austenite is converted into bainite

R. Martempering→Austenite is converted into martensite

Example 14.44

With a solidification factor of 0.97×10^6 s/m^2, the solidification time (in seconds) for a spherical casting of 200 mm diameter is

(A) 539 (B) 1078 (C) 4311 (D) 3233

GATE 2003

Solution

Solidification time is given by

$$t = c_m\left(\frac{V}{A}\right)^2$$

For sphere, $$t = c_m\left(\frac{\frac{4}{3}\pi r^3}{4\pi r^2}\right)^2 = c_m\left(\frac{d}{6}\right)^2$$

or $$t = 0.97\times10^6\times\left(\frac{0.2}{6}\right)^2$$

$$t = 1077.7\,\text{s}$$

Example 14.45

A shell of 100 mm diameter and 100 mm height with the corner radius of 0.4 mm is to be produced by cup drawing. The required blank diameter is

(A) 118 mm (B) 161 mm (C) 224 mm (D) 312 mm

GATE 2003

Solution

Given: $D_p = 100$ mm, $h = 100$ mm and $r = 0.4\,\text{mm}$.

Let D_b be the diameter of blank.

Volume of work material

$$\frac{\pi}{4}D_b^2 t = \frac{\pi}{4}D_p^2 t + \pi D_p t\,h; \qquad \left[\frac{D_p}{r} = 25 > 20\right]$$

or $$D_b = \sqrt{D_p^2 + 4D_p h} = \sqrt{100^2 + 4\times100\times100}$$

$$D_b = 223.6\,\text{mm}$$

Example 14.46

A brass billet is to be extruded from its initial diameter of 100 mm to a final diameter of 50 mm. The working temperature of 700°C and the extrusion constant is 250 MPa. The force required for extrusion is

(A) 5.44 MN (B) 2.72 MN

(C) 1.36 MN (D) 0.36 MN

GATE 2003

Solution

Reduction ratio (extrusion ratio), $r_x = \frac{A_o}{A_f}$

True strain, $\varepsilon = \ln r_x = \ln\left(\frac{A_o}{A_f}\right) = 2\ln\left(\frac{r_o}{r_f}\right)$

$$\varepsilon = 2\ln\left(\frac{100}{50}\right) = 1.38$$

At working temperature 700°C;

Average flow stress, $\bar{\sigma}_f = \frac{K\varepsilon^0}{1+0} = K = 250\,\text{MPa}$

Ram pressure, $p = \bar{\sigma}_f\varepsilon = 250\times1.38 = 345\,\text{MPa}$

Force required for extrusion, $F = pA_o$

$$F = 345\times\frac{\pi}{4}\times100^2 = 2709623.6\text{ N}$$

$$F = 2.7\,\text{MN}$$

Example 14.47

A metal disc of 20 mm diameter is to be punched from a sheet of 2 mm thickness. The punch and the die clearance is 3%. The required punch diameter is

(A) 19.88 mm (B) 19.94 mm

(C) 20.06 mm (D) 20.12 mm

GATE 2003

Solution

Punch diameter $= D_b - 2c = D_b - 2at$

$$= 20 - 2 \times \frac{3}{100} \times 2 = 19.88$$

Punch diameter = 19.88 mm

Example 14.48

The height of the down sprue is 175 mm and its cross-sectional area at the base is 200 mm^2. The cross-sectional area of the horizontal runner is also 200 mm^2. Assuming no losses, indicate the correct choice for the time (in seconds) required to fill a mold cavity of volume 10^6 mm^3 (using $g = 10$ m/s^2)

(A) 2.67 (B) 8.45 (C) 26.72 (D) 84.50

GATE 200

Solution

Head available at the base of sprue, $H = 175$ mm

Velocity of stream at base $v = \sqrt{2gH} = \sqrt{2 \times 10^4 \times 175}$

$$v = 1870.8 \text{ mm/s}$$

Time required to fill cavity

$$T = \frac{\text{Volume of cavity}}{\text{Flow rate}} = \frac{10^6}{200 \times 1870.8}$$

$$T = 2.67 \text{ s}$$

Example 14.49

For rigid perfectly-plastic work material, negligible interface friction and no redundant work, the theoretically maximum possible reduction in the wire drawing operation is:

(A) 0.36 (B) 0.63 (C) 1.00 (D) 2.72

GATE 2001

Solution

Area reduction, $r = \dfrac{A_o - A_f}{A_o}$

True strain, $\varepsilon = \ln\left(\dfrac{A_o}{A_f}\right) = \ln\left(\dfrac{1}{1-r}\right)$

Drawing stress, $\sigma_d = \bar{\sigma}_f \varepsilon = \bar{\sigma}_f \ln\left(\dfrac{1}{1-r}\right)$

The maximum possible draw stress is equal to yield strength of material. Therefore,

$$\frac{\sigma_d}{\bar{\sigma}_f} = 1 = \ln\left(\frac{1}{1-r_{max}}\right)$$

or $$\frac{1}{1-r_{max}} = e^1 = 2.71$$

$$r_{max} = 0.63$$

Example 14.50

Resistance spot welding is performed on two plates of 1.5 mm thickness with 6 mm diameter electrode, using 15000 A current for a time duration of 0.25 s. Assuming the interface resistance to be 0.0001 Ω, the heat generated to form the weld is

(A) 5625 W-s (B) 8437 W-s

(C) 22500 W-s (D) 33750 W-s

GATE 2001

Solution

Heat generated, $Q = I^2Rt$

$$Q = 15000^2 \times 0.0001 \times 0.25$$

$$Q = 5625 \text{ W-s}$$

Example 14.51

The "Jominy test" is used to find

(A) Young's modulus (B) Hardenability

(C) Yield strength (D) Thermal conductivity

GATE 2016

Solution

The "Jominy test" is used to find hardenability.

Example 14.52

Under optimal conditions of the process the temperatures experienced by a copper work piece in fusion welding, brazing and soldering are such that

(A) $T_{Welding} > T_{Soldering} > T_{Brazing}$ (B) $T_{Soldering} > T_{Welding} > T_{Brazing}$

(C) $T_{Brazing} > T_{Welding} > T_{Soldering}$ (D) $T_{Welding} > T_{Brazing} > T_{Soldering}$

GATE 2016

Solution

$$T_{Welding} > T_{Brazing} > T_{Soldering}$$

Example 14.53

The non-traditional machining process that essentially requires vacuum is

(A) Electron beam machining
(B) Electro chemical machining
(C) Electro chemical discharge machining
(D) Electro discharge machining

GATE 2016

Solution

Vacuum is required electron beam machining.

Example 14.54

A hypothetical engineering stress-strain curve shown in the figure has three straight lines PQ, QR, RS with coordinates $P(0,0)$, $Q(0.2,100)$, $R(0.6,140)$ and $S(0.8,130)$. 'Q' is the yield point, 'R' is the UTS point and 'S' the fracture point.

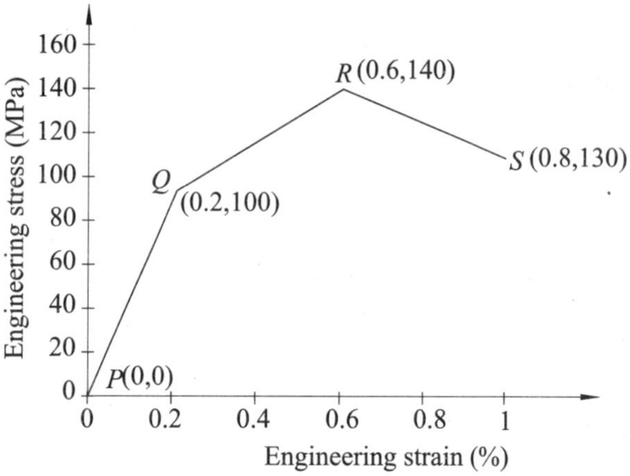

The toughness of the material (in MJ/m^3) is _____.

GATE 2016

Solution

Toughness of the material = Area under curve up to fracture point.

$$\text{Toughness} = \frac{1}{2}\left(100\times\frac{0.2}{100}\right)+\frac{1}{2}\left[(140+100)\times\left(\frac{0.6-0.2}{100}\right)\right]+\frac{1}{2}\left[(140+130)\times\left(\frac{0.8-0.6}{100}\right)\right]$$

$$\text{Toughness} = 0.85\ \text{MJ/m}^3$$

Example 14.55

A cylindrical job with diameter of 200 mm and height of 100 mm is to be cast using modulus method of riser design. Assume that the bottom surface of cylindrical riser does not contribute as cooling surface. If the diameter of the riser is equal to its height, then the height of the riser (in mm) is

(A) 150 (B) 200 (C) 100 (D) 125

GATE 2016

Solution

Using modulus method of riser design, let d and h be the diameter and height of riser respectively.

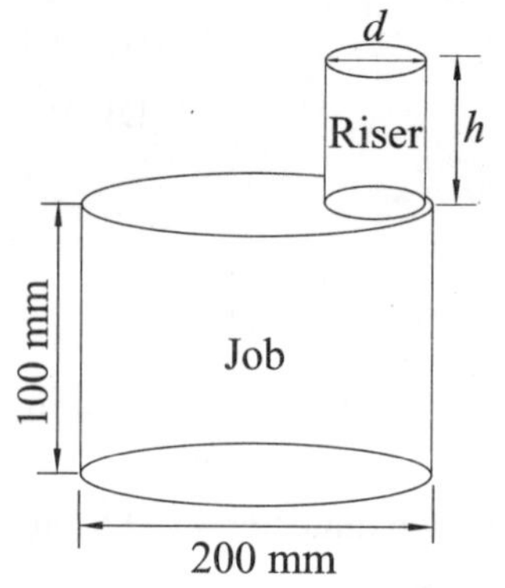

Solidification time of riser = 1.2 × Solidification time of job

$$c_m\left(\frac{V}{A}\right)_{\text{riser}} = 1.2\times c_m\left(\frac{V}{A}\right)_{\text{job}}$$

$$c_m\left(\frac{\pi\left(\frac{d}{2}\right)^2 h}{\pi dh+\frac{\pi}{4}d^2}\right) = 1.2\times c_m\left(\frac{\pi\left(\frac{200}{2}\right)^2\times 100}{\pi\times 200\times 100+2\times\frac{\pi}{4}\times 200^2}\right)$$

Substituting $d = h$ gives

$$d = h = 150\ \text{mm}$$

Example 14.56

A 300 mm thick slab is being cold rolled using roll of 600 mm diameter. If the coefficient of friction is 0.08, the maximum possible reduction (in mm) is ______.

GATE 2016

Solution

Maximum draft is given by

$$d = t_o - t_f = \mu^2 R$$

Substituting roll radius, $R = \frac{600}{2} = 300$ mm and $\mu = 0.08$, we have

$$d = (0.08)^2\times 300$$

$$d = 1.92\ \text{mm}$$

Example 14.57

In the phase diagram shown in the figure, four samples of the same composition are heated to temperatures marked by a, b, c and d.

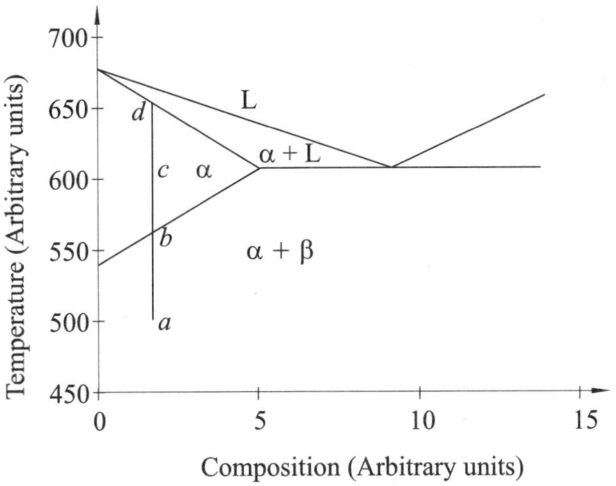

At which temperature will a sample get solutionised the fastest?

(A) *a* (B) *b* (C) *c* (D) *d*

GATE 2016

Solution

Fastest is solutionised at *c*.

Example 14.58

The welding process which uses a blanket of fusible granular flux is

(A) Tungsten inert gas welding

(B) Submerged arc welding

(C) Electroslag welding

(D) Thermit welding

GATE 2016

Solution

Submerged arc welding

Example 14.59

The value of true strain produced in compressing a cylinder to half its original length is

(A) 0.69 (B) 0.69 (C) 0.5 (D) 0.5

GATE 2016

Solution

$$\text{True strain, } \varepsilon = \ln\left(\frac{h_o}{h}\right) = \ln\left(\frac{h_o}{h_o/2}\right)$$

$$\varepsilon = \ln 2 = 0.69$$

Example 14.60

In a binary system of *A* and *B*, a liquid of 20% *A* (80% *B*) is coexisting with a solid of 70% *A* (30% *B*). For an overall composition having 40% *A*, the fraction of solid is

(A) 0.40 (B) 0.50 (C) 0.60 (D) 0.75

GATE 2016

Solution

Weight of liquid *A*; $W_{LA} = l_a \times W_l = 0.2 W_l$

Weight of solid *A*; $W_{SA} = 0.7 \times (W_T - W_l)$

$$W_A = 02 \times W_l + 0.7 \times (W_T - W_l)$$

or $$\frac{W_A}{W_T} = 0.7 - 05\left(\frac{W_l}{W_T}\right)$$

or $$0.4 = 0.7 - 0.5\left(\frac{W_l}{W_T}\right)$$

or $$(\% W_l) = \frac{W_l}{W_T} = \frac{3}{5}$$

$$(\% W_s) = 1 - \frac{3}{5} = 0.4$$

$$(\% W_s) = 0.4$$

Example 14.61

Gray cast iron blocks of size 100 mm × 50 mm × 10 mm with a central spherical cavity of diameter 4 mm are sand cast. The shrinkage allowance for the pattern is 3%. The ratio of the volume of the pattern to volume of the casting is______.

GATE 2016

Solution

Ratio of volume of pattern to casting

$$= \frac{(0.97 \times 100)(0.97 \times 50)(0.97 \times 10)}{100 \times 50 \times 10}$$

Ratio of volume of pattern to casting $= 0.913$

Volume of cavity is assumed to be small and negligible.

Example 14.62

The voltage-length characteristic of a direct current arc in an arc welding process is $V = (100 + 40l)$, where l is the length of the arc in mm and V is arc voltage in volts. During a welding operation, the arc length varies between 1 and 2 mm and the welding current is in the range 200 to 250 A. Assuming a linear power source, the short circuit current is ______ A.

GATE 2016

Solution

For arc length $l = 1\,\text{mm}$; $V_{l=1\,\text{mm}} = 140\,\text{V}$, $I_{l=1\,\text{mm}} = 250\,\text{A}$

For arc length $l = 2\,\text{mm}$; $V_{l=2\,\text{mm}} = 180\,\text{V}$, $I_{l=2\,\text{mm}} = 200\,\text{A}$

Arc voltage and current are related to open circuit voltage

V_o and short circuit current I_s as:

$$V_{arc} = V_o\left(1 - \frac{I}{I_s}\right)$$

$$140 = V_o\left(1 - \frac{250}{I_s}\right) \quad \text{(i)}$$

$$180 = V_o\left(1 - \frac{200}{I_s}\right) \quad \text{(ii)}$$

Equations (i) and (ii) give

Short circuit current, $I_s = 425$ A

Example 14.63

Engineering strain of a mild steel sample is recorded as 0.100%. The true strain is

(A) 0.010% (B) 0.055% (C) 0.099% (D) 0.101%

GATE 2016

Solution

Relation between engineering strain (E) and true strain (e) is

$$e = \int_{l_1}^{l_2} \frac{dl}{l} = \ln\left(\frac{l_2}{l_1}\right)$$

or $$e = \ln\left(\frac{l_1 + \Delta l}{l_1}\right) = \ln\left(1 + \frac{\Delta l}{l_1}\right) = \ln(1 + e)$$

or $$e = \ln\left(1 + \frac{0.1}{100}\right)$$

$$e = 0.0999\,\%$$

Example 14.64

Equal amounts of a liquid metal at the same temperature are poured into three moulds made of steel, copper and aluminum. The shape of the cavity is a cylinder with 15 mm diameter. The size of the moulds are such that the outside temperature of the moulds do not increase appreciably beyond the atmospheric temperature during solidification. The sequence of solidification in the mould from the fastest to slowest is (Thermal conductivities of steel, copper and aluminum are 60.5, 401 and 237 W/m-K, respectively. Specific heats of steel, copper and aluminum are 434, 385 and 903 J/kg-K, respectively. Densities of steel, copper and aluminum are 7854, 8933 and 2700 kg/m^3, respectively.)

(A) Copper - Steel - Aluminum
(B) Aluminum - Steel - Copper
(C) Copper - Aluminum - Steel
(D) Steel - Copper - Aluminum

GATE 2016

Solution

Let A and V be the surface area and volume of body respectively.

Heat transfer from body by convection = Heat loss by body

$$h\,A(T - T_a) = -\rho V c\frac{dT}{dt}$$

or $$\frac{dT}{dt} = -\frac{h\,A}{\rho Vc}(T - T_a)$$

or $$\frac{dT}{dt} = -\frac{h\,l}{k}\frac{1}{l^2} \times \frac{k}{\rho c}(T - T_a)$$

where $l = \frac{V}{A}$ (Characteristic length)

or $$\frac{dT}{dt} = \left(-\frac{Bi}{l^2} \times (T - T_a)\right)\frac{k}{\rho c}$$

where $Bi = \frac{hl}{k}$ (Biot number)

Cooling rate $\frac{dT}{dt} \propto \frac{k}{\rho c}$

	k	c	ρ	$\frac{k}{\rho c}$
Steel	60.5	434	7854	1.7749×10^{-5}
Copper	401	385	8933	1.1659×10^{-4}
Aluminum	237	903	2700	9.720×10^{-5}

$$\left(\frac{k}{\rho c}\right)_{copper} > \left(\frac{k}{\rho c}\right)_{alum} > \left(\frac{k}{\rho c}\right)_{steel}$$

The sequence of solidification in the mould from the fastest to slowest is

Copper - Aluminum - Steel

Example 14.65

Spot welding of two steel sheets each 2 mm thick is carried out successfully by passing 4 kA of current for 0.2 s through the electrodes. The resulting weld nugget formed between the sheets is 5 mm in diameter. Assuming cylindrical shape for the nugget, the thickness of the nugget is_____mm.

Latent heat of fusion for steel	1400 kJ/kg
Effective resistance of the weld joint	200 μΩ
Density of steel	8000 kg/m^3

GATE 2016

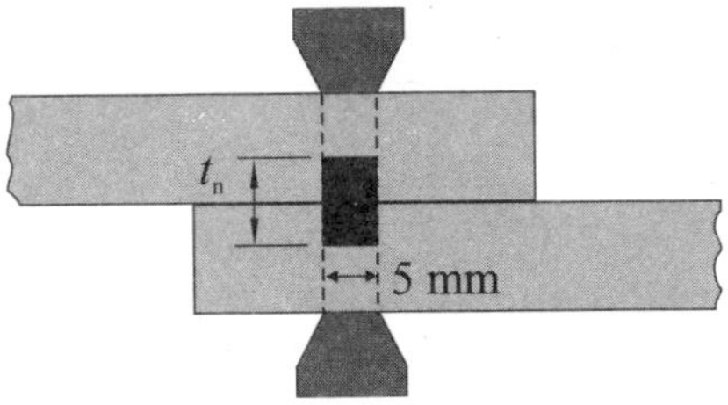

Solution

Heat supplied, $Q = I^2 R\tau$ (i)

Energy required for melting

$$= mL = \left(\rho \frac{\pi}{4} d^2 t_n\right) L \quad \text{(ii)}$$

Equating Equations (i) and (ii), we have

$$I^2 R\tau = \left(\rho \frac{\pi}{4} d^2 t_n\right) L$$

$$t_n = \frac{4 I^2 R\tau}{\rho \pi d^2 L}$$

Substituting given values $I = 4\,\text{kA}$, $\tau = 0.2$ s, $d = 5$ mm, $L = 1400\,\text{kJ/kg}$, $R = 200\,\mu\Omega$ and $\rho = 8000$ kg/m^3, we have

$$t_n = \frac{4 \times 4000^2 \times 200 \times 10^{-6} \times 02}{8000 \times \pi \times \left(\frac{5}{1000}\right)^2 \times 1400 \times 10^3}$$

$$t_n = 2.91\,\text{mm}$$

Example 14.66

In a sheet metal of 2 mm thickness, a hole of 10 mm diameter needs to be punched. The yield strength in tension of the sheet material is 100 MPa and its ultimate shear strength is 80 MPa. The force required to punch the hole (in kN) is ______.

GATE 2016

Solution

Force required to punch the hole is

$$F = \tau_s A_s = \tau_s \pi d t$$

Substituting $t = 2$ mm, $d = 10$ mm and $\tau_s = 80\,\text{MPa}$, we have

$$F = 80 \times 10^6 \times \pi \times \frac{10}{1000} \times \frac{2}{1000}$$

$$F = 5026.5 \text{ N}$$

$$F = 5.026 \text{ kN}$$

Example 14.67

In an arc welding process, welding speed is doubled. Assuming all other process parameters to be constant, the cross-sectional area of the weld bead will

(A) increase by 25% (B) increase by 50%

(C) reduce by 25% (D) reduce by 50%

GATE 2017

Solution

Rate of heat energy delivered $HR_w = f_1 f_2 VI = U_m A_w v$

$$A_w \propto \frac{1}{v} \quad \text{other parameters constant}$$

$$A_1 \propto \frac{1}{v_1} \quad \text{(i)}$$

$$A_2 \propto \frac{1}{(2v_1)} \quad \text{(ii)}$$

From equations (i) and (ii), we have

$$\frac{A_2}{A_1} = \frac{1}{2}$$

$$A_2 = \frac{A_1}{2}$$

By doubling welding speed area reduce by 50%.

Example 14.68

A 10 mm deep cylindrical cup with diameter of 15 mm is drawn from a circular blank. Neglecting the variation in the sheet thickness, the diameter (upto 2 decimal points accuracy) of the blank is ____ mm.

GATE 2017

Solution

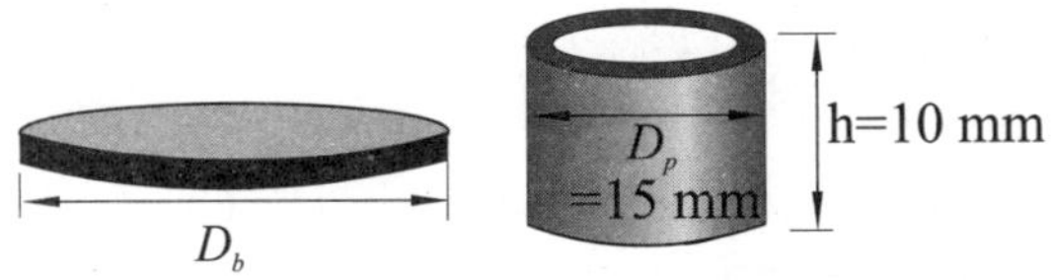

$$\text{Volume } V = \frac{\pi}{4} D_b^2 t = \frac{\pi}{4} D_p^2 t + \pi D_p t\, h$$

or $$D_b = \sqrt{D_b^2 + 4D_p h}$$

$$D_b = \sqrt{15^2 + 4 \times 15 \times 10}$$

$$D_b = 28.72\,\text{mm}$$

Example 14.69

A sprue in a sand mould has a top diameter of 20 mm and

height of 200 mm. The velocity of the molten metal at the entry of the sprue is 0.5 m/s. Assume acceleration due to gravity as 9.8 m/s^2 and neglect all losses. If the mould is well ventilated, the velocity (upto 3 decimal points accuracy) of the molten metal at the bottom of the sprue is _____ m/s.

GATE 2017

Solution

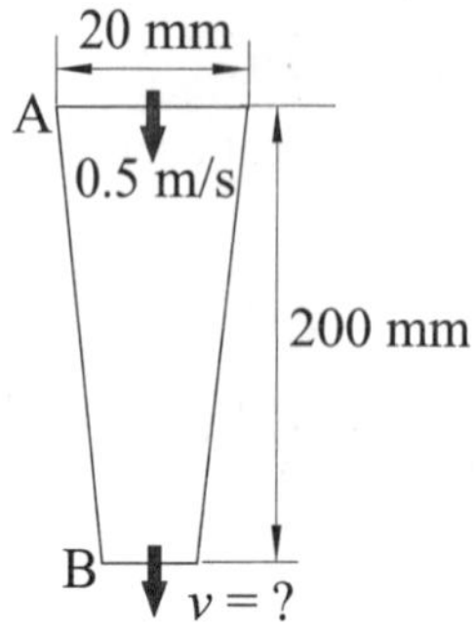

Applying Bernoulli's equation between A and B

$$\frac{p_A}{\rho g}+\frac{v_A^2}{2g}+z_A=\frac{p_B}{\rho g}+\frac{v_B^2}{2g}+z_B$$

$$\frac{p_{atm}}{\rho g}+\frac{0.5^2}{2g}+0.2=\frac{p_{atm}}{\rho g}+\frac{v}{2g}+0$$

$$v = 2.043 \text{ m/s}$$

Example 14.70

The crystal structure of aluminium is

(A) body-centred cubic (B) face-centred cubic

(C) close-packed hexagonal (D) body-centred tetragonal

GATE 2017

Solution

The crystal structure of aluminium is face-centred cubic.

Example 14.71

Given the atomic weight of Fe is 56 and that of C is 12, the weight percentage of carbon in cementite (Fe_3C) is_____ .

GATE 2017

Solution

Percentage of Carbon by weight in cementite (Fe_3C)

$$=\frac{12}{56\times 3+12}\times 100$$

Percentage of Carbon in cementite (Fe_3C) = 6.67 %

Example 14.72

A strip of 120 mm width and 8 mm thickness is rolled between two 300 mm-diameter rolls to get a strip of 120 mm width and 7.2 mm thickness. The speed of the strip at the exit is 30 m/min. There is no front or back tension. Assuming uniform roll pressure of 200 MPa in the roll bite and 100% mechanical efficiency, the minimum total power (in kW) required to drive the two rolls is_____.

GATE 2017

Solution

Given: $w = 120$ mm, $t_o = 8$ mm, $R=\frac{300}{2}=150$ mm, $t_f = 7.2$ mm, $V_f = 30$ m/min, $p = 200$ MPa

Rolling force $F = w\int_0^L p\,dL = wpL$

Contact length $L=\sqrt{R(t_0-T_f)}$

Power required to drive the two rolls is

$$P = 2\times 2\pi NFL = 4\pi\left(\frac{V_f}{2\pi R}\right)wpL\times L$$

$$P=\frac{4\pi V_f wpR(t_0-T_f)}{2\pi R}$$

$$P=\frac{4\pi\times\frac{30}{60}\times\frac{120}{1000}}{2\pi\times\frac{150}{1000}}\times 200\times 10^6\times\frac{150}{1000}\times\frac{(8-7.2)}{1000}$$

$$P = 9.6 \text{ kW}$$

Example 14.73

The number of atoms per unit cell and the number of slip systems, respectively, for a face-centred cubic (FCC) crystal are

(A) 3, 3 (B) 3, 12 (C) 4, 12 (D) 4, 48

GATE 2018

Solution

Number of atoms per unit cell in FCC = 4

Number of slip system = 12

Example 14.74

The maximum reduction in cross-sectional area per pass (R) of a cold wire drawing process is

$$R = 1-e^{-(n+1)}$$

where n represents the strain hardening coefficient. For the case of a perfectly plastic material, R is

(A) 0.865 (B) 0.826 (C) 0.777 (D) 0.632

GATE 2018

Solution

Condition for maximum reduction per pass,

Maximum possible draw stress = Yield strength

$$\bar{\sigma}_f \ln\left(\frac{A_o}{A_f}\right)=\sigma\ln\left(\frac{A_o}{A_f}\right)=\sigma$$

or $$\ln\left(\frac{A_o}{A_f}\right)=1$$

or $$\frac{A_o}{A_f}=e$$

or $\dfrac{1}{1-R}=e$

Maximum reduction in area $R=\dfrac{e-1}{1}=0.632$

$$R=0.632$$

Example 14.75

The percentage scrap in a sheet metal blanking operation of a continuous strip of sheet metal as shown in the figure is_______.

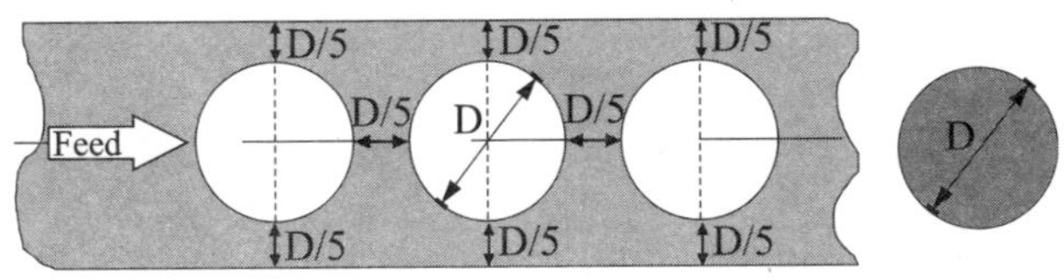

GATE 2018

Solution

Consider rectangle *ABCD*.

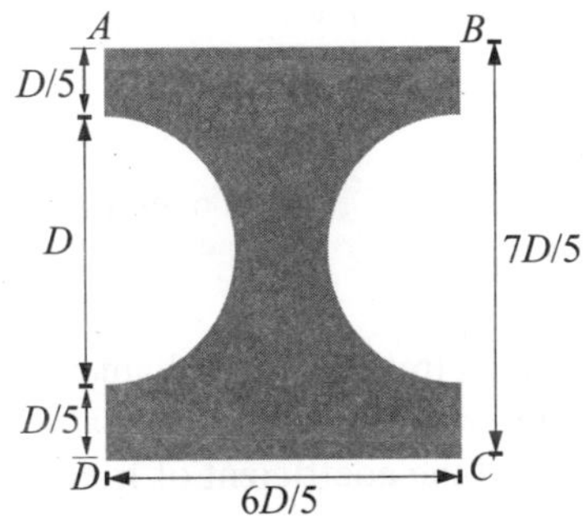

Rectangle *ABCD* is continuous repeated.

Area of rectangle *ABCD*, $A_t=\dfrac{7}{5}D\times\dfrac{6}{5}D=\dfrac{42}{25}D^2$

Area of blanking disc, $A_b=\dfrac{\pi}{4}D^2$

$$\% \text{ of scrap}=\frac{A_t-A_b}{A_t}\times 100\%$$

$$\% \text{ of scrap}=\frac{\frac{42}{25}D^2-\frac{\pi}{4}D^2}{\frac{42}{25}D^2}\times 100\%$$

$$\% \text{ of scrap}=53.25\%$$

Example 14.76

The true stress (σ) - true strain (ε) diagram of a strain hardening material is shown in figure. First, there is loading up to point A, i.e., up to stress of 500 MPa and strain of 0.5. Then from point A, there is unloading up to point B, i.e., to stress of 100 MPa. Given that the Young's modulus E = 200 GPa, the natural strain at point B (ε_B) is________.

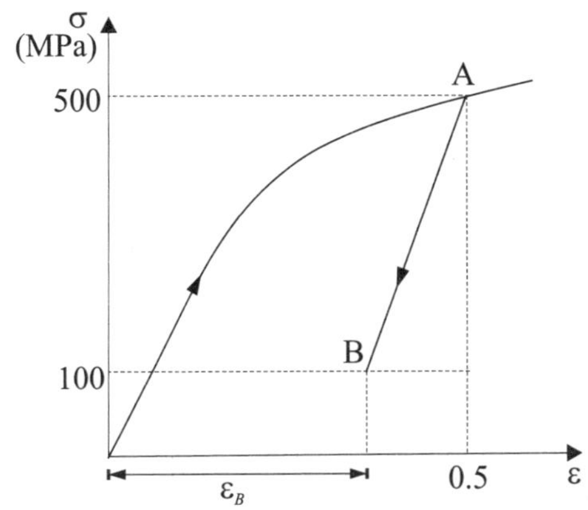

GATE 2018

Solution

We know that slope of line AB is equal to Young's Modulus E.

$$E=\frac{500-100}{0.5-\varepsilon_B}$$

$$200\times 10^3=\frac{500-100}{0.5-\varepsilon_B}$$

$$\varepsilon_B=0.498$$

Example 14.77

A bar is compressed to half of its original length. The magnitude of true strain produced in the deformed bar is_________ .

GATE 2018

Solution

True strain, $\varepsilon=\ln\left(\dfrac{L}{L_o}\right)$

Substituting $L=\dfrac{L_o}{2}$, we have

$$\varepsilon=\ln\left(\frac{L_o/2}{L_o}\right)=\ln(0.5)$$

$$\varepsilon=-0.693$$

$$\text{True strain } \varepsilon=0.693$$

Example 14.78

Denoting *L* as liquid and *M* as solid in a phase-diagram with the subscripts representing different phases, a *eutectoid* reaction is described by

(A) $M_1 \rightarrow M_2 + M_3$ (B) $L_1 \rightarrow M_1 + M_2$

(C) $L_1 + M_1 \rightarrow M_2$ (D) $M_1 + M_2 \rightarrow M_3$

GATE 2018

Solution

$$M_1 \rightarrow M_2 + M_3$$

Example 14.79

During solidification of a pure molten metal, the grains in the casting near the mould wall are

(A) coarse and randomly oriented

(B) fine and randomly oriented

(C) fine and ordered

(D) coarse and ordered

GATE 2018

Solution

During solidification of a pure molten metal, the grains in the casting near the mould wall are fine and randomly oriented.

Example 14.80

Match the following products with the suitable manufacturing process

	Product		Manufacturing Process
P	Toothpaste tube	1	Centrifugal casting
Q	Metallic pipes	2	Blow moulding
R	Plastic bottles	3	Rolling
S	Threaded bolts	4	Impact extrusion

(A) P-4, Q-3, R-1, S-2 (B) P-2, Q-1, R-3, S-4

(C) P-4, Q-1, R-2, S-3 (D) P-1, Q-3, R-4, S-2

GATE 2018

Solution

Toothpaste tube → Impact extrusion

Metallic pipes → Centrifugal casting

Plastic bottles → Blow moulding

Threaded bolts → Rolling

Example 14.81

The true stress (in MPa) versus true strain relationship for a metal is given by

$$\sigma = 1020\varepsilon^{0.4}$$

The cross-sectional area at the start of a test (when the stress and strain values are equal to zero) is 100 mm^2. The cross-sectional area at the time of necking (in mm^2) is______.

GATE 2018

Solution

Load $P = \sigma A \quad \Rightarrow \quad dP = A\,d\sigma + \sigma\,dA$

At ultimate point, $dP = 0 \Rightarrow \quad \dfrac{d\sigma}{\sigma} = -\dfrac{dA}{A}$ (i)

Since $Al = \text{constant} \quad \Rightarrow \quad \dfrac{dl}{l} = -\dfrac{dA}{A} = d\varepsilon$ (ii)

From Equations (i) and (ii) we obtain

$$\frac{d\sigma}{\sigma} = d\varepsilon \quad \Rightarrow \quad \frac{d\sigma}{d\varepsilon} = \sigma$$

Substituting $\sigma = 1020\varepsilon^{0.4}$;

$$\frac{d}{d\varepsilon}1020\varepsilon^{0.4} = 1020\varepsilon^{0.4}$$

$\varepsilon = 0.4$ Neck formation start at ultimate point

$$\ln\left(\frac{A_o}{A_f}\right) = 0.4$$

$$A_f = \frac{A_o}{e^{0.4}} = \frac{100}{e^{0.4}} = 67.032$$

Cross-section area at the time of necking = 67.032 mm^2

Example 14.82

A steel wire is drawn from an initial diameter (d_i) of 10 mm to a final diameter (d_f) of 7.5 mm. The half cone angle (α) of the die is 5° and the coefficient of friction (μ) between the die and the wire is 0.1. The average of the initial and final yield stress $[\sigma_Y)_{avg}]$ is 350 MPa. The equation for drawing stress σ_f, (in MPa) is given as:

$$\sigma_f = (\sigma_Y)_{avg}\left\{1 + \frac{1}{\mu \cot\alpha}\right\}\left[1 - \left(\frac{d_f}{d_i}\right)^{2\mu\cot\alpha}\right]$$

The drawing stress (in MPa) required to carry out this operation is _________ .

GATE 2018

Solution

Substituting given values $d_i = 10$ mm, $d_f = 10$ mm, $\alpha = 5°$, $\mu = 0.1$ and $[\sigma_Y)_{avg}] = 350$ MPa

$$\text{Drawing stress } \sigma_f = 350\left\{1 + \frac{1}{0.1\cot 5}\right\}\left[1 - \left(\frac{7.5}{10}\right)^{2\times 0.1\cot 5}\right]$$

$$\sigma_f = 316.25 \text{ MPa}$$

Example 14.83

For sand-casting a steel rectangular plate with dimensions 80 mm × 120 mm × 20 mm, a cylindrical riser has to be designed. The height of the riser is equal to its diameter. The total solidification time for the casting is 2 minutes. In Chvorinov's law for the estimation of the total solidification time, exponent is to be taken as 2. For a solidification time of 3 minutes in the riser, the diameter (in mm) of the riser is ______ .

GATE 2018

Solution

Chvorinov's law, Solidification time $t = k\left(\frac{V}{A}\right)^2$

$$\frac{t_{\text{casting}}}{t_{\text{riser}}} = \left(\frac{V}{A}\right)^2_{\text{casting}} \times \left(\frac{A}{V}\right)^2_{\text{riser}}$$

$$\frac{t_{\text{casting}}}{t_{\text{riser}}} = \left(\frac{lbh}{2(lb+bh+hl)}\right)^2 \times \left(\frac{2\pi r^2 + 2\pi rh}{\pi r^2 h}\right)^2$$

$$\frac{2}{3} = \left(\frac{80\times 120\times 20}{2(80\times 120 + 120\times 20 + 20\times 80)}\right)^2 \times \left(\frac{3}{r}\right)^2$$

$r = 25.92$ mm

Diameter of riser = 51.84 mm

Example 14.84

A welding operation is being performed with voltage = 30 V and current = 100 A. The cross-sectional area of the weld bead is 20 mm^2. The work-piece and filler are of titanium for which the specific energy of melting is 14 J/mm^3. Assuming a thermal efficiency of the welding process 70%, the welding speed (in mm/s) is __________.

GATE 2018

Solution

Rate of heat energy delivered to the operation $= U_m A_m v$

$$\eta \times VI = U_m A_m v$$

Welding speed $v = \frac{\eta \times VI}{U_m A_m}$

Substituting $V = 30$ V, $I = 100$ A, $A = 20$ mm^2, $U_m = 14$ J/mm^3 and $\eta = 0.70$. We have

$$v = \frac{0.70\times 30\times 100}{14\times 20} = 7.5$$

Welding speed $v = 7.5$ mm/s

Example 14.85

In a casting process, a vertical channel through which molten metal flows downward from pouring basin to runner for reaching the mold cavity is called

(A) blister (B) sprue (C) riser (D) pin hole

GATE 2019

Solution

Sprue

Example 14.86

Which one of the following welding methods provides the highest heat flux (W/mm^2)?

(A) Oxy-acetylene gas welding

(B) Tungsten inert gas welding

(C) Plasma arc welding

(D) Laser beam welding

GATE 2019

Solution

($\approx 10^9$ W/cm^2) Laser beam welding

Example 14.87

Match the following sand mould casting defects with their respective causes.

	Defect		Cause
P	Blow hole	1	Poor collapsibility
Q	Misrun	2	Mold erosion
R	Hot tearing	3	Poor permeability
S	Wash	4	Insufficient fluidity

A) P-4, Q-3, R-1, S-2 (B) P-3, Q-4, R-2, S-1

(C) P-2, Q-4, R-1, S-3 (D) P-3, Q-4, R-1, S-2

GATE 2019

Solution

P-3, Q-4, R-1, S-2

Example 14.88

Hardenability of steel is a measure of

(A) the ability to harden when it is cold worked

(B) the maximum hardness that can be obtained when it is austenitized and then quenched

(C) the depth to which required hardening is obtained when it is austenitized and then quenched

(D) the ability to retain its hardness when it is heated to elevated temperatures

GATE 2019

Solution

the depth to which required hardening is obtained when it is austenitized and then quenched

Example 14.89

The fluidity of molten metal of cast alloys (without any addition of fluxes) increases with increase in

(A) viscosity (B) surface tension

(C) freezing range (D) degree of superheat

GATE 2019

Solution

degree of superheat

Example 14.90

The cold forming process in which a hardened tool is pressed against a workpiece (when there is relative motion between the tool and the workpiece) to produce a roughened surface with a regular pattern is

(A) Roll forming (B) Strip rolling

(C) Knurling (D) Chamfering

GATE 2019

Solution

Knurling

Example 14.91

The binary phase diagram of metals P and Q is shown in the figure. An alloy X containing 60% P and 40% Q (by weight) is cooled from liquid to solid state. The fractions of solid and liquid (in weight percent) at 1250°C, respectively, will be

(A) 77.8% and 22.2% (B) 22.2% and 77.8%

(C) 68.0% and 32.0% (D) 32.0% and 68.0%

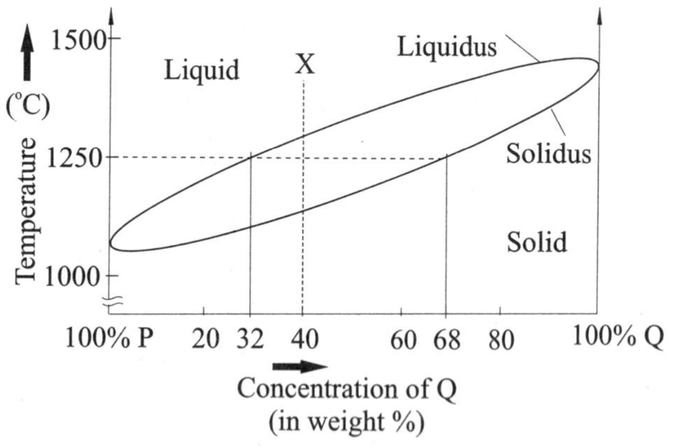

GATE 2019

Solution

Applying Lever Rule

$$\% \text{ Solid} = \frac{\text{Length of tie - line on opposite side}}{\text{Total length of tie - line}} \times 100$$

$$\% \text{ Solid} = \frac{40-32}{68-32} \times 100 = 22.22\ \%$$

$$\% \text{ Liquid} = \frac{68-40}{68-32} \times 100 = 77.77\ \%$$

22.22% and 77.77%

Example 14.92

The figure shows a pouring arrangement for casting of a metal block. Frictional losses are negligible. The acceleration due to gravity is 9.81 m/s^2. The time (in s, round off to two decimal places) to fill up the mold cavity (of size 40 cm × 30 cm × 15 cm) is ________.

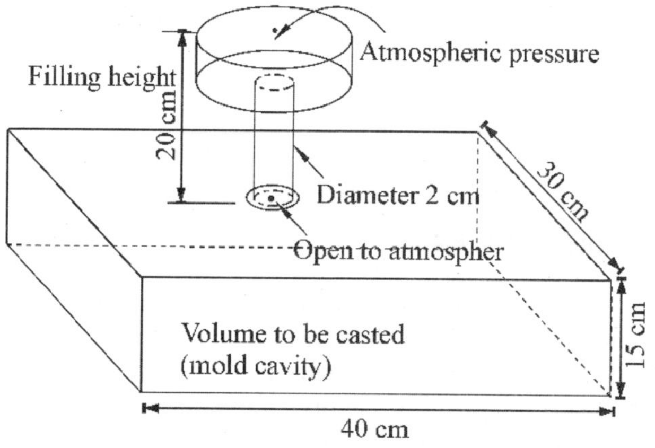

GATE 2019

Solution

Time to fill up the mold cavity;

$$T = \frac{\text{Volume of cavity (V)}}{\text{Volume flow rate of metal (Q)}}$$

$$T = \frac{l \times b \times w}{A \times V} = \frac{l \times b \times w}{\frac{\pi}{4} \times d^2 \times \sqrt{2gh}}$$

Substituting given values $l = 40$ cm, $b = 30$ cm, $w = 15$ cm, $d = 2$ cm and $h = 20$ cm, we have

$$T = \frac{40 \times 15 \times 30}{\frac{\pi}{4} \times 2^2 \times \sqrt{2 \times 981 \times 20}}\ \text{s}$$

$T = 28.94$ s

Example 14.93

A gas tungsten arc welding operation is performed using a current of 250 A and an arc voltage of 20 V at a welding speed of 5 mm/s. Assuming that the arc efficiency is 70%, the net heat input per unit length of the weld will be________ kJ/mm (round off to one decimal place)

GATE 2019

Solution

Rate of heat energy delivered $HR_w = f_1\ VI$ J/s

Rate of heat energy delivered per unit length

$$= \frac{f_1\ VI}{v} \text{ J/mm}$$

Substituting given values $I = 250$ A, $V = 20$ V, $v = 5$ mm/s and $f_1 = 0.7$, we have

Rate of heat energy delivered per unit length

$$= \frac{0.7 \times 250 \times 20}{5} = 700 \text{ J/mm}$$

Rate of heat energy delivered per unit length $= 0.70$ J/mm

Example 14.94

The thickness of a sheet is reduced by rolling (without any change in width) using 600 mm diameter rolls. Neglect elastic deflection of the rolls and assume that the coefficient of friction at the roll-workpiece interface is 0.05. The sheet enters the rotating rolls unaided. If the initial sheet thickness is 2 mm, the minimum possible final thickness that can be produced by this process in a single pass is _______ mm (round off to two decimal places).

GATE 2019

Solution

Maximum possible draft for the given coefficient of friction is

$$d_{max} = \mu^2 R$$

or $$t_o - t_f = \mu^2 R$$

Substituting given values $t_o = 2$ mm, $R = 300$ mm and $\mu = 0.05$, we have

$$2 - t_f = 0.05^2 \times 300$$

$$t_f = 1.25 \text{ mm}$$

Minimum possible thickness, $t_f = 1.25$ mm

14.3 PRACTICE PAPER

Time: 3 hours **Max. Marks: 100**

Q.1 to Q.30 carry one mark each

Q.1 to Q.20 Multiple Choice Questions

Q.1 Consider the following quenching media

1. Oil
2. Water
3. Water + NaOH
4. Brine

The correct sequence of these media in order of increasing hardness of steel undergoing heat treatment

(A) $1 \to 3 \to 2 \to 4$ (B) $2 \to 1 \to 3 \to 4$

(C) $1 \to 2 \to 3 \to 4$ (D) $4 \to 3 \to 2 \to 1$

Q.2 Match List-I (crystal structure) with List-II (Atomic packing factor) and select the correct answer using the codes given below lists.

List-I		List-II	
(P)	Simple cubic	(1)	74 %
(Q)	Body-centered cubic	(2)	74 %
(R)	Face-centered cubic	(3)	52 %
(S)	Hexagonal close packed	(4)	68 %

(A) P-3, Q-4, R-2, S-1 (B) P-4, Q-3, R-2, S-1

(C) P-4, Q-3, R-1, S-2 (D) None of these

Q.3 A 50 mm diameter disc is to be punched out from a carbon steel sheet 1.0 mm thick. The diameter of the punch should be

(A) 49.925 mm (B) 50.00 mm

(C) 50.075 mm (D) None of these

Q.4 A compound die will be used to blank and punch a washer out of aluminum alloy sheet stock 3 mm thick. Dimensions of washer are shown in figure. The clearance is 6% of plate thickness. Shear strength of material is 300 MPa. The size of punch and die in blanking operations are, respectively

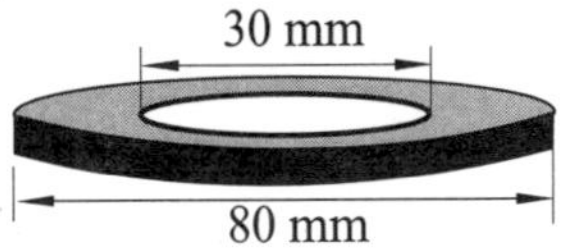

(A) 80.00 mm, 79.64 mm (B) 80.00 mm, 80.36 mm

(C) 79.64 mm, 80.00 mm (D) 79.64 mm, 80.36 mm

Q.5 A 50 mm flat plate is to reduced to 35 mm in a single pass cold rolling operation. The roll diameter is 600 mm.

The minimum coefficient of friction that would make this rolling operation possible is

(A) 0.135 (B) 0.192 (C) 0.223 (D) 0.324

Q.6 Two castings of the same metal have the same surface area. One casting is in the form of a sphere and the other is a cube. The ratio of the solidification time for the sphere to that of the cube is

(A) 1 (B) $\frac{6}{\pi}$ (C) 2π (D) $\frac{7}{\pi}$

Q.7 The voltage (V) - length (l) characteristic of DC arc is given by $V = 20 + 4l$ V (l in mm). During welding operation, the arc length is expected to vary between 4 mm and 6 mm with the welding current limited between 450 A and 550 A. The power source has a linear characteristic. The arc power (in kW) at an arc length of 5 mm is

(A) 15 kW (B) 20 kW (C) 22 kW (D) 18 kW

Q.8 The height of the down-sprue is 175 mm and its cross-sectional area of the base is $200\,\text{mm}^2$. The cross-sectional area of the horizontal runner is also $200\,\text{mm}^2$. Assuming no losses, indicate the correct choice for the time (in seconds) required to fill a mold cavity of volume $10^6\,\text{mm}^3$.

(A) 2.67 (B) 8.45 (C) 26.72 (D) 84.50

Q.9 A blanking operation has to be performed on a 2 mm thick sheet to obtain 80 mm diameter piece. The shear strength of the sheet material is 450 MPa. The blanking force (in kN) required for this operation is

(A) 450.0 kW (B) 226.2 kN

(C) 210.5 kN (D) 160.81 kN

Q.10 A screen with 300 mesh count has wires with a diameter of 0.0012 inch. The maximum particle size that will pass through the wire mesh, is

(A) 0.0081 (B) 0.006 (C) 0.0012 (D) 0.00213

Q.11 The stress-strain behaviour of a material is shown in figure. It resilience and toughness in Nm/m^3, are respectively

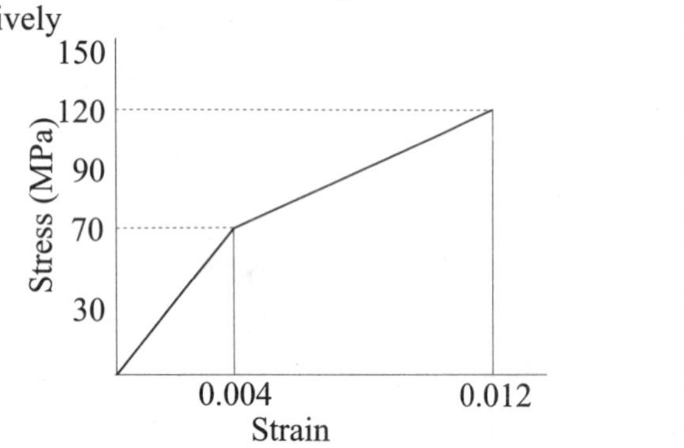

(A) $28 \times 10^4, 76 \times 10^4$ (B) $28 \times 10^4, 48 \times 10^4$

(C) $14 \times 10^4, 90 \times 10^4$ (D) $76 \times 10^4, 104 \times 10^4$

Q.12 The constant c_m in Chvorinov's rule is given as $3\,\text{s/mm}^2$ and is used to produce a cylindrical casting with a diameter of 50 mm and a height of 100 mm. The time for the casting to fully solidify is

(A) 260 s (B) 300 s (C) 606 s (D) None of these

Q.13 A series of rolling operations are to be used to reduce the thickness of a plate from 60 mm down to 30 mm in a tandem rolling mill as shown in figure.

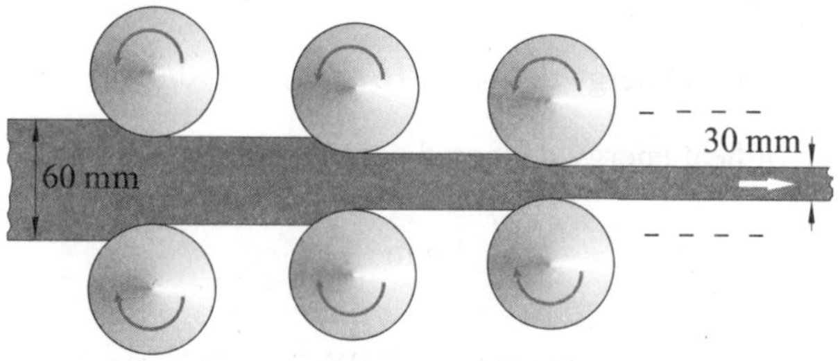

Roll diameter = 750 mm and coefficient of friction between rolls and work = 0.15. The specification is that the draft is to be equal on each pass. The minimum number of passes required

(A) 2 (B) 3 (C) 4 (D) 5

Q.14 A spherical drop of molten metal of radius 2 mm was found to solidity in 10 minutes. A similar drop of radius 4 mm would solidify in

(A) 40 s (B) 28.30 s (C) 20 s (D) 14.14 s

Q.15 A compound die will be used to blank and punch a washer out of aluminum alloy sheet stock 3 mm thick. Dimensions of washer are shown in figure. The clearance is 6% of plate thickness. Shear strength of material is 300 MPa. The size of punch and die in punching operations are, respectively

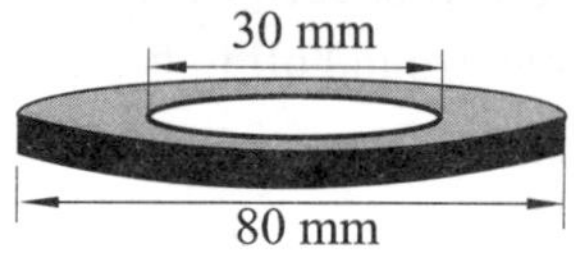

(A) 30.36 mm, 30 mm (B) 29.64 mm, 30 mm

(C) 30 mm, 30.36 mm (D) None of these

Q.16 A strip is to be rolled from a thickness of 30 mm to 15 mm using a two-high mill having rolls of diameter 300 mm. The coefficient of friction for unaided bite should nearly be

(A) 0.31 (B) 0.5 (C) 0.25 (D) 0.07

Q.17 A cylindrical billet that is 200 mm long and 40 mm in diameter is reduced by indirect extrusion to a 20 mm diameter as shown in figure.

Die angle = 90°. If the Johnson equation has $a = 0.8$ and $b = 1.5$, and the flow curve for the work metal has

$K = 800$ MPa and $n = 0.15$. The extrusion strain is.

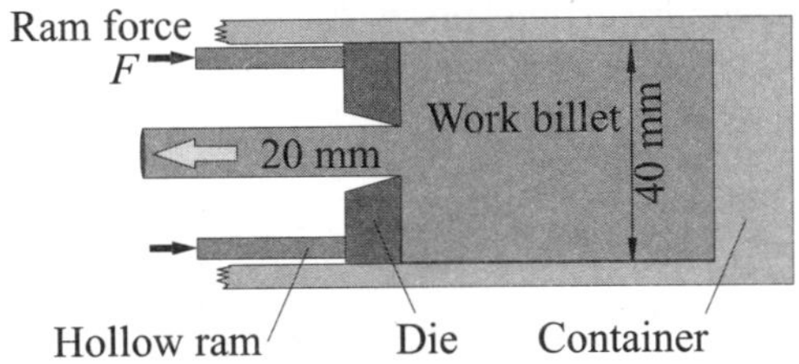

(A) 2.76 (B) 2.07 (C) 1.54 (D) 2.88

Q.18 The value of the strain hardening exponent for a metal that will cause the average flow stress to be $\frac{3}{4}$ of the final flow stress after deformation, is

(A) 0.233 (B) 0.333 (C) 0.392 (D) 0.40

Q.19 Match the properties in Column-I with the options in Column-II.

Column-I		Column-II	
(P)	Toughness	(1)	Resistance to plastic deformation
(Q)	Resilience	(2)	Time dependent permanent deformation under constant load
(R)	Creep	(3)	Total elongation of failure
(S)	Hardness	(4)	Area under the stress-strain curve
		(5)	Area under the elastic part of the stress-strain curve

(A) P-4, Q-5, R-1, S-2 (B) P-4, Q-5, R-2, S-1
(C) P-5, Q-3, R-2, S-1 (D) P-3, Q-2, R-5, S-1

Q.20 A strip with a cross-section $150\,\text{mm} \times 4.5\,\text{mm}$ is being rolled with 20% reduction of area using 450 mm diameter rolls. The angle subtended by the deformation zone at the roll centre is (in radians)

(A) 0.01 (B) 0.02 (C) 0.03 (D) 0.06

Q.21 to Q.30 Numerical Answer Questions

Q.21 Two casting, a cube and a slab of the same material solidify under identical mold conditions. The volumes of the castings are equal but the slab dimensions are in the ratio of 1:2:4. The ratio of the solidification time of the cube to that of the slab is__________.

Q.22 A cylindrical billet of 100 mm diameter is forged from 50 mm height to 40 mm at $1000°$C. The material has a constant flow stress of 80 MPa. The work (in Nm) of deformation is______ .

Q.23 A 50 mm thick plate is to be reduced to 40 mm in pass in a rolling operation. Entrance speed of plate is 20 m/min. The plate is widen by 2% during the operation. The exit velocity of the plate is ______.

Q.24 A hot upset forging operation is performed in an open die. A cylindrical workpart has a diameter $= 25$ mm and a height $= 50$ mm. The part is upset to a diameter $= 50$ mm. The work metal at this elevated temperature yields at 85 MPa ($n = 0$). Coefficient of friction at the die-work interface $= 0.4$. The final height (in mm) of the part is___________.

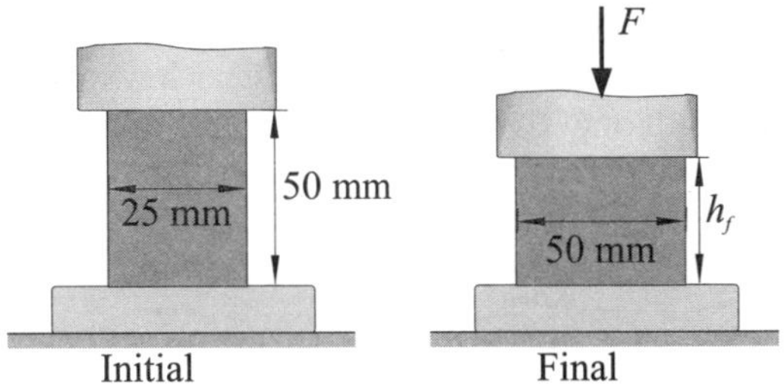

Upset forging operation

Q.25 A hot rolling mill has rolls of diameter $= 600$ mm. It can exerts a maximum force $= 2000$ kN. It is desired to reduce a 40 mm thick plate by the maximum possible draft in one pass. The starting plate is 250 mm wide and in the heated condition the average flow stress is 140 MPa. The maximum possible draft (in mm) is________.

Q.26 In a rolling process, thickness of a strip is reduced from 4 mm to 3 mm using 300 mm diameter rolls rotating at 100 rpm. The velocity of the strip (in m/s) at the neutral point is _______.

Q.27 A cylindrical test specimen of diameter 10 mm and gage length 50 mm is extended to 65 mm. Neglect the elastic deformation. The ultimate strength occurs at and a force of 25000 N and at an extension of 70 mm. The strain hardening exponent n is________.

Q.28 The shape $ABCD$ shown in figure is to be produced by blanking operation from a large sheet of 4 mm thickness. The material is an alloy steel having ultimate shear strength of 600 MPa. The force required (in kW) for the blanking operation is___________.

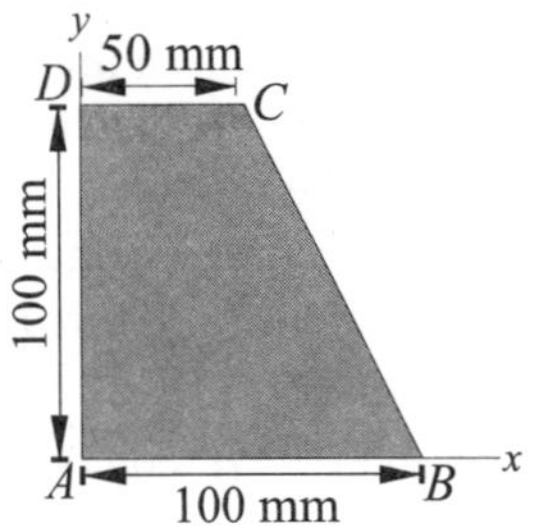

Q.29 A circular sheet of diameter 150 mm has to be deep drawn to a cup with 123 mm inner diameter. The thickness of sheet is 3 mm and the ultimate strength of the sheet material is 300 MPa. The deep drawing force (in kN) is__.

Q.30 The aspect ratio of a cube particle shape is_______.

Q.31 to Q.65 carry two mark each

Q.31 to Q.50 Multiple Choice Questions

Q.31 The shape factor of cubic shape metallic particle is

(A) 6.0 (B) 7.0 (C) 7.4 (D) 8.2

Q.32 The shape *ABCD* shown in figure is to be produced by blanking operation from a large sheet of 4 mm thickness. The material is an alloy steel having ultimate shear strength of 600 MPa. The coordinate of the center of pressure during operation with origin at *A* is

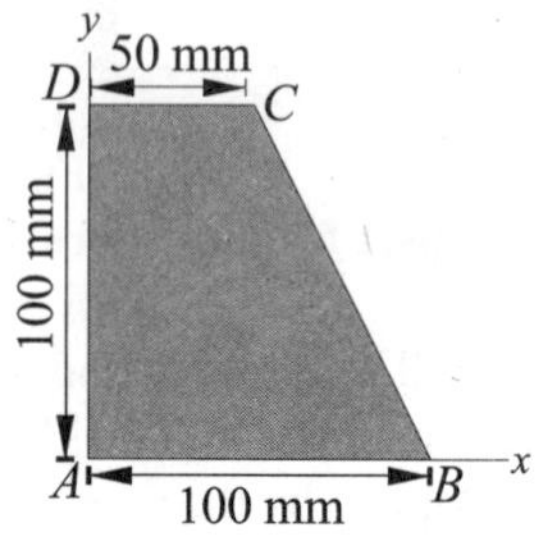

(A) 40.45 mm, 43.09 mm (B) 40.45 mm, 47.32 mm

(C) 44.24 mm, 40.8 mm (D) 44.24 mm, 47.32 mm

Q.33 For a certain metal, strength coefficient = 600 MPa and strain hardening exponent = 0.20. During a forming operation, the final true strain that the metal experience = 0.73. The flow stress at this strain and average flow stress are respectively

(A) 563.4 MPa, 469.5 MPa (B) 363.4 MPa, 469.5 MPa

(C) 233.4 MPa, 469.5 MPa (D) 563.4 MPa, 439.5 MPa

Q.34 A metal of strength coefficient 900 MPa and strain hardening exponent 0.40 used in a forging operation in which the work part is reduced in cross-sectional area by stretching. The average flow stress on the part is 600 MPa and initial cross-sectional area is 100 mm^2. The final cross-sectional area (in mm^2) of part is

(A) 43.1 (B) 74.3 (C) 69.6 (D) 95.2

Q.35 A cylindrical work part has a diameter = 50 mm and height = 40 mm. It is upset forged to height = 20 mm. Coefficient of friction at the die-work interface = 0.2. The work material has a flow curve defined by $K = 600$ MPa and $n = 0.12$. The instantaneous force (in kN) in the operation at height = 30 mm, is

(A) 35708 (B) 4234 (C) 9238 (D)1558

Q.36 For the case of molding, it is decided to replace a spherical riser of diameter 100 mm by a cylindrical riser. Assume blind risering and ratio of height to radius of cylinder is 2. The height and diameter (in mm) of the cylindrical riser that will have the identical solidification time, respectively

(A) 100, 100 (B) 150, 150 (C) 50, 50 (D) 75, 75

Q.37 A cylindrical billet that is 200 mm long and 40 mm in diameter is reduced by indirect extrusion to a 20 mm diameter as shown in figure.

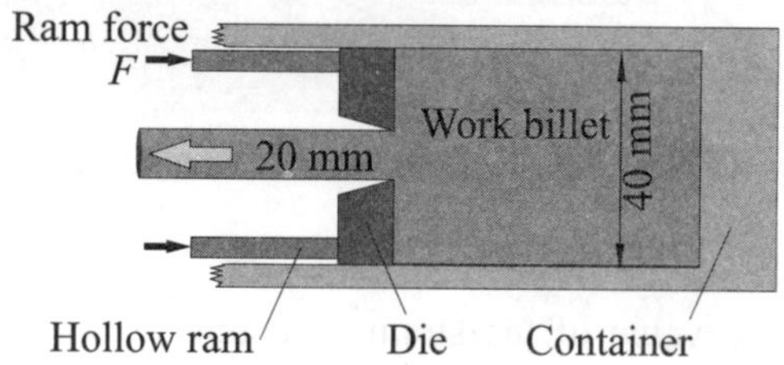

Die angle = 90°. If the Johnson equation has $a = 0.8$ and $b = 1.5$, and the flow curve for the work metal has $K = 800$ MPa and $n = 0.15$. The ram force (in kN) is nearly

(A) 9281 (B) 5324 (C) 3254 (D) 2644

Q.38 A cylindrical billet of 100 mm diameter is forged from 50 mm height to 40 mm at 1000°C. The material has a constant flow stress of 80 MPa. If a 10 kN drop-hammer is used to complete the reduction in one blow, what will be the height (in mm) of the wall?

(A) 628.3 (B) 248.3 (C) 928.3 (D) 528.3

Q.39 A 4.0 mm diameter wire is drawn to a diameter of 3.5 mm. The stress-strain cuve of wire material is given by $\sigma_f = 500\varepsilon^{0.3}$ MPa. The draw stress required for the operation is

(A) 500 MPa (B) 250.6 MPa

(C) 78.5 MPa (D) 69.1 MPa

Q.40 A 75 mm long billet that has a 35 mm diameter is reduced to a diameter of 20 mm through direct extrusion. The flow curve for the work metal is defined by $K = 750$ MPa and $n = 0.25$. The ram pressure is

(A) 690.2 MPa (B) 750 MPa

(C) 375 MPa (D) 268 MPa

Q.41 A riser of spherical shape is to be designed for a sand casting mold. The casting is a rectangular plate, with length = 200 mm, width = 100 mm and thickness = 18 mm. The solidification time of casting is 3.5 minutes. What is the diameter of the riser so that it will take 25% longer for the riser to solidify?

(A) 54.2 mm (B) 50.4 mm (C) 47.5 mm (D) 53.5 mm

Q.42 An L-shaped structure section shown in figure is direct extruded from an aluminum billet in which $L_o = 300$ mm and $D_o = 80$ mm. Die angle = 90°. What will be the length of the extruded section if the butt remains in the container at the end of the ram stroke is 25 mm.

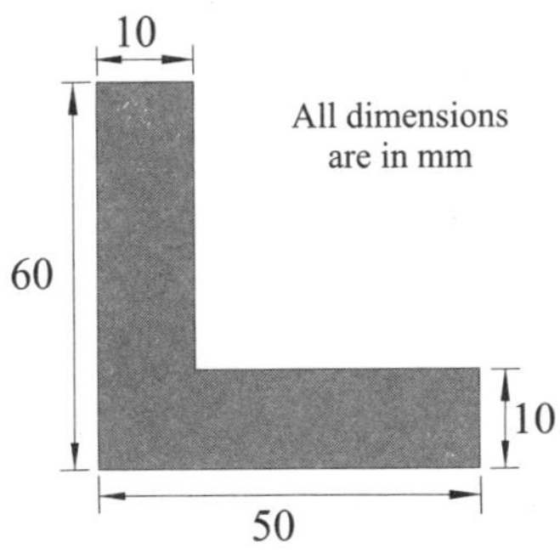

(A) 348.5 mm (B) 726.5 mm

(C) 954.4 mm (D) 1382.3 mm

Q.43 A cylindrical riser is to be used for a sand casting mold. For a given cylinder volume, what is the diameter to length ratio that will maximise the time to solidify?

(A) 0.5 (B) 1 (C) 1.5 (D) 2

Q.44 A 35 mm thick plate will be rolled down to 32 mm. The width of the plate is 150 mm and rotational speed is 15 rpm. The material properties are given as $K = 480$ MPa, $n = 0.22$ and $\mu = 0.16$ at the roll-workpiece interface. The minimum roll radius (in mm) to have initial grasping is

(A) 243 (B) 240 (C) 120 (D) 265

Q.45 A cylinder with a height-to-diameter ratio of unity solidifies in four minutes in a sand casting operation. What is the solidification time if the cylinder height is doubled?

(A) 8.75 min (B) 6.52 min

(C) 5.76 min (D) None of these

Q.46 A bending operation is to be performed on 4.0 mm thick and 30 mm width sheet. The part drawing is given in figure. The size (length) of blank is

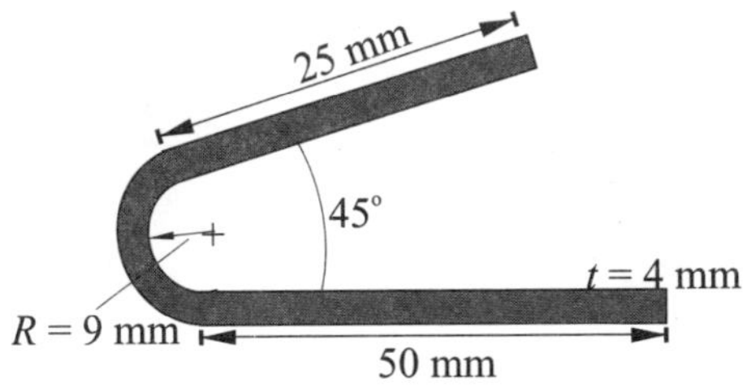

(A) 100.91 mm (B) 80.20 mm

(C) 89.64 mm (D) 9 89.41 mm

Q.47 A series of rolling operations are to be used to reduce the thickness of a plate from 60 mm down to 30 mm in a tandem rolling mill as shown in figure.

Roll diameter $= 750$ mm and coefficient of friction between rolls and work $= 0.15$. The specification is that the draft is to be equal on each pass. The draft for each pass is:

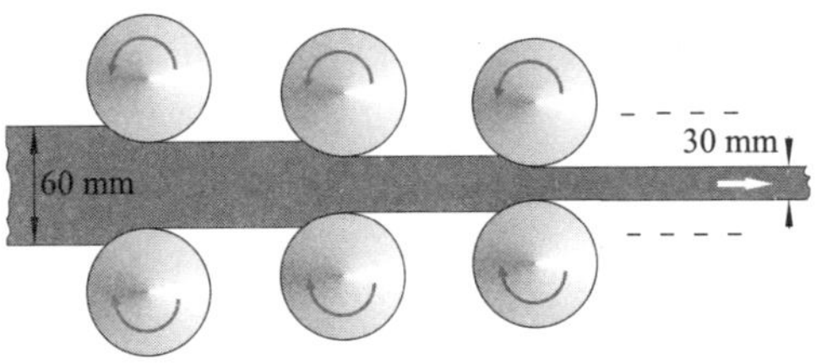

(A) 7.5 mm (B) 8.20 mm (C) 5.4 mm (D) None of these

Q.48 Match List-I (steel) with List-II (application) and select the correct answer using the code given below the lists:

List-I (Steel)		List-II (Application)	
(P)	Mild steel	(1)	Ball bearing
(Q)	Tool steel	(2)	Cold chisels
(R)	High carbon steel	(3)	Shaft and axles
(S)	Medium carbon steel	(4)	Rolled steel sections

(A) P-2, Q-1, R-4, S-3 (B) P-4, Q-3, R-2, S-1

(C) P-2, Q-3, R-4, S-1 (D) P-4, Q-1, R-2, S-3

Q.49 A sheet-metal blank is to be bent by V-die as shown in figure. The tensile strength of metal is 450 MPa. V-die opening width $= 25$ mm, Width of sheet $= 50$ mm. The bending force (in kN) required is

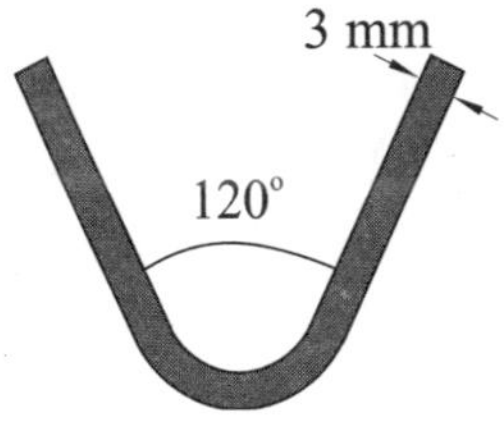

(A) 10.77 (B) 234.8 (C) 2312.7 (D) 465.9

Q.50 From tensile of a particular alloy, the following values are obtained. The material exhibits linear work hardening as shown in the figure given below:

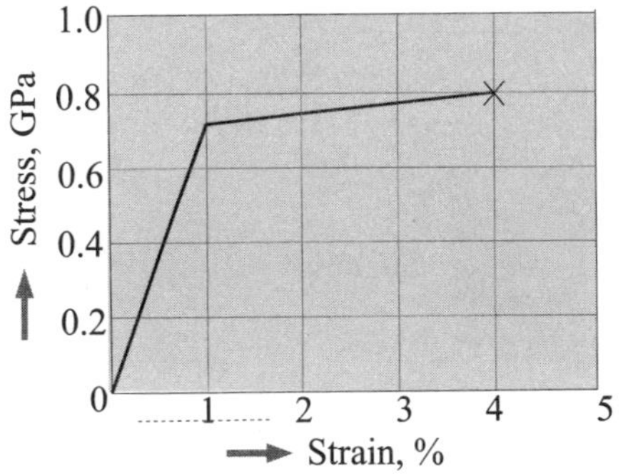

	At yield	At fracture
Stress, GPa	0.7	0.8
Strain, %	1	4

If the cylindrical specimen had a dimension of diameter 10 mm and length 50 mm, find the length of the specimen at the yield point, in mm.

(A) 52.5 mm (B) 54.3 mm (C) 50.5 mm (D) 53.00 mm

Q.51 to Q.65 Numerical Answer Questions

Q.51 A cup-shaped part is backward extruded from an aluminum slug, that is, 40 mm in diameter. The final dimensions of the cup are shown in figure. The flow stress of metal is 300 MPa and constant in the Johnson extrusion strain equation are $a = 0.8$ and $b = 1.5$. The extrusion force (in kN) is ________.

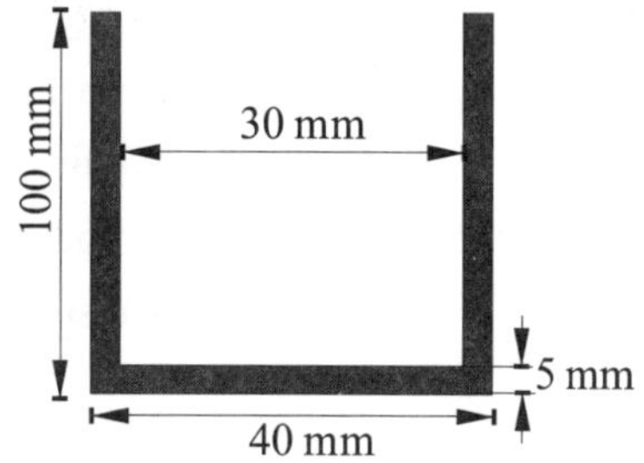

Q.52 A 10 mm diameter rod of a metal that has true stress-true strain relationship $\sigma = 900\varepsilon^{0.5}$ MPa, is subjected to tensile force. The minimum diameter (in mm) that can be achieved before break, is________

Q.53 A 20 mm plate is to be reduced to 18 mm in a single rolling pass. The diameter of roll is 500 mm and the true stress-true stain curve of the plate material is $\sigma = 600\varepsilon^{0.22}$ (MPa). The roll force per unit width (in N/mm) is ____.

Q.54 A hot upset forging operation is performed in an open die. A cylindrical work part has a diameter = 25 mm and a height = 50 mm. The part is upset to a diameter = 50 mm. The work metal at this elevated temperature yields at 85 MPa ($n = 0$). Coefficient of friction at the die-work interface = 0.4. The maximum force (in kN) in the operation is_______

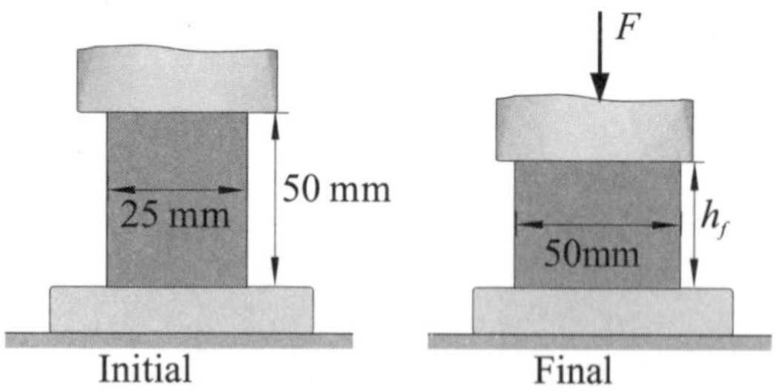

Upset forging operation

Q.55 A cylindrical test specimen of diameter 10 mm and gage length of 50 mm is expended to 65 mm. Neglect the elastic deformation. The ultimate strength occurs at a force of 25000 N and at an extension of 70 mm. The strength coefficient (in MPa) of the material is________.

Q.56 An electron beam welding (EBW) operations uses the following process parameters:

Accelerating voltage = 50 kV

Beam current = 50 mA

Diameter of circular area on which beam is focused = 0.3 mm

Heat transfer efficiency f_1 = 0.85

The average power density (PD) in the area (in W/mm^2) is ____.

Q.57 Wire is drawn through a draw die with a entrance angle 12°. The coefficient of friction at the work die interface is 0.06. The average flow stress of metal is 150 MPa. Wire of starting diameter is 3 mm and final diameter is 2.5 mm. The draw force (in N) required for the operation is _________.

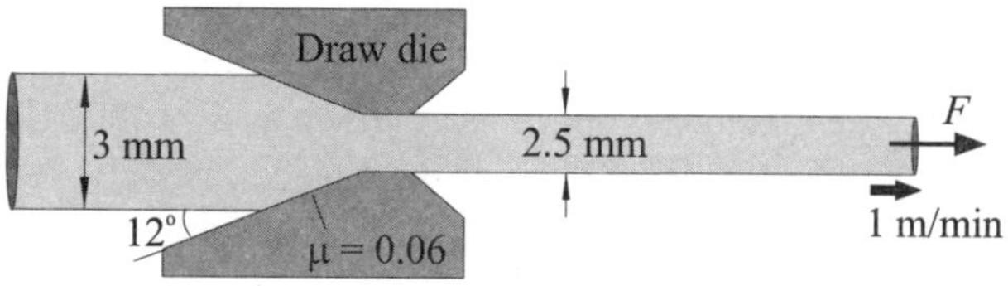

Wire drawing operation

Q.58 A cold heading operation (shown in figure) is to produce the head on steel nail. The coefficient of friction at the die-work interface is = 0.10. The strength coefficient for this steel is $K = 550$ MPa and strain hardening exponent $n = 0.24$. The maximum force (in kN) that the punch must apply to form the head in this open die operation, is____________.

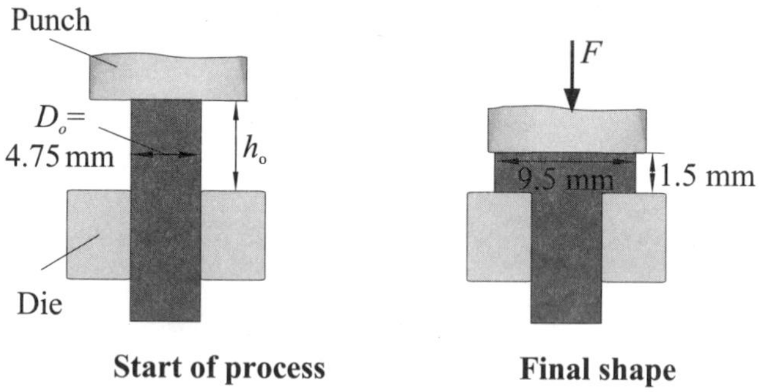

Q.59 A plate that is 300 mm width and 7 mm thickness is rolled to a thickness of 5 mm. The roll radius is 200 mm and rotates at 180 rpm. The average flow stress of the material is 200 MPa. The power (in kW) required for the process is ____.

Q.60 In a certain welding operation to make a groove weld, weld cross-section area $A_w = 20$ mm^2, welding speed $v = 6$ mm/s, heat transfer efficiency $f_1 = 0.95$, melting efficiency $f_2 = 0.5$, melting temperature of metal $T = 1000°C$. Heat generation rate required at the welding source to accomplish this weld is____.

Q.61 The DC power source for an welding has the characteristic $3V + I = 240$, where V = Voltage and I= current in ampere. For maximum arc power at the electrode voltage should be set at

(A) 20 V (B) 40 V (C) 60 V (D) 80 V

Q.62 The extrusion pressure in direct extrusion is given by

$$p = K_x \bar{\sigma}_f \left(\varepsilon_x + \frac{2L}{D_o} \right)$$

The value of shape factor K_x of given cross-section of extruded part (shown in figure) is________.

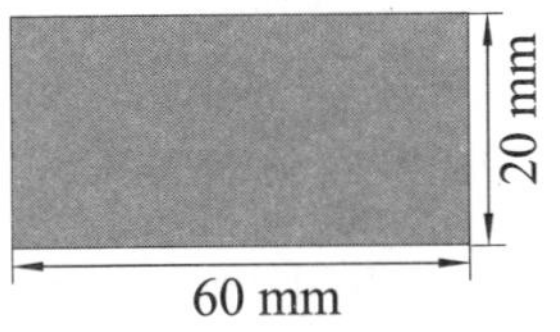

Q.63 A flat bottom cup of inside diameter 100 mm and height 60 mm is to be deep drawn from a blank of 3 mm thickness. The diameter (in mm) of blank is ________.

Q.64 A 10 mm diameter annealed steel wire is drawn through a die at a speed of 0.5 m/s to reduce the diameter by 20%. The yield stress of the material is 800 MPa. Neglecting friction and strain hardening, the power required for the drawing process (in kW) is_________.

Q.65 Wire is drawn through a draw die with a entrance angle 12°. The coefficient of friction at the work die interface is 0.06. The average flow stress of metal is 150 MPa. Wire of starting diameter is 3 mm and final diameter is 2.5 mm. The exit velocity of wire is 1 m/min. The power (in W) required to perform the operation is ______.

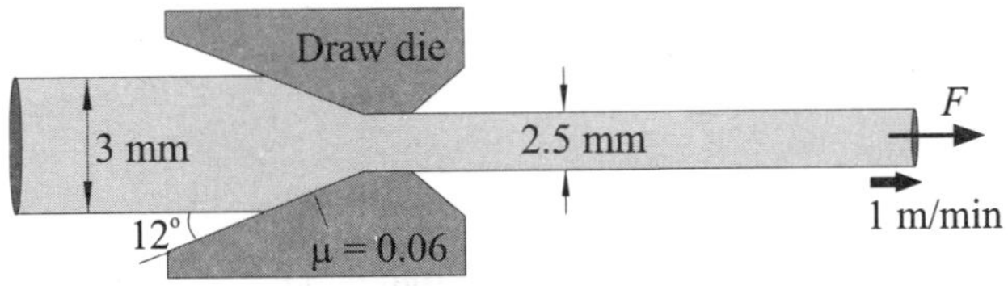

Wire drawing operation

14.4 SOLUTION TO PRACTICE PAPER

Q.1 Ans:(C)

Correct sequence of media

Oil→ Water → Water + NaOH→ Brine

Q.2 Ans:(A)

Correct matching P-3, Q-4, R-2, S-1

Q.3 Ans:(B)

Diameter of hole, $D_h = 50\,\text{mm}$

Diameter of punch in punching operation $= D_h = 50\,\text{mm}$

Diameter of punch $= 50\,\text{mm}$

Q.4 Ans:(C)

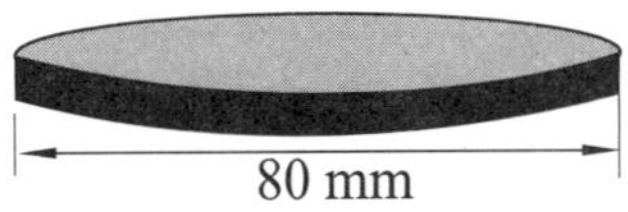

Blank

Clearance, $c = \frac{6}{100} \times 3 = 0.18\,\text{mm}$

Blanking operation:

Diameter of blank, $D_b = 80\,\text{mm}$

Diameter of punch in blanking operation

$= D_b - 2c = 80 - 2 \times 0.18$

Punch diameter $= 79.64\,\text{mm}$

Diameter of die in blanking operation $= D_b = 80$

Diameter of die $= 80\,\text{mm}$

Q.5(C)

Maximum draft is given by $d_{max} = \mu^2 R$

or $t_o - t_f = \mu^2 R$

or $\mu = \sqrt{\frac{t_o - t_f}{R}} = \sqrt{\frac{50 - 35}{300}} = 0.223$

$\mu = 0.223$

Q.6 Ans:(B)

Let r and a be the radius of sphere and side of cube respectively.

Surface area of sphere = Surface area of cube

$$4\pi r^2 = 6a^2$$

$$\left(\frac{r}{a}\right)^2 = \frac{6}{4\pi}$$

Solidification time is given by $t = c_m \left(\frac{V}{A}\right)^2$

Ratio of solidification times

$$\frac{t_{\text{sphere}}}{t_{\text{cube}}} = \left(\frac{V}{A}\right)^2_{\text{sphere}} \times \left(\frac{A}{V}\right)^2_{\text{cube}} = \left(\frac{\frac{4}{3}\pi r^3}{4\pi r^2}\right)^2 \times \left(\frac{6a^2}{a^3}\right)^2$$

or $$\frac{t_{\text{sphere}}}{t_{\text{cube}}} = 4\left(\frac{r}{a}\right)^2 = 4 \times \frac{6}{4\pi}$$

$$\frac{t_{\text{sphere}}}{t_{\text{cube}}} = \frac{6}{\pi}$$

Q.7 Ans:(B)

Power, $P = VI$

Substituting $V = 20 + 4\,l$, we get

$$P = (20 + 4l)I$$

Current 450 A at arc length 4 mm and current 550 A at arc length 6 mm.

Substituting current $I = 500\text{A}$ for arc length 5 mm, we have

Arc power for arc length of 5 mm is

$$P = (20 + 4 \times 5) \times 500$$

$$P = 20\,\text{kW}$$

Q.8 Ans:(A)

Velocity of molten metal at inlet of runner

$$v = \sqrt{2gh}$$

$$v = \sqrt{2 \times 981 \times 17.5} = 185.29\,\text{cm/s} = 1852.9\,\text{mm/s}$$

Let t be the time required to fill a mold cavity.

$$\text{Volume of cavity} = avt$$

or $$t = \frac{\text{Volume of cavity}}{av} = \frac{10^6}{200 \times 1852.9}$$

$$t = 2.67\,\text{s}$$

Q.9 Ans:(B)

The blanking force, $F = \sigma_s A_s$

or $F = \sigma_s \pi d\, t$

Substituting $\sigma_s = 450 \times 10^6$ Pa, $d = \frac{80}{1000}$ m, $t = \frac{2}{1000}$ m,

We get $F = 450 \times 10^6 \times \pi \times \frac{80}{1000} \times \frac{2}{1000} = 226194.6\,\text{N}$

$$F = 226.2\ \text{kN}$$

Q.10 Ans:(D)

Given: Mesh count $MC = 300$, wire thickness $t_w = 0.0012$ inch.

Particle size, $PS = \frac{1}{MC} - t_w$

$$PS = \frac{1}{300} - 0.0012$$

Particle size, $PS = 0.00213$ inch

Q.11 Ans:(C)

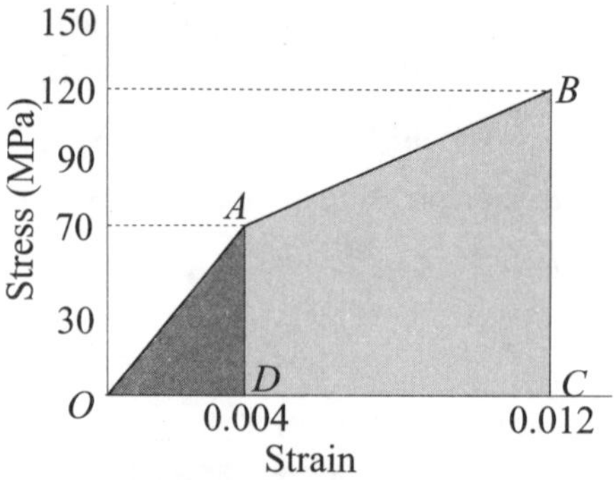

Resilience is the ability of a material to absorb energy under elastic deformation and to recover this energy upon removal of load. Resilience is indicated by the area under the stress-strain curving to the point of elastic limit.

Resilience = Area of OAD

$$\text{Resilience} = \frac{1}{2} \times 70 \times 10^6 \times 0.004$$

$$\text{Resilience} = 14 \times 10^4\ \text{Nm/m}^3$$

Toughness is the energy of mechanical deformation per unit volume prior to fracture.

Toughness = Area of $OABCDO$

$$= \frac{1}{2} \times (70 \times 10^6 \times 0.004) + \frac{(120 + 70) \times 10^6}{2}(0.012 - 0.004)$$

$$\text{Toughness} = 90 \times 10^4\ \text{Nm/m}^3$$

Q.12 Ans:(B)

Solidification time, $t = c_m\left(\frac{V}{A}\right)^2$

$$t = c_m\left(\frac{\frac{\pi}{4}d^2h}{\pi dh + 2 \times \frac{\pi}{4}d^2}\right)^2 = c_m\left(\frac{dh}{2(2h + d)}\right)^2$$

Substituting $c = 3\ \text{s/mm}^2$, $d = 50$ mm and $h = 100$ mm

$$t = c_m\left(\frac{50 \times 100}{2(2 \times 100 + 50)}\right)^2$$

$$t = 300\,\text{s}$$

Q.13 Ans:(C)

Maximum draft, $d_{\max} = \mu^2 R$

$$d_{\max} = (0.15)^2 \times \frac{750}{2}$$

$$d_{\max} = 8.4375 \text{ mm}$$

$$\text{Minimum number of passes} = \frac{t_o - t_f}{d_{\max}} = \frac{60-30}{8.4375} = 3.55$$

Therefore, minimum number of passes = 4

Q.14 Ans:(A)

Solidification time, $t = c_m\left(\frac{V}{A}\right)^2$

$$t = c_m\left(\frac{\frac{4}{3}\pi r^3}{4\pi r^2}\right)^2 = c_m\frac{r^2}{9}$$

For spherical drop of $r = 2$ mm;

$$10 = c_m\frac{2^2}{9} \qquad \text{(i)}$$

For spherical drop of $r = 4$ mm;

$$t = c_m\frac{4^2}{9} \qquad \text{(ii)}$$

Equations (i) and (ii), give

$$t = 40 \text{ s}$$

Q.15 Ans:(C)

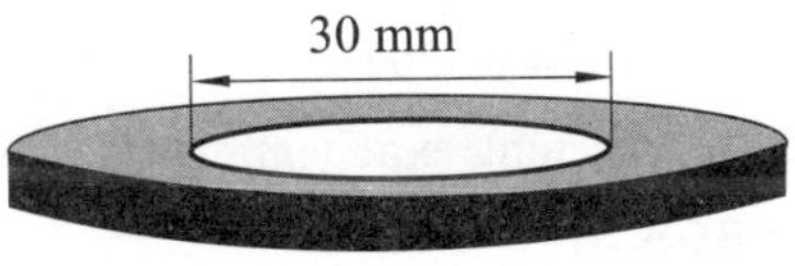

Clearance, $c = \frac{6}{100} \times 3 = 0.18$ mm

Punching operation:

Diameter of hole, $D_h = 30$ mm

Diameter of punch in punching operation

$= D_h = 30$ mm

Punch diameter $= 30$ mm

Diameter of die in punching operation

$= D_h + 2c = 80 + 2 \times 0.18$

Diameter of die $= 30.36$ mm

Q.16 Ans:(A)

Draft d is given by

$$d = t_o - t_f = \mu^2 R$$

or $$\mu = \sqrt{\frac{t_o - t_f}{R}} = \sqrt{\frac{30-15}{150}}$$

$$\mu = 0.35$$

Q.17 Ans:(D)

Reduction (extrusion ratio) $r_x = \frac{A_o}{A_f}$

$$r_x = \left(\frac{D_o}{D_f}\right)^2 = \left(\frac{40}{20}\right)^2 = 4$$

The true stain, $\varepsilon = \ln r_x = \ln 4 = 1.386$

The extrusion strain, $\varepsilon_x = a + b\ln r_x$

$$\varepsilon_x = 0.8 + 1.5\ln 4 = 2.88$$

$$\varepsilon_x = 2.88$$

Q.18 Ans:(B)

Average flow stress ($\bar{\sigma}_f$) $= \frac{3}{4}$ flow stress (σ_f)

or $$\frac{K\varepsilon^n}{1+n} = \frac{3}{4}K\varepsilon^n$$

Strain hardening exponent, $n = 0.333$

Q.19 Ans:(B)

Correct matching P-4, Q-5, R-2, S-1

Q.20 Ans:(D)

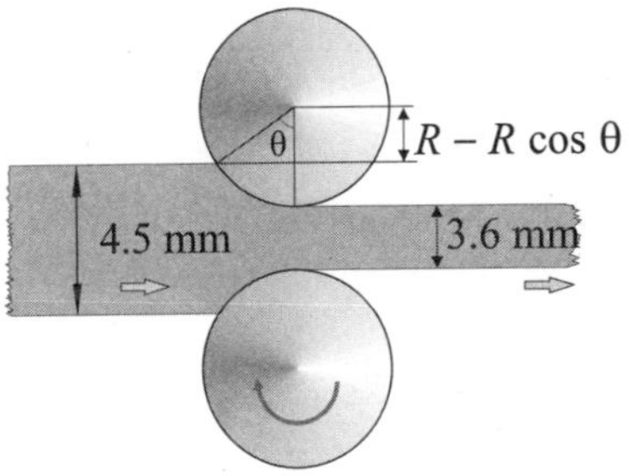

From the geometry of figure

$$R - R\cos\theta = \frac{t_o - t_f}{2}$$

Substituting initial thickness $t_o = 4.5$ mm, final thickness $t_f = 0.8 \times 4.5 = 3.6$ mm and rolls radius $R = \frac{450}{2} = 225$ mm.

We get

$$225(1-\cos\theta) = \frac{4.5-3.6}{2}$$

or $$\theta = 3.624^\circ$$

$$\theta = 0.063 \text{ radians}$$

Q.21 Ans:[1.36]

Let a be the side of cube and x be the thickness of slab.

Volume of cube = Volume of slab

$$a^3 = x \times 2x \times 4x \Rightarrow \frac{a}{x} = 2$$

Solidification time is given by $t = c_m\left(\frac{V}{A}\right)^2$

Ratio of solidification time,

$$\frac{t_{\text{cube}}}{t_{\text{slab}}} = \left(\frac{V}{A}\right)^2_{\text{cube}} \times \left(\frac{A}{V}\right)^2_{\text{slab}} = \left(\frac{a^3}{6a^2}\right)^2 \times \left(\frac{28x^2}{8x^3}\right)^2$$

or $$\frac{t_{\text{cube}}}{t_{\text{slab}}} = \left(\frac{28}{6\times 8}\right)^2 \times \left(\frac{a}{x}\right)^2 = \left(\frac{28}{6\times 8}\right)^2 \times 2^2$$

$$\frac{t_{\text{cube}}}{t_{\text{slab}}} = \frac{49}{36} = 1.36$$

Q.22 Ans:[6283]

The forging force is, $F = \sigma_f \frac{\pi}{4}d^2 = 80 \times \frac{\pi}{4} \times 100^2$

$$F = 628.3\text{ kN}$$

Work of deformation, $W = F\Delta h$

$$W = 628.3 \times 10^3 \times \frac{(50-40)}{1000}$$

$$W = 6283\text{ Nm}$$

Q.23 Ans:[24.51]

Volume of metal entering = Volume of metal exiting

$$t_o w_o v_o = t_f w_f v_f$$

Exit velocity, $v_f = \frac{t_o}{t_f}\frac{w_o}{w_f}v_o$

or $$v_f = \frac{50}{40} \times \frac{w_o}{1.02\,w_o} \times 20$$

$$v_f = 24.51\text{ m/min}$$

Q.24 Ans:[12.5]

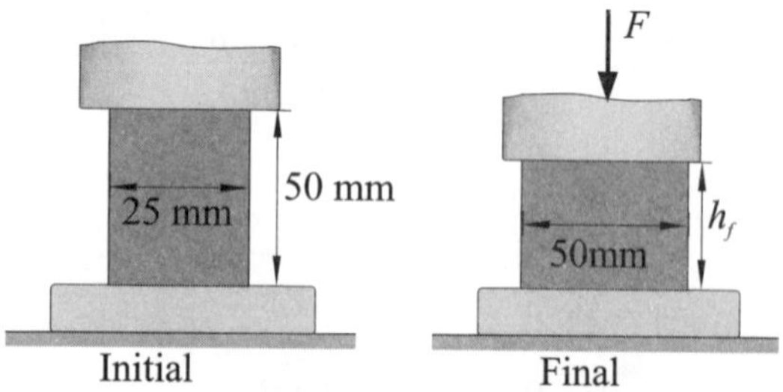

Upset forging operation

Volume of workpiece $= \frac{\pi}{4}D_o^2 h_o = \frac{\pi}{4}D_f^2 h_f$

Final height of the part, $h_f = \frac{D_o^2}{D_f^2}h_o = \left(\frac{25}{50}\right)^2 \times 50$

$$h_f = 12.5\text{ mm}$$

Q.25 Ans:[10.88]

Draft, $d = t_o - t_f = 40 - t_f$

Contact length, $L = \sqrt{R(t_o - t_f)} = \sqrt{300\,d}$

The roll force is, $F = \bar{\sigma}_f wL$

$$2000 \times 10^3 = 140 \times 250 \times \sqrt{300d}$$

$$d = 10.88\text{ mm}$$

Q.26 Ans:[1.57]

The roll velocity and work velocity is same at neutral point. Therefore, the velocity of strip at neutral point,

$$v = \omega r = \frac{2\pi N}{60} \times \frac{D}{2} = \frac{2\pi \times 100}{60} \times \frac{300}{2}$$

$$v = 1.57\text{ m/s}$$

Q.27 Ans:[0.3364]

The true strain at extension of 70 mm (strain at ultimate strength) is

$$\varepsilon = \ln\frac{70}{50} = 0.3364$$

Therefore, value of $n = 0.3364$

Strain hardening exponent, $n = 0.3364$

Q.28 Ans:[868.3]

Perimeter of sheet, $L = AB + BC + CD + DA$

$$L = 100 + \sqrt{50^2 + 100^2} + 50 + 100 = 361.8\text{ mm}$$

Shear area, $A_s = 361.8 \times 4 = 1447.2\text{ mm}^2$

Force required, $F = \sigma_{us}A_s = 600 \times 1447.2 = 868320\text{ N}$

$$F = 868.3\text{ kN}$$

Q.29 Ans:[180.7]

Deep drawing force, $F = \pi D_p t \sigma_{ut}\left(\frac{d_o}{D_p} - 0.7\right)$

Substituting $D_p = 123$ mm, $t = 3$ mm, $\sigma_{ut} = 300$ MPa and $d_o = 150$ mm

$$F = \pi \times 123 \times 3 \times 300\left(\frac{150}{123} - 0.7\right) = 180672.9\text{ N}$$

$$F = 180.7\text{ kN}$$

Q.30 Ans:[1.732]

Let L be the edge of cube.

Maximum dimension of the cube = Length of diagonal

$$= \sqrt{L^2 + L^2 + L^2} = \sqrt{3}\, L$$

Minimum dimension of the cube = Side of cube = L

$$\text{Aspect ratio} = \frac{\text{Maximum dimension of the cube}}{\text{Minimum dimension of the cube}}$$

$$\text{Aspect ratio} = \frac{\sqrt{3}L}{L} = 1.732$$

Aspect ratio $= 1.732:1$

Q.31 Ans:(C)

Let L = edge of one face.

Surface area of cube $A = 6L^2$, Volume of cube $V = L^3$

Let D be diameter of a sphere of equivalent volume.

$$V = \frac{4}{3}\pi\left(\frac{D}{2}\right)^3 = L^3 \quad \Rightarrow D = \left(\frac{6}{\pi}\right)^{\frac{1}{3}} L = 12407\, L$$

$$\text{Shape factor, } K_s = \frac{A}{V} \times D = \frac{6L^2}{L^3} \times 1.2407\, L$$

Shape factor, $K_s = 7.444$

Q.32 Ans:(A)

The shear area can be divided into four parts (Part-1 is AB, Part-2 is BC, Part-3 is CD and Part-4 is AD).

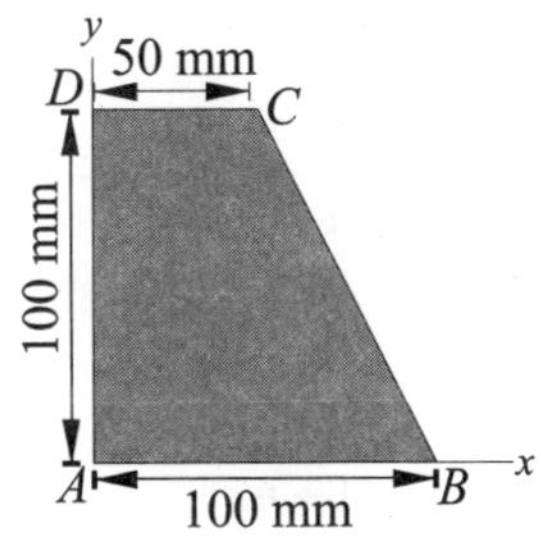

For part-1; $l_1 = 100\,\text{mm}$, $x_1 = 50\,\text{mm}$, $y_1 = 0$

For part-2

$l_2 = \sqrt{50^2 + 100^2} = 111.8\,\text{mm}$,

$x_2 = 75\,\text{mm}, y_2 = 50\,\text{mm}$

For part-3 $\quad l_3 = 50\,\text{mm}$, $x_3 = 25\,\text{mm}$, $y_3 = 100\,\text{mm}$

For part-4 $\quad l_4 = 100\,\text{mm}$, $x_1 = 0$, $y_4 = 50\,\text{mm}$

x-coordinate of centre of pressure,

$$\bar{x} = \frac{\sum lx}{\sum l} = \frac{100 \times 50 + 111.8 \times 75 + 50 \times 25 + 100 \times 0}{100 + 111.8 + 50 + 100}$$

$$\bar{x} = 40.45\,\text{mm}$$

x-coordinate of center of pressure,

$$\bar{y} = \frac{\sum ly}{\sum l} = \frac{100 \times 0 + 111.8 \times 50 + 50 \times 100 + 100 \times 50}{100 + 111.8 + 50 + 100}$$

$$\bar{y} = 43.09\,\text{mm}$$

Coordinate of the center of pressure is 40.45 mm, 43.09 mm.

Q.33 Ans:(A)

Flow stress, $\quad \sigma_f = K\varepsilon^n$

Substituting given values $K = 600\,\text{MPa}$, $n = 0.20$ and $\varepsilon = 0.73$.

$$\sigma_f = 600\,(0.73)^{0.20}$$

Flow stress, $\sigma_f = 563.4\,\text{MPa}$

$$\text{Average flow stress, } \bar{\sigma}_f = \frac{K\varepsilon^n}{1+n}$$

$$\bar{\sigma}_f = \frac{600 \times (0.73)^{0.20}}{1 + 0.2} = 469.5$$

Average flow stress, $\bar{\sigma}_f = 469.5\,\text{MPa}$

Q.34 Ans:(B)

$$\text{Average flow stress, } \bar{\sigma}_f = \frac{K\varepsilon^n}{1+n}$$

$$600 = \frac{900\varepsilon^{0.4}}{1 + 0.4}$$

$$\varepsilon = 0.8416$$

$$\text{The true strain, } \varepsilon = \ln\left(\frac{A_o}{A_f}\right) = 0.8416$$

or $\quad \dfrac{A_o}{A_f} = 2.32$

or $\quad A_f = \dfrac{A_o}{232} = \dfrac{100}{2.32}\,\text{mm}^2$

$A_f = 43.1\,\text{mm}^2$

Q.35 Ans:(D)

$$\text{True strain, } \varepsilon = \ln\left(\frac{40}{30}\right) = 0.287$$

Flow stress, $\sigma_f = K\varepsilon^n = 600\,(0.287)^{0.12} = 516.6\,\text{MPa}$

$$\text{At } h = 30\text{ mm, } A = \frac{V}{h} = \frac{\frac{\pi}{4}(50)^2 \times 40}{30} = 2617.9\,\text{mm}^2$$

or $\quad A = \dfrac{\pi}{4}D^2 = 2617.9\,\text{mm}^2$

or $\quad D = 57.73\,\text{mm}$

Forging shape factor (at $h = 30$ mm);

$$K_f = 1 + \frac{0.4\mu D}{h} = 1 + \frac{0.4 \times 0.2 \times 57.73}{30} = 1.154$$

The forging force is, $\quad F = K_f \sigma_f A$

$$F = 1.154 \times 516.6 \times 2617.9 = 1558811\text{ N}$$

$F = 1558\text{ kN}$

Q.36 Ans:(A)

Let d and h be the diameter and height of cylindrical riser respectively.

Solidification time is given by $t = c_m\left(\frac{V}{A}\right)^2$

For spherical riser;

$$t_{\text{sphere}} = c_m\left(\frac{\frac{4}{3}\pi r^3}{4\pi r^2}\right)^2 = c_m\left(\frac{r}{3}\right)^2 = c_m\left(\frac{50}{3}\right)^2$$

For cylindrical riser ($h = 2r = d$);

$$t_{\text{cyl.}} = c_m\left(\frac{\pi\left(\frac{d}{2}\right)^2 h}{\pi d\,h + 2\pi\left(\frac{d}{2}\right)^2}\right)^2 = c_m\left(\frac{\pi\left(\frac{d}{2}\right)^2 d}{\pi d \times d + 2\pi\left(\frac{d}{2}\right)^2}\right)^2$$

or $$t_{\text{cyl.}} = c_m\left(\frac{d}{6}\right)^2$$

Since solidification time is same; $c_m\left(\frac{50}{3}\right)^2 = c_m\left(\frac{d}{6}\right)^2$

$$d = 100\,\text{mm}$$

$$d = h = 100\ \text{mm}$$

Q.37 Ans:(D)

Reduction (extrusion ratio), $r_x = \frac{A_o}{A_f}$

$$r_x = \left(\frac{D_o}{D_f}\right)^2 = \left(\frac{40}{20}\right)^2 = 4$$

True stain, $\varepsilon = \ln r_x = \ln 4 = 1.386$

Extrusion ratio, $\varepsilon_x = a + b\ln r_x = 0.8 + 1.5\ln 4 = 2.88$

Average flow stress,

$$\bar{\sigma}_f = \frac{K\varepsilon^n}{1+n} = \frac{800 \times 1.386^{0.15}}{1+0.15} = 730.56\,\text{MPa}$$

The ram pressure is

$$p = \bar{\sigma}_f\,\varepsilon_x = 730.56 \times 2.88 = 2104\,\text{MPa}$$

The ram force is

$$F = p\left(\frac{\pi}{4}D_o^2\right) = 2104 \times \frac{\pi}{4}(40)^2 = 2643964\ \text{N}$$

$$F = 2644\ \text{kN}$$

Q.38 Ans:(A)

The forging force is $F = \sigma_f \frac{\pi}{4}d^2 = 80 \times \frac{\pi}{4} \times 100^2$

$$F = 628.3\,\text{kN}$$

Work of deformation,

$$W = F\Delta h = 628.3 \times 10^3 \times \frac{(50-40)}{1000}$$

$$W = 6283\,\text{Nm}$$

Let h be the height of blow.

Work of deformation, $W = mgh$

or $6283 = 10 \times 10^3 h$

or $h = 0.6283\,\text{m}$

$$h = 628.3\,\text{mm}$$

Q.39 Ans:(D)

Reduction, $r = \frac{A_o - A_f}{A_o} = 1 - \left(\frac{d_f}{d_o}\right)^2$

or $$r = 1 - \left(\frac{3.5}{4.0}\right)^2 = 0.2343$$

True strain,

$$\varepsilon = \ln\frac{l_f}{l_o} = \ln\frac{A_o}{A_f} = \ln\left(\frac{d_o}{d_f}\right)^2 = \ln\left(\frac{4.0}{3.5}\right)^2 = 0.267$$

Average flow stress,

$$\bar{\sigma}_f = \frac{K\varepsilon^n}{1+n} = \frac{500 \times (0.267)^{0.3}}{1+0.3} = 258.8\,\text{MPa}$$

The draw stress is

$$\sigma_d = \bar{\sigma}_f \ln\frac{1}{1-r} = 258.8 \times \ln\left(\frac{1}{1-0.2343}\right)$$

$$\sigma_d = 69.09\ \text{MPa}$$

Q.40 Ans:(A)

Reduction ratio or extrusion ratio,

$$r_x = \frac{A_o}{A_f} = \left(\frac{d_o}{d_f}\right)^2 = \left(\frac{35}{20}\right)^2 = 3.06$$

True strain, $\varepsilon = \ln r_x = \ln(3.06) = 1.1192$

Average flow stress,

$$\bar{\sigma}_f = \frac{K\varepsilon^n}{1+n} = \frac{750 \times (1.11192)^{0.25}}{1+0.25} = 617.13\,\text{MPa}$$

The ram pressure is $p = \bar{\sigma}_f \ln r_x$

$$p = 617.13 \times \ln 3.06$$

$$p = 690.2\,\text{MPa}$$

Q.41 Ans:(C)

Let d be the diameter of riser.

Volume of riser; $V = \frac{4}{3}\pi\left(\frac{d}{2}\right)^3$

Surface area of riser; $A = 4\pi\left(\frac{d}{2}\right)^2$

$$\frac{V}{A} = \frac{\frac{4}{3}\pi\left(\frac{d}{2}\right)^3}{4\pi\left(\frac{d}{2}\right)^2} = \frac{d}{6}$$

Solidification time of riser,

$$t_{\text{riser}} = 1.25\, t_{\text{casting}} = c_m\left(\frac{d}{6}\right)^2 \qquad \text{(i)}$$

Solidification time of casting, $t_{\text{casting}} = c_m\left(\frac{V}{A}\right)^2$

or $$t_{\text{casting}} = c_m\left(\frac{200\times100\times18}{2(200\times100+100\times18+200\times18)}\right)^2$$

$$t_{\text{casting}} = c_m(7.0866)^2 \qquad \text{(ii)}$$

Equations (i) and (ii) give

$$1.25 = \left(\frac{d}{6}\right)^2\left(\frac{1}{7.0866}\right)$$

$$d = 47.5\,\text{mm}$$

Q.42 Ans:(D)

Starting volume,

$$V_o = \frac{\pi}{4}D_o^2L_o = \frac{\pi}{4}\times80^2\times300 = 1507964.4\,\text{mm}^3$$

Area of cross-section,

$$A_{\text{L-section}} = 50\times10+50\times10 = 1000\,\text{mm}^2$$

The final volume consists of two sections: (i) butt (circular section), and (ii) extruded L-section.

Let L be length of the L-section.

Final volume, $V_f = \frac{\pi}{4}D_o^2\times25 + A_{\text{L-section}}\times L = V_o$

or $$\frac{\pi}{4}80^2\times25+1000\times L = 1507964.4$$

Thus,

Length of extruded section, $L = 1382.3\,\text{mm}$

Q.43 Ans:(B)

Volume of cylindrical riser, $V = \frac{\pi}{4}d^2h$

$$h = \frac{4V}{\pi d^2}$$

Surface area of riser, $A = \pi dh + 2\times\frac{\pi}{4}d^2$

or $$A = \pi d\left(\frac{4V}{\pi d^2}\right)+2\times\frac{\pi}{4}d^2$$

or $$A = \frac{4V}{d}+\frac{\pi d^2}{2}$$

Condition for maximum solidification time;

$$\frac{dA}{d(d)} = -\frac{4V}{d^2}+\pi d = 0$$

or $$\frac{4V}{d^2} = \pi d$$

or $$\frac{4}{d^2}\times\frac{\pi}{4}d^2h = \pi d$$

$$\frac{d}{h} = 1$$

Q.44 Ans:(C)

From the geometry of figure.

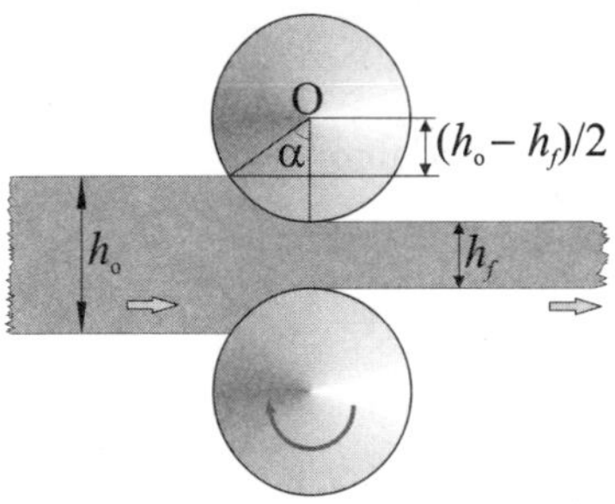

$$R - R\cos\alpha = \frac{h_o-h_f}{2}$$

$$R = \frac{h_o-h_f}{2(1-\cos\alpha)}$$

To find $R_{\min}$ for initial grasping, we should first find the α value.

For grasping the condition, $\tan\alpha \le \mu$ should be satisfied.

$$\tan\alpha \le 0.16 \Rightarrow \alpha \le 9.09$$

$$R \ge \frac{35-32}{2(1-\cos 9.09)} = 119.4\,\text{mm}$$

$$R_{\min} = 120\ \text{mm}$$

Q.45 Ans:(C)

Solidification time, $t = c_m \left(\frac{V}{A} \right)^2$

$$t = c_m \left(\frac{\frac{\pi}{4} d^2 h}{\pi dh + 2 \times \frac{\pi}{4} d^2} \right)^2 = c_m \left(\frac{dh}{2(2h + d)} \right)^2$$

Substituting $\frac{d}{h} = 1$ and $t = 4$ min

$$4 = c_m \left(\frac{d}{6} \right)^2 \qquad \text{(i)}$$

Now substituting $h = 2d$,

$$t = c_m \left(\frac{d \times 2d}{2(2 \times 2d + d)} \right)^2 = c_m \left(\frac{d}{5} \right)^2 \qquad \text{(ii)}$$

Equations (i) and (ii) give

$$t = 5.76 \text{ min}$$

Q.46 Ans:(A)

Size of blank, $l = 50 + BA + 25$

Bending allowance, $BA = \theta(R + k_{ba} t)$

For $R \geq 2t$; $BA = \theta(R + 0.5t)$

$$BA = 2\pi \frac{135}{360}(9 + 0.5 \times 4)$$

$$BA = 25.91 \text{ mm}$$

Therefore, the size of blank,

$$l = 50 + 25.91 + 25 = 100.91$$

$$l = 100.91 \text{ mm}$$

Q.47 Ans:(A)

Maximum draft, $d_{max} = \mu^2 R = (0.15)^2 \times \frac{750}{2}$

$$d_{max} = 8.4375 \text{ mm}$$

Minimum number of passes $= \frac{t_o - t_f}{d_{max}} = \frac{60 - 30}{8.4375} = 3.55$

Therefore, minimum number of passes = 4

Draft per pass $= \frac{60 - 30}{4} = 7.5$

Draft per pass = 7.5 mm

Q.48 Ans:(D)

Correct matching P-4, Q-1, R-2, S-3

Q.49 Ans:(A)

The bending force is given by

$$F = \frac{K_{bf}\, \sigma_t w t^2}{D}$$

For V-bending, $K_{bf} = 1.33$

Substituting given values
$\sigma_t = 450$ MPa, $w = 50$ mm, $t = 3$ mm and die opening width $D = 25$ mm.

$$F = \frac{1.33 \times 450 \times 50 \times 3^2}{25} = 10773 \text{ N}$$

$$F = 10.77 \text{ kN}$$

Q.50 Ans:(C)

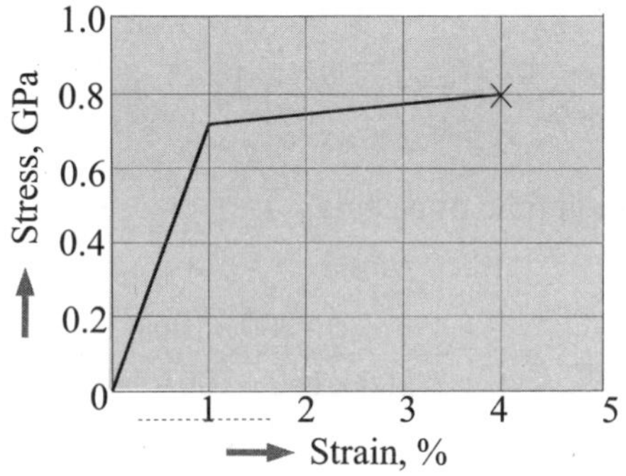

Strain $\varepsilon = \frac{\text{Final length} - \text{Initial length}}{\text{Initial length}}$

From the stress-strain curve; strain at yield point is 1%

$$\varepsilon = \frac{1}{100} = \frac{L - 50}{50}$$

Length of the specimen at the yield point, $L = 50.5$ mm

Q.51 Ans:[886.2]

Extrusion ratio, $r_x = \frac{A_o}{A_f} = \frac{\frac{\pi}{4} \times 40^2}{\frac{\pi}{4} \times (40^2 - 30^2)} = 2.28$

Extrusion strain, $\varepsilon_x = a + b \ln r_x$

$$\varepsilon_x = 0.8 + 1.5 \times \ln 2.28 = 2.03$$

Perimeter of the extruded cross-section,

$$C_x = \pi(40 + 30) = 219.9 \text{ mm}$$

Extruded cross-section area,

$$A = \frac{\pi}{4}(40^2 - 30^2) = 549.7 \text{ mm}^2$$

Radius of circle, $R = \sqrt{\frac{A}{\pi}} = \sqrt{\frac{549.7}{\pi}} = 13.22$ mm

Perimeter of circle,

$$C_c = 2\pi R = 2\pi \times 13.22 = 83.11\,\text{mm}$$

The shape factor is given by $K_x = 0.98 + 0.02\left(\dfrac{C_x}{C_c}\right)^{2.25}$

$$K_x = 0.98 + 0.02\left(\frac{219.9}{83.11}\right)^{2.25} = 1.158$$

$$p = K_x \bar{\sigma}_f \varepsilon_x = 1.158 \times 300 \times 2.03 = 705.22\,\text{MPa}$$

Extrusion force, $F = pA_o = 705.22 \times \dfrac{\pi}{4} \times 40^2 = 886208$

$$F = 886.2\ \text{kN}$$

Q.52 Ans:[7.78]

The rod can be stretched upto the point of instability where the rate of increase in load due to strain-hardening is just balanced by the rate of decrease in load due to diminishing area of cross-section since the load is maximum, that is, $dP = 0$.

$$P = \sigma A \quad \Rightarrow \quad \frac{dP}{dl} = A\frac{d\sigma}{dl} + \sigma\frac{dA}{dl} = 0 \qquad \text{(i)}$$

Volume of rod Al = constant; $\dfrac{dA}{A} + \dfrac{dl}{l} = 0$

$$\frac{dA}{dl} = -\frac{A}{l} \qquad \text{(ii)}$$

From Equations (i) and (ii), we get

$$A\frac{d\sigma}{dl} + \sigma\left(-\frac{A}{l}\right) = 0 \Rightarrow \frac{d\sigma}{\sigma} = \frac{dl}{l} = d\varepsilon$$

or $$\frac{d\sigma}{d\varepsilon} = \sigma$$

Substituting $\sigma = 900\varepsilon^{0.5}$, we get

$$\frac{d900\varepsilon^{0.5}}{d\varepsilon} = 900\varepsilon^{0.5}$$

or $\varepsilon = 0.5$

True train, $\varepsilon = \ln\left(\dfrac{l_f}{l_o}\right) = \ln\left(\dfrac{A_o}{A_f}\right) = 2\ln\left(\dfrac{d_o}{d_f}\right) = 0.5$

or $$2\ln\left(\frac{10}{d_f}\right) = 0.5$$

Minimum diameter, $d_f = 7.78$ mm

Q.53 Ans:[6702.8]

Roll force per unit width is given by $F = \bar{\sigma}_f L$ (N/m)

Substituting average flow stress,

$$\bar{\sigma}_f = \frac{K\varepsilon^n}{1+n} = \frac{K\left(\ln\dfrac{t_o}{t_f}\right)^n}{1+n}$$

and contact length $L = \sqrt{R(t_o - t_f)}$, we get

$$F = \frac{K\left(\ln\dfrac{t_o}{t_f}\right)^n}{1+n} \times \sqrt{R(t_o - t_f)}$$

$$F = \frac{600\left(\ln\dfrac{20}{18}\right)^{0.22}}{1+0.22} \times \sqrt{250(20-18)}$$

$$F = 6702.8\,\text{N/mm}$$

Q.54 Ans:[273.7]

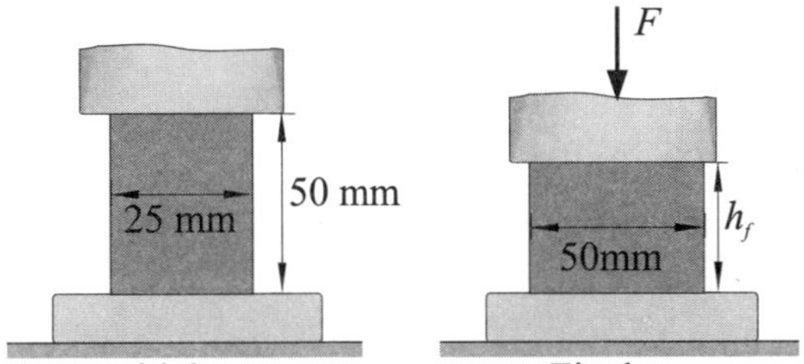

Upset forging operation

Volume of workpiece $= \dfrac{\pi}{4}D_o^2 h_o = \dfrac{\pi}{4}D_f^2 h_f$

Final height of the part,

$$h_f = \frac{D_o^2}{D_f^2}h_o = \left(\frac{25}{50}\right)^2 \times 50 = 12.5\,\text{mm}$$

The true strain, $\varepsilon = \ln\left(\dfrac{h_o}{h_f}\right) = \ln\left(\dfrac{50}{12.5}\right) = 1.38$

The flow stress, $\sigma_f = K\varepsilon^n = 85(1.38)^0 = 85\,\text{MPa}$

Force is maximum at largest area volume

$$A_f = \frac{\pi}{4}D_f^2 = \frac{\pi}{4} \times 50^2 = 1963.5\,\text{mm}^2$$

$$K_f = 1 + 0.4\frac{\mu D}{h} = 1 + 0.4 \times \frac{0.4 \times 50}{12.5} = 1.64$$

The forging force is $F = K_f \sigma_f A_f$

$$F = 1.64 \times 85 \times 1963.5 = 273712\ \text{N}$$

$$F = 273.7\ \text{kN}$$

Q.55 Ans:[445.63]

The true strain at extension of 70 mm (strain at ultimate strength) is

$$\varepsilon = \ln\frac{70}{50} = 0.3364$$

Therefore, value of $n = 0.3364$

The true strain at extension of 70 mm is

$$\varepsilon = 0.3364 = \ln\frac{A_o}{A}$$

$$A = \frac{A_o}{e^{0.3364}} = 0.7143A_o = 0.7143\times\frac{\pi}{4}\times 10^2$$

$$A = 56.10\,\text{mm}^2$$

$$\text{True ultimate strength} = \frac{25000}{56.10\,\text{mm}^2} = 445.63\ \text{W/mm}^2$$

Strength coefficient = 445.63 MPa

Q.56 Ans:[30099]

The power density is given by $PD = \frac{f_1 VI}{A}$

Area in which beam is focused,

$$A = \frac{\pi}{4}D^2 = \frac{\pi}{4}(0.3)^2 = 0.0706\,\text{mm}^2$$

Substituting $f_1 = 0.85$, $V = 50\times 10^3$ V and $I = 50\times 10^{-3}$ A, we get

$$\text{Power density, } PD = \frac{0.85\times 50\times 10^3\times 50\times 10^{-3}}{0.0706}$$

$$PD = 30099\ \text{W/mm}^2$$

Q.57 Ans:[395.89]

Draw stress is given by

$$\sigma_d = \bar{\sigma}_f\left(1+\frac{\mu}{\tan\alpha}\right)\phi\ln\frac{A_o}{A_f}$$

Substituting, $\bar{\sigma}_f = 150$ MPa, $\mu = 0.06$, $\alpha = 12°$, $d_o = 3$ mm, $d_f = 2.5$ mm and

$$\phi = 0.88 + 0.12\left(\frac{D}{L_c}\right) = 0.88 + 0.12\left\{\frac{\left(\frac{3+2.5}{2}\right)}{\left(\frac{3-2.5}{2\sin 12}\right)}\right\} = 1.154,$$

We get,

$$\text{Draw stress, } \sigma_d = 150\left(1+\frac{0.06}{\tan 12}\right)1.154\ln\left(\frac{\frac{\pi}{4}\times 3^2}{\frac{\pi}{4}\times 2.5^2}\right)$$

$$\sigma_d = 180.65\,\text{MPa}$$

$$\text{Draw force, } F = \sigma_d\times\frac{\pi}{4}d_f^2 = 180.65\times\frac{\pi}{4}2.5^2 = 395.89$$

$$F = 395.89\,\text{N}$$

Q.58 Ans:[52.83]

$$\text{Volume of nail head, } V = \frac{\pi}{4}D_o^2\,h_o = \frac{\pi}{4}D_f^2\,h_f$$

$$\text{or}\quad h_o = \frac{D_f^2}{D_o^2}h_f = \left(\frac{9.5}{4.75}\right)^2\times 1.5 = 6\,\text{mm}$$

$$\text{The true strain, } \varepsilon = \ln\frac{6.0}{1.5} = 1.3863$$

$$\text{Flow stress, } \sigma_f = K\varepsilon^n = 550(1.3863)^{0.24} = 594.8\,\text{MPa}$$

$$K_f = 1 + 0.4\frac{\mu D}{h} = 1 + 0.4\times\frac{0.1\times 9.5}{1.5} = 1.2533$$

$$A_f = \frac{\pi}{4}\times(9.5)^2 = 70.88\,\text{mm}^2$$

The forging force is $F = K_f\sigma_f A_f$

$$F = 1.2533\times 594.8\times 70.88 = 52838.4\ \text{N}$$

$$F = 52.83\ \text{kN}$$

Q.59 Ans:[904.6]

Power required for the process, $P = 2\times(2\pi NFL)$

Substituting rolling force,

$$F = \bar{\sigma}_f wL = 200\times 10^6\times\frac{300}{1000}\times\frac{20}{1000} = 120\times 10^4\ \text{N}$$ and

contact length, $L = \sqrt{R(t_o - t_f)} = \sqrt{200(7-5)} = 20\,\text{mm}$.

we get

$$P = 2\times\left(2\pi\times\frac{180}{60}\times 120\times 10^4\times\frac{20}{1000}\right)\text{W}$$

$$P = 90.46\times 10^4\ \text{W}$$

$$P = 904.6\ \text{kW}$$

Q60 Ans:[1363.3]

Unit energy required to melt the metal,

$$U_m = 333\times 10^{-6}T_m^2$$

$$U_m = 3.33\times 10^{-6}(273+1000)^2 = 5.39\ \text{J/mm}^3$$

Rate of heat energy delivered to the operation,

$$HR_w = U_m A_w v$$

$$HR_w = 5.39\times 20\times 6 = 647.56\ \text{J/s}$$

Heat energy available for welding,

$$H_w = f_1 f_2 HR = 647.56\ \text{J/s}$$

Heat generation rate by the welding power source,

$$HR = \frac{647.56}{0.95\times 0.5}$$

$$HR = 1363.3\ \text{W}$$

Q.61 Ans:[40]

Power, $P = VI$

Substituting $V = \dfrac{240 - I}{3}$, we have

$$P = \left(\frac{240 - I}{3}\right) I = 80\,I - \frac{I^2}{3}$$

For maximum power; $\dfrac{d}{dI}(P) = 0$

$$\frac{dP}{dI} = 80 - 2\frac{I}{3} = 0$$

$$I = 120\text{ A}$$

Electrode voltage, $V = \dfrac{240 - 120}{3} = 40$

$$V = 40\text{ V}$$

Q.62 Ans:[1.016]

The shape factor is given by

$$K_x = 0.98 + 0.02\left(\frac{C_x}{C_c}\right)^{2.25}$$

The perimeter of the extruded cross-section

$$C_x = 2(60 + 20) = 160\text{ mm}$$

Cross-section area of extruded cross-section

$$A_x = 60 \times 20 = 1200\text{ mm}^2$$

Area of circle, $A_x = \pi R^2 = 1200\text{ mm}^2$

Radius of circle, $R = \sqrt{\dfrac{1200}{\pi}} = 19.544$ mm

Perimeter of a circle of the same area as the extruded shape,

$$C_c = 2\pi R = 2\pi \times 19.544 = 122.79\text{ mm}$$

Shape factor, $K_x = 0.98 + 0.02\left(\dfrac{160}{122.79}\right)^{2.25}$

$$K_x = 1.016$$

Q.63 Ans:[184.39]

Let D_b be the diameter of blank.

Volume of blank = Volume of cup

$$\frac{\pi}{4}D_b^2\,t = \frac{\pi}{4}D_p^2\,t + \pi D_p h t$$

or $D_b = \sqrt{D_p^2 + 4D_p h}$

or $D_b = \sqrt{100^2 + 4 \times 100 \times 60}$

Diameter of blank, $D_b = 184.39$ mm

Q.64 Ans:[8.97]

Draw force is given by

$$F = A_f \bar{\sigma}_f\left(1 + \frac{\mu}{\tan\alpha}\right)\phi \ln\frac{A_o}{A_f}$$

Neglecting friction and strain hardening, the draw force is

$$F = A_f\,\sigma \ln\frac{A_o}{A_f} = \frac{\pi}{4}d_f^2 \times \sigma \times 2\ln\frac{d_o}{d_f}$$

$$F = \frac{\pi}{4}8^2 \times 800 \times 2\ln\frac{10}{8} = 17946.26\text{ N}$$

Power required for the drawing process,

$$P = Fv = 17946.26 \times 0.5$$

or $P = 17946.26 \times 0.5 = 8973.13$ W

$$P = 8.97\text{ kW}$$

Q.65 Ans:[6.6]

Draw stress is given by $\sigma_d = \bar{\sigma}_f\left(1 + \dfrac{\mu}{\tan\alpha}\right)\phi \ln\dfrac{A_o}{A_f}$

Substituting $\bar{\sigma}_f = 150$ MPa, $\mu = 0.06$, $\alpha = 12°$, $d_o = 3$ mm, $d_f = 2.5$ mm and

$$\phi = 0.88 + 0.12\left(\frac{D}{L_c}\right) = 0.88 + 0.12\left\{\frac{\left(\dfrac{3 + 2.5}{2}\right)}{\left(\dfrac{3 - 2.5}{2\sin 12}\right)}\right\} = 1.154,$$

We get,

Draw stress,

$$\sigma_d = 150\left(1 + \frac{0.06}{\tan 12}\right)1.154\ln\left(\frac{\frac{\pi}{4} \times 3^2}{\frac{\pi}{4} \times 2.5^2}\right) = 180.65\text{ MPa}$$

Draw force,

$$F = \sigma_d \times \frac{\pi}{4}d_f^2 = 180.65 \times \frac{\pi}{4}2.5^2 = 395.89\text{ N}$$

The power required for wire drawing operation $P = Fv$

or $P = 395.89 \times \dfrac{1}{60}$

$$P = 6.6\text{ W}$$

15 Manufacturing Science-II

GATE Mechanical Engg.

GATE Syllabus

Machining and Machine Tool Operations: Mechanics of machining; Basic machine tools; Single and multi-point cutting tools, tool geometry and materials, tool life and wear; Economics of machining; Principles of non-traditional machining processes; Principles of work holding, design of jigs and fixtures.
Metrology and Inspection: Limits, fits and tolerances; Linear and angular measurements; Comparators; Gauge design; Interferometry; Form and finish measurement; Alignment and testing methods; Tolerance analysis in manufacturing and assembly.
Computer Integrated Manufacturing: Basic concepts of CAD/CAM and their integration tools.

Chapter Outline

15.1 KEY CONCEPTS AND FORMULAS

Metal Removal Processes

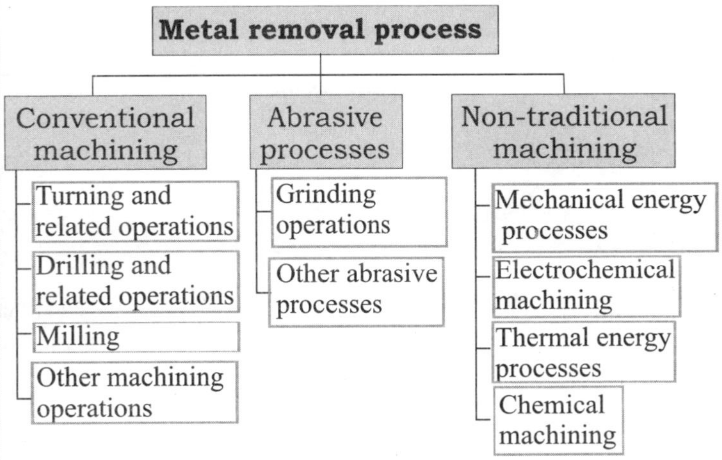

Metal Cutting Theory

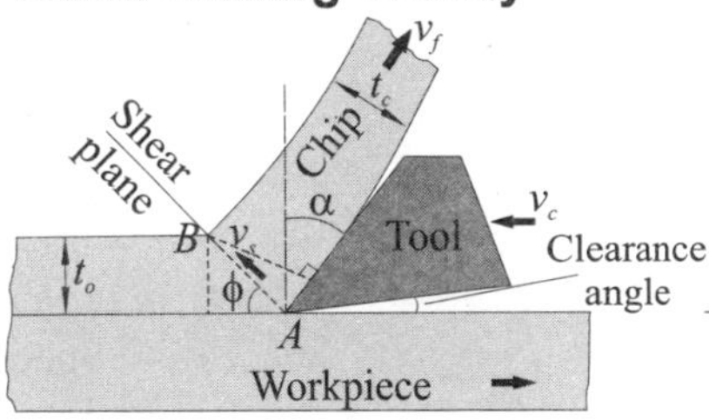

Orthogonal cutting tool model

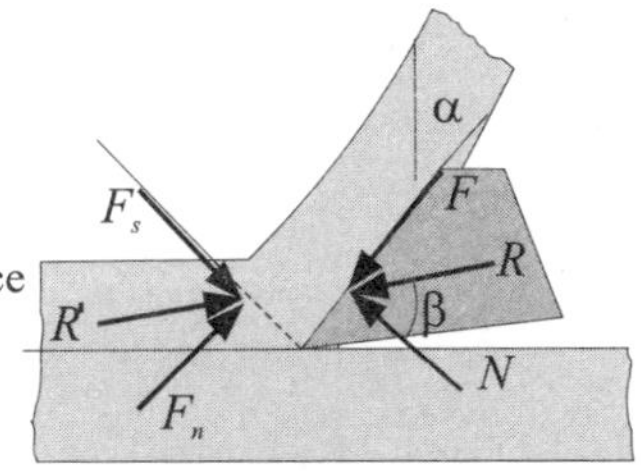

Forces in metal cutting

Chip thickness ratio, $r = \dfrac{t_o}{t_c} = \dfrac{AB\sin\phi}{AB\sin[90-(\phi-\alpha)]}$

or $r = \dfrac{t_o}{t_c} = \dfrac{\sin\phi}{\cos(\phi-\alpha)}$;

where ϕ = Shear angle, α = Rake angle

$$r = \frac{l_c}{l_o} \quad \begin{matrix} \leftarrow \text{Length of chip} \\ \leftarrow \text{Corresponding length of material from workpiece} \end{matrix}$$

This can be rearranged to determine ϕ as follows:

$$\tan\phi = \frac{r\cos\alpha}{1 - r\sin\alpha}$$

Velocity relationships:

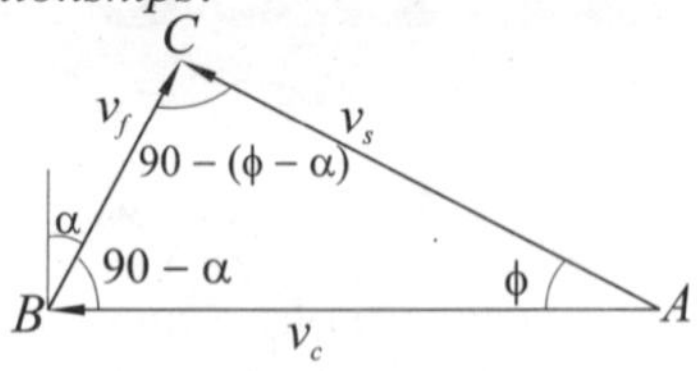

From trigonometric relations,

$$\frac{v_f}{\sin\phi} = \frac{v_s}{\sin(90 - \alpha)} = \frac{v_c}{\sin[90 - (\phi - \alpha)]}$$

or $$v_s = v_c \frac{\cos\alpha}{\cos(\phi - \alpha)}$$

or $$v_f = v_c \frac{\sin\phi}{\cos(\phi - \alpha)} = v_c r$$

Shear Strain

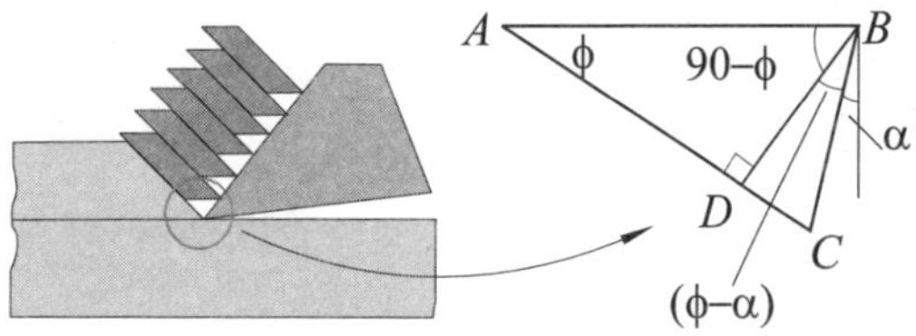

Shear strain, $$\gamma = \frac{AC}{BD} = \frac{AD + DC}{BD}$$

$$\gamma = \tan(\phi - \alpha) + \cot\phi$$

Force Relationships

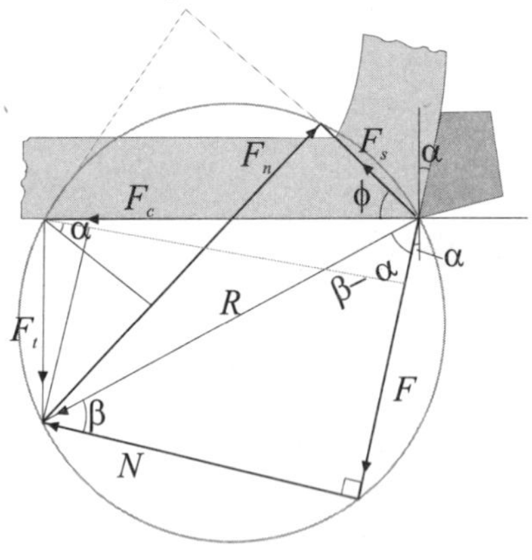

Merchant's circle

F_c = Cutting force, and F_t = Thrust force

Friction force, $F = F_c \sin\alpha + F_t \cos\alpha$

Normal force, $N = F_c \cos\alpha - F_t \sin\alpha$

Shear force, $F_S = F_c \cos\phi - F_t \sin\phi$

Normal force to shear,

$$F_N = F_c \sin\phi + F_t \cos\phi$$

Coefficient of friction, $\mu = \tan\beta = \frac{F}{N}$

Friction angle,

$$\beta = \tan^{-1}\left(\frac{F_c \sin\alpha + F_t \cos\alpha}{F_c \cos\alpha - F_t \sin\alpha}\right)$$

Shear stress, $\tau = \frac{F_s}{A_s}$

where A_s = Area of shear plan $= \frac{t_o w}{\sin\phi}$

$$F_c = R\cos(\beta - \alpha)$$
$$F_s = R\cos(\phi + \beta - \alpha)$$
$$F_t = R\sin(\beta - \alpha)$$

Cutting force, F_c and thrust force F_t are related to the shear strength of the work material.

$$F_c = F_s \frac{\cos(\beta - \alpha)}{\cos(\phi + \beta - \alpha)}$$

$$F_t = F_s \frac{\sin(\beta - \alpha)}{\cos(\phi + \beta - \alpha)}$$

$$\frac{F_t}{F_c} = \tan(\beta - \alpha)$$

The Merchant's analysis is based on the minimisation of rate of energy consumption which is equal to $F_c\, v_c$.

$$\frac{d}{d\phi} F_c\, v_c = 0; \text{ which give}$$

$$2\phi = \frac{\pi}{2} + \alpha - \beta \quad \text{(Merchant equation)}$$

Power in Machining

The rate of energy (power) consumption during machining

$$P = F_c v_c$$

Specific cutting energy/pressure,

$$U = \frac{P}{MRR} = \frac{F_c v_c}{t_o w\, v_c} = \frac{F_c}{t_o w}$$

$$U = \frac{F_c}{A_o} \ (\text{Nm/mm}^3)$$

Cutting Temperature

The energy dissipated in metal-cutting operations gets converted into heat.

Three regions (shear zone 80-85%, chip tool interface 15-20%, tool-work interface 1-3%) where heat is generated.

Average shear plane temperature increases,

$$\Delta T = \beta \frac{F_s v_s}{\rho c v t b}; \text{ where } \beta \text{ may be assumed to be 0.8.}$$

$$\Delta T = \frac{0.4U}{\rho c}\left(\frac{v_c t_o}{k}\right)^{0.333}; \text{ where } U = \text{Specific energy,}$$

v_c = Cutting speed, t_o = Chip thickness before cut, k = Thermal diffusivity, ρc = Volumetric specific heat of work material.

Turning Operation

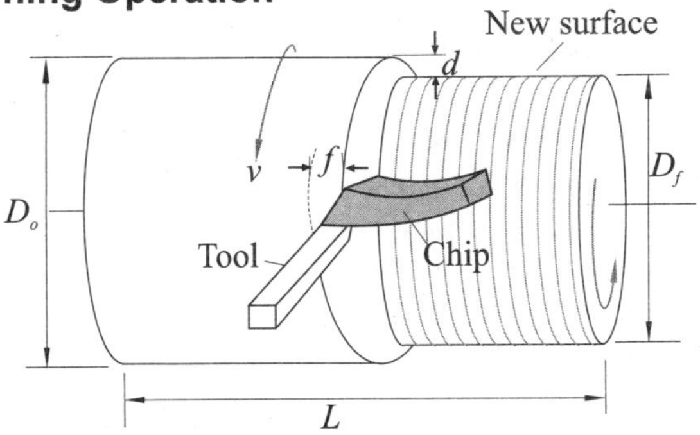

Cutting speed, $v = \pi D_o N$

Dept of cut, $d = \dfrac{D_o - D_f}{2}$

Feed rate, $f_r = Nf$ (mm/min) where f = feed (mm/rev)

Machining time, $T_m = \dfrac{L}{f_r}$

where L = Length of cylindrical work part

Material removal rate, $MRR = vfd$

Operations Related to Turning

(i) Facing, (ii) Taper turning, (iii) Contour turning, (iv) Form turning, (v) Chamfering, (vi) Cut-off, (vii) Threading, (viii) Boring, (ix) Drilling, (x) Knurling.

Drilling Operation

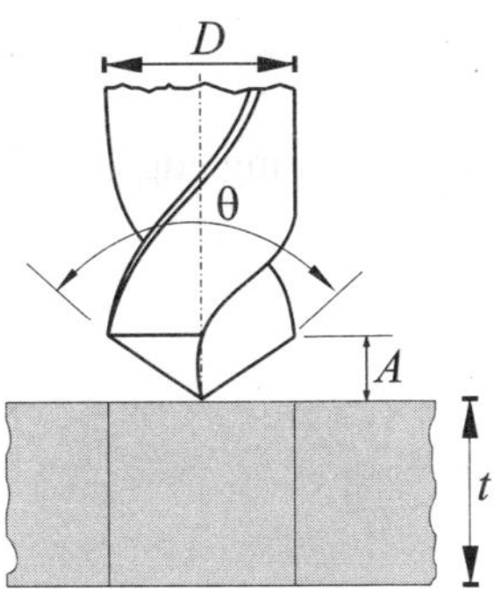

Through hole

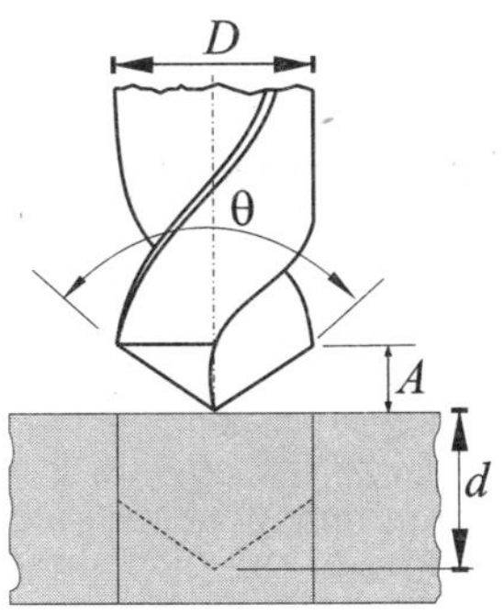

Blind hole

Cutting speed, $v = \pi DN$

Feed rate, $f_r = Nf$

Drill time, $T_m = \dfrac{t+A}{f_r}$ (For through hole) and $T_m = \dfrac{d}{f_r}$ (For blind hole)

where $A = \dfrac{D}{2}\cot\dfrac{\theta}{2}$, t = Work thickness, d = Hole depth, θ = Drill point angle.

Material removal rate, $MRR = \dfrac{\pi}{4} D^2 f_r$

Operations Related to Drilling

(i) Reaming, (ii) Tapping, (iii) Counterboring, (iv) Countersinking, (v) Centering, (vi) Spot facing.

Milling Operation

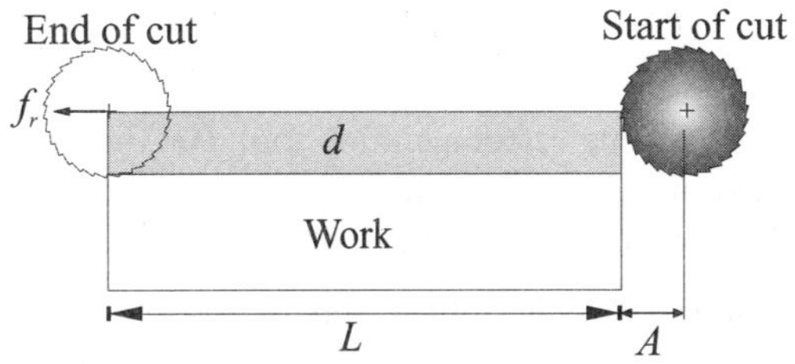

Slab milling

Cutting speed, $v = \pi DN$

Feed rate, $f_r = N n_t f$

where n_t = Number of teeth on cutter, f = Chip load in mm/tooth (or feed per cutter tooth)

Material removal rate, $MRR = wdf_r$

where w = Width, d = Depth (in slab milling)

Machining time, $T_m = \dfrac{L+A}{f_r}$ (for slab milling)

where $A = \sqrt{d(D-d)}$

Machining time, $T_m = \dfrac{L+2A}{f_r}$ (for face milling); where $A = \sqrt{w(D-w)}$

Types of Milling Operations

(A) Peripheral Milling

(i) Slab milling, (ii) Slot milling, (iii) Side milling, (iv) Straddle milling.

(B) Face Milling

(i) Conventional face milling, (ii) Partial face milling, (iii) End milling, (iv) Profile milling, (v) Pocket milling, (vi) Surface contouring.

Shaper

The shaper is a machine having reciprocating tool that takes a straight-line cut.

Average cutting speed, $v_c = \dfrac{2LN}{12C}$; where $L =$ Stroke length,

$N =$ Stroke per minute, and $C =$ Cutting time ratio.

$$\text{Cutting time ratio} = \frac{\text{Cutting time}}{\text{Total time}}$$

$$\text{Number of strokes, } S = \frac{W \leftarrow \text{Width of work}}{f \leftarrow \text{Feed}}$$

$$\text{Machining time, } T = \frac{S}{N} = \frac{SL}{v_c \times 6C} \text{ (min)}$$

Tool Life

Tool life is a measure of the length of time a tool will cut satisfactory.

Types of wear that effect a cutting tool: (i) Abrasion wear, (ii) Adhesion wear, (iii) Diffusion wear, (iv) Chemical and electrolytic wear, (v) Oxidation wear.

Relationship between tool life and cutting speed:

$$VT^n = C \quad \leftarrow \text{Taylor's tool life equation}$$

$$VT^n f^m d^p H^q = k\, T_{\text{ref}}^n f_{\text{ref}}^m d_{\text{ref}}^p H_{\text{ref}}^q$$

Where $f =$ Feed, $d =$ Depth of cut, $H =$ Hardness.

$$VT^n f^m = k\, T_{\text{ref}}^n f_{\text{ref}}^m$$

Tool Materials

Properties require in a tool-material: (i) Toughness, (ii) Hot hardness, (iii) Wear resistance.

Cutting tool materials: (i) High-speed steel and its predecessors, (ii) Cast cobalt alloys, (iii) Cemented carbide, cermets and coated carbides, (iv) Ceramics, (v) Synthetic diamond and cubic boron nitride.

Singel-point tool specifications (ASA):

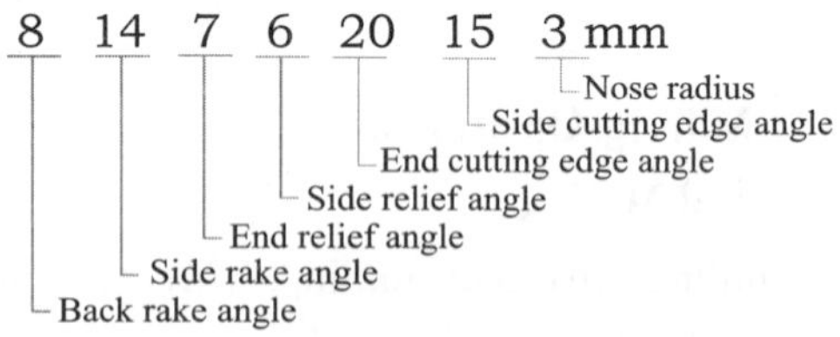

Surface Finish in Machining

Maximum surface roughness is given by

$$H_{\max} = \frac{f}{\tan C_s + \cos C_e} \text{ and } R_a = \frac{f}{4(\tan C_s + \cos C_e)}$$

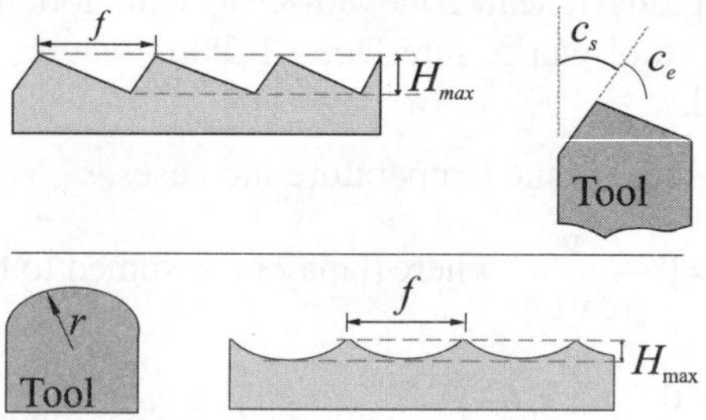

Surface geometry models

where $f =$ Feed, $C_s =$ Side angle, $C_e =$ End angle,

$H_{\max} = \dfrac{f^2}{8r}$ and $R_a = \dfrac{f^2}{32r}$; $r =$ Nose radius of the tool.

Optimizing Cutting Speed

Total time per unit product, $\quad T_C = T_h + T_m + \dfrac{T_t}{n_p}$

where $T_h =$ Part handling time (time of loading the part), $T_m =$ Machining time, $T_t =$ Tool change time, $n_p =$ Number of pieces cut in one tool life.

$$T_C = T_h + \frac{\pi DL}{vf} + \frac{T_t(\pi DL v^{\frac{1}{n}-1})}{fC^{\frac{1}{n}}};$$

$$n_p = \frac{T}{T_m} = \frac{\left(\dfrac{C}{v}\right)^{\frac{1}{n}}}{\dfrac{\pi DL}{vf}} = \frac{fC^{\frac{1}{n}}}{\pi DL v^{\frac{1}{n}-1}}$$

For minimum cycle time; $\dfrac{dT_C}{dv} = 0$

Cutting speed for maximum production;

$$v_{\max} = \frac{C}{\left[\left(\dfrac{1}{n} - 1\right)T_t\right]^n} \text{ and tool life } T_{\max} = \left(\frac{1}{n} - 1\right)T_t$$

Total cost per unit product,

$$C_c = C_o T_h + C_o T_m + C_o \frac{T_t}{n_p} + \frac{C_t}{n_p}$$

Where $C_o =$ Cost rate, $C_t =$ Cost per cutting edge.

$$C_c = C_o T_h + C_o \frac{\pi DL}{vf} + \frac{(C_o T_t + C_t)\pi DL v^{\frac{1}{n}-1}}{fC^{\frac{1}{n}}}$$

For minimum cost per piece; $\dfrac{dC_c}{dv} = 0$

Cutting speed for minimum cost,

$$v_{min} = C\left(\frac{n}{1-n} \times \frac{C_o}{C_o T_t + C_t}\right)^n$$

Tool life, $T_{min} = \left(\frac{1}{n} - 1\right)\left(\frac{C_o T_t + C_t}{C_o}\right)$

Grinding

Peripheral speed, $v = \pi DN$

Material removal rate, $MRR = v_w w d$

where d = Depth of cut (infeed), w = Cross feed (width of grinding path) and v_w = Work feed.

Length of the chip, $l_c = \sqrt{Dd}$; where D = Wheel diameter, d = Depth of cut.

Grinding wheel specification

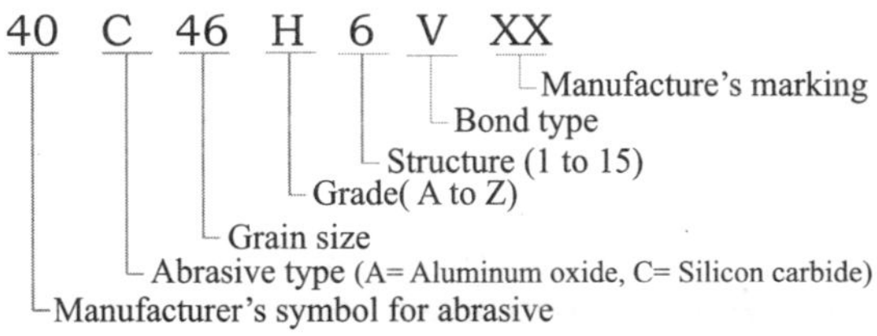

Non-traditional Machining

Classification according to principal form of energy used to effect material removal.

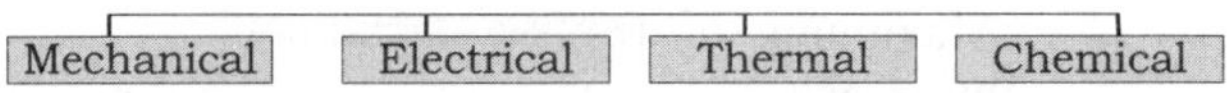

Mechanical

Ultrasonic machining (USM)

USM is the process of material removal by repetive impacts of high frequency abrasive particles against the workpiece.

Abrasive jet machining (AJM)

AJM is mechanical process for cutting, deburing, and cleaning hard brittle materials.

Water jet cutting (WJC)

WJC is a process that utilises a high velocity stream of water as the cutting agent.

Electrical

Electrochemical machining (ECM)

ECM utilises the principle of metal removal by electrochemical means and the rate of metal removal is governed by Farade's laws of electrolysis.

Thermal

Electrical Discharge Process (EDM)

EDM is the process of removal metal by controlled erosion through a series of electric sparks.

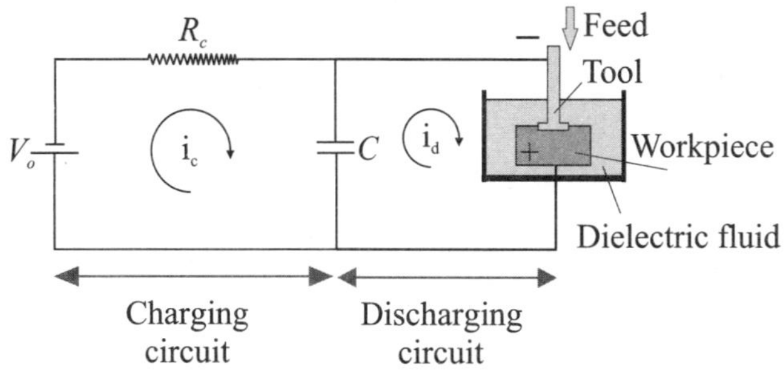

Charging current, $i_c = \frac{V_o - V_c}{R_c} = C\frac{dV_c}{dt}$

Charged voltage of the condenser,

$$V_c = V_o\left(1 - e^{-\frac{t}{RC}}\right)$$

Energy delivered in each spark, $= \frac{1}{2} C V_c^2$

Total energy delivered per second $= \frac{1}{2} C V_c^2 f_c$;

where f_c = Number of sparks/second.

Material removal rate, $MRR \propto \frac{1}{2} C V_c^2 f_c$

Electron beam machining (EBM)

In electron beam machining, heat is generated by high speed electron impinging on the workpiece, the beam being converted into thermal energy.

Laser beam machining (LBM)

LBM is the process of removing metal by focussing the laser beam on the work surface.

Chemical

Chemical machining (CHM)

In CHM material is removed from selected area of the workpiece through controlled chemical dissolution of material in contact with strong chemical reagents or etchants such as acids or alkaline solutions.

Mechanics of electrochemical machining

Metal removal rate is determined by Farade's first law, which states that the amount the chemical change produced by an electric current is proportional to the quantity of electricity passed.

Metal removal rate, $MRR = CIt$; where C = Specific removal rate, I = Current, t = Time.

$$I = \frac{E}{R};\ E = \text{Voltage and } R = \text{Resistance} = \frac{g\,r}{A}$$

where g = gap between electrode and work, r = resistivity of electrolyte, and A = surface area between work and tool.

$$MRR = C\frac{E}{R}\,t = \frac{CEA}{gr}\,t$$

Linear travel rate, $f_r = \dfrac{MRR}{At} = \dfrac{CE}{gr} = \dfrac{CI}{A}$

Jigs and Fixture

Jig: It is a device which holds and locates a workpiece, and guides and controls one or more cutting tools. Jigs are used in drilling, reaming or tapping operation.

Fixture: It is a device which holds and locates a workpiece but does not guide the cutting tool. Fixture are used in milling, grinding, planning, welding and turning.

Principles of Jigs and Fixture

(i) Reduction of idle time, (ii) Rigidit,y (iii) Clearance between Jig and component, (iv) Swarf clearance, (v) Locating points and supports, (vi) Easy loading and unloading of jig, (vii) Clamping, (viii) Fool proofing, (ix) Design for safety, (x) Components should ejected, (xi) Spring locations, (xii) Jig base, (xiii) Accuracy, (xiv) Jig buses.

Degrees of Freedom

A work piece in space, free to move in any direction can move in 12 directions

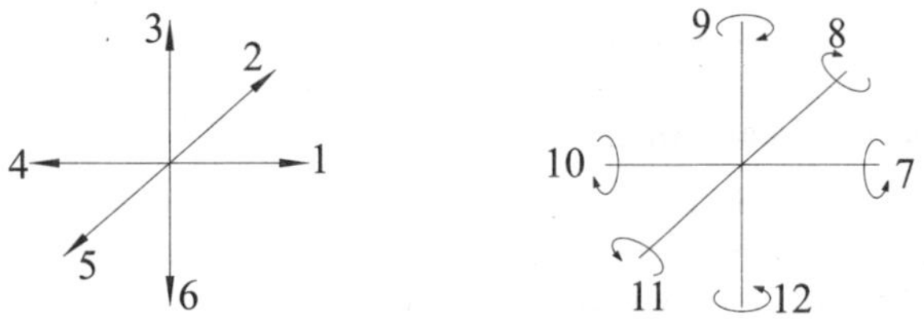

Principles of Location

3-2-1 Method of location, Principle of least points, Principle of extreme position, Principle of mutually perpendicular plane, Location of accurate work, Small locating surfaces, Replacement a necessity.

Metrology and Inspection

Metrology is the science of measurement. The science is concerned with six fundamental quantities; length, mass, time, electric current, temperature and light radiation.

Principle of Measurement

Accuracy: Accuracy is the degree to which the measured value agrees with the true value of the quantity of interest.

Precision: It is the degree of repeatability in the measurement process. Good precision means that random errors in the measurement procedure are minimised.

Limit, Fits and Tolerance

Limits: The maximum and minimum permissible sizes within which the actual size of a component lies are called limits.

Fits: Fit is defined as the degree of tightness or looseness between two making parts to perform a definite function when they are assembled together.

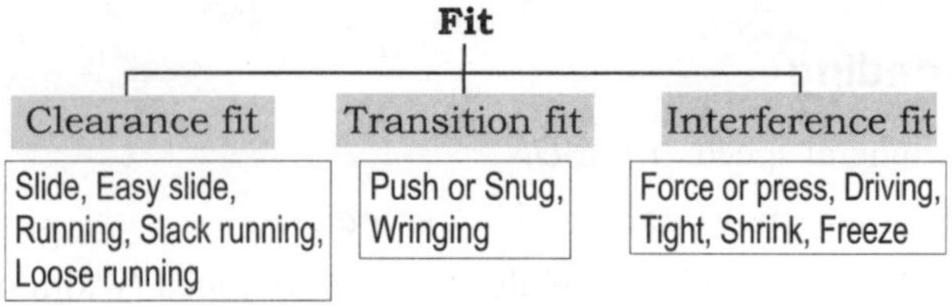

Tolerance: Tolerance is the permissible variation in the dimension of a part as it is not possible to produce a part to exact specified dimension. It is the differences between higher and lower limits of dimension of a part. It may be unilateral and bilateral.

Types of Fits

System of Fits

Hole basic system: The size of the hole is kept constant and shaft size is varied to obtain various classes of fit.

Shaft basic system: The size of the shaft is kept constant and the variation is only done in the hole size to obtain various classes of fit.

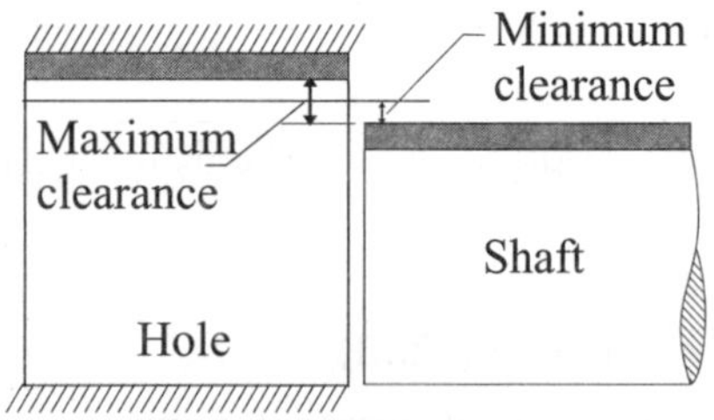

Clearance fit

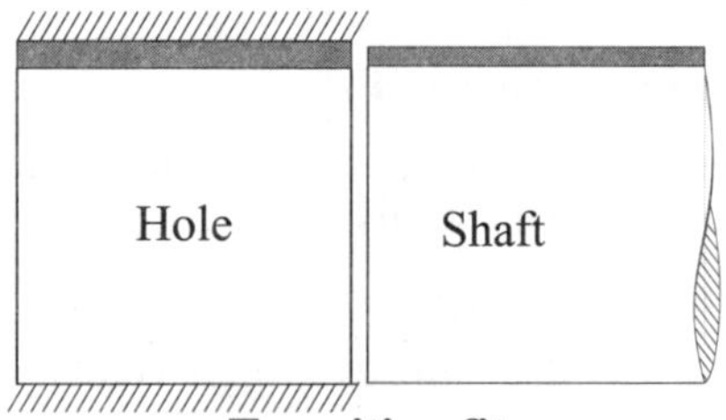

Transition fit

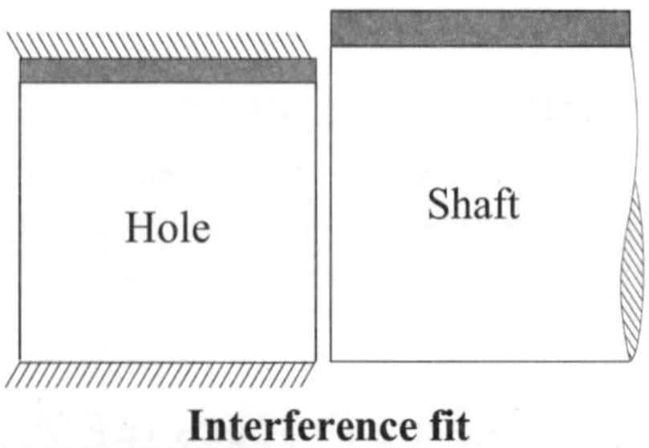

Interference fit

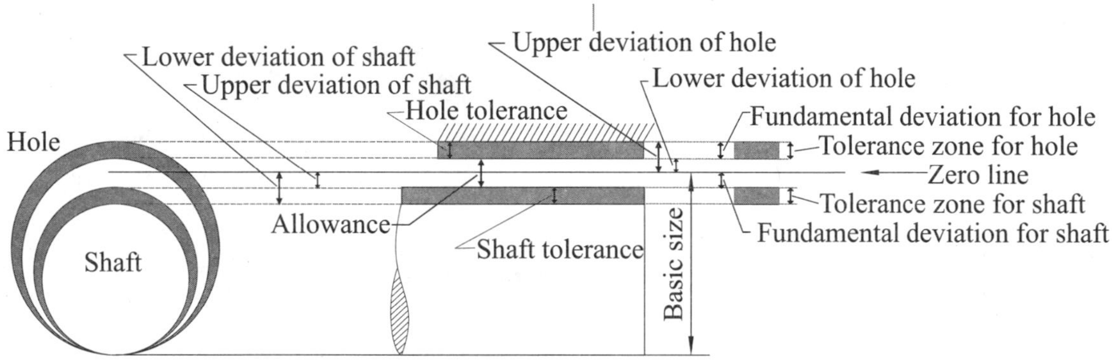

Limit, fit and tolerance

Allowance

Allowance is the prescribed difference between the dimension of two mating parts for any type of fit. The allowance may be positive or negative. The positive allowance is called clearance and negatice allowance is called *interference*.

System of tolerance

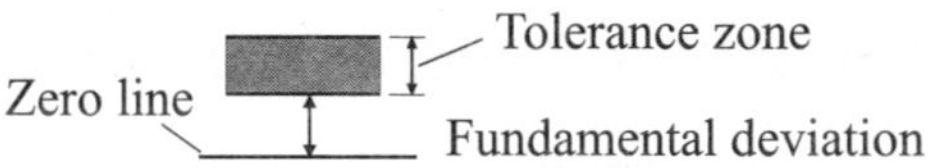

Grade is a measure of the magnitude of the tolerance. Lower the grade, the finer the tolerance. There are total of 18 grades of fundamental tolerances and 25 types of fundamental deviation. The fundamental tolerances are IT01, IT0, IT1, IT2, ... IT16. Tolerance value corresponding to grades are determined using the standard tolerance unit (i, in μm), which is a function of basic size.

$$i = 0.453\sqrt[3]{D} + 0.001D \text{ microns;}$$

where $D = \sqrt{D_{max} \times D_{min}}$ and size up to 500 mm (for IT5 to IT16)

For IT01, $i = 0.3 + 0.008D$

For IT0, $i = 0.5 + 0.012D$

For IT1, $i = 0.8 + 0.020D$

The position of the tolerance zone from zero line is determined by fundamental deviation. The ISO system defines 28 classes of basic deviation for holes and shafts.

Tolerance Grade	IT5	IT6	IT7	IT8	IT9	IT10
Values	7i	10i	16i	25i	40i	64i
Tolerance Grade	IT11	IT12	IT13	IT14	IT15	IT16
Values	100i	160i	250i	400i	640i	1000i

Linear Measurements

Linear measuring instruments are categorised depending upon their accuracy. The two categories are non-precision instruments and precision instruments.

Non-precision instruments: Steel rule, caliper, divider, Depth Gauge and telescopic gauge that are used to measure to the line graduations of a rule.

Precision instruments: Micrometers, vernier calipers, height gauges and slip gauges.

Slip gauges: Slip gauges are supplied as a set comprising of rectangular steel blocks of different dimension with opposite faces lapped flat and parallel to a high degree of accuracy.

Comparators: Comparators are classified on the basis of type of the amplification method used.

(a) Mechanical comparators, (b) Optical Comparators, (c) Pneumatic comparators, (d) Electrical comparators.

Angular Measurements

Direct Angular Measurement

Vernier Bevel Protractor (Universal Bevel Protractor): It is a simplest instrument for measuring the angle between two faces of a component. It consists of a base plate attached to a main body and an adjustable blade which is attached to a circular plate containing vernier scale.

Face Standard Angular Measuring Devices

Sine bar: It is simple device used either for accurately measuring angles or for locating work to a given angle.

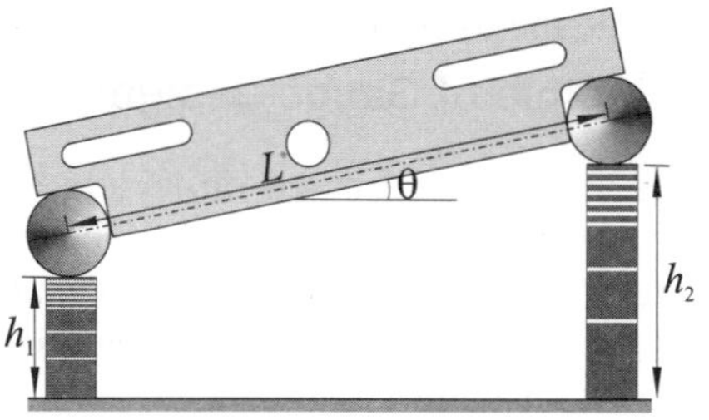

$$\theta = \sin^{-1}\left(\frac{h_1 - h_2}{L}\right)$$

Measurement of Inclines

Spirit level: It is one of the most commonly used instruments for inspecting the horizontal position of surfaces.

Clinometer: A clinometer is a special case of application of spirit level, in which it is mounted on a rotary member carried on housing. A semicircular scale is used to measure the angle of inclination of the rotary member carrying the spirit level relative to its base. Clinometer is mainly used to measure the included angle between two adjacent faces of the workpiece.

Angle Comparators

Autocollimators: It is an angle comparator based on the principle of reflection of light. Least measurement given by autocollimator is up to 1'.

Measurement of Internal and External Tapers

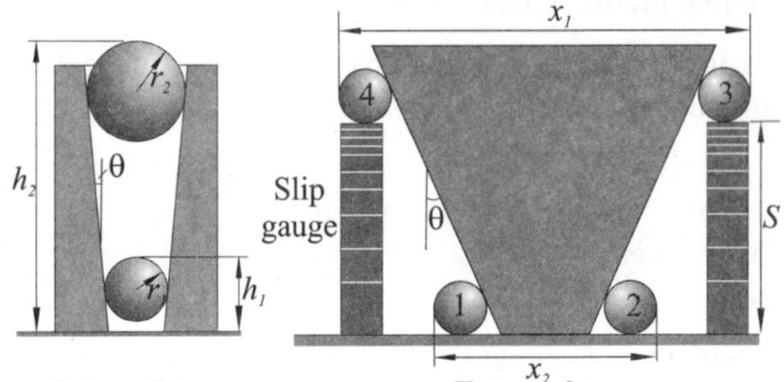

Internal taper External taper

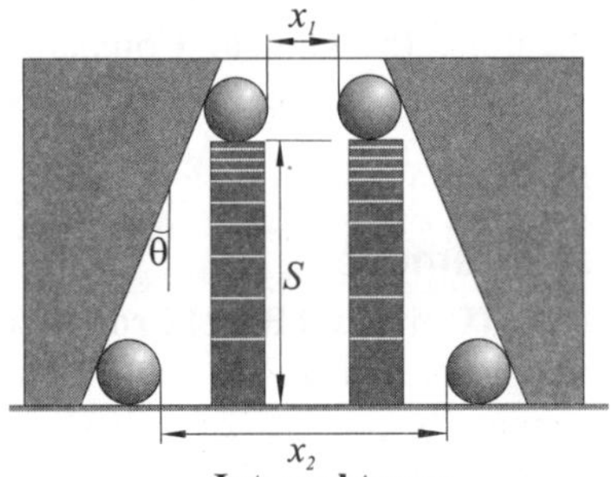

Internal taper

Gauge Design

A gauge is a device for determining the relative size or shape of a component. It determines whether, the part is inside or outside the tolerance zone.

Taylors Principle of Gauge Design:

Limit gauges are designed based on taylors principle. It states that, (i) GO gauges should be designed to check the maximum materials limit while the NOGO gauges should be designed to check the minimum material limit of shaft/hole, (ii) GO gauges should check all the related dimensions simultaneously whereas NOGO gauge should check only one element of dimension.

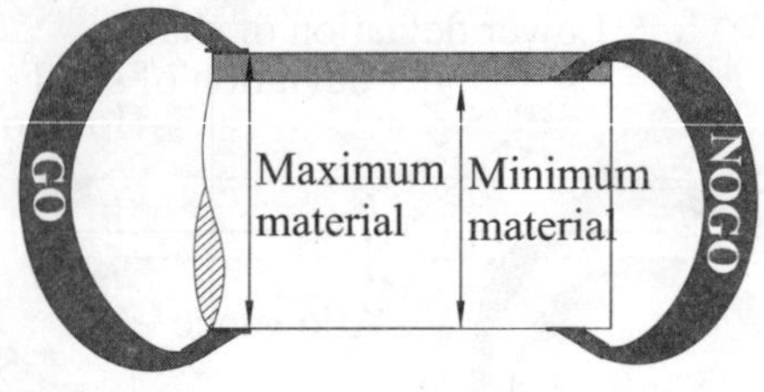

Interferometers

Interferometers are optical instruments used for measuring flatness and determining minute differences in length by direct reference to the wavelength of light. Basically, an interferometer is constructed using the same principle as of an optical flat.

Types of Interferometer

The various types of interferometers are: (i) Michelson interferometer, (ii) Fabre parrot interferometer, (iii) Fringe counting interferometer, (iv) N.P.L. flatness interferometer, (v) Pitter NPL gauge interferometer, (vi) Zeiss gauge block interferometer, (vii) Multiple beam interferometer, (viii) Laser interferometer.

Inspection of Screw Threads and Gears

Gauging of screw threads: (i) Shop measurement of the screw threads, (ii) Direct measurement.

Shop measurement of screw threads: (i) Ring screw gauges, (ii) Plug screw gauges, (iii) Thread calliper gauges.

Direct measurement of the screw threads: (i) Measurement of major and minor diameter, (ii) Measurement of pitch or effective diameter, (a) Two wire method (b) Three wire method.

Two-wire Method and Three-wire Method

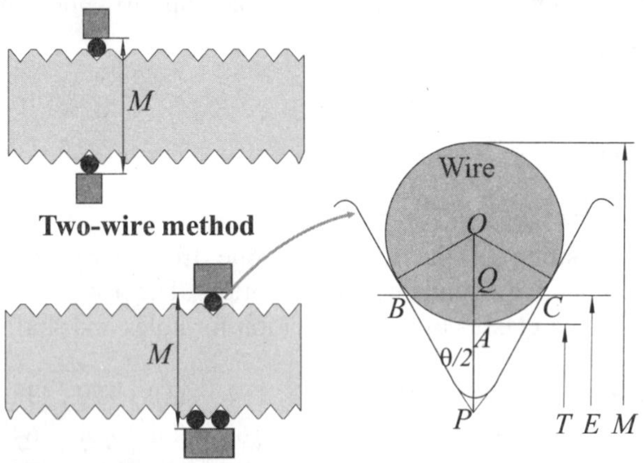

Three-wire method

Distance below wire, $T = M - 2d$

Effective diameter, $E = M - 2d + 2\,AQ$

where d = diameter of wire.

$$AQ = PQ - PA = QC\cot\left(\frac{\theta}{2}\right) - \left(OP - \frac{d}{2}\right)$$

$$AQ = \frac{p}{4}\cot\left(\frac{\theta}{2}\right) - \left(\frac{d}{2}\operatorname{cosec}\frac{\theta}{2} - \frac{d}{2}\right)$$

Effective diameter, $E = M - d + \frac{p}{2}\cot\frac{\theta}{2} - d\operatorname{cosec}\frac{\theta}{2}$

Best Size Wire Method

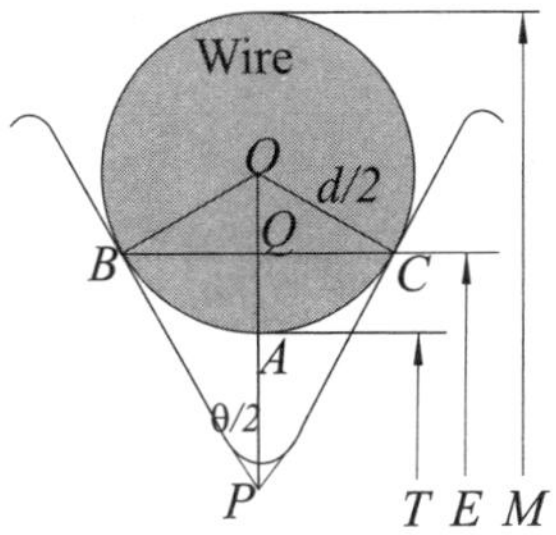

Best wire method

$$CQ = \frac{\text{Pitch}}{4} = \frac{p}{4}$$

In ΔPCO, $\cos(\theta/2) = \frac{(p/4)}{(d/2)}$

Diameter of wire, $d = \frac{p}{2}\cos\frac{\theta}{2}$

For American metric thread, $d = 0.577p$

For Whitworth, $d = 0.564p$

Surface Roughness

Surface texture: Surface texture is repetitive or random deviation from the nominal surface. Surface texture includes roughness, waviness, lay lines and flaws.

Roughness and waviness: The irregularities on the surface can be broadly grouped into two categories: (i) Primary texture (roughness), (ii) Secondary texture (waviness).

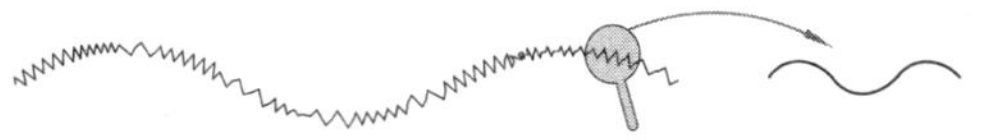

Micro geometrical error (Waviness) Micro geometrical error (Roughness)

RMS and CLA values: Surface roughness in described by either: (i) CLA (centre line average) or RMS (root mean square) values.

CLA value (or arithmetic mean value), $Ra = \frac{\sum h}{N}$

Root mean square (RMS) value, $\text{RMS} = \sqrt{\frac{\sum h^2}{N}}$

Roughness grade symbols:

Ra value (in mm)	Roughness grade symbol
50	∼
12.5-25.0	▽
1.6-6.3	▽▽
0.2-0.8	▽▽▽
0.025-0.1	▽▽▽▽

Computer Integrated Manufacturing (CIM)

CIM is the automated version of the manufacturing process, where the three major manufacturing functions, product and process design, planning and control, and the manufacturing process itself are replaced by the computer automated technologies. All these technologies are tied together using a network and integrated database.

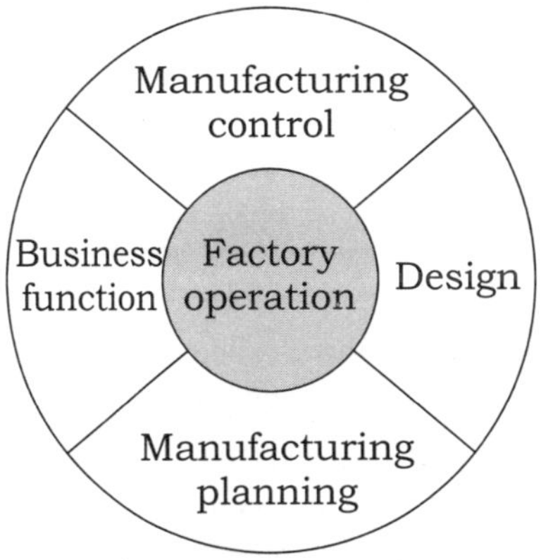

Elements of CIM

Benefits of CIM System

(i) Increased machine utilisation, (ii) Reduced direct and indirect labour, (iii) Reduce manufacturing lead time, (iv) Lower in process inventory, (v) Scheduling flexibility, etc.

CAD/CAM

CAD/CAM (computer-aided design and computer-aided manufacturing) refers to computer software that is used to both design and manufacture products. CAD uses computer technology for design and design documentation.

The effective use of computer technology in manufacturing planning and control is known as *computer aided manufacturing* (CAM). Manufacturing engineering functions such as process planning and numeric control (NC) are included in CAM. The application of CAM is divided in two categories: (i) manufacturing planning, and (ii) manufacturing control.

Numerical Control (NC)

Numerical control (NC) is a form of programmable

automation in which the mechanical actions of a piece of equipment are controlled by a program containing coded alphanumerical data.

Components of an NC system

(i) Data input device

(ii) Machine control unit (MCU)

(iii) Machine tool operative member

(iv) Servo drives for each axis of motion

(v) Feed back devices

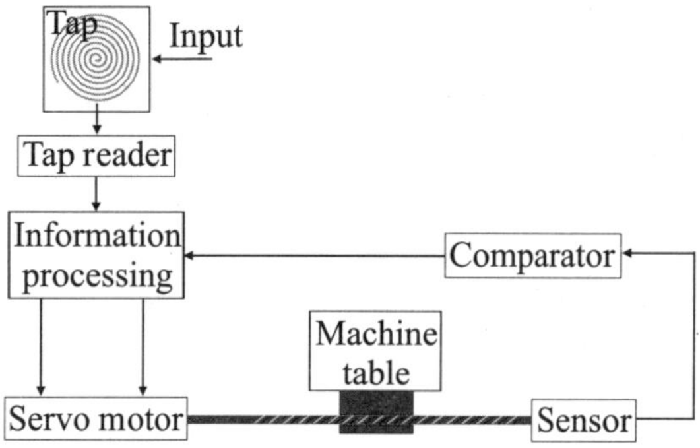

1. Part program: It is the detailed set of commands to be followed by the processing equipment.

2. Machine control unit (MCU): It is a microcomputer that stores the program and executes it by converting each command into actions by processing. equipment. MCU consists of both hardware and software.

3. Processing equipment: It accomplishes the sequence of processing steps to transform the starting work part into a completed part.

NC Programming

The program is prepared by listing the coordinate values *X, Y, Z* of the entire tool path as suited to machine the component. The coordinate values are prefixed with preparatory codes to indicate the type of movement required from one coordinate to the other. The coordinates are also suffixed with miscellaneous codes for initiating functions like start, stop, coolant on/off, etc.

NC part Programming

Manual part programming: It uses basic numerical data and special alphanumeric code to define the steps in the process.

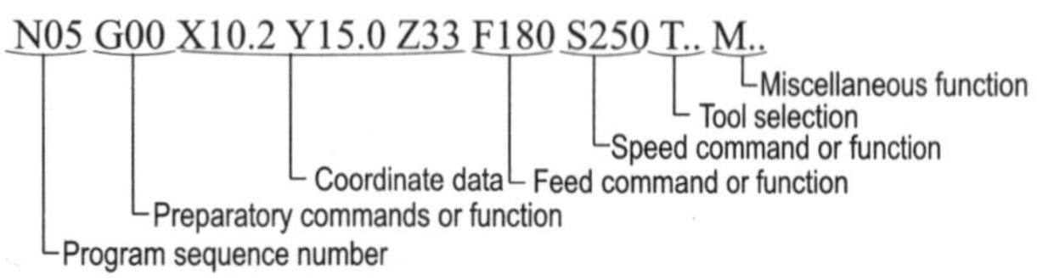

Common letter address specifications	
Type	**Function**
N-word	Sequence number: Used for line identifications
O-word	Program number: Used for program identification
G-word	Preparatory function
M-word	Miscellaneous/auxiliary function
F-word	Feed rate designation
S-word	Spindle speed designation
T-word	Tool designation
Z-word	*Z*-axis designation (similar for *X* and *Y* axes)
H-word	Tool length offset designation
Only two letters H and L are unassigned G and M-words examples	
G00	Prepare for a point-to-point operation
G01	Linear interpolation in contouring system
G03	Circular interpolation, counterclocwise
M00	Stop machine
M03	Starts spindle in clockwise direction

Computer-Assisted Part Programming (APT)

APT is divided into two steps:

(i) definition of part geometry

(ii) specification of tool path and operation sequence.

For example: APT geometry statements

$$P1 = \text{POINT} / 30.0,\ 90.0$$

$$L1 = \text{LINE} / P1,\ P2$$

where point P1 located at $x = 30\,\text{mm}$, $y = 90\,\text{mm}$, L1 is line that goes through points P1 and P2.

APT motion statements

GOTO/P1

This directs the tool to move from its current location to a position defined by P1.

GORGT/L3, PAST, L4

This direct the tool to go right along line L3 until it is positioned just past line L4.

NC Positioning System

Open-loop positioning system:

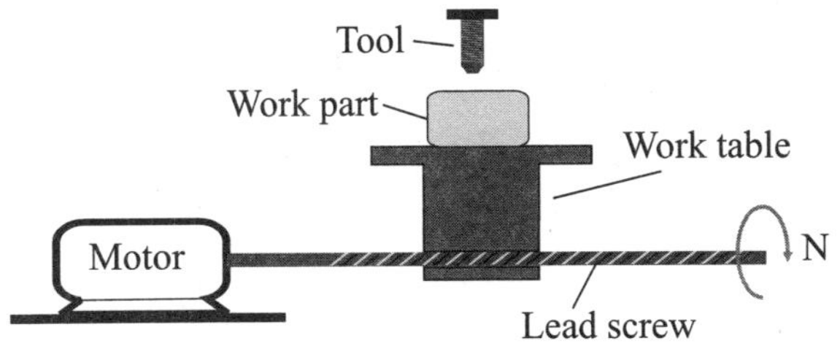

Step angle, $\alpha = \dfrac{360}{n_s}$; where n_s = Number of step angles for the motor.

Angle of lead screw rotation, $A = \alpha\, n_p$;

Where n_p = Number of pulse received by the motor.

Movement of table, $x = p\dfrac{A}{360}$; where p = Pitch of the lead screw mm/rev.

or $$x = \frac{p\alpha\, n_p}{360}$$

Number of pulses required to achieve a specified x-position increment in a point-to-point system can be found

$$n_p = \frac{360x}{p\alpha}$$

Rotational speed of the lead screw, $N = \dfrac{360 f_p}{n_s}$

where f_p = Pulse train frequency, n_s = Steps/rev.

Table travel speed, $V_t = f_r = Np$; where f_r = Table feed rate.

Pulse train frequency, $f_p = \dfrac{V_t\, n_s}{60p} = \dfrac{f_r\, n_s}{60p}$

15.2 SOLVED EXAMPLES

Previous Years GATE Questions

Example 15.1

A resistance capacitance relaxation circuit is used in an electrical discharge machining (EDM) process. The discharge voltage is 100 V at a spark cycle time 25 μs, the average power input required is 1 kW. The capacitance (in μF) in the circuit is

(A) 2.5 (B) 5.0 (C) 7.5 (D) 10.0

GATE 2015

Solution

Energy stored in capacitor, $U = \dfrac{1}{2}CV^2$

or $$U = P_{av}t = \frac{1}{2}CV^2$$

Substituting given values of $V = 100$ V, $t = 25\times10^{-6}$ s and $P_{av} = 1\times10^3$ W.

$$1\times10^3 \times 25\times10^{-6} = \frac{1}{2}C\times100^2$$

or $$C = 5\times10^{-6}\,\text{F}$$

$$C = 5\ \mu\text{F}$$

Example 15.2

A single point cutting tool with 0° rake angle is used in an orthogonal machining process. At a cutting speed of 180 m/min, the thrust force is 490 N. If the coefficient of friction between the tool and the chip is 0.7, then the power consumption (in kW) for the machining operation is___.

GATE 2015

Solution

Given: $\alpha = 0^o$, $v = \dfrac{180}{60}$ m/s, $F_t = 490$ N, $\mu = 0.7$

Friction angle, $\beta = \tan^{-1}\mu = \tan^{-1}0.7 = 35°$

Power consumption in machining operation is $P = F_c v$

$$P = \frac{F_t}{\tan(\beta-\alpha)}v$$

$$P = \frac{490}{\tan(35-0)}\times\frac{180}{60} = 2100\ \text{W}$$

$$P = 2.1\,\text{kW}$$

Example 15.3

A drill is positioned at point P and it has to proceed to point Q. The coordinates of point Q in the incremental system of defining position of a point in CNC part program will be

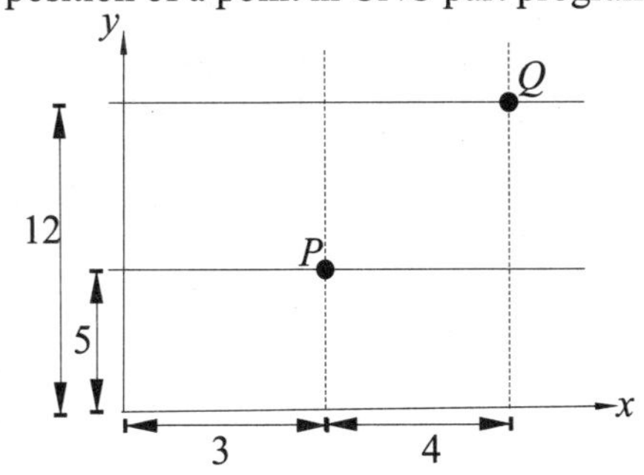

(A) (3, 12) (B) (5, 7) (C) (7, 12) (D) (4, 7)

GATE 2015

Solution

Coordinates of point Q in the incremental system is (4, 7).

Example 15.4

In a CNC milling operation, the tool has to machine the circular arc from point (20, 20) to (10, 10) at sequence number 5 of the CNC part program. If the center of the arc is at (20, 10) and the machine has incremental mode of defining position coordinates, the correct tool path command is

(A) N 05 G90 G01 X-10 Y-10 R10

(B) N 05 G91 G03 X-10 Y-10 R10

(C) N 05 G90 G03 X-20 Y-20 R10

(D) N 05 G91 G02 X-20 Y-20 R10

GATE 2015

Solution

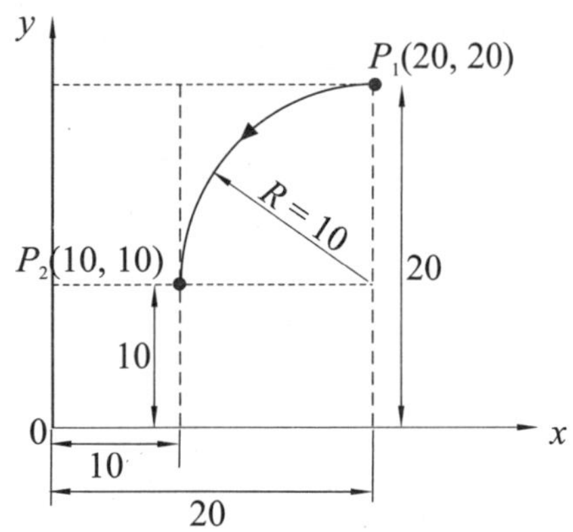

N05 G91 G03 X10 Y10 R10

- N05 — Sequence number
- G91 — Incremental coodinate system
- G03 — Circular interpolation CCW
- X10 Y10 — Coordinates
- R10 — Radius

Example 15.5

Orthogonal turning of a mild steel tube with a tool of rake angle 10° is carried out at a feed of 0.14 mm/rev. If the thickness of the chip produced is 0.28 mm, the values of shear angle and shear strain will be respectively

(A) 28° 20' and 2.19 (B) 22° 20' and 3.53

(C) 24° 30' and 4.19 (D) 37° 20' and 5.19

GATE 2015

Solution

Given: $\alpha = 10°, f = 0.14$ mm/rev, $t_c = 0.28$ mm

In turning operation feed, f = Uncut chip thickness, t_o

Chip thickness ratio, $r = \dfrac{t_o}{t_c} = \dfrac{0.14}{0.28} = 0.5$

$$\tan\phi = \frac{r\cos\alpha}{1 - r\sin\alpha} = \frac{0.5\cos 10}{1 - 0.5\sin 10} = 0.5392$$

$$\phi = \tan^{-1} 0.5392 = 28.33°$$

Shear strain, $\gamma = \cot\phi + \tan(\phi - \alpha)$

$$\gamma = \cot 28.33 + \tan(28.33 - 10)$$

$$\gamma = 2.186$$

Example 15.6

Hole of diameter $25.0^{+0.040}_{+0.020}$ mm are assembled interchangeably with the pins of diameter $25.0^{+0.005}_{-0.008}$ mm. The minimum clearance in the assembly will be

(A) 0.048 mm (B) 0.015 mm

(C) 0.005 mm (D) 0.008 mm

GATE 2015

Solution

Minimum clearance in the assembly is

= Lower limit of hole – Higher limit of pin

$= (25 + 0.020) - (25 + 0.005)$

Minimum clearance = 0.015 mm

Example 15.7

Under certain cutting conditions, doubling the cutting speed reduces the tool life to $\left(\dfrac{1}{16}\right)^{th}$ of the original. Taylor's tool life index (n) for this tool workplace combination will be______.

GATE 2015

Solution

Taylor's tool life equation, $VT^n = C$

$$2V\left(\frac{T}{16}\right)^n = VT^n$$

or $16^n = 2$

$$n = \frac{1}{4} = 0.25$$

Example 15.8

An orthogonal turning operation is carried out under the following conditions; rake angle = 5°, spindle rotational speed = 400 rpm, axial feed = 0.4 m/min and radial depth of cut = 5 mm. The chip thickness t_c is found to be 3 mm. The shear angle (in degree) in this turning process is____.

GATE 2015

Solution

Given: $\alpha = 5°$, $N = 400$ rpm, $f_r = 0.4$ m/min, $d = 5$ mm, $t_c = 3$ mm

Feed rate, $f_r = Nf \Rightarrow 0.4 = 400f$

or $f = \frac{0.4}{400}$ m/rev = 1 mm/rev

In turning operation: Feed = Uncut chip thickness = 1 mm

Chip thickness ratio, $r = \frac{1}{3}$

$$\tan\phi = \frac{r\cos\alpha}{1 - r\sin\alpha} = \frac{\frac{1}{3}\cos 5}{1 - \frac{1}{3}\sin 5} = 0.34199$$

$$\phi = 18.88°$$

Example 15.9

In the assembly shown below, the part dimensions are:

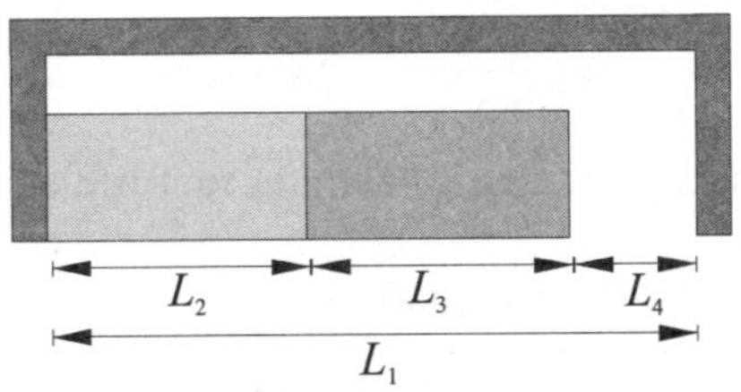

$L_1 = 22.0^{\pm 0.01}$ mm, $L_2 = L_3 = 10.0^{\pm 0.005}$ mm

Assuming the normal distributions of part dimensions, the dimension L_4 in mm for assembly condition would be

(A) $2.0^{\pm 0.008}$ (B) $2.0^{\pm 0.012}$ (C) $2.0^{\pm 0.016}$ (D) $2.0^{\pm 0.020}$

GATE 2015

Solution

$$(L_4)_{max} = (L_1)_{max} - (L_2)_{min} - (L_3)_{min}$$

$$(L_4)_{max} = (22.0 + 0.01) - (10.0 - 0.005) - (10.0 - 0.005)$$

Maximum dimension of $L_4 = 2.02$ mm,

$$(L_4)_{min} = (L_1)_{max} - (L_2)_{max} - (L_3)_{max}$$

$$(L_4)_{min} = (22.0 - 0.01) - (10.0 + 0.005) - (10.0 + 0.005)$$

Minimum dimension of $L_4 = 1.98$ mm

Therefore, the dimension L_4 is $2^{\pm 0.02}$

Example 15.10

The main cutting force acting on a tool during the turning (orthogonal cutting) operation of a metal is 400 N. The turning is performed using 2 mm depth of cut and 0.1 mm / rev feed rate. The specific cutting pressure (in N/mm^2) is

(A) 1000 (B) 2000 (C) 3000 (D) 4000

GATE 2014

Solution

Specific cutting energy is given by

$$P_u = \frac{F_c}{tw}$$

Substituting feed $t = 0.1$ mm, depth of cut $w = 2$ mm and $F_c = 400$ N

$$P_u = \frac{400}{0.1 \times 2} = 2000$$

$$P_u = 2000 \text{ N/mm}^2$$

Example 15.11

During pure orthogonal turning operation of a hollow cylindrical pipe, it is found that the thickness of the chip produced is 0.5 mm. The feed given to the zero degree rake angle tool is 0.2 mm/rev. The shear strain produced during the operation is_______.

GATE 2014

Solution

Chip thickness ratio, $r = \frac{0.2}{0.5} = 0.4$

$$\tan\phi = \frac{r\cos\alpha}{1 - r\sin\alpha} = \frac{0.4\cos 0}{1 - 0.4\sin 0} = 0.4$$

$$\phi = 21.8°$$

Shear strain, $\gamma = \cot\phi + \tan(\phi - \alpha)$

or $\gamma = \cot 21.8 + \tan(21.8 - 0)$

Shear strain, $\gamma = 2.9$

Example 15.12

For the given assembly: 25H7/g8, match Group A with Group B

Group A	Group B
(P) H	(I) Shaft type
(Q) IT8	(II) Hole type
(R) IT7	(III) Hole tolerance grade
(S) g	(IV) Shaft tolerance grade

(A) P-I, Q-III, R-IV, S-II (B) P-I, Q-IV, R-III, S-II

(C) P-II, Q-III, R-IV, S-I (D) P-II, Q-IV, R-III, S-I

GATE 2014

Solution

H7 is for hole where 7 indicates its tolerance grade.

g8 is for shaft where 8 indicates its tolerance grade.

Correct match:

P-II, Q-IV, R-III, S-I

Example 15.13

If the Taylor's tool life exponent n is 0.2, and the tool changing time is 1.5 min, then the tool life (in min) for maximum production rate is_______.

GATE 2014

Solution

The tool life for maximum production rate is

$$T_{max} = \left(\frac{1}{n} - 1\right) T_t$$

$$T_{max} = \left(\frac{1}{02} - 1\right) 15$$

$$T_{max} = 6 \text{ min}$$

Example 15.14

A metric thread of pitch 2 mm and thread angle 60° is inspected for its pitch diameter using 3-wire method. The diameter of the best size wire in mm is

(A) 0.866 (B) 1.000 (C) 1.154 (D) 2.000

GATE 2013

Solution

The diameter of the best size wire is $d = \frac{p}{2}\sec\frac{\theta}{2}$

or $$d = \frac{2}{2}\sec\frac{60}{2}$$

$$d = 1.154 \text{ mm}$$

Example 15.15

A steel bar 200 mm in diameter is turned at a feed of 0.25 mm/rev with a depth of cut of 4 mm. The rotational speed of the workpiece is 160 rpm. The material removal rate (in mm^3/s) is

(A) 160 (B) 167.6 (C) 1600 (D) 1675.5

GATE 2013

Solution

Metal removal rate in turning operation is

$$MRR = fdv$$

or $$MRR = fd\frac{pDN}{60}$$

Substituting given values, $D = 200$ mm, $f = 0.25$ mm/rev, $d = 4$ mm and $N = 160$ rpm, we have

$$MRR = 0.25 \times 4 \times \frac{\pi \times 200 \times 160}{60}$$

$$MRR = 1675.5 \text{ mm}^3/\text{s}$$

Example 15.16

Two cutting tools are being compared for a machining operation. The tool life equations are:

Carbide tool $VT^{1.6} = 3000$

HSS tool $VT^{0.6} = 200$

where V is the cutting speed in m/min and T is the total life in min. The carbide tool will provide higher tool life if the cutting speed in m/min exceeds

(A) 15.0 (B) 39.4 (C) 49.3 (D) 60.0

GATE 2013

Solution

For the same cutting speed V, the tool life (T_1) of carbide tool will be equal to that of HSS tool;

$$\frac{VT_1^{1.6}}{VT_1^{0.6}} = \frac{3000}{200}$$

$$T_1 = 15 \text{ min}$$

Substituting $T_1 = 15$ min in carbide tool life equation, we have

$$V(15)^{1.6} = 3000$$

$$V = 39.38 \text{ m/min}$$

Example 15.17

In a CAD package, mirror image of a 2D point $P(5,10)$ is to be obtained about a line which passes through the origin and makes an angle of 45° counter clockwise with the x-axis. The coordinates of the transformed point will be

(A) (7.5, 5) (B) (10, 5) (C) (7.5, – 5) (D) (10, – 5)

GATE 2013

Solution

The point $P(5,10)$ and its mirror image Q is shown in the figure.

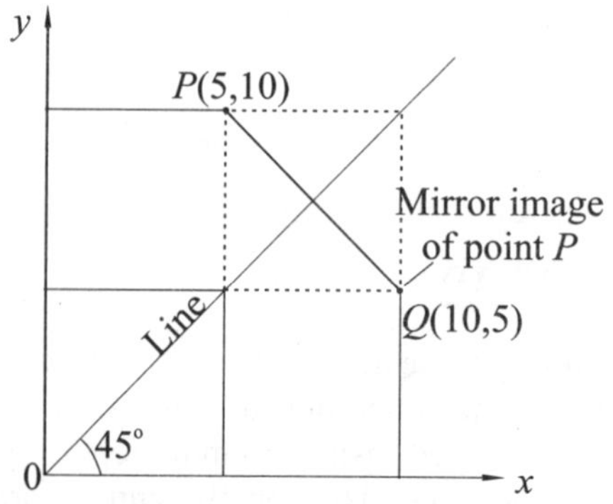

The coordinate of Q is (10,5)

Example 15.18

Cylindrical pins of $25^{+0.020}_{+0.010}$ mm diameter are electroplated in a shop. Thickness of the plating is 30^{+2} micron. Neglecting gauge tolerances, the size of the GO gage in mm to inspect the plated component is

(A) 25.042 (B) 25.052 (C) 25.074 (D) 25.084

GATE 2013

Solution

The size of the cylindrical pin after plating can be

$$25^{+0.020}_{+0.010} + 0.030^{+2} = 25.03^{+0.022}_{+0.012}$$

The maximum size of the pin for GO gauge is

$$25.03 + 0.022 = 25.052$$

$$25.052 \text{ mm}$$

Example 15.19

During the electrochemical machining (ECM) of iron (atomic weight = 56, valency = 2) at current of 1000 A with 90% current efficiency, the material removal rate was observed to be 0.26 gm/s. If titanium (atomic weight = 48, valency = 3) is machined by the ECM process at the current of 2000 A with 90% current efficiency, the expected material removal rate in gm/s will be

(A) 0.11 (B) 0.23 (C) 0.30 (D) 0.52

GATE 2013

Solution

The metal removal rate in ECM process is:

$$MRR = \frac{\eta IA}{Fv\rho}$$

where A is the atomic weight, v is the valency, F is Faraday's constant = 96500 C/mol, ρ is the density of the alloy.

$$\frac{(MRR)_{\text{iron}}}{(MRR)_{\text{titanium}}} = \frac{\eta_1 I_1 A_1}{\eta_2 I_2 A_2} \times \frac{F v_2 \rho_2}{F v_1 \rho_1}$$

$$\frac{0.26}{(MRR)_{\text{titanium}}} = \frac{0.9}{0.9} \times \frac{1000}{2000} \times \frac{56}{48} \times \frac{3}{2}$$

Metal removal rate of titanium $(MRR)_{\text{titanium}} = 0.297$

$$(MRR)_{\text{titanium}} = 0.297 \text{ g/s}$$

Example 15.20

Linked Answer Questions

In orthogonal turning of a bar of 100 mm diameter with a feed of 0.25 mm/rev, depth of cut of 4 mm and cutting velocity of 90 m/min, it is observed that the main (tangential) cutting force is perpendicular to the friction force acting at the chip-tool interface. The main (tangential) cutting force is 1500 N.

Q(a) The orthogonal rake angle of the cutting tool in degree is

(A) Zero (B) 3.58 (C) 5 (D) 7.16

Q(b) The normal force acting at the chip-tool interface in N is

(A) 1000 (B) 1500 (C) 2000 (D) 2500

GATE 2013

Solution

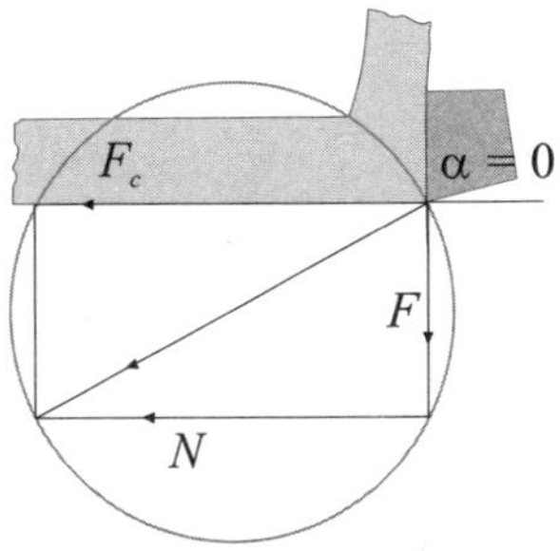

The rake angle α is shown in the Merchant's diagram as shown in the figure.

(a) Since cutting force F_c is normal to friction force F, hence the rake angle $\alpha = 0$.

(b) The normal force at the chip tool interface,

$$N = F_c \cos\alpha - F_t \sin\alpha$$

$$N = 1500 \cos 0 - F_t \sin 0$$

$$N = 1500 \text{ N}$$

Example 15.21

In an interchangeable assembly, shafts of size $25.000^{+0.040}_{-0.010}$ mm mate with holes of size $25.000^{+0.030}_{+0.020}$ mm. The maximum interference (in macrons) in the assembly is:

(A) 40 (B) 20 (C) 30 (D) 10

GATE 2012

Solution

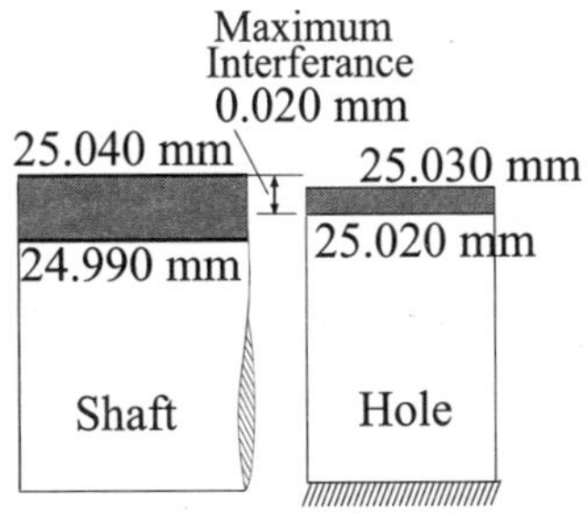

Maximum interference

= Maximum size of shaft − Minimum size of hole

Maximum interference = 25.040 − 25.020 = 0.020 mm

Maximum interference = 20 μm

Example 15.22

A CNC vertical milling machine has to cut a straight slot of 10 mm width and 2 mm depth by a cutter of 10 mm diameter between points (0,0) and (100, 100) on the x-y plane (dimensions in mm). The feed rate used for milling is 50 mm/min. Milling time for the slot (in seconds) is

(A) 120 (B) 180 (C) 170 (D) 240

GATE 2012

Solution

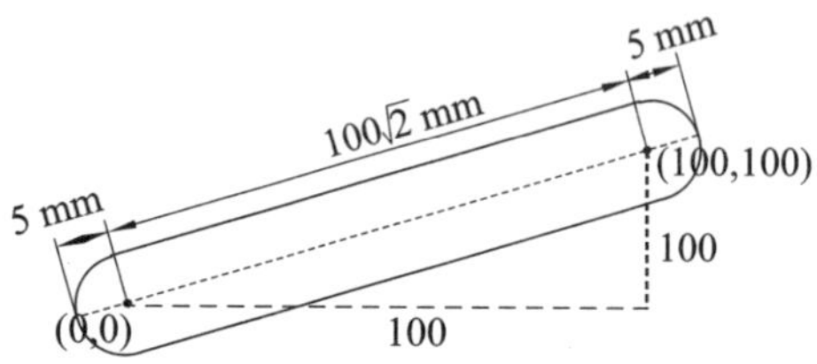

Milling time, $T = \frac{L}{f}$

$$T = \frac{100\sqrt{2}+5+5}{50}\ \text{min}$$

or $T = 3.028\ \text{min}$

$$T = 181.7\ \text{s}$$

Example 15.23

In a single pass drilling operation, a through hole is 15 mm diameter is to be drilled in a steel plate of 50 mm thickness. Drill spindles speed is 500 rpm, feed is 0.2 mm/rev and drill point angle is 118°. Assuming 2 mm clearance at approach and exit, the total drill time (in seconds) is

(A) 35.1 (B) 31.2 (C) 32.4 (D) 30.1

GATE 2012

Solution

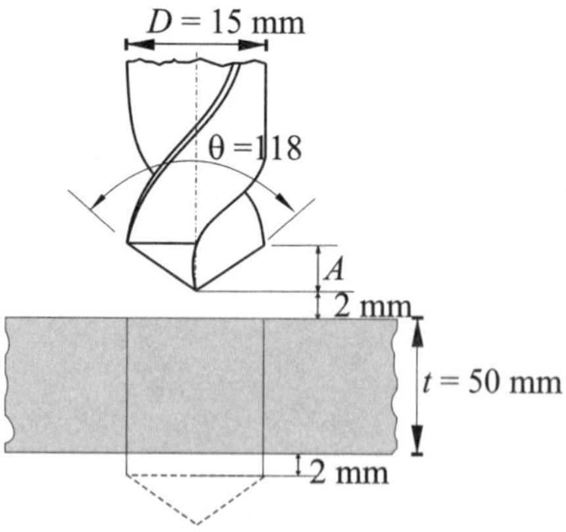

Feed rate, $f_r = Nf$

or $f_r = \frac{500}{60} \times 0.2 = 1.667\ \text{mm/s}$

Drill time, $T_m = \frac{t + A + a_{apra} + a_{exit}}{f_r}$

$$T_m = \frac{50 + \frac{15}{2}\cot\frac{118}{2} + 2 + 2}{1.667}\ \text{s}$$

$$T_m = 35.09\ \text{s}$$

Example 15.24

Details pertaining to an orthogonal metal cutting process are given below:

Chip thickness ratio	0.4
Undeformed thickness	0.6 mm
Rake angle	+10°
Cutting speed	2.5 m/s
Mean thickness of primary shear zone	25 microns

The shear strain rate in s^{-1} during the process is

(A) 0.1781×10^5 (B) 1.0104×10^5

(C) 0.7754×10^5 (D) 4.397×10^5

GATE 2012

Solution

Given: $r = 0.4$, $t_o = 0.6\ \text{mm}$, $\alpha = 10°$, $v_c = 2.5\ \text{m/s}$ $t_m = 25\ \mu\text{m}$.

Shear angle, $\phi = \tan^{-1}\left(\frac{r\cos\alpha}{1 - r\sin\alpha}\right)$

or $\phi = \tan^{-1}\left(\frac{0.4\cos 10}{1 - 0.4\sin 10}\right)$

$$\phi = 22.94°$$

Shear strain rate,

$$\dot{\gamma} = \frac{v_c \cos\alpha}{t_m \cos(\phi - \alpha)} = \frac{2.5\cos 10}{25 \times 10^{-6}\cos(22.94 - 10)}$$

$$\dot{\gamma} = 1.01049 \times 10^5\ \text{m/s}$$

Example 15.25

A hole is of dimension $\phi\, 9^{+0.015}_{+0}$ mm. The corresponding shaft is of dimension $\phi\, 9^{+0.010}_{+0.001}$ mm. The resulting assembly has

(A) Loose running fit (B) Transition fit

(C) Close running fit (D) Interference fit

GATE 2011

Solution

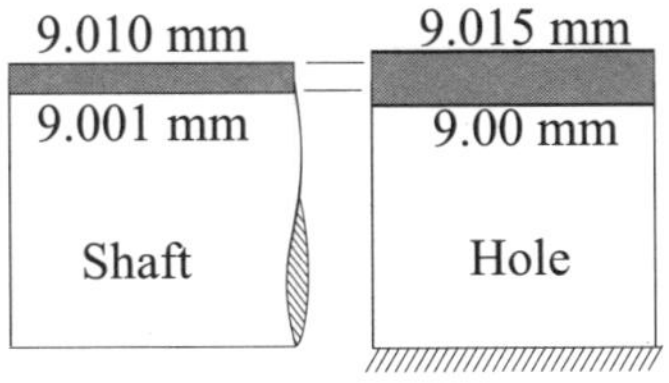

Transition fit

Shaft size and hole size are shown in figure.

The resulting assembly is transition fit.

Example 15.26

A single-point cutting tool with 12^0 rake angle is used to machine a steel work-piece. The depth of cut, that is uncut thickness is 0.81 mm. The chip thickness under orthogonal machining condition is 1.8 mm. The shear angle is approximately

(A) 22°   (B) 56°   (C) 26°   (D) 76°

GATE 2011

Solution

Given: $\alpha = 12°$, $t_o = 0.81\,\text{mm}$, $t_c = 1.8$ mm

Chip thickness ratio, $$r = \frac{0.81}{1.8} = 0.45$$

$$\tan\phi = \frac{r\cos\alpha}{1 - r\sin\alpha} = \frac{0.45\cos 12}{1 - 0.45\sin 12} = 0.4855$$

Shear angle, $$\phi = \tan^{-1} 0.4855$$

$$\phi = 25.90°$$

Example 15.27

For tool A, Taylor's tool life exponent (n) is 0.45 and constant (C) is 90. Similarly for tool B, $n = 0.3$ and C is 60. The cutting speed (in m/min) above which tool A will have a higher tool life than tool B is

(A) 26.7   (B) 42.5   (C) 80.7   (D) 142.9

GATE 2010

Solution

Taylor's tool life equation, $$VT^n = C$$

For tool A; $$VT_A^{n_A} = C_A$$

$$T_A = \left(\frac{C_A}{V}\right)^{\frac{1}{n_A}}$$

For tool B; $$VT_B^{n_B} = C_B$$

$$T_B = \left(\frac{C_B}{V}\right)^{\frac{1}{n_B}}$$

Tool life of tool $A >$ Tool life of tool B

$$\left(\frac{C_A}{V}\right)^{\frac{1}{n_A}} > \left(\frac{C_B}{V}\right)^{\frac{1}{n_B}}$$

$$\left(\frac{90}{V}\right)^{\frac{1}{0.45}} > \left(\frac{60}{V}\right)^{\frac{1}{0.3}}$$

$$V > 26.66 \text{ m/s}$$

Example 15.28

A taper hole is inspected using a coordinate measuring machine, with a probe of 2 mm diameter. At a height, $z = 10\,\text{mm}$ from the bottom, 5 points are touches and a diameter of circle (not compensated for probe size) is obtained as 20 mm. Similarly, a 40 mm diameter is obtained at a height $z = 40\,\text{mm}$. The smaller diameter (in mm) of hole at $z = 0$ is

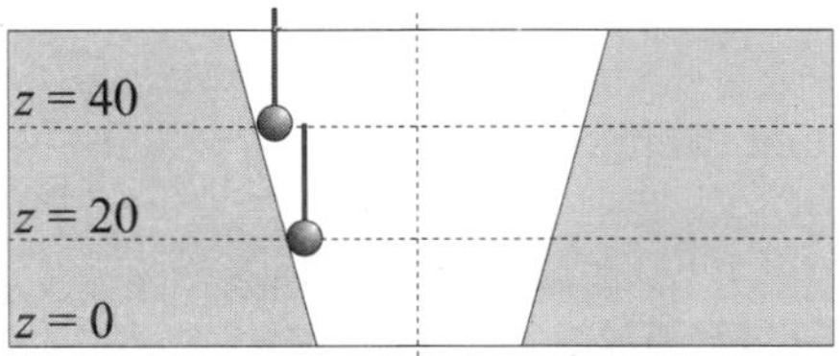

(A) 13.334 (B) 15.334 (C) 15.442 (D) 15.542

GATE 2010

Solution

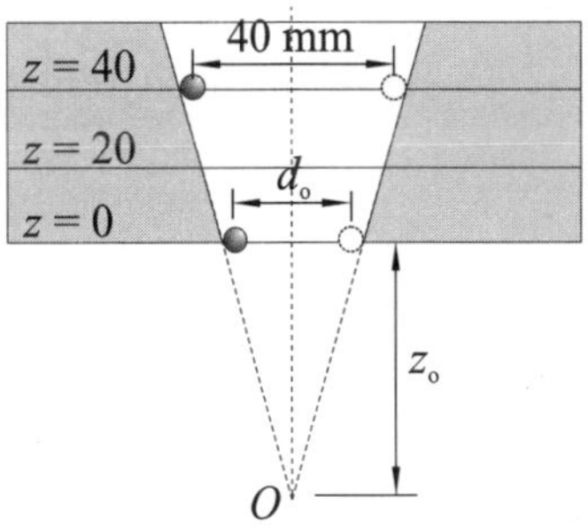

Let z_o be the height of bottom from apex O. Let d_o be the smaller diameter of hole.

From the geometry of figure,

$$\frac{40/2}{z_o + 40} = \frac{20/2}{z_o + 10} = \frac{d_o/2}{z_o}$$

From which we get

$$z_o = 20\,\text{mm},\ d_o = 13.33\,\text{mm}$$

$$d_o = 13.33\,\text{mm}$$

Example 15.29

Electrochemical machining is performed to remove material from an iron surface of $20\,\text{mm} \times 20\,\text{mm}$ under the following conditions:

Inter electrode gap $= 0.2$ mm

Supply voltage (DC) = 12 V
Specific resistance of electrolyte = 2 Ω cm
Atomic weight of iron = 55.85
Valency of iron = 2
Faraday's constant = 96540 C
The material removal rate (in g/s) is

(A) 0.3471 (B) 3.471 (C) 34.71 (D) 347.1

GATE 2009

Solution

Electric resistance, $R = \frac{\rho l}{\text{Area}}$

$$R = \frac{2 \times \frac{1}{100} \times 0.2 \times 10^{-3}}{20 \times 20 \times 10^{-6}} = 0.01\ \Omega$$

Current, $I = \frac{V}{R} = \frac{12}{0.01} = 1200\ \text{A}$

Material removal rate, $MRR = \frac{AI}{FZ} = \frac{55.85 \times 1200}{96500 \times 2}$

$$MRR = 0.34711\ \text{g/s}$$

Example 15.30

Match the following:

NC code	Definition
(P) M05	(1) Absolute coordinate system
(Q) G01	(2) Dwell
(R) G04	(3) Spindle stop
(S) G09	(4) Linear interpolation

(A) P-2, Q-3, R-4, S-1 (B) P-3, Q-4, R-1, S-2
(C) P-3, Q-4, R-2, S-1 (D) P-4, Q-3, R-2, S-1

GATE 2009

Solution

Correct match:

NC code	Definition
(P) M05	(3) Spindle stop
(Q) G01	(4) Linear interpolation
(R) G04	(2) Dwell
(S) G09	(1) Absolute coordinate system

Example 15.31

Linked Answer Questions

In a machining experiment, tool life was found to vary with the cutting speed in the following manner:

Cutting speed (m/min)	Tool life (min)
60	81
90	36

Q(a) The exponent (n) and constant (C) of the Taylor's tool life equation are:

(A) $n = 0.5$ and $C = 540$ (B) $n = 1$ and $C = 4860$
(C) $n = 1$ and $C = 0.74$ (D) $n = -0.5$ and $C = 1.155$

Q(b) What is the percentage increase in tool life when the cutting speed is halved?

(A) 50% (B) 200% (C) 300% (D) 400%

GATE 2009

Solution

(a) Taylor's tool life, $VT^n = C$

Substituting $V = 60, T = 81$ and $V = 90, T = 36$, we have

$$60 \times 81^n = C$$
$$90 \times 36^n = C$$

Solving for n and C, we have

$$n = 0.5 \text{ and } C = 540$$

(b) Taylor's tool life, $VT^{0.5} = 540$

$$V_2 T_2^{0.5} = V_1 T_1^{0.5}$$

Cutting speed is halved; $V_2 = \frac{V_1}{2}$

$$\frac{V_1}{2} T_2^{0.5} = V_1 T_1^{0.5}$$

or $T_2 = 4T_1$

Thus, the percentage increase is

$$= \frac{4T_1 - T_1}{T_1} \times 100$$

Percentage increase tool life = 300%

Example 15.32

In orthogonal turning of a low carbon steel bar of diameter 150 mm with uncoated carbide tool, the cutting velocity velocity is 90 m/min. The feed is 0.24 mm/rev and the depth of cut is 2 mm. The chip thickness obtained is 0.48 mm. If the orthogonal rake angle is zero and the principal cutting edge angle is 90°, the shear angle in degree is

(A) 20.56 (B) 26.56 (C) 30.56 (D) 36.56

GATE 2007

Solution

Shear angle, $\phi = \tan^{-1}\left(\frac{r\cos\alpha}{1 - r\sin\alpha}\right)$

Substituting rake angle $\alpha = 0$ and chip thickness ratio

$$r = \frac{\text{Feed}}{\text{Chip thickness}} = \frac{0.24}{0.48} = 0.5, \text{ we have}$$

$$\phi = \tan^{-1}\left(\frac{0.5\cos 0}{1 - 0.5\sin 0}\right) = \tan^{-1} 0.5$$

$$\phi = 26.56^o$$

Example 15.33

In orthogonal turning of medium carbon steel, the specific machining energy is 2.0 J/mm^3. The cutting velocity, feed and depth of cut are 120 m/min, 0.2 mm/rev and 2 mm respectively. The main cutting force (in N) is

(A) 40 (B) 80 (C) 400 (D) 800

GATE 2007

Solution

Specific cutting energy (pressure) $U = \frac{P}{MRR}$

$$U = \frac{F_C v_c}{t_o w v_c} = \frac{F_c}{t_o w} = \frac{F_c}{A_o}$$

Substituting $U = 2.0 \text{ J/mm}^3$, $A_o = 0.2 \times 2 \text{ mm}^2$, we have

$$2 = \frac{F_c}{02 \times 2}$$

or $F_c = 0.8 \text{ Nm/mm} = 0.8 \times 1000 \text{ Nmm/mm}$

Cutting force, $F_c = 800$ N

Example 15.34

A hole is specified as $40^{0.050}_{0.000}$ mm. The mating shaft has a clearance fit with minimum clearance of 0.01 mm. The tolerance on the shaft is 0.04 mm. The maximum clearance in mm between the hole and the shaft is

(A) 0.04 (B) 0.05 (C) 0.10 (D) 0.11

GATE 2007

Solution

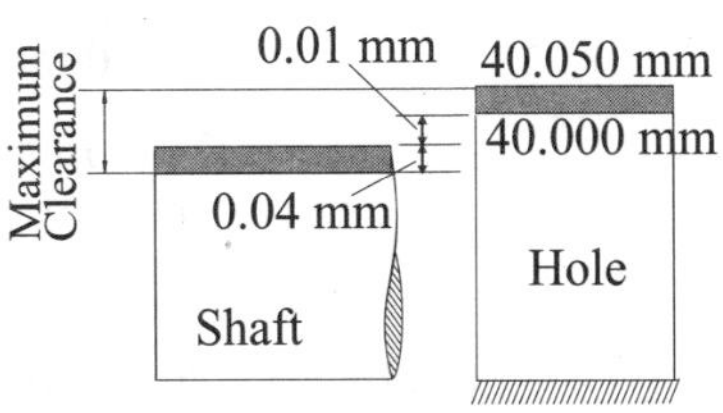

Maximum clearance $= 0.01 + 0.04 + 0.050$

Maximum clearance $= 0.10$ mm

Example 15.35

In orthogonal turning of low carbon steel bar with principal cutting edge angle of $90°$, the main cutting force is 1000 N and the feed force is 800 N. The shear angle is $25°$ and orthogonal rake angle is zero. Employing Merchant's theory, the ratio of friction force to normal force acting on the cutting tool is

(A) 1.56 (B) 1.25 (C) 0.80 (D) 0.64

GATE 2007

Solution

Using Merchant's equation $2\phi = \frac{\pi}{2} + \alpha - \beta$

Substituting given values $\alpha = 0, \phi = 25°$, we have

$$2 \times 25 = \frac{\pi}{2} + 0 - \beta$$

$$\beta = 40°$$

The ratio of friction force to normal force, $\frac{F}{N} = \tan\beta$

$$\frac{F}{N} = \tan 40$$

$$\frac{F}{N} = 0.84$$

Example 15.36

Linked Answer Questions

A low carbon steel bar of 147 mm diameter with a length of 630 mm is being turned with uncoated carbide insert. The observed tool lives are 24 min and 12 min for cutting velocities of 90 m/min and 120 m/min respectively. The feed and depth of cut are 0.2 mm/rev and 2 mm respectively. Use the unmachined diameter to calculate the cutting velocity.

Q(a) When tool life is 20 min, the cutting velocity in m/min is

(A) 87 (B) 97 (C) 107 (D) 114

Q(b) Neglect over-travel or approach of the tool. When tool life is 20 min, the machining time in min for a single pass is

(A) 5 (B) 10 (C) 15 (D) 20

GATE 2007

Solution

Given: $T_1 = 24$ min, $V_1 = 90$ m/min, $T_2 = 12$ min, $V_2 = 120$ m/min, $D = 147$ mm and $L = 630$ mm.

(a) Using Taylor's tool life, $VT^n = C$

$$V_1 T_1^n = V_2 T_2^n \Rightarrow 90 \times 24^n = 120 \times 12^n$$

$$n = \frac{\ln\left(\frac{120}{90}\right)}{\ln\left(\frac{24}{12}\right)} = 0.411$$

For tool life, $T = 20\,\text{min}$

$$V \times 20^{0.411} = 90 \times 24^{0.411}$$

$$V = 97\ \text{m/min}$$

(b) Cutting velocity, $V = \pi DN$

$$N = \frac{V}{\pi D} = \frac{97}{\pi \times \frac{147}{1000}} = 210.04\ \text{rpm}$$

Machining time, $t_m = \dfrac{L}{Nf} = \dfrac{630}{210.04 \times 0.2}$

Machining time, $t_m = 15\ \text{s}$

Example 15.37

Common Data Questions

In an orthogonal machining operation:

Uncut thickness	= 0.5 mm
Cutting speed	= 20 m/min
Rake angle	= 15°
Width of cut	= 5 mm
Chip thickness	= 0.7 mm
Thrust force	= 200 N
Cutting force	= 1200 N

Assume Merchant's theory

Q(a) The values of shear angle and shear strain, respectively, are:

(A) 30.3° and 1.98 (B) 30.3° and 4.23

(C) 40.2° and 2.97 (D) 40.2° and 1.65

Q(b) The coefficient of friction at the tool chip interface is

(A) 0.23 (B) 0.46 (C) 0.85 (D) 0.95

Q(c) The percentage of total energy dissipated due to friction at the tool chip interface is

(A) 30% (B) 42% (C) 58% (D) 70%

GATE 2006

Solution

Given: $t_o = 0.5\,\text{mm}$, $v_c = 20\,\text{m/min}$, $w = 5\,\text{mm}$, $t = 0.7$ mm, $F_T = 200\,\text{N}$, $F_c = 1200\,\text{N}$ and $\alpha = 15°$.

(a) Chip thickness ratio, $r = \dfrac{t_o}{t} = \dfrac{0.5}{0.7} = 0.714$

Shear angle, $\phi = \tan^{-1}\left(\dfrac{r\cos\alpha}{1 - r\sin\alpha}\right)$

$$\phi = \tan^{-1}\left(\frac{0.714\cos 15}{1 - 0.714\sin 15}\right)$$

$$\phi = 40.23°$$

Shear strain, $\gamma = \cot\phi + \tan(\phi - \alpha)$

$$\gamma = \cot 40.23 + \tan(40.23 - 15)$$

$$\gamma = 1.65$$

(b) Using Merchant's theory,

$$2\phi = \frac{\pi}{2} + \alpha - \beta$$

or $2 \times 40.23 = \dfrac{\pi}{2} + 15 - \beta$

or $\beta = 24.6°$

Coefficient of friction, $\mu = \tan\beta = \tan 24.6°$

$$\mu = 0.457$$

(c) Friction force, $F = F_c \sin\alpha + F_t \cos\alpha$

or $F = 1200\sin 15 + 200\cos 15$

or $F = 503.76\,\text{N}$

Heat generated due to friction, $Q_f = Fv_f = F \times r\,v_c$

$$Q_f = 503.76 \times 0.714 \times 20 = 7193.8\ \text{J/min}$$

Total heat generated,

$$Q = F_c v_c = 1200 \times 20 = 24000\ \text{J/min}$$

Percentage of energy dissipated due to friction

$$= \frac{Q_f}{Q} \times 100 = \frac{7193.8}{24000} \times 100$$

Percentage of energy dissipated due to friction = 30%

Example 15.38

A 600 mm × 30 mm flat surface of a plate is to be finish machined on shaper. The plate has been fixed with the 600 mm side along the tool travel direction. If the tool over-travel at each end of the plate is 20 mm, average cutting speed is 8 m/min, feed rate is 0.3 mm/stroke and the ratio of return time to cutting time of the tool is 1:2, the time required for machining will be

(A) 8 min (B) 120 min

(C) 16 min (D) 20 min

GATE 2005

Solution

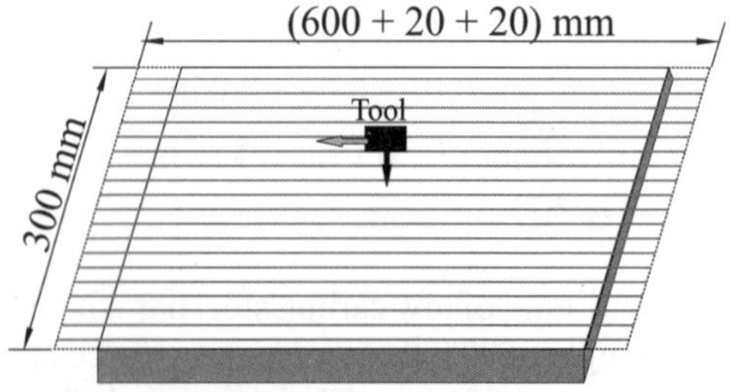

Machining timing for each stroke,

$$t = \frac{640}{8 \times 1000} = 0.08 \text{ min}$$

Number of stroke, $n = \frac{300}{0.3} = 1000$

Total cutting, T = cutting time + return stroke time

$$T = 0.08 \times 1000 + \frac{1}{2} \times 0.08 \times 1000$$

$$T = 120 \text{ min}$$

Example 15.39

A tool of an NC machine has to move along a circular arc from (5,5) to (10,10) while performing an operation. The centre of the arc is at (10, 5). Which one of the following NC tool path commands performs the above mentioned operation?

(A) N010 G02 X10 Y10 X5 Y5 R5

(B) N010 G03 X10 Y10 X5 Y5 R5

(C) N010 G01 X5 Y5 X10 Y10 R5

(D) N010 G02 X5 Y5 X10 Y10 R5

GATE 2005

Solution

The desired movement of tool is shown in figure.

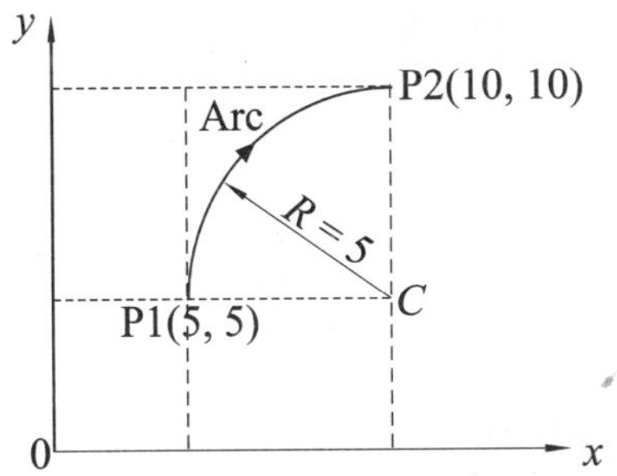

The movement is in clockwise direction. The preparatory word G02 is used for circular interpolation in clockwise.

Correct command: N010 G02 X5 Y5 X10 Y10 R5

Example 15.40

In an interchangeable assembly, shafts of size $25.000^{+0.040}_{-0.0100}$ mm mate with holes of size $25.000^{+0.020}_{-0.000}$ mm. The maximum possible clearance in the assembly will be

(A) 10 microns (B) 20 microns

(C) 30 microns (D) 60 microns

GATE 2004

Solution

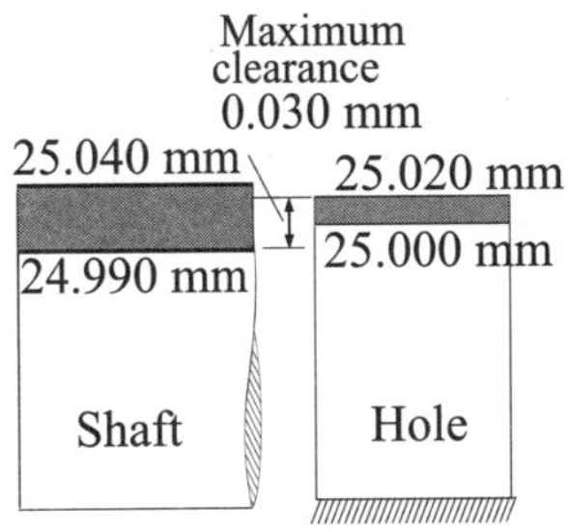

Maximum clearance

= Maximum size of hole – Minimum size of shaft

Maximum clearance = 25.020 – 24.990 = 0.030 mm

Maximum clearance = 30 microns

Example 15.41

During the execution of a CNC part program block

NO20 GO2 X45.0 Y25.0 R5.0

The type of tool motion will be

(A) Circular interpolation in clockwise

(B) Circular interpolation in counter clockwise

(C) Linear interpolation

(D) Rapid feed

GATE 2004

Solution

The preparatory word G02 is used for circular interpolation in clockwise direction.

Tool motion will be circular interpolation in clockwise

Example 15.42

GO and NOGO plug gauges are to be designed for a hole $20.000^{+0.050}_{+0.010}$ mm. Gauge tolerance can be taken as 10% of the hole tolerance. Following ISO system of gauge design, size of GO and NOGO gauge will be respectively

(A) 20.010 mm and 20.050 mm

(B) 20.014 mm and 20.046 mm

(C) 20.006 mm and 20.054 mm

(D) 20.014 mm and 20.054 mm

GATE 2004

Solution

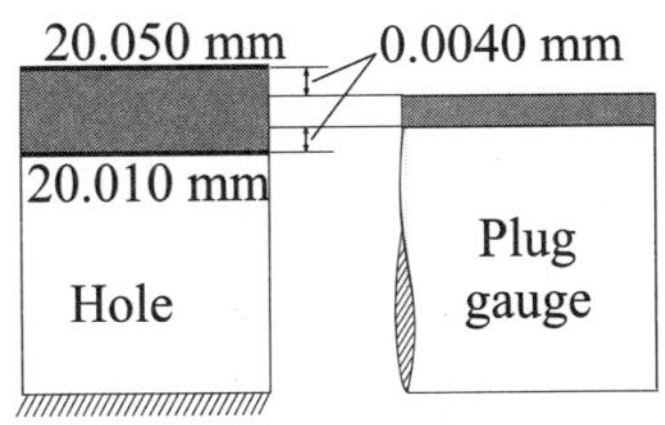

Hole tolerance $= 20.050 - 20.010 = 0.040$ mm

Gauge tolerance $= 10\%$ of $0.040 = 0.0040$ mm

Size of GO gauge $= 20.010 + 0.0040 = 20.014$ mm

Size of NOGO gauge $= 20.050 - 0.0040 = 20.046$ mm

Example 15.43

Through holes of 10 mm diameter are to be drilled in a steel plate of 20 mm thickness. Drill spindle speed is 300 rpm, feed 0.2 mm/rev and drill point angle is 120°. Assuming drill over-travel of 2 mm, the time for producing a hole will be

(A) 4 s (B) 25 s (C) 100 s (D) 110 s

GATE 2004

Solution

The tool has to travel through tool point height, plate thickness and over travel, therefore, time for drill

$$T = \frac{\dfrac{d/2}{\tan\theta/2} + t + t_o}{Nf} = \frac{\dfrac{10/2}{\tan 60} + 20 + 2}{300 \times 0.2} \text{ min}$$

$$T = 24.8 \text{ min}$$

Example 15.44

In a 2-D CAD package, clockwise circular arc of radius 5, specified from $P_1(15,10)$ to $P_2(10,15)$ will have its center at

(A) (10,10) (B) (15,10) (C) (15,15) (D) (10,15)

GATE 2004

Solution

The diagram of circular arc is shown in figure.

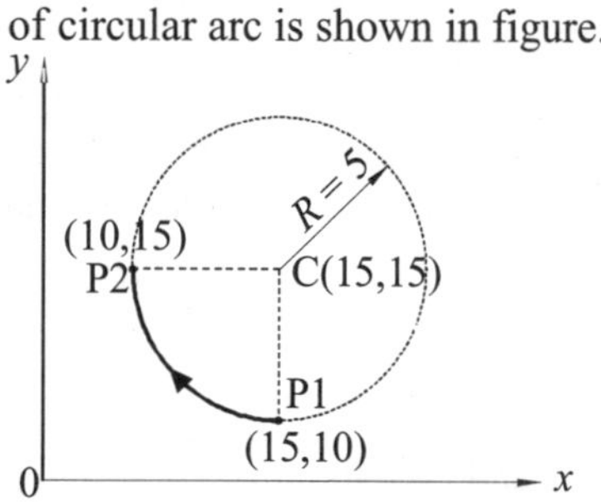

The centre of the arc is (15, 15).

Example 15.45

In an orthogonal cutting test on mild steel, the following data were obtained:

Cutting speed $= 40$ m/min

Depth of cut $= 0.3$ mm

Tool rake angle $= +5°$

Chip thickness $= 1.5$ mm

Cutting force $= 900$ N

Thrust force $= 450$ N

Using Merchant's analysis, the friction angle during the matching will be

(A) 26.6° (B) 31.5° (C) 45° (D) 63.4°

GATE 2004

Solution

Coefficient of friction, $\mu = \tan\beta$

$$\tan\beta = \frac{F_t \cos\alpha + F_c \sin\alpha}{F_C \cos\alpha - F_t \sin\alpha}$$

$$\tan\beta = \frac{450\cos 5 + 900\sin 5}{900\cos 5 - 450\sin 5} = 0.6147$$

Friction angle, $\beta = 31.56°$

Example 15.46

In a machining operation, doubling the cutting speed reduces the tool life to $\frac{1}{8}$ th of the original value. The exponent n in Taylor's tool life equation $VT^n = C$, is

(A) $\frac{1}{8}$ (B) $\frac{1}{4}$ (C) $\frac{1}{3}$ (D) $\frac{1}{2}$

GATE 2004

Solution

The Taylor's tool life equation, $VT^n = C$

$$VT^n = 2V\left(\frac{T}{8}\right)^n \quad \text{or} \quad 8^n = 2$$

$$2^{3n} = 2^1$$

$$n = \frac{1}{3}$$

Example 15.47

A batch of 10 cutting tools could produce 500 components while working at 50 rpm with a tool feed of 0.25 mm/rev and depth of cut of 1mm. A similar batch of 10 tools of the same specification could produce 122 components while working at 80 rpm with a feed of 0.25 mm/rev and 1 mm depth of cut. How many components can be produced with one cutting tool at 60 rpm?

(A) 29 (B) 31 (C) 37 (D) 42

GATE 2003

Solution

Batch I: 10 cutting tools, 500 components, 50 rpm, feed 0.25 mm/rev, $d = 1$ mm.

Batch II: 10 cutting tools, 122 components, 80 rpm, feed

0.25 mm/rev, $d = 1$ mm.

Batch III: 1 cutting tools, x components, 60 rpm, feed 0.25 mm/rev, $d = 1$ mm.

Using Taylor's equation,

$$V_1T_1^n = V_2T_2^n = V_3T_3^n$$

Let K be the tool constant

$$50\times 0.25\left(\frac{500}{10}K\right)^n = 80\times 0.25\left(\frac{122}{10}K\right)^n$$

$$= 60\times 0.25\left(\frac{x}{1}K\right)^n$$

From which, we get,

$$n = \frac{\ln\left(\frac{80}{50}\right)}{\ln\left(\frac{500}{122}\right)} = 0.3332$$

$$50\times 0.25\left(\frac{500}{10}K\right)^{0.3332} = 60\times 0.25\left(\frac{x}{1}K\right)^{0.3332}$$

$$x = 28.9$$

Example 15.48

A threaded nut of M16, ISO metric type, having 2 mm pitch with a pitch diameter of 14.701 mm is to be checked for its pitch diameter using two or three numbers of balls or rollers of the following sizes

(A) Rollers of 2 mm ϕ (B) Rollers of 1.155 mm ϕ

(C) Balls of 2 mm ϕ (D) Ball of 1.155 mm ϕ

GATE 2003

Solution

Diameter/size of ball or roller $d = \frac{p}{2}\sec\frac{\theta}{2}$

$\theta = 60°$ for metric thread

$$d = \frac{2}{2}\sec\frac{60}{2}$$

$$d = 1.154 \text{ mm}$$

Example 15.49

A part shown in the figure is machined to the sizes given below:

$$P = 35.00 \pm 0.08 \text{ mm}$$

$$Q = 12.00 \pm 0.02 \text{ mm}$$

$$R = 13.00^{+0.04}_{-0.02} \text{ mm}$$

With 100% confidence, the resultant dimension W will have the specification

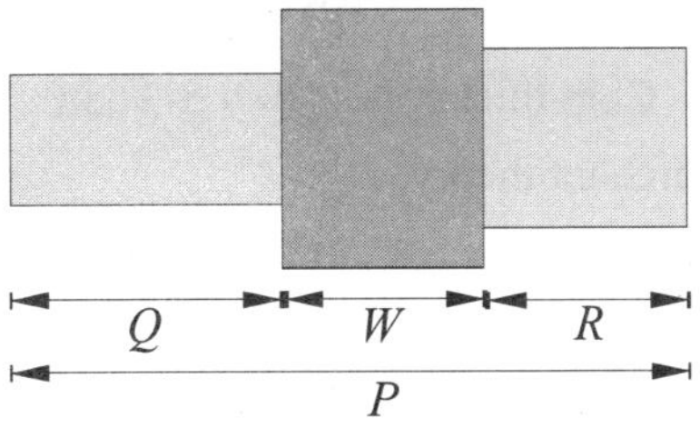

(A) $9.99^{+0.13}_{-0.13}$ mm (B) $10.00^{+0.13}_{-0.13}$ mm

(C) $9.00^{+0.13}_{-0.13}$ mm (D) None of these

GATE 200

Solution

From the geometry of figure,

$$W = P - Q - R$$

$$W_{max} = P_{max} - Q_{min} - R_{min}$$

$$W_{max} = (35.00 + 0.08) - (12.00 - 0.02) - (13.00 - 0.02)$$

$$W_{max} = 10.12 \text{ mm}$$

$$W_{min} = P_{min} - Q_{max} - R_{max}$$

$$W_{min} = (35.00 - 0.08) - (12.00 + 0.02) - (13.00 + 0.04)$$

$$W_{min} = 9.86 \text{ mm}$$

$$W^{max}_{min} = 9.99^{+0.13}_{-0.13} \text{ mm}$$

Example 15.50

Common Data Questions

A cylinder is turned on a lathe with orthogonal machining principle. Spindle rotates at 200 rpm. The axil feed rate is 0.25 mm per revolution. Depth of cut is 0.4 mm. The rake angle is $10°$. In the analysis it is found that the shear angle is $27.75°$.

Q(a) The thickness of the produced chip is

(A) 0.511 mm (B) 0.528 mm

(C) 0.818 mm (D) 0.846 mm

Q(b) In the above problem, the coefficient of friction at the chip tool interface obtained using Ernst and Marchant theory is:

(A) 0.18 (B) 0.36 (C) 0.71 (D) 0.982

GATE 2003

Solution

Given: $N = 200$ rpm, $f = 0.25$ mm/rev, $d = 0.4$ mm, $\alpha = 10°$ and $\phi = 27.75°$.

(a) Chip thickness ratio, $r = \frac{t_o}{t_c} = \frac{\sin\phi}{\cos(\phi - \alpha)}$

Chip thickness before cut, $t_o = f = 0.25$ mm

$$\frac{0.25}{t_c} = \frac{\sin 27.75}{\cos(27.75 - 10)}$$

Chip thickness, $t_c = 0.511\,\text{mm}$

(b) Ernst-Marchant theory,

$$2\phi + \beta - \alpha = \frac{\pi}{2}$$

Friction angle, $\beta = \frac{\pi}{2} + \alpha - 2\phi$

$$\beta = \frac{\pi}{2} + 10 - 2 \times 27.75 = 44.5^\circ$$

Coefficient of friction, $\mu = \tan 44.5^\circ$

$$\mu = 0.982$$

Example 15.51

The time taken to drill a hole through a 25 mm thick plate with the drill rotating at 300 rpm and moving at a feed rate of 0.25 mm/rev is:

(A) 10 s (B) 20 s (C) 60 s (D) 100 s

GATE 2002

Solution

Drilling time, $t = \frac{L}{f_r} = \frac{L}{Nf}$

Substituting, $L = 25$ mm, $N = 300$ rpm and $f = 0.25$ mm/rev, we have

$$t = \frac{25}{300 \times 0.25} = 0.33\,\text{min}$$

Drilling time, $t = 20$ s

Example 15.52

In an orthogonal cutting process, the tool used has rake angle of zero degree. The measured cutting force and thrust force are 500 N and 250 N, respectively. The coefficient of friction between the tool and the chip is _________.

GATE 2016

Solution

Given: Rake angle $\alpha = 0^\circ$, cutting force $F_c = 500\,\text{N}$, and thrust force $F_t = 250\,\text{N}$.

Relation between cutting force F_c and thrust force F_t is

$$\tan(\beta - \alpha) = \frac{F_t}{F_c}$$

$$\tan(\beta - 0) = \frac{250}{500}$$

or $\tan\beta = 0.5$

Coefficient of friction, $\mu = \tan\beta = 0.5$

Example 15.53

Match the following:

(P) Feeler gauge	(I) Radius of an object
(Q) Fillet gauge	(II) Diameter within limits by comparison
(R) Snap gauge	(III) Clearance or gap between components
(S) Cylindrical plug gauge	(IV) Inside diameter of straight hole

(A) P–III, Q–I, R–II, S–IV (B) P–III, Q–II, R–I, S–IV

(C) P–IV, Q–II, R–I, S–III (D) P–IV, Q–I, R–II, S–III

GATE 2016

Solution

Correct match:

P. Feeler gauge	III. Clearance or gap between components
Q. Fillet gauge	I. Radius of an object
R. Snap gauge	II. Diameter within limits by comparison
S. Cylindrical plug gauge	IV. Inside diameter of straight hole

Example 15.54

The tool life equation for HSS tool is $VT^{0.14} f^{0.7} d^{0.4} = \text{Constant}$. The tool life ($T$) of 30 min is obtained using the following cutting conditions: V = 45 m/min, $f = 0.35$ mm, $d = 2.0$ mm. If speed (V), feed (f) and depth of cut (d) are increased individually by 25%, the tool life (in min) is

(A) 0.15 (B) 1.06 (C) 22. 50 (D) 30.0

GATE 2016

Solution

The tool life equation, $VT^{0.14} f^{0.7} d^{0.4} = \text{Constant}$

$$V_1 T_1^{0.14} f_1^{0.7} d_1^{0.4} = V_2 T_2^{0.14} f_2^{0.7} d_2^{0.4}$$

Substituting $T_1 = 30$ min, $V_2 = 1.25\ V_1$, $f_2 = 1.25 f_1$ and $d_2 = 1.25\ d_1$. we have

$$V_1 \times 30^{0.14} \times f_1^{0.7} d_1^{0.4} = 1.25 V_1 \times T_2^{0.14} \times (1.25 f_1)^{0.7} \times (1.25 d_1)^{0.4}$$

From which, we get,

$$T_2 = 1.055\,\text{min}$$

Example 15.55

The following data is applicable for a turning operation. The length of job is 900 mm, diameter of job is 200 mm, feed rate is 0.25 mm/rev and optimum cutting speed is 300 m/min. The machining time (in min) is ______.

GATE 2016

Solution

Given: $L = 900\,\text{mm}$, $D_o = 200\,\text{mm}$, $f_r = 0.25$ mm/rev and

$v = 300$ m/min.

Machining timing, $T_m = \frac{L}{f_r} = \frac{L}{fN}$

Cutting velocity, $v = \pi D_o N \quad \Rightarrow \quad N = \frac{v}{\pi D_o}$

$$T_m = \frac{L}{f\left(\frac{v}{\pi D_o}\right)} = \frac{L\pi D_o}{fv}$$

$$T_m = \frac{900 \times \pi \times 200}{0.25 \times 300 \times 1000} \text{ min}$$

$$T_m = 7.54 \text{ min}$$

Example 15.56

In an ultrasonic machining (USM) process, the material removal rate (MRR) is plotted as a function of the feed force of the USM tool. With increasing feed force, the MRR exhibits the following behaviour:

(A) Increases linearly

(B) Decreases linearly

(C) Does not change

(D) First increases and then decreases

GATE 2016

Solution

With increasing feed force, the MRR first increases and then decreases.

Example 15.57

For a certain job, the cost of metal cutting is Rs. $18C/V$ and the cost of tooling is Rs. $270\ C/(TV)$, where C is a constant, V is the cutting speed in m/min and T is the tool life in minutes. The Taylor's tool life equation is $VT^{0.25} = 150$. The cutting speed (in m/min) for the minimum total cost is_____.

GATE 2016

Solution

Given: Cost of metal cutting $= \frac{18\ C}{V}$, cost of tooling $= \frac{2700\ C}{TV}$, and Taylor's tool life equation $VT^{0.25} = 150$.

$$\text{Total cost} = \frac{18\ C}{V} + \frac{2700\ C}{TV}$$

Substituting $T = \left(\frac{150}{V}\right)^{\frac{1}{0.25}}$, we have

$$\text{Total cost} = \frac{18\ C}{V} + \frac{2700\ C}{\left(\frac{150}{V}\right)^{\frac{1}{0.25}} V} = \frac{18\ C}{V} + \frac{2700\ CV^3}{150^4}$$

Condition for minimum total cost $\frac{d}{dV}(\text{Total cost}) = 0$

$$-\frac{18\ C}{V^2} + \frac{2700\ C \times 3V^2}{150^4} = 0$$

From which, we get

$$V = 57.9 \text{ m/min}$$

Example 15.58

The surface irregularities of electrodes used in an electrochemical machining (ECM) process are 3 μm and 6 μm as shown in the figure. If the work-piece is of pure iron and 12 V DC is applied between the electrodes, the largest feed rate is __________ mm/min.

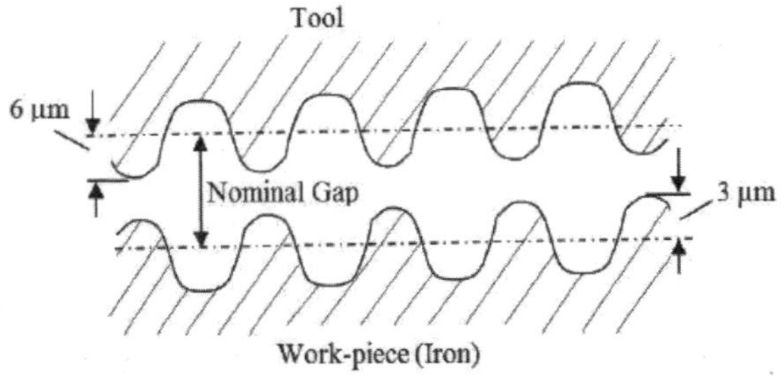

Conductivity of the electrolyte	$0.02\ \text{ohm}^{-1}\ \text{mm}^{-1}$
Over-potential voltage	1.5 V
Density of iron	$7860\ \text{kg/m}^3$
Atomic weight of iron	55.85 gm

Assume the iron to be dissolved as Fe^{+2} and the Faraday constant to be 96500 C.

GATE 2016

Solution

Given: Conductivity $= \frac{1}{\sigma} = 0.02\ \text{ohm}^{-1}\text{mm}^{-1}$, $A = 55.85$ g, $L = 3 + 6 = 9 \mu$m, $Z = 2$, $F = 96500$ C.

Resistance, $R = \frac{\sigma L}{\text{Area}} = \frac{\frac{1}{0.02} \times 0.009}{\text{Area}} = \frac{0.45}{\text{Area}}$

$$I = \frac{V}{R} = \frac{12 - 15}{R} = 23.333 \times \text{Area}$$

$$\text{MRR} = \frac{AI}{\rho ZF} = \frac{55.85 \times 23.333 \times \text{Area}}{7860 \times 10^{-6} \times 2 \times 96500}$$

$$\frac{\text{MRR}}{\text{Area}} = \frac{55.85 \times 23.333}{7860 \times 10^{-6} \times 2 \times 96500} = 0.8589 \text{ mm/s}$$

$$\frac{\text{MRR}}{\text{Area}} = 51.53 \text{ mm/min}$$

Example 15.59

For the situation shown in the figure, the expression for H in terms of r, R and D is

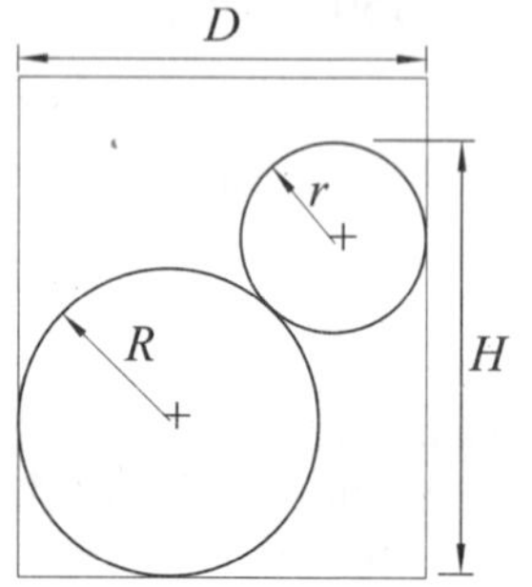

(A) $H = D + \sqrt{r^2 - R^2}$

(B) $H = (R + r) + (D + r)$

(C) $H = (R + r) + \sqrt{(D^2 - R^2)}$

(D) $H = (R + r) + \sqrt{2R(R + r) - D^2}$

GATE 2016

Solution

From the geometry of figure.

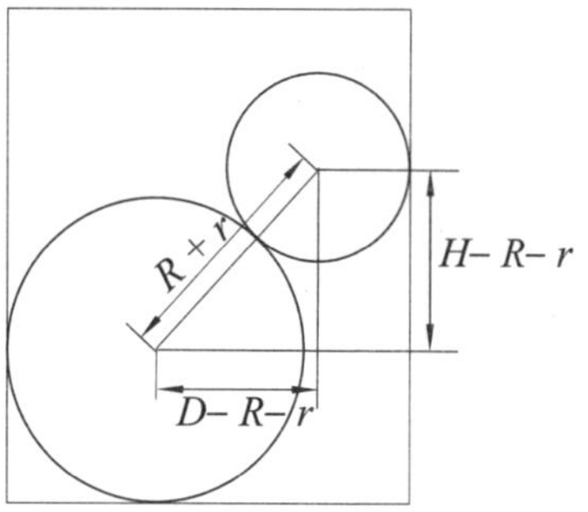

$$(R + r)^2 = (H - R - r)^2 + (D - R - r)^2$$

or $$(R + r)^2 = (H - R - r)^2 + D^2 - 2D(R + r) + (R + r)^2$$

or $$(H - R - r) = \sqrt{2D(R+r) - D^2}$$

$$H = R + r + \sqrt{2D(R + r) - D^2}$$

Example 15.60

In a wire-cut EDM process, the necessary conditions that have to be met for making a successful cut are that

(A) Wire and sample are electrically non-conducting

(B) Wire and sample are electrically conducting

(C) Wire is electrically conducting and sample is electrically non-conducting

(D) Sample is electrically conducting and wire is electrically non-conducting

GATE 2016

Solution

(B) Wire and sample are electrically conducting

Example 15.61

Internal gears are manufactured by

(A) Hobbing (B) Shaping with pinion cutter

(C) Shaping with rack cutter (D) Milling

GATE 2016

Solution

Internal gears are manufactured by shaping with pinion cutter

Example 15.62

Match the following part programming codes with their respective functions

Part programming codes	Functions
(P) G01	(I) Spindle stop
(Q) G03	(II) Spindle rotation, clockwise
(R) M03	(III) Circular interpolation, anti-clockwise
(S) M05	(IV) Linear interpolation

(A) P – II, Q – I, R – IV, S – III

(B) P – IV, Q – II, R – III, S – I

(C) P – IV, Q – III, R – II, S – I

(D) P – III, Q – IV, R – II, S – I

GATE 2016

Solution

Correct match:

Part programming codes	Functions
(P) G01	(IV) Linear interpolation
(Q) G03	(III) Circular interpolation, anti-clockwise
(R) M03	(II) Spindle rotation, clockwise
(S) M05	(I) Spindle stop

Example 15.63

For an orthogonal cutting operation, tool material is HSS, rake angle is 22°, chip thickness is 0.8 mm, speed is

48 m/min and feed is 0.4 mm/rev. The shear plane angle (in degree) is:

(A) 19.24 (B) 29.70 (C) 56.00 (D) 68.75

GATE 2016

Solution

Given: Rake angle $\alpha = 22^\circ$, $t_c = 0.8$ mm, $v = 48$ m/min, $f = 0.4$ mm/rev $= t_o$.

Chip thickness ratio, $r = \frac{t_o}{t_c} = \frac{0.4}{0.8} = 0.5$

$$\tan\phi = \frac{r\cos\alpha}{1 - r\sin\alpha} = \frac{0.5\cos 22}{1 - 0.5\sin 22}$$

$$\phi = \tan^{-1} 0.5704$$

$$\phi = 29.7^\circ$$

Example 15.64

In a single point turning operation with cemented carbide tool and steel work piece, it is found that the Taylor's exponent is 0.25. If the cutting speed is reduced by 50% then the tool life changes by ______ times.

GATE 2016

Solution

The Taylor's tool life equation, $VT^{0.25} = C$

$$V_1 T_1^{0.25} = 0.5V_1 \times T_2^{0.25}$$

$$T_2 = 16T_1$$

Example 15.65

Two optically flat plates of glass are kept at a small angle θ as shown in the figure. Monochromatic light is incident vertically.

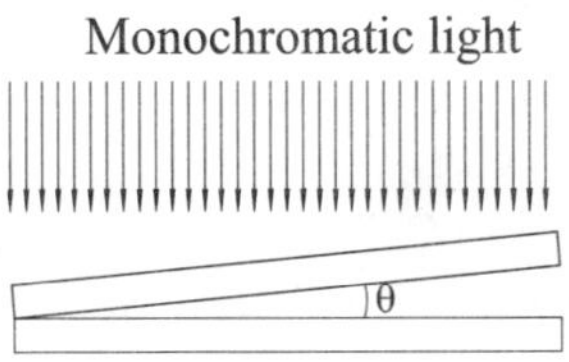

If the wavelength of light used to get a fringe spacing of 1 mm is 450 nm, the wavelength of light (in nm) to get a fringe spacing of 1.5 mm is _________.

GATE 2016

Solution

Let N be number of fringe over a width l mm.

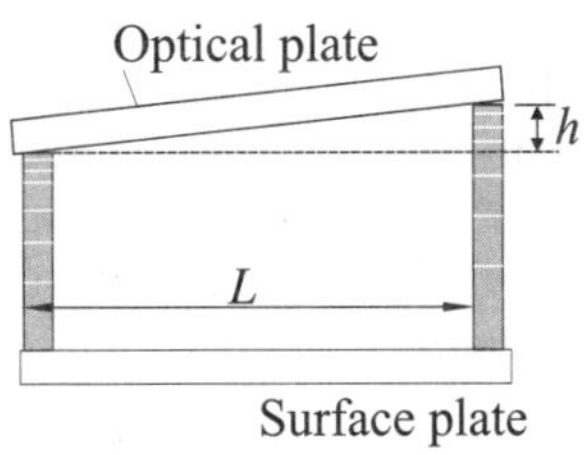

$$h = \frac{\lambda LN}{2l}, \qquad \frac{l}{N} = \text{fringe spacing}$$

$$\frac{\lambda_1}{\left(\frac{l}{N}\right)_1} = \frac{\lambda_2}{\left(\frac{l}{N}\right)_2} \Rightarrow \frac{450}{1} = \frac{\lambda_2}{1.5}$$

$$\lambda_2 = 675 \text{ nm}$$

Example 15.66

The figure below represents a triangle PQR with initial coordinates of the vertices as $P(1, 3)$, $Q(4, 5)$ and $R(5, 3.5)$. The triangle is rotated in the x-y plane about the vertex P by angle θ in clockwise direction. If $\sin\theta = 0.6$ and $\cos\theta = 0.8$, the new coordinates of the vertex Q are:

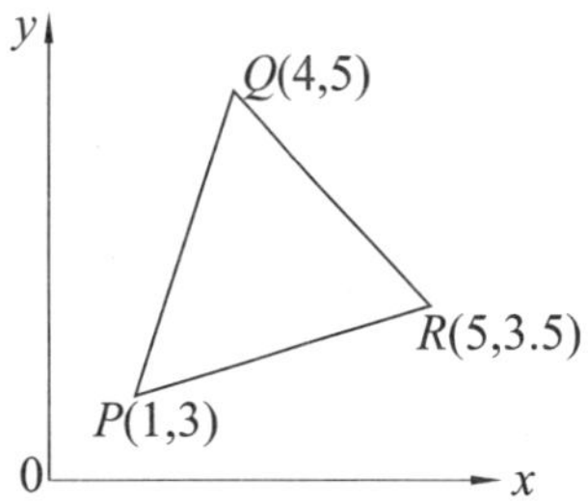

(A) (4.6, 2.8) (B) (3.2, 4.6)

(C) (7.9, 5.5) (D) (5.5, 7.9)

GATE 2016

Solution

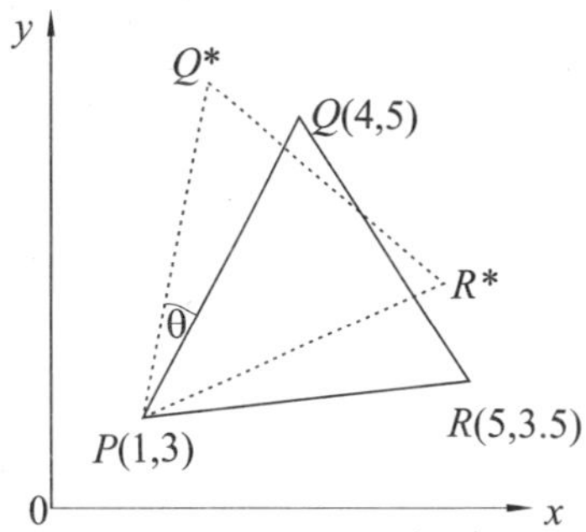

The vertex Q is rotated anti-clockwise by angle θ about vertex P.

New coordinate of the vertex Q^* is given by

$$[x_{Q^*} - x_P \quad y_{Q^*} - y_P] = \begin{bmatrix} \cos\theta & \sin\theta \\ -\sin\theta & \cos\theta \end{bmatrix} \begin{bmatrix} x_Q - x_P \\ y_Q - y_P \end{bmatrix}$$

or $$[x_{Q^*} - 1 \quad y_{Q^*} - 3] = \begin{bmatrix} 0.8 & 0.6 \\ -0.6 & 0.8 \end{bmatrix} \begin{bmatrix} 4-1 \\ 5-3 \end{bmatrix}$$

or $$[x_{Q^*} - 1 \quad y_{Q^*} - 3] = \begin{bmatrix} 0.8 & 0.6 \\ -0.6 & 0.8 \end{bmatrix} \begin{bmatrix} 3 \\ 2 \end{bmatrix}$$

or $$[x_{Q^*} - 1 \quad y_{Q^*} - 3] = [3.6 \quad -0.2]$$

$$x_{Q^*} = 4.6, y_{Q^*} = 2.8$$

Example 15.67

Cylindrical pins of diameter $15^{\pm 0.020}$ mm are being produced on a machine. Statistical quality control tests show a mean of 14.995 mm and standard deviation of 0.004 mm. The process capability index c_p is

(A) 0.833 (B) 1.667 (C) 3.333 (D) 3.750

GATE 2017

Solution

Upper limit $USL = 15 + 0.020 = 15.020$ mm

Lower limit $LSL = 15 - 0.020 = 14.980$ mm

$$\sigma = 0.004 \text{ mm}$$

Process capability index $C_p = \dfrac{USL - LSL}{6\sigma}$

$$C_p = \frac{15.020 - 14.980}{6 \times 0.004}$$

$$C_p = 1.666$$

Example 15.68

Match the processes with their characteristics

Process	Characteristics
P: Electrical Discharge Machining	1. No residual stress
Q: Ultrasonic machining	2. Machining of electrically conductive materials
R: Chemical Machining	3. Machining of glass
S: Ion Beam Machining	4. Nano-machining

(A) P-2, Q-3, R-1, S-4 (B) P-3, Q-2, R-1, S-4

(C) P-3, Q-2, R-4, S-1 (D) P-2, Q-4, R-3, S-1

GATE 2017

Solution

(A) P-2, Q-3, R-1, S-4

Example 15.69

Metric thread of 0.8 mm pitch is to be cut on a lathe. Pitch of the lead screw is 1.5 mm. If the spindle rotates at 1500 rpm, the speed of rotation of the lead screw (rpm) will be________.

GATE 2017

Solution

Speed of rotation of lead screw $= \dfrac{1500 \times 0.8}{1.5} = 800$

Speed of rotation of lead screw = 800 rpm

Example 15.70

Circular arc on a part profile is being machined on a vertical CNC milling machine. CNC part program using metric units with absolute dimensions is listed below:

```
N60 G01 X30 Y55 Z-5 F50
N70 G02 X50 Y35 R20
N80 G01 Z5
------------------------
```

The coordinates of the centre of the circular arc are:

(A) (30, 55) (B) (50, 55) (C) (50, 35) (D) (30, 35)

GATE 2017

Solution

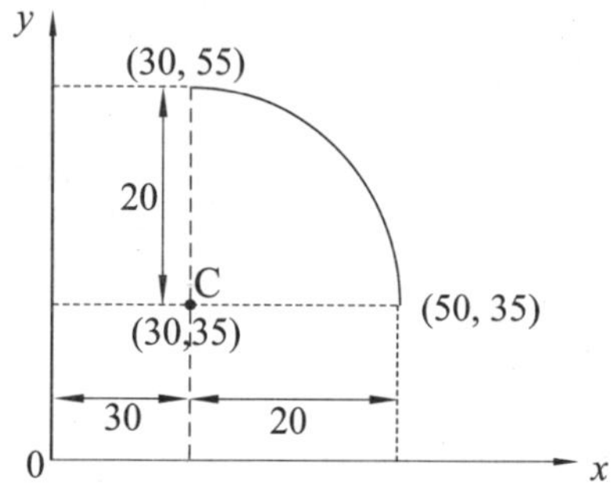

The coordinates of the centre of the circular arc C is (30, 35)

Example 15.71

Assume that the surface roughness profile is triangular as shown schematically in the figure. If the peak to valley height is 20 μm, The central line average surface roughness R_a (in μm) is

GATE 2017

(A) 5 (B) 6.67 (C) 10 (D) 20

Solution

$$R_a = \frac{20}{4} = 5 \,\mu\text{m}$$

$$R_a = 5 \,\mu\text{m}$$

Example 15.72

A block of length 200 mm is machined by a slab milling cutter 34 mm in diameter. The depth of cut and table feed are set at 2 mm and 18 mm/minute, respectively. Considering the approach and the over travel of the cutter to be same, the minimum estimated machining time per pass is_______ minutes.

GATE 2017

Solution

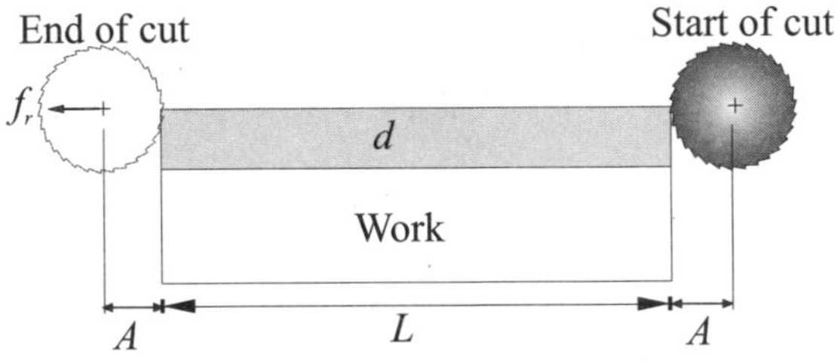

Slab milling

Machining time,

$$T_m = \frac{L+2A}{f_r} = \frac{L+2\sqrt{d(D-d)}}{f_r}; \quad \text{for slab milling}$$

Substituting $L = 200$ mm, $D = 34$ mm, $d = 2$ mm, $f_r = 18$ mm/min.

$$T_m = \frac{200+2\sqrt{2(34-2)}}{18} = 12 \text{ min}$$

Machining time per pass $T_m = 12$ min

Example 15.73

Two cutting tools with tool life equations given below are being compared:

Tool 1: $VT^{0.1} = 150$

Tool 2: $VT^{0.3} = 300$

Where V is cutting speed in m/minute and T is tool life in minutes. The breakeven cutting speed beyond which Tool 2 will have a higher tool life is_______ m/minute.

GATE 2017

Solution

Tool life equations

Tool 1: $VT^{0.1} = 150$

Tool 2: $VT^{0.3} = 300$

At breakeven point $T_1 = T_2$

$$\left(\frac{150}{V}\right)^{\frac{1}{0.1}} = \left(\frac{300}{V}\right)^{\frac{1}{0.3}}$$

We obtain

$$V = 106.121 \text{ m/min}$$

Example 15.74

The standard deviation of linear dimensions P and Q are 3 μm and 4 μm, respectively. When assembled, the standard deviation (in μm) of the resulting linear dimension $(P+Q)$ is ______.

GATE 2017

Solution

Standard deviation of linear dimensions P is 3 μm.

Variance of linear dimensions P is 9 μm.

Standard deviation of linear dimensions Q is 4 μm.

Variance of linear dimensions Q is 16 μm.

Variance of linear dimensions $(P+Q)$ = Variance of linear dimensions P + Variance of linear dimensions Q

Variance of linear dimensions $(P+Q) = 9 + 16 = 25$

Standard deviation of linear dimensions $(P+Q) = \sqrt{25} = 5$

Standard deviation of linear dimensions $(P+Q) = 5$ μm

Example 15.75

A cylindrical pin of $25^{+0.020}_{+0.010}$ mm diameter is electroplated. Plating thickness is $2.0^{\pm 0.005}$ mm. Neglecting the gauge tolerance, the diameter (in mm, up to 3 decimal points accuracy) of the GO ring gauge to inspect the plated pin is_____.

GATE 2017

Solution

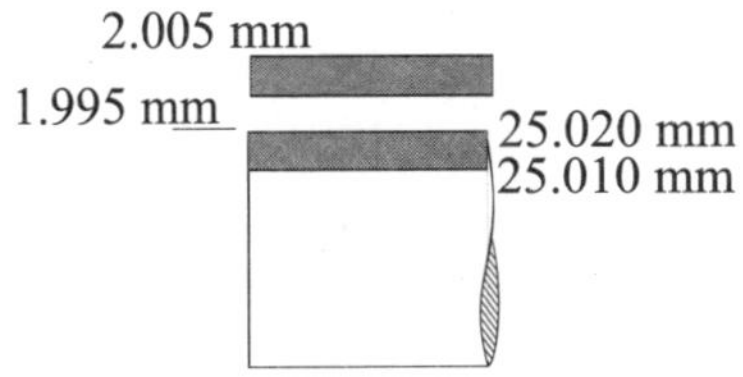

Diameter of GO ring gauge $25.020 + 2 \times 2.005 = 29.030$

Diameter of GO ring gauge = 29.030 mm

Example 15.76

During the turning of a 20 mm-diameter steel bar at a spindle speed of 400 rpm, a tool life of 20 minute is obtained. When the same bar is turned at 200 rpm, the tool life becomes 60 minute. Assume that Taylor's tool life equation is valid. When the bar is turned at 300 rpm, the tool life (in minute) is approximately.

(A) 25 (B) 32 (C) 40 (D) 50

GATE 2017

Solution

Tool life equation $VT^n = C$

$$\frac{V_1}{V_2} = \left(\frac{T_2}{T_1}\right)^n \Rightarrow \frac{D_1N_1}{D_2N_2} = \left(\frac{T_2}{T_1}\right)^n$$

$$\frac{20\times 400}{20\times 200} = \left(\frac{60}{20}\right)^n \Rightarrow 3^n = 2$$

$$n = \frac{\ln 2}{\ln 3} = 0.63$$

$$\frac{V_1}{V_2} = \left(\frac{T_3}{T_1}\right)^{0.63} \Rightarrow \frac{20 \times 400}{20 \times 300} = \left(\frac{T_3}{20}\right)^{0.63}$$

$$T_3 = 31.57 \text{ min}$$

Example 15.77

In an orthogonal machining with a tool of 9° orthogonal rake angle, the uncut chip thickness is 0.2 mm. The chip thickness fluctuates between 0.25 mm and 0.4 mm. The ratio of the maximum shear angle to the minimum shear angle during machining is____.

GATE 2017

Solution

Given: Rake angle $\alpha = 9°$, $t_o = 0.20$ mm, $t_c = 0.25$, $t_c = 0.40$ mm

Chip thickness ratio $r = \frac{t_o}{t_c}$, $r_{min} = \frac{0.20}{0.40} = 0.5$

$$r_{max} = \frac{0.20}{0.25} = 0.8$$

Shear angle, $\phi = \tan^{-1}\left(\frac{r\cos\alpha}{1 - r\sin\alpha}\right)$

$$\phi_{min} = \tan^{-1}\left(\frac{0.5\cos 9}{1 - 0.5\sin 9}\right) = 28.18°$$

$$\phi_{max} = \tan^{-1}\left(\frac{0.8\cos 9}{1 - 0.8\sin 9}\right) = 42.08°$$

$$\frac{\phi_{max}}{\phi_{min}} = \frac{42.08}{28.18} = 1.493$$

$$\frac{\phi_{max}}{\phi_{min}} = 1.493$$

Example 15.78

Using the Taylor's tool life equation with exponent $n = 0.5$, if the cutting speed is reduced by 50%, the ratio of new tool life to original tool life is

(A) 4 (B) 2 (C) 1 (D) 0.5

GATE 2018

Solution

Taylor's tool life equation $VT^{0.5} = \text{Constant}$

$$V_1 T_1^{0.5} = V_2 T_2^{0.5}$$

$$V_1 T_1^{0.5} = \frac{V_1}{2} T_2^{0.5}$$

Tool life ratio, $\frac{T_2}{T_1} = (2)^{\frac{1}{0.5}} = 4$

$$\frac{T_2}{T_1} = 4$$

Example 15.79

A grinding ratio of 200 implies that the

(A) grinding wheel wears 200 times the volume of the material removed

(B) grinding wheel wears 0.005 times the volume of the material removed

(C) aspect ratio of abrasive particles used in the grinding wheel is 200

(D) ratio of volume of abrasive particle to that of grinding wheel is 200

GATE 2018

Solution

Grinding ratio is defined as

$$= \frac{\text{Volume of work material removed}}{\text{Volume of wheel wear}}$$

$$200 = \frac{\text{Volume of work material removed}}{\text{Volume of wheel wear}}$$

Grinding wheel wears 0.005 times the volume of material removed

Example 15.80

Interpolator in a CNC machine

(A) controls spindle speed

(B) coordinates axes movements

(C) operates tool changer

(D) commands canned cycle

GATE 2018

Solution

Interpolator in a CNC machine coordinates axes movements

Example 15.81

The height (in mm) for a 125 mm sine bar to measure a taper of 27°32′ on a flat work piece is _______ .

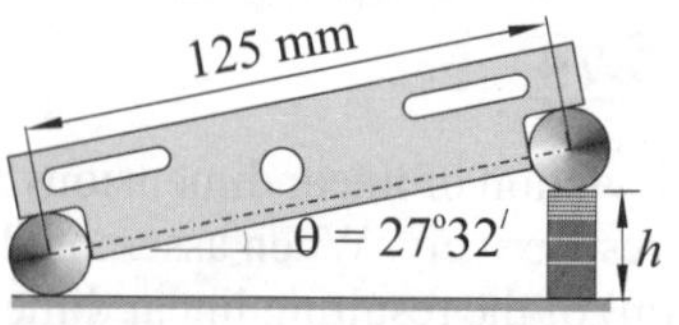

GATE 2018

Solution

$$\theta = 27°32' = \left(27 + \frac{32}{60}\right)^{\circ} = 27.533°$$

In Sine bar, $\sin\theta = \dfrac{h}{125}$

$$h = 125 \sin 27.533$$

$$h = 57.782 \text{ mm}$$

Example 15.82

An orthogonal cutting operation is being carried out in which uncut thickness is 0.010 mm, cutting speed is 130 m/min, rake angle is 15° and width of cut is 6 mm. It is observed that the chip thickness is 0.015 mm, the cutting force is 60 N and the thrust force is 25 N. The ratio of friction energy to total energy is __________ .

GATE 2018

Solution

Given: $t_o = 0.010$ mm, $v_c = 130$ m/min, $\alpha = 15°$, $b = 6$ mm, $t_c = 0.015$ mm, $F_c = 60$ N and $F_t = 25$ N.

Chip thickness ratio $\quad r = \dfrac{t_o}{t_c} = \dfrac{0.010}{0.015} = 0.666$

Friction force, $\quad F = F_c \sin\alpha + F_t \cos\alpha$

$$F = 60 \sin 15 + 25 \cos 15 = 39.6773 \text{ N}$$

Ratio of frictional energy to total energy $= \dfrac{F\, v_f}{F_c\, v_c}$

$$= \frac{F\, v_c r}{F_c\, v_c} = \frac{F}{F_c} r$$

$$= \frac{39.6773}{60} \times 0.666 = 0.4408$$

Ratio of frictional energy to total energy = 0.4408

Example 15.83

An electrochemical machining (ECM) is to be used to cut a through hole into a 12 mm thick aluminum plate. The hole has a rectangular cross-section, 10 mm × 30 mm. The ECM operation will be accomplished in 2 minutes, with efficiency of 90%. Assuming specific removal rate for aluminum as 3.44×10^{-2} mm^3/(A s), the current (in A) required is __________ .

GATE 2018

Solution

Volume of metal to be removed $= 10 \times 30 \times 12$

Energy required $= \dfrac{10 \times 30 \times 12}{3.44 \times 10^{-2}} = 104651.16$ A·s

Actual energy required $= \dfrac{104651.16}{0.9} = 116279.07$ A·s

Current $\quad I = \dfrac{116279.07}{2 \times 60} = 968.99$ A

$$I = 968.99 \text{ A}$$

Example 15.84

Feed rate in slab milling operation is equal to

(A) rotation per minute (rpm)

(B) product of rpm and number of teeth in the cutter

(C) product of rpm, feed per tooth and number of teeth in the cutter

(D) product of rpm, feed per tooth and number of teeth in contact

GATE 2018

Solution

Feed rate in slab milling $f_m = f_t\, Z\, N$, where f_t = feed per tooth, Z = Number of teeth in the cutter, N = rpm

Example 15.85

Metal removal in electric discharge machining takes place through

(A) ion displacement (B) melting and vaporization

(C) corrosive reaction (D) plastic shear

GATE 2018

Solution

Metal removal in electric discharge machining takes place through melting and vaporization.

Example 15.86

The preferred option for holding an odd-shaped workpiece in a centre lathe is

(A) live and dead centres (B) three jaw chuck

(C) lathe dog (D) four jaw chuck

GATE 2018

Solution

The preferred option for holding an odd-shaped workpiece in a centre lathe is four jaw chuck.

Example 15.87

Following data correspond to an orthogonal turning of a 100 mm diameter rod on a lathe. Rake angle: +15°; Uncut chip thickness: 0.5 mm; nominal chip thickness after the cut: 1.25 mm. The shear angle (in degrees) for this process is _______ .

GATE 2018

Solution

Shear angle $\phi = \tan^{-1}\left(\dfrac{r\cos\alpha}{1 - r\sin\alpha}\right)$

Substituting $r = \dfrac{t_o}{t_c} = \dfrac{0.5}{1.25} = 0.4$ and $\alpha = 15°$, we have

$$\phi = \tan^{-1}\left(\frac{0.4\cos 15}{1 - 0.4\sin 15}\right)$$

$$\phi = 23.32^\circ$$

Example 15.88

Taylor's tool life equation is used to estimate the life of a batch of identical HSS twist drills by drilling through holes at constant feed in 20 mm thick mild steel plates. In test 1, a drill lasted 300 holes at 150 rpm while in test 2, another drill lasted 200 holes at 300 rpm. The maximum number of holes that can be made by another drill from the above batch at 200 rpm is ______ .

GATE 2018

Solution

Time required for drilling one hole $t = \dfrac{L}{f\,N}$

Here, f and L is constant, N is variable

First test $T_1 = 300\,t_1 = 300 \times \dfrac{L}{f \times 150}$ min

$$V_1 = \pi D \times 150 \text{ mm/s}$$

Second test $T_2 = 200\,t_2 = 200 \times \dfrac{L}{f \times 300}$ min

$$V_2 = \pi D \times 300 \text{ mm/s}$$

Taylor's tool life equation $V_1 T_1^n = V_2 T_2^n$

$$(\pi D \times 150) \times \left(\frac{300 \times L}{f \times 150}\right)^n = (\pi D \times 300) \times \left(\frac{200 \times L}{f \times 300}\right)^n$$

$$2^n = 2 \times \left(\frac{2}{3}\right)^n$$

$$n = 0.6309$$

Let x be the number of holes drill at speed 200 rpm.

$$V_1 T_1^{0.6309} = V_x T_x^{0.6309}$$

$$(\pi D \times 150) \times \left(\frac{300 \times L}{f \times 150}\right)^{0.6309} = (\pi D \times 200) \times \left(\frac{x \times L}{f \times 200}\right)^{0.6309}$$

$$150 \times 2^{0.6309} = 200 \times \left(\frac{x}{200}\right)^{0.6309}$$

$$x = 253.53$$

Example 15.89

A circular hole of 25 mm diameter and depth of 20 mm is machined by EDM process. The material removal rate (in mm^3/min) is expressed as

$$4 \times 10^4 I\, T^{-1.23},$$

where $I = 300$ A and the melting point of the material, $T = 1600°$C. The time (in minutes) for machining this hole is ________

GATE 2018

Solution

Metal removal rate,

$$MRR = \frac{\text{Volume of metal required to remove}}{\text{time}}$$

$$4 \times 10^4 \times 300 \times 1600^{-1.23} = \frac{\frac{\pi}{4} \times 25^2 \times 20}{t}$$

Time $t = 7.143$ min

Example 15.90

The length, width and thickness of a steel sample are 400 mm, 40 mm and 20 mm, respectively. Its thickness needs to be uniformly reduced by 2 mm in a single pass by using horizontal slab milling. The milling cutter (diameter: 100 mm, width: 50 mm) has 20 teeth and rotates at 1200 rpm.The feed per tooth is 0.05 mm. The feed direction is along the length of the sample. If the over-travel distance is the same as the approach distance, the approach distance and time taken to complete the required machining task are

(A) 14 mm, 18.4 s (B) 21 mm, 28.9 s

(C) 21 mm, 39.4 s (D)14 mm, 21.4 s

GATE 2019

Solution

Given: $l = 400$ mm, $w = 40$ mm, $t = 20$ mm, $d = 2$ mm, $D = 100$ mm, $n_t = 20$ teeth, $f = 0.05$ mm/teeth, $N = 1200$ r pm.

Feed rate, $f_r = N\,n_t f$

$$f_r = 1200 \times 20 \times 0.05 = 1200 \text{ mm/min}$$

$$f_r = 20 \text{ mm/s}$$

Approach distance, $A = \sqrt{d(D-d)} = \sqrt{2(100-2)} = 14$ mm

Approach distance, $A = 14$ mm

Machining time $T_m = \dfrac{A+l+A}{f_r} = \dfrac{14+40+14}{20}$

$$T_m = 21.4\text{ s}$$

Example 15.91

The position vector $\vec{OP}$ of point P(20,10) is rotated anti-clockwise in X-Y plane by an angle $\theta = 30°$ such that point P occupies position Q, as shown in the figure. The coordinates (x, y) of Q are

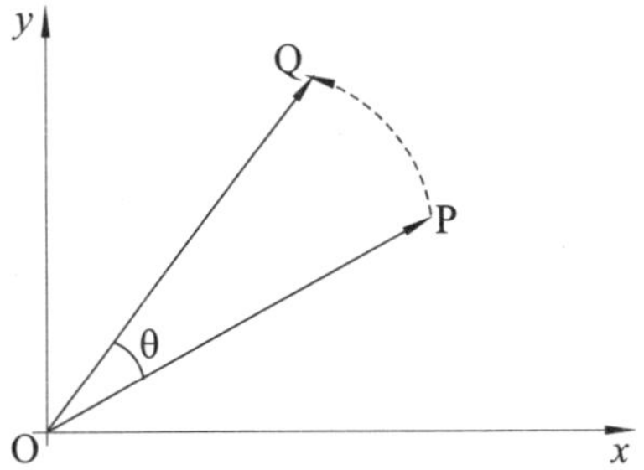

(A) (13.40, 22.32) (B) (22.32, 8.26)

(C) (12.32, 18.66) (D) (18.66, 12.32)

GATE 2019

Solution

Let (x', y') be the coordinates of position Q.

$$\begin{bmatrix} x' \\ y' \end{bmatrix} = \begin{bmatrix} \cos\theta & -\sin\theta \\ \sin\theta & \cos\theta \end{bmatrix}\begin{bmatrix} x \\ y \end{bmatrix}$$

$$\begin{bmatrix} x' \\ y' \end{bmatrix} = \begin{bmatrix} \cos 30 & -\sin 30 \\ \sin 30 & \cos 30 \end{bmatrix}\begin{bmatrix} 20 \\ 10 \end{bmatrix}$$

$$\begin{bmatrix} x' \\ y' \end{bmatrix} = \begin{bmatrix} 12.32 \\ 18.66 \end{bmatrix}$$

$$x' = 12.32,\ y' = 18.66$$

Example 15.92

In orthogonal turning of a cylindrical tube of wall thickness 5 mm, the axial and the tangential cutting forces were measured as 1259 N and 1601 N, respectively. The measured chip thickness after machining was found to be 0.3 mm.The rake angle was 10° and the axial feed was 100 mm/min. The rotational speed of the spindle was 1000 rpm. Assuming the material to be perfectly plastic and Merchant's first solution, the shear strength of the material is closest to

(A) 722 MPa (B) 920 MPa

(C) 200 MPa (D) 875 MPa

GATE 2019

Solution

Given: $F_t = 1259$ N, $F_c = 1601$ N, $t_c = 0.3$ mm, $\alpha = 10°$, Feed rate $f_r = 100$ mm/min, $N = 1000$ rpm, $w = 5$ mm.

Feed rate $f_r = N f \Rightarrow$ Feed $f = \dfrac{f_r}{N} = \dfrac{100}{1000} = 0.1$ mm/rev

Since it is orthogonal machining $t_o = f = 0.1$ mm

Chip thickness ratio, $r = \dfrac{t_o}{t_c} = \dfrac{0.1}{0.3} = 0.33$

$$\tan\phi = \frac{r\cos\alpha}{1 - r\sin\alpha}$$

$$\phi = \tan^{-1}\left(\frac{0.33\cos 10}{1 - 0.33\sin 10}\right) = 0.348$$

$$\phi = 19.18°$$

Shear force $F_s = F_c\cos\phi - F_t\sin\phi$

$$F_s = 1601\cos 19.18 - 1259\sin 19.18$$

$$F_s = 1098.42\text{ N}$$

Shear stress $\tau = \dfrac{F_s}{(t_o w / \sin\phi)} = \dfrac{1098.42}{(0.1 \times 5 / \sin 19.18)}$

$$\tau = 721.74\text{ MPa}$$

Example 15.93

A circular shaft having diameter $65.00^{+0.01}_{-0.05}$ is manufactured by turning process. A 50 μm thick coating of TiN is deposited on the shaft. Allowed variation in TiN film thickness is ± 5 μm. The minimum hole diameter (in mm) to just provide clearance fit is

(A) 65.01 (B) 65.12 (C) 64.95 (D) 65.10

GATE 2019

Solution

Shaft size $= 65.00^{+0.01}_{-0.05}$ mm $\Rightarrow$ 65.01 mm - 64.95 mm

Coating thickness $= 50.00^{+5}_{-5}$ μm $\Rightarrow$ 0.055 mm - 0.045 mm

Maximum size of shaft with coating

$$= 65.01 + 2 \times 0.055 = 65.12\text{ mm}$$

Minimum hole diameter (clearance fit) = 65.12 mm

Example 15.94

In ASA system, the side cutting and end cutting edge angles of a sharp turning tool are 45° and 10°, respectively. The feed during cylindrical turning is 0.1 mm/rev. The center line average surface roughness (in μm, round off to one decimal place) of the generated surface is ________.

GATE 2019

Solution

Center line average surface roughness (CLA)

$$R_a = \frac{f}{4(\tan C_s + \cos C_e)}$$

Substituting $f = 0.1$, $C_s = 45°$ and $C_e = 10°$

$$R_a = \frac{0.1}{4(\tan 45 + \cos 10)}$$

$$R_a = 3.747 \times 10^{-3}\text{mm}$$

$$R_a = 3.747 \ \mu\text{m}$$

Example 15.95

Taylor's tool life equation is given by $VT^n = C$, where V is in m/min and T is in min. In a turning operation, to tools X and Y are used. For tool X, $n = 0.3$ and $C = 60$ and for tool Y, $n = 0.6$ and $C = 90$. Both the tools will have the same tool life for the cutting speed (in m/min, round off to one decimal place) of _______.

GATE 2019

Solution

Taylor's tool life equation; $VT^n = C$

Tool X; $V_X T_x^{0.3} = 60$

Tool Y; $V_Y T_Y^{0.6} = 90$

For same tool life $T_X = T_Y$ $(V_X = V_Y = V)$

$$T_X = T_Y \Rightarrow \left(\frac{60}{V}\right)^{\frac{1}{0.3}} = \left(\frac{90}{V}\right)^{\frac{1}{0.6}}$$

Solving equation $\ln V = 2\ln 60 - \ln 90 \Rightarrow V = \dfrac{60^2}{90}$

$$V = 40 \text{ m/min}$$

Example 15.96

The transformation matrix for mirroring a point in $x - y$ plane about the line $y = x$ is given by

(A) $\begin{bmatrix} 1 & 0 \\ 0 & -1 \end{bmatrix}$ (B) $\begin{bmatrix} -1 & 0 \\ 0 & 1 \end{bmatrix}$ (C) $\begin{bmatrix} 0 & 1 \\ 1 & 0 \end{bmatrix}$ (D) $\begin{bmatrix} 0 & -1 \\ -1 & 0 \end{bmatrix}$

GATE 2019

Solution

$$\begin{bmatrix} 0 & 1 \\ 1 & 0 \end{bmatrix}$$

Example 15.97

In an electrical discharge machining process, the breakdown voltage across inter electrode gap (IEG) is 200 V and the capacitance of the RC circuit is 50 μF. The energy (in J) released per spark across the IEG is _______.

GATE 2019

Solution

Energy released per spark

$$= \frac{1}{2}CV^2 = \frac{1}{2} \times 50 \times 10^{-6} \times 200^2$$

$$\text{Energy released per spark} = 1\text{ J}$$

Example 15.98

A through hole is drilled in an aluminum alloy plate of 15 mm thickness with a drill bit of diameter 10 mm, at a feed of 0.25 mm/rev and a spindle speed of 1200 rpm. If the specific energy required for cutting this material is 0.7 N.m/mm^3, the power required for drilling is ______ W (round off to two decimal places).

GATE 2019

Solution

Metal removal rate $MRR = \dfrac{\pi}{4}D^2 f_r = \dfrac{\pi}{4}D^2(Nf)$

Power required for drilling, $P = MRR \times \text{Specific energy}$

$$P = \frac{\pi}{4}D^2(Nf) \times \text{Specific energy}$$

$$P = \frac{\pi}{4} \times 10^2\left(\frac{1200}{60} \times 0.25\right) \times 0.7$$

$$P = 274.88 \text{ W}$$

Example 15.99

In an orthogonal machining with a single point cutting tool of rake angle 10°, the uncut chip thickness and the chip thickness are 0.125 mm and 0.22 mm, respectively. using Merchant's first solution for the condition of minimum cutting force, the coefficient of friction at the chip-tool interface is _____(round off to two decimal places).

GATE 2019

Solution

Given that $\alpha = 10°$, $t_o = 0.125$ mm, $t_c = 0.22$ mm

Chip thickness ratio $r = \dfrac{t_o}{t_c} = \dfrac{0.125}{0.22} = 0.568$

$$\tan\phi = \frac{r\cos\alpha}{1 - r\sin\alpha}$$

$$\phi = \tan^{-1}\left(\frac{r\cos\alpha}{1 - r\sin\alpha}\right) = \tan^{-1}\left(\frac{0.568\cos 10}{1 - 0.568\sin 10}\right)$$

$$\phi = 31.706°$$

Using Merchant's equations; $2\phi = 90 + \alpha - \beta$

$$2 \times 31.706° = 90 + 10 - \beta$$

$$\beta = 36.59°$$

$$\mu = \tan\beta = \tan 36.59°$$

$$\mu = 0.74$$

15.3 PRACTICE PAPER

Time: 3 hours **Max. Marks: 100**

Q.1 to Q.30 carry one mark each

Q.1 to Q.21 Multiple Choice Questions

Q.1 Chip thickness ratio is the ratio of

1. Chip thickness to uncut thickness
2. Uncut thickness to chip thickness
3. Cutting speed to chip velocity
4. Chip velocity to cutting speed

Of these

(A) 1 alone is true (B) 2 alone is true

(C) 2 and 4 are true (D) 1 and 3 are true

Q.2 A fit on a hole shaft system is specified as H7- s6. The type of fit is

(A) Clearance fit (B) Running (sliding) fit

(C) Transition fit (D) Interference fit

Q.3 Match List-I (machining processes) with List-II (Operating media) and select the correct answer using the codes given below the lists.

List-I (Machining processes)	List-II (Operating media)
(a) Abrasive jet machining	(1) Dielectric
(b) Electron beam machining	(2) Electrolyte
(c) Electro-chemical machining	(3) Abrasive slurry
(d) Electro-discharge machining	(4) Vacuum
	(5) Air

(A) a-3, b-4, c-2, d-1 (B) a-3, b-4, c-1, d-2

(C) a-4, b-5, c-2, d-1 (D) a-4, b-5, c-2, d-1

Q.4 In Taylor's tool life equation $VT^n = C$, the constants n and C depend upon

1. Work piece material
2. Tool material
3. Coolant

(A) 1, 2 and 3 (B) 1 and 2 only

(C) 2 and 3 only (D) 1 and 3 only

Q.5 Clearance in a fit is the difference between

(A) Maximum hole size and Minimum shaft size

(B) Minimum hole size and Maximum shaft size

(C) Maximum hole size and maximum shaft size

(D) None of these

Q.6 Match List-I with List-II and select the correct answer using the code given below the lists.

List-I (Unconventional machine process)	List-II (Basic process)
(a) Electro polishing	(1) Thermal
(b) Electrochemical machining	(2) Mechanical
(c) Abrasive jet machining	(3) Electrochemical
(d) Electrical discharge machining	(4) Chemical

(A) a-4, b-3, c-2, d-1 (B) a-2, b-1, c-4, d-3

(C) a-4, b-1, c-2, d-3 (D) a-2, b-3, c-4, d-1

Q.7 A 50 mm diameter shaft and hole pair of 50 H7g6, the type of fit is

(A) Clearance fit (B) Transition fit

(C) Interference fit (D) None of these

Q.8 The best size wire for ISO metric thread for measuring pitch diameters of screw thread in terms of its pitch is

(A) $0.75p$ (B) $0.6p$ (C) $0.5773p$ (D) $0.5p$

Q.9 The standard tolerance unit is equal to

(where D = Geometric means of the lower and upper diameters of a particular diameter step.)

(A) $i = 0.45(\sqrt[3]{D}) + 0.001D$ (B) $i = 0.45(\sqrt[4]{D}) + 0.001D$

(C) $i = 0.45(\sqrt[3]{D}) + 0.01D$ (D) $i = 0.45(\sqrt[4]{D}) + 0.01D$

Q.10 Match List-I with List-II and select the correct answer using the codes given below the lists.

List-I (Measuring device)	List-II (Parameter measured)
(a) Diffraction grating	(1) Small angular deviations on long flat surfaces
(b) Optical flat	(2) On-line measurement of moving parts
(c) Auto collimators	(3) Measurement of gear pitch
(d) Laser scan micrometer	(4) Surface texture using interferometry
	(5) Measurement of very small displacements

(A) a-5, b-4, c-2, d-1 (B) a-4, b-1, c-5, d-2

(C) a-3, b-5, c-4, d-1 (D) a-5, b-4, c-1, d-2

Q.11 A shaft has a dimension, $\phi\, 35^{-0.009}_{-0.025}$. The respective values of fundamental deviation and tolerance are:

(A) –0.025, ± 0.008 (B) –0.025, 0.016

(C) –0.009, ± 0.008 (D) –0.009, 0.016

Q.12 The value of chip thickness ratio is

(A) Greater than one (B) Greater than two

(C) Less than one (D) Less than zero

Q.13 A hole and mating shaft are to have a nominal assembly size of 50 mm. The assembly is to have a maximum clearance of 0.15 mm and a minimum clearance of 0.05 mm. The hole tolerance is 1.5 times the shaft tolerance. By using hole basis system. The limits of size for the shaft is

(A) $50^{-0.05}_{-0.09}$ mm (B) $50^{-0.04}_{-0.05}$ mm

(C) $50^{-0.08}_{-0.06}$ mm (D) None of these

Q.14 In metal cutting operation, the approximate ratio of heat distributed among chip, tool and work, in that order is

(A) 80 : 10 : 10 (B) 33 : 33 : 33

(C) 20 : 60 : 10 (D) 10 : 10 : 80

Q.15 Match List-I (machining process) with List-II (Associated medium) and select the correct answer using the codes given below the lists.

List-I (Machining process)	List-II (Associated medium)
(a) Ultrasonic machining	(1) Kerosene
(b) EDM	(2) Abrasive slurry
(c) ECM	(3) Vacuum
(d) EBM	(4) Salt solution

(A) a-2, b-3, c-4, d-1 (B) a-2, b-1, c-4, d-3

(C) a-4, b-1, c-2, d-3 (D) a-4, b-3, c-2, d-1

Q.16 In a single-point turning operation of steel with a cemented carbide tool, Taylor's tool life exponent is 0.25. If the cutting speed is halved, the tool life will increase by

(A) Two times (B) Four times

(C) Eight times (D) Sixteen times

Q.17 The sequence of markings "S14K14S" on a grinding wheel represents respectively

(A) Bond type, structure, grade, grain size and abrasive type

(B) Abrasive type, grain size, grade, structure and bond type

(C) Bond type, grade, structure, grain size and abrasive type

(D) Abrasive type, structure, grade, grain size and bond type

Q.18 Match List-I with List-II and select the correct answer using the codes given below in the lists.

List-I	List-II
(a) Surface profilometer	(1) Calibration
(b) Light section microcsope	(2) Form tester
(c) Microkater	(3) Film thickness measurement
(d) Interferometer	(4) Center line average
	(5) Comparator

(A) a-4, b-3, c-5, d-1 (B) a-4, b-2, c-5, d-1

(C) a-2, b-3, c-3, d-5 (D) a-2, b-2, c-3, d-5

Q.19 The value of surface roughness R_a obtained during the turning operation at a feed f with a round nose tool having radius r is given as:

(A) $\frac{f}{8r}$ (B) $\frac{f^2}{32r}$ (C) $\frac{f^2}{8r}$ (D) $\frac{f^3}{8r^2}$

Q.20 Consider the following forces acting on a finish turning tool

1. Feed force, 2. Thrust force, 3. Cutting force

The correct sequence of the decreasing order of the magnitudes of these forces is:

(A) 1, 2, 3 (B) 2, 3, 1 (C) 3, 1, 2 (D) 3, 2, 1

Q.21 to Q.30 Numerical Answer Questions

Q.21 A threaded nut of M16, ISO metric type, having 2 mm pitch with a pitch diameter of 14.701 mm is to be checked for its pitch diameter using two or three numbers of balls or rollers of sizes (diameter in mm)________.

Q.22 In turning a solid round bar, if the travel of the cutting tool in the direction of feed motion is 1000 mm, rotational speed of the workpiece is 500 rpm, and rate of feed is 0.2 mm/rev, then the machining time (in seconds) will be__________.

Q.23 Given that the peripheral speed of the grinding wheel of 100 mm diameter for cylindrical grinding of a steel workpiece is 30 m/s, what will be the estimated rotational speed of the grinding wheel in revolution per minute (rpm)?_________.

Q.24 A stainless steel rod of diameter 10 mm and of length 125 mm is being reduced in diameter to 9 mm by turning on a lathe. The spindle rotates at 360 rpm, and the tool is travelling at an axial speed of 175 mm/min. The cutting time (in min) is__________.

Q.25 An orthogonal cutting operation is being carried out under the following conditions: cutting speed = 2 m/s, depth of cut = 0.5 mm, chip thickness = 0.6 mm. Then the chip velocity (in m/s) is________.

Q.26 The time taken (in minutes) to face a work-piece of 72 mm diameter, if the spindle speed is 80 rpm and crossfeed is 0.3 mm/rev, is_________.

Q.27 Dimension (in mm) of hole and shaft of mating parts are: $20^{+0.05}_{+0.00}$ mm and $20^{-0.02}_{-0.05}$ mm. Tolerance of shaft is ___.

Q.28 In the measurement of surface roughness, height of successive 10 peaks and troughs are measured from a datum and are 30, 24, 29, 21, 18, 24, 22, 23 and 26 microns. The measurements are obtained on 10 mm length. The value of surface roughness Ra (in microns) is_______.

Q.29 A medium carbon steel workpiece is turned on a Lathe at 50 m/min cutting speed, 0.8 mm/rev feed and 1.5 mm depth of cut. What is the rate of metal removal (in mm^3/min)?__.

Q.30 In orthogonal cutting test, the cutting force = 900 N, the thrust force = 600 N and chip shear angle is 30°. Then the chip shear force (in N) is_______.

Q.31 to Q.65 carry two marks each

Q.31 to Q.50 Multiple Choice Questions

Q.31 If α is the rake angle of the cutting tool, ϕ is the shear angle and v_c is the cutting velocity, then the velocity of chip sliding along the shear plane is given by

(A) $v_c \dfrac{\cos\phi}{\cos(\phi-\alpha)}$ (B) $v_c \dfrac{\sin\phi}{\cos(\phi-\alpha)}$

(C) $v_c \dfrac{\cos\phi}{\sin(\phi-\alpha)}$ (D) $v_c \dfrac{\sin\phi}{\sin(\phi-\alpha)}$

Q.32 A tapered surface is to be turned on an automatic lathe. The length of workpiece is 750 mm and diameters at one end is 100 mm and other end is 200 mm. The automatic controls on the length permit the speed to be maintained at a constant value of 200 m/min by adjusting the rotational speed as a function of workpiece diameter. Depth of cut = 3.0 mm and feed = 0.25 mm/rev. The rough geometry of the piece has already been formed, and this operation will be the final cut. The rotation speeds (rpm) at beginning and end of the cut is (respectively)

(A) 468.5, 318.3 (B) 300.8, 150.4

(C) 636.6, 318.3 (D) None of these

Q.33 The radius of concave surface can be easily determined by a depth micrometer as shown in the figure. The radius of curvature R is equal to

(A) $\dfrac{d^2}{8h}+\dfrac{h}{2}$ (B) $\dfrac{d^2}{8h}-\dfrac{h}{2}$ (C) $\dfrac{d^2}{4h}+h$ (D) $\dfrac{d^2}{8h}+h$

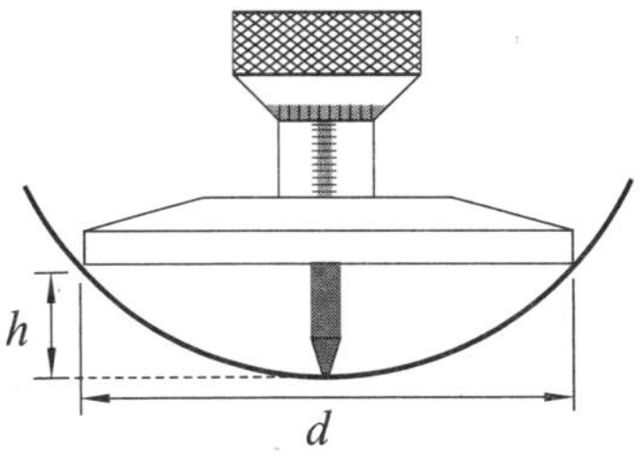

Q.34 A hole is specified as $45^{+0.050}_{+0.000}$ mm. The mating shaft has a clearance fit with minimum clearance of 0.01 mm. The tolerance on the shaft is 0.04 mm. The maximum clearance in mm between the hole and the shaft is

(A) 0.04 (B) 0.05 (C) 0.10 (D) 0.11

Q.35 The best size wire diameter for an M20 × 2.5 screw is

(A) 2.5 mm (B) 1.25 mm (C) 20 mm (D) 1.443 mm

Q.36 A fit is specified as 25 H8/e8. The tolerance value for a nominal diameter of 25 mm in IT8 is 33 microns and fundamental deviation for the shaft is –40 microns. The maximum clearance of the fit in microns is

(A) –7 (B) 7 (C) 73 (D) 106

Q.37 In the measurement of surface roughness, height of successive 10 peaks and troughs are measured from a datum and are 30, 24, 29, 21, 18, 24, 22, 23 and 26 microns. The measurements are obtained on 10 mm length. RMS value of surface roughness is

(A) 24.5 microns (B) 22.6 microns

(C) 23.9 microns (D) 21.6 microns

Q.38 In orthogonal cutting, the depth of cut is 0.5 mm at a cutting speed of 2 m/s. If the chip thickness is 0.75 mm, the chip velocity is

(A) 1.33 m/s (B) 2 m/s (C) 2.5 m/s (D) 3 m/s

Q.39 In an orthogonal cutting test, the cutting force and thrust are observed to be 1000 N and 500 N respectively. If the rake angle of tool is zero, the coefficient of friction in chip-tool interface will be

(A) $\dfrac{1}{2}$ (B) 2 (C) $\dfrac{1}{\sqrt{2}}$ (D) $\sqrt{2}$

Q.40 Tool life tests on a lathe have resulted in the following data :

(i) V = 100 m/min, T = 10 min

(ii) V = 75 m/min, T = 30 min

The value of exponent n in the Taylor tool life equation is

(A) 0.2617 (B) 0.2619 (C) 0.2639 (D) 0.3319

Q.41 A straight teeth slab milling cutter of 100 mm diameter and 10 teeth rotating at 200 rpm is used to remove a layer of 3 mm thickness from a steel box. If the table feed is 400 mm/min, the feed per tooth in this operation will be

(A) 0.2 mm (B) 0.4 mm (C) 0.5 mm (D) 0.6 mm

Q.42 A cylindrical workpart made of titanium alloy is to be turned. The starting diameter = 500 mm and the length = 1000 mm. Cutting conditions are: feed f = 0.4 mm/rev, and depth of cut d = 3.0 mm. The cut will be made with a cemented carbide cutting tool whose Taylor tool life parameters are C= 400 and n = 0.23. (In Taylor equation units of T is min and V is m/min). What is the cutting speed that will allow the tool life to be just equal to the cutting time for this?

(A) 32.64 m/min (B) 105.83 m/min

(C) 150.31 m/min (D) 202.18 m/min

Q.43 Tool life tests on a lathe have resulted in the following data:

(i) V = 100 m/min, T = 10 min

(ii) V = 75 m/min, T = 30 min

The tool life for a speed of 90 m/min is:

(A) 15.13 min (B) 14.9 min

(C) 10.15 min (D) 10.22 min

Q.44 The rake angle of a cutting tool is 15°, shear angle 45° and cutting velocity 35 m/min. What is the velocity of chip along the tool face?

(A) 28.5 m/min (B) 27.3 m/min

(C) 25.3 m/min (D) 23.5 m/min

Q.45 In an orthogonal cutting operation, the following observations are made:

Cutting force = 1470 N

Rake angle = 5°

Width of cut = 5.0 mm

Chip thickness before the cut = 0.6 mm

Chip thickness ratio = 0.38

The coefficient of friction in the operation is:

(A) 0.42 (B) 0.42 (C) 1.291 (D) 1.6

Q.46 A stainless steel rod of diameter 10 mm and of length 125 mm is being reduced in diameter to 9 mm by turning on a lathe. The spindle rotates at 360 rpm, and the tool is travelling at an axial speed of 175 mm/min. Material removal rate (in mm^3/min) is:

(A) 235.51 (B) 2610.08 (C) 3101.28 (D) None of these

Q.47 The radius R of a pulley block is measured as shown in the figure is calculated by

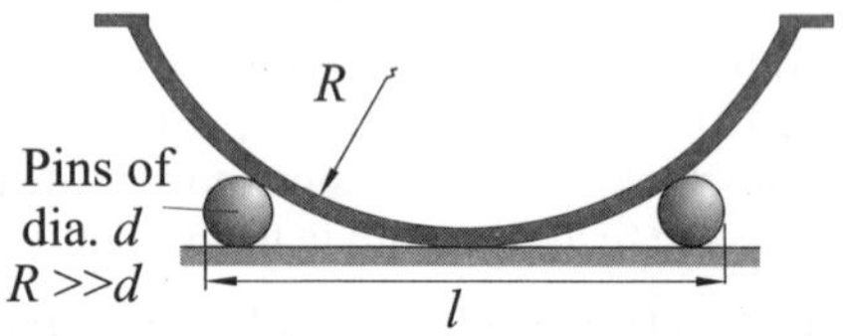

(A) $R = \frac{l-d}{8d}$ (B) $R = \frac{(l-d)^2}{4d}$

(C) $R = \frac{(l-d)^2}{8d}$ (D) $R = \frac{(l-d)^2}{2d}$

Q.48 A hole and mating shaft are to have a nominal assembly size of 50 mm. The assembly is to have a maximum clearance of 0.15 mm and a minimum clearance of 0.05 mm. The hole tolerance is 1.5 times the shaft tolerance. By using hole basis system. The limits of size for the hole is:

(A) $50^{+0.03}_{+0.00}$ mm (B) $50^{+0.02}_{+0.00}$ mm

(C) $50^{+0.06}_{+0.00}$ mm (D) None of these

Q.49 In an orthogonal cutting operation, the following observations are made:

Cutting force = 1470 N

Thrust force = 1589 N

Rake angle = 5°

Width of cut = 5.0 mm

Chip thickness before the cut = 0.6 mm

Chip thickness ratio = 0.38

The shear strength of the work material is:

(A) 87.6 MPa (B) 95.9 MPa

(C) 133 MPa (D) None of these

Q.50 A cylindrical workpart made of titanium alloy is to be turned. The starting diameter = 500 mm and the length = 1000 mm. Cutting conditions are: feed f = 0.4 mm/rev, and depth of cut d = 3.0 mm. The cut will be made with a cemented carbide cutting tool whose Taylor tool life parameters are C = 400 and n = 0.23. (In Taylor equation units of T is min and V is m/min). The cutting time is

(A) 19.42 min (B) 26.14 min

(C) 34 min (D) 102.5 min

Q.51 to Q.65 Numerical Answer Questions

Q.51 In an orthogonal cutting, the cutting tool has a rake angle = 10°. The chip thickness before the cut = 0.5 mm. and the chip thickness after the cut = 1.125 mm. The shear plane angle (in degree) is______.

Q.52 Two balls of diameter 30 mm and 15 mm are used to measure the taper of a ring gauge. During inspection, the ball of 30 mm diameter was protruding by 2.5 mm above the surface of the ring. This surface is located at a height of 50 mm from the top of the 15 mm diameter ball. The taper angle (in degrees) of ring gauge is________.

Q.53 A tapered surface is to be turned on an automatic lathe. The length of workpiece is 750 mm and diameters at one end is 100 mm and other end is 200 mm. The automatic controls on the length permit the speed to be maintained at a constant value of 200 m/min by adjusting the rotational speed as a function of workpiece diameter. Depth of cut = 3.0 mm and feed = 0.25 mm/rev. The rough geometry of the piece has already been formed, and this operation will be the final cut. The time required (in minutes) to turn the taper is________.

Q.54 Using the Tayer equation ($VT^{0.5} = 400$) for tool life, what is the value of the percentage increase in tool life when the cutting speed is reduced by 50%?

Q.55 In a machining operation, chip thickness ratio is 0.3 and the rack angle of the tool is 10°. What is the value of the shear strain?

Q.56 For a certain tool it is found that the relationship between cutting speed (V) and tool life (T) is as follows:

$$V = \frac{1540}{2.73 + T} + C$$

If for a cutting speed of 80 m/min the tool life is 19.27 min, the cutting speed (in m/min) corresponding to tool life of 6.27 min should be______.

Q.57 A brass pin has a length of 500 mm and job of 40 mm diameter. The pin is to be reduced to 38.8 mm in one pass, when cutting speed is 60 m/min and feed is 0.8 mm/rev. The machining time (in min) is_________.

Q.58 A 18 mm hole is to be drilled in a work-piece having thickness of 50 mm. The cutting speed is to be 12 m/min and feed 0.2 mm/ rev. The cutting time (in min) will be___.

Q.59 A conventional lathe and a CNC lathe are under consideration for machining a given part. The relevant data are shown below:

	Preparation cost (Rs.)	Production time per part (min)	Machine and operator cost (Rs.)
Conventional lathe	30	30	75
CNC lathe	150	15	120

What is the break-even quantity, above which CNC lathe is economical?

Q.60 The lives of two tools A and B, are governed by the equations $VT^{0.125} = 2.5$ and $VT^{0.250} = 7$, respectively in a certain machining operation, where V is the cutting speed in m/s and T is the tool life in seconds. The speed V^*(in m/s) at which both the tool will have the same life ___.

Q.61 The bore diameter D, of the plain ring having a height of 35 mm is measured using two spherical balls, each of diameter d = 25.000 mm. The ring is placed on a surface table and then both the balls are placed inside the ring. In this position, the height h of the top of the upper ball from the surface table is found to be 42 mm. The bore diameter D (in mm) of the plain ring is_________.

Q.62 When milling a slot 20 mm wide 10 cm long in a rectangular plate 10 cm × 20 cm. The cutting conditions used are:

Cutting speed = 60 m/min

Diameter of end mill = 20 mm

Number of flutes = 8

Feed = 0.01 mm/fluate

Depth of cut = 3 mm

The cutting time (in seconds) for this operation is_____.

Q.63 During orthogonal machining of a 25 mm diameter steel bar at 300 rpm with an HSS tool, a tool life of 10 min is obtained. When the same bar is turned at 250 rpm, the tool life increased to 52.5 min. Tool life (in min) at a speed of 275 rpm is_____.

Q.64 Figure shows the 3-wire method of inspecting screw threads. Assuming ISO metric threads of size M16 with pitch = 2 mm and effective diameter = 14.701 mm. Diameter of the roller used for the measurement is 1.155 mm. The wire measurement M (in mm) is______

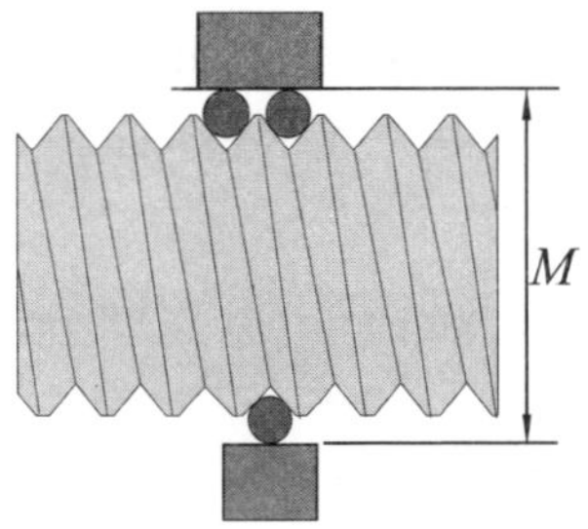

Q.65 During orthogonal machining of a steel workpiece with a single point cutting tool of 10° rake angle, the following data are recorded:

Chip thickness = 1.5 mm

Uncut chip thickness = 0.6 mm

Cutting force = 980 N

Thrust force = 440 N

width of cut = 1.8 mm

The shear strength (in N/mm^2) of the material is_____.

15.4 SOLUTION TO PRACTICE PAPER

Q.1 Ans:(C)

Chip thickness ratio, $r = \frac{t_o}{t_c} = \frac{v_{chip}}{v} = \frac{\text{Chip velocity}}{\text{Cutting velocity}}$

Q.2 Ans:(D)

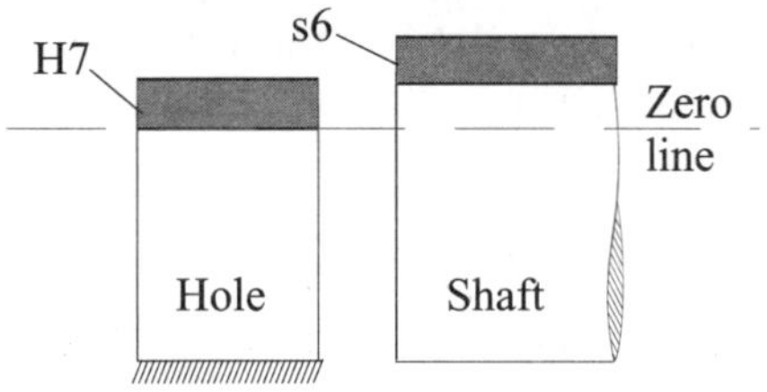

Tolerance zone and fundamental deviation of H7-s6 are shown in figure.

H7-s6 is interference fit

Q.3 Ans:(A)

Correct match:

List-I (Machining processes)	List-II (Operating media)
(a) Abrasive jet machining	(3) Abrasive slurry
(b) Electron beam machining	(4) Vacuum
(c) Electro-chemical machining	(2) Electrolyte
(d) Electro-discharge machining	(1) Dielectric

Q.4 Ans:(A)

Exponent n and constant C depend upon

1. Work piece material, 2. Tool material, 3. Coolant.

Q.5 Ans:(B)

Clearance = Minimum hole size – Maximum shaft size

Q.6 Ans:(A)

Correct match:

List-I (Unconventional machine process)	List-II (Basic process)
(a) Electro polishing	(4) Chemical
(b) Electrochemical machining	(3) Electrochemical
(c) Abrasive jet machining	(2) Mechanical
(d) Electrical discharge machining	(1) Thermal

Q.7 Ans:(A)

Tolerance zone and fundamental deviation of 50 H7g6 are shown in figure.

50 H7g6 is clearance fit

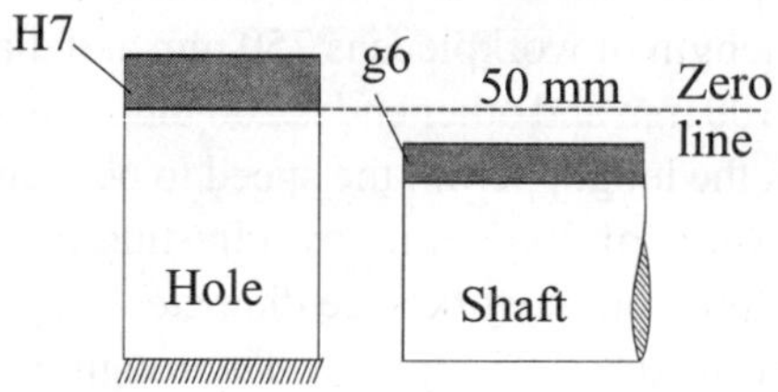

Q.8 Ans:(C)

Best size wire diameter, $d_w = \frac{p}{2}\sec\theta$

For metric thread $2\theta = 60°$; $d_w = \frac{p}{2}\sec 30$

$d_w = 0.5773\,p$

Q.9 Ans:(A)

Tolerance $i = 0.45(\sqrt[3]{D}) + 0.001D$

Q.10 Ans:(B)

Correct match:

List-I (Measuring device)	List-II (Parameter measured)
(a) Diffraction grating	(4) Surface texture using interferometry
(b) Optical flat	(1) Small angular deviations on long flat surfaces
(c) Auto collimators	(5) Measurement of very small displacements
(d) Laser scan micrometer	(2) On-line measurement of moving parts

Q.11 Ans:(D)

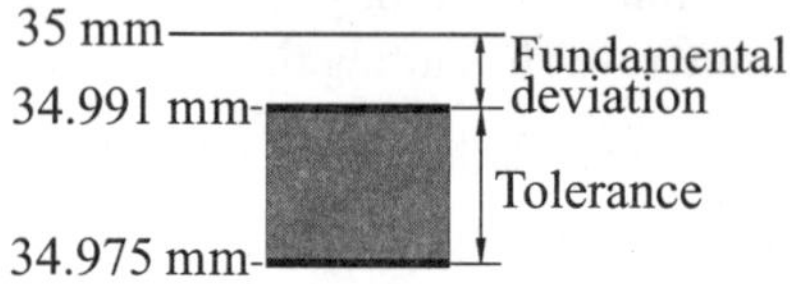

Fundamental deviation $= 35 - 34.991 = -0.009$ mm

Tolerance $= 34.975 - 34.991 = 0.016$ mm

Fundamental deviation and tolerance are –0.009 mm, 0.016 mm.

Q.12 Ans:(C)

Chip thickness ratio, $r = \frac{t_o}{t_c} < 1$

Q.13 Ans:(A)

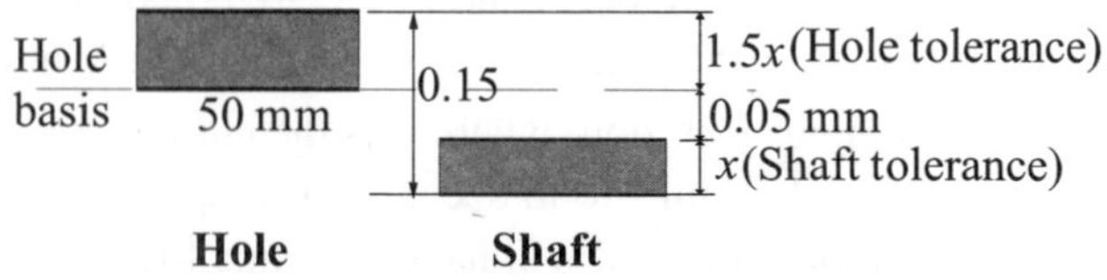

Let x be the shaft tolerance.

$$x + 0.05 + 1.5x = 0.15$$

$$x = 0.04\text{ mm}$$

Size of shaft

Maximum size $= 50 - 0.05$

Minimum size $= 50 - 0.05 - 0.04 = 50 - 0.09$

$$50^{-0.05}_{-0.09}\text{ mm}$$

Q.14 Ans:(A)

Heat distribution

chip, tool and work :: 80 : 10 : 10

Q.15 Ans:(B)

Correct match:

List-I (Machining process)	List-II (Associated medium)
(a) Ultrasonic machining	(2) Abrasive slurry
(b) EDM	(1) Kerosene
(c) ECM	(4) Salt solution
(d) EBM	(3) Vacuum

Q.16(D)

Taylor's tool life equation, $VT^{0.25} = C$

$$V_1 T_1^{0.25} = \frac{V_1}{2} T_2^{0.25}$$

$$T_2 = 16T_1$$

Q.17(B)

S 14 K 14 S

- S – Abrasive type
- 14 – Grain size
- K – Grade(A to Z)
- 14 – Structure (1 to 15)
- S – Bond type

Q.18(A)

Correct match:

List-I	List-II
(a) Surface profilometer	(4) Center line average
(b) Light section microcsope	(3) Film thickness measurement
(c) Microkater	(5) Comparator
(d) Interferometer	(1) Calibration

Q.19 Ans:(B)

Surface roughness, $R_a = \dfrac{f^2}{32r}$

Q.20 Ans:(D)

Cutting force > Thrust force > Feed force

Q.21 Ans:[1.155]

Given: pitch $p = 2$ mm and $d_p = 14.701$ mm

Best size wire diameter, $d_w = \dfrac{p}{2}\sec\theta$

For metric thread $2\theta = 60°$; $d_w = \dfrac{2}{2}\sec 30$

$$d_w = 1.155\text{ mm}$$

Q.22 Ans:[10]

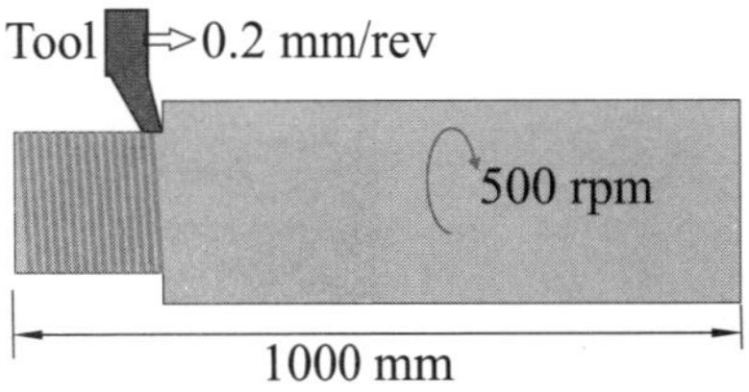

Given: $L = 1000$ mm, $N = 500$ rpm and $f = 0.2$ mm/rev

Machining timing, $T_m = \dfrac{L}{fN}$

$$T_m = \frac{1000}{02 \times 500}$$

$$T_m = 10\text{ min}$$

Q.23 Ans:[5729.5]

Rational speed, $N = \dfrac{V}{\pi D} \times 60$ rpm

$$N = \frac{30}{\pi \times \frac{100}{1000}} \times 60\text{ rpm}$$

$$N = 5729.5\text{ rpm}$$

Q.24 Ans:[0.715]

Cutting time, $T_m = \dfrac{\text{Length of rod}}{\text{Axial speed of tool}}$

$$T_m = \frac{125}{175}$$

$$T_m = 0.715\text{ min}$$

Q.25 Ans:[1.66]

Given: Cutting speed $v_c = 2$ m/s, depth of cut $t_o = 0.5$ mm, chip thickness $t_c = 0.6$ mm.

Chip thickness ratio, $r = \dfrac{t_o}{t_c} = \dfrac{0.5}{0.6} = 0.833$

Chip velocity, $v_f = r\,v_c$

$$v_f = 0.833 \times 2$$

$$v_f = 1.66\text{ m/s}$$

Q.26 Ans:[1.5]

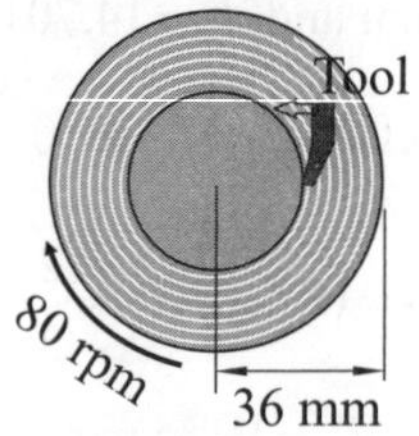

Machining time, $T_m = \dfrac{L}{fN}$

$$T_m = \frac{72/2}{0.3 \times 80}$$

$$T_m = 1.5\ \text{min}$$

Q.27 Ans:[0.03]

Tolerance of shaft

= Maximum size of shaft – Minimum size of shaft

Tolerance of shaft = (20 – 0.02) – (20 – 0.05)

Tolerance of shaft = 0.03 mm

Q.28 Ans:[23.7]

Surface roughness *Ra*

$$= \frac{\sum h}{N} = \frac{30+24+29+21+18+24+22+23+26}{10}$$

$$Ra = 23.7\ \text{microns}$$

Q.29 Ans:[60000]

Given: Cutting speed $v_c = 50$ m/min, feed $f = 0.8$ mm/rev, depth of cut $d = 1.5$ mm.

Metal removal rate, $MRR = vfd = 50 \times 10^3 \times 0.8 \times 1.5$

$$MRR = 60{,}000\ \text{mm}^3/\text{min}$$

Q.30 Ans:[497.42]

Given: Cutting force = 900 N, thrust force = 600 N and shear angle = 30°

Shear force, $F_s = F_c \cos\phi - F_t \sin\phi$

$$F_s = 900\cos 30 - 600\sin 30$$

$$F_s = 479.42\ \text{N}$$

Q.31 Ans:(D)

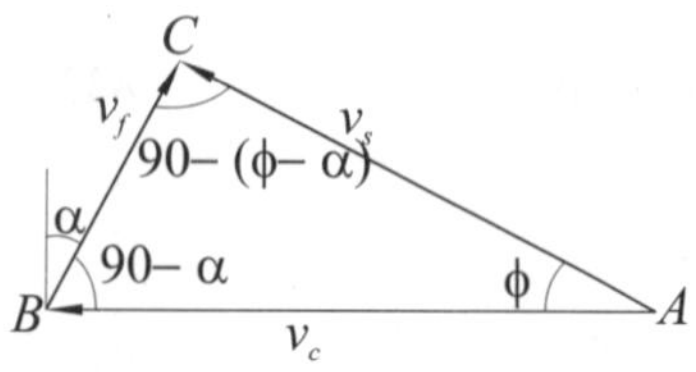

Cutting velocity and chip velocity are shown in figure.

Chip thickness ratio, $r = \dfrac{t_o}{t_c} = \dfrac{\sin\phi}{\sin(\phi - \alpha)} = \dfrac{v_f}{v_c}$

$$v_f = v_c \frac{\sin\phi}{\sin(\phi - \alpha)}$$

Q.32 Ans:(C)

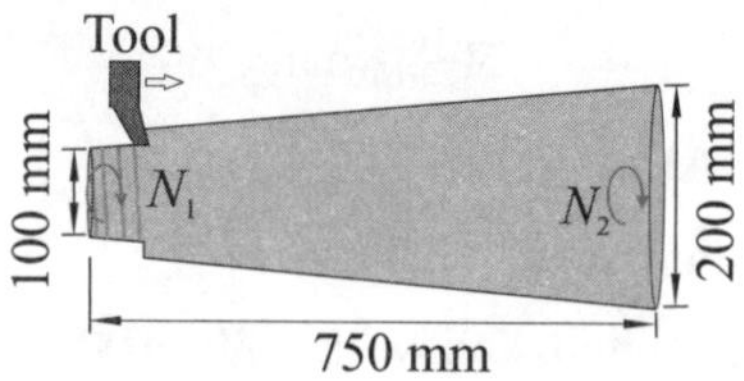

Rotational speed, $N = \dfrac{V}{\pi D} = \dfrac{200 \times 1000}{\pi D}$

At beginning of cut (D_1 = 100 mm);

$$N_1 = \frac{V}{\pi D_1} = \frac{200 \times 1000}{\pi \times 100}$$

$$N_1 = 636.6\ \text{rpm}$$

At beginning of cut (D_1 = 200 mm);

$$N_2 = \frac{V}{\pi D_2} = \frac{200 \times 1000}{\pi \times 200}$$

$$N_2 = 318.3\ \text{rpm}$$

$$N_1 = 636.6\ \text{rpm},\ N_2 = 318.3\ \text{rpm}$$

Q.33 Ans:(A)

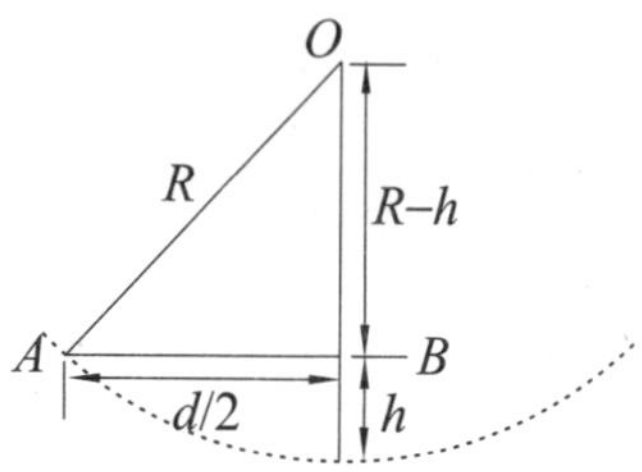

Let *R* be the radius of curvature.

In Δ *OAB*,

$$R^2 = \left(\frac{d}{2}\right)^2 + (R-h)^2$$

or $$R^2 = \frac{d^2}{4} + R^2 + h^2 - 2Rh$$

$$R = \frac{d^2}{8h} + \frac{h}{2}$$

Q.34 Ans:(C)

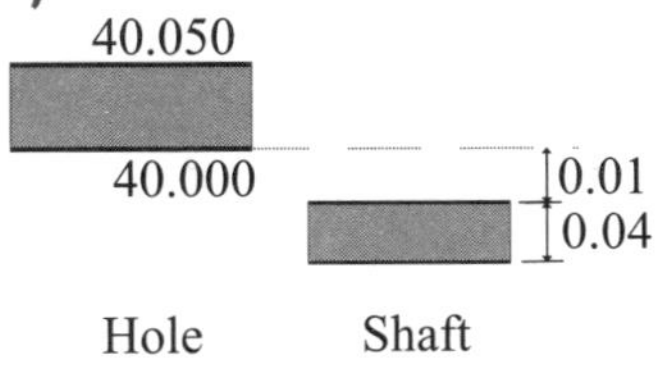

Maximum clearance = (40.05 – 40.00) + 0.01 + 0.04

Maximum clearance = 0.10 mm

Q.35 Ans:(D)

Pitch of M20 × 2.5 screw is $p = 2.5$

Best size wire diameter, $d_w = \frac{p}{2}\sec\theta$

For metric thread $2\theta = 60°$; $d_w = \frac{2.5}{2}\sec 30$

$d_w = 1.443$ mm

Q.36 Ans:(D)

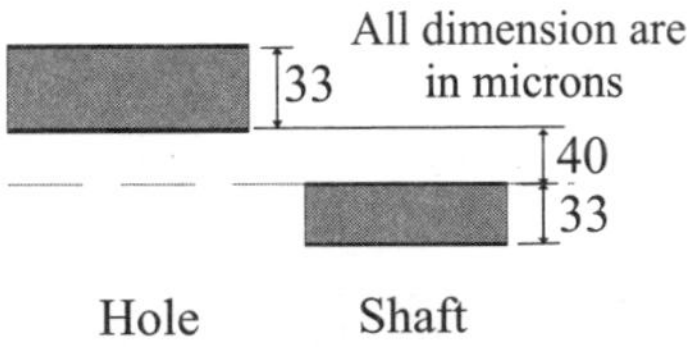

Maximum clearance = 33 + 40 + 33

Maximum clearance = 106 microns

Q.37 Ans:(C)

RMS value of surface roughness $= \sqrt{\frac{\sum h^2}{N}}$

$$= \sqrt{\frac{30^2 + 24^2 + 29^2 + 21^2 + 18^2 + 24^2 + 22^2 + 23^2 + 26^2}{10}}$$

RMS value of surface roughness = 23.9 microns

Q.38 Ans:(A)

Given: $d_o = t_o = 0.5$ mm, $v_c = 2$ m/s, $t_c = 0.75$ mm

Chip thickness ratio, $r = \frac{t_o}{t_c} = \frac{0.5}{0.75} = 0.666$

Chip velocity, $v_f = r\,v_c = 0.666 \times 2$

Chip velocity, $v_f = 1.33$ m/s

Q.39 Ans:(A)

Given: Cutting force, $F_c = 1000$ N, thrust force $F_t = 500$ N and rake angle $\alpha = 0$.

Friction force, $F = F_c \sin\alpha + F_t \cos\alpha$

$$F = 1000\sin 0 + 500\cos 0 = 500\text{ N}$$

Normal force, $N = F_c \cos\alpha - F_t \sin\alpha$

$$N = 1000\cos 0 - 500\sin 0 = 1000\text{ N}$$

Coefficient of friction, $\mu = \frac{F}{N} = \frac{500}{1000}$

$\mu = 0.5$

Q.40 Ans:(A)

Taylor's tool life equation, $VT^n = C$

(a) V = 100 m/min, T = 10 min;

$100 \times 10^n = C$ (i)

(ii) V = 75 m/min, T = 30 min;

$75 \times 30^n = C$ (ii)

Equations (i) and (ii) give

$$n = \frac{\ln\left(\frac{100}{75}\right)}{\ln\left(\frac{30}{10}\right)}$$

$n = 0.2617$

Q.41 Ans:(A)

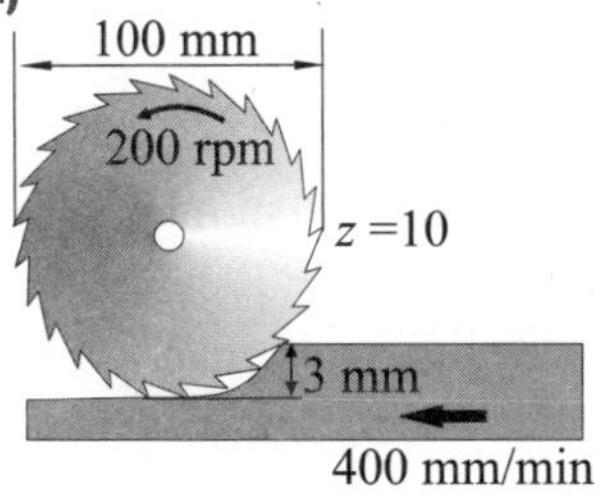

Given: $D = 100$ mm, $z = 10$ teeth and $N = 200$ rpm.

Feed per tooth $= \frac{f}{NZ}$

Feed per tooth $= \frac{400}{200 \times 10}$

Feed per tooth = 0.2 mm

Q.42 Ans:(D)

Given: $D = 500$ mm, $L = 1000$ mm, $f = 0.4$ mm/rev, $d = 3.0$ mm, $n = 0.23$ and $C = 400$

Cutting time, $T_m = \frac{L}{fN} = \frac{L}{f\frac{V}{\pi D}} = \frac{\pi DL}{fV}$ (i)

Taylor's tool life equation, $VT^{0.23} = 400$

Tool life, $T = \left(\frac{400}{V}\right)^{\frac{1}{0.23}}$ (ii)

Cutting time T_m = Tool life T

or $$\frac{\pi DL}{fV} = \left(\frac{400}{V}\right)^{\frac{1}{0.23}}$$

or $$\frac{\pi\times\frac{500}{1000}\times\frac{1000}{1000}}{\frac{0.4}{1000}V} = \left(\frac{400}{V}\right)^{\frac{1}{0.23}}$$

From which

$$V = 202.18 \text{ m/min}$$

Q.43 Ans:(B)

Taylor's tool life equation, $VT^n = C$

(i) $V = 100$ m/min, $T = 10$ min;

$$100\times 10^n = C \qquad \text{(i)}$$

(ii) $V = 75$ m/min, $T = 30$ min;

$$75\times 30^n = C \qquad \text{(ii)}$$

Equations (i) and (ii) give

$$n = \frac{\ln\left(\frac{100}{75}\right)}{\ln\left(\frac{30}{10}\right)} = 0.2617$$

$$C = 100\times 10^{0.2617} = 182.68$$

The tool life for a speed of 90 m/min is

$$T = \left(\frac{182.68}{90}\right)^{\frac{1}{0.2617}}$$

$$T = 14.9 \text{ min}$$

Q.44 Ans:(A)

Given: $\alpha = 15°$, $\phi = 45°$ and cutting velocity $V_c = 35$ m/min.

Velocity of chip along the tool face, $V_f = V_c\dfrac{\sin\phi}{\cos(\phi-\alpha)}$

$$V_f = 35\frac{\sin 45}{\cos(45-15)}$$

$$V_f = 28.57 \text{ m/min}$$

Q.45 Ans:(C)

Shear angle, $\phi = \tan^{-1}\left(\dfrac{r\cos\alpha}{1-r\sin\alpha}\right)$

$$\phi = \tan^{-1}\left(\frac{0.38\cos 5}{1-0.38\sin 5}\right) = 21.38°$$

Using Merchant equation,

$$2\phi = \frac{\pi}{2}+\alpha-\beta \quad \text{or} \quad \beta = \frac{\pi}{2}+\alpha-2\phi$$

$$\beta = 90+5-2\times 21.38 = 52.24°$$

$$\mu = \tan 52.24$$

$$\mu = 1.291$$

Q.46 Ans:(B)

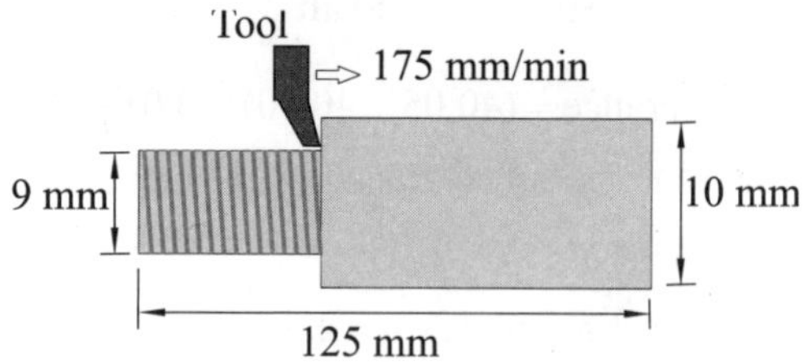

Given: $l = 125$ mm, $D_1 = 10$ mm, $D_2 = 9$ mm, $N = 360$ rpm and feed $f = 175$ mm/min.

Depth of cut, $d = \dfrac{10-9}{2} = 0.5$ mm

Feed, $f = 175 \text{ mm/min} = \dfrac{175}{360}$ mm/rev

Metal removal rate, $MRR = \pi D_{avg} d f N$

$$MRR = \pi\left(\frac{10+9}{2}\right)\times 0.5\times\frac{175}{360}\times 360$$

$$MRR = 2610.08 \text{ mm}^3\text{/min}$$

Q.47 Ans:(C)

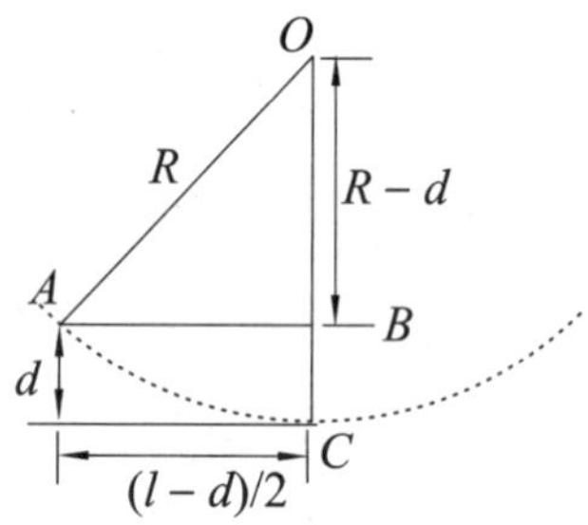

Let R be the radius of curvature of pulley block.

In ΔOAB, $$R^2 = \left(\frac{l-d}{2}\right)^2 + (R-d)^2$$

or $$R^2 = \left(\frac{l-d}{2}\right)^2 + R^2 + d^2 - 2Rd$$

or $$\left(\frac{l-d}{2}\right)^2 + d^2 - 2Rd = 0$$

Since $R >> d$, term d^2 can be neglected.

$$2Rd = \left(\frac{l-d}{2}\right)^2$$

$$R = \frac{(l-d)^2}{8d}$$

Q.48 Ans:(C)

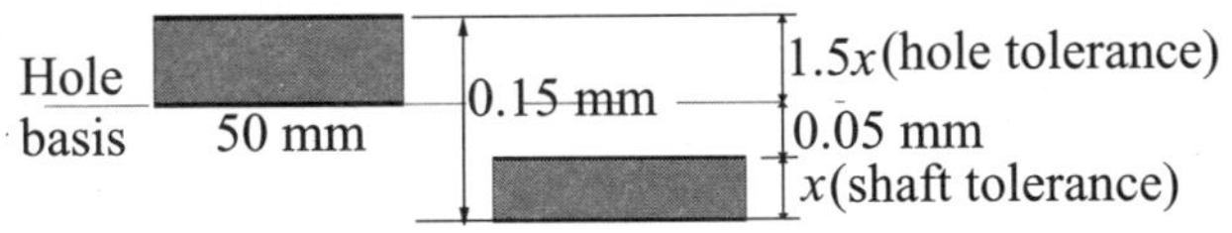

Let x be the shaft tolerance.

$$x + 0.05 + 1.5x = 0.15$$

$$x = 0.04 \text{ mm}$$

Size of hole

Minimum size = 50 (hole basis system)

Maximum size $= 50 + 1.5 \times x = 50 + 0.06$

$$50^{+0.06}_{+0.00} \text{ mm}$$

Q.49 Ans:(B)

Shear angle, $\phi = \tan^{-1}\left(\dfrac{r\cos\alpha}{1 - r\sin\alpha}\right)$

$$\phi = \tan^{-1}\left(\frac{0.38\cos 5}{1 - 0.38\sin 5}\right) = 21.38^\circ$$

Shear force, $F_s = F_c \cos\phi - F_t \sin\phi$

$$F_s = 1470 \cos 21.38 - 1589 \sin 21.38$$

$$F_s = 789.3 \text{ N}$$

Shear area, $A_s = \dfrac{w\,t_o}{\sin\phi} = \dfrac{5 \times 0.6}{\sin 21.38} = 8.23 \text{ mm}^2$

Shear strength, $\tau = \dfrac{F_s}{A_s} = \dfrac{789.3}{8.23} = 95.9 \text{ N/mm}^2$

$$\tau = 95.9 \text{ MPa}$$

Q.50 Ans:(A)

Given: $D = 500$ mm, $L = 1000$ mm, $f = 0.4$ mm/rev, $d = 3.0$ mm, $n = 0.23$ and $C = 400$.

Cutting time, $T_m = \dfrac{L}{fN} = \dfrac{L}{f\dfrac{V}{\pi D}} = \dfrac{\pi DL}{fV}$ (i)

Taylor's tool life equation, $VT^{0.23} = 400$

Tool life, $T = \left(\dfrac{400}{V}\right)^{\frac{1}{0.23}}$ (ii)

Cutting time, T_m = Tool life, T

or $\dfrac{\pi DL}{fV} = \left(\dfrac{400}{V}\right)^{\frac{1}{0.23}}$

or $\dfrac{\pi \times \dfrac{500}{1000} \times \dfrac{1000}{1000}}{\dfrac{0.4}{1000}V} = \left(\dfrac{400}{V}\right)^{\frac{1}{0.23}}$

From which, $V = 202.8$ m/min

Taylor's tool life equation, $VT^{0.23} = 400$

Tool life for $V = 202.8$ m/min; $T = \left(\dfrac{400}{V}\right)^{\frac{1}{0.23}}$

$$T = 19.42 \text{ min}$$

Q.51 Ans:[25.4]

Given: $\alpha = 10^\circ$, $t_o = 0.5$ mm, $t_c = 1.125$ mm

Chip thickness ratio, $r = \dfrac{t_o}{t_c} = \dfrac{0.5}{1.125} = 0.444$

Shear angle, $\phi = \tan^{-1}\left(\dfrac{r\cos\alpha}{1 - r\sin\alpha}\right)$

$$\phi = \tan^{-1}\left(\frac{0.444\cos 10}{1 - 0.444\sin 10}\right)$$

$$\phi = 25.4^\circ$$

Q.52 Ans:[19.18]

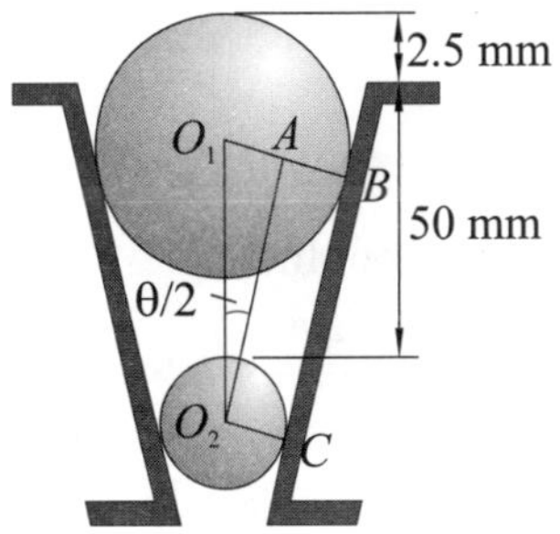

Let θ be the taper angle of ring gauge.

Given: $O_1B = \dfrac{30}{2} = 15$ mm, $O_2C = \dfrac{15}{2} = 7.5$ mm

From the geometry of figure,

$$O_1O_2 = 50 + 2.5 - 15 + 7.5 = 45 \text{ mm}$$

$$O_1A = 15 - 7.5 = 7.5 \text{ mm}$$

In ΔO_1O_2A,

$$\sin\frac{\theta}{2} = \frac{O_1A}{O_1O_2} = \frac{7.5}{45} = 0.166$$

$$\frac{\theta}{2} = 9.6^\circ$$

$$\theta = 19.18^\circ$$

Q.53 Ans:[7.08]

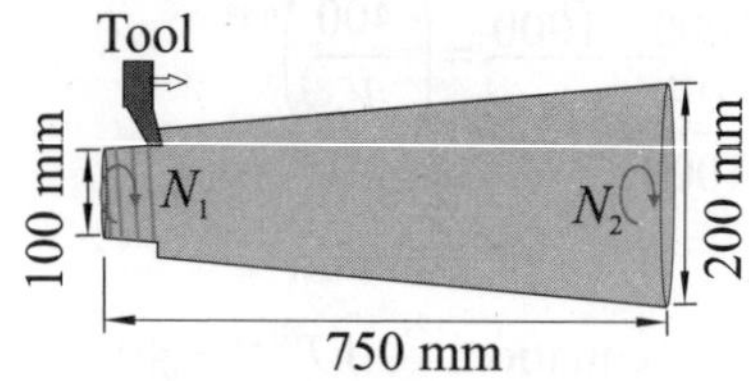

Given: $L = 750$ mm, $v_c = 200$ m/min, $f = 0.25$ mm/rev, $d = 3.0$ mm, $r_1 = 50$ mm, $r_2 = 100$ mm.

Metal removal rate, $MRR = vfd$

$$MRR = 200 \times 1000 \times 0.25 \times 3 = 15000 \text{ mm}^3/\text{min}$$

Frustum area of cone, $A = \pi(r_1 + r_2)\sqrt{L^2 + (r_2 - r_1)^2}$

$$A = \pi(50 + 100)\sqrt{750^2 + (100 - 50)^2}$$

$$A = 354214 \text{ mm}^2$$

Volume of cut, $V_{vol} = Ad = 354214 \times 3 = 1{,}062641 \text{ mm}^3$

Machining time, $T_m = \dfrac{V}{MRR} = \dfrac{1062641}{15000}$

$$T_m = 7.08 \text{ min}$$

Q.54 Ans:[300]

Taylor's tool life, $VT^{0.5} = 400$

$$V_1T_1^{0.5} = V_2T_2^{0.5}$$

$$V_1T_1^{0.5} = (0.5V_1)T_2^{0.5}$$

or $T_2 = 4T_1$

Percentage increase in tool life

$$= \frac{T_2 - T_1}{T_1} \times 100 = \frac{4T_1 - T_1}{T_1} \times 100$$

Percentage increase in tool life = 300%

Q.55 Ans:[5.8]

Given: Chip thickness ratio $r = 0.3$ and rack angle $\alpha = 10°$

Shear angle, $\phi = \tan^{-1}\left(\dfrac{r\cos\alpha}{1 - r\sin\alpha}\right)$

$$\phi = \tan^{-1}\left(\frac{0.3\cos 10}{1 - 0.3\sin 10}\right)$$

$$\phi = 17.31°$$

Shear strain, $\gamma = \tan(\phi - \alpha) + \cot\alpha$

$$\gamma = \tan(17.31 - 10) + \cot 10$$

$$\gamma = 5.8$$

Q.56 Ans:[181.1]

Tool life equation, $V = \dfrac{1540}{2.73 + T} + C$

Substituting $V = 80$ m/min, $T = 19.27$ min, we have

$$C = 80 - \frac{1540}{2.73 + 19.27} = 10$$

Therefore, $V = \dfrac{1540}{2.73 + T} + 10$

Cutting speed for tool life, $T = 6.27$ min;

$$V = \frac{1540}{2.73 + 6.27} + 10 = 181.1$$

$$V = 181.1 \text{ m/min}$$

Q.57 Ans:[1.308]

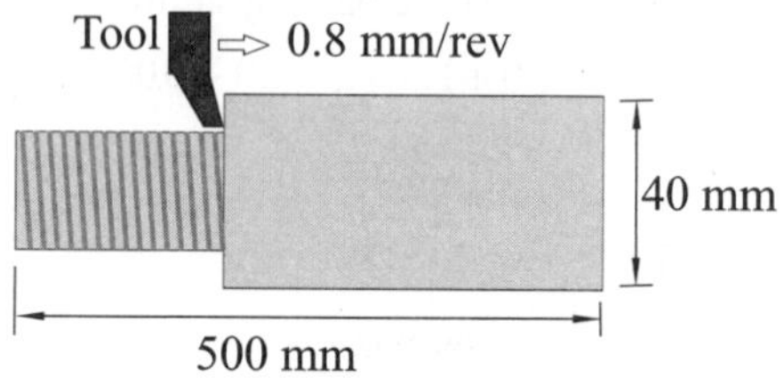

Machining time, $T_m = \dfrac{L}{fN}$

Cutting speed, $V = \pi DN \Rightarrow N = \dfrac{V}{\pi D}$

$$T_m = \frac{L}{fN} = \frac{L\pi D}{fV}$$

Substituting given values $V = 60$ m/min, $f = 0.8$ mm/rev, $D = 40$ mm and $L = 500$ mm

$$T_m = \frac{500 \times \pi \times 40}{0.8 \times 60 \times 1000} \text{ min}$$

$$T_m = 1.308 \text{ min}$$

Q.58 Ans:[1.18]

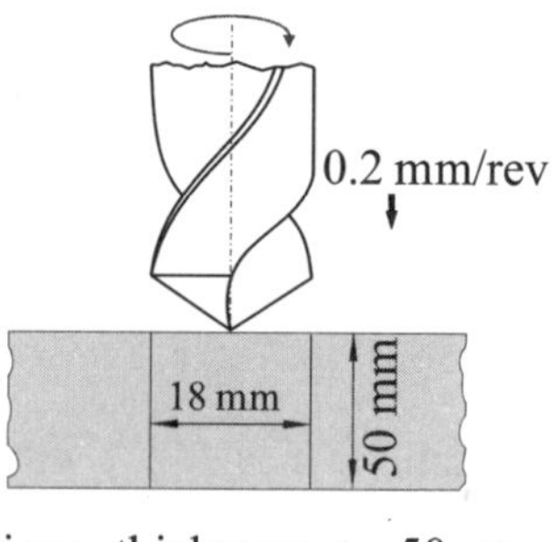

Given: Workpiece thickness $t = 50$ mm, cutting speed $V = 12$ m/min, feed $f = 0.2$ mm/rev and diameter of hole $D = 18$ mm.

Cutting speed, $V = \pi DN$ m/min

$$N = \frac{V}{\pi D} = \frac{12 \times 1000}{\pi \times 18} = 212.2 \text{ rpm}$$

Cutting time, $T_m = \dfrac{t}{fN}$

$$T_m = \frac{50}{0.2 \times 212.2}$$

$$T_m = 1.18 \text{ min}$$

Q.59 Ans:[16]

Let x be the break-even quantity.

Total cost;

$$= \text{Preparation cost} + \left(\frac{\text{Machine and operator cost} \times \text{Production time per part}}{60}\right)x$$

For conventional lathe;

$$\text{Total cost} = 30 + \left(\frac{75 \times 30}{60}\right)x \qquad \text{(i)}$$

For CNC lathe :

$$\text{Total cost} = 150 + \left(\frac{120 \times 15}{60}\right)x \qquad \text{(ii)}$$

At break-even point;

$$30 + \left(\frac{75 \times 30}{60}\right)x = 150 + \left(\frac{120 \times 15}{60}\right)x$$

From which, we get

Break-even quantity $x = 16$

Q.60 Ans:[0.892]

Tool life equation for tool A; $VT^{0.125} = 25$

Tool life equation for tool B; $VT^{0.250} = 7$

Let speed V^* be the cutting speed at which tool life same.

$$T = \left(\frac{25}{V^*}\right)^{\frac{1}{0.125}} = \left(\frac{7}{V^*}\right)^{\frac{1}{0.250}}$$

or $$\frac{1}{0.125}\ln\left(\frac{25}{V^*}\right) = \frac{1}{0.250}\ln\left(\frac{7}{V^*}\right)$$

or $$\ln\left(\frac{25}{V^*}\right)^2 = \ln\left(\frac{7}{V^*}\right)$$

or $$V^* = \frac{25^2}{7} = 0.892$$

$$V^* = 0.892$$

Q.61 Ans:[43.33]

From the geometry of figure,

$$x = \sqrt{d^2 - \left(h - \frac{d}{2} - \frac{d}{2}\right)^2}$$

or $$x = \sqrt{2hd - h^2}$$

and $$D = \frac{d}{2} + x + \frac{d}{2} = d + x$$

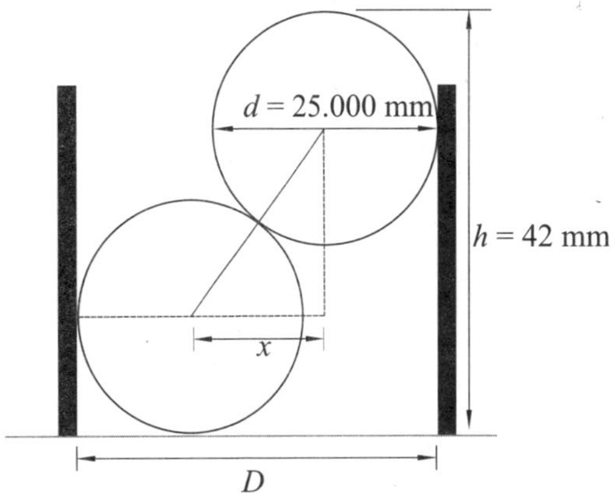

$$x = D - d = \sqrt{2hd - h^2}$$

$$D = d + \sqrt{2hd - h^2}$$

$$D = 25 + \sqrt{2 \times 42 \times 25 - 42^2}$$

$$D = 43.330 \text{ mm}$$

Q.62 Ans:[86.4]

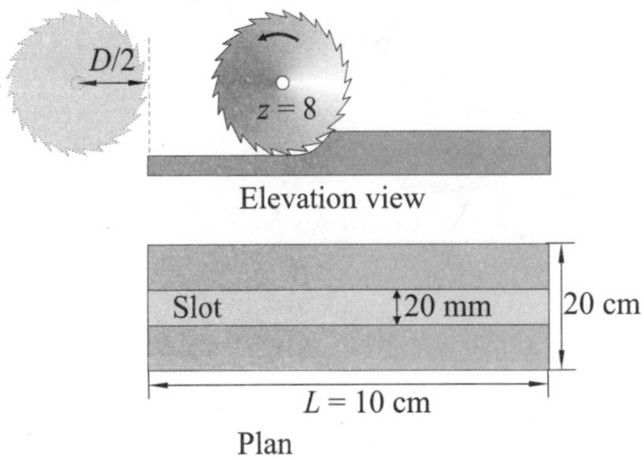

Distance travelled by cutter:

$$L = 100 + \frac{D}{2} = 100 + \frac{20}{2} = 110 \text{ mm}$$

Feed of cutter, $f_r = 0.01 \times 8 = 0.08$ mm/rev

$$f_r = 0.08 \text{ Nmm/s}$$

Cutting speed, $V = \pi DN$

or $$N = \frac{V}{\pi D} = \frac{60 \times 1000}{\pi \times 20} = 955 \text{ rpm}$$

$$f_r = 0.08 \times \frac{955}{60} = 1.273 \text{ mm/s}$$

Cutting time, $$T_m = \frac{L}{f_r} = \frac{110}{1.273}$$

$$T_m = 86.4 \text{ s}$$

Q.63 Ans:[22.07]

Taylor's tool life equation, $VT^n = C$

$$\pi DNT^n = C$$

$$NT^n = C_1$$

For $N_1 = 500$ rpm, $T_1 = 10$ min;

$$500 \times 10^n = C_1 \quad \text{(i)}$$

For $N_1 = 250$ rpm, $T_1 = 52.5$ min

$$250 \times 52.5^n = C_1 \quad \text{(ii)}$$

Equations (i) and (ii) give

$$n = 0.1099 \text{ and } C_1 = 386.38$$

$$NT^{0.1099} = 38638$$

Tool life for, $N = 275$ rpm,

$$T = \left(\frac{386.38}{275}\right)^{\frac{1}{0.1099}} = 22.07$$

$$T = 22.07 \text{ min}$$

Q.64 Ans:[16.434]

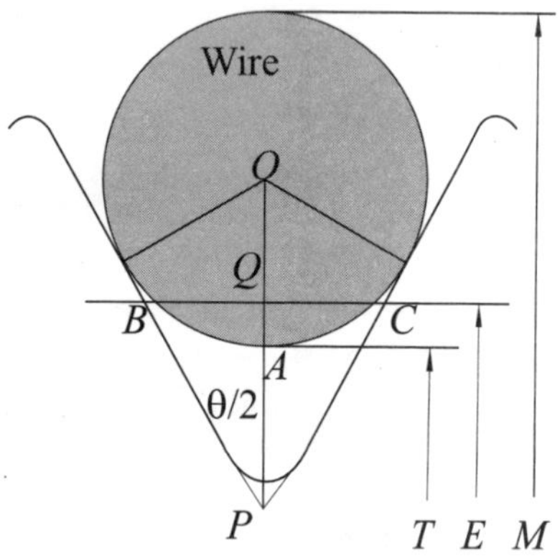

Given: Pitch $p = 2$ mm, effective diameter $E = 14.701$ mm, diameter of roller $d = 1.155$ mm.

Distance below wire, $T = M - 2d$

Effective diameter, $E = M - 2d + 2\,AQ$;

where d = diameter of wire.

$$AQ = PQ - PA = QC \cot\left(\frac{\theta}{2}\right) - \left(OP - \frac{d}{2}\right)$$

$$AQ = \frac{p}{4}\cot\left(\frac{\theta}{2}\right) - \left(\frac{d}{2}\operatorname{cosec}\frac{\theta}{2} - \frac{d}{2}\right)$$

Effective diameter, $E = M - d + \frac{p}{2}\cot\frac{\theta}{2} - d\operatorname{cosec}\frac{\theta}{2}$

Substituting $p = 2$ mm, $E = 14.701$ mm, $d = 1.155$ mm, we have

$$14.701 = M - 1.155 + \frac{2}{2} \times \cot\frac{60}{2} - 1.155 \times \operatorname{cosec}\frac{60}{2}$$

$$M = 16.434 \text{ mm}$$

Q.65 Ans:[263.9]

Chip thickness ratio, $r = \frac{t_o}{t_c} = \frac{0.6}{1.5} = 0.4$

Shear angle, $\phi = \tan^{-1}\left(\frac{r\cos\alpha}{1 - r\sin\alpha}\right)$

$$\phi = \tan^{-1}\left(\frac{0.4\cos 10}{1 - 0.4\sin 10}\right) = 22.94^\circ$$

Shear force, $F_s = F_c\cos\phi - F_t\sin\phi$

$$F_s = 980\cos 22.94 - 440\sin 22.94$$

$$F_s = 731 \text{ N}$$

Shear area, $A_s = \frac{wt_o}{\sin\phi} = \frac{1.8 \times 0.6}{\sin 22.94} = 2.77 \text{ mm}^2$

Shear strength, $\tau = \frac{F_s}{A_s} = \frac{731}{2.77} = 263.9$

$$\tau = 263.9 \text{ N/mm}^2$$

Industrial Engineering

GATE Syllabus

Production Planning and Control: Forecasting models; Aggregate production planning; Scheduling; Materials requirement planning; Inventory Control: Deterministic models; Safety stock inventory control systems.

Operations Research: Linear programming; Simplex and duplex method; Transportation; Assignment; Network flow models; Simple queuing models, PERT and CPM.

Chapter Outline

16.1 KEY CONCEPTS AND FORMULAS

Production Planning and Control

Production planning and control can be defined as the process of planning the production in advance, setting the exact route of each item, fixing the starting and finishing dates for each item, to give production orders to shops and to follow up the progress of products according to orders. The principle of production planning and control lies in the statement 'First Plan Your Work and then Work on Your Plan'.

Forecasting Methods

Qualitative Methods (or Opinion and Judgmental Methods)

(i) Forecasts by individual sales people, (ii) Forecasts by division or product-line managers, and (iii) Combined estimates of the two.

Quantitative Forecasting Methods (or Time Series)

(i) **Moving average (MA)**: A moving average is obtained by summing and averaging the values from a given number of periods repetitively, each time deleting the oldest value and adding a new value.

$$\text{MA} = \frac{\sum x}{\text{Number of periods}}$$

(ii) **Freehand curve**: A freehand curve (or hand fit) is simply a plot of a representative line that (subjectively) seems to best fit the data points.

(iii) **Least squares**: Least squares are a mathematical technique of fitting a trend to data points. The resulting line of best fit has the following properties: (a) the summation of all vertical deviations about it is zero, (b) the summation of all vertical deviations squared is a minimum, and (c) the line goes through the means x and y.

Best fit line $y = a + bx$

Where a and b are determined from solving equations $\sum y = na + b\sum x$ and $\sum xy = a\sum x + b\sum x^2$.

(iv) **Exponential smoothing**: It is a moving average forecasting technique that weights past data in an exponential manner so that the most recent data carry more weight in the moving averge.

Current period forecast, $F_t = F_{t-1} + \alpha(D_{t-1} - F_{t-1})$

where F_{t-1}= last period forecast, D_{t-1}= last periods actual demand and α = smoothing constant.

(v) **Regression and correlation methods**: Regression and correlation techniques quantify the statistical association between two or more variables: (a) Simple regression expresses the relationship between a dependent variable y and a independent variable x, and (b) Simple correlation expresses the degree or closeness of the relationship between two variables in terms of a correlation coefficient.

Aggregate Production Planning

Aggregate production planning is concerned with the determination of production, inventory, and work force levels to meet fluctuating demand requirements over a planning horizon that ranges from six months to one year.

Break-Even Analysis

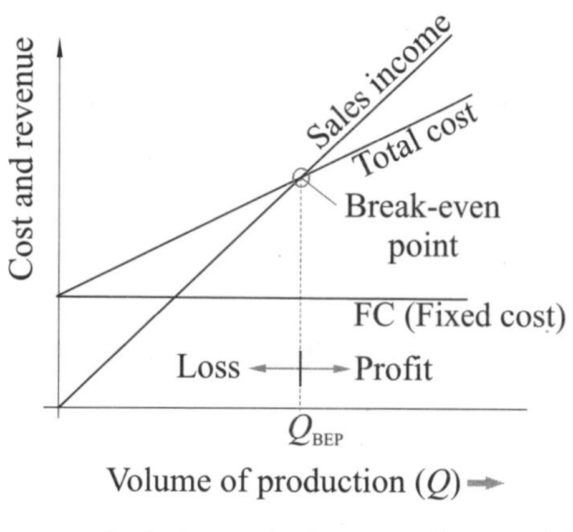

Break-even analysis is an algebraic and/or graphic model for describing the relationship between costs and revenues for different volume of production.

Total cost, $TC = FC + V \times Q$

Total revenues, $TR = S \times Q$

Profit $= TR - TC$

$= S \times Q - (FC + V \times Q)$

The quantity at break-even point (profit = 0) is then

$$Q_{BEP} = \left(\frac{FC}{S - V}\right)$$

Scheduling

Scheduling is the process of arranging, controlling and optimizing work and workloads in a production process or manufacturing process. Scheduling is used to allocate plant and machinery resources, plan human resources, plan production processes and purchase materials.

Shortest Processing Time (SPT) Rule

In single machine scheduling problem, sequencing the jobs in increasing order of processing time is known as the *shortest processing time (SPT) sequencing*. Shortest processing time rule minimises the mean flow time.

Weighted Shortest Processing Time (WSPT) Rule

In single machine scheduling problem, sequencing the jobs in increasing order of weighted processing time is known as *weighted shortest processing time (WSPT) sequencing*. The weighted processing time of a job is obtained by dividing its processing time by its weight.

Earliest Due Date (EDD) Rule

The lateness of a job is defined as the difference between the completion time and the due date of that job. The maximum job lateness and the maximum job tardiness are minimized by earliest due date sequencing. In a single machining scheduling problem, sequencing of jobs in increasing order of due date is known as *earliest due date Rule*.

Sequencing

Johnson's algorithm for 2 machines and *n* jobs:

Johnson's algorithm is used for sequencing of n jobs through two machines (or work centres). The purpose is to minimise idle time on machines and reduce the total time taken for completing all the jobs. The algorithm can be fulfilled in the following steps.

Jobs	Machine *A*	Machine *B*
1	t_{1A}	t_{1B}
2	t_{2A}	t_{2B}
3	t_{3A}	t_{3B}
n	t_{nA}	t_{nB}

Step 1: Find the minimum among the time taken by machine A and B for all the jobs.

Step 2a: If the minimum processing time is required by machine A to complete the job, place the associated job in the first available position in the final sequence. Then go to Step 3. (If it is a tie you may choose either of them, for applying the above rule.)

Step 2b: If the minimum processing time is required by machine B to complete the job, place the associated job in the last available position in final sequence. Then go to Step 3. (If it is a tie you may choose either of them, for applying the above rule.)

Step 3: Remove the assigned job from consideration and return to step 1 until all the positions in the sequence are filled.

Inventory Control

Inventory control is a planned approach of determining what to order, when and how much to order so that costs associated with buying and storing are optimal without interrupting production and sales.

Techniques of inventory control: (i) ABC analysis, (ii) HML analysis, (iii) VED analysis, (iv) FSN analysis, (v) SDE analysis, (vi) GOLF analysis, and (vii) SOS analysis.

Economic Order Quantity (EOQ)

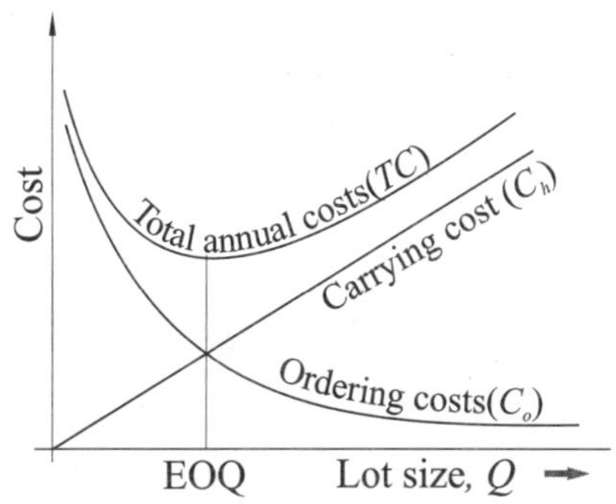

Economic order quantity (EOQ) is the order quantity of inventory that minimises the total cost of inventory management.

Inventory costs are ordering costs and carrying costs.

Ordering and setup costs for placing orders, expediting, inspection, and changing or setting up facilities to produce in-house.

Carrying costs on invested capital, handling, storage, security, insurance, taxes, spoilage and data processing costs.

Let A = Anual demand, Q = Order quantiy,

C_o = Ordering cost, C_h = Holding (carrying) cost,

C = Purchase cost

Total cost = Ordering cost + Carrying cost + Purchase cost

Where, Ordering cost = $\frac{A}{Q}C_o$, Carrying cost = $\frac{Q}{2}C_h$ and

Purchase cost = AC

Total cost, $TC = \frac{A}{Q}C_o + \frac{Q}{2}C_h + AC$

Total cost is minimum $\frac{d}{dQ}TC = 0$; $-\frac{A}{Q^2}C_o + \frac{1}{2}C_h = 0$

Optimal quantity (EOQ), $Q^* = \sqrt{\frac{2AC_o}{C_h}}$

Optimum number of order, $N^* = \frac{A}{Q^*}$,

Optimum order interval, $t = \frac{365}{N^*}$ in days

Average yearly cost, $TC = \sqrt{2C_oC_hA}$

Safety Stock

Safety stock is the stock held by a company in excess of its requirement for the lead time. Companies hold safety stock to guard against stock-out.

Safety stock = (Maximum daily usage – Average daily usage) × tead time

Lead time is the time which supplier takes in ordering the items.

Operations Research

Operations research (OR) is an analytical method of problem-solving and decision-making that is useful in the management of organisations.

Application Area of OR

(i) Marketing and sales, (ii) Production management, (iii) Inventory control, (iv) Finance, investments and budgeting, (v) Defence, (vi) Personnel management, (vii) Research and development.

Methodology of OR

(i) Formulation the problem, (ii) Constructing a model to represent the system under study, (iii) Deriving a solution from the model, (iv) Deriving a solution from the model, (v) Testing the model and the solution derived from it, (vi) Establishing controls over the solution, (vii) Putting the solution to work, i.e., implementation.

OR Model

Mathematical techniques, Statistical techniques, Inventory models, Allocation models, Sequencing models, Routing models, Competitive models, Queuing models, Dynamic programming models, Simulation techniques, Decision theory, Replacement models, Heuristic models, Goal Programming, Reliability theory, Markov analysis, and Combined methods.

Linear Programming

Linear programming is a mathematical technique for minimising or maximising an objective function subject to bounds, linear equality, and inequality constraints.

Structure of linear programming model: (i) The activities (variables) and their relationships, (ii) The objective function and (iii) The constraints.

General Mathematical Model of an LPP

Optimise (Maximise or Minimise)

$$Z = c_1x_1 + c_2x_2 + c_3x_3 + c_4x_4 + - - - - + c_nx_n$$

Subject to constraints,

$$a_{11}x_1 + a_{12}x_2 + a_{13}x_3 + - - - - + a_{1n}x_n (\le = \ge) b_1$$
$$a_{21}x_1 + a_{22}x_2 + a_{23}x_3 + - - - - + a_{2n}x_n (\le = \ge) b_2$$
$$a_{31}x_1 + a_{32}x_2 + a_{33}x_3 + - - - - + a_{3n}x_n (\le = \ge) b_3$$
$$- -$$
$$a_{m1}x_1 + a_{m2}x_2 + a_{m3}x_3 + - - - - + a_{mn}x_n (\le = \ge) b_m$$

and $x_1, x_2, x_3 - - x_n \ge 0$

Graphical Solution of Two Variable LP Problems

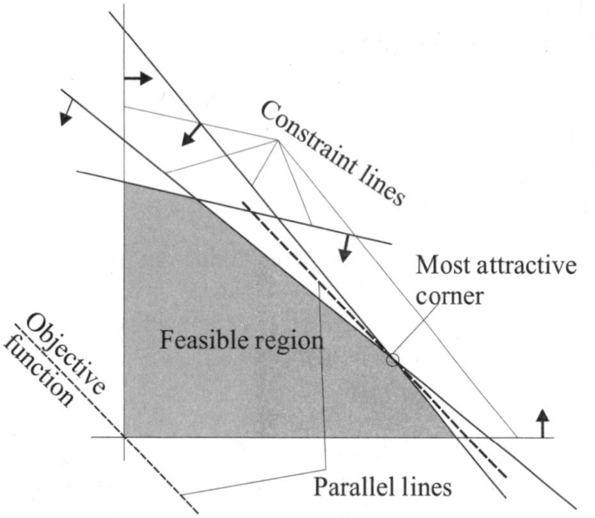

Step 1: Formulate the LP problem.

Step 2: Construct a graph and plot the constraint lines.

Step 3: Determine the valid side of each constraint line.

Step 4: Identify the feasible solution region.

Step 5: Plot objective function line to determine the direction of improvement.

Step 6: Find the most attractive corner.

Step 7: Determine the optimal solution by algebraically calculating coordinates of the most attractive corner.

Step 8: Determine the value of the objective function for the optimal solution.

Basic Steps of the Simplex Algorithm

Step 1: Convert the LP problem to a system of linear equations.

Step 2: Set up the initial tableau.

Step 3: Select the pivot column.

Step 4: Select the pivot in the pivot column.

Step 5: Use the pivot to clear the pivot column in the normal manner. This gives the next tableau.

Step 6: Repeat Steps 3-5 until there are no more negative numbers in the bottom row (with the possible exception of the answer column).

Transportation

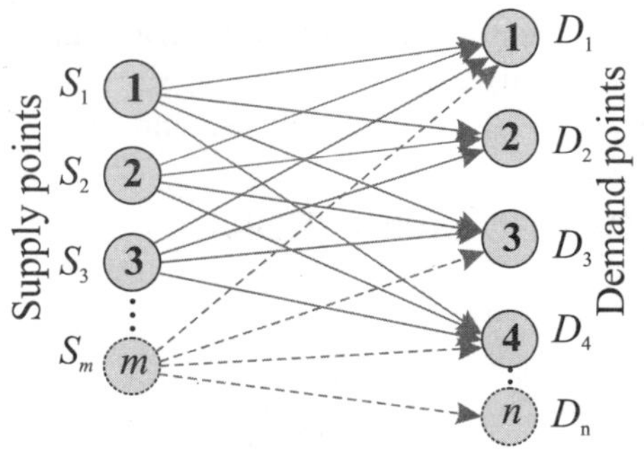

Destinations (Demand points) Availability

Supply (sources)	D1	D2	D3	D4	---	D_n	Availability
S1	c_{11}	c_{12}	c_{13}	c_{14}		c_{1n}	a_1
S2	c_{21}	c_{22}	c_{23}	c_{24}		c_{2n}	a_2
S3	c_{31}	c_{32}	c_{33}	c_{34}		c_{3n}	a_3
⋮							
S_m	c_{m1}	c_{m2}	c_{m3}	c_{m4}		c_{mn}	a_m
Requirement	b_1	b_2	b_3	b_4		b_n	

Transportation (distribution model) is special type of linear programming problem that involves transportation or physical distribution of goods and services from supply points (sources) to demand point (destinations). The objective is to determine how much should be shipped from each source to each destination so as to minimize the total transportation cost.

Let a_i = availability at the *i*th source, b_i = requirement at the *i*th demand point, c_{ij} = cost of transportation per unit from *i*th source to *j*th destination and x_{ij} = quantity of the commodity transported from *i*th source to *j*th destination.

The problem is to determine the values of x_{ij} such that cost of transportation is minimised.

We assume that the total quantity available is the same as the total requirement, $\sum a_i = \sum b_j$.

Include a dummy source or a dummy destination having a supply d or demand d to convert it to a balanced transportation problem.

Solution of transportation problems: The solution procedure is an iterative one that begins with an initial solution that is feasible, but not necessary optimal.

Initial Solutions	Optimal Solutions
(1) Minimum cost	(1) Stepping-stone
(2) Northwest corner	(2) Modified distribution (MODI)
(3) Vogel's approximation method (VAM)	

Assignment

Assignment problem is one of the special cases of transportation problems. The goal of the assignment problem is to minimise the cost or time of completing a number of jobs by a number of persons.

Solution of Assignment Model

Hungarian Assignment Method:

Step 1: Find the minimum cost each row of the $m \times m$ cost matrix.

Step 2: Construct a new matrix by subtracting from each cost the minimum cost in its row.

Step 3: For this new matrix, find the minimum cost in each column.

Step 4: Construct a new matrix (reduced cost matrix) by subtracting from each cost, the minimum cost in its column.

Step 5: Draw the minimum number of lines (horizontal and/or vertical) that are needed to cover all the zeros in the reduced cost matrix. If m lines are required, an optimal solution is available among the covered zeros in the matrix. If fewer than m lines are needed, proceed to next step.

Step 6: Find the smallest cost (c) in the reduced cost matrix that is uncovered by the lines drawn in Step 5.

Step 7: Subtract (c) from each uncovered element of the reduced cost matrix and add k to each element that is covered by two lines. Return to Step 5.

Simple Queuing Models

Queuing theory is a mathematical study of waiting lines. It is a tool to make business decisions about the resources provided for services. Queuing models suggests ways and means to improve the efficiency of the services. Its objective is to find out the optimum service rate and the number of servers so that the average cost of being in queuing system and the cost of service are minimised.

Assumptions: Independent arrivals, exponential distributions, customers do not leave or change queues, large queues do not discourage customers.

Mathematical notation: λ = Mean arrival rate, μ = Mean service rate per channel, n = Number of customer in the

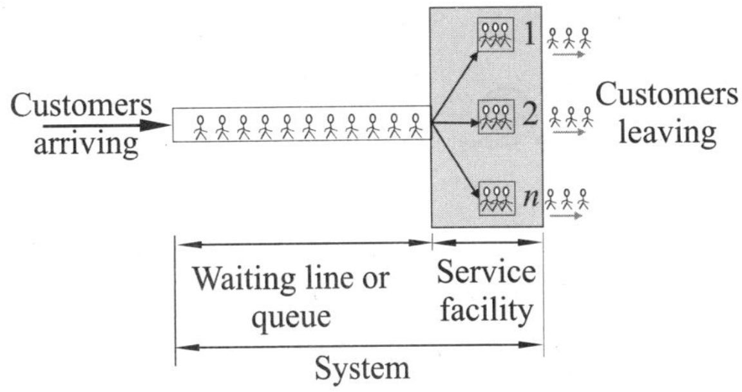

system (Waiting line + Service facility).

Queuing model: Single channel Poisson arrivals with exponential service infinite-population M/M/1.

Traffic intensity or utilisation factor, $\rho = \dfrac{\lambda}{\mu}$.

Expected number of customers in the system (waiting + being served), $L_s = \dfrac{\lambda}{\mu - \lambda}$

Expected number of customers in the queue,

$$L_q = \frac{\lambda}{\mu} \times \frac{\lambda}{\mu - \lambda}$$

Expected time a customer spends in the system,

$$W_s = \frac{1}{\mu - \lambda}$$

Expected waiting time a customer spends in queue,

$$W_q = \frac{\lambda}{\mu} \times \frac{1}{\mu - \lambda}$$

Average number of non-empty queue $= \dfrac{\mu}{\mu - \lambda}$

Probability of queue length being greater than or equal to n, the number of customers, $p(\geq n) = \left(\dfrac{\lambda}{\mu}\right)^n$.

PERT and CPM

PERT (programme evaluation review technique) and CPM (critical path method) are the two most popular network analysis technique used to assist managers in planning and controlling large scale projects.

Network

In a PERT network diagram each activity is represented by an arrow that is called a *branch* or an *arc*. The beginning and end of each activity is indicated by a circle that is called a *node*. The term event is also used in connection with the nodes. An event represents the completion of the activities that lead into a node.

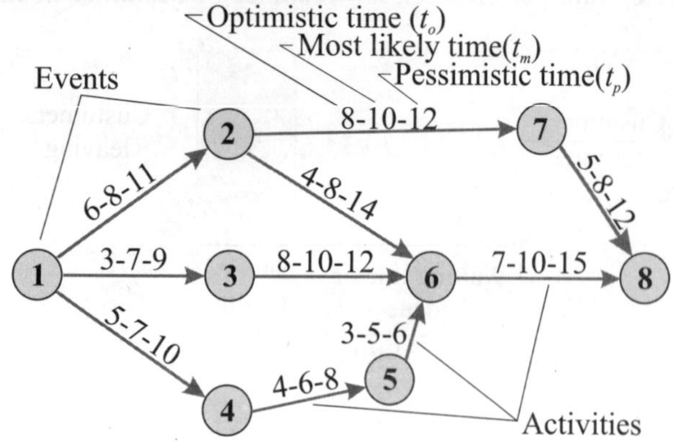

Network

Network analysis: (i) Network analysis is a techniques which can be used for the planning, management and control of projects, (ii) Network is a graphical representation of all the activities and events arranged in a logical and sequential order, (iii) Network analysis plays an important role in project management, (iv) A project is a combination of interrelated activities all of which must be executed in a certain order for its completion.

Main objectives are: (i) Complete the project within stipulated period, (ii) Optimise resources utilisation, (iii) Better coordination in interdependent activities.

Expected Activity Time

(i) Optimistic time (t_o): Everything has to go perfectly to achieve this time.

(ii) Most probable (likely) time (t_m): The time required under normal circumstances.

(iii) Pessimistic time (t_p): The maximum time.

Expected activity time, $t_e = \dfrac{t_o + 4t_m + t_p}{6}$

Standard Deviation of an Activity Time

The standard deviation of an activity time is estimated by assuming that there are six standard deviations between the optimistic and pessimistic times.

Estimate of the standard deviation of activity time,

$$\sigma = \left(\frac{t_p - t_o}{6}\right)$$

Variance of the activity times, $\sigma^2 = \left(\dfrac{t_p - t_o}{6}\right)^2$

Probability of Completing the Project on Time:

Standard normal variate, $z = \dfrac{t - t_e}{\sigma}$

From the table of normal distribution, we find the required probability.

Earliest finish time (EF) = Earliest start (ES) + Expected activity time.

Earliest start time rule: The ES time for an activity leaving a particular node is the largest of the EF times for all activities entering the node.

Latest start time (LS) = Latest finish time (LF) – Expected activity time

Latest finish time rule: The LF time for an activity entering a particular node is the smallest of the LS times for all activities leaving that node.

Slack: Slack is the amount of time an activity can be delayed without affecting the completion date for the overall project.

$$\text{Slack} = \text{LS} - \text{ES} = \text{LF} - \text{EF}$$

The critical path activities are those with zero slack.

Critical path: The (estimated) project duration equals the length of the longest path through the project network. This longest path is called the *critical path.*

16.2 SOLVED EXAMPLES

Previous Years GATE Questions

Example 16.1

Customers arrive at a ticket counter at a rate of 50 per hour and tickets are issued in the order of their arrival. The average time taken for issuing a ticket is 1 min. Assuming that customer arrivals form a Poisson process and service time are exponentially distributed, the average waiting time in queue in minute is

(A) 3 (B) 4 (C)5 (D) 6

GATE 2013

Solution

Given that:

Customer arrival rate, $\lambda = 50$ per hour

Ticket issuing rate, $\mu = 60$ per hour

Waiting time in queue is, $t_p = \dfrac{\lambda}{\lambda(\mu - \lambda)}$

$$t_p = \frac{50}{60(60-50)}\text{ h}$$

or $$t_p = \frac{50}{60 \times 10} \times 60 \text{ min}$$

$$t_p = 5 \text{ min}$$

Example 16.2

A linear programming problem is as follows:

Maximise $3x + 7y$

Subject to $3x + 7y \leq 10$

$4x + 6y \leq 8$

$x,\ y \geq 0$

It has

(A) An unbounded objective function

(B) Exactly one optimal solution

(C) Exactly two optimal solutions

(D) Infinitely many optimal solutions

GATE 2013

Solution

The feasible region for this problem is as shown in the graph.

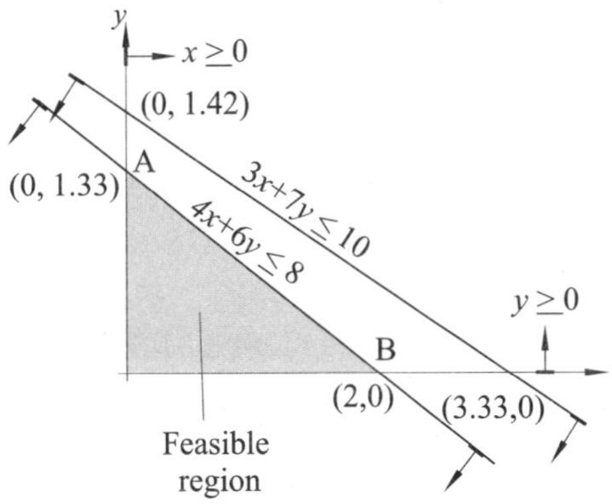

The feasible region has only two corners A and B.

The value of $3x + 7y$ at these points are:

$$z_A = 3 \times 0 + 7 \times 1.33$$

$$z_A = 9.31 \quad \Rightarrow \quad z_{\text{maximum}} = 9.31$$

$$z_B = 3 \times 2 + 7 \times 0$$

$$z_B = 6$$

z attains the maximum value at the point A.

Therefore,

Problem has exactly one optimal solution.

Example 16.3

Linked Answer Questions

For a particular project, eight activities are to be carried out. Their relationships with other activities and expected durations are mentioned in the table.

Activity	Predecessors	Durations (days)
a	-	3
b	a	4
c	a	5
d	a	4
e	b	2
f	d	9
g	c, e	6
h	f, g	2

Q(a) The critical path for the project is

(A) a - b - e - g - h (B) a - d - f - h

(C) a - c - g - h (D) a - b - c - f - h

Q(b) If the duration of activity f alone is changed from 9 to 10 days, then the

(A) Critical path remains the same and the total duration to complete project changes to 19 days.

(B) Critical path and the total duration to complete the project remain the same.

(C) Critical path changes but the total duration to complete the project remains the same.

(D) Critical path changes and the total duration to complete the project changes to 17 days.

GATE 2012

Solution

(a) First of all the network diagram is drawn for the given problem.

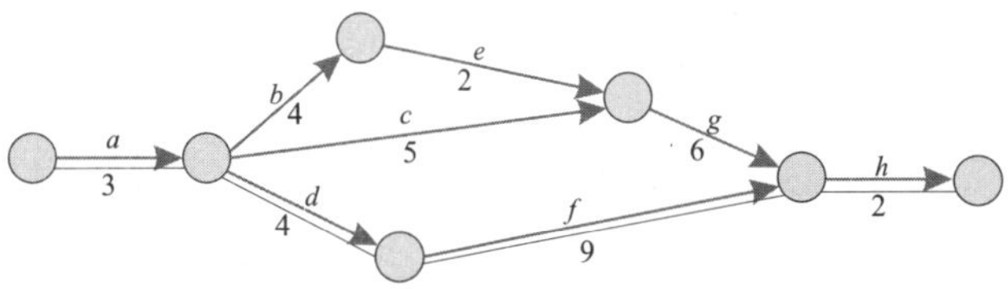

There can be three paths in the problem, namely,

Path-I: a - b - e - g - h time taken 17 days

Path-II: a - c - g - h time taken 16 days

Path-III: a - d - f - h time taken 18 days

Thus, critical path a - d - f - h is with maximum target time of 18 days.

Maximum target time, $T_e = 3 + 4 + 9 + 2 = 18$ days

(b) If the duration of activity f alone is changed from 9

days to 10 days, then critical path remains same a - d - f - h and

$$T_e = 3 + 4 + 10 + 2 = 19 \text{ days}$$

Example 16.4

Common Data Questions

One unit of product P_1 requires 3 kg of resource R_1 and 1 kg of resource R_2. One unit of product P_2 requires 2 kg of resource R_1 and 2 kg of resource R_2. The profits per unit by selling product P_1 and P_2 are Rs. 2000 and Rs. 3000 respectively. The manufacturer has 90 kg of resource R_1 and 100 kg of resource R_2.

Q(a) The manufacturer can make a maximum profit of Rs.

(A) 60000 (B) 150000 (C) 135000 (D) 200000

Q(b) The unit worth resource R_2, i.e., dual price of resource R_2 in rupees per kg is

(A) 0 (B) 1500 (C) 1350 (D) 2000

GATE 2011

Solution

(a) Let x and y be the number of product P_1 and P_2 respectively.

Maximise: $z = 2000x + 3000y$

Constrains:

$$3x + 2y \leq 90$$

$$x + 2y \leq 100$$

$$x,\ y \geq 0$$

Constrains are shown on graph

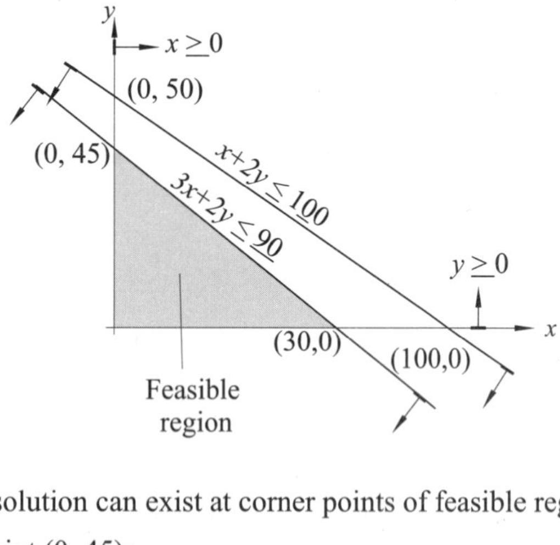

The solution can exist at corner points of feasible region.

At point (0, 45);

Profit, $z = 2000 \times 0 + 3000 \times 45$

$$z = 135000$$

At point (30,0);

Profit, $z = 2000 \times 30 + 3000 \times 0$

$$z = 60000$$

Therefore, maximum profit is Rs. 135000 at (0, 45)

(b) For maximum profit, the manufacturer has to produce $y = 45$ number of product P_2.

Given that 2 kg of resource R_2 is utilised for each product P_2.

Therefore, unit worth of resource R_2 is:

$$\text{Unit worth} = \frac{135000}{45 \times 2}$$

$$\text{Unit worth} = \text{Rs. } 1500/\text{kg}$$

Example 16.5

The demand and forecast for February are 12000 and 10275, respectively. Using single exponential smoothing method (smoothing coefficient $= 0.25$), forecast for the month of march is:

(A) 431 (B) 9587 (C) 10706 (D) 11000

GATE 2010

Solution

Forecast by exponential smoothing method is:

$$F_{\text{March}} = F_{\text{Feb}} + \alpha\,(D_{\text{Feb}} - F_{\text{Feb}})$$

Substituting $D_{\text{Feb}} = 12000$, $F_{\text{Feb}} = 10275$ and $\alpha = 0.25$, we have

$$F_{\text{March}} = 10275 + 0.25\,(12000 - 10275)$$

$$F_{\text{March}} = 10706$$

Example 16.6

Annual demand for window frames is 10000. Each frame costs Rs. 200 and ordering cost is Rs. 300 per order. Inventory holding cost is Rs. 40 per frame per year. The supplier is willing to offer 2% discount if the order quantity is 1000 or more, and 4% if order quantity is 2000 or more. If the total cost is to be minimized, the retailer should

(A) Order 200 frames every time

(B) Accept 2% discount

(C) Accept 4% discount

(D) Order economic order quantity

GATE 2010

Solution

Given that:

$$A = 10000$$

$$C_o = \text{Rs. } 300 \text{ per order}$$

$$C_h = \text{Rs.} 40 \text{ per frame per year}$$

Frame cost, $p = \text{Rs. } 200 \text{ per frame}$

Economic order quantity, $Q^* = \sqrt{\dfrac{2C_o A}{C_h}}$

$$Q^* = \sqrt{\frac{2\times 300\times 10000}{40}}$$

$$Q^* = 387.29$$

Then the total cost of purchase and inventory,

$$T(Q^*) = \frac{A}{Q^*}C_o + \frac{Q^*}{2}C_h + p\times A$$

$$T(Q^*) = \frac{10000}{387.29}\times 300 + \frac{387.29}{2}\times 40 + 200\times 10000$$

$$T(Q^*) = 2.015\times 10^6$$

For the first offer:

Frame cost, $p = \text{Rs. } 200\times 0.98$ per frame

Order quantity, $Q = 1000$

Total cost of purchase and inventory,

$$T(Q) = \frac{A}{Q}C_o + \frac{Q}{2}C_h + p\times A$$

$$T(Q) = \frac{10000}{1000}\times 300 + \frac{1000}{2}\times 40 + 200\times 0.98\times 1000$$

$$T(Q) = 1.983\times 10^6$$

For the second offer:

Frame cost, $p = \text{Rs.}200\times 0.96$ per frame

Order quantity, $Q = 2000$

Total cost of purchase and inventory,

$$T(Q) = \frac{A}{Q}C_o + \frac{Q}{2}C_h + p\times A$$

$$T(Q) = \frac{10000}{2000}\times 300 + \frac{2000}{2}\times 40 + 200\times 0.96\times 10000$$

$$T(Q) = 1.9615\times 10^6$$

From which

Last offer (4% discount and order quantity 2000) cost is minimum.

Example 16.7

The project activities, precedence relationships and durations are described in the table. The critical path of the project is

Activity	Precedence	Duration (in days)
P	–	3
Q	–	4
R	P	5
S	Q	5
T	R, S	7
U	R, S	5
V	T	2
W	U	10

(A) P-Q-T-V (B) Q-S-T-V

(C) P-R-U-W (D) Q-S-U-W

GATE 2010

Solution

First of all the network diagram is drawn for the given problem.

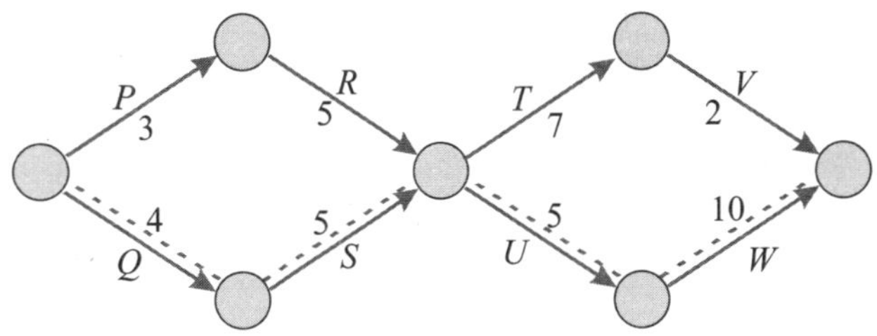

There can be four paths namely

Path-I: P-R-T-V, time taken 17 days

Path-II: P-R-U-W, time taken 23 days

Path-III: Q-S-T-V, time taken 18 days

Path-IV: Q-S-U-W, time taken 24 days

Thus, critical path (Q-S-U-W) is with maximum target time of $(4+5+5+10)$ 24 days.

Critical path of network is Q-S-U-W

Example 16.8

Common Data Questions

Four jobs are to be processed on a machine as per data listed in the table.

Job	Processing time (in days)	Due date
1	4	6
2	7	9
3	2	19
4	8	17

Q(a) If the earliest due date (EDD) rule is used to sequence the jobs, the number of jobs delayed is:

(A) 1 (B) 2 (C) 3 (D) 4

Q(b) Using the shortest processing time (SPT) rule, total tardiness is:

(A) 0 (B) 2 (C) 6 (D) 8

GATE 2010

Solution

(a) Job with the earliest due date will be first processes, therefore, following sequence occurs.

Job	Processing time (in days)	Flow time	Due date	Tardiness
1	4	4	6	–2
2	7	11	9	2 ← Delay
4	8	19	17	2 ← Delay
3	2	21	19	2 ← Delay

Therefore, total three jobs (2, 4, 3) will be delayed.

(b) Job with the earliest due date will be first processes, therefore, following sequence occurs.

Job	Processing time (in days)	Flow time	Due date	Tardiness
3	2	2	19	–17
1	4	6	6	0
2	7	13	9	4 ← Delay
4	8	21	17	4 ← Delay

Therefore, total tardiness $4+4=8$ days.

Example 16.9

A company uses 2555 units of an item annually. Delivery lead time is 8 days. The reorder point (in number of units) to achieve optimum inventory is

(A) 7 (B) 8 (C) 56 (D) 60

GATE 2009

Solution

Annual requirement $=2555$ items

or Per day requirement $=\dfrac{2555}{365}$ items

Therefore, 8 days quantity is

$$\text{Reorder level} = \frac{2555}{36} \times 5$$

Reorder level $=56$

Example 16.10

Consider the following linear programming problem (LPP).

Maximise: $z = 3x_1 + 2x_2$

Subject to: $x_1 \le 4$

$x_2 \le 6$

$3x_1 + 2x_2 \le 18$

$x_1 \ge 0, x_2 \ge 0$

(A) The LPP has a unique optimal solution

(B) The LPP is infeasible

(C) The LPP is unbounded

(D) The LPP has multiple optimal solution

GATE 2009

Solution

The feasible region is shown in the graph.

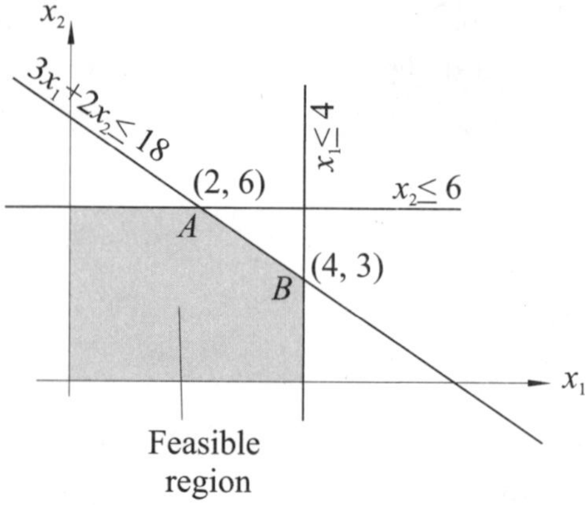

The feasible region has four corners. The value of z at these points are:

Value of z at A (2,6); $z = 3\times 2 + 2\times 6 = 18$

Value of z at B (4,3); $z = 3\times 4 + 2\times 3 = 18$

Therefore, LPP has multiple optimal solution.

Example 16.11

Six jobs arrived in a sequence as given in the table.

Jobs	Processing time (days)
I	4
II	9
III	5
IV	10
V	6
VI	8

Average flow time (in days) for the above jobs using the shortest processing time rule is

(A) 20.83 (B) 23.16 (C) 125.00 (D) 139.00

GATE 200

Solution

The shortest processing time rule is based on the principle that the shortest job is handled first and completed.

Jobs	Processing time (days)	Cumulative time (days)
I	4	4
III	5	9
V	6	15
VI	8	23
II	9	32
IV	10	42
		Sum **125**

The average flow time (AFT) is:

$$\text{AFT} = \frac{125}{\text{Number of jobs}} = \frac{125}{6}$$

$$\text{AFT} = 20.83$$

Example 16.12

Common Data Questions

Consider the following PERT network.

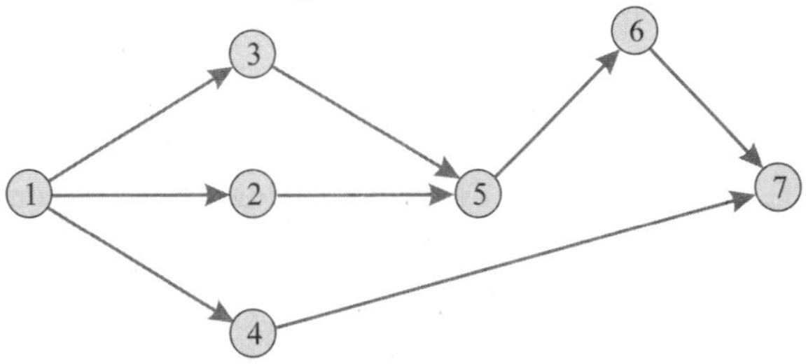

The optimistic time, most likely time and pessimistic time of all the activities are given in the table.

Activity	Optimistic time (days)	Most likely time (days)	Pessimistic time (days)
1–2	1	2	3
1–3	5	6	7
1–4	3	5	7
2–5	5	7	9
3–5	2	4	6
5–6	4	5	6
4–7	4	6	8
6–7	2	3	4

Q(a) The critical path duration of the network (in days) is

(A) 11 (B) 14 (C) 17 (D) 18

Q(b) The standard deviation of the critical path is:

(A) 0.33 (B) 0.55 (C) 0.77 (D) 0.88

GATE 2009

Solution

(a)

Activity	Optimistic time t_o (days)	Most likely time t_m (days)	Pessimistic time t_p (days)	Pessimistic time t_e (days)
1–2	1	2	3	2
1–3	5	6	7	6
1–4	3	5	7	5
2–5	5	7	9	7
3–5	2	4	6	4
5–6	4	5	6	5
4–7	4	6	8	6
6–7	2	3	4	3

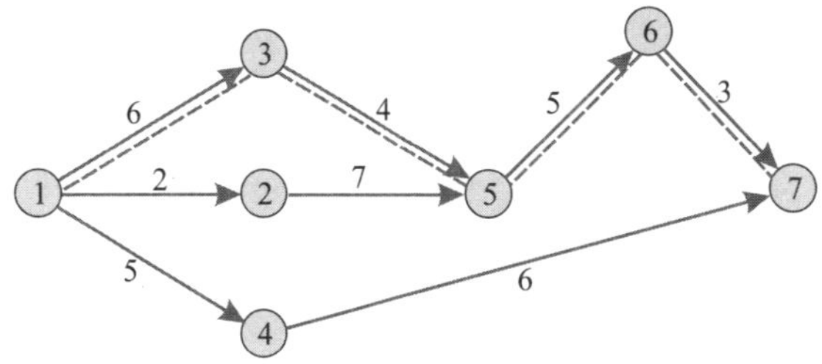

Longest duration path is 1–3–5–6–7

Critical path duration $= 6 + 4 + 5 + 3 = 18$ days

(b)

Activity	Optimistic time t_o (days)	Most likely time t_m (days)	Pessimistic time t_p (days)	$\left(\frac{t_p - t_o}{6}\right)^2$
1–3	5	6	7	$\left(\frac{1}{6}\right)^2$
3–5	2	4	6	$\left(\frac{2}{3}\right)^2$
5–6	4	5	6	$\left(\frac{1}{3}\right)^2$
6–7	2	3	4	$\left(\frac{1}{3}\right)^2$
				$\sum\left(\frac{t_p - t_o}{6}\right)^2 = \frac{7}{9}$

Standard deviation of critical path,

$$\sigma = \sqrt{\sum\left(\frac{t_p - t_o}{6}\right)^2} = \sqrt{\frac{7}{9}}$$

$$\sigma = 0.8819$$

Example 16.13

A set of 5 jobs is to be processed on a single machine. The processing time (in days) is given in the table. The holding cost for each job is rupees. K per day.

Job	Processing time
P	5
Q	2
R	3
S	2
T	1

A schedule that minimises the total inventory cost is:

(A) T- S- Q- R- P (B) P- R- S- Q- T

(C) T- R- S- Q- P (D) P- Q- R- S- T

GATE 2008

Solution

Job	Processing time
T	1
S	2
Q	2
R	3
P	5

Sequence of job is T- S- Q- R- P

Example 16.14

A manufacturing shop processes sheet metal jobs, wherein each job must pass through two machines (M_1 and M_2, in that order). The processing time (in hours) for these job is:

Machine	Jobs					
	P	Q	R	S	T	U
M_1	15	32	8	27	11	16
M_2	6	19	13	20	14	7

The optimal make-span (in hours) of the shop is:

(A) 120 (B) 115 (C) 109 (D) 79

GATE 2006

Solution

By examining the rows, we find the smallest value. It is job P and machine M_2. Thus, we schedule job P last as shown below:

Job						P

The reduce set of machine and jobs becomes

Machine	Job				
	Q	R	S	T	U
M_1	32	8	27	11	16
M_2	19	13	20	14	7

The small value is M_2 and job U. Thus, we schedule job U second last.

Job					U	P

The reduce set of machine and jobs becomes

Machine	Job			
	Q	R	S	T
M_1	32	8	27	11
M_2	19	13	20	14

Similarly, we obtained

Job	R	T	S	Q	U	P

The optimal make-span of the shop is found using the following table:

Job	Machine M_1		Machine M_2	
	Time in	Time out	Time in	Time out
R	0	8	8	21
T	8	19	21	33
S	19	46	46	66
Q	46	78	78	97
U	78	94	97	104
P	94	109	109	115

The optimal make-span (in hour) of the shop is 115 h.

Example 16.15

Consider the following data for an item.

Annual demand: 2500 units per year, ordering cost: Rs. 100 per order, inventory holding rate: 25% of unit price.

Order quantity (units)	Unit price (Rs.)
< 500	10
≥ 500	9

The optimum order quantity (in units) is:

(A) 447 (B) 471 (C) 500 (D) $\geq$ 600

GATE 2006

Solution

Given that:

$A = 2500$ units per year, $C_o = 100$ per order and $C_h = 25\%$ of unit price

Assuming EOQ (Q *) less than 500

$$C_h = 0.25 \times 10 = 2.5$$

$$Q^* = \sqrt{\frac{2C_o A}{C_h}} = \sqrt{\frac{2 \times 100 \times 2500}{2.5}}$$

$$Q^* = 447.21$$

Assuming EOQ (Q *) more 500

$$C_h = 0.25 \times 9 = 2.25$$

$$Q^* = \sqrt{\frac{2C_o A}{C_h}} = \sqrt{\frac{2 \times 100 \times 2500}{2.25}}$$

$$Q^* = 471.4 \quad \text{which is not true}$$

Thus,

$$Q^* = 447.21$$

Example 16.16

A firm is required to procure three items (P, Q, and R). The prices quoted for these items (in rupees) by suppliers $S1$, $S2$ and $S3$ are given in table. The management policy requires that each item has to be supplied by only one supplier and one supplier supply only one item. The minimum total cost (in rupees.) of procurement to the firm is

Item	Supplies		
	$S1$	$S2$	$S3$
P	110	120	130
Q	115	140	140
R	125	145	165

(A) 350 (B) 360 (C) 385 (D) 395

GATE 2006

Solution

Subtract the minimum element of each row from all the elements of the row.

Item	Supplies		
	$S1$	$S2$	$S3$
P	0	10	20
Q	0	25	25
R	0	20	40

Now, subtract the minimum element of remaining row.

Item	Supplies		
	$S1$	$S2$	$S3$
P	0	0	10
Q	0	0	0
R	0	0	20

Minimum cost allocation, $P - S1$, $Q - S3$, $R - S2$

Minimum cost $= 110 + 140 + 145$

Minimum cost = Rs. 395

Example 16.17

The table gives details of an assembly line.

Work station	I	II	III	IV	V	VI
Total task time at the workstation (in minute)	7	9	7	10	9	6

What is the line efficiency of the assembly line?

(A) 70% (B) 75% (C) 80% (D) 85%

GATE 2006

Solution

Work station	I	II	III	IV	V	VI
Total task time at the workstation (in minute)	7	9	7	10	9	6

Maximum time

Line efficiency of the assembly line is given by

$$\eta = \frac{\sum t_i}{\text{Number of station} \times t_{max}} = \frac{7+9+7+10+9+6}{6 \times 10} \times 100$$

$$\eta = 80\%$$

Example 16.18

A component can be produced by any of the four processes I, II, III and IV. Process I has a fixed cost of Rs. 20 and variable cost of Rs. 3 per piece. Process II has a fixed cost Rs. 50 and variable cost of Re. 1 per piece. Process III has a fixed cost of Rs. 40 and variable cost of Rs. 2 per piece. Process IV has a fixed cost of Rs.10 and variable cost of Rs. 4 per piece. If the company wishes to produce 100 pieces of the component, from economic point of view it should choose

(A) Process I (B) Process II

(C) Process III (D) Process IV

GATE 2005

Solution

Process	I	II	III	IV
Fixed cost (F)	20	50	40	10
Variable cost per piece (V)	3	1	2	4
Total cost of 100 piece ($F + nV$)	320	150	240	410

Hence, minimum cost is Rs.150 in process II.

Example 16.19

The annual demand for an item is 10,000 units. The unit cost is Rs.100 and inventory carrying charge is 14.4% of the unit cost per annum. The cost of one procurement is Rs.2000. The time between two consecutive orders to meet the above demand is____month(s).

GATE 2016

Solution

Economic order quantity is given by

$$\text{EOQ} = \sqrt{\frac{2C_o A}{C_h}}$$

Substituting given value, $A = 10{,}000$ unit, $C_o = 2000$ and $C_h = 0.144 \times 100$, we have

$$\text{EOQ} = \sqrt{\frac{2 \times 2000 \times 10000}{0.144 \times 100}}$$

$$\text{EOQ} = 1666.67 \text{ units}$$

The time between two consecutive orders,

$$T = \frac{\text{EOQ}}{A}$$

$$T = \frac{1666.67}{10000} = 0.1667 \text{ years}$$

$$T = 2 \text{ months}$$

Example 16.20

Maximise: $z = 15x_1 + 20x_2$

Subject to:

$$12x_1 + 4x_2 \geq 36$$
$$12x_1 - 6x_2 \leq 24$$
$$x_1, x_2 \geq 0$$

The above linear programming problem has

(A) Infeasible

(B) Unbounded

(C) Alternative optimums

(D) Degenerate

GATE 2016

Solution

Constrains are shown on graph.

Since, there is no limitation of boundary for the feasible rigion, therefore, the LPP has unbounded solution.

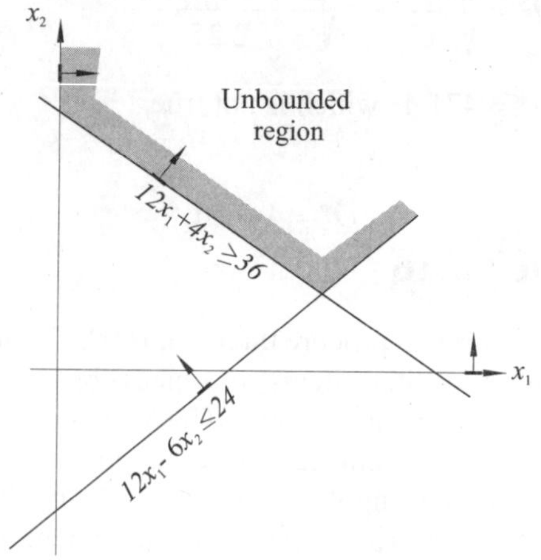

Example 16.21

In a single-channel queuing model, the customer arrival rate is 12 per hour and the serving rate is 24 per hour. The expected time that a customer is in queue is ______ minutes.

GATE 2016

Solution

Given: Arrival rate $\lambda = 12$ per hour, and service rate $\mu = 24$ per hour

$$\rho = \frac{\lambda}{\mu} = \frac{12}{24} = 0.5$$

Expected numbers of people in the system,

$$L_s = \frac{\rho}{1-\rho} = \frac{0.5}{1-0.5} = 1$$

Expected numbers of people in the queue,

$$L_q = L_s - \rho = 1 - 0.5 = 0.5$$

Waiting time in queue, $W_q = \frac{L_s}{\lambda} = \frac{0.5}{12} = 0.04166$

$$W_q = 2.5 \text{ min}$$

Example 16.22

A project consists of 14 activities, A to N. The duration of these activities (in days) are shown in brackets on the network diagram. The latest finish time (in days) for node 10 is _______.

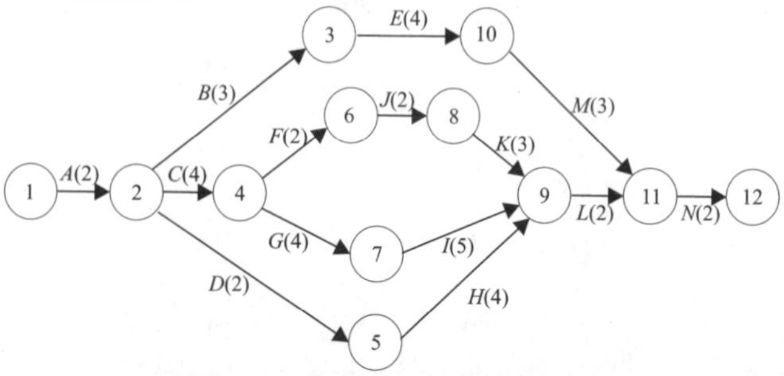

GATE 2016

Solution

T_E and T_L values are determined for all the events. The network with the T_E and T_L values for all events is shown in figure.

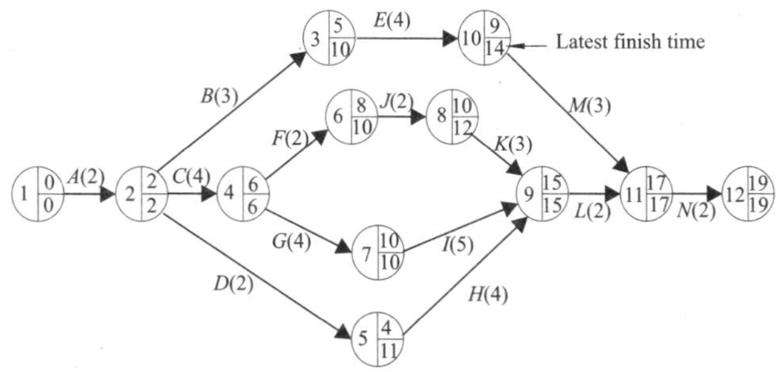

Example 16.23

In PERT chart, the activity time distribution is

(A) Normal (B) Binomial (C) Poisson (D) Beta

GATE 2016

Solution

In PERT chart, the activity time distribution is beta.

Example 16.24

The demand for a two-wheeler was 900 units and 1030 units in April 2015 and May 2015, respectively. The forecast for the month of April 2015 was 850 units. Considering a smoothing constant of 0.6, the forecast for the month of June 2015 was:

(A) 850 units (B) 927 units (C) 965 units (D) 970 units

GATE 2016

Solution

	Demand	Forecast
April	900	850
May	1030	

Smoothing constant, $\alpha = 0.6$

Forecast by exponential smoothing method was

$$F_{May} = F_{April} + \alpha\,(D_{April} - F_{April})$$

$$F_{May} = 850 + 0.6\,(900 - 850)$$

$$F_{May} = 880$$

$$F_{Jun} = F_{May} + \alpha\,(D_{May} - F_{May})$$

$$F_{Jun} = 880 + 0.6\,(1030 - 880)$$

$$F_{Jun} = 970$$

Example 16.25

A firm uses a turning center, a milling center and a grinding machine to produce two parts. The following table provides the machining time required for each part and the maximum machining time available on each machine. The profit per unit on parts I and II are Rs. 40 and Rs. 100, respectively. The maximum profit per week of the firm is rupees._____.

Type of machine	Machining time required for the machine part (minutes)		Maximum machining time available per week (minutes)
	I	II	
Turning center	12	6	6000
Milling center	4	10	4000
Grinding machine	2	3	1800

GATE 2016

Solution

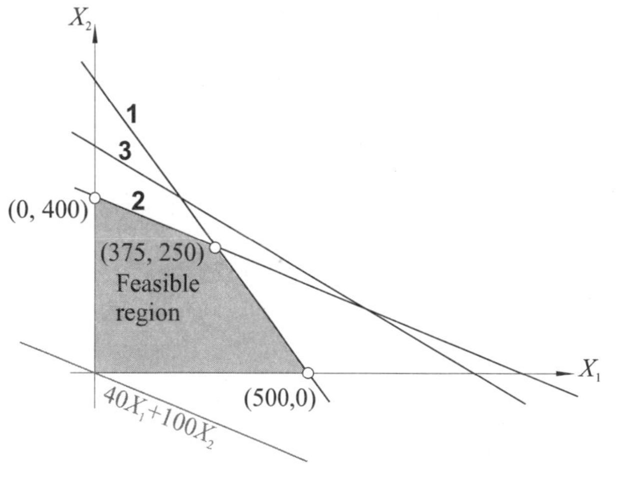

Let X_1 and X_2 be the two parts I and II respectively.

Profit, $Z = 40X_1 + 100X_2$

Constraints:

$$12X_1 + 6X_2 \le 6000 \quad \text{(i)}$$

$$4X_1 + 10X_2 \le 4000 \quad \text{(ii)}$$

$$2X_1 + 3X_2 \le 1800 \quad \text{(iii)}$$

$$X_1, X_2 \ge 0$$

$$Z_{(0,400)} = 40 \times 0 + 100 \times 400 = 40000$$

$$Z_{(375,250)} = 40 \times 375 + 100 \times 250 = 40000$$

$$Z_{(500,0)} = 40 \times 500 + 100 \times 0 = 20000$$

$$Z_{max} = 40{,}000$$

Example 16.26

A food processing company uses 25,000 kg of corn flour every year. The quantity-discount price of corn flour is provided in the following table.

Quantity (kg)	Unit price (Rs./kg)
1-749	70
750-1499	65
1500 and above	60

The order processing charges are Rs. 500/order. The handling plus carry-over charge on an annual basis is 20% of the purchase price of the corn flour per kg. The optimal order quantity (in kg) is_____.

GATE 2016

Solution

Economic order quantity, $Q^* = \sqrt{\dfrac{2AC_o}{C_h}}$

Consider unit price 60,

$$Q^* = \sqrt{\frac{2 \times 25000 \times 500}{60 \times 0.2}} = 1443.37 < 1500$$

$$\text{Total cost, } TC_{Q=1500} = \frac{25000}{1500} \times 500 + \frac{1500}{2} \times 60 \times 0.2 + 25000 \times 60$$

$$\text{Total cost, } TC_{Q=1500} = 15{,}17{,}333$$

Consider unit price 65,

$$Q^* = \sqrt{\frac{2 \times 25000 \times 500}{65 \times 0.2}} = 1386.75$$

$$\text{Total cost, } TC_{Q=1386.75} = \frac{25000}{1386.75} \times 500 + \frac{1386.75}{2} \times 60 \times 0.2 + 25000 \times 65$$

$$\text{Total cost, } TC_{Q=1386.7} = 16{,}423{,}343$$

$$\text{Total cost, } TC_{Q=1500} < \text{Total cost, } TC_{Q=1386.7}$$

Therefore, the optimal order quantity (in kg) is 1500.

Example 16.27

Following data refers to the jobs (P, Q, R, S) which have arrived at a machine for scheduling. The shortest possible average flow time is_______days.

Job	Processing time(days)
P	15
Q	9
R	22
S	12

GATE 2017

Solution

Job	Processing time(days)	In	out
Q	9	0	9
S	12	9	21
P	15	21	36
R	22	36	58

$$\text{Shortest possible average flow time} = \frac{58}{4} = 17$$

Example 16.28

Two models, P and Q, of a product earn profits of Rs. 100 and Rs. 80 per piece, respectively. Production times for P and Q are 5 hours and 3 hours, respectively, while the total production time available is 150 hours. For a total batch size of 40, to maximize profit, the number of units of P to be produced is________.

GATE 2017

Solution

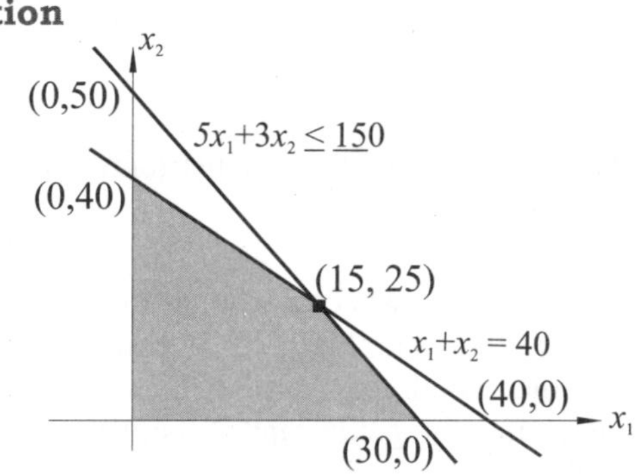

Let x_1 = number of units of P, x_2 = number of units of Q.

Maximize $z = 100x_1 + 80x_2$

$$5x_1 + 3x_2 \le 150$$

$$x_1 + x_2 = 40$$

$$z_{(0,40)} = 100 \times 0 + 80 \times 40 = 3200$$

$$z_{(15,25)} = 100 \times 15 + 80 \times 25 = 3500$$

$$z_{max} = 3500$$

Example 16.29

For a single server with Poisson arrival and exponential service time, the arrival rate is 12 per hour. Which one of the following service rates will provide a steady state finite queue length?

(A) 6 per hour
(B) 10 per hour
(C) 12 per hour
(D) 24 per hour

GATE 2017

Solution

Arrival rate $\lambda = 12$ /hour, Service rate $= \mu$

For steady state finite queue length $\mu = \lambda$

Service rate $\mu = 12$ per hour

Example 16.30

A product made in two factories P and Q, is transported to two destinations, R and S. The per unit costs of transportation (in Rupees) from factories to destinations are as per the following matrix:

Factory \ Destinations	R	S
P	10	7
Q	3	4

Factory P produces 7 units and factory Q produces 9 units of the product. Each destination requires 8 units. If the north-west corner method provides the total transportation cost as X (in Rupees) and the optimized (the minimum) total transportation cost Y (in Rupees), then (X – Y), in Rupees, is

(A) 0 (B) 15 (C) 35 (D) 105

GATE 2017

Solution

	R	S	
P	10	7	7
Q	3	4	9
	8	8	

By North-West corner rule

	R	S
P	10 (7)	7
Q	3 (1)	4 (8)

Total cost $x = 10 \times 7 + 3 \times 1 + 4 \times 8 =$ Rs. 105

By Vogel's approximation method (VAM)

		$v_1 = 6$	$v_2 = 7$	
		R	S	
$u_1 = 0$	P	10	7	7 (1)
$u_2 = -3$	Q	3	4	9 (1)
		8 (7)	8 (3)	

Total cost $y = 3 \times 8 + 4 \times 1 + 7 \times 7 =$ Rs. 77

$$x - y = 105 - 77$$

$$x - y = 28$$

Example 16.31

A project starts with activity A and ends with activity F. The precedence relation and durations of the activities are as per the following table:

Activity	Immediate predecessor	Duration (days)
A	-	4
B	A	3
C	A	7
D	B	14
E	C	4
F	D,F	9

The minimum project completion time (in days) is___.

GATE 2017

Solution

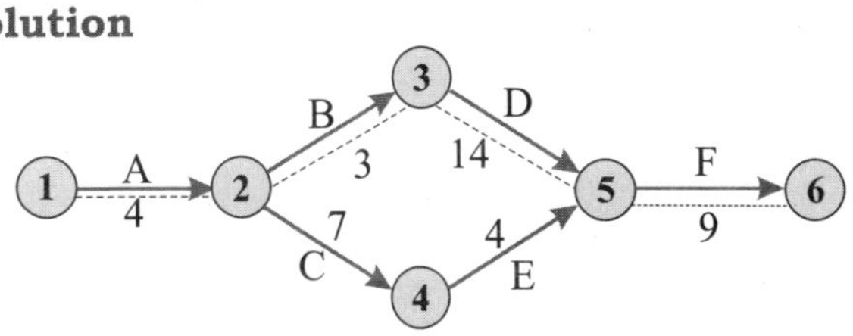

Minimum project completion time $= 4 + 3 + 14 + 9 = 30$

30 days

Example 16.32

The time series forecasting method that gives equal weightage to each of the m most recent observations is

(A) Moving average method

(B) Exponential smoothing with linear trend

(C) Triple Exponential smoothing

(D) Kalman Filter

GATE 2018

Solution

Moving average method

Example 16.33

The minimum value of $3x + 5y$

such that:

$$3x + 5y \le 15$$

$$4x + 9y \le 8$$

$$13x + 2y \le 2$$

$$x \ge 0,\ y \ge 0$$

is _______.

GATE 2018

Solution

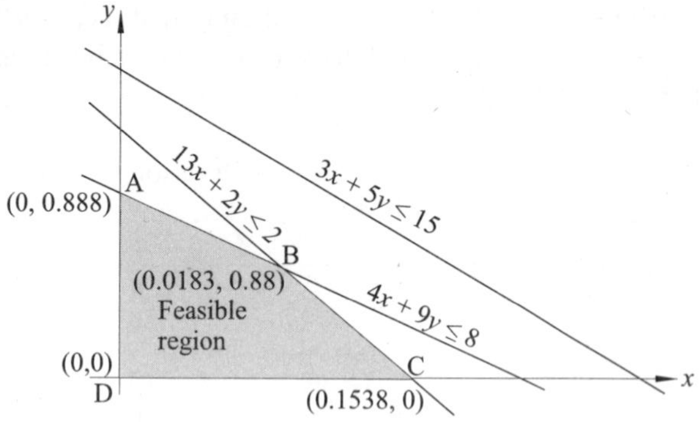

The feasible region has four corner A, B, C and D. The value of $z = 3x + 5y$ at these points are:

$$z_A = 3 \times 0 + 5 \times 0.888 = 4.44$$

$$z_B = 3 \times 0.0183 + 5 \times 0.88 = 4.46$$

$$z_C = 3 \times 0.1538 + 5 \times 0 = 0.4614$$

$$z_D = 3 \times 0 + 5 \times 0 = 0$$

Minimum value of $z = 0$ at D (0, 0)

Example 16.34

Processing times (including setup times) and due dates for six jobs waiting to be processed at a work centre are given in the table. The average tardiness (in days) using shortest processing time rule is ___________ .

Job	Processing time (days)	Due Date (days)
A	3	8
B	7	16
C	4	4
D	9	18
E	5	17
F	13	19

GATE 2018

Solution

By using Shortest Processing Time (STP) rule

Job	Processing time (days)	Due Date (days)	Job Flow Time	Tardiness
A	3	8	$0+3=3$	0
C	4	4	$3+4=7$	3
E	5	17	$7+5=12$	0
B	7	16	$12+7=19$	3
D	9	18	$19+9=28$	10
F	13	19	$28+13=41$	22
Total				**38**

$$\text{Average tardiness per job} = \frac{\text{Total tardiness}}{\text{No. of Jobs}} = \frac{38}{6}$$

Average tardiness per job $= 6.33$

Example 16.35

A local tyre distributor expects to sell approximately 9600 steel belted radial tyres next year. Annual carrying cost is Rs. 16 per tyre and ordering cost is Rs. 75. The economic order quantity of the tyres is

(A) 64 (B) 212 (C) 300 (D) 1200

GATE 2018

Solution

Economic Order Quality, $\text{EOQ} = \sqrt{\dfrac{2DC_o}{C_h}}$

Substituting $D = 9600$, $C_h =$ Rs. 16/year and $C_o =$ Rs. 75/year. We have

$$\text{EOQ} = \sqrt{\frac{2 \times 9600 \times 75}{16}}$$

EOQ $= 300$

Example 16.36

The arrival of customers over fixed time intervals in a bank follow a Poisson distribution with an average of 30 customers/hour. The probability that the time between successive customer arrival is between 1 and 3 minutes is_____ .

GATE 2018

Solution

Given: Arrival rate $\lambda = 30$ customer/hr

$$\lambda = \frac{1}{2} \text{ customer/min}$$

Probability $P = 1 - e^{-\lambda T}$

$$P(1) = 1 - e^{-\frac{1}{2}\times 1} = 0.393$$

$$P(3) = 1 - e^{-\frac{1}{2}\times 3} = 0.7768$$

$$P(1 \le T \le 3 \text{ min}) = 0.7768 - 0.393$$

$$P(1 \le T \le 3 \text{ min}) = 0.383$$

Example 16.37

The problem of maximizing $z = x_1 - x_2$ subject to constraints $x_1 + x_2 \le 10$, $x_1 \ge 0$, $x_2 \ge 0$, $x_2 \le 5$ has

(A) no solution (B) one solution

(C) two solutions (D) more than two solutions

GATE 2018

Solution

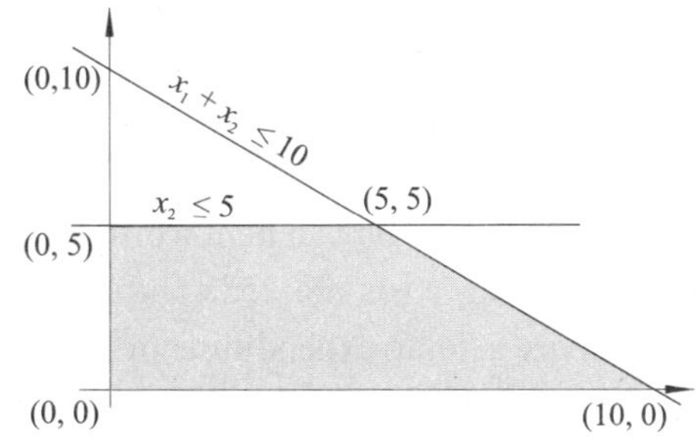

$z = x_1 - x_2$

$z_{(0,0)} = 0, z_{(0,5)} = -5, z_{(5,5)} = 0, z_{(10,0)} = 10, z_{max} = 10$ at $(10,0)$

The problem has one solution.

Example 16.38

The arc lengths of a directed graph of a project are as shown in the figure. The shortest path length from node 1 to node 6 is _____.

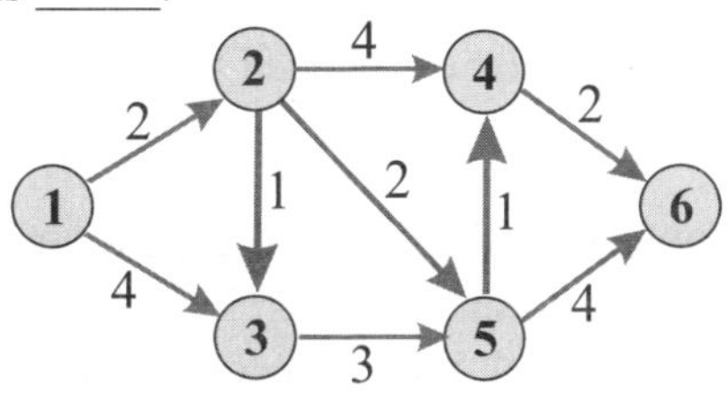

GATE 2018

Solution

Shortest path $1 \xrightarrow{2} 2 \xrightarrow{2} 5 \xrightarrow{1} 4 \xrightarrow{2} 6$

Shortest path= 7

Example 16.39

The table presents the demand of a product. By simple three-month moving average method, the demand-forecast of the product for the month of September is

Month	Demand
January	450
February	440
March	460
April	510
May	520
June	495
July	475
August	560

(A) 490 (B) 510 (C) 530 (D) 536.67

GATE 2019

Solution

Forecast of the product for the month of September

$$= (495 + 475 + 560) / 3 = 510$$

Forecast of the product for the month of September = 510

Example 16.40

The annual demand of values per year in a company is 10,000 units. The current order quantity is 400 values per order. The holding cost is Rs. 24 per valve per year and the ordering cost is Rs. 400 per order. If the current order quantity is changed to Economic Order Quantity, then the saving in the total cost of inventory per year will be Rs.____ (round off to two decimal plances).

GATE 2019

Solution

Givent: $A = 10000$ units, $Q = 400$ valve/order, $C_o =$ Rs. 400 per order, $C_h =$ Rs. 24 per valve per year

Economic order quantity, $Q^* = \sqrt{\dfrac{2\,C_o\,A}{C_h}}$

$$Q^* = \sqrt{\frac{2 \times 1000 \times 400}{24}}$$

$$Q^* = 577.35$$

Then the total cost, $T(Q^*) = \dfrac{A}{Q^*}C_o + \dfrac{Q^*}{2}C_h$

$$T(Q^*) = \frac{10000}{577.35} \times 400 + \frac{577.35}{2} \times 24 = \text{Rs. } 13856.41$$

Order quantity, $Q = 400$

Total cost of purchase,

$$T(Q) = \frac{10000}{400} \times 400 + \frac{400}{2} \times 24 = \text{Rs. } 14800$$

Saving $= T(Q) - T(Q^*) = 14800 - 13856$

Saving $= T(Q) - T(Q^*) =$ Rs. 943.60

16.3 PRACTICE PAPER

Time: 3 hours Max. Marks: 100

Q.1 to Q.30 carry one mark each

Q.1 to Q.21 Multiple Choice Questions

Q.1 When the ordering cost is increased to 4 times, the Economic order quantity (EOQ) will be increased to:

(A) 2 times (B) 3 times (C) 8 times (D) Remain same

Q.2 Consider the following statements:

The break-even point increases if the

1. Fixed cost per unit increases
2. Variable cost per unit decreases
3. Selling price per unit decreases

Which of the above statements is/are correct?

(A) 1 only (B) 1 and 2 (C) 2 and 3 (D) 1 and 3

Q.3 Economic order quantity is taken at the point where the cost of carrying equals the cost of:

(A) Ordering the materials

(B) The material

(C) The safety stock

(D) Both the material and the safety stock

Q.4 Match List-I with List-II and select the correct answer using the code given below the lists:

List-I	List-II
(a) Transportation problem	(1) Critical path
(b) Assignment problem	(2) Stage coach
(c) Dynamic problem	(3) Vogel's approximate method
(d) PERT	(4) Hungarian method

(A) a-2, b-1, c-3, d-4 (B) a-3, b-4, c-2, d-1

(C) a-2, b-4, c-3, d-1 (D) a-3, b-1, c-2, d-4

Q.5 A production system has a product type of layout in which there are four machines laid in series. Each machine does a separate operation. Every product needs all the four operations to be carried out. The designated capacity of each of the four machines is 200, 175, 160 and 210 products per days. The system capacity (in product per day) would be

(A) 210 (B) 200 (C) 175 (D) 160

Q.6 If t_o is the minimum or the optimistic time and t_p is the maximum or the pessimistic time for the completion of an activity, then standard deviation σ for β-distribution curve is

(A) $\sigma = \frac{t_p - t_o}{6}$ (B) $\sigma = \frac{t_p - t_o}{3}$

(C) $\sigma = \frac{2t_p - t_o}{3}$ (D) $\sigma = \frac{t_p - t_o}{2}$

Q.7 Manufacturing a product requires processing on four machines A, B, C, D in the order A- B-C-D. The capacities of four machines are $A = 100, B = 110, C = 120$ and $D = 130$ units per shift. If the expected output is 90% of the system capacity, then what is the expected output?

(A) 90 units (B) 99 units (C) 108 units (D) 117 units

Q.8 If the fixed cost of the assets for a given period doubles, then how much will the break-even quantity becomes?

(A) Half the original value

(B) Same as the original value

(C) Twice the original value

(D) None of these

Q.9 If demand is doubled and ordering cost, unit cost and inventory carrying cost are halved, then what will be the EOQ?

(A) Half (B) Same (C) Twice (D) None of these

Q.10 Every year DPS Ltd. buy an item worth Rs 1,00,000. The inventory carrying costs are 25% and each ordering procedure involves a total expenditure of Rs.500. How much (Rs) of the item should DPS Ltd. order every time?

(A) 20,000 (B) 10,000 (C) 5,000 (D) 1000

Q.11 The following figures relate to a small manufacturing company.

Selling price per unit = Rs. 12.50

Fixed cost = Rs. 60,000

Variable cost per unit = Rs. 7.50

The number of units to be produced to break-even is:

(A) 10,000 (B) 12,000 (C) 15,000 (D) 14,400

Q.12 The three time estimates of a PERT activity are: Optimistic time = 8 min, most likely time = 10 min and pessimistic time = 14 min. The expected time of the activity would be:

(A) 10.00 min (B) 10.33 min

(C) 10.66 min (D) 11.00 min

Q.13 If the earliest starting time for an activity is 8 weeks, the latest finish time is 37 weeks and the duration time of the activity is 11 weeks, then the total float is equal to:

(A) 18 weeks (B) 14 weeks

(C) 56 weeks (D) 40 weeks

Q.14 At a self-service store, a cashier can serve 10 customers in 5 min. On an average 15 customers arrive every 10 min. If the arrivals are as per Poisson distribution and services as per exponential distribution, the probability that the cashier would be idle is:

(A) 0.5 (B) 0.75 (C) 0.25 (D) 0

Q.15 The earliest occurrence time for event A is 8 weeks and the latest occurrence time for even A is 26 weeks. The earliest occurrence time for event B is 32 weeks and the latest occurrence time for event B is 37 weeks. If the activity time is 11 weeks, then the total float will be:

(A) 11 (B) 13 (C) 18 (D) 24

Q.16 The earliest time of the completion of the last event in the below network in weeks is:

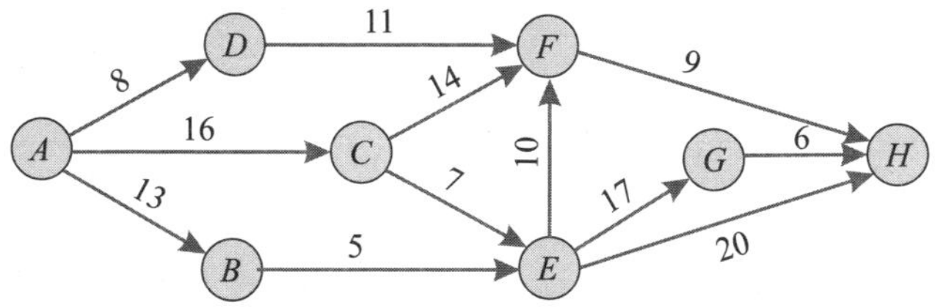

(A) 41 (B) 42 (C) 43 (D) 46

Q.17 The demand data of sales for the months January, February, March and April are 11, 10, 12 and 14 thousand rupees. The forecasted sales for the month of May by three periods moving average is:

(A) 10 (B) 12 (C) 16 (D) 20

Q.18 Item *B* requires four numbers of item *C*. Product *P* requires two numbers of items *B* and five numbers of item *C*. If five number of product *P* is to be manufactured, the number of item *C* required will be:

(A) 65 (B) 55 (C) 45 (D) 35

Q.19 The estimated duration of times for an activity, in the PERT network under the worst and best environment are as 9 and 3 days. The variance of this activity is:

(A) 6 days (B) 1 days (C) 2 days (D) None of above

Q.20 The demand for April, May and June are 100, 200 and 300 units. The minimum initial inventory required for maintaining constant rate of production is:

(A) Zero (B) 100 (C) 200 (D) 300

Q.21 to Q.30 Numerical Answer Questions

Q.21 The demand during the month April, May and June are 10, 20 and 30 tonne and the weight assigned are 1, 2 and 3 respectively. The forecast (in ton) for July is___.

Q.22 If critical path of a project is 20 months with a standard deviation 4 months, what is the probability (in %) that the project will be completed in 24 months?

Q.23 In a forecasting situation, exponential smoothing with a smoothing constant $\alpha = 0.2$ is to be used. If the demand for nth period is 500 and the actual demand for the corresponding period turned out to be 450, what is the forecast for the $(n+1)$th period?

Q.24 In the production of a product, the fixed costs are Rs. 6000 and the variable cost in Rs. 10 per product. If the sale price of the product is Rs.12, the break-even volume of products to be made will be ____.

Q.25 A product is manufactured by processing on the four work-stations (WS). The capacity of each machine on these work-stations is given in the diagram as shown. In the diagram M1, M2A, M2B, M3, M4A and M4B are the machines and 500, 275, 560, 200 and 200 are their capacities in number of products made per shift. If the products made in this system are 5% defective, then what will be the output from this system?

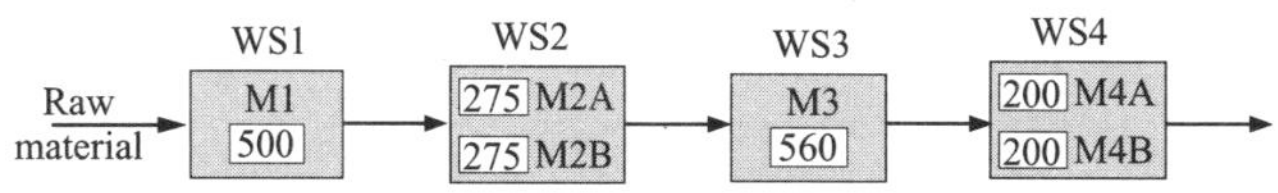

Q.26 A PERT activity has an optimistic time estimate of 3 days, a pessimistic time estimate of 8 days, and a most likely time estimate of 10 days. What is the expected time(in days) of this activity?

Q.27 An operation consultant for an automatic car washer plans for enough capacity of stalls to handle 60 cars per hour. Each car will have a wash time of 3 min, but there is to be a 20% allowance for set-up time, delays and payment transactions. How many car wash stalls should be installed?

Q.28 Process *X* has a fixed cost of Rs. 40,000 per month and a variable cost of Rs. 9 per unit. Process *Y* has a fixed cost of Rs. 16,000 per month and a variable cost of Rs. 24 unit. At what production quantity, total costs of processes *X* and *Y* will be equal?

Q.29 Given below is a critical path network with the duration time of each activity. The completion time of the network is________.

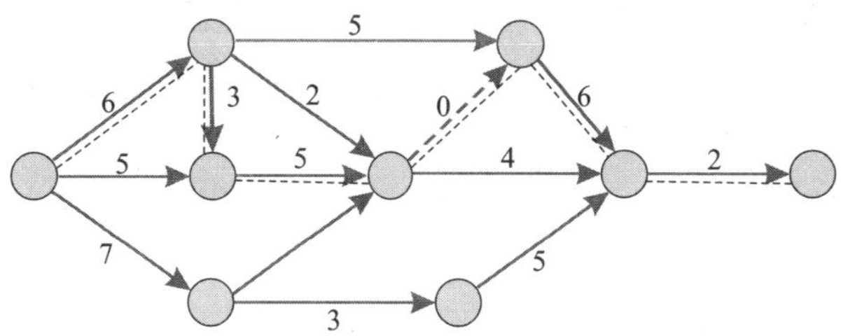

Q.30 The demand for four months are 150, 100, 250 and 300. The rate of production is maintained as constant and equal to 200. If the initial inventory is 100 unit, the final inventory is________.

Q.31 to Q.65 carry two marks each

Q.31 to Q.50 Multiple Choice Questions

Q.31 The break-even point can be lowered by:

(A) Increasing the fixed costs

(B) Increasing the variable costs

(C) Decreasing the slope of the income line

(D) Reducing the variable cost

Q.32 The following table lists the jobs of a network along with their time estimates:

Jobs	Duration (in days)		
	Optimistic	Most likely	Pessimistic
1-2	3	6	15
2-3	6	12	30
2-4	5	11	17
3-4	3	9	27
3-5	1	4	7
5-6	2	5	8
3-6	4	19	28
4-6	2	5	14

Critical path for the network is:

(A) 1-2-3-6 (B) 1-2-3-4-6

(C) 1-2-3-5-6 (D) 1-2-4-6

Q.33 The network for a certain project is shown in figure.

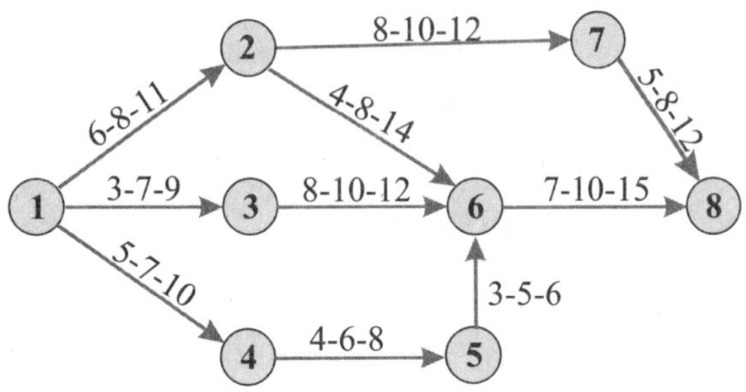

The critical path is:

(A) 1-2-7-8 (B) 1-2-6-8

(C) 1-3-6-8 (D) 1-4-5-6-8

Q.34 Estimated time T_E and variance of the activities V on the critical path in a PERT network are given in the following table:

Activity	T_E (days)	V (days)^2
a	17	4
b	15	4
c	8	1

The probability of completing the project in 43 days is:

(A) 15.6% (B) 50.0% (C) 84.1% (D) 90.0%

Q.35 A small workshop undertaking repair of damaged cars has one denter and one painter. Presently there are six cars need repair. The following estimates in hours of time needed for denting and painting on the cars are available:

Car	1	2	3	4	5	6
Denting time (h)	4	7	3	12	11	9
Painting time (h)	11	7	10	8	10	13

What is the sequence of cars that completes all the jobs in minimum time?

(A) 3→1→2→6→5→4 (B) 4→2→6→5→3→1

(C) 3→1→5→2→6→4 (D) None of these

Q.36 A military equipment is to be transported from origins, *P*, *Q*, *R* to destinations *a*, *b*, *c* and *d*. The supply at the origins, the demand at the destinations and cost of shipment are shown in the following table:

		Destinations				
		a	*b*	*c*	*d*	Supply
Origins	*P*	10	22	0	22	8
	Q	15	20	12	8	13
	R	20	12	10	15	11
	Demand	5	11	8	8	

Supply of military equipment from origin *Q* to destinations *a*, *b*, *c* and *d* (by least cost method) are:

(A) *a*-5, *b*-0, *c*-0, *d*-8 (B) *a*-3, *b*-2, *c*-0, *d*-8

(C) *a*-5, *b*-0, *c*-3, *d*-5 (D) *a*-2, *b*-,3 *c*-5, *d*-3

Q.37 In the network diagram shown in the figure. The critical path is along

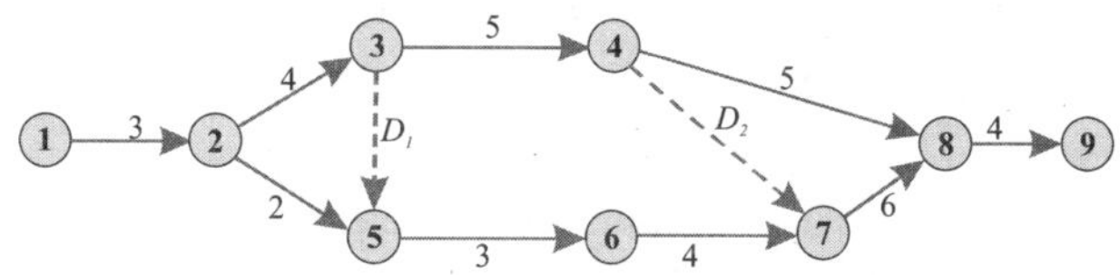

(A) 1→2→ 3→4→8→9

(B) 1→2→3→5→6→ 7→8→ 9

(C) 1→2→ 3→4→7→8→9

(D) 1→2→5→6→7→ 8→9

Q.38 It is given that the actual demand is 59 units, a previous forecast 64 units and smoothing factor 0.3. What will be the forecast for next period, using exponential smoothing?

(A) 36.9 units (B) 57.5 units

(C) 60.5 units (D) 62.5 units

Q.39 A company has four work centres *A*, *B*, *C* and *D*, with per day capacities of 450 units, 390 units, 360 units and 400 units respectively. The machines are laid down in order *A*, *B*, *C* and *D* and product has to be operated on all these machines for getting converted into finished product. The actual output turns out to be 306 units per day. What is the system efficiency?

(A) 68% (B) 78% (C) 80% (D) 85%

Q.40 Which one of the following information combinations has lowest break-even point ?

	Fixed cost	Variable cost/unit (in Rs.)	Revenue unit (in Rs.)
(A)	30,000	10	40
(B)	40,000	15	40
(C)	50,000	25	40
(D)	60,000	30	40

Q.41 The following figures relate to a small manufacturing company.

Selling price per unit = Rs. 12.50

Fixed cost = Rs. 60,000

Variable cost per unit = Rs. 7.50

The number of unit to be produced to earn a profit of Rs.12000, is

(A) 10000 (B) 12000 (C) 15000 (D) 14400

Q.42 There are five jobs, each of which has to go through the two machines A and B in the order AB. Processing times (in h) are given in the table:

Job	Machine A (h)	Machine B (h)
1	5	2
2	1	6
3	9	7
4	3	8
5	10	4

The sequence (order) for the five jobs that will minimise the total elapsed time for the completion of all the jobs, is

(A) $1\to2\to3\to4\to5$ (B) $2\to4\to3\to5\to1$

(C) $3\to4\to2\to5\to1$ (D) None of these

Q.43 There are five jobs, each of which has to go through the two machines A and B in the order AB. Processing times (in h) are given in the table below:

Job	Machine A (h)	Machine B (h)
1	5	2
2	1	6
3	9	7
4	3	8
5	10	4

The minimum total time elapsed to complete five jobs, is:

(A) 30 h (B) 23 h (C) 27 h (D) 28 h

Q.44 A standard machine tool and an automatic machine tool are being compared for the production of a component. Following data refers to the two machines.

	Standard machine	Automatic machine
Setup time	30 min	2 h
Machine time per piece	22 min	5 min
Machine rate	Rs. 200/h	Rs. 800/h

The break-even production batch size above which automatic machine tool will be economical to use will be

(A) 4 (B) 5 (C) 24 (D) 225

Q.45 A new facility has to be designed to do all the welding for 3 products: A, B and C. Per unit welding time for each product is 20 s, 40 s, and 50 s respectively. Daily demand forecast for product A is 450, for B is 360 and for C is 240. A welding line can operate efficiently for 220 min a day. Number of welding lines required is:

(A) 5 (B) 4 (C) 3 (D) 2

Q.46 The variance (V) for critical path

$a\to b=4$ time units

$b\to c=16$ time units

$c\to d=4$ time units

$d\to e=1$ time units

The standard deviation of the critical path $a\to e$ is:

(A) 3 (B) 4 (C) 5 (D) 6

Q.47 A manufacturer produces two types of products, 1 and 2, at production levels of x_1 and x_2 respectively. The profit and production constraints are:

Profit: $z=2x_1+5x_2$

Constraints: $x_1+3x_2\le 40$

$3x_1+x_2\le 24$

$x_1+x_2\le 10$

$x_1>0,\ x_2>0$

The production level of products 1 and 2 for maximum profit is:

(A) $x_1=3,\ x_2=7$ (B) $x_1=7,\ x_2=2$

(C) $x_1=4,\ x_2=12$ (D) $x_1=0,\ x_2=10$

Q.48 In a single channel queue, the mean waiting time in the system is 50 min, the mean waiting time in the queue is 30 min, the mean rate of service will be______.

(A) 3/h (B) 2/h (C) 1/h (D) None of these

Q.49 The mean and standard deviation of project completion time are 16 days and 2.44 respectively. The probability that the project would be completed with 15 days, will be:

(A) 19 % (B) 34 % (C) 43 % (D) 66 %

Q.50 Last year, a manufacturer produced 15000 products which were sold for Rs. 300 each. At that volume, the fixed cost were Rs. 15.2 lacs and total variable costs were Rs. 21 lacs. The break-even quantity of product would be:

(A) 4500 (B) 5000 (C) 9500 (D) 2560

Q.51 to Q.65 Numerical Answer Questions

Q.51 Three jobs *A*, *B*, *C* are to be assigned to 3 machines M_1, M_2 and M_3. The processing cost per unit for each job-machine combination is shown in matrix.

	Machines		
Jobs	M_1	M_2	M_3
A	17	25	31
B	10	15	16
C	12	14	11

What is the minimum processing cost for assignment?

Q.52 A capstan lathe is used to mass-produce, in batches of 200, a particular component. The direct material cost is Rs. 4 per piece, the direct labour cost is Rs. 3 per piece and overhead costs are 400% of the labour costs. What is the production cost per piece?

Q.53 The following table lists the jobs of a network along with their time estimates.

Jobs	Duration (in days)		
	Optimistic	Most likely	Pessimistic
1-2	3	6	15
2-3	6	12	30
2-4	5	11	17
3-4	3	9	27
3-5	1	4	7
5-6	2	5	8
3-6	4	19	28
4-6	2	5	14

The length (expected completion days) of critical path is (in days)_________.

Q.54 Consider the network given in the figure.

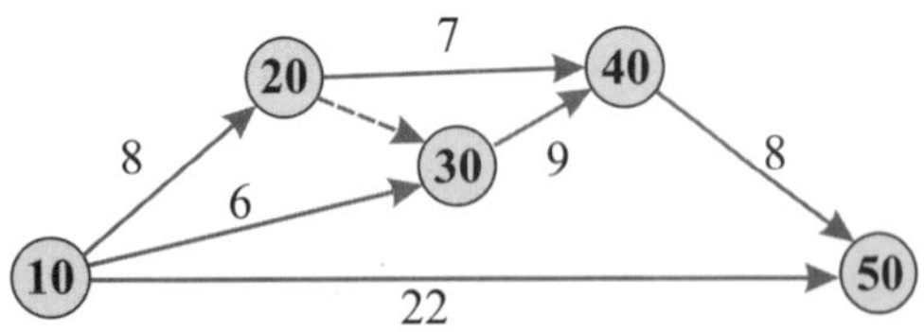

Activity times are given in the number of days. The earliest expected occurrence time (T_E) for the event 50 is______.

Q.55 Time estimates of an activity in a PERT network are optimistic time $t_o = 9$ days, pessimistic time $t_p = 21$ days, most likely time $t_l = 15$ days. The approximate probability (in %) of completion of this activity in 13 days is______.

Q.56 Using the exponential smoothing method of forecasting, what will be the forecast for the fourth week if the actual and forecasted demand for the third week is 480 and 500 respectively and $\alpha = 0.2$?

Q.57 The indirect cost of a plant is Rs. 4,00,000 per year. The direct cost is Rs. 20 per product. If the average revenue per product is Rs. 60, the break-even point (number of product) is_________.

Q.58 For the network shown in the figure, the variance along the critical path is 4. The probability (in %) of completion of the project in 24 days is_______.

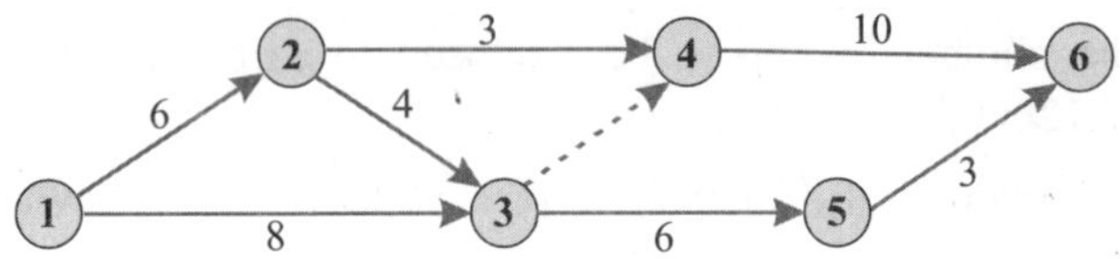

Q.59 The network for a certain project is shown in figure.

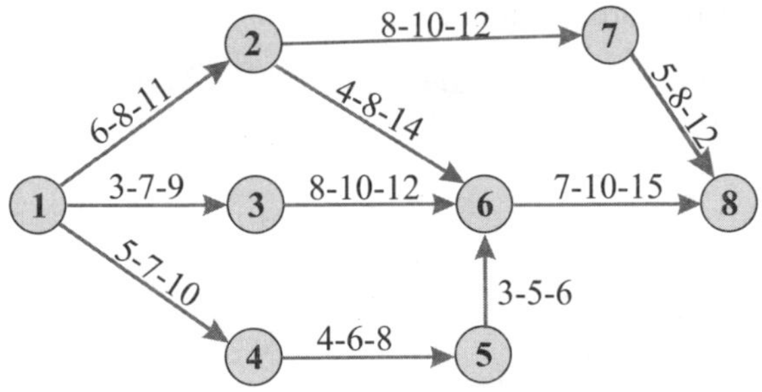

The expected time for the path 1- 4- 5- 6 -8 is_____.

Q.60 An operation consultant for an automatic car washer plans for enough capacity to handle 60 cars per hour. Each car will have a wash time of 4 min, but there is to be a 25% allowance for setup time, delays and payment transactions. How many cars wash stalls should be installed?

Q.61 A small workshop undertaking repair of damaged cars has one denter and one painter. Presently there are six cars need repair. The following estimates in hours of time needed for denting and painting on the cars are available:

Car	1	2	3	4	5	6
Denting time (h)	4	7	3	12	11	9
Painting time (h)	11	7	10	8	10	13

If the sequence of car is 3- 1- 6- 5- 4- 2, then the time (h) for complete all the jobs will be_____.

Q.62 The demand for a product in the month of March turned out to be 20 units against an earlier made forecast of 20 units. The actual demand for April and May turned out to be 25 and 26 units respectively. What will be the forecast for the month of June, using exponential smoothing method and taking smoothing constant α as 0.2? ______.

Q.63 A military equipment is to be transported from origins, *P*, *Q*, *R* to destinations *a*, *b*, *c* and *d*. The supply at the origins, the demand at the destinations and cost of shipment is shown in the following table:

		Destinations				
		a	*b*	*c*	*d*	**Supply**
Origins	*P*	10	22	0	22	8
	Q	15	20	12	8	13
	R	20	12	10	15	11
	Demand	5	11	8	8	

The cost of shipment (by least cost method) is_______.

Q.64 In a single server infinite population queuing model, arrivals follow a Poisson distribution with mean $\lambda = 4$ per hour. The service times are exponential with mean service time equal to 12 min. The expected length of the queue will be______.

Q.65 The arrival is Poisson, with the mean rate of 5 units per hour. The service time is exponential with mean rate of 8 units per hour. The service is valued as Rs. 150 per hour. The average idle time cost per day of 8 hours will be___.

16.4 SOLUTION TO PRACTICE PAPER

Q.1 Ans:(A)

Economic order quality is given by

$$\text{EOQ} = \sqrt{\frac{2\,C_o\,A}{C_h}} \qquad \text{(i)}$$

Ordering cost is increased by 4 times, then

$$\text{EOQ}' = \sqrt{\frac{2\times((4C_o)A}{C_h}} \qquad \text{(ii)}$$

Equations (i) and (ii) give

$$\text{EOQ}' = 2\times\text{EOQ}$$

Q.2 Ans:(D)

Break-even quantity is given by

$$Q = \frac{F}{S-V}$$

where F = Fixed cost, S = Selling price, and V = Variable cost.

Break-even point increases if the

1. Fixed cost per unit increases

3. Selling price per unit decreases

Q.3 Ans:(A)

Let A = Annual demand, C_o = Ordering cost per order, C_h = inventory carrying cost per unit and Q = Order quantity.

Total cost of managing the inventory = Ordering cost + Inventory carrying cost

That is,

$$E = C_o\frac{A}{Q} + \frac{1}{2}Q\,C_h$$

E is minimum; when $C_o\dfrac{A}{Q} = \dfrac{1}{2}Q\,C_h$

Ordering cost = Inventory carrying cost

Q.4 Ans:(B)

Correct match:

(a) Transportation problem (3) Vogel's approximate method

(b) Assignment problem (4) Hungarian method

(c) Dynamic problem (2) Stage coach

(d) PERT (1) Critical path

Q.5 Ans:(D)

A production system of four machines in series is shown in figure.

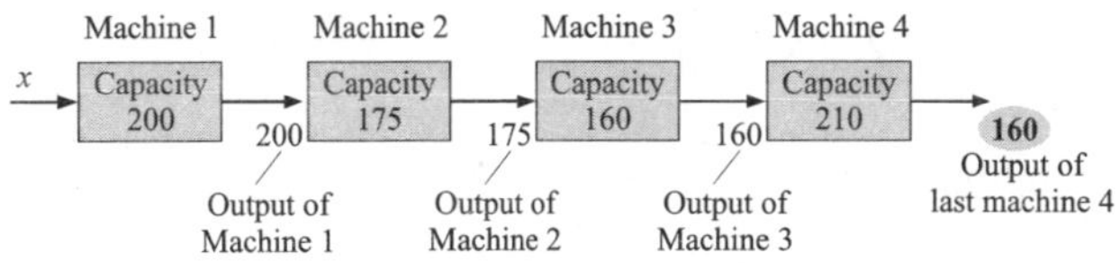

Therefore, the system capacity (in product per day) would be 160.

Q.6 Ans:(A)

$$\text{Standard deviation, } \sigma = \frac{t_p - t_o}{6}$$

Q.7 Ans:(A)

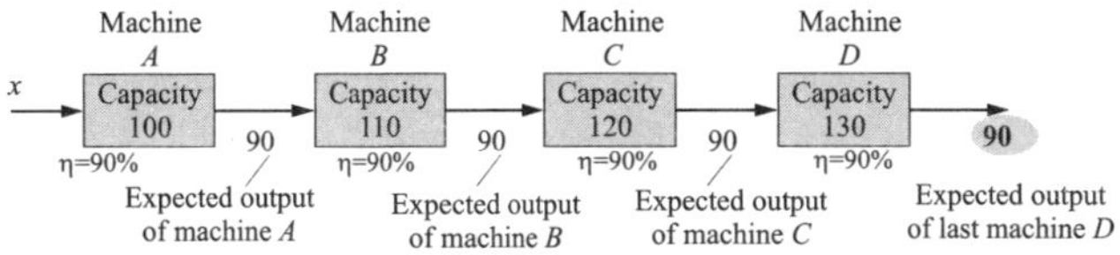

Four machines A, B, C, D in the order A- B- C- D (in series) is shown in figure.

From which

$$\text{Expected output} = 90$$

Q.8 Ans:(C)

Let F, V and S be the fixed cost, variable cost per unit and selling price per unit respectively.

Break even quantity, $q = \dfrac{F}{S-V}$ (i)

If the fixed cost is double, then the break-even quality,

$$q' = \frac{2F}{S-V} \quad \text{(ii)}$$

From Equations (i) and (ii), we have

$$q' = 2q$$

Q.9 Ans:(D)

Economic order quality is given by

$$\text{EOQ} = \sqrt{\frac{2C_o A}{C_h}} \quad \text{(i)}$$

If A is doubled, C_o and C_h are halved, then the new EOQ is

$$\text{EOQ}' = \sqrt{\frac{2 \times \frac{C_o}{2} \times 2A}{\frac{C_h}{2}}}$$

or $$\text{EOQ}' = \sqrt{2} \times \sqrt{\frac{2C_o A}{C_h}} \quad \text{(ii)}$$

From Equations (i) and (ii), we have

$$\text{EOQ}' = \sqrt{2} \times \text{EOQ}$$

Q.10 Ans:(A)

Annual requirement, $A = 1{,}00{,}000$

Inventory carrying cost, $C_h = 0.25$

Order cost per order, $C_o = 500$

Economic order quality in Rs. is given by

$$\text{EOQ (Rs.)} = \sqrt{\frac{2C_o A}{C_h}}$$

$$\text{EOQ (Rs.)} = \sqrt{\frac{2 \times 500 \times 100000}{0.25}}$$

$$\text{EOQ (Rs.)} = 20{,}000$$

Q.11 Ans:(B)

Given that

Selling price per unit, S = Rs. 12.50

Fixed cost , F = Rs. 60,000

Variable cost per unit, V = Rs. 7.50

Let n be the number of units to produce.

For break-even; $F + nV = nS$

$$60000 + n \times 7.5 = n \times 12.5$$

or $$n = \frac{60000}{12.5 - 7.5}$$

$$n = 12000$$

Q.12 Ans:(B)

Given that:

Optimistic time $t_o = 8$ min, most likely time $t_m = 10$ min, and Pessimistic time $t_p = 14$ min.

Expected time of the activity, $t_e = \dfrac{t_o + 4t_m + t_p}{6}$

$$t_e = \frac{8 + 4 \times 10 + 14}{6}$$

$$t_e = 10.33 \text{ min}$$

Q.13 Ans:(A)

Given that:

Earliest starting time, $E_S^i = 8$ weeks

Latest finish time, $L_C^j = 37$ weeks

Activity time, $t_E^{ij} = 11$ weeks

Total float is the difference between the maximum time available to perform the activity and activity duration time. The maximum time available for any activity is from the earliest start time to the latest completion time.

Total float: $T_F^{ij} = T_C^j - E_S^i - t_E^{ij}$

Total float: $T_F^{ij} = 37 - 8 - 11$

$$\text{Total float} = 18 \text{ weeks}$$

Q.14 Ans:(C)

Mean arrival rate, $\lambda = \dfrac{15}{10} = 1.5$ customers/min

Mean service rate, $\mu = \dfrac{10}{5} = 2$ customers/min

Probability that cashier would be idle, is

$$P = 1 - \frac{\lambda}{\mu} = 1 - \frac{1.5}{2}$$

$$P = 0.25$$

Q.15 Ans:(C)

Given that: $T_E^i = 8, T_L^i = 26, T_E^j = 32, T_L^j = 37$ and $t_{ij} = 11$

Total float, $T_F^{ij} = T_L^j - T_E^i - t_{ij}$

Total float, $T_F^{ij} = 37 - 8 - 11$

Total float, $T_F^{ij} = 18$

Q.16 Ans:(D)

Critical path A - C - E - G - H is shown in network diagram.

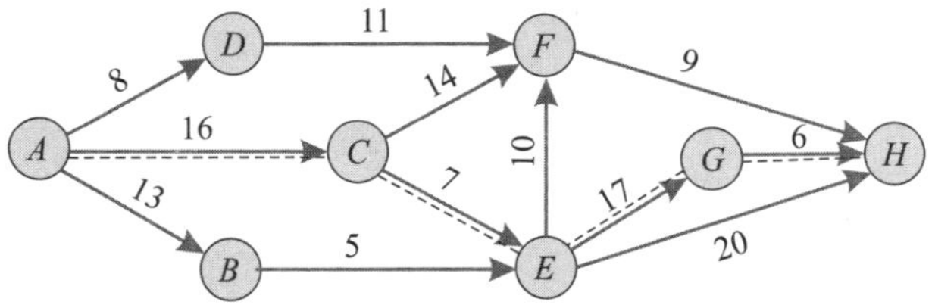

The completion time is $T = 16 + 7 + 17 + 6$

Completion time, $T = 46$ weeks

Q.17 Ans:(B)

It is for three months (periods) moving average. Hence, the last three values are to be taken.

Hence, moving average $= \dfrac{10 + 12 + 14}{3} = 12$

Forecast for the month of May $= 12$

Q.18 Ans:(A)

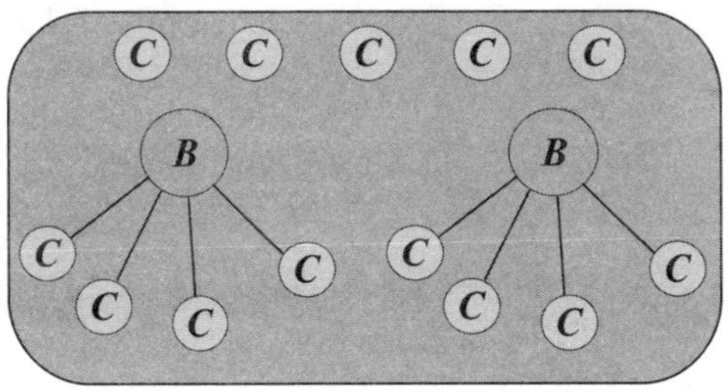

Product P

Number of C required per product P

$P =$ Number of C in item $B +$ Number of C

$P = 4 \times 2 + 5 = 13$

Number of item C required for 5 product of P

$P = 5 \times 13 = 65$

Q.19 Ans:(B)

Duration under worst environment is the pessimistic time, $t_p = 9$ days

Duration under best environment is the optimistic time, $t_o = 3$ days

Variance of activity, $V = \left(\dfrac{t_p - t_o}{6}\right)^2 = \left(\dfrac{9-3}{6}\right)^2$

Variance of activity, $V = 1$

Q.20 Ans:[0]

Total demand $= 100 + 200 + 300 = 600$

Constant rate of production

$$= \frac{600}{3} = 200 \text{ units per month}$$

Cumulative production	200	400	600
Cumulative demand	100	300	600
Excess/shortage	100	100	0

There is no shortage and no need for initial inventory.

Hence, initial inventory required = Zero

Q.21 Ans:[23.5]

The forecast for July is to be calculated by weighted moving average method.

Weighted moving average $= \dfrac{\sum w_i x_i}{\sum w_i}$

Forecast for July, $F_{\text{July}} = \dfrac{\sum w_i x_i}{\sum w_i}$

Forecast for July, $F_{\text{July}} = \dfrac{10 \times 1 + 20 \times 2 + 30 \times 3}{1 + 2 + 3}$

Forecast for July, $F_{\text{July}} = 23\frac{1}{3}$ ton

Q.22 Ans:[84.1]

Given that:

Expected completion time for the project, $T_E = 20$ months

Scheduled completion time for the project, $T_S = 24$ months

Standard deviation $\sigma = 4$ months

Therefore, normal deviate, $z = \dfrac{T_S - T_E}{\sigma}$

or $z = \dfrac{24 - 20}{4} = +1$

From the probability function table, the probability corresponding to $z = +1$, is 84.1%.

84.1% probability that the project will be completed in 24 months.

Q.23 Ans:[490]

Given that:

Smoothing constant, $\alpha = 0.2$

Demand for n th period, $= 500$

Actual demand for nth period, $= 450$

Forecast for $(n+1)$th period

$$= \text{Actual demand} \times \alpha + \text{demand} \times (1-\alpha)$$

Forecast for $(n+1)$th period

$$= 450 \times 0.2 + 500 \times (1-0.2)$$

$$\text{Forecast for } (n+1)\text{th period} = 490$$

Q.24 Ans:[3000]

Given that:

Fixed cost, $F = \text{Rs. } 6000$

Variable cost, $V = \text{Rs. } 10$ per product

Selling price, $S = \text{Rs. } 12$ per product

Let n be the break-even volume of product.

At break-even point; $F + n \times V = n \times S$

Volume at break-even, $n = \dfrac{F}{S-V} = \dfrac{6000}{12-10}$

$$n = 3000$$

Q.25 Ans:[380]

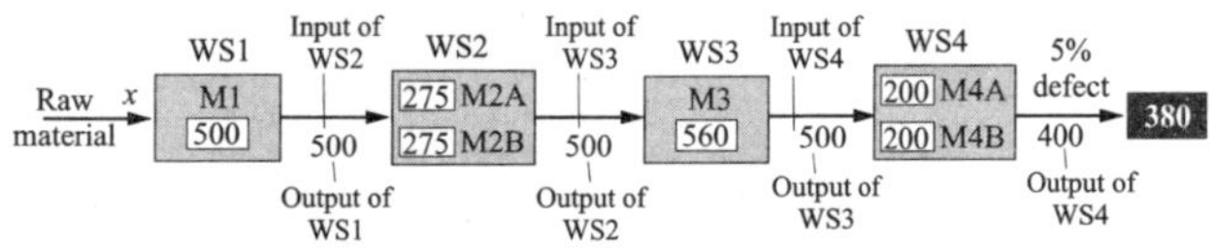

Q.26 Ans:[8.5]

Given that:

$$t_o = 3 \text{ days}, t_p = 8 \text{ days and } t_m = 10 \text{ days}$$

Expected time, $t_e = \dfrac{t_o + 4t_m + t_p}{6}$

$$t_e = \frac{3 + 4 \times 10 + 8}{6}$$

$$t_e = 8.5 \text{ days}$$

Q.27 Ans:[4]

Total time for wash one car, $t = 3 + 0.2 \times 3$

$$t = 3.6 \text{ min}$$

Number of car wash in one hour is:

$$n = \frac{60}{3.6}$$

Number of car wash stalls, $N = \dfrac{60}{\left(\dfrac{60}{3.6}\right)} = 3.6 \approx 4$

$$\text{Number of car wash stalls, } N = 4$$

Q.28 Ans:[1600]

	Process X	Process Y
Fixed cost (F)	Rs. 40,000	Rs. 16,000
Variable cost (V)	Rs. 9 per unit	Rs. 24 per unit

Let Q be the quantity of units.

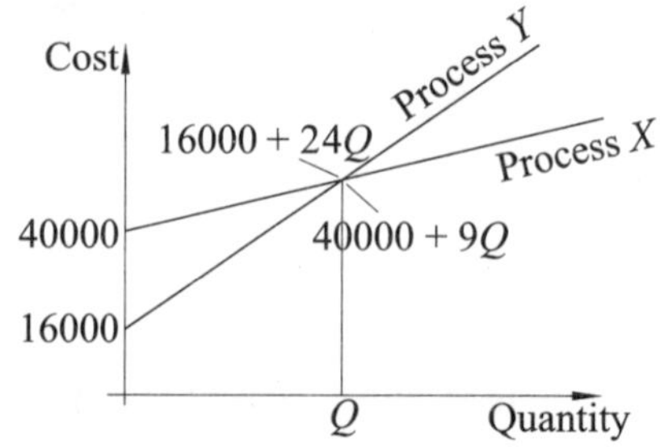

Total cost of process X = Total cost of process Y

$$40000 + 9Q = 16000 + 24Q$$

$$Q = 1600$$

Q.29 Ans:[22]

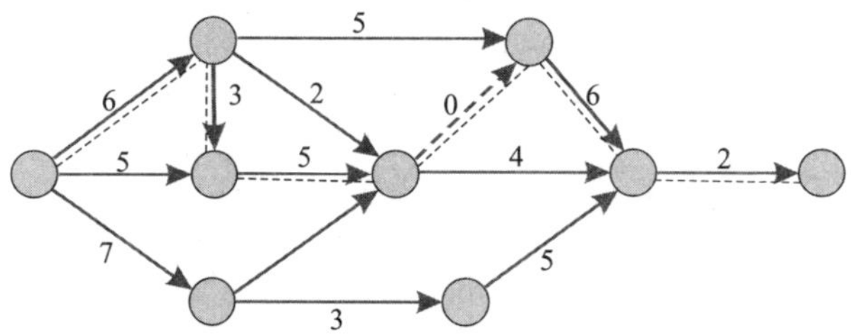

$$\text{Completion time, } T = 6 + 3 + 5 + 0 + 6 + 2 = 22 \text{ days}$$

Q.30 Ans:[100]

Total demand for four months,

$$D = 150 + 100 + 250 + 300 = 800 \text{ units}$$

Total production for four months,

$$P = 200 \times 4 = 800 \text{ units}$$

As demand and production for four months are same, there will be no change in the inventory.

Final inventory = Initial inventory = 100 units

Q.31 Ans:(D)

Let F, V and S be the fixed cost, variable cost per unit and selling price per unit respectively.

Break-even point (quality), $Q = \dfrac{F}{S-V}$

From which

Break-even point can lowered by reducing the variable cost (V).

Q.32 Ans:(A)

Jobs	Duration in days			Expected time
	Optimistic t_o	Most likely t_m	Pessimistic t_p	$t_e = \frac{t_o + 4t_m + t_p}{6}$
1 - 2	3	6	15	7
2 - 3	6	12	30	14
2 - 4	5	11	17	11
3 - 4	3	9	27	11
3 - 5	1	4	7	4
5 - 6	2	5	8	5
3 - 6	4	19	28	18
4 - 6	2	5	14	6

The network for the data is given in the figure.

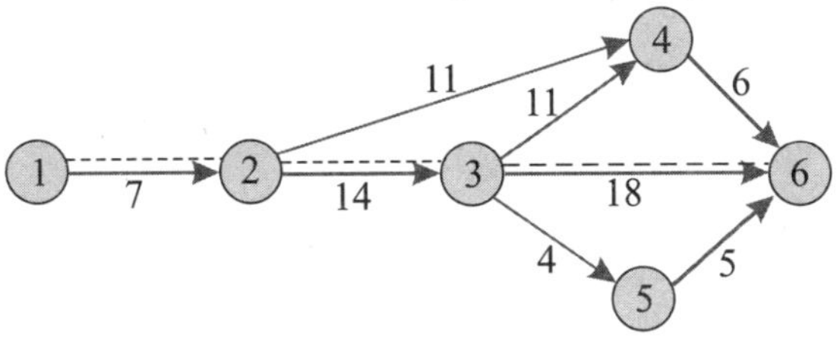

Critical path (1- 2- 3- 6) is with maximum target time of $T_{1\text{-}2\text{-}3\text{-}6} = 7 + 14 + 18 = 39$ days

Q.33 Ans:(D)

Path	Optimistic time t_o	Most likely time t_m	Pessimistic time t_p	Expected time t_e
1 - 2 - 7 - 8	19	26	35	26.34
1 - 2 - 6 - 8	17	26	40	26.83
1 - 3 - 6 - 8	18	27	36	27.00
1 - 4 - 5 - 6 - 8	19	28	39	28.33

Critical path (1-4-5-6-8) is with maximum time of 28.33.

Critical path is 1-4-5-6-8

Q.34 Ans:(C)

Activity	T_E (days)	V (days)^2
a	17	4
b	15	4
c	8	1
	$\sum T_E = 40$	$\sum V = 9,\ \sigma = \sqrt{\sum V} = 3$

$$\sum T_E = 40 \text{ and } T_S = 43 \text{ days}$$

Normal deviate, $z = \dfrac{43 - 40}{3}$

or $z = 1$

From the probability function table, the probability corresponding to $z = 1$ is 84.1%.

Probability of completing the project in 43 days is 84.1%

Q.35 Ans:(A)

Car	1	2	3	4	5	6
Denting time (h)	4	7	3	12	11	9
Painting time (h)	11	7	10	8	10	13

By examining the rows, we find the smallest value. It is denting time of 3 h for car 3. Thus we schedule car 3 first as shown below:

Car	3					

The reduced set of denting and painting time becomes:

Car	1	2	4	5	6
Denting time (h)	4	7	12	11	9
Painting time (h)	11	7	8	10	13

The smallest value is denting time of 4 h for car 1. Thus we schedule car 1 next to car 3 as shown below:

Car	3	1				

The reduced set of denting and painting time becomes:

Car	2	4	5	6
Denting time (h)	7	12	11	9
Painting time (h)	7	8	10	13

The smallest value is denting time 7 for car 2. Thus, we schedule car 2 next to car 1,

Similarly, we obtain

Car	3	1	2	6	5	4

Q.36 Ans:(A)

Least cost method consists in allocating as much as possible in the lowest cost cell and then further allocation is done in the cell with the second lowest cost and so on.

Solution obtained by least cost method.

	Destinations				Supply
	a	b	c	d	
P	10	22	0 (8)	22	~~8~~
Q	15 (5)	20	12	8 (8)	~~13~~
R	20	12 (11)	10	15	~~11~~
Demand	~~5~~	~~11~~	~~8~~	~~8~~	

Supply of military equipment from origin Q to destination a, b, c and d are $Q - a = 5$, $Q - b = 0$, $Q - c = 0$ and $Q - d = 8$.

$a - 5,\ b - 0,\ c - 0,\ d - 8$

Q.37 Ans:(B)

Critical path is 1-2-3-5-6-7-8-9

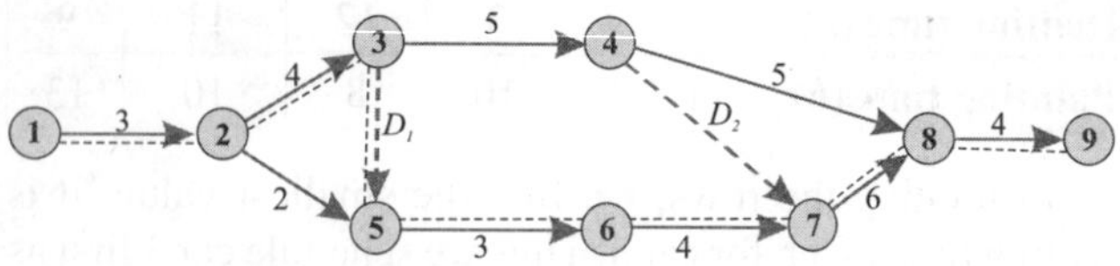

Q.38 Ans:(D)

Given that:

Previous forecast, $F_{t-1} = 64$

Previous actual demand, $D_{t-1} = 59$

Smoothing factor, $\alpha = 0.3$

Forecast for next period is:

$$F_t = F_{t-1} + \alpha(D_{t-1} - F_{t-1})$$

$$F_t = 64 + 0.3 \times (59 - 64)$$

Forecast for next period, $F_t = 62.5$

Q.39 Ans:(D)

Maximum output = 360 units per day

Actual output = 306 units per day

$$\text{System efficiency, } \eta = \frac{\text{Actual output}}{\text{Maximum output}} = \frac{306}{360}$$

System efficiency, $\eta = 85\%$

Q.40 Ans:(A)

	Fixed cost F	Variable Cost/unit (Rs.) V	Revenue per unit (Rs.) S	Break even quantity $Q = F/(S-V)$
(A)	30,000	10	40	1000 ← minimum
(B)	40,000	15	40	1600
(C)	50,000	25	40	3333
(D)	60,000	30	40	6000

Q.41 Ans:(D)

Given that:

Selling price per unit, S = Rs. 12.50

Fixed cost, $F = 60,000$

Variable cost per unit, V = Rs. 7.50

Let N be the number of unit produce

Profit = Selling cost − (Fixed cost + Variable cost)

$$12000 = 12.5N - (60000 + 7.5N)$$

Number of unit produce, $N = 14400$

Q.42 Ans:(B)

Job	Machine A (h)	Machine B (h)
1	5	2
2	1	6
3	9	7
4	3	8
5	10	4

By examining the columns, we find the smallest value. It is machine A and time 1 h for job 2. Thus, we schedule job 2 first

Job	2				

The reduced set of machine time becomes:

Job	Machine A (h)	Machine B (h)
1	5	2
3	9	7
4	3	8
5	10	4

The smallest value is machine B of time 2 h for job 1 in the second column. Thus, we schedule job 1 last as shown below.

Job	2				1

Similarly, we get the optimal sequence as:

Job	2	4	3	5	1

Sequence for jobs $2 \to 4 \to 3 \to 5 \to 1$

Q.43 Ans:(A)

Job	Machine A (h)	Machine B (h)
1	5	2
2	1	6
3	9	7
4	3	8
5	10	4

By examining the columns, we find the smallest value. It is machine A and time 1 h for job 2. Thus, we schedule job 2 first

Job	2				

The reduced set of machine time becomes

Job	Machine A (h)	Machine B (h)
1	5	2
3	9	7
4	3	8
5	10	4

The smallest value is machine B of time of 2 h for job 1 in the second column. Thus we schedule job 1 last as shown below:

Job	2				1

Similarly, we get the optimal sequence as

Job	2	4	3	5	1

The optimal time of the sequence is found using the following table:

Job	**Machine A (h)**		**Machine B (h)**	
	Time in	Time out	Time in	Time out
2	0	1	1	7
4	1	4	7	15
3	4	13	15	22
5	13	23	23	27
1	23	28	28	30

Total time to complete jobs = 30 h

Q.44 Ans:(D)

Let N be the number of component at break-even.

Total cost of N component by standard machine,

$$T_{\text{stand-m/c}} = \left(\frac{30}{60} + \frac{22}{60}N\right)200 \qquad \text{(i)}$$

Total cost of N component by automatic machine

$$T_{\text{auto-m/c}} = \left(2 + \frac{5}{60}N\right)800 \qquad \text{(ii)}$$

From Equations (i) and (ii), we have

$$T_{\text{stand-m/c}} = T_{\text{auto-m/c}}$$

$$\left(\frac{30}{60} + \frac{22}{60}N\right)200 = \left(2 + \frac{5}{60}N\right)800$$

From which

$$N = 225$$

Q.45 Ans:(C)

Time required to weld product A;

$$t_A = \frac{20}{60} \times 450 = 150 \text{ min}$$

Time required to weld product B;

$$t_B = \frac{40}{60} \times 360 = 240 \text{ min}$$

Time required to weld product C;

$$t_C = \frac{50}{60} \times 240 = 200 \text{ min}$$

Hence, total time required by one line

$$T = t_A + t_B + t_C$$

$$T = 150 + 240 + 200 = 590 \text{ min}$$

Number of welding line required $= \frac{590}{220} = 2.68$

Number of welding line required = 3

Q.46 Ans:(C)

Activity	**Variance (V)**
$a \to b$	4
$b \to c$	16
$c \to d$	4
$d \to e$	1
	$\sum V = 25$

Standard deviation, $\sigma = \sqrt{\sum V} = \sqrt{25}$

$$\sigma = 5$$

Q.47 Ans:(D)

The feasible region is as shown in figure.

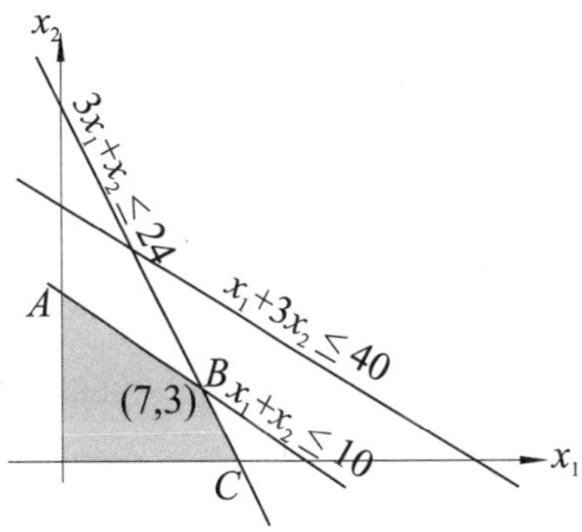

The feasible region has three corner A, B and C

The value of profit $z = 2x_1 + 5x_2$ at these points are:

$$z_A = 2 \times 0 + 5 \times 10 = 50$$

$$z_B = 2 \times 7 + 5 \times 3 = 29$$

$$z_C = 2 \times 8 + 5 \times 0 = 16$$

$$z_A = 50$$

Q.48 Ans:(A)

Let T_s, T_q and μ be the mean waiting time in the system, mean waiting time in queue and mean service rate respectively.

$$T_s = T_q + \frac{1}{\mu}$$

or $$50 = 30 + \frac{1}{\mu}$$

$$\mu = \frac{1}{20} \text{ / min} = 3/\text{h}$$

Mean rate of service $\mu = 3/\text{h}$

Q.49 Ans:(B)

Given that:

$T_E = 16$ days

$\sigma = 2.44$

$T_s = 15$ days

Normal deviate, $z = \dfrac{T_s - T_E}{\sigma}$

$$z = \frac{15 - 16}{2.44} = 0.41$$

From the probability function table, the probability corresponding to $z = 0.41$ is 34%

34% probability of completion in 15 days

Q.50 Ans:(C)

Given that:

Fixed cost, $F = 1520000$

Variable cost per product, $V = \dfrac{2100000}{15000} = 140$

Selling price per piece, $S = 300$

Let n be the break-even quantity

$$F + nV = nS$$

or $n = \dfrac{F}{S - V} = \dfrac{1520000}{300 - 140}$

or $n = 9500$

Break-even quantity, $n = 9500$

Q.51 Ans:[43]

	Machines		
Jobs	M_1	M_2	M_3
A	17	25	31
B	10	15	16
C	12	14	11

Subtract the minimum element of each row from all the elements of the row.

	Machine		
Job	M_1	M_2	M_3
A	0	8	14
B	0	5	6
C	1	3	0

Now subtract the minimum element of each remaining row.

	Machine		
Job	M_1	M_2	M_3
A	0	8	14
B	0	0	1
C	1	3	0

Therefore, optimal assignment is $A \rightarrow M_1$, $B \rightarrow M_2$, $C \rightarrow M_3$

Minimum cost $= 17 + 15 + 11$

Minimum cost =Rs. 43

Q.52 Ans:[19]

Material cost $= 4 \times 200 =$ Rs. 800

Labour cost $= 3 \times 200 =$ Rs. 600

Overhead cost $= \dfrac{400}{100} \times 600 =$ Rs. 2400

Total cost = Material cost + Labour cost + Overhead cost

Total cost $= 800 + 600 + 2400 =$ Rs. 3800

Cost per piece $= \dfrac{3800}{200}$

Cost per piece = Rs. 19

Q.53 Ans:[39]

Jobs	Duration (in days)			
	Optimistic (t_o)	Most likely (t_m)	Pessimistic (t_p)	Expected (t_E)
1- 2	3	6	15	7
2- 3	6	12	30	14
2- 4	5	11	17	11
3- 4	3	9	27	11
3- 5	1	4	7	4
5- 6	2	5	8	5
3- 6	4	19	28	18
4- 6	2	5	14	6

The network is drawn below:

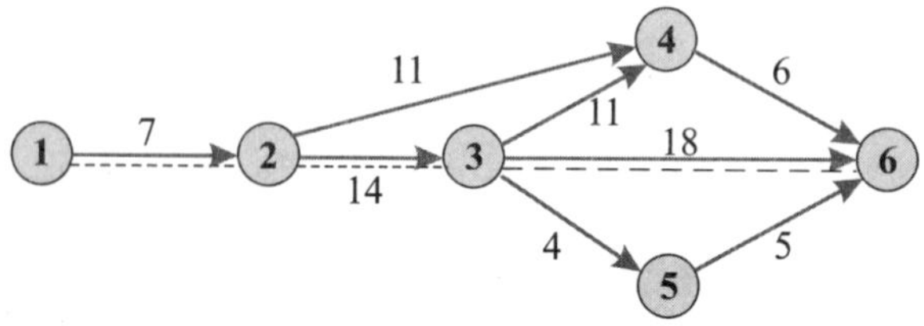

Critical path (1→2→3→6) is shown by double line on the diagram.

Expected completion time, $T_E = 7 + 14 + 18$

$$T_E = 39 \text{ days}$$

Q.54 Ans:[25]

The network for the given data is given below:

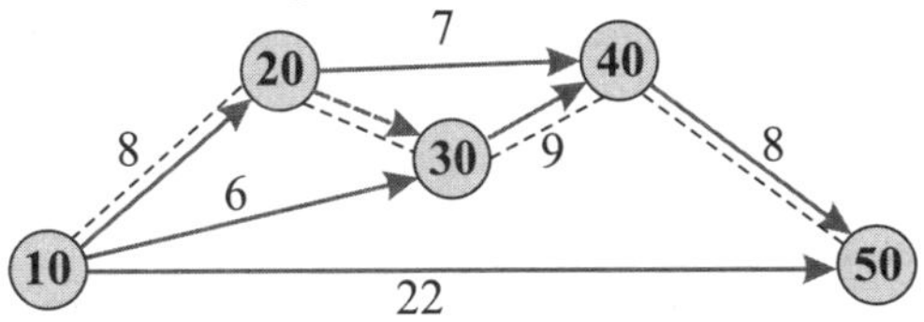

Critical path (10-20-30-40-50) is shown by dotted line on the diagram.

Expected completion time, $T_E = 8 + 0 + 9 + 8$

$$T_E = 25$$

Q.55 Ans:[16]

Given that:

Optimistic time, $t_o = 9$ days

Pessimistic time, $t_p = 21$ days

Most likely time, $t_l = 15$ days

Completion time, $t_s = 13$ days

Expected completion time, $t_E = \frac{t_o + 4t_l + t_p}{6}$

$$t_E = \frac{9 + 4\times 15 + 21}{6} = 15 \text{ days}$$

Standard deviation, $\sigma = \sqrt{\left(\frac{t_p - t_o}{6}\right)^2} = \left(\frac{21-9}{6}\right) = 2$

Normal deviation, $z = \frac{t_s - t_E}{\sigma} = \frac{13-15}{2}$

$$z = -1$$

From the probability function table, the probability corresponding to $z = -1$ is 16%.

16% probability of completion in 13 days

Q.56 Ans:[496]

Given that:

$$D_t = 480, F_t = 500 \text{ and } \alpha = 0.2$$

Forecast for period $(t+1)$ is:

$$F_{t+1} = F_t + \alpha(D_t - F_t)$$

$$F_{t+1} = 500 + 0.2 \times (480 - 500)$$

Forecast for period $(t+1)$, $F_{t+1} = 496$

Q.57 Ans:[10000]

Given that:

Fixed cost, $F =$ Rs. 400000

Variable cost, $V =$ Rs. 20 per product

Selling cost, $S =$ Rs. 60 per product

Let x be the numbers of product at break-even.

$$F + x V = x S$$

$$x = \frac{F}{V - S} = \frac{400000}{60 - 20}$$

$$x = 10000$$

Q.58 Ans:[97.7]

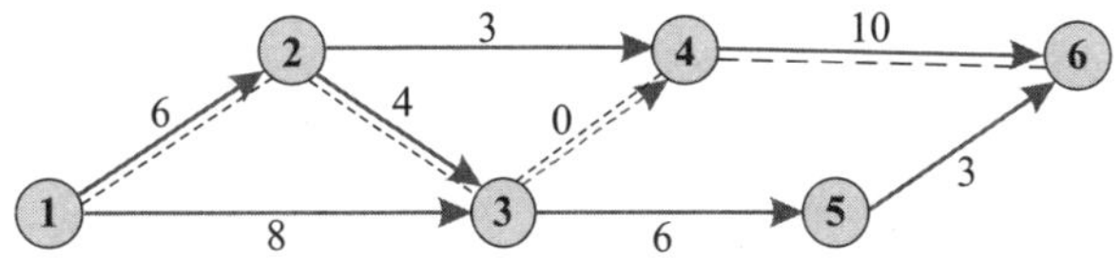

Critical path (1-2-3-4-6) is shown by dotted lines on the diagram.

Expected completion time, $T_E = 6 + 4 + 0 + 10 = 20$ days

and given $T_s = 24$ days

$$\sum V = 4$$

$$\sigma = \sqrt{\sum V} = 2$$

Standard deviation, $z = \frac{T_s - T_s}{\sigma} = \frac{24-20}{2} = 2$

From the probability function table, the probability corresponding to $z = +2$ is 97.7%.

97.7% probability of completion of the project is 24 days.

Q.59 Ans:[28.33]

Path	Optimistic time (t_o)	Most likely time (t_m)	Pessimistic time (t_p)	Expected time $t_E = \frac{t_0 + 4t_m + t_p}{6}$
1-4-5-6-8	19	28	39	28.33

Expected time for the path 1–4–5–6–8 is 28.33 days

Q.60 Ans:[5]

Time required for handling one car is

$$t_{wash} = 4 + 4 \times 0.25 = 5 \text{ min}$$

Each stall handle $= \frac{60}{5} = 12$ cars in one hours

Therefore, the number of stalls $= \frac{60}{12} = 5$

Number of stalls = 5

Q.61 Ans:[62]

Sequence of car for denting and painting is given by

$$3 \to 1 \to 6 \to 5 \to 4 \to 2$$

Car	Denting time		Painting time	
	in	out	in	out
3	0	3	3	13
1	3	7	13	24
6	7	18	24	37
5	18	29	37	47
4	29	41	47	55
2	41	48	55	62

From which

Completion time = 62 h

Q.62 Ans:[22]

Given that:

$D_{march} = 20$ units, $F_{march} = 20$ units, $D_{April} = 25$ units, $D_{May} = 26$ units and $\alpha = 0.2$.

Forecast for the month $(t+1)$ is given by

$$F_{t+1} = F_t + \alpha(D_t - F_t)$$

Forecast for the month April

$$F_{April} = F_{March} + \alpha(D_{March} - F_{March})$$

or $F_{April} = 20 + 0.2 \times (20 - 20) = 20$

Forecast for the month May

$$F_{May} = F_{April} + \alpha(D_{April} - F_{April})$$

or $F_{May} = 20 + 0.2 \times (25 - 20) = 21$

Forecast for the month June

$$F_{June} = F_{May} + \alpha(D_{May} - F_{May})$$

or $F_{June} = 21 + 0.2 \times (26 - 21)$

$$F_{June} = 22$$

Q.63 Ans:[271]

Least cost method consists in allocating as much as possible in the lowest cost cell and then further allocation is done in the cell with the second lowest cost and so on.

Solution obtained by the least cost method.

	Destinations				Supply
	a	b	c	d	
P	10	22	0 (8)	22	~~8~~
Q	15 (5)	20	12	8 (8)	~~13~~
R	20	12 (11)	10	15	~~11~~
Demand	~~5~~	~~11~~	~~8~~	~~8~~	

Cost of shipment $= 0 \times 8 + 15 \times 5 + 8 \times 8 + 12 \times 11$

Cost of shipment = 271

Q.64 Ans:[3.2]

Mean arrival rate, $\lambda = \dfrac{4}{60}$ per minute

Mean service rate, $\mu = \dfrac{1}{12}$ per minute

$$\rho = \frac{\lambda}{\mu} = \frac{4}{60} \times \frac{12}{1} = 0.8$$

Length of queue is, $L_q = \dfrac{\rho^2}{1-\rho} = \dfrac{(0.8)^2}{1-0.8}$

$$L_q = 3.2$$

Q.65 Ans:[450]

Mean arrival rate, $\lambda = 5$ units/h

Mean service rate, $\mu = 8$ units/h

$$\rho = \frac{\lambda}{\mu} = \frac{5}{8} = 0.625$$

Portion of time that service being idle

$$= 1 - \rho = 1 - 0.625 = 0.375$$

Average idle time cost of service /day

= portion of service being idle × Number of hours per day × idle time cost per hour

Average idle time cost of service /day $= 0.375 \times 8 \times 150$

Average idle time cost of service /day = Rs. 450

17 General Aptitude

GATE Syllabus

Verbal Ability: English grammar; Sentence completion; Verbal analogies, Word groups; Instructions; critical reasoning and verbal deduction.

Numerical Ability: Numerical computation; Numerical estimation; Numerical reasoning and data interpretation.

Chapter Outline

17.1 KEY CONCEPTS AND FORMULAS

Sentence

A sentence is a combination of words including a subject and a verb which express a complete idea. A sentence begins with a capital letter and ends with a period, question mark or exclamation mark. A sentence consists of two parts, i.e., subject and predicate.

Subject: The part of sentence which performs some action in a sentence is called *subject.*

Predicate: The part of sentence which tells about the subject is called *predicate.*

Kinds of Sentences

There are four kinds of sentences.

(i) Assertive or declarative sentence: A sentence that makes a statement or assertion is called an *assertive* or *declarative sentence*. Assertive sentence ends with a period.

(ii) Interrogative sentence: A sentence that asks a question is called an *interrogative sentence.* Interrogative sentence ends with question mark.

(iii) Imperative sentence: A sentence that expresses a request, command or advice is called an *imperative sentence*. It ends with a period.

(iv) Exclamatory sentence: A sentence that expresses strong feelings or emotions is called an *exclamatory sentence*. These sentences express surprise, joy, sorrow, appreciation, love excitement, frustration, anger, etc. An exclamatory sentence ends with exclamation mark.

Kinds of Sentences According to Structure

Simple sentence: A simple sentence consists of only one independent clause containing a subject and a verb and it expresses complete thought. There is no dependent clause.

Compound sentence: A compound sentence consists of at least two independent clauses joined by coordinating conjunctions. There is no dependent clause in compound sentence.

Complex sentence: A complex sentence consists of one independent clause and at least one dependent clause joined by subordinating conjunction (because, although, since, when, unless etc.) or relative pronoun (that, who, which etc).

Complex compound sentence: A complex compound sentence consists of at least two independents and one or more dependent clauses.

Tense

An aspect of verb which tells the time of an action is called *tense*. There are mainly three kinds of tenses:

(i) Present tense, (ii) Past tense, and (iii) Future tense.

Each of present, past and future tense is further divided into four kinds:

(i) Simple (Indefinite), (ii) Continuous (Progressive), (iii) Perfect, and (iv) Perfect Continuous (Perfect progressive).

Present Tense

(i) Present simple tense, (ii) Present continuous tense,

(iii) Present perfect tense, (iv) Present perfect continuous tense.

Past Tense

(i) Past simple tense, (ii) Past continuous tense, (iii) Past perfect tense, (iv) Past perfect continuous tense.

Future Tense

(i) Future simple tense, (ii) Future continuous tense, (iii) Future perfect tense, (iv) Future perfect continuous tense.

Numerical Ability

Numbers

Natural numbers → {1, 2, 3, 4, ...}

Whole numbers → {0, 1, 2, 3, 4,. . . . . .}

Integers → {–3, –2, –1, 0, 1, 2, 3, ...}

Rational numbers → $\left\{\frac{1}{2}, \frac{3}{5}, -\frac{3}{4}, 0, 3, 2, -5, \ldots\right\}$

Irrational numbers → $\{\pi, \sqrt{2}, \sqrt{5}, \ldots\}$

Test for Divisibility of Numbers

Divisibility by 2: If the last digit is an even number or it has zero '0' at the end.

Divisibility by 3: If the sum of the digit given number is divisible by 3.

Divisibility by 4: If the number formed by the last two digits of the given number is divisible by 4 or if the last two digits are '00'.

Divisibility by 5: If the last digit of the given number is 0 or 5.

Divisibility by 6: If the given number is divisible by both 2 and 3.

Divisibility by 8: If the number formed by the last three digits of the given number is divisible by 8 or if the last three digits are '000'.

Divisibility by 9: If the sum of the digits of the given number is divisible by 9.

Divisibility by 11: If the difference of the sum of its digits in odd place and sum of its digits in even place is either zero (0) or multiple of 11.

Division and Remainder

Divisor) Dividend (Quotient

Remainder

$$\text{Dividend} = \text{Divisor} \times \text{Quotient} + \text{Remainder}$$

Number Series

A series is a sequence of numbers. These numbers are called terms of the *sequence*. All the terms of sequence are arranged according to a certain predefined rule. Following are the important rules or order on which the number can be made.

(i) Pure series (perfect square, perfect cube, ...)

(ii) Difference series, (iii) Mixed series, (iv) Geometric series, (v) Two-tier arithmetic series, and (vi) Three-tier arithmetic series.

Progressions

Arithmetic Progression (A.P.)

A sequence whose terms increase or decrease by a fixed number is called an *arithmetic progression*. The A.P. can be written as $a, a+d, a+2d, a+3d, \ldots a+(n-1)d$

$$\text{Sum of } n \text{ terms, } S_n = \frac{n}{2}[2a + (n-1)d]$$

Geometric Progression (G.P.)

A sequence (finite or infinite) of non-zero numbers in which every term, except the first one, bears a constant ratio with its preceding term, is called a *geometric progression*. The G.P. can be written as a, ar, ar^2, $ar^3, \ldots ar^{n-1}$.

Sum of n terms, $S_n = \dfrac{a(r^n - 1)}{r - 1}$

Sum Rules

Sum of n terms

$$1 + 2 + 3 + \ldots\ldots = \frac{n(n+1)}{2}$$

$$1 + 3 + 5 + 7 + \ldots\ldots = n^2$$

$$2 + 4 + 6 + 8 + \ldots\ldots = \frac{n(n+1)(2n+1)}{6}$$

$$1^2 + 2^2 + 3^2 + \ldots\ldots = \left[\frac{n(n+1)}{2}\right]^2$$

HCF and LCM

Highest common factor (HCF): If two or more numbers are broken into their prime factors, then the product of the maximum common prime factors in the given numbers is the HCF of the number.

Lowest common multiple (LCM): The LCM of two or more than two numbers is the product of the highest powers of all the prime factors that occur in these numbers.

Common multiple: A common multiple of two or more numbers is a number which is exactly divisible by each one of them.

$$\text{LCM} = \frac{\text{LCM of the number in numerators}}{\text{HCF of the numbers in denominators}}$$

$$\text{HCF} = \frac{\text{HCF of the number in numerators}}{\text{LCM of the numbers in denominators}}$$

Product of two numbers

= LCM of the numbers × HCF of numbers

Simplification

$$a^m \times a^n = a^{m+n}$$

$$a^m \div a^n = a^{m-n}$$

$$(a^m)^n = a^{mn}$$

If $x = n(n+1)$, then

$$\sqrt{x - \sqrt{x - \sqrt{x - \sqrt{x - \ldots\ldots\infty}}}} = n$$

$$\sqrt{x + \sqrt{x + \sqrt{x + \sqrt{x + \ldots\ldots\infty}}}} = n + 1$$

Algebraic Formula

$$(a+b)^2 = a^2 + b^2 + 2ab,\ (a-b)^2 = a^2 + b^2 - 2ab$$

$$(a+b)^2 + (a-b)^2 = 2(a^2 + b^2)$$

$$(a+b)^2 - (a-b)^2 = 4ab$$

$$(a+b)^3 = a^3 + b^3 + 3ab(a+b)$$

$$(a-b)^3 = a^3 - b^3 - 3ab(a-b)$$

$$a^3 + b^3 = (a+b)(a^2 - ab + b^2)$$

$$a^3 - b^3 = (a-b)(a^2 + ab + b^2)$$

$$a^3 + b^3 + c^3 - 3abc$$
$$= (a+b+c)(a^2 + b^2 + c^2 - ab - bc - ca)$$

Logarithms

If for positive real number $(a \neq 1)$ $a^m = b$, then $\log a^b = m$.

$$\log_a mn = \log_a m + \log_a n$$

$$\log_a\left(\frac{m}{n}\right) = \log_a m - \log_a n$$

$$\log_a (m^n) = n \log_a m$$

$$\log_n m = \frac{\log_a m}{\log_a n}$$

So, $\log_n m = \dfrac{\log m}{\log n}$, where m, n, a are positive and $n \neq 1$, $a \neq 1$

$\log_b a \times \log_a b = 1$, where a, b are positive and not equal to 1.

$a^{\log_a x} = x$, where, a and x are positive, $a \neq 1$.

Percentage

To convert any fraction to rate per cent, multiply it by 100 and put (%) sign.

To convert a rate per cent to a fraction, divide it by 100 and remove the (%) sign.

Average

$$\text{Average} = \frac{\text{Sum of quantities}}{\text{Number of quantities}},\ x_{\text{avg}} = \frac{\sum x}{n}$$

$$\text{Average of } 1, 2, 3, \ldots\ldots n = \frac{n+1}{2}$$

If a certain distance is covered at a speed of x km/h and the same distance is covered at a speed of y km/h, the average speed during the entire journey is $\left(\dfrac{2xy}{x+y}\right)$ km/h.

Ratio and Proportion

A ratio is a comparison of two quantities by division. The equality of two ratios is called *proportion*.

$$\frac{a}{b} = \frac{c}{d} \quad \text{or} \quad a:b::c:d$$

If $\frac{a}{b} = \frac{c}{d}$ then $\frac{a+b}{a-b} = \frac{c-d}{c-d} = \frac{a}{b} = \frac{c}{d}$

Chain Rule

$$\frac{\text{Man}_1 \times \text{Days}_1 \times \text{Work rate}_1}{\text{Amount of work done}_1} = \frac{\text{Man}_2 \times \text{Days}_2 \times \text{Work rate}_2}{\text{Amount of work done}_2}$$

Time and Work

If A can do a piece of work in X days and B can do the same work in Y days, then both of them working together will do the same work in $\frac{XY}{X+Y}$ days.

If A, B and C, while working alone, can complete a work in X, Y and Z days respectively, then they will together complete the work in $\frac{XYZ}{XY+YZ+ZX}$ days.

There are two groups of people with same efficiency. In first group M_1 persons can do W_1 works in D_1 time and in the other, M_2 persons can do W_2 works in D_2 time. The relationship between two groups is given by

$$M_1 D_1 W_2 = M_2 D_2 W_1$$

Simple and Compound Interest

Simple interest, $\text{SI} = \frac{P \times R \times T}{100}$

Amount = Principal + Simple interest

Compound interest, $\text{CI} = P\left[\left(1+\frac{R}{100}\right)^n - 1\right]$

If the interest is compounded n times a year, then

Amount, $A = P\left(1+\frac{R}{100 \times n}\right)^{nt}$

Pipes and Cisterns

If an inlet can completely fill the empty tank in X hours, the part of the tank filled in 1 hour $= \frac{1}{X}$.

If an outlet can empty the full tank in Y hours, the part of the tank emptied in 1 hour $= \frac{1}{Y}$.

If both inlet and outlet are open, net part of the tank filled in 1 hour $= \frac{1}{X} - \frac{1}{Y}$.

Time and Distance

$$\text{Speed} = \frac{\text{Distance travelled}}{\text{Time taken}}, \quad V_{\text{avg}} = \frac{\sum d}{\sum t}$$

$$V_{\text{avg}} = \frac{\sum Vt}{\sum t}, \quad V_{\text{avg}} = \frac{\sum d}{\sum\left(\frac{d}{t}\right)}$$

Boats and Streams

If the speed of boat (or swimmer) be x km/h and the speed of the stream be y km/h, then

(i) Speed of boat (or swimmer) downstream = $(x + y)$ km/h

(ii) Speed of boat (or swimmer) upstream = $(x - y)$ km/h

Mensuration

Triangle

Area, $A = \frac{1}{2}ah$

$A = \sqrt{s(s-a)(s-b)(s-c)}$

where $s = \frac{1}{2}(a+b+c)$

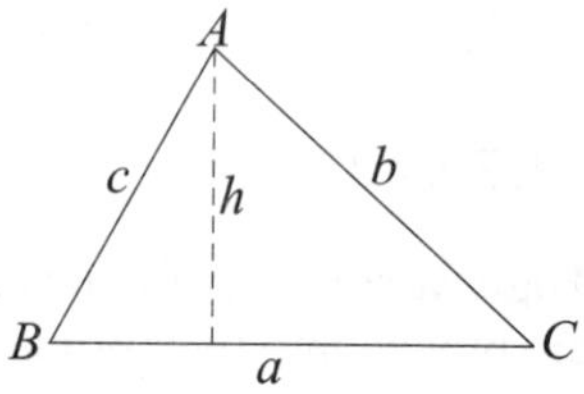

Perimeter, $P = a + b + c$

Regular Polygon

If all the sides of a polygon are equal, it is called a *regular polygon*.

Sum of exterior angles $= 2\pi$

Sum of interior angles $= (n-2)\pi$

Cube

Volume of cube $= a^3$, Surface area $= 6a^2$

Right Circular Cylinder

Volume of cylinder, $V = \pi r^2 h$

Area of curve surface $= 2\pi rh$

Total surface area $= 2\pi r^2 + 2\pi rh$

Right Circular Cone

Volume of cone, $V = \frac{1}{3}\pi r^2 h$

Curve surface area $= \pi rl = \pi r\sqrt{h^2 + r^2}$

Total surface area $= \pi r(r + l)$

Sphere

Volume of sphere $V = \frac{4}{3}\pi r^3$, Surface area $= 4\pi r^2$

Data Interpretation

The process of evaluating data using analytical and logical reasoning to examine each component of the data provided. Techniques for interpretation of data are:

(i) Ratio, (ii) Percentage, (iii) Rate, and (iv) Average

Type of Data Representation

(i) Tables, (ii) Line graphs, (iii) Bar graphs, (iv) Pie charts and (v) Venn diagram.

Quadratic Equation

Quadratic equation, $ax^2 + bx + c = 0$

Roots are: $\alpha = \dfrac{-b + \sqrt{b^2 - 4ac}}{2a}, \beta = \dfrac{-b - \sqrt{b^2 - 4ac}}{2a}$

$$\alpha + \beta = -\frac{b}{a}, \qquad \alpha\beta = \frac{c}{a}$$

Quadratic equation of given roots α and β is

$$x^2 - (\alpha + \beta)x + \alpha\beta = 0$$

Permutation and Combination

Permutations (represented by ^nP_r) can be defined as the number of ways in which r things at a time can be selected and arranged at a time from the amongst n things.

$$^nP_r = \frac{n!}{(n-r)!}$$

Combinations (represented by ^nC_r) can be defined as the number of ways in which r things at a time can be selected from the amongst n things available for selection.

$$^nC_r = \frac{n!}{r!(n-r)!}$$

Probability

Probability, $P(A) = \dfrac{\text{Number of cases favourable to } A}{\text{Number of possible outcomes}}$

Operations on Sets

Union of sets: Let A and B be two given sets. Then the union of A and B is the set of all those elements which belong to either A or B or both.

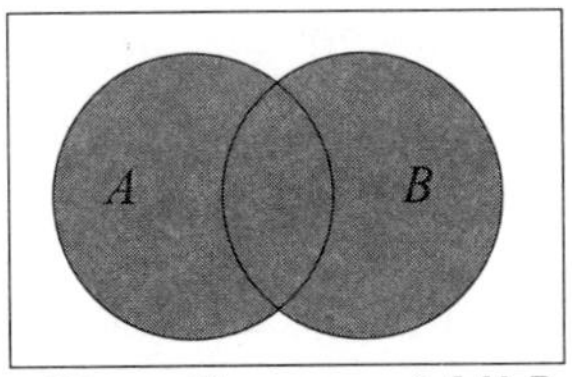

Venn diagram of $A \cup B$

Intersection of sets: Let A and B be two given sets. Then the intersection of A and B is the set of elements which belong to both A and B.

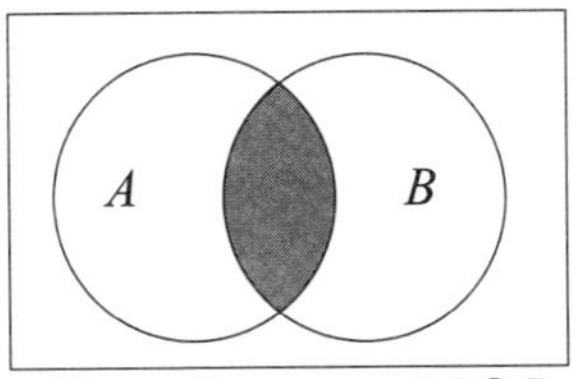

Venn diagram of $A \cap B$

17.2 SOLVED EXAMPLES

Previous Years GATE Questions

Example 17.1

The total exports and revenues from the exports of a country are given in the two pie charts below. The pie chart for exports shows the quantity of each item as a percentage of the total quantity of exports. The pie chart for the revenues shows the percentage of the total revenue generated through export of each item. The total quantity of exports of all the items is five lakh tonnes and the total revenues are 250 crore rupees. What is the ratio of the revenue generated through export of Item 1 per kilogram to the revenue generated through export of Item 4 per kilogram?

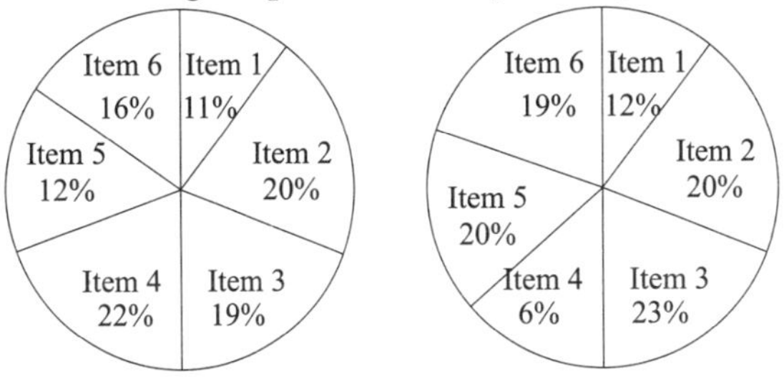

Exports **Revenues**

(A) 1:2 (B) 2:1 (C) 1:4 (D) 4:1

GATE 2014(BT)

Solution

Items	Exports		Revenues		Rs./kg
Item 1	11%	55×10^6	12%	Rs. 3000×10^6	54.45
Item 2	20%		20%		
Item 3	19%		23%		
Item 4	22%	110×10^6	6%	Rs. 1500×10^6	13.63
Item 5	12%		20%		
Item 6	16%		19%		
Total		500×10^6 kg		Rs. 25000×10^6	

The ratio of the revenue generated through export of Item 1 per kilogram to the revenue generated through export of Item 4 per kilogram is

$$= \frac{54.45}{13.63} = 4$$

4:1

Example 17.2

X is 1 km to the northeast of Y. Y is 1 km to the southeast of Z. W is 1 km to the west of Z. P is 1 km to the south of W. Q is 1 km to the east of P. What is the distance between X and Q in km?

(A) 1 (B) $\sqrt{2}$ (C) $\sqrt{3}$ (D) 2

GATE 2014(BT)

Solution

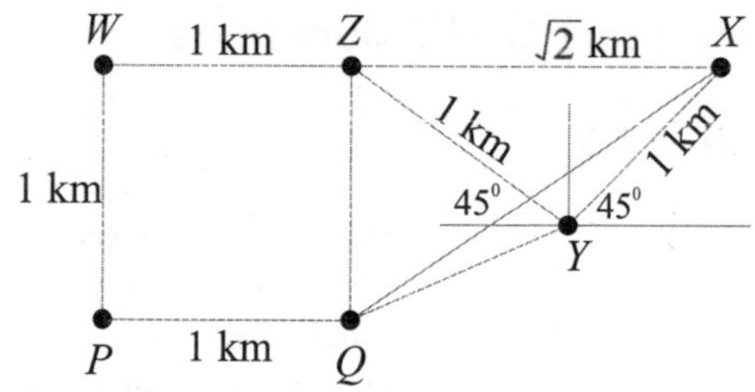

$$QX = \sqrt{(\sqrt{2})^2 + 1^2}$$

$$QX = \sqrt{3} \text{ km}$$

Example 17.3

The volume of a sphere of diameter one unit is ___ than the volume of a cube of side one unit.

(A) least (B) less (C) lesser (D) low

GATE 2016(BT)

Solution

Volume of sphere, $V_{\text{sphere}} = \frac{1}{6}\pi d^3 = \frac{1}{6}\pi \times 1^3 = 0.52$

Volume of cube, $V_{\text{cube}} = a^3 = 1^3 = 1$

From which

$$V_{\text{sphere}} < V_{\text{cube}}$$

Example 17.4

A window is made up of a square portion and an equilateral triangle portion above it. The base of the triangular portion coincides with the upper side of the square. If the perimeter of the window is 6 m, the area of the window in m^2 is

(A) 1.43 (B) 2.06 (C) 2.68 (D) 2.88

GATE 2016(BT)

Solution

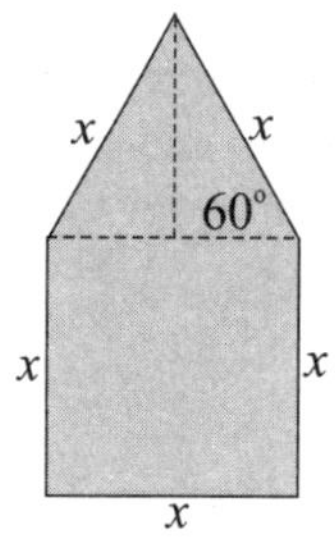

Let x be the side of triangle.

Perimeter of window $= 5x = 6$

or $\quad x = \frac{6}{5}$ m

Area of window, $A = x^2 + \frac{1}{2}x \times (x \sin 60)$

$$A = x^2 + \frac{\sqrt{3}}{4}x^2 = \left(\frac{6}{5}\right)^2\left(1 + \frac{\sqrt{3}}{4}\right)$$

$$A = 2.06 \text{ m}^2$$

Example 17.5

Find the missing sequence in the letter series.

B, FH, LNP,. . .

(A) SUWY (B) TUVW (C) TVXZ (D) TWXZ

GATE 2016(BT)

Solution

ABCDEFGHIJKLMNOPQRSTUVWXYZ

Skip → 3words 5words 7words

TVXZ

Example 17.6

Find the odd one in the following group:

ALRVX, EPVZB, ITZDF, OYE IK

(A) ALRVX (B) EPVZB

(C) IT ZDF (D) OYEIK

GATE 2014(CE)

Solution

ALRVX ← **one** vowel

EPVZB ← **one** vowel

ITZDF ← **one** vowel

OYEIK ← **Three** vowel

Example 17.7

The smallest angle of a triangle is equal to two thirds of the smallest angle of a quadrilateral. The ratio between the angles of the quadrilateral is 3:4:5:6. The largest angle of the triangle is twice its smallest angle. What is the sum, in degrees, of the second largest angle of the triangle and the largest angle of the quadrilateral? _______

GATE 2014(CE)

Solution

Let the angles of quadrilateral are 3α, 4α, 5α and 6α.

Sum of angles, $\quad 3\alpha + 4\alpha + 5\alpha + 6\alpha = 180(4-2)$

$$\alpha = 20°$$

Therefore, angles of quadrilateral are 60°, 80°, 100° and 120°.

The smallest angle of triangle $= \frac{2}{3} \times 60° = 40°$

The largest angle of triangle $= 2 \times 40° = 80°$.

So, angles of triangle are 40°, 60° and 80°

The second largest angle of triangle + The largest angle of quadrilateral $= 60° + 120° = 180°$

180°

Example 17.8

One percent of the people of country X are taller than 6 ft. Two percent of the people of country Y are taller than 6 ft.

There are thrice as many people in country X as in country Y. Taking both countries together, what is the percentage of people taller than 6 ft?

(A) 3.0 (B) 2.5 (C) 1.5 (D) 1.25

GATE 2014(CE)

Solution

Let number of people in country $Y = 100$

number of people in country $X = 3Y = 300$

One percent of people in country $X = 3$

Two percent of people in country $Y = 2$

Total numbers of people taller than 6 ft in both the countries $= 3 + 2 = 5$.

% of people taller than 6ft in both the countries

$$= \frac{5}{300 + 100} \times 100 = 1.25$$

$1.25\,\%$

Example 17.9

If ROAD is written as URDG, then SWAN should be written as:

(A) VXDQ (B) VZDQ (C) VZDP (D) UXDQ

GATE 2015(CE)

Solution

$R \xrightarrow{R+3} U$ $\quad$ $S \xrightarrow{S+3} V$

$O \xrightarrow{O+3} R$ $\quad$ $W \xrightarrow{W+3} Z$

$A \xrightarrow{A+3} D$ $\quad$ $A \xrightarrow{A+3} D$

$D \xrightarrow{D+3} G$ $\quad$ $N \xrightarrow{N+3} Q$

VZDQ

Example 17.10

A function $f(x)$ is linear and has a value of 29 at $x = -2$ and 39 at $x = 3$. Find its value at $x = 5$.

(A) 59 (B) 45 (C) 43 (D) 35

GATE 2015(CE)

Solution

Let $f(x) = ax + b$

Value of $f(x)$ at $x = -2$ is 29; $\quad -2a + b = 29 \quad$ (i)

Value of $f(x)$ at $x = 3$ is 39; $\quad 3a + b = 39 \quad$ (ii)

Equations (i) and (ii) give $a = 2, b = 33$

Therefore, $\quad f(x) = 2x + 33$

Value of $f(x)$ at $x = 5$; $\quad f(x) = 2 \times 5 + 33 = 43$

$$[f(x)]_{x=5} = 43$$

Example 17.11

The exports and imports (in crores) of a country from the year 2000 to 2007 are given in the following bar chart. In which year is the combined percentage increase in imports and exports the highest?

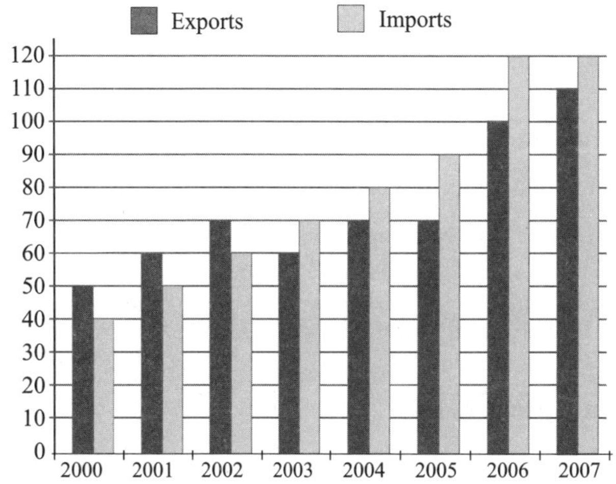

GATE 2015(CE)

Solution

$$\text{Increase in exports in 2006} = \frac{100 - 70}{70} \times 100 = 42.8\,\%$$

$$\text{Increase in imports in 2006} = \frac{120 - 90}{90} \times 100 = 33.3\,\%$$

Imports and exports in 2006 is more than any other year.

Example 17.12

Choose the most appropriate equation for the function drawn as a thick line, in the plot below:

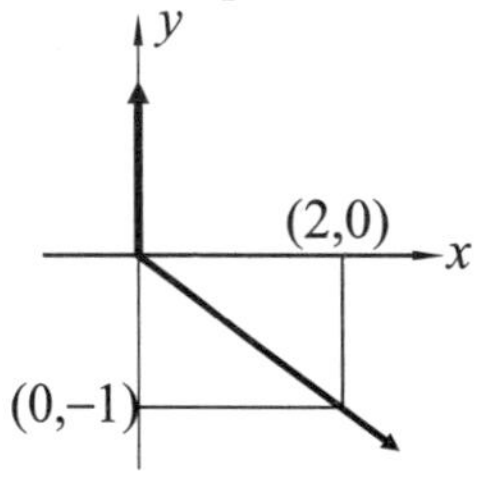

(A) $x = y - |y|$ (B) $x = -(y - |y|)$

(C) $x = y + |y|$ (D) $x = -(y + |y|)$

GATE 2015(CE)

Solution

From the graph

For $y \geq 0$; equation of line $x = 0$ (i)

For $y \leq 0$; equation of line $x = -2y$ (ii)

Equations (i) and (ii) give

$$x = y - |y|$$

Example 17.13

Four cards are randomly selected from a pack of 52 cards. If the first two cards are kings, what is the probability that the third card is a king?

(A) 4/52 (B) 2/50

(C) 1/52 × (1/52) (D) 1/52 × (1/52) × (1/50)

GATE 2015(CE)

Solution

There are 4 kings in a pack of 52 cards.

If 2 cards are selected and both are kings, remaining cards will be 50 out of which 2 will be kings.

Probability that the third card is a king, $P = \dfrac{2}{50}$

Example 17.14

How many four digit numbers can be formed with the 10 digits 0, 1, 2, ... 9 if no number can start with 0 and if repetitions are not allowed?

GATE 2015(CE)

Solution

In thousand place, 9 digits except 0 can be placed.

In hundreds place, 9 digits can be placed (excluding one used in thousand place).

In tens place, 8 digits can be placed (excluding one used in thousand place and hundred place).

In ones place, 7 digits can be placed (excluding one used in thousands, hundred place and tens place).

Therefore, total number of combinations $= 9 \times 9 \times 8 \times 7 = 4536.$

Example 17.15

There are 16 teachers who can teach Thermodynamics (TD), 11 who can teach Electrical Sciences (ES), and 5 who can teach both TD and Engineering Mechanics (EM). There are a total of 40 teachers, 6 cannot teach any of the three subjects, i.e., EM, ES or TD. 6 can teach only ES. 4 can teach all three subjects, i.e., EM, ES and TD. 4 can teach ES and TD. How many can teach both ES and EM but not TD?

(A) 1 (B) 2 (C) 3 (D) 4

GATE 2015(CE)

Solution

First we draw a Venn diagram as shown in figure.

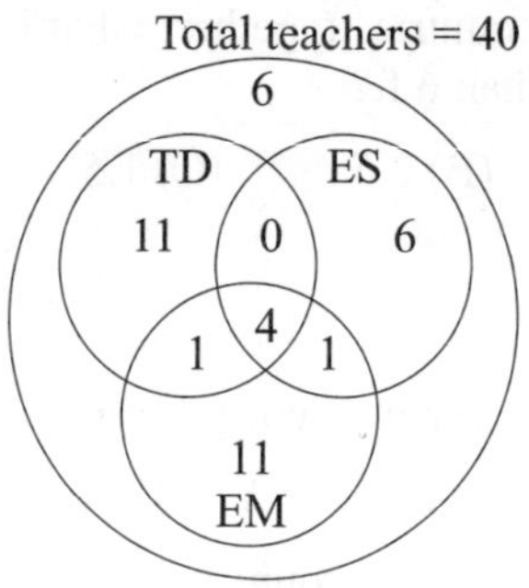

Number of teachers can teach both subjects ES and EM is $= 4 + 1 = 5$

Number of teachers can teach both subjects ES and EM but not TD is $= 5 - 4 = 1.$

Number of teachers can teach both subjects ES and EM but not TD is 1.

Example 17.16

Read the following table giving sales data of five types of batteries for years 2006 to 2012.

Year	Type-I	Type-II	Type-III	Type-IV	Type-V
2006	75	144	114	102	108
2007	90	126	102	84	126
2008	96	114	75	105	135
2009	105	90	150	90	75
2010	90	75	135	75	90
2011	105	60	165	45	120
2012	115	85	160	100	145

Out of the following, which type of battery achieved the highest growth between the years 2006 and 2012?

(A) Type V (B) Type III (C) Type II (D) Type I

GATE 2015(CE)

Solution

Year	Type-I	Type-II	Type-III	Type-IV	Type-V
2006	75	144	114	102	108
2012	115	85	160	100	145
Growth	$\dfrac{115-75}{75}$ 53.33%	$\dfrac{85-144}{144}$ −40.9%	$\dfrac{160-114}{114}$ 53.33%	$\dfrac{100-102}{102}$ −1.96%	$\dfrac{145-108}{108}$ 34.25%

Type-I achieved a growth of 53.33% in the period which is higher than other type of battery.

Example 17.17

The given question is followed by two statements. Select the most appropriate option that solves the question.

Capacity of a tank A is 70% of the capacity of tank B. How many gallons of are in tank A and tank B?

Statements:

I. Tank A is 80% full and tank B is 40% full.

II. Tank A is full if it contains 14,000 gallons of water.

(A) Statement I alone is sufficient

(B) Statement II alone is sufficient

(C) Either statement I or II alone is sufficient

(D) Both the statements I and II together are sufficient

GATE 2015(CE)

Solution

Given: $Q_A = 0.7Q_B$

Statement-I : $[Q_A]_{\text{actual}} = 0.8Q_A$ and $[Q_B]_{\text{actual}} = 0.4Q_B$

Statement-II : $Q_A = 14000$ gallons

To find gallons in tank A and tank B;

Both the statements I and II together are sufficient.

Example 17.18

A cube is built using 64 cubic blocks of side one unit. After it is built, one cubic block is removed from every corner of the cube. The resulting surface a rea of the body (in square units) after the removal is _______

(A) 56 (B) 64 (C) 72 (D) 96

GATE 2016(CE)

Solution

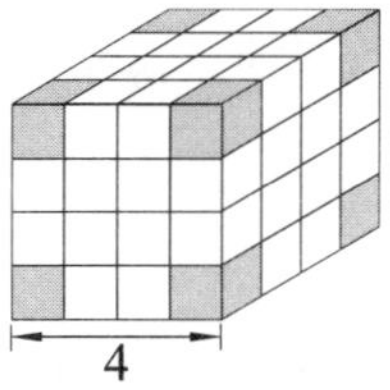

Total surface area of cube $= 6 \times 4^2 = 96$

Surface area after removal of blocks from each corner

$$= 96 - (8 \times 3 \times 1^2) + (8 \times 3 \times 1^2)$$

Surface area after removal of blocks $= 96$

Example 17.19

If $f(x) = 2x^7 + 3x - 5$, which of the following is a factor of $f(x)$?

(A) $(x^3 + 8)$ (B) $(x - 1)$ (C) $(2x - 5)$ (D) $(x + 1)$

GATE 2016(CE)

Solution

Substitute $x = 1$ in $f(x) = 2x^7 + 3x - 5$;

$$f(x) = 2 \times 1^7 + 3 \times 1 - 5 = 0$$

Therefore, $(x - 1)$ is one factor of $f(x)$

Example 17.20

(x % of y) + (y % of x) is equivalent to

(A) 2 % of xy (B) 2 % of (xy/100)

(C) xy % of 100 (D) 100 % of xy

GATE 2016(CE)

Solution

$$(x \% \text{ of } y) + (y \% \text{ of } x) = \frac{x}{100} \times y + \frac{y}{100} \times x$$

$$(x \% \text{ of } y) + (y \% \text{ of } x) = \frac{2}{100} xy$$

(x % of y) + (y % of x) is equivalent to 2 % of xy

Example 17.21

Two finance companies, P and Q, declared fixed annual rates of interest on the amounts invested with them. The rates of interest offered by these companies may differ from year to year. Year-wise annual rates of interest offered by these companies are shown by the line graph provided below:

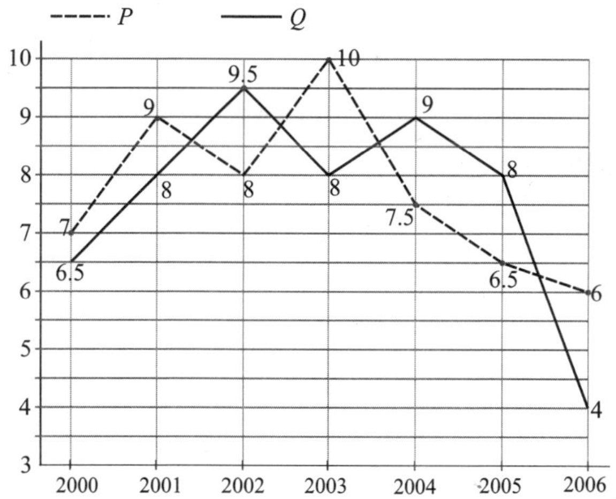

If the amounts invested in the companies, P and Q, in 2006 are in the ratio 8:9, then the amounts received after one year as interests from companies P and Q would be in the ratio:

(A) 2:3 (B) 3:4 (C) 6:7 (D) 4:3

GATE 2016(CE)

Solution

Let the deposited money in the company P is $8x$

and the deposited money in the company Q is $9x$

Interest after one year from the company $P = 8x \times \dfrac{6}{100}$

Interest after one year from the company $Q = 9x \times \frac{4}{100}$

$$\text{Ratio of interest} = \frac{8x \times \frac{6}{100}}{9x \times \frac{4}{100}} = \frac{4}{3}$$

$$\text{Ratio of interest} = \frac{4}{3}$$

Example 17.22

The sum of the digits of a two-digit number is 12. If the new number formed by reversing the digits is greater than the original number by 54, find the original number.

(A) 39 (B) 57 (C) 66 (D) 93

GATE 2016(CE)

Solution

Let the original number be $(10x + y)$

$$x + y = 12 \quad \text{(i)}$$

$$(10y + x) - (10x + y) = 54$$

$$9y - 9x = 54 \quad \text{(ii)}$$

Equations (i) and (ii) give

$$x = 3 \text{ and } y = 9$$

Thus, original number $(10x + y) = 39$

Example 17.23

A square pyramid has a base perimeter x, and the slant height is half of the perimeter. What is the lateral surface area of the pyramid?

(A) x^2 (B) $0.75x^2$ (C) $0.50x^2$ (D) $0.25x^2$

GATE 2016(CE)

Solution

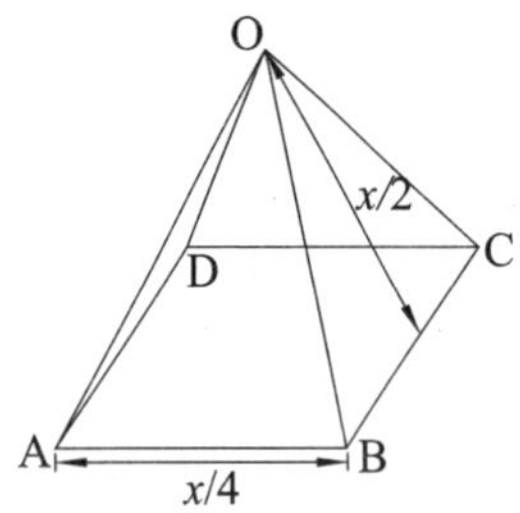

Area of triangle OBC,

$$= \frac{1}{2} \times \frac{x}{4} \times \frac{x}{2} = \frac{x^2}{16}$$

Lateral surface area of pyramid

$$= 4 \times \frac{x^2}{16}$$

Lateral surface area of pyramid $= 0.25x^2$

Example 17.24

Ananth takes 6 h and Bharath takes 4 h to read a book. Both started reading copies of the book at the same time. After how many hours is the number of pages to be read by Ananth, twice that to be read by Bharath? Assume Ananth and Bharath read all the pages with constant pace.

(A) 1 (B) 2 (C) 3 (D) 4

GATE 2016(CE)

Solution

Ananth covers $\frac{1}{6}$ of the book in 1 h.

Bharath covers $\frac{1}{4}$ of the book in 1 h.

Let n be the number of hours.

$$\frac{\left(\frac{1}{6}\right)n}{\frac{1}{4}} = 2$$

$$n = 3 \text{ h}$$

Example 17.25

If $\log_x(5/7) = -1/3$, then the value of x is

(A) $\frac{343}{125}$ (B) $\frac{12}{343}$ (C) $-\frac{25}{49}$ (D) $-\frac{49}{25}$

GATE 2015(CH)

Solution

$$\log_x(5/7) = -1/3 \quad \Rightarrow \quad x^{\frac{1}{3}} = \frac{7}{5}$$

or

$$x = \left(\frac{7}{5}\right)^3$$

$$x = \frac{343}{125}$$

Example 17.26

A cube of side 3 units is formed using a set of smaller cubes of side 1 unit. Find the proportion of the number of faces of the smaller cubes visible to those which are NOT visible.

(A) 1 : 4 (B) 1 : 3 (C) 1 : 2 (D) 2 : 3

GATE 2015(CH)

Solution

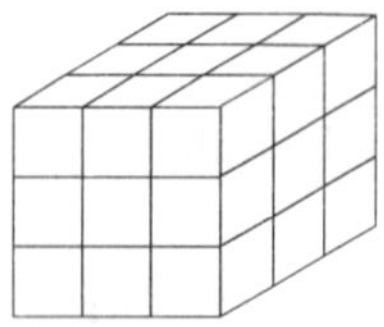

Number of faces per cube =6

Total number of cubes $= 3^3 = 27$

Total number of faces $= 27 \times 6 = 162$

Total number of visible faces $= 9 \times 6 = 54$

Total number of non-visible faces $= 162 - 54 = 108$

$$\frac{\text{Number of visible faces}}{\text{Number of non-visible faces}} = \frac{54}{108}$$

$$\frac{\text{Number of visible faces}}{\text{Number of non-visible faces}} = \frac{1}{2}$$

Example 17.27

Fill in the missing value.

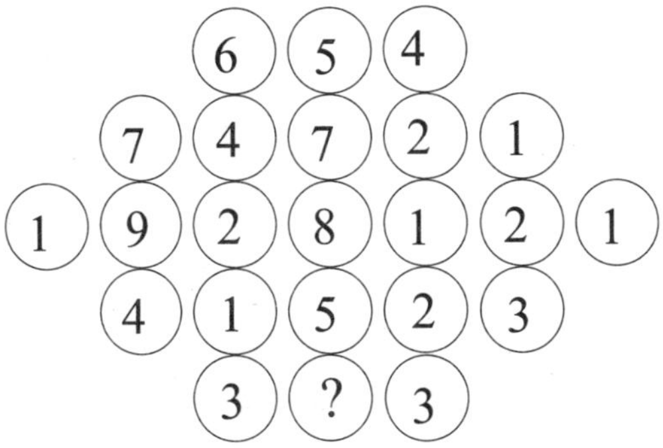

GATE 2015(CH)

Solution

Middle number is the average of the numbers on both sides.

Therefore, average of 3 and 3 is 3.

Example 17.28

Find the sum of the expression

$$\frac{1}{\sqrt{1}+\sqrt{2}} + \frac{1}{\sqrt{2}+\sqrt{3}} + \frac{1}{\sqrt{3}+\sqrt{4}} + - - - + \frac{1}{\sqrt{80}+\sqrt{81}}$$

(A) 7 (B) 8 (C) 9 (D) 10

GATE 2013(CS)

Solution

$$\frac{1}{\sqrt{1}+\sqrt{2}} + \frac{1}{\sqrt{2}+\sqrt{3}} + \frac{1}{\sqrt{3}+\sqrt{4}} + - - - + \frac{1}{\sqrt{80}+\sqrt{81}}$$

Multiply and divide each term by conjugate of denominator. We get,

$$-(\sqrt{1}-\sqrt{2}) - (\sqrt{2}-\sqrt{3}) - (\sqrt{3}-\sqrt{4}) \ldots . -(\sqrt{80}-\sqrt{81})$$

$$= \sqrt{81} - \sqrt{1} = 8$$

$$\frac{1}{\sqrt{1}+\sqrt{2}} + \frac{1}{\sqrt{2}+\sqrt{3}} + \frac{1}{\sqrt{3}+\sqrt{4}} + \ldots + \frac{1}{\sqrt{80}+\sqrt{81}} = 8$$

Example 17.29

A tourist covers half of his journey by train at 60 km/h, half of the remainder by bus at 30 km/h and the rest by bicycle at 10 km/h. The average of the tourist in km/h during his entire journey is

(A) 36 (B) 30 (C) 24 (D) 18

GATE 2013(CS)

Solution

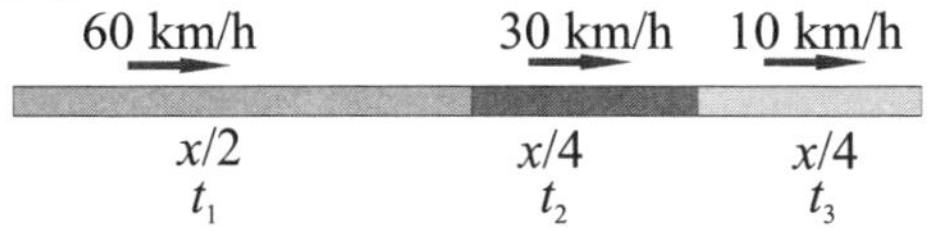

Let the total distance covered $= x$

$$\text{Average speed} = \frac{x}{\text{Total time taken}}$$

$$\text{Average speed} = \frac{x}{\frac{\left(\frac{x}{2}\right)}{60} + \frac{\left(\frac{x}{4}\right)}{30} + \frac{\left(\frac{x}{4}\right)}{10}} = \frac{120}{5}$$

Average speed = 24 km/h.

Example 17.30

Out of all the 2-digit integers between 1 and 100, a 2-digit number has to be selected at random. What is the probability that the selected number is not divisible by 7?

(A) 13/90 (B) 12/90 (C) 78/90 (D) 77/90

GATE 2013(CS)

Solution

The number of 2-digit multiples of 7 (14, 21, 28, 35, 42, 49, 56, 63, 70, 77, 84, 91, 98) = 13

Therefore, probability of choosing a number not divisible by 7 is

$$= \frac{90-13}{90} = \frac{77}{90}$$

Example 17.31

What will be the maximum sum of 44, 42, 40, ... ?

(A) 502 (B) 504 (C) 506 (D) 500

GATE 2013(CS)

Solution

The maximum sum is the sum of 44, 42, 40, ... ,2.

Sum of n terms of an A.P., $S = \frac{n}{2}[2a + (n-1)d]$

Number of terms, $n = \frac{44-2}{2} + 1 = 22$, $a = 44$ and $d = 2$

Maximum sum of 44, 42, 40, ... is

$$S = \frac{22}{2}[2 \times 44 + (22-1) \times -2]$$

$$S = 506$$

Example 17.32

If $\left(z+\frac{1}{z}\right)^2=98$, compute $\left(z^2+\frac{1}{z^2}\right)$.

GATE 2014(CE)

Solution

$$\left(z+\frac{1}{z}\right)^2=z^2+2\times z\times\frac{1}{z}+\frac{1}{z^2}=98$$

$$z^2+\frac{1}{z^2}=98-2=96$$

$$z^2+\frac{1}{z^2}=96$$

Example 17.33

What is the average of all multiples of 10 from 2 to 198?

(A) 90 (B) 100 (C) 110 (D) 120

GATE 2014(CS)

Solution

Number of 10 from 2 to 198 are 10, 20, 30, ... ,190.

Number of terms, $n=\frac{190-10}{10}+1=19$

$$a=10,\ d=10$$

$$\text{Average}=\frac{\frac{n}{2}[2a+(n-1)d]}{n}=\frac{1}{2}[2a+(n-1)d]$$

$$\text{Average}=\frac{1}{2}[2\times 10+(19-1)\times 10]$$

$$\text{Average}=100$$

Example 17.34

The value of $\sqrt{12+\sqrt{12+\sqrt{12+\sqrt{12+...}}}}$ is

(A) 3.464 (B) 3.932 (C) 4.000 (D) 4.444

GATE 2014(CS)

Solution

Let $y=\sqrt{12+\sqrt{12+\sqrt{12+\sqrt{12+...}}}}$

$$y=\sqrt{12+y}\quad\Rightarrow\quad y^2-y-12=0$$

$$(y-4)(y+3)=0\quad\Rightarrow\quad y=4,\ y=-3$$

$$\sqrt{12+\sqrt{12+\sqrt{12+\sqrt{12+...}}}}=4$$

Example 17.35

If x is real and $\left|x^2-2x+3\right|=11$, then possible values of $\left|-x^3+x^2-x\right|$ include

(A) 2, 4 (B) 2, 14 (C) 4, 52 (D) 14, 52

GATE 2014(CS)

Solution

Given that $\left|x^2-2x+3\right|=11\ \Rightarrow\ x^2-2x+3=\pm 11$

$x^2-2x+3=11;$ $\qquad$ $x^2-2x+3=-11$

$x^2-2x-8=0;$ $\qquad$ $x^2-2x+14=0$

$(x-4)(x+2)=0$ $\qquad$ Roots are imaginary

$x=4,\ x=-2$

Value of $\left|-x^3+x^2-x\right|$

at $x=4$; $\quad\left|-4^3+4^2-4\right|=52$

at $x=-2$; $\quad\left|-(-2)^3+(-2)^2-(-2)\right|=14$

Possible values of $\left|-x^3+x^2-x\right|$ include

14, 52

Example 17.36

The ratio of male to female students in a college for five years is plotted in the following line graph. If the number of female students doubled in 2009, by what percent did the number of male students increase in 2009?

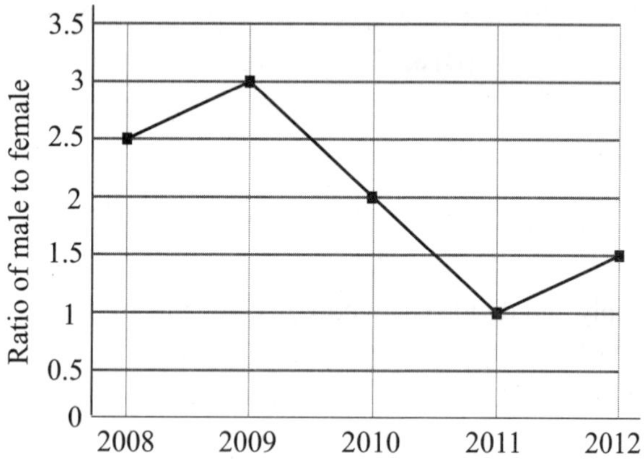

GATE 2014(CS)

Solution

Let f =Number of female in 2008

Number of female in 2009 $f'=2f$ (i)

From graph:

Male-female ratio in 2008; $\frac{m}{f}=2.5$ (ii)

Male-female ratio in 2009; $\frac{m'}{f'} = 3$ (iii)

Equations (i), (ii) and (iii) give

$$\frac{f'}{m'} \times \frac{m}{f} = \frac{3}{2.5} \Rightarrow \frac{f'}{2m} \times \frac{m}{f} = \frac{3}{2.5}$$

or $$\frac{f'}{f} = \frac{6}{2.5}$$

or $$\frac{f'-f}{f} = \frac{6-2.5}{2.5} = 1.4$$

% increase male in 2009 ; $\frac{f'-f}{f} \times 100 = 1.4 \times 100 = 140$

140%

Example 17.37

The pie chart below has the breakup of the number of students from different departments in an engineering college for the year 2012. The proportion of male to female students in each department is 5:4. There are 40 males in Electrical department. What is the difference between numbers of female students in the Civil department and the female students in the Mechanical department?

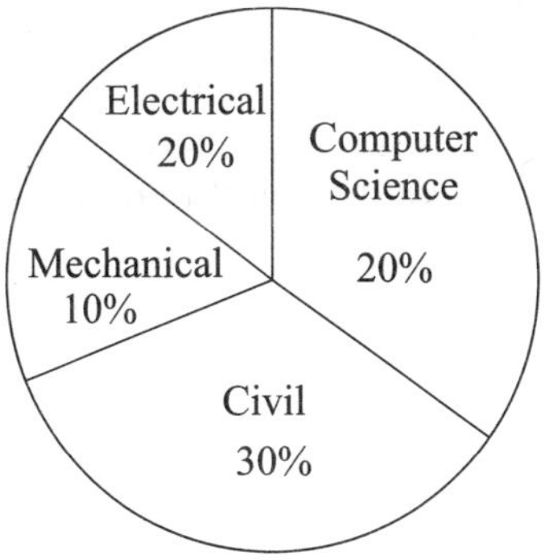

GATE 2015(CS)

Solution

Electrical male students = 40

Electrical female students $= \frac{4}{5} \times 40 = 32$

Total number of electrical students = 40 + 32 = 72

Total number of students in college, $N = \frac{72}{0.2} = 360$

Mechanical strength $= 0.10 \times 360 = 36$

Civil strength $= 0.30 \times 360 = 108$

Female strength in mechanical $= \frac{4}{9} \times 36 = 16$

Female strength in Civil $= \frac{4}{9} \times 108 = 48$

Difference of female student of civil to female students of mechanical is

$$48 - 16 = 32$$

Example 17.38

The number of students in a class who have answered correctly, wrongly, or not attempted each question in an exam, are listed in the table below. The marks for each question are also listed. There is no negative or partial marking.

Q. No.	Marks	Answered correctly	Answered wrongly	Not attempted
1	2	21	17	6
2	3	15	27	2
3	1	11	29	4
4	2	23	18	3
5	5	31	12	1

What is the average of the marks obtained by the class in the examination?

(A) 2.290 (B) 2.970 (C) 6.795 (D) 8.795

GATE 2015(CS)

Solution

Average marks obtained by the class

$$= \frac{21 \times 2 + 15 \times 3 + 11 \times 1 + 23 \times 2 + 31 \times 5}{21 + 15 + 11 + 23 + 31}$$

Average marks obtained by the class = 2.970

Example 17.39

In a quadratic function, the value of the product of the roots $\alpha\beta$ is 4. Find the value of $\frac{\alpha^n + \beta^n}{\alpha^{-n} + \beta^{-n}}$

(A) n^4 (B) 4^n (C) 2^{2n-1} (D) 4^{n-1}

GATE 2016(CS)

Solution

$$\frac{\alpha^n + \beta^n}{\alpha^{-n} + \beta^{-n}} = \frac{\alpha^n + \beta^n}{\frac{1}{\alpha^n} + \frac{1}{\beta^n}} = \frac{\alpha^n + \beta^n}{\frac{\alpha^n + \beta^n}{\alpha^n \beta^n}} = \alpha^n \beta^n$$

$$\frac{\alpha^n + \beta^n}{\alpha^{-n} + \beta^{-n}} = \alpha^n \beta^n = (\alpha\beta)^n = 4^n$$

$$\frac{\alpha^n + \beta^n}{\alpha^{-n} + \beta^{-n}} = 4^n$$

Example 17.40

Among 150 faculty members in an institute, 55 are connected with each other through Facebook and 85 are connected through WhatsApp. 30 faculty members do not have Facebook or WhatsApp accounts. The number of faculty members connected only through Facebook accounts is______.

(A) 35 (B) 45 (C) 65 (D) 90

GATE 2016(CS)

Solution

Venn diagram is shown in figure.

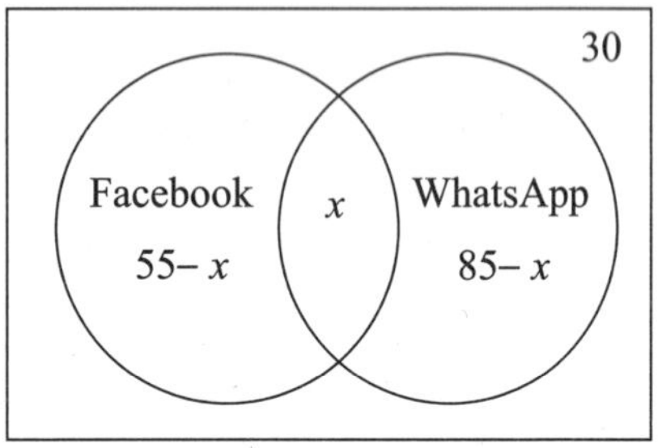

Total faculty $= 150 = (55 - x) + x + (85 - x) + 30$

$$x = 20$$

Number of faculty members connected only through Facebook $= 55 - x = 55 - 20 = 35$

Example 17.41

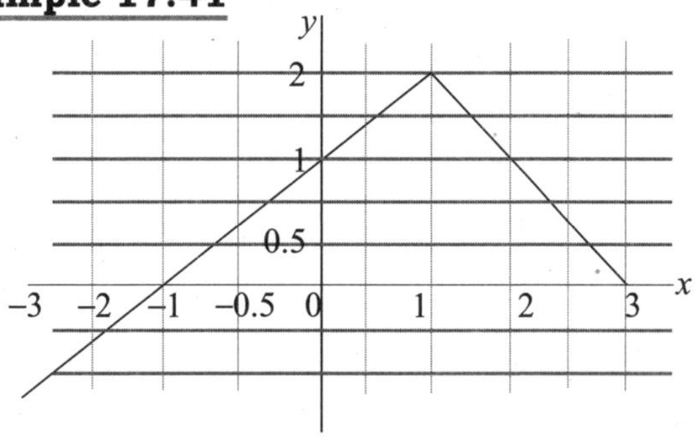

Chose the correct expression for $f(x)$ given in the graph.

(A) $f(x) = 1 - |x - 1|$ (B) $f(x) = 1 + |x - 1|$

(C) $f(x) = 2 - |x - 1|$ (D) $f(x) = 2 + |x - 1|$

GATE 2016(CS)

Solution

Equation of line:

For $x > 1$; $f(x) = 3 - x$

For $x < 1$; $f(x) = x + 1$

Which gives

$$f(x) = 2 - |x - 1|$$

Example 17.42

In the summer of 2012, in New Delhi, the mean temperature of Monday to Wednesday) was 41°C and of Tuesday to Thursday was 43°C. If the temperature on Thursday was 15% higher than that of Monday, then the temperature in °C on Thursday was

(A) 40 (B) 43 (C) 46 (D) 49

GATE 2013(EC)

Solution

Let T_{MON} = Temperature of Monday

$$\frac{T_{MON} + T_{TUE} + T_{WED}}{3} = 41$$

or $$T_{MON} + T_{TUE} + T_{WED} = 123 \quad \text{(i)}$$

$$\frac{T_{TUE} + T_{WED} + T_{THU}}{3} = 43$$

or $$T_{TUE} + T_{WED} + T_{THU} = 129 \quad \text{(ii)}$$

$$T_{THU} = 1.15\,T_{MON} \quad \text{(iii)}$$

Equations (i), (ii) and (iii) give

$$T_{THU} - T_{MON} = 6$$

Substituting $T_{THU} = 1.15\,T_{MON}$

$$T_{THU} - \frac{T_{THU}}{1.15} = 6$$

$$T_{THU} = 46\text{°C}$$

Example 17.43

A car travels 8 km in the first quarter of an hour, 6 km in the second quarter and 16 km in the third quarter. The average speed of the car (in km/h) over the entire journey is

(A) 30 (B) 36 (C) 40 (D) 24

GATE 2013(EC)

Solution

Average speed, $$v = \frac{8 + 6 + 16}{\left(\frac{1}{4} + \frac{1}{4} + \frac{1}{4}\right)}$$

Average speed $v = 40$ km/h

Example 17.44

Find the sum to n terms of the series 10 + 84 + 734 + ...

(A) $\frac{9(9^n + 1)}{10} + 1$ (B) $\frac{9(9^n - 1)}{8} + 1$

(C) $\frac{9(9^n - 1)}{8} + n$ (D) $\frac{9(9^n - 1)}{8} + n^2$

GATE 2013(EC)

Solution

$S = 10 + 84 + 734 + ... + n$ terms

$S = (9 + 1) + (9^2 + 3) + (9^3 + 5) + . . . + n$ terms

$$S = (9 + 9^2 + 9^3 + \ldots) + (1 + 3 + 5 + \ldots)$$

$$S = (9 + 9^2 + 9^3 + \ldots) + (1 + 3 + 5 + \ldots)$$

$$S = \frac{9(9^n - 1)}{9 - 1} + \frac{n}{2}[2 \times 1 + (n-1) \times 2]$$

$$S = \frac{9}{8}(9^n - 1) + n^2$$

Example 17.45

What is the next number in the series?

12 35 81 173 357 ____

GATE 2014(EC)

Solution

357+368

12 35 81 173 357 = 725

Difference → 23 46 92 184 368

725

Example 17.46

A train that is 280 m long, travelling at a uniform speed, crosses a platform in 60 s and passes a man standing on the platform in 20 s. What is the length of the platform in metres?

GATE 2014(EC)

Solution

Given: Length of train = 280 m

Let x be the length of platform.

$$\frac{x + 280}{v} = 60 \qquad \text{(i)}$$

$$\frac{280}{v} = 20 \qquad \text{(ii)}$$

Equations (i) and (ii) give

$$\frac{x + 280}{280} = \frac{60}{20}$$

$$x = 560$$

Length of platform $x = 560$ m

Example 17.47

The exports and imports (in crores) of a country from 2000 to 2007 are given in the following bar chart. If the trade deficit is defined as excess of imports over exports, in which year is the trade deficit 1/5th of the exports?

(A) 2005 (B) 2004 (C) 2007 (D) 2006

GATE 2014(EC)

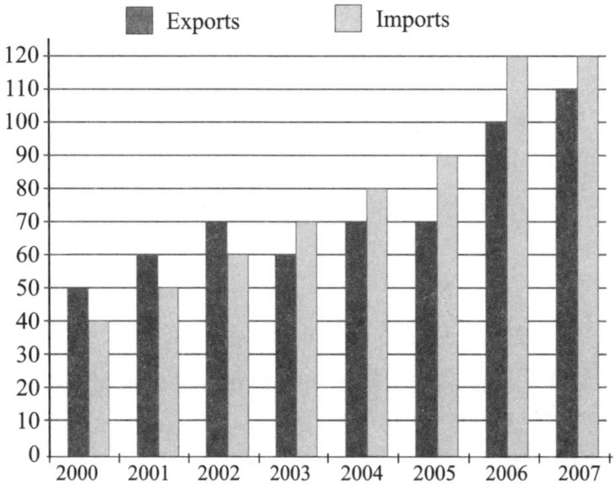

Solution

In Year 2004 ; $\dfrac{\text{Imports} - \text{Exports}}{\text{Exports}} = \dfrac{80 - 70}{70} = \dfrac{1}{7}$

In Year 2005 ; $\dfrac{\text{Imports} - \text{Exports}}{\text{Exports}} = \dfrac{90 - 70}{70} = \dfrac{2}{7}$

In Year 2006 ; $\dfrac{\text{Imports} - \text{Exports}}{\text{Exports}} = \dfrac{120 - 100}{100} = \dfrac{1}{5}$

In Year 2007 ; $\dfrac{\text{Imports} - \text{Exports}}{\text{Exports}} = \dfrac{120 - 110}{110} = \dfrac{1}{11}$

Example 17.48

Find the odd one in the following group:

Q,W,Z,B B,H,K,M W,C,G,J M,S,V,X

(A) Q,W,Z,B (B) B,H,K,M

(C) W,C,G,J (D) M,S,V,X

GATE 2014(EC)

Solution

Q, W, Z, B	B, H, K, M	W, C, G, J	M, S, V, X
8 6 4	8 6 4	8 6 4	8 6 2

Example 17.49

The sum of eight consecutive odd numbers is 656. The average of four consecutive even numbers is 87. What is the sum of the smallest odd number and the second largest even number?

GATE 2014

Solution

Let eight consecutive odd numbers are

$$a - 6, a - 4, a - 2, a, a + 2, a + 4, a + 6, a + 8.$$

The sum of eight consecutive odd numbers is

$$8a + 8 = 656$$

$$a = 81$$

The smallest odd number $a - 6 = 75$

Average of four consecutive even number

$$\frac{(x-2) + x + (x+2) + (x+4)}{4} = 87$$

$$x = 86$$

The second largest even number $x + 2 = 88$

Therefore, sum of the smallest odd number and the second largest even number is $(75 + 88) = 163$.

Example 17.50

The total exports and revenues from the exports of a country are given in the two charts shown below. The pie chart for exports shows the quantity of each item exported as a percentage of the total quantity of exports. The pie chart for the revenues shows the percentage of the total revenue generated through export of each item. The total quantity of exports of all the items is 500 thousand tonnes and the total revenues are 250 crore rupees. Which item among the following has generated the maximum revenue per kg?

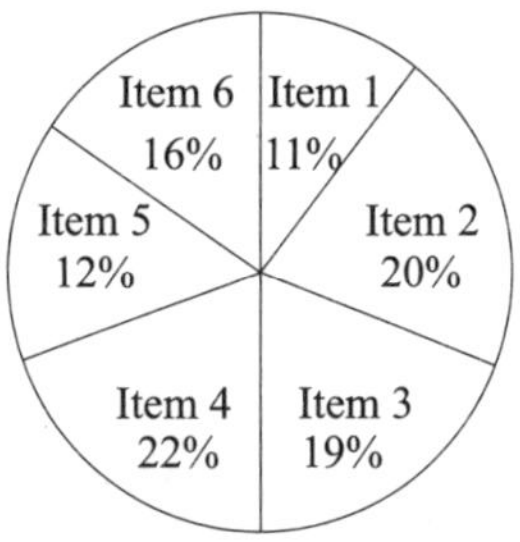

Exports

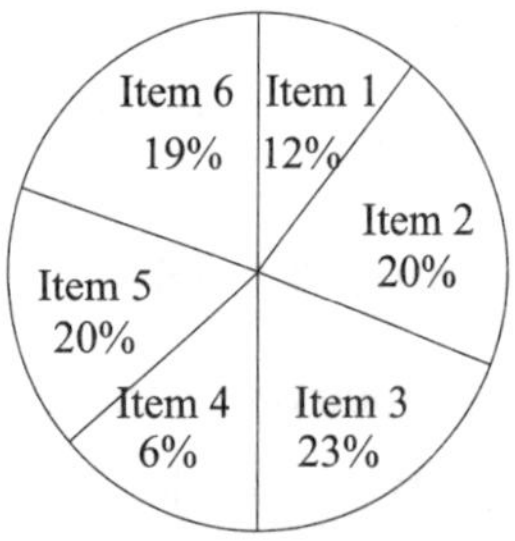

Revenues

(A) Item 2 (B) Item 3 (C) Item 6 (D) Item 5

GATE 2014(EC)

Solution

Items	Exports		Revenues		Rs./kg
Item 1	11%		12%		
Item 2	20%	100×10^6	20%	Rs. 5000×10^6	50
Item 3	19%	95×10^6	23%	Rs. 5750×10^6	60.5
Item 4	22%		6%		
Item 5	12%	60×10^6	20%	Rs. 5000×10^6	83.33
Item 6	16%	80×10^6	19%	Rs. 4750×10^6	59.37
Total		500×10^6kg		Rs. 25000×10^6	

Example 17.51

Find the next term in the sequence: 7G, 11K, 13M, ___

(A) 15Q (B) 17Q (C) 15P (D) 17P

GATE 2014

Solution

Prime numbers

7G, 11K, 13M, 17Q

Words location $7^{th}, 11^{th}, 13^{th}$ and 17th

Example 17.52

A man can row at 8 km/h in still water. If it takes him thrice as long to row upstream, as to row downstream, then find the stream velocity in km/h.

GATE 2014(EC)

Solution

Let v be the velocity of stream.

Speed of man in upstream $= 8 - v$

$$\text{Time taken, } t_1 = \frac{x}{8-v} \quad \text{(in upstream)}$$

Speed of man in downstream $= 8 + v$

$$\text{Time taken, } t_2 = \frac{x}{8+v} \quad \text{(in downstream)}$$

$$3 \times \frac{x}{8-v} = \frac{x}{8+v}$$

Stream velocity, $v = 4$ km/h

Example 17.53

Let $f(x, y) = x^n y^m = P$. If x is doubled and y is halved, the new value of f is:

(A) $2^{n-m}P$ (B) $2^{m-n}P$ (C) $2(m-n)P$ (D) $2(n-m)P$

GATE 2014(EC)

Solution

Given : $f(x, y) = x^n y^m = P$

Now x is doubled and y is halved.

$$f'(x, y) = (2x)^n \left(\frac{y}{2}\right)^m$$

or $$f'(x, y) = 2^{n-m} \times x^n y^m$$

$$f'(x, y) = 2^{n-m}P$$

Example 17.54

In a sequence of 12 consecutive odd numbers, the sum of the first 5 numbers is 425. What is the sum of the last 5 numbers in the sequence?

GATE 2014(EC)

Solution

Let 12 consecutive odd numbers be

$$a - 10, a - 8, a - 6, a, \ldots, a + 10, a + 12$$

Sum of first five numbers $5a - 30 = 425$

$$a = 91$$

Sum of last 5 numbers

$$(a+4)+(a+6)+(a+8)+(a+10)+(a+12)$$

$$= 5a + 40 = 5 \times 91 + 40 = 495$$

495

Example 17.55

Industrial consumption of power doubled from 2000-2001 to 2010-2011. Find the annual rate

(A) 5.6 (B) 7.2 (C) 10.0 (D) 12.2

GATE 2014(EC)

Solution

Let r = annual rate.

Number of years from 2000-2001 to 2010-2011; $n = 10$

$$P_n = P_0(1+r)^n \Rightarrow 2P = P(1+r)^{10}$$

or $$\ln(1+r) = \frac{\ln 2}{10} = 0.0693$$

or $$1 + r = 1.07177$$

or $$r = 0.07177$$

$$r = 7.17\%$$

Example 17.56

A five-digit number is formed using the digits 1,3,5,7 and 9 without repeating any of them. What is the sum of all such possible five digit numbers?

(A) 6666660 (B) 6666600 (C) 6666666 (D) 6666606

GATE 2014(EC)

Solution

Number of 5 digits numbers $= 5! = 120$

Sum of numbers are:

$$S = 97531 + \ldots + 13579 \quad \text{(120 terms)}$$

or $$S = 13579 + \ldots + 97531 \text{ (in reverse order)}$$

$$2S = 111110 + 111110 + \ldots + 111110 \text{ (120 terms)}$$

$$S = \frac{111110 \times 120}{2}$$

$$S = 6666600$$

Example 17.57

From a circular sheet of paper of radius 30 cm, a sector of 10% area is removed. If the remaining part is used to make a conical surface, then the ratio of the radius and height of the cone is ________.

GATE 2015(EC)

Solution

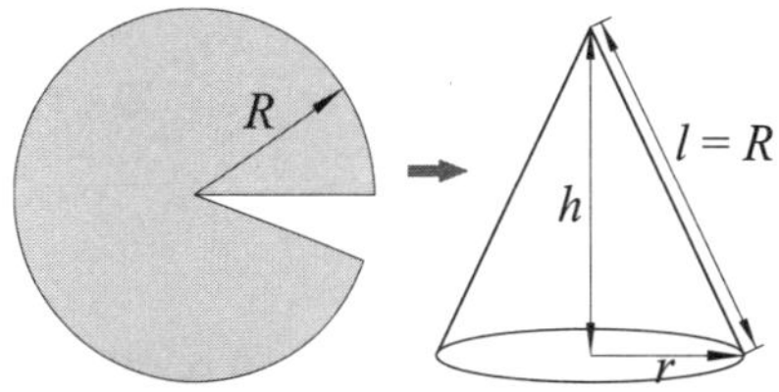

Surface area of cone, $\pi r l = 0.9\pi R^2$

$$\pi r R = 0.9\pi R^2$$

or $$r = 0.9R$$

or $$h = \sqrt{l^2 - r^2} = \sqrt{R^2 - (0.9R)^2}$$

or $$h = \sqrt{l^2 - r^2} = \sqrt{R^2 - (0.9R)^2}$$

or $$h = 0.4358R$$

$$\frac{r}{h} = \frac{0.9R}{0.4358R} = 2.06$$

Ratio of radius to height of cone is 2.06

Example 17.58

$\log\tan 1° + \log\tan 2° + \ldots + \log\tan 89° + \ldots$

(A) 1 (B) $\frac{1}{\sqrt{2}}$ (C) 0 (D) -1

GATE 2015(EC)

Solution

$$\log\tan 1° + \log\tan 2° + \ldots + \log\tan 89° + \ldots$$

$$= \log(\tan 1° \times \tan 89°) + \log(\tan 2° \times \tan 88°) + \ldots$$

$$= \log[\tan 1° \times \tan(90 - 1°)] + [\log\tan 2° \times \tan(90 - 2°)] + \ldots$$

$$= \log[\tan 1° \times \cot 1°] + [\tan 2° \times \cot 2°] + \ldots$$

$$= \log 1 + \log 1 + \ldots + \log 1 + \ldots = 0 + 0 + 0$$

$$\log\tan 1° + \log\tan 2° + \ldots + \log\tan 89° + \ldots = 0$$

Example 17.59

The Venn diagram shows the preference of the student population for leisure activities.

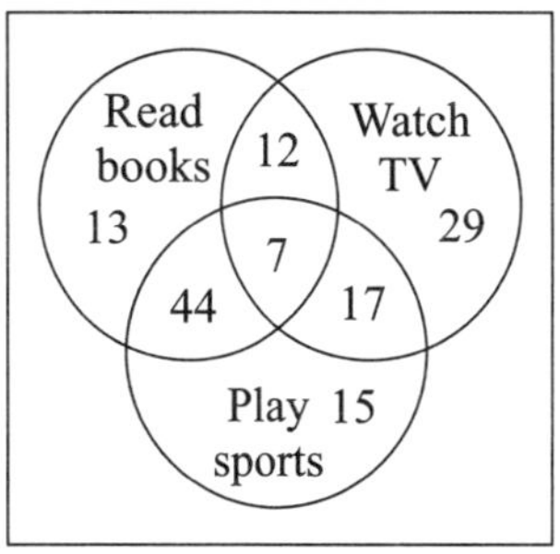

From the data given, the number of students who like to

read books or play sports is

(A) 44 (B) 51 (C) 79 (D) 108

GATE 2016(EC)

Solution

From Venn diagram,

Number of students who like to read books or play sports $= (13+12)+(15+17)+(44+7) = 108$

Example 17.60

The velocity V of a vehicle along a straight line is measured in m/s and plotted as shown with respect to time in seconds. At the end of the 7 s, how much will the odometer reading increase by (in m)?

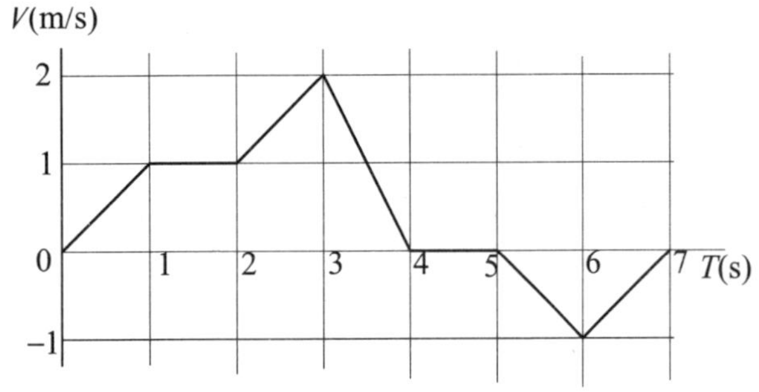

(A) 0 (B) 3 (C) 4 (D) 5

GATE 2015(EC)

Solution

Odometer reading (total distance)

$$= |\text{Area under } V\text{-}T \text{ curve}|$$

$$= \frac{1}{2}\times 1\times 1 + 1(2-1) + 1\times\left(\frac{1+2}{2}\right)$$

$$+\frac{1}{2}\times 2\times(4-3) + \frac{1}{2}1\times(7-5)$$

Odometer reading = 5 m

Example 17.61

Consider a function $f(x) = 1-|x|$ on $-1 \le x \le 1$. The value of x at which the function attains a maximum, and the maximum value of function is:

(A) 0, −1 (B) −1, 0 (C) 0,1 (D) −1, 2

GATE 2015(EE)

Solution

Graph of function $f(x) = 1-|x|$ is sketched.

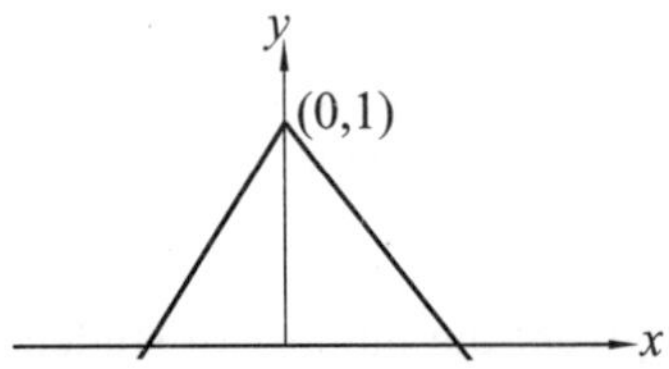

From the graph, we can easily see that it has maximum value 1 at $x = 0$

0, 1

Example 17.62

In the given figure angle Q is a right angle, $PS:QS = 3:1$, $RT:QT = 5:2$ and $PU:UR = 1:1$. If area of triangle QTS is 20 cm^2, then the area of triangle PQR in cm^2 is____.

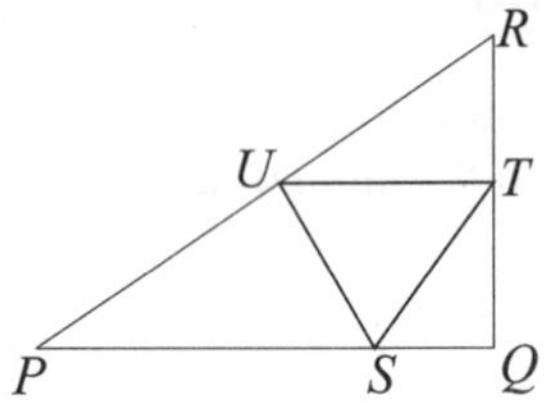

GATE 2016(EE)

Solution

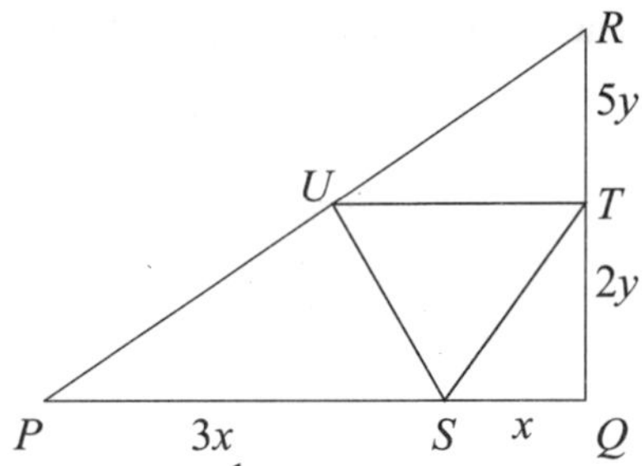

Area of triangle $QTS = \frac{1}{2}x\times 2y = xy = 20$

Area of triangle PQR

$$= \frac{1}{2}(3x+x)\times(5y+y) = 12xy = 12\times 20$$

Area of triangle $PQR = 240\text{ cm}^2$

Example 17.63

A right-angled cone (with base radius 5 cm and height 12 cm), as shown in the figure below, is rolled on the ground keeping the point P fixed until the point Q (at the base of the cone, as shown) touches the ground again.

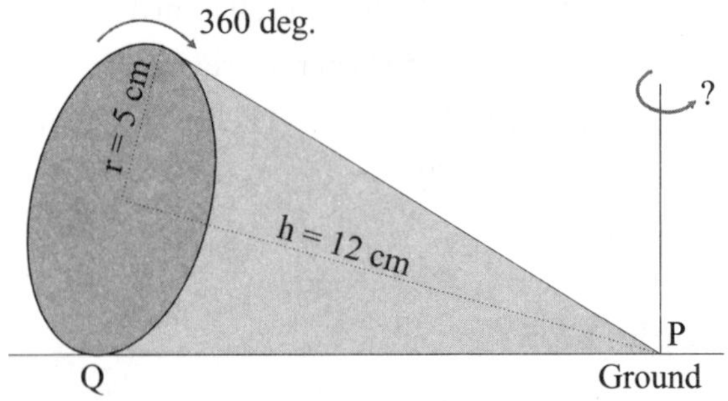

By what angle (in radians) about P does the cone travel?

(A) $\frac{5\pi}{12}$ (B) $\frac{5\pi}{24}$ (C) $\frac{24\pi}{5}$ (D) $\frac{10\pi}{13}$

GATE 2017

Solution

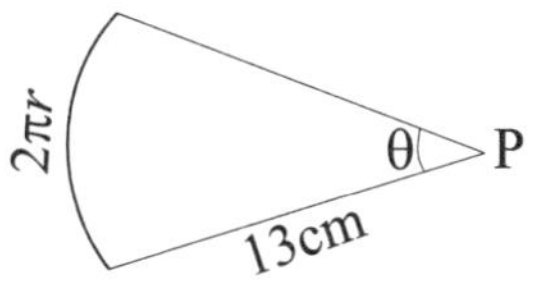

Angle of cone travel $\theta = \frac{2\pi r}{l} = \frac{2\pi \times 5}{13}$

$$\theta = \frac{10\pi}{13}$$

Example 17.64

In a company with 100 employees, 45 earn Rs. 20,000 per month, 25 earn Rs. 30,000, 20 earn Rs. 40,000, 8 earn Rs. 60,000, and 2 earn Rs. 150,000. The median of the salaries is

(A) Rs. 20,000 (B) Rs. 30,000

(C) Rs. 32,300 (D) Rs. 40,000

GATE 2017

Solution

All values put either in ascending or descending order first.

Median = Average of two middle most value.

$$= \frac{30000 + 30000}{2}$$

$$\text{Median} = 30000$$

Example 17.65

The growth of bacteria (lactobacillus) in milk leads to curd formation. A minimum bacterial population density of 0.8 (in suitable units) is needed to form curd. In the graph below, the population density of lactobacillus in 1 litre of milk is plotted as a function of time, at two different temperatures, 25°C and 37°C

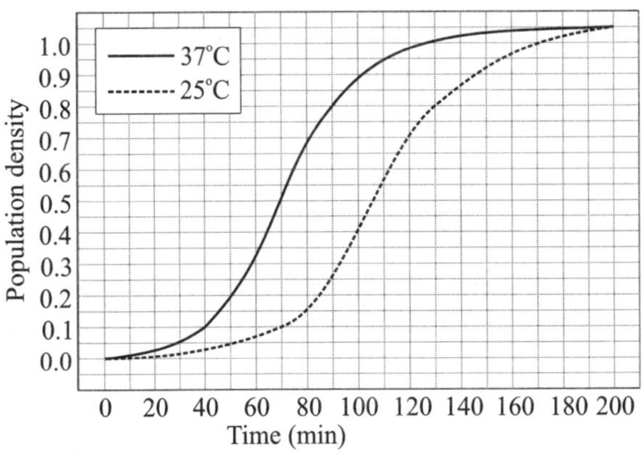

Consider the following statements based on the data shown above:

(i) The growth in bacterial population stops earlier at 37°C as compared to 25°C

(ii) The time taken for curd formation at 25°C is twice the time taken at 37°C

Which one of the following options is correct?

(A) Only i (B) Only ii

(C) Both i and ii (D) Neither i nor ii

GATE 2017

Solution

(A) From graph, statement (i) is correct

The time taken for curd formation at 25 °C = 120 min

The time taken for curd formation at 37 °C = 80 min

Hence (ii) is incorrect

Example 17.66

If a and b are integers and $a - b$ is even, which of the following must always be even?

(A) ab (B) $a^2 + b^2 + 1$ (C) $a^2 + b + 1$ (D) $ab - b$

GATE 2017

Solution

$$a - b = \text{even}$$

$$\left.\begin{aligned} \text{odd} - \text{odd} &= \text{even} \\ \text{even} - \text{even} &= \text{even} \end{aligned}\right]$$

$$ab - b = b(a-1) = \text{odd} \times \text{even} = \text{even}$$

$$= \text{even} \times \text{odd} = \text{even}$$

Example 17.67

A couple has 2 children. The probability that both children are boys if the older one is a boy is

(A) 1/4 (B) 1/3 (C) 1/2 (D) 1

GATE 2017

Solution

$$\text{Probability} = \frac{\text{No. of favaurable cases}}{\text{Total number of possible cases}} = \frac{1}{2}$$

Example 17.68

X bullocks and Y tractors take 8 days to plough a field. If we halve the number of bullocks and double the number of tractors, it takes 5 days to plough the same field. How many days will it take X bullocks alone to plough the field?

(A) 30 (B) 35 (C) 40 (D) 45

GATE 2017

Solution

$X + Y$ = work (plough a field) in 8 days

or $8X + 8Y$ = work (plough a field) in 1 days (i)

$$\frac{X}{2} + Y = \text{work (plough a field) in 5 days}$$

or $$\frac{5X}{2} + 5Y = \text{work (plough a field) in 1 days} \quad \text{(ii)}$$

Equations (i) and (ii) gives

$$8X + 8Y = \frac{5X}{2} + 5Y = \text{work (plough a field) in 1 days}$$

or $$Y = \frac{11}{4}X$$

From equation (i)

$$8X + 8 \times \frac{11}{4}X = 30X = \text{work (plough a field) in 1 days}$$

30 bullocks alone plough the field in 1 day

Example 17.69

There 4 women P, Q, R, S, and 5 men V, W, X, Y, Z in a group. We are required to form pairs each consisting of one woman and one man. P is not to be paired with Z, and Y must necessarily be paired with someone. In how may ways can 4 such pairs be formed?

(A) 74 (B) 76 (C) 78 (D) 80

GATE 2017

Solution

If P is paired with Y, then

Q has 4 choices

R has 3 choices

S has 2 choices

Total 24 choices

or If Q is paired with Y, then

P has 3 choices

R has 3 choices

S has 2 choices

Total 18 choices

or If R is paired with Y, then

P has 3 choices

Q has 3 choices

S has 2 choices

Total 18 choices

or If S is paired with Y, then

P has 3 choices

Q has 3 choices

S has 2 choices

Total 18 choices

$$\text{Total} = 24 + 18 + 18 + 18 = 78$$

Example 17.70

In the graph below, the concentration of a particular pollutant in a lake is plotted over (alternate) days of a month in winter (average temperature 10°C) and a month in summer (average temperature 30°C).

Consider the following statements based on the data shown above:

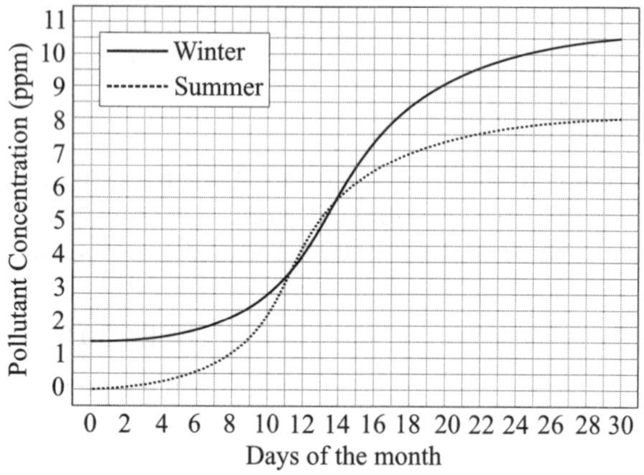

(i) Over the given months, the difference between the maximum and the minimum pollutant concentrations is the same in both winter and summer.

(ii) There are at last four days in the summer month such that the pollutant concentrations on those days are within 1 ppm of the pollutant concentrations on the corresponding days in the winter month.

Which one of the following options is correct?

(A) Only (i) (B) Only (ii)

(C) Both (i) and (ii) (D) Neither (i) nor (ii)

GATE 2018

Solution

The difference between the maximum and the minimum pollutant concentrations

(i) in winter $= 8 - 0 = 8$ ppm,

(ii) in summer $= 10.5 - 1.5 = 9$ ppm

(i) is false & (ii) is correct from the graph.

Example 17.71

Seven machines take 7 minutes to make 7 identical toys. At the same rate, how many minutes would it take for 100 machines to make 100 toys?

(A) 1 (B) 7 (C) 100 (D) 700

GATE 2018

Solution

7 machines make → 7 toys in→ 7 minutes

1 machines make → 1 toys in→ 7 minutes

So, 100 machines make → 100 toys in→ 7 minutes

7 minutes

Example 17.72

A rectangle becomes a square when its length and breadth are reduced by 10 m and 5 m, respectively. During this process, the rectangle loses 650 m^2 of area. What is the area of the original rectangle in square meters?

(A) 1125 (B) 2250 (C) 2924 (D) 4500

GATE 2018

Solution

Let l and b be the length and breadth respectively.

Given: $l-10=b-5$

$l-b=5$ (1)

Given: $l\times b-(l-10)\times(b-5)=650$

$5l+10b=700$ (2)

Equations (1) and (2) give $l=50$ m and $b=45$ m

Area of original rectangle $= lb = 50\times 45$

Area of original rectangle $= 2250\ \text{m}^2$

Example 17.73

A number consists of two digits. The sum of the digits is 9. If 45 is subtracted from the number, its digits are interchanged. What is the number?

(A) 63 (B) 72 (C) 81 (D) 90

GATE 2018

Solution

Let xy be two digit number. ($10x + y$ be the number)

$x+y=9$ (1)

$(10x+y)-45=10y+x$

$x-y=5$ (2)

Equations (1) and (2) give $x = 7$ and $y=2$.

Number is 72

Example 17.74

For integers , and , what would be the minimum and maximum values respectively of $a+b+c$ if $\log|a|+\log|b|+\log|c|=0$?

(A) –3 and 3 (B) –1 and 1

(C) –1 and 3 (D) 1 and 3

GATE 2018

Solution

Given: $\log|a|+\log|b|+\log|c|=0$

It is possible only if $|a|$, $|b|$ and $|c|$ are equal to 1.

So, $|a|$, $|b|$ and $|c|$ may be equal to ±1, ±1 and ±1 respectively.

Maximum value of $a+b+c=1+1+1=3$

Minimum value of $a+b+c=-1-1-1=-3$

$-3<(a+b+c)<3$

Example 17.75

Given that a and b are integers and $a+a^2b^3$ is odd, which one of the following statements is correct?

(A) a and b are both odd

(B) a and b are both even

(C) a is even and b is odd

(D) a is odd and b is even

GATE 2018

Solution

Given that a and b are integers and $a+a^2b^3$ is odd.

$a(1+ab^3)$ is odd

$$\underbrace{a}_{\text{odd}}\underbrace{(1+\overbrace{ab^3}^{\text{even}})}_{\text{odd}} \text{ is odd}$$

$$\overbrace{\underbrace{a}_{\text{odd numer}} \times \underbrace{b^3}_{\text{even number}}}^{\text{even number}}$$

a is odd and b is even number

Example 17.76

From the time the front of a train enters a platform, it takes 25 seconds for the back of the train to leave the platform, while travelling at a constant speed of 54 km/h. At the same speed, it takes 14 seconds to pass a man running at 9 km/h in the same direction as the train. What is the length of the train and that of the platform in meters, respectively?

(A) 210 and 140 (B) 162.5 and 187.5

(C) 245 and 130 (D) 175 and 200

GATE 2018

Solution

Let L_p and L_t be the length of plateform and train respectively.

$$\frac{L_p+L_t}{(54\times 000/60\times 60)}=25$$

or $$L_p+L_t=\frac{54\times 1000}{60\times 60}\times 25 \qquad \text{(i)}$$

$$\frac{L_t}{\{(54-9)\times 000/60\times 60\}}=14$$

or $\qquad L_t = \dfrac{45\times 1000}{60\times 60}\times 14 \qquad$ (ii)

Equations (i) and (ii) give $L_p = 200$ m, $L_t = 175$ m

Length of train = 175 m, Length of plateform = 200 m

Example 17.77

Which of the following functions describe the graph shown in the below figure?

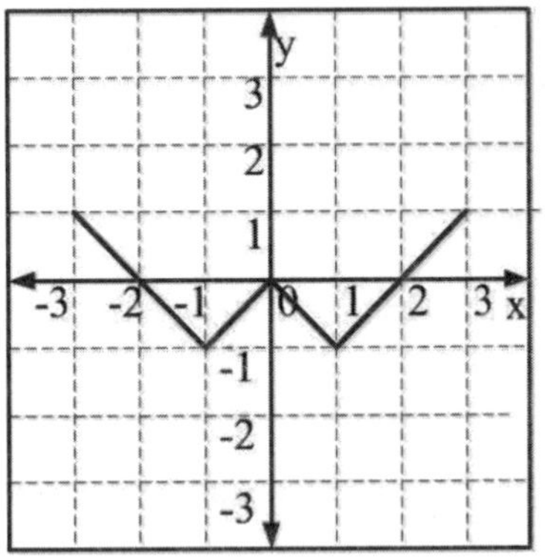

(A) $y = ||x|+1|-2$ $\qquad$ (B) $y = ||x|-1|-1$

(C) $y = ||x|+1|-1$ $\qquad$ (D) $y = ||x-1|-1|$

GATE 2018

Solution

Values of x and y from graph are given in table.

x	0	± 1	± 2
y	0	-1	0

Option (A) $y = ||x|+1|-2$ Not satisfied

Option (C) $y = ||x|+1|-1$ Not satisfied

Option (D) $y = ||x-1|-1|$ Not satisfied

Option (B) $y = ||x|-1|-1$ Satisfied

Example 17.78

Consider the following three statements:

(i) Some roses are red.

(ii) All red flowers fade quickly.

(iii) Some roses fade quickly.

Which of the following statements can be logically inferred from the above statements?

(A) If (i) is true and (ii) is false, then (iii) is false.

(B) If (i) is true and (ii) is false, then (iii) is true.

(C) If (i) and (ii) are true, then (iii) is true.

(D) If (i) and (ii) are false, then (iii) is false.

GATE 2018

Solution

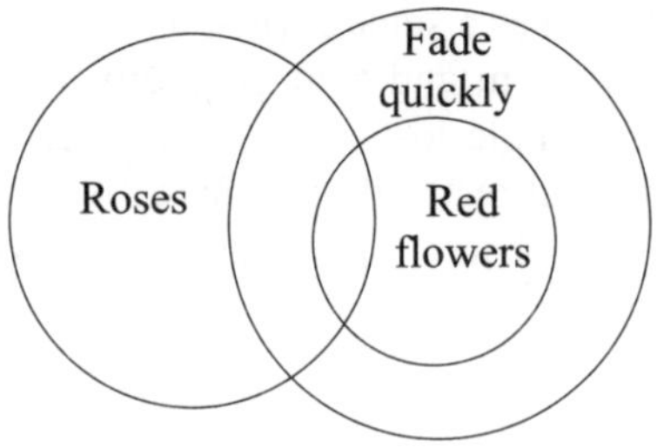

(C) If (i) and (ii) are true, then (iii) is true.

Example 17.79

Find the missing group of letters in the following series:
BC, FGH, LMNO, _____

(A) UVWXY $\qquad$ (B) TUVWX

(C) STUVW $\qquad$ (D) RSTUV

GATE 2018

Solution

TUVWX

Example 17.80

The perimeters of a circle, a square and an equilateral triangle are equal. Which one of the following statements is true?

(A) The circle has the largest area.

(B) The square has the largest area.

(C) The equilateral triangle has the largest area.

(D) All the three shapes have the same area.

GATE 2018

Solution

Perimeter $\quad P_c = P_s = P_T \quad \Rightarrow \pi D = 4a = 3s$

Area of circle $\quad A_c = \dfrac{\pi}{4}D^2 = 0.78D^2$

Area of square $\quad A_s = a^2 = \left(\dfrac{\pi}{4}D\right)^2 = 0.61\,D^2$

Area of triangle $\quad A_T = \dfrac{\sqrt{3}}{4}s^2 = \dfrac{\sqrt{3}}{4}\left(\dfrac{\pi}{3}D\right)^2 = 0.47\,D^2$

Area of circle > Area of square > Area of triangle

The circle has the largest area

Example 17.81

The value of the expression

$\frac{1}{1+\log_u vw}+\frac{1}{1+\log_v wu}+\frac{1}{1+\log_w uv}$ is ________.

(A) −1 (B) 0 (C) 1 (D) 3

GATE 2018

Solution

$$\frac{1}{1+\log_u vw}+\frac{1}{1+\log_v wu}+\frac{1}{1+\log_w uv}$$

$$=\frac{1}{\log_u u+\log_u vw}+\frac{1}{\log_v v+\log_v wu}+\frac{1}{\log_w w+\log_w uv}$$

$$=\frac{1}{\log_u uvw}+\frac{1}{\log_v vwu}+\frac{1}{\log_w wuv}$$

$$=\log_{uvw} u+\log_{uvw} v+\log_{uvw} w$$

$$=\log_{uvw} uvw=1$$

$$\frac{1}{1+\log_u vw}+\frac{1}{1+\log_v wu}+\frac{1}{1+\log_w uv}=1$$

Example 17.82

Forty students watched films A, B and C over a week. Each student watched either only one film or all three. Thirteen students watched film A, sixteen students watched film B and nineteen students watched film C. How many students watched all three films?

(A) 0 (B) 2 (C) 4 (D) 8

GATE 2018

Solution

Venn diagram is shown in figure.

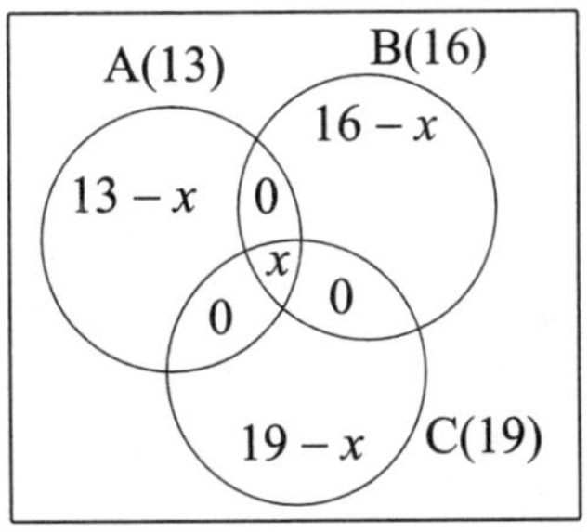

Total = 40

Let x be the number of students watched all three films.

$$(13-x)+(16-x)+(19-x)+x=40$$

$$48-2x=40$$

$$x=4$$

Example 17.83

A wire would enclose an area of $1936\ \text{m}^2$, if it is bent into a square. The wire is cut into two pieces. The longer piece is thrice as long as the shorter piece. The long and the short pieces are bent into a square and a circle, respectively. Which of the following choices is closest to the sum of the areas enclosed by the two pieces in square metres?

(A) 1096 (B) 1111 (C) 1243 (D) 2486

GATE 2018

Solution

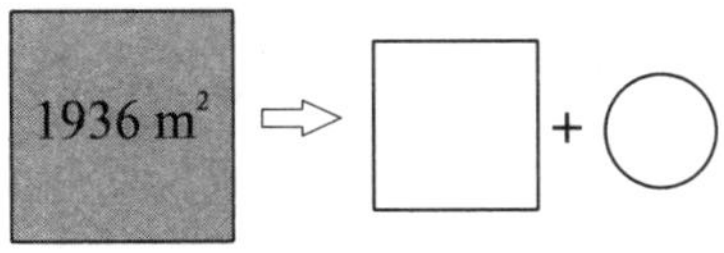

Area of square $a^2=1936$

$a=44\ \text{m}$

Length of wire $=4a=4\times 44=176\ \text{m}$

Length of wire Part-1 $L_1=3\times 44=132\ \text{m}$

Length of wire Part-2 $L_2=1\times 44=44\ \text{m}$

Long wire (part-1) is bent in square shape.

Side of square $a_1=\frac{132}{4}=33\ \text{m}$

Area of square $=33^2=1089\ \text{m}^2$

Long wire (part-2) is bent in circle shape.

Diameter of circle $D=\frac{44}{\pi}=14\ \text{m}$

Area of circle $=\frac{\pi}{4}14^2=153.94\ \text{m}^2$

Total area enclosed = Area of square + Area of circle

Total area enclosed = 1089 + 153.94

Total area enclosed = $1243\ \text{m}^2$

Example 17.84

A contract is to be completed in 52 days and 125 identical robots were employed, each operational for 7 hours a day. After 39 days, five-seventh of the work was completed. How many additional robots would be required to complete the work on time, if each robot is now operational for 8 hours a day?

(A) 50 (B) 89 (C) 146 (D) 175

GATE 2018

Solution

Fifth-seventh of work $\frac{5}{7}W = 125 \times 39 \times 7$

$$W = 47775 \text{ robots-hrs}$$

Remaining work $= 47775 - 125 \times 39 \times 7$

$$= 13650 \text{ robots-hrs}$$

Let x be the number of robots complete the work in $52 - 39 = 13$days.

$$x \times 13 \times 8 = 13650$$

$$x = 131.25$$

Additional robots required $= 131.25 - 125$

$$= 6.25$$

Additional robots required =7

Example 17.85

An unbiased coin is tossed six times in a row and four different such trials are conducted. One trial implies six tosses of the coin. If H stands for head and T stands for tail, the following are the observations from the four trials:

(1) HTHTHT (2) TTHHHT

(3) HTTHHT (4) HHHT__ __.

Which statement describing the last two coin tosses of the fourth trial has the highest probability of being correct?

(A) Two T will occur.

(B) One H and one T will occur.

(C) Two H will occur.

(D) One H will be followed by one T.

GATE 2018

Solution

For remaining two trials highest probability is, that

HH

HT

TH

TT

Out of four possible cases one head (H) and one tail (T), will highest probability occurence.

One H and one T will occur.

Example 17.86

The sum and product of two integers are 26 and 165 respectively. The difference between these two integers is_____.

(A) 2 (B) 3 (C) 4 (D) 6

GATE 2019

Solution

Let x and y be the numers

$$x - y = \sqrt{(x+y)^2 - 4xy}$$

Substituting given value $x + y = 26$ and $xy = 165$, we have

$$x - y = \sqrt{26^2 - 4 \times 165}$$

or $x - y = 4$

Difference on numbers = 4

Example 17.87

A firm hires employees at five different skill levels P, Q, R, S, T. The shares of employment at these skill levels of total employment in 2010 is given in the pie chart as shown. There were a total of 600 employees in 2010 and the total employment increased by 15% from 2010 to 2016. The total employment at skill levels P, Q and R remained unchanged during this period. If the employment at skill level S increased by 40% from 2010 to 2016, how many employees were there at skill level T in 2016?

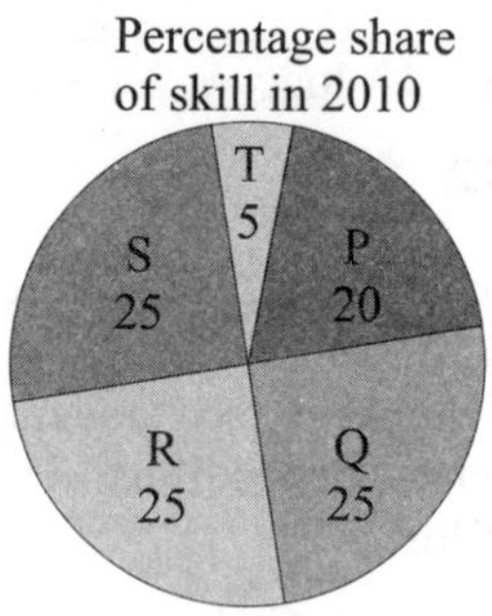

(A) 30 (B) 35 (C) 60 (D) 72

GATE 2019

Solution

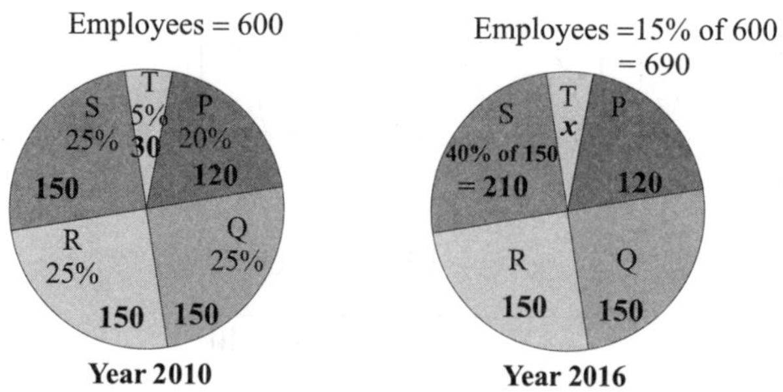

Number of employees at skill level T

$$x = 690 - (120 + 150 + 150 + 210) = 60$$

Number of employees at skill level T = 60

Example 17.88

A person divided an amount of Rs. 100,000 into two parts and invested in two different schemes. In one he got 10% profit and in the other he go 12%. If the profit percentages are interchanged with these investments he would have got Rs. 120 less. Find the ratio between his investments in the two schemes.

(A) 9:16 (B) 11:14 (C) 37:63 (D) 47:53

GATE 2019

Solution

Let x and y be the parts of investment.

$$x + y = 10000 \qquad \text{(i)}$$

Let z = profit before interchange

$$1.1x + 1.12y = z \qquad \text{(ii)}$$

$$1.12x + 1.1y = z - 120 \qquad \text{(iii)}$$

Solving Equations (i), (ii) and (iii), we get

$$x = 47000 \text{ and } y = 53000$$

$$\frac{x}{y} = \frac{47000}{53000}$$

$$\frac{x}{y} = \frac{47}{53}$$

Example 17.89

If IMHO = JNIP ; IDK = JEL ; and SO = TP, then IDC = ______.

(A) JDE (B) JED (C) JDC (D) JCD

GATE 2019

Solution

IDC = JED

Example 17.90

The product of three integers X, Y and Z is 192. Z is equal to 4 and P is equal to the average of X and Y. What is the minimum possible value of P?

(A) 6 (B) 7 (C) 8 (D) 9.5

GATE 2019

Solution

Given: $xyz = 192$, $z = 4$, $P = \frac{x+y}{2}$

Now, $$xy = \frac{192}{z} = \frac{192}{4} = 48$$

We know that Arithmetic mean≥ Geometric mean

$$\frac{x+y}{2} \geq \sqrt{xy} \quad \Rightarrow \quad P \geq \sqrt{xy}$$

$$P \geq \sqrt{48} \quad \text{or} \quad P \geq 6.92$$

Possible value of $P = 7$

Example 17.91

Fiscal deficit was 4% of the GDP in 2015 and that increased to 5% in 2016. If the GDP increased by 10% from 2015 to 2016, the percentage increase in the actual fiscal deficit is ___.

(A) 37.50 (B) 35.70 (C) 25.00 (D) 10.00

GATE 2019

Solution

Let x be GDP in 2015.

Year	GDP	Fiscal deficit
2015	x	$0.04x$
2016	$1.1x$	$0.05 \times 1.1x$

Percentage increase in the actual fiscal deficit

$$= \frac{0.05 \times 1.1x - 0.04x}{0.04x} \times 100$$

Percentage increase in the actual fiscal deficit = 37.5%

Example 17.92

Mola is a digital platform for taxis in a city. It offers three types of rides- Pool, Mini and Prime. The Table below presents the number of rides for the past four months. The platform earns one US dollar per ride. What is the percentage share of revenue contributed by Prime to the total revenues of Mola, for the entire duration?

	Month			
	January	February	March	April
Pool	170	320	215	190
Mini	110	220	180	70
Prime	75	180	120	90

(A) 16.24 (B) 23.97 (C) 25.86 (D) 38.74

GATE 2019

Solution

	Month					
	Jan	Feb	Mar	Apr	Total no. of rides	Revenue ($)
Pool	170	320	215	190	895	895
Mini	110	220	180	70	580	580
Prime	75	180	120	90	465	465
					Total revenue	1940

Percentage share of revenue contributed by Prime

$$= \frac{\text{Revenue of prime}}{\text{Total revenue}} \times 100 = \frac{465}{1940} \times 100$$

Percentage share of revenue contributed by Prim = 23.97%

17.3 PRACTICE PAPER

Time: 3 hours **Max. Marks:100**

Q.1 to Q.30 carry one mark each

Q.1 to Q.20 Multiple Choice Questions

Q.1 Choose the most appropriate word from the options given below to complete the following sentence.

A person suffering from Alzheimer's disease__ short-term memory loss.

(A) experienced (B) unexperienced

(C) is experiencing (D) experiences

Q.2 The Tamil version of ________John Abraham-starrer Madras Café ______ cleared by the censor board with no cuts last week, but the film's distributors _____ no takers among the exhibitors for a release in Tamil Nadu _______ this Friday.

(A) Mr., was, found, on (B) a, was found, at

(C) the, was, found, on (D) a, being, find, at

Q.3 Fact: If it rains, then the field is wet.

Read the following statements:

(i) It rains

(ii) The field is not wet

(iii) The field is wet

(iv) It did not rain

Which one of the options given below is NOT logically possible, based on the given fact?

(A) If (iii), then (iv) (B) If (i), then (iii)

(C) If (i), then (ii) (D) If (ii), then (iv)

Q.4 Choose the most appropriate word from the options given below to complete the following sentence. The official answered _____ that the complaints of the citizen would be looked into.

(A) respectably (B) respectfully

(C) reputably (D) respectively

Q.5 If m and n are whole numbers such that $m^n = 121$, then $(m-1)^{n+1} = ?$

(A) 10 (B) 10^2 (C) 10^3 (D) 10^4

Q.6 The value of $\frac{1}{1\cdot 2} + \frac{1}{2\cdot 3} + \frac{1}{3\cdot 4} + \ldots + \frac{1}{9\cdot 10}$ is:

(A) $\frac{11}{10}$ (B) $\frac{8}{9}$ (C) $\frac{9}{10}$ (D) $\frac{25}{1089}$

Q.7 If $\left(x+\frac{1}{x}\right) = 3$, then the value of $\left(x^6 + \frac{1}{x^6}\right)$ is:

(A) 927 (B) 414 (C) 364 (D) 322

Q.8 If $a^2 + b^2 = 45$ and $ab = 18$, then $\left(\frac{1}{a} + \frac{1}{b}\right)$ equal to

(A) $\frac{1}{3}$ (B) $\frac{2}{3}$ (C) $\frac{1}{2}$ (D) Cannot be determined

Q.9 Fill the missing number

5, 8, 12, 17, 23, ____ , 38

(A) 29 (B) 30 (C) 32 (D) 25

Q.10 If $a + b + c = 0$, the value of $\left(\frac{a^2}{bc} + \frac{b^2}{ca} + \frac{c^2}{ab}\right)$ is:

(A) 1 (B) 0 (C) -1 (D) 3

Q.11 The value of:

$(1^3 + 2^3 + 3^3 + \ldots + 15^3) - (1 + 2 + 3 + \ldots + 15)$ is

(A) 14280 (B) 14400 (C) 12280 (D)13280

Q.12 A man can swims 3 km/h in still water. If the velocity of the stream be 2 km/h, the time taken by him to swim to a place 10 km upstream and back, is

(A) $8\frac{1}{3}$ h (B) $9\frac{1}{5}$ h (C) 10 h (D) 12 h

Q.13 If $\frac{1}{\log_x 10} = \frac{2}{\log_a 10} - 2$, then $x =$

(A) $\frac{a}{2}$ (B) $\frac{a}{100}$ (C) $\frac{a^2}{10}$ (D) $\frac{a^2}{100}$

Q.14 If $\sqrt{3-2x} = \sqrt{2x} + 1$, then, $4x^2 =$

(A) 4 (B) $2-2x$ (C) $4x-2$ (D) $6x-1$

Q.15 *A* can do a piece of work in 30 days while *B* can do it in 40 days. *A* and *B* working together can do it in

(A) $15\frac{2}{7}$ days (B) $17\frac{1}{7}$ days

(C) $18\frac{3}{7}$ days (D) None of these

Q.16 *A* and *B* can do a piece of work in 6 days and *A* alone can do it in 9 days. The time taken by *B* alone to do the work is:

(A) 20 days (B) 18 days

(C) 24 days (D) None of these

Q.17 Two trains of equal length are running on parallel line in the same direction at speeds of 46 km/h and 36 km/h. The faster train passes the slower train in 36 s. The length of each train is:

(A) 50 m (B) 80 m (C) 72 m (D) 82 m

Q.18 If three positive real number *x, y, z* are in arithmetic mean such that $xyz = 4$, then what will be the minimum value of *y*?

(A) $2^{\frac{1}{3}}$ (B) $2^{\frac{2}{3}}$ (C) $2^{\frac{1}{4}}$ (D) $2^{\frac{3}{4}}$

Q.19 A lucky man finds 6 pots of gold coins. He counts the coins in the first four pots to be 60, 30, 20 and 15, respectively. If there is a definite progression, what would be the numbers of coins in the next two pots?

(A) 12, 9 (B) 12, 10 (C) 10, 8 (D) 10, 9

Q.20 A tap can filled a tank in 48 min, whereas another tap can empty it in 2 h. If both the taps are opened at 11:40 A.M., then the tank will be filled at

(A) 12:40 P.M. (B) 1:30 P.M.

(C) 1:00 P.M. (D) 1:20 P.M.

Q.21 to Q.30 Numerical Answer Questions

Q.21 Raju has 14 currency notes in this pocket consisting of only Rs. 20 notes and Rs.10 notes. The total money value of the notes is Rs. 230. The number of Rs.10 notes that Raju has is_______.

Q.22 If $(1.001)^{1259} = 3.52$ and $(1.001)^{2062} = 7.85$, then $(1.001)^{3321} =$_________.

Q.23 Given that $f(y) = \frac{|y|}{y}$, and q is any non-zero real number, the value of $|f(q) - f(-q)|$ is______.

Q.24 The sequence $a_1, a_2, a_3, \dots, a_n \dots$ is such that

$a_n = \frac{a_{n-1} + a_{n-2}}{2}$ for all $n \geq 3$. If $a_3 = 4$ and $a_5 = 20$

What is the value of a_6?

Q.25 A turtle starts swimming from a point *A* located on the circumference of a circular pond. After swimming for 4 m in a straight line it hits point *B* on the circumference of the point. From there it changes direction and swims for 3 m in a straight line and arrives at point *D* diametrically opposite to point *A*. How far is point *D* from *A*?

Q.26 25 persons are in a room. 15 of them play hockey, 17 of them play football and 10 of them play both hockey and football. Then the number of persons playing neither hockey nor football is ______.

Q.27 A 16.2 m long wooden log has a uniform diameter of 2 m. To what length the log should be cut to obtain a piece of 22 m^3 volume?

Q.28 A number *x* equals 80% of the average of 5, 7, 14 and a number *y*. If the average of *x* and *y* is 26, the value of *y* is______.

Q.29 In a class, 20 opted for Physics, 17 for Maths, 5 for both and 10 for other subjects. The class contains_____ students.

Q.30 In the figure shown, what is the value of

$v + x + y + z + w$?

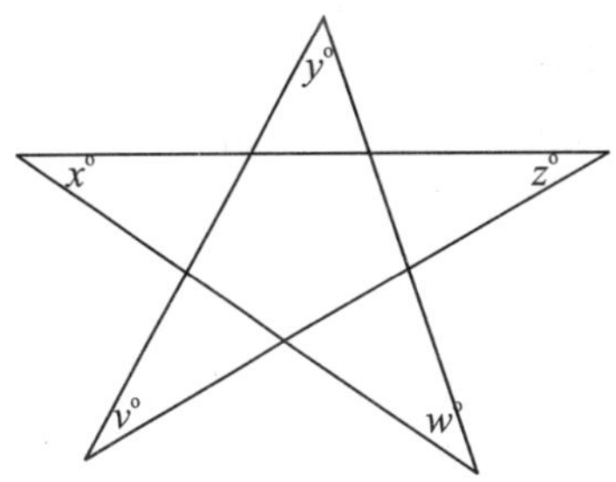

Q.31 to Q.65 carry two marks each

Q.31 to Q.50 Multiple Choice Questions

Q.31 If $3 \leq X \leq 5$ and $8 \leq Y \leq 11$, then which of the following options is TRUE?

(A) $\frac{3}{5} \leq \frac{X}{Y} \leq \frac{8}{5}$ (B) $\frac{3}{11} \leq \frac{X}{Y} \leq \frac{5}{8}$

(C) $\frac{3}{11} \leq \frac{X}{Y} \leq \frac{8}{5}$ (D) $\frac{3}{5} \leq \frac{X}{Y} \leq \frac{8}{11}$

Q.32 Velocity of an object fired directly in upward direction is given by $V = 80 - 32t$, where *t* (time) is in seconds. When will be the velocity be between 32 m/s and 64 m/s?

(A) (1, 3/2) (B) (1/2, 1) (C) (1/2, 3/2) (D) (1, 3)

Q.33 A point is chosen at random from a circular disc shown below. What is the probability that the point lies in the sector OAB?

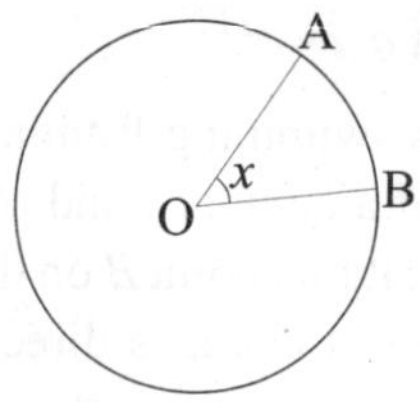

(Where $\angle AOB = x$ radians)

(A) $\frac{2x}{\pi}$ (B) $\frac{x}{\pi}$ (C) $\frac{x}{2\pi}$ (D) $\frac{x}{4\pi}$

Q.34 The capacity of the conical vessel shown above is V. It is filled with water upto half its height. The volume of water in the vessel is:

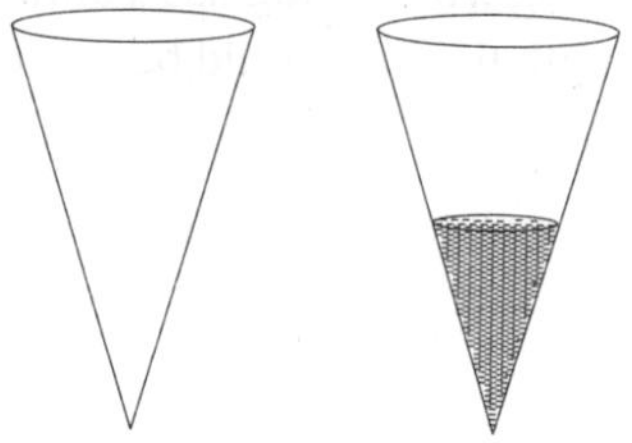

(A) $\frac{V}{2}$ (B) $\frac{V}{4}$ (C) $\frac{V}{8}$ (D) $\frac{V}{16}$

Q.35 A large tank filled with water is to be emptied by removing half of the water present in it everyday. After how many days will there be closest to 10% water left in the tank?

(A) One (B) Two (C) Three (D) Four

Q.36 If the average of a, b, c be M and $ab + bc = -ca$, then the average of a^2, b^2, c^2 is:

(A) M^2 (B) $3M^2$ (C) $9M^2$ (D) $27M^2$

Q.37 If the sum of first n natural number is one-fifth of the sum of their squares, then n is:

(A) 5 (B) 6 (C) 7 (D) 8

Q.38 A person walks downhill at 10 km/h, uphill at 6 km/h and on the plane at 7.5 km/h. If the person takes 3 h to go from a place A to another place B and 1 h on the way back. The distance between A and B is:

(A) 15 km (B) 23.5 km (C) 16 km

(D) Given data is insufficient to calculate the distance

Q.39 The triangle formed by the lines $y = x$, $y = 1 - x$ and $x = 0$ in a two-dimensional plane is (x and y axes have the same scale)

(A) Isosceles and right-angled

(B) Isosceles but not right-angled

(C) Right-angled but not isosceles

(D) Neither isosceles nor right-angled

Q.40 A vessel is partially filled with water. More water is added to it at a rate directly proportional to time $\left[\text{i.e.,} \frac{dV}{dt} \propto t\right]$. Which of the following graphs depicts correctly the variation of total volume V of the water with time t?

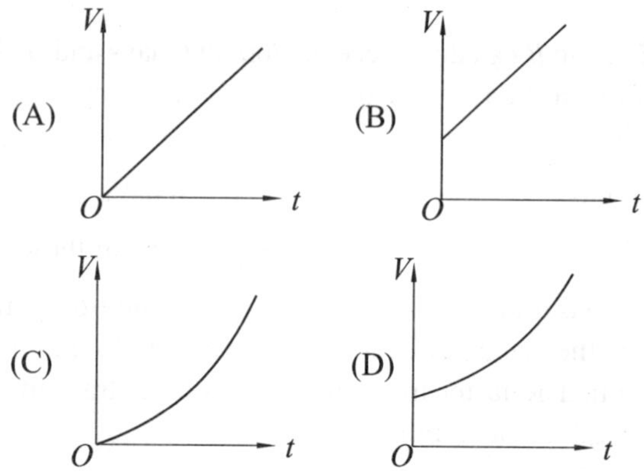

Q.41 How many numbers greater than 5000 can be formed with four of the digits 3, 4, 5, 6, 7 (no digit is to be repeated)

(A) 32 (B) 36 (C) 72 (D) None of these

Q.42 There are two buckets A and B. Initially A has two litres of water and B is empty. At every hour one litre of water is transferred from A and B followed by returning $\frac{1}{2}$ litre back to A from B half an hour later. The earliest A will get empty is in

(A) 5 h (B) 4 h (C) 3 h (D) 2 h

Q.43 In how many ways 5 letters can be posted in 3 letter boxes in the locality?

(A) 15 (B) 36 (C) 243 (D) 360

Q.44 Following table gives data on tourists from different countries visiting India in the year 2011.

Country	Number of Tourists
USA	2000
England	3500
Germany	1200
Italy	1100
Japan	2400
Australia	2300
France	1000

Which two countries contributed to the one-third of the total number of tourists who visited India in 2011?

(A) USA and Japan (B) USA and Australia

(C) England and France (D) Japan and Australia

Q.45 The sum of n terms of the series

$4 + 44 + 444 + \ldots$ is

(A) $\frac{4}{81}[10^{n+1} - 9n - 1]$ (B) $\frac{4}{81}[10^{n-1} - 9n - 1]$

(C) $\frac{4}{81}[10^{n+1} - 9n - 10]$ (D) $\frac{4}{81}[10^{n} - 9n - 10]$

Q.46 Four circles of unit radius each drawn such that each one touches two others and their centres lie on the vertices of a square. The area of the region enclosed between the circles is:

(A) $\pi - 1$ (B) $\pi - 2$

(C) $3 - \pi$ (D) $4 - \pi$

Q.47 The population of a new city is 5 million and is growing at 20% annually. How many years would it take to double at this growth rate?

(A) 3-4 years (B) 4-5 years

(C) 5-6 years (D) 6-7 years

Q.48 Percentage of male, female, literate and illiterate

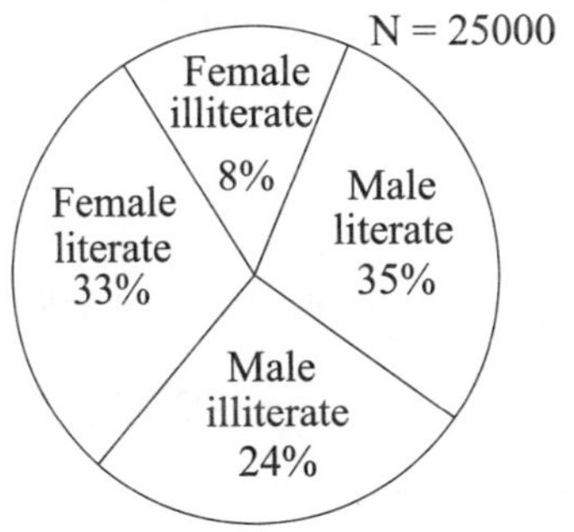

What is the difference between the number of literate male and that the literate female?

(A) 7500 (B) 1500 (C) 500 (D) 50

Q.49 If $|9y - 6| = 3$, then $y^2 - \frac{4}{3}y$ is_______

(A) 0 (B) $-\frac{1}{3}$ (C) $\frac{1}{3}$ (D) Undefined

Q.50 If $\frac{a^2 + b^2}{c^2 + d^2} = \frac{ab}{cd}$, then $\frac{a+b}{a-b}$ equal to

(A) $\frac{c+d}{c-d}$ (B) $\frac{c+d}{d}$ (C) $\frac{c+d}{c}$ (D) $\frac{c-d}{c+d}$

Q.51 to Q.65 Numerical Answer Questions

Q.51 A king ordered that a golden crown be made for him from 8 kg of gold and 2 kg of silver. The goldsmith took away some amount of gold and replaced it by an equal amount of silver and the crown when made, weighed 10 kg. Archimedes knew that under water gold lost $\frac{1}{20}$th of its weight, while silver lost $\frac{1}{10}$th. When the crown was weighted under water, it was 9.25 kg. How much gold was stolen by goldsmith?

Q.52 In a Science talent examination, 50% of the candidates fail in Mathematics and 50% fail in Physics. If 20 % fail in both these subjects, then the percentage who pass in both Mathematics and Physics is________.

Q.53 The figure shows an aerial view of a piece of land. If all angles shown are right angles, what is the perimeter (in m) of the piece of land?

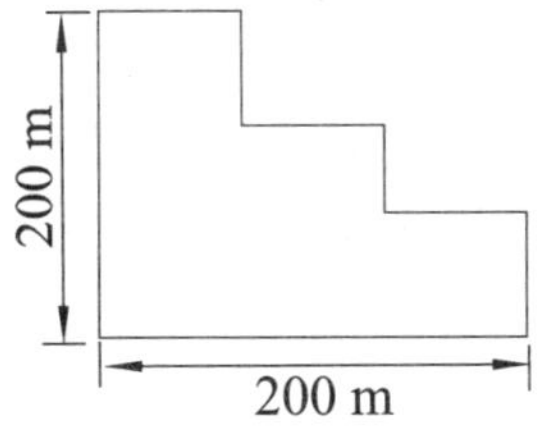

Q.54 The value of $\frac{2^{-14} + 2^{-15} + 2^{-16} + 2^{-17}}{5}$ is how many times the value of 2^{-17}?

Q.55 Positive integer y is 50 % of 50 % of positive integer x, and y percent of x equal 100. The value of x is_______.

Q.56 A can complete a job in 9 days, B in 10 days and C in 15 days. B and C start the work and are forced to leave after 2 days. The time taken to complete the remaining work is_______days.

Q.57 Density of a rice grain is 1.5 g/cc and bulk density of rice heap is 0.8 g/cc. If a 1 l container is completely filled with rice. What will be the approximate volume (in cc) of pore space in the container?

Q.58 In a community of 175 persons, 40 read the Patrika, 50 read the Dainik and 100 do not read any. How many persons read both the papers?

Q.59 The ages of Amit and Sanjay are in the ratio 2:3. After 12 years, their ages will be in the ratio 11:15. The age of Sanjay is _______.

Q.60 In a survey, it was found that 65% of the people watched news on TV, 40% read in news paper, 25 % read newspaper and watched TV. What percentage of people neither watched TV nor read newspaper?

Q.61 A bee leaves its hive in the morning and after flying for 30 min due south reaches a garden and spends 5 min collecting honey. Then it flies for 40 min due west and collects honey in another garden for 10 min. Then it returns to the hive taking the shortest route. How long was the bee away from its hive? (Assume that the bee flies at constant speed).

Q.62 A bird perched at the top of a 12 m high tree sees a centipede moving towards the base of the tree from a distance equal to twice the height of the tree. The bird flies along a straight line to catch the centipede. If both move at the same speed, at what distance (in m) from the base of the tree will the centipede be picked up by the bird?

Q.63 In any given year, the probability of an earthquake greater than magnitude 6 occurring in the Garhwal Himalayas is 0.04. The average time between successive occurrences of such earthquakes is _______ years.

Q.64 A foundry has a fixed daily cost of Rs. 50,000 whenever it operates and a variable cost of Rs. 800Q, where Q is the daily production in tonnes. What is the cost of production in Rs./tonne for a daily production of 100 tonne?

Q.65 A wire of length 340 mm is to be cut into two parts. One of the parts is to be made into a square and the other into a rectangle where sides are in the ratio of 1:2. What is the length of the side of the square (in mm) such that the combined area of the square and the rectangle is a MINIMUM?

17.4 SOLUTION TO PRACTICE PAPER

Q.1 Ans:(D)

Q.2 Ans:(C)

Q.3 Ans:(C)

Q.4 Ans:(B)

Q.5 Ans:(C)

Given that $m^n = 121 \Rightarrow m^n = 11^2 = 121$

Hence $m = 11$, $n = 2$, substituting these values

$(m-1)^{n+1} = (11-1)^{2+1} = 10^3$

$$(m-1)^{n+1} = 10^3$$

Q.6 Ans:(C)

$$\frac{1}{1\cdot 2}+\frac{1}{2\cdot 3}+\frac{1}{3\cdot 4}+\ldots+\frac{1}{9\cdot 10}$$

$$=\left(\frac{1}{1}-\frac{1}{2}\right)+\left(\frac{1}{2}-\frac{1}{3}\right)+\left(\frac{1}{3}-\frac{1}{4}\right)+\ldots+\left(\frac{1}{9}-\frac{1}{10}\right)$$

$$=\frac{1}{1}-\frac{1}{10}=\frac{9}{10}$$

$$\frac{1}{1\cdot 2}+\frac{1}{2\cdot 3}+\frac{1}{3\cdot 4}+\ldots+\frac{1}{9\cdot 10}=\frac{9}{10}$$

Q.7 Ans:(D)

$$\left(x+\frac{1}{x}\right)^3 = 3^3 = 27$$

or $$x^3+\frac{1}{x^3}+3\times x\times\frac{1}{x}\left(x+\frac{1}{x}\right)=27$$

or $$x^3+\frac{1}{x^3}+3\times 3=27$$

or $$x^3+\frac{1}{x^3}=18$$

Now, $$\left(x^3+\frac{1}{x^3}\right)^2=18^2$$

or $$x^6+\frac{1}{x^6}+2=324$$

$$x^6+\frac{1}{x^6}=322$$

Q.8 Ans:(C)

$$\frac{1}{a}+\frac{1}{b}=\frac{a+b}{ab}=\frac{\sqrt{(a+b)^2}}{ab}$$

$$=\frac{\sqrt{a^2+b^2+2ab}}{ab}=\frac{\sqrt{45+2\times 18}}{18}=\frac{9}{18}$$

$$\frac{1}{a}+\frac{1}{b}=\frac{1}{2}$$

Q.9 Ans:(B)

5, 8, 12, 17, 23, __, 38

Difference → 3 4 5 6 7 8

Missing number $= 23 + 7 = 30$

Q.10 Ans:(D)

$$a^3+b^3+c^3-3abc$$

$$=(a+b+c)(a^2+b^2+c^2-ab-bc-ca)=0$$

or $$a^3+b^3+c^3=3abc$$

$$\left(\frac{a^2}{bc}+\frac{b^2}{ca}+\frac{c^2}{ab}\right)=\left(\frac{a^3+b^3+c^3}{abc}\right)=\left(\frac{3abc}{abc}\right)$$

$$\left(\frac{a^2}{bc}+\frac{b^2}{ca}+\frac{c^2}{ab}\right)=3$$

Q.11 Ans:(A)

We know that $\sum n^3 = \left[\frac{n(n+1)}{2}\right]^2$ and $\sum n = \frac{n(n+1)}{2}$

$$(1^3+2^3+3^3+\ldots+15^3)-(1+2+3+\ldots+15)$$

$$=\left[\frac{15(15+1)}{2}\right]^2-\frac{15(15+1)}{2}$$

$$=120^2-120$$

$$(1^3+2^3+3^3+\ldots+15^3)-(1+2+3+\ldots+15)=14280$$

Q.12 Ans:(D)

Speed of man in upstream $= 3 - 2 = 1$ km/h

Speed of man in downstream $= 3 + 2 = 5$ km/h

Total time taken $= \left(\frac{10}{1} + \frac{10}{5}\right) = 12$ h

Total time taken $= 12$ h

Q.13 Ans:(D)

$$\frac{1}{\log_x 10} = \frac{2}{\log_a 10} - 2$$

or $\log_{10} x = 2\log_{10} a - 2$

or $\log_{10} x = 2(\log_{10} a - 1)$

or $\log_{10} x = 2(\log_{10} a - \log_{10} 10)$

or $\log_{10} x = 2\log_{10} \frac{a}{10}$

or $\log_{10} x = \log_{10}\left(\frac{a}{10}\right)^2$

$$x = \left(\frac{a}{10}\right)^2$$

Q.14 Ans:(D)

$$\sqrt{3-2x} = \sqrt{2x} + 1$$

$$(\sqrt{3-2x})^2 = (\sqrt{2x} + 1)^2$$

or $3 - 2x = 2x + 2\sqrt{2x} + 1$

or $1 - 2x = \sqrt{2x}$

or $(1-2x)^2 = (\sqrt{2x})^2$

$$4x^2 = 6x - 1$$

Q.15 Ans:(B)

Here $X = 30$ days, $Y = 40$ days

A and B working together can do the work in

$$= \frac{1}{\frac{1}{X} + \frac{1}{Y}} = \frac{XY}{X+Y} = \frac{30 \times 40}{30 + 40} = \frac{120}{7}$$

$17\frac{1}{7}$ days

Q.16 Ans:(B)

Here $X = 6$ days, $Y = 9$ days

B alone will complete the work in

$$= \frac{1}{\frac{1}{X} - \frac{1}{Y}} = \frac{XY}{Y - X} = \frac{9 \times 6}{9 - 6} = 18$$

18 days

Q.17 Ans:(A)

Let x be the length of each train.

Relative speed, $v_r = \frac{x + x}{T}$

$$(46 - 36) \times \frac{1000}{60 \times 60} = \frac{2x}{36}$$

Length of train, $x = 50$ m

Q.18 Ans:(B)

For real number; Arithmetic mean $\geq$ Geometric mean

$$\frac{x + y + z}{3} \geq (xyz)^{\frac{1}{3}}$$

or $x + y + z \geq 3(xyz)^{\frac{1}{3}}$

or $x + y + z \geq 3 \times 4^{\frac{1}{3}}$

x, y, z are in arithmetic mean; $y = \frac{x + z}{2}$

or $2y = x + z$

$y + 2y \geq 3 \times 4^{\frac{1}{3}}$

$y \geq 4^{\frac{1}{3}}$

Minimum value of y is $2^{\frac{2}{3}}$

Q.19 Ans:(B)

Pot-1	Pot-2	Pot-3	Pot-4	Pot-5	Pot-6
$\frac{60}{1}$	$\frac{60}{2}$	$\frac{60}{3}$	$\frac{60}{4}$	$\frac{60}{5}$	$\frac{60}{6}$
60	30	20	15	12	10

Q.20 Ans:(C)

In one minute, $\frac{1}{48} - \frac{1}{2 \times 60} = \frac{1}{80}$ of tank can be filled.

The whole tank can be filled in 80 min.

The tank will be filled at 1:00 P.M.

Q.21 Ans:[5]

Let x be the number of Rs. 10 notes.

Total money $10x + 20(14 - x) = 230$

$$-10x + 280 = 230$$

$$x = 5$$

Q.22 Ans:[27.64]

Given that $(1.001)^{1259} = 3.52$ and $(1.001)^{2062} = 7.85$

$$(1.001)^{3321} = (1.001)^{1259+2062}$$

$$= (1.001)^{1259} \times (1.001)^{2062}$$

$$= 3.52 \times 7.85$$

$$(1.001)^{3321} = 27.64$$

Q.23 Ans:[2]

Given that $f(y) = \dfrac{|y|}{y}$

$$f(q) = \frac{|q|}{q} = 1$$

$$f(-q) = \frac{|-q|}{-q} = -1$$

$$|f(q) - f(-q)| = |1 - (-1)| = 2$$

$$|f(q) - f(-q)| = 2$$

Q.24 Ans:[28]

$$a_n = \frac{a_{n-1} + a_{n-2}}{2} \Rightarrow a_5 = \frac{a_4 + a_3}{2}$$

Substituting known values, we get

$$20 = \frac{a_4 + 4}{2}$$

or $a_4 = 36$

Now, $a_6 = \dfrac{a_5 + a_4}{2}$

or $a_6 = \dfrac{20 + 36}{2}$

$$a_6 = 28$$

Q.25 Ans:[5]

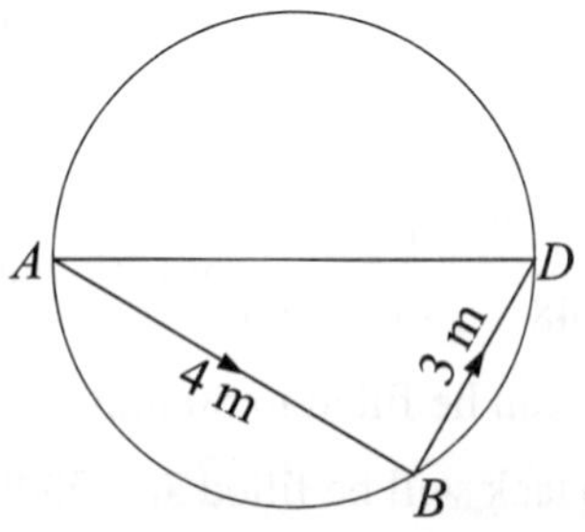

$$AD = \sqrt{AB^2 + BD^2}$$

$$AD = \sqrt{4^2 + 3^2} = 5$$

$$AD = 5\text{ m}$$

Q.26 Ans:[3]

Given that: 25 persons in room

15 persons play hockey

17 persons play football

10 persons play both hockey and football.

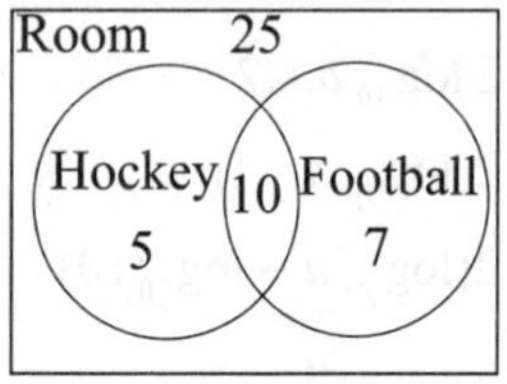

Number of persons play hockey and football

$$= 5 + 7 + 10 = 22$$

Number of persons playing neither hockey nor football $= 25 - 22 = 3$

Q.27 Ans:[7]

Volume of piece, $V = \dfrac{\pi}{4} d^2 l$

or $22 = \dfrac{\pi}{4} \times 2^2 \times l$

or $l = \dfrac{22 \times 4}{\pi \times 2^2}$

$$l = 7.0\text{ m}$$

Q.28 Ans:[39]

$$x = \frac{80}{100} \times \left(\frac{5 + 7 + 14 + y}{4}\right)$$

$$x = \left(\frac{y + 26}{5}\right) \quad \text{(i)}$$

Average of x and y; $\dfrac{x + y}{2} = 26$ (ii)

From Equations (i) and (ii), we get

$$52 - y = \left(\frac{y + 26}{5}\right)$$

$$y = 39$$

Q.29 Ans:[42]

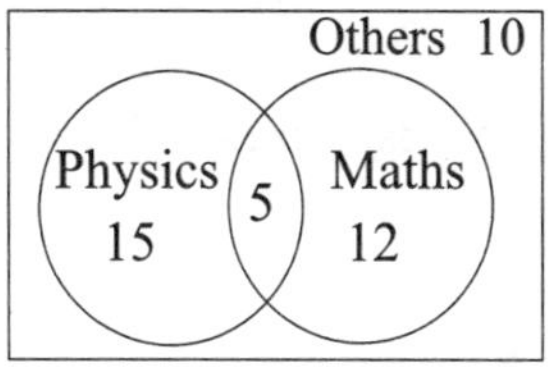

Total number of students $= 15 + 5 + 12 + 10 = 42$

Q.30 Ans:[180]

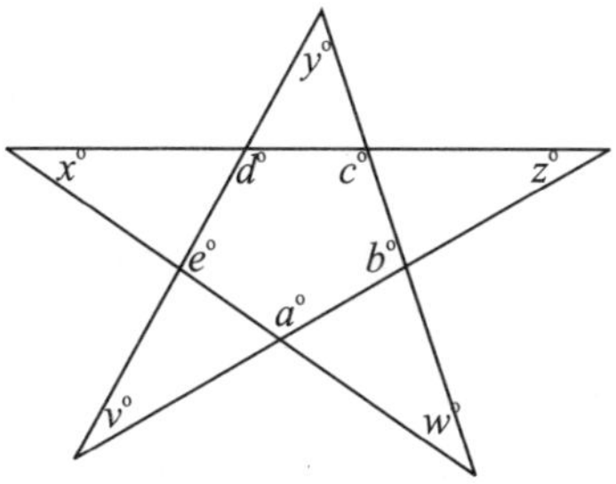

The sum of the interior angle of any polygon is $180(n-2)$, where n is the number of sides. Thus,

$$a+b+c+d+e=180(5-2)=540$$
$$a+x+z=180$$
$$b+y+v=180$$
$$c+x+w=180$$
$$d+v+z=180$$
$$e+y+w=180$$

Summing above equations, we get

$$a+b+c+d+2(x+y+z+v+w)=900$$
$$540+2(x+y+z+v+w)=900$$
$$x+y+z+v+w=180$$

Q.31 Ans:(B)

$$3 \le X \le 5 \quad \Rightarrow X_{max}=5, X_{min}=3$$
$$8 \le Y \le 11 \quad \Rightarrow Y_{max}=11, Y_{min}=8$$
$$\left(\frac{X}{Y}\right)_{max} = \frac{X_{max}}{Y_{min}} = \frac{5}{8}$$
$$\left(\frac{X}{Y}\right)_{min} = \frac{X_{min}}{Y_{max}} = \frac{3}{11}$$

Thus,

$$\frac{3}{11} \le \frac{X}{Y} \le \frac{5}{8}$$

Q.32 Ans:(C)

Velocity of object, $V = 80 - 32t \Rightarrow t = \frac{80-V}{32}$

Substituting $V = 32$ m/s and $V = 64$ m/s, we have

$$t = \frac{80-32}{32} = \frac{3}{2}\text{ s and } t = \frac{80-64}{32} = \frac{1}{2}\text{ s}$$

$$\left(\frac{1}{2}, \frac{3}{2}\right)$$

Q.33 Ans:(C)

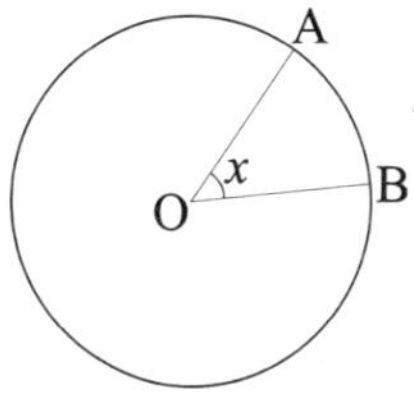

Area of circle, $A = \pi r^2$

Area of sector AOB, $A_x = \frac{\pi r^2}{2\pi} x$

Probability that the point lies in the sector OAB,

$$P = \frac{A}{A_x} = \frac{\frac{\pi r^2}{2\pi} x}{\pi r^2}$$

$$P = \frac{x}{2\pi}$$

Q.34 Ans:(C)

Volume of conical vessel, $V = \frac{1}{3}\pi R^2 H$

Volume of water, $V' = \frac{1}{3}\pi\left(\frac{R}{2}\right)^2 \frac{H}{2}$

$$V' = \frac{1}{3}\pi R^2 H \times \frac{1}{8}$$

$$V' = \frac{V}{8}$$

Q.35 Ans:(C)

First day water present $= 50\,\%$

Second day water present $= 25\,\%$

Third day water present $= 12.5\,\%$

Fourth day water present $= 6.25\,\%$

Third day 12.5% (closest to 10%) water present

Q.36 Ans:(B)

Average of a, b, c, $\frac{a+b+c}{3} = M$

$$a+b+c=3M$$

We know $(a+b+c)^2 = a^2+b^2+c^2+2(ab+bc+ca)$

$$(3M)^2 = a^2+b^2+c^2+2(-ca+ca)$$

$$a^2+b^2+c^2 = 9M^2$$

Average of a^2, b^2, c^2 is

$$\frac{a^2+b^2+c^2}{3} = \frac{9M^2}{3}$$

$$3M^2$$

Q.37 Ans:[C]

Sum of the first n natural numbers $= \frac{n(n+1)}{2}$

Sum of the squares of the first n natural numbers

$$= \frac{n(n+1)(2n+1)}{6}$$

$$\frac{n(n+1)}{2} = \frac{1}{5}\left[\frac{n(n+1)(2n+1)}{6}\right]$$

$$2n+1 = 15$$

$$n = 7$$

Q.38 Ans:(D)

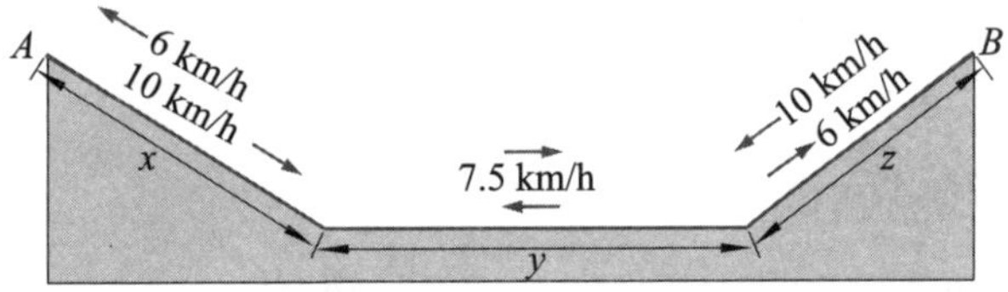

Total time from place A to place B; $t_x + t_y + t_z = 3$

$$\frac{x}{10} + \frac{y}{7.5} + \frac{z}{6} = 3$$

Total time from place B to place A; $t_x + t_y + t_z = 1$

$$\frac{z}{10} + \frac{y}{7.5} + \frac{x}{6} = 1$$

Distance between place A to place B $(x + y + z)$ cannot be calculate from given data.

Q.39 Ans:(A)

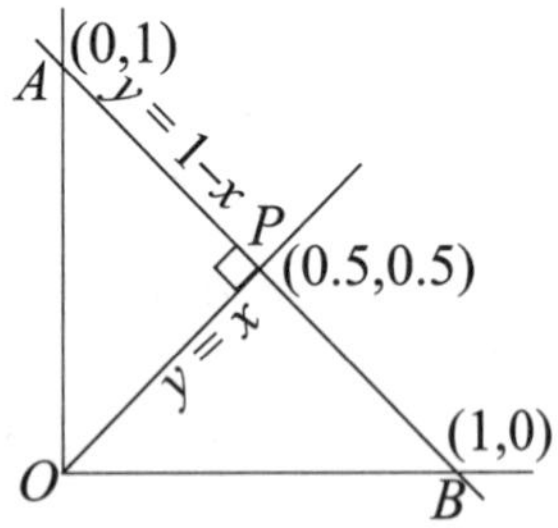

Straight lines $y = x$ and $y = 1-x$ are drawn, which are intersect at $P\left(\frac{1}{2}, \frac{1}{2}\right)$.

$$OP = AP = \frac{1}{\sqrt{2}} \text{ and } \angle APO = 90^\circ$$

The triangle is isosceles and right-angled

Q.40 Ans:(D)

Given that: $\frac{dV}{dt} \propto t$

or $\frac{dV}{dt} = kt$

or $\int_{V_o}^{V} dV = \int_0^t kt\,dt$

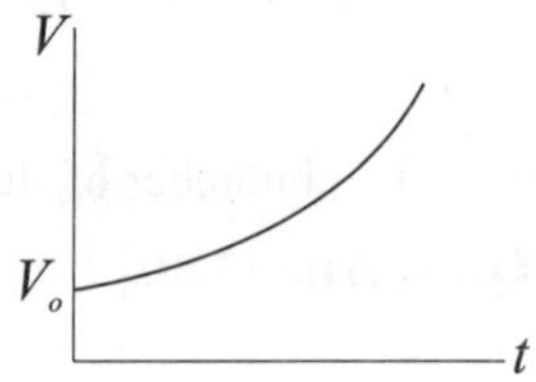

Graph of $V = V_o + \frac{k}{2}t^2$ is shown in figure.

Q.41 Ans:(C)

1st digit 5, 6, 7	Last 3 digit
$^3p_1$ ways	$^4p_3$ ways

The left most place digit can be filled in $^3p_1$ ways. Remaining 3 places can be filled in $^4p_3$ ways (since no repetition is allowed).

Required numbers greater than 5000

$$= {}^3p_1 \times {}^4p_3 = 72$$

Q.42 Ans:(C)

	0 h	1 h	$1\frac{1}{2}$ h	2 h	$2\frac{1}{2}$ h	3 h
Bucket A	2 l	1 l	$1\frac{1}{2}l$	$\frac{1}{2}l$	1 l	0 l
Bucket B	0	1	$\frac{1}{2}l$	$1\frac{1}{2}l$	1 l	2 l

Bucket will get empty in 3 h

Q.43 Ans:(A)

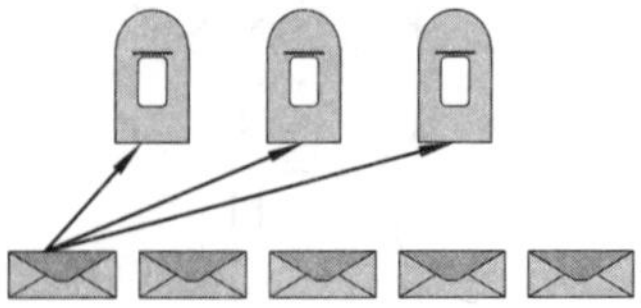

Each letter can be posted in 3 letter boxes in 3 ways.

Required number of ways $= 3+3+3+3+3$ (or $^5c_3$)

Required number of ways $= 15$

Q.44 Ans:(C)

Total number of tourists $= 13500$

$\frac{1}{3}$ of total number of tourists = 4500

Number of tourist (England + France)

$$= 3500 + 1000 = 4500$$

England and France

Q.45 Ans:(C)

Given series $4 + 44 + 444 + ...$

$$S = 4 + 44 + 444 + ... + n \text{ term}$$

$$S = 4(1 + 11 + 111 + ... + n \text{ term})$$

$$S = \frac{4}{9}(9 + 99 + 999 + ... + n \text{ term})$$

$$S = \frac{4}{9}(9 + 99 + 999 + ... + n \text{ term})$$

$$S = \frac{4}{9}[(10-1) + (100-1) + (1000-1) + ... + n \text{ term})$$

$$S = \frac{4}{9}[(10 + 100 + 1000 + ... + n \text{ term})$$

$$- (1 + 1 + 1 + ... + n \text{ term})]$$

$$S = \frac{4}{9}\left[\frac{10(10^n - 1)}{10 - 1} - n\right]$$

$$S = \frac{4}{81}(10^{n+1} - 9n - 10)$$

Q.46 Ans:(D)

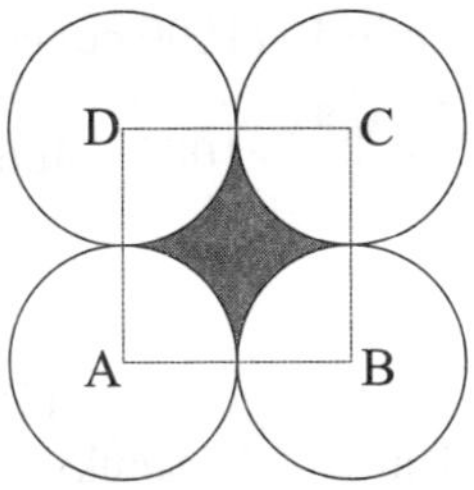

Side of square $a = 2$ units

Area of the region enclosed between the circle

$$A = a^2 - 4 \times \frac{1}{4}\pi r^2$$

$$A = 2^2 - 4 \times \frac{1}{4}\pi \times 1^2$$

$$A = 4 - \pi$$

Q.47 Ans:(A)

Let n be the number of years.

Population after n years, $2P = P(1 + r)^n$

or $2 = (1 + 0.2)^n$

or $2 = (1.2)^n$

or $n = \frac{\ln 2}{\ln 1.2} = 3.8$ years

$$n = 3\text{-}4 \text{ years}$$

Q.48 Ans:(C)

Number of literate male $= 0.35 \times 25000 = 8750$

Number of literate female $= 0.33 \times 25000 = 8250$

The difference between the number of literate male and literate female is $= 8750 - 8250 = 500$

Q.49 Ans(B)

$9y - 6 = 3$: For $9y - 6 > 0 \Rightarrow y > \frac{2}{3}$

$y = 1$ ← which is greater than $\frac{2}{3}$

$6 - 9y = 3$: For $9y - 6 < 0 \Rightarrow y < \frac{2}{3}$

$y = \frac{1}{3}$ ← which is less than $\frac{2}{3}$

Value of $\left(y^2 - \frac{4}{3}y\right)$ at $y = 1$; $\left(1^2 - \frac{4}{3} \times 1\right) = -\frac{1}{3}$

Value of $\left(y^2 - \frac{4}{3}y\right)$ at $y = \frac{1}{3}$; $\left[\left(\frac{1}{3}\right)^2 - \frac{4}{3} \times \frac{1}{3}\right] = -\frac{1}{3}$

$$\left(y^2 - \frac{4}{3}y\right) = -\frac{1}{3}$$

Q.50 Ans:(A)

Given: $\frac{a^2 + b^2}{c^2 + d^2} = \frac{ab}{cd} \Rightarrow \frac{a^2 + b^2}{c^2 + d^2} = \frac{2ab}{2cd}$

$$\frac{a^2 + b^2 + 2ab}{c^2 + d^2 + 2cd} = \frac{a^2 + b^2 - 2ab}{c^2 + d^2 - 2cd} = \frac{2ab}{2cd}$$

$$\frac{(a+b)^2}{(c+d)^2} = \frac{(a-b)^2}{(c-d)^2}$$

$$\frac{a+b}{a-b} = \frac{c+d}{c-d}$$

Q.51 Ans:[3]

Weight of gold $= m_G$

Weight of gold in water $= (m_G)_W = m_G - \frac{m_G}{20} = \frac{19}{20}m_G$

Weight of silver $= m_S$

Weight of gold in silver $= (m_S)_W = m_S - \frac{m_S}{10} = \frac{9}{10}m_S$

Let x kg gold be stolen

Weight of crown in water

$$(m_G)_W + (m_S)_W = \frac{19}{20}(m_G - x) + \frac{9}{10}(m_S + x)$$

$$9.25 = \frac{19}{20}(8 - x) + \frac{9}{10}(2 + x)$$

$$x = 3 \text{ kg}$$

Q.52 Ans:[20]

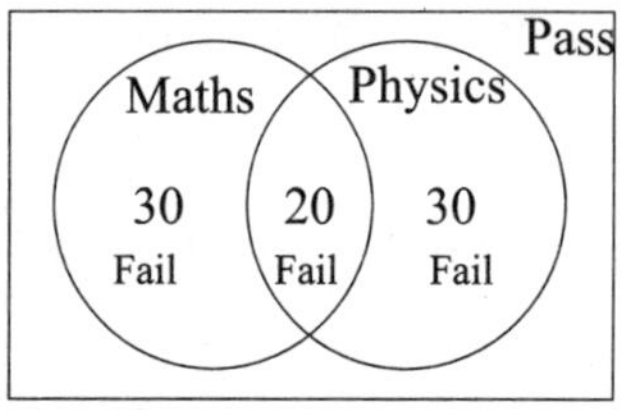

Number of students passed in both the subjects

$$= 100 - (30 + 20 + 30)$$

$$20\,\%$$

Q.53. Ans:[800]

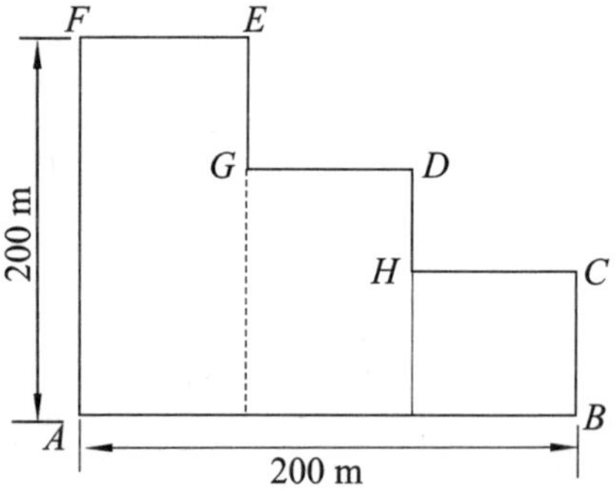

If all the angles are right angles, then

$FE + GD + HC = AB$ and $EG + DH + CB = FA$,

Hence, the Perimeter of the land is

$= AB + (BC + HC + HD + GD + EG + FE) + FA$

$= AB + FA + (HC + GD + FE) + (BC + HD + EG)$

$= 2AB + 2FA = 2 \times 200 + 2 \times 200$

Perimeter = 800 m

Q.54 Ans:[3]

Let the value of $\dfrac{2^{-14} + 2^{-15} + 2^{-16} + 2^{-17}}{5}$ be n times the value of 2^{-17}.

$$n \times 2^{-17} = \frac{2^{-14} + 2^{-15} + 2^{-16} + 2^{-17}}{5}$$

$$n = \frac{2^{-14+17} + 2^{-15+17} + 2^{-16+17} + 2^{-17+17}}{5}$$

$$n = \frac{8 + 4 + 2 + 1}{5}$$

$$n = 3$$

Q.55 Ans:[200]

According to problem,

$$y = 0.50 \times 0.50x \Rightarrow y = 0.25x \quad \text{(i)}$$

and $\dfrac{y}{100} \times x = 100 \quad \Rightarrow xy = 10000 \quad$ (ii)

Equations (i) and (ii) give

$$0.25x^2 = 10000$$

$$x = 200$$

Q.56 Ans:[6]

$$(B + C)\text{'s 2 days work} = 2\left(\frac{1}{10} + \frac{1}{15}\right) = \frac{1}{3}$$

$$\text{Remaining work} = 1 - \frac{1}{3} = \frac{2}{3}$$

$\frac{1}{9}$ work is done by A in 1 day

Therefore, remaining $\frac{2}{3}$ work is done by A in $\frac{2}{3} \times \frac{9}{1} = 6$ days

Q.57 Ans:[466]

Density of rice grain = 1.5 g/cc

Density of rice heap = 0.8 g/cc

Volume of pore space in 1 l (1000 cc) container is

$$= \frac{(1.5 - 0.8)}{1.5} \times 1000 = 466 \text{ cc}$$

Q.58 Ans:[15]

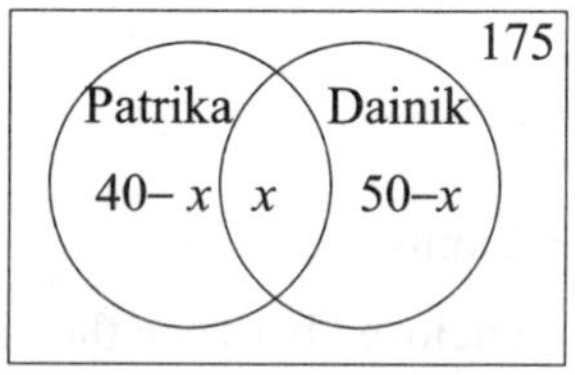

$$(40 - x) + x + (50 - x) = 175 - 100$$

or $\quad x = 15$

Number of persons read both paper = 15

Q.59 Ans:[16]

Let x be the present age of Sanjay.

Present age ratio: $\dfrac{\text{Age of Amit}}{\text{Age of Sanjay}} = \dfrac{2x}{3x}$

Age ratio after 12 years: $\dfrac{2x+12}{3x+12}=\dfrac{11}{15}$

$3x=48$

Age of Sanjay, $x=16$ years

Q.60 Ans:[20]

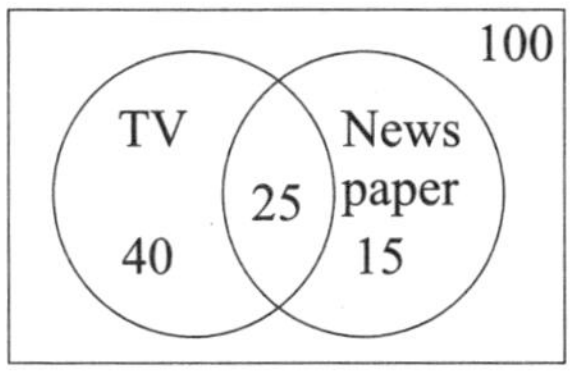

% of people neither watched TV nor read newspaper

$=100-(40+25+15)$

20%

Q.61 Ans:[135]

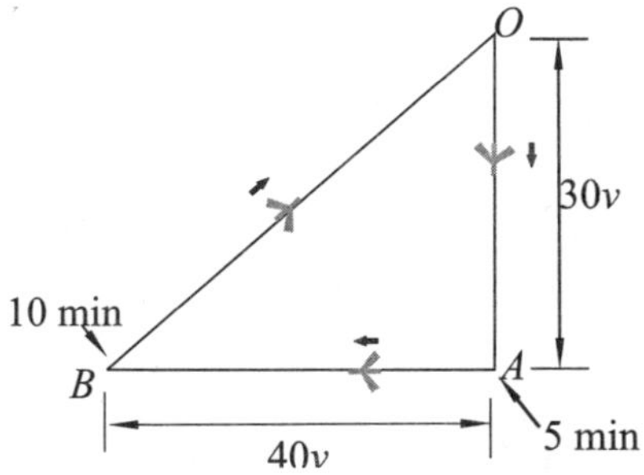

Let v be the speed of bee.

Distance, $OA=30v$

Distance, $AB=40v$

Distance, $OB=\sqrt{(40v)^2+(30v)^2}=50v$

Total time, $T=30+5+40+10+\dfrac{50v}{v}$

$T=135$ min

Q.62 Ans:[9]

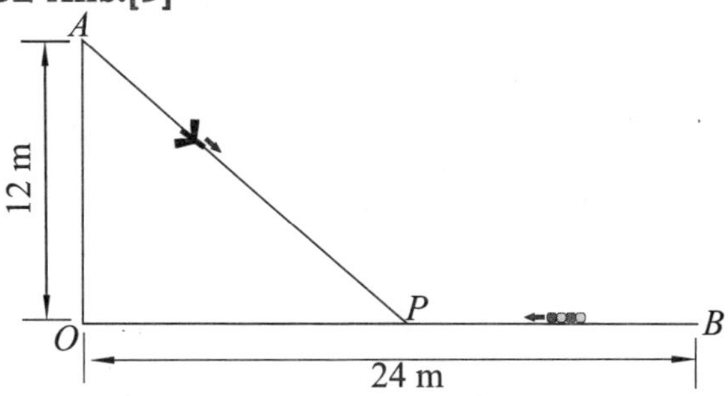

Let v be speed of bird and centipode.

From the geometry of figure.

$AP=BP=vt$

In ΔOAP; $AP^2=OA^2+OP^2$

$$(vt)^2=12^2+(24-vt)^2$$

or $$vt=\frac{12^2+24^2}{2\times 24}=15$$

or $$OP=24-BP$$

or $$OP=24-vt=24-15$$

$OP=9$ m

Q.63 Ans:[25]

Number of earthquake in one year is 0.04.

or One earthquake in $\dfrac{1}{0.04}=25$ years

Therefore, the average time between successive occurrences of such earthquakes is 25 years.

Q.64 Ans:[130000]

Fixed cost = Rs. 50,000

Variable cost = Rs. $800\times Q$

Cost of production of 100 tonnes = Rs. $50{,}000+800\times 500$

Cost of production of 100 tonnes = Rs. 130,000

Cost of production per tonne of 100 tonnes = Rs. 1300.

Q.65 Ans:[40]

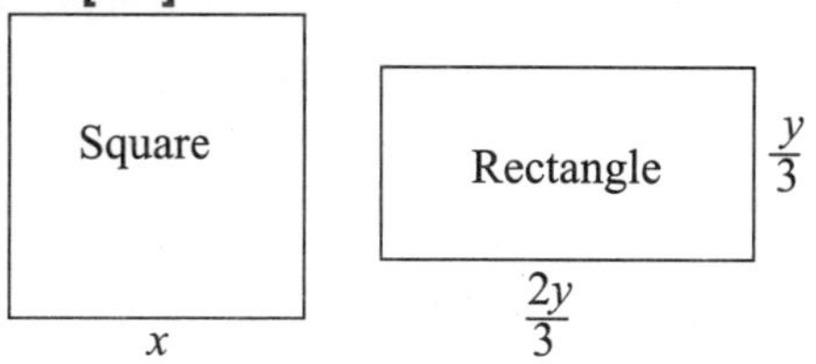

Length of wire,

$$4\times x+2\left(\frac{y}{3}+\frac{2y}{3}\right)=340$$

or $$y=170-2x$$

Total area, $$A=x^2+\frac{2}{9}y^2$$

$$A=x^2+\frac{2}{9}(170-2x)^2$$

$$\frac{d}{dx}A=2x+\frac{2}{9}\times 2(170-2x)\times -2=0$$

or $$x=40\text{ mm}$$

Length of side of square, $x=40$ mm